C000125920

ISBN 978-0-656-33651-7
PIBN 10786800

HANSARD'S
PARLIAMENTARY DEBATES,

THIRD SERIES

COMMENCING WITH THE ACCESSION OF

WILLIAM IV.

27° VICTORIÆ, 1864.

VOL. CLXXIV.

COMPRISING THE PERIOD FROM

THE FIFTEENTH DAY OF MARCH 1864,

TO

THE THIRD DAY OF MAY 1864.

Second Volume of the Session.

LONDON:
PUBLISHED BY CORNELIUS BUCK,
AT THE OFFICE FOR HANSARD'S PARLIAMENTARY DEBATES,
23, PATERNOSTER ROW [E.C.]

1864

LONDON : CORNELIUS BUCK, PRINTER, 23, PATERNOSTER-ROW.

TABLE OF CONTENTS

TO

VOLUME CLXXIV.

THIRD SERIES.

BEING ALSO AN ABSTRACT OF THE LORDS' "MINUTES OF PRO-
CEEDINGS," AND THE COMMONS' "VOTES AND PROCEEDINGS,"
IN RELATION TO THE PUBLIC BUSINESS OF THE SESSION.

[*The * indicates that there was no Debate at that Stage of the Bill.*]

LORDS, TUESDAY, MARCH 15.

MINUTES.]—PUBLIC BILLS—*First Reading* —Mutiny*.
Second Reading — Malt for Animals (No. 16); Marine Mutiny*.
Referred to Select Committee—Insane Prisoners Act Amendment* (No. 14).

Select Committee — Insane Prisoners Act Amendment *appointed*. (List of Committee, *see* p. 3.)
Committee—Vestry Cess Abolition (Ireland) (No. 19); Inclosure* (No. 25).
Report—Inclosure.*

DENMARK AND GERMANY—IDENTICAL NOTE OF AUSTRIA AND PRUSSIA—Question, The Earl of Ellenborough; Answer, The Duke of Somerset   ..

Insane Prisoners Act Amendment Bill (No. 14)—

Order of the Day for the House to be put into Committee *discharged*, and Bill referred to a Select Committee. And on *Monday, April 25th*, the Lords following were named of the Committee :—Ld. Chancellor, Ld. President, D. Richmond, E. Carnarvon, E. Romney, E. Cathcart, V. Eversley, L. Wodehouse, L. Cranworth, L. Wensleydale, L. Chelmsford, L. Kingsdown.

Malt for Animals Bill (No. 16)—

Moved, That the Bill be now read 2ª.—(*Lord Stanley of Alderley.*)   ..   3
After Debate, Motion *agreed to* :—Bill read 2ª accordingly, and *committed* to a Committee of the Whole House on *Friday* next.

VOL. CLXXIV. [THIRD SERIES.]   [*b*]

TABLE OF CONTENTS.

LORDS, WEDNESDAY, MARCH 16.

MINUTES.]—PUBLIC BILLS—*First Reading* — Consolidated Fund (£584,650) (No. 33) ; Consolidated Fund (£4,500,000) (No. 34).

Second Reading—Mutiny (*Committee negatived*).
Committee—Marine Mutiny .
Reported—Marine Mutiny .
Third Reading—Inclosure (No. 25).

Their Lordships met, and having gone through the business on the Paper
without debate,

House adjourned at a quarter past Four o'clock.

COMMONS, WEDNESDAY, MARCH 16.

MINUTES.]—NEW MEMBER SWORN—Henry Edward Surtees, esquire, *for* Hertford County.
SELECT COMMITTEE—Schools of Art, *nominated* (*List of Committee*), *see* p. 1703, vol. clxxiii.
PUBLIC BILLS—*Resolution in Committee* — Bank Notes (Scotland) .
First Reading — Chief Rents (Ireland)

(*Lords*) [Bill 52] ; Bank Notes (Scotland) [Bill 53].
Second Reading — Judgments, &c., Law Amendment [Bill 3]; Tests Abolition (Oxford) [Bill 18]; Election Petitions [Bill 17].
Third Reading — The Consolidated Fund (£584,650) ; The Consolidated Fund (£4,500,000) .

TABLE OF CONTENTS.

TABLE OF CONTENTS.

Government Annuities Bill [Bill 11]—

Order read, for resuming *Adjourned Debate*, on Question [4th March], "That Mr. Speaker do now leave the Chair:"—Question again proposed:—Debate *resumed*   211

Amendment proposed,

To leave out from the word "That" to the end of the Question, in order to add the words "the Bill be committed to a Select Committee,"—(*Sir Minto Farquhar*,)—instead thereof   211

Question proposed, "That the words proposed to be left out stand part of the Question."

After long Debate, *Moved*, "That the Debate be now adjourned:"—(*Mr. Ayrton :*)—Motion *agreed to :*—Debate adjourned till *To-morrow.*

SUPPLY—Order for Committee read; Motion made, and Question proposed, "That Mr. Speaker do now leave the Chair:"—

MR. STANSFELD AND THE GRECO CONSPIRACY—Amendment proposed,

To leave out from the word "That" to the end of the Question, in order to add the words "the statement of the Procureur Général on the trial of Greco, implicating a Member of this House and of Her Majesty's Government in the plot for the assassination of our Ally the Emperor of the French, deserves the serious consideration of this House,"—(*Sir Henry Stracey*,)—instead thereof   250

Question proposed, "That the words proposed to be left out stand part of the Question."

After long Debate, Question put:—The House *divided*; Ayes 171, Noes 161; Majority 10.

            Division List—Ayes and Noes   284

DENMARK AND GERMANY—POSTPONEMENT OF NOTICE—Observations, Viscount Palmerston; Reply, Mr. Bernal Osborne   ..   *   286

Main Question put, and *agreed to.*

SUPPLY *considered* in Committee—CIVIL SERVICE ESTIMATES   ..   .   289

(In the Committee.)

£1,866,000, on Account of certain Civil Services.

After short Debate, Vote *agreed to:*—Resolution to be reported *to-morrow.*

Factory Acts Extension Bill—

On Motion of *Mr. Bruce,* Bill for the Extension of the Factory Acts, *ordered* to be brought in by Mr. Bruce and Sir George Grey :— Bill *presented*, and read 1°. [Bill 55.]

Life Annuities and Life Assurances Bill—

On Motion of *Mr. Chancellor of the Exchequer,* Bill to provide for the investment and appropriation of all monies received by the Commissioners for the reduction of the National Debt, on Account of Deferred Life Annuities and payments to be made on Death, *ordered* to be brought in by Mr. Chancellor of the Exchequer and Mr. Peel: —Bill *presented*, and read 1°. [Bill 56.]

                                            House adjourned at Two o'clock.

Page

LORDS, FRIDAY, MARCH 18.

COMMONS, FRIDAY, MARCH 18.

TABLE OF CONTENTS.

COMMONS, MONDAY, APRIL 4.

LISBURN ELECTION PETITIONS COMMITTEE—House informed, That the Committee
met on Tuesday, the 22nd day of March last, pursuant to adjournment,
when they were informed that Mr. Stirling, one of the Members of the
Committee, was prevented by severe illness from attending; and that the
Committee had adjourned until Tuesday, the 5th day of April, at Eleven.
Whereupon, the House being informed that Mr. George Harrison, the medical
attendant of Mr. Stirling, attended at the door, he was called in, and at the
bar examined upon oath in relation to the state of Mr. Stirling's health on
the 22nd day of March last; and then he withdrew.

Motion made, and Question proposed,

"That Mr. Stirling be excused for not attending the said Committee upon Tuesday, th
22nd day of March last, and be discharged from further attendance on the said Committee."—(*Mr. Adair*)   391

After Debate, Debate *adjourned* till *To-morrow.*
Report to be *printed*—(*Parl. Paper,* No. 182.)

TABLE OF CONTENTS.

House adjourned at a quarter after Ten o'clock.

LORDS, TUESDAY, APRIL 5.

MINUTES.]— PUBLIC BILLS — *Committee*— of Chancery (Despatch of Business) * [H.L.]
Court of Chancery (Despatch of Business) (No. 18); Conveyancers, &c. (Ireland) *
[H.L.] * (No. 18); Conveyancers, &c. (Ire- (No. 17).
land) * (No. 17). *Third Reading*—Bills of Exchange and Pro-
Report—Malt for Animals * (No. 16); Court missory Notes (Ireland) * (No. 26).

METROPOLITAN RAILWAYS—

TABLE OF CONTENTS.

LORDS, THURSDAY, APRIL 7.

House adjourned at a quarter before Six o'clock.

COMMONS, THURSDAY, APRIL 7.

THE FINANCIAL STATEMENT OF THE CHANCELLOR OF THE EXCHEQUER—
Resolution—

1. Sugar Duties—
"That, towards raising the Supply granted to Her Majesty, on and after the undermentioned dates, in lieu of the Duties of Customs now charged on the articles undermentioned, the following Duties of Customs shall be charged thereon, on importation into Great Britain or Ireland (that is to say) :
On and after the fifth day of May, one thousand eight hundred and sixty-four—
Sugar—namely,
Candy, Brown or White, Refined Sugar, or Sugar, rendered by any process equal in quality thereto
the cwt. £0 12 10
On and after the sixteenth day of April, one thousand eight hundred and sixty-four—
Sugar—namely,
White Clayed Sugar, or Sugar rendered by any process equal in quality to White Clayed, not being refined, or equal in quality to refined . . . the cwt. 0 11 8

Yellow Muscovado and Brown Clayed Sugar, or Sugar rendered by any process equal in quality to Yellow Muscovado, or Brown Clayed, and not equal to White Clayed . . . the cwt. 0 10 6
Brown Muscovado Sugar, or Sugar rendered by any process equal in quality thereto, and not equal to Yellow Muscovado, or Brown Clayed . . the cwt. 0 9 4
Any other Sugar not equal in quality to Brown Muscovado
the cwt. 0 8 2
Cane Juice . . . the cwt. 0 6 7
Molasses . . . the cwt. 0 3 6
Almonds, paste of . the lb. 0 0 1
Cherries, dried . . the lb. 0 0 1
Comfits, dry . . the lb. 0 0 1
Confectionery . . the lb. 0 0 1
Ginger, preserved . the lb. 0 0 1
Marmalade . . . the lb. 0 0 1
Plums preserved in Sugar the lb. 0 0 1
Succades, including all fruits and vegetables preserved in Sugar, not otherwise enumerated the lb. 0 0 1."

After long Debate, Committee report Progress.

[In order to present a complete view of The Chancellor of the Exchequer's Financial Plan, the Resolutions which he had given notice to move in Committee of Ways and Means are here added as they stood on the Notice Paper.]

TABLE OF CONTENTS.

THE BUDGET — FINANCIAL PLAN.

CUSTOMS DUTIES.

1. Sugar Duties.

That, towards raising the Supply granted to Her Majesty, on and after the undermentioned dates, in lieu of the Duties of Customs now charged on the articles undermentioned, the following Duties of Customs shall be charged thereon, on importation into Great Britain or Ireland (that is to say):

On and after the fifth day of May, one thousand eight hundred and sixty-four—

Sugar—namely,

Candy, Brown or White, Refined Sugar, or Sugar, rendered by any process equal in quality thereto, the cwt. £0 12 10

On and after the sixteenth day of April, one thousand eight hundred and sixty-four—

Sugar—namely,

White Clayed Sugar, or Sugar rendered by any process equal in quality to White Clayed, not being refined, or equal in quality to refined . . . the cwt. 0 11 8

Yellow Muscovado and Brown Clayed Sugar, or Sugar rendered by any process equal in quality to Yellow Muscovado, or Brown Clayed, and not equal to White Clayed . . . the cwt. 0 10 6

Brown Muscovado Sugar, or Sugar rendered by any process equal in quality thereto, and not equal to Yellow Muscovado, or Brown Clayed . . . the cwt. 0 9 4

Any other Sugar not equal in quality to Brown Muscovado.	the cwt.	0 8 2
Cane Juice . . .	the cwt.	0 6 7
Molasses . . .	the cwt.	0 3 6
Almonds, paste of .	the lb.	0 0 1
Cherries, dried . .	the lb.	0 0 1
Comfits, dry . .	the lb.	0 0 1
Confectionery . .	the lb.	0 0 1
Ginger, preserved .	the lb.	0 0 1
Marmalade . . .	the lb.	0 0 1
Plums preserved in Sugar	the lb.	0 0 1

Succades, including all fruits and vegetables preserved in Sugar, not otherwise enumerated the lb. 0 0 1

2. Drawbacks on Sugar.

That, on and after the undermentioned dates, in lieu of the Drawbacks now allowed thereon, the following Drawbacks shall be paid and allowed on the undermentioned descriptions of Refined Sugar, on the exportation thereof to Foreign parts, or on removal to the Isle of Man for consumption there, or on deposit in any approved Warehouse, upon such terms and subject to such regulations as the Commissioners of Customs may direct, for delivery from such Warehouse as Ships' Stores only, or for the purpose of sweetening British Spirits in Bond (that is to say):

On and after the fifth day of May, one thousand eight hundred and sixty-four—

Upon Refined Sugar in loaf, complete and whole, or lumps duly refined, having been perfectly clarified, and thoroughly dried in the stove, and being of an uniform whiteness throughout; and upon such Sugar pounded, crushed, or broken in a warehouse approved by the Commissioners of Customs, such Sugar having been there first inspected by the Officers of Customs in lumps or loaves as if for immediate shipment, and then packed for exportation in the presence of such Officers, and at the expense of the exporter; and upon Candy . for every cwt. £0 1

Upon Refined Sugar unstoved, pounded, crushed, or broken, and not in any way inferior to the Export Standard Sample No. 1 approved by the Lords of the Treasury, and which shall not contain more than five per centum moisture over and above what the same would contain if thoroughly dried in the stove . . for every cwt. 0 11

And on and after the twenty-first day of April, one thousand eight hundred and sixty-four—

Upon Sugar refined by the Centrifugal, or by any other process, and not in any way inferior to the Export Standard No. 3 approved by the Lords of the Treasury for every cwt. 0 12

Upon Bastard, or Refined Sugar unstoved, broken in pieces, or being ground, powdered, or crushed, not in any way inferior to the Export Standard Sample No. 2 approved by the Lords of the Treasury for every cwt. 0 10

Upon Bastard, or Refined Sugar being inferior in quality to the said Export Standard Sample No. 2 . . for every cwt. 0 8

3. Continuing the Duty on Tea—

That, towards the raising the Supply granted Her Majesty, the Duties of Customs now charged on Tea shall continue to be levied and charged and after the 1st day of August, 1864, until the 1st day of August, 1865, on importation into Great Britain or Ireland.

4. Altering the Duty on Corn—

That, in lieu of the Duties of Customs now charged on the undermentioned Articles, on the importation into Great Britain or Ireland, the following Duties of Customs shall be charged (that is to say):

Wheat, Barley, Oats, Rye, Pease, Beans, Maize, or Indian Corn, Buck Wheat, Bear or Bigg . the cwt. £0 0

COMMONS, MONDAY, APRIL 11.

VOL. CLXXIV. [Third Series.]　　[*d*]

LORDS, TUESDAY, APRIL 12.

COMMONS, TUESDAY, APRIL 12.

COMMONS, WEDNESDAY, APRIL 13.

WAYS AND MEANS—Order for Committee read; Motion made, and Question
proposed, "That Mr. Speaker do now leave the Chair:"—

THE SUGAR DUTIES AND THE MALT DUTY—

Amendment proposed,

To leave out from the word "That" to the end of the Question, in order to add the
words "the consideration of the Duties upon Sugar be postponed until the House
shall have had the opportunity of considering the expediency of the reduction of the
Duty upon Malt,"—(*Colonel Barttelot*,)—instead thereof 972

Question put, "That the words proposed to be left out stand part of the
Question:—The House *divided*; Ayes 347, Noes 99; Majority 248

Division List—Ayes and Noes 1053

WAYS AND MEANS *considered* in Committee:—

Resolution on Sugar Duties (April 7) again proposed 1057

Question again proposed:—

"That, towards raising the Supply granted to Her Majesty, on and after the undermentioned dates, in lieu of the Duties of Customs now charged on the articles undermentioned, the following Duties of Customs shall be charged thereon, on importation into Great Britain or Ireland (that is to say):
On and after the fifth day of May, one thousand eight hundred and sixty-four—
Sugar—namely,
Candy, Brown or White, Refined Sugar, or Sugar, rendered by any process equal in quality thereto
the cwt. £0 12 10
On and after the sixteenth day of April, one thousand eight hundred and sixty-four—

Sugar—namely,
White Clayed Sugar, or Sugar rendered by any process equal in quality to White Clayed, not being refined, or equal in quality to refined . . . the cwt. £0 11 8

Yellow Muscovado and Brown Clayed Sugar, or Sugar rendered by any process equal in quality to Yellow Muscovado, or Brown Clayed, and not equal to White Clayed . . . the cwt. 0 10 6

Brown Muscovado Sugar, or Sugar rendered by any process equal in quality thereto, and not equal to Yellow Muscovado, or Brown Clayed . . . the cwt. 0 9 4

[*April* 14.]

WAYS AND MEANS—RESOLUTIONS—*continued*.

Any other Sugar not equal in quality to Brown Muscovado

		£	s	d
	the cwt.	£0		2
Cane Juice	the cwt.	0		7
Molasses	the cwt.	0		6
Almonds, paste of	the lb.	0		1
Cherries, dried	the lb.	0		1
Comfits, dry	the lb.	0		1
Confectionery	the lb.	0		1
Ginger, preserved	the lb.	0		1
Marmalade	the lb.	0	0	1
Plums preserved in Sugar	the lb.	0	0	1
Succades, including all fruits and vegetables preserved in Sugar, not otherwise enumerated	the lb.	0	0	1

—(*Mr. Chancellor of the Exchequer*.)

Motion, by leave, *withdrawn*.

Then on the Motion of *Mr. Chancellor of the Exchequer*—

(1.) *Resolved*,

That, towards raising the Supply granted to Her Majesty, on and after the undermentioned dates, in lieu of the Duties of Customs now charged on the articles undermentioned, the following Duties of Customs shall be charged thereon, on importation into Great Britain or Ireland (that is to say):

On and after the fifth day of May, one thousand eight hundred and sixty-four—

Sugar—namely,

Candy, Brown or White, Refined Sugar, or Sugar, rendered by any process equal in quality thereto, and Manufactures of Refined Sugar . . : the cwt. £0 12 10

On and after the sixteenth day of April, one thousand eight hundred and sixty-four—

Sugar—namely,

White Clayed Sugar, or Sugar rendered by any process equal in quality to White Clayed, not being refined, or equal in quality to refined . . . the cwt. 0 11 8

Yellow Muscovado and Brown Clayed Sugar, or Sugar rendered by any process equal in quality to Yellow Muscovado, or Brown Clayed, and not equal to White Clayed . . . the cwt. 0 10 6

Brown Muscovado Sugar, or Sugar rendered by any process equal in quality thereto, and not equal to Yellow Muscovado, or Brown Clayed . . . the cwt. 0 9 4

Any other Sugar not equal in quality to Brown Muscovado. the cwt. 2

		£	s	d
Cane Juice	the cwt.			7
Molasses	the cwt.			6
Almonds, paste of	the lb.			1
Cherries, dried	the lb.	0	0	1
Comfits, dry	the lb.	0	0	1

Confectionery, not otherwise enumerated . . . the lb. £0 1
Ginger, preserved . : the lb. 0 1
Marmalade . . . the lb. 0 0 1
Plums preserved in Sugar the lb. 0 0 1
Succades, including all fruits and vegetables preserved in Sugar, not otherwise enumerated the lb. 0 0 1

(2.) *Resolved*,

That, on and after the undermentioned dates, in lieu of the Drawbacks now allowed thereon, the following Drawbacks shall be paid and allowed on the undermentioned descriptions of Refined Sugar, on the exportation thereof to Foreign parts, or on removal to the Isle of Man for consumption there, or on deposit in any approved Warehouse, upon such terms and subject to such regulations as the Commissioners of Customs may direct, for delivery from such Warehouse as Ships' Stores only, or for the purpose of sweetening British Spirits in Bond (that is to say):

On and after the fifth day of May, one thousand eight hundred and sixty-four—

Upon Refined Sugar in loaf, complete and whole, or lumps duly refined, having been perfectly clarified, and thoroughly dried in the stove, and being of an uniform whiteness throughout; and upon such Sugar pounded, crushed, or broken in a warehouse approved by the Commissioners of Customs, such Sugar having been there first inspected by the Officers of Customs in lumps or loaves as if for immediate shipment, and then packed for exportation in the presence of such Officers, and at the expense of the exporter; and upon Candy . for every cwt. £0 12 10

Upon Refined Sugar unstoved, pounded, crushed, or broken, and not in any way inferior to the Export Standard Sample No. 1 approved by the Lords of the Treasury, and which shall not contain more than five per centum moisture over and above what the same would contain if thoroughly dried in the stove . . for every cwt. 0 12 2

And on and after the twenty-first day of April, one thousand eight hundred and sixty-four—

Upon Sugar refined by the Centrifugal, or by any other process, and not in any way inferior to the Export Standard No. 3 approved by the Lords of the Treasury for every cwt. 0 12 10

Upon Bastard, or Refined Sugar unstoved, broken in pieces, or being ground, powdered, or crushed, not in any way inferior to the Export Standard Sample No. 2 approved by the Lords of the Treasury for every cwt. 0 10 10

TABLE OF CONTENTS.

TABLE OF CONTENTS.

COMMONS, WEDNESDAY, APRIL 20.

LORDS, THURSDAY, APRIL 21.

COMMONS, THURSDAY, APRIL 21.

LORDS, FRIDAY, APRIL 22, 1864.

TABLE OF CONTENTS.

LORDS, MONDAY, APRIL 25.

MINUTES.]—Public Bills—*Second Read-ing* — Warehousing of British Spirits * (No. 46).

Select Committee—On Insane Prisoners Act Amendment, *nominated* (see p. 3).
Third Reading — The Consolidated Fund (£15,000,000) * (No. 54), and *passed*.

Their Lordships met; and having gone through the business on the paper, without Debate,

House adjourned at half past Five o'clock.

COMMONS, MONDAY, APRIL 25.

MINUTES.]—Select Committee—On Bank-ruptcy Act, *nominated* (see p. 1482).
Ways and Means—*Resolution* [April 21] *re-ported*.
Public Bills—*Ordered*—Court of Chancery (Ireland).
First Reading—Court of Chancery (Ireland) * [Bill 78].
Second Reading — Customs and Inland Re-venue [Bill 73]; Thames Conservancy [Bill 60]; Partnership Law Amendment [Bill 68].

Committed to Select Committee—Thames Con-servancy.
Committee — Civil Bill Courts (Ireland) *re-committed* [Bill 79]; Court of Chancery (Despatch of Business) (*Lords*) * [Bill 69]; Charitable Assurances Enrolments (*Lords*)* [Bill 72].
Report — Civil Bill Courts (Ireland); Court of Chancery (Despatch of Business) * ; Cha-ritable Assurances Enrolments (*Lords*) *.
Withdrawn—Penal Servitude Acts Consoli-dation * [Bill 23].

COMMONS, TUESDAY, APRIL 26.

COMMONS, WEDNESDAY, APRIL 27.

SUPPLY—Order for Committee read; Motion made, and Question proposed,
    " That Mr. Speaker do now leave the Chair :"—

UNITED STATES—SEIZURE OF THE " TUSCALOOSA"—
    Amendment proposed,
    To leave out from the word "That" to the end of the Question, in order to add the
    words "the instructions contained in the Despatch of the Duke of Newcastle to Sir
    P. Wodehouse, dated the 4th day of November, 1863, and which remain still unre-
    voked, are at variance with the principles of International Law," — (*Mr. Peacocke,*)—
    instead thereof   1777
    Question proposed, "That the words proposed to be left out stand part of
    the Question."
    After long Debate, Question put :—The House *divided ;* Ayes 219, Noes 185;
    Majority 34.

Main Question put, and *agreed to.*

SUPPLY *considered* in Committee :—Committee report Progress; to sit again
    this day.

Customs and Inland Revenue Bill [Bill 73]—

Bill *considered* in Committee   1859
                        (In the Committee.)
Clause 1 *agreed to.*
Clause 2—Amendment (*Mr. Crawford*); after short Debate, Amendment *withdrawn.*
Clause *agreed to.*
Remaining Clauses *agreed to.*
Schedule C.
Amendment (*Mr. Hennessy*)—Amendment *withdrawn.*
Bill *reported,* as amended; to be considered on *Monday* next, and to be
    printed. [Bill 82.]

Union Assessment Committee Act Amendment Bill—

On Motion of *Mr. Villiers,* Bill to amend the Union Assessment Committee Act, *ordered*
    to be brought in by Mr. Villiers and Mr. Gilpin :—Bill *presented,* and read 1°. [Bill 83.]
                        House adjourned at Two o'clock.

TABLE OF CONTENTS.

Page

LORDS, FRIDAY, APRIL 29.

COMMONS, FRIDAY, APRIL 29.

TABLE OF CONTENTS.

TABLE OF CONTENTS.

LORDS.

SAT FIRST.

THURSDAY, APRIL 21.

The Viscount Sidmouth, after the Death of his Father.

TOOK THE OATH.

TUESDAY, APRIL 12.

The Lord Bishop of Ossory.

COMMONS.

NEW WRITS.

MONDAY, APRIL 4.

For *Oxford City, v.* The Right Hon. Edward Cardwell, one of Her Majesty's Principal Secretaries of State.

WEDNESDAY, APRIL 6.

For *Lancaster Borough, v.* William James Garnett, Esq., Manor of Northstead.

Thursday, April 7.

For *Fifeshire*, *v.* James Hay Erskine-Wemyss, Esq., deceased.

Tuesday, April 12.

For *Devizes*, *v.* The Hon. W. W. Addington, now Viscount Sidmouth.

Friday, April 15.

For *Pontefract*, *v.* Hugh Culling Childers, Esq., Commissioner of the Admiralty.

Monday, April 18.

For *Merthyr Tydvil*, *v.* Henry Austin Bruce, Esq., Vice President of the Committee of Privy Council on Education.

NEW MEMBERS SWORN.

Wednesday, March 16.

Hertford County—Henry Edward Surtees, Esq.

Monday, April 4.

Coventry—Morgan Treherne, Esq.

Wednesday, April 6.

Armagh—John Matthew Stronge, Esq.

Monday, April 11.

Oxford City—The Right Hon. Edward Cardwell.

Friday, April 15.

Lancaster Borough—Edward Mathew Fenwick, Esq.

Monday, April 18.

Barnstaple—Richard Bremridge, Esq.

Tuesday, April 19.

Devizes—Sir Thomas Bateson, Baronet.

Thursday, April 21.

Pontefract—Hugh Culling Eardley Childers, Esq.

Friday, April 22.

Fifeshire—Sir Robert Anstruther, Baronet.

Wednesday, April 27.

Merthyr Tydvil—Right Hon. Henry Austin Bruce.

HANSARD'S

PARLIAMENTARY DEBATES,

IN THE

Sixth Session of the *Eighteenth Parliament* of the
United Kingdom of *Great Britain* and *Ireland*,
Appointed to meet 31 May 1859, and from thence Con-
tinued till 4 February 1864, in the Twenty-seventh
Year of the Reign of

HER MAJESTY QUEEN VICTORIA.

SECOND VOLUME OF THE SESSION.

HOUSE OF LORDS,

Tuesday, March 15, 1864.

MINUTES.]—Public Bills—*First Reading—*
Mutiny*.
Second Reading—Malt for Animals (No. 16);
Marine Mutiny*.
Referred to Select Committee—Insane Prisoners
Act Amendment* (No. 14).
Select Committee—Insane Prisoners Act Amend-
ment *appointed.* (List of Committee, *see* p. 3.)
Committee — Vestry Cess Abolition (Ireland)
(No. 19); Inclosure* (No. 25).
Report—Inclosure.

DENMARK AND GERMANY—IDENTICAL
NOTE OF AUSTRIA AND PRUSSIA.

QUESTION.

THE EARL OF ELLENBOROUGH :
My Lords, I wish to give notice, that
on the Motion for the adjournment of the
House on Friday, I shall call the attention
of your Lordships to the actual state of
affairs between Germany and Denmark.
In the absence to-night of the noble Lord
the Secretary of State for Foreign Affairs
and the Lord President of the Council, I
wish to ask the noble Duke (the Duke of
Somerset), Whether the identical Note that
appears in the newspapers of to-day from
Austria and Prussia, making an amended
proposal relative to an armistice and a

Conference, is authentic? The difference
between the present proposition and that
which was formerly made is, that the latter
was a separate proposal made by Prussia
and Austria severally, while the Note now
published is an identical proposition on the
part of both to the effect that the Danes
may elect either to have an armistice,
providing that there shall be a mutual
evacuation of the Island of Alsen by the
Danes and of Jutland by the allies, or an
armistice on the basis of the *uti possidetis.*
That is, in fact, a proposition to the effect
that hostilities shall cease, that the prizes
taken on both sides shall be restored, and
that the embargo upon ships on both sides
shall be taken off. Now, supposing this
Note to be authentic, I must express my
earnest hope that the Danish Government
will accept the proposal of an armistice
on the basis of the *uti possidetis.* With
respect to further operations at sea, I
think it very probable that at the present
moment the Danes have the temporary
advantage at sea. But great questions
must be decided on great and not on little
views. It is not possible that any advantage that Denmark may gain at sea can
have any effect on the ultimate result of
this war; and, therefore, I trust that she
will agree to that condition also, and that

we shall have the happiness to see the great Powers of Europe assembled in Conference with this armistice first established: for without the establishment of that armistice there can be no hope of a successful result from the Conference. And I do hope at the same time, that when Austria and Prussia forwarded that identical Note, they at the same time forwarded by telegraph instructions to Marshal Wrangel not to commit the army to any further military operations; for it will be a most criminal act if, while these Powers held out the hope of a pacific settlement, they do anything to endanger the lives of more men than have already unfortunately fallen in this most unrighteous war.

THE DUKE OF SOMERSET: In the absence of my noble Friend the Secretary for Foreign Affairs, I will only say that, without vouching for the exact words of the Note published to-day, the statement made is substantially correct. It would be very inconvenient for me, under present circumstances, to give any further answer to the question.

INSANE PRISONERS ACT AMENDMENT BILL—(No. 14.)—SELECT COMMITTEE.

THE LORD CHANCELLOR said, that as this Bill had been the subject of a good deal of discussion, the Government thought the best mode of dealing with it in that House was to refer it to a Select Committee.

Order of the Day for the House to be put into Committee *discharged*, and Bill referred to a Select Committee.

And on *Monday, April 25th*, the Lords following were named of the Committee—

Ld. Chancellor.	V. Eversley.
Ld. President.	L. Wodehouse.
D. Richmond.	L. Cranworth.
E. Carnarvon.	L. Wensleydale.
E. Romney.	L. Chelmsford.
E. Cathcart.	L. Kingsdown.

MALT FOR ANIMALS BILL—(No. 16.)
SECOND READING.

Order of the Day for the Second Reading read.

LORD STANLEY OF ALDERLEY, in the absence of the noble Lord the President of the Council, moved that it be read a second time *pro formâ*, with the understanding that the discussion should be taken on Thursday next.

Moved, That the Bill be now read 2ª.

The Earl of Ellenborough

LORD BERNERS said, that some provisions ought to be introduced into the Bill which would render it more acceptable to the agricultural classes, and prevent it from becoming a dead letter. He must be allowed to say that he did not believe the farmers were likely to avail themselves of its provisions, and he would, therefore, suggest that some modification should be made in the clauses which would render the measure more beneficial to the farmers whilst it would not materially injure the revenue. He would suggest an addition to Clause 2 to the following effect:—

"That every such maltster, on application in writing from any feeder of animals, that on a certain day he shall require a given quantity (not less than —— quarters) for the feeding of animals, shall give notice to the Excise officers to attend at the day and hour named, and see that such quantity of malt is duly mixed in his presence with the quantity of linseed meal, or other substance, as is required by this Act; and the exciseman shall there and then deliver to the said feeder of animals, or his servant, a certificate permitting the removal of such malt, to be used for feeding purposes only (subject to such fines or penalties as may be fixed by this Act); and shall deliver to such maltster a certificate allowing the drawback of the duty so sold and delivered."

LORD STANLEY OF ALDERLEY said, he really knew nothing of the details of the Bill, and therefore was unable to state the views of the Government. But the existing clauses had been carefully drawn, and alterations such as those contemplated by the noble Lord would scarcely be consistent with the precautions indispensable to be observed. The best course for the noble Lord would be to give notice of Amendments, which should be carefully considered.

EARL GREY felt bound to express his regret that the Bill had been introduced. With all the regulations that could be adopted, he believed it would be impossible to make the malt revenues under the new system as safe as they now were. He was sorry that Her Majesty's Government, with a view to the protection of those revenues from the agitation that was being raised against them, had brought in the Bill; and with still greater surprise and regret he should see that agitation countenanced by any gentleman calling himself a friend to the landed interests; for he was persuaded that no measure more injurious to the landed interests than the repeal of the malt duties could possibly be adopted by Parliament. What were the malt duties? It was altogether a delusion to suppose that they were paid by the farmer or the landed proprietor; they were paid neither by the one nor the other, but by the consumer of beer. At this moment, according to the relative prices of different kinds of corn, barley was the most remunerative crop that a farmer could grow; there was a market for any quantity the farmer could deliver, and he did not believe that the repeal of the malt duties would improve his position in that respect —on the contrary, any difference that resulted would probably consist in the importation of a greater quantity from abroad. But if the duties were repealed it was perfectly clear that a heavier charge would be thrown upon the landed interest in the shape of increased income tax—an impost falling most unfairly, land being the only interest which paid on the gross income instead of upon the net. No doubt it would be impossible to repair that injustice without giving room for evasion and destroying the efficiency of the law, but practically the proprietor of land contributed more largely to the income tax than the owner of any other income of equal amount. There could be no doubt that the repeal of the malt duty must necessarily lead to an increase of that impost. Of all the indirect taxes there was probably none so unobjectionable as the malt tax; for though it was an Excise duty it was not like the duty on bricks, or glass, or articles of that description, for it interfered with no manufacture capable of being carried on or susceptible of improvement upon a great scale. The production of malt was a very simple process—it was used only in connection with beer, and if the duty were taken off to-morrow he doubted whether any corresponding stimulus would be given to the trade. Then as to its effect upon the consumer. The duty fell upon an article of luxury; and though, no doubt, it would be very desirable to make beer cheap for the working man, there were many other articles—such as tea and sugar—that it would be still more desirable to cheapen. And if, under the name of facilitating the feeding of cattle with malt, we were to sweep away the whole of this revenue of £6,000,000, we should be driven irresistibly to make further reductions upon other articles, and a further increase of direct taxation. Our army and navy had to be maintained at great cost; any very large reductions of public income were, therefore, impossible. Therefore, those who were agitating against the malt duties were virtually agitating for the increase of the income tax. He hoped that this would be understood by those who took a real interest in the welfare of the owners and occupiers of land, and that no man who called himself a real friend to them would encourage this agitation. He thought it right, as one who had had some experience in the other House of Parliament of the mode in which taxes were discussed, to express his opinion upon this subject; but it would be a great satisfaction to him if the advice which he had ventured to give to the landed interest could be enforced by the far more powerful authority of the noble Earl who sat on the opposite side of the House (the Earl of Derby.)

THE DUKE OF ARGYLL said, he was glad that the noble Earl had taken the opportunity of expressing the opinion he entertained, which was no doubt shared by a great majority of the House, with respect to the retention of the malt duty. The noble Earl said that the Government, in order to meet some of the objections urged against the malt duty, had brought in a Bill which would prove dangerous to a large portion of the public revenue. He could assure his noble Friend that the Chancellor of the Exchequer would not have introduced the Bill had he not been assured by the highest practical authorities that he could do so without endangering an important source of revenue. But while we retain the tax it was desirable to give to the farmer every possible advantage which was consistent with the maintenance of the revenue. He (the Duke of Argyll) was himself connected with a large barley growing district in Scotland; and it often happened that in wet seasons barley was rendered useless for the higher purpose of malting; and in many such cases of damaged barley the farmers might take advantage of the permission given by this Bill to malt it for cattle. All the clauses of the Bill were specially directed to the protection of the revenue. The noble Lord opposite (Lord Berners) had given notice of his intention to move an Amendment; but he hoped their Lordships would not agree to any step which would diminish the securities provided for by the Bill.

THE EARL OF HARDWICKE said, that as the Bill was only to remain in force for five years it would, unless some such Amendment as that suggested by his noble Friend behind him was introduced into it, be entirely inoperative. Neither landlords nor tenants would construct malt houses for barley under this Bill, which could not be considered worth more than five years' purchase; and he therefore hoped that the Government would consider the Amendment before the House went into Committee.

LORD REDESDALE said, that the argument of the noble Earl on the cross benches (Earl Grey) would not hold, because we had of late years seen indirect taxes equal in amount to the malt duty taken off without their abolition necessarily leading to any increase of the income tax. Nor was it necessary that the malt tax should be totally abolished at once. If the surplus was not large enough to admit of the adoption of such a step, part of it might be remitted, and such partial remission would, he believed, lead to an increase of consumption, which would make up some of the loss to the revenue. If, therefore, the noble Earl's argument to the contrary was to be taken as valid, it was good against all reductions of taxation whatever. Both theoretically and practically the malt tax was the most unjust duty that could be levied. It was a duty levied upon one of the commonest productions of this country with regard to one of the commonest manufactures. It tended most seriously to prevent the brewing of good beer by the poor, who were thus prevented from obtaining the most nutritious and wholesome beverage which they could enjoy. There was no duty upon cider, nor upon any other of our home manufactures except spirits. He believed that it was most desirable to encourage the use of beer rather than spirits. The argument that the duty was paid by the consumer and not by the producer applied to almost every other tax. Was not the duty on printed cottons paid by the consumer? And yet it was the producers who procured its abolition. Was not the duty on beer paid by the consumer? And yet it was the brewers who got it taken off. The malt duty was indefensible both in principle and in practice, and some portion of revenue might desirably be sacrificed in order to effect its reduction. There was no reason why the duty should be dealt with as a whole. It ought to be treated in the manner most likely to contribute to the benefit of the people and to the ultimate abolition of what he must consider a most unjust tax.

LORD WODEHOUSE said, he did not join in the regret which had been expressed

by the noble Earl (Earl Grey), that the Bill should have been introduced at all; but he was disposed to think that if it was not amended so as to extend its operation beyond five years it would be inoperative. It was only fair to the farmers that the experiment should be tried, whether it was possible, while retaining the malt duties, to allow them to use malt for the feeding of cattle. He himself lived in a part of England where barley was an important agricultural produce. He did not understand his noble Friend on the cross benches, as the noble Lord the Chairman of Committees appeared to have done, to argue that because this tax was paid by the consumer they ought never to look to its abolition. His noble Friend pointed out that the tax fell principally upon the consumers, and was not of serious injury to the producers. He also called attention to the fact—and it was a most important one—that an important portion of the public revenue was raised from this duty, and that if it was swept away recourse must be had to an increase of the income tax. He was himself far from denying that the farmers might derive some benefit from the abolition of this tax; but there were several considerations which must limit that advantage. In the first place, there was no doubt that there would be a largely increased importation of barley, and probably also of malt. There was also the still more serious consideration that, although he would not go so far as to say that no more barley could be grown, he believed that on the best soils in the country, and with the best system of cultivation, it was doubtful whether you could get more barley than was now produced. These were considerations which the farmers ought to bear in mind. But there was another which was even still more important. If the malt tax was repealed, several other important branches of revenue would be affected. The spirit duties, the wine duties, and the malt duties were so intimately connected that you could not meddle with one without affecting the others. In his opinion it was exceedingly undesirable that an agitation should be got up against the malt tax, as if by repealing it great benefits would be obtained, without bearing in mind that its repeal must seriously injure the revenue of the country, and probably lead to the increase of the income tax—a tax which pressed more heavily than any other upon the farmer, and which it was not desirable to raise to a high pitch in time of peace, because by that means you would anticipate the use of a most powerful instrument for the raising of a large revenue in time of war.

Motion *agreed to :* Bill read 2ᵃ accordingly, and *committed* to a Committee of the Whole House on *Friday* next.

VESTRY CESS ABOLITION (IRELAND) BILL—(No. 19.)

SECOND READING.

House in Committee (according to Order).
(In the Committee.)
Clauses 1 to 3 *agreed to.*
Clause 4 (Guardians of Poor of Unions, &c., to provide Coffins for Interment of Poor Persons dying in such Union.)
Moved, To omit Clause 4.

THE EARL OF DONOUGHMORE *moved* the rejection of the 4th clause on the ground that the same provision had been fully discussed in Parliament two years ago, and rejected, and that practically the levying of vestry cess in Ireland for any purpose whatsoever was now restricted to certain parishes in the City of Dublin, and one or two others. Under those circumstances, it was proposed by the clause to throw an additional burden upon the whole of Ireland, by enabling the Boards of Guardians to levy a taxation for which there was no necessity, inasmuch as he never knew an instance in which any poor person had been buried without a coffin— a contingency against which the clause seemed intended to provide.

THE EARL OF ST. GERMANS said, that if the clause were omitted the corporation of Dublin would not unnaturally complain of having been unfairly treated, inasmuch as no compensation would be secured for those officers, whose places would be abolished under the Bill. The effect of the Amendment, if carried, indeed would probably render it inexpedient that the Bill should be proceeded with.

THE EARL OF CORK said, the object of the Bill was to abolish véstries in Dublin, and to provide compensation for the officers. He objected to a clause, affecting the whole country, being introduced into a Bill of this nature.

THE EARL OF DESART also opposed the clause. He thought it scarcely fair to subject all the ratepayers in Ireland to an unnecessary burden for the sake of compensating some sixty or seventy persons in Dublin.

THE EARL OF LEITRIM suggested that as their Lordships had had but a small opportunity of discussing the Bill, which was very important to Ireland, its further consideration should be postponed till after Easter.

After a few words from The Earl of DONOUGHMORE and The Earl of St. GERMANS,

On Question, That the Clause stand Part of the Bill, their Lordships *divided:* Contents 27 ; Not-Contents 34 : Majority 7.

Amendment *agreed to.*

Report thereof to be received on *Thursday* next.

CONTENTS.

Westbury, L. (*L. Chancellor.*)	Crewe, L.
	Dartrey, L. (*L. Cremorne.*)
Somerset, D.	De Tabley, L.
	Ebury, L.
Camden, M.	Foley, L. [*Teller.*]
	Hunsdon, L. (*V. Falkland.*)
Airlie, E.	Keane, L.
De Grey, E.	
Harrowby, E.	Panmure, L. (*E. Dalhousie.*)
Innes, E. (*D. Roxburghe.*)	
	Sefton, L. (*E. Sefton.*)
Saint Germans, E. [*Teller.*]	Seymour, L. (*E. St. Maur.*)
Sommers, E.	Stanley of Alderley, L.
	Sundridge, L. (*D. Argyll.*)
Stratford de Redcliffe, V.	Wodehouse, L.
Sydney, V.	Worlingham, L. (*E. Gosford.*)
Torrington, V. .	
Cranworth, L.	

NOT-CONTENTS.

Salisbury, M.	Chelmsford, L.
	Clements, L. (*E. Leitrim.*)
Derby, E.	Colchester, L.
Desart, E.	Colville of Culross, L.
Devon, E.	Delamere, L.
Graham, E. (*D. Montrose.*)	Dunsany, L.
Grey, E.	Feversham, L.
Hardwicke, E.	Inchiquin, L.
Lucan, E.	Lismore, L. (*V. Lismore.*)
Malmesbury, E.	
Stanhope, E.	Monson, L.
Tankerville, E.	Monteagle of Brandon, L.
Verulam, E.	Redesdale, L.
Exmouth, V.	Saltersford, L. (*E. Courtown.*)
Hawarden, V.	
Hutchinson, V. (*E. Donoughmore.*) [*Teller.*]	Silchester, L. (*E. Longford.*)
Belper, L.	Somerhill, L. (*M. Clanricarde.*)
Berners, L.	
Boyle, L. (*E. Cork and Orrery.*) [*Teller.*]	Sondes, L.

House adjourned at a quarter past Six o'clock, till To-morrow Four o'clock.

HOUSE OF COMMONS,

Tuesday, March 15, 1864.

MINUTES.]—PUBLIC BILLS—*First Reading*—
Borough Franchise* [Bill 47]; Jersey Court*
[Bill 48]; Registration of County Voters (Ireland)* [Bill 49]; Union Relief Aid Acts
Continuance* [Bill 50]; Poor Law (Ireland)
Acts Amendment [Bill 51].
Committee — Consolidated Fund (£4,500,000)*;
Consolidated Fund (£584,650)*.
Report—Consolidated Fund (£4,500,000)*; Consolidated Fund (£584,650)*; Chain Cables and
Anchors* [Bill 46], and *re-committed*.

DUTY ON FIRE INSURANCES.
QUESTION.

MR. HUBBARD said, he would beg to
ask the hon. Member for Dudley, Whether
he will postpone his Motion for a Bill to
reduce the Duty on Fire Insurances until
after the Budget?

MR. H. B. SHERIDAN said, in reply,
that the Notice of Motion which stood in
his name, and the Notice of Amendment
given by the Chancellor of the Exchequer,
raised the same issue which was submitted
to the House last year, and on which the
House expressed an opinion by a large
majority, that the Duty on Fire Insurances
should be one of the first duties repealed
or reduced. He thought he should be
wasting the time of the House if he again
brought forward the question without giving the Chancellor of the Exchequer an
opportunity in his statement on the Budget
of carrying out the expressed wishes of
the House, and he would therefore, with
the permission of the House, postpone his
Motion on the subject until after the Financial Statement of the Chancellor of
the Exchequer.

DOE PARK RESERVOIR, BRADFORD.
QUESTION.

MR. FERRAND said, he rose to ask
the Secretary of State for the Home Department, If he will direct the engineer
appointed to examine the Bradfield Reservoir to visit and report upon the Doe Park
Reservoir, belonging to the Corporation of
Bradford, which is in a leaky and dangerous state? He had, about two years ago,
called the attention of the right hon. Gentleman to the dangerous state of this Reservoir, when the right hon. Gentleman
communicated by telegraph with the Mayor
of Bradford, the reservoir being the property of the corporation. The answer of
the latter was, that care should be taken
to preclude the possibility of accident, but
since then the reservoir had been repeatedly filled, and the lives of the inhabitants
were in consequence in imminent peril.
He (Mr. Ferrand) saw the reservoir about
a month since, when it was leaking in
three places. ["Order!"] He thought
that, after what had happened at Sheffield,
he might be permitted to add a few words
in explanation of his Question. A month
since he saw this reservoir, when it was
quite full and leaking in three places, one
stream being sufficient to work a large
mill. He now asked, whether the right
hon. Gentleman would be so good as to
send the engineer who had been despatched
to Sheffield on to Bradford, which was only
a few miles distant, with orders to report
on the state of the reservoir at that place?

SIR GEORGE GREY stated, in reply,
that about two years ago the hon. Member
addressed to him a letter on the state of
the reservoir, which the hon. Gentleman
considered to be in a dangerous state.
In consequence, he communicated, not by
telegraph but by letter, with the Mayor
of Bradford, expressing a confident expectation that the corporation of that town
would take every measure in their power
with a view to insure the safety of the
public. He received an immediate answer,
describing what had been done with respect
to the reservoir at that time, and stating
that it was intended to have it carefully
examined by the engineer. A few days
afterwards he received a Report from the
engineer as to the measures taken, and
that Report appeared quite satisfactory.
From that time he had not heard one
word on the subject of the reservoir, and
he regretted that the matter had not
been brought under his notice earlier if the
hon. Gentleman thought that the reservoir
was again dangerous. He had received
a letter that day on the subject from the
hon. Gentleman, and he had written to
the Mayor of Bradford calling for a Report.

NATIONAL EDUCATION (IRELAND).
QUESTION.

SIR HUGH CAIRNS said, he wished to
ask the Chief Secretary for Ireland, When
the Returns relative to National Education
(Ireland), ordered in the present Session,
will be laid upon the table; for what reason the Annual Report of the Commissioners of National Education (Ireland) for
the year 1862 has not yet been presented

to Parliament ; and whether he will take steps to have that Report, and also the Report for 1863, laid upon the table before the Vote for National Education (Ireland) is moved. He also wished to know, whether there will be any objection to lay on the table any Official Communications which has passed between the Irish Secretary and the Education Commissioners on the subject of the recent alteration in the Rules with respect to Convent Schools ?

SIR ROBERT PEEL, in reply, said, all the Returns referred to would be laid on the table in the course of the evening. As to the Annual Report of the Commissioners for 1862, that was laid on the table of the House on the 23rd of July last year. With regard to the Report of 1863, he had learnt from the First Commissioner that the Annual Report, but not the Appendix, would be ready on the 1st of June ; and with respect to the correspondence between himself and the Commissioners on the subject, there was no objection to lay Copies on the table.

SIR HUGH CAIRNS said, he wished to know, whether the right hon. Baronet is aware that, in July last, under the name of a Report of the Commissioners, there was laid on the table what was called in that House a "dummy," and nothing in the shape of a Report was laid on the table. He desired to know, when the second Report will be laid on the table ?

SIR ROBERT PEEL said, he must admit that on the 23rd of July it was a "dummy" that was laid upon the table. It was at a time when Members were going away for the holydays. The Report was now laid on the table.

EXPENDITURE WITHOUT ACCOUNT.
QUESTION.

LORD ROBERT MONTAGU said, he would beg to ask Mr. Chancellor of the Exchequer, Whether a sum of money is ever issued by direction of the Lords of the Treasury as "Expenditure without Account ;" and, if so, in what manner the same is brought under the consideration of the Commissioners for the Audit of Public Accounts ; and whether the Expenditure is passed by them after due examination of the vouchers for the subordinate items of expenditure included in that sum. What he wanted to know was whether, if £10,000 were given to a person "without account," the Auditing Officer would have to put up simply with the receipt for that sum, or whether he could exact receipts for the various items of expenditure and follow the sum of £10,000 to its appropriation ?

THE CHANCELLOR OF THE EXCHEQUER said, he was at a loss to understand what the noble Lord meant by "Expenditure without Account," unless he meant expenditure upon interest, which was constantly going on. It was advances for various services, which were advances made to meet the exigencies of the public service before any final account could be rendered. In all cases where expenditure of that kind took place, the persons to whom it was made were strictly accountable to the Commissioners of Audit. It was the business of the Commissioners of Audit to see that proper vouchers were given.

THOMAS'S RIFLED CANNON.
QUESTION.

LORD FERMOY said, he would beg to ask the Under Secretary of State for War, Whether the trial of Mr. Lynal Thomas's system of rifling large guns is completed, and whether he has any objection to produce the Report of the trials ?

THE MARQUESS OF HARTINGTON said in reply, that in 1862 a large gun was constructed at Woolwich for the purpose of trying Mr. Lynal Thomas's system of rifling, on the distinct understanding that it was to be at that gentleman's own expense. A very large outlay had been incurred, which had not yet been paid by Mr. Thomas. The gun had been fired against iron plates, and Mr. Thomas had repeatedly requested that further trials should be made. The Ordnance Select Committee had, however, recommended that no more trials should take place against iron plates until the general merits of the gun had been more accurately determined. All experiments had since been suspended by order of Earl de Grey until an arrangement could be come to with the view of deciding whose property the gun really was at the present moment. During last year, Mr. Lynal Thomas was declared bankrupt. He had been allowed a certain time to pay for the gun manufactured for him at the Royal factory, and if he did not pay within that period, steps would be taken to determine who should have possession of the gun. It would, under present circumstances, be extremely inconvenient to publish the Report of trials which had not been concluded.

POOR LAW—CASUAL POOR.
QUESTION.

MR. KEKEWICH said, he wished to ask the President of the Poor Law Board, Whether his attention has been called to the great increase of applications for relief by the casual poor, especially in the Southern Districts; and whether he proposes to issue any instructions to the Boards of Guardians on the subject, or whether he thinks it desirable that all vagrants making application for relief should have their names entered in a register by the Police?

MR. C. P. VILLIERS replied, that his attention had been drawn to the applications for relief by the casual poor, but not to a great increase in their number, for that had not occurred. With respect to the southern districts, to which the hon. Member especially referred, they were usually classed as south-western and south-eastern, each division containing five counties, and being the subject of a separate Report. In the south-eastern division the number of vagrants relieved on the 1st July, 1863, was 286, and on the 1st of January, 1864, 214; and in the south-western 128 on the 1st of July, and 136 on the 1st of January. There was, therefore, a diminution in the first case, and in the other an increase of only eight. He did not propose to issue any instructions; but he had, during the winter, called the attention of the guardians in the metropolis to the subject, and had directed the Inspectors to do the same throughout the country. He had been induced to do so very much in consequence of the very satisfactory statement on the matter in Major General Cartwright's Report. The gallant officer said—

"Relief to vagrants has each year been reported upon, and, deeply impressed with the great advantage of placing this duty in the hands of the police, I venture again to bring it before the public. The appointment of trustworthy police officers to administer the tickets to the applicants for vagrant relief has been largely extended during the year, and as it becomes more universal it proves itself to be more beneficial . . . As far as practice informs me, nothing can be acting better than this system, both to the destitute wayfarer or the public; the former when in distress and want of relief immediately obtains it, the latter are protected by proper examination from the imposition of the professional mendicant."

The policemen were employed in about ninety unions at present as relieving officers; and he had directed the attention of the guardians to the importance of adopting the practice generally. As to the last part of the hon. Member's question, the Police, when employed as relieving officers, were already in the habit of entering on the register the names of vagrants who applied to them.

BISHOPRICS IN IRELAND.
QUESTION.

MR. DILLWYN said, he would beg to ask the Chief Secretary for Ireland, When a Return relative to Bishoprics, &c., in Ireland, ordered on the 7th of May last, and another relative to the Dioceses of Cashel, Emley, Waterford, and Lismore, ordered on the 5th of May last, and which, not having been presented to the House in the course of last year, were again ordered on the 9th of February last and the 12th of February last respectively, will be laid upon the table of the House?

SIR ROBERT PEEL, in reply, said, the Return ordered on the 7th of May would be laid on the table that evening. The other Returns had been made out in an improper form, and had been returned to Dublin for correction.

DIETARY IN WAKEFIELD PRISON.
QUESTION.

LORD FERMOY said, he would beg to ask the Secretary of State for the Home Department, What was the effect of the late change of dietary in Wakefield Prison on the Health of the Prisoners; and whether he will lay a Copy of the Correspondence on the subject, together with the Report of the Medical Officer, upon the table of the House?

SIR GEORGE GREY said, in reply, that a change had been made in the dietary in Wakefield Prison as an experiment. At the end of six months the visiting justices said that it had not been long enough in operation for them to form a decided opinion on it. The medical officer, however, gave such an unfavourable report of the effect of the diet in lowering the health of the prisoners and in increasing the mortality, that he had ordered it to be suspended. An inquiry was at present going on into the whole question of prison dietary?

LORD FERMOY: Upon whose Report was the dietary discontinued?

SIR GEORGE GREY: It was the Report of the Medical Officer to the Visiting Justices.

METROPOLITAN RAILWAYS.
QUESTION.

MR. CRAWFORD said, he wished to ask the President of the Board of Trade, in reference to the following passage in the Report of the Select Committee on Metropolitan Railways—

"The Committee are of opinion that some of the provisions of 'The Companies Clauses Consolidation Act, 1845,' require revision in relation to Metropolitan arrangements, and they recommend the introduction of a Bill for that purpose."

Whether it be the intention of the Government to introduce such a Bill ?

MR. MILNER GIBSON, in reply, said, the subject was under consideration. Such a Bill as was referred to would probably be introduced during the Session, but not until after the inquiry before the Select Committee on Metropolitan Railways had taken place.

COLLECTION OF TAXES BILL.
QUESTION.

In reply to Mr. HANBURY,

THE CHANCELLOR OF THE EXCHEQUER said, that in all likelihood he would propose that this Bill should be passed through Committee *pro formâ* on Friday, with the view of introducing some Amendments. No contested step would be taken on that evening.

MR. HUNT wished to know when the discussion would be taken on the principle of the Bill ?

THE CHANCELLOR OF THE EXCHEQUER said, it was not his fault if, on the second reading, there had been only a moderate amount of discussion. Any hon. Member who chose could again discuss the principle of the Bill, on the Motion for its re-committal, after it had been passed through Committee *pro formâ*.

THE CIVIL SERVICE ESTIMATES.
QUESTION.

LORD ROBERT MONTAGU said, the Secretary of the Treasury had given notice that he would ask for Votes on account of the Civil Service Estimates on Thursday. Only No. 6 and No. 2 had yet been presented. He trusted the right hon. Gentleman would give an undertaking that the course pursued the last year should not be taken again—namely, the voting of sums on account in the early part of the evening and the balance at a later period.

MR. PEEL said, the Vote on account which he proposed to move on Thursday was similar to the Vote taken last year at the same time. It was necessary to provide for the first quarter's payments in the ensuing year, and not to provide for any new service.

CASE OF COLONEL CRAWLEY.
PAPERS MOVED FOR.

MR. DUDLEY FORTESCUE rose to call attention to the court-martial on Colonel Crawley ; and to move an Address for copies. The hon. Member said, he had a painful sense of the disadvantages under which he laboured in doing so, for he was fully aware of the reaction of feeling which, at all events, in the higher classes of society had taken place on the subject ; and if he were at liberty to consult his own inclination, he should gladly have abstained from reverting to it. But after the distinct pledge which he gave last year, and after the strong appeal which had been made to him by Colonel Crawley himself, in his defence at Aldershot, when he said that some public explanation was due alike to the honour of Mr. Fortescue and to the dignity of Parliament, he felt it was impossible to remain altogether silent. Perhaps he had the stronger claim to the indulgence of the House from the opportunity, which he sought some time ago, having been denied him of explaining and vindicating in the leading organ of the press his original statement, an opportunity which, if it had been afforded to him, would in all probability have saved both himself and the House from the infliction of the present address. At the outset, however, he wished to disclaim any intention of calling in question the verdict of the late court-martial. That verdict he believed to have been honestly arrived at. There was a conflict of evidence, on which, in accordance with the just and well recognized principles of our law, the construction most favourable to the accused might fairly be put ; and whatever, after a closer study of that evidence than probably any other Member had thought it worth his while to bestow upon it, his own individual opinion might be, he was not in any way called upon to pronounce that opinion there, nor should he presume to obtrude it upon the House. In any remarks, therefore, he might make on the present occasion, he wished once more distinctly to disclaim any intention to reflect upon Colonel Crawley, or to impugn the decision of that tribunal before which he had been tried and acquitted. But as the acquittal of a prisoner arraigned for certain acts was quite compatible with the commission of those acts by other parties, though the person accused might have been free from all responsibility for them, and as the language which had been held respecting his statements, and of which he might take as a sample the expression used in another place of "a ridiculous delusion," had placed him on his defence, he trusted he should not appeal in vain to the House to give him a hearing while he stated why, though prepared to modify, he could not retract his original statement altogether. Now, in the first place, great exaggeration had been imputed to his description of the quarters in which Sergeant Major Lilley was confined, and great pains had been taken to show that they were spacious and commodious beyond the average of those provided for soldiers of his rank. Such really appeared to have been the case with respect to the quarters in which Sergeant Major Lilley was first confined ; but he begged to remind the House that his remarks were intended to apply solely to those to which the prisoner was removed, and in which he died. The fact of Sergeant Major Lilley having occupied two distinct sets of quarters, differing so widely in the amount of accommodation they afforded, had given rise to much misconception, and had led him into various errors of detail, such as must almost inevitably arise in describing events in the absence of eye-witnesses, and at a distance of several thousand miles from the scene of their occurrence. Considering the distance of India from England, he did not think that the slight errors and inaccuracies into which he had fallen were much to be wondered at, and they were much less surprising when one remembered the amount of error and mis-statement into which those parties had been betrayed who, from being on the spot, had the best possible opportunities of insuring absolute correctness in their assertions. For instance, Sir Hugh Rose stated in one of his despatches, on the authority of communications from Mhow, that the first quarters occupied by Sergeant Major Lilley consisted of three rooms, and that his second quarters consisted of two rooms and a verandah on each side. The plans produced at the court-martial showed that the first quarters, instead of only three, contained five rooms ; and that what was called a second room in the

last quarters was nothing but a small enclosed verandah, six feet wide, a mere passage in fact, in which the sentry was posted. Again, the Assistant Adjutant General, Major Champion, who was at Mhow during the whole period of the arrest, and through whom all the correspondence relative to it passed, when examined at Aldershot, with the plans and models before him, not only made several mistakes as to their dimensions, but actually stated that when he left Mhow, the quarters in which Sergeant Major Lilley died, were occupied by another married man ; and it was only on the following day that the fact was extracted from him, that the man referred to occupied, in addition, the whole of the adjoining quarters, or more than double the amount of accommodation allotted to Lilley and his wife. After so striking an example of official inaccuracy, he thought he might claim plenary absolution for any mistake into which, at so great a distance from the spot, and with such inferior opportunities of ascertaining the truth, he might have fallen. It would be recollected that in speaking of the inconvenience and suffering inflicted upon Lilley and his wife, by the position in which the sentry was posted, he had made a statement which naturally excited the greatest horror and indignation throughout the country. That statement, undoubtedly, required some modification. The same cause to which he had already referred—the change of quarters during the arrest—had misled him to a certain extent on this point ; but it was to be remembered that the fact of the sentry having been posted within two feet from his wife's bed was sworn to by Lilley, before the Mhow Court Martial, in the presence of Colonel Crawley, who did not dispute it, but, on the contrary, distinctly admitted it in his official reply, when he said the fault lay with the adjutant. Now he (Mr. D. Fortescue) had applied that statement unwittingly to the second quarters, whereas, in reality, it applied to the first. These, it appears, were provided with the ordinary conveniences of a dwelling, while the second were entirely destitute of them. To the extent, therefore, involved in the removal of the sentry to the adjoining passage, instead of being in the same room, that statement must be modified. It only remained for him to express his regret if, either from any defect in the information supplied to him, or from any unconscious perversion of it

Mr. Dudley Fortescue

on his part, he had been led, in however small a degree, to overstate the facts of the case, and to add one darker shade to a picture which, in his opinion, assuredly required no such assistance.

But, turning from these details, he could not sit down without saying a word on the subject of the arrest itself. The question of the illegality of the arrest, involving, as it did, no less a principle than the competency of an officer to suspend at his own will and pleasure the clear and distinct provisions of the Articles of War, he believed was now, to most persons, by far the most serious subject for consideration. It would be recollected that the Horse Guards, in framing their charges against Colonel Crawley, had carefully limited themselves to the details of the arrest, leaving out of view the much graver question involved in the arrest itself. That course, he was certain, had given rise to very general dissatisfaction. On the subject of arrest the language of the Articles of War was plain and explicit. The Articles provided that no officer or soldier was to be kept in arrest or confinement beyond a period of eight days without being brought before a court-martial. [" No, no !" *and cheers.*] He would be glad to be corrected by hon. Gentlemen opposite if he were wrong in his reading of the Articles, but he contended that any officer who kept a soldier in arrest for more than eight days without trial was liable to be cashiered. ["No, no!" "Read the Article," *and cheers.*] What, then, were the circumstances of this case ? Three non-commissioned officers, who had been regularly subpœnaed as witnesses for the defence of a prisoner on trial at Mhow, were summoned, before they could give their evidence, before their commanding officer, in his own house, and after a very unusual private examination were put under arrest, and kept in close arrest for several weeks, on a vague charge of conspiracy, which his Royal Highness the Commander-in-Chief, after a perusal, he presumed, of all the documents, had declared to be without a shadow of foundation. It was true this plain and outspoken expression of opinion had been somewhat qualified in one of the later and contradictory Memorandums issued from the Horse Guards ; but, at all events, His Royal Highness had never retracted the condemnation he had so strongly expressed upon the course pursued in keeping three non-commissioned officers in

arrest without bringing them to trial. He was quite aware that an attempt had been made to justify that high-handed and arbitrary act on the ground of necessity. In the defence at Aldershot the following language was used:—

" It was a question of mutiny or no mutiny."

" A crisis had arrived ; the danger was imminent ; one step more and the flame might have kindled in the ranks, and the famous regiment of the Inniskilling Dragoons would have broken out into open mutiny."

And again—

" Close arrest may be a severe measure, but it is better than blowing your soldiers from the guns."

No doubt, if reduced to such a Hobson's choice as that, it was ; but did any one really believe that such an alternative was ever dreamt of ? Did any one believe that the Inniskilling Dragoons, as gallant and loyal a regiment as ever wore Her Majesty's uniform, was really on the brink of mutiny, that there was ever a question of blowing any of them from the guns ? Neither the evidence nor the documents gave any indication of such a state of things. He saw opposite an hon. and gallant Officer (Captain Archdall) who had served in that corps, and he would ask him whether he was prepared to endorse that statement ? Did the confidential inspection Reports, for which he had moved, and which he was sure his noble Friend below him (the Marquess of Hartington) would be eager to produce, give any indication of such a state of things ? If so, it was the strangest commentary upon them that an officer who had brought the regiment to such a state of disorganization should have been appointed to the 4th Dragoons, when that regiment was just emerging from the crisis of the court-martial on Captain Robertson. The only offence alleged against the non-commissioned officers was founded upon their reading of the defence of Mr. Smales, a proceeding which, if he had rightly understood the answer of his right hon. Friend the other night, they had as clear and unquestionable a right to take, as Colonel Crawley had to communicate freely with his own witnesses on his own trial ; and he believed that the attempt to stifle all communication between Paymaster Smales and his witnesses was one of the many grounds which had led to the reversal of the decision of the notorious Mhow Court Martial. The other offence alleged against the sergeant-majors was the unsupported assertion of one of their comrades that they had used improper language in speaking of their commanding officer. The credence due to that assertion might be judged of from the fact that Sir William Mansfield, after going through all the documents bearing upon it, stated that the men could not be put on their trial, and yet for weeks after the receipt of that letter they were kept in confinement, with what deplorable consequences everybody was now acquainted. The question now was, Who was to blame for all that? It appeared that the sanction and approval of his superiors had absolved Colonel Crawley in the matter of the arrest, while the verdict of the court-martial acquitted him of undue severity in its enforcement. The result was, that for all that had occurred no one was responsible, no one was to blame. He was sure that that view of the case was not acquiesced in by the country; he was certain it had given rise to great and general dissatisfaction. It had confirmed the general distrust in courts-martial and the administration of military justice. It had strengthened the general impression that in any issue between an inferior and his superior officer every principle of justice, every consideration of fair play, was postponed and rendered subordinate to the one paramount object of what was called "supporting authority." How false and erroneous such ideas of supporting authority were, he need hardly stop to discuss. In that House there were hon. and gallant Gentlemen who had themselves held command, some of whom were now commanding regiments with distinction and success. He appealed to them whether their experience had not shown that the best and surest mode of maintaining their authority was to inspire every officer and private soldier under them with a full reliance on their strict and impartial justice —with a perfect confidence that the Articles of War were in their hands no instrument of uncertain and arbitrary application, applicable in all their severity as against the private soldier, but powerless, and capable of being wholly set aside, if their provisions affected his superior officer? That a feeling of distrust, such as he had described, generally existed, must be patent to every one who had either studied the language of the press on this subject, or listened to the comments of that outer world which lay beyond the circle of the contribution to the Crawley Defence Fund. Not long ago he had read a letter sent to a newspaper on

Mr. Dudley Fortescue

this subject, the authenticity of which, as the production of a non-commissioned officer, was guaranteed by the editor of the paper. That letter put the case so clearly, and yet so temperately, in the point of view from which it was regarded by the inferior ranks of the army, that it deserved the serious attention of all who had the interests of that service at heart. The writer expressly avoided what might be called the sensational part of the question, and confined himself strictly to the points involved in the arrest; and, after indicating how each successive step of that arbitrary and illegal proceeding had obtained the approval, first of Major General Farrell, then of Sir William Mansfield, and afterwards of Sir Hugh Rose, he described, in forcible language, how the Articles of War —the *habeas corpus* of the army, the soldier's only protection against the unlimited abuse of the authority of those above him —had been set at defiance and trampled under foot by those who were most strictly bound to maintain them; he showed how detrimental to the interests of the service such a course must be; how it must discourage recruiting, and tend to neutralize the good effects of all that system of rewards and bounties by which, of late years, the Horse Guards had endeavoured to encourage the deserving and well-conducted soldier. And finally, expressing, as he said, the sentiments of every non-commissioned officer with whom he had conversed — and they were many — the writer testified from his own experience, both as a private and as a sergeant, that it was the almost universal feeling of the ranks that it was worse than useless to complain of any wrong suffered from a superior officer, or to expect redress for an injustice sustained at his hands. Such a feeling, if it really prevailed among so important and influential a class as the non-commissioned officers, the very mainstay of discipline in the army, the indispensable link, as our army is constituted, between the officer and the soldier, was a grave matter for consideration. He need hardly remind the House how the whole of our army depended for its supply of men on voluntary enlistment, nor how in these times of rapidly increasing material prosperity, when every day new and tempting avenues of employment presented themselves to those classes on whom we relied for recruits, it was more than ever necessary not only to multiply inducements to attract them into the ranks, but, above all, to beware of repelling them from enlistment by the impression, that there existed no protection for the person of the soldier, such as the common law of the land cast around that of every one of Her Majesty's meanest subjects. He believed that the mischief which had been done by all that unhappy business was incalculable. He believed that the death of Sergeant Major Lilley and the illegal imprisonment of his comrades would for many a day supply a fruitful theme for the publichouse agitator, and furnish a powerful antidote to the blandishments of the recruiting sergeant. He believed it would take years of strict and impartial administration at the Horse Guards to counteract those evil effects and to restore that confidence in military justice, which, if it ever existed, must, by the circumstances to which he had referred, have been shaken to its very foundations. He had no wish to see Colonel Crawley placed again on his trial, nor Major General Farrell, nor Sir William Mansfield, nor Sir Hugh Rose placed upon theirs. But he did hope that their recent experience would not have been lost on any one of them. And if the public scandal which had been caused by these events, and which no verdict of acquittal, no social, and no financial triumph on the part of one of the chief actors in them could do away with—if it awakened in the minds of the military authorities a deeper sense of responsibility, a firmer determination to do right and justice to all, no matter at what cost to individuals, no matter at what apparent sacrifice of authority ; but, most of all, if it should lead, as he did not despair that it might, to some sweeping and radical change in those cumbrous and antiquated forms of procedure, with their fatal temptations to perjury, and their fatal experience, how readily those temptations were succumbed to, then the late court-martial, costly and barren of results as many might think it, would have conferred great and lasting benefit on the army. The hon. Member then moved for the papers, according to his notice.

MR. H. R. GRENFELL rose to second the Motion. He should have preferred rising at a somewhat later stage of the debate if his hon. Friend had not communicated to him his intention to call the attention of the House to some points in the late court-martial, and also to make some personal explanations with regard to his own conduct in the matter. That, he thought, left it open for an independent Member to say something as to what the duties of that House were with respect to these unfortunate occurrences. He was aware that it was most absurd for a civilian to say anything whatever on subjects of military discipline ; it was, perhaps, still more absurd for gallant officers to attempt to attain their objects by resorting to any legal quibbles of whatever description ; but it was most absurd of all, for a man who was neither a soldier nor a lawyer to attempt to throw any light on a question which, in its military features, might puzzle an Adjutant General, and in its legal aspects might call for the interposition of an Attorney General. His only excuse for interfering in the matter was that he was a taxpayer, and the representative of a large body of taxpayers. He had a right to know—and at some time he might perhaps be called upon to give an explanation —of the reasons for the Return he held in his hand, certifying that £18,000 had been spent on this court-martial. Every one who had listened to his hon. Friend's speech must feel that it was utterly impossible for him to have made the statements he did last year without being himself firmly convinced that, to a certain extent, they were true. He was sure also that his hon. Friend was not the man likely to make statements without having taken the best means he could to find out whether those who had given him information were or were not worthy of credit. But the best justification of the course which his hon. Friend then pursued was the speech made by the noble Marquess (the Marquess of Hartington) last year, and which, in fact, scarcely differed from the speech then made by his hon. Friend. The best justification for his subsequent course was to be found in the admissions made by the Judge Advocate General in that House, and by the Secretary of State for War in another place. Those admissions were, first, that the arrest was illegal ; and secondly, that the court-martial at Mhow was unfair ; and the statement made by the Secretary of State for War was, that if any one was to blame for the information as to the falsity of the charges of cruelty not having been given to the House last year it was Colonel Crawley—who, so long as he thought he could use the fact of this cruelty as a weapon against his adjutant, took no pains to refute the charge, but who, when he found that weapon was a boomerang which would recoil on himself, declared, in his own defence, that the cruelty had never existed. Like his hon. Friend he should be sorry to question the verdict of the court-martial—he was quite certain it had been arrived at after a fair hearing of the evidence which was brought before it; but, although Colonel Crawley should be considered not guilty on that evidence, he was morally responsible for the illegality of the arrest, and also for being a principal party to an unjust court-martial. He hoped that some hon. and gallant Member would tell the House what those who objected to the course adopted by the military authorities in this country would have done had they been in their position? Would they have refused the court-martial on Colonel Crawley? He very much doubted it. It was well known that there were different opinions as to the best mode of administering the army in this country. Some thought it ought to be administered absolutely by the Horse Guards; others, that it should be administered by the Secretary of State for War, with a Board of military officers around him; others thought that the military administration was bound to consult certain irresponsible authorities who were supposed to have a monopoly of the expression of feelings of the officers. For himself, he maintained the Commander-in-Chief was bound to see justice done to all ranks of the army. His Royal Highness was not only the Commander-in-Chief of generals, colonels, majors, and captains, but also of non-commissioned officers and privates—and he was bound to consider the feelings of one class as much as those of the other. He (Mr. H. R. Grenfell) would go further than that, and say he believed that if all the colonels, majors, and captains in the army were swallowed up to-morrow by an earthquake, the Commander-in-Chief would have no difficulty in finding very efficient officers to supply their places; but if the same earthquake swallowed up all the non-commissioned officers of the army, officers would find very great difficulty in finding men to substitute for them. Therefore he believed the Commander-in-Chief was right in ordering this court-martial, because it showed that he had due consideration for the feelings and wrongs of the non-commissioned officers in the army equally with those of the superior ranks. But if that were true of the Commander-in-Chief, it was still more the case of the Secretary of State. He (Mr. H. R. Grenfell) could not forget that the Secretary of State for War had

Mr. H. R. Grenfell

once been a liberal Member in that House, and that, when he discussed the subject of promotion by purchase in the army, he founded almost all his arguments on the efficiency of non-commissioned officers, and the very few rewards vouchsafed to them. There could, therefore, have been no excuse for the noble Earl if, on the first occasion that presented itself of injustice done to non-commissioned officers, he had thrown around the delinquent the mantle of his dignity, and interposed between the victim of that wrong and the light of justice that cold shade of the aristocracy about which he was wont to be so fluent. The question now before the House was, whether they should call on the Government to produce any further papers with reference to this court-martial. He could not help thinking they had got almost enough papers on this subject. But he confessed he was somewhat astonished to find the right hon. and gallant General the Member for Huntingdon (General Peel) had moved that the House should declare it had had enough papers, seeing that, at an early day of the Session, the hon. and gallant Member placed a notice on the paper asking for the production of a very voluminous pamphlet on this subject. There was nobody admired more than he (Mr. Grenfell) did the pamphlets of the gentleman in question, who had written on various subjects, and many hon. Gentlemen opposite would do well to read some of his lucubrations on international law; but he had never before heard in that House of any Member asking for the production of a paper of an advocate—an *ex post facto* argument—after the whole case was finished. It appeared to him, that if all the papers connected with the case were produced before the House, it would become very much like the Schleswig-Holstein question, and they would all get very much confused in looking them over. He had stated that he thought there were certain public considerations, apart from Colonel Crawley and apart from his hon. Friend (Mr. Dudley Fortescue), that it would be a very good thing for the House to notice. His hon. Friend had made some allusion to those points, and he trusted the House would not think he was dwelling too long upon the subject if he ventured to express a hope that they would receive an assurance from the Government that the whole question of courts-martial would be taken under their consideration. He was quite certain that the working of that tribunal was eminently unsatisfactory to the public. He need not call attention to the Aldershot court-martial, which seemed to him to be somewhat analogous to a case which occurred some time ago in our Lunacy Court —he meant the Wyndham case, in which from, he would not say the incompetency, but the small calibre, of the Judge—it was found that the counsel on each side took every sort of liberty. But in that case it seemed to him that justice did not suffer, because the liberties were taken on both sides, and the only people who suffered were the unfortunate litigants. But in the case now under consideration, he thought the liberties were all taken on one side. On one side there was the gentleman connected officially with the prosecution ; the official prosecutor was an officer highly distinguished in Her Majesty's service, but he believed he was no great judge of the law of evidence ; and he (Mr. Grenfell) was informed that the counsel for the prosecution was not even assisted by a solicitor. On the other side, there was an enormous array of legal talent. There was a member of that House, a Chancery lawyer, the writer of the pamphlet and a solicitor, and there was also the prisoner himself, who, after all, must have known more about the case than anybody else. He hoped, therefore, they should have an assurance from the Government, that the constitution of tribunals of this kind should be taken into consideration. There was one more subject to which he wished to make an allusion, and that was the consequence to officers of giving evidence. They had had placed in their hands a memorandum of his Royal Highness the Commander-in-Chief on the late court-martial, in which the reasons were given for the dismissal of Major Swinley from his regiment. He did not wish to pass any opinion upon this document, but he apprehended that it was the duty of Major Swinley to tell the whole truth — and he thought it would have been much better, if it were to be considered part and parcel of military discipline that such a memorandum should be sent out at the conclusion of a court-martial, at all events that it should not be laid on the table of the House, where it would be sure to meet with some discussion. He hoped that the case of Major Swinley would be taken into consideration by the Government. He was informed, and as he had seen the story in the newspapers there could be no indiscretion in alluding to it, that the only portion of Major Swinley's evidence which might appear to have shown an *animus* against his commanding officer was given on his return into the court for the purpose of filling in a certain expletive which he need not name in his evidence; that he did not so return of his own accord, but was called upon in terms which no officer or gentleman could refuse to obey, to go back and complete his evidence. He (Mr. Grenfell) had searched in vain through the evidence of that officer for anything like *animus* with that one exception ; and he hoped, therefore, that the House would be assured by the Government that some justice should be done to Major Swinley. He knew it would never do for that gallant officer to go back into the same regiment with Colonel Crawley—but he might be placed in some other regiment. Before he sat down he would appeal to hon. and gallant Members who had had the honour of commanding regiments, and would ask any of them whether, if they were placed in the same position as Colonel Crawley, they would have acted in the way that that officer had done ? He would ask, whether any of them believed that there was anything like a conspiracy in the regiment ? If they really believed there was a mutiny, then, of course, there was an end of the question ; but he had not yet seen a tittle of evidence to show that anything of the kind existed. In conclusion, he should only express his hope that Her Majesty's Government would be able to give the House some satisfactory statement respecting the points he had referred to, and also that some hon. and gallant Gentleman would tell the House what he would have done had he been placed in circumstances similar to those in which Colonel Crawley was placed. He would further hope that the Government would give some intimation that in witnesses giving evidence before courts-martial, truth was the thing necessary, and not the favour of sergeant, colonel, or even of Commander-in-Chief.

Motion made, and Question proposed,

" That an humble Address be presented to Her Majesty, that She will be graciously pleased to give directions that there be laid before this House, Copies of a Letter from Lieutenant Colonel Crawley, announcing, for the information of Sir William Mansfield, the arrest of Sergeant Majors Lilley, Duval, and Wakefield, on a charge of conspiracy ; together with any Documents in support of such charge.

" Of the last half-yearly Confidential Inspection Report on the 6th Dragoons, prior to Colonel Shute's resigning the command.

" And, of first half-yearly Confidential Inspection Report subsequent to Colonel Crawley's assuming the command of that regiment."—(*Mr. Dudley Fortescue.*)

LORD LOVAINE, who had given notice of an Amendment, to move an Address for Copy of Correspondence and Legal Opinions forwarded by Sir William Mansfield from India to the Secretary of State for War and the Commander-in-Chief, relating to the legality of the Mhow Court Martial, said, Sir, I have had the advantage of having served some few years in Her Majesty's army; I feel, therefore, that I am not altogether disqualified from entering into this Question, and giving an opinion upon the case. I am perfectly well aware that it is some time since I retired from the service, and that my experience does not quite justify me in trespassing very long upon the attention of the House. There is, however, some advantage in knowing something of military discipline when we come to discuss a question of this sort. Now, as regards the case of the hon. Member who brought forward this Motion, and the statements of the hon. Gentleman who seconded it, I have two or three observations to make. In the first place, the hon. Member who commenced the discussion said, that he did not intend to go into the evidence or impugn in any way the result of the courtmartial at Aldershot; nevertheless it appeared to me that the hon. Gentleman did comment upon the evidence, and tried to make out that the manner in which the place where Sergeant Major Lilley was confined had been wrongly described. To that I give a complete contradiction. If there were any truth in the statement of the witnesses it was evident that the bungalow in which Sergeant Major Lilley was confined had one small room, one large room, and two verandahs communicating with one another. The hon. Gentleman said he was partially mistaken in what he had said regarding the position of the sentry over his prisoner. I think the hon. Gentleman might have gone further, and said that he was grossly mistaken in the matter. It was clearly proved that the sentry had never obtruded himself upon Mrs. Lilley, and that he never saw her. The witness was asked whether he saw the bed in which the Sergeant Major and Mrs. Lilley slept; and his answer was that he could not see it, as there was a screen between him and

the door leading into the bedroom. There was no complaint whatever on this subject made to Colonel Crawley, except the first complaint after the sentry had been posted in room No. 2 of the first bungalow, nor could she be seen in the second bungalow. Then the hon. Member says that according to the military law no soldier can be kept in confinement for more than eight days without a court-martial. If the hon. Gentleman would but read a little further upon the subject he would find that he is mistaken. The real fact is, that according to military law no soldier shall be kept eight days in confinement without a charge of some military offence being brought before a higher authority, with a view to his being brought to a court-martial. ["No, no!"] I believe that that is so. And if that be the case I contend that the law has been carried out in the present instance. Before the expiration of eight days' confinement of the Sergeants Major, the charge was sent in to the Commander-in-Chief, and they were continued in confinement until the receipt of a letter from Sir William Mansfield ordering them to be released. Up to that moment, at all events, it must be admitted that the confinement was legal. The hon. Gentleman then said that the Sergeants Major were kept six weeks in confinement. Now what is the case? They were imprisoned the 26th April. The receipt of the letter from Sir William Mansfield ordering their release was the 6th May; and, therefore, the only charge of illegality of confinement could apply to the period between the 26th April and the 6th May, which was three weeks instead of six. Now, I think it would be well if the hon. Gentleman, when making charges against a man who might have erred in the performance of his duty, had taken care to be well informed as to the facts, and had recollected that Colonel Crawley had a most arduous duty to discharge, under circumstances of great responsibility.

MR. DUDLEY FORTESCUE: When I said six weeks I meant that six weeks was the duration of the whole of the imprisonment, and that it was illegal because these men had never been brought to trial at all.

LORD LOVAINE: If the meaning of the Articles of War be that the prisoner should not be confined eight days without the charge being laid before the Commander-in-Chief, the confinement in this case was legal. The moment the Commander-in-Chief had reported on the subject it ceased to be legal to keep the prisoner in confinement without bringing him before a court-martial or discharging him. So far as my recollection goes that reading of the law is correct. Then, as to what has been stated in respect to Major Swinley, I have no particular observation to make, except this :—When the acquittal took place it does appear to me that the actions of a man who has been twice reproved before the Mhow Court Martial and once before the Aldershot Court Martial for the *animus* he had shown in his manner of giving his evidence—when these things are recollected, I think it would be just as well if the hon. Member had been a little more moderate in his remarks upon the man who has been acquitted, and shown a little less affection for a man whose conduct has been reproved. I can only say, once for all, that Colonel Crawley has been brought to trial, not for the illegal confinement of those prisoners, as the hon. Gentleman who seconded the Motion appears to think. [Mr. GRENFELL: I never said anything of the kind.] If I misunderstood the hon. Gentleman I am sorry for it. Colonel Crawley has been tried, and exposed to a great degree of obloquy. Few men have suffered more in his position. He has been prosecuted—I might almost say persecuted —before the court-martial for an alleged crime with a virulence and an animosity which I really believe to be unparalleled since the days of Admiral Byng! Is it not time that Colonel Crawley should enjoy the advantages of his full and complete acquittal, instead of suggesting doubts as to his possible criminality? The Motion which stands in my name relates to the Mhow Court Martial, because I think that the authorities in India have not received fair play in that matter. I observed, in the report of the court-martial on Colonel Crawley, that charges have been made most distinctly of unfair dealing, illegality, incompetence and of injustice on the part of the Indian authorities. We have never seen the reply given to these charges, although such a reply certainly exists, as is proved by the letter of Sir Hugh Rose, dated the 6th of April, 1863. It is certain, however, that the trial was fully approved of by the Commander-in-Chief. The Judge Advocate, indeed, stated that that trial was not illegal, but that it was unfair. Now, I confess that I do not understand the great difference which exists

between what is illegal and what is unfair, and I should be glad if the learned Gentleman would enlighten me upon the subject. But this is very certain that, whether it was illegal, or whether it was unfair, the Commander-in-Chief at home wrote his approval of it in his Memorandum of the 18th of December, 1862. In that document his Royal Highness stated, that the court had come to the proper verdict as regarded the insubordinate tone of the letter written by Paymaster Smales to his commanding officer ; and he stated that in this decision he was fortified by the opinion of the Judge Advocate General. Again, on the 3rd June, 1863, six months after the events had occurred, the noble Lord the Under Secretary of State for War stated that the proceedings of the Mhow Court Martial had been submitted to the Judge Advocate General, who gave his opinion that the sentence was legal. The extraordinary part of the case is—that after it had been submitted to the Judge Advocate General, and after an opinion expressed upon it by the Commander-in-Chief, who passed one of the highest rebukes ever passed on a commanding officer on Colonel Crawley, it was suddenly discovered, on the 3rd June, that the proceedings were unfair and irregular, and that finding of the court-martial must be reversed. One of the reasons given for so doing was the discredit thrown unfairly on the evidence of certain witnesses. Surely this was a question for the court itself, but if it was wrong, it was certainly a most singular coincidence that the court-martial at Aldershot, as well as that at Mhow, agreed in commenting severely on the very irregular and evasive manner in which the evidence of these witnesses was given. According to the papers, the confinement of the witnesses was another of the reasons given for saying that the court martial was irregular. But what is the charge made by Captain Smales with regard to the detention of his witnesses? He protested against the proceedings. Three highly respectable non-commissioned officers, he said, had been placed under close arrest, and he asked for the protection of the Court, because, if they continued placing witnesses under arrest he would have no witnesses to produce. Captain Smales does not say that he could not communicate with his witnesses. He never applied to see them, and there is no proof that, if he had done so, he would have been refused. That being the case, on what rests the illegality caused

by the imprisonment of these witnesses?
And though I do not feel myself capable
of bandying legal arguments with the right
hon. Gentleman opposite, I consider the
circumstances are so remarkable and so
extraordinary, that I am justified in asking
for further papers. The fact that we are
now discussing this matter is attributable
to calumnies and falsehood, as are now
admitted to be, which were circulated by
the Indian press, and which, unfortunately,
were echoed in this country, and found a
mouthpiece in this House in the hon.
Member for Andover (Mr. Dudley Fortescue). Besides that, the case has been
brought before the House with every species
of exaggeration. Last Session, the noble
Lord the Under Secretary for War, came
down to this House and said it would have
been a great deal more satisfactory to himself, and doubtless to the House also, if he
could have come down that night and have
handed them over a victim. That was the
whole secret. A victim was required, and
a victim was found; and I must say that
it was not the fault of the Judge Advocate
General, if the victim was not brought to
the knife. Another most extraordinary
thing was the unprecedented fact, that a
pension had been given to the parents of
Sergeant Major Lilley, who had been reduced in rank by Sir William Mansfield
for misconduct, and who, it had since
been proved, was given to drink. An outcry was raised in this country, and it was
thought necessary to yield to the pressure from without; and, therefore, the
Government without further investigation
directed the court-martial which was held
in this country. The Indian authorities,
by that proceeding, have seen all their actions reviewed, and an officer brought to a
court-martial on the *ex parte* statements
of persons whose evidence had been discredited. It was necessary that the Indian authorities should have the means of
making themselves heard, for the whole of
the Indian army had by that proceeding
been placed under discredit and a slur;
that in all the Indian army,· from the
Commander-in-Chief down to the youngest
subaltern, it was impossible to compose a
tribunal that would do justice and act impartially in this matter. The court-martial, as I have said, took place in England,
under the plea that the English people
would not be satisfied with an inquiry
elsewhere, or, in other words, the venue
was changed from the place where it was
most natural that the inquiry should take

Lord Lovaine

place, to a country where the greatest
amount of ill-feeling against the party accused existed, and where he would have
the least possible chance of escaping. My
right hon. and gallant Friend (General
Peel) has a Motion on the paper, that it is
inexpedient that any further papers shall
be produced in connection with this matter, and perhaps that is the best thing to
be done; but I have thought it necessary
to make this statement from a sincere belief that it is the duty of the Government
to give information of the most full and
ample description, and not give a part here
and a part there. Nevertheless, I agree
with my right hon. and gallant Friend,
that, in this, as in all other matters connected with the army, it is the worst thing
in the world for the army to make this
House a tribunal of appeal in matters relating to the discipline of the service. I
know that my gallant Friend's feelings are
very strong upon that point, and if I could
feel assured that Her Majesty's Government intend to pursue anything like a firm
course with regard to any interference by
this House in the discipline of the army,
by refusing the papers moved for, I would
say that my Motion ought to be withdrawn.
Perhaps it will be better that I should do
so, but I wish it to be clearly understood
that, unless this case is finally closed, so
far as the War Office and the Horse
Guards are concerned, I shall reserve to
myself the right of moving for papers hereafter. I therefore beg leave to withdraw
my Motion.

GENERAL PEEL: I have always deprecated any interference by this House with
the military command and discipline of
the army, and I have always been opposed to the inquiries constantly made
by hon. Members on both sides of the
House—including, I am sorry to say, military men — why such an officer has got
a regiment, and why such an officer has
been passed over, as questions which the
House of Commons has nothing to do with.
I draw a distinction between questions relating to discipline and promotion, and
everything relating to the civil administration and Government of the army. This
is no distinction of my own; it will be
found introduced into the patent of the
First Secretary of State for War. Everything is there handed over to him with the
express exception of military command—
the discipline of the army and promotions
and appointments. That exception was
deeply and seriously considered by the

Committee on Military Organization, which was presided over by the late Sir James Graham, and although that Committee came to the conclusion that it was not wise to continue that reservation in future patents, for it was impossible to entirely divest the Secretary of State for War of all responsibility in regard to the action of the Commander-in-Chief, they were unanimous in thinking that any Secretary of State who interfered with the Commander-in-Chief would not be a wise man. The Committee report—

"The Secretary of State does not interfere in any way with the ordinary routine administration of the discipline of the army. That is left to the military authorities, aided by the legal knowledge of a Parliamentary officer—namely, the Judge Advocate. The army is thus enabled to feel assured that the patronage of the army as regards the first commissions and the ordinary promotions and appointments, other than those which are self regulated by purchase or seniority, will not be distributed with a view to political objects, or to the necessities of successive governments. Nor will the discipline of the army, as daily administered, vary in its character with each change in the civil department. Your Committee think that the introduction of any system which shall shake this reliance on the part of the army would be prejudicial to the efficiency of the service, by introducing doubt and dissatisfaction where confidence should exist."

In the next paragraph the Committee quote the opinion of the late Secretary of War, Lord Herbert—

"In his opinion some regulation is necessary, as pointing out to the Secretary of State the necessity of not invading the province of the officer who has the military command of the army intrusted to him."

If that is necessary with reference to the Secretary of State for War, how much more so is it with regard to this House, composed of upwards of 650 Members, the great majority of whom must be very imperfectly acquainted with what is necessary to insure the discipline of the army? And I say this in no disrespect to them, but from a firm belief that the obedience required from a soldier—and in that word I include the whole of the army, from the second in command down to the lowest drummer boy in the service—cannot be compared with any other obedience, or be judged by any ordinary rules. I may be asked if I wish to remove from the House the control of everything relating to the discipline of the army? Certainly not that proper constitutional control which the House possesses. You have a Minister of the Crown who is responsible for the administration of the army : and if you are not satisfied with his administrative conduct you have the means of ensuring his removal by a vote of want of confidence. But whatever you do, do not attempt yourself to interfere with the administration and government of the army, for if you do, you will lead to the belief that every man in the army who has, or supposes he has, a grievance, may come to this House for redress, instead of looking to his officers and the Commander-in-Chief for it. If you set yourselves up as a court of appeal from every military tribunal, the end of it will be to diminish the power and authority of the Commander-in-Chief, and make him subservient to public opinion, which is very often hastily formed, and on very insufficient grounds, as it seems to have been in the present instance. Above all, and worse than all, you will do that which the Committee on Military Organization thought the most detrimental to the public service—namely, the introduction of doubt and dissatisfaction where confidence ought to exist. Your soldiers will not have that confidence in their officers which I believe firmly every good soldier possesses, and they will not look up to them for that justice which they are certain, in my opinion, to obtain. I know the difficulty of getting the House of Commons to agree to this system of non-intervention with regard to military affairs. I have heard it said to those who have expressed this opinion, that no doubt it is a very beneficial system, but that the House of Commons will never agree to it—that they vote the supplies, and therefore they think they have a right to interfere. That is a doctrine I think the hon. Gentleman who has seconded the Motion now before the House (Mr. H. R. Grenfell) has laid down ; but it is an excuse I have often heard offered for a man who does a foolish thing at his own expense —such as when a man is his own architect, and builds a frightfully ugly house ; or when he is his own lawyer, and makes a very bad will. It is often said of them in language more expressive than elegant, that "the man who pays the fiddler has a right to call the tune." I perfectly admit, that not only have you a right to call the tune, but I say you actually exercise your right—for you nearly did the other night, when you narrowly escaped making a material alteration in the Mutiny Bill ; and if you do not like the manner in which the tune is played, you can insist upon changing the fiddler ; but do not attempt to play it yourself, for if you do, depend upon it you will produce a discord that will astound you. Having laid down my opinions as to the rule the House ought to observe with regard to military command and discipline, I come now with the greatest possible regret to the consideration of the question before the House, which in my opinion is, from the beginning to the end, an exception to all rules, and which, I trust, will never be looked upon hereafter as a precedent. It has done more, in my opinion, to weaken confidence in the governing powers of the army, and to expose a system of want of discipline, than I could have considered possible. I am not going to follow the hon. Gentleman into Colonel Crawley's court-martial, nor re-try him nor any of the parties referred to; on the contrary, I think the parties on their trial are Her Majesty's Government, for the manner in which they have acted. I was not the least surprised, when first those exaggerated accounts were received of the treatment of Lilley and his wife, at the general indignation that existed in this country. Neither was I surprised at the hon. Gentleman bringing it under the notice of the House. But although those exaggerated accounts received a kind of confirmation from the Memorandum of the 18th December, which, however, has since been so modified, so explained, and so apologised for, that not one line of it remains — notwithstanding the assumed confirmation it received, I could not believe that any officer in Her Majesty's service could be guilty of the cruelties charged against Colonel Crawley; and still less could I believe that such distinguished officers as Sir William Mansfield and Sir Hugh Rose, who were upon the spot, and must have seen a description of those cruelties in the Indian newspapers, would not have caused an instant inquiry to be made into the matter, and justice done to the parties. It is my belief, that if these officers did not do it they are not fit for their position, and that they belie that high character which they have attained during their glorious career. But Her Majesty's Government were not prepared to give them even a fair trial. On the contrary, when the noble Marquess (the Marquess of Hartington) replied to the hon. Gentleman who brought forward the question, he attached so much blame to General Farrell and General Mansfield, that, if that was the deliberate opinion of Her Majesty's Government, they were bound to have brought those officers to a court-martial. The noble Marquess, how-

General Peel

ever, concluded his speech by twice expressing his regret that he had not a victim to offer; and I recollect the late hon. Member for Brighton (Mr. Coningham) observing that it was not a victim that was demanded, but justice. And if the Secretary of State for War had promised that the strictest inquiry should be made and justice done, even if it was necessary in doing it to censure or punish the highest in command in India, if the House had that confidence in him which I am inclined to give him, they would have been perfectly satisfied with such a statement. But instead of that the victim must be Colonel Crawley. He was the victim pointed out, and the Government did everything in their power to sacrifice him. I was astonished when I heard the Secretary of State for War give his reasons in another place why Colonel Crawley had been brought to a court-martial. That noble Lord said that the case stood in a peculiar position in consequence of the course taken by Colonel Crawley himself, who had used language which it was impossible to interpret at that time in any other sense than that something had been done which shocked Colonel Crawley, which he considered improper, and, I think, he said inhuman. He said the blame of that proceeding was not attributable to him, but to his adjutant and his lieutenant. You had that speech in your possession from the previous October or November, and if you believed something inhuman had been done, and that Lieutenant Fitzsimon was the cause of it —and up to that time they had never heard him contradict the statement—why did you not bring Lieutenant Fitzsimon to a court-martial? You no sooner received, in a most irregular manner from Captain Smales, a letter that had been addressed by Lieutenant Fitzsimon to the Commander-in-Chief in India, and afterwards withdrawn, than, upon the unsupported testimony of Lieutenant Fitzsimon, you determined to try Colonel Crawley upon it, and to prefer his word to Colonel Crawley's, and to try him for a crime which you had looked over in Lieutenant Fitzsimon. I do not wish to be considered an admirer of Colonel Crawley. On the contrary, one of the great proofs of want of discipline this case produced was produced by Colonel Crawley himself in the course of his defence, when he brought forward in a triumphant manner, and proved it in evidence, that the Colonel of another regiment visited him on the morning when he was under arrest, and about to proceed to England to be tried by a court-martial, and told him that his men were turned out and ready to give him a cheer. Instead of his pointing out the impropriety of such a proceeding, Colonel Crawley not only received that ovation, but similar cheers from the witnesses who were coming over to attend the court-martial. That was a very improper proceeding. If these men had turned out to cheer a comrade coming up for a court-martial, no one would doubt that they would have been guilty of a great want of discipline. All I can say is, that if this is a specimen of the present state of discipline of the army, it must have been materially altered since I was a regimental officer. But the case came on. It was decided to try Colonel Crawley, and to try him in this country, the ground alleged for that course being the great excitement which the case had created here, and that no trial in India would be satisfactory to the English public. This was exactly the reverse of the course taken in ordinary legal proceedings, as a trial is generally removed from a place in which great excitement exists. Fortunately, however, for Colonel Crawley, he was brought before that much maligned tribunal a court-martial instead of a jury in Westminster Hall. If he had been tried before a Westminster jury, Colonel Crawley, whatever the evidence might have been, would have had a very bad chance. I, at the time of the trial, had no means of knowing what was going on beyond reading the evidence published in the daily papers; and it appeared to me that the evidence of the witnesses called for the prosecution was conclusive as to the innocence of Colonel Crawley to such an extent, that I thought on several occasions those witnesses were giving their evidence for the defence and not for the prosecution. When the case for the prosecution was closed I considered that it would have been a wise thing if the Government had withdrawn from the prosecution, confessed that the case had broken down, and offered to pay Colonel Crawley his expenses. If they had done that at that time they would have saved the country from the scandal of officers on full pay, headed by your own Commander-in-Chief in Ireland, entering into subscriptions for the purpose of relieving a brother officer from the expenses, not of a military prosecution, but of a military persecution. And sure I am, if the noble Lord had not expressed the in-

tention of the Government to pay the expenses up to a certain point, that subscription would have risen to a much larger amount. But the Government did not adopt that course. You called upon the accused for his defence; and after he had concluded it, after his mouth was shut and he had not a single opportunity of saying anything more, the prosecution answered by a reply which I will not venture to designate. You had tried Colonel Crawley upon two charges, so narrow in themselves that he had actually objected to them from the first, because he said they did not give him the opportunity of vindicating himself from the vile aspersions which had been cast upon him. He was anxious to show the grounds upon which the sergeant-majors were arrested. You said, "No; so far as you are concerned, the arrest was perfectly legal, and we do not allow you to enter into the question; we confine you to the two charges." Thus you prevented Colonel Crawley from entering upon this question; and then in your reply, you brought forward this very question of the illegality of the arrest upon which you had prohibited him from entering. Now, who is responsible for this reply? It has been repudiated by the Horse Guards and the War Office. It is said that it is to be looked upon as a speech of counsel; but I always understood that counsel were not responsible for what they utter, because they are merely acting from their instructions. Certainly in this case the counsel was counsel, attorney, prosecutor, and judge also. But the gallant officer, who acted as official prosecutor upon that occasion, I understand did exercise a certain degree of responsibility, for he positively refused to read three-fourths of the reply—

"His generous tongue disdained to speak
The thing his heart disproved."

He positively refused to be the mouthpiece of the Captain Smales's and the Jacob Omniums, who were anxious, notwithstanding all the evidence that had been brought forward, to repeat those refuted calumnies which had appeared in the Indian press, and in articles in magazines. They attempted to obtain a verdict by bringing forward the topics which the prisoner had not been allowed to reply to in his defence. Fortunately for Colonel Crawley, all these attempts had no effect upon the honourable men who constituted the court-martial, and who, on the contrary, came to the conclusion that he was fully and honourably acquitted upon the charges which were brought against him. Surely one would have thought that that was quite sufficient, and that there would have been an end of the case—at all events, that the War Office would have adopted the very wise determination of His Royal Highness the Commander-in-Chief expressed in the Memorandum at the close of these proceedings, in which he said that the object of the inquiry having been attained, it was not his intention to continue the discussion respecting the circumstances under which this court-martial arose. What a pity it was that the Secretary for War had not followed the example of the Commander-in-Chief. When called upon to lay the proceedings before Parliament with this reply attached to it, the reply recollect becomes a Parliamentary document and remains for ever upon your proceedings, and it is a reply in which the prosecutors were not content with assailing Colonel Crawley, but dragged before the Court the highest military names in India who had no opportunity of defending themselves, and who were not even aware that their conduct would be impugned. How, under these circumstances, I ask, is it possible that the discipline of the Indian army can be maintained? The hon. Member is surprised that I have moved for the production of a pamphlet. But the author of the pamphlet has informed me that he has made an official document of it by forwarding it both to the Horse Guards and to the War Office, and it is as a public document that I have moved for it. What has been produced by agreeing to lay these papers before the House? You have produced a discussion which had far better have been avoided, and you have produced three separate Motions for further papers, two of which are by hon. Members who move for confidential Reports. I am sure that if the House of Commons was aware of the nature of those confidential Reports, they would not insist upon their being produced. Many an officer has had his character taken away behind his back in these confidential communications; and if they are to be laid on the table of this House and sold for a penny throughout the whole world, no inspecting field officer will address such reports with confidence again. I trust that the House will not agree to that, and will come to the conclusion that the production of any further papers is inexpedient.

General Peel

Amendment proposed,

To leave out from the first word "That" to the end of the Question, in order to add the words, "the production of any further Papers relating to the court-martial on Colonel Crawley is inexpedient,"—(*General Peel,*)

—instead thereof.

The Marquess of HARTINGTON said, he rose to state the course which the Government intended to take. The Government gave a most cordial assent to the Amendment just moved by the right hon. Gentleman, agreeing in the necessity of not producing more papers, and of avoiding further discussion. He should have occasion by-and-by to state why he disagreed with the right hon. Gentleman in thinking that the papers already produced had done harm to the discipline of the army; but surely no one could now say that this question had not been fully and amply discussed, and he thought a large majority in the House would agree with the right hon. Gentleman that the time had at last come when this controversy should be brought to an end. He was happy to find that the hon. Member who brought this subject forward (Mr. D. Fortescue) had responded to the appeal which he had made to him, and did not invite the House to go through all the proceedings of the trial. Considering the very strong opinion held by the hon. Gentleman upon this subject, he had acted in a very fair and manly way in declaring that he would not call in question the justice of the finding of the court-martial. But he had alluded to that which one would have thought had long ago been discussed and decided—the speech of the hon. Gentleman being a repetition of that which he had made last Session, calling in question the original legality of the arrest of the sergeants, and the further illegality of the continued arrest of Sergeant Major Lilley. In reply to the hon. Gentleman last year, he (the Marquess of Hartington) admitted, and still admitted, that in the opinion of the Law Advisers of the Crown, and of the military authorities at the Horse Guards, Sir William Mansfield's decision in continuing the arrest of the three sergeant-majors, while allowing that no sufficient ground existed upon which they could be brought to trial, was not to be justified, and that Sir William Mansfield committed an error in judgment when he sanctioned this continued arrest. The hon. Gentleman had concluded by saying that he did not wish to see Sir

William Mansfield, General Farrell, or Colonel Crawley tried over again. But what, then, was his object in raising this question? He thought last year, and he continued to think it a most unfortunate circumstance that, owing to a series of mistakes and a series of misunderstandings, the sergeants had been kept in confinement for three weeks beyond the time they could have been legally confined; but he stated last year that, though Colonel Crawley might be morally responsible for the occurrence, yet, as he was covered by the order of his superior officer, he could not be held legally responsible for the continued and, as the Government thought, illegal confinement. Again, he then admitted that, on the other hand, Sir William Mansfield was technically responsible for that continued arrest. But it must be remembered that Sir William Mansfield was placed under great difficulties, for he was 400 miles from the place where the occurrence took place, and, consequently, he had not an opportunity of making constant references to know how those proceedings were going on. He was, unfortunately, under the impression, when he sanctioned the confinement, that the trial would terminate in a few days. If he had not been under that impression he would not have sanctioned it. The hon. Member had disclaimed the idea of wishing to see the Horse Guards put Sir William Mansfield on his trial; and he did not think that any Member of that House would have considered the Government justified in arraigning an officer of such distinguished services and talents upon his trial for his share in this unfortunate transaction, for they might be quite certain that no court-martial would have found him guilty of any military offence. Therefore, though the Government held him legally responsible for what had taken place, they at the same time held that morally he was guiltless. He said last year that, though they would not put the gallant officer on his trial, the opinion which the Commander-in-Chief had formed of the mistake he had committed would be forwarded to him; and it had since been sent to him. To such an officer he thought the receipt of such an opinion was a full and ample punishment—if punishment it might be called—for any error of judgment which might be laid to his charge in connection with those men. The hon. Member who seconded the Motion (Mr. H. R. Grenfell), had made some observations with reference to the proceedings of the court-martial in this case and to courts-martial in general, and had expressed a hope that the Government would be able to state that some alteration was to be made in respect to the practice of courts-martial. In reply, he might say that the subject of the practice and procedure of courts-martial was under the consideration of the Government, but he could not say what alterations would be proposed, or at what time they would be in a position to make any proposition on the subject. It was one of great importance and difficulty, and the Government would not be justified in acting hastily in the matter. As to the observations of the hon. Member with reference to Major Swinley, the House would remember that the gallant officer had been censured by the court-martial for the evidence he gave against Colonel Crawley. Whether that evidence had been elicited from him in any particular manner, he was not prepared to say; whether Major Swinley tried to make the worst of the case against his commanding officer it was not for him to say; but it was quite manifest from the evidence he did give before the court-martial, that his feeling towards Colonel Crawley was such as to make it impossible he could be allowed to remain in the regiment of which that gallant officer was the commanding officer. Major Swinley had not exactly been placed upon half-pay—he was permitted to exchange to half-pay. The other officers whom it had been thought necessary to censure were engaged in arranging their exchanges, and no doubt before long they would be gazetted. The proceedings of Dr. Turnbull had been made the subject of investigation by a Court of Inquiry at Chatham, and though the result was that the charges against him were not substantiated, it was thought necessary that he should leave the Inniskilling Dragoons, and he would shortly be appointed to another regiment.

The other speeches delivered during the present discussion had gone more to attack the Government for the course they had pursued. It was urged that they had yielded unduly to popular clamour in trying Colonel Crawley in England, and it was argued that they had conducted the trial unfairly, and that they had acted unwisely in imparting to the House of Commons the amount of information which they had laid before it. Last year the hon. Member for Andover (Mr. Dudley Fortescue), in a speech of great moderation and ability, brought forward the case of Sergeant Major Lilley. In no exaggerated terms he told the House a tale which he was not surprised created a strong impression and a feeling of great excitement throughout the country. It was argued by hon. Members on the other side of the House, that those who had to answer for the Government on that occasion should have been able to refute all the statements and exaggerations, as they called them, of the hon. Gentleman with respect to Colonel Crawley. But at that time the Government were not in possession of materials by which the statements of the hon. Member for Andover could have been refuted. A constant correspondence had been going on between the Horse Guards and the authorities in India ; many points had been pressed on the consideration of the Commander-in-Chief, but there was nothing in the possession of His Royal Highness that would have enabled the War Department to answer in any manner, satisfactory to the House, the statements made by the hon. Member for Andover on that occasion. The speech of the hon. Member was principally directed to the illegality of the imprisonment—that was, at least, the point to which he (the Marquess of Hartington) in his reply chiefly adverted. In commenting on the statements of the hon. Member he stated — what it was impossible to deny then, and what it was now equally impossible to deny—namely, that in the opinion of the Government, Sergeant Major Lilley died while he was confined in an illegal imprisonment, and that his death under such circumstances was a lamentable occurrence, calculated to raise feelings of horror and indignation in the country. He explained, as well as he could, the circumstances under which the Sergeant Major's death had taken place, and his words gave occasion for much criticism on the part of hon. Members opposite. It had been stated that he said that he deeply regretted not being able to come down to the House with a "victim" to atone for the death of Sergeant Major Lilley. It was quite true the Government had not then a victim to give, and they did not go out of their way to look for one. He stated that the fact undoubtedly was that the Sergeant Major died while in illegal imprisonment, and that Colonel Crawley was not legally responsible for that imprisonment ; but he further informed the House that there was a conflict of evidence as to the severity, or the

The Marquess of Hartington

degree of the severity, with which the detention had been carried out, and that it was necessary the matter should be inquired into. That promise had been fulfilled, and it was the only promise ever made, or which it had appeared necessary for the Government to give. When it had been determined that there should be an inquiry, it became necessary to consider how it should be conducted. The whole affair was involved in so much mystery, and it seemed so difficult to get at the facts, that the Government thought a court-martial would be the most satisfactory tribunal before which the circumstances could be investigated. In reference to what had been said as to the injustice towards Colonel Crawley involved in such a decision on the part of the Government, he had to observe that there were instances of courts-martial being allowed to officers in order to give them an opportunity of clearing themselves ; and the character of Colonel Crawley had been so seriously impugned, both in India and at home, that it was thought desirable that he should be allowed to appear before a court-martial with the view of exculpating himself. In short, the court-martial on Colonel Crawley was authorised on the most direct and straightforward manner of getting at the real facts of the case. Besides that, the military authorities had evidence which had great weight on their minds in deciding to bring Colonel Crawley before a court-martial. They had the sworn testimony of Sergeant Major Lilley before the Mhow Court Martial, never contradicted, as to the manner in which the sentry was placed in his room. They had also Colonel Crawley's reply, in which he admitted the existence of undue severity and inhumanity in the circumstances of the imprisonment of Sergeant Major Lilley, although he said that he was not responsible for it, and that reply was not given until nearly a month after that statement had been made. Was it not remarkable that Colonel Crawley should have allowed that period to elapse during which he might have ascertained for himself whether the facts were true or not, and that at the conclusion of that period he should have appeared before the court-martial, and have stated publicly his conviction that severity and inhumanity had accompanied the imprisonment of Sergeant Major Lilley, though he was not responsible for it ? They had also the letter of Lieutenant Fitzsimon directly contradicting the statement of his commanding officer. The

right hon. Gentleman (General Peel) said
that that letter came before the Commander-in-Chief in an irregular manner.   He
(the Marquess of Hartington) acknowledged that the manner in which that
letter was obtained was somewhat unusual; but if it had not come before him
in an irregular manner, it never would
have come before him at all.   The House
ought not to forget the circumstances attending that letter.   When Sir Hugh
Rose's remarks were published, reflecting
on Lieutenant Fitzsimon's carelessness in
posting the sentries, Lieutenant Fitzsimon
protested against the statement made
against him by his commanding officer,
and sent his letter in the usual way
through the acting adjutant to the commanding officer, that it might be by him
forwarded to Sir Hugh Rose.   Colonel
Crawley placed that letter in the hand of
General Farrell, who sent for Lieutenant
Fitzsimon, and told him that the letter
was an exceedingly improper one, that it
would be detrimental—indeed, ruinous to
his future prospects.   Not unnaturally,
Lieutenant Fitzsimon then wrote to the
General, requesting that this letter, which
was to bring such ruinous consequences to
him, might be withdrawn, and he stated
that he did so because, in the opinion of
General Farrell, the letter was an insubordinate one.   This, however, he was not
allowed to do in that way.   He was not
allowed to say that it was on account of
General Farrell's opinion, but he was compelled to ask for its withdrawal without
assigning any reason.   When that letter
came before the Commander-in-Chief, in
an irregular manner, it turned out that, in
the opinion of the Judge Advocate General and all the military authorities, both
at the Horse Guards and the War Office,
without exception, it did not contain one
improper or insubordinate sentence or word.
Therefore, if there was anything irregular
in the manner in which that letter came
before the Commander-in-Chief, there was
also something extraordinary in the manner in which it was prevented reaching Sir
Hugh Rose.   The circumstances attending
the suppression of this letter—for he could
call it nothing else—did weigh upon the
minds of the Commander-in-Chief and the
Secretary of State in thinking that something had occurred, which Colonel Crawley
confessed had occurred, but which great
pains appeared to have been taken to suppress, and for which it appeared Colonel
Crawley was responsible.   Those were the

grounds on which it seemed that the trial
would be justifiable.   It was true that they
had statements from India in explanation;
but none of those statements went to disprove any one of the statements made by
the hon. Member for Andover.   If he made
any exception to that general assertion, it
would be to express his regret for one
omission in his speech of last year.   The
military authorities were certainly then
aware—and he had intended to explain it
—that there was nothing unfit for human
habitation in the house in which Sergeant
Major Lilley was confined, and that, whatever the quarters were, they were the
quarters he would have occupied even if
he had not been arrested.   But though he
regretted not having made that statement,
he could not see that it would have made
any difference.   Colonel Crawley was tried,
not for having imprisoned Sergeant Major
Lilley in a dungeon unfit for human habitation, but for carrying out his imprisonment in his own house with unnecessary
severity.   On the other hand, Sir Hugh
Rose had taken exception to some remarks
in the Memorandum of the Commander-in-
Chief with reference to the quantity of
brandy stated to have been consumed by
Sergeant Major Lilley.   The Commander-
in-Chief acknowledged that explanation,
and said that he then understood what
were the reasons which had induced Sir
Hugh Rose to make his remarks on Lilley's intemperate habits.   But in that
letter, which was before the House, the
Commander-in-Chief never modified his
originally expressed opinion that, up to
the time of his imprisonment, Lilley had
been a man of temperate habits.   The
evidence, he said, which supported the
allegation of the habits of intoxication of
Lilley was of a doubtful character, but the
evidence which represented him as having
been previously a man of a temperate character was undoubted, and had never been
shaken.   After Sir Hugh Rose's explanation the Commander-in-Chief acknowledged
that he now understood the grounds on
which he had acted; but he never changed
his opinion upon the two essential points
touched upon in his Memorandum—that
the imprisonment was illegal, and that
there was no foundation for the allegation
that Lilley's death was caused by the
quantity of spirits he consumed.   [Lord
LOVAINE intimated dissent.]   What further
explanation did the noble Lord desire ?

LORD LOVAINE said, he did not understand his Royal Highness to go quite

so far as that. The words of the Memorandum were—

"Having ascertained the quantity of brandy consumed in the house of the non-commissioned officer, that shows the probability of his symptoms having been aggravated by drinking; at the same time his Royal Highness must remark, that the allegation of habitual drunkenness rests on very doubtful evidence, while the evidence was undoubted of previous good conduct and sobriety."

He confessed he could not see clearly what was the effect of that passage.

THE MARQUESS OF HARTINGTON said, he was not engaged in defending the language of the Memorandum, he was merely stating that his Royal Highness had never modified the opinions originally expressed in the first Memorandum of the 16th September. The military authorities also received from India explanations as to the nature of the bungalow, and statements made in a casual and summary manner about the severity of the arrest. He maintained that the Government had not at that time in their possession sufficient materials for confuting the statements made in the press and by the hon. Member for Andover. Then the Government had been attacked because they ordered the court-martial to be held in this country. The reason for doing so was that the proceedings at the Mhow trial had very much agitated the minds of all the military authorities in India, and especially in the Bombay Presidency, and that the Commander-in-Chief in that presidency and Sir Hugh Rose were both, to a certain extent, mixed up, in public opinion, with the transactions which had taken place in connection with that court-martial. It seemed to the Government, when charges of the very gravest nature had been brought against Colonel Crawley, that it would be much better for that officer and for all concerned, and much more satisfactory to the public, that the trial should take place in some place where the superior military authorities were not involved in the case to the extent of those in India. It certainly never entered into the mind of his Royal Highness the Commander-in-Chief, or to his noble Friend the Secretary of State for War, that Colonel Crawley would not have had a fair trial in India; but only that it would be more satisfactory to the Colonel himself, and to the public in England, that it should take place here. The very first incident of the Aldershot Court Martial showed what would have been the inconvenience of holding the trial at Mhow. In drawing up the charges, the legality or

Lord Lovaine

illegality of the arrest was specially and studiously excluded, because it was held that so far Colonel Crawley was covered by the sanction of Sir William Mansfield. The very first thing, however, which Colonel Crawley did when on his trial in England was to appeal against the very narrow issue raised in the charges, and to ask to be permitted to go into the whole question, in order to show what were the reasons which induced him in the first instance to order the arrest of the Sergeant Major. If the Court had been sitting at Mhow to whom would that reference have been made? Why, the application would have had to be made to Sir William Mansfield, who would thus have had to decide a question involving the legality of his own act. Such inconveniences would repeatedly have occurred if the trial had taken place at Mhow; and surely if it were not to take place at Mhow there was no other Court in India in which the trial could properly have taken place. To have removed it to any other part of India would have been to cast an apparent slight on the officers of the Bombay Presidency. If the court-martial was not to meet in its natural place, then it was much less painful to the officers in India that it should be taken to England. He could not believe that hon. Members were serious in desiring that the trial should have taken place, if at all, in India. Everybody, he thought, had acknowledged that the public mind was, and very naturally, much excited by the accounts received from India. Surely, then, if there was to be an investigation, it would have been throwing away their pains and trouble to have held it at such a distance as India. It would at once have been said that the Government were trying to shield the Indian authorities from the publicity of a full and searching inquiry. The right hon. Gentleman opposite had condemned the Government for giving any papers on the subject. He quite agreed with the right hon. Gentleman (General Peel), that it was highly undesirable that the House of Commons should habitually make itself a court of appeal for the revision of the proceedings of courts-martial: it was quite as undesirable that it should constitute itself into a court of appeal in any case, whether affecting military or civil affairs. It was, however, useless to argue, when a case had caused very wide-spread popular excitement, when the public believed, whether rightly or wrongly, that injustice and oppression had been committed, that the

Government ought to try and suppress discussion on the subject in the House of Commons. He would have been very glad to have been able at the outset to have given a full explanation of all the circumstances of the case; but when he was unable to do so, he thought the House was perfectly entitled to all the information upon the subject which the Government had it in its power to give. He really could not see in what way the Government could be held responsible for encouraging discussion unduly. The late hon. Member for Brighton (Mr. Coningham) insisted on reading extracts from a book purporting to be a report of the Mhow Court Martial, and when called to order for so doing, the Speaker decided that the hon. Member was at liberty to read from the publication. The Government felt, under these circumstances, that if the proceedings of the Mhow Court Martial were to be cited in the House, it would be well that the House should have a correct and authentic statement of what had taken place. His noble Friend at the head of the Government appealed, but in vain, to the late hon. Member for Brighton not to raise a discussion on the matter until the trial of Colonel Crawley had been concluded. He was confident that no word or act of the Government last Session could be construed into an encouragement of a public discussion on these points. As to laying the proceedings of the Aldershot Court Martial on the table, as he explained the other night, it seemed only just and reasonable that the House should be in possession of a report of the trial on which Colonel Crawley was acquitted as well as of that which had led to his being accused of oppression and injustice. The remaining papers had been laid on the table at the desire of His Royal Highness the Commander-in-Chief, in order to explain the course he had taken in the matter, particularly with regard to the discussions which had arisen with Sir Hugh Rose. He fully agreed with the right hon. Gentleman in what he said, as to the inexpediency of producing many of the papers that had been asked for; but it was not from one side of the House only that such demands were made. He was astonished to see on the paper a notice of a Motion by the noble Lord the Member for the East Riding (Lord Hotham), for the production of a confidential Report. He hoped that, as the noble Lord had not yet risen, he had abandoned his intention of proceeding with that Motion; but it was very extraordinary that such a notice should have been given at all by any one who knew what a confidential Report was. Hon. Members opposite had certainly taken a strange method of showing their solicitude for the discipline of the army. A noble Lord asked for a confidential Report. Another hon. Member, supposed to represent the officers of the army, impugned the decision of the Commander-in-Chief, and his right to bring the commanding officer of a regiment to a court-martial whenever and on whatever charges he deemed proper. It was indeed an extraordinary way of maintaining the discipline of the army to assail the authority of the Commander-in-Chief. He did not intend to follow the observations which had been made upon the conduct of the prosecution. The Judge Advocate General was prepared to speak upon that point. He had stated the grounds upon which it was thought necessary by the Government to summon Colonel Crawley home to stand his trial; he had explained why it was thought necessary to produce the papers which had already been laid on the table; and he had also explained the reasons why it was deemed expedient to try Colonel Crawley in this country rather than in India. It only remained for him to say, that, in the opinion of many military authorities, that which had occurred had not been in any manner prejudicial to the discipline of the army. Hon. Gentlemen opposite had never explained in what way discussion was fatal to discipline. What was the discipline which had been so grievously injured by the conduct of the Government? He imagined that discipline consisted in summary but strict justice, and he could not see how it should be hurtful to its interests that it should be sometimes discussed in the House of Commons, or why it should be necessary to hide everything connected with the army in the Horse Guards, or in the records of the Judge Advocate General's office. There was something which would be far more fatal to discipline than the procedure adopted in Colonel Crawley's case. It would be fatal, indeed, if the discipline of the army should be allowed to degenerate for a moment into tyranny. The suspicion even that it had ever degenerated into tyranny would be most injurious. He believed that the army ought to be as jealous of the purity of the administration of military justice, of the purity of its discipline, as it was of its honour and of its reputation for courage.

A most serious stain was cast upon the purity of military justice by the statements made in the newspapers and repeated in that House last year; and there was no way in which that discipline could be vindicated except by a full, complete, and impartial investigation. Such an investigation had taken place at Aldershot, and no Member of that House rejoiced more than he did that Colonel Crawley had been able to relieve himself from the imputations which had been cast upon him, and that the discipline of the army and the reputation of its commanding officers had been so clearly vindicated.

Lord HOTHAM said, he wished to say a few words, as he had been so pointedly alluded to by the noble Lord. The noble Lord would have done better if, to quote a homely proverb, he had looked at home and addressed himself rather to the hon. Member for Andover than to him. He could assure the noble Lord and the House that if the hon. Member for Andover had not moved for two confidential Reports, no notice of a Motion would have been given by him for papers of that kind; but when he saw the notice given by the hon. Member for Andover, he imagined that the hon. Member expected to find in those Reports some information favourable to the cause he supported, he thought it was better, instead of objecting to the production of two confidential Reports, to move for all such Reports as had been made, so that they might have all the information that could be afforded to them. That was the sole reason for his having given the notice which the noble Lord had pleased to censure. He never for a moment believed that a Government could have been found weak enough to produce confidential Reports ; but, at the same time, he was not disposed to leave them at liberty to present such a case as might have suited the hon. Member for Andover, and to keep back information possibly throwing light on the other side. He concurred in the general principle which had been laid down by his right hon. Friend the Member for Huntingdon (General Peel) ; but it had been admitted that this was entirely an exceptional case, and exceptional diseases always required exceptional remedies. He admitted fully the value of the right hon. Gentleman's principle, but when such things were done as had been done in this case, there was more to fear from mystery and secresy than from letting the whole truth be known to the country. He should

be glad to withdraw his Motion for the production of the confidential Reports, if the hon. Member for Andover would do the same. With reference to the other notice he had given, he had felt that great injustice had been done to two most distinguished officers, Sir Hugh Rose and Sir William Mansfield, and his notice of an Amendment on that point stood on a different footing from the other. The question related to the arrest of the sergeant-majors, and also to the keeping them under arrest. When the hon. Member for Andover moved for papers relating to the arrest only, he thought, in justice to Sir William Mansfield, that he should have an opportunity of showing the grounds on which he acted in ordering those men to be kept under arrest. If the hon. Member had made neither of those Motions, he should not have moved in the matter. If he thought great injustice would have been done to Sir William Mansfield if only the Reports moved for by the hon. Gentleman had been produced, he thought so now still more after the depreciatory remarks which the noble Lord (the Marquess of Hartington) had made in speaking of Sir William Mansfield. He had never had the honour even of seeing Sir William Mansfield, and, therefore, he made this statement from no motive of private friendship. The noble Lord had spoken of the necessity of upholding the authority of persons filling high situations; but how little had the noble Lord acted in accordance with his own proposition, when he spoke in the manner he had done with regard to the Commander-in-Chief at Bombay. That alone would prevent him withdrawing that part of the Motion which had reference to Sir William Mansfield. It was impossible to suppose, knowing the source from which the hon. Member from Andover got his information, that he was ignorant that the question of the legality or illegality of the imprisonment of the sergeants was about to be tried by a Court of Law. If the hon. Gentleman was not ignorant of that, he thought it would have been more decorous and gracious, and more in accordance with custom, if he had abstained from bringing before the House a question that was about to be tried in Westminster Hall.

The MARQUESS OF HARTINGTON said, he was quite unaware what observations of his were referred to by the noble Lord. He had stated that it was not wonderful if in one particular instance, and under circumstances of great difficulty, Sir William Mansfield had committed an error of judgment ; but the Commander-in-Chief had expressed an opinion that, all through these trying circumstances, the gallant General had been actuated by a wish to do justice, and to promote the interests of the service. He (the Marquess of Hartington) had already admitted that Sir William Mansfield was an officer of the highest distinction, and he had stated that it was that which made it the more extraordinary that in this one instance he should have committed what the Government thought was an error of judgment. Not one syllable of what he had said was intended to depreciate the character of Sir William Mansfield. On the contrary, through all this transaction he considered that Sir William Mansfield had acted in a most straightforward and generous manner. The gallant General had been, as he felt certain he would now be, the last man in the world to support hon. Gentlemen on the other side in questioning the opinion of the Commander-in-Chief.

MR. O'REILLY said, that he had no desire to question the finding of the tribunals which had tried Paymaster Smales and Colonel Crawley, and he should as little ask the House to canvass the verdict of a jury in Westminster Hall. He also quite agreed with the right hon. Gentleman (General Peel), that the discipline of the army and the conduct of the military authorities in particular cases should not be canvassed in that House. There was, however, one thing most essential in order to maintain the discipline of the army, and that was that the certainty — the known certainty — that the rules of the law and of universal justice would be observed equally by the highest and lowest authorities in the army. When these rules appeared to be infringed, it was the duty of that House to see that the law of the land and the majesty of justice were sufficiently vindicated. He had submitted two questions to the Under Secretary of State for War which the noble Marquess told him he could not answer within the ordinary limits, and he had, therefore, reserved them for the present occasion. One of those questions the noble Marquess had virtually answered in the speech he had just made. It was, whether the 18th Article of War was still and had been in force during the last two years. This Article was as follows:

"No officer or soldier who shall be put in arrest or confinement shall continue in such arrest or confinement more than eight days, or until such time as a court-martial can be conveniently assembled."

The noble Marquess had answered this question in the affirmative. The last clause implied, that when more than eight days elapsed there must be charges standing against the person under arrest, and that steps must be taken to assemble a court-martial. His second question was, whether the placing Regimental Sergeant Major Lilley, and Troop Sergeants Major Wakefield and Duval, of the 6th Inniskilling Dragoons, under close arrest for an indefinite period—namely (according to the terms of the order of Sir William Mansfield, dated May 6, 1862), "until the proceedings in the trial of Captain Smales are entirely closed," a period which proved to be one of more than twenty-eight days —was contrary to the first quoted of the Articles of War, and illegal. He had also inquired whether it was lawful in the army to prevent a prisoner on his trial from having access to the witnesses who were to be called for his defence. He had put that question to the highest authority on military law, and had been informed that some high military authorities held that there were cases in which a prisoner on his trial might be lawfully debarred from access to his witnesses. The Judge Advocate General, however, stated that there was no clearer principle of law and justice than that a prisoner was entitled to have the freest access to the witnesses he wished to call in his defence. An order of Major General Farrell was on record, dated April 26, 1862, at which date Captain Smales was on his trial, and the names of the three sergeant-majors had been given in as witnesses for the defence. It was as follows:—

"You are to keep the Regimental Sergeant Major Lilley and Troop Sergeants Major Wakefield and Duval in close arrest, under sentries, to forbid any one to have access to them, except under your own express permission."

The second order was Sir William Mansfield's, and dated May 6:—

"The sergeants-major are not to be released from arrest until the proceedings in the trial of Captain Smales are entirely closed."

He thought the House must now be convinced that Mr. Smales, when on his trial, had not enjoyed free and entire access to all the witnesses for his defence. He now came to the question, who was accountable for these breaches of military law! For the first part of the arrest of Lilley, General

Farrell appeared to be responsible, and for the latter part General Mansfield. Inferring that the military authorities at home considered it undesirable to bring to trial such distinguished officers as General Farrell and General Mansfield, he wished to know what steps had been taken by the authorities to render it certain that such conduct would not be repeated, and to let the soldiers in the army know that they would not again be subject to such illegal and unjust proceedings. Nothing was more important than that every officer and soldier should have instilled into him a feeling of entire confidence that he would receive perfect justice. The proceedings in the case of Colonel Crawley had been read and commented on in every barrack-room in the kingdom. Soldiers knew perfectly well the rules of the service, and there was not a private in the army who did not know that the sergeants-major were confined under arrest for more than eight days, without any charges against them, or steps being taken to bring them to a court-martial. It was equally well known in the army, that to deny a prisoner free access and communication with his witnesses was illegal and unjust. The House would, therefore, feel it desirable that the soldiers of the army should know that steps had been taken to prevent a repetition of this interference with law and justice. It was not for him to suggest what steps ought to be taken; but if, among the endless memoranda and appendices to verdicts and findings growing out of this case, there had been one short General Order, stating that it had come to the knowledge of the Commander-in-Chief that through inadvertence and without ill-motive a violation of the law and an interference with the course of justice had unhappily occurred, and that his Royal Highness, therefore, wished to call the attention of commanding officers of troops to what the law really was under the 18th Article of War, and to remind them that it could not be violated—had such an order been written and read on the parade ground of every battalion of Her Majesty's troops, it would have done more to confirm and extend the confidence of the army in the administration of military justice than a thousand discussions such as those which had taken place in the House of Commons could do to shake it.

Sɪʀ JAMES FERGUSSON said, he did not think it possible that the scandal affecting the 6th Dragoon Guards, which had

Mr. O'Reilly

caused so much excitement out of doors, and with regard to which so extraordinary and exceptional a course had been taken, could fall into oblivion without seriously committing the reputation of many valuable public servants of the Crown. The discussions, at the same time, which had taken place in that House must have taught a serious lesson to persons in high position, and have shown them that the best course in difficult cases was to follow established usage. For himself, and those by whom he was surrounded, he disclaimed the imputation thrown out by the noble Lord (the Marquess of Hartington) that they represented only one portion of the army. Some Gentlemen wished to deduce from the unfortunate and painful circumstances of this case the conclusion that some change was required in the law and practice of courts-martial. On the contrary, he thought it discreditable to persons in high positions that they should seek to escape by such a course; for he ventured to think that the position of perplexity, difficulty, and discredit in which so many in high positions now found themselves was to be attributed to their departure from all previous custom and usage. He was not going to narrate over again all the incidents of the Mhow Court Martial; it could hardly have passed from the minds of hon. Gentlemen how moving were the terms and how extravagant the statements with which the case was introduced to the House. In fact he should have passed them over altogether had it not been for the disingenuous manner in which the noble Marquess had thought fit to gloss over the very remarkable speech of the hon. Member for Audover made in June last; but having had a recent opportunity of refreshing his memory with regard to the terms then used, he must say that the hon. Member for Andover owed an explanation to the House very different from any which he had yet offered. The noble Marquess would have it inferred that the hon. Member's charge strictly referred to the illegal imprisonment of the three sergeant-majors; whereas the gravamen of the hon. Member's charge consisted in the cruel treatment to which it was alleged that the three non-commissioned officers had been subjected in the course of a long and illegal imprisonment. The hon. Member told the House that

" The place where Sergeant Major Lilley was confined was a single room in a bomb-proof building, formerly used as cavalry stables, and which had since been pulled down as unfit for the occupation of European troops. It was almost impossible that the roof of this building could get cool, as it was so formed that the amount of heat absorbed by it in the day could not be carried off by night. In a room, then, more like an oven than a human habitation was Sergeant-Major Lilley imprisoned, and that room was shared by his wife, who was confined to her bed by a diarrhœa attending the last stage of consumption."—[3 *Hansard,* clxxi. 434-5.]

Further on he added that, "incredible as it might appear, Colonel Crawley ordered the sentry to be stationed inside the room;" and the picture was completed in these words :—

"There, in the presence of strange men, renewed from day to day and from hour to hour, and posted three feet from her bed, all the functions of nature had to be performed by this dying woman."

From the observations of the hon. Member it might have been supposed that the confinement of Sergeant Major Lilley was continuous in one single building; but subsequent explanations showed that he had been confined in two separate buildings, the first of which was equal to that occupied by a captain in his own regiment. On a subsequent occasion the hon. Member certainly explained that

"Sergeant Major Lilley was at first confined to his own quarters, where he had several apartments; but that when he was ordered under confinement he was removed from his proper quarters to others where he was confined to a single room. It was in the single room that the sentry was posted. On that point he spoke from the testimony of two eye-witnesses."—[3 *Hansard,* clxxi. 1442.]

Mr. DUDLEY FORTESCUE asked, where the hon. Gentleman had procured these statements ?

Sir JAMES FERGUSSON said, he had copied the extracts which he had read from *Hansard's Parliamentary Debates,* and he had no objection to place the papers in the hands of the hon. Member for the purpose of verification. [3 *Hansard,* clxxi. 432.] He had also in his possession the report as it appeared in *The Times.* The order for the release of the sergeant-majors, according to the hon. Member, "found one of them a raving lunatic, and he was conveyed to the hospital suffering from brain fever." But what he wanted to fix upon the hon. Member was the statement that Sergeant Major Lilley was confined in a single room, in which the sentry was posted within two or three feet of Mrs. Lilley's bed. And he called on the hon. Gentleman, if he valued his word—if he valued the honour of the House, in which unguarded and unsupported statements ought not to be made—to give the names of the two eye-witnesses to whom he had referred. He was persuaded the

hon. Gentleman believed every word he had stated, and that he was incapable of exaggeration—the reputation which he enjoyed in the House placed him above such a suspicion; but unwittingly he had made himself the organ of most false and utterly unsupported statements, which all the evidence adduced upon oath in this country had refuted, and therefore he owed an explanation to the House different from any which had yet been given. The case of Sergeant Major Wakefield might be disposed of in two words. He had been suffering from excitement caused by drink taken during his imprisonment, and the name of the sergeant was known through whose instrumentality he obtained it. He certainly received medical treatment; on the first day after his release he had a seidlitz powder given him, on the next day a black draught, and on the third day he was dismissed well, without having been confined to hospital at all. The statements of the hon. Gentleman naturally did not rest. They were repeated and amplified day after day by clever and, perhaps, unscrupulous pens writing in the public press —though he would not say unscrupulous, because many of the persons repeating the statements believed them as much as the hon. Member did — but his statement being quoted again and again in leading articles in powerful journals, he thus lent his name to the dissemination of charges altogether unfounded. In particular, the case was taken up by a very able writer, whose reputation was deservedly wide, and whose literary *sobriquet* was so well known as almost to have acquired an individuality. Judging that gentleman merely by his public writings and without reference to private acquaintance, he believed him to be actuated by a sincere desire to oppose wrong in every shape; and if he had been betrayed into extreme statements—and he had been betrayed into very extreme statements—he still held him to be incapable of writing a word which he did not believe to be true. Unfortunately the tissue of falsehoods put forward without contradiction for several weeks did all the mischief. There was very great excitement when the hon. Member brought forward the Motion of which he had given notice, and within a fortnight afterwards a most important circumstance took place. The War Office had not far to go for suggestions. There were then in this country gentlemen more than any others interested in the reversal of the decision of the Mhow Court Martial and in the ruin of Colonel Crawley; and one of them, a clever, and, as he believed, most unscrupulous man, was suffering under the sentence of the court-martial at Mhow, by which he had been dismissed. The ways of the War Office were not unknown to him; he had suffered vicissitudes in his career, he had fallen and risen again, and he knew how to besiege the War Office day after day till the door was opened to him. Late in 1862 the proceedings of the court-martial which had condemned him arrived in England, and in November of the same year the Judge Advocate General —as had been elicited by a question in that House—passed on the proceedings of that court-martial to the Commander-in-Chief. The noble Marquess said that he had not approved those proceedings; at any rate, he had not said one word against them which appeared in any public record. His Royal Highness the Commander-in-Chief founded two Memoranda on what he at least took to be the consent and approval of the Judge Advocate General, for it was impossible to mistake the manner in which His Royal Highness dealt out his opinion, in no measured terms, to the officers concerned. For months after Mr. Smales had been gazetted out of the service all his solicitations were vain; but after the statement of the hon. Member for Andover in that House a fresh proceeding was concocted by the Judge Advocate General, and, without a due regard to the importance of such a step, the Queen was advised to pardon Mr. Smales. He should like to know what reasons could be given for the right hon. and learned Gentleman's change of opinion, except the pressure caused by the *ex parte* statements which were so movingly repeated in that House. Upon the reversal of Mr. Smales's sentence followed the order for the court-martial upon Colonel Crawley. And here he must notice two absolute novelties as startling, and even more dangerous to the due administration of justice and to that confidence in the military authorities which it was desirable to preserve than that which had reference to Mr. Smales's case. It was now on record, and could not be doubted, because they had it, in addition to all the previous evidence, on the admission of the noble Marquess that night, that that court-martial was ordered on *ex parte* statements, and the *ex parte* statements, too, of those who had more reason than anybody else to wish for Colonel Crawley's ruin. Before he was

Sir James Fergusson

put upon his trial, no opportunity was afforded to Colonel Crawley of answering the charges made against him; although it was the practice of the service to give such an opportunity to any private soldier who might be accused by a comrade. Officers of the army had a right to look to their superiors to sustain them, and did not expect to be condemned unheard. It had not been their practice hitherto to rush to the press as a means of defending themselves. It was on record, however, that Colonel Crawley, on hearing a statement which accused him of inhuman conduct towards Mrs. Lilley, sent an officer immediately to ascertain whether it was true that a sentinel was posted within her room, and found that that was not and never had been the fact; and, moreover, the sentinel was removed still further from the outside of her door. There had, then, in this case been a plain disregard of the fundamental rule of the service, that no one should be brought to trial till he had had an opportunity of offering explanations in answer to the charges made against him. With regard to Adjutant Fitzsimon's letter of complaint against his commanding officer, it was said that there had been a refusal to forward it; but there had been no refusal—its withdrawal had been advised by Major General Farrell entirely out of regard for the writer's prospects—that he, a young officer, might not do a foolish thing and fly in the face of authority. The letter, at all events, was insubordinate; and it was not shown that in urging its withdrawal Major General Farrell was actuated by anything but good feeling towards the writer. At any rate, Colonel Crawley was not in fault in the matter, but forwarded the letter to his superior, as he was bound to do, accompanying it, as was the ordinary course, by his own remarks upon it. Moreover, what was the practice when a junior officer forwarded a letter to head-quarters in any way except through his commanding officer? Why, that it was immediately sent back to that commanding officer for his comments. What was the reason that Lieutenant Fitzsimon's letter, with Colonel Crawley's remarks upon it, was not sent for from India before the extreme and extraordinary course was adopted of ordering him home to take his trial? It had been said, forsooth, that India was so far off. But why, in the name of justice, was one measure to be meted out to an officer who might be stationed in Edinburgh, and another to an officer who was stationed abroad? It might, indeed, have caused a few weeks' delay, but when they saw how long the Government left a trial like that of the *Alexandra* hanging over, to the grievous prejudice of the parties concerned, let them not say that time and distance prevented their following the ordinary course of justice in regard to Colonel Crawley. Colonel Crawley, however, was brought home. The noble Marquess had not been very ingenuous in pointing out that Sir William Mansfield would have had to pronounce in a case in which he was implicated, because the noble Marquess must have known that it was not Sir William Mansfield, but Sir Hugh Rose, the Commander-in-Chief in India, who possessed the power of dealing with such cases. The noble Marquess must be sensible how precipitate and hasty the conduct of the Government had been. Had they waited three weeks or a month after the court-martial was ordered, they would not only have had the letter of Sir Hugh Rose, answering every part of the statement of the hon. Member for Andover, but the letter of Adjutant Fitzsimon, if forwarded in the ordinary course. Moreover, they would have had the very Indian newspapers, the first channels of the slander, recanting and repairing their error, and stating that they had been deceived by the letter of Mr. Smales. [The hon. and gallant Member here read an extract from *The Times of India* withdrawing all the charges made in that paper against Colonel Crawley.] He did not wish to enter upon the subject of the court-martial's decision, although some hon. Gentlemen desired to make that House a court of appeal against the decision, and the noble Marquess did not seem to treat that as an improper proceeding. But Colonel Crawley, with every disadvantage, with the issue narrowed in a way which he complained made it impossible that full justice could be done him, although prosecuted with zeal and ability, and although denied the production of documents essential for his case, yet triumphed so completely over every allegation that there was not a question as to his unanimous acquittal. One act of public honour he must do to the learned counsel who conducted the prosecution. The learned counsel had been, he must say, dealt with. It had been the Deputy Judge Advocate acted, by a most impartial as the counsel assist-

ing the official prosecutor. A gentleman of his eminence at the bar employed for such a purpose, and opposed as he was by able counsel on the other side, would naturally think it his duty to leave no stone unturned in order to procure that conviction which to his mind no doubt seemed consistent with justice. With respect to the hon. Member for Andover, that hon. Gentleman had two courses open to him—he had to offer an apology to that House for having, unwittingly he believed, been the vehicle of gross slander and unscrupulous falsehood.

MR. DUDLEY FORTESCUE rose to protest against the hon. and gallant Gentleman's language. He did not think it was at all parliamentary that an hon. Member who had been in error on some points, and who had acknowledged that he had been so, should have such epithets as "gross slanders" and "unscrupulous falsehoods" coupled with the mention of his name, because in the discharge of his duty he had called the House's attention to a very grave public scandal, and which, as he would at a later period point out, had a great deal more foundation than the hon. and gallant Gentleman appeared to suppose.

SIR JAMES FERGUSSON said, he did not retract a word. He believed the hon. Member for Andover sincerely believed all he said, but he had been made the vehicle of falsehood. He would not make quotations from the proceedings at the court-martial for the purpose of proving this; he would leave hon. Gentlemen to satisfy themselves on the point. The hon. Member had two courses before him — to apologize to the House, or take exception to the proceedings of the court-martial. He had not adopted either, but raised fresh issues. That was a course not consistent with what he thought fair in regard to this case. He hoped and believed that the credit and position of the officers impugned would not suffer from what had been said, but he still thought great and grievous injustice had been done to them. There was no department on which that injustice rested more heavily than on that of the Judge Advocate General, and he did the right hon. Gentleman no wrong in saying so, as he had the full opportunity of reply.

MR. HEADLAM said, that before entering upon the subject to which the attention of the House had been called that night—namely, the Crawley Court

Martial—he would in a few words answer what had been said by the hon. and gallant Baronet opposite (Sir James Fergusson), with respect to the Mhow Court Martial. There had been a little confusion here by the mixing up of two opinions he had given on the subject with the observations made by his noble Friend the Under Secretary for War. The course he had taken on that occasion was a clear and simple one ; he only regretted that it was not in accordance with the practice that the opinions of the Law Officers of the Crown should be produced, inasmuch as they would have made this evident. The facts were these :—The proceedings of the Mhow Court Martial were sent to him without any additional evidence or statement of facts whatever. He gave an opinion simply on the face of the proceedings, that opinion being founded on various objections which he thought applied to the whole course of the proceedings. At the same time, he felt, that as the proceedings had been confirmed in India, there were only two courses open—the one to advise Her Majesty to grant a pardon, the other to take no notice of what had occurred, but to hold the finding good, inasmuch as there was no power of revision. He stated, in his first opinion, that if it had come before him in the ordinary course of business in this country, he should have recommended that it be sent back to the Court ; but he could not say that it was illegal. At the same time, he stated his opinion, which he still retained, that Captain Smales had been guilty of a grave military offence in writing the letter, and he arrived at this opinion independently of the charge. Upon that opinion his noble Friend stated what took place in this House, and upon it Captain Smales was gazetted out of the regiment. Afterwards, further papers were laid before him, showing the manner in which Captain Smales's witnesses had been treated ; and he then considered the proceedings so unfair that he advised that Her Majesty should be advised to grant that officer a pardon. These were the circumstances of the case. It was, of course, competent to any one to question the opinions which he gave ; but he entertained no doubt with respect to them either when he gave them or at the present time.

He now came to the question which was immediately before the House. He could assure the right hon. and gallant General opposite (General Peel) that, in common with

him and with every one who had anything to do with the administration of justice in the army, he deprecated the discussion of the proceedings of courts-martial in that House, but he was individually glad that his hon. Friend the Member for Andover (Mr. Fortescue) had made his Motion, because it gave him an opportunity of laying before the House the steps which he had taken with reference to this particular inquiry, and the principles upon which he had acted, and, at the same time, of answering the objections which had been urged against himself and against the office with which he was connected. If he understood the right hon. and gallant General rightly, he said that the Government were wrong from the first—wrong in ordering the court-martial, wrong in holding it in this country, wrong as to the manner in which it was conducted, and wrong in the course which they had since pursued with reference to the production of papers. On all of these charges he would make a few observations. As to the papers, he must remind the right hon. and gallant General that the proceedings of a court-martial were in reality the record of a great public trial. Now, if there was one principle which was more characteristic of our Constitution than another it was that there should be nothing of the nature of secrecy connected with a public trial ; and although he deprecated in the strongest terms the discussion of the proceedings of courts-martial in that House, the abstinence must proceed from the discretion of the House itself, and it was neither desirable nor possible that the Government should, by any arbitrary exercise of power, stop discussion by refusing to lay the record of a great public trial upon the table. The other papers laid before the House were memoranda, or documents of that description. He (Mr. Headlam) agreed that there was a difficulty about laying them on the table, for one of them led to another, and it was difficult to say when they were to stop. It was possible that in their production the Government might have gone too far, but if an error had been committed it was not one of a serious description. With reference to such courts-martial as these at Mhow, and on Colonel Crawley in England, it was not for the Government, when so strong an opinion had been expressed, to stop discussion by refusing to produce the papers. The next point was, whether the Government were right or wrong in ordering a court-martial on Colonel Crawley, and in deciding that it should take place in this country. Let him carry the recollection of the House back to the time when the court-martial was ordered. There were then a few plain, broad, simple facts which had excited much attention in the public mind, and exercised considerable influence in that House—a few broad and simple facts which the Government were not in a condition to contradict, and which they were not at this moment able to contradict. He alluded to the facts that Sergeant Major Lilley was up to the time of these occurrences a perfectly good soldier, of the highest possible character; that he came to his end, and his wife almost contemporaneously, under circumstances signally calculated to excite compassion in the public mind ; that he and the other sergeants who were put in prison were never brought to a court-martial ; and that no very clear grounds were then stated, nor could be now stated, why they were incarcerated. In addition to all this, there stood out the fact, that the name not only of the commanding officer of the regiment, but the names of officers of still higher rank in India, were mentioned in connection with these facts. Suppose the Government had adopted the course which he supposed the right hon. and gallant General would have pursued, and, acting public opinion at defiance, had said, " We will trust entirely to the officers of India. We will not have an investigation in this country, but will leave it to them to say whether there shall be a court-martial." [General PEEL : That is not at all the doctrine which I laid down.] He understood the right hon. Gentleman to object most strongly to the interference of the Government and the order that the court-martial should take place in this country.

GENERAL PEEL explained that what he said was, that if the Secretary of State had come to Parliament, and declared upon his responsibility that he would have an inquiry, in which justice should be done to all parties, that House would have been satisfied.

MR. HEADLAM said, that was exactly what was done ; but the noble Lord the Secretary of State, having promised an inquiry, was bound to have it in such a form as he considered best calculated to elucidate the whole case and satisfy the public. He put it to the House what would have been the consequence if the Government had refused to hold the court-martial in this country. If the court-

martial had taken place in India, the proceedings would not have been known in this country; the inquiry would have taken place under the immediate control and superintendence of the very officers whose names had been mixed up with the charges. Those officers would have been placed in a position of the greatest doubt and difficulty ; they would have been subjected to grave and unjust suspicions, and in the end there would have remained in this country a strong impression that a deed of cruelty and oppression had been committed in a distant land. Mark what had been the result of the proceedings as they had actually taken place. There had been a trial conducted under the superintendence of men of the highest rank and position in the army, who were entirely unconnected with the charges, and whose verdict was entitled to the highest possible confidence from the country. The proceedings of each day were published by the press ; and the result was that the impression which had been produced by the facts to which he had referred was gradually obliterated until at the end, owing to the manner in which the trial had been conducted, there was a general acquiescence in the verdict which was returned. Under those circumstances, he had no hesitation in saying that the decision of the Government, that the trial should take place in this country, was a wise one. He did not wish to underrate the evils which were inseparable from these proceedings. The trial of a commanding officer for the abuse of his powers, whether he proved innocent or guilty, was in itself a very serious thing; nor did he wish to underrate the less important consideration of the cost of the investigation or the hardship to Colonel Crawley, although against that must be set off the additional value to him of an acquittal in this country ; but looking at the matter from the highest point of view, and having regard to the importance of maintaining the public confidence that justice was well administered by military tribunals, he maintained that it was infinitely better that the trial should have taken place in this country than in India. He now came to that part of the question for which he was more especially responsible—namely, the manner in which the trial was conducted; and the simplest course would be for him to state frankly to the House every step which he took in the matter, and leave it to them to say whether he could have acted in a more suitable manner. Let him, however, first say a word or two about the functions of his office, with respect to which some confusion appeared to exist. The duties of that office, as its name partially indicated, were somewhat anomalous. Certain of them were judicial and others connected with the functions of a prosecution. The judicial duties were to advise Her Majesty after the proceedings were over as to their legality, and to advise the Court upon any point which might arise in the course of a trial. These were the only judicial duties, the examination of the evidence and the consideration of the verdict rested entirely with the Court, and the Judge Advocate had nothing to do with them. On looking back to the history of his office, he found that it had been much more a prosecutor's office than a judge's. For instance, in the trial of General Whitelock for his failure at Buenos Ayres, at the beginning of this century, the then Judge Advocate, Mr. Ryder, himself conducted the prosecution, performing the part which was on the late occasion performed by Sir Alfred Horsford, assisted by the Deputy Judge Advocate. He had no doubt that Mr. Ryder, in General Whitelock's case, acted in conformity with the spirit of the time, but he appeared to have pressed the case in a manner hardly consistent with the practice of the present day. Coming to what took place upon the present occasion, he had to inform the House that after it had been determined by the higher authorities that Colonel Crawley should be tried in this country, instructions were sent to him (Mr. Headlam) to draw the charges. The evidence that was laid before him seemed to be such as would justify the placing of an officer upon his trial. Drawing the charges was, of course, a duty of the prosecution; but, at the same time, this duty was a part of the ordinary functions of his office. After having drawn the charges, he had next to give advice upon some points of evidence. After these steps a considerable interval elapsed during the reference to India, and at last, in October, Colonel Crawley arrived in this country, together with a large body of persons, who, it should be observed, were not divided into witnesses for the defence and witnesses for the prosecution, but were simply sent over from India under a general order from Sir Hugh Rose to the effect, that anybody who knew anything about the matter should be sent to England. He then communicated with the Deputy Judge Advocate, and it was agreed between them that he should take the part of officiating Judge Advocate at the trial. It had not been customary for the Deputy Judge Advocate to take an active part in a trial, but it was thought that the importance of the present trial made it an exception to the general rule. The Horse Guards appointed Sir Alfred Horsford to conduct the prosecution, but did not give him the assistance of an attorney or counsel. A few days afterwards he received a letter from the Deputy Judge Advocate stating, that very naturally Sir Alfred Horsford had come to him for advice as to the manner in which the prosecution should be conducted. Now, let the House consider the position in which Sir Alfred Horsford, a gallant officer and a straightforward English gentleman, was placed. He was called upon, without the aid of counsel or attorney, to prepare a prosecution involving an immense complication of facts, and a great variety of evidence. Moreover, from the manner in which the witnesses were sent over from India, he had no knowledge of what each individual could state. In circumstances of such difficulty it is not to be wondered at that he went to the Deputy Judge Advocate for advice; who first gave him general advice, which afterwards became particular advice; and ultimately the Deputy Judge Advocate wrote to him (Mr. Headlam) that he was expected to give so much assistance to the prosecution that he could not follow out the original arrangement under which he was to be officiating Judge Advocate on this trial. In consequence of that he (Mr. Headlam) appointed Colonel Pipon, who had written a book upon the subject, and who was well acquainted with the duties of officiating Judge Advocate, and requested him to undertake that duty which he had discharged to the satisfaction, he believed, of all parties. After that arrangement the objection to the Deputy Judge Advocate General assisting Sir Alfred Horsford did not continue, and, therefore, he did assist him in getting up the case. Then came the question of how the trial was to be managed, and who was to assist Sir Alfred Horsford. He (Mr. Headlam) consulted the noble Lord at the head of the War Office and the Commander-in-Chief upon the subject. His first impression was that in a case of that magnitude it would be proper that an attorney should be appointed to collect evidence, to instruct counsel, and to assist the Horse Guards. Objections

Mr. Headlam

were made to that course, on the ground that there was no precedent for it in the whole history of the army. That objection might have been got over had it not been further urged that there was a strong feeling in the army against introducing the practice of employing lawyers to conduct military trials. He did not himself entertain that feeling, but he considered it his duty on all occasions to consider the feelings of the army, and he accordingly, on this occasion, gave up his own opinion and consented that the Deputy Judge Advocate General should assist the prosecution at the trial. There were other reasons which induced him to come to this conclusion. The Deputy Judge Advocate had practised at the common law bar and in criminal courts with success, and had considerable experience. He was also aware of that gentleman's earnest desire that the trial should be a perfectly fair one in all respects —fair towards the accused, the prosecution, and the public, and with the usual zeal of civil servants on behalf of their departments, he was desirous that the duty intrusted to the office with which he was connected, should be properly performed. Strong language had been used upon this subject, but he would like to hear from any hon. and gallant Gentleman, what other course could have been taken. To have left Sir Alfred Horsford without assistance to conduct the whole case, with counsel of great eminence arrayed against him, would have been manifestly unfair, and would have made the trial a mockery. It was very easy to find fault with what had been done; but it was exceedingly difficult to say what better course could have been taken; and, after hearing all that had been said, he (Mr. Headlam) did not see what other course he could have taken for the public service.

In conclusion, he would wish to say a few words upon the subject of courts-martial in general. During the time he had held his present office he had had an opportunity of reading the proceedings of some thousands of courts-martial, and he was glad to be able to say that in ninety-nine out of one hundred, or even a larger proportion, justice had been well administered in the army, and in such a form as to do credit to the good sense and intelligence of the officers. No doubt there were some defects, such as want of uniformity in the punishments; but, speaking generally, the public had a right to place confidence in the mode in which military justice was administered. At the same time, the legal machinery at the command of the Judge Advocate was most insufficient. There did occasionally occur cases, such as the case under consideration and that which occurred in Dublin two or three years ago, where the legal machinery at the disposal of the Horse Guards was found to be insufficient. In such cases, of course, the prisoner, from his station and the importance of the issues involved, would be able to obtain the best legal assistance. Therefore, in such cases, for justice to be done, the prosecutor or military man ought to have legal assistance also, but no provision for that assistance existed. Even if a prisoner should be provided, and the prosecutor also should be assisted by counsel, then the Court would be in a difficulty. The President, a military man, the head of a Court whose members were unacquainted with law, would be called upon to decide nice questions of evidence mooted by opposing counsel. As the law now stood, therefore, the Judge Advocate was scarcely in a position to grapple with success with great cases such as that under discussion, and it behoved the Government to consider whether or not it was desirable to introduce some change. All he could say was that he had made the best arrangement he could under the circumstances, and, in favour of that arrangement he might urge that it separated the duties of prosecutor from the judicial duties of Judge Advocate. In reference to any change which might be made in the present system, he would, for his own part, observe that he believed the ordinary criminal courts of this country were the most perfect tribunals that ever existed for the trial of great and complicated causes. In those courts the evidence was in the first place collected and sifted by men whose profession made them conversant with the duty ; it was then laid before counsel ; and when the trial came on it was conducted by men somewhat in the position of his hon. and learned Friend the Attorney General, who managed it with the utmost gravity, dignity, and decorum ; while the accused, on the other hand, had at his command all the ability and eloquence which the bar of England could afford. The result was that the trial proceeded without any wrangling between counsel, under the auspices of a Judge who would be sure to put a stop to any irregularity that might arise, and who, at the close of the proceedings, marshalled the facts of the case in the clearest possible manner for the consideration of the jury.

That so perfect a mode of procedure could
ever be attained by our courts-martial we
had perhaps no right to expect; but he
could not, at the same time, refrain from
expressing his opinion, that if any change
were made in the present system, the object held in view ought to be to make it
approximate as nearly as possible to the
standard of excellence which he had just
described.

MR. MOWBRAY said, he was quite
sure that there was one point in his right
hon. Friend's statement which all would
agree in—that he had stated with perfect
fairness and frankness to the House that
night all the proceedings in his own office
connected with the court-martial on Colonel
Crawley. But with respect to the Mhow
Court Martial, he thought the House had
a right to expect a further reference than
that which his right hon. Friend had
given. With respect to that court-martial, his right hon. Friend said that his
course was clear and simple; but what was
alleged in reference to that court-martial
was, that the vacillating judgments which
had been pronounced upon it tended very
much to subvert the administration of
military justice in India. Now, let him
call attention to the particular dates of
that court-martial. It was, he believed,
concluded on the 9th of June, 1862, and
its proceedings were confirmed by Sir
Hugh Rose on the 11th of July, and
they reached this country about the month
of October, 1862. Some time in the
month of November, those proceedings
having come to my right hon. Friend's
office, and full time for its consideration
having been afforded him, he advised that
the proceedings, and the sentence passed
in accordance with those proceedings, were
legal; and acting upon that opinion, the
memorandum of the Commander-in-Chief
was issued, and Captain Smales was gazetted out of the regiment on the 18th
December, and his name disappeared from
the *Army List* in January, 1863. Now,
what he (Mr. Mowbray) complained of was
that his right hon. Friend, while professing to make to the House a clear
statement that evening on the subject,
had given it no information with regard
to the interval which elapsed between
December, 1862, and June, 1863, and of
the circumstances which were brought before him by the importunity of Captain
Smales's friends, who were continually
knocking at the door of the Judge Advocate's office. He (Mr. Mowbray) wanted

Mr. Headlam

to know what were the circumstances
which led him to change his mind, and
having pronounced in November, 1862,
that the proceedings were legal, and the
sentence legal, that he should have advised that the proceedings should be set
aside, and that a free pardon should be
given to Paymaster Smales in June last
year. If ever, he might add, there was
a case in which his right hon. Friend
should be careful that the proceedings of
his department should not be marked by
vacillation, it was the case of Indian
courts-martial. He said so for a reason
which had been well explained by His
Royal Highness the Commander-in-Chief,
who stated that—

"Whereas the Commander-in-Chief in England
submits to Her Majesty the name of any officer
who, having been tried by court-martial, is sentenced to be cashiered, and the actual cashiering
does not take place until the Queen's pleasure has
been taken, in India the fiat of the Commander-
in-Chief in that country is absolute, and no reference is made to the Queen's pleasure."

That being the state of things, it was all
the more requisite that his right hon.
Friend should have acted with the greatest
caution and deliberation before he attempted to call in question the sentence of a
court-martial so approved. If he thought
that Captain Smales had been really guilty
of a military crime, what was the evidence
which had induced him to change his
mind? But, be that as it might, his right
hon. Friend had paid a very well-deserved
tribute to the proceedings of courts-martial
in general—a tribute to the justice of which
he (Mr. Mowbray), though he had not had
the good fortune of his right hon. Friend
in being connected for so long a time with
his office, could, from his own experience
in the office of Judge Advocate, bear
testimony. In ninety-nine cases out of
one hundred their proceedings were very
satisfactory; but he must say that if
there were any courts-martial in reference
to which, more than others, according to
his experience, technical accuracy was observed, it was those held in India. Indeed,
so much so was this the case, that he had
frequently seen proceedings sent back for
revision on points which he (Mr. Mowbray) should hardly have deemed of sufficient importance to require such a step.
Unless, then, the proceedings of Indian
courts-martial had very much changed
within the last six years, his right hon.
Friend, in impeaching the sentence of the
Mhow Court Martial, took a step calculated
very seriously to shake our military sys-

tem in that country. His right hon. Friend had alluded to the question of the conduct of Sergeant Major Lilley. He (Mr. Mowbray) did not wish to enter into that question, which was a very painful one, but his right hon. Friend should have recollected, when speaking of him as a man of such high character, that the evidence at Aldershot showed that Sergeant Major Lilley was openly hostile to Colonel Crawley, and that he used violent language against him to the other sergeants, thereby increasing the ill-feeling already existing in the regiment against the commanding officer. Now he (Mr. Mowbray) said that evidence, which he held to be unimpeachable, did not bear out the exemplary character which had been given to Sergeant Major Lilley, There was a question put by the hon. and gallant Member for Longford (Major O'Reilly) which his right hon. Friend did not touch upon, and which, from the manner in which it had been treated that night, promised anything but an end to the controversy—the question of the legality or illegality of the arrest. That was a question which appeared likely to be tried by the Courts in this kingdom. The noble Lord (the Marquess of Hartington) repeating the opinion derived from his right hon. Friend, had again stated that there could be no doubt as to the legality of the arrest; but his right hon. Friend could not have forgotten the opinion of the Judge Advocate of Bombay as to its legality. Stress had been laid on the Article of War that was read by the hon. and gallant Member for Longford; but was his right hon. Friend aware of the construction put by the highest military authority of the age (the late Duke of Wellington) upon that very Article? In 1844 the case of the imprisonment of two officers of the 76th Regiment of Foot was brought before the House, and Lord Hardinge was asked whether under that Article any officer could be kept in arrest more than eight days without being brought to a court-martial. Lord Hardinge said, "Certainly an officer can be kept under arrest for a longer time by order of the Commander-in-Chief." He (Mr. Mowbray) ventured to think that what could be done by order of the Commander-in-Chief in England could be done by order of the Commander-in-Chief in Bombay, and he would like to have had some more explicit statement of the grounds upon which the noble Lord gave so decided an opinion that the order for arrest was illegal. He

(Mr. Mowbray) now came to the latter part of the speech of the right hon. Gentleman, with respect to the manner in which the trial had been conducted by the department over which his right hon. Friend presided. In doing so, he could assure the House that he did not at all wish to lay himself open to the imputation which now-a-days was usually flung out by Gentlemen on the Ministerial side of the House about attacking an absent man. He was not going to attack the Deputy Judge Advocate. In all the commendations passed by his right hon. Friend upon that zealous, indefatigable, and most learned public servant, he most entirely concurred. When in office he had the pleasure of seeing how thoroughly he had mastered both the principles and practice of military law; he knew how assiduous he was in the discharge of his duties; he knew how impartial he was in his mind; and he was quite sure that if the Deputy Judge Advocate had erred at all it was through an earnest desire to do his duty to the department with which he was connected. As his right hon. Friend had said, among all those indefatigable men who served the Crown without the hope of that distinction which rewarded more public servants, not one was more zealous, more learned, or more able than the Deputy Judge Advocate. He would rather take issue with his right hon. Friend with reference to what he described as the difficulties with which he had to contend, and say that the fault rested with his right hon. Friend who seemed to have felt the difficulty, but had not the boldness to hold his own opinion against the Horse Guards. With respect to the mode of conducting the proceedings on the trial, his right hon. Friend said that the office and the duties were anomalous, and that in times past the post was more of a prosecuting than a judicial nature. He (Mr. Mowbray) rather thought that the proper definition of the *judex advocatus* would be rather the other way—that it implied that the *judex*, or judicial part, was the more predominant, and that the *advocatus* had not the meaning which was commonly ascribed to it. His right hon. Friend referred to the case of Whitelock, and to a case when one of his predecessors, Sir C. Morgan, conducted the prosecution; but his right hon. Friend should recollect that it was through his instrumentality the change was made by which not only the Judge Advocate was not prosecutor, but that he cannot be a witness for the prosecution. But what was his duty with respect to the prisoner? He found the law thus laid down in the last edition of *Simmons on Courts Martial*, a book of admitted authority—

"Mr. Tytler considers that the Judge Advocate is bound to assist the prisoner in the conduct of his defence; but it is more in consonance with the custom of the service that the Judge Advocate should only interfere to the extent to which the Court itself is bound to interpose, to take care that the prisoner shall not suffer from a want of knowledge of the law, or from a deficiency of experience or of ability to elicit from witnesses, or to develop by the testimony which in the course of the trial may present itself, a full statement of the facts of the case as bearing on the defence. To this end the court-martial and Judge Advocate are bound, it is conceived, to offer their advice to the prisoner. Justice is the object for which the Court is convened and the Judge Advocate appointed. To this aim all their inquiries ought to be directed; and if in the prosecution of this design the prisoner should be benefited, the efforts of the Court or of the Judge Advocate will have been satisfactorily and legitimately exerted."

What he said was, that in the part which his right hon. Friend allowed the Deputy Judge Advocate to take in the prosecution his right hon. Friend lost sight of the functions of his own office as Judge Advocate, because it was impossible to distinguish between the chief of the Department and its permanent official, or to forget the close and confidential relations which must usually subsist between them. His right hon. Friend said, that when Sir Alfred Horsford was appointed prosecutor the War Office gave him no counsel or attorney. Was he to understand that the right hon. Gentleman made the request that he should have counsel and attorney? [Mr. HEADLAM: No!] Then that was the very omission for which he blamed his right hon. Friend; because, in so exceptional a case, where the eyes of every one, not only in England but in India, were fixed upon the proceedings, it was of the greatest possible importance that the prosecution should be fully and efficiently conducted, so that no ground for finding fault should have been left, either as to the appliances with which the prosecution was got up, or as to the mode in which it was conducted. The right hon. Gentleman did not seem to have consulted the Horse Guards; and as to the taxpayers, the first complaint of their representative, the Member for Stoke-upon-Trent, was that no solicitor was employed. Many hon. and gallant Friends might differ from him, but, if he had been in office, he should have deemed it absolutely indispensable to have

Mr. Mowbray

funds to employ solicitor and counsel versed in criminal law, so that the prosecution should be fully and efficiently conducted. And in a prosecution where an expenditure of upwards of £18,000 had already been sanctioned, it was surely worth while to incur this trifling additional legal charge with a view to the greater regularity of the proceedings. His right hon. Friend said, that a great deal of strong language had been used with respect to the proceedings at the court-martial. He (Mr. Mowbray) was sorry to say, that if he were to venture to travel into that matter he should be compelled to assent to much of the criticism which they had heard and read in respect to it. He read day by day in *The Times* what passed, and it did not appear to him that the prosecution was conducted as, from his knowledge of criminal procedure, he should have expected that it would have been. There was not enough candour and fairness, and there was too much effort to gain a verdict. The introduction of new matter in a highly rhetorical and exceedingly ingenious and astute reply, though creditable to the intellect and ability of the hon. and learned Gentleman, could not carry any greater condemnation than was contained in the closing words, that he had tried to lead the Court through a gate unknown to the public and by a way avoided by the prisoner. If there was one thing which he had learnt from his experience in criminal courts, it was that the part of counsel for the prosecution in his opening speech was to be fair, candid, explicit, and above-board, never to introduce new matter after the mouth of the prisoner's counsel was closed, to avoid highly rhetorical language, and to always understate rather than overstate the facts with which he had to deal. With respect to the future, he could not but fear that both the proceedings at Mhow and at the Crawley Court Martial might have induced a feeling in the public mind that some change in the law of courts-martial was necessary. The noble Lord (the Marquess of Hartington) said, that "discipline should be summary but strict, not hid in the Horse Guards nor kept in the office of the Judge Advocate General." But in this case discipline, it was said, was neither summary nor strict; it had languished from October, 1862 to June, 1863; it was hid in the records of the Judge Advocate's office; and all the discussions and the questions asked in this House had failed to clear up this part of the transaction.

He regretted that it was not proposed to make some change in the Articles of War, so that in future the Deputy Judge Advocate should not take the course which he had taken in these proceedings. If a new system were adopted it was doubtful whether in 99 cases out of 100, perhaps in 999 out of 1,000, you would have justice on the whole better administered. But if you are to replace the old system by a new one, you must still bear in mind that the procedure at courts-martial could not be as technical as in other courts of justice ; the feelings and traditions of the service must be respected ; and besides this, the House should remember the words of Lord Macaulay—.

" A strong line of demarcation must be drawn between soldiers and the rest of the community ; they must be subject to a sharper code and to a more stringent form of procedure than are administered by the ordinary tribunals. For of all maladies incident to the body politic military insubordination is that which requires the most prompt and drastic remedies."

Whatever changes were introduced should be introduced with deliberation, and he hoped that nothing which his right hon. Friend might have done would tend to shake the confidence felt in the administration of justice in our army either here or in India.

MR. SMOLLETT said, he thought that the present debate was more a personal explanation of the Member for Andover than a Motion for papers, and in his judgment the statement made by the hon. Gentleman (Mr. Fortescue) last Session was not capable of modification. He thought the hon. Gentleman ought to have retracted the statement he made then, and that an apology was due to the House and to the country ; for it was owing to that " sensation speech" of the hon. Member that the court-martial was ordered at Aldershot, and that £20,000 of public money had been thrown away. The hon. Gentleman had told them of the arrest of Sergeant Major Lilley on April 24, and said that he had been detained for thirty days ; that the detention was illegal ; that the sergeant was confined in a single bomb-proof room, so ingeniously constructed that it resembled a furnace, being heated by the sun during the day, and never cool during the night. He had said that his wife was imprisoned along with him, a woman so reduced by diarrhœa that she was unable to rise from her bed, and he complained of the indignity put upon her by the sentinels being placed in her apartment ; and that

in this place, more like an oven than a human habitation, Sergeant Major Lilley was baked to death.

MR. DUDLEY FORTESCUE protested against misquotations of his speech. He should be perfectly satisfied if the hon. Member quoted either from *Hansard* or *The Times*, but he had never used the expression "baked" to death.

MR. SMOLLETT said, the hon. Gentleman had spoken of the prison as an oven, and confinement in an oven implied baking. The hon. Member told them, that so convinced were the relatives of Sergeant Major Lilley that he had been judicially murdered, that his relatives were determined to take criminal proceedings against the offender if he set his foot in England, and he stated that there were abundant witnesses to speak to the truth of that statement. That would be found reported in *The Times*. And the hon. Gentleman went on to ask if the person who had committed such acts was fit to command a cavalry regiment. Now, who that had heard that statement would have believed that Sergeant Major Lilley, during his arrest, had lived in a house of four rooms, and this was denominated a "bomb-proof cell, so heated that it resembled an oven." The hon. Gentleman had explained since that he alluded to the second house in which the Sergeant Major was confined. But this was not bomb-proof—it was a tiled house ; and he (Mr. Smollett) begged to say, that both the houses occupied by Sergeant Major Lilley were better than many of those in which he had resided for months during the hot weather in India. Almost every allegation made by the hon. Member had proved unfounded ; and he (Mr. Smollett) repeated that, in his opinion, the hon. Gentleman was bound to have made a retractation of statements reflecting upon an officer serving in a high position in India. He would not go into the details of the trial, or consider whether Colonel Crawley was an officer of tact and discretion, or whether that House should be constituted a court of appeal from courts-martial ; but he would ask, who was really responsible for the discipline of the army ? Was the Commander-in-Chief solely responsible ; or was his responsibility shared with the Secretary for War ? He thought that was a very important question. In illustration of this question, he wished first to advert to the case of Paymaster Smales, who was attached to the 6th Dragoons. He was found fault with by

Colonel Crawley, upon whom he retorted, that any slight irregularities of his were as nothing compared with those which the colonel was constantly in the habit of committing, and that the colonel made false certificates of his presence at musters and parades. That was a sort of letter that could not remain unanswered. It did not appear, however, that Colonel Crawley wished to treat Paymaster Smales with undue severity; but the latter declined to withdraw the letter, and seemed to have constituted himself the mouthpiece of the discontented officers of the corps. A court-martial was held upon Captain Smales, and the sentence of the Court was, that Paymaster Smales should be cashiered, and that sentence was confirmed by the Commander-in-Chief in India. A memorial was sent up from Paymaster Smales, which was unsuccessful, and he was removed from the army. Up to this time everything seemed to have been correct and consistent, if not just. When the matter was first mooted in that House, the authorities seemed to be resolute; the noble Lord (the Marquess of Hartington) told them that Paymaster Smales had been guilty of insubordination, and that he had been removed; and when the matter was brought forward by Mr. Coningham, he repeated that statement. But soon after a great commotion was got up, sensation speeches were made, and it seemed as if the Ministers had lost their wits, and they were then told that an inquiry should take place, and that the matter was referred to the Judge Advocate General. The Judge Advocate General was a legal gentleman, and legal gentlemen could generally be reckoned on to give such opinions as their clients might desire. After the adjournment of the House in July it was stated that Paymaster Smales had, under the advice of the Judge Advocate General, received a free pardon. Whilst the friends of Paymaster Smales were congratulating themselves on their success, Sir Edward Lugard, on the part of the Horse Guards, declared that His Royal Highness the Commander-in-Chief would pay no attention to the pardon, and that Paymaster Smales would not be reinstated, and would not receive his half-pay. Three months afterwards, just as Colonel Crawley was beginning his defence, the name of Paymaster Smales re-appeared in the *Gazette* as captain, and it turned out that he was to receive his half-pay from the date at which he was removed from his paymastorship. Now he would ask the

Mr. Smollett

House whether such an unseemly mass of capricious orders had ever before been issued in any matter of serious business? It was clear that one or two, if not three, Departments were at cross purposes with each other. This was apparent too from the way in which Colonel Crawley had been attacked. When the hon. Member for Andover made his sensation speech last year, the noble Lord the Under Secretary of State for War declared that he would not offer up Colonel Crawley or Sir Hugh Rose to satisfy public indignation. But in a short time a different course was adopted. The late hon. Member for Brighton (Mr. Coningham) attacked the authorities every night, stating that he did not want to see Colonel Crawley punished, but declaring that the Commander-in-Chief ought to be punished, and that execution ought to be done on Sir William Mansfield and Sir Hugh Rose. The noble Lord at the head of the Government at length consented that further inquiries should be made; and a week afterwards it was stated that Colonel Crawley was to be put on his trial in India. After a little more agitation it was intimated that he would be brought to trial in this country; and if some more pressure had been applied from below the gang-way, perhaps the command of the army would have been taken out of the hands of the Commander-in-Chief, and the entire regiment would have been ordered home from India. Now he should like to know to what Department of the State the country was indebted for this contradictory and incoherent course of conduct. If the various orders were issued by the Commander-in-Chief of his own free will, then he must be a person made of very squeezable materials. If his opinion was set aside by the Office of the Secretary for War, and he was coerced into that course of conduct, and if the War Office was influenced by the political demonstrations on that side of the House, the fact ought to be admitted, and then the blame could be placed on the proper Department. In whatever way the proceedings were viewed it appeared to him that not one single Department of the Government was free from blame. It had been said that it was an excellent thing that the court-martial had taken place at Aldershot, and that it was most desirable to disabuse the public mind of the erroneous impression which existed. He altogether demurred to that opinion, and did not think there was any necessity at all for holding the court-martial. The hon. Member who had introduced the subject (Mr. Fortescue) was the cause of that court-martial, and nothing had struck him (Mr. Smollett) more than the absence of all notice of the salient points of his speech by the noble Lord the Under Secretary for War. The noble Lord took no notice of baking one soldier to death and driving another to a lunatic asylum, and altogether passed over the hard treatment to which it was said Mrs. Lilley had been subjected. If the noble Lord did not know these facts, he ought to have informed the House that he would institute inquiries into the matter. It might have been said that such inquiries could only have been made in India; but the hon. Member had declared that all the necessary witnesses were already in this country: if, therefore, a Commission had been appointed, it would have been clearly ascertained that the hon. Member for Andover had discovered a series of mares' nests. He repeated, that he could not absolve the Government from blame, but no doubt the chief offender was the hon. Member for Andover, who, by his exaggerated and inflated statements, made without authority and without proof, had driven the Government into proceedings most mischievous to the discipline of the army and fatal to the interest of those whom he had wished to serve.

MR. DUTTON said, he desired to express his satisfaction at the handsome manner in which Sir William Mansfield had been spoken of, and thought the explanation of the noble Lord the Under Secretary, with reference to his previous remarks on that distinguished officer, perfectly satisfactory. With reference to the allegation that Captain Smales had been deprived of a proper opportunity of getting up his evidence by the arrest of the sergeants, he was of opinion that it was disproved by the dates. Now, what were the dates of these transactions? The court-martial commenced on the 1st of April, 1862. Captain Smales commenced his defence on the 21st of April, and the men were not arrested until the 26th; so that if he did not get up materials for his defence he had ample time to see his witnesses, and, therefore, it was quite clear that he could not have been prejudiced by the men having been placed under arrest. With reference to the duration of the men's imprisonment, it was impossible to manage such matters in India in the same manner as they were managed in this country; and

he did not see how Sir William Mansfield could have acted otherwise than he had done, seeing that it took eight days to communicate from the place where he was to the scene of the court-martial. He found that grave suspicions existed of insubordination, and from the evidence of Sergeant Morton it appeared that the three parties who were arrested had been in the habit of holding meetings with closed doors. As Commander-in-Chief he was responsible for the discipline and safety of his regiment, and only acted with the decision which was the characteristic of a good soldier.

MR. E. P. BOUVERIE said, he wished to protest against the attacks upon his hon. Friend the Member for Andover (Mr. D. Fortescue), by the hon. and gallant Member for Ayr (Sir James Fergusson), and the hon. Member for Dumbarton (Mr. Smollett). The language used towards his hon. Friend was perfectly unjustifiable. If facts were brought to the knowlege of any hon. Member which, to the best of his judgment, gave *primâ facie* ground for believing that there had been a default in the administration of justice, either civil or military, at home or in any of our colonial possessions, he had a right, and it was his duty to bring those facts before the House that they might be inquired into. He had heard the speech of the hon. Member for Andover last year, and he was bound to say that though his statements had been proved to be unfounded in their material parts, yet in the first instance his hon. Friend had grounds for making those statements to the House. He was not the first man to originate those statements. He had himself, and he had no doubt other hon. Members had received a printed statement and correspondence, in which the same facts were given as distinctly and as broadly as they had been stated by his hon. Friend. In that pamphlet it was stated that the friends of Sergeant Major Lilley, when Colonel Crawley gave them the opportunity, meant to have him arrested and tried for manslaughter. It was, therefore, for the interest of Colonel Crawley that the facts should be sifted as they had been. The right hon. Gentleman the Member for Huntingdon (General Peel) had complained of the course taken by the Government, but they really at that time had as little means of judging of the truth or falsehood of these allegations as any other Member of the House. They had certainly the Memorandum of the Commander-in-Chief before them, in which his Royal Highness passed his judgment on the facts—

"There are points of Lieutenant Colonel Crawley's conduct of which his Royal Highness cannot speak in too strong terms; he alludes to the confinement under arrest of certain non-commissioned officers during the trial, on a charge of conspiracy, which he never attempted to prove against them, and for which there does not appear to be the shadow of a foundation. He has also reason to believe that the Commander-in-Chief in India, if he had been better acquainted with the circumstances, would have taken a different view, and would not have attributed the death of that non-commissioned officer to excess."

Now, whether it might not have been better to wait for the explanations of the Commander-in-Chief in India before sending such a Memorandum to be read before the soldiers of the Inniskilling Dragoons he would pronounce no opinion; but after such an opinion so publicly expressed, when such rumours were rife, and public opinion throughout the country was so much excited, it was absolutely necessary that the Government should institute a further inquiry. It was all very well to say that the inquiry had resulted in disproving all the allegations; but nevertheless the inquiry had tended to the interest of Colonel Crawley, and the advantage of the public. Last year he was the only Member who, while he was of opinion that there should be an inquiry, expressed his conviction that in all probability a British officer like Colonel Crawley would be able to disprove the charges made against him if he had an opportunity. That opportunity he had had, and the public would rejoice, as he rejoiced, that such a scandalous stain as would have rested on the character of a British officer had those charges been proved had been entirely removed, and that Colonel Crawley had been shown never to have done anything approaching to that which was attributed to him. He was convinced, from what had fallen from the hon. Member for Andover, that he was satisfied that he had been the result of the inquiry; if he was not satisfied, he was not the man he took him to be.

COLONEL GILPIN said, his object in rising upon that occasion was to make an appeal to the Under Secretary for War and the Government generally, in favour of an officer who had been worse treated than any officer of the British service similarly situated. He knew nothing of Colonel Crawley. He had never seen him to his knowledge, nor had had any communication

Mr. E. P. Bouverie

with him. The other night, when he put a question to the noble Lord the Under Secretary for War relative to Colonel Crawley's expenses, he was told that the usual expenses would be paid by the Government, and that Colonel Crawley would not be put to more expense than if his regiment were quartered in this country. But it should be recollected that Colonel Crawley had to break up his establishment in India, and to dispose of his effects, and that the only free quarters he received were during the three weeks of the court-martial at Aldershot. He (Colonel Gilpin) knew that it was not usual to recognize the legal expenses of prisoners so situated; but he would ask, whether this was a usual court-martial? Was it usual to bring a man 10,000 miles to trial? Was it usual to hunt him down before trial as so many had done in this country? Was it usual to hear speeches made in this House conveying imputations of the gravest character against a man before his trial? As an example of some of the speeches that had been made upon the subject in that House, he would refer to what had fallen from the hon. Member for Stafford (Mr. Alderman Sidney) to show the groundlessness of the charges which had been made against Colonel Crawley. That hon. Gentleman said the wife of Sergeant Major Lilley was placed in the same cell with her husband, and died in her confinement, which took place under circumstances of the greatest indecency. He (Colonel Gilpin) regretted that that hon. Gentleman was not then in the House, but he had given him notice of his intention to quote one extract from the speech which he had made on this subject. Now, the statement of the hon. Gentleman was utterly at variance with the facts, and was contrary to the rules of the service. If he were in his place he would have asked him upon what grounds he made such a statement. The facts were, that Mrs. Lilley was never placed under any sort of restraint. She went in and out of her husband's quarters when she pleased. She attended his funeral, and died of consumption in about six weeks afterwards. But that was not all. In another place, a noble Earl, who was celebrated for his philanthropy and benevolence, added fuel to the flame, and did not think it inconsistent with his Christian benevolence to say that such was the feeling of the people of England upon the subject, that it was absolutely necessary a court-martial should take place in this country. After all that excitement it would be easily seen that an acquittal was a matter of existence to Colonel Crawley. Now, what chance had he alone and unassisted against the legal advisers of the Crown? It has been said that Colonel Pipon was Judge Advocate, and Sir Alfred Horsford prosecutor. Nominally, that was so; but he had it on the highest authority that in everything that distinguished officer (Sir Alfred Horsford) did, he was guided entirely by counsel. Who was the counsel? The Deputy Judge Advocate, whose duty it was to prepare the charges, to consider the proceedings after the sentence; and this last act led him to watch over the fair interests of the prisoner as well as of the Crown. Sir, I hope this is the last time we shall see that Gentleman acting in the double capacity of judge and prosecutor. He appealed to the noble Lord at the head of the Government to act liberally on this occasion, and to pay the whole of the expenses of Colonel Crawley, including the legal expenses, being convinced that such liberality would meet with the approval of the public. Colonel Crawley not only stood acquitted of every particle of charge against him, but he was also, he believed, acquitted in the mind of every honourable man in the country. He concurred in opinion with the right hon. Gentleman the Member for Huntingdon (General Peel), and regretted the moment that the court-martial was over that Her Majesty's Government did not pay every sixpence of the expenses of Colonel Crawley, and thus save the scandal of British officers putting their names to a subscription list, in the performance, as they believe, of a duty entirely neglected by those in authority over them.

MR. NEATE said, that the Deputy Judge Advocate did not deserve any of the censure that had been cast upon him for his conduct in this matter. His right hon. and learned Friend the Judge Advocate General had already explained that when the Deputy Judge Advocate had the duty cast on him of assisting the prosecution, he threw aside all the duties and responsibilities of his official position, and acted merely as any other legal gentleman who appeared would have done. He had known the Deputy Judge Advocate for thirty years, and there was no man more scrupulously exact in his observance of the rights of others, or more prompt to resent or repel any wrong done to himself or those

whom he felt it his duty to defend. If the energy of that learned Gentleman's character had carried him beyond the limits which a cooler mind would have set to itself, that was an error of a generous description. The prosecution seemed to have one arm tied behind its back, because it was thought desirable not to call in question the legality of the conduct of Sir William Mansfield and Sir Hugh Rose, and the advisers of Colonel Crawley had taken advantage of that circumstance. He thought the military Gentlemen on the other side had better let the matter rest. He had nothing to say against Colonel Crawley's acquittal, and even before the court-martial was over, he had come to the conclusion that the evidence would not justify a conviction. It did not, however, follow, on that account, that Colonel Crawley had acted in a manner in which it was desirable a commanding officer should act; and if hon. Gentlemen, on the other side, thought their opinions on this matter were the opinions of the British public, they deluded themselves very much.

CAPTAIN ARCHDALL said, that the hon. Gentleman who brought forward this Motion had appealed to him to say something as to the state of discipline of the Inniskilling Dragoons. He was happy in bearing testimony to the efficiency and high character of the regiment. He could appeal to the flattering terms in which His Royal Highness the Commander-in-Chief had spoken of the Inniskilling Dragoons; and he could also appeal to the testimony of Lord Cardigan, the most particular, and, perhaps, the most efficient Inspector General of Cavalry, who ever rode down the ranks of a regiment, and who, at the last inspection before its departure for India, reported of its efficiency in higher terms than he had ever before reported of any regiment. As he was on his legs, he would say, that no one deprecated more than he did the irregular and frequent discussions in that House on matters connected with the discipline of the British army. At the same time, to borrow the expression of the noble Lord at the head of the Government, he confessed he was unable to "go the whole hog" with his hon. and gallant Friends around him in condemning the hon. Member for Andover (Mr. D. Fortescue). What was the state of things when the hon. Gentleman brought the question under the consideration of the House? A blight had fallen on the Inniskilling Dragoons, the scandal of a court-martial on an officer had visited it, and the death of a non-commissioned officer under illegal arrest had excited a strong feeling throughout the country. The subject had already been referred to on more than one occasion. The public believed the most improbable and impossible statements in regard to the treatment which a non-commissioned officer was said to have received from his commanding officer; for no man who knew anything of the army could believe that any officer would have dared to act towards his subordinate as it was alleged Colonel Crawley had acted. The country being in a state of indignation at the supposed cruelty practised towards Sergeant Major Lilley, the hon. Member for Andover, not being well acquainted with the rules of the army, gave to the accusation an easy credence, and brought forward those allegations under the belief that they could have been supported. An opportunity was thus afforded to the Under Secretary at War to explain or contradict these statements; but the noble Lord being unable to give such contradiction at the time, made a statement remarkable for the absence of official circumlocution and obscurity; he held nothing back; he admitted that irregularities had taken place, that much blame was due for such irregularities, but that that blame must be distributed among a number of individuals; and he promised that there should be further inquiry. It was to be regretted that the authorities at the Horse Guards did not wait the result of that inquiry before bringing Colonel Crawley to court-martial. Misled, however, by the statements of Mr. Smales, who had been dismissed from the service, and of Lieutenant Fitzsimon, (who, he was glad to say, had received his military education in the Austrian and not in the British army), the military authorities ordered the court-martial upon Colonel Crawley. Colonel Crawley was acquitted of the charge preferred against him—namely, of having used unnecessary severity towards Sergeant Major Lilley; but at the same time there was no doubt that Colonel Crawley had carried out the imprisonment of Sergeant Major Lilley with the utmost rigour, with a severity most unusual in India, and such as was only had recourse to when a prisoner threatened to commit some act of violence, or attempted to break his arrest. And, as regarded Mrs. Lilley, without a sufficient regard to decency, much had been said about the eighth clause in the Mutiny Act. It appeared, however, to him to be per-

Captain Archdall.

fectly clear that a man could not legally be kept in confinement beyond eight days, or until he should be brought before a court-martial; that was to say, until a decision was come to whether he could be tried by court-martial upon the charges brought against him or not. It was found that there was not sufficient evidence to bring the sergeant-majors to trial, and from that moment their arrest was illegal. It was true Colonel Crawley had been honourably acquitted by the court-martial of the charges preferred against him. He congratulated him on his acquittal; but notwithstanding that acquittal, and the statement of the right hon. and gallant Member for Huntingdon, that " not a rag of the Memorandum of last year remained," he believed that the censure passed by the Commander-in-Chief upon Colonel Crawley, of being wanting in that tact, temper, and judgment so essential in a commanding officer, remained undisturbed. He (Captain Archdall) entirely agreed with the noble Lord opposite, that it was time this controversy should end; he regretted the end was not more satisfactory. The law had been broken; had it been vindicated? Colonel Crawley, one of the chief actors in the drama, had been tried and acquitted; acknowledged illegalities and irregularities had taken place at Mhow, which by being allowed to remain unpunished had been condoned. The court-martial at Aldershot had cost the country £18,000. Altogether the result seemed to be, that in this case the Government had sustained the character given to it by a noble Earl in another place, of having " meddled and muddled."

COLONEL DICKSON said, he had heard with astonishment the speech just delivered; but he should not have risen but for the taunts thrown out on the other side of the House against those who were designated the military defenders of the abuses of the Horse Guards. He stood there as the representative of an important constituency, and he felt that he was not acting inconsistently with his duty in taking the part of a maligned and ill-used officer. The right hon. Member for Kilmarnock (Mr. Bouverie) was the only man who had as yet stood up in a fair and honourable manner, avoiding all the technicalities of the law, and spoken in favour of the much injured and persecuted Colonel Crawley. The hon. Member for Andover (Mr. Dudley Fortescue), not satisfied with being one of the originators of this great scandal, and accepting the verdict of the court-martial, had made a speech full of insinuations against Colonel Crawley, suggesting that he was morally guilty of the charges made against him, though in the beginning of his speech he confessed that he had been misled, and held out the hope that he was going to atone for the mistake he had made. The hon. Gentleman who followed the hon. Member for Andover said, that those who stuck up for discipline in that House were the first aggressors on the authority of the Commander-in-Chief, who instituted the court-martial; and he challenged them to stand up, if they dared, and say that the court-martial ought not to have taken place. He (Colonel Dickson) said boldly that the charge against Colonel Crawley was unfounded, and that the trial ought not to have been ordered. He did not question the conduct of the Commander-in-Chief, but he thought the trial had never been called for by the circumstances of the case or by the opinion of the country. It had been said that the regiment was in a state of mutiny. But by whom had this been said? Not by Colonel Crawley; never by the military authorities. He had served in the regiment upwards of twenty years. The hon. and gallant Member (Captain Archdall) stood up for the regiment to which he had belonged; but circumstances had changed since the hon. and gallant Member was an officer of the Inniskillings; and no doubt, when Colonel Crawley joined his regiment he found his officers deteriorated in discipline. At all events, there was high authority for the allegation. Colonel Crawley, on joining his regiment, was met by those who ought to have supported him, with the most determined hostility and was worried. He was met at the outset by the most determined opposition, the reason for which was known to many in the House, arising from circumstances of former years. One of those was a man who, a hope had been expressed that night, might be re-instated, but who he (Colonel Dickson), for the credit of the British army, hoped would never be restored to his former position. Monstrous rumours, one-twentieth part of which it was impossible could be true of any colonel in the British army, had been sent home, implicating not only Colonel Crawley but Sir Hugh Rose and Sir William Mansfield. Who behaved better in the Indian Mutiny than Sir Hugh Rose? If not fit for the command of the British army in India,

why did not the Government at once remove him? But if fit to command the British army in India, surely he was fit to decide on a question concerning an individual sergeant of dragoons. The next person against whom the rumour was directed was Sir William Mansfield. He thought the House owed all three an ample apology. The Under Secretary for War said he thought that what was said to Sir William Mansfield, was a greater punishment than if he had been tried by a court-martial. But was his conduct illegal or not? According to the opinion of the Judge Advocate General, it was not. We knew what we owed these officers. We knew the difficulties of their position at a distance from home. How could they perform their duties if on every turn their conduct was on rumour sent home, to be taken up in that House, censured, and branded? He thought the interference of the House had been detrimental to the discipline of the army. He believed that if the army were polled to-morrow, not one of them would express the slightest condemnation of the course which was pursued by Colonel Crawley in India. He hoped an end would be put to this kind of interference—if not, a heavy blow would be struck at the discipline of our army. He trusted this was the last time such rumours would be acted upon, to the annoyance of an efficient officer, who owed his position to no aristocratic influence, but rose to his present rank by the aid of his own merit.

SIR PATRICK O'BRIEN wished to say nothing disrespectful of Colonel Crawley, who was a King's County man, and one of five sons who had served Her Majesty with credit and distinction, but only to express his opinion on the large public question at issue. Certain officers of the Inniskilling Dragoons had been compelled to give evidence before the court-martial, and in consequence of that evidence were liable, without having an opportunity of defending themselves, to be put on half-pay or sent to the West Indies. That was, in his opinion, very hard and unjust usage. His own opinion was that His Royal Highness the Commander-in-Chief acted with great pluck in the matter; and whilst Generals Rose, Mansfield, and Farrell were the persons who ought really to have been held accountable for Sergeant Lilley's unjust imprisonment, Colonel Crawley had been made their scapegoat. He regretted that the particulars connected with the affair had been much exaggerated, the extravagant language made use of at first having led to a reaction in the popular feeling in the opposite extreme.

SIR WILLIAM FRASER would repeat the observation of the hon. Member for Stoke-upon-Trent (Mr. H. R. Grenfell), that if the Inniskilling Dragoons were in a mutinous state when Colonel Crawley joined them, the charge against Colonel Crawley fell to the ground. Sir William Fraser thought that nothing produced so great an effect on the public mind during the long and painful investigation at Aldershot as the alleged state of the Inniskilling Dragoons before Colonel Crawley joined. He had formerly two near relatives in this regiment, and he would not say a single word against the gallantry of the regiment in former days, or its discipline in later days; but the House should have before it some evidence of the condition of the regiment at the time Colonel Crawley joined. It would be found that when Colonel Crawley joined, the regiment was in a very unsatisfactory condition. That officer put a question which was very pertinent when he asked the Horse Guards to produce the letter of Colonel Shute to His Royal Highness the Duke of Cambridge; every one expected that letter would have been produced, the Court having decided that it was relevant, and were astonished when it was not produced. He would be the last to demur to the course His Royal Highness the Duke of Cambridge took in declining to produce that letter, as he had no doubt whatever that His Royal Highness believed it was to the best interest of the British army that it should not be produced; but there could be no doubt whatever that the absence of that letter had a material effect on the interests of Colonel Crawley; and the public felt that although the prosecution was not identified with the Ministers of the Queen, the withholding of this letter was not fair. He firmly believed that it would have shown that the regiment was not in so perfect a state as it was believed to be when Colonel Crawley joined it, and his ground for this was the letter of His Royal Highness the Duke of Cambridge to Sir Hugh Rose, dated 14th January, 1864, the statements in which were to the effect that the regiment when Colonel Crawley joined had materially changed from what it had formerly been, and that the discipline of the regiment, so far as the officers were concerned, was impaired. The Duke of Cambridge added, that this bad state of feeling among a

Sir Patrick O'Brien

portion of the officers appeared to be beginning to affect the non-commissioned officers; and this was how Colonel Crawley was induced to suspect a conspiracy amongst the three Sergeants Major against his authority, and that the conduct of the Sergeants Major strengthened the assumption, but there was no legal evidence by which they could be brought to trial. That was the effect of the letter. It had been stated over and over again that Colonel Crawley locked these men up in order to prevent their giving evidence against him on the trial. That was not true; these men had committed a specific military offence, in using obscene and mutinous language against their colonel; and he asked any hon. Member of the House who was a magistrate, if a man were brought before him for a burglary, would he refuse to commit him because he had received a subpœna to attend as a witness at a trial on a totally different subject at the next assizes? and this was what it was in effect urged Colonel Crawley should have done. Something had been said as to the hon. Gentleman who had made the Motion last year, and he trusted that hon. Gentleman would respond to the appeal Colonel Crawley made to him in his eloquent defence. The statements of the hon. Member for Andover had been distinctly contradicted by the witnesses, and Colonel Crawley appealed to the hon. Gentleman, for the sake of his own honour and for the dignity of Parliament, to expose the parties of whom he had been made the dupe. It was the practice of political partisans in that House to back up those who thought with them, and to go great lengths to support them; but he appealed to the House in the name of all that was gentlemanlike and manly, and asked was it fair that the hon. Member for Andover should sit smiling during the whole debate without making an explanation as to the charges which he had made against Colonel Crawley.

MR. DUDLEY FORTESCUE wished, before the debate closed, to give some answer to the remarks which had been addressed to him, especially to the appeal of the hon. Member for Ayrshire (Sir James Fergusson)—an appeal which, if not at variance with strict Parliamentary usage, was certainly not in accordance with that courteous and gentlemanlike spirit which was one of the most honourable characteristics of the House of Commons, and which he thought the hon. Member might study with great advantage in the improvement of his manners. When he decided on bringing this matter before the House a second time, he had at first intended going through the evidence taken before the court-martial, and showing how far it confirmed and how far it refuted his original statement ; and, as far as he was concerned, he would have been very glad to have taken that course. On consideration, however, he thought it better not to weary the House with unnecessary details, and he had contented himself with a general admission that, on some points, he had been led into error, while stating the reasons. which prevented him from altogether retracting, though he was quite prepared to modify, his original statement. That course, he believed, had been considered satisfactory by the House in general, but as some hon. Members opposite had insisted on dwelling on these details, he trusted he should now be excused if, in answer, he briefly referred to one or two points of the evidence in justification of his statement. First, with regard to the allegation that the quarters in which Sergeant Major Lilley died consisted only of one room, it would be seen, on referring to the evidence, that, for all practical purposes, they were so considered. Major Swinley, in answer to a question (Page 35, Q. 468), whether he had not sought to give the impression that Lilley and his wife were shut up in one room, said distinctly—

" If I ever did speak about it to other people I should have done so, not during the whole course of the arrest, but during the latter part of the arrest, as from the recollection of my own sergeant major's quarters I believe them to have been shut up in one room."

Again, Major Champion, in the following passage (Page 19, Q. 130), described as a single room a set of quarters exactly corresponding to those in which Lilley died, with the addition of a passage between them. Major Champion questioned by the Prosecutor—

" With reference to the evidence you gave yesterday in cross-examination (extract read), were any additional quarters given to Quarter Master Sergeant Dibble besides those occupied by Sergeant Major Lilley ? Answer : I am glad to have the opportunity of stating that I forgot to mention yesterday that Quarter Master Sergeant Dibble inhabited the quarters Lilley died in, and also a room on the north side of the model of similar dimensions. The passage of communication (pointing to the model) is seen on the north side of Lilley's quarters in lighter coloured wood."

He had entirely abstained from saying anything about the treatment of Mrs. Lil-

ley ; but if hon. Gentlemen turned to the evidence of Dr. Barnett, they could not fail to come to the conclusion that in the details of the arrest, whoever might have been responsible for it, there was a needless disregard of decency and humanity. After some preliminary questions, Dr. Barnett was asked—

" Could the sentry see into Mrs. Lilley's bedroom ?—From No. 2 room he could see into No. 3, Mrs. Lilley's bedroom. I should say not distinctly, without removing the chick that was on the door.

" Could you see the sentry through the chick ? —Yes, I have frequently seen the sentry over the lining of the chick ; the chick was lined halfway up with a sort of red cotton. I could see the sentry's head over that.

" Could he hear anything that was going on in the bedroom ?— The conversation carried on in the bedroom could be heard in the other room distinctly, unless it was in an undertone; in my visits to Mrs. Lilley I always spoke to her in an undertone in asking her professional questions, lest it should be overheard by the sentry."

" Was Mrs. Lilley ever confined to her bed during the confinement in either bungalow ?— Yes, she was ; she was a great part of each day in bed ; sometimes she was much better, and then she sat up part of the day, but many days she was confined the whole day."

Dr. Barnett stated in answer to other questions—

" In your opinion, as a medical man, was the sentry at any time during the arrest placed in a position where he could not interfere with or annoy Mrs. Lilley ?—I never observed any change in the position of the sentries in either bungalow, with the exception of the occasion I have already stated, when I met the sentry at the door of No. 4 room in the first bungalow."

Question repeated—

" I consider that the position of the sentry during the whole period of the sergeant major's arrest must have been an annoyance to Mrs. Lilley.

" Do you remember the inconvenience to Mrs. Lilley being rendered less at any time during the arrest, from the alteration of the position of the sentry ?—No, I do not.

" Did you after the 7th of May observe any diminution of the inconvenience to Mrs. Lilley ?—I observed no diminution of the inconvenience after the 7th of May."

With the exception of one or two points, which he had unintentionally misunderstood, he thought he could appeal to the evidence that had been given to prove the substantial accuracy of the statements he had made. With regard to his Motion for confidential Reports, it had been in a manner forced upon him by the right hon. and gallant Gentleman (General Peel), who had made it a condition to his not opposing the proceedings of the court-martial being laid on the table, that he should make a Motion. So he had moved for the papers; and considering how Colonel Shute's character had been reflected upon in what had been said as to the state of the regiment, he thought it only fair to him to do so. If he had committed an error in moving for Confidential Reports he was glad to find he had done so in such good company as that of the noble Lords the Members for Northumberland and the East Riding (Lords Lovaine and Hotham). At the same time, after the discussion that had taken place, he would not press his Resolution.

CAPTAIN ARCHDALL said, he could only speak as to the discipline of the Inniskillings when they left this country. He did not know what had happened afterwards.

Question, " That the words proposed to be left out stand part of the Question," put, and *negatived.*

Words *added.*

Main Question, as amended, put, and *agreed to.*

Resolved,

That the production of any further Papers relating to the court-martial on Colonel Crawley is inexpedient.—(*General Peel.*)

POOR LAW (IRELAND) ACTS AMENDMENT BILL—[BILL 51.]

LEAVE. FIRST READING.

MR. HENNESSY moved for leave to introduce a Bill to Amend the Irish Poor Law. As there was to be no opposition he would reserve his statement.

LORD NAAS protested against the introduction of a measure of such importance without some statement of the provisions. Two years ago a Committee sat to consider the Irish Poor Law, and decided that it was not desirable to change its leading provisions. Many alterations of a minor kind were recommended, and were carried out. He thought after that declaration by the Committee, and after the general expression of opinion the other night in favour of the principles of the Irish Poor Law, it was only wasting the time of the House now to introduce a Bill which had not the slightest chance of being passed.

MR. HENNESSY said, that the Bill simply embodied the clause in the English Act.

Motion *agreed to.*

Mr. Dudley Fortescue

Bill to amend the Irish Poor Law Acts, *ordered* to be brought in by Mr. HENNESSY and Mr. POLLARD-URQUHART.

Bill *presented*, and read 1°. [Bill 15.]

BOROUGH FRANCHISE BILL.

On Motion of Mr. BAINES, Bill to extend the Parliamentary Franchise in Cities and Boroughs in England and Wales, *ordered* to be brought in by Mr. BAINES, Mr. BAZLEY, and Mr. SCHOLEFIELD.

Bill *presented*, and read 1°. [Bill 47.]

REGISTRATION OF COUNTY VOTERS (IRELAND) BILL.

On Motion of Mr. AGAR-ELLIS, Bill to amend the Laws which regulate the Registration of Parliamentary Voters in Counties in Ireland, *ordered* to be brought in by Mr. AGAR-ELLIS and Colonel FRENCH.

Bill *presented*, and read 1°. [Bill 49.]

JERSEY COURT BILL.

On Motion of Mr. LOCKE, Bill to amend the constitution, practice, and procedure of the Court of the Island of Jersey, *ordered* to be brought in by Mr. LOCKE, Mr. HADFIELD, and Mr. AYRTON.

Bill *presented*, and read 1°. [Bill 48.]

UNION RELIEF AID ACTS CONTINUANCE BILL.

On Motion of Mr. C. P. VILLIERS, Bill to continue for a further period certain provisions of the Union Relief Aid Acts, *ordered* to be brought in by Mr. VILLIERS and Mr. GILPIN.

Bill *presented*, and read 1°. [Bill 50.]

House adjourned at Twelve o'clock.

HOUSE OF LORDS,

Wednesday, March 16, 1864.

MINUTES.] — PUBLIC BILLS—*First Reading*—
　Consolidated Fund (£584,650)* (No. 33);
　Consolidated Fund (£4,500,000)* (No. 34).
Second Reading--Mutiny* (*Committee negatived*).
Committee—Marine Mutiny*.
Reported—Marine Mutiny*.
Third Reading—Inclosure* (No. 25).

Their Lordships met ; and having gone through the business on the paper without debate,

　　House adjourned at a quarter past
　　　　Four o'clock, till To-morrow,
　　　　　　Twelve o'clock.

HOUSE OF COMMONS,

Wednesday, March 16, 1864.

MINUTES.]— NEW MEMBER SWORN — Henry Edward Surtees, esquire, *for* Hertford County. SELECT COMMITTEE—Schools of Art, *nominated* (*List of Committees*), *see* p. 1703, vol. clxxiii. PUBLIC BILLS—*Resolution in Committee*—Bank Notes (Scotland)*.
First Reading—Chief Rents (Ireland)* (*Lords*) [Bill 52] ; Bank Notes (Scotland)* [Bill 53].
Second Reading—Judgments, &c., Law Amendment [Bill 3]; Tests Abolition (Oxford) [Bill 18]; Election Petitions [Bill 17].
Third Reading—Consolidated Fund (£584,650)*; Consolidated Fund (£4,500,000)*.

JUDGMENTS, &c., LAW AMENDMENT BILL—[BILL 3.]—SECOND READING.

Order for Second Reading read.

Moved, "That the Bill be now read a second time."—(*Mr. Hadfield.*)

MR. HADFIELD said, he rose to move the second reading of this Bill, the object of which was to put an end to one of the greatest abuses that existed in connection with the law. At present, when a purchase or transfer of land was made, the purchaser had to make search for any judgments that might exist before the purchase could be completed. No matter in what part of England he might be, he had to search every register for possible incumbrances, and to continue the search down to the very morning on which the purchase was completed. That, of course, was only done at great expense, and was a great abuse and hardship. He had communicated with the hon. and learned Attorney General on the subject, and he believed that the Government would not object to the second reading of the Bill on the understanding that it should be referred to a Select Committee. He felt justified in assenting to that proposal, and he trusted that the result of the deliberations of the Committee would be satisfactory. He might state that the proposed measure would not in any way affect Ireland.

MR. BAZLEY begged to second the Motion.

SIR GEORGE GREY stated, on the part of the Attorney General, that he had no objection to the Motion, so that the Bill might afterwards be referred to a Select Committee.

MR. SCULLY said, he had no objection to the Bill as far as it went, though it was but a very small instalment of a much larger measure. In his opinion, a registration of titles would be the best machinery for the purpose of facilitating the sale and transfer of land. He hoped there would be as few lawyers as possible on the Committee, as he considered them the obstructors of all legal reforms. When they saw that resistance would be in vain, they assisted in the carrying of such measures with the view of mutilating them as much as possible.

Bill read 2° and *committed* to a Select Committee.

TESTS ABOLITION (OXFORD) BILL. [BILL 18.] SECOND READING.

Order for Second Reading read,

MR. DODSON, in moving the Second Reading of the Bill, said : Two tests are now required at Oxford as necessary conditions for the degree of Master of Arts or of Doctor of any Faculty. The one is a subscription to the Thirty-nine Articles, the other a subscription to the Three Articles of the 36th Canon. This last involves assent to the whole of the Prayer Book, and further a promise, absurd enough when required of a layman, that he will use that book only in public prayer, and administer the Sacrament according to its rites. These tests are accompanied by a declaration that the graduate subscribes to them heartily, willingly, and to their fullest extent. The Bill proposes to abolish these subscriptions on taking any degree. It does not even except degrees in divinity, for these degrees are only conferred upon persons in holy orders, or at all events upon such as have been pronounced by the bishops qualified to take holy orders. A test in such a case appears superfluous, and therefore better omitted. Let it, however, be distinctly understood, that the Bill does not interfere with the discipline or religious teaching of the University. It leaves untouched the declaration of conformity to the liturgy which the Act of Uniformity requires of all heads of houses, fellows, and tutors. It leaves untouched those University statutes which require such persons or any professors to be members of the Church of England, or, at all events, to teach nothing contrary to her doctrines. The Bill itself provides that no graduate shall in virtue of his degree take any office in or out of the University hitherto confined to churchmen, unless he shall have made a declaration of membership with the Church. The form of declaration is borrowed from Cambridge, was framed by that University, and is by her required of her own untested graduates as a sufficient qualification for such offices. There is then no occasion for alarmists to conjure up pictures of the University converted into an arena for the conflicts of contradictory theologians, or a stage for divinity lectures from which all divinity has been eliminated for fear of offending the susceptibilities of some sect of hearers.

It would be wasting the time of the House to advance objections to these stringent and complicated subscriptions. If they be looked upon as legal tests, they are nugatory because they cannot practically be enforced. If as moral tests they must be construed either literally or conventionally. If literally, they are too onerous to be exacted from young men, the majority of whom have only a knowledge in theology sufficient for the schools. If conventionally, then, all other difficulties apart, you must entirely ignore the declaration which states that they are made heartily, willingly, and explicitly. I will not say that the University confers at once a degree in arts and a license in mendacity ; but I do say that you can only escape the unreasonable stringency of the tests by a correspondingly unreasonable laxity of interpretation.

The Oxford Commissioners in 1853 reported that those tests were morally injurious and engendered a habit of playing fast and loose with solemn obligations. Those eminent and experienced teachers in the University who signed the petitions last year presented to both Houses, repeated that statement, adding that these tests troubled the consciences of some, prevented others who would be valuable members of the University from joining her, and failed to promote religious harmony. If any confirmation of this were needed we had it in the extraordinary spectacle presented at Oxford only yesterday week. But I do not anticipate that any one will venture upon a defence of these subscriptions. Last year, when the petitions referred to were presented, debates ensued in both Houses ; the petitions were much criticized, the petitioners still more. Indefinite dangers to the Church and the University from some unknown quarters were apprehended if their prayer were granted ; but no one defended the subscriptions themselves. But the Bill not only abolishes these stringent subscriptions; it allows degrees to be taken without any religious test whatever. Well, that is the case now at Cambridge, at Dublin, and at the Scotch Universities. Are the Members for Cambridge or Dub-

Mr. Dodson

lin, or Scotch Members, therefore, prepared to admit that their Universities are godless institutions, divorced from religious teaching ? But, precedent apart, how is it reconcilable to common sense that a lay University should say to a man, as Oxford does now, you have distinguished yourself in mathematics, in classics, in history, or in science, but I refuse you the higher degrees which should be the reward of your competency and your conduct ; I will not give you the degree that should be your passport into the world, unless you make a profession of holding certain religious opinions.

These tests were imposed in times when religious opinions were indissolubly associated with political opinions, and when the triumph of one faction meant the destruction of another. We do not live in the 17th century. All opinions are now not only tolerated, but recognized as having as good a right to exist as those of the Establishment. There are men who conform to the Church yet are not prepared to give a formal approval to all her doctrines. There are others just outside her pale who do not wish openly to declare themselves dissidents. Is it just or politic to call upon such men to take their stand on one side or the other of a rubicon of orthodoxy. It is the duty and the interest of the Church to invite all to avail themselves of her teaching and her ministrations without stopping to investigate the soundness of their creed. She does so, and why is a lay University to be more religiously exclusive than the Church herself ?

It may be said the Bill will admit to the University avowed dissidents from the Church. The Church and the University should rejoice that they have something to offer that can attract young men of that class within the sphere of their influence. If dissenting parents, attracted by the advantages of an Oxford career, care to expose their sons to its influences and associations, surely the Church should be the last to complain. The University cannot fear their numbers, and will scarcely admit that she stands in dread of the learning and ability of her own pupils. Granting, however, that the presence of Dissenters would be a difficulty, it is one the University ought not to shrink from. She boasts of being a seminary of orthodoxy ; but it is a cheap boast if she takes care to discourage all from coming, except those who come with a foregone conclusion to accept all her teachings. Some schoolmasters acquire a fleeting reputation for their schools by keeping none but docile and clever boys; but the master who really does his duty and is deserving of honour is he who takes all comers and makes the best of the disposition and abilities of each. Much more is such a course the duty of the University. The University has great privileges bestowed upon her and secured to her by the State, not in order that she should shut herself up in dignified indolence, but that she should bravely bear her part in the work of the age, and grapple with its difficulties, of which, from the point of view of that Church with which the University is connected, Dissent is one of the greatest.

After all, the Bill introduces no new principle. In 1854, the Legislature pronounced that the advantages attending education at Oxford should be open to all, irrespective of their religious professions. This change formed no part of the original scheme of the Oxford Reform Act. It was hastily introduced and imperfectly carried out. The subscriptions then required at matriculation and on taking the degree of B.A. were abolished; but the even more objectionable subscriptions, required for subsequent degrees, were left subsisting. But it is obvious that the attractions of a University career consist not only in the education, but still more in the degrees which stamp the man as having received and profited by that education. When the Cambridge Reform Act was passed two years later with more experience and more deliberation, the error committed in the case of Oxford was seen and avoided, and the requirement of religious tests was abolished in the case of all degrees. Perhaps the objection will be made that the Bill would allow the untested Masters of Arts, among whom might possibly be some Dissenters, to vote in Convocation, or, according to the phrase often employed, would admit them to the governing body of the University. How far can Convocation be properly styled the governing body of the University? It is the parliament of the University, or rather, perhaps, the electoral body, for its legislative powers are very limited indeed. Be this as it may, the vote has hitherto always accompanied the degree, and has been one of its attractions and privileges; and it has not appeared to the promoters of the Bill necessary, in order to secure the position and teaching of the Church in the University, to interpose, for

the first time, a disfranchising test between the degree and the vote. But, if this be an objection, still it affords no reason for refusing the second reading of the Bill. It is a question for Committee, and one which, although I confess I prefer the Bill as it stands, although I believe I shall be able to show good cause for maintaining it as it stands, I shall be ready fully to discuss and consider in Committee.

Sir, a petition has been presented against this Bill, under the seal of the University. I do not know whether the hon. Baronet who moves that the Bill be read this day six months will be very anxious to direct attention to that petition, but I am. One paragraph states—

"That this Bill, should it become law, would destroy to a great extent the existing securities that the government, teaching, and discipline of the University, and of its colleges and halls, shall be intrusted to members of the Church of England. That as to the colleges generally, it would remove the most important of those securities, whilst with respect to the University as a whole it would abolish them altogether."

When that paragraph was adopted, the University must have been still under the influence of that hurricane of religious frenzy and panic which has recently swept over it, for calmer reflection would have shown that the Bill does not interfere with the colleges at all; that it does not impair the existing securities for the discipline or religious teaching of the University; but, on the contrary, made assurance doubly sure, by providing that no untested graduate should hold any office hitherto tenable only by a member of the Church, until he should have made the declaration of membership. Another paragraph states—

"That such a change would not tend to promote the efficiency, harmony, and general interests of the University, but would, on the contrary, as your petitioners believe, be injurious both to the University and to the Church."

The harmony intended is no doubt religious harmony, but when Convocation speaks of that, one is tempted to think that that grave body is, to use a vulgar expression, "poking fun" at the House of Commons. It talks of religious harmony, when within the last few days we have seen one member of Convocation saying to another "We do not believe in the same God." If Discord and all her serpents were summoned from Pandemonium and admitted to Convocation they would find they had nothing to teach but possibly much to learn. As to the interests of the University, her true interest is to show that she is not what her enemies would have her to be, a monkish and effete institution, but to prove that, while preserving her own identity, and asserting her own distinctive principles, she can adapt herself to altered circumstances, and encounter the difficulties of the times as they arise. It does not, moreover, appear to have occurred to the petitioners, that there were any interests but those of the University to be considered. Now, the University is not a mere creature of the State; she is a great corporation; but she enjoys great privileges from the State which she is not slow to claim and to insist upon; but she is placed in her high position, not solely for her own benefit, but for that of the country at large, whose interests are in such a case as this not to be forgotten. Yet another paragraph states—

"That the Oxford University Act, 1854, whilst it abolished all subscriptions and declarations at matriculation, and on taking the Bachelor's degree, left untouched the conditions required for taking those degrees which confer a share in the government of the University as a corporate and educating body. And that no cause has since arisen for depriving the University of the power then left in its hands, of retaining or modifying those conditions as may in its deliberate judgment be best for the interests intrusted to its care."

An unanimous petition against any concession scarcely indicates a spirit of concession; and probably most persons will think that if the matter be left to the judgment of the University, that judgment will indeed be deliberate. Possibly Oxford might even be tempted to follow the example of a sister University which, when a Bill of a character somewhat similar to this was impending over it, petitioned Parliament that the subject might be left to the University; and, when the question was submitted to the University, rejected it on the plea that it ought to have been dealt with by the Legislature. It would, however, scarcely be fair, even if the desired result could be so obtained, to leave this subject to the discretion of the University. In her different legislative bodies the clerical element, and still more clerical power and influence, vastly predominate. The persons composing them have subscribed these tests, and have undertaken that their teaching shall be in accordance with them. Such persons cannot propose the abolition of the tests without exposing themselves to the taunt, however unjust and unfounded such a taunt would be, that they had themselves misgivings as to the subscriptions they had made.

The Bill seeks to render education at Oxford really free, and to abolish the pre-

Mr. Dodson

sent stringent tests. That proposition is made in the interests of all, whether Churchmen or Dissenters, who now do, or who may hereafter, resort to Oxford. It is made in the interest of the country at large, which is directly concerned in seeing that the utility and popularity of its greatest educational institution be not marred and diminished by unnecessary trammels; it is made in the interest of the Church; it is made in the interest of the University, lest defences erected for her protection in times of dynastic dangers and political convulsion, but which have long ceased to be safeguards, should remain as barriers to restrict the just liberties of those within her walls, and to deter others, who would come to add to her strength and to her honour, from entering her gates. The hon. Member then moved the second reading of the Bill.

MR. NEATE begged to second the Motion. He confessed that he entered into the question of the tests with the greatest reluctance. His long and still continued connection with the University of Oxford, although it would not allow him to shrink from the task of bearing testimony to, he believed, the justice of the proposed Bill, nevertheless brought him in direct opposition to several persons whom he had ever regarded with feelings of respect and affection. Whatever pleasure he might have felt in his association with such men, he now felt proportionate pain in opposing them. He did not concur with all that had been said by his hon. Friend in reference to the character of the Oxford Convocation and of their petition. The University of Oxford—he spoke of the resident body of it—was composed of men who were not only eminently just and virtuous, but also a very wise and tolerant body. He could well understand how reluctant they might be to adopt a measure which, though it might not destroy, yet they felt it might seriously impair, the character of the University in its connection with the Church of England—a measure which might seem to give to religious teaching a less definite and authoritative character than it now possessed. It was not, however, his intention to enter into the objections urged against this Bill. Before he took leave of that part of the subject he would willingly distinguish the resident body of the University from that extraneous element, which, however glad they were to see them at their commemorations, when they added so much to the dignity and pomp of the celebrations, and also when they saw them at the elections, when they brought their assistance and the benefit of their experiences, the weight of their position and wealth, and their numbers in the country, but yet they would most willingly that they stayed away when the University was managing its own affairs. And he said that as one of the resident body. He pointed out the direct compromise that was suggested and devised by all those who represented the piety, learning, and wisdom of the University, which, however, failed on a recent occasion by the tumultuous intrusion of most unwelcome visitors, who were responsible for that act, and to whom the discredit and remorse of that victory belonged. They were, however, indebted to the opposition then displayed for this, that it would be a strong argument for the House to interfere and enlarge the spirit of that Convocation which had so unwisely set itself in opposition to the better sense of the great English public. His hon. Friend had shown that the real character of the University was, that it was a lay and public corporation. At one time, indeed, it was a question whether it was not to be an ecclesiastical corporation, and the Pope, with the bishops under him, claimed jurisdiction over it ; but, happily for us, the University resisted that claim, and asserted its right not to be subjected to ecclesiastical jurisdiction, but to have the benefit, as all other corporations had, of the protecting control of the Court of Queen's Bench. The University, however, could not expect to have it both ways. They would be glad to be fenced in by the hedges of the Church, and they claimed, at the same time, immunity from her jurisdiction ; but if they chose—and they did choose—to shut out episcopal jurisdiction, they must consequently let in the principle upon which the House of Commons and the public generally acted. The University was no more a Church of England corporation than every corporation in the kingdom was before the repeal of the Test and Corporation Act ; and he could not see any good reason why the University, from its character, should have been exempted from the effect of those tests, except that it was too powerful a body, or that it would have answered no good purpose to have made the attempt. The House perhaps did not accurately understand what was the exact position of Dissenters in reference to the University. There was no exclusion from the benefits of all the studies, but they did not go beyond the degree of B.A., which really amounted to hardly any admission at all ; and if such young men were to be cut off in their career there, just at the time when others were about to enter upon theirs, very few would avail themselves of such privileges ; for what young man of spirit, he asked, would enter into the public career of official life if he was never to aspire beyond the office of a Lord of the Treasury ? That was about the position of Dissenters in our Universities. By the University Act, no man could open a hall unless he was a member of Convocation —that was to say, that a Roman Catholic or a Dissenter (although the Universities had wisely altered their examination so as to admit them) were only admitted on the condition that they would place themselves under the tuition and direction of members of the Church of England. So far as the Universities were considered, there could be very little doubt of the propriety of such a measure, but only its justice. He would not shrink from considering what might be the effect of the present measure on the colleges. He admitted that it would be but of little value unless it was to pave the way to full admissions and to emoluments. With regard to the professorships, which were in the gift of the University, there would be little difficulty, but it would be a very difficult and delicate question how to deal with the colleges. The colleges were eleemosynary corporations, while the University was a lay corporation. There was nothing inconsistent in having a University not founded exclusively upon the basis of the Church of England, and there was an instance of it in the University of London. By the charter of King's College, London, an extract from which he had obtained by the kindness of the principal, it was provided that no person who was not a member of the United Church of England and Ireland, as by law established, should be competent to act as governor by virtue of his office, or to be nominated or act as life governor, member of the council, or fill any office in the college except the two professorships of Oriental and Modern Literature. He should, however, add, that the reverend divine who had given him that information stated in the letter which accompanied it, his most earnest hope that the House of Commons would not pass this Bill. He, however, availed himself of the information so conveyed (in relation to the University of London) to show that it was conceivable to have a Church of England college within a University not founded on that exclusive basis; but whether it was desirable to maintain that distinction was another thing. If the present Bill should become law, he believed it would be made a handle for gaining admission into the colleges, and he admitted that one of the reasons why the petition in its favour was not opposed by a more numerous majority was, that the Bill as it stood failed to answer that object. A few, however, protested against it, and there would have been many more if the Bill had been more decided in its character. That brought him to the consideration of how far the colleges in the University of Oxford should be allowed to retain their exclusive character. All charitable endowments were to a certain extent for the public benefit, and so long as they answered their original purpose, and they were useful, so long the conditions upon which they were founded should be preserved, and he should be sorry to say anything that would impair the great principle of charitable endowments; but he admitted it might be a question hereafter whether, as they were now bringing our Universities into harmony with our other institutions, they might not at no distant time bring the colleges into harmony with the Universities. He thought the practical difficulty of attaining that object was greatly exaggerated. He did not see why there should not be an Act passed for securing the religious teaching and worship of the colleges according to the doctrine of the Church of England. At present no test was imposed upon undergraduates, and it was only the prospective test which seemed to have the effect of imposing on all members an education in the doctrine of the Church of England, and practically he could see no difficulty in the colleges retaining their Church of England character and education without any such tests. At present the test with regard to the colleges did not depend on the subscription of the Articles. That was enforced by the Act of Uniformity, or rather it would be so if the operation of the Act was not annually suspended by an Act of Indemnity. According to the Act of Uniformity there was an obligation to subscribe to a certain declaration, but in practice it was never made. He next came to what he considered to be the most difficult and the most delicate

Mr. Neate

part of the subject — the delicate question whether the University should admit Members of other persuasions than that of the Church of England. That question might involve great difficulty; but the real difficulty was, that members of the Church of England were not willing to pledge themselves to that large amount of dogmatic theology which was contained in the Thirty-nine Articles. There was a great difference between subscriptions as carried out in former years and now. In those days, subscription was a sort of ceremony gone through by a youth of eighteen or nineteen, who was told to look upon it in that light. At the present time it was imposed on men of twenty-four or twenty-five, accustomed to think seriously and look at the act of subscription as a solemnity. He apprehended that many were deterred from completing their University career by the subscription. He was aware that both in and out of Oxford there prevailed a considerable amount of laxity of religious belief. Although he thought that young men were sound in essentials, still there were many doubts about points of subscription, and they objected to it as an unjust exaction. But whatever might be the difficulty and danger that might arise from that laxity of belief in certain points, was any good done by continuing the distinction of tests? Had the existence of tests prevented the growth of that spirit of unbelief? And would their continuance restrain it? If it were to be cured at all, it must be, not by the restraint of tests, but by the example of life. In that respect, nothing could be beyond the example set at Oxford. And there must also be the authority of learning as well as life. The progress of the spirit of unbelief was never effectually restrained by the impositions of tests. What would be the inevitable result of driving young men from the University from the necessity imposed upon them of taking a test which they could not approve? Would it not be to swell the ranks of conscientious Dissenters? The minds of the undergraduates could not fail to be influenced by the spectacle of conscientious dissent, regardless of personal sacrifice, on the part of those who were many of them the brightest and best trained intellects in the University; and to what would the men turn who were thus excluded? They would most probably recruit the ranks of the press, which, with one or two exceptions, although not of an irreligious character, certainly shrank from any acceptance of dogmatic theology ; and what was now only a friendly scepticism would be converted into severe and bitter hostility. That consideration brought him to the brink of a question, compared to which the usual subjects for discussion brought before that House sank into comparative insignificance. He hoped that hon. Gentlemen on the other side of the House would not treat the present as a party question. He knew very well that there was a disposition to assume or affect a patronage of the Church. There was also in a portion of the Church a willingness to accept that patronage. But the alliance would be prejudicial to both. It would not be in the interests of the Church to connect itself with any political party, and whatever advantage hon. Members opposite might derive at the next election, and perhaps the next but one also, by the support of the Church, many of them would hereafter regret to find that they had weakened the Church by leaning too heavily on it. So far as the test produced the exclusion of Dissenters, it was unjust ; so far as it imposed acceptance on reluctant members of the Church, it was immoral ; and the Bill was therefore recommended to adoption by the principle of justice and the principle of morality; and if it had justice and morality on its side, it was hard and dangerous to say that religion was against it.

Motion made, and Question proposed, "That the Bill be now read a second time."—(*Mr. Dodson.*)

SIR WILLIAM HEATHCOTE said, that he rose to move an Amendment, of which he had given notice. The Bill bore on its face the avowal of the principle, that there should be a disruption of the connection which had hitherto prevailed between that which, with all deference to the mover, he must call the governing body of the University of Oxford and the Church of England. If there had been any doubt as to the real intention of the measure, it would have been removed by the remarks of his hon. Friend who had charge of the Bill, and still more by the very able speech of his hon. and learned Friend the Member for Oxford City (Mr. Neate). Notwithstanding the disclaimer of his hon. Friend the Member for East Sussex (Mr. Dodson) he held Convocation to be the governing body at Oxford. It was the court of ultimate resort ; it passed the

laws ; it appointed the officers; it regulated the relations of the University to the Church. Consequently, he was bound to consider how far such a body could safely be dissociated from the Church. His hon. Friend, while he did not disguise his desire to carry out the Bill as it stood, held out hopes that if the House would agree to the second reading, it might be so modified in Committee as to place certain guards on it. In the early part of his argument his hon. Friend said his object was to place the University of Oxford in the position of the University of Cambridge ; but there was really a great difference between the situation of the latter and that in which Oxford would be placed by the Bill. At Cambridge the degree of M.A.—that was the mere title to affix those letters to the end of a man's name—could be taken without any declaration at all ; but the mere degree gave the possessor no weight in the University. No one could become a member of the Senate who had not submitted to a certain test, showing that he was a member of the Church of England. Now, the principle of the Bill was to break altogether the connection between the government of the University of Oxford and the Church of England. His hon. Friend's proposal as to the subsequent modification of the measure simply amounted to saying, " If you will only agree to the principle of the Bill now, when we go into Committee we will cut out that principle and put in something very different, or, at least, I will discuss the question with you whether we shall do so or not." He was satisfied that it would not be prudent to accept the advice of his hon. Friend. Had the Bill been brought in originally for the purpose of placing the University of Oxford on the same basis as Cambridge, although he could not approve of the change as being altogether satisfactory, still he should have been under considerably greater difficulty in opposing it. He owned that in his opinion uniformity in the regulations of the two Universities would be in itself a great advantage. On that ground he opposed the very regulation in question when first brought forward. There was, no doubt, a very great attraction in the idea of avoiding the necessity of imposing on any lay members of an institution terms which were more stringent than the ordinary conditions of lay communion. There were good reasons, however, why the Oxford system was best. He knew perfectly well that the uniformity of the two University systems.

had no attraction for his hon. Friend opposite, or else he would not have proposed in his Bill to establish at Oxford a regulation different from that at Cambridge. The fact was that if the Bill were carried, it would only furnish an argument for another advance in the same direction, and for pushing Cambridge forward to the position which Oxford would then occupy. A Bill which struck at the root of the principle of association between the governing body of the University and the Church was not one about which it was wise or necessary to argue at any length. It depended very much on the broad principles on which hon. Members had made up their minds. From certain points of view everything was clear, and the very same facts and arguments might lead to precisely opposite conclusions, according to the aspect in which they were regarded. He assumed that the Universities were Church institutions, not only in theory but in fact. They threw open their education, their honours, and their first degree to all who could get the use of them, but, in point of fact, nineteen-twentieths of those who were in a position to avail themselves of these advantages were Churchmen. Taking his stand on that assumption, he could not agree to a Bill which would dissociate the Church from these institutions. As to the proposal of his hon. Friend which (without meaning any personal offence) he must characterize as insidious, to pass the second reading and amend the Bill in Committee, he had had some experience as to the dangers of such a concession. He and other hon. Members had more than once, already, consented to the second reading of a Bill in the hope, and sometimes on the understanding, that it would be modified in the next stage. The result had been that, although they failed in getting the desired Amendments, they had never heard the last of their assenting to the second reading. The only justification for giving way on the present occasion would be the conviction that the suggested Amendment would not only improve the Bill, but also the existing state of things, and that he did not think it would do. He must, therefore, meet the Bill by direct opposition. It might be desirable to state to the House how the matter actually stood at Oxford with regard to these tests. After the B.A. degree at Oxford everything remained open as at the commencement. It was only on taking the M.A. degree that any difficulty arose. He could not but believe that the distinction

Sir William Heathcote

at Cambridge between the two classes of masters—those who had merely the degree and those who had taken the test, and were members of the Senate—was an evil. At Oxford the consequences of the change would be more serious than some supposed. Since the University Act of 1854 numbers of lay fellows of colleges and lay tutors had entered. These gentlemen were B.A.'s, who had not taken the declaration. The statutes of the colleges, however, required their fellows to proceed as soon as possible to the higher degree, on taking which they were, of course, identified with the Church through the subscription. If, however, the declaration were made conditional merely on admission to Convocation, many would be able to hold the fellowships and tutorships without ever identifying themselves with the Church. When laymen voluntarily put themselves in the position of teachers, of whom a great number were clergymen, he did not think that they had any right to complain if they were subjected to more definite obligations as to the Church than the ordinary terms of lay communion. That was an important consideration. If, then, he could not believe that any Amendment would put this Bill into a better shape, it was too much to ask him to assent to the second reading, and, to use a common expression, to be "dragged through the dirt," by admitting a principle which could not be afterwards modified by any improvement at a further stage. On these grounds he begged to move that the Bill be read a second time that day six months.

Mr. SELWYN begged to second the Amendment.

Amendment proposed, to leave out the word "now," and at the end of the Question to add the words "upon this day six months."—(*Sir William Heathcote.*)

Mr. GRANT DUFF: Sir, I regret to find that the hon. Baronet who has just sat down has no intention of accepting the conciliatory proposal of my hon. Friend the Member for East Sussex. That proposal should not be misunderstood. We have no idea of yielding the point about the vote in Convocation ; all we say is that that point, although an important one, is but a single point, and not the principle of the Bill, and we think that the fight over it might well be postponed till we go into Committee ; but before I go further, Sir, there is one assertion of the hon. Baronet so novel and extraordinary, that I must really draw attention to it. Where is his authority for the statement that the University of Oxford is a Church institution? Every one knows that, from accidental circumstances, it has been very closely connected with the Church; but it is a lay corporation, and if any evidence can be given in favour of the view put forward on the other side, I hope we shall hear something more about it from succeeding speakers. I have allowed my name to be put on the back of this Bill for three reasons. First, because I think it makes a reasonable concession to the claims of the Liberal party within the Church. Secondly, because it makes a concession too slight, but still a concession, to the claims of Nonconformists; and thirdly, because, independently of its influence on the fortunes of any sect or party, I think it will be useful to the University. My hon. Friend's Bill echoes, as has been said, the petition presented last Session; from 106 members of the University of Oxford, a number considerable in itself, but far more significant when we recollect who were the petitioners, and how strong were the motives to induce them not to sign. These 106 represent a very large and very influential section of University men, but above all, they represent a growing party—a party which is becoming stronger with every succeeding term. In the years between 1827 and 1833 it became sufficiently evident that the movement which had rolled all over Europe, and had in this country carried successively the repeal of the Test Act, Catholic Emancipation, and the Reform Bill, had reached at last even the University of Oxford, and there seemed not a little chance that that great corporation might awake from the sleep in which it had been long held, and make at least some steps forward, carrying the Church of England along with it. No sooner, however, had the first symptoms of a desire for progress shown themselves, than some of the most intelligent men of the University began, compelled by the influences amidst which they had been brought up, to look about and see whether it was altogether necessary to yield to this movement from without; whether there were no forces other than the mere high and dry church and king Toryism which could be brought into the field. They fell back upon the Laudian theology, and called to their aid the church principles of the 17th century. The principles which they enunciated in the "Tracts for the Times" had infinitely greater charms for the minds of young men at the University than the dull and lifeless theology which had previously been in fashion there, or than the productions of another school which was widely popular in that day in various parts of the country, but which, for reasons to which it is unnecessary to allude, never flourished in the atmosphere of Oxford. The great majority of the ablest young men who were educated there during that period fell under the influence of the new teachers, who succeeded not only in damming back but even altering the direction of the current of thought in Oxford for twelve years. Well, time passed on; "the merciless logic" of the leader of the movement brought its natural results to him and to others. The great secession to Rome took place. Then came a change at Oxford. A few followed, one by one, with hesitating steps, but many paused, and listened to other voices before they went further. And other voices soon made themselves heard. Men who had been formed under Arnold at Rugby were just old enough to speak with some authority in the University, and hardly had they begun to fill the void than the new burst of liberal opinion, which shook half the thrones of the Continent, came to scatter mediæval fancies. Those who were at Oxford in those days will not readily forget the abiding change which the events of that year produced, increasing tenfold the interest in and knowledge of the Continent—its social, political, and religious modes of thought. Since February, 1848, the history of opinion in Oxford is merely a branch of the general history of religious opinion in Protestant Europe. It has lost altogether the curiously local and exceptional character which it had during the so-called Oxford movement. Any one could foresee what would be the end of that movement who had read the history of the great storm of the 17th century, or had observed the ripples of reactionary opinion in Italy, France, or Germany, in the first half of this century. But he who presumes to say how and when the present movement will end, must be able to look far down through history, and calculate the results of influences such as have never before been called into action. Point out to me any Protestant community in Europe in which reforming agencies are not being set to work as powerful as any of those which heralded the revolt of the human mind against the Latin Church. In England, in Scotland, in Germany, in France,

in Switzerland, in Holland, I see everywhere the same questions being raised,
and becoming the property no longer
of a few thinkers but of the great public.
It is not as if it were a new movement;
it is a very old one, and can be traced year
by year, name by name, from the days of
Bacon to our own. Do you deny that it
has made itself felt powerfully in Oxford?
Do not look merely to this petition, or to
this Bill, go down to Oxford and talk there
with those who know what men are really
thinking in the place. Is it really seriously
maintained that the obligation of adopting
the Thirty-nine Articles and the Prayer
Book which now exists, preserves anything
like uniformity of opinion amongst members of Convocation? Rome and Geneva,
Tubingen and Canterbury, are hardly further apart than were many of the groups
which gathered on Tuesday the 8th in the
Sheldonian Theatre. Is there not something extremely absurd in the idea that
Dr. Pusey and Mr. Maurice, Professor
Jowett and Dr. Cotton, have all signed
the Thirty-nine Articles and accepted the
Prayer Book, and are, no doubt, perfectly
ready to sign them again on the shortest
notice? I dare say many who hear me
read at the time the famous tract 90.
Well, after the publication of the views
therein contained—views which are still,
as every one knows, the views of not a few
clergymen of the Church of England—
what, I would venture to ask, can you
expect from the Thirty-nine Articles? If
the very views against which they were
chiefly directed can be held in the teeth
of them, how, in the name of wonder, are
they, or the Prayer Book either, to exclude
from the governing body of your Universities persons whose heresies were never
dreamt of in the days of Queen Elizabeth?
We ought not to forget, Sir, that neither
professors nor tutors, nor clergymen in
pulpits, are now the true teachers of Oxford. Books are its teachers, as they are
ours; and I am ready to stake my whole
case upon this assertion, that there is no
one book written by any author living or
lately dead which is now powerfully influencing men's minds, either in London or in
Oxford, which breathes a spirit in the
slightest degree favourable to the sort of
views which commend themselves to the
minds of those who are in favour of theological tests in learned institutions. Is it
worth while urging the immorality of a
system which teaches men to think so little
of what once was supposed to be a solemn

engagement? Is it worth while to show
that any man who can deliberately and *ex
animo* adhere to every clause in the Thirty-
nine Articles and the Prayer Book must
either be talking of what he does not understand, or must not only have mastered
the results of all the controversies of the
era of the Reformation, but must have
thought himself, wonderful to relate, precisely into the intellectual attitude of the
two different and opposing sets of men who
drew up these forms 300 years ago? Every
one gives himself a little latitude in subscribing, some more, some less, and must
do so from the very nature of things. Is
it worth while to point out to how many
scrupulous people these tests are a cruel
snare, or that the great originators of
heresies are after all the test-bound clergy?
Turning, Sir, to the case of the Nonconformists, I pass over numerous powerful
arguments which have been, or will be,
urged in the debate, such as, that this
exclusion from the Universities is one of
the last vestiges of persecution, that the
Universities are the property of the nation,
and not of any particular religious body
or set of persons in it; that it is infinitely
important for the whole nation as well as
for the Nonconformists, that they should
obtain that higher culture which Oxford
gives, and which they at present find it
difficult to obtain; that religion has only
to gain by the disappearance of sectarian
hatreds; that, with a view to the maintenance of our position in the world, everything that promotes the unity of the nation is infinitely desirable; that certain
sects of Nonconformists, the Methodists,
for example, cannot be said to have deserved ill of the Church; that in our Scotch
Universities, not only is the governing
body of the University open to all creeds,
but all the professorships except the divinity professorships have been freed from
tests, without the slightest bad effect upon
the religious character of the nation. I
will dwell, however, for a moment upon
two other arguments which ought to have
some weight with the hon. Gentlemen
opposite. Have they really so little faith
in the attractions of the Church of England as to doubt that it will rob many of
the Nonconforming sects of some of their
most distinguished young men, if once the
obligation of passing under the yoke of
the Thirty-nine Articles and of the Prayer
Book considered as a test at their M.A.
degree is done away. Can any one doubt
that many who go up Nonconformists will

come away Churchmen in their hearts, if they are not compelled to an ignominious retractation? Again, Sir, can any one doubt that those hon. Gentlemen upon the other side who dislike and fear the Liberal or movement party within the Church more than they fear and dislike almost any Nonconformists, will find in "the orthodox Dissenters," if admitted to convocation, most useful allies against their dreaded foes? Oxford has not been always so jealous about her tests. She was not even so jealous in days when toleration had made but little progress. Towards the end of the 17th century, a Greek College was established in Oxford for students of the Oriental Churches, and I do not read of any attempts having been made to proselytise the young men who attended it. This College was soon broken up, but from casual circumstances, and not from any religious motives—chiefly, I believe, because greater facilities were offered to Greek students in Halle and in Paris. From twenty to thirty years later, there was the case of Courayer, who was made a D.D. of Oxford, with all and each of the privileges appertaining to the doctorate in sacred theology. Courayer was then a Roman Catholic, and a Roman Catholic he remained to the day of his death, in spite of his Protestant or Anglican inclinations. Lastly, Sir, I support this Bill, because I think it will be useful to the University. Experience has taught us that Oxford has always most flourished when clerical influence has been weakest there. Every improvement which has been made in the place in our times, and in all other times, has been made in the teeth of clerical opposition. With almost every humiliation that has befallen the University, from the earliest times down to the disgraceful scene which took place upon the 8th March, clerical influence has been closely connected. Public opinion, acting either directly or through Parliament, has, on the other hand, always been her best friend, and assuredly she wants all her best friends at present. No one is a more attached or loyal member of that great corporation than I am, but I am obliged to confess, with sadness—when I consider her vast wealth, her unequalled prestige, and her enormous influence—that there is scarcely a University in Christendom which, in proportion to her means, is doing so little for science and good learning.

MR. NEWDEGATE said, he had felt at the close of last Session, from the movement in that House with regard to subscription to those formularies which had hitherto constituted the membership of the Church of England for laymen as well as ecclesiastics, that there were about to be introduced into the House proposals for changes of the greatest magnitude. The course of the present debate had shown that his anticipations were not ill-founded. When, towards the close of the last Session, the hon. Member for East Sussex (Mr. Dodson) drew attention to a petition signed by 106 persons, among whom he (Mr. Newdegate) was willing to admit were distinguished members of the University of Oxford, he felt perfectly convinced—although the ostensible object of the hon. Member was to place that University, with regard to subscription and church membership, on the same footing as the University of Cambridge—that he would be dragged far beyond the limits he intended, and that his proposals would be made the vehicle of carrying forward objects in which he would fain believe the hon. Member did not participate. He thought the course which the present debate had taken, clearly showed that the anticipations he had ventured to entertain were not unfounded. The hon. Member for Elgin (Mr. Grant Duff) stated, at the close of the Session, that as an advanced Liberal he felt himself placed in a very difficult position. The hon. Member for Rochdale (Mr. Cobden) had declared that the system of free imports could be carried no further; the Earl Russell had stated that the question of Reform was to be allowed to sleep, so the hon. Member for Elgin appealed to the Government in order to ascertain to what measures such ultra-Liberals as himself were to resort for the sake of action to his class of politicians, whether for good or for evil, essential as the air they breathe. In short, the hon. Member described himself as a "frozen out gardener." He hinted that in an attack upon the Church might be found agreeable occupation for those who abhorred inaction in the cause of extreme change and destruction. The Bill before the House was introduced as one of those various changes which, under the guise of moderate principles, went far beyond the scope of those who would reform rather than destroy; it appeared to him not of a very candid nature. What did that Bill propose? It proposed to abolish the well known and well understood declarations of Church membership as a condition of the admission of a member of the University of Oxford to the degree of Master of Arts. It nevertheless proposed that these well known subscriptions should still be retained as an essential security that the clergy should adhere to the true doctrines of the Church, and teach in accordance with those doctrines. The Bill had not the honesty to abolish the declaration for the laity altogether, but it proposed that while the ecclesiastical Master should continue to subscribe the well known articles and formularies of the Church, the lay Master should only declare himself a *bonâ fide* member of the Church of England. He trusted the House would carefully observe this declaration of *bona fide* membership of the Church of England, and consider in what it originated, and what desires and feelings it was intended to satisfy. It was perfectly clear that if no one objected to any portion of the articles or formularies of the Church, there could be no reason for the change now proposed—namely, a declaration that they were simply *bona fide* members of the Church. The proposal, therefore, implied, under a vague generality, that the House were unwilling to admit to the governing body of the University of Oxford men who did not concur in all the Articles or all the formularies of the Church of England as hitherto subscribed by every person admitted to the degree of Master of Arts, which it was proposed should still be hereafter subscribed by the clerical Master. The Bill of the hon. Member for East Sussex (Mr. Dodson) established a distinct difference between the terms of Church membership for the laity and the clergy. The hon. Member for the City of Oxford (Mr. Neate) said that there had been too much clerical influence in the government of the University of Oxford, and the hon. Member for East Sussex (Mr. Dodson) said there had been a monkish spirit displayed in the government of the University. But what was now proposed? It was proposed to assimilate the terms of Church membership in the governing body of the University of Oxford to the terms of the Church membership which existed in the Church of Rome. In the Church of Rome the governing body meant the clergy. The laity were placed in an inferior position; they were the subjects of the clergy, and it was now proposed to degrade the lay members of the Church of England, who willingly subscribed the Articles and formularies of

the Church, into a position similar to that of the Roman Catholic laity, by enacting that the declaration now required of the lay Masters shall be superseded, and that, for the purpose of governing the Church, they ought to be placed on a level with men who did not accept the tests, which had always been required, and were still to be enforced in the case of the clergy. The result was that if they assented to this Bill they would constitute a governing body with the lay element stamped as unsound. That was the position in which the governing body of the University of Oxford would be placed if the power of legislation was retained to them. They would constitute the clergy a separate class still abiding and bound by the declaration which he believed nine-tenths of the lay Masters of the University were willing and anxious to subscribe. He could conceive nothing more dangerous, and nothing more dishonourable, than that proposal. He would much rather that such subscriptions and declarations were done away with altogether. But let the House look at the extreme illiberality and intolerance produced by latitudinarian opinions. The hon. Member for Oxford City (Mr. Neate) stood before the country as an advanced Liberal; and what was his proposal? He complained that the University of Oxford, the great nursing mother of the Church, was free from Episcopal supervision and control. He was discontented that that intelligent and learned constituency, that that first of all corporations, should continue to govern the University according to the will of its majority as at present constituted. What was the ground of his discontent? It was because a proposal recently submitted to Convocation had not been passed, out of the usual course, for the endowment of a Professor appointed by the Crown, not by Convocation; a Professor who, unfortunately, held opinions which had been condemned as latitudinarian, which were disapproved by the Episcopal bench as well as by the nearly unanimous feeling of the members of the Church of England. A petition had been presented to that House, signed by 106 members out of 800, and that House was asked to compel the majority to bend to the will of that small minority. They were told that that was a growing minority; but it was not denied that it was a minority, and that the feeling of the majority of the Masters of Arts, as well as the general feeling of the Church of England, was against the change. Of all the strange phases of liberalism he regarded the present as one of the strangest—that it should be deemed Liberal, that a small minority should seek to overbear the voices of the great majority of the educated classes of the country. In point of fact the liberty now claimed was not claimed on the part of the great majority, but liberty for a few talented and ambitious men to enforce the arbitrary dictates of their own wills, it might be their capricious fancies, as the ruling principle of the University, in opposition to an overwhelming majority of men equal in learning and superior in principle to themselves. Such was the tendency of the proposal before the House, and he trusted the House would reject it as unsound and deceptive in itself, and dangerous in the consequences to which it was likely to lead. As to the proposed declaration of *bona fide* Church membership, he held that words "*bona fide*" were worth nothing if the terms of the membership were not those hitherto recognized by the University and the country. He had rejoiced in hearing the able, temperate, statesmanlike speech of the hon. Member for the University of Oxford (Sir William Heathcote), in defence of the freedom of the University of which he was the honoured representative. That University was now the only seminary limited exclusively to the Church of England. Were they then to subject this University to a measure of Reform still more extensive than the Act which now governed the University of Cambridge? He would ask the Members for the University of Cambridge what hope they could have if this measure passed for Oxford, but that Cambridge would be secularized after the manner of the University of London, which, though it might have produced men distinguished in learning and science, had not yet given proof that it was likely to rise to the position of the two great Universities which were now condemned because in them was taught the pure Protestant faith of the Church of England, whereby those great principles of true freedom were inculcated which had rendered the people of this country fit for the freedom they enjoyed. This had been effected by providing them with teaching, untrammelled by the narrowness of bigotry and untainted by the wildness of latitudinarian speculation. He knew that many hon. Members would vote for the second

reading of this Bill in very different senses. If there were a division he was satisfied that this would prove to be the case. He addressed the moderate Liberals on the other side of the House, and would ask them to consider, before they sanctioned this Bill, whether they were willing to commit themselves to an extreme policy. Let them look at the history of the world, and of the great national changes which had been effected. If analogy could teach them anything, they would see that if they took this step they would be urged onward by an irresistible power, and he entreated them to have the courage to resist a measure which would commit them far beyond their intentions. He trusted that the right hon. Gentleman the Chancellor of the Exchequer who, he saw, was about to address the House, would not countenance a measure distasteful to the constituency which he had so long represented, which had been so proud of being represented by him, which had exhibited towards him a forbearance and a confidence that he himself would be the first to acknowledge. [The CHANCELLOR of the EXCHEQUER: Hear, hear!] And he would ask the right hon. Gentleman what had that constituency—what had that governing body done that they should be degraded as was now proposed? Had they proved intolerant? Certainly not: against that imputation the Chancellor of the Exchequer ought to be their witness. On the contrary, it had been used as a reproach that, within the University of Oxford, there was a freedom of thought, a latitude of opinion, an extent of speculation which amounted to absolute dissoluteness. It was difficult to imagine what more could be wanted. Surely, some valid objection could be urged, when the House was asked to disturb a system which had done so much to maintain the Protestant character of our religion. He had heard the honoured name of Arnold appealed to. He admitted that Arnold was a bold thinker, whose mind was endowed with rare powers of discrimination. Rejoicing in the fulness of his intellect, he had enunciated maxims which were now misunderstood and perverted by those who falsely professed themselves his disciples; because, if there was any principle to which Arnold adhered, it was that all Government in this country should be Christian, and distinctively Christian. And yet it was now proposed to use his authority for the purpose of breaking down the safeguards of that great corporation which had proved itself the best defender of the Christian faith—the Church of England—the best defender of the Christianity which should rule the nation—and all this in the name of Arnold ! It pained him to hear the memory of the illustrious dead dishonoured. He would only further express the hope that this Bill would be rejected on the second reading. He regarded the Bill as hypocritical, tending to purposes which had not been avowed ; but the result of which must be to overthrow an organisation which had worked most satisfactorily, and which would not be succeeded by a better. Against such an innovation he begged to enter his earnest protest.

THE CHANCELLOR OF THE EXCHEQUER : Sir, we are invited to reject this Bill on the second reading by the Motion of my hon. Friend and Colleague the Member for the University (Sir William Heathcote), and if there is any voice and any authority in this House which would weigh with me to adopt such a course, they are the voice and the authority of my hon. Friend. For many years we have represented the University in common, and I do not know that on any great question involving her interests or the interests of the Church, although we have sat during those years on different sides of this House, we have ever materially or widely differed. But, Sir, I am not able on this occasion to follow the call of my hon. Friend, and I cannot help expressing the regret with which I heard the conclusion at which he had arrived, and that he was to move the rejection of this Bill. My hon. Friend must not underrate through his natural modesty the importance of his own position. If I view these questions aright, I believe they are questions that can only be settled by the mediating influence of intelligent minds, and the weight of character; and the judgment and intelligence of my hon. Friend, and the deservedly great weight attaching to his character, qualify him, perhaps more than any other, so to mediate and bring about a kindly accommodation of these difficult and contested questions. But my hon. Friend refuses to accept that task, and invites us to reject this Bill on the second reading. Let us consider, then, a little, the position in which we stand. It has been said—and said, I think, with irrefragable truth — by my hon. Friend who is the main author of this Bill, that the question of the application of religious tests in the University of Oxford has been partially considered, but never has been

settled by Parliament. In 1853 my noble Friend Earl Russell—then the leader of this House under the Government of the Earl of Aberdeen—and the whole of that Cabinet determined, and as I think wisely, that when they were attempting to deal with the multitude of questions connected with the discipline, the studies, and the property of the University and the Colleges, it was far better for them to prevail on Parliament, if they could, to lay aside altogether that class of considerations which might very materially have disturbed that general reform which they contemplated. But in one of the very last stages of that measure, when all the numerous and complicated questions properly connected with it had been disposed of, a Motion was made in this House and carried after a single discussion, which had the effect of abolishing the application of religious tests on admission to the University and on admission to a bachelor's degree ; and it was intimated, on what was thought to be a very good authority by a noble Lord sitting in this House, that that Motion would not be effectually opposed by the predominating influences in another place. Well, it is hardly possible, I think, to say that a decision of that kind carried within itself *prima facie* evidence of being a complete solution of the question. But we have more conclusive evidence, because, when only two years afterwards the question connected with the reform of the University of Cambridge came to be discussed, then Parliament, on full consideration, and I think at the instance of the mover of this Bill, and the Government of my noble Friend now at the head of the Administration, adopted a system materially different from that of the University of Oxford. It is with the recollection of these circumstances that my hon. Friend and Colleague invites us to reject this Bill. Now, I ask, is he acting wisely in assuming an attitude of indiscriminate resistance, or is he taking a course altogether consistent even with the argument he has used ? He does not hesitate to admit that there is great advantage in a general correspondence between the two Universities in the regulations relating to this vital question ; but that advantage he proposes to forego by the rejection of this measure. My hon. Friend, by what, I must confess, seems to me a very forced assumption, undertakes to declare that the admission of Dissenters to the governing body is in such a sense the principle of this Bill that everything else which it contains is altogether subordinate ; and that is the proposition on which my hon. Friend justifies the Motion he has made. Now, is that statement not palpably contrary to the true construction of this Bill ? Is it not true that the Bill involves a question, of which I am sure he would not depreciate the importance, which is totally unconnected with the admission of Dissenters to the governing bodies, or even to degrees ? Sir, there are many questions involved in this Bill, but there are two which are not only distinct in themselves, but which are each of sufficient importance to justify, if need be, the introduction of a distinct and separate measure. One of those questions is, whether the restraints of the University ought to be relaxed as regards Dissenters ; the other is the question whether, as regards the membership of the Church of England, the tests now apply a proper means of ascertaining it. If we are of opinion that the tests applied in the University of Oxford for the purpose of ascertaining membership in the Church of England are tests which are not fit to be applied under all the circumstances of the day, and in the present state of our law, to the laity and the large and somewhat miscellaneous body which constitutes the Convocation, that is a state of facts which amply justifies us in voting, and even imperatively requires that we should vote, in favour of the second reading of this Bill. The hon. Gentleman who has just spoken grapples with this question, as is his custom, in his usual frank and manly way. He takes his objection outright and on principle to any proposal for substituting a declaration of *bonâ fide* membership for the present declaration respecting the Articles and the Prayer Book. My hon. Friend, if I may so presume to call him, has gone the length of saying that this declaration of *bonâ fide* membership of the Church of England is a hypocritical system. [Mr. NEWDEGATE : As standing by the side of the existing tests.] Well, I am ready to let him have the benefit of that explanation, whatever that may be. But when I heard that language, although I took some pains, Sir, to secure your eye, I was not without apprehension that the hon. and learned Member for the University of Cambridge (Mr. Selwyn), whose great institution is administered on this system, would in his vehemence have risen to anticipate me and to reply to the hon. Gentleman who sits beside him, because this

declaration of *bonâ fide* membership in the Church of England, although undoubtedly its scope has been extended by Parliamentary legislation, was yet not due in its origin to such legislation. It is the University of Cambridge itself, I believe, to which is due the whole credit or discredit, as the case may be, of having invented this hypocritical system of dealing with one-half the consciences of the laity and those of a great portion of the clergy of the Church of England. My hon. Friend and Colleague was, in my opinion, indistinct and unsatisfactory in this vital branch of his argument. He told us that in a certain part of his speech he would show that it is fitting in the University of Oxford to apply the test of subscription to the Thirty-nine Articles and the Prayer Book, as contained in the canon, to the case of lay membership in the Church of England; and I vainly listened to him with the utmost eagerness in order to discover what demonstration he would give us on that subject. For he admitted the strength of the *primâ facie* reasoning that there ought not to be in the University of Oxford alone a mode of ascertaining membership in the Church of England which is totally unknown to our law and practice everywhere else throughout the kingdom. Well, what is the argument adduced by my hon. Friend and Colleague to justify this singular state of things ? It is simply this, that there are in Oxford a certain number of lay fellows and teachers, and that with respect to such lay fellows and teachers, when you consider the character and traditions of the University, and that they educate a large portion of the clergy, it is fair to require of them something more than a bare declaration of membership in the Church of England. This I understand to be the argument, and the whole argument, of my hon. Friend on that point. Now, there may be twenty, thirty, or forty gentlemen —I do not believe there are so many— standing in the category thus described by my hon. Friend—that is to say, of laymen who are, nevertheless, teachers of future clergymen ; and I do not prejudge at this moment the question of what course you ought to adopt with them. [Mr. NEATE : There are not, I believe, over half-a-dozen.] Well, I have probably overstated the number ; but let that pass. The question I have to put is this :—Granted that there may be a score or so of lay teachers at Oxford who are training future clergymen —granted, if you like, that it may be right to ascertain from these teachers that they are not merely *bonâ fide* members of the Church of England in a general sense, but also specifically acquainted with and adherents to its doctrines. I ask is that a reason why the same test of adherence to the Thirty-nine Articles and to the Prayer Book, why the teachers' test of the Church of England, why the clerical test of the Church of England, should be applied to the 3,000 laymen constituting the majority of Convocation? I venture to say that there is no answer to that question. My hon. Friend did not attempt to provide an answer to it, and there is none to be found. I am not aware of any valid reason whatever why a special and exceptional rule is to be maintained in the University of Oxford for the purpose of ascertaining the Church membership of the lay members of Convocation, which is, as I have said, totally unknown to our law and practice elsewhere. I submit that that consideration is an ample justification for us to vote in favour of the second reading. But, Sir, I am not prepared to adopt this Bill without amendment. I could not support it on the third reading as it now stands in respect to certain of its provisions. I do not think it quite consistent or becoming in us, for example, to lay down by law the principle that no test shall be applicable to the taking of degrees in divinity, because, although the degree of divinity may be restricted by the present practice to persons in orders, yet I do not know that that restriction rests on any broad and universal principle; and the question whether such degrees should be accompanied with a test is a matter which I think it better to leave open, and not close by law. I admit it to be a very fair subject for consideration what test should be required from persons who are to teach in the University; and I am bound to say that, as regards the governing body of the University, I think, with my hon. Friend, that that governing body should not be thrown open irrespective of religious distinctions. It is not possible to decide a question of that kind on abstract principle. We must look at the general state of the country, at the division of religious communities, at the manner in which that division crosses the division of the classes of which society is formed. When I take that survey, I find in the first place that the education of Oxford is, and always has been, and I trust ever will continue to be, a strictly and formally religious education. Since the passing of

the Act of 1853 the University has, in my opinion, with very good judgment, endeavoured to provide that the liberal enactments of that measure relating to Dissenters should in no respect affect the course of its tuition with regard to members of the Church of England. That being so, and such being the character of the education in the University, on whom does the maintenance of that character depend? On the governing body of the University. It is needless to enter into the question whether or not the governing body consists of Convocation; and for this reason, that the governing body, if it does not consist of Convocation, does consist of it together with the Hebdomadal Council; but no test is to be left for the Hebdomadal Council that is not to be applied to Convocation, and therefore these bodies will go together. We have, then, to consider whether the governing body itself is, or is not, to be composed of members of the Church of England. When we take into view the character of the education at Oxford, and likewise consider that the enormous majority of all classes which are likely at any period within our view to partake of the benefits of the University are members of the Church of England, it is, I think, not unreasonable to say that the governing body shall be composed of such members. What right have you to expect of those who do not belong to the Church of England that they shall, as members of that governing body, give themselves to the careful and jealous maintenance of the religious teaching of the University? It is not even fair, I think, to call upon such gentlemen to discharge duties for which by their religious profession they are necessarily in a great degree disqualified? But, besides that, I must take this into view :—In my opinion, the great justification for now opening this question, and also one great difficulty in the way of those who would have us refuse this Bill a second reading, lies in the state of the legislative arrangement deliberately adopted by Parliament for the University of Cambridge. I venture to say, that in the present circumstances, the best course which we can take—the course which would be fairest to those members of the Church of England who desire relaxation—the course most conducive to the interests both of the Church and of the Universities generally, and most just also as regards the Nonconformists, is to adopt for Oxford in the main the system already adopted for Cambridge. I, for one, am not able to defend the present legislative arrangement of Oxford. I would greatly have preferred that the University herself, by the exercise of her own powers, should have made the changes which are reasonable. There are, I think, five points on which changes might be fairly made at Oxford, all of which have been made at Cambridge ; some of them must be made by the Legislature, and the rest might be made by the University herself. I confess I do not see how you are to justify the exclusion of Dissenters from lay degrees, nor how you are to justify the maintenance of the lay test for Churchmen; and I hope that those who may follow me in this debate will address themselves to the solution of that difficulty, which I venture to say was left, if not wholly untouched, yet wholly unsolved, by my hon. Friend. In the third place, I must confess I think it would be very well if those who govern the University had the power of admitting, even into the governing body, by special decrees made for that purpose, persons whom it might be desirable to introduce upon special or exceptional grounds, although they might not individually belong to the Church of England ; just as at King's College, as has been mentioned by the hon. Member for the City of Oxford, certain professorships are thrown open to particular persons, irrespectively of their religious communion. There is another point which, although it has not been distinctly referred to in this discussion, is yet of great practical importance, and one with regard to which Oxford and Cambridge are under a different legislative arrangement. I mean the question of private Halls. As far as I am acquainted with the feelings of the Nonconformist bodies—and especially with the feelings of some among them—I believe that what they are most anxious for is to be allowed to found private Halls in the Universities under masters of their own persuasion. The provisions of the Oxford University Act as to private Halls have proved almost entirely inoperative, and if somewhat amended after the manner of the Cambridge University Act, advantage might be anticipated from them. The difference between the two Acts in this respect is apparently very slight. But the Oxford Act provides by its 25th section, that any Member of Convocation—that is, of the governing body—having obtained a license for the purpose, may open a private Hall. This confines the superintendence

of private Halls entirely to members of the Church of England, and consequently imposes on the Members of other religious denominations this disability — that they must either refrain from sending their children to the University altogether, or place them under the direct control of persons belonging to the Church of England. Now, the exaction of these terms might be justifiable if absolutely necessary for the welfare of the University ; but I own I do not see what mischief or danger could arise from allowing young gentlemen of other persuasions than the Church of England to come to Oxford and be placed under the disciplinary care of persons of their own denomination. That is not my opinion only, but the opinion of the Legislature ; because by the Cambridge Act of 1856, there is this modification introduced, that the privilege of establishing private Halls in that University is given, not to the members of Convocation, but to members of the University. Therefore, gentlemen, having taken the proper degrees and qualified themselves in other respects in such manner as to conform to any general rules laid down, may open private Halls at Cambridge without being members of the Church of England. That is a matter of great practical importance, and one the solution of which would depend not at all on our adopting this Bill as it stands, but on our adopting that provision of it which liberates degrees from the application of any religious test. Then, with regard to college emoluments, it is difficult and somewhat invidious to maintain the existing law at the University of Oxford after the concession which has been made at the sister University. At Cambridge you have made this concession, that no declaration shall be taken or required on admission to any college emolument which is made the means of assisting a young man in going through his course as an undergraduate ; and I confess I do not know why admission to such emoluments should be by law restricted, excepting as far as it involves admission to the governing body either of the University or of the Colleges. If that be the state of the law—if these are the points which remain open for discussion without interfering with the exclusive possession of the governing body by the Church of England, I confess that I am quite at a loss to understand how my hon. Friend can, even to himself, reconcile the course of undiscriminating resistance to which he commits himself. I do not think it is wise, as regards the interests of the University, to exhibit her in such a position. It is not for those who petitioned against the Bill to take distinctions between the second reading and the Committee; and I cannot wonder that the authorities at Oxford should have expressed their objections to the opening of the governing body. But it is for us to reconcile in the best way we can the various conflicting claims and interests with which Parliament is appointed to deal. Lately it has been too much the fashion to adopt a policy of indiscriminate resistance. I cannot conceal my own opinion on that subject. If you look back upon history you will find that the greatest vice and misfortune of the Church of England has been that, for many generations past, on questions not of temporal but spiritual interest, her friends, or those who thought themselves her friends, have shown a great deal too much tenacity in clinging to their privileges to the very last moment that it was practicable, and at length only had them positively wrenched from their grasp when concession had lost all possible grace and value, and when consequently nothing could be obtained in return. Sir, if I take my present course, it is not because I believe that this is an easy time for the Church of England, or a time without its dangers. On the contrary, as regards the religion of that Church, I admit that these are days when it is subject to peculiar and, perhaps, unprecedented dangers. But these dangers will not be averted or even mitigated by declining to make concessions which do not touch her faith, but indicate her desire to live in good will with every branch and section of the community—to consult, as far as possible, the feelings of all Christians and of all persons, be they Christians or not, to whom it is possible for the Universities to impart a portion of their benefits; and thus to show that when she does take a course of resistance it is from no narrow or hasty impressions, but because she is convinced that the vital interests are at stake of that faith which is committed to her charge. That is the policy upon which I desire to act. I am not here to seek for favour by holding language which would allow it for one moment to be believed that I think the maintenance of the definite religion of the Church of England is a matter of small or secondary importance; on the contrary, I believe that there is no higher object which any member of that Church could set before himself than that; and especially for me, in my position as one of the repre-

sentatives of the University of Oxford, to depart from that duty would be one of the basest acts of desertion of which any man could be guilty. But, nevertheless, while I do not question the sincerity, I do question the wisdom of the disposition which for several years past we have seen evinced. No doubt it is natural to bodies of men—and the history of all religious sects and parties shows it—to make use of the day of prosperity not as, I think, true wisdom would dictate, for the purpose of accommodating difficulties and removing grounds of offence, but for the extremest assertion of every right and every privilege to which it still remains within their strength to cleave. I was once, Sir, taken to task for questioning the judgment of this House, but I think it is quite competent for us, in a manner consistent with all due respect, to lament any decision at which this House may have arrived. It is not necessary now to enter into particulars, but various Bills have been proposed involving concession in one shape or another to Dissenters and persons who desire the relaxation of tests; and it appears to me that the readers of our discussions and those who learn the decisions to which this House has come during the last two or three years will have concluded with regret, if they are readers of wise and dispassionate mind, that very precious opportunities—golden opportunities, have been lost of uniting and knitting together the minds and hearts of men by reasonable concession, and that the assertions of right by majorities, which have been perhaps somewhat ruthlessly and certainly sternly made, are by no means calculated to diminish those dangers which lie in the future —that they procure, indeed, the gratification of a triumph for the moment, but that they store up difficulties for those who are to sit on these benches in this House hereafter. With that policy of indiscriminate resistance to almost every measure aiming at relaxation or relief, even down to the poor little measure—for so I must call it— of my hon. Friend the Member for Sheffield (Mr. Hadfield), which, I think, we carried through this House only by a majority of four, merely to undergo very shortly the miserable fate which too certainly awaited it in another place—with that policy I must say it is not simply as a Minister of the Crown, and not only as a Member sitting on this side of the House, that I decline to associate myself, but because I believe that, however sincerely, however honourably intended—and that I do not for one moment

The Chancellor of the Exchequer

question—it is a policy no more fatal to the application of the principles of civil and social justice than to the best interests of the Church of England herself.

MR. SELWYN said, he had not intended to take part in that debate, but, as the hon. Member for East Sussex (Mr. Dodson) had appealed to him, and as the right hon. Gentleman the Chancellor of the Exchequer had referred to the case of the University of Cambridge, and by a mistaken application of that case, had endeavoured to lead the House away from the matter before it—namely, the principle of the Bill, he felt called upon to offer a few remarks, with the view of bringing the House back to the proper subject of their discussion. In answer to the appeal of the hon. Member for East Sussex he was ready to admit that the Act of 1856 had not in any degree severed the connection between the University of Cambridge and the Church of England ; but he could not endorse the assertion of that hon. Member, which had been repeated by the Chancellor of the Exchequer, that the effect of the Bill before them would be to assimilate the condition of the two Universities. On the contrary, they had only to compare two statements made in the able and temperate speech of the hon. Gentleman in introducing the Bill, to see how wide a difference there would be between the two Universities under a measure like the present. The first of those statements was that the object of the Bill was the admission of persons to all degrees without any religious test whatever. With regard to that statement, the hon. Member for Sussex was correct, but the Chancellor of the Exchequer quite as incorrect. The second statement of the hon. Member for East Sussex was to the effect that the Bill would admit persons without any religious test to the Convocation, which was the Parliament of the University. Let them take together these two statements, the accuracy of which he acknowledged, and contrast them with the speech of the Chancellor of the Exchequer, who admitted that it would be a great evil to admit persons to the governing body of the University without a religious test. But was not the Parliament of the University its governing body? If so, would not the very evil which the right hon. Gentleman had deprecated, directly follow from the Bill which he had so earnestly supported ? Then they were told that, under the Act, the University of Oxford would be in the same position as that of Cambridge. But what was the position of Cambridge ? True, in the Cambridge Act of 1856 the mode in which the declarations constituting the test were to be made was left to the discretion of the governing body of the University, but the essential principle of that Act was, that no person should be admitted to the Senate unless he had, in the manner prescribed by the University, signed some declaration or made some statement that he was a *bond fide* member of the Church of England. What was the effect of that ? Why, that the governing body of that University must necessarily consist exclusively of members of the Church of England. Now, he would read a few lines of the Bill, the object of which had been fairly stated by its introducer, and then again ask the House to compare them with the Chancellor of the Exchequer's speech. The Bill provided that no person should be required, to enable him to take the degree of M.A., or any other academical degree, to subscribe any formulary of faith, or to make or subscribe any declaration or take any oath concerning his religious profession. The right hon. Gentleman complained of his own Colleague for not grappling with the question before the House ; but how had he dealt with it himself ? Why, he invited them, in a debate on the principle of this Bill, to follow him into a discussion of five favourite points of detail of his own, and particularly into the question of private Halls, which had nothing whatever to do with the principle of the Bill now before the House. The hon. Member who seconded the Motion very candidly stated what was the object of the Bill. The House, however, did not require that statement. On the presentation of petitions on that subject last year, the House was clearly and distinctly told that the object was not merely to introduce persons of any religious persuasion and without any test into the governing body of the University itself, but also to enable them to hold fellowships, and to introduce them into the governing bodies of all the individual colleges. And that had been stated again to-day. Last year, indeed, they said they would not go so far as to make every one eligible as a head of college. There might, according to this proposal, be a body of fellows all Unitarians, and who might govern a College according to their own views, except that when they came to elect a head, they must turn to a member of the Church of England. That was the limit of last year ; but it was obvious that the religious test, if confined to the headship, could not be maintained, and in the Bill before them that condition had been removed. The hon. Member for Sussex drew a picture of what, in his opinion, was a properly constituted educational establishment. He said a good schoolmaster should be one who did not limit his scholars to those not difficult to deal with, but that he ought to admit all who came, and deal with each of them as the urgency of the case required. Well, apply that to the Universities. Was there any exclusion? He maintained that there was no exclusion of persons of any denomination from the Universities, which were open to all who desired to obtain the advantages of academical education and academical degrees. There was, therefore, an absolute absence of any grievance to justify the adoption of the dangerous principle embodied in the measure. It was said that a Dissenter was deprived of the passport and stamp to his character for learning which a degree afforded, and which might help him in his future career. Was that the fact? Happily there were several cases where Dissenters had distinguished themselves at the University, and if such a person became a Senior Wrangler at Cambridge, or took a first class degree at Oxford, he was admitted to the degree of B.A. without any test whatever. Did he not, then, thus possess his passport and stamp of character to show how he had succeeded in his academical career? Would anybody care or inquire whether he afterwards went on to take the formal degree of M.A., which was the mere result of the payment of certain fees and the lapse of a few years. The real passport was obtained by the competitors for the B.A. degree and the honours thus conferred. He thought it would be wasting the time of the House to endeavour further to refute the statements so confidently made by the Chancellor of the Exchequer, when he said that the effect of the Bill would be to assimilate the practice at Oxford to what now existed at Cambridge. Far from it. The real effect of the Bill, as described by its seconder, would be to do that for Oxford which no dissenting body would permit to be done in the case of any school or college instituted for the religious education of the members and ministers of a particular persuasion—namely, that the members of the governing body of that institution should be admitted without any religious test or qualification whatever. That, and that

Mr. *Selwyn*

only, was the simple proposal of the Bill, and that reason alone, for no substantial grievance existed, ought to lead to its rejection. The very fact that the two Universities had gone so far as they had done, in opening their doors to Dissenters, and all other persons, without any religious test or qualification, was urged as an argument against them. They had recently had at Cambridge the scion of a distinguished Jewish family, and a Dissenter, the son of a dissenting minister, had lately obtained high honours there; but this only rendered it the more necessary that they should be cautious when they came to the consideration of the question, who were to be members of the governing body? He could not help regretting that here, as in the case of the small schools, they were continually being compelled to contest such questions, when within a few years the whole matter had been settled by the wisdom of Parliament. It was not consistent with what was due to the real prosperity of those educational establishments that they should be perpetually harassed by such attacks. More than anything else they required a period of repose, and it was only in cases of some pressing emergency, where there was a real and substantial grievance, that that House should interfere with the internal arrangements of bodies such as these. The evil effects of a measure like that before them would not be limited to members of the Church of England. These persons who were receiving the benefit of admission to the Universities would themselves be the greatest possible sufferers; for supposing the schemes which had been advocated in that House were carried into execution to the fullest extent—supposing they brought the Universities, he would not say down to the level, but to the condition of the University of London, what would be the inevitable result? His hon. Friend the Member for the University of Oxford had said, and the Chancellor of the Exchequer had also said, that nineteen-twentieths of those who desired and were in a position to reap the benefit of a University education were and would for a long time be members of the Church of England. He believed they might go further and say that that was the case with ninety-nine out of every hundred. What would be the necessary result if they carried into execution these measures? It would be that the parents and guardians of those young men who desired to see them educated in the principles of the

Church — if the connection between the Church and the Universities were rudely severed, as it would be by the passing of the Bill—would at once set about the establishment of some other body with features of exclusion so cardinal and fundamental as effectually to keep out the sons of Dissenters. The sons of Dissenters went to the Universities not merely to acquire classics or mathematics but also for the sake of that social distinction which arose from being members of the University ; they would not be willing to be confined to private Halls of their own; and the inevitable result of severing the connection between the Church and the Universities would be that some other exclusive Church of England institution would be founded, which would deprive the sons of Dissenters of the great social advantages they now enjoyed. But they were told by the Chancellor of the Exchequer that it was wrong to oppose the second reading of this Bill — that they were engaged in a course of indiscriminate resistance, of which they would some day rue the consequences and see the folly. He confessed he differed entirely from the right hon. Gentleman on that point, and he appealed to the experience of the last five Sessions as to which was the wiser course to take. They had tried both courses—they had tried the system of concession. They had themselves proposed measures of concession, and they had accepted them from the other side of the House. What had been the result ? They had tried the policy recommended by the Chancellor of the Exchequer in the case of the Endowed Schools Bill and in the case of the Burials Bill. In that case the Chancellor of the Exchequer, as in the case before them, picked out one difficulty, some minute matter of detail, and because the state of the law was not altogether perfect, he said he would vote for the second reading and discuss the Bill in Committee. On every occasion when they had taken a single step in the path of concession it had not led to the settlement of the question, but had been treated as a steppingstone to further aggression. That proved the wisdom of the course they had determined to take in reference to that and similar questions. And when they were told that the object and effect of the Bill would be to admit persons to the governing body at Oxford without any religious test at all ; when they were told that afterwards the same principle was to be applied to the University of Cambridge, and that afterwards it was to be applied to all colleges with the exception of the headship of those colleges, they were bound, if they wished to preserve the connection of the Universities with the Church, to reject a measure involving such a principle. There was one portion of the speech of the hon. Member for East Sussex which he had heard with great regret. That hon. Member, who usually spoke with great ability and moderation, towards the close of his speech had thought it right to allude to what had recently taken place at the University of Oxford, and, summoning spirits from Pandemonium, spoke of the discord and disunion which prevailed at the University. That was certainly not the proper time to discuss such matters, but if the University was in the condition he described, the passing of such a Bill as that must tend to promote that disunion, and perpetuate that discord. If the measure were carried, every evil he described would be aggravated, and every meeting of Congregation would necessarily become an arena of religious discussion and acrimonious controversy. He deprecated the revival of such discussions in that House. They had had five Wednesdays without anything of the kind, and he had trusted that the Session would have passed without the introduction of any such measures. It was with great regret he found the hon. Member for East Sussex, usually so moderate, embarked in these religious controversies. He regretted still more to hear him refer to the disunion which had existed in the Church, more or less, since Apostolic times. If that disunion existed, it was rather a reason for moderation and abstinence from attack than an argument for the introduction of such a Bill. There was abundance of work to be done by all, both within and without the pale of the Church, who wished to advance the cause of religion and morality. Heathenism and infidelity were increasing around them at home—the infant Church in the colonies was struggling under great difficulties—the vast field of missionary labour was unoccupied ; and while all that work remained necessarily to a great extent, unperformed, it was a great pity to enter upon such discussions and dissensions, especially when no real grievance existed. *Bella geri placuit nullos habitura triumphos.* It was not merely because he felt satisfied that the measure would be dangerous to the University which he represented—that it would be injurious to the cause of religion and religious education, and to the best interests of the Church of England, but because he believed it would be deeply injurious to those sons of Dissenting parents who were now receiving the benefits of a University education, that he called on the House to reject the Bill.

Mr. SCULLY said, that personally he might be thought in a dilemma with regard to the measure before the House, being bound by his duty as a Catholic to do nothing to strengthen, and by the oath he had taken as a Catholic Member to do nothing to weaken the Church of England ; yet he should support the second reading of the Bill, which he did not think would impair its legitimate strength. It did not strengthen the Church of England to see three distinguished Members for the Universities out of four opposing indiscriminately the second reading of a Bill which would only enable those who could write B.A. after their names to write M.A. To that extent only the Chancellor of the Exchequer went in his support of the Bill. He was sorry the right hon. Gentleman was Member for the University of Oxford ; if he were free from that incubus there could be little doubt he would soon go the length of advocating the admission of Dissenters to the University as members of Convocation. He did not see what mischief that could do to the Church of England. He would not go into the religious question. The hon. and learned Member who last spoke gave no reason whatever why the degree of M.A. at Oxford should be placed on a different footing from that in which it stood at Cambridge. Both Universities should act on the same principle. He believed the mere teaching and preaching of the Church of England were open to the members of all persuasions, to Dissenters, Turks, or Infidels, who were all rigidly excluded from the loaves and fishes. The admission of Dissenters into Convocation was not a question of religion, but of loaves and fishes. Nothing was talked of but mixed education for Ireland ; why should not the same system be adopted in Oxford ? Two years ago he accompanied a deputation to the Government for the purpose of securing a charter for the Catholic University of Ireland. The noble Lord at the head of the Government talked in a strain of great liberality of mixed education, and would not countenance anything exclusive, although he took the liberty of reminding him that in the public schools of Eton, Harrow, Rugby,

Mr. Selwyn

and at the University of Oxford, the system was exclusive and carried on exclusively by Protestant clergymen. Those who represented Oxford need be under no apprehension if the second reading of this Bill were carried. It would probably be so curtailed in Committee that it will only assimilate the law at Oxford to that at Cambridge. The Bill, however, involved an important principle which he thought the House ought to affirm.

Lord ROBERT MONTAGU said, he would not detain the House for more than two or three minutes. It seemed to him that the difference between the two sides of the House would be completely bridged over if the author of the Bill would only insert in it three words, placing Oxford exactly on the same footing as Cambridge. The arguments which had been used went to that extent ; and those which had been used by the Chancellor of the Exchequer were very strong—he thought totally irrefragable. Some hon. Members, he was aware, went a great deal further than that, and would have no tests at all, not even a subscription for clergymen ; but with such he could not agree. He did not think the hon. Member for Sussex, who moved the Bill, would go so far as that. The hon. Member for the City of Oxford had said that all he wanted was to proceed upon the same principle as the House of Commons and the State acts upon. When Members took their seats, they must all take an oath abjuring certain doctrines as injurious to the State. Even the Queen on the throne took an oath, and submitted to a test without which a Stuart would now be on the throne. They had no business to inquire into the private opinions of a man. In his private capacity he had a perfect right to hold what opinions and notions he chose ; but it was a different matter when he became a public teacher. When he took upon him a national office he was bound to teach only those doctrines which had been approved by the nation. The nation considered it a duty to give religious education to the people. The State paid for that education; for endowments, educational endowments, although originally established by individuals, were dealt with at the time of the Reformation as national property, and must now be so considered; they paid so much money for having certain religious principles instilled into the people. It was therefore necessary to define accurately what should be taught; or rather, to guard against what should not be taught. There would otherwise be nothing but confusion and vagaries in doctrine. Would they have the teachers in one parish contradicting and perhaps anathematizing another in the adjoining parish ? The State, therefore, imposed certain tests, and said, " Those only may teach who will teach according to the articles which we impose. Into your private opinions we don't inquire; but your public teaching must be in accordance with these articles." That was the principle which had been laid down by the Lord Chancellor in the judgment which he had pronounced the other day in the case of the *Essays and Reviews.* His words were these—

"That only is matter of accusation, which is advisedly taught or maintained by a clergyman, in opposition to the doctrine of the Church."

The doctrine of the Church was determined in that trial by the Articles of the Church. It was, therefore, only where the teaching was openly and advisedly in opposition to the doctrines of the Church that it could form matter of accusation against any public teacher. *A fortiori* those who train youths in the University must teach according to the Articles. If that were not so, they would have every clergyman setting himself up as the sole arbiter of doctrine; and there would be an Ecclesiastical tyranny as intolerable as that of the Star Chamber. Public opinion again would establish a penal system, and the basis of the Church would be narrowed. Already public opinion was more narrow than the Articles. Thus a sum of money had been raised, not for the prosecution, but the persecution of Bishop Colenso, and a subscription had been also got up for the prosecution of Mr. Wilson and Dr. Williams. Still more recently there had been an attempt made by private individuals to impose certain tests ; and if any clergyman did not sign the paper which was sent round for signature, he was hunted down by the religious papers of the day as a heretic. Yet this paper condemned the decision of the Privy Council, and was against the law of the land; it set up an *imperium in imperio.* With respect to the Bill, if the hon. Member for East Sussex would only agree to the same simple test for the governing body of the University of Oxford which was imposed at Cambridge, he would meet most of the difficulties on that (the Opposition) side of the House. The Chancellor of the Exchequer had allowed that the governing body ought not to be free for every Dissenter, but only for those who held the doctrines of the nation. He hoped the hon. Gentleman would give them an undertaking, that if the Bill passed the second reading he would in Committee introduce words such as he had indicated.

MR. BUXTON said, that hon. Gentlemen opposite argued that the House ought to adopt their views because they represented the opinions of the majority of Members of Oxford University. But could the House forget what had occurred a few day since, when the whole governing body of Oxford was overcome by an irruption of angry bigots from every corner of the land ? And yet hon. Gentlemen opposite invited the House to submit to the judgment of a mere numerical majority like that ! In his opinion no attempt had been made either by the hon. Baronet or the hon. and learned Member for Cambridge University, to meet the great argument in favour of the Bill—that the present system weighed with cruel oppression upon the consciences of many young men. According to the present system, if a young man hesitated to accept the tests, he was marked as a Dissenter or a sceptic, and consequently in most cases men forced themselves to swallow the tests, although with reluctance. Thus the University tempted the young men whom it fostered to tamper with their consciences by pretending to accept that concerning which they entertained serious doubts. Coming to the Bill itself, they had been told that the real aim of this proposal was to assail the Established Church. That he denied. Practically, the hold of the Church of England on the University would remain exactly what it was then. Even should a few Dissenters make their way into Convocation, they would be an almost imperceptible minority, and under the provisions of the Bill every functionary of the University, and every one actually engaged in teaching, would still have to declare himself a *bona fide* member of the Established Church. In fact, it was a delusion to suppose that this was in the main a Dissenter's question. No doubt the Bill might relieve a certain number of Dissenters, but its main effect would be to relieve those who, while still loyal members of the Church, were yet unable to subject their minds to every part of her dogmatic teaching. And there lay the very gist of the whole question. The strife was between the principle of religious subjection and the principle of religious liberty. It was impossible to understand the meaning of these tests, or even to imagine any possible plea for them, unless they were regarded as parts of a great system which emanated in days gone by, from the idea that uniformity of belief was the first essential, and that it was therefore the bounden duty of the people to submit their minds to the religious teaching of the national Church. That idea could not be more vividly expressed than in the words of the declaration, which was incorporated by law with the Thirty-nine Articles, as a constituent part of them. In that declaration the Sovereign says—

"It is most agreeable to our Kingly office not to permit unnecessary disputations, or questions to be raised. . . . We do, therefore, require all our loving subjects to continue in the uniform profession of the Articles of the Church, and we prohibit the least difference from the said Articles." Again, it says that, "From the doctrine and discipline of the Church of England we will not endure any varying or departing in the least degree;" the conclusion—the logical conclusion—being that "if any person in either of our Universities shall hold any public disputations upon the Thirty-nine Articles, he shall be liable to our displeasure, and we will see there shall be due execution upon him."

There was expressed in the plainest of words, the idea from which these tests naturally issued. That idea 300 years ago led the Government of almost every land in Christendom to attempt the extermination by fire and sword of all who broke through the required uniformity of belief, and who dared to dissent from the national Church, whatever that Church might be. By degrees humanity revolted from that course, but still even in England, within two centuries, imprisonment and banishment were not thought too harsh penalties for those who worked out their own faith for themselves. A length even those measures were found, in England at least, unbearable. But even till our own day that idea so far wrought upon the law of the land that no one might serve the State in any way unless he had declared himself a subject of the national Church. That oppression had also disappeared. But this test, still inflicted on the laymen educated at Oxford, was in fact nothing else but a miserable rag and tatter of the system which issued from the idea that uniformity of belief was essential, and that all men ought to bow the knee to the religion established by the State. And those who would maintain these tests were, one could plainly see, swayed mainly by the feeling that the national Church ought by right to enjoy

the undoubting, uncompromising, loyal allegiance of the whole people, and that no acknowledgment should be made which could be staved off of men's right to reject her supremacy over their mind and conscience. Now, on the one hand, he was sure that his hon. Friend (Mr. Dodson), and most of those who supported his Bill, were fully alive to the unspeakable value of the Established Church, and fully admitted, not merely the utility, but the absolute necessity of doctrinal teaching and the means of worship being offered for men's acceptance. And strongly as he (Mr. Buxton) detested the tyrannical stringency of the existing subscription required of the clergy, he entirely allowed that those who were to preach from the pulpits of the Church, and to serve at her altars, must in some way be ascertained to be true members of that Church. But, when he came to a test thus thrust upon laymen, he could not but see that it was nothing but an expression of the right of the Church to a dominion over men's minds, and he advocated the abolition of that test distinctly upon the principle of religious freedom—the principle, namely, that every man had an absolute, indefeasible right, with which no other man and no law of man could be entitled to interfere, to think out his own faith, to believe or to disbelieve, to accept in part or to accept as a whole the religious teaching that was set before him. Holding that right to religious freedom to be among the first and foremost of the natural rights of man, and perceiving that these tests were a trespass upon that freedom—upon that ground, far more than upon the ground of the oppression they caused, he demanded their repeal. He was well aware that this was not a popular view to take, but, at least, they might have the satisfaction of feeling that in founding themselves upon it they were conforming themselves to the realities of the life around them. They were not, like hon. Gentlemen opposite, clutching vainly at an ideal state of things, but were seeking to bring the law of the land into harmony with actual facts. It was happily the fact that such uniformity of belief, such subjection of men's minds and consciences to the dogmatic teaching of others, was quickly becoming a mere dream of the past. The younger generation of men, those who would stamp the age, were grappling more and more boldly with religious truth, throwing their own minds upon it, and working their way to their own conclusions. Some looked on that state of things with alarm; others, to his mind wiser, rejoiced in it as a sign of vigorous life—life far higher than any which was possible in the dead level of uniform belief. But, whether they thought of this with hope or with awe, at any rate nothing could be more futile than the endeavour to keep down that strong movement in men's minds by such poor and decayed trammels as those which it was the aim of the Bill to sweep away.

SIR STAFFORD NORTHCOTE said, he had no wish to detain the House by entering deeply into the somewhat desultory discussion to which the Bill had given rise, but before a division took place he wished to recal the minds of hon. Members to the exact position in which they stood, and to justify the position they had taken upon that side of the House. They had been censured by very high authority for what had been called "indiscriminate resistance" to measures of this kind. The justification for indiscriminate resistance on the present occasion was to be found in what he must call the indiscriminate nature of the attack. Let the House remember what was the exact position of the Bill. It was a remarkable fact that there had been no less than three distinct views taken as to the intentions and object of the Bill. The hon. Gentleman who introduced the Bill, in a speech of great moderation, said that he was about to introduce no new principle, but simply to complete what had been begun in 1854; that the principle of 1854 was, that education at the Universities should be thrown open to Dissenters, and this Bill was simply the complement of what was done in 1854. The hon. Gentleman said that it was not only the education but the degree which stamped that education which was of importance. Upon that point the hon. Gentleman was set right by the seconder of the Motion, who was himself practically acquainted with the subject, who said in effect that it was a delusion to say that the conferring a degree of M.A. was giving a stamp to the education that had been received. That stamp was given when, after passing through the curriculum, a man obtained the degree of B.A. The hon. Gentleman who seconded the Motion, however, said he wanted something more—that the prizes of the Universities should be open to Dissenters, a step which the mover did not seem to wish to take, nor the Bill to contemplate. Then there was the view taken by the hon. Member for Maidstone (Mr. Buxton), who reproved Members on that side of the House for saying that the Bill would weaken the connection of the University with the Church of England. But that expression had been first used by the hon. Member for Oxford (Mr. Neate), who knew the practical working of Convocation. That hon. Member had told them that he was aware that if this measure was passed it would, if not destroy, certainly impair the connection between the Church and the University; that it would have the effect of rendering less definite, less authoritative, the teaching of the Church at the University. When such arguments were brought forward by such authority it was time for the party with which he had the honour to act to ask, before going to a division, what was really the principle of the Bill, and what were they going to vote upon. The Chancellor of the Exchequer said he wished to pare the measure down to a minimum, that he was ready to defend the colleges and to keep the prizes in the hands of the Church; that he was decidedly of opinion that the governing body must be retained in the hands of the Church, thus far differing *in toto* from the hon. Gentleman who moved the second reading of the Bill. But the right hon. Gentleman then said he thought that the House ought to take the step of assenting to the principle of the Bill with the view of placing the University of Oxford on the same level as that of the University of Cambridge. Now that view of the Chancellor of the Exchequer was wholly different from the view put forth by the mover and seconder of the Bill, and the Bill itself. Was there, he (Sir Stafford Northcote) asked, anything whatever in the Bill that would lead the House to suppose that its object was simply to place the two Universities upon the same footing? The Bill, on the contrary, was well calculated to revive the rivalry which in the course of advance some time ago existed between the two Universities. For nearly a century there had been a marked distinction observed between the two Universities. At one time it was thought desirable that Oxford should obtain a step in advance of Cambridge. At another time it was considered prudent that Cambridge should obtain a step in advance of Oxford. The result was a constant desire on the part of each to obtain an advantage of the other. The present measure, if carried, would have the effect of reproducing that restless and unnatural competition between the Universities of Oxford and Cambridge. While it would be consistent for Gentlemen who held the views which the promoter of this Bill held to support a measure that would have that effect; the party with whom he had the honour of acting felt themselves not only justified, but actually bound by their principles, to resist the progress of such a measure. If they did not wish to be false to their principles they must take their stand in opposition to the measure. They could not accept the advice tendered them, of assenting to the second reading of the Bill in the hope that in Committee, by the cutting out of all its most important provisions, they might bring it to such a miserable fragment as the Chancellor of the Exchequer wished to reduce it. They knew very well what the consequences of such a course would be. If they assented to the second reading with that view it would be said that they admitted the main principle of the Bill, and their standing ground would be cut away from them. He hoped that they would take no such course, and that they would continue to stand upon the firm ground they then occupied. The Chancellor of the Exchequer entreated them to consider the position in which they stood, and he reminded the House that some years ago the Government of which he was a principal organ came forward with a measure to settle the status of the University of Oxford. That was a great measure, embracing a large number of questions, which were kept distinct from any plan for admitting Dissenters; but that towards the close of the discussion, a private Member brought forward a clause for the admission of Dissenters to the University. That clause was passed at a single discussion, and in that way the present state of things was inaugurated at Oxford. But the right hon. Gentleman went on to say that that was no solution of the question. He (Sir Stafford Northcote) maintained it was a solution of the question by Parliament deliberately proposed and amply discussed. Two clauses were proposed which were deliberately discussed. One of them was accepted and the other was rejected. The Chancellor of the Exchequer said that some years afterwards a Bill was proposed with much more deliberation in regard to the University of Cambridge, and very different from the hasty measure respecting the University of Oxford, and passed into a law. The right hon. Gentleman then

Sir Stafford Northcote

called upon the House to agree to a Bill which gave rise to such conflicting opinions, even amongst its promoters, and said that the Government would make it the means of introducing a settlement of the question, by making the measure hastily passed consistent with the measure deliberately passed. If that were so, why had not the Government taken the subject in hand, and proposed a measure on their responsibility, instead of leaving it to a private Member? But he (Sir Stafford Northcote) would venture to ask whether the settlement arrived at in respect to Cambridge was so satisfactory that the House was prepared to stand by it? Were the Dissenters in Cambridge University satisfied? Why, the right hon. Gentleman the Member for Kilmarnock (Mr. E. P. Bouverie) last year came down to the House and said that the position of the Dissenters at Cambridge was intolerable—that Parliament had no doubt granted them an A.M. degree, but that it shut them out from what the hon. Member for Cork (Mr. Scully) called the loaves and fishes. The right hon. Gentleman then went on to argue upon the propriety of giving the Dissenters in the University of Cambridge admission to the prizes of that University, and asked the House to do by them what the hon. Member for the City of Oxford wished to be done by this Bill. Now, as a matter of justice to those with whom he (Sir Stafford Northcote) acted, he was determined that the House should not go to a division upon any such understanding as that to which he had referred, and that it should not be supposed, though the party with whom he acted were opposed to the principle of the Bill, that they were prepared to offer an indiscriminate resistance, as the right hon. Gentleman said, to any measure that might be presented for altering the position of the University of Oxford. They had never shown a disposition to offer an indiscriminate resistance to what was really good and proper. But when an important measure was brought forward, in respect of which there were three distinct and contradictory views taken by its supporters, when they heard the ablest and the best amongst its supporters say that they looked upon it as a step for throwing open the prizes to Dissenters, and for weakening the connection of Church and State, they (the Conservatives) would be betraying their principles and not doing their duty as members of the Church if they did not stand up and say that they were determined to resist the further progress of the measure. If it was desired to place Oxford upon the same footing as Cambridge, and to deal with the five points referred to by the Chancellor of the Exchequer, let the Bill be withdrawn or negatived, and then let the Government take the matter into their own hands ; or, if the Government should shrink from the task, let any hon. Member who was anxious for that settlement bring forward a measure for that purpose. But with regard to this Bill, he called upon the House not to be deluded into thinking that it was wrong to offer indiscriminate resistance to indiscriminate attack, and therefore he appealed to them not to assent to the second reading.

MR. WALTER said, it was very discouraging to Members who, like himself, felt great difficulty in making up their minds upon the subject to find, upon looking for guidance and information to those Gentlemen who from their position might be supposed to understand the question, that they were rather at cross purposes upon it. Such was certainly the case in the present discussion. Whatever might be the intentions of the hon. Member for East Sussex, there could be no doubt that the Bill, as it stood, went the whole length of throwing open Convocation or the governing body of the University of Oxford to all persons indiscriminately, without the application of a theological test. But the Chancellor of the Exchequer, in supporting the second reading, told the House that that was not what he meant ; that he did not want to throw open Convocation ; that he thought the connection of the Church of England with the governing body of the University should be maintained as it at present existed. When, however, that element was taken out of the Bill nothing would remain in it. The only grievance to be dealt with, then, was of so slight and imperceptible a nature that it was difficult to understand what it was. He had himself been a Master of Arts of Oxford University for twenty years, but he had not considered it a privilege of so extraordinary a nature that he should go far out of his way to obtain it. When the whole object of the Bill, as weeded by the Chancellor of the Exchequer, would be to confer the barren privilege of being a Master of Arts without a right of voting, upon certain individuals not members of the Church of England, he did not think such an object was worth the time or trouble of

discussion in that House. He admitted that the question as to members of Convocation was very difficult and important. He was himself entirely opposed to maintaining the existing test of subscription to the Thirty-nine Articles, and he thought the hon. Member for Oxford University (Sir William Heathcote) went almost as far when he said that he saw no reason for imposing upon laymen the same tests of Church membership as were required of ministers of the Church. He would be content with such declaration as was to be found in one part of the Bill, that any person becoming a member of Convocation should declare he was *bonâ fide* a member of the Church of England. But that was not what was brought before the House. The Bill proposed, if anything, that all theological tests whatever should be withdrawn as regarded members of Convocation. That raised a still more difficult question, whether it was possible to take away from the University of Oxford, as distinguished from the colleges, that distinctive character of being identified with the Church of England which at present it assumed to possess. He would be sorry to commit himself at present to any definitive opinion upon that point, but it seemed to him that a very complicated position might arise if the University of Oxford were placed in the position of the University of London with a number of Church colleges attached to it. Let any one consider what would be the position of the University of London if a number of Church colleges were to be attached to it, and then they could form a notion of what the University of Oxford might become if the Bill passed in its present shape. While he was prepared to support any measure for substituting a declaration of *bonâ fide* membership of the Church for the test at present applied to members of Convocation, he could not support the Bill in its present shape, and he did not think it would be worth while going into Committee upon it if it was, as he gathered from the Chancellor of the Exchequer, his intention to weed it entirely of that portion which hon. Gentlemen opposite regarded as the mischievous part of the Bill. He hoped, therefore, the measure would be withdrawn, but should it be pressed to a division he would be compelled to vote against the second reading.

MR. GOSCHEN said, the hon. Member who had last spoken was in error in saying that the principle of the Bill was to admit to the government of the University persons who could not sign a declaration of Church membership. The Chancellor of the Exchequer had also spoken upon that point, and it had been argued that the Bill contained no other principle. To say that was to overlook one of the chief motives for bringing forward the Bill, which was to get rid of a system which distressed conscience, promoted dishonesty, impeded learning, discouraged theological study at the University, and on the whole was unjust, intolerant, and inquisitorial. The Bill proposed to remove the evil by abolishing tests for academical degrees. The question of honesty had not been noticed by the opponents of the Bill. When it was stated that the cause of learning was endangered by the test, the cry in answer was, "The Church in danger." But let hon. Gentlemen opposite consider how they could deal with the case of a man who came to the University with a superficial form of adherence to the Church, and, under the stimulus of the very learning and study which it is the duty and highest privilege of the University to enforce, found that although he wished to believe certain things, yet honestly he could not. Was such a man to be told, "Stifle that morbid craving after truth; if you cannot give an intelligent adhesion to the Church, give it anyhow?" Or would they say to him, "You ought to have arrived at one conclusion only from your study, and you have arrived at another. We wished you to listen and not to reflect. Your learning is great, your genius undeniable, your character unblemished, but you dissent from one of the 500 propositions contained in the Thirty-nine Articles, you are weak enough to confess it, and you can never be a member of that University, which otherwise you are so fitted to adorn?" He left the opponents of the measure the benefit of the choice between these two answers.

MR. WALPOLE : The hon. Gentleman who has just spoken has his name on the back of the Bill, but he has certainly not made more clear than it was before what is its principle. The principle announced by the Mover, and which is contained in the Bill itself, is exactly that which was so clearly stated by my hon. Friend the Member for Oxford University (Sir William Heathcote) —namely, to admit to the governing body of the University persons who are not members of the Church of England. That is the principle contained in the Bill. The principle contended for by the hon. Seconder is to go still further; and to admit

Dissenters, not only to the governing body of the University, but to all the endowments of the colleges. The Chancellor of the Exchequer supports the Bill, not on the principle of the Bill itself, not upon the principle of the Mover, nor on that of the Seconder, but upon the principle that he wants simply to place the University of Oxford upon the same footing as the University of Cambridge. And then the hon. Gentleman who has just addressed the House, with his usual acuteness and ability, starts another principle quite different from all the others—namely, that you ought to import into this Bill the question of subscription. I have a strong objection to Bills, professing to contain certain principles, being brought in and the sanction of the House asked to their second reading, with the intention afterwards of adopting and carrying into effect totally different principles. The Chancellor of the Exchequer calls our resistance to Bills of this kind, " indiscriminate resistance to all improvement." No, it is anything but indiscriminate resistance to all improvement. It is the application of a practical rule of wisdom to be observed in this House, where we have had previous experience of similar propositions on former occasions. I will explain what I mean. We have had three measures submitted to us of late years. One related to the great question of church rates, which was mainly argued at first upon the ground that Dissenters had a grievance in being required to pay for a Church which they did not frequent, and with which they were not in communion. We attempted to meet that grievance. I myself proposed a Bill to relieve Dissenters from it ; but that Bill was opposed, and measures for the total abolition of church rates were advocated instead, because the promoters had ulterior views as against the Church Establishment itself. Then came the Bill relating to endowed schools. That Bill was ostensibly brought in because it was said that the children of persons not belonging to the Church did not have fair play in religious instruction if they went to endowed schools. The objection was removed by a conscience clause, and yet other measures were still persisted in because their promoters would be content with nothing less than that Dissenters should become managers and trustees of those schools, though they never belonged to them. Then take the third question of burying-grounds. It was said that it was a grievance that the body of a person who

Mr. Goschen

in his lifetime had not been a member of the Church could, if the law were strictly enforced, be refused interment in the churchyard, where his remains might rest near those of his own relations. We offered to relieve Dissenters from that grievance, but they were not satisfied ; they required the use of the Church and the churchyard, as if they were their own ; and they demanded the right to have any ceremonies performed in them, other than those of the Church of England. And now we have a Bill which the House is asked to pass upon the ground that it is to assimilate Oxford University to Cambridge University, while we know well, from what we have heard, that such is not really the object in view. Now, in my humble judgment, that is not a fair way of dealing with the House. If it be intended merely to assimilate the two Universities, let Her Majesty's Government bring in a Bill for that purpose and I venture to say that little or no opposition will be made to it on this side of the House. But if a measure is introduced professing one object, but really having another, then, I say, we are not only justified, but absolutely called upon to give our opposition to such a proposal.

SIR GEORGE GREY : I only wish to say that, in voting for this Bill, I distinctly disavow doing so upon the assumption that its principle is such as has been described by hon. Gentlemen on the opposite side— the severance of the connection between the Church and the University. I do not find that principle in the Bill. If we were reading this Bill now a third time, that might be the effect of it. But we are not reading the Bill a third time. We shall have to go into Committee upon it if this stage is passed. I have now only to look to the principle, and that I take to be that there shall no longer be any test upon taking academical degrees with certain qualifications. In the Cambridge Act the qualifications are enumerated. It says that an M.A. degree taken without test shall not enable any person to become a member of the Senate or to fill certain offices. My hon. Friend proposes to consider in Committee the question of adding the qualifications which are not now inserted in the Bill, to the effect that an M.A. degree shall not entitle any person to become a member of Convocation without test. No one can deny that it will be competent to add that qualification when the Bill gets into Committee.

MR. DODSON said, he thought he had cause to complain that the principle of his Bill had been misrepresented by hon. Gentlemen opposite. The principle of the Bill was not the admission of Dissenters into the governing body of the University, but the completion of the opening of University education by the removal of all unnecessary tests, at the same time maintaining the offices of the Church in the hands of members of the Church. The grievance created by the test had not been denied. The test itself harassed those who went to the University, deterred others from going there at all, provoked religious disunion, and added fuel to religious discord. To refuse to allow the second reading of the Bill would be to refuse to the laity a concession which by common consent was pronounced necessary in the case of the clergy.

Question put, "That the word 'now' stand part of the Question."

The House divided :—Ayes 211 ; Noes 189 : Majority 22.

Main Question put, and agreed to.

Bill read 2°, and committed for Wednesday, 1st June.

AYES.

Acton, Sir J. D.
Adair, H. E.
Adam, W. P.
Agnew, Sir A.
Alcock, T.
Antrobus, E.
Athlumney, Lord
Ayrton, A. S.
Aytoun, R. S.
Baines, E.
Baring, H. B.
Baring, rt. hn. Sir F.T.
Baring, T. G.
Barnes, T.
Bass, M. T.
Bazley, T.
Beale, S.
Beaumont, W. B.
Beaumont, S. A.
Bellew, R. M.
Berkeley, hon. H. F.
Berkeley,hn.Col.F.W.F.
Berkeley, hon. C. P. F.
Biddulph, Colonel
Black, A.
Blake, J.
Blencowe, J. G.
Bonham-Carter, J.
Bouverie, rt. hon. E. P.
Bouverie, hon. P. P.
Brand, hon. H.
Bright, J.
Bruce, Lord E.
Bruce, H. A.
Buchanan, W.
Buller, J. W.

Buller, Sir A. W.
Butler, C. S.
Butt, I.
Buxton, C.
Caird, J.
Cardwell, rt. hon. E.
Castlerosse, Viscount
Childers, H. C. E.
Cholmeley, Sir M. J.
Churchill, Lord A. S.
Clay, J.
Clifford, C. C.
Clifton, Sir R. J.
Clive, G.
Cobden, R.
Collier, Sir R. P.
Cox, W.
Crawfurd, E. H. J.
Crawford, R. W.
Crossley, Sir F.
Davey, R.
Dering, Sir E. C.
Dillwyn, L. L.
Douglas, Sir C.
Duff, M. E. G.
Duke, Sir J.
Dunbar, Sir W.
Dundas, F.
Dundas, rt. hon. Sir D.
Enfield, Viscount
Evans, T. W.
Ewart, W.
Ewart, J. C.
Fenwick, H.
Fermoy, Lord
Finlay, A. S.

Fitzroy, Lord F. J.
Forster, C.
Forster, W. E.
Fortescue, hon. F. D.
Fortescue, C. S.
French, Colonel
Gaskell, J. M.
Gavin, Major
Gibson, rt. hon. T. M.
Gilpin, C.
Glyn, G. C.
Goldsmid, Sir F. H.
Gower, hon. F. L.
Greene, J.
Greenwood, J.
Gregson, S.
Grey, rt. hon. Sir G.
Gurdon, B.
Hadfield, G.
Hanbury, R.
Hankey, T.
Hardcastle, J. A.
Hartington, Marquess of
Headlam, rt. hon. T. E.
Henderson, J.
Henley, Lord
Herbert, rt. hon. H. A.
Hibbert, J. T.
Hodgkinson, G.
Hodgson, K. D.
Howard, hon. C. W. G.
Ingham, R.
Jackson, W.
Jervoise, Sir J. C.
Johnstone, Sir J.
Kershaw, J.
King, hon. P. J. L.
Kinglake, A. W.
Kinnaird, hon. A. F.
Knatchbull - Hugessen, E.
Layard, A. H.
Langton, W. H. G.
Lawson, W.
Leatham, E. A.
Lefevre, G. J. S.
Lewis, H.
Lindsay, W. S.
Lloyd, T.
Locke, J.
Lowe, rt. hon. R.
Lysley, W. J.
MacEvoy, E.
Mackinnon, W. A. (Lymington.)
Mackinnon, W.A.(Rye.)
M'Mahon, P.
Marjoribanks, D. C.
Martin, P. W.
Merry, J
Mildmay, H. F.
Miller, W.
Mitchell, T. A.
Moffatt, G.
Moncreiff, rt. hon. J.
Morris, D.
Morrison, W.
Neate, C.
North, F.
Ogilvy, Sir J.
Onslow, G.
O'Reilly, M.W.
Owen, Sir H. O.

Packe, Colonel
Padmore, R.
Paget, C.
Paxton, Sir J.
Peel, rt. hon. Sir R.
Peel, rt. hon. F.
Pender, J.
Peto, Sir S. M.
Pilkington, J.
Pinney, Colonel
Pollard-Urquhart, W.
Ponsonby, hon. A.
Potter, E.
Pugh, D.
Robartes, T. J. A.
Robertson, D.
Russell, H.
Russell, A.
Russell, Sir W.
St. Aubyn, J.
Salomons, Mr. Ald.
Scholefield, W.
Scott, Sir W.
Scully, V.
Seely, C.
Seymour, H. D.
Seymour, A.
Shelley, Sir J. V.
Sheridan, R. B.
Sheridan, H. B.
Smith, J. B.
Smith, A.
Smith, J. A.
Stacpoole, W.
Staniland, M.
Stanley, hon. W. O.
Stansfeld, J.
Steel, J.
Stirling, W.
Stuart, Colonel
Sykes, Colonel W. H.
Talbot, C. R. M.
Taylor, P. A.
Tite, W.
Tollemache, hon. F. J.
Tomline, G.
Tracy, hon. C. R. D. H.
Turner, J. A.
Vane, Lord H.
Verney, Sir H.
Vernon, H. F.
Villiers, rt. hon. C. P.
Vivian, H. H.
Warner, E.
Watkins, Colonel L.
Western, S.
Westhead, J. P. Brown-
Whalley, G. H.
Whitbread, S.
White, J.
White, L.
Wickham, H. W.
Williams, W.
Winnington, Sir T. E.
Wood, rt. hon. Sir C.
Woods, H.
Wyld, J.
Wyvill, M.

TELLERS.
Mr. Dodson.
Mr. Goschen.

NOES.

Adderley, rt. hon. C. B.
Addington, hon. W. W.
Angerstein, W.
Arbuthnott, hon. Gen.
Archdall, Captain M.
Astell, J. H.
Baillie, H. J.
Baring, T.
Barrow, W. H.
Barttelot, Colonel
Bathurst, A. A.
Bathurst, Colonel H.
Beach, W. W. B.
Bective, Earl of
Beecroft, G. S.
Bentinck, G. W. P.
Benyon, R.
Beresford, rt. hon. W.
Bernard, hon. Col.
Bernard, T. T.
Bond, J. W. M'G.
Bramston, T. W.
Bridges, Sir B. W.
Briscoe, J. I.
Bruce, Major C.
Bruce, Sir H. H.
Burghley, Lord
Burrell, Sir P.
Cave, S.
Cecil, Lord R.
Chapman, J.
Codrington, Sir W.
Cole, hon. H.
Collins, T.
Cubitt, G.
Curzon, Viscount
Dalkeith, Earl of
Damer, S. D.
Dickson, Colonel
Disraeli, rt. hon. B.
Du Cane, C.
Duncombe, hon. A.
Duncombe, hon. W. E.
Du Pre, C. G.
Dutton, hon. R. H.
Edwards, Colonel
Egerton, hon. A. F.
Egerton, E. C.
Egerton, hon. W.
Elphinstone, Sir J. D.
Estcourt, rt. hon. T.H.S.
Fane, Colonel J. W.
Farquhar, Sir M.
Farrer, J.
Fellowes, E.
Fergusson, Sir J.
Ferrand, W.
FitsGerald, W. R. S.
Fleming, T. W.
Floyer, J.
Franklyn, G. W.
Gallwey, Sir W. P.
George, J.
Getty, S. G.
Gore, W. R. O.
Gower, G. W. G. L.
Graham, Lord W.
Greenall, G.
Grey de Wilton, Visct.
Grogan, Sir E.
Hamilton, Lord C.

Hamilton, Viscount
Hamilton, I. T.
Hardy, G.
Hardy, J.
Hartopp, E. B.
Harvey, R. B.
Hervey, Lord A.
Hay, Sir J. C. D.
Henley, rt. hon. J. W.
Heygate, Sir F. W.
Heygate, W. U.
Hodgson, R.
Holford, R. S.
Holmesdale, Viscount
Hotham, Lord
Humberston, P. S.
Hume, W. W. F.
Hunt, G. W.
Ingestre, Viscount
Jermyn, Earl
Jervis, Captain
Jolliffe, rt. hon. Sir W. G. H.
Jolliffe, H. H.
Kekewich, S. T.
Kelly, Sir FitzRoy
Ker, D. S.
Kerrison, Sir E. C.
King, J K.
Knatchbull, W. F.
Knight, F. W.
Knox, Colonel
Langton, W. Gore
Leeke, Sir H.
Lefroy, A.
Legh, Major C.
Legh, W. J.
Lennox, Lord G. G.
Lennox, C. S. B. H. K.
Leslie, C. P.
Leslie, W.
Liddell, hon. H. G.
Longfield, R.
Lovaine, Lord
Lygon, hon. F.
Lytton, rt.hon.Sir G.E. L. B.
Mainwaring, T.
Malcolm, J. W.
Malins, R.
Manners, right hon. Lord J.
Manners, Lord G. J.
Miles, Sir W.
Miller, T. J.
Mills, A.
Mitford, W. T.
Montagu, Lord R.
Montgomery, Sir G.
Mordaunt, Sir C.
Morritt, W. J. S.
Mowbray, rt. hon. J. R.
Murray, W.
Naas, Lord
Newdegate, C. N.
Newport, Viscount
Noel, hon. G. J.
North, Colonel
Northcote, Sir S. H.
Packe, C. W.
Pakington, rt hn. Sir J.

Papillon, P. O.
Patten, Colonel W.
Peel, rt. hon. Gen.
Pennant, hon. Colonel
Pevensey, Viscount
Powell, F. S.
Powys-Lybbe, P. L.
Repton, G. W. J.
Ridley, Sir M. W.
Rogers, J. J.
Rolt, J.
Rowley, hon. R. T.
Salt, T.
Sclater-Booth, G.
Scott, Lord H.
Scourfield, J. H.
Smith, A.
Smith, S. G.
Smyth, Colonel
Somerset, Colonel
Somes, J.
Stanhope, J. B.
Stuart, Lieut.-Col. W.
Stracey, Sir H.
Surtees, H. E.
Taylor, Colonel
Tempest, Lord A. V.
Thynne, Lord E.

Tollemache, J.
Tottenham, Lieut.-Col.
    C. G.
Trefusis, hon. C. H. R.
Turner, C.
Vance, J.
Vansittart, W.
Verner, Sir W.
Verner, E. W.
Vyse, Colonel H.
Walcott, Admiral
Walker, J. R.
Walpole, rt. hon. S. H.
Walsh, Sir J.
Walter, J.
Waterhouse, S.
Watlington, J. W. P.
Welby, W. E.
Whitmore, H.
Woodd, B. T.
Wyndham, hon. P.
Yorke, hon. E. T.
Yorke, J. R.

TELLERS.
Sir W. Heathcote.
Mr. Selwyn.

ELECTION PETITIONS BILL—[BILL 17.]

SECOND READING.

Order for Second Reading read.

Moved, "That the Bill be now read a second time."—(*Mr. Hunt.*)

SIR GEORGE GREY said, a similar Bill had been introduced last year and referred to a Select Committee. The Bill, however, as now introduced, was considerably different from the shape in which it was reported by that Committee, and its details would require great consideration. He should, however, not oppose the second reading.

SIR FRANCIS GOLDSMID said, he feared that the effect of the Bill would be to discourage *bona fide* petitions. Parliament could not make a petitioner proceed against his will. He believed it would be impossible ever to make the Bill efficient, and in not opposing the second reading he wished to reserve to himself the liberty of moving its rejection on going into Committee.

MR. COLLINS said, he was of the same opinion, and he hoped it would be understood that, in assenting to the second reading, the House did not pledge itself to the principle of the Bill.

Motion *agreed to.*

Bill read 2°, and *committed* for *Wednesday,* 20th April.

VOL. CLXXIV. [THIRD SERIES.]

BANK NOTES (SCOTLAND) BILL.

Resolution *considered* in Committee.

(In the Committee.)

Resolved, That the Chairman be directed to move the House, That leave be given to bring in a Bill to authorise and regulate the issue of Bank Notes in Scotland by Banking Companies.

Resolution *reported.*

Bill *ordered* to be brought in by Sir JOHN HAY, Sir EDWARD COLEBROOKE, Mr. DUNLOP, and Mr. FINLAY.

Bill *presented,* and read 1°. [Bill 53.]

CHIEF RENTS (IRELAND) BILL [*Lords*].

Bill *presented,* and read 1°. [Bill 52.]

House adjourned at a quarter
before Six o'clock.

~~~~~~~~

HOUSE OF LORDS,

Thursday, March 17, 1864.

MINUTES.]—PUBLIC BILLS—*Second Reading*—
Bills of Exchange and Promissory Notes (Ireland)* (No. 26) ; Consolidated Fund (£584,650)*
(No. 33) ; Consolidated Fund (£4,500,000)*
(No. 34), (*Committee negatived*).
Third Reading—Consolidated Fund (£584,650)*
(No. 33) ; Consolidated Fund (£4,500,000)*
(No. 34) ; Mutiny* ; Marine Mutiny.*

THE MHOW COURT MARTIAL—SIR
WILLIAM MANSFIELD.

NOTICE OF MOTION WITHDRAWN.

LORD CHELMSFORD, who had given Notice

"To call the Attention of the Secretary of State for War to the Court Martial held at Mhow in the East Indies on Paymaster Smales, of the Inniskilling Dragoons, with reference to the Part alleged to have been taken in that Proceeding by His Excellency Sir William Mansfield, Commander-in-Chief at Bombay."

said, that in the discussion which had taken place elsewhere, such ample justice had been done to Sir William Mansfield, that the object which he had in view had been fully attained. He could not himself say anything half so satisfactory as the statements which had been made on that occasion ; and as he was unwilling to run the risk of effacing by repetition the effect which had been produced, he would withdraw his Notice.

EARL DE GREY AND RIPON said, he was glad the Notice had been withdrawn, as he thought it very desirable that discussions connected with the discipline of the army should be avoided as much as pos-

G

sible. Although it had been his duty to differ upon one point from Sir William Mansfield, he fully believed that the distinguished officer was actuated solely by a desire to serve the public interests and to maintain the discipline of the army.

ARMY—TEN YEAR ENLISTMENT ACT.
QUESTION.

THE EARL OF DESART asked the noble Lord the Secretary of State for War, Whether the Government have made any Preparation to meet the Difficulties which seemed likely to ensue in consequence of the Operation of the Ten Year Enlistment Act? Those difficulties were so notorious that he thought it would be useful and would tend to quiet the public mind, before Parliament separated for the Easter holydays, to know whether the Government had in view any plan for mitigating the dangers that were apprehended. Unless measures were promptly taken, the army might be reduced to a state yet more inefficient than it was before the Crimean War. In one regiment of Guards alone a loss of 700 men was anticipated. If that were so with the Guards, it was impossible to conjecture what might be the case with respect to the Line regiments, especially those on foreign stations. These soldiers might be replaced as far as numbers went, but it would only be with raw material in place of disciplined troops, and at least £20 must be expended upon a recruit before he was efficient. England at present was regarded in Europe as undecided and untrustworthy. If we could not obtain the number of men necessary to recruit our army we might become objects of contempt to the world, and be unable to meet the consequences which might arise in the present unsettled condition of affairs throughout the world.

EARL DE GREY AND RIPON thought the magnitude of the evils to be apprehended had been very much overstated by the noble Lord. It was quite true that a period of ten years having all but elapsed since the Crimean War, a considerable number of men, under the operation of the Limited Enlistment Act, would be entitled to their discharge next year; but it by no means followed that the services of the whole number, or anything like the whole number, would be lost to the State. Judging by what had taken place in previous years, there was every reason to

believe that not more than half—probably less than half—of those entitled to their discharge would avail themselves of the opportunity. The question was not one of such magnitude as the noble Earl supposed; still, no doubt, a much larger number of men would take their discharge this year and next than would do so under ordinary circumstances; and measures were under the consideration of Her Majesty's Government for holding out inducements to old soldiers to re-engage, either immediately or within a limited period, and giving them certain advantages which they would have enjoyed had their services been continuous. It was not in his power to state the exact steps which might be necessary for the purpose, as the subject was one requiring a good deal of consideration, but he could assure the noble Earl that the circumstances of the time had not escaped attention. If the noble Lord alluded to legislative measures, he was not at all inclined to admit that the operation of the Limited Enlistment Act had disappointed expectation. The termination of the period of service at a given time was one of the features of the Act, and formed one of the grounds on which its adoption was originally recommended to the House. In exceptional periods, such as that now approaching, it was quite right that the Government should take measures to mitigate the inconveniences with which the operation of the Act was attended, and to prevent an unusually large diminution of the army. But those measures should be suited to the emergency, and it was not necessary to accompany them with any reflections upon the Act itself. He had no detailed information as to the case to which the noble Earl (the Earl of Desart) had specially referred. It was true, however, that the Guards were in an exceptional position, and owing to the facilities which they possessed for obtaining employment, probably a larger number of them would take their discharges than would be the case in other regiments. The regiments of the Guards were composed one of three and the others of two battalions each; and he could scarcely believe that so large a number as 700 men were in a position to claim their discharge from a single regiment of the Guards.

VISCOUNT HARDINGE desired to know whether the noble Earl would lay upon the table Returns showing what had been the operation of the Ten Year Enlistment Act up to the present time; and he should also like to know how the proposed reduction of 2,000 men in the strength of the Royal Artillery was intended to be effected. For his own part, he was greatly surprised that any reduction of that arm of the service should have been proposed. Considering that Parliament had just sanctioned an extensive system of fortifications, the importance of trained gunners, and the fact that it took three years to train an artilleryman, this was the very last force in which any reduction ought to be made. Did the noble Earl intend to effect the reduction by discharging trained men or by stopping recruiting?

EARL DE GREY AND RIPON said, that he should be glad to lay before their Lordships the fullest information which he could afford. With reference to the Artillery, it was not intended to discharge any men but those of bad character; but only to suspend recruiting; and to allow those men who were entitled to their discharge to leave the service. His noble Friend had greatly overstated the amount of the reduction which was to be effected. Instead of 2,000 men, it would amount to only 1,200 in the garrison Artillery, and 100 more in consequence of a re-arrangement of the Horse Artillery, making altogether 1,300. His noble Friend and the House must recollect, that in the course of last year a brigade of field Artillery was brought home from India without relief and converted into garrison Artillery, and that after the lapse of a few months we should have at home the garrison Artillery from the Ionian Islands. The Infantry battalions were last year reduced to the minimum strength at which he and the military authorities thought they could be kept; but the companies of garrison Artillery had been retained at their war strength. [A noble LORD : The Gold Coast Corps?] The Gold Coast Corps was disbanded in consequence of a mutinous and dangerous spirit which had broken out in it, and there had been substituted for it another West Indian Regiment.

THE EARL OF HARDWICKE said, that the noble Lord had spoken of the garrison and field Artillery as distinct and separate, but he took them to be the same body of men.

EARL DE GREY AND RIPON said, that the Artillery was all one regiment, but it was formed into separate brigades. The garrison Artillery was distinct from field Artillery, and its organization was different.

THE EARL OF HARDWICKE : But they served for both. Garrison Artillery was often converted into field Artillery, and *vice versâ.*

THE IRISH CONSTABULARY.
QUESTION.

THE EARL OF DONOUGHMORE asked Whether the Government have in contemplation any Measure for the Reform and Improvement of the Irish Constabulary? He thought the question was a very important one, because the condition of that force had often been incidentally alluded to in both Houses of Parliament, and had for several years occasioned considerable dissatisfaction in Ireland. Grand juries, magistrates, and public bodies had presented addresses to the Government upon the subject, and Judges had often complained of the inefficiency of the police as a means of preventing and detecting crime. At the Spring Assizes of 1862, Baron Fitzgerald and Justices Keogh, Christian, and Ball delivered charges in which they complained of the manner in which the police performed their duties, and their inefficiency for the protection of the interests of the public by the prevention and detection of crime. At the last Spring Assizes similar charges were delivered to which he would more particularly call their Lordships' attention. At Roscommon Mr. Justice Christian, after complaining of the large number of crimes which were committed, and the small number of persons who were arrested, continued—

" The result of this whole analysis is, that in the large number of forty-nine cases, with but one solitary exception, and even he ultimately escaped, there has been no detection. These are results of a startling description, and for which two causes only can be assigned ; either that the injured parties were influenced by intimidation, or by disinclination to assist justice ; or—and the other cause is more for you than for me—that the Constabulary of your county, although in other respects effective, are deficient in energy and skill in that most delicate and important part of their duties, the detection of offenders, which I greatly fear is not popular in the force—particularly in the higher grades—resulting, perhaps, from too high military training of the constabulary."

At Limerick, Mr. Justice Keogh said—

" The Constabulary are the parties who ought to look to it, and it is not creditable to the Constabulary force of this county that so many offences should remain undiscovered, and that the persons by whom they have been committed should escape with impunity. Now, the police force of this country is of great magnitude. In a military point of view it is a considerable army, and in a pecuniary point of view it is a considerable expense.' It costs the country £715,000 annually. That is the sum charged to the Consolidated Fund for the maintenance of the Constabulary force. I have seen from the observations of a learned brother that a similar state of things exists in another county ; that offences have been committed, and that the perpetrators remain undiscovered, and investigation abandoned. Military display may be a very useful thing, and, no doubt, it is, in its proper place ; but I beg leave to say, if the Constabulary apply their attention solely to that, and neglect their primary and more appropriate duties, the object for which the Constabulary were established by Parliament and the Legislature is lost sight it."

At Cavan, Baron Fitzgerald used almost the same language. The right hon. Gentleman the Chief Secretary, in speaking of these Judges, said they had been "disporting themselves" in Ireland, abusing the police and the magistrates ; but there was not in any of these charges a word of complaint against the magistrates. Of course, none of these learned persons had taken any notice of these accusations ; but at Cork, Mr. Justice Keogh reiterated his statement, and called the attention of the Grand Jury to the ratio of offences and offenders. There could be no doubt that there was general discontent in Ireland at the conduct of the Constabulary. The admission of the noble Lord the Secretary for Foreign Affairs, he might add, the other evening, to the effect that 600 men had been carried off in one day to be made food for powder at the other side of the Atlantic, and that detection was impossible, clearly showed that the police were not efficient. In making these observations he wished nevertheless distinctly to be understood as regarding the Irish Constabulary as a force of great merit. He was acquainted with a great number of the officers of the force, and constantly came in contact with them in the discharge of his magisterial duties, and he freely admitted that they were an excellent body of men. He desired, therefore, to cast no blame upon them, but rather upon the organization under which they acted. With improved organization the force might be made quite efficient. It cost the country £715,000 for the force, and for that amount the country had, he thought, a right to expect an efficient police. If it was meant that the police should take the place of a standing army in Ireland, let that at once be stated, and the matter then would be understood. But the Constabulary in Ireland was clearly located there, not as an armed force, but to prevent crime, and assist in its detection, and he now came to the point why so many complaints

The Earl of Donoughmore

were made against it in its character of a police force. The first reason was, in his opinion, that the force had too much of a military organization. In making that statement, he did not mean to contend that it should have nothing of that kind, because when, arms were put in men's hands, it was desirable that they should have some amount of discipline and order. That afforded no good ground, however, for clothing them in handsome uniforms, and furnishing them with all the *minutiæ* of equipment which in the case of a regular force was highly desirable. His first suggestion, therefore, was that the military organization of the police should be reduced to the point where it was absolutely necessary, and that it should not be carried a step beyond. He was also of opinion that all the nonsense about parading here and parading there, presenting arms to the Judges when they came into a town, and touching their caps to their officers in the way of salute, should be abolished. Such things tended to make the force a military one when such was not really the case. The next and the most important point connected with the subject was the spirit of centralization which prevailed. When the police were first established in Ireland they were put under the control and direction of the local magistrates, and were bound to take orders from them. But how stood the matter now ? There was a body consisting of seventy or seventy-two stipendary magistrates, whose members were located all over the country, and who were in immediate communication with the Government, and when the local magistrate endeavoured to use the force, every sort of difficulty was thrown in his way. This centralization should be done away with, and the police placed more under the control of the local magistracy. With reference to another point, he might observe that in a town with which he was acquainted in the South of Ireland, the corporation were anxious to obtain the services of some of the Constabulary for the purpose of watching the town, as was the case in London and all large cities. A good deal of difficulty was made about the matter ; but fortunately his noble Friend Lord Naas was at the time Chief Secretary, and when it was urged that the performance of the duty in question would destroy the discipline of the force, he said "You are policemen and must do policemen's duty ; you are not paid to walk about and wear fine clothes." As soon, however, as his noble Friend's back was turned, the police spirit became predominant, and from that time to the present the corporation of the borough of Clonmel were unable to procure the police to watch the town. A similar state of things prevailed in several towns in the North of Ireland. The other day, he might add, it appeared that an order was issued that the Constabulary were not to arrest drunken men at the railway stations—he had always understood that it was the duty of the police to prevent drunken men from annoying the Queen's subjects anywhere—and from a Return which had been submitted to the other House of Parliament, he learnt that the Constabulary authorities in Dublin had taken upon themselves the power of construing the Game Act of last Session with respect to poachers, who, if caught by the Metropolitan Police in Dublin, were at once brought before the magistrates ; but, if by any of the Constabulary, were let go, because the men received positive orders from their superiors not to seize the poacher unless they were certain that he was the man who took the game. · One would have thought that the constable who had been most instrumental in preventing crime or in apprehending offenders would have been the man selected for promotion ; but, on the contrary, the constable who was smartest at drill, who kept his accoutrements in the neatest order, and best understood all the mysteries of red tape, as developed in filling up returns, was the man who got forward. The man who had a natural aptitude for the service was left in the ranks until he got tired of the service, and his fellows were not encouraged to follow his example. To crown all, the mode of selecting the officers was absurd. He admitted that there must be great difficulty in getting good officers for such a force, but all anxiety was got rid of by throwing the whole thing into a competitive examination, where a knowledge of *Cæsar's Commentaries*, trigonometry, the differential calculus, and French spoken with an incurable Irish accent, was the requisite qualification. The sharp, intelligent young man, who could ·ride well, who understood something of the language of the people, and who was well up to all their tricks and contrivances, was the sort of person for an officer of the police, and not a youth fresh from school, with his head crammed by a tutor with accomplishments useful only for other purposes. He readily admitted that the organization of the police in Ireland must differ in some respects from the organization of the police in England ; yet they might adopt some points from the English system. The English police was a local police, with its chief constables responsible in each county to the magistracy, and not responsible to any external authority. The Irish police must be responsible to an external authority, but they ought in some degree to be also responsible to local authority. He would read to their Lordships one or two extracts from letters which would show what the Irish police thought of themselves. Of course he could not give the names of the writers, because they wrote anonymously, lest they should at once be dismissed. The first was an extract from a letter to the *Cork Examiner*, dated March 10, 1864 :—

" In 1859 a code of Enfield Rifle Drill was issued, with strict orders to men and constables to learn it off as quick as possible. We were drawn to head-quarters thrice a week in order to exercise ; our weapon at the time was the short carbine, the only fit one, I may say, for the Constabulary. Well, away we worked till the issue of the Enfield, when, lo and behold ! it was found we were all the time under an incorrect course of instruction. At it we went again under the new style, till a still more improved system of drill was issued, to which, of course, we were obliged to change ; but judge our dismay, when, about two months since, just as we were beginning to think ourselves very smart fellows, a new work was sent forth, completely superseding all previous issues. . . . Why need a policeman hunt up what he will never be questioned about, to the neglect of that which is the only road to promotion ? . . . When a county or sub-inspector visits a station he thoroughly examines the men in drill, points out their errors, records their defects in the visiting journal, and gives a caution as to improvement. Does he also inquire into the return of crimes committed in the district, their number, and the result in each case ? Does he question the men as to the best mode of discovering the offenders ? Not at all. He must be above such trifles. A knowledge of the different parts of the beautiful Enfield is of more importance. He sets himself down, unfastens the lock from the stock, unscrews the spring, and requires each man to name the various parts of lock, stock, and barrel. Woe to the unfortunate policeman who is wanting in this all-important examination ; his chance of promotion is gone. . . In the time of Inspector General M'Gregor, our patrols left their barracks at night without exciting the least suspicion. They carried their accoutrements under their greatcoats. . . . Now, they must carry all those traps outside the greatcoat, and march as soldiers to the battlefield, giving by the parade due notice to all intending burglars who may be on the watch to carry on their operations in some other quarter. . . . What sane man will endanger his neck by crossing hedges and ditches at night, holding his long sword in one hand and his natty rifle in the other, trembling lest they shall get a scratch which will show and be punished at the next examination ? He can have but little care of his own poor body, and small blame to him, under the circumstances, to keep the fair road and leave the fields and the bypaths to the plunderer and the robber, who would not ply their trade with such impunity if the Constabulary were armed with good smart sticks and a pair of Colt's revolvers." . .

The next letter referred to a point upon which he had not touched, the introduction of competitive examination, not for the appointment of officers, but for promotion in the service. It was an extract from a letter from a retired member of the force in the same newspaper—

. . . " The introduction of competitive examination for promotion in the service, established during the command of the late Inspector General, was a deathblow to the efficient working of the force in the detection of offenders. By this mode of obtaining promotion some of the most useless members have been raised over the heads of hardworking good men,—members who were never known to perform a creditable turn of duty, and were generally to be found interrupting the cook in her passage to the fire with a slate and pencil, or a book in hand, and feet placed on the fender, instead of being usefully employed. This has caused inactivity among the men, and has also caused the best and most active members to leave, and good men who were unable to leave became so disgusted and disheartened at the promotion of useless, idle men over them, for no other cause but that they could work sums in decimal fractions more expertly, have also become, in many instances, as useless as the men promoted. . . . . Instead of the men being seated constantly at the fire, poring over books, or with the national or parochial teachers, they should be employed in the prevention of crime and the detection of offenders. . . . Four men are generally ordered to Dublin to compete. I maintain that the least qualified, in point of literary qualifications, frequently happens to be the most respectable, and in every way, for what is required, the best man ; notwithstanding the man who gains the most marks succeeds." . .

He should like to know what the illustrious Duke, the Field Marshal Commanding-in-chief, would say to such a system in the army. He quite admitted that a certain amount of increased education was necessary for the higher rank—that the corporal should know more than the private, and the sergeant more than the corporal; but promotion from the ranks of any force ought to be given for service. He apologized to their Lordships for having detained them so long, but the complaints were general from all parts of Ireland, and from all sorts of people, and he hoped the noble Earl would be able to assure them that the subject would be taken soon into consideration, with the desire to make the Irish police force much more efficient than it was at present.

The Earl of Donoughmore

EARL GRANVILLE said, he did not rise to reply to the speech just made in anything of an antagonistic spirit, because of course there could be but one object— to give this force the most efficient character. He felt some difficulty in following the noble Earl in the observations he had made, in consequence of his great local knowledge on the subject ; but he must observe that he did not attach very great importance to some of the evidence which he had brought forward. Anonymous letters from persons alleging themselves to be members of the police force was not the sort of evidence to which he thought their Lordships would attach much weight. But there was other evidence, no doubt, of a more important character. The noble Earl had, however, made some admissions which were of weight. The noble Earl said, it appeared to him that it was desirable that the force should be armed ; and if so it followed as a matter of course that it should to a certain extent be disciplined. This was so obvious that it would be a waste of time to prove it. The Irish Government had the very highest possible opinion of the spirit, loyalty, and efficiency of this branch of the service. The noble Earl, however, had brought some objections to their efficiency, one or two of which were not very formidable. The noble Earl had stated that Earl Russell—whom he (Earl Granville) might name, as he was not present— had admitted to their disfavour that they could not help 500 or 600 men leaving the shores of Ireland for the purpose of serving in the Federal cause in America. But suppose there had been several hundreds of the detective police force of London present, how could they have assisted in preventing people from embarking from Ireland, there not being any law to prevent their emigration, and the men being engaged as labourers, whatever might have been their ultimate destination? Hence it was quite childish to lay the charge of the noble Earl as to the impossibility of dealing with this state of things, to the inefficiency of the Irish police. Then it was complained that the Government at Dublin had issued an order that the constables should not have power to interfere with drunken people at the railway stations. But what was the fact ? Why, that in so doing they would, contrary to the practice in England, be interfering with the duties of the railway police, who were made constables expressly for the purpose of dealing with such matters, and it was very expedient that the functions of the two bodies should be kept separate. Then the noble Earl remarked that two different constructions had been put upon one and the same statute ; and he said that there was too much centralization. He (Earl Granville) had no greater wish for centralization than the noble Earl; but it must be remembered that both governing bodies were under one law ; and the remedy was not to be found in subdividing the command further than it existed at present. Then as to certain parts of the country—in Tipperary, in Lowth, in Cork, in the county of Leitrim, and in Roscommon — complaints had been made about the number of undetected crimes. But one thing was to be considered— namely, that with regard to the detection of crime there were facilities in England which did not exist in Ireland. One branch of crime, especially—that of sending threatening letters—it was not very easy to detect in Ireland. Unless persons were willing in some shape to give evidence, it was almost impossible to prosecute this species of crime to conviction. Not even a man's own tenants or servants would give the slightest assistance. It was far different in this country. But in considering this question of the failure to detect crime, he thought it was of some importance to observe what had been said by some of the learned Judges in their charges on circuit through the country. Now, in Kerry, the learned Judge said that the circumstances to which he referred were a fair indication that the state of crime in the country did not arise from the non-detection of crime. A similar satisfactory statement was made with regard to the counties of Donegal, Londonderry, Monaghan, Carlow, Kildare, Kilkenny, Meath, Westmeath, and Galway. This showed that the charges against the police were not capable of proof. In every county a certain portion of the force was set apart as a detective police. The whole subject was, however, deemed to be so important that the Home Secretary was about to communicate with the Irish authorities, with a view of ascertaining whether any mode could be adopted of placing the Irish Constabulary in a higher degree of efficiency.

THE EARL OF DESART thought that his noble Friend (the Earl of Donoughmore) could hardly have procured better evidence as to police grievances than that of statements by policemen themselves, and it was not very likely that a policeman would make his grievances otherwise than by anonymous letters. He doubted the absolute necessity of arming the police force in Ireland ; and thought that it was not desirable to show to the people of Ireland that they thought that they could not govern them except by what was in fact a military force.

THE MARQUESS OF CLANRICARDE said, that the statements referred to by his noble Friend the Lord President, were very gratifying as regarded the character of the country, but they did not show that the absence of crime in Ireland was owing to the efficiency of the police. He did not at all deny what the noble Earl had said as to the state of the country ; for he believed that the people of Ireland, on the whole, were better behaved than any population of the same number in any other country. It was said that the police were unsuccessful in detecting crime because persons would not come forward and offer them assistance. It was no doubt true that at times, and in districts where a bad spirit happened to prevail, both peasants and farmers—nay, persons in a much higher position than either—were often very backward in giving information to the Constabulary. Why was this? He thought the circumstance, in a great degree, might be attributed to the fact that they felt the criminals were more powerful than the Irish Government and the police force ; and the people thought that it was better to keep on terms with those who might injure them, than trust to the protection of the police. He recollected the time when there was no difficulty in procuring the assistance of farmers and peasants to detect crime ; but at that time the Constabulary was not a military force. The noble Earl the Lord President said, that the Irish Government were very well satisfied with the Constabulary. But who were the Irish Government? The Earl of Carlisle, the Lord Chancellor of Ireland, Sir Robert Peel, and Major General Larcom. Did their Lordships think those four Gentlemen, communicating with no one but their own police officers, were sufficient authorities as to what was going on in the interior of Ireland? Did they know as much about it as the numerous grand juries who had petitioned on the subject in the spirit of the observations of the Irish Judges? His right hon. Friend Chief Justice Monahan had made some observations to the effect, that he did not concur in what had been said by some of his learned brethren with regard to this matter; but his right hon. Friend had not stated facts to bear out his opinion, while the comments of one of the other Judges had been called forth by the fact, that in one county out of eighty-eight cases of crime there were only thirty-three in which persons charged with offences were in gaol. Again, he wanted to know if so little crime existed in Ireland, why was a Constabulary of 12,000 men kept up there at an annual expense of £750,000 ? It might be said that the Constabulary, trained and drilled as they were, would be useful in the event of an invasion. No doubt they might be so. But there a very awkward question arises. The police were not under the Mutiny Act, and so they were no more a safe body of soldiers than they were good constables. It was sometimes argued that those who entertained objections to the present constitution of the force wished to abuse the police. He certainly had no such idea. He believed that the Irish Constabulary was composed of as good a body of men, for their number, as could be found anywhere. The stuff was there, but it was not properly made use of. The men did the duty they were ordered to do; but that duty was not what it ought to be. He thought this subject deserved the attentive and serious consideration of the Government.

THE EARL of LEITRIM said, he did not intend to cast the slightest slur upon the persons of whom the Constabulary was composed; but he also complained of the present condition of the force, and thought there must be an inquiry before there could be a proper reform of the Constabulary. The force might be a popular one, but it was not popular, for it was badly got up and badly officered. He thought that the practice of the police patrolling two and two with arms was not warranted except in certain exceptional cases, and then only by the special direction of the superior officers. Of the necessity of those cases the magistrates were the best judges, and he contended that the magistrates in quarter sessions ought to have the power of making regulations for their own county in regard to the arming of the police. At present, the police were very much what they had been described by a statesman at the end of the last century—namely, a political tool; and complaints such as were now rife would continue to be made until Ireland was governed on constitutional principles. When

The Marquess of Clanricarde

that time arrived, and not before, Ireland would be like England.

THE EARL OF DONOUGHMORE said a few words in reply.

House adjourned at a quarter past Seven o'clock, till To-morrow, Twelve o'clock.

HOUSE OF COMMONS,

Thursday, March 17, 1864.

MINUTES.]—SUPPLY—*considered in Committee* — CIVIL SERVICE ESTIMATES — £1,866,000 on Account.
PUBLIC BILLS — *First Reading*— Factory Acts Extension* [Bill 55]; Life Annuities and Life Assurances* [Bill 56].
Committee — Government Annuities [Bill 11]. *Debate,* March 4, *resumed,* and *further adjourned;* Warehousing of British Spirits* [Progress, 7th March] [Bill 54].
Report — Warehousing of British Spirits* *recommitted.*

OFFICERS OF THE INDIAN ARMY— THE ROYAL COMMISSION.

QUESTION.

CAPTAIN JERVIS said, he would beg to ask the Secretary of State for India, When he will be prepared to state to the House the measures he proposes to adopt in order to remedy the grievances of the Officers of the Indian Army, stated by the "Royal Commission on Memorials of Indian Officers" to have arisen by departures from the assurances given by Parliament?

SIR CHARLES WOOD said, in reply, that when the hon. and gallant Gentleman last asked him the question, he (Sir Charles Wood) said, that the Indian Government hesitated about taking what might be the most effectual measure—namely, the cancelling the promotions in the staff corps which had been given. After consultation, with some of the best military authorities, it was considered that such course would be a great hardship. Any other measure required the fullest consideration, because it would affect not only the Officers of the Indian Army, but also the Officers of the Line serving in India. He hoped early after Easter, however, to be able to lay on the table of the House the Despatch which would contain the details of the measure which the Government proposed.

SALISBURY CATHEDRAL.

QUESTION.

MR. HENRY SEYMOUR said, he would beg to ask Mr. Walpole, If he could, on the part of the Ecclesiastical Commissioners, lay upon the table of the House any Reports of Mr. Gilbert Scott or other architects upon Salisbury Cathedral, upon which the Ecclesiastical Commissioners made a Grant of £10,000 for the repair of the Cathedral? He also wished to know, Whether the right hon. Gentleman could, on the part of the Commissioners, lay on the table a Return moved for last year by the hon. Member for Surrey, with respect to Grants sanctioned by the Ecclesiastical Commissioners for the purpose of other Cathedrals?

MR. WALPOLE replied, that it was not correct for the hon. Member to say that the Commissioners made a grant. What they did was to sanction a grant. When a commutation of estates took place, then the Chapter laid a statement before the Commissioners, stating the conditions on which the commutation was proposed. The Commissioners then had to consider whether they could take the estate with propriety on those conditions. The document, giving the approbation of the Commissioners for the commutation of the estates of the Salisbury Cathedral Chapter, contained an extract from the Report of Mr. Gilbert Scott, relative to the amount of money required for the repair of the cathedral and spire, and stated that sum to be about £10,000. The Commissioners, in commuting the estates, sanctioned the grant of that sum of £10,000 as part of the conditions on which the estates were to be conferred on them. The Return referred to by the hon. Member was made last year; but, for some reasons unknown to him, the hon. Member for Surrey never moved that it should be printed. It ought to be in the library of the House, and he believed it would give all the information required; if not, he should be ready to concur in any Motion by which that information could be more fully supplied.

GOVERNMENT ANNUITIES BILL.

QUESTION.

MR. THOMSON HANKEY said, he would beg to ask Mr. Chancellor of the Exchequer, with reference to his proposed insurance of lives in connection with the Savings Banks, To state what is the amount of a Single Premium proposed to be charged on the Insurance of £100 on lives of the following ages—namely, 20, 30, 40, 50; and also the Annual Premium to be charged for Insurance on lives of the same ages; and whether he will lay upon the table of the House a paper giving the above information? He would also beg to ask what is the smallest amount proposed to be insured?

THE CHANCELLOR OF THE EXCHEQUER said, in reply, that in the statement he had made last week he had said it was probable that there would be felt much interest, and even jealousy, on the subject of the rules by which the Government proposed to give effect to the provisions of the Bill now before Parliament, in case of its being adopted; and he added that he had no objection to lay those provisions in detail on the table, and to make the operation of the Act contingent on their being so laid. Of course, it was in the power of the House to interfere, and stop the action of them, if they should think fit. The question connected with supplying tables was one of considerable importance. He had not the least doubt that it was a matter entirely practicable, but at the same time it would be necessary to obtain the assistance of actuaries and professional gentlemen of the highest skill and experience, in addition to the Government Actuary; and he would not be justified in going to the expense of employing those gentlemen on the part of the public in framing tables before he knew whether it was the pleasure of the House to adopt the general principles of the Bill. At the same time, the House was entitled to know upon what rules the Government proposed to proceed. No decision had been arrived at with respect to the minimum amount proposed to be insured.

THE INDIAN BUDGET.

QUESTION.

MR. J. B. SMITH said, he would beg to ask the Secretary of State for India, When he intends to present the Indian Budget to the House; and whether, considering the importance of bringing the affairs of India under the review of Parliament, he cannot arrange the Indian Financial Year in such a manner as to be able to present the Budget in the early part of the Session instead as heretofore in the last week of the Session to an empty and exhausted House?

Sir CHARLES WOOD replied that it was his intention to present the Indian Budget as early as he could after the receipt of the necessary information from India. Of course it was the object of the House to have the most complete information on the subject. The Budget statement in India was made in the month of April, and the Parliamentary Papers were laid on the table by the 14th of May; so that, time being allowed for Members to read them, the end of May, or the early part of June, was the earliest period when the Indian Budget could be brought forward in that House. The financial year in India very nearly corresponded with the English financial year; and he could not see that it would be worth while to alter the whole arrangements in India in order to make in that House the financial statement in reference to India at an earlier period than usual. Such a course would, besides, very much interfere with the business of that House at a time when its attention was required for the affairs of this country.

Mr. J. B. SMITH said, he wished to know whether the right hon. Gentleman would bring forward the statement in May or in August?

Sir CHARLES WOOD said, he must repeat that the financial accounts, which formed the basis of the statement, were by Act of Parliament laid on the table by the 14th of May. They had then to be printed, and he apprehended that hon. Members would not wish him to make a statement on papers which they had not had time to read.

Mr. H. BAILLIE said, he wished to know whether the right hon. Gentleman intended to bring forward the Indian Budget in the beginning of June?

Sir CHARLES WOOD said, the accounts only reach here in April. They were very voluminous, and took a certain time to print and prepare. It was also necessary that after they were printed the House should have a certain time to consider them. So far as he was concerned he should be glad to make the statement at as early a period after the 14th of May as possible. The state of the public business might, however, prevent him from proceeding with the matter as early as he desired.

Mr. HENRY SEYMOUR said, he did not understand the right hon. Gentleman's answer. He begged to ask him whether he would undertake to bring forward his

Budget within fourteen days after the papers had been presented?

Sir CHARLES WOOD said, he could only repeat that personally he should be ready to do so, but that it would depend on the business of the House whether it would be in his power.

NEW SOUTH WALES IMPORT DUTIES.

QUESTION.

Mr. W. MILLER said, he rose to ask the Under Secretary of State for the Colonies, If advice has been received at the Colonial Office of the Legislative Assembly of New South Wales having followed the example of Canada in imposing a heavy Duty on British as well as Foreign manufactured goods; and, if so, if that has been done with a view of protecting their own manufacturers, or for the purpose of raising Revenue by means of indirect taxation; and if he is aware of its being the intention of other communities in Australia to follow the same course in regard to their Fiscal Laws through their respective Legislative Bodies elected on the principle of Manhood Suffrage?

Mr. CHICHESTER FORTESCUE, in reply, said, the question was one of considerable importance, and he would endeavour to give the House full information concerning it, although the Report of the Governor of New South Wales on the new tariff had not yet been received. The Government of that Colony had found themselves obliged, for purposes of revenue, to impose a considerable addition on its taxation in order to make up a deficit which would amount to about £900,000, at the end of the next year, on an ordinary revenue of £1,500,000. That deficit had been mainly produced by over-expenditure on the part of the Central Government on public works in the Colony, which now cost about £700,000 a year. It was the opinion of the soundest colonial politicians that that expenditure on public works ought to be transferred to the municipal and local taxation of the Colony. The Ministry had, however, to supply the actual deficit, and with that object they proposed an *ad valorem* duty on the importation of various articles to the extent of 10 per cent on some of them. That proposal, he understood, was supported by a very noisy, but limited, body of agitators for protection, but it had failed. The Ministry had, however, since made a similar proposal, imposing duties on the importation of a variety

Mr. J. B. Smith

of articles, in some cases amounting to a considerable percentage. Spirits, wine, rice, furniture, and certain manufactures were, by this plan, rendered subject to taxation when imported. The Colonial Minister, in introducing his tariff, took great pains to prove that its object was not protection, but revenue. At the same time he spoke of "incidental protection" —a phrase which was sometimes used in Colonial Assemblies, especially in Canada —as one of the consequences which he rather expected to follow from the new tariff. The idea had excited a certain degree of protectionist feeling among the artisan electors, and colonial politicians were apt to flatter that feeling by certain small concessions. For instance, in the present case, when they found themselves obliged, for purposes of revenue, to increase their taxation, they selected as subjects of an import duty such articles as leather goods, furniture, and so on, rather than tea or sugar, which did not come into competition with colonial manufactures. He had, however, reason to believe, from official information, from the debates in the Colonial Assembly, and from the newspapers, that the good sense of the colonists would prevent this coquetting with protection from developing into a regular and permanent system.

LORD JOHN MANNERS said, he wished the hon. Gentleman would explain the observations he had made. He had attacked the Governor and Parliament of New South Wales for some legislative enactment they had passed, and he wished to know whether, in that attack, the hon. Gentleman intended to deny the right of the Parliament of New South Wales to arrange their system of taxation as they themselves thought most advantageous?

MR. CHICHESTER FORTESCUE said, he did not know what the noble Lord meant by accusing him of an attack on the Colonial Government. He had said nothing that could be construed into an attack either on the Government or Parliament. He had merely endeavoured to give what information he could to Gentlemen who were naturally interested in the question. If he had had to announce to the House that the Parliament of New South Wales had deliberately imposed protective duties on the import of British manufactures, it would have been with sincere regret. He had stated, however, that the Colonial Ministry had prepared the tariff for the purposes of revenue, but that words

had been used implying a certain degree of coquetting with Protectionist principles, for the purpose of gratifying a certain class of electors in the Colony.

LORD JOHN MANNERS said, the hon. Gentleman had left unanswered his question as to whether he denied the right of the local Government and Legislature to arrange their taxation as they deemed most expedient.

NEW PATENT OFFICES—FIFE HOUSE.

QUESTION.

LORD ALFRED CHURCHILL said, he rose to ask the First Commissioner of Works, Whether, taking into consideration the great inconveniences of the present Patent Office, it is the intention of Her Majesty's Government, in accordance with the recommendation of the Patent Commissioners, to afford facilities for erecting suitable Patent Offices, including library and museums, &c., upon the site of Fife House, Whitehall, it appearing that the Crown lease of this property has recently expired, and that the Commissioners of Patents have ample funds at their disposal for building purposes?

MR. COWPER said, in reply, that he had been in communication with the Commissioners of Patents with the view of finding more extended accommodation both for their offices and museum. There was, however, great difficulty in making a suitable arrangement. The offices ought to be in a situation where there would be ready access to those professional gentlemen who were engaged in legal proceedings in regard to patents; and the museum was required to be accessible to the general public, and particularly to those who were interested in inventions. At present, no site had been found. That to which his hon. Friend alluded, between Fife House and the intended embankment of the Thames, was not at present available, and could not be disposed of until the river works had made greater progress, and streets had been laid out on each side in connection with the embankment.

SIR JOHN HAY asked, if the House was to understand that Fife House was to be taken from the United Service Institution?

MR. COWPER said, his reply was that no decision had been come to as to the use to which Fife House was to be applied. The matter was at present under consideration.

THE CHANCERY FUND COMMISSIONERS.

MR. MURRAY said, he would beg to ask the Secretary of State for the Home Department, Why the Report of the Chancery Fund Commissioners, laid upon the table of the House, has not been delivered to Members?

SIR GEORGE GREY said, in reply, that he was not aware of the reason why the circulation of the Report had been delayed, but he believed it would be delivered very shortly.

IMPROVEMENTS NEAR THE VICTORIA TOWER.—QUESTION.

MR. T. MILLER said, he wished to ask the First Commissioner of Works, Whether it is his intention to proceed with the Improvements adjacent to the Victoria Tower, as recommended by the Royal Commission of last year, principally on the ground of the danger to which the Houses of Parliament are at present exposed from fire and other causes?

MR. COWPER said, in reply, that the Report of the Thames Embankment Commissioners last year contained a very valuable recommendation for the enlargement of the open space in the neighbourhood of the Victoria Tower, by the extension of Old Palace Yard and the embankment of the river to the south of that tower. Thus the wharves which were now filled with destructible materials would be removed, and a source of danger to the Houses of Parliament avoided. That recommendation, however, would, if carried out, involve the expenditure of a very large sum of money, and he was unable at the present moment to inform his hon. Friend that he had any proposal to make on the subject.

MR. HENRY SEYMOUR said, he wished to know, when the Return he had moved for last Session, showing the duration of the leases of Crown property between the Houses of Parliament and Trafalgar Square, would be ready?

MR. COWPER said, he would inquire into the matter.

THE "TUSCALOOSA."

MR. PEACOCKE said, he would beg to ask the First Lord of the Treasury, Whether he will lay upon the table of the House the opinion of the Law Officers of the Crown upon the subject of the *Tuscaloosa,*

Mr. Cowper

which was forwarded to the Admiral at the Cape of Good Hope?

VISCOUNT PALMERSTON replied, that it was well known that, for very good reasons, it was not the custom to lay on the table of the House the opinions given by the Law Officers of the Crown. Those opinions were confidential, and intended for the guidance of the Government. The Government could act on them or not as they saw fit, in the exercise of their own discretion and on their own responsibility; and it was obvious that for professional as well as political reasons that it was not proper to lay such papers before Parliament.

CHURCH BUILDING ACTS.

MR. F. S. POWELL said, he wished to ask the Attorney General, Whether it is intended to introduce a Bill for consolidating and amending the Church Building Acts and New Parishes Acts, during the present Session; and, if such be the case, whether it is proposed to introduce the measure at an early day?

THE ATTORNEY GENERAL was understood to say that he would introduce a Bill for the Consolidation of the Church Building Acts and New Parishes Acts after Easter.

THE IRISH CONSTABULARY.

SIR HERVEY BRUCE said, he rose to ask the Chief Secretary for Ireland, Whether he considers the Instructions issued to the Constabulary in that Country in May, 1860, relieve them from the duties of properly watching the towns of Ireland by night, which appears clearly to have been their duty under the Instructions issued in October, 1837.

SIR ROBERT PEEL replied, that he had examined the Instructions issued in May, 1860, and in October, 1837, and he could discover no difference between them. If there was any difference he would be glad, on the hon. Gentleman conferring with him, to take steps to put the two sets of Instructions in accord one with the other.

MEDICAL OFFICERS IN INDIA.

MR. BAZLEY said, he would beg to ask the Secretary for India, Why Medical Officers of Her Majesty's British and Indian Armies are deprived of the substantive pay of their rank in India ; why Medical Officers of the Indian army of ten and fifteen years' service, ranking with captains, receive when on sick furlough merely the pay of a subaltern ; and when the 900 Medical Officers of the late Company's Army, whose services were transferred to the Crown in 1857, will be informed what their future prospects are to be as regards rank, pay, and pension ?

SIR CHARLES WOOD replied, that Medical Officers in India were paid upon a totally different scale from Medical Officers in this country. The whole subject had been under the consideration of himself and Council, and not long ago he stated that they were prepared with a general plan which would put things, he hoped, on a more satisfactory footing. Some further steps, however, required to be taken before that plan could be carried out.

DOE PARK, &c., RESERVOIRS, BRADFORD.—QUESTION.

MR. FERRAND said, he rose to ask the Secretary of State for the Home Department, To communicate to the House the Reply he has received from the Mayor of Bradford, relating to the state of the Doe Park Reservoir ; whether other store reservoirs belonging to the Bradford Waterworks have not been, and are not still, in a leaky and dangerous state when filled with water ; and whether the Sheffield Reservoir, which has just burst, and the Bradford Store Reservoirs have not been constructed by the same engineer ?

SIR GEORGE GREY: Sir, the Mayor of Bradford acknowledged yesterday the receipt of my letter of the 15th, and informed me that he would immediately confer with the engineer of the corporation with reference to it ; and, having since come to town, he has to-day informed me, that the fears expressed by the hon. Member are much exaggerated, that some repairs are going on at the reservoir, and that, with the concurrence of the engineer, instructions have been given to draw off the water, so as to prevent the possibility of accident while the repairs are going on. He further informs me that the engineer of the Bradford corporation is Mr. Leather, of Leeds, and that he had nothing whatever to do with the construction of the Sheffield Reservoir. I have no information as to any other reservoirs belonging to the Bradford Waterworks.

MR. FERRAND said, that to-morrow evening he should consider it is duty to make a statement, with respect to the alarming condition of the Bradford reservoirs.

TREASURY REGULATIONS.
QUESTION.

LORD ROBERT MONTAGU said, he wished to ask the Secretary to the Treasury, Whether it is the practice of the Lords of the Treasury to direct in any case that issues be made as final payments, "without account," to any person; whether, in such a case, the Audit Officers would be satisfied with that person's receipt for the total issue, or whether they would have the power to require to see Vouchers for the items of the expenditure ; and whether the Lords of the Treasury themselves examined the Vouchers ; and whether the Audit Office is bound to submit to the declaration of the Treasury as to the proper appropriation of the money ?

MR. PEEL said, in reply, that in certain cases where payments were made the issues were made "without account." In such cases the Audit Office would be satisfied, provided a due receipt were given for the total issue, and if authority were produced from the audit accountant. Those were all the cases in which a claim had to be submitted before a direction was given for payment. The examination of the vouchers was not made by the Lords of the Treasury. The examination of the salaries of Foreign officials was made by the Foreign Office.

THE COVENANTED CIVIL SERVICE— INDIA.—QUESTION.

MR. SMOLLETT said, he would beg to ask the Secretary of State for India, Whether it be true that Sir Charles Trevelyan has recently proposed, that all parties hereafter appointed to the Covenanted Civil Service of India, under the system of competitive examination, shall be required to spend one or more years at an English University, there to acquire the habits and demeanour suitable for Gentlemen who may be called upon to fill the highest positions under the Crown in Her Majesty's Indian Possessions ; and, if so, he wished to ask if steps are being taken to carry into early operation Sir Charles Trevelyan's proposition ?

SIR CHARLES WOOD said, in reply, that he had received no such proposal from Sir Charles Trevelyan, and had no intention of taking any steps to carry into effect a proposition of which he had not previously heard.

DISTRICT LUNATIC ASYLUMS (IRELAND)
QUESTION.

COLONEL GREVILLE said, he rose to ask the Chief Secretary for Ireland, If he has received the Resolutions passed by the Grand Juries of the different counties affected by the changes proposed in the District Lunatic Asylums; and, if so, Whether it is the intention of the Government to persevere in the contemplated changes?

SIR ROBERT PEEL replied that no Resolutions passed by the Grand Juries had yet been received by him. When he had received them he would communicate with the hon and gallant Gentleman.

SUB-INSPECTORS OF FACTORIES.
QUESTION.

COLONEL EDWARDS said, he would beg to ask the Secretary of State for the Home Department, with reference to the statements made by him on the subject of the Memorial of Sub-Inspectors of Factories, and the recent increase of their salaries sanctioned by the Treasury, Whether it was intended to convey to the House that the Sub-Inspectors' salaries had been raised to £700 per annum after certain years of service; and, if not, whether he would state the exact nature and extent of the change sanctioned by the Treasury?

SIR GEORGE GREY replied that it was certainly not intended to convey to the House that the salaries of the Sub-Inspectors of Factories had been raised to £700 a year. What he did say was that the Estimate for the ensuing financial year would be increased by £600. The salary of these officers hitherto had been £300 a year, with the exception of the six senior Sub-Inspectors, who received £350. By the new scale, the salary would rise after a service of ten years by a progressive increase of £50 each at certain intervals to the maximum of £500 a year after thirty years' service. Travelling and personal expenses were allowed in addition to the salary.

Mr. Smollett

DENMARK AND GERMANY.
THE PROPOSED CONFERENCE.
QUESTION.

LORD ROBERT MONTAGU: I wish, Sir, to ask the noble Lord at the head of the Government, Whether any arrangement has been come to with the other leading European Governments in respect to the proposed Conference on the Danish Question; and, if so, when the Conference is likely to meet? Perhaps the noble Lord will also state, supposing a Conference has been arranged, on what basis the parties will negotiate—whether it will be the *uti possidetis*, or the basis mentioned in the Despatch of Earl Russell which is given towards the end of the recently published Blue Book?

VISCOUNT PALMERSTON: Sir, Her Majesty's Government, as is well known, have obtained the consent of Austria and Prussia to a Conference, and we are waiting for an official answer from Denmark upon the same question. We have good reason to believe, however, that Denmark will consent to the Conference, though we have not yet received any official intimation to that effect. With respect to the basis mentioned by the noble Lord opposite—*uti possidetis*—that refers rather to an armistice than to a Conference. What we have proposed is — whereas it was found impossible to bring the parties to agree to an armistice upon any terms likely to be accepted by both, we suggested a Conference without an armistice, trusting that when the Conference met, the first question it would have to consider would be the establishment of an armistice. What the basis will be is, of course, a matter for subsequent consideration; but I wish the House to understand that the state of the matter at present is, that we have good reason to hope that we shall get from the Danish Government a consent to the Conference.

SWEDEN AND DENMARK.
THE CORRESPONDENCE.—QUESTION.

LORD JOHN MANNERS: Sir, I wish to ask what further Papers will be presented to the House relative to the Danish Question. I understand that a statement has been made in the Swedish Parliament to the effect, that the Papers hitherto presented to the English Parliament did not fully represent the whole state of the case as regards the action taken by Sweden. I wish, therefore, to ask the Under Secretary of State for Foreign Affairs, Whether the additional Papers to be placed before us will include those relating to the course proposed by Sweden in February last, and whether they will be laid on the table previous to the Motion of the hon. Member for Liskeard ?

MR. LAYARD: The utmost I can do will be to present the Papers referred to by the noble Lord to-night in "dummy." They shall be printed without delay, and distributed as soon as possible after the adjournment of the House for the recess.

MR. STANSFELD AND THE GRECO CONSPIRACY.

SIR HENRY STRACEY: Sir, I have placed a Notice on the paper to move—

"That the statement of the Procureur Général, implicating a Member of this House of Commons and of her Majesty's Government in the plot for the assassination of our ally the Emperor of the French, deserves the serious consideration of the House."

I wish to ask the noble Lord at the head of the Government, Whether he will allow this Notice to take precedence of the other Notices ?

VISCOUNT PALMERSTON: I have no power over the order of business in the House.

SIR HENRY STRACEY: I did not hear the noble Lord's answer to my Question; will he be good enough to repeat it ?

VISCOUNT PALMERSTON: The hon. Baronet asked me if I would consent to his Notice having precedence of the other Notices ; and I answered that I had no command over the business of the House. It is for the House itself to say, whether or not it will give precedence to the Motion of the hon. Baronet.

MR. DISRAELI: I do not wish, Sir, to give any opinion on the propriety or impropriety of the suggestion of the hon. Baronet, but I do wish to vindicate the privileges of the individual whose duty it is to lead the business of this House ; and I must say that I do not understand how the noble Lord on a Government night has not the power of arranging the order of business. I should like to understand from the noble Lord, whether he has abdicated and given up that privilege which hitherto the leader of this House has been supposed to possess of arranging on Government nights the order of business.

VISCOUNT PALMERSTON: The Notice given was of a Motion on going into Committee of Supply, and I do not myself see any reason for disturbing that arrangement.

MR. DISRAELI: I merely desire to say, in my own justification for rising, that while I admit that the noble Lord may be the best judge as to what is the best course for proceeding with the business of the House, yet I understood him in his explanation to state that he had no power of arranging the order of business on a Government night.

SIR HENRY STRACEY said, he would move that the Orders of the Day be postponed until after his Motion.

MR. SPEAKER: That will not be the proper course for the hon. Member to take. If the hon. Member could claim the ground of Privilege, that would give his Question precedence without postponing the Orders of the Day. It is for the House to say whether this is a question of Privilege of that nature which should take precedence over all the other business. The hon. Member did me the favour of speaking to me in private on this point. A matter of Privilege which claims this precedence should be some subject which has recently arisen, and which clearly involves the privileges of this House and calls for its immediate interposition. I stated to the hon. Baronet that as this subject has already been twice under the notice of the House—as questions have been asked twice in this House upon it—it did not appear to me to come under the character of something which had recently arisen, and required the immediate interposition of the House without notice. I therefore told the hon. Gentleman that in my opinion the course which he proposed to himself of raising any question which he might deem fitting upon it on going into Committee of Supply was the right course for him to follow. It is for the House to decide whether it thinks, under the circumstances, that is the proper course to be pursued. The House has the power of directing the course which it may think right in this case.

VISCOUNT PALMERSTON: I would offer a suggestion, Sir, which may, perhaps, meet the views of all parties—namely, that after my right hon. Friend the Chancellor of the Exchequer's Bill on Government Annuities, the Penal Servitude Bill should be postponed, to give the hon. Baronet the opportunity he desires.

GOVERNMENT ANNUITIES BILL,
(MR. H. B. SHERIDAN.)

PERSONAL EXPLANATIONS.

THE CHANCELLOR OF THE EXCHE-QUER : Sir, I rise before the reading of the Orders of the Day with reluctance, but without any hesitation, to refer to the statements made by the hon. Gentleman the Member for Dudley (Mr. H. B. Sheridan) on this day week. The House is naturally jealous of the character of its Members, and would very justly resent observations made by any one, and especially if made by a Minister of the Crown, which purported to relate to matters of fact that appeared to reflect upon the character of any one of its Members, and which might afterwards be found not to be fully sustained by the real state of the case. I wish, therefore, to acknowledge, in the fullest manner, to the House, that if I made any statement of facts implicating, in any degree, the character and conduct of the hon. Gentleman (Mr. H. B. Sheridan), and if I am not able to sustain that statement, I not only owe to him a full and humble apology, but I deserve, at the hands of the House, the severest censure. On that principle I propose to refer to what has taken place. The hon. Gentleman made partial explanations—very fairly stating that he had had no notice on this subject—partial explanations with regard to allegations that proceeded from me on the nights of the Monday and Tuesday of last week. As far as respects the question of notice, it is but due to him I should say that I only became acquainted with the facts of the case of the British Provident Association, in such a manner as to make me feel it to be my duty to notice them in debate, on the morning of the Monday, when the debate came on. At the same time it would be to me matter of the deepest regret if, in consequence of the want of notice, the hon. Member suffered any prejudice. However, the explanations offered by him on the Monday and Tuesday of last week did not appear to me to make it necessary for me to proceed further with a subject from which I not unnaturally shrank. But on Thursday the hon. Gentleman made a statement in which he distinctly impugned and contradicted various allegations of fact which I had submitted to the House. He concluded with the assumption—which would have been justifiable on the supposition upon which it proceeded—the assumption that he had disposed of those allegations ; and he kindly assured me, that although I had misrepresented the facts he was quite sure that I had done it unintentionally. That was on Thursday last. I thought it my duty to lose no time in examining into the statement which I had made—for I had no right to keep a matter of that kind hanging any longer than was necessary over the head of the hon. Member, and I may add over my own head also. On Friday afternoon I therefore addressed a note to the hon. Member to this effect—

" 11, Carlton House Terrace.

" The Chancellor of the Exchequer presents his compliments to Mr. Sheridan, and is prepared to reply to Mr. Sheridan's statement of yesterday in the House of Commons. He will, as Mr. Sheridan may prefer, either postpone his reply until Thursday, when the Bill comes on, or, request the Speaker to permit him to make it on Monday, at the commencement of public business, as a matter of personal explanation."

I did not receive any written answer to that letter, but I received a verbal message through my hon. Friend the Member for Lewes (Mr. Brand), from which I gathered that, on the whole, the hon. Gentleman would prefer that I should make the statement to-day. Now, I wish the House to have in the most distinct manner present to its mind the actual issues that were raised. I stated that an institution called the British Provident Association had existed for eleven years. I perceive that I am reported as having stated that it did business for eleven years. I did not use that expression. I stated that only for three years did it register its accounts, as required by law, and that those three years were from 1853 to 1856. I stated that its receipts in those years were £10,600, and that its expenses were £15,700—that is to say, being chiefly at least a Life Assurance Society with immediate receipt and with postponed liabilities, its expenses in those three years were about 50 per cent above its receipts. I said that it was taken into Chancery, and that the shareholders were called upon to meet the demands of the policy-holders. I stated that an action was brought against the manager, and that the substance of the action was that he was charged with interpolating words into a deed, the effect of which was to transfer the liability in respect of unpaid calls from himself to the portion of the shareholders from whom he bought them ; and, lastly, I stated two names, one of which appeared to be, and has proved to be, the name of a Member of this House.

MR. H. B. SHERIDAN: I beg pardon; but do I understand the right hon. Gentleman to say that the second name he mentioned had anything to do with the trial?

THE CHANCELLOR OF THE EXCHEQUER: I have stated precisely the allegations which I made on Monday week. I never said anything whatever in relation to the connection of any person with the trial except Mr. John Sheridan. I come now to the contradictions. But as the hon. Member wishes me to enlarge—I was desirous rather to contract my reference to that—I ought to say that I did state that the name of the hon. Member appeared first as auditor and then as trustee of that society. The hon. Member, Sir, contradicted me as follows:—He said the society did business for eight years only, from 1852 to 1850. He said it registered its accounts in the years 1852, 1853, and 1854; he said the Act was then accidentally repealed which required the registration of accounts, and that the Registrar refused to receive them; he said, so far from being a bad concern, that—but I had better read his own words upon both these points. He said that it registered its balance-sheet for the years 1852, 1853, and 1854, but that it was then held that the Act of Parliament which compelled their registration was repealed—unintentionally repealed—and that the Registrar refused to receive the balance-sheet after that date. Then with reference to the goodness of the concern the hon. Member stated that—

"So far from the company being compelled to go to Chancery to make provision for the policy-holders from the resources of the shareholders, and so far from their affairs being in a bad state, the fact was that when their business was transferred to another office in 1859 a bonus of £6,000 was paid to the shareholders for the business thus transferred."

Lastly, Sir, the hon. Member said that—

"No action was ever brought against Mr. John Sheridan, and that no charge was ever made by any shareholder against the manager."

MR. H. B. SHERIDAN: I rise, Sir, to order. I made no such statement.

THE CHANCELLOR OF THE EXCHEQUER: I am quoting the words as they are reported, but of course it is quite open to the hon. Gentleman to question their accuracy, and I should make a similar claim.

MR. H. B. SHERIDAN: My words were not reported in the same way as the words of the right hon. Gentleman were

reported. My words were only given generally, as observations, but his were given literally.

THE CHANCELLOR OF THE EXCHEQUER: I cannot tell the exact force of that distinction, but I make no difficulty about that matter, if the hon. Gentleman says the report is inaccurate.

MR. H. B. SHERIDAN: What I said was that no action was brought against the manager charging him with interpolating words in a deed.

THE CHANCELLOR OF THE EXCHEQUER: On the whole, the upshot of it was that this society while it existed had obeyed the law, had transacted a reputable business, and had been unfortunate, but had not been guilty. Now, Sir, I applied no epithets in my description of the doings of that society; but I frankly own that I consider that the facts which I stated to the House made out the case of a dishonest or fraudulent society. And I am not at all surprised at, and I do not at all disclaim, the interpretation, if this were the interpretation given to my statement. Sir, I will go back to the facts, and endeavour, if possible, to avoid the use of a single epithet. And first, as to the existence of the society, it was provisionally registered in the name of "The United Trades and General Life and Fire Assurance Association," in the month of September, 1849. On the 26th of September, 1850, its name was changed to "The British Provident Life and Fire Assurance Company." The hon. Member has stated that it did no business until the year 1852. I hold in my hand a tract published on behalf of the British Provident Life and Fire Assurance Company, containing the tables of the company, dated 1850, and bearing among the names of the auditors the name of the hon. Member. It assumed the name of the British Provident on the 26th of September, 1850. It was completely registered on the 14th of December of that year. In 1859 it made arrangements for transferring its business, and an order for winding up was made by the Court of Chancery, on the 8th of March, 1861. Therefore, in stating that the existence of the society reached over eleven years, I am rather within than beyond the mark. So much as to the duration of the society. The hon. Member says it registered its accounts in 1852, 1853, and 1854.

MR. H. B. SHERIDAN: I rise to order. I never made any such statement.

I said from 1853 to 1856, the accounts being from March to March in each year.

THE CHANCELLOR OF THE EXCHE-QUER: It certainly is rather a misfortune that the figures of the hon. Member were misapprehended by those who reported them. I pass that by. But he does not contradict my statement, which is to the effect that the society registered its accounts from 1853 to 1856—that is, from March, 1853, to March, 1854, March, 1855, and March, 1856. I have said the society was completely registered in 1850. It was bound to register its accounts every year from that time, and consequently it now stands confessed that this society registered no accounts till it came to the year March, 1854. Then comes the question of the repeal of the Act. The hon. Gentleman stated, as I understood him, that the Act was repealed in 1854; but as he now explains it the Act was repealed in 1856. Sir, the Act was not repealed in 1856; but there is this colourable ground for the statement of the hon. Gentleman—that an impression prevailed that it was repealed in 1856. That impression, however, continued only for ten months, until a certain date in 1857. At that time other Assurance Societies resumed the registration of their accounts; but no further accounts were registered by the British Provident until it transferred its business in 1859. At any rate my statement is completely borne out that it registered its accounts during three years only of its existence. Even according to the statement of the hon. Gentleman, it appears that during five or six years it did business without registering its accounts. The Act requiring registration of the accounts of Joint Stock Companies was repealed in 1862. I have stated that the expenses of the society were £15,700. Its receipts were £10,600. The hon. Gentleman appears, however, to contradict me indirectly, by saying that, so far from being a bad business, a bonus of £6,000 was paid to the shareholders. That obliges me to inquire what was the position of the shareholders if a bonus of £6,000 was paid to them. That is not sufficient to show it was not a bad business, because the question is, what had the shareholders paid? Now, that is very difficult to ascertain, but I think I can ascertain enough to bear out the statement that this was a bad business; that it was taken into Chancery; and that it was necessary to make large calls on the share-

Mr. H. B. Sheridan

holders in order to meet the claims of the policy-holders, which I believe up to this moment have not been completely settled. In the three years for which the society registered its accounts, the shareholders paid £7,584. There were about 17,000 shares of £10 each taken up. Before the society was wound up a further call was made of £2 10s. per share, and if that £2 10s. was paid the sum must have amounted to about £38,000. After the society got into Chancery, the Vice Chancellor found it necessary to make a further call in 1862 of £5 per share, and in 1863 another call of £5 per share. So that this much appears clear, that besides the £7,584 originally paid, £12 10s. was called on these 17,000 shares. I leave any one to add up the sum, and ask whether I am not justified in representing this as a rotten unsound concern, to use the mildest term, even if it be true that £6,000 was paid to the shareholders. What I find is, according to Mr. Turquand, the eminent accountant, the debts acknowledged amounted to £9,000. There were £39,000 of claims registered under examination; and as to payments to shareholders, I am only able to trace £2,069 subject to taxation for costs; and it appears, according to a printed statement, that £5,000 were paid to Mr. John Sheridan, but what further became of it I have not been able to ascertain. I have gone into these details because the hon. Gentleman represented the state of this society as one in which the shareholders had particularly benefited. The hon. Member says—and here he has the advantage over my ignorance or carelessness in legal phraseology—that no action was brought against Mr. John Sheridan. How the gentlemen connected with the Chancery bar must have smiled when I said that an action was brought against Mr. John Sheridan when I spoke of a matter of Chancery jurisdiction! I was quite wrong in the expression I used. What I intended to convey to the House, and what I believe every one who heard me knew I intended to convey, that which was clearly apprehended from what I said was this—that there was a legal proceeding in which the substantial issue was whether, for the benefit of Mr. John Sheridan, or for his exoneration from a pecuniary charge and to throw that on another shareholder, certain interlineations were made in a deed after it was executed. I am now referring to that part of the hon. Gentleman's personal explanation in which he thought fit to contradict my statement. I hold in my hand a statement of the proceedings in this very case, extracted from *The Times* newspaper, and which some 100,000 persons have read before me. I will read to the House only a few lines. Mr. Sheridan was examined upon that occasion, the formal issue of which was between Mr. Harben, the complaining shareholder, and the official manager of the company. But Mr. John Sheridan was the party really involved in the transaction, and that was what I intended to convey in my original statement. The account in *The Times* says :—" Mr. Sheridan, the managing director, was examined. He distinctly swore that he had no doubt that the interlineations were made before the execution." A statement was made that the interlineations were made by the clerk; but Mr. Knight, the clerk, "positively swore that he never made and never would make any interlineation after the execution of any document for Mr. Sheridan or any other person." "Mr. Orpen swore distinctly as to the transfer of the shares in question being executed after Mr. Sheridan had agreed to give him £50 for them and take them himself, these two only being present at the agreement." Mr. Serjeant Shee then addressed the jury in reply in an able speech.

MR. H. B. SHERIDAN: Surely the opinion of counsel ought not to be taken against the character of one of the parties?

THE CHANCELLOR OF THE EXCHEQUER : I am sustaining my statement by the evidence of public documents, which have been read by 100,000 persons in this country, and are matters of perfect public notoriety. Besides, from whom am I to know the real issue if not from the counsel in the cause?

MR. H. B. SHERIDAN : From the Vice Chancellor.

THE CHANCELLOR OF THE EXCHEQUER : Well, you shall have his opinion directly. I quote the statement of a friendly counsel. Mr. Serjeant Shee insisted on the utter improbability of two persons like Mr. Sheridan and Mr. Knight conspiring together to commit one of the grossest frauds that could be imagined without the least apparent motive; for in the case of Mr. Knight there was an instance of an attesting witness to a deed afterwards lending himself to interline it, when many a man had been executed for

a less matter : the jury must be perfectly certain that the interlineations had been made after the execution of the deed before they could find a verdict in favour of Mr. Orpen, and must weigh well before, upon a case of suspicion only, they took a course entailing such very serious results to two persons. The jury consulted for a short time, and stated that they were unanimously of opinion that the interlineations in question were made after the deed of transfer had been executed. The Vice Chancellor said "that the public and the parties were very much indebted to the jury for the patience and intelligence which they had shown, and he saw no reason to be dissatisfied with their verdict." Then I again state that every allegation I have made against the British Provident Society has been either admitted or proved by the facts of the case; and, I submit, the counter allegations of the hon. Gentleman I have overthrown, with the exception of the trivial verbal question of the word "action." Every statement I made on the subject of the British Provident Society remains unshaken and unquestioned. I have not stated any matters now on the authority of any private information or from any knowledge of my own; I have stated what is recorded in public documents, and has been for the most part published in the journals of the day. Under these circumstances I leave the matter in the hands of the House.

MR. H. B. SHERIDAN : Sir, the right hon. Gentleman seems much astonished to find that he cannot so much rely upon the report of the words used by me in this House as upon the elaborate report of his own speech in reference to this matter. There is this material difference between our positions. The right hon Gentleman addresses this House in a twofold capacity —it is a tribunal in which he is not only listened to but his words are stereotyped on the public mind. The words of the right hon. Gentleman are stereotyped in the minds of the people of this country. But of course, with an humble individual like myself, that advantage is not enjoyed, and the defence I make is so dwarfed and briefed, that when read in the public prints, it links so horribly as to become merely a string of detached quotations. The right hon. Gentleman has used the name of Sheridan so frequently that it would not be surprising if hon. Members were led to believe that I was the person to whom he referred in connection with all these proceedings. Almost every other word used by him was the name of Mr. Sheridan. Public documents, or newspaper reports rather, were read, and the right hon. Gentleman's notion of fairness under the circumstances was that he could do nothing better than read the speech of the counsel for the official manager in order to show the character of the issue. The right hon. Gentleman has said this was an action against the manager of this company for interlining words in a deed. That I distinctly dispute and deny. No action whatever was brought against the manager. I stated the other day that an issue was raised upon the trial as to which that gentleman was called as a witness, but it was no part of the charge to the jury that Mr. John Sheridan had interpolated those words. I knew nothing about these matters until the right hon. Gentleman threw them at me the other night ; but I have since informed myself concerning them, and I find that the whole of the writing in that deed was in the hand-writing of another person, and not in that of Mr. John Sheridan, the manager of the society. The right hon. Gentleman also says that the trial was a trial by jury. It was rather a trial by inuendo than a fair trial by jury of a person accused of an offence. The meanest subject of these realms is entitled to be tried by a jury when a charge is made against him. But then, what are the circumstances attending such a trial ? The accused must first be summoned to take his trial by a writ of summons, or by some form of process in the name of the Sovereign or of some person who charges him. That enables him to prepare his defence, to retain his own private attorney, to collect witnesses, to select counsel, and in all the thousand and one ways connected with such proceedings he takes whatever steps he thinks necessary to defend himself. None of these incidents were to be found in connection with the trial to which the right hon. Gentleman refers, and it will be time enough to launch all the charges made by him against this gentleman when he has been fairly tried and a jury has pronounced a verdict against him. The right hon. Gentleman admits that in point of form, or according to the ordinary meaning to be attached to language, he was in error when he said that Mr. John Sheridan was the manager of this company, and that an action was brought against him for interpolating words in a deed. I say, I accept the statement of

Mr. H. B. Sheridan

the Chancellor of the Exchequer that that statement was an error in point of form ; but there was an error in something else than form. I had myself nothing to do with that trial. When the right hon. Gentleman attacks me for something supposed to be done by my brother or by anybody else, it is difficult to see what that can have to do with this House. But if he would look about him more carefully he could find other game of the same sort to fly at. If personal charges of this kind, or what appear to be personal charges, are to be thus bandied about, it is highly necessary that the person making them should take care that he is fully conversant with the facts, and he should look about and see if he is the person to make them. There is an adage that persons who live in glass houses ought not to throw stones, and if such a person does throw a heavy stone he must expect to have one in return. The right hon. Gentleman says this was a trial against Mr. John Sheridan. If it was, then that gentleman was undefended at it. I find in the *Post Magazine*, from which the right hon. Gentleman himself has quoted, it is stated that at the conclusion of the trial the counsel for the defendant announced their intention of appealing to the Lords Justices, the defendant being the official manager of the company. Another point upon which the right hon. Gentleman had not correctly informed himself, or respecting which his memory had failed him, is, that there was a second trial, and that there had been a previous proceeding of a similar character, though not before a jury. Now it is very well known to all persons conversant with legal proceedings, that nineteen out of twenty cases in the Court of Chancery are tried in Chambers before the representatives of the Vice Chancellors. Hon. Members who are acquainted with the practice in Chancery know that the Judge's deputy in chambers does nearly all the real business in a manner somewhat resembling the proceedings before common law Judges in chambers. Those gentlemen are accustomed to hear charges of fraud banded about with freedom whenever shareholders are called upon as contributories, and in the case which has been referred to, the presiding authority, who represented the Vice Chancellor, was informed that there had been an interlineation in the deed. He heard all the facts the witnesses had to say upon that point, and his decision I will read from the same document to which the Chancellor of the Exchequer has referred—

"In March, 1861, an order was made to wind up the society, and the official manager included Orpen's name in the list of contributories. Orpen insisted that he had transferred his shares, but on producing the instrument of transfer two interlineations appeared in it that the transfer was to Sheridan, ' on behalf of the Society,' and these Orpen, by an affidavit, stated were not in the instrument at the time of its execution, and Mr. Sheridan and Mr. Knight, a clerk, were examined *vivâ voce* before the Chief Clerk, who decided the interlineations were in the deed of transfer when it was executed."

It is very odd that the right hon. Gentleman should have forgotten this circumstance, for if he had made himself acquainted with all the facts, he must have known that there was a preliminary proceeding, and that the second proceeding to which he referred was an appeal from the first. I think, so far as relates to the so-called trial by a jury, I have at all events restored the balance. We all know what the inclination of juries is when the parties to the proceedings they are inquiring into are, on the one hand, an objecting shareholder, and on the other a company or the representative of a company. I do not doubt that in this case the jury was composed of intelligent, careful men ; but all who are acquainted with such matters know that juries, whenever there is an opportunity, prefer an individual to a company or the representative of a company. I shall say no more of this so-called trial, except that I believe if Mr. John Sheridan had really been put upon his trial the result would have been very different. Now, as to the filing of the balance sheet. The right hon. Gentleman is mistaken. He said on the former occasion that this company was in existence eleven years; but towards the end of his statement he admitted, inadvertently I believe, that the company was only in existence for nine years, having been started in 1850, and the business transferred to another company in 1859. The right hon. Gentleman stated—and that was the only statement uncontradicted — that the accounts of the company were only registered for three years, and that no other accounts but those referring to those three years from 1853 to 1856 were to be found at the registration office. It must be borne in mind that I had nothing to do with these accounts beyond auditing them on two occasions; but the fact is that all the cash accounts and other proceedings of the company up to 1856 were registered. So little business was done up to 1853 that all their business up to that time was included in the first balance sheet. The object of registration is to set forth the state of the company, its financial position, and the business it has done. All these facts, from the commencement of the society to 1856, are to be found in the balance sheets registered in the proper office. But, says the Chancellor of the Exchequer, the society did not register its balance sheet after that date, and he denies that the Act 7 & 8 Vict. was repealed. He referred to my statement upon that point as an attempt to mislead the House. I have in my hand the Act of Parliament which was said to have repealed the 7 & 8 Vict. c. 110. It is dated the 14th of July, 1856, and it repealed the former Act, and the Law Officers of the Government must have declared so, or the Government would not subsequently have re-enacted the former statute. In part 5, paragraph 107, of the General Act of 1856, I find that the 7 & 8 Vict. c. 110, is repealed, and in the margin, under the head of "Acts repealed," is the entry "7 & 8 Vict. c. 110." Yet, notwithstanding this fact, the right hon. Gentleman says I mislead the House when I said the Act was repealed in 1856. But it is clear that the Act must have been repealed in 1856, when we find that another statute was passed in 1857 re-enacting the 7 & 8 Vict. If the Government and their Law Officers were led to believe that the first Act had been repealed, was it surprising that the managers of companies should have thought so too, especially when they found the registration office refused to accept their balance sheets ? The Chancellor of the Exchequer admitted that this society did file its accounts up to 1856.

THE CHANCELLOR OF THE EXCHEQUER : No, for three years only.

MR. H. B. SHERIDAN : I will quote the right hon. Gentleman's words—

"I mean the British Provident. It was founded in 1851, and carried on business for eleven years, and only for three of those years did it register its accounts as required by law. These were the years from 1853 to 1856."

The right hon. Gentleman says "No !" but, I repeat, up to 1856 the whole of the accounts of the company were registered. After 1856 the Act of Parliament under which the accounts were registered was repealed, and considerable confusion was occasioned in consequence of that state of the law for one or two years afterwards ; so that the balance sheets, not of this company only but those of other offices, were not filed, and before 1858 and 1859 the business was transferred to another office. The very utmost the right hon. Gentleman made out, therefore, was that the last balance sheet for 1858-9 was not filed. The Government, on the re-enactment of the registration clause ; did not send round to the other offices and inform them that the blunder had been rectified, and to request them to continue the registration of their accounts. A great difference of opinion also existed at the time in the country upon the question of registration, and there were some of the largest offices who did not during that time file their balance sheets. The Act of Parliament under which they were filed was a partial one— friendly to some offices and not to others, and it was not a proceeding which found so much favour with them as to induce them to go in shoals to register their accounts. The registrar was not empowered to take them in the years he had mentioned. I contend that I have fully substantiated the statement, that it is not true the British Provident was in existence for eleven years, and that for three of these years only had it filed its accounts, and that I have shown, that in every particular so far as that is concerned my statement was correct. With respect to the third statement, that this policy business must have been bad, because two years afterwards the shareholders got into difficulties, and the business was transferred. What has that to do with me ? It is well known that shareholders are many of them great speculators and adventurers. They do not take shares for the mere dividend of $3\frac{1}{4}$ per cent, but they often make 500, 600, and 700 per cent premium. I know shares at this time that are at a high premium, and the London and Liverpool Company paid last year 40 per cent dividend. The House has nothing to do with the difficulties of unhappy shareholders : if they lose on some shares they make it up on others ; but all the House has to do is with questions of public policy. The right hon. Gentleman, in illustration of his argument for a change, said the British Provident, amongst others, had failed to pay those poor persons who had intrusted their savings to them. I deny that statement, or that he has in any way answered the statement I made the other night. The right hon. Gentleman said the other night—

Mr. H. B. Sheridan

" Of course it was necessary that the society should be brought to book, and called on to make provision from the resources of the shareholders for the demands of the policy holders. The society was in Chancery in 1862. An action was brought against the manager of the society for interpolating words in a deed in order to alter its character."

But no such demand was ever made. Two years before the society went into Chancery, its business was transferred to an office of character and standing, which paid something like £6,000 for the goodwill, showing that it was not considered to be worthless by those who understood it. But the right hon. Gentleman insinuates that, although the business might have been transferred for that sum, probably Mr. John Sheridan might have had some of it. That is a new issue ; the right hon. Gentleman finds he cannot sustain his former statement, and he prefers a new indictment in the hope of carrying away the attention of the House. What if Mr. John Sheridan might have had £5,000 out of that sum. He is not a Member of this House. I have heard the right hon. Gentleman has been engaged getting up this case ever since I denied his statement, and I have heard from an hon. Member on the opposite side of the House that the right hon. Gentleman has sent for a copy of the shorthand writer's notes of what took place in Chancery, and every effort has been made during the past week to get up a complete and crushing reply to my statements ; but I do not think that up to this time it has been done. I will read a letter to the House which I have received from the cashier and accountant of the office which took the transfer of the business from the British Provident. He says—

" British Nation Life Assurance Association, Chief Offices, 316, Regent Street, W., London, 16th of March, 1864.
" Re British Provident.
" Dear Sir,—The amounts paid by this Company for the policy business and goodwill of the British Provident were something between £7,000 and £8,000, the whole of which was paid to the credit of the shareholders of the British Provident Company, and no part of which was paid to the manager or officers of the Company, or in any way, directly or indirectly, paid to their use or benefit.
" I am, dear Sir, yours truly,
" JOHN MADDEN, Cashier and Accountant.
" H. B. Sheridan, Esq., M. P."

That letter I am willing to place in the hands of the right hon. Gentleman, should he think it necessary to test its accuracy. Now the right hon. Gentleman thinks to insinuate again his charges against a gentleman who is not before the House; but surely every hon. Member of this House who has the least regard for the responsibility of his position, ought to be careful how he attacks the reputation and character of persons who are not before them. There was, indeed, a time when statements and attacks like these might have been made with impunity—when you debated with closed doors; but now, when every such statement is stereotyped out of doors in millions of ways, these attacks come under the notice of all, and are read everywhere. Therefore, neither the right hon. Gentleman, nor any one else ought to have the same protection when he attacks private and individual character now as was given in former days. He ought not to have the same privileges as in former days, because there is not the same reason for it. The statements are not now made to Members only, but to the whole world. And I say that such insinuations as the right hon. Gentleman threw out just now, in order to answer the strongest part of the case he had to deal with, are not worthy of the dexterity of so great and so renowned a debater. I have answered all these points, and I have proved that the statements which I made on a former occasion were correct, and that the right hon. Gentleman was wrong in every one of his. I have proved that the right hon. Gentleman was wrong in each and every one of his charges, and I should like to know with respect to other statements which the right hon. Gentleman made the other night, whether he is willing to divest himself of the shield of privilege which surrounds and protects him here, and repeat boldly out of doors what he has said in the House, so as to take upon himself the civil responsibility for these depreciatory statements? I now ask the right hon. Gentleman, what was the object of his statements with respect to the British Provident Society? Why did he intrude that question upon the attention of the House? I think the House has good reason to demand an answer. Was it as an illustration of his argument? The letter I have just read proves that the business of the society was conducted in such a way that a large sum of money was paid for it. What was his object in making the charge with regard to the non-filing of the accounts? What has that to do with the business turning out ultimately bad? Is it that he thought to damage me in any way, by associating the name of the Member for Dudley with

this society? I never acted as a trustee, but only as an auditor many years ago. Is any Member of this House who happens to be honourably connected, as trustee or otherwise, with a public company, to be the next person to be selected for such attacks? Is it come to this — that in these days of joint stock enterprise any one connected with a public company is to be assailed in this House as if he were responsible for its actual management and for the details of its transactions? I repeat it is most unfair, and that the argument cannot be sustained on any grounds. The right hon. Gentleman introduced the subject in reference to Friendly Societies. But the British Provident was not a Friendly Society, and did no friendly business. All the right hon. Gentleman professed to do was to introduce a Bill to provide for the better regulation of Friendly Societies; why, therefore, did he bring forward the British Provident Society, which was not in existence, and which left behind it no heritage of woe? I should like to ask the right hon. Gentleman that question, and if he can give a good reason for having done so, then I shall be very much surprised indeed. I should like to know how it was that the right hon. Gentleman forgot to mention other institutions with which he might be supposed to be more familiarly acquainted. The right hon. Gentleman spoke, indeed, of the European Office in language which requires a more ample apology than I have heard in this House. He described their transactions as equivalent to wholesale robbery; and—I beg it to be observed that I make the statement in the full belief and knowledge—there is not a more high and honourable institution, and it would be no disgrace to any one to be connected with it. The right hon. Gentleman must have believed otherwise, or he would never have made use of such remarkable and never-to-be-forgotten words; but he forgot to mention, when something in connection with the European must have appeared to him so monstrous as to raise his indignation against it to the utmost, to state that the right hon. Gentleman the President of the Board of Trade was the President of that society. I have no wish in saying that—no one would wish—to give pain to so high-minded, amiable, and honourable a man, and it is right I should say that he is not the President of that company now—neither am I the auditor of a society that ceased to exist three or four years ago. A more flourishing and honourable company than the European does not exist; but I want to know how it is the right hon. Gentleman has overlooked the fact that a Gentleman sitting in the Cabinet with him was once the President of an institution which he described in such terms; how it was the right hon. Gentleman forgot to mention that fact to the House, and yet drew out of the ruins of the British Provident my name and laid it on the floor of the House. I cannot understand it, nor can I understand how it was the right hon. Gentleman forgot to mention another of these Benefit Societies, which, in the language of the noble Lord the Member for North Leicestershire (Lord John Manners), "has come to grief." I am not about to drag before the House the names of hon. Members in connection with matters with which this House has nothing to do; but there is one of these companies, which has the names of twelve M.P.'s and ex-M.P.'s on its direction and connected with it—not that there is anything dishonourable in it; not only were there ten or twelve M.P.'s and ex-M.P.'s connected with it, but there are at this time three of them holding high offices under the Crown, two of them are in the Cabinet, and one of them holds a very high position indeed. I will not refer to the names. ["Name!"] I am in the hands of the House, and will do so if they wish, but I would rather not. Now, the right hon. Gentleman forgot to mention that, but he did not forget to mention a more insignificant person like the Member for Dudley. Was it that the fire insurance question was coming on? It could not be that; but it must have been something that would give the Member for Dudley more significance than twelve Members of Parliament, including three Members of the Cabinet. There must be something more than meets the eye in this outburst of invective, and this torrent of indignation. Another circumstance connected with the European is, that the hon. Member for Walsall (Mr. Charles Forster) is a director. He is a gentleman of the highest estimation in this House, and his character will not be diminished by the fact of his being a director of this company, for it is a first-class institution. The hon. Member for Walsall deserves well of the Government; he is in direct communication with them, and attends a great deal to the private business of the House. I think he is a gentleman whose claims to notice should not have been overlooked. The right hon. Gentleman has a facility in forgetting his

Mr. H. B. Sheridan

friends, it is very clear. I want to know how it is that the right hon. Gentleman did not look still nearer home in his Quixotic research after rotten companies. I believe that there are some hon. Gentlemen in this House who have to avenge themselves yet in reference to particular companies, and the right hon. Gentleman will find that every statement he made on Monday week affecting the financial condition of the institutions he referred to, and generally all those sweeping charges he ventured on with respect to their fraudulent transactions, will be successfully denied. I do not wish to trespass too long on the attention of the House, though I could say a good deal more; but I believe further explanations will be given to-night by other hon. Gentlemen, and I do not wish to anticipate them. I want to know, however, how it is that the right hon. Gentleman, under these circumstances, with his mind so much incensed, forgot the Protective Burial Company in Liverpool, in the prospectus of which Mr. Robertson Gladstone is described as "justice of the peace and treasurer." Yes, he is described "justice of the peace," in order to induce poor people to part with their money to this Insurance Company. I do not mean to sink to the level of abusing institutions which I know nothing about, and I am not prepared to say that this is not a first-rate institution —I believe it is—but it is odd that the right hon. Gentleman should have forgotten it, particularly when he inveighed so much on the sin of paying 20 or 25 per cent to agents. The right hon. Gentleman spoke of the expenses of certain companies being about 13 per cent on their receipts; but in respect to this company to which Mr. Robertson Gladstone belonged, the very first item is 25 per cent to agents. I find that the expenses of this institution, which probably formed the model of those which the right hon. Gentleman regarded with so friendly an eye, as his brother's name was connected with it, though I do not say that it now is, are 45 to 46 per cent on the receipt. The figures are £2,132 13s. 11d. for expenses out of £5,890 11s. 9d. for receipts; yet the right hon. Gentleman the other night said, or implied, that anybody going beyond 13 per cent for expenses was driving headlong to destruction. I will not go further in this matter, for I think I have shown the House that there was some partial selection of these companies on the part of the right hon. Gentleman; but I wish to know what he meant by associating my name with the trial of Mr. John Sheridan. I will forgive him forgetting his brother's company and certain other companies, though there is nothing dishonourable about them that I know of. I also forgive him remembering that I was auditor of the British Provident Company in 1856. The fact of my being auditor does not imply that I had anything to do with the management. I was auditor, or accountant, in fact—that is, I inspected the items of account; but no accountant is responsible for the bankruptcy of the persons whose accounts he audits. But I do not understand why the hon. Gentleman should drag into the House the name of John Sheridan in consequence of some quarrel with the shareholders of his company into which he was only incidentally a party. Why was his character as a witness attacked, and why did the right hon. Gentleman put him and me side by side? I have looked into Mr. May's *Law and Practice of Parliament.* I find that it is an offence against the privileges of this House to reflect against any hon. Member by name. The person so acting must either give good reason for what he says or retract. This is a matter affecting the privileges of the House, and good reason should be given for associating my name with remarks of a sweeping nature. I think that the right hon. Gentleman should give some account of his conduct to this House if he will not condescend to do so to me. Does he mean to say that I am connected with the management of the society to which he alluded? It is, however, a question of a much larger and wider character—it is a question affecting the freedom of debate in this House. You take care of Members on their approach to this House, and on their exit from it, and protect them from arrest; but that is not sufficient if when they get here the frowns of the right hon. Gentleman or the threats of any one should intimidate them from doing their duty to their country. I have been the humble means of getting an expression of opinion from the House with respect to one item of taxation; and I had given notice of opposing the Government Annuities Bill. I may have suffered for that; but it is for this House to decide whether, when a person in the high position of the Chancellor of the Exchequer has worked up the House to a great degree of excitement, he should not say what is his object in making the comments he did reflecting on an individual Member. I

maintain that some apology is necessary to this House for the hon. Gentleman's unwarrantable personal attack on me. ["Hear, hear!"] I accept that cheer as evidence that I have established the position which I undertook to establish.

THE CHANCELLOR OF THE EXCHEQUER: It appears to me that the hon. Member for Dudley has considerably widened the scope of this discussion. I do not complain of that; but if I do not follow him into matters that do not appear to me —["Order!"] I think I am justified— ["Order!"]

MR. ROEBUCK: I rise to order. If the right hon. Gentleman is allowed to address the House a second time, I hope the House will accord the same privilege to the hon. Member for Dudley.

THE CHANCELLOR OF THE EXCHEQUER rose again, but was stopped by cries of "Order!"

MR. SPEAKER: The right hon. Gentleman is at liberty to make any observation, but it must be confined to explanation, and not be a reply.

THE CHANCELLOR OF THE EXCHEQUER: I am not going to reply to the statement of the hon. Member, but to answer a few questions which have been put to me; and I should have been wanting in respect to the House if I had not risen to do so. The hon. Gentleman asks why on a previous occasion I did not name other societies. I can only say, with respect to those to which the hon. Gentleman referred, that as far as I was acquainted with them —and I was very imperfectly acquainted with them—they did not appear to me to bear the character of fraudulent institutions. With respect to the case of the British Provident Society I have not disguised my reason for selecting that case. I thought it my duty not to deal simply with anonymous charges, vague and unparticularized, against societies many of which I deemed to be great disgraces to the age. I selected the British Provident Society, because I deemed it to be the case of a society which was necessary to justify the description I gave; and it seemed to me a far more manly course to choose a society with which was connected, in some manner, the name of a Member of this House than to deal with a society which had no representative here. The hon. Gentleman has asked me a third question —why I have connected his name with that of Mr. John Sheridan? What I did was simply this—I described to the House the history of this society as far as I had been able to learn it, and not one of the essential particulars I mentioned has, in my opinion, been shaken. I then stated the hon. Member's connection with this society, and I was in hopes that the hon. Gentleman would have explained that connection—and he has explained it, in a manner of which I leave the House to judge. I do not know whether I should express concurrence with the hon. Gentleman on one point. He has said that an apology is due to the House. ["Hear, hear!"] In answer to that cheer from hon. Gentlemen opposite I may remind them that I began by stating, that if the allegations I made were not sustained, not only was an apology due from me to the hon. Member, but that I deserved the severe censure of the House. By that issue I intend to stand or fall.

GOVERNMENT ANNUITIES BILL.

[BILL 11.]—COMMITTEE.

ADJOURNED DEBATE.

Order read, for resuming *Adjourned Debate* on Question [4th March], "That Mr. Speaker do now leave the Chair."

Question again proposed.

Debate *resumed.*

SIR MINTO FARQUHAR, in rising to move the Amendment of which he had given notice, begged to ask the indulgence of the House, for he especially felt the difficulty of his position after the very extraordinary and exciting scene which had just occurred. He could not refrain from expressing his deep regret that personal feeling should have formed so large an element in this debate. The motives of the right hon. Gentleman were, he was satisfied, thoroughly pure and honest in bringing forward this measure, and no doubt he had done so with the feelings that it would be for the benefit of the industrial classes. The right hon. Gentleman had stated, that the Report of the Registrar of Friendly Societies was the foundation of the Bill; that Report having recorded many failures, and many very gross abuses. He (Sir Minto Farquhar) had referred to that Report, and he found that most of the complaints from members of Friendly Societies in different parts of the country had reference to the expenditure of funds in beer, dinners, processions, and what might be called outside charitable subscriptions. The Registrar had brought this question under the notice of the late Attorney General (Sir William Atherton), who had given a distinct opinion that such expenditure was illegal, and that proceedings might be taken against any officers of a Friendly Society who might pay away a portion of the common funds for such purposes. He thought that the knowledge of this fact would lead to much improvement in some of the Friendly Societies, in many of which, however, if the members chose to have an annual dinner, they provided it at their own expense. The right hon. Gentleman had taken credit to himself for the unpresuming and unaggressive manner in which he had introduced his Bill. The truth was, that at first hon. Members did not know what to make of the Bill, the object of which appeared to be simply to give additional facilities with reference to Government Annuities, to which no one could be opposed. It was at the opening of the Session that his hon. Friend the Member for Lewes (Mr. Brand), had given notice of the intention of the Chancellor of the Exchequer to bring in this Bill, and on the 11th of February, the right hon. Gentleman introduced it, and stated that it would deal with small Life Insurances as well as with Annuities. Before that statement, not a soul in the House had the least idea that the Bill had reference to Life Insurances. He (Sir Minto Farquhar) had read the Bill, and put it aside, supposing it to be simply an amending Bill relating to Government Annuities. It was the hon. Baronet the Member for Evesham (Sir Henry Willoughby), who, with his usual sagacity, at once saw the necessity of deferring the second reading of the Bill long enough to give the country time to consider its provisions. The Bill was nevertheless read a second time on the 15th February. It was only on Monday week last that an explanation of the proposed machinery of the Bill was given by the right hon. Gentleman, and he (Sir Minto Farquhar) did not think that he had made out his case. The Chancellor of the Exchequer said that Parliament had interfered for the regulation of factories, and of companies, and had introduced sanitary Acts. These were totally different cases to the present one, and it was very questionable how far the Government ought to undertake such a measure as this. The right hon. Gentleman had said that—

"The Bill had grown, not out of the case of Life Assurance Societies, but out of a considera-

The Chancellor of the Exchequer

tion of the case of Friendly Societies, and of the wholesale error, but not error only, along with error, deception, fraud, and swindling, which are perpetrated upon the most helpless portions of the community who find themselves without defence."

Yet he had not omitted to assail certain smaller Insurance Offices in sweeping terms, and they should be permitted to vindicate their character if they could, and ought not to be condemned unheard. He maintained that if those Friendly Societies were not on a proper footing the law ought to be remedied, and as such a vague and general attack had been made, the parties ought to have an opportunity of coming before this House, and showing that they were not in the condition which the right hon. Gentleman said they were. He had no personal interest whatever in this question. The Company with which he had the honour to be connected was indifferent to the measure. It was an old office, and one of those first-class institutions to which the right hon. Gentleman referred. But was it to be said that the old Insurance Offices, because they were not affected by this Bill, were to turn round and say they would not lend a helping hand to those offices of a later origin, and which had done a great deal of good by enlarging the application of the principle of Insurance among the people and making it more freely known? It would be too bad on the part of the old offices if they did not express their desire that all the offices affected by this Bill should at least have an opportunity of stating their case. There was not one of them which did not declare that the right hon. Gentleman had overstated his case. The right hon. Gentleman said he was not to be frightened by the clamour against centralization. What did he mean by that? Was it to be said that hon. Gentlemen were not to protest against such a measure as that introduced? He (Sir Minto Farquhar) would, for one, join in the clamour against centralization, because he was opposed to it. The right hon. Gentleman had made use of the words "fraud and swindling" in reference to certain societies. No doubt there were some fraudulent societies. He acknowledged with regret that there were societies which had disgraced themselves; but that was no reason why those who desired should not be allowed to defend themselves. Take the invested capital in Life Insurance Offices generally, and it would be found to amount to £100,000,000, while the risk was £375,000,000, and the interest and premiums no less than £14,000,000 a year.

That, indeed, was a vast and wonderful fact. The right hon. Gentleman had spoken of the subsidy which the Friendly Societies received from the Government in the shape of interest on their investments, the rate which at the National Debt Office the Government was compelled to pay such Friendly Societies as existed before 1828 being £4 11s. upon every £100, and to those founded before 1844, £3 16s. per annum. It must be admitted that the Government subsidy, as the right hon. Gentleman had termed it, was a boon; but he had the authority of an eminent actuary for saying, that by far the greater number of existing societies received no benefit from it. What did he say?—

"No doubt this must be admitted as a boon and as a government subsidy, but how many of the existing societies are entitled to those benefits? It appears that in 1857 out of 3,073 societies which gave returns of their duration, 1,672 were under twenty years of existence, and 2,714 under forty; so that if this proportion holds good as to other societies the returns of which are not sent in, by far the greater number are not receiving the benefit of either rate to which the statement refers. Under the Act 1850 this privilege only amounts to an investment with the Commissioners for the reduction of the National Debt at a rate of interest of £3 0s. 10d. per cent."

He (Sir Minto Farquhar) could not agree with the right hon. Gentleman that the present proposal was analogous to the Post Office savings banks system. In the case of a Post Office savings bank, a man made his deposit and he was without difficulty paid again; there was little or no risk of fraud and personation. But take the case of a man insuring his life. A number of forms had to be gone through; certain printed questions had to be sent by the office to a friend and to the medical man of the insurer for reply. Those questions related specially to the health, (habits whether active and sober), and the profession of the insurer. The printed questions were then returned to the office, and he had afterwards either to appear before the medical officer of the office, or if he lived in the country he had to be examined by a doctor appointed by the office, and at last before he was accepted his case had to be considered and approved by the board of directors. Then he had to pay the premiums upon his policy, and when he died, the office, upon the probate of his will, and the certificate of his death, paid the money. If the money happened by some mischance not to be paid to the proper person, the office was liable to have to pay it again.

He would like to know whether the right hon. Gentleman thought that attendance to all the requirements of an Insurance Office was a task the Government could undertake ? and how he was going to regulate all that he could not understand, either from the Bill or the speech of the right hon. Gentleman ? Now, if the measure were referred to a Select Committee, they would at least have the advantage of having before them Sir Alexander Spearman, Mr. Scudamore, and Mr. Chetwynd, who, as he understood, were the promoters of this Bill, and who could then show how they proposed to carry it out. In the second place they would give opportunity, which fair play and justice demanded, to the offices which had been attacked to come forward and offer an explanation. He (Sir Minto Farquhar) was sure that every hon. Member must regret to have heard what passed to-night. He saw opposite the hon. Members for York and Bradford, two Gentlemen of the highest position, and of great commercial knowledge and standing, and yet if one might believe the statement of the Chancellor of the Exchequer, who surely could not have intended it, they were, one the chairman, the other a director of a company, capable of entering into a fraudulent understanding with a bankrupt concern. It was only fair that individuals and associations, attacked in such terms, should be heard before a Select Committee. There were no fewer than 3,000,000 persons connected with Friendly Societies, and the Chancellor of the Exchequer could not be ignorant that his statement had excited among them great alarm and apprehension. Only a full and impartial investigation could quiet their fears. The right hon. Gentleman had said a good deal about the activity of insurance agents ; he called them "Touters !" Was an agent to sit in his office twiddling his thumbs, or was it not rather his duty to get as much business as he could for his employers ? There was not the slightest doubt that against these Insurance Offices there was a certain amount of fraud and personation constantly attempted. That was an important point, and one which would require the utmost caution on the part of the House in dealing with the subject. The noble Lord the Member for King's Lynn, the other night, put his finger upon that point in a moment ; and no doubt this was the real difficulty and great defect of the Bill. Now, the agents of some

Sir Minto Farquhar

of these societies were obliged to go from house to house collecting the weekly and fortnightly pence required to keep up the policies of the persons insured ; they thus became acquainted with all the insured, and, as they were responsible for their identification after death, they gave their employers a very valuable degree of security. How was it possible for the Government to transact such a business, to protect themselves against fraud—a point of so great importance, and to meet the convenience of the poorer classes as it was met by the existing societies. He could mention one of these companies connected largely with the industrial classes, which had frequently suffered from personation, and from numerous misstatements of age. He was informed that it was the custom of that office to pay the claims each Board day, but this was found so objectionable that it was compelled to adopt the system of paying claims every day which were delivered in the office before a certain hour. He understood that this company was necessarily obliged to have proper certificates as full as those for ordinary insurances, and the agents, who visited the houses of the assured regularly, had no difficulty in identification, and in the payment of claims at the head office. To a certain extent, the strict rules observable in the ordinary insurances had to be disregarded, and the claims were paid by what is called rule-of-thumb principle. If the assurers removed from one town to another, there were what are called transfer sheets, and the agents at that town soon became as familiar with the assured as he who introduced them. In a Government system, unless they adopted (which was not likely) the plan of collecting the premiums from door to door, the difficulty of identification would be incalculable, and in cases of removal from town to town all idea of identity must be cast aside, and the Government, or any company which did not adopt similar rules, would be exposed to very great loss. Another question which would affect all Government Assurances would be, that while their rates were calculated at £3 per cent, it was well known that if companies were to be restricted to £3 per cent for their investments, little if any margin could be secured. It was only by the power to advance money at £4, £4½, and £5 per cent, which companies possessed, that they were enabled to accomplish great results. Now, as to lapsed policies, the truth was they were almost valueless until they had run a considerable number of years. What was termed the surrender value of a policy was known to all Insurance Offices; and it meant that the policy after a certain time acquired a certain value, and that if the holder wished to surrender it, the office would give him back a certain proportion of the premiums he had previously paid. As to the lapsed policies, which the right hon. Gentleman referred to on a former occasion, most of them could only have been a short time in force, and when they were allowed to lapse only a few pence or shillings could have been paid; and, after considering the risk of death during the continuance of the policies in question, in which case the office must have paid the full amount, it would be seen that the policies lapsing under such circumstances, had absolutely no surrender value at all. The Chancellor of the Exchequer had said something about returning the amount of five years' premiums on surrender, but he would find it rather difficult to carry that out. He (Sir Minto Farquhar) would ask for further information on this point, which he (Sir Minto Farquhar) probably misunderstood, for what would become of the claims on death in the mean time? for premiums were meant to provide for claims. The right hon. Gentleman spoke also of the romance connected with amalgamations. No doubt, in the case of the amalgamation of some offices, there had been circumstances of mismanagement or even fraud; but bankers and merchants sometimes failed as well as Assurance Companies, and as long as this continued the wicked world it was, there would always be rogues and scheming speculators whose only object was to rob innocent people of their money. That, however, did not prove that two companies might not honestly and advantageously coalesce, and be carried on at much less expense than if they remained separated. He would not dwell on the case of the Royal Liver Friendly Society, which the right hon. Gentleman had attacked, as the hon. Member for Liverpool, who was to second his present proposition, was well able to deal with that matter; but a petition from that society alleged that its rules had been submitted to the late Attorney General and approved by the Registrar of Friendly Societies; that they had also been sanctioned by Mr. Samuel Brown, Mr. Neison, and other well-known and experienced actuaries. The petition-

ers, moreover, courted the strictest and most searching investigation into the state of the affairs of their institution, and wound up by praying to be heard at the Bar of that House, or, at least, in a Select Committee. The right hon. Gentleman said that many of these offices insisted on having their arbitrations in London; but it turned out that the Royal Liver Society had its arbitrations at Liverpool. [The CHANCELLOR of the EXCHEQUER said, the society he had named was the Friend-in-Need Society.] He was not the defender of these societies, but he thought they were entitled to an opportunity of rebutting, if they could, the grave charges which had been made against them. If they were found, on proper investigation, to deserve the bad character imputed to them, they would suffer the consequences. If, on the other hand, they had been accused unfairly, the House should afford them the opportunity of exculpating themselves. Mr. Harben, an officer of the British Prudential Society, had written to *The Standard* impugning the accuracy of the right hon. Gentleman's statements, and a similar complaint had appeared from the secretary of the Friend-in-Need Society. Surely these gentlemen should receive a hearing before a Select Committee. Moreover, if the right hon. Gentleman's picture of the state of so many of these institutions proved on full inquiry to be correct, a much more radical remedy for the evil would be demanded than this Bill could supply. The machinery of the measure should also be closely examined in a select Committee, and care should be taken that its working was not likely to involve any risk to the public exchequer, as the taxpayers would have to make good any possible loss. The principle of insurance on lives was directly contrary to that of cancelling the public debt by terminable or Life Annuities. The former was in fact creating a new debt by undertaking to pay a certain sum at death in return for sums paid in, and unless there were some care in the selection of lives, and unless the premiums were accurately calculated and ample, there must be a loss, and who was to pay?—the public. It was clear that the prime motive which induced a poor man to join Friendly Societies, and Offices more particularly connected with the working classes, was that he might obtain assistance when ill—the sick pay was the attraction, that which especially helped him when perhaps on a bed of sickness, when his family were hanging on his hands, and when it was possible that without such aid they might be thrown upon the workhouse. The Government surely could not think of adding a plan for giving sick pay to their proposed measure. If it were contended that these societies were not able, under existing arrangements, to keep their promises to those who joined them, let the regulations affecting them be amended, but let them not, by a measure of this kind, deprive such societies of the very elements of success. He (Sir Minto Farquhar) had had a good deal to do with the working classes. He should not be in the House of Commons but for the support of the industrial classes and small tradesmen. They had sent him to Parliament, although he was a Tory. Although he questioned the policy of Government interference, and although opposed, as he had already said, to centralization, yet if it could be clearly proved to him that the Government could undertake to work the machinery of this Bill, and that it would really be a benefit to the working classes, he should be prepared to waive his objections; and he believed that the Chancellor of the Exchequer was under the impression that the proposition was a good one. Let the question, however, be fully gone into. Let Parliament and the country know by the means of a Select Committee's investigations the whole machinery and working of the measure, and let that Committee have before it those who had been attacked. It was for these reasons that he must persist in his determination to move that the Bill be referred to a Select Committee, and that Motion he accordingly made.

Mr. HORSFALL said, he rose to second the Motion. He could not quite concur with the hon. Baronet who had just sat down in believing that there had been any intention to mislead the House on the introduction of the Bill.

Sir MINTO FARQUHAR: I do not make the imputation. I said the other night that I did not impute any such intention.

Mr. HORSFALL: Looking, however, at the important interests affected by the Bill, and the large amounts which had been invested in Friendly Societies by the humbler classes of the country, he would urge upon the House that the greatest caution ought to be observed in dealing with the subject. The pleasure with which he had listened to the Chancellor of the Exchequer's eloquent speech the

Sir Minto Farquhar

other evening, was in some degree marred by the conviction he then had in his mind, that the statements put forward by the right hon. Gentleman could not altogether be substantiated. It was easy to bring very serious charges in a very few words, but it often took time and some documentary evidence to rebut them. He must, therefore, ask the indulgence of the House if he referred to documentary evidence at greater length than was his wont in addressing them. The right hon. Gentleman said in his speech, "I am very anxious to have it understood that I state these things as I gather them from the published records, and not as matters privately or personally known to myself." Accordingly, he took it for granted that the right hon. Gentleman referred to the Report of the Registrar of Friendly Societies, and on taking up that volume he was very much surprised to find that a large portion of it consisted of fifty to an hundred anonymous letters, with no names, no places, and no dates, and of five extracts from leading articles in provincial papers. The book was edited, he believed, by Mr. Tidd Pratt; and one of the articles opened in these terms—

"Mr. Tidd Pratt, the Registrar of Friendly Societies, has rendered many a good service to the working classes of England, but none more likely to accomplish greater ends than that which he has just achieved with regard to the legal expenses which a Friendly Society may incur."

He opened the volume hoping to obtain some valuable information, but with the exception of these leading articles, anonymous letters, and one or two balance-sheets, the Report was good for nothing. The right hon. Gentleman singled out for comment two societies existing in considerable strength in the town he had the honour to represent—the Royal Liverpool Friendly Society and the Liverpool United Legal Friendly Burial Society. As regards the first of these the right hon. Gentleman had misstated—he was sure unintentionally —some of the facts connected with the society. In the first place, he had taken the number of policies to the end of the year 1863, whereas he had only taken the accumulated fund down to June, 1863. The right hon. Gentleman said, "The Royal Liver last year made 135,000 policies; the number which lapsed in the same time was 70,000." He did not state that the rules of the society provided against the forfeiture of any policies in consequence of non-payments through omissions or derelictions on the part of the officers of the society. Its rules also were most favourable to members in arrear of payments. Only members who by their own default were fourteen weeks, or more than a quarter of a year, in arrear were wholly excluded and out of benefit. All the large societies allowed but twenty-one days' grace, whereas the Royal Liver gave a quarter of a year to enable members to recover their policies. The right hon. Gentleman, perhaps, was not aware that great difference of opinion existed as to the state of the law. Parliament had not given to Friendly Societies the power of buying up lapsed policies. Parliament defined the payments Friendly Societies should make, and limited those payments to fixed contingencies. The fact that a large proportion of lapsed policies accrued in the Liver as in all other large Friendly Societies was not owing to any want of consideration for the depositors, but chiefly to the state of the law. The right hon. Gentleman, therefore, had not acted quite fairly in bringing a charge of want of consideration against the society. [The CHANCELLOR of the EXCHEQUER : I brought no such charge.] The charge had not been made in terms, but by implication. The right hon. Gentleman said—

"There is a rule in the regulations of the Royal Liver which authorizes the Committee of Management to grant to the widow or relations of any member dying out of benefit, in cases of want of employment, sickness, or anything else whereby he was necessarily rendered unable to pay, any sum not exceeding £5. The discretion is given to the committee ; but," he added, " it is not for me to say how much has been distributed in that way."

Again, the Chancellor of the Exchequer stated the premium income of the society to be £77,000 a year ; and asked what did the House suppose to be the expense of management in raising and dealing with the income —£36,000 ! The whole cost of management, properly so called—namely, salaries to agents, treasurer, collectors, clerks, and committee of management would be found not to be a large percentage on a gross receipt of £83,000. The society's accounts were swollen by items for 'commission' and costs of collection, which scarcely ought to be regarded as a part of the cost of management at all. These commissions were, in effect, payments made by the depositors themselves to the collectors, who saved them the trouble and loss of time and labour incident to attendance at an office, to pay in their deposits. The commissions were cheerfully paid by the depositors to the collectors, who called at their houses for their money. In the accounts of many societies the commissions were not thus accounted for; but the Royal Liver Society, since its reconstruction, had always kept those items on the face of its accounts, feeling that the true interests of Friendly Societies required that nothing whatever should be concealed from the members, but that every item of receipts and every item of expenditure, to the smallest fraction, should be brought into the balance-sheet. Such Friendly Societies as the Royal Liver wholly depended upon a system of house-to-house collection of small sums, not exceeding 1d. in the majority of cases, and rarely amounting to 1s. in any case. The commission was calculated for in the tables of the Royal Liver Society, and did not exceed the amount so allowed for. It could be wished that commissions for collection might be dispensed with. But how was that to be effected ? Habits of providence and thrift had to be brought home to the dwellings and families of the poor; and when agents of the societies collected the money at the dwellings of depositors, regularity of payment was promoted and public-house temptations avoided. The right hon. Gentleman said that the Royal Liver held its meetings in public-houses, but that assertion he (Mr. Horsfall) denied. Then, as to the accumulated assets of the society, which the right hon. Gentleman stated at £39,000, with an income of £77,000, after fourteen years' existence. The Royal Liver Friendly Society had however, only in its present form, an existence of four years. In 1860 the members themselves entirely reconstructed the board of management, and that board caused to be framed new and most excellent rules, which were settled by Her Majesty's late Attorney General, and instituted a continuous and rigid audit of the accounts through Messrs. Harmood, Banner and Son, public accountants, of Liverpool. The result was, that the society had since enjoyed great prosperity. In 1861, its income was £27,000; in 1862 it had risen to £64,900 ; in 1863 to £83,000 ; and by July, 1864, at its then rate of increase, it would be £100,000. In 1861, the assets of the society were £18,000; in 1862, £25,600; in 1863, £39,000; and in the six months between July, 1863, and January, 1864, they increased to £50,000. Such were the true facts connected with the Royal Liver Society, which conducted the whole of its proceedings in public. There was no concealment or hurrying up to London in case of arbitration. An application to the nearest magistrate was all that was necessary, and by him an arbitrator was appointed. The trustees of the society were well known to the right hon. Gentleman; they were Mr. Rathbone, of Liverpool, Mr. Rawlings, of Liverpool, and his hon. Friend the Member for South Lancashire. These names ought surely to be guarantee sufficient for the manner in which the affairs of the undertaking were conducted. But that was not all. He held in his hand a document signed by a gentleman whom the Chancellor of the Exchequer had deservedly complimented a few evening ago —the actuary of the Guardian Fire Life Assurance Company—and what said that gentleman?

"I have examined the burial branch benefit tables, and also the endowment and sick branch tables of the Royal Liver Friendly Society, and on the perusal of the rules of the said society, and ascertaining therefrom the restricted liability of the society under such rules, on information furnished me by a Committee of the said society appointed for such purpose, together with the statistics produced to me by such Committee, and in comparison of their rates of charges with the usual assurance rates, and taking into account the nature of their insurance and the class assured, and the modes of paying the premiums for securing benefits from the funds of the said society; and further taking into consideration the results of the previous and present working of the said society under such tables, so far as can be judged of by their balance-sheets for the last two years produced to me, and the continued progressive improvement of the said society in a pecuniary point of view, and also allowing a rate of working expenditure not exceeding 40 per cent per annum, I hereby certify, that I consider the said burial branch, endowment, and sick branch tables of the said Royal Liver Friendly Society perfectly safe, and calculated at rates which may be beneficially retained by the members of the said society.

It was not necessary that he should say more with reference to the Liver Society, and he now came to the other society—the Liverpool United Legal Friendly Burial Society. The title of that society, as quoted by the right hon. Gentleman, was differently reported in different papers. In *The Times* it was called the Liverpool United Loyal Friendly Burial Society, in the other papers it was rightly called the Liverpool United Legal Friendly Burial Society.

THE CHANCELLOR OF THE EXCHEQUER: It was the Liverpool Victoria that I quoted.

MR. HORSFALL: It was not so reported in any paper, and they could scarcely all be wrong.

Mr Horsfall

THE CHANCELLOR OF THE EXCHEQUER: This is the programme I quoted from (holding up a prospectus).

MR. HORSFALL said, the right hon. Gentleman must have quoted then the title of one Company, and the balance-sheet of another. Of course, when the subscribers to the Liverpool United Legal Friendly Burial Society read the Chancellor's statement, they went to the Committee and said, "You must be putting forth a false balance-sheet, as the Chancellor of the Exchequer says that your business is £10,000 a year, and after twenty-one years your accumulations are only £3,900." The Committee were naturally very indignant, and they had written to him (Mr. Horsfall) with a statement of their accounts, from which it appeared that, instead of the income of the society being £10,130, and its accumulated capital only £3,900 as stated by the right hon. Gentleman, its income was £12,725 and its accumulated capital £14,158. He was very glad that the right hon. Gentleman had withdrawn his accusation against this society, and he had no doubt that that withdrawal would be perfectly satisfactory to its members. The hon. Member for Dudley had referred to a society in Liverpool called the Liverpool Protective Burial Society, of which Robertson Gladstone, Esq., was the treasurer. Now, he (Mr. Horsfall) would not have alluded to that at all if it had not been for the difference between the statement put forward by that society and the statement of the Chancellor of the Exchequer. The right hon. Gentleman calculated the working expenses of that society at something like 48 per cent. The society made it—[The CHANCELLOR of the EXCHEQUER: I never mentioned it.] He was perfectly well aware of that, but the hon. Member for Dudley had mentioned it; and upon the mode of calculation adopted by the right hon. Gentleman, the expenses of the management of that society would amount to from 45 to 48 per cent of the receipts, but according to the calculations of the managers of the society themselves, they were only about 10 per cent. It would be for the right hon. Gentleman to explain how he made the amount between 40 and 50 per cent. Now that it was proposed that the business of all these societies should be taken under the patronage of the Government, it would be well to know a little of the results of Government management. He had in his hand a book published by an hon. Member opposite, in which it was stated that the expenditure in the Post Office for the year 1861 amounted to £3,154,000, against a gross receipt of £3,530,000, leaving only £376,000 to be properly carried to revenue—a pretty large percentage for the cost of management. He had also a curious document relating to the "Customs' Insurance Benevolent Fund," the balance-sheet of which, he did not hesitate to say, was the most extraordinary one that was ever submitted to the public. The accounts were all mixed up together, but the receipts for the year ending the 5th of January, 1864, were estimated, subject to correction, at £33,000. These receipts were derived from a variety of sources. One was what was called "The Bill of Entry Income," which was estimated to produce from £25,000 to £27,000. Although this society had no office to pay for, the expenses of management of this branch of the society were something above 50 per cent. But what was its most remarkable feature was, that, although every Customs' officer was bound to contribute one penny in the pound of his salary to it, there were certain members who did not receive a farthing of benefit from it. As an illustration of the opinion which was entertained of the measure by those who were acquainted with the subject, he would read what was said of it by a gentleman who was evidently, an admirer of the right hon. Gentleman. Mr. George Smyth, who described himself as having been for twenty years mixed up with Insurance Companies and Friendly Societies, said—

" When I read the speech of the Chancellor of the Exchequer—as I did over and over again—in support of his Annuities Bill, I was perfectly astounded. No one can admire more than I do the learning, the eloquence, the financial ability, and political integrity of the hon. Gentleman; but I did not think that by such a Bill he was capable of offending the feelings of self-help, self-respect, and self-reliance of, I may say, the entire working population of England; that he would despise and ridicule the mighty work which, almost unaided by legislative protection, they alone have done to provide against the afflictions of sickness and death; that he could mistake or misrepresent important facts with respect to that work, the Friendly Societies of England; that he would sneer at or undervalue the good they have done, as it were, by stealth; and that, all of a sudden, he would introduce a Bill, not to reform these institutions, not to give protection to the members of them, and perpetuate them as a prominent feature of our social system and the loftiest and holiest objects of finance—in my mind an easy work for the Legislature—but that he should ask the representatives of the working

men of England in Parliament assembled to help the Government to establish a Friendly Society of its own, which proposes, not to insure persons under sixteen years of age, being rather a risky and troublesome as well as an unprofitable class of lives—not to insure against sickness, an unprofitable business also—but a society that, by virtue of the security it would offer, might induce the best lives of the working classes to become policy holders in it, leaving to the existing Friendly Societies all the sick business, which is bad, and all the bad lives in the life branch, without offering to the members that must remain by these societies the slightest hope of that legislative protection, the want of which alone has led to the evils of which the right hon. Gentleman complains."

All the objections to the Bill were summed up in that sentence. It did not go to the amendment of the Friendly Societies Act, as it ought to have done. It went to sapping them all; taking the best Life Assurance business to be managed by the Government, leaving the rest to the managers of these societies, and depriving three millions of their members of the best portion of the receipts which should accrue to them. He had, therefore, great pleasure in seconding the Amendment.

Amendment proposed,

To leave out from the word "That" to the end of the Question, in order to add the words "the Bill be committed to a Select Committee," —(*Sir Minto Farquhar,*)

—instead thereof.

Question proposed, "That the words proposed to be left out stand part of the Question."

MR. HODGKINSON said, that he failed to discover in the observations of the hon. Member for Liverpool and the hon. Baronet the Member for Hertford any reason why the Bill should be referred to a Select Committee. They had both adduced reasons why a Select Committee should be appointed to consider the management of Friendly Societies and Life Assurance Companies, but none why the Bill should be referred to such a Committee. It was quite immaterial to the consideration of the measure whether the Royal Liver or any other Friendly Societies were solvent or insolvent, or whether their affairs were well or ill-managed. It was impossible to have read the recent Reports of the Registrar of Friendly Societies without being aware that many of these societies were in a very unsound state. But those which were unsound were generally confined to certain districts. He was happy to be able to bear testimony to the general management of most of the Friendly Societies in his own district. He could speak of the careful way in which their accounts were kept, the prudence with which their resources were husbanded, the economical and remunerative manner in which their savings were invested, the sound principle on which their benefits were granted, and consequently the great amount of good they had effected. It was true that the Bill would, in some degree, interfere with private enterprize, and it was equally true that the rule that Government should not interfere with private enterprize was a sound one, but it was not of universal application. Like most other rules it admitted of exceptions, and it should be remembered that Friendly Societies already owed much of their security to the interference which for some time had existed with respect to them; and he, for one, should be glad to see that interference go one step further. Something in the shape of an official audit or examination of their accounts should be —he would not say, forced upon them, but placed at their disposal. He did not mean an audit year by year, but a periodical valuation of their assets and liabilities. He believed every sound, well managed society would gladly avail itself of the offer, and those which refused must either have a character far above suspicion or they would very soon become powerless for evil. It was said this Bill would enable the Government to enter into active competition with Friendly Societies and Assurance Companies. In his opinion, it would do so to a very limited extent. It was only with reference to small Life Assurances that the Bill introduced any innovation. It had been stated, in the course of the debate on the subject which had taken place a few evenings before, that the Chancellor of the Exchequer would subsidize his Insurance Offices, because he had the National Exchequer at his back, and that he would thus be able to defy all competition. The House, however, had the assurance of the right hon. Gentleman that nothing of the kind was intended, and even if that assurance had not been given, it might be safely conjectured, that if a Vote were asked for such a purpose it would be almost unanimously rejected. But it was said that the scheme was to be self supporting, and the Chancellor of the Exchequer had himself stated that the rate of interest at which he could accumulate his premiums would be 3¼ per cent. From that amount, however, he

Mr. Hodgkinson

would have to deduct the expenses of carrying on the business, which would absorb at least a quarter per cent, and he would ask whether, accumulating his premiums at the remaining 3 per cent, he would be able effectually to compete with private companies? He did not believe that such would be the case, while he was of opinion that the Bill would have some operation, and that that operation would be beneficial in those districts in which the Benefit Societies had been badly managed, as well as advantageous to persons whose habits were migratory, and who would have an opportunity of paying their premiums at a post office. He maintained, however, that, like the Post Office savings banks, the measure would not have the effect of supplanting, but of supplementing existing societies. The Post Office savings banks, for instance, had not prejudicially affected any well managed savings banks which were previously in existence, and which, so far as his experience went— and he knew a great many of those institutions—were doing as great a business now as before. Taking, for instance, the new deposits in Newark savings bank, and he meant to speak simply of new accounts, he found that those for the year ending the 20th of November, 1860, were £11,841; for the year ending the 20th of November, 1861, 12,484; 1862, 11,324; 1863, 11,997; while for the period from the 20th of November last to the present date they exceeded those for the corresponding period of any former year. But, although his opinion of the probable operation of the present, which was a somewhat similar scheme to the Post Office savings banks, was such as he had indicated, he could not agree with the Chancellor of the Exchequer in his estimate as to the expense of working out the proposal, which the right hon. Gentleman seemed to think would be very trifling. Now, the first expense attendant on the insurance of lives was that for medical examination. The right hon. Gentleman stated, that the Government had already a most efficient staff of medical officers connected with the administration of the Poor Law, who might be called Government officers, and be made available for the purposes of the Bill. It was no doubt true that these medical men were, to a certain extent, Government officers; they were elected by the Poor Law Guardians; their election had to be confirmed by the Board in London; and one-half their salaries was repaid out of the Consolidated Fund. But then their pay was fixed with reference to the special services which they had to perform, and the right hon. Gentleman would, he thought, find that he had got into a hornet's nest if he set about delegating the delicate task of examining lives for insurance to those gentlemen without giving them additional pay. Then the right hon. Gentleman seemed to think that it would cost little or nothing to collect his premiums, inasmuch as that could be done through the Post Office. Now, the hon. Member for Liverpool, at all events, did not seem to look upon that as an economic mode of collection, but although he did not agree with him in the opinion that the Post Office was the most expensive of our institutions, yet he would go the length of saying that if an addition were made to the labour of any department the allowance to the labourers must also be increased. It should, moreover, be borne in mind that policies of Insurance were subject to transfer; that in the case of a policy which remained in operation for twenty or thirty years, the transfer might take place, as in existing institutions, a great many times, and that many delicate questions must very frequently arise as to who the persons were to whom the money should be paid. Such were the difficulties which Insurance Offices had new to encounter, and he felt convinced that when the Chancellor of the Exchequer had got his scheme fairly at work, adhering to the principle that it was to be self-supporting, he would find that, so far as pounds, shillings, and pence were concerned, he would not be able to compete with those societies already in operation. The right hon. Gentleman in his speech had alluded to the enormous expense at which some of those offices were conducted, as the rock on which so many of them split, instancing specially the high premiums paid. There were, however, other expenses even still higher. There was often an unnecessarily large staff maintained, either to give the appearance of a large business being done or patronage to the directors. There were, besides, expensive buildings, and above all a system of advertising on a scale the most extravagant. In saying so he did not allude to the legitimate advertising in the newspapers, but to the custom of inundating men's tables with books and pamphlets, and placarding the walls of towns with statements, to the effect that Mr. So-and-So was a director of the particular office

named. He found, for instance, that the cost of advertising in an office which he would not mention, but which stood first in the list of the blue-book delivered in June last, was no less than £7,359 12s. 3d., the income of the office being £311,000, and its expenses of management £74,000, or 24 per cent on its receipts. The managers of those offices, he might add, were not satisfied with advertising in the way to which he referred, but sent about almanacks containing puffs of their several establishments. Another office which had an establishment in Pall Mall and one in Oxford Street, went beyond advertising, for it kept a poet to sing the praises of Life Insurance. He might be permitted to read an extract from a poem commencing—

> "When dear Papa was ta'en to Heaven,
> And Ma was left to strive for seven,
> With scarce enough for burial fees,
> (So lingering was poor Papa's disease),
> Tho' full of grief, we'd no despair,
> Relations spoke so very fair."

After describing how advice and a kiss was all the benefit derived from relations, the poem went on to show how a policy of Life Insurance in a certain office was found, and concluded—

> "They took it to the office, and wasn't it funny,
> When they got there they received the money!"

There was one point upon which he was not quite clear, that the Chancellor of the Exchequer was correct. He doubted whether there was any royal road for the ascertainment of the solvency or otherwise of Insurance Offices. The Chancellor of the Exchequer seemed to think that giving the age of the office, the amount of the premial income, and the extent of the accumulation, it was easy to determine whether the society was solvent or not. The right hon. Gentleman instanced two offices of the same age, having been established in 1825. One office had a premial income of £247,000, and accumulations to the extent of £2,133,000, or between eight and nine years' income. That office was safe, according to the view of the Chancellor of the Exchequer. The other office had a premial income of £44,000, and an accumulated fund of £780,000, or seventeen years' premial income. Both offices professed to divide their profits among the assurers, so that if one was safe the other must have defrauded its deceased policy holders of a large amount of bonuses. However, the truth was that there was no royal road to ascertain solvency, as in the cases referred to one office might have done a large business at first, and very little lately, while the other might have done quite the reverse. He was himself a director of an office which was established in 1823. It had already paid £6,000,000 to its policy holders, it had an income of £500,000, of which £283,000 was derived from premiums, and had accumulations to the extent of £5,200,000, or the amount of eighteen years' premial income; while the best feature was the fact that the total expenses of management, including agents' commission and directors' fees, was under 4½ per cent of its income. He could not but think the Bill might do much good, and could do no harm, and as he did not see any advantage that could accrue from sending it to a Select Committee, he should vote against the Amendment of the hon. Baronet.

MR. SALT said, that having taken a deep interest in the objects of Friendly Societies, he differed from many hon. Members on that side of the House in regarding the Bill as a small matter. He believed the principle of that and all Bills of a similar character was simply to declare that there were occasions when it was necessary for the Legislature to interfere for the protection of certain classes of the community, who either from poverty or want of education, or the peculiarity of their position, were unable fully and adequately to help themselves. But the protection which the State afforded in cases of that description was necessarily limited by another principle of equal importance—namely, that the Government ought never to interfere with the business and the commercial transactions of private companies, unless such an interference were absolutely necessary and for the benefit of the community at large. He believed that principle applied to the Bill before the House. The first clause of the present Bill related to what were called Deferred Annuities, which were better understood by the term of "old age pay." The principle of giving old age pay under the guarantee of the Government was no new one, and the clause simply extended an already existing power by permitting Deferred Annuities to be paid for by periodical contributions instead of, as at present, in one lump sum. He could not conceive a greater boon that could be offered to the poor labouring man than a measure of the kind. There were certain things which the poor man required. The provision usually made for him was usually for old

age pay, sick pay, and pay for medical attendance; and the question was, whether Life Assurance Societies were competent to deal with all these matters, or whether there were any of these particular requirements with which the Government should interfere. It was the opinion of authorities who were experienced in such matters, that Government interference was necessary where the payments were long deferred, or where the benefit was not immediate. But as to payments at death and Deferred Annuities there were some difficulties which required the interference of the Government to be overcome. He had taken great interest in small parish societies, founded in pure honesty and good faith, and some of them dating seventy or eighty years ago; and he was satisfied that, under a proper system, safe societies might be established by which sick pay could be adequately provided for poor men. Much evil had arisen, however, from the true principles of Life Assurance not being properly understood, and from the funds not being kept up through young men not being induced to enter. They had young men beginning at the age of twenty with their small payments, thinking that when they reached the age of sixty, they would be possessed of sick pay and all the advantages these societies were supposed to possess. But too often, when forty years had elapsed, the shillings and the pence, which had been hardly wrought for and which economy and self-denial had treasured up, were found to have vanished, and the poor man's hopes of independence were doomed to disappointment. He was unable to tell any poor man who came to him for advice where he could deposit his earnings with safety. The old savings banks had not done what they should have done in that respect; and in one instance when he had written to a manager about a small annuity he received for answer that they knew nothing about it. He was connected with one Friendly Society which he believed to be perfectly stable. Its rules had been carefully considered. It was under excellent management. The clergyman and the gentry took an interest in it, but where was the security that forty or fifty years hence the members would have the services of such able administrators? For these reasons he thought the subject was one which eminently demanded the interference of Government, and that it was the duty of the Government to popularise and systematise a plan of

Mr. Hodgkinson

old age pay. He was sorry that in that Bill the phrase of Deferred Annuities was used, because it was apt to mislead and withdraw attention from the real point to be considered—namely, the benefit of the labouring classes. For the grounds he had stated, however, so far as Clause 1 was concerned, he gave it his hearty and unqualified support. As to the Life Assurance Clause he did not believe that the Bill would interfere in the least with long established companies. The Government savings banks had in no way interfered with well established Banking Companies, and beyond providing £3 or £4 for burial expenses, he never knew or heard of a poor labouring man entertaining the notion of Life Assurance. The small insurers for £50 or £100 at death were men earning £2 or £3 a week—men who could reason acutely, and in matters of business were quite as well able to take care of themselves as those in the higher classes. He accepted with unfeigned thankfulness and heartfelt satisfaction the first clause of the Bill. He believed it would confer one of the greatest boons which could possibly be given to the poor, and was likely to bring comfort and plenty to many an aged couple in their declining years, as well as preventing as many aged couples spending the last days of their life in the solitude of the Union Workhouse. He was not quite so certain about the operation of the second clause, but on the whole he thought it would be of benefit, and when the Bill passed, he hoped steps would be taken to make its provisions fully and efficiently known to those whom it was calculated so materially to benefit. If a scheme could be devised which would secure to poor men old age pay, with a moderate sum at their death for burial, with the possibility of repayment of premiums according to the scheme already adopted by the Government, and by no other office, an incalculable benefit would be offered to the working men of this country.

SIR FRANCIS GOLDSMID said, he was of opinion that the House ought not hastily to proceed with the Bill. If working men were discouraged from insuring by the loss which they might sustain through the failure of Insurance Societies, and it was suggested that the mischief might be remedied by legislation, any measure introduced for that purpose was certain of receiving favourable consideration, particularly when it was recommended by so eloquent a speech as that of the right hon. Gentleman the Chancellor of the Exchequer. But he must say that when he ceased to listen, and began to reflect, he felt that the right hon. Gentleman had failed to satisfy him, either that the business proposed to be undertaken was one that could be transacted by the State with safety to the public—with safety to the finances of the country, or that the scheme of the Chancellor of the Exchequer would really serve the interest of the classes for whose benefit it was proposed. First, with regard to the finances : it was said that the insurance business intended to be carried on under the Bill was identical in its character with the business of Deferred Annuities. The two were quite distinct. In the case of Deferred Annuities, all that was required was to ascertain the age of the person and to receive the money. In the case of Life Assurance it was necessary to inquire into the state of health of the party whose life was to be insured, and that was attended with more difficulty than the right hon. Gentleman seemed to suppose. Indeed, when introducing the measure he informed the House that it was easy to ascertain all that it was requisite to know when it was proposed to insure the life of a working man. The right hon. Gentleman said the only things necessary to be known were the age, the employment, and the habits of the man.

THE CHANCELLOR OF THE EXCHEQUER : And there is the medical examination.

SIR FRANCIS GOLDSMID : A medical examination was the main security at present, and it now appeared to be admitted that there could be no simplification in that respect. Then it was said that a periodical Report would be laid before Parliament, showing the nature of the business transacted, and enabling the House to put a stop to operations with which it might be dissatisfied. But was this a matter over which it was possible for the House of Commons to exercise any effective control? They knew that in ordinary Insurance Offices, the business was, as a general rule, managed by the directors, and that the shareholders could not interpose except in cases of the grossest abuse. It was vain to expect that as to transactions of this character the House of Commons could do what was found impracticable by shareholders. The next consideration was whether the scheme was for the benefit of the working classes. With reference to that point, two arguments were used which were the twin offspring of the same fertile brain, but which appeared to him to be fratricidal. First it was admitted that the Government ought not to undertake the business except for the advantage of the classes for whom it was intended, and then it was admitted that there were many companies at present engaged in the business which were of a solid character; but it was said those offices would not suffer by the Bill. If they told him that the working classes did not understand, and could not be made to understand, the difference between solvent and insolvent companies, then he contended that by interfering with Life Insurances in the way proposed by the Bill, they must withdraw support from both sound and unsound offices in an equal measure. If, on the other hand, he was told that the working classes were capable of distinguishing or being taught to distinguish between sound and unsound offices, then he said the whole foundation of the Bill disappeared. He believed the latter supposition to be the true one. He thought it was an unfair imputation on the working men, looking at the advances they had made of late years, to say that they could not be taught to make the distinction between sound and unsound societies, and he contended that it was the duty of statesmen not to pass such a Bill as this, but to spread among the people that knowledge of insurance which would enable them to make a judicious selection of an office or a society. As one means of enabling them to do so, Parliament ought to require the publication of accounts and rules as recommended by Mr. Tidd Pratt. Employers, both in towns and in country, would also do great service by helping to find for Friendly Societies places of meeting, distinct from public-houses. In a letter to *The Times*, a clergyman of much experience—the Rev. Mr. Girdlestone —stated that in his opinion the principle of the measure was a most valuable one; but he added that it would bestow no real benefit upon working men, unless the Chancellor of the Exchequer applied his proposal to relief in sickness as well as to a sum paid down at death; but how was this to be done by the right hon. Gentleman? In the Report on Friendly Societies for 1862 it appeared that a member of one of these societies had, after joining it, taken to keeping pigeons, and that he had had a severe fall when going

Sir Francis Goldsmid

on the roof in the snow to tend his birds; and Mr. Tidd Pratt was consulted whether payment should be made to the sick man "after him meeting with his accident with his own foolish excursions after his pigeons." Let the House only imagine the right hon. Gentleman adding to his already multifarious occupations the duty of sitting as supreme arbiter in cases like that of the unlucky pigeon-fancier. Yet the Life Assurances of those societies were only a subordinate part of their business; and therefore a measure applying only to insurances could not possibly check the main evils arising from abuses connected with such institutions. He thought that no sufficient case had been made out for departing from the great general principle, that the Government ought not to undertake business which the people were capable of conducting themselves.

Mr. GREGSON said, he should support the Bill as he believed it to be essential for the security of the working classes. At present they did not know where to go if they wished to insure their lives— did not know which of the small offices were sound and which unsound. The Bill would supply that want, and allowing the premiums to be paid by small instalments it would give a great incentive to Life Assurance. He agreed with the hon. Baronet who had just spoken, that the position of existing societies would be much improved if compelled to publish their accounts. He declined to follow the hon. Baronet (Sir Francis Goldsmid) into the question of the clergyman's view of sick pay, or into the hypothesis of the pigeons, because there was no necessary connection between Life Assurance and sick clubs. When Life Assurance Societies were first established, some seventy or eighty years ago, the principle of them was so little understood that the same premium was taken for all ages. But the principle was now understood, and that class of business could be conducted with perfect safety. As to the examinations, he did not attach much importance to them. He had often found in his experience of Life Assurance that the most robust persons died the soonest, simply because they thought they could take liberties with their constitutions, whereas persons whose health was less robust took more care of themselves and lived the longer. If, therefore, a great number of lives were insured, and the date of birth, the occupation, and the habits of the insurers were ascertained, he would just as soon take those lives as others selected with more care by the great Insurance Companies. It was well known that men entered these existing societies generally when young, and when they arrived at the age of sixty or seventy years they found themselves utterly disappointed in their hopes of receiving a substantial benefit from them in their old age. He therefore hailed the measure of the Chancellor of the Exchequer as a great boon to the industrial classes, who knew very well that, if they availed themselves of its advantages, they would have the most unquestionable security for their money. He objected altogether to refer the Bill to a Select Committee. All the circumstances were known, and a Select Committee would delay the Bill to another year, which would be very undesirable. The effect of the Bill would be, in his opinion, largely to increase the appreciation of Life Assurance in this country. Persons insured their houses, though these might not be burnt down, while they did not insure their lives, though they were sure to die. He believed that the Bill, while interfering with the large offices or the substantial provident societies, would largely increase the number of insurers, and so tend greatly to the welfare of the community. In his opinion it was a wise and a sound measure, and he hoped that the Chancellor of the Exchequer would persevere with it, and would decline to refer it to a Select Committee.

MR. SOTHERON ESTCOURT said, I think, Sir, that the main object of this Bill appeals to the feelings of all men, and that if we were only to listen to our feelings we should at once declare ourselves in favour of the measure. But if we listen for a moment to our judgment, and consider the means by which it proposes to carry its object out, I am afraid we cannot assent to the Bill. If I have rightly collected the intentions of the hon. Gentlemen who have addressed this House in favour of the proposition, I believe I have expressed what was in the mind of every one of them. The object of the Bill commends itself to the benevolence and kindness of every gentleman, but I doubt whether the means which are proposed to effect that object are such as we can approve. I certainly listened with attention to the eloquent statement of the Chancellor of the Exchequer, and so far as my humble tribute of admiration goes I willingly tender it to him. But however great my admiration of the eloquence of the right hon.

Gentleman, I confess my admiration is far greater for the courage which he manifested in attempting to deal with so hazardous and difficult a subject. I cannot help thinking, however, that if the right hon. Gentleman had been less courageous he would have been much more successful; and that he has raised up a great amount of opposition in the work he has undertaken by the mode in which he unfolded his story in introducing the Bill. Upon one point I entertain a strong opinion. I think that this Bill, if carried into law, will do little or no harm to Friendly Societies properly so called. If I venture, then, to criticise any of the details of the measure, I wish to say that it is not because I anticipate any sort of opposition will result between the offices it proposes to establish and those institutions in which for many years I have taken a great interest. I repeat, I do not think that this Bill will interfere with the existing Friendly Societies, and for several reasons. It is perhaps enough to give one reason, and that is—I do not believe that the working classes, scattered as they are over the face of this country, will take advantage of the Bill if it should become law. I do not believe that those classes enter into Friendly Societies or clubs for the sake of the benefits of such societies so much as companionship. And of the benefits which they offer to them, the only one I think they much care about is the provision in time of sickness. I have also read in the public papers the letter which has been referred to in the course of this debate. That letter was written by a worthy clergyman, a neighbour of mine, and he, while approving the object of the right hon. Gentleman, says—"the Chancellor of the Exchequer will do nothing at all unless he introduces some mode of amending sick clubs." That gentleman, I am sure, speaks the opinions of the greater part of the clergy of this country. But no Chancellor of the Exchequer, nor any Member of this House, will venture to undertake so gigantic an operation as that of dealing with the sickness of the working classes. Why, it is as much as any of the ordinary clubs can do, with all their local and personal knowledge, and all the local checks and restraints exercised by those who manage the club, to prevent imposition in the matter of sickness. How then would it be possible for the Government, without any such local knowledge or local checks, to prevent fraud? There is another view of this matter deserving attention. If this Bill comes into operation it will to a certain degree affect all the working men in this country, and unless it is more guarded in its provisions than it is at present, it will greatly interfere also with the independence of individual action. This was the point raised the other day by the hon. and learned Member for Sheffield (Mr. Roebuck), and I entirely concur in the conclusion to which he arrived. I believe that the only safe mode in which his Bill can be brought into operation will be to limit it with due regard to the amount and character of its operation, to that species of business which is not profitable even to solvent societies. If you trench upon the field of profit you will do harm to those institutions already established, and to that extent interfere with the self-action of the people for whose benefit the Bill is intended. But if you had an opportunity of moulding the clauses of this Bill in such a manner as to avoid that difficulty, all would be well. You ought so to draw your Bill as neither to run the risk of interfering with the independence and self-action of the people, or of interfering with the real business of Assurance Offices. But if you take the Bill in its present shape, you will have no guarantee against the evils to which I have called attention. I think it will be more than the Chancellor of the Exchequer can expect that we should pass this Bill in its present shape. The Bill on the face of it gives us very little information of its object. It is drawn in such technical language that any person reading it would suppose that its object was to amend the Act passed seven or eight years ago giving the Government the power of granting annuities. The whole language of the Bill from first to last bears reference to that former Act. Now, if we are able to do that good which Gentlemen opposite expect from carrying out the professed object of the Bill, assuredly it would be better for the character of the House and the Government, and for the good of the people, that that object should appear plainly upon the face and in the Preamble of the Bill. Our object, I believe, is this—that whereas, not annuities only, but assurances of a sum of money to be paid on the occurrence of death, form the business of certain societies, many of which are insolvent, we are desirous of affording the working classes the offer of a secure payment however long the day to which such benefit may be postponed. I think it is far better

that the Government should go further in this direction, and that the principle upon which it is to act should be distinctly enunciated in the preamble. It should also be distinctly stated, that it was not contemplated by the Bill to carry on any business of a profitable nature which might be conducted by a solvent company. If they were to go beyond the point where profit began, wherever that point was, then, assuredly, they would do harm. There is one evil which I think is likely to arise from the discussion of last week and perhaps of this evening. I am afraid it will be supposed that the observations of those who have pointed out certain glaring defects in certain existing societies will apply to existing solvent societies; and, partly in order to set this right, my hon. Friend (Sir Minto Farquhar) proposes to send the Bill to a Committee. I do not know how far he proposes that reference to be extended; but I should object to the Bill being sent to the Committee if the reference would allow a committee to take evidence upon the conflicting claims of different societies. That would introduce not merely a temporary delay, but would cause the entire postponement of the Bill. I am entirely with the right hon. Gentleman the Chancellor of the Exchequer in his object to afford the working man a security which he cannot obtain otherwise. So far I am favourable to the Bill. I hope the Chancellor of the Exchequer will succeed in carrying it; but I hope it will receive considerable alteration before we are called upon to pass it. I understand it is not the intention to ask permission to take evidence. If the intention is to give the Committee a reference to the other matters, of inquiry into the solvency of a number of small Insurance Societies, I should object; but no doubt we shall have this fully explained. In giving my consent to the Select Committee, I wish that the order of reference to the Committee should be a simple direction to amend the Bill. For what is the alternative? It is either to agree to that proposition, or to pass the Bill in its present shape. Many Amendments have been suggested. The hon. Gentleman who last spoke has an important Amendment to propose—to fix a maximum for the operation of these Government annuities. There is no proposition — I think there ought to be a proposition—to fix a minimum, because it was most important that they should not transfer to Government the furnishing of the expenses of burial.

Mr. Sotheron Estcourt

I think it is impossible to arrive at a satisfactory conclusion on these points in this House. I think it is a question that fairly ought to go to a Committee, and therefore I shall vote for that proposition. I have heard no answer to another point not admitting of easy solution, namely, the great risk which the Government is about to undertake. That, I think, has not been fairly considered or satisfactorily explained by the right hon. Gentleman the Chancellor of the Exchequer. Observe, now, what is his position. What the Chancellor of the Exchequer is doing is to place himself in the position of a young actuary, who proposes to set up a large Insurance Office. The first few years will probably seem years of success and triumph. You do not know the risk that you run till after many years of business—perhaps the whole of the present generation may be swept away before you find out your risk. You cannot fairly say that because your Post Office savings banks have been a great success the like result will attend your annuity scheme, as if the one were germane to the other. In the savings banks you at all times know the amount of your liabilities. The risk in the savings bank is of a different description, and altogether unlike the risk of an Assurance Office. There was a sum of £40,000,000 belonging to the old savings banks, and supposing that in a few years there should be £40,000,000 in the new savings banks, then, with regard to the last £40,000,000, the risk was that the Government might be called on at any moment to return the amount received in gold; but with regard to the repayment of the other £40,000,000, notices were required and delay intervenesd; besides, the name and character of the managers, known in their own locality, would act as a buffer in case of a panic. But whatever the risk is you know the amount of it. But when you come to insurance it is a case of estimate. The liabilities of to-day may not be in proportion to what you have received. You may have received a premium of £3 or £4 and be called on to pay an assurance of £100. Therefore, this is a new career on which the Government is entering, and it will have difficulties and liabilities of a more extended kind. If it is to be a boon to the country, it is of the greatest importance that all these points should be well turned over in the Committee upstairs. I do not at all despair of seeing the Bill put into a shape in which it will realise the anticipations of the hon. Member who last addressed the House. The Bill is fraught with difficulty. I do not see the mode of getting over it; and I do not think we have heard any satisfactory solution of the difficulty. Grant us the permission to discuss the matter in Committee, and we may arrive at the conclusion not only that by means of Government agency the working classes may have the opportunity afforded them of providing for themselves and their relations an annuity in old age, and furnishing them with what some of them so much want—but which many of them, I am afraid, will not avail themselves of—a provision for their wives and families after their decease. By means of this Committee you may get rid of that important objection to the Bill—namely, that you may seriously interfere with the independent action of the people; and, in the next place, you may avoid the danger which at present stares you in the face, that while you seek to do good you may do great injury to the Friendly Societies and Insurance Societies spread all over the country.

MR. GOSCHEN said, that he felt himself unable to give a silent vote on that occasion, though personally he had every reason to be silent; for he was not only a director of an Assurance Company himself, but he probably represented more directors and managers of Assurance Societies than any other Member of the House. But so convinced was he of the wisdom and policy of the measure, that he felt it to be his duty to do the little he could in answering the objections to it which had been raised. It was universally admitted that the bearings of the question had been scarcely exaggerated—that it was a measure of the greatest consequence and importance; and no one could suppose that the great anxiety that was felt and the strong opposition which was manifested in certain quarters to the Bill was entirely owing to the efforts of those who fancied it would deal a blow at their own private interests. The Bill, no doubt, had some strong and weighty objections to it, and they must be fairly met; but he thought that they might be fairly disposed of, and that the Bill would be one which was well worthy of the character of the right hon. Gentleman and of the House, and leave a mark upon the history of the Session. Although the Bill was laid on the table at the commencement of the Session, it was not till the statement of the Chancellor of the Exchequer was made that the House saw that a great measure was about to be proposed. The statement of the right hon. Gentleman the Chancellor of the Exchequer was so luminous, so complete, and to his mind so exhaustive, that the House, notwithstanding the novelty of the proposition, saw the full extent of the question, and the points on which the measure rested were accurately understood. No argument had been used in the course of the discussion which had not been shadowed forth and anticipated by the Chancellor of the Exchequer himself. The Bill was opposed on five different grounds. There was an objection to the principle of the Bill; there was an objection to the practicability of the Bill; there was an objection to the necessity of the Bill; there was an objection to the evidence on which that necessity was grounded; and there was an objection that it clashed with private interests. He did not propose to enter into the objections raised to the evidence, and he was glad that the discussion had latterly lost the somewhat personal character it assumed in the beginning of the evening. He did not think that the evidence with regard to the existing Friendly Societies and Insurance Companies should be too rigorously sifted. It was not so much a question as to which of these societies was solvent; that was an important matter for the societies themselves; but the passing of a necessary Bill ought not to be made dependent on particular evidence respecting particular Friendly Societies or Insurance Offices. The question was, whether it was possible to find that absolute security and honesty in Friendly Societies to which every man who made a painful sacrifice of the present for the sake of the future—for such it was to the working man—was entitled. He did not propose to go into the question of the insolvency of these Friendly Societies. But he proposed to deal with the objections on other grounds. There were two points which he would mainly deal with — the objection against Government interference and the argument against the practicability of the Bill. He thought it perfectly natural and legitimate that hon. Members who thought as he did, that the interference of Government should be jealously watched, should require that most satisfactory evidence should be brought before they sanctioned any unwarrantable interference with private enterprise. It was quite natural,

Mr. Goschen

also, that hon. Gentlemen acquainted with the difficulties of administration should feel rather anxious lest the State should prove unequal to the task about to be imposed upon it. But these two arguments were in themselves quite distinct. No one had spoken with more force about the anticipated loss to the revenue than the hon. Member for Dudley, whose imagination was so excited at the idea of a loss to the revenue, that he talked of an addition of £200,000,000 to the national debt. Sharing the belief of the hon. Gentleman that every possible encouragement should be given to insurance, and that not even considerations of Imperial taxation should be placed side by side with it, he voted in the majority against the Government on the question of the Fire Insurance duty. Now, however, the hon. Member and the Chancellor of the Exchequer had changed positions, and while the latter was the patron of insurance the former was the champion of the revenue. He himself held that they ought, as far as they could, to foster the tendency of all classes to insure. Every policy taken out by a working man was a guarantee, not only to himself but to the community, upon whom otherwise the care of his family would fall. As long as the Poor Laws existed in their present state, and every parish or union was bound to provide a minimum support for those who had no other means of existence, so long every working man who bought an annuity or insured his life was doing a service not only to himself or family, but also to his parish, his county, and even to the nation at large. From self-interest, therefore, as well as from philanthropy, they ought to support this measure. It did not force anything on the working classes, and that was quite right, for they ought not to be regarded as mere clay in the hands of the potter. Without, however, interfering with their liberty of action in any way, it gave them help to be self-helpful. The opposition to the Bill had rested, in a considerable degree, on the probable loss to the revenue which would result from it. Now, the elements on which the success of a system of insurance would depend were these — the scale of premiums, value of lives, rate of interest at which the premiums were invested, the expenses and the profits which accrued to the shareholders. Assuming, in the present case, that the scale of premiums of the Government would be identical with that of the Insurance Offices —although it was fair to argue that if the risk, as was said, was greater, the premiums should be higher—and that the value of the lives would be the same, then the Government would lose on the rate of interest, but would gain the commissions paid to agents, and the 10, 12, 20 per cent, or whatever it might be which constituted the shareholders' profits. Thus the Government would have advantages as well as disadvantages to deal with, and if they were put together it would be found, on the whole, to have a margin in its favour. The average of lives, not of working men, but of general policy-holders in the offices was, he was told, about fifteen years, and he would assume that the Government invested at $3\frac{1}{4}$ per cent, and the companies at $4\frac{1}{2}$. Meanwhile the Government saved at least 6 per cent. in commissions paid to agents, and had besides the margin of at least 10 per cent, which he had been told by persons of experience was the minimum rate of profits on insurances paid to the shareholders. Balancing these profits and savings against the loss of interest, it would be found that on policies running fifteen · years there was a margin of 6 per cent in favour of Government to cover any increased expenditure. In an adverse statement which had been circulated and seen by many hon. Members, it was estimated that the Government were likely to issue 1,000,000 of policies, and these would require 1,000 additional clerks. Now, 6 per cent on a million policies, bearing £3 premium each, would give Government £180,000, which, if they even knocked off £80,000, would leave £100,000 saved. They had already 3,000 post-offices which were savings banks, and he believed that on the average a third of a clerk additional at each post-office would be sufficient to meet the demands of the case, and the margin he had referred to would be amply sufficient to cover the increased outlay as well as that for the medical officers. Fears were entertained that the postmasters would not be competent for the work. He saw no reason why postmasters should not be as efficient in the discharge of the duties as the tradesmen who often acted as agents of Friendly Societies. Even if they were not very competent, all they would have to do was to keep the accounts, and the other duties might be left to the medical officers of the union, and partly to the Guardians of the Poor. It seemed to him that the Government could exercise greater supervision than the agents of the offices, who were, moreover, personally interested in bringing lives to the offices for which they acted. With regard to identification, there was a vast number of persons in the country receiving pensions for service in the army or navy, but there was no particular difficulty in identifying them, and fraud happened but rarely. There must be regulations, and those regulations must be enforced. It was said that the working classes would not be able to understand them. That he could not believe, because he knew that the working classes were able to understand the most difficult and intricate questions of settlement better than many hon. Gentlemen who were then listening to him. A working man knew his rights as well as possible, and he would not find more difficulty in mastering the simple regulations which Government must impose with respect to identification of policies than he found in acquainting himself with all the details of settlement. Nor did he think that the valuation of the lives of working men would present greater difficulties than that of the lives of persons moving in a higher sphere. The disorders of the working classes were more simple, and Union officers would, in their cases, be more reliable authorities than London physicians who pronounced upon the value of lives after a brief conversation with the persons proposing to insure. It had been said that the present Bill had a centralising tendency, that it was new, that it was un-English. Why, even in Anglo-Saxon times, the people were compelled to insure, not only their properties against theft, but their souls against eternal perdition. But he did not wish to rest upon an antiquarian argument, though, at the same time, he hoped the *doctrinaire* argument would not be pushed beyond its due limits. He agreed that the Government ought never to interfere so long as private enterprise could do the business as well. He quite accepted that proposition, but he doubted whether Friendly Societies could do that as well which the Government proposed to do. The Government proposed to give something which no one else could give—absolute security. He did not wish to say a word against Friendly Societies, except that he would not insure his own life in one, and why should they not try to give the working classes every advantage in the way of insurance that hon. Members would desire for themselves? But it was said to be quite easy for work- .

ing men to discern between a good and a bad society. For his own part, however, he did not see how they could possibly distinguish between the two. ["Divide."] He trusted the House would allow him to proceed. They had already had one personal discussion that evening, and it was only human nature that they should desire to proceed to the other which they were expecting; but the Bill before them was a most important one, and he trusted they would not vote against it upon arguments which they did not wish to hear refuted. There was one other point on which he desired to offer a few remarks. He considered that the measure before the House involved no real interference on the part of the Government. A man that took out a policy would be no more under the control of the Government than one that bought Consols. [*Cries of* "Divide."] He must yield to the feeling of the House, but, in sitting down, he might be allowed to add that the Bill had this further advantage, that it would create among the working classes a numerous body of State creditors, who would have a not less deep interest in the national welfare and tranquillity than those who, at present, were too apt to regard themselves as the only persons who had what was called a stake in the country.

MR. AYRTON moved the adjournment of the debate.

THE CHANCELLOR OF THE EXCHEQUER: The House had an understanding at the commencement of the evening, that this debate should be brought to a conclusion in time for another matter to be discussed, and therefore I comply with that understanding by assenting to the adjournment of the debate. I wish, however, to say one word in justice to a respectable body of men. A deputation from the working men of London waited upon me this morning under the presidency of a gentleman of the most distinguished philanthropy, to assure me that those trades' unions, to which I referred on a previous occasion as involving in their system a principle of coercion towards the minority of their own body, were working themselves out of what they—or at all events those who came to me—seemed to feel to be a vicious system. I cannot refrain from taking the earliest opportunity of expressing the very great gratification which I feel at learning that such was the case. As to what fell from my right hon. Friend (Mr. Sotheron Estcourt), my right hon. Friend stated—

Mr. Goschen

and he appeared to express the opinion of many hon. Gentlemen sitting near him—that he was not disposed to connect this Bill with a general inquiry into the condition of Friendly Societies and Insurance Offices; but that he thought that it would be better considered in a Select Committee on clauses, as such committee is generally understood, and as distinguished from a committee to inquire into the subject. If we had been debating this as a contested matter, my hon. Friend the Member for Hertford (Sir Minto Farquhar) will admit that his Motion, though in terms only it is a Motion to refer the Bill to a Committee, yet that his speech and the speech of the hon. Member who seconded it, proceeded entirely upon the supposition that it was to go to a Committee in order that various societies should be examined into and investigated. To that proposition we entertain the most insuperable objection. Nothing would induce me to encounter the responsibility of undertaking to carry forward this Bill in such a shape. I do not say that there may not be a Committee on Friendly Societies, but I am aware of no analogy or precedent that will warrant the appointment of a Committee to call before it an insurance officer, even though the rules on which they act may not be altogether such as can be approved and endorsed. They enjoy no exemptions, they take no special benefit from the law, they are acting upon the privileges of British subjects, and I am not prepared to be a party to calling them before a Committee, and to examining into the state of their concerns. We should consider such a Committee entirely foreign to our object. As to a judicious inquiry into the question of Friendly Societies, apart from this Bill, that is a different character, and upon it I do not wish to give any opinion whatever. If I understand from my hon. Friend (Sir Minto Farquhar) that he is satisfied to prosecute elsewhere, or in any other way, those inquiries in reference to these Societies in general, and that the desire entertained by many gentlemen is for considering the clauses of the Bill in a Committee upstairs rather than in a Committee of the House, I can only say that if we could conclude at present upon a Motion of that kind, and be able shortly after the financial statement to go into that Committee, I should be very willing to close on those grounds. I wish the House to very clearly understand the position in which I stand in reference to existing Societies. I quoted the cases of various Societies, and of those which I cited, I think there were four which I mentioned only for the purpose of commendation. I quoted several other Societies, the British Prudential among others; but I did not presume to take upon myself to say that they were insolvent societies. I pointed out facts connected with their balance-sheets, and merely went to the point of saying that they were not societies which carried with them sufficient evidence to guarantee the minds of the public, and entitle them to say to the Government " Don't enter upon · our field, which is satisfactorily occupied already." I admit that I quoted the case of societies not existing, which had not been solvent, and that I said one was a case of a fraudulent society. As regards the present question, I hope that what I have said is distinctly understood, that to a general committee I have an insurmountable objection, but that if the desire is to go into a committee upon the clauses, not taking evidence upon the general question, I am willing to accede to such a proposition.

MR. SOTHERON ESTCOURT said, that it would be for the convenience of the House, and would save time, to adopt the course proposed. The proposition now made by the right hon. Gentleman was a very fair one, and he trusted that the House would agree to it.

MR. THOMSON HANKEY said, that he could not vote for sending the Bill to a Committee, because he objected to the principle of it. There was no evidence to satisfy him that the business was such as could be safely undertaken by the Government; and he did not wish to see the Post Office have another heavy business annexed to it.

LORD STANLEY: I entirely understand the objection to inquire into the general question of the constitution and solvency of Friendly Societies in a Committee upon this Bill. Such an inquiry would be one of almost interminable length; it would render impossible the passing of the Bill in the present Session, and there are other reasons which would make such an investigation difficult in the present Parliament, if it is meant to be complete and thorough-going. There seem then to be but two alternatives. We must either proceed with the Bill after a continuance of the debate, or else accept the compromise of the Chancellor of the Ex-

chequer and go into Committee, not upon the subject of Friendly Societies but upon the clauses of the Bill. I confess that, for my own part, I should be very glad if that compromise could be arranged. Obviously, however, it is a thing that can only be done by the general consent and understanding of the House, and it is impossible not to see that there are a number of hon. Members who wish to postpone the debate in order that they may have an opportunity of expressing their opinions. I, therefore, think it better that we should accept the proposition for adjournment, and that the question should be again raised at the earliest opportunity after the House meets. The right hon. Gentleman may then be able to carry his Bill without the necessity of sending it upstairs.

THE CHANCELLOR OF THE EXCHEQUER: I have no objection to the adjournment of the debate, but it must be understood that if the debate is adjourned the Government will be entirely free to take their own course.

Debate *adjourned* till *To-morrow.*

SUPPLY.

Order for Committee read.

Motion made, and Question proposed, "That Mr. Speaker do now leave the Chair."

MR. STANSFELD AND THE GRECO CONSPIRACY.

SIR HENRY STRACEY: In introducing the motion which I have placed upon the paper for to-day, I do it as an individual Member, and because I feel that the dignity of this House has been assailed in consequence of information having been withheld by her Majesty's Government upon a serious question, which affects not only the Government but also the country at large, and certainly concerns the dignity of the House. I wish the House distinctly to understand that the task I have undertaken is to me by no means an agreeable or a pleasant one, and I do it purely as a matter of duty. I am surprised, however, on looking along the front bench opposite, not to see that Member of the Administration who is chiefly concerned in this question. It is far from my disposition to take any advantage of any Member of the Government, or to take him by surprise; but is it not singular that the Government itself should not have taken care that that Member was present? I think that to the House and the country it will be surprising indeed that that Member should not himself have taken care to be here. Nevertheless, I repeat I am influenced by no animus whatever against him. I have not the honour of his personal acquaintance, and I cannot therefore have any feeling or wish but to support in my humble capacity the dignity of the House, in which, though unworthy, I have a right to feel as much interest as any other person. It will be in the recollection of the House that the hon. Member for Finsbury (Mr. Cox), put a question to the hon. Member for Halifax (Mr. Stansfeld), well worded, temperate, and well judged, but the question was not answered in that satisfactory way which I am sure the House required to be answered. [Mr. Stansfeld here entered the House.] But that answer introduced that which, at any rate so far as the question was concerned, appeared to be perfectly superfluous, and which I saw very clearly astonished the hon. Member who put the question. It introduced a considerable eulogy and a great panegyric of M. Mazzini. This surely was uncalled for, but if it be in accordance with the views and opinions of the hon. Member he felt that he was called upon to make this defence of Mazzini, to make this kind of eulogy and panegyric upon him—if he entertains those Mazzinian opinions honestly and fairly, all I can say is that, however erroneous I know them to be, and however wrong as fatal to good order and government I believe them to be, I nevertheless respect a man who feels honestly and sincerely the opinions he professes. But the hon. Gentleman the Member for Halifax, when this question was put to him by the hon. Member for Finsbury, said he felt great astonishment, mingled with indignation, that his name should be mentioned in association with that of an assassin. Well, now, why should this extraordinary indignation and astonishment have occurred to the hon. Member? I allude merely to reports and what I have also read, for which those who publish it are answerable. But the House is bound to receive those statements if they are not contradicted. All I can say is, I beg to ask the hon. Member whether he forgets—and I am sure he will not deny it if he remembers it—that his name was mixed up with certain conspirators in the year 1857? Does he forget that in a certain conspiracy, called the

Sir Henry Stracey

"Orsini conspiracy," in 1858, his name was also mixed up? These periods are only a few years antecedent to the present, and so one does not see under these circumstances why he should be so affected with extraordinary astonishment and indignation. Now, Sir, in the year 1857 there was in the courts an acte d'accusation, and in it I find the following words: —"Two other names are still to be cited: that of the Sieur James Stansfeld, brewer, of London, who was also made the banker of Mazzini," &c. In fact the term is made use of—I say no more—"Two other assassins," for the acte d'accusation went on to say that two "other" assassins were proposed by Massarenta at Genoa, where he was; and Campanella and Massarenta were invited to call for money at the brewer's Stamfield (Stansfeld). It finished by saying that, at the same time, the authorities seized in the portfolio of Tibaldi the address of the "brasseur Stansfeld." Now, I only mention this as having read it, and I put a question to the hon. Gentleman, has he forgotten those trials of Tibaldi and Orsini in 1857 and 1858, because if he has not forgotten them, why should he be so wonderfully surprised, and feel such indignation as he showed the other day? Still, as I said before, if the hon. Member honestly avows and participates in those opinions, I can only find fault with him for an error in judgment. Now the hon. Member said upon that occasion, in reply to the hon. Member for Finsbury, that he believed his friend of eighteen years' standing to be incapable of assassination. Upon my word I do not mean to say that he is capable of assassination, and I think it very possible on that point the hon. Member may be right. But that is not the question. Does he not instigate to assassination? That is the question. Does the hon. Member for Halifax remember the name of Gallenga alias Mariotti. If the name does not remain in his memory I will take the liberty to call his attention to an account given in the *Révue des Deux Mondes*—an unsuspected Liberal authority—of December, 1856, wherein it was said—

"As to the home politics of Piedmont, they are summed up in an incident merely personal to all appearance, and yet of some significance. A man mixed up in political life, a writer and a deputy, a whilom friend of M. Mazzini, and subsequently an adherent of the Monarchy of Savoy and of the existing Government, M. Antonio Gallenga, wrote some time ago a history of Piedmont. M. Gallenga does not show himself altogether favourable to the sect of Young Italy; more particularly he relates a fact which dates more than twenty years back. At that time a young man named Mariotti, furnished with a dagger received from the hands of the Chief of Young Italy, is said to have arrived one day at Turin, with the fixed design of slaying the King, Charles Albert. The regicide was overtaken by weakness, or did not find in his friends the support which he expected, and the enterprize failed. M. Mazzini, no doubt, was far from content with his old pupil's method of writing history, and published a letter, not, of course, to blame the idea of the crime, but to relate that the narrative was all the more exact, inasmuch as Mariotti and M. Gallenga were only one and the same person. M. Gallenga has himself confirmed this identity. The revelation has produced an extraordinary sensation. The result has been that M. Gallenga has been obliged to resign his place as deputy, to replace in the King's hands the Cross of SS. Maurice and Lazarus, which he had received, and to retire from political life."

I will now read a letter, which is really very interesting, from Mazzini, but which having been published, may have been met with by some hon. Members—

"Not long" says Mazzini, "before the expedition to Savoy, after the shooting down of our friends in Genoa, Alessandria, and Chambery, towards the end of 1833, there came to me one evening at the Hotel de la Navigation at Geneva, a young man whom I did not know. He brought me a note from L. A. Melegari, now a professor and ministerial Deputy at Turin (then one of us) [some committee], who recommended his friend to me with words more than warm, as one who was bent upon doing a lofty deed, and wished to come to an understanding with me about it. The young man was Antonio Gallenga. He came from Corsica. He was affiliated to the "Giovane Italia." He told me that from the moment the proscription commenced, he had resolved to avenge the blood of his brethren, and to teach tyrants, once for all, that guilt was followed by expiation; that he felt himself called to strike down, in the person of Charles Albert, the traitor of 1821, and the butcher of his brethren; that he had brooded over the idea in the solitude of Corsica, until it had grown gigantic and too strong for him. And more besides. I raised objections, as I have always done in similar cases, discussed the matter, and put everything before him that might change his purpose. I said that I thought Charles Albert deserving of death, but that his death would not save Italy; that in order to assume the ministry of expiation one should be free from every low feeling of revenge, and from everything unworthy of that mission; that one should feel himself capable, after accomplishing the act, of folding his hands on his breast and giving himself up as a victim; that in any case he would die in the attempt; that he would die branded by men as an assassin; and so on, for a good while."

Well, now, why did Mazzini do this? I think I shall show that he had his object in so doing, as he said he had done on similar occasions. It was for nothing else than to try the steadfastness of these young men, and see whether they had courage and nerve enough for what they proposed to take in hand. The letter continued—

"He replied to all, and his eyes sparkled while he spoke,—Life was nothing to him, he would not retreat a step; the act being accomplished, he would cry *Vive l'Italia!* Tyrants were too audacious, because secure through other men's cowardice; that barrier should be broken through. He felt himself destined for the work. He had kept a picture of Charles Albert in his room, and by constantly looking at it had given more and more predominance to his idea. He ended by convincing me that he was one of those beings whose purposes are a matter between their own consciences and God, and whom Providence from time to time lets loose upon earth (like Harmodius of yore) to teach despots that the limit of their power rests in the hand of one single man. And I asked him what he required of me? 'A passport and a little money.' "

Well, what did M. Mazzini give him? He said—

"I gave him a thousand francs, and said he would get a passport in Ticino. While passing the St. Gothard he wrote me a few words full of enthusiasm; he had prostrated himself on the side of the Alps, and had turned towards Italy, swearing to do the deed. He got a passport in Ticino, in the name of Mariotti. Arrived in Turin, he had an interview with a member of the committee of the association, whose name I had given him. The offer was accepted. Projects were decided upon. The deed was to done in a long passage at the court, through which the King passed every Sunday when going to the Royal Chapel. Some persons who got a special ticket, were allowed there to see the King. The committee was able to procure a ticket. Gallenga went with this, without arms, to study the ground; he saw the King, and was more determined than ever—at least he said so. It was decided that the act should be accomplished on the following Sunday."

Then came a passage which the House will do well to bear in mind—

"Then being afraid in those moments of organized terror to look out for a weapon in Turin, they sent a member of the committee, Sciandra, a merchant now dead, through Chambery to Geneva to ask me for arms and notify the day to me."

The House ought to understand that M. Mazzini, according to the hon. Member for Halifax, is incapable of assassination. But the hon. Gentleman did not also add that he is incapable of instigating to assassination; for what I have already read proves, that the hon. Gentleman's friend is not incapable of instigating to that deed. But let the House be good enough to mark the next passage—

"A poniard with a *lapis lazuli* handle, a gift which I cherished much, was on the table; I pointed to that. Sciandra took it and went away."

With reference to the work on "The Dagger," which was alluded to the other evening by my hon. Friend the Member for the King's County, I understand that

M. Mazzini has written a letter to *The Times*, in which he spoke of something being intended to be the moral dagger. The House will however, I think, agree with me, that that poniard with the *lapis lazuli* handle was certainly not meant to be the "moral dagger." The letter went on—

"But the committee, learning that the Carabineers were posted two doors from that of the regicide, and knowing nothing of Angelini, concluded that the Government had been warned of the plot and were in search of Gallenga. They therefore made him leave the city, and sent him to a country house outside Turin, telling him that the attempt could not be made on that Sunday, but that if things got quiet, they would call him in for one of the Sundays following. One or two Sundays afterwards they sent for him; he was not to be found; he had gone off, and I saw him again in Switzerland. . . . He put his name to circulars printed in Turin, intended to magnify the Piedmontese Monarchy. He was selected by the Government for some petty embassy in Germany; later he was, and is, a deputy."

I really think that if confirmation be wanted of the disposition of M. Mazzini to instigate to assassination, none could be supplied of a stronger kind than that which I have just quoted. If further confirmation, however, be needed, it is only necessary to refer to the correspondence to which my hon. Friend the Member for King's County had also alluded, between Daniel Manin, the ex-dictator of Venice, and M. Mazzini, in which M. Mazzini defends and glorifies on principle the acts which, in the case of Gallenga and King Charles Albert, he had sanctioned in practice. There was another point which I shall be obliged to the hon. Member for Halifax if, in his reply to me, he will be good enough to answer. M. Mazzini, in his letter to *The Times* of the 16th, states that a speech which was delivered in this House on this subject was unsupported by legal evidence. Now, Sir, the Members of this House are men of honour in every respect, and do not require legal evidence on all occasions. Moral evidence, and strong probability, will in general be enough for us. I think I may state in this House composed of Gentlemen of honour, that we do not want legal evidence upon all occasions, but that moral evidence is enough for us. I will take the liberty of putting another question to the hon. Gentleman. The leading journal mentions a bank note which was issued in the name of the Italian Liberation Society, and at the foot of that note there is given a London agent, and that agent is James Stansfeld; and there is also given a direction to 2,

Sir Henry Stracey

Sydney Place, Brompton. Now it will be satisfactory if the hon. Gentleman will tell us whether he ever lived at 2, Sydney Place, Brompton, or if he ever had any connection with that address. It is not an old matter, and perhaps the hon. Gentleman may have had an opportunity of referring to it; because, according to *The Times*, not only this note, but others emanating from the same source, can be produced. Under these circumstances, I am not wrong in feeling that the Motion which I now submit is not altogether superfluous. In those remarks of the Procureur Général which were mentioned by the hon. Member for Finsbury (Mr. Cox) the other night, the name of Mr. Flower was given. Now we have never had a straightforward or direct answer. The only direct answer which has been vouchsafed has come from him who is the reputed instigator of plots to assassination—M. Mazzini; but from the hon. Gentleman, one of the Ministers of the Government opposite, I do not think there has come any explanation in answer to the question of the hon. Gentleman the Member for Finsbury. But the explanation which we received from the instigator of conspiracies himself, M. Mazzini, is that certain letters were sent for him to the hon. Gentleman's house, and that they were sent with various others by his (Mazzini's) friends. A question was put by my hon. Friend the Member for King's County (Mr. Hennessy), who wished to know whether Mr. Flower was in truth M. Mazzini, and the hon. Member for Halifax answered, "I can have no knowledge of that. I know nothing of it." Afterwards the noble Lord the Member for Tyrone (Lord Claude Hamilton) put the following question, to which no reply was given. The noble Lord said, "I should like to know from the hon. Member for Halifax whether M. Fuori is not an intimate acquaintance of the hon. Gentleman, whether he has not visited at his house, and whether he is not in fact the secretary of Mazzini." I have further to ask whether M. Fuori is that Mr. Flower mentioned by Greco, and to whom the letters were to be addressed, and I have no doubt when the hon. Gentleman gets up he will give us an answer to these particular questions, and further to say whether "Mr. Flower," to whom letters were to be addressed, was the "Mr. Flower, of 35, Thurloe Square." But, in the absence of explanation, the strange silence observed with respect to such direct questions as have been put, creates the impression either that the hon. Gentleman has not the power or the means to clear up the mystery, or else his lips are sealed by friendly feeling for this instigator of conspiracies. The hon. Gentleman indeed said that he "had not been the medium which some gentlemen seemed to imagine." Well; that is a very easy way of answering, but it is not an answer as direct as the House has a right to expect. It is not by showing indignation that Members of this House are to be satisfied. I may take the liberty of saying that generally when a man is afraid to answer a particular charge —that nine cases out of ten, when the matter will not bear probing—that man will put himself into a rage. That is a general feeling. This much is clear, I think, that with respect to Greco—who was, doubtless, an enthusiastic patriot in Mazzini's estimation, but of whom latterly he was rather ashamed, and, perhaps, when his diabolical designs were promulgated to the world he endeavoured to shake off— that when questions connected with so serious a plot were addressed to the hon. Member for Halifax and the Under Secretary for Foreign Affairs, instead of "repelling such remarks with contempt," or declaring it "unworthy of the Government to notice such insinuations," they would have acted more worthily in speaking out plainly like honourable men. Members were sent to Parliament by their constituents to sift and inquire into public matters of every kind, to investigate everything concerning the welfare of the country, and it was unbecoming in gentlemen filling high official positions to return evasive or other than straightforward answers. I cannot help thinking it would have been more becoming on the part of the hon. Member for Halifax if he had expressed his regret to this House, instead of putting himself into a defiant attitude and adopting an irritable manner, and, if I may make use of the term, a swaggering tone. Allow me to say, sir, that the Emperor of the French having shown so friendly a feeling and exhibited so generous a disposition towards this country, Englishmen generally felt he ought to have been treated with greater courtesy than has been manifested in the silence and indifference with which the remarks of the Procureur Général were received. Surely it was incumbent upon Her Majesty's Government, for the sake of their own dignity, to ask for explanations as to the right of the Procureur Général to

make these remarks, and rather to compel him to substantiate his charges, or at once openly and straightforwardly to refute his statements. But who has given any information at all? Certainly not the Government as represented by the hon. Member for Halifax, nor by the hon. Gentleman the Under Secretary for Foreign affairs. I beg to say that, so far as my opinion is concerned—and I have consulted others upon the subject — I believe that the conduct of the Government will be looked upon neither as English-like nor straightforward, nor will it add to the respect in which we are held abroad. On the contrary, I fear it will add to the load of humiliation which we are suffering in foreign estimation. Now, sir, were there any just grounds for the remark of the Procureur Général? Let us think for a moment. A letter is found which belongs to a man convicted of a conspiracy to murder—there is a letter found amongst his papers that directed him to apply for money at the house of an English gentleman, now a Member of this House, and now one of Her Majesty's ministers. That gentleman has himself acknowledged that he is the intimate friend of Mazzini—that he is a friend of eighteen years' standing. Surely, sir, with such a chain of evidence was not the Procureur Général justified in making these remarks? I was sorry to hear the Under Secretary for Foreign Affairs deny that he had had any correspondence with France upon the subject, and I only trust that such correspondence may be thought to be more necessary in the future than in the past; and I also trust that the hon. Member for Halifax will in point of candour take a lesson out of the book even of this instigator to murder. I prefaced my remarks with those with which I desire to conclude, and I hope I have not trespassed a moment longer than necessary, but I beg to assure the hon. Gentleman that these remarks are not made with any kind of animus on my part. It is, I assure you, a painful duty to me to make them, because they reflect upon a man whom I may call young, and who has shown considerable talent in this House, and who is, at any rate, ascending the ladder of advancement, and has reached a certain distinction—and I cannot but feel that I may by this Motion— for a time at least—imperil that advancement. [*Laughter.*] It may be a laughing matter to some gentlemen of unfeeling principles, but I do not treat it as a

K

laughing matter, nor do I think it is so felt by the hon. Gentleman himself. I introduced this question because the replies which have been made have been most unsatisfactory. I think the dignity of the House has been compromised, and in consequence the dignity of the country. I will state nothing further, but will only beg leave to move,

"That the statement of the Procureur Général on the trial of Greco, implicating a Member of this House and of Her Majesty's Government in the plot for the assassination of our ally the Emperor of the French, deserves the serious consideration of this House."

Lord CLAUD HAMILTON seconded the Motion.

Amendment proposed,

To leave out from the word "That" to the end of the Question, in order to add the words "the statement of the Procureur Général on the trial of Greco, implicating a Member of this House and of Her Majesty's Government in the plot for the assassination of our Ally the Emperor of the French, deserves the serious consideration of this House,"—(*Sir Henry Stracey.*)

—instead thereof.

Question proposed, "That the words proposed to be left out stand part of the Question."

Mr. STANSFELD : Sir, it is not my intention to say one word in reply to the strictures of the hon. Baronet upon the character of Signor Mazzini. I have already fulfilled that which I believe to be a duty in bearing my testimony to the character of a man whom I have known for many years. As far as I am concerned, I do not think it fitting that that discussion should be continued, and as far as I am concerned it is now at an end. I will now address myself to the Motion of the hon. Baronet so far as it concerns myself and my character. The very terms of that Motion appear to me to justify the course which I pursued when this question was first introduced to the notice of the House. The hon. Baronet taking up this statement of the Procureur Général, moves that "that statement, implicating a Member of this House and a Member of Her Majesty's Government, in a plot for the assassination of the Emperor of the French, deserves the serious consideration of the House." Now, Sir, right or wrong, I put the same construction upon the statement of the Procureur Général which has been put upon it by the hon. Baronet. I hold in my hand a copy of *The Times* of the 1st of March, and in it I find the statement

Sir Henry Stracey

of the Procureur Général given in these words—

"I searched in the *London Commercial Almanack* and in the *Post Office Directory* to ascertain who could be the person placed in correspondence with Greco. At page 670 I found the answer, and it is not without sorrow that I recognize the name of a Member of the English Parliament, who already in 1857 had been constituted by Mazzini treasurer to the Tibaldi plot which was directed against the Emperor's life."

I must say, Sir, that it appeared to me then, and it still appears to me, that an imputation so odious, and, as I shall presently show, so utterly unsupported by the evidence adduced upon this trial, was one which I could only fittingly meet by a denial which, although general, I believe to have been complete, and which I do not think the House will consider it unnatural should be accompanied by some expression of indignation and contempt. What, Sir, was the evidence adduced upon this trial ? The hon. Baronet has supposed—I cannot believe that he has read the evidence—but he has supposed that it was to this effect, —that Greco was directed to apply to some person at my address for money for the purpose of this plot. Why, Sir, even supposing the letter which was found upon Greco's person to have been Signor Mazzini's production, that letter did not refer him to my address, but to another address, for money. Upon him was stated to have been found a slip of paper on which was written — it does not appear in whose handwriting—" Mr. Flower, 35, Thurloe square." Now, that is the whole extent of the evidence from which the Procureur Général chose to draw these extraordinary inferences. The Procureur Général also refers to Tibaldi's plot in 1857, and states that I had been constituted by Mazzini treasurer of that plot. What was the evidence with respect to that, not brought forward in this trial, but quoted by the Procureur Général ? It was two supposed excerpts from notes of Signor Mazzini, referring persons in vague terms to my address for money if they required it. That was the whole extent of the evidence as far as the Tibaldi plot was concerned. Now I am perfectly free to admit that with that evidence before the Procureur Général, he or his Government would have been perfectly justified in asking for explanations upon a question of that kind ; but I cannot admit for a moment that any man accustomed to consider evidence and inclined to fair play would have been led to the conclusion which the Procureur Général was induced to express upon that occasion. [*Cries of* " Deny, deny !" *and* " Order, Order !"] I am about to deny. I am about to say that I did not think it fitting that I should give any other but a general denial to a statement of that kind. But the circumstances are now entirely changed. The whole subject is before the House by virtue of the Motion of the hon. Baronet. I have, therefore, no longer any hesitation or any difficulty. I feel it, of course, no indignity to offer to the House any explanations which the House may think requisite or fitting, or to answer any questions which the House may think it desirable that I should answer. Let me take the statement of the Procureur Général. He states that I was a person placed in correspondence with Greco. Now, Sir, neither directly nor indirectly, neither by letter nor personally, have I ever had any communication with that person. I never even heard his name, nor knew of his existence, until I saw in the papers the report of his arrest with his accomplices for the late conspiracy. [An hon. MEMBER : That is not the question.] [*Cries of* " Question !" *and* " Order !"] To go back to the case of Tibaldi. Signor Mazzini has already voluntarily written to the press, stating that no such supposed fund or plot ever existed, and that, of course, he never asked me to act as treasurer to any such fund. It is hardly necessary, I hope, for me to say that which I now do say very distinctly, that I have never held any funds, that I have never advanced any money, for any such purpose or for any purpose whatever, to the persons who were named in connection with that conspiracy. It is one thing to have had a long personal intimacy with a man, and another thing to be implicated in his undertakings, whether of a character which will bear investigation or of a character such as those which have been attributed to M. Mazzini. The hon. Baronet has referred to the trial of Orsini, and has suggested that my name was connected with that trial. I do not know how to reply to that assertion, because it is the first time that I have heard that my name was ever connected with it. If the hon. Baronet, or any other Member of this House will adduce any evidence or make any statement in corroboration of that assertion, I shall be ready to answer it. Then the hon. Baronet has referred to ʌrtain notes—and here he approached the

region of something like facts. In the year 1850, immediately after the fall of the Roman Republic, I was requested to allow my name to be placed on the back of these notes as a reference in case persons might apply to take them, their object being to aid in the accomplishment of Italian unity and independence. I am perfectly ready to admit that I assented to my name being so used, but very shortly after giving my consent—I believe within a very few weeks—I saw reason to question the propriety, and even the legality, of that step. I thought I was justified in taking the counsel and opinion of a very old friend of mine, a very eminent member of the legal profession, Mr. Serjeant Manning. I took his opinion, and, acting upon his opinion and advice, I requested, and my request was, of course, immediately complied with —that my name should be withdrawn from those notes. These are the simple facts —I have nothing to state to-night but simple facts—these are the simple facts, as far as I know them, in which the House can be interested in this matter. I have no objection if any other question occurs to the mind of any hon. Member to answer it. [*Cries of* " Flower, Flower."] I can have no hesitation in answering any questions which may be put by the House. I therefore now leave the subject. [" Flower, Flower."] I should add this if the House will allow me. I have omitted to notice one important part of the matter —the use to which my house has been put. Well, of course the natural consequences of the intimate personal relationship with M. Mazzini, which I have never for a moment hesitated to acknowledge, accounts for that. M. Mazzini's letters, as the House will easily understand, have not for many years been able to reach him through the foreign post if addressed in his own name. He has, therefore, very naturally asked his various English friends —of whom I am one—to allow letters to be addressed to their houses. Letters for him have in that way been addressed to my house among others. Those letters to him have been addressed to my house under a name which has been mentioned here. They have been addressed to my house under the name, among others, of " Signor Fiore." I need not say, that of the contents of those letters I have always been entirely ignorant. The name Flower is, as the House of course understands, the translation of the word Fiore ; but I do not believe that any letter was ever addressed to my house for M. Mazzini in the name of Flower. I entirely admit, at the same time, that it is not advisable, that it is not fitting, whatever may be the nature of M. Mazzini's correspondence, that it should be addressed to the residence of a person occupying the position which I have the honour to hold. It has not been necessary for me to make any suggestion of that kind to M. Mazzini—he has himself volunteered to state that he has taken measures to prevent his letters being addressed to my residence. I have contented myself with a simple statement of facts. I repeat that I have no knowledge of any of those transactions to which the hon. Baronet refers, and I now leave this question without any further remark in the hands of the House.

LORD HARRY VANE: Sir, I am one of those who have heard with regret some of the explanations which have been just offered by the hon. Gentleman. I certainly think the House will admit that the explanations which the hon. Gentleman has given us to-night is of a more satisfactory character than that which we heard the other night. What he stated the other night was no explanation at all. It was simply a defence of the character of M. Mazzini. Now, we have nothing to do here with the character of Mazzini. Certainly, it is not our duty to defend it. We have no right to go against the whole moral sense of Europe. We are not called upon, and we ought not to set ourselves against the opinions of united Europe. I say, without fear of contradiction, that in every part of Europe—among all classes—among all ranks—among all men of honourable feeling, there is but one feeling, but one sentiment, with respect to the general conduct, feelings, principles, and actions of M. Mazzini. It is a mistake to suppose that that opinion with respect to him is confined alone to the Imperialist party in France. I speak from personal knowledge, and from a large acquaintance with the people of France. I have discussed this subject elsewhere. I know that of men of all sides, of all principles, of all colours, except, perhaps, the remnant of the party of 1793, including even the republicans, who were supporters of General Cavaignac, all condemn the principles of M. Mazzini. There is no one whose ideas and whose name are now held in such abhorrence throughout Europe. No one ever suspected that the hon. Gentleman himself has been guilty of participation

in the horrible plot which has been referred to. But no one can deny that the hon. Gentleman has been guilty of great imprudence in allowing, according to his own admission, letters to be addressed to his house in order that correspondence might be carried on from the Continent with M. Mazzini. The hon. Gentleman not having had cognizance of the exact nature of the correspondence, how was he to answer for the consequences? I say that the French Government, the French people, and the French Chamber, have a perfect right to complain of the conduct on the part of an Englishman, who having the honour of a seat in this House should, by his feelings for Italian liberty, have been betrayed into such an act of imprudence—and I do not impute any more serious fault to the hon. Gentleman. But nothing could produce a more unfortunate effect on the Continent than the statement he formerly made; but I am happy to think ho has now altogether admitted that he has broken off all connection with M. Mazzini. The hon. Gentleman may remain the permanent friend of Mazzini—may even sympathize with him in his opinions, but he has no right to found upon these opinions acts that tend to compromise this House—or to compromise, as I think he has compromised, the Government with which he is connected—and even, in my opinion, the English people. When a man in a situation like that the hon. Gentleman occupies acts as he has done, opinions are naturally imputed to him which he does not entertain. Certainly, he has unwarily made himself the agent of doctrines and opinions which he should be the first to repudiate. I am happy he has given us his explanation. Knowing the effect elsewhere, I think the matter is in many respects to be deplored. I hope, however, the hon. Gentleman has had a lesson for the future, and that he will show more prudence than he has hitherto exhibited.

LORD HENRY LENNOX: No one is more averse than I am to enter into any controversy in this House which can be considered of a personal nature. But there are some questions which, though immediately personal in appearance, are of great and paramount interest to the country, and I venture to say that the question now before the House is of that kind. The hon. Gentleman has stated that, on the first occasion, he expressed his feeling of indignation and astonishment at the speech of the Procureur Général. His indignation can well be felt and sympathized with; but I own the astonishment of the hon. Gentleman astonishes me. Until I heard the speech of the hon. Gentleman to-night, I was not aware that this was the first time he had learnt that his name had ever been implicated in any of the attempts of M. Mazzini. [Mr. STANSFELD: I said Orsini.] But I hold in my hand a statement, which I copied from a newspaper of the day, in which the facts are narrated — the *acte d'accusation*, which translated into English, may be called the bill of indictment against Orsini in August, 1857, and in which the name of Mr. Stansfeld occurs. It is an extract—I translate it from the *Moniteur*—

"Two other names more ought to be cited—that of Mr. James Stansfeld, brewer, of London, who has made himself banker of Mazzini. *Enfin*, two new assassins were to be proposed by Massarenti at Genoa, where he was. Mazzini charged Campanella to judge in his place if they ought to be admitted to assist in their detestable design, and in case Campanella accepted them, he invited him, as well as Massarenti, to get money from the brewer Stansfeld. At the same time, the address of the brewer Stansfeld of London was seized in the portfolio of Tibaldi."

The prisoner, according to the French law, is examined and allowed to criminate himself. Tibaldi was asked—

"In your portmanteau was found the address of a brewer (le Sieur James Stansfeld) known as being the banker of Mazzini?"

The answer was of a very peculiar nature. It was this—

"Yes, but because he was to introduce me to some English opticians for the sale of my goods."

That was the answer given in that solemn inquiry. I have no further knowledge than I have derived from the public journal of the day; but I agree in the general principles touched on by the noble Lord. There can be no doubt these events have produced a most painful effect on the mind of Europe. I am one of those who think that it is a great disgrace to this country, that when any trial occurs for some detestable crime upon the person of a foreign Sovereign, it is always said to be in England, in London, that the plot is hatched and the money obtained. The Motion, therefore, of the hon. Baronet I think well timed. We should recollect that, on a previous occasion, the great cry was — This House can do nothing, because there has been a pressure put on it by a foreign Government. We are now told, "Oh, you are discussing a question here which has been forgotten in France," but I beg to assure the House that such is not the case. I have had letters from countrymen of our own residing in Paris, who inform me that the feeling there is most deep on the subject, and that nothing but the strong hand of the Emperor has been able to suppress such public ebullitions of feeling as would greatly endanger the peace and good understanding which it is so desirable should continue to exist between the two countries. I can assure the House that I have it from Englishmen, and not from Frenchmen, or from men whose sympathies are Imperialist, that the feeling in France is deep set, and that nothing, as I said before, but the power of the Emperor could keep it in check, ready as it is to burst forth under this renewed proof that plots and assassinations have their nest and original hiding place in this—I am happy to think—abode of freedom for the people of all nations.

MR. P. A. TAYLOR said, he thought the House would scarcely be likely to receive any increase of dignity from the fact of its becoming the sounding board for the scandalous tittle-tattle of the police courts of Paris. For his own part, he had no hesitation in stating that he had, for many years, been the intimate friend of Signor Mazzini. He stood, therefore, in some respects, in the same relation to that gentleman as his hon. Friend the Member for Halifax, and wished to explain to any further extent which might be necessary, in order that the House might thoroughly understand the matter, the question of the way in which letters to M. Mazzini, while in this country, happened to be addressed. It would be easily comprehended by all those who were acquainted with the relations which subsisted between the Post Office and the Governments of Europe, that any one engaged, as M. Mazzini had been, in politics and political conspiracy against tyranny, might as well have any letters posted to him from Italy burnt as expect that they would be delivered to him in London, if addressed in his own name. He, therefore, was ready to acknowledge that, in common with other friends of Signor Mazzini, he had for years past placed his address at that gentleman's disposal. Hon. Members would, however, he had no doubt, have the candour at once to perceive and to admit that that circumstance not only did not imply the slightest possibility of conspiracy for assassination on the part of those who thus granted the privilege which he mentioned, but not even the slightest knowledge of what the letters so addressed might contain. For his own part, he had had letters for M. Mazzini addressed to his house under a variety of names, and had sometimes smiled at the simple means used to avoid suspicion, means which would be of little avail if the writers had the English Post Office to deceive. If anybody asked him whether any of the letters which came to his house for M. Mazzini were addressed M. Flower, he could not undertake to say whether such was or was not the case. He had letters addressed to himself which contained certain indications inside to show that they were meant for M. Mazzini. Some were addressed in Italian, which, he was sorry to say, he did not understand, and those he had forwarded to M. Mazzini, stating that being written in Italian, they were probably intended for him, adding, "If not, you will return them to me and tell me what is in them." He was not at all astonished to find that surprize was expressed that English gentlemen and Members of Parliament should have such confidence in a person such as hon. Members opposite believed M. Mazzini to be; while he regretted extremely to hear the observations which had been made by the noble Lord who had spoken, and to find the House of Commons made the vehicle for the miserable calumnies of the reactionary party in Europe. He might add that to those who knew M. Mazzini only from the calumnious reports of the press for the last twenty years, the respect, esteem, and affection which those who had the honour of his aquaintance entertained for him were, no doubt, matter of astonishment, but for that it was easy to account.

SIR JOHN PAKINGTON : I will detain the House but a very few moments. I should be very glad if I could avoid intruding on its attention at all, for during my not very short experience in this Assembly, the present is one of the most painful occasions which I can recollect. I cannot agree with the noble Lord the Member for Hastings (Lord Harry Vane) in the opinion he has expressed, that the explanations which we have heard tonight from the hon. Member for Halifax may be regarded as satisfactory, while I do concur with the noble Lord in thinking that the language and explanation which we first heard from the hon. Gentleman were both unsatisfactory and ill judged. That being so, I cannot see how what has fallen from him this evening has very

much altered the position of affairs. I speak, I am sure, with no prejudice against the hon. Gentleman. I recognize the ability which he has displayed in this House, and I quite agree with the noble Lord, that there is not a man among us who would for a single moment think of imputing to the hon. Gentleman any intentional complicity with assassins. But what are the facts of the case as they stand? Signor Mazzini is the avowed associate and adviser of the assassin Greco. He is the avowed associate of the assassin Gallenga, and for years the hon. Gentleman opposite has been the intimate friend and associate of this friend and adviser of assassins. These are the plain facts of the case, and I cannot help thinking that something is due to the dignity of this House and to the feelings of our French allies, who are naturally irritated and angry at finding these foul plots one after another brought to maturity in this country. It is painful to us, and must be painful to our neighbours, to learn that a person holding the high position of a Member of Parliament and a situation in Her Majesty's Government has now lived for years as the intimate associate of Mazzini. On this subject, however, I do not wish to dwell at greater length than simply to address an inquiry to the noble Lord at the head of the Government. I think the statement made by the Procureur Général at the trial of Greco, implicating, as it did —whether rightly or wrongly I do not now stop to inquire—a Member of Her Majesty's Government, required that some communication should be made and some explanation offered by the head of the Government of England to the Government of France with respect to a circumstance of a character so singular and unsatisfactory. I wish, therefore, to ask the noble Lord the First Minister whether, on the part of the English Government, he has taken any notice in communicating with the French Government of the statement in question; and, if not, whether it is his intention to do so? It must, in my opinion, depend on the answer of the noble Lord to that inquiry what part this House ought now to take; and if the noble Lord's reply is not satisfactory, I am sorry to say that, in my opinion, it will be the duty of my hon. Friend to press his Motion to a division.

VISCOUNT PALMERSTON : Nothing, no doubt, can in general be more painful than personal discussions in this House. I cannot at the same time express any regret that the hon. Baronet opposite has brought this subject to-night under our consideration, because it has drawn from my hon. Friend beside me an explanation which, differing from the right hon. Gentleman who has just spoken, I think perfectly satisfactory, conveying as it did an absolute and total denial of the only charge which has been insinuated against him—that of having any cognizance whatsoever of the plot against the Emperor of the French which had recently been the subject of investigation in France. The right hon. Baronet asks me whether Her Majesty's Government have deemed it right to make any communication to the Government of France with respect to a passage in the speech of an advocate at the trial. Well, Sir, my answer is "No." We have no right to take cognizance of what takes place in a court of justice in France. If there was an opinion that anything which passed upon that occasion amounted to a charge against my hon. Friend, that he had any connection, direct or indirect, with that assassin, an answer to the imputation, to the insinuation, was given by my hon. Friend to this House, and publicly to the world—a complete refutation even to suspicion. But I will fairly own that I should have felt humiliated if I had been a party to a communication to the French Government to tell them that an English gentleman, a Member of Parliament holding office under the Government, was not connected with an infamous plot against the Emperor's life. I congratulate hon. Gentlemen opposite upon the feelings and sentiments which seem to actuate them upon the present occasion. We have been told that the imputations—false as they were—of the Procureur Général have excited the indignation of the French nation, and that something is due to the feelings of France to remove the impression which they entertain, that something or other has taken place in this country which is equal to—if not an acquiescence—at least to an absence of disclaimer of any participation in the attempt that was to have been made. We have been reminded of the Orsini conspiracy in the year 1858. Then there was an attempt upon the life of the Emperor, not suspected, not intercepted, but actually made. What did the Government of that time do? We spontaneously proposed to the House a measure which was intended to prevent a recurrence of similar attempts. Hon. Gentlemen oppo-

site formally, publicly expressed their approval of the step and promised their support. But when they found that, by a combination of circumstances, a dereliction of their promises and the absolute abandonment of their own opinions might lead to a change of Government, they threw over their promises, they cast their indignation to the winds, and joined in condemning that of which before they had expressed their approval. In point of fact, they refused to grant the satisfaction which they now say is due to the French people. I say then, Sir, that the language they hold on the present occasion, directed against a Member of the Government, needs no explanation, except by referring to the events of that time. With regard to my hon. Friend, I say that if I thought for a moment that my hon. Friend could have had the slightest participation in the transaction to which this discussion refers, I should have represented to him that it would be more becoming that he should cease to be a Member of the Government. I have not done so; and I have not done so because I know my hon. Friend to be incapable of participation in any such abominable and atrocious a transaction. Therefore, I say I do not regret the Motion of the hon. Baronet, because it has afforded to my hon. Friend an opportunity of repeating the disclaimer which, I think, he sufficiently made upon the former occasion; but as that is not considered to have been sufficient, then I think what he has said this evening ought to be conclusive reason to the House and to the country why the Motion of the hon. Baronet should not be deemed acceptable.

MR. DISRAELI: Sir, I confess I am disappointed at the tone which has been adopted by the noble Lord. I think the noble Lord to-night had an opportunity—a golden opportunity—of extricating the House from a painful position, and to place it in relation to an ally of this country in one which would have become him, and in which he might have done justice not only to his colleagues but to the character of the House in which he has sat so long, and in which he must take a deep interest. The noble Lord, instead of taking the line which my right hon. Friend (Sir John Pakington), animated by the most proper spirit, indicated as one he believed the House expected the noble Lord to follow, unfortunately seems to have taken refuge in that vein to which he is too accustomed to resort. He said they had not applied to the French Government because they could not submit to the humiliation. The noble Lord, however, forgets that he is the head of a Government who when they have felt it to be their duty have not permitted the word "humiliation" to induce them to refrain from a course which they deemed to be expedient. I thought it was very unfortunate that the noble Lord, after telling the House that he would submit to no humiliation —the act of humiliation being a friendly representation to a friendly foreign Government—I thought it very unfortunate that the noble Lord should immediately recal to the recollection of the House the circumstances of 1858. I think some regard to the feelings of the President of the Board of Trade should have restrained him. I think he should have shown some regard to the feelings of one "absent" Member, Earl Russell. The noble Lord should be ashamed of attacking by innuendo an absent man. But, says the noble Lord, with heedless rhetoric, What had we to complain of? Are we to apply to a foreign Government, because one of my colleagues has been accused by some foreign official of that which he did not perpetrate, and which he has openly denied? Why, Sir, this leads us, after all the noise of the noble Lord, to recur to the real question before us. The statement of the noble Lord proved that he did not understand the very point upon which of all others he should have directed the judgment of the House. Let us see, in the first place, what occurred. The Procureur Général, the Attorney General of a foreign country, makes a public statement in a court of the highest consideration in France, and what is the statement? He says that a Member of the British Parliament—and what, perhaps, he was not aware of at the time, a Member of the Administration—had been, he was sorry to say, the medium by which Mazzini communicated with the conspirators against the life of his Sovereign. Did the hon. Member for Halifax deny the statement? Why he admitted it, and he explained it. He told us the letters came to his house— he, sitting by the side of the noble Lord who has misstated his whole case, does not deny that letters did come, and that his house in Thurloe Square was the medium for communication between Mazzini and his correspondents. Does he deny that? [Mr. STANSFELD: What correspondents?] What correspondents? You know them better than I do, I suppose. "What cor-

respondents?" asks the Member for Halifax. Why, the assassins of Europe. "What correspondents?" asks the Member for Halifax. Why, the advocates of anarchy throughout the Continent. "What correspondents?" asks the Member for Halifax. Why, the men who point their poniards at the breast of our allies. Why, Sir, this is the most unfortunate movement on the part of the noble Lord I have ever witnessed. Still smarting under the successful combination of his present Colleague the President of the Board of Trade in 1858, labouring under a confused idea that the course he then pursued towards a foreign Power was a great blunder, he is now positively inert, and will not perform the first duty which civilization, if no other reason, demands. Why, the charge made by the highest legal authority in France against the hon. Member for Halifax is one which the hon. Member has himself admitted. It is that his house was the medium of communication between Mazzini and his correspondents, and yet the noble Lord says the hon. Member for Halifax has denied the charge, and Under Secretaries of State and others have treated with contempt this charge which is now admitted. I am willing to give to the hon. Member for Halifax, or to any Gentleman who sits in this House, the most favourable interpretation of their conduct. I say that, even to those who have listened with scandalous levity to charges of so grave a character. But nobody denies that sufficient has occurred to require on the part of the Government a friendly, temperate, dignified, and, if necessary, confidential communication to the foreign Government. Take our own case. Supposing the Attorney General here had made a statement, after an important State trial in this country, that he regretted to find that one of the most eminent members of the Chamber of Deputies in France had made his house the machinery of communication between foreigners and conspirators against our Sovereign, would you be surprised if the representative of the French Emperor were to ask for some explanation of such statement, and if proof had been given of the accuracy of such statement, as has been so lavishly admitted by the noble Lord, would it not have been his duty to have expressed his deep regret that such circumstances should have occurred — that such incidents should have happened? Judge by your own feelings what you would have expected the representatives of your Sovereign to do. But what is the course which the Government now wishes us to follow ? It is the universal feeling of this country that the dignity of this House is compromised, and I am sorry to say, after the speech of the noble Lord, that the dignity of the Government is also compromised. What my right hon. Friend suggested in no spirit of unfriendliness would have avoided division, and would have afforded the noble Lord an opportunity, while vindicating the dignity of this House, to come forward and take those steps, so easy for a person of his great position, which would have removed the extreme apprehension and disquietude which this affair has occasioned. After the speech of the hon. Member for Halifax he had only to come forward and say that, from this evening, he should feel it his duty to make communications by which regret should be expressed, that even unconsciously the house of one who is considered to be a Minister of the Crown should be made the medium and machinery of the communications of conspirators and assassins. The offer has been refused —the noble Lord will not assert the dignity of the House of Commons, and I think the House of Commons ought to assert its own. The noble Lord has rejected the proposition of my right hon. Friend, made in a becoming spirit, and it is for the House of Commons to conduct itself in a spirit equally becoming. After the rejection of our proposal by the noble Lord, I see no course to take sufficient to maintain the dignity of this House, and to place it in its proper position before Europe, but to support the Motion of my hon. Friend.

Mr. BRIGHT : Sir, I wish I could persuade myself that the excitement manifested by hon. Gentlemen opposite to-night had so good a foundation as might be built upon a strong anxiety to preserve friendly relations with France, and to maintain the honour and dignity of this House. But I think I discern in the temper which they have manifested very different motives, which make me believe that they are not in a condition to take a very impartial and just view of this case. What is that which we are now called upon to consider ? I do not say that the circumstances which have arisen are not such as to excite some surprise and some dissatisfaction. But let us in considering them not be unjust or ungenerous to a Member of this House. We all sit here by equal right. I confess—and

I do so with much pleasure—that during the twenty years I have had a seat in this House, although there has been temporary passion, yet in the end, and sometimes after only a few minutes' consideration, the House has been willing to do justice to every one of its Members. Let us not, then, treat this question, in which the hon. Member for Halifax is so deeply involved, and in which his feelings, no doubt, have been greatly excited—let us not discuss it in a spirit which is unfair and ungenerous to him. What are the facts ? We know that in this country and for many years past, there has been a great enthusiasm amongst certain persons, sometimes amongst considerable classes of the people, in favour of political refugees—refugees here sometimes from the oppression and from the wrongs of the Governments from which they fled—refugees sometimes, it may be, for offences against those Governments that could not easily be defended. We have had the questions of Poland, of Hungary, and of Italy. Who is there in this House who was here ten years ago that does not recollect the late Lord Dudley Stuart? He was a man of the most amiable character, but he had a burning, an unquenchable enthusiasm with regard to the Poles. Take the hon. and learned Gentleman the Member for the King's County, who during the last twelve months has made himself distinguished by his advocacy of the claims of Poland. We have had a very eminent man in this country who for several years was connected with the politics of Hungary. He had zealous friends amongst us—and we have had also refugees, and not a few, from Italy. Who is there who will say he never felt any sentiment of sympathy with some at least of the Italian refugees? Now, I am one of those who on the whole rather discouraged the course which has been taken by some English enthusiasts in this House with regard to those exiles from abroad. I thought that their conduct was likely on some occasion to embarrass the Government, to embarrass Parliament, and to embarrass our diplomacy abroad ; and therefore I have given generally very little favour to the enthusiasm I have seen. But still, if I did not feel sympathy for the refugees that have been driven here I would despise myself ; and if there be any man in this House who will stand up and say he never felt a particle of sympathy for the refugees that have been driven to our country, I say I despise him. Take the precise case of the hon. Member for Halifax and Mazzini. I believe there is no man acquainted with Mazzini who will not acknowledge that, so far as can be known of his character from personal association with him, he is a man of the most profound devotion. [An hon. MEMBER: "To the dagger!"] That devotion may not be to the principles of some hon. Gentlemen opposite, but he has a profound devotion to the principle of the unity and independence of Italy. Every one who has been associated with him will admit that he is a man of a character powerful and fascinating, and that he obtains over those with whom he associates a singular influence. There are few persons that ever were acquainted with him who, apart from this special question we are now discussing, would not express for him the highest admiration. One of the statements that the hon. Baronet opposite read refers, I believe, to thirty years ago. I don't know Mazzini's age, but I believe that he might be at that time five and twenty. Consider what his compatriots in Italy have suffered. I think I have read that the right hon. Gentleman who just sat down, in one of his early writings, expressed opinions—it may be merely to excite a sensation amongst his readers—but still opinions very much like those to which the hon. Baronet has alluded to-night.

MR. DISRAELI: There is not the slightest foundation for that statement. I give it the most unequivocal contradiction.

MR. BRIGHT: Doubtless, then, those who quoted writings said to be the right hon. Gentleman's were in error. I accept the right hon. Gentleman's statement freely, but I was not about to blame him. It is that kind of writing that comes often in youth from great enthusiasm and from an acquaintance with what at school we are taught to regard as the heroic deeds of ancient days. I did not rise for the purpose of saying a single syllable in defence of Mazzini. The observations I have made in regard to him are for this purpose—to explain, and if it be necessary, in some degree to justify the friendship that has existed between the hon. Member for Halifax and Mazzini, and many other eminent foreigners, for many years past. But, Sir, there is not a man in this House who believes now that the hon. Gentleman on any occasion has ever had the slightest intimation that any plot of this nature was being concocted, or about to be carried into effect. I undertake to say that if Mazzini

Mr. Bright

were connected with any of those plots he would himself feel it was utterly impossible that he could discuss them with the hon. Member for Halifax, or with any person of his intelligence, or occupying his position in this country. ["Oh, oh!"] Hon. Gentlemen opposite may feel differently, I am willing to show to the hon. Member for Halifax that fairness and justice which if I were in his place I would ask for myself. I am not defending—understand me —the enthusiasm under which any Englishman allows himself to be so intimately and personally connected with a gentleman who is the soul of conspiracy throughout the various countries of Europe. I always discouraged it—I condemn it now—I think it full of embarrassment; and my hon. Friend at this moment feels the embarrassment. The embarrassment is not confined solely to himself, but affects, of course, to a certain extent the Government of which he is a Member. But making all these allowances—granting everything that has been said on the other side—I do not mean about Mazzini, because I admit nothing on his account, and say nothing in his defence —but admitting everything that has been said in regard to the hon. Member for Halifax, and everything that he has said—considering that his friendship began with Mazzini when he was a very young man, and through the enthusiasm to which young men are liable—and I should be ashamed of myself if I had never felt it—I ask the hon. Gentlemen opposite whether the course they are taking is one worthy of a great party. Do you believe that your leader, now practising upon the House with simulated horror, really tells what he felt in regard to this transaction in Paris? I do not believe that you wish to become the helpers of the police of Paris. Do not suppose that I differ from any of you who have expressed disgust and horror at the attempt on the life of the Emperor of France. I believe there has never been a ruler on the throne of France who has been so friendly to this country, or more anxious to preserve peace with this country. I have said it when some of you said the very opposite. I look with indignation and horror at attempts coming from any quarter, and under any provocation whatever, to plunge that great nation into the anarchy from which it is possible his life only saves it; but, at the same time, it is not necessary to make yourselves in this House the instruments of adding fuel to whatever fire may exist, thus exasperating the state of things that now prevails in France. Have you another object hardly less worthy—that of worrying the existing Government? I need not tell you that I am no partisan of that Government—that I never have been —that I have never, since a short time after its formation, looked forward with dismay to its dissolution; but if I were as hungry as the hungriest person to place myself on that Bench, I would be ashamed to make my way to it over the character, the reputation, the happiness, and the future of the last appointed and youngest Member of that Government.

Lord ROBERT CECIL: The hon. Member who has just resumed his seat accused this side of the House of a number of unworthy motives. Among others, he has charged us with showing excited feelings, directed apparently by motives which we will not avow in supporting the Motion of the hon. Baronet. I will venture to say, for hon. Members on this side of the House, that there would have been no excitement, no vehement prosecution of the charge, if it had not been for the speech of the noble Lord at the head of the Government, who tried by topics totally irrelevant, and by the repetition of the merest claptrap, to draw away the attention of the House of Commons from the real gravity of the charge brought against his Colleague the hon. Member for Halifax. We have travelled over a great variety of subjects, we have been brought back to the Conspiracy Bill, we have had allusions to the French Treaty—there have been a great number of insinuations of all kinds, but very little from the opposite side has been said with respect to the actual Motion before the House. The point is this:—If the documents read this evening by the hon. Baronet are true, and if the documents quoted by my hon. Friend the Member for the King's County the other night are true, Mazzini is, in intention, a murderer. These publications were before the world, and the hon. Member for Halifax trusted Mazzini as few would trust another. He allowed him, knowing he was an agent for sowing discord in every country—knowing he was the prime instrument of every revolution that was being organized in every nation in Europe—he allowed him to make his house an instrument for the prosecution of his schemes. He has a right to any sympathies he may think fit to indulge in, but it was his duty, when trusting M. Mazzini to such an extent, to make him-

self acquainted with his views and with the schemes which he was likely to pursue. He ought to have known as well as any hon. Member in this House, that Mazzini was the advocate of political assassination; but knowing the force of extracts quoted by my hon. Friend the Member for King's County — knowing the doctrines of M. Mazzini — he allowed him to make his house the instrument of schemes which he did not know—allowed him, for aught he knew, to make his house an instrument for promoting a scheme of political assassination. Unless he was certain of the schemes in which M. Mazzini was engaged, he ought not to have permitted him to have his letters directed to his house. The question now is, whether he can undo what he has done. No one accuses him of complicity in the crime; what we accuse him of is imprudence which is deeply culpable, and which may seriously compromise this country. An imputation has been made abroad that schemes of this kind are encouraged in this country, and for that imputation the imprudence of the hon. Member for Halifax has given ground. It is open to the Government to refute the charge; it is open to them to disavow in a particular manner any connection or sympathy with schemes of this kind. They have refused to do so; they have gone back on subjects totally irrelevant; they have endeavoured to blind the House of Commons and the people; and the duty of the House of Commons is to declare by its Vote to-night that it has no complicity in such schemes as those with which the conspirators have been charged, and that it deeply deplores the culpable conduct of the hon. Member for Halifax.

The CHANCELLOR of the EXCHEQUER: Sir, I apprehend that the duty which we are now performing—whatever way it turns—is of a judicial character, and therefore at the risk of being exceedingly dull, I shall endeavour to confine myself, as far, at all events, as good intention goes when beginning a speech— which I know is not always carried out in the course of it—to a treatment of the question in that spirit. With regard to M. Mazzini, I am not in the position of the hon. Gentleman who has been acquainted with him for many years. I never saw M. Mazzini. I do not partake in his opinions with regard to Italy, and those whom I have been accustomed to look upon as authorities on Italian politics have differed vitally from M. Mazzini as regards his views and measures. But I am bound, at the same time, to say that I never knew one of those men who did not accord to M. Mazzini on the one hand great talents and force of character, and on the other hand the most perfect truth and integrity. That is an important point in the present discussion; and therefore, until the contrary is shown to be the case, I shall assume that M. Mazzini is to be believed on his word. How does that apply to the case which the noble Lord who has just addressed the House stated with considerable fairness? He threw overboard very fairly the idea that it is our duty to inquire very minutely as to who has intercourse with every one that comes from a foreign country. My hon. Friend the Member for Birmingham has pointed out the difficulties that arise from such an intercourse. The noble Lord stands up for perfect freedom of action. He does not complain of the Member for Halifax, because he was in friendship with M. Mazzini; but he says, if my hon. Friend allowed M. Mazzini to make use of his house, it was his duty to make himself acquainted with M. Mazzini's views, and to ascertain that he was not applying his command over the hon. Member's house for the purpose of concocting schemes of assassination. If M. Mazzini is a man to be believed, it is not necessary for me to say that my hon. Friend is to be implicitly believed; and that being so, I say that my hon. Friend has done precisely what the noble Lord says he ought to have done. My hon. Friend has told the House that he believes in the truth of M. Mazzini's declaration in the newspapers, and knows this to have been the feeling of M. Mazzini during all the years in which he has had a friendship for him. Therefore, he has brought himself to as high a certainty as a man can possess, according to his own conscientious conviction, that M. Mazzini never has made, and never could make, use of his house for the purposes which the noble Lord has justly denounced, because he thinks he knows that M. Mazzini is incapable of entertaining these views. That is with respect to the general ground stated by the noble Lord. It is not enough for us in a case of this kind to have a general impression that my hon. Friend has acted indiscreetly, and therefore to adopt the Motion which is proposed without examining its terms. For what are its terms? We are invited to vote a Resolution that the statement of the Procureur Général on the trial of Greco,

implicating a Member of this House, and of Her Majesty's Government in a plot for the assassination of our ally the Emperor of the French, deserves the serious consideration of this House. Now, I put it to this House that a statement by the Procureur Général does not deserve, and cannot fitly become, the basis of consideration by this House. What is the Procureur Général? He is the distinguished advocate who pleads the cause of the Crown in the court where Greco was tried. What is his duty? His duty is to raise the case to the very highest against Greco, against Mazzini, and against every one he can touch. It is not the obligation of the Procureur Général to take a calm, unbiassed, and dispassionate view of the merits of every individual with whom he may deal. His duty is to state the case at the highest point; without any disrespect to him or imputation on the French Government, his statement is essentially an *ex parte* statement, which ought to be subjected to the full and searching scrutiny of a judicial procedure before it can, with propriety, become the subject of consideration here. If the hon. Member is content to wait until the finding of the Court of Justice in France shall establish any such charge as the hon. Baronet thinks the Procureur Général has established, then, I grant you, is the time when the state of things described by my noble Friend behind me would altogether have passed away; because it is one thing to take notice of the statement of counsel, whose duty it is to bring out one particular side of the question, and it is another thing to take notice of the solemn judicial finding of a court in which I think we, as a friendly Government, irrespectively of the high character of French Courts of Justice, should be bound to place the utmost confidence. Upon that ground, therefore, it is not fitting that the statement of the Procureur Général should become the subject of consideration by this House. But that is not all. I am not now entering into the question whether the statement of my hon. Friend was perfectly sufficient or not. The feelings of gentlemen differ so much with regard to parties on the Continent, that there is room for much difference of opinion on this point. Let us look, however, at what the Procureur Général has said, and how it has been met. And now I come to what I think is the issue placed before the House—stated in the most positive manner that I can possibly state it. Here are the words—I think they are correctly given— of the Procureur Général:—I searched in the *London Commercial Almanac*, and in the pages of the *Post Office Directory*, to ascertain" — what? "to ascertain who could be the person thus placed in communication with Greco." What is the charge of the Procureur Général? Not that my hon. Friend's house was used for the reception of M. Mazzini's letters. Upon that subject my hon. Friend has told you he is convinced that M. Mazzini was incapable of writing such letters or of entering into such plots. But that is not the matter in issue. That is not the charge made by the Procureur Général. His charge is, that a certain person was placed by M. Mazzini in communication with Greco. By looking into the *London Directory* he finds, as he thinks, that that certain person is my hon. Friend. Well, is this true? I am sure that my noble Friend on the back bench will not say that my hon. Friend's explanation was unsatisfactory. Was it possible for my hon. Friend to have given a more distinct and uncompromising denial to this charge. I unhesitatingly appeal to the candour of a body of English Gentlemen to say whether my hon. Friend is not entitled to the benefit of this denial? [An hon. MEMBER: No!] The interruption of the hon. Member is far less creditable to himself than to my hon. Friend, and is a somewhat unmannerly proceeding. I say that my hon. Friend has met the specific declaration of the Procureur Général with a denial as specific as a man can give; and, under these circumstances—the House having received this direct denial from one of its own Members — a man of unimpeached honour and integrity—you are invited to vote that the declaration of the Procureur Général deserves our serious consideration. Those are the circumstances under which you have to vote. God knows that if I thus speak it is not because I am indifferent to the feelings of irritation which subsist, if they do subsist, in France. On that subject, I confess I have great doubts. I believe that there is a growing intimacy and cordiality, and increasing relations of friendship between these two countries. I believe that every day of extended communications and friendly intercourse is laying deeper, and widening more and more, that strong basis of reciprocal confidence between the two peoples which, in my opinion, forms the only effectual security for the peace of Europe and the world.

I say, that if I thus speak, it is not on account of any indifference in that respect; it is not on account of insensibility to the many claims which the Emperor of the French possesses not only upon the forbearance, but upon the respect and cordial goodwill of this House. I have not forgotten his many good offices, and at no period have I been slow to recognize them. I will not enter into the question whether all parties and persons have been equally forward to pursue a similar course, but this I will say, that I am very glad to see this feeling towards the French Government prevail in this House; and it is not because we do not share this feeling that we decline to adopt the Motion. It is because, called upon to take a course essentially judicial in its character, we find the allegations upon which the Motion rests entirely fail, inasmuch as a full denial has been given to the statement of the Procureur Général by the speech of my hon. Friend.

LORD CLAUD HAMILTON said, he could not rest silent under the unjustifiable imputations of the hon. Member for Birmingham, who had deliberately charged the Opposition with being actuated by most improper motives and by party objects in bringing forward this Motion. What right had the hon. Member to interfere in a proceeding which, as the right hon. Gentleman had said, was of somewhat a judicial character, by casting such unworthy and wholesale imputations? He appealed to the right hon. Gentleman in the chair, whether such imputations were not forbidden by the usages of the House. For himself, he disclaimed any such motives; but he had a painful feeling that it was the duty of the House to purge itself from the unfortunate position in which the hon. Member's indiscretion had placed it. The hon. Member had had more than one opportunity of making a full explanation of his conduct. Instead of doing so he had risen and delivered a bombastic declaration against assassination, but he had denied nothing. The right hon. Gentleman had spoken of candour, but he could see nothing candid in the conduct of the hon. Gentleman. He himself had asked the hon. Member a distinct question, which he hoped might have elicited a satisfactory explanation, but in vain. Two days afterwards Mazzini, through *The Times*, published to all Europe the real facts of the case, and that evening, the hon. Member had confirmed the statement. The hon.

Gentleman had admitted an acquaintance of eighteen years with the notorious Mazzini, and had openly expressed an admiration for that person. He therefore stood before the country and before Europe as either the dupe or the accomplice of Mazzini. The House knew he did not stand well abroad. There was a time when the name of England was a tower of strength, but since she had left Denmark in her present position all that was changed. He believed the hon. Member to have been the ignorant dupe of Mazzini. He should at some future time feel it his duty to put some questions to the hon. Gentleman which he hoped would be explicitly answered.

MR. COX said, he had only two or three words to say. The Chancellor of the Exchequer had stated that the hon. Member for Halifax had denied the charge of the Procureur Général. To his (Mr. Cox's) mind, he admitted every word of it. These were the words:—

" He, Greco, if he were in want of money, was to apply to an address in London. That address was 35, Thurloe Square, Brompton. I turned to the *London Directory*, and at page 670, I am sorry to say, I found the name of a Member of Parliament."

Seeing that statement, he (Mr. Cox) thought it his duty to put a question to the hon. Member, and he was by no means satisfied with the answer. He therefore once more, in seconding the Motion of the hon. Member for the King's County, put a question as to letters addressed to Mr. Flower, and the hon. Gentleman replied, " I had no knowledge of them." And when he wished to know whether this Mr. Flower was not the true Mazzini, the hon. Member replied, " I have no knowledge of that. I don't know anything about it." He should like the hon. Member to explain which was the true answer—was it the answer he gave the other evening, or the admission which he made that night.

MR. STANSFELD: What I said was this—that M. Mazzini had letters addressed to him under the name of Fiore, and I said that Flower was the translation of that name; but I added that to my knowledge no letters had been received at my house in that name.

Question put.

The House *divided*:—Ayes 171; Noes 161: Majority 10.

Lord Claud Hamilton

AYES.

Adam, W. P.
Agar-Ellis, hon. L. G.F.
Angerstein, W.
Antrobus, E.
Aytoun, R. S.
Baines, E.
Baring, H. B.
Baring, T. G.
Barnes, T.
Bass, M. T.
Beale, S.
Beaumont, S. A.
Berkeley, hon. C. P. F.
Blencowe, J. G.
Bonham-Carter, J.
Bouverie, rt. hon. E. P.
Bright, J.
Bruce, H. A.
Buchanan, W.
Buller, J. W.
Buller, Sir A. W.
Bury, Viscount
Butler, C. S.
Butt, I.
Buxton, C.
Caird, J.
Cardwell, rt. hon. E.
Castlerosse, Viscount
Childers, H. C. E.
Clay, J.
Clifford, C. C.
Clive, G.
Colebrooke, Sir T. E.
Collier, Sir R. P.
Cowper, rt. hon. W. F.
Cranfurd, E. H. J.
Crawford, R. W.
Crossley, Sir F.
Davey, R.
Denman, hon. G.
Doulton, F.
Duff, M. E. G.
Dunbar, Sir W.
Dundas, F.
Dundas, rt. hon. Sir D.
Enfield, Viscount
Evans, T. W.
Ewart, W.
Ewart, J. C.
Fenwick, H.
Fermoy, Lord
Forster, C.
Forster, W. E.
Fortescue, hon. F. D.
Fortescue, C. S.
Gibson, rt. hon. T. M.
Gilpin, C.
Gladstone, rt. hon. W.
Glynn, G. C.
Glynn, G. G.
Goldsmid, Sir F. H.
Goschen, G. J.
Gower, hon. F. L.
Gower, G. W. G. L.
Gregson, S.
Grenfell, H. R.
Grey, rt. hon. Sir G.
Gurdon, B.
Hanbury, R.
Hankey, T.

Hardcastle, J. A.
Hartington,Marquess of
Headlam rt. hon. T. E.
Henderson J.
Henley, Lord
Herbert, rt. hon. H. A.
Hibbert, J. T.
Hodgkinson, G.
Hodgson, K. D
Howard, hon. C. W. G.
Hutt, rt. hon. W.
Ingham, R.
Jackson, W.
Kershaw, J.
King, hon. P. J. L.
Kinglake, A. W.
Kinglake, J. A.
Kinnaird hon. A. F.
Layard, A. H.
Leatham, E. A.
Lefevre, G. J. S.
Lee, W.
Lewis, H.
Lindsay, W. S.
Lloyd, T.
Lowe, rt. hon. R.
Lysley, W. J.
Mackinnon, W. A.
Marjoribanks, D. C.
Massey, W. N.
Merry, J.
Mildmay, H. F.
Miller, W.
Mills, J. R.
Moffatt, G.
Montagu, Lord R.
Morrison, W.
Norris, J. T.
Ogilvy, Sir J.
Osborne, R. B.
Packe, Colonel
Padmore, R.
Paget, Lord C.
Paget, Lord A.
Paget C.
Palmer, Sir R.
Palmerston, Viscount
Peel, rt. hon. Sir R.
Peel, rt. hon. F.
Pender, J.
Peto, Sir S. M.
Pilkington, J.
Pinney, Colonel
Ponsonby, hon. A.
Potter, E.
Pritchard, J.
Pugh, D.
Robartes, T. J. A.
Robertson, D.
Robertson, H.
Roebuck, J. A.
Russell, A.
Russell, Sir W.
St. Aubyn, J.
Salomons, Mr. Ald
Scholefield, W.
Scott, Sir W.
Seely, C.
Seymour, H. D.
Seymour, A.

Sheridan, R. B.
Sheridan, H. B.
Smith, J. B.
Smith, M. T.
Smith, A.
Smith, J. A.
Stacpoole, W.
Stansfeld, J.
Steel, J.
Sykes, Colonel W.
Taylor, P. A.
Thornhill, W. P.
Tite, W.
Tollemache, hon. F. J.
Tracy, hn. C. R. D. H.
Turner, J. A.
Villiers, rt. hon. C. P.
Vivian, H. H.

Warner, E.
Watkins, Colonel L.
Weguelin, T. M.
Western, S.
Westhead, J. P. B.
Whitbread, S.
White, J.
White, L.
Williams, W.
Wood, rt. hon. Sir C.
Woods, H.
Wyld, J.

TELLERS.

Brand, hon. H. B. W.
Knatchbull-Hugessen, E.

NOES.

Acton, Sir J. D.
Adderley, rt. hon. C. B.
Addington, hon. W. W.
Archdall, Captain M.
Astell, J. H.
Bailey, C.
Baillie, H. J.
Barttelot, Colonel
Bathurst, A. A.
Bathurst, Colonel H.
Beach, W. W. B.
Bective, Earl of
Beecroft, G. S.
Bentinck, G. W. P.
Bernard, T. T.
Bond, J. W. M'G.
Bovill, W.
Bowyer, Sir G.
Bramley-Moore, J.
Bramston, T. W.
Bridges, Sir B. W.
Bruce, Major C.
Bruce, Sir H. H.
Burghley, Lord
Cairns, Sir H. M'C.
Cargill, W. W.
Cave, S.
Cecil, Lord R.
Chapman, J.
Clifton, Sir R., J.
Codrington, Sir W.
Cole, hon. H.
Collins, T.
Cox, W.
Cubitt, G.
Dalkeith, Earl of
Damer, S. D.
Dickson, Colonel
Disraeli, rt. hon. B.
Duncombe, hon. W. E.
Edwards, Colonel
Egerton, hon. A. F.
Egerton, E. C.
Elcho, Lord
Elphinstone, Sir J. D.
Estcourt, rt. hn.T.H.S.
Fane, Colonel J. W.
Farquhar, Sir M.
Ferguson, Sir J.
Ferrand, W.
FitzGerald, W. R. S.
Fleming, T. W.
Floyer, J.

Fraser, Sir W. A.
Gallwey, Sir W. P.
George, J.
Greaves, E.
Greenall, G.
Greene, J.
Greville, Colonel F.
Griffith, C. D.
Grogan, Sir E.
Haliburton, T. C.
Hamilton, Lord C.
Hamilton, Viscount
Hamilton, I. T.
Hardy, G.
Hartopp, E. B.
Harvey, R. B.
Hassard, M.
Hay, Sir J. C. D.
Henley, rt. hon. J. W.
Hennessy, J. P.
Heygate, Sir F. W.
Heygate, W. U.
Holford, R. S.
Holmesdale, Viscount
Horsfall, T. B.
Hotham, Lord
Humberston, P. S.
Hume, W. W. F.
Humphery, W. H.
Hunt, G. W.
Jervis, Captain
Jolliffe, rt. hon. Sir W. G. H.
Kerrison, Sir E. C.
King, J. K.
Knight, F. W.
Knox, Colonel
Knox, hon. Major S.
Laird, J.
Leader, N. P.
Legh, Major C.
Legh, W. J.
Lennox, Lord G. G.
Lennox, C. S. B. H. K.
Lovaine, Lord
Lygon, hon. F.
Lytton, rt. hon. Sir G. E. L. B.
M'Cann, J.
Malcolm, J. W.
Malins, R.
Manners, rt. hn. Lord J.
Miles, Sir W.

Miller, T. J.
Mitford, W. T.
Montgomery, Sir G.
Moor, H.
Mowbray, rt. hon. J. R.
Naas, Lord
Nicol, W.
Noel, hon. G. J.
Northcote, Sir S. H.
O'Reilly, M. W.
Packe, C. W.
Pakington, rt. hn. Sir J.
Parker, Major W.
Patten, Colonel W.
Paull, H.
Peacocke, M. G. W.
Peel, rt. hon. General
Pennant, hon. Colonel
Pevensey, Viscount
Powell, F. S.
Repton, G. W. J.
Ridley, Sir M. W.
Rowley, hon. R. T.
Salt, T.
Sclater-Booth, G.
Scott, Lord H.
Selwyn, C. J.
Smith, Abel
Smith, S. G.
Smollett, P. B.
Somerset, Colonel

Somes, J.
Stanhope, J. B.
Stanley, Lord
Stuart, Lieut.-Col. W.
Surtees, H. E.
Taylor, Colonel
Tempest, Lord A. V.
Thynne, Lord E.
Tollemache, J.
Tomline, G.
Torrens, R.
Trefusis, hon. C. H. R.
Turner, C.
Vance, J.
Vandeleur, Colonel
Vansittart, W.
Vyse, Colonel H.
Walcott, Admiral
Walker, J. R.
Walsh, Sir J.
Waterhouse, S.
Whitmore, H.
Wyndham, hon. P.
Wynn, C. W. W.
Yorke, hon. E. T.
Yorke, J. R.

TELLERS.

Lennox, Lord H. G. C. G.
Stracey, Sir H. J.

DENMARK AND GERMANY—POSTPONEMENT OF NOTICE.—OBSERVATIONS.

VISCOUNT PALMERSTON: I have to make an appeal to my hon. Friend the Member for Liskeard, who has given notice that to-morrow evening he will call attention to the affairs of Denmark. The papers bringing down the history of the question to the latest period will be delivered only to-day. As I am able to tell my hon. Friend that negotiations are still pending, it is the opinion of myself and of my noble Friend at the head of the Foreign Office, that there would be considerable inconvenience to the public service if the matter were brought under discussion in the House before that question is finally decided. I would submit to my hon. Friend, therefore, whether it would not be better that he should postpone what he has to say upon the subject until the other papers are in the hands of hon. Members, and until after the recess. In making this appeal I must again repeat that in my own opinion, and in that of my noble Friend, it would be inconvenient, and, indeed, injurious to the public interests, that the discussion should take place with the imperfect knowledge which the House has of the transactions which have taken place.

MR. BERNAL OSBORNE: Of course, I am always anxious to forward the interests of the public service, and on this occasion I place myself entirely in the hands of the House. Entertaining however, as I do, a very strong conviction that this House ought not to separate for a recess of three weeks in the present juncture of affairs in Denmark without some discussion, and some definite expression of the views of the Government as to what their proposed action is to be, I can hardly think that the House will be of opinion that the noble Lord has assigned sufficient reasons for me to give way to him. If I understand the noble Lord rightly, he grounds his request on the fact that conferences are about to ensue. On that point I take a very different opinion, perhaps, from some hon. Members. I cannot but regard these conferences, which failed when coupled with an armistice, but appear to be coming off now without one, to be very much in the nature of a Parliamentary manœuvre, more for the amusement of the people who live on the banks of the Thames than for the advantage of those in the neighbourhood of the Eider. Holding that view, dissenting totally from the policy pursued by the noble Lord's Government to the unfortunate inhabitants of the Duchy of Schleswig Holstein, and believing that these people have been sacrificed by an iniquitous and unjust treaty conducted by the noble Lord at the head of the Government, unless I am moved by other hon. Gentlemen, I do not feel inclined to give way on this occasion. If I am told by the noble Lord that he has very good reason to suppose that by the mystery which is being used he will promote, not a temporary and patched-up peace but a permanent peace, then I think I might conscientiously give way; but as at present advised, unless I hear some strong reasons to the contrary, I do not think sufficient motives have been assigned why this debate should not come on, or why some more definite explanation of the views of the Government should not be given. But, as I said before, I am in the hands of the House, and if hon. Gentlemen on both sides are of opinion that I am bound in honour to withdraw, I shall cheerfully consent to whatever course they choose to point out to me.

VISCOUNT PALMERSTON: The hon. Member asks me whether we expect to be able to arrange a permanent peace. Of course, our desire is to make an arrangement that should be permanent, but as

Mr. Bernal Osborne

the arrangement, whatever it may be, depends, not upon us only, but also upon the other Governments who will be parties to the Conference, I can only state what the views and wishes of Her Majesty's Government are. It is impossible that I can say what the result of the proposed negotiations may be.

MR. KINGLAKE: Will the noble Lord state what is the basis of the Conference?

VISCOUNT PALMERSTON: I have already stated that we have not yet got an official answer from the Danish Government. Of course, therefore, it is impossible to say what basis may be adopted. Until we get a formal answer from Denmark, we must remain in the same state in which we have been for the last week.

MR. DISRAELI: My own opinion is, that it is much to be regretted that the early period at which Easter falls this year, and what I think is the very bad custom which we have fallen into of late years of having very long holydays at Easter, render it necessary that Parliament should adjourn at the present moment. It is highly expedient that a discussion should take place upon the recent negotiations conducted by Her Majesty's Government; but what we have to decide to-night is, whether it is more convenient that a discussion should take place with ample information or with scanty information. Now, I do not myself think that on the last night of our meeting — that is, to-morrow—we could really do full justice to the subject. It must be, comparatively speaking, a brief debate. Many hon. Gentlemen who are anxious to address the House would not have an opportunity of speaking, and probably it would end without an expression of opinion on the part of the House of any decided character upon any definite point. What would happen then? We should have to recommence our discussions after the recess on a greater scale; and if that be the case, is it not better that we should not to-morrow begin an imperfect debate, but should at the earliest convenient opportunity commence the discussion with the advantage of that information for which I myself have asked before, and which it is desirable should be in the hands of hon. Members? The negotiations, though spread over a considerable period, are all connected together, and it is of great importance that we should have a clear conception of the motives and views with which Her Majesty's Government have favoured this plan of a Conference. That it is impossible we can have to-morrow, and although I am always unwilling to interfere between hon. Members and the opportunities they have obtained, still I think, considering the position of the hon. Member for Liskeard, the importance of the subject, and the very brief space of time that can be given to the discussion, that on the whole it would be better if the hon. Member did not proceed with his Motion to-morrow.

COLONEL DICKSON said, he trusted that if the hon. Member withdrew his Motion he would secure a very early day after the recess for bringing it forward again.

MR. BERNAL OSBORNE said, he believed a Motion was to be brought forward in another place to-morrow on the subject. However, as he had put himself into the hands of the House, he would bow to their decision.

Main Question put, and *agreed to.*

SUPPLY—CIVIL SERVICE ESTIMATES.

Civil Service Estimates, Class I., *considered* in Committee.

(In the Committee.)

MR. PEEL said, he had to move a Vote of £1,256,000, on account of the Civil Service Estimates. It was absolutely necessary to pass the Vote before the House separated for the Easter recess.

£1,866,000, on account of certain Civil Services :—

Class I.

Royal Palaces......	£12,000
Public Buildings	30,000
Furniture of Public Offices	5,000
Royal Parks and Pleasure Gardens	25,000
New Houses of Parliament	10,000
British Embassy Houses Abroad	1,000
New Foreign Office, Buildings	20,000
Probate Court Registries	3,000
General Register House, Edinburgh	1,000
Public Record Repository	7,000
Westminster Bridge Approaches	5,000
New Westminster Bridge	3,000
Holyhead Harbour	10,000
Public Buildings, Ireland	25,000
New Record Buildings, Dublin...	5,000
Rates for Government Property	7,000

Class II.

Two Houses of Parliament, Offices	18,000
Treasury...	14,000
Home Office	7,000
Foreign Office	19,000
Colonial Office	8,000
Privy Council Office	7,000
Board of Trade, &c.	17,000
Privy Seal Office	1,000
Civil Service Commission	3,000
Paymaster General's Office	5,000

VOL. CLXXIV. [THIRD SERIES.]

Exchequer (London)	2,000
Office of Works and Public Buildings	9,000
Office of Woods, Forests & Land Revenues	8,000
Public Records, &c.	6,000
Poor Law Commissions...	20,000
Mint, including Coinage	14,000
Inspectors of Factories, Fisheries, &c...	9,000
Exchequer and other Offices in Scotland	2,000
Household of Lord Lieutenant, Ireland	2,000
Chief Secretary, Ireland, Offices	5,000
Inspection, &c., of Lunatic Asylums, Ireland	1,000
Office of Public Works, Ireland	6,000
Audit Office	9,000
Copyhold, Tithe, and Inclosure Commission	5,000
Ditto, Imprest Expenses	4,000
General Register Offices, England, Ireland, and Scotland	17,000
National Debt Office	4,000
Public Works Loan Commission & West India Relief Commission	1,000
Lunacy Commissions	2,000
Registrars of Friendly Societies	1,000
Charity Commission	4,000
Local Government Act Office, and Inspection of Burial Grounds	2,000
Landed Estates Record Offices...	1,000
Quarantine Expenses	1,000

Secret Service	8,000
Printing and Stationery	90,000
Postage of Public Departments	35,000

Class III.

Law Charges, England	9,000
Criminal Prosecutions, &c.	50,000
Police, Counties and Boroughs, Great Britain	60,000
Crown Office, Queen's Bench	2,000
Admiralty Court Registry	3,000
Late Insolvent Debtors' Court...	2,000
Probate Court	21,000
County Courts	40,000
Land Registry Office	2,000
Police Courts (Metropolis)	6,000
Metropolitan Police	40,000
Bankruptcy Court Compensations	5,000
Lord Advocate and Solicitor General, Salaries	1,000
Court of Session	5,000
Court of Justiciary	3,000
Prosecutions under the Lord Advocate.	2,000
Exchequer, Scotland, Legal Branch	1,000
Sheriffs and Procurators Fiscal not paid by Salaries, and Expenses of Prosecutions in Sheriff Courts	9,000
Procurators Fiscal, Salaries	6,000
Sheriff Clerks	4,000
Register House, Edinburgh, Salaries and Expenses of Sundry Departments	5,000
Law Charges and Criminal Prosecutions	16,000
Court of Chancery	2,000
Courts of Queen's Bench, Common Pleas, and Exchequer	3,000
Process Servers	3,000
Registrars to the Judges, and Clerk of the Court of Errors	2,000
Manor Courts Compensations	1,000
Registry of Judgments	1,000

L

Court of Bankruptcy and Insolvency ...	2,000
Court of Probate	3,000
Landed Estates Court	4,000
Dublin Metropolitan Police and Police Justices	13,000
Constabulary of Ireland...	200,000
Four Courts Marshalsea Prison ...	1,000
Inspection and General Superintendence	5,000
Prisons and Convict Establishments at Home	90,000
Maintenance of Prisoners in County Gaols, &c., and Removal of Convicts	70,000
Transportation of Convicts	10,000
Convict Establishments in the Colonies	50,000

Class IV.

Public Education, Great Britain ...	184,000
Science and Art Department	38,000
Public Education, Ireland	80,000
University of London	2,000
Universities, &c., in Scotland	6,000
Queen's Colleges, Ireland	2,000
Belfast Theological Professors, &c..	1,000
British Museum...	22,000
National Gallery...	5,000
Scientific Works and Experiments ...	2,000

Class V.
NORTH AMERICA.

Bermudas	1,000
Clergy, North America	1,000

WEST INDIES, &c.

Governors and others, West Indies, &c.	3,000
Justices, West Indies	1,000

AFRICA.

Western Coast	4,000
St. Helena	2,000

MISCELLANEOUS.

Falkland Islands	2,000
Labuan	2,000
Emigration	3,000
Treasury Chest	5,000
Captured Negroes, Bounties on Slaves, &c.	15,000
Commissions for Suppression of Slave Trade	3,000
Consuls Abroad	42,000
Services in China, Japan, and Siam ...	5,000
Ministers at Foreign Courts, extraordinary Expenses	10,000
Special Missions, Outfits, &c	10,000
Third Secretaries to Embassies... ...	1,000

Class VI.

Superannuation and Retired Allowances	60,000
Polish Refugees & Distressed Spaniards	1,000
Merchant Seamen's Fund Pensions ...	4,000
Relief of Distressed British Seamen ...	9,000
Miscellaneous Charges, formerly Civil List	1,000
Public Infirmaries, Ireland	1,000
Westmoreland Lock Hospital	1,000
House of Industry Hospitals	2,000
Cork Street Fever Hospital	1,000
Dr. Steevens's Hospital	1,000
Concordatum Fund, and other Charities and Allowances, Ireland	3,000
Non-conforming and other Ministers, Ireland	11,000

Class VII.

Temporary Commissions	4,000
Patent Law Expenses	8,000

Fishery Board, Scotland	4,000
Local Dues on Shipping, under Treaties of Reciprocity	16,000
Inspectors of Corn Returns	1,000
Miscellaneous Charges from Civil Contingencies	1,000
Total... ... ... £1,866,000

MR. AUGUSTUS SMITH said, he had protested last year against the system of taking Votes on account before the Estimates were in the hands of hon. Members, and he wished to repeat that protest. The practice was irregular and unconstitutional.

THE CHANCELLOR OF THE EXCHEQUER said, he hoped the Committee would not suppose it was asked to do anything irregular. The course of public business rendered it almost impossible to get Votes in Supply regularly passed before Easter, and thus Votes on account became indispensable.

SIR MATTHEW RIDLEY said, he wished to ask, Why it was that the production of the whole of the Civil Service Estimates was so long delayed, the Army and Navy Estimates having been already placed in the hands of Members?

THE CHANCELLOR OF THE EXCHEQUER said, the Civil Service Estimates embraced so many points, and were governed by so many considerations, that it was impossible to get them ready at an equally early date. The Army and Navy Estimates were governed by comparatively few considerations, and were within the control of the Departments.

Vote *agreed to.*

House *resumed.*

Resolution to be reported *To-morrow.*

Committee to sit again *To-morrow.*

FACTORY ACTS EXTENSION BILL.

On Motion of *Mr. Bruce*, Bill for the Extension of the Factory Acts, *ordered* to be brought in by Mr. BRUCE and Sir GEORGE GREY.

Bill *presented*, and read 1°. [Bill 55.]

LIFE ANNUITIES AND LIFE ASSURANCES BILL.

On Motion of *Mr. Chancellor of the Exchequer*, Bill to provide for the investment and appropriation of all monies received by the Commissioners for the reduction of the National Debt, on Account of Deferred Life Annuities and payments to be made on Death, *ordered* to be brought in by Mr. CHANCELLOR of the EXCHEQUER and Mr. PEEL.

Bill *presented*, and read 1°. [Bill 56.]

House adjourned at
Two o'clock.

HOUSE OF LORDS,

Friday, March 18, 1864.

MINUTES.]— PUBLIC BILLS — *First Reading* — Settled Estates Act Amendment [H.L.] (No. 35); Improvement of Land, 1864 [H.L.] (No. 36).
Second Reading—Court of Chancery (Despatch of Business)* (No. 18) ; Conveyancers, &c. (Ireland)* (No. 17).
Committee—Bills of Exchange and Promissory Notes (Ireland)* (No. 26) ; Malt for Animals* (No. 16).
Report—Bills of Exchange and Promissory Notes (Ireland)* (No. 26).
Royal Assent — Consolidated Fund (£584,650) [27 & 28 *Vict.* c. 5].
Consolidated Fund (£4,500,000) [27 & 28 *Vict.* c. 6].
Sir John Lawrence's Salary [27 & 28 *Vict.* c. 2].
Inclosure [27 & 28 *Vict.* c. 1].
Mutiny [27 & 28 *Vict.* c. 3].
Marine Mutiny [27 & 28 *Vict.* c. 4].

DENMARK AND GERMANY.
POSTPONEMENT OF NOTICE.

EARL RUSSELL : Seeing that the noble Earl opposite (Earl of Ellenborough) has given notice of his intention, on the Motion for Adjournment, to call the Attention of the House to the actual State of Affairs in Germany and Denmark, I rise on public grounds to request the noble Earl not at present to bring on that discussion. I do not expect that anything that could fall from him will tend to increase the difficulties which surround the settlement of this question; and, for my own part, I must say that I should have been very glad to render the fullest explanation of the conduct of the Government in respect to the affairs of Denmark and Germany. There are, however, reasons of public policy which make it desirable that there should be no discussion at the present moment. In the first place, I have now to present, by command of Her Majesty, various papers in continuation of those which were presented a few weeks ago. These papers contain the further correspondence which has taken place up to a very recent period. In the next place, there has been a correspondence lately carried on with regard to the holding of a Conference and a proposed armistice, and I have good hopes that the Danish Government will agree to that Conference. If that should be the case, I should hope that an armistice, on the grounds of humanity and on the basis already proposed, would be acceptable to all parties. But that matter is still in doubt, and your Lordships will see that the discussion of this subject, at a time when these matters are still in doubt, would be very undesirable. I do therefore trust that the noble Earl, on grounds of public policy, will postpone the discussion until all the papers which have been presented are in your Lordships' hands. Although, as I have stated, I have no fear that anything the noble Earl might say would interfere with the settlement of this question, yet any discussion at the present moment might be liable to misapprehension by the parties now engaged in war, and might thus tend to the public injury, and prevent the success of the negotiations which are now being carried on.

THE EARL OF ELLENBOROUGH : Under the circumstances stated by the noble Earl, I cannot take upon myself the responsibility of bringing on at the present moment a discussion on the existing state of affairs in Germany and Denmark. At the same time, I cannot come to the conclusion at which he arrives. I by no means participate in the noble Earl's opinion, that a discussion on the subject in this House would have an injurious effect. On the contrary, I am very much afraid that if we adjourn this discussion we shall postpone it until a period when it will be too late to produce any beneficial effect.

THE EARL OF DESART : I regret that your Lordships are always met with the same excuse—that negotiations are still going on — negotiations "never ending, still beginning," until the result is absolute failure.

VISCOUNT STRATFORD DE REDCLIFFE : It affords me much gratification to find that the noble Earl, whose Notice appears on the Votes of the House, feels himself at liberty to acquiesce so cheerfully in the request addressed to him by the Secretary of State for Foreign Affairs; but I cannot refrain from expressing, at the same time, my concern at that part of what has fallen from my noble Friend the Foreign Secretary, which states that considerable uncertainty still hangs over the prospect of a Conference on Danish affairs. Ten days have elapsed since the last conversation upon that important subject in your Lordships' House, and the official language respecting a Conference is still confined to an expression—a stronger one perhaps—of hope. It appears, moreover, that if the Danes consent to a Conference, there is little reason to expect that they will agree to have it accompanied with an armistice, and it also appears that no basis of negotiating in the Conference has been established by common arrangement. Under such circumstances, with every wish for a pacific settlement, and with all due feelings of deference to Her Majesty's Government, I cannot look forward to the issue of the pending difficulties without a sentiment of deep and painful apprehension.

THE EASTER RECESS.
ADJOURNMENT OF THE HOUSE.

On the Motion of Earl GRANVILLE, it was *agreed* "That the House at its rising do adjourn till Tuesday, the 5th of April next."

THE "KEARSARGE" — FEDERAL ENLISTMENTS IN IRELAND.
ADDRESS FOR PAPERS.

THE MARQUESS OF CLANRICARDE rose to ask a question of the noble Earl the Secretary of State for Foreign Affairs, of which he had given private notice. In a recent debate his noble Friend read to their Lordships a letter addressed by Captain Winslow, the Commander of the United States steamer *Kearsarge*, to the American Consul at Queenstown, which was to the following effect :—

"A party of the men, either by the connivance of the crew or otherwise, were concealed on board this vessel on the night of her departure from Queenstown. These men, I learn, were in expectation of being enlisted in the service of the United States, after the *Kearsarge* had proceeded to sea ; but found their mistake. To have turned them ashore at Brest would have been to expose them to temptation to enlist on board the *Florida*. I therefore determined to leave them at Queenstown as soon as it was practical. You will please notify Admiral Jones, as I informed him that no enlistment should be made at Queenstown. I have, therefore, sent on shore this party that no charge of subterfuge may be alleged against me."

When these men were brought back and landed at Queenstown, they were indicted for having enlisted in this very ship, the captain of which, by saying that "they found their mistake," distinctly implied that they did not enlist. Sworn depositions were taken, in which it was stated that when they landed in France, they were told that if they liked to enlist they might do so, and that all but one accepted the offer. The Attorney General for Ireland thought it necessary to prosecute, and upon those depositions they were indicted for having so enlisted. At the trial the

Viscount Stratford de Redcliffe

men saw that the evidence was too strong against them, and they every one of them pleaded guilty to the very offence to show that they could not have committed which the noble Earl read that letter—and concluded by saying, "I do not know that the captain could have acted otherwise than he did." What said the Judge who tried these persons? Referring to the leniency which he was about to show, he said that he pitied these men very much, and wished that he had before him those who were more guilty than the prisoners. And that there might be no mistake as to who those were, he said, "unfortunately that can not be done, because it is known that the vessel had proceeded to sea," — clearly showing that the persons who entrapped and induced the men to enlist were the officers of the ship or persons connected with it. More than that, it was stated in the sworn informations that when the party first went on board the *Kearsarge* in Queenstown, there was a person there who was said to be representing the American Consul. It appeared to him that this was a most serious proceeding. When his noble Friend heard of the transaction, he applied to Mr. Adams, and it was from that Minister that he had received the letter which his noble Friend had read to their Lordships. He had no doubt that Mr. Adams placed implicit reliance in the veracity of the gentleman who wrote it. There might be some circumstances of which he was ignorant, which might explain the circumstances, but he thought that an explanation was due to the House, to which his noble Friend had read the letter, to the United States' Government, to the United States' navy, and to the character of Captain Winslow. There were other circumstances connected with the late trial to which he wished to call attention. The prisoners having pleaded guilty, the Attorney General for the Crown very naturally and properly stated that there was no wish to press for a severe sentence, and the Judge bound the men over in recognizances of £20 to appear when called upon. Let the House see how the Americans treated an analogous case, in which a British subject was charged—not with enlisting men directly into a regiment, or on board a ship, but with merely "retaining and hiring a British subject to go into British territory in order that he might enter the service of the British Crown." One Wagner was charged with retaining and hiring Abraham Cook, who there was no doubt was a British subject, to go beyond the limits of the United States to enlist into the service of his own country, and the case having been heard and the prisouer convicted, the Judge sentenced him to imprisonment for two years and a fine of 100 dollars. His noble Friend the Secretary for Foreign Affairs had lately told the House that the Government had for some time been aware that enlistment for the Federal army was going on in Ireland, and that remonstrances on the subject had been addressed to the American Minister. But if that enlistment were going on against the wishes of the Government, why was it that the offenders were not punished ? It was said, indeed, that no evidence on the subject could be procured. It appeared from the statement which had been made by the responsible officer of the Crown—the Attorney General—on the occasion of the trial to which he had adverted, that the law on the subject in Ireland had never been made known to the people, and that they were in total ignorance of the provisions of the Foreign Enlistment Act as set forth in the Queen's Proclamation. The Attorney General said, " I take this occasion to announce to the people what are the provisions of the Act ; " and the Judge added that considering the prisoners were ignorant of the law, he was disposed to let them off easy. Now, everybody who had lived for any time in Ireland knew that there was not a proclamation issued offering a reward of £5, which was not stuck up at every police barrack throughout the country, and yet the Government, which professed to be so anxious to prevent recruiting for the Federal service, left, according to the Attorney General, the people of Ireland for two and a half years in entire ignorance of the law and proclamation on the subject. He begged leave to move for a copy of the information on which the indictment in the case of certain persons for enlisting for the Federal service was founded, for the matter was a very serious one, and the House ought to be placed in possession of all the requisite details with respect to it.

EARL RUSSELL said, that so far as the Government were concerned, he did not think his noble Friend had any reason to complain. Constant statements were made to the effect, that the people in Ireland were being recruited for the Federal service, and that the offending parties were not prosecuted. But in the instance to which the noble Marquess alluded, certain persons were taken on board a ship of war of the United States, who were afterwards landed and had been proceeded against by the Government ; nor did his noble Friend seem to find any fault either with the Attorney General who prosecuted, or with the Judge. The noble Marquess, however, called upon him to explain the letter of the commander of the Federal vessel denying the enlistment. He (Earl Russell) would only say that it was that very day that he had learnt that the men had pleaded guilty, and that it was not likely he should have received any fresh communication from that officer on the subject. He found, at the same time, in the papers which had just been presented, that there was not only the letter from which his noble Friend had quoted, but one from Lieutenant Commander Thornton to Captain Winslow, in which he said —

" I beg leave to state, in accordance with your request, that on or about the 3rd of November, 1863, several men from Queenstown came on board of this ship as applicants for enlistment in the naval service of the United States. In the absence of yourself, and of any definite instructions in regard to such applications, I told the men that if they were physically qualified for enlistment they might remain on board until your return, when you would decide. Upon your return your instructions were not to enlist them ; they were accordingly sent out of the ship."

How it was that the lieutenant commander had acted upon those instructions, and that notwithstanding these men were said to have been enlisted, he could not explain. It was very proper that the United States' Minister should be informed of the circumstances of the case, and that he should be asked to account for them. For his own part, he could only say that in his opinion, when a captain in the United States' naval service and a lieutenant serving under him alleged certain facts to have occurred, the Government were not to blame if they did not at once declare that they did not believe a word of the statement, and that those gentlemen must be telling falsehoods. With respect to the general question, that sufficient pains were not taken to make the law known in Ireland, he should simply assure the House that so far as the Foreign Office were concerned, they had not only some time ago directed papers containing extracts from the Foreign Enlistment Act to be circulated, but had again repeated the instruction last autumn. The Irish Government had, of course, its own method of making those announcements public, and he would only say that he recollected the late Mr. O'Connell having once observed—it having been stated that some officer of the Government had put a notice in the *Dublin Gazette*—that there was no such sure way of keeping the matter secret. The Irish Government had, no doubt, taken those steps which they deemed proper in the present instance.

THE EARL OF DONOUGHMORE said, it was quite evident that the men had been enlisted, and he was surprised that the noble Earl should be deceived by such transparent falsehoods as those which had been put forward. It was not true that the men were sent on shore at once, for they were taken to Brest, and it was not till after the lapse of thirty-six hours, the American Minister having probably telegraphed to the captain meanwhile not to trifle about these men, that they were taken back to Cork, where they were landed in the uniform of the United States' navy. He would, under these circumstances, ask the noble Earl whether he believed the captain's story? He should like to know what the noble Duke at the head of the Admiralty would think if any captain in our service were to tell him that fifteen men had got on board his ship, and that he had not found out that they were there until he had been at sea three or four days? The fact was that the United States' captain had in the present instance either stated what was a transparent falsehood, or else he was not fit for his post, and did not know how to command a ship. He would ask their Lordships to contrast the noble Earl's satisfaction with the explanation of the American captain on the subject with the manner in which he had received the assurances of the Messrs. Laird and other British merchants, who had pledged their honour not to send a vessel which had been seized by the Government to sea without a week's notice, and yet who had their promises disbelieved. The fact, however, was, that any transparent falsehood seemed to be a sufficient excuse for a particular line of conduct when it came from the Federal Government.

EARL RUSSELL said, that the reports both of the captain and the lieutenant of the *Kearsarge* stated that the ship put to sea on the night of the 5th November, 1863; it was blowing hard and very stormy, and on the following day it was found that several were strangers on board, and on

Earl Russell

inquiring it was found that they had come on board at Queenstown in the hope of being enlisted. They were landed at Brest, but afterwards re-embarked, and were landed at Queenstown in the pilot boat. This was the statement of the captain and the lieutenant, and he confessed he did not see the discrepancy to which the noble Earl that had just spoken had referred.

THE MARQUESS OF CLANRICARDE then moved an Address for

Copies of the Informations and Depositions upon which an Indictment was framed against certain Persons for having enlisted on board the United States Ship of War *Kearsarge*, and of the Indictment to which those Persons pleaded Guilty at the last Assizes for the County of Cork.

Motion *agreed to.*

SETTLED ESTATES ACT AMENDMENT BILL
[H.L.]

A Bill to amend the Settled Estates Act, 1856 —Was *presented* by The Lord CRANWORTH, and read 1ª. (No. 35.)

IMPROVEMENT OF LAND, 1864, BILL [H.L.]

A Bill intituled the Improvement of Land Act, 1864—Was *presented* by The LORD CHANCELLOR, and read 1ª. (No. 36.)

House adjourned at Six o'clock, to Tuesday the 5th of April next, a quarter before Five o'clock.

HOUSE OF COMMONS,
Friday, March 18, 1864.

MINUTES.]—SELECT COMMITTEE — On Schools of Art, Mr. Salt *added*.
Report — Railway Companies' Powers, *Report* (No. 141).
SUPPLY—*considered in Committee*—Committee—R.P.
Resolutions [March 17] *reported*.
PUBLIC BILLS—*First Reading*—Costs Security* [Bill 58].
Second Reading—Fish Teinds (Scotland)* [Bill 45]; Union Relief Aid Acts Continuance* [Bill 50].
SELECT COMMITTEE — Cattle, &c., Importation [Bill 28], and Cattle Diseases Prevention [Bill 27] *nominated*.
Committee — Government Annuities* [Bill 11], *Debate* [March 17] *resumed* and *further adjourned*; Collection of Taxes* [Bill 57].
Report—Collection of Taxes* [Bill 57], and *recommitted*.

THE FACTORY ACT—SCUTCH MILLS.

QUESTION.

MR. BENTINCK said, he wished to ask the Secretary of State for the Home Department, Whether Scutch Mills came within the definition of a "Factory;" whether the Law Officers of the Crown have given any opinion on that point; and, if so, whether that opinion supports the conclusion at which the Factory Inspectors have arrived on that point?

SIR GEORGE GREY replied, that he did not understand that any opinion on the subject had been given by the Law Officers of the Crown, but the question arose some years ago, and it was held by the Inspectors that ordinary Scutch Mills did not come within the Factory Act; but that other Scutch Mills, with a particular sort of machinery attached, did come within the Act.

HUDSON'S BAY COMPANY'S TERRITORY.—QUESTION.

SIR EDWARD GROGAN said, he wished to ask the Under Secretary of State for the Colonies, Whether the Hudson's Bay Company had any ownership in the soil or any right, except that of taking wild animals, to the district of country lying between Lake Superior and British Columbia, comprising the only prairie and some of the most fertile land in British America; and, if the Company had no right, whether the said district should not be opened for settlement under the Crown, and thus invite the emigrants who now leave this country for the United States to settle in our own Colony?

MR. CHICHESTER FORTESCUE said, in reply, that the Hudson's Bay Company had always claimed and still claimed territorial as well as trading and hunting rights over the country referred to in the question of the hon. Baronet, and those claims had been twice submitted to the Law Officers of the Crown under two different Governments, and pronounced by them to be valid. Under these circumstances, and considering the length of time —200 years—during which the claims of the Hudson's Bay Company had been unquestioned, his noble Friend the Duke of Newcastle did not think it his duty, except in the case of most extreme necessity, to question those claims. With respect to opening out the country to settlement, he must say that he did not think that the country had hitherto been closed against settlement by the fact of its being in the hands of the Hudson's Bay Company. He believed that it was its situation, and the natural difficulties of that region which separated the territory in question from Canada, together with its distance beyond the settled territory of the United States, that had constituted the real reasons why population had not made its way and was not likely to make its way there in considerable numbers until the more desirable prairie land of the United States was opened out. Still, the period was approaching when it would be desirable to remove every obstacle to the settlement of the district in question, and his noble Friend was in communication with the authorities of the Hudson's Bay Company in the hope of arriving at some agreement by which the territory might be transferred from the Company to the Crown.

THE SUEZ CANAL.—QUESTION.

MR. DARBY GRIFFITH said, he would beg to ask the First Lord of the Treasury, Whether the Sultan has authorised the Pacha of Egypt to submit the questions at issue relative to the Suez Canal to the arbitration of the Emperor of the French; and, whether, among such questions considered to be at issue, the requirement of the supply of forced labour for the execution of the works of the Canal is presumed to be included?

VISCOUNT PALMERSTON said, in reply, that all that the Government knew about the matter to which the hon. Member referred was that which was contained in the *Moniteur*, where it was announced that a Commission had been appointed by the Emperor of France, at the request or with the consent of the Pacha of Egypt, to arbitrate between the Lesseps Company and the Pacha. The Government had no official information on the matter, and therefore he could not say on what points the arbitration was to take place.

THE "AGINCOURT"—CHAIN CABLES.
QUESTION.

MR. LAIRD said, he wished to ask the Secretary to the Admiralty, Whether it is correct that the 5½-inch rolled iron armourplate manufactured by the Mersey Steel and Iron Company for the *Agincourt* was only classed "A 4;" and if he has had any applications from Chain Cable and Anchor Manufacturers, whose private certificates are received by Lloyd's until the 1st of July, 1864, requesting the Transport Department of the Admiralty to place them on the same footing as Messrs. Brown, Lennox, and Co. were placed by the advertisement of the 19th of January last; and, if such applications have been made, whether the Admiralty are prepared to agree to their request by issuing a similar advertisement to that of the 19th January?

LORD CLARENCE PAGET, in reply to the first question, said, that it was not a correct statement that the armour-plate referred to was only classed A 4. It was classed A 1. With regard to the second question, several applications had been made by Chain Cable and Anchor Manufacturers to the effect alluded to by the hon. Members, and the Admiralty had referred the question to the Committee of Lloyd's. It was the desire of the Admiralty that all the principal Anchor Manufacturers should be put on the same footing. If the hon. Member would repeat his question after Easter, perhaps he would be enabled to give him a more definite answer.

BANKRUPTCY COURT, DUBLIN.
QUESTION.

MR. VANCE said, he wished to ask the Secretary to the Treasury, If any arrangements are in progress to give better accommodation for the transaction of public business in the Bankruptcy Court in Dublin?

MR. PEEL, in reply, said, attention had been directed to the object of giving better accommodation in the Bankruptcy Court by means of an improved building, and in the Civil Service Estimates a Vote would be asked for in order to make provision for a commencement of the work.

DENMARK—ORDER OF SUCCESSION IN HOLSTEIN AND SCHLESWIG.
QUESTION.

MR. BERNAL OSBORNE said, he rose to ask the First Lord of the Treasury, Whether Her Majesty's Government has grounds for believing that the order of succession in Holstein and Schleswig, which was contemplated by the Treaty of London, will be consented to by the Assemblies of Estates in those Duchies?

VISCOUNT PALMERSTON, in reply, stated that, in the first place, the Government had no certain knowledge that the Estates of those Duchies were to be assembled. He was aware that there existed a wish that they should be assembled on the part of some portion of Germany. [Mr. BERNAL OSBORNE: The whole of Germany.] But if there were any legal or competent au-

Mr. Laird

thority to assemble them, he confessed he could not see what they were likely to do when assembled.

MR. BERNAL OSBORNE said, he wished to know. whether he was to understand that it was the noble Lord's opinion that those Duchies were not entitled to any assembly of the Estates.

VISCOUNT PALMERSTON said, he did not quite understand the question. The Duchies had Estates which were liable to be summoned by a competent authority. He believed, however, there was a doubt whether there existed any competent authority at present.

MR. BERNAL OSBORNE: In consequence of the Treaty of 1852.

VISCOUNT PALMERSTON: The Treaty 1852 had nothing to do with the matter. Holstein and Schleswig were now occupied by Foreign Powers. The authority of the Sovereign of the Duchies had been suspended by those Foreign Powers, and it was doubted whether there was any authority competent to summon the Estates.

SIR HARRY VERNEY said, he wished to know, Whether it is to be understood that no steps would be taken with regard to Holstein and Schleswig without obtaining the opinion of the inhabitants of those Duchies in some way that would be deemed legal and constitutional?

VISCOUNT PALMERSTON said, that was a question of policy which he really could not undertake to answer.

SIR HARRY VERNEY said, he would beg to ask, Whether the noble Lord was not aware that by the Constitution of Denmark the Duchies of Schleswig and Holstein were placed on the same constitutional footing as the Estates of Denmark; and whether he was not aware that the consent of the Rigsraad having been asked to the new Constitution, it was not competent to ask the same assent from the Estates of Holstein and Schleswig?

VISCOUNT PALMERSTON was understood to say that he supposed his hon. Friend referred to the Treaty of 1852, and that that treaty was confirmed by the Powers of Europe.

IRISH CONSTABULARY.
QUESTION.

SIR HERVEY BRUCE said, he wished to ask the Chief Secretary for Ireland, Whether he considers the omission of the words "by night" after the words "by day," in second line of sixth paragraph of the instructions issued to the Constabulary in May, 1860, which words occur in the second line of the fifth paragraph of the instructions issued to the same force in October, 1837, relieves them from the properly watching of the towns in Ireland by night, or, if he did not consider it relieves, why they do not perform that duty as they formerly did?

SIR ROBERT PEEL said, in reply, that the words used in the last set of instructions were almost a literal repetition of those used in the former one, and that there was no substantial alteration.

LORD NAAS said, he wished to know if it is the intention of the Government to issue any fresh instructions as to watching towns in Ireland?

SIR ROBERT PEEL replied, that after the discussion which took place the other night, he would endeavour to meet as far as he could the wishes of hon. Gentlemen as expressed on that occasion.

GOVERNMENT ANNUITIES BILL—MR. H. B. SHERIDAN.—PRIVILEGE.

SIR JOHN HAY, who had given notice of a Motion—

"That this House sees with regret that the Chancellor of the Exchequer has not considered it his duty, after the explanation given last night, to withdraw the imputations which he has cast upon the hon. Member for Dudley"—

said, I rise for the purpose of bringing before the House a question of Privilege. It will be in the recollection of the House that a challenge was given very recently, in reference to certain allegations made by the Chancellor of the Exchequer against the hon. Member for Dudley (Mr. H. B. Sheridan). The right hon. Gentleman said that if the allegations he had made were not sustained, not only was an apology due from him to the hon. Member for Dudley, but that he should deserve the censure of the House. "Upon that issue," added the right hon. Gentleman, "I intend to stand or fall." Now I am anxious to bring under the consideration of the House the circumstances which led to that challenge. Certainly I owe an apology to the House for intruding upon them on this matter; but I venture to think—

MR. SPEAKER: The question of Privilege having been raised, that must be decided before the hon. and gallant Member can proceed to address the House.

THE CHANCELLOR OF THE EXCHEQUER: I wish, as the person mainly concerned, to make only one observation. I do not set myself up as an authority on the rules of the House, but I may perhaps be permitted to say, that it would be most acceptable to me if the hon. Baronet could be allowed to proceed with his Motion, and that every facility should be afforded for its discussion.

MR. SPEAKER: I think the House will be of opinion, that it would not be a convenient course to extend the area of privilege without due consideration: as regards the occurrence being a recent one, so far the hon. Member is in order. But I should say, on looking at the terms of his Motion, that what has occurred in the House does not fulfil other conditions as regards privilege. In my opinion, it does not distinctly concern the privileges of the House, or call for the present interposition of the House. At the same time, I should be sorry to give any opinion to the House which is not perfectly fair and candid; and I must admit that the challenge referred to on the part of the right hon. Gentleman the Chancellor of the Exchequer does materially complicate this question. After what has been stated, if it should be the general desire of the House to pursue this discussion, I would venture to recommend that the area of privilege should not be extended; and I would suggest that it would be a more convenient course, if the House deems this a matter which it would be proper at once to entertain, if the noble Lord will consent, not to deal with it as a question of privilege, but to postpone the other Orders until after the Motion of the hon. Member has been disposed of.

VISCOUNT PALMERSTON: Sir, in accordance with the recommendation you have just given, I beg to move that the Orders be postponed till the Motion of the hon. Baronet the Member for Wakefield has been disposed of.

MR. E. P. BOUVERIE: Sir, there are two points of order which I would respectfully submit for your consideration. I understand that the intention of the hon. Baronet the Member for Wakefield, is to submit to the House a Resolution of which he has given notice. As I read his Resolution, it seems to me to be a vote of censure on a Member of the House for words spoken in a past debate. Now, there are two rules of the House which I have always understood were strictly observed. One is, that we have no right in this House to refer to a past debate in the same Session. The other rule is still more important and absolute, and is necessary for the protection of Members of the House and for the freedom of debate. It is that no Member is to be called upon to answer for words spoken in this House unless it be immediately moved that the words used be taken down by the clerk at the table. Therefore I want to know, Sir, whether the House can now be called on to pass a vote of censure on a Member of this House for statements made by him, and "imputations conveyed," to quote the phrase of the Resolution, in the course of a speech spoken by him nearly a fortnight ago? [A MEMBER: Only last night.] I understood that the "imputations conveyed" were those originally made in a speech on Monday week—nearly a fortnight ago. I can only say that if the House comes to a vote of censure on a Member for words used at that distance of time, no matter what these words may have been or how open they were to censure at the time, it will be distinctly contravening what has been the universal rule and order of the House in such a case. This is a matter not of mere form, but of substance. It is a practice essential to the protection of the liberty of debate in this House, and if it be broken through, any Member may be liable to be censured and ill-treated for words which were never really spoken by him, at the will of a majority of the House. As far as I can judge, it seems to me that the House would be committing a breach of our most respected orders if it were to go into a debate on words spoken by the Chancellor of the Exchequer on a previous occasion.

MR. ROEBUCK: I think, Sir, the object of the hon. Baronet is not to find fault with any particular expression used by the right hon. Gentleman, and therefore the words could not be taken down. That to which he wishes to draw attention is the whole tone and spirit and temper and behaviour of the right hon. Gentleman in the discussion to which he refers.

MR. SPEAKER: It appears to me that the view taken by the hon. and learned Member for Sheffield is the correct one. This is not a question of words liable to objection used in debate. If it had been, the words, no doubt, ought to have been taken down at the moment. The House will, however, remember that last night the time of the House was occupied for nearly two hours by a matter of personal explanation, extending far beyond the ordinary limits of such explanations; and a series of statements and facts were

Mr. E. P. Bouverie

brought under discussion. My understanding is that it is on these statements that the challenge was offered, and the challenge has been accepted. At the same time, I think the House has been judicious in not considering the question as one affecting the established rules of privilege.

MR. H. BAILLIE: I think the view taken by the right hon. Member for Kilmarnock (Mr. Bouverie) is the correct one —namely, that if we are to have a discussion at all, it must be upon words recorded by the Clerk at the table, and not upon the mere tone of a speech. Holding that opinion, I shall take the sense of the House upon any Motion for postponing the Orders of the Day.

MR. NEWDEGATE: I think it must be perfectly apparent to common sense, that when the House is asked to act judicially, the exact substance of the indictment upon which we are invited to give a judgment should be laid before us, and after notice, unless the words to which exception is taken have just been spoken, and are quite fresh in the memory of the House. I am sure the hon. Member for Wakefield (Sir John Hay) would not wish to induce the House to enter upon an inquiry to discover what were the objectionable passages in a speech which is not before us. It seems to me that we are asked to pass an opinion upon the temper manifested by a Member of this House in debate, without having any evidence of the temper of which the hon. Baronet complains. I do not see, therefore, how the House can, in the present state of circumstances, without having any distinct issue before us, express an opinion creditable to itself.

COLONEL FRENCH: I hope it will not be forgotten that a challenge has been given to the House by the Chancellor of the Exchequer. The complaint, as I understand it, is not that any particular words have been spoken, but that certain words have not been spoken. Let us hope that, under the circumstances, the right hon. Gentleman will relieve the House from the necessity of going into this debate, by withdrawing the imputations upon the hon. Member for Dudley.

LORD STANLEY: I think the House is in danger of getting into great difficulty if it proceeds further in this matter. The question is not merely of form, but of substance also. There seems to be great weight in the observations of the right hon. Member for Kilmarnock

(Mr. Bouverie), and it certainly would not be worth while—I say so with all respect to the Chancellor of the Exchequer and the other party concerned—for the sake of bringing this particular question to a satisfactory issue to establish a precedent that might become in times more troubled than these a source of considerable inconvenience. There is another point that I would recommend to the consideration of the House. I confess I do not see how we are to come to a satisfactory solution of the points in dispute—if they are still in dispute—between the Chancellor of the Exchequer and the hon. Member for Dudley. If we are to be called upon to adjudicate upon these matters, we cannot do so merely upon an *ex parte* statement from either side. I, for one, utterly disclaim the responsibility of undertaking to decide who is right and who is wrong in such matters as those which were the subject of discussion yesterday upon a mere *ex parte* statement on each side, with no evidence, no witnesses to examine, no means of satisfying ourselves upon the points on which we might desire further information. I do not think there could be any satisfactory issue to this discussion if it were to take place, and I am persuaded it would be better that the matter should be allowed to remain where it is.

LORD ROBERT CECIL: If the House should refuse to go into this discussion to-night, it must follow that hereafter, when a Minister of the Crown or any other Member, having uttered words affecting the reputation of another Member, challenges the judgment of this House, that challenge must be held to be a mere idle and futile flourish. The Chancellor of the Exchequer closed the debate last night by distinctly challenging the judgment of the House. Are we now to say, by allowing the matter to end here, that the judgment so challenged shall not be given? There is another point. The reputation of a private Member of this House has been, in the opinion of many of us, cruelly dealt with. For that great wrong, if it be a wrong, there is, if you refuse to go into this matter to-night, absolutely no redress. Protected by the privileges of this House, the Chancellor of the Exchequer cannot be sued before the ordinary courts of the land for having, as it is assumed, slandered and calumniated another Member. I do not say that he has actually slandered and calumniated any man, but I do say that if he has done so he cannot be subjected to those processes of law to which every person has a right, in ordinary cases, to resort when he feels his reputation has been wrongfully and foully injured. It appears to me that if we maintain this privilege of protecting Members of this House from all actions at law—and we must maintain it—and if we do that by the side of the fact that words spoken here are published over the length and breadth of the land, and are soon known to the whole world, we must make up our minds, when imputations affecting the character of a Member are made in this House, and are denied, and when the judgment of the House is challenged, not to refuse to pass the judgment so demanded.

LORD ROBERT MONTAGU: I think the noble Lord the Member for King's Lynn (Lord Stanley) has shown a great deal more wisdom than the noble Lord who has just spoken. If it were intended to raise a discussion upon certain words which had been uttered in this House, those words, as the right hon. Member for Kilmarnock has said, ought to have been taken down at the time by the clerk, so that there should be no doubt as to the words which had been actually used. If, on the contrary, certain allegations of fact were to be called in question, and we were to invite the Chancellor of the Exchequer to withdraw imputations if we decided that they were unfounded, then it would be necessary that at the outset we should come to a solemn judgment as to whether those imputations are true or false. Has any one Member in this House compared the speech of the Chancellor of the Exchequer with the reply of the hon. Member for Dudley? Has any one Member set the imputations against the answer which had been given to them? If not, then not a single Member of the House is in a position to give judgment in the matter. But, even supposing that hon. Members had compared the speeches in question, item with item, and statement with reply, then they must, moreover, take some evidence to prove whether the imputations of the Chancellor of the Exchequer, or the answers of the hon. Member for Dudley are true or false. Both the Chancellor of the Exchequer and the hon. Member for Dudley, I have no doubt, have stated and would always state what they believed to be true. Yet either the one or the other may be mistaken, and, therefore, we cannot give judgment upon their statements alone. For these reasons I entirely agree with the noble Lord the

Member for King's Lynn, and I shall vote against the Motion of the noble Viscount at the head of the Government.

THE CHANCELLOR OF THE EXCHE-QUER: I rise, Sir, in the hope that in the fewest possible words I may be able to assist the House in what undoubtedly appears to be a serious dilemma. I do not feel very confident upon that subject, but I think it my duty to offer the few remarks which I have to make. They may, at any rate, help the House to a conclusion on the question whether they would proceed to the consideration of this matter in full detail —which would be the course most agreeable to myself—or whether they should take some other step in conformity with the general rules which regulate our proceedings. My hon. and gallant Friend the Member for Roscommon (Colonel French) appealed to me to relieve the House by withdrawing what he called my "imputations." I think the House will feel that no man being a Member of this House, not to say a Minister of the Crown, can, except in vague and general terms, deny what is only vaguely and generally imputed. The hon. Baronet the Member for Wakefield (Sir John Hay) is met with this difficulty—that he did not cause the words to be taken down at the time they were spoken. My sincere object is to help the hon. Baronet out of that difficulty, and, at the same time, to avoid saying what is offensive to anybody. I shall endeavour to avoid repeating anything that would give pain, but I shall also endeavour to define, as far as I can, the state of the case. Let me distinguish between what was said of a certain company or institution and what was said of the hon. Member for Dudley. I have never shrunk from avowing, I have never attempted to conceal, I thought it part of my duty to make manifest, that I described in my speech a certain company or institution, which need not now be named, as a company of a certain character. [An hon. MEMBER: Fraudulent.] My object at present is to state the case without using offensive expressions, or allowing a syllable to pass my lips calculated to give offence. I showed that the company or institution was of a certain character by a series of allegations of facts, and, with the exception of a verbal matter, I am not able to recede from any one of those allegations. I shall not now enter into any detail, but I may say that I am perfectly prepared with conclusive documentary evidence to re-establish any one of my

Lord Robert Montagu

allegations impugned in the statement which followed mine last night. That is my position. Two questions, I think, arise—are the allegations true; in other words, was the character attempted to be fastened upon the company or institution just? Or is the House prepared to affirm that the allegations are untrue and the character unjust? Upon the first question I cannot promise to do more than I have done, because, in my opinion, the allegations have been sustained; but I may point out to the noble Lord the Member for Stamford (Lord Robert Cecil) that if he thinks they have not been sustained, and if he desires to make them the subject of inquiry, it is competent to him or any other Member to move words of instruction to a Committee of this House which would completely open up the question of the truth or falsehood of the allegations. Or, if the noble Lord prefers a shorter course to his object, and thinks fit to move a Resolution that the company described by me was a company which, although perhaps unfortunate, did nothing to forfeit moral confidence and respect, it is open to him to move such a Resolution; and although I could not vote for it, yet, if it were the sense of the majority of the House, I should at once express my regret for having been so unfortunate originally as to form an opinion at variance with that of the high authority of the House, and should promise that thereafter my mouth would be for ever closed on that subject. So much, therefore, as far as the vindication of the company is concerned. Now I come to what concerns the hon. Member; and if I have been apparently prolix upon what concerns the company, it was that I might cut off and clearly separate that portion of my remarks from what concerns the hon. Member. Well, no one has given me any assistance by referring to any words or terms used by me respecting the hon. Member for Dudley; and, therefore, in the sincere attempt which I wish to make to facilitate the proceedings of the House, I have no course open to me but to state my own view—which, I grant, is totally without authority—of the bearing of the description given by me of the company upon the hon. Member. I am sure the House will receive it with indulgence. I found a company that bore in my mind a certain character. I deemed it, whether erroneously or not, a part of my duty to open up, by a single specimen at any rate, the character of a certain portion of these companies. I found in the advertisements of that company a name, as auditor, which appeared to be the name of a Member of this House, although, of course, I was not absolutely justified in concluding that it was the name of that hon. Gentleman; but I adverted to it as probably being the name of a Member of this House; and I stated, in terms for which I claim no praise at all, but terms such as decency required, that I had no doubt he was in a situation to make a satisfactory explanation to the House upon the subject. It may be asked of me what did I mean to convey by that reference to the hon. Gentleman. That is a perfectly fair question, and I will give to it, not only a sincere answer, but the clearest answer that I can offer. But, observe, that everything except the reference to the hon. Member was part of the *res gestæ* from which I sought to prove the character of the company—another portion of this question, although I do not say that he will not be justified in raising that also before the House if he thinks it to be his duty to do so; because I hold that those who are outside of this House are as much entitled, though perhaps, not in the same form, to our protection, as those who sit within its walls. Now, my view of the case in its bearing on the hon. Member I left at the time to be inferred simply from the words which I used; but I think it was this—that when the name of an hon. Gentleman is found bearing a responsible office in a company which appears to be of the character to which I have referred, the effect is twofold. In the first place there arises against him a certain amount of adverse presumption that he is implicated in the transactions of that company; and in the second place there arises this patent and important fact, that his name as connected with these offices in the company has gone out to the world, and has presumably served in the eye of the public as a guarantee of the soundness and respectability of that company. Now, Sir, that is precisely what I intended to convey with regard to the hon. Member. I should be ashamed to say that I do not think my words are calculated to establish against him a certain amount of adverse presumption. I should also be ashamed to say that I do not think it is most unfortunate that many gentlemen are in the habit of permitting their names unhappily to become guarantees to the public on behalf of institutions of which they do not, perhaps, know the real character in many cases— which they may in many cases believe, and which they do in many cases believe, to be thoroughly respectable and solvent, but which, at the same time, may be quite otherwise. And I do not deny that I think a certain amount of blame is to be attached to any one who, as an officer or trustee of a company such as I believe that company was, whether he has direct cognizance of its transactions or not, allows his name to be held out as a guarantee. I hope that that is an explicit statement of what I conceive to be the effect of my speech. With respect to a name given on behalf of a company that is bad, if the House thinks that the company is good, and chooses to say so by its vote, of course the charge entirely disappears, and I have already stated the course which I should take in that case. With regard to the adverse presumption against a Member of this House, of course it is obvious that it is for him to rise and purge himself by his denial of any knowledge or any complicity in any transaction connected with that company which is not according to the laws of honourable commercial enterprize. Now, I did not understand the hon. Member—but I submit myself to the judgment of this House if I am wrong—I did not understand the hon. Gentleman in the course he took on Thursday night to adopt the method of purgation which I have described. The hon. Member questioned my allegations, stated that they were utterly untrue, touched many of them in detail, and said nothing, as far as I could gather, with respect to the admission even that there was anything whatever to blame in the proceedings of this company; and, of course, if that be so, he did not require to disclaim—

MR. H. B. SHERIDAN: I rise to Order. I distinctly stated, when the right hon. Gentleman made his first speech, that —[*Cries of* "Order!" *and* "Chair!"] Sir, I cannot allow the right hon. Gentleman to make a statement to the House which is not founded on fact. ["Order!"]

MR. SPEAKER: The hon. Member will have an opportunity of explaining.

THE CHANCELLOR OF THE EXCHEQUER: I really had no intention to misstate what the hon. Gentleman said. I am speaking of what he said on Thursday. I thought I was only stating what was patent and obvious to all. Perhaps, when the hon. Member is perfectly cool he will see that my remark does not in any way call for either that or any other interruption. Undoubtedly, to state it moderately, the main staple of the hon. Gentleman's explanation was his objection to the truth of the allegations of fact which I had made. On that my statement was, that what I felt was that if I had made allegations not founded on fact I had committed a grave offence and deserved the severest censure of the House. I am still of that opinion, and I do not mean to interpose any obstacle, if it depends upon me, to the trial of that question, if it is to be tried. And now I come to the purely personal part of the matter. If the hon. Member has made the denial to which I have referred, declaring—without committing himself, if he pleases, about this company—that he knew nothing of, and that he had no share in, any transactions except such as were legitimate, I can only say that I have not been fortunate enough to hear that declaration. But, if that declaration was made, my duty is plain, and I cannot hesitate to perform it. I heard him say that the duties of an auditor were of a definite character, and that he had given his name as trustee in various instances. I will not attempt to quote, because I do not recollect precisely the effect of what he stated ; but I did not hear from his mouth that distinct declaration applicable to the whole state of the case. If he could, indeed, entirely or generally disprove the allegations of fact which I made, I do not say that it would be necessary for him to make such a declaration ; but if he did make such a declaration, I would not for one moment hesitate to admit that so far as I am concerned that declaration made in this House and accepted by this House is absolute and conclusive, and entirely disposes of whatever adverse presumption might have arisen out of the facts stated by me—whether they be true or not true —as far as regards the hon. Gentleman. Can I say more than that ? If the hon. Gentleman has made that declaration, I must say that I did not fully apprehend its purport and meaning, and I make an apology for not having done so. If he makes that declaration now I will abide by my word, and that declaration shall be final and conclusive upon me; and if accepted by the House it disposes of whatever adverse presumption there might have been against him, and leaves him, as far as my statement is involved, exactly as if that statement had never been made. Perhaps, if hon. Members should think that there is

more which I ought to state in this matter [" No !"], and should suggest it to me in debate, I am sure the House, in its kindness, will not prevent me, on the ground of form, from rising again to make good any deficiency in my present remarks. I have endeavoured to give the bearing of the case in the clearest light, to separate effectually what I think are the two distinct parts of it, to explain my position in relation to it, to vindicate myself and the statements of fact which I made, and at the same time to do justice to the hon. Member.

VISCOUNT PALMERSTON : I should hope, after the explanation of my right hon. Friend, that it will be unnecessary for the hon. Gentleman opposite to make the Motion which has been suggested. I am sure the House will all concur in regretting a discussion which has given pain to the hon. Member for Dudley — pain which I am certain that my right hon. Friend must, like myself, regret should have been given, and which arose out of the statements which he deemed it his duty to make. But I should really trust, that after the statement which my right hon. Friend has just made, and the frank and handsome manner in which he has accepted the declaration of the hon. Member for Dudley, it will not be thought necessary for the House to go on with this Motion.

MR. H. B. SHERIDAN : Sir, I have been challenged by the right hon. Gentleman to say whether or not in the course of the debate raised by him I denied certain allegations which he made. I never heard any allegations made of the nature to which he evidently alludes ; but immediately after the speech to which this discussion refers I did rise and state that I had acted as an auditor of the company many years ago ; that the position of the company was then of such a character that the business was both sound and profitable ; that I knew of no transaction of the company that deserved any censure ; that I ceased to hold office immediately after 1856 ; that I was in entire ignorance of any of the other incidents by which he characterized the company ; that I was not responsible for any of the conditions which attached to its management; and that neither then nor last night could I understand how or why my name was brought forward in connection with the company.

THE CHANCELLOR OF THE EXCHEQUER : The hon. Gentleman has made the declaration to which I referred, and has stated explicitly that he knew of no transaction of the company deserving censure. If he did the same thing on a former evening, I regret that I did not gather its effect. The House will, I am sure, forgive me if it should prove that I have been misled on a particular point. He stated that he ceased to hold office in the company in 1856. I quoted his name as trustee, I think, in 1859. But it was from what purported to be an advertisement of the company itself. However that may be, accepting the declaration of the hon. Gentleman, and accepting it also as made on the first night of the debate, I must add my sincere regret if he has suffered pain owing to my failure to perceive the effect of his statement on that occasion.

SIR JOHN HAY: I think, Sir, after the very satisfactory explanation which has just fallen from the right hon. Gentleman, it would be very unfair indeed to proceed further with this matter. I had not the acquaintance of the hon. Member for Dudley, and my only object was to obtain what appeared to be necessary, in the first assembly of gentlemen in Europe, from the right hon. Gentleman, whom we all respect for his talents and eloquence. I myself felt, and others felt, that after the explanation I understood to be made by the hon. Member for Dudley there was something cruel, as it were, in the right hon. Gentleman not rising in his place and accepting it freely and frankly in the manner he has done to-day. The House, I am sure, will forgive me for the intrusion; but I feel I have done a service to it by placing this matter on a proper footing.

THE EASTER RECESS.

VISCOUNT PALMERSTON *moved*, "That the House at its rising do adjourn till *Monday*, 4th April."

DOE PARK &c. RESERVOIRS, BRADFORD.
OBSERVATIONS.

MR. FERRAND said, he rose to call attention to the dangerous state of the Doe Park and other reservoirs, belonging to the Bradford Corporation Waterworks. This was a question of great importance to a large number of people residing in his own immediate neighbourhood. He put a Question the other evening to the right hon. Baronet the Secretary of State for the Home Department, in respect to the dangerous state of those reservoirs; and the right hon. Gentleman replied by saying that he would communicate on the subject with the Mayor of Bradford. On a subsequent evening the right hon. Baronet informed him (Mr. Ferrand) that he had made the communication referred to, and that he had received a letter from the Mayor of Bradford, informing him that his (Mr. Ferrand's) statement in regard to the Doe Park Reservoir, was exaggerated. Instead of that being the case, he now asked the indulgence of the House while he endeavoured to prove that, so far from his statement being exaggerated, it was considerably within the mark. The Bradford Corporation had expended nearly £750,000 on those waterworks, a large item of which money was expended in repairing leaking and dangerous reservoirs. The engineer of the Bradford Corporation Waterworks held his appointment under an Act of Parliament, and received 5 per cent of all the money expended on those waterworks. The corporation had no power of dismissing him, therefore he was a paramount master over the corporation and over the waterworks. In his (Mr. Ferrand's) immediate neighbourhood there were three reservoirs belonging to those waterworks. The highest of these is, he believed, in a perfectly safe state. The second, called the Doe Park Reservoir, which, when full, contained 110,000,000 gallons of water, was completed about two years ago. Soon after it was filled the immense volume of water forced its way through the embankment, and there was every probability of the embankment giving way, and the water in such case would have burst down the valley, carrying death and desolation wherever it spread. A messenger arrived at his house one evening, informing him of this alarming state of things. He (Mr. Ferrand) immediately dispatched a messenger on horseback to Bradford to inform the Mayor, and at the same time he addressed a letter to the Home Secretary on the subject. The Waterworks Committee happened to be sitting at the time, and by great exertions they were enabled to stop the leak. Since that period this reservoir had been frequently repaired, and the embankment had been repuddled seven different times. About a month ago he himself visited the reservoir, and he found the water within a few feet of the top of it. In the centre of the embankment a large number of men

were employed driving a shaft twenty
yards long from the summit to the bottom
for the purpose of stopping the leakage.
Another shaft was being driven outside
the embankment for the purpose of discovering the leakage, where a large body
of water flowed out sufficient to turn a
good-sized mill. During the last two years,
when this reservoir was full of water, the
corporation employed men during the night
to watch it and to report to the inhabitants
when there was danger of the embankment
giving way. The contractor gave up repairing it some months ago and threw it
upon the hands of the corporation, who,
for a considerable time, had been endeavouring to stop the leaks. It was under
these circumstances that he had called the
attention of the Home Secretary to the
dangerous state of this reservoir. The
Mayor had stated that the reservoir had
been run dry, and at present there was no
further danger. Below this reservoir there
was another which held 11,000,000 cubic
feet of water. If the higher reservoir
broke down upon the second, both embankments would go, and the water would
rush through the valley and would probably occasion as much destruction as the
Sheffield reservoir had recently done. If
the catastrophe occurred during the night,
the probability was that every person residing in the valley would perish. Last
Monday week the water of the second reservoir, notwithstanding the bywash and
the perpendicular culvert, rose five feet
above the culvert and bywash, and if it
had only risen a few feet more, it would
have overflowed the embankment, and the
most disastrous consequences would have
ensued. In the valley there were five or six
mills. There were seven or eight tenants
with their families on his own property
besides about 300 people residing in the
valley. A short distance below this valley the railway crossed the river Aire
with a wooden bridge upon a high embankment, and the Leeds and Liverpool
Canal was carried across it by an aqueduct.
If the embankment gave way the manufacturing town of Shipley would be a scene
of ruin—in fact, there was a danger of the
waters rushing even as far as Leeds itself,
where the damage would be frightful.
There was another reservoir in the valley
of the Aire—the Silsden Reservoir—to
which also he wished to draw attention;
this had also been in a dangerous state,
and the embankment would have given way
on one evening but for the timely warning

Mr. Ferrand

given by a person who discovered the leakage. At the time, there were 2,000 or
3,000 persons residing in its immediate
vicinity. In that case the embankment
was taken down and a new one constructed.
There was another reservoir in a neighbouring valley also in a dangerous state,
and notwithstanding that the engineer of
the waterworks had a few months ago certified on oath that it was in a secure state,
he (Mr. Ferrand) was informed that that
reservoir had since given way. He thought
he had now made out a strong case to justify the right hon. Gentleman the Home
Secretary in sending down a good engineer.
He would now ask leave to read the following letters from a gentleman at Bradford,
for the purpose of showing that he had not
made an exaggerated statement, as he had
been charged with having done:—

"Bradford, Yorkshire, March 16, 1864.
"Sir,—I see by the paper this morning that Sir
George Grey stated last night in the House of
Commons, in reply to your question about the
Doe Park Reservoir, that he had written to the
mayor of Bradford for information on the subject
of its alleged insecurity.
"Without at all wishing to cast any reflection
on our worthy mayor, it may be important to you
to know that any statement he may make, if even
affirming its safety, will not have the slightest
effect in re-assuring the minds of a large portion
of the public hereabouts. The present mayor has
always been in the corporation the most prominent
and assiduous promoter of the corporation waterworks schemes; and it is almost unnecessary that
I should tell you that in every respect the public
have reason to complain of the whole management
of these matters. Not only have the original estimates of cost been very far exceeded, but wholly
unlooked for delays in the completion of the works
have taken place, and it is well known in the town
and neighbourhood of Bradford that these delays
have mainly arisen from the defective character of
the workmanship in the various stages of construction, and especially so in the reservoirs. I
am not at present a resident of Bradford, having
removed from the borough about four months ago,
and it might, perhaps, be said that I meddle with
what does not now concern me; but as the safety
of human life concerns every man, I do not hesitate
to say that any reply the mayor of Bradford may
send to Sir George Grey will not be deemed sufficiently reliable by thousands of the inhabitants
and ratepayers of Bradford; not that the mayor
would willingly state any untruth, but because he
has been so often identified with waterworks mistakes."
"W. Ferrand, Esq., M.P.

He had also received the following telegram
from a merchant of Bradford, residing in
the valley below the Doe Park embankment:—

"March 17.—The Doe Park embankment since
it was made has been repuddled in seven different

places, and is still leaking. Hughenden reservoir which must receive the water from Doe Park, rose five feet last Monday week, notwithstanding the bywash and culvert being in full play. The arch under the Hughenden embankment is considerably out of . . . I say these reservoirs are unsafe. The Silsden culvert is three feet out of perpendicular."

What he desired to know was, whether a Government Inspector would be sent down to places where danger was apprehended?

Sir GEORGE GREY thought it would have been more convenient if the hon. Gentleman had brought the facts he had just mentioned under the notice of the Government in a different manner. If the hon. Gentleman would be good enough to place upon paper the facts which he had now mentioned and communicate with him (Sir George Grey), he would consider whether they were sufficient to require that a Government Inspector should be sent down to the place in question. He did not dispute the facts stated by the hon. Gentleman, because he only now heard them for the first time, and therefore could not say that the reservoirs referred to were not in a dangerous state ; but certainly no previous communication to that effect had been made to him.

COLLECTION OF TAXES BILL.

QUESTION.

Sir HENRY WILLOUGHBY inquired of the Chancellor of the Exchequer, Whether it was intended to proceed that evening with the Collection of Taxes Bill?

The CHANCELLOR of the EXCHEQUER said, that the course he proposed to take would, he thought, be convenient and satisfactory to the House. He proposed to go into Committee *pro formâ* that evening, with a view to introduce a number of Amendments. These Amendments would relate to the meetings of the Commissioners, to granting to present collectors fair considerations for their vested interests, to compensations to collectors whose services would not be continued, and also to a mode of enabling persons resident in country districts to pay their taxes by means of money orders instead of being required to visit the market town. In order that those Amendments might be intelligible it would be necessary to reprint the Bill. That course he proposed to take, and to fix the Committee for a distant day, say about the middle of April.

M. MAZZINI—THE GRECO CONSPIRACY. —POSITION OF MR. STANSFELD.

QUESTION.

LORD ELCHO : Sir, I wish to put a question to my noble Friend at the head of the Government, of which I have privately given him notice. It is a question which I think naturally follows from the very painful discussions which we have had in this House, arising out of the unfortunate friendship which exists between the hon. Member for Halifax and M. Mazzini—a friendship which is, I think, unfortunate in its consequences as regards the hon. Member for himself, for the Government of which he is a Member, and for this House. I do not wish to revive the painful discussion of last evening, nor to express any opinion upon the course which has been taken by the hon. Gentleman the Member for Halifax since the question was first brought before the House by the hon. Member for Finsbury. I do not say whether it would have been better if the hon. Gentleman the Member for Halifax had at once expressed his regret for what had occurred, instead of attempting to defend a man who I consider is, in many respects, incapable of being defended. All I wish to say is this : looking calmly and dispassionately at the whole question, it appears to me that the hon. Gentleman has been guilty, to say the least, of a grave indiscretion—an indiscretion which amounts to a public scandal. The indiscretion of the hon. Gentleman is this — that he, a Member of Her Majesty's Government, allowed, and has allowed up to a very recent time, his name to be used as a cover for the secret correspondence of M. Mazzini. Now, I say, that is a grave indiscretion, amounting to a great public scandal—a scandal affecting not only the character of the hon. Gentleman, but of the Government of which he is a Member, the character of this House, and of this country—one which is calculated to cause a bad understanding and bad feeling, even if such have not already been created, between this country and a friendly foreign country. That being so, it appears to me that the division of last night, so far from placing the House in a better position, has rather put us in a worse position, because a question which was not in itself a party question, was by the issue made to depend upon it by the hon. Member made a party question. I voted with the minority last night, but I say I did not vote as a party

M

man for a party move, but as the only means presented to me as a Member of this House, as one to whom the honour of this House and the country is dear—the only means of expressing my opinion that a great public scandal had taken place; and whether the explanation of the hon. Gentleman might or might not have been deemed satisfactory, still something appears to be wanting beyond what has already been said or done upon this subject. Any further Resolution upon this subject would unquestionably be made the subject of a party division—such a colour would be given to it on this side of the House. But when the last division is said to have been a party division, I may say that I have heard many men on either side of the House express their regret that they found themselves obliged to vote one way or the other upon this question. I am confident that I express the public opinion out of doors and the opinion of Members in this House when I say, that I and most if not all the Members of this House most bitterly regret the position in which we are placed. But if that division cannot place the House in a right position there is one course which, if it had been taken at the very outset, would have placed the Members of this House right with the country and with a Foreign Power. That is, if the hon. Member for Halifax at once, when he saw the position in which his indiscretion, his culpable indiscretion I must call it, had placed this House and this country, and the Government of which he is a Member, had immediately tendered his resignation as a Member of the Government. Now, the question which I wish to ask the First Lord of the Treasury is this, whether the hon. Member for Halifax has at any time since this subject was first brought under the notice of the House by the hon. Member for Finsbury (Mr. Cox) formally tendered his resignation to Her Majesty's Government, and, if so, whether the resignation has been refused. Since I came down to the House this evening I have been privately informed that the hon. Gentleman has done so. When I first thought it desirable to ask this question I was in utter ignorance that any such offer had been made. But the fact was there was an almost universal opinion last night in the House, that the only course for the hon. Gentleman to take was to tender his resignation, and that opinion was not confined to hon. Gentlemen opposite, for the friends of the hon. Member himself expressed themselves to that effect. With reference to the refusal of the Government to accept the resignation I do not wish at present to express any opinion. What I wish to do now is to ask my noble Friend, Whether, at any time since the question has been discussed, the hon. Member for Halifax has tendered his formal resignation?

VISCOUNT PALMERSTON: I cannot but regret that my noble Friend, in asking the question which he might have put simply, has thought fit to revive the discussion of last night, which I certainly hoped had been concluded. I shall, however, abstain from following my noble Friend's example, and will simply answer the question which he has put. The noble Lord asks whether my hon. Friend has at any time subsequent to the introduction of the subject by the hon. Member for Finsbury, tendered the resignation of his office. My hon. Friend immediately after the question was brought forward made a communication to me through a common friend, that he placed his office entirely at the disposal of the Crown, and that at the slightest intimation from me he would formally tender his resignation of that office. My answer was I did not wish him to take that step, that I wished him not to take it—and if there is any responsibility attaching to that decision I am perfectly willing to take that responsibility upon myself.

MR. W. E. DUNCOMBE: After hearing the statement made by the noble Lord at the head of the Government, I must express my surprise at the decision at which he has arrived. I confess I think it is unworthy the position of Her Majesty's Government that a Member of this House who has committed so grave an indiscretion as that charged against the hon. Member for Halifax should be allowed to retain his position in that Government. I think Her Majesty's Government stand in a very unenviable position in permitting a gentleman to remain a Minister of the Crown who has been for seventeen years the intimate friend of Mazzini—a man who has not the courage to carry out his diabolical schemes, but who skulks under that protection which this free country affords to political refugees and exiles, to abuse that hospitality and conspire against the crowned heads of Europe and the established Governments of Europe, to send forth his emissaries into every capital to produce anarchy, and, if possible, to

Lord Elcho

overthrow Governments with which we are in alliance. Is it, I again ask, worthy of the position of Her Majesty's Government that they should have as a Colleague, sitting on that bench, one who admits that he has been for many years the intimate friend of Mazzini—a man who has been excluded from France and other countries —and who, I believe, dare not show his face in Italy, because he is known to be the plotter and a conspirator of Europe, and a disgrace to his nation ; and who, I must say, does bring down on every person who has any dealings with him, directly or indirectly, a portion of that disgrace.

MR. ALDERMAN ROSE : It will, I think, be heard with some surprise, not only throughout this country but on the Continent, that the Government have thought proper to endorse, if I may use the expression, the conduct of the hon. Member for Halifax. I have this afternoon seen a letter from a person of some eminence at Paris, and judging from the description which he gave, the effect of this discovery will not be laid at rest quite as soon as Ministers appear to think it will. Such a feeling has been created in France that I believe the First Minister of the Crown will have cause very much to regret that he has thought fit to adopt the conduct of his Colleague in this matter, and not to accept his resignation. For what is the state of the case ? Here is a man whose business has been for years to conspire against all constituted Governments and authorities in other countries, and who has, through the instrumentality of a Minister of the Crown, been carrying on a secret correspondence which he could not have done under the auspices of a less important personage. I think, therefore, that Her Majesty's Government, in not accepting the resignation of the hon. Gentleman, do, to a very great extent, adopt the responsibility of his conduct; and when they come to know the effect of that conduct throughout France, they will very much regret that they did not accept his resignation.

MR. W. E. FORSTER : I regret that this subject has been again renewed ; but it now certainly stands on a much more tangible ground than on last evening. Last evening we were asked whether we thought that the remarks of the Procureur Général deserved our serious consideration, so far as they regarded the hon. Member for Halifax. We decided that they did not. This evening my noble Friend the Member for Haddingtonshire (Lord Elcho) in ask-

ing the noble Lord at the head of the Government whether the hon. Member for Halifax has tendered his resignation, says that he considers that what he has done is a public scandal. He is followed by an hon. Member opposite, who says that the fact of my hon. Friend having been the friend of M. Mazzini for many years is a reason why he should not be a Member of the Administration. I trust that that Motion will be brought definitely before us, and that we shall be asked to decide, whether the fact that a man has been the friend of such a person as M. Mazzini does make it improper that he should be a Member of the Government. I do not agree with M. Mazzini in his views. I disagree with almost all the views I believe he now holds on foreign matters. I believe that he has done harm as well as good not only to the cause of order, but also to the cause of liberty throughout Europe; but I am not ashamed to say, whatever may be the feeling of some Members of this House, that I believe him to be a most earnest and sincere man, and a devoted patriot ; and I say, moreover, that I believe that one of the great reasons for the hostility shown to him, and through him to my hon. Friend the Member for Halifax is, that whatever may have been his faults he has been one of the great instruments in effecting the resurrection of Italy. There is a difference of opinion about that, but this I do say— and I do not think that any Member of the House, when he calmly considers the matter, will doubt it—that though we may not agree with M. Mazzini in his views, we may have a high opinion of his character. Then comes this question—my hon. Friend having had a personal friendship for M. Mazzini, and also an agreement with him in opinion that Italy should be a nation, and a prosperous nation, ought he to have disowned and rejected his friendship with him because he became a Member of the Administration ? I should not be ashamed of being the friend of M. Mazzini. I am not ashamed of being his acquaintance, but I should have been ashamed of my hon. Friend the Member for Halifax if, when he was appointed a Member of the Government, he had said to M. Mazzini, " I will have nothing more to do with you, and I disown the friendship of past years." I now come to what the noble Lord said about a public scandal. What is this public scandal ? Does any Member suppose that my hon. Friend is implicated in this plot, or so-called plot, which has been, I will not say discovered, but lately tried in Paris? Almost every Member who has spoken has acknowledged that he does not believe he was implicated. Does any one suppose that he was unconsciously concerned in it, or made use of in any way for the purpose of this conspiracy? I have not heard any hon. Gentleman say so. What, then, does all this excitement arise from? It arises from this—that among the papers of Greco were the few words, "Mr. Flower, 35, Thurloe Square." There was no proof nor allegation that Greco ever wrote a letter to that address. My hon. Friend states candidly and acknowledges with regret that M. Mazzini, being unable to receive letters from the Continent in his own name, he allowed his letters to be directed to his house, as they were to the houses of other of M. Mazzini's friends; but my hon. Friend does not know that M. Mazzini ever gave the name of Mr. Flower, and does not suppose he ever did. Now, the whole of this scandal comes to this. My hon. Friend says he has been acquainted with M. Mazzini for many years, that he did not refuse him access to his house, and that not having refused him access to his house, he did not tell him he should get no letters there, and that it was possible that letters may have been intended to be sent by some one to his house in the name of Flower. I quite grant that my hon. Friend did commit an indiscretion in allowing M. Mazzini's letters to be continued to be addressed to his house. He has expressed his regret for that. Is the House prepared to say that they think this ought to prevent my hon. Friend from continuing in the Administration, of which he is a credit and an ornament—that he ought no longer to remain a Member of the Government because he has the friendship of Mazzini, and has committed this indiscretion, which he now regrets? That is the simple question; and the noble Viscount, with that courage and generosity which makes him so popular in this House and the country, has declared that he will not be the instrument of driving my hon. Friend away from office because he has committed that indiscretion. I am persuaded that that is also the feeling of this House; and that, although the House may not agree with my hon. Friend in his opinion of Mazzini, it will assent to no proposal intended to drive my hon. Friend from office because he is a friend of Mazzini, because he owns his friendship, and because he has com-

Mr. W. E. Forster

mitted what, after all, is a very pardonable offence. And in this, I feel sure, that the opinion of the country will support the opinion of the House.

SIR JOHN WALSH: Sir, it appears to me that the hon. Gentleman who has just sat down (Mr. W. E. Forster), has scarcely stated the case with perfect correctness as regards the hon. Member for Halifax. And it appears to me there is a great difference between the hon. Gentleman being a friend of Mazzini for a great many years and his having given him facilities for carrying on a clandestine correspondence by permitting him to have letters addressed in a false name to his address. It appears to me there is the widest possible distinction between the two cases. I think it is most unfortunate that any gentleman holding a conspicuous office in the Administration should have been so long connected with a person like Mazzini, who has been implicated in such grave conspiracies against all the States of Europe. At the same time, I think the hon. Member, by his admission that he permitted Mazzini to have letters addressed to him in a false name to his house, and that he was so much implicated in Mazzini's conspiracy on a former occasion as to permit his name to be printed at the foot of a kind of bank-note which Mazzini circulated, greatly aggravates his false position. Hon. Members opposite have thought it necessary to pronounce very great eulogies on Mazzini's character. I have no wish to go into that question further than to say that Mazzini has been known to be a conspirator all his life. We have had proof of it on several occasions, and that he has encouraged assassination on several occasions. His was the head that plotted if his was not the hand which tried to execute these abominable plots; and it does appear to me that the very circumstance that he was the head to plot, though not the hand to execute, is in itself a very grave aggravation of the charges that are made against him. With regard to the noble Lord at the head of the Government, I have always observed that one of his noblest characteristics is, that he never deserts a friend in a strait, however great it may be; and however much the noble Lord in his mind feels that he is making a personal and political sacrifice in sustaining a friend, that one of his principal characteristics is to always sustain a friend and pull a Colleague through the mire if he can. I really think the noble Lord has been guided on this occasion more by that chivalrous feeling than by any deliberate approval of the conduct of the hon. Member for Halifax; for the noble Lord must know, as every hon. Member must feel convinced, that it is a great blow to his Administration. And I feel certain that in this House, with the country, and on the Continent, it will place Her Majesty's Government in a very embarrassing and unfortunate position. Now, I do not think the noble Lord has given a perfectly distinct answer to the question put to him by my noble Friend the Member for Haddingtonshire, which was, whether, the hon. Member for Halifax had thought fit, since this unfortunate question arose, to tender his resignation? The reply of the noble Lord at the head of the Government I understand to be, that the hon. Member for Halifax did not tender formally his resignation, but that through a third party—a mutual friend—he privately conveyed to the noble Lord an intimation that he was ready to resign if the noble Lord requested him to do so. That appears to me to be the substance of the reply. But, Sir, I think circumstances are now in some degree changed, and the hon. Member for Halifax does not now stand exactly in the same position as he did. The very small majority—which, if my noble Friend's explanation of their motives be taken as a correct one, was rather an equivocal one—has to a certain degree reestablished or whitewashed the hon. Member for Halifax; and I, therefore, ask him whether, considering the position in which he is placed with reference to this House, and the position in which he has placed the Government, whether it does not occur to him as a gentleman and a man of honour, that it would be a proper and becoming course for him to adopt—not to intimate through a third party—not merely to suggest that he was ready to resign his place if the noble Lord asked him, but to tender in a frank, manly, and direct manner his resignation positively and absolutely to the noble Lord at the head of the Government.

VISCOUNT PALMERSTON: What I intended was that my hon. Friend the Member for Halifax, through a common friend, placed himself and his office entirely in my hands.

MR. HALIBURTON: Perhaps the noble Lord will favour the House with his reasons for not accepting the hon. Gentleman's resignation—the reasons which operated with him when he declined to accept it. Now, I think the matter was debated last night on either side in a spirit which was not altogether becoming. On one side many of the remarks which were made with respect to Mazzini were received with a levity which I think unbecoming, and on the other side of the House a warmth of passion was exhibited which was very much out of place. As a public body, sitting in a *quasi*-judicial capacity, we have a great duty to perform, both towards the people of this country and the Emperor of the French. This is not the first time we have been charged with permitting conspiracy to be hatched for the purpose of taking the life of a monarch with whom we are in friendly alliance. Now, I think I am not saying too much when I state there is not a man in Europe whose life is so valuable to Europe at large, and—with the exception of our own gracious Sovereign—so valuable to us as that of the Emperor of the French. We owe to him and to his philosophic mind—to the calmness and clearness with which he considers the politics of the world—the repression of those rivalries, jealousies, and animosities which for ages past have existed in France against England. We know that in 1858, when that abominable conspiracy was hatched in this country by Orsini, such were the feelings of the French nation, and the French army in particular, that certain French Colonels addressed His Majesty, and besought him to lead them forth to drag the assassins from London, a place that harboured the villains of the world. Nor is the feeling less intense at the present moment, particularly connected with a man of Mazzini's character. We are told that this is only an indiscretion on the part of the hon. Member for Halifax. Indiscretion! It appears to me that there have been a succession of blunders. I do not think that any man possessing proper feelings ought to have gone into an Administration carrying with him the friendship of a man like Mazzini. Nor do I think that the noble Lord at the head of the Government should have invited a friend of Mazzini—not a secret friend, but a man who avows and glories in his friendship as one of the greatest philanthropists and patriots of the day—to take part in his Administration. Lord Russell, when he was a Member of this House, in discussing the Conspiracy Bill, spoke of him as "the assassin Mazzini," and he told a story to illustrate the character of that person. The noble Lord said—

" I will relate another instance, which became known last year. Mazzini, who is one of the persons who, they say, preach assassination, stated that a person holding a high station in the Piedmontese army came to him when a young man, and proposed to him to assassinate Charles Albert, the King of Sardinia. Mazzini told him he was hardly worthy to commit such an action ; but he gave him instructions, sent him to Turin, and gave him his own dagger wherewith to commit the crime."—[3 *Hansard*, cxlviii. 1041.]

Talk of the hon. Gentleman's indiscretion ! Did he hear that speech ; did he ever read that speech ; did he ever hear of it ? It is something more than an indiscretion to have the friendship of a felon of that kind. It is well known in this country that he is the father of assassins—that he is a man who sends assassins out with poisoned daggers. For men to claim him, as two hon. Gentlemen have done here, with pride, as a glorious man of fine intellect, as a noble character above the ordinary prejudices of the world, is that a mere indiscretion ? Is it an act of indiscretion to make his house a post office for the receipt of treasonable letters sent from different parts of the Continent to the great arch-agitator of the world ? Is that an indiscretion ? It is something more than an indiscretion ; it would form in an indictment a very strong feature in evidence. The hon. Baronet the Member for Yarmouth (Sir Henry Stracey) read last night extracts from Mazzini's own writings, in which he teaches the doctrine of assassination. Did the hon. Gentleman (Mr. Stansfeld) know that before or during his long friendship with Mazzini ? If he did it was his duty to cast him off. Talk of indiscretion ! There was another act of something more than indiscretion. When the noble Viscount the First Lord of the Treasury, on account of the hon. Gentleman's talents and abilities, tendered him a seat in the Cabinet—I mean in the Government — the hon. Gentleman should have explained to the noble Lord that by his complicity, or through his friendship, with Mazzini he would bring disgrace on the Administration ; or he should have said to Mazzini, "I am now in connection with Her Majesty's Government, and I cannot cover your treasonable correspondence. I will not bring discredit on an honourable Administration. I cannot continue the association without bringing into the Government contamination from the company I keep." Talk of a friendship with Mazzini ! A man certainly might by a strong effort of moral courage manage to associate with Calcraft. I shall not de-

Mr. Haliburton

tain the House longer. Every man has made up his mind on this matter. I believe that in respect of the transaction the mind of the public runs all one way. Indeed, I might go further and say that the private opinion of every Member of the Cabinet is in the same direction. We find the hon. Member the particular and intimate acquaintance of Mazzini, the man who advances him money, who endorses his name on the back of Mazzini's bank-notes to give them currency abroad ; and I believe the miserable majority of ten against the Motion of the hon. Baronet last night is in reality a condemnation of what the friends of the hon. Member call " an indiscretion." I now want to know whether the noble Lord will state the reasons why he retains the hon. Gentleman in his Government, knowing as he does how very offensive to the people of the Continent has been the fact of his favouring and harbouring that most wretched man, Mazzini. I ask the noble Lord whether he will state to the House the reasons which induce him to keep the hon. Member in his Government, contrary to the hon. Gentleman's own wishes.

LORD HOTHAM : Before the business is finally disposed of, I am anxious to ask a question of the noble Lord at the head of the Government. It is, what business the House will be called upon to proceed with on the first meeting of Parliament after the recess ; whether it is the intention to go into Committee of Supply, and, if so, whether the Army Estimates will be taken ?

MR. HENLEY : I should not have taken any part in these discussions, because painful they must be to every one who hears them, whatever his opinion of the particular transaction, if the statement made by the noble Viscount had not placed the matter, if possible, in a more painful and disagreeable position than it stood in before : because, if there be one thing more than another in the feeling of the country, it is to the mode and manner in which this question was treated and answered in this House—first, when the hon. Member for Finsbury (Mr. Cox) made an inquiry of the hon. Gentleman the Member for Halifax, and, next, when the affair was made the subject of a debate arising out of an inquiry put by the hon. Baronet (Sir Lawrence Palk) to the Under Secretary for Foreign Affairs. I am one of those who think that the noble Viscount, who, it appears, was then cognisant of the whole of the facts, should have caused a different course to be adopted. If the hon. Member for Halifax, when the question was first asked of him, had made that avowal which he did not make voluntarily, but which I must say has been dragged out of him by a protracted inquiry—if he had said it was true that he had given M. Mazzini leave to have his letters sent to his house, and had added, "I am sorry for it ; I was not aware how the privilege might be used"—if the question had been frankly answered in that way this matter would have stood in a very different light. But, if I may use the phrase, the facts were studiously kept from the knowledge of the House. No man could guess from the reply of the hon. Member for Halifax to the first inquiry, and still less from the answer of the hon. Gentleman the Under Secretary for Foreign Affairs to the second, that it was perfectly plain and true that the house of the hon. Member for Halifax had been at the disposal of a man, whose character has been sufficiently designated in the course of these debates, to serve as a receptacle for his correspondence. After what has taken place one might be tempted to ask, whether the bags of the Foreign Office are not at the service of M. Mazzini? One might be disposed to ask the question, because both the hon. Gentlemen stood up for M. Mazzini. {Mr. LAYARD dissented.] The hon. Member for Southwark shakes his head. I am only saying the question might be asked, because both hon. Gentlemen entertain similar opinions respecting the man whose correspondence was covered by the hon. Member for Halifax. [Mr. LAYARD : No !] It now appears clear that the house of the hon. Member for Halifax was at the disposal of M. Mazzini for letters coming to him. Now, that was just the question raised in the first instance. No one pretended to believe for a moment that the hon. Member for Halifax was mixed up with any conspiracy to murder. To make that the issue was only to throw dust in the eyes of the House and the country. The question was whether the hon. Member had subjected himself to the imputation of allowing letters, which he knew nothing about, and which probably he took care to know nothing about, to pass through his house. If that had been frankly avowed when the matter was first brought under the notice of this House—if there had not been an attempt to keep it back—the matter would have

been on a different footing, and, in my opinion, the noble Viscount would have stood in a much higher position—because he seems to me to have been a party to keeping it back. It appears that at the time of the hon. Member for Finsbury asking his question, the noble Viscount had had the whole matter brought to his knowledge ; and I regret that in his usual frank manner he did not at once make the statement we have since heard from him—there should have been a disclaimer to the country and the world, and it should have been acknowledged that an indiscretion had been committed, and I believe that if the hon. Member for Halifax had at first made a frank avowal of the indiscretion with which he had acted, the whole affair would have passed away. If a man commits an indiscretion and frankly owns it, no one in the country is disposed to go further than to say, "You have been a foolish fellow," and the matter is at an end ; but if he gets up and talks of character, and raises all sorts of false issues and dodges, and has not the manliness to acknowledge that he has committed a fault, no one in the world will feel sure that there is not something behind that you have not got hold of, and you cannot trust the man for a statement of the whole transaction from beginning to end.

MR. LAYARD : I do not wish to prolong this discussion, but as reference has been made to a previous conversation which took place in this House, and the nature of it has been misrepresented by the right hon. Gentleman and others, I must say a few words with respect to it. The question, then, put to me the other evening by the hon. Baronet the Member for Devonshire (Sir Lawrence Palk) had nothing whatever to do with Mazzini or with letters sent to my hon. Friend's house, and I did not answer, as I could not, whether letters had been sent or not. Next, it is said that I made use of terms with respect to Mazzini the same as those used by the hon. Member for Halifax. I distinctly and utterly deny that anything of the kind took place. What did take place was this:—The hon. Baronet got up and asked me whether, in consequence of the statement made by the public prosecutor in France, on such evidence as he thought might have justified the assertion, that a Member of the Government had been implicated in a plot to assassinate the Emperor of the French, Her Majesty's

Government had thought fit to make a representation to the French Government on the subject; and my answer was nothing but this—that I thought it not consistent with the dignity of Her Majesty's Government to make a representation founded on a statement made by the public prosecutor of France in a court of justice in the course of a trial. That is my opinion still, and I believe it is the opinion of this country. I said nothing with respect to Mazzini's opinions. I said that the French Government had made no communication to this country, and that it was for the French Government to make a communication, if they wished for an explanation; but that I was convinced that the French Emperor, who is well acquainted with this country, felt the accusation so monstrous, whether made against a Member of the Government, or a Member of this House, or against any English gentleman, that he had not thought fit to make a representation on the subject, and it was not for us to make a representation in the sense indicated by the hon. Member for Devonshire.

MAJOR STUART KNOX: I wish to ask the hon. Member for Halifax, whether it is true that his name appears in the majority of 10, who voted last night; and whether it is not contrary to the practice of the House that he should have taken part in the division?

MR. BERNAL OSBORNE: The right hon. Gentleman the Member for Oxfordshire (Mr. Henley) commenced the few remarks he made by saying that this was a very painful subject. Well, it is a painful subject; but, somehow or other, I recollect noticing, in the course of my Parliamentary experience, that there is nothing in which this House so much delights, nothing which will attract such a numerous attendance of Members, as a purely personal and painful subject. I think that my noble Friend the Member for Haddingtonshire (Lord Elcho), when he addressed himself with so much unction to-night to this painful subject, might have reflected that the painful subject is somewhat assuming the aspect of a painful persecution, for no two lads recently escaped for the holidays from school could have presided over the impalement of a cockchafer with greater glee than the civic dignitary the hon. Member for Southampton (Alderman Rose) and the hon. and gallant Member for Dungannon (Major Knox) have shown in the attack upon the hon. Member for

Mr. Layard

Halifax. The civic dignitary on a late occasion, not satisfied with hunting Mazzini through every gyration, put the question whether Mazzini had ever lived at the house of the hon. Member for Halifax, and made an inquiry after his washing. To-night the hon. Member for Dungannon (Major Knox) rises and persecutes the hon. Member for Halifax, asking whether he voted in the majority last night. Why should he not have voted in the majority? I have no sympathy whatever with the views of the hon. Member, but I beg leave to correct the statement just made on the other side of the House, that the noble Lord at the head of the Government has given him a seat in the Cabinet. He only fills a very humble seat in the Admiralty barge; and what I say is, that, after all, you are only persecuting a clever young man who holds a minor office in the Admiralty. It would seem from the discussion last night that there is so little to do in the way of real business, that we make it a business to debate personal questions, and to get up with hypocritical faces and declare that these are "painful subjects." Why you all delight in them, and next to roasting a Bishop possibly nothing is so agreeable to the House as baiting a Member of the Administration. I have no particular confidence in Her Majesty's Government, or in the Members of the Administration, but I should be ashamed to pitch upon one of its Members, and that a very humble Member, who has made his way without any aristocratic connections, and has made his position solely by his own abilities, and hunt him, and use opprobrious expressions towards him. I do lament the indiscretion he committed. I know nothing of Mazzini, and, as far as I have heard of his views, I do not much like them; nor am I anxious to meet him at dinner or to defend him in this House. But let it be recollected that Mazzini has not yet been put on his trial. He has yet to undergo a trial in Paris on this very business that we are debating. If we were —what we are not—a judicial assembly, for we are perfectly incapable of acting in a judicial spirit in consequence of our passions, and we incline, therefore, to these painful subjects—but if we were a judicial assembly we would not condemn a man unheard, and without having the facts of the case before us. With regard to this indiscretion of the hon. Member for Halifax, I would ask the House, in sober sadness, are we not carrying this matter

too far? We have had this question debated, and the Baronets have come out
upon it very strong. First of all, there
was the hon. Baronet the Member for Devonshire (Sir Lawrence Palk), and after him
last evening another came out, and I never
heard a melodramatic part played so well
as that of the "Dagger and the Bowl" by
the hon. Baronet the Member for Yarmouth
(Sir Henry Stracey), who not only spoke
but looked the character to perfection. We
had an animated debate last night; and
came to a division. I voted in the majority, not approving altogether of the conduct of the hon. Gentleman the Member
for Halifax; but I felt bound to take the
denial he gave, which I think explicit, and
not to take a dirty advantage by wreaking
vengeance on a small member of Her
Majesty's Government. An hon. Gentleman on the other side of the House—
Member for some place in Cornwall—(Mr.
Haliburton) referred to that legal functionary Mr. Calcraft, why or wherefore I
cannot understand. All I can say is, that
if every indiscretion of hon. Members in
their youth is to be visited on them,
would hon. Gentlemen on the other side of
the House escape? I think that the
course we are pursuing is unworthy the
character of English Members of Parliament. With regard to the hon. Gentleman
the Member for Halifax, I think that the
position he holds in the Ministry is unworthy of his talents, and if I were in his
position I would at once resign. If I were
the hon. Gentleman, I would not consent
to hold my seat on the Treasury bench
with any imputation hanging over me. If
he were to resign, he must return to office
again, and in a better place; and sure I
am that it is unworthy of us as Members
of Parliament, and such conduct will not
be responded to by the great public out of
doors, to go on baiting, night after night,
a junior Lord of the Admiralty.

MR. SEYMOUR FITZGERALD: Sir,
I have taken no part in this discussion.
The right hon. Gentleman behind me (Mr.
Henley) has said what I am sure everybody has felt—that this is a very painful
subject; but when the hon. Gentleman
who has just sat down says that it is a
painful question, I would remind him that
it is a serious question also, seeing that he
has addressed a speech to the House in
which he seeks to turn the case into ridicule. In one sentence which he uttered I
cordially agree—that we are not fulfilling
our duties as Members of Parliament.

Now, Sir, I must confess that the answer
given to the Question of the noble Lord
(Lord Elcho) has somewhat altered the
condition of affairs; and I am glad rather
to put aside the personal matter, as regards
the hon. Gentleman the Member for Halifax, because the answer of the noble Lord
puts this Question in a much more serious
position, and brings it before us upon the
deliberate judgment of the Prime Minister
of England. I do not, of course, impute
to the hon. Member for Halifax any complicity with this plot. When the Question
was first mooted, the hon. Gentleman met
it with an indignant denial. But he did
more—at the very moment when Mazzini
is accused of attempting the life of our
ally, the Emperor of the French, he passes
the most studied eulogium on him, and
then sits down side by side with the Prime
Minister of England. It is that which
has made the question serious. But it is
doubly serious when we know that the hon.
Member for Halifax has expressed his readiness to tender his resignation to the noble Lord, and that the noble Lord not only
said he did not desire it, but that if offered,
he would refuse to accept it. The present
state of affairs is serious to this House.
It compromises the Government, it compromises the character of the country; it
compromises our relations with our allies.
The position we stand in is this: that when
a Member of the Government has passed
a studied eulogium upon the person who is
accused of having conspired against the
life of a Sovereign ally, that Member is
not only not called upon to resign, but receives the approval of the noble Lord at
the head of the Government, and an avowal
that if he tendered his resignation he would
not receive it. We are told that we are
hunting—to use a phrase of the hon. Member opposite (Mr. Bernal Osborne)—a subordinate Member of the Government. That
is not now the question. We have now to
deal with a much more serious question—
not with the position of a subordinate Member of the Government, but with the position which the head of the Government has
chosen to assume in sanctioning the eulogium which the hon. Gentleman passed
upon Mazzini, and in not doing that which
I think he was bound to do—doing his best
to remove the imputations under which, as
the results of the first night's debate, his
Administration rests.

MR. NEWDEGATE: I regret that the
debates during the last few nights should
have assumed a personal character, origina-

ting on this side of the House to an extent positively painful. What, Sir, has passed this evening? There has been a futile attempt to pass a censure upon the Chancellor of the Exchequer—and on what ground? Because, in pursuance of his duty, he has thought fit to use strong terms of reprobation with regard to a company, which, I must say, appears to deserve the term of fraudulent. An hon. Member's name is connected with that company, and the House has been occupied night after night in raking up an expression used by the Chancellor of the Exchequer, which after all might have been indiscreet as regards the individual towards whom it was employed, but just towards the company with which it was connected. What is the second part of these proceedings? A great part of two nights have been spent in attacking a Member of the Government, because he had the indiscretion to consort in former years with a person who has been charged with instigating assassination; but who, he says, abominates assassination. My opinion of M. Mazzini's course and character must be the same as that of every right-minded person. But I would ask hon. Members on this side of the House, who are so very zealous in condemning the hon. Member for Halifax, whether hon. Members on this side of the House can really pretend to be so very nice? whether, if a similar course were pursued towards them, imputations quite as grave might not be brought against some who sit on their own side. Have we not heard, Session after Session, from Members of the Opposition, the defence of the brigands of Italy — men who have burnt their prisoners, men who gouge, men who rape, men who have committed every atrocity? Have we not heard Members on their side proclaim these men patriots? It seems as though they were so accustomed to such laudation on crime as to have become insensible to it when proceeding from one side of the House; they might, I think, show a little more forbearance when they find that some of the associates of hon. Members opposite are fit to be placed at the bar with the brigands of Italy. I hope the House will forbear from such personalities. I do not understand that it is the duty of the Opposition to spend the time of the House in such matters, to the interruption of the useful business of the country.

Mr. DARBY GRIFFITH wished to draw attention to a rather singular incident in connection with the very small majority in favour of the Government on the previous evening. He had always understood that when a Member was personally interested in any question before the House he ought to abstain from voting. He would not express an opinion as to whether the peculiar nature of the debate last night justified the hon. Member for Halifax in continuing present after he had made his statement, but he must own he was very much surprised to observe the name of the hon. Gentleman in the division list as forming one of the small majority. He was afraid that this might be made a precedent on some future occasion, and begged leave to ask the Speaker whether such a proceeding was in accordance with the usages of the House.

Mr. SPEAKER said, that no doubt the rule was that no Member could vote on a question in which he was peculiarly interested; and, also, there were occasions when it was becoming for a Member to leave the House before the division, although there was no positive charge against him. The vote of the previous evening, however, was whether or not certain matters did not require the serious consideration of the House, and it could not be said, on any interpretation of the rules of the House, that the hon. Member for Halifax ought not to have voted on that question.

Mr. DENMAN said, he believed it to be the opinion of that side of the House, that when the hon. Member for Halifax was first questioned on this subject he would have done better if he had replied categorically, and not allowed his feelings to lead him into an eulogium on M. Mazzini. He must, however, remind the House, that when the hon. Gentleman on that occasion showed a desire to give more detailed information on the subject, he was met with cries of "No," which prevented him from continuing his explanation. These cries, in which he (Mr. Denman) joined, he interpreted as the expression of an apprehension, that if the House were to force on these explanations, it would be playing into the hands of the French police, by eliciting information for the purpose of compromising all the correspondents of Mazzini. He doubted whether it was reasonable or desirable that after such a matter as this had been discussed as it was last night, they should be again deliberating upon it, again casting imputations upon the hon. Member for

Mr. Newdegate

Halifax, again questioning the purity of his motives and the honesty of his statements. The sole scrap of evidence against him was a piece of paper found upon a man in France, not dated, which might have been left in his pocket for years, which was thoroughly accounted for by the fact that the hon. Member had once, indiscreetly if you will, allowed his name to be placed upon notes issued to raise money for certain patriots abroad. That paper contained the address of Flower, at the house of the hon. Member for Halifax. The answer of the hon. Member was, that he never, until now, knew that the name of "Flower" was used on letters intended to reach Signor Mazzini. There was absolutely nothing in the evidence at the trial, or in the statements of the Procureur Général, to show when or under what circumstances that scrap of paper came into the hands of Greco, how it was used by him, or whether he used it at all or not. For his own part, he did not pretend to know what the doctrines of Mazzini were, but this he did know, that on the Continent, when a man evinced a passionate desire for liberty, however pure his patriotism might be, and however he might abhor assassination, one of the ordinary practices of despotic Governments was to brand him with opprobrious epithets, and to say that he was a conspirator and an assassin. It was said that Earl Russell once spoke of Mazzini as "that assassin Mazzini;" but there was nothing, except the current statement abroad, to prove that Mazzini approved assassination. The hon. Member for Halifax had declared that Mazzini abhorred assassination as much as any Gentleman in that House, and that being his belief, he would have shown himself a coward, unworthy of his position, if he had cast off his friend for fear of compromising himself. Moreover, the hon. Gentleman had stated that his house would not be used again as it had been; and so the only importance of the charge against him fell to the ground. He had done right in tendering his resignation when his conduct was made the subject of discussion and inquiry, and the noble Lord at the head of the Government had also done right in refusing to accept it, because it would have been wrong to turn out an innocent man in order to please his political enemies and the Procureur Général of a foreign Power. It would have been contrary to the dignity of the House if the Government had taken that course, and hon. Gentlemen opposite would have been the first to fly at their throats if they had done so. A miserable scrap of paper and a miserable bit of a charge of indiscretion on the part of the hon. Member for Halifax had been used to get up a serious, grave, and, as the hon. Member for Liskeard had called it, "painful" allegation of conspiracy. Hon. Members opposite thought to weaken the Government, but he believed the attack made upon the hon. Member for Halifax would greatly strengthen the Government when it was known that they had the fortitude to disregard the speech of the Procureur Général, and to refuse to discard a useful public servant on such evidence.

SIR JAMES FERGUSSON said, that the discussion was in one sense important, and that it ought not to terminate in the issue attempted to be raised by the hon. and learned Gentleman. The hon. and learned Member and his Friends might regard this as a question of slight importance, but in no other country in Europe would such an opinion be entertained. He had talked of a miserable scrap of paper, but the scrap of paper bore the address of a Lord of the Admiralty, which was found sewn in the clothes of a person on the eve of the committal of a horrible outrage, and the matter had been referred to by the representative of the French Government in a proceeding of the greatest gravity. The hon. Member for Halifax was then asked a question upon the subject in that House, but he did not at once own all that was elicited last night. The hon. and learned Gentleman had talked of the want of evidence, as if the importance of this question depended on the amount of evidence and not upon the seriousness of the imputation. It came out by close questioning and from other sources, that the hon. Member had placed his House at the disposal of Mazzini, and had permitted a correspondence to go on under false names—names that were not always known to M. Mazzini himself, and with respect to which the hon. Gentleman had never asked any questions. It was now owned that the name upon this alleged miserable scrap of paper was one of those by which Mazzini was known in this country. [Mr. STANSFELD: A translation of a name.] If an hon. Member thought proper to have such intimate relations with a man who philosophized on the theory of the dagger, the Members of the House would not conceive themselves entitled to interfere. It was only when a Member who had accepted an office under the

Crown was accused of being the medium between the authors of the moral and immoral theory of the dagger that the House, with a dissatisfaction approaching to disgust, saw the hon. Gentleman sitting beside the First Lord of the Treasury.

Motion *agreed to.*

House at rising to adjourn till *Monday*, 4th April.

GOVERNMENT ANNUITIES BILL.
QUESTION.

SIR MINTO FARQUHAR asked, What course the Government intended to pursue in regard to this Bill? Many hon. Members were under the impression that the Chancellor of the Exchequer had consented to adjourn the debate until that day, with a view of fixing some day after Easter for the resumption of the debate.

MR. MILNER GIBSON said, that his right hon. Friend was under the impression that an understanding had been come to in regard to referring this Bill to a Select Committee. The Chancellor of the Exchequer was prepared to agree to a Select Committee upon the clauses of the Bill, but not a Committee to hear evidence on the whole subject. He thought that after what had passed there was an agreement to refer the Bill to a Select Committee after Easter on its clauses.

MR. HUNT wished to know, whether it was intended to refer the financial calculations of the Bill to a Select Committee?

MR. MILNER GIBSON: No; it will be referred to the Select Committee as it stands.

SUPPLY.

Motion made, and Question proposed, "That Mr. Speaker do now leave the Chair."

THE IONIAN ISLANDS.
PAPERS MOVED FOR.

MR. GREGORY in rising, pursuant to notice, to call attention to the demolition of the fortress of Corfu and the neutralization of the Ionian Islands, said, he should despair of obtaining the attention of the very few Members now present in the House, were it not that the proceedings to which he was about to refer were attended with injustice, violence, and bad faith. It was because the nation in question was weak and unprotected that he

Sir James Fergusson

appealed to the House of Commons to assist him in obtaining justice for it. He was convinced that what the Chancellor of the Exchequer had, a few minutes previously, called "an adverse presumption" against the foreign policy of the Government existed, and that public opinion was not in favour of a system under which a kind of balance-sheet was maintained, exhibiting on one side concessions to the strong and on the other violence towards the weak. If they turned their eyes upon the map of the whole world now they would hardly find a spot where the name of England was regarded with friendly feeling—a state of things which was almost entirely owing to the manner in which foreign countries had been treated by our Foreign Office—yet there was one spot where the name of England was cherished and revered only a few months ago, and that was Greece and the Ionian Islands. Now, however, owing to circumstances to which he was about to refer, all that was changed; and he believed there were few parts of the world where this country was viewed with greater distrust and dislike. It was recently remarked in the French Legislative Assembly by Monsieur Thiers, that France never interfered with Greece after her revolution, and was honoured and liked in that country now; whereas England, which had professed herself to be the friend and patron of Greece from the commencement, was now regarded with peculiar aversion. He taxed the Foreign Office with illegality, with violence, and with bad faith upon this question; and, although the papers which, in his opinion, ought to have been produced were refused by that Department, he believed he had in his possession sufficient information to bring home that charge. Had the Ionian Islands belonged to us, had they been a colony with which we were about to part company, as some day we might have to part company from Canada, it would have been bad taste and bad policy to destroy their fortifications and to devastate their country before bidding them farewell; but we are actually now blowing up and laying waste property over which we have not, and never had, the smallest right, and against the destruction of which the owners protest. We addressed strong language to Austria and Prussia about the "outrage and injustice" of which they had been guilty towards the weak and unprotected Denmark, whilst we ourselves had been equally guilty towards a weaker Power. The impression which prevailed that those Islands formed part of the possessions of England was utterly unfounded. From the time when the French were driven out in 1800, and they were erected into a republic with the Sultan for their suzerain, their rights as an independent State had been recognized in successive treaties; and when England took possession of them in 1809 the official despatches and proclamations declared that we went "not as conquerors, but as allies," and recognized "the independent Government of the Septinsular Republic." The 6th article of the Treaty of Vienna was to this effect—

"His Britannic Majesty contends that a convention with the Government of the Ionian Islands should regulate all matters in relation to the maintenance of the fortresses and as regards the keep and pay of the troops."

It contained a distinct recognition of the right of the Ionians to the fortresses, which clearly revived as soon as the Protectorate of England came to an end. Even in those high-handed days His Britannic Majesty consented that a convention with the Government of the Ionian Islands should regulate everything relating to the maintenance of fortresses and to the keep and pay of British garrisons. Yet now the Ministers of the Queen proceeded to demolish those fortresses not only without the consent but against the protest of the people of that country. But has this independence ever been denied? Some years ago a Lord High Commissioner stated in a memorable despatch, that the population was so hostile to the English Protectorate, that it would be better to hand over the whole of them to Greece with the exception of Corfu. In replying to that suggestion, the noble Lord now at the head of the Foreign Office said, "it would be a breach of good faith to a State under our protection to take any portion and make it an element of our strength." If we could not retain any portion of the country without breach of faith, whence comes the right to destroy any portion of the country without equal breach of faith. He was present at a debate in the House of Lords on the 16th of April last, when Lord Malmesbury, in speaking of the cession of the Ionian Islands to Greece, gave it as his opinion that it was desirable the fortresses should be destroyed and that the Islands should be neutralised; and he recollected the tartness which Lord Russell infused into his reply. Lord Russell said that, although, no doubt, Lord Malmesbury

understood the subject on which he had spoken, yet from what had fallen from him one might imagine quite the reverse; that the noble Earl had referred to Corfu as if it were one of Her Majesty's colonial possessions which it was proposed to cede; that, on the contrary, the Ionian Islands were a free and independent republic, under a British protectorate, and that they were in no sense a possession belonging to Her Majesty. Then Lord Russell used these important words: — "If the people of the Ionian Islands were united to Greece, it would be for them to decide whether the fortress of Corfu should be maintained." After that the hon. Gentleman the Under Secretary of State could hardly, without something like sheer blasphemy towards his Chief, deny the illegality of the acts we were committing. It might be said that we had spent considerable sums of money on these fortifications; but so also the Ionians had done. On the 19th of March, 1825, the Lord High Commissioner, in an address to the Ionian Legislature, represented to them the ruinous condition of these fortresses, and specially of Vido; whereupon they voted £164,000 to restore and complete them. In 1833 the Ionian Parliament voted £15,000 more for the same purpose. In 1836 their regular contribution for the maintenance of the fortresses and the support of the garrisons was fixed at £35,000, which was afterwards diminished to £25,000. It was said that the Ionians had not paid up their contributions. He admitted that it was so; but if it was an argument in this case it ought to have been brought forward against the Ionians before they were called upon to vote "aye" or "no" to the annexation. Instead of that these people were told by the Lord High Commissioner at the time the annexation was proposed, that they would receive a full acquittance for all the arrears then due from them to Her Majesty. But even if we had spent millions, and the Ionians had not spent one farthing on these fortifications, still, when we gave up the protectorate we were in the position of outgoing tenants, who had no right to create rack and ruin on the property they were about to leave. He maintained then from these facts, that in this matter our Government had been guilty of violence and illegality towards these people. Moreover, he accused the Government of bad faith in its dealings with the Ionian Islands. It was not till

November, 1863, that the Ionians knew anything of the treaty by which their fortresses were to be demolished and the Islands neutralized; and it was not till the same period that the young King George, having made the cession of these Islands a *sine quâ non* to his acceptance of the throne of Greece, heard one word about these conditions so calculated to make him unpopular at the very outset with his new subjects. At the Conference held in London on the 14th November, 1863, everybody had representatives but Greece and the Ionian Islands. True, Greece was invited to send a plenipotentiary; but when he arrived the whole affair was over and the first treaty signed, leaving the four Powers afterwards to make a distinct treaty with Greece and thereby imposing on her King the humiliation of accepting a treaty with conditions so galling to his future subjects the islanders. Our Government had thus dealt with the interests of Greece, without Greece, and against Greece. They had sedulously concealed from the Ionians what the conditions were that would be attached to the annexation, and they had also concealed from the young King of Greece conditions the execution of which had excited a painful feeling against His Majesty among his people. The despatch from Lord Russell to Lord Bloomfield, of June, 1863, had not one word about the neutralization of these Islands or the demolition of their fortresses, neither was there such a word in the treaty of August, on the faith of which the young Danish Prince was induced to accept the throne of Greece. By the terms of that instrument the young Prince accepted the throne on the express condition that the Ionian Islands were to be "effectively united" with the Hellenic kingdom. Was the neutralisation now spoken of the way to make the union with Greece "effective?" But on the 3rd of October, little more than a month before the treaty of November last was promulgated, when the Lord High Commissioner put it to the Ionian Legislature to say "aye" or "no" whether they would be annexed to Greece, His Excellency told them that they were then fully cognizant of all the conditions attached to the proposed annexation; and as if to show that there were to be no after-claps, he specified certain conditions, among which was a Vote of £10,000 for the King of Greece's Civil List, and a stipulation that all previous contracts were to be observed, and that

the English cemeteries should be protected. The last act in that disreputable drama was the treaty of the 14th of November last. By it the King of Greece and the Ionians were informed of the decision of the great Powers. No wonder the new King of Greece was astonished and deeply pained when he heard of it. He might quote to the House the letter of the 9th of December, 1863, from Count Sponneck, the Greek Minister for Foreign Affairs, to the President of the Ionian Parliament. In this letter the Count stated that His Majesty had heard of the dismantlement of the fortress with profound grief, and that the Government had taken steps to obtain a modification of the Resolutions come to by the five Powers in London on the 14th of November. Of course, the King had heard of the measure with grief. Our Government had induced him to accept a throne which they had made ridiculous by hawking it round Europe; and now they made him unpopular in the eyes of the Ionians and odious to his own subjects for accepting terms which they thought derogatory to the dignity of the Crown and of their country. And what had been the result? Already the words "traitor" and "treason" were being applied to the person and the conduct of the King; pamphlets were being published recommending him not to tolerate this disgraceful and perfidious treatment, but to abdicate the throne and return to Denmark; and if another revolution broke out in Greece and a catastrophe occurred, it would be all in consequence of this disreputable proceeding. He would now say a few words about the Articles of the treaty. By the second Article, inserted, he believed, to meet the requisitions of Austria and some English partisans of Turkey, these Islands were to be neutralised; but he now understood that that measure was to be confined to Corfu and Paxo. What advantages would Europe in general and Turkey in particular gain from that neutralization? It was said that Corfu was neutralized because it was so near the mainland of Turkey—but in that case why were not the provinces of Phthiotis and Acarnania dealt with in the same manner? He did not know what was the exact meaning of the word "neutralization." It was explained by the treaty to some extent, because the second article said, "consequently no armed force, either naval or military, shall at any time be assembled or stationed upon the territory or in the waters of those Islands." What would be the effect of the condition if Greece were involved in war? Are not Greek vessels to take refuge in Corfu? Are they forbidden to enter Corfute ports? Or have they only the same right of entry and departure as the enemy's vessels? It was clear, at all events, that it was not a measure which rendered necessary the destruction of the fortresses, because, although Belgium was neutralized in the year 1831, the fortress of Antwerp was not destroyed, and Belgium now had a large army, and might, if she pleased, have a fleet. If the whole country was neutralized he could understand it, but he could not understand the neutralization of one limb, leaving the rest in a different position. The real object of all these conditions seems to have been to prevent the consolidation of this new people, and to afford a pretext for the interference of the protecting Powers. How clearly this was the case was shown by the proposal of Russia, in connection with the fourth Article, that the Greeks and Ionians should have separate flags. The fifth Article, stipulating for the tolerance of different religions, was most insulting to the sovereignty of the King and utterly unnecessary, because it was notorious that in no country in the world was there greater toleration for all religious opinions than there was in Greece, and that not merely a legal tolerance but a tolerance arising from the feeling and sentiment of the people. The third Article provided for the destruction of the fortresses; and this, he understood, was attributable to the fears and jealousy of Austria, who was afraid lest these fortresses should be taken by a *coup de main* by the Italians, and become the bases of hostile operations in the Adriatic. Never was argument more illogical. In this country we were erecting fortifications at Portsmouth, Chatham, and elsewhere, to avoid a *coup de main*, and in the Ionian Islands, to avoid the same thing, we were destroying them. And to put the climax to the absurdity and stupidity of this treaty, it was notorious that, as soon as our troops marched out, the Ionians might, if they could get the money, restore all those fortifications. He thought he had now shown that Her Majesty's Government had been guilty of illegality, violence, and bad faith towards the Ionians. The treaty was offensive to the Ionians themselves, lowering to the dignity of their King, whom we had inveigled into accepting the throne; dangerous, because of the pretext it would give for foreign interference; and a notable specimen of bad policy. He was ready to admit, for the sake of argument, that, unless these fortresses had been destroyed, Austria would not have consented to the abandonment of the protectorate. But, if that was so, let Austria take all the discredit of this proceeding, which was stigmatized in every part of Europe in language much stronger than any which he had employed. Why should we allow our name to be execrated, our good faith impugned, and our influence impaired wherever the Greek tongue is spoken, in order to satisfy Austrian apprehensions and jealousies. Was the oppressor of Venetia and the invader of the Danish duchies so dear to England, that we ought to take all this odium upon ourselves in order to please her. It was at this moment of great importance that the name of England should stand high among the Christian populations of the East. They were restless and discontented, and it was most desirable that we should be able to press upon them counsels of peace and moderation. A little while ago we had that power. When, on the 10th of December, the Acroceraunian mountains opposite Corfu were lit up with fire, fires of joy, in answer to the illuminations in that island, they were as the lighting up of hope in the breasts of the oppressed at the deliverance of their brethren, and the people of the East believed in the generosity and disinterestedness of England, and would have obeyed her councils. Now the feeling was exactly the reverse. We had lost all hold on the popular mind in Greece, and that was a great misfortune with reference to the future settlement of that country. Yet how easily all this might have been prevented. If the Lord High Commissioner had gone before the Legislative Assembly at Corfu before the Vote for annexation had been taken, if he had said, "My Government has all along been willing to abide by the clear understanding which it had with you, but Austria is afraid of the dangers which may arise to Europe by the existence of your fortifications, and she insists on their destruction, and the neutralization of your islands. It is for you to decide whether you are willing to accept annexation on these terms, and, if so, be your own executioners, for we are not prepared to devastate your Islands to gratify Austria;" that would have spared us all the odium which had been heaped on our heads. He had been recently on the Continent, and he must say that no transaction among all our numerous failures that had lately occurred had created so strong a feeling in Italy and France as this. If an Englishman wishes to be comfortable abroad, he must divest himself of the very senses which God has given him. If he goes into the streets, he must shut his eyes to avoid the caricatures which flaunted in every window representing this country as debasing herself before the strong and indemnifying herself by bullying weak Ionia and weak Brazil, and receiving with complacency the retributive castigations of Prince Menschikoff and Secretary Seward. If he goes into a club he must close his ears, or he will hear on every side comments on his country as painful as they are unjust. He knew that our wish was to be honest and courteous in all our dealings —to act as gentlemen; but the impression that prevailed abroad, since Lord Russell had been at the head of the Foreign Department, was, that we were acting in a very different manner. He asked his hon. Friend to give him the papers up to November 14, 1863. He had refused them before on the ground that negotiations were pending, but he (Mr. Gregory) asked them now only to the date of the treaty which had been signed. It was by our willingness to become the instruments of carrying out that treaty that we had brought upon ourselves the stigma of violence without law, and of diplomacy without faith; and he wanted to ascertain from the papers what on earth could have been the pressure that could induce Lord Russell thus to have dirtied the character of his country. The hon. Member concluded by moving for papers connected with the demolition of the fortresses of Corfu and the neutralization of the Ionian Islands.

CAPTAIN JERVIS seconded the Motion.

Amendment proposed,

To leave out from the word "That" to the end of the Question, in order to add the words "an humble Address be presented to Her Majesty, that She will be graciously pleased to give directions that there be laid before this House, Copy of any Correspondence up to the Treaty of the 14th day of November, 1863, on the subject of the annexation of the Ionian Islands to Greece, between the Foreign Office and the Governments of Austria, Prussia, Russia, France, and Greece,"—(*Mr. Gregory*,)

—instead thereof,

Mr. Gregory

Question proposed, "That the words proposed to be left out stand part of the Question."

MR. SMOLLETT said, he was not one of those who thought the renunciation of the protectorate of the Ionian Islands by Great Britain was a matter to be much lamented. It had existed for nearly fifty years, and had been exercised with such singular incapacity, that our withdrawal would not leave fifty persons in the Islands who were friendly to British rule. Yet *primâ facie* it did not seem a difficult matter for a maritime Power like Great Britain to manage successfully seven small islands with a population of 160,000 souls, and yet the Government had signally failed. Our withdrawal, however, was justifiable on two grounds. In the first place, our Governments had been odious to the people, and none more so than since Colonel Storks had become Lord High Commissioner; secondly, we were right in withdrawing, because our protectorate had always been a source of expense to this country. That fact, however, although true, was most discreditable to us. The Treaty of Paris provided that the Islands should defray the expenses of their civil administration, and they had done so. By the treaty it was also provided that a garrison of 3,000 men should be maintained—a force that was more than sufficient for the occupation of the Islands. In 1824 the revenue of the Islands amounted to £140,000, which was sufficient to defray all the civil charges and the military expenses if we had only acted with common sense; but owing to our own extravagance, the protectorate had come to be a considerable charge upon the British Exchequer. The Islands contained a population hardly exceeding that of a London parish, and yet this little dependency was provided with a Senate, a House of Representatives, a Speaker, and all the paraphernalia of representative governments, and they paid these persons salaries for creating mischief. Large sums were spent upon palaces, more was wasted upon fortifications that were useless. A Lord High Commissioner was maintained with a salary equal to that of the President of the United States, and the office was bestowed not upon men with colonial experience, but upon decayed politicians. He did not include the Chancellor of the Exchequer among decayed politicians, but he had been Commissioner and a bad one for a short time. The office was jobbed away to parties to whom a good palace and a residence in a fine climate, with £6,000 a year, was a godsend. Now thirty years ago Sir Charles Napier had pointed out how these Islands should be governed. He recommended the appointment of a governor with a salary of £2,000 or £3,000, to reside at Cephalonia, that all the pomp and paraphernalia of the House of Representatives should be suppressed, and that a small body of ten or twelve representatives of the people should be appointed to assist the governor. If the semi-regal Court of Corfu, the Senate, and the House of Representatives had been got rid of, and the waste of money upon fortifications stopped, we might have had a Government respected and respectable. But as such a wise arrangement could not be expected after fifty years of folly, he was rejoiced that we were ridding ourselves of the responsibility; his only wonder was that the Protectorate had continued so long. For the last fifteen or twenty years the Islanders had been clamouring for annexation to Greece, as they, like King Otho, had a notion of some future great Greek kingdom in the Levant. Emissaries were sent into the Islands to foment discontent, in which they were successful; but King Otho was unfortunate in his endeavours to extend his dominions, having been unlucky enough to incur the antipathy of the noble Viscount at the head of the Government. The House would remember how the late King Otho was snubbed by the noble Lord, and a British fleet was sent to the Piræus, not for the protection of English citizens, but to enforce the preposterous claims of a Maltese Jew named Don Pacifico. That was, he believed, a monstrous swindle. A national quarrel, too, was nearly being forced upon King Otho, because he claimed a small island called Sapienza, lying off the coast of Greece. That island was about the size of Palace Yard, and was quite uninhabited. The House, too, would remember the odium which was incurred by King Otho during the Crimean war, because he wished to enlarge his dominions at the expense of Turkey, then apparently on the eve of dissolution. The Greeks were a quick-witted people, and when they saw that King Otho was an obstacle in the way of the accomplishment of their cherished objects, they intimated to him that "it was no longer "— to use the expression of the noble Lord the Foreign Secretary—"expedient that he should reign over them."

No sooner had King Otho taken his departure from Greece, than the noble Earl (Earl Russell) intimated to the Provisional Government at Athens, through Mr. Elliott, the fact that England was perfectly ready to relinquish the Protectorate of the Ionian Islands in favour of Greece, on condition—first, that its government should be monarchial; secondly, that the new King should rule constitutionally; thirdly—and the condition was a very hard one—that he should be a person *omni exceptione major*, a person to whom no exception could be taken; and lastly, that he should not seek to extend his territories or entertain insidious designs against his neighbours the Turks. The Greeks were perfectly delighted with the proposal. Their revolution had been perfectly successful, and from the fact that the offer to which he referred was made so soon after the departure of Otho it would seem as if that revolution had been brought about by English intrigue. In the enthusiasm of the moment the vacant throne was offered to a scion of the Royal House of England, who was at the time a young gentleman serving on board one of Her Majesty's ships. This offer, which did not savour altogether of absolute wisdom, was, however, graciously declined; and then overtures were, with the concurrence of the English Government, made to the male scions of almost every petty Court in Germany; but not even one of that hungry lot would accept the throne on any conditions whatever. In the extremity of their distress, however, the present King of Denmark accepted the throne for his second son, William Christian, but only on certain conditions, the first being that the cession of the Ionian Islands to Greece should be made *pari passu* with the accession of the new King; the second, that pocket-money to the extent of £12,000 a year should be provided for the young gentleman by the great Powers of Europe. It took some months to obtain the assent of the protecting Powers to those conditions; but they were finally agreed to, and then — and not till then—the Prince, who was now called George, proceeded to Athens, where he was introduced to his constituents and thanked them for his election, but told them what Members of that House never told their constituents—that he had come among them without the slightest capacity and without any experience. It was folly to contend that a young gentleman, then seventeen and now eighteen, who accepted the throne under these conditions was a constitutional monarch. He would ask whether, under these circumstances, the conditions which Earl Russell had in contemplation when he made the offer to cede the Ionian Islands had been in any way complied with. We were, he supposed, under the impression that we had been governing those Islands constitutionally, though our rule there was a perfect despotism ; but so far from its being his opinion that the King of the Greeks was a person to whom no exception could be taken, he must confess he knew very little which could be said in his favour. He believed, indeed, that any Gentleman selected by lot from the benches opposite—any Philhellene—for instance, the hon. Member for Galway (Mr. Gregory), if he came under that category—would fill the throne of Greece much more ably, and keep under control much more effectually than the present King the most licentious and intriguing population in Europe. Be that, however, as it might, he felt perfectly assured that if we expected that that young Prince would settle down quietly in Athens, drawing £12,000 a year, giving dinners and fattening on his pay, without entertaining any desire to extend his dominions, or any insidious designs against the territories of his neighbours, we should find ourselves much mistaken. If he were to do so, his Government would become contemptible in the eyes of his subjects ; the treaty which placed him on the throne of Greece, accompanied, as it was, with a mass of diplomatic rubbish, would not last so long as that which placed his father on the throne of Denmark, and which was now violated by two of the parties to it, and was not thought worth defending by the remainder. With respect to the fortifications, he must say that he was very glad that they were to be destroyed. He had heard it said that a great deal of Ionian money had been expended on them; but he did not believe it. They were in ruins when we took them, and Sir Thomas Maitland who was one of the first Lord High Commissioners, and who was one of the very few persons who held that office who knew his business, never expended a shilling on them. He went by the name of "King Tom," and was a very excellent ruler. During his sway from 1816 to 1824, a sum of £87,000 a year was upon the average spent upon the civil administration of these Islands, but this sum did not include the expenses of

Mr. Smollett

3,000 men, which they ought to maintain. Sir Thomas Maitland left behind him at his death in the treasury of Corfu a large sum of money; and when his successor, Sir Frederick Adam, came into office, an arrangement was entered into with the English Government to the effect, that if the Greeks would vote the amount in the Treasury, £160,000, for the repair of the fortresses, then entirely neglected, the Government would ask for no further sum for the maintenance of troops due up to that date. The arrangement proved to be satisfactory to the Parliament of the Ionian Islands, then entirely subservient to the Lord High Commissioner, and they at one sitting, he believed, voted the whole amount to be spent on fortifications. The sum so spent was, however, really and truly British money, which should have been paid into the British Treasury in part payment for keeping up 3,000 men. That statement he made on the authority of Sir Charles Napier, and he never heard of the Greeks having spent any other money on those fortifications, while we had expended something like half a million sterling. If they were to be kept up they would be a source of great expense ; but if they were to fall into other hands—and could they insure the throne of Greece to the young King who now occupied it for two years, even in one of the Government offices—then they would be a menace to Turkey, the maintenance of which country in its present integrity many statesmen deemed to be essential to the preservation of the peace of Europe. Under all these circumstances, he was very glad that the Ionian Islands were made over to Greece—whether to a monarchial or a Republican Government he did not care, but he was heartily glad that we had got rid of them.

Mr. LAYARD said, his hon. Friend the Member for Galway (Mr. Gregory) seemed to have made himself the mouthpiece of all the discontent and disaffection which existed in the East. He did not, certainly, mean to imply, that he in any way supported or countenanced the intrigues which there prevailed; there was, however, a kind of sweet simplicity about his hon. Friend which made him take for gospel almost everything which was told him; and, as he was not a man to do anything by halves, he did not hesitate to accept every kind of exaggeration as truth, and every report which happened to reach him as a fact. It was no matter of surprise that there should be persons in the East who had an object in making it appear that the act of generosity—if so he might be allowed to call it—performed by Her Majesty's Government had in it some deep design; he was not surprised that there should be persons in the East, jealous of the influence and good name of England, who endeavoured to counteract the effect likely to be produced by the surrender of the Ionian Islands, because, as his hon. Friend ought to know, there was in the East a host of petty intriguers, who were constantly attempting to make political capital out of every event which happened in that quarter. But he was surprised that a man like his hon. Friend, an English Gentleman and a Member of the English Parliament, should come forward to support those views, and to make Europe believe that we were not actuated by an honest policy and by the most sincere desire to promote the interests of Greece, but by some unworthy and underhand motives which we did not dare avow. Our surrender of those Islands was an act of generosity unprecedented in history. We had voluntarily surrendered a territory, and that surrender was made in good faith and with the utmost loyalty. [Mr. GREGORY said, he did not deny it.] Yet the hon. Gentleman accused the Government of pursuing towards Greece a policy of "injustice, violence, and bad faith." His hon. Friend had argued, although disclaiming the intention of doing so, as if the Ionian Islands were a possession or colony of this country. But the Ionian Islands were placed under the protection of Great Britain by a solemn treaty made with the concurrence of the great Powers, and especially of Austria, and we held them upon certain conditions to which those Powers were parties. When we undertook the Protectorate, we were bound to govern the Islands as a separate State, in a liberal and constitutional manner. In the early times of our connection with them he was ready to admit that we did not carry out all our promises, for after the termination of the great war an order of ideas reigned in Europe not very favourable to liberal government. The hon. Member for Dumbartonshire (Mr. Smollet) had alluded to Sir Thomas Maitland, more generally known as "King Tom," who certainly ruled somewhat despotically, but who, nevertheless, did a great deal of good for the Islands. In his time roads were made, other public works were carried on, and

the Islands attained to a great state of prosperity. After some time public opinion began to make itself felt, and a liberal constitution was granted to the Islands—a more liberal one it would be difficult to conceive. These concessions, instead of having promoted a good understanding between the Ionian people and the protecting Power, had increased disaffection. The liberal institutions granted to the Islands were made use of by local intriguers, who in a short time got up movements not only in the Islands, but in Greece. At that time the question of nationalities began to be much agitated in Europe. The claims of the Islands to be united to Greece, on the ground of a common nationality, were put forward; but the singular thing was that those who were at the head of the party which put forward these claims were not Greeks at all. There was scarcely one who had not an Italian name, and who was not descended from the Venetian settlers in the Islands. The town of Corfu and a considerable part of the Islands was not inhabited by people of the Greek race. Over and over again the Ionian Parliament voted annexation to Greece; but, of course, this country could not consent to an annexation, and the Parliament was prorogued or dissolved. At that time it was nearly impossible to give the Islands to Greece. Greece was then almost verging on bankruptcy [An hon. MEMBER: She is still]; brigandage prevailed, and the country was in a state of complete disorganization. A fixed policy of the Greeks too, at this time, was aggression on Turkey, which had put against them the great Powers of Europe. It would have been most unfair, therefore, to hand over the Islands to Greece. What we had always foreseen happened at last, and the Greek people, exasperated by bad government, compelled the King to leave. What took place in Greece ought to be a warning to his hon. Friend. For a long time we had been held up to odium in the East as the chief obstacle to the prosperity of Greece, and Sir Thomas Wyse, our representative at Athens, a Philhellene in the truest sense of the word, had incurred great disfavour by constantly warning the Greek Government of what would take place, exhorting them to abstain from aggression upon their neighbours, and to devote their attention to developing the resources of the country. The King fell; and then, notwithstanding the bad name which accord-

ing to some we had earned for ourselves
in Greece, the Greeks united as one man
to offer their throne to an English Prince,
thus showing their belief that our policy
had always been directed to promoting
their true interests. It was not considered expedient that the throne should
be accepted for an English Prince ; but
after the tribute which had been paid
to this country we felt under a moral
obligation to assist the Greeks in finding
a Prince competent to fill the throne.
At that time Mr. Elliot was sent to
Athens to explain to the Greek Government the reasons why their offer of
the crown to Prince Alfred could not be
accepted ; and at the same time he was
instructed to advise them to retain a monarchial and constitutional form of Government, to give up aggressive designs upon
Turkey, and to develop the resources of the
country. If the Government would pledge
themselves to this policy, he was instructed
to promise that England, with the assent
of the great Powers, would give up the
Protectorate of the Ionian Islands in favour
of Greece. It was true that from various
circumstances it was not easy to obtain a
person eligible in every way to fill the
throne. The three great protecting Powers
had determined that it should not be filled
by any member of their Royal families,
and that of course limited the number of
eligible persons. At length the throne
was offered to Prince William of Denmark,
and accepted, on his behalf, by his guardian, and the choice was subsequently
ratified by all the great Powers. To carry
out the change of dynasty, it was necessary first of all that a treaty should be
concluded between the three Powers who
had made Greece what she was and had
guaranteed her independence. Her Majesty's Government succeeded in obtaining the consent of Russia and of France
to the change of dynasty, and in placing
Prince William on the throne as King
George. In the treaty it was agreed
that the Ionian Islands should be surrendered to Greece, and it was further agreed
that the three Powers should each give up
£4,000 a year of interest due to them
upon the Greek debt, and that £10,000 a
year should be appropriated to the civil
list of the King from the revenue of the
Islands. The next step was to obtain the
assent of the parties to the Treaty of
1815 to a new treaty which gave up the
Protectorate of the Ionian Islands, confided by the great Powers to this coun-

Mr. Layard

try. His hon. Friend said that the conditions contained in that treaty were unknown to the new King of Greece and to
Count Sponneck, and to the people of the
Ionian Islands, and of Greece, until after
October. This was an extraordinary statement, for the fact that the fortifications
were to be destroyed and the Islands neutralized was a matter of common notoriety all over the East. Moreover, he
held in his hand despatches which showed
that in August the matter was discussed
at Copenhagen long before the King left
that city ; and both His Majesty and
Count Sponneck were well aware of what
was proposed to be done, Count Sponneck
in the middle of the summer not only acceding to the proposal, but suggested that the
whole of Greece should be declared a neutral State. On the 30th of June his noble
Friend (Earl Russell), speaking in another
place, spoke of the probable destruction
of part of the fortifications, because Greece
maintained a very small army, and therefore large fortifications would be only a
temptation to a foreign Power to take
them. Our Minister at Copenhagen had
had a conversation with Count Sponneck
upon this very question, so that he was
perfectly justified in saying that it was
well known both to the King and his
Minister, that the demolition of the fortifications was one of the conditions of the
cession of the Islands. His hon. Friend
said that Her Majesty's Government were
doing the dirty work of Austria in this
matter. But his hon. Friend forgot that
Austria had a perfect right to a voice respecting the conditions on which the Islands should be surrendered, for she was a
party to the original treaty which gave England the Protectorate, and we were bound
to consult her. Austria said, "You are going to give a very strong place to a country
which we believe to be incapable of defending it. These Islands will be exposed to
a *coup de main*, and if taken by a strong
Power at enmity with us, our possessions in
the Adriatic might be endangered. They
may also be a great source of danger to
Turkey ; and on all these grounds we
think it dangerous to the peace of Europe
that these fortifications should remain as
they are." She had a perfect right to start
these objections. His hon. Friend said
that if Austria did not assent to the conditions of the treaty she might have been
left out. But Her Majesty's Government
had reason to know that the views of Austria were shared by both Russia and Prus-

sia, both of which would have refused to accede to the treaty if Austria had declined to do so. France also entirely approved the views of Austria. Would it have been an advantageous arrangement for Greece to have left Austria and the other Powers, or even Austria alone, out of the treaty? Suppose Prussia, Russia, and Austria had said, "We decline to have anything to do with the treaty, we decline to accept the responsibility of handing these Islands over to Greece, we shall reserve our rights, and when the time comes shall take care to vindicate them." If the Islands had been conceded under these conditions the gift would have been a fatal one to Greece and a source of constant anxiety to Europe. Another point submitted by Austria was that the Islands should be declared neutral, which in some respects might have been an advantage to Greece and to the Islands themselves, and was not altogether an unreasonable proposal, although its value may be doubtful. Another condition was that the conventions of Austria as to commerce and trade with the Ionian Islands should not be affected by the annexation to Greece. To this condition Austria was entitled, because there was a clause in the Treaty of 1815 which guaranteed these rights to her. She was the only Power in the east of Europe which had extensive commercial relations with the Ionian Islands. The Austrian Lloyds' boats touched at Corfu, and the other Islands. The trade was to a certain extent a coasting trade, and had no reservations been introduced in favour of Austria, great injury might have been done to an important commercial company. Well, then, there was the clause as to religious toleration. It was well known that the Greek was not the most tolerant of religions. The great antagonism in the East was between the Roman Catholics and Greeks, and as the French Government had obtained certain rights in favour of Roman Catholics in the Ionian Islands, there was a natural wish on its part that those rights should be guaranteed by treaty. His hon. Friend (Mr. Gregory) said, it was a most unexampled thing to declare the independence of a country and destroy part of its fortifications, and he quoted the case of Belgium. But he could not have quoted a more unlucky instance, because the treaty which gave independence to Belgium provided for the destruction of five fortified places. Then his hon. Friend said they ought to have delayed the signa-

ture of the treaty until the people of the Ionian Islands had agreed to the conditions. But the people had really no voice in the question. It was their duty to say "aye" or "no," whether or not they assented to the union with Greece. They had no right to go further and interfere in European arrangement arising out of a European treaty. It was, therefore, not necessary to lay the conditions of the treaty before the Ionian Parliament. Her Majesty's Government thought it best, for the interests of the Islands and of Greece, to put a stop to the state of uncertainty then existing, and to have the treaty signed as soon as possible. It was true that the Greek Government objected to the terms of the treaty; and the English Government had steadily, faithfully, and loyally endeavoured to serve Greece by inducing the Powers to make the modifications which she desired, and render the stipulations of the treaty as little onerous to her as possible. Accordingly, many modifications had been effected. In the first place, instead of the whole of the Islands being neutralized, the neutralization was confined to Corfu and another. Again, Her Majesty's Government had succeeded in inducing Austria to give up altogether her demand, that only a certain number of troops should be maintained in the Islands, and now there was to be no limit to the number of troops. The original agreement was that all the fortifications should be destroyed; but we represented to Austria that this was not necessary, and that in the work of destruction and dismantling no more need be done than would remove the danger to which the Islands would be exposed if the present fortifications were maintained. Accordingly, the old fortifications would remain untouched. Only two forts would be destroyed and another dismantled. With regard to Fort Neuf, he might observe that for several years there had been an agitation to get the British Government to destroy that fort, in order that a certain road uniting the town and a suburb might be made; and now the agitators in the Island made its destruction a grievance. As to the question between the Ionian Islands and Austria, with regard to a separate flag under which the Ionian commerce was to be carried on, we had explained to Austria the objections to carrying out what she wished for, and that when the Ionian Islands came to be united to Greece, a distinction could not be made with respect to flags, but that the Ionian should be merged in the Grecian flag. It had been at length agreed that Austria should enjoy her commercial privileges for a limited period, and that when that period expired other arrangements should be made. Next, as to the £10,000 which was to have been paid annually out of the revenue of Corfu to the civil list of the Islands, that proposal had been modified by allowing the Greek Government to make that sum chargeable upon the whole revenue of the kingdom. He contended that the destruction of the fortifications would be no loss to Greece. The fortifications of Corfu, if defended properly, would take about 10,000 men. Would it be desirable to call upon a young Power like Greece to incur such an expenditure as that force would involve? If, on the other hand, the fortifications were not defended, at any moment a lawless band might take possession of them, and hold the Island against the Greeks themselves. It had been said, in the course of this debate, that the destruction of the fortifications was a violation of the 4th, 5th, and 9th Articles of the treaty; but it was not so, for the fourth Article of the treaty referred to recited that the cession of the Islands to Greece should take place with the concurrence of Austria, France, Russia, and Prussia; and the destruction of the fortifications was to take place in fulfilment of one of the conditions on which that concurrence had been obtained. The destruction of the fortifications was, therefore, a literal fulfilment of the 4th Article; and it was no violation whatever of either the 5th Article or the 9th. The hon. Member would have the House believe that all this was a trick on the part of the British Government, and that we had no intention of benefiting Greece by giving up these Islands. But if the British Government was not acting in good faith in this matter, we might have taken advantage of the objections made to the conditions as a ground for backing out of our proposal; but, on the contrary, we had acted most loyally to Greece throughout in carrying out our intentions.

Mr. GREGORY: What right had you to destroy the fortifications?

Mr. LAYARD: There was no article in the Treaty of 1815 about giving up the fortifications, either in the condition we received them or in any other condition, and the spirit of the Treaty of 1815 required that they should be destroyed. Among

Mr. Layard

the many complaints that were now brought forward against us, one was that we were removing the historical Venetian guns from Corfu. But that was not true—the guns we were removing were guns we had put there; and he did not think we were called upon to make a present of these guns to Greece in addition to giving up arrears amounting to £90,000. The hon. Member for Dumbartonshire (Mr. Smollett) had characterized the Government of England in the Ionian Islands as one of odious oppression, and the only Government he lauded was that of "King Tom." [Mr. SMOLLETT: He acted constitutionally and with the Senate.] He did not think that was the character generally given of "King Tom's" rule; but, be that as it might, the hon. Gentleman had gone on to speak of our having employed none but decayed politicians as Lord High Commissioners. Now, Sir Henry Storks was not a decayed politician. [Mr. SMOLLETT: His government is most odious to the people.] He had known the gallant gentleman for a very long time, and he could assure the House that he did not know whether Sir Henry Storks was a Liberal or a Conservative. All he knew was, that he had been employed in most important public services, and had well deserved the rewards which his country had bestowed upon him. The hon. Member said Sir Henry Storks was the worst governor the Islands had ever been ruled by; but the government of Sir Henry Storks did not deserve the character which the hon. Gentleman had given it. In a time of great difficulty, and in the face of great opposition, he performed his duties in a manner that deserved the gratitude of the country; and his memory would be cherished in the Islands themselves when the names of the intriguers who found mouthpieces in this House were forgotten. It had been said that there were not twenty persons in the Islands who would regret the departure of the English. His impression was quite otherwise. He believed their departure would be deeply regretted. There might be persons who lived by agitation who would not regret it; but the great bulk of the people would regret it, for his belief was, they would never be so prosperous and happy as they had been under English rule. His acquaintance with the Islands taught him that there was no people on the face of the earth who might have been more happy, prosperous, and truly free than the people of the Ionian

Islands under our Protectorate, had they not been misled by designing and unprincipled men. He only trusted the time might not come when they would deeply regret that they had ever acceded to the wishes of a few persons to withdraw from our protection. His hon. Friend had spoken of the noble Lord at the head of Foreign Affairs in terms which he ought to have blushed to use, for he said that Lord Russell had "dirtied the character of England." He (Mr. Layard) believed the noble Lord had raised the character of this country. He had had some opportunity of judging of the policy and opinions of his noble Friend, and he believed there was no man in this country who had more truly liberal opinions and was more anxious to promote them, while, at the same time, maintaining due respect for treaties. It seemed to him (Mr. Layard) that liberalism in these days was supposed to consist in an entire disregard for international obligations and international treaties. But let hon. Members look at the career of the noble Lord at the head of the Foreign Office. While promoting to the best of his power all over Europe liberal opinions and constitutional government, he had endeavoured to maintain treaties in perfect good faith. What his hon. Friend charged the noble Lord with was this—that, instead of violating treaties, he had acted in accordance with them in consulting Austria, Russia, and Prussia about the cession of the Ionian Islands. He would say, as regarded Greece herself, they had done the best for her interests. They had her interests only at heart; they desired that she should have a constitutional Government, that would develop her resources, and contribute to the welfare and liberty of her people. They deprecated aggression upon other States, and they took only a wise and just course when they made it one of the conditions of the cession of the Islands to Greece, that she should renounce all attempts at aggression upon her neighbours. Those Islands, inhabited by an industrious and intelligent population, might add much to the strength of Greece; but if Corfu were to be made a nest of intrigue, and to become the basis for carrying on aggressions on neighbouring countries, then the cession could only tend to make her position worse, and to embroil her with the nations of Europe. With respect to the papers, he thought it would be advisable to give them to the end of November, and he hoped after Easter that the treaty would be signed, and that

he should be able to give the rest of them.

CAPTAIN JERVIS said, he had heard with surprise the admission of the hon. Gentleman the Under Secretary for Foreign Affairs, that this country had handed over, at the instigation of a few individuals, a happy and contented people to a country that was in a state of bankruptcy and anarchy. He had always protested against handing over these Islands to Greece; but he had done the Foreign Office the justice of supposing that they believed that, by so doing, they were about to add to the happiness of these Islands and not to their misery. They had been under our rule for the last forty-five years, and they had enjoyed a state of contentment and civilization, which was unknown to the rest of Europe; but now it seems they had been handed over to a country which was in a state of anarchy and bankruptcy, overrun with brigands, and in so turbulent and disorderly a condition, that the foreign Ambassadors had three times threatened to leave the country. But having agreed to hand these Islands over to Greece, Her Majesty's Government ought to have acted in a straightforward and honourable manner. They had no right to enter into a treaty with a young prince, stating that those Islands were to form an integral portion of his dominions, and then emasculate them as they were about to do. If the Islands were to form part of a constitutional and independent State, as would appear from Article 3, what was meant by laying it down that an army or navy was not to be kept on the Islands? He had looked into the various treaties and protocols that bore upon the question of our Protectorate, and he had been unable to discover any authority which would entitle us to insist upon such a condition. The hon. Gentleman (Mr. Layard) had said, that the noble Lord at the head of the Foreign Office, had distinctly stated in the House of Lords that the fortifications were

that it was doubtful whether some of them should not be destroyed, because Greece had but a small army, and it would be a temptation to some foreign Power to seize upon the fortifications if they were allowed to stand. But the noble Lord had stated quite the contrary of what the hon. Gentleman had alleged. It was true there were fortifications, such as those of St. George, in Cephalonia, and fortifications in Zante and Cerigo, which might be demolished, but these were to remain untouched.

It had been said that having paid for the fortifications at Corfu, we had a right to destroy them; but he held in his hand a Return made by the Board of Ordnance in 1848, from which it appeared that, of the total expenditure from 1815 to 1848 of £456,000, the sum of £307,000 had actually been contributed by the Islands themselves. It was all very well to say that a part of the money expended ought to have gone to the payment of the troops; but by the Treaty of 1815 we were bound to see the fortresses maintained in a state of efficiency, and with regard to the men themselves, by whom the Ionian Islands were to be protected, they might have been much better protected by a small body of police. Was it right, because we had required a strong force in these Islands for our own purposes, that the people there should be called upon to pay for them when they did not require a single man for their own protection? He should like to ask what precautions had been taken for the protection of the English officials in these Islands and the retention of their pensions? He believed that not a single measure had been taken for this purpose, but that we had done our best to crush the interests of the people. We had not taken a single step to protect the claims of those who had served us for years; and he should like to know, what was the real state of Greece and of these Islands as to fortifications, and also as to the interests of those personally concerned, when we handed them over to Greece?

Mr. CHICHESTER FORTESCUE said, he could relieve the mind of the hon. and gallant Member with regard to security of pensions and compensations when the Protectorate should cease. The British Government had made provision in the treaty for those pensions with great care; but, with reference to meeting present payments when quarter-day should arrive, representations on the subject had been made at the Colonial Office, and the answer was that we were in communication with the Lord High Commissioner upon that point, and though at this moment of great political change the finances of the Ionian Islands were temporarily affected and diminished, yet Sir Henry Storks was using every exertion to provide for the salaries and pensions, and there was every reason to believe that they would be punctually paid. With respect to the future pensions and compensations of British subjects who

Captain Jervis

would lose their offices in consequence of the cession, he explained fully to the House not long ago the course that had been taken. He stated that the Greek Government would be bound by the treaty to pay those pensions and compensations regularly in the case of the former to the British Consul at Corfu, and in the case of the latter to the British Minister at Athens. The greater part of the hon. and gallant Gentleman's remarks had been answered by anticipation by his hon. Friend (Mr. Layard). The hon. and gallant Gentleman took it for granted that everything in the treaty between the Great Powers was to be carried out literally. But his hon. Friend had explained that by the friendly exertions of the British Government many of the restrictions which were at first sought to be imposed on Greece had been relaxed, and that the conditions that were now being actually carried into effect were of a much less stringent character. Without debarring the Crown of Greece from sending soldiers and ships to the Ionian Islands, and keeping them there, provision was made for their general neutrality, and that was a much greater advantage to a weak Power than it could be to any other. His hon. Friend the Member for Galway (Mr. Gregory) was a warm and sincere friend of the Greek people, and it was well known that they had proved their sense of his friendship by electing him a vice-president of a society for the union between the Islands and Greece. His hon. Friend, however, might have employed that exceptional position much more usefully than he had done by acting rather as a mediator between the parties concerned than as the advocate of one. His hon. Friend might have pointed out to the Ionians that when they made up their minds to demand a great change of this sort and had at last attained their wishes, they could not expect everything to be *couleur de rose.* He might have pointed out the difficulty of a great Power carrying out a thing unexampled in history—the voluntary cession of a territory in its own hands—when there were other Powers whose consent was necessary, and various conflicting interests to be reconciled. He might have told them that they had after all but a trifling price to pay for that condition of national life which they had been so long demanding, and their agitation for which had made all useful British rule in the Islands impossible. He (Mr. C. Fortescue) must remind his hon. Friend that this was a critical moment in the history of the Ionian Islands. It could not but happen that so great and serious a political change must greatly affect the interest of many persons in the Islands. It affected for the time being the credit of the country; it diminished its commerce and revenue, and no doubt had a prejudicial influence on the livelihood of many in Corfu who had long been dependent upon the Protectorate and the garrisons; it spoilt the trade of the political agitator, who found himself " cursed by a granted prayer," and led to a temper on the part of the Ionians which rendered them not very easy to please, and made them ready to find fault with those conditions which England had found necessary in order to carry out the cession. Under these circumstances, it would have been satisfactory if his hon. Friend had shown a temper more English and less Ionian in this matter. His hon. Friend seemed disposed to treat the pecuniary part of the question as of little or no importance ; but the fact was that the amount of Ionian or British money expended on the fortifications was an element of considerable importance in the equitable question between the two Governments. He spoke, of course, of the modern works, and not of that venerable structure the citadel of Corfu, which it was not intended to touch. In annual instalments spread over many years, the Ionian Government had spent on the fortifications of Corfu some £250,000. [Captain JERVIS: £300,000 up to 1848.] The hon. and gallant Member was mistaken. The amount he mentioned included other military expenses besides the cost of fortifications. [Captain JERVIS : It is for fortifications alone.] He believed the hon. and gallant Gentleman was under a mistake. The amount of Ionian money expended on the fortifications could not have exceeded £250,000, while the amount of English money expended for the same purpose was much larger. The fact was, that the British Government had not enforced the rights they enjoyed under the Treaty of Paris to the full extent, and had, on the whole, been extremely moderate in their demands for military expenses. Taking the whole period of the Protectorate, the British Government had not obtained from the Ionian Islands above £25,000 a year, upon the average, for their military purposes of every kind, fortifications included, while they had expended three or four times as much. He would now say a word as to the administration of these Islands by the Colonial Office, and the position in which they parted company with them. He was far from saying that that administration had been free from errors and blots, or that in all respects it would bear a strict and rigid scrutiny. Judging it fairly, however, and comparing it with the conduct of other Governments under similar circumstances, there was no reason why it should be condemned by Parliament, or by the Ionians themselves in their calmer moments. The difficulties under which England undertook the management of these Islands should be remembered. We found the people corrupted by centuries of misgovernment and a long period of anarchy ; life and property were insecure ; agriculture and commerce were almost in abeyance, and there was scarcely anything resembling law and order in the country. For some time our Government was, no doubt, despotic enough, but it was firm, efficient, and on the whole unselfish. The object of the British Government had always been to promote the welfare of the Ionians, and Ionian interests had seldom, if ever, been sacrificed to those of the protecting Power. At length, in consequence of a desire manifested by the Ionians themselves, a constitution of an ultra-Liberal character was conferred on them. It was an anomalous form of Government, but the intention was good. The first use that the islanders made of the new system was to turn it against the protecting Power. After some experience of the operation of this state of things, Her Majesty's Government, then under the guidance of Lord Derby, sent the right hon. Gentleman the Chancellor of the Exchequer (Mr. Gladstone) to visit the Ionian Islands, and through him proposals were made for an amended constitution to the Ionians ; but they refused to accept it, with the view of hastening that consummation which had at length arrived. Under that state of things what was left for the British Government to do? We had very little, if any, active power. The position of the representative of the British Crown was passive rather than active. He could only try faithfully and loyally to carry out the constitution, and endure with as much patience as he could muster, the irritations and provocations to which he was constantly subjected. Such had been the behaviour of Lords High Commissioners for some years past, and especially of his gallant friend Sir Henry Storks. He did not know whether hon. Members had read an interesting account which was to be found in one of our Parliamentary papers written by a leading member of the Greek Assembly, who had visited Cephalonia at a time when a general election was going on. He says that he found some of the candidates bitterly hostile to the protecting Power. He expresses his astonishment to find that the protecting Power, which was all powerful if it chose to exert its strength, was absolutely impartial between the contending parties. He found that the voters voted as they pleased, and that the Returns were honestly made. He says that this state of things would have been utterly impossible in his own country under the late *régime*. He expressed his astonishment and admiration at a state of things he never saw before — the excellent roads — the good order of the villages—the happy smiling appearance of the country — and he contrasts with this, as he says with tears in his eyes, the condition of his own country. That was an instance of the kind of testimony that might be produced, of what, with all its shortcomings, was the well meant and unselfish efforts of the British Government to carry out the Protectorate of the Ionian Islands. Well, the time had now come when the British Government had seized a favourable opportunity of granting the prayers which had been so long urged upon them. No doubt the Ionian people would have to make some sacrifice of ease, comfort, and security for the sake of obtaining the object of their patriotic wishes—wishes which, though stimulated by political agitators for their own purposes, were, he had no doubt, sincerely felt both by many enlightened Ionians, and by the simple and well-disposed peasantry of the Islands in general. Her Majesty's Government hoped and believed that the Ionians would soon pass through their crisis of trial, and that by union with a kindred race they would be developed into a prosperous and well governed people. It was their hope also that the irritation attending the change, and caused by the conditions which the British Government had been compelled to impose would pass away, and that the Ionians would look back with good and kindly feelings to the Power which had so long ruled them, and at last had granted them that which they so warmly desired. It was to be hoped that they would

Mr. Chichester Fortescue

forget those invectives against England which they still heard from certain parties in the Islands, and from some to-night in that House. His advice to the Ionian people was that they would put out of their minds those eloquent incentives to ill-feeling towards this country which they had heard that night from his hon. Friend the Vice President of the Union Society.

MR. SEYMOUR FITZGERALD : Sir, I regret very much that a question of so much importance should have been discussed to-night in so thin a House. The question is one of importance not only to this country — not only as regards our relations with foreign Powers, but of particular importance to the country of which the hon. Gentleman who has just sat down has spoken, and which—fatally, I think, to its own prosperity—the noble Lord at the head of the Foreign Office had taken under his own special protection. We are now discussing this question probably for the last time, and therefore I am unwilling to allow this opportunity to pass without some observations. I am not going to discuss at all the propriety of this cession of the Ionian Islands. Upon that question I have a very, very strong opinion, and I have expressed that opinion very strongly in this House. But this has now passed—it is a matter of history, and I am not going to revive the question. But the hon. Member who spoke last (Mr. Chichester Fortescue) has referred to a portion of the history of the Ionian Islands, and he has said that the result of English dominion there has been to establish a kind of Paradise. [" No, no !"] Will the hon. Gentleman allow me to proceed ? He said this—that, where there had been disorder, where there had been no regular Government, we had established a regular Government, that agriculture had flourished, that roads had been made, which had conferred the greatest benefits on the inhabitants. The hon. Gentleman contrasted this state of things with the condition of Greece. But has there been that freedom ? Has there been that constitutional government developed ? Has there been that agricultural prosperity ? Have public improvements been made ? The very reverse. Of all countries in Europe there is not a country where so little has been done for the prosperity of the people as in Greece. And yet the hon. Gentleman, for the glorification of the policy of his Government, has pointed out this as the result of their policy—that whereas we have made the

Ionian Islands specially prosperous under our rule, and whereas their condition was particularly contrasted with the condition of Greece, we have now severed our connection with the Islands, we have deprived them of the benefits of that established and regularly-organized government which gave them all those benefits, and we have united them to a country which has long been in a state of anarchy, in which, whilst it had a Government, according to the description of those who found fault with the late Greek Government, no improvement had been made, and which, since the late Government has been overthrown, has gone far to relapse into that anarchy and disunion which so lately distinguished it under the Ottoman Government. I come now to deal with the Motion of the hon. Member for Galway (Mr. Gregory), which is, to call the attention of the House to the demolition of the fortresses of Corfu and the neutralization of the Ionian Islands. I am entirely in accordance with his opinion in reference to those points, and I regret the more, on this ground, that the House is so thin, because I think this is one of the many instances of the policy of the Foreign Secretary and the Government altogether—for the noble Lord at the head of the Government said the other night that he identified himself with the policy of the noble Earl. I say that the policy of the Government on this question is just one of those they have meddled, and where in meddling they have done no good to those in whose favour they have interfered. On the contrary, I say they have compromised the character of this country. First, let me point out the course of the Government in reference to the Greek question, in reference to the abdication of the late King. I pass over the fact that the Government went all over Europe hawking the Crown of Greece to any body whom we could find willing to make a good bidding; that they offered it first to one and then to another; and I say that Her Majesty's Ministers greatly compromised our own position by allowing the name of one of the members of our Royal Family to be introduced into the discussion, it being well known that the Prince would never accept it, and that his name was only put forward for the moment to oust the claims of a Prince who might have been put forward by the Court of Russia. But having hawked the Crown of Greece all over Europe, at length we obtained a candidate; we

obtained somebody who would accept it, the present King of Greece. Upon what terms did that Prince accept the throne of Greece? It was specially provided that he only accepted it upon the condition of an effective union of the Ionian Islands with Greece. Well, of course, that Prince was perfectly entitled to lay down that position, and we were entitled, as far as we could, to carry out that agreement; but we were not entitled—that agreement having been made and that condition having been laid down—to take any step, which, on the one hand, would compromise the position of the future King of Greece, or which, on the other hand, should disappoint the expectations of the Greek people, or of the people of the Ionian Islands. But what has been done? The agreement being that the crown should be accepted only on the condition of the effective union of the Ionian Islands with Greece, what was done? The present King of Greece was induced to hurry off to Greece before that effective union was completed. And the British Government ought to have known, that at the time it was stipulated that the union should take place, that was a condition which they had no power to make and an engagement which they had no power to fulfil, without the consent of the other Powers of Europe. And not only that, but it was expressly stated by the noble Lord opposite, and by the noble Earl who is at the head of the Foreign Office, that the effective union of the Ionian Islands with Greece could not be accepted without the adhesion and consent of the other Powers of Europe. You induced the present King of Greece to go to Greece, there being no union effected between the Ionian Islands and Greece, and then your difficulties arose; because you were perfectly well aware that you could not unite the Ionian Islands with Greece of your own mere motion. It was quite out of your power to do it. You induced the King of Greece to go there, and then your difficulties arose. You applied to the other Powers of Europe, the parties to the Treaty of 1815, and what was the answer? At first they were not inclined to agree; but other great political questions being at the time pending, they did not raise difficulties, and therefore they agreed to the union of the Islands to Greece on certain terms—and those terms you have been compelled to carry out. The first fault I find with the policy of the Government is that they were unable to fulfil their promise that the King of Greece should go to Greece under an effective union of the Ionian Islands with Greece, they not having first obtained the assent to it of the great Powers of Europe. [Mr. LAYARD: No, no!] It is not a courteous way for the hon. Gentleman to answer me in that manner; he should rather give any information he possesses to the Chancellor of the Exchequer, who, as I see he is taking notes, is to follow me in this debate, who, no doubt, will give me a suitable answer. I now come to the terms upon which this effective union has been completed, and here I may say Her Majesty's Government have conducted themselves more blameably than in the instance to which I have already alluded. The Ionian people and the Greek Government were told that there was to be a union effected between them, but not one word was said to them as to the condition, and that it was to be one that would turn out to both parties, not an advantage, but a disgrace. You had to enter into negotiations with Austria and the other Powers of Europe, and they have made stipulations under which alone the Ionian Islands can be united to Greece. The first is the demolition of the fortresses. Now, I ask you to point out to me under what treaty, or on what stipulation in any treaty, rests your right to destroy those fortresses. Under the treaty by which you became possessed of the Protectorate of those Islands, and under which you were entitled to occupy the fortresses, you were bound to apply certain monies you received from the Ionian people towards the maintenance of the fortifications, and I want you to show me your right to demolish them. I entirely deny that you have any such right whatever. I perfectly admit that it would be legitimate on the part of the Austrian Government to say they would not consent to the union of the Ionian Islands with Greece unless they were demolished; but when that proposition was made to you, it was your duty to say that, under such circumstances, the union of the Ionian Islands to Greece was impossible, because we have no right whatever to destroy those fortresses. The hon. Gentleman the Under Secretary for the Colonies has argued that we have a right to destroy what we have built up for a number of years past with British money; but I entirely deny it. By destroying what you have built up you do not restore the forts to their original position, but by pulling your improvements

Mr. Seymour FitzGerald

down you make those forts that remain valueless. And what I say is, that you have presumed on your power to do that which you have no right to do, and in this respect. the Ionian people and the Greek people have the greatest grounds of complaint against you. Further, when you spoke of the union of the Ionian Islands with Greece, you told neither the Ionian people nor the Greeks that they were to have a possession where all that which we had been doing for a series of years, and which we considered to be of importance for the security of the Islands, was to be destroyed, and that we were going to hand over to them not great military strongholds, but mere heaps of ruins. What, again, is the state of the case as regarded the neutralization of the Ionian Islands? You told the Ionian people that they were to be united to Greece; you told the Greeks that they were to have this great addition to their kingdom; but you did not tell them that in order to preserve it they would not be entitled to send a single regiment there beyond what was necessary for police purposes; nor did you tell the Ionians that, except a few policemen, they were not to have that which, of course, after a long occupation such as ours, they would look forward to —namely, a garrison, with all the dignity and splendour which naturally attached to the presence of a garrison. But there is something even worse and more objectionable behind. I refer to the commercial stipulations annexed to the cession of the Islands. When you said you would cede these Islands to Greece, the Greeks naturally considered that you intended that they should be joined to Greece as a part of the kingdom, subject to the same laws, having the same relations with foreign Governments, with the like aspirations and interests for the future. But you have done nothing of the kind. You have told the Greek Government that, with respect to commercial arrangements and the admission of foreign vessels to the ports of the Ionian Islands, they were to be absolutely powerless. You had no right to do that. To sum up the whole matter, you have abused your power as regarded the fortresses. With respect to the neutralization of the Ionian Islands, you have done that which is dangerous to them and dangerous to Europe, while in the matter of commercial regulations you have done your best to impede the future prosperity of the Islands. You had done all this without a shadow of authority, without any ground of right. In doing it you have deceived at once the Greeks and the Ionian people; and the result will be that you would hand over that which had been a prosperous possession of the British Crown to a long future of anarchy and revolution.

THE CHANCELLOR OF THE EXCHEQUER : Sir, I am afraid it would not be for the convenience or advantage of the House that the debate should be carried on in the manner which has characterized it hitherto—that is to say, by hon. Gentlemen who, appearing at one portion of the evening, were not present during the other portions, who reply to speeches they have not heard, and who advance arguments which, totally out of place, they would have spared if they themselves, instead of being also out of place, had been in their seats during the speeches of the responsible officers of the Crown. I am always glad to hear the hon. Gentleman who has just spoken (Mr. S. FitzGerald), but I believe the House would have been deprived of a great portion of the immense advantage of hearing his speech, if he himself had been present when my hon. Friends the Under Secretary for Foreign Affairs, and the Under Secretary for the Colonies addressed the House. I admit that I am somewhat in the same condition myself ; but I am not volunteering to instruct the House — I am simply rising, on the part of the Government, to notice the observations which fell from the hon. Gentleman. At any rate, I had the advantage of hearing the excellent speech of my hon. Friend the Under Secretary for the Colonies ; and I must say, so far as I can recollect the terms of that speech, I would wish to be bound by it as a manly, just, impartial, and liberal exposition of our policy with respect to the Ionian Islands, worthy of my hon. Friend, myself, and of the Department which he represents in this House. The hon. Gentleman opposite appears to think that there was a great inconsistency in the representation made by my hon. Friend. The representation was this—that the people of the Ionian Islands had reaped great benefits and advantages under British rule, and yet, notwithstanding, they were seized with a kind of itch for political union with Greece. That appears to the hon. Gentleman opposite to be a paradox and inconsistency ; I contend, on the contrary, that there is no paradox or inconsistency in those statements. It is perfectly true that

the English Government has conferred great benefits on the Ionian Islanders, and yet they may cherish a sincere desire for union with Greece. For after all it is not material advantages that form the entire life of a people. There is something in the heart, the mind, the traditions, and the history of man, and I have always maintained that these Ionians being of the same blood with the Greeks, the great parents of civilization, would have been the basest of human kind if they had entertained no desire to share their political and national fortunes. No doubt the base men of the Ionian Islands traded on that rooted sentiment of the honest and good portion of the Ionian people ; but having mixed with all classes, all political sects, and all ranks of that people, I never found any distinction between them, except in this — that all men professed the desire of union with Greece, that the good men felt it, and the bad men traded on it. The policy of Her Majesty's Government with reference to the Ionian Islands has long been before the country. When the resolution was first taken by the Cabinet it was not concealed, but was at once made known to the country and to Parliament. There was a disposition in some quarters to complain that this matter was going to be transacted in the dark and done in a corner, and that England was going to be cheated out of the possession of the Protectorate. But the facts confute that allegation. All last Session the intention of the Government was as notorious as day. If hon. Gentlemen objected to the cession, why did they not address the Crown on the subject ? There was no premature engagement to bind the Crown, until long after it was in the power of Parliament to interfere and check the action of the Executive. Why was not the opinion of Parliament fairly challenged at an earlier day ? It is quite possible that hon. Gentlemen opposite were not of one mind on the subject. There is one eminent and distinguished man who sits on the opposite benches, and with whom I was brought into relation on this subject. He ought to be the organ of hon. Gentlemen opposite if he objects to the cession of these Islands. I refer to the Colonial Secretary in the Government of Lord Derby (Sir E. Bulwer-Lytton). Why is he not in his place to-night ? Why does he leave to the hon. Gentleman (Mr. S. FitzGerald), and to the noble Lord the First Commissioner of Works in the Government of Lord Derby, to vindicate the title of the Ionian people to remain under the British Crown? The right hon. Gentleman the Member for Hertfordshire has never opened his mouth in objection to the policy of the Government upon the cession of the Ionian Islands; yet he is the person who, if he had objected, should have been in his place to-night—and from my knowledge of his high character and feeling he would have been in his place.—to impeach the proceedings of Her Majesty's Government. The hon. Gentleman has flinched from grappling with this question, and with the policy of the Government, but he made objections to certain particulars of our proceedings. He says that it was the condition of these arrangements that the Ionian Islands should be effectively united with Greece, and that we undertook to affix conditions which it was not in our power to fulfil. It is undoubtedly difficult in this, as in other transactions, to make a satisfactory arrangement of details. We had many parties to consult, who were standing in a different category. We had to consult first the people of the Ionian Islands, then the people of Greece, who were for the moment without a regular and organized Government; we had to deal with the person who was about to become the Sovereign of Greece; we had to deal with the various Powers who were parties to the treaty of protection, who entertained widely different views, and stood in widely different positions. How were we to do otherwise than fix our eyes on the main question, whether it was or was not the desire of the Ionian Islanders to be united to Greece? Would it not be paltry and frivolous, when we had ascertained that this desire really existed, if we had, on account of any minor questions, shrunk from giving effect to that desire? I do not, however, admit that there has been any failure in the details, or that any one has been induced to act by expectations that have turned out to be delusive. I do not admit that the hon. Gentleman has made out the charge which it was perhaps his ex-official duty to bring against Her Majesty's Government. The hon. Gentleman says that it is not in the power of the Government to fulfil their promise to the Ionians of an effective union with Greece. But is not that promise about to be fulfilled? Are we to be told, because Corfu is to be neutralised, that the union of these Islands with Greece is ineffective? You may tell me that the neutralization of Corfu is a

The Chancellor of the Exchequer

bad arrangement. On that point there may be much to be said; but if Her Majesty's Government had enforced the completion of these arrangements without the neutralization of Corfu, the hon. Gentleman would have been quite as eloquent in pointing out the danger of allowing Islands to pass into the possession of Greece, which are remote from her territory, one of which is divided by only two miles of sea from the territory of the Ottoman Porte, and contains a fortress capable of holding 20,000 men. Then there is the question of the demolition of these fortresses. As regards the works that have been erected by England, I must confess that if the Austrian Government had confined its demand to the demolition of Fort Neuf, it might reasonably have been expected that the feelings of the people of Corfu would have been effectively consulted, and that none of those powerful sentiments which have been enlisted in this matter would have been excited. I will not say that Austria has inflicted any injury on the people of Corfu; but they are particularly attached to those fortifications—they are bound up with their traditions; they remind them of the times of the Ottoman domination; and to see the mine driven, the axe, and the mattock at work in destroying them must undoubtedly be painful to the population of the Island. I do not think that the course taken by the Austrian Government has been injurious, but I do admit that it has been painful. But would Her Majesty's Government have been justified in making such a condition a ground for withdrawing the assent of Great Britain from the fundamental points of the arrangement, and thus defeating the great desire of the people for union with their neighbours and fellow citizens? Clearly what we had to do was to act in perfect good faith in giving effect to what we believed to be the desire of the people as far as was compatible with the general objects of European policy; and to sacrifice all interests of a secondary character to the attainment of that end. Although I must confess that I look with suspicion and with some degree of aversion on the policy of Austria towards the Christians of the East—which I do not consider to have been at any time a fraternal, a generous, or a confiding policy—in this particular instance I do not believe that it has been the means of inflicting a wrong or a wound on the real political interests of the people of the Islands. It is not for their interests, or for those of the people of Greece, to be in delusive possession of the attractions of a great fortress, lest they should feel themselves prematurely stimulated or driven into the political arena, and urged to anticipate, by forced and unnatural efforts, what may, in the counsels of Providence, possibly be the future fortunes of their race. As one who is sincerely attached to that people, I confess my earnest desire that they may be induced resolutely—and it will require resolution— to lay aside every dream of conquest, to cast away every temptation to aggression, that they may set themselves to the prosecution of peaceful industry, to the establishment of good laws, to the cultivation of union among themselves, and to the peaceful development of the resources of their people. And I further hope that in this important crisis of their history they may eschew that vain ambition and pride of military establishments which, undoubtedly, was the great misfortune and vice of the late Government of Greece, and which might be stimulated to even a higher intensity if that people, numerically so small, were enabled to boast of possessing fortresses of so high a rank even among the great fortresses of Europe. But there was another point more distinctly put by the hon. Member — he seems to think that a delusion was practised, first on the King of Greece, and, secondly, on the Ionian Assembly, by our keeping back the knowledge of these important conditions of union until both these parties were effectually committed to them. My information on this point is not as full as I could wish, for my mind has not recently been given to the subject, but I hope to be able to make the matter clear to the House. The acceptance by the Ionian Assembly of the proferred union with Greece is dated last October. The King did not commit himself finally by taking his departure until a later date—in fact, His Majesty did not arrive in Greece till November. The treaty was made in August, and in that month the King was perfectly aware of its conditions.

Mr. SEYMOUR FITZGERALD asked, if the conditions of the demolition of the fortresses and the neutralization of the Islands were made known in the month of August?

The CHANCELLOR of the EXCHEQUER: That was so. The conditions were communicated to Copenhagen from the British Government in the month of July; and as early as the 10th of August despatches written from Copenhagen recited in detail conversations of the British Minister with the Danish Government on these two subject. This was before the preparation of the final treaty, before the Ionian Assembly was invited to commit itself by an acceptance of the union, and long before the King committed himself by setting out for Corfu. The hon. Gentleman has referred to certain conditions with reference to commerce. Perhaps he had chiefly in view the important line of steamers, called the Austrian Lloyds. I believe it was originally asked that a perpetual concession should be granted, guaranteeing the possession of their privileges in perpetuity to that line. Such an arrangement would have been, I think, very disparaging to the kingdom of Greece, and in itself essentially a deviation from the rules of justice. The terms of the agreement, as it now stands, I am informed, continue the line for fifteen years, and at the end of that time the Greek Government will be bound to negotiate for the renewal of the general covenant; but the conditions of that renewal will be as free to the Greek Government as to any independent Crown. With regard to the Ionian Assembly, Her Majesty's Government accepted the declaration of the will of the Assembly as the most competent organ of the people in those Islands; and I do not think they could do more. Her Majesty's Government did not invite, and I do not think by their acts they have ever given their sanction or expressed concurrence in the favourite modern doctrine of *plebiscite*, or, as we should call it, national suffrage. I think I may fairly appeal to the right hon. Gentleman whether, with the complexity of affairs and the diversity of persons and interests we had to deal with, he could have pointed out any order of proceedings more reasonable in itself, more conformable to public law, or more likely to attain the object in view than that which we actually followed.

Lord JOHN MANNERS said, the right hon. Gentleman commenced his speech by a violent attack on his hon. Friend (Mr. Seymour FitzGerald) for the indiscretion — a word of which they had heard much that night—he had shown in speaking in a debate during the whole of which he had not been present; but the right hon. Gentleman then proceeded to admit that he had not himself been present through the debate, and that therefore he was himself guilty of the very same offence with which he charged his hon. Friend. And really from the speech which he had delivered it was to be inferred that he had spent very little of his time in the House during the debate which had been raised by the hon. Member for Galway. Did the right hon. Gentleman require to be told that this question was raised, not upon the great question of the policy of the cession, but as to the manner in which the Government were carrying it out? One would have supposed, listening to the right hon. Gentleman, that the debate had been originated by his hon. Friend or himself, and that they had come down to raise a great debate on the policy of the cession of the Ionian Islands. On the contrary, it had been raised by those who, unlike them, had not objected *in limine* to the cession of these Islands, but who, like the hon. Member for Galway (Mr. Gregory), had been among the most forward and determined supporters of that foolish policy — and a foolish policy he (Lord John Manners) did not hesitate to say it was, as he had taken the proper occasion to say so last year, almost at the commencement of the Session. The right hon. Gentleman taunted them with not having challenged the policy of the Government at the proper time, alleging that no step which had been taken by the Government previous to the meeting of Parliament would have prevented Parliament from giving a formal vote. Did the right hon. Gentleman mean to say that Her Majesty's Government had not announced to Europe that negotiations were pending for the cession of the Ionian Islands to Greece before Parliament met? Did he mean to tell them that the noble Viscount, almost in as many words, had not denied the right of Parliament to interfere in the matter of the cession of these Islands, which had come under the protectorate of the Crown merely by virtue of a treaty? In what circumstances, then, were those placed who objected to the policy of that cession? and with what justice could the right hon. Gentleman taunt them with not having brought forward a Motion on that subject? If the right hon. Gentleman had been in his place he must have known that the question raised that night was raised by the hon. Member for Galway impugning the mode and manner in which the cession was subsequently carried out. After all the virtuous indignation which the Chancellor of the Exchequer had expended upon his hon. Friend

he had not condescended to answer his arguments and facts. He had not made any reply to his hon. Friend's argument as to the right of the Government to demolish these fortifications; but he gave reasons why the Ionian people might be unwise in retaining fortifications requiring 20,000 men. The arguments of the right hon. Gentleman went to the length of asserting that it was bad policy on the part of the Ionians to wish to maintain them. What, however, his hon. Friend had contested was the right of the English Government to destroy those fortifications. He would not himself give any opinion on that point; for, entertaining the views which he did of the cession of these Islands, he did not wish to mix himself up with these—as he held them to be—minor questions. But the right hon. Gentleman had made no answer to the challenge of his hon. Friend; and as to these considerations of policy, surely the Ionian people and the Greeks might be allowed to be the best judges. If, as the right hon. Gentleman said, they were so well adapted to spread the name and fame of their Greek ancestry throughout a remote posterity, why might they not be trusted to decide these questions for themselves? He confessed he was a little amused at finding that the right hon. Gentleman who lectured his hon. Friend for not being present at the whole of the debates, had in one of those eloquent speeches in which he so often delighted to indulge, enlarged upon the virtuous determination of the present Ionian population to recover the connection with their own glorious Greek ancestry. Surely the right hon. Gentleman could not have been in the House when the Under Secretary for Foreign Affairs was enlightening them on that very question about half an hour before, taking care to tell them that these modern Ionians were in reality nothing better than Venetians.

MR. LAYARD begged the noble Lord's pardon. What he might have said was that some of the leaders and a good part of the population of Corfu were so.

LORD JOHN MANNERS: If they took away Corfu from the Ionian Islands they took away a considerable portion of the subject-matter of that debate. Having done what the right hon. Gentleman had not done—namely, listened to the greater part of that discussion, he came to the conclusion that in the cession of these Islands a very foolish thing had been done, and done, too, in the most ungracious manner, in a manner which had dissatisfied everybody and contented nobody. They had heard from the hon. Member for Galway (Mr. Gregory) a statement of the grievances and the feelings of the Greek and the Ionian people in that matter. The statement had been corroborated on that (the Opposition) side in an amusing speech, which the right hon. Gentleman did not hear, by the hon. Member for Dumbartonshire (Mr. Smollett), who did not dissent from the policy of the cession. They had seen, also, in all the public papers the feeling which animated the King of Greece and his Ministers. On the other hand, three official Gentlemen had expressed satisfaction that night with the cession. The chief ground of the satisfaction expressed by the Under Secretary for Foreign Affairs amounted to this—that the Ionian Islanders were a most discontented, turbulent, bad Venetian people, who were, however, extremely happy under the rule of England, but who, he seemed rather to anticipate, would find that they had made a bad bargain by the exchange. That was the hon. Gentleman's only proof of the political sagacity of Her Majesty's Government, and the only ground of his satisfaction. The other Under Secretary who had spoken had dilated on the happiness, the contentment, the liberty, the material, moral, and social development which these Islands had enjoyed under our Protectorate, and therefore the satisfaction that he could feel in handing them over to a State in which, as he said, freedom was unknown, the Under Secretary himself could best explain. And, lastly, they had heard from the Chancellor of the Exchequer himself—as he humbly believed, the real cause of the cession of the Ionian Islands—one of those glowing harangues which he doubted not would greatly please people out of doors, concluding with a very sensible piece of practical advice to the Ionians and Greeks generally, which, it was much to be questioned, from all that had been seen of their antecedents, whether they were very likely to profit by. But the sum of it all was, that a very foolish and imprudent thing had been done in a most unsatisfactory and ungracious way ; and he believed that neither the people of Greece nor the Ionian people, nor those who were interested in the welfare and prosperity of the Greeks, would have cause to bless Her Majesty's Government for having ceded these Islands at all, and still less for ceding them in the manner they had done.

VOL. CLXXIV. [THIRD SERIES.]

MR. CHILDERS said, that hon. Gentlemen opposite not having committed themselves in any way on this question last year derived one advantage perhaps from that course—namely, that they were able now that the cession had taken place and the thing was done, to take whatever side they pleased in the matter. But although last Session there had been no formal debates on that question in that House, in the other House the distinguished leader of the Conservative party had expressed definite opinions with regard to the conditions of the cession of these Islands. He was bound to say, that if anybody was to blame about those conditions to which the hon. Member for Horsham (Mr. Seymour FitzGerald) had just objected it was Lord Derby himself. Speaking in a debate on the 30th of June last—a debate antecedent to the signature of the treaty, and still more so to the imposition of the terms complained of by Count Sponneck, Lord Derby was, he believed, historically the first English statesman who referred to the neutralization of these Islands, as being one essential condition for the proper carrying out of the proposed cession. His hon. Friend the Member for Horsham complained of the disgust felt by the Ionians at their ceasing to have the advantages of garrisons and military expenditure; but Lord Derby had foreseen this and " wished the Ionian Islands joy of the change." The demolition of the fortifications was suggested by Lord Derby as necessary to the proper carrying out of the cession. The noble Lord said—

" There is another point of minor importance on which I should like some information from the noble Earl. I presume that when we cede the Islands we shall not hand over the extensive works which we have constructed at Corfu at so much expense. Those works will probably be demolished, for it is obvious that the Greek army, which, I am told, consists of 8,000 men and 4,000 officers, will find it very difficult to garrison these extensive works." [3 *Hansard*, clxxi. 1726.]

And, so far from the Greek nation and the people of the Ionian Islands being taken by surprise, the course to be pursued was indicated in the reply of Earl Russell, who said—

" With regard to the fortifications, it is doubtful whether some of them should not be destroyed, because Greece maintains a very small army, and therefore large fortifications in the Ionian Islands would only be a temptation to a foreign Power to take them." [3 *Hansard*, clxxi. 1733.]

That was long before the date of the treaty, so that the Greeks had ample information of what was intended to be done. Who-

O

ever was in fault it was not Her Majesty's Government, and it seemed rather hard that they should be taunted for carrying out suggestions made by their opponents. As to the general question, he was confident that the country was satisfied that considering the expense to which we were put and the complications in which we were involved by the Protectorate of these Islands, their cession was a great boon ; and if hon. Members opposite or his hon. Friend behind him (Mr. Gregory) would put that question to the House, he had no doubt that it would by an overwhelming majority pronounce, as the country had already pronounced, in favour of the policy of Her Majesty's Government.

MR. CAVE said, that his hon. Friend (Mr. Seymour FitzGerald) did not object either to the neutralization of the Ionian Islands or to the demolition of the fortresses, that the Resolutions in regard to those matters, which were come to at an early period, were not sooner communicated to those who were most interested in them. He (Mr. Cave) had already expressed his opinion fully on this question, and he should not have risen had it not been for the attack which had been made upon Sir Henry Storks by the hon. Member for Dumbartonshire. He should be the last to object to perfect freedom of debate, and he entirely dissented from the doctrine that a public servant should be spared because absent. The character of public servants was the property of the country which employed them, and it was the duty as well as the right of the representatives of that country to discuss it. Still, moderation was necessary. It was not right that a public man whose acts had been adopted by the Government should be spoken of as Sir Henry Storks had been in the last Session of Parliament in terms which Cicero might have employed in denouncing Verres, or Burke have applied to Warren Hastings. Perhaps, therefore, even at that late hour, the House would give him a few minutes to defend an absent man ; and as he had heard some of the circumstances which had been referred to discussed upon the spot, he might, perhaps, be allowed to give his view of the matter. Before Lord Seaton's Reform, the Administration of the Ionian Islands was practically in the hands of the Lord High Commissioner. Afterwards it was thrown, or intended to be thrown, into the hands of the Ionian people, or rather of their Parliament, which, perhaps, was

Mr. Childers

not quite the same thing. The intention was that there should be government by party, but that, in a small community, was obviously impossible. In England each class is divided, and class not arrayed against class (though some have endeavoured to bring this about); but in the West Indies for instance, party conflict would be conflict of races ; in the Ionian Islands that of classes. If, therefore, the party system were impossible, the Government would be in the hands of one class, and become oligarchy or ochlocracy, unless controlled by a strong hand for the good of all. The Lord High Commissioners before Sir Henry Storks, instead of holding this position, governed the country by the great families into whose hands they threw all the offices, and who made things comfortable, ruling by monopoly of patronage but causing great and just discontent in the mass of the people. Sir Henry Storks went out in troublous times. He had a perfect knowledge of the Oriental and semi-Oriental races, and was determined to put an end to that state of things, and not only to reign but to govern. That caused great discontent against him among the higher classes, who immediately began to intrigue against him, and who raised the cry of union with Greece, not that they wanted it, but in order to obtain a return to the old *régime*, in order to get rid of a master. They wanted, to use an apt illustration, though it sounds like a bad joke, they wanted to get King Log instead of King Stork. But who were they who thus conspired against the Lord High Commissioner ? Were they in open opposition ? No ; the people who got up this agitation were actually Members of the Government. It was as if one-half of the present Cabinet, which was said not to be quite in accord upon all questions, was plotting to turn out the noble Lord at the head of the Government. Under such circumstances, how was it possible that the Government should be carried on ? He mentioned this among many instances to show the difficulties with which the Lord High Commissioner had to contend. The man who had to govern diverse races under such highly exceptional circumstances as those under which Sir Henry Storks had to rule those Islands ought to be treated like the general commanding an army, and to be judged by the results. We should not look at such transactions from an English point of view. We had done mischief enough already, by supposing our English system to be like a general fitting saddle which would suit the back of any horse. Vigour and justice were the qualities which, in the eyes of all Eastern races, constituted the beau ideal of a ruler. These qualities characterized the first, and he believed they characterised him who was apparently to be the last of the English Presidents of the Septinsular Republic; and as the name of Sir Thomas Maitland was a household word throughout the seven Islands where his administration was regarded as a kind of golden age, so he believed that the present Lord High Commissioner would be remembered with no unkindly feelings by the great majority of the Ionian People, when they regretted, as they would do a thousand times, the just and beneficent Protectorate of England.

MR. DARBY GRIFFITH said, it did not follow, though they might be in favour of the cession, that they were, therefore, precluded from objecting to the mode in which it had been carried out. The objection which he had taken last Session to the policy of the Government was that the House was kept in the dark with respect to it. He complained that Her Majesty's Government had thought proper, instead of consulting Parliament, to act upon the prerogative of the Crown; and that this had given rise to most of the difficulty which had arisen. If Parliament had been consulted there would have been a probability of avoiding the vacillating policy which had been pursued. Her Majesty's Government had first demanded £10,000 for the late King, and the repayment of £90,000 to this country; but the first demand had been modified so as to be nearly abandoned, and as to the £90,000 that demand was abandoned altogether. These were instances of the vacillating policy to which he had alluded.

MR. GREGORY said, he would withdraw his Motion.

Amendment, by leave, *withdrawn.*

Main Question put, and *agreed to.*

SUPPLY.

SUPPLY *considered* in Committee. House *resumed.* Committee report Progress; to sit again on *Monday*, 4th April.

CATTLE, &c. IMPORTATION BILL, AND CATTLE DISEASES PREVENTION BILL —NOMINATION OF COMMITTEE.

MR. H. A. BRUCE moved that the Select Committee to which these Bills are referred should consist of seventeen Members.

MR. FERRAND complained that no Members representing manufacturing districts were nominated upon the Committee, and, with a view to supply the omission, moved that the Committee consist of nineteen Members.

MR. H. A. BRUCE assented to the Motion, and undertook to confer with the hon. Member as to the additional names to be placed upon the Committee.

Motion *agreed to.*

Ordered, That the Cattle, &c. Importation Bill and Cattle Diseases Prevention Bill be committed to the same Committee.

Ordered, That the Committee do consist of nineteen Members : — Committee *nominated :*—

Mr. BRUCE, Lord NAAS. Mr. CAIRD, Mr. LEADER, Mr. MILLER, Mr. LESLIE, Mr. HODGKINSON, Mr. HUNT, Mr. THOMPSON, Colonel BARTTELOT, Mr. HOLLAND, Mr. BENTINCK, Mr. COX, Sir WILLIAM MILES, Mr. Alderman SALOMONS, Mr. ALGERNON EGERTON, and Sir THOMAS BURKE :—Power to send for persons, papers, and records ; Five to be the quorum.

COSTS SECURITY BILL.

On Motion of *Mr. Butt*, Bill to amend the Law relating to the giving of Security for Costs by Plaintiffs resident out of the jurisdiction of the Courts, *ordered* to be brought in by Mr. BUTT and Mr. MURRAY.

Bill *presented*, and read 1°. [Bill 58.]

House adjourned at a quarter before One o'clock, till Monday, 4th April.

HOUSE OF COMMONS,

Monday, April 4, 1864.

MINUTES.] — NEW WRIT ISSUED— *for* Oxford City *v.* The Right Hon. Edward Cardwell, one of Her Majesty's Principal Secretaries of State.

NEW MEMBER SWORN—Morgan Treherne, esquire, *for* Coventry.

SUPPLY—*considered in Committee*—NAVY ESTIMATES.

PUBLIC BILLS — *Committee* — Union Relief Aid Acts Continuance* [Bill 50].

Report—Union Relief Aid Acts Continuance.

LISBURN ELECTION.

House informed, That the Committee met on Tuesday, the 22nd day of March last, pursuant to adjournment, when they were informed that Mr. Stirling, one of the Members of the Committee, was prevented by severe illness from attending ; and that the Committee had adjourned until Tuesday, the 5th day of April, at Eleven.

Whereupon, the House being informed that Mr. George Harrison, the medical attendant of Mr. Stirling, attended at the door, he was called in, and at the bar examined upon oath in relation to the state of Mr. Stirling's health on the 22nd day of March last ; and then he withdrew.

Mr. ADAIR, as Chairman of the Committee, begged to move that Mr. Stirling be excused for non-attendance at the Committee on the 22nd of March, and that he should have leave to absent himself from any of its further sittings.

Motion made, and Question proposed,

"That Mr. Stirling be excused for not attending the said Committee upon Tuesday, the 22nd day of March last, and be discharged from further attendance on the said Committee." — (*Mr. Adair*.)

Mr. HUNT said that, as regarded the first part of the Motion; which was to excuse the hon. Member for Perthshire (Mr. Stirling), for non-attendance on the 22nd of March, there could be no objection; but, as regarded the latter part, he thought the House ought not to assent to it, for upon it another question arose, whether, in consequence of the adjournment which had taken place, the Lisburn Election Committee was now in existence. The proceedings of Election Committees were regulated by an Act of Parliament, the 11 & 12 *Vict.* c. 98, which was very strict and precise in its terms, and by which the Committee was bound at almost every step. He would suggest to the House that the Lisburn Election Committee had inadvertently transgressed the rules laid down by that Act, and had, in consequence, ceased to exist as an Election Committee. The Committee began its sittings before the House adjourned for the Easter recess ; and, as it was bound to do, continued them till the 22nd of March, when it adjourned in consequence of a Member's illness. On the 22nd of March the hon. Member for Perthshire (Mr. Stirling) did not attend the Committee, who were, under the provisions of the Act, unable to continue their sittings until the excuse of the hon. Member was allowed by the House. The 73rd section stated that an Election Committee—

"Shall meet at the time and place appointed for that purpose, and shall proceed to try the merits of the election petition so referred to them, and they shall sit from day to day, Sunday, Christmas-day and Good Friday only excepted ; and shall never adjourn for a longer time than twenty-four hours, unless a Sunday, Christmas-day, or Good Friday intervene, and in such case not more than twenty-four hours, exclusive of such Sunday, Christmas-day, or Good Friday, without leave first obtained from the House, upon Motion, and special cause assigned, for a longer adjournment ; and if the House be sitting at the time to which such Select Committee is adjourned, then the business of the House shall be stayed, and a Motion shall be made for a further adjournment for any time to be fixed by the House ; provided always that if such Select Committee have occasion to apply or report to the House, and the House be then adjourned for more than twenty-four hours, such Select Committee may also adjourn to the day appointed for the meeting of the House."

Now the House, on the 22nd of March, stood adjourned for more than twenty-four hours, and therefore the Committee might adjourn for a longer period than twenty-four hours—namely, until the day of the meeting of the House, when it would be necessary for them to apply to the House in consequence of the hon. Member's illness. It appeared, however, that the Committee had adjourned until "to-morrow," and he would suggest, that the adjournment to an unlawful day was equivalent to an adjournment *sine die*, and that the Committee by that Act, having committed *felo de se*, had ceased to exist. There was only one case reported of an unlawful adjournment. That was the St. Alban's case on the 10th of April, 1851, and it appeared from the Report of Mr. John Clerk, well known for his cognizance of the duties of Election Committees, that—

"In a recent case the Committee on a Monday informed the parties that they should apply to the House for leave to adjourn until eleven o'clock on the following Thursday. They then adjourned until the next day, Tuesday, at eleven o'clock, in case the House did not give them power to adjourn till Thursday. The House gave the Committee power to adjourn, and the Committee omitted to meet on the Tuesday, in order formally to adjourn, thinking that the leave given by the House operated as an adjournment. The following entry was made in the Minutes :—'The House having given the Committee power to adjourn, the Committee stands adjourned until Thursday.' The irregularity was not known to the parties at the time. Some days afterwards the counsel for the sitting Member were about to object to any further proceedings on the part of the Committee on account of the flaw in the proceedings, but the point was not discussed, for upon the application of the counsel for the petitioners for further time to procure the attendance of witnesses, the Committee refused to grant it and reported the sitting Member duly elected."

According to the opinion of the accomplished lawyer, Mr. Clerk—

"It would appear that in the case of an illegal adjournment such as that alluded to before, the Committee was dissolved by operation of law. Their powers lapsed from their not having been continued in accordance with the statutable authority. If this opinion be correct, that the powers of the Committee lapsed in consequence of the flaw in their proceedings, it seems quite clear that the House could give no relief. Their control over Election Committees is strictly defined by the Act of Parliament. They could not have appointed a second Committee, for that can only be done in the case alluded to in section 78."

The House, doubtless, would be very reluctant to stop the proceedings of an Election Committee on mere technical grounds; but hon. Members must bear in mind that, supposing the present Committee to continue its sittings and its Report to be adverse to the sitting Member, it might happen that the sitting Member might, nevertheless, be advised to take his seat and to vote in that House. An action might then be brought against him for penalties, and the case taken into a Court of Law, which might decide that the powers of the Election Committee had ceased under the Act. In the meantime a new writ might have been issued to elect a new Member for Lisburn, and the sitting Member be, notwithstanding, entitled by law to retain his seat. He had brought the matter to the notice of the House, and he now left the House to deal with it as it thought best.

MR. ADAIR said, that the hon. Member had referred to the 73rd section of the Act, but had overlooked the 75th, which provided that when one of the Members was prevented attending on account of illness, an Election Committee was obliged to adjourn and report the Member's absence to the House; and the section further stated that the Committee should not sit again until the excuse of the Member so absenting himself was allowed by the House, when the four remaining Members of the Committee would proceed with the investigation. It therefore appeared to the Lisburn Election Committee that they were no longer a Committee for any purpose whatever, until the excuse of the hon. Member for Perthshire (Mr. Stirling), for not attending the Committee on the ground of illness, was allowed by the House; and if the Committee had adjourned till the present day, they would not then, on meeting, have been a Committee for sitting, deliberating, deciding, or even adjourning to the following day. Seeing that their last act as a Committee, before they entered, as it were, into a state of trance, was to adjourn, they did not think there could be any use in meeting again at a time when, as no Report had been made to the House, they would not be a Committee for any practical purpose whatever. He might mention, incidentally, that the counsel for the petitioners had stated that if the Committee had met to-day, he should respectfully have declined to attend on behalf of his clients. Under those circumstances, believing that they were acting in accordance with the spirit, if not with the strict letter of the law, they had deemed it best to adjourn till to-morrow As to the opinion of the learned gentleman, whose works on election law commanded great respect, that was, after all, only the view of the writer, and not the decision of a Court of Law. He would not enter into the question of the further consequences which might attend the proceedings, but he believed it had been held in Courts of Law, that where words were merely directing, and were not followed by a statement that all proceedings taken in contradiction to those words would be null and void, any departure from these words would not be held sufficient to render nugatory any previous proceedings in the case.

SIR GEORGE GREY said, that the question was one of considerable importance, and he felt with the hon. Member for Northamptonshire (Mr. Hunt) that it should not be hastily decided. Had it been generally known that the question would have come on for discussion that day, many hon. Members who were not present would have been in their places, and the Law Officers of the Crown also would have been in attendance. He thought the best course of proceeding would be for no discussion on the subject to take place that night, but that it be postponed till the following day, and that then the Report should be brought up by the Chairman of the Committee and printed, and then the House would have the question distinctly before it. The Motion, that the hon. Member for Perthshire (Mr. Stirling) be discharged from attendance on the Committee, should not be adopted, as it would prejudge the question to be discussed by the House.

MR. HUNT observed, that the first part of the Motion, excusing the hon. Member for Perthshire (Mr. Stirling) from further attendance, might be agreed to at once.

MR. WALPOLE said, he understood that the Committee stood adjourned till eleven to-morrow, and therefore they must consider the course the Committee should then take, as well as what the House should do to-day. He concurred with the right hon. Baronet (Sir George Grey), that the matter had better be postponed for the attendance of the Law Officers of the Crown, and he thought, therefore, that the question had better be deferred until to-morrow. The Motion consequent upon the Report of the Committee had better be deferred till to-morrow, and the House could then take the whole subject into its consideration. He apprehended, however, that the Committee had better meet to-morrow, or they might involve themselves in new difficulties, and then adjourn till the following day, reporting what they had done to the House.

SIR GEORGE GREY begged to move that the Report brought up by the Chairman of the Committee be printed and considered to-morrow.

Debate *adjourned* till *To-morrow*.
Report to be *printed*.

MALTA DOCK.—QUESTION.

MR. CORRY said, he wished to ask the Secretary to the Admiralty, Whether, as the papers respecting the New Dock at Malta are not in the hands of hon. Members, he will postpone asking for the Vote till next week?

LORD CLARENCE PAGET stated, in reply, that he should postpone Vote 11, in which the expense for the Malta Dock was included, until hon. Members had had a reasonable time for considering the papers on that subject, which he regretted to say, were not yet in their hands.

DENMARK AND GERMANY.
THE CONFERENCE.—QUESTIONS.

MR. BERNAL OSBORNE: I wish, Sir, to put three Questions to the noble Lord at the head of the Government, of which I have given him notice. The first is, Whether all the Powers who were parties to the Treaty of London of 1852 have consented to attend the Danish Conference; the second is, whether the German Confederation have consented to send representatives to that Congress, and if any basis has been settled for this Conference to discuss; and the third is, whether an Armistice has been agreed upon?

Mr. Hunt

VISCOUNT PALMERSTON: All the parties who signed and concluded the Treaty of 1852 have consented to send representatives to the Conference. No answer has yet been received from the German Diet, who have been invited to send a representative. The basis proposed for the Conference to start from is an endeavour to restore peace to the North of Europe. We have not thought it desirable, upon the plea of establishing a basis, to endeavour to settle beforehand those subjects which can more properly be the subjects of consideration when the Conference shall be assembled.

MR. BERNAL OSBORNE: As to the armistice?

VISCOUNT PALMERSTON: No armistice has yet been agreed to.

RESIGNATION OF MR. STANSFELD.

MR. STANSFELD (who sat on the second bench below the gangway on the Ministerial side of the House) said, Sir, I crave the indulgence of the House while I offer some explanations of a personal character; and in order to admit of discussion, if discussion be desired, on the subject with which I have to deal, I shall conclude by moving the adjournment of the House. Since the House last sat I have taken a step which the place from which I speak will have already sufficiently indicated to the House. I have felt it to be my duty to send in my resignation to the noble Lord at the head of Her Majesty's Government. The House will recollect that upon a former occasion I tendered that resignation, and that the noble Lord refused to accept it. I thank the noble Lord for the implicit credence which he gave to the statements that I made to him and to the House, and I thank him likewise for the courage he showed upon a former occasion in standing by me. But, Sir, there are occasions on which, I think, it becomes a man to consult his own conscience and his own sense of right as to the course which he should adopt, and the present appears to me to have been one of those occasions. I have become convinced, from what I have seen, heard, and read, that I have ceased to be—if I could ever believe myself to have been—any accession to the strength of Her Majesty's Government, and that I have become—or, at any rate, I have reason to fear I may have become—a source of difficulty and a cause of embarrassment to them. Under those circumstances, I felt—as I am sure every honourable man would feel—that it was for me, and not for others, to take upon myself the responsibility of saying that I could not, by any possibility, consent to be an enduring cause of embarrassment to a Government which I desired to support. There is another reason which has induced me to resign my appointment, and which the House will perhaps allow me to state. The House will remember that on the first occasion, when the subject (which I need not name) was discussed here, fault was found with me for dealing too seriously, or, as it was said, in a tone of too much indignation, with a speech of the late Procureur Général of France. Now, Sir, after what has happened—after the speech of the successor of that late Procureur—I do not think any person will repeat that blame. I think the House will agree with me that I was fully justified in the interpretation which I put upon the *animus* of that discourse. The attack having been renewed, I have to say to the Government and to the House, with all respect, that I prefer to meet it here alone rather than on that bench sheltered beneath the protecting ægis of the noble Lord. I desire to say a few words on the present occasion, because the House will understand that nothing can be more important to one of its Members than his relations with the general body. It has been said that I did not originally deal candidly with the House. Nothing could by possibility be—I mean in the sense of being mistaken—more unjust. I do not wish to say it by way of boast, but I do think that among my faults a want of courage to avow my own opinions, or to accept the responsibility of any act of mine past or present, is not one which any Member of this House could seriously lay to my charge. The explanation of that which may have appeared at first to be want of candour—for on occasions like the present almost any misunderstanding is possible — must be extremely simple to those who believe what I say. I felt, with respect to the speech of the Procureur, as I have already stated to the House. I then defended a personal friend of mine from an accusation of which I believed—of which I still believe—him to be unjustly the object. Some questions were then put to me by hon. Members. As my hon. and learned Friend the Member for Tiverton (Mr. Denman) explained afterwards, the House evidently had a disinclination that those questions should be addressed to

me; I think there was a feeling that, though it might not be so intended, it might bear the aspect of something like a Parliamentary cross-examination for the purpose of eliciting evidence for a criminal trial in a foreign court. I assure the House it was solely because such seemed to me to be the general feeling that at the moment I did not offer the distinct and explicit explanation which I submitted on a subsequent occasion. Now, I wish to look back and consider honestly what were my motives at the time I spoke. I think there was another motive. I felt it to be due to M. Mazzini, and I may say that I also felt it was due to myself, that from him first should come public statements and explanations as to the use to which he, and not I, had put my house, which had been more or less at his disposal as an address. That was another reason for my not then having made the statement which I subsequently made; and I think it will be an answer to the imputation which I have heard—I think in this House—that that explanation was dragged from me by the letter of Signor Mazzini published in *The Times* newspaper. Now, I wish to offer a word in reference to what I said about M. Mazzini. I said that from long and intimate personal relationship with him I believed him, in fact I knew him to be, incapable of this kind of low and odious criminality which is laid to his charge, and I now repeat that statement. And I would ask the House at least to allow me to say that I refuse to abandon the hope that in some calmer moments of the future to which I look, some perhaps of those who now hear me may cast their thoughts back to this night, and say that that man's testimony could not have been worthless, who gave the pledges which I have given of the sincerity of his convictions. Now let me state to the House, not at too great length, but with the greatest frankness, the nature of my relations with Signor Mazzini, and with the cause with which his name is connected, and to which his life has been devoted. I have long been personally and intimately associated with him. I have long had a very deep general sympathy with that which has been the object of his life—the unity and independence of Italy. If I am asked whether I have always agreed with the methods which have seemed to him wisest from time to time to achieve or progress towards that end, why, Sir, I should have to give the answer which may easily be anticipated—

that I have sometimes agreed with them, and that at other times I may have thought his views, his practical views, were less wise than they were sanguine and giving evidence of a great and strong hope. But that is not the question which has been raised in this case. The speeches of the two French Procureurs point distinctly, not only to his implication, but—let there be no mistake about the matter—they suggest my implication—at least as far as some kind of knowledge is concerned—in plots against the life of the French Emperor. Now, statements of that kind are to be met in two ways—general and specific. I will deal with those statements first generally, but completely, in the most explicit manner ; and I would desire to use the plainest language which the forms of this House permit me to use. I say, then, that every insinuation of that nature is untrue ; and I put it to the House, to those who may care to consider it, to look into the evidence upon which those speeches have been based, and to say whether, in their opinion, any honest man could upon that evidence have ventured to come to the conclusion that such insinuations could be put forth with any show or any pretence of truth. I come next to specific matters. Without detaining the House too long, I will deal with certain names, because, after all, the question seems to be what I have known of certain persons implicated in those French criminal proceedings. Now, the first name is that of Greco. I think I have already stated to the House that I never heard his name, that I neither knew of his existence, nor of the names or the existence of any of his supposed accomplices, until I saw in the newspapers, as every other Member of this House saw, the account of their arrest. Can anything be more explicit than that ? I will go back to the year 1857—to the Tibaldi case. I cannot venture to say that I never saw Tibaldi, but I am utterly unconscious of ever having seen him. I have seen too many Italian refugees to be able to say that I have never seen this man or that man, or to pretend to remember the names of all the men I have ever seen; but I can say this, that I never saw any man, call him Tibaldi or call him by any other name, who in 1857 ventured to come near me to suggest the notion of plots like this. Two other names have been mentioned in connection with the affair of 1857—one of them is the name of Massarenti. I knew him very well. He was famous in re-

Mr. Stansfeld

lation to the small commerce carried on by Italians in this city. He lived in the neighbourhood of Hatton Garden, and dealt in maccaroni and Italian pastes. He has certainly received money from me, but only in the shape of very moderate payments for the goods in which he dealt. The second name is Campanella, who, I believe, was condemned at the trial in 1857. I knew him well. He was a gentleman and a scholar, a student, almost a recluse. He was a man utterly incapable of soiling his fingers in dirt of this kind. And I know as a fact—because the House is perfectly aware that these things have been the subject of talk in France, Italy, and England—I pledge my knowledge of that man to the House, and I do him this act of justice to-night, when I say that he was one who expressed his utter contempt for plots of this description. Two extracts have been given of alleged letters, of which the House will understand that if they be genuine I am prepared to take the whole responsibility that may attach to them. I do not know—it is impossible for me, or for any one connected with me, to say—whether those extracts are genuine or not; but I will say this, that there is nothing in them that I have the slightest desire to deny. As far as I can judge, they may be genuine extracts of letters, which, by means to which I will not further refer, came into the possession of the French authorities. What do these extracts prove ? The extract from the first letter proves nothing except the relation of friendship which I have admitted, and which it is perfectly well known has long subsisted between Signor Mazzini and myself. What is the purport of the second extract ? It states that a remittance has been received, and will be applied according to instructions. Now, it is said that this House is not a court of justice, but, at least, it is a court of honour ; and we speak here upon our honour. The House will believe me when I say that I am utterly unable, and those with whom I am connected by family ties are utterly unable, to imagine or recollect to what that passage—if it be a veritable passage—refers. But this I am enabled to assert, that it did not refer, because it could not refer—for that would imply knowledge—it did not refer to anything that would not bear the test of the closest examination ; and that, as far as I can judge, upon my honour and upon my conscience, I believe it must have referred either to some mere private transaction or to the distribution of some probably moderate or trifling sum for a charitable purpose. Sir, I trust that I have now made an explanation which will not be unsatisfactory to the House. I have only to add that if any doubts remain upon the minds of any hon. Members, I not only am ready but I invite them to give expression to those doubts, and to enable me at once completely to satisfy them and to answer any questions which they may have to put to me. Meanwhile I leave this subject, and I throw myself upon the House, and I may add upon my countrymen, with reference to a question in which is involved that which is every man's dearest inheritance—an unblemished character and a fair name.

Motion made, and Question proposed, "That this House do now adjourn."—(*Mr. Stansfeld.*)

VISCOUNT PALMERSTON: Sir, my hon. Friend has reminded the House that on the former occasion when he tendered his resignation I declined to accept it and requested him to continue in office. Upon the present occasion, as he has now stated, he left me no option. I can only say that I am convinced that the motives which led my hon. Friend to make that peremptory decision were highly honourable to him. He no doubt thought, having an explanation to make, which he has now made, and which I am persuaded the House will deem perfectly and entirely satisfactory, that such explanation would come from him with a better grace and with more effect if holding an independent position than if he made it from the bench on which we now sit. Sir, I can only express the great regret which I and my Colleagues feel at having lost the official assistance of a man whose great ability, whose untiring industry, whose perfect truthfulness, and whose unswerving integrity of mind rendered him a most valuable Member of the Administration to which he belonged, and endeared him to all those who had the advantage of his friendship. With regard to those insinuations and aspersions to which he has referred, I can only say that with him I repudiate them with disdain. I am firmly convinced, and I am sure all those who know my hon. Friend must be equally convinced, that any charge of implication in those base proceedings, which charge I think had been basely thrown out against him, is altogether unsupported by proof and is utterly devoid of foundation.

I will not go into details, but I will say that I am convinced that my hon. Friend attaches the same value to the welfare and personal safety of that Sovereign who reigns over the Empire of France which any hon. Member of this House can attach to it; that he is as sensible as we are that that great Sovereign has upon many grave and important occasions proved himself to be a true friend and faithful ally of this country; and we all feel that his personal security and his dynastic welfare are not only of the utmost value to the loyal and attached people he governs, but are equally essential to the general interests of Europe.

Motion, by leave, *withdrawn.*

SUPPLY.

Motion made, and Question proposed, "That Mr. Speaker do now leave the Chair."

THE MAILS IN THE PROVINCES.
MOTION FOR A SELECT COMMITTEE.

MR. R. LONG said, he rose to move for a Select Committee of inquiry respecting the operations of the Post Office, with an especial view to the improvement of the existing arrangements for the transmission of mails in the provincial districts. His object was only to point out the defects in our postal system within the kingdom, and he hoped that the instances which he would lay before the House would be sufficient to convince hon. Members of the reasonableness of his Motion. Some time ago he had put a question to Her Majesty's Government on the subject, but the answer he had received appeared to him so ambiguous that he thought himself justified in now asking the House to assent to a Committee of Inquiry. He had no wish to make any attack on the leading principles of the postal system. On the contrary, he did not think that anything could be better than the general arrangements made some twenty-five or thirty years ago for the transmission of our mails from London to the most extreme points of the kingdom. Too little attention had, however, been paid to the public convenience in regard to the postal communications between certain provincial towns in which the arrangements still observed were of an extremely objectionable character. When it was considered what an enormous increase had taken place of late years in the number of letters transmitted through the post, it became the more necessary to accelerate as much as possible the communication between one provincial town and another. Now, it was undeniable that in many of our provincial towns advantage was not taken of facilities which really existed for the speedy despatch and delivery of letters, and the mails were still despatched by a horse and cart and sometimes even by messengers on foot. Notwithstanding the existence of railways, such clumsy arrangements were still adhered to, whereby three days were required for a letter to be received and an answer returned to the writer between towns of only a few miles distance from each other. Such facts proved distinctly a great want of supervision and of progress in the postal department. Remonstrances had been made over and over again against the continuance of such a system; private interest had likewise been brought to bear but without effect. That was the state of things in a district with which he was connected, and though improvements had been suggested they had been unable till January last to obtain the opinion of the Post Office on the subject. It was not, in fact, until February last, when a few hon. Members warmly took up the question, that the Treasury conceded certain facilities for the transmission of letters between some of those towns which complained of the inconvenience and delay of the then existing system. In many other provincial towns, however, the evil continued unabated. A memorial from Hereford had been forwarded to him, of which a copy had been presented to the noble Lord at the head of the Government. In that document it was stated that, notwithstanding the existence of railway communication between Hereford, Ross, and Gloucester, the mails were still conveyed through the district of those important towns by horse and cart along the turnpike road, which ran nearly parallel with the railway. That was, in his opinion, a gross piece of mismanagement, for which no defence could be set up. Again, he had received a letter from a gentleman residing near Newport, in South Wales, complaining of similar defects in the postal arrangements in that district. Between Newport, Cardiff, Merthyr, and other important towns, the mails were still conveyed by horse and cart, instead of by the railway, which communicated directly with them. With regard to the postal communications between Shrewsbury and Dublin, he had been informed by a gentleman, resident at the former, and having

Mr. R. Long

large trade transactions with the latter place, that in consequence of the Irish mails arriving at Stafford one hour after the down mails left Shrewsbury, twenty-four hours' delay occurred in the despatch and receipt of letters between Shrewsbury and Dublin. That was an inconvenience to which the public had no right to be subjected. Then, again, with regard to the postal arrangements between Shrewsbury and Liverpool. A passenger could be conveyed from Shrewsbury to Liverpool in three hours, but it required twenty-four hours for a letter to reach Liverpool and for an answer to be received in Shrewsbury. That was a great grievance, and one which the public had a right to call upon the Post Office authorities to remedy. Coming nearer to London, he had received a letter from a gentleman, dated from Ash, near Sevenoaks, in Kent, complaining that letters from that place were sent by the South Eastern Railway by Croydon to Tunbridge, thence by omnibus to Sevenoaks, to Wrotham by mail cart, and the last seven miles to Ash by messenger. Remonstrances had been made over and over again to the Post Office, but the inhabitants could get no redress. Another letter from a magistrate resident at Uckfield, in Sussex, on behalf of the inhabitants of his locality, stated that it took two days to send a letter to a place only seven or nine miles distant. The letters were first sent to London, and then by a circuitous route to their destination, and when there happened to be a heavy fall of snow they were delayed several hours longer. Notwithstanding all their complaints they could get no redress from the Post Office authorities, and it was therefore to be inferred that no better arrangements could be made than that four days should be wasted in communicating with parties residing at a distance of only nine miles from each other, and in receiving an answer, in fact as long a time as would be required for a communication with Paris or Edinburgh. It would be easy to multiply instances of delay, but he had no wish to occupy the time of the House unnecessarily, in order to show that some beneficial change was absolutely necessary, and that the country generally had a right to expect to be provided with rapid and frequent postal communication. But the right hon. Gentleman the Secretary of the Treasury would, no doubt, ask what remedies he proposed to remedy the evils pointed out. Such remedies appeared to him very simple. First, let the Post Office authorities adopt the railway system in its entirety ; and secondly, let them place the central Post Office in the heart of the railway system. If the chief and central Post Office was removed from St. Martin's-le-Grand to Charing Cross, the old building might be advantageously sold, and thus a large sum might be placed at the Chancellor of the Exchequer's disposal, either for the building of a worthy national gallery, or for other purposes. Then there ought to be post offices at all the railway stations, and the letter boxes should be cleared and the letters forwarded by every train. Such a plan would multiply communications indefinitely between different places on the line, in which case all delays arising from cross posts would be obviated. The adoption of such a system would greatly increase the revenue and give great satisfaction to the public. There should also be a free delivery of letters all over the country, the same as in the metropolitan districts, and an additional expense should not be thrown on remote districts, as was now the case. Local newspapers ought to have the privilege of transmission through the Post Office, as well as newspapers generally, by the issue of a cheap postage stamp. The ability now displayed in the conduct of the cheap press, the increased intelligence of the people who read those newspapers, and the immense number now in daily circulation throughout the country, rendered it necessary that such accommodation of cheap and easy transit should be given to the public. But so far from the Post Office authorities having done anything to assist the diffusion of knowledge in that respect, they levied 100 per cent tax on every penny newspaper transmitted through the Post Office. Hitherto the Post Office had allowed the mail carts to take packages of newspapers into the rural districts, but an order had recently been issued prohibiting the continuance of that arrangement unless each paper bore a stamp. So far from the present system being advantageous to the revenue it was the reverse, but the issue of a cheap stamp such as he had referred to would, he was certain, add considerably to the Post Office returns. In that opinion he was borne out by a passage in the last Post Office Report, which stated, that whilst the Post Office had incurred additional expense by reason of the improved arrangements throughout the country to the amount of 1½ per cent, the increase of revenue in 1862 over 1861 was 3 per cent; clearly showing, he contended, that every

advantage given to the public was appreciated, and was made a means of usefulness and a positive benefit to the revenue. He hoped he should not plead in vain to the House for that support which he now ventured to ask for his Motion for a Select Committee.

MR. CLIVE begged to second the Motion, and said, when he came down to the House he was under the impression that the hon. Member for Chippenham (Mr. Long) would not have brought it forward until to-morrow, and he was, therefore, not prepared with the facts which he had intended to bring forward in order to fortify the arguments of the hon. Member. He might state, however, that several complaints of delay in the transmission of letters through the post had come under his own personal knowledge. He particularly referred to Hereford and its neighbourhood, where the greatest inconvenience was experienced, owing to the mails being sent round through Shrewsbury. He had been in constant communication with his constituents on the subject for the last two years, and had made several representations to the Postmaster General, but without success. They were much obliged to the Postmaster General for some improvements he had effected, but grievances remained unredressed which subjected the public to much inconvenience. He hoped that the statements that had been made would have some influence on the mind of the noble Lord Her Majesty's Postmaster General.

Amendment proposed,

To leave out from the word "That" to the end of the Question, in order to add the words " a Select Committee be appointed to inquire into the Post Office, with an especial view to the improvement of existing arrangements for the transmission of Mails in the provincial districts,"— (*Mr. Richard Long*,)

—instead thereof.

MR. PUGH said, the country was much indebted to the hon. Gentleman the Member for Chippenham (Mr. Long) for having brought forward the subject. Great dissatisfaction had existed in the neighbourhood of Carmarthen for some years past relative to the postal arrangements of the district The great cause for complaint was that sufficient use was not made of the facilities afforded by railways for the transmission of letters ; and he was able to endorse the statements of the hon. Member with regard to the insufficiency of the arrangements at Gloucester and Carmarthen. He could give other instances but he thought it unnecessary, feeling satisfied that right would be done on the proposed Committee. He was sure that the districts in South Wales, especially Carmarthen, would derive great benefit from the labours of such a Committee.

MR. AYTOUN said, he could corroborate the statements that had been made with reference to the great dissatisfaction that prevailed in country districts with regard to the present postal arrangements. The inhabitants of the rural districts of Scotland had also great reason for complaint, and he hoped the Committee would not be refused. The indifference shown by the Post Office authorities to the convenience of important places in the country, and the great delay in remedying a grievance when stated, were universally condemned. He brought a grievance complained of by his constituents before the notice of Her Majesty's Postmaster General in October last ; and though the remedy for the same was, in itself, but a simple matter—an additional post in the middle of the day—five months elapsed before it was applied. The insufficiency of the present system was complained of in all parts of the country, and he hoped the Committee would be granted.

MR. WYLD said, he hoped the right hon. Gentleman the Secretary to the Treasury would accede to the Motion. The hon. Member for Chippenham (Mr. Long) had not complained so much of Post Office mismanagement as of the persistent non-adoption of modern facilities offered by railways for improved postal arrangements. He spoke for the inhabitants of a large portion of the West of England, and though they were very thankful for what had already been done—and they knew how much they owed to the great man, who had till very recently held a high position in the General Post Office—still much remained to be accomplished, in order to give even absolutely necessary accommodation. He believed, that so far from Her Majesty's revenue losing by the improvements which were suggested for facilitating the delivery of letters, it would be greatly augmented thereby.

MR. LIDDELL begged to remind the House that the subject of the postal arrangements of the country was a very wide one. In 1853 he obtained a Select Committee of Inquiry, similar to the one now asked for, and they found it an Herculean task. He, therefore, ventured to

suggest the expediency of defining, as correctly as possible, the precise branches of inquiry into which the Committee ought to enter. Without such definition, our postal arrangements were so extensive that several Sessions would elapse before the inquiry would be concluded. It was now urged that our postal arrangements had not kept pace with the requirements of the times, and he, as the representative of a large commercial community, could add his testimony to many of the statements of the hon. Member for Chippenham (Mr. Long) with regard to the great complaints that were made in many parts of the country, that our present postal arrangements did not meet the requirements and growing wants of the public. The right hon. Baronet the present Home Secretary (Sir George Grey) gave some valuable information before the Committee of 1853 relative to his own locality, and some of the suggestions he then made had, he believed, been since carried out. He had received a letter from the largest journalist in his neighbourhood, complaining of the serious inconvenience to which the public had been put, in consequence of the order recently issued by the Post Office, forbidding the Post Office messengers from taking parcels of newspapers into the rural districts, without each paper were stamped. He would urge the Government to grant the Committee which had been asked for, the scope of its inquiry being strictly limited to the matters of grievance which were wished to be remedied.

MR. HENRY SEYMOUR begged to corroborate what had fallen from the hon. Member for Bodmin (Mr. Wyld), as to the dissatisfaction which prevailed in the West of England respecting the present postal arrangements. Scarcely any use was there made of the railways for postal purposes, and the inhabitants were at present absolutely worse off, with regard to the transmission of letters, than they were before the age of railways. In one district there was only one post a day where formerly there were two. A few years ago, he brought before the House the case of a parish in Wilts, where a letter received from a place only five miles distant, occupied four days in its journey, having been taken round by Bristol, London, and possibly to other places. He had hoped that the Post Office authorities might have been able to improve the system, but nothing whatever had been done. He had been on deputation after deputation to the Postmaster General, having for their object the facilitation of the conveyance of letters, but no remedy had been devised. He, therefore, thought it time that a Committee should be appointed to inquire into the existing arrangements, and to suggest improvements therein.

COLONEL SYKES said, that the postal communication with Aberdeen had been thrown into the greatest confusion in consequence of the discontinuance of the direct mails from Aberdeen. The railway companies were always ready to make the most liberal arrangements for the conveyance of the mails, and which would ensure the convenience of the district, but they were met by the remark, "Oh, you are too costly ; the Post Office cannot afford it." But, in his opinion, whether the arrangements were costly or not, they ought to be adopted if the convenience of the public would be thereby enhanced. He thought that out of the large revenue of the Post Office a portion might well be devoted to remedying the grievances now complained of.

COLONEL FRENCH said, that in many cases improved arrangements had not been carried out, in consequence of the extravagant sums demanded by railway companies for the conveyance of mails. With regard to the complaints which had been made, he believed that the Post Office authorities had made great efforts to meet the wants of the public, but in so widely extended a system there must always be some particular cases of grievance, and it was impossible to satisfy every one.

MR. PEEL said, the Motion of the hon. Member for Chippenham (Mr. Long) sought to establish two propositions, first, that country places and provincial districts were not well and satisfactorily served with regard to their local correspondence ; and secondly, that it was expedient to appoint a Committee to consider what improvements could be made, and in what manner they could be carried out. He thought that country places, generally speaking, had no great reason to complain of the present postal arrangements. The hon. Gentleman admitted that they had shared to the full extent with other parts of the country the advantages of a low and uniform rate of postage, and all the other improvements with regard to the registration of letters, money order offices and Post Office savings banks; and there was scarcely a place, however out of the way

and remote, that a letter did not reach its destination in the course of a single night. The hon. Gentleman had complained of the restriction on free delivery of letters at the residence of the persons to whom they were addressed ; but the Report of the Post Master General stated that more than 95 per cent of all letters were delivered free at the residences to which they were addressed, and that this percentage was being continually enlarged. He by no means wished to imply that the system was perfect, or that there might not be ground for complaint in particular cases. Indeed, if it were possible to perfect the system to-day, change of circumstances would render it imperfect to-morrow. What was wanted, however, was not the enunciation of some new principle within the scope of a recommendation of a Committee of Inquiry, but rather arrangements in detail for the consideration of the heads of the Post Office Department. The hon. Member for Chippenham had cited a number of particular cases with the view of showing that there was ground for inquiry on the part of the House ; but it was very difficult to form any positive opinion as to whether those cases proved defective management, for the House had not the contrastatement of the Post Office, nor could they have had it, because the hon. Gentleman's notice did not state the cases on which he intended to rely. Doubtless, as the hon. Member had stated, there were isolated cases in which the arrangements were not perfect; but probably the inconveniences resulting therefrom were greatly outweighed by the advantages of the general system on which the business of the Post Office was conducted, from which some inconveniences could not be severed. The hon. Gentleman had complained of want of expeditious communication between contiguous places. But he did not think it was the duty of the Post Office to establish communications between places merely because they were near, and without taking into consideration the correspondence which passed between them. The places might be very near, and the number of letters very small; and, in that case, the Post Office would not be justified in incurring a large expense to meet the demands of a very small correspondence. Again, it was conducive to the general convenience that the mails of the different localities should arrive at the same time as the London mails. The correspondence between London and any particular locality had to be considered in the first place; and the delivery of letters in rural districts must be regulated in connection with that correspondence. Complaints had been made of the few deliveries in the country; but it must be remembered that letters could not be delivered on the arrival of every mail without an army of letter carriers. The arrangements must be so contrived as to make one or two deliveries suffice for all the correspondence of the place. It sometimes happened that the mail course between two places near each other might be circuitous and yet not inconvenient, as for instance when mails were dispatched by an up-train on one line to be met and brought back by a down-train on another. Another complaint had been that the facilities afforded by railways were not sufficiently made use of by the Post Office. The Post Office had power in some cases to demand the running of a mail train; in others, to arrange for the use of particular trains; and in others to make use of all the trains, letter carriers being sent as passengers carrying the mail bags with them. It was for the public convenience that the Post Office should make a large use of railways; but the Post Office had to consider also the amount of the expense, and in the Scotch case referred to by the hon. and gallant Member for Aberdeen (Colonel Sykes) the charge was considered too high, and the inconvenience complained of arose from the Post Office and the railway company not being able to agree to terms. It was the duty of the Post Office authorities to provide as much public accommodation as possible; but it was likewise their duty to obtain as large a revenue as possible, and to guard against useless expenditure. If an inflexible rule were laid down that the Post Office must use every railway as soon as constructed, a greatly increased tax would be laid on the public. The time in which the mails were in transit was principally at night, a period when railway companies might fairly urge that a train would have few passengers, and could not be remunerative. What was wanted, then, was to get the train on moderate terms. The case of the Shrewsbury and Aberystwith Railway had been instanced. In that case, if the Post Office had demanded mail trains on the opening of the line they would have had to pay a heavy charge. They waited till the traffic had been somewhat developed; and then arrangements were easily concluded by which the mails

Mr. Peel

were carried at fair rates. The Post Office acted on a fair rule. When a country place claimed increased postal accommodation, the question asked was, whether such increase would be likely to be self-supporting? He did not think that the surplus revenue of one part of the country should be employed in defraying the expenses of another. If the question of remunerative postal arrangements were to be ignored, the Post Office would speedily cease to bring in any revenue at all. He was far from saying that there was not room for improvement in details, but he thought that the desired improvement could be best effected by the Post Office authorities. In point of fact, improvements were constantly being made. The annual Report of the Post Master General gave an account of the improvements effected during the year. They consisted mainly of acceleration of the mails and extensions of delivery. The Post Office authorities had special facilities for obtaining local information. They had surveyors constantly travelling about the country, making personal inquiries as to the operation of the Post Office, and wherever improvements were needed they were introduced as speedily as possible. The suggestions which had been made in the course of the debate were entitled to consideration, but he did not think the appointment of a Committee of Inquiry would be the best means of remedying the defects complained of.

MR. H. BAILLIE said, that the county which he had the honour to represent, enjoyed fewer facilities, in the way of postal communication, than any of the districts to which allusion had been made in the course of the debate. The question to be considered was entirely one of principle. It was, whether the Post Office ought to give increased accommodation to those districts only the inhabitants of which were able and willing to pay for it; or whether, having a large surplus revenue, the business was so to be conducted as to be altogether at the service of the country, although some of the correspondence wouldnot be remunerative. The rule of the Post Office was to give increased accommodation only where it could be proved that it would pay, or where a guarantee was given against a possibly accruing deficit. He had presented a petition praying for increased postal facilities from the Isle of Skye, where, with a population of 20,000 inhabitants, there was a mail only three times a week. The answer of the Post Office was, that a daily service would cost £1,200 a year, and that they had not been assured that what was demanded would be attended with adequate returns. He had likewise presented a similar petition from Fort William, which had only a mail twice a week, and though distant only sixty miles from Inverness the mail was forty-eight hours on the road, and the request was for a mail which would take only twelve hours. The Post Office authorities made a similar reply in this case —it would not pay. He thought these cases worthy of consideration by a Select Committee. Was the Post Office established for the occasion of revenue, or for the general benefit of the public ? Believing the latter to be the case, he would support the Motion.

SIR MATTHEW RIDLEY said, the right hon. Gentleman the Secretary to the Treasury (Mr. Peel), had complained that specific cases of grievances had not been adduced. In a case represented to him as occurring in the district which he had the honour to represent, he thought there was a substantial grievance. By recent orders of the Postmaster General, the letter carriers were no longer to carry penny newspapers unless they were stamped. The consequence was that those papers were thereby doubled in price. It had been suggested that a smaller stamp might be adopted. That was altogether another matter. A grievance of that nature—which was entirely in opposition to the assistance which the Post Office ought to give to the diffusion of information—might very well be inquired into by the proposed Committee. He considered he had furnished the right hon. Gentleman with a specific case of grievance, and he should certainly support the Motion.

MR. BENTINCK thought that the arguments used by the right hon. Gentleman, the Secretary to the Treasury (Mr. Peel) favoured, rather than otherwise, the Motion which he intended to oppose. The hon. Member for Chippenham (Mr. Long), who brought forward the Motion, had no wish to pass any censure on the general conduct of the Post Office ; but, being fully aware of the enormous difficulties attendant on the successful working out the complicated details of the system of the Post Office, he had moved that a Select Committee be appointed to inquire into those difficulties, and also into the best means of affording facilities to the Post Office for meeting the evils

the existence of which scarcely a Member of that House would venture to doubt. He complained, in the first place, that the facilities for transit afforded by railways were not made the most of, and secondly that, in consequence, localities within a few miles of each other might as well, for purposes of postal communication, be 500 miles apart.

But the real grievance was, that in the present, as in most other cases, the convenience and the advantage of the metropolis and large towns was studied before that of rural and thinly peopled districts. He admitted the difficulties of the case; and that the order of reference to a Committee such as had been proposed, ought to be very carefully worded, lest the subject should become unmanageable. But there were two points which, he thought, would well repay investigation, and both related to money. The right hon. Gentleman had spoken of losses sustained by the Post Office through the employment of railways. He thought that, considering the practical monopoly which the railway companies had obtained, they ought to be compelled to carry the mail bags at a reasonable rate. The other question was, whether in cases where it could be shown that the correspondence would not be sufficient to pay the extra expense, the Post Office might not be empowered to charge additional rates ? [An hon. MEMBER : No, no!] An hon. Member said "No." He thought it a question well worthy of serious consideration whether, in such cases, the inhabitants of these districts might not be allowed to decide whether they would not pay an increased postage-rate in order to obtain the advantage of improved postal communication. A Select Committee, he was convinced, would facilitate the labours of the Post Office authorities, and he would therefore support the Motion.

MR. KINNAIRD thought the Post Office authorities were sometimes in error, proceeding as they did upon the principle, that because the number of letters for a particular locality would not pay the expense of conveyance and delivery, therefore increased postal facilities should not be extended to that locality. At the same time, he was of opinion that the attention of the Treasury should in the first instance be drawn to the subject, and then, if that Department refused to provide remedies for the grievances complained of, recourse might be had to a Select Committee of Inquiry.

THE CHANCELLOR OF THE EXCHEQUER said, the hon. Member for Inverness (Mr. Baillie) had broadly and fairly laid down the principle that the Post Office ought not to be considered as a source of revenue to the Government, but that the surplus revenue derived from it ought to be expended in providing increased postal accommodation. For his own part, however, he should be very reluctant, by acceding to the proposal before the House, to commit himself to the acceptance of such a principle. The Post Office now yielded a net revenue of a million and a half; that million and a half was received in return for services, and stood in the place and performed the functions of a million and a half raised by taxation. If, therefore, the suggestion were acceded to that that million and a half was to be laid out in providing additional accommodation, the result would be that there would be a gap to that extent which would have to be stopped by the levying of a new tax, or by the augmentation of some tax already in existence. Now it was desirable to know, whether the principle involved in such a scheme was one upon which hon. Members were prepared to proceed, because any Committee appointed to try a particular case, would evidently derive the greatest possible light and assistance from the possession of information as to whether the House did or did not deem it right that the funds of the Post Office should be applied freely and without stint to the extension of local accommodation. Independently of that objection, which he naturally felt, as the person who would be expected to discover the unpleasant substitute for the revenue which was now raised without taxing anybody, he was disposed to doubt and question the justice of the doctrine which had that evening been laid down by more than one hon. Member; for what did it amount to, and where would it lead them? It would lead them to the conclusion that, while a large revenue was raised in populous districts, in connection with the Post Office, that revenue might be appropriated to supplying the wants of remote districts with isolated houses difficult of access. Under that seemingly popular proposition, that the Post Office should not be a source of revenue, was concealed, not intentionally of course, a doctrine of a very different nature—namely, that one portion of the country ought to be taxed for the purposes of another. He did not agree with the doctrine that the Post

Mr. Kinnaird

Office was never to extend the facilities for communication, except when there was a moral certainty of a remunerative return. Such a doctrine, in his opinion, involved a most narrow, undue, and improper view of the functions of the Department. The Post Office ought to consider particular cases in a liberal spirit, and if the hon. Member was correct in stating that the Post Office excluded from its view the extension of the means of communication, that was wrong; but he thought his hon. Friend was misinformed. He wished, at the same time, to remark that the Department of the Post Office was not directly represented in the House of Commons, and it, therefore, devolved on his right hon. Friend the Secretary for the Treasury (Mr. Peel), or upon himself, to speak on behalf of that Department when it became the subject of discussion in that House. Consequently the means at the disposal of his right hon. Friend and himself, as regarded forming a correct opinion and expressing their views to the House, must entirely depend on whether they had, or had not, been put in possession beforehand of the nature of the complaints to be made; if that had not been done, to invite the House to appoint a Committee of Inquiry, was to pass by the Executive Government. He did not deny the right of the House to take that step if it pleased; it had rather been to refer executive questions to be dealt with by the Executive; and if the redress sought was not obtained, then to bring the matter before the House. He would suggest to the hon. Member for Chippenham (Mr. Long), that the best course to pursue would be for him to bring before the Treasury, by way of appeal, some of the cases which he had cited, and thus give that Department an opportunity of seeing how the difficulties could be best met. If, after reviewing the matter, in conjunction with the Post Office, they declined to act in the direction which he indicated, then it would be open to him to appeal to the House, and to call upon it, through the medium of a Committee, or otherwise, to take the question into its own hands. The hon. Member for West Norfolk laid down a reasonable doctrine, that localities should be allowed to contribute where they were not sufficiently large to render them remunerative to the Post Office, and that was to some extent already done. He hoped the hon. Member for Chippenham would adopt this suggestion, and give the Treasury an opportunity of reviewing the matter.

MR. W. WILLIAMS hoped that no consideration would induce either the House or the Government to increase the rate of postage, or to make in any district the slightest variation from the uniform rate that now prevailed. Of all financial reforms that had taken place, the reduction in postage rates was the most important.

MR. HENLEY said, he should not have taken any part in that discussion but for an observation of the right hon. Gentleman the Chancellor of the Exchequer. He told the House that the Post Office gave a revenue of a million and a half; and if that were taken away he must find some other means of raising that sum. He understood the right hon. Gentleman to say, that it would not be just to the taxpayers at large to call on them for that amount in order to give the convenience of additional postal communication to sparsely populated districts that would not pay the expenses.

THE CHANCELLOR OF THE EXCHEQUER: I expressly guarded myself against saying that in no case should there be increased accommodation unless the service were remunerative. My argument went to the extent of controverting the principle that the revenue of the Post Office ought generally to be applied to furnishing such accommodation to thinly inhabited localities.

MR. HENLEY said, he perfectly understood that the right hon. Gentleman did not say in no case; but he thought if the principle were to be applied to the packet service different results to those which existed would be produced. He apprehended that the packet service was not included in the expense of the Post Office. He did not think the right hon. Gentleman had so flourishing a figure as a million and a half after deducting the packet service, which was only for the advantage of those persons using it. He hoped the principle would not be carried too far, that districts were to be deprived of postal privileges because they were not sufficiently populated to make them remunerative to the Post Office. Not only was there the local advantage, but the advantage to the sender, and it must be remembered that a great deal of the Post Office business was the carrying of circulars from populous places, and where there were not postal facilities for delivering these circulars, private individuals in large towns were put to considerable expense to deliver them. He should be the last person to say that the

Post Office was not an immense advantage to the community in all parts of the country, but those persons who had not its advantages, seeing others in possession of them, of course became dissatisfied. He hoped the Government would not draw the line too tightly. He, for one, did not think it unreasonable that all those cases should be brought before the notice of the Treasury, because, if they could not provide an adequate remedy, an appeal could then be made to the House ; in fact, he considered that course the most likely to be attended with success.

MR. T. BARING said, he did not agree with the right hon. Gentleman the Member for Oxfordshire (Mr. Henley), that the packet service was merely for the benefit of those persons who sent letters by it ; it was an advantage to the whole country. That service involved an outlay, whether too large or not was not then the question, which was not merely for the advantage of the individuals who sent those letters, but for the good of the community at large. Any other view of steam communication would be narrow and one sided, seeing that the advantages extended to the whole productive industry of the country.

Question, " That the words proposed to be left out stand part of the Question," put, and *agreed to.*

Main Question put, and *agreed to.*

SUPPLY—NAVY ESTIMATES.

NAVY ESTIMATES *considered* in Committee.

(In the Committee.)

1. £1,164,100, Naval Stores.

SIR JAMES ELPHINSTONE said, with reference to the item £120,000 for gunboats to be built by private contract, he should be glad of some explanation. Our former gunboats had been such lamentable failures, that he thought the noble Lord the Secretary for the Admiralty ought to state the nature of the gunboats he intended to build.

MR. C. BERKELEY begged to call attention to the number of ships removed from the effective list of the navy since the Return dated Feb. 1, 1863. At that date the number was 669, but at present was represented as 630, thus showing that thirty-nine vessels had been removed from the effective list ; and he thought, as there had been some vessels added, the number might be larger. Some were sailing vessels, which it was possible had been transferred to the harbour list; but, looking into the details, thirty-three or thirty-four he found to be steam vessels struck off during the past year. Many, if not all those vessels, were quite unseaworthy, and the reason he called the attention of the House to them was that he thought it desirable that the noble Lord the Secretary of the Admiralty should explain if any others now in the service, especially gunboats, were in a similar condition. Some of them were gunboats built about ten years ago. One of the vessels condemned was the *Victor*, and as there were five other ships of the same class built at the same time, it was desirable that the House should be informed as to the present condition of those vessels. Perhaps, too, the noble Lord would explain under what circumstances it was that two frigates which were now upon the stocks—the names of which he did not know—were to be pulled down. A system had lately sprung up of putting into the *Navy List*, and allowing to remain there for some time, the names of vessels on which little or nothing had been expended. Such cases were those of the *Sappho* at Deptford, the name of which was published in the list for three years, and then disappeared, and of the *Alligator*. He should like to have some explanation of these circumstances. It would be convenient if the noble Lord would give the House some more information than had yet been vouchsafed with regard to the character and form of the vessels building on Mr. Reed's plan. In successive *Navy Lists* vessels not only appeared and disappeared, but the same vessels seemed to alter their tonnage. It was stated, for instance, that the frame of the *Circassia*, of 950 tons, had been appropriated to the *Enterprise*, building on Mr. Reed's plan, in July, 1862; but in the *Navy List* for 1861 a vessel called the *Enterprise* was included as well as the *Circassia*, and since the appropriation referred to another vessel called the *Circassia* had appeared on the scene. Different tonnages and armaments were given in every case with regard to these vessels. He was not to be understood, however, as insinuating that any wasteful or improvident practices existed in any of the dockyards. The very best guarantee against anything of the kind was afforded by the appointment of such men as Sir Baldwin Walker and Admiral Robinson.

Mr. W. WILLIAMS said, he must complain that there was no real reduction in the Navy Estimates for the present year. No credit was due to the Admiralty, for the only apparent reduction was in the Vote for material. But if the Admiralty wanted more materials of any kind it would, without hesitation, purchase them, and then submit a supplementary Estimate to the House. The Vote for wages was £170,000 more than it was last year.

Mr. CORRY said, as he had been prevented from attending in his place when the Navy Estimates were under discussion, he was anxious to make a few remarks on this occasion, and there was no part of those Estimates—not even the reduction of 4,000 men—which he had read with greater dissatisfaction than the diminution of about £200,000 in the sum proposed for the building of armour-plated ships. From the statement of his noble Friend the Secretary to the Admiralty, he concluded that it was not intended at present to exceed the number of the twenty-five now built or in progress. Of these, they were told nineteen would be available next year, and in the following year the whole number would be ready for service. He appealed to hon. Members whether, if armour-plated ships were to supersede wooden ships, that was a force adequate to the wants of the British navy, or one with which it would be possible to carry on a great war. In the event of a war occurring in 1866, he would like to know how the noble Lord would propose to appropriate those vessels? How many of the twenty-five would he allot for the defence of the Channel; how many to the Mediterranean, where we have interests at stake not less important; how many to the Baltic; how many to the North Sea, to the West Indies, to the coasts of China and India, and how many to the Pacific, where a large and important colony had lately sprung up? It was nonsense to talk of defending our vast interests on those stations with twenty-five ships, when it was well known that all the principal nations of Europe were acquiring large fleets of armour-plated ships; and America, too, was largely increasing her strength in ships of that description. His noble Friend had abstained this year from speaking of what the French were doing, but the information had been furnished by France herself. In a letter from the Paris correspondent of *The Times*, he found that—

"According to statistics recently published the French Government possesses at present,

Mr. C. Berkeley

either finished or in progress of completion, 43 screw iron-plated vessels, being altogether of the force of 24,000-horse power, and 1,356 guns; of these, four are liners (of which England has none), 19 frigates, 19 gunboats, and 1 ship with a spur."

We were promised twenty-five ships and six gunboats, of the united horse-power of 23,000, against the French forty-three vessels of 24,000-horse power. It was true that many of the French vessels were of a small class, but among them they were told there were four line-of-battle ships and 19 frigates. In former days an opinion was entertained that it was necessary for the interests of England that she should possess a far larger navy than that of France; but in the present day, as far as armour-plated ships were concerned, all that we aimed at was equality. He did not think that condition of things safe; and he complained of the policy of the Admiralty in not during the present year laying down additional armour-plated ships, because, as two years were required to build a large armour-plated ship, it would now be impossible to add to the number of twenty-five till the year 1867. There could be no difficulty about a good model, because, according to his noble Friend, the *Bellerophon* was the perfection of what an armour-plated vessel should be. The right hon. Gentleman the Chancellor of the Exchequer being in easy circumstances, his noble Friend would do well to induce him to increase the Vote for contract-built ships to the amount taken last year, and thus obtain the means of laying down two or three vessels similar to the *Bellerophon* during the present year. But, although he disapproved of the policy of the Admiralty in respect of armour ships, he rejoiced to learn, from reading his noble Friend's speech, that some attention was about to be paid to our steam reserves. In the opinion of some persons, wooden ships were at the present time altogether useless; but that was a view which he did not share. If we had the great misfortune to be engaged in a war with France, did anybody suppose that all her sailing ships would not be employed to cripple our trade, or that we should keep ours in harbour while hers were scouring the ocean? An efficient steam reserve was therefore necessary, and from all the information he had been able to collect, nothing could be more unsatisfactory than the state of our steam reserve at this moment. His attention had been drawn to this subject by a paragraph which appeared last year in *The Times*, under the head of "Naval and Military Intelligence." The writer was a gentleman possessing accurate means of information, for he was, he believed, the correspondent of *The Times* at Portsmouth. He asserted, that of the whole of the "steam reserves" not more than seven or eight vessels could be pronounced ready to proceed to sea; that others would take months to get ready, and the remainder could never be made available under any circumstances. "In proof that no part of this statement was exaggerated," the writer added, "let one port be selected as an example—say Portsmouth." The substance of his statement was as follows:—That, exclusive of gunboats, the first division of the steam reserve at Portsmouth consisted of one line-of-battle ship and two screw corvettes; that the line-of-battle ship, the *Duncan*, could not be got ready for sea in three months; that one of the corvettes, the *Esk*, was ready for sea, but that the other was rotten; that in the second division there were four line-of-battle ships, three screw corvettes, and one paddle sloop; of these, the four liners would each take three months to make ready; that two of the corvettes were rotten, and the third of iron, so slight as to be unfit for war service, and that the paddle sloop might be placed in the useless category; that in the third division there were seven line-of-battle ships, eight first-class frigates, six sloops, and two troopships, all screws, and screws with a vengeance, for of these one of the line-of-battle ships had never been to sea, but would take six months to complete, and that the remainder would engage the whole of the resources of the yard six or eight months to make them ready for sea; that the hulls of the six sloops were all half rotten and their machinery in want of heavy repairs, and that the five paddle sloops were all useless; that the two troopships had both seen long foreign service, and required repairs; that in the fourth division the *Penelope* and the *Retribution*, paddle frigates, were both rotten from the keel to topsides. The writer added—

"Out of all the vessels so enumerated in the four divisions there is only one vessel—the *Esk*, of 17 guns, and 250 horse-power—that is ready for sea."

He then went on to say that the annual cost of the "preservation and repair" of these vessels, exclusive of wages to stokers and engineers, was £45,000, and that for that sum Portsmouth possessed only one vessel ready for sea, and it would require years to complete the remainder. That was the state of things last year. This statement naturally excited great alarm in his mind, and he had made it his business to make inquiries as to the state of the steam reserves at the other dockyards; and he found that the state of the steam reserves last autumn was much the same as at Portsmouth, at Devonport, and at the Nore. Of forty-three line-of-battle ships, exclusive of gunboats, composing the first, second, and third divisions of the steam reserve, only six were ready. Of twenty-six frigates in the three divisions, only two were ready. Of six corvettes in the three divisions, none were ready. Of twenty-six sloops, only three were ready; and of thirteen gun vessels only one was ready. The general result was, that of 115 ships of the above classes in the three divisions, all of which ought to have been in a seaworthy state, only twelve were ready for sea. That was a most unsatisfactory state for the steam reserves to be in, especially as he could state that means were taken when Lord Derby was in office to place them in good condition. He should be glad to hear that matters were not so bad as he had been led to suppose, and that the Admiralty would make every effort to place the steam reserve in a proper state of repair. The hon. Member for Halifax (Mr. Stansfeld), in explaining Vote 8, said that it was the intention of the Admiralty to bring up some of the arrears of the first division of the steam reserve. He trusted that the noble Lord the Secretary to the Admiralty would tell the Committee that it was the intention of the Admiralty to place the whole of the three divisions in a substantial state of repair, for if war broke out, and our steam reserves were not in an effective condition, the country would run great risk of disgrace and disaster.

Mr. LINDSAY said, he had observed that *The Times'* correspondents abroad were usually very accurate in their statements. Did the right hon. Gentleman give the stamp of his own authority to the statement that France at that moment possessed 43,000 tons of armour-plating?

Mr. CORRY said, that the statement he had quoted was that the French now had ready or in process of completion forty-three armour-plated ships of 24,000 horse power.

Mr. LINDSAY said, that this statement was still more startling. No hon.

Mr. Corry

Member ought to make such statements unless he was prepared to vouch for their accuracy. If the figures were correct, the navy of this country was in a most unsatisfactory position. Although he had long opposed an excessive naval expenditure, he was ready, if the statement just made was accurate, to support the Government in any Votes to increase the number of armour-plated ships. England ought to possess a navy, not merely equal to that of France, but equal to that of France and any other great European Power combined; and he should not be satisfied unless England maintained that position, for the protection of our commerce and the safety of our homes to a great extent depended upon the strength of our fleet. He trusted that the noble Lord the Secretary to the Admiralty would tell the Committee what number of armour-plated ships France really did possess. Perhaps the number quoted in the paragraph referred to was simply that of French ships ordered to be built, the construction of which might be spread over a great number of years. He believed that the Admiralty could now send to sea armour-plated ships equal to those of any two European Powers. As long as that was the case the House and the country would be satisfied. With regard to wooden ships it would be found that they would be worthless in action against armour-plated ships. But he did not therefore hold that the Admiralty ought to sell their wooden ships. We ought to keep the same proportion of wooden vessels with respect to other countries as we did of iron-plated ships. What he objected to was the repair of obsolete wooden ships to be laid up in ordinary. In his opinion it would be far better to employ the money in building vessels as fleet and as powerful as the *Alabama*, which might act as the police of the seas. He saw in the Votes a large sum for stores for the Government dockyards. It would be more satisfactory if these Votes were given more in detail, and stating how the stores were to be appropriated. Having visited the Chatham Dockyard, which was 100 acres in extent, and refreshed his memory by going to see the private yard of the Messrs. Laird Brothers, which covered a space of only twelve acres, he had no hesitation in saying that the Messrs. Laird turned out a larger amount of work—and of splendid work too—than was done in the Chatham Dockyard. Hon. Members knew now the money voted for wages for the Chatham

Dockyard and the expense of the permanent staff; but they had no idea of the amount of money sunk in that yard in the shape of plant, timber, and materials. That was a thing which they ought to know, and on the opposite side of the account they ought to have the amount of work turned out in the yard in the course of twelve months. If they had that they could get the sums expended in private yards and the amount of tonnage turned out, and in that way they would have the materials for useful comparison. In Messrs. Laird's yard for instance, every piece of timber was cut by machinery, and the saw-mills were situated in the most convenient place, quite close to the water. But in Chatham Dockyard the timber was even now to a very great extent sawed by hand, at an enormous extra cost, and a saw-mill was placed on the top of a hill—of all places in the world the most inconvenient. All the timber had to be drawn up by ingenious machinery and then let down to the water's edge again. The circumstance put him in mind of an officer in Somerset House, whom the Admiralty appointed to answer the questions that were put to his department. He was an efficient officer, but he was deaf and dumb. Much had been said about the excellence of the work turned out from Her Majesty's dockyards, but that was all matter of opinion. He had seen an iron ship building in the yard of Messrs. Laird; it was sister to another which was being built in Her Majesty's dockyards, and he could say that so far from being in any way inferior to the latter, in strength and in seasoned timber it was quite equal and in some respects superior. He regretted that the Committee should be called upon to Vote this year £246,000 less for building in private yards, because the meaning was that £246,000 more would be devoted to building in Her Majesty's yards. That involved a question of policy. He did not wish Her Majesty's Government to give up shipbuilding. But supposing the country were to be suddenly involved in an European war, how could dependence be placed upon private yards to supply the necessary vessels especially treated as they always were by the Admiralty? Though the private yards might be able to produce gunboats and ordinary vessels, they would not be able to build those large classes of armour-plated ships that would then be required, because for that purpose they would require to have a large sum of money invested in the necessary plant. But Messrs. Laird's dock would be as valuable to Her Majesty's Government in the event of war as any dockyard for which the Committee might be asked to vote a large sum of money. That firm had created an establishment which might be of great value to the country in time of need. It was a dangerous thing, then, to throw overboard the private yards. Foreign nations were obliged to come to the private yards of this country, but Her Majesty's Government were shutting the door against a class of men who might be of the utmost value to the nation. He begged, therefore, to enter his protest in the strongest possible manner against the proposed increase of the plant in Her Majesty's dockyards.

MR. CORRY said, his hon. Friend the Member for Sunderland (Mr. Lindsay) sought to make him responsible for the statistics with regard to the French navy which he had quoted, but he had taken them from a letter of *The Times'* correspondent, who stated that they had been recently published. He had often heard hon. Members say that every statement of that kind published by the French Government was most accurate.

COLONEL SYKES: Does he say they were published by the Government?

MR. CORRY: He says the statistics were recently published.

COLONEL SYKES: Aye, but not by the Government.

SIR FREDERIC SMITH said, he was very glad to find that his hon. Friend the Member for Sunderland had been employing his time in the recess last autumn so profitably. He could have wished that he had been with his hon. Friend on the occasion of his visit to Chatham, as he had no doubt he should have come to a different conclusion from his hon. Friend as to the amount and quality of the work turned out there. His hon. Friend had not said that the *Achilles* was not of admirable shape; he had been unable to find a flaw in her; but not content to let the case stand on its own merits, he had proceeded to compare this ship with another built in a private yard. And for once in his life, somewhat illogically, his hon. Friend had argued, that if the Government did not at the present time apply to the private yards, it would not be able to have recourse to them in times of emergency. Yet it was admitted that those private yards were building now men-of-war for all the other maritime Powers of Europe. No doubt Mr. Laird's was an excellent establishment, but was it fair on that account to say that there was no good work turned out of the Government dock-yards? He believed that the ships that were being constructed by Mr. Reed were giving fair employment to the private yards. It was not fair to say, therefore, that the Government was not giving fair play to the private yards. His hon. Friend had carried his criticism upon Chatham so far as to object to the position of the saw mill. That position was selected forty-five years ago. He was there when it was constructed, and he remembered that the mill was placed there by the elder Brunel, the inventor of the system of block machinery, and the then very able Surveyor of the Navy (Sir Robert Seppings) thought it not desirable to fix it close to the water's edge ; but the timber was floated up a channel to a point under the saws, then lifted by hydraulic pressure, and sent down an inclined plane to the water's edge when converted. The process was very simple, and was not justly liable to the criticism passed on it by his hon. Friend. The interruption of the naviga-tion of the Medway was thus left unob-structed, as the mast pond was in an in-ternal basin, instead of in the river. If his hon. Friend said that ships built in the Government yards were built on a defective construction, on a defective plan, he re-plied that that objection would be equally applicable to ships when built in private yards, as the designs in both cases were those of the chief constructor of the Navy. There was great variety of opinion as to what constituted the strength of ships; but his hon. Friend had not been able to assert that the *Achilles* was built upon defective lines. She was designed upon the most scientific principles, with the aid of the most practical shipbuilder in Her Majes-ty's service. Mr. Lang, in the Chatham dockyard, was a very remarkable man and a practical shipbuilder, and there was no doubt that if that gentleman had had any objections to make to the designs of the Controller, the latter would have listened to them. If there were any improvement in any vessel of the Messrs. Laird over the *Achilles*, it must be owing to their having had the advantage of first seeing the *Achilles*. Mr. Lang no doubt was origi-nally a wooden shipbuilder, but he had had the advantage of the science of Mr. Samu-da, one of the most experienced authorities on iron shipbuilding. These two gentle-

Sir Frederic Smith

men had been schoolfellows together, and when any difficulty occurred, Mr. Lang invariably had recourse to Mr. Samuda's assistance, and *vice versâ*. He believed that the Government were right in em-ploying in private yards a certain amount of men to supplement the labour in the public yards ; and as far as he could judge of the *Northumberland*, built in a private yard, he should say that she would be a most perfect ship.

Colonel SYKES said, the system which the hon. Member for Sunderland (Mr. Lindsay) wished to see carried out — namely, that the dockyard authorities should be accountable for all their receipts and outgoings and that there should be pe-riodical stock takings—was in contempla-tion by the junior Lord of the Admiralty, whose services the Government had just now had the misfortune to lose, and whose indefatigable inquiries during the last au-tumn had resulted in laying down a system which was explained in what was called the "labour chart." That hon. Member was possessed of an acute mind and unbounded zeal, and his services had been in the highest degree advantageous to the Go-vernment. It was to be hoped that he would be replaced by another officer of equal capability. As the Estimates were now framed, no one could properly judge whether the sums asked for were founded on a proper basis, or whether it was not all guess-work ; for the sums were asked for in a lump, without the slightest expla-nation of the quantities or of the cost of the materials. Nothing short of the plan projected by the hon. Member for Halifax (Mr. Stansfeld) would be satisfactory to the House or to the country. He had been very much astonished to hear the hon. Gentleman the Member for Tyrone (Mr. Corry) quote a paragraph from a newspaper in reference to the relative strength of the French and English navies. If the hon. Member had referred to the French Es-timates for 1865 or for 1864, he would have seen that the ships of the English navy were, both in number and power, be-yond all comparison superior to those of the French navy. There had never been a time when our navy, in regard either to ships or men, was so powerful as at present.

Mr. BENTINCK begged to express a hope that in future the Votes would be so arranged as not under one head to embrace such a multiplicity of questions, the effect of which was to lead to debate desultory and somewhat confused. He agreed with his hon. Friend the Member for Tyrone

(Mr. Corry) in his observations on the armour-plated ships, which to the number of twenty-five were promised to be in readiness next year. He did not imagine that his noble Friend (Lord Clarence Paget) was prepared to tell the Committee that because a great revolution had taken place in the construction of the navy, therefore wooden vessels were to be entirely dispensed with, nor did he think that he would be prepared to state that twenty-five armour-plated ships were as many as would be required for fulfilling all the duties of the navy of this country. It was obvious that either our navy must for the future be confined to iron sheathed vessels, or that we should have to draw very largely on the services of our wooden ships. Now, he wanted to know in what position the country stood; if it was understood that in future we were to be solely dependent on iron-plated ships, why, in that case, were not immediate orders given for the construction of a much larger number? And, on the other hand, if it was admitted that there was still occasion for the services of a very large number of wooden vessels, he wished to be informed why a more satisfactory account of the state of the Naval Reserve with regard to those ships had not been presented. It was said that iron-plated ships were not fit to fulfil all the duties required—and the Committee ought to know whether iron-plated ships were to be depended on exclusively, or whether wooden and iron-plated ships should be combined. He wanted his noble Friend to define the policy of the Government on that subject, and to state what the future navy of Great Britain was to consist of, so that the House might know with what they were dealing. With respect to the somewhat old question of the amount of reliance that ought to be placed upon the public and private yards for supplying the requirements of the navy, he must say that he differed from the views of the hon. Member for Sunderland (Mr. Lindsay). He believed that nothing could be more injurious to the interests of the British navy than in any way to restrict the operations of the public dockyards. It was utterly impossible that this country, with the demands which existed upon her naval power, should ever be reduced to a total dependence upon the resources of private yards, without being placed in a most defenceless state. The more work that was done in public dockyards the more was this country likely to be placed in a position to meet any possible emergency,

and the true principle was to execute all the work possible at those establishments, leaving the surplus to be performed by the private yards. What he deprecated was this annual discussion as to the comparative merits of the two systems, because he believed that a feeling of rivalry ought not to be encouraged and ought not to exist. As to the difference in the cost which his hon. Friend desired to see equalized, it must be borne in mind that in the private yards the employers of labour have a direct interest in obtaining the largest possible return from the labour employed—an element which they could never have in the public yards. For that reason alone, he did not think that any amount of ingenuity would ever enable Government establishments to work as cheaply as the private yards could; but that, he contended, was a fact which ought not to weigh with the Committee in comparison with the efficiency of the public service.

SIR MORTON PETO said, he could not think with the hon. Member for West Norfolk (Mr. Bentinck), that the hon. Member for Sunderland (Mr. Lindsay) was to be blamed for calling attention to the comparative merits of the two systems. Great service was done by the discussion as to the comparative merits of public and private dockyards, as it had the effect of keeping the Government up to the mark, and urging them on to improvements. He quite agreed that in the Government dockyards such a number of ships should be built as would render the country prepared for any emergency; but, at the same time, he wanted the accounts of the Admiralty to be so presented that hon. Members might know the cost of building every single vessel, with the amount of tonnage accurately defined, so that having the same data in the case of a vessel constructed in a private yard, a comparison might be instituted between the two. It would then be seen what was actually doing, whether the country was obtaining value for its money. He agreed with the hon. Member (Mr. Bentinck), that it was important that they should know the future policy of the Government with respect to iron and wooden vessels. Were they prepared to vote money for the repairs of an immense number of wooden vessels which, at the present moment, were practically useless, and which nobody imagined could be sent out against an enemy? With regard to those which were coming home, he trusted that his noble Friend the Secretary to the Admiralty would follow the practice which was adopted by the hon. Member for Sunderland (Mr. Lindsay) in his own case—namely, when he had a vessel that did not suit his purpose, to break her up and dispose of her, and substitute better in her place.

LORD CLARENCE PAGET said, he did not blame hon. Members for drawing comparison between public yards and private establishments. It was right that those things should be inquired into, and that, indeed, was the reason for the Admiralty for the last four years endeavouring to place their accounts on such a footing as would enable them to lay before Parliament the sums expended on each ship. They were now in a position to do so, and he was prepared to challenge the hon. Member for Sunderland (Mr. Lindsay) to move for a Return for any or all of the dockyards, of the number of ships built in 1862-3 and their tonnage, the expenditure on the one side, and on the other the progress made in their construction, showing in fact the value obtained for money. The hon. Gentleman would then be able to express an opinion to the Committee, but it was not fair that he should persist in making broad statements without proofs as to the superior workmanship and administration of the private yards as compared with the public establishments. No doubt the work in the latter was more costly ; but he believed that the repairs of the wooden vessels built in the public dockyards were not on so large a scale—not so expensive—as those of similar ships constructed by private traders. At all events, he was ready to repeat the offer made by the hon. Member for Halifax (Mr. Stansfeld)—who, unfortunately, was no longer his Colleague, and who was a great loss to the Admiralty—that all those matters should be carefully gone into with any mercantile man who might chose to undertake the business. Certainly, the Admiralty would be only too happy if they could improve their system by a comparison with that in vogue in private yards. The hon. Member for West Norfolk (Mr. Bentinck) had asked him a difficult question as to the future policy of the Government with regard to the construction of ships. He must protest against having to look into futurity in a matter of such magnitude. First of all, it must depend a good deal upon foreign countries, and especially upon France, because the great object of Her Majesty's Government was to maintain at all times the navy of this country in such a state of efficiency as to enable us to cope successfully

Sir Morton Peto

with foreign Powers. One could not advert to the subject without more or less dealing with foreign nations, and especially with France. He generally avoided as much as possible any statement of the actual numbers of the French navy, but he could not allow the alarming picture drawn by the right hon. Gentleman the Member for Tyrone (Mr. Corry) to pass without notice. He did not know the source from which the right hon. Gentleman obtained his information, but he believed that on the 8th of February the French had eight armour-cased frigates afloat, and eight building, making together sixteen. They had also of new floating batteries—a small class of vessels for the defence of their coast—four afloat and seven building ; also one turret-ship building ; making, with the foregoing, a total of twenty-eight ; besides which they had five small iron gunboats, of a kind that could be taken to pieces. That was all that Her Majesty's Government knew of the French navy. The hon. Member for West Norfolk (Mr. Bentinck) asked what their policy was. It would be to go on building armour-plated vessels which were undoubtedly the class that must take the place of line-of-battle ships, and to build them in such numbers as would enable this country always to be in a proper position as regarded foreign Powers. That, he believed, was their position at the present moment, and it was that belief which justified the Government in not asking this year for a very large Vote on account of contract-built ships. The Admiralty had a high opinion of the private shipbuilding firms of the country, and relied on them in a great measure for the construction of its armour-plated fleet. Although it should not be unnecessary to enter into any large contracts during the present year, yet those firms might rest assured that recourse would be had to them as the construction of that fleet proceeded. The vast majority of the armour-ships now in existence, taking into consideration the tonnage, had been built in private yards. The hon. Baronet the Member for Portsmouth (Sir James Elphinstone) asked for some description of the armour-plated gunboats about to be constructed by contract. Those vessels would be of over 700 tons, their engines of 160 horse-power, their length 160 feet, their speed was expected to be about 9½ knots, and they would carry an armament, as at present advised, of two 100-pounder guns, of 125 cwt., and two 24-pounder howitzers.

Although he had before alluded to the intention of the Admiralty to build six of those vessels, he might state that they now proposed to set about the construction of two, both of them being vessels on the twin-screw principle, and being likewise an experiment of a wooden bottom combined with an iron frame. It was manifest that if they could combine wood and iron in that way, they would overcome one of their greatest difficulties — namely, the defects of wooden construction in regard to the liability to rot. That liability to rot existed, not so much in the planking as in the frame. Our iron-armour ships, though so near home that they could be continually docked, soon got so foul as to lose their speed and become unmanageable. Therefore, the system of wooden planks with an iron frame was about to be tried. The hon. Member for Tyrone (Mr. Corry) drew his information from sources which were often very accurate —namely, the articles of newspaper correspondents at the ports; but, undoubtedly, those gentlemen sometimes used very highly coloured language in describing the defects in ships and the state of our fleet at those places. Perhaps his noble Friend would be good enough to look at the Return of the state of the steam reserve for March. [Mr. CORRY had spoken of it last June.] He would admit frankly that our reserves were not in a satisfactory state; and that was the reason why they asked for upwards of £100,000 increase on Vote 8, to bring them up to the condition in which they ought to stand. At the same time, he must protest against the statement that the reserves in the home ports were in a most disgraceful and inefficient state. The hon. Member for Gloucester (Mr. Berkeley) asked what had become of two ships —namely, the *Sappho* and the *Alligator*. They had been removed from the list in common with a good many others. A custom had prevailed of putting the name of a ship in the *Navy List* when it was contemplated to build her, and before she was in actual existence. That practice had been brought under the notice of the Admiralty by the Controller, and, accordingly, a number of ships had this year been removed from the list, which had no existence except on paper. With regard to the *Enterprise* and the *Circassia*, which had been referred to, those two vessels had exchanged names. With regard to the lengthening and altering of vessels, where wooden ships had been converted into iron-plated ships, the Admiralty had

been obliged to enlarge the frames and alter the floors, in order to give the additional floatation necessary for carrying armour-plates. With those explanations, he trusted the Committee would allow the Vote to pass. He would again request the hon. Member for Sunderland (Mr. Lindsay) to cease making these sweeping accusations against the management of the dockyards, but, instead thereof, to move for a Return of the cost of any ship built there during the past year; and then let the hon. Member for Birkenhead (Mr. Laird) persuade his talented son either to give a similar Return from their yard, or to allow the Admiralty to inspect their premises and institute a comparison between the cost of the two establishments. The Admiralty had no desire to shirk this question. The *Achilles* would soon be at sea, and the hon. Member for Sunderland (Mr. Lindsay) might then get at every shilling that had been expended upon her construction.

MR. LAIRD said, that having been challenged by the noble Lord the Secretary to the Admiralty, he thought it right to state that, although the building of ships in the Royal dockyards and by contract had been a good deal discussed in that House, he was not prepared to admit that the principle of building by contract had ever yet been fairly tested. The present system was a bad one. The designs were all made by the Controller of the Navy, assisted now by Mr. Reed, and until lately by Mr. Watts. The entire designing power for the navy of this country was, therefore, concentrated in one man. The plans were made by the Government, and the contractors were not allowed to exercise their own talent or their own ingenuity, but were bound down in every way to carry out the precise orders issued to them. He did not at all depreciate the talents of the Controller of the Navy or his assistants, but he did say it would be much better for the Government, if they determined to go on building ships by contract, to throw open the designs for the vessels to the whole talent of the country than to waste the public money on a school of naval architecture. He had never thought it desirable that the ships of our navy should be built altogether by private contract. He thought it would be madness to propose such a system. · It would be injudicious to altogether discontinue the present system, but the Government should import into it all the talent of the country. What did Government do in the engine department?

When they contracted for a pair of engines they did not send any particular plan with the order, but requested those persons who were allowed to tender to send in designs. When sent in, these were referred to the head engineer of the department, who, as he was not allowed to compete himself, was able to give his important judgment as to whether the engines were likely to answer the object for which they were designed. The question was decided not by mere reference to price, but on the merits of the designs and the capability of the party to carry out the work. And what had been the result of that system of competition? That all other countries came to us for their machinery. If the Government adopted the same course with reference to their ships, a much greater amount of talent would be brought to bear, and they would have vessels of a much more perfect character than heretofore. There was an advantage in doing a portion of their work out of the Government dockyards. In time of war, the Government could not do all their work in their dockyards. But by doing part of their work in private building yards in time of peace, there would always be a number of men who knew how the Government work should be done, and the amount of dockyard accommodation would be thus doubled or trebled, and the facilities for repairs necessary in case of war would be greatly increased. It would be much better to keep a staff of workmen employed during peace on the Mersey or the Clyde than to have to import men to Portsmouth and Plymouth in time of war. He had not intended to make these remarks; but having been called on by the noble Lord the Secretary to the Admiralty to say whether parties were allowed to visit the building yard at Birkenhead, he must be allowed to observe that he believed private yards were open to the inspection of any body, and if private individuals were allowed to inspect the Government accounts in their building yards much good would result.

Sir JAMES ELPHINSTONE said, he quite agreed with his hon. Friend the Member for Birkenhead (Mr. Laird), that it would be a great advantage if the Government could be assisted in their designs for the navy by the whole available talent of the country. The country had suffered by placing the construction of ships in the hands of individuals. Uncontrolled by any supervision, or by the operation of contemporary science, the ships of Sir W. Symonds had cost the country dear. He did

Mr. *Laird*

not doubt that Mr. Reed was a very clever and talented man, but he very much doubted the policy of letting him enter upon such large works perfectly uncontrolled. It was not fitting that such vast sums of money should be expended upon the knowledge and experience of a single individual, especially when that individual had not, up to the present moment, sent a single ship afloat. He had seen in *The Times* newspaper a list of the number and description of ships Mr. Reed had designed and had under construction without having had an opportunity of trying a single one of them. They were all in progress, and many of them exhibited features in their construction in a great degree foreign to all previously received ideas of shipbuilding. Those might be steps in the right direction, but they might also be steps in the wrong direction; and he maintained it was not proper thus to expend the money of the country on the sole responsibility of one individual. He should be one of the last to imitate American example in anything; in fact, he thought America one of the most unfortunate countries on the face of the earth; but we might do worse than borrow from America her plan formerly acted on, of submitting designs for shipbuilding to Congress, taking the opinion of the best shipbuilders in the country as to the merits of those designs, and very good ships had been built in that way. He did not wish the Government to act precisely in that manner, but he certainly did think, in the present transition state of the navy, that they should avail themselves of all the scientific assistance they could possibly command.

Mr. LINDSAY said, he had found no difficulty in ascertaining at Birkenhead the amount of money expended in wages, materials, rent, insurance, plant, &c., but he had sought in vain for similar information with regard to Chatham Dockyard. He was, therefore, driven to make general charges for want of specific information. The noble Lord the Secretary to the Admiralty himself had resorted to general charges. Five years ago, it would be recollected, he had spoken of a mysterious sum of £5,000,000. He had been five years in office, however, without giving those data which would enable hon. Members to ascertain the relative cost of those ships constructed in private yards and those in Her Majesty's dockyards. With respect to the article of coal, the Admiralty was also to blame. In the present Estimates there was a charge of £275,000 for coal.

The coalowners of the North had called the attention of the Admiralty over and over again to the unnecessary expenditure under this head. Nothing but Welsh coal was used for ships of war, under the impression that it caused no smoke, while North of England coal caused a great deal. The Welsh coal was delivered in large lumps, which ground the small into dust, which thereby became utterly worthless and could not be used. By adopting a mixture of one-half Welsh coal with one-half North of England coal, the dust of Welsh coal, which hitherto had been worthless, could be made as available as larger coal, while by that mixture the quantity of smoke emitted would be as small as that from an equal quantity of Welsh coal. For two years those facts had been laid before the Admiralty without result, and persons who complained of the present system were taunted with making general charges without stating details. Some months ago the Government had instituted a trial between those two kinds of coal, and the result proved the correctness of what he had, years ago, said on the subject. But now that the Government officers had certified to those facts, and tenders had been issued, the Admiralty, instead of asking for tenders for half Welsh and half North country coal—which mixture had been proved to be the best—asked for tenders to supply only one-third North of England coal. Another point he would urge on the noble Lord was the different qualities of the various kinds of coal on the Admiralty list. There were some thirty different sorts of North of England coal, and perhaps twenty different kinds of Welsh coal on the Admiralty list; yet the contractors were allowed to ship any one of the kinds specified in the Admiralty list, though these kinds differed in value, some being as low as 7s. a ton, while others could not be got for 10s. A contractor would, of course, supply the cheapest and the least valuable coal that was included in the Admiralty list. He hoped the noble Lord the Secretary to the Admiralty would go further into that question, and allow the different kinds of coals to be classified and tested as to their relative qualities, and that in future only the best kind of Welsh and of North of England coal would be placed on the Admiralty list. A few years ago they were told that only two firms could build engines for the Government, though they discovered afterwards that twenty or thirty firms could build

them. The result had been a considerable reduction in the cost of engines, and he hoped the number would be still further increased. If the Returns he had asked for were faithfully made, he would undertake to prove to the House that, quality considered, they had been paying too much for ships built in Her Majesty's dockyards, and that, therefore, it was neither wise nor just to the taxpayers that they should go on increasing the plant in Her Majesty's dockyards, and thus create great establishments for the building of ships which could be built as efficiently and more economically in the private yards of the country.

MR. BENTINCK said, that the noble Lord the Secretary for the Admiralty, had not exactly dealt with the question raised by the hon. Member for Tyrone (Mr. Corry) and afterwards alluded to by himself. That question related to the number of iron-plated ships about to be commissioned, either in private or in Her Majesty's dock-yards. In asking the noble Lord what the future policy of the Admiralty was to be, he wished to place no restrictions on the noble Lord. He only desired to know the views which the Admiralty entertained on so important a question as the future construction and state of the navy of this country. On a former occasion the noble Lord said that it was not intended to continue to build wooden ships, but to devote larger sums to the building of iron-plated vessels. But nothing confirmatory of that statement was to be found in the present Estimates. If the noble Lord thought that wooden ships would be useless against iron-plated ones—and the noble Lord had admitted that much—he wished to know what his ideas were as to our navy for the future. With the exception of one vessel, not a shilling was asked for in the present Estimates for the building of any additional iron-plated ships. Was our navy to be limited to the twenty-five iron-plated ships at present in existence, or were more to be built?

MR. LAIRD said, that as there had been a discussion as to the respective number of ships in the French and English navies he would quote what he believed to be an accurate statement of the strength of the French navy. He found that our neighbours possessed four iron-cased ships of 3,750 tons and 900 horse-power, two of 4,200 tons and 1,000 horse-power, and ten of 3,780 tons and 1,000 horse-power, making together sixteen vessels, built, or which would be ready in the course of the present year. In addition, the French had five floating batteries of about 10 ft. draught of water, four of from 8 ft. to 10 ft. draught, and seven of 6 ft. 6 in. draught, all in an advanced stage of construction. Then, they had five small batteries, built in sections, but not armour-plated, thus making a total of 37 iron-cased ships or batteries built or building in France. In this country we had 17 iron-plated ships built or in course of construction — eight upon Mr. Reed's plan and seven floating batteries, or a total of 32 against the French 37. Now, there was certain information which the Committee ought to have. It appeared that for wages, materials, and dockyard expenses we should spend this year about £3,000,000. They ought to know how much was for iron-plated ships, how much for wooden vessels for the police of the sea, and how much for repairs. Without such information the accounts before them were useless. They had at the present time a large number of ships which would cost as much to repair as to build. He wished to learn how many ships of various classes they were to have for the £3,000,000, and how large a sum was to be expended on the repairs.

MR. SOMERSET BEAUMONT said, he begged to express his satisfaction that the coal question had been brought before the Committee, and hoped the noble Lord would tell them what he proposed to do in reference to the future supply of coal. It was only by incessant, he might almost say persecution of the Admiralty, that the Government had granted the prayer of the coalowners of the North of England. The coalowners had not obtained their requests as matters of favour, for the reports of the engineers of the Admiralty were, in all respects, favourable to them.

SIR MORTON PETO said, it would be desirable if the noble Lord would state the intentions of the Admiralty with regard to the repairs of iron-coated vessels. When the hon. Member for Tyrone (Mr. Corry) stated the proportion between our iron-clads and those of France to be as thirty-seven French and thirty-one English, he ought to have mentioned the difference in their tonnage. The largest of the French vessels was 4,000 tons—most of them were of 2,000 tons—while in our own navy many of the ships were from 5,000 to 7,000 tons.

Mr. Laird

LORD CLARENCE PAGET said, he believed that it was understood in the House that the Government could not do away with their wooden ships, as they required a vast number of such vessels to perform the duties of what might be termed the police at sea, and at the present time they had not arrived at the position of being able to do without frigates and corvettes. They were obliged, to a great extent, to put their forces upon the same footing as those of other countries. With regard to the question of coal, of which the hon. Gentleman the Member for Sunderland (Mr. Lindsay) had made such a grievance, and in connection with which he showed so much antipathy towards the Government—

MR. LINDSAY begged to disclaim the idea of having either a grievance or an antipathy. He was merely performing his duty to his constituents by seeing that they obtained a fair return for the money they were called upon to expend.

LORD CLARENCE PAGET said, that the Admiralty exhibited no partiality in the choice of their coal. The naval officers certainly preferred the Welsh to the North country material; and to test the value of each the Admiralty had instituted a series of careful experiments, the result of which was already before the House in a report which he had lately laid on the table. He could only inform the hon. Member for Sunderland (Mr. Lindsay), and also the North country coal owners, that the Government had no desire to employ the Welsh coal exclusively, but simply to obtain the most satisfactory mixture they could for the use of the fleet, and orders had been given to supply the Fleet with both descriptions, which were to be combined in various proportions, and careful reports to be made. The hon. Gentleman the Member for Birkenhead (Mr. Laird) wished to know in what manner the Admiralty proposed to devote so large a sum of money to shipbuilding during the forthcoming year. Their proposal was to build of iron armour ships, 6-8ths; of wood armour large ships, 15½-8ths; of wood armour corvettes, 8¾-8ths; of frigates, 5¾-8ths; of despatch vessels, 7½-8ths; of gunboats, 12½-8ths; of a fast vessel of new design, which he might term a species of *Alabama*, 6-8ths; and one tank vessel, for Simon's Bay. There was also some work to be done upon smaller vessels. He did not pledge himself for the Government's following out that programme in its entirety, because, as the House well knew, they were influenced in a great measure by their repairs, which, if heavy, would largely disturb their building operations. They were in arrears as to repairs, and it was proposed by the end of the year to have the reserve in a satisfactory state. He acknowledged that the figures he had given to the House did not represent the ultimate number of armour vessels, because, although the amount of building was considerable, he had no hesitation in saying that if greater exertions were made elsewhere, it would be his duty to ask the House for additional supplies. The Government believed that the progress that was now being made, was so far satisfactory, that this country- might be said to occupy the position to which she was entitled as compared with Foreign Powers.

MR. LAIRD said, that it might be found necessary to take men engaged in shipbuilding from their duties and to place them upon repairs, but that fact would not prevent the noble Lord from replying to his question. He would again ask how many ships were to be built for the money that was about to be voted?

LORD CLARENCE PAGET said, he would give the hon. Member the names of the ships it was proposed to construct.

SIR JAMES ELPHINSTONE, though he did not personally anticipate such an event, considered that six-eighths of a vessel like the *Alabama* would be of very little service in case of the war with America, which the occupants of the Ministerial bench appeared to regard as so probable. If hostilities really were imminent, they ought to construct twenty ships like the *Alabama*, or at the present moment to be in possession of twenty-five such vessels.

LORD CLARENCE PAGET, in reply to Mr. Laird, said, that the wooden ships, not armour-plated, to be completed during the year 1864-5 were the *Endymion*, screw-frigate at Deptford; a tank vessel for Simon's Bay; the *Helicon*, despatch, paddle steamer; the *Minstrel*, gunboat; the *Cherub*, gunboat; and a fast vessel of the *Alabama* class, of new design.

Vote *agreed to.*

(2.) £662,212, Steam Machinery.

MR. CORRY observed, that the item "for engines ordered to be built," £17,000, seemed very small, and did not seem to indicate that any great effort was to be made.

LORD CLARENCE PAGET said, that the Admiralty were making very good progress with their engines.

SIR JAMES ELPHINSTONE asked what were the iron gunboats for which there was an item of £120,000?

LORD CLARENCE PAGET said, that the Admiralty were going to build two of those boats in the first instance, and not to commence any more until it was seen how those two answered.

Vote *agreed to.*

(3.) £64,350, Medicines and Medical Stores.

SIR MORTON PETO asked what steps the Admiralty intended to take with respect to mitigating the prevalence of a disease which was at present so great an evil in the navy?

MR. ALDERMAN SALOMONS observed, that the announcement of the intention of the Government to do away with the dockyard at Deptford had given rise to a good deal of alarm among the men employed there and in the vicinity. He hoped, if such was the intention, that the claims of those men would be taken into consideration.

LORD CLARENCE PAGET said, that the subject referred to by his hon. Friend the Member for Finsbury (Sir Morton Peto) had engaged the serious attention of the Government, and he hoped that at a later period of the Session a proposal would be brought before the House with the view of checking that frightful disease which was so great an evil in the navy. With reference to the matter brought forward by his hon. Friend the Member for Greenwich (Mr. Alderman Salomons), he was afraid it would be a considerable period before Deptford dockyard could be done away with; but when the time arrived the interests of the men employed in that yard would be duly considered.

Vote *agreed to.*

(4.) £102,320, Naval Miscellaneous Services.

COLONEL SYKES observed, that there was an item of £2,000 for subsistence and travelling expenses of dockyard officers and others superintending ships building by contract. He would beg to ask how many of those persons were there, how often in the year did they make their superintendence, and what was their allowance?

LORD CLARENCE PAGET said, there were Inspectors in the employ of the Government at all the large armour makers and shipbuilders, to see that the contracts were properly carried out.

SIR JAMES ELPHINSTONE begged to urge the expediency of establishing sailors' homes, and of combining therewith recruiting offices. There was a great want of the former as temporary barracks when the men came on shore; and with regard to the latter, he must say that recruiting was conducted on the primitive style of a hundred years ago, and that the public-houses were the recruiting offices of the navy. He would suggest that some money might be advantageously expended in improving the system?

MR. LINDSAY remarked, that different plans of fitting prevailed in the different public dockyards, and when the officers from those yards were sent out to inspect work under contract in private establishments, each carried with him the system that prevailed in the particular dockyard from which he had been sent. Much inconvenience was thereby caused to contractors when the Inspectors were changed during the progress of a contract. Could not an arrangement be made for leaving the one Inspector in charge throughout the execution of a contract, or for introducing a uniform system of fitting?

SIR HARRY VERNEY asked, Whether it was the intention of the Admiralty to appoint a Chaplain General to the navy in accordance with the recommendations of the Select Committee which had recently reported in favour of the appointment of such an official?

LORD CLARENCE PAGET, in reply to the hon. and gallant Member for Chatham (Sir James Elphinstone), said there was an increase over last year of £200 for contributions in aid of sailors' homes and charitable institutions in the neighbourhood of the dockyards. If the gallant Member proposed to have sailors' homes all over the coast, a new principle would be involved which could not be adopted without asking the House to consent to it. The scheme would entail considerable expenditure, since if carried out in England it must also be in Scotland and Ireland. In reply to the hon. Baronet the Member for Buckingham (Sir Harry Verney), he might say that the Duke of Somerset had taken into consideration the evidence laid before the Select Committee, and had found that, although it would be advantageous in some respects that a Chaplain General should be appointed, yet the arrangement had

Lord Clarence Paget

corresponding disadvantages, as the appointment might interfere with the discipline in ships if the chaplain had any other superior than the captain to look to.

SIR JAMES ELPHINSTONE said, he wished to explain that his question referred only to sailors' homes in dockyards.

Vote *agreed to.*

(5.) £697,790, Half Pay, Reserved Half Pay, and Retirement Officers of Navy and Royal Marines.

MR. LINDSAY wished to know when the noble Lord the Secretary to the Admiralty intended to bring forward his plan for the increase of pay in the navy.

LORD CLARENCE PAGET said, the matter was not yet fully matured, but due notice would be given.

Vote *agreed to.*

(6.) £490,201, Military Pensions and Allowances :—*agreed to.*

(7.) £193,983, Civil Pensions and Allowances.

LORD ROBERT MONTAGU asked, Why the full superannuation allowance of £1,000 a year granted to Sir Richard Bromley, the retired accountant general of the navy, was not included in this Vote? That pension had been allowed under a Treasury Minute of 1863, and the amount now asked was only £481 12s.

LORD CLARENCE PAGET said, it was true the Treasury had awarded Sir Richard Bromley a pension of £1,000, but the appointment which he now held at Greenwich, to the advantage of the public service, entitled him to receive £600 a year, and the amount on the Vote was to raise his pay to that which he would have received as accountant general. When he resigned his present appointment, he would be entitled to draw the entire pension fixed by the Treasury.

Vote *agreed to.*

(8.) £314,230, Freight of Ships, &c.

COLONEL SYKES begged to call attention to the increase in several items over the Estimates for last year.

LORD CLARENCE PAGET said, this was owing to the war in New Zealand and the surrender of the Ionian Islands. That step had rendered necessary the transport home of the stores hitherto collected there. Other portions of the increase were caused by the large force which had to be kept up in Canada and the local disbursements in China.

MR. LINDSAY said, a Committee had sat on the transport service, which recommended the consolidation of the several departments, and that the responsibility should be fixed. He regretted that those recommendations had not been carried out.

LORD CLARENCE PAGET said, that the Admiralty, as he had on more than one occasion before stated, were perfectly ready to carry out the transport service in connection with the Colonial Office, but that owing to the very weighty reasons which had been urged by the Duke of Newcastle against any alteration in the present system the change had not been made. Negotiations were, he might add, now going on with a view to bringing the Indian transport service between this country and Alexandria under the control of the Admiralty.

SIR JAMES ELPHINSTONE remarked, that while the *Himalaya* and *Orontes* were very good ships for the transport service, that was not the case with other vessels so employed. He wished, therefore, to know whether the Government intended to increase the number of vessels of the *Himalaya* class, and whether they proposed to lay on the table any Returns with respect to the transport of men in private ships and in those belonging to the Admiralty, specifying the expense in each instance? He asked the question, because he fancied it would be found that such vessels as the *Himalaya* would convey men at a much smaller cost than any vessel which the Government might hire.

LORD CLARENCE PAGET said, he was glad to hear the hon. Baronet bear testimony to the economical working of the Admiralty transports. The *Tamar* and *Orontes*, which had been built by the hon. Member for Birkenhead (Mr. Laird) for the service, were very fine vessels. He could not say that it was the intention of the Admiralty to do anything further in that direction at present, but it was under consideration to build two large Government transports for the Indian Government.

MR. LINDSAY observed, that however the matter might now stand, the last Returns which had been published on the subject clearly showed that the conveyance of troops in the Government transports cost just double that which was expended on private ships.

SIR JAMES ELPHINSTONE begged to repeat his question as to whether there would be any objection to give the Return to which he had alluded, stating the relative cost of the conveyance of men in the vessels employed.

LORD CLARENCE PAGET said, if the hon. Baronet would visit him at the Admiralty, he would endeavour to procure for him such information as he required.

Vote *agreed to*.

House *resumed*.

Resolutions to be reported *To-morrow*.

Committee to sit again on *Wednesday*.

House adjourned at a quarter after Ten o'clock.

~~~~~~~~

HOUSE OF LORDS,

Tuesday April 5, 1864.

MINUTES.]—PUBLIC BILLS—*Committee*—Court of Chancery (Despatch of Business) [H.L.]* (No. 18); Conveyancers, &c. (Ireland)* (No. 17).

Report—Malt for Animals* (No. 16); Court of Chancery (Despatch of Business)* [H.L.] (No. 18); Conveyancers, &c. (Ireland)* (No. 17).

Third Reading—Bills of Exchange and Promissory Notes (Ireland)* (No. 26).

METROPOLITAN RAILWAYS.

PETITION.

THE EARL OF DERBY *presented* a Petition from the Vestry of St. George's, Southwark, praying for the compulsory establishment of cheap trains upon Metropolitan Railways. The noble Earl said that, in so doing, he desired to say a few words in reference to the Metropolitan Railway system, as it was now being introduced and sought to be still further introduced in the crowded suburbs of London. The Petition emanated from the Vestry of a parish which contained about 53,000 persons, mostly of the poor and labouring classes. The parish was already densely crowded, and that overcrowding was continually increased by the destruction of dwellings by the railways which passed through the district, while there could be no corresponding construction of new houses, the district being already densely covered. One railway alone had destroyed 100 houses, recently occupied by 300 families, the rateable value of these houses being £1,179. The petitioners, therefore, prayed for some measure of relief at the hands of their Lordships. Some time since a noble Friend of his, not now present (the Earl of Shaftesbury), made a proposition that all Metropolitan Railway Companies should be compelled to erect additional buildings as a compensation for those taken down. That was found to be impracticable, and he was afraid that the Resolution which the House came to, that all railways should provide such buildings, had proved to be no protection at all. The petitioners prayed (and it was not unreasonable or unworthy of serious consideration) that those Railway Companies which had obtained permission to construct metropolitan *termini* should be compelled to run at least one train in the morning and one in the evening at a very low rate of charge, at hours most suitable to the working classes, in order to accommodate those persons who might wish to be taken out into a more healthy neighbourhood to reside, and be brought back again to their work. The petitioners suggested that the fares should be as low as 1*d.* per trip, whatever the distance might be. He (the Earl of Derby) believed that there was one Railway Company that had already intimated their intention to start such trains at a rate not higher than 1*s.* per week for any distance not exceeding ten miles ; that company was the London, Chatham, and Dover. He thought the suggestion was one worthy of their Lordships' consideration ; and also whether it would not be right to insert a clause in each of the Bills before Parliament requiring that such trains in and out of London should be run morning and evening at such hours as might be suitable to the labouring classes, for limited distances—such as ten miles. If that were done, it would give an immense relief to the large population of this and other parishes, and enable the people to return to their homes without much loss of time. He was not prepared to move anything on the subject, but he hoped his noble Friend the President of the Council and Her Majesty's Government would consider the matter, and would confer with his noble Friend the Chairman of Committees, and see whether it would not be possible, and, if so, desirable, that some such clause should be introduced into all the Metropolitan Railway Bills passing through the House in the course of this Session.

THE EARL OF MALMESBURY said, that a system as nearly as possible like that recommended by his noble Friend was carried out with great success in Paris. The railways there were obliged to carry

The Earl of Derby

the working men, many of whom lived in the suburbs, into town and back at a certain low rate.

EARL GRANVILLE said, that the railways, no doubt, might be made much more available for the purpose recommended by the noble Earl than they were at present. He should communicate with the President of the Board of Trade, and he hoped in the course of the Session some steps would be taken to give effect to the views of his noble Friend.

EARL RUSSELL said, he had been informed by the Bishop of London, who had fully considered the subject, that the great difficulty was with regard to who was to purchase the land for building the houses; for the Railway Companies were at present prevented by law from purchasing land for such a purpose.

THE EARL OF DERBY : I do not mean that these companies should be bound to provide the land, but that they should be compelled to provide facilities for carrying the working classes to and from the outskirts of the metropolis at low fares.

Petition to lie on the table.

UNITED STATES.
FOREIGN ENLISTMENT ACT—THE
"KEARSARGE."—QUESTION.

THE EARL OF DONOUGHMORE said, that at the last Cork assizes certain persons pleaded guilty to an indictment charging them with having violated the Foreign Enlistment Act, and they were released upon their own recognizances. The offence was having enlisted subjects of Her Majesty on board the United States ship of war *Kearsarge.* The captain of that vessel stated that the men came on board without his knowledge, and he was not aware of their being on board until he had got to sea, and that when he went into Brest he put them on shore ; but as they were without the means of subsistence he took them on board again and conveyed them back to Cork. When this subject was last alluded to, the noble Earl opposite (Earl Russell) made what certainly appeared to be a very extraordinary statement, for he said that he could not see what else the captain could have done. That was a very remarkable statement, because it appeared from the evidence that had been taken, that the men were actually put into the uniform of the United States' Navy by order of the officers of the ship. Now, what he (the Earl of Donoughmore) wished to know was, Whether the noble Lord had required any explanation from the American Minister with regard to this circumstance ?

EARL RUSSELL said, that at an early period of the discussion of this matter he had complained to the United States' Minister of the conduct of the officers on board the *Kearsarge.* After what had passed in that House, and after what occurred in the Court of Justice in Ireland, he had again called the attention of the United States' Minister to the subject, and had asked him to refer to the newspapers and to the opinion given by Mr. Justice Keogh. The United States' Minister informed him that in the month of November last he had received instructions from his Government, that if the Consul had been at all instrumental in violating the Foreign Enlistment Act he should be at once dismissed, and that, with regard to the officer in command of the ship, if the Minister found that he was to blame he was to be reported to the Government, in order that the proper notice might be taken. Mr. Adams did not act upon those instructions, because he did not consider that there was any blame due either to the Consul or the officer in command of the ship in enlisting these persons into the service of the United States. The Correspondence was not yet concluded, but when further explanations had been given the despatches would be laid on the table.

THE EARL OF DERBY said, that unless Mr. Adams denied the statement that these men were examined by the surgeon and attested, that their names were entered on the books of the ship, and that they were clothed in the uniform of the United States' Navy, it was impossible that the officers of the ship should not be cognizant of the men being on board.

THE MARQUESS OF CLANRICARDE said, there could be no difficulty in ascertaining the truth, if it was desired that the truth should be elicited. He believed the *Kearsarge* was now repairing at one of our ports. If so, why should not the officers at once come to London, and make such a statement of the real facts as the American Minister would be prepared to vouch for ? It was rather too much to extend to them the hospitality of this country in the face of such statements as were made on the trial at Cork. Either these gentlemen had stated the truth or not. If they had told the truth, let them come forward and verify the facts. No one who knew Mr. Adams would dispute whatever he was prepared

to vouch for from his own personal knowledge.

NORTH AMERICA—BRITISH CONSULS IN THE CONFEDERATE STATES.

THE MARQUESS OF CLANRICARDE, in rising, pursuant to notice, to move for

" A Copy of any Correspondence that may have taken place between Her Majesty's Government and the Government of the Confederate States of North America relating to the Removal of British Consuls from those States, or the Cessation of the Functions of the Consuls or any of them therein ; and of the Correspondence with the Consuls thereupon : Also, for Copies of all Correspondence with any Agents of the Confederate Government in this Country up to this Date, in continuance of that already before the House,"

said, that if he had rightly understood the noble Earl the Secretary for Foreign Affairs on a previous occasion, British subjects in the Confederate States had been compelled to enter the army and to fight the battles of those States against their will ; and that the British Consuls having been driven from the country, there was no one in those States to whom they could appeal for redress. That was a very serious charge to bring against the Confederate Government; and he thought that his noble Friend who had touched not only lightly but very curtly on the point, would now admit that he had spoken somewhat in haste, if not in anger, and that the circumstances of the case did not bear the aspect which he had given to them. The means open to their Lordships of informing themselves as to the true facts were very imperfect. Some papers had been presented to the House last Session with regard to one of the Consuls lately residing in the Confederate States, and some correspondence, alleged to have taken place with the authorities of the Confederate States, had been published in a London newspaper, which correspondence he hoped his noble Friend would not object to lay upon the table. Of the five principal Consulships existing at the outbreak of the war, in New Orleans, Charleston, Richmond, Mobile, and Savannah, that at New Orleans might be put out of the question, the town having since fallen into the hands of the Federals. As soon as the Confederate Government was organized, it at once acknowledged the Consuls resident in those ports upon the authority of the *exequaturs* issued to them by the former Government; it did not stand on the formality of requiring letters of credence, but at once admitted them to full access, and treated those Consuls as long and as far as possible with

Q

friendship and cordiality. The existence of the blockade of course rendered communication with this country and with Lord Lyons, under whom the Consuls were originally appointed, extremely difficult, but that intercourse had been carried on by means of private persons travelling between Southern States and New York. Our Consul at Charleston accordingly intrusted a bag of letters to the care of a private individual, who, however, took with him other letters addressed to persons in the Federal States, which by the law of the country he might do without illegality, provided he took no payment for conveying them. That gentleman was arrested by the agents, not of the Confederate, but of the Federal Government, and the certificate which he produced, that he was a bearer of despatches for the English Government, not being regarded as any protection whatever, he was thrown into gaol. The bag of despatches, however, was sent forward, and its contents, among other papers, included letters forwarding bills of exchange to pay dividends in England. The arrest was regarded as so outrageous a proceeding, that ultimately the United States apologised for it; but they withdrew the *exequatur* of the Consul, who up to that time had conducted the negotiations with which he was charged in a manner entirely satisfactory to the British Government and to the Confederate States, with whom he had communicated in the most friendly way. The next case to which he wished to draw their Lordships' attention was that of Mr. Magee, our Consul at Mobile. This gentleman also had been received with the greatest cordiality and treated with the utmost respect by the Confederate authorities, and he too had been the means of preserving British subjects from injustice at the hands of the subordinate agents of the Confederate States. Mr. Magee was appointed in 1861, and in 1862 he was called on by the Bank of Mobile to afford facilities for the transshipment of specie in payment of dividends due by the State of Alabama to creditors in London. Of late years the doctrine had been advanced that State payments to private creditors ought not to be liable to the accidents of war. During the Russian War we had faithfully performed our undertakings, even to the Government of Russia; and, in like manner, the State of Alabama, being anxious to pay British creditors the money due to them, applied to the Consul to know whether he could assist in forwarding the

amount to London. The Consul wrote to his colleague at New Orleans, understanding that a British ship-of-war was there, and without any secrecy or intrigue suggested that that vessel might, with the consent of the Federal commander on the station, call at Mobile, and take on board the money for England. The Consul at New Orleans was of opinion that she might; but as the *Rinaldo* did not come into harbour, another ship, the *Vesuvius*, commanded by Lieutenant Croke, was communicated with, and to that officer the transaction also seemed perfectly legitimate. He communicated with the Federal commander, and told him that he wanted to go into Mobile to transact business with the Consul, who had money for him to take back to England. There could be no doubt about the matter, because the letter of the Federal commander, Captain Hitchcock, had been printed since the transaction was taken up by his own Government, and to the honour of commanding officers in the United States' navy the instances were very rare in which any statements, inconsistent with fact, could be attributed to them. The Federal commander avows that he was informed that money was about to be sent, and Mr. Magee went on board Her Majesty's ship with the money, and the commander of the vessel received it. After that, however, a telegram arrived from Lord Lyons forbidding the Consul to transport the money; but it had already been shipped; and thereupon his noble Friend had dismissed this gentleman from his post. With the exact ground of that dismissal he was not acquainted. In one of the despatches it was stated to be that he had violated the blockade; while in a letter from the noble Earl to Mr. Mason the reason assigned was that Her Majesty's Government considered that the shipment of this money was an act which gave aid to one of the belligerents against the other. If the Consul had given aid to either, it was to the Federals by sending money out of the Confederate States; but the parties really benefited by the act of the Consul were the creditors resident in England. At all events, offence was taken at Washington, and in truth it was upon the demand of the United States' Government that Mr. Magee was dismissed. Another gentleman was sent to Mobile by Lord Lyons, and he deeply regretted what he had now to state to their Lordships. Mr. Cridland, who had occasionally acted for the Consul at Richmond, seemed to have received a Commission and instructions from Lord Lyons, and an article appeared in the *Richmond Whig,* stating that he had got such a Commission and likewise an *exequatur* from Washington, and that he was accredited to Mr. Lincoln and not to the Confederate Government. Thereupon, Mr. Cridland went to Mr. Benjamin, the Confederate Secretary of State for Foreign Affairs, denied that statement, and assured him that he was proceeding to Mobile to look after British interests unofficially, and without any commission or *exequatur* whatever ; and he procured the insertion in the *Richmond Whig* of a similar contradiction of its first statement. Mr. Benjamin was, therefore, as he himself had stated in a despatch—

"Quite surprised at receiving from the Secretary of the Navy the official communication of a telegram received by him from Admiral Buchanan, informing him that Mr. Cridland had been introduced to him by the French Consul as the acting Consul at Mobile, and had shown an official document signed by Lord Lyons appointing him English Consul at Mobile."

He thought that after this their Lordships would not think that Mr. Benjamin or President Davis acted unbecomingly in at once forbidding Mr. Cridland to exercise any of the functions of a Consul within the Confederate States, and intimating that it would not be displeasing to them if he chose another residence. Since that time, no attempt had been made to appoint another consul at Mobile. Mr. Moore, also, who was our Consul at Richmond, had been dismissed by President Davis, not capriciously to get rid of his protection of British subjects, but because he had used disrespectful language towards the Confederate Government, and had especially misconducted himself with respect to two individuals whom he claimed as British subjects, but who, upon investigation by a proper tribunal, were proved not to be such. At all events, there was alleged against him a special grievance, and he was not driven out because he afforded protection to British subjects, but in consequence of misconduct, or what was considered to be misconduct on his part. In point of fact, then, when the dismissal of Consuls complained of by his noble Friend took place, there were in these States only two regular Consuls, one at Savannah and the other at Charleston. Why were they dismissed? The war began in 1861. In 1862 a very stringent law was passed to enable the States to raise Militia. The British residents remonstrated against serv-

ing in it ; and in the autumn of that year the noble Earl the Secretary of State for Foreign Affairs wrote a despatch, which was communicated to the Confederate Government, in which he laid down sound principles about the injustice of *ex post facto* laws and the necessity of exempting from their operation foreigners who were residing in the country, unless they had had notice of the intention to enact them. At that time, however, the necessity did not arise for the strict enforcement of the law, and 'nothing more seemed to have taken place. But in 1863 matters took such a turn, that it appeared probable that the statute would be put into operation, and the alarm of the British residents revived. From the statement of Mr. Benjamin, in his letter to Mr. Fullarton, it would appear that the consular agents of the British Government had been instructed to assume the power of determining for themselves whether British soldiers who had enlisted under the Confederates were bound to serve, or whether they might not with propriety throw down their arms in the face of the enemy. It was hardly credible that any Englishman had, and quite impossible that a British Government could have made such a suggestion. But he (the Marquess of Clanricarde) could not think that British subjects, after enjoying all the privileges of citizens in a foreign country, were justified in claiming the excuse of the Foreign Enlistment Act and the Queen's Proclamation ; at any rate, such an attempt at interference as that attempted by the two Consuls was intolerable in any functionary, and naturally led him to make the inquiry, why all the confusion to which he had referred was allowed to prevail ? Why was there not some better understanding on the subject between our Government and the *de facto* Government of the Confederate States? He would not go to the length of saying that there should at this moment be an immediate recognition of those States, although it might be a question for graver discussion whether if, a year and a half ago, the European Governments had taken counsel together, and recognized the Confederate States, looking steadily in the face all the consequences of that recognition, torrents of blood and hundreds of thousands of lives might not have been saved, and not only that ruin and misery which had already arisen out of the war, but that which was yet to come might not have been avoided. He would admit that the present time did not appear favourable for that recognition; but he hoped that before long a proper occasion might arise for such recognition, because he was anxious to see peace, which that recognition would lead to, restored. He might further observe that it appeared, even from the correspondence between Earl Russell and Mr. Mason, that it would have been perfectly easy to have had our Consuls in the Confederate States ; we had consular agents in the Spanish American State before the year 1820, although it was not until the year 1826 that their independence was acknowledged. But, be that as it might, Mr. Benjamin, in commenting on the conduct of some of the Consuls to whom he had alluded, instructed Mr. Mason to call the attention of the British Government to the expediency of instituting a renewed examination of the subject as connected with the relations between the two Governments, with the object of placing those relations on a footing more in accordance with accomplished facts. In reply to the representations of the Confederate Government on the subject, his noble Friend the Secretary for Foreign Affairs, in a despatch dated the 19th of August, said he was—

"Willing to acknowledge that the so-styled Confederate States are not bound to recognize an authority derived from Lord Lyons, Her Majesty's Minister at Washington," adding, "but it is very desirable that persons authorized by Her Majesty should have the means of representing at Richmond and elsewhere in the Confederate States British subjects who may be in the course of the war grievously wronged by the acts of subordinate officers. This has been done in other similar cases of States not recognized by Her Majesty, and it would be in conformity with the amity professed by the so-styled Confederate States towards Her Majesty and the British nation if arrangements were made for correspondence between agents appointed by Her Majesty's Government to reside in the Confederate States and the authorities of such States."

Now, that was exactly what Mr. Benjamin had previously suggested through Mr. Mason, and, that being so, why was it, he should like to know, that we were left without proper persons to afford protection to British subjects in that quarter ? Under all the circumstances of the case, and assuming the statements to which he had alluded to be correct, his noble Friend was not, in his opinion, justified in making the other evening a curt declaration to the effect that our fellow-subjects in the Confederate States were driven into the ranks of the army and deprived of protection because Consuls were not permitted

The Marquess of Clanricarde

by the Government of those States to reside there. It appeared now, from a report in the newspapers, that his noble Friend, in consequence of certain complaints, had directed our Consul at the Havannah to go to Richmond and remonstrate with the Confederate Government. He was not aware whether this report were true, but it would be very advisable for the noble Earl to state what the fact was. A document had recently been published in the Federal newspapers and forwarded to this country by Lord Lyons, which purported to be the Annual Report of the Confederate Secretary of the Navy. In a London newspaper it had been stated that all the Confederates in Europe asserted this document to be a forgery; and, judging from internal evidence, he could not believe in its genuineness. In the first place, it was addressed to the Speaker of the House of Representatives of the Confederate States. That was a form of Departmental Report which no one had ever seen adopted before in any country. In the same paper there was a report from the War Secretary, which was addressed to the President, Mr. Jefferson Davis, which was the invariable form in which these documents were addressed. Then, again, in this supposed Report there was an account of the capture of a United States' gunboat off Galveston by a party of naval officers. That affair had been reported more than a year ago, and was well known as one of the most dashing affairs of the war. It was performed not by naval officers, but by two engineer officers and a party of infantry who were serving under General Magruder. Reading a little further down the Report, however, it became evident what was its object. In a later paragraph the Secretary of the Navy reported that he had ordered the steam rams at Liverpool and the other vessel about which so much contention had lately arisen—a very likely fact certainly for the Confederate Secretary of the Navy to wish to have published abroad, over America and Europe. It was clear that the object of the Report was to prejudice the mind of the British Secretary of State and British Courts of Justice. So long as his noble Friend encouraged the Federal Government as he had encouraged them, treating them as if they were the superior Power, and must win in this tremendous conflict, so long would there be very little chance of an accommodation between the two parties. The noble Earl ought to have observed a fair neutrality, but over and over again he had perceived in his noble Friend's action evident signs of Federal influence. If the *Kearsarge* had belonged to any other Government, her officers would not have been allowed to come into our ports convicted, as they had been, of breaking our laws. He hoped that the noble Earl would lay before the House the last Reports from our Consul at Boston. It was notorious throughout America that the moment the Irish recruits, about whom there had been a conversation the other night, landed at Boston, the utmost efforts were made to compel them to enter into the American service. The noble Earl had submitted to too many of these things, and he certainly ought not to have spoken of the Confederate Government in the tone he used the other night. The noble Marquess concluded by moving an Address for the Papers.

EARL RUSSELL : It is rather difficult to make out the exact object which my noble Friend has in view ; but with regard to the various circumstances to which he has alluded, I will detain your Lordships a short time by a few remarks. In the first place, my noble Friend said it was not right to say that the Confederate Government had sent away our Consuls, nor that many British subjects had been compelled to serve in the Confederate armies. I can only speak of the facts reported to me, and to the Government of which I am a member, and as I thought quite notorious. There have been complaints over and over again from different parts of the Confederate States, that British subjects were obliged to serve in their militia and armies. We have had to consult the Law Officers of the Crown, who have said that it was not fair to make British subjects, not being American citizens, serve in the armies of either belligerent without giving them time to leave the country if they thought fit. I have acted on that opinion, and it seems to me not only law, but fair and equitable. My noble Friend may think they ought to be compelled to serve; on that point, as well as on others, he and I differ. Then, as to the question of the various Consuls. My noble Friend enters into the question of the withdrawal of Mr. Bunch's *exequatur*, which was taken away, I think, very unfairly by the United States' Government, on the ground that he had communicated with the enemy. Then he enters into the case of Mr. Magee, who sent specie in a British ship of war, and he blames Lord Lyons for what he did in that matter. I believe Lord Lyons has taken the utmost pains in his most responsible position, to behave fairly and impartially between both parties. Permission was obtained by Lord Lyons from the American Government, that British ships of war should be allowed from time to time to go to blockaded ports ; but Lord Lyons thought it an abuse of the privilege that specie should be sent from a Confederate port in a British ship of war, inasmuch as such specie might afford means of carrying on war against a State friendly to Great Britain. He accordingly stated that opinion ; and if he had not done so the American Government might have withdrawn the privilege; and I think there is nothing in the law of nations that would have deprived them of the power to do so. I thought that Lord Lyons was right ; and I sent out an order that the Consul who had sent the specie should not be continued in his functions. But my noble Friend gave a rather detailed account of the conduct of Mr. Cridland. Now, while that gentleman was acting as Consul at Richmond, I believe he enjoyed the confidence and respect of everyone for the manner in which he performed his duties. He was desired to go to Mobile, not as Consul, but to act as Consul—to defend and protect British property and interests. My noble Friend complains of what, I agree with him, was a very unjustifiable act on the part of one of our Consuls—his advice to British subjects that they were not to resist their enlistment in the Confederate army, but to desert their colours in the moment of action. I think that very improper advice on the part of a Consul ; and I do not think there was any instruction given to our consular agents which could justify any of them in giving that advice. I do not find either in the opinion of the Law Officers of the Crown, or in any directions that I gave myself, anything that would justify that course ; and if the Secretary of the Confederate States had written to this country to complain of that conduct, I should have thought it right to reprimand and even to dismiss the Consul who had acted in so improper a manner. Instead of that, the President of the so-called Confederate Government sent away our Consuls, though these are the persons to whom British subjects would naturally have recourse, in order to obtain redress for grievances. The only remedy they would have when the Consuls were removed was that suggested by Mr. Benjamin—namely, that when pressed as soldiers they should apply to the tribunals of the country. Now a man may easily write to his Consul to claim redress, but that a man marching about should go to a court of law—that was a suggestion that I thought entirely futile. I therefore thought that was a very harsh and unfriendly proceeding on the part of the Confederate Government. At the same time it ought to be remembered, likewise, that the Confederate Government had good reason to complain of our Consul, and our Consul saying that he had been so instructed, the Confederate Government might at first have believed him. Therefore, I did not enter into any complaint or angry remonstrance; but I asked Mr. Mason whether, if consular agents, or persons under any other name, were sent to the Confederate States, intercourse might not be carried on and negotiations opened, by which we might be able to obtain redress where redress ought to be given, or have reasons stated for its refusal. My noble Friend does not complain of that. There has no doubt been a delay in carrying that arrangement into effect. It was thought necessary to send a letter to Richmond to know whether such persons would be received; and that letter the Federal Government would not allow to be sent. But I think it is quite right of the British Government to endeavour to open communications with the so-called Confederate States, without recognising them; yet, as being States of considerable extent, in which civil war is carried on, and in which there is a considerable number of British subjects, I say there can be nothing wrong in endeavouring to enter into communication with those States. My noble Friend has addressed your Lordships on various other subjects. I desired Mr. Crauford, when he arrived at Richmond, to call the attention of the Government to the intercepted correspondence—a correspondence which I believed at the time to be genuine, and which showed that a party in the country had been employed by the Confederate Government to procure means of carrying on war against a State in amity with us. My noble Friend is aware that Her Majesty declared at the beginning of this war her determination to preserve a strict neutrality, and prohibited her subjects from taking part on one side or the other. I am sorry to say the injunction of Her Majesty has not been obeyed, and that English subjects have enlisted in the Federal service, and that others have supplied the means of war to the Confederates. I

Earl Russell

have thought it right on every occasion, when it appeared to me that there was ground of complaint against the United States, to remonstrate with the Federal Government, and, generally speaking, our remonstrances have received a respectful attention. With regard to the document to which my noble Friend alluded, it has been the subject of a great deal of inquiry. It is said to have been published in a New York paper as genuine; but Mr. Seward states that, having made further inquiry, he finds it to have been altogether a forgery. It was supposed to have been issued by the Secretary of the Confederate Navy, but it was, in fact, an invention of some gentlemen in New York. Certainly, I should not think of making any complaint on that subject to the so-called Confederate Government. There was a question with regard to which my noble Friend made inquiries before the holydays—I mean the case of the *Saxon*. That is before the Courts; and the ship and the cargo have been released. It is alleged that a British subject was murdered; and the American Government have ordered that a court-martial shall try the officer accused of the murder. With regard to the Motion of my noble Friend, I suppose he will not depart from the usual form and object to the introduction of the words " or Extracts " after the word " Copies," and also that he will not object to the insertion of the words " so-called " before " Government of the Confederate States." Otherwise it might seem as if the House recognised the Confederate States, although Her Majesty had not done so.

THE MARQUESS OF CLANRICARDE said, he had no objection to the Amendments proposed by his noble Friend.

Address for—

Copies or Extracts of any Correspondence that may have taken place between Her Majesty's Government and the Government of the so styled Confederate States of North America relating to the Removal of British Consuls from those States, or the Cessation of the Functions of the Consuls or any of them therein; and of the Correspondence with the Consuls thereupon: Also, for Copies or Extracts of all Correspondence with any Agents of the so styled Confederate Government in this Country up to this Date, in continuance of that already before the House.

—*agreed to*

House adjourned at a quarter before Seven o'clock, till To-morrow, a quarter before Two o'clock.

HOUSE OF COMMONS,

Tuesday, April 5, 1864.

MINUTES.]—SELECT COMMITTEE—on Turnpike Trusts *nominated (see* March 8).
Report—Kitchen and Refreshment Rooms (House of Commons)° (No. 175).
Resolutions [April 4] *reported.*
PUBLIC BILL— *Considered as amended* — Union Relief Aid Acts Continuance° [Bill 50].

LISBURN ELECTION.

House informed, That the Committee met . this day, pursuant to adjournment, and as no leave had been granted or excuse allowed in the case of the absence of Mr. Stirling, a Member of the Committee, the Committee had further adjourned until To-morrow, at Eleven o'clock.

Order read, for resuming *Adjourned Debate* on Question [4th April],

" That Mr. Stirling be excused for not attending the said Committee upon Tuesday, the 22nd day of March last, and be discharged from further attendance on the said Committee."—(*Mr. Adair.*)

Question again proposed.

Debate *resumed.*

THE ATTORNEY GENERAL : A question of considerable importance as regards the practice of the House and to Members of Election Committees was incidentally raised upon this Motion by my hon. Friend the Member for Northamptonshire (Mr. Hunt) yesterday, and it is a question, I think, of very much too great importance for the House to dispose of in a hasty or informal manner. It appears that a petition was presented against the validity of the return for Lisburn, a Committee was appointed to try the merits of that Petition, and in a Report which we have from that Committee they simply mention the absence, on the day of the last meeting before the recess, of one of the Members, on the ground of illness, and they make the usual application to the House to accept the excuse of that hon. Member, and to relieve him from further attendance upon the Committee. The House yesterday examined evidence at the Bar, and satisfied itself as to the validity of the excuse, but the hon. Member for Northamptonshire took notice that the Committee had adjourned to a day, which, according to the view he took of the Act of Parliament under which they were acting, was a day to which it was not in their power to adjourn. That raised the important question

whether, such an error having been committed, the further and subsequent proceedings of the Committee would be valid. The House is aware of the importance of proceeding with the utmost circumspection and regularity in a matter of this kind ; and it becomes necessary, therefore, to consider anxiously the proper course to be taken. The conclusion to which hon. Members will come will, I think, probably be, that they have not before them at present in any such formal or regular shape as will entitle them, under this Act of Parliament, to take cognizance of a matter of so much importance, the facts upon which the question which has been suggested may arise. It has appeared to myself—and I hope it will appear to the House—that the proper course of proceeding will be to accept the excuse of the hon. Member for Perthshire, of the sufficiency of which there can be no doubt— and to abstain from going on with the other words of the Motion, which are in truth superfluous, because they only express that which is, under the terms of the Act of Parliament itself, the consequence in law of the acceptance of the excuse—to accept the excuse now, and so remove the mere formal impediment, and enable us to proceed in any way which may be competent to us by law. The effect of adopting that course will be, as I anticipate, that as soon as the. Committee, being free from the impediment of the absence without excuse of a Member, assembles and proposes in the ordinary course to go on with the business before them, it will be suggested to them, probably by those who represent one or both of the parties before them, that a question has arisen as to the legal effect of their adjournment upon their competency to proceed any further. In that case, unless I am greatly mistaken, it will probably appear necessary to the hon. Gentlemen who compose the Committee to consider what is the proper course for them to take, and to give serious consideration to the objection, and if it should appear of sufficient importance to demand the consideration of the House, I cannot doubt that they will think it right, without further proceeding in the business before them, to make such a Report to the House as would enable the House to take formal cognizance of the matter. When that is done, it will be for the House to consider what would be the proper course of proceeding upon the Report. Perhaps it would be improper for me to anticipate the decision of the House, but my strong impression is that, under circumstances in any degree similar, it has been the usual course of the House to appoint a Committee to search for precedents, and to inquire into and report upon the matter, so that the House may ultimately arrive at a conclusion on the subject, with the greatest deliberation and the greatest possible assistance. I therefore humbly suggest that so much of the Motion should be adopted as proposes to accept the excuse of the hon. Member for Perthshire, and that at present no further action should be taken in the matter.

SIR HUGH CAIRNS: I certainly concur, generally, in the advisability of the course which my hon. and learned Friend the Attorney General has proposed, and in the observations which he has made. It is quite true that the objection which has been raised is of a highly technical character, but it must be remembered that the whole of the Act of Parliament is technical in its character. Good reasons can no doubt be assigned for the stringent rules laid down for the meeting and proceedings of an Election Committee; but any one who consults the Act of Parliament will find that the rules are of a most imperative and precise character. Another reason why we should act with great caution and deliberation is, that it is obvious that this is a matter in which the House, unless it acts with great care, may bring itself into collision with the other House of Parliament and with the Courts of Law. Certain proceedings may be taken or suggested on the Report of an Election Committee constituted by Act of Parliament, provided the other House of Parliament agree; but the other House may say that the proceedings of the Committee are irregular, and may decline to assent to them. Again, actions for penalties in the Courts of Law may raise embarrassing questions as to whether the return of the Committee has been legal or not. As the Attorney General has pointed out, we possess only an incidental knowledge of the difficulty that exists. We have no Report from the Committee stating that objections have been raised to their proceedings, or that they feel a difficulty on the subject. All that they have done is to report the illness of one of their members, and to ask that the usual order of the House in such a case should be made. We are told that the Committee have met to-day, and have taken

The Attorney General

upon themselves the responsibility of adjourning till to-morrow. Of course, the House will not at present express an opinion whether that course was open to the Committee, but I think we can have little doubt, after what has been said in this House, that to-morrow, if the Committee should propose to transact business, an objection will be taken by one or other of the parties to their competence to proceed; and if the Committee appeal to the House, the House will then have before them all the facts necessary to raise the question. I should question, however, whether this is a question in which precedents could be searched for with any advantage. That may be the proper course where a question of privilege or practice is raised, but this does not seem to me to be a case where the privilege or the practice of the House will be involved; it is simply a question of the interpretation of an Act of Parliament. At the same time, it may appear desirable to the House that such a question should be considered by a Committee, who can perhaps approach it in a more judicial spirit than the House itself, and that consequently a Committee should be appointed. However, I quite concur with the Attorney General in thinking that it will be advisable for the House to do nothing more to-night than excuse, if it thinks fit, the non-attendance upon the 22nd of last month of the hon. Gentleman, whose illness we all deplore, without going on to say that he is to be excused from further attendance upon the Committee, which, by recognizing the existence of the Committee, would in reality be to decide a question in dispute. I assume that the Attorney General proposes to omit the words, "And be discharged from further attendance on the said Committee."

MR. HENLEY: I have no wish, after what has fallen from the two hon. and learned Gentlemen, than to make the observation that I do not feel quite clear what the position of the House will be after to-morrow. The formal attention of the House was called yesterday by the hon. Member for Northamptonshire to the question that, in his opinion, the Committee had adjourned to a day to which it was not competent for them to adjourn. I understand now that the House has received a Report from the Committee, which, by its adjournment from day to day, is to meet to-morrow, and when the Committee is to take action on some supposed proposal, which may be made by one or both parties as to its power to proceed further. The point that I do not feel clear upon is, whether this House, having, by acting on the recommendation of the Attorney General, sanctioned, as it were, the meeting of the Committee to-morrow, would or would not be making itself a party to the mistake already committed by the Committee, if mistake there has been. That is a point upon which neither the Attorney General nor the hon. and learned Member for Belfast have touched at all, and yet it appears to me a very important one. It strikes me that the Committee might be in a difficulty to-morrow if, after having by their action to-day to a certain extent precluded themselves from forming any opinion, they should choose to go on to-morrow to try the case. If they were to do that, what would be our position? I do not give any opinion, but doubtless if there be a difficulty there are many hon. and learned Gentlemen present who can aid in helping us out of it.

THE SOLICITOR GENERAL said, the question at issue was a pure question of law, and he apprehended that the course taken by the House to-night would not affect it in the slightest degree.

MR. GATHORNE HARDY remarked, that the reason why the latter part of the Motion was to be left out was to prevent the House committing itself upon the question of law. All the House was asked to do was to excuse the non-attendance of the hon. Member for Perthshire on the 22nd of March, and the Committee would meet the next day on its own responsibility. The meeting might turn out to be a meeting of four gentlemen having no authority, or, if the House so decided, it might be a meeting of a properly constituted Committee.

MR. LYGON said, he could not understand how the question had come before the House. If the Committee was in existence it could, of course, Report; but if, as some thought, it was defunct, it could make no Report at all. Supposing the House were, as suggested, to refer the matter back to the Committee, and supposing the Committee were to decide, at its meeting on the next day, that it was competent to it to go on, it might proceed without reporting to the House at all. On the other hand, if the Committee was really defunct, the House should not allow its power to slip away from it into the hands of four Gentlemen, who were no more entitled to be called the Lisburn Election Committee than any other four Members of the House.

MR. W. E. FORSTER said, that as an unfortunate Member of the Committee, he would express a hope that the House would not create any difficulty which might increase their embarrassment. The Attorney General and the hon. and learned Member for Belfast seemed to proceed upon the supposition, that if the Committee met on the following morning it would certainly happen that objection would be made by one or both of the parties to their proceeding. It was, however, by no means certain that that contingency would arise, and he trusted that the House would continue the discussion so as to aid the Committee with its order or advice. He trusted that the Committee would be left with some idea of what they were to do in the event of a different result- from that which appeared to be contemplated by the two hon. and learned Gentlemen.

MR. MACDONOGH said, he thought the course proposed by the hon. and learned Attorney General was full of peril. In the first place it was a strange proceeding to empower the Committee to correct its own mistake, if a mistake had been committed; and, in the next place, neither of the contingencies which had been suggested might arise. There might be no objection taken by either party, and it did not follow that the Committee would make a Report to the House. The whole thing might thus be left at sea. He had no hesitation in asserting as a lawyer, that the proceedings of the Committee were illegal. The Committee had no power to adjourn for so long a period, and the inquiry was at an end. Nothing could be more plain and distinct than the mandatory language of the statute. The object of requiring adjournments from day to day was obvious. If a Committee could adjourn for a week or a fortnight, that very adjournment by enabling the party petitioned against to retain his seat and vote, might turn the fate of a Ministry. There was nothing technical in the question; his hon. and learned Friend was well skilled in the proceedings of Courts of Equity, but he did not appear so often in a Court of Law, or he would have known that it was not technical to say that every inferior tribunal must follow the conditions attached to its existence by statute; and there was not a country gentleman present who did not know the importance and necessity of proper adjournments from sessions to sessions. The House had before it all the facts of the case. On the 22nd of March, Parliament stood adjourned, on that day the Lisburn Committee was sitting, on that day a report was made to it of the illness of one of its members, and on that day it adjourned until the 5th of April. It did so, no doubt, through inadvertence; he believed the adjournment was pressed by the counsel for the petitioner. Those facts having been reported to the House, it was in a condition to dispose of them. He dissented from the proposition that a Committee should be appointed to search for precedents. It was not a question of precedent or privilege; it was a question on the construction of a statute; it was a matter of principle, and, he repeated, the adjournment was contrary to the Act—against both its letter and its spirit. The House could not do away with the prohibitions of the statute, it had no dispensing power, nor could it by searching for precedents which did not exist, throw light upon the subject. He told the House that the Committee was incompetent after that day to make a report; there was an end of it. The statute, which was a reiteration of the 9 *Geo*. IV., provided that the sittings of these Committees should be from day to day, and in emphatic and unambiguous language it enacted that they never should adjourn except for twenty-four hours. But there was a proviso, that in case they should have occasion to report to the House —as, for example, on the misbehaviour of a witness, or the illness of a member—then the public business of the House, if the House were sitting, should be stayed, and the subject-matter of the report be inquired into; but that if the House were not sitting, the Committee should adjourn till the very day on which Parliament met, in order to approach that House at the very earliest opportunity. That being so, would any lawyer get up and say that an adjournment of even one day beyond that was legal? He would refer the House to what he considered an authority upon the point. A case had arisen in which a man had been convicted at quarter sessions upon a day to which they had been improperly adjourned. That man was sentenced to transportation. The law officers of the Crown having, however, seen the mistake, caused the prisoner to be again tried under the proper legal forms. The accused set up the plea

Mr. Macdonogh.

autre fois convict. After a legal discussion the Court held that that plea could not be presented as a bar to the second trial, and on the ground that there had not been any legal trial or conviction of the prisoner. In another section of the statute of the 9 *Geo*. IV. there was this provision:—Suppose the case of a prorogation of Parliament, and that a Committee was then sitting, what was the Committee then to do? There was no occasion to report to the House, or to complain of the misbehaviour of a witness. It was, therefore, not under the necessity of approaching Parliament in the first instance, and accordingly that section provided that, on the prorogation, there should be no dissolution of the Committee, but that it should adjourn not to the day of the meeting but to the next day after the meeting of Parliament. That provision was incorporated in the 11 & 12 *Vict*., the statute they were now dealing with. The language of the statute was perfectly plain upon this subject, and it was impossible for them to put any other interpretation upon it, than that which was its obvious meaning. No person had ventured to assert the legality of any future meetings of the Committee. It could not make any Report to the House, for it had lost its power of framing a Report. An inferior tribunal like that must act strictly up to the conditions of its existence, otherwise that existence was at an end. Why, therefore, should that House give any recognition to the existence of a body that, by its own act, had ceased to exist? He had no idea that such a course would be proposed, and had heard with surprise the Attorney General and his hon. and learned Friend the Member for Belfast describe the objection taken against the Committee as a mere technical one, which might be removed by that House. He totally dissented from that view of the case. He considered that the proceedings of the Committee had become illegal, and being so, that that body had ceased to exist. He contended that they could not resuscitate that Committee, and the House ought not to take it upon itself to receive from it that day any single species of report. The Committee should be left in this position—that being dissolved, and the opinion of the House to that effect being delivered, it might meet the legal gentlemen at the trysting-place to-morrow, or it need not, for there was an end of it. He, therefore, submitted respectfully to the House that it should hold its hands in this matter. The House could not possibly dispense with a statute. An Election Committee was bound to observe the law, and if it improperly refused to proceed, it might be liable, like other inferior tribunals, to a mandamus from the Court of Queen's Bench. Of course, such a mandamus would not lie against the House itself.

SIR GEORGE GREY reminded the House that the course which was recommended by his hon. and learned Friend the Attorney General, and concurred in by the hon. and learned Member for Belfast, was one which did not recognize in any degree the present legal existence of the Committee. The only Motion submitted was, that the hon. Member for Perthshire (Mr. Stirling) should be excused for his non-attendance on the Committee on a day when it undoubtedly had a legal existence. But his hon. and learned Friend proposed, under the peculiar circumstances of the case, that the Committee should be allowed to act for itself; and that when it met on the following day, if an objection should be made to its competence, or if it had doubts as to its power to proceed, it might then come with a Report to the House and ask for its guidance and direction. He concurred with the hon. and learned Gentleman who had last spoken in the opinion, that the House ought to be most cautious in their conduct as regarded a Committee which was not sitting under the authority of that House, but under that of an Act of Parliament. He agreed with the hon. and learned Gentleman in thinking that it was a case in which the House had really no power to interfere. The wisdom of the course suggested seemed to him to be more prudent since he had heard the speeches of hon. Gentlemen on the other side. It might turn out that they would ultimately have to express an opinion on the matter, although he hoped they would not; but it would be inexpedient to commit themselves by any hasty resolution. If the present suggestion of the Government were adopted, it would not render valid the proceedings of the Committee on the following day. If its proceedings might be legally questioned in a court of law, no Resolution of the House could prevent it.

MR. PAULL said, he was a Member of this unfortunate Committee, and he thought it right to offer some observations in reply to the suggestions made by the Attorney General and the hon. and learned Member for Belfast. It appeared to him that the House ought to know what had taken place before the Committee that day, and what was likely to transpire the next morning. He wished to make a similar appeal to that made by the hon. Member for Bradford (Mr. W. E. Forster.) He confessed he felt somewhat humbled in what had taken place; and, as far as he was concerned, he would most laboriously endeavour to redeem the error into which the Committee had fallen. But he did not consider that they would be in a better position to solve their difficulty on the following than they were on that day. It was suggested that the Committee should meet when it was considered probable that an objection would be taken, and arguments raised on the competency of the tribunal to proceed further; that in such case the Committee should take issue upon the question raised and act upon their own responsibility. But he did not think that any such objection would be raised the next day. What had occurred that day before the Committee was this :—No person representing the sitting member appeared in the Committee-room. The only persons present were those who appeared on behalf of the petitioner. After a short pause the counsel for the petitioner, not having seen the Votes, but presuming that the House had taken on the previous day the step they were asked to take that day—namely, to accept the excuse offered for the non-attendance of one of the Members of the Committee, rose and said he claimed the right to be heard. Now, that was what would be, probably, done again on the following day. Nobody would object, and he (Mr. Paull), therefore, asked the House whether they really meant to cast the responsibility upon the Committee of deciding the question. He would respectfully suggest that that was not a responsibility which the House ought to cast upon the Committee. Without meaning to praise himself, he must say that he had never sat with Gentlemen who had bestowed greater pains or attention on the discharge of their duty than had been done by his Colleagues in that Committee, and he believed they would continue to evince the same spirit ; but in the difficulty in which they were placed, they ought to receive some guidance from the House. On the following morning the Committee would again meet, and, no doubt, there would be nobody there to represent the sitting Member. The counsel for the sitting Member would not, of course, be anxious to render any assistance to the Committee, but would feel quite satisfied to leave the Committee in the difficult position in which it was placed. Now, the House in effect told the Committee that they might remain where they were and get out of their difficulty the best way they could. The same proceeding as that which had just taken place before the Committee might go on from day to day, without any power on the part of the Members to relieve themselves. With such a prospect before them, he trusted that the House would take such a step as would guide the Committee towards some definite conclusion.

MR. AYRTON said, he entirely concurred with the Attorney General that they ought to pass a Resolution expressing no opinion, but that the hon. Gentleman who had been absent from the Committee should be excused for non-attendance. But, unfortunately, the Attorney General had coupled that sound advice with a suggestion that something might be done in the future, and he ventured to express his humble dissent from that suggestion. What was the object of the Act? To divest the House of Commons as a body of all right to intervene in the proceedings of an Election Committee. They had set up Election Committees and remitted to them the whole question, without reserving the smallest control over their proceedings. Such being the law, the usage and rights of Parliament entirely fell to the ground. The whole matter was a question of the construction of a statute, and there was no part of that statute which vested in the House any right to give any direction whatever to an Election Committee. The House had no such power. The Committee must go on at their peril, and finish their work as they best could, if they thought they could go on; but one thing they had no right to do—to bring back the question to the House and ask them to decide, or give them any direction how they should decide in the matter.

MR. MONTAGUE SMITH said, that having looked into the Act of Parliament, he considered the Committee defunct, and the House could neither give nor take away jurisdiction from such a body. The jurisdiction of an Election Committee stood entirely on the Act of Parliament, which prescribed a most rigid code of procedure.

Mr. Paull

The time an Election Committee should sit and adjourn was imperative. This Committee, according to the Report made to the House, had adjourned from the 22nd of March till to-day, being a day beyond that on which the House sat. The House, in his opinion, ought not to have received that Report. By receiving it they sanctioned the existence of the Committee, which, according to the best consideration he had been able to give to the Act, appeared to him to have no longer any existence. What would be gained by requiring the Committee to sit again and make another Report? His feeling of pity was moved by the lamentation of the only two Members of the Committee who had spoken. They complained that they had been put to considerable difficulty. His humble advice to them was this, to follow the example of the sitting Member, and not to appear at all. The best course, in his opinion, would be to adjourn the debate.

MR. LOCKE said, it appeared to him that the hon. and learned Member for Truro (Mr. Montague Smith) had given an opinion upon this question which he had no right to give. The hon. and learned Gentleman said the Committee was defunct, and he called upon the House to declare it to be defunct. [Mr. MONTAGUE SMITH: No, no!] That House should not constitute itself a jury to sit upon the body of the Committee. It was evident that the House had no power whatever to act in the matter. He considered that the proposition made by the Attorney General was the right one to act upon under the circumstances. Let the House wait until the Committee had put them in possession of some tangible facts, and then they would do nothing. He was opposed to the adjournment of the debate.

LORD STANLEY: Sir, it seems to me that the House is getting itself into a little difficulty about this matter. It appears quite clear from the terms of the Act, that the Committee has in effect put an end to its own existence, by adjourning to an illegal day, and consequently any act subsequently performed by it will have no validity in law. On the other hand, it appears equally clear that the powers of the Committee, being derived from the statute and not from any Resolution of Parliament, no Resolution which we might pass can in the slightest degree influence the future proceedings of the Committee or the state of the law. We cannot, therefore, directly interfere in any way in the matter. At the same time, it does not seem quite fair to call upon the Members of the Committee to meet day by day under such circumstances, to decide at their own risk whether they constituted a legal tribunal or not, and to take upon themselves the responsibility that may follow such a decision. Now if the House were simply to decline to proceed at all in the matter, and to adjourn the discussion, not for a day, but for a period of six months, the sole result would be that the Committee would not be able to sit any longer, because by the statute it was laid down that " such Select Committee shall never sit until all the Members to whom leave has not been granted, nor excuse allowed, are met." The Committee would be disqualified for meeting, and the matter in that way would be brought to the only legal conclusion—namely, that the whole proceeding would fall to the ground. I do not urge this proposition of an adjournment on the ground of its being a solution altogether satisfactory; but we are in a difficulty every way, and really that is the only means which I can see of getting out of the difficulty. I, therefore, move that this debate be adjourned to this day six months.

Motion made, and Question proposed, " That the Debate be now adjourned."

MR. WALPOLE: I subscribe to every word stated by the noble Lord the Member for King's Lynn with so much clearness and force in the commencement of his speech, but, in the latter part, he pointed out the great difficulty in which the House is placed, and I am rather doubtful whether it will not be increased by the course proposed by my noble Friend. By adopting it the House will come to no decision upon the subject; the Committee may consider that they are bound to meet, and the friends of the petitioner and also those of the sitting Member may consider they are perfectly entitled to have the petition heard out. The proceedings may go on from day to day, expenses be incurred, and nothing be decided, and the matter will have to come back to the House for advice and guidance in a worse form than it is at present. For that reason, I doubt if the House had better adopt the Amendment for the further adjournment of the question. Some of the observations made by the hon. and learned Member for the

Tower Hamlets (Mr. Ayrton) appear to me to put the case on its proper footing, with one exception, that he has not contemplated that there may and must be cases in which the House must decide on this particular Act of Parliament. If that be so, and for the reason the hon. and learned Member has pointed out, the great thing we have to take care of is that the functions of the House are not brought to bear so as to interfere with the functions of the Committee. The object of the Act of Parliament is to take away all such inquiries from this House in order to avoid party and political discussions relative to election petitions; but how can we accomplish the double object of leaving the House to decide only those matters which are brought before it, and of leaving to the Committee all the functions which, by the statute, are delegated to them? That, I think, can be accomplished, and accomplished in the best way by the Motion of the learned Attorney General, than by any other mode that has been suggested. The House has only one question now to determine, and one proposition brought before it — namely, whether the hon. Member for Perthshire is to be excused for his non-attendance on the Committee on the 22nd of March last; and, until you decide it, the hon. Member is in contempt. It is, therefore, right towards him that you should decide it, and it should be borne in mind that in deciding that question you decide nothing more than simply saying that on the 22nd March last there was a legitimate excuse for the non-attendance of a particular member of that Committee. If that be so, and you assent to it, you leave the matter exactly where it would have been left by the Act of Parliament, and the Committee will have to take action in the matter. It is for them to decide how they shall proceed in future. They have taken upon themselves to adjourn the Committee till to-day. That course, probably, will be found to be in excess of their power, but it is for them to decide and not for this House, in the first instance, whether or not they can properly and legally proceed with the inquiry. If they think they cannot proceed, they can report to the House according to the view they are induced to take on the subject, after hearing counsel on one or both sides. Suppose, however, they should not hesitate to go on after counsel have appeared on both sides, and suppose they should unseat the sitting Member, what will be the consequence? Why, that this House must then interfere; because it must take action should the sitting Member still continue, in violation of the Committee's Report, to assert his right to the seat. It is clear, therefore, that there are matters which must ultimately come before the House as a Court of Appeal, but, until we get to that point, my earnest recommendation to the House is to leave the whole matter in the hands of the Committee until the difficulty is brought before the House on a specific Motion, and then you will have no difficulty in dealing with it.

THE ATTORNEY GENERAL: The noble Lord the Member for King's Lynn appears to me to have overlooked two things, one of which has been pointed out by my right hon. Friend opposite. The other is the effect of his Motion on the position of the hon. Member for Perthshire. The present position of the hon. Member is this, that up to this moment he has been absent from the Committee without leave —his excuse not having been allowed by the House. The Act states that any Member of a Committee who absents himself without leave or excuse, shall be directed to attend the House at its next sitting, and he shall then be taken into the custody of the Serjeant at Arms. If, therefore, you adjourn this matter for six months you will be, in the first place, directly superseding the Act; and secondly, you will leave the hon. Member for Perthshire in this unpleasant and improper situation, that he will be liable to be taken into the custody of the Serjeant at Arms. The House must either reject or accept the excuse, and if you reject it you must proceed against the hon. Member under the terms of the Act. The noble Lord has evidently overlooked the latter part of the 75th clause, which deals with the sittings of a Parliamentary Committee during the absence of a Member. Such a Committee, although it cannot sit for business during the absence of a Member, can sit for the purpose of adjourning daily, and that was the view of those who thought the Committee had done wrong in this instance in adjourning over till the re-assembling of the House after the Easter holydays, instead of adjourning from day to day until the matter had been settled by the acceptance or rejection of the excuse for the hon. Member for Perthshire's absence. If the

Mr. Walpole

noble Lord's view be correct, the Committee has not miscarried, because an Act of Parliament cannot require that to be done which is impossible. I think that, considering all the circumstances, the course which I have suggested is the proper one to be adopted. As to the further course of proceeding by that Committee, I will not presume to suggest what they should do. I have only ventured to suggest what I think it possible they may do to bring the question before the House. · If the Committee should think it desirable to state the facts to enable the House to consider whether it should do anything or not, the mode of doing so will be by a formal Report of the Committee. If that be done, then the House can determine whether the matter has reached that stage at which it would be consistent with its own functions and duties to enter into an inquiry upon the subject.

MR. ADAIR said, as Chairman of the Committee, he wished to say that after all he had heard he believed the course suggested by the Attorney General would be the best course for the Committee to pursue. He ventured to say on behalf of the Committee, that they would undertake to consider the question with what small amount of wisdom they might find amongst them, and come to some conclusion upon it. Should it occur to them that their proceedings had become unintentionally invalid, then they would be prepared to state the fact, and if they should see reason for drawing the attention of the House to anything that might occur the next day, it would be in their power to make a Report to the House. The Committee, he was sure, regretted that through an inadvertence the discussion had been rendered necessary, but at the same time he was also sure they would not hesitate to take upon themselves the responsibility of any further proceedings.

LORD STANLEY said, he had proposed his Amendment as a means of disembarrassing the House from an inconvenient responsibility; but, as it did not meet the approval of the hon. and learned Gentleman who was mainly responsible for the management of such questions, he would not press it.

Motion and Original Question, by leave, *withdrawn.*

Ordered,

That Mr. Stirling be excused for not attending the said Committee upon Tuesday, the 22nd day of March last.—(*The Attorney General.*)

DEPARTURE OF MAILS FROM SOUTHAMPTON.—QUESTION.

MR. H. BERKELEY said, he would beg to ask Mr. Chancellor of the Exchequer, Whether it is the intention of the Government to change the port of departure of the Mails from Southampton; and whether, since a Committee of the House decided in favour of Bristol as a port of departure, but did not consider there was sufficient accommodation for ships and passengers, and those requirements being now obtained by a Railway to Portishead, and the projection of Docks, a Bill for which is before Parliament, he would take the case of Bristol into consideration?

MR. PEEL replied, that there was no present intention of changing the port of departure of any of the Mails which now left Southampton. In consequence of some memorials which had been received, inquiries were being made as to what would be the advantage in point of time, and as to what additional subsidy would have to be given if the West India Mail Packets which left Southampton were required to call at some port more southerly than Southampton, with the view of landing and embarking Mails. He imagined that Bristol, as a port of call for vessels starting from Southampton, would be unsuited. As to its being available as a port of departure, when any contracts had to be renewed the Government would be unfettered with regard to the acceptance of an offer on that subject, and such an offer would, of course, be taken into consideration.

UNITED STATES—SEIZURE OF THE "SAXON."—QUESTION.

COLONEL SYKES said, he rose to ask the Under Secretary of State for Foreign Affairs, Whether he can give any information to the House of the results of the reference to the American Government respecting the seizure of the *Saxon* and the conduct of Lieutenant Donoghue?

MR. LAYARD said, in reply, that from a Report of Her Majesty's Consul at New York, the Government had learnt that the Judge of the District Court had directed that the *Saxon* and her cargo should be delivered to their respective owners, free from all costs, charges, and expenses, reserving the questions of salvage and probable cause of seizure. With respect to Lieutenant Donoghue, he believed that he

was to be tried, but did not know under what circumstances.

SIR JAMES ELPHINSTONE said, he wished to ask, whether any proposal has been made to pension the widow of the chief officer of the *Saxon*?

MR. LAYARD said, he had no information upon the subject beyond rumour.

WAR DEPARTMENT CLERKS.
QUESTION.

MR. ALDERMAN ROSE said, he would beg to ask the Under Secretary of State for War, Why the Privilege of Medical Attendance for the Wives and Families of Clerks and others in the War Department, granted by Circular dated 19th of March, 1857, was not extended to the Wives and Families of the Civil Assistants of the Ordnance Survey Branch of that Department; and why the Privileges contained in the Medical Circular, No. 849, and dated 30th January, 1864, have not been applied to the Wives and Families of the permanent Civil Assistants and others of the Ordnance Survey Branch of the War Department?

THE MARQUESS OF HARTINGTON said, in reply, that the Circular referred to by the hon. Member was not framed for the purpose of conferring any fresh privileges, but only with a view to regulating the manner in which those already existing should be exercised. The wives and families of the Clerks in some of the Civil Departments of the Army had long been entitled to receive medical assistance under certain circumstances, but it was not considered advisable to extend that system further. He had no objection to lay upon the table Copies of the Circular.

DISMISSAL OF MR. MORELL.
QUESTION.

LORD ROBERT CECIL said, he rose to ask the Vice President of the Council, If he will state to the House the grounds upon which Mr. Morell has been dismissed from the office of Her Majesty's Inspector?

MR. LOWE: I am sorry, Sir, that the noble Lord has thought it necessary to put this question, because the punishment of dismissal is a very severe one, and I am unwilling to add to the pain of it by a public discussion in this House. It would be scarcely fair to Mr. Morell if I were to undertake to state *ex parte* the grounds on which he was dismissed; but, if the noble Lord thinks it requisite that I should do so, he can move for the Correspondence which terminated in Mr. Morell's dismissal.

CHAIN CABLES AND ANCHORS.

QUESTION.

MR. LAIRD said, he wished to ask the Secretary to the Admiralty, Whether it is correct that the Transport Board of the Admiralty have decided to withdraw the Advertisement, dated the 19th January last, notifying that they would accept the Private Proof Certificates of Messrs. Brown, Lennox, and Co., for Chain Cables and Anchors for Vessels hired by the Transport Board, and that in future they intend not to hire any Vessels the Chain Cables and Anchors of which are not proved at a public testing machine; and if this will be notified by public advertisement?

LORD CLARENCE PAGET, in reply, said, the Admiralty had decided to withdraw the advertisement notifying that they would accept the private proof certificates of Messrs. Brown, Lennox, and Co., and that in future they did not intend to hire any vessels the chains, cables, and anchors of which had not been proved at a public testing machine, and that the same would be notified by advertisement. At the same time, he was bound to state, with reference to Messrs. Brown, Lennox, and Co., that the change had not been made on account of any dissatisfaction with regard to their chains and anchors, but in order that they might be put on the same footing with other makers.

PUBLIC LANDS AND BUILDINGS (LOCAL RATES).—RESOLUTION.

MR. ALDERMAN SALOMONS said, he rose to call attention to the exemption from Local Taxation now claimed on account of property in the occupation of Government Departments; and to move that all Lands and Buildings used and occupied for Public purposes should be assessed to Local Rates, and pay Rates accordingly. The question was one which affected not only his own constituents, but more or less every district throughout the kingdom. Exemption from local rating was claimed for all premises in the occupation of Government for public purposes, but he was at a loss to understand why they should be relieved of their fair share of the local burdens. The local taxation of the United Kingdom amounted to about

Mr. Lowe

£18,000,000 sterling—a sum rather under the annual revenue of Spain, but about equal to that of Prussia, and superior to that of several of the States of Europe. These burdens ought to be equally distributed, but in every town they found a building occupied by the Post Office or some other Government establishments, for which, although occupying excellent situations and sharing in all the advantages of well-directed local management, the Government claimed the privilege of not contributing anything towards the necessary local expenses, which in England and Wales alone amounted to £14,500,000. Petitions had been presented from various parts of the country complaining of this grievance, and showed that it was not a question merely of limited but of general importance. In 1858 a Committee, moved for by the hon. Member for Portsmouth, sat to inquire into the question which he brought forward. It was presided over by the eminent, and much to be regretted statesman, Sir George Lewis; and the Report which was drawn up stated that, in the opinion of the Committee, all Government buildings, whether occupied for public purposes or not, ought to be liable to rates. The exemption was claimed on the plea that the occupation of such buildings was not a beneficial occupation—the term beneficial meaning an occupation from which the occupiers derived a profit—and yet the smallest national school in the kingdom, where the children paid their pence, could not claim exemption upon a similar pretext. He considered that where a building was used as a Post Office, where stamps were sold, and money orders issued at a profit, where money on deposit was received, in competition with Friendly Societies, and where soon, probably, a competition would be carried on with Insurance Offices, by granting annuities, such building was really to all intents and purposes beneficially occupied. Union houses, which above all others should be exempt, were liable to rate, as being considered in law beneficially occupied; and he saw no reason why public establishments should not also be rated. The most recent case which he might instance was tried at Birmingham in 1856 or 1857, for the purpose of showing how great was the difficulty in defining a beneficial occupation. Two houses were taken for the Post Office of that town, and were rated by the parish. The rating was resisted and the case carried to the Court of Queen's Bench on appeal, and it was then argued before the full Court, and maintained that the Post Office authorities in the course of their duties were engaged in competition with private individuals and public companies, and were therefore rateable. They were, to all intents and purposes, deriving profit from their occupation. The rating was overruled, and the appeal dismissed, but Lord Campbell said—

"I certainly should be well pleased if it were made part of the general law that, whenever property subject to rates is taken for a public purpose, it should remain subject to the same burden while it is applied to those public purposes. I think this would be but equitable; for the existing law is very hard upon the occupiers of the rest of the parish, upon whom an increased burden is thrown. But, as the law now stands, if property is in the occupation of the servants of the Crown for public purposes, it is exempt from rates. It is wholly immaterial whether it be part of the hereditary property of the Crown, or be obtained for this purpose, having before been in the occupation of a subject."

Justice Erle said—

"I also am of opinion that land occupied by the servants of the Crown, exclusively for the performance of a public duty, is not rateable. I agree in thinking that it would be just in future to make such land rateable, on some equitable principle; but it is the province of the Legislature to alter the law; it is our province to declare the law as it is; and under the existing law such property is exempt."

Justice Crompton said—

"I am clearly of opinion that this property is within the rule which exempts from rates property occupied for public purposes. It is said this rule works hardship on the rest of the parish; and this may be, although the Legislature do not seem as yet to be of that opinion. In early canal acts there often was a provision that property occupied for the canal should be rateable, but at the same rate as if occupied as before. Without some such qualification, it might be injurious to make property, taken for the Crown, rateable in the occupation of its servants."

To show how the existing law acted upon the metropolis, he could not point to a stronger case than that which had recently occurred with regard to Portman Street Barracks, from which the Guards had just removed. While the Guards remained there the property was not subject to rate, but now that the barracks were removed to Chelsea, a large area in Marylebone parish would become available for building purposes and be subject to rates. In Chelsea, however, the land occupied by the new barracks went out of rating, and thus

Marylebone adds to its rate and Chelsea loses. A similar case was likely soon to arise on the removal of Knightsbridge Barracks, and it was impossible for any one to approve a system of that kind. Shortly after the meeting of the present Parliament, the then Home Secretary, Sir George Lewis, announced that the Government would propose a Vote in the Civil Estimates for the purpose of meeting some of the local charges from which property occupied for public purposes was exempt. That pledge was fulfilled, but he must say that the dissatisfaction created by the way in which the money voted was distributed, had really almost made the outcry greater than before. It had been contended that various localities derived great benefit from the Government establishments situated in them; but with regard to Deptford, which had had a dockyard for 150 years, no place had a greater appearance of impoverishment than the locality where that dockyard was situate, which was a small parish of about eighty acres, upwards of forty of which were occupied by the dockyard itself. For years the Government property had never contributed to the poor rate, though a large number of labourers were employed there at low weekly wages, and a great many poor were being constantly supported by the parish. It was proved before the Committee upstairs, that in the parish where the dockyard was situated, 10s. in the pound was the amount of the poor rate, and 2s. the amount of the other local rates; and not one single sixpence had been contributed to the local rates for 150 years by the Government for occupying the dockyard for public purposes. Such was the benefit which Deptford had derived from the occupation by the Government for so many years of all the best waterside portion of the district. The Government had for years escaped all contribution to the rates for local improvements, to which all the other holders of property had contributed. The consequence was, that the rates so swelled the rents that many of the smaller houses were shut up, and many of the men employed in the dockyard had to reside and had to buy their provisions out of the parish. In recent years there had been a great increase in the local rates throughout the country, though not in the poor rate, nor, he was happy to say, in the number of the poor. There was nothing so remarkable as the fact established by statistical accounts that, while the pauper class throughout the country amounted in 1841 to upwards of 1,000,000, the number of persons receiving in and outdoor relief in 1859-60 had diminished to between 800,000 and 900,000. Yet, though the number of paupers had diminished, the improved condition of the workhouses, the adoption of sanitary measures, of better drainage and sewerage, had a tendency to increase the rates, while the aid offered by the Government—under the arrangement by which they gave some modified assistance to the poor rate on account of property occupied by public establishments—consisted of a most miserable sum. The Government had for a couple of years, in certain cases, contributed to the poor rates, but at the end of that time they reduced their subscriptions very considerably, on the ground that the rates included charges for other objects than the relief of the poor, which they could not recognize. They maintained that they ought not to pay a share of any expenses except those which were strictly for the relief of the poor. He wished the House to observe the extraordinary increase in the county rate levy of the kingdom within the last fifty or sixty years, not for the use of the poor, but owing to the increasing multiplication of county charges for police, lunatic asylums, gaol improvements, and other purposes unconnected with poor relief, but which are collected through the poor rate. In 1792, the year of the first authentic Return, the amount of the county rate was £218,185; in 1800, £292,280; in 1810, £436,447; in 1820, £698,868; in 1830, £708,007; in 1834, £691,548; in 1841, £1,091,427; in 1851, £1,563,949; and in 1862, £2,218,207. No doubt a large proportion of the increase arose from the police rate and the improvement in gaols: these charges were included in the poor rate, and under these circumstances it was very hard upon the local ratepayers that the Government should refuse to bear their fair share of taxation on account of the buildings which they occupied for public purposes. It was not just that one part of the country should have to pay for another; but that was the result of the present system. The whole liability should be distributed equally over the country. He had taken the trouble to write to Paris to inquire into the mode in which these things were managed there. The largest part of the revenue of Paris was derived from the Octroi, but the Go-

vernment of France had an arrangement with the municipality at Paris, by which it paid one lump sum as the contribution of the Government towards paving and other local charges. Now, Gentlemen frequently argued in that House that London ought to pay for its own improvements, and that the Consolidated Fund should not pay anything. That was exactly what he contended. He fully admitted the justice of the demand that the other towns and cities should not be called on to contribute to the improvements of London. On the other hand, however, Liverpool, Dublin, Manchester, &c., ought not to be relieved from any taxation at the expense of the metropolis, which was indirectly the effect of exempting Government property from rates. There was one other point to which he would call attention, and that was, that the Government fixed upon the best localities for their establishments. No doubt many had noticed that all the small steamers crowded together at London Bridge; but the reason for that was, that just below was the Custom House with its long quay, where steamers were not allowed to stay, and below that again was the Tower; so that practically there was no place for the steamers between a short distance below London Bridge and the Docks. But the Government, however, contributed nothing to the rates when occupying these valuable sites. He might draw the attention of the House to other instances of the same kind, but he trusted he had already made out a case which warranted him in having brought the question before them, and which would induce them to agree to the Motion. The hon. Member concluded by moving in the terms of his Notice.

Mr. MORRISON, in seconding the Motion, said, his constituency was much interested in the subject, because although in some places the Government had paid a share of the poor rates, they had refused to give even that relief to Plymouth. The case of his constituents might be briefly stated. The Committee which sat in 1858 declared that the ordinary principle of rating for Poor Law purposes was not applicable to Government establishments, because it was impossible to say what a fort or a dockyard might let for, and they recommended the appointment of arbitrators. In 1859 Mr. Wilson, then Secretary of the Treasury, put himself in communication with the authorities of Plymouth, and eventually surveyors were instructed to value the Government establishments. The valuation was approved by both parties, and the Government paid its quota of a rate of 1s. 6d. in the pound, levied in the autumn of 1860. In the following June another rate was laid, and an application was made to the Treasury for its contribution. The Treasury not only did not send the money, but did not even acknowledge the receipt of the letter. In the following November a further rate was levied upon the town, and an application was made to the Treasury; and again no notice was taken of the application. At last, in the autumn of that year, a letter was received by the guardians stating that it was not considered advisable to continue the contribution to the parish rates, inasmuch as the Government property bore so small a proportion to the entire property of the parish. In 1862 he (Mr. Morrison) and his Colleague had an interview with Mr. Hamilton, of the Treasury, upon the subject. The only explanation they could obtain of the singular discontinuance of the Government contribution after an arrangement specially made was, that as the money came out of the annual Vote passed by that House, the Treasury were not bound by the arrangement for more than one year. His constituents felt strongly upon the question, not because of the amount involved, but because they felt that they had been put in a different category from other parishes. As to the argument that the Government establishments were beneficial to the localities, he thought it was fair to say that they consisted in Plymouth of marine barracks, which were occupied by soldiers, whose pay was very small. If the same land were occupied by ordinary buildings it would contribute a much larger sum to the poor rates. Then the very uncertain position in which soldiers were placed, their liability to be suddenly sent on foreign service, involved the necessity of a large increase to the poor rates, because their wives and children very often became chargeable upon the rates. In a garrison town there were many other evils which it was not necessary to specify, and which tended directly, and indirectly, to increase the rates. He thought they were entitled to claim some contribution from the Government towards the rates. The Government enjoyed the benefit of the roads, gaslight, paving, and so on, and caused a large increase in the police rates

by necessitating the maintenance of a large police force in garrison towns; and they ought therefore to make some contribution towards these expenses.

Motion made, and Question proposed,

"That, in the opinion of this House, all Lands and Buildings used and occupied for Public purposes should be assessed to Local Rates, and pay Rates accordingly."—(*Mr. Alderman Salomons.*)

MR. THOMSON HANKEY said, he differed entirely from the recommendation of the Committee which had been referred to. He considered that it was not a wise determination, and that it would entail upon the country a large and unnecessary expenditure. These buildings were for the public convenience, and were useful to the localities where they were placed. As to the argument about the land being covered by other buildings, he doubted if there were no Government establishments whether the land would be covered at all. He thought it would be a great waste of public money to tax buildings which were for the general convenience, and he hoped the Government would not assent to the Motion.

MR. SCLATER-BOOTH said, that the Government, at all events, could not use the argument urged against this proposal by the hon. Gentleman who had last spoken, because they had conceded the principle at issue. He did not wish to enter into first principles, or to discuss the question whether property ought to be liable to rates in proportion to its being beneficially occupied or not; but he took his stand on the Report of the Select Committee of 1858, which was presided over by the lamented Sir George Lewis. When this Parliament met in the summer of 1859, the question was put whether the Ministry proposed to introduce a Bill to render Government property subject to rates, and Sir George Lewis answered that he hoped to carry out an arrangement for giving some of the principal parishes concerned, some compensation for the non-payment of rates on the Government property situated in them. He had himself drawn attention to the position of the town of Aldershot, and asked whether it was not as fully entitled to participate in the grant on that account as any other place. Sir George Lewis treated the question as a large and general one, and distinctly admitted the principle that the Government inflicted an injustice by occupying property of that description with-

R 2

out paying rates on it. In the case of the parish of Alverstoke an enormous additional burden had been thrown upon the ratepayers by the Government establishments there. The Government had accordingly submitted in the year 1861 to an assessment of £10,800, and had paid rates upon that amount including county and police rates. In the year 1862, however, a change of policy seemed to have taken place at the Treasury and the Alverstoke ratepayers were told, not only that no more contributions would be made towards county and police rates but that the year's rate already paid on those accounts must be refunded. How the ratepayers there had got out of their difficulty with the Government he did not know; but certainly the county had not repaid the money which they had rightfully received. No principle had, as far as he was aware, been laid down by the Government as to what parishes should receive the State contribution and what should not; nor did he know that in the matter any distinction in principle had ever been established in that House between poor rate, county rate, police rate, and other local rates. Certainly, he could see no distinction in principle between them. He could understand the Government refusing any contribution at all, because the law supported them in it; but, having once admitted the principle to which he had referred, they ought to apply it fairly and equally, and thereby relieve the ratepayers from the uncertainty in which they were placed.

Mr. WYKEHAM-MARTIN said, he would put it to the hon. Member for Peterborough, who spoke of the national and general objects served by the Government establishments, whether it was fair that the cost of those objects should be defrayed out of the pockets of individual parishes. As to the benefit which those establishments conferred on their immediate neighbourhood, he could state that it was greatly over estimated. The truth was, that in the district which he represented there was property which the Government would themselves neither beneficially occupy nor let others do it. They kept a bare common for strategical purposes. There was but one public institution in the parish, the Military Lunatic Asylum, and that was a burden to the neighbourhood. Within his recollection it was the practice that so long as a soldier was in sound health in the bar-

Mr. Solater-Booth

racks of Chatham their Chatham neighbours got the benefit of him; but the moment he became hopelessly insane he was removed from Chatham parish to the unfortunate parish of St. Margaret, Rochester, and at ten o'clock at night turned loose into the street, with a notice sent to the proper authorities to catch him and keep him until his settlement was ascertained. The only other public building was a large convict establishment. He thought that so far from these places being a benefit to the locality they were a positive curse.

Mr. PEEL said, the House had been told that the Government could not contend for the fullest assertion of the right of public property to be exempt from local rates, because they had for several years past obtained an annual Vote for making contributions to certain parishes in respect to the Government property situated in them. Now, there were circumstances in the present day, in his opinion, which, though they did not raise the question as to the propriety of the exemption of public property from local rating, yet justified the Government in making exceptions to the application of that principle. There was no doubt that the Government property was now more extensive than it used to be; and, on the other hand, the local rates had very considerably increased. Local undertakings and drainage works were conducted on a much larger and more expensive scale than formerly, and the ratepayers felt more severely any contraction of the area of rating. But because the principle of exemption should be suspended in certain cases he did not think they ought to go to the other extreme, and say that all public property should pay rates, just as if it were private property. It would be quite as unreasonable and unfair that public property should be rated in every case, as that it should be exempt in every case. If it was right that public property should pay rates, the rule should be subject to great exceptions, that would go far to neutralize the purpose which his hon. Friend had in view. He did not think, for instance, that property then in possession of the Government ought to be liable to rates. It should be remembered that occupiers were by no means a fixed body. Premises did not usually remain in the same hands for a long time, and where property for a considerable period had been exempt from rates it was quite evident that in such a place leases were made and sales of land took place, full allowance being made for the fact that rates were levied on a much less area than the parish itself. Therefore, it would be improper that a large sum of money should be paid at the expense of the taxpayers of the country to the existing owners of property and ratepayers of the parish. Taking the case of Chelsea, could it be doubted that in that parish property was purchased and held on the full understanding that the Royal hospital and asylum were not to be rated? To discontinue the present exemption, therefore, would be to make a present of the rates to the existing owners. The great exception which he would make was this, that if any property acquired by Government was to be rated, it should be assessed only according to its value when it was so acquired, and not according to the increased value which it might receive from any additional outlay on the part of the Government. The parish in which Netley Hospital was situated was assessed at £7,000. A few years ago the Government bought 130 acres of land there, which, for purposes of assessment, was worth £150 a year, and on that property they had built a hospital which cost £355,000. Now, if they were to pay on the value of the property as it had been improved by that great outlay, they would pay not in the proportion of £150 to £7,000, but actually two-thirds of the rates of the parish. So, again, at Shoeburyness, the land occupied by Government was about one-third of the parish, which was an agricultural one, and the outside it ought to demand from the Government was that they should pay one-third of the rates. The Government had expended on buildings in that parish upwards of £100,000, and if they were to pay rates as on private property they would pay not one-third, but five-sixths. And so in the case of Alverstoke, in which the Government had built three forts at an expense of about £100,000 each, which caused no addition to the pauperism of the parish. The plan upon which the Government proceeded in the application of the Parliamentary grant was this :—They recognized two classes of cases. The first was where parishes made application in respect of the large extent of Government property within them. There were cases where the Government had also manufacturing establishments, which brought a large resident population into the neighbourhood. It was conceded that in such cases the Govern-

ment establishments would probably add largely to the charge for the relief of the poor, and that being very extensive, they shared in the benefits derived from the expenditure of the parish for various purposes, such as paving, lighting, &c. In these cases they had agreed to contribute, and, as it was necessary to draw the line somewhere, they had, with the concurrence of the late Sir George Lewis, who was Chairman of the Committee to which the hon. Gentleman had referred, agreed that where the value of the Government property was one-eighth of the value of the rateable property of the parish they would make a contribution, and they measured the extent of their contribution by the value of the property combined with the expenditure of the parish upon the relief of the poor. With respect to Deptford and Rochester, they found that other parishes in the country made application to the Government for contributions out of the annual grant, on the ground that they had a similar amount of property to Deptford and Rochester. On inquiry, it was found that Deptford and Rochester fell far below the proportion of one-sixth, and they were, therefore, no longer to receive assistance from the grant. The other class of cases was where the Government had purchased land which had formerly paid rates. In such cases, they were willing to proceed on the principle of indemnifying parishes against actual loss. In the case of Chelsea, for example, the Government, in order to build a barrack, purchased twelve acres of land which formerly contributed to the rates of the parish.. While, then, the Government did not think that the parish had any claim upon them on account of Chelsea Asylum or Hospital, they did admit its claim in respect of the twelve acres according to the provisions of the recent Defence Act. In the Defence Act and other Acts it was provided that property purchased by Government should continue to pay the same rates as were paid before the Government bought it, but no more. He would ask the House also to look to the liability to undue charges the Government would be under supposing their property was made liable to be trade. In the Government buildings in most cases there would be no occupier, no person who would have any interest in checking the assessment made by the parish ; and it should be borne in mind that the Government would have no voice in the expenditure of the money.

It was unreasonable that the Government should be rated like a private person. A private person went into a parish because he saw it was his interest to do so, but the Government went there for public purposes only. It would not be right, therefore, that the ratepayers of the parish should make any profit out of the accidental presence of a public establishment; it was quite sufficient if they were indemnified against actual loss. It had been said that if the Government buildings were removed they would make room for private ones, and these latter would be rateable. But it should be remembered that if such buildings increased the rateable value of the parish, they would in all, probability, increase likewise its chargeability. The hon. Member in his Resolution alluded to the exemption from local taxation now "claimed" on account of Government property, as if the claim of the Government were doubtful, whereas nothing could be clearer than that the Government had a legal foundation for the exemption. It was not an exemption conferred by statute, but because the property of the Government was not a beneficial occupation, and did not, therefore, fulfil the conditions that made it the subject of rating. The latter part of the hon. Member's Resolution did not go the full length of the recommendation of the Committee, for he only wished that Government land, &c., should be assessed to local rates, and "pay rates accordingly." The Committee, on the other hand, recommended that all land and building held by corporations, charities, and trustees for any purposes whatever, should be deprived of the immunity such property enjoyed from the absence of what was called beneficial occupation. He must, however, remind the House that a Bill had recently been brought in to give effect to that principle, but that it had met with so much opposition that it did not proceed to a second reading. The late Sir George Lewis was thereupon of opinion that the plan then pursued ought to be adopted. It was an experimental plan, and might, in some points, profitably undergo revision. In some cases it might be found to be hard upon the taxpayers, while in others parishes received larger sums than could be justified if the matter were looked into. He scarcely thought, however, it would be right at that time to agree to a Motion that all the land and buildings in the occupation of the Government should pay rates accordingly.

Mr. Peel

Sir JAMES ELPHINSTONE said, he thought that a powerful case had been made out for the Motion. In 1858 he had moved for a Committee on the same subject, which was granted, and the Government had stated their intention of adhering to the principle contained in the Report of that Committee. When the right hon. Member for Wiltshire brought in the Bill which had been referred to, the reason why it was not pressed to a second reading was not so much on account of the opposition to the proposal as from an understanding that the Government intended fairly to apply and carry out the recommendations of the Committee. The recommendations of the Committee included all rates, but the Government had substituted an arbitrary assessment, of which they themselves calculated the terms, and that was the substitute for the larger measure recommended by the Report. There were two classes of Government property—forts, hospitals, &c., which did not create a pauper population, and docks and barracks, which not only created a pauper population, but polluted and deteriorated a locality by cases of bastardy, disease, and poverty. Such establishments often threw very heavy rates on the population not of the parish in which the Government property was situate, but of the contiguous parish. On the other hand, the Government, by attempting the functions of manufacturers, deprived the localities of the rates those parishes would receive if the work of the dockyards was carried on by private individuals. If the Government were to lease Portsmouth dockyard to private contractors to build ships for Her Majesty's service, the whole of the extensive property would be rated to the relief of the poor; but, under the present system, the Government, although they had a beneficial interest in these buildings as manufacturers, threw the bulk of the rates on the inhabitants of the localities. He could not see, therefore, why the Government should refuse to take their share of the local burdens upon them. The system which had lately been introduced of periodically discharging men from the dockyards and re-entering them, was one that loosened the ties which had formerly existed between the Government and their employés, and it appeared to have been adopted for the very purpose of enabling the Admiralty to repudiate any claims for superannuation allowance that might be made upon them. Only the other day a well-conducted man who had been seventeen years in the Portsmouth dockyard, but who was club-footed and deformed, had been dismissed, owing to the particular nature of the occupation. This man had come to him and said, "I have a wife and six children, and have been discharged at a week's notice. What is to become of me?" He inquired into the case, found him a deserving man, whose health had been injured, and who with his family would probably become a burden on the parish of Portsea. Considering that the Resolution of his hon. Friend (Mr. Alderman Salomons) did not ask for more than common justice demanded, he should give it his support.

MR. LOCKE said, that he also had been a Member of the Select Committee of 1858, and he had heard no argument to induce him to alter the opinion to which he had then given expression, that all public property should be included in the general rating. He would ask what was the popular meaning of the words "beneficial occupation," and whether there was any occupation that was not for some one's benefit. A Government dockyard, for example, was occupied for the benefit of the public at large, and a hospital for the benefit of its inmates, and was that particular locality in which these institutions were situated justly called upon to pay a larger proportion towards the rates than other portions of the community? It was proved over and over again before the Committee, that it was no benefit to parishes, but rather detrimental to them, that they contained Government establishments. The same ground, if occupied by private establishments, would pay rates, and why should there be one rule for the Government and another for the public at large? When the Committee was moved for in 1858, the right hon. Gentleman the Member for the University of Cambridge, who was then Secretary for the Home Department, had agreed with him that the principle of rating should be extended to all public buildings whatever, and had upon his suggestion enlarged the reference to the Committee, so as to include public buildings of every description, whether belonging to the Government, or to any institutions, charitable or otherwise; and the right hon. Gentleman the Member for Wilts, in accordance with the Report of the Committee, brought in a Bill the principle of which was clear and plain, that all property whatever of a public description should be rated to the relief of the poor and other burdens. He

felt confident that the Chancellor of the Exchequer, considering the line he took last year with reference to the taxation of public charities, would be the last man to say that the principle adopted by the Committee should not be carried out. He sincerely hoped the words of the Committee's Report would be taken in their clear and full meaning. Why should they not legislate on the broad principle? Where could be the inconvenience? He saw no reason why the Court of Quarter Sessions, which had to adjudicate on the rights of private persons, should not also be able to adjudicate on the rights of the Government. It was not the amount of money which had been laid out, but what a property would let for, that was the rule of assessment; and objections had often been raised in consequence of the very small rate which was levied on the owners of large mansions; but the answer always was, that if they were to be let, the rent offered would be comparatively small, and upon the rent which they would let for, the sum at which they were to be rated must be assessed under 6 & 7 *Will.* IV. c. 96, upon the net annual value, that is to say, of the rents at which the premises might reasonably be expected to let from year to year with certain deductions mentioned in the Act. The Government could not, then, be the losers, even if they had expended large sums on their establishments.

THE CHANCELLOR OF THE EXCHEQUER said, he had understood that it was not the intention of his hon. Friend to take the sense of the House, but having heard within the last few minutes that such was his intention, he was reluctantly obliged to call attention to the precise question upon which they were about to divide. It appeared that by his Motion, in the mind of the hon. Baronet the Member for Portsmouth, and others, the hon. Member was about to give effect to the recommendation of the Committee of 1858, which recommendation was supported by the high authority of Sir George Lewis, though Sir George Lewis afterwards somewhat modified his views. But nothing could be more different than the proposition of the Committee of 1858 from the Motion of his hon. Friend. His hon. Friend who last spoke was somewhat inconsistently about to support the Motion, having himself indicated the principle on which they ought to proceed. He said, let there be no exceptions—let them carry out the principle that everything was of value. That principle was good for churches, Dissenting chapels, and buildings for any other purpose. That was the ground on which his hon. Friend the Member for Southwark proceeded. Let it be understood in its full breadth by those who were prepared to accept the principle. His hon. Friend's argument was, there could be no difficulty; they had a perfect test of value, and everything ought to be rated alike. His hon. Friend appealed to him in complimentary terms, and said he was sure, having recommended the taxation of charities, he would be the last to flinch from the application of this principle. Did his hon. Friend think the reception his proposal for the taxation of charities met on the other side, and from many Gentlemen of very popular principles sitting on that (the Ministerial) side, was such as to induce the House, on a very complicated matter, and with its eyes but partially opened, to commit itself at once to the principle laid down by his hon. Friend the Member for Greenwich? His hon. Friend the Member for Southwark drew no distinction between matters sacred and profane —Trojan and Tyrian were alike to him —ecclesiastical, municipal, or charitable— he would treat all alike. But what did his hon. Friend the Member for Greenwich say? He knew very well if he came to attack municipal bodies, instead of being surrounded by a number of Gentlemen who represented docks and yards, and who very naturally came forward to support the claims of their constituents, he would have been confronted by a phalanx of a very different kind, and he shrunk from making a proposal that, on the ground of justice, all these buildings should be rated. But it was a very easy thing to make claims on the part of particular parishes against the Treasury, and, selecting buildings belonging to the State, he claimed that they should be rated. He believed that a hospital for dogs had been created in the metropolis. Was that in the eye of the law a charitable establishment not to be rated, while a building belonging to the State, which had been exempted from time immemorial by the common law of England, was to be brought within the reach of his proposition? He invited the House to say that "all lands and buildings used and occupied for public purposes should be assessed to local rates, and pay rates accordingly." He understood his hon. Friend by "public purposes" to mean State purposes. How,

The Chancellor of the Exchequer

then, did they stand in relation to this matter? It was a subject which must be thoroughly and fairly scanned; but it was one of extreme complication. The difficulty of letable value, his hon. Friend would not deny, although slight in principle, was serious in practice. It was very serious in practice even with regard to mansions of noblemen and gentlemen throughout the country; but it would be infinitely more serious in practice when it came to be applied to St. Paul's, to the Abbey at Westminster, to the Tabernacle of Mr. Spurgeon, and all the endless variety of other buildings which might be drawn in; or, excluding them, to the Museum, the Houses of Parliament, and other buildings, which it was hardly possible to describe. He invited them to commit themselves without qualification or exception to this abstract principle. His hon. Friend took only one part of the Resolution of the Committee, entirely drawn and severed from and losing all relation to the rest, and what would be the case under it? They would find a parish in the country where, perhaps, one half of the area and one half of the buildings were Government property—and had been so for 100, 200, or 300 years—where every proprietor holding land or houses in the parish had taken his property subject to that condition of things, where there had been no change in the area occupied by the Government, and where, therefore, the rates payable by the portion of the parish not belonging to the Government were perfectly well known to those who paid them, and where it was understood from time immemorial that the burden of the rates should fall only on that part of the parish. His hon. Friend asked the House to pledge itself by an abstract Resolution that property which was now and had been for hundreds of years in the hands of the Government should be thrown into rating. The effect would be to endow the ratepayers of that parish with a large sum out of the pockets of the tax-payers of the country. ["No, no!"] He would prove it in spite of the emphatic negative. The hon. and gallant Baronet opposite (Sir James Elphinstone) had quoted the position of the dockyards at Portsmouth, and had said that if the dockyards were not there the land would be occupied by private persons, and would be assessed to the poor.

Sir JAMES ELPHINSTONE explained that what he said was, assuming for the sake of argument that the Government were to let those premises at Portsmouth to contractors to do the business which was at present done there, those premises, which now paid a very partial rate, would then come fully and entirely upon the rates of the parish.

THE CHANCELLOR OF THE EXCHEQUER said, the fact that there was a dockyard in Portsmouth at all was entirely due to the action of the Government, but for which the work now performed there would have been carried on at Liverpool or upon the Clyde. In the case which he had taken for convenience, of a parish where half the property was Government property, he contended that to throw the Government property into rating was simply to relieve the rest of the parish of a certain charge which had been placed upon it from time immemorial, and that was what he called the endowment of the ratepayers of that particular parish out of the pockets of the ratepayers of the country. That would be the consequence of adopting a Motion in the terms of that to which they were now asked to accede. He did not wish to lay down any rigid rule upon the subject, because he thought time should be allowed to the House to see their way through the difficulties with which it was surrounded. Some progress had already been made in that direction. In the case of the barracks at Chelsea and various other cases, the Treasury had given its sanction to a principle which he considered a very fair one, that the parish should be no loser by throwing land into Government occupation, but that the assessment should continue the same as before. The Government were at present engaged in working out that difficult question, and endeavouring to frame just, fair, and equitable rules with regard to it. It was a very serious matter which would have to be considered, whether they should make a proposal involving buildings other than Government buildings to the House. He was prepared to admit that he did not think the present system satisfactory. He could not, however, agree with those who said that the House had committed itself to any line of action upon the subject. The House had done nothing except by way of annual Vote, for the express purpose of reserving the matter, and keeping it in its own hands. But when the Government had arrived at clear views, and had solved the difficulties of the case in the most practical manner they were able, it would be proper to apply a legislative remedy. The old practice rested upon the law, and alterations in that practice ought to receive a form equally permanent. Nothing could be more absurd than, on account of an abstract principle, to throw upon the taxpayers of the country generally the burden of sustaining out of their pockets charges which had theretofore been borne by certain portions of the property in particular places, and which had so continued, without change, for a long period of time. It was only yesterday that they were arguing a question of an exactly opposite character, and he was so far glad that his hon. Friend had improved upon that discussion. The proposal then was to spend £1,500,000 of postal revenue derived chiefly from populous districts, to provide accommodation for rural districts; in the present case his hon. Friend reversed the principle, proposing, however, to act upon a reduced scale. But he contended that his hon. Friend's proposal was simply in effect to throw upon rural parishes and those which had not Government establishments a new and gratuitous burden for the purpose of bestowing a gratuitous relief not founded in justice upon those parishes in which there were Government buildings. Although his hon. Friend had announced his intention of dividing, he did not think he could seriously desire to establish by such means a new and perfectly gratuitous burden. If he believed that State buildings ought to be taxed, and that municipal and charitable buildings ought not, let him say so boldly, and bring in a Bill giving effect to his views. They would then see the *modus operandi*, and how the hon. Member addressed himself to all the practical questions which would arise. The question was one which could only be settled by patient and careful examination in detail, and he trusted the House would not commit itself to a proceeding so precipitate and so questionable in point of principle as that involved in the Motion of his hon. Friend.

SIR FRANCIS BARING said, he would suggest to his hon. Friend that, after the remarks of the right hon. Gentleman, it might not be advisable to divide. He did not agree with all the charges which had been made — sometimes seriously, and sometimes in jest—against the Administration of the day; on the contrary, he thought both Governments had behaved with remarkable good faith towards the naval ports. He advised the hon. Member to be very careful how he accepted the invitation of the right hon. Gentleman to bring in a Bill; and, above all, how he mixed up the question of charities with that of dockyards; otherwise, by raising the feeling of the country, he might rather imperil than improve the position at present held by the naval ports. He had the benefit of the Chancellor of the Exchequer's admission that the present state of things was not satisfactory, and with that admission it would be much better to leave the task of finding a suitable remedy on the shoulders of the right hon. Gentleman than to take it upon his own.

MR. DUTTON said that, however much certain parishes like those of London might be benefited by the existence within them of Government buildings, that argument did not apply to a great many small parishes in the country. He knew of a parish near Aldershot where large barracks and a lunatic asylum had been erected, and where, consequently, the rates pressed with undue severity on the parishioners.

MR. BONHAM-CARTER said, he should regret if a Vote were agreed to in a thin House, with the prospect of having it reversed afterwards in a full House; though he quite agreed with the principle that public buildings of a certain class should be liable to local taxation. He, however, thought, after what had fallen from the Chancellor of the Exchequer, that it would not be wise to press the Motion to a division.

MR. ANGERSTEIN said, the Resolution of his hon. Colleague only applied to public buildings occupied by the Government, and did not refer at all to buildings used for charitable or sacred purposes. It was left to the right hon. Gentleman to deal with that larger subject, if he were so disposed. The right hon. Gentleman had dwelt upon the fact that much of the Government property had been used for public purposes for long periods, and therefore ought not, after a lapse of years, to be suddenly called upon to bear the local burdens. But, although Deptford dockyard had been long established, it had been enlarged from time to time. The same could be said in stronger terms of Woolwich dockyard and arsenal. In consequence of the Government establishments, the population of the parish of Plumstead had increased within the last ten years from 8,000 to 26,000. Last year 4,000 workmen had been discharged from the Government establishments at

Sir Francis Baring

Woolwich, and it was not just to leave the burden of distress thus caused to be borne wholly by the ratepayers of the parishes. He hoped the subject would receive the favourable consideration of the Government; and, if such a pledge were given, no doubt his hon. Friend would withdraw the Motion.

MR. ALDERMAN SALOMONS, in reply, expressed his disappointment at the speech of the Secretary to the Treasury, who had been misinformed upon some points. There was, he believed, no instance in which the Government had made any contribution in respect of any other charge but that for the relief of the poor. With respect to what had fallen from the Chancellor of the Exchequer, he would only observe, that churches and chapels were exempted by the statute from local taxation. He was in the hands of the House, and if it was their wish that he should not press his Motion to a division, he would be willing to withdraw it.

Question put.

The House *divided:*—Ayes 30; Noes 52: Majority 22.

TURNPIKE TRUSTS—NOMINATION OF COMMITTEE.

MR. CLIVE moved that the Select Committee on Turnpike Trusts consist of twenty-one Members.

Motion *agreed to.*

Then it was moved that the following hon. Members be Members of the said Committee:—

Mr. BRUCE, Colonel HUSSEY PACKE, Mr. ALCOCK, Mr. FENWICK, Mr. MILDMAY, Mr. WRIGHTSON, Lord HENLEY, Mr. DODSON, Mr. CLIVE, Colonel PENNANT, Colonel BARTTELOT, Colonel SMYTH, Mr. SCLATER-BOOTH, Colonel Stuart (Bedford), Sir JAMES FERGUSSON, Sir WILLIAM JOLLIFFE, Colonel GILPIN, Mr. WALTER, Colonel FRENCH, Mr. WILLIAM LEGH, and Mr. WESTERN.

MR. FERRAND said, that the Committee moved for by the hon. Member for Hereford did not contain in its list any representative of the agricultural interests in the neighbourhood of the manufacturing districts. He would therefore request the hon. Gentleman to postpone the Motion for a week, to enable the right hon. Gentleman the Secretary of State for the Home Department to place some unprejudiced Member of the House upon the Committee.

MR. CLIVE said, he must deprecate the idea of any prejudice existing in the minds of the Members nominated. Originally, he proposed that there should be seventeen

Members on the Committee, but at the suggestion of the hon. Member (Mr. Ferrand) he had increased them to nineteen, and afterwards to twenty-one. He had succeeded in inducing the hon. Member for South Lancashire (Mr. W. Legh) to serve upon the Committee, but he could not get any other hon. Members, representing manufacturing counties, to do so.

MR. FERRAND said, he objected to the name of Mr. Western, and would suggest instead the appointment of Sir John Ramsden.

MR. SPEAKER said, that the hon. Member could not then oppose Mr. Western's appointment, but that he could do so by giving notice.

MR. H. A. BRUCE said, that Mr. Western was eminently qualified to act as a Member of the Committee, from the fact that he represented a county which was peculiarly situated with regard to turnpikes.

Motion agreed to.

Committee *nominated :—*Power to send for persons, papers, and records; Five to be the quorum.

Instruction to the Committee, that they do limit their inquiry to the Turnpike Trusts of England and Wales.

SUPPLY—NAVY ESTIMATES.

Resolutions [April 4] *reported.*

MR. YORKE said, he wished to ask the Secretary of the Admiralty, Whether he is aware that ten of the captains of 1846 who were compulsorily placed on the retired list on attaining the age of sixty, without having served in their present rank, have refused an offer of retirement on 18s. a day made to them at the age of fifty-five; whether he is aware that such offer of retirement was refused by them on the distinct understanding, founded on a former Order in Council, that they should on arriving at their flag, or reaching the age of sixty, rise to the pay of 25s. per diem, which has since been reduced to 20s.; and whether it is the intention of the Government to consider the claim of those ten officers to the 25s. pay?

LORD CLARENCE PAGET said, that it was true that there were some gallant officers who were rather disadvantaged than advantaged by the Order in Council of 1860, but their case was not so bad as the hon. Member supposed. Under the old Orders they had the option of retiring at the age of fifty-five or of remaining on the active list with all its chances, when

in accordance with the regulations of the service they would at some future and distant period have risen to a rate of 25s. a day. The Order in Council of 1860, which was greatly for the benefit of the whole naval service, had produced a greater flow of promotion to the flag list, and had entirely altered the position of those officers, who arrived at a position on the flag list at a much earlier date than they would otherwise have done. That order provided that officers who had not served at all should on their arrival at the age of sixty be at once placed upon retired pay at the rate of 18s. and 20s. a day. Thus, although these officers lost the ultimate chance of rising to 25s. a day, they had the advantage of a more immediate increase from 10s. 6d. or 12s. 6d. to 18s. and 20s. The Duke of Somerset considered their case, but came to the conclusion that there was no reason for treating them exceptionally; nor did the Committee on retirement and promotion, which carefully investigated all the circumstances, think that any ground had been shown for making any special recommendation that the Order in Council, in this case, should be altered.

Resolutions agreed to.

House adjourned at a quarter
before Nine o'clock.

HOUSE OF LORDS,

Wednesday, April 6, 1864.

The House sat for Judicial Business only.

House adjourned at a quarter before
Five o'clock, till To-morrow,
half past Ten o'clock.

HOUSE OF COMMONS,

Wednesday, April 6, 1864.

MINUTES.]—NEW WRIT ISSUED—For Lancaster Borough, *in the room of* William James Garnett, esquire, Manor of Northstead.
NEW MEMBER SWORN—*For* Armagh, John Matthew Stronge, esquire.
PUBLIC BILLS—*Ordered*—Copyright (No. 2)[*].
First Reading—Copyright (No. 2)[*] [Bill 50].
Second Reading—Jersey Court [Bill 48]; Registration of County Voters [Bill 49].
Committee—Chain Cables and Anchors [Bill 46] *re-committed.*
Report—Chain Cables and Anchors.
Third Reading—Union Relief Aid Acts Continuance[*] [Bill 50], and *passed.*
Withdrawn—Copyright [Bill 46].

COPYRIGHT BILL—[BILL 46.]

BILL WITHDRAWN.

On Order for Second Reading of the Copyright Bill,

MR. BLACK asked permission to withdraw the Bill in order to substitute a Bill for the consolidation and amendment of the law on the subject.

Order for Second Reading read and *discharged.*

Bill *withdrawn.*

COPYRIGHT (No. 2) BILL.

Then, Bill to consolidate and amend the Acts relating to Copyright in Works of Literature and the Fine Arts, *ordered* to be brought in by Mr. Black, Mr. Stirling, and Mr. Massey.

Bill *presented*, and read 1°. [No. 59.]

CHAIN CABLES AND ANCHORS (*re-committed*) BILL.—[Bill 46.]—COMMITTEE.

Order for Committee read.

Bill *considered* in Committee.

(In the Committee.)

Clause 1 (The Board of Trade may grant Licenses for proving Chain Cables and Anchors, and may suspend or revoke Licenses).

MR. HUMBERSTON, in the absence of Mr. Liddell, moved the omission from the clause of the words " person or persons." The object of the alteration was that the testing machines which were to be established under the clause should be in the hands of public companies or bodies, and not in those of private individuals. He believed it was the wish of the trade generally that such an alteration should be made in the Bill.

MR. AYRTON hoped the words would not be omitted, because if they were, a serious injustice would be done to the very respectable persons engaged in the manufacture of chain cables and anchors. Those manufacturers were in the habit of testing their own work, and sending it forth with a guarantee of its fitness for the purpose intended. Other people engaged in the same trade made and sold bad and unsound chain cables, and it was necessary to prevent the continuance of that evil; but in doing so they should not so alter the Bill as to prevent those who had earned a reputation for doing right carrying on their lawful business. Moreover, in his opinion greater responsibility attached to an individual than to a company, which was the creature of law and without any responsibility whatever.

MR. MILNER GIBSON said, that the point now raised had been carefully considered by the Select Committee to which the Bill was referred, and they were unanimous in thinking that the same rule, whatever it might be, should be applied equally to persons and companies. They saw no distinction between a private partnership and that description of partnership known as a joint stock company. Any body of persons could, if they thought fit, by adopting certain forms, constitute themselves into a joint stock company; and it seemed to him that the principle of disqualifying private partnerships from being licensed to test chain cables must also extend itself to partnerships known as companies. The Committee considered that they must either exclude both or retain both, and they decided in favour of the Board of Trade granting licenses to companies, persons, or individuals of whom they approved. But there were other considerations which rendered it necessary that the clause should remain as it stood. It was requisite that after a certain date no chain cable should be sold in this country which had not undergone the test of a testing machine, and they ought then, therefore, to throw no obstacle in the way of establishing such machines, especially as there might be a doubt whether there would be a sufficient number for the wants of the trade. That was a reason for retaining the words which it was proposed to omit. He thought it would be extremely impolitic to strike them out of the clause, and he should object to their omission. The Select Committee viewed the possibility of the manufacturers themselves testing the chains which they had made or in which they were interested. Security would be given for the efficiency of the test, because another clause provided, first that the testing machine should be certified to be efficient, and secondly that the testing operations should be carried on under some public officer, who should be responsible for their being honestly made. He hoped the Committee would support the decision of the Select Committee, which had fully discussed this particular point.

SIR JAMES ELPHINSTONE hoped the Attorney General would give the Committee his opinion on the effect of the clause. It appeared to him, that according to the argument of the right hon. Gentleman the President of the Board of Trade, the words objected to were surplusage, inasmuch as any body of persons numbering seven could form themselves into a limited joint stock company, and could if these words were omitted exercise the powers given by the Bill. Under those circumstances, it might meet the general wish expressed by the chain cable makers in the country if they struck out the words as proposed.

MR. HENLEY thought that the reasoning of the hon. Baronet conclusively showed that they ought to support the recommendation of the Select Committee. The hon. Member said that private parties consisting of seven in number might form themselves into a company with "limited" stuck to their names and avail themselves of the powers of the Bill. In that case they might get a company of seven persons, with no responsibility at all, instead of private individuals who were responsible for their actions. He (Mr. Henley) thought that was a great change for the worse. He confessed he had not great faith in this legislation—he very much doubted whether it would do any good; but if the Bill passed they ought to give every facility to respectable persons to set up testing machines. They ought to try and prevent a monopoly in these machines, which would be good neither for the buyers nor sellers. He should much prefer to have a substantial responsible man though his name might be "John Brown," than one of those companies that were so readily got up now-a-days with the word "limited" stuck to their names, without any responsibility at all.

MR. LAIRD said, that since the Bill passed through the Select Committee he had been waited upon by a deputation representing all the large manufacturers of chain cables and anchors in this country, with the exception of one firm, and they were in favour of these particular words being struck out of the clause, although they admitted that it was beneficial to them to have the privilege of testing cables and anchors on their own premises. Lloyds' Committee had also intimated their wish that the words should be struck out, and they had decided that in future they would not accept tests from any private manufacturers, and that all cables and anchors must be certified by a public board. He felt bound to mention these facts; but if it was the feeling of the Committee that

the clause should pass in its present shape he should not offer any opposition.

MR. JACKSON said, that the Select Committee were engaged two hours in discussing this clause, and that they unanimously decided that the words "person or persons" should be introduced as well as "company;" because several respectable chain cable makers stated that it would be a great inconvenience to them if they had to send their chains to be tested by a public machine. He should vote for the clause as it stood.

MR. LIDDELL rose to defend the Amendment of which he had himself given notice, although unfortunately he did not arrive in time to move it. The professed object of the measure was to secure a good article, and that was the reason why he wished to see the Amendment adopted. It was obvious that the testing authority should be an independent body who were wholly above the suspicion of being actuated by any motives of private interest, and for that reason it was desirable that these words should be removed from the clause. The mode of dealing with the precious metals appeared to him to be a somewhat analogous case. The precious metals were assayed by the Goldsmiths' Company, who affixed their stamp upon them. The purchaser of gold and silver had therefore the security of such stamp to satisfy him that the article in question was such as was represented. Here the value of a public proof was clearly shown, and there was no reason why a similar arrangement should not be adopted in the case of chain cables and anchors. He hoped, therefore, that the Amendment would be assented to.

MR. RICHARD HODGSON expressed a hope that the Committee of the House would not overrule the opinion of the Select Committee upon the point under consideration. The great objection to the supposed working of the Bill was the absence of good testing machinery; it was, therefore, an important object to provide a sufficient number of testing machines. Now, if this proposition were agreed to, it would have the effect of limiting greatly the number of testing machines. There was a discretionary power given under this Bill. No obligation would exist for the erection of testing machinery. A chain manufacturer by this Bill would not be compelled to erect a testing machine, but he would be allowed to do so if he pleased under certain conditions; first, he must obtain a license from the Board of Trade ; next, he must submit to the inspection of a supervising officer from the Board of Trade.

Mr. HENLEY said, that the arguments used in regard to the striking out of the words, went upon the supposition that those testing machines were to be private machines. But it should be recollected that the Bill provided that a public officer should be appointed to see the working of this machinery. Therefore, the argument of the hon. Member for Northumberland (Mr. Liddell) as to the Goldsmiths' Company, did not properly apply here. He (Mr. Henley) did not think that this was a bit more private test whether the machinery was erected by an individual or a company, inasmuch as there would be a public officer present to see it put in force. If they were to strike the word "companies" also out of the clause, and leave all these matters to be done by public bodies, there would then be some consistency in the arguments urged; but, at present, he confessed he was at a loss to see any.

Mr. BENTINCK said, it appeared to him that the Committee had really only one point to decide, and that was in what manner the most efficient test could be established. He had been a Member of the Committee to which the Bill was referred, and he was bound to say he preferred the Bill in its original state, believing that it was better calculated to promote an efficient mode of testing chain cables. But, since then, the position of affairs had become altered. In the first place, they had had the opinion of all the principal chain makers in this country, with but one exception, that the proposed mode of testing these cables was unsatisfactory. Well, then, assuming that which was generally assumed in this country, though he confessed he thought it was an error, that majorities were always in the right, it might be reasonably supposed that the majority of the chain cable makers were the best able to form an opinion as to the most effectual mode of testing the article. But they had the opinion of Lloyds' expressed on this subject—a very high opinion it would be admitted—and Lloyds', as he understood, declined to accept the testing system in the shape proposed by this Bill. The noble Lord the Secretary of the Admiralty had further informed them that the Board of Admiralty were opposed to the proposed system. If, therefore, they were to pass this Bill in its

present shape, it was obvious that this principle of testing would prove objectionable to the great majority of chain makers, and to the Board of Admiralty. He should certainly much rather see adopted the suggestion of the right hon. Gentleman the Member for Oxfordshire, that the companies also should be left out of the clause.

Mr. HENLEY : It is no suggestion of mine.

Mr. BENTINCK understood the right hon. Gentleman to say that he considered the omission of the companies would be a better mode of proceeding on this subject. It appeared to him that there would be a difficulty in finding a sufficient number of testing machines. He should certainly be glad to see the proposition of the hon. Member adopted.

Mr. THOMSON HANKEY said, he was sorry that the hon. Member for Huntingdon (Mr. T. Baring) was not in his place, because he was sure he would be able to offer some sound reasons against the adoption of the proposed Amendment. He (Mr. Thomson Hankey) certainly objected to the whole Bill. He objected especially to the retention of the word "companies." The great object was to secure the most independent body possible for the testing of those cables. He did not think it ought to be left to any individuals who pleased to set up a testing machine, inasmuch as it would be impossible to exercise such an efficient control over such persons as over public bodies.

Amendment *negatived*.

Clause *agreed to*.

Clause 2 (Whenever License granted, a resident Inspector to be appointed by Board of Trade).

Mr. AYRTON desired to ask his right hon. Friend the President of the Board of Trade, whether he was responsible for this clause, and what its precise effect would be; for it appeared to him that the tester was not to be appointed upon the responsibility of the persons licensed to carry on the testing work, but by the Board of Trade? If that were the case, it followed that those who undertook the business of testing would incur no responsibility whatever as to the cables being what they were represented to be; and practically the responsibility would be thrown upon the Board of Trade or its officer. Supposing that the person appointed by the Government to inspect those chains had given an improper certificate as to the efficiency of certain chain cables, which afterwards broke, the Board of Trade might find itself, on the principle that an employer was responsible for the acts of his servant, placed in a very serious dilemma. Considerable inconvenience of this kind had already been experienced in the case of licensed pilots. He wished the right hon. Gentleman to explain the precise measure of responsibility which the Board of Trade were prepared to accept in such cases. Unless the right hon. Gentleman the President of the Board of Trade could give a satisfactory answer to the question, he thought the clause ought to be struck out.

MR. THOMSON HANKEY considered the word "resident" Inspector ought to be omitted from the clause. If it was retained it would tend to prevent the employment of men of a superior class, and would moreover add materially to the expense of the working of the Bill, because it would prevent one Inspector from superintending three or four joint stock or private testing machines in the same neighbourhood.

MR. MILNER GIBSON said, this was not a Government Bill, but one brought in by the hon. Member for Birkenhead (Mr. Laird) which had been sent before a Select Committee, and now came before a Committee of the Whole House in its present form. He had not taken any practical part in the matter; but it was thought desirable by the Committee that some public officer should be appointed to superintend the operation of testing, in order to see that it was honestly performed, and that no fraud was committed. In order to provide for the particular difficulty suggested by the hon. and learned Member for the Tower Hamlets (Mr. Ayrton), he had introduced a clause at the end of the Bill providing that chain and anchor makers, shipowners, &c., should not be relieved by the provisions of the Bill from any responsibility which at present attached to them in respect of any chain cable or anchor made, sold, or used by them. They would, therefore, retain their present responsibility even after the passing of this Bill. Without at all questioning the principle of inspection, he thought it was susceptible of improvement. The Bill had not become a reality till the present time, and they had not viewed it as one likely to become law, but merely as a matter under discussion. It was not entirely matured, neither had it been adopted as, or made in any way, a Government

measure. The House sanctioned its second reading, and on the part of the Board of Trade he felt it his duty, as it appeared to be the wish of the House that some legislation should take place on the subject, to assist in making it, if possible, a good working measure. He should be very glad to consider what Amendment could be made in the clause, and on the Report, if any different and better mode of inspection could be devised, either by the omission of the word "resident," or otherwise, he should be ready to consider it; but he did not wish to be a party to the overthrowing of the Bill. If they permitted the establishment of testing machines, he thought there should be some security, not only for the efficiency of the tests, but also their honest use. He did not wish to say one word against the principle of some kind of Government inspection, but he reserved to himself the right of deciding whether the best mode was adopted by the Bill. He hoped the hon. and learned Member for the Tower Hamlets, seeing that the responsibility of the manufacturers and others was retained by the clause to which he (Mr. Milner Gibson) had referred, would not press his opposition to the whole of the clause.

MR. RICHARD HODGSON said, he was surprised to hear the remarks of the right hon. Gentleman, because he had looked upon the Bill as a reality, and one that would pass into a law.

MR. MILNER GIBSON explained. He stated that hitherto the Bill had not been considered a reality, but it had become something like it now.

MR. RICHARD HODGSON said, that if he had wanted any explanation of the observations of the right hon. Gentleman, he probably should have found it in the memorandum which had been that morning issued by an officer of the Board of Trade Department, which commented on the proceedings of the Select Committee, and also on the provisions of the measure. If he was wrong in ascribing the authorship of the document to that gentleman he was sorry for it; but the gentleman to whom he had particularly alluded was before the Committee, and it was then open to him, and that was the time when he ought to have stated his objections to the Bill, and not privately and by circular after the Bill had left the Select Committee, and still less should he have adopted the course of issuing the circular partially, sending several copies to a Member of tho Committee who was adverse to the Bill, and none to those who, like himself, (Mr. Hodgson) desired the Bill to pass. He (Mr. Hodgson) moved the clause in the Select Committee, to which an exception had been taken by the hon. and learned Member for the Tower Hamlets, and he could assure the Committee that he did not intend, neither did he believe he had affected, in the slightest, the present responsibility of the manufacturers or the shipowners. On the contrary, what he intended, and what he believed the clause effected, was the most efficient possible mode of supervision by an Inspector appointed by and responsible to the Board of Trade. He did not, however, under the circumstances, object to the suggestion of the hon. Member for Peterborough (Mr. Hankey) for striking out the word "resident" Inspector, provided the Inspector were appointed by the Board of Trade, and subject to removal by it, on a sufficient cause of complaint being made out against him. The clause followed the phraseology adopted by Lloyds' relative to the appointment of the Inspector at Newcastle, and he hoped the Committee would not alter it, otherwise than in the manner proposed by the hon. Member for Peterborough.

Mr. THOMSON HANKEY then moved the omission of the word "resident."

Mr. AYRTON said, the right hon. Gentleman the President of the Board of Trade had not answered his question, and the clause to which the right hon. Gentleman had referred did not meet his objection. The question he put was, Whether the Government intended to undertake the responsibility of testing the chains, &c.; or whether it was intended to continue it as at present, on the manufacturers?

THE ATTORNEY GENERAL thought that the clause required no Amendment in this respect. It was the most common thing in the world for a Government officer to superintend the performance of an operation in which the public had an interest. Thus, for instance, a railway could not be opened without a Government inspection. Nothing in the clause indicated that the slightest responsibility was to be undertaken by the Board of Trade or its officers; and, by reference to the 10th clause, it would be seen that any maker or dealer in chains and cables was not relieved from any responsibility which attached to him.

Mr. HENLEY said, he thought that this clause was the valuable part of the

Bill. If they had a machine for weighing or testing, they should have some one to see that it was applied to properly testing or weighing the things which the machine was intended to test. He thought the Amendment of the hon. Member for Peterborough was a good one. It was most difficult to tell what "resident" might mean. The clause the right hon. and learned Gentleman had referred to was a wonderful one. Hitherto, if a dealer in chains gave a warranty he was responsible, and he presumed he would continue under the same circumstances responsible.

Mr. INGHAM suggested that, to prevent misunderstanding, the same words should be employed here as were used in the section of the Mining Act under which Inspectors were appointed.

Mr. CAVE said, he quite approved of the Amendment, and had himself prepared one to the same effect, but he had no doubt that of his hon. Friend would do quite as well. It was absolutely necessary, especially as the first clause had been retained intact, including manufacturers, in conformity with an Amendment he had himself moved last year. The idea of every manufacturer having his own resident Inspector was like a distiller or brewer having his own private exciseman; and it would be impossible for the Board of Trade to work the Act satisfactorily with such machinery.

Mr. HODGKINSON said, he was quite unable to put any interpretation on the word "resident," and suggested that if it was to be continued in the Bill, they must have an interpretation clause.

Amendment *agreed to.*
Clause *agreed to.*

Clauses 3 to 7 *agreed to,* with Amendments.

Clause 8 (After 1st July, 1865, it shall be unlawful for Makers and Dealers to sell unproved Chain Cables and Anchors).

Mr. HUMBERSTON pointed out, that the effect of the clause was to prevent any maker of chain cables or anchors from selling them unless they were previously tested and stamped. The Amendment he proposed was to limit the clause to all seagoing vessels and coasters. The effect of the clause as it stood would be prejudicial to the trade generally in regard to the manufacture of small anchors for boats and river craft. In the case of boat anchors, for instance, it would press very harshly. The charge for testing was 20s.

a ton, but for a single hundredweight it would be 10*s.*, and this would be a heavy charge on each anchor. He quite agreed with the Bill so far as it applied to sea-going vessels and coasters, to which he proposed that the clause be limited.

MR. MILNER GIBSON said, he did not object to the Amendment.

MR. HENLEY said, he did not object to the Amendment, but doubted whether they ought not to go further. Would it not be better for the right hon. Gentleman to consider the matter between this and the Report, and decide whether it was not desirable that the word "vessel" should be more strictly defined? There was at present no interpretation clause, and he would suggest the introduction of one to define the meaning of vessels.

MR. J. EWART suggested, that the word "vessel" should be omitted, and that a provision should be made that anchors of a certain weight should be tested.

MR. MILNER GIBSON thought the suggestion of the right hon. Gentleman (Mr. Henley) worthy of consideration, and that it might be desirable to introduce an interpretation clause, describing the vessels whose chains and anchors were required to be tested, on bringing up the Report.

MR. BENTINCK also approved of the suggestion. The question was one of a somewhat comprehensive character. The term "fishing boats" was almost as comprehensive as the term "vessels." The omission of the words "fishing boats" would not be sufficient.

MR. MILNER GIBSON suggested the propriety of letting the clause stand over for consideration on bringing up the Report.

MR. LAIRD preferred the suggestion which had been made by the hon. Member for Liverpool.

MR. THOMSON HANKEY inquired whether the clause would apply to the sale of anchors to foreigners?

MR. LIDDELL suggested the insertion of the words "United Kingdom" to meet the difficulty.

MR. RICHARD HODGSON said, he could not recognise the propriety of any distinction being made between anchors and chains intended to be supplied to foreigners and those intended for English vessels. All chain cables and anchors should be tested and stamped for whatever service they might be intended.

MR. LAIRD said, that he had sent a copy of the Bill to the principal chain-

makers at Newcastle and in Staffordshire, who held a meeting and appointed a deputation, which had waited on him. This clause was fully discussed, and they came to the conclusion that it should pass in its present form. He believed if anchors and cables were allowed to be exported without having had the test applied to them, it would be opening a door to the use of anchors and cables of an inferior quality in this country.

MR. HENLEY said, he should be sorry to see the House admit a legislation authorizing the sale to foreigners of anchors and chain cables that were not deemed fit for our own use. It was like getting up two classes of razors, those for our own shaving being required to cut, but those for foreigners being intended only to sell. If we secured good articles for ourselves, we should give foreigners the same advantage.

MR. CAVE said, he thought the trade of this country would derive great advantage from foreigners knowing that they could only get good articles here. He rose to ask, whether it would not be better to follow the original Bill, and to exempt ships of war and other public vessels from its provisions? It was well known that the Admiralty and other public bodies had their own testing machines in Government dockyards, and it seemed an unnecessary expense and trouble to oblige chains and anchors made for them to be sent also to a licensed testing machine. He thought the President of the Board of Trade should remember that such vessels were omitted from the former Bill, and were included in the present.

MR. HUMBERSTON said, that after the intimation which had been given by the President of the Board of Trade, he would withdraw his Amendment.

Amendment, by leave, withdrawn.

SIR JAMES ELPHINSTONE suggested that fifty tons might be the limit of the vessels whose chains and anchors should be required to be tested.

MR. BENTINCK remarked that the limit of fifty tons would exclude a very large class of vessels.

SIR MORTON PETO regarded the object of the Bill to be to give the public a guarantee that chain cables, when sold in the first instance, were made of good materials. To permit the exportation of chain cables without the test mark, would be to open a shop on the other side of the Channel for the sale of a bad article. He hoped the Bill would pass in its integrity.

Clause *agreed to.*

Clause 9 (Persons committing certain Offences to be guilty of a Misdemeanour.)

In answer to Mr. AYRTON,

MR. MILNER GIBSON said, that as he read the Bill, after a certain time, parties having untested chain cables and anchors would not be able to sell them without the mark ; but he hoped the delusion or misunderstanding would not get abroad that this testing would give all the qualities and security required.

SIR MORTON PETO observed, that at least this guarantee would be given to the public—that the chains and anchors which had undergone the tests were originally made of suitable material, and such as ought to be manufactured.

MR. MILNER GIBSON: So far as tensile strain went.

SIR MORTON PETO thought the measure imperatively called for, and he hoped it would be applied to all anchors and chains, whether intended for exportation or not.

SIR JAMES ELPHINSTONE said, that a chain re-tested was more to be trusted than one that had never been tried. After a time chains might become worthless, but in well-regulated ships the chains after a voyage were cleaned, put in a dry place, and ought not to be deteriorated.

MR. LAIRD said, he had framed the Bill originally on the Admiralty standard, which had been tried for many years, and been found efficient. It was hardly fair, then, in the right hon. Gentleman to imply that the test adopted by the Government for the protection of ships of war, and troops sent in transports, would not work advantageously for the public.

MR. MILNER GIBSON remarked, that a chain cable might stand the tensile strain, and yet not be in all respects a good chain.

Clause *agreed to.*

Clause 10 *agreed to.*

Preamble.

ADMIRAL WALCOTT congratulated his hon. Friends the Member for Birkenhead and the Member for Portsmouth, on the great intelligence and zeal they had displayed in this matter. He believed such a measure was much wanted, and it would

Sir Morton Peto

no doubt, have the effect of saving life and property to a large extent.

House *resumed.*

Bill *reported ;* as amended, to be considered on *Friday.*

JERSEY COURT BILL—[BILL 48.]
SECOND READING.

Order for Second Reading read.

MR. LOCKE : I rise, Sir, to move the second reading of this Bill. I am hardly aware whether the Government intend to offer to it any opposition or not, but I can hardly suppose they do, inasmuch as the Bill has already been before the House, and they have admitted the existence of the evils which it proposes to remedy. It is precisely the same Bill that was introduced in the year 1861, and I believe at that time it met with the general approbation of the House. It is not my intention to go into the grounds upon which it has been agreed on all hands that a reform is necessary in the Royal Court of Jersey. It would be needlessly taking up the time of the House were I to state the instances which have occurred, and which have, on a former occasion, been brought before the attention of the House, of the great inconvenience which suitors, and not only suitors but other persons who have gone to the Island of Jersey to take up their residence there have been put to in consequence of the law procedure of that Island. I shall content myself with pointing out the recommendations of the Royal Commissioners sent in the year 1859, and which were reported to this House in the year 1860 and the commencement of 1861. Complaints had been made before the sitting of this Commission and also of a previous Commission which sat in 1846. The question was fully gone into in 1846, I believe, as to the Criminal Procedure in the Island of Jersey, and, subsequently, this second Commission was appointed in 1859 fully to consider the laws of the Island, and likewise to Report upon the procedure of the Courts of the Island. The latter Commissioners made their Report partly, as I have stated, in 1860, and fully in 1861 ; and on the 1st of May, 1861, Mr. Sergeant Pigott introduced a Bill into this House, founded entirely upon the Report of the Commissioners ; and, in June of that year, the Bill was read a second time. The Bill which I have now the honour to introduce is precisely the same Bill that was introduced by Mr.

Sergeant Pigott. When that Bill was read a second time in June, 1861, Sir George Lewis, who was then the Secretary for the Home Department, stated that he entirely approved of the provisions of the Bill, but inasmuch as the States of the Island of Jersey had not had sufficient time to consider the Report of the Commissioners, he thought it was too soon for this House to legislate upon the subject, and upon his expressing that view, Mr. Sergeant Pigott did not go on with the Bill, or seek to pass it that Session. He did not, however, say he would not proceed any further with the Bill, but, on the contrary, he pledged himself to bring it in again on a future occasion, and he has only been prevented from doing so by having been appointed by Her Majesty one of the Judges of the land. Sir George Lewis upon that occasion fully admitted the necessity of reform in the Royal Court of Jersey, and stated that his only objection to proceeding with the Bill was, that scarcely six weeks had elapsed since the Report of the Commissioners had been laid before the House, and that the authorities of the Island of Jersey had not had sufficient time to consider what they would do with regard to the recommendations of the Commissioners. Now such an argument as that cannot by any possibility be brought forward on this occasion, because the Report, as I have stated, was made in the year 1861, and we are now in the year 1864. The Report has been brought to the attention of the States of the Island of Jersey, and the Bill which was brought in by Mr. Sergeant Pigott has likewise been brought under their consideration. They know full well what the intention of the Government of this country is, and if they have not proceeded as they had the opportunity of doing, by the withdrawal of the Bill in 1861, they have nobody but themselves to blame ; and I think I shall be justified in saying that this House ought to agree to the second reading of this Bill on the present occasion. As I have already said, I shall not go at length into a statement of the grievances which have been alleged and redress for which is demanded at our hands by persons who have become residents in the Island of Jersey. But I will shortly call the attention of the House to the Report of the Commissioners of 1859. The Commissioners thus classify the legislative sources of the laws of Jersey :—First, Royal Charters ; second,

Orders of the Sovereign in Council ; third, laws passed by the States or, before 1771, by the Royal Court, and allowed by the Sovereign in Council ; fourth, local ordinances by the States, in force for three years without the express allowance of the Crown, if not expressly disallowed ; and fifthly, Acts of the Imperial Parliament. Now the reason, the obvious reason, why the proper mode of dealing with this question is by a Bill in Parliament, I think, will appear from the Report of the Commissioners themselves, because they say, with regard to the Sovereign in Council, those Orders might be resorted to in order to effect the desired reform, though they admit that that position is disputed by many legal authorities in Jersey. I think, therefore, it is better that a course should be adopted which is open to no objection. As to the third mode, laws passed by the States, there is no doubt that the States, if they like, have the power, with the sanction of the Crown, of reforming this Court at Jersey. But is there any hope whatever that they will adopt that course ? Time was given them in the year 1861, at the instance of Sir George Lewis, it being said that they were not then prepared. They have had plenty of time since, and I shall presently state to the House the mode in which they have recently acted. In my opinion, no hope whatever can be entertained that the States of the Island of Jersey will entertain this question, and pass any bill that shall effect the reforms which we all desire. Therefore, the only mode that suggests itself to me is by an Act of the Imperial Legislature, and the Commissioners say that the competency of Parliament to legislate for Jersey is unquestionable, nor do I find that any of the authorities in the Island of Jersey have ever disputed that proposition, although they say the Imperial Parliament ought not to interfere with them inasmuch as they are not represented. Various acts, however, have been passed by the Legislature of this country with reference to Jersey, and such acts are now in force, and consequently no legal question can by possibility be raised as to whether or not this House has the power of legislating for the island.

SIR GEORGE GREY : They may not register the Act.

MR. LOCKE : That is true, but if they do not register, an order may be given by the Crown that they must register, and they cannot disobey that order. Therefore, to all intents and purposes, this House has full power to legislate for the Island of Jersey. That being so, I come to the question of what the Bill contains. Though many of the inhabitants of Jersey are most anxious that this Bill should pass, I think the House will be somewhat astonished that any should object when they find how very small are the dimensions of the Bill. It is a Bill which does not interfere with the constitution of Jersey in any way whatever. It does not interfere in the slightest degree with any of their rights and privileges. If it interferes with the rights and privileges of anybody, it is simply the rights and privileges of twelve men, and the question is whether they have performed their duty, and whether they ought not to be got rid of. It interferes with the constitution of the Royal Court of Jersey. Now, how is that Court constituted? At the head of it is the Bailiff. He is appointed by the Crown, and he has a salary of, I think, £300 a year, and he is entitled to perquisites, amounting altogether on the average to £650 a year. He has likewise other duties to perform; he is a member of the States. But no complaint is made with regard to the Bailiff; he is a person who has had a legal education, and I believe that he has, as far as lies in his power, seeing how he is trammelled by the Jurats, performed his duties most satisfactorily. But now we come to the clog of the system in this Royal Court of Jersey, which is caused by these twelve persons called Jurats. Now, how are they paid, and what is their qualification? The qualification is, that they must be assessed at a rent of a little over £30 a year; so that any person in the Island of Jersey, with a few exceptions — the exceptions being those who carry on the trade of a brewer, a butcher, a baker, or a tavernkeeper—may be elected one of these Jurats, the sole qualification being that he occupies premises of the rental of £30 15s. 3d. a year. Now, upon the face of it, is it right that twelve Jurats should be thus appointed, who are not jurymen judging merely of the facts, but of the law? But, even if they were, it would be most objectionable to have only these twelve men, persons of no legal education whatever, trying everything in a place like Jersey and having the authority of Judges. I may here say that I do not found my observations upon statements made by persons living in Jersey, who have suffered inconvenience from

the mode in which justice is there administered, but all I state is founded on the Report of the Commissioners. Now, the Commissioners state that they have no complaint to make of the Bailiff; but the Bailiff cannot rule in his court according to law. He must rule along with the majority of the Jurats, so that, in point of fact, here are twelve men who have received no legal education, a majority of whom can enforce their view in opposition to the only man belonging to the court who is supposed to know anything about law, and he is bound to give a decision directly contrary to law on many occasions, because the majority of the Jurats chose to think that he should do so. Can anything be more absurd than that such a system as this should be allowed to go on in a place where there is now a population of 60,000 persons, and where they have vessels belonging to the island amounting to a tonnage of 50,000 tons. Important questions arise from time to time, shipping questions, questions between persons residing in this country and persons residing in Jersey, who must submit to the decision of these twelve Jurats, who, it is admitted on all hands, by everybody, I believe, in the Island, do not necessarily know anything about law, and I have never heard that they do. And who are these Jurats? They are elected, and they hold their office for life, and are members of the States. They receive no salary, but they receive fees, and it is their direct interest, and the Commissioners state that such is the fact, that the cases should be delayed as long as possible. There are instances, I believe, where cases have been delayed for an immense number of years. I do not impute that entirely to a desire on the part of the Jurats to accumulate fees, but to the fact that the same Jurats must attend upon every occasion, supposing it is a case where evidence is to be taken. They sit only for a short time; they are Members of the States as well as of the court, and they have many duties to perform. A certain number of them can attend only on particular days, the cases cannot proceed on any subsequent occasion, unless the same Jurats can come again, and the consequence is that from time to time the course of justice is delayed, and the greatest inconvenience arises to the suitors. There is another point. The Crown law officer is likewise essential to the constitution of this court; not that it is necessary that he should do anything.

but the court cannot go on unless he is present. This again causes great delay, because his duties often require him to be elsewhere. The quorum of the court is the Bailiff and seven Jurats, but in the first instance the case is brought before a smaller tribunal, consisting of the Bailiff and two or three Jurats. It is alleged that inconvenience arises from the irregularity of the attendance of the Jurats. Now, what are the recommendations of the Commissioners? They recommend that the Bailiff shall still remain, that his salary shall be increased, and, in addition to the Bailiff, there shall be two Judges of £1,000 a year each. They recommend that all the fees should be paid into a fund in the Island, that the salary of the Judges in future shall be paid out of that fund, if it be sufficient, and there are certain other provisions for the purpose of paying them. The proposed expenditure is £3,200 a year, and that is all. Now, really it does seem to me very extraordinary that with a proposition like this, made in 1861, and well understood by the States of the Island of Jersey at that time, that they should not have made up their minds to adopt this Bill. I can only come to the conclusion, as they have not done so, that their great object is to set themselves against any reform whatever. [Mr. HADFIELD: Hear, hear!] Now, what has recently taken place? I do not know exactly the course which the right hon. Gentleman the Secretary of State intends to pursue, but I may state for the information of the House that the right hon. Gentleman expressed himself in approval of the principle of this Bill so far back as 1846, when he filled the office which he now holds. I may also state for the information of the House, that his late predecessor, Sir George Cornewall Lewis, fully approved of the Bill introduced by Mr. Sergeant Pigott, and that a petition very numerously and respectably signed, has been sent to Her Majesty, which expressed the approval by the petitioners of the principle of this measure. What I am now about to state is not taken from the Report of the Commissioners, but from a letter of the Lieutenant Governor of the Island of Jersey, in which he states the character of the persons who have signed the petition, expresses his approval of the prayer of the petition, &c., and urges exactly those arguments which we urge in favour of this Bill. I have no desire to found this Bill upon the statement of any private individual, or upon any of the objections which may have been brought forward in that way. I found the measure entirely upon the Report of the Commissioners, upon the opinion of the great bulk of the people of Jersey, as expressed in their petition, and also upon the authorities there. I will read to the House a few passages from the letter of the Lieutenant Governor to Sir George Grey. The Lieutenant Governor says—

"I have the honour, at the request of a deputation of influential gentlemen of the Island, who waited upon me yesterday, to transmit the accompanying petition to the Queen, praying for a reform of the constitution of the Royal Court, in accordance with the recommendations of the two last Royal Commissions, and to solicit Sir George Grey to lay the same before Her Majesty. This petition humbly prays that the elections to supply the vacancies on the Bench may be suspended by Her Majesty in Council until measures are taken to separate the Judicial from the Legislative functions of the Jurats, and for ensuring a better administration of Justice. The Petitioners, in accordance with the Royal Commissioners' recommendations — 'that no member of this branch (Jurats) of the Legislative Body should form part of the Judicial Body,' urge that the Jurats should be relieved from the Judicial office, retaining their present positions as members of the States and of the corporate body called the Administrators of the Impot. The petitioners forcibly exhibit that the ancient system of an elected and unpaid Magistracy, fulfilling the double functions of Judges and Legislators, and not qualified by any description of legal training to administer the laws, however well such a system may have been adapted to the times in which it was instituted, is entirely unsuited to the requirements of the present day, and is adverse to the true interests of the Island. The petition contains the names of many of the largest landed proprietors, and of the most educated and influential native and resident gentlemen of the Island; and I am informed by the deputation that all the petitioners, with a few solitary exceptions, are ratepayers; that, moreover, the Island has not been generally canvassed, but that the people have been left to come forward spontaneously and affix their signatures. Sir George Grey will, doubtless, expect me to offer some comments on the contents of the petition. I cannot, for my part, but admit the reasonableness of its scope and prayer, directed, not against individuals, but against a system the working of which appears to have produced widespread dissatisfaction for the last thirty years at least, and to have kept this community in a state of agitation for a long period, and which, apparently, will not cease until the recommendations of the two last Commissions are adopted. I am induced to believe that the time is come when the necessity for the proposed change in the judicature of the Island is more and more felt and desired, and that the present conjuncture of circumstances offers a most favourable opportunity for introducing it, by separating the judicial from the legislative functions of the Jurats, and assigning the former to men of competent legal attainments, as the only guarantee for the proper administration of the laws."

In reply to the Lieutenant Governor's communications, Mr. Waddington, on the 9th of last March, wrote—

I am directed by Secretary Sir George Grey to inform you that the Lords of the Committee of Council for the Affairs of Jersey and Guernsey, having taken the whole of the case into careful consideration, would be prepared to recommend to Her Majesty that the prayer of the Petition from the Landowners, &c., should be granted, and to advise the Queen to accept the resignation of these two Jurats, and to direct that their places should not be filled up, on receiving a distinct assurance from the States of Jersey that they are prepared to take the necessary measures for carrying into effect, in whole or in part, the recommendations of the Commissioners appointed to inquire into the Civil, Municipal, and Ecclesiastical Laws of Jersey, with regard to the constitution of the Royal Court. And I am to request that you will inform Sir George Grey what steps the States are ready to take as regards the furtherance of reform in the mode of administering justice in the Island.

Well, after the receipt of that letter, what do they do? They call the States together, and instead of setting themselves to work to comply with the suggestions contained in the letter received from Sir George Grey, they take a course which evinces their decided opposition to all reform whatever in the Island. I have here a report of a debate which has just occurred in the States upon this very subject. It was introduced by the Attorney General there, who was anxious that a reform should take place, that the Report of the Commissioners should be acted upon, and that a Bill, similar to that now before the House, should be passed. I will not trouble the House with quotations from the speeches of Gentlemen who took part in that debate, but it is perfectly obvious that they entirely set themselves against any reform whatever. In all probability, if Her Majesty's Government decide upon waiting until the States of the Island of Jersey adopt the recommendations of the Commissioners, and refuse to pass any Bill in the meantime, they will have to wait till the Greek Kalends. The States intend doing nothing of the sort. What have they done? They have referred the matter to a committee to report upon it, and have adopted the course of sending a deputation over to this country to oppose the Bill I have introduced. Already they have waited upon the Secretary of State for the Home Department and have made their representations to him. I am informed, not by the right hon. Gentleman, but by others, that they have induced him to oppose this Bill on the second reading. Upon what grounds

I cannot by any possibility understand, unless he chooses to hand himself over to the authorities of the States of Jersey and say "I delight to be imposed on. I wish with all my heart to believe those I have no right to believe when they say they are anxious to come forward and make those reforms which can never be made unless the Legislature of this country make them." Unless the right hon. Gentleman wishes to be imposed on, the only course he can pursue is to allow this Bill to be read a second time. What real objection can there be to the course I propose? This is no new measure. The Bill was read a second time in 1861.

SIR GEORGE GREY: I beg my hon. Friend's pardon. That is a mistake. The objection of Sir George Lewis was taken to the second reading.

MR. LOCKE: The Government expressly state in the letter which they have sent over to Jersey that they approve of the principle of the Bill. In that case I do not see how they can object to the second reading. The reason the Bill was not proceeded with in 1861 was that Sir George Lewis raised an objection, which was that the States of Jersey had not had sufficient time to consider the recommendations of the Commissioners. He thought the Bill came too soon. That objection does not apply now. We have given them three years, and still they have done nothing. The Government told them they must do something, and what have they done? They have simply appointed a Committee for the purpose of devising the means of evading all reform whatever. Under these circumstances, I ask the House to read the Bill a second time, and I am willing to place myself in the hands of the House as to the time when it shall go into Committee. If the Government will intimate that they intend to introduce a Bill themselves—if they will take the labour off my hands, I shall be most happy to resign the duty to them. Indeed, I think the question is one which would be much better dealt with by the Government than by an independent Member. I believe there is not the slightest objection to any one of the enactments of this Bill on the part of the Government. As I have already stated, its object is simply to reform the Court of the Island of Jersey. It does not interfere with the rights or privileges of a single individual in that Island, but it will give them such a Court as every civilised people ought to have, and will abolish that which up to the present time has been considered by every right feeling person in the island to be a nuisance. I beg now to move that the Bill be read a second time,

MR. HADFIELD : I rise to second the Motion of my hon. Friend for the second reading of the Bill. Already two Royal Commissions have been issued to inquire into the state of the administration of the law in Jersey—one in 1846, and the other in 1859. Both of those Commissions have recommended most important alterations, but as yet none of those alterations have been carried into effect. Some slight and unimportant legislation may have taken place in the Island ; but I believe I am correct in saying, that not one of the important recommendations of either of the Commissions has yet been carried into effect by the States. Unless the whole of the inquiries which have hitherto taken place be a farce, it is necessary that something should be done to carry out the recommendations of the Commissioners. The issuing of a Royal Commission is no farce. On the contrary, it is a very serious step for this House to take. The expense of the last Commission was something like £5,000. And, after waiting now for five years, we are in this position ; we have been required to wait until the matter has approached the present stage, and now we are asked to wait still further. I cannot conceive anything more unjust to the Island than the present condition of the law there. In my humble opinion they are not removed from a state of barbarism ; they are only adapted to a place to which civilization has not extended. I believe it is a fact that you may arrest a man there for an imaginary debt on the mere *ipse dixit* of a complainant. In one case a gentleman was imprisoned for three years, and it was only after he had endured that amount of imprisonment that it was discovered that there was not the shadow of foundation for the claim. That could not have happened in this or any other civilised country. There are no less than sixteen recommendations contained in the Report of the last Royal Commissioners. The House is aware that a previous Commission sat in 1846. Perhaps the right hon. Gentleman the Secretary of State will allow me to remind him that the proceedings of that Commission met with his entire approval. If my memory serves me aright, he then filled the office he so ably fills at the present time. When they remonstrated with

him from the Island of Guernsey concerning any interference with the law by the Government, the right hon. Gentleman addressed a letter to the authorities there, in which he announced his intention of persevering with the reform of the law of the Islands. As I have already stated, there are no less than sixteen recommendations contained in the Report of the last Commission, and if these recommendations were carried out, and if law and justice were properly administered in Jersey, the value of property would increase in that Island to a very considerable extent. I forget what the exact calculation was, but I think I am within the limit when I say it was estimated that, by a proper administration of the law, the value of property would increase at least 30 or 40 per cent. The hon. Member for Leicestershire has presented a petition to this House, in which he states that his rights have been greatly prejudiced and interrupted, solely because the laws are in such an inefficient state that it is impossible for him to obtain redress. The Court which the hon. and learned Member for Southwark proposes to reform is conducted in a manner which shows that there is altogether a want of authority on the part of those who have charge of it. Not only are irregularities of every description committed, but even acts of violence, of discourtesy, and impropriety are constantly taking place. The most improper language is used by the advocates who attend the Court, and altogether the proceedings are conducted in a discreditable way. As regards property there, if you wish to build a church you must vest the property in trustees, and the wives of trustees are entitled to dowers out of it, while the property itself is liable to be seized for the debts of trustees who are appointed for its protection. The inefficiency of the laws of that Island is so great as to render the value of property uncertain. The delays which take place in the administration of law are disgraceful, and the constant complaints which have been made on the subject demand, in my opinion, the serious consideration of this House with the view of passing some legislative enactment for the removal of the grievances now complained of. I should like to know what possible objection there can be to sending this Bill before a Committee. If the right hon. Gentleman (Sir George Grey) has not had time to attend to all the recommendations of the Commission, let us adopt some other course. Let us send the Bill to a Select Committee for the purpose of having its provisions fully considered. Eighteen years have now elapsed since the first Commission was issued, and nothing important has yet been done. Are we not, I would ask, to take this matter into consideration for ages ? Is it right that the civil laws of Jersey should continue to exist in their present state ? Is it right that, having issued a Commission in 1859—five years ago—we should now be called upon for further delay before legislating upon the subject ? The propriety of introducing legal reforms into Jersey has been admitted on both sides of the House. The Commission of 1846 was issued by what was considered the Liberal side of the House, when the right hon. Gentleman the present Home Secretary was in office. But in 1859 another Commission was issued, and at that time the Government of Lord Derby were in office. The appointment of the Commission had the sanction of the right hon. Member for the University of Cambridge (Mr. Walpole), who was then Home Secretary, although he retired from office before the Commission was actually appointed. The right hon. Gentleman the Member for Wiltshire (Mr. Sotheron Estcourt) actually pleaded in this House the propriety of issuing the Commission. It was issued, therefore, by the authority of the Government of Lord Derby. The Commissioners in the last Commission, in the two visits which they paid to the Island, spent three months in investigating these matters, and in collecting evidence on the subject. They presented their Report to the House in 1860, in an enormous volume of more than 800 pages, much of it closely printed. That Report is now before the House, and all we are asked to do is to pass this simple measure. The measure my hon. Friend has brought before the House I can only regard as the beginning of important regulations. Until the Royal Court is reformed, and put into more intelligent hands, into the hands of those thoroughly conversant with the law, nothing can be done. Until that is done we can have no real reform in Jersey. We have waited for a reform of the criminal law of Jersey for eighteen years, and, as nothing material has been done on the part of the States themselves to reform these great abuses which the excellent Reports of these Commissioners point out, I do hope and trust, after such an expendi-

Mr. Hadfield

ture of money as this country has incurred, that the House will feel it necessary without further delay to take up the question seriously. I would put it to the House, if it is not time that we should have some effective legislative enactment for the purpose of remedying the evils which have been so justly complained of. If this Bill should pass, it would be the commencement of the reforms which are so much needed, and the beneficial result to the people of Jersey would be very great indeed. I have already had the honour of presenting petition after petition in favour of some measure of reform, and I have urged on the Government to take the matter into their careful consideration with the view of bringing in some measure that would be satisfactory to the people of Jersey. This Bill would be regarded as a great boon, and it would tend materially to enhance the value of property in Jersey ; and if the right hon. Gentleman the Home Secretary would take it in hand, I think he would be fairly entitled to the thanks of the people of the Island. Under these circumstances, I have great pleasure in seconding the Motion for the second reading of the Bill.

Moved, " That the Bill be now read the second time."—(*Mr. Locke.*)

SIR GEORGE GREY said, the hon. and learned Gentleman who had moved the second reading of this Bill was right in anticipating that the Government would raise no objection to the principle of the Bill. He agreed with the principle ; but he wished to guard himself against approving all the clauses contained in the Bill, especially those relating to the mode of payment of the Judges, which he thought would require further consideration. As far as the Bill aimed at the reform of the constitution of the Royal Court, a separation of the judicial from the political functions, and the appointment of paid Judges, he approved its object. The hon. and learned Gentleman was not correct in saying that the Bill relating to this subject, introduced two years since by Mr. Serjeant Pigott, was read a second time, because it would be found, upon reference to the records of the House, that the Bill was withdrawn in consequence of objections made to it by the Government upon the ground that sufficient time had not been allowed to the States to act upon the recommendations of the Royal Commission. That objection did not arise now ; but until yesterday he would have been disposed to request the hon. and learned Gentleman to postpone the measure to give the States a further opportunity of carrying out the reforms which were needed. The late Governor of Jersey (Sir Percy Douglas) had in 1861 pressed upon the States the expediency of effecting the reforms which had been suggested by the Royal Commission, and, in fact, some reforms were effected in the mode of administering the Criminal Law, and especially as regarded summary jurisdiction. The present Governor (Major General Cuppage), animated by the same spirit, had also urged the necessity of further reforms; and letters had been referred to by the hon. and learned Gentleman which showed the opinion of the Government here upon the subject. Not long ago two Acts were passed by the States providing for the resignation of two jurats, and the election of others. These Acts were referred to the Privy Council, together with a memorial signed by a large number of the inhabitants of Jersey, praying for reforms of the constitution of the Court and in the administration of justice. After consulting the Law Officers of the Crown, the Privy Council decided to advise Her Majesty to confirm those portions of the Acts relating to the resignation of Jurats, but to withhold assent from the portions relating to the election of other Jurats; and further suggested that the Lieutenant Governor should call upon the States to consider what steps should be taken to carry out the recommendations of the Royal Commissioners. The memorial was subsequently sent to Jersey to be communicated to the States. A copy of the present Bill had also been sent to the Governor, who, while he approved of it generally, suspended the expression of any decided opinion until it was seen what determination the States had arrived at. Only yesterday, however, he (Sir George Grey) had received a letter from the Chairman of the Committee of the States announcing that it had been merely resolved to appoint a Committee to take such measures as they might think necessary to resist any attempt to invade their privileges. There was no desire whatever to interfere with their privileges, but he confessed that this letter had held out no hope that the States would do anything effectually in the matter. The Government here had shown a forbearing spirit, and had wished to leave the requisite reform to be carried out by the States themselves; but as the States declined to take any steps in that direction, it could not be said that Parliament was not entitled to interfere. He should, therefore, not object to the second reading of the Bill, on the understanding that the Committee upon it would be postponed for a considerable time to allow the States to take any steps which might appear to them proper under the circumstances.

Motion *agreed to.*

Bill read 2°, and *committed* for *Wednesday, 4th May.*

REGISTRATION OF VOTERS (IRELAND) BILL—[BILL 49.]—SECOND READING.

Order for Second Reading read.

MR. AGAR-ELLIS moved the second reading of the Bill. The object of the Bill was simply to assimilate the registration and the polling districts, the one being at present regulated by the baronies, and the other not. It also gave the clerk of the peace additional powers, in order that he might carry out the additional duties imposed on him.

Moved, "That the Bill be now read a second time."—(*Mr. Agar-Ellis.*)

MR. WHITESIDE said, he did not desire to impede the Bill, but he thought a measure of this kind should be in the hands of the Government. Perhaps the Attorney General for Ireland would take it up, for if any mistake were made in a Bill of this kind, it might in future lead to great inconvenience.

MR. O'HAGAN (ATTORNEY GENERAL FOR IRELAND) said, as far as he was concerned, he would give any assistance to his hon. Friend he could. The difficulty had arisen from the system of registration in baronies, and as it was occasioned by the Bill introduced by his hon. Friend (Mr. Ellis) himself, he had thought it desirable that that hon. Gentleman should have charge of this Bill. For his own part, he must say he quite agreed with the Bill, and should be quite willing to accept any responsibility with reference to it, or to promote it in any way he possibly could.

Motion *agreed to.*

Bill read 2°, and *committed* for *Wednesday* next.

LISBURN ELECTION.

MR. ADAIR informed the House, That the Select Committee appointed to try and determine the merits of the Petitions complaining of an undue Election and Return for the Borough of Lisburn, having met this morning pursuant to adjournment, a protest was entered on behalf of the sitting Member against the competence of the Committee to proceed with the case; whereupon the Committee having heard Counsel for the Petitioners, considered the circumstances of the adjournment of the Committee made from the 22nd day of March last until Tuesday, the 5th day of April, being the day after that to which the House had been adjourned, and came to the conclusion that they are no longer legally empowered as a Committee to proceed further in the matter of the said Petition.

House adjourned at a quarter after Three o'clock.

HOUSE OF LORDS,

Thursday, April 7, 1864.

MINUTES.]—SELECT COMMITTEE—Journal Committee — Ninety-fifth Volume (Session 1863), with Index, reported ready for Delivery.
PUBLIC BILLS—*First Reading* — Charitable Assurances Enrolments [H L.]* (No. 38); Union Relief Aid Acts Continuance* (No. 39).
Second Reading—Settled Estates Act Amendment [H.L.] (No. 36).
Third Reading—Malt for Animals* (No. 16); Conveyancers, &c. (Ireland)* (No. 17).

DENMARK AND GERMANY.
BOMBARDMENT OF SONDERBORG.
QUESTION.

THE EARL OF SHAFTESBURY: My Lords, seeing my noble Friend the Secretary of State for Foreign Affairs in his place, I will take the liberty of putting a Question of which I have given him private notice. Your Lordships are well aware that the attention of the public has been drawn to a very sad occurrence which has taken place in the Danish war, a telegraphic report of which appeared in the newspapers of the 5th, and also of the 6th inst. I will read the telegram upon which I wish to put the Question. It is dated Ulkeböl, and says—

"The Prussians have bombarded Sonderborg for forty-eight hours without any previous intimation. Eighty townspeople, women and children, have been killed or wounded, fifty houses in the centre of the town were burnt, and 1,500 shells thrown into the town, which is now deserted."

Mr. Adair

Now, my Lords, it is possible that this statement may be altogether untrue. We may hope so. But if true, it puts before us one of the most cruel—one of the most outrageous—acts ever perpetrated, or ever recorded in the history, I do not say of a civilized, but even of an uncivilized country. Consider, my Lords, that the laws of war, as I believe, and certainly the modern usages of war, have laid it down that no bombardment is to take place without previous notice, and also that no undefended place or unwalled town is ever to be bombarded at all. But in the present instance both these usages have been violated. An undefended town, without walls or bulwarks of any kind, and without any previous notice, has been bombarded for forty-eight hours, and eighty women and children have been made the victims of that atrocity. Now, my Lords, I must say, that if this be so, it is a state of things which will bring us to believe that the Prussian Government, which is responsible, and the Prussian military, which are the instruments, are not fit to be counted in the list of civilized men or civilized nations. I will not go further, upon the supposition that all this may prove untrue, than to express my hope that the Government will be able to give us information upon this subject; and that if it be true, as stated in this telegram, they will be good enough to tell us what steps they have taken upon the matter. I will only repeat now what I said before—that I do sincerely hope and trust—and I am sure since the time I had last the honour of addressing your Lordships the feeling of the country has grown much more intense—I do sincerely hope that the British fleet will appear in those seas to prevent the occurrence — it may be the recurrence—of these most cowardly and frightful atrocities.

EARL RUSSELL: My Lords, in regard to the question of my noble Friend, I can only say, that I saw in the newspapers the account which he has read, and I sent a telegram to Sir Andrew Buchanan, our Minister at Berlin, with a view to ascertain what might be the truth. But I cannot find that Sir Andrew Buchanan can give me any intelligence at present on the subject. It is impossible but that in a very few days we should know what are the actual facts of the case. I should not think myself warranted in giving an opinion until we know the real facts.

UNITED STATES—FOREIGN ENLIST-
MENT ACT—THE "KEARSARGE."

EXPLANATION.

THE EARL OF DERBY said, he wished
to correct a mistake which had appeared
in all the reports he had seen, to the effect
that he had stated that the men on board
the *Kearsarge* were examined by the medical officers, had been placed on the books
of the ship, and that they were clothed in
the uniform of the United States navy.
On the contrary, he had only stated, in
answer to the noble Earl, that if Mr.
Adams did not deny the placing of the
men on the books and clothing them in
the uniform, then it was impossible that the
officers could not have known those facts.

EARL RUSSELL said, he had called the
attention of Mr. Adams to the statements
that had been made, and he had also called
the attention of the Home Secretary to
them.

DENMARK AND GERMANY—DISCUSSION
ON THE AFFAIRS OF DENMARK.

QUESTION.

EARL GREY said, he wished to ask the
noble Earl, with reference to the notice
which had been given by a noble Lord not
now in his place (Lord Campbell) of his
intention to bring on the question of Denmark on Monday evening. Whether his
noble Friend would make an objection to
any discussion on the subject, just as he
had done before the Easter holydays; and
in the event of his doing so, whether that
objection would apply as well to the transactions which preceded the invasion of
Schleswig by the Prussians and Austrians
as to the present state of affairs? He
asked the question upon this ground—that
as the papers containing an account of those
transactions had been laid upon the table
by command of Her Majesty, if they were
allowed to remain without any notice being
taken of them, it might virtually imply that
their Lordships approved the course taken
by Her Majesty's Government. Now, as
he for one was of opinion that the policy of
Her Majesty's Government in this matter
was not entitled to approval, he thought it
would not be right that the House should
be debarred of the opportunity of expressing its views upon the subject.

EARL RUSSELL: In answer to the
Question of my noble Friend, I beg to
say that when it was proposed to bring on
the discussion before Easter, I took upon
myself the responsibility of asking that it
should not at that time take place, for two
reasons — one was that I was about to
present by command of Her Majesty further papers, containing part of the Correspondence which had taken place on the
subject of the war; and the other was,
that very delicate negotiations were going
on with various Powers on the subject of
a Conference. He could not say that
either of those reasons now existed, because the papers presented were complete, and there were now no negotiations going on with respect to the Conference. All the parties to the Treaty of
London had already accepted the proposal
of a Conference, and the only question
that remained was with regard to the Diet
of Frankfort, which body had received a
communication on the subject on the 27th
of March, inviting them to send a representative, but had not yet had time to
reply. He did not wish, therefore, to take
upon himself the responsibility of saying
that the subject should not be discussed.
But it was another question whether the
House, seeing that the Conference was
about to meet, would wish to enter upon
a protracted discussion on those affairs.
That was a matter for the consideration of
the House. But he did not think it possible to separate the early part of the Correspondence from that which had afterwards taken place.

SETTLED ESTATES ACT AMENDMENT
BILL—[H.L.] (No. 43.)—SECOND READING.

LORD CRANWORTH, in moving the
second reading of this Bill, said, that the
object of the Bill was to amend an Act
which had been passed some six or seven
years ago — the 19th and 20th of the
Queen, c. 120—the object of which was to
facilitate leases and sales of settled estates.
It often happened that marriage and other
settlements contained no power to the
trustees to grant leases for building and
other purposes, and it became necessary
to apply to Parliament for a Private Act
to enable them to do so; and the object
of the statute was to enable trustees to
grant such leases by a summary application to the Court of Chancery. Owing,
perhaps, to some obscurity in the wording
of the Act, the Courts of Chancery had
put an interpretation upon it which prevented the intention of the Act from being
fully carried out. The object of the present measure was to render it unnecessary
to comply with certain conditions which

the Court of Chancery had held to be required by the Act, unless the Court should see some special reason why the compliance with such conditions was necessary or expedient.

Moved, " That the Bill be now read 2ª."
—(*Lord Cranworth.*)

THE EARL OF MALMESBURY said, he had been a considerable sufferer from the interpretation put upon the 19 & 20 *Vict.* He happened to own a considerable tract of land which had suddenly become valuable, owing to its proximity to a fashionable watering-place. Owing to the Act to which the noble and learned Lord had alluded, he found that every lease that he had to grant he had to apply for through his solicitor to the Court of Chancery. This was a process involving much expense and great delay; but it had other ill effects. A gentleman living very near to him was in a much better position. There were numerous applications for the land for building purposes. The consequence was, that builders when applying to him (the Earl of Malmesbury), found that they would have to wait some weeks before the lease could be made out. They would immediately say they could not wait so long. His neighbour was in the condition to give a lease within a few days, and of course the builders and contractors went to him. In this manner, the value of his property was sometimes greatly diminished.

THE LORD CHANCELLOR said, that the case of the noble Earl was by no means singular. He believed there was a great deal of property in the country so situated, particularly in the neighbourhood of large manufacturing towns. Several cases had come within his own experience. The Act did not, it would appear, state explicitly the intention which the noble and learned Lord who introduced it had in view. As to the delay, there was considerable delay involved in the fact that a solicitor had to be employed for such a purpose as an application to the Court of Chancery, more particularly solicitors who lived in remote parts of the kingdom, who had, of course, to conform to the rules of the Court. He approved of the present measure, and considered that it would be most beneficial in its operation.

Motion *agreed to:* Bill read 2ª accordingly, and *committed* to a Committee of the Whole House *To-morrow.*

House adjourned at a quarter before Six o'clock, till to-morrow, half past Ten o'clock.

Lord Cranworth.

HOUSE OF COMMONS,
Thursday, April 7, 1864.

MINUTES.]—NEW WRIT ISSUED—For Fifeshire *in the room of* James Hay Erskine-Wemyss, esquire, deceased.
WAYS AND MEANS—*considered* in Committee—R.P.
PUBLIC BILLS—*Second Reading*—Naval Agency and Distribution [Bill 39]; Naval Prize Acts Repeal* [Bill 40]; Naval Prize* [Bill 41].

PRUSSIAN BREECH-LOADING RIFLES.
QUESTION.

MR. ONSLOW said, he wished to ask the Under Secretary of State for War, Whether his attention has been called to the vast superiority of the Prussian Breech-loading Rifles in the Danish Campaign, as described in the Letter of *The Times'* Correspondent from Sönderborg ?

THE MARQUESS OF HARTINGTON, in reply, said, the arm in question was well known to the Ordnance Select Committee. There were two or three specimens of it in their possession, and some years ago it was tried at Woolwich. The arm was very efficient for a limited number of rounds, but after that the escape of gas was so great that the weapon would have been dangerous for use. It was possible that improvements had since been made in it. They had no reason, however, to suppose that the breech-loading rifles of the Prussian army was superior to the Westley Richards' rifles, of which a supply had been ordered, and which were to be issued to several regiments for the purpose of trial. There were a great number of difficult questions connected with the breech-loading rifles for the use of the army, and it had been deemed advisable, before the general adoption of any weapon, to have a thorough trial by regiments in all parts of our possessions.

WAYS AND MEANS.
THE FINANCIAL STATEMENT.

WAYS and MEANS *considered* in Committee.

(In the Committee.)

THE CHANCELLOR OF THE EXCHEQUER : Mr. Massey—With a view, Sir, to gather fully the purport of the figures which I am about to submit to the House, it may be well that we should notice, in the first instance, though in a very few words, the particular circumstances which have recently affected the condition of the country. In the financial year 1862-3, we had but an indifferent harvest; Ireland was suffering under lamentable depression, and Lancashire had been afflicted beyond all example. In 1863-4, on the contrary, England at least was blessed with a harvest of unusual abundance; the distress of Ireland was in some degree mitigated, at any rate as regarded the consuming powers of the country, by the low price of grain; and, in respect to Lancashire, the distress which there prevailed had been very considerably reduced, although the district still continued in a condition far below, and sadly different from, that of its usual prosperity and vigour. On the whole, therefore, after considering, on the one hand, the advantages, and, on the other hand, the drawbacks of the year, we may, perhaps, arrive at the conclusion that its circumstances did not differ materially as a whole from those of an average financial year. With this brief preface, I proceed to lay before the Committee the particulars of the statement I have to submit.

And first, in regard to the financial year which has just expired. The expenditure of that year, as it was estimated on the 16th of April, 1863, was £67,749,000; but augmentations, chiefly in consequence of the New Zealand War, and partly in consequence of the payment for the Scheldt Tolls, have been made during the present Session, which raised the amount voted by Parliament to £68,283,000. The actual expenditure under the authority of Parliament was, however, only £67,056,000; or less by nearly a million and a quarter than the sum which the various Departments had been authorized to lay out. As respects the Army, its Estimates amounted to £15,469,000; but its actual expenditure was not more than £14,638,000; and this although a war has, unhappily, been raging in New Zealand, which cannot be deemed to have added less, and may, perhaps, be estimated to have added more, than half a million of money to the military expenditure of the country. As regards the Navy, the Votes for that service amounted to £10,736,000, and the expenditure to very nearly the same sum, or £10,821,000. The Miscellaneous Services were estimated at £7,805,000, and the expenditure was £7,702,000.

Here, Sir, perhaps, it may be well that I should pause for a moment to disabuse the minds of some portion of the House of an impression that has gone abroad with regard to a constant, rapid, and still continuing increase in the Miscellaneous Estimates of the country. The Miscellaneous Services for the year 1859-60 amounted to £7,721,000. In 1863-4 they were £7,702,000; and these Estimates in the present year as they now lie on the table amount to £7,628,000. On the whole, therefore, this portion of the public expenditure has been now for some time almost stationary; for the slight tendency to decrease shown to the extent of £93,000 is too small to be relied on, or to be stated as a fact of much significance. There is another important item of the civil expenditure, which at one period was viewed with peculiar and just jealousy by the House; I mean that called the Packet Estimate. In 1860-1 the House was called upon to vote on that account £1,069,000. I need not say that it is an Estimate upon which it is difficult to operate for the purpose of reduction, as the outlay takes place under contracts which endure for a considerable term of years; but the Estimate which we propose to submit in the present year does not amount to more than £883,000; showing a decrease of £186,000 during the last four years. I do not seek to attach an exaggerated value to these facts, nor do I say we should rest content with them; but I have stated them in order to correct a prevailing impression.

Now, Sir, it is I think desirable that the House should understand what has been the state of our expenditure during the last year in comparison with the expenditure of former and recent years. I will therefore take the expenditure as it appears in the Exchequer accounts, only placing to the debit of the proper years respectively the sums of money called "Excesses," which in those accounts appear under a later year than that to which they properly belong. Taking this view of our expenditure, I find it was in 1862-3, £69,302,000, and in 1863-4, £67,056,000; showing a decrease of £2,246,000. In 1861-2 the expenditure was £70,838,000, and the decrease, estimated in the same manner, would stand at £3,782,000. In 1860-1, when the charges on account of hostilities in China were very heavy, the expenditure was £72,504,000; and the expenditure of the year that has just expired, when compared with that sum, shows a decrease of £5,448,000. If, lastly, I go back to the year 1859-60, which may be called the first of our years of high expenditure, I find that in that year we spent £70,017,000; and the expenditure of 1863-4, as compared with 1859-60, shows a diminution of £2,961,000.

But in order to come more accurately at the state of this important portion of the case, it is necessary to take into view two circumstances. We must bear in mind, upon the one hand, that we have incurred of late years certain charges for fortifications; and, upon the other hand, that both our expenditure and our Revenue have included during the past year a considerable amount—not less than about £1,125,000 —which does not appear at all in the accounts of previous years. When I rectify the balance by the removal of those new charges appearing upon both sides of the account, and therefore forming no real part of the expenditure for the purposes of comparison, and likewise by the addition of the charge for fortifications, the account will stand as follows. In 1859-60 our expenditure was, as I have said, £70,017,000; and in 1863-4, fortifications included, it was £66,731,000; showing, therefore, a decrease, as compared with 1859-60, of £3,286,000.

I do not know whether I need trouble the Committee with a comparison drawn upon the same basis between the year 1863 and the intermediate years since 1859-60. Perhaps that would be laying before them figures that may be dispensed with, when I have quite enough of that commodity to present; and, therefore, I shall not enter into the particulars. But in order to exhibit the case with perfect clearness to the Committee I must not overlook this important element, that in the year 1860 we received, through the providence of our forefathers, the benefit of a very considerable relief from the annual charge of the National Debt. The permanent annual relief which we have been enjoying since 1860 is £2,146,000; but in the year 1859-60, owing to a peculiar arrangement, with which I need not now trouble the Committee, the charge on account of those Terminable Annuities, which ceased altogether in 1860, exceeded that amount. As I stated to the House in the Budget of 1859—and I need not now correct the statement — the charge in 1859-60 on account of Terminable Annuities was £2,540,000. Deducting that sum from the expenditure of 1859-60 for the purpose of comparison with 1863-4, and in

order to ascertain how we should have stood relatively if it had not been for that important relief, we find that the expenditure of 1859-60, independent of the charge for these annuities, was £67,471,000, as against £66,731,000 expended last year. That I believe to be a fair comparison. In this point of view the expenditure of last year, as compared with that of 1859-60, shows an absolute diminution of £740,000, independently of the relief obtained by the cessation of the Long Annuities. This sum of £740,000, although it is not a large one, is yet a sum worth taking into notice; and it is the more material because this is the first year in which I have been enabled to state to the House that, after allowing for the relief we have obtained by the cessation of the Long Annuities, our actual expenditure, including fortifications, has been less than was the charge in 1859-60.

I now come to compare the expenditure of the year which has just expired with the Revenue of that year. Here, of course, I refer simply to the Exchequer account; but I will endeavour to supply every needful explanation at each stage, so that, whatever figures I submit, the precise effect of them may be understood by the Committee. The expenditure of the year 1863-4, as it appears on the Exchequer account, is £67,056,000. The Revenue of the same year, as represented in the same account, is £70,208,000, showing a surplus of Revenue over expenditure amounting to the sum of £3,152,000. But, again, in order to estimate that surplus aright, we must take into view the expenditure upon fortifications; because, although the House has deliberately, and as a matter of policy, made a completely separate arrangement for dealing with that expenditure, yet, in point of law, it must appear upon the balance-sheet; and, in point of practical effect, we cannot exclude it from the account. The expenditure upon fortifications for the year has been £800,000; and if we deduct that amount from the surplus of £3,152,000, there still remains a surplus of Revenue over expenditure amounting to £2,352,000.

Perhaps the Committee will now desire to know in what degree the receipt of Revenue has corresponded with the anticipations which last year they were encouraged to entertain. Last year, with a view to greater precision, I restified, at the period of the Appropriation Act, near the close of the Session, the estimates which I had made in submitting the financial statement. I then put the Revenue at £68,171,000; the actual receipt has been £70,208,000. The surplus, therefore, of receipt beyond the anticipated amount of income is £2,037,000. More or less, that surplus appears in every branch of Revenue; that is to say, in all the heads of receipt which can properly be called heads of Revenue. The Customs, estimated at £22,737,000, yielded £23,232,000, or an excess of about half a million. The Excise, estimated at £17,624,000, actually produced £18,207,000; showing an excess of £583,000. The Stamps, estimated at £9,000,000, yielded £9,317,000. The Income Tax, estimated at £8,600,000, gave us £9,084,000; and there are surpluses of smaller amount upon the remaining items of Revenue, with one slight exception, to which I shall presently advert, under the head of China. So much for the general result. But further, I am aware that the House naturally looks with a peculiar interest not only to the aggregate, but also to the detailed receipt of the Revenue from Customs. Because, undoubtedly, whatever may have been the case with the Excise in former years, upon the whole the Customs must be taken as the branch of Revenue which now gives us the greatest number of significant criteria for judging of the condition of the people. The total estimated decrease upon the revenue of Customs last year, as compared with the previous year, when the tea duty had been levied at 1s. 5d. per pound, was £1,297,000. The actual decrease was only £802,000; and this, notwithstanding that the important article of sugar, including molasses, was affected by a partial scarcity, which became sensibly operative during the latter portion of the year. This article, therefore, instead of increasing with the improved condition of the country, has shown a positive decrease of £253,000. Again, there is another branch of Revenue, the decrease of which I always refer to with satisfaction; the Revenue which is derived from the duty upon corn. This item was less in the year that has just expired than in the year which immediately preceded it, by the sum of £225,000; and I need hardly stop to observe that this reduction bears happy testimony to the abundance of our domestic produce, and to the moderation of the price at which the first necessary of life was supplied to all classes of the community.

The article of wine exhibits an increase of £104,000, which I conceive to be, with reference to the recent change in that branch of Revenue, a very satisfactory increase. Spirits show an increase of £285,000, and tobacco an increase of between £200,000 and £300,000. The article of tea, which had been estimated to leave at the end of the year a loss to the Revenue amounting to £1,300,000, shows a loss amounting to only £930,000.

The excess of revenue from the Excise over the estimate has been large. It has been owing substantially to two causes. In consequence of the partial improvement in the condition of the country, the article of spirits—I mean spirits distilled at home—exhibits an increase of £250,000; and the important item of Revenue which we derive from malt, in consequence of the almost unparalleled excellence of the barley harvest, shows a greater receipt than was ever known before, and an increase upon the immediately preceding year of £710,000. That, of course, is not an augmentation upon the continuance of which, to an equal degree, we can count in future years; and the Committee ought always to bear in mind that the Estimate of Revenue from the Excise does not appear in the same relation now to the actual Revenue as it did before the malt credits were shortened. In former times, when it was the practice to give from six to eight months' credit upon the Revenue derived from malt, the malting of any given year supplied the revenue for the year following. The effect was that the Chancellor of the Exchequer, when he made his financial statement, knew the amount that was coming due to him, and was in a condition to inform Parliament what his Revenue from malt would be for the coming year. At present, he only knows about one half of it; and to that extent an element of uncertainty has been introduced into the Estimates annually laid before the House on this important and variable article, for which some considerable allowance must necessarily be made.

The only other item of receipt to which I think it right to refer is the China indemnity. The China indemnity was estimated at £450,000; the actual receipt is £435,000. We might have made it larger if it had not been that we have not taken the receipt up to the latest moment to which we might, perhaps, have taken credit for it; and that we have likewise made, under the auspices and through the medium of the hon. Member for Lancaster (Mr. Gregson), an arrangement with the merchants interested in the indemnity for the final liquidation of their claims, which is, I think, equitable to them and highly advantageous to the country, but which, inasmuch as it has brought on a final settlement with them at an earlier period than we anticipated, tends to diminish the receipt available at the moment for the Exchequer.

Sir, if I now proceed to compare the Revenue of the year which has passed with the Revenue of former years, it is because I think—and I believe the Committee will concur in that opinion—that, in the growth of the Revenue of the country, after making due allowance for the effect of any casual circumstances, and of all legislative changes, we have, upon the whole, a pretty sure test of the growth of its strength and its resources. I proceed, then, to compare the Revenue of this country for 1863-4 with that of the previous year 1862-3 as it stands in the Exchequer account; and the result is this :—that, although taxes of between three and four millions sterling were remitted last year, the decrease of income would appear to be no greater than £394,000. But such a statement would be, in some degree, delusive. It is necessary to allow for a considerable increase on the two last heads of our receipts, which ought not to be regarded properly as heads of Revenue for the purpose which I have just described; I mean that which is called the Miscellaneous Revenue, which is the 8th head of receipt, and also the China Indemnity, which constitutes the 9th head. Well, the Revenue for 1862-3, after deducting those two heads, was £67,850,000; and the Revenue of 1863-4, after making a similar deduction, stands as £67,173,000. There is, therefore, a decrease in the actual Revenue of the country in 1863-4, as compared with that of the year 1862-3, which may justly be stated at £677,000. But, Sir, when it is considered that the remission of taxes in 1863 was £3,703,000, and that the loss which was anticipated from that remission was £3,343,000, the actual loss being £677,000, it will be seen that the recovery has been no less than £3,026,000.

But now let us look back somewhat further, for the purpose of ascertaining the growth of the Revenue of the country not merely in a twelvemonth, inasmuch as the circumstances of a particular year

are liable to very considerable fluctuation in comparison with the year which may immediately precede or follow it, but during a longer period. We will then, if we go back to the year 1860-1; and I select that year because, since that period, we have laid on no new taxes; I do not speak of charges altogether insignificant, which may have been on the one side repealed and on the other side imposed; but I mean none that have a sensible influence on the account. We shall find, Sir, that the Revenue of 1860-1 showed a gross total of £70,283,000; and, after deducting the receipt of which I spoke — namely, the Miscellaneous, it was £68,830,000. But of this amount no less than £1,111,000 was due to Malt Credits taken up, which did not of right belong to the Revenue of the year. After we have deducted this sum, the Revenue of 1860-1 stands at £67,719,000. The Revenue of the year 1863-4, estimated in the same way, was £67,173,000, showing a decrease of Revenue since 1860-1 of only £446,000. But then, in that period, we have taken 3*d.* from the Income Tax, which withdraws from the Revenue £3,525,000; we have taken off the Paper duty, which may be taken to withdraw from the Revenue a gross sum of £1,340,000 ; we have reduced the Tea duty at a gross expense to the Revenue of £1,660,000; and we have repealed the charges on shipping at a cost of £143,000; thus showing a diminution of taxes to the extent of £6,668,000. I have omitted here to add to the list certain other and minor diminutions of taxes which I might have introduced, and which I place against some partial augmentations, also of a secondary character, that have been adopted by the House. The real diminution of taxes since 1860-1, but, of course, not including the legislation of that year— in fact, extending over a period of three years, from April, 1861, to April, 1864— has been £6,668,000. Against that sum we find that the Revenue has decreased by £446,000. The effect of these figures is to show that the increase of the Revenue from the same or from equivalent sources, in those three years, has been £6,226,000, or at the rate of about two millions sterling per annum. But then the year 1860-1, from which I have been measuring our progress, was a year of considerable depression. If I were to go back somewhat further and compare the Revenue of the year that has just closed with the Revenue of the year 1858-9, which is as follows:—

The total Revenue of 1858-9 was	£65,477,000
Or, deducting Miscellaneous Receipt.	2,126,000
The Revenue properly so called was	63,350,000
Revenue of 1863-4 as above .	67,173,000
Increase . .	3,823,000
Add, balance of taxes repealed over taxes laid on since 1858-9	2,703,000
Together	£6,530,000
Or, per annum	£1,306,000

But I will not now trouble the Committee with the details—the annual increment of the Revenue during those five years would appear not to be so great. As well as I can calculate it, it appears to me that since 1858-9 the Revenue has grown at a rate somewhat exceeding £1,300,000 for each year, taking one year with another. If, again, we go still further back—namely, to 1853 — and I do not go beyond that date, because it would be difficult for me to calculate with the requisite precision the effect of all the changes that were adopted in the years preceding that period—it would appear that since 1853 the Revenue of the country, always reckoning it as from the same or equivalent fiscal sources, has grown on the average at the rate of a full million sterling per annum. Even in the worst years of which I have, as Finance Minister, had to encounter the results—namely, 1860-1 and 1861-2, the annual increment of the Revenue was about £900,000. In better years, such as that which has now elapsed, it has been, as I have shown, nearly or about £2,000,000. And upon the whole— not necessarily for each particular year, but reckoning upon the probable course of events over a series of years—it is certainly no unsafe calculation that our Revenue, independently of additional sources of taxation, increases from its own proper and inherent vigour; that is to say, from the growth of wealth and population, as well as from improvements in the law, at a rate exceeding a million per annum. I do not venture, however, to expect that the rate of increase would be the same, were Parliament to hold its hand from the work of improving legislation.

Sir, having stated these particulars with reference to the Revenue of the country, I will now state the condition of our cash account, and our operations within the year touching the National Debt. The

balances in the Exchequer on the 31st of March, 1863, were £7,263,000. On the 31st March, 1864, they were £7,352,000. That is an ample but not excessive amount. With respect to the liquidation of debt within the year, it has been considerable. £1,000,000 of Exchequer bonds have been paid off; nearly £2,000,000—or, in precise figures, £1,994,000 — of Exchequer bills have been paid off; and, besides what I have stated, there have been redeemed, under the operation of the law relating to surplus Revenue, Exchequer Bills, and a very small portion of stock to the extent of £366,000. These sums taken together, make up a total of £3,360,000 out of the capital of the debt, liquidated within the year. Independently of this amount, it is only fair that the House should take into view the fact, that a very large sum has annually been paid in the shape of Terminable Annuities towards the liquidation of the debt. That portion of our annual payments for Terminable Annuities, which represents not interest but capital, is not less than £1,400,000 a year. And there are other payments of a minor description for the same purpose, which amount to £205,000. Therefore, our account for the Debt would, on the whole, stand as follows:—First, on the side of reduction. The total amount of the figures which I have given is £4,966,000. But then a debt for fortifications has been incurred, amounting to £820,000; so that the net approximate total sum which has been applied, from the proceeds of the taxes of the country, during the year, to the liquidation of the Debt, is £4,146,000.

Sir, the House was pleased last year, and as I think discreetly pleased, to give its sanction to a measure, or, indeed, to more than one measure, intended for the purpose of furthering and renewing that policy which aims at the reduction and extinction of the Debt by the conversion of Perpetual into Terminable Annuities. And I have to acquaint the House that in consequence of those measures we have during the last year converted Perpetual into Terminable Annuities to the extent of £433,000 per annum.

Next, Sir, as regards the huge total of the Debt itself, it is always interesting to the House to know what is the present state of the capital, and of the charge upon that capital, as compared with former years; because, although it may have been the opinion of some, or the caprice of others, that in consequence of our great wealth we might afford to look on the National Debt as a matter of trivial moment, I must say I never have been at all able to acquiesce in any such view of the matter, nor do I believe that it is generally approved by Parliament. The Debt of this country appears to me to be a very inflexible and formidable fact; grave and serious even in the midst of our wealth and prosperity; and likely to become still more grave and serious in its pressure if our prosperity should turn out to be less permanent and less stable than most of us are disposed to believe.

The actual capital of the National Debt at present stands thus. The stock (that is, the sum total of the Perpetual Annuities) amounts to £740,793,000. The book debts, by which I mean the capital sums repayable in money, not the mere redemption-value assigned to stock by Act of Parliament, are £37,645,000. Then there are Exchequer Bonds, £2,600,000, and Exchequer Bills £10,536,000. Thus, the total Debt is now £791,574,000. In the year 1853-4, which exhibited the lowest point that the Debt has reached since the close of the great Revolutionary War, it was £769,082,000. The Russian War, of course, produced an important change in these figures; and the Debt now stands at £22,492,000 more than it was in the year 1853-4. In 1856, immediately after the close of the Russian War, it stood at £808,108,000. It now stands, as I have stated, at £791,574,000; showing a decrease, since the last-named year, of about sixteen and a half millions sterling. In the year 1815, which gives the maximum point of the Debt, it was £861,039,000. At the present moment it shows a decrease of £69,465,000 from its amount in 1815.

Next as to the annual charge. In 1815 the annual charge was £32,646,000; in 1863-4 it was £26,211,000, showing a decrease in the amount payable from year to year of £6,435,000. And, therefore, we stand with a reduction of £69,465,000 in the capital, and of £6,435,000 in the charge of the National Debt, as the result of the efforts and experience of a great nation, of its Ministers, and of its Parliaments throughout half a century. But we also stand with a capital of £791,574,000 facing us in the future, and with an annual charge which still must remain for the present at between

£26,000,000 and £26,500,000. Nor must we omit to bear in mind that the half century, during which the measure of our exertions has been as above, was a half century following upon the greatest war of modern times, and one during which England has had far less participation in European conflicts than at any time during the last two hundred years.

Now, Sir, having heard this account of the state of the country as far as depends on its expenditure, its Revenue, and its public engagements, the Committee may wish to know what is the state of that trade and industry upon which our future prosperity and strength must mainly depend. The general state of the trade of the country is certainly of a vigour and strength that is surprising when we consider that it has been subject to such peculiar and serious drawbacks. The figures are indeed so enormous that they are almost staggering to believe. I will give them in the largest and simplest form for the years 1861, 1862, and 1863, and I will include in my statement of the exports of British produce the exports of foreign and colonial produce, of which this country has become more and more the entrepôt. In 1861 our imports were estimated at £217,485,024; including, however, an enormous importation of corn; in 1862 they were £225,716,976; and in 1863, the year when we were almost wholly deprived of the largest and most valuable of all our imports, the cotton of America, our imports stood at £248,980,942. Our exports of British produce stood for the first of those three years at £125,102,814; in 1862 their amount was £123,992,264; and in 1863 they rose to £146,489,768. Our exports of foreign and colonial produce for the first year stood at £34,529,684; in the second year they stood at £42,175,870; and in 1863 at £49,485,005. The total exports of the country in 1861 were £159,632,498; in 1862 they were £166,168,134; and in 1863 they were £195,974,773. The total movement of the foreign trade of the country, our imports and exports being taken together, stood thus:—In 1861 our total imports and exports were £377,117,522; in 1862 they were £391,885,110; and in 1863 they were £444,955,715. That astonishing sum I will only illustrate by these two statements; in the first place, it may be taken to be about three times the trade of the country as it stood at a period which I may call comparatively recent—namely, in the year 1842, when

The Chancellor of the Exchequer

Parliament first began deliberately and advisedly to set itself to the task of reforming our commercial legislation; and, in the second place, the sum may be taken to represent not far short, in round numbers, of £1,500,000 sterling for every working day in the year—a magnitude of industry and of operations connected with industry so vast that if it did not stand upon incontrovertible figures it hardly could receive belief. But, in my judgment, not only are these figures remarkable when we consider them as they exhibit the progress and energy of Englishmen, and as they prove the strength of that country, which is dear to all our hearts; they mean much more than this—though that, too, of itself, were much —they mean that England is becoming more and more deeply pledged from year to year to renounce every selfish view, and every scheme of violence or aggression; to be the champion of peace and justice throughout the world; and to take part, with no view to narrow or inferior interests, but only with a view to the great object of the welfare of humanity at large, in every question that may arise in whatever quarter of the globe.

Now, Sir, I referred but a minute ago to the year 1842, and stated that it was since 1842—since the commencement of the great work of Parliament with respect to commercial legislation — that these great results have taken place. I do not for a moment overlook the fact that other elements have been at work—elements of immense power and of immense utility; of such power and utility that there are some who think that the same effects would have been produced even if our commercial legislation had remained precisely as it was. ["Hear!"] I hear a solitary cheer from an hon. Member opposite, and I accept it as the proof of my somewhat paradoxical assertion. Well, Sir, it is a matter of great national and public interest—a matter of interest, let me add, to other countries as well as our own— that we should satisfy ourselves in some degree, and by approximate evidence, of the truth on this question. Now, I do not at all deny that other countries which have made changes comparatively slight in their commercial laws have likewise partaken largely in the benefits I have described, and have made great progress in trade and industry. I do not undervalue for one moment the great advantage of the vast powers of locomotion which have been set in action, and of many other causes which have co-operated to produce the astonishing development of modern commerce; but then I find—and here I take my stand on facts—take the evidence, at any rate, for what it is worth—I find that if I select several years in which Parliament has with firm and unsparing hand addressed itself to the business of liberating commerce, these operations have been immediately followed by striking augmentations in the trade and industry of the country. Whatever has been due to improvements in locomotion, to the electric telegraph, to cheap postage, to the progress of machinery, or to other like causes, the effect has, on the whole, been equally manifested from year to year. Allowance must, of course, be made for good and bad harvests; but still, if I find this feature meeting me on the examination of the case—that the legislation of Parliament in certain cases where it has been marked and comprehensive, has also been immediately followed by striking and great results — I think we may conclude that we have not been feeding ourselves by an empty dream when we have held, that in giving freedom to the energy, capital, and skill of Englishmen, we were adopting the true means of extending our commercial prosperity. I will only instance three years in which changes of that kind have taken place. In 1853 important changes of that description were made. The exports of British produce in 1852 had been £78,076,000. Now, recollect that 1852 was a year of great prosperity—a year of an excellent harvest, and of the cheapest capital ever known in this country. The year 1853 was a year of a bad harvest, but it was also a year of legislation in behalf of freedom of trade. Well, Sir, while the exports of 1852 were £78,076,000, the British exports of 1853 were no less than £98,933,000. In 1860 we had something of the same kind. The exports of 1859 were £155,692,000. Here I include exports of foreign and colonial produce; I could not include them in the figures 1853, because at that date there was no official standard of valuation in this department of our commerce. In 1859, as I have said, the British exports of all kinds were £155,692,000. The year 1859 was a prosperous year, and a year of a rich and abundant harvest; the year 1860 was a year of the worst harvest known for half a century; and yet our exports increased, even under these most unfavourable circumstances, from £155,692,000 to £164,521,000. In 1863, again, it was in the power of Parliament to grant considerable measures of relief, and the exports, which in 1862 were £166,168,000, rose in 1863 to £195,974,000. The general circumstances of the latter year were in this case more favourable than those of the former; but room is left for the operation of legislative causes too. Of course, I do not desire—I do not think it is possible—to lay down any such rule or dogma as to say that these figures, and no others, represent the precise influence of your legislation; but what they show is this, that there has been an essential and vital connection between the growth of the industry of the country.and the legislative process pursued within the last quarter of a century.

Now it is, I think, due to the interests concerned, and likewise to the feelings and opinions of the Committee, that I should refer to some of those particular subjects that have been dealt with in the fiscal and commercial legislation of recent years; with a view to show that we are not, at any rate, indifferent to the interests and complaints—if complaints there be—of those who think they have been hardly treated in the sacrifice of their particular interests to the general good. The first subject I will refer to is the long-contested, though in a legislative sense now settled question, with reference to the Paper duty. It is impossible for me to give a complete and clear view of the present condition of the paper manufacture; because we have lost the special means of information which at other times the Government possessed, and I can only attempt to present to the House facts which in themselves are fragmentary and partial, though they are indisputable as far as they go, and they may also, as I think, be considered satisfactory. It is said—with satisfaction on the one side, and perhaps with dissatisfaction on another side, but the fact is undeniable—that there has been an immense increase in the importation of foreign paper. The importation of foreign paper in 1859, the last year before any practical question had been raised respecting the repeal of the duty, was 18,000 cwt. In 1864 it has arisen to the enormous amount of 197,000 cwt. But although we have no means of judging conclusively, yet the official figures before us would lead us

to infer that there has not been, in consequence of that increased importation, any diminution in the production of British paper. At all events, we have before us the evidence which I shall now state. If we look to the rags and other materials for making paper which are imported into this country, and if we deduct from these figures the quantities re-exported in each year, the figures stand thus. In 1859 we imported materials for papermaking to the extent, according to a strictly drawn official statement, of 115,000 cwt., and in 1864 we imported, of the same materials, no less than 731,000 cwt. And here let me say that whatever pressure or distress may have existed at home, yet there has been a positive increase in the amount of British paper and paper goods exported. By paper goods I mean chiefly paper hangings. In 1859 the amount of paper and paper hangings exported amounted to 115,000 cwt., and in 1864 the amount had increased to 190,000 cwt. Of quality I cannot speak, but about the same quantity of paper of British manufacture was exported as the quantity of foreign paper imported into this country. Then comes the question of price. Now, the price has been very greatly reduced. The price of paper has been reduced by an amount even exceeding that indicated by the duty. In 1859, taking printing paper, which is, perhaps, the fairest test, the price of printing paper was 6½d. to 8½d. per lb.; in 1864 the price ranges from 4¼d. to 6¼d. per lb.:—so that, in fact, six farthings of duty having been taken off, the reduction in price has been from seven to nine farthings per lb.; and the fall in the price of writing paper, of which I need not trouble you with the particulars, has been almost equally great. There is another very curious result, although I do not say that the fact is sufficiently developed to enable us to come to a positive conclusion regarding it. I am very far from representing, as I will show by-and-by, that the state of the papermaking trade is at present one of the prosperity in which we should all desire to see it, because it is affected—and I think and hope affected for the time only, by very serious drawbacks; but the figures I have given up to the present moment, like those I am about to give, even if they be liable to any construction different from mine, yet they are, I believe, unquestionable as matters of fact. Now as to the number of paper manufacturers. There was a good

The Chancellor of the Exchequer

deal of good humoured banter in this House, at the time when rather sanguine expectations were formed, that the manufacture of paper being, from the atmospheric conditions it requires, very suitable for rural districts, upon the repeal of the duty there would arise a large number of rural paper mills. All of us must remember how much was made of that topic; but it is one on which I have for three years abstained from opening my lips. Nor am I going now to present any very highly coloured picture of the state of things. But there is, at least, before us this rather remarkable circumstance—that the diminution in the number of papermakers, which was steadily and rapidly going on as long as the duty existed, may now be said to have ceased. The papermakers of this country in 1838—excluding a small number of cardboard manufacturers, who, although they paid the same license, were not exactly papermakers—numbered 505; in 1848 the number was 427; in 1858, 366; in 1859, 365; in 1861, 364; and in 1863, 360. Therefore it is the fact, as far as it goes, that the number of papermakers in this country, which before had been rapidly declining, has since the repeal of the duty, notwithstanding the presence of foreign competition, and notwithstanding other causes operating severely upon the trade, been very nearly a stationary number. There has been another circumstance which I admit has been a peculiar disadvantage to the manufacturers. The paper trade was in no small degree dependent upon the cotton trade for its material; and the consumption of paper used for the purpose of packing in the export of cotton goods was enormous. And you must recollect that while the value of our cotton goods exported, being, from their almost doubled price, very high in amount, may tend to diminish the apparent loss of trade, yet the dear cotton goods require no more paper for wrapping than the cheap cotton goods; and therefore a large demand for paper has, since the repeal of the duty, and from causes quite unconnected with that repeal, been very greatly reduced. This is quite independent of the further fact, that the papermakers have suffered greatly in the withdrawal of an important element in the supply of materials—the refuse of cotton and cotton rags upon which they formerly depended to a very considerable degree. But what is really the case of the papermakers? Is it not the same case to which, one after an-

other, almost every branch of British industry has been subjected? They grew up under the influence of protection. Protection, in a greater or a less degree, unnerved their energies. They adopted, or were content to depend upon, imperfect and wasteful methods of manufacture; and when the protection, which had thus beguiled them into security, was by Act of Parliament withdrawn, considerable suffering ensued. That suffering gradually threw them back upon the exercise of their invention and skill. The restorative process next commenced, and after a short interval every one of those branches of industry, I believe with scarcely more than a single exception, has become more healthy, more vigorous, and more profitable than before. May not the case be the very same with the makers of paper? I am now going to give the House one single case of what has happened in the paper trade, the facts of which are supplied to me by a gentleman who is himself engaged in the trade. He is a partner in a mill which has been erected and set to work since the repeal of the duty. He has not authorized me to make use of his name in the House, but he has authorized me to say that, if the facts are doubted, he is willing to communicate in confidence with any hon. Gentleman who may entertain such doubts. His statement is this. His mill is almost a new one. For the four months ending October 31, 1863, he found that he made his paper at a cost of £57 per ton, and that commodity, made at such a cost, did not pay him. He did not complain; he joined in no agitation for the re-imposition of the paper duty, or for other purposes, equally unattainable; but he and his partners set themselves to work to see what could be done by improvements in the processes of manufacture and by the more skilful and economical use of chymical agents, so essential in the manufacture of paper. The results, as they have been told me, were surprising indeed. In October, 1863, the firm had produced paper, as I have said, at a cost of £57 per ton. In December they produced at a cost of only £47, and at the present moment they are producing at a cost of £39 per ton; and this gentleman declares to me that the article now produced is better than what he produced last summer for £57 per ton. For my own part, I cannot say I believe that the condition of the paper trade essentially depends upon the laws of foreign countries, with regard to the export of rags. Those laws, no doubt, form an element, and no unimportant element, in the case of the papermakers: but I am convinced they would be ill-advised if they were taught to depend upon anything but their own energies. In the case of no other trade have we consented to look to the legislation of foreign countries as a guide for our own. Our system of freedom in trade is a system which is grossly unjust unless it is uniformly and universally applied. It would be monstrous to say to any branch of industry or class of British producers, "We will expose you to foreign competition," unless we likewise say to them, "All you want at home we will take care you shall have on terms of perfect equality as far as our own laws are concerned, and on the best terms that we can get for you as far as relates to the laws of foreign States." That is the principle of justice, and to that length the Government goes with the papermakers. We lament that Foreign Governments should maintain restrictions of any kind upon the export of raw material. No doubt, it is an element in the case of the papermakers, and to those who have been accustomed to depend upon it, for the moment at least, it is a very essential element. Therefore, it is with great satisfaction that I say we are expressly authorized to hope and believe that concessions will be made by the Government of France in this particular, by a favourable change in the export duty now levied on rags in that country.

I go next to a very important question —the question of the Spirit duties. The Committee will be aware how important that question is when I remind them that, not from strong liquors taken as a whole, but from the single article of what is called "ardent spirits," we are enabled to raise nearly one-fifth of the entire Revenue of the country. It will be in the recollection of the Committee that in the year 1860 the duty upon spirits was raised to the very high point of 10s. per gallon. Anticipations were then expressed that, although there must necessarily be a considerable diminution in the consumption, yet, from the augmentation of the duty, there would be a considerable increase in the Revenue. That increase has not been so great as was expected. The question at once arises—to what cause is the partial failure due? Whether it is due to smuggling? or to a change of taste? or

The Chancellor of the Exchequer

to distress? or lastly, to the operation of the duty? But, whatever may be the cause, I wish to point out to the Committee that those persons are in error who imagine that the augmentation of the duty has been unaccompanied by an increase of receipt. In point of fact, a considerable increase in the Revenue has been obtained from spirits; and I think the policy upon which the House adopted that measure was this—that in respect to this particular article it is our business to derive from it the largest possible amount of Revenue, without the same regard which we pay in other cases to the encouragement of the manufacture, or to augmented consumption. The Revenue arising from British and foreign spirits for the financial year 1859-60 amounted to £12,301,000. That has been stated in a Return made at the instance of my hon. Friend the Member for Stamford (Sir Stafford Northcote). But I perceive that the Inland Revenue Department has very properly explained, in that Return, that the Revenue of 1859-60 includes a large sum which was due to what I may call the premature delivery of spirits from bond, in the month of February, 1860, when an expectation prevailed that the duties upon spirits were about to be increased. The effect of that was that about £340,000 was received, and went to the account of 1859-60, which really belonged, according to the best calculation that can be made, to 1860-1. The impression that has gone abroad, that no increased Revenue has yet been derived from British spirits, is due in some degree to this, that the circumstance to which I have referred has been overlooked. Now, when we allow for that anticipation, the real Revenue for the year 1859-60 must be estimated, for the purposes of comparison, as follows:— First of all, deduct from the duty received on British spirits in that year, the sum of £340,000; and secondly, deduct also from the receipt of that year on foreign spirits, a further sum of £225,000, in consequence of the great diminution which near the end of the year 1859-60 was enacted by Parliament in the duty on foreign spirits, and in particular in the duty upon French brandy. The corrected total of the Revenue on foreign, colonial, and British spirits for 1859-60 for the purpose of comparison with the Revenue for the present year will then stand at £11,756,000; namely, on British spirits

£9,458,000, and on foreign and colonial spirits £2,298,000 ; making together £11,756,000. In 1860-1 the Revenue, from the three sources together, was £12,168,000; in 1861-2 it was £12,267,000; in 1862-3, when the Lancashire distress had reached its utmost intensity, it fell to £12,102,000; and in 1863-4, when the distress had partially abated, it rose to £12,638,000. So that the real state of the question, considered as a fiscal question, is no other than simply this : the Revenue of 1859-60, properly belonging to the year, may be taken at £11,756,000; and in 1863-4 it is £12,638,000, an increase in the receipt from spirit duties above the amount at the former period reaching the considerable sum of £882,000. Now, Sir, this being a question of great interest, I have sought for the means of throwing light upon it. Why is it that the Revenue from spirits has not risen more largely still ? Is it owing to smuggling, to distress, or to change of taste? It is not owing to smuggling. The evidence on that subject, I think, is clear. It is quite true that in Ireland at this moment there is, in consequence of the very low price and condition of the oat crop, an increase of smuggling as compared with the three preceding years; but it is not true that there is an increase in smuggling, even in Ireland, as compared with what it was when the duty was 8s. a gallon. Is then the shortcoming to be ascribed to distress? We have tolerable means of judging whether distress has operated in this matter or not; because the circumstances of the three countries, as connected with the consuming power, have materially differed during the last four years. Ireland has, unhappily, been afflicted with a succession of bad harvests. The harvest of 1864 was better, not, perhaps, as regards the seller, but as regards the consumer of agricultural produce ; but the three previous harvests had been lamentably deficient. England, at least, in one great focus of consumption of this kind—in Lancashire—has suffered in a peculiar degree. Scotland, having but a small cotton trade, and having had its industry in a generally flourishing condition, may be said hardly to have suffered at all. Now, it is curious that the spirit Revenue of the three countries has varied in the precise proportion of their distress, thus represented. In England the Revenue may be said to have been stationary since 1859-60. In that year it was £4,341,000. In 1863-4 it was £4,390,000, being an increase of £49,000, or about 1 per cent on the total amount. In Ireland, where the pressure of distress has been greatest, the Revenue in 1859-60 was £2,685,000 ; in 1863-4 it had sunk to £2,322,000 : that is to say, there was a reduction of about 14 per cent on the whole, which may be mainly accounted for, not only by the gradual change of taste which operates in all the three countries, but by the special distress under which Ireland has been labouring. In Scotland, where the pressure of distress has been much less felt—I do not know whether hon. Members from Scotland may take it as a compliment or not, but certainly the Revenue from spirits has increased in a manner not at all unsatisfactory, considering the nature of the changes that have been made in it. In 1859-60, although unduly swollen by premature deliveries, it was £2,973,000, and in 1863-4 it was £3,332,000, showing an increase of upwards of £350,000. This may be considered a very satisfactory result—as a result pretty fully answering to the computations made when Parliament reduced the duty. But in truth another cause besides distress has been at work, and it is one the operation of which we must contemplate with satisfaction. The truth is that a great change of taste is going forward, which is not to be indicated by one circumstance or another, but by careful comparison of an aggregate of facts, and by a multitude of observations. There is a very steady process, and a very happy process in operation—a gradual translation of taste from stronger and more ardent liquors to milder and more wholesome liquors, and we cannot understand what is going on with reference to the spirit duty unless we keep that essential element in view. But I am glad to say that, as far as distillers of spirits are concerned, although they have had a considerable diminution of home demand, an export trade is rapidly creating itself. Some ten or twenty years ago the quantity exported was very trifling. In 1859, however, the export trade had risen to 1,941,000 gallons; and in 1863 it had risen to 4,071,000 gallons. If I am correctly informed, the Scotch distillers, in addition to a tolerably liberal supply for home consumption, put forth the energy and sagacity usual with their countrymen, and have vindicated to themselves a considerable portion of this export trade.

With respect to wine, the figures stand

as follows:—In 1859 the quantity of wine imported from Portugal was 2,106,000 gallons; in 1864 it reached 2,669,000 gallons; showing an increase of somewhat over 25 per cent. The wine imported from Spain is, however, apparently more in favour than the Portuguese wine. In 1859 the quantity imported was 2,884,000 gallons; in 1864 it had risen to 4,799,000 gallons, or there was an increase of about 70 per cent. The wine imported from France in 1859—the last year before the change of duty—was 597,000 gallons; in 1864 it was 1,965,000 gallons, showing an increase of 230 per cent. As regards the import of wines from other countries, which are generally made up of light qualities, the quantity in 1859 was 577,000 gallons, and in 1864 it was 1,184,000 gallons; so that there was an increase of over 100 per cent. The import of colonial wines alone has largely decreased, distinctly proving that nothing but the bounty—a bounty perfectly artificial, extravagant in amount, and totally unreasonable in principle—a pure endowment in effect, taken out of the pockets of the people of England — was really the principal basis of the trade in the colonial wines of the Cape which formerly came to this country. If the wine trade can extend by natural means, and on the footing of equal advantage in the Colonies, by all means let it do so. But my opinion is, that even in those colonies the climate of which is best adapted to the growth of wine, the rate of labour is much too high to enable those communities to apply with profit any considerable portion of their strength to this peculiar manufacture. On the whole, the increase in the consumption of wines of all kinds in this country is most satisfactory. In 1858-9 it was 6,974,000 gallons, and in 1863-4 it was 10,729,000 gallons; showing an increase of about 55 per cent. I ought to add that the figures which I have given for the financial year 1863-4 are not precisely accurate as regards units or hundreds of gallons, but for every substantial purpose they are sufficiently to be relied on.

There is another subject which I wish to mention to the Committee, because it was the subject of legislation during last year, and is also a subject of fiscal and of much commercial importance. I mean the subject of the Tobacco duties. During the last year an Act was passed for the purpose of reconstructing our system with regard to the duties and drawbacks on

The Chancellor of the Exchequer

manufactured tobacco; the joint objects being to diminish smuggling, to increase trade, and to augment the Revenue; and I think the Committee will be of opinion that where those objects can be satisfactorily combined, the result is one well worth having. As regards the effect upon those descriptions of tobacco which were formerly smuggled, the case, up to the present time, stands as follows. The descriptions of tobacco which were most largely smuggled into this country were cigars and Cavendish. Of cigars imported legally from abroad in the eleven months from April, 1862, to February, 1863, there were 2,316,000 lbs. The cigars imported in the corresponding eleven months of 1863-4 were 3,976,000 lbs.; thus showing a very large increase in the legal trade. With respect to Cavendish, the manufacture of which in this country had been previously prohibited, but which was allowed by the Act of last year to be manufactured in bond, six manufactories have been since established by way of a commencement of the trade. But the increased importation which I have described of the foreign manufactured article has not been attended with a diminution of the manufacture of tobacco at home; for, whereas it appears that in 1863 there were entered for home consumption, that is to say for home use, after manufacture in one form or another, 35,735,000 lb. of raw tobacco, in 1864, after the duty had been lowered, and after the British manufacturer, I may add, had been put through his usual paroxysm of apprehension and alarm — after the usual announcements had gone forth that several hundreds and thousands of workmen, employed in the tobacco trade, were about to be dismissed, if they had not been actually driven out destitute into the streets, instead of 35,735,000 lb. in the year preceding the change, the British manufacturer entered for consumption in the year ending March 31, 1864, 36,590,000 lb. And he is even beginning to have some hope or glimmering of an export trade; for, whereas in six months of 1862-3 the exports amounted to only 50,000 lb., the quantity exported in the same period of 1863-4 was 123,000 lb. Lastly, I am happy to say that, as regards Revenue, the results of the Act are very satisfactory. This duty has long been a growing duty. About 1843 it was deemed that the smuggler had got the better of the Revenue Department. But his triumph, if it was real, was only temporary. Smuggling has been kept, comparatively at least, within bounds from that time to this; while I trust now that it is in the way of being more than kept within bounds, and that it will be greatly reduced. The average annual growth of the Revenue from tobacco in this country for twenty-one years, beginning with 1842 and ending with 1862, has been £105,000. But last year, when the change of duty was adopted, I am glad to say that the increment of our receipt rose from an average of £105,000 up to £290,000.

Lastly, Sir, the working of the change in the Tea duties, which was made last year, has up to this time been entirely satisfactory. Our consumption of tea was, in the financial year 1857-8, 77,069,000 lbs. In 1862-3, it had only risen to 77,437,000 lbs. But in 1863-4, it has been 90,362,000 lbs. As regards Revenue, the receipt from tea was in 1862-3, £5,485,000. In 1863-4, it was £4,554,000. In other words, whereas I estimated that the loss from the reduction of duty would be £1,300,000, it was only £931,000. As respects price, it may be stated in general terms, that the consumer has had the full benefit of the change; and the price in bond is now lower than in February, 1863, by from 1*d.* to 3*d.* per lb.

Now, Sir, the House will be glad to be informed in a few words what is the position of our trade with France. In the year 1859, immediately before our Treaty of Commerce with France, our imports from that country amounted to £16,870,000. In 1863, they had risen to £24,024,000. Our exports to that country in 1859—I will not go into details about the proportion of foreign and colonial goods included in this Estimate—were £9,561,000. In 1863 there had risen to £22,963,000. I am very glad to say that the French manufacturers are beginning to discover the futility of their alarms, just as the traders of this country have so frequently found it by experience on their side. And at this moment the French spinners of flax, who were in such a state of apprehension when my hon. Friend the Member for Rochdale (Mr. Cobden) was negotiating the French Treaty, have become exporters of linen yarns to this country, and have sent cargoes of that commodity to the port of Dundee, amounting during a part, and a part only, of last year, to £500,000. With all this, I may remind the Com-

mittee that the pauperism of the country, excluding the pauperism of Lancashire, which is of an exceptional and temporary character, has not only not been stationary, but has actually decreased since the year 1848-9. In that year the total number of paupers, indoor and outdoor, was 981,330; in 1863-4 it was 828,320. In 1848-9 there were 61 paupers for every 1,000 of the population. In the year 1863-4 there were 46 in every 1,000. In other words, in the former year there were 939 of working population out of every 1,000 of the community, and in the latter year there were 954 persons of a working and self-supporting population out of every 1,000 of the community.

Such is the general state of things as regards the year 1863-4, through which we have just passed.

I now come to the Estimates for 1864-5. We find that the charge for the Funded and Unfunded Debt may be taken at £26,400,000. The increase which appears in this charge is owing to the operation of the measures, to which I have recently referred, for converting Perpetual into Terminable Annuities. The Consolidated Fund charges, other than those for the Public Debt, amount to £1,930,000. The Estimates for the Army are £14,844,000, and those for the Navy, £10,432,000. But the latter will probably be subject to a certain amount—not a very large amount—of increase on account of a plan now under consideration for improving the condition of some classes of officers and men in the Navy. The collection of the Revenue is estimated at £4,692,000, and the Packet Estimates are £883,000. The Miscellaneous Estimates may be taken for present purposes at £7,628,000. It is probable that will not ultimately be the precise figure; and I have made a reserve of £80,000 for any variation, in the way of increase, which may occur in the Navy and Miscellaneous Estimates taken together. The total estimated expenditure of the country for 1864-5 will, therefore, stand at £66,890,000; that is an amount lower than the estimated expenditure of 1863-4 by £1,393,000, and lower than the actual expenditure of that year by £166,000; but it is higher than the estimated expenditure of 1858-9—which is the last year before we come to the years of a very high expenditure—by £2,226,000; or, if we correct the comparison by debiting ourselves with the amount of the Long Annuities, which we have saved, and also the expenditure for fortifications, but deducting £1,125,000 which now appears on both sides of the account, but did not so appear in 1858-9, there is an aggregate increase of £4,047,000. I am anxious to draw the attention of the Committee to these figures, because they may be taken as a fair statement of the actual, present, and still remaining growth of our expenditure since the time when we returned from the Russian war to a peace establishment.

I now come, Sir, to the estimates of the Revenue for the year; first, I take the Customs at £23,150,000; secondly, the Excise, at £18,030,000; thirdly, the Stamps at £9,320,000; fourthly, the Taxes, £3,250,000; fifthly, the Income Tax, £8,600,000; sixthly, the Post Office, £3,950,000; seventhly, the Crown Lands, £310,000. That is the whole of the Revenue properly so-called. For the eighth head, that of "Miscellaneous Receipts," we estimate a sum of £2,250,000; and the last or ninth head is that of Indemnities: the estimate under this head is £600,000, of which £500,000 is from China, and the other £100,000 we have already received from Japan but have not yet brought to account. These sums make up a total estimated Revenue of £69,460,000, and an estimated expenditure of £66,890,000, leaving a probable surplus of income over expenditure of £2,570,000.

Sir, among the proposals which the Government are about to make, there are several which have no very great bearing on the Revenue, but to which I may call attention, first, to put them out of the way of the more material question as to the manner in which the substance of the surplus is to be dealt with. Perhaps the Committee may be surprised when I commence by saying, that we propose to submit to Parliament a plan for altering the present duty on corn. The duty upon corn is now levied by measure, while almost all transactions, I believe I may say all, connected with the foreign corn trade, are carried on by the rules of weight. In consequence of this discrepancy, and the inconvenience resulting from it, the merchants connected with the corn trade made representations to the Government, I think about twelve months ago, in order that the mode of levying the duty might be altered. Accordingly, we propose to change it from an uniform rate of 1s. a quarter, to an uniform rate of 3d. per cwt. This change will take effect immediately on the passing of the Act. It is not necessary that it should take effect before. We also propose that lentils and two or three other articles of small importance which now pay no duty, should be put upon the same footing as corn; as it is the opinion of the trade that there would be some convenience in such an arrangement. I ought further to mention it has been proposed by some persons connected with the trade to modify the duty on corn in a more important degree; by laying a duty of 3d. per cwt. on wheat only, and of 2d. per cwt. on other kinds of corn. It has been very justly stated that this would be a fairer arrangement, having regard to the value of the article on which the duty is imposed. But there are two reasons which have withheld the Government from adopting it. One is that it would cause a considerable loss to the Exchequer, which we do not think the Government, after taking other claims into view, are now in a condition to afford. But another reason is this—that it would appear as if we were deliberately setting about the construction of a regular system of corn duties; as if we regarded duty on corn as a permanent portion of our finance. That in my opinion would be wrong. When the great change in the Corn Laws was proposed in 1846, this duty was imposed as a nominal duty; but it has produced a considerable Revenue which it has not been found convenient to part with heretofore, and I am not prepared to say it would be prudent to part with it at the present moment; but I confess, on the other hand, I should be reluctant to see Parliament committed to any plan which might appear to assume that a duty of this kind on corn—not a very heavy impost, but still something more than a nominal one in amount, and one which in principle it would be difficult to defend—should be regarded as a permanent imposition upon the greatest article of human subsistence among us.

Next, Sir, I purpose to make a change, which I hope will be agreeable to the House, in the charges paid for licences by dealers of tea in certain cases. It is well known that these licences operate with stringency in some cases; I mean especially in rural districts, where the trade of the shopkeepers is exceedingly small, and where they are obliged to combine a great number of branches in order to constitute a business that will yield a remunerative return. Now, no person in a village or hamlet can sell tea without paying a licence duty of 11s. 6d. It is supposed that this rate of duty amounts to 10 per cent on a sale of from 30 lb. to 35 lb. of tea in the year; and it will be seen that such a change may tend to narrow the supply of the commodity to the rural populations, although it is not felt as an obstruction in the towns. I think it would be good policy even if we are to put it on no other ground than the furtherance of the great change adopted last year, to make a reduction upon that duty with regard to all the more thinly populated districts. We therefore propose in all houses under £10 a year rating, and not being in a municipal or Parliamentary borough, to reduce the duty from 11s. 6d. to 2s. 6d. We calculate that this reduction will cause a loss to the Revenue of about £10,000.

Two years ago we adopted some useful regulations with regard to hawkers. We legislated with respect to hawkers on foot and hawkers having one horse. We reduced the duty from £8 to £4 for one horse; but we overlooked the case of hawkers with two horses. The result is that a hawker with two horses pays £4 on one horse and £8 on the other. We propose to place both horses on the same footing.

We propose also to modify and reduce the stamp duty now payable on admission to ecclesiastical benefices of small value. At present there are two rates. There is a rate for rectories and vicarages on the one hand, and a rate for perpetual curacies on the other. There is no ground for that distinction. We propose, therefore, to abolish it. Perpetual curacies will henceforward be charged like rectories and vicarages. The scale of duties now in force imposes an uniform rate of £7 upon presentation and institution together to all benefices of less than £300 a year. In lieu of this uniform charge, we propose a scale of duties, which will diminish gradually from the £7 rate down to the value of £50, under which rate there will be no charge whatever for stamp duty.

Next, Sir, I have to announce with pleasure to the hon. Member for Devizes (Mr. Darby Griffith), that I cordially agree to a proposal which he has suggested, and which I think is founded on good sense and practical utility. It is this: that the duty on proxies to vote at the meetings of Joint Stock Companies, which heretofore has been 6d., and which some years ago was as high as 30s., should be re-

duced to 1d. Joint Stock Companies are assuming a character and function of vast importance in the commerce of this country. It may be, indeed, that they are at the present moment extending their character and function—I hope it may not be so—even beyond what properly belongs to them. But they are at all events coming to be essentially and permanently so important, that it is worth the while of Parliament to give every facility in its power to enable the members of these companies to exercise an effective control over their management.

Besides these changes, I propose also to make a certain reduction in the duties upon letters of attorney for the receipt of dividends; and to make a change in the stamp duties upon settlements, the effect of which will be the removal of a singular anomaly, to this effect—that, as the law now stands, a settlement including foreign coin, and shares and stocks in foreign companies, is not liable to any stamp in respect to that foreign property. It appears to me that that exception is improper and absurd, and I propose to place all such property on the same footing with other property. We likewise propose to declare the law with respect to the liability of policies of Life Insurance to the stamp duty. I propose also to legalize the practice, universally established practice, although now an illegal one, of what is known as marine re-insurance. That, I believe, is a practice almost essential to the conduct of Insurance Offices; still it is not allowed by the law; and we propose to legalize it on the payment of a shilling stamp, as is now done in the case of Fire Insurance. Lastly, Sir, I propose to extend—of course under the control of the magistrates—to refreshment houses and sellers of beer the benefit of what are called occasional licences for the sale of the commodities in which they deal, just as it is now enjoyed by publicans.

Last year, Sir, as it will be remembered, the Government made a proposal with respect to the taxation of charities. As I shall be silent, or, at least, as our proposals will be silent, upon the subject this year, I do not wish the Committee to lie under the impression that there has been any change of views on the part of the Government. Certain directions have, however, been given by the Secretary for the Home Department for the collection of information, which will be laid before Parliament, but which is not yet fully in our

possession. That information, we think,
will tend to enlarge such means of judgment as Parliament already possesses, and
will be useful at the time when its attention shall be again directed to the subject.

With the insignificant exception of the
sum of £10,000 for tea duties, I reckon
that these minor changes, which I have
briefly and somewhat hurriedly gone over,
will leave the surplus pretty nearly as
it stood. Deducting this £10,000 from
the surplus of £2,570,000, we still have
a surplus of £2,560,000 upon which to
operate.

And now, Sir, as regards the disposal
of that surplus. The present year is one
which has produced an unusual number of
formidable claimants for the appropriation
of the surplus. Relying on the kindness
and patience of the Committee, I shall
endeavour to deal fairly with the most
important of these cases, or, at least, with
such of them as I think it will not be possible to pass over. As regards the first, and
likewise the largest, of the operations we
propose, there is no reason why I should
keep the Committee in suspense. I do not
think that when the matter is seriously
considered apart from prejudice, apart from
interest, and apart from any promise or
pledge, there can be any doubt as to the
first claim upon the surplus. In my clear
judgment, and in that of all my Colleagues,
the first claim is that of the article of
Sugar. I need scarcely remind the Committee of the enormous importance of
that article to trade and to consumption.
I believe that in its importance, in reference to the comforts of the people, it may
be said to stand next to corn. I believe
it may also be said with probable truth
that, next to the subject of corn, the question of the sugar duty is, to the mass of
the people, the question of the liveliest
interest. That duty was raised for the
purposes of war; it was readjusted after
the peace, in the year 1857: but the principal part of what had been imposed with
a view to the exigencies of war, has never
been removed. We have had at various
times claims either more urgent, with reference to the general wants of the people, or offering promise of greater public
advantage to follow upon remission or reduction; but I know of no such claim at
the present moment. We propose, therefore, to the Committee, to make a considerable change and reduction in the
sugar duties. There is but one considerable objection to the measure, as far as I

The Chancellor of the Exchequer

am aware; and that is, that at the present moment we are labouring under what
may be called a quasi-scarcity in consequence of diminished production and increased price. At the present moment
there is an increase which may be stated
at from 8s. to 10s. per cwt. over the prices
of 1863. That is a considerable augmentation; and the increase is about 6s. per
cwt. above the price of 1861-2. Perhaps,
we may say that the last named sum
represents the excess of price at this period
above the fair average level of prices. I
wish, however, to present this observation
to the Committee; that in the case of sugar,
we can hardly say that the existence of this
partial and relative dearness is simply a
reason for refraining from legislation. In
a case like that of tea it might be so, because in the case of tea, in the first place,
you are dependent upon one source of supply, and in the next place you are yourselves the great consumers of the world,
exceeding all other consumers in so great
a degree, that what you can hope to draw
over from other quarters by giving peculiar inducements in your own market at a
given moment would be a comparatively
small supply. But that is not the case
with regard to sugar. Our consumption,
vast as it is, is comparatively small with
reference to the total consumption of the
world. Sugar is produced in a multitude
of countries, it is sent to a multitude of
markets; and the consequence is, that if
at a particular time the supply be diminished, an alteration in our law, made at
that particular crisis, is likely to have the
effect of attracting to the markets of this
country a large quantity of sugar which
would otherwise find its way to other
countries, and consequently of mitigating
any inconvenience we might feel from
scarcity. It may also be said that increased
price has already in great measure done
its work and very considerably restrained
consumption; and that, consequently, the
stock in bond, on which we have to draw,
offers to us a prospect by no means unsatisfactory. On the last day of February,
1862, the stock of sugar in the country was 1,707,000 cwt.; in 1863 it had
risen to 2,038,000 cwt., and in 1864 it
was 2,272,000 cwt.; so that, as regards our
supplies in hand, we are actually in excess
over preceding years, and it is only what
is known with respect to the late crops
which makes us apprehend that, on the
whole, we cannot look forward to an abundant provision.

I come now to the subject which is the most formidable part of my task this evening. I have said that we propose to deal with the sugar duties. But how are we to deal with them? There arises here a question which is grave in two senses—it is grave in the sense of being important, and it is grave, also, I am afraid, in the sense of being irremediably dull. The question, whether sugar is to be taxed by uniform or classified duties, is one of great fiscal moment, and also of great importance to an immense amount of trade and breadth of cultivation throughout the world. I am bound, therefore, to treat it as thoroughly and conclusively as I can. On the other hand, it is a subject which, as to details, abounds, I may say, in every element of repulsiveness. It is bad enough to talk about "muscovado," "treacle," and "molasses;" it is a great deal worse to be immersed in "Dutch numbers," "glycose," "tehaur," and "jaggery;" and such is the technical phraseology of the sugar trade. I will endeavour to avoid it as much as may be practicable and to state intelligibly the views of the Government on the subject.

At present, Sir, we have in form a system of classified duties upon sugar; approved by many, a scandal and offence to many others. Now, I am not able to deny that this system of classified duty appears to have been the gradual growth and product of experience. When the sugar market of this country was the monopoly of the colonial producer, we had a system of uniform duty. That system of uniform duty was gradually modified and departed from in proportion as improvements in this manufacture were introduced; as our market was opened to all the sugars of the world; and as we found that we had to deal with a multitude of varieties and classes of sugar, of which previously little or nothing had been known. Neither again am I able to say that this system of classified duty has been condemned by our experience of its practical working. Let us look at the consumption of sugar per head of the population. In 1841—which was, however, a period of relative scarcity — the consumption of sugar in this country amounted to no more than seventeen pounds per annum per head. In 1851, when there had been a change to a period of almost entire free trade, the consumption had risen to 26¼ lbs. per head. In 1861 we had been for ten years under the operation of this classified system, but Parliament had not had it in its power between 1851 and 1861 to give the consumer any such signal and decisive boon as it had conferred between 1841 and 1851; yet the growth of consumption had by no means stopped, but it had increased from 26¼ lb. in 1851, to 35¼ lbs. in 1861, and in 1863—although that year was, as I have stated, a year of comparative scarcity—it had increased to 35¼ lbs. per head.

Neither can it with truth be said that the system of classification has been condemned by authority. I speak in the presence of my hon. Friend the Member for Rochdale (Mr. Cobden), who, among living men, on a question of free trade, has not only a right to be heard, but to be heard among the very first. He has been manfully challenged by his constituents—I am revealing no secret now, but only repeating what I have seen in the newspapers—and he has answered them like a man. A portion of them make an appeal to him to be the champion of uniform duty as a thing required by the principles of free trade. His answer is to the effect that, in his opinion, *ad valorem* duties, or an approximation to that method such as we have in the case of sugar, is not in point of principle to be condemned. I say in point of principle, because in the application of that principle to practice, there are several considerations which must govern our proceedings.

Again, Sir, on questions of this nature the authority of *The Economist* newspaper is one which carries great weight among the most intelligent and instructed commercial classes. That journal has taken the side of classification. But I shall not attempt to describe by reference what I may call the literature of the subject. It has been perfectly enormous. To keep abreast of that literature, I laboured and struggled as long as I was able; and I thought — I conscientiously believed — until within the last fortnight, with something like success. Up to that time, I believe, I had conscientiously fulfilled the duty of making myself acquainted with the whole product of the press of the country, so far as the sugar duties are concerned; but at last I was compelled to abandon the attempt. I have, however, had the advantage of seeing the very able publication of Professor Leone Levi, of King's College, who without being, as far as I am aware, actuated by any bias on the subject, distinctly gives judgment in favour of the principle of a classified duty on sugar. Speaking in this House, however, I may now allude to an authority on the question, to which it will perhaps be deemed more to the purpose that I should refer. Two years ago a Select Committee was appointed on the Motion of my hon. Friend the Member for the City of London (Mr. Crawford). That Committee was constituted with great care. It was presided over, on the part of the Government, by my right hon. Friend now the Secretary for the Colonies (Mr. Cardwell); and that Committee, after a patient and impartial investigation of the question under their consideration, pronounced distinctly in favour of the present system of classifying sugars for the purposes of duty. Nor is even this all; for last year we had what may be called an international discussion on the subject. Chosen officers from the Customs and commercial departments of the European countries most interested in the sugar trade—namely, England, France, Belgium, and Holland—met in Paris to discuss the matter, with especial reference to the systems of drawbacks in use in the several countries; and not only did the representatives of England find no reason to recede from our system, but the representatives of France, and also, I think, the representative of Holland, actually came to the conclusion that they would do well to abandon the system of an uniform duty, and come over to the system of classification. Therefore, Sir, so far as authority is concerned, there is, I think, a very considerable mass on the side of the system now embodied in our law.

I admit, however, Sir, that authority though it is a considerable element in the case is not the only nor even the main consideration which should guide us. Let us turn, then, to argument. And here we are told by those who recommend uniform duty, that classification is protection; while on the other hand the West Indian colonists says, "No, classification is not protection, but uniformity is protection." Well, according to the old proverb, "Give a dog a bad name, and hang him," it is, I confess, somewhat satisfactory to find that, at this time of day, we have nothing to do but to fasten on any doctrine the name of "protection," in order to demonstrate to any reasonable man that we have fastened upon it the worst and most conclusive condemnatory charge to which any

The Chancellor of the Exchequer

plan can possibly be open; so much so, indeed, that no man will have the courage to defend a legislative proposal under such a stigma. But there is another argument against classification, which purports to be drawn from the analogy of our tariff, and the mode in which we deal with other articles. It is said, "You never dream of imposing different duties on different qualities of tea, and why should you do it in the case of sugar?" The fact, however, is that we did impose different duties on teas of different qualities, and that we abandoned that system, not because it was false in point of principle, but simply because, from the nature of the commodity itself, the principle was found inapplicable in practice. But is it true that uniformity of duty is the general characteristic of our tariff? That tariff, I am happy to say, now reaches only to such moderate dimensions, that it is not easy to produce very numerous instances of the soundness or unsoundness of the view taken upon the one side or the other with regard to this point. The instances, however, although few, are nevertheless almost all distinctly in favour of classification. The wine duty is a rude and partial and very far from being a consistent approximation—but still in a degree it is an approximation—to a duty on value; for there can be no doubt that, upon the whole, the light wines consumed in this country are much cheaper wines than the stronger. Take, as a clearer example, the case of coffee; when it comes here in its raw state it pays a duty of 3*d.* per lb.; when roasted the duty is 4*d.* per lb.; and this instance is particularly applicable to the case of sugar, because the differences between different sugars is little, if anything, more than a difference in the degree of manufacture; yet we are told that if we impose a greater duty on sugar in its more manufactured state, we depart from the analogy of the tariff, besides being guilty of the high crime and misdemeanour of protection. Again, what do we do with respect to cocoa? When the pure raw material comes into our market we lay upon it a tax of a farthing per lb.; but when it has gone one stage further, and the husk is removed, the charge is raised to 1*d.*; when it has made a further advance, and reaches the condition of cocoa paste, we tax it at the rate of 2*d.* per lb. The duty on corn is a shilling a quarter, and we are now about to levy upon it 8*d.* a cwt.; but on flour, which is simply corn manufactured in part, and rid of a certain portion of refuse, we impose 4½d. per cwt. There is also the case of wood; the raw material, the tree as it is cut, pays a shilling a load, but let it be sawn up into planks before it comes here and it pays 2s. a load. These things being so, it will, I think, be seen that the analogy drawn from the tariff is completely in favour of the system of classification.

Let us now look at the plans proposed, and endeavour to judge them by their respective merits. Sir, I know that the Committee has a peculiar aversion to deal with any question in respect to which there are three courses which it might be possible to follow. I am extremely glad, therefore, to be able to say that in the present instance there are not three but four courses, so that I am thus relieved from a great dilemma. The plans suggested are these :—One is to have two rates of duties, the first on refined sugar and the second on unrefined. Refined and unrefined, however, are not the only categories with which we have to deal, because both those descriptions come under the head of solid sugar. There is besides these a class of sugar which, in unscientific language, may be specified as liquid, and which comes hither under the title of either " melado " or " molasses." There are those who say, " Let us have one duty for refined, and a second for unrefined solid sugar; with a third duty for liquid sugar." But that does not accord with the doctrine of uniformity. Another plan is to have one rate of duty only on refined and unrefined sugar, but still to have a second rate for liquid sugar. Neither does this plan in any manner satisfy or give effect to the arguments for an uniform duty. A third plan is, to have one rate of duty only for both solid and liquid; and the fourth is to adopt a system aiming at an approximation to value, upon the principle of the existing system, but without adhering altogether to its details. Now, I beg to throw overboard, in the most ruthless manner, the two first of these plans. It appears to me that the advocates of an uniform rate have not—to use a homely phrase—" a leg to stand on " when they draw a distinction between refined and unrefined sugar. I am confident that the proposal to compound together all classes of unrefined sugar, but still to recognize a distinction between them at a particular moment when the article becomes, what

we chose to call, refined, cannot be upheld in argument, or in practice. I reject in the same way the distinction sought to be drawn between solid sugars on the one side, and liquid sugars on the other. When it becomes the interest of a man to narrow and confuse the line between these two classes, the only difference being that the one contains more moisture than the other, you will not be able to mark the distinction between them. All sugar contains some moisture. One principle governs the whole matter. Any distinction drawn must be purely arbitrary, and could not possibly bear the stress we should have to lay upon it, if we were to adopt this form of legislation. If we are to have a uniform duty, it must be upon the footing of a principle which will cover alike the cane juice as first expressed from the cane and the refined sugar consumed at the breakfast or dinner-tables of our families. The question, therefore, simply lies between a really and rigidly uniform duty on the one hand, and a classified duty on the other, founded on the principle of the present scale. How, then, do we deal with the point at issue? I deal with it in the first place by making an admission. I do not contend that the present scale is a perfect one. Nor do I adopt the principle on the authority of the Select Committee. Though authority is in favour of the principle of the present system, yet, if the weight of argument were the other way, the Government would not, I admit, be justified in sheltering themselves under that authority. But, moreover, it is to be borne in mind that it was pointed out by the Committee that the existing scale operated unjustly at two points. It constitutes, as they think, an almost prohibitive duty on the lower descriptions of sugars which may come here to be refined for consumption; and it operates severely, also, on the higher descriptions of unrefined sugar which come from the Mauritius, the East Indies, and elsewhere. Again it has been suggested that the difficulties of the case may be ultimately met by giving permission to refine in bond. I do not know how that is. But, for the purposes of the present discussion, I put aside altogether the question of refining in bond.

In endeavouring to grapple practically with the subject, I think we ought to come to the resolution that no class interests ought to govern the adjustment of the question; and I further admit that, although there would be certain difficulties connected with the system of drawbacks in the event of our adopting a uniform rate of duty, yet those difficulties may not be of sufficient weight to call upon us to reject that principle, if in other respects we should come to the conclusion that it was sound. The general proposition which I lay down, and which I invite the Committee to proceed on, is this—that the form of our duty should be such as will least interfere with the natural course of trade, and be the least open to the charge of offering to the producer or manufacturer a premium on doing something different from that which he would do if there were no duty at all. Now, let us try on that principle how we are to proceed. I am quite willing to accept in general terms the doctrine laid down by the Manchester Chamber of Commerce, and in which, I may add, that the Liverpool Chamber of Commerce have concurred. I received the other day an address from the Manchester Chamber of Commerce, to which was attached a name distinguished in the annals of free trade—that of Mr. Henry Ashworth—and which I think contains sound doctrine on this question. It says—

"Your memorialists are most desirous that the duties on sugar should be fixed at as low a rate as possible, and that in the interests of the consumer no impediments should be opposed to the importation of any class of sugar, from the very lowest quality to the finest loaf sugar; and in order that no one class of persons should be protected at the expense of another, it is, in the opinion of your memorialists, needful that the duties be assessed upon the article in proportion to the amount of crystallizable saccharine matter which it contains."

I believe that that is a sound principle, inasmuch as it indicates the main basis of just legislation, which should, in our opinion, take the amount of crystallizable saccharine principally for its rule. Now, let me try the case by an example; and here I will, for once, introduce one of those barbarous and outlandish words to which I have referred, namely, "jaggery," which signifies the lowest description of sugar made in the East Indies. Let us suppose that there are in the market of the East Indies, at a given moment, 2 cwt. of jaggery, each of which contains 50 per cent, not of saccharine matter, because in saccharine matter they will perhaps not differ very much from other and far better sugar, but of what is called crystallizable saccharine matter; that is to

The Chancellor of the Exchequer

say, saccharine matter of a description that can be profitably extracted by the refiner, or what I would call extractible sugar. These 2 cwts. will, when refined, yield, without including the minor products of the refinery, 1 cwt. of sugar. The question is, who is to manufacture the article, the refiner in India, or the refiner in England? The sugar is, by the supposition, just as it has come from the cane and undergone the first process; the point for our decision is, how are we to adjust our law in such a way that we shall, by means of the duty, give no inducement to any man to refine in England rather than in India, or in India rather than in England? That, I think, is a fair way of stating the case. Now, what will the Indian refiner do if we have an uniform duty, which we are told is the way to do justice and to avoid the scandal of protection? The Indian refiner buys these 2 cwts. of jaggery, refines them, and sends the refined sugar to this country; and if the duty in this country is 10s. a cwt., he pays 10s. for the introduction of his 100 lb. of refined sugar. What is the British refiner to do? He buys these 2 cwts. in India on the same terms as the Indian refiner. Very good. He sends them at a greater expense to England. With that greater expense we have nothing to do. We must not undertake to reimburse him for a single farthing of it. It is his affair, not ours. But when he has brought his 2 cwts. here, that he may refine them, he has to pay 10s. duty upon each. So that while the English refiner, to get his 100 lb. of sugar into the market, has to pay 20s., the Indian refiner sends it in for 10s.; and yet we are told that that is the way to do justice and escape the stigma of protection.

Now, Sir, our sincere, impartial desire has been to consider the question entirely without prejudice; but there is no doubt what the operation of such a duty as that would be. It would be simply equivalent to a bounty approaching more or less nearly to 10s. a cwt. upon refining in India, as against refining in England. And it might be that, although from the dearness of skilled labour, the dearness of capital, and the dearness of machinery in India, refining in that country might cost some shillings, say 2s.—say, if you like, 5s.—a cwt. more than in England, it would still be worth a man's while to refine in India rather than send the sugar to be refined in this country, because of the heavy fine imposed upon him by our fiscal law. That is the view which Her Majesty's Government take of the matter. We are not willing to give any premium for the employment of labour and capital in England rather than in India; but certainly we are not willing to be parties to imposing a penalty upon the employment of labour and capital in England, as compared with India; and this it is which would in our view be the effect of an uniform duty. We have therefore sought to amend the duty in general conformity with the principle laid down in the memorial of the Manchester Chamber of Commerce.

The present duties upon sugar—I reject for a moment the liquid or semi-liquid classes, which it is not at this moment necessary to keep in view—the present duty upon sugar is distributed into four classes: refined sugar, which is charged 18s. 4d. per cwt.; white clayed, 16s.; brown clayed, 13s. 10d.; Muscovado, or below brown clayed, 12s. 8d. And here for a moment I must make a further reference to what are called "Dutch numbers," because, although that may be speaking in a foreign tongue before a general audience in England, yet the Dutch numbers are, in point of fact, the only universal language of the sugar trade of the world. If you tell a man of any nation what your duty is according to the Dutch numbers, that statement is construable into the trade terms of every tongue, and he knows exactly on what qualities of sugar your duty of any given amount will fall. Our "refined" corresponds with the best of the Dutch numbers, the highest of which is 20. It includes numbers 19 and 20. The "white clayed or equal to white clayed" corresponds with the numbers from 15 to 18 inclusive; the class which we describe as "brown clayed and equal to brown clayed" corresponds with the numbers 11 to 14; our class, No. 4, "not equal to brown clayed," corresponds with the Dutch numbers 7 to 10; and nothing under 7 can, I believe, ordinarily pay the duty which we now impose.

In proceeding to revise the scale thus established, we have, in the first place, had to consider whether it was desirable for us to alter essentially the present dividing points between these classes. There are four classes, and there are, therefore, three dividing points. Those dividing points have not been fixed with reference to any abstract principle. They

rest upon knowledge and experience, and they are now pretty well understood—at any rate, as well as they are capable of being understood—all over the world. We have, therefore, thought that it would be very undesirable to recast the duties *in toto*, and to establish a completely new set of distinctions. Consequently, we adhere to the dividing points between the classes which are now established; but we meet the grievance of the better unrefined sugars by diminishing the intervals of duty at the upper end of the scale; and we meet the grievance of the lower class of sugars by establishing a new class at the lower end of the scale, with a lower rate of duty than the rest, for the purpose of making those sugars practically admissible which are now excluded. The drawbacks, of course, will have to be altered in proportion to the duties. I should say also, with regard to a collateral point of some importance, that in order to make this change fair as it affects the refiners, we shall propose to postpone the reduction of the duty upon foreign refined sugar for four weeks from the present day; whereas I hope that, if the House is disposed to accede to our proposal, and should think it reasonable to proceed upon this day week with the Resolution relating to sugar, the new law will be generally in operation as early as on Saturday week.

I will now, Sir, proceed to give the new scale of duty:—Refined sugar, instead of 18s. 4d., will, if our proposal be adopted, stand at 12s. 10d. per cwt.; white clayed, or equal to white clayed, instead of 16s., at 11s. 8d.; brown clayed, or equal to brown clayed, instead of 13s. 10d., at 10s. 6d.; Muscovado, instead of 12s. 8d., at 9s. 4d.; and a new class will be constituted for inferior sugars, corresponding with the Dutch numbers under and up to No. 6, which will be liable to a duty of 8s. 2d. The duty on molasses will be 3s. 6d. per cwt., and that on melado 6s. 7d. The effect of these changes I will describe as well as I can. At present, the interval between "brown clayed" and "refined" is, I think, the chief subject of complaint. It is so great that it certainly does, in our judgment, somewhat disturb and divert the natural course of trade. It is now 4s. 6d. a cwt. We reduce it to 2s. 4d. The fifth class provides for the low sugars now excluded. The smallest reduction we make upon any description of sugar is 3s. 4d. a cwt., the largest

5*s*. 6*d*., the average is over 4*s*.; and although it is very difficult to compare classified duties which do not run upon precisely the same terms, I think I may say that the effect of this change will be to reduce the duty on sugar to 1*s*., or to more than 1*s*. per cwt. beneath any point at which it has stood before during the present century. Finally, Sir, I have to add that we propose to make the sugar duty the subject of a permanent Act, and to leave the tea duty leviable from year to year.

I will now state to the Committee what I think will be the financial result of this plan. The Revenue from sugars for 1864-65, as we estimate it, would, if left without alteration, amount to £6,555,000. The reductions of duty, as I have stated them, will cause a first loss of £1,719,000; but, allowing for the entry of sugars that are now practically excluded, and taking credit for an increase of consumption amounting to 6 per cent, which I think is a moderate estimate, £361,000 of that sum would be recovered, and the loss to the Revenue in twelve full months would be £1,358,000. Again, however, allowing a trifling sum for the fraction of a year which has passed, I take the net loss for 1864-5 at £1,330,000. That, as the Committee will see, has reduced my surplus from £2,560,000 to £1,230,000. So much for the question of sugar.

And now, Sir, I come to a subject which, considering the circumstances of the time, it is impossible for Her Majesty's Government, whatever their view of it may be, to pass by without notice. I allude to the demand which has been made for the reduction or repeal of the Malt duty. That is a subject of very great importance. It involves a Revenue of about £6,000,000, and its reduction by one-half would, in the first instance, involve a loss very considerably larger than the great reduction which I have just proposed upon sugar. Now, Sir, I do not disguise the fact, that this has become a question apparently of great political importance. A great victory has recently been won in Hertfordshire. A gentleman I believe highly competent not only to take a share in our proceedings, but even to adorn this House, has failed to obtain a seat in Parliament because he was not ready to accede to the demand for the repeal of the Malt duty. The successful candidate, if we may rely upon

The Chancellor of the Exchequer

the declarations ascribed to him, saw no difficulty in the way; and on the list of his committee appeared a name most highly and justly respected in this House, the name of a person of great political influence, that of my right hon. Friend the Member for Hertfordshire, Secretary of State for the Colonies in the late Administration, (Sir Edward Bulwer-Lytton). A Motion from the opposite side of the House has also been hanging over our heads, and is now only for a short time suspended, which declares that the Malt duty has a paramount claim on the consideration of Her Majesty's Government, with a view to remission or reduction. Now, Sir, I do not suppose the Committee would allow us to keep that surplus of a million and a quarter, which I have named, in our own hands. Are they disposed to give it to the malt duty? [Several hon. MEMBERS: No!] I am very much obliged to my hon. Friends who said "No," for relieving me of that portion of my labours. But I wish, at the same time, seriously to say—because it is a serious matter when the country is agitated on a question of this kind, and when prospects involving such an amount of financial change are held out to persons and classes who believe themselves to be deeply interested—that it is desirable we should ascertain whether these are prospects of which it is reasonable to expect the fulfilment, or whether they are wholly of a visionary and delusive character. It is commonly said that if you reduce the malt duty one-half there will be little or no loss. But, Sir, it is, unfortunately, part of my duty to defend all taxes; and I find myself constantly confronted with a corresponding assertion. It is a most convenient assertion for a man who demands the reduction of a tax. He gives his opinion, and I give mine; I think mine is the best, and he adheres to his own; but there is no mode of settling the question between us. If, however, Parliament adopts the change, and it is followed by a great loss, no one is responsible, which is not satisfactory to the public, nor advantageous for the general welfare. In the case of malt, however, we have fortunately some means of determining whether a reduction of one-half in the amount of the duty will or will not entail a loss to the Revenue; because a reduction, not precisely of one-half the malt duty, but sufficiently near that proportion for my purpose, took place when the removal of the beer duty was sanctioned. The removal of the beer duty was adopted not only because it was a moiety practically of the whole tax, but I imagine also because, apart from the inequality of its imposition, it may have been thought to be the most burdensome moiety. A period of no less than thirty-five years has elapsed since the beer duty was removed; and although last year the malt duty exceeded by £700,000 the amount levied the year before, to this hour the malt duty has not replaced to us the loss of the beer duty. In 1829, the last year of the beer duty, the joint produce of the two taxes was £7,286,000. The malt duty for the last year was £6,091,000, and the average of the malt duty might, perhaps, be stated at about £5,500,000. So that, having taken off practically about one-half of the malt duty, after the lapse of thirty-five years there is a gap of a million and three-quarters not yet filled up. I ask, after finding such a state of facts, can it be maintained that little loss will be felt, even at the first moment, if we again reduce the malt duty one-half? No, Sir, the case stands far otherwise. If you choose to take that step, you may tell your little children now growing up that the longest lived among them may witness a recovery of the duty to its present figure ; but pray give up the idea of ever seeing it yourselves within the term of your natural lives.

After all, Sir, as I conceive, I am not here to defend the malt duty specially; whether as a tax, or as an excise tax, I have no peculiar love for it : but in looking at the claims of various interests to remission, we must look at their comparative grievances. What is the grievance of the grower of barley ? Has free trade been a severe infliction upon him ? It is not here, as in the case of the paper-maker, who is knocked down and put under sharp suffering before he gets on his feet again. The grower of the fine barleys in this country is possessed almost of a natural monopoly. He has had no pressure at all to undergo. He cannot move our compassion by pointing to decreased and still decreasing prices for his commodity. What was the price of barley before the abolition of the Corn Laws ? From the time when the sliding scale began, and averages were taken under that law—that is to say, from the period from 1827 to 1846—the average price of barley was 32s. 6d. ; and

for the seventeen years since the repeal of the Corn Laws the average had been 33s. 11½d. Even that statement hardly represents the case, because the rise established has not I apprehend been in fact so much a rise on bad barleys, as on the good ; and if I could separate the good from the bad I should probably be able to show you that the growers of good barley who are now so obstreperous for relief, are the very men whose produce has most increased in value. [" No, no !"] Well, then let it simply stand that the whole of them have increased in price; and my belief is that the position of the grower of good barley is the most favourable of all. Let me, however, carry the elucidation one point farther. The years which have elapsed since the repeal of the Corn Laws include a few years when the mind of the country was possessed by uncertainty and panic of such a character that the transactions of those years hardly form a secure test; but if I were to take the last eleven years, from 1853 to 1864, the average price of barley would be no less than 36s. 1d., or 3s. 7d. a quarter more than for the twenty years preceding the alteration in the law.

I have another point to mention ; one of considerable interest, and the only point I shall call attention to in further vindication of the intentions, or non-intentions, of the Government as regards the malt duty. I always feel comparatively at my ease when I can legitimately refer to considerations which, besides appealing to such broad sentiments of nationality and patriotism as we all entertain on behalf of the country at large, induce English, Scotch, and Irish gentlemen to bear in mind, not the selfish interests, but the fair respective claims of each of the three countries. The question of the malt duty has never been laid before the House from that point of view, and, in my opinion, it is high time that it should be so presented. When the hon. Member for the North Riding (Mr. Morritt) or any one else, proposes to surrender five or six millions of Revenue, derived from the malt duty, let us reflect how that proposal will bear, if it should be adopted, on the interests of the three countries, and how the amount of relief will be divided between them.

If we take together the Revenues received into the Exchequer from spirits and from malt, we find that England pays

£10,500,000, or about 10s. per head of its population; Scotland pays £3,620,000, or about 22s. per head; and Ireland, though unhappily not so wealthy as either of the other two countries, pays £2,653,000, or 10s. per head; Ireland, in fact, pays almost exactly the same proportion that is paid by England. What would be the effect of giving away these £5,000,000 or £6,000,000 of malt duty? It would be a distinct boon to England, and the gap created by it must be filled by means of general taxation on the three countries. Scotland and Ireland, while obtaining hardly any appreciable relief, would be of course liable to pay their fair share of any augmented Income Tax, or of any other tax you might choose to impose for the purpose of meeting the deficiency. The malt duty paid by England in the financial year that has just expired was £5,722,000; by Scotland, £263,000; and by Ireland, £300,000. Scotland and Ireland pay their strong liquor tax, and pay it largely; but they pay it in the shape of the duty upon spirits, which the hon. Member has not proposed, and which I hope the House would not consent, to reduce. But the fact stands that his proposal would, in its operation, be egregiously and grossly partial. And if the hon. Member for the North Riding will accept a friendly suggestion from me, I advise him before he makes the Motion of which he has given notice, and which I have no doubt he will submit to the House with great ability, and evidently with most powerful and influential support, well to digest the figures which I have now given with reference to the relative bearing of the malt duty upon the three countries. Her Majesty's Government, not insensible to the evils attending on the application of a system of Excise to any manufacture, have notwithstanding come to the conclusion that they would not fulfil, but, on the contrary, that they would be betraying their duty to the country under the circumstances in which we stand, if they were to apply any part of the limited surplus at our command to the reduction of the malt duty.

There is another question that it is my next duty to bring under the view of the House; it is the question of the Income Tax. For this is not only the largest subject in amount of Revenue upon which it is in the power of any Minister of Finance to address Parliament, but it is for other reasons by far the most impor-

The Chancellor of the Exchequer

tant. It is the most important, because it is associated with the strength and security of the country in times of emergency, in a manner that belongs to no other tax, and because it involves social questions touching the relations of class to class and their relative susceptibility of taxation, and moral questions—especially in their relation to certain Schedules of the tax—which are of a moment far transcending the topics that bear on ordinary questions of taxation. It is, in fact, a subject so large that it might be made the foundation not only of a particular proposition, but even of a policy. Now, Sir, it is, I think, beyond all dispute that the country ought to be dealt with fairly and plainly on the subject of the Income Tax. The country ought to consider and Parliament ought to decide what course it will take. Will it maintain the Income Tax at its present level? will it abolish the tax altogether? or will it reduce it in amount? Will the Legislature consent to regard the Income Tax as an instrument of ordinary finance, for the satisfaction of ordinary purposes; or will it decline to employ it in times of peace, and in the absence of great national emergencies, except it be for the special purpose of effecting further reforms in its general financial policy? These questions have all, perhaps, been mooted from time to time: but they have never been definitely decided by Parliament. In 1842 the Tax was proposed with a view to commercial reforms. In 1845 it was renewed with a view to further commercial reforms. In 1848 it was renewed, on the proposition of my right hon. Friend the Secretary of State for India (Sir Charles Wood), in a time of considerable public apprehension, though not perhaps of absolute danger, but it was renewed only after he had consented to make a great abatement from the rate at which he originally proposed to revive it. In 1851 Parliament refused to renew it, except on the appointment of a Parliamentary Committee which was appointed to inquire into all its bracings and into the possibility of entirely reconstructing it. In 1853 it was renewed for the longest period that Parliament has ever granted the Tax, upon a statement of figures and upon calculations which at the time appeared to me, I confess, as they also appeared to others, to afford a reasonable promise of its extinction. In 1860 it was again renewed, and even raised, for the purpose of meeting the necessities of the country in connection with its establishments for defence, but likewise in the same spirit in which it had been originally conceived, and with a view of carrying boldly onwards the great work of commercial reform. Since 1860 Parliament has taken no definite Resolution on any question of policy connected with the Income Tax; but it was well content last year, on the proposition of the Government, to reduce the rate from 9*d.* in the pound to the same rate at which it was originally imposed—namely, to 7*d.* in the pound. These things being so, we find ourselves, in fact, at the point at which we stood in 1842 in reference to this matter. The questions, however, which I lately mentioned, are questions on which Parliament ought to have an opinion. It is not desirable that they should be disposed of in an indirect or equivocal manner, or that the Income Tax should creep unawares into perpetuity; that it should be continually dealt with simply by renewals from twelvemonths to twelvemonths, founded on and perhaps sufficiently justified by the exigencies of the moment, but having no reference to policy, and announcing to the country no clear, distinct, and decided views on the part of Parliament with respect to the proper mode of dealing with this great instrument of taxation.

There are many arguments, without doubt, which may be urged in favour of the permanent maintenance of the Income Tax as a source of ordinary revenue. Its efficacy is enormous; and I do not know any tax by which in the same degree as by the Income Tax you would be able to get at the vast reserved incomes of the country. You get at them, it is true, unequally and roughly, for you refer it, in a large majority of such cases, pretty nearly to the conscience of each taxpayer to decide what his standard of payment shall be; but still you get at them, and in a greater degree than by any other engine of taxation with which I am acquainted. On the other hand, the House is aware of the stringent mode in which the Income Tax operates on the lower class of incomes, though its effect in that way was very much mitigated by the measure adopted last year for the deduction of £60 from incomes below £200. And, no doubt, those who desire to see the permanent maintenance of the Income Tax have reason to congratulate themselves on the ope-

ration of a plan which relieves the impost of much of the hardship with which it pressed on the lower classes of incomes. Nevertheless, it is indisputable that the tax still bears severely on small fixed incomes, on what may be called the non-elastic incomes of the country. It is also unquestionable, that it imposes a serious burden on the taxpayer in the shape of time, trouble, and annoyance; especially I am afraid in a year like this, when the new assessments are made. It has been my disagreeable duty in this House to perform the invidious task of deprecating the complaints of Members who complain of the injustice involved in the way in which this tax falls on many of their constituents; and I have done so, not because I do not sympathize with those who so complain, but because I know that much annoyance and trouble are inseparable from the ordinary operation of the tax at the period when the year arrives for the renewal of the assessments. The evil of inquisition into private affairs is a serious one; and the use of a war tax in time of peace, by which a portion of our last reserve is expended, are subjects well deserving the notice of the House. To the opinion of the inequality and injustice of the Income Tax which is maintained by some, and of which my hon. Friend the Member for Buckingham (Mr. Hubbard) is, perhaps, the most ardent champion in this House, I do not accede; but it cannot be denied that that opinion is widely spread among many large classes; and such a conviction or impression, prevailing so widely, is no doubt, a matter to be considered in reference to any means of taxation. As to fraud, it is needless to enter on that topic; it is a sad and perplexing subject, and I am afraid that the extent to which encouragement is given to fraud through the imposition of the Income Tax is evil of the most formidable kind, and of an extent which it would be difficult to measure. But there is one operation of the Income Tax which I cannot help frankly stating to the House, and that is its operation with respect to public economy. That is a topic which I do not think has been fully, or perhaps ever, discussed in Parliament. An experience, which I may now call long, in the office which I have now the honour to hold, and the necessity of placing myself in conflict at all times, by day and by night, in all places and all circumstances, with every sort of demand for increased public expenditure, have brought me by steady degrees very nearly to a grave conclusion on this subject. My growing belief is, that if it is the desire of the House to see re-established in public administration those principles of reasonable thrift—I do not speak of wholesale changes or wholesale reductions, in which I have little faith—but those principles of reasonable thrift which directed the Government of this country from about the period of the Duke of Wellington's Administration until the time of the Russian war, it is most questionable whether that object can be accomplished compatibly with the affirmation of the principle that the Income Tax is to be made a permanent portion of the fiscal system of the country, with the view of satisfying, not the particular exigencies of the moment, or of working out particular reforms, but of satisfying the ordinary every day expenses of the nation.

But now, Sir, it may be said, "Why all this idle talk about economy? Have you not declared to us the wealth of the country? Have you not shown the enormous development of our trade?" Yes, I have; but I hold this opinion as a matter of principle — that public economy now remains just as much the bounden duty of this House as it was before we commenced our commercial legislation, or reaped the benefit of our vast railway system, or before the country achieved the vast material, and the considerable social and moral progress, of which we are now the rejoicing witnesses. For, in the first place, it may be said that in this country you have still and will always have an enormous mass of paupers. Just now I read, amid the cheers of the House, the statement that our paupers are reduced in number to somewhere about 840,000. That amount, however, does not include persons who are dependent upon charitable establishments; or who are relieved by private almsgiving; but only comprises those who are driven to the last necessity of resorting to the poor-house. And surely even the reduced number which I stated is a great, aye, an enormous number. But, besides all those whom it comprises, think of those who are on the borders of that region — think how many of the labouring classes are struggling manfully but with difficulty to maintain themselves in a position above the place of paupers. I saw but yesterday a clergyman whose

The Chancellor of the Exchequer

sphere of duty is laid in the east end of London; and he told me that he had the charge of 13,000 people, of whom 12,000 were ever on the verge of actual want. I read but last week the letter of a philanthropist well-known in this country, in which he said—and, I believe, said with perfect truth—that there are whole districts in the east end of London in which you cannot find an omnibus or a cab, and in which there is no street music, nor even a street beggar. What shall I say with respect to Ireland? When we think of the population of Ireland, and when we hear the Members from that country rise in this House and complain of the bearing of unequal taxation, not because they object to bear their fair share of taxation, but because they say, and they see, that the taxes press too severely on the country of whose interests they are the special and chosen champions, there surely remains no room for doubt that it is our duty to practise public economy. Again, and yet more at large, what is human life, but, in the great majority of cases, a struggle for existence; and if the means of carrying on that struggle are somewhat better than they were, yet the standard of wants rises with the standard of means, and sometimes much more rapidly, and it does not follow that because you have made additions to the means of subsistence and comfort of the people of this country, that you can safely cease to care for the supply of other wants which demand your consideration. Happily, much already has been done. In many places wages have much increased, though in many other places they have not. Had we, however, achieved much more than all that has been done, ample room would still remain, and ample necessity for public thrift. If this be doubted, need I say that we have authority in our favour, independent of general argument. Two years ago the House of Commons wisely assented to the following Motion, proposed by the noble Lord at the head of the Government:—

"This House, deeply impressed with the necessity of economy in every department of the State, is at the same time mindful of its obligation to provide for the security of the country at home and the protection of its interests abroad, and observes with satisfaction the decrease which has already been effected in the national expenditure, and trusts that such further diminution may be made therein as the future state of things may warrant."

I consider that we are bound to observe

the spirit of that Resolution. And for my own part I must say that, quite independently of all proof of need among the people, and of all citation of authorities, it is the duty of the Legislature constantly to study the enforcement of thrift in the public expenditure.

After all I have said, I certainly am not the man who ought to oppose on principle any proposal that the Income Tax should run over a term of years; but I have been sufficiently warned of the danger of making such a proposition. We now ask the House to adopt no general conclusion on the subject. We do not propose a plan which is to adopt the Income Tax as an ordinary means of Revenue, neither do we propose as a principle its abolition; but we propose that we should aim at and pursue as a policy its reduction, as circumstances may allow, to that which was once, or which may hereafter be taken for, its legal minimum; and that we should now at once proceed to take the first of the steps for bringing us to that result. Our proposal is to take off 1*d.* from the Income Tax, which now stands 7*d.* in the pound. If it should happily be in the power of the Committee at any time to repeat that operation, and to reduce the tax to 5*d.*, our position might then be described as follows. The proceeds of the tax at that rate would be about a trifle over £6,000,000; and then it would be perfectly possible for Parliament to proceed even to the extinction of the Income Tax. But it could only do so, firstly taking into view the elasticity and growth of the Revenue to which I have referred; secondly, if it were prepared steadily to exercise in the manner described in the Motion of my noble Friend two years ago the spirit of economy; and thirdly, if it thought fit to make what would, I apprehend, be alike just and necessary, namely, some addition to the direct taxation of the country in other forms. Or, it will be possible for the House, if it shall think fit, to adopt another mode of operation. It would be possible for Parliament to say, "We will recommence another round of change, treading that circle in which so much good has been achieved; and will take away portions of the burdens which are still imposed in the form of indirect taxation." Or, lastly, it might come to the conclusion that the Income Tax was fit to be retained, without any special justifying

cause, as part of the ordinary financial machinery of the country. But that conclusion would, as I have observed, be one far from favourable, in my judgment, to the practical enforcement of economy. The principal point, however, to which I would call attention at present is this; that if we can reach the standard of 5*d.*, then we shall establish ourselves in a position from which Parliament will have it in its power to consider deliberately and on principle what course it shall thereafter pursue, with a view either to the maintenance or the abolition of the tax.

We propose then, Sir, to make a reduction in the impost to 6*d.* The ultimate loss from the removal of that 1*d.* I estimate at £1,230,000, the immediate loss, or loss for the financial year, being £800,000. The case of Schedule B in Scotland and Ireland will be dealt with precisely as in the Act of 1853; £430,000 of the entire loss will be postponed.

The surplus, which began with £2,570,000, is now brought down to no more than £430,000. And here it would have been the wish of the Government to stop. There is, however, still another subject demanding our attention. In consequence of the formal intimation given by the vote of the House, we have deemed it our duty, limited as are our means, to consider whether we could submit a measure which, whatever else it might do, would do good as far as it went, and which would indicate at least our desire to meet with deference and respect the convictions entertained by the House of Commons, even although we did not entirely and absolutely share them, if it could be done without a vital sacrifice of the public interests. I refer to the duty on Fire Insurances. We do not think that we should have been justified in entertaining the idea of a large operation with regard to that duty, to the displacement or prejudice of either of the proposals we have made; nor are we prepared—as, indeed, I should hope the Committee will not ask us—to assent to any such proceeding if it should be proposed from any other quarter. Now, how does the duty on Fire Insurances stand? The amount of the Fire Insurance duty is £1,700,000, and it increases at the rate of about £50,000 a year. Here, again, we are met with a difficulty that we have before encountered. There is the greatest possible difference of opinion as to what I may call the self-recovering power of the Fire Insurance duty in the event of a reduction. For my own part, I am not very sanguine on that score, at least as regards the greater part of the duty. On examination it will be obvious to the Committee that the duty divides itself into two portions, the larger of which is a tax on property, and the other, and smaller portion, a tax on industry and trade. Two-thirds of it may be said to be levied on buildings and furniture; so much of it is a tax on property. The remaining third, as nearly as it is possible to make a conjectural estimate, is levied on stock-in-trade. My hon. Friend the Member for Bradford (Mr. W. E. Forster), in the presence of an important deputation from the Chambers of Commerce, a short time ago, expressed publicly to me a strong opinion that in respect of stock-in-trade, as far as his observation went in those branches of commerce with which he is connected, or acquainted, the reduction of the Fire Insurance duty would be followed by a rapid and even by a complete recovery. I go thus far with the hon. Member—that it may be taken for a general rule that taxes on trade, industry, and labour when reduced, rapidly recover; while taxes on property when reduced, recover slowly. We have seen this rule exemplified in the assessed taxes and in other instances; the reason being, as I apprehend, that taxes, which are substantially taxes on property, are, in the main, paid by the rich, who do not feel their burdens seriously, and whose proceedings are therefore not materially affected by their removal. We have felt that there is this doubt as to the self-recovering power of the Fire Insurance duty, and it will be very desirable to arrive at least at a partial solution of it by the trial of an experiment. The proposal we have to make is, therefore, to reduce the duty to half its present amount—that is, from 3s. to 1s. 6d., as far as stock-in-trade is concerned. We shall then see what the energy of commerce will effect in regard to that portion of the tax, and we may thus find ourselves in a more favourable position for forming a judgment as to the amount of loss likely to result from dealing with the residue. [Mr. WHITE: Will fixtures be stock-in-trade?] I do not see how fixtures can be included without considerable difficulty; but utensils and machinery will be deemed stock-in-

The Chancellor of the Exchequer

trade. I would, however, refer hon. Members to the language of the Resolution which I am about to lay upon the table

In making this proposal, we have been partly prompted by another consideration. There is, we are aware, something very invidious in the position of farm stock in relation to stock-in-trade. They are essentially the same and they ought to be treated in the same manner. But although we think the exemption unfair, we do not propose to abolish it. We can only mitigate the inequality by a reduction of the duty on stock-in-trade generally of one-half, but even this appears to be a change of considerable value.

We propose that the Act on this subject should take effect from the 1st of July next. There will be provisions with regard to returns of the duty on altered policies, which will, of course, be at the lower rate only; but I need not enter now into the details. The financial result will probably be as follows:—The produce of the Fire Insurance duty on stock-in-trade is estimated at £566,000. The first loss by the diminution would be £283,000 for the year; but as it will operate for only nine months it will be no more than £213,000. Allowing for an increase of insurances to the extent of 10 per cent, or £21,000, the net loss for 1864-5 may be stated at £192,000.

We have now, Sir, gone to the full extent of the discretion permitted us. To sum up, the effect of the changes will be this. The surplus before any reductions was £2,570,000. The relief afforded during the year by the proposed changes will be as follows. On Sugar it will be £1,719,000, on Income Tax £800,000, on Fire Insurance duty £213,000, on Tea Licences £15,000:—£2,747,000. In 1865-6, there will be a further loss of £28,000 on Sugar: so that the total will amount to £433,000 on Income Tax, and £70,000 on Fire Insurance duty, making £531,000. The financial loss on which we must reckon in the present year will be as follows:—On Sugar £1,330,000, on Income Tax £800,000, on Fire Insurance duty £192,000, on Tea Licences £10,000—total £2,332,000. The actual relief from taxation in the current year will, however, be greatly augmented by the reductions of last year. The relief by the present proposals will be to the extent of £2,747,000, and by the remissions in 1863, £898,000. The total relief for 1864-5 will, therefore, amount to £3,645,000, and the estimated loss by the proposals of the year will, as we estimate, amount to £2,332,000. The surplus after these deductions is £238,000. It has grown "fine by degrees and beautifully less;" but I need not say to the Committee that it is no longer a surplus on which we could possibly contemplate any further operations.

We have proposed these plans, which I have submitted to the Committee, in the discharge of our responsibility, and not at all as being of opinion that they ought to be or can be compared in point of magnitude with the remissions and changes of some former years; but yet they are, as we think, steps towards the accomplishment of the great purposes which Parliament has taken in hand. Looking at the proposals of a particular year, they may, perhaps, be likened to the stones cast singly by the passing traveller on a heap. Each separate contribution is small; but the general result is that in the course of time a pile arises which is found worthy to commemorate some renowned action or some glorious death. It is in this sense that we offer these proposals to Parliament. We believe them to be good. We trust that they will meet with your acceptance, and that you will receive them as pledges, on our part, of an earnest desire to co-operate with the Legislature in carrying yet further forward those purposes, the steady prosecution of which has already done so much for the strength and security of England, for the comfort and happiness of the people, for the honour of the age in which we live, and for the hopes we entertain on behalf of the times that are to come.

Sir, I now place in your hands the first of the Resolutions which we shall submit to the House in order to give effect to the financial measures of the year.

1. Sugar Duties—

"That, towards raising the Supply granted to Her Majesty, on and after the undermentioned dates, in lieu of the Duties of Customs now charged on the articles undermentioned, the following Duties of Customs shall be charged thereon, on importation into Great Britain or Ireland (that is to say):

On and after the fifth day of May, one thousand eight hundred and sixty-four—

Sugar—namely,

	£	s.	d.
Candy, Brown or White, Refined Sugar, or Sugar, rendered by any process equal in quality thereto . . . . the cwt.	0	12	10

On and after the sixteenth day of April, one thousand eight hundred and sixty four—

Sugar—namely,

	£	s.	d.
White Clayed Sugar, or Sugar rendered by any process equal in quality to White Clayed, not being refined, or equal in quality to refined . . . the cwt.	0	11	8
Yellow Muscovado and Brown Clayed Sugar, or Sugar rendered by any process equal in quality to Yellow Muscovado, or Brown Clayed, and not equal to White Clayed . . . . . the cwt.	0	10	6
Brown Muscovado Sugar, or Sugar rendered by any process equal in quality thereto, and not equal to Yellow Muscovado, or Brown Clayed . . . the cwt.	0	9	4
Any other Sugar not equal in quality to Brown Muscovado. the cwt.	0	8	2
Cane Juice . . . the cwt.	0	6	7
Molasses . . the cwt.	0	3	0
Almonds, paste of . . the lb.	0	0	1
Cherries, dried . . the lb.	0	0	1
Comfits, dry . . the lb.	0	0	1
Confectionery . . the lb.	0	0	1
Ginger, preserved. . the lb.	0	0	1
Marmalade . . . the lb.	0	0	1
Plums preserved in Sugar the lb.	0	0	1
Succades, including all fruits and vegetables preserved in Sugar, not otherwise enumerated the lb.	0	0	1"

[In order to present a complete view of The Chancellor of the Exchequer's Financial Plan, the Resolutions which he had given notice to move in Committee of Ways and Means are here added as they stood on the Notice Paper.] (*See following pages.*)

[1. The Sugar Duties—

CUSTOMS DUTIES.

1. Sugar Duties—

That, towards raising the Supply granted to Her Majesty, on and after the undermentioned dates, in lieu of the Duties of Customs now charged on the articles undermentioned, the following Duties of Customs shall be charged thereon, on importation into Great Britain or Ireland (that is to say):

On and after the fifth day of May, one thousand eight hundred and sixty-four—

Sugar—namely,

Candy, Brown or White, Refined Sugar, or Sugar, rendered by any process equal in quality thereto,		the cwt.	0	12	10

On and after the sixteenth day of April, one thousand eight hundred and sixty-four—

Sugar—namely,

White Clayed Sugar, or Sugar rendered by any process equal in quality to White Clayed, not being refined, or equal in quality to refined . . . the cwt.			0	11	8
Yellow Muscovado and Brown Clayed Sugar, or Sugar rendered by any process equal in quality to Yellow Muscovado, or Brown Clayed, and not equal to White Clayed . . . the cwt.			0	10	6
Brown Muscovado Sugar, or Sugar rendered by any process equal in quality thereto, and not equal to Yellow Muscovado, or Brown Clayed . . . the cwt.			0	9	4
Any other Sugar not equal in quality to Brown Muscovado.	the cwt.		0	8	2
Cane Juice . . .	the cwt.		0	6	7
Molasses	the cwt.		0	3	6
Almonds, paste of .	the lb.		0	0	1
Cherries, dried . .	the lb.		0	0	1
Comfits, dry	the lb.		0	0	1
Confectionery . .	the lb.		0	0	1
Ginger, preserved. .	the lb.		0	0	1
Marmalade . . .	the lb.		0	0	1
Plums preserved in Ginger	the lb.		0	0	1
Succades, including all fruits and vegetables preserved in Sugar, not otherwise enumerated	the lb.		0	0	1

2. Drawbacks on Sugar—

That, on and after the undermentioned dates, in lieu of the Drawbacks now allowed thereon, the following Drawbacks shall be paid and allowed on the undermentioned descriptions of Refined Sugar, on the exportation thereof to Foreign parts, or on removal to the Isle of Man for consumption there, or on deposit in any approved Warehouse, upon such terms and subject to such regulations as the Commissioners of Customs may direct, for delivery from such Warehouse as Ships' Stores only, or for the purpose of sweetening British Spirits in Bond (that is to say):

On and after the fifth day of May, one thousand eight hundred and sixty-four—

Upon Refined Sugar in loaf, complete and whole, or lumps duly refined, having been perfectly clarified, and thoroughly dried in the stove, and being of an uniform whiteness throughout; and upon such Sugar pounded, crushed, or broken in a warehouse approved by the Commissioners of Customs, such Sugar having been there first inspected by the Officers of Customs in lumps or loaves as if for immediate shipment, and then packed for exportation in the presence of such Officers, and at the expense of the exporter; and upon Candy . for every cwt.	£0	12	4
Upon Refined Sugar unstoved, pounded, crushed, or broken, and not in any way inferior to the Export Standard Sample No. 1 approved by the Lords of the Treasury, and which shall not contain more than five per centum moisture over and above what the same would contain if thoroughly dried in the stove . . for every cwt.	0	11	9

And on and after the twenty-first day of April, one thousand eight hundred and sixty-four—

Upon Sugar refined by the Centrifugal, or by any other process, and not in any way inferior to the Export Standard No. 3 approved by the Lords of the Treasury for every cwt.	0	12	4
Upon Bastard, or Refined Sugar unstoved, broken in pieces, or being ground, powdered, or crushed, not in any way inferior to the Export Standard Sample No. 2 approved by the Lords of the Treasury for every cwt.	0	10	10
Upon Bastard, or Refined Sugar being inferior in quality to the said Export Standard Sample No. 2 . . for every cwt.	0	8	2

3. Continuing the Duty on Tea—

That, towards the raising the Supply granted to Her Majesty, the Duties of Customs now charged on Tea shall continue to be levied and charged on and after the 1st day of August, 1864, until the 1st day of August, 1865, on importation into Great Britain or Ireland.

4. Altering the Duty on Corn—

That, in lieu of the Duties of Customs now charged on the undermentioned Articles, on their importation into Great Britain or Ireland, the following Duties of Customs shall be charged (that is to say):

Wheat Barley Oats Rye Pease Beans Maize, or Indian Corn Buck Wheat Bear or Bigg	the cwt. £0 0 3

5. Imposing a Duty of Customs on Lentils, Millet Seed, and Dari—

That the following Duties of Customs shall be charged on the undermentioned Articles, on importation into Great Britain or Ireland (that is to say):

Lentils Millet Seed Dari	the cwt. £0 0 3

And that the Duties be paid on first Importation; and such Goods shall not be warehoused either for Home Consumption or Exportation.

INLAND REVENUE.

6. Income Tax—

That, towards raising the Supply granted to Her Majesty, there shall be charged, collected, and paid for one year, commencing on the 6th day of April, 1864, and in respect of all Property, Profits, and Gains mentioned or described as chargeable in the Act passed in the 16th and 17th years of Her Majesty's reign, chapter 34, for granting to Her Majesty Duties on Profits arising from Property, Professions, Trades and Offices, the following Rates and Duties (that is to say):

For every twenty shillings of the annual value or amount of all such Property, Profits, and Gains (except those chargeable under Schedule (B) of the said Act), the Rate or Duty of sixpence.

And for and in respect of the occupation of Lands, Tenements, Hereditaments, and Heritages chargeable under Schedule (B) of the said Act, for every twenty shillings of the annual value thereof,

In England, the Rate or Duty of three pence, And in Scotland and Ireland respectively, the Rate or Duty of twopence farthing.

Subject to the provisions contained in section 3 of the Act 26 *Vict.* chapter 22, for the exemption of Persons whose whole Income from every source is under £100 a year, and relief of those whose Income is under £200 a year.

7. Fire Insurance Duty—

That, in lieu of the yearly per-centage Duty now chargeable for or in respect of any Insurance from loss or damage by Fire only, which shall be made or renewed on or after the 1st day of July, 1864, of or upon any Goods, Wares, or Merchandise, being stock in trade, or of or upon any Machinery, Implements, or Utensils used for the purpose of any manufacture, there shall be charged and paid yearly a Duty at and after the rate of one shilling and sixpence per annum for every £100 insured; and that no return or allowance of Duty, except at and after the last-mentioned rate, shall be made in respect of time unexpired, or otherwise, on any such Insurance as aforesaid which shall have been made or renewed before the day or time aforesaid.

8. Excise Duty on Licences to sell Tea, &c.—

That, towards raising the Supply granted to Her Majesty, there shall be charged and paid on the Licences hereinafter mentioned, the following Duty of Excise in lieu of the Duty now payable thereon (that is to say):

For and upon any Licence to be taken out yearly by any person to trade in or sell Coffee, Tea, Cocoa Nuts, Chocolate, or Pepper, in any house rated to the relief of the Poor, at a sum less than ten pounds per annum, and not being within the limits of a Municipal or Parliamentary Borough, the Duty of two shillings and sixpence.

9. Stamp Duties on Letters of Attorney and Proxies—

That, towards raising the Supply granted to Her Majesty, there shall be charged and paid for and upon the several matters and things hereinafter mentioned, the following Stamp Duties, in lieu of the Stamp Duties now chargeable thereon respectively (that is to say):

For and upon any Letter or Power of Attorney, Commission, Factory, Mandate, or other Instrument in the nature thereof, For the receipt of Dividends or Interests of any of the Government or Parliamentary Stocks or Funds, or of the Stocks, Funds, or Shares of or in any Joint Stock Company, or other Company or Society whose Stocks or Funds are divided into Shares, and transferable.	
If the same shall be for the receipt of one payment only . . .	£0 1 0
And if the same shall be for a continuous receipt, or for the receipt of more than one payment . .	0 5 0
For the receipt of any sum of money, or any Cheque, Note, or Draft for any sum of money not exceeding £20 (except in the cases aforesaid), or any periodical payment (other than as aforesaid) not exceeding the annual sum of £10. . .	0 5 0
For the sole purpose of appointing or nominating a Proxy to vote at any one Meeting of the Proprietors or Shareholders of any Joint Stock or other Company, or of the Members of any Society or Institution, or of the Contributors to the Funds thereof . . .	0 0 1

10. Stamp Duties on Appointments to Ecclesiastical Benefices, &c.—

That, towards raising the Supply granted to Her Majesty, there shall be charged and paid for and upon the several matters and things hereinafter mentioned, the following Stamp Duties, in lieu of the Stamp Duties now chargeable thereon respectively (that is to say):   Duty.

For and upon any Donation or Presentation, by whomsoever made, of or to any Ecclesiastical Benefice, Dignity, or Promotion.

Also, for and upon any Collation by any Archbishop or Bishop, or by any other Ordinary or competent authority, to any Ecclesiastical Benefice, Dignity, or Promotion.

Also, for and upon any Institution granted by any Archbishop, Bishop, Chancellor, or other Ordinary, or by any Ecclesiastical Court, to any Ecclesiastical Benefice, Dignity, or Promotion proceeding upon the Petition of the Patron to be himself admitted and instituted, and not upon a presentation.

Also, for and upon any nomination by Her Majesty, Her Heirs or Successors, or by any other Patron, to any Perpetual Curacy.

Also, for and upon any Licence to hold a Perpetual Curacy not proceeding upon a nomination.

Where the net yearly value of any such Benefice, Dignity, Promotion, or Perpetual Curacy shall not amount to £50	Nil.
Where the same shall amount to £50 and not amount to £100 . .	£1 0 0
Where the same shall amount to £100 and not amount to £150 . .	2 0 0
Where the same shall amount to £150 and not amount to £200 . .	3 0 0
Where the same shall amount to £200 and not amount to £250 . .	4 0 0
Where the same shall amount to £250 and not amount to £300 . .	5 0 0
And where such value shall amount to £300 or upwards . .	7 0 0
And also, for every £100 thereof over and above the first £200, a further Duty of	5 0 0

11. Hawkers and Pedlars—

That, for and upon any Licence to be taken out by a Hawker or Pedlar to travel and trade with more than one horse or other beast bearing or drawing burthen, there shall be charged and paid for every such horse or beast over and above one, the sum of four pounds in addition to the Duty now chargeable on a Licence to a Hawker and Pedlar to travel and trade with one such horse only.

12. Ad Valorem Stamp Duties on Settlements—

That, towards raising the Supply granted to Her Majesty, the ad valorem Stamp Duties granted and made payable under the head of "Settlement" in the Schedule to the Act passed in the thirteenth and fourteenth years of Her Majesty's reign, chapter ninety-seven, shall be deemed to extend to and shall be chargeable upon or in respect of any definite and certain principal sum or sums of money of any denomination or currency, whether British, Foreign, or Colonial, and any definite and certain share or shares in the Stocks or Funds of any Foreign or Colonial Government, State, Corporation, or Company whatsoever, as well as upon or in respect of the Shares, Stocks, and Funds in the said Schedule mentioned.

And that where any principal sum of money secured or contracted for by, or which may become due or payable upon, any Bond, Debenture, Policy of Insurance, Covenant or Contract, shall be settled or agreed to be settled, or such Bond, Debenture, Policy, Covenant or Contract shall be settled or assigned or transferred by way of settlement, or shall be agreed so to be, then and in any of such cases the same shall be deemed to be a Settlement of such principal sum of money, and shall be chargeable with the said ad valorem Stamp Duties on the amount thereof accordingly.

And that where the subject of any Settlement chargeable with the said Duties shall be any share or shares in any such Stocks or Funds as aforesaid, or any sum or sums of money secured by any Foreign or Colonial Bond, Debenture, or other security, bearing a marketable value in the English Market, then the value of such share or shares, and of such Bond, Debenture, or other security respectively shall be ascertained and determined by the average selling price thereof on the day or on either of the ten days preceding the day of the date of the Deed or Instrument of Settlement; or if no sale shall have taken place within such ten days, then according to the average selling price thereof on the day of the last preceding sale, and the said ad valorem Duties shall be chargeable on such Settlement in respect of the value so ascertained and determined; and the value of any sum or sums of money expressed in coin of a Foreign or Colonial denomination or currency, shall be determined by the current rate of exchange on the day of the date of the Deed or Instrument of Settlement, and the said ad valorem Duties shall be chargeable in respect of the value so determined as last aforesaid.

13. Excise Duties on Occasional Licences to Refreshment House Keepers, Wine Retailers, Beer Retailers, and Tobacco Dealers—

That, towards raising the Supply granted to Her Majesty, there shall be charged and paid the following Duties of Excise for and upon the Occasional Licences hereinafter mentioned (that is to say):

For and upon every Occasional Licence to the Keeper of a Refreshment House, for each and every day for which such Licence shall be granted	Nil.
For and upon every Occasional Licence to retail Foreign Wine to be consumed at the place where sold, for each and every day for which the same shall be granted . . .	£0 1 0
For and upon every Occasional Licence to retail Beer to be consumed at the place where sold, for each and every day for which the same shall be granted	0 1 0
For and upon every Occasional Licence to deal in or sell Tobacco or Snuff, for each and every day for which the same shall be granted . . .	0 0 2

14. Inland Revenue Laws Amendment—

That it is expedient to amend the Laws relating to the Inland Revenue.

[MR. CRAWFORD

MR. CRAWFORD said, he should not presume to add anything in the shape of criticism upon the comprehensive speech they had just heard from the Chancellor of the Exchequer. He thought the statement of the right hon. Gentleman would be received throughout the country with great satisfaction, and he thought that, on the whole, the mode in which the Chancellor of the Exchequer had dealt with the surplus would be viewed with approval. With respect to the mode in which the right hon. Gentleman proposed to deal with the sugar duties, he thought he would find very many Members—at any rate on that side of the House—who would be disposed to think, with him, that the mode in which the duty was proposed to be dealt with was unsatisfactory. If no other hon. Member would take up the matter, he should be prepared to state on a future occasion his views for a settlement of the sugar question at variance from those of the right hon. Gentleman.

MR. CAVE said, he should not have risen but for the observations of the hon. Member for the City of London. He thought his hon. Friend a bold man to wish to re-introduce the subject of uniform duties to the House after the speech of the Chancellor, and the luminous pamphlet of Professor Leone Levi, which had been distributed to Members; and he begged to assure the hon. Gentleman that when the subject again came on for discussion he (Mr. Cave) and those who thought with him upon it would be ready to meet him. With regard to the proposed alteration of the tea licences, he reminded the Chancellor of the Exchequer that the borough which he (Mr. Cave) represented, though it was called a parliamentary borough, was as large as the county of Rutland, and remote villages within its boundary were as much country places as any that were to be found in England. There were other boroughs of similar nature. He hoped, therefore, that the Chancellor of the Exchequer would take the matter again into his consideration, and introduce some other definition of those small traders who were to benefit by the reduction of the license duty.

MR. HUBBARD said, he was sorry to have to make any remarks that might appear an exception to the general feeling of satisfaction with which the statement of the right hon. Gentleman had been received; but he could not help expressing his extreme regret that, after the expression of the opinion of the House on the question of the Fire Insurance duties, the right hon. Gentleman should have minimised his proposals by limiting his alteration to the duty on stock-in-trade only. He (Mr. Hubbard) thought that the distinction the right hon. Gentleman had made between stock-in-trade and other property was wholly untenable. Fire Insurance was the most uncertain and indiscriminating in its operation, and it was a tax not only on the property of the rich but on those who could not afford to run the risk of fire. He must express his extreme disappointment at the suggestion, and he felt certain the House would not be satisfied with it.

SIR JAMES FERGUSSON begged to ask the right hon. Gentleman for further information upon one point respecting the Income Tax. The right hon. Gentleman had referred to the prospect of a new assessment under schedules A and B of the Income Tax in the present year, but he had not stated to the House what was the increase of revenue upon which he reckoned from that source. Judging from the experience of the past, a very large increase was to be expected from that operation; and if the increase on the present re-assessment equalled that realized on former occasions, and corresponded with the advancing prosperity to which the right hon. Gentleman had himself referred, it would probably tend to increase his surplus considerably beyond the sum he had stated of £238,000, and he would not be entitled to point afterwards to such an enhanced source of revenue unless he now should explain to the Committee the amount he calculated to gain from it.

MR. WHITE said, he shared but partially in the satisfaction with which the Committee generally had heard the able and lucid statement of the Chancellor of the Exchequer. The apparently paradoxical task which the right hon. Gentleman had set himself—namely, to take nothing from the rich, and yet to give a good deal to the poor, was one that had already to a great extent been performed; and indeed no Government could solve a nobler problem. The policy of the last twenty years, while it had made the rich richer, had left the poor less poor. The right hon. Gentleman had referred to the marvellous results of that policy—a policy which had raised the combined imports and exports of the country from £172,000,000 to the prodigious sum of £440,000,000 a year. He trusted that these results would encourage him to persevere in the same course and courageously to insist upon applying the same free trade principles to land and to labour. When that was done the spectacle which this country would present was one that might well challenge the admiration and the envy of the world. He should have been glad if the right hon. Gentleman had stated how much of the public revenue was contributed by the working classes. It had been calculated from the actual receipts at co-operative stores, that an artisan with a wife and three children, who was earning £50 or £60 a year, contributed to the public burdens at the rate of 20 per cent upon his wages. At Chester the right hon. Gentleman had observed that each man's share of taxation might be fairly stated at an eighth of his income; and if that was the case the labouring classes were palpably aggrieved, seeing that they pay not an eighth but a fifth. He could not think that the country was in a satisfactory state when a million of its inhabitants—or one in thirty of its gross population — were paupers, one-fifth of those paupers being able-bodied persons, and three or four millions more being on the verge of pauperism. He would have much preferred a reduction in the duties on some articles which were more closely connected with the comfort, and indeed the healthful existence, of the working classes, to the alteration which the right hon. Gentleman proposed to make upon the Income Tax. He believed the amount of taxation imposed upon the poorer classes to be grossly inequitable. The right hon. Gentleman would pardon him for saying that the proposal to reduce the Income Tax was not out of place in the quarter from which it proceeded, as it was only appropriate that the burden should be lightened by the same hand which had been instrumental in augmenting it. When the right hon. Gentleman came into office, the taxation per head throughout the country was 39s. 6d., while it had now increased to 45s. Nor was that all. In 1853, what had been called the optional expenditure of the country was 15s. per head per annum. It now amounted to 26s. 8d., showing an increase of 80 per cent, or more than double the increment of the national wealth which had occurred during the same period. While he believed that with our present limited system of representation the Chancellor of

Mr. White

the Exchequer could not do more than he had done, still he must record his opinion that it was not as much as the country was entitled to, nor as the right hon. Gentleman himself would gladly have attempted if he had found himself under more favourable circumstances.

MR. DUNLOP rose, as the representative of a constituency largely engaged in the sugar trade, to say that he thought the right hon. Gentleman had adhered to the right principle in dealing with the sugar duties; and he applauded the right hon. Gentleman for having stripped off the pretended disguise of free trade which had covered a system of bounty and premium, whereby the Colonies had obtained advantages which they never would have had if there had been no duty at all. He thought that when the admirable speech which they had just heard had gone over the land, it would produce such an impression that the hon. Member for the City of London (Mr. Crawford) would find little encouragement to proceed with the Motion which he had just threatened. He hoped, however, that the right hon. Gentleman would defer bringing the proposed changes into operation than a longer period of four weeks.

MR. WHITESIDE said, he was disappointed with that part of the financial statement which dealt with the Spirit duties—a question in which Ireland was deeply interested. In 1860 the Chancellor of the Exchequer commenced his unfortunate policy of raising the duties upon spirits. The right hon. Member for Buckinghamshire (Mr. Disraeli) had equalized them, leaving them where the most eminent persons connected with the trade in Ireland thought they ought to be left. But the Chancellor of the Exchequer wanted to pay the expenses of a war in China, and so he increased the spirit duties by 1s. 11d. a gallon, indulging in an anticipation which, like some others, had not been verified—namely, that after making all deductions he thought he might reckon upon an additional million. All the arguments used by the right hon. Gentleman on that occasion were, in his opinion, fallacious. One of these arguments was, that the duties had been several times raised advantageously; but, if a duty were raised four or five times, that rather furnished an argument against any further increase. Then the right hon. Gentleman said he was quite sure that illicit distillation would not be likely to take place in Ireland, because the duty of protecting the revenue was to be transferred from the Excise to the constabulary. In the following year, however—1861—he was obliged to make this statement:—

"The Committee will be anxious to hear what is to be said with regard to the spirit duties. We anticipated an increase in the Revenue from the duty imposed in July last on British spirits of £650,000, whereas there has been altogether a diminution in the actual yield of the spirit duty, as compared with the Estimate, of no less than £910,000, or £250,000 more than the whole increase at which we aimed." [3 *Hansard,* clxii. 560.]

That certainly, as the right hon. Gentleman added at the time, was "an astounding diminution." But, in 1862, the right hon. Gentleman gave a better account of the matter—not that he had much to boast of, because the produce of the duty was still considerably less than his Estimate. In 1860-1 he got £2,269,000 from Ireland; in the following year he got only £2,461,000. The argument ordinarily used by the right hon. Gentleman was, that by diminishing a duty you increased the consumption; but in this case he increased the duty and diminished the consumption. Under those circumstances, he would have done wisely if he had given some relief. In 1863 his Estimate was £10,000,000 for the spirit duties; his receipts were only £9,394,000, being a deficiency compared with his Estimate of upwards of £600,000. He explained the deficiency by a reference to the condition of the lower classes, owing to the failure of the cotton supply, and drew a picture of Ireland admirable for its truthfulness. Yet, on the present occasion, when the circumstances of Ireland were as bad, if not worse, he had not said one word upon that important subject—or, at all events, very little to the point, and he had suggested no measure of relief. In the debate on emigration at the beginning of the Session, the facts were denied by the Chief Secretary for Ireland in his usual argumentative manner, and likewise by the Attorney General, who invented for the occasion a poetic Ireland. Had the right hon. Gentleman looked into the facts to see if the increase in the duty on spirits might not have had something to do with the present state of things? On proposing to raise the spirit duties, the Chancellor of the Exchequer, as already stated, felt quite satisfied that there would be no increase of illicit distillation. There never was a time when illicit distillation

was more rife in Ireland than it was at the present moment, in consequence of the excessive duty put upon the article by the Chancellor of the Exchequer. In one town in Donegal there were recently no fewer than thirty-one persons in gaol for offences against the Revenue, and the Judge of assize adverted in his charge to the difficulty of repressing crime in that county, owing to the amount of illicit distillation which prevailed. The anticipation of the Chancellor of the Exchequer had not been realized, and upon his own reasoning, he ought to reduce the duty to what it was in 1858. It was quite true, as the right hon. Gentleman had said to-night, that very little of the good article which the Irish distillers manufactured was sold in a pure state by the retailers and small dealers. That was on account of the excessive duty. The dealers first watered the spirit, they then put treacle in it, they then strengthened it with vitriol, and an eminent distiller had informed him it was going to be called "Gladstone's Cordial." Such stuff must be very unpleasant to swallow, and it might be said that the only effect of the increase of duty had been to endanger the health of Her Majesty's subjects. But there was still a point in morals remaining. When the learned Judge to whom he had referred asked the grand jury whether they could assist in repressing crimes against the revenue, the answer he received was, that it was quite impossible while the high duty remained on spirits. Those who were acquainted with Ireland—unfortunately there were none such in the Government—knew that wherever there was an illicit still there was Ribandism. The persons engaged in that confederacy liked the neighbourhood of a private still. It united and stimulated them, and it brought them together to conspire against the very existence of society. There was thus a combination of reasons why the right hon. Gentleman should reduce the spirit duties. A large distiller in Cork, who had sent statistics to the right hon. Gentleman, stated that his legislation had caused a decrease of 18 per cent in the home consumption of Ireland. The quantity distilled in Ireland from 1859 to 1861 was reduced by nearly one-half. The colonial distiller had not gained much, but the foreigner had. Again, between 1863 and 1859 there was a falling off of 19 per cent in the quantity of spirits retained for home consumption;

while there was, on the other hand, an increase of 47 per cent in the quantity of brandy imported from France. Supposing the right hon. Gentleman himself were a large distiller who had embarked some £80,000 or £100,000 in establishing a spirit manufactory with an expensive machinery and a large staff, from which he had been accustomed to derive an excellent income—what would he say to receiving, as had actually happened, from his cashier at the end of one twelvemonth the nominal sum of £50, instead of several thousands a year, and at the end of another twelvemonth, perhaps, an account showing a balance on the wrong side? The mischief and injustice done by first inducing men to invest their skill and capital in any branch of business under a particular state of law, and then by entirely changing the basis of that law, could scarcely be exaggerated. The distillers of Ireland and Scotland had in that way suffered grievous hardship. Hitherto the brewers had escaped, but perhaps the sword of Damocles would yet be suspended over their heads, and they might hereafter have to complain, as the distillers did now, that a great injustice had been done them. He would not ask for any exclusive advantage for Ireland, but he believed that what was stated in the leading journal that morning was strictly true—namely, that the people were flying from that country in masses, and its consuming power was consequently in that sense diminishing. If the spirit duty were reduced to what it was in 1858 it would be a great benefit to an important manufacturing industry in both Ireland and Scotland, and also a boon to the agricultural interest who used the grain for feeding their cattle in the winter, and whose supply had been reduced. As the right hon. Gentleman's experiment on this matter had failed, he ought, in candour, to admit his mistake, and endeavour to retrace his steps—a course which would give an impulse to trade without in the end impairing the public revenue.

MR. MORRITT said, he had been asked by hon. Members whether, after the Chancellor of the Exchequer's statement, he meant to go on with his promised Motion relating to the Malt tax. It was certainly his full intention to persevere with that Motion. He did not think the right hon. Gentleman's assertion, that a reduction of the duty on malt would benefit England far more than Ireland or Scotland, was a sufficient argument against the adoption of

Mr. Whiteside

such a measure. He did not see that that fact, if fact it were, should induce him to lessen his efforts towards England. He should be glad to take the advice which had been tendered, but he could not; and so it was his full intention to carry on his Motion, and he hoped to show that he was proposing that which was right, and that he was acting from no political feeling or party purpose, or from any private feeling; and, above all, it had nothing to do with elections or political capital in his own county. He had never, and should never, use matters of that kind for any such purpose. He simply should propose the Motion because he thought it a right and just thing to do.

MR. KINNAIRD hoped that the Chancellor of the Exchequer would not yield to the appeal made to him by the right hon. Member for Dublin University (Mr. Whiteside), in favour of a reduction of the duty on spirits. High moral considerations were involved in that subject, and if there was any part of the Chancellor of the Exchequer's policy which had been especially beneficial to the country, it was his mode of deriving a large revenue from a branch of trade which, instead of being stimulated, ought rather to be subjected to some degree of restraint.

LORD CLAUD HAMILTON confirmed the statement of his right hon. Friend (Mr. Whiteside). The learned Judge to whom his right hon. Friend referred, took a different view from the last speaker, for the whole effect of his charge was that the demoralization throughout the whole population was caused through temptation given to illicit distillation. In the recent bad harvests, the corn not being in a state to be brought to market, the rural population had been tempted to use it for the manufacture of a valuable article of commerce. The Judge stated that this should not be viewed as a fiscal question, and he invited magistrates and others to consider it as a moral question; for not only were the persons having an illicit still breaking the law, but they made the whole of their neighbours *particeps criminis* by bribing them to keep the secret and give warning on the approach of the police. He (Lord Claud Hamilton) maintained that a reduction of the present high duty on spirits was imperatively demanded in the interests of public morality, to which all fiscal considerations were matters of minor importance.

MR. NORRIS wished to throw out a

[U 9, *page* 608 *b follows.*]

hint for the consideration of the right hon. Gentleman in relation to licenses. Under the 9 *Geo.* III. c. 61, magistrates gave their approval for licenses to certain houses to sell beer, and through the medium of the excise the beer license so obtained was, or at least had been, the key to the obtaining of a license for the sale of spirits and beer. Subsequently to the passing of that act, the 1 *Will.* IV. c. 64, called the Beer Act, came into operation. That Act imposed a payment of 60*s.*, and 5 per cent, for a beer license, while under the old Act of George III. the charge was £1 2*s.* 6*d.* The result was that in half the borough towns of England there were some persons who paid 63*s.* for their license, whilst there were others living in the very same street who paid only £1 2*s.* 6*d.* This was so unequal and unjust, that he thought it demanded the consideration of the right hon. Gentleman. The right hon. Gentleman had referred to the various joint stock companies which have been recently called into existence, and hon. Members were aware that Lords and Members of the Lower House were advertised as directors of many of those joint stock companies. Among these were hotel companies on a gigantic scale. If one of these companies erected a magnificent edifice for the purpose, or with the effect, of absorbing eight or ten of the ordinary taverns, he thought a larger amount of license might fairly be demanded of it than was paid by the ordinary road-side taverns. One of these great hotels would absorb the custom of twelve or thirteen respectable hotels, or drive them out of the field, and it would be only fair to see whether they might not be made more largely available than at present for fiscal purposes. If in the case of sugar it was right that the unmanufactured article should come into the country at a lower rate than the manufactured, would it not be well by means of some arrangement with foreign countries to enable our manufacturers of paper to obtain the raw material of their industry untaxed? On one point the right hon. Gentleman had been misinformed. He stated that the import of rags during the past year was far larger than the import of rags had been during any previous year, and he appeared to think that all these rags were intended for the manufacture of paper. The right hon. Gentleman had quoted from the Board of Trade Returns the number of tons of rags imported last year; but probably he was not aware that within the

last eighteen months, owing to the dearth of cotton material, the manufacturers of Lancashire and Yorkshire had been driven to import the refuse of the woollen clothing of France, Belgium, and Italy, in order to remanufacture it into articles of clothing, and not for papermaking purposes. These importations had appeared in the Board of Trade Returns as importations of rags, and the right hon. Gentleman had supposed that the papermakers had the benefit of them. He begged to congratulate the right hon. Gentleman on the excellent Budget which he had produced, and which would add to his popularity, and be acceptable both to the House and the country.

MR. M'MAHON said, he joined the right hon. Gentleman the Member for the University of Dublin (Mr. Whiteside) and the noble Lord the Member for Tyrone (Lord Claud Hamilton) in their expression of regret that the spirit duties had not been reduced. He spoke not in the interest of the distillers, nor on moral grounds, but in the interest of tillage only. In the county which he represented, perhaps more barley and oats were grown than in any other county in Ireland. These kinds of grain were formerly largely used for the purposes of distillation; but the excessively high duties imposed on spirits by the Chancellor of the Exchequer had reduced the cultivation of both barley and oats, and thrown the land out of tillage and the people out of employment. The result was emigration, or a condition of destitution and discontent at home. The right hon. Gentleman was going to reduce the sugar duties, but he ought to take into consideration the case of agriculturists at home. Since 1843 the policy of our legislation had been to impose excise duties on home manufactures equivalent to the customs duties on imported sugars, the consequence of which was that the production of beetroot sugar in Ireland had been entirely annihilated. The foreign manufacturer, for instance, might make 1,000 cwt. of sugar, of which he might sell 900 cwt. untaxed anywhere he pleased, and he might bring only a tenth of the whole manufacture into the London market; but the Irish manufacturer would be exposed to the constant supervision of the Excise, and would have to pay on every pound that he manufactured. How, then, could the Irish compete with the Cuban manufacturer? The right hon. Gentleman had done much to promote freedom of trade;

he (Mr. M'Mahon) thought that free tillage was of greater importance to society than freedom of exchange. During the last twenty years the efforts of Parliament had been directed to the removal of restrictions on the interchange of commodities, while not a burden had been removed from tillage. All that the farmer could do at present was to let grass grow on his farm. If he grew barley and oats, and attempted to convert the grain into spirits, he was met by the exciseman; if he grew beetroot, and attempted to convert it into sugar, he was also met by the exciseman. The growth of tobacco was altogether prohibited. In the county which he represented £60 or £70 per acre was formerly made by the growth of tobacco. If free trade was of such importance, why was it not extended to tillage? Why should not the farmer grow tobacco, make beetroot sugar, and distil spirits from grain? In other words, why should not the farmer be as free with the produce of his land as the potter with his clay?

Mr. BENTINCK said, that while, in common with every Member of the Committee, he had listened with pleasure to the eloquent statements of the Chancellor of the Exchequer, he need hardly remind the Committee that what contributed to their pleasure was the studied manner in which all that right hon. Gentleman's speeches were prepared. Every word which he addressed to the Committee was intended to convey its special meaning, and in some instances its special sting. He could not, therefore, forbear remarking on the tone with which the right hon. Gentleman had referred to protection. The right hon. Gentleman thought proper to speak of the subject of protection probably for the purpose of eliciting a cheer from hon. Members below the gangway on his own side of the House; he had thought proper—not to imply—but to assert that there was something amounting to a stigma in the very word, and that it was one of those questions now supposed to be scouted in every part of the world. He (Mr Bentinck) objected to the tone in which the right hon. Gentleman thought proper to deliver himself upon that subject. Now, while he was prepared to admit that disrepute ought to attach and did attach to those who, for personal and sordid motives, had raised the question in this country, and whose political conversion on the subject was so sudden that doubts

were entertained as to their sincerity, he was not prepared to admit that those who under all circumstances adhered to their opinions were to be attacked in the manner in which the right hon. Gentleman thought proper to attack them. Now, what had free trade done? It had half ruined Ireland. ["No, no!"] Hon. Members might say no; but he would undertake to say, that if that country were polled, nine out of every ten would attribute the ruin of Ireland to free trade. With all his political legerdemain the right hon. Gentleman had never been able to prove, except on the old principle of *post hoc ergo propter hoc*, that protection had done any good to England, and when the right hon. Gentleman wished to raise the question he must do more than assert that such was the consequence of the figures he quoted. It did not surprise him that the right hon. Gentleman had not shown any inclination to take into account the agricultural interest. It was not his wont so to do, but he touched upon the question of the repeal of the malt duty. He (Mr. Bentinck) admitted that it was difficult to decide how far this duty affected various soils; but though the lands which grew the finest kinds of barley might not derive any benefit from its remission, the lands which grew an inferior kind would surely obtain an enormous advantage. The question was not to be so easily shelved as the right hon. Gentleman supposed. He (Mr. Bentinck) could not but be surprised with what the right hon. Gentleman called his strong arguments against dealing in any way with the malt duty. He said the repeal would only benefit England, while Scotland and Ireland would hardly receive any advantage from it; while those countries would have share in the taxes which would have to be substituted. What was this but an admission that England had been bearing a much larger share of taxation than she ought to bear, and he (Mr. Bentinck) hoped that this admission would enlist the sympathies of English Members when the question came on for discussion. With regard to the income tax he was glad to find the right hon. Gentleman returning to the views of some years ago, in favour of a great diminution, if not the entire abolition, of that tax. He only hoped this might be taken as a prelude to the right hon. Gentleman's return to his former opinions on other subjects, which those on that (the Opposition) side of the House would all hail with delight. The right hon. Gentleman had thought proper to introduce the question of the paper duty. With all his talents as a financier and his great skill in debate, he could not help thinking that the Chancellor of the Exchequer would have done much better if he had left that subject alone. In the minds of the great majority of the nation the repeal of the duty on paper was one of the most unfortunate measures to be found in the financial history of this country, and, if any proof were wanting respecting the impolicy of that remission, it would be found in the daily account of the state of the paper manufacturers. The duty was an increasing one, and the right hon. Gentleman should not forget that no one was interested in the repeal unless it was a few persons who had investments in penny papers, and who brought a strong pressure to bear on a weak Government. He (Mr. Bentinck) trusted that the first act of a strong patriotic Government would be to reimpose the duty on paper.

MR. CHILDERS thought the hon. Gentleman (Mr. Bentinck), who complained of the tone of his right hon. Friend with regard to protection, was hardly justified in saying, almost in the same breath, that those who advocated free trade were actuated by sordid and personal motives. He did not rise, however, to answer the hon. Gentleman, but to express the feeling which actuated so many Members as to the satisfactory character of the Budget, taking it as a whole. He thought the reduction of the income tax from 7d. to 6d. in the pound would give satisfaction, and he trusted they might expect its reduction to 5d. next year. He however inclined to believe the Chancellor of the Exchequer had over-estimated the amount of loss on sugar. He also felt doubtful whether, if they were to abide by the classified system of sugar duty, the proposal now made was altogether in the right direction. It was more logical than the existing scale, and on the whole in accordance with the Resolutions of the Committee two years ago; but he could not but think that, before long, the graduated scale would have to be abandoned. He thought that the reduction of Fire Insurance was not exactly that which would be the most satisfactory. The restriction of the reduction to a part only of the duties—those payable on insurances of stock-in-trade—would be disappointing

to the country, and he feared that this second exemption would tend to perpetuate the high rate on house and other property. It would have been better if the right hon. Gentleman had proposed to reduce the whole duty by 6d. this year, and a prospective 6d. in following years. The loss to the revenue would not, in that case, have been more than £50,000 in excess of the right hon. Gentleman's calculations. He would suggest that, as the Chancellor of the Exchequer proposed to continue the malt duty at its normal figure, he should take off the excrescence of an additional 5 per cent, which had been removed from almost every other excisable and customable article. That reduction of 5 per cent would be a decided relief, and would be recovered in two or three years. He could assure his hon. Friend the Member for Abingdon (Mr. Norris), that the Chancellor of the Exchequer had correctly stated the figures relative to the importation of rags, and that he had not included the woollen rags that were not used for paper. He was informed that persons who, two or three years ago, excited by statements of the cheapness of foreign paper, went through the foreign markets, were now so satisfied of their mistake that they had come back to the English market, and were now buying nothing but English paper. The Return for which he had moved, relative to the export of paper to our Colonies, would show this conclusively. Reserving the details of the proposal with regard to sugar for further consideration, he thought that the Chancellor of the Exchequer's present Budget would add considerably to his character and reputation.

MR. HENLEY said, he had no wish to remark upon the general character of the Budget, which would come before the House on a future occasion; but he wished to advert to the arguments of the Chancellor of the Exchequer in regard to the impossibility, according to his reasoning, of any increase in the consumption of malt if the duty were reduced. The right hon. Gentleman founded this argument on the fact, that thirty-five years ago the beer duty was taken off, and that during those thirty-five years the malt duty had not recovered what the malt and beer duty together then produced. He could not say that the right hon. Gentleman had misunderstood the question, but he had certainly misrepresented it. What was the real state of the case? The parties most anxious to have a reduction of the malt duty were not those who grew the highest qualities of barley, and unquestionably not the brewers, but those who did not wish to drive all the poor of this country to the beerhouses, as had been done by recent legislation. Those persons believed that a great deal of barley, which would not bear the high duty, would be malted, and that the cottager would thus be enabled to brew his own beer and share it with his family, instead of being driven to a beerhouse, where he certainly did not improve his morals. He could not see, therefore, how the reduction of the beer duty bore on this question. It had comparatively nothing to do with it, because the complaint was that the malt duty shut out those who would grow the lower qualities of barley, which would make a wholesome beverage at a moderate duty. The malt duty was mainly a consumer's question, but to those to whom it was both a consumer's and a producer's question, it was unsatisfactory to be told that it was mixed up with the old beer duty. When he heard the Chancellor of the Exchequer speculating upon a reduction of the duty on sugar being followed by an increase of consumption, he did not see why a reduction in the malt duty should not lead to a corresponding increase in the consumption of malt. There would certainly be an increased growth of the inferior qualities of barley with a moderate duty.

Mr. MAGUIRE regretted to find that Ireland was but little favoured by the plan of the Chancellor of the Exchequer. The right hon. Gentleman had represented that the alarm which existed last year among those who were engaged in the manufacture of tobacco in Ireland was an unreasonable alarm, and took credit to himself for the success of the changes he then introduced; but he forgot to mention that it was the very alarm which was excited and the pressure which it induced that led to the measure turning out a successful experiment, instead of a measure of ruin and confiscation, as it would otherwise have been. Coming to the subject of spirits, he must say for himself that he did not wish to encourage in any way the consumption of ardent spirits; but if people were to drink them at all they should be enabled to have pure ardent spirits, and not poison. He had been informed that to such an extent was adulteration practised in Ireland, that it was positively dangerous to drink,

Mr. Henley

stuff that was sold in the public-houses of that country. If the right hon. Gentleman made inquiries he would find that lunacy was on the increase in Ireland, mainly attributable to the poisonous quality of the spirits which the high duty had compelled the poorer people to drink. The right hon. Gentleman had almost given a pledge that the advanced duty would not increase illicit distillation; but the hon. Members for Dublin University and Tyrone County had shown, what the Attorney General for Ireland could confirm, that illicit distillation was greatly on the increase—and no wonder when the duty was so enormous. There could be no greater cause of crime and demoralization than illicit distillation. The revenue had not been increased, the trade had been almost destroyed, and a poisonous beverage had been substituted for a less injurious article. It might be too late now to make any change this year, but it was to be hoped that early next Session the right hon. Gentleman would deal efficiently with this subject, or what was, unhappily, almost the only branch of industry remaining to Ireland would be annihilated. With respect to the paper trade, he did not agree with the hon. Member for West Norfolk (Mr. Bentinck), because he believed the repeal of the paper duty had been a wise and beneficial measure, which had resulted in a wider diffusion, not only of political information, but also of general literature. He therefore congratulated the Chancellor of the Exchequer upon the success of that measure; but what he blamed the right hon. Gentleman for was that he had sacrificed the paper trade of his own country to the paper trade of foreign countries. It was a wise step to remove the Excise duty on paper manufactured in this country, so far having free trade; but having it in his power to retain the Customs duty of 1*d.* until foreign Governments reduced their export duties upon rags, the right hon. Gentleman had rashly and madly sacrificed that screw, and thus enabled the foreign manufacturer to obtain an advantage of 15 or 16 per cent over the papermakers of England, Scotland, and Ireland. He knew nothing of the imaginary case which the right hon. Gentleman had introduced with so much delicacy, and abstaining to give the name, but stating that the gentleman would give the facts in confidence to any one who desired to know them. But he would like to know the gentleman's name, in order that the paper manufacturers of this country might be able to examine his facts. If that gentleman had succeeded in reducing the cost of production by 50 or 60 per cent, he was indeed a wonderful man. The right hon. Gentleman had told them that he expected the French Government would reduce the export duty upon rags, and he rejoiced to hear it; but would that example be followed by the Belgian and German Governments? He could not understand that it was free trade for Englishmen to give up all to the foreigner and to receive nothing from him. Whether it were free trade or not, it certainly was not wise or patriotic in a Minister of this country to play into the hands of the foreigner to the destruction of a native industry. The right hon. Gentleman ought to persevere in his efforts to induce foreign Governments to act reciprocally. He hoped, therefore, that next year the Chancellor of the Exchequer would give due consideration to the case of Irish spirits and to the claims of the papermakers to equal justice with the foreign manufacturer.

MR. BASS, referring to the Chancellor of the Exchequer's statements respecting the malt tax, said, he thought the right hon. Gentleman had rather understated at £3,000,000 what would be the first loss at a reduction of the tax. The present revenue from malt being £6,200,000, one-half would be rather more than £3,000,000, to which must be added the return of duty paid upon stock in hand, which would be at least a million and a half more. The Chancellor of the Exchequer had, however, wholly ignored the elasticity of the tax, to use a term of his own. The right hon. Gentleman the Member for Oxfordshire (Mr. Henley) had clearly shown that the Chancellor of the Exchequer had overlooked some very important considerations in relation to the beer tax, which was removed in 1830. It was not probable that brewing by individuals would be carried to any great extent except in rural districts. With regard to the recuperative power of the malt tax, it had been shown during the Russian war that a high additional rate of duty did not by any means produce a corresponding increase in the amount of revenue, while a reduction of duty was not followed by anything like a corresponding loss of revenue. At that time—in 1854—an additional duty of 2s. a bushel, or nearly 75 per cent, was imposed on malt, and the increase of revenue was only 21 per cent. In 1856 the war duty was taken off, and the result was an increase of more than double that percentage. The right hon. Gentleman had laid great stress on the result of a reduction of the malt duty, as it would affect Ireland. Now, the fact was that the malt duty was so excessive that they could not in Ireland afford to drink beer. The natural energy of their character did not require that the Irish should drink whisky, and if the malt duty were reduced they would probably drink the more lethargic beverage, to which we were accustomed in this country. It appeared from the right hon. Gentleman's speech, that in the consumption of French wine there had been an increase amounting to 300 per cent. Could any body doubt that if the malt duty were adequately reduced, the consumption of good, sound beer would show as large an increase? Considering how largely the consumption of every article had increased on the reduction of the duty on it, he could not see how, with justice, the malt duty could be retained on its present scale. The brewers were quite content with things as they were. Their policy as brewers was *quieta non movere*. They made a living and were satisfied. Those who insisted that brewers would benefit from a reduction in the malt tax were, in his opinion, quite mistaken; for if the trade were asked whether they would prefer the reduction or an additional duty of 10s., he believed they would prefer the latter.

MR. MALINS said, that whilst one part of the Budget had given him entire satisfaction, he must say that he was much disappointed with another part of it. The part with which he was thoroughly satisfied was the proposal for the reduction of the Income Tax, because, though the present proposal was the reduction of a penny only, it was an earnest of an intention gradually to annihilate a tax, which seemed to him on every principle objectionable. But as to the Fire Insurance duty, he thought that the proposal was as unsatisfactory a one as could possibly be made. The right hon. Gentleman, in the face of two Resolutions of the House that the duty on Fire Insurance generally should be reduced, had proposed that it should be partially and most unfairly reduced. In April, 1862, the House, by a majority of 11, gave the hon. Member for Dudley-(Mr. Sheridan) leave to introduce a Bill for the reduction of Fire Insurance duty, and in July last a majority of 36 affirmed that the duty

X 2

ought to be reduced. The meaning was, that it should be reduced generally. But the proposal of the right hon. Gentleman was, that the duty should be reduced, not on furniture, houses, and buildings, but only with respect to stock-in-trade. If the right hon. Gentleman could only part with £200,000 of revenue, he should still have applied it to a general, and not a partial reduction of the duty. Indeed, one part of the right hon. Gentleman's own speech condemned the course he proposed to take, for he said that he had always thought that the reduction of duty upon agricultural property was unfair because it was partial. In face of this he proposed to take off the duty in reference to stock-in-trade only. A great trader, who had £100,000 of stock-in-trade would have to pay a duty of 1s. 6d. only, whilst his next-door neighbour, who had no stock, would have to pay 3s. duty on the insurance of his furniture. He (Mr. Malins) himself would, for instance, have to pay the full amount of 3s. duty upon the insurance on his furniture and books. [Mr. WHITESIDE: Your law library would be stock-in-trade.] He did not know how that might be, but clearly his furniture in his private house would not come under that category. The right hon. Gentleman had taken off the paper duty, and the paper trade was well nigh ruined, because he said the House had decided twice against the duty; but the House had, in general terms, voted the same as to Fire Insurance duty, and yet the right hon. Gentleman proposed not a general, but a partial reduction in it. The class of persons the right hon. Gentleman proposed to benefit was the class least requiring relief. It was the non-trader, bound to insure his property under covenant, who ought to receive consideration. He was sorry that in a Budget, the general principles of which he considered satisfactory, and to the tone of the observations introducing which he assented, a proposal with respect to Fire Insurance should be inserted benefiting not the bulk but only a small portion of the community.

SIR FRANCIS GOLDSMID said, that the Chancellor of the Exchequer had said that, by reducing the duty on Fire Insurance of stock-in-trade, he wished to try the recuperative force of a reduction in the duty on Fire Insurance. Now it appeared to him, that the experiment was about to be made in the direction from which there was the least chance of suc-

Mr. Malins

cess. If a man was insuring his furniture, which generally he could do at the ordinary rate, it became a matter of importance to him whether he had to pay 1s. 6d. or 3s. duty; but to a man who had to pay a rate of perhaps 12s. or 13s. for insuring his stock-in-trade, it was almost a matter of indifference whether the duty was 1s. 6d. or 3s.

COLONEL SYKES said, that having twice voted in favour of reducing the duty on Fire Insurances, he had certainly expected that any measure on the subject would have been general, and not partial. The present duty of 3s. was a barrier to insurance on the part of the occupiers of small houses; but if the duty were reduced to sixpence, the recuperative principle would have a chance of coming into operation.

MR. CAIRD said, that that part of the Chancellor of the Exchequer's propositions, by which he stated that lentils and other articles of the same description would be placed in the same position as corn, would not be received with favour by agriculturists. Those articles did not come into competition with corn, but some of them were useful for the purposes of distillation in Ireland and Scotland, and hitherto the right hon. Gentleman had not done much in favour of that class of manufacturers. He trusted the right hon. Gentleman would reconsider the point.

THE CHANCELLOR OF THE EXCHEQUER said, that the proposal to which his hon. Friend (Mr. Caird) had just referred, was made at the suggestion of the trade; but it was a matter on which he thought it quite right that all parties should be heard. By passing the Resolution in Committee, the House would not be bound to the imposition of the duty, and there would be time for a further consideration of the subject before a Bill was brought in. The question was one with respect to which he was in no way prejudiced. He had to observe that the debate of that evening had been rather less of a conversational character, and rather wider in range than those which generally followed the Financial Statement of the Chancellor of the Exchequer; but he had no reason to complain of the tone of the discussion, which was very satisfactory to him. After having detained the Committee so long, while making his statement, he would only refer to one or two of the points which had been adverted to. He was sorry that the hon. Member for West Norfolk (Mr. Bentinck) should have supposed that anything which had fallen from him had been uttered in disrespect of those who had been the consistent champions of protection. It was the wish to relieve the dullness of a very dry subject which had induced him to refer to the matter at all; but certainly he had not intended to cast any reflection, personally or otherwise, on the gentlemen who advocated the policy of protection. With regard to the duty on beer, while he was glad that the point referred to by the right hon. Gentleman the Member for Oxfordshire (Mr. Henley) had been brought under the consideration of the House, his own opinion was, that whether the malt duty was reduced or not, the capital and other advantages possessed by that class of manufacturers, of which his hon. Friend the Member for Derby (Mr. Bass) was commander-in-chief, must every day narrow the demand for private brewing. He did not, therefore, attach much weight to the argument; but he was glad that the right hon. Gentleman had brought it forward. His hon. Friend the Member for Derby said that the Irish did not drink beer, because of the heavy duty. He did not altogether understand the argument, and he did not think the Irish Members, to whose consideration he had submitted his argument, would derive much advantage from it. The hon. Member said, that if they would reduce the duty, the Irish would drink beer. He could not concur with his hon. Friend, seeing that the duty on beer was only 25 or 27 per cent, while the habitual drink of the Irishman was whisky, on which the duty was 400 per cent. He was bound also to say, with respect to the suggestion of the hon. Member for Pontefract (Mr. Childers), that if they could not effect a large reduction in the malt duty they should take off the 5 per cent which was imposed some time ago. The hon. Member said it was the only case in which that 5 per cent still remained. That, however, was not so. The 5 per cent additional duty was still levied upon tobacco and on some other articles. It was true that when they had dealt with the duty upon any article, they had endeavoured to get rid of that 5 per cent: but he objected altogether to taking off the 5 per cent upon malt. In his opinion, if they wanted to devise a plan, which would effect a minimum of good and a maximum of evil in taxation, it would be by taking off the 5 per cent on

the duty on malt. He believed that the imposition of the 5 per cent was a hardship at the time, but that had long since righted itself. On the same ground he should object to the reduction of the duty on Fire Insurances by 6d. In his opinion, if the House of Commons could not go further than that it had much better leave the duty as it at present stood. The hon. and learned Member for Wallingford (Mr. Malins) said, that the Votes of the House on the subject of Fire Insurance, would not be satisfied by the proposal which he (the Chancellor of the Exchequer) had made. But he contended that these Votes would be far better satisfied by dealing effectively with one particular branch of the subject than by making a general reduction so small as to have no material operation in the way of extending insurance, and thus in no degree to replace the loss of revenue. Whether there was any force in the hon. and learned Gentleman's distinction between the tax upon property and the tax upon trade and industry, was a matter for the Committee to consider: but he trusted that they would not consent to any ineffective reduction such as had been suggested. An hon. Baronet opposite (Sir James Fergusson) complained that he had given a fallacious estimate of the Income Tax, and had not taken into account the re-assessment, which, in course of law, must take place in the present year. The hon. Baronet could scarcely have attended to the figures, which were very remarkable. Last year his estimate of the Income Tax for the year at 7d., with one quarter at 9d., was £8,600,000. This evening he had again submitted an estimate for the tax at 7d., but without the assistance of the quarter at 9d., and yet he had stated the probable result at the same amount—£8,600,000. The Committee would see, therefore, that he had allowed, and allowed liberally, for the re-assessment, which he agreed was likely to have a greater effect this year than on any previous occasion.

Sir JAMES FERGUSSON: I did not presume to say that the right hon. Gentleman had made a fallacious estimate. I asked him to state what he estimated would be the amount due to the re-assessment.

The CHANCELLOR of the EXCHEQUER said, it would be very difficult to distinguish between that portion of the tax which was likely to be due to the re-assessment and that which would be the amount without the re-assessment. It was a matter of pure details. A rough estimate might, perhaps, be obtained by calculating the value of the penny tax as compared with that of last year. If, however, he could find any means of giving more detailed information which he thought worthy of being submitted to the House, it should be very much at the service of the hon. Baronet. As to illicit distillation, it was necessary to bear in mind that they had to deal not only with the three portions of the United Kingdom, but with foreign as well as with home-made spirits. There had been on the whole a considerable augmentation of the revenue from this source, though it was true that there had been no increase at all in Ireland. When the right hon. Gentleman opposite (Mr. Whiteside) recommended that we should reduce the duties on spirits in Ireland, with a hope of recovering revenue by increased consumption, he forgot that that was a principle on which Parliament had never acted with reference to spirits. Unless it could be shown that the revenue was failing through illicit distillation, the argument that decreased duty would lead to increased consumption had never been held to be applicable. He had stated that there had been an increase of illicit distillation in Ireland; but the right hon. Gentleman must be perfectly aware that in Ireland every year when there was a large quantity of grain at a low price and in bad condition there was invariably an increase of illicit distillation. But he was prepared to show that that increase of illicit distillation had not been produced by the increased duties. When, in speaking of the paper duties, he had referred to the abolition of the export duty on rags by the French Government, he was under the impression that that export duty had been removed by the Italian Government, but not being certain of the fact he had not alluded to it. Since then he had referred to the papers, and had found that such was the case, and he hoped that the example would be followed by other Governments. The suggestion of the hon. Member for Shoreham (Mr. Cave) as to the licenses on the sale of tea should have his best attention. The right hon. Gentleman concluded by moving that the Chairman report Progress.

House *resumed.*

Committee report Progress; to sit again *To-morrow.*

The Chancellor of the Exchequer

SUPPLY.

Order for Committee read.

Motion made, and Question proposed, " That Mr. Speaker do now leave the Chair."

JAPAN—THE 20th REGIMENT.

QUESTION.

COLONEL SYKES rose to call attention to a recent statement in *The Times*, to the effect that the 2nd Battalion of the 20th Regiment on its arrival at Calcutta had immediately been transferred to other transports and been despatched to Japan. It would be said that the object of this transfer of troops to Japan—of the probable financial consequences of which he warned the Chancellor of the Exchequer in the strongest manner—was to insist upon the fulfilment of guarantees which the Japanese Government had given us by treaty. To that he replied that we had no treaty with the Emperor of Japan. We had, indeed, a treaty with one of the Princes of the empire, who was called by us the Tycoon of Yeddo, though, in fact, there was no such person known to the Japanese as the Tycoon. The name originated in this way. When the American Commodore Perry went to Japan he had with him a Cantonese interpreter, who, not knowing how to describe the Prince of Yeddo, called him Tycoon, which, in the Cantonese dialect, meant Great Prince. His proper title was Ziogoon, or Siogoun, meaning Generalissimo. A gentleman who seemed to possess good sources of information, in writing to the editor of the *Japan Herald*, expressed it to be his opinion that the Tycoon's Government was the cause of the serious difficulties with which we had to contend in that quarter, adding that the result of the relations which had been established with Japan was, that in the first instance two Russians were killed in the streets; then the British diplomatic residence was attacked, and Mr. Oliphant dangerously wounded; that event was followed by the attack on a party, one of whom, Mr. Richardson, was killed while riding on the high road; and lately a French officer was attacked while taking a ride, and different chiefs have fired upon foreign vessels from their forts; in short, the principle was maintained that it was a good thing to kill foreigners. Now that it appeared was particularly the feeling in the immediate vicinity of Yokohama, whither we were sending a regiment of

Europeans. And what, he would ask, were our prospects for the future when we got our regiment there? Why, in all probability, that some fine morning some of the officers would go out on a shooting excursion, that they would be seized; would endeavour to defend themselves, like Mr. Moss; that a struggle would ensue; that they would be maltreated, put into a Black Hole, and ultimately, perhaps, be surrendered to our Consuls. With a regiment at hand we should not submit to what we might deem an outrage, and should take the law into our own hands. We should in short be likely to get into a contest with all the Princes of the empire in succession, all of whom were opposed to us, and thus we should have in Japan a renewal of our China policy, which, as the Chancellor of the Exchequer had informed the House, had cost us seven millions sterling and an enormous sacrifice of human life. That, he contended, was a prospect which was not likely to lead to a diminution of our expenditure, while another element of discord and consequent loss was to be found in the probability that attempts would be made to smuggle opium into the country; that it would be seized, and then we should feel ourselves called upon to demand redress. Was it consistent with our professions of humanity to seek to hold our ground in Japan by means of force, against a people who were inimical to us? Under all the circumstances of the case, he hoped the House would look upon the question in a cautious and earnest spirit, so that we might be saved from falling into the same groove as in China. He would beg, in conclusion, to ask the Under Secretary of State for War, Whether he has made any provision in the Estimates for the charge of the 2nd Battalion 20th Regiment, transferred in December from the Indian Establishment for service in China or Japan, and whether other regiments are under orders for service in China or Japan?

VOLUNTEER ARTILLERY CORPS.

OBSERVATIONS.

MR. H. BERKELEY rose to call the attention of the House to the armament of the Volunteer Artillery force. The Royal Artillery were not inferior to any similar force in any country in Europe; but they were not a large force and they were scattered over the face of the world. It was, therefore, considered an excellent arrangement when, six years ago, a large part of the Volunteer force enrolled themselves into artillery corps. As regarded the Rifle Volunteers, they were promised, and they had received, the best arms the country possessed. But that was not the case with the Volunteer Artillery. When they were enrolled, they were informed that they must take such weapons as the War Office could provide, but the Secretary of State promised that they should ultimately be armed as effectively as the Royal Artillery. The Volunteers accepted that promise, and the Royal arsenals were ransacked to find guns wherewithal to arm them. They received six-pounders which, for ought he knew, might have been with Wolfe on the Heights of Abraham; field artillery which had seen service at Fontenoy and Culloden, and certainly numerous guns which had followed Wellington throughout his campaigns from Assaye to Waterloo. At first the Volunteers were satisfied with these weapons. They could learn their drill with them, and that was all that they then wanted. Six years had, however, now elapsed, and not the slightest improvement had been made in their armament. Let the House suppose the case of an invasion, an attempt by means of a flotilla to make a descent upon our shores. The noble Lord the Secretary for the Admiralty understood this part of the question, because with the noble Marquess the Under Secretary for War, to whom, in virtue of their offices, he was united in a bond of red tape, he formed a perfect Siamese twin of artillery—he would ask the noble Lord and the noble Marquess, against such a flotilla, consisting of gunboats carrying the heavy artillery of the day, what could our Volunteers effect with their old rotten 18-pounders, which had been disused for forty years? There were artillery officers enough in the House to tell them what would be the result of such a contest. At a range of a mile with smooth bored guns hit the bull's-eye about once in thirty shots, while with rifled ordnance it was struck twice out of three times. Some Volunteer Artillery corps were so disgusted with the guns which had been supplied to them that they had armed themselves. Messrs. Horsfall and Clay, of Liverpool, had for some time been making 12-pounder breech-loading guns on the pattern of Captain Forbes, a very distinguished artillerist. Four of these guns had been either purchased by or presented to the 8th Lancashire Artillery Volunteers, of which Mr. Clay, a member of the firm, was commander, and with these they were able to hit the bull's-eye at a mile range twice out of three times. It might be asked why such guns were not noticed by the Government, and the only reason that he could imagine was that they were too cheap. It seemed as though in the eye of the Government quality signified nothing. These guns without appurtenances cost only £95 a piece, while the price of similar weapons of the Armstrong pattern was £125. They might, however, at least be admitted to a trial; but it seemed that anything which came into competition with Sir William Armstrong's productions was regarded with the greatest disfavour by the Government. Perhaps he should be told that guns could not be made fast enough to arm the Volunteers; but it seemed to him that six years was quite long enough for the accomplishment of that object. The refusal to supply these corps with proper weapons savoured very much of that ignorance which characterized the Ordnance Department at the time of the Crimean war, when our army was sent into the field to contend with guns of inferior calibre against the 32-pounders of the Russians. At the battle of Inkerman two 18-pounders, which had probably been sent out by mistake for pork or cocoa, or something of that sort, turned up at the right moment, and did the work which the poor little 6-pounders could not effect. A remarkable instance of the importance of efficient artillery was afforded by the present war. The Danes had neglected their artillery, and, being armed for the most part with old smooth-bore guns, were cut to pieces by the Germans with their improved artillery. The able writing of the two Correspondents of *The Times*, one with the Danish and the other with the Prussian army, established the inferiority of the old Danish artillery and the superiority of the modern Prussian guns. Were we to wait till war came to our own shores? If the Volunteers were only for show, let the force be abolished; but if, as he believed, they were the best force which could be relied on for the support of the army, let justice be done to them by providing arms with which in case of need they could do themselves honour. Expense, no doubt, would be urged as a reason against furnishing this improved artillery; but he might mention that a proposition had been

Mr. H. Berkeley

made to rifle all the brass ordnance in this country in the same manner that the Emperor Louis Napoleon had done, at the cost of less than £2 a gun. He begged to ask the noble Lord the Under Secretary whether any steps had been taken, or were likely to be soon adopted, for arming the Volunteer Artillery in the same manner as the Royal Artillery?

INSTRUCTION AND EMPLOYMENT OF SOLDIERS.—RESOLUTION.

SIR HARRY VERNEY, in introducing the Resolution of which he had given notice, said, that in 1860 the Government instructed General Crawford to proceed to the French camp at Chalons, and to make a Report upon the work carried out by the soldiers of that army. General Crawford reported that men on attaining a certain age were instructed in some trade, and taught to shift for themselves when placed in difficult circumstances; and suggested as a point worthy of consideration, that something of the same kind might be effected for the improvement of the British soldier. The late Sir George Lewis, on receipt of this Report, appointed a Committee, and it was the recommendations of this tribunal to which he was anxious to give effect. The hon. Baronet having read evidence given before the Committee on this subject, concluded by moving his Resolution.

MR. BERNAL OSBORNE seconded the Motion.

Amendment proposed,

To leave out from the word "That" to the end of the Question, in order to add the words "it is expedient that the recommendations contained in the Report of the Committee on the proper means for the Instruction and Employment of Soldiers and their Children in Trades, and of the Under Secretary of State in a Letter to the Quartermaster General, Horse Guards, dated 23rd May, 1862, be carried into effect, with due regard to the duties and discipline of the Army,"
—(*Sir Harry Verney*,)
—instead thereof.

Question proposed, "That the words proposed to be left out stand part of the Question."

THE MARQUESS OF HARTINGTON said, that with regard to the Question put to him by the hon. and gallant Member for Aberdeen (Colonel Sykes), he was under some misapprehension with reference to the 20th Regiment. The first battalion of the regiment was doing duty in India, and therefore was not provided for in the Estimates. The second battalion, which was intended for India, but was afterwards diverted for service either in China or Japan, had been provided for in the Estimates. He did not think that he need on that occasion follow the hon. and gallant Member into his fears and prophecies with regard to our military force in Japan. It was not at all correct to suppose that the regiment was or was intended to be quartered in Japan. At one time the aspect of affairs in that country was extremely threatening. Several residences belonging to Europeans there were burnt down, and it was not unlikely that other hostile demonstrations would be made against the Europeans. Colonel Neale accordingly applied to General Brown for a small force of soldiers to protect Yokohama, but General Brown refused to send them without the sanction of the Home Government. That was afterwards given, and 160 men were sent there; and it was now expected, from the present peaceful aspect of affairs in that country, that they would soon be able to withdraw them; and then there would be no English soldiers at all in Japan. No other regiment was under orders for service in China.

With regard to the question of the hon. Member for Bristol (Mr. H. Berkeley), the Volunteer Artillery was not raised with the intention of their acting as field artillery, but almost entirely and exclusively as garrison artillery. He was not aware that they had been armed with the extremely imperfect and antiquated weapons described by the hon. Member; on the contrary, the only guns supplied to the Volunteer Artillery were 18, 24, and 32-pounders. It was true that one or two corps had provided themselves with field guns at their own expense, but he was not aware if the particular corps referred to had done so. The Newcastle corps had done so, not, however, because they were dissatisfied with the guns supplied to them by the Government, but because they wished to be able to take part in reviews as field artillery. Up to the present time no field batteries had been granted to Volunteer Artillery Corps; but it was intended in the present Estimates to take a sum of money to enable the Government to provide for a limited number of those corps with field guns. Still it was not intended that the Volunteer Artillery should act generally as field artillery, the main object being that they should take a part, if necessary, in the

defence of the coasts as garrison artillery. The guns that had been supplied, although not equal in precision and range to the rifle guns of the present day, were all that was necessary for teaching the Volunteers their gun-drill. With regard to Mr. Clay's gun, he could state that if it had ever been submitted to the consideration of the War Office it would have met with a fair trial. In all that had been said as to the beneficial nature of the recommendations contained in the Report of the Committee on the instruction and employment of soldiers he entirely concurred, and it was intended that a trial of those recommendations should be made as an experiment in the first instance. He trusted that the House would now go into Committee, for though the number of men for the army had been agreed to, not one shilling of the necessary money had yet been voted.

GENERAL PEEL thought, that when the House had once voted the number of men, it was bound to vote the money for them; but the first Vote which would be proposed embraced several important points, and he thought it was now too late (twenty minutes past eleven o'clock) to proceed with the discussion of them.

COLONEL DUNNE and COLONEL DICKSON also stated, that if the House went into Committee at that time of night, it would be impossible to get through any Votes.

VISCOUNT PALMERSTON hoped that the House would go into Committee to-morrow.

Amendment, by leave, *withdrawn.*

Question again proposed, "That Mr. Speaker do now leave the Chair."

Motion, by leave, *withdrawn.*

Committee *deferred* till *To-morrow.*

NAVAL AGENCY AND DISTRIBUTION
BILL—[BILL 39.]
SECOND READING.

Order for Second Reading read.

LORD CLARENCE PAGET moved the second reading of this Bill, which with the two following Bills on the Orders of the Day—the Naval Prize Acts Repeal Bill, and the Naval Prize Bill—was proposed for the purpose of consolidating the Acts relating to naval prizes. One point in which it was intended to alter the law had reference to ransom, and it would be left to the Privy Council to decide at the commencement of any war, whether the question of ransom should be entertained. After the Bills were read a second time, he would move that they be committed *pro formâ*, for the purpose of receiving alterations, and then that they be reprinted with the Amendments.

Moved, "That the Bill be now read a second time."—(*Lord Clarence Paget.*)

Sir JOHN HAY said, he did not oppose the Bill; but he rose to draw the attention of the noble Lord that the Repeal Act professed to deal with a number of Bills in force since the reign of Queen Anne; but five or six were omitted that should have been included. A number of Acts were also repealed in part, but he thought, with some care, these statutes might be wiped off, and what was valuable put in another Act. Confusion would arise in respect of the Acts repealed in part; they referred to pay and prize, and they were repealed as regarded prize and not as regarded pay. He thought those subjects should be separated. There were six Acts with reference to the slave trade, which might be dealt with in the same way. He thought it very undesirable that the whole of the law with regard to prize should be left to be settled by Royal Proclamation, or Orders in Council, as proposed by the 13th, 14th, and 15th clauses.

Motion *agreed to.*

Bill read 2°, and *committed* for *Thursday* next.

Then, NAVAL PRIZE ACTS REPEAL BILL, and NAVAL PRIZE BILL read 2°, and *committed* for *Thursday* next.

House adjourned at a quarter before Twelve o'clock.

HOUSE OF LORDS,

Friday, April 8, 1864.

MINUTES.] — PUBLIC BILLS — *Committee* — Settled Estates Act Amendment [H.L.]° (Nos. 35 and 43).
Third Reading—Court of Chancery (Despatch of Business) [H.L.]° (No. 18), and *passed.*

Their Lordships met; and having gone through the business on the paper, without debate,

House adjourned at a quarter past Five o'clock, to Monday next, Eleven o'clock.

Lord Clarence Paget

HOUSE OF COMMONS,

Friday, April 8, 1864.

MINUTES — SELECT COMMITTEE — on Public Accounts—Mr. Cobden *discharged*, Lord Robert Montagu *added.*
SUPPLY—*considered in Committee* °—Committee —R.P.
PUBLIC BILLS—*Select Committee*—Cattle Importation and Cattle Diseases Prevention, Mr. Joseph Ewart and Mr. Beecroft *added.*
Committee—Warehousing of British Spirits ° (*recommitted.*
Report—Warehousing of British Spirits°.

UNITED STATES — COMPULSORY ENLISTMENT OF BRITISH SUBJECTS.

QUESTION.

SIR ANDREW AGNEW said, he must beg leave, in asking the Question of which he had given notice, to make a brief statement of facts. Two months ago a gentleman at Kingston-upon-Thames received a letter from his son, dated New York, January 22, in which he expressed himself as extremely well pleased with his ship and his captain, under whom he had served with great comfort for eight years. A few days ago the father received a letter from his son's captain, dated New York, March 11, saying—

"We arrived at this port on the 20th of January; your son was missing a few days after. He went on shore a little the worse for drink, and has not since returned. I fear he has been kidnapped by some of the runners of this port, and sent to sea. . . I have forwarded his effects to the Board of Trade, in London. . . . You will obtain all information about effects, &c., at —, Mark Lane."

The wretched father hurried to Mark Lane, where he received a confirmation of the captain's story, the agent adding that New York had become a horrible place; hundreds of young men had been kidnapped, and never after heard of. Of his own son's fate this gentleman was still in entire ignorance. He, therefore, begged to ask the Under Secretary of State for Foreign Affairs, Whether Her Majesty's Government have received any Reports from Consular Officers in the United States of America, stating that British Subjects have been kidnapped, detained, or otherwise outraged with the object of forcing them to serve as soldiers in the Federal Army?

MR. LAYARD said, he must beg to state, in answer to his hon. Friend, that Her Majesty's Government had received Reports from our Consuls at Boston, Portland, and New York, on the subject of the kidnapping of Irishmen who had been induced to go to the United States on various pleas. These Reports agreed in the main with the information which the public had been able to derive from the newspapers. At Portland 7 and at Boston 102 British subjects had, it appeared, been kidnapped. Those persons had been tempted, under various pretences, to leave Ireland, and on arriving in the United States were actually imprisoned for some time, kept without sufficient food, and then plied with whisky. When in a state of intoxication they were prevailed upon to enter the army of the United States. Lord Lyons had already made a Report on the subject to Her Majesty's Government. As soon as the Government received information of what had taken place at New York, instructions were sent to Lord Lyons to make inquiry and to ask for redress ; and further, to call on the United States' Government, in future, to protect British subjects who might be induced, under false pretences, to proceed to the United States. He trusted soon to receive from Lord Lyons an account of what he had been able to do in the case of the persons who had been so ill-used at New York.

TOBACCO JUICE FOR SHEEP-DRESSING.

QUESTION.

LORD JOHN BROWNE said, he would beg to ask Mr. Chancellor of the Exchequer, Whether, as tobacco juice for sheep-dressing is allowed to be made at Glasgow from tobacco free of Duty, he will allow the same privilege to be granted to parties applying therefor in Dublin, Belfast, Cork, and the other principal ports of Ireland ?

THE CHANCELLOR OF THE EXCHEQUER replied, that he was glad the noble Lord had put the question, as it might, perhaps, draw the attention of parties interested to an arrangement with which it was possible they might not be sufficiently acquainted. The Treasury had extended the privilege to which the noble Lord had referred, and which was originally granted by way of experiment to a particular individual, to tobacco manufacturers and other persons who might apply for it in Glasgow, Leith, or any other port at which tobacco might be legally imported, under the regulations laid down in the first instance, and on condition that suitable premises were provided, and that the Crown

was put to no additional expense thereby. That privilege was common, in principle, to all the ports of the three Kingdoms at which tobacco could be imported, and Dublin, Belfast, and Cork were among the number.

CONVICTS IN COUNTY GAOLS.

QUESTION.

MR. J. R. ORMSBY GORE said, the Government having increased the allowance towards the maintenance in County and Borough Gaols of Convicts sentenced to Penal Servitude from a maximum of 4s. per head per week to a maximum of 8s., for such a period as they may be detained in prison, beyond two calendar months from the time of conviction, he wished to ask the Secretary of State for the Home Department, Whether it is intended to keep such Convicts in County Gaols for any time longer than at present, as it will in Shropshire necessitate an increase of accommodation and in staff, there being no means of giving hard labour for any greater number than at present ?

SIR GEORGE GREY, in reply, said, it was certainly not intended to detain convicts sentenced to penal servitude for a longer time than at present in county or other local prisons ; but, on the contrary, it was hoped that they would be kept there for a shorter time. In consequence of the increase of penal servitude sentences in 1861-2, it was difficult to provide for the convicts in the Government prisons, and some of them were therefore detained longer than usual in the local gaols. Last year, however, there was some decrease in the number of penal servitude sentences, and it was expected that arrangements would be made to remove convicts from the local prisons at an earlier period than hitherto.

THE BRADFORD RESERVOIRS.

QUESTION.

MR. FERRAND said, he rose to ask the Secretary of State for the Home Department, Whether he has received Mr. Rawlinson's Report on the state of the Bradford Reservoirs ; if so, whether he has reported them to be safe ; if not, which are reported unsafe ; and, in the event of any of them being unsafe, whether the Government will take immediate steps to protect those persons whose lives are endangered;

and whether he will lay the Report upon the table of the House.

SIR GEORGE GREY said, in reply, that Mr. Rawlinson had not yet made his detailed Report of the result of his inspection of the Bradford Reservoirs, which are eleven in number, but he intended to do so as soon as he could. He was at present engaged in his other duties. He had, however, informed him (Sir George Grey) that in two out of the eleven Reservoirs—Doe Park and Bradfield—the embankments were imperfect, but, the water having been drawn off while they were repairing, there was no present danger, and the corporation undertook that they should not be filled again till they were made properly safe. All the rest Mr. Rawlinson deemed to be sound.

MR. W. E. FORSTER said, he should be glad to know whether when Mr. Rawlinson's Report is sent in it will be laid on the table?

SIR GEORGE GREY said, he should think there could be no objection to presenting it.

DENMARK AND GERMANY—THE CONFERENCE.—QUESTION.

SIR HARRY VERNEY said, he would beg to ask the First Lord of the Treasury, Whether, at the Conference about to assemble on the affairs of Germany and Denmark, the interests of the inhabitants of the Duchies of Holstein and Schleswig will be represented and protected?

VISCOUNT PALMERSTON: Sir, I can assure my hon. Friend that the interests of the people of Schleswig and Holstein will be sufficiently cared for. In the first place, there will be in the Conference a representative of their lawful Sovereign; and that Sovereign, no doubt, will have equally at heart the interests of all his subjects. In the next place, there will be in the Conference the representatives of the two German Powers who have taken up arms on the alleged ground of enforcing engagements connected with these two Duchies. Thirdly, the Diet will, we hope —but no answer has yet been received— be represented at the Conference, and although the Diet has nothing whatever to do with the Duchy of Schleswig, that not being a portion of the Confederation, the representative of the Diet will take good care of the interests of the Duchy of Holstein, which is under the Confederation.

Mr. Ferrand

FACTORY INSPECTORS.
QUESTION.

COLONEL EDWARDS said, he would beg to ask the Secretary of State for the Home Department, Whether Sub-Inspectors of Factories must be at least twenty-five years of age before being appointed; whether it is true that the new scale of salary to be paid does not give them any annual increase of pay, but requires thirty years of service before the scale of £500 a year is reached, and limits the recipients of £500 a year to two Sub-Inspectors out of twenty; and whether it is true that the allowance for personal expenses when absent from home is only 12s. a night for a Sub-Inspector of Factories, while the same allowance in other Departments is 15s., and in some instance £1 per day; and, if so, why this allowance to Sub-Inspectors of Factories has not been raised to the average standard?

SIR GEORGE GREY replied, that it was required by the Factory Regulations that Sub-Inspectors should be at least twenty-five years of age at the time of their appointment. The new scale of salaries recommended by the Chief-Inspectors, and submitted to the Treasury, would not give an annual increase of pay; but there were five classes, the lowest beginning with £300 a year, with an increase at the rate of £50 per annum in each case, after a certain number of years' service, and reaching £500 after thirty years' service. It was true that only two could be at the same time in the highest class. As to the allowance for expenses, Sub-Inspectors received in addition to their travelling expenses, 12s. a day, which was the same allowance as that granted to Inspectors of Mines, and he had no reason to believe that it was insufficient.

LORD JOHN MANNERS said, he wished to know, whether the increased scale of salaries has received the recommendation of the two Chief Inspectors?

SIR GEORGE GREY believed it was adopted on the joint recommendation of the two Chief Inspectors.

SUPPLY.

Order for Committee read.

Motion made, and Question proposed, "That Mr. Speaker do now leave the Chair."

ST. MARY'S BURIAL GROUND, SYDENHAM.

SELECT COMMITTEE MOVED FOR.

Mr. NEWDEGATE said: Mr. Speaker, it will be in the recollection of those Members of the House and of the Government, who were present here at the close of last Session, (I mean during the two last days of the Session,) that I gave notice of my intention to put a question to the right hon. Gentleman the Secretary of State for the Home Department, with respect to the circumstances under which the right hon. Gentleman had granted a licence for the use of a certain piece of ground at Sydenham, for the purposes of burial by a religious community known as the Oratorians, who possess an establishment at Brompton, and declare themselves to be of the Roman Catholic order of St. Philip Neri. In order that I might have an opportunity of entering into an explanation of the circumstances which had led me to think it my duty to put this question (the statement of which appears to excite some feelings of irritation among Members on the other side of the House, and on this side of the House, who are connected with the Roman Catholic body), I moved the adjournment of the House. This afforded the right hon. Member for the County of Limerick (Mr. Monsell), and the hon. and learned Member for Dundalk (Sir George Bowyer), an opportunity to speak, and the right hon. Member for Limerick thought fit to accuse me of having hounded to death a Mr. Turnbull, who had been appointed one of the Calendarers in the State Paper Office, but was afterwards removed, through the intervention of the noble Lord at the head of the Government, at the instance of a large number of gentlemen, who thought that Mr. Turnbull's antecedents, particularly as connected with certain Roman Catholic publishing societies, were not such as to render it advisable that he should be continued in that office. This House being summoned to the House of Lords for the purpose of prorogation, prevented my then replying to the accusation which had been levelled against me, but in a letter, which after the close of the Session I addressed to the right hon. Member for Limerick, and which appeared in *The Times* and other newspapers, I think I completely disposed of the imputation that I had joined in "hounding Mr. Turnbull to death." I believe, Sir, that that gentleman died under the pressure of difficulties that affected his health; but these were caused by his connection with these Roman Catholic publishing societies. I wish now to call the attention of the House to the subject of the Motion before it, which is connected with the circumstances that induced me to put the question at the end of last Session, to which I have alluded, since by the termination of the last Session the discussion of this subject was then precluded. There are some singular circumstances connected with this burial ground at Sydenham, and with the burials which have taken place within it. And, first, let me state that so secretly was the application made for licence to perform burials in this ground—made at the instance of the late Duke of Norfolk—that none but the parties immediately concerned was aware of the application having been made to the right hon. Baronet at the head of the Home Department. It appears, Sir, the right hon. Baronet sent down an Inspector, who subsequently reported that, as the burials were likely to be few—those only of members of the community of St. Philip Neri—he thought that the piece of ground might be used with safety, although the situation of the soil was not eminently favourable for the purpose. Thereupon the right hon. Baronet granted a licence, but that licence was never published in the *Gazette*, and I have the authority of Mr. Saxton, whose property and land adjoin the ground belonging to this community, that neither he nor the incumbent of the parish of Sydenham, nor the rate-collectors, nor any of the neighbours, nor, as I have been informed, the persons who have conducted the ordnance survey of that vicinity, had the slightest idea that the application had been made, or that the licence had been granted for the use of this piece of ground, or any part of it, as a burial ground. Now, in the Acts of Parliament which regulate burials, particularly within the metropolitan district, there are very stringent provisions that notice shall be given to the neighbouring proprietors and to the residents in the immediate neighbourhood, of any ground which is to be constituted a burial ground, in order that if there are any valid objections to the use of such ground, the persons who will be affected should have the opportunity of stating them. In the present case, no such opportunity was afforded; and, Sir, this matter might have passed without notice, but that a Mr. William Hutchison, who was brother-in-law of Mr. Smee, the medical officer to the

Bank of England, died, and was buried in this piece of ground at Sydenham. I believe that many Members of the House are by this time familiar with the circumstances under which this Mr. William Hutchison joined the community of St. Philip Neri. He was the relative of the late Mr. Smee, who was formerly a well known officer of the Bank of England, the eminent accountant in that great establishment. Mr. Smee, whose petition I presented, was brought up in his father's house with Mr. Hutchison, on terms of the greatest intimacy and affection: to use his own expression, they lived together as brothers; and eventually Mr. Smee married the sister of Mr. Hutchison. Well, Mr. Hutchison, after studying at King's College, and reading with an eminent Conveyancer in London, entered the University of Cambridge, and there he came into contact with the Rev. Mr. Faber, who, I am informed, is now no more. Here I may observe, that I remember this person (Mr. Faber) when I was an undergraduate at Christ Church, Oxford; he was one of the tutors of the College, and passed for a clergyman of the Church of England. There were surmises, however, that he was not in heart a member of that Church; his opinions were extreme; and finally he declared himself to be a member of the Church of Rome, and became a Roman Catholic priest. But, during his transition from one Church to the other, he seems to have been actively employed; for five or six of my own contemporaries at the University changed their religion, and one of them at least became a priest. I can easily understand, therefore, the influence which this Mr. Faber may have exercised on the mind of Mr. Hutchison. Suffice it, that he persuaded him to become a Roman Catholic. He then persuaded him to go to Birmingham, to the house of the Roman Catholic Bishop there. He next persuaded him, or rather Faber and his allies persuaded Mr. Hutchison, that it was his duty to leave his family; and then Mr. Faber took Mr. Hutchison to Rome, impressed with the idea that his eternal salvation depended upon his implicit obedience to Mr. Faber. And when they returned, Mr. Hutchison became a priest of the Church of Rome, and entered this community of St. Philip Neri. The attachment of Mr. Smee to his brother-in-law never failed. At all times his house was open to him: at all times his family were but too anxious to

Mr. Newdegate

receive him back. About the period in this sad history to which I have brought my narrative, Mr. Smee, himself an eminent medical man, became very apprehensive that the discipline to which his relative was being subjected was undermining his health. Moreover, he became apprehensive, that the religious excitement to which he was exposed was affecting his intellect; he prayed him to come to his old home were it but for a short time. But no: Priest Faber's influence was supreme; obedience was exacted; there must be no change of life. The disease increased, and the health of Mr. Hutchison gradually failed under this process. About this time Mr. Faber told Mr. Hutchison that he would die, and that in virtue of the obedience which Mr. Hutchison owed him as head of the Oratory he must make his will, and Mr. Faber made Mr. Hutchison's will at first in favour of the late Duke of Norfolk, no doubt with the intention that the Duke of Norfolk should be trustee for the Order; but owing to some legal difficulties, I know not what, the intention was changed, and the will was made in favour of Mr. Faber by himself as the head of this Community. Now observe: a member of this Community, bound by this implicit obedience, makes a will at the bidding of his Superior, the document being witnessed by two other members of this Community in favour of whose Superior this instrument is executed. Now if this is a Community in the sense of having a community of property, every one of these persons— the person who made the will and the witnesses who attested it—had an interest in the property bequeathed under that document. In my belief there is in that establishment no community except the community of implicit obedience to the Superior, and the circumstances which are stated in the petition presented this night from Mr. Harrison, whose son, when captain of Westminster School, was induced by this same Mr. Faber to join the Oratory, convince me that there is no community but a community of implicit obedience to the Superior in this so-called Community, and that he has as much the sole control of the property, which may be devised to that Community, as if it were devised to him in his capacity of being the head of it. Thus, Sir, the will was executed, and the illness of Mr. Hutchison increased; but I will do the Oratorians the justice of saying, that when Mr. Hutchison's illness was near its climax, they permitted his relative, Mr. Smee, as an eminent medical man, to attend him in .this, which proved to be his last illness. Two years after Mr. Faber had told Mr. Hutchison that he would die, Mr. Hutchison did die, and was buried in this private burial ground — private as it is called, secret as I think I can show you that it should be termed—because, as I have stated to the House, before its inauguration none of the means of publicity were afforded which are by law treated necessary before a piece of ground is constituted a burial ground within the limits of the metropolitan district were used. At the funeral of this poor man there was, indeed, a ceremony. Mr. Smee states that members of the family of the Duke of Norfolk attended, but that when all was over, a day or two afterwards, as the representative of the nearest of kin to Mr. Hutchison, Mr. Smee adopted the course which is usual with the Bank of England and all the great Insurance Companies. He applied for an extract of the register of burials kept within this place, or a certificate of the burial of his relative contained therein. Mr. Smee, who is a person perfectly cognizant of the usual practice in these matters from his position as medical officer of the Bank of England, had observed and was distressed by this fact, that when he went to visit the grave of his relative, he found that his was the third burial in this secret burial ground. There was the mark of the grave of some one, but no tombstone to tell the antecedents of that man, or what his name had been. Mr. Smee inquired who was there buried. The Oratorian in attendance only said, "Oh! that is the grave of a lay brother." One grave with a tombstone was there previous to the burial of Mr. Hutchison, that of a Mr. Wells, whose real names were "Frederick Fortescue Wells," which were the names in his will, and by which he was known previous to his joining this Community; but the names on the tombstone are simply "Albanus Wells." And so with Mr. Hutchison's tombstone. The names were not simply "William Hutchison," the name by which he had been christened, the name on his will, but the name "Anthony" had been interpolated between the true christian name and the surname, and so it read, on the tombstone, "William Anthony Hutchison." Now, any man who is cognizant of the practice in the courts will easily see the immense confusion

that might be caused by the interpolation of another christian name. The public means, the simplest public means, of identifying the dead, was destroyed by this change of name on the tombstone. Cases have been known where heirs of law have been enabled to discover and prove their right to large properties by means much less likely to afford information than the correct statement of a name upon a tombstone. But it appears that when persons join this Community or Order of St. Philip Neri, they are expected to adopt another christian name, a proceeding which is typical of the fact that they have left the world, abandoned their families, and cut themselves off from all the natural relations which endear the life of man, for the purpose of absolute devotion to this Order and absolute submission to the obedience which it exacts. Such is the character of the proceeding recorded on the tombstone of this Mr. Hutchison by the change of his name. And all these circumstances raise the presumption that this Community, this Order, established at Brompton, with its country house and secret burial ground at Sydenham, is one of those Orders which under the clauses of the liberal Act of 1829, which gave relief from their civil disabilities to all the laity of the Roman Catholic persuasion in the kingdom, is illegal within this country. Beyond what I have stated, also, there is presumptive evidence for believing that those who have founded, those who inhabit, and those who have devised property to this establishment or community, are perfectly aware that it is illegal. For I am told that the trust deed or settlement, designate it as you will, under which this property is held is of a most complicated nature, evidently drawn up by the hand of some skilful lawyer intent upon evading some provisions of the general law. Now, all the circumstances to which I have ventured to call the attention of the House render this narrative peculiarly significant, and the number of petitions which I have to-day presented show that the people of England, in common with the people of Italy, and in common with the Legislature of France, are of opinion that the existence, the increase, and the nature of these Establishments, Societies, Communities, or Orders, which are now on the increase in England and Wales, are matters that ought to be inquired into; because there is in all the actions which I have detailed the exhibition of a desire to evade the general operation of the law. For what is the law of England with respect to burials? Why, Sir, it is felony to tamper with the register of burials. In every public burial ground there must be kept a register of burials, free of access to every one upon payment of one shilling. For the same fee we can obtain a certificate from the authority in charge of the register, and if that register or the authorised certificate is tampered with, the crime is felony. That is the provision under the Burial Laws. But how stands the matter under the Forgery Laws? If any one tamper with a register of burials; if any one tamper with, change, or alter a certificate of burials for the purpose of presenting it, in order to deal with property in any court, the penalty is at the discretion of the court, varied from penal servitude for life to a minimum of penal servitude for three years. It is clear, therefore, that the law of England attaches no small importance to the registration of burials, for it was said to me by a competent authority, the registration of death may be evaded. It is sometimes difficult to prove the identity of the person who is dead. Therefore the Bank of England and the large Insurance Companies are not satisfied with the mere register of death, but insist upon the production of certified extracts from the register of the burial, because the means of identification after death are most important with a view to the due transmission of the property of the deceased to his heirs. Thus the practice of the great institutions of this country which deal with property and the law agree that the preservation of proper registers of burials and the due production of certificates is of the last importance to the transmission of property; aye, and it may be to the tracing of the cause of death. I ask the House, then, to grant a Committee; because, from the best advice I have been able to obtain, this place, this private, this secret burial ground has not been contemplated by the law and is beyond the law. I believe that no register is kept there. I believe there can be no legally produced certificates; and, unless the Legislature shall interpose, this burial ground may be a place for secret burials for ever, and others may be established characterized by the same objectionable features. That is one ground on which I ask for a Committee to inquire into the state of the law as to Burial. My belief is, that this burial ground and this community

are both beyond the purview of the law, and that it is not consistent with the safety of England, that it is not right, that it is not safe, that any large number of persons combined under a rigid discipline should exist in this free country of England beyond the purview of the law. Sir, I come now to what may be termed the second part of the case. I have stated all I have to say with respect to the St. Mary's Sydenham Burial Ground, with respect to the late Mr. Hutchison, and with respect to Mr. Smee. Of the latter gentleman, however, I would add, that having been brought into contact with him by accident, he appears to me to be a person who is well deserving the confidence which is reposed in him by that great establishment whose servant, whose competent servant, he is. Mr. Smee has written a letter and published it yesterday which certainly grieves me; that letter he has addressed to the Duchess of Norfolk. Well, Sir, I think that that letter ought to have been written. I think that a man who has had such bitter experience of the effects of the practices of this Order in his own family, does right in publicly warning others to beware how they intrust the members of their families to the keeping of such Bodies. But, then, the letter should have been addressed to Mr. Hope Scott and Mr. Sergeant Bellasis, the guardians of the daughter of the Duchess of Norfolk, who has been consigned to a convent not in England but in Paris. Had Mr. Smee remonstrated with these gentlemen, he would have done right; I think, however, he has made a mistake in addressing his letter to the Duchess of Norfolk. I knew nothing of it myself, and deeply lament it. But I say this, that as a man versed and employed in so many matters connected with the transmission of property after death, having this sad experience in his own family, and knowing that Mr. Hutchison was a friend of the late Duke of Norfolk, Mr. Smee pursued a manly course in beseeching those who have charge of this poor lady not to allow her to fall a victim to the fate which is the lot of so many nuns, for a short-lived race are nuns. This I say upon the authority of Mr. Hobart Seymour, a gentleman and clergyman, who, some years ago, prosecuted a close inquiry in Italy with regard to the dowering of nuns who enter convents, and the terms upon which unhappy ladies were consigned to those establishments. He found that, on a calculation of their average lives, the dowry, on the average, was so large, and the lives of the nuns so short, that a very handsome profit was left from year to year to these Communities, as they are called, and in the Papal States, through these Communities, to the Papal Treasury. Now all these nice calculations and details as to what may be got by the safe keeping, as it is called, but, as we believe, the imprisonment of these helpless women, grate upon our English feelings ; and let me say to the Roman Catholic Members of this House that they must make allowance for those feelings. I sometimes think that they are uncharitable. They may be of opinion, that the consigning of ladies to these convents is, on the part of their families, a sacrifice grateful to their religion. They may think, when they procure a change of religion in the members of some of our families, when they induce those who were once Protestants, as in the case of Mr. Hutchison, to enter such a Community as that of St. Philip Neri, that it is a sacrifice which is due to religion. But that is not our feeling. Our feeling is, that a person who is consigned to one of these establishments is a dead loss to his family ; is a dead loss to his country ; is a dead loss to himself. Gentlemen who are of the Roman Catholic persuasion must therefore make allowance for the point of view in which we, Protestants, regard these establishments and their inmates. Now, last August, Cardinal Wiseman attended the Roman Catholic Congress which was held at Malines, and since I suppose the Roman Catholic Members of the House will accept him as an authority, with the permission of the House, I will show that Cardinal Wiseman boasts of the vast increase of these establishments of late years in England, Wales, and Scotland, where their existence, in the case of monasteries, is contrary to law. I hold in my hand the translation of part of the speech made by Cardinal Wiseman during the Roman Catholic Congress which sat at Malines from the 18th to the 22nd of August last. In that speech he said—

" Allow me now to present to you, by means of statistics, a rapid view of the effect produced by these different measures. The Census gives the population in England—

For the year 1831 13,896,797
  ,,   ,,   1841 15,914,148
  ,,   ,,   1851 17,927,609
  ,,   ,,   1861 20,066,224

an increase of about two millions in each decennial period from 1831 to 1841. The population,

therefore, increased 14 per cent. In the same period the number of priests increased about 25 per cent, or nearly double. During the following 10 years the population increased 13 per cent, the number of priests 45 per cent. Lastly, from 1851 to 1861, while the population increased 12 per cent, the number of priests increased about 37 per cent. Here, again, are the precise statistics which will allow you to judge of the continued increase of the Roman Catholic Church in England. In 1830 we numbered but 434 priests for the whole of England. At present, we have 1,242, that is to say, three times as many. The number of our churches which was 410 has now increased to 872; from 16 convents which we possessed in 1830 in the United Kingdom, we have now, in 1863, 162. Lastly, in 1830 we had not a single religious house of men, in 1850 there were already 11, and to-day their number is 55."

He then goes on to mention other societies, such as the Society of St. Vincent de Paul, which I shall have to refer to afterwards, showing the enormous proportion by which the priests and the Communities of the Church of Rome had exceeded the rate of the increase of the population of this country. Sir, Cardinal Wiseman's statement is borne out by the facts. I have here an account taken from the Roman Catholic Directory of these religious houses—of these monasteries and convents. I find that the numbers given in this record exceed the numbers stated by the Cardinal at Malines, for it gives for England, Wales, and Scotland, 186 convents and 58 monasteries, or communities of men ; this, Sir, betokens a vast change and a great increase in those organizations, part of which continues illegal by the declaration of law. This is one of the characteristics of the present times, not only in England, but in France and Germany. I have no doubt that the attention of the Government has been drawn to the Report of a Committee of the Legislature of France in 1861, of which M. Dupin, then Procureur Général, was the chairman. This Committee, in their Report, advert in strong terms to the enormous increase, not of the communities—the orders, monasteries, and convents—which are sanctioned by law in France, but those which are unauthorized. I have made inquiries as to what are the terms of authorization in France ; that is, the terms upon which, under the constitution of France, these establishments may be formed, and are protected by the law. France, be it remembered, is a Roman Catholic country, and I find, that under the law of 1852, the existence of monastic vows is recognized as rightful in the inhabitants of those convents and monasteries, but only for a period of five years. Five years after the acceptance of the vow, it ceases to be operative, and it is especially provided that if any person have taken these vows, whether monk or nun, may leave the convent and marry, aided by the civil power, which would have enforced that person's remaining within the convent during the five years for which the profession had been made. There are many other provisions, I have them all here, but I will not detain the House by reading them, which go to secure in every way the safe establishment of these religious houses. But with all this, what do we find? Why, that the ambitious spirit which now guides the Roman Catholic hierarchy and organisations in France will not accept the assistance of the State upon these terms, and that the number of unauthorized communities has vastly increased in that country. We see the same thing in England. Now, three works have lately been published in Paris, to which I wish particularly to draw the attention of the Government, and of Members of this House. The first of these is a work by M. Charles Habeneck, entitled *Les Jesuites en* 1861. The second is a work by M. Cayla, published by Dentu, intituled *Ces bons Messieurs de St. Vincent de Paul*; and the third is a work by M. Charles Souvestre, *Instructions secretes des Jesuites*. Now, in all these works, and they support each other by independent evidence, it is clearly shown that this Society of St. Vincent de Paul is organized on the principle of the ancient League, which existed in the 16th century, and like the League is under the auspices of the Jesuits. I need not remind the House how many troubles on the Continent, how many religious wars that League produced. This society is organized upon the principle of the Congregation des Messieurs, of which Louis XIV. became a member, and history records the ambition of that prince, the wars which he carried on, and the intolerance of which he was guilty. This society is organized upon the principle of the Congregation which was so active after the close of the war ended in 1816, that it obtained influence with the Court and Ministers of Charles X., and by its operation upon the people of France, its everlasting interference with their families, its rapacious spirit, its bigotry and its tyranny, brought about the Revolution of 1830. I think, Sir, it is clearly proved in these works that these unauthorized societies, particularly the society of St. Vincent de Paul, al-

Mr. Newdegate

though that was formed originally by certain law students in the sacred cause of charity, have become subjected to a political influence, that of the Jesuits, of which it is enough to say that the strong Government of the Emperor of the French stands somewhat in awe of; and the proof of that fact is recorded in the Circular, Order, or Decree of M. Persigny, by which he strikes down, so far as the withdrawal of the legal authorization can do so, the central power of this association, declaring it to be unnecessary for the purposes of charity, and that politically it was inconsistent with the authority of the Emperor. Let me now come back to the community of St. Philip Neri, near our own doors—the establishment of the Oratory. When I heard that these persons were members of the society of St. Philip Neri, I asked myself, "Who was this St. Philip Neri?" I thought I could learn something of the character of the community from that of their patron saint, and so I did. I found in a work by Mr. Samuel Phillips Day, who was himself formerly a member of the order of the Presentation, that Neri or Nerius, who was afterwards canonized, was born in Florence in the year 1515, during the pontificate of Leo X.; that his father followed the occupation of an attorney, and was a great friend of the monks, especially the Dominicans; and that his mother was the descendant of a noble family who held distinguished offices in the state in the time of the republic. It appears to me that these Oratorians, by the acquisitive disposition they have shown, manifest that they have succeeded to some of the "sharp practice" which their patron saint may be supposed to have derived from his father's occupation. The present Superior of this society, M. Dalgairns, has declared that its members are not bound by religious vows; but that seems to me an evasion, for we know that they are bound by that extraordinary obligation of obedience which seems stronger than any vow, and is especially characteristic of the Jesuit system. We see that they are subjected to all the influence by which the strict discipline of the regular orders in the Church of Rome has ever been maintained. And, Sir, I believe that M. Faber, in his work on this very Order of St. Philip Neri, told the truth when he said it is a society eminently adapted to work its way under the free constitution of this country, and to establish a power as alien to our laws, no less alien to our constitution, than this same power has proved itself to the Government of France in the political organisation of the society of St. Vincent de Paul, which has a central organisation conducted under the auspices of a Cardinal at Rome, and extends its ramifications throughout the Continent. The society of St. Vincent de Paul was founded on the pretence of charity, but is used for the dissemination of those Jesuit doctrines, and the extension of that Jesuit power, which have proved so often —aye, and are proving now —fatal to the peace of Europe, and destructive of human happiness, and I am convinced that this order of St. Philip Neri is of the same stamp and character. Then, I inquired, what are the laws in Germany and in Prussia with respect to these religious Communities, and what do I find? That in Prussia, up to the Revolution of 1850, due security had been taken by law for tracing these establishments, for ascertaining their property, and so far as may be necessary for limiting the operation of their discipline. But in 1850 a wild spirit of liberalism prevailed. All the former laws were swept away, and subsequently there has been an enormous increase of these establishments under laws so lax that the Prussian Government can no longer exercise the control essential for the preservation of the peace. and good feeling among the various religionists of the country. The Jesuits have established themselves again in Prussia; and I ask this House whether they have heard nothing of the difficulties of the Prussian Government, and of their incapability to restrain the outburst of popular violence? Have we not had the weakness of that Government tendered to us as an excuse for the outrage which has been committed by that Prussian Government upon inoffensive Denmark, our neighbour just across the channel? That is the disposition which has grown up with the increase of these establishments. But now let us see what the Italians are doing. I have in my hand a copy of the Bill for suppressing many, and regulating some, of the Roman Catholic establishments which is now before the Italian Parliament, and with the permission of the House I will read a few words from the preamble to that Bill, which will best explain to the House the feelings of the Roman Catholic population of Italy, and the measures that they deem it necessary to take, with a view to preserving among themselves the blessings of peace and that sanctity of the family which these

religious orders have been too often known to violate. It says—

" The Government (of Italy) is not induced to promote the suppression of religious houses by motives of hostility or anger, but by the conviction that the nature and effects of such institutions are repugnant to the spirit of the times, and burdensome to the new political and economical position of the nation, against which tendency the Government, and you yourselves, gentlemen (addressing the Italian Parliament) desire to guard yourselves in tranquillity, and free from the prepossessions of party."

Thus we have the Italians, as a means of consolidating peace among themselves, suppressing many of these establishments, in no spirit of blind hostility, but, as it appears to me, acting much in accordance with the advice of the Rev. Canon Wordsworth, who has written an able book on the present state of Italy, recommending the retention of some few of these institutions, which are thought to be really useful for the purposes of charity or of education, but suppressing those which they find to be the organs of a power that is hostile to their domestic peace, hostile to their freedom, hostile to their national independence, and likely to bring them in collision with the other nations of Europe.

Sir, I have to apologize to the House for the length of the remarks into which I have been drawn in directing your attention to the very peculiar circumstances which characterize the establishment of this secret burial ground at Sydenham; and in showing, that if you would avoid the establishment of other burial grounds under similar circumstances, it is necessary that a Committee of this House should consider and review the law of burials. Within the last ten years there has been an unprecedented increase of these monastic and conventual establishments in this country—of monastic establishments that are contrary to law—and I humbly trust that the House and the Government may be warned, may be induced by these circumstances and by the conduct of Foreign Governments — the other Governments of Europe—to follow the example of the Government of France; and that, bearing in mind the misfortunes that are opening up to Prussia, for they are misfortunes, and the measures which the Italians find necessary for consolidating their polity, that this House will permit a Select Committee to examine these matters, with a view to their reporting the evidence taken before them, and their opinion thereon for the further consideration of the House.

Amendment proposed,

To leave out from the word "That" to the end of the Question, in order to add the words "a Select Committee be appointed to inquire into the Allegations contained in the Petition of Mr. Alfred Smee, which was presented upon the 19th day of February last, relative to the Saint Mary's, Sydenham, Burial Ground; and further into the existence, increase, and nature of the Conventual and Monastic Communities, Societies, or Institutions in England, Wales, and Scotland."—(*Mr. Newdegate.*)

—instead thereof.

SIR GEORGE GREY said, it appeared to him that the petition of Mr. Smee, which had been printed upon the Motion of the right hon. Gentleman opposite, the Member for North Warwickshire (Mr. Newdegate), upon which this Motion was founded, did not in itself afford sufficient reasons for the appointment of the Committee which had been asked for. He must express the same opinion with regard to the correspondence which had taken place between Mr. Smee and the Home Office which had been laid before the House. At the same time, he could not but sympathize with that gentleman's feelings when he found that a near relative with whom he had been brought up on terms of intimacy, and with whom he afterwards became closely connected by ties of marriage, had been induced to change the religion in which he had been brought up, and to adopt the creed of a Church from which Mr. Smee, no doubt, conscientiously dissented. Referring to the other circumstances mentioned by the hon. Gentleman, it was much to be regretted that a youth imperfectly instructed in the truths and doctrines of his own Church should, on his first entrance into active life, be exposed to the influence of a man of deep learning, great persuasive powers, and very attractive manners, such as was the late Dr. Faber; but he scarcely thought the House could be recommended to agree to a Committee for the purpose of considering and suggesting measures to counteract such influence. The only practicable way of counteracting that influence would be by taking care that, as far as possible, the youth of this country should be well grounded in the doctrines and truths of their own Church before sending them out into the world, and should thus be better enabled to resist such influence. Having said this, it appeared to him that the hon. Gentleman had wrongly interpreted the object and effect of the Act for the regulation of Burial Grounds, an Act which was framed entirely on sanitary grounds, and solely for the pur-

Mr. Newdegate

pose of affording protection to the health of the public; and that he also entertained an erroneous opinion as to the powers by that Act vested in the Secretary of State. Although the Secretary of State was required to give his consent to the opening of burial grounds within the metropolitan district, it was never intended that this power should be exercised arbitrarily, and still less that it should be exercised with reference to the religious creed of the persons applying. The approval of cemeteries had never been granted or withheld by the Government on account of the religious creeds of the parties for whose use they were intended. In this case the requisite application had been made to the Home Office, and referred to an Inspector, who, after examining the ground, made, as was usual, a detailed Report, from which it appeared there was no objection to the burial ground in a sanitary point of view. Mr. Smee was evidently under the impression that some extraordinary course had been adopted with regard to the cemetery at Sydenham, and that the permission of the Government had been unfairly obtained. That was not the case, and he hoped the publication of the correspondence would remove the impression. He regretted that the hon. Member should have thought it necessary to associate the name of the late Duke of Norfolk with these proceedings. The facts were simply as follows:—Dr. Faber, being at the time the principal of this Roman Catholic College at Brompton, made application to the Home Office to be permitted to open a burial ground for the use of the college. On receipt of the application the matter was referred in the usual manner to the Inspector, who, being then occupied with other matters, did not make his Report for some time. The Duke of Norfolk then wrote a letter, which was now before the House, calling attention to the application, and stating the importance which the members of the Roman Catholic Church attached to the privilege of having such a burial ground. That letter was sent to the Inspector, who afterwards reported in detail and showed that, as regarded sanitary objects, there was not the slightest cause for apprehension; and accordingly, as in several other cases, both Roman Catholic and Protestant, the burial ground was granted for the exclusive use of the religious community on whose behalf the application was made. The hon. Gentleman had said that the members of the community referred to had belonged to the order of St. Philip Neri. He did not know whether the statement was correct or not; but there was nothing on the face of the proceedings to show him that the college for which the burial ground was required was an institution not recognized by law, or that the members were of the order of St. Philip Neri. In order to establish the illegality of such a society, it would be necessary to ascertain by whom vows were administered and by whom they were received before any proceedings could be taken against them for a violation of the law. Last year, upon Mr. Smee making a complaint as to certain irregularities in the management of the burial ground, the Inspector was ordered to report upon that complaint; but the Report was to the effect that, in the course of seven years, only three interments had taken place in the cemetery, so that persons living in the neighbourhood could not have been at all affected on account of their proximity to the ground. So far, therefore, there was no reason for the appointment of a Committee. He was informed that access was given to the friends of persons buried there, as in any other burial ground. With respect to the inscriptions upon the tombstones, that was a matter with respect to which the Government had no right to interfere. If real names were not inscribed upon the graves, no doubt that might be productive of inconvenience in cases where it might be necessary to establish a title to property. But they all knew the inconvenience was much greater when no names at all were inscribed upon them, and there was no law in this country compelling the erection of tombstones, or providing for the nature of the inscription to be put upon them if erected. The hon. Gentleman had alluded to the case of Mr. Hutchison, who, according to Mr. Smee's account, was possessed of considerable property, and had been induced by undue spiritual influence to dispose of it in a manner different from that in which he would otherwise have done had he been free from that influence. That might, or might not, be true; but, if correct, the law provided a remedy.

MR. NEWDEGATE said, he rose to explain. He believed the law to be totally inefficient in the present case.

SIR GEORGE GREY said, that could only be so if the Court should decide that no undue influence had been exercised upon the mind of Mr. Hutchison. If undue influence of a spiritual nature were exercised upon a man in his dying moments for the purpose of affecting the disposal of his property, that would be a reason for setting aside the will. The hon. Gentleman had stated that the Italian Parliament had legislated for the suppression of monasteries, but he must remember that this country possessed a remedy in the statute of Mortmain against the serious evils which had arisen in Italy from the large amount of property acquired and held by monasteries. He did not think that any good results would arise from an inquiry into the subject, but that it would rather tend to foster religious discussions and disputes; and, so far as the documents before the House were concerned, he did not consider that there was any ground for granting the Select Committee asked for by the hon. Gentleman.

LORD EDWARD HOWARD: Sir, I would willingly have been spared intruding myself upon the House on this occasion. I beg to observe that in anything I may say, it will be remembered I speak in defence. I, and those connected with me, have been attacked, and it is proper I should defend my family from the charges brought against it. No one can deprecate more than myself the introduction of discussions on religious subjects into this House; but if they are to be brought on at all, they ought to be conducted in the same manner as other discussions, and to be accompanied by the same gentlemanlike feeling and propriety of bearing which characterize all the proceedings of the House, and which are more or less adhered to in all ranks and conditions of life. Even prize-fighters shake hands before they begin their contest, and give some semblance of an adherence to formality and decorum. In the present case, however, there has been manifested a most remarkable want of that propriety, inasmuch as a violent personal attack has been made upon a family to whom I am nearly related; but not one word of previous intimation has been given to me on the matter, and the broadest assertions have been made by the hon. Member for Warwickshire, without any attempt at proof. Not only have the hon. Gentleman's calumnies been aimed at the gentlemen who lived at the Oratory, but they have been, by implication, extended to myself. I feel sure that the House will, with its usual generosity and kindliness of feeling, permit me to reply, which I wish to do in no strenuous manner, to the slanderous statements which the hon. Gentleman has been made the vehicle for publishing. In this petition, with which the hon. Gentleman by presenting it to the House has identified himself, the statement has been made, that the family of the Duke of Norfolk has been, and is, in close connection with the members of the Order of St. Philip Neri, at Brompton, and assist them in their various schemes. A little further down it adds, that young men of position and wealth are concealed from their friends by the members of that Order. What is this but an assertion that the family to which I have the honour to belong, is engaged with others in conspiracy, in fraud, and in concealment? Upon this part of the case I shall really dwell no further, because I do trust that both my family and myself have many valued friends among members of all religious persuasions; and I am quite sure that no person in this country, except Mr. Smee and the hon. Gentleman, would give any member of my family, or myself, credit for taking part in such disgraceful proceedings. In another clause of the petition it is stated that the heir to the dukedom of Norfolk—and I think it says his brother also—have been seen assisting in ecclesiastical garments in the public performance of services at the Oratory. Now, I think the hon. Gentleman stated that he belonged to the University of Oxford. I myself belonged to Cambridge, and when I went to the chapel in the University, which I did, I was in the habit of putting on a surplice, and I should suppose that the hon. Gentleman also wore his surplice on the same occasions. Is there anything disgraceful in assisting in the public service of a public Church? And, if not, if the hon. Gentleman wore a surplice while attending his College chapel service, might not other people, in a public church like the Oratory at Brompton, also take part in the service clad in the same way? I have seen my nephew assisting there; and, perhaps I may also say, that on that occasion when I saw him assisting there—perhaps more than once—I then had a little boy who had grown to an age when one's feelings are bound up very deeply with his well-being, as a son who promised to be a hope to one's family, and a prop to one's declining years. I am proud to say that that little boy also assisted in the service with my nephew, dressed in the garments which the hon. Gentleman has described. That little boy died within a short period

Lord Edward Howard

of so assisting at the public services of the church; and I can tell the hon. Gentleman that, so far from being ashamed of it, it is the greatest possible comfort to me that, at the solicitation of his mother, I allowed him to pay that small meed of devotion and service to his Creator. He has passed to his account, into a purer world, where certainly there is no malignity like that to which my family has been to-night exposed. I do not believe he has a less bright place there because in that instance he paid his little meed of homage to his God; nor do I believe that his mother, who since then has also died, has a less bright place there, because she wished that he should take that part in the service of the church. The grief which I have had to sustain in the loss of these two loved ones, coupled within the short space of twenty months with the loss of the father of the young Duke, one of the best of brothers—that grief is to be ripped open, the lids of the coffins of those who are gone are, as it were, to be torn away, and their graves are to be exposed to public desecration because such a person as Mr. Smee chooses to allege these untruths in a petition for which the hon. Member for Warwickshire becomes the sponsor to this House. Having said so much on matters which affect me personally, although I am not at all undertaking the defence of the Oratory, still it is, perhaps, fair that I should advert to one or two points mentioned by the hon. Gentleman. He stated the case of a Mr. Harrison. As I understand it, Mr. Harrison was brought to the Oratory by an elder brother, who was an officer in the army; he became a convert, returned to Westminster School the same night, and a very short time afterwards he returned to his father's house. What took place was clear and open. Respecting the case with which Mr. Smee's name is connected in the petition, it certainly does seem to me extraordinary that an hon. Gentleman, in the position of a county Member, should endeavour, by animadversions in this House, to influence a case which is before the ordinary tribunals of the country. Whatever the will to which reference has been made may be, and I know nothing of it, it will no doubt be properly decided upon by the high authorities before whom it has now been placed. Then the hon. Gentleman endeavoured to make a strong case out of the omission of names on the tombstones in the burial ground at Sydenham. But it is the register of deaths by the properly certified officers, and not the names on tomb-stones, which are resorted to for the purposes of identification. On his way to this House, the hon. Member must have walked over the churchyard of St. Margaret's, where upon many of the stones not a single name can be traced. This is the same in other places. The tombstone inscription may be obliterated by time, and it is the public and official record by which identification is established.

I pass now from the petition to one of the most extraordinary documents which I certainly ever read—"The Public Appeal to the Duchess of Norfolk," dated from Finsbury Circus, April 9. I had been detained in the country, and on arriving in town last night, I found to my great surprise a copy of this letter. I believe it has been published elsewhere. The hon. Gentleman says, he does not object to the writing of this letter; but, while he condemns its address to the Duchess, he thinks it should have been addressed to two gentlemen of the learned profession whom he inaccurately described as the guardians of a certain person. [Mr. NEWDEGATE: I said they were the trustees.] One of the statements in the letter is—

" But the high position of your Grace's family has been used to assist the schemes of the members of the Oratory, to obtain his money from his family."

Now, the truth no doubt was, that Mr. Hutchison, whose fortune has been exaggerated, was a charitable and generous man, and chose to give his money accordingly. Some persons squander their money; others dispose of it in charity. Some even sacrifice their lives in works of charity. But who blames Howard for such a sacrifice? Who blames Wilberforce and Clarkson for their efforts in the cause of the slave? And who blames those benevolent persons who give bountifully of the means at their disposal to promote works of charity? Why, we do not even blame those persons who leave their money to help to pay off the National Debt, and why should Mr. Hutchison be blamed because he chose to give some of his fortune in charity, and some of it to the Oratory for certain purposes indicated? Sir, I deny that, so far as the Duchess of Norfolk is concerned, there is the smallest ground for this calumny, which is so improperly brought forward in this letter, and with which, in some degree, the hon. Gentleman identifies himself.

MR. NEWDEGATE: I knew nothing about the letters.

LORD EDWARD HOWARD: I am glad to hear it, and I trust, then, that this will be a caution in future to the hon. Member as to the company in which he trusts himself, and the use to which he allows himself and his name to be put by others. We all hear of young men coming to the metropolis and there being taken advantage of by designing persons; but I should hardly have expected that a Gentleman of the age of the hon. Member would get into such a position as this. Allow me, Sir, in the most friendly way, to suggest to the hon. Member, that if he has not been prudent hitherto, he should henceforth take care that he is not led by others into such a position as to be made the medium for advancing, if not of countenancing, accusations of the most flagrant and unfounded character. In a further part of this letter—I am not quoting the words—the Duchess of Norfolk is accused by direct implication of the murder—the prospective murder—of her daughter, by immuring her in a certain convent into which she had gone. I should not, of course, think of saying a word in refutation of that. That young lady is my niece; and this I will say, that I never saw any person more anxious to enter a religious order than she was to enter the one which she has adopted. She was perfectly aware of the practice of that order, and she was most anxious to attach herself to it. I am quite sure, and all Catholics know, that there are many young women who could never be happy in the tumult of the world, but elect of themselves to enter a convent. This was the case with my niece; and no young woman ever took that step or any other with a greater prospect of happiness. Mr. Smee then goes on to say, " Your grace stood by the grave of my relative as the cold clay, sod by sod, was thrown upon his noble form, in a sort of ecstasy at the music of the *requiem*." Surely, if the Duchess attended this funeral she must have done so from the most praiseworthy motives. How absurd are those observations! Having taken the trouble to go down, was the Duchess to have laughed during the solemn ceremony? Is that the hon. Member for North Warwickshire's idea of the kind of behaviour becoming at a funeral? I do not know what his experience on those occasions has been, but mine would lead me to think that the observations contained in this letter with reference to the conduct of the Duchess of Norfolk are not only uncalled for, but absurd. Then the hon. Member talks of the increase in the number of convents in this country. Now, this is a point on which, with the permission of the House, I should wish to say a word. The fact is. that in 99 cases out of 100, convents are established in this way:—Two or three nuns are invited by some philanthropic persons to come and teach at a school which may have been set up in their neighbourhood. Catholic ladies and gentlemen know by experience that nuns are the best instructors of children — that they generally succeed in winning them from evil courses, and accordingly they are glad to induce nuns to commence such schools. The hon. Member for North Warwickshire and other persons of his way of thinking are always accusing Catholics of keeping their people in ignorance and allowing them to become drunkards and commit offences which bring them before the police magistrates; but when Catholic gentlemen are doing all they can to make the poor of their creed good members of society, the hon. Gentleman and his friends not only will not help them, but seem to be actuated by a desire to hinder them from effecting that object. I wish to apologize to the House for the length of the statement I have made. It really has been a most painful one to me. Circumstances that have caused me sorrow deeper than can be described have been raked up in a manner most unjustifiable, and my duty was clear that I ought to come down to the House and defend my family and myself from such attacks. If I had allowed a feeling of diffidence to prevail, and had not relied on that kindness which the House has so generously extended to me, I must have submitted to be browbeaten by those statements which the hon. Member has made in so positive a tone. The hon. Gentleman has spoken of those whom I feel it my duty to defend. Unfortunately my family has been diminished considerably of late by successive casualties; but I am happy that I have been spared to defend it from calumny; and I should have hoped that no hon. Member of this House would have stood godfather to such statements as those which the hon. Member for North Warwickshire has sanctioned. I can, however, assure him on behalf of my family, whether on the part of those who are now living, or of those who have departed from this life, that we

Lord Edward Howard

wish him no further harm than that he may see the error of his ways, and that as he becomes an older he may also become a wiser, juster, and fairer man. Again, thanking the House most cordially for the manner in which it has received my explanation, I beg to express my confidence in the fairness and justness of the British public. It will know in what quarter to bestow its sympathy, and where to place its confidence; for, though the judgment of the people of this country is sometimes misled, it is, in the main, solid and sound. With the utmost confidence, I leave this case in the hands of the House.

MR. NEATE said, that the hon. Gentleman the Member for North Warwickshire (Mr. Newdegate) was not, in his opinion, fairly open to the charge made by the noble Lord the Member for Arundel (Lord Edward Howard), that he had brought on the present Motion without due notice. He had had no communication with the hon. Member, but he knew all the circumstances of this case, and that it would be brought forward; and the noble Lord himself seemed to know more about it than the hon. Member. It was no sufficient legal reason for setting aside a will that such will had been made under religious influence. The only question was whether such cases as that brought forward by the hon. Gentleman were sufficiently numerous to call for legislative interference; for, as the law stood, he believed it was quite possible to bring to bear upon a dying person religious influence which it might be found difficult to resist, and which might result in great injury being done to the relatives of a testator. He thought that, so far from deserving blame, the hon. Member for North Warwickshire was entitled to the thanks of the House for calling attention to an institution which in his opinion, in this and other similar instances, deserved the just reprobation of the House.

MR. O'HAGAN (THE ATTORNEY GENERAL FOR IRELAND) said, that the observations made by the hon. and learned Gentleman the Member for Oxford City (Mr. Neate) required a reply, and he thought it not unbecoming that he should give one. It had not been his intention to have interfered at all in the discussion, especially after the touching and beautiful address of the noble Lord the Member for Arundel, but that he had the honour and happiness of knowing some of the Members of that Community which, to adopt the words of the noble Lord, had been grossly slandered in the House that night. He would not follow the speech with which that discussion opened, in regard either to the living or the dead who had been assailed in that speech ; he would not say a word in reference to the character of the late Father Faber, who, he believed, whether as a man of intellect or a man of conscience, or a distinguished Englishman, would always be spoken of with extreme respect. Every one belonging to his religious creed knew that which it was no shame to the hon. Member for North Warwickshire if he did not know, that the constitution of the Community at Brompton did not, in the smallest degree, bring them within the purview of the law. Persons who belonged to the Oratory at Brompton—those who belonged to any Community of that distinguished order— were not bound by vows such as the hon. Member appeared to suppose. It was a matter of perfect notoriety that they lived together in Community—they were secular priests associating voluntarily, not bound to remain together for a single hour, each holding his property, and able to dispose of it just as he desired. He would say nothing as to the burial ground ; that point had been answered conclusively by the right hon. Baronet the Secretary for Home Affairs, although he could not for the life of him see that there was any illegality or ground for suspicion in the fact of the name adopted at confirmation being the one inscribed upon the tombstone of one of the members of the Oratory. He wished to reply to an observation made by the hon. and learned Member for Oxford City (Mr. Neate), that according to the law of this land no amount of spiritual influence would nullify a will. It was notorious, that in the Probate Courts of England as well as in Ireland, cases constantly arose where the question for the jury and the Court was whether undue religious influences had been exercised. The hon. Member for North Warwickshire (Mr. Newdegate), who introduced this Motion, had referred to the case of Father Hutchison, a man of intellect and an accomplished scholar. That gentleman was forty years of age at the period of his death ; he had been eighteen years a member of the Oratory, and died in full possession of his faculties. When he joined that Community he possessed a fortune of £30,000 or thereabouts. It was entirely under his own control. Portions of this property he devoted to the establishment of ragged schools in Holborn, and to the support of charities of various kinds ; and at the period of his death, in his fortieth or forty-first year, he had by these acts of charity and benevolence denuded himself of the whole of the property, with the exception of £4,000 or £5,000. He was the friend of Father Faber, to whom he was deeply attached, and with whom he had lived for many years, trusting him, not only as a friend, but as a religious man ; and he bequeathed this £4,000 or £5,000 to Father Faber, and that bequest was at this moment undergoing consideration in the Court of Probate. Was it not then monstrous that members of that distinguished religious Community—men of the highest character, men of the brightest accomplishments, men of the greatest devotion to their own religion, and also men of great devotion to the poor—should be assailed in the manner they had been, when the question upon which the charges were founded was before the properly constituted tribunal, to be determined there, not upon suggestion, not upon insinuations, not upon assertions without a particle of proof such as had been presented to the House and to the country that night, but on solemn inquiry and legal evidence ? It did appear very monstrous. If, in this kingdom of England, twelve or twenty gentlemen of any other religious denomination than Roman Catholic chose to live together, no man would have ventured to assail those twelve or twenty gentlemen, as the priests of the Oratory had been assailed in that House. It was not manly thus to assail persons who were unable to defend themselves, who from their position, their character, and their profession had to be defended by others. So far as the present case went there was no evidence before the House, and no ground for the proposition of the hon. Member for North Warwickshire. It was a principle of British law that we had no right to assume guilt against any man ; that we were not to assume that any individual of any Community whatever had broken the law of the land without hearing evidence in support of the charge, and afterwards what he had to say—in defence. Speaking now only of his own country he would say that if there was one thing which more than another mitigated the miseries of Ireland, it was the existence among its poor and wretched people of religious Communities, always ready to administer consolation and relief, to teach, to comfort, and to support the poor. Unless the Community of the Oratory at Brompton could be proved to be contrary to the law of the land, he trusted that the day was far distant when that House would assent to such a proposition as that of the hon. Member for North Warwickshire.

SIR GEORGE BOWYER said, he would occupy the attention of the House for a few minutes only. One of the allegations of the hon. Member for North Warwickshire was that the Christian name of Father Hutchison inscribed on the tombstone was not the name by which he was baptized. The fact was that Father Hutchison changed his name at confirmation, or rather added to his existing name that of his particular patron saint. And he must tell the hon. Member for North Warwickshire that the law of England allowed any person to change his name at confirmation. If he would look into the highest legal authority, *Coke upon Littleton*, he would find it there laid down that any one could lawfully change his name at confirmation, and an instance was cited of a learned Judge who had done so, and the change was held valid in law. He would briefly touch upon one other point. It seemed to be inferred by the hon. Member for North Warwickshire, that some advantage of Father Hutchison in his dying moments was taken by the Oratorians. The fact was that the will of Father Hutchison, so far from being a death-bed will, was made three years before his death. He lived for fifteen years at the Oratory. And he would ask, what was more natural than that he should wish to leave his remaining property to those with whom he had so long lived, and from whom he had received daily acts of kindness for many years, rather than to Mr. Smee, between whom and himself there had long existed, in consequence of his change of religion, a want of cordiality.

MR. R. LONG said, that as his hon. Friend the Member for North Warwickshire was precluded, by the forms of the House, from replying, it was due to him that some hon. Member should stand up in his behalf, and say that nothing was further from his intention than to state anything that could be construed and twisted even by the disingenuous and tortuous practices of Roman Catholics into anything savouring of disrespect towards any member of the noble family of Howard. His hon. Friend's Motion was directed, not against individuals, but against institutions. At the outset of his remarks, his hon. Friend stated that he knew nothing of the letter alluding to the Duchess of Norfolk; and the noble Lord's speech, painful as it was to listen to, was a most ingenious perversion of the remarks of his hon. Friend. The points chiefly dwelt on by his hon. Friend were that there was no registrar's certificate, and that the name on the tombstone had been falsified. Were he a Roman Catholic he would not oppose the appointment of the Committee for an inquiry into conventual and monastic establishments. He thought the country was entitled to have evidence of the practices carried on within their walls. That very morning he had received a paper, which, no doubt, other hon. Members had seen, and which, if not true, was a libel. It was entitled "Facts; or, Nuns and Nunneries." Many instances were given of the maltreatment of unfortunate females in these establishments, he would call them prisons, in which their property was confiscated. These assertions were either true or false; and if he were a Roman Catholic he would defy the most bitter Protestant, as the Catholics would call him, to prove them. Instead of keeping those establishments hermetically sealed, he would have light let into them. At all events, let England have the same opportunity as was possessed in France, and even in bigoted Austria, of knowing what was going on in those establishments, and ascertaining whether any of the inmates were confined against their will, by the legal visitation of the civil power. That was all that was asked by the Motion of the hon. Member for North Warwickshire. Let the Committee be appointed, and he would undertake to prove instances of innocent, unfortunate, trusting females being seduced—he did not mean to use the word in its offensive sense — but cases of innocent, trusting girls drawn from their families by clever designing priests — drawn into establishments, shut up there, kept there contrary to their will, their property confiscated, and their persons denied to their relations. Appoint a Committee, and they would prove that those assertions were facts. He did not wish to say anything offensive to Roman Catholic Members; but, were he a Catholic, that was the course he would take. He could not sit still and hear the observations of his hon. Friend misrepresented and himself abused without offering those remarks.

Mr. O'Hagan

LORD EDWARD HOWARD: I ask the hon. Member whether, in using the phrase "disingenuous and tortuous practices peculiar to Roman Catholics," he meant to apply it to me? [*Cries of* "Order!" *and* "Chair!"]

SIR PATRICK O'BRIEN said that, as a Roman Catholic, he could not allow the observations of the hon. Member for North Wilts (Mr. Long) to pass without expressing the contempt which he felt for them. The hon. Member for North Warwickshire was a follower of the right hon. Gentleman the Member for Buckinghamshire (Mr. Disraeli). If the hon. Member had studied the speeches of his political leader, he might have seen in one of them a maxim which it would have been well for him to have borne in mind on the present occasion—namely, that "insolence is not sarcasm, and that violence is not invective." [*Cries of* "Order!" "Chair!" "Divide!"]

MR. NEWDEGATE [*amid renewed cries of* "Order!" *and* "Chair," said: A violent attack has been made on me. I beg to explain that the Motion which I submit to the House is, as expressed in the terms of it, "for an inquiry into certain allegations made in the petition of Mr. Smee, the medical officer of the Bank of England;" and further, that this Motion is "for an inquiry into the——[*Cries of* "Chair!"]

MR. SPEAKER: If the hon. Member has been misunderstood on any point an opportunity of explanation is afforded to him. But he cannot go beyond explanation.

MR. NEWDEGATE: I beg your pardon, Sir, if I have erred; but I have been misrepresented, and I beg to explain that the Motion I submit to the House is a Motion for an inquiry into Monastic and Conventual establishments, and it is substantially the same as those which have been repeatedly supported by majorities in this House. ["No, no!"]

Question put, "That the words proposed to be left out stand part of the Question,"

The House *divided* :—Ayes 113; Noes 80 : Majority 33.

AYES.

Acton, Sir J. D.
Agar-Ellis, hon. L. G. F.
Alcock, T.
Anson, hon. Major
Ayrton, A. S.
Bagwell, J.
Baring, T. G.
Beamish, F. B.
Beaumont, W. B.
Beaumont, S. A.
Beecroft, G. S.
Bellew, R. M.
Bowyer, Sir G.
Brady, Dr.
Bright, J.
Browne, Lord J. T.
Bruce, H. A.
Butt, I.
Castlerosse, Viscount
Clay, J.
Clifton, Sir R. J.
Cochrane, A. D. R. W. B.
Coke, hon. Colonel
Collier, Sir R. P.
Collins, T.
Cowper, rt. hon. W. F.
Cox, W.
Crawford, R. W.
Cubitt, G.
Dalglish, R.
Davey, R.
Dent, J. D.
Dillwyn, L. L.
Disraeli, rt. hon. B.
Doulton, F.
Duff, M. E. G.
Dunkellin, Lord
Ewart, J. C.
Fitzroy, Lord F. J.
Forster, C.
Forster, W. E.
Fortescue, C. S.
French, Colonel
Gibson, rt. hon. T. M.
Gladstone, rt. hon. W.
Glynn, G. G.
Goschen, G. J.
Gregory, W. H.
Grey, rt. hon. Sir G.
Hardcastle, J. A.
Hartington, Marquess of
Headlam, rt. hon. T. E.
Henley, rt. hon. J. W.
Herbert, rt. hon. H. A.
Heygate, W. U.
Hibbert, J. T.
Hodgson, K. D.
Horsman, rt. hon. E.
Howard, Lord E.
Humphery, W. H.
Hutt, rt. hon. W.
Jackson, W.
Kinglake, A. W.
Kingscote, Colonel
Layard, A. H.
Lefevre, G. J. S.
Lewis, H.
Liddell, hon. H. G.
Locke, J.
Lygon, hon. F.
M'Cann, J.
MacEvoy, E.
M'Mahon, P.
Maguire, J. F.
Malins, R.
Manners, rt. hn. Lord J.
Martin, J.
Moffatt, G.
Norris, J. T.
North, F.
O'Brien, Sir P.
O'Conor Don, The
O'Hagan, rt. hon. T.
O'Loghlen, Sir C. M.
Packe, Colonel
Paget, C.
Paget, Lord C.
Palk, Sir L.
Palmer, Sir R.
Palmerston, Viscount
Peel, rt. hon. Sir R.
Pinney, Colonel
Pollard-Urquhart, W.
Potter, E.
Ricardo, O.
Russell, A.
Russell, F. W.
Seymour, H. D.
Sidney, T.
Smith, J. B.
Stansfeld, J.
Taylor, P. A.
Thornhill, W. P.
Tottenham, Lieut.-Col.
C. G.
Tracy, hn. C. R. D. H.
Vane, Lord H.
Vernon, H. F.
Walpole, rt. hon. S. H.
Walter, J.
Whitbread, S.
Wood, rt. hon. Sir C.
Woods, H.
Yorke, J. R.

TELLERS.
Brand, Mr.
White, Colonel

NOES.

Adderley, rt. hon. C. B.
Agnew, Sir A.
Archdall, Captain M.
Aytoun, R. S.
Bentinck, G. W. P.
Beresford, rt. hon. W.
Bramley-Moore, J.
Bridges, Sir B. W.
Burghley, Lord
Burrell, Sir P.
Butler, C. S.
Caird, J.
Calthorpe, hon. F. H.
W. G.
Carnegie, hon. C.
Clive, Capt. hon. G. W.
Craufurd, E. H. J.
Du Cane, C.
Duncombe, hon. A.
Dunlop, A. M.
Edwards, Colonel
Elphinstone, Sir J. D.
Ewing, H. E. C.
Fane, Colonel J. W.
Fellowes, E.
Fleming, T. W.
Foley, H. W.
Gard, R. S.
Gore, J. R. O.
Gray, Captain
Grogan, Sir E.
Gurney, J. H.
Gurney, S.
Haliburton, T. C.
Hardy, J.
Holland, E.
Holmesdale, Viscount
Horsfall, T. B.

Hunt, G. W.
Kendall, N.
Knightley, R.
Knox, hon. Major S.
Langton, W. H. G.
Leslie W.
Lopes, Sir M.
Lysley, W. J.
Mackie, J.
Maxwell, hon. Colonel
Miller, W.
Mills, A.
Mills, J. R.
Montagu, Lord R.
Murray, W.
Neate, C.
North, Colonel
O'Neill, E.
Parker, Major W.
Pease, H.
Peel, J.
Robertson, D.
Rose, W. A.
Selwyn, C. J.

Shirley, E. P.
Smith, A.
Somes, J.
Stuart, Lieut.-Col. W.
Stracey, Sir H.
Stronge, J. M.
Sykes, Colonel W. H.
Tempest, Lord A. V.
Thynne, Lord H.
Torrens, R.
Treherne, M.
Vance, J.
Verner, Sir W.
Walcott, Admiral
Watlington, J. W. P.
White, J.
Willoughby Sir H.
Wynne, W. W. E.
Yorke, hon. E. T.

TELLERS.
Mr. Newdegate
Mr. R. Long.

Question again proposed, "That Mr. Speaker do now leave the Chair."

SCIENTIFIC INSTITUTIONS OF DUBLIN.

OBSERVATIONS.

MR. GREGORY, who had given notice to move for a Select Committee to inquire into the Scientific Institutions of Dublin which were assisted by Government aid, said, that after the division which had just taken place it was not, he believed, possible for the Speaker to put the Motion which it had been his intention to submit to the House. What he proposed, therefore, to do was to take the discussion on his Motion at once, and if the Government should signify their readiness to assent to it, then to move for the Committee, *pro formâ*, on some future occasion. In the year 1862, applications were made to the Treasury by the Royal Dublin Society for a sum amounting in round numbers to £10,000, to put the Museum, the Botanic Gardens, and the agricultural department of the society into an efficient state, but, before entertaining the application, the Treasury considered that a Commission should be appointed to report upon the Royal Dublin Society and other scientific institutions in Dublin, and also into the system of scientific instruction in Ireland. It is unnecessary, at present, to enter into any general discussion of the Report of this Commission. It is sufficient to say that the main features of it are two recommendations, the first, a very proper one—namely, to increase the powers of the executive council acting on behalf of the society, inasmuch as it did not possess adequate control over the general management of the affairs of the society, and in particular over its officers, while its decisions were liable to be overruled and reversed by the accident of the popular vote of the whole body. On more than one occasion there has been a conflict between the Government, whose annual subsidy is the main support of the institution and the society; and there have also been conflicts between the council and the general body, in which the decisions of the council have been overruled. It was clear that such a state of things could not be continued, nor could it be suffered that large sums of public money should be annually voted, when at any moment the society might place itself in collision with the Government. With the view of having these chances of collision, increased power was recommended to be placed in the hands of the council, which thus became a central and executive authority, able to act immediately and without the necessity of consulting the members at large. No one could dispute the propriety of this suggestion. The second recommendation was very different—namely, that the Museum of Irish Industry should be totally abolished, with the exception of the Professors of Geology and Botany, who should be transferred to the Royal Dublin Society. That the Geological and Paleontological Collections should be transferred to Marsh's Library, belonging to the society, and the Technological collection distributed throughout the country. There was also this ominous sentence at the end of the Report—

" Some advantage would be gained if all the Parliamentary grants in aid of science and art at Dublin were included in the estimate of the Royal Dublin Society, and were paid through its medium, inasmuch as they would annually be brought under consideration in one point of view, and the council of the Royal Dublin Society would have an opportunity of making any representation which the circumstances of the time might render proper in reference to them."

When this astounding recommendation got wind, alarm rose high among the scientific institutions in Dublin, more especially as this summary mode of extinguishing their independence had been adopted without any evidence whatever having been taken from them or about them. In fact, evidence seems to have been quite a secondary consideration with the Commissioners, who conclude their Report with the following extraordinary passage, perhaps one of the most extraordinary that was ever submitted in a Report to Her Majesty : —

" We submit the evidence taken by us, but it is proper to add that in the conclusions at which we have arrived we were partly influenced by a variety of documentary information as well as by our own knowledge of facts."

It would be difficult to find an instance in which the House of Commons was looked on to acquiesce in a Report based on documentary evidence of which it knew nothing, and on facts of which, though doubtless familiar to the Commissioners, and of great weight in their opinion, the House was equally ignorant. The Royal Irish Academy and other scientific institutions at once protested against the high-handed proceedings which were threatened, and the first-named society published a series of resolutions, and very stout and excellent resolutions they were, namely—

"That the Royal Irish Academy regards with surprise and alarm the suggestion contained in the Report of the Commissioners of Inquiry respecting scientific instruction in Ireland, that the academy should be placed under the superintendence, and to some extent under the control, of the council of the Royal Dublin Society.

"That the Commissioners appointed by the Treasury to inquire into a number of scientific institutions, including this Academy, have made the above recommendation without examining any of its officers, or even notifying their intention of taking evidence affecting its interests.

" In fact, the objections to such an arrangement felt by the members of the Royal Irish Academy are such as would be felt by the members of the Royal Society of London to a proposal to submit them, in any degree, to the control of the Society of Arts.

"That the Academy entirely dissents from the opinion expressed in the Report of the Commissioners, to the effect that real public benefit would ensue from affiliation of this Academy to any other society.

"That the only other reason assigned by the Commissioners for an innovation which would thus compromise the honour and interests of an important national institution is an alleged official convenience of the most inconsiderable kind."

It was felt quite clearly by the Government that this was a little too strong a measure even for Ireland, and accordingly these societies were re-assured by a pledge that the recommendation of the Report would not be applied to them. They were not to be devoured then, at all events. As regards the Museum of Irish Industry, however, there was to be no surrender—its destruction was resolved on by the Treasury and the Department of Science and Art, and the capital of Ireland, as regards scientific institutions, was to be reduced to the level of a provincial town. When, however, the fate that impended over this institution became known, general indignation prevailed. Petitions flowed in from all parts of Ireland, protesting against the destruction of an institution from which such benefit had been derived, and the utility of which was daily becoming more and more acknowledged. These petitions came from the Town Commissioners of Dundalk. Lismore, Ballymoney, Maryborough, Rathkeale, Guilford, Ballyshannon—from Dundalk, from the Limerick Athenæum, Tralee, Waterford, and Clonmel Mechanics' Institute—Drogheda, Omagh, Cork, Croom, and Bandon. The Lord Lieutenant saw at once the unpopularity and the extreme impolicy of the measure. He objected to the details of the Report and to its tendency, stating, in a letter from Sir Thomas Larcom, February, 1863,

" That the consolidation of the Museum of Irish Industry and of the scientific lectures in the Royal Dublin Society would be considered, as regards industrial education, a reversion of the original intention, and of the policy which has been pursued for the last eighty years in Ireland." " As to the provincial lectures, his Excellency recognizes the merits of the system described in the Report as successful in England, but doubts whether Ireland is yet sufficiently advanced to receive it with advantage, and that it is more fitted to produce mediocrity in the many than high acquirements in individuals."

And representations were made to the Chancellor of the Exchequer by about sixty Irish Members, which clearly indicated the feeling of the country. The petitioners had good ground for their remonstrances. They argued against the recommendation on general grounds; but they argued also against it on the special ground of the composition of the Commission, and on the composition of the witnesses, and the House of Commons would be rather astonished when they heard the allegations. They were these:—That the Committee was essentially a packed Committee. It was composed of the representative of the Treasury, Sir Charles Trevelyan, and the Treasury had already determined on this amalgamation. No proof is required of this; the correspondence proves it; nor does there appear to be the least desire on the part of the Treasury to conceal that determination. The second member was Captain Donnelly, of the Department of Science and Art, also intent on the suppression of the Irish Industrial Museum, as it is also, not without reason, suspected of being equally intent on the suppression of the kindred institution in Jermyn Street. The policy of that Department has been to centralize everything at Kensington; to make Kensington, and it alone, the Central College of Science, leaving only secondary institutions to the provincial towns, among which it is intended that, ere long, Dublin should be reckoned. The other two Members of the Commission were actually both of them at the time members of the Royal Dublin Society. As this society had an immediate benefit in the increase of its sphere, its importance, and its funds by this amalgamation, it was natural enough that these gentlemen should be objected to. The objection was the more valid, as the Royal Dublin Society had invariably looked on the Museum of Irish Industry as a rival institution to be got rid of. Not to make allegations without proof, it would be sufficient to quote the letter of the Royal Dublin Society to the Government, in 1854, protesting against even the establishment of the Museum—

"It is a matter of great surprise and regret to the society that Government should have deemed it necessary or economical to have established in close proximity, and for nearly similar objects, such an Institution as the Irish Museum."

He wished to guard himself against anything that could give rise to the imputation of wishing to ascribe unfairness to Sir Richard Griffith, or Chief Justice Blackburn, of both of whom it was his desire to speak with the respect to which their eminent position and character entitled them. He wished to say nothing more than that the Commission was not impartial —on the contrary, that it was eminently partial, and the Chancellor of the Exchequer would support him in his objections to such a Commission when he recalled the discussion which took place on the Holyhead Committee of 1863. These were Mr. Gladstone's words—

"What I said was, that in my opinion, and in the opinion of the Government, the Committee had not been impartially constituted. I referred to the position occupied by many hon. Members on it."

The right hon. Gentleman refused to be bound by the Report of that Committee, assuring the House, at the same time, that he entertained the highest respect for the character of the Members composing it. But if this objection held good as regards the composition of a Committee, it was ten times worse as regards the composition of a Commission, because the right hon. Gentleman had the opportunity of objecting to the Committee at the time of its nomination, whereas no opportunity is given for objection to a Commission appointed by the

Crown until the Report becomes the subject of discussion. The composition of the Commission was a pretty strong affair; but what would the hon. Gentleman think of the examination pursued — that, out of the seventeen witnesses examined, sixteen were connected with the Royal Dublin Society, eight members of Council, six officials, and two committee men. Sir Robert Kane was the only other person examined. No other persons were summoned to give evidence. Professor Jukes, the lecturer on geology to the Museum of Irish Industry, and the local director of the Geological Survey, never heard of the Commission save by report, nor was there a single person summoned from the other scientific societies, although the Report recommends, from the Commissioners' knowledge of facts, that these institutions should be affiliated, or, in reality, placed under the Royal Dublin Society. There was nothing like an illustration. Suppose a Commission were appointed to inquire into the London corporation with a view to ascertain whether that body should have its funds increased, whether it should retain its own police and have the police of the other districts of the metropolis put under its jurisdiction—suppose that Commission to be composed of two aldermen and of two Government officials, whose departments had notoriously and avowedly prejudged the question favourably—suppose the evidence as to the advisability of the annexation to have been derived from seventeen witnesses only, sixteen of whom were the Lord Mayor, aldermen, common council men and civic officials —could there be doubts of the result— and yet such a case would not be one whit more flagrant than the present. What is the institution that it is now proposed should be destroyed? One would suppose that it was some old outworn institution no longer adapted to the wants of the present age, but it is precisely the reverse. It is a new and vigorous institution, eminently successful, every day increasing in its efficiency and popularity, and the functions of which, instead of being smothered in the Royal Dublin Society, ought to be greatly extended. This Irish Museum was established by Sir Robert Peel, no mean judge of the requirements of Ireland, at the time when the Queen's Colleges were established, as, in deference to Trinity College, Dublin, a Queen's College was not established in that city, and I believe I have good reasons for stating that it was the intention of Sir

Mr. Gregory

Robert Peel to make this institution essentially a college for scientific instruction. The Museum galleries have only been finished ten years at great expense. Now it is proposed to dismantle them, and Professor Jukes will tell you that it will take three years to re-arrange them. The Museum of Irish Industry was originally called the Museum of Economic Geology, based on the same plan as that of Jermyn Street on the operation of the Geological Survey, but with a wider range. The suppression of this Museum would be to the Irish branch of the survey the same thing as the suppression of the Museum of Practical Geology to Great Britain. One of the main objects connected with the educational or instructional part of this institution was the carrying out of investigations connected with the industrial arts, and in deciding on the establishment of this museum. Lord Lincoln, then Secretary, said that one principal reason was, that it should be a school of instruction and research in the industrial arts. For that end a school of chemistry was established, and now two courses of systematic instruction in practical chemistry are given —one in the laboratory by day, the other in the evening, and the evening classes are generally composed of artisans and persons employed in shops. Now, let me show the progress of this institution as compared with another most successful institution, that of Jermyn Street. From 1855 to 1861 the Jermyn Street pupils increased from 104 to 140; from 1855 to 1861 the Irish Museum pupils increased from 15 to 50. Jermyn Street, 1861—cost of maintenance, £6,387; visitors 24,151; laboratory students, 140; students' school of science, 6; occasional students, 124; attendance on lectures 2,400. Stephen's Green Museum, 1861—cost of maintenance, £4,062; visitors 28,843; laboratory students, 50; visitors to library, 140; attendance at lectures, 8,010. Now as to results. One example will suffice. Mr. Dowling was a clerk in a humble establishment in Dublin. He became a pupil in the practical chemical class in the Irish Museum. Having passed the examination necessary for his qualification, he became a teacher under the art and science department, and established a school of chemistry at Cork; and what has been the success of that school?—why, something almost incredible. On reference to the 9th Report of Science and Art, it will be seen that at the science examinations

for 1861, there were given for chemistry, one gold, two silver, and three bronze medals. Mr. Dowling's pupils carried away two silver and two bronze medals, leaving only two to be contended for by competitors from the whole of Great Britain. He also took eight first classes out of seventeen, although twenty-two other teachers of the United Kingdom brought up their schools. In the 10th Report we find these words, as regards the next year's examination of 1862—

"It exhibits the remarkable fact that the students of Irish schools, numbering only 374, were successful in obtaining 149 prizes, and 12 out of a total of 689 prizes and 34 medals."

In chemistry, out of the six medals of 1862 —namely, one gold, two silver, and three bronze, Mr. Dowling's pupils took one gold, two silver, and one bronze. This is indeed incredible, and on a witness, a member of the Royal Dublin Society, being asked how this extraordinary success was to be accounted for, he said it was due to the taste being imparted to the young men of Ireland by lectures, and he instanced, in particular, the popularity of those of Professor Jukes at Belfast, Professor Jukes being professor of practical geology at the Irish Museum. We should pause before sweeping away a system marked with success, and the efficiency of which might be infinitely increased; but my Lords of the Department of Science and Art see no reason why this latent talent of Ireland should be encouraged, or why more than the merest elementary education should be given in Ireland. If that country is to obtain a higher education, let her children spend their money in London, and come to Jermyn Street and Kensington for their training. They and the Commissioners and the advocates of amalgamation, contend that the work might be done somewhat cheaper if the Irish Industrial Museum were abolished. One witness—namely, Mr. Foot, a vice-president of the Society—objects to the Museum because it has not the public confidence and regard—that the collections are in some respect duplicate collections. Mr. Steele, one of the Secretaries of the Society, says—

"There are, certainly, collections at the Irish Museum illustrative of the manufactures of porcelain, glass, iron, and various clays, which are of no practical value, as there are no manufactures in Ireland."

Of course, the witness presumed there never would be any. Sir Thomas Larcom is of a different opinion. He says—

"It is dangerous to measure the industrial character of a country merely by its present condition. The remarkable circumstance mentioned by Sir R. Kane in his evidence of the German chemists finding occupation in the manufacturing establishments is a practical commentary on the importance of giving facilities for high industrial education, and his Excellency cannot but feel that it would be highly advantageous if young Irishmen were trained to fill such places, a career which has already been opened to one or more students from Stephen's Green."

Professor Haughton, who has the arrangement of the museum of the Society, thinks—

"That collections made by geological surveys ought not to be left together, but that all fossils should be brought together and arranged according to their zoological affinities without reference to where they came from."

That the Royal Dublin Society had for its members very many persons of high rank; that many people visit one museum, and few visit two; that you have the same lecturers giving the same class of lectures on the same subjects in both establishments. These are the objections to the existence of the Irish Museum. To these objections it is replied that the two institutions were founded for different purposes —the Royal Dublin Society for the encouragement of husbandry, which might fairly bring under its scope everything connected with agriculture, the vegetable and the animal kingdom. The Irish Museum was for economic geology—the one for all that is on the surface of the earth, the other for all that is below it. That it is admitted even in one of the Reports of the Society that the lectures of the Royal Dublin Society, when they trench on the province of the Irish Museum, are intended only to give popular elementary instruction in science, whereas the lectures of the Irish Museum are to give more advanced and technical instruction. That the numbers of persons visiting a museum, though it may be a test of its popularity, is no test of its utility; and, as such, Madame Tussaud is more popular than Jermyn Street. That when the Report speaks of many persons visiting one museum—few having time to visit two, one would imagine that the writer of the passage had an idea that a scientific museum was a raree show, and that good and profit were to be obtained from one visit to it—that scientific museums are not supported for the sake of having files of visitors passing through them, but for the use of scientific men or of students intending to become so, so that they repay their expense by additions which they make

Mr. Gregory

to the intellectual wealth of the country. That, as regards the composition of the society being of the salt of the earth, the very great personages of the land, there is no gain in that—that it is not a scientific Society — that it is a private Society, though maintained chiefly at the public expense—that it is entirely anomalous in its functions and principles, and has no parallel in England, Scotland, or Continental Europe, as in no country in the world are Botanic Gardens, schools of science and art, supported by the State —yet handed over to a private society —but that this experiment is characteristically reserved for Ireland; that the governing staff of the Irish Museum consists wholly of scientific men who are obviously the only persons to whom the management of a scientific institution can properly be trusted, and that there is nothing in the Report which hints at giving to the scientific officers of the Museum any place among the governing body of the Royal Dublin Society; that these scientific officers would be perfectly ready and proud to serve under a man eminent in science like Sir Roderick Murchison, but not under a shifting unscientific body as the Royal Dublin Society, which says of itself—

"They do not profess to be a scientific body nor to endeavour to enforce the vigorous co-operation of the lovers of abstract science. They do not see 'why the co-operation of eminent men of science should be estimated more highly by the Government than that of the landed professional and mercantile gentry of Ireland, with whom the society originated.'"

In the evidence before the Committee of 1836, they say that their scientific professors were not intended to make scientific discoveries, but were only for the purpose of giving popular scientific lectures. The original salaries of professors were £300 annually, they were subsequently reduced to £200, and then to £150. The idea of what a professor should be capable of was rather magnificent. On the death of Sir Charles Gesecke, it was resolved—

"That the new Professor should possess a thorough knowledge of mineralogy, geology, zoology, conchology, and comparative anatomy; he should also be practically acquainted with coal and metallic mining."

This was pretty well for £150 per annum, considering also that a rule was framed that he should pay for any gallipots he might break. So much for the scientific capabilities of the Society into which a really scientific institution is to be merged.

That, as regards the mixing together of the rocks and fossils of both museums, no recommendation could be more prejudicial to science, or evince greater ignorance of the objects of the two institutions. The Royal Dublin Society's Museum is arranged according to biological affinities for the physiologist. The Irish Museum is arranged for the study of practical geology in stratigraphical order, according to the relative position of rock groups, and the fossils according to their position in the various strata, the history of which they illustrate. In London the first arrangement is that of the British Museum, the second arrangement is that of the Museum in Jermyn Street, and Sir Roderick Murchison would be as aghast if he were called on to amalgamate his collections with the British Museum, as Professor Owen would be if called on to transfer his to Jermyn Street. Each, in fact, assists and supplements the other, and their very distinctness of arrangement constitutes their value. Lastly, as to the allegation that the Museum has not the public confidence and regard, as stated by Mr. Foot, the best reply to that are the remonstrances addressed to the Treasury, not only by the Irish Executive and by Irish Members, but by all the chief towns in Ireland, where scientific education has been commenced, and its good effects have made themselves felt. He (Mr. Gregory) could state from his own knowledge that this Report had given great alarm in Ireland, and that it had raised, and justly raised, great indignation, and that the composition of such a Commission as this, and such an examination as was pursued, would not for one moment have been tolerated in England or in Scotland. He (Mr. Gregory) protested against this summary manner of depriving Ireland of a high course of scientific instruction. He protested against Dublin, which he once represented, being reduced to the level of a provincial town, and compelled to seek the most elementary instruction at the hands of a clique at Kensington, which had become most odious to England, and wished to extend its offensiveness to Ireland. He rejoiced to find in the late correspondence with the Treasury and the Dublin Society, that the Society had had the wisdom and good taste to ask for the aid it required on the basis of its absolute exigencies, and not on the basis of aggression on a kindred institution. He wished well to the Royal Dublin Society with all his heart. He was convinced that

if a fair inquiry was granted, it would be able to substantiate its claims for assistance, and that arrangements might be recommended defining the functions of each institution, putting an end to further temptations at aggression which are so craftily suggested to it, and laying the foundation for a material addition to the intellectual advancement of Ireland.

Sir ROBERT PEEL said, it might tend to curtail unnecessary discussion if, in the absence of his right hon Friend the Chancellor of the Exchequer, he announced at once that the Government were prepared to agree to the Committee for which the hon. Gentleman the Member for Galway (Mr. Gregory) had just moved. He had no doubt that the result of the full inquiry which would take place as to the character of the institutions in question would be to place them in a different position from that which might have followed from the decision of the Commission of 1862. He agreed in very much which had fallen from his hon. Friend, but there were two points in which he was in error. His hon. Friend had repeatedly declared that the Government were desirous of making Dublin a provincial town and of destroying the Museum of Irish Industry by amalgamating it with the Royal Dublin Society. He was totally unaware of any such designs being entertained on the part of the Government in regard to Dublin, and he could state that they had come to no decision whatever with respect to the amalgamation of the two museums. It was true that the Commission of 1862 had in their Report recommended such a proceeding, but the Government had not resolved to adopt it. He owned frankly that the feeling against amalgamation was very strong in Ireland; and that, for his own part, he had never approved of the recommendation of the Commission. From the first he had deemed the constitution of the Commission rather singular, and he thought that the result of the inquiry was very partial; for, while several representatives of the Dublin Society had been examined, no one had been examined on the part of the Museum of Industry It was under that conviction that the Government were now willing to grant the Committee. The objects of the Royal Dublin Society and of the Museum of Irish Industry were quite separate, the former being, as he might say, exhibitional, while the other was intended to give education for industrial purposes. He should be very sorry to see the latter lose its distinctive character, and he hoped the House would never sanction a measure which would deprive the country of the valuable services of so eminent a man as Sir Robert Kane.

SIR EDWARD GROGAN said, the statement of the right hon. Baronet the Member for Tamworth would relieve the question of a great deal of difficulty. He had intended to second the Motion of his hon. Friend the Member for Galway. He felt that one of the institutions in question had not been fairly dealt with. The Government had agreed to contribute towards the erection of a new museum on ground belonging to the Royal Dublin Society, but the building was still in an unfinished condition. The shell had been erected, but all the internal fittings, the glass cases and other arrangements necessary to display the objects and specimens in the possession of the Society were wanting, and the educational means at the command of the Society were thus rendered valueless. In 1861, Captain Donelly, who had been sent over to Dublin by the Government on a mission of inquiry, reported in favour of making a grant to the society, but suggested that the constitution was not so perfect as it might be. Immediately afterwards the society were informed by the Treasury that the introduction of the changes proposed by Captain Donelly might be made a condition of the continuance of the public aid given to the institution. From that day to the present not a farthing had been given to the society, notwithstanding their frequently expressed readiness to assent to every condition which the Government might think fit to impose, and notwithstanding also that the Commission, appointed subsequently to the mission of Captain Donelly, had re-echoed his recommendation that a grant should be made. The Society had shown the utmost readiness to comply with the recommendations of the Commissioners. A special Committee to consider the changes to be made in the constitution and powers of the Council had been appointed; the Society agreed to adopt them; and, if the alterations in the constitution of the society had not been completed, it was only because the society had been requested by the Treasury not to proceed further, as the Government wished to institute an inquiry with respect to the proposal of amalgamation with the Mu-

Sir Robert Peel

seum of Irish Industry. Within the present year the society had represented to the Treasury that they took no interest in the question of amalgamation, but simply wished for means to enable them to carry out the objects for which the society was founded. It would thus be seen that the society was not in fault. The absolute necessity of this grant to enable the Society to discharge its duties to the public had been admitted on all hands. They had over and over again intimated their willingness to meet the views of the Government with respect to a change in their constitution, but all their applications for pecuniary aid had been refused; because the Government were determined, in order to save a few pounds, to carry out the scheme of the amalgamation with the Museum of Irish Industry. The Dublin Society was made to suffer, in fact, for official indecision and procrastination. No such niggardliness was shown to public institutions in England. During the last few years enormous sums had been given to the British Museum and other establishments of a similar kind, though the private contributions were comparatively inconsiderable. But that was not the case with the Royal Dublin Society, for on one occasion, while the sum voted by Parliament for its support was only £5,500, no less than £6,198 was collected for it among its own members. When people were found so liberal in supporting such an institution, they had reason to complain of the Government for withholding so small a sum as £10,000, to enable them to put to a proper use the large stores which they had collected for the public benefit.

MR. WHITESIDE said, he must complain of the extraordinary conduct of the Government in relation to the matter under discussion. The Royal Commission appointed by the Government had recommended a grant of public money amounting to only £10,000, in order to put a most valuable public institution in efficient working order. Notwithstanding which, the right hon. Baronet the Member for Tamworth (Sir Robert Peel) had now thrown overboard the Report of that Commission, and had proposed to refer the whole subject to the investigation of a Parliamentary Committee. That, in his opinion, was one of the most extraordinary proceedings in the present extraordinary age of which he had ever heard. Even the right hon. Baronet had said that the constitution of the Commission was somewhat curious, but he must remember that the Commissioners were of the Government's own selection. [Sir ROBERT PEEL: I merely referred to the opinion expressed by the hon. Member for Galway.] He certainly understood, as did other hon. Members, the right hon. Baronet to express that as his own opinion. The Commissioners had fully dealt with the subject; they had examined most competent witnesses, such as Professor Haughton and Lord Talbot de Malahide, than whom there was not a more patriotic nobleman in Ireland, and they had deliberately recommended the amalgamation between the Royal Society and the Museum of Industry. He could not understand why the Government should not carry out the recommendation which would enable them to maintain, at the least possible expense, an efficient national institution. And yet it had been said that there was not evidence to justify the recommendations of the Commissioners Why. Sir Robert Kane himself, the President of the Museum of Irish Industry, had been summoned before the Commission, and in his evidence he made use of the following remarkable words : — "I fully believe if the amalgamation took place to-morrow the public would not lose by the change, and the country would not look upon it unfavourably." [Mr. GREGORY: His whole evidence was against it.] What could be stronger than the words he had quoted? He quite agreed with the right hon. the Member for the city of Dublin (Sir Edward Grogan), that the proper course to be taken would be for the Government to place on the Estimates for the present year the grant which the Royal Commission had recommended to be given to the Royal Dublin Society. The Royal Dublin Society did not shrink from inquiry; but, in the present proposal, what he complained of was the waste of time and money that would be involved, and the inconsistent conduct of the Government.

MR. VANCE said, he must complain of the tone of the hon. Member for Galway (Mr. Gregory) and of the right hon. Baronet the Member for Tamworth (Sir Robert Peel), for they had both prejudged, to a certain extent, the recommendations of the Committee which it was proposed to appoint, when all they had to do was to make out a case for inquiry. The hon. Member for Galway had hardly spoken of the Royal Dublin Society with the same kindness as he would have shown had he continued a Member for the City. But that society had obtained the approval of successive Governments and Parliaments; it took a range of scientific inquiry more extensive than any other learned body in Europe, and was, to a certain extent, self-supporting. It had obtained a grant of something like £6,000 a year, but it collected more than that sum among its supporters. It had expended £4,700 upon a permanent agricultural hall, and £5,000 upon the building of a museum of natural history, and it only asked the Government for £6,000. It had a school of arts and a school of design, exhibited agricultural shows and gave large rewards, and now it was almost *in extremis* in consequence of the non-fulfilment of the promises of the Government. The Government had promised that, if the society complied with certain conditions, the grant should be made; they did comply with those conditions, and the Government, notwithstanding. had changed their minds on the most vital point, and had refused the grant. The citizens of Dublin and the people of Ireland demanded of that House that there should be some satisfactory settlement of the question. That a valuable collection of natural history, fine libraries, and a splendid museum of mineralogy should be left in such a state that it was impossible to exhibit them, was a perfect scandal to the Government. If Ireland had its own Parliament, which formerly made grants of £10,000 and £12,000 a year to that institution, the interests of the institution would have been protected, and he thought that the Imperial Government and Parliament ought not to refuse the small assistance now asked of them.

MR. LEFROY said, he would not enter upon the question of the amalgamation of the two societies, but would simply state that he believed they had been of great advantage to the people of Ireland. The present position of affairs was, however, most deplorable. There were fine collections of natural history scattered about the rooms and covered with dust, and many valuable books of the society had to be stowed away in the rafters for want of fitting accommodation. He hoped no delay would take place on the part of the Government in settling the question.

MR. ADDERLEY said, the primary question before the House was, whether those two institutions should be amalgamated. The Royal Commission had re ported in favour of their amalgamation. He had been surprised that the right hon. Baronet the Member for Tamworth (Sir Robert Peel) should have said that he quite acknowledged the justice of the argument against that Report of the hon. Member for Galway (Mr. Gregory). The right hon. Baronet appeared only too eager to throw over the recommendations of the Commission appointed by the Government of which he was a Member, and to appeal from their Report to a SelectCommittee of that House. The Report of the Government's own Commission was distasteful to Dublin, and therefore also to the right hon. Baronet; and no doubt they might constitute a Committee which would reverse that Report, and substitute for it another that would be more palatable. Of course, it was an unpopular measure in any locality to stop up one of two existing avenues to the Exchequer, but the broader interests of the public should not be forgotten in this House. He confessed he was surprised at not seeing the Vice President of the Committee of Privy Council in his place, for that question referred to his Department. But why was that right hon. Gentleman not there? Because he had compromised himself and expressed a strong opinion in favour of the Report of the Commission, and he therefore could hardly have taken the part so boldly taken by the right hon. Baronet. The right hon. Baronet, moreover, proposed to proceed in a somewhat Irish fashion, for he expressed his desire that they should have an inquiry, and then he went on to pronounce by anticipation the most decided opinions as to what the issue of that inquiry should be. He strongly condemned the Report of the Commissioners, by way of an argument for an inquiry into its subject, and professed himself astounded that anybody should recommend the amalgamation of the two societies, which is one of its alternative conclusions. The inquiry was thus to be a sham one, starting with a foregone conclusion. It could not be denied that those institutions were, to a great extent, identical. Neither could it be denied that both institutions had done a great deal of good, but the question was, whether they would not have done a great deal more if they had been amalgamated. If the argument of the hon. Member for Galway were good for anything, then, instead of amalgamating those institutions, the House ought to double or triple their number. He could not agree with the hon. Member that the metropolis of Ireland

Mr. *Adderley*

would be affronted or reduced to the level of a provincial town if those two identical institutions had one staff of officers and one principal by whom they might communicate with the Government, and one sucker to the Treasury. He was sorry the Government had thrown over the Report of their own Commission which had so recently inquired into the subject. All the evidence that could be useful had been taken, and the facts of the case were fully known, and it would be a waste of public money to ask the same witnesses to come to London and give their evidence over again. He feared that the Committee would be called together not for any practical object, but to assist in carrying out a foregone conclusion. The duplication of this institution was a simple and notorious job ; the verdict of the Royal Commission was the only one impartial judges could give; and packing a Committee to reverse it would maintain, but in no way justify, a public imposition.

NEW BANKRUPTCY ACT.

OBSERVATIONS.

Mr. MOFFATT, who had given notice "To call the attention of the House to the working of the new Bankruptcy Act, and to move for a Select Committee to inquire and report thereon," said, the House could hardly be aware of the strong feeling that existed throughout the country with reference to the unhappy working of the new Bankruptcy Act. Since he had given notice of a Motion on the subject, his table had been covered with notes, letters, and communications, all complaining of the operation of the Act, exposing the gross frauds which it encouraged, and making suggestions for its amendment, which might usefully be considered by the Committee for which he moved. The transactions governed by the Bankrupt Act had attained an amount so marvellous as scarcely to be measured by figures. Taking the way in which the imports were turned over and over again in articles manufactured, sold and resold, passing from wholesale dealers to retail dealers, and thence to the consumer, in the daily trade of the kingdom, their aggregate value could scarcely be expressed in hundreds of millions. On the authority of an acute actuary, he believed that the amount of insolvency in this country annually exceeded £50,000,000 —a sum approaching the yearly expenditure of the nation. That was a tax which fell exclusively on the mercantile classes, who did not, however, ask to be relieved of the burden, though they did ask Parliament not to increase it by such a mischievous legislation as now governed the whole question of debtor and creditor in this country. Only a few of this country's transactions rested immediately on a money basis. Most of them arose out of credits more or less extensive. In a trading country like England one would have supposed it to be the first duty of the Government to make the Law of Bankruptcy more perfect than any other part of the Commercial Code. Instead of that they had a law so inoperative and so prejudicial to the creditor, and often also to the debtor, that traders endeavoured to avoid its operation, as much as possible. Creditors had in many cases submitted to be wronged or robbed by their debtors, rather than avail themselves of the law as it stood prior to 1860-61. In that year the first Law Officer of the Crown gave his attention to this subject, and denounced the cost and delay of the then existing system; he showed how the costs reduced the assets 30 per cent, and how the officers of the court were obstructed in the administration of the law. In 1858 the total amount of money liabilities proved in bankruptcy was £8,200,000. In the same year the amount received by the official assignees was £1,800,000. The amount of the dividends declared was only £980,000, or about 2s. 4½d. in the pound on the proved debts. In 1860, the last year under the old Act, the debts proved were £4,479,000, the amount received by the official assignees £1,250,000, and the amount of dividend declared was only £590,000, or about 2s. 7½d. in the pound. Out of the whole amount received, that was the sum which, after months of delay, found its way into the pockets of the creditors. But that was a happy state of things, compared with what took place under the new Act. By the last Return the total amount received by the official and trade assignees was £650,000. In another direction an enormous increase had taken place under the new Bill. Instead of the number of bankruptcies being moderate, as in 1858, when they were 1,080, or as in 1860, when they were 1,430, they were nearly 10,000 — the exact figures showed that 9,663 persons obtained quittance from their pecuniary liabilities, of whom nearly 7,000 paid not one farthing of dividend. With that enormous increase

in the number of applications to Courts of Bankruptcy, the total amount of assets realized was only £616,000. The new Bankruptcy Act came into operation in 1861, and in a year nearly 10,000 persons availed themselves of its provisions; and the whole amount of receipts under those bankruptcies was only £600,000. He thought that when those figures were placed side by side, they formed the most complete and satisfactory proof that the Bankruptcy Law had better be eliminated from the statute book altogether than remain in its then form. If the Legislature could produce nothing better than that, it would be well to leave the trade and commerce of the country to shift for themselves. The only thing then a man would have to trust to, would be the character of him with whom he did business. That was really very much the case at present. If the creditor demurred to the terms proposed, the debtor replied, "If you don't accept I will go into the Bankruptcy Court;" and it was remarkable that out of 9,000, who had gone into that court, only 700 had gone in on petition of the creditors. The new Bankruptcy Bill, as brought into the House, had, he thought, very great merits. It was laid on the table, and amended after due consideration. It was a very great improvement on the old Bill. It grappled boldly with the question of the bankrupt's property. It gave every facility for agreements out of court; it had the great merit of clearing the gaols of insolvent debtors; it assimilated proceedings in insolvency and bankruptcy. It proposed a machinery by which all that it proposed would probably have been effected. After much discussion, the Bill left that House and went to another place. There it shared something like the fate of "the man who journeyed from Jerusalem to Jericho," for it returned to them in a very different state. The provisions, which would have tended to render the Bill effective, were cut out of it. The enactment, that there should be a High Court of Bankruptcy, with a Chief Judge in bankruptcy, was gone; whilst, on the other hand, the old machinery was retained, and every facility afforded to debtors to pass through the court without any effective check. The result was soon shown, for whilst in 1858 the total number of insolvents and bankrupts was 4,580, and in 1860 it was 4,250, the number in the year following the passing of the Bill was nearly 10,000.

The Bill also originally proposed to deal very effectively with trust deeds, but nothing could be more defective than the provisions as they now stood. The mode of operation was this :—The debtor finding it to his advantage to come to some reckoning with his creditors, prepared a list of what he was pleased to call his debts and assets, placed the matter in the hands of a solicitor, telling him that certain persons who were set down as creditors had agreed to accept a composition of, say five shillings in the pound. It frequently happened that the persons so designated were sufficient in number and amount to bind the other creditors ; and he (Mr. Moffatt) had been assured by commercial men that they had, under such circumstances, felt compelled to accept the composition, although their conviction was that the debts of the majority were mainly fictitious, and though it was clear that, at all events, they were not trade debts ; in such cases all that could be done was for a creditor to insist on bankruptcy; but probably the whole assets were only £80 or £100, whilst the very initiation of proceedings in bankruptcy would cost £30, a cost to which the creditor might become personally liable, and for which risk he could ensure no corresponding advantage. It might be said that the creditors had a remedy, because the 197th section provided, that if it could be proved that a single false debt were inserted the whole arrangement was null ; but the Commissioners, instead of examining the insolvent upon that matter, cast upon the creditors the onus of proof, and this made the enactment a sham and a delusion. In reference to compositions, the practice formerly was for the debtor to notify his difficulty to his creditors, and they appointed a solicitor to look into the matter and say whether there ought to be a bankruptcy or not ; but now the course was, for the firm that was under the necessity of stopping payment to place their affairs in the hands of a friendly accountant, or a still more friendly solicitor, who signified to the creditors that he had their affairs in hand. The creditors were summoned, the accountant or solicitor made a statement for those who employed him. Having looked into the affairs, he assures the creditors, " though there has been misfortune, and perhaps indiscretion, there it is, and the best thing that can be done is to accept the composition of 5s. 10d. ; if they don't, the thing must inevitably go into bankruptcy." If a

Mr. Moffatt

demur be made, he says he will look again into the case : he does ; the creditors think the matter over, and in the end the composition is accepted. These things were increasing, and would continue to increase unless the law put a stop to them. Dishonest debtors were reaping the benefit of the wonderful facility which the law now gave them. He should, then, like to know from the Attorney General, whether he was prepared to approve such a state of things, or whether, on the contrary, he agreed with him, that the law imperatively required inquiry and amendment ? He believed they could scarcely overrate the importance of this subject to the trade, industry, commerce, and character of the country. The present law operated not only against creditors, but against honest debtors. When the law was found to give no security, it operated to limit the extent of credit. His belief was that the measure had been a thorough failure. It required entire re-organization, and it was the duty of the Government to take the initiative at the earliest opportunity. He moved the appointment of a Select Committee to inquire and report on the subject.

MR MURRAY said, that in seconding the Motion, he wished to raise no objection to the principle of the Act of 1861, which he thought was a good one ; but he did object to the mode in which the Act had been administered. Returns of the business in Bankruptcy during two years ending October 11, 1863, had been laid before the House, from which it appeared that 18,133 persons had become bankrupt, and of this number only 1,546, or 8½ per cent, had paid dividends. Of the 18,133 only 1,442 were made bankrupts by their creditors, while the remainder went to the court of their own motion. Upon looking to ascertain what became of these bankrupts, he found, that of the gross number he had mentioned, 12,844 had had their discharges granted, 913 or 5 per cent, had their discharges suspended, and only in 276 cases or 1½ per cent, were the discharges refused. Comparing these figures with the calculations made by the Attorney General in introducing the Bill of 1861, it was clear that, under the old system, certificates were refused to a greater extent than discharges were now withheld from bankrupts. The law, too, as at present administered, would not, unfortunately, reach many of the dishonest debtors. Every Commissioner exercised a separate judgment, and there was no

fixed rule by which dishonesty could
be detected, or, if detected, punished.
That was not, however, the only evil, for
the assets had considerably diminished.
It was an extraordinary thing that out
of the 18,133 who had passed through
the Bankruptcy Court, 699 only had paid
dividends under half-a-crown in the pound,
456 had contrived to pay dividends under
5s., and 212 under 7s. 6d., making a total
of 1,367 out of the 1,546 to whom he
had previously alluded. In the course
of two years, five only had paid 20s.
in the pound. The Act had also increased the expenses instead of diminishing them, for the charges at the court
in the two years amounted to £183,214
8s. 8d. In that sum was included £4,933
paid to the registrars of the county
courts, so that the cost of administering
the Bankruptcy Law in this country was
£178,281 8s. 8d. During the same period
the retiring annuities and compensations
had amounted to £45,325 10s. 6d., making a total of £224,000, or equal to a
sixth of the value of all the bankrupts'
and insolvents' estates in England and
Wales. On the other hand, the figures he
had cited had no reference to the legal,
auctioneers', or other charges connected
with the ordinary administration of a
bankrupt's estate. In addition to these
financial defects, the present system of
audit was altogether inefficient. It was a
matter of public notoriety that not long
since one of the official assignees was a
defaulter to the extent of several thousand
pounds. As he understood the case, the
excuse of the official assignee was that his
accounts had not been properly audited by
his Commissioner. He did not consider
that that was an excuse which could be
entertained for a moment for making away
with the property of creditors, although it
might serve to show that the Commissioner had not performed his duty. The
instance he had alluded to, however, was
not a solitary one, nor was it a solitary
case in which the accounts had not been
audited. There was no correct or satisfactory system of auditing Bankruptcy accounts in practice in this country, and it
would be advisable if auditing were properly
carried out on some system similar to that
employed in Scotland, where an officer,
called an accountant in Bankruptcy, not
only examined every account, but also
ascertained how much had been collected
from the estate, and the cause why any
property or debts was outstanding, and

for this duty he and his clerks received
£1,500 a year. In England there existed nothing of the kind, for the duty of
looking after the estate was not confided
to any one. If a better system were instituted, they would not hear of the defalcations of creditors' assignees, or of official
assignees. He, therefore, cordially seconded the Motion, in the hope that some
advantage might accrue from an alteration
of the present system of the Bankruptcy
Law in its administration, and that it
might better enable creditors to obtain
that to which they were justly entitled.

THE ATTORNEY GENERAL said,
though it was not possible to put the Motion to the House, he could assure them
that the Government felt that the subject
brought forward by the hon. Member was
one which deserved the fullest and most
searching inquiry. It was the earnest
desire of the Lord Chancellor that the
bankruptcy system should be thoroughly
investigated and understood by the country, and that with the assistance of the
House its working might be made as
perfect as possible. The Act referred to
by the hon. Gentleman contained several
useful provisions, and with respect to
some of them he believed that it had undoubtedly succeeded, while with respect to
some of the others it could not be denied
that its effect had not been so satisfactory
as was desirable. The House would remember that one most important step in
advance was effected by the Bill; he referred to the abolition of the distinction
between bankruptcy and insolvency. That
had been done once and for ever, and he
had no hesitation in saying that if nothing
else had been effected by the Act, that
would still have been an important contribution to the cause of legal advancement.
The remarkable figures quoted by the hon.
Gentleman were, in the main, attributable
to the fact of their having included among
the bankrupts those who were formerly
classed under the head of insolvents, and also
to the fact that prolonged imprisonment for
debt was done away with. He regarded as
one of the chief benefits of the Act the opportunity it afforded a man of clearing himself
in the world and getting rid of the load of
debt hanging upon his shoulders. Although
a man might not be able to satisfy the demands of his creditors, he believed it to be
a benefit to society for him to have the
means at his disposal of getting free in the
world, and endeavouring for the future to
earn his title to a name for honesty. He

did not, therefore, look either with alarm or dissatisfaction upon the number of persons who had taken advantage of the Act without paying any dividend. The next point aimed at by the Act was to get rid of oppressive and unnecessary imprisonment of small debtors for debt. As the House was aware, under the provisions of that statute, the gaols were visited every fort night, and their inmates if confined for debt were compulsorily adjudged bankrupts, and then released. The result of that provision was that the Queen's prison had been entirely closed, and that imprisonment for debt was now all but abolished. The Lord Chancellor had in view an amendment of the law for the purpose of enabling some debtors to become bankrupts in *formâ pauperis* without the necessity of going to prison, a plan which he believed many of them at present adopted for that purpose. Another object sought to be attained was the suitable regulation of estates administered under trust deeds: for in many instances the creditors as well as the debtors had no desire to incur too much publicity in respect to their business transactions. His hon. Friend was not satisfied with the operation of that portion of the Act, but he (the Attorney General) doubted whether the unsatisfactory trust deeds which had of late years become prevalent were fairly attributable to the operation of the law. He thought the mercantile community had a great deal to answer for in that respect. The object of the Act was to bring all such transactions under the cognisance of the court; and, in this respect also, if further improvements might still be made, a valuable step had been taken, and the Act might fairly be stated to have been successful. The number of these deeds had been continually increasing; and if it happened, as it sometimes did, that persons not really creditors signed deeds, or signed them for amounts not really due to them, the clauses in the Act bearing on that point furnished easy means of bringing those frauds under the notice of the Court. With regard to the discharge of bankrupts, it appeared that the provisions on the subject had on the whole worked well. But in two other respects he admitted that the Act seemed to be deficient. For one of the changes he referred to—the system of administering the bankrupt's estates by trade assignees instead of by official assignees—the mercantile community were mainly responsible. They had desired that the management of the property should be left in their hands,

on the ground that they could get in the assets better and more cheaply than was done before. But hitherto that change had not worked well; and, though he was far from saying that they ought to return to the old system of official assignees without any improvement, inasmuch as the want of an efficient audit was a blot upon that system, experience did not encourage them to persevere with the present plan of putting the whole collection of the assets into the hands of creditors' assignees. In the first place, he believed it was shown that assets were not better got in, that the amounts were not greater, and that the expenses of collection were not diminished. On the contrary, the ordinary operation was this:— A creditor's assignee was chosen, and he at once appointed a solicitor to do, with less responsibility and less security, and at greater cost, business which the official assignee before did better. He hoped that the inquiry of the Committee, to the appointment of which the Government did not object, would assist them in the correction of this evil. Another great feature originally contemplated in the Act of 1861, and one without which, as was pointed out at the time, it became nugatory to the public and was deprived of its fair chance of success, was the appointment of a chief Judge in bankruptcy. One of his first duties as Law Officer of the Crown was to endeavour to persuade that House to adhere to its decision in favour of a chief Judge, against the opinion of the House of Lords. He then said, "You are cutting off the head of the Bill; you are taking out the main spring of the machine, and the system cannot be expected to work well if you deprive it of its controlling and superintending power." The system of Commissioners had been found to work in a most unsatisfactory manner. The expense of that system was very great, and though he did not like to make any personal allusions, and though, no doubt, all the Commissioners intended to discharge their duties satisfactorily, the number who were able to discharge their duties with efficiency was by no means great, from health, age, and otherwise. The whole system wanted fresh blood infused into it; and, with all the imperfections in this measure—imperfections inseparable from a new machinery—if there had been an efficient and vigorous mind, addressing itself to the improvement and amendment of the administration in bankruptcy centrally in London, he believed that by that time we should have been deriving from the new Act benefits which everybody would be able to appreciate. Unfortunately, the country was deprived of that chance, and that had contributed materially to the disappointment of its expectations. He believed that if the Committee extended its inquiry into the matter they would find it cheaper and better for the country to assimilate the administration in bankruptcy to the administration of deceased person's estates in Chancery; and if even it were necessary to go to greater expense than could be involved in the appointment of one superior Judge (though one Judge would, he believed, be all that was necessary), still, in dispensing with, or greatly reducing the present enormous staff of Commissioners and Registrars throughout the country, there would be a saving of money along with a gain of real efficiency. The Lord Chancellor, as the author of the Act of 1861, was most desirous of seeing all the evils corrected which were complained of, and quite acceded to the desire for inquiry. His Lordship was most sensible that the expenses of bankruptcy administration were intolerably great, and ought to be diminished. These expenses arose from various causes. Among other things required was a greatly reduced scale of costs for attorneys and solicitors, and his Lordship had been directing his attention to that subject. No vote could be taken now upon the appointment of the Committee, but the Government would be glad to see it appointed at some future time.

MR. MALINS said, that having been a strong supporter of the Bill of 1861, he was sorry that it had not worked more satisfactorily. But he entirely agreed with the Attorney General that the failure was mainly owing to the powers given to the creditors' assignee and the non-appointment of a chief Judge. His own opinion was so strong, that when the House of Lords declined to sanction the appointment of a chief Judge, he had recommended the Lord Chancellor to abandon the Bill altogether, rather than fail to secure the coherence and the one uniform system which a chief Judge alone could give, and which alone could make the Act successful. It was now high time the House should take the matter in hand, and revert to the principle sanctioned by it in 1861, but unfortunately rejected by the other House. He was glad to have a Committee, for the principle of the Bill

was sound, and the machinery only was defective.

THE STEAM RAMS AT BIRKENHEAD.

QUESTION.

SIR LAWRENCE PALK said, he rose to call the attention of Mr. Attorney General to—

"A rule obtained for a Commission to examine the Pacha of Egypt and other witnesses at Cairo, to obtain evidence against the Steam Rams detained at Birkenhead; and to ask how long this investigation is likely to take, and the probable expense of it: Whether the trial of the Birkenhead iron-clads will be postponed from May next, until this information be obtained: And, why this rule was not applied for when the vessels were first detained?"

He believed the Foreign Enlistment Act was framed to prevent armed ships from leaving our ports with the intention of taking part in a war against belligerents in amity with England. The question was intimately connected with the question of neutral and belligerent rights, and of these rights he could not give a better definition than was contained in a letter from Earl Russell to Lord Lyons, dated March 27, 1863. Now, Earl Russell wrote to Lord Lyons—

"I said to Mr. Adams that the most stringent orders had been given long ago to watch the proceedings of those who might be suspected of fitting out vessels of war for Confederate purposes; that if there were six vessels, as it was alleged, fitting out in British ports for such purposes, let evidence be forthcoming, and the Government would not hesitate to stop the vessels, and to bring the offenders before a court of justice; and that Mr. Adams was no doubt aware that the Government must proceed according to the regular process of law, and upon sworn testimony."

Now, although the Foreign Enlistment Act was framed in good faith, it was certainly not intended that the Government of the neutral should be bound to issue a roving Commission for the purpose of finding evidence to convict those who were connected with the supposed war vessel; but as Earl Russell expressed it, the evidence was to be forthcoming upon which the Government was to act in the matter. The evidence, in short, was to be brought before the neutral. Earl Russell wrote to Mr. Adams on the 14th of September—

"When the United States' Government assumes to hold the Government of Great Britain responsible for the captures made by vessels which may be fitted out as vessels of war in a foreign port, I have to observe that such pretensions are entirely at variance with the principles of international law, and with the decision of American Courts of the highest authority ; and I have only, in conclusion, to express a hope that you may not be instructed again to put forward claims which Her Majesty's Government cannot admit to be founded on any grounds of law or justice."

It appeared to him that before the neutral Government could legally seize a ship on any grounds whatever, it was for the Government asking for the seizure to prove that the vessel was built, fitted out, and intended for the purpose of taking part in the war with a belligerent State. He thought it must be admitted that the *onus probandi* rested with the Government making the claim, and not with the neutral Government ; but in the case of the iron-clad vessels there could not be any pretence for asserting that they had been built for any underhand purpose, because the Messrs. Laird had published a correspondence between them and Her Majesty's Government, ranging over a considerable period, and giving the Government the fullest information it was possible to give, affording them free access to the vessels whenever it was required, and pledging the Messrs. Laird, as mercantile men of honour, station, and repute, that no advantage should be taken of the Government. The Messrs. Laird had at all times faithfully performed that promise ; and therefore he could not think they could be accused of having in any way misled the Government. A letter was written by the Secretary of the Treasury to those gentlemen on the 7th of October, which really was somewhat of a curiosity in literary correspondence. It stated—

"Gentlemen,—Referring to your ready acceptance of the offer of Her Majesty's Government to prevent any attempt at the forcible abduction of your property, the iron-clad vessel now nearly completed at Birkenhead, and understanding that the trial trip which has been the subject of former correspondence has been abandoned, I am directed by the Lords Commissioners of Her Majesty's Treasury to acquaint you that, from information which has been received, it has become necessary to take additional means for preventing any such attempt."

The House would observe that in the latter part of the letter a supposition was expressed that steps might be taken which the former part stated to have been abandoned. On the 1st of September, Earl Russell wrote to Mr. Adams—

"In the first place, Her Majesty's Government are advised that the information contained in the depositions is in great measure mere hearsay evidence, and generally that it is not such as to show the intent or purpose necessary to make the building or fitting out of these vessels illegal under the

Sir Lawrence Palk

Foreign Enlistment Act. Secondly, it has been stated to Her Majesty's Government at one time, that these vessels have been built for Frenchmen, and at another that they belonged to the Viceroy of Egypt, and that they were not intended for the so-called Confederate States. It is true that in your letter of the 25th of July you maintain that this statement as regards French ownership is a pretence, but the inquiries set on foot by Her Majesty's Government have failed to show that it is without foundation. Whatever suspicion may be entertained by the United States' Consul at Liverpool as to the ultimate destination of these vessels, the fact remains that M. Bravay, a French merchant, residing at Paris, who is represented to be the person upon whose orders these ships have been built, has personally appeared, and has acted in that character at Liverpool. There is no legal evidence against M. Bravay's claim, nor anything to affect him with any illegal act or purpose ; and the responsible agent of the Customs at Liverpool affirms his belief that these vessels have not been built for the Confederates. Under these circumstances, and having regard to the entire insufficiency of the depositions to prove any infraction of the law, Her Majesty's Government are advised that they cannot interfere in any way with these vessels."

Therefore, on the 1st of September, Her Majesty's Government were of opinion that, whatever suspicion might be entertained by the Government of the United States, the fact remained that a French merchant had ordered those vessels. He wanted to prove that, from the beginning to the end of this affair, Mr. Laird had stated that M. Bravay had ordered those vessels, and that as far as they were concerned the transaction was a *bonâ fide* one. He would show that by the despatches of the noble Earl the Secretary for Foreign Affairs, as also by a speech of the noble Lord at the head of the Government. He also contended that if there was any justification for the seizure in the first instance, that justification was still the same ; and it was both unfair and prejudicial to the interests of commerce that delays should take place to obtain information in foreign countries where that information could not have anything to do with the question, and could not prove anything that might be alleged against those ships. On the 5th of September Mr. Adams, in an angry tone, wrote—

"In my belief, it is impossible that any nation retaining a proper degree of self-respect could tamely submit to a continuance of relations so utterly deficient in reciprocity. I have no idea that Great Britain would do so for a moment."

On the 11th of September, Earl Russell observed—

"But law, as you are well aware, is enforced here as in the United States, by independent Courts of Justice, which will not admit assertion for proof, nor conjecture for certainty. . . . With respect to the Egyptian Government, it was only on the 5th instant that Her Majesty's Government received a despatch from Mr. Colquhoun, Her Majesty's Consul General in Egypt, which is conclusive on the subject."

He should like to ask the Attorney General what had taken place since the 11th of September to render it desirable that a roving Commission should be sent to seek evidence in Egypt. On the 27th of October, after some more angry correspondence had taken place between Mr. Adams and the Foreign Office, the cupola ships were detained ; and many months after a rule was obtained to issue a Commission to examine the Pasha of Egypt and other witnesses to find evidence against those vessels. On the 23rd of July, 1863, on the question that the Appropriation Bill do pass, the noble Lord at the head of the Government said—

"Now, what is the duty of a neutral in regard to two belligerents, and what are the rights of neutrals ? The American Government have laid down the position for themselves, because they have declared that a neutral is at liberty to furnish a belligerent with anything that the belligerent may choose to buy, whether it be ships, arms, or anything else. I cannot, in the abstract, concur with my hon. Friend in thinking there is any distinction in principle between muskets, gunpowder, bullets, and cannon on the one side, and ships on the other. Those are things by which war is carried on, and you are equally assisting belligerents by supplying them with muskets, cannon, and ammunition as you are by furnishing them with ships that are to operate in war."

If it was the duty of a neutral to send a roving Commission to Egypt to obtain evidence, one would suppose it was their duty to act when there could be no difficulty in obtaining evidence at home that arms, cannon, and men were shipped for a belligerent. It appeared from a correspondence between Mr. Hammond, of the Foreign Office, and Mr. Hamilton, of the Treasury, that the Collector of Customs at Liverpool had stated to Messrs. Klengender and Co. that, if certain fort guns which they intended to ship on board the *Gibraltar* were for the Federal Government no obstacle would be placed in the way, and that such shipments to New York were very common. It appeared from the explanation given by Mr. Hamilton, that the collector referred to guns shipped as merchandise, and not as part of an armament of a vessel-of-war, so that, according to the policy of Her Majesty's Government, guns might be shipped as merchandise to New York—and were commonly—but that if the guns were intended for the Confederates, they would be contraband, and liable to seizure. So common was this shipment of guns and ammunition to the Federal States become, that it was only the other day that he had read an account of how the *Germania* was detained at Southampton for some time, shipping some heavy siege guns from the Low Moor Ironworks. If it was the duty of the Government to send out roving Commissioners to seek for evidence against the Confederate States, he should like to hear the Attorney General's idea of neutrality as regarded the Federals. As the hon. and learned Gentleman was so anxious to strain the law in all its fulness, strength, and majesty against the Confederates, he (Sir Lawrence Palk) should like to know upon what principle of justice and of law the permission was given to the Federals to ship guns and ammunition in the broad light of day ? So long as the policy of England was plain, straightforward, and honest, the people would support the Government in sustaining neutrality, as long as it appeared conducive to the interests of the country. But he believed that nothing would be so unpopular or so distasteful to the country as to see a different measure of justice dealt out to the two belligerent parties. If he had a feeling for one more than another it was towards the Confederates, who were fighting for liberty, while the Federals were fighting to enslave them ; but that was merely a matter of feeling, and had nothing to do with the merits of the case. He begged the noble Lord to look around him, and to observe where his foreign policy was leading him. He supported freedom where it cost nothing, but when his assistance was most wanted he deserted his friends, as he had deserted Poland. The Government professed to hate treachery, and to dislike the company of those who consorted with conspirators, but it was but the other day that the friend of Mazzini had been a member of the Government. They had given advice to Denmark on all occasions, and led her to believe that she would receive from us actual co-operation ; but in the hour of danger the Government had deserted her, as they had deserted Poland. The consequence was that at that moment England had not an ally in the world, and all nations were anxious to avoid her friendship. The English spirit of this nation was the only thing left for them to insult, but he was perfectly convinced, that if the partiality to which he had referred were continued, the English people would arise as one man, and scatter the Government and their policy to the winds.

THE ATTORNEY GENERAL: As I have already spoken, I will promise not to make a speech in answering the hon. Baronet.

MR. SPEAKER: It is only by the express permission of the House that the hon. and learned Gentleman can again address it. ["Go on!" "Go on!"]

THE ATTORNEY GENERAL: I only thought of giving a simple answer to the question of the hon. Baronet, for I had no idea he would take so wide a circuit over all human affairs. My answer to him is that we did not send out a roving Commission, but having certain evidence—

SIR LAWRENCE PALK said, he rose to order. If the Attorney General by the rules of the House could not fully answer his questions, he would rather take another opportunity of raising the question.

MR. SPEAKER: By the indulgence of the House, the Attorney General was replying to the hon. Baronet.

THE ATTORNEY GENERAL: I will simply reply to the hon. Baronet's questions. With regard to his first question, I have to say that, of course, my attention has been called to a step which has been taken under my advice. The hon. Baronet seems to think that the Commission is a roving Commission to discover evidence. That probably arises from the fact that he does not understand the nature of these proceedings. There are persons in Egypt who, we believe, are able and willing to be witnesses for the Crown. Of course, we know perfectly well already what their evidence is, and when we got the Commission we were obliged to give particulars, and we gave a pretty full note to the other side. The hon. Baronet asks how long the investigation will take, and my answer to that is that the Commission is returnable on the 10th of May, which is earlier than the earliest day on which the trial could take place. Therefore, if the arrangements of the Court will permit of the trial taking place after next Easter Term, we shall be perfectly ready, and the Commission will cause no obstacle or delay. As to the expense of the proceedings, I really cannot undertake to say. The Crown has taken the least expensive mode of proceeding. A single Commissioner has been sent out —a consul from a neighbouring country. Of course, if the other side go to more expense, that is a voluntary action on their part. As to why we did not apply for a

Sir Lawrence Palk

rule when the vessels were first detained, my answer is that we were not ready to proceed to trial at an earlier period than we are actually now proceeding to trial; and to apply for a rule earlier would have been unnecessary and useless.

BOMBARDMENT OF SONDERBORG.
QUESTION.

MR. DILLWYN said, he rose to call the attention of the House to a telegraphic despatch which appeared in *The Times* newspaper of the 6th instant, relative to the bombardment of Sönderborg by the Prussians without previous intimation, and to ask the First Lord of the Treasury, If Her Majesty's Government have received information whether the account given in that despatch is substantially correct; and, if so, what steps have been taken by Her Majesty's Government to recall the Prussian Government to a sense of the necessity of carrying on war in accordance with the usages of civilized nations? He should endeavour to disassociate the question of the bombardment, to which his question referred, as far as possible from that of the war which had unfortunately broken out between the allied Powers and Denmark. So far as the war was concerned, he did not wish, on the present occasion, to come forward as the advocate of one side or the other, further than to say, that, in his opinion, the Danes by not fulfilling the conditions of the Treaty of 1852 gave the Prussians the first cause of quarrel. At the same time, he could not help thinking that the demands of the Prussians on Denmark had been prosecuted in a violent and unjustifiable manner—a view of the case in which he was supported by no less an authority than that of the First Lord of the Treasury. He entertained no doubt that the existing feeling throughout the country was one of sympathy with the Danes, and detestation of the conduct of the Prussians. Indeed, he believed the feeling of the country would have been much more strongly expressed on the subject had it not been for the assurances of the noble Lord, as well as those of the Secretary for Foreign Affairs, taken in conjunction with the near relations which existed between the Prussian Court and the Royal family of this country. Had not the country thought that the arbitrary course of Prussia would have been stayed by those considerations and the brave words of the noble Lord, there would have undoubtedly been a stronger feeling of sympathy with the Danes. As it happened, however, the noble Lord had hardly condemned the conduct of Prussia when it became more outrageous and violent ; and this state of things had been going on so long, that a strong feeling was arising throughout the country in favour of taking a more decided part in favour of the Danes. There had been a good deal said indeed, of late, about a Conference ; but, for his own part, he did not much believe that it tended to good results. The country generally, however, entertained the hope, that if the great Powers were to enter into a Conference with the avowed desire of peace, the Prussians would in all probability become more amenable to the ordinary usages of civilized nations. That expectation had now been very rudely dispelled by a telegram which had appeared in *The Times* newspaper of the 6th of April, which was dated Ulkebol, April 4, and which came from the special correspondent of that paper, whose information was usually correct, and to which, therefore, the country at large attached great importance. The telegram to which he alluded described such a state of proceedings as had never been, he thought, laid before the House, and it was to the following effect—

" The Prussians have bombarded Sonderborg for forty-eight hours without any previous intimation. Eighty townspeople, women, and children, have been killed or wounded. Fifteen hundred shells have been thrown into the town, which is deserted. The cannonade suddenly and completely ceased this morning ; it has, however, recommenced. The Danish position is uninjured."

Now, he did not know that an account of so dastardly an outrage—for he could call it by no other name—had ever been read in that House before ; an outrage perpetrated by one civilized nation upon another, with whom they were not even at war, but whom they had professed to have taken under their protection. After that outrage, he would like to know, if the opinion of the people of Sönderborg could be taken, whether they would prefer to be under the dominion of the Prussians to that of the Danes. The concluding portion of the telegram was very significant, for it stated that the Danish position was uninjured, which showed that the attack could not have been made for any military purpose. The destruction of the town, in fact, could neither be looked upon as a military operation nor as the result of accident, because the Danish position, so far as he could make out from the map, was about two miles from the town of Sönderborg. Now, he thought that both our interests and our honour required that we should enter a most energetic protest against the conduct of a war in the manner to which he had drawn the attention of the House. We had a vast seaboard, and it was most assuredly our interest to recall to the mind of other countries the necessity of waging war in accordance with the usage of civilized nations. If we were not prepared to accept that principle, France or any other nation with which we happened to have a quarrel might send a fleet to bombard Brighton or any other of our towns which was exposed. Our honour was also to some extent involved. Our Government had made representations to the Danes which they had accepted and acted upon, and we were therefore bound to protect them against utter destruction. The allies had invaded Jutland upon one pretext, and, as they would never want a stick to beat a dog, they would probably soon find another, and cross over and attack the other Danish provinces. It was difficult to say what we ought to do. No man was more anxious to avoid war than he was; but he desired to see some measures adopted to prevent the rest of Denmark being swallowed up as Schleswig and Holstein had been. It was vain to hope that we should go to war to recover those Duchies. He supposed that Prussia meant to keep them for herself, but he should be sorry to see the rest of Denmark fall into the clutches of that unprincipled Power. What was the use of our Ambassador at Berlin ? The noble Lord at the head of the Government had condemned the conduct of the Prussians in the strongest language, and they could not doubt that his condemnation was followed by remonstrances addressed to the Ministry at Berlin. If our remonstrances, instead of doing good, operated directly to the contrary, we had better recall our Ambassador, and with all his heart he wished that such a step might be taken. He should also like to see a portion of our fleet sent to the Baltic to help the Danes to protect their territory. He was for peace, but that would not be an act of war. We were told that Prussia was not at war with Denmark, she was only carrying out a little friendly intervention; and if that was so, it certainly could not be an act of war on our part to send a fleet to assist the Danes to protect their territory against an uncalled-for aggression without the excuse of war. He did not see how any one could say that that would be an act of war. At all events, it would not be half so hostile a measure as the invasion of the Danish territory by the Prussians. It was high time that the question was brought before the House, and he, for one, should be prepared to back the Government in any measures however strong to prevent the further decimation of the unfortunate Danes.

Mr. BERNAL OSBORNE : Sir, when I first read the notice of the very proper question which has been put by my hon. Friend, I had no idea that it was about to lead to such warlike results. The question is a natural one for a Member of the House of Commons to put with reference to what appears to be an outrage on humanity, and I had hoped that my hon. Friend, although he was somewhat confused in his argument, because he began by saying that he was against Denmark, but that, somehow or other, he was opposed to the Prussians.

Mr. DILLWYN explained that he had said that he thought Denmark was wrong in the first instance—in the first quarrel—but that the conduct of Prussia was unjustifiable.

Mr. BERNAL OSBORNE : I was under the impression that the hon. Gentleman would have contented himself with a simple protest ; but, like the lion lashing himself into a fury with his own tail, he has imitated the example which was set him in another place, to the horror of the Chancellor of the Exchequer, who was thinking of his surplus, which we disposed of, or shall dispose of, I hope, last night [*Laughter*]—or shall dispose of on a future evening ; though I am sure that the right hon. Gentleman's speech last night would have convinced any one that we might have passed the Budget the same evening. But what was my astonishment to hear the hon. Gentleman, who had announced himself as a Dane, calmly propose that we should send our fleet to the Baltic for the protection of Denmark, without any discussion whatever having taken place in this House. The House will recollect that at the meeting of Parliament—and I must beg the attention of the junior Lord of the Treasury, the hon. and gallant Member for Kidderminster (Colonel White), who has lately addressed his constituents upon this question, and who has such confidence in her Majesty's Government — at the meeting of Parliament there was no subject of such absorbing interest as the complication of affairs in the North of Europe. Various skirmishes occurred upon this subject, and enormous interest was taken in it by the leaders of the great party that I see opposite. But what has happened since ? The House sat for six weeks, and no opinion whatever was expressed as to the policy of Her Majesty's Government ; and to this day the House is liable to be led away by the raw head and bloody bones statements made by my hon. Friend. I contend that it is positively necessary that this question should be examined fully and calmly by this House in the face of the country. At first it was said, and said with great truth, that it was impossible to discuss this Dano-German question in the absence of the papers bearing upon it. It was complained that those papers were most unaccountably delayed. I have since seen the reason, and am able to give an explanation of that. Negotiations having been going on for months, it was not too much to expect that at the meeting of Parliament papers would have been immediately laid upon the table of this House. No such course was adopted by Her Majesty's Government. After a considerable interval had elapsed, a bulky volume was produced—Nos. 1, 2, 3, and 4 ; but when a debate was about to take place upon those interesting papers, the noble Lord interposed with that specious plea which we so often hear from the Treasury Bench, of its being prejudicial to the interests of the country — and for " country," we may sometimes read " Ministry." The noble Lord deprecated any discussion, and announced to the House that a Conference—in which even the hon. Gentleman who has so much confidence in the noble Lord has no confidence—was about to take place upon the subject. Well, Sir, I yielded to the appeal of the noble Lord. On the re-assembling of Parliament after the holydays, other papers were laid upon the table—volume No. 5. These papers have issued from the press like the novel of *Sir Charles Grandison*, which was published in separate volumes. They are as lengthy, and certainly, on the whole, I may say as dull. But on reading No. 5 I perfectly acquit the Government. I quite understand the reasons for the delay in presenting the previous volumes. In fact, I will go further. I think the hon. Under Secretary of State for Foreign Affairs deserves great credit for his assiduity in revising, suppressing, and clipping these papers into a state in which they shall be fit for the Parliamentary mind. I believe there never was an instance where so many important papers have been subjected to such a clipping process as in this Dano-German correspondence. All the important documents—and they must have caused my hon. Friend a great deal of trouble—have been what is vulgarly called "through the mill," until they assume the shape of "elegant extracts." Well, Sir, and what is the present position of this matter? These papers strongly remind one of the character of the month which has just passed. The correspondence in Parts 1, 2, 3, and 4 was conducted by the Foreign Office with leonine vigour; No. 5, Sir, has concluded with most lamb-like bleating. In studying what I may call the early style of the Foreign Office, I was impressed with fear lest the Government, in their hysteric fussiness and irritating industry in reading lectures to Germany and the Great Powers generally, might anticipate the suggestion of my hon. Friend the Member for Swansea, and immediately send a fleet to the Baltic. Luckily, No. 5 has been produced, and I am relieved, at least, of that anxiety; for in those papers their new style is perceptible, and I must say that a more striking contrast to the first four volumes, or a more remarkable avidity for feasting on humble pie, has never been displayed by any Government or any Ministry which has swayed the foreign destinies of this country. Let the House, before I put the question I am about to do, calmly consider the matter, and not be led away by the exciting statement of my hon. Friend; but let the House, I say, calmly consider what have been the results, I will not say of our policy, because it would be an affront to the word, but of our bungling diplomacy. We are told that we are to have a Conference, and the extraordinary thing is that, directly this Conference is announced, the war, which had hitherto languished, has become most sanguinary; so much so that in the same telegram announcing that M. Quaado and another Danish Minister are about to start to attend the Conference, the intelligence is continued that Sönderborg has very nearly been laid in ashes. The immediate effect of the approaching Congress upon the North of Europe, which we seek by its means to pacify, has been to lead the Prussians to redouble their attacks, adding immensely to the slaughter. Let us go a little further, and see what this Conference is. We are told that the attendance of all the signataries to that remarkable Treaty of 1852 has been promised; and, what is more, that a Plenipotentiary of the German Diet will attend—a Power, by-the-by, which has been treated by the Government of the noble Lord heretofore very much in the light of a poor relation—that is to say, not taken into account at all. Suddenly—and let the House mark that it was at the suggestion of the French Government, which declined, if there be any truth in the papers contained in No. 5, to be present without a plenipotentiary from the Diet attended—we have a statement that a plenipotentiary from the German Diet was also invited. Whether that plenipotentiary will attend or not we do not know exactly, but from the nature of the German Diet I think that we can foresee that, whatever day the noble Lord has named for his Conference, the German Diet, by reason of their sluggish mode of proceeding, will not be in a position to send an answer to the noble Lord's invitation for some weeks, if not for some months later. They will have to refer the matter to the 37 States which they represent; these will refer it back again, and the subject will then be entertained by a Select Committee; so that at the end of the Session. probably, the noble Lord will have an answer from the German Diet. The French Minister, with more foresight than our own, suggests that the protocol might be left open for the German plenipotentiary; and that, perhaps, might be the best course to pursue. But suppose the Conference meets, I want the House calmly to consider what it is to do. It appears to me that this Conference is nothing more nor less than a means of escape for Her Majesty's Ministers from their bungling proceedings and uncalled-for meddling in the North of Europe. It is, in fact, a political pic-nic given by the noble Lord, to which every country will be allowed to bring its basket of suggestions, with no *pièce de resistance* provided in the shape of a basis, but with perfect freedom —and indeed agreement—on the part of each one present to differ upon every point from everybody else. All this time, when the noble Lord is sending out his general invitations for an "At home" on a certain day—I want to know what the Foreign Office are about to do with the London Treaty of May 8, 1852? We hear a great deal about this treaty in the early style of the Foreign Office; but by some extraordinary transmutation in No. 5, as laid upon the table of the House, the Treaty of 1852 has vanished altogether from the consideration of Her Majesty's Government. So thoroughly is this the case, that having put upon the paper a Motion for the 19th instant, relating to the Treaty of 1852, I now am seriously at a loss to know whether that treaty any longer applies to the treatment of this Dano-German question. It is really a curious study to trace what is the main thought running through the mind of Her Majesty's Government in their handling of this subject. In their place in Parliament I find them speaking what my hon. Friend called brave big words of menace to Germany, and clinging with desperate tenacity to what I call that ill-omened, unfortunate, and unjust Treaty of 1852; a treaty which I shall prove was made at the instigation of Russia, which compromised the interests of Denmark, and which, I think, compromised the honour of this country, in ignoring the liberties and rights of a free people. That treaty, however, as I will endeavour to prove, has been entirely laid ·aside. I will not inflict upon the House a passage from the blue-book, but if they will turn to page 732 of Part No. 5, they will perceive that in despatch 1,040, of February 23, the Foreign Minister, running away from his previous promises, wrote to Lord Bloomfield at Vienna, proposing a Conference without a basis. He had first insisted on a basis, but in that despatch he gives it up. I leave it to any sensible man to say, in the present state of feeling between the Powers, whether there is any likelihood of their coming to an agreement at such a Conference, even though the anxiety of the noble Lord to get them all into one room, like the Kilkenny cats, may be gratified. The despatch to which I have referred was dated February 23, and on February 26 a proposal in accordance with its terms was first made to the Danish Ministers by Sir A. Paget; and what was the state of things in the Danish Cabinet when that proposal was made? Why, so great was the consternation created among those unfortunate Danes, whom we have been leading astray all through with false hopes, and then deserting them in their extremity, so great, I say, was the consternation among them, that they said to Sir A. Paget, "For God's sake don't call on us for any immediate answer." Like gallant men, who do not think of themselves merely, they said, "If we agree at once to a Conference without a basis,

not merely will our places be at stake, but probably the dynasty which you have taken so much trouble to set up." That is the feeling created at Copenhagen among the Danish Ministry by this proposal of a Conference without a basis. On the 9th of March—I go on to page 706—a fresh pressure was put on Denmark. It appears to have been felt that affairs had come to such a point in this House, that Her Majesty's Government could no longer resist taking action and putting a fresh pressure on Denmark. On March 15, Austria declares to our Ambassador, that though she had formerly agreed to the basis of the Treaty of 1852, she will now no longer be satisfied with the fulfilment by the Danes of the engagements of 1851-2; and that if she meets in Conference she will demand further engagements. On March 16, Denmark still asserts that she will only meet in Conference on the basis of the engagements of 1851-2; but she takes very little by this, for on the 17th of March, Sir Andrew Buchanan, at Berlin, announces to M. Bismark, that Her Majesty's Government had altogether given up the engagements of 1851-2 as the basis for the meeting of the Conference. But what happens after that? It is a most extraordinary thing, and it must strike every hon. Member with astonishment, that whenever we want any real information on foreign affairs we are not furnished with it by our own Government, who, while they do not pretend to legislate for home affairs, yet appeal to us for our support on account of the vigour and foresight of their foreign policy. Well, when anything remarkable is to be learnt respecting foreign policy, we do not find it in this blue-book. No. We must go to the foreign papers, and in the second edition of *The Times* published yesterday there appears a despatch from the French Minister for Foreign Affairs to the French Ambassador in London, which is not to be found in the blue-book, though the despatch is dated as far back as March 20. The contents of that despatch are of so extraordinary a nature, that I think that some detailed statement is due from the noble Lord the Prime Minister, as to whether the Government are agreed to take the suggestion contained in that despatch as the basis of the Conference. The proposition of the French Minister involves such a serious principle, that I think the House should take it into consideration if the Government does not. M. Drouyn de Lhuys says he wishes to acquaint the Cabinet of London with the

course intended to be taken by the French
Government in reference to the Conference;
and he goes on to say that, if the French
Plenipotentiary attend, he thinks it his
duty to inform Her Majesty's Government
that he will propose as a basis, for the
consideration of the Conference, the propriety of consulting the wishes of the population of Schleswig and Holstein, as to
who should be their Sovereign. I take it
that this is really a *bonâ fide* despatch, and
that is the purport of it. I want to know,
then, why it is not given in the blue-book,
and whether the Government will lay a
copy of it on the table of the House? I
wish, too, that the noble Lord will tell the
House whether he, or the representative of
the British Government at the Conference,
is prepared to concur in that basis laid
down by the French Minister? In fact,
the further we look into this question of
the Conference, it appears impossible to
hope that any good will result from it.
None of the representatives about to enter
the Conference, with the exception of the representatives of Austria and Prussia, who
will of course be together, appear to have
any settled ideas of any sort or kind, and
they seem to have given up all previous
pledges to abide by the Treaty of 1852.
The Conference, therefore, so far from
settling the peace of the North of Europe is
more likely to embitter matters, and instead
of localizing the war, is likely to extend
it even over a larger area. I would wish to
draw the attention of the House to the
remarkable answer given by the noble Lord
the Foreign Secretary to this country to
the invitation to attend the Conference,
which was proposed by the Emperor of the
French to be held at Paris. The very reasons given for refusing to attend that Congress apply with equal force to the assembly of the Conference which is shortly to
meet. I will only read two passages from
the despatch of the noble Lord, but they
are of so much importance that I am sure
the House will excuse the time I shall occupy in doing so. At the same time, I
must say that I shall always lament that
the invitation to attend the Congress was
not accepted; and I think, also, that it
might have been responded to with somewhat more courtesy, without the answer
being first published in *The Times* newspaper. But what were the reasons given
for not attending that Conference? Earl
Russell stated in last November to Earl
Cowley that the British Government would
feel more apprehension than confidence

from the meeting of a Congress of Sovereigns and Ministers without fixed objects,
ranging over the map of Europe, and exciting hopes and aspirations which they
might feel themselves unable either to
gratify or to quiet. But the noble Lord
goes further. Let the House remember
that the present Conference is to be held
during a state of war and without an armistice or basis, and then consider how
applicable to it are these words, used in
reference to the Congress proposed by the
French Emperor. The noble Lord, the
Foreign Secretary, wrote, in November
last, to Earl Cowley—

"Indeed it is to be apprehended that questions
arising from day to day, coloured by the varying
events of the hour, would give occasion rather for
useless debate than for practical and useful deliberation in a Congress of twenty or thirty representatives, not acknowledging any supreme authority, and not guided by any fixed rules of
proceeding."

That language held by the noble Lord in
refusing to join the Congress for the pacification of Europe, and for lessening our
armaments, is, I am afraid, more applicable on this occasion than when it was
addressed to the Emperor of the French.
I am very much inclined to believe that
this whole Conference will only turn out a
Parliamentary hoax, and it would have
been much better, instead of meeting on
the 12th of April, if the noble Lord had
postponed it till the 1st of April next.
But I really wish to know when this Conference will assemble? At present, it
stands for the 12th of April, but I see
by the foreign newspapers that it has no
chance of meeting then. I want only to
know what prospect there is, if it does
meet at all, of any report of its proceedings being made before this House is dismissed for the long vacation. I can well
understand that if this case is brought before the House in any shape, the plea will
be urged that it would be prejudicial to the
public service to discuss the question while
the Conference is sitting; but, in my opinion, and in the opinion, I believe, of a
great many Members of this House who
take the trouble to read the papers on the
subject, we should be strengthening the
hands of the Government by having a proper discussion on these questions. I want
to know, and I hope the noble Lord at the
head of the Government will give some
proper account to the House, as to what
has become of this Treaty of 1852. Does
Her Majesty's Government intend to abide
by that treaty, or are we to have another

state of affairs by which there will be a temporary patching up of this system on the Continent, condemning these poor unfortunate Schleswig-Holsteiners to what the noble Lord calls the away of their lawful Sovereign, but whom they do not acknowledge as their lawful Sovereign. It certainly is surprising that any man who pretends to lead a Liberal party should endeavour to force a Sovereign on a people who have never been consulted as to their choice. I hope the noble Lord will give an explanation, and not evade any of these points ; but of this I am sure, that, whatever may be the present opinion of the country, in ignorance of the transactions which have taken place, it will hereafter regret that Germany has been irritated, Denmark cajoled, and England humiliated.

VISCOUNT PALMERSTON : Sir, it is difficult to satisfy my hon. Friend, for he finds fault with the past, with the present, and with the future. I shall not, therefore, attempt to alter his opinions, but shall simply answer the questions which have been put to me. Now, Sir, my hon. Friend accuses Her Majesty's Government of having misled Denmark, and of having excited expectations which have not been fulfilled. I utterly deny these allegations. There is not a syllable in the blue-books with which my hon. Friend pretends to be familiar, but which I cannot believe he has read, which bears out the assertion he has made. Our policy, Sir, has been plain and simple from the beginning, and, as I think, honourable throughout. Our object has been first of all to prevent war, and, and, hostilities having commenced, to restore peace. My hon. Friend says we have thrown over the Treaty of 1852. No such thing. Again, I say my hon. Friend has not read a word of the blue-books, for there is not a syllable in them to justify such a statement. On the contrary, not only do we maintain the Treaty of 1852, but every one of the Powers who concluded that treaty equally maintains it. Therefore my hon. Friend must have been in a dream on this matter, and comes down here to expound his illusions, instead of telling us what he would have discovered if he had perused those documents which seem to weigh so much on his mind, but to dwell so little on his memory. My hon. Friend has fallen into some of those contradictions which men of his genius and imaginative powers are occasionally apt to stumble into. He has critized the Conference, and very naturally, being of an inquisitive turn of

mind, he wants to know what the Conference will do when it assembles. I am not able to gratify his curiosity. If he wishes to know the past I furnish him with the blue-books. If he wishes to know the future he must apply somewhere else. My hon. Friend ridicules the Conference, which, by the way, he has invested with a function which I was not aware naturally belonged to it. He says a Conference cannot meet without a basis. When two Powers—two nations—two Governments begin to treat for peace it is, no doubt, essential that the plenipotentiaries should settle the terms on which they are to negotiate, and agree whether it is to be on the principle of *uti possidetis* or the *status quo ante bellum.* It is not, however, the peculiar function of a Conference to have a basis. A Conference is an assembly of plenipotentiaries of different powers, who meet for the purpose of ascertaining what is the state of things, and how they can be set right. That is a Conference. My hon. Friend objects to the Conference, which is to meet for the purpose of endeavouring to put an end to the hostilities that are raging, but which he says will only create more mischief. He pledges his political sagacity—and I beg you to bear that in mind—that the Conference can lead to no good result. I can only say I trust that next year on the day he has mentioned—namely, the first of April, he will remind us of what he has now predicted. My hon. Friend says we are wrong to agree to the Conference, but that we were equally wrong not to have agreed to the Congress. He thinks the reason we gave for not going to the Congress was absurd. I said there was no object for the Congress to deal with. Well, there was no object for the Congress, because there was no war which it was to bring to a close, and there was no particular subject to which the Congress was to direct attention. Here, however, there is a distinct object—to endeavour to reconcile parties who are differing, and to put an end to hostilities now raging. The cases are utterly different, and my hon. Friend would, I think, have shown more discrimination of mind if he had not drawn this distinction, which was exactly the wrong way. I repeat that all the parties who concluded the Treaty of 1852 agree in holding that they are bound by it to acknowledge King Christian as the Sovereign of Denmark, and to respect and maintain the integrity of that kingdom. You may say that is not a basis ; at least it is an agreement. The Powers have all agreed that that is the condition on which they enter into the Conference with a view to reconcile the differences which have arisen between Denmark and Germany. My hon. Friend confounds two things which are in themselves entirely separate—the agreements of 1851-2, and the Treaty of May, 1852. There are differences between Germany and Denmark as to the agreements of 1852, the main facts of which were that whereas, on the one hand, the German Powers agreed not to require what had formerly been demanded, namely, the administrative and political union of Holstein and Schleswig; on the other hand, the Danish Government agreed not to do anything which could tend to incorporate Holstein with Denmark. But these agreements are totally different and distinct from the Treaty of 1852, and it is quite essential to our understanding of the matter, that the distinction should be borne in mind. The agreements of 1851-2 may be settled either way, without at all infringing the Treaty of 1852, and the Treaty of 1852 may be adhered to by those who entertain different opinions as to the engagements which preceded it. Then my hon. Friend asks when the Conference is to meet. We have the assent of all the Powers who concluded—I do not say of those who acceded to the treaty—France, Austria, Prussia, Russia, Sweden, and Denmark. The German Confederation was not a party to that treaty. [Mr. BERNAL OSBORNE: The Confederation was not asked.] No; and some of the Powers of Germany objected to proposing to the German Diet to become a party to the treaty. At one time Prussia was against it, although she afterwards changed her mind, and wished the treaty to be communicated to the Diet. The other Powers, however, would not consent to that, because they considered the questions which were to be settled by this treaty, namely, the succession to the Danish Crown, and the integrity of the Danish monarchy, to be European and not German questions. We have asked the Diet to send a plenipotentiary to the Conference. Whether they will be as long in giving an answer as my hon. Friend imagines, I cannot say; but in deference to the desires of Austria and Prussia, who are anxious to give them a little more time to consider their answer, the meeting of the Conference will be postponed from the 12th to the 20th of April. France, it is true, wishes the Diet to send a representative to the Conference, but does not make that a *sine qua non*. Even if the Diet does not appear in the Conference, it will still be possible to proceed with it, as the protocol may be left open for the Diet to accede to it. My hon. Friend alluded to a despatch from the French Government to the French Ambassador here, containing the suggestions of an appeal to the populations of Holstein and Schleswig. That is not, however, put forward as a basis, but is thrown out merely as a suggestion. There are obvious objections which may be raised to any such proceeding, and it is not likely that the other Powers will fall into the suggestion; nor, indeed, does France require it. The French Government state distinctly that they stand on the Treaty of 1852, and hold themselves bound by its engagements. Well, Sir, that is the state of the case. My hon. Friend has his opinions, but I do not think they are partaken by the country at large. Although my hon. Friend is very abundant in his criticisms, I am really quite at a loss to understand what he would have done if he had had the management of affairs. [Mr. BERNAL OSBORNE: Let it alone.] My hon. Friend, therefore, would have been a party to a treaty—[Mr. BERNAL OSBORNE: I would not have made it]—by which this country was bound to acknowledge a certain Sovereign as King of the countries under the sway of the Danish Crown, and to respect the integrity of the Danish monarchy; and in spite of the general opinion that this country was bound in honour and in interest to endeavour to maintain that treaty, he would have done nothing but sit still with his hands in his pockets as he is doing now. I do not think that such a course would have been to the credit of the Government or to the satisfaction of the country at large. We may be wrong and he may be right, but such, at least, is our opinion of the matter. We endeavoured to persuade other countries to fall into our views, and we trust we have accomplished, or are about to accomplish, a considerable step in assembling a Conference with the object of restoring peace. That is the answer to my hon. Friend, and at this late hour I cannot go into the other matters to which he referred. My hon. Friend who opened the question to-night, referred to a transaction at Sönderborg, which I am afraid there is no reason to doubt really took place. We have no official or authentic information, but we have reason to believe, without knowing the extent to which lives were sacrificed, that a bombardment of Sönderborg did take place, and that some of the citizens were killed. The invasion of Danish territory was, in our opinion, unjust and unjustifiable, and I am sorry to say that circumstances have occurred in connection with the conduct of the German troops during the invasion which are not in keeping with the practice of civilized nations in modern times. We have made an inquiry at Berlin, but we have not yet got an answer — an inquiry, first, as to whether the thing did take place; and next, by what authority, and under what orders, the bombardment was carried out. I do not think the British Government can presume to dictate to the Prussian army the manner in which they should conduct their operations, but there are opinions which men may express as to conduct pursued in violation of ordinary rule and humanity, though I hope we shall be allowed to determine what we shall say when we get an answer from the Government of Berlin.

Mr. KINGLAKE said, he thought that if it should turn out that the Prussians had been guilty of bombarding Sönderborg in the manner described, and that the bombardment had taken place without provocation, they would find no defenders either in the House of Commons or in any part of the United Kingdom. But he would take leave to say, on the present occasion, something analogous to what he took the liberty of saying when the House was dealing with the affair at Kagosima. He then said that before passing a censure upon Admiral Kuper, it would be well for the House to hear in the first instance what Admiral Kuper might have to say for himself, and he thought the result in that case, which he now knew, entitled him to hold that the course thus suggested was the proper one to take. Certainly, he should be sorry to abandon the hope that the Prussians might have something to say either in disproof or in extenuation of an act which at present, seemed to be highly discreditable to them. He could not agree with the hon. Member for Liskeard (Mr. Bernal Osborne), in endeavouring to pass a censure upon the Government for refusing to enter into the Congress proposed by the Government of France; nor could he concur with him in thinking that there was any analogy between that case and the present, because the objection which the Government took to going into a Congress was founded upon the supposition that the parties invited to send representatives could

not see clearly what the objects sought to be attained were; whereas here, though he admitted that there was the greatest difficulty as to the bases of negotiation, yet on one point all Europe was agreed, because all Europe desired to see the restoration of peace. He presumed it was almost part of the duty of the noble Lord at the head of the Government to, in some manner, misunderstand the arguments and statements of the hon. Member for Liskeard; but what the hon. Gentleman endeavoured to convey to the House was this—That in the earlier stages of the negotiation the Government had, in the most earnest and persistent way, put forward the first Treaty of 1852 and then the integrity of the Danish monarchy as conditions without which nothing like a successful negotiation could take place. Then the hon. Member, perceiving that in the later portion of the papers the language used by the Government in this respect was moderated—and, perhaps, the House would think, properly moderated — permitted himself to quarrel with the change in their policy. He could not follow his hon. Friend in this, because the change, if any, was one which he hailed with great satisfaction. No doubt Her Majesty's Government had obtained the assent of foreign Powers to a Conference, but almost every Power which had so agreed, had annexed a distinct condition, and, therefore, the hon. Member for Liskeard very much understated his case when he said that there was an attempt to go into a Conference without a basis. The difficulty in which the Government were placed was not that there was no basis, but that there were three or four different bases, totally dissimilar the one from the other — nay, absolutely inconsistent one with the other. In language anxiously employed for the purpose of preventing any such misrepresentation, as was from time to time attempted, the Danish Government had declared that under no circumstances would they go into a Conference except upon the condition that the basis of the Conference was the arrangements of 1851 and 1852. On the other hand, both Austria and Prussia had said in terms equally distinct, that they would not go into the Conference if the arrangements of 1851 and 1852 were to be made the basis. It was, therefore, clear that no two parties agreeing to differ in terms as precise as possible, could find any language more perfectly representing the impossibility of their coming together than the language used by the Government of Copenhagen on the one side and by the Governments of Berlin and Vienna on the other. The matter consequently stood thus: That the Danish Government insisted that the basis should be the arrangements of 1851 and 1852, that the two great German Powers insisted that the Conference should take place without any such basis, and that England was proceeding upon the principle, or, at all events, in the hope, that the Conference was to have ultimately for its basis, though not as a preliminary, an adherence to the Treaty of 1852. Certainly the noble Lord at the head of the Government had to-night put that view of the case in a way which he ventured to say would tend to inflame the anger of the whole of Germany, for he had said, in terms as distinct as could be used, that the King of Denmark was the only lawful Sovereign of the two Duchies. There was going on what was virtually a war of succession — for he did not care for the pretences put forward by Austria and Prussia—and in the midst of that war, it being the avowed object of Her Majesty's Government to restore peace, they arrayed themselves, heroically it might be, on the side of one of the disputants, declaring in language which must be extremely displeasing to the German Powers, that the King of Denmark was the only lawful Sovereign of the Duchies. To hear the noble Lord one might imagine that he was a representative of Lord Liverpool's Government, announcing to the House that a congress of Sovereigns had disposed of nations and peoples by an arrangement which they had determined should last for ever. It so happened that within a few minutes from the moment when the noble Lord made that rash statement to the House there was put into his hands a paper which showed that the King of Denmark, the "lawful Sovereign" of the noble Lord —had not only very difficult subjects to deal with, but had also a very disloyal Parliament. The Parliament of Schleswig-Holstein—if so he might term the estates —had by a unanimous vote determined to protest before Europe against the notion that they were to be handed over by foreign Powers to any Sovereign whom the Powers assembled in London might please to select. He deeply regretted that the noble Lord had used that language, for he had looked forward to the proposed Conference in the hope that if it could ever turn out of any use at all, it might

be useful as furnishing a graceful mode of retreat for Her Majesty's Government, enabling them to recede from a long and persistent adherence to the Treaty of 1852, which, in his judgment, had been the cause of the disturbance ; an adherence which was not required by the terms of the treaty itself, because the way in which the treaty was put forward was founded upon a misinterpretation of it. Be that, however, as it might, he thought it was very unfortunate that a policy most English—a policy which he should have thought most acceptable to the Liberal party in this country, had been recommended, not by Her Majesty's Government, but by a foreign Sovereign. He could only trust that the Conference might be found a mode of enabling the Government to retreat from the position into which they had got, because he believed that to put forward the Treaty of 1852 in the way they did, and to endeavour to force it upon those who had never been consulted, was a policy entirely inconsistent with the principles which they themselves had loudly proclaimed.

GENERAL PEEL : I rise merely to say that the subject before the House is not a fit subject for ridicule. There is no portion of it at which the British House of Commons has any reason to laugh. The hon. Member for Swansea asked whether it was true that Sönderborg was bombarded without notice, and eighty of its inhabitants killed. He was followed by the hon. Member for Liskeard, who asked very proper questions, some of which have not been answered at all. Then the noble Lord got up, and the world will hear of the House of Commons being convulsed with laughter. I say that is adding insult to injury. The noble Lord at the head of the Government said there was nothing in the blue-books that could lead the Danes to believe they might expect assistance from this country. I am afraid there is a great deal that will not be found in the blue-books ; but I well remember the words used by the noble Lord himself at the end of last Session, when he said, that if the Duchies were invaded Denmark would not stand alone. I thought at the moment that that was a very indiscreet declaration for the Prime Minister to make, but I entirely relied on it. I was abroad during the recess, and when I heard Germans talk very angrily about enforcing their claims against Denmark, I used to say, "Take care ; we are bound to resist it." But their reply was, "Oh, no ; you will not resist. Denmark·

will be left alone." And it appears they knew the noble Lord much better than I did. My only object in rising is this. I do not think that upon a question being asked on a Motion for going into Committee of Supply, whether a telegram addressed to a newspaper is true or not, is the proper time for entering into a discussion of a great question of this kind. I thought the omission of an assurance of our friendly relations with foreign Powers in the speech from the Throne at the opening of the Session very significant, and that that circumstance made it absolutely necessary for this House to inquire why the usual assurance was left out. Is it because Her Majesty's Government was no longer able to declare that they had received those friendly assurances? And has that arisen from any one act of the Government, or is it the natural consequence of the whole of the foreign policy which they have adopted since they came into office? These are questions which the House has a right to know, and I venture to promise the Government that they will get an opportunity of answering them.

SIR HARRY VERNEY said, he would not presume to give any answer to the question which was addressed to the noble Lord with respect to the bombardment of Sönderborg. He feared that the reply had been by no means satisfactory. He wished, however, to give an explanation which he had seen as to the cause of that bombardment. He had seen it stated in a Hamburg paper, that there was an understanding between the Danes and the Prussians that there should be no bombardment of Sönderborg or of West Dybböl, as the latter contained the sick and wounded of the Prussians, and the former was full of women and children. But, subsequently, a Danish officer was sent with a flag of truce to say that the Danes were going to bombard West Dybböl, and the reply was, "If you do so we will bombard Sönderborg." He did not defend the bombardment, because he believed it added to the horrors of war, but he was merely giving the account which he had seen in a paper from Hamburg, and there was one circumstance which made him hope that account was true. Hon. Gentlemen would recollect that about a month ago a shot was fired at a Danish vessel, and it went into Sönderborg. Immediately a flag of truce was sent by the Prussians to say that it was a mere accident, and the Danes were asked to take care that their vessels should not

come in a line with Sönderborg. The noble Lord said he would stand upon the basis of the Treaty of 1852, but that treaty reserved the rights of the German Bund. One of those rights was, to reject any one who proposed to come into the Bund, and, therefore, they had the right to reject the King of Denmark coming into it as Duke of Holstein. His hon. Friend had said, and the right hon. Gentleman opposite (General Peel) repeated, that Her Majesty's Government had been making representations to Denmark, the effect of which had been to induce the Danish Government to rely upon the assistance of England. But he would ask any hon. Gentleman who had read the blue-books, whether the representations of Her Majesty's Government to Denmark had not been over and over again to this effect, "Perform your promises." The patience of Earl Russell, and the earnestness with which he had addressed these representations to the Danish Government, were beyond all praise; and his own opinion was that the despatch of September, 1862, was one of the wisest and most moderate of despatches, and really contained the basis of an arrangement which might have settled everything. But this country was not entirely without blame, for he believed the Danes would have acceded to the proposal of September, 1862, had they not believed there was such a strong Danish party in this country and the House of Commons that they might refuse the proposition of Earl Russell without exposing themselves to danger. But whatever they felt with regard to the war—and he did not defend the conduct of Austria and Prussia in the matter—they were bound to recognize the fact that it was caused by the Danes. There was one party, however, against whom nothing could be said, and that was the German inhabitants of Holstein. They had been the victims of oppression, and he trusted, that whatever they did, they would not lend themselves to a policy which would lead to the infliction of greater oppression and injury upon them. It appeared to him that the proposal of the Emperor of the French was more likely to lead to a happy result, and he must press upon Her Majesty's Government to give an answer to the question of his hon. Friend behind him, and state whether they would produce the despatch of the French Government. If not, he should feel it his duty to move for its production.

MR. PEACOCKE said, he believed that the country had been deeply disappointed that the House had so far abdicated its functions as not to have raised a discussion on that question since it met in February. He was extremely disappointed at the tone adopted by the noble Lord that evening, and also on a former occasion. The noble Lord told them that Austria and Prussia had commenced a most aggressive, unjust, and unnecessary war. The noble Lord also said that he considered we were bound, as parties to the Treaty of 1852, to guarantee the integrity of the Danish monarchy. Now, if the opinions of the noble Lord were that it was the duty of Her Majesty's Government to guarantee the integrity of the Danish monarchy, and if he believed that Austria and Prussia had commenced a most aggressive and unjust war, he (Mr. Peacocke) was very much surprised that the noble Lord did not, in opposition to his policy as displayed in the blue-book, give active aid to Denmark. He (Mr. Peacocke) did not advocate a war policy, for this reason—because he believed that Denmark was originally in the wrong, and that she had never put herself in the right. But he thought it most impolitic that the noble Lord should come down and use such strong and aggravating expressions towards Austria and Prussia at the very time that he was about to meet them at the table of a conference, with a view to settle the dispute in an amicable manner. If the noble Lord's language towards those Powers had been more conciliatory, it would have rendered more likely the attainment of a practical and pacific result. He believed that these Conferences would have no result at all, and for this reason. In the papers before the House, Denmark distinctly told them that she would make no concessions whatever—that she would agree to nothing like a union between Schleswig and Holstein until she was utterly exhausted. On the other hand, the German Powers distinctly told them that they could not consent to treat on the basis of the engagements of 1851-2. He regretted that the noble Lord had not felt it his duty to state whether it was true or not that the French Government had communicated to Her Majesty's Government the fact, that it intended at the Conference to advocate that which was virtually the principle of an appeal to nationalities by universal suffrage? The noble Lord stated that all the Powers which had accepted the Conference had agreed to the mainte-

nance of the integrity of the Danish monarchy; but how could a Power which advocated the application of the principle of universal suffrage to the Duchies be said to agree to the maintenance of the integrity of the Danish monarchy? Was it to be believed that the answer of the population of Schleswig and Holstein would be in favour of the integrity of the Danish monarchy? He thought it was the duty of the Government to endeavour to maintain the integrity of that monarchy, but in doing so to call upon Denmark to fulfil the promises she made to the German Powers in 1851 and 1852. The difficulties of that question were indeed great, but they would not be lessened by the irritating language which the noble Lord habitually employed.

MR. SOMERSET BEAUMONT said, that the noble Lord had talked of delusions; but when, at the end of last Session, he told Denmark that in case of the invasion of her territories she would not stand alone, he imparted to Denmark what she had since found out to be a delusion. He agreed with what had fallen from the hon. Member for Bridgwater (Mr. Kinglake), and had hoped that they would that night have heard from the noble Lord something to indicate that he meant to represent the feelings of what ought to be the Liberal party on that question—something to indicate that he desired to consult the wishes of the people of these States before giving additional authority to treaties which had been the cause of so much disturbance in Northern Europe. It was difficult to get accurate information as to the state of feeling in Schleswig and Holstein; but, if they read the official papers before them, they could not help seeing that the people of those Duchies had substantial grounds for discontent with their "lawful Sovereign." He thought there was a great deal to be said both for Denmark and for the German Confederation on that question. It seemed to him that a country like Denmark, having attached to it two provinces under subjection to foreign Powers, occupied a very unfair and anomalous position; and he was not surprised that Denmark, with the spirit and courage which she had exhibited, should wish to free herself from a burden that was almost too much for her to bear. And if the noble Lord, instead of seeking to give further authority to treaty stipulations which had produced so much confusion, had sought to withdraw Denmark and the German Confederation from their unnatural relation, he would have better deserved the thanks of the country than he now did. He had hoped that something might have come from these Conferences, but from what had been said that night he feared, with the hon. Member for Liskeard, that when the House sat there on the 1st of next April it would have nothing to do but make speeches over their decent burial.

Question put, and *agreed to.*

SUPPLY.

SUPPLY *considered* in Committee.

House *resumed.*

Committee report Progress; to sit again on *Monday* next.

LIFE ANNUITIES AND LIFE ASSURANCES BILL—[BILL 56.]
SECOND READING.

Order for Second Reading read.

Moved, " That the Bill be now read a second time."—(*Mr. Chancellor of the Exchequer.*)

THE CHANCELLOR OF THE EXCHEQUER, in moving the second reading of this Bill, said, the object of its first and most important clause was to provide that all stock received by the Commissioners for the reduction of the National Debt, either on account of Life Assurances or on account of Deferred Annuities, should not be cancelled as it was under the provisions of the present law, but should be held by those Commissioners and kept alive, and dividends received upon it, so that there should be an adequate fund to meet the prospective obligations on those annuities or assurances when they arose.

Motion *agreed to.*

Bill read 2°, and *committed* for *Friday,* 29th *April.*

House adjourned at half after Twelve o'clock till Monday next.

~~~~~~~~

HOUSE OF LORDS,
Monday, April 11, 1864.

MINUTES.]—PUBLIC BILLS— *First Reading*— Regius Professorship of Greek (Oxford) [H.L.] (No. 44).
Second Reading—Charitable Assurances Enrolments [H.L.] (No. 38).

Mr. Somerset Beaumont

REGIUS PROFESSORSHIP OF GREEK (OXFORD) BILL—[H.L.] (No. 44.)
FIRST READING.

THE LORD CHANCELLOR: My Lords, I rise for the purpose of presenting to your Lordships a Bill which I sincerely trust will meet with a favourable reception from the House. It is a Bill for the better endowment of the Regius Professorship of Greek in the University of Oxford. As your Lordships are aware, in the time of King Henry VIII., five Royal Professorships were founded in that University, and the Regius Professorship of Greek was one of the number. Similar foundations were also made in the University of Cambridge. The holders of the other four Regius Professorships at Oxford which accompanied the Regius Professorship of Greek have been more fortunate than the occupiers of that chair. To every one of them has been attached some ecclesiastical preferment, or some mastership or other endowment. To the Greek Professor there is nothing but the original stipend of £40 a year. That sum was at that time adequate, but it continues to the present moment, the only remuneration given for the Professor's labours and exertions in the cause of Greek literature. To each of the Regius Professorships of Greek and Hebrew in the University of Cambridge a statute, passed in the year 1840, has annexed a canonry in Ely Cathedral. Now, your Lordships are aware that in the ecclesiastical patronage of the Lord Chancellor are included several canonries—I think they are twelve in number—in the cathedral churches of Norwich, Rochester, Bristol, and Gloucester. The average vacancies are generally one in every six years; and as there has not been a vacancy for four years, there would be, according to the average, a vacancy in somewhat more than a twelvemonth from the present time. In consequence of recent circumstances, to which I will not further allude, it appears to me that it would be an act of justice, and also an act of general expediency, if one of those canonries in the patronage of the Lord Chancellor were annexed to the Greek Professorship at Oxford University. But in bringing in this measure I have not for a moment presumed to attempt to come to any understanding—much less to make any bargain—with the University of Oxford. In that body, and in its sense of justice, I have the greatest confidence; to it I bear the highest possible reverence and gratitude, and I have no doubt that a Bill which proposes to accomplish this endowment will be received by the University in the same spirit in which it is offered by the Crown and by the Ministers of the Crown; and I may be permitted to express a hope, and even an expectation, that the University of Oxford will, if this measure passes, hasten to provide for the present Regius Professor of Greek an adequate endowment until that canonry shall have fallen vacant, which, by the passing of this measure, I trust he will receive. In conclusion, I beg leave, my Lords, to move the first reading of the Bill.

Bill for the better Endowment of the Regius Professorship of Greek in the University of Oxford, *presented* and read 1ª. [No. 44.]

CHARITABLE ASSURANCES ENROL-MENT BILL—[H.L.] (No. 38.)
SECOND READING.

LORD CRANWORTH, in moving the second reading of this Bill, said, its object was to extend to a further period of two years the time of enrolment for charitable assurances, as provided under the 24 *Vict.* c. 9 and 25 *Vict.* c. 17. Within the last two years 1,146 more deeds had been enrolled than before, and there was a continual progress of enrolment going on. He also proposed that where the original deeds had been lost, as was often the case, and therefore where it was impossible to enrol them, the Clerk of Enrolments shall be required to enrol any deed appointing trustees of property the subject of such charitable trusts, or any deed reciting the original deed of conveyance, provided the deed required to be enrolled shall not bear date less than thirty years prior to such intended enrolment, and the enrolment shall be as effectual as if the original deed of conveyance had been duly enrolled.

THE LORD CHANCELLOR suggested that it would be necessary to ascertain beyond doubt that the original deeds had been lost, and sufficient time should be allowed to elapse before the right proposed by the Bill could be exercised.

LORD REDESDALE thought that the time in which deeds might be enrolled should not be extended beyond one year. Under the first Bill one year was given, then two, and now it was proposed to give two years more. If they went on in that way they would never come to an end.

Motion *agreed to:* Bill read 2ª, and *committed* to a Committee of the Whole House *To-morrow.*

DENMARK AND GERMANY.
RESOLUTIONS.

LORD CAMPBELL rose to call the Attention of the House to the Correspondence upon Denmark and Germany which has been presented to Parliament; and to move—

"That, in the Opinion of this House, if the Demand made by Denmark for Mediation, according to the Principle laid down in the Protocol of Paris, 1856, had been more decidedly supported by Her Majesty's Government, the Bloodshed and the other Evils already occasioned by the War in Denmark might have been prevented, and there would have been less Danger than there now is of a more extensive Disturbance in the Peace of Europe:

"That, in the Opinion of this House, a Conference upon the Danish Question in order to lead to a practical Result ought to be accompanied by such Steps as may convince the Powers of Europe that Her Majesty's Government adhere to the Treaties in which the Duchy of Schleswig has been guaranteed to Denmark by Great Britain."

My Lords, before adverting to the Resolutions I have put upon the paper, I cannot but thank the noble Earl on the cross benches (Earl Grey), for the declaration he elicited from the noble Lord the Foreign Secretary on Thursday last. I shall venture also to congratulate that noble Lord himself, on having, by what he then said, withdrawn, so far as it depended on him, all obstacles to Parliamentary debate upon this question. At no time, looking to the facts, was debate more practical and called for. A Conference impends. The very day is mentioned. As things stand, all the world proclaims its uselessness, and counts upon its failure. And it is certain that nothing will be done to give it better prospects of succeeding, unless Parliament is brought to bear on the Executive. Can it be said that Parliament by interfering will embarrass a proceeding which is doomed to fail, unless Parliament in some degree controls it. We cannot forget either that debate was long averted because the papers were not all completed; that the last of the series has only just been given to us at the very moment that the Conference is mentioned. If, under such circumstances, the Conference were made a pretext for arresting all discussion, it might well appear to be intended for that purpose; unequal as it seems to the accomplishment of any other.

My Lords, the first Resolution merely recites that, if the principle of arbitration laid down in the protocol of Paris 1856 had been insisted on more gravely by Great Britain, the existing bloodshed might have been prevented. And it cannot be denied, that the Danish Government impressed that principle upon our own. They did so in a despatch from Bishop Monrad, the First Minister at Copenhagen, to M. Bille, the Danish representative in London, dated January 5, 1854, to be found at page 523, of No. 4 in the correspondence. It cannot be said from what appears before us—it might, perhaps, from what is hidden —that Her Majesty's Government have acted on the doctrine so enforced. The despatch of Bishop Monrad is given both in French and English, and, therefore, we have no excuse for overlooking it. My Lords, this Resolution would not, I trust, appear an exaggerated tribute to the principle laid down in the Treaty of Paris. It cannot escape the House that that principle has never yet been recognized in action. There seems to be a steady disposition to overlook and to ignore it, whenever any opportunity occurs of giving it effect. The second Resolution states what is very obvious, that some further steps are necessary to give the Conference the prospect of succeeding it does not now enjoy. But in order to pave the way for such a proposition, it seems but natural and just to pass a guarded and a moderate opinion on the past diplomacy which this transaction has elicited. Had that diplomacy been one unbroken scene of tact, of energy, and of achievement, it might be uncalled for in the House to betray solicitude about the issue of the Conference. Unless what has lately happened afforded topics of regret, it might seem harsh to give an admonition on the future. Abrupt and irrelevant advice no doubt verges upon censure, at least it claims superiority. At the same time—harmonising as they do—the Resolutions are independent of each other. The second may commend itself to those whose feelings are a bar to the reception of the other, and as the second bears upon the vital question of what ought to be done, my subsequent remarks shall be exclusively directed to it. And the very first point to be remarked is that the Conference abounds in elements of failure. What Power goes into it with any disposition to assist us? Austria and Prussia no longer profess a regard for the Treaty of 1852.

Lord Campbell

The Cabinet of St. Petersburg is too much allied with those of Berlin and Vienna to be counted on. Prince Gortschakoff has declared in the very papers now before us, that they are acting, and that they ought to act in concert. All Europe recognises the alliance, and sees that Poland is its victim. While Austria and Prussia are essential to the Czar, as regards the insurrection he is struggling with, he is not likely to control them. Can we rely on France when the language of its Government has more than once discouraged any Conference as useless; when they disclaim adherence to the Treaty of 1852, and point to universal suffrage in the Danish Duchies as the means of a solution? Sweden, no doubt, may be faithful to the objects we pursue. But it is clear, in spite of her support, that if France and Prussia and the German Powers are adverse or indifferent, the burden of the Conference is thrown upon Great Britain. The burden might not be too great, if the other Powers were convinced of her unalterable loyalty to the treaties which were framed to secure the integrity of Denmark. But can they do so at this moment? The language of the noble Lord the Foreign Secretary, in this House on February 15, and his despatch of February 19 about the guarantee of Schleswig, make it utterly impossible. They may be chosen from a mass of evidence converging to the point that Her Majesty's Government, although they are not ready to dispute the obligations of the treaties, are not obedient to their spirit, or prepared for their demands. But as a crowning test of how far a satisfactory solution can be expected from the Conference, have we any reason to suppose that the Danish Government anticipate it? Are there not abundant signs of the despair with which they enter it? And do they not correctly represent the Danish people in that feeling. The temper of that people is not a melancholy or desponding one. Hope seems to have a larger place than fear in their complexion. But in all climes and all societies, men fighting against odds, and overwhelmed by embarrassments, will catch at frail, inadequate, and evanescent means of a deliverance. The scepticism with which the Danish Government and people look upon this measure augurs badly for its efficacy; since they would be the first to overrate the chances it includes. It is not irrelevant to ask, therefore, will the obligations of Great Britain be answered by an unsuccessful

Conference ? The obligations of the country, no doubt, are founded upon treaties. But these books contain facts which seriously heighten them. It is now seen that the despatch of September, 1862, raised the German spirit of encroachment, and acted in a manner most disastrous to the interests of Denmark. It is seen that the Danish Government were eager for the Congress which the Emperor of the French proposed, and to which Great Britain was an obstacle. In deference to our views, and in reliance on our action, the Danish Government revoked the proclamation upon Holstein of March 30, and made concessions well remembered by the world. The attack of the noble Lord on the Danish Constitution of November 18, and which is found in a despatch to Lord Wodehouse dated December 17, could not but do much to aggravate their difficulties, and to encourage their assailants. It certainly appears a harsh and also a gratuitous proceeding, since the question is most intricate, is altogether Danish, and one on which the Foreign Office has no mission to decide. Can it be said that we have any measures in reserve to provide against the failure of the Conference ? And if it cannot, will an unsuccessful Conference fulfil the obligations which the treaties have imposed and circumstances have extended. But will the dignity of the country bear an unsuccessful Conference. Our diplomacy has now gone through a series of reverses on this question, which it would be invidious to enumerate and dangerous to increase. The Conference is not a French, a Russian, a German, or a Danish, but a British proposition. The reluctant and desponding Powers are dragged into it, not indeed by British force, but British importunity. Its failure will not be divided. But there is also this to be considered. To meet the Austrian and Prussian representatives, while the aggression we denounce is still proceeding to its climax, while Schleswig is disorganized and trampled on, while Sönderburg is under a bombardment, is not entirely consistent with the attitude of protest and remonstrance. It verges more upon indulgence of the crime which is going on. Success is indispensable to requite Great Britain for the loss of pride she undergoes in entering the Conference, and to guard against the new misfortune which its failure would imply.

But will the tranquillity of Europe lose nothing by an unsuccessful Conference ? If no result arises from it, the war in Denmark only seems to have a choice of dangerous terminations. If it ends in the dismemberment of that ancient monarchy, Europe receives a blow, the balance of power suffers, and new causes of hostility arise. If France or Russia intervenes, no man can calculate the limits of the struggle. Again, unless it ends in a solution, a Conference—according to the reasoning of the noble Lord upon the project of the Emperor—must leave behind it seeds of animosity and discord. An unsuccessful Conference would therefore seem to menace the general tranquillity of Europe, as well as to run counter to the duties and impeach the honour of this country.

My Lords, I have already ventured to advert to the conditions of succeeding—namely, that as all depends upon Great Britain in the Conference, the other Powers should be convinced of her unwavering adherence to the treaties by which Schleswig is maintained. And there is more than one mode by which the condition may be satisfied. A diplomatic manifesto, wholly different in its spirit from that of the noble Lord on February 19th, or an instruction to British representatives at Berlin and Vienna, similar to that which Lord Westmoreland received in 1848, might very possibly inspire the necessary confidence. But after the despatches which have already gone abroad, such expedient would hardly be admissible. At least, the presence of the noble Lord as Foreign Secretary, would be a fatal bar to their effect. The noble Lord is now associated with the despatch of September 1862, which all the world regarded as a German one in spirit—with the despatch of February 19th, which tries to evade the guarantee when Denmark had insisted on it—with the attack upon the Danish Constitution, which he hurled against it in December—with the refusal of the Congress, at which the whole of Germany rejoiced. Right or wrong, the noble Lord is not regarded as the friend of Denmark on the Continent of Europe. Diplomatic measures would not, therefore, have the necessary influence. But does it follow that the noble Lord ought to deprive the country of his assiduous services and well meaning exertions ? Another course presents itself. A British fleet appearing in the Baltic—although the noble Lord was still the Foreign Secretary—would make the powerful impression which is wanted, assure the world that our engagements to Denmark had not been forgotten, and so pave the way for the results to which the Conference aspires. But having barely indicated such a course, I would ask leave to guard myself against absolute concurrence in all that has been said in this House and elsewhere upon the subject. Some noble Lords have recommended, that in order to protect Sönderborg, a fleet ought to be despatched into the Baltic. It has also been advanced that the Austrian and Prussian ships, if they appear, ought to be watched, pursued, and hindered, in those waters. Intelligent observers out of doors have held that a naval force established in the Little Belt would be a proper step to guard the island of Funen. By some who have lately quitted it, it is thought that Flensburg might be usefully selected as a maritime position for our vessels. But all these measures are attended with a hazard of collision. Such a remark would not be applicable to the presence of a British fleet in the port of Kiel, unless the Danish Government objected to the proceeding. No one will deny, that were this course pursued, Great Britain would command a higher aspect at the Conference than belongs to her at present. But there is also this distinct consideration. It is known to every one conversant with the subject, and it is clear too from these papers, that Prussia has been drawn into this war, in some degree by other motives, but in a great degree by maritime ambition, to which Kiel is indispensable. As soon as it is seen that that point is wholly unattainable, maritime ambition ceases to prolong the strife; the motives which govern Prussia no longer exceed the motives which govern Austria; both the German Powers are impelled against Denmark by the fear of a popular opinion, which gradually exhausts itself. Neither are lured on by the hope of a material advantage, which sentiment would otherwise remain. The upshot appears to be, that Great Britain would rise in power to control the war, as much as Prussia sank in aspiration to pursue it. The Conference would then have, what it now appears to want, the prospect of succeeding. Would such a mode of acting lead to war? As I contend, it would be more likely to avert it. Those who raise a pacific cry the moment any naval demonstration is suggested, assume this paradox as granted —namely, that timid counsels always lead to peace, and that decisive measures always tend to conflagration. Would such a paradox if nakedly advanced, instead of co-

Lord Campbell

vertly assumed, be tolerated for a moment? Have not the events of our own time sufficiently refuted it? If timid schemes, or fair spoken despatches, or amiable remonstrances were a security for peace, why is Northern Europe now in flagrant war, and Southern Europe looking for it? Can we forget that, in 1826, Mr. Canning and his colleagues averted war by sending an expedition to the Tagus? Can we forget that the reserve and hesitation, not unconnected with sagacity which in 1853 withheld the fleet from the Black Sea when Colonel Rose demanded it, never led to the advantages they counted on; and that the ships of the Allies were only in the Bosphorus when the disaster of Sinope made war with Russia unavoidable. No one who reflects upon American affairs and the constant risks to which their civil war exposes us, and which in 1862 were narrowly escaped, could recommend a step adapted to involve Great Britain in a war upon the Continent. But to send a fleet to Kiel may have a very different operation. Suppose, in consequence of our slackness and inertness, the German Powers, indirectly sheltered by the Czar, were to gain possession of that harbour. Regard to interests and treaties would forbid Great Britain to acquiesce in such an occupation, and war would then be necessary to dislodge it. But would the step be open to exception as regards public law and international propriety? Can it be an act of illegality or violence to despatch a fleet into the harbour of a Power which is friendly, of a Power which is outraged, of a Power you have guaranteed, of a Power which invokes the aid it is entitled to receive from you? Day by day we are initiated in the secret that it is not an act of illegality or violence to plant a devastating army in his territory. If Austria and Prussia are entitled to a material possession upon land in order to pursue a shadowy and doubtful right, has Great Britain no title to a material possession on those waters, in order to discharge a clear and undisputed obligation? If they, without making war, may overrun a line of defence, revolutionize a Duchy, besiege Duppel, and force the Danish army into Alsen; if in a friendly spirit and with a peaceable design they can dismiss the servants of the King of Denmark, arrest his subjects, forbid his currency, bombard his towns, insult his flag, and alienate his revenues, might not either France or Great Britain, or the two together, irreproachably possess a single harbour on the Baltic, with the sanction of the Power it belongs to. Except as regards material possession, the cases would not have indeed a similarity. They have moved through the path of wrong, of spoliation, and of bloodshed to gain a maritime position on that coast ; Great Britain would move in the path of law, of policy, and treaties to prevent them.

I have but a further view to submit upon this measure; and it addresses itself in no way to the sympathies but to the coldest calculations of the House. A few ships in the Baltic might enable Great Britain to become a party to arrangements which European interests may sanction, and which existing difficulties may require, but which she could not entertain unless her faith to treaties and her loyalty to Denmark had been previously asserted. Supposing it were found essential as a safeguard against future wars to make the Eider the southern boundary of Denmark, and to form a clearer line than is observed between the German and Scandinavian territories, our present attitude disqualifies us for going into such questions. If Great Britain had a certain status on the Baltic, she would have the power to resist, and power to concede; at present, she has neither. At the same time, my Lords, although such a course appears to be the one which circumstances indicate, the Conference requires and the guarantee imposes, these Resolutions in no way bind the House to an approval of it, should any other line of action be preferred as safer or as more effectual. They only ask your Lordships to affirm that the principle of 1856 might have been usefully insisted on with greater firmness and tenacity, a proposition few as yet have ventured to dispute. But should it be deemed unnecessary or imprudent to declare it; at least no difference of opinion can well exist upon the second—namely, that the Conference does not meet under just auspices, or promise satisfactory results, while Europe doubts our loyalty to those treaties of which Schleswig has been so long and so conspicuously the object. With equal truth it might be said, perhaps, that in such circumstances a Conference is likely to bring on Denmark further wrongs, on Great Britain new humiliations, and on Europe darker clouds than those which menace its horizon. The noble Lord concluded by moving to resolve :—

"That, in the Opinion of this House, if the Demand made by Denmark for Mediation, according to the Principle laid down in the Protocol of Paris, 1856, had been more decidedly supported by Her Majesty's Government, the Bloodshed and the other Evils already occasioned by the War in Denmark might have been prevented, and there would have been less Danger than there now is of a more extensive Disturbance in the Peace of Europe.

"That, in the Opinion of this House, a Conference upon the Danish Question, in order to lead to a practical Result, ought to be accompanied by such Steps as may convince the Powers of Europe that Her Majesty's Government adhere to the Treaties in which the Duchy of Schleswig has been guaranteed to Denmark by Great Britain."

THE DUKE OF ARGYLL said, that before proceeding to the discussion of the noble Lord's Motion, he wished to call their Lordships' attention for a few moments to the circumstances under which it was brought forward. The other evening his noble Friend on the cross bench (Earl Grey) asked the noble Earl the Foreign Secretary, whether the same objections which existed before Easter to a discussion of the Dano-German question still applied. To that the Foreign Secretary replied that he had no wish to interfere with the discretion of the House. Under the circumstances, no other reply could have been given ; but it was a great mistake to suppose that it was ever either the desire or for the advantage or the interest of a Government, for its own sake, to interfere with a Parliamentary discussion on a question such as that now brought under their Lordships' consideration. The Constitution of this country gave to the responsible executive Government the most formidable power which could be given to any body of men — the power of committing the honour and the credit of the country, either for peace or war, without the previous knowledge or consent of Parliament ; and not only did the executive Government possess the power, but Parliament had occasionally shown itself jealous of any attempt on the part of the Government to cast off that responsibility. On the very first night of the Session, the noble Earl opposite (the Earl of Derby) had declared that it was the business of a Government to have a policy of their own, and not to seek one from Parliament ; and in that doctrine he (the Duke of Argyll) fully concurred. The Government, therefore, were bound in these matters to exercise the greatest amount of caution and circumspection, and it was no hardship, but an immediate advantage to the Government to have a discussion of these questions before Parliament; and his noble Friend (Earl Russell) had always courted, rather than deprecated, discussion on matters of public interest. Still, the

Government were called on to enter into this discussion under circumstances very disadvantageous to themselves. In a few days they were about to meet in conference the representatives of Europe, called together by themselves, for the purpose of restoring peace to the North of Europe. It would be inexcusable, therefore, for them to appear as partisans either of one side or the other, or to say one word which would lessen the chances of peace. There must be, then, many parts of the subject on which the Government were bound to hold their peace, or to speak with the greatest caution. The history of the noble Lord's Resolution seemed a curious illustration of the Darwinian theory of development. Some days ago the Notice on the paper was "to call attention to the Correspondence recently presented to Parliament." On Thursday last the second Resolution, having reference to the Guarantee of 1720, made its appearance in the paper; and the day following, after the conversation of that night, the full-blown Resolution, as it was now placed before their Lordships, appeared. On the subject of the Guarantee of 1720, the noble Lord had already addressed their Lordships some weeks ago—that subject was his own, and no doubt the second Resolution, which had reference to that question, was his own. But in the first Resolution he had not the least hesitation in saying he recognized the hand of his noble Friend near him (Earl Grey). With regard to the speech and Motion of the noble Lord (Lord Campbell) he had some difficulty in following all his arguments, because the greater part of them referred to the future —to the manner in which the Conference was to be conducted. Now he (the Duke of Argyll) was of opinion that it was the duty of the Government, under the circumstances, as far as possible to avoid a discussion of the future, and confine themselves to the discussion of the past. As to the second Resolution—his noble Friend's own Resolution —the wording of it was not quite correct, for the Guarantee of 1720 was not a guarantee of the whole of Schleswig, but only of that part of it which then belonged to the Sovereign of Denmark. It would hardly, therefore, be for the interest of Denmark that instructions should be given to the Government to insist upon that guarantee. His noble Friend to whom he attributed the drawing up of the first Resolution (Earl Grey) had on various occasions spoken very freely of the conduct of

The Duke of Argyll

the Government. He had given the House what was called "a bit of his mind" on the subject, and he wished very much that he would give them the whole. He was anxious to hear what his noble Friend meant by more decided action in support of the Protocol of 1852? What did the noble Earl mean by "more decided" measures? He had no doubt that the noble Earl meant that the Government might have prevented the war altogether, if, in fact, they had only threatened to take part in it. The question put was, Why did not the Government prevent the war? but the real question which his noble Friend wished to put was, Why had not the Government taken part in it? The critics of the Government had always one story; they never avowed that they were in favour of a war policy; but they said, that if the Government had done this or the other, they would have prevented war. But it was equally open to the Government to say, that if they had adopted a different course they would have increased the chances of bloodshed and the miseries that have resulted. He maintained that it was sufficient for the Government to show that they had adopted and had adhered to some definite line of policy, which they were able to support and maintain in that House of Parliament and to justify before the country. He submitted that the Government had a ready answer to the charge made against them, because they had not prevented war, or since they could not prevent it that they hadn ot taken part in it. He protested against the doctrine that, *primâ facie*, there was any case against the Government of this country for not preventing a continental war, even supposing it might have broken out under circumstances of much injustice. England had a great position in Europe—the noble Earl smiled—England had a great position in Europe, not only on account of her material power, but from the just impression which prevailed that, on the Continent at least, she had no selfish interests whatever to serve; and that so far as our interests, which were principally commercial, were concerned, they were bound up with the prosperity of the whole world. But England was not the general arbitress in the quarrels of continental nations. There might be wars under circumstances of the greatest injustice waged there; but that was not a *primâ facie* case against the English Government for not having interfered in them. He would take the case of the Italian war. It so happened that at that time the Liberal party were not in office, but rather a party more opposed to the objects of that war than we were; yet the noble Earl then at the head of the Foreign Office (the Earl of Malmesbury), did everything in his power to prevent that war; and he believed that no Minister ever acted more earnestly or faithfully as far as that object was concerned. The hand of the noble Earl was hardly ever off the telegraphic wires; his messages jostled each other on their way to the various capitals of Europe. And not only did he exercise all his influence in deprecation and remonstrance, but the noble Earl then at the head of the Government (the Earl of Derby) also made a powerful speech in their Lordships' House, in which he went very near to threaten that the power of England would be brought into action, if that war broke out. Noble Lords now present would doubtless remember the intimation conveyed in that remarkable speech to France and to the Government at Turin, that if we were to be neutrals we must be in a position of armed neutrality; and that England had interests in the Adriatic which they were determined to defend. Noble Lords would remember that this speech was received with cheers from both sides of the House. But what was the effect? The language ended in nothing—and the war took place in spite of all their efforts. He (the Duke of Argyll) never heard that the noble Earl felt any humiliation at having failed to prevent that war, though it was one which in its circumstances was considered by them to be unjust. Then he maintained that it was no *primâ facie* case against the existing Government that they had not prevented the present war, and any case against the Government must arise from special obligations in respect to the position of Germany and Denmark. Consequently, in order to see whether there was any case against the Government, it was necessary to refer to the documents in which the obligations of the English Government were defined. Now, if noble Lords would look into the documents, they would find that we were under no such obligations. He was surprised that the noble Lord (Lord Campbell) should have said that those obligations were mainly to be found in the guarantee of 1720. He (the Duke of Argyll) denied that, and asserted that they were to be found in the Treaty of 1852, which was not a treaty of guarantee,

but simply of recognition, signed not by England alone or even principally. It was a treaty in which we were co-signataries with all the great Powers of Europe, and some of the smaller Powers. There was, indeed, a passage in the preamble which referred to a question of policy, and announced as a principle that the existence and integrity of Denmark formed a necessary part of the balance of power; but to that declaration all the other Powers were signataries. Therefore the duties and obligations of the English Government, arising from that treaty, are duties and obligations which run exactly parallel with those of the other Powers; and nothing in that document could compel or induce the Government to go in advance or in front of the other Powers, or to act independently of them. This, then, was the principle on which Her Majesty's Government founded their policy—to rally the other Powers to act with them in this matter, but not to advance before them. He asked the House whether they could conscientiously say that the Government had failed in this duty? His noble Friend (Earl Grey) said yes—he (the Duke of Argyll) called upon him to prove it. Without troubling the House with a mass of quotations from the blue-books, he would direct attention to a few facts, which would prove that the Government had done all they could to ally themselves with the other great Governments of Europe, and induce them to act along with this country in preventing the war. Those who had attended to the Schleswig-Holstein quarrel must know that one of the transactions which had most tended to complicate the matter, and to render war almost inevitable, was the resolution of the German Diet to assume authority, not merely with respect to Holstein, but also with respect to Schleswig. This Resolution was dated the 25th March, 1852, at a time when public attention was very little directed to the subject. The moment that his noble Friend at the head of the Foreign Office was aware of that, he addressed to the great Powers a despatch directing attention to this Resolution of the German Diet, and soliciting a joint protest against that assumption of power. This communication was sent to the two great non-German Powers—France and Russia—and it expressed a hope that an intimation would be conveyed from them to the German Diet respecting the gravity of the step they had taken. That attempt, on the part of his noble Friend failed, because France and Russia declined to join in the proposed protest, which Russia, at least, thought might seem to assume somewhat of a threatening nature. Therefore, if that joint action failed, it was not owing to want of vigilance on the part of his noble Friend. In November last occurred the death of the King of Denmark; and then arose the question about the right of succession. It was mainly due to the exertions of his noble Friend that the principle of the Treaty of 1852 had been recognized as a surviving principle by the two great German Powers, in spite of the disputes which had arisen. No one who had read the papers could doubt or deny that there were the gravest apprehensions that the two great German Powers were about to retreat from their former position and call in question the Treaty of 1852, and, on the other hand, that it was mainly owing to the remonstrances of his noble Friend, seconded no doubt by the Emperor of the French, that these two great Powers had admitted that the principle was still in force. In the present year his noble Friend made still greater efforts to avert any hostile action on the part of the German Powers. He would refer the House to the propositions made to the Russian and French Governments on the 5th, 10th, and 18th of January. The answer of the French Government was given on the 19th of January, and in still greater detail on the 30th; and though he did not wish to cast any blame on the French Government for declining to co-operate, because they had the right if they chose to keep the issues of peace and war in their own hands, yet he could not help thinking that if the two great non-German Powers had accepted the proposals of his noble Friend, the danger of war would have been averted. It would be admitted by any candid person who read the correspondence, that if Her Majesty's Government had been ready, to use the language of his noble Friend, to take any "more decided measures"—if they had thought it their duty to threaten, that in the event of the German Powers crossing the Eider a *casus belli* would arise, they would have had to make that declaration alone, and we should have involved ourselves in the danger of war with the whole of Germany, and especially with the two great military Powers, Austria and Prussia, without any ally to fight on our side. He would not waste the time of the House in pointing out the many objections which militated against

many of these. Such a course would readily occur to the mind of every noble Lord. With respect to the assumption that such a declaration would have prevented war, it should be remembered that we were not dealing with the Governments of Germany alone. We were dealing to a great extent with forces which took their origin in the revolutionary passions which were now existing on the Continent; in short, he did not believe it would be too much to say that we were dealing with two fanatical democracies. These were not Powers accessible to reason; and he was therefore convinced, in spite of the arguments of his noble Friend, that if we had taken that course, we not only should not have averted war, but we should have been forced to join in the war, should have increased the bloodshed, and brought on new and complicated dangers. It would be admitted that any course which isolated us from France would be very dangerous. As long as both countries went together there were few things which they could not secure in the way of peace; but if isolated action were once adopted by either, there were contingencies which might impel them more and more in opposite directions, and might lead to the greatest perils to the peace of Europe. He should be guilty of great affectation if he were to say that he apprehended any danger to the Government from these Resolutions. The aspect of the benches opposite did not indicate that the noble Earl (the Earl of Derby) had any intention of giving a very active or warm support to the Motion, unless, indeed, the noble Earl's forces had been routed by General Garibaldi. But whatever opinion might be expressed by the House upon the Resolutions, he hoped that one opinion only would be expressed by every Member who might speak that night upon one part of the subject, and that was the lamentable bloodshed which was now taking place. He was sure it was with feelings of absolute affliction that every Member of the House read the daily accounts of the cruel and useless slaughter which was going on. It was absolutely certain that every object sought by the war might have been obtained by negotiation. During the last ten years we had witnessed three great wars in which there had been great bloodshed, but in respect of all three great issues had been at stake. In the case of the Russian war, in which we were parties, the question was whether the same

Sovereign should reign at St. Petersburg and Constantinople. In case of the Italian war the question was whether one of the greatest nations in Europe, with an ancient literature and a noble history, and the highest capacities for political life, should continue to be for ever nothing but the favourite camping ground of German soldiers. With regard to the war now raging on the other side of the Atlantic, however they might deplore it, extending as it did over such a vast territory, and as yet giving no indications of its approaching end, no man could deny that there were great issues raised, all of which probably could only be settled by the results of war. But, in contrast to these, the war in Denmark had for its object issues that could certainly be settled by other means. What was the object set before them by the German Powers? He did not depreciate to the Schleswig-Holsteiners the value they set upon their liberties; they had as good a right to their liberties as we had to ours; but was there a single object in respect to them which could not be as well obtained by negotiation and without any effusion of blood? We were going to the Conference with three great objects. The first was to restore peace to the North of Europe; the second to secure the legal rights of the Duchies; and, the third, to reconcile with those rights the integrity and independence of Denmark. There was one argument which might be fairly urged against taking what was called a "more decided course," and that was that there was some doubt as to the merits and justice of the original quarrel. He would not dwell upon the weak points of the Danish case. The Danes were a gallant people, more sinned against than sinning. But those who had read the papers must remember that we had been compelled to make admissions on the subject of the constitution which was the immediate cause of the war—admissions which raised some doubts as to whether the Germans might not have had some fair grounds of dispute with the Danish people. But feeling the duty of impartiality in the present position of the Government, he was much more disposed at present to point to just grounds of complaint against the German Powers. He did not know whether many noble Lords had read the engagements of 1851-2, which Denmark was accused of having broken. In those engagements, Denmark had made two promises to the German Powers, the one that a common constitution should be

provided for the whole monarchy, the two Duchies included; and the other, that certain local liberties should be guaranteed to the people of Schleswig and Holstein. There was also a third, that Denmark should not incorporate, or take any steps to incorporate, Schleswig. It had been vehemently asserted by Germany that the Danes had broken those three engagements. But what he wished to direct the attention of the House and the country to was this—that, in his opinion, it was equally demonstrable that the promises made by Germany to Denmark had not been faithfully adhered to. The Germans said that the correspondence of 1851-2 constituted a series of diplomatic engagements. If they were diplomatic engagements, however, they were equally binding on both parties. He had selected three distinct promises made to Denmark, all of which had been more or less violated. The first promise went to the whole root of the matter, and it was this—that what was called the theory of Schleswig-Holsteinism should be abandoned. That declaration was not only conveyed by Germany to Denmark in general terms, but was also made in the most explicit manner. He would ask whether the Germans had abided by that promise? Was it not the fact that the theory of Schleswig-Holsteinism had been made a perpetual engine against Denmark from day to day, and was it not the real cause of most of the difficulties that had occurred? Another most solemn promise had been given by the Emperor of Austria, to which he was anxious to direct their Lordships' attention. It was to the effect that the Austrian Government would never allow the Federal Power to be exercised in Holstein in any manner in which it might not be equally exercised in every other part of the Confederation. Her Majesty's Government had admitted, and indeed could not deny, the legal right of the German Diet to put in "execution" in Holstein; but he would ask the German Powers to say whether, in the circumstances which had occurred, they had faithfully adhered to the promise of the Emperor of Austria? That execution took place by way of securing to the people of Holstein certain local privileges and rights. But were there not in other parts of the German Federation local privileges and rights which had been violated, and did the German Diet exercise their power in respect to those rights? Why should the Diet enforce against the Duke of Holstein powers which they did not dare to enforce against the King of Prussia? So long as they acted unequally and unfairly in this respect they not only violated their promises, but also the fundamental principles of all Federal Constitutions. The object of the Federation was the mutual defence of its members; but if the power of the majority was always to be brought to bear against the weaker members, then the Federation would become the means of anarchy, and the Great Powers would be setting the most dangerous precedent against themselves. The third promise was a distinct and emphatic repudiation of any right or competence on the part of the German Diet in the Duchy of Schleswig. The Diet had, however, now asserted its competence. In all these respects Germany had violated the promise of 1851-2 more certainly and more clearly than the Danes. It was the desire of Her Majesty's Government to go into the Conference, not as partisans of one side or the other, but impartially. They desired nothing but to restore peace to Europe—no doubt compatibly with the local rights of the two Duchies, and consistently if possible with the integrity of the Danish monarchy. They wished the balance of power in Europe to be maintained, and the rights of all the parties to be preserved. These were the objects which Her Majesty's Government had in view in times past; and in their efforts to avert war he believed they had had the approbation of the country, and would have the support of Parliament.

EARL GREY said, his noble Friend who had just sat down (the Duke of Argyll), had taken very unnecessary trouble to prove what he (Earl Grey) had no wish to deny or conceal, that he had advised the noble Lord (Lord Campbell) to add the first Resolution to that which he had originally proposed to move, and he would now state why he thought their Lordships ought to agree to it. In doing so, it would be necessary for him to give some slight account of the proceedings which had led to the war now going on, but he would do so as shortly as possible. Fortunately, he need not weary their Lordships with the long and complicated question, as to what were the respective rights of Germany and Denmark and of the Duchies themselves with reference to the matters in dispute; it was sufficient to say that, on the 1st of October last, the dispute had arrived at such a point that the German Diet thought it necessary to adopt a resolution for

The Duke of Argyll

enforcing its demands against Denmark by what was called "execution," which meant the military occupation of Holstein. In the interval before this decree was carried into effect, Her Majesty's Government exerted themselves strenuously to avert its being acted upon; nor had he any fault to find with that part of their proceedings. It seemed not impossible that they might have succeeded in their efforts when, unfortunately, the death of the late King of Denmark occurred. That event produced an immediate change in the state of affairs. A violent agitation arose in Germany with respect to the right of succession in the Duchies, and a large party insisted that Prince Frederick of Augustenburg was the rightful heir. Into that question, however, he was happy to say it would not be necessary for him to enter; but, whatever might be the truth on the subject, it was clear that the Austrian Government, at all events, held that the title of the present King of Denmark was a good one; because their Lordships would find in the papers a very remarkable diplomatic correspondence between the Governments of Austria and Bavaria, in which the former Government showed—or considered that it showed — by reference to various documents, that the present King of Denmark was the rightful Duke of Holstein, not by virtue of the Treaty of 1852, but by virtue of a law legally passed by the late King of Denmark as Duke of Holstein, regulating the future succession to the Duchy. The Austrian Government went on to say that the validity of this law was by implication recognized by the Diet itself. He would farther remark, that to the present moment the German Diet— the only competent authority in Germany —had never decided against the right of the present King of Denmark to the Duchy of Holstein. When it ordered the federal troops to occupy Holstein, it professed to do so under the resolution of the 1st of October, which had decreed "execution" for the purpose of enforcing the performance of his engagements by the King of Denmark, with an express declaration that his rights to the Duchy were to be maintained. But, though these were the professions of the Diet, what was done was little in accordance with them. There was a good description of what had taken place in one of the despatches of Sir Augustus Paget. He stated that, when the German troops entered Holstein, the Federal Commissary declared that they did so to enforce certain orders of the German Diet, that they did not intend to interfere with the rights of the Sovereign, that those rights were reserved, and that eventually his power was to be restored. Notwithstanding this, the Federal troops entered Holstein with bands playing the revolutionary air ; they allowed the Augustenburg colours to be displayed in all directions, while they removed the arms of Denmark from the public buildings and took away every symbol of Danish authority ; and while nominally prohibiting any attempt to assert the rights of the Pretender, they allowed the proclamation of the Prince Augustenburg, as Duke of Holstein, to take place in the presence of the Federal Commissary and of the Federal troops. He confessed that he regarded these proceedings as utterly irreconcilable with good faith. At the same time, he was not sure that it would have done much harm to Denmark had matters stopped here, and certainly there would have been no war if the German measures of spoliation had been confined to Holstein, because the Danes, acting upon our advice, had wisely determined not to resist by force the occupation of that Duchy, and as the Federal troops advanced those of Denmark retired. But, unfortunately, before the Federal troops entered Holstein another cause of quarrel had arisen. His noble Friend (the Duke of Argyll) had informed their Lordships that one of the main subjects of dispute was as to how a joint Legislature for the different divisions of the Danish monarchy should be established. After the failure of many attempts to form such a Legislature, the King, in the year 1855, established such a body under the name of the Rigsraad. His authority to do this in the manner in which he did it was contested ; but the Assembly continued to meet, and until the year 1858 members from Holstein, as well as those from Schleswig and Denmark, sat in it, and the Rigsraad did practically act for the whole of the Danish Monarchy. In that year the representatives of Holstein withdrew, but the Rigsraad continued to be the joint Legislature for Denmark and Schleswig. Holstein was thus practically separated, so far as legislation was concerned, from the rest of the kingdom. In the beginning of last year the late King of Denmark determined formally to establish this state of things, and he issued the patent of the 30th of March, which separated Holstein, for legislative purposes, from

the rest of the monarchy, and gave it power to manage its own affairs. Great objections were raised to this measure, but he need not discuss the question of its justice or injustice, because the patent was ultimately revoked. Later in the year the patent was followed by the presentation to the Rigsraad of a Bill for altering the constitution of that body. This Bill made no change in the respective functions of the Rigsraad and the provincial assemblies; it left to the States of Schleswig, and the Legislature of Denmark Proper, precisely the same powers they had previously exercised, and made no alteration or increase in those assigned to the Rigsraad in acting for the common interests of these two divisions of the kingdom. All it did was formally to sanction the exclusion of the Holstein members from the Rigsraad, and to make important changes in the manner in which the members of that body were appointed. The Bill, which was in fact a Reform Bill, was introduced in the autumn of last year. It underwent considerable discussion, but with some difficulty the necessary majority of two-thirds—that is, the majority necessary to authorize a constitutional change—was obtained, and at the death of the late King it had been read a third time, and only required the signature of the Sovereign to make it law. The King died on the 15th of November ; and on the 16th the Prussian Envoy presented to the Danish Government a despatch protesting against this law being allowed to come into force. It could only be stopped by the refusal of the Royal Assent, and that assent was not refused. On the 17th of November the new King signed the Bill, and on the 18th it was proclaimed as the law of the land. It was acknowledged on all hands that the King of Denmark had practically no option in the matter. When in a constitutional country a measure of reform has after much debate passed the Legislature, it is no easy matter for the Sovereign to refuse his assent. Every one knew that in 1832 William IV. had practically no power to withhold his assent from the Reform Bill, and the King of Denmark was equally precluded from refusing his sanction to this Bill. If he had done so, the result would have been an immediate revolution and his expulsion from the country. Was that the reason for the presentation of the Prussian despatch ? We could not look into men's hearts and see what were their motives ; but if were to judge the motives of the Prussian Government by their acts we could hardly resist the conclusion that the reason why this protest was presented at that particular moment was that Prussia desired to pick a quarrel with Denmark, which she could not escape. What were the facts? The Bill had been under discussion for six weeks, and all that was going on was perfectly well known at Berlin, and yet not a hint of an objection had previously been let fall. Nay, more; only three weeks before the protest was delivered, M. Bismark held language which induced both the English and Danish Envoys at Berlin to believe that this Bill was the very thing that he desired. Sir Augustus Paget, in his despatch of the 18th of November, reported distinctly that his opinion was that this Bill would carry into effect precisely the arrangement which M. Bismark described as most desirable—namely, a free and united Denmark up to the Eyder, and a free Holstein beyond that river. Having thus allowed the Bill to pass, not only without objection, but with implied approval, no sooner was it known that the power of arresting the measure, except by refusing the Royal signature, was gone by, and that in Copenhagen the greatest excitement had been created by the mere doubt that the King might refuse his assent, than the Prussian Envoy presented a peremptory and overbearing despatch protesting against the law coming into force. Was it possible to understand this conduct otherwise than as intended to produce a rupture? Sir Augustus Paget, in his despatch of the 18th of November, reported that he had had· a conversation with the Prussian Envoy, and that when he pointed out how inconsistent his protest was with the previous conduct of the Prussian Government, he did not attempt to deny the accuracy of this statement, but said that he must act upon his instructions. There could be no doubt what those instructions were. They must have been to keep back the objections to this Bill until it was out of the power of Denmark to deal with them, and when the power to yield had passed away to press them with the greatest possible violence. That was what took place. From the moment that the despatch of November 16 was presented, Prussia continued to urge this demand upon Denmark. Somewhere about the close of December the first intimation of which he found any notice in the papers was given to Den-

Earl Grey

mark that those demands would be enforced by an armed occupation of Schleswig. On the 28th of December a formal motion to that effect was made in the German Diet by Austria and Prussia, and was referred to a committee. It was again brought before the Diet on the 14th of January, when the proposition of Prussia and Austria was rejected; but these Powers declared they would proceed with the measure they contemplated, notwithstanding the decision of the Diet, and that Schleswig would be at once taken possession of as "a material guarantee." Much negotiation took place before that measure was carried into effect. These negotiations were continued until the beginning of February, when the German army crossed the Eyder; and in the course of them Denmark applied for the mediation of England and other friendly Powers under the Protocol of 1856. Their Lordships would no doubt remember that, during the Congress of Paris in 1856, the representatives of the European Powers recorded in a Protocol the wish of these Powers that in future, when serious differences arose between nations, an attempt should be made to settle them by the good offices of a friendly State before appealing to arms. Referring to this Protocol, Denmark asked for the mediation of England and other European Powers. The noble Duke who had just spoken (the Duke of Argyll) indeed disputed the accuracy of that statement; but if he referred to the papers he would find that they contained a despatch addressed by the Prime Minister of Denmark to the Danish Envoy in this country, dated the 5th of January, and communicated to his noble Friend the Secretary for Foreign Affairs on the 13th of that month, in which there was distinct reference made to the Protocol of 1856 and application made under that Protocol for the mediation of England. A similar despatch was also sent to France. Her Majesty's Government supported the application, and proposed that a Conference should take place, and that in the meantime no appeal should be made to force. The proposal was, however, rejected—he might almost say contemptuously rejected —by Austria and Prussia. Then followed an application that if the German Powers would not consent to that, time, at least, should be given to Denmark, in order that she might obtain a legal repeal of the law that had given so much offence; but that proposal was also summarily rejected, although Her Majesty's Government had gone so far as to tell Prussia that the continuance of friendly relations with this country would be endangered by the rejection of the proposal. But the Prussian Government, having apparently a very just notion how little real resolution was implied by these big words, treated the remonstrance with utter disregard, and proceeded with their preparations for the invasion of the Duchies. While these preparations were going on, there was a whole series of despatches from his noble Friend opposite, not, he thought, written in a tone which became a Minister of this country. The British Minister complained in a tone of great irritation of the conduct of the German Powers, but, at the same time, made it clear that no interference on the part of England would take place. In the meantime, Her Majesty's Government had been pressing hard upon the Danes in order to induce them to repeal the law of November 18, which afforded the pretext for the threatened invasion. His noble Friend whom he saw on the bench below (Lord Wodehouse) was instructed to inform the Danish Government that, if they did not accede to what was proposed, they could not look for support from us. Now, if it had been intended to aid Denmark in the event of her adopting our advice, his noble Friend the Secretary of State would no doubt have been perfectly justified in laying before her the terms on which that aid would be granted. He might have said to her, "We intend to take up your quarrel ; but there are certain weak points in your case, and we should wish to see them removed before we can give you our support." That, however, was not the course which his noble Friend had taken, and he (Earl Grey), for one, could not think it either generous or just towards a little nation like Denmark, unwarrantably attacked by two great Powers, unless we meant to assist her in the end, to embarrass her by such advice as we had given, and to place her at the moral disadvantage of having communicated that advice to Germany, thus encouraging Germany to proceed by telling her that Denmark was in the wrong. The reply of the Danish Minister that the law afforded no just ground of complaint to Germany, as it made no substantial alteration in the relations of Schleswig and Denmark, was, he might add, in his opinion, quite unanswerable. He did not mean to say that it was prudent on the part of Denmark to pass the law of November, or

that Her Majesty's Government might not very fairly have represented to her that it would be well to repeal it ; but it seemed to him that the argument of the Danish Government, to show that this law gave no valid ground of complaint to Germany, had never been answered, and, at all events, even if the law were one to which Germany might, in the first instance, have fairly taken exception, the fact that no objection had been made to it at the proper time, that on the contrary the Prime Minister of Prussia had used language implying his approval of it, destroyed all claim on the part of the German Powers to insist on its immediate repeal. It was, therefore, most extraordinary that, while this country was acting as the self-constituted friend of Denmark, and while we were professing to give her our assistance, that by far the strongest point in her case had never been adverted to. When his noble Friend (Lord Wodehouse) passed through Berlin in his way to Copenhagen, on his special mission, he had a long conversation with M. Bismark, of which he has given a very able Report. In this conversation, respecting the demands made upon Denmark by the German Powers, not the slightest allusion was made by his noble Friend to the remarkable statement in Sir A. Paget's despatch of the 18th of November, as to the implied assent given by Prussia to the new law until it was practically irrevocable, nor is this statement noticed in any of the other communications between our Government and the German Powers that he could find recorded in the papers. He repeated, it was neither just nor generous towards Denmark thus to play the part of an over-candid friend, to give up in argument with her opponents the strong points in her case, to make the admissions most damaging to her, to force her to act against her own judgment, by saying that if she refused to follow our advice she must not look for our support; and then, after all, when she had taken our advice, and when the German Powers still persevered in their aggression—an aggression which we had declared to be an outrage—to refrain from raising a single finger in her defence ! If we were determined to give Denmark no aid beyond words, it would have been far better for her that we should have abstained from interfering at all ; that we should have imitated the wise and dignified conduct of France, whose Minister, when congratulating the King of Denmark on his accession, told him frankly that France did not intend to go to war for his protection, and that they had no advice to give except that Denmark should act in a conciliatory manner. It would have been better for Denmark, and still more would it have been better for our own dignity, if Her Majesty's Government had taken that course. Instead of this, after holding language towards Prussia, going to the very verge of threats—indeed, the Prussian Government said we had gone beyond the verge—we passively looked on while the outrage we had condemned was perpetrated, and this country had thus been lowered in the eyes of the whole civilised world. The effect of such conduct had been the more damaging to our reputation, because the Prime Minister, in his place in the House of Commons, had said in the last Session of Parliament that, if Denmark should be attacked by Germany she would not find herself alone. His noble Friend who spoke last (the Duke of Argyll), had defended our policy on the ground that we could not have acted differently without the risk of war. He could not admit this argument to be sound; he was convinced there was a course open to us by which we should have escaped all the indignity we have endured, and have prevented the oppression of Denmark, without incurring so much danger of being involved in war as we are now exposed to by the consequences of the policy that has been pursued. Denmark, as he had mentioned, had claimed the application to the disputes between herself and Germany of the rule laid down by the Congress of Paris, that in case of differences arising between nations an attempt ought, in the first place, to be made to settle them by the good offices of a friendly State. We supported this demand, and proposed that the differences should be referred to a Conference, all hostile operations being in the mean time suspended. We might have made this proposal in such a manner as to command respect, instead of to invite rejection. We should have been fully entitled to say that this was a case which came directly within the rule laid down by the Congress of Paris; and that looking to the great interests involved, and to the great importance of preserving the peace of Europe, we required of the German Governments that no hostile operations should be commenced until the good offices of friendly Powers had been tried. He was quite aware that we could not have held that language without being prepared for action. We must, of course, have been

Earl Grey

prepared, if the necessity for it had arisen, to send a British force to the Eyder to assist the Danes in defending their territory. But he utterly denied that any such contingency was probable. Such a policy could only have led to hostilities in the almost impossible event of Germany being insane enough to make an offensive war against England. All that was necessary was that we should have made Germany clearly understand that if she attempted to cross the Danish frontier she would find that frontier defended by English troops. There would have been no difficulty in defending that frontier. It was less than fifty miles in extent, strong by nature, and strengthened by strong fortifications; and though the Danes were not able to man those fortifications themselves, no great force would be necessary on our part to enable them to defend them. Nor would England have been alone in the matter. For even if no other great Power had joined us, Sweden was prepared to do so. In these papers there were several despatches in which the Swedish Government state that, though they were unable to protect Denmark themselves, they were perfectly willing to stand by the side of any great Power in doing so; and he was persuaded that a force such as England, Denmark, and Sweden could have easily raised, would have been amply sufficient to defend the frontiers of Schleswig against any force that Germany could have employed. The seat of war was but two days' steam from the mouth of the Thames, and unless our naval and military establishments were in a very different state from that in which they ought to be, considering the very large grants Parliament had made for their support, and very different also from that in which he trusted they were, there would have been no difficulty in sending out a force amply sufficient for the purpose. It would have been an easy operation compared with that undertaken by Mr. Canning in 1826, when he met a threatened aggression on Portugal by Spain by sending, at a very brief notice, a British expedition to Portugal, which had the desired effect. But, in truth, there never would have been the slightest chance of a war. It would have been sufficient to make Germany clearly understand that if she attacked the Danes she would find the warning of Lord Palmerston made good, and that she would not have to fight with them alone. He was quite persuaded that the statesmen of

Austria would have thought twice before they sent a larger part of their army than had been necessary to contend with Denmark only, (and a much larger force would have been required) to so great a distance from their own territory to attack a British army upon the Eyder. They would have reflected that the first shot fired at a British army would necessarily have been the signal for the appearance of a British fleet in the Adriatic. They would have remembered that the whole population of Venetia is ready to rise as one man to seize the first favourable opportunity to throw off the yoke of this new champion of nationality; that the army of Italy now raised to 300,000 men, is panting with impatience to assist in freeing their fellow-countrymen from their galling bondage; that the whole Italian nation,—King, Parliament, and people,—are burning with desire for the moment when prudence will allow them to release this gallant army from the restraint which now prevents its rushing forward to drive the hated foreigners from the soil of Italy; that a state of siege is necessary in Galicia; that Hungary is discontented; and that the Austrian finances are in such a state that the first sound of a war with England would have produced a national bankruptcy. In such a state of things, he firmly believed that prudence would have prevailed, and that the rulers of Austria would not have been so reckless, and so deaf to the dictates of common sense, as to commit an act of aggression obviously unjust and in direct violation of the understanding of 1856. And if Austria would not have acted thus, he thought it was pretty certain that Prussia would not have done so single-handed. Neither the internal nor the external situation of Prussia were such as to encourage her to enter upon such a contest, and she would hardly have ventured, under such circumstances, to send her army to conquer for the people of Schleswig those constitutional rights which she refused to her own people. These considerations convinced him, that even without other assistance than that which was offered by Sweden, we had it completely in our power to protect Schleswig from invasion without any real risk of war. But he must add, that the correspondence laid before them left little doubt in his mind that we might have obtained the support of France. He was aware that when General Fleury was sent to compliment the new King of Denmark on his accession, he was instructed to say that France did

not intend going to war for the protection of Denmark. He was also aware that when the French Government was asked by our own to concur in giving a vague assurance of material aid to Denmark in certain circumstances very obscurely described, this request was refused, and it would have been matter of surprise to him if any different answer had been returned to such an application by so sagacious a ruler as the present Emperor of the French. But he did not find in these papers that France was ever asked to join with us in requiring both parties to adhere to the understanding come to by the Powers of Europe in 1856, and to postpone, at all events, an appeal to arms till an attempt had been made to settle the dispute by friendly mediation. This he thought was all that there was any occasion for asking, or that it would have been right to ask. He was no such partizan of Denmark as to pretend that she stood altogether free from blame in the controversy that had led to the war. On the contrary, he believed that if from the year 1852 to the present time Denmark had governed the Duchies more wisely, and in a more conciliatory spirit, the circumstances never would have arisen which gave Germany a plausible pretence for interfering; but as the noble Duke (the Duke of Argyll) had observed, if Denmark was wrong, Germany was still more wrong, especially in insisting on deciding this question by the sword. The more clear it was that there were faults on both sides, the more clearly was the case one for the interference of friendly Powers; and if France had been asked to join in prohibiting hostilities till endeavours had been made to settle the dispute in a peaceable manner, he thought she would have done so, and that we should have succeeded in preventing war. He wished to call their Lordships' attention to some facts bearing upon that point. They would find a remarkable despatch from Lord Cowley, bearing date the 5th of January, in which his Lordship recounted a conversation he had had with the French Minister of Foreign Affairs. He had been instructed to ask the French Minister to join him in making a strong remonstrance against a resort to arms. In the course of their conversations, M. Drouyn d'Lhuys asked, "If the Germans refuse, what then?" Lord Cowley must have been deeply mortified that his instructions did not allow him to answer that question as it ought to have been answered. But, of course, he was bound by his instructions, and all that they enabled him to say was, "In that case it seems to me further deliberations will become necessary; but why anticipate difficulties which may never be realized?" That answer was characteristic of the policy of Her Majesty's Government throughout the whole of these negotiations. "Why anticipate difficulties?" Was it not the great object of a statesman's life to anticipate possible difficulties? He made or ought to make no move whatever without considering what counter moves might be made on the other side. To talk of a statesman not anticipating difficulties, was as if one talked of a chessplayer not anticipating difficulties, but always making his moves on the supposition that his opponent would not endeavour to defeat them. Not a whit more senseless would be the conduct of a statesman who should not attempt to foresee the possible consequences of the policy he adopted. He was not in the least surprised that after receiving such an answer, M. Drouyn de Lhuys dropped the conversation and said he would report it to the Emperor. A few days afterwards the conversation was renewed, when M. Drouyn de Lhuys reminded Lord Cowley of the answer which France and England had received in the case of the remonstrances they addressed to Russia in reference to the Polish insurrection, when having represented to Prince Gortschakoff that if Russia did not adopt a certain policy towards Poland, she would be held responsible, the Prince replied that Russia accepted the responsibility before God and man, and the French minister added that he was not willing to again expose himself to such a rebuff as that. He must say he thought M. Drouyn de Lhuys was right, and he was surprised that his noble Friend the Secretary for Foreign Affairs, when he determined to abstain from all serious measures, did not at the same time give up writing the sort of despatches they found in the papers. Why go on making proposal after proposal to the German Powers and remonstrance after remonstrance, which only served to provoke answers, in which sneering contempt is hardly concealed by the mere form of diplomatic politeness. It was clear beforehand all this writing would be fruitless, for to do the Prussians justice they had been candid, and had never concealed their real objects. M. Bismark told his noble Friend (Lord Wodehouse) in so many words, that there never could

be a good feeling between Prussia and Denmark while the latter maintained her democratic institutions, and he therefore recommended a *coup d'état*. In another conversation with Sir A. Buchanan he said that the honour of Prussia would not be satisfied till she had proved that she was not afraid to draw the sword, thus clearly avowing that a peaceable settlement was not the object of Prussia. But to return to the question as to how far France would have been disposed to join us in restraining the German Powers from the use of force against Denmark, he would remind their Lordships of a further conversation between M. Drouyn de Lhuys and Lord Cowley on the 19th of January, in which the former, after saying in reply to Lord Cowley that France had already used diplomatic means to maintain the integrity of Denmark, and would continue to do so, proceeded to ask—

"Does your proposal go further, and have you the application of force in contemplation? We must reserve our answer; we do not say no, but we cannot say yes. We are not bound by any guarantee to maintain the stipulations of that treaty. For instance, if we have to choose between its modification and the commencement of a war, uncertain as to its duration, and dubious as to its results, to speak frankly we prefer the former alternative."

This was a judicious answer, and certainly did not imply that we should have met with a refusal if the proposition then submitted to the French Government had been the one which, he (Earl Grey) contended, ought to have been made. What in his opinion this country ought to have asked France, was to join in saying to Prussia and Austria, "We think this is a case for compromise, and we insist on it that there shall be no fighting until an attempt has been made to bring about a peaceable settlement." He believed there would have been no danger of war if that course had been taken. But who could say there was not much danger to Europe in the present position of affairs? A war commenced in bad faith had been carried on in a manner which could only be described as savage. The pretence had been that Schleswig was to be taken as a guarantee; Austria had had the hypocrisy to say that it was taken in the interest of Denmark; and then, because Denmark resisted with our concurrence, (for their Lordships must remember we had expressly disclaimed offering her any advice against resistance to the invasion), they proceeded to treat Schleswig as a conquered country, and to remove in that Duchy, as they had done in Holstein, every semblance of Danish rule. They removed all the local officers who were loyal to the Danish Crown, and they warred even against the dead, pulling down the monument erected to the Danes, who had in the former war fallen in the service of their country. This was a perfectly wanton and gratuitous outrage to the feelings of the population. They invaded Jutland and went beyond the sternest rules of war in cruelty and violence, compelling the inhabitants to support the troops by whom they were oppressed, levying large contributions not only of food and forage, but of money, and enforcing the payment by arresting and threatening to shoot the principal inhabitants of the villages if the contributions were not paid. Nothing more marked the spirit with which the war was carried on by the Prussians, than an account he read in the newspapers the other day, describing the manner in which they had revenged themselves for a military disadvantage on the unarmed population. By a well planned and well executed surprise a small detachment of Prussian cavalry was captured by a Danish force, and this feat of arms, as fair as it was bravely done, the Prussians, by their own account, punished by burning the farms and laying waste the property of the inhabitants of the district where it occurred, because the troops by whom it was effected were beyond their reach. Was that the way in which honourable soldiers carried on even a just and necessary war ? Then, again, there was the bombardment of Sönderborg, which his noble Friend (the Earl of Shaftesbury) denounced the other evening in just terms ; and he perceived that the second edition of that day's *Times* contained a letter describing the atrocious barbarity of that bombardment, and the wanton cruelty inflicted thereby on the unarmed and peaceful population as having been even worse than his noble Friend supposed. It was now said that the Austrian fleet was to go to the Baltic ; but were the Germans to be allowed to use their forces both by land and by sea to the absolute destruction of Denmark ? He believed that a little moderation and firmness in the first instance might have prevented affairs reaching their present condition ; but now, when the passions of the contending parties have been inflamed, and all the difficulties increased by the German troops being in possession both of Schleswig and Holstein, it was

difficult to see how, without the actual use of force, it would be possible for this country to arrest or limit the barbarous war that was going on, before it had led to consequences most dangerous to the general peace of Europe. This danger is greatly increased by the fact that those transactions have had a most unhappy effect on the opinion entertained of this country in the world. A great nation cannot forfeit her reputation for courage, and for a determination to maintain her rights and her honour—cannot become suspected of irresolution and timidity, without provoking wrongs and insults which she cannot always continue to endure. He could not, therefore, believe it to be of good augury for our permanent enjoyment of the blessings of peace, that the conduct of our Government as to Denmark, following so closely what had occurred with respect to Poland, should have created, as it notoriously had, a general impression on the Continent of Europe, that this country is no longer animated by its old spirit, and is so afraid of the pecuniary losses and sacrifices which war would impose upon it, that it would prefer submitting to almost any wrong or any insult rather than appeal to the sword. No doubt this impression is a false one— there cannot be a more complete misconception of the real feeling of the nation, but unhappily the mischief such a belief may do depends little upon its being correct, and that it generally prevails at this moment among foreign nations is too certain to admit of doubt. Thus the timid and vacillating policy pursued by Her Majesty's Government in their too great fear of war, is directly calculated to bring upon us in the end the very evil they have been anxious to escape, and which a more manly policy would, in all probability, have averted.

Earl RUSSELL : My Lords, it now appears clearly, I think, from my noble Friend's speech, that we are arraigned, not for not having prevented the war between Austria and Prussia, and Denmark, but for not having ourselves joined in it. The real substance of my noble Friend's arraignment is, that we are now at peace. My noble Friend has read most discreetly the papers laid before Parliament, referring only to those parts which told in favour of his own views, and omitting to notice anything which militated against them. My noble Friend began by saying that he would not enter into a long discussion of what is called the Schleswig-Holstein question; but I must say that without a consideration of that question it would be difficult to say why the German and Danish Powers should now be at war. It has been my task to attend to this question. In the year 1862 I offered proposals for the settlement of that question, which if they had been accepted would, I believe, have prevented the possibility of the war which is now being waged. But I was then told that it was really a matter which had no danger or importance, and that I was interfering in a question which might very well be allowed to sleep for a century, or half a century, without the fear of disturbing the present state of affairs. My Lords, I never took that view of the subject. I always thought it was a serious matter, which, unless satisfactorily disposed of in time, might lead to deplorable eventualities. In looking into the history of this question, it seemed to me that the arrangements made in 1851 between Prussia and Austria on the one side, and Denmark on the other, were most unfortunate and almost contradictory. They gave not only to Austria and Prussia, but to the Powers of Germany, either a right, or, at all events, a pretext for interference in the internal and domestic concerns of the Danish Monarchy, which, unless perfect good temper and a spirit of the greatest conciliation were shown on both sides, could not but engender discussion and controversies of the angriest kind, and perhaps the ultimate outbreak of war. That, my Lords, has been the history of these transactions for the last ten years. For my own part, looking carefully at this subject, I will say that with regard to this matter, as with regard to other matters of great importance in which this country has been interested, I have deemed it my duty, holding the post of Secretary of State for Foreign Affairs, to divest my mind of all partisanship, to endeavour to view the question, between the Powers at enmity with each other, with a fair and impartial mind, so as, if possible, to form a clear and just judgment upon it. Nothing, I think, would be more discreditable to English statesmen than to rush at once into a strong decision on the one side or the other, without carefully investigating all the circumstances of the case. Now, with regard to this treaty, the Danish Government promised, in 1851, that it would hold Schleswig very much as a separate State—that it should have separate provincial Estates

Earl Russell

for its own affairs, and a representative body; that it should have a Minister, and that its administration should be conducted solely in Schleswig. It was very difficult to keep to all these engagements; Denmark had entered into them in a moment of necessity, when foreign troops occupied part of her soil. I will not now, in this time of her distress, point out in detail where I think that her promises were not fulfilled. Instances of it are to be found in the papers on your Lordships' table, and I will not further refer to them. But Germany, on the other side, took the most unfair advantage of what was done in detail by Denmark, on every occasion putting forward propositions to which it would have been impossible for Denmark to accede, because they would, in fact, have set up a German authority at the very seat of her rule, and thus would have destroyed not only the nominal integrity, but the real independence of Denmark. Well, my Lords, such being the unfortunate state of affairs, neither party, I think, having been entirely in the right, and neither being able to say that it was free from all blame, the dispute went on until, on the 1st of last October, Germany resolved on a Federal execution in Holstein. That decree for Federal execution, according to the opinion of Her Majesty's Government, the Diet had a right to issue, on the ground of the Federal pact. But whatever might have been the previous difficulties on that subject, they were aggravated tenfold on the death of the late King of Denmark. It might have been supposed — those who thought favourably of the pretensions of Germany might well suppose—that the late King, having been governed by counsellors of what might be deemed ultra-Danish principles, and having himself not only a great love for his country but taking a somewhat prejudiced view of the question with respect to Danish and German interests, might have judged partially on these matters. But the new King was not liable to that suspicion; and I am persuaded even to this moment, that if Germany had temperately urged the claims of the German subjects of the King of Denmark to certain rights and privileges which Denmark had agreed to maintain, King Christian IX. would have so governed and so administered his dominions that all real ground of complaint would have been removed by fair discussion and reasonable concession. But the course taken was very different, and I confess it appears to me, as it has been argued by my noble

Friend who has just sat down, that the Powers of Germany did seem rather disposed to excite a quarrel than to exhibit a conciliatory temper. Well, as we wished above all to prevent the outbreak of war in Europe, it was our object so to counsel both parties that an amicable settlement might be arrived at. My noble Friend finds fault with the advice that we gave to Denmark to abolish the November Constitution; but as the engagement of Denmark was such as I have just stated to your Lordships—namely, that Schleswig should have a separate Constitution, and should not part with that Constitution unless with the consent of her own Estates, it appeared to us, upon study and examination, that the November Constitution was inconsistent with the obligations which Denmark had taken to Germany. My noble Friend (Lord Wodehouse) who proceeded to Copenhagen, and who had no prejudice in favour of Germany and against Denmark, came to the same conclusion, and urged it, as his own opinion as well as the opinion of Her Majesty's Government, on the Government of Denmark. Surely, even in befriending the cause of Denmark by negotiation, it was our part to see that she was in the right. We could hardly go to Germany, to Prussia, and Austria, and say, "Denmark is quite in the wrong, but we beg you not to insist on her doing right." We could not urge that course; and, therefore, to enable us to make due representations to Germany we proposed that that Constitution should be revoked. My noble Friend found great fault throughout his speech with our making representations without being at once ready to commence hostilities. It is clear that where your honour is attacked, and the representations you make are not listened to, you must defend your honour. If you have great interests at stake, and wish to prevent their being sacrificed, you must defend those interests. But where you only seek to pursue the benevolent design of maintaining peace between other Powers, and enabling each State to maintain its own sovereign rights, I cannot think there is any humiliation; indeed, I think there is a decided advantage, in urging over and over again as we have done by friendly advice, that peace should be preserved, and that those Powers should not injure one another. Well, my Lords, in viewing this subject, it seemed to me that unless we were prepared alone to make ourselves the defenders of the liberties of Europe,

unless we were to take a course which no great statesman who had adopted a European policy for England has ever advocated, we were bound on a question of European policy to endeavour to obtain allies. Now, the allies to whom we naturally looked were France and Russia. I am now maintaining that it would have been unwise for the Government of this country to have committed itself to hostilities without having the aid and assistance of other European Powers. My noble Friend read part of the correspondence which we carried on with other Courts; and he read up to the 5th of January, when he found that Lord Cowley, having been asked by M. Drouyn de Lhuys what more we proposed besides a Conference, stated that he was unable to answer that question, and that it was unnecessary then to consider more than the present proposition. But as we heard that the French Government desired to know what it was that Her Majesty's Government proposed to do, I immediately wrote a despatch conveying the intentions of Her Majesty's Government. I also wrote a similar despatch to Russia. What I said in effect was this:—There is a project evidently conceived in Germany for depriving Denmark of the States of Holstein and the Duchy of Schleswig. Supposing that project is persevered in, will you, France, will you, Russia, agree with us in giving material assistance to Denmark? That is my answer to my noble Friend's reproach. The very thing which he blamed us for not doing, if he had had the goodness and the patience ·to read a few pages further on, he would have found that we actually did.

Earl GREY: I expressly mentioned that despatch, and said its terms were so vague that the application could have had no other answer than that it received.

Earl RUSSELL: My despatch referred distinctly to a plan conceived for the dismemberment of Denmark, and went on to say, that to prevent the execution of that plan we sought the co-operation of France, of Russia, and of Sweden, in order to give material assistance to Denmark in resisting that dismemberment. My noble Friend calls that vague, and says that we did not propose to give material assistance. Certainly we did not specify the number of troops and ships that we proposed to give, but what we did propose to give was material assistance. It appears to me that nothing could be more clear and plain than the proposal of Her Majesty's Government, and the French Government so considered it, because M. Drouyn de Lhuys spoke at great length to Lord Cowley on the subject, and stated that the Emperor of the French expressed his approval, and more than that, he wrote a long despatch, of which you will find a summary in the papers; but the answer of France was to this effect, that France was not opposed to the integrity of Denmark, but she thought it might be that some change would, perhaps, be preferable to the maintenance of that integrity, just as in 1831 it appeared to the British Government that the setting up of Belgium, as an independent country, was preferable to the maintenance of the integrity of the Netherlands. It went on to say that the question of war with Germany was a very serious question for France, and that France would prefer to keep herself at perfect liberty as to any future measures she might take if the balance of power were actually in danger; but, at present, she did not think it necessary to give the assistance required. My noble Friend then makes a most extraordinary supposition. He says, that if instead of asking France whether she would assist us in preventing the dismemberment of the Danish monarchy, she had been asked whether she would give material assistance in preventing the Austrian and Prussian troops from entering Schleswig, we should have obtained her aid. A more extraordinary, a more wild or unfounded supposition I never heard made in this or the other House of Parliament. The answer of Russia was not so plain and distinct, but the effect of it was clear—that she wished to preserve her liberty of action; that she wished to know exactly what the proposition of England was, but she did not feel at present that her means and resources would admit of the policy of giving material assistance to Denmark. And then the question comes to this—which, however, my noble Friend never put —whether England, France, Russia, and Sweden having made a treaty, by which they did not guarantee or agree to guarantee the integrity of the Danish Monarchy, but to respect and acknowledge the Prince who was to succeed to the throne of all the Danish states and dominions, we alone, without France and Russia, should take upon ourselves to maintain the integrity of Denmark. Now observe, our object was to maintain the balance of power and the peace of Europe;

Earl Russell

but the balance of power and the peace of Europe are questions of as serious importance to France and Russia as to England, and, therefore, it was not the business of England alone to undertake their defence. But when I heard my noble Friend explain the manner in which this was to be done, I own I was much more impressed than before with the danger of the alternative course which he thinks we ought to have pursued. In the first place, my noble Friend thinks that in the month of January we should have sent a squadron to the Baltic. We might have done so in the month of March, for in that month we sent an expedition to Copenhagen, and in the Crimean war we sent a fleet to the Baltic; but if you were to send a fleet to the Baltic in the month of January, you would have destroyed your ships and lost your fleet. My noble Friend also says that Venetia was panting to go to war with Austria, that Gallicia was disturbed, and that Hungary was disaffected. But, my Lords, only consider in what a state Germany was. It was in a state of violent enthusiasm, bent upon having Schleswig and Holstein separated from Denmark, looking to that end above all, not caring much, perhaps, about the Prince of Augustenburg, but putting him forward to serve as her instrument for that purpose. This was also to be taken into account— that Prussia and Austria, afraid of altogether thwarting the wishes of Germany, were executing them in such a way as they thought would be still conducive to peace and order in Germany, while they made Denmark suffer from their attacks. Well, then, we should have had on one side Germany, carrying, at least, Prussia, if not Austria, along with her, invading Denmark, and we there to defend it; we should have had Venetia making war in the Adriatic, and should have had the people of Hungary rising in delight that England was at war with Germany; and every violent and revolutionary plot coming to its completion under English auspices. And all this disturbance in Europe—this general war—a general war was to be undertaken in the name of peace, and in order to prevent Schleswig from being invaded. Not the least consideration in this matter was that France was taking a very different view from ours. While we looked to the integrity of Denmark, France was looking to the interests of nationalities, and what should be done for the people of Schleswig and Holstein. I do not blame

France for that, but that was another element of danger ; for, while we were supporting nothing but Denmark, and supporting her right or wrong in the things which she maintained, France might have taken an opposite view, and then these two nations, whose united action is of so much importance to Europe, might have been brought into collision, though having no interests that were rival, but, ou the contrary, the utmost interest in living at peace. Well, that is the prospect which my noble Friend holds out ; and I can only rejoice the more that we have not thrown the firebrand into Europe, and not caused the extensive conflagration which my noble Friend has indicated. Now, my Lords, it is necessary to consider a little what we have effected. All those representations which my noble Friend holds so cheap, and which he says produced no result, as they have not prevented the war from breaking out, have, at all events, produced this effect—that on the 31st of January, before they went into Schleswig, those Powers who had been constantly thinking and suggesting that the maintenance of the Constitution of November had dissolved the Treaty of 1852, and set themselves quite free to take any course they liked — the Powers who held these views did, on the 31st of January, inform England, France, and Russia that they held to the Treaty of 1852,. and respected the integrity of Denmark. Well, that, I think, is a very great point gained. It appears to me that, instead of the total dismemberment of Denmark, we can now go into the Conference with every Power except the Confederation, clearly bound to respect the Treaty of 1852, and clearly bound to respect the integrity of Denmark. We have made great steps in advance since the month of January. I own when I heard the language talked in London, and still more at Berlin, I was constantly afraid that the King and Government of Prussia would declare that the Treaty of 1852 was at an end. But by the firmness and moderation of our language, we have obtained from them the declaration that they will maintain that treaty, and in the Conference will consider that as the object to be always kept in view. My noble Friend has contrasted the position we are now in with that of Mr. Canning in 1826. Well, there is a very great difference between the power of Spain in 1826 and that of Germany in 1863. Austria and Prussia and the whole of Germany, with 44,000,000 of people, are very different from Spain

at that time. But, besides this, England was bound by treaty to defend Portugal as if she were England, and Mr. Canning felt under that treaty, and very justly felt, that the honour of England required that she should send her troops there, and that where the English standard was no invasion should come. He was perfectly justified. With regard to Spain, I recollect perfectly well hearing Mr. Canning say, "I am told that we must have war sooner or later. If that be the case, I say later." My noble Friend says just the reverse. He says, "We must have war sooner or later, and I say sooner." I say with Mr. Canning, "later," and I am quite content to abide by that. As the Conference is to meet on the 20th of this month, I know not that I need enter—or, indeed, that it would be right for me to enter—upon the questions that must there be agitated. The object of England is, and, I think, ought to be, to modify the extreme pretensions and, if possible, abate the animosities of different nations. I hold that to be a fitting object for England to endeavour to attain ; but if I wish to do that, I must not begin by laying severe blame on the different parties to this war. With regard to the conduct of this war by Austria and Prussia, I entirely agree with much that has been said by my noble Friend. But we have already stated in our despatches our opinion on this point, and my noble Friend at the head of the Government has declared that this is an iniquitous aggression on the part of Austria and Prussia, and that the resistance of Denmark is justified by the conduct of Austria and Prussia. I know not that anything stronger could have been said, even by my noble Friends opposite. With regard to the whole subject, I must consider the many interests we have spread over the whole face of the globe, and the danger that if we were at war with Germany that other wars might spring out of it, that our commerce might be intercepted by privateers sailing under any name or flag, and scouring the ocean to destroy our commerce. It may be a low and unworthy consideration in the eyes of my noble Friend, but when I reflect on the exposition made by my right hon. Friend the Chancellor of the Exchequer the other night of the magnificent situation of this country, I am not inclined to hazard and imperil that situation without a clear case of honour, or without great and mighty interests being at stake, calling for our armed intervention. Also, we must consider that by the side of that exposition of flourishing trade, and of the improvement of our finances and all our material interests, there remains the fact, which was stated then, and must be stated every year, that there is more than £26,000,000 interest of debt to pay, and that that £26,000,000 interest of debt has been caused almost entirely by war, the greater portion of it having been caused by the two last wars which this country undertook. In 1764 the interest of our debt was £4,600,000; it is now £26,200,000. May we not be unwilling —may we not fairly be cautious—before we add to that debt? One of those wars, the American war, was one which no man in these days will defend. The other of those wars, the father of my noble Friend (Earl Grey) most eloquently opposed as unjust and unnecessary. Whether these wars were justified or not, the cost and burden of them have been immense; and, while that is no reason why we should desert any cause in which we are bound to go forward, or why we should abandon any friend whom we have obligations to support, they are reasons, I think, why we should pursue a pacific, and not a warlike course. I confess, for my own part, that while I have the authority and adopt the policy of the great men to whom I have referred, and who held that the balance of power ought to be maintained, I likewise agree with them when they sought alliances in order to support the balance of power, and in thinking that the destruction of one of the States of Europe is not only a great outrage, but a peril to the independence of all the other States. But at the same time, I do think that a policy the least hostile that we can make it, and the least disposed to make a quarrel where it can be avoided, ought to be pursued by this country. I cannot, therefore, agree with my noble Friend in his Motion, that, "in the opinion of this House, if the demand made by Denmark for mediation, according to the principle laid down in the Protocol of Paris, 1856, had been more decidedly supported by Her Majesty's Government, the bloodshed and the other evils already occasioned by the war in Denmark might have been prevented." Now, I do not believe that that is the opinion of this House, and I shall, at all events, feel it to be my bounden duty to oppose that part of the Motion. With regard to the other Resolution of my noble Friend, " that such steps ought to be taken as may convince

the Powers of Europe that Her Majesty's Government adhere to the treaties," it is unnecessary to attempt to convince them that we adhere to the treaties. The Treaty of 1720 is, indeed, one which has been disputed by persons of great learning, and we are not called upon to assert the validity of that treaty. But, with regard to the Treaty of 1852, it is our object to maintain that, and to have it recognized by the Powers of Europe. I trust that will be the result of the Conference. With respect to the policy of France, I shall say this one word — that we were not ready last year to adopt the course proposed by France—namely, to send an identical note to Russia, and afterwards to concert measures in case Russia did not agree to our proposal. We were rather satisfied with the terms proposed by Austria, and which would leave upon Russia the responsibility of her refusal. We did not think it wise to go to war with Russia in the cause of Poland, and we therefore informed France of our determination not to do so: the French people have great sympathy with the Poles. There is besides the tie of religion, which makes a close connection between France and Poland. With regard to Denmark again, we have a great feeling with a gallant people—a maritime people like ourselves, professing the same religion with ourselves, and constantly connected with us by maritime commerce. Therefore, while France sympathized more with Poland, the sympathies of England have been more with Denmark; and while we refused to join France in the proposal regarding Poland, she refused to join us in the proposition with regard to Denmark. We have no reason to find fault with France on that ground; but still I must say, that if we are to interfere—if we are to defend Denmark on the grounds of the interests of Europe and the balance of power, the Powers of Europe ought to go together, and not to leave that great task to be undertaken by us alone. There are other matters requiring consideration. My noble Friend alluded to one—that of the Austrian fleet going to the Baltic. That is a question on which Her Majesty's Government have made representations to the Austrian Government. At present, the Austrian Government have promised that they have no intention to send their fleet into the Baltic. They say they are about to send their fleet into the North Sea to protect the commerce of the German Powers, which is very extensive. That is a legiti-

Earl Russell

mate object. England is quite free to act in such cases ; and, while we will not act without it is absolutely necessary, and while I am fully conscious of the power of England, yet we do not wish to hurry into war without necessity. And, for my own part, I think that a pacific policy is our true policy.

THE EARL OF DERBY : My Lords, as this discussion has turned upon the policy and conduct of the Government, and as many Peers are absent from town, I think it is a matter of regret that the noble Lord (Lord Campbell) did not give longer notice of his intention of bringing forward this subject. But I apprehend — and I am confirmed in my opinion by the state of the House—that it is not the intention of the noble Baron to ask the House to pronounce any opinion, but that his object was to express his own individual opinion, and to enable any other Members of your Lordships' House to express their opinion, on the policy and conduct of the Government as they appear from the voluminous papers on the table. That being the case, I apprehend that the peculiar wording of his Motion is a matter of minor consideration, and in the few words which I shall address to your Lordships I will confine myself not to the terms of that Motion, but to a consideration of the state of affairs as they now stand. I have gone through the dreary waste of these interminable papers ; I have plodded through them with the greatest possible patience ; I have gone through the greater part of the 800 and odd pages which comprise those extracts which Her Majesty's Government have been pleased to lay before us from the correspondence which has taken place upon this subject during the past year ; and I can assure the noble Duke (the Duke of Argyll) that the last accusation which I should think of making against the Secretary of State is one of want of diligence—because I perceive that the noble Earl has during the last year written, exclusive of duplicates, no less than 170 despatches upon the subject of Denmark and Germany. And although certainly I have not been struck with admiration of the style of these despatches—although I have seen them characterised by what I consider a most forcible weakness—I must say that I have been struck with astonishment and admiration at the persevering industry with which the noble Earl has gone on spinning day after day thread by thread his political cobwebs, utterly regardless of every single thread

being swept away one after another—spinning, spinning, spinning on, but at the same time not making the slightest progress towards the completion of his web, and not having been able to catch a single diplomatic fly. I have no great fault to find with the tone and character of the noble Earl's speech, and I have no wish to increase the difficulties of the position, great and serious as they are, in which Her Majesty's Government and Europe are placed. I entirely concur in what the noble Earl has said with regard to the policy of this country being essentially a peace policy —a policy of avoiding the horrors of war ; but I think that the noble Earl placed that policy on the lowest and humblest ground when he rested it simply upon pecuniary considerations. There are considerations which impress me with a greater horror of war than does the risk of impairing the flourishing state of Her Majesty's Exchequer ; and although I consider war a great and grievous evil, yet there are evils greater than war, and among them are the sacrifice of the honour of the country and the abandonment of the interests of a friend who has placed himself in your hands. The question is, what is a warlike policy ? Is the course which Her Majesty's Government has pursued under the auspices of the noble Earl more likely to aggravate the danger or to remove from us the evil of war ? I am afraid that the course which the Government have pursued is one which in the end is more likely to lead to serious complications and a general disturbance of the peace of Europe, than if they had in the first instance taken a more decided, a more straightforward, and a more determined course. It is, of course, impossible, looking back at these negotiations, to say that a particular course taken at a particular time would have produced this or the other effect. It is, of course, open to the noble Earl to hold his opinion, that if we had made stronger remonstrances, with the view, of course, of acting upon them, we should have been more likely to incur danger of war ; and, on the other hand, it is open to the noble Earl on the upper bench (Earl Grey) to argue that if we had adopted a more resolute tone, the probability is that it would have imposed upon Europe the obligation and necessity of maintaining peace. But, my Lords, that of which we do complain, and which we feel to be the course least creditable to this country, is that of holding out menaces, threats, and remonstrances to foreign countries, and at the same time conveying to those countries and to Europe generally the impression that they may safely set at defiance our representations, our threats, and our remonstrances, because nothing will induce us to give any material aid, or to take any part further than these querulous remonstrances with which the noble Earl is assailing every Court in Europe. I admit fully the great danger of the position, and I admit what was stated by the noble Duke—and it is a consideration which ought not to be lost sight of—that its dangers are greatly aggravated, because they are not under the control of statesmen and monarchs who act under the guidance of reason, but are under the control of democratic influences and revolutionary parties, who are acting not upon reason, but from passion, who are desirous of driving all matters to extremity, and who, I am afraid, are exercising great influence at the present time. I admit that there is something of that same feeling on both sides ; but what is the mainspring of the course of action which is pursued by Austria and Prussia ? It is not that Prussia and Austria—certainly it' is not that Austria—desire to pursue an aggressive policy ; but, it is this, that there is a revolutionary party abroad who are anxious to create disturbance throughout Europe for the purpose of their own selfish and revolutionary ends. They are exercising an influence upon the minor Powers of Germany, partly of persuasion, partly of ambition, partly of fear; and these minor Powers, carried away by a torrent which they are unable to stem, have placed themselves in a perilous position for their own interests at the head of the democratic movement, fomenting and encouraging plans which can only be fraught with the most imminent danger to themselves. Well, but two great Powers like Austria and Prussia might, one would think, safely defy this revolutionary influence. They might, but there are many motives which operate with them. Prussia may have—we know she has—motives of personal ambition to be gratified by the extension of her possessions and the acquisition of a naval harbour. Prussia also entertains great jealousy of Austria ; and Prussia desires to take the sting out of the democratic movement by placing herself at the head of it, and, strange to say, placing herself at the head of that movement, being herself a despotic country, for the purpose of putting down the liberties

of a neighbouring country which she considers too democratic. That is the anomalous position of Prussia ; what is that of Austria ? Why, Austria fears that if Prussia is allowed to take this lead, Prussia will, in point of fact, be the ruling Power, and maintain a paramount influence in the Confederation over these minor Powers, and that she herself will be hereafter compelled to play a subordinate part. Therefore, it is first the power of the revolutionary party acting on the small States ; next, the small States acting on the mutual jealousies of Austria and Prussia ; and lastly, those jealousies themselves which will not allow either to take a single step in which the other shall not go side by side with her. These are the circumstances which really constitute the great and imminent danger to the peace of Europe, whatever course of policy any Government may pursue. I do not quarrel with the way in which the noble Earl has spoken of the case as between Denmark and Germany, nor will I enter into a discussion of the Schleswig-Holstein question, which I think he has stated very fairly. There have been violations of the engagements entered into on both sides ; neither party is free from blame, and any British Minister is perfectly justified in holding the balance evenly between the two, and not throwing himself and the weight of his authority exclusively into the scale of either. With respect to the obligations entered into by Denmark, I recollect that the noble Earl on a previous occasion used the expression that it was not open to Denmark to use the *argumentum ab inconvenienti*, because if she had entered into these obligations she was bound in honour to fulfil them. But if Denmark has entered into engagements which, taken in the sense put upon them by Germany, places her in a state of absolute paralysis as to her internal condition, and practically subordinate the whole Monarchy to one portion which happens to be a part of the German empire, it is not an *argumentum ab inconvenienti*, but there is a manifest impossibility of fulfilling to the letter the conditions entered into. Denmark has made many efforts to relieve herself, with justice to her subjects, from the painful position in which she has been placed ; but every one of her propositions has been rendered futile by the positive refusal of Holstein to enter into any compromise whatever, and the persistent manner in which Prussia has backed Holstein in these extreme views, and has maintained that, without her assent, no arrangement can be entered into. What can be more absurd than that there should be four portions of one monarchy—one of which contains 1,500,000, and the other three about 500,000 inhabitants — but that each of these several divisions should have an equal voice in the administration of the affairs of the whole monarchy, and that upon the ground that no one of these divisions should be made wholly subordinate to another? I am glad to see that the noble Earl recognizes the monstrous injustice of that proposition; but here is another, which is not less impracticable—that is to say, that if Holstein (or Lauenberg, which would be a stronger case) if Holstein refuses her assent in any one of these four assemblies to any measure passed by Denmark, or the other three portions of the monarchy, for the general advantage of the whole country, not only shall that measure not take effect with regard to the whole country, but it shall not take effect with regard to those three divisions which have passed it and adopted it, because the fourth refuses to accept it; and that fourth claims that there shall be one constitution for the whole; the consequence of which is that every measure, great or small, must be based upon the separate convenience of the four several divisions. If that is the case, Holstein, as a fief of Germany, exercises an absolute prohibitory influence on all legislation in Denmark. Denmark is placed at the foot of Holstein, and Holstein is at the foot of Germany. Now, my Lords, I care not that that may be the literal or technical interpretation of engagements entered into. No court of equity would say that such engagements could be supported to the letter. It is obviously a case not for intervention by arms, but for friendly negotiation by a friendly Power; and that is the course which Germany ought to have taken. I will not repeat what the noble Earl has said this evening with regard to the ungenerous way in which Germany availed herself of the increasing difficulties which pressed upon Denmark, with a view to cause her to accede to conditions with which it was impossible that she could legally comply. I think the course taken by Germany in that respect was wholly unjustifiable. But the question with which we have now to deal is the effect which was produced by the policy which Her Majesty's Government pursued in the endeavour to prevent or mitigate the danger which threatened Denmark, and the position in which our influence and interests stand in Europe, owing to the positive declaration made by the noble Earl of pacific principles. In looking through those papers, I find that to almost every country we have addressed successively representations, remonstrances, and threats, going almost to the length of a warning that non-compliance with our recommendations would be followed by a war. We have gone to the very verge of saying to Denmark, "if you act on our recommendations"—as she studiously did — "you will have our material aid." We went thus far, I maintain, by putting the converse to her, and telling her that if she did not obey our instructions we could render her no assistance. Now, would it not, I would ask, have been more generous and fair, and candid to say to Denmark, "We advise you, as friends, to take such a course; but, at the same time, you will adopt that which, in your own judgment, you consider the best; for you must bear in mind that from us you are to expect nothing more than our moral influence." I entirely concur with the noble Earl in the opinion that we were not bound by the terms of the treaty to come forward to protect and maintain Denmark, or called upon to support the integrity of an instrument which our co-signataries were not prepared to uphold. But, then, we ought not to have held out to Denmark the expectation that it was our resolve to see that the treaty was preserved, and the Prime Minister ought not, in his place in Parliament, to have stated that in the event of her territory being invaded she would not stand alone. By making that statement the noble Earl conveyed something more than an intimation; he gave a distinct and direct pledge, on which the Danes placed reliance; and from that moment they said to themselves, "No matter though there are 40,000,000 against two; we know the power of England: we have the promise of the Prime Minister of England that that power will be exerted in our defence in the case of exigency. The honour of England has hitherto been held inviolable, and we have the utmost confidence that it will be so on the present occasion." When, however, we look to the other Powers of Europe, we find that they do not judge us quite so favourably as Denmark. Here are a few of the representations made by the noble

Earl opposite, and of the answers which he received. On the 31st of August, 1863, he writes as follows :—

" I have caused M. Katte to be informed . . . that if Austria and Prussia persist in advising the Confederation to make a Federal Execution now, they will do so against the advice already given by Her Majesty's Government, and must be responsible for the consequences, whatever they may be."—*Correspondence*, No. 2 (1864), p. 125.

" Responsible for the consequences " seems to be a favourite phrase of the noble Earl's ; but the States of Europe have learnt to regard it as nothing more than a mere *brutum fulmen*, which he is on every occasion ready to launch. The noble Earl is informed, in answer to his representation, that the matter was in the hands of the Confederation, that Austria and Prussia would not further interfere, and that execution would go on. The next application is one in which still stronger language is used, and in which the tone assumed is of a more warlike character. It is addressed to the Diet, and a copy of it was ordered to be presented officially to the President of the Diet on the part of Her Majesty's Government. In this despatch the noble Earl says—

" Her Majesty's Government could not see with indifference a military occupation of Holstein, which is only to cease upon terms injuriously affecting the Constitution of the whole Danish monarchy. . . . Her Majesty's Government could not be indifferent to the bearing of such an act upon Denmark and upon European interests. Her Majesty's Government, therefore, earnestly entreat the German Diet to pause."—*Correspondence*, No. 2 (1864), p. 145.

Now the phrase, " Could not see with indifference " is one which in diplomatic language assumes very serious import ; but the German Diet nevertheless treated it with profound indifference, because they quietly say in reply, that " they are not in a position to take any action on the communication of Her Majesty's Minister," and request the President to communicate a copy of their decision and of the report of the Committee in answer to it. Such is the simple reply of the Diet which amounts to this—that they did not deem it necessary to take any notice of the noble Earl's communication. On the 9th of November the noble Earl writes—

" As matters now stand, Her Majesty's Government have come to the conclusion, that it is inexpedient for them, at least for the present, to make any further proposal to the Diet. . . . . At present Her Majesty's Government can only leave to Germany the responsibility of risking a general war in Europe, which the Diet seems to be so bent

on provoking."—*Correspondence*, No. 3 (1864), p. 199.

Again, we have the noble Earl writing as follows to the Government of France :—

" If the Government of the Emperor of the French are of opinion that any benefit would be likely to follow from an offer of good offices on the part of Great Britain and France, Her Majesty's Government would be ready to take that course. If, however, the Government of France would consider such a step as likely to be unavailing, the two Powers might remind Austria, Prussia, and the German Diet that any act on their part tending to weaken the integrity and independence of Denmark would be at variance with the Treaty of the 8th of May."

M. Drouyn de Lhuys having a lively recollection of the case of Poland last year, when the French Government had joined us in making strong representations— [Earl RUSSELL : Joined in the proposals with Austria.] Yes ; but they took the step conjointly of throwing upon the Emperor the responsibility of the course they were about to take ; and M. Drouyn de Lhuys, no doubt bearing all this in mind, replies to the noble Earl that the offer of good offices would, in his opinion, be useless. He adds—

" The second mode of proceeding suggested by his Lordship would be in a great measure analogous to the course pursued by Great Britain and France on the Polish question. He had no inclination to place France in the same position with regard to Germany as she had been placed with regard to Russia. The formal notes addressed by the three Powers to Russia had received an answer which literally meant nothing, and the position in which those three great Powers were now placed was anything but dignified ; and if England and France were to address such a reminder as that proposed to Austria, Prussia, and the German Confederation, they must be prepared to go further, and to adopt a course of action more in accordance with the dignity of two great Powers than they were now doing on the Polish question."

[Earl RUSSELL : That has reference to Poland.] He draws a contrast between the case of Poland and that of Denmark. France has strong Polish sympathies, as I have already observed, and England has strong Danish sympathies; and if we did not show ourselves inclined to join France with regard to Poland, it was not unnatural that France should show a disinclination to join us with reference to Denmark. Now, I never did call upon the noble Earl to make war for Poland ; but then I think that when one great Power calls upon another and demands the fulfilment of treaty obligations, which was what the noble Earl did last year in reference to Poland, that Power must naturally expect either to be called upon to give effect to its menaces, or to withdraw them under such humiliation as the noble Earl's policy on that, as on too many other occasions, has entailed on this country. There is another paragraph in the document to which I have referred that does not relate to Poland, but to the great Powers; and I am surprised, after the rebuff which he had received from M. Drouyn de Lhuys, the noble Earl should again have pursued precisely the same course. As to what the noble Earl said about "the heavy responsibility," if by any precipitate measures the Powers should break the peace of Europe, M. Drouyn de Lhuys observes that he has not forgotten that when the case of Russia in reference to Poland was under the consideration of France, Great Britain, and Austria, she was warned of the "heavy responsibility," and that Prince Gortschakoff replied that he was quite ready to accept that responsibility; and that he (M. Drouyn de Lhuys) did not wish to provoke another such answer, or to be again treated with such indifference. I do think M. Drouyn de Lhuys has shown a much truer sense of what is due to a great country than the noble Earl has. M. Drouyn de Lhuys said—

"I will anticipate a difficulty; I will look forward and see what is to take place in the event of an unfavourable answer, and if I can see that you will continue your course notwithstanding an unfavourable answer I will act with you; but if in the event of an unfavourable answer you are to get out of the strait and leave me in the difficulty, I must say—though you may not think much of it, because you are so used to it, yet that I do not look upon it in the same light."

Now as to the amount of influence which this country has, under the noble Earl, exercised in Europe, let me say that a good deal of light is thrown upon this subject by a despatch of Sir Andrew Buchanan. When the noble Lord, whom I see in his place (Lord Wodehouse), left Berlin on his way to carry out his hopeless negotiations, Sir Andrew Buchanan was left behind, and received some instructions as to applications to be made to the German Powers in obedience to the noble Lord. Sir Andrew Buchanan says—

"I regret also, with reference to representations which I have made by your Lordship's order to M. Bismark during the last fortnight, on other subjects connected with the question, that I have failed in obtaining compliance with the wishes of Her Majesty's Government. I was instructed to suggest that time should be given to Lord Wodehouse to negotiate with the Danish Government before the Federal execution is carried into effect. The execution will take place within six days of

his Lordship's arrival in Copenhagen. I was instructed to express the hope of Her Majesty's Government that no disputed territory on the frontier or at Rendsburg would be occupied. Rendsburg will be occupied, with the exception of that portion which is on the north side of the Eider."

And here I must remind the noble Earl that his geography is rather weak, and that the mouth of the Eider is not in the Baltic.

EARL RUSSELL: I never said it was.

THE EARL OF DERBY: I beg the noble Earl's pardon. My noble Friend near me had been speaking of the ease with which a British fleet might be sent to the Eider; and the noble Earl replied that it was impossible to do that because of the extreme difficulty of sending ships into the Baltic at this time of year. Sir Andrew Buchanan then went on to say—

"I was instructed to state that the execution should only take place for Federal obligations violated. The execution will take place in virtue of a decree of the German Diet, against which Her Majesty's Government have formally protested at Frankfort, by a despatch communicated officially to the Governments of Austria and Prussia. Lastly, I was instructed to request that the Prussian Government would consult with that of Austria, and state to Lord Wodehouse precisely what Austria and Prussia will require to bring about a friendly disposition on both sides, but they have declined to give any explanation of the arrangements which they would accept from Denmark."

Here, then, are four or five points on which the noble Earl has desired Sir Andrew Buchanan to make strong representations in the hope of staying the war, every one of which is contumeliously rejected by the German Powers. And here I find two lines on which I think it would have been wiser if the noble Earl had employed his scissors, which have been so freely applied in other parts of the papers. I find Sir Alexander Malet writing thus to the noble Earl from Frankfort—

"There is an absolute persuasion that England will not interfere materially, and our counsels, regarded as unfriendly, have no weight."

I think the noble Earl did succeed in frightening for a moment one Minister—the Prussian Minister. On the 14th of January the noble Earl thus describes, in writing to Lord Bloomfield, what had passed between him and Count Bernstorff—

"I had spoken on a former occasion in the sense that Denmark would resist such an occupation (of Schleswig), and might be aided by Great Britain. He wished to have an explanation. It is to be observed that, in speaking to Count Bernstorff on the occasion referred to, I had expressly declared that I could not say what the decision

of the Government might be, as the Cabinet had not yet deliberated, and consequently not submitted any opinion to the Queen; but that, judging from the general current of feeling in Parliament and in the nation, I thought an invasion of Schleswig by Germany might lead to assistance to Denmark on the part of this country. . . . . .
Her Majesty's Government could not wonder that the King of Denmark was ready to defend Schleswig, and to consider its hostile occupation as a fatal blow to the integrity of his dominions. But I could not doubt that he would be assisted by Powers friendly to Denmark in that defence.— *Correspondence*, No. 4 (1864), p. 534.

Now the charge made against the Government is that, being without any decided policy of their own, they came to Parliament for a policy, and without having formed any judgment of their own, they deliberately resolved to be guided by the apparent views of Parliament and the country. Here is a statement which throws the strongest light on this charge. We have the noble Earl informing the Prussian Minister that Her Majesty's Cabinet had not consulted on the subject, and that consequently they were not prepared to recommend any policy to the Queen. To Denmark, therefore, we have the noble Earl holding out expectations that if she complied with certain advice she will obtain material assistance, and to Prussia we have him saying—and he caused this apprehension in the mind of the Prussian Minister—that in the event of Schleswig being occupied, Denmark would find herself assisted in her defence by friendly Powers. The Prussian Minister seemed rather startled at first, having in the course of the correspondence pressed upon the noble Earl the special evils of Germany. To that the noble Earl replied that he was quite aware of that; but that Germany had had plenty of time to consider that, and must take all the responsibility. As soon as Count Bernstorff heard the old familiar words, "take all the responsibility," he was relieved at once, and drew the very natural conclusion—England will never interfere, and will content herself with throwing on us the responsibility. So it has been throughout all these transactions. Step by step the measures protested against in the strongest terms by the noble Earl and his Government, are adopted; the modest application for delay that the King might do that legally which he could not do otherwise, was rejected; the Federal execution grows into a material guarantee, and at last into an invasion and occupation of the country without a declaration of war, and accompanied with

The Earl of Derby

scenes of barbarity and ferocity almost unparalleled in civilised war. I regret to find that that spirit of destruction is not yet extinct in the Prussian army, which caused so much anxiety to the Duke of Wellington in 1814, and which he had so much difficulty in restraining. The bombardment of Sönderborg is an act of unparalleled ferocity if it be true, as I have heard, that after the bombardment had once ceased, and the inhabitants were tempted to return to seek among the ruins for the remnants of their property, they found themselves in a trap, and the bombardment was again opened on them. I hope the noble Earl will be able to tell us, that from the information forwarded to him he knows that this atrocious story is not true, or, at least, that it is greatly exaggerated, and that the Prussians have not drawn upon their arms the ineffaceable stain which would rest on them if this atrocity had been committed. I wish I could see in the proposed Conference any prospect of a prosperous issue. It certainly does not assemble under the most favourable auspices. The two principal parties concerned come out with declarations diametrically opposed to each other. One party declares that she will not listen to any proposal for the abrogation of the Treaty of 1852, and the others insist that Denmark shall perform the engagements of 1851-2, yet say that they will be by no means satisfied to leave Denmark in so desirable a position as she was left in by that treaty. Now the engagements of 1851 and 1852 were different. [Earl RUSSELL: They were one arrangement.] No; the arrangement of 1851 was between Russia, Austria, and Denmark; whilst that of 1852 was between all the great Powers, and did not make the slightest reference to the previous arrangement. Besides, one was a treaty, and the other was a sort of agreement, sanctioned by a correspondence of a very loose character, capable of various interpretations, and by no means a sound basis for such an important matter. Therefore, while I hold that the engagements of 1851-2 are very fair and legitimate grounds for conference negotiation, and mediation if necessary, they must never be confounded with the Treaty of 1852, the sole and only object of which was to settle the succession, and to ensure the continuance of the Danish dominions under one sovereign. I was glad to hear that the noble Earl used the expression which showed that he did not confine himself to what should be done to maintain the integrity of Denmark, but that the object was also to ensure the independence of that country. I can conceive that there might be arrangements to secure the dominions under the same sovereign, and yet those arrangements might be such that the independence of Denmark might be altogether sacrificed. From the statement of the noble Earl we are entitled to hope that England will go into this Conference with no undue preference for either party, and that her whole endeavour will be to secure fair and equitable terms for both sides. I wish I could feel the same confidence with regard to some of the other Powers, and in the motives and objects with which they will enter into the Conference. Above all, I wish the Conference had not been delayed so long, and that if an armistice could not have been obtained before the Conference assembled, it had been determined that at its first sitting, and as a preliminary, terms should be proposed by which an end would be put to this bloodthirsty war. I do justice to the motives which have actuated the noble Earl throughout the whole of this correspondence. I cannot, however, conceal from myself my conviction that, by the strength of his remonstrances, and the feebleness of his acts, he has confirmed the impression so prevalent throughout Europe, that we have ceased to be a great Power, that our military and naval position has been made subordinate to our trading and commercial interests; and that, however England may bluster, and however loudly she may talk, there is not the slightest danger of her interfering materially to exercise the slightest influence or control in the affairs of Europe.

Lord WODEHOUSE: My Lords, as I have been referred to several times in the course of this debate for the part I have taken in some part of these transactions, I must be allowed to say a very few words by way of explanation, without wishing to enter at length into the discussion which has taken place. The noble Earl who has just sat down referred several times to the assurances which, he said, though they might not have been directly given, were to be inferred from the language which I held at Copenhagen — assurances that the Danish Government might expect the material support of this country if they followed our advice. The noble Earl said that care had been taken not to give direct assurances. Now, I think the best proof that the Danish Government have not understood my language in this sense, is to be found in a despatch written by Sir Augustus Paget to the noble Earl the Foreign Secretary, on the 22nd of December. In that despatch you will find that the Danish Minister had never inferred that such a promise was given to him, for Sir Augustus Paget mentions that in the interview he had with M. Hall, immediately after the joint interview M. d'Ewers and myself had with him, M. Hall complained that " there was no promise of support if Germany continued her aggressions; there was no prospect even of the execution being arrested." My instructions, certainly, were not to give any such promise, and if I had done so, I should not have obeyed my instructions. I think a conclusive proof that no such assurances were given, is to be found in the constant complaints of the Danish Government that Her Majesty's Government would not give them a promise of support, although they advised them to make certain concessions to Germany. I wish to say a word or two on another point. My noble Friend the Secretary for Foreign Affairs has said, I not only advised that the Constitution should be revoked, but he thought my own opinion was the Constitution ought not to be carried into effect. In that supposition he is quite correct. My noble Friend, knowing that my sympathies were not very strong with Germany, asked me to examine carefully the Constitution of November, and, having done so, I came to the conclusion that it was expedient for the Danish Government to revoke it. My sympathies were with the Danes, and I would not have undertaken the mission which Her Majesty was pleased to confide in me, if I thought the advice which I was authorized to give was not such as Denmark ought to follow. I think no advice was given to her which it would not have been for her advantage to follow; but, though she did ultimately consent to follow the advice we gave her, unfortunately she consented too late. Throughout those negotiations—not only those which took place while I was discharging my mission, but throughout the whole of them—all the concessions made by Denmark have invariably been made when they were too late. I pressed that very strongly on the Danish Government. I said, "If you make concessions, make them early;" but I cannot conceal from myself, while no man admires more the courage and constancy of the Danish people, that they have not been well advised by the Government which has presided over their destinies. In the first place, the Danish Government attempted more than Denmark could accomplish; they attempted to bring Schleswig into closer union with Denmark, in order to consolidate the kingdom, but not remembering that, however desirable, as regards Denmark, that might be, they had entered into engagements with Germany, the non-fulfilment of which, however onerous and inconvenient they might be, must lead to a very unequal contest. The opinion which I held when I was advising the Danish Government I now, viewing matters with the light of subsequent events, hold more strongly still. I think that it would have been far better for the Danish Government, by making timely concessions, to have entered into negotiations, while in the possession of Schleswig, than to have provoked a war and been compelled to enter into them with Schleswig in the hands of the German Powers. It may be very fairly said in reply, that the conduct of the German Powers has been bad. I admit that it has been marked by great duplicity as well as violence; but I still think that if Denmark had pursued another course, she would have had a fair chance of obtaining a Conference before Schleswig passed out of her hands. My noble Friend (Earl Grey) expressed his surprize, that in my conferences with M. von Bismark, and others, I did not make use of an argument which he suggested. I am exceedingly sorry that it did not occur to me, as perhaps it might have produced more effect than those which I did use. I used a great many arguments, but, I regret to say, they appeared to make very little impression upon M. Von Bismark. I think the fact is that the Prussian Government materially changed their policy at the last moment. When the death of the late King of Denmark took place, the Prussian Government, alarmed at the strong democratic feeling of the party which was making use of this Schleswig-Holstein question for its own ulterior purposes, thought that the best way out of the difficulty was to attack Denmark. Having acquiesced in the proceedings of Denmark with regard to the new constitution up to the King's death, Prussia found out suddenly that she could not acquiesce in them for a single day longer. The noble Earl who has just sat down (the Earl of Derby) pointed out most

truly that it would be a complete mistake and most impolitic to admit that the engagements of 1851 were to be connected with the Treaty of 1852. The engagements of 1851-2 were entered into by Austria and Prussia with Denmark, and the other Powers of Europe were not parties to them; whereas the treaty of 1852 was a European engagement, entered into by the Great Powers, in which no reference was made to the engagements of 1851-2. It might be all very well for the German Powers to argue, that it was because they entered into certain engagements in 1851-52 that they signed the Treaty of 1852. That might have been in their minds; but it was not in the treaty, and by that treaty they were bound. I now wish to say one or two words with respect to the difficult question as to what ought or ought not to have been done to prevent the war. In alluding to that subject, I must say that I cannot conceal from myself that the position of the Government has been materially injured by the policy pursued with respect to Poland. When that policy was under discussion in your Lordships' House, I abstained from saying anything on the subject; but it then seemed to me from the first that serious consequences must follow if, after entering into a diplomatic correspondence with Russia in conjunction with Austria and France, the Government should be compelled to withdraw — wisely, I admit, but under circumstances which could not but weaken, to some extent, the good understanding which exists between this country and France; an understanding which I deem essential, particularly in the present state of Europe, to the maintenance of treaties and the balance of power. At the time, I thought it not probable that Russia would give way to any mere remonstrances with respect to the Poles; and that being so, it would in my opinion have been far better if our Government had confined itself to a protest and had not exposed itself to that rebuff. I hope that in the case of Denmark this country will have again the full co-operation of France, without which I despair of seeing this question satisfactorily and speedily settled. If this co-operation should not be obtained, and if the Conference should unfortunately fail in settling the question, a grievous shock will be given to the whole system under the protection of which the treaties of Europe exist; because these treaties exist and are preserved by the concert and understanding which exist among the Great Powers of Europe; and if that understanding be permanently impaired, Europe will be thrown into a state of anarchy. I do not agree with my noble Friend (Earl Grey), that it would have been better to have attempted, by a display of force, to prevent the attack by the German Powers on Schleswig, and I concurred in all that has fallen from the noble Secretary for Foreign Affairs, as to its not being obligatory on this country to interfere alone. It may be said that the despatch of a body of British troops to the scene of action would have stopped the German invasion; but a wise statesman would consider what must have been the result if that policy failed. Neither the interest nor the honour of this country was engaged in such a manner that the Government ought to have incurred so great a risk as a war with Germany. It is, of course, possible that we might have averted the war by announcing our determination to take a part in it if it should be commenced by Germany; but we had no right to presume that such a result would have followed; and the Government were quite right not to come to any such resolution upon the mere chance that it would have saved us from responsibilities which we were not absolutely prepared to encounter. The position in which this country, France, and Russia are now left inspire me with considerable doubt as to the expediency of such treaties as that of 1852, which, although they have not directly the character of guarantees, are quasi-guarantees, the non-fulfilment of which casts a certain amount of discredit on those Powers who are parties to them. The reputation of this country on the Continent has been referred to, and I entirely concur in the remark that this country should not unnecessarily interfere in the various affairs of Europe. My opinion is that the British Government should interfere in them as seldom as possible; but, if led to interfere, it should be in a manner to make the country respected.

EARL GRANVILLE: My Lords, when my noble Friend the Secretary for Foreign Affairs appealed the other night to the discretion of this House, I own it appeared to me that on this question there was one of two courses to be taken. If the House were of opinion that the present Ministers have so entirely neglected the interests and honour of the country in the negotiations which have been carried on, and are likely to neglect them for the future, then the House should take some strong mea-

sure for the purpose of removing them from office; but if the House were not of that opinion, the other course, obviously, is to endeavour to strengthen their hands in the Conference in which they will have to meet the representatives of the other Powers. The speech of the noble Earl opposite (the Earl of Derby) gave me in many respects great satisfaction. The noble Earl certainly showed a desire not to raise difficulties in the way of the success of the Conference; but, at the same time, I must say I think the noble Earl would have done better if he had abstained from throwing doubt on the probability of the Conference terminating successfully. I must express my satisfaction at hearing the noble Earl declare that he had read the whole of the papers laid on the table. We all know what an acute eye the noble Earl has to discover a flaw, and, therefore, it was very satisfactory to find that the blame attributed to my noble Friend the Foreign Secretary, and to the Government, was so very small. The noble Earl opposite began with the regular cut and dry phrase about my noble Friend's style, and then he gave my noble Friend credit for diligence; and, though the noble Earl spoke with something like contempt of the continued attempts of the Government to prevent the war and bloodshed which have taken place, and to stop it for the future, I think that he would have expressed great indignation if it had appeared that we had not used every exertion in our power to prevent so unfortunate a state of things. The noble Earl says we are perpetually spinning cobwebs and never catching flies. I entirely deny that, and I say we have caught some flies. In the first place, we secured those declarations from Austria and Prussia with regard to the Treaty of 1852, and the maintenance of the integrity and independence of Denmark which, I think, are of very considerable importance. By our endeavours we also got Austria and Prussia to agree to an armistice, although Denmark, for reasons of her own, declined to accede to that armistice. Moreover, chiefly, I believe, owing to the exertions of my noble Friend, seconded as he has been by France and Russia, we are going in a few days into a Conference, and it is the opinion of Her Majesty's Government, and the opinion, also, not only of France and Russia, but of Prussia and Austria, that one of the first objects of the Conference should be to secure an armistice. The noble Earl has tried to pick out the plums from an enormous cake; but he has sought to draw some inferences from these papers which I entirely dispute. He says he could not find in them anything to show that we had given any pledge of assistance to Denmark. That is sufficiently disposed of by the speech of M. Hall, to which my noble Friend has referred. With regard to another most important point—namely, that we had given the Germans to understand that by no means and on no score would we go to war on this question, I defy the noble Earl to point out any passage in the papers before Parliament, indicating that we have given any such assurance whatever. On the contrary, these papers show that we actually pledged ourselves that, if France and Russia would agree with us, we would render material aid to Denmark. That was a species of combination which, I believe, would have tended entirely to avert the existing difficulties. The noble Earl (Earl Grey), speaking certainly without any evidence derived from the papers, thinks that France was prepared to give material aid. Now, I believe that France was quite determined from the beginning to do nothing of that kind; and when the noble Earl says that we ought to have used menace, and grounded his opinion principally on the assumption that that menace would have been effectual for its purpose, I must say I cannot at all concur with him. How has this war been decided upon by Germany? It is a remarkable fact that various reasons, some of them aristocratic, and some democratic, have combined to carry away these States into a war which is deeply to be deplored, but which I think it would have been impossible for any statesman to prevent; and I am not in the least convinced that the menace of sending a few men to Denmark and ordering a squadron to cruise outside —for it would not have been able to go into—the Baltic would itself have sufficed to stop all chance of war, especially when the States of Germany were intoxicated with delight at finding that there existed one subject on which there was perfect union among them; and when, moreover, they knew that France was determined not to join us, and that Russia, too, was unwilling to separate herself entirely from Austria and Prussia. Then the noble Earl (Earl Grey) told us that this country has lowered itself in consequence of its unwillingness to go to war.

EARL GREY: I never said anything of the sort.

Earl Granville

EARL GRANVILLE: The noble Earl in a previous debate gave me a similar contradiction to this, and I found afterwards, on looking at the report of his speech, that I had correctly quoted him. Now, I cannot help feeling struck by the contrast presented by the language held by the noble Earl on this question and that which he has for many years held with respect to the policy which ought to be adopted by this country. If any Member of this House has more strongly than another condemned menaces of war, or uttered more eloquent denunciations against the Quixotic idea of England's undertaking to redress injuries and injustice throughout the world, it is the noble Earl himself. I have heard him argue that this country was all the stronger not only for abstaining from going to war, but even for not spending her money to prepare the armaments necessary for war; yet now, he comes down and twits us because we have acted in consonance with the language held by every statesman who has governed this country for close upon half a century, every one of whom having announced in the clearest way to Europe and the world that, although they should always be prepared to uphold the honour and interests of the nation at all hazards, said that nothing but urgent necessity should draw them into war. The noble Earl referred to Mr. Canning's conduct in respect to Portugal. In the very speech in which he defended the expedition to Portugal I think Mr. Canning distinctly stated, that but for the necessity imposed by treaty engagements, he would not have gone into that war—that he felt that war ought not to be undertaken because it was just, but, to justify entering into it, it must also be urgent and expedient. The noble Earl's father, whether in Opposition or in office, clung on every possible occasion to the policy of maintaining peace. Lord Aberdeen's earnestness in the same endeavour is well known; and the noble Earl opposite (the Earl of Derby) and his Colleagues when in power exhibited equal anxiety in their foreign policy for the preservation of peace. I am surprised, then, at the noble Earl coming down to the House and holding up the Government to derision for having hitherto kept their hands quite free, as I maintain they now are, to take any part in European matters which they may think fit. By our carefully avoiding to involve ourselves in war up to this moment, I believe that much advantage is gained to the country and to

Europe. We wish it to be understood that we are desirous for peace ; that we are unfettered by any engagement which could prevent us from taking any course that we might deem expedient ; but that as long as we can see any chance of securing our object without war, we will not depart from a policy which has been perfectly consistent both before and since the meeting of Parliament.

EARL GREY wished to explain. His objection to the policy of the Government was, that it was a policy of expedients, which could lead to no useful result. He held that if we had taken a more decided part in the first instance we should have rendered an attack unlikely, and have been in a position to speak to the Powers of Europe with greater weight and authority.

EARL RUSSELL wished to say a few words relative to the bombardment of Sönderborg. There was no doubt as to the fact of that bombardment ; the only question was as to the notice given. It was stated by the Prussian Government that they had given a general notice—I think, some weeks ago—that Sönderborg being part of the fortress of Duppel was liable to bombardment. It appeared to him that that justification—if so it was called—was perfectly insufficient, because the people of Sönderborg naturally would not act on a general notice, but supposed they would have received, according to the usages of war, a special notice of twenty-four hours.

LORD CAMPBELL said, he could not expect to gain the indulgence of the House at so late an hour, as they were not expecting a division and none was likely to occur. The remarks of a noble Duke, now absent from his place (the Duke of Argyll), called imperatively for a word of observation, or he (Lord Campbell) would be silent. The noble Duke, a Member of the Cabinet, had openly endeavoured to overthrow the guarantee of Schleswig, as bearing only on a portion of that duchy. It was true that in one of the instruments containing it, it was confined to that part of Schleswig "now in the possession" of the King of Denmark. But in other instruments there was no such limit. And those who had referred to this ancient point were of opinion that the whole mainland was in possession of the King of Denmark in 1720. Beyond this, it was admitted on all hands that the guarantee applied to the southern portion of the Duchy. It came into force, therefore, the moment that the Eider was crossed by an invader. If the position of

the noble Duke was tenable, the guarantee would not have found fifteen years ago, in the First Minister and Foreign Secretary of the present day, unreserved and unhesitating champions. Whatever the noble Duke had urged, if applicable now, was applicable to that period. As regards the debate, he (Lord Campbell) saw no reason to regret it. Not one noble Lord had answered his remarks as to the necessity of further measures to give the Conference a prospect of succeeding. And neither the noble Lord the Foreign Secretary, nor the noble Lord the President of the Council, had objected to the specific course which he proposed, namely, that of occupying Kiel by British vessels.

Motion (by leave of the House) *withdrawn.*

House adjourned at a quarter before Eleven o'clock, till To-morrow, half past Ten o'clock.

HOUSE OF COMMONS,

Monday, April 11, 1864.

MINUTES]—NEW MEMBER SWORN—The Right Honourable Edward Cardwell, *for* Oxford City.
SELECT COMMITTEE—Scientific Institutions (Dublin).
SUPPLY—*considered in Committee*—ARMY ESTIMATES.
PUBLIC BILLS — *Ordered*— Church Building and New Parishes Acts.
First Reading—Thames Conservancy * [Bill 60] ; Church Building and New Parishes Acts Amendment * [Bill 61].
Second Reading—Common Law Procedure (Ireland) Act (1853) Amendment * [Bill 43].
Referred to Select Committee—Government Annuities [Bill 11], Adjourned Debate [17th March] *resumed.*
Third Reading—Warehousing of British Spirits * [Bill 54], and *passed.*

THE HIGHWAYS ACT.—QUESTION.

MR. LIDDELL said, he would beg to ask the Secretary of State for the Home Department, Whether it is the intention of Her Majesty's Government to move for the appointment of a Committee of Inquiry into the operation of the Highways Act, previous to introducing further legislation on the subject, or any amendments of the said Act?

SIR GEORGE GREY, in reply, said, he thought an inquiry would be desirable before they attempted to make any extensive change in the law relating to Highways; but although the Act was in operation in a great many parts of the kingdom, yet it had not been so for a sufficiently long period to test its effects. He was, therefore, afraid that an inquiry by a Committee would necessarily be an imperfect one, owing to the want of experience of the working of the measure. He could not, therefore, propose a Committee of Inquiry in the present Session. The amended Bill, which he hoped to introduce, would not be an extensive measure, but only intended to remedy some defects found to exist in certain districts of the country, and which were said to interfere with the useful operation of the law.

DENMARK AND GERMANY—THE CONFERENCE.—QUESTION.

MR. HORSMAN: Sir, I have a question to put to the noble Lord at the head of the Government with respect to the coming Conference on the affairs of Denmark. I assume that in the Conference our representative may undertake certain engagements on the part of England which will not be valid until ratified by the Crown in the exercise of its prerogative under the advice of its responsible Ministers. The question I have to ask is, Whether Ministers, before they determine upon the advice they shall give to the Crown, will submit such engagements to the consideration of Parliament, so as to obtain the consent of Parliament before they advise their ratification by the Crown?

VISCOUNT PALMERSTON: Sir, my right hon. Friend is no doubt well aware that, in a mixed Constitution like ours, each branch has its separate functions, though those functions are very often so interwoven with one another that it is very difficult to draw a definite line between them. Nothing but great forbearance on the part of each branch enables the aggregate whole to work harmoniously as a Government. But there are matters in respect to which the line is distinct, precise, understood, and acknowledged. Such is the case with regard to the functions of negotiating and making treaties with Foreign Powers. That function is known to be distinctly with the Crown, acting under the advice of its responsible Ministers; and if the case should arise which is contemplated by my right hon. Friend, of which I am not at all aware, we should deem it our duty to adhere

Sir George Grey

strictly to the spirit and practice of the Constitution.

MR. HORSMAN: I hope the noble Lord will excuse me, but I am afraid I have not made my question quite intelligible. I know, of course, that the Government would adhere, in whatever course they may adopt, to the principles and practice of the Constitution; but my question has reference to the practice of the Constitution so far as this, that the Crown exercises its prerogative under the advice of its responsible Ministers, and that those Ministers act under the control and advice of Parliament. I therefore wish to know whether Her Majesty's Ministers, before tendering their advice to the Crown, will give Parliament an opportunity of considering it?

VISCOUNT PALMERSTON: I thought my answer went precisely to that point. It is not the practice, nor is it in accordance with the principles of the Constitution, that the Crown should ask the advice of its Parliament with respect to engagements which it may be advised are proper to be contracted. I ought, perhaps, to have added something with regard to the question of my right hon. Friend, whether, if the Plenipotentiary of England in the Conference should agree to certain engagements which would afterwards have to be ratified by the Crown, Parliament would be consulted between those two events. My right hon. Friend must be aware, that by international usage, the only ground upon which a Sovereign can refuse to ratify engagements made by a duly authorized Plenipotentiary, acting of course upon instructions, is that he has entered into such engagements either without instructions or against instructions. There is a Conference to be held in London, and it is not to be supposed that my noble Friends who are to represent this country will act either without instructions or against instructions.

MR. HORSMAN: Is there any case of exceeding instructions?

VISCOUNT PALMERSTON: If a Plenipotentiary goes beyond his instructions he does that which is not authorized by his instructions, and therefore he acts either without instructions or against instructions.

THE ARMY ESTIMATES.—NOTICE.

THE MARQUESS OF HARTINGTON said, he wished to give notice, that in the event of his not being able to get Votes to-night in Committee of Supply on the Army Estimates, he should ask the House to pass a Vote on account to-morrow evening.

LORD HOTHAM said, he wished to know whether the noble Lord intended to limit himself to-morrow night to asking for a Vote on account, or whether he proposed to take his chance of the double event of getting a Vote in Supply and taking a Vote on account?

THE MARQUESS OF HARTINGTON said, they hoped to be able to get a Vote in Supply that night, but if they were not able to do so, he would ask the House to give them a Vote on account.

GOVERNMENT ANNUITIES BILL—
[BILL 11].
COMMITTEE. ADJOURNED DEBATE.

Order read, for resuming Adjourned Debate on Amendment proposed to Question [17th March], "That Mr. Speaker do now leave the Chair;" and which Amendment was, to leave out from the word "That" to the end of the Question, in order to add the words "The Bill be committed to a Select Committee," — (*Sir Minto Farquhar,*)—instead thereof.

Question again proposed, "That the words proposed to be left out stand part of the Question."

Debate *resumed.*

MR. AYRTON said, he should be glad to promote any proceeding which might lead to practical legislation on the subject of Insurances for the working classes, but the question before the House was not whether they should legislate for the evils that had long existed in regard to the conduct of Assurance Societies, but whether they should at once pass the Bill of the Chancellor of the Exchequer without any inquiry, and without satisfying themselves by any authentic means or evidence of the reasonable character and necessity for passing that Bill. He was in favour of the proposition of the hon. Gentleman opposite for a Select Committee. The Chancellor of the Exchequer had thought proper to make important statements involving very grave imputations upon existing institutions. No doubt hon. Members connected with those institutions would be able to defend whatever admitted of defence in the conduct of their affairs, but he was bound to ask himself whether, supposing the statements of the Chancellor of the Exchequer were true, they afforded

any reason for the Bill under consideration. Supposing, as stated by the Chancellor of the Exchequer, there had been an immense collapse of Life Assurance Companies within the last eighteen years, it only proved that there had been great eagerness to carry on that business; for, besides that great collapse, no less than 220 companies were projected in the same time, and did not even take root so far as to be regarded as having been founded. It proved that thousands of persons had been ready to embark in business of assurance of all kinds, but the market was so overstocked by the companies already formed, of standing and position, that they were not able to obtain sufficient custom to keep them alive. But if that was so, what necessity was there for the Government to interfere in that business? The right hon. Gentleman said that many of these societies conducted their business badly, but he really had not entered sufficiently into the merits of the question. Many Assurance Societies with large capital, and resting on a solid foundation, rejected for the most part the small premiums paid by the working classes, because they knew that that branch of business was attended with such risks and difficulties as would probably involve more loss than gain to them. Surely, then, the State ought to hesitate before it embarked in operations which men accustomed to large undertakings shrank from. The right hon. Gentleman sought to enlist the favour of the House for the measure by citing the success attained by his Post Office savings banks; but so far from the results of their legislation relating to savings banks affording any support to the Bill, they went rather to establish an opposite conclusion. There used, no doubt, to be great abuses in the management of savings banks, and it was necessary to legislate on the subject. Chancellors of the Exchequer, some time ago, without correcting these evils, brought forward measures which those who managed these institutions thought necessarily tended to put an end to them. Consequently, the proceedings of those Chancellors of the Exchequer were opposed in that House; and the right hon. Member for Wiltshire (Mr. Sotheron Estcourt), in order to defeat the late Sir George Lewis, moved for a Committee of Inquiry. The Committee sat, and found that the savings of the whole body of the working classes were, to a considerable extent, imperilled from defective legislation. The Government ought at once to have taken the Report of that Committee into consideration, and proposed a law giving adequate protection to the deposits of the people. But, though asked to bring in a Bill founded on that Report, the Chancellor of the Exchequer refused; and why? Because he had conceived the project of establishing Post Office savings banks. He, therefore, felt himself at liberty to neglect all the warnings given by that inquiry, and contented himself with setting up a rivalry between the Government and the existing savings banks. That was an abandonment of the duty incumbent on a responsible Minister of the Crown, of watching over the general interests of the people; and it ought to operate as a caution to them against a repetition of the same error in regard to Friendly and Benefit Societies. It had been left to him and one or two other private Members to deal with the subject which the Chancellor of the Exchequer ought to have taken up, and they had to bring in a Bill to amend and consolidate the law relating to savings banks. The first difficulty they had to encounter was the impossibility under which private Members laboured of passing through the House a Bill of that character, unless they cut it down to the narrowest possible limits; and, therefore, they were obliged to reject several valuable provisions for a reform of these institutions. The hon. Member for Oldham (Mr. Hibbert) had proposed that the savings banks might be made to facilitate the system of small Life Assurances for the people; but the promoters of the Bill were unable to entertain that suggestion. The Chancellor of the Exchequer did not undertake the responsibility of dealing with it; and so the people were deprived of that most legitimate opportunity of using the savings banks effectually for carrying out the very objects which the right hon. Gentleman now had in view. That illustrated the necessity of keeping the Government from operations like this, which could be and were managed by institutions wholly apart from the State. But the right hon. Gentleman said the Post Office savings banks had been very successful, and by their rivalry had improved the administration of private institutions. Now, he denied that proposition. In 1858, when the agitation which had existed against the savings banks generally was put an end to, the deposits in the savings banks were

Mr. Ayrton

£36,200,000; and from 1858 to 1860, being a period of only two years, after confidence had been restored, they increased no less than five millions sterling. From 1860 to the present time, since the Chancellor of the Exchequer declined to take upon his shoulders the responsibility of watching over these institutions, and set up as a rival in their business instead, what had been the result? In 1860 the gross capital was £41,258,000; and in 1863 that gross capital was £41,237,000; being a decrease of £21,000. It was a great question, then, whether the Post Office Savings Banks Bill had been any great advantage at all. But a possible future evil might arise from the Post Office savings banks. Let them once reach the position of having a capital such as could be felt in the money market in London; let them be as successful as other savings banks had been, and let there be 40 millions accumulated and payable on demand, and he ventured to predict that it would be in the power of any man, however insignificant, in a time when the interest for money was high and the wealthy got 5 or 6 per cent, to raise a cry that the poor were only getting $2\frac{1}{2}$ per cent, and that cry would re-echo through the kingdom, and there was not a merchant or banker in that House who would not go down on his knees and beg that that $2\frac{1}{2}$ per cent should be made 3 or 4 per cent to save the country from the consequences of the demand that must necessarily arise for the payment of that money. The danger incident to that mode of legislation was that it brought the people face to face with the Government, and there would be no intermediate moral influence operating such as existed in regard to all other savings banks, in the case of which, moreover, there were legal restrictions which would prevent such a contingency arising. The whole tendency of these transactions with reference to savings banks warned them to be careful as to what they should do on the present occasion. To his mind they afforded a conclusive argument in favour of the most full and complete investigation of the merits and application of the Bill before them. He wished the Chancellor of the Exchequer, in moving the second reading, had not made any reference to the efforts of working men for improving the condition of their fellows; for, whatever he might think of the labours of such persons, there could be no doubt they had been far more useful than extreme freetraders were apt to imagine. No doubt there had been an immense development of industry as the result of free trade; but, to use the language of Adam Smith, the higher they carried organized industry the greater the degradation they might inflict on the people; and he believed that result would have been seen in England but for the labours of those who had associated themselves for the purpose of having their labour respected, and compelling employers to conduct themselves with some regard to moral restraints. It was a pity, then, that the Chancellor of the Exchequer had spoken in so disparaging a tone of Mr. Potter, a man who was admired and respected by the working classes, and those who were associated with him. Such remarks were likely to give reason to suspect the motives for the introduction of the measure, and it was to be regretted that the right hon. Gentleman had not made a more complete and frank apology to the House than he had yet done. He had evinced an amount of ill-feeling which was wholly unnecessary for the purposes of his Bill. With respect to that class of Assurance Societies that were likely to be affected by the Bill, the Chancellor of the Exchequer had thrown a cloud of odium upon them by speaking of them as creatures of the State, subsidized by considerable bounties; but he did not explain in his usual clear manner what he meant by those statements. Friendly Societies received, some of them, rates of interest higher than those which now prevailed; but that was only the result of past errors of the right hon. Gentleman's predecessors in office, and was not to be regarded as a boon given at the present moment. The Government had no alternative but to adhere to its engagements to these societies. These were founded upon the then current rate of interest, and no precautions had been taken that, when it was reduced, the societies should submit to a corresponding reduction in the rate they received. It could not, therefore, be said that these institutions were subsidized by the State, but that the country was paying for the errors of past legislation. It could not be said that these institutions were really subsidized by the State in the shape of small exemptions from taxation; they were rather relieved from what would otherwise be an unjust and oppressive burden. When it was recollected for what purpose they were established, he did not think these institutions should be described as protected societies, using the old shibboleth of Protection in its invidious signification. They were not protected in the sense of an abuse of protection; they only enjoyed the requisite securities for carrying out their most beneficent design. But these institutions, it was said, were badly managed, and the only way to remedy that evil was for the Chancellor of the Exchequer to have a model institution of his own, and leave some 20,000 institutions, in which hundreds of thousands of persons were interested, entirely at the mercy of accident and circumstances on the grand principle that free trade would bring about a cure. That was a most dangerous doctrine to accept in all the latitude of its announcement by the Chancellor of the Exchequer. What were the evils of the Friendly Societies? If they carefully and minutely examined into the matter, they would be able to arrive at the conclusion that there were specific general heads of mismanagement, which being cured, all the rest that was necessary would follow as a consequence. They might be summed up in two or three remarks, and illustrated in a thousand different ways, but they would result in two or three simple points in the end. He granted that it was true that they were ignorantly established with insufficient tables to accumulate the funds necessary to meet liabilities; and great loss and misery had in some instances ensued. But was there no remedy? If the Chancellor of the Exchequer's Bill was sound, they would be told there was an ample remedy. The Chancellor of the Exchequer, it was said, had arrived at a theory and a principle that he could construct a table for working men's assurance that would operate of itself without any special knowledge of circumstances, and free from all risk and danger. If there was that patent table—if the nation could adopt it and make it the foundation of a new law, and work it out for all the people of England, was it not the duty of the House to see that the same table was made compulsory on these Assurance Companies? But others would say that the Bill was unsound, and that they could not have a universal table that would be self-working without loss or inconvenience. If so, there was an end of the argument. That was one difficulty. Then it was said the people suffered on account of lapsed policies.

He was really surprised to find the Chancellor of the Exchequer had fallen into this error of puffing Assurance Companies. The objection was evidently unsound when it came to be examined in detail. Of course, every one who paid and allowed his policy to lapse contributed something and got nothing in return; the accumulated fund was thus greatly increased; and if there was no lapse the companies would be obliged to charge a great deal more. In order to show how fallacious was the great argument about lapsed policies, he would refer to what had taken place under the present system. By the existing law a man could purchase an annuity absolutely, without any claim to a contingent return of payments, or he might purchase one upon certain conditions, giving him the power to receive back a certain amount. Thus it appeared from the Government tables, that if a man aged twenty-two wished to secure himself an annuity of £12 when he attained the age of sixty, and was willing to run the risk of the policy lapsing before the time of his receiving the benefit derived, he would have to pay 2s. per month. If, however, he desired to reserve to himself the power of getting back, under any contingency, the money he had paid, he would be required to pay 3s. per month. Thus, by the Government system, as it now existed, a man who chose to run the risk of his policy lapsing, could insure for 50 per cent less than under the other arrangement. But if there was a doubt of the view taken by the great bulk of the people as to this great evil of lapsing policies, he would again refer to the practice under the existing system. There had been, up to the present time, 10,800 annuities granted, amounting to £219,000 per annum, for which no less than £2,522,000 had been paid. But under the other arrangement, of insuring against the lapse of policies, only £59,000 had been paid for annuities. It was plain, therefore, that the boon of guarding against lapse of policies was regarded by the public as merely nominal and illusory. Then, again, it had been said that the expense of the management of the Friendly Societies had been very great. That was true, but he feared that it was impossible for any society to avoid large expenses when engaged in minute transactions with the people. It was impossible to persuade people that it was for their interest to take their pence every week or month to the Insurance Office to pay the premiums; but they would have a collecting agent to call at their houses, although the cost of such a proceeding entailed upon them a charge of 25 per cent. If the officers of any of those societies were asked upon that point, they would state that if they did not go themselves to gather the pence, their business would speedily come to nothing. It was the same with these offices as it was with the baker, and although it was possible for him to make a 4lb. loaf, the people were not satisfied they had their weight unless they had a bit of bread over. It was impossible to alter the habits of the people, and it was useless to complain that the present mode of insuring was expensive, nor was that a reason for Government interference. Another objection, and a strong one, was that the smaller Friendly Societies conducted their business at public-houses. That was an objectionable state of things, but it was not an evil that could not be got rid of. If Parliament were to enact that it should be illegal for these societies to hold their meetings at public-houses, an end would at once be put to the system, and school - houses and similar places would be selected instead. But it must be recollected that the working classes were not without excuse in the example of other classes who met in taverns to discharge their business. In the City of London there was a great corporation which seemed to exist only for the purpose of feeding people; and, in our courts of justice, the Judges and barristers had to qualify themselves by the processes of eating and drinking, and a Queen's Counsel could not rise to the dignity of the Bench unless he almost swam in wine up to the table at which he sat. These things no doubt had an effect upon the people, but they were no arguments for the Chancellor of the Exchequer setting up an opposition establishment. He wished, however, to call the attention of the Chancellor of the Exchequer to what was really the source of this proposal — the opinion of Mr. Tidd Pratt. That gentleman was invested with the authority over all the Friendly Societies, but from want of moral influence he was incapable of exercising that authority. He was, doubtless, an active and intelligent gentleman, but the people all over England would not be governed by a person in an office in London. The consequence was that Mr. Tidd Pratt's communications were disregarded.

Mr. Ayrton

But there was a remedy other than this Bill. If the moral weight of a recognized officer of the Crown holding a position in the country was brought to bear upon the Friendly Societies, there could be no doubt but that those societies would be managed as well as the Poor Law Board, or any other Government department was managed. When it was found that the Manchester Unity Friendly Society was badly managed, their central committee having great influence, remonstrated with the branch offices, the result of which was that reforms were introduced which made the society the best managed in the country. But what kind of a remedy would the Bill be for the evils now complained of? Were all the existing members of these societies to be left exposed to those evils, or were private Members of Parliament to be expected to take up that subject? It seemed to him that Mr. Tidd Pratt himself had suggested a scheme which was worthy of consideration. That Gentleman had proposed a Bill to place the supervision of those societies in the Boards of Guardians. The Bill was introduced into the other House, but as it was to some extent a taxing Bill it could not be passed; and he (Mr. Ayrton) had intended to introduce it with some modifications into this House. It would be well that the provisions of the Bill should be explained to the Committee before any decision was come to as to the Bill now under discussion. The area over which the system would extend would be enormous, though not so large as the Chancellor of the Exchequer had stated. He believed, however, that without limitation or diminution it would include 9,500,000 persons. If the Bill were successful, the result would be that in every parish and hamlet a stipendiary officer of the Crown would be located, whose duty it would be to institute an examination into the private affairs of individuals. The services of medical men and employers of labour would also be enlisted in the same direction, and such an organization would, he believed, be an unfortunate thing for all classes in the country. The Government would pursue a much better plan if they were to encourage the establishment of associations among the people themselves, for it was through the exercise of local administration that a nation became most fitted for the enjoyment of political rights. What they needed was a thorough and searching inquiry into the real character of the Bill, and not an examination into the mis-doings of all the Insurance Societies in the country, the result of which would only afford matter for contention, and tend to the gratification of rival companies. The Committee ought to examine such men as Mr. Tidd Pratt, to have the evidence of practical and independent persons who had made such subjects the study of their lives. There was no reason why that course should not be adopted, because there was not the slightest necessity for passing the measure hurriedly through Parliament. The measure did not press; it did not matter whether the Bill were passed in three months' or twelve months' time. He did not desire to defeat legislation on the subject. On the contrary, the Bill he had intended to bring in might be considered as hostile to the Friendly Societies now existing, but it was on a principle different from the present Bill, and more in accordance with the character and spirit of our institutions.

MR. HUBBARD considered, that much of the hostility displayed towards the Bill, was excited in consequence of its being introduced under a title which neither explained its real nature and character, nor the intentions of the Government in bringing it forward. He believed, however, that the defect had been atoned for by the right hon. Gentleman's speech, in which he had given the requisite information. Any prejudice which had existed against the measure arising out of the mode of its introduction had passed away, and there was much in it that commended it to the acceptance of the House. The principle that Government should not interfere with schemes which could not be satisfactorily undertaken by individuals or private societies was generally good, but there were undoubtedly cases in which the interference of Government would be attended with benefit. The establishment of banks for the receipt of the small savings of the labouring classes was an instance of this, for the security elsewhere could not be so great as that afforded by the Government, and the increased security would probably be the occasion of attracting more deposits, the result of thrift and frugality. He therefore thought it was a measure the House might fairly entertain. He looked upon it as an extension of the Post Office savings banks principle, which had received the sanction of the country. When Government proposed to establish a rate of interest which could in any way be supposed to compete with the operations of other societies, jealousy would not unnaturally be excited; but in a case of that kind such a feeling need not arise. At present the Government paid upon these deposits the moderate rate of 2½ per cent interest, and repaid the capital in only one way—namely, at call. They now proposed to leave to the depositors the choice of receiving their money in the form of deferred annuities, or in a sum payable at death. No doubt, Government would incur a strong risk, but he did not regard that as an objection to the measure. If the Government thought they could accept the responsibility, and carry out the system without endangering the finances of the country, he for one should not object; but he would strongly impress upon the Government the advisability of paying the same rate of interest upon the deposit money, in whatever form it was to be withdrawn. It was his intention to support the Motion of his hon. Friend the Member for Hertford (Sir Minto Farquhar), but he believed that there would be no difficulty in so framing the Bill as to meet at once the purpose of the Government and the views of those who were at present opposed to the measure.

COLONEL SYKES said, that he had received many letters both for and against the Bill, and in this conflict of testimony he must necessarily pause before he gave his vote. The question ought to be considered dispassionately in a Committee, and the House would be better able to form a judgment after that Committee had reported. One of the soundest principles of political economy was that the Government should never do that for the people which the people could do for themselves; and the question was whether the maxim had not been violated by the Government measure. On the other hand he was quite sure it would be to the advantage of the working classes to get the Government security, because the Government would be able to pay. He should vote for the Amendment.

MR. THOMSON HANKEY said, he objected altogether both to the inquiry proposed and to the principle of the Bill. According to the practice of the House, to vote for a Committee was to sanction the principle of a measure, and that he was not prepared to do. There was great danger, if the Bill passed, of overloading that already

Mr. Hubbard

overloaded department—the Post Office, and of incurring great risks and liabilities hereafter on the part of the State. His vote would be given both against the Committee and against going on any further with the Bill.

THE CHANCELLOR OF THE EXCHEQUER: This discussion appears to have arrived now at its natural close, and this is the less to be regretted because possibly the Amendment of my hon. Friend does not present to the House any difference of opinion. The effect of the Amendment will be that the House, at its discretion, will name a competent number of Gentlemen as a Select Committee. These Gentlemen will meet and probably will appoint me, as the author of the Bill, the Chairman of the Committee. I should then have the opportunity of giving all the information which it is in my power to afford respecting the Bill, and the views with which I should endeavour to act upon it, assisted by such officers of the Government as were able to render me assistance. After the Committee had been nominated, a further question would arise—namely, whether the Committee should have power to send for persons, papers, and records. Upon this proposal would arise practically the question, whether the Committee shall be a Committee upon the clauses of the Bill, or a Committee of general inquiry into the subject of the Bill. I certainly could not agree to any general inquiry, and it is but right we should have a clear understanding upon the point. I see no mode by which if "persons, papers, and records" were to be sent for, the Committee could avoid falling into great difficulty. The officers of the Government, and persons favourable to the Government plan, who would be examined, would give evidence upon a very complex question, involving an immense amount of detail, and then the Committee would say very naturally that they were bound to hear persons of intelligence and information who entertained opposite views. Now, that is a kind of investigation which it would be totally impossible to undertake. In the first place, it would amount on my part to an entire abnegation of the regular and ordinary duties of my office were I to become in any degree the organ of the Government in conducting an investigation of this sort. In the next place, great practical evils would arise from an investigation which it would be impossible to separate from a great deal of controversial matter. It would be said that it was necessary to inquire into the manner in which the Bill would operate upon the interests of existing societies, and this would essentially involve the inquiry how these societies were conducted, and whether it was a good part or a bad part of their management which would be affected. We should thus in effect become a Committee of investigation and inquisition into the management of these societies, and Her Majesty's Government are not prepared to become responsible for such an inquiry. But we may accept the Amendment as it stands, with the limitation I have mentioned, the fact being, I believe, that the appointment of a Committee is supported by some hon. Gentlemen who agree in thinking that a general investigation would be far from expedient. I will now notice two or three of the points which have been touched upon, with his usual ability, by my hon. and learned Friend (Mr. Ayrton). Let me remind the House that this Bill was met by a powerful concerted and organized opposition. There is nothing in the fact discreditable to the parties with whom the opposition originated, for they had a perfect right to organize an opposition if they thought right. But I certainly never remember a case of a Bill which was the subject of such an opposition out of doors, and yet gained ground by long delay. Generally speaking a long postponement is fatal, but in this instance during the considerable interval which has elapsed since the Bill was introduced there has been a remarkable development of public opinion in its favour. I appeal to the opponents of the Bill as well as to its supporters, and I ask whether the opinion of the press has not been declared in a very singular degree in favour of the measure, irrespective, so far as I know, of party interests and opinions. Certainly, in my public life of thirty years, I have never received so many letters upon any one measure as I have with reference to this Bill, expressing approval and even gratitude from all classes of the community, and especially from those who have a strong interest in the question. At the commencement of the discussion upon the Bill there was a great number of petitions against it, many of them drawn up in a common form. Now, meetings are held in favour of the Bill, and petitions in its favour are coming forward—petitions from working men, who can have none but the most disinterested motives in supporting it. My hon. Friend (Mr. Ayrton) lately

presided over a great meeting at Exeter Hall, called in opposition to the measure; but the independent working men mustered so strongly on the other side, that my hon. Friend could not determine on which side the majority lay, though some who favoured the Bill said that, had they been in the chair, they should not have been at all doubtful. And lastly, I must say, I have observed with peculiar satisfaction, that not only some public meetings, but also boards of guardians in the country are beginning to give their minds to this matter, and from many places petitions have been presented on behalf of the boards of guardians, expressing a hope that this House will not withhold so great a boon to the working classes as they think this law will prove. Under these circumstances, I most cordially wish to return to the position in which we stood when this Bill was introduced, and to free the discussion from the controversial element. It was not of my will that this element crept into our debates on the Bill, and what I did afterwards I did under the pressure of a public necessity. I think, however, that this necessity has passed away, and therefore I have not a word of accusation or reproach to utter against any society or public company. But I wish to define the precise extent to which I meant to carry my remarks in respect of living societies. I do not mean dead societies, of which I introduced examples, but such societies as the Royal Liver, the British Prudential, and other societies. I did not presume to attach, nor do I think I should be justified in attaching to any of these societies a fraudulent character. What I meant to do was this—the societies adopted certain language. They said, "We are quite aware there is a great field for insurance among the people of England; it is quite true that there is a great portion of that field unoccupied; it is quite true that the Friendly Societies, notwithstanding the large numbers of their members, leave the unoccupied portion of that field untouched;" but they also said, "we are ready to do the work, and therefore we claim that you should leave us to do it, and not have the Government enter upon it." That being so, as against that exclusive claim, I thought it right, by reference to the manner in which the most staple and respectable Life Assurance Companies were conducted, to show that those societies were not entitled to set up so high a claim, and that they could

not give the working man so positive a
security after his twenty, or thirty, or
forty years' payments as the great Insurance Societies give to the wealthy classes
where they made a judicious selection of
an office for that purpose. That is the
extent to which I went. I would not be
justified in saying that any of the existing societies were fraudulent societies. I
disclaim the imputation that I said so
before, and certainly I do not say so now.
But, when I used language which I regret
to say I am not prepared to retract respecting the heartless iniquity that had been
at work, I did not mean it to be understood
that any such language was applicable to
existing societies. I further said, and I
repeat it now, regarding the Professional
Society, and every other society to which I
alluded, that, though I believe all my statements to have been correct, no one shall
be better pleased if it can be shown that
the construction I put on my facts was
an erroneous one, and that although there
may have been a want of prudence and a
want of care, still no corrupt motives have
been at work. I am told by my hon.
Friend the Member for York that he is of
that opinion with respect to the Professional Society, and I am glad to accept
my hon. Friend's opinion on the point.
I think the case was one of the most reckless, hazardous, and even unjustifiable
management; but still I am willing to
believe that the facts are not incompatible
with the absence of fraudulent intention
on the part of the managers. My hon.
Friend the Member for the Tower Hamlets
has alluded to what I said on the subject
of working men's trades unions, and expressed his regret that I had not made a
full explanation and apology. My reason
for not having made a more full explanation is, that I have not had the opportunity of doing so since I first spoke on
the subject, though I intimated in two
words my wish to do so. The explanation
is briefly this:—On a former occasion I
adverted to a meeting which had been held
under the presidency of Mr. Potter, at
Exeter Hall; and, as far as my memory
serves me, I stated that the name of
Mr. Potter had been very much connected
with that sort of agency, and those proceedings on the part of trades unions
which were believed by the public to imply
the coercion of the minority of the working
class by the majority of the working
class. I have been assured since I made
that statement that my description would

not be a true description of trades unions
as they exist at present. I am told that
there was a great deal of that character
attachable to them in former times; but
that the real advances which the working
class has been making, not only in intelligence and in the means of existence, but in
the whole view of their social duties, has
essentially and materially altered the character of these societies, and that there are
few of them, if any, against which the
charge would lie. I can only say I made
those observations out of no hostility or
indifference to the working class. I believe that to this hour, in certain cases and
in certain parts of the country, there are
instances in which a portion of the working class still tyrannizes over its own
members. Those proceedings, I am glad
to hear, are certainly alien to the views
and feelings of the trades unions of London;
and, therefore, I am extremely glad to believe that there is no foundation for any
charge of that description being made
against them. My hon. Friend has also
referred to two other points. He mentioned the question of tables. He said I
had not overcome the difficulty which
arose on that point, and he then referred
to a plan by which it might be overcome
—namely, by proposing to this House to
enact that the use of a certain set of tables
should be compulsory; but my hon. Friend
seemed to lose sight of a grand distinction
between assurance by Government and
assurance by private societies. The grand
difference in favour of private societies
arises from the fact that, after all, the rate
at which assurance business can be done
depends in the main upon the rate at
which the managers can, with prudence
and propriety, be allowed to make investments. Private societies working for
themselves can make investments at a
rate which it is impossible to aim at.
You cannot say to the Chancellor of the
Exchequer of the day and those who advise him that they are prudent men, and
you will allow them to go into the money
market and invest the public money to the
best advantage. You compel them to invest
in securities on which they can get only
3 or 3¼ per cent; but it would be a very
great hardship if we were to come down to
this House with a set of tables which
would absolutely preclude any private
societies from adopting any other investment. My hon. Friend, moreover, anti-
cipates great danger from the successful
working of this Bill, and he denies that

the Post Office savings banks have succeeded, alleging that all the money they have got has been filched from the old savings banks. Now, I take the liberty of saying that this last conclusion of his is one which he will not be able to prove by figures. Then, he says, if the time ever comes when a vast sum of money is in the hands of the Government on account of the Post Office savings banks, and if at the same time the rate of interest is high, there will be what the right hon. Gentleman the Member for Oxfordshire once called, I think, "an ugly rush," and we shall be called on to reimburse those funds which will be only bearing 2¼ per cent interest. [Mr. AYRTON: Or to pay a higher interest.] Yes, of course, that is an alternative. The rate of interest allowed on money deposited in the Post Office savings banks is now 2½ per cent; and I am not prepared to say it ought ever to be higher. At the same time, I do not altogether exclude from my mind the hope that some addition may yet be made in that respect, compatibly, of course, with the essential requisite that the public is not to subsidize the Post Office savings banks to the extent of a single farthing, but should even reserve to itself a margin sufficient for its own perfect security. Within the last few months we have had a singular example of the preference of the public for low interest on Government security, rather than high interest in other quarters. The Birmingham Savings Bank determined, in consequence of the Act of last year, to close their establishment. At that moment the rate of discount in London was 8 per cent, and there were, of course, plenty of people in Birmingham to make by advertisement to the depositors offers of high interest, to the extent of 5 and even 6 per cent for the money at call. There were 35,000 depositors, but I believe two-thirds of the whole number and of the entire capital, went to the Post Office banks, giving only £2 10s., rather than to other banks giving much higher terms. I feel the greatest confidence in the political security of these banks, and even if the argument of the hon. Member were good as regards these institutions, it would not hold good in regard to the present measure. If a man chooses to insure with the Government a sum of money payable on death, he cannot very well fulfil the necessary condition and claim his money just because there happens to be a high rate of interest in the market. I

judge from the tone of the debate that the House thinks we have gone sufficiently into this subject, and I hope my hon. Friend opposite understands exactly from my explanation what the Government is prepared to do.

SIR MINTO FARQUHAR said, that supposing they agreed to the Committee without a division, he should at a future period propose the Committee to the House, and, in doing so, should follow it up by asking for leave to send for persons, papers, and records. He thought it desirable that the Committee should examine such gentlemen as Sir A. Spearman, Mr. Chadwick, Mr. Scudamore, Mr. Tidd Pratt, several actuaries, and three or four gentlemen connected with Friendly Societies and Industrial Insurance Offices. He should like that evidence to be distinctly taken and printed for the benefit of the House, so that they might be assisted to come to a decision on the subject.

SIR FITZROY KELLY said, he rose to say a few words on behalf of certain societies to which the Chancellor of the Exchequer had made allusion on more than one recent occasion in that House. The right hon. Gentleman had indulged in a series of observations regarding these societies which the House was little accustomed to. He stated that the Professional Society had transferred its business to the European Society, but that, in order to make themselves safe, the European made it a condition that the amount of liability should be inscribed on each policy, in a manner and under circumstances which the right hon. Gentleman described. This, the Chancellor of the Exchequer said, was no better than wholesale robbery. And wholesale robbery it would have been if there had been a particle of truth in the right hon. Gentleman's description of the transaction. The Chancellor of the Exchequer went farther, and said that a good many of these proceedings were worse than wholesale robbery, and that many persons who had never seen the inside of a gaol were fitter to be there than many a rogue convicted ten times over at the Old Bailey. Did the right hon. Gentleman apply this to the European?

THE CHANCELLOR OF THE EXCHEQUER said, he had applied that expression to many transactions of the kind, namely, amalgamations, but not to that particular case.

SIR FITZROY KELLY said, it was then a misfortune that so great a master of language should have expressed himself in such a way that there was not a man of common understanding who would not imagine that the right hon. Gentleman had referred to one or the other of those societies, or to both; but he was glad to receive the explanation of the right hon. Gentleman. The right hon. Gentleman would, he was sure, feel gratified when he (Sir FitzRoy Kelly) stated that there was no ground whatever for imputing the slightest impropriety of conduct to either of those two societies. He did not understand what the right hon. Gentleman meant by saying that, supposing there was a policy for £1,000, the outstanding value was £600, and the premiums paid £200. How could a policy of assurance, while the person was in life, be worth more than the aggregate amount of premiums paid upon it? The Professional, owing, perhaps, to undue expenditure in the management, and the misfortune of having a defaulting secretary, who embezzled a large sum of money, was obliged to suspend its payments and resort to the Court of Chancery for winding up. The affairs of the society were investigated by the Master of the Rolls, and the very transactions which the right hon. Gentleman had condemned— the combination of the Professional and European — was made with the express sanction of that learned Judge. That transaction did not involve the principle that a policy of the value of £600 should be treated as worth a great deal less. At the time the Professional Society was wound up there were outstanding policies to the amount of £1,500,000, and debts amounting to £150,000, £100,000 of which was for ordinary liabilities and money borrowed, and £50,000 necessary to make up to the European the difference between the value of the policies upon which certain premiums had been paid and the policies upon which for the first time the European should then assume a liability. And this, so far from coming to anything like 60 per cent, if there had been any loss, which there was not, would amount to only 3 or 4 per cent. That which the right hon. Gentleman described as loss to the extent of 60 per cent amounted to only between 3 and 4 per cent, but was no loss at all, for the directors, who must have considered themselves in some respects responsible, in a pecuniary point of view, for the misdeeds of their officers, advanced £50,000 to meet their liabilities; and out of the £150,000 of liabilities £100,000

— *Sir FitzRoy Kelly*

had already been discharged, a contribution of 2s. 6d. in the pound had been paid on the other £50,000, and a further call had been made under which every shilling would be eventually paid. He (Sir FitzRoy Kelly) was not a defender of all these Insurance Societies. He listened to the opening speech of the right hon. Gentleman, when introducing the measure, with much gratification. He thought the Bill, if it passed, would effect a very great public benefit if judicious amendments were introduced into it in Committee. All that could be said in favour of the Bill he was prepared to say, with some modifications and qualifications; but, with regard to the Professional Society, there was no ground for imputing to the managers misconduct of any kind, or anything beyond that misfortune which might happen to any company. He was quite sure the right hon. Gentleman would take some opportunity of doing justice to those gentlemen.

THE CHANCELLOR OF THE EXCHEQUER said, he had paused for a moment before rising to reply, in the hope that some Gentleman would say something about the society to which the hon. and learned Gentleman had referred, but he regretted that superior attractions had drawn Gentlemen away from the performance of that duty. He trusted, therefore, that after what the hon. and learned Gentleman had said, the House would allow him to make a few remarks by way of explanation. In the strongest part of the language which the hon. and learned Gentleman had quoted he did not refer particularly to the Professional Company, but alluded to other societies, which he did not think it necessary to name. When he spoke of the wholesale loss inflicted upon holders of policies of the Professional Company he meant to describe the effect of rash and reckless speculation, without imputing any improper motives. It too frequently happened that persons of great respectability involved themselves in undertakings of this kind, which had the effect of deluding and robbing others, without the smallest impurity of motive on their own part. He believed, after what the hon. and learned Gentleman had stated, that there was no impurity of motive on the part of the Professional directors. It was also to be hoped—and might, indeed, be believed—that nothing would ultimately be lost to such of the policy-holders as might have kept their policies alive; while he did not think that the ruinous loss inflicted upon the shareholders was in the slightest degree attributable to any intention on the part of the Directors.

Question put, and *negatived.*

Words *added.*

Main Question, as amended, put, and *agreed to.*

Ordered, That the Bill be committed to a Select Committee.

SUPPLY—ARMY ESTIMATES.

SUPPLY *considered* in Committee.

(In the Committee.)

(1.) £5,708,983, General Staff and Regimental Pay, Allowances and Charges.

GENERAL PEEL said, he rose to make a few remarks on the subject of recruiting for the army. It might appear to some that the question was one of those respecting the discipline of the army with which that House ought not to interfere, but the recruiting for the army was governed by an Act of Parliament, and it was to the effect of that Act he wished to draw attention. He regretted that a Return for which he had moved had not been laid upon the table, because it would have shown whether the alarm which had been expressed with respect to the working of the Limited Enlistment Act was well founded or not. On a previous occasion, the Under Secretary for War had stated that the War Office had no alarm whatever on the subject, because there were only about 4,000 men who would claim discharges on expiration of service during the year. For his own part, however, when he looked at the manner in which it was proposed to meet the requirements of the service, he confessed he felt the greatest possible alarm. If it was necessary in time of peace to reduce the standard of the army by one inch—in other words, if the ten years' service men were to be replaced by recruits of a lower standard—he thought things could not be regarded as in a satisfactory condition. He did not mean to say that good men could not be got at 5ft. 5in.; but his alarm arose from the War Office being obliged in time of peace to resort to a measure which ought to be reserved for some great emergency. Nor did he believe it to be absolutely necessary to reduce the standard at the present moment. Additional men were not wanted for the Artil-

lery. Recruiting for that corps might be checked by raising the standard; and then the standard for the line might be kept at 5ft. 6in. But, looking to the inevitable consequences of the Limited Enlistment Act, he should wish to see a more intimate relation established between the militia and the regular army, and he thought it could be established with advantage to both. Hitherto the line alone had derived all the advantage. He well recollected the great benefits which the line derived during the Indian mutiny from the volunteers and the militia; but he wanted to see those advantages increased and made reciprocal. Was it impossible to obtain for the militia the services of those limited service men who, after the expiration of their service, should decline to re-enter the line? By this means the militia would get many good non-commissioned officers, and a reduction could be made in the permanent staff, in the corps of enrolled pensioners, and in that army of reserve of which he never saw anything except in the Estimates. At present, by the Limited Enlistment Act, men for the artillery and the cavalry were enlisted for twelve years, whereas men for the line and for the Guards were enlisted only for ten. He did not see why they should not all be enlisted for twelve years, the men in the line at the expiration of ten years being allowed to commute their two years' remaining service in the regular army for five years' service in the militia. The expenses of recruiting for India were very high. He found, on reference to the Estimates, that although the regular army in India was only one-third of the whole army, the expense of recruiting for that portion was larger than for the remaining two-thirds. That might be because of the great wear and tear of the regiments in India. If so, nothing could be worse than reducing the number of the depôts to a hundred men. If a regiment was ordered to India, any man within a year and a half of the expiration of his ten years' term of service was not allowed to go out, because the Indian Government would have to pay his passage there and back. But why should not such a man be passed into a militia regiment? The estimate for furlough pay was £130,000 last year, and for the ensuing year was £137,000. With respect to the capitation rate of £10, he could not help thinking that it would be found, if the matter were strictly examined into, that they had now to pay more than the £10 would cover. With respect to men volunteering in India, he admitted the propriety of offering men who volunteered there from one regiment into another more inducements than the ordinary bounty; but who paid the expense for men who volunteered in India? There was a small sum put down in the Estimates for enlistments in the colonies, but that could not apply to India. He wished to ask, what were the items covered by the capitation rate; and what, after two years' experience, was the opinion of the War Office as to its being sufficient to cover the amount now paid by that department?

COLONEL DUNNE thought it extraordinary that the War Department remained ignorant of the fact known to every officer of the army, that there were something like 20,000 men whose period of service expired in each year. They had no right to calculate upon these men re-enlisting, and there was not an officer in the service who would not recommend that the first enlistment should be for twelve years for the line as well as for cavalry and artillery. The suggestion of the right hon. and gallant Member who had just spoken, for securing a more intimate and advantageous relation between the regular army and the militia, was one well worthy of the attention of the Government. It was one of the most important subjects that could engage their consideration. As things stood, a great number of men were discharged from the army, perhaps without a pension, and then spread discontent where they resided. At any rate they were entirely lost to the service. As the ten years' men were not sent out to India with their regiments if they had only a year or two of their term to serve, and as a year or a year and a half was required to make soldiers of them, it was clear that the country enjoyed but a short period of efficient service from them.' If these men who could not be sent out to India were transferred to militia regiments, they would improve the efficiency of the militia, and be retained in the service of the country. The capitation rate was, he thought, a very bad bargain for this country. He noticed at page 12 of the Estimates, an item of £44,500 for the clothing of two Indian regiments in China. He wished to have some explanation of that item. The whole of the clothing system was in a most unsatisfactory state. No army in Europe was clothed in so expensive a manner as ours;

General Peel

and no commanding officer could at that moment tell what was the price of a single article of clothing; and the department, though presided over by an officer of great talent for organisation and great experience, was not in the condition it ought to be. He believed that the work would be better done by contract, and that the large Government clothing establishments should only exist as a check to extravagant outlay. He thought it quite practicable to make a large reduction in these Estimates without at all diminishing the efficiency of the army. With reference to the purchase of horses, they would require to alter their system, or the cavalry would soon be dismounted. But he felt it was perfectly useless going over items; they talked there year after year on the subject, but nothing was done.

MR. O'REILLY said, that although reduction could not be well looked for that year, he had no doubt that a proper, well conducted inquiry would lead to very considerable economy in the general expenditure on the Army Estimates; but instead of reduction he saw symptoms of their increase. In the observations he was about to make, it might appear that he differed from two axioms laid down by high authorities. The first was that of the right hon. and gallant General opposite (General Peel), that the cost of the army might be taken to be, in round numbers, £100 per man; but he presumed the gallant General did not mean that such was the necessary calculation, but only that of late years it might be accepted as a fact. If they went on as at present, he believed the gallant General would agree with him that the expenditure would not be limited to £100 per man. The second maxim was laid down by the late lamented Secretary of State for War, that there was nothing whatsoever to be gained by a comparison with other services. He could not agree that a careful comparison in particular items between the administration and management of the French army and our own would be altogether futile. The totals were certainly sufficiently striking. The British army might be taken in round numbers to consist of 147,766 men; the number of horses, 13,693, or one horse to every 11 men. The total estimated cost was nearly £15,000,000; but if they deducted Votes 8, 9, 10, and 11, for auxiliary forces, £1,209,509; Vote 14, for fortifications, £73,000; Vote 16, for surveys, £88,345; and Vote 27, for disembodied militia, £31,213 — in all, £1,402,167, they would arrive at the conclusion that £13,442,721 represented the cost of the army, which gave £92 2s. 6d. per man. The total number of men in the French army was 400,000; horses, 85,705, or one horse to 4¾ men. The total Estimate was 430,260,367f., which was equal to £17,210,414, or about £43 per man. The causes generally assigned for the greater cost of the English troops were:—1st, higher pay and allowances; 2nd, the cost of recruiting as compared to conscription; 3rd, the extra expenses of troops in the colonies; and 4th, the extra cost of transport of troops to and from colonies. He would discuss the first cause, which was the main one, later. The total cost of the recruiting service was £102,471, or very nearly 14s. per man. The French *recrutement et réserve* was 739,479f., or 1f. 80c., or 1s. 6d. per man; therefore the extra cost of recruiting was 12s. 6d. per man. The extra cost of our troops in the colonies comprehended, as allowance for high price of provisions and allowance for wives whose husbands were abroad, a sum of £47,000, and extra allowance for China, £49,395. This amounted to 13s. per man. But in the French budget, under the head *solde et entretien des troupes*, he found allowances special to Africa—namely, allowance to officers entering on campaign and indemnity for campaign rations a sum of 2,822,859f., which was 7f., or 6s. per man. Therefore the extra cost of English troops in the colonies was 7s. per man. Then, as to the extra cost of the transport of troops to and from our colonies, the total English transport service, as given at page 17, was £179,330. To this should be added allowance to discharged soldiers to take them home, £18,000, and travelling expenses of officers, £7,000, making the whole £188,759, or equal to about £1 8s. per man. The total of the French *service de marche* was equal to 14s. per man. Therefore the extra cost of English troops was 14s. per man. The amount of excess in the English Estimates, accounted for under these heads, was:—Cost of recruiting, 12s. 6d. per man; troops in colonies, 13s. per man; transport to colonies, 14s. per man—in all, £1 19s. 6d. The cost of the British soldier—namely, £92, might be divided into the heads of the Votes; but this would neither enable them to compare it with the French, nor, in some cases, give an accurate idea. Thus the Vote for regimental pay and allow-

ances might give the idea that it meant all that the men received; but, in reality, for this purpose they must add the item, "cost of provisions above amount of stoppages," which came under the Vote for Commissariat, but which was substantially an addition to the men's pay. So also Vote 1, "General Staff," to be compared with French Vote for Etats Majors, must be augmented by 159 generals who came under Vote No. 20, and by the honorary colonels commandant of regiments, because the French Vote comprised all "generals in reserve," and all officers except those serving with their regiments. And the French of "Etats Majors" must be diminished by "Intendance Militaire," which corresponded to part of Vote 18, and by several items which corresponded to parts of our Votes for "manufacturing departments," "works," and "education." The House would understand that he was making a comparison of the items which were common to both services. Thus the expense of the general staff was about the same in each country—£2 a head. Regimental pay and allowances for food cost in England £41 15s. per man, and in France £20. The Commissariat charges were in England £1 1s. per man, and in France 14s. Clothing was a remarkable item, for it could not be said that we were disadvantageously placed in that respect, and certainly the French soldier was as well clothed as the English; but while the cost of the former was only £2 2s. 6d., the latter cost £4 6s. When the Committee came to discuss those Votes in detail, he would take an opportunity of pointing out the differences of cost with greater minuteness; but he believed one all pervading cause of greater expense here, was to be found in what was called the establishment. He might, however, instance some other difference between the cost of similar items in the two armies. Thus martial law in England cost 6s. per man, and in France only 2s. 6d. But the cost of medical attendance was more nearly alike, being £1 16s. in the English army, and £1 10s. in the French, proving that on those matters which concerned the well-being and efficiency of the soldier, the French were not behind us. In the article of stores there was a remarkable difference — the cost being in the French army £1 10s. per man, while in the English army it was about £8 10s. The total of the votes would give a sum of £10 10s. per man; but he had made a deduction for the amount supplied to the navy based on a calculation of the late Sir G. C. Lewis. Small arms in England cost £1 6*s.* per man, and in France only 7*s.* 2*d.*; while gunpowder which cost us £1 8*s.* per man, only cost the French 16*s.*, although they were not more sparing of that article than we were. Then came an item of considerable importance. The House would admit that French military education was quite equal to ours, and yet the cost there was 6*s.* as against £1 4*s.* here. Probably if any one was asked what would be the cause of any greater charge for military education in this country as compared with the cost in France, the answer given would be that our young men were more expensively lodged and fed. The fact, however, was, that the cost of living and clothing in the French colleges was as great as it was in England, but the cost of teaching and administration in our military colleges was double that of the French. The administration of the French army cost 4*s.* 6*d.* per man, as compared with £1 7*s.* in England. Rewards and pensions cost us £14 4*s.*, and the French only £6 6*s.*, but he thought we got value for our greater expenditure in that respect. These facts certainly required consideration, for there could be little hope that the cost of the pay of the army would be reduced. On the contrary, it was more probable that it would become politic as well as just to increase the pay as the general prosperity of the country increased, but that fact rendered increased economy in the administration of the army more necessary. The cost of a French army of 400,000 men if paid, lodged, and pensioned as well as the English army, with as costly medical attendance, would be, instead of £17,200,000, as at present, £31,050,000, or an additional cost of £34 12*s.* 6*d.* per man. And if to that were added the English rate of clothing, law, stores, education, and administration, the cost of the French army would be £5,350,000 more. On the other hand, if our Estimates were reduced to the French standard, with regard to these items the difference on 147,000 men would be a sum of £1,966,123. Allusion had been made to the charge for horses, and he had found that horses cost as much in France as here; but, while the cost of our staff for purchasing was one-ninth of the whole sum expended, in France it was only one thirty-fifth, although the expenses of maintaining the College of Alfort was included. The cost of the transport service

Mr. O'Reilly

in this country was large, simply because no pains were taken to look clearly into the subject. In one instance 200 men had to be removed from Yarmouth to Deptford, and they were sent by way of London on their return. It was, however, suggested by an officer that the troops should be embarked on board a steamer which would stop opposite the barracks at Deptford, and this course was adopted at a saving of about three-fourths of the expenses which would by the other route have been incurred. A similar case occurred in Ireland, where it was proposed to remove a regiment from a town on the eastern coast to Aldershot by sending them by rail to Dublin, marching across the town, then going by rail to Kingstown, and then by steamer to Liverpool, instead of at once embarking the troops at the port where they were stationed for Liverpool, a plan which was ultimately adopted with much less expense. He also might refer to a case in Ireland where the War authorities paid £500 to obtain lodgings for some of the troops, while within an hour's distance there was an unoccupied barracks. He was not prepared to propose the reduction of any specific Vote, for nothing was easier on the part of Government than to meet such a proposition. If he pointed to any particular clerk as one whose services might be dispensed with, the Government would find no difficulty in proving that that particular clerk was the most important man in the service. The duty of individual Members of the House was to point out the grounds on which reforms should be introduced, but to leave their management to those with whom the responsibility rested. It was by those means that the reduction in the Customs had been effected. The simplest method of accomplishing this end would be through the agency of a great Minister, one sufficiently long at his post to be so thoroughly master of all the details as to resemble Carnot, the organizer of victory. Another would be by means of a Royal Commission, which had produced such valuable results in connection with the Indian army. The last course would be the appointment of a Committee of the House. The last plan, however, he considered to be undesirable, as a Committee of the House was always belligerent, and he did not think any good would result from its inquiry. He believed that the Government would act in the matter if the country, supported by the House, were to call upon them to do so.

COLONEL NORTH said, he wished to call attention to a recent regimental order, which he could only characterize as a piece of contemptible economy. It appeared that the veterinary surgeon at Aldershot, who looked after the horses of the staff and the mounted officers of regiments, had applied for assistance, and that, after a long correspondence, an assistant was granted to him, who was to receive 1s. 1d. a day, or £18 5s. a year. They were now dealing with a Vote which amounted in the whole to nearly £6,000,000. The Committee would scarcely credit it, but it was the fact, that an order was issued for the deduction from the pay of every officer receiving forage at Aldershot, a farthing a week, or a penny a month towards the payment of the salary of £18 5s. of the assistant to the staff veterinary surgeon. He did not know who had suggested that reduction, but whoever the person was, he showed that he might take a first-rate place in a competitive examination on the subject of practical economy. There was also an item of £1,460, allowance to an instructor for the men in cookery. He wished to know whether there were more than one instructor? He would also observe that the hon. Member who had just spoken was in error in attributing the mismanagement he had referred to the negligence of the Horse Guards. The Horse Guards only superintended the discipline of the army, and the facts mentioned by the hon. Member would come within the province allotted to the Secretary for War.

MR. W. WILLIAMS said, that having voted the number of men, it was not possible to reduce materially the amount of the Vote; but he could not help thinking that the policy of Her Majesty's Government being to keep the country out of a war, the sum which was now demanded for the army was an extravagant one, and that a much smaller force and a much smaller outlay would be sufficient for the defence of the country. He also wished for some explanation as to the item of £1,435 for the director of gymnastics and fencing, and for sergeant instructors. He saw no necessity for such an expenditure.

SIR HENRY WILLOUGHBY said, he wished to call attention to the inconvenience of discussing so large a Vote as £5,708,000, and to suggest that it should be subdivided. It was utterly impossible for private Members to do more than express their opinions upon the Vote in its present shape. It appeared that the British troops in India were 146,700; but according to a marginal note, 1,532 Indian troops had to be added, making a slight increase over the number last year. He wished to know whether the 1,532 were to be considered as British troops, subject to the Mutiny Act.

SIR FREDERIC SMITH said, he knew no reason why the Vote should always appear in its present gigantic form. It certainly could be more easily discussed in separate items. He was quite prepared to point out how an extensive economy might be practised; and if the noble Lord would turn his attention to the various items he was sure a reduction of £500,000 might be made in the Vote. He regretted very much the intention to make a reduction in the number of the Royal Artillery. The line might, perhaps, be reduced to a small extent, but a reduction of the Royal Artillery affected the most important element in the service; and yet this was, it seemed, to be attempted for the sake of a miserable economy. It required two or three years to make even an intelligent man a good gunner. When the last attempt of this sort was made, many of the men went into the Life Guards; but, of course, the experience they had gained as gunners was not of much use to them as cavalry soldiers. If the noble Lord desired to weed the Artillery he should take care not to lose efficient men. Why was it that our service was deficient in staff knowledge? The fact was that we had not selected a sufficient number of men from the higher ranks to receive instruction in staff experience, but in consequence of the arrangements now being carried out we should have a class of staff officers second to none in Europe. In the Peninsular war, no doubt the staff was equal to all the service it was called to fulfil, but they were placed under the direction of a great captain. The expenditure on that branch of the service might not appear to be useful at the moment, but at a critical moment, and in the present state of Europe no one could tell how soon that time might arrive, its use would be made apparent. The Crimean war was a war of siege and not of campaign, and there was no movement of troops there which could teach a single lesson. He approved very much of the establishment at Aldershot, which was an excellent strategic position, for troops could be transported thence to the most important points on the coast in a few hours, and on that very ground it was singled out by Lord Hardinge. He hoped the Government would keep up that establishment in efficiency; it was an admirable school for the army, and many officers who had visited the continental armies had expressed peculiar admiration of the way in which the troops were moved at Aldershot.

THE MARQUESS OF HARTINGTON said, he rose to reply to the questions he had put to him. As he did not then see the right hon. and gallant Member for Huntingdon in his place, he would defer for a time his reply to the observations of the gallant General, as he hoped to be able in some degree to calm the apprehensions which he entertained in regard to the probable effect of the Limited Enlistment Act. The hon. and gallant Member for Queen's County (Colonel Dunne) asked what was the meaning of the Vote for pay and clothing for certain native Indian troops. The fact was, that the Home Government did not pay the expenses of these regiments in detail. The Indian Government sent in the account and the amount was paid in a lump sum. It had been alleged that the great source of extravagant military expenditure was the establishments. That was a very vague term, but he had a Return of the expenses of what he might call the establishments, and he had ascertained that the commissariat staff cost £104,000; clothing staff, £24,000; barrack staff, £53,000; purveyor's staff, £28,000; stores, £218,000; War Office and Horse Guards, £202,000; and the chaplains, if they could be included in the list, £50,000, making in all £679,000. That was, no doubt, a large item, but not so great as the sweeping assertions which had been made would lead one to imagine. It was obvious that any reduction in the establishments would not make much impression on the total amount of the Estimates. He should be glad if any hon. Gentleman would inform him whether he had omitted any establishment from his list, and how any diminution could be effected. Reference had also been made to the depôt battalions which had been described as one of the most extravagant parts of our system. It was, no doubt, a question well worthy of discussion, whether some more economical system could not be devised, and he did not know any on which the attention of gallant Members could better be bestowed. He had not, however, as yet heard from them any practical suggestions on the subject, or, indeed, anything more than wide general statements.

Sir Frederic Smith

He concurred in the laudatory remarks on the speech of the hon. Member for Longford, who appeared to have entered deeply into the question of the comparative cost of the French and English armies. That was a subject which had not escaped the attention of the War Office; and he agreed with the hon. Member, that although it did not follow that we could reduce our expenses in the same proportion as the French, a comparison of the accounts of the two armies would disclose where our expenditure was in excess and might lead to useful results. But, as he had said, his noble Friend at the head of the War Office had not overlooked the importance of such an inquiry, and had received valuable assistance in conducting it. However large the cost of our army might be, it would not be difficult to show that the additional expense was to be attributed, not to extravagance, but to causes easily accounted for. With respect to the relative cost of a French and an English soldier, it was very difficult to arrive at an exact comparison, because he believed the French Budget did not include all the expenses which were incurred for the army, and which were embraced in our Estimates. It was necessary to take out of other parts of the French Budget some expenses which were properly chargeable to the army in order to make a fair comparison. The general conclusion at which the War Office had arrived was not very different from that which had already been stated to the Committee. It was that the French soldier cost about £47 18s. 10d. per annum, while the English soldier cost about £91 17s. 2d. In France the expense of the staff, putting together various items scattered through the French Budget, might be stated at £1 12s. 11d. per man, whereas in England it amounted to £2 5s. 7d. The great secret of the higher expenditure in England as compared with that of France was to be found in the fact that not only our soldiers but also all persons connected with the administration of military affairs, were better remunerated for their services than the same class in France. In the French War Office, for example, there were 479 *employés*, with salaries ranging from £72 to £1,000. There were no fewer than 382 whose salaries did not exceed £144 per annum. He did not know whether any hon. Member was prepared to say that we could find gentlemen capable of performing the responsible duties intrusted to the officials in our War Office for so small an *a*mount of remuneration. He did not believe we could; at any rate, it had hitherto been found impossible to do so. Again, taking the items in the French Budget for pay, allowances, beer and wine, recruiting service, gymnastic and musketry instruction, good conduct money, and other matters, and comparing them with the corresponding items in our Estimates, the result was, that the French soldier cost £18 4s. 10d., and the English soldier £30. It thus appeared that the cost of the English soldier was very nearly double that of the French soldier; and that proportion might be said to run through the whole comparison. Moreover, it ought to be borne in mind that a great part of the administration of the French army was carried out regimentally, and not departmentally, as with us, and hence the charge for actual pay and allowances should be taken at a lower rate as regarded the French army and at a higher rate as regarded the English than appeared on the face of the comparisons laid before the Committee. The hon. and gallant Member for Oxfordshire (Colonel North) had referred to a charge of one farthing per week against infantry officers, and, in connection with it, had accused the Government of practising a miserable economy. It would be found, however, on inquiry, that the charge in question had been in existence for a great many years.

COLONEL NORTH: Not with respect to infantry officers. The date of the order applicable to them is the 16th of October last.

The MARQUESS OF HARTINGTON said, the deduction had been made in the case of cavalry officers ever since 1815, and it had only been extended to infantry officers when the latter received the advantages for which it was originally enforced. The hon. and gallant Member had also asked him a question with respect to cooking. In reply, he had to state that the greater part of the item—£1,460—would go in extra pay to sergeants-instructors, of whom there were now 170, and the number was being increased. A considerable saving had been effected in the article of fuel, chiefly in consequence of the improvements made in cooking, which improvements were mainly due to the exertions of the sergeants-instructors. The hon. Baronet opposite (Sir Henry Willoughby) suggested that the Vote might be very advantageously subdivided. He did not exactly see how. A great many of these items were very small, and they were given in great detail.

It would be perfectly competent to move that the Vote be reduced by any one of them, if it was considered desirable; but the great bulk of the Vote was for the pay of the men, and he did not see how that could be advantageously subdivided. The form of the Estimates had been altered only two years ago. Hon. Members were generally agreed that a great improvement had been effected in the form in which the Estimates were now presented to the House; but if it was thought that any real advantage would be obtained by a greater subdivision, he did not suppose there would be any great difficulty in carrying it out. The hon. Member for Lambeth had asked a question about gymnastics. They had taken a very small Vote under that head, but he believed it was the commencement of a system to the army which he thought would be most important. A Committee had inquired into the whole subject of gymnastics as carried out in the armies of other nations, and they had reported that they were of opinion that it would be of immense advantage to the soldier if we had facilities for putting recruits through a regular course of gymnastics as part of their drill. Gymnastics for the amusement of the soldier were, no doubt, beneficial, and they were good in the way of providing a healthy recreation; but what was really required was that the soldier should go through a certain course in proportion to his strength as a part of his drill. It was difficult to estimate the advantage that would be attained by developing the muscles of our troops, and enabling them to undergo hardships to which many now succumbed. He regretted very much he had not been able to lay on the table the Return for which the gallant General (General Peel) had moved, and which he certainly did hope to be able to produce before proceeding with the Estimates. But if that right hon. and gallant General had been present, and he was sorry he was not, he would he was sure have agreed with him, that it was not desirable to postpone the Committee on the Army Estimates until he was able to lay on the table a Return which had been longer in preparation than he anticipated. The fact was, that although it was very easy to tell the number of men enlisted in particular years, it did not at all follow from these numbers that that was the number of men who would be entitled to take their discharge at the end of ten years. For instance, ten years ago, during the Crimean war, a very large number enlisted under the

Ten Years Act, but a very large number of these men died in the Crimea; a very large number, when discharged, were re-engaged, and a considerable number had died since then. Therefore, the large number of men enlisted that year did not represent the number of men entitled to take their discharge this year. The right hon. and gallant General said he had felt considerable apprehensions in regard to the number of men taking their discharge this year. Their information was not complete up to the present time, and the only way in which they could estimate the number that would probably be entitled to their discharge would be by considering the effect of the Limited Enlistment Act on previous years. They had Returns of the effect of the Enlistment Act up to the year 1860. Up to that time, 7,335 men had completed their term of service, and were therefore entitled to take their discharge. Of these, 3,845 were re-engaged; leaving 3,490 who were discharged. Of these 3,490, 650 re-enlisted within six months, and the total loss up to 1860 was only 2,340 men. This had been going on three years and a quarter, the annual loss was therefore only 860 men. There was no reason, he was aware of, to suppose that a larger proportion of men were about to take their discharge than in the three first years when the Act came into operation. They might assume that the same proportions would be maintained. It was quite true, as stated by the right hon. and gallant General, that considerable apprehensions were felt by the Commander-in-Chief and the officers of the army as to the number of men the army was likely to lose; but, although they were under some apprehension, the Commander-in-Chief and the Adjutant General had not estimated the number of men who would be entitled to take their discharge this year at more than 10,400. Now, applying the calculations he had just made to that number, the army was not likely to lose more than 4,000, retaining 6,000 of that number in the ranks; 4,000 would be the total loss at all likely to occur in the ensuing year, owing to the operation of the Limited Enlistment Act; and he asked the Committee to consider for a moment the advantages they had up to the present time enjoyed connected with it. By the Returns of 1850, 1851, and 1852, it appeared that the annual deaths in the army were over 29 per 1,000, while according to the same Returns of 10 years subsequent, 1860,

1861, and 1862, the deaths were reduced to 18 per 1,000, showing in the death vacancies of the army a reduction of 11 per thousand. Now, the average number of men serving during the last years was 195,730, and the difference of the two rates of mortality would cause in these numbers an annual saving in death vacancies of 2,200 men. He was quite aware that they could not attribute all that saving to any particular cause. No doubt, the improved sanitary and medical regulations had done something, and he hoped a great deal; but the great bulk of the saving of 2,200 in the death vacancies annually was to be attributed to the fact that in 1860, 1861, and 1862, we had a much younger class of men than in 1850, 1851, and 1852. After our army had suffered great losses in the Crimea and the Indian mutiny, a very large number of young men joined it. Still it was quite evident that the army was to a certain extent composed of younger men, and, therefore, of a class of men less likely to die rapidly. In that view he was borne out by some medical statistics which had been drawn up, from which it appeared that in the army the number of deaths of men under 30 years of age was 7.06 per 1,000, while of men between 30 and 40 it was 15.99 per 1,000. In India the comparison was still more striking, for serving in India and China the mortality of men under 30 was 25.66 per 1,000, and of men between 30 and 40 it was 43.79 per 1,000. It was clear, therefore, that in an army composed of younger men the mortality was less than among older men. Against the loss occasioned by the discharge of the 10 years' service men, must be set the saving arising from the diminished mortality. As he had before said, some years' further experience of the working of the Act would be necessary to ascertain what were its actual results. When the Legislature passed that Act it must have intended that a certain number of soldiers should take their discharge under it at the expiration of 10 years' service. But, besides the actual gain to the service by the diminished mortality, there were many other ways in which that subject must be regarded. There could be no doubt that men who had served for 10 years in the army must have been improved by the training they had received, and as they would generally remain in the country they might be available for re-enlistment, should an emergency arise. Still, in the uncertainty which ex-

The Marquess of Hartington

isted as to the actual number who would take their discharges, and the certainty that a larger number than hitherto would be entitled to avail themselves of their right, Lord De Grey had had under his consideration a measure which, he hoped, would have the effect of inducing a larger proportion to re-enlist. It was hoped that the necessity for such additional inducement would only be temporary, but it had been decided to offer to the soldier who re-enlisted, not only the bounty which he would now receive, but also an additional £1, which would be the cost of a recruit to replace him. It was also intended to encourage the re-enlistment of soldiers who had taken their discharges, by extending the period of re-enlistment for six months after the discharge to twelve months, and then to allow them to reckon all their past service towards a pension on twenty-one years' service. The right hon. and gallant General (General Peel) had said he thought that alarm must have existed upon the subject, or the authorities would not have been induced to lower the standard in a time of peace. That measure, perhaps, was hardly necessary, and was not caused by the expectation of a greater number of vacancies, but the recruiting was proceeding at a slower rate than was desirable. Much of that slowness was attributable, he believed, to the stringency of the medical regulations, which threw the whole travelling expenses of a recruit rejected by the regimental surgeon upon the surgeon who had originally passed him. The consequence of that regulation was that the surgeons attached to the recruiting staff were over careful in passing recruits, and in order to encourage recruiting so as to obtain the ordinary number, it was intended to relax the regulation he had referred to, and to reduce the standard by one inch. The right hon. and gallant General had alluded to the item of levy money. It must be admitted that that item was not so clearly stated in the Estimates as it might have been. The item was made up in the following manner: — The levy money at home, £32,200, was for 15,000 recruits, and was the real expense of raising that number. The £5,800 for Indian depôts was the same charge for 2,700 men. But the item of £27,000 to make good casualties in India, ought not properly to have been called levy money. Of that amount only £9,000 was really levy money for 4,000 men, but the remaining £18,000 was for the passage of men to India. The

gallant General had inquired whether it was intended to pay the extra bounty to men who re-enlisted in India. The fact was, the Indian Government did pay the extra bounty, and it was right they should, as they saved the cost of the passage home of the men who re-enlisted. With respect to the capitation charges, they were, as the gallant General was aware, the result of a comparison of the gross charges paid by the Indian Government with the total number of men stationed in India. That rate would expire in April, 1866, when they could revise it on much more correct data than they had possessed at the time that the rate was first adopted. They sometimes thought at the War Office that they were losing money by it; but he believed that they would find that there had not been much either gained or lost. The explanation of the great increase of furlough pay was that the furlough regular turns for officers only came into force just before the Indian Mutiny. Of course, during the Indian Mutiny, very few of the officers took advantage of those regulations, and, therefore, it was impossible in the first year to arrive at any correct estimate.

GENERAL PEEL said, he wanted to know whether the supplementary Estimate of £40,000 for the yeomanry, was the exact sum that appeared in the original Estimate. The ground upon which the noble Lord had consented to call out the yeomanry was that the war in New Zealand was nearly at an end, and he should like to hear whether the sum of £40,000 was the saving from that cause.

LORD HOTHAM said, he desired to say a word upon the Limited Enlistment Act. The opening observations of the noble Lord upon that subject had afterwards been materially diluted by the statement, that in consequence of the number of men who might claim their discharge at the end of their period of service, the Secretary for War had thought it necessary to offer inducements to these men beyond those to which they would have been previously entitled. The inducements that would have to be given, would depend very much upon the service on which the men were engaged. One of the objections which he had always entertained to the Act, that it might be the cause of the country being taken by surprise by great numbers of men leaving the army at times when it was very inconvenient to part with them, had, at length, been acknowledged by the Government. At the close of the Peninsular war a large number of men, whose service had expired, claimed their discharge, and he well remembered being employed for three days in the duty of counting out the bounty monies to the men to induce them to re-enlist, at the rate of £16 16s. per man. He had the honour two or three years ago to be employed as Chairman of the Royal Commission on the subject of recruiting for the army, and after a good deal of information had been obtained, it appeared to the Commissioners that, although there might not be any necessity for repealing the Limited Enlistment Act as it stood, yet inasmuch as a man was, perhaps, in the best of his soldier's life when he could claim his discharge under that Act, there was no reason why those who were willing to enlist for fifteen or sixteen years, should not have the opportunity of doing so. It was a mistake to suppose that men enlisted from a military feeling, or from a fondness for military life; they enlisted, for the most part, under the pressure of private circumstances; and there were very few who cared for what period they were to serve, or to whom it would be any inducement to enter for ten years rather than for fifteen. On the contrary, many were deterred from entering the army, now that the period of service was only ten years, by the fear that at the end of the time they would be thrown upon the world without any means of support. The Government might, without the slightest interference with the Limited Enlistment Act, to which they were very much attached because it was a favourite project of Lord Panmure's, carry out this recommendation of the Commission.

COLONEL DICKSON said, that when he found that there was a reduction of only £215,000 upon an expenditure of nearly £15,000,000, and that the supplementary Estimates for the embodied militia amounted to a much larger sum, he thought they could not look with much favour upon the economy of a Government, the Chancellor of the Exchequer of which had, the other night, given them so severe a lesson upon the subject, especially when they found that that economy was accompanied by the reduction of 1,500 men belonging to the most valuable portion of the service. In the War Office the increase for clerks was £4,000, and in that monstrous establishment 409 clerks were employed at an average salary of £270 a year. There were

two kinds of economy—the one of expenditure and the other of management—and he wished to call the attention of the noble Lord to the advisability of not making the reduction of six men and four horses per troop of cavalry, and he hoped the noble Lord would take the matter into his most serious consideration. If the army really was to be reduced, 816 trained cavalry soldiers and 1,372 artillerymen were not exactly the men who should be selected for that purpose. The proposal only showed that they ought not to have at the War Office men unconnected with the service. The noble Lord would acquit him of any personal allusion, for when they considered the noble Lord's position — when they remembered that, with the whole world at his feet, the noble Lord had renounced the frivolities of life—they could not but regard such a course as being alike honourable to himself and advantageous to the country. He considered, however, that when men who had no practical knowledge came to decide upon such arrangements as the one proposed, they ought to consult those whose professional experience and education would have enabled them to form a trustworthy opinion upon the subject. The reduction of six men and four horses per troop would be most disadvantageous to the efficiency of the cavalry regiments. It might appear anomalous to say that horses were the less important part of a cavalry regiment, and it would have been better to have taken off double the number of horses to the same number of men. At present the strength of a cavalry regiment was 621 men and 400 horses, and yet it was almost impossible —the casualties averaging from 160 to 200 men—on any occasion to mount the whole of the horses. The fewer horses there were, the more they could be attended to, and the better instruction would the men receive. A horse, too, could be purchased at any time, and it would be ready for the ranks in six weeks or two months; but a man could not be replaced under a year and a half. If reduction were essential, it would be better to reduce six horses and four men, but it would be still better to leave the men as they were.

THE MARQUESS OF HARTINGTON said, that the proportion of men to horses in which the reduction was being made was the proportion previously existing in the cavalry, so that if it were wrong, then it must have been wrong before. He quite admitted that at the War Office they were not always qualified to judge of these matters, but when that was so they sought advice from those at the Horse Guards who were competent to judge. He did not mean to say that the Commander-in-Chief or the Adjutant General would recommend the reduction of the army. But, when once that reduction was decided upon, the purely military authorities were consulted as to the best way of carrying it out. In this case, the Adjutant General, than whom he did not think there could be any better authority, was of opinion that the efficiency of these cavalry regiments was not impaired by the proposed reductions, further, of course, than by the numerical decrease which would take place in their strength. Since the Crimean war, there had been a great change in the organisation of our cavalry force, and a considerable increase in the strength of the regiments. Formerly a regiment of cavalry consisted of three squadrons; now it consisted of four. In 1853 the number of privates in the regiment was 304; in 1863 it was 504, and the reduction proposed would bring it down to 456. The force of cavalry was 9,132 in 1853, and in 1863 it was 11,331. He did not think that any just complaint could be made as to the manner in which the reduction was to be effected. With regard to the artillery, it was the fact that in the enormous French army there were no more than 30,000 or 40,000 artillerymen, while in our army there were 20,000.

COLONEL NORTH said, the noble Lord seemed to forget the fortifications, and how they were to be manned.

THE MARQUESS OF HARTINGTON: By the militia and Volunteers.

COLONEL NORTH: The militia and Volunteers! Oh, oh!

SIR FREDERIC SMITH said, he wished to ask the reason for the increase of the Vote for fire brigade, musketry warders, works in the field, &c., from £500 in the last year to £3,700 in the Estimates before them.

THE MARQUESS OF HARTINGTON said, his only explanation was that he supposed the sum taken last year was not found sufficient.

Vote *agreed to.*

(2.) Motion made, and Question proposed,

"That a sum, not exceeding £1,319,047, be granted to Her Majesty, to defray the Charge of the Commissariat Establishment, Services, and Movement of Troops, which will come in course of payment during the year ending on the 31st day of March, 1865, inclusive."

SIR FREDERIC SMITH said, that the Vote stood upon the Estimates at £1,352,047.

THE MARQUESS OF HARTINGTON said, that was one of the Votes alluded to by the noble Lord at the head of the Government, when he stated that the extra cost involved in calling out the Yeomanry would not cause an increase on the total Estimates. The Vote had been reduced by £33,000—a reduction warranted, as the Government thought, by the accounts from New Zealand. That reduction was chiefly in the items for commissariat transport to the colonies, which was taken at a very high rate indeed, because while the army was actively engaged in New Zealand, the cost of transport was enormous. There might be a considerable saving on the Estimates which had reference to war in New Zealand, although the war might not come to a conclusion for some little time. The Estimates were framed on a supposition that the war would continue over the whole of the financial year; and though the war was not yet at an end, there was reason to believe that it would not last for more than a year from the date of the last accounts, which dated back for a considerable period. The Government had estimated that the war would continue to April, 1865, and its cessation before that period would cause a corresponding decrease in the Estimates.

SIR FREDERIC SMITH said he wished to ask, what was the reason of the great increase of £46,000 in the cost of forage?

MR. W. WILLIAMS said, he thought the item for buildings and incidental expenses connected with the commissariat excessive.

THE MARQUESS OF HARTINGTON said, that the increase in the item for forage was due to the high price of it in New Zealand. There were commissariat branches in all parts of the world, and the officers had a variety of duties to perform, and the amount referred to by the hon. Member for Lambeth was very reasonable.

MR. HUNT said, he thought it desirable they should report Progress. For the sake of regularity he would suggest that, as an alteration had been made in the amount of the Vote, an amended Estimate should be submitted.

MR. AUGUSTUS SMITH said, he took the same view. He would also observe that the charge for provisions was very high.

THE MARQUESS OF HARTINGTON said, an explanatory paper had been published on the subject of the increased price of provisions in certain parts.

COLONEL BARTTELOT said, he was quite surprised at the amount charged for forage. How many horses were there in New Zealand?

THE MARQUESS OF HARTINGTON said, he could not tell the exact number of horses there, but there could be no doubt that forage was very scarce, as it had been found necessary to send out a certain kind of it from this country.

MR. ARTHUR MILLS urged the Government to prepare an amended Estimate. He believed the cost of the New Zealand war had been much underrated, and at the end of the year it would be found to be nearer a million than half a million.

MR. HUNT said, he would move that the Chairman should report Progress.

THE MARQUESS OF HARTINGTON said, the original Estimate was framed on the supposition that the war would last for three quarters of a year from that month, but later advices had led them to believe that it would be concluded in a shorter time.

MR. AUGUSTUS SMITH said, he wanted to know the items on which a reduction had been made.

VISCOUNT PALMERSTON said, he hoped the Committee would not insist upon reporting Progress. Estimates of future expenses were necessarily conjectural, as were those of savings. The fact simply was that they thought, from the latest advices, that the war would not continue as long as they at first imagined.

MR. HUNT said, he wanted an explanation of the items of reduction.

THE MARQUESS OF HARTINGTON said, the chief reduction was in the item for commissariat transport. There was further a reduction in the cost of forage for the colonies, and also in the charge for provisions.

MR. ARTHUR MILLS said, there would be a difficulty in comparing the items with those of the last and of the next year, if no new Estimate were prepared.

VISCOUNT PALMERSTON observed, that there would be a sum total for this year to be set against that for next year.

Mr. Hunt

ADMIRAL DUNCOMBE said, he thought previous notice ought to have been given of the reduction of an Estimate.

SIR STAFFORD NORTHCOTE said, that the remark of the noble Viscount opposite, though true as regarded the Appropriation Act and the total amounts, yet, on a comparison of the Estimates of one year with those of another, it was more convenient that they should know what the items were.

Motion made, and Question, "That the Chairman do report Progress, and ask leave to sit again,"—(*Mr. Hunt,*)—put, and *negatived.*

Original Question put, and *agreed to.*

(3.) £596,694, Clothing.

COLONEL DUNNE said, he had tried for the last three or four years to obtain from the Government the prices at which the army was clothed, but he had never received any satisfactory reply on that point. He believed the reason was that the accounts were not kept as they ought to be. The system of a great central establishment for clothing the army was a very costly one, and that, under the existing system, the clothing for the army cost double what it otherwise would. Mr. Hume used to find fault with the system of Government establishments, and used to protest that, except in special cases, Government should not undertake any manufacture. He wished to know whether the accounts of these establishments were kept on any system, and whether the noble Lord could state the prices of the articles manufactured?

MR. W. WILLIAMS said, he wished for an explanation of the item of £13,000 for the purchase of buildings for inspecting contract clothing. He agreed with the hon. and gallant Member that the cost of clothing the army was excessive, and ought to be diminished.

MR. O'REILLY said, he gave a preference to the system of clothing adopted in the French army, where the materials were supplied to the different regiments and manufactured by the men themselves. The result was that the clothes of the French soldier were of better materials than those of our troops—they fitted better, and were supplied at a more economical rate. In the Sanitary Report on the Indian army it was proved that the men suffered very much from the misfits of shoes sent out by the contractors. He would press on the Government the advantage of employing the soldier in his idle hours in some trade. From the Report of the Committee it appeared that all the officers examined were in favour of this except Sir George Brown, who maintained that when the soldier was not on drill he might spend his time in the canteen. Sir George Brown was decidedly opposed to the soldier being employed in trade. [An hon. MEMBER: He said nothing about the canteen.] He said that after drill the soldier should have his time to himself. It would be a great improvement if the clothing were made, as in other armies, by the soldiers themselves. He besought hon. Gentlemen who objected to Government establishments to have a care what they did. It was desirable to keep up a system of promotion in the army, and these central establishments offered to soldiers a sort of promotion to which the degree of their attainments rendered them eligible.

MR. CARNEGIE observed, that when the hon. Member for Longford drew a comparison between the French army and ours, it should be recollected that the French army was raised by conscription and ours by voluntary enlistment. The French army, therefore, had a much larger number of skilled mechanics than our own. He had always found there had been ample employment for all tailors and shoemakers in making alterations and repairs, without setting them to actual making of regimental clothing. If the clothing were attempted to be made in the regimental workshops, he believed it would not be attended with good results. He quite agreed as to the advisability of rewarding efficient non-commissioned officers, but he did not see how the introduction of the system of manufacturing in regiments the clothes to be worn by the soldiers would at all tend to that desirable end.

COLONEL NORTH said, that the duty required from the English soldier was much more than that required from the foreign soldier. He would also observe that if there was one thing more than another which would give offence to officers and soldiers in the army, it would be interfering with the buttons and facings of their uniforms. Civilians had no idea what were the feelings in the army on that subject, and he therefore hoped the day was far distant when the Government would interfere in such matters.

SIR FREDERIC SMITH said, he believed it to be the opinion of many French officers that their own system was a bad

one. No fewer than 30,000 men were employed in making up clothing and shoes for the French army, and about 1,000 in making caps. These men never took part in action, or left the depôts of the different regiments. Was the clothing of our army badly made just then? He did not think so. It was much better made than it used to be when the colonels of regiments had it made up and got a profit by it. Then nearly every suit had to be unmade and made up again in order to fit the men. It would be much better to leave the present system as it was, than attempt to make the clothing and shoes of a regiment by those who ought to be fighting men.

MR. W. WILLIAMS said, he wished to know whether it would not be more economical to hire buildings for their manufactures than to build great establishments at Pimlico?

THE MARQUESS OF HARTINGTON admitted that the sum required for new buildings in Pimlico was very large, but those buildings were finished, and he could not see how it could be more economical to hire buildings when they had got what they wanted. It was said they could not tell the cost of any article; but they knew the cost of materials and the other expenses, and, therefore, they could calculate the cost of the articles made. Since they had manufactured clothing themselves, the cost of that portion which was still got from contractors was materially diminished. In 1859 the contract price of a private's tunic was £1 1s., but in 1863 it was only 16s. 5d., such reduction being caused by the Government competition. Comparisons had been made between the cost of clothing in the English and the French armies; but, even admitting that the French soldier was equally well clothed as our men, it was certain that he did not receive so many articles of clothing, and had to wear them much longer. He really thought the clothing of the English soldier was the point least open to attack.

GENERAL PEEL said, he was surprised to hear complaints of the clothing, as he had thought that if there had been any improvement in any department of the army, it was in the clothing. When he established the Pimlico manufactory he believed experience would prove what it had done, that by that means army clothing would be produced both better and cheaper. He thought that the Royal Artillery had always made their own clothes.

When he filled the position of War Secretary he had caused Returns to be made, showing the expense of the clothing in every regiment in the army, and he should be glad if such a Return were placed before Parliament every year. It would afford much useful information.

COLONEL DUNNE said, he believed that the establishment at Pimlico clothed 30,000 men, besides the Irish constabulary and the London police, but he did not think that one establishment would be sufficient to clothe the whole army; Although he did not object to a moderate establishment to operate as a check upon contractors, he deprecated too large an establishment as uselessly expensive.

MR. HUNT said, there appeared to be a reduction in the cost of the clothing. Tunics that formerly were charged a guinea, were now supplied at 16s. 5d. If they had had published the cost of the clothing in 1859 in the present Estimates, they would have been able to have formed some idea whether the new clothing department had had any effect in reducing the expenses in that department.

MR. CARNEGIE said, he wished to call attention to the item with regard to clerks. The military store clerks appeared to have been got rid of and pensioners employed in their stead.

SIR STAFFORD NORTHCOTE asked, what was the meaning of the entire abolition of the military store clerks? A number of clerks had been engaged for a considerable time as temporary clerks, but he believed it was the feeling of the late Sir George Lewis and former Secretaries for War, that it was desirable to absorb them as much and as often as possible into permanent clerks. He asked if all the temporary clerks in the department had been so absorbed, or if they had been disposed of in any other way. Temporary clerks, so called, but who had discharged their duties as such for a number of years, and as such they were deserving of much consideration, should be dealt with tenderly.

MR. AUGUSTUS SMITH said, that taking the number of men in the Estimates, and dividing with them the cost of the clothing, it gave a sum somewhat less than £4 for each man. He, however, admitted that that was not a fair way of arriving at the individual cost.

THE MARQUESS OF HARTINGTON said, there had been no alteration in the Pimlico staff. Some of the store clerks had been removed, and absorbed in other departments, as vacancies occurred; but he was not aware until that moment, that any of them had been only temporary clerks.

Vote agreed to.

(4.) £611,165, Barracks.

COLONEL NORTH asked, to what cause the saving in the use of fuel, referred to in the Vote, was to be attributed?

COLONEL DUNNE said, he wished for an explanation of the alteration with regard to the payment of the ranger of the Curragh of Kildare.

THE MARQUESS OF HARTINGTON said, that as the Curragh had become a military station, it was thought better to transfer the charges to the military department, instead of continuing them with the office of Woods and Forests. The Curragh, up to that time, had hitherto been held by the Crown at a nominal rent, but now it was proposed to take a lease of the property. In answer to the question of the hon. and gallant Member for Oxfordshire (Colonel North), the saving in the fuel had been effected partly by the use of improved grates in the barracks, and, still more, by better management in the cooking department. The plan of allowing the men a profit upon the price of the fuel burnt under the regulation quantity had in many cases been eminently successful.

COLONEL NORTH asked the amount of the pay and allowances of the Inspector.

THE MARQUESS OF HARTINGTON said, the Inspector's (Mr. Marriner's) salary was £150 a year, and his travelling expenses actually expended. Captain Ross, Assistant Quartermaster General at Aldershot, who was not exclusively employed in the cooking department, was included in the general staff, the expense of which, when completed, would be about £1,750.

Vote agreed to.

(5.) £45,433, Divine Service.

(6.) £40,549, Martial Law.

LORD HOTHAM said, that although he could count a length of service in the House, only exceeded by that of the noble Lord at the head of Her Majesty's Government, and, he believed, by that of two other hon. Members, he could truly say he had never risen with so much reluctance as he felt on the present occasion. That reluctance proceeded from many causes, but he would trouble the Committee with only two—one was, because the question was one of military discipline, and

General Peel

the other, because he had to take exception to the conduct of the two high individuals to whom the Queen, in the exercise of her Prerogative as head of the army, had confided its management, and who it had always been both his desire and his habit to support. He felt, as he always had felt, that except under circumstances of an extraordinary nature, questions of military discipline were not adapted to the consideration of popular assemblies; but Her Majesty's Government, having asked for a grant of money to cover the expenses of the late court-martial at Aldershot, had created the necessity for a discussion, which it was impossible to avoid. If any hon. Member were of opinion that the money so asked for had been unnecessarily or wastefully expended, or that in its expenditure the efficiency of the service for which the House was called upon annually to sanction the disbursement of such enormous sums had been injured, it would be his imperative duty to say so. He was glad to be able to say (and this was the only occasion when he would thus express himself) that to Sir Hugh Rose, Sir William Mansfield, and Colonel Crawley, he was a total stranger. He could, therefore, be influenced by no personal feelings in the course he was taking. He wished it also to be borne in mind that he stood there to speak his own sentiments, and not those of any one else. He had been asked by no one to be his mouthpiece, or to say a word on the subject. And, above all, he desired to disclaim all wish to shelter any one from the consequences of his misconduct; for in his (Lord Hotham's) opinion, every soldier should do his duty properly, and if he did it not, he should be compelled to do it. He believed that both the House and the country had great reason to complain of the conduct of the military authorities in withholding information which they must have had in their possession, and which ought, on every principle of justice, to have been published. He did not mean to impute any intentional error to those high authorities to whom he had already referred, but he believed that they were appalled by the fire of the battery opened upon them by the hon. Gentleman the late Member for Brighton (Mr. Coningham) and others, that they thus became victims to the common misfortune of over-anxious and over-sensitive minds, and that they did injustice from the fear of being thought not willing to do justice, and

wrong, from the fear of being accused of not doing right. It would be remembered that great excitement prevailed in the country during the last year, in consequence of information which came from India respecting the Mhow Court Martial, and that the subject was brought forward in this House by the hon. Member for Andover (Mr. Dudley Fortescue), on the 5th of June last year. On that occasion, appeals were made by the hon. Gentleman to the sensibilities of every one, and attention was particularly attracted to such sentences as these:—"The prisoners had been confined in a bomb-proof building, unfit for habitation," "more like an oven than a human habitation," that "these facts were not imaginary, but that he had drawn them from documents placed in the hands of the military authorities." The hon. Member also stated that as to the brandy which it was said Sergeant Major Lilley had consumed, "the evidence of the sentries and of the medical officers proved conclusively that there was not the slightest symptom of excess, and that this had been endorsed by His Royal Highness the Commander-in-Chief." With regard to the prisoner's quarters, it was now a matter of public notoriety that General Sir William Mansfield, the Commander-in-Chief in Bombay, was at Mhow in March, 1863; and that being so, he must have reported to the military authorities upon what he saw and knew to be the case on the subject, and information supplied by General Mansfield contradictory of the account given by the hon. Member for Andover must have been in possession of the Government at the time. Unless the noble Lord stated, of his own personal knowledge, that no such information was then possessed by the Government, he must be excused for remaining of that opinion. The noble Lord confirmed the greater part of what th hon. Member for Andover had said, and further stated — though his statement, strange to relate, seemed to have made no impression—"that the sergeant major had grossly derogated from his duty in not bringing to the knowledge of his commanding officer what was going forward in the regiment," and he assured the House that, "although he could not produce to them a victim, nothing would induce the Secretary of State to depart a hair's breadth from the strict rules and principles of justice." Soon after, it was announced that Colonel Crawley would be tried by a court-martial; and subsequently, that he would be tried—not in India, but in England. A portion of the press took credit for having caused this change. It was monstrous, said they, that Colonel Crawley should be tried by a court nominated by Sir Hugh Rose, who had approved the proceedings of the court-martial at Mhow; and yet these lovers of justice said it was quite proper that the members of the court should be named by His Royal Highness the Commander-in-Chief, by whom Colonel Crawley had been condemned, in language such as he (Lord Hotham) never remembered being used towards an officer of Colonel Crawley's position, and to which it would be his (Lord Hotham's) duty, before he sat down, to allude. Several inquiries were then made as to the propriety of the course announced. The hon. Member for West Norfolk asked if it was legal, and if legal, whether it did not involve a reflection on, if not an insult to, the officers of the army in India. The hon. and gallant Member for Limerick (Major Gavin) said that he had, not long ago, served in India, and that he considered it as an insult to say that the case could not be tried fairly there. The right hon. Gentleman (Mr. Disraeli), with the natural feeling of an ex-Chancellor of the Exchequer, asked whether the expenses would not be very great. Of this there was no doubt, as was shown by the Vote of upwards of £18,000, now under consideration. On the 25th of June it was asked by the Member for Brighton, whether a second memorandum, embodying the opinion of His Royal Highness the Commander-in-Chief on the Mhow Court Martial, had not been issued, to which the noble Lord (the Marquess of Hartington) answered in the negative, adding, "no public memorandum at least." Following these inquiries, a right hon. Gentleman (Mr. Bouverie) said, he wished to know distinctly whether any communication had been addressed to Sir Hugh Rose, through the Adjutant General, the purport of which was to qualify the memorandum issued by the Commander-in-Chief on the 18th of the previous December. And now he (Lord Hotham) came to a point of very serious importance—a point involving not only the proceedings of which he had spoken, but involving the relations of the Government with the House of Commons. In replying to the question of the right hon. Gentleman, the noble Lord stated that if he would put

Lord Hotham

the question on another day he would answer it, but he apprehended that he should be compelled to repeat the answer he had already given, "that there was no public or official memorandum existing on the subject excepting that which had been published." The inquiries made about the second memorandum attracted the attention of the public, and, curiously enough, on the very day when the noble Lord denied the existence of any second memorandum, there appeared in *The Times* a letter signed "Civilian," in which the writer said—

"I believe I can assist Mr. Bouverie in describing the document bearing on the Mhow Court Martial which he asks the War Office to produce. Two memoranda, emanating from the Horse Guards, have been read by Colonel Crawley to the assembled officers of the 6th Dragoons. They are, therefore, clearly not private letters, but public documents, which the House of Commons is entitled to see. The first of them is dated December 18, 1862, and has been published; the second, which was communicated by Colonel Crawley to the regiment at Mhow about the end of April or the beginning of May, 1863, is probably the document which Mr. Bouverie wishes to elicit. I have a *resumé* of it before me. It cannot possibly be identical with the letter dated 'Horse Guards, February, 1863,' privately sent to the Commander-in-Chief in India by the Duke of Cambridge, which has since been produced, inasmuch as a private document of that nature would certainly not have been formally read to the assembled officers of any regiment."

He believed that there was no public office the heads of which were not promptly informed of anything which appeared in the papers affecting or reflecting upon them; and therefore it was impossible to surmise that not one of the numerous gentlemen employed in the War Office had called the noble Lord's attention to that letter, and that he should not have renewed his inquiries whether he had not been misled as to the existence of the document in question. On the 29th of June—four days afterwards—the right hon. Gentleman (Mr. Bouverie) repeated his inquiry, so worded as apparently to prevent all possibility of mistake. He asked whether any communication or memorandum signed by the Adjutant General has been sent to the Commander-in-Chief in India modifying the opinion on the proceedings of the court-martial at Mhow contained in the memorandum of His Royal Highness the Commander-in-Chief, now upon the table of the House, or in any way relating to the same subject. To that inquiry the noble Lord replied—

"The only document which at all answers the description of it given by my right hon. Friend is a communication or memorandum which was last March forwarded by the Adjutant General to the Commander-in-Chief in India, and which was covered by private letters to Sir William Mansfield and Sir Hugh Rose. The private letters that covered the memorandum were marked 'Private,' and they were addressed, 'My dear Mansfield,' and 'My dear Rose.' . . . I hope I have made it sufficiently clear to the House that when I stated there was no 'public memorandum' on this subject I was perfectly correct."

This question touched very importantly the relations between the House and the Government. It would be recollected that Government had a great advantage in respect of the production of papers. It was the practice to give implicit credence to the assurance of any Member of the Government in such cases. If a paper were asked for, and the Government said it was prejudicial to the public interest to produce it, then it was taken for granted that the answer was a proper one, and no Member would venture to push his inquiry farther; but it was a matter touching the relations of the House of Commons and the Government if it should turn out, after repeated denials of the existence of a particular paper, that that paper had been in the possession of the Government at the time its existence was denied. With respect to this document nothing further took place until the present Session, when he moved for the production of "any paper or memorandum other than the one previously presented," and the Committee would be surprised to learn that the Return to that Motion was the very identical paper for which the right hon. Member (Mr. E. P. Bouverie) had made such repeated applications last year, and the existence of which was so constantly and perseveringly denied. He could carry the matter a step further, because they now knew that the paper of March the 14th was an answer to a letter of Sir Hugh Rose of the 20th of January, which, as hon. Members would doubtless remember, appeared in the proceedings of the Mhow Court Martial. The importance of the paper was very great, for if it had been produced, the statement of the hon. Member for Andover, as to there never having been any suspicion, either before or during Lilley's confinement, that he had taken spirits, could have been flatly contradicted. It was written in reply to the letter of Sir Hugh Rose, enclosing the addendum of the medical officer of the Inniskilling Dragoons, dated the day after the *post mortem* examination, which said—

"In addition to my report of yesterday, I have the honour to add that it has been brought to my notice that the deceased was in the habit of drinking a considerable quantity of brandy daily while in arrest, and on inquiry I find this to be true. It is my opinion that this, in conjunction with the other exciting causes before stated, was calculated to increase the predisposition to apoplectic seizure of which he died."

Having stated these things, the conclusion which he drew was, that this court-martial need not, ought not, and if the whole truth had been told, would not have taken place in England. The noble Lord would no doubt refer to the excitement which existed, but to this, he (Lord Hotham) would reply, that that excitement was mainly created by the silence of the Government upon these points. If they had told the House and the country what they knew, but what they carefully concealed, he did not believe that there would have been half the excitement, or any of the scandal which they had witnessed during the last twelve months, nor should they have had to pay a Bill of £18,000. But other reasons had been given for holding the court-martial in this country. One was, that "grave charges had been brought against Colonel Crawley in the public press and in Parliament on the authority of persons entitled to confidence." The hon. Member for Andover was entitled to be implicitly believed as to anything which he stated of his own knowledge, but as in this instance he had received his information from others, and as the Government had responsible officers whose reports they had already received, he did not think that that was any reason for departing from the ordinary course. Then it was said, that the refusal to hold the court-martial here would have operated against recruiting, but there might be found in the proceedings of the court-martial at Aldershot ample evidence to set at rest any such apprehension. Again, the Secretary of State for War and the noble Lord (the Marquess of Hartington) had given as another reason for holding the court-martial in England, that Colonel Crawley had admitted and confessed that he had committed an act of inhumanity. But any one who would take the trouble of looking at the Mhow Blue Book would see that what Colonel Crawley said was that "if" he had been guilty of the act imputed to him, or had had any knowledge of it, it would have been an act of inhumanity on his part. Was that a reason for holding the court-martial in this country? It was also said that another reason was to be found in a letter from Lieutenant Fitzsimon, complaining of Colonel Crawley, which Paymaster Smales had delivered to His Royal Highness the Commander-in-Chief. It was well known to be one of the first principles of military discipline, that no complaint should be forwarded otherwise than through, and accompanied by, the explanation of the commanding officer. And yet the Commander-in-Chief had received the letter in question from the hands of one, then only known as one just cashiered by the sentence of a court-martial, and had acted upon it without any previous communication with the Commander-in-Chief in India. And this was the more extraordinary, inasmuch as only a year before, on March 18, 1862, His Royal Highness had directed Sir William Mansfield to inform this same officer (Smales) that "he had been guilty of a great error and breach of discipline in forwarding a letter to the Secretary of State for War direct, instead of through his immediate commanding officer." When the court-martial met, Colonel Crawley earnestly prayed that he might be tried on every charge that had been made against him, but his prayer was not granted. Colonel Crawley then appealed again to the Commander-in-Chief, who replied, coldly, that it was not proposed to make any addition to the charges. Colonel Crawley then naturally thought that, at least, he would be allowed to show why he had done certain things of which he had been accused. The prosecutor objected, on the ground —first, that it would be irrelevant to go into these matters, and that if they did "the inquiry would be altogether endless." This was an unfortunate observation to proceed from the prosecutor. What would have been said of the Solicitor General if, when recently prosecuting seven foreigners (of whom five had since been executed) for piracy, he had made use of such language? He would have been execrated from one end of the country to the other; and yet, of what value would Colonel Crawley's life have been to him if he had been convicted of such charges as were brought against him? Then again, as to the prosecutor's reply. How was that to be characterized? He (Lord Hotham) had the advantage of possessing a large acquaintance among lawyers, and he had availed himself of it to ask whether the course pursued at the court-martial on Colonel Crawley would have been tolerated

Lord Hotham

in any court of law. They one and all declared that any attempt on the part of the prosecutor to introduce new matter in the reply would have been instantly stopped, and most probably reprehended, by the bench. What could have been the object of attacking, in the reply, the Commander-in-Chief in India and the Commander of the Forces in Bombay, who were not there to defend themselves, except to make a last expiring attempt to obtain on any terms a conviction, and to make such conviction apply to all that had been said and done against Colonel Crawley? When the result of the court-martial was known, every one expected that the Commander-in-Chief, in announcing it to the army, would deal handsomely with Colonel Crawley. He had been acquitted in the fullest and most honourable manner, without any defence except that which the prosecutor had made for him, and after a trial which would have been stopped in Westminster Hall, at the end of the prosecution, on the ground that there was nothing to go to the jury. He (Lord Hotham) felt sure that the Commander-in-Chief would take a wide and extended view of the whole of the proceedings, from their commencement to their end, and if it appeared that he had previously said against any persons that which they did not deserve, or in favour of others more than they deserved, he would take that opportunity of setting matters right, and putting everything before the army and the country in a way which no one could misunderstand. The object of military, like that of civil, punishment was not vengeance, but to deter others from committing the like offences. If a regiment or its officers were proved to be guilty of extraordinary misconduct, the fact ought to be published to the whole army. If, as in the present case, the commanding officer of a regiment was put on his trial and honourably acquitted, common justice required that the whole army also should be made cognizant of the fact. Cases of this kind were fortunately rare, but there were two which he would mention. In 1814, the commanding officer of the 10th Hussars was brought before a court-martial on the complaint of his officers, and although reprimanded on a point of small importance, the charges substantially failed. The proceedings of the Court being laid before the Prince Regent, he ordered the Commander-in-Chief, the Duke of York, to announce His Royal Highness's opinion on the subject, which was that all the officers should be removed, and that the letter embodying his Royal Highness's commands should not only be read at the head of each regiment, but be entered in its order book. In the case of the 85th Regiment, also, in 1813, there was a solemn adjudication of the Prince Regent to the same effect. Surely, if there had ever been held a court-martial, the result of which ought to have been notified in the most solemn and formal manner, the late court-martial at Aldershot was one. No such notification, however, had been made to the army, nor had any thing appeared but a memorandum published in the newspapers—addressed, apparently, to no one, and remarkable for its deviation from the ordinary course of proceeding in being signed by the Military Secretary; whereas the universal rule was that all letters and orders on the subject of discipline should be signed by the Adjutant General. And when he looked at the contents of this memorandum, he (Lord Hotham) could not help saying that, considering that Colonel Crawley had been fully and honourably acquitted of the charges preferred against him, considering also the character he had received from innumerable witnesses—a character of which any officer might well be proud, it would have been more generous, and certainly more conducive to the good of the service, if instead of speaking of Colonel Crawley in the way he had done, His Royal Highness had seen fit to signify to the army his determination to support him in the exercise of his just authority, and to convey, privately, any further admonition which the case might have seemed to require. But how have matters been left by this memorandum? There remained the recorded and unrevoked opinion of the Commander-in-Chief that the regiment had always been in excellent order until Colonel Crawley took the command of it. The Committee, however, could not have forgotten a question which was put on the court-martial to which the prosecutor objected, and a letter which was asked for by Colonel Crawley, and of which, after two days delay, it was stated that it would be "detrimental to the public service" to admit the production. It was clear, therefore, what were the contents of that document, but in addition to this, it was also clear that His Royal Highness had been misled on this point, inasmuch as it was now matter of general notoriety

in India that, from the period of the arrival of the Inniskillings in that country, or shortly after, the state of its officers had been reprobated by Sir Henry Somerset, then Commander-in-Chief in Bombay, and by every, or nearly every, other general officer who had had the regiment under his command. And yet it was left on record that the Commander-in-Chief considered the regiment to have been in perfect order until it got into the hands of Colonel Crawley. And how stood the case as regarded Sir Hugh Rose and Sir William Mansfield? Personal compliments had, indeed, been paid them, and credit for good intentions given; but in no instance that he (Lord Hotham) had been able to discover, had any reliance been placed on their judgment. Sir Hugh Rose had reported, on the authority of Dr. Turnbull, Assistant Surgeon Barnett, and Mrs. Lilley, that the unfortunate Sergeant Major had, during his confinement, drank daily a sufficient quantity of brandy to "compromise" his life; and this was corroborated by two Inspectors General of Hospitals, Dr. Beatson and Dr. Linton. His Royal Highness gave his opinion that

"Had Sir Hugh Rose been better acquainted with some of the facts of the Sergeant Major's case, he would have taken a different view of it."

And again, His Royal Highness said that "there was no proof that he took brandy to such an extent as to cause his death." Sir William Mansfield had reported that the

"Clandestine, unsoldierlike, and improper proceedings of the three non-commissioned officers might be fairly interpreted by Colonel Crawley into a conspiracy."

And Sir Hugh Rose, in a letter dated April 16, 1863, referred to

"Evidence in proof of a cabal on the part of the three non-commissioned officers having been already forwarded to the Horse Guards."

His Royal Highness had given publicly his opinion that there seemed " not to have been a shadow of foundation for a charge of conspiracy." Again, Sir Hugh Rose had reported that Sergeant Major Lilley

"Had, on more occasions than one, acted with great impropriety, and want of discipline ; that he was not by any means the superior non-commissioned officer described by the Commander-in-Chief to have been."

And that Sir William Mansfield had stated that he was " a very ill-behaved non-commissioned officer." And that there exists

" An official, recorded, and public proof of his misconduct already forwarded to the Horse Guards."

Sir William Mansfield had also reported the use by Sergeant Major Lilley, of

" Objectionable and opprobrious language, in presence of other non-commissioned officers, towards Colonel Crawley."

That he

" Hoped that there might be some mistake as to the use of those beastly and abominable expressions against his commanding officer, which had been attributed to him."

And that he had ordered him to be deprived of his " situation of regimental sergeant major." Of these serious reports, the Commander-in-Chief had taken no other public notice than to say that

" The character of Sergeant Major Lilley for sobriety and good conduct, previous to his arrest, seems to have been undoubted.

All these circumstances were well known in the regiment, and every hon. Member could judge what effect was likely to be produced on the minds of the officers, noncommissioned officers, and men, when they found that the Commander-in-Chief had thought them undeserving of notice. But a great question still remained to be considered—namely, on what principles was the army, henceforward, to be governed. If it was to be governed on the principles which had been applied to this case, he (Lord Hotham) had no hesitation in stating that, before many years had elapsed, its discipline would be such as, to quote an expression of the Commander-in-Chief, "to render it worse than useless." An officer who received a commission in the army was bound to devote his best energies of mind and body to the service of his Sovereign, but he had a right to expect something in return. He had a right to expect that a liberal interpretation should be put on his actions — that allowance should be made for the difficulties under which he might be placed, and that he should receive protection and support from the Crown, at all events, until it had been proved that he had been guilty of any crime. That rule had clearly not been acted upon in the case of Colonel Crawley. The Government had had it in their power to protect him from much of the obloquy which had fallen upon him, but they had stood by, and by their silence allowed him to be condemned by public opinion for almost every offence, except cowardice and desertion, of which an officer could be guilty. He (Lord Hotham) need not tell the Committee how much,

Lord Hotham

in military operations, may depend on the exercise of promptitude and vigour in times of emergency. How could they expect officers to act with vigour and decision in such times, if they had to stop and think, not what should be done, but what the hon. Members for Brighton or Andover would say of them, and how much protection or support they would receive from their superiors!

Sir Hugh Rose and Sir W. Mansfield were not " bloated aristocrats ; " they had not got to their present high positions by influence or high connections, but as the result of their services in the field. They were officers who had rendered good service to their country at the time when the fate of the Indian Empire hung trembling in the balance, and to whom the country would look in any future war. He (Lord Hotham) took leave to say, that if they had been so utterly deficient in judgment as the orders issued from the Horse Guards had, not unnaturally, led the public to consider them, they ought, long since, to have been recalled. But although the authorities had not thought fit to remove them, they had allowed their representative at the courtmartial to discredit the authority and to damage the character of these officers in the estimation of the army and the nation, by perverting their language and misrepresenting their conduct. He entirely agreed with the author of an able pamphlet, to which much reference had been made, in asking whether

" It is in this manner that the authority and influence of Commanders-in-Chief are to be maintained in the eyes of their subordinates, and whether such treatment of such men is compatible with the well-being of the English army, or the safety of the Indian Empire."

He (Lord Hotham) was deeply grieved to be compelled to make these observations, but the subject to which they referred was much too important to be allowed to pass unnoticed. What had been done by the Government had created general regret in the army, and it would require a long time, and a very different course of action, to restore to the Executive that confidence in its firmness and in its decisions which it ought to possess, and which had been so rudely and so lamentably shaken by its conduct in this case.

The Marquess of HARTINGTON said, he hastened to dissipate the very natural apprehension of the Committee by stating at the outset that he did not intend to follow the noble Lord through the able but very long statement he had made on the question of the trial of Colonel Crawley. It was with some surprise that he recollected that the noble Lord on a former occasion, when the Amendment was put that it was not expedient to produce any further correspondence on the subject, did not make a point of being present to return a negative to that question. [Lord HOTHAM: I was in my place.] Then he was still more astonished that the noble Lord did not cry " No ! " [Lord HOTHAM: Does the noble Lord mean to say I did not ?] At any rate, the noble Lord did not call for a division. No one could have assented to the Motion of the right hon. Gentleman opposite without also assenting to the principle he laid down, that such subjects ought not to be discussed in the House. Moreover, the noble Lord had an opportunity of expressing his views, but he made only a short speech, saying, as he understood, that he would not ask for more papers, and that he thought further discussion of the matter unadvisable. [Lord HOTHAM: No, no !] The noble Lord would not make his statement then, but waited for two or three weeks, and then delivered a very long speech, replying to many of the arguments used on the former occasion. What would be said if the hon. Member for Andover (Mr. D. Fortescue) took a week or two to consider the noble Lord's remarks, and then came down and answered them ? The noble Lord asserted that the Government, when the subject was first brought before the House, were in the possession of information which ought to have enabled them to refute the great part of the hon. Member for Andover's charges. The other night he stated that the Government and the Horse Guards were no doubt in the possession of evidence which showed that the dwelling in which Sergeant Major Lilley died was one similar to that in which he would have lived if not in confinement. He regretted to find, in regard to his speech last year, that he either omitted to state that to the House, or, at least, that he mentioned it in such a manner that it escaped the notice of the reporters. He certainly never understood that the hon. Member for Andover wished to assert that Sergeant Major Lilley was confined in a black hole, or that the house differed from his ordinary dwelling. He was sorry, however, that he did not put the point to the House with sufficient distinctness last year. That was the only portion of the statement of the hon Mem-

ber for Andover which last June he was in a position to dispute. As to the essential charge against Colonel Crawley, and that on which he was eventually tried—that he caused sentries to be posted in Lilley's quarters so as to render the punishment unnecessarily aggravating and severe—he had not then the materials on which he could contradict it. It was further said that there was a great deal of hesitation and delay about the production of papers. The fact was, that having to deal with such a mass of correspondence, the Government had great difficulty in knowing exactly what were the documents asked for. It had been asserted that it was wrong to give any papers at all ; but the Government certainly desired to give only those which would enlighten the House. They were quite aware that the publication of one led to a demand for another, and that, therefore, it was very essential that none should be given except those which were absolutely necessary. As to the memorandum asked for, speaking on the authority of the Commander-in-Chief, he stated he did not know of any memorandum answering the description given of that required, except a private one. He believed that the memorandum asked for in the House was stated very clearly to be one in which the Commander-in-Chief modified the opinion given on the whole case in the first memorandum. His Royal Highness, conscious that he had never materially modified his first opinion, very naturally said he did not know of any memorandum of the kind. [Lord HOTHAM: What is the meaning, then, of the words, " very much modified ?"] It was, he owned, unfortunate that these words were ever used, for they had led to great misapprehension. He believed many hon. Members and the public read those words without perusing the rest of the memorandum. The second memorandum modified was the Commander-in-Chief's opinion on Sir Hugh Rose's remarks ; but he did not think any document existed that materially modified his Royal Highness's view of the general merits of the case. As to the letter on which the noble Lord opposite laid so much stress, it was not a memorandum at all. His Royal Highness undoubtedly did not know what was the document which hon. Members wished to obtain when the delay arose as to the production of the memorandum. His Royal Highness, as he had told the House, was most anxious that all he had written to Sir Hugh Rose modifying his opinion should be made known, and that led him to desire that certain passages of the letter referred to should, if possible, be given. The noble Lord was not correct in stating that the court-martial would cost £11,000 more than the House had yet heard of. He did not believe there was any sum including even the Indian allowances for witnesses in this country, of the slightest importance which was not comprised in the account already laid on the table. The noble Lord had complained of the narrow charge upon which Colonel Crawley was tried. Last year it was stated over and over again that Colonel Crawley was not responsible for the arrest. In that respect he was covered by the orders of his superior officer, but it was thought that there were circumstances connected with the manner in which the arrest had been carried out which ought to be made the subject of further investigation. Eventually that investigation assumed the form of a court-martial, and even before Parliament was prorogued last autumn the charges upon which it was intended to try Colonel Crawley were known. The noble Lord had also referred to the fact that the result of the court-martial was not promulgated in a general order. He did not know whether it would have been in accordance with precedent to issue a general order, but, at all events, the Commander-in-Chief had published a document in which the full and complete nature of the acquittal of Colonel Crawley was recorded, in which several hostile witnesses were severely censured, and in which others were subjected to punishment. It was not his intention to follow the noble Lord further. The whole question had already been decided, and he did not think any useful object would be gained by re-opening it.

SIR WILLIAM FRASER said, he wished to call the attention of the Advocate General to what he submitted was the inexpediency of making the colonel of the regiment the prosecutor in the event of a court-martial upon an officer of his regiment. The practice was, in his opinion, most objectionable, as putting, it might be, a distinguished officer in an unpleasant position, and likely to breed ill-feeling in regiments. Supposing that an adjutant was brought before a court-martial and acquitted, how could the business of the regiment be properly carried on with the adjutant in daily communication with his

The Marquess of Hartington

colonel who had tried, without success, to convict him of what had been laid to his charge. He trusted that some other arrangements would be adopted in future.

MR. HUNT said, he thought that the whole question of the administration of military law required investigation. The present system worked well enough in ordinary cases, but, as had recently been proved, it broke down under unusual pressure. The duties of the Judge Advocate, he thought, wanted revision, for it was his duty to advise the prosecutor, whilst, at the same time, he was legal assessor to the tribunal that had to adjudicate on the matter. Surely a person who acted as assessor should not be connected with the prosecution; and probably it would be better to have a legal assessor to give his assistance to the court. It was also desirable that the practice of writing out questions should be done away with, and that witnesses should be subjected, when necessary, to a sharp cross-examination. There was another point as to the assistance given to a prisoner by legal gentlemen. If legal assistance was allowed to be given, why should it not be regularly recognized by the Court? In the case of Colonel Crawley, he was reprimanded by the Court for putting a certain question to a witness, and he was obliged to explain that the question was not drawn up by him, but was first placed in his hands by the gentleman who sat next to him—his legal assistant. Then the prisoner had to read a long defence, which was written for him by a legal gentleman the day before; but he did not see why, when the defence was to be made, the legal gentleman should not make his speech as in any other court. He thought the whole question of sufficient importance to be dealt with by a Royal Commission.

LORD LOVAINE observed, that the recent trial had shown the great inconvenience of the present procedure; because words had been placed in the mouth of an officer attributing injustice to one of the highest military authorities in India, and folly to another. With reference to the speech which had been read by the prisoner in this case, that it was quite clear, from a note that subsequently appeared in *The Times*, it had been sent to that newspaper before it was delivered in court. As published, it contained passages which were omitted when the speech was actually read before the court.

COLONEL DICKSON said, he thought that the worst thing that could happen would be the introduction of an extra legal authority into courts-martial. He trusted that the time would never come when regimental or military courts-martial would be conducted by other than the colonel of the regiment ; for, however much courts-martial were blamed for their decisions, it generally turned out that they had been right after all. He hoped they had heard the last of the court-martial on Colonel Crawley. The continued discussion of the question was calculated to have a very deleterious effect upon the discipline of the army.

MR. HEADLAM said, that when the subject was formerly before the House, he had expressed his opinion that in ordinary cases justice was well administered by courts-martial, but that the legal machinery of the Judge Advocate General's office was not sufficient to conduct such a trial as had lately taken place. At the same time, he could not admit many of the statements which had been made as to the manner in which that trial had been conducted ; but that was a subject he would not go into at that time. It might be very easy to say that no legal assistance should be given, but he did not see how it was possible to preclude it. The whole subject of courts-martial was under consideration, and every effort would be made to place it on as sound and satisfactory a basis as possible.

MR. HUNT said, he hoped that the noble Lord would take care that the Votes were amended in consequence of the favourable news from New Zealand.

Vote *agreed to*.

House *resumed*.

Resolutions to be reported *To-morrow*.

Committee to sit again on *Wednesday*.

CHURCH BUILDING AND NEW PARISHES ACTS AMENDMENT BILL.

LEAVE. FIRST READING.

THE ATTORNEY GENERAL moved for leave to bring in a Bill to consolidate and amend the Church Building and New Parishes Act.

MR. HADFIELD said, he believed that the measure was intended to secure the payment of church rates in certain parishes. He thought that the Attorney General ought to explain its objects before he asked for leave to introduce such a Bill.

THE ATTORNEY GENERAL said, the Bill was recommended by a Select Committee and the same as introduced last year. It would not in any way interfere with church rates. The law would be left as it stood. If any Amendments could be suggested he would be most happy to consider them.

Leave given.

Bill to consolidate and amend the Church Building and New Parishes Acts, *ordered* to be brought in by Mr. ATTORNEY GENERAL and Sir GEORGE GREY.

Bill *presented*, and read 1°. [Bill 61.]

LISBURN ELECTION.

MR. ADAIR said, he rose to move as a Resolution—

"That the Minutes of the Proceedings of, and the Evidence taken before the Select Committee on the Lisburn Election Petition be laid before this House."

The petition on the subject had been referred to a Committee, of which he was the Chairman. Up to the 22nd of March, the day on which the Committee adjourned, the proceedings had been regular and legal, and the evidence on both sides had been completed, and all that remained to be done was to hear the reply of the Petitioner's counsel on the whole case ; but in consequence of the adjournment having been made to a day which the statute did not authorize, a Report could not be made to the House, and the Committee also decided that they were unable to pass any Resolution. The Committee felt great regret at the position in which both parties had been placed. The petitioner had incurred great expense without obtaining that which he conceived he had a right to expect, the decision of the Committee as between himself and the sitting member, and owing to circumstances over which he had no control, he was afraid that the petitioner was without redress. With regard to the sitting member, he ventured to say that the result could hardly be satisfactory to him and his friends. He had been induced to make those observations because the circumstances attending the Committee had been such as were worthy of the consideration of the House, and it was for the House to decide whether some legislation was not necessary to remedy such a state of things.

MR. HUNT seconded the Motion.

Motion made, and Question proposed,

"That the Minutes of the Proceedings of, and the Evidence taken before, the Select Committee on the Lisburn Election Petition be laid before this House."—(*Mr. Adair.*)

MR. MACDONOGH said, the subject was one of considerable importance. He did not object to the production of the proceedings of the Committee, but resisted the production of the evidence as a thing unheard of and illegal. The Committee had not reported the evidence to the House, and, therefore, it would be irregular to lay such evidence before them. No sufficient reason had been urged for the adoption of the Motion. The proceedings of the Committee, and also of that House, with reference to Election Committees, were regulated by statute, and Mr. May's excellent work stated that the House had parted with its functions by the passing of the Act 11 *Vict.*, and had delegated it to a Committee, and he would put it to the Attorney General to state whether the present proceeding was regular or not, and whether in these days of economy the House should be called on at ten minutes past one o'clock to discuss a subject which if carried would be irregular and entail useless expense. It was no party question, for the Motion had been moved by an hon. Member on the Government side of the House, and seconded by a Gentleman on the Opposition side. It was impossible to resuscitate that defunct Committee, and he objected to the publication of the evidence that had been taken in relation to a variety of matters connected with the election, unless it was strictly regular to do so. Two cases only of a similar character had occurred since the passing of the Act. One was the case of Great Yarmouth and the other Beverley. In the first case, the Committee declared the election void, and reported to the House that the place ought to be disfranchised. It was then ordered that the evidence should be laid upon the table of the House, but that was ordered to be done to enable the House to say if they would disfranchise the borough or not. With regard to Beverley, a similar course was taken in order to instruct the Attorney General to prosecute Mr. Glover for signing a false declaration. The Report of the Committee in each case was first laid upon the table, and the evidence was afterwards ordered to be printed and submitted to the House.

THE ATTORNEY GENERAL said, he so far agreed with his hon. and learned Friend that this was no party question, and he hoped the House would not make it so. It appeared to him not to be irregular but in the highest degree regular and proper that the evidence taken by the Committee should be laid upon the table of the House, and there was not one word in the Act which was an obstacle to its being done. There was a much greater reason for its being done in this case than there was in those which had been referred to, because an occurrence of an unprecedented nature had taken place. The Committee, with the best possible intentions, had miscarried, and were unable to come to a Report after they had taken all the evidence which had been adduced before them; and after the case, upon the evidence, was closed on both sides. What, therefore, was the House to do? Was the House not to inform itself of everything that had taken place regularly before that Committee whilst its powers were perfect and legal and nothing had occurred to suspend them? They had taken evidence to show whether bribery or corruption was or was not practised by the sitting Member; and it might be that it completely exonerated him and his friends and the constituents of the borough, or it might be that a state of things had prevailed in the borough which deserved the attention of the House. Under circumstances so unprecedented, it would be a dereliction of duty if the House did not take care to have all the information which the publication of the proceedings before the Committee could give them.

MR. WHITESIDE said, he would appeal to the right hon. Gentleman the Speaker whether the Committee had not ceased to exist, and whether the present proposal was irregular. The Act said the Committee might report, and by the next clause they were permitted, after having first reported, to bring any matter in connection with their inquiry before the House, and take their opinion upon it, but it must be as a Committee. The Committee had ceased to exist, and therefore this proceeding was irregular. In the other House of Parliament it was enacted that if a Committee reported the existence of corrupt practices the House should recommend the appointment of a Royal Commission. But in this case there was no Report. Still, the hon. and learned Gentleman opposite said the House had the same authority to proceed as if there was a Report. If so, the last Act was useless. Was there, he asked, any precedent for taking steps on the Report of a Committee which had ceased to be a Committee?

MR. COLLINS saw no reason why the evidence should not be laid before the

House, for the use of those Members who desired to peruse it. No action could be founded on the evidence without a special Act of Parliament, and he did not think that any case would be made out for dealing by Act of Parliament with the borough of Lisburn. Still, if the House thought they ought to know all the circumstances of the case, the evidence could be printed and afterwards become lumber.

MR. GEORGE said, he had no objection to the Committee setting themselves right with the House, but he did object to the evidence being printed. The Committee, when once appointed by the House, derived its power from the statute, and was no further under the control of the House. If a Committee neglected to perform its duties, and thereby became defunct, there was an end of it, and its proceedings. The very counsel for the petitioning Member in his book on election law said that in the case of an illegal adjournment the Committee was defunct. The Committee had never expressed an opinion. The investigation was in the nature of a criminal proceeding; and the law presumed the innocence of a man whose guilt was not proved.

SIR GEORGE GREY said, there was no question of the appointment of a second Committee, nor as to the validity of the last election for Lisburn. The question was whether the Chairman, having reported that the Committee were not competent to proceed, the House had not a right to know what were their proceedings while they were a competent Committee under the Act of Parliament. The House did not call on the extinct Committee for the evidence, but upon the officer of the House, in whose custody that evidence was.

MR. LYGON contended that the evidence and the proceedings altogether of the Committee were all null and void. No action could be taken by the House except on the Report of the Committee, and in that case there was no Report. The Minutes ought to be laid before the House, because grave inconvenience might follow if that were not done. Upon that ground he was anxious that they should be produced, so that then they might take action, in order to prevent the recurrence of a similar failure of justice. He would move, as an Amendment, the omission of the words "and the evidence taken before."

Amendment proposed, to leave out the words "and the Evidence taken before."—(*Mr. Lygon.*)

SIR HERVEY BRUCE said, he was of opinion that the evidence could not be produced, because no one was in a position to say that the inquiry had been completed.

MR. HUNT said, he hoped the hon. Member for East Worcestershire would withdraw his Amendment. This was a very anomalous and exceptional case. The evidence was complete. The sitting Member was not in this country, but his father, who was in the House, was anxious that the evidence should be printed.

MR. WHITESIDE said, no answer had been given to the argument. The question for the House to consider was upon what ground it was that the evidence should be printed. He asked for information from the Speaker, the highest authority on the subject.

MR. NORTH said, he considered it would be advisable to print the real facts that had come out during the inquiry, because they had already appeared in the newspapers in a garbled form. The House might possibly, on receiving the evidence, address the Crown for a Commission to inquire into the corruption of the borough.

MR. SPEAKER said, that it was for the House to decide the question. If he had seen anything in the proposition contrary to the rules of the House he should have considered in his duty to call attention to it.

MR. HASSARD said, he should support the Amendment on the ground that the Committee alone could decide upon the value of the evidence.

Question put, "That the words proposed to be left out stand part of the Question."

The House *divided* :—Ayes 114; Noes 22 : Majority 90.

Main Question put, and *agreed to*.

Ordered,

That the Minutes of the Proceedings of, and the Evidence taken before, the Select Committee on the Lisburn Election Petition be laid before this House.—(*Mr. Adair.*)

THAMES CONSERVANCY BILL.

On Motion of *Mr. Hutt*, Bill to amend the Laws relating to the Conservancy of the River Thames; and for other purposes relating thereto, *ordered* to be brought in by Mr. HUTT and Mr. PEEL.

Bill *presented*, and read 1°. [Bill 60.]

SCIENTIFIC INSTITUTIONS (DUBLIN).

Motion made, and Question proposed,

" That a Select Committee be appointed to inquire into the condition of the Scientific Institutions of Dublin which are assisted by Government aid."—(*Mr. Gregory.*)

Debate arising,

Motion made, and Question, "That the Debate be now adjourned."—(*Mr. Whiteside,*)—put, and *negatived.*

Original Question put, and *agreed to.*

Ordered,

That a Select Committee be appointed, "to inquire into the condition of the Scientific Institutions of Dublin which are assisted by Government aid."—(*Mr. Gregory.*)

And, on Monday, April 18, Committee *nominated* as follows :—

Mr. GREGORY, Lord HENRY LENNOX, Sir ROBERT PEEL, Mr. LUKE WHITE, Mr. LYGON, Sir COLMAN O'LOGHLEN, Mr. COGAN, The O'CONOR DON, Mr. O'REILLY, Mr. DILLWYN, Sir EDWARD GROGAN, Mr. GEORGE, Mr. LEADER, Mr. LEFROY, and Mr. WALDRON :—Power to send for persons, papers, and records ; Five to be the quorum.

House adjourned at Two o'clock.

~~~~~~~

HOUSE OF LORDS,

Tuesday April 12, 1864.

MINUTES.]—*Took the Oath*—The Lord Bishop of Ossory.
PUBLIC BILLS—*Second Reading*—Punishment of Rape (No. 52).
Committee—Charitable Assurances Enrolments * (No. 38).

PUNISHMENT OF RAPE BILL—(No. 22)

SECOND READING.

Order of the Day for the Second Reading read.

THE MARQUESS OF WESTMEATH, in moving the second reading of the Bill, said, the frequency of the crime to which the Bill referred, particularly in the manufacturing districts, and a case which had been tried at the late spring assizes in the county of Sligo, in Ireland, had induced him to bring forward the present measure. In the case to which he had referred, a young woman had been taken off by some men, who had confederated for the purpose, and extreme violence had been offered to her with a view to get possession not only of her person, but of her money, and in order to prevent any respectable man from having anything to do with her. The punishment inflicted by the Court for that offence was only two years' imprisonment ; and he now proposed by the present Bill to give power to the Judge, where more persons than one were concerned in the crime, to order the infliction of corporal punishment, and if that punishment were inflicted publicly, so that it might be known to those who were not in the habit of reading the newspapers, so much the better.

Moved, That the Bill be now read 2ª.

LORD RAVENSWORTH opposed the Motion on the ground that the additional punishment contemplated by the Bill would have no additional deterrent effect. The offence in question was commonly committed by persons who were in company together, upon a casual encounter with their victim, and without premeditated design.

EARL GRANVILLE said, that though he was very much opposed to the increase of the system of flogging, and had much doubts of its efficacy, at the same time he was not prepared, on the part of the Government, to oppose the second reading of the Bill.

EARL GREY said, that there could be no doubt that some of the sentences recently inflicted for this offence were scandalously insufficient ; but the fault did not lay with the law, but with the administration of the law, and an expression of the opinion of the Legislature might lead to better results. Different Judges awarded different measures of punishment, and the consequence was a great scandal on the inequality of the sentences awarded. He was afraid that it would be an insuperable difficulty to define by law the exact measure of punishment to be given to different degrees of crime ; but still he thought that something might be done, under the authority of the Lord Chancellor, if the Judges were to meet together to lay down some common rule of action in order to establish greater uniformity in the administration of the law.

LORD WENSLEYDALE said, that last year he had ventured to propose that the Lord Chancellor should write to the Judges and ask them to meet together in order that they might come to some common understanding in regard to the sentences which should be passed in cases of a similar kind. Objections were taken to that course ; but he agreed to the want of uniformity, and the lenient sentences which were now frequently passed were a scandal and a disgrace and ought to be put an end to. He thought it highly desirable that the Judges should agree to some common principle in passing sentences.

THE LORD CHANCELLOR said, that the subject was one of very great difficulty. He felt unwilling to take the course suggested by his noble and learned Friend. If he called upon the Judges to define the law with a view of limiting their discretion, he should be calling upon them to do that which would be better performed by an enactment of the Legislature.

LORD CRANWORTH said, that the Bill was open to many objections. The Judges were necessarily intrusted with almost unlimited discretion ; but the noble Marquess proposed to add a new element of uncertainty and a new element of difference in the sentences of the Judges. Since the abolition of capital punishments in so many cases, there had been a gradual system of inflicting too lenient punishments in ordinary convictions. He remembered thirty years ago his noble and learned Friend on the cross benches (Lord Wensleydale), remarking that the effect of taking away capital punishment would lead to the diminution of punishment all down the scale. Unfortunately that prediction had turned out to be too true, and it was a great misfortune, in his opinion, that punishments were not more severe in many cases than they now were. He could not, however, concur in the proposal that the Judges should meet and lay down any general rules ; because crime admitted of such an infinite variety of shades of guilt that it was impossible to say beforehand what the punishment on any given offence ought to be. The only way in which punishments would eventually be more uniformly inflicted would be through the agency of public opinion. He saw no other means of arriving at that result.

THE MARQUESS OF WESTMEATH trusted that their Lordships would pass the Bill through its present stage.

Motion *agreed to* : Bill read 2ª accordingly, and *committed* to a Committee of the Whole House on *Thursday* next.

CONVICT GEORGE HALL—THE PREROGATIVE OF MERCY.

ADDRESS FOR CORRESPONDENCE.

THE EARL OF CARNARVON, in moving that an humble Address be presented to Her Majesty for Copy of Correspondence relative to George Hall, convicted of Murder at the Warwick Assizes, and respited on the 13th of March, said, he wished it to be distinctly understood that he did not attach any blame to the Home Secretary

for the decision at which he had thought fit to arrive ; what he did find fault with was the mode and steps by which that decision had been arrived at. The object in making this Motion was to elicit from Her Majesty's Government some statement as to the principle on which the prerogative of mercy was exercised ; for in previous instances similar divergence between decisions first arrived at and those ultimately acted upon were observable. When Townley was removed to a lunatic asylum on the ground that insanity had supervened, a formal and distinct assurance was given by the Secretary of State to the magistrates of Derbyshire that his sentence was only respited, and not commuted. Yet, within a fortnight from that time, without any fresh circumstances having supervened to throw doubt either upon the guilt or sanity of the prisoner, the sentence of capital punishment was commuted. In Wright's case, which followed a very few days afterwards, strong efforts to obtain a respite were made ; but Sir George Grey decided, and he thought very rightly, that the law must take its course. By contrast with the course taken in the previous case, however, a strong and painful impression was made upon the public mind. [He then alluded to the case of Jessie McLachlan, at Glasgow, and quoted an extract from Sir George Grey's speech, to the effect that the exercise of this power must be conformed to the popular feeling of the time.] This was a dangerous innovation on the Constitution, and proved the necessity that some principle of action should be laid down for future guidance. In the case of George Hall, that to which the papers he was now asking for referred, it was shown that the man had received grievous provocation, and that it was one in which the extension of the prerogative of mercy would be perfectly defensible ; but the Home Office remained immovable, and on the 11th of March the Home Secretary wrote a letter to the Mayor of Birmingham announcing his decision, and the grounds on which it was founded. Sir George Grey stated, that after most careful and anxious consideration, he felt that this could only be viewed as a deliberate and premeditated murder, and that the most dangerous consequences to society must ensue if provocation such as the prisoner had received were held sufficient to excuse the act which he had committed. That letter was received in Birmingham on the 12th ultimo, and the intimation which it conveyed was final; but those who had to deal with Sir George Grey knew him better than he appeared to know his own mind. A very strong pressure was exerted, and in thirty-six hours after the receipt of that letter, a reprieve came down from the Home Office, and the sentence was commuted to penal servitude for life. With the reprieve itself he had no fault to find; but he asked whether the Secretary of State having, after "full and anxious" consideration, as he himself stated, arrived at a particular decision, he was not doing something which appeared to require explanation when after the lapse of a few hours he took a course diametrically opposite. In the discussions arising out of Jessie McLachlan's case, Sir George Grey had argued that, if capital punishment is to exist, public feeling in each case must be taken into account, and the prerogative of mercy exercised in accordance with that feeling. Public feeling was in many subjects a safe and most reasonable element of consideration; but he entirely denied that it was a reliable guide, or should be allowed to influence the mind of a Secretary of State in reviewing punishment, inasmuch as public opinion in ninety-nine out of every hundred such cases meant the public opinion of the particular district, or county, or town, where the murder was committed, where the history and antecedents of the prisoner were known, and where consequently a prepossession in his favour or a prejudice against him existed almost invariably. Those who took the office ought not to shrink from the performance of its duties; the only consideration which ought to weigh with them was that of the due administration of justice. If any fresh fact transpired it was the duty of the Secretary of State to consider it; but it was entirely a matter between him and his conscience, and he was not justified in shifting the burden of responsibility to the shoulders of any one else, still less to so inconvenient, so vague, and so irresponsible a body as was expressed in the words "public opinion." Before he sat down he should like to ask the noble and learned Lord on the Woolsack, referring to the fact that as a general rule in cases in which persons had been sentenced to penal servitude for life they received a ticket-of-leave at the expiration of twelve years, not only whether Townley would be entitled to a ticket-of-leave at the end of that period, but whether, according to the existing rule,

The Earl of Carnarvon

there would be any objection to the Secretary of State granting such a remission of his sentence. The noble Earl concluded by moving—

"That an humble Address be presented to Her Majesty for Copy of Correspondence relative to George Hall, convicted of Murder at the Warwick Assizes, and respited on the 13th of March."

THE LORD CHANCELLOR said, he was sure that the noble Earl would be one of the last persons to act unfairly towards the Secretary of State for the Home Department; but, without intending it, few things could be more unfair than the course which he had pursued. The case of Townley had been twice before their Lordships. On an occasion it was made the subject of a Motion by the noble Earl; and as that Motion was withdrawn, he presumed that the noble Earl was satisfied with the explanations which were given.

THE EARL OF CARNARVON said, that the reason he withdrew that Motion was that on the same evening on which he gave notice of it, the Home Secretary introduced a Bill to remedy the defects of the law, and he thought that it would be unfair to the right hon. Gentleman to enter into the discussion of the circumstances in that House when he was about to explain them in another place.

THE LORD CHANCELLOR thought that for the same reason the noble Earl should have abstained from passing that censure upon the Secretary of State which was contained in the words that he had made a promise to the magistrates of Derbyshire with respect to the convict Townley, and had afterwards departed from its terms. No such assurance was given beyond the simple statement that the transfer of the convict to the lunatic asylum did not involve the commutation of the sentence. The noble Earl complained that it was afterwards commuted. Did the noble Earl know that after the convict was once lodged in the lunatic asylum, whither he was compelled by force of law to be sent, he could not be taken out of it except upon a certificate that he had recovered his reason and was restored to sanity? The result was that it was necessary to go through a process, which, in the eye of the law, admitted that the man had once been insane before he could be removed from the asylum. His right hon. Friend came to him and asked his opinion whether, under these circumstances, it was possible to send him back to Derby to be executed. They found that no case of the kind had occurred in which the convict was afterwards executed, and therefore he (the Lord Chancellor) gave the advice—for which he was responsible in the sense of having given it —and his right hon. Friend acted upon it, that under the circumstances it would be impossible to permit Townley to undergo the last sentence of the law. He was compelled to come to that conclusion most unwillingly by the circumstances which had occurred, and he believed that the course which was adopted was taken with the concurrence of all reasonable and well informed men. The noble Earl had contrasted Townley's case with that of Wright. In Wright's case the prisoner pleaded guilty, and although he (the Lord Chancellor) would have been glad if the sentence had not taken effect so rapidly, that was the result of the present state of the law. He would now pass to the immediate subject of the Motion—namely, the case of the convict Hall. He was glad that the noble Earl had brought this matter before the House, not on account of the case itself, but on account of the important subject connected with it, to which he had properly referred, and concerning which he only regretted that his observations were so concise. In Hall's case his right hon. Friend referred the papers to him, and after examining them he arrived at the conclusion that there was no reason whatever for the exercise of mercy. He persevered in that opinion, being perhaps firmer than his right hon. Friend, who adopted his language in the letter which he wrote to the Mayor of Birmingham. What afterwards occurred? Hundreds of persons whose representations were entitled to the greatest consideration, besieged the Home Office, and implored his right hon. Friend to remit the sentence. There appeared to be a combination of opinions that the execution of the sentence would be unjust and unbecoming, and that it would shock the moral sense of the community. Those opinions came to this—that there was in truth so much moral provocation that the offence ought to be regarded as having been committed under such provocation as would reduce murder to manslaughter. He begged the noble Earl to place himself in the situation of the Secretary of State for the Home Department. The Secretary of State had his own judgment and the verdict of the jury ; but against that there was an array of opinions which were entitled to respect, all assuring him that if this man

were hanged the object of capital punishment would be defeated, and he would be regarded as a martyr. He lamented that that should be the state of things, but he confessed that he was most happy to hear that in his absence his right hon. Friend had arrived at the conclusion that Hall ought to be respited, and he was sure that if the noble Earl had been Secretary of State he would have acted in the same manner, and would have felt as he did, that a great weight was taken off his mind by the opinion which he entertained being overborne and overpowered by the amount of argument and the amount of conviction expressed by persons who were entitled to the highest consideration. So much with regard to the particular cases. He would now make a few remarks on that part of the subject which had long engaged his attention, and to which he desired to take the opportunity of directing that of their Lordships—namely, the state of the law on this subject ; for it was of that, and not of the mode of its administration, that complaint ought to be made. To administer it otherwise was impossible. The present practice had grown up in a long series of years. The right hon. Gentleman who now with so much credit to himself filled the office of Home Secretary, and who had succeeded to it with all its traditions and practices, said that we, at no very remote period, possessed a code in all respects sanguinary. That character had in some degree been taken from it by the exercise of the prerogative of the Crown; and then succeeded a period of too much remission and gentleness in the administration of the criminal law. At present the prerogative of mercy was vested in the Crown, and administered under the advice of the Secretary of State. In the exercise of that prerogative the Secretary of State was called upon to pay regard to the moral aspect of the case, as contrasted with the legal. He had to deal with the representations made to him with respect to undue influence having been allowed to particular facts—that some particular facts had been withheld—that fresh evidence had been discovered, and that, in short, there had been a failure of justice. He had also to deal with appeals of the most unscrupulous character made by persons who seemed to be of opinion that they were, under all circumstances, bound to advocate the remission of capital punishment. Indeed, one of the most difficult points with which any man could have to deal was to know how to administer the particular functions of a Secretary of State in that particular, and he should like to see connected with the Home Office some kind of quasi tribunal which should be auxiliary to the Secretary of State in the exercise of the great powers with which he was intrusted. The prerogative of mercy must, of necessity, be left to the Crown ; but when the Secretary of State was called upon to advise the Crown it was quite clear that he had not the means of making a satisfactory investigation. There ought, therefore, in his opinion to be some constituted authority for relieving the Secretary of State of the duty which thus devolved upon him, and discharging it in a satisfactory manner. As matters at present stood the Secretary of State was in the position of a court of criminal appeal, but of one at the same time constructed in the worst of all possible ways. There were no certain rules laid down for his guidance, and the decision depended in a great measure on the character of the individual. A man of sterner nature would be guided by certain views, while a man of a gentler disposition might meet with a number of modern arguments by which his mind might be influenced. There was, therefore, in our present institution with respect to the dispensation of the prerogative of mercy, nothing but a vast discretion invested in the individual, and then that individual discharging in the best possible manner the power invested in him, which, however it might be discharged, was always exposed to criticism. It was, he might add, impossible to lay before the public all the reasons which influenced the Home Secretary; but he should, at the same time, submit to the House that nothing could be more unsatisfactory than to have the decisions of courts of justice set aside on grounds of the nature of which they were ignorant, and the sufficiency of which there were no means of ascertaining. He was, therefore, obliged to the noble Earl for having drawn to the question the attention of the House, and he wished he could at once proceed to state that the remedy for the evils of which he complained was clear and easy. He had not, however, been able to solve the problem himself, nor had he been able to obtain any satisfactory solution of the question as to how the limits of the prerogative of the Crown in those cases were to be fixed on a satisfac-

The Lord Chancellor

tory basis. As our trials were public, so the discussions on the cases which came before our tribunals ought to be equally public, in order that there might be no mistrust entertained with respect to the due administration of the law. It was said that the definition and classification of our law with respect to the several degrees of murder were most imperfect ; and if the noble Earl were to take the trouble of contrasting the definition on the subject in the English law with that in the French, or the more accurate definition of the several States of America, he would find the various degrees of murder laid down and defined in the case of the latter countries, with the punishments affixed, and that was the only mode in which at present he was able to say anything like an approximation to limiting the amount of uncertain discretion vested in the Home Secretary could be arrived at. If we could satisfactorily define beforehand what constituted murder in the first instance, and what, in the second place, was the appropriate punishment of the offence as classified, half the evil of the present state of things would be removed, and then we might have something like a public inquiry in cases in which by accident material circumstances happened not to be submitted to the jury, making it auxiliary to the functions of the Secretary of State. Had he, he might add, been aware that the noble Earl would have drawn attention to the case of Townley that evening, he would have taken care to bring down to the House more detailed information on the subject ; while, with regard to the papers which more particularly related to his Motion, he could only say that, being of a private nature, their production would be attended with inconvenience.

THE DUKE OF MARLBOROUGH said, he thought the noble and learned Lord had not given a satisfactory answer to the question with regard to the remission of punishment. As matters at present stood, the Home Office exercised an autocratic jurisdiction almost unprecedented in the remission of sentences. It would be of little use for the Judges to meet together to agree as to some mode by which regularity of sentences could be ensured, if the Home Secretary was able to interfere by arbitrary regulations, made or unmade at his own arbitrary pleasure. He hoped when the Bill which was now before the House of Commons, to carry out the recommendations of the Commission over which the noble Earl (Earl Grey) presided, came up to their Lordships' House, that care would be taken to regulate the manner in which the remissions of sentences were to be carried out.

EARL GREY said, that an express distinction had been drawn between sentences for life and sentences for terms of years. Those sentenced for a term of years were considered to have a claim to remission after a given time if their conduct had been good; but with regard to convicts sentenced for life no claim was recognized, though each case had to be considered on its own merits. The noble Duke was somewhat mistaken as to the amount of discretion now exercised by the Home Secretary, as compared to what was the former practice. Instead of being greater, that was now actually much less than in former years. In the old days of transportation it was the invariable practice for the Home Secretary to remit a portion of the sentences of those sentenced to short terms who were not actually sent out of the country, and it was also the practice to remit a portion of the sentences in the colony, and this was done according to no clear and certain rule, but on vague reports from the officers in charge of criminals. Now, on the contrary, there was a regular scale laid down on certain definite rules, by which remissions of punishment were granted according to what each criminal had earned by his conduct, which was recorded from day to day; and when the Act of Parliament was passed, under which this system was adopted, a circular had been addressed by the Secretary of State to the Judges, explaining to them what proportion of the sentences they passed might be remitted for good conduct, so that they allow for this in determining what punishment to award for different crimes.

THE EARL OF CARNARVON said, he expressed himself satisfied with the explanation of the noble and learned Lord on the Woolsack, and would withdraw his Motion.

Motion (by leave of the House) *withdrawn.*

House adjourned at half past Six o'clock, to Thursday next, half past Ten o'clock.

HOUSE OF COMMONS,
Tuesday, April 12, 1864.

MINUTES.]—NEW WRIT ISSUED—For Devizes v. The Hon. W. W. Addington, now Viscount Sidmouth.
PUBLIC BILL—*Ordered*—Joint Stock Companies (Voting Papers)°.

BARNSTAPLE ELECTION.

MR. WALPOLE *reported* from the General Committee of Elections, the names of the Members of the Select Committee appointed to try and determine the matter of the Petition complaining of an undue Election and Return for the Borough of Barnstaple, to which they had annexed the Petition referred to them by the House relating thereto, and the List of Voters severally delivered in to the Committee on behalf of the Petitioner and of the sitting Member:—ALEXANDER MURRAY DUNLOP, esquire; Sir FRANCIS HENRY GOLDSMID, baronet; WILLIAM HENRY HUMPHERY, esquire; GEORGE SCLATER-BOOTH, esquire; EDWARD HOWES, esquire, Chairman.

Report to lie upon the Table.

EGYPT—THE SUEZ CANAL—QUESTION.

MR. DARBY GRIFFITH said, he would beg to ask the First Lord of the Treasury, Whether the Sultan has recently ordered the Pacha of Egypt to discontinue the supply of forced labour to the works of the Suez Canal; and whether Her Majesty's Government will support the Sultan in that determination?

VISCOUNT PALMERSTON: Sir, the hon. Gentleman is well aware, and so is the House, that some time ago the Sultan gave an order that forced labour should be discontinued in Egypt, as it has long been in every other part of the Turkish Empire. The parties engaged in the Suez Canal, who had been employing forced labour to a great extent, petitioned for a prolongation of time, which has been, I believe, twice granted to them. No doubt it is very much to be regretted in the interest both of England and of France that, when both countries are much in need of cotton, 30,000 or 40,000 people who might be usefully employed in the cultivation of cotton in Egypt, are occupied in digging a canal through a sandy desert and making two harbours in deep mud and shallow water. I should hope that so useless an occupation will soon be put an end to.

IRELAND—DAUNT'S ROCK.—QUESTION

MR. MAGUIRE said, he rose to ask the President of the Board of Trade, As to the intentions of the Government with respect to Daunt's Rock; whether they intend to take immediate measures to have it removed by blowing it up, or whether they have resolved on at once giving the usual notice of the intention to place a Light Ship, with fog bell and signal gun, near it; and, if so, out of what sources do they propose that the cost of such Light Ship is to be defrayed?

MR. MILNER GIBSON: Sir, there is no intention, on the part of the Board of Trade, to take the measures referred to by the hon. Gentleman. Considerable difference of opinion exists as to whether it would be desirable to place a Light Ship upon Daunt's Rock. If it should be decided that such a ship should be placed there, the Elder Brethren of the Trinity Corporation are of opinion that, considering the proximity of the Rock to Cork Harbour, the expense of supporting the Light Ship should be borne by the vessels frequenting or otherwise using Cork Harbour. Inman's Company, one of the ships of which was recently lost upon the Rock, signified their willingness—not lately, but some time ago — to pay any toll upon their ships which it might be necessary to impose for the support of a Light Ship. Although the Government has no intention to place a Light Ship at present, it has been recommended that an improvement should be made in the light on Roche's Point. That proposition has been sanctioned by the Board of Trade, and will shortly be carried into effect. It is such that the light exhibited on Roche's Point will indicate to a ship making for Cork Harbour when she is approaching Daunt's Rock, so as to warn her against running into that danger.

MR. MAGUIRE: Is not Daunt's Rock five miles off the extreme point of the entrance to Cork Harbour? I also wish to know, Whether the attention of the Government has been directed to the necessity of removing Daunt's Rock altogether, and whether there has been any survey made with that object in view?

MR. MILNER GIBSON: There has been no Government survey of Daunt's Rock with a view to ascertain the expense of its removing by blowing it up, but I am informed that a private survey is now going on, and that the opportunity is being taken of the steamer lying upon the Rock to ascertain its exact dimensions, and to arrive, if possible, at an estimate of what the cost would be of removing it by blasting. I cannot say whether such a scheme is practicable or not, but I hope the survey now going on will throw some light on that question.

MR. MAGUIRE: The right hon. Gentleman has not yet answered my question. I desire to know, Whether Daunt's Rock is not five miles off the extreme point of the entrance of Cork Harbour?

MR. MILNER GIBSON: I believe the Rock is between four and five miles from the entrance of Cork Harbour, but there are two lights visible, the light upon the Head of Kinsale and the light upon Roche's Point. The latter is visible in clear weather in the neighbourhood of the Rock. Provided, therefore, the weather be clear, there are sufficient lights to enable any prudent navigator to avoid Daunt's Rock.

MR. MAGUIRE: I have only one question more. Is it not a fact known to the right hon. Gentleman that Robert's Head shuts out the light on Roche's Point?

MR. MILNER GIBSON: Only in the case of a ship being so close in to the Rock as to be out of her proper track would the light on Roche's Point be screened by Robert's Head.

BURIAL GROUNDS.—QUESTION.

MR. NEWDEGATE said, he rose to ask the Secretary of State for the Home Department, Under what provisions of the Law is the power to grant Licences for Private Burial Grounds or Places vested in the Home Secretary, and should not such Licences be published; where does the Law require the Registers of Burials performed within such Private Burial Grounds or Places to be kept, and are there specified by Law any means by which, or conditions subject to which, the Public have the right of access to and inspection of such Registers; who are the Persons or Officers whom the Law holds responsible for the Registration of Burials in such Private Burial Grounds or Places within the Metropolitan District; the same questions with respect to Places beyond the Metropolitan District; who are the Persons or Officers whom the Law requires to make, or to afford facilities for making, extracts from such Registers, and to certify such extracts; and which of the Statutes relating to Burials apply to the

Registration of Burials in such Private Burial Grounds or Places; and, if no Statute applies or is sufficient to enforce such Registration, does the Government intend to introduce a Bill to amend the Law in these respects?

SIR GEORGE GREY: Sir, there is no express power given by law to the Secretary of State to grant licences for Private Burial Grounds; but, by the 15 & 16 *Vict.* c. 85, s. 9, it is enacted—

" That no new Burial Ground shall be provided or used in the Metropolis, or within two miles of it, without the previous approval of the Secretary of State."

And by 16 & 17 *Vict.* c. 134, s. 6, power is given by Order in Council to prohibit the opening of a new Burial Ground beyond the Metropolis, within the limits mentioned in the order, without the same approval. Before the Act passed as to the Metropolis any Burial Ground might be opened without any approval, and this is the case still beyond the Metropolis in any place with regard to which no prohibitory Order in Council has been passed. By the *52 Geo.* III. c. 146, s. 5, it is enacted that, where the burial is performed in any other place than the Parish Church, and by any other person than the incumbent, the officiating minister shall transmit to the clergyman of the parish a certificate of the burial, and the clergyman of the parish is to register it in the parish register. The same Act provides for access to and search of parish registers. The parish clergyman is charged with the custody of the register and with the duty of registering. I believe this Act is in force with regard to all Burial Grounds not provided by Burial Boards under Burial Acts, and with regard to which there are special provisions. This is independent of the registration of death required in all cases by law.

MR. NEWDEGATE: Do I understand the right hon. Gentleman to say, that a clergyman of the Church of England of the parish is the person responsible for the registration of burials performed by other ministers?

SIR GEORGE GREY replied in the affirmative.

CHANCERY FUNDS.—QUESTION.

MR. MURRAY said, he wished to ask Mr. Attorney General, Whether he intends to introduce this Session any Bill to carry into effect the improvements in the management of the business of the Court of Chancery in the Accountant General's Office, as recommended by the Report of the Chancery Funds Commission, and in other respects to carry into effect the other recommendations of the Commissioners?

THE ATTORNEY GENERAL said, in reply, that it was not the intention of the Government to introduce a Bill of that character this Session. The Report of the Commissioners was .not unanimous, and it was necessary that it should receive the most careful consideration. If, however, there were any improvements in this matter which could be carried out by virtue of the powers belonging to the Lord Chancellor, the Lord Chancellor would no doubt be glad to adopt them.

LICENSED HOUSES IN THE METRO-POLIS.—QUESTION.

SIR JOHN SHELLEY said, he would beg to ask the Secretary of State for the Home Department, Whether the Government have come to any determination in reference to an alteration of the Law regarding the regulations as to the hours at which Licensed Houses in the Metropolis should be closed during the night?

SIR GEORGE GREY, in reply, said, he had received strong representations from some parts of the metropolis of the evil arising from certain public-houses and refreshment houses being kept open during the whole of the night. It was suggested that it would be desirable to make such an alteration in the law as would compel the closing of such houses between the hours of one and four o'clock in the morning. He believed that such an alteration would be of great benefit to the public, and in accordance with the wishes of the majority of licensed victuallers. The right hon. Gentleman was understood to say that a measure was in course of preparation on the subject.

UNITED STATES—THE BARQUE "SCIENCE."—QUESTION.

MR. HASSARD said, he wished to ask the Under Secretary of State for Foreign Affairs, If the case of the barque *Science*, seized at Matamoras on the 5th November last, has yet been adjudicated upon; and, if it has not been adjudicated upon, if he will take steps to have such case disposed of without further delay?

MR. LAYARD said, in reply, that the case of the *Science* was still under adjudication, and nothing had yet occurred, as far as he was aware, to authorize any interference with the usual proceedings of the Prize Court. All the proceedings relating to seizures at Matamoras were under consideration by Her Majesty's Government.

ARMY—GARDEN ALLOTMENTS TO SOLDIERS.—QUESTION.

MR. W. EWART said, he would beg to inquire of the Under Secretary of State for War, What steps have been taken, or are about to be taken, to enable soldiers in camp (or elsewhere, where it is possible) to employ themselves in the cultivation of gardens ?

THE MARQUESS OF HARTINGTON, in reply, said, he had very little to add to, and he did not think he had anything to retract in, the answer which he gave to the hon. Gentleman on this question some time since. He then stated that his noble Friend (Earl de Grey) had every disposition to afford facilities to soldiers desiring to employ themselves in the cultivation of gardens, and that a commencement had been made in the matter, and would be extended as much as possible. The Horse Guards had received a Report from the officer commanding the Artillery at Aldershot, that two batteries of Artillery had been for some time cultivating ground as gardens, and that the very best results had followed. Occupation had been afforded to the men, and their comfort also greatly increased by the production of vegetables for their mess. The land had also been allotted for that purpose for the Military Train at Aldershot, but owing to a question having arisen as to the payment of rates by the soldiers, it had not yet been cultivated. At Warley three acres had been allotted for that object. In the southeastern division, in the neighbourhood of Brighton and Dover, some of the troops had had allotments made to them. In Woolwich also some allotments were in existence, and more were being provided. At Colchester arrangements of a similar nature were in progress. No general rule could be laid down on that subject, and each case must be dealt with as it arose. In some places land was easily procured, and in others not so readily; and it became a question, of course, whether the soldiers were not to pay rent for land taken out of

Mr. Hassard

occupation ; but he could assure the hon. Member that every representation made by the Generals commanding at the different stations would be taken into consideration by the War Office, and that every disposition existed to encourage this system.

LAW AND EQUITY COURTS (IRELAND).
QUESTION.

MR. BUTT said, he wished to ask the Attorney General for Ireland, Whether it is intended to bring in any measure to assimilate the proceedings of the Law and Equity Courts in Ireland to those of the English Courts; and, if so, when such Bill will be introduced ?

MR. O'HAGAN replied, that he hoped in a very few days to introduce a Bill for assimilating the constitution and procedure of the Courts of Equity in Ireland to those of the English Courts of Equity, and also to assimilate the practice and procedure of the Courts of Law in Ireland to those of the English Law Courts.

DENMARK AND GERMANY — THE CONFERENCE.—QUESTION.

MR. BERNAL OSBORNE said, he rose to ask the Under Secretary of State for Foreign Affairs to be good enough to inform him, Whether Her Majesty's Government have any objection to lay on the table the Despatch of the French Government of the 30th of March, suggesting that the wishes of the population of Schleswig and Holstein should be consulted ; also, whether he will lay on the table the answers to the invitation to join the Conference about to assemble, which has been sent out by Her Majesty's Government?

MR. LAYARD, in reply, said, with regard to the first part of the hon. Member's question, that to the best of his belief that despatch was only read and not communicated in copy to Her Majesty's Government. Perhaps the hon. Gentleman would repeat his question to-morrow, and he would then be able to answer it.

MR. BERNAL OSBORNE said, he wished for an answer to his second question.

MR. LAYARD said, he would request the hon. Gentleman to repeat that question also to-morrow.

INDIA—INDIAN OFFICERS.
RESOLUTION.

CAPTAIN JERVIS, in rising to bring forward the question of which he had given notice, said, he was aware how careful the House always was in entering upon subjects connected with the details of military affairs, not to interfere with the prerogatives of the Crown. The body of officers, however, to whose case he wished to draw attention, were dealt with by his Motion in their capacity of late servants of the East India Company. Ever since the formation of the East India Company, their military as well as civil servants had been protected by the House; and in consequence of the Report of a Committee, which sat more than a century ago, an Act of Parliament was passed which pointed out how promotion in the Indian army should be carried out. Subsequently, in 1794, a memorial was sent home from the officers of the Bengal army, complaining of certain grievances under which they suffered. That memorial, by order of the House, was brought to the bar, and its subject taken into consideration. It was then referred to the Board of Control who undertook that justice should be done to the memorialists. The Board of Control thereupon, in 1796, laid upon the table of the House the principles upon which the East India Company were to carry out promotions and other matters relative to the service; and the regulations which were then put in force may be said to have emanated from that House. In 1832, the Committee of the House appointed to investigate the state of the East India Company, inquired most fully and carefully into the organization and administration of the Indian army, and, in consequence of its Report, the organization of 1796 was ordered to be continued. In 1858 it having been considered desirable to put an end to the administration of the East India Company, and to transfer it to the Crown, so careful was the House that no injustice should be done, that it enacted that the officers of the Indian army should retain the whole of the rights and privileges which they enjoyed under the East India Company; and in 1860, when it was considered desirable to abolish the local Indian army, the right hon. Gentleman the Member for Oxfordshire (Mr. Henley) insisted on the introduction of a clause reiterating that pledge, for fear of its being otherwise broken— a pledge which that House distinctly affirmed— namely, that the original instructions given by the East India Company for the protection of their officers should be carried out by the Secretary of State for India. It was therefore, with no little astonish-

ment, that shortly after the passing of the Act containing that clause, that the officers of the East Indian army found, from a despatch published by the Governor General in Council, that the whole of those privileges and advantages had been entirely destroyed. They at once took the usual steps for memorialising through their commanding officers, the Governors of the various Presidencies, and through them the Governor General, and through him the Secretary of State for India; but for two years they had been unable to obtain any redress. At last the Secretary of State, on the recommendation, or at least in accordance with the unanimous feeling of the House, appointed a Commission, composed of some most eminent and able men, to inquire whether the promises made in 1858, and renewed in 1860, had or had not been departed from; and that Commission, after a careful and anxious inquiry which extended over several months, decided that they had been departed from, and reported accordingly on the 9th November last. Six months had elapsed since the presentation of that Report, without anything being done by the Government, and petition after petition was still being presented to that House for a redress of grievances. Now, if the organization of the Staff Corps, which had been put in force, and had caused so much difficulty, had not previously been inquired into or thought of, or if there had been but a mere attempt made to enact something better than had hitherto existed, perhaps some excuse might be found; but for years the East India Company had been anxious to carry out a Staff Corps as proposed, and been unable to do so. In 1833 the question had been fully gone into by the Committee, who examined Sir John Malcolm and every other eminent and able officer who had served in India, and in whom the country at that time placed reliance. The Committee reported that from the peculiar organization of the Indian army the arrangement for the formation of the proposed Staff Corps could not be carried out without injuring the prospects of those whom the Government had promised should be confirmed in all their privileges and advantages. When, in 1860, the Act was brought in for the stoppage of the recruiting for the Indian army, and the clause was to be inserted for the fulfilment of the promise contained in the Act of 1858, a Committee had been appointed, which was presided over by the noble Lord the Member for the East Riding (Lord Hotham), to inquire whether the proposal intended to be carried out by the Secretary of State for India would be within the guarantee given by Parliament. That Committee reported on the 30th July, 1860—the day on which the right hon. Baronet accepted, in the fullest possible manner, the pledge asked of him of inserting a clause—that if the right hon. Baronet carried out his proposition for the re-organization of the Indian army, it would be contrary to the pledge that had been given by Parliament. The question had been fully gone into by a Commission, of which the noble Lord the Member for King's Lynn (Lord Stanley) and the then Secretary of State for War (General Peel) were members, and that Committee distinctly reported that the Crown could not interfere in any way with the re-organization of the army, because if it did it would interfere with the pledges that had been given by Parliament. It was now high time that something should be done to allay that feeling of irritation which had been felt by so many of these gentlemen ; and it was only right and just, when they asked a body of noble and gallant men to serve for years in a foreign land, and to be ready at a moment's notice to sacrifice their lives and their interests for the good of their country on the faith that certain pledges should be scrupulously adhered to and carried out, to act fairly and honestly by them. He should not enter into what might be called the details of military organization, but merely confine himself to the pledge that was given. The main point in the whole of these Reports and Acts of Parliament to which he had referred was, that any man entering the Indian army and agreeing to serve a certain number of years, did so upon condition that he should not be superseded by others in his profession, and that at the end of a certain number of years he should retire on a fixed pension. This was, however, completely set aside by the formation of a Staff Corps. When, also, the Committee of that House, which sat in 1833, were investigating the affairs of the East India Company, it directed the Company to turn its attention to the fact that their officers did not retire at a sufficiently early age to enable them to obtain active and intelligent men to command their regiments. The Company not only granted increased retiring pensions, but induced their officers to form a fund amongst themselves, to induce men, when they attained a certain age, to accept the pensions offered by

Captain Jervis

the Company. This has lately been declared by the right hon. Gentleman the Secretary of State for India to be illegal, and the large sums of money which these gentlemen have advanced are not to be held as giving them a claim in equity to compensation. When discussing the point last year with the Commission appointed by himself, the right hon. Baronet said they must assimilate the practice of bonus in the Indian army to the practice which prevailed in the British army. But what was the fact ? The Queen's Regulations warned any officer who gave against giving more than regulation prices for Commissions ; that he did it on his own risk, as it was contrary to law, for if more was given than the regulation price it was a misdemeanour, and on its coming to the notice of the Commander-in-Chief, he was bound to prosecute ; and if the person was convicted, he, in addition to other penalties, lost his commission. But what was the case with regard to the officers of the Indian army ? It was publicly announced in 1838 by the Governor General of India in Council, that the East India Company fully recognized their junior officers subscribing to regimental funds for the purpose of buying out their seniors. The East India Company could do nothing without the sanction of the Board of Control, and that sanction had been given in this instance. So far as India and the Indian army were concerned, any order of the Governor General of India in Council had the force of law. The Secretary for India, in reply to these statements submitted to the Royal Commissioners, said that they were not facts. But if orders from the East India Company, agreed to by the Board of Control and published by the Governor General, were not facts, it was difficult to know what were facts. He also said that the facts, if facts, were not recognized by the Board of Directors. But what was the fact ? In 1855, a case having occurred in a Court of Law by which the practice he had described was decided to be contrary to law, the Directors of the East India Company entered into correspondence with the Government of India and the Board of Control with a view to the introduction of a Bill into that House to make the practice lawful. He would urge upon the House that it was highly necessary that some arrangement should be made to put an end to a state of things which was very unsatisfactory. If our countrymen abroad were to be required to observe the discipline and obey the regulations prescribed, they were entitled to demand fair treatment. The present position of those officers was not of their seeking, but it was the result of an act of the Government, and therefore it was the duty of the Government to see that justice was done to them. The hon. and gallant Member concluded by moving—

"That this House, having by the Acts 21 & 22 *Vict. c.* 106, and 23 & 24 *Vict. c.* 100, guaranteed to the Officers of the late East India Company's Service that their advantages as to 'pay, pensions, allowances, privileges, promotions, and otherwise,' should be secured to them, has learnt with regret, from the Report of the Royal Commission on Memorials of Indian Officers, that in certain cases this assurance has been departed from, and is of opinion that full and speedy reparation should be made to those who have suffered by such departure."—(*Captain Jervis.*)

SIR DE LACY EVANS said, he cordially seconded the Motion, as he considered the subject brought under the notice of the Government and the House was of very great importance. The grievance of which these officers complained was one that ought to be removed, and he was astonished that the Government should for so long have continued to overlook their complaints. Perhaps an explanation might be found in the fact that these officers were a long way off, and therefore their complaints might safely be treated with neglect. Not long ago the privates of the Indian army were induced to believe that the Government had not behaved well towards them. When it was proposed to identify the privates of the Indian army with the Queen's army, the noble Lord at the head of the Government stated in that House that the men, if they preferred to remain in their former positions, would be entitled to an additional bounty; but when the time came for payment of that bounty, the Government in India refused to give it. He believed that after some time Lord Canning had thought it was advisable that the bounty should be paid; but in the meantime a great deal of indiscipline, approaching to mutiny, took place among the men. He had more than once in that House reminded the noble Viscount that he was in some measure the cause of that mutinous feeling, as he had led the men to understand that they would be entitled to receive an additional bounty whenever they transferred their services to the Queen's army. The noble Lord had not given any reply to any of these representations. Then, as to the officers of that army, there certainly did prevail among them a feeling that they could not rely upon being treated with good faith by the Government. He had had considerable experience with armies in different services, and he knew no surer way of promoting indiscipline and even mutiny, than by raising a belief in an army that they would not be fairly dealt with by the Government. When the Government decided that the two armies should be amalgamated, some of the most experienced officers of the Indian army declared that it would be a very difficult operation to carry out; and so it had proved. An equitable arrangement had not yet been come to, although if the Government deemed it right to carry out the amalgamation, they ought also to have done justice to those who were affected by that determination. After more than a year since the amalgamation took place, complaints still continued to be made, and at last the right hon. Baronet caused a Commission to inquire into them. He had not seen the Report, but he was told that that Commission declared the officers had not been treated with good faith. He hoped, now that the subject had been formally brought before the House, the right hon. Baronet and the noble Viscount would admit the necessity of setting at rest all doubts as to the treatment of officers belonging to the late Indian army.

Motion made, and Question proposed.

COLONEL SYKES: Sir, I rise to support the Motion of the hon. Member for Harwich; and, as the question is of great gravity, affecting the rights of some thousand British officers, and affecting the policy of the proposed military organization of the native armies of India, I will beg the indulgence of the House for some little time. As an old Indian officer who has passed through all the grades of the service, I naturally feel a strong interest in the subject before the House; but probably on that account not much weight would be attached to my testimony. When, however, the House saw two officers of the Queen's army taking the initiative, he hoped they would accept that fact as an evidence of the importance of the subject and of the justice of the complaints. Let the House consider how large a number of officers were affected. It was shown by a Return before the House that, at the time of the annexation, or re-organization, or amalgamation, that the establishment of the Indian army comprised 6,333 officers, and the number absolutely on the roll on the 1st January, 1861, was 5,121. Surely, when complaints were made by a great proportion of so large a body of officers, that they felt themselves aggrieved and their prospects blighted by the non-fulfilment of the promises of the Government, the House would give them a ready hearing, and grant them that redress which a Resolution of that House alone could give them. In the first place, it is necessary to have a distinct idea of what the several Parliamentary guarantees have been. They are as follows: that by 21 & 22 *Vict.* c.106, Clause 56, August 2, 1858, it was enacted that—

"The Indian military and naval forces of Her Majesty shall be under the same obligations to serve Her Majesty as they would have been under to serve the said Company, and shall be liable to serve within the said territorial limits only, and be entitled to the like pay, pensions, allowances, and privileges, and the like advantages as regards promotion, and otherwise, as if they had continued in the service of the said Company."

That by the Act of the 23 & 24 *Vict.* c. 100, 1860, it was further enacted that—

"The advantages as to pay, pensions, allowances, privileges, promotions, and otherwise, secured to the military forces of the East India Company by the former Act, should be maintained in any place for the re-organization of the Indian Army."

That on the 18th January, 1861, the Secretary of State for India addressed a military despatch, dated India Office, London, to the Governor General of India, containing the following paragraph:—

"In the execution of these measures, the amalgamation, the pledge that due regard shall be paid to the rights and claims of the officers of Her Majesty's Indian forces will be scrupulously adhered to."

I would beg to call my right hon. Friend's particular attention to the terms "scrupulously adhered to;" and the Governor General of India in a General Order, dated Fort William Military Department, 10th April, 1861, assured the army that—

"In the execution of the measures to bring about the proposed amalgamation, it is the intention of Her Majesty's Government that the pledge that due regard shall be paid to the rights and claims of the officers of Her Majesty's Indian Forces, shall be scrupulously adhered to."

That notwithstanding these several guarantees by Acts of Parliament, and pledges by the Secretary of State for India, and the Governor General, numerous grievous violations, consequent upon the amalgamation, have taken place, affecting the pay,

Colonel Sykes

allowances, privileges, rights of promotion, or otherwise, of the officers of the East India Company's late forces. The most vital and important of these is the fundamental right of the armies of India to *regimental* promotion by seniority up to the rank of major; and, after that, promotion by seniority in a general list of field officers; and so rigid was supersession guarded against, that on a lieutenant-colonel obtaining his coloneley, in either of the three armies of India, all the senior lieutenant-colonels, both in the Indian and Royal armies, had the brevet rank of colonel given to them to prevent supersession. Two Acts of Parliament have made this rule a law, and both Lord Hotham's and Lord Cranworth's Commissions have declared that, in the amalgamation of the Indian and Royal armies, this rule must be carried out; and Lord Cranworth's Commission have reported that it has not been carried out, and, consequently, there has been a violation of two Acts of Parliament. The fact being that the Secretary of State for India has sanctioned, upon his own authority, a new system of promotion to substantive rank from length of service, and independently of seniority, which is contrary to the system guaranteed by the two Acts of Parliament, and is, therefore, contrary to law. I maintain, therefore, that all the promotions made in the Staff Corps are *ipso facto* null and void; for the Secretary of State for India was destitute of the legal power to make them. He has stated on former occasions that he has only exercised the power which the East India Company could have exercised; but I deny that they had any such powers; and even if they had had the power, they never would have exercised it in the extensive and crushing manner my right hon. Friend has done. But independently of the injustice done to Royal and Local Officers by the multiplying supersessions consequent upon these promotions, the Staff Corps system is repugnant to public policy. The promotions made on the completion of a prescribed period of service in the Army and in the Staff Corps are necessarily cumulations of the higher ranks. The lieutenant-colonels and majors having substantive rank and pay, together with staff allowances, have no motive for retiring; and their number is ceaselessly increasing to the great embarrassment of the Government which cannot find suitable employment for officers of their rank, and is consequently constrained to continue them in the performance of duties which should be limited to captains or subalterns; and the pay of the substantive rank of the field officers is, in fact, an unnecessary waste of the public money. The Staff Corps also, as at present constituted, causes injury to the public interests, as they were not obliged to join their regiments when in the field. Under the old system, all Staff Officers were morally obliged to join their regiments when taking the field (or be sent to Coventry), to give proper efficiency to Native regiments, which, in a line-of-battle or in a storming party, all experience proves are efficient precisely in the proportion of the number of European officers accompanying the men. European regiments need to be fully officered in the field; Native troops need it ten times more. Formerly, also, officers absent from their regiments on the staff contributed to the band and mess funds, and to the retiring funds of their respective regiments. They no longer continue to do so, and great injury is consequently done to the remaining officers of their regiments. Now, as the supersession injuries inflicted by the promotions in the Staff Corps are to be remedied, the question arises of how it best can be done. There are three methods—

First, by giving substantive rank, and consequently pay, to all officers superseded.

Secondly, by throwing all the officers of the army of each presidency into one general list, both regimental and staff, putting the superseded officers into their proper places, and then promoting by seniority or from length of service.

Thirdly, by abolishing the Staff Corps ; allowing the present Staff Officers to hold their present appointments, but promoting them only regimentally.

The first method would occasion very great expense, and would not remedy the evil of the cumulative rank and expense in the present Staff Corps system, and would occasion endless promotions to remedy supersessions which are occurring and must occur almost daily—not by ones and twos, but in shovelsful, as is shown in the following recent general orders :—

The Madras Services—Military General Orders.

. (*From 19th Feb. to 4th March* 1864.)

PROMOTIONS AND APPOINTMENTS. — Lieutenant D. Standen having completed twelve years' service, four of which were on permanent Staff employ, to be captain.

The undermentioned officers having completed twenty years' service, six of which were on permanent Staff employ, to be majors :—Captains Robert Renton, Edward Bannerman Ramsay, James Langford Pearse, Edward Herbert Harington, Goodson Adey.

The undermentioned officer having completed twelve years' service, four of which were on permanent Staff employ, to be captain :—Lieut. G. A. A. Warner.

Major F. J. B. Priestley, having completed twenty-six years' service, eight of which were on permanent Staff employ, to be lieutenant colonel.

The Bengal Services—Military General Orders.

(*From 3rd to 17th Feb.* 1864.)

PROMOTIONS AND APPOINTMENTS, &c.—The undermentioned officers having completed twenty years' service, six years of which were on permanent Staff employ, to be majors :—Captains J. Fendall, E. J. Spilsbury, T. A. Corbett.

Bombay Services.

(*From 15th to 20th Feb.* 1864.)

The undermentioned officers having completed twelve years' service, four of which were on permanent Staff employ, to be captains :—Lieutenant A. F. Danvers and Lieutenant T. Kettlewell.

(*From 13th to 28th Dec.* 1863.)

The undermentioned officer having completed twenty years' service, six of which were on permanent Staff employ, to be major from the date specified, under the Royal Warrant of the 16th January 1861, subject to Her Majesty's approval :—Captain (Brevet Major) Henry Hastings Affleck Wood, 9th December, 1863.

The undermentioned officers having completed twenty-six years' service, eight of which were on permanent Staff employ, are promoted to be lieutenant colonels, under the Royal Warrant of the 16th January, 1861, subject to Her Majesty's approval :—Majors William Edmonstone MacLeod and Samuel Thacker, from 11th December, 1863.

The undermentioned officers having completed twelve years' service, four of which were on permanent Staff employ, to be captains from the date specified, under the Royal Warrant of the 16th January, 1861, subject to Her Majesty's approval : Lieutenants Claude Malet Ducat and Henry Rivett Mandeville Van-Heythuysen, 12th December, 1863 ; Lieutenants Charles Frederick Boulton and Trevenen James Holland, 13th December, 1863.

Most of these promotions having occurred so recently as the last and the preceding months, the House can judge of the rapidity of the cumulative process to constitute the Staff Corps a body of majors and lieutenant-colonels only, at an early period. The total number of officers who joined the Staff Corps on the 18th of February, 1861, from the Native Infantry alone were :—Bengal, 586 ; Madras, 319 ; Bombay, 229: total, 1,134 ; but transfers to the Staff Corps from the other branches of the armies raised the number to 1,297. So that these officers had a privilege conferred upon them to the prejudice of their brother officers, not only of the local Service, but to those of the Royal Army.

The first method would be very expensive, but he concurred with a noble Lord who said in another place that the "redress of India's wrongs must not be a question of money."

The second method, though it might restore all officers to their right position, would abolish regimental succession and regimental organization, and destroy that *esprit de corps* which is the foundation of discipline, the bond of friendly regimental social relations, and the emulative stimulus between regiments so usefully applied to the army.

The third method is the simplest and most effectual. That is the abolition of the Staff Corps and the cancelling all promotions made in it, which are, in fact, illegal. Officers at present on the Staff Corps would only be too happy to keep their appointments and be promoted in their regiments as formerly, and, in fact, revert to their former conditions of service; and they would have little right to complain of losing that illegal rank which has been accompanied by the solace and advantage of superior pay, but to which they had no proper title, at the expense of their brother officers (often their seniors) of the local armies.

Sir, the grievances of the officers of the Indian armies were arranged under twelve different heads, but the Royal Commission has reported that the Parliamentary Guarantees have only been departed from in the following instances :—

First.—That the supersession of local officers by officers who have entered the Staff Corps, is a departure from the Parliamentary Guarantee.

Second.—Retaining the names of officers who have joined the new Line regiments from Native Cavalry and Infantry regiments on the lists of their old corps, and thereby obstructing promotion therein, is a similar departure from the guarantee.

Third.—Retaining the names of lieutenant colonels who have retired from the service on the list governing promotion, and thereby obstructing and delaying promotion long since due, is a departure from the guarantee.

Fourth.—That the average time fixed for regulating the promotion of lieutenant colonel to colonel, namely, twelve years, is too much.

Fifth.—That the Royal Warrant, dated 1st January, 1862, amalgamating the general and field officers of the Regular Army, with officers of similar rank in the Indian Army is inapplicable, and may cause injury to the latter officers.

Unfortunately the Commission has not viewed favourably (under a misconception,

Colonel Sykes

I assume) a very serious grievance, namely, the loss of the Regimental Retiring Funds, which, for many years past, had frequently been sanctioned, not only by the Court of Directors, but by the Board of Control, and consequently by the Government of the country. The establishment of the Staff Corps has broken down these funds, because the staff officers will not contribute to them, as they are promoted independently of regimental seniority. Some officers have lost sums to which they would have been entitled of £3,000 up to £5,000 upon their own retirement, and towards which they had contributed for many years; and yet the Secretary of State looks without sympathy upon these serious sacrifices, and the discomfort, indeed deprivation in old age, which the loss will occasion to worn-out officers. My right hon. Friend has said the practice was pronounced by a Court of Law illegal, and therefore he could not accept its breaking down as a grievance. No doubt by the Act of *Geo.* III. the sale of commissions or offices was, and is, prohibited. But the Retiring Funds of regiments could never have been contemplated by the Act, and their operation, neither in law nor equity, should come within the prohibitory clauses of the Act. In the Indian retiring system there is no bargain or sale between any two individual officers. All the officers of a regiment according to their rank subscribe to a common fund; out of this fund, when a senior officer wishes to retire upon his pension and return to Europe, usually after twenty-five to thirty years service, a bonus is given to him, to alleviate his condition after retirement; and without this bonus he would be obliged to continue in India, probably in bad health and with a broken down constitution, to the detriment of the efficiency of the army and the public interests, for the pension of his rank would not support him and his family in Europe. The practice should rather be encouraged than denounced. Independently, however, of the twelve grievances enumerated by the petitioners to the House of Commons, new grievances have arisen consequent upon the so-called re-organization of the Bombay army, which converts the old regular regiments into irregular regiments, and attaches six European officers to each regiment, instead of the regimental establishment of twenty-five as heretofore. Secondly, in posting officers to take command, and do duty with regiments to which they do not belong, and with which they had never served, to the disgust of the old native officers and men. Thirdly, in divorcing Native regiments from their old European officers. Fourthly, in appropriating, or rather confiscating, the mess plate and property belonging to the old regimental officers, and giving it to the six officers attached to the irregular regiment, and to which they may never have belonged at all ; and fifthly, in reducing the former pay and allowances of cavalry officers to the infantry scale ; and sixthly, giving the commanding officer and second in command of regiments, authority over the other four officers, although some of them may bear senior commissions. With respect to the conversion of the regular regiments of the Bombay army into irregulars, and attaching to them six officers only who may not belong to the regiments, and giving them regimental rank and authority, notwithstanding the Parliamentary guarantees, but as I have a separate Motion on the subject I will not at present trespass upon the House on this additional grievance. In regard to the third additional grievance, the divorcing regiments from their officers. Strange as the phrase may seem to military men, it is nevertheless quite true. A regular Native regiment had its number in the line, and its twenty-five officers. By the General Bombay Orders, dated the 28th December, 1863, the Commander-in-Chief, Sir William Mansfield, carries out what he is pleased to call the re-organisation of the army; that is to say, he converts the native regiments, whether the native officers and men like it or not, into irregulars; posts six officers to each regiment, whom he selects at his pleasure from Line or local officers; and the real officers of each regiment whom he may not have selected, he permits to exist upon papers in the army list, but to have no right to join the regiment with which they may have served from the date of their first commission, or to have authority or status therein. They are literally, therefore, only paper officers. I have presented to the House a petition from Captain C. F. Grant of the 3rd regiment, of twenty-seven years' service, to this effect; and there are scores of others similarly circumstanced. Why, Sir, an owner of cattle could not dispose of his animals with less ceremony. The fourth additional grievance relates to the disposal of the mess plate and property, and the following extract of a letter from a field officer will best explain its nature :—

"We are, for the most part, justly enraged at the cool order issued by the Chief on the formation of the old native infantry corps into irregulars; and without our knowledge or consent making over all our mess property to the half-dozen officers who have been appointed to the different corps; for instance, the flower vase which cost me £25, which I gave to my mess (the old 19th), is now by this order the property of the officers who now compose the 19th irregular corps, and who, with only one exception, never belonged to the corps on its original footing !"

The fifth additional grievance is the reduction of the former pay and allowances of cavalry officers to the infantry scale of pay, with the addition of the staff pay of any command they may hold in an irregular regiment. The infantry pay and the staff allowance together, it is said, do not amount to the pay and allowances guaranteed by the two Acts of Parliament ; but as official information has not, I believe, been yet received at the India Office of this new arrangement, I would hope the paltry saving is not really contemplated. The sixth additional grievance is of a very serious character, as it abrogates the power of an officer's commission; but the following order of the Commander-in-Chief, Sir William Mansfield, appeared in *The Overland Times*, of the 20th February to the 14th March, 1864 :—

"The Commander-in-Chief is pleased to intimate that it has been ruled by the Government of India, that in all cases the officer appointed to the command of a regiment organised under the new system, the commandant in virtue of his appointment commands the regiment, the second in command will rank next in the corps, the other officers taking rank regimentally according to army standing."

By the above extraordinary order, any junior officer selected by favouritism, or any other cause, to command or to be second in command of a regiment, is to nullify the commissions of any senior officers who may be in the regiment, but who have not had influence enough to obtain the command, or second in command.

In conclusion I must add a few words of appeal to the House and to the country. The East India Company's armies, in conjunction with a comparatively small proportion of Royal troops, in the course of 100 years, annexed an empire of nearly 200 millions of souls to the British crown. Distinguished loyalty and gallantry had been manifested by the native troops for more than 100 years, with the melancholy exception of the mutiny of the greater part of the Bengal army in 1857, attributable, however, chiefly to British ignorance, disregard of caste, pre-

judices, and want of tact; but, at that
critical period, the Madras and Bombay
armies, with the exception of two Bombay
regiments, remained faithful and actively
efficient, and preserved the British dominion in the west and south of India. These
armies are surely, therefore, officers and
men, entitled to the gratitude and confidence of the British Government and to
the maintenance of their former status and
proud distinction of regular troops; and it
is equally impolitic and unjust to make
such changes in their ancient organization, as wounds their self-respect, and, by
shaking their reliance upon the stability
of their rights, jeopardizes their attachment
to the State.

SIR CHARLES WOOD: I quite admit
the importance of the subject which has
been introduced in so temperate a manner
by the hon. and gallant Member (Captain
Jervis). There is, however, not the least
reason for supposing that the Government
has been disinclined to do justice to the
officers of the Indian army. We have
all along admitted that they are entitled
not only to justice, but to the most
liberal and generous treatment on the
part of the Government. I have never
denied that for a moment, nor have I a
single syllable on this matter to retract.
Our object has been to adhere scrupulously
to the Parliamentary guarantee given to
these officers. I need hardly remind the
House that the whole of these arrangements
were sanctioned by a great majority—
indeed, by almost the whole—of the council of India, who naturally sympathize
with the officers of the Indian army, and
were little likely to withhold anything to
which they were fairly entitled. I can
assure the House that the very last thought
in our minds was the idea of doing any injustice to the Indian officers. After the
statements which have been made, I hope
I may be permitted, without going into
details, to say that a very large measure of
consideration was given to the army of India.
We adopted, of course, those arrangements which we deemed best calculated
to promote the efficiency of the public service; but in doing so we endeavoured to
give to the Indian officers every possible
consideration. The very first step that was
taken in regard to pensions, pay, and allowances, imposed an additional annual
charge of a quarter of a million on the
Indian revenue. We cannot, therefore, be
accused of having stinted our measures by
mere considerations of economy. When

Colonel Sykes

the question was raised in the House I
felt that Parliament had a right to see
that the guarantee which they had given
was fairly carried out, and I recommended the appointment of a Commission to inquire into the subject. The
testimony which the hon. and gallant
Officer has borne to the character of that
Commission justifies, I think, the selection
which was made. I did not endeavour to
choose those who were prejudiced on my
side of the question, but did my best to
secure an unbiassed inquiry. We owe our
best thanks to the noblemen and gentlemen who served on this Commission for
the exceeding pains which they have taken
in considering the subject, and for the impartiality with which they have drawn up
their Report. When the question was
under consideration by my Council, we
certainly did not think that we were in
any way infringing the Parliamentary
guarantee. In order to make ourselves
sure on that question we submitted the
whole of the despatches to the then Law
Officers of the Crown, who reported that we
had done nothing which might not have
been done by the East India Company, and
which, therefore, we were not justified in
doing. Being fortified by that authority,
I hope the House will not suppose me to be
exceedingly obstinate in continuing to be
unconvinced that we have departed from
the guarantee. At the same time, I defer
to the opinion expressed by the Commission,
and frankly and fully accept their Report.
The Commission, it will be observed, have
classed the complaints made under thirteen different heads. In regard to eight
out of that number they have reported
that the Parliamentary guarantee has not
been violated; in regard to two they say
that there may be an infringement; and in
regard to three that a departure from the
assurance of Parliament has taken place.
With respect to the retiring fund, to which
allusion has been made by the hon. and gallant Gentleman, it was a Court of Law
which declared that it was illegal; and I
only cited that decision. The Commission
very justly remark that it is impossible to
suppose that Parliament could have intended
to guarantee the continuance of a practice
contrary to law. The Court of Directors,
in a despatch to the Bombay Government,
in 1838, expressed disapprobation of their
having received payment of subscriptions
even provisionally, or given any encouragement to the service to expect a sanction to
the system. It is, however, not worth while

going into that question now. The hon. and gallant Member for Aberdeen (Colonel Sykes) has said that the majority of officers of the Indian army, whom he stated correctly enough to be below 5,000 and 6,000, have cause for complaint ; but that is far, indeed, from being the fact. The officers who volunteer into the Line are benefited by the change, and so are the officers of the Staff Corps, and of the Artillery and Engineers. Those officers who were appointed on the distinct understanding that they would be subjected to any change which might be made, have no just cause of complaint. In fact, instead of a majority of the officers in the Indian army having complained, the utmost number who can be injuriously affected by the changes, and can have possible cause of complaint, is about 1,500. Moreover, I must be permitted to say that there is a good deal of unfairness in many of those who complain, for although they gain on the whole, they say nothing about their gains, but insist only on what they lose. For instance, an officer complains that he has to remain lieutenant-colonel longer than would have been the case under the old system, but suppresses the circumstance that he reaches that grade more speedily. If a major becomes a lieutenant-colonel four years sooner than he would otherwise have been, but remains a lieutenant-colonel two years longer, it is clear that he is a gainer by the change. He gains four years' pay as lieutenant-colonel, instead of as major, and actually obtains a colonel's allowances two years sooner than under the old system. In complaining of the delay in getting beyond the rank of lieutenant-colonel, it is, therefore, not fair to keep back the fact that promotion to that grade is much accelerated. If you deduct the cases of that kind from the whole number of complaints, you will see that no very large proportion of the 1,500 Indian officers have any real cause to complain. The hon. and gallant Member for Aberdeen says, that promotion by regimental seniority was the legal right of the officers of the Indian army. If that is so, of course there can be no question of the promotions complained of being illegal ; but all I can say is, that in the time of the Company many promotions and appointments were made in utter derogation of regimental seniority. [Colonel SYKES: They were exceptions.] I do not deny they were exceptions, but you cannot have an exception to that which is a legal right. Besides, no person will tell me that the occurrences which took place two years ago were not of a very exceptional character. It was certainly an exceptional state of affairs when sixty-two regiments mutinied in Bengal and disappeared entirely from the service. So, too, the great reduction which has been made in the Indian army was an exceptional measure, because, up to very recently, the number of Native troops had always been on the increase. When the Indian army was reduced to the extent of 130,000 men, the necessary result was, that there were far more officers than were required to officer the existing army. I apprehend nobody will maintain that it was not as competent to the Crown as it would have been to the Company, or that it was not as much the duty of the Crown as it would have been the duty of the Company, to reduce the army. But then came the question, how the officers were to be dealt with ? The hon. and gallant Gentleman says that the officers of the Indian army had a right to pay and promotion just as if they had continued to be employed. But is that the case with any other army in the world ? When reductions were made in the English army the officers are put on half pay for life. In the case of the Indian army, the pay and promotion up to the rank of General still go on just as if the officers continued to be employed; so that a young gentleman who was appointed in December, 1861, will be promoted up to the rank of General, with the pay of the rank which he may hold, though he had never served at all when the change was made. Surely that is not dealing hardly with the Indian officers ? Reference has been made to certain cases mentioned in the Report of the Commissioners of some retardation of promotion in consequence of the reduction. The Commissioners say it was competent to the Crown to reduce the Indian army, and they add it was the duty of the Crown to show every consideration to the officers. I think when we have continued to them the whole of their pay and promotion, although the regiments to which they belonged have ceased to exist, it cannot be fairly said that we have evinced any want of consideration for them. But there are three cases in which the Commissioners have reported a breach of the guarantee. I am prepared to give redress in those cases. It has not been from any want of attention, of thought, or of care, that the measures for this purpose have not been completed. I solemnly declare that these questions connected with the Indian army have cost me more time and trouble ten times over than all the rest of Indian affairs put together. The House must not forget that it was necessary to consult a great number of people—because no step can be taken in giving promotion which affects the Indian army alone. Nothing could be more simple than the course suggested by the hon. and gallant Member for Aberdeen, that the whole of the promotions to the Staff Corps should be cancelled; but, as I stated on a former occasion, I must hesitate before adopting a measure of that kind. The officers of the Staff Corps have not been selected by the Government at home. They are tried and experienced men, selected at various times by the Indian Government, and it would be extremely hard to them to cancel the rank which they have now held for three years. That would be inflicting an injustice upon them without doing good to other persons, for I believe that many of the officers who complain of the supersession actually gain by the others being on the Staff Corps. If the promotions are not cancelled, however, it becomes a difficult question to determine what can be done. It is extremely difficult to devise any mode which will even approximate towards remedying the breach of guarantee without entailing injury and hardship upon another class of officers. The hon. and learned Member for Aberdeen talked about promoting all the officers in the same way as the officers on the Staff Corps; but what, I ask, would be the effect of that upon the officers of the Line? They have not complained of the promotion of the officers in the Staff Corps, but if they are to be superseded by all the officers of the old Indian army they will have a just and legitimate cause of complaint. What is the best mode of dealing with the cases of breach of guarantee I am at present unable to say. Shortly before Easter we devised a measure which, upon the whole, we thought would answer the purpose; but difficulties occurred, and it became necessary to consult again with the military authorities in this country. The plan is at present under the anxious consideration both of the Government and of the military authorities, and it will be brought forward as soon as possible; for I need hardly say I am as anxious as anybody can be to fulfil every pledge I have

Sir Charles Wood

given. I do not, of course, complain of the hon. and gallant Gentleman opposite for submitting this matter to the House, but after what I have said I hope he will not think it necessary to press it to a division.

CAPTAIN JERVIS said, that after the clear admission of the right hon. Gentleman that he accepted the Report of the Commissioners, and that it would be carried out *bonâ fide*, he would withdraw his Motion.

MR. BASS wished to know, why the grievances of the medical officers of the Indian army had not also been brought under the consideration of the Commission?

LORD STANLEY: May I be allowed to ask, whether the plan to be proposed will be produced in time to be discussed this Session?

MR. AYRTON asked, Whether there was any scheme under consideration for the employment of Indian officers when they returned home after serving in India?

MR. HENRY SEYMOUR said, he questioned what had fallen from the right hon. Gentleman with respect to the retiring funds of Indian officers. He could not understand how the practice could be called illegal, considering the approving despatch of the Court of Directors in November, 1837, and the adoption of the recommendations by previous Governments.

SIR CHARLES WOOD said, it was not for him to pronounce what was legal or illegal—the practice was declared to be illegal by a Court of Law before which the point was raised. He was perfectly aware of the despatch which the hon. Gentleman had quoted, which, however, did not affect the opinion of the Court of Law in any way. With regard to the question of the hon. Member for the Tower Hamlets, it was quite true that several Indian Engineer officers had been employed in this country, and there was no reason why Indian officers should not be employed here on general service on their return from India. As to the noble Lord's question, he hoped in a very short time to be able to announce that a conclusion had been come to upon the point. He was in hopes that he should have been able to submit his proposal before Easter, but unforeseen difficulties of detail had arisen, causing some delay. He hoped, however, to lay the proposal on the table in a short time. With regard to the question of the hon. Member for Derby, the case of the medical officers was a totally separate one. It had been under consideration for some time, but difficulties had arisen with the War Office. He had great hopes, that as far as the existing service was concerned, the difficulties would soon be removed.

Motion, by leave, *withdrawn*.

EDUCATION.
REPORTS OF INSPECTORS OF SCHOOLS.
RESOLUTION.

LORD ROBERT CECIL, in bringing forward the Resolution of which he had given notice—

"That, in the opinion of this House, the mutilation of the Reports of Her Majesty's Inspectors of Schools, and the exclusion from them of statements and opinions adverse to the educational views entertained by the Committee of Council, while matter favourable to them is admitted, are violations of the understanding under which the appointment of the Inspectors was originally sanctioned by Parliament, and tend entirely to destroy the value of their Reports,"

said, at this interesting time of the evening, I beg to promise the House that I will be exceedingly brief in dealing with the matter which I desire to bring before its attention. It may seem to some hon. Members to be a matter of small importance; but I do not think they will be of that opinion when they reflect that it involves the truth and purity of the information on which the House sanctions the payment of large sums of money taken out of the taxes paid by the people. What I wish to bring under the notice of the House is this:—The Inspectors of Schools make, as the House is aware, Reports annually to Parliament, containing, or professing to contain, the facts which those Inspectors have had under their cognizance, and the information which they have gathered with respect to the progress of education in those districts of the country which fall under their observation. Upon that information the House legislates, or rather it passes the Estimates for Education which are submitted to it. The Estimate for Education is, as the House wells knows, an Estimate of enormous amount; it has increased for many years, until it has now reached, I think, something like £800,000. The only information which the House possesses to enable it to judge whether the grant is rightly or wrongly dispensed is derived from the Reports of those Inspectors who are appointed for that purpose, and who make their Reports to the Committee of Privy Council, and through that Com-

mittee to Parliament. Now, what the right hon. Gentleman the Vice President of the Committee of Council on Education claims to do, and what I traverse his right to do, is this:—He claims to expunge from those Reports all opinions which differ from his own, and at the same time to retain in them those opinions which agree with his own. It will be at once plain to hon. Members that such a practice entirely destroys the value of the Reports as any guide to the House in the course it should take on educational matters. Nor is this all. What I want to point out to the House is that this is not only an injurious plan, but is a breach of the original understanding upon which those Inspectors were appointed. They were appointed in the year 1840, after, as some hon. Members may remember, very fierce contests, in which all parts of the Government scheme were sharply called in question. They were appointed under a Minute that was afterwards laid before Parliament; and when that Minute had been laid before Parliament the general feeling was that so satisfactory had the arrangement which the Government had made turned out, that all the antagonism which had been raised disappeared at once, and the scheme of the Government was allowed to go on without further resistance. Since that time the Inspectors have held their office without any opposition on the part of Parliament, they have increased largely in number, and have been relied on by this House as its source of information. Now, that Minute, I maintain, is the contract between the Government and the House, and I want to call the attention of hon. Gentlemen to its terms. It was passed in January, 1840, and says—

"The Reports of the Inspectors are intended to convey such further information respecting the state of elementary education in Great Britain as to enable Parliament to determine in what mode the sums voted for the education of the poorer classes can be most usefully applied. Your Reports will be made to the Committee, but it is intended that they shall be laid before both Houses of Parliament. The Committee doubt not that you are duly impressed with the weight of the responsibility resting upon you, and they repose full confidence in the judgment and discretion with which your duty will be performed."

Now, the House of Commons, knowing that that was the understanding on which the Inspectors were appointed, and receiving their Reports from year to year, have become accustomed to look to those Reports for a true account of the state of Education as it actually existed, and on the faith of them have made the enormous grants for which the Minister applied on behalf of the Educational Department. What I wish the House particularly to notice is this :— The right hon. Gentleman the Vice President of the Committee of Council claims—I believe in a Minute which he passed—to exclude from the Reports all " matters of opinion." But that is not what he really does. What he really does is to exclude all matters of opinion hostile to himself. Of course, for reasons which the House will well understand, the right hon. Gentleman is rather a formidable man for his subordinates to deal with, and I cannot afford to quote any information which I may have received from them for fear of the vengeance which might descend on the head of the unfortunate wight who supplied it. But I ask the House to believe me without asking me for proof—and I can give proof if I am challenged—I ask the House to believe that the sort of things cut out of the Reports are of this character. Supposing, for instance, that there is something in the construction of a school which is, in the opinion of the Inspector, injurious to the condition of the children, and that it is desirable that, in regard to it, the Privy Council should relax its rule —that is an opinion to which the right hon. Gentleman does not accede, and it is ruthlessly cut out. Supposing that the right hon. Gentleman has to meet opponents in Parliament ; supposing, for example, he has to meet an opponent so formidable to him as the hon. Member for Berkshire (Mr. Walter), and that that hon. Gentleman gathers together some very cogent arguments against the views of the Vice President of the Education Department, and supposing that some unfortunate Inspector should in his Report state facts or opinions which would seem in any way to support the proposition which such an opponent as I have indicated would bring forward, then that passage is ruthlessly cut out by the right hon. Gentleman the Vice President. But suppose some Inspector of more docile and loyal mind, knowing the duty he owes to his Department, knowing the allegiance he bears to the right hon. Gentleman, makes it his business so to construct his Report that the Vice President of the Council shall have available materials for the next speech which he may have occasion to deliver, and shall be able to cite the opinion of that In-

Lord Robert Cecil

spector of Schools against such a Motion as that of the hon. Member for Berkshire, then the Report is received with open arms and appears with all the honours. The right hon. Gentleman tells us he excludes matters of opinion. Let us test that assertion. I will quote from Mr. Stewart's General Report for 1862. Mr. Stewart is a keen opponent of the views of the hon. Member for Berkshire, and the consequence is that his Report is unmutilated, and finds its way into the blue-book. He says—

" It is not unusual to represent the schools of the class just mentioned as institutions in which an unnecessarily high quality of instruction is given to the scholars, and at the same time to make out as a grievance that your Lordships' system ignores the very existence of 15,000 schools which stand in great need of assistance, but get nothing, although, without the services of educated teachers, they really contrive to teach children the simple elements of education."

Mr. Stewart then goes on at length to refute that opinion—

" There are, of course, examples in which the general regulations of all public departments press with severity and apparent inequality ; but, on the whole, it is not correct to say that schools are unaided because your Lordships require an impossible standard of school management and instruction."

Now, that is a direct opinion on the objections raised by Gentlemen in this House and elsewhere, and it states that those objections are futile ; but, of course, it is put in by the Vice President of the Council, because it states an opinion which he himself entertains. I will now just merely read the sentence with which this Report concludes, to show how boldly Mr. Stewart advances his opinions regarding certificated teachers, and how far the right hon. Gentleman gives expression to opinions with which he concurs. He says—

" This state of things is neither due to the enticements of public grants nor wholly to individual exertion ; highly-trained teachers have obtained a fair trial, and experience has shown that they are not only the best, but the only persons qualified, as a class, to conduct schools in which the poor are to be thoroughly, although plainly, educated."

That, of course, is a direct negative to the Motion of the hon. Member for Berkshire ; it is a direct opinion on the subject of a legislative change yet under the consideration of the House of Commons; it is an opinion in sympathy with the views of the Vice President of the Privy Council; and you have the remarkable fact that it appears, while the opinions of Inspectors who adopt the other view of the question are excluded. Of course, if I had the opinions of the mutilated Inspectors, I have no doubt I should be able to make my case a great deal stronger. The House will see that, and appreciate my difficulty. I know the ferocity, almost, with which the right hon. Gentleman exercises his powers; and I am not disposed to subject any one with whom I am acquainted to the exercise of those powers. I submit to the consideration of the House this question: —Will you trust to Reports that have been subjected to this expurgating process, by which the Minister, who represents the Department in this House, excludes all that is hostile and retains all that is favourable to himself? I ask hon. Gentlemen to apply to the case the test of their own experience. What would the owner of a distant estate think if he ordered his bailiffs to report to the land steward, and if when the bailiffs had sent in their reports he found some day that some of them containing some strong opinions on the management of land were absent, while some maintaining the particular views of the steward himself were carefully preserved? The steward might be a man entertaining opinions in which many other persons did not concur. He might entertain strange, quaint, and crotchety opinions on agricultural questions. He might be of opinion that you ought to put all your manure on rich land, and none of it on poor land. Well, supposing him to entertain those opinions, and to argue them out on letters from bailiffs which supported them, while he suppressed those letters from bailiffs which opposed them, I ask, does any Gentleman who is the owner of land think the steward would retain his situation? Sir, the remedy is in the hands of the House. They are intrusted with the expenditure of vast sums of money; and usually when they grant large sums they guard by Acts of Parliament the expenditure of that money; but in the case of Education they hand over enormous sums to a Minister who conducts his department, not on regulations which the House itself can control, but on Minutes which the Government are always introducing, and which, if defeated, they can reintroduce with illusory modifications by which the opinion of the House is defied or eluded. The House of Commons, in dealing with a Department so constituted, is bound to its constituents to use a double amount of caution. It is bound to insist that the channels of information on which it depends shall be pure, and that it shall not be called upon to legislate for such

vast interests as are now at stake on unfaithworthy and garbled statements. The noble Lord concluded by moving his Resolution.

MR. WALTER: Sir, as I may be unable to address the House at a later period of the evening. I beg to say a few words in seconding the Motion of the noble Lord. If the question which my noble Friend has raised was simply one affecting the order and discipline of the Department, I should be the last to join in supporting it; but the case is of a serious character; and the noble Lord has stated very fairly that by adopting the course it has been pursuing in garbling the Reports of the Inspectors, the Education Department deprives this House of the information which it ought to possess when dealing with this question. If the Inspectors were merely correspondents of the Department; if those who have charge of the Department receive the Reports of the Inspectors merely to grind up in order to make a report of their own, that would be quite a different question, and I should not object to their garbling those Reports. But I think the Inspectors stand in a very different position. They are gentlemen of very superior education; they get high salaries; and I think I may say it is believed by this House, that of all others they are eminently competent to guide the House on this subject. Well, what is the position of any Member who entertains views of his own—it may be crotchety, but at all events deliberate views—on this question? My noble Friend has truly reminded the House that it has been my lot to address the House on the question of certificated masters. That question has undergone discussion here in two successive Sessions. I find in the Reports of two Inspectors—Mr. Norris and Mr. Stewart—opinions to the effect that I have entirely failed by my arguments to show that the system of certificated masters is not the best one. And I find in the same Reports statements that in the uncertificated schools are good-for-nothing masters—old crippled persons, eighty years of age, paupers, and all the rest of it; and, in short, that I have not a leg to stand on if I bring the matter forward. I do not complain of that. On the contrary, I say the Inspectors have a right to make those statements; but when I have reason to know that in a Report of a different character, by a gentleman holding different opinions—a Report which speaks of a particular school as being the very beau-ideal of what an infant school ought to be, of its being the best school in the Inspector's district—when I find the whole passage containing that statement struck out because the Inspector thought it right to state that the school was conducted by an uncertificated mistress, I say it is not fair, because it deprives me, and any gentleman holding the same views, of the opportunity of bringing our case before the House in a proper manner. When we read the Inspectors' Reports as they appeared in the Report of the Commissioners, we felt that they were not writing under the fear of the Department. Now, I have looked through all the evidence I could find in all the volumes of that Report, and I find that those gentlemen hold very different views ; and there is enough to satisfy me that I have a strong *primâ facie* case ; but if I am told that in any opinions which may be expressed by the Inspectors in future those parts that support the views I put forward are to be struck out, then I say I have no chance of bringing my case properly before the House. Mentioning this particular case, I call on the House, if they wish to have accurate information on the subject, to encourage the Inspectors by all means to state their opinions fully.

Motion made, and Question proposed,

"That, in the opinion of this House, the mutilation of the Reports of Her Majesty's Inspectors of Schools, and the exclusion from them of statements and opinions adverse to the educational views entertained by the Committee of Council, while matter favourable to them is admitted, are violations of the understanding under which the appointment of the Inspectors was originally sanctioned by Parliament, and tend entirely to destroy the value of their Reports."—(*Lord R. Cecil.*)

MR. LOWE : Sir, I assure the House that the case mentioned by the hon. Member for Berkshire is entirely new to me ; I have not the least idea to what the hon. Member alludes. The noble Lord the Member for Stamford (Lord Robert Cecil) has spoken of the "ferocity" which we displayed in a recent instance. I quite understand what he means. On Thursday last the noble Lord asked me to state the grounds on which Mr. Morrell had been dismissed from the office-of Inspector. I said I did not think it would be right to make an *ex parte* statement on the subject ; but if the noble Lord chose to move for the Correspondence it would be at his service as an unopposed Return. The noble Lord has not thought right to move for it [Lord ROBERT CECIL : I am going to

Mr. Walter

do so], but, without having the documents in his hands, the noble Lord attributes to the Lord President the course of conduct which he has just mentioned to the House. The House must judge of the justice of that course. The noble Lord asks us to assert two opinions. The House is asked to assert two facts ; first, that the Reports of Her Majesty's Inspectors of Schools are mutilated ; and secondly, that statements and opinions adverse to the educational views entertained by the Committee of Council are excluded from the Reports, while matter favourable to them is admitted. The noble Lord then calls upon the House to declare, as matters of opinion, that that is a violation of the understanding under which the appointment of the Inspectors was originally sanctioned by Parliament, and that it tends entirely to destroy the value of their Reports. Now, I maintain that those two facts are untrue, and that those two opinions are absurd. Let me state again to the House, as I stated last year, the practice of the Office on the subject, and then the House will be able to judge whether what is done amounts to mutilation or not. The matter which first drew attention to this subject was a Report of a Roman Catholic Inspector, which we inadvertently allowed to be laid on the table of the House, and a considerable portion of which was devoted to a statistical inquiry into the comparative state of Roman Catholic and Protestant countries, in order to demonstrate that illegitimate births, capital crimes, and other offences were more frequent in Protestant than in Roman Catholic countries. That Report was too offensive a document to be laid on the table of the House and to be printed at the public expense, and I felt ashamed at having been a party to its production, for it is not the business of our Department to interfere in these religious controversies. It therefore appeared to us necessary to take some steps to prevent a recurrence of such a proceeding. What were we to do ? No doubt the obvious expedient would have been what the noble Lord calls mutilation —namely, to read over the Reports of the Inspectors, and to strike out the passages considered improper to be laid before Parliament. These Inspectors are appointed under the Privy Council, and the directions given to them are that they should report on the state of the schools which they inspect, and offer practical suggestions for their improvement. There is not any exclusion of opinion. On the contrary, opinion is perfectly admissible, if directed to the practical object of the improvement of the schools inspected. Such are the instructions under which the Inspectors act. Well, then, if the Inspectors, having received those instructions, do not write their Reports in conformity with them, they obviously commit a breach of duty; and the simple question we had to consider was, what would be in such a case the proper remedy to be applied. As I said, I could have garbled and mutilated these Reports; but I did not think it right or fair to do so—because if a sentence was struck out it might very well be argued that not only was that particular sentence expunged, but its removal might materially alter the contents of the Report. Therefore, it appeared to be the safest course to make the Inspectors their own censors, to send back, in case of need, the Reports to them, with a copy of the instructions as to the manner in which the Reports were to be drawn up, and to leave it to them to bring their Reports into conformity therewith, and informing them if that was not done the Reports would be put aside as documents not proper to be printed at the public expense. That is the course which the Office has uniformly observed. It does not point out in any case passages to which objections are made, but merely lays down the rule and principle on which the Inspectors are to proceed, and leaves them to apply that rule and principle to their own Reports. The Inspectors are, as has been most truly observed, gentlemen of great intelligence, and, if they will, they can perform the office of removing what seems to be improper in their Reports. We do not proceed in any narrow spirit, but allow a considerable latitude, and it is only in extreme cases that we have thought it necessary to act on the determination I have just mentioned. I would ask the House, then, after it has now heard the statement I have made, what does it think of the assertions of the noble Lord that the Vice President of the Committee of Council cuts out this, revises that, and excludes the other? What does it think of the allegation of the hon. Member for Berkshire, that a particular statement with respect to a particular school was omitted at my instance? The House is informed of the invariable principle on which the Department proceeds, and I ask hon. Gentlemen how can they, with any degree of fairness or consistency, vote, in the face of my statement, that I am a person who mutilates these Reports, when the aim and object of the Committee of Council are, that mutilation should not be the work of the Department, but that the Inspector himself, who may have inadvertently made his Report not in accordance with his instructions, should have the power of setting it right? Therefore, I cannot conceive with what face the noble Lord can ask the House to agree to his Motion, which he supports with statements at variance with the facts of the case, to the effect that the heads of the Office cut out passages from the Reports. It is next said that we exclude from the Reports what is unfavourable to our views, and leave in what is favourable. That assertion is liable to the same answer. We neither strike out nor retain anything. The noble Lord says that he has information to that effect; but, judging from what has fallen from that noble Lord, I should say that the information is of very little value. It is not our wish that the Inspectors should write in favour of the Department or against it; and we do not strike out passages either because they are favourable or unfavourable, if they only come within the Minute of instructions, and offer practical suggestions for the improvement of schools. What is objected to is general controversial matter, not matter of opinion within the Minute, but matter of opinion which does not bear on the subject the Inspector has to report upon; but I do not feel it my duty to erase from a Report any argument in favour of retaining certificated teachers, because that is a matter which has to do with the improvement of the schools under inspection. It is as germane to the argument as an argument in favour of doing away with certificated teachers. I never have had occasion to notice any such argument since the Inspectors are unanimous the other way. I think I have shown the House pretty good reason why it should not vote that these Reports are mutilated or are not fair, and it now remains for me to deal with the noble Lord's two matters of opinion. First of all, it is said that the course pursued is contrary to the understanding on which the Inspectors were directed to report, and the noble Lord quotes a letter of 1840. [Lord ROBERT CECIL: A Minute.] No, it is not a Minute. All who are familiar with these matters at the beginning, know that in 1840 the only assistance which the Privy Council gave to schools consisted of grants for building, there being then no annual grants; and the Inspector's duty was not to interfere with the instruction and management or discipline of schools, or press on the managers any suggestions which they should not be inclined to receive. The office of Inspector at that time was quite different from what it now is. The noble Lord quoted a passage as to the Reports of the Inspectors, and he said they were to report on the state of particular districts, and how far it would be expedient for Government or Parliament to provide additional means of education in those districts. But the Reports which were then contemplated are not the least like what our Inspectors make now. These former Reports were to be made on the general state of education, in order that the Government, which had not then made up its mind as to the manner in which assistance ought to be given to schools, should have their attention directed to the state of education. Our present Reports, on the other hand, are Reports on schools, and on matters which occurred to the Inspectors in connection with those schools. The one class of Reports has become obsolete in course of time, and the other class is substituted for it. I admit to the noble Lord that it is the understanding, and always has been, that the Reports of the Inspectors should be laid before Parliament. That is the object with which they report, and when we call on them to report, we do so with the intention of laying their Reports before Parliament. The Reports, however, are not made directly to Parliament, but to the Privy Council under instructions, and are then laid before Parliament if they fairly and reasonably agree with those instructions. That is the practice of my Office, and it is not peculiar to the Committee of Privy Council, but prevails in other public offices having Inspectors, such as the Home Office. It is not everything that a gentleman chooses to write which is to be laid on the table of the House of Commons, or we might have an account of every quarrel and controversy in which he had embarked, and a record of every indiscreet expression which he may have penned. It is quite open to the House to express an opinion that the Inspectors should report directly to Parliament, and not to the Privy Council, and thus exonerate us from all responsibility in the matter. I have not the slightest objection to any amount of report which the House may then choose to require; but only while we

have the responsibility we are bound to exercise a control. The matter which first drew attention to the subject was the Report of Mr. Fletcher in 1849. That gentleman drew up a Report of more than 200 pages, which referred not only to education, but went into the statistics of crime, and into the amount of committals for offences; and all this was printed at the public expense. That was considered an abuse, and a circular was issued to prevent the recurrence of such cases. But, if the House thinks it advisable that a number of very clever men should exercise their faculties in giving greater latitude to these Reports, and that they should be printed at the public expense, nothing can be easier. Let the House give its orders, and they shall be obeyed. No delusion can be greater than that the Privy Council Office is in any way afraid of any criticism of their proceedings. We have undergone every criticism that the whole of a highly educated class could bring upon us. Every one of these Inspectors can write what he likes, not in a Parliamentary blue-book, which nobody reads, but in the Reviews, which everybody reads. There is no soreness at anything that can be said. You have heard the worst of us, and we are not the least afraid of any facts that can be brought against us. But what we are anxious for, what we do wish, is to keep the Office in discipline; if we do issue instructions, to see that they are not disobeyed, and to keep the officers within the limits of those instructions. The House may itself undertake the duty of those by whom the Revised Code is to be administered; but, in that event, relieve us from the responsibility. I shall then be happy to congratulate the noble Lord on the triumph he has obtained, and I hope the House will not grow tired of the task. There is one more matter of opinion expressed by the noble Lord—that the effect of the exercise of our jurisdiction over these Reports is entirely to destroy their value. The noble Lord appears to consider the whole and sole value of the Inspectors' Reports to consist in their being damaging and derogatory to their superiors, and furnishing arguments to those who always talk of the largeness of the Education Estimates, but have done everything to make them larger and less efficient. The sort of thing the noble Lord contemplates may be very delightful, but it is scarcely practicable. He seems to contemplate a department, nominally responsible to Parliament for large sums of money, living under an Aulic Council of Inspectors, criticising its action, condemning its conduct, and furnishing arms to any one who may attack it. That, according to the noble Lord, may be the *beau ideal* of a public department; but such a department must necessarily end in perfect anarchy. Responsibility would be utterly frittered away and destroyed, and your Inspectors, having their own way, you would have a bad system of inspection. I think, therefore, I have shown that it is not true that these Reports are mutilated as the noble Lord says; nor is it true—at any rate the noble Lord is quite unable to adduce any evidence on which the House can act—that there is any capricious or unfair dealing with the Reports in order to make them pleasing to the Department. Nor can it be said with any justice that the withholding, in some cases, of these Reports is a violation of any understanding; for whoever said it was the intention of the Department that they should all be laid before Parliament? To make that out it should be shown that the Privy Council bound themselves to lay these Reports in every case on the table of the House, which no one has ever asserted. And as to the opinion that these Reports are only valuable so far as they are condemnatory of the Office under which the Inspectors act, I think that is an assertion which it will not do the House much credit to take from the lips of the noble Lord. One thing more I have got to say, and I hope it will give satisfaction to the noble Lord; it is this, that this policy of vivisection, or mutilation, or whatever he may call it, has been entirely successful. I have the greatest pleasure in telling the House that, in the present year, we have now got in all the Reports of the Inspectors, and I am proud to say it has not been necessary to send a single Report back to the Inspectors. The noble Lord will, of course, say that the reign of terror had prevailed; but I can assure him that is not the case. The noble Lord appears to think that it should be a source of the greatest satisfaction to the House and the country to find the Department in a state of civil war, and the public service in jeopardy; but there is nothing of the kind. I can assure him that the Inspectors—a very valuable body of men, who have undertaken, no doubt, duties which press very heavily on some of them—are doing good service, and the system is worked with a smoothness and success which surprise us. We really see no rock ahead, except such Motions and speeches as are made by the noble Lord, which would lead the House to suppose that the system was really founded on the principle of having antagonistic influences at work—those representing the Department in Parliament and the Inspectors—and that the best thing they can do for the public service is that it shall be torn in pieces between them. I sincerely hope that the House will not listen to the Motion of the noble Lord, because it will be fatal to the present organization of the Office, and because the two statements which it expresses are utterly untrue, and his two opinions absurd.

Mr. W. E. FORSTER: Having brought forward this question last year, I wish to say a very few words to show the position in which the great educational question, which we have all at heart, now stands. The right hon. Gentleman has made great changes—I am not going to say whether they are advantages or disadvantages—but no doubt great changes have been made. A crisis has arisen in the question; and just at this moment, when we are most anxious to get all the information possible as to facts, the right hon. Gentleman comes forward and pleads for the discipline of his Office—what none of his predecessors found it necessary to do—by saying that it was not the original understanding that all the Inspectors' Reports should be produced. Those who knew the history of the Education movement understood that when the Government gave State aid they were to receive information from impartial and educated gentlemen as to how that State aid was applied. It was never more important that we should know the facts; but no facts are given which run counter to the view of the right hon. Gentleman. He says it is very easy to print these facts elsewhere; but I say the place where they ought to appear is that in which by the arrangement of the Office they ought to appear—I mean in the Reports of the School Inspectors. There is another point. Perhaps the House is not aware that this year the right hon. Gentleman only gives Reports for half the kingdom—the Reports are only from half the Inspectors in the course of the year. I do not suppose that he has taken care to pick the half most favourable to himself, but at the present time, when information from all parts of the country is so much required, he steps forward and says, "I will save the country a few pounds in the printing of these Reports." Never was there a more penny wise and pound foolish policy. If, as he says, the Inspectors send foolish Reports, let us see them; it may be a reason for getting rid of them. Then the right hon. Gentleman said the Reports did not contain practical suggestions:—let him be good enough to produce those Reports which he says were not mutilated, but sent back to the Inspectors;—let us see them, whether with or without the marginal marks upon them, and then the House will form its own opinion on the subject. There is another reason why the Office which is concerned in the distribution of the Educational Grant does, to use plain language, want watching and control. The right hon. Gentleman has issued a new Code himself in the shape of supplementary rules. I say that is a reason why we ought to know as well as we possibly can from those gentlemen who go through the country, and whose business it is to report the local circumstances of the schools, what it is that the great central bureaucratic establishment is doing in the matter. The right hon. Gentleman, in the conclusion of his speech, gave the strongest possible argument in favour of the Motion. He said, that while the last thing the Office was afraid of was opinions, yet that he could not work the Office if these gentlemen were allowed to give us their opinions and practical suggestions.

MR. LOWE explained that he did not mean to say that if the present system were abolished the Office would not work, but he intended to imply that the Government of the Office would be taken out of their hands. With respect to the reduction in the number of Reports—under the original system they had head Inspectors and assistant Inspectors, and the head Inspectors only made reports; but the system had been changed, and now all were Inspectors and made Reports. According to the present plan of one-half of the Inspectors reporting this year, the same number of Reports would be presented as in former times.

MR. LIDDELL said, there was an old saying that hard words did not always constitute sound argument; and the speech of the right hon. Gentleman (Mr. Lowe) showed the truth of the saying. He had said that the noble Lord's (Lord R. Cecil) assertions were untrue, and his opinions absurd; but how had he proved what he

Mr. W. E. Forster

had said? To prove the first part of his assertion he had said that the Reports were not mutilated by the Department, but by the Inspectors themselves. Now, the Government of Japan, when it was wished to punish an officer did not punish him themselves, but called upon him to commit suicide;. and this was precisely the course which the right hon. Gentleman had taken. The right hon. Gentleman had also said that the Reports contained opinions which ought not to be printed; but surely the best way would be to give the House an opportunity of judging of that, and then, probably, an expression of opinion would correct the evil.

SIR GEORGE GREY said, that as the practice of other Departments had been adverted to, he felt bound to state, as the result of considerable experience, that he thought it was absolutely necessary for the interests of the public that the heads of Departments should exercise some degree of control over the Reports of Inspectors. He had had occasion at the Home Office, as had been the case with his predecessor (Sir James Graham), to call the attention of Inspectors to the nature of their Reports, in which, after stating facts, they proceeded to enter upon controversies upon disputed points. In those cases the Reports were not mutilated, but sent back to the Inspectors, exactly in the same way as he understood from his right hon. Friend the Vice President the Reports of the Inspectors of Schools had been dealt with. He considered that it was absolutely necessary that the head of a Department should exercise a power of that kind.

Question put—

The House *divided:* — Ayes 101; Noes 93 : Majority 8.

AYES.

Annesley, hon. Col. H.	Gallwey, Sir W. P.
Astell, J. H.	Gard, R. S.
Barrow, W. H.	George, J.
Beecroft, G. S.	Getty, S. G.
Bridges, Sir B. W.	Gilpin, Colonel
Brooks, R.	Gore, J. R. O.
Cargill, W. W.	Greenall, G.
Cartwright, Colonel	Greene, J.
Cochrane, A. D. R. W. B.	Gregory, W. H.
Collins, T.	Grey de Wilton, Visct.
Cubitt, G.	Griffith, C. D.
Disraeli, rt. hon. B.	Grogan, Sir E.
Du Cane, C.	Haliburton, T. C.
Dunne, Colonel	Hamilton, Major
Fane, Colonel J. W.	Hardy, G.
Farquhar, Sir M.	Hardy, J.
Fergusson, Sir J.	Hay, Sir J. C. D.
FitzGerald, W. R. S.	Henley, rt. hon. J. W.
Forster, W. E.	Horsfall, T. B.
Fraser, Sir W. A.	Hotham, Lord

Hubbard, J. G.
Hunt, G. W.
Kekewich, S. T.
Kennard, R. W.
Knatchbull, W. F.
Knightley, R.
Lacon, Sir E.
Leader, N. P.
Leeke, Sir H.
Lefroy, A.
Legh, W. J.
Leslie, W.
Liddell, hon. H. G.
Lovaine, Lord
Lowther, hon. Colonel
M'Cann, J.
M'Cormick, W.
MacEvoy, E.
Maguire, J. F.
Malins, R.
Manners, right hon.
 Lord J.
Mills, A.
Mowbray, rt. hon. J. R.
Nicol, W.
Noel, hon. G. J.
North, Colonel
Northcote, Sir S. H.
O'Conor Don, The
Packe, C. W.
Pakington, rt. hn. Sir J.
Peacocke, G. M. W.
Pease, H.

Peel, J.
Powell, F. S.
Quinn, P.
Repton, G. W. J.
Ridley, Sir M. W.
Rose, W. A.
Scott, Lord H.
Selwyn, C. J.
Seymour, H. D.
Shirley, E. P.
Smith, Sir F.
Somes, J.
Stanhope, J. B.
Stanley, Lord
Stracey, Sir H.
Sullivan, M.
Surtees, H. E.
Taylor, Colonel
Tomline, G.
Torrens, R.
Turner, C.
Vance, J.
Vansittart, W.
Vyse, Colonel H.
Walpole, rt. hon. S. H.
Waterhouse, S.
Whiteside, rt. hon. J.
Williams, W.
Woodd, B. T.

Pinney, Colonel
Pollard-Urquhart, W.
Price, R. G.
Ramsden, Sir J. W.
Salomons, Mr. Ald.
Scholefield, W.
Sidney, T.
Smith, J. B.
Smith, A.
Sykes, Colonel W. H.
Trelawny, Sir J. S.
Turner, J. A.

Verney, Sir H.
Villiers, rt. hon. C. P.
Warner, E.
Weguelin, T. M.
Whitbread, S.
White, L.
Wood, rt. hon. Sir C.
Woods, H.

TELLERS.
Brand, hon. H. B. W.
Dunbar, Sir W.

TELLERS.
Cecil, Lord R.
Walter, J.

NOES.

Acton, Sir J. D.
Ayrton, A. S.
Bagwell, J.
Baring, T. G.
Bass, M. T.
Bazley, T.
Black, A.
Blencowe, J. G.
Bouverie, hon. P. P.
Bramston, T. W.
Briscoe, J. I.
Bruce, Lord E.
Bruce, H. A.
Buller, Sir A. W.
Buxton, C.
Cardwell, rt. hon. E.
Clay, J.
Clifford, C. C.
Cobbett, J. M.
Cobden, R.
Collier, Sir R. P.
Cowper, rt. hon. W. F.
Cox, W.
Crossley, Sir F.
Dalglish, R.
Davey, R.
Denman, hon. G.
Dillwyn, L. L.
Dodson, J. G.
Duke, Sir J.
Dundas, rt. hon. Sir D.
Evans, Sir De L.
Ewart, W.
Ewart, J. C.
Finlay, A. S.
Forster, C.
Fortescue, C. S.

French, Colonel
Gibson, rt. hon. T. M.
Gilpin, C.
Gladstone, rt. hon. W.
Gower, G. W. G. L.
Grenfell, H. R.
Grey, rt. hon. Sir G.
Hadfield, G.
Henderson J.
Hodgkinson, G.
Hutt, rt. hon. W.
Ingham, R.
Knatchbull-Hugessen,
 E.
Layard, A. H.
Lefevre, G. J. S.
Lindsay, W. S.
Lowe, rt. hon. R.
Mackie, J.
Martin, P. W.
Martin, J.
Mills, J. R.
Moor, H.
Morris, D
Neate, C.
Norris, J. T.
O'Brien, Sir P.
Ogilvy, Sir J.
O'Hagan, rt. hon. T.
O'Loghlen, Sir C. M.
Osborne, R. B.
Padmore, R.
Paget, Lord A.
Palmer, Sir R.
Palmerston, Viscount
Peel, rt. hon. F.
Ponder, J.

JOINT-STOCK COMPANIES (VOTING PAPERS).—LEAVE.

MR. DARBY GRIFFITH, in moving for leave to bring in a Bill to afford shareholders in joint-stock companies facilities for voting by means of Voting Papers, explained that under the present system the vast majority of shareholders could vote only by anticipation. Shareholders in public companies, unless they were able to be personally present, which was often physically impossible, for no room could be found large enough to contain perhaps 18,000 or 20,000 people, were in the habit of delegating their authority and voting by proxy. The consequence was that the proxies being necessarily given in anticipation, the question was decided before it could be discussed by the meeting of shareholders. The Bill which he asked to be allowed to introduce would effect but a very slight alteration in the present state of the law. The great charter of railway companies was the well-known Clauses Consolidation Act, the 8 & 9 *Vict.* c. 16, and his proposal was merely subsidiary to that Act, and all the powers which directors and shareholders possessed under it would remain in full operation. What he proposed to enact was this, that when at a meeting of a company a poll should be demanded upon a question put and seconded, Voting Papers should be sent to the shareholders, who should be allowed to vote by means of them. When it was remembered that an instance had occurred in which a great company, being apprehensive of attack, thought themselves called upon to send out something like 10,500 proxies before the report was issued (and they actually received proxies representing £8,000,000 of money) and the shareholders were thus called upon to vote in the dark and by anticipation, he thought it would be admitted there were good grounds for such a measure as this. The principle of voting by papers was familiar to the House ; it had been assented to in the case of the Universities, and was sought to be enacted in the Bill for restricting the use of spirituous liquors. He begged to move for leave to bring in the Bill.

MR. HADFIELD seconded the Motion, and said that the question was one of great importance, and the lowering of the duty on proxies proposed by the Chancellor of the Exchequer would be a great advantage to shareholders.

MR. INGHAM suggested that the scope of the Bill should be extended.

Motion *agreed to.*

Bill to afford Shareholders in Joint Stock Companies facilities for Voting by means of Voting Papers, *ordered* to be brought in by Mr. DARBY GRIFFITH, Mr. HADFIELD, and Mr. VANCE.

MUSEUM AND LIBRARY OF PATENTS.
OBSERVATIONS.

MR. DILLWYN rose to call attention to the insufficiency of the accommodation at present provided for Patents and Models of Inventions in the Museum at South Kensington. He said it was of the greatest importance that those who had invented machinery should have a ready means of seeing what had been already done in the same way. The present Museum of Patents was quite inadequate for the purpose, and, in fact, had been originally intended to be only temporary.

Notice taken, that 40 Members were not present;—Committee counted, and 40 Members not being present,

House adjourned at Eight o'clock.

HOUSE OF COMMONS,
Wednesday, April 13, 1864.

MINUTES.] — SELECT COMMITTEE — On Dockyards, Mr. Stansfeld *discharged,* Lord Clarence Paget *added.*
SUPPLY—*Resolutions* [April 11] *reported.*
SUPPLY—WAYS AND MEANS— *considered in Committee*[*].
PUBLIC BILLS—*First Reading*—Joint Stock Companies (Voting Papers)[*] [Bill 62].
Second Reading — County Franchise [Bill 33], *Previous Question negatived.*
Committee — Trespass (Ireland) [Bill 13]—R.P.; Registration of County Voters (Ireland)[*] [Bill 49].
Report — Registration of County Voters (Ireland)[*].

Mr. Darby Griffith

COUNTY FRANCHISE BILL—[BILL 33.]
SECOND READING.

Order for Second Reading read.

MR. LOCKE KING, in moving the second reading of his Bill to extend the franchise in counties in England and Wales, said, that there had never been a measure with regard to the principle of which such singular unanimity had prevailed among the leaders on both sides of the House. The history of the progress of the measure which he had given on moving for leave to introduce the Bill, must have convinced every Member that such was the case. It was a happy omen to all supporters of the Reform, that its justice had been admitted by those who, to their honour and to the benefit of the country, had led parties in the House for something like a quarter of a century. If he understood the matter rightly, the House must be taken to represent the mature views of the nation at large ; and it must be admitted that the opinions of the majority were, to some extent, represented within those walls; in this view the history of the measure was an undeniable proof that there existed a demand for the extension of the franchise. It might, however, be asked why, if such were the case, some of the measures in which the extension of the county franchise was included did not pass? The answer was, that in these Bills the question he advocated was in evil company. There had been, as it were, a binding together of the living and the dead. The Bills with which his was associated had all perished unheeded and unmourned, while the extension of the county franchise remained a living principle. It had been repeatedly proposed and had found the greatest acceptance in the country. It might, indeed, be likened to a bud which was now and then nipped by chilling blasts, but which had so much vigour and strength in its constitution that, sooner or later, it would be sure to blossom ; and if by any accident the measure did not succeed on this occasion, it would certainly be passed at last. The Bill of 1852 was, as they all knew, a compromise; it was unsatisfactory to the country, and after a little while no more was heard of it. The Bills of 1854 and 1859 contained the very principle he was now contending for ; but they happened to be unpopular and came to an untimely end. The Bill of 1860, which he might call the Bill of the noble Lord the present First Minister, also disappeared in some unaccountable way. It seemed to him that it was like a child badly nursed. It was never allowed to take the air in any way. It vanished before it had received any ventilation or discussion in the House, and few of them knew how the unfortunate passed away. He was quite prepared whenever the question of the representation of the people was brought before the House, to hear a great many lectures delivered by hon. Gentlemen opposite on the subject of interests, what interests are, and what interests ought to be represented, and especially on the necessity of doing justice to one interest in particular. It appeared to him that all who loved the Constitution must desire to see it maintained in an efficient condition, and improved where that was possible; not to limit or deteriorate the noble result of so many ages of wisdom, and of conflict. This Bill had for its object to improve that portion of the Constitution on which the healthy action of the whole so much depended. Those who imagined that it was intended merely to increase the number of electors wholly misunderstood the proposal. That was not its sole object. Owing to the vast expansion of trade, the enormous accumulation of wealth, and the growing spread of education in the country, a great number of interests had sprung into existence since the Bill of 1832, for which, consequently, there was no provision in that measure. Hence, any system of representation from which these interests were excluded must naturally be imperfect. Hon. Members opposite, who were so fond of talking about interests, rather ignored the new ones which had arisen. Had the new classes which had come into existence no right to claim representation? And if that claim were admitted, what reason was there to fear that they would overturn the balance of the grand structure of the Constitution? He was satisfied that the classes whom he proposed to admit to the franchise would be as anxious to preserve the Constitution as those now in possession of the privilege. To the principle of the Bill no objection could be raised. It was no novelty. In 1832 the principle of an occupancy franchise in counties as well as boroughs had been fully recognised by the introduction of the celebrated Chandos Clause. There being no objection in principle, the question was reduced to one of limit. The line had been drawn at £50; and there it might have been allowed to remain if trade, manufactures, and all that tended

to make the country great, had continued stationary and unprogressive. The country had, however, developed in an extraordinary manner, and to retain the limit of 1832 would be most unwise and unfair. It would be as bad as binding a strong man down with cords and then bidding him be up and doing. The principle of the Bill was essentially that of the representation of interests. In any redistribution of political power, interests must be held in primary respect, and the Bill would give admission to interests which were now almost entirely shut out. The term "interests" had a vague meaning, but he might define it as implying property of various kinds, and would divide it into four heads — agriculture, commerce, manufactures, and professions. Now, there were in England 338 borough Members, and 160 county Members, giving a total of 498 Members. Speaking generally, there might be said to be about 129 Members to each of the classes he had mentioned. He did not wish, however, to apply the "short division" and "rule of three" mode of reasoning to the question, with any intention of testing the representation by the rules of arithmetic or geometry. He desired merely to show that some of the interests were over-represented, and others under-represented. Was it not the case that one of the interests — the first and most powerful of them, agriculture, was represented by more than 129? In the first place, there were the 160 county Members who were specially charged with the duty of representing the political interests of agriculture. It might, perhaps, be held that considering the importance of these interests, thirty-one additional Members was not an excessive representation. It must be recollected, however, that there were many boroughs, the interests of which were mainly agricultural. All boroughs were not great centres of trade like Southwark with its 10,000 electors and £1,500,000 of rateable property; Finsbury, with its 20,000 electors and £2,000,000 of rateable property; or Marylebone, with its 21,000 electors, and £6,000,000 of rateable property. It might be truly said that all interests were represented in these boroughs except agriculture. He did not expect that all boroughs should come up to the same standard, or that those which did not should be disenfranchised. Far from it: what he wanted to call the particular

attention of the House to was the fact
that there were a great number of boroughs in which the interests represented
were mainly agricultural. In regard to
the boroughs, he was quite at a loss to
know what principle had guided the framers
of the Act of 1832. They had been dealt
with without reference to their size.
Some, like Bridport and Dorchester, covering only one square mile, were placed
on the same footing as regarded representation as Wenlock, which extended
over seventy-three square miles. What
limit should be assigned to boroughs not
mainly agricultural? Should it be three
square miles as in the case of Southwark,
or seven as in the case of Marylebone or
Finsbury? He had no objection to be as
liberal as possible, and would, therefore,
suggest as a limit, twelve square miles.
He would take the boroughs of twelve
square miles where the interests represented were nearly, if not purely, agricultural, Taking that standard, he found
that 38 boroughs returning 52 Members,
were more than 12 square miles, omitting
12 Welsh boroughs which were also mainly
agricultural. There were 15 between 12
and 20 square miles, nine between 20
and 30, eight between 30 and 40, three
between 40 and 50, and one, Wenlock,
as already mentioned, amounting to 73
square miles. He had no desire to speak
of these boroughs invidiously. The electors were men of high character and intelligence, and returned some of the most
valued Members in the House. Thus a
considerable addition must be made to
the Members representing the agricultural interests in that House. It might be
said there were counties in which other
interests were blended with those of agriculture; but he had taken no note of the
twelve Welsh boroughs he had referred
to, and also of a great many boroughs
under twelve miles in area, which were
mainly interested in agriculture. He had
also omitted Aylesbury, as he did not know
its extent. The one deduction might, therefore, be set off against the other. In
the agricultural boroughs there was a
vast number of agricultural holdings of
between £10 and £50. Why should a
small farmer, rated between £10 and £50
rent, be directly represented within a
borough, while without its limits that
qualification would give no representation
at all? The argument that the Bill
would reduce the county constituencies to
a dead level was quite erroneous. It

Mr. Locke King

was the present system which had the
effect of creating a dead, dull, uninte-
resting level. He would not say a word
against the £50 voters. They were
very intelligent, respectable men, but it
must be owned that they had a knack
of looking at everything in one way. It
was also said that the county Members
under the Bill would be lowered to the
condition of mere delegates; but there
was no ground for that apprehension.
Speaking roughly, there were about
520,000 county electors, of whom 100,000
held occupation votes. The object of
the occupancy clause in the Reform Bill
was to give a new element to the county
representation, but it had signally failed.
It had to some extent multiplied the number of electors, but had not introduced any
new interests. The only advantage it had
conferred was the recognition of the principle of an occupancy franchise in counties.
A grievous error was committed in not
going below £50, because there was
scarcely any difference between the old
county qualification and the new one. The
men entitled to vote under each occupied
much the same social position, shared the
same kind of views, and were susceptible to
much the same influences. This Bill was
intended to remedy this great and glaring
defect, by introducing a large number of
interests which were entirely shut out
from the franchise at present. But it
was alleged that many of those who were
at present without the franchise were
nevertheless indirectly represented. The
suggestion was absurd. Who were some
of these men who were said to be indirectly represented? There were in counties many persons occupying houses rented
at £25, £30, and up to £50—ministers
of religion, retired officers of the army or
navy, commercial or professional men, who
possessed education, intelligence, and respectability. How could they say to such
men, "Oh, be content, you are represented by your neighbour in a £50 house."
Then, were the interests of the class living
in houses between £10 and £25 per annum to be lightly passed over? They
were, many of them, men who had risen
by their own endeavours from the condition of being employed to that of employers; and was it to be said that they
were directly represented under the present system? Those were anomalies that
ought to be removed, and would be removed by the adoption of his Bill. Estimates were constantly made of the num-

bers who would be introduced by his Bill; but those who talked of the county constituencies being "swamped," made that statement on fallacious information—on Parliamentary Returns of the number of houses rated to the poor between £10 and £50 per annum. One sought to make out that 300,000 new electors would be added to the roll. He was sorry to say that his Bill would add nothing like that number to the county constituencies. The total number of persons rated above £50 was about 200,000, but only 100,000 were actually on the register. Of the persons rated below £50, probably not more than 250,000 would be affected by his Bill; but from that number there must be large deductions, as a considerable proportion of the small shopkeepers in the counties, lodging-house keepers, heads of schools, and many others paying between £10 and £30 per annum rent were widows and spinsters; besides the 40s. freeholders already on the register, not to speak of double returns in parishes. Even, however, if 250,000 were added, the House should bear in mind that the county constituencies had for a long time been in a state of decay; they had not in any degree kept up in numbers with the population and wealth of the country. In a country like this, standing still was going to decay; but the county constituencies had actually decreased, and it was high time they should be reinforced. Many persons said that £50 was too high and £10 too low, and that there ought to be a compromise. His own opinion was that, whatever might have been the case in former times, the day had gone by when a compromise could be effected. Both sides of the House were committed to the principle of a £10 franchise in counties, and it would be next to impossible to stop at a qualification above £10. If the class whom he wished to bring within the pale of the Constitution were tainted with a revolutionary or seditious spirit there might be some reason for rejecting his Bill; but the whole country was never more peaceful or loyal—in the full sense of the word, more Conservative—than at the present moment, and he did not think any attempt at a compromise would be attended with the slightest success. He might also derive an argument in favour of his Bill from the peculiar state of the times. At no period were our relations with Foreign Powers in such a delicate and difficult position as they were now; but at this critical juncture there could be no doubt the country feels the greatest confidence in and gratitude to the Government for the manner in which they had carried us through—not entirely—but would get us out of those difficulties. But when the great question of peace or war came to be decided, would it not be desirable that a larger body of electors should be consulted? It might be necessary to increase taxation, and, if so, surely it would be satisfactory to the Government to know that their measures had been submitted to the great mass of persons whom he desired to introduce, and that those who were great payers of direct taxation had had a voice in any proposal that rendered necessary an increase in our taxation. It had been urged on a former occasion, and would probably be so again, that this Bill should be postponed till some more convenient time, or a more comprehensive measure was proposed. The postponement of the Bill on either of those points would be degrading to the House, especially as the leaders on both sides of the House had pledged themselves to Reform, and had introduced measures for that purpose. He would remind hon. Members on the Liberal side of the House, that many of them were elected at the last general election on the cry of Reform, and the Members of the present Government were placed on the Treasury benches solely on the distinct pledge and promise that they would do their best to carry a measure of Reform. Was chucking a Bill on the table of the House and getting it printed, he asked, doing the best a Government could to get Reform? But he was not without hopes that the noble Lord at the head of the Administration would do something more. Were the Liberal Members to tell their constituents at the next election that the Government whom they had placed in office had neither helped Reform themselves, nor permitted others to do so? He trusted the noble Lord would assist him to pass his Bill, which, though a fragment, would yet go far to remove a great and crying injustice. The hon. Gentleman concluded by moving the second reading of the Bill.

Motion made, and Question proposed, "That the Bill be now read a second time."

MR. AUGUSTUS SMITH, on rising to move the Previous Question, expressed his regret that the subject of Reform should have been again brought under the notice of the House during the present Session. The first two Sessions of the present Parliament were wasted by their attention being diverted from their ordinary and proper business to measures for reconstructing the constitution. They were now in the "sere and yellow leaf," and what remained of their time ought not to be consumed in profitless discussions, but should be devoted to the real business of the country. On the occasion of the introduction of this Bill, after he had given notice of his intention to move the Previous Question, the hon. Member for East Surrey (Mr. Locke-King) was kind enough to advise him to consult his constituents on the subject. The fact was that he consulted his constituents at the last two general elections, when he told them plainly and frankly, in answer to questions, that he had the greatest objection to the proposed alteration of the county franchise, and could not support it. But he wished to ask his hon. Friend, whether it was constitutional for Members of that House to consult their constituents upon all the questions that came before them. He had no hesitation in saying, for his own part, that since he had occupied a seat in the House he had never once allowed the thought to cross his mind what his constituents might think of any opinion he might express in that House, or any vote he might give. [Lord HENLEY: Oh, oh!] The hon. Member for Northampton and others might choose to follow a different course, but he should be ashamed of himself if he allowed considerations such as those he had indicated to influence his votes, and, what was more, he believed his constituents would be ashamed of him if he did so. He dwelt on this the more, as when the hon. Gentleman showed how little he understood such a fundamental principle of our Constitution, he was a very unsafe guide as to any changes to be adopted ; and he, for one, was not disposed to place himself at his feet as his constitutional Gamaliel. Further consideration had strengthened his conviction of the unreasonableness, danger, and impolicy of the Bill under discussion. He regarded it as one that must inevitably lead to a series of changes which, when completed, would entirely alter the character of our Constitution. The fundamental principle of our Constitution was, and always had been, the equal representation of interests—of separate and independent interests. Just as an elector, no matter

what his property might be, had only one vote, so each interest, provided it was sufficiently important to be represented at all, ought, as near as possible, to have an equal voice and share in the Legislature. Many centuries ago, when our Constitution first assumed its present form, Simon de Montfort summoned two knights from every shire, two citizens from every city, and two burgesses from every borough. All the important interests which then existed were required to send the same number of representatives. This principle of duality singularly prevailed, and does so still through a great portion of our civil polity. It was rather Norman than Saxon, and by these same Normans was introduced, much about the same period of history, into Sicily and Hungary. It was unfortunately lost sight of by the Reform Act of 1832, which gave three Members to some places, and one Member to others ; and thus, to a certain extent, admitted that the principle of representation should be regulated according to population ; but it still regulated the elections to the American Senate. Rhode Island, with a population of not 200,000, about equal to that of Hertfordshire or Oxfordshire, returned the same number of representatives to the Senate as the great State of New York, with a population of 3,000,000, equal to what are comprised in our metropolitan districts. One result was that the Senate stood higher in the estimation of the American people than the House of Representatives. If we were to have a reconstruction of our Constitution, the principle of equal representation of interests ought to be kept steadily in view. He wished to say a few words as to the operation of the measure before them. The hon. Member for East Surrey had said that the county constituencies had been gradually decreasing. He would take the county the hon. Gentleman himself represented. A few years ago the number of electors in East Surrey was about 6,000 or 7,000 ; it was now 10,000. [Mr. LOCKE-KING said his remark referred to the counties generally.] Then the hon. Member should recollect that the county electors greatly outnumbered the borough electors. There were upwards of half a million county voters, with only 160 representatives, whereas there were about 460,000 borough electors, who returned 338 Members. He objected to great, overgrown; bloated constituencies, because in many respects they operated most prejudicially. Let the House consider what the effect of the present Bill would be. In East Surrey there were 35,000 houses irrespective of those within boroughs, rated for the relief of the poor, and about 20,000 of those were in the immediate vicinity of the metropolis, forming the outskirts of the boroughs of Lambeth and Southwark, such as Battersea, Streatham, Kennington, &c., together with about 7,000 congregated together as a town at Croydon. Thus the Bill would simply give the House two more metropolitan Members. Far be it from him to call in question the merits of the metropolitan Members. They were energetic, well-informed, and industrious; but he might say, at least, that the county Members were possessed of merits which, though different, were not of less value to the deliberations of the House, and well qualified them to hold the candle on occasions to the others. It was to be remembered, moreover, that the metropolitan Members had great advantages over the rest of the House. They, for the most part, lived in London, and had only to walk from their counting-houses or offices to attend to the interests of their constituents in the House and elsewhere. Sydney Smith once said that Bishop Bloomfield, from his residence in London, monopolized all the business of the Ecclesiastical Commission; and embodied in himself the Church of England militant here on earth. In like manner, he was afraid that if the number of metropolitan Members was increased, the proceedings of the House would come to be governed almost entirely by that body of representatives. Another effect of establishing an uniformity of franchise for counties and boroughs might be illustrated by the case of West Surrey. The number of electors in West Surrey at present was between 4,000 and 5,000. In Guildford the voters numbered 500 or 600, each returning the same number of two Members. Nobody objected to that, because the Guildford electors had separate interests of their own; but if by lowering the franchise to £10 the voters of West Surrey were increased to 12,000 or 14,000, the anomaly would become so glaring and absurd that a great cry would be got up for some further change, and a call for an equalisation as to Members in the several electoral areas, the franchise being the same, and no longer an expression of separate and distinct interests, which it would be difficult to resist. He believed, indeed, that the Bill now on the table must necessarily lead to electoral districts, which would swamp all the small towns. The small towns might be called the heart of the Liberal interest; they were more independent, and acted under a greater sense of responsibility, than the enormous masses congregated in great cities, and it would be a mistake to allow them to be swamped. On the occasion of both the two last Reform Bills, an agreement seemed to have been come to by the territorial and manufacturing magnates, to allow the remaining nomination boroughs—such as Launceston, Tavistock, Calne, Arundel, and the rest— to stand intact; but he, for one, thought with the late Mr. Hume, that towns above a certain population should be joined together for electoral purposes. Hon. Gentlemen who command these nomination boroughs may rest assured they cannot be retained much longer. They are not strong enough to stand by themselves; but if they are united with other places, while the objectionable principle of individual nomination will be neutralized, if not got rid of, they will become sufficiently large and powerful to preserve their existence. The hon. Member for East Surrey had referred to the fact, that the present Parliament was elected under the promise that they would consider the question of Parliamentary Reform. But it could not be disguised that the general apathy on the subject was such that no blame could attach either to the Government or the Parliament for the course they had taken in reference to that question. He thought the hon. author of this Bill and the House itself would do far better if they applied their skill and diligence to the reduction of the expenditure rather than to devising schemes for remodelling the franchise. In return for the advice his hon. Friend had been pleased to give him, he would venture, in conclusion, to offer him, therefore, this advice—namely, to take care to be more frequently in his place when Estimates were under discussion. It, to be sure, was not a very glorious struggle, but still much was to be done by the machinery which exists. He begged to move the Previous Question.

MR. KNIGHTLEY agreed with the last speaker in thinking that the House could be more usefully employed than in engaging for the twentieth time in flat, stale, and unprofitable discussions which could lead to no practical result. He had no wish to attribute improper motives to the hon. Member for East Surrey, whom everybody respected; but he could not help suspecting that his real object in bringing forward this Motion, was to give himself and his friend something to talk about at the next general election. The hon. Member was evidently afraid that his constituents might ask him how the question of Reform had been dealt with, or why, since the Government had abandoned all their pledges, he had given them so steady and systematic a support. He, doubtless, wished to be able to tell them that he and his party had done their best, and that the censure of the country ought to fall upon the obstinate, wrong-headed, retrograde Members on both sides who had opposed even the mildest measure of Reform, and refused to take a single step in the right direction. No doubt the hon. Member and his friends were entitled to supply themselves with as good an answer to disagreeable questions as they could find; but he, for one, would do what he could to prevent them indulging in frothy claptrap at the expense of the rest of the House. With that view he would endeavour to show that the Bill as it stood, so far from being a step in the right direction, was opposed to all the fundamental principles of Reform laid down by hon. Gentlemen opposite at the last general election. The principles upon which, according to all the authorities, a measure of Reform ought to be based were—first, a more equal distribution of the representation in respect to property and population; and next, the recognition of the rights of the labouring classes to some share of political power. How did the Bill propose to deal with those two principles? First, as to a more equal distribution of the representation. It seemed a strange anomaly that small unimportant places, like Ripon, Richmond, or Tavistock, for example, with a nominal constituency of 200 or 300 electors, and which were really under the dictation of a single individual, should have as many Members of Parliament and as much political power as the whole county in which they were situated, with a population of hundreds of thousands, and an amount of property to be estimated only by millions; and that in divisions in that House the votes of the county representatives of Devonshire or Yorkshire should be absolutely neutralized by the nominees sent from two or three insignificant villages. But how did the hon. Member for East Surrey seek to rectify that anomaly? Did he propose to enlarge the area of boroughs or to increase the representatives of coun-

Mr. Knightley

ties? He proposed to do precisely the reverse; he proposed enormously to increase, possibly to double, the constituencies of Yorkshire and Devonshire, and to leave the pocket boroughs exactly as he found them. Was that a step in the right direction—was that their enlightened policy—was that consistent with the principles of their Reform programme? But it might be said he had taken an extreme case, and that there were some very large towns and some small counties. The hon. Member for East Surrey did not want to go into arithmetic, but he (Mr. Knightley) did. By the last census it appeared that every county Member in England and Wales represented 71,423 inhabitants, while every borough Member represented only 25,557. That was to say, every county Member on an average represented very nearly three times as large a population as every borough Member. That was an important fact, which he could impress on the attention of the rural districts. Representation and taxation were convertible terms, and those who were least represented in that House would almost infallibly find themselves most overburdened with taxes. But not only did the hon. Gentleman propose nearly to double the number of the county electors, while what the counties required was a very large increase in the number of their Members, but he sought completely to alter the character of the county constituencies. That brought him to another very important point — namely, how the Bill affected the rights of the labouring classes? Hon. Gentlemen opposite, and many also on his side of the House, said at the last general election that, by their improved intelligence and increased respectability, the working classes were fairly entitled to some share of that political power from which they were excluded by the operation of the first Reform Bill. That might be perfectly true in regard to the boroughs for which the hon. Member did not propose now to legislate; but it was not true in regard to the counties. The county franchise was very much lower than the borough franchise. Those who had not looked closely into the matter talked as if the county constituencies consisted mainly of the class to which the hon. Gentleman alluded—namely, the £50 occupiers, or tenants at will under the Chandos Clause That was an entire fallacy. In round numbers the total county constituency was about 500,000 electors. Less than 100,000 voted in the counties by reason of occupation, and more than four-fifths voted in respect of freehold and independent property of their own. Of those freeholders a considerable number belonged to the labouring population—to men who were not of the professional or trading class, but who earned their daily bread by the sweat of their brow and the labour of their hands. A 40*s.* freehold was in these days an extremely low franchise; it was about 10*d.* a week. They could not well go much lower than that. He did not say it was too low; for he thought the 40*s.* freeholders constituted a most valuable element in our representative system. The fact of their retaining their small patrimony of garden ground, or little cottage, or whatever it might be, was strong presumptive evidence at least that those people were industrious and steady in their habits, and as such they were well qualified to exercise some share of political power. Nevertheless, it was an exceedingly low franchise, and it did include a large proportion of the labouring class. He spoke from personal knowledge as to his own county, and he had no reason to suppose it differed in that point from other counties. No doubt, the county Members also represented the large territorial interests of the landed proprietors; but there was nothing incompatible in that. Notwithstanding what the hon. Member for Birmingham (Mr. Bright) might be pleased to assert, there was no antagonism of interest or hostility of feeling between the labouring agricultural class and the great landed proprietors. And if any one doubted the fact that the country Gentleman in that House was the poor man's truest friend and best ally, let him look to the division lists for those who carried the Ten Hours' Act, the Bleaching Works' Bill, and other measures for regulating the duration of labour, and relieving the working class, and he would find that one and all of those measures were passed by the votes of the country Gentlemen. He might be told, perhaps, that these were town questions ["" Hear, hear! ""] in which the county constituencies had no concern. The hon. Member who cheered, it was clear, did not know much about it. The county Members represented the artisans in the large towns quite as much as the agricultural labourers in the villages. That was a matter of fact, not of mere inference. Take the town of Birmingham, which he selected, because one of its Members had made himself somewhat conspicuous on this subject, and he would bring the question

home to his own door. He found from a Return laid on the table some time ago, that in that borough there were 1,910 electors, or in round numbers 2,000, who voted for small property of the value of £2 and upwards of yearly rental. Among them were included a great number of the common operative class; but they were the constituents not of the hon. Member for Birmingham, but of the hon. Member for North Warwickshire (Mr. Newdegate), and, as such, undoubtedly exercised a very considerable influence in all county contests. No man could vote for the borough Members of Birmingham unless he occupied a house of £10 and upwards rental; this, of course, excluded all the working men in the sense in which he used the term. Therefore, the hon. Member for North Warwickshire did represent a very considerable number of the labouring class in Birmingham, while the hon. Member for that borough did not represent one of them. But if Parliament passed this Bill, it would completely alter the relation that now existed between the county Members and the labouring classes, because it was quite obvious that if to the 100,000 county electors, who now voted by reason of occupation, they added all the £10 occupiers, not one of whom belonged to the working class, properly so called, they would swamp all the small freeholders. Thus they would deprive the poor man of his only political power in the counties, without giving him any equivalent in the boroughs, where they said he ought to have some. Was that their enlightened policy ? — was that a step in the right direction ? Was that compatible with the principle of Reform? He might be told that that was not their only measure ; that they were all, as one man, in favour of the Bill of the hon. Member for Leeds (Mr. Baines), for a £6 borough franchise. He declined to listen for one moment to that argument ; he declined to debate a Bill before the House on the vague assumption that another measure not then before them might be brought forward. Nay, he said, the object of the two measures was not only distinct, but absolutely conflicting. The Bill then under discussion would place the occupier in the county in the same position as the occupier in the borough. The Bill of the hon. Member for Leeds would entirely destroy that principle ; and the House could not go on tinkering the Constitution in that way. The other day he read in an ably-conducted periodical these remarks on those Bills—

"Such proposals as that of Mr. Baines and of Mr. Locke-King are simply a nuisance, and nothing more. It is absurd to suppose that they can ever be allowed to pass so long as any kind of statesmanship exists in either House of Parliament. Unless they are stupid blunderers, they are grossly insincere. They are measures in effect revolutionary, and yet even in that sense incomplete ; and they are proposed under the plea that no great change would come of them. It may be right that the Constitution should be recast, and that a new class should be installed in power, but no statesman of any party will endure that it should be done surreptitiously by measures of professed innocence and under the guise of sham moderation."

That was the opinion of the *Saturday Review*. He was far from saying that that proposal might not properly form part of a large, a comprehensive, a statesmanlike, and well-considered measure of Parliamentary Reform ; but in its present bare and bald state, and as an isolated proposition, he objected to it, because it would be most unjust to the rural districts, and detrimental to the political influence of all the small freeholders. He begged to second the Motion.

Previous Question moved, "That that Question be now put."—(*Mr. Knightley.*)

VISCOUNT ENFIELD said, it was useless to deny that hon. Members sitting on his side of the House were placed in considerable embarrassment by the Bill of the hon. Member for East Surrey ; and he was not ashamed to own that he was one of that number. It would be very easy for those who merely wished to give a vote which might please their constituents, or which might, perhaps, have reference to a general election, to vote simply for the second reading of that Bill. But he was one of those who was anxious that the vexed question of Reform should not year after year be dragged through the dirt, and really desirous that, if possible, some definite solution of it might be attained. He was not afraid to own that he thought such a solution was almost hopeless at the present moment. And why did he think so ? He looked to the two measures of Reform which were severally introduced by the Government of Lord Derby and by the Government of the noble Lord the Member for Tiverton. Neither of those measures received Parliamentary assent ; they were hardly even accepted with any feelings of satisfaction by either side of the House. He would say nothing about the Bill brought in by Lord Derby's Government, except this—and he was not averse to make the confession — that it

Mr. Knightley

contained, in his judgment, the elements of a solution that would have been more practical, and perhaps more satisfactory, than the measure proposed by the Government of the noble Viscount. But the Bill of the present Government had met with a reception equally unfavourable at the hands of its so-called supporters and opponents ; indeed, its professed friends and adherents had treated it with as little favour and courtesy as those who were its declared enemies. In one of the most able and powerful speeches which he had ever heard in that House, the hon. Member for Salford (Mr. Massey) exposed in all their hollowness whatever faults that measure contained, and after the delivery of that speech the fate of the Bill was sealed. If Members on his side had not supported the Bill with all the readiness and zeal which they should have shown, considering how they were returned at the last general election, it was hardly becoming that they should now find fault with those who attempted anew the solution of that question. But, even supposing the second reading of the present Bill acceded to, what was the chance of its becoming law ? He, for himself, confessed that he was not prepared to support the extension of the county franchise as low as £10, but he should be ready to agree to £20, on the ground that taxation and representation would then go together. The hon. Member for East Surrey said, that the days of compromise were past. He denied that assertion. He believed that a reasonable compromise had never been fairly suggested, except by one right hon. Gentleman, whose position and popularity were deservedly great in that House—the Member for the University of Cambridge (Mr. Walpole); and that proposal had been endorsed by one whose memory would ever be green in that House—the late Lord Herbert. Both of those high authorities said, that if they extended the franchise to £20 occupiers in the counties a satisfactory solution would be attained. He entirely concurred in that view. £20 was the point at which taxation ceased, because below that sum a man did not pay the house tax, and was not qualified to serve on a jury. If, therefore, they went below that point they would not satisfy the reasonable expectations of those who wished to see the county franchise fairly extended, but not too far reduced. What course, then, ought he to take on that occasion ? He was anxious to see this question settled, but despaired of its being finally set at rest by his hon. Friend's Bill. The Previous Question had been moved, but he confessed that he did not like that way of getting out of the difficulty. It was hardly fair, and did not accurately represent the feelings either of those who supported or of those who wished to object to the Bill. If the measure went into Committee, he meant to propose that the limit should be £20. He had little expectation of seeing the Bill arrive at that stage; but, considering the importance of the question, and also considering the way in which those especially who sat on his side were returned at the last election, he could not give either an adverse or a silent vote. He could not agree with the hon. Member for Truro (Mr. Augustus Smith) in saying that the question ought not to be put. He thought it ought to be put, and, if possible, carried to a satisfactory solution, and he should therefore support the second reading of the Bill, with such reservations and modifications as he had ventured to shadow forth.

LORD ROBERT MONTAGU thought that the arguments of the noble Lord were sound, but the result at which he had arrived was a very lame conclusion to his able speech. His own great objection to the Bill was that it was founded on a delusion. It assumed that the representation of the country was a real thing. This was a hallucination. He begged the House to consider two facts. The first was that the representation of the counties was in the hands of the large landowners. It was chiefly in the hands of the Peers. Every one, he thought, would confess that—even the country Gentlemen themselves. This was certainly an anomaly; but this he must say, that he did not disapprove of that so much as he did of that to which he was about to allude. It was right that it should be so to a certain extent, because it secured an adequate representation for the wealth of the country. The other proposition, which he thought would be equally accepted, was this, that the borough representation was in the hands of the "whips" on the two sides of the House. ["No!"] If a man wanted a seat, it was well known that he applied to one of the "whips;" and that, he supposed, was the way in which every Member got in for a borough. Sometimes, when a vacancy occurred in a borough, if no candidate had been already provided, then a deputation was sent up by train to an office in London for a candidate. Then some gentleman, whose name had been previously placed on a list kept by the "whip," went down to the constituency and was, perhaps, returned for the borough, although he had never been heard of before. That the borough seats should be in the hands of the two "whips" on each side of the House, was very objectionable. If the representation was in the hands of patrons, faction was sure to be nourished. For the question put to the constituencies was merely, "Whom will you have for Prime Minister—the leader on this side, or the leader on that side?" So that the whole matter at issue was one of men and not of measures. The electors were asked to decide on the names, not on the policy of the Administration. He called this a mummy franchise, or representation embalmed in parties. This could not be rectified except in one way. For there was only one thing which the people of England cared about, and that was to accumulate wealth. They desired to have their hands free and unshackled in order to amass riches. Hence their worship of free trade; for restrictions on trade were restraints on the increase of wealth. When men had accumulated wealth sufficient, then their only object was to enjoy it in peace and security. They invested it in land and became conservatives, and thought of handing it down to posterity. Sometimes manufacturers, who had heaped up riches, purchased estates with a fine park and mansion, and came to that House to support the Ministry of the day and obtain a peerage. Thus they acquired the power in the country which belonged to landed property, which was, indeed, inseparable from wealth. If they did separate wealth and political power, with the intention of putting a real franchise in the hands of the electors, they would only be generating a constant conflict. Wealth would strive to increase its power, and the mob would attempt to grasp at wealth, by seeking to confiscate the property of those who possessed it. The hon. Member for East Surrey tried to alter that state of things, and to make the county representation a reality by means of lowering the franchise. But that would not divert power into other channels besides property; it would increase the power of the landowners; it would give a greater hold to the aristocracy. In the counties they would buy up the votes of the mob; and the lower the franchise the easier these votes could be bought. The effect of that would be that the landowners would degrade and corrupt the people. The leaders of Parties would seek power by the same means—by moral degradation and corruption. They also would bribe the electors; they would moreover not only maintain but create offices to give to their friends in return for support. Such would be the results of a lowering of the franchise—the moral degradation of the people. At first the franchise might be good-humouredly exercised amid beer and blarney; by-and-by the elections would be carried on, as in America, with the aid of bludgeons, until at last the reign of bayonets and despotism came in. The present electors, moreover, would not like to have their heels trodden on by a class now inferior; they already repudiate the notion of being swamped. The candidate would not trouble himself to enter the trim little parlour of the farmer when he could secure the votes of half a dozen labourers in the dung-yard. But how, then, were they to separate wealth from power? The only way of doing it was the plan lately suggested by the hon. Member for Rochdale (Mr. Cobden). It was most consistent in that hon. Gentleman to make such a suggestion. The only thing he had wondered at was that when he had chalked it up on the wall he ran away and denied it. The only mode of doing it was by abolishing the law of primogeniture, by subdividing property, by breaking up wealth into many hands, and thus pounding power into little impalpable atoms. But then they must remember that they changed the whole face of the nation; it would then become democratic. They would then give the farm of the freeholder, the estate of the gentry, the funds of the merchant, and the stock of the trader, to be taxed by an ignorant and indigent mob. This would rob men of the fruits of their industry, and therefore discourage industrial pursuits. That was why, if there were a true Conservative party, there could be no other party at all; because there would be on the one side all the wealth and power, which is conservative, and on the other side only the democratic mob, which would be penniless and politically powerless. Since the Reform Act of 1832, neither wiser legislators nor acuter statesmen had appeared on the stage to act their parts. The only difference now was that they heard, not that certain principles should be supported, but that the people desired so-and-so, and that their desires must be submitted to. Yet they knew how opinions were bred. They knew how desires and passions in the people were fanned. Men did not think

Lord Robert Montagu

for themselves, but read their newspapers; and those newspapers, with but very few exceptions, were in the hands of the leaders of parties; and thus they came round to the point from which they first started. He objected to the measure of the hon. Member because it proceeded on a hallucination—namely, that a real franchise was in the hands of the constituencies, whereas it was really in the hands of the large landowners or the leaders of parties in that House; and because the only effect of lowering the franchise would, therefore, be to lower the moral feeling of the people.

LORD HENLEY thought that a Bill like the present might have been allowed to pass that House without much opposition from either side, and particularly from the Opposition, for a provision very much resembling it was contained in the measure of Reform, which the right hon. Member for Buckinghamshire introduced. The Bill might, therefore, be permitted to go into Committee, and might there be thoroughly discussed. It was a step in the right direction—in the direction of that Reform which those on his side were taught to believe was part of their creed. The measure was a safe one. Our commerce and prosperity had largely increased since 1832, and the country had been kept clear, to a great extent, of foreign wars. That was, he believed, mainly due to the beneficial effects of the Reform Act of that year, and to the manner in which it had brought public opinion to bear on the conduct of national affairs. The Bill now before the House, however, required the addition of a few clauses, and then it would be a very valuable measure. As it stood it would increase the power of the landlords, from its admitting a small class of voters who were utterly dependent on their landlords. He had learnt for the first time that day, from the noble Lord the Member for Huntingdon (Lord Robert Montagu), that it was a very beneficial thing that the Peers should have influence in the elections to that House.

LORD ROBERT MONTAGU had not said that that was beneficial, but that it was not so injurious as that the boroughs should be in the hands of the leaders of that House.

LORD HENLEY could assure the noble Lord that the boroughs were not in the hands of the leaders of that House, but that their Members were returned because the electors thought they would support their views in Parliament. Not one hundredth part of the boroughs chose their Members because any "whip" in that House told them to do it. Any man of political standing was almost certain to find a borough to return him if his opinions coincided with those of the constituency. The present Bill would enfranchise occupiers of houses between £50 and £10 rent in towns—a class of men wholly unexceptionable. They consisted chiefly of tradesmen, ministers of all denominations, clerks, and men of business. Such tenants, for the most part, were as independent of their landlords as their landlords were independent of them. But when they came to the agricultural districts they found a very different state of things. Those who paid rents of between £10 and £50 were mostly very small farmers, the most dependent class which it was possible to imagine. If intrusted with the franchise they would be brought up to the poll in droves, to vote entirely at the beck of their landlords. The hon. Member for Northamptonshire (Mr. Knightley) had remarked on the wide disparity between the average amount of population represented by each county and by each borough Member respectively; but there was a good reason for that inequality—namely, that while the borough electors were independent, the county electors were dependent, and not allowed to have an opinion of their own. On another point this Bill did not go far enough—it totally excluded the labouring classes. The line which it drew would pass over the heads of labouring men, scarcely any of whom occupied £10 houses. Why, he would ask, were they to be excluded? These men paid taxes and were able to hold opinions on political subjects. Efforts were being made to ameliorate their condition in every respect, except giving them a voice in the representation of the country. It would be better, in his opinion, to have a household franchise than a £10 one. If they were to take the definition of a house as laid down by the Census Commissioners in their last Report, and if they were to admit each occupier of such a house to the right of voting, they would obtain a clear and decided criterion, which would admit almost every respectable occupier to the franchise. Considering the great addition which this Bill would make to the constituency, he thought his hon. Friend who brought it forward should have proposed in it some means by which the expense of county elections might be reduced

—for instance, by increasing the number of polling places, by providing that votes should be taken by voting papers, or by some other such machinery. He did hope that the subject would not be lost sight of. They must keep their eyes upon it, and even if this Bill were not carried in the form in which it now stood, he trusted they would have the opportunity of again discussing the subject, and that discussion would eventually lead to the adoption of some measure which would be for the good of the country.

MR. NEWDEGATE rejoiced at the tone and temper of the debate. He thought it showed that the House had made great and effectual progress in the consideration of the question of Reform. It was well known that he was a Conservative according to the meaning of that word in 1842—too decided a Conservative he feared for hon. Members who sat on the front bench on that side of the House. But why was he a Conservative? Because he was anxious to preserve that form of Constitution which secured our freedom, and because he did not believe that freedom—too often won by violence—could be defended against the aggressions that were directed against it without violence, except by law. Now, no subject, in his estimation, could be better worthy of the deep deliberation of the House than the constitution of the body which was to frame the laws that should defend our freedom; and it would be unworthy of that House to declare that they were not ready to examine and consider whether they in that House duly represented the intelligence, the power, the whole elements of the nation, the action of which it was the intention of the Constitution to elicit for the government of the Empire. He had felt the force, the truth, and the sound judgment manifested in the speech of the noble Lord the Member for Middlesex (Viscount Enfield), one of whose constituents he had the honour to be, and representing as he did another constituency which might be considered metropolitan—a constituency embracing almost as great a variety of interests as that which the noble Lord the Member for Middlesex represented, he agreed with the noble Lord that it would become neither of them to reject summarily every proposal for the re-arrangement of the legislative machinery of the nation, and to declare that they considered it immutable, and incapable of being accommodated to the change of circumstances and the altered position of the country in the vast progress which it was making. But he totally differed from the conclusion at which the noble Lord appeared to have arrived. The noble Lord condemned the Bill as containing an objectionable proposal, and as insufficient in itself. He agreed with the noble Lord that the proposal contained in the Bill was objectionable, and that the Bill was insufficient, and, therefore, he should vote for the Previous Question, hoping that when next the hon. Member for East Surrey submitted a proposal of this nature to the House he would submit it rather more in detail, and with more clauses and machinery in it, to enable the House to judge what would be its practical effect. The hon. Member proposed a Bill containing but one element in a very few clauses; but the House must all feel that if this change was effected others must follow. He thought they had a right to expect that when a proposal of this sort was submitted the immediate consequences which must follow from the adoption of the principle of the Bill, should be provided for in the machinery of the Bill itself. Otherwise, the House was asked practically to take a leap in the dark. He thought they should not be called upon to scramble for results in the mere chance medley of a Committee. The Bill practically proposed a uniformity of franchises between the counties and boroughs. He thought that this uniformity of franchises would be greatly objectionable, because the representative constitution of this country, which had been pre-eminent in its success, was characterised more by its variety than by any other quality. We had a hereditary House of Lords, and we had a House of Commons, returned by constituencies of various character, ensuring the representation not only of all classes but of a great variety of personal characteristics within these classes; while a due representation of those interests on which the wealth and industry of the people depended was also ensured. He also objected to the Bill on a point which was touched by the noble Lord the Member for Northampton (Lord Henley). He (Mr. Newdegate) represented a large body of 40s. freeholders, and if this Bill passed they would be completely swamped, just as the tenant farmers would be. He did not think it would be right to swamp those two elements, because he did not consider that those two elements had proved unworthy of confidence. The 40s.

freeholders formed the most independent portion of the county constituencies; and he could say this in vindication of the tenant farmers, that he was returned by them at one period in direct opposition to the majority of the landowners of the division. Therefore, when he heard the independence of that class impugned, he replied that he sat for one Parliament in that House as the direct representative of their independence. He deprecated bit by bit Reform, on the ground that it was simply cheating the House and the country into the adoption of measures which, taken by themselves, must inevitably prove unsatisfactory. It was clear, as the case stood, that the majority of the people of this country ought to have a fuller representation in that House. He did not say this in the sense of merely wishing to favour the agricultural interest. He represented a county constituency which was a mixed constituency. A Return issued in the year 1851, after the Census of 1851, showed that in the counties the annual value of real property was £60,564,288. The inhabited houses were 2,053,998; the population was 10,495,930; and the Members returned were 159. The annual value of real property in the boroughs and cities in 1851 was £42,898,247, the inhabited houses were 1,383,000; and the population 7,431,679; the Members returned by this minority being 337, or more than double the number of those returned by the majority. He had wished to see whether this state of things had changed in 1861, and he found by a Return issued in that year, that the annual value of real property in the counties, exclusive of boroughs, was £66,208,505; the number of inhabited houses was 2,290,061; the population was 11,427,775; and the number of Members returned was 160. In the boroughs and cities the annual value of real property was £47,850,033, the number of inhabited houses was 1,449,444, the population 8,638,469, and the number of Members returned 338. According to that calculation each county Member represented an average population of 71,423, and each borough Member represented a population of 25,657. Thus the proportions were virtually unchanged; and he held that the House ought not to deal with the representation of the people unless it was prepared to adjust that representation, in some degree, to the number of the constituents. That was the principle of the Bill of 1832, and of the Bills

Mr. Newdegate

introduced by Lord Russell in 1851 and 1854. There were some objections to the Bill of 1854, but that was taken, as a whole, the best of the schemes of Reform that had, of late years, been submitted to the House. It did not contemplate merely an addition to the representation of the agricultural body, but it proposed to give additional representatives to those county populations which had increased more rapidly than the average borough populations, thus increasing the primary disproportion of representation to the disadvantage of the inhabitants of the counties. He thought no man could deny this fact, that by collecting voters into large constituencies they did not provide for the elicitation and expression of the real intelligence of those large constituencies which could only be elicited by due subdivision, and the establishment of a direct relation between the representatives and the inhabitants of well-defined localities. It was confessed that these vast masses were governed by cliques, and he thought if the House would consider the exhibition made where universal suffrage prevailed—if they would remember how easily undue influence had been made predominant through *plebiscites* for the establishment of despotism abroad, and if they had regard to the fact that democracy had established two despotisms in America, it would be evident that they should exercise great care in dealing with this question. Those who loved freedom as he did, would manifest the greatest care in dealing with the representation, which ought to be so regulated as to elicit the general sense of the people in such a manner as to render it worthy of being deemed public opinion.

MR. WARNER did not much like the Bill, but he thought there were reasons why the House ought not to dismiss it in the summary manner which was proposed by the Amendment. The Bill was an attempt to remedy an acknowledged defect in the representation. If he might say so without offence, he thought it was a clumsy and an impracticable attempt. For that very reason, and in order to clear the way for future reform, he wished to see it thoroughly discussed in Committee. It had been admitted by all parties at different times, that the basis of the franchise was too narrow and ought to be enlarged. The great question in dispute, which had paralysed the action of Parliament for many years, was the question how to en-large the basis wisely and safely, and consistently with the traditions of the nation. Large measures of reform had been introduced, but they had failed because they were too large for consideration. Members looked at these subjects from so many different points of view, that it was found impossible to agree upon any common principles for legislation. The great merit of the present Bill was, that it raised one definite point — that of uniformity in the franchise. He did not approve of uniformity. He believed that the diversity of our existing franchise, the distinct character of different constituencies, was the great safeguard of liberty against the tyranny of majorities. He hoped Parliament would never consent to abandon that safeguard. If we did so, we should have to try under difficulties to establish some other protection for our liberties in place of it ; some one, perhaps, of the many forms which had been proposed of plural voting ; or even the scheme known as Mr. Hare's, the most perfect system that had ever been devised for a theoretical constitution. But in this country it was very difficult to introduce innovations of this nature. It was easier to maintain the advantages we possessed than to introduce new securities for our protection. He was very anxious to have this question of uniformity in the franchise set at rest. If he might venture to offer a suggestion to the House, it would be to allow this Bill to pass a second reading, and to refer it to a Select Committee, where the questions which it raised might be thoroughly examined. He did not believe any Committee would approve of a uniform franchise ; but a negative decision might be of great value. It might perhaps be said that it was inconsistent to affirm the principle of the Bill at the second reading, and then leave it to be negatived by a Committee. But this was not what he proposed. If the House agreed to the second reading, the only principle it would affirm was, that the £50 qualification in counties was excessive, and ought to be reduced. He thought there were few Members on either side of the House who would think that a very dangerous doctrine. A Select Committee might perhaps recommend a qualification intermediate between the existing £50 and the £10 proposed by the Bill ; and if the House was dissatisfied with the decision of the Committee it would still be in its power to reject the Bill. He thought the course he had suggested would be more respectful to the expressed opinions of large numbers of hon. Members' constituents than the course which had been recommended by the Amendment.

MR. BENTINCK said, he would assure the hon. Gentleman who brought forward this measure, that the last thing he would do was to use a single expression in any way discourteous to him. He deserved, on the contrary, the tribute of every hon. Member in that House for the combined courtesy and ability with which he had always treated this question; and, therefore, in any remarks he might make, he hoped the hon. Gentleman would clearly understand that he was speaking solely with reference to the measure, and not in any way discourteously to himself. He must say, in the first place, that the hon. Gentleman occupied a somewhat false position in that House as the advocate of this measure; and, in the next place, he thought he had brought forward some most remarkable arguments in favour of it. First, as to the position of the hon. Member. Highly and deservedly respected as he was, both in the House and in the district he represented, he must beg to remind the House that, practically speaking, he was not a county Member. Nominally, he was so; and that he was worthy to represent any constituency in the country he fully admitted; but circumstances over which he had no control practically did not place him in that House in the position of a county Member. He was virtually one of that dangerous class of metropolitan Members who never rose without making the House tremble to its very centre, for it was always expected that they were about to press some unjustifiable and piratical attack on the public purse. He hoped never to see their number increased. The House was entitled to have some misgiving as to the sincerity of the hon. Member's views when he told them he came forward as the champion of the rural interest. The first argument he used to induce the House to receive his proposal favourably, was that all other measures of Reform had been cast aside unheeded. That was true; but was there anything in this measure that entitled it to more favourable regard? So far from that, it was open to even more objections than most of the unfortunate Reform Bills that had been already rejected by the House. He said all who loved the Constitution desired to improve its efficiency; and how did he proceed? Why, by taking away that very small share of

Mr. Warner

representation which a large proportion of the wealth, knowledge, and influence of the country now possessed. It had been said that objections were made to the Bill because it would be injurious to the interests of certain classes. He did not know what classes were referred to, but certainly the Bill, if passed, would deprive one particular class of all share of influence in the House, because it would entirely swamp the rural districts, which were already so imperfectly represented. The hon. Member said the Bill was intended to give a share in the representation to those who were now excluded; but that was not so. The real object was to increase the power of a class already unduly powerful in that House. The hon. Member said he had not based his measure upon any mere arithmetical calculation; and that was true, for if he had paid regard to the Liberal maxim that numbers should be represented, he would not seek to diminish the small amount of power possessed by the most numerous and wealthy class in the country. He (Mr. Bentinck), therefore, congratulated the hon. Member for his discretion in giving up the arithmetical argument, for as his hon. Friend behind him (Mr. Knightley) had clearly shown, any reliance on that argument would have left him not a leg to stand on. But the most extraordinary argument of all in favour of this Bill was that of the noble Lord the Member for Northampton, that the Bill ought to be passed because the Members on both sides of the House were pledged, through their leaders, to reform. How had the House dealt with those who were spoken of as its leaders? If an onslaught was made upon the Government from that (the Opposition) side of the House, under the guidance of its leaders, the attack was easily repelled; but if made by independent Members it was almost sure to be successful. It was a known fact that those who were called the leaders on both sides of the House could not rely upon more than fifty or sixty men to follow them at all times. [*A laugh.*] Hon. Members need not laugh at that. Only last year there was a remarkable instance of the fact. Upon a question of great importance, as it was held to be, the leaders on the Ministerial Bench and those on the front Opposition Bench joined their forces, but the result was that they were beaten by an increased majority by the independent Members on both sides of the House. Thus it was useless to talk of the House being bound by the promises of its leaders whom nobody followed. The noble Lord the Member for Northampton (Lord Henley) had spoken of the political creed of the great Liberal party, but did not go into detail upon that subject. Now, if any one would tell him what the creed of the great Liberal party was, it would solve one of the greatest mysteries of the time. The noble Lord also referred to the beneficial effects which he believed the Reform Act of 1831 had had upon the foreign policy of 1864. Now, if he (Mr. Bentinck) could believe that, he would become one of the most ardent Reformers. The noble Lord had not, however, explained how the connection could be proved between the Reform Bill of 1831 and the political events of foreign countries in 1864. The noble Lord had apparently misunderstood an expression of his noble Friend the Member for Huntingdonshire (Lord Robert Montagu), who had not said that Peers ought to exercise influence over the elections of Members of Parliament, but merely that Peers must necessarily exercise a certain influence at elections, not as Peers but as the owners of large properties. But among other dogmas of reform one was that Peers should not interfere at elections, and that prohibition required explanation. Why upon any principle of equity and justice, should not a Peer be allowed to take part in elections so long, at least, as the other House of Parliament was prevented from having any voice in matters of taxation? If that were the practice of the Constitution, the only thing they could do was to say to the Peers, "You shall have·no voice in the taxation of the country, for by a parity of reasoning you are exempted from all taxation, otherwise you would be deprived of your rights as citizens." Until that principle was recognized by law he, for one, was prepared to say that the right of the Peer to vote for a Member of that House was indisputable, and any attempt to dispute that right was a gross and clear act of injustice. The noble Lord had spoken of the greater independence in boroughs as compared with counties; but that point was not admitted. In times of great public excitement the electors in boroughs were driven by popular clamour, and an amount of coercion was practised which contrasted strongly with the proceedings in counties, such as had been described by his hon. Friend behind him. It was well known, that in one-half the boroughs

of this country, the question at a time of election was what candidate had the most money. The experience of that House proved that nearly all the bribery cases which had arisen referred to boroughs and not to counties. Therefore, the effect of increasing the borough constituencies would be simply to increase the area of corruption. He concurred with the hon. Member for Truro in his objections to these bit-by-bit reforms. The inevitable consequence of admitting such measures as this—would be that, to the prejudice of the public business ·of the country, the House would be engaged every Session discussing some favourite reform project of particular Members. He now told the hon. Member for East Surrey that it was impossible to devise any measure, or to suggest any proposal more entirely destructive of the interests of the rural districts than that which he had introduced. The hon. Gentleman said his object was to increase the area of the rural franchise. The effect of his Bill would be precisely the reverse. The effect would be to flood every rural district in this country with an enormous infusion of what he might term the urban element. The rural districts were now unfairly and insufficiently represented, and the effect of the proposed measure would be to destroy in that House what little share of representation the rural districts at present possessed, by flooding every county in England with an enormous number of urban voters residing in the small towns. He appealed to the representatives of the rural districts to bear in mind that the only real existing grievance of which any reformer had a right to complain was the insufficient representation of the rural districts. All other complaints were only got up for the purpose of creating political capital and talking political claptrap.

MR. NEATE said, that three-fourths of the representation was really in the hands of the landed aristocracy, and therefore it was a mistake to complain of the rural districts being not fairly represented. There were but few towns except the metropolis, one or two commercial ports, and some particularly independent constituencies, such as that which he had the honour to represent, which were not more or less under the influence of the landed aristocracy. And even Oxford, up to the time of his own return, was in part under the influence of the landed aristocracy. It had been imputed to him that he had accused the aristocracy of insensibility towards the wants and feelings of the poor. He had never made such a charge, which would be unjust ; but when the efforts of the landed aristocracy on behalf of the factory operatives was held up for admiration, he would remark that, although it was kind to ask their neighbours to treat their servants well, yet it would be kinder still to attend to the wants of their own servants. He hoped that when the question of union rating came under consideration, the landed aristocracy would consider the interests of the labourers rather than their own.

MR. TREHERNE said, that although not the youngest, yet he was one of the newest Members of the House, and therefore asked their indulgence while he addressed a few remarks to them. He did not rise to abuse the landed aristocracy, nor to discuss whether they exercised too much influence in the smaller towns, because those matters had nothing to do with the question before the House. He only ventured to speak now, because, when he was a candidate at the last and previous elections, he had been rigidly questioned upon one point, and he had then declared it to be his deliberate opinion that, in order to calm the agitation and misunderstanding that prevailed, a £20 franchise in counties and a £10 rental franchise in boroughs was an arrangement which should have his support. [*A laugh.*] He assured hon. Members that he did not come into that House as a delegate, but as an independent Englishman, to express his opinion, whether it pleased or displeased Gentlemen on the opposite side of the House. An hon. Gentleman had asked what was the political creed of the great Liberal party: and upon that point he (Mr. Treherne) was equally ignorant, notwithstanding the fact that although he was but a young Member he was a candidate of thirty-two years' standing. He was not indebted for his seat to any of the landed aristocracy, but he sat in that House in consequence of the death of a very eminent gentleman who had been called "the Master of Whiggery." Had that right hon. Gentleman (Mr. Ellice) lived he (Mr. Treherne) might not have been now a Member of that House ; but he had been returned by a triumphant majority over a gentleman bearing a name that was worthily honoured in Parliament and in the country. At his frequent elections he had always been questioned upon this subject of county representation, and if the hon. Member for Surrey had stuck to his text he would

Mr. Neate

have had his support. But the hon. Member had departed from his text. He had not had the prudence of introducing the thin end of the wedge, but he had sought to ram it home at once. He did not know what the opinions of hon. Gentlemen opposite might be, but to him it appeared that there was a considerable difference between £10 and £20. He thought this measure was both premature and inconsistent, but he was aware that it was a matter of policy just before a general election to revive the cry of " Reform ;" and even to proclaim the name of Tory, which he had already heard several times in that House. When the elections came on the electors were puzzled to find out what was a Tory. They made antediluvian researches to discover the origin of Tories ; they regarded them sometimes as bipeds of some abnormal shape—perhaps with a tail and hoofs—but they were always led to believe that they were men with the worst possible designs. He had been returned to that House as a Tory, and he rejoiced in the name, for he had achieved a greater victory than if he had come there under the name of a Liberal Conservative or a Liberal. A Tory was a gentleman of independent means, of independent mind, who would speak the truth, and would not be deterred by the laughter of one party or the frowns of another. With regard to the Bill under discussion, he thought there had been much assertion but little argument in its favour. This was not the time for a party one-sided measure. One Member ought not to come with a Bill for a £10 or £20 franchise, another with a Bill for the Ballot, and another with a Bill for something else ; but there should be some comprehensive attempt to settle this vexed question, and to relieve parties from much of that asperity of feeling which unfortunately was so often exhibited.

MR. PEASE said, he did not know nor care to inquire which political party would be gainers by this measure, but he regarded it broadly as a question whether there were not large numbers of persons who were well qualified to exercise the franchise and who did not yet possess it. Every one would admit that, since the franchise was first established upon its present basis, there had been great advances made in respect of intelligence and wealth, and it was inconsistent to allow the representation to remain exactly as it was when other and different circumstances existed. Every hon.

Member must be aware that in his own neighbourhood there were many persons qualified to vote, who nevertheless had no share in the representation. Objections were made to partial reforms; but because a complete measure could not be obtained, that was no reason why an instalment should not be accepted. When a complete measure of Reform was proposed it was rejected; and when a mere bit of Reform was asked for it was refused, because a complete measure was not presented. Such a state of things could not continue for ever. He had been sorry to be obliged to draw an inference from the discussion that many hon. Members had no confidence in their neighbours, and he must also deprecate the argument that those Members who supported Reform measures were indulging in political claptrap or making mere hustings speeches. The strength of that House depended upon its being a full, free, and hearty representation of the views and opinions of the country, and until the representation was placed upon that footing, Members must be expected to bring in Bills for the removal of admitted evils.

Sir JOHN WALSH said, he thought they were much obliged to the hon. Member for Coventry (Mr. Treherne) for enlivening a debate which before had been remarkable only for its dull gravity and repose—a feeling he might remark which seemed fully shared in by people out of doors on this subject. There had been no gathering on Kennington Common or Primrose Hill in favour of Reform—almost no petitions to the House on the subject. This apathy on a question which once convulsed the country was not a little surprising. Another singular circumstance was that the Bill had not found a single supporter in that House, and it was doubtful whether even the hon. Member for East Surrey was a hearty admirer of his own Bill. Not one of those who had spoken that evening and said that they intended to vote for the second reading, had done so without qualification; every one of its professing supporters had found fault with it as imperfect, defective, or inadequate—and intended to vote for it only in order that they might alter and modify it. Another objection to the Bill was that it was not designed to be a final measure, but only as a prelude to future legislation. At present, however, it seemed to be brought forward merely as a matter of habit. The noble Lord the Member for Northampton had in his remarks argued very much on the *post hoc propter hoc*

principle. The noble Lord appeared to believe that all the progress that the country had made since the passing of the Reform Bill was attributable to that measure. Did the noble Lord, however, believe, that the introduction of railroads and steamboats, and the discovery of the goldfields of Australia and California were the results of the adoption of the Reform Bill? The real fact was, that not only had humanity in general made great progress, but the English nation itself had exhibited a growing conviction that the views and opinions upon which the Reform Bill had been founded were fallacious. He believed that the first Reform Bill was promoted by a number of Gentlemen who entertained, and, for ought he knew, might still entertain the idea that the true secret of progress was embodied in the extension of democratic principles. He was quite certain that the experience of France, and more recently that of America, had convinced many of the fallacy of those opinions, and that they no longer regarded as models the Constitutions of those two countries.

Mr. COLLINS said, he believed that the Bill was one which would not be supported by any hon. Member with sincerity. There were no two Members among those who supported the Bill supported it on the same grounds. One noble Lord had intimated his intention of supporting the second reading in order that the rate fixed by the Bill might be reduced, and another noble Lord also proposed giving it his support in order that he might double the amount. He maintained that the various Reform measures which had been introduced during the last fourteen years had all been in direct hostility to the principles of the Bill. Those measures had dealt with the questions of borough and county representation and the re-distribution of seats; but the Bill introduced by the hon. Member for East Surrey dealt only with one of those questions. The hon. Member for Leeds (Mr. Baines) also had a Bill bearing upon borough suffrage, which he had proposed bringing forward, but it was understood that he now intended to abandon it. [Mr. BAINES: No!] His reason for that statement was, that the hon. Member for Huddersfield (Sir Francis Crossley) had said that the Bill was only brought forward for the purpose of inducing the Government to transfer the assizes to Leeds instead of to Wakefield. The Bill of 1852 had an opposite effect to that of the one now brought forward by the hon. Member for East Surrey, because it took out of the county a number of towns and grouped them together, so that, instead of extending town influence in the county representation, its effect was exactly the reverse. The Reform Bill of 1854 was in like manner unfavourable to the principle at present proposed, because, while making a most considerable addition to the number of county Members, it selected a number of towns which had formerly shared in the county representation, and gave them the power of electing their own Members; thus doubly enhancing the county interest by the reduction of the urban element. The Reform Bill introduced by the present Government in 1860, although he believed it to be the worst of its kind that had been framed, dealt with the respective claims for representation to a limited extent in the same way. The Bill of 1859, proposed by Lord Derby's Government, made some addition to the number of county Members, and diminished the number of unenfranchised large towns. The Bill of 1854 was, in his opinion, the most statesmanlike attempt that had ever been made to grapple with this complex and difficult question. The real object of the hon. Member for East Surrey, as expressed in the Bill he had brought forward, was to disfranchise the rural element. He protested against the idea that the Bill had been supported by successive Governments. He believed that its second reading had only been approved in order to allow it to be sent into Committee. He was convinced that the majority of the House had never entertained the principle of extending the suffrage to all £10 county householders. It was said that hon. Members on his side of the House were bound by the Bill of Lord Derby. He did not, however, believe that they were averse to the principle of £10 householders in the country receiving the franchise, but they held that their voice in the representation should have effect in the town and not in the county elections. If it is thought desirable that the £10 householders in counties should be enfranchised, they should be annexed to the towns where they transacted their business, and the smaller towns ought to be grouped together, as was the case in Wales and Scotland. He would assume as correct the statement regarding the Members who sat for boroughs while they virtually represented county interest, though he believed that statement to be exaggerated. Supposing that statement

Mr. Collins

to be correct, there would only be 210 such Members in the House as compared with something like 280 representing the boroughs; so that the borough interest would still be much better represented than that of the county. The question ought to be looked at fairly, and not be brought forward just at the close of Parliament as a mere hustings' cry, which, in reality, it was, because, during the last four years, with a majority in the House favourable to liberal opinions, it had not been attempted to introduce the subject. The effect of the Bill in Middlesex, if it were to come into operation, would only be to add another metropolitan borough to those already existing—a thing against which, in the year 1861, this House had most emphatically protested. The question of Reform was one, he was convinced, which would be looked at one day in a statesmanlike point of view; but he should oppose the Bill, because he believed it was calculated to create a dominant town interest in county constituencies—an interest which was already too great.

MR. HIBBERT said, he for one should go into the lobby with the sincerest desire that the measure should succeed; and he believed that was the feeling on his side of the House. He would support a proposition for the grouping of boroughs in certain cases, or any similar measure which would help on the cause of Reform. The hon. Member (Mr. Knightley) said that the county Members represented on the average 75,000 inhabitants, while the borough Members represented only 25,000, but the hon. Gentleman need not hold that conclusive against giving more voting power to the county Members. For his own part, he neither believed that the influence of Peers in the county representation was greater than it must naturally be; nor, on the other hand, that the borough Members were returned by the influence of the "whips" on either side. He believed that this measure would strengthen, and not weaken the Constitution, and he considered that many persons were unjustly treated in being excluded from the franchise.

VISCOUNT PALMERSTON: Sir, I am anxious, before the House comes to a division, to state in a very few words the reasons for the vote which I intend to give. I cannot vote against the Bill of my hon. Friend, because that might warrant the supposition that I am indisposed to any change in the county franchise. Undoubtedly, I am of opinion that there might be some change effected. At the same time, it is but fair and candid to my hon. Friend and to the House to say that I cannot vote for the £10 franchise proposed by the Bill. It appears to me that the object we ought all to have in view is to form a legislative machine in which all interests in the country shall be fairly represented. The two leading interests of this country are on the one hand the trading and the commercial interests, and on the other the agricultural interest ; and any alteration of our system which tends to introduce too largely the trading and commercial, or the town, element into the agricultural, or country element, would I think injuriously disturb the balance which it is essential for the interests of the country that we should maintain. That is the view which I take of the measure of my hon. Friend, and therefore, if it should go into Committee, I shall not be prepared to vote for the particular franchise which he proposes to introduce. It will be time enough when we are in Committee to consider what the franchise should be. Then, Sir, I venture to differ from my hon. Friend as to the expediency of the course which he has determined to pursue. It is quite natural, that having fixed his mind upon his particular measure, he should take every fair opportunity of bringing it under the consideration of the House. But I think it would have been better if he had abstained from mooting the question. It is plain to every man, I think, who attends at all to the indications of public opinion in this House and in the country, that there does not exist at the present moment in this House or out of it the same interest in such changes as existed some time since. The fact is, that organic changes have been looked to not as a mere end so much as a means to an end. They were looked to as a means of effecting great alterations and improvements in our internal system, our commercial system, our laws, procedure, and other matters. Many of those improvements have been made. Commerce has been freed from its shackles, the industry of the country has been encouraged by liberty, and many of those alterations and improvements which were to be the result of organic changes have been accomplished by the Legislature as it stands ; and therefore there is a less ardent desire for change than existed before those improvements were made. There are also other considerations connected with external affairs which have tended

to allay the desire for organic changes— I mean considerations arising from the events which have occurred in other countries, and which are attributable, in a great measure, to the influence of organic arrangements in those countries. Those examples seem to indicate danger from interfering with the organic system of the country, and have rendered us less anxious for changes that might possibly approximate to such a state of things as now exist abroad. I am not going to enter further into this question. I am merely anxious to state, that in voting for the second reading of my hon. Friend's Bill, I must not be understood as assenting to the particular franchise he has proposed, but as reserving to myself in Committee the right to take any view I please on the consideration of what amount of franchise it may be desirable to introduce into the measure.

Previous Question put, "That that Question be now put."

The House *divided* :—Ayes 227 ; Noes 254 : Majority 27.

TRESPASS (IRELAND) BILL—[BILL 13.]
COMMITTEE.

Order for Committee read.

Motion made, and Question proposed, "That Mr. Speaker do now leave the Chair."—(*Mr. W. Ormsby Gore.*)

MR. BAGWELL, in moving that the House will resolve itself into the said Committee on that day six months, alluded to the evidence taken before the Select Committee of 1846, as shewing the demoralizing tendency of the Game Laws. This Bill was to repeal a section of the old Irish Game Act of *Geo.* III., whereby the prosecutor in the case of trespassers upon land must be the occupier, and it was now proposed to give this power to the landowner. He was surprised that the Chief Secretary for Ireland should have given his support to such a Bill ; but from the right hon. Baronet he appealed to the Attorney General for Ireland, who might one day be a Judge in the country, and who, if this law passed, would have to deal with a frightful increase of crime in that capacity.

Amendment proposed,

To leave out from the word "That" to the end of the Question, in order to add the words "this House will, upon this day six months, resolve itself into the said Committee," — (*Mr. Bagwell,*)

—instead thereof.

Mr. W. R. ORMSBY GORE said, that his object in bringing forward this Bill was not to make the existing law at all more stringent than it was before.

CAPTAIN ARCHDALL said, that the hon. and learned Gentleman was under a complete misapprehension as to the effect of the Bill, which he might say he had brought forward, not for the sake of the landlords of Ireland, but for the sake of tenants. All the Bill did was to enable the landlords who had reserved the right to the game to prosecute trespassers, instead of placing the onus on the occupier as was the law at present. The Bill did not introduce any increased stringency into the Game Laws.

Mr. DAWSON said, the Bill was a harmless one, of purely a defensive character. If game preservation was to be permitted in Ireland at all, why circumscribe the only means by which the destruction of game could be prevented and punished? If the occupier of land was disinclined to become a public prosecutor, he ought to be rejoiced that under this Bill the property of his landlord would be protected without risk or injury to himself.

Mr. M'MAHON said, that if it was a good argument in favour of the Game Laws, that game was property produced at the expense of the landlord, woodcocks, quails, and landrails were certainly not in the category. He complained that the Bill extended to those birds, and said that under its provisions a person killing wild ducks or teal on a part of the seashore claimed as private property might be imprisoned for two months. The English law did not extend to these birds, and as he believed that game was very well protected in Ireland by the existing law, he should support the Amendment.

Mr. BRIGHT: I wish to make a few observations on this Bill. I will not go into the general question of the Game Laws, though it is one to which I have paid a good deal of attention. Every English Member will recollect with surprise, and every Irish Member with pleasure, that in Ireland there have been far fewer of contests and bloody adventures in connection with the Game Laws than in England. I suppose every Irish Member will congratulate himself and his country on that fact. Now, as far as I understand this Bill, the object of it is to give additional powers to the proprietors of land for the preservation of game. It gives them additional powers for the prosecution of poachers, and, in

point of fact, removes the obstacles to their prosecution that now exist in the present state of the law, by which it is necessary that the prosecution shall be carried on by the tenant and not by the proprietor. The Bill also includes several definitions of birds as game which have not hitherto been admitted to be of the nature of game. I put it to the Irish Gentlemen—I do not know whether they are past listening to any appeal—but I remember that it is stated, in a book written under the direction of an Irish Lord Chancellor, that 200 Acts of Parliament had been made for the landowners, and not one for the tenant. I call on Irish Gentlemen to recollect, that at this moment there is not in any country of Europe so great a state of suffering as in Ireland. The people are fleeing from that country —from every port from which a ship sails to the West. And not the poorest only, but the class of persons which, in my opinion, it is for the interest of the landed proprietors especially to retain. If there be any Irish proprietors here who think it is for their interest and for the interest of their country to introduce into Ireland such an approximation to the law of England with regard to game, as shall induce a greater preservation of game, and add to the elements of discord in that country —if there be such a man in this House from my heart I pity him—I pity his heart as well as his head, and I pity the country that is represented by such men in the Imperial Parliament.

Mr. WHITESIDE said, he was afraid that the hon. Member for Birmingham, in consequence of not having spoken in favour of Parliamentary Reform, was indemnifying himself by taking this opportunity of venting his indignation upon something connected with Ireland. This was really a most innocent Bill. There were, and always had been, different opinions as to the principle of the Game Laws; but if the objections urged with regard to the particular game which should be included in the Bill were well founded, they would form a subject for consideration in Committee. The Bill was in no way likely to increase those bloody adventures which the fervid imagination of the hon. Member had conjured up as likely to occur if the measure were adopted. It merely provided that where a tenant took land, and agreed that the exclusive right to the game should be vested in his landlord, in that case, and in none other, if some friend of humanity in the shape of a poacher took game on the land, the landowner might take him before the magistrate and get a penalty inflicted. The tenant was relieved from all annoyance and vexation. The landlord must make out his case as well as he could ; and he would not be able to proceed at all against the person who had illegally trespassed unless, by express bargain with the tenant, the exclusive right to the game on the farm was vested in him. If he (Mr. Whiteside) thought that this Bill would create unpleasantness in Ireland he would not support it. But, under the operation of laws to which the hon. Member for Birmingham had given his cordial assent, a great part of the West of Ireland had been deserted by the people and been made fit for game ; and he hoped that the hon. Member would give his aid to counteract the effect of those laws, and to remedy the evils which he was able so eloquently to point out.

SIR ROBERT PEEL said, that he had agreed to the second reading of the Bill on the understanding that he should propose Amendments in Committee, and he had now an Amendment on the paper, to reduce the penalties imposed by the Bill to the maximum penalties enforced in England. He saw no objection to the proposal to go into Committee on the Bill, if it was clearly understood that full opportunity would be given for the discussion of the Amendments which it would be necessary to propose when the Bill got into Committee.

CAPTAIN ARCHDALL said there was a great deal of poaching in Ireland, but the class of poachers was quite different from the English poachers. Very often the sub-Inspector of police was a poacher.

MR. M'CANN said that, under the Bill, a farmer's child who on his father's land took a landrail's nest would be liable to a penalty. The measure would create a great deal of ill-blood, and he hoped it would not be persevered with.

Question put, "That the words proposed to be left out stand part of the Question."

The House *divided* :—Ayes 158 ; Noes 45 : Majority 113.

Main Question put, and *agreed to*.

Bill *considered* in Committee.

House *resumed*.

Committee report Progress ; to sit again on *Wednesday*, 27th April.

WAYS AND MEANS.

WAYS AND MEANS *considered* in Committee.

(In the Committee.)

Resolved,

" That, towards making good the Supply granted to Her Majesty, the sum of £15,000,000 be granted out of the Consolidated Fund of the United Kingdom of Great Britain and Ireland."

House *resumed*.

Resolutions to be reported *To-morrow*.

Committee to sit again *To-morrow*.

THE MALT TAX AND THE SUGAR DUTIES.

PRECEDENCE OF MOTIONS.

COLONEL BARTTELOT appealed to the hon. Member for the City of London (Mr. Crawford) to postpone his Motion with reference to the adjustment of the sugar duties which stood for to-morrow, as an Amendment to the Motion for the Speaker to leave the Chair. He made this request in order that the Motion of which he had given notice in reference to the malt tax, might be disposed of. The latter was also on the paper for the same day, as an Amendment to the Motion for going into Committee, but the Motion of his hon. Friend (Mr. Crawford) had priority.

THE CHANCELLOR OF THE EXCHEQUER said, that the sugar trade was one of immense importance to the general interests of the country, and it was necessarily hung up in almost entire suspense during the deliberation on the sugar duties which were now pending. His hon. Friend the Member for the City of London (Mr. Crawford) wished to raise a question of very great importance, not at all contesting the principle of the proposed alteration in those duties, but contesting the manner in which that alteration was proposed to be carried out. That being so, it was for the convenience of the sugar trade and of the public generally, that the sense of the House should be taken on the Motion of the hon. and gallant Member (Colonel Barttelot) as soon as possible. He should therefore, hope that his hon. Friend the Member for the City of London would yield to the appeal made to him by the hon. and gallant Gentleman ; and as the public was expecting that the alterations in the sugar duties would take effect on Saturday, if the proposed alteration was recognized by the House, he hoped hon. Members would be moderate in the exercise of the privilege on Friday, in order to give his hon. Friend an opportunity of bringing on his Motion.

MR. CRAWFORD said, that on the understanding that he would not be placed in a worse position by giving up his place on the paper to-morrow, he was willing to accede to the request of his hon. and gallant Friend. But he hoped the House would show him some consideration on Friday. He supposed the Committee of Ways and Means would be taken next after Supply on Friday.

THE CHANCELLOR OF THE EXCHEQUER : It will.

MR. CRAWFORD, under those circumstances, would give precedence to the Motion of his hon. and gallant Friend.

House adjourned at seven minutes before six o'clock.

HOUSE OF LORDS,

Thursday, April 14, 1864.

MINUTES.] — PUBLIC BILLS—*First Reading*— Joint Stock Companies (Foreign Countries) [H.L.]* (No. 45); Warehousing of British Spirits* (No. 46).
Committee—Punishment of Rape (No. 52).
Report—Settled Estates Act Amendment [H.L.]* (No. 47); Vestry Cess Abolition (Ireland)* (No. 48); Charitable Assurances Enrolments* (No. 49).
Withdrawn—Leases and Sales of Settled Estates Act Amendment* (No. 30).

PUNISHMENT OF RAPE BILL.—(No. 52.)
COMMITTEE.

House in Committee (according to Order).

Clause 1 (In Convictions for Rape, Whipping may be added to other Punishment).

LORD WENSLEYDALE proposed, in line 2, to omit the word "may" for the purpose of inserting the word "shall," so as to render the punishment compulsory.

LORD RAVENSWORTH objected to the proposal to make the punishment compulsory. However effectual flogging might be in certain cases, he did not think it was likely to have a deterring effect with respect to a crime which was generally committed without premeditation, and under the influence of a sudden impulse. He would prefer vesting a discretionary power to order that punishment in the hands of the Judge, which might be exercised where great violence was used, or where persons aided and abetted in the offence.

The Chancellor of the Exchequer

LORD CRANWORTH thought it a system fraught with inconvenience to legislate in this piecemeal manner. He should much prefer that some general view should be taken as to the cases in which flogging could be effectually applied. Why, for example, should not the punishment of whipping be inflicted in a class of cases which would easily occur to their Lordships, or for the crime of sending letters threatening to charge persons with infamous offences? Instead of considering the whole subject, one noble Lord took up one class of offences, and another some other, and the result would be to import into the Criminal Law the same discordancy and difficulty from which they thought they had relieved the statute-book three or four years ago.

THE MARQUESS OF WESTMEATH said, he stated the other night, and he would repeat, that there was no analogy whatever between the crime of rape and any other.

THE EARL OF CARNARVON said, he agreed with the noble and learned Lord that there was great inconvenience in piecemeal legislation of this kind. He remembered, however, that last year, when he asked the House to agree to a Bill for inflicting the punishment of whipping upon garotters, the noble and learned Lord pointed out that such a punishment was peculiarly applicable to the crime of rape. The object of applying this punishment was not to inflict torture, but simply to make the punishment of rape more determinate. Having sat upon one of their Lordships' Committees last Session, which had before it gaolers from various parts of the country, he could state their testimony in regard to whipping, which was, that one single infliction of corporal punishment was so effective with some of the most hardened offenders that no repetition of the offence took place. Almost every Judge upon the Bench stated that, in regard to the class of crimes which were committed by young lads and boys when they were hurried away by the impulse of the moment, no form of punishment exercised such a deterrent effect as corporal punishment. The measure was, he admitted, not so perfect in form as could be desired, but he should be sorry to see the Bill dropped. He would propose to subject to the provisions of the Bill not only persons convicted of rape, but also those convicted of assault with intent to commit a rape.

THE LORD CHANCELLOR said, that the crime of rape was so serious, and the law attached to it so heavy a penalty, that the Legislature would, he feared, only diminish the gravity of the crime by superadding the present additional punishment. He should think it better to confine the punishment now proposed to cases of assault with intent to commit a rape. In that case it might be desirable not to make the punishment of whipping compulsory. No doubt it would be very much better if the whole subject of the Criminal Law and the punishment of whipping were comprehensively considered ; but as that was impossible at the present time, he did not see why their Lordships should abstain from doing that which was desirable, although it was not so general or so extensive as it might be.

LORD CRANWORTH desired to repeat his opinion, that it was very unadvisable to raise questions of this nature, when only three years ago they had passed, with the greatest deliberation, some six or eight Bills in reference to the Criminal Law ; at which time the punishment of flogging was considered and rejected.

THE LORD CHANCELLOR said, he did not remember that Parliament had at the time expressed any opinion adverse to whipping for such an offence as was now under their Lordships' consideration.

LORD CRANWORTH said, he well remembered that the propriety or impropriety of inflicting this punishment was a matter of great deliberation at the time to which he had referred.

THE EARL OF MALMESBURY said, it was quite true the Criminal Law had been consolidated three years ago ; but, unlike the Medes and Persians, their Lordships, he thought, would be willing to modify former legislation upon good cause shown.

THE EARL OF DERBY said, that having listened carefully to the debate, both upon that and a former evening, he was unable to agree entirely with either of the views expressed by noble Lords who had made proposals to the House. He suggested that a compromise might be effected, according to which, while it would be compulsory to inflict punishment of the nature referred to in cases where the offence had actually been completed, its infliction should be left to the discretion of the Judges where there was only an attempt. He did not think it wise to place both classes of offenders upon the same footing.

THE EARL OF CARNARVON gladly accepted the compromise suggested by his noble Friend. He begged to withdraw the

Motion which he had proposed, and gave notice that he should move a separate clause when the Report was brought up.

Amendment *agreed to* (with a consequent Amendment).

Clause *agreed to.*

Remaining clauses *agreed to.*

The Report of the Amendment to be received on *Tuesday* next.

SHIPS OF WAR—PETITION OF MR. JAMES CHALMERS.

THE EARL OF HARDWICKE *presented* a Petition from Mr. James Chalmers in favour of an Invention by the Petitioner in Naval Armour, and praying for compensation. The noble Earl said, he trusted that, in bringing under the notice of the House similar petitions from time to time in the case of inventors who thought themselves aggrieved, he would not be supposed to be trespassing unduly on its attention. In the present instance, the petitioner stated that he was the inventor of a new and improved mode of building and fortifying ships of war, and that he had applied to the Admiralty with respect to it ; that they had refused to his plan the consideration which they had freely extended to those of others, and that, though his target had been officially promised a fair trial, it had been subjected to a test which had never been resorted to in the case of any other armour target ; that the representatives of the press and all those who had witnessed the trial had regarded it as unsatisfactory; that the plan had in its main features been ultimately pirated by the Chief Constructor of the Navy in the building of the *Bellerophon,* and that the Chairman of the Ironplate Committee had declared such to be the case. The petition concluded with the prayer that the House would be disposed to take the matter into its favourable consideration.

THE DUKE OF SOMERSET said, nothing could be more fair than that the noble Earl should, if he thought fit, bring under the notice of the House any grievance to which an inventor might think he had been subjected. With respect to the question of targets generally, he would state that it might be quite possible to produce one which could resist shot, and yet which could not with advantage be used in building the side of a ship. As to the particular plan of Mr. Chalmers in August 1862, Mr. Chalmers made application to the Admiralty to give it a trial. That application the Admiralty referred to the Iron-plate Committee, who reported that the plan was so like another which was under their consideration, that they did not think it worth trying. The trial was accordingly refused, but Mr. Chalmers again and again renewed his application. Ultimately, the Admiralty told him, that if he constructed a target, he must do so at his own expense, and on the express understanding that they were not committed to any engagements for the future. Mr. Chalmers undertook that his target should be superior in every way to the *Warrior* target—that it should be lighter, of simpler construction, and more economical. But when it was made and tried it was proved to be heavier, to be more complicated in its construction, and to be more costly. The *Warrior* target weighed 347 lb. per square foot, but Mr. Chalmers' target was 385 lb. per square foot, without its supports, the weight of which brought it up to 485 lb. per square foot. As to the system of construction, the object sought was, as he had often stated to the House, that the iron plates should contribute to the strength of the structure of the ship. The *Warrior* target consisted of five parts, two only of which did not add to the structural strength of the ship; but the Chalmers' target consisted of seven parts, of which four did not add to the structural strength of the ship. In fact, the target was very complicated in construction, and he had been told by various persons connected with shipbuilding (to whom he had spoken on the subject) that it would be extremely difficult to build a ship on that principle, even without regarding expense. In point of resistance, no doubt, the Chalmers' target did resist shot better, in some respects, than the *Warrior* target. It did not resist the 68-pounder quite so well. It was quite true that the target was very severely tried ; but every target was submitted to the progress of gunnery. They submitted Mr. Chalmers' target to shot from guns of new construction, and Sir William Armstrong's 300-pounder sent a steel shot right through it ; but the Admiralty did not condemn it on that account. The Admiralty agreed to pay the cost of the target, and did pay £1,200 when the account was sent in ; but Mr. Chalmers, being very much dissatisfied, wrote several letters to the Admiralty, asking them to make new targets and try further experiments on them. The Admiralty, however, having other series of experiments on hand, did not choose to go

The Duke of Somerset

on trying experiments with a principle which they did not mean to adopt. The great fault he had to find with inventors was, that they did not invent. They often make small adaptations of previous constructions and proclaim the result as a great discovery. It was very easy for people when they saw a new idea at work to suggest alterations which might be improvements ; but if everybody who did that paraded his suggestion as a great invention, it would be impossible for the Admiralty to make any progress with their experiments. Then Mr. Chalmers asked to have his target back again, and when the Admiralty consented to that — being apparently by their assent deprived of a grievance — he wrote back angrily to say that they had no right to give it him back as it was public property, and that the Admiralty had made use of his improvements in other constructions. But that was not the case. A great many minor improvements had been adopted from time to time, but it could not be said that any particular person was entitled to claim them as his inventions. No doubt improvements had been made on the *Warrior* target. When that was first built the plates were only 4½-in. thick—for the manufacturers then could not roll plates any thicker. It was many months before the manufacturers could roll 5½-in., and months before they could turn out 6-inch plates. Then the *Minotaur* target was tried ; in some respects it showed inferior resistance to the *Warrior*, but the fact was that the plates at that time were inferior. Now, however, so much improvement had been made in the manufacture of iron, that in three months he could get more iron plates, and of a better quality, than he could have got in two years before. He had no doubt that in another year or so they would get still better plates. With regard to the statement that the *Bellerophon* target was not submitted to the same test as Mr. Chalmers' target, that was true in some respects, but in others it was submitted to a severer test, and besides other trials to which it was subjected, it was experimented on with the 68-pounder gun, the Armstrong 110-pounder, and the Whitworth 70 and 150-pounders. The statement that anything was copied from Mr. Chalmers' target for the *Bellerophon* target was quite a mistake. Mr. Chalmers said there was a stringer of iron edge-ways round the vessel, but that was to some extent the case with the *Warrior*, which had iron stringers at a distance of 3ft. 9in. apart. They might as fairly say that Mr. Chalmers had copied his stringer from the *Warrior*, as Mr. Chalmers could say they had taken his stringer for the *Bellerophon*. There had, indeed, been very little advance since the construction of the *Warrior*, except that they now got thicker plates and better iron. People complained of the cost of these experiments, but he was told by iron manufacturers that they had an immense effect in improving the manufacture of iron ; and the result of the experiments was that there was an increased supply of good iron. It was not at all his wish to do any injustice to inventors, but on the contrary, he would be glad to see any inventions brought forward that were calculated to be useful.

Petition to lie on the table.

JOINT STOCK COMPANIES (FOREIGN COUNTRIES) BILL [H.L.]

A Bill to enable Joint Stock Companies carrying on Business in Foreign Countries to have official Seals to be used in such Countries—Was *presented* by The Lord REDESDALE ; and read 1ª. (No. 45.)

House adjourned at a quarter before Seven o'clock, Till to-morrow a quarter before Five o'clock.

HOUSE OF COMMONS,
Thursday, April 14, 1864.

MINUTES.]— SELECT COMMITTEE — On Bankruptcy Act, *appointed.*
SUPPLY—WAYS AND MEANS—*considered in Committee.*
Resolution [April 13] *reported.*
PUBLIC BILLS—*Resolutions in Committee*—Partnership Law Amendment*.
Ordered—High Court at Bombay*.
First Reading — High Court at Bombay* [Bill 67] ; Consolidated Fund (£15,000,000)* ; Partnership Law Amendment* [Bill 68] ; Court of Chancery (Despatch of Business) *Lords* [Bill 69]
Committee — Naval Agency and Distribution* [Bill 39] ; Naval Prize Acts Repeal* [Bill 40] ; Naval Prize* [Bill 41], *committed, considered, reported,* and *re-committed* [Bills 64 and 65] ; County Courts (Ireland)* [Bill 12] ; Common Law Procedure (Ireland) Act (1853) Amendment* [Bill 43].
Report—Naval Agency and Distribution, and *re-committed ;* County Courts (Ireland)*, and *re-committed ;* Common Law Procedure (Ireland) Act (1853) Amendment.*

INDIAN MEDICAL DEPARTMENT.
QUESTION.

MR. BAZLEY said, he would beg to ask the Secretary of State for India, How many candidates for employment in the Medical Department for India were presented, and how many were the vacancies at the time of the competitive examination in January last, and again how many at the recent examination ?

SIR CHARLES WOOD was understood to state, in reply, that for two or three years there had been no examination of candidates for the Indian Medical Service.

CITY OF LONDON BYE-LAWS.
QUESTION.

MR. ALDERMAN SALOMONS said, he would beg to ask the Secretary of State for the Home Department, If he has yet approved the proposed bye-laws for the City of London, and especially if he intended to sanction bye-law No. 12, which virtually proposes to withhold the common-law right of way through the principal streets of the City from dealers in fruit, fish, and vegetables !

SIR GEORGE GREY replied, that the bye-laws made by the City had not yet been approved, and for this reason, that a question arose as to whether some of them were not in excess of the powers given by the Act of Parliament. Upon the City authorities being informed of the doubt existing on the subject, they took the opinion of their own Law Officers, who reported that the bye-laws were within the powers of the Acts. So much doubt existed, however, on the subject, that he had thought it right to submit the question to the Law Officers of the Crown, and it was now under their consideration ?

THE HIGHWAY ACT.—QUESTION.

MR. R. LONG said, he would beg to ask the Secretary of State for the Home Department, Whether Magistrates resident in places which are exempted from the operation of the Highway Act are, or are not, *ex officio* members of the General Highway Board of the district in which they reside ?

SIR GEORGE GREY stated, in reply, that the law required that magistrates, in order to be *ex officio* members of the General Highway Board, should reside within the highway district ; and it was held that Magistrates residing in a place exempted from the operations of the Highway Act were not within the district contemplated in the Act, and therefore not *ex officio* members of the Highway Board. Several representations had been made to him on the subject, and it was one of the points which, in the amended Bill, would have to be considered.

THE CONSTABULARY (IRELAND).
QUESTION.

CAPTAIN ARCHDALL said, he rose to ask the Chief Secretary for Ireland, If the Irish Government have directed the Inspector General of Constabulary to recall the instructions issued to the police on the 27th of October, 1862, with reference to the Act 25 & 26 *Vict.* c. 114, and to issue fresh instructions in conformity with the provisions of the said Act?

SIR ROBERT PEEL, in reply, said, the question raised by the hon. and gallant Member had been submitted to the Law Officers of the Crown in Ireland, who were of opinion that the instructions that had been issued were in accordance with the Act of Parliament.

THE MERCHANT SEAMEN'S ACT.
QUESTION.

MR. BENTINCK said, he wished to ask the President of the Board of Trade, Whether any penalty attaches to Vessels not carrying the proper Lights prescribed by the Merchant Seamen's Act; and, if Vessels infringing those regulations are subject to penalties, what those penalties are, and what is the proper course to take for recovering them?

MR. MILNER GIBSON said, in reply, that by the Merchant Shipping Act a wilful non-observance of the regulations as to Lights constituted a misdemeanour, and the offending parties might be indicted and punished by fine or imprisonment. But it was considered that this was not so convenient a way of enforcing those regulations as a more summary procedure. There was also another penalty which might be enforced against persons who had failed to comply with the regulations. The owners of ships not carrying regulation Lights, in case of collision were considered to be in default, and therefore liable to damages for the injury occasioned by their neglect.

MR. BENTINCK said, he wished further to ask, whether, in reference to the matter, the right hon. Gentleman intends to

Sir George Grey

take any steps to facilitate the observation of those regulations?

MR. MILNER GIBSON said, that the subject was under consideration.

HOLYHEAD HARBOUR.—QUESTION.

MR. STANLEY said, he wished to ask the President of the Board of Trade, What steps are being taken to mark more distinctly the Platter Rocks in the Refuge Harbour of Holyhead?

MR. MILNER GIBSON said, in reply, that buoys were placed there to mark distinctly the situation of those rocks, and he was not aware that anything more was necessary. It had been suggested that some kind of Light should be placed upon them, but at present no plan for that purpose was matured. All that existed there were the ordinary buoys for marking shoals.

MR. STANLEY said, he wished to know if there had not been some plans submitted to the Board of Trade by which something better than buoys could be placed on the rocks?

MR. MILNER GIBSON believed there had been plans submitted, but nothing had as yet been decided upon.

COST OF PROSECUTIONS.—QUESTION.

SIR JERVOISE JERVOISE said, he would beg to ask the Secretary of State for the Home Department, Whether his attention has been directed to the charge of the Chairman of the Quarter Sessions for Cumberland, showing the cost of prosecutions at the Sessions and Assizes to be an average of rather more than £12 for each prosecution; while under the Criminal Justices Act the average was rather more than £1 6s. per head; whether his attention has been called to a case tried at the last Assizes at Winchester, in which the prisoner had elected to be tried at the Assizes, where, after lying nearly two months in prison, at the cost of the county, he was sentenced to fourteen days' imprisonment, his companion in crime having agreed to be tried at Petty Sessions, and having been there sentenced to fourteen days' imprisonment; and whether it is in contemplation to propose any course tending to a more uniform mode of proceeding and to the extension of the Act?

SIR GEORGE GREY, in reply, said, he had not seen the charge of the Chairman of Quarter Sessions until a copy had been sent to him by the hon. Baronet. He had no doubt that the statement of the hon. Baronet was correct—that the expenses of a prosecution at the Sessions or Assizes were very much higher than under the Criminal Justices Act. With regard to the case tried at the Winchester Assizes, he supposed that the Judge in passing the sentence of fourteen days' imprisonment must have taken into consideration that the prisoner had been already two months in gaol, which would account for the apparent disproportion between the sentence being nominally the same as that passed upon his associate in crime. He had no doubt that the Criminal Justices Act had been very beneficial in its operation. The Government, however, had no intention at present to extend its provisions.

VOLUNTEER DRILL INSTRUCTORS.

QUESTION.

GENERAL BUCKLEY said, he wished to ask the Under Secretary of State for War, Whether it is in contemplation to provide the Drill Instructors of Volunteer Corps clothing and accoutrements in the same manner as if they were in a Regiment of the Line?

THE MARQUESS of HARTINGTON, in reply, said, the pay of 2s. 7d. a day which Drill Instructors of Volunteers Corps, not Pensioners, received was constituted as follows:—2s. 1d., which was the sum they would receive if they were Sergeants in the Line; 4d., lodging allowance; and 2d., compensation for clothing. If in addition to compensation for clothing the Government undertook to clothe the Instructors, the latter would be in a better position than Sergeants in the Line, which was not intended. There was, therefore, no intention to provide them with clothing.

GENERAL BUCKLEY said, that in the Artillery the Sergeants were clothed.

THE MARQUESS OF HARTINGTON stated that the Sergeants in the Artillery Corps were still attached to the army.

IRELAND—ADDITIONAL POLICE AT LISBURN.—QUESTION.

MR. WHITESIDE said, he wished to ask the Chief Secretary for Ireland, By whose directions, and whether upon the recommendation of any Local Magistrate, and whether upon any representations of breaches of the peace committed or apprehended, 150 additional Police were recently ordered to proceed to the town of Lisburn, and there to remain? The right hon. and learned Gentleman read a communication which he had received, in which the writer stated that the inhabitants considered that a great insult had been given to this pre-eminently loyal and peaceful town, and that during the last week a large body of Police was observed patrolling the town as if it were in a state of siege, whereas it was more like one on an ordinary Sunday.

SIR ROBERT PEEL said, in reply, that disturbances were apprehended at Lisburn as the result of the petition against Mr. Verner. The facts were these: —Everybody who knew what the excitement at elections was knew that they sometimes threatened a good deal of disturbance. Well, on the 23rd of March, 1,000 persons, men, women, and children, marched through the town of Lisburn with drums, fifes, shouting, and even the firing of pistols. That, of course, even in a town like Lisburn, created some excitement, and a magistrate of the counties of Down and Antrim on the 30th of March made a solemn declaration that disturbances were to be apprehended. He said that he had just arrived from London, and found a great crowd of people assembled round his house, shouting, "Verner for ever!" "To hell with the petition!" and "To hell with Richardson!" Shots were also fired in the vicinity of that magistrate's house. In the belief that riots would take place, and the reports being that what was called the Vernerite party were very indignant, a request was made to the Government that some assistance should be given; and every sensible person in that part of Ireland thought the Government in granting it acted with prudence and discretion. Accordingly 107 (not 150) of the Police were sent to Lisburn, and they afforded protection to the timid inhabitants of that place. The right hon. and learned Gentleman was wrong in saying the police were retained there. They arrived, he (Sir Robert Peel) believed, on the 4th of April, and were removed on the 11th. Not only did that magistrate of the counties of Down and Antrim make that declaration as to the apprehension that the peace would be broken, but another magistrate in Petty Sessions at Lisburn expressed his belief that the Government exercised a wise discretion in anticipating any probable disturbances. If actual disturbances had taken place, he was sure that the right hon. and learned Gentleman would have been the first to blame the Government for not having provided against their occurrence. He (Sir Robert Peel) was informed by several magistrates in the north of Ireland that they viewed with great satisfaction the course followed by the Government on that occasion.

Mr. WHITESIDE said, the right hon. Baronet had not answered his question. Was it on the recommendation of any local magistrate that the police were sent to what, according to his knowledge of it, was a peaceful town? What was the name of the gentleman who arrived from London? And was there any breach of the peace in point of fact?

Sir ROBERT PEEL said, there was no breach of the peace in point of fact, because they prevented it. But there was an information sworn to, and a local magistrate did request assistance.

Mr. WHITESIDE: Was there any person "bonnetted?"

STAMP ON PROXIES.—QUESTION.

Mr. DARBY GRIFFITH said, he would ask Mr. Chancellor of the Exchequer, Whether the penny stamp on Proxies would be the common receipt stamp?

The CHANCELLOR of the EXCHEQUER replied there would be an Inland Revenue stamp for both purposes.

THE INCOME TAX.—QUESTION.

Mr. HUBBARD said, he would beg to ask Mr. Chancellor of the Exchequer, Whether he proposes to re-enact the Income Tax as it stood at the close of 1863, or whether he proposes any, and, if any, what change in its provisions?

The CHANCELLOR of the EXCHEQUER said, in reply, that Government had no intention whatever of making any material change in the provisions of the Income Tax Act. A point of some consequence was raised last year relating to Railway Companies ; but it had since been settled by the Courts of Law. He was not aware of any other point requiring legislation.

DENMARK AND GERMANY—THE
CONFERENCE.—QUESTION.

Mr. BERNAL OSBORNE said, he wished to repeat the question which he put the other night to the Under Secretary of State for Foreign Affairs—namely, Whether he will lay on the table the French Despatch of the 20th of March, and also

the answers received by Her Majesty's Government to their invitations to a Conference?

Mr. LAYARD said, in reply, that, as he had stated the other night, the French despatch was not communicated to Her Majesty's Government, but only read to the noble Lord at the head of the Foreign Office. No official copy was left with the Government. As to the other part of the hon. Member's question, there was no intention of laying any further papers on the table at present.

Mr. BERNAL OSBORNE: Not the answers?

WAYS AND MEANS.

Order for Committee read.

Motion made, and Question proposed, " That Mr. Speaker do now leave the Chair."

THE SUGAR DUTIES AND THE MALT DUTY.

Colonel BARTTELOT rose to make the Motion which stood in his name—

"That the consideration of the Duties upon Sugar be postponed until the House shall have had the opportunity of considering the expediency of the reduction of the Duty upon Malt."

In rising to submit this Motion, he should first thank the hon. Member for the City of London (Mr. Crawford), who had kindly given way to him on the present occasion. He must also thank the Chancellor of the Exchequer for the courtesy he had shown him in enabling him to bring on the discussion of this important question that evening. In venturing to submit this subject to the consideration of the House, he only wished that it had been placed in abler hands than his, and that it had been brought forward by his hon. Friend the Member for East Suffolk, who had always taken so active a part on that subject in the House. However, it was thought that one who was not identified with the former Government in that House, as his hon. Friend had been, and who represented an agricultural district and a barley-growing country, should be selected to make the Motion which stood in his name. In doing so he ventured to state distinctly that his proposition was one to take a part of the surplus which the Chancellor of the Exchequer now had at his disposal, and to apply it to the reduction of the malt duty instead of applying it to the reduction of the sugar duties. The claims of sugar in comparison with those of malt he had no doubt would be fairly and fully discussed. He could safely say that he approached the discussion with no party feeling. It was no party question, but one bearing on the general interests of the country. It was equally a question for agriculturists and consumers, the latter of whom he believed would get the greatest share of the benefit, which might accrue from the change he contemplated. The measure would also unfetter a branch of trade greatly shackled by the very heavy taxation now imposed upon it, and which those sharing his opinions thought ought to be removed. He would venture to say one word to his hon. Friend the Member for the North Riding of Yorkshire (Mr. Morritt), who had a Motion on the paper somewhat similar to that of his (Colonel Barttelot's). He had interposed his Motion in no hostile spirit to that of his hon. Friend. They were both unanimous upon this question. But it had been the desire of those acting with him to avail themselves of the earliest opportunity of placing to their credit some portion of that surplus which the right hon. Gentleman had now at his disposal. With those few remarks he ventured to draw attention to the claims which, he thought, malt had on their consideration.

He would first remind the House and the right hon. Gentleman opposite, the Chancellor of the Exchequer, that he had some short time ago moved as an Amendment to the Motion of the hon. Member for Dudley (Mr. Sheridan) the following Resolution:—

" That this House is unwilling to proceed upon any Motion respecting the surrender of the large amount of public revenue which is yielded by the duty upon Fire Insurances until it shall have learned the probable state of receipt and charge for the coming financial year, and until, if there shall then appear to be a likelihood of a surplus income available for the remission of taxes, it shall have had an opportunity of considering together the several claims for reduction, and of determining in what manner such a surplus may best be disposed of, with a view to the general relief and welfare of the people."

It was with regard to that Resolution that he now called the attention of the House to the claims of the taxpayers. And he would first ask the question, which would benefit the community most, the reduction of the malt or of the sugar duties? In the first place, the reduction of the malt duty—particularly with a surplus in the hands of the Chancellor of the Exchequer, which might give them a reasonable hope that it might be reduced further in future years, with a view to a total abolition—

would show to the people that the House regarded no class interest at all, but looked to the general benefit of the labouring population. He had no hesitation in saying that no reduction such as was proposed by the Chancellor of the Exchequer in the sugar duties, though it might benefit a certain class, would benefit to the same degree or extent the population generally as the reduction of the malt tax. The proposed reduction would not reach the general consumers, but would go into the pockets of a limited class. He would appeal to those connected with the rural districts, whether the remission now proposed to be made on sugar would enable the small shopkeeper to sell his goods at such a reduced price as would benefit the labouring man in the least visible degree? Although sugar had still some of the war duties of 1854, nevertheless those duties had been materially decreased of late years. They did not stand in the same position as they did many years ago. Formerly there was a great difference made in the duties on East and West India sugars. But in 1854 the duties were made uniform. In 1840 the East India sugar duty was £1 13s. 7d. per cwt., whilst the West India sugar duty was £1 5s. 2d. What were these duties at the present moment. They had been very much reduced ; whereas the tax on malt had greatly increased since its first imposition ; and if they went back to 1703, they would find that the tax on malt had increased from 6d. to 2s. 8½d. During the Crimean war the tax no doubt was 4s. per bushel, but the consumption of malt was very greatly reduced in consequence. The consumption of malt had not kept pace with the population of the country. In early years a vast quantity of good beer was drunk in this country, and he appealed to the hon. Gentleman opposite the Member for Derby (Mr. Bass), who he was sure would endorse his opinion, that a vast quantity of miserable and horrible stuff was poured down the throats of the labouring population. The hon. Member shook his head ; but he knew well that he could not rise and state in his place in that House that such was not the fact. And not only was it the fact, but that also with the reduction of the sugar duties worse beer still would be brewed. A vast amount of sugar was used in all our breweries (he did not include the hon. Member's), because it could be used cheaper than the best malt. A vast amount of sugar and molasses was also used in the manufacture of whisky; for whilst the best Islay and Campbeltown whiskies were made from malt, the inferior distillers used a great quantity of molasses, because they could make whisky cheaper from it than they could from malt at its present high rate of duty. He was not going to say that with a reduction of the malt duty there would not necessarily be a reduction in the consumption of spirits, and therefore in the revenue derived from spirits, but he thought no man would say that if such were to be the result it would not be a great blessing to the general community; for the use of spirits was the greatest curse we had in this country. They had been invited to discuss the bearing of the proposed reduction in the malt duty on the relative taxation of England, Ireland, and Scotland. Now, suppose the tax were taken off malt, and the English consumer was the person principally benefited by it, what then? They must not consider the amount of the reduction per head, but the general taxation of the three countries— they must see whether or not they were fairly taxed in other respects—or why not give to England the benefit of the reduction of the tax which she now principally paid? The Returns showed an increased consumption of malt in Ireland, and he found in Sir Morton Peto's book on Taxation, that the consumption of malt in Ireland had increased from 1,691,157 bushels in 1857 to 2,513,760 bushels in 1862; showing a great increase in the consumption of malt in that country, and showing also that the people of that country were not so wedded to whisky but that they would drink good beer when they could get it. He asked the House how it was with the Customs duty on cotton. The Customs duty on cotton was repealed at the instance of the cotton manufacturers; were they to be found all over England, Ireland, and Scotland? So far from their being found all over the three kingdoms, they were almost confined to Lancashire, Yorkshire, and Cheshire; he considered that that which would benefit the whole of the community was a proper and fair tax to take off. He was anxious that all manufactures should, if possible, be relieved from taxation; but agriculture ought to be relieved equally with them. Those who represented agricultural districts thought they had formed a strong bond of union with the manufacturers. They had sympathised with and assisted them in

Colonel Barttelot

their distress, and they believed they deserved every thing that had been done for them, and all the praise that had been bestowed on them. That being so, that whatever the tax might be the remission of which would most benefit the community, that was the tax which was the most proper and fair to be reduced, and he believed the reduction of the malt tax would benefit the whole community. Let them first consider the subject in the light of a landlord's question. In this view it would be most beneficial. A tenant could cultivate the land better if the tax were removed, and a great advantage would be indirectly given to the landowner, whilst the tenant would also derive a direct benefit if he could use his produce in such a way as to turn it to the best account. He need hardly appeal to those hon. Members who farmed their own land to say what a direct advantage it would be to a tenant if he could crop his land in a manner that would be most productive to him. The tax on malt caused them to depart from the usual rotation of crops, because if they thought they could not grow good malting barley — they would not grow inferior barley — they had recourse to wheat and oats, preferring crops that might not always prove remunerative to so uncertain a crop as barley, particularly in a bad season. Besides benefiting the landlord and the tenant-farmer, it would also benefit the labourer, by enabling him to have pure wholesome beer to drink in his own cottage, which was the natural beverage of every Englishman, instead of the unwholesome beverage that was retailed at the public-house. At harvest time hon. Members knew that the men preferred beer, and they had a better chance of getting their work done by giving the men beer than by sending them out tea and sugar. Every one who could do so now brewed his own beer, and the effect of the remission of the malt tax would be to enable every man who had a good copper to brew good wholesome beer at 4d. per gallon—a very superior article to that now to be had in the country pot-house for 4d. per quart. He did not say that taking off the tax would prevent men from going to the beer-shop; but he believed that if they could have a good wholesome beverage at home, many of them would abstain from going to the pot-house, and a stop would be put to a corresponding amount of crime and misery at present existing amongst the lower classes. What harm, he asked, had been done to the revenue by the remission of the duties on glass, bricks, soap, paper, and hops? Was not the revenue more flourishing than ever? And he thought the Government should so control the expenditure as to be able to remove a tax which pressed so heavily and grievously on the agricultural interest. It had been said that if a portion of the malt tax was taken off there would not be a proportionate increase in the consumption, and the history of the beer duty had been appealed to as an argument in support of that proposition. The beer duty was taken off in 1829, at which time the malt tax realized £3,026,126; but in 1831, after the beer tax had been removed, the malt duty rose to £4,257,781, being an increase of £1,231,655; which showed the malt tax was elastic and would bear reduction, and give, at the same time, a largely increased revenue. He did not for a moment pretend to say that if they reduced the duty one-half there would be an immediate increase of a very large amount; but in the course of a very short time there would be a rebound the same as they had witnessed with regard to every other tax. He might be told it was very easy for him to make that statement, but that it was much more difficult to prove; but one thing he thought was certain, that if they could reduce the tax on malt so that inferior barley might be made into wholesome beer, the injurious and deleterious articles now used in the manufacture of bad beer would be to a great extent superseded. The malt tax was a most expensive tax to collect, but he was not going to enter into that question; but if the general consumers paid four or five times as much as the tax when collected, it surely was an argument why a part if not the whole of the tax should be taken off. A good deal had been said about the Hertfordshire election; all he wished to say about it was that the electors had a right to elect whomsoever they pleased. They ought not to be dictated to, and because a Member was rejected at one place that was no reason why he might not be returned or rejected at another, whatever influence was brought to bear and whatever might be said about it. He was informed that at the recent election for that county large placards were posted on the omnibuses and cabs containing the words, "Cowper and the repeal of the Malt Tax." His belief was that the hon. Gentleman used that which he thought would do him the most good, and he believed the addresses of the two candidates were so equally significant in that respect, that there was little to choose between them, and it was difficult to say which would have gone the furthest with regard to the malt tax. It was, therefore, impossible to say whether the election was lost or won by raising the cry on this question. The Herts election had nothing to do with it, nor with the Budget. He was surprised at the leading journal, in noticing the debate that was coming on on the malt tax, using such expressions as those he was about to read, because he had hitherto been willing to believe that that journal fairly and honestly represented the case to the country. That journal said, "The glorious prospect of cheap beer fires the bucolic imagination and inspires with delightful visions the brains of the coldest agriculturist." Now, he did not know its meaning here—but if the House came to a Resolution to provide beer at the public expense for the whole of England, he could understand his agricultural friends running to the beer barrel; but he did not understand that a Motion for the repeal or partial repeal of the malt tax would inspire such views in the brains of any agriculturist; but they might think, that with a reduction of the duty, they might be able to supply themselves with that beverage which he believed they all desired. Upon what principle could the tax be maintained? Surely not upon the principles of free trade, because the tax had been condemned by the highest authorities. When the Corn Laws were repealed Sir Robert Peel said, "If the Corn Laws are repealed the malt tax cannot be sustained;" and the hon. Member for Rochdale used the same, or nearly the same, words at a meeting he attended in the Midland counties. But the malt tax still existed; and unless some determined action was taken he (Colonel Bartelot) feared it would continue, because it was such a convenient tax, but one that could not be supported on any other principle than that it was a revenue tax. Surely, at the present time, and with the vast resources of this country, the House would not say that the tax should not be repealed on account of the money it returned, and that nothing was to be done to remove a tax which was considered one of the greatest injustice. He would not, however, detain the House longer. He had run his horse as straight at the fence as he could. He believed he was on a good horse; but it was for the House to say if he was to win the race that day. Should he, however, be beaten, his horse would "come again," for he was not likely to be bowled out of time. He believed that in introducing the Motion he had not done an unwise or foolish thing: he did not wish to set one party against the other; what he desired was, to elicit the opinion of the whole House upon a subject which affected the whole community—not the barley-grower only, but the labouring man and all who consumed beer; and he believed that the reduction of the malt tax would be far more beneficial to the community than the reduction of the sugar duties. He had, therefore, no hesitation in asking the House to appropriate the Chancellor of the Exchequer's surplus rather towards the reduction of the malt tax. The hon. and gallant Gentleman concluded by moving his Amendment.

Mr. COBBETT said, he had much pleasure in seconding the Motion, because it afforded him an opportunity of stating fully his opinion with regard to the malt duty. He did not speak as a landowner or as an occupier of land, but as one who regarded the question as it affected the labouring man. He had often heard the labouring man's cause quoted in that House, he was afraid sometimes for party purposes; and, at the same time, he had often seen that as soon as the party question had been disposed of, the labouring man had been entirely forgotten. When he first entered that House the question under consideration was, whether Lord Derby's administration should be dismissed or not, and he heard several Members on the then Opposition side of the House stand up and in very vehement and just terms urge the cause of the labouring man. It was said that the labouring man was forgotten, and that there was an iniquity in the mode in which our taxes were imposed, and that the burden was laid more heavily in proportion on the poor man than it was on the rich. He was not sure that the present Lord Chief Justice was not one of those who made a very animated appeal to the House on the subject. The consequence was that Lord Derby's Government was dismissed, and he was sorry to say the labouring man was dismissed also. Upon a more recent occasion, when Lord Derby's Administration was again in

peril, he remembered hearing several hon. Members speaking on the Reform Bill introduced by the noble Earl's Government urge that the labouring man had been forgotten, and he believed it was the late Sir James Graham who said that as the labouring man paid very nearly the whole of the interest on the National Debt, he ought to have been more considered in that Bill. He (Mr. Cobbett) quite concurred in that opinion; and he considered it wrong that the labouring man's case should not have been considered in 1832, and the taxes paid by him lightened, and the taxes on gentlemen a little more heavily imposed. He also thought that although Lord Derby's Reform Bill ought to have been read a second time, it was a Bill in which the labouring man had been too much forgotten. He felt sure the House of that day would have given him something more in Committee than was proposed in the Bill; but, unfortunately, the Liberal side of the House thought it better to stifle the Bill by not reading it a second time. He cordially joined his hon. and gallant Friend (Colonel Barttelot) in asking the House to postpone dealing with the sugar duties until they had had an opportunity of considering that iniquitous impost which placed on the poor man so heavy a burden as a tax which doubled the price of the beer he drank. This was no party question; and if it had been he should have most probably voted for it, for sometimes one was compelled to vote even upon a party question; but he should not have put himself so prominently forward as to almost volunteer to second the Motion, if he had thought it was brought on as a party question and for a party purpose. He did not design it as a party question, nor did he believe it was so designed by his hon. and gallant Friend. His case was the case of the poor man. He was not a landowner, and scarcely a land occupier, but such as he was he had never ventured to grow barley. He seconded the Motion from his intimacy with the condition of the labouring man, both in the factories in the North, and at the plough in the South. He had inquired into his condition on all occasions when he thought he could gain information, and he believed he was capable of describing the labouring man's cause. The effect of the malt tax was more than to double what he considered to the labouring man, one of the necessaries of life, because they had to pay about 8s. per bushel for malt, and 4s. per bushel for barley, and, in addition to that, the profits of the brewer and the publican had to be added. There were many persons, however, who argued that beer was not a necessary of life; but he hoped there were not many of that opinion in that House. He remembered hearing the right hon. Gentleman the Member for Buckinghamshire distinctly avow on one occasion, and also the right hon. Baronet the Member for Hertfordshire (Sir E. Bulwer Lytton), do the same, that beer was a necessary of life, and it afforded him much gratification to hear two such eminent men make that declaration. He had frequently visited the working man at his work, and he knew from conversation with him much about him, and he could give the House many instances in which it was perfectly clear to him that the working man suffered very much when he was deprived of his necessary quantity of wholesome beer. He himself knew an instance of a labouring man, of good character, with a wife and three children, who was obliged to give up his work because he could not afford to purchase a quart of porter a day, which he found was necessary for his strength, in order that he might keep up to his work with younger men. He would not trouble the House by going more minutely into the question, but he assured the House that many cases had come to his knowledge in which he had seen the greatest detriment to the working man caused by not having the support of beer. He did not believe the working man could get on with his work and do justice to his master unless in addition to his bread and his piece of bacon, he had also something to sustain him in his work. For want of beer he had known instances of men reduced to so low a condition that what would otherwise have been a trifling illness had carried them off. He recently read in a Sussex newspaper a report of an inquest on a labouring man who dropped down dead while returning from his work through Cowdray Park. The verdict was, "Died from natural causes, accelerated by want." Now, "accelerated by want," if it meant anything, meant starvation. The *post-mortem* examination showed that the man was at work without a sufficiency of food. The evidence of the wife was that he had been ill; that he had then gone to work; that as he did not return home at the time expected she thought what had taken place, and went to seek him across Cowdray Park, to the parish of Heyshot,

and found him dead by the roadside. It happened that this was the parish of the hon. Member for Rochdale (Mr. Cobden). He (Mr. Cobbett) consequently mentioned the case to the hon. Member, who said he knew the man, and that if he or his wife had applied for assistance, nourishment would probably have been given him in the shape of beer. Reducing the duties on tea and sugar was not what the labouring man wanted. The labouring man ought not to depend on tea and sugar. There was no nutriment in tea or sugar, and could not be said to be of much value as food. He believed, on the other hand, that they were very expensive, and considering that the fire had to be kept up both in winter and summer for the preparation of this tea, he thought they would in the long run cost more to the labourer than if he contented himself with beer of his own brewing. He had been frequently applied to by the parish doctor for beer, port wine, mutton and beef tea, for the relief of labourers suffering from severe illness; but never in the course of his life had application been made to him for tea and sugar. He regarded that fact as a convincing proof that beer was a necessary of life to the labouring man. Supposing the fact established that beer was a necessary of life, what sort of beer was it that the labouring man got? In towns, tolerably good; but in the remote parts of the country, the beer which the brewers supplied was excessively bad. He knew this personally from having walked part of the Home Circuit in Sussex, Surrey, and Kent. On one or two occasions, he and his friend had taken lunch in a public-house, and not being able to drink the beer, had been obliged to take gin and water as a substitute. But this was the sort of beer that was supplied to the labouring man about the country. Another bad effect of the malt tax was that it drove the working man to the beer-house or public-house. As those who lived in the country knew, nothing was more destructive to a labouring man than the habit of going to the public-house. If the malt tax were repealed, he would be able to brew at home, and drink the beer with his family. The subject merited their attention, if that were the only argument in its favour, because the policy which compelled a labouring man to frequent the beer shops and public-houses was a most destructive one. Formerly, as he had stated a short time since, the labouring man brewed his own beer, and if his wages at present were higher he would do so still. If they could do anything which would have the effect of again inducing the labourer to brew his own beer, they would do more towards regenerating the working part of the population than could be done in any other way. He believed that a large number of people, especially those with incomes ranging from £500 to £1,500 a year, would receive more advantage from the repeal of the malt duty than they would from the reduction of the income tax by a penny. He seconded the Motion of the hon. Member for West Sussex, because he regarded it as the first step towards a total abolition of the tax. The Chancellor of the Exchequer had now a million and a half of surplus at his disposal, and he proposed to apply a portion of it towards the reduction of the sugar duties; but, in his opinion, the right hon. Gentleman could not do better than commence the reduction of the malt tax, and make provision for taking off the whole in four or five years' time.

Amendment proposed,

To leave out from the word "That" to the end of the Question, in order to add the words "the consideration of the Duties upon Sugar be postponed until the House shall have had the opportunity of considering the expediency of the reduction of the Duty upon Malt,"—(*Colonel Barttelot,*)

—instead thereof.

Mr. SURTEES (who rose with several other hon. Members) said, that being a new Member, he felt indebted to the kindness and courtesy of the House for the opportunity of addressing it; but he felt that the House was so well informed upon all the points relating to the question under consideration, that it was scarcely possible for him to afford any information with which the House was not already acquainted. Having, however, the honour to represent a county which produced a large quantity of barley, he was anxious, in promising his cordial support to the Motion of the hon. Member for West Sussex, to offer one or two remarks on the subject. He should have been glad if the right hon. Gentleman the Chancellor of the Exchequer had been able so to frame his Budget as, consistent with the efficiency of the defences of the country and the honour and welfare of the nation, to have introduced a measure for the repeal of the Malt Tax, or, at any rate, for its immediate reduction, with an assurance

Mr. Cobbett

that, as far as his influence went, any future surplus of revenue should be devoted to the reduction and ultimate repeal of that duty. The right hon. Gentleman, in his financial statement, had done him the honour of making a personal allusion to him, the good taste of which—or the contrary—he would leave to the opinion of the House. In referring to the repeal of the Malt Tax, the right hon. Gentleman had stated that he (Mr. Surtees) did not perceive any difficulty which lay in the way of its removal. He would now remind the right hon. Gentleman that where there was a will there was a way. The right hon. Gentleman, however, did not possess the will, or he would not have abandoned one million and a quarter of revenue by the abolition of the Paper Duty in 1860. He had not the will, or he would not have abandoned under the French Treaty of Commerce above a million of revenue. He had not the will, or he would now devote the surplus of revenue at his disposal to the object which was so anxiously desired by many of Her Majesty's subjects. He (Mr. Surtees) confessed that he was not a little astonished, remembering the recent financial measures with regard to paper and the French Treaty of Commerce, to hear the right hon. Gentleman say that, "in its importance to the comforts of the people, sugar might be said to be next to corn." Why, then, did not the right hon. Gentleman reduce the duty on sugar in 1860, instead of reducing the duties on paper and on wines? Adding together the amount of the Paper Duty, £1,250,000, the amount sacrificed under the French Treaty, £1,090,000, the present surplus of £2,500,000, the drawback on beer and malt, £220,000, and the expense of collecting revenue, the House would find that the result was a total of between £5,000,000 and £6,000,000. Therefore, when the right hon. Gentleman said that he (Mr. Surtees) saw no difficulty in the way of the repeal of the Malt Tax, he was much mistaken. He confessed that he did see a great difficulty in the way of the repeal of the Malt Tax, and that difficulty was the Chancellor of the Exchequer himself. The right hon. Gentleman, speaking of the Hertfordshire election, alluded in complimentary terms to his hon. opponent. With those sentiments he cordially agreed. But, who was his opponent? He was a near relation of the right hon. Member for the Borough of

Hertford, a Member of Her Majesty's Government (Mr. Cowper), of whose presence on more than one occasion during his canvass he had the advantage; he was also a near connection of the noble Viscount at the head of the Government. And what did his hon. Opponent say in his address respecting the Malt Tax? He said—

"I should vote for the repeal of the Malt Tax, in preference to that of any other. Looking forward to the ultimate abolition of this tax, I should gladly hail any measure by which for the time its pressure upon agriculture might be mitigated."

The right hon. Gentleman the Chancellor of the Exchequer would admit that it was a legitimate object to endeavour to obtain relief from this tax—a tax which, since the British farmer had been compelled to compete with the producers of corn from all parts of the world, was felt to be most unjust in principle, as well as burdensome and oppressive in its operation. Suppose that a maltster bought four quarters of the best barley, which when converted into malt would supply the brewer with the saccharine principle that he required as completely as five quarters of malt made from inferior barley, the total cost of the four quarters of best barley and five quarters of inferior barley being about the same. Now, as each quarter of malt must pay a duty of £1 1s. 8½d., did it not follow that the maltster would prefer purchasing the best barley, because he naturally chose to pay only four times £1 1s. 8½d., instead of paying five times that sum, which he would have to do if he bought the five quarters of inferior barley? The inferior barley, therefore, was neglected, and consequently depreciated in value. The Malt Tax fettered capital and restricted trade, and consequently depreciated the value of barley; because, notwithstanding the malt credits, which were very short, unless the maltster could sell his malt soon after it was made, which frequently was not possible (for brewers were not always buyers, and frequently refrained from buying malt until about the time that the duty was payable), he would be obliged to advance out of his capital the amount required by the Excise Officers; or, if he had no spare capital, he was often obliged to dispose of a portion of his malt at any sacrifice in order to be able to pay the duty. This often affected the value of the malt held in stock by other maltsters. The Malt Tax also caused a mo-

nopoly, and thus depreciated the value of barley. He believed there were not in 1862 above 6,100 licensed maltsters in England, Ireland, and Scotland; and when the restrictions caused by the Excise Laws were considered, it was only astonishing that there were so many. On behalf of the consumer, as well as of the producer, he said that if the Malt Tax were repealed and the licence abolished, thousands of persons would come into the market and purchase small quantities of barley for the purpose of making their own malt, and brewing their own beer with pure malt and hops; and that important article barley would then be brought to a free and unfettered market, which, on every principle of freedom in trade, and on every principle of justice, ought to be permitted. He begged to offer to the House his grateful thanks for the kindness and forbearance with which it had listened to him.

MR. JOHN PEEL said, he had presided for several years in his own neighbourhood over an association of tenant-farmers, comprising some of the most intelligent farmers in the Midland counties. Now, there was no class of Her Majesty's subjects more patriotic and more willing to bear their fair share of taxation than the farmers of England. As a body he was sure they would repudiate all claim to special immunities or privileges for their own class. All they desired was, to be put on the same footing as other interests, and that the same principle of free trade which had been so happily adopted with regard to commerce and manufactures should be extended to agriculture. The Chancellor of the Exchequer, in his recent financial statement, laid down the proposition that the form of our duties should be such as would least interfere with the natural course of trade, and would be least open to the charge of offering to the producer a premium for doing something different from that which he would do if there were no duty at all. Now, he thought that the malt tax was in direct opposition to the principle here laid down by the right hon. Gentleman, because the tax did interfere with the ordinary course of the farmer's trade, and compelled him to produce that which he would not produce if there were no duty. A short extract from a letter addressed to him by an intelligent farmer would illustrate this statement. The writer said —

"Respecting the derangements of agriculture caused by the tax on malt, we all know that it has a bad effect upon our course of cropping. Barley would be more extensively grown if the crop in the Midland counties were a safe one. A good deal of our soil being strong, and a large portion of the crop now grown being always of second-class character, it goes for grinding, and not for malting; and on account of the risk of the crop, you know that more wheat is grown than would or ought to be. My own farm is a specimen of many; the land is too strong for first-class barley, but I could grow a good fair sample, and if I could sell it for malting I should grow more than I do instead of wheat. I plough 300 acres, and if the trade were unfettered, I should sow quite sixty acres with barley. Now, I seldom grow more than twenty-five acres annually, and the other thirty-five I sow with spring wheat."

In his opinion the representatives of agriculture in this House had neglected their duty in not bringing this question sooner before the House. Had they done so, he thought they might have adduced reasons for the reduction of the tax which it would have been impossible to resist. Every one knew that for a man to cultivate a farm up to the standard of the present day required a considerable amount of capital, great industry, and no small amount of intelligence; yet there was no calling which at present offered so small a return as farming did for this outlay of skill and capital. During the last few years the profits of the farmers had been unusually small, and it was not, therefore, surprising that they should now rise up as one man to protest against the injustice to which they were subject. He trusted that the House would not refuse to consider their case, and would apply to agriculture the same principles which had been applied to trade and commerce. The right hon. Gentleman the Chancellor of the Exchequer, the other evening, said—

"I find that if I select several years in which Parliament has with firm unsparing hand addressed itself to the business of liberating commerce, those operations have been followed by striking success."

And he (Mr. John Peel) believed that if the same liberal policy were extended to agriculture in this instance the same results would follow. It might be that at this the eleventh hour the Chancellor of the Exchequer would be unwilling to interfere with his financial arrangements, and the House hesitate to disappoint the expectations which had been held out of certain reductions in the income tax and other matters; but he hoped that the farmer would know that he had had a fair consideration given to his claims, and that the right hon. Gentleman, if unable to

Mr. John Peel

give him any relief in the present year, would, at all events, give him an assurance that any future surplus should be applied to relieve him from a portion of the burden under which the industry in which he was engaged now languished.

MR. BANKS STANHOPE said, there was one point on which every hon. Member was agreed, and that was that the Chancellor of the Exchequer had a surplus to dispose of; and he (Mr. Stanhope) thought he should be able to show, by contrasting the claims of malt with the claims of sugar, that malt had a prior claim for a remission of duty. By the statement of the Chancellor of the Exchequer, they had a gross surplus of £2,570,000. Out of the surplus the Chancellor of the Exchequer devoted to the reduction of sugar duties the sum of £1,330,000. This would represent about one quarter of the duty on malt. He would ask the House to compare the case of malt as against that of sugar. There was a great similarity in several points between the two cases—sugar and malt. Both were articles of general consumption among the lower as well as the higher classes; both were articles which were subject to indirect taxation, but there was this difference—that sugar was subject to a Customs duty and the malt to an Excise duty. He must say that, as a general rule, it was preferable to take off an Excise rather than a Customs duty. It was to be remembered that when you took off a Customs duty, you helped the consumer, who was an Englishman, and the producer, who was a foreigner; but when you took off an Excise duty you helped the consumer who was an Englishman, and the producer who was an Englishman also. Comparing the articles of malt and sugar he asked the House to go back a few years, in order to see what had been the process of our legislation with regard to the two articles. He should go back to 1841 and to 1861 to see what the Legislature had done in respect of the duties on malt and sugar in the period between those two years. He should first show what was the amount of taxation on sugar in 1841 and what it was in 1861. He should then take the year 1841, and see what was the average consumption per head of sugar in Great Britain and Ireland, and he should do the same with respect to 1861. Before making this comparison he begged to mention that in 1821 the average consumption of sugar per head was 16lb.; in 1831,

17lb.; in 1841, 17lb. The House would see, therefore, that during the years between these two periods the consumption of sugar was stationary. In 1821 the consumption of malt per head was a bushel and a half, in 1831 there was a little increase; in 1841 it was again a bushel and a half. It appeared, therefore, that the consumption of both sugar and malt was stationary during the 20 years between 1821 and 1841. They must now see what had been the process of legislation in regard to each commodity; for if in 1861 the relative claims of malt and sugar had remained the same as they were in 1841, although he felt strongly for the agricultural interests, he should not have considered himself justified in making his speech, or in supporting the Motion of his hon. and gallant Friend. Between the years 1821 and 1841 the beer duty was taken off; but as regarded sugar there had been hardly any difference at all. In one sort of our sugar there had been a reduction of 2s. per cwt., in another 4s. per cwt., and in another 12s. per cwt. They must now look to what had occurred between 1841 and 1861. The duties paid by unrefined sugars in 1841 were:—West Indian, £1 5s. per cwt.; East Indian, £1 5s.; other British possessions, £1 13s. Foreign, £3 6s.; refined, £8 16s.; brown candy, £5 17s.; white candy, £8 16s. Molasses—foreign, £1 4s.; British ditto, 9s. 5d. In 1861 the duties were:—Unrefined, equal to white clayed, 16s.; brown, 13s. 10d. not equal to brown, 12s. 8d.; refined, 18s. 4d.; molasses, 5s. The malt duty, 2s. 8½d. per bushel, was precisely the same in each of the years 1841 and 1861. He asked, then, which was the petted interest? While malt in 1861 paid the same duty as it had in 1841, refined sugar, which had paid £8 16s. per cwt. in 1841, only paid 18s. 4d. in 1861. He must now trouble the House with figures to show what had been the average consumption of each commodity at several periods between the years to which he was referring. He quoted from a Parliamentary Return moved for in 1862. First, as to malt. In 1841 the consumption of malt was 36,164,403 bushels; in 1851, 40,337,416; in 1859, 42,759,065; in 1860 37,453,907; in 1861, 43,065,088. The average number of bushels per head was in 1841 1·35; in 1851, 1·47; in 1859, 1·49; in 1860, 1·3; in 1861, 1·49. It therefore appeared that the average consumption per head of malt through those

years was almost completely stationary; but if they came to sugar, the figures were marvellous. In 1841 the consumption of sugar was 4,057,900 cwts.; in 1851, 6,571,626; in 1859, 8,884,299; in 1860, 8,771,996; in 1861, 9,180,969; showing an increase of about 4,000,000 cwts.; between 1841 and 1861, or in other words, the consumption had doubled between the two periods. The average consumption per head was in 1841 17 lb.; in 1851, 26·73; in 1859, 34·59; in 1860, 33·9; in 1861, 35·21. There was another point to which he begged to direct the attention of the House. Practically, there was no difference in what was received per head for the duty paid on malt in 1841 and 1861 respectively, because the consumption was stationary; but what was the case with sugar? In 1841 the consumer of 17 lb. of sugar paid 3s. 10d. duty; in 1861 the consumer of 35 lb. paid only 4s. 2½d. He paid 4½d. more duty, but for that he had 18 lb. more sugar. This was said to be a consumer's question, and as such he would treat it. He had not said a word for the producer. When they were told to consider the case of the poor man, they must admit that the consumer of sugar, who had been able so largely to increase his consumption, was less worthy of sympathy than the consumer of malt, whose supply was restricted by the high duty. He would now say a word or two as to molasses. In 1841 the consumption was 401,000 cwt.; in 1851, 772,000 cwt.; in 1859, 678,000cwt.; in 1860, 557,000cwt.; and in 1861, 1,079,232 cwt. They might, perhaps, be told that the consumers of molasses had gained nothing. In 1841 the average payment per head for molasses was 1¼d., and in 1861, 1¾d. The difference was not very much, but at any rate the consumer of molasses paid a smaller contribution than in 1841, though he consumed a great deal more than double the quantity of the article. Such being the facts of the case, in the name of justice and common sense, when there were two claimants for relief, why should they give it to the one that required it least, and deny it to the other that was so much in need of it? The consumer of malt paid as much as he did in 1841, while the relief to the consumer of sugar had been doubled since then. An argument which was represented as very formidable by those who supported the reduction of the sugar duty was that a portion of it was a war impost. ["Hear!"] Hon. Gentlemen opposite were ready to cheer now; but why did they not remember that in 1860 and 1861 ? There were then war duties on tea and sugar, but hon. Gentlemen opposite preferred to take off the paper duty. What were the duties on sugar before, during, and since the war? In 1854 the duties were as follows : — Refined, 16*s.*; white clayed, 14*s.*; brown, 12*s.*; not equal to brown clayed, 11*s.* In 1855 the duties were respectively 20*s.*, 17*s.* 6*d.*, 15*s.*, and 13*s.* 9*d.*, and they were now 18*s.* 4*d.*, 16*s.*, 13*s* 10*d.*, and 12*s.* 8*d.* Next, he would ask, what had been the effect of the rise of duty on the consumption? In 1854 the consumption was 8,404,551 cwt. ; in 1855, when the high war duty was in force, there was a decrease to the amount of 724,210 cwt. ; in 1856, there was a decrease of 904,000 cwt., and in 1857 a decrease of 758,000 cwt. In that year there was a reduction from the high war duties to the present rates. Had the existing scale caused a decrease or increase of consumption ? In 1858 there was an increase over 1854 of 599,517 cwt. ; in 1859 there was an increase of 744,000 cwt. ; in 1860, of 556,000 cwt. ; in 1861, of 996,000 cwt.; in 1862, of 1,312,000 cwt. ; and in 1863 of no less than 1,496,481 cwt. [Mr. R. W. CRAWFORD : What is the consumption per head of the population ?] He was sorry he could not give the precise amount. The fact, however, remained, that in 1854 there was a duty of 16*s.* per cwt., and in 1863 of 18*s.* 4*d.* ; and yet, with the higher duty, there was a large increase of consumption. He was justified, therefore, in saying that the sugar duty was not a burdensome tax, and did not possess the first claim, above all other imposts, for reduction. In the case of malt, the Chancellor of the Exchequer had offered an argument quite unprecedented. The right hon. Gentleman told those who advocated the reduction of the duty on malt that the consumption of malt was so small in Scotland and Ireland that the lowering of the duty would be a relief only to England, and scarcely any at all to the other two divisions of the kingdom. They had heard a great deal about "oppressed nationalities" in connection with foreign politics; but this was the first time the cry had been raised in regard to finance. He agreed with his hon. and gallant Friend who introduced the subject, that the doctrine had not been followed even by the right hon. Gentleman himself in former years. For instance, when the duty on cotton was

Mr. Banks Stanhope

taken off, to the great advantage of the manufacturers of England, Ireland was never thought of at all. Then, when the right hon. Gentleman was in Sir Robert Peel's Government, the duty on bricks was removed ; but that was no relief to Scotland, where bricks were scarcely ever used. In fact, similar instances might be cited almost *ad infinitum.* The Members for Scotland and Ireland might, perhaps, be tempted to accept this new and dangerous doctrine, but if they did they must expect to find it adhered to in regard to every other duty, and would probably repent of the bargain before long. The sum paid per head for malt was 5*s.* 6*d.* in England, in Scotland 1*s.* 5*d.*, in Ireland 1*s.* 1*d.* The reduction of the duty by a fourth would give a relief per head in England of 1*s.* 5*d.*, in Scotland of 4*d.* and in Ireland of 3*d.* It might be worth while, for the sake of argument, to consider the spirit duty in the same light. It was now 10*s.* a gallon throughout the United Kingdom. The consumption of spirits in England was 4*s.* 6*d.* per head, in Scotland, 20*s.* 6*d.*; and in Ireland 8*s.* 11*d.* Let them take off one-fourth of the duty and see what the effect would be upon the respective countries. The relief in England would be 1*s.* 1*d.* per head, in Ireland 2*s.* 3*d.*, and in Scotland 5*s.* 1*d.* He hoped the Irish and Scotch Members would clearly understand that the rule laid down with respect to malt must be adopted in the case of spirits, and that before they voted against the Motion for reducing the malt tax they would weigh well the effect of the principle when applied to spirits. The statistics of the question possessed almost a mournful importance. To what cause must be ascribed the enormous consumption of spirits in Scotland and Ireland; partly, undoubtedly, to a damp climate ; partly to bad habits of drinking handed down from father to son ; partly to the prevalence of illicit distillation in former times; but also partly to our vicious legislation. Our oppressive malt tax caused an enormous amount of whisky-drinking in both Scotland and Ireland. And here he would venture to tell the House a Scotch story. Some years ago there lived in Edinburgh a certain individual whose only fault was that he was too much addicted to the drinking of whisky-toddy. In fact, he was drinking himself to death, and his friends remonstrated with him. He thereupon took a partial pledge of temperance, and joined the Total Abstinence from

Spirits Society. For two years all went on well; but in the third he began drinking whisky and water more than ever. On being accused of his backsliding, this person said, "I own I have broken the pledge, but my only excuse is that I am a very poor man, and cannot afford it. The Total Abstinence from Spirits is too much for me, as I cannot get drunk under 6s. a day." The argument applied equally to beer. The malt tax so increased the price of beer that the people of Ireland and Scotland drank spirits because they could not afford ale. The case of the producer was a very simple one. He agreed with the Chancellor of the Exchequer that the best barley had the monopoly of the market; but the second rate barley was shut out—not the sort that would be used by the hon. Member for Derby or Mr. Allsopp, but still a sort that might be used for a respectable sort of beer. And how did the impost work? The malt tax was practically an increase of the expenses of the farmer. He paid so much a year to his ploughman, and gave him his lodging, food, and drink. The drink consisted of beer, and the price of beer was increased by the malt tax. In thrashings and harvests it was the custom to give a labourer beer as part of his wages. On his own farm, instead of giving beer, he gave the labourer 3d. a day, but if beer cost 2d. and not 3d. a quart, he would give the smaller sum and save the difference. Thanking the House for the kind way in which they had heard him, he would very briefly state the reasons why he gave his cordial support to this Motion. He supported it on the grounds of justice and common sense. The consumer of sugar had been the favoured child of legislation, and the consumption of sugar had doubled in amount; but it was not right, under the present system of free trade, to place this tax on farmers for the purposes of revenue. He supported the Motion because he regarded it as the beginning of a new system, and as an earnest that if we remained at peace and the country was flourishing, the tax would be got rid of altogether; he supported it because he thought that the agricultural interest had a right to have at last a share in the reduction of taxation; and finally, he supported it because he believed that the removal of this tax would be beneficial to all classes of Her Majesty's subjects.

SIR EDWARD DERING said, that the hon. Member for Sussex, and those who followed him in the debate, had dis-

cussed this subject so ably and so fully in all its details, that it was not only unnecessary, but almost a difficulty to adduce fresh arguments in addition to those which they had already pressed on the consideration of the House; still, as large agricultural constituencies, such as that which he represented, felt most warmly on the subject, he would avail himself of this opportunity to make a few observations, and would endeavour to avoid the ground which had been already trodden. It was, he thought, much to be regretted, that so important a question as the reduction of the malt duty should be presented to them in a form which made it impossible that they could arrive at a satisfactory conclusion. He did not mean to convey that it was possible, by the adoption of any particular form of words, to have achieved a parliamentary success this year, but he contended that the advocates for the reduction of the malt tax were placed in a most disadvantageous position in having to encounter the united opposition of those who objected on financial grounds, as well as of those who opposed it as the representatives of the sugar interest. The disadvantage would be felt thus—many hon. Members, of which he was one, were ready to record their opinion that the malt duty was oppressive, that it was as injurious to the comforts of the poorer classes as to the interests of agriculture; that it was against the first principles of free trade; and that it was most desirable to remove it at the earliest opportunity—but again, there were many hon. Members, representatives of large towns, who would have gladly voted in favour of an abstract Resolution to that effect, and yet who felt unwilling to vote on the direct issue raised by this Motion of malt *versus* sugar. He alluded to this, because, as he foresaw that they should be in a minority, he hoped neither the House or the country would suppose that the Members who would go into the lobby would comprise all those who were in favour of the reduction of the malt duty. Some remarks had been made on the instability of abstract Resolutions. If this had come from the Chancellor of the Exchequer, it would have been intelligible, but he was surprised to find it in the mouth of the advocates of the repeal of the duty. The experience of the last few years was all in favour of abstract Resolutions. He would point to the Resolutions on the paper duty, and the duty on Fire Insurances as the best evidence, that no Chancellor of the Exchequer, however gifted or powerful, could long venture to ignore the recorded opinion of that House. As it had been with these other subjects, so it would be with malt. If the people were in earnest on this subject—if this question was not taken up merely for party purposes, to be dropped as soon as they were answered, if, he repeated, the people persevered in pressing this upon their representatives, and their representatives upon Parliament, he cared not from what section of the House the Ministers of the Crown were taken, it would be totally and entirely impossible for them to turn a deaf ear to the remonstrances of the representatives of the people. He should vote with the hon. and gallant Member, but he should have gone into the same lobby with much greater satisfaction, if the question had been raised on its own intrinsic merits, instead of being brought forward in direct antagonism to the great sugar consuming mass of the community.

Mr. BEACH said, that the opponents of the malt tax claimed that a fair issue should be raised, and that a definite decision should be come to, and he thought that the Motion of the hon. and gallant Member for West Sussex raised that issue and challenged the decision in no inconvenient manner. In the present day when unrestricted competition was the law of the country, and our agriculturists had to compete with all the world, it was difficult to justify the retention of an oppressive tax like that on their produce. It was only by the application of an unprecedented amount of skill, energy, and capital, that the British farmer was able at all to hold his ground against his foreign rival; but even now wheat was being poured into the country in such profusion that it could scarcely be cultivated here at a remunerative price. In such a state of things was it not monstrous that barley, the second product of the soil, in which Englishmen were supposed to excel the cultivators of every other country, should be subject to such a heavy impost? Five quarters of barley was a very moderate quantity to be grown on an acre of land; and yet on that quantity no less than £5 10s. was imposed by the State, or probably about five times the amount of rent per acre which the tenant paid to his landlord. The repeal of the tax, it was said, would only relieve the cultivators of light soils, because heavy soils would not produce barley successfully. That he thought was an error, for the reason why heavy soils would not produce barley successfully was that, in land of that description, it did not vegetate with sufficient rapidity to conform with the Excise regulations. Some asserted that the repeal of the malt tax would do no good to the producer, others that it would do no good to the consumer. To whom, then, would it do good? He believed that the truth lay between two extremes, and that the repeal would benefit both the producer and the consumer. It was alleged that the tax could not be got rid of, because it yielded so large a revenue. That was a feeble argument, because if the tax was unjust, means ought to be taken to lessen its amount as soon as possible, and then they might see their way more clearly to its ultimate extinction. The Chancellor of the Exchequer stated the other night that they could not look for an increased consumption of malt from a reduction of the duty. That assertion required him to enter into a few statistics. That tax was imposed at a memorable epoch — namely, .1697. The scale was first fixed at 6¼d. per bushel, and remained at that rate for about sixty years. Now what was the rate of consumption under those duties. Under the low scale of duty the average consumption from 1700 and 1710 was 23,672,504 bushels ; and in 1759 it had increased to 28,090,254 bushels. But the population only increased from 5,475,000 in the year 1700 to 6,467,000 in 1750. Thus in 1750 there was an increase of over four million bushels of malt, although there was only an increase of a million of population. It was an increasing revenue even at that time. But in 1760, during the Seven Years' War, it was found necessary to raise the duty to 9¼d. Indeed it seemed that Financial Ministers had generally looked to an increase of the malt tax in times of war and difficulty ; but, unfortunately, when peace was restored, the Finance Minister of the day usually had forgotten to reduce it again. The scale which was raised to 9¼d. in 1760, was again raised in 1780, during the American war, to 1s. 4¼d., and the consumption increased from 28,090,252 bushels in 1759 to only 29,432,584 in 1802 ; although the population had increased from 6,467,000 to 8,892,536. That was surely a proof that during the last century an increase in the rate of duty made a vast difference in the consumption of malt. But coming to the

Sir Edward Dering

period of the great war, he found that the duty was raised in 1802 to 2*s.* 5*d.*; in 1803 to 4*s.* 5½*d.*; in 1816 it was reduced to 2*s.* 5*d.*; in 1823 it was raised to 2*s.* 7*d.*; and in 1840, 5 per cent was added, making the duty 2*s.* 8⅜*d.* Under those fluctuations the consumption increased from 29,432,584 bushels in 1802 to 34,638,214 bushels in 1851. The increase of consumption was trifling during that time, considering that the population had nearly doubled, being in 1801, 8,892,536, and in 1851, 17,922,768. But the Chancellor of the Exchequer told them that the beer duty had been repealed without being followed by much increase in the consumption of malt. That might be true if they took a long series of years for their calculation; but if they took a short period, the reverse was the case. During 1812 the consumption of malt actually fell to 18,092,965 bushels. In 1829, the year before the beer duty was repealed, the consumption was 23,428,135 bushels; and in 1830 the consumption was 26,900,902 bushels. Immediately after the beer duty was repealed, it increased in 1831 to 32,963,470. Surely an immediate increase of 6,000,000 bushels was no unsatisfactory result. The increased consumption of malt certainly did not recoup the loss occasioned by the reduction of the beer tax, which was in the nature of an adventitious addition to its amount; but this was only another proof how oppressive in itself the malt tax was, and no expedient they could adopt would increase the consumption of malt, except the repeal or reduction of the tax. The hon. Member for London (Mr. Crawford) had asked the hon Member for Lincolnshire (Mr. Banks Stanhope), what was the consumption per head of sugar as compared with that of malt. He had seen it stated in a recent Return that the consumption of sugar per head in England was 36lb. The duty might fairly be taken at 13*s.* per cwt.; so that the amount of tax which each consumer of sugar paid was 4*s.* 4*d.*; but taking the average consumption of malt to be about two bushels per head, the proportion of tax paid by every consumer was 5*s.* 6*d.*, or about 1*s.* 2*d.* more than the tax on sugar. This was an important element in the consideration of the relative claims of these two taxes to reduction. During the last few years they had repealed other taxes of more or less amount, and no doubt they had given great relief to certain classes of the community. But what had they done for the poorer consumers? The repeal of the tax on foreign wines was exclusively for the benefit of the higher classes. The tax on tea, no doubt, was distributed equally over the community. The tax on paper also was abolished. He would have preferred to the repeal of those duties the reduction of the malt tax, whose gigantic proportions would then have become "small by degrees and beautifully less." He could only say that in the interest of all classes of the community, producers and consumers, he should cordially support the Motion of the hon. Member for West Sussex.

MR. ALCOCK said, he remembered that when in 1833 Sir William Ingilby brought forward a Motion to repeal one-half of the malt tax, and carried it by a majority of 10 in a House of 314, Lord Althorp came down next day, and stated that if the House did not reconsider the Resolution, he should be obliged to propose a property tax of £10,000,000 or £11,000,000, and he persuaded them to rescind the vote. He contended that the Government of that day had committed a breach of faith with the country; they had never done anything to repeal the malt tax, and a subsequent Government did impose a property tax. The Government was bound to carry out the vote of the House—repealing the malt duty—or they ought never to have proposed a property tax. Not that he was an enemy to the property tax; it was only fair and right that they should have a certain amount of direct taxation; but what he should have liked was, that the Chancellor of the Exchequer should have put on 2*d.* additional, making the income tax 9*d.* in the pound, which, with his present surplus, would have enabled him entirely to repeal the malt duty. Instead of this, he had made a perfectly ridiculous proposition, which could only bamboozle the country—he allowed farmers to malt barley for feeding cattle, provided they mixed it with linseed. He did not believe that any farmer in the country would thank him for it; while the right hon. Gentleman, no doubt, calculated that he would be enabled to retain his malt tax of £6,000,000 for the next ten or twenty years. He would retain it till the country compelled him to give it up; and there had not been that amount of movement and remonstrance against it which would secure its repeal. He should, at all events, vote for this Motion, and should on every occasion vote for the repeal of the malt tax, whatever party or Government might be in power.

LORD ROBERT MONTAGU would detain the attention of the House for a few moments only. He wished to say a few words, chiefly in answer to the remarks which fell from the hon. Member for Oldham (Mr. Cobbett), and to explain the vote which he intended to give upon the present occasion. He, in the first place, disputed the hon. Member's statistics. The hon. Member had stated, somewhat rashly it seemed, that if the malt tax were repealed, beer would be reduced to half its present price. The hon. Member had given the House no grounds for such a belief; he had not favoured them with the calculations by which he had arrived at such a result. He (Lord Robert Montagu) thought he could give sufficient reasons for not accepting such a statement without strict investigation. He had read in the *Economist*, a paper which was always accepted as an undoubted authority on such matters, that the total value of beer annually consumed in England and Wales, amounted to £60,000,000. The malt tax amounted to £6,000,000, or one-tenth of the price of the beer and ale consumed. Taking the labourer's pot of beer at 3*d.*, the amount of tax which he paid was about one farthing. This was, however, an erroneous calculation; it was far too favourable to the case of those who desired the repeal of the malt tax. That calculation was made on the assumption that all the malt in the kingdom was used for brewing beer. Yet fully one-half, he supposed, was employed in the distillation of spirits. If so, the proportion of malt tax paid by the labourer in the price of a pot of beer, was about one-eighth of a penny. But even this calculation was too favourable to the malt tax repealers, for it proceeded on the assumption that the whole of the reduction would go to the consumer. Yet, one-half of it, he supposed, would go in profits to the retailer of beer. This reduces the amount of malt tax contained in the price of a pot of beer to one-sixteenth of a penny. This, therefore, represented the utmost reduction which could take place if the malt tax were totally repealed. If the labourer drank a gallon of beer daily, he would hardly save one farthing. The hon. Member for Oldham had used an *ad misericordiam* argument in favour of the reduction of the malt tax. He had spoken eloquently of

Mr. Alcock

the poor labourer's toil and sweat, of his low condition, and hard work. There were others, however, besides the labourer, whom the House had to consider. The labourer might enjoy his beer, and it might be very good for him, but he had a wife and children, who could enjoy far more their tea and sugar, which would be better for them. The Chancellor of the Exchequer had considered the benefit and happiness of the greater number, and had taken off the war taxes on tea and sugar. Then the hon. Member said that if the malt tax were repealed, the poor man would brew his own beer, and drink it at home. Now he (Lord Robert Montagu) could not see how the repeal of the malt tax would enable the poor man to brew his beer at home. The maltster and brewer have large capital, they have every convenience and appliance, and are able to malt and brew a large quantity at a time. The poor man has none of these advantages; perhaps not even a room to brew in. Any way, if the malt tax were repealed, the superiority of advantage in favour of large maltsters and brewers would remain exactly where it was now, and the poor man would labour under the same disadvantages. But would the poor man even drink his beer at home? Not at all. The poor man liked company as well as those who resorted nightly to gilded saloons. He sought the society of his fellows. Would he drink his beer at home, with perhaps a scolding wife by his side, and squalling babies around him? or would he still go to the public-house, to be surrounded by jovial fellows, to be supplied with daily papers, clay pipes, a blazing fire, political discussions, and every comfort that could serve to attract him? Hon. Gentlemen had appealed to the principles of free trade to forward their cause. He heartily congratulated those hon. Members on their conversion. Yet he thought that their conversion, though it might be from interest, was certainly not from knowledge. One of the principles of free trade was to reduce a tax wherever the consumption would thereby be so increased that the revenue would be recouped. But if this tax were reduced by half, would the revenue be recouped by an increased consumption? Did hon. Members suppose that England and Wales could drink £120,000,000 worth of beer in a year? Another principle of free trade was, that if a tax were oppressive, so that the consumption was dwindling away year by year—so that trade laboured heavily and gradually declined, then the tax should be at once reduced, because it shackled trade. But was that the case with the malt tax? Not at all; for the consumption had every year been increasing. Free trade principles had not, therefore, in this case, been applied with knowledge. The hon. Member for Lincolnshire (Mr. B. Stanhope) had said that more malt had not been annually consumed since 1841. He (Lord Robert Montagu), in the first place, denied that statement. The malt tax was an increasing tax. They had, moreover, to take other matters also into consideration. Malt is used only for the manufacture of drinks. But the nation now enjoyed many other drinks besides beer. The taxes had been taken off light wines, tea, and coffee, and the use of all these drinks had largely increased. Now, it is impossible to drink more than a certain amount; and therefore, when men drink more claret, tea, or coffee, they require less beer. This argument, therefore, did not carry much weight. But the hon. Member had said that if the tax were repealed there would be an increase in the consumption of malt. Now, malt is made from barley. But where is the increased amount of barley to come from? Where will that barley be grown? Barley was now grown only on light soils, which were unsuitable to wheat. Would the hon. Member desire to supplant the wheat on heavy soils, or to plough up pasture lands to grow barley? Truly those hon. Members were free traders! It was supposed that they were against all importation of corn from foreign countries; but it appears that they would rob the British farmer by importing barley from abroad! The hon. Member had also said that the repeal of the malt tax would lessen the consumption of spirits, and had then continued in this strain, "Look at the moral effect of repealing the tax; you will diminish the consumption of spirits." He (Lord R. Montagu) ventured to prophesy that the effect would be the very opposite. Every one knows that it is impossible to malt secretly. Malting requires much room, and many appliances to effect the process. It can be smelt across the road. In a county, the exciseman who knows how much has been malted, can follow the malt to its destination. But if it were allowed to malt free of tax, any one could then malt without the interference or knowledge of the exciseman. He could then take his two bushels of malt up a moun-

tain, or behind a wall, or into a garden, and distil his gallon of spirits. For it was very easy to distil without being detected. Therefore, if they repealed the malt tax, they would degrade the people by inducing them to distil spirits illicitly; they would also favour the consumption of ardent spirits. This, of course, would also diminish the consumption of beer. The hon. Member had also said that if the tax were reduced the number of excisemen would also be reduced, and that the revenue would thereby be saved. But if they reduced the tax, how could they get rid of a single exciseman? If they were even to repeal the tax altogether, how many excisemen could be knocked off the civil list? How many could be spared? Very few; for they had numerous other duties to perform. This was, however, a question which only the Chancellor of the Exchequer could well answer. He was not against the repeal of the malt tax if he saw his way to it. He would have pleasure in voting for the Motion of the hon. Member for the North Riding (Mr. Morritt), for as soon as the indirect taxation could again be reduced, the malt tax would have a first claim upon their attention. It was an odious tax, and they must seize upon the earliest available opportunity for reducing it. There was, however, one thing which he greatly disliked, and that was this — that because there was an agitation got up among the constituents upon this subject, they should come down to the House and say, "Oh, repeal the tax!" although they said all the time in private that they knew very well it could not be done. They who acted thus were deceiving their constituents. They were sent there by their constituents to investigate the details of every case, to look after the real interests of their constituents, and to tell their constituents what was possible and what was not. But they should not help to delude their constituents, or fan the flames of an interested agitation. Hon. Members knew how an agitation was always got up. It was a regular science, which was learned as practitioners learned the medical science. It was carried on by a regular set of professional people in London. These persons got up petitions, which were all drawn up in the same language. Meetings were held all over the country. At these meetings statements were made, which there was no one there to expose; and arguments were used, which there was no one to refute. Thus any pretended facts which were put forward were believed by the "bucolic mind." It was dishonest and dishonourable to foster such an agitation, when they knew that the malt tax could not now be taken off, and when they felt that it would be more beneficial to their constituents to repeal the war tax upon sugar. He would take the bolder, more honest course, and trust to the support of honest Englishmen. He knew his constituents to be straightforward, bold, and candid men. They would not think the worse of him for taking a true and honest part.

MR. POLLARD-URQUHART said, he regretted that a rivalry should have been raised between sugar and malt. He admitted that the malt tax was injurious to agriculture; but sugar had peculiar claims on their consideration, and it would almost be a breach of faith to the sugar producers not to attend to them. In consequence of the emancipation measure of 1834, and of the free trade measures of 1845 and 1847, the British sugar grower had had great difficulties to contend with. His own opinion was that the sugar duties had the first claim upon Parliament with a view to their reduction, and especially so as almost every producing interest, except the West India interest, had recovered from the injury suffered during the transition from protection to free trade; and he also thought that hon. Gentlemen who were in favour of repealing the malt duty would very much facilitate the acquirement of their object by supporting the Government proposition, and thus getting out of the way of the superior claims of the sugar duties. If the Motion of the hon. Member for the North Riding (Mr. Morritt) had been brought forward, he should have supported it, for he thought that, from the instances of the advertisement duty, the paper duties and other taxes that had been repealed, the passing of an abstract Resolution of the House at the proper time, would lead to the repeal of the malt duty; but, anxious as he was to see the malt tax repealed, he could not on the present occasion vote for the Motion of the hon. and gallant Colonel.

COLONEL NORTH said, he should not have risen, but he could not avoid noticing the language of the noble Lord the Member for Huntingdonshire (Lord Robert Montagu), who had thought it right to call in question the motives, feelings, and honour of men as honourable as himself.

LORD ROBERT MONTAGU said, that he did not mean to call in question the motives of the hon. and gallant Gentleman, nor those of the mover of the Resolution; he had only stated what were his own motives.

COLONEL NORTH said, he did not know what the noble Lord meant, but he certainly seemed to convey the notion that hon. Members who supported the Resolution were hounded on by their constituents, that they were driven like a flock of sheep to vote against the malt tax. As far as he was himself concerned, that was not the case. His constituents did think that they had a right to ask for a reduction of this tax; but their feeling was that if the financial state of the country was such as to allow of any reduction of taxation, the malt duty had the first claim to consideration. They were quiet, orderly people, not prone to agitation, and were willing to bear just taxation; but when they had seen such taxes as the paper duties and wine duties repealed or reduced, they felt that a tax affecting the drink of the working classes deserved the attention of the House. The noble Lord was quite mistaken in the remarks he had made. He could not understand how it was that the noble Lord, himself a county Member, could turn round upon a body of Gentlemen who represented the largest constituencies in the country, and especially upon a question in which the noble Lord's own constituents had a deep interest.

MR. PUGH said, that he should always be glad to be able to vote for a reduction, or even repeal, of the malt duty; but he could not do so on the present occasion, because it was put in competition with others which certainly did press with some severity upon the poorer classes. He must say, however, that he felt certain the time would come when it would present strong claims for consideration. It was the boast of the late Sir Robert Peel, after he had succeeded in repealing the Corn Laws, that the working man would eat his bread no longer leavened with the sense of injustice, and so it might be said that the repeal of the malt duty would enable the working man to drink his beer unembittered by a similar feeling. When the repeal of the malt duty was discussed in 1833, one of the arguments used by the leading opponents of that measure—Lord Althorp and Lord John Russell—was that if the malt duty were repealed it would be necessary to impose an income tax. Some years after that an income tax was imposed, and since then a vast amount of money had been derived from that source. The agriculturists, therefore, naturally felt that the time was come either for the repeal of the malt duty or a reduction of the income tax. For his own part, he must confess he was in favour of a properly graduated income tax, which would enable the State to tax stores of wealth which otherwise could not be reached. In the debates on the malt tax in 1833, to which he had already alluded, Sir William Ingilby, who proposed the repeal, expressed an opinion in favour of an income tax, saying that one advantage of an income tax was that by means of it you were able to reach some rich men, who otherwise would contribute but little to the purposes of the State; and he gave an instance of one who had died worth £800,000, but who could not be said to have added much to the public funds by the payment of taxes, as he kept only an old woman and a tom cat. Of course it would be useless to ask for a reduction of taxation unless the money could be spared; but if we should happily remain at peace, if we steadily maintained the ties of amity with the great and gallant nation across the water, if the beneficent provisions of the Treaty of Commerce, one of the most admirable measures ever adopted, were allowed fairly to operate, and if a prudent retrenchment were exercised, he was convinced that before long we might reduce not only the malt tax but the income tax to an inappreciable amount. He, as intending at some future time to support the reduction or repeal of the malt tax, thanked the hon. and gallant Member who had brought forward this Motion for the opportunity which he had thus afforded for the expression of opinion upon the subject; but he (Mr. Pugh) thought that if the hon. and gallant Member could do so consistently with his duty, he would do well to retreat from his position on the present occasion, so that he might in a short time again advance with a better prospect of success.

MR. WESTERN said, that being connected with an agricultural county, he desired to state his reason why he could not support this Motion. He could not do so because this Motion for the reduction of the malt duty was made in professed opposition to the proposal of the Chancellor of the Exchequer for the reduction of the sugar duties. Nearly every Member of the county with which he was connected (Essex) and the county adjacent was favourable to the repeal of the malt tax. He felt that they were masters of agriculture, and the farmers certainly would rather see the malt tax reduced than any other. He must add that he desired the repeal of the malt tax as much as any one, so soon as the state of the revenue would permit of doing so; and he trusted that the Government would be able to make such further reductions in the expenditure as would enable the Chancellor of the Exchequer to repeal the tax altogether in a very short time. He was, however, convinced that the present proposal for reducing the malt duty one-fourth would be of no benefit to the agricultural interest, though that interest might be greatly benefited by the total repeal; and he thought, moreover, that the hon. and gallant Member had done considerable damage to his cause by pitting malt against sugar. If he had brought it forward as a substantive Motion, many hon. Members would have voted for it who now felt bound to oppose it.

VISCOUNT INGESTRE said, he could not agree with the noble Lord the Member for Huntingdonshire (Lord Robert Montagu), that it was either dishonest or dishonourable on the part of any Member of that House to advocate the claims of his constituents. In the county which he had the honour to represent (Staffordshire), a very large meeting of landowners and tenant farmers had been held, at which resolutions were unanimously agreed to in favour of the entire repeal of the malt tax. He admitted that he was not aware of the strong feeling that existed in regard to the malt duty, and when he received an invitation to attend the meeting, he wrote to say that £5,000,000 was a large sum for any Chancellor of the Exchequer to give up, but that he was ready to support any measure for lessening a burden that pressed so heavily on the agricultural interest. However, when he heard the Chancellor of the Exchequer dilate on the elasticity of the public revenue, with a surplus of £2,500,000, and hold out the hope that, if the country prospered in the same degree, Parliament would have an increasing surplus to deal with, he could not help thinking that the right hon. Gentleman had passed over the repeal of the malt duty rather too lightly; because, in the counties of England interested in the growing of barley, the matter was one of very great importance. The right hon. Gentleman seemed to imply that the question was being used as a means of political agitation, and he alluded to the recent election for Hertfordshire. Now, in his county, the matter had been taken up by landlords and tenant farmers without regard to political feeling, and simply as a great agricultural question. The farmers held that it would only be carrying out the principle of free trade fairly to repeal the malt tax, and they called upon the Chancellor of the Exchequer to relieve them from that burden, even if he substituted something else in its place. He believed that the right hon. Gentleman was misinformed in asserting that the repeal of the malt tax had had anything to do with the result of the late election for Hertfordshire, for, as he understood, both candidates were in favour of a repeal of the tax. The cause of Mr. Cowper's defeat, he was informed, was, that when he stood for Tamworth he was in favour of the abolition of church rates; but that when he came forward for Hertfordshire he could not make up his mind as to what he wished to be done. One great advantage of taking off the malt tax would be that the working classes would get better beer —that would be a great benefit, for, at present, the rule was that in the agricultural villages you could not get a glass of beer that was worth drinking. He liked a glass of beer himself; but if a traveller pulled up in a country village, a good glass of beer, as a rule, was not to be got. If the malt tax were taken off, the poor man would have a chance of brewing his beer at home, and he need not go to the public-house. A great cause of crime was drink, and especially the drinking of ardent spirits. As a member of the grand jury, he had observed that most cases of assault were committed under the influence of ardent spirits; and he did not doubt that spirits were consumed because the beer was so bad, and so much adulterated, that the poor man took to what was more pleasant and more potent. He should cordially support the Motion of his hon. and gallant Friend.

SIR BROOK BRIDGES said, he would hardly have risen to address the House but for the extraordinary description of an agricultural constituency which had been given by the noble Lord the Member for Huntingdonshire, and to congratulate him on the peculiar character of the constituency with which he was connected. It

was quite new to him (Sir Brook Bridges) to hear that an agricultural constituency could be driven to do that which in their conscience they disapproved of, and he entirely repudiated the description of the noble Lord. As to the merits of the general question, he thought that there were two considerations which were very strong in favour of a remission of the duty. In the first place, it pressed heavily upon one particular class of agricultural produce; and he believed that inferior barley would be put in a very much better position if the duty were less. The second consideration was, that it was upon what was peculiarly the beverage of the working man that so large an amount of taxation was levied. He thought that there was just as much ground for the remission of this duty as there had been for others which were now taken off, and that the farmers had a right, upon the modern principles of free trade, to demand the repeal of the malt duty. He felt sure that they must all be deeply indebted to the hon. and gallant Member for West Sussex for having brought forward his Motion, and he should certainly, as far as he was concerned, give it his cordial support.

SIR FRANCIS CROSSLEY said, that he had already on a previous occasion ventured to express his opinion that the malt tax caused no injury to the agricultural interest. The right hon. Gentleman the Member for Oxfordshire (Mr. Henley), in admitting that it was a consumer's question, maintained, also, that it was one affecting the producer, and retorted upon him by asking how the manufacturers would like a duty placed upon their produce? That question was very easily answered. In this country the extent of land was limited, and was not enough to produce sufficient barley for our home consumption, so that not only could we not export, but we were compelled to supply our own wants by importation from abroad. If barley had formed one of our exportable products, the argument, he admitted, would have been a powerful one. The tax would certainly weigh rather heavily upon that portion of the agricultural community who paid for their work partly in money and partly in beer; but he ventured to say that the chief portion of the revenue resulting from the duty was contributed not by the agricultural, but by the manufacturing districts. The hon. Gentleman the Member for Oldham (Mr. Cobbett) had said that the price of beer was doubled by the malt duty, because malt was worth twice as much as barley. If malt could make itself into beer without the aid of manual labour and without the combination of hops, the statement of the hon. Member would be correct. But malt was only one particular article employed in the manufacture of beer, and a difference in price consequently could not be affected to so great an extent. The hon. Gentleman also said a great deal about beer being a necessary of life. Now he distinctly denied the assertion. He had himself been for twelve years, though not of late, a total abstainer; and there were in the employment of the firm with which he was connected some hundreds if not a thousand persons who were total abstainers from intoxicating liquors, and those men did as much or more work than those who drunk beer. To say that beer was a necessary of life to a working man was all moonshine. He denied also that there was any necessity for agricultural labourers to use beer during harvest time, for the use of beer rather tended to excite than to quench thirst; while with tea and coffee the men would be much better able to get through their work. In answer to the argument of the hon. Member for Oldham, who had instanced some cases in which it was believed that death had resulted from the non-employment of beer, it was certain that for one death which occurred in that way at least ten would be attributable to excessive drinking.

MR. PACKE said, he was glad to see the hon. Baronet who had just spoken looking so well, but he echoed the sentiment of the hon. and learned Member for Oldham (Mr. Cobbett) when he said that it was impossible to get in the harvest in hot weather, and when men were worked very hard, without a certain quantity of beer to renew their wasted energies. Doubtless, some persons abstained from malt liquor and thrived very well upon it; but the labouring man who worked from early in the morning till late at night, especially in harvest time, could not get on without the stimulus of such a drink. He thought the agricultural classes had a fair right to ask that a portion of the surplus revenue which the Chancellor of the Exchequer intended to apply to the lowering of the sugar duties, should be applied to lowering the duty on malt; but whenever there was to be a

remission of taxation the farmers went to the wall; and the right hon. Gentleman dealt with some taxes in which they were in no way concerned. He should give his cordial support to the Motion of the hon. and gallant Member for West Sussex.

MR. DU CANE said, that as one of the representatives of an agricultural constituency greatly interested in the question before the House—an interest in which he fully sympathized—he desired to offer his thanks to the hon. and gallant Member for West Sussex for the very able, temperate, and judicious manner in which he had raised the issue before the House. He had no wish in the abstract to dispute the principle on which the Budget was based — the same apparently which the Chancellor of the Exchequer enunciated three years ago when he said that he looked upon the direct and indirect taxation as two fair sisters to whom in his official capacity he was privileged to pay an equal amount of attention. He supposed there was no one who would object in the abstract to the remission of the 1*d*. off the income tax, to such moderate benefits as might be gained from the proposed reduction of the Fire Insurance duty, or to the doubtful cheapening of sugar resulting from the reduction of duties upon that commodity. But the principles of justice and fair play ought to guide the House in all impositions or remissions of taxation; and, in spite of the elaborate self-laudation of his own policy by the right hon. Gentleman when introducing his financial scheme, he believed those principles had not been carried out in the present instance, and that, if carried out, the claims of those affected by the reduction of the duty on sugar would have been found subservient to the large claims of those affected by the reduction of the malt tax. It had been urged by various speakers, and by the right hon. Gentleman himself, that the duty on sugar, being a war tax, had therefore a priority of claim. That principle had been altogether broken through when the paper duty was taken off, in preference to reducing the duty on tea and sugar. But, going back to the early history of the malt tax, what was it, he wished to know, but a war tax? It was originally imposed, and again increased, for the purposes of war long before Mr. Pitt ever called the income tax into existence, and something like a century before the exigencies of the Crimean War required the sugar duties to be raised. Surely, then, if the principle were to obtain that war taxes were the first to be removed, the malt tax claimed priority. He would go further, and say that there never was a tax which, after the lapse of 100 years, bore on its face such marks of its early origin, or exhibited more strongly the peculiar oppressiveness of all taxes imposed in stormy times. In spite of the enormous increase in our population, and the corresponding development of the resources of the country, and in spite of the relief given to the brewers by the abolition of the beer duty, the consumption of malt per head had enormously diminished, and the manufacture of malt was at this moment entirely stationary. Admitting that for the last few years the statistics had been rather more favourable, it must be remembered that these were times, upon the whole, of great national prosperity, and that the barley harvest for last year was one of the most remarkable, if not the most remarkable of any during the past half century. But in spite of all these considerations the fact remained that the consumption of malt had enormously diminished out of all proportion to the population of the country. He did not attribute this altogether to the operation of the malt tax—a more general use of tea and coffee no doubt had its share in bringing about this anomalous state of things; but, in the main, he agreed with the opinion expressed by no mean authority on all matters of taxation, Mr. M'Culloch. In commenting on what he calls this "anomalous" result, he observes—

"There cannot be a question that it is mainly owing to the exorbitant duties with which malt and the ale and beer manufactured from it have been loaded, and the oppressive regulations imposed on the manufacture of malt and the sale of beer."

As a war tax good grounds, therefore, existed for saying that the malt duty had a paramount claim to consideration, and as far as the necessaries of the people were concerned, the farmers of England had an ample right to assert the prior claim of the malt tax to reduction over the sugar duties. But, in his mind, there was another and a stronger argument in favour of their claims. At the time of the greatest financial and commercial excitement which the country ever witnessed the sugar duties were entirely reduced and remodelled, while the malt duties were left wholly untouched. Language was held at that period by the free trade leaders which, in his mind, was

Mr. Du Cane

tantamount to a direct pledge, that if the farmers would consent to a repeal of the Corn Laws the repeal of the malt tax would follow as a matter of course. But long before the free trade era it was over and over again asserted that if the Corn Laws were repealed the malt duty should be also abolished. In 1831 a Royal Commission was appointed to inquire into the Excise laws. Sir Henry Parnell, who was chairman of that Commission, expressed the opinion that so long as the Corn Laws remained untouched the malt tax would also remain untouched, because otherwise the effect would be to produce a great monopoly in the barley trade; and he added, that if ever the Corn Laws were repealed, then, as a matter of necessity, the malt tax should be reduced at least one-half. Now, perhaps Sir Henry Parnell, when uttering that language, never contemplated the establishment of the free trade principle in this country. But as that great financial change drew nigh that great statesman's opinions were reiterated by the most zealous and distinguished free traders. The right hon. Gentleman the Member for Wolverhampton (Mr. C. P. Villiers), who might be considered the great originator of that change, asked—

"Would the landed interest be willing, if the malt tax was taken off, to release the country from the tax of the Corn Laws; for of this he was sure, that all those were now injured by the existence of the monopoly, which he might term the community at large, would be ready, nay, be anxious, to get rid of it."

The late Sir Robert Peel, who afterwards carried the great measure of Corn Law repeal, said—

"Repeal the Corn Laws, and you must allow the agriculturist to grow his own tobacco and to grow and manufacture his own malt."

That was strong enough; but the language used by Sir James Graham was still stronger—

"It enhanced the price of beer; this enhanced price of beer diminished the demand for it, and the diminished demand caused a smaller quantity of barley to be cultivated, and the lessened price of barley was, *pro tanto*, a tax on the barley land or as Adam Smith, he believed, said, it had the same effect as if the barley land had been stricken with barrenness. If the Corn Laws were repealed, not a single year would elapse before the malt tax would also be repealed."

The hon. Member for Rochdale (Mr. Cobden) who would, he hoped, express his opinions on this question to-night, in a speech delivered to his constituents in the West Riding in 1849, said—

"We sympathise with the farmers. We never will tolerate one shilling duty on corn; but we will co-operate with them in getting rid of that obnoxious tax, the malt duty. We owe the farmers something, and we will endeavour to repay them in kind."

These were the opinions held by almost every distinguished free trade leader; and such language, coming from men of such eminence, must, he contended, be regarded as tantamount almost to a pledge to the farmers and consumers of this country— a pledge almost as binding as if this House had passed a formal Resolution that, after the Corn Laws were repealed, the repeal of the malt tax should follow. If at that time the farmers of England, instead of giving themselves up to a most gallant and prolonged, but to what at this interval must be admitted to be a most hopeless struggle for protection—if they had devoted one-tenth of the energy which they had bestowed upon that question to an endeavour to obtain the repeal of the malt tax, that tax would long ago have been numbered with the past. Grasping at the shadow, however, they lost the substance. When his right hon. Friend the Member for Buckinghamshire came into office in 1852, acting upon the previously experienced opinion of all the free trade leaders, proposed to remit half the malt duty, how was he met? He was told that the hour of compromise was past, and the very statesmen who had lured the farmers on by holding out this bait of a promise of their support in the reduction of the malt duty, were the first to turn round in a body and resist his proposal. From that moment to the present the question of malt tax repeal had been kept in abeyance. The nation had passed through times of war and of war expenditure, but now that it had happily arrived at days of reduced expenditure and prosperity budgets the language he had quoted amply justified the farmers in renewing their claims for a reduction of the duty. The hon. Baronet who had just spoken (Sir Francis Crossley) said that the malt tax was paid entirely by the consumer, and that the farmers had very little to do with the question. But if, as he had shown, during more than 100 years the effect of this tax had been to check consumption and restrict the cultivation of the raw material, the hon. Baronet must admit that there was no good *primâ facie* ground for saying that, although this tax was paid directly by the consumer, indirectly it was a tax which came out of the

pockets of the producer. The Chancellor of the Exchequer laid great stress on the argument that the price of the best barley had been slowly increasing since the repeal of the Corn Laws, and said that the farmers could not expect a remission of the tax in the face of that fact. But this fact, to his mind, furnished the strongest argument that could be urged in favour of the remission. He was ready to admit that the repeal or reduction of this tax was not demanded by growers of the best barley. They, as a class, if not altogether hostile, were at least indifferent to repeal or reduction. But the growers of the best barley, after all, were only a very limited portion of the agricultural community. Those who asked for a repeal of the malt tax were the growers of inferior barley, who complained with great justice, that while on the one hand great monopoly was caused in effect by the present Excise law, and the best barleys were maintained at an artificial price, there was no demand for barley of inferior quality, which was a complete drug in the market. This inferior barley might, it was true, be converted by the farmers into a wholesome and sound beverage for their labourers, or it might be used as a condiment for their cattle; but by the Excise laws they were not allowed to use it at all for the first of these purposes, and they were only at liberty to use it for the second under such restrictions as, in the opinion of all practical men, amounted to virtual prohibition. This, however, was not the only injustice. The right hon. Gentleman said that the average price of barley was higher now than when the Corn Laws were repealed. But that average was altogether fictitious. It was based on the finest samples of barley, inferior samples being almost entirely excluded from the calculation. Hence resulted this great injustice—that while inferior barley was worth no more than from 20s. to 25s. a quarter, the farmer was bound to pay tithes or a corn rent, if he were unfortunate enough to hold a farm on a corn rent, at the full average of the best barley, from 33s. to 34s. a quarter. Well, then, what was the position of the farmers at the present moment with regard to the foreigner? A drawback was allowed in respect of the duty and cost of collection upon all malt and beer exported from this country. Now the quantity of malt exported last year was about 65,000 quarters, and during the same period 470,000 barrels of beer were exported, the declared value of both being about, £1,600,000. He believed that he was not overstating the case when he said that the value of the drawback upon the malt and beer thus exported amounted to at least £500,000 ; so that while, on the one hand, the home produce were fettered with a duty which rendered consumption almost stationary, the foreigner was not only allowed to receive our malt duty free, and feed his cattle abroad with it, but he was also allowed to enter our markets duty free, and to undersell the farmers here with cattle fed on English barley. Thus under this system the foreigner received, as it were, a present of £500,000, which was wrung from the pockets of the British farmer and the home consumer. This anomaly and injustice was in existence seventeen years after free trade, so called, had become law, and was justified by the Chancellor of the Exchequer, who the other night detained the House for two hours while he dilated on the wisdom and justice of this free-trade policy. He would not, however, rest the case solely upon the benefit which the reduction of the malt tax would confer upon the farmer. Great as that benefit would be, it would be nothing compared with that which would result to the consumer, and especially to the whole mass of the labouring classes. There was a time when every British labourer had his barrel of home-brewed beer in his own cottage. About the year 1839 a labourer named James Kershaw, then ninety-one years of age, was examined before the Poor Law Committee, and was asked whether he remembered the condition of the labourer during the earlier period of his life ? The old man answered yes ; and stated that when he was married he could buy a bushel of malt for half-a-crown, and every poor person had a barrel of beer to drink, instead of water ; but the price soon rose to 3s. 6d. In reply to further questions, he stated that at that time, as a general rule, all labouring men brewed ; that they had left it off ever since the tax raised the price of malt so high that they could not afford to buy it ; and that when he was examined no poor man brewed his own beer. That was, that instead of each man having a cask of home-brewed, they were driven to purchase the adulterated and poisonous stuff which was generally sold in the village beershop. Did the House know what sort of poisonous decoction it

Mr. Du Cane

was that was retailed to the working classes under the name of beer, in the vast mass of the beershops throughout the country and in London—in the country districts especially ? A few days ago a constituent of his, a member of the Council of the Royal Agricultural Society—Mr. Fisher Hobbs—made a tour through his neighbourhood, and by way of practical experiment collected thirteen or fourteen samples of beer from different beer shops. These he brought to London, and submitted them to a celebrated analytical chymist. Professor Voëlcker for analysis. The Professor having analyzed them, stated that one-half of them were extensively drugged with deleterious substances, intended to produce either unnatural thirst or premature intoxication, while the other half could not be dignified with the name of beer, being merely a sort of malt washings mixed up with a large quantity of molasses. That was the case in the country districts. What was the sort of beer generally sold by the smaller publicans in London ? Dr. Letheby, the medical officer of health for the City of London, stated .that there could not be a doubt that adulteration of beer extensively prevailed in the metropolis. "The chief ingredients," he said,

" Are a saccharine body—as foots and liquorice, to sweeten it ; a bitter principle—as gentian, quassia, sumach, and terra japonica—to give astringency ; a thickening material."

And this he should, had he been in the House, have commended especially to the notice of the Chancellor as illustrative of the probable operation of the Malt for Animals Bill—

" As linseed, to give body ; a colouring matter, as burnt sugar, to darken it ; cocculus indicus, to give a false strength ; and common salt, capsicum, copperas, and Dantzic spruce to produce a head ; as well as to impart certain refinements of flavour."

And he added the statement that the loss to the revenue in consequence of these adulterations amounted in London alone to nearly £100,000 per annum. And what price did the labouring classes pay for this villanous decoction ? He believed that he was under rather than overstating the case when he said that on every quarter of barley converted into malt 126 per cent was charged before it reached the labouring man in the form of beer. Of this, 66 per cent was attributable to the duty, and the remainder represented the respective profits of the maltster, brewer, and publican. · There might be some who would say that the reduction of the malt tax would extend the consumption of beer and increase drunkenness. That was, to some extent, the objection of the hon. Baronet the Member for the West Riding (Sir F. Crossley), who said that for one man to whom beer did good ten died of it; and after the facts which he (Mr. Du Cane) had stated, he did not wonder at it. But his answer to that argument was, get rid of the malt tax, and you will knock the country beer-shop nuisance on the head, and give a greater stimulus to sobriety and morality among the labouring classes than will be accomplished by years of compulsory liquor laws, or any amount of agricultural meetings, speeches from waggons, and rewards to farm labourers. He had, during the present Session, presented at least 100 petitions in favour of the repeal of the malt tax, and it was a most significant fact, almost all those petitions had been signed, in most instances they had been headed, by the signature of the clergyman of the parish. The ground on which these gentlemen signed was, that they believed the beershop nuisance to be the cause of at least nine-tenths of the crime, drunkenness, and immorality among the working classes, and the great difficulty which they had to contend with in any movement which they made for their advancement. So much for the case of the labouring classes. He would next say a word upon what he might call the Chancellor of the Exchequer's "separate nationality" argument. The right hon. Gentleman told the Committee that England was the only country really concerned in the repeal of the malt tax; and, of course, he expected that the Scotch and Irish Members would unite to oppose any Resolution moved with that object. It might be true that the repeal of the malt tax would benefit England more than Ireland and Scotland; but why, when he gave those statistics, did not the right hon. Gentleman explain the incidence of taxation generally on the three countries? Why did he not tell the Committee to what extent England relieved Ireland and Scotland of spirit duties, and in what proportion, as compared with those countries, she contributed to the Income Tax and Customs duties? The right hon. Gentleman based his estimate of the amount which each of the three countries contributed to the malt tax speciously, but unfairly, upon the quantity of malt actually manufactured in each of the three countries; but he never said a word of the quantity of malt and beer which was exported from England to both Ireland and Scotland. He believed that there was a large exportation of malt to Ireland, for the purposes of brewing and distilling, and in Scotland there was hardly a small village in which that excellent beverage brewed by the hon. Member for Derby and other English brewers was not to be found in great abundance. The argument of the right hon. Gentleman went to the effect that all the malt manufactured in England was consumed in England. But to estimate the amount contributed by each of the three countries to the malt tax, upon the amount of malt actually manufactured in each of them, was as absurd as to suppose that all the coals of Northumberland and calicoes of Lancashire were consumed within the precincts of those two counties. He could not help thinking that it would be rather dangerous for the Irish and Scotch Members to adopt and act upon this "separate nationality" doctrine. The malt tax was described as solely an English grievance; but had the House never heard of grievances which were solely Irish or Scotch? He had repeatedly, at the request of Scotch or Irish friends, remained in the House till some unheard of hours, to vote on questions which were of no interest personally to him, but which were considered of the most vital consequence to the Gentlemen from those kingdoms; and acting on the principle of doing to others what we would have done to ourselves, he had often waited in that House to a weary hour in the morning, for the purpose of performing the service asked of him. But if this separate nationality doctrine was to be acted upon, and in two or three years there should arise an Irish or Scotch question, such as the reduction of the spirit duties, for instance, hon. Members who represented English agricultural constituencies, when appealed to for aid, would be apt to say, "No; remember how you treated us in the case of the malt tax. Our constituents don't drink whisky, and we will leave you to fight your own battle with the Chancellor of the Exchequer." Would then the Scotch and Irish Members expose themselves to such a retaliation, by refusing to assist their English brethren on this question, and say, "It's no affair of ours; our constituents don't drink beer; their beverage is whisky." Such a course

would be equally ungenerous and dangerous. The right hon. Gentleman, in describing the demand as one for the entire
repeal of the malt tax, had altogether
misrepresented the appeal which they
were making. None of them in that
House, and he believed no Member in the
country, had raised the question of the
immediate repeal of the whole of the malt
tax, though, no doubt, the meaning of the
movement was to bring about an extinction
of the impost. All they wanted to do
was to put the malt tax on the same footing as other taxes, and to have in this case
the benefit of such reductions as the Chancellor of the Exchequer could spare from
his surplus, until the happy day arrived
when the entire Excise charge upon malt
should be abolished. He was not so sanguine as to believe, that if one-half the
tax was taken off to-morrow the revenue
would immediately recover it; but the
consumption would keep *pari passu* with
the reduction, and the past history of the
tax was no exception to that remarkable
vigour and elasticity which the Chancellor
of the Exchequer delighted in the other
night as distinguishing the other branches
of the revenue; but he thought it was
utterly impossible for any one who looked
attentively at the past history of the malt
tax, from its first imposition, in the year
1697, up to the present time, to avoid
coming to the conclusion that in proportion as the duty had been increased the
manufacture and consumption of malt
had diminished, and in proportion as the
duty had been lowered the manufacture
and consumption had been increased. If
they went into individual years they
would find, first of all, that in 1750 the
duty on malt was only 6*d.* a bushel, and
the consumption was 29,284,000 bushels, or at the rate of five bushels per
head. In 1781 the duty rose to 1*s.* 4*d.* a
bushel, when, notwithstanding a thirty
years' increase of population, the amount
manufactured fell short of that manufactured in 1750 by 3,000,000 bushels.
In 1803, the duty was 2*s.* 5*d.* a bushel,
and the amount which paid duty was
29,562,000 bushels. In that year the
duty was raised to 4*s.* 5¼*d.* a bushel—the
highest, he believed, it had ever reached—
and the consumption sank next year to
22,000,000 bushels, being a decrease of
7,000,000 bushels in a single year. In
1818, the duty had again dropped to 2*s.* 5*d.*,
and the consumption rose to 24,700,000;
but in 1819, the duty was again raised to

Mr. Du Cane

3*s.* 7¼*d.* a bushel, and the quantity then
fell to only 22,600,000 bushels. They
came next to the year 1840. In that
year the duty was at 2*s.* 7*d.* a bushel, and
the consumption was 36,652,000 bushels;
but 5 per cent was then added to the tax,
and the effect was that in 1842 the
consumption had dropped to 30,790,000
bushels. It recovered slowly during the
next ten years; but in 1852 it was only
35,000,000 bushels, or, with a twelve
years' increase of population, actually less
than it had been in 1840. And lastly—
and that perhaps was the greatest case
in point—in the year 1854, when the
Crimean war broke out, the duty was
raised from 2*s.* 7*d.* to 4*s.* per bushel, when
consumption dropped from 36,245,847
bushels in 1853 to 31,869,000 bushels in
1854, and in spite of the large increase
of duty the amount of revenue remained
nearly stationary. Now let the House
glance for a moment at the other side of
the picture, and see what the effect had
been of reduction of the duty on consumption. In 1821 the duty was reduced from
3*s.* 7*d.* a bushel to 2*s.* 7*d.*, and the consumption gradually and steadily increased,
till in 1830 it had increased some 6,000,000
bushels; and on the beer duty being taken
off, another steady increase of 5,000,000
bushels took place in the next seven years.
And finally, in 1856, the year when peace
with Russia was concluded, the duty was
reduced from 4*s.* to 2*s.* 7*d.*, when the consumption immediately increased by nearly
4,500,000 bushels, and the amount of
revenue literally exceeded that of the
previous year of high duty by no less
than £100,000. He was unfeignedly glad
that his hon. and gallant Friend had put
this issue to-night, once for all, fully and
fairly before the House. If they really
wished to produce any effect in respect of
the reduction or the repeal of the malt
tax, there was no use in going on holding
county meetings, and waiting on the right
hon. Gentleman the Chancellor of the
Exchequer with exceedingly numerous
deputations to receive exceedingly cautious
and diplomatic replies, or in inundating
the House with petitions. If they wanted
to produce any effect on the right hon.
Gentleman, they must — as they were
doing that night—submit their proposition
fairly to the House, and take the sense of
the House fairly upon it. If they could
judge by the expression of opinion in the
country, and by what had been said in
that House a few weeks ago, when the

Malt for Cattle Bill was before them, and what had been said in the course of the present discussion, his hon. and gallant Friend ought to be successful; but whether he was successful or not they would have effected this great good—they would have shown that there were men in the House and in the country, however small their number might be, who were thoroughly in earnest on this question, and who did not advocate it merely for the sake of a party division, or as an election war-cry, but because they conscientiously believed that the reduction would be not only fair and just, but most beneficial to all classes of the community.

MR. COBDEN: Sir, I listened to the speech of my hon. and gallant Friend—and I may say my representative—who opened this debate with great pleasure. He brought forward his Motion with much ability, and I have not a word to say in opposition to the views he advocates. But as an experienced agitator, I must be allowed to tell him that he has erred grievously in the mode in which he has introduced this subject for the first time formally to the House. There is no rule more deserving the attention of any one who takes charge of a question in this House than this—that he should never allow it to jostle or to become entangled with another question, good in itself, but with which it has no necessary connection. The mode in which this Motion is introduced into the House is such as absolutely to preclude a fair division upon its merits; because my hon. and gallant Friend asks the House to consider not merely the merits of the malt tax, but the merits of another tax which he proposes to remove out of the way in order that the malt tax may occupy its place. With regard to the sugar duty, looking at the matter only as a question for the consumer—although I am not going to deal with the malt tax solely in the light of a consumer's tax—I confess I should infinitely prefer abolishing the sugar duty to abolishing the malt tax. Perhaps there is no tax — after the tax upon bread—upon which there may be so much said to justify total repeal as the duty on sugar. We live in a country where we have not so much of the sun's rays as more southern climes are favoured with. We know that it is the solar heat which bestows sugar upon the earth, and the consequence is that our fruits want the flavour which in other and more genial climes they possess. We require, therefore, more sugar as an admixture to our food. Again, the people of this country are large consumers of tea. We are denied the wine which they have in France and other countries, and the people consequently drink tea in larger quantities than any other in Europe. That consumption of tea implies the necessity of the consumption of sugar. Then, again, sugar appeals to the sympathies of all — not merely to the working man, for whose benefit alone, in seeking for a reduction of the malt tax, our sympathies are invoked, but to his wife and children—not merely to the man in health, but to the invalid and to helpless infancy. I am very sorry, therefore, that this question, which is most important in itself, and excites so much interest, has been injudiciously complicated with another question, so as to deprive us of a fair vote upon its merits. In dealing with the malt tax, I said I would not regard it solely as a consumer's question. Standing here as an advocate of free trade, and having applied free trade principles with so much rigour to the farmer and the landowner, whom I will not separate in this matter, I am fairly bound to admit that, if they come before this House and state that the operation of the malt tax is such as to impede the processes of scientific husbandry and to interfere with the most desirable rotation of crops—that if they establish the truth of that upon the judgment of practical farmers—this is a question that affects the interests of the producer as well as the interests of the consumer. I am bound to say that we have never lost sight of the producer in the great changes which we have been effecting in our fiscal system during the last twenty years. We all know that Sir Robert Peel began his commercial reforms, which have been followed up to the present day, by laying down and acting upon the maxim that it was necessary, before exposing the manufacturers of this country to competition with the manufacturers of the rest of the world, to relieve them in every possible way from all disadvantages in the supply of their raw material and in the processes of manufacture. I was surprised that the hon. Baronet the Member for the West Riding (Sir F. Crossley), in his speech, rather lost sight of this principle, which we have always claimed in the interests of the manufacturer. He said, that as the farmers of this country did not produce sufficient barley for its consumption they were not entitled to the removal of the difficulty and impediment which the malt tax imposed upon them. I consider that the fact that they do not produce enough of barley for this country is no argument why they should not have the full application of the economical fiscal system which we have been carrying out for the last twenty years. We admit the foreigner to free competition with them; the foreigner may not have this malt tax to interfere with his husbandry; and therefore I repeat it is no sufficient answer to say that the landowners and farmers of this country do not produce the full quantity of barley necessary for the consumption of the people. The question really is:— What is the force and validity of the plea put forward by the producer? I have inquired of the most intelligent farmers with whom I am acquainted, and I will mention one because he lives in a county which has lately been the theatre of a great contest turning upon this question. I have had the great pleasure and advantage of being acquainted with Mr. Latimore, one of the best farmers in Hertfordshire, for more than twenty-two years. He stood by my side at the commencement of the movement for free trade in corn, and much to his credit and greatly in proof of his enlightenment, was always an advocate of that principle. Mr. Latimore is now one of the most ardent advocates of the removal of the malt tax; and, as one to whom I owe more than to any one for the information I acquired with reference to agriculture and its bearing upon free trade, I cannot but regard with the greatest respect the evidence he offers me upon the subject. Mr. Latimore has stated publicly —and I believe he has stated to the Chancellor of the Exchequer and the Prime Minister—that the operation of the malt tax tends to interfere with the proper and judicious rotation of crops. Some soils are not so well suited as others for the growth of barley. Thus, taking Norfolk, where the soil is of a superior character for the growth of barley, and then taking those districts where the soil is not peculiarly suited for that kind of grain, and where the crop is of an inferior quality, you cannot sell that inferior barley for malting purposes, because the duty being the same upon barley of high quality as of low quality, it acts as a prohibitory duty in the sale of inferior grain for malt. Besides that, Mr. Latimore tells me that he finds malt a necessary article for the consumption of stock, particularly lambs and

Mr. Cobden

sheep, at particular seasons. I have visited his farm, and I have seen his lambs at Easter season feeding upon malt dust brought from Ware. He was at that time paying, weight for weight, as much for his malt dust as he was selling his wheat for; and he tells me that he has been obliged to abandon the purchase of this malt dust, because it was so dear that he could no longer use it. I take the evidence of such men to be conclusive in the matter. The farmers stand, in my opinion, precisely in the same position with regard to barley, from which the malt is made, as they did with regard to hops before the hop duty was repealed. We all know that in Kent a very superior quality of hops is grown, and that in Sussex the quality is inferior. The duty being the same in both cases, its effect was to operate most oppressively upon the inferior quality of hops grown in Sussex. It was, in fact, a protective duty upon the superior hops grown in Kent; and it was on that ground that the hop-growers raised an agitation for the repeal of the duty. It was not an agitation in which the consumers were the movers. The movement originated exclusively with the hop-growers of Sussex, because they wanted to escape from the severe disadvantage under which they were labouring in consequence of the duties pressing upon them so heavily. Such is the position in which the farmer is now placed, and it appears to me that he has good grounds to come here and to ask that the trade in malt should be made free, as a complement to those free trade measures and that economical policy which has been enforced in every other direction during the last twenty years. It may be said that there has been a measure proposed for the purpose of enabling malt to be manufactured for the consumption of cattle. Well, I believe it is generally understood that that device will be a failure. I believe the farmers attach very little importance to it. But, independently of regarding the question merely as a consumer's question, I maintain that it would be a great relief to the very poorest part of the community if the malt tax could be abolished. I say the very poorest part of the community, because I think the consumption of beer, probably more than of any other article, belongs to the very poorest of our labourers —I now speak of the male labourers more than any other. I am of this opinion, because all of us who are acquainted with rural life know that, if they could, the agricultural labourers of this country would all enjoy the beverage of beer. With their limited wages, and with the general habit of agricultural labourers to be married men, I think there is very small danger of these men ever carrying the indulgence too far. But, depend upon it, it would contribute very much to the contentment of that class, and to make them less dissatisfied when comparing their lot with that of the rest of the community, if instead of being obliged to resort to the brook or the spring for their beverage they could enjoy some share of the produce of the land on which they are employed in the shape of a draught of beer. I am not one myself who attaches very much importance to the beverage which men may take. I think more depends upon what they eat than upon what they drink. But I would like to lay down this as a rule in dealing with this question and with all other questions—that we do not sit here to legislate with the view of passing sumptuary laws either with respect to drink, or meat, or clothing. We do not pretend by our fiscal regulations to make men moral, and I think it is quite out of place to introduce the subject at all in discussions like the present. I should say that it would be a disadvantageous argument, in treating this question, to contend that by repealing the malt tax you would necessarily have a very much larger individual consumption of beer. If I, instead of my hon. and gallant Friend, were dealing with this question, I would never put the case upon that argument. It does not follow if you take the duty off malt that the present beer drinkers will increase their consumption of beer. You may have many mouths drinking beer that now cannot get it at all, and you may have those who now drink beer consuming the same quantity at a very much less expense. Hon. Gentlemen will find a passage in Adam Smith upon this very subject. He says in a passage which is well worthy of consideration, speaking as an advocate of the repeal of the malt tax, just as he would have advocated a repeal of the Corn Law, that it does not follow that because intoxicating drinks are cheap therefore the people in the country where they are cheap should be necessarily intemperate; and he mentions the fact, that in those countries where wine is cheap there the population is generally the most sober. And he states as a fact, that though the regiments in France that had been brought from the northern provinces into the southern portion of the

country were found at first to indulge their appetites to some excess, yet that familiarity with the cheap wines of the South speedily produced an effect rather sober than otherwise. Now, who are the sober people amongst us at the present moment? Why, doubtless, the great progress in sobriety in this country during the last thirty or forty years has been precisely amongst those classes who have had in abundance the means of intoxication always at their hands. My hon. Friend here (Mr. Lawson), who, I believe, wishes, with strictly benevolent views, to put temptation out of the working man's way by the regulation of the number of public-houses, would not pretend to say that he would deprive any one of the fullest opportunities of indulging in his wine or his beer in his own house. I therefore think it would be wrong to assume that necessarily there would be a greatly increased consumption of beer arising out of a change in this law. I tell you what would happen if you abolished the malt tax. I have no doubt there would be a great consumption of other excisable and duty-paying articles. If beer were cheaper the families of working men would consume more tea, sugar, tobacco, and other things that pay duty. Therefore, it is quite possible that you might have a very large increase in your revenue, arising from these other sources, without necessarily implying any large increase in the consumption of intoxicating liquor. Well, we now come to consider the question of the financial difficulty of this great problem. I assume that whatever is proposed to be done would be done with the view of the ultimate abolition of this tax. I do not say that any Chancellor of the Exchequer would be likely to propose to do this in any one year; but if I were dealing with this question out of the House, I should look to total repeal, and nothing less, as my ultimate object. Now where is the difficulty in the way of accomplishing this? I exhort my hon. and gallant Friend opposite not to think of ever putting on a substitute in the form of another tax in the place of this. Let him depend upon it that this House will never put on any other tax as a substitute for the malt tax. How, then, are you to meet this case? Well, in the first place, if you abolished this tax, you would not lose that amount of revenue, because there would be a decided increase from other sources. In the next place, you do not intend to abolish it all in one year—

that is certain. Well, then, I maintain you must all steadily look to a reduction of our expenditure. I consider that we have been running riot in our extravagance. For the first five years after I entered this House, when Sir Robert Peel was at the head of affairs, we spent £20,000,000 a year less than the average of the last five years. Will anybody pretend to tell me there is not a margin for saving and economy in that? This Parliament has been unparalleled in its extravagance. Names have been given to different Parliaments. One was called " the Long Parliament," another was called " the Unlearned Parliament," and this ought to be called for ever " the Prodigal Parliament." Well, then, you have an opportunity for economy, in watching stringently your expenditure, and you have the natural growth of revenue which comes from reduction of taxation; and if you remain at peace you will have the growth arising from the elasticity and buoyancy of your finances which leaves you every year with a surplus of two or three millions. All this leads me to conclude, that if hon. Gentlemen opposite are in earnest about this matter they may ultimately accomplish what they have now in hand. What I should recommend to my hon. and gallant Friend is, that he should not take the opinion of the House on this Motion. If he does, I should be in the same predicament as three or four other Gentlemen who have spoken, who, while favourable to the Motion, tell us that they shall be obliged to vote against it, inasmuch as it has been put in antagonism with the reduction on sugar. I should hope that my hon. and gallant Friend will withdraw the Motion, having the advantages of the discussion, which is all that he can hope for at this moment, bearing in mind, too, that these are questions which are not carried in a Session. One or two Gentlemen have spoken of free trade in corn as if it were carried straight off; but I know, to my cost, that that question took us seven years of weary labour. You have now only just begun. You have only to press this question as a producer's question in addition to the interests of the consumer, and with that perseverance which I think will characterize hon. Gentlemen opposite, when they are once roused to a question, and they are sure soon to accomplish their object, to the great benefit not only of that part of the community which they represent, but also to the

Mr. Cobden

satisfaction of all classes of the community.

MR. BARROW said, he thanked the hon. Member for Rochdale for the eloquent speech he had made in condemnation of the malt duty, and for the plain manner in which he had shown that some time or other the malt tax must be abolished. It was only a question with the hon. Gentleman whether they should make the remission now or not. He (Mr. Barrow) was unwilling that they should neglect any opportunity of making a beginning. He had presented petitions signed by 7,000 or 8,000 persons, the greater portion of them householders, in favour of the abolition of the tax. The farmers in his county unanimously supported the abolition, and they were actuated as much by a consideration for the benefit of their labourers as of themselves. He had taken no part in the agitation which had been got up on the subject, but he entirely concurred in the opinions expressed by the petitioners, that the existence of this tax was a serious evil for the consumer as well as the producer.

MR. MILNER GIBSON said, it appeared to him not to be very clear what was the precise proposal now submitted to the House; whether it was intended to take an opportunity that night to express generally the views of the House on the malt tax question, or whether it was intended to raise some definite issue as to the precise reduction which the House should agree to in the malt tax, and whether such reduction was to take the place of the proposed reduction of the sugar duties. The Resolution was exceedingly vague and indefinite, and the speeches of hon. Gentlemen who supported it had not made it very intelligible. The hon. Mover of the Resolution stated that what he meant by postponing the repeal of the duty on sugar, and dealing with the duty on malt, was that we ought now to reduce the duty on malt one half.

COLONEL BARTTELOT: What I stated was, and I thought I stated it distinctly, that I wished to reduce the duty on malt to the extent of the reduction of the duty on sugar proposed by the Chancellor of the Exchequer.

MR. MILNER GIBSON: Then he had not caught the exact proposition of the hon. and gallant Gentleman, but he was clear that some other hon. Gentleman had proposed to reduce the duty by one quarter. He (Mr. Milner Gibson) was not particularly friendly to the malt tax or to any other tax, nor was he altogether disposed to condemn the eliciting an expression of opinion by the medium of a Resolution. But he did say this, that when they were asked to pass by a proposition of relief to the consumers of sugar in this country which had been submitted by the Chancellor of the Exchequer—a proposition capable of being carried into effect with the surplus at the disposal of the Chancellor of the Exchequer—the House ought not lightly to agree to such a proposition, without considering whether they could, with the means at hand, deal with the malt tax in the way proposed by hon. Gentlemen opposite. What was the amount which his right hon. Friend the Chancellor of the Exchequer had to dispose of? He understood that hon. Gentlemen opposite meant to accept the proposed reduction of 1*d*. in the pound on the Income Tax—that this was to be retained; he understood they were to retain other taxes proposed to be reduced; but that they refused to accept the reduction in the duty on sugar, and proposed to substitute a reduction of one quarter of the present malt tax. He found, however, that the loss on the proposed reduction in the duty on sugar, according to the statement of the Chancellor of the Exchequer, was £1,300,000.

THE CHANCELLOR OF THE EXCHEQUER: £1,330,000.

MR. MILNER GIBSON: He had made a calculation, and he found that the reduction of one quarter of the malt tax would occasion a loss in the present financial year, after providing for the payment of drawbacks, of no less than £1,880,000; and this calculation was made after allowing for an increase of 10 per cent on the consumption of malt arising from the reduction of duty. The question, then, was—how were they going to pay £1,880,000 with £1,330,000? The only argument that could be adduced in favour of the malt tax, according to the hon. and gallant Mover, was that it produced a great revenue—as if taxes were put on for any other purpose than that of producing revenue. There could not be a stronger argument in favour of a tax than that it yielded a very large return. He admitted the evils of an Excise duty, although he had been informed by competent authority that the regulations of the Excise did not materially—perhaps not at all—interfere with the malting of barley. And, whatever might be said concerning competition with the foreigner, it must be borne in mind that there was a

duty on the importation of foreign malt more than sufficient to countervail the Excise duty and to meet the disadvantage to the maltsters arising from their having to malt under Excise regulations. When the right hon. Gentleman the Member for Buckinghamshire attempted to deal with the malt tax in 1852, he laid down the proposition that it was idle to deal with it in a small way. The right hon. Gentleman was then of opinion that it was not worth while to make any reduction less than one-half, "because, recollect, you are going to retain your Excise system and the principal evils that belong to this tax, very much as they are, giving by a small reduction an inappreciable advantage to the consumer." The right hon. Gentleman laid down a doctrine with reference to malt which he (Mr. Milner Gibson) thought was perfectly sound, and he thought it ought to guide the House at the present moment—that the House ought not to deal with the malt tax until they were in a position, in reference to revenue and surplus, to be able to give an appreciable benefit to the consumer and to the farmer, if benefit were to be derived by dealing with this tax. If, said the right hon. Gentleman, we deal with the malt tax in a small manner, the House will probably accomplish none of those objects to which he had alluded; the consumer would not be benefited—there would neither be cheap beer, nor would there be freer cultivation of the land of the country. Seeing, then, the position in which they were placed, he asked the House, was it reasonable to reject the advantageous proposition as to sugar for the purpose of giving a reduction in malt, which the right hon. Gentleman the Member for Buckinghamshire stated in 1852 would neither benefit the consumer nor the farmer? What would be the reduction in a quart of beer if the malt tax were altogether repealed? He believed that it would not exceed a halfpenny a quart in the average beer, taking the quantity of malt used in the manufacture of beer. He believed a farthing a pint would be about the amount of the relief. To make the reduction now proposed we must lose a large revenue—no less than £1,880,000 —and the relief to the consumer would only be a quarter of a farthing on a pint of beer. He asserted, then, that the trifling advantage to the consumer would be purchased at too great a sacrifice of the revenue. When we considered the taxation upon malt, and its effect upon the price of beer, which was said to have caused the consumption of malt to stand still for some years past, there was another matter worthy of consideration. He had been told that one reason why malt was not now so extensively consumed, measuring the consumption per head of the population, was that a description of beer had come into use of late years in which was introduced a smaller quantity of malt. The fashionable and popular beers of the day, he believed, did not contain so large a proportion of malt as the old English beer of former days; not that it was thought the worse for that circumstance, but, in point of fact, the taste was somewhat altered, and what was called pale or bitter beer, he was told, did not contain so large a proportion of malt as beer contained in former times. If he were wrong he hoped his hon. Friend the Member for Derby (Mr. Bass) would correct him. He would like to call attention to the taxation on beer, through the malt tax, in comparison with the taxation on food arising from the imposition of Customs and Excise duties. He found the percentage of duty on the market value of coffee from Ceylon to be 33 per cent; upon tea from China, 83 per cent; upon sugar, yellow muscovado, Cuba, and West India, 61¼ per cent; brown muscovado from Cuba and the West Indies, 59 per cent; and from the Brazils, 65 per cent. Upon wine from France, 22 per cent; from Portugal, 30 per cent; and from Spain, 29 per cent. But in the case of porter, allowing that two bushels of malt made 36 gallons, or 144 quarts of porter, and putting the porter at 4*d.* per quart, the duty was only 12½ per cent on that beverage. If, then, the duty on sugar ranged from 59 to 65 per cent on the value, and the duty on beer caused by the malt tax was only 12½ per cent— and probably on other kinds of beer it might rise to 15 per cent—he said it was a case of dealing with sugar before dealing with malt. He thought there were many duties upon the food and the beverages of the people of this country that ought to be considered before those on malt tax, because the malt tax was in itself so light an *ad valorem* tax on the article consumed compared with the tax on those articles of food and drink to which he had referred. Several hon. Gentlemen thought it was a great evil to have repealed the paper duty. Probably many hon. Gentlemen thought that if that duty had been retained there would have been a greater chance of get-

Mr. Milner Gibson

ting the duty off beer. He did not for an instant dispute the right of every hon. Gentleman to express freely his opinions on such questions, nor did he quarrel with those opinions; but he differed from them because he thought it was more desirable, by the repeal of the paper duty, to promote education and the diffusion of knowledge—more desirable by the repeal of the paper duty that this object should be accomplished rather than by a reduction of the duty on malt to cheapen an intoxicating drink like beer. He might be wrong. He did not say that the repeal of the malt tax would not in itself be a benefit. He distinctly said it would be a benefit. But it was not because he held an abstract opinion in favour of the abolition of the malt tax as beneficial in itself that he advocated caution in dealing with the revenue. Sugar was more extensively used than beer. It was used by a larger number of people, taking the whole population of the country, than beer. Sugar entered into the consumption of man, woman, and child, down to the merest infant; it entered into the consumption of every family, from the highest to the lowest, and of every age, both old and young. This could not be said of beer. But, further, he said it was a mistake to merely consider that sugar was consumed for domestic use. It was extensively used for distilling purposes; it was even extensively used in brewing, as well as for other manufacturing purposes. He ventured to say that there was no article in our tariff of greater commercial importance than the article of sugar. He hoped the House, under all these circumstances, would accept the proposal of the Chancellor of the Exchequer, seeing that there was no intention on the other side of the House to make any reduction in the expenditure which would enable the House to deal largely with the malt tax. ["Oh! oh!"] It was new to him to hear that hon. Gentlemen opposite were disposed to make such a reduction in the expenditure as would enable the Government to deal largely with the malt tax. Seeing that the House generally was inclined to support the reduction of the Income Tax, and that the surplus did not admit of any further dealing with taxation, he thought that common sense required something a little more definite and intelligible than a Motion for rejecting the proposals of the Government in order that the expediency of reducing the malt duty might be considered. The expediency of a reduction of the duty on malt was purely a question of revenue. We had not the means at present of dealing with the tax, even if there were not other taxes with preferable claims. Under these circumstances, he had no doubt that the House would support the proposals of the Chancellor of the Exchequer by a large majority.

MR. BASS said, he admitted that the hon. Member for Rochdale (Mr. Cobden) was a great logician, but if his logic had not failed that night logic was a matter of which he (Mr. Bass) knew nothing. The hon. Gentleman had argued that a reduction in the price of beer would not be followed by an increased consumption, though, at the same time, it would bring the article within the reach of those who could not afford it at present. Assuming, then, that those persons who could not get beer now would get it then, was the House to conclude that those who used it now would give it up because they could buy it so much cheaper? With regard to the Motion of the hon. and gallant Member for West Sussex, he (Mr. Bass) confessed that he took the same view as the right hon. Gentleman who had just sat down—that it was somewhat indefinite. No doubt the object of the hon. and gallant Member was either now or hereafter to repeal the malt tax; but his Resolution did not deal with the manner in which the malt tax should be reduced or repealed. He could not but think that the Resolution of which the hon. Member for the North Riding (Mr. Morritt) had given notice was better calculated to attain that object. Both the House and the country had adopted the Budget of the right hon. Gentleman. The organs of public opinion on every side not only approved of the reduction of the Income Tax, but they were unanimous in opinion that it was right to take off the war duties on sugar. Probably if he (Mr. Bass) had been asked before the right hon. Gentleman had declared his intentions, he would have preferred a reduction of the malt tax; but now he could only look to the future for that. With regard to a partial reduction of the malt tax, it would be impossible to accommodate the trade to a small reduction, nor would the benefit to the consumer be considerable. The right hon. Gentleman who had just sat down (Mr. Milner Gibson) was not altogether accurate in his estimate of the reduction in the price of beer by a repeal of the duty, because it should be observed that the trade obtained a profit on the duty they paid, as well as on the price of barley; and in the event of the reduction or repeal of the duty, competition would infallibly compel them not only to give up the duty, but the profit they at present obtained upon it. Many hon. Gentlemen opposite were in the habit of supporting the proposition of the hon. Member for Carlisle (Mr. Lawson) for reducing the number of public-houses; but he would ask what would be the use of taking off the duty on malt if at the same time they deprived the population of the means of getting beer. It was all very well for the hon. Member to go about saying that brewers were a mischievous class of persons who were not fit to sit in that House, because they manufactured a poison which destroyed the bodies and souls of men, but hon. Gentlemen opposite, while they cried out for a reduction of the malt duty, should not encourage him in his teetotal notions. He thought the right hon. Gentleman opposite (Mr. Disraeli) was quite right when in 1852 he declared that they could not take off less than one-half the malt tax at a time. They could not accommodate the rule of the trade to a smaller reduction. He would tell the right hon. Gentleman how he could facilitate the movement for a repeal if the Chancellor of the Exchequer should have another surplus of two or three millions, and that was not to date the repeal from the 1st of April, but from the 1st of October, because at the former date the duty would have to be taken off the stocks in hand, which would amount to probably one-half of the repeal beyond the actual amount repealed. On the 1st of October, however, the payment on stocks in hand would be a mere bagatelle. If the hon. and gallant Gentleman had framed his Motion that it would be expedient for the Chancellor of the Exchequer, on the first opportunity, to reduce the malt tax, he (Mr. Bass) would have gone heartily with him. With regard to the argument about the labourers and the humbler classes brewing their own beer, he was persuaded that was false. He had seen it recommended that they should brew in tea-kettles, as it was said was the case in America. Now, the man who brewed a couple of bushels could not do it so cheaply by 10 per cent as the man who brewed 50 bushels, and the man who brewed 50 bushels could not brew so cheaply as the man who brewed 500 bushels. It was, therefore, quite obvious that it was preposterous to expect that there would be a large amount of private brewing. Moreover, the bulk of the labouring population lived in towns. Now, the greater part of the profit of private brewing was derived from what were called the outcasts of brewing. It was of no use for a poor man to brew without he had a pig to take his grains, and he must bake his own bread in order to employ the yeast. These were conditions which would preclude the great bulk of the labouring classes from private brewing. On the whole, he could not support the Motion now before the House, but he most heartily agreed with the hon. Member for the North Riding (Mr. Morritt), that the malt tax should be dealt with at the first favourable opportunity.

MR. BENTINCK said, that although his right hon. Friend the President of the Board of Trade had spoken with his usual ability and eloquence, he thought he had been wanting in his usual discretion, for he touched upon two very dangerous subjects. The right hon. Gentleman had laid great stress upon the fact that a reduction of the duty on malt would not effect the reduction of a halfpenny a quart in the price of beer. Now, he (Mr. Bentinck) recollected the time when the right hon. Gentleman used to lay great stress on the enormous benefit that would accrue to the poor by a reduction of the duty on corn affecting the quartern loaf. He regretted that the right hon. Gentleman had forgotten the arguments he then used. The right hon. Gentleman had also touched on the dangerous subject of the paper duty. He would have done wisely not to have alluded to that subject, and still more wisely if he had not called attention to those remarkable arguments which were once used in the teeth and laughter of the House, that the repeal of the paper duty was necessary to increase the number of penny newspapers. The right hon. Gentleman had quoted various opinions, but he should have recollected that there was hardly a public man on either side of the House who could not be quoted both for and against any question. He (Mr. Bentinck) would not appeal to the House, because it appeared to be wild on the subject of sugar; but he would make an appeal to those Gentlemen who had at heart the agricultural interests, and he would ask them to look at this question as a matter of business. Agreeing with them

Mr. Bass

that there was no possible ground for a retention of the malt duty under a system of free trade, he would venture to suggest to them that no Member who had spoken up to that moment had fairly put before the House the difficulties which they had to contend with. In the first place, the advocates of a repeal of the malt tax must take care that if they succeeded they did not get the same amount of taxation reimposed in a worse shape. Let them also take care that they did not find themselves working hand in hand with those gentlemen who would substitute the principle of direct for indirect taxation. There was another difficulty that stared them in the face. He wished to deal frankly with the whole question. He believed that a partial repeal of the duties on malt would not benefit the rural districts—that they would do nothing if they did not take steps to procure their total repeal. He went farther, and contended that the total repeal under our present financial system was an utter impossibility. If they carried out free trade and repealed the duties on malt, the consequence would be national bankruptcy. They must look for a total repeal by a revision of our whole system of taxation. If the advocates of the abolition of this tax directed their efforts to a mere agitation in the counties for that purpose, he believed the result would be failure. They must do this:—There are many districts in England that had no interest in the malt duties because the soil was not capable of growing barley, but which, nevertheless, were laid under a large amount of onerous and unjust taxation. What he wanted to see was—not meetings in the various counties for the professed purpose of obtaining a reduction in the duty on malt, but every county in England banded together for the purpose of obtaining a repeal or modification of that unjust amount of taxation which now pressed upon the rural districts. If they carried out the question in that way he pledged himself to the success of the attempt. They had not only the advantage of numbers and property, and every possible facility which could be required for the agitation of a great question, but they had more—they had right and justice on their side; and he contended that they were not doing justice to those they represented in that House when they confined themselves to a mere attempt to repeal the duty on malt, and shut their eyes to the fact that there was a most unfair and onerous amount of taxation borne by the agricultural districts. The question must be fought out on the hustings ; it must be fought where the battle of reform was fought. The whole question of the repeal of the malt duties was involved in the question of the paper duties. So long as they had in the House of Commons men who were prepared for mere party purposes— for the mere purposes of a small faction who from a combination of circumstances were dominant—to tamper with the taxation of this country, so long would the great interests of the country be neglected. His test of the sincerity of any Government to do justice to the rural districts would be the making the re-enactment of the paper duties a part of their financial arrangement. [*A laugh.*] Hon. Gentlemen opposite were pleased to laugh. Let them wait a little, and let those laugh that win. The hon. Member for Rochdale (Mr. Cobden) had bestowed great praise on an informant of his resident in Hertfordshire; but the best thing the hon. Member could have done for his informant was not to have called attention to the information supplied in reference to the Corn Laws, because all the information of that sort which the hon. Member received prior to the repeal of the Corn Laws had been falsified by the result. The hon. Member for Rochdale was again at his old game : he was trying to create bad blood and dissension in the agricultural districts. He wanted to commence a renewal of that system of agitation of which he was so expert a professor for many years for objects of his own; but on this occasion the hon. Gentleman had let the cat out of the bag, by showing that his object was not to benefit the rural districts, but to renew the agitation in which he had in former years shown himself so expert a professor for a sweeping reduction of expenditure. He could, however, assure the hon. Member that nobody in the rural districts was disposed to sacrifice the honour of this country even for the sake of cheapening his beer. He counselled those hon. Gentlemen who moved in this matter to rely upon their resources, and not to expect help from either front bench in that House, because these matters of finance were made party questions for party purposes.

THE CHANCELLOR OF THE EXCHEQUER : Sir, the hon. Gentleman who has just sat down has made a speech which appears to me to be honourable to his candour and frankness ; but I confess that I feel some surprise that he should propose, as a practical proposition, that which he exacts as a first condition in the policy of any Government—that is, to receive his confidence and support—namely, that they shall found their whole financial system upon the re-imposition of the paper duty. It is not because I think there is the smallest probability of the adoption of such a measure in any part of this House that I refer to that portion of the hon. Member's speech, but I cannot help expressing my regret that, whatever may have been his opinion about the repeal of the paper duty, the hon. Gentleman, with so much acuteness and intelligence as he undoubtedly possesses, is insensible of the enormous advantage that has resulted from the establishment of a cheaper newspaper press in this country. I do not know — I may be right or I may be wrong — but my belief is—speaking not from antecedent expectations, but from experience—that few measures ever have been adopted in Parliament which have had a more powerful effect in attaching the lower part of the community to the laws and institutions of the country than the establishment of the cheap press, which has taken the labouring population out of the hands of a class of newspapers that formerly abounded, and were most exceptionable in their character—I mean many of the weekly and Sunday papers—and which has made that population from day to day partakers in every subject of public interest, and thereby in my opinion greatly raised their intelligence. Contenting myself with making that protest, I now address myself to the immediate subject before us. I will not attempt to enter into a full discussion of the arguments upon the malt tax, nor even into a full discussion of those arguments which have been touched to-night. But upon that matter I shall only venture to say two things. In the first place, I would really recommend hon. Gentlemen who are so ardent in their advocacy of the removal of the malt tax, to study that memorable statement which was put upon record by the late Sir Robert Peel in the year 1835. And I frankly own that I think the perusal of that speech, even at this time of day, after nearly thirty years, would very considerably tend to narrow the range of our debates on this question. The only other thing I shall say on this subject is that I venture to tender my thanks to the hon. Member for Derby (Mr. Bass), for the wise and practical opinion he has given us, that it is vain to look upon the repeal of the malt tax to encourage an extensive system of private brewing—what may be called kettle brewing—that will come into competition with the regular trade. I feel convinced that there never was an opinion expressed more founded on practical experience and common sense than the opinion given by my hon. Friend, that, whether there be a malt tax, or whether there be no malt tax, it is idle to expect a revival of that inferior and more wasteful system of production to come into competition with the scientific and economical operations of the large brewers. I wish to refer for a moment to an argument that has been noticed in this debate, because I was myself the cause of its introduction a few evenings ago. It has been treated as a matter which is very strange, that the subject of nationalities should be introduced into a discussion on the malt tax. I quite agree that it is only in a very extreme case that it is likely any such point should be urged; but I have not heard of any hon. Member from Scotland or from Ireland who has taken the view adopted by some hon. Gentlemen on the other side—namely, that the point is irrelevant to the present question. Why is it that we are happily enabled on almost every occasion to exclude the subject of nationality from our financial debates, and to forget that there is such a thing as separate nationalities in the three kingdoms? It is because of the general equity and justice with which our system of taxation bears upon the three kingdoms. And the moment that any doubt on that score is raised, such as we have seen expressed this year in the speech of the hon. and gallant Gentleman opposite (Colonel Dunne), the House admits that it is a fair subject for argument. I say with great submission, but with the utmost confidence, that this is a case in which it is impossible to move without taking some regard of the very glaringly different manner in which your measures would operate in the three kingdoms. You have got a system of taxation upon strong liquors. Those strong liquors, as far as the people are concerned, overlooking the insignificant quantity of wine consumed among them—and I admit that it is comparatively insignificant—those strong liquors are two—beer and ardent spirits. Ardent spirits are consumed in Scotland and in Ireland, partly neat and partly diluted, but to such an extent that we may almost ignore, as far as the people of those countries are concerned, the consumption of beer. Most of the beer now

The Chancellor of the Exchequer

consumed in Ireland, and I apprehend also in Scotland, is not consumed by the people, but by the wealthier classes. In England, on the contrary, you have the consumption of strong liquors by the people composed of two elements—beer and ardent spirits; but beer is by far the more important of the two. And, at the same time, it so happens that while you tax your beer to an extent which may be variously estimated at 12 or 15 or 20 per cent, you tax ardent spirits at the rate of between 300 and 400 per cent. In that way the balance is already cast to a very considerable degree in favour of England, and against Ireland and Scotland. And I venture to say that it is not while we are engaged in debating these matters in the manner we are debating them to-night, but whenever the subject of the repeal of the malt tax becomes a practical question of financial reform, that you may rely upon it you will have in some way to look at the question of how it bears upon the three kingdoms, and in what position the people of the three kingdoms would be left relatively to each other after its repeal. Some hon. Gentlemen have said that they will be satisfied if we proceed to make a very moderate contribution towards the reduction of the malt tax on the present occasion, provided it is understood that by that act we pledge our future surpluses to the further prosecution of this work in future years. Now, I hope whatever course the House may take, it will steadily refuse to pledge its future surpluses. If the House has thought—and I think this year it has shown that it has thought—that it would be unwise to anticipate the disposal of the surplus, even of the current year, until the usual financial statement has been received, and the whole subject of the finance of the year can be comprehensively considered, how much more unwise and unstatesmanlike would it be if it were now to give a vote affecting directly, it is true, but a moderate portion of our revenue, but which would be announced to the country as involving a foregone conclusion in respect to the manner in which we shall devote millions of pounds in future years which we do not know whether we shall ever possess or not? I am persuaded, Sir, that the House of Commons will never give a pledge involving any such principle. Well, is it in our power to make an effective reduction of the malt tax at this moment? You cannot at present reduce it, at the outside, by more than one-fifth.

My right hon. Friend (Mr. Milner Gibson) stated, and stated, I believe accurately, that to reduce it one-fourth would take away £1,860,000 of your revenue; and one-fifth, or even one-sixth, is all, if the change were to take immediate effect, that it would be in your power to remit. Now, if the subject of the malt tax is to be approached at all, it ought not to be approached in a manner so petty, so trivial in its scale, and so inadequate to the objects in view. Nay more, I venture to say that you cannot approach the subject of the malt tax without considering the relation of that tax—I am not now speaking of objections on the ground of nationality —but without considering the relation of this tax on a particular beverage to your whole system of taxation upon beverages and some other articles. An ineffective reduction of this kind is a reduction which ought on no account to be made. When we look fairly at this subject we find that, after all, one great part of the objection to this tax—an objection of which I have never denied the force—is the system of the Excise. Well, whether the reduction be of one-fourth or one-fifth of the malt tax, it leaves the Excise system precisely where it was—it leaves also all the expenses of collection exactly where they were, and would only make a certain application of an amount of the public revenue, not small indeed in itself but exceedingly small in relation with this particular tax, and most unlikely to be made up to you by the reproductive energies of the country. But this question lies much deeper than it seems. It is closely connected with and cannot be dissevered from the policy which you are to adopt and maintain with regard to the taxation on spirits, on tea, on sugar, on tobacco, and, in fact, on the luxuries of the people. I listened with great attention to the speech of my hon. Friend the Member for Rochdale, who certainly stated, with very great force, all that can be stated—and I, for one, am by no means the person to deny that a great deal can be stated—against the malt tax. But look at the way in which he dealt with the question. Do not suppose there is any prospect of any long alliance between my hon. Friend and hon. Gentlemen opposite. How did he begin? He named the article of sugar, and having done so, he went on to repudiate altogether the tampering with a mere fraction of the malt tax. He said if dealt with it must be dealt with by a determined policy of repeal. He was met

with this demand. If the malt tax be repealed what substitute is to be provided? My hon. Friend answered that question with perfect consistency. His answer consisted of three points. First of all he said you will save the expense of collection. That is quite true. The expense of collection, as stated by Sir Robert Peel— and it is about the same now—amounted to £150,000. That does not go far to replace £5,000,000. Then he said another portion of the remitted tax would be repaid in duty-paid commodities. Very good—let us make an allowance for that. It is possible that a few thousands may come back; but still £5,000,000 would be withdrawn by the repeal, and you must be prepared to answer the question how your accounts are to be squared when that withdrawal takes place. My hon. Friend knew the difficulty, and, in entire consistency with everything he ever said and did, he said, "I am an economist; I am for a large reduction of establishments. £20,000,000 have been added to the expenditure of the country," and he intimated here, as elsewhere, that he thought the whole or the greater part of that had been unnecessarily added to the expenditure. Therefore, he comes into court with perfectly clean hands; not tampering with small reductions, he will repeal the tax, and he will meet it by economy—not adopted for the occasion, but the profession, I may say the labour, of his life. He is a good deal more sanguine than I am. Till he reaches that point he may possibly walk in harmony with the Mover of this Resolution and with other hon. Gentlemen on the opposite side; but that harmony is destined to be sadly and sharply broken when he reaches the point of reductions. ["No, no!"] I can only say that I judge from all the indications that have been given during the present Session. It is possible that there may be 200 or 250 Gentlemen on that side of the House who have in silence been brooding, with anxious and eager expectations, over the subject of public economy, who warmly applaud what has been done during the last few years in that sense, and who look forward to much greater things; but it is a great pity that those Gentlemen do not give the world the benefit of their opinions. Very unfortunately the speaking minority on that side held, especially during this Session, very different language. I have heard various proposals made during this Session; I should like to know which of them was in favour of economy. The Estimates were somewhat smaller than those of last year, and have they not in almost every point been made the subject of complaint? Notices have been brought forward by Gentlemen opposite with respect to the Estimates of the year, directly or indirectly complaining of these reductions, as they think, unwisely made. I cannot help mentioning an instance, because it is really worthy of record. When the Navy Estimates were under consideration, we heard the hon. Baronet the Member for Radnorshire (Sir John Walsh) lamenting and denouncing the saving of a quarter of a million in the Estimates. I heard that with some surprise, but the testimony of my ears is not to be discredited. I heard him declare that, considering the immense power and responsibility of England, and the vast amount of work to be done by its navy, it would not be unreasonable that the Navy Estimates should be double their present amount. It would be very difficult, I think, under these circumstances, to make any arrangement for steady co-operation between the hon. and gallant Gentleman who brought forward this notice in a manner so acceptable to the House and my hon. Friend the Member for Rochdale. But, Sir, the question that is immediately proposed to us is a question of comparison between malt and sugar. Well, now, I have no doubt the hon. and gallant Gentleman is perfectly sincere in the proposal he has made, and yet I confess I think that he himself must feel that he is struggling against the fixed conviction of the House, as well as the fixed conviction of the country. I think he must feel that not this or that party only—not by any means the front bench alone on this or that side, both of which stand so low in the estimation of the hon. Member for West Norfolk—but that the real opinion, persuasion, and expectation of the people of England have all of them unequivocally pointed to the conclusion which Her Majesty's Government have adopted on this subject. I believe that if on Thursday last I had, on the part of my Colleagues, announced that we had come to the conclusion to pass by the claims of the sugar duties for reduction, and propose, in lieu, to take off one-fifth of the duty on malt, the great bulk of hon. Gentlemen opposite, including those on the front bench, would have been the first to raise the outcry against us, and it is highly probable the hardihood—I will not call it courage—which could induce

The Chancellor of the Exchequer

any Government to make such a proposal would have ended not only in the discomfiture of the plan, but the total evaporation of those who proposed it. It is very material to consider what is the history of this question. It is quite true that in 1860 we proposed the repeal of the paper duties in preference to the reduction of what were called the war duties on sugar and tea. The reasons, right or wrong, that led us to that conclusion, were stated to the House; they were finally accepted by the Legislature. I revive no question about them now, but the question I put is this—and I put it not only to the front bench opposite, for the front bench is accused by the hon. Member for West Norfolk of not supporting the Motion, but I put it to the second, third, fourth, and fifth benches—for a straightforward course was then taken by the whole party—what was it? They said—

"Notwithstanding the Resolution which pledged the House, you are wrong in proposing the repeal of the paper duties; there are claims which come before them."

What were they? Were they the claims of malt? No; we were told, both with consistency and perfect justice, that the claims of the tea and sugar duties were altogether superior to the matter of malt. The sugar duty is not yet disposed of. It is now proposed to put by the claim of sugar and to prefer the claim of malt. It is quite fair to refer to a Notice which it was perfectly understood at the time expressed the sense of the whole opposition, because I think that Notice may be said to have expressed the sense of the whole House. On the 3rd of June, 1862, my right hon. Friend the Member for the University of Cambridge (Mr. Walpole), had pledged himself to move an Amendment on the subject of the reduction of expenditure distinctly pointing to retrenchment, and he indicated in that Notice not merely retrenchment in general, but the specific purpose with which retrenchment was to be pursued. And what was that specific purpose? It was—

"The accomplishment of such further reduction as may not only equalize the revenue and expenditure, but may also afford the means of diminishing the burden of those taxes which are confessedly of a temporary and exceptional character."

My right hon. Friend, I know, would bear me out in stating that it did not mean the malt tax. That is not compatible with its words. It meant the Income Tax, which had been raised to 9d. in the pound, and which, therefore, might be fairly described as temporary and exceptional; and it meant the tax on tea and sugar, which in the strictest sense were exceptional. Were those terms excepted to on account of the sentiments they conveyed? Certainly not. They were objected to on political grounds by my noble Friend at the head of the Government; but the sentiments which my right hon. Friend sought to express with respect to the particular merits of those taxes prevailed universally on both sides of the House; and in making a proposal last year with respect to the tea duties, and this year with respect to sugar and for the reduction of the Income Tax, we have, in my judgment, pursued not only a sound policy, but we have taken steps which might be with substantial accuracy described as a redemption of that solemn pledge. We have got the last part of that redemption as regards sugar to accomplish and carry into effect, and I feel confident that by no mere party majority we shall be supported in that measure. I feel also confident that—quite apart from any such pledge, quite apart from party interests—the choice made is the right choice, equitable in itself, so intimately connected with the welfare and comfort of the people, that it is entitled on every ground of public interest and policy to the first place in the selection; and I am quite persuaded that the vote pronounced by the House by a conclusive majority on this occasion will receive universal ratification in the mind and judgment of the people of England.

Mr. DISRAELI: Sir, although the Resolution of my hon. and gallant Friend the Member for West Sussex, which I may be permitted to say he has brought forward, not only with great ability, but with peculiar candour, is very simple in its character, still the discussion in the House to-night has branched out into three distinct subjects. We have had to consider the expediency of the total repeal of the malt tax; we have had to consider the expediency of a remission of that tax proportionate to the amount of surplus which the Chancellor of the Exchequer proposes to apply to the reduction of the sugar duty; and thirdly, we have been called upon to consider, but not so fully, I think, as the circumstances require, the engagements which this Parliament has entered into with the country as to the remission of taxation generally. Now, with regard to the first subject—namely, the expediency of getting rid of the malt tax, I am, I think,

as much alive as most people are to the objections to that impost. I am not surprised, too, that many of my hon. Friends should, at this moment in particular, be excited to attack the character and incidence of that tax. As they have listened now year after year to the most eloquent denunciations from the Treasury bench of all Excise duties, and the consequences of those duties — I can easily comprehend that when they find almost every Excise impost has been terminated, and that they are left with one that brings, it is true, the largest amount of money into the Treasury, but which is peculiarly burdensome to the interests with which they are intimately connected—I am not surprised, I say, that they should think the time had arrived when they were called upon to consider whether it was possible to obtain relief from that impost. Irrespective of that, there is another part of our recent legislation which has naturally called the attention of my hon. Friends and of their constituents to this subject. We have now for some time been lessening the prices of articles of drink to the superior classes—at least to the wealthier classes—but especially, I may say, to the wealthy middle class; and when we find that brandy, the only spirit used by the rich, is very much reduced in price, and that wine is greatly cheapened, so that it has come into considerable consumption by the middle class, I think it is a natural conclusion, and one of a very grave character, that we should inquire whether it is not in our power to lighten the pressure which the price of beer imposes upon the limited resources of the humbler classes. I think those are two conclusions which may be drawn from our financial policy of late years, and which would easily account for the considerable—I will not call it agitation, for that is rather an odious word in this House—but for the great attention which has been given to the exigency of the tax upon malt. I am alive, and have ever been, to the great disadvantage of this tax as regards the welfare and comfort of the labouring classes. But I have always been of opinion that it is inexpedient, if we should attempt to deal with it, to deal with it in any other way than a large manner. I retain the opinion which I expressed in 1852, and which the President of the Board of Trade has referred to to-night, that if this tax is to be dealt with, it must be grappled with in a manner which may at least insure some considerable alleviation of the public burdens. No one, at present, of those who talk very largely of the reduction and almost of the total repeal of this tax has come forward in this House with any proposition of that kind ; and, therefore, I will not dwell longer upon this subject. I come now to the second point, and that is, whether it would be expedient to apply the amount of surplus which the Chancellor of the Exchequer contemplates applying to the reduction of the sugar duties to a proportionate remission of the malt tax ; and I will treat of that now, and only for a moment, without any reference to the particular and exceptional character of the duties upon sugar, to which the Chancellor of the Exchequer has just referred. Now, in the first place, re membering what I have ventured to say to the House, that in dealing with the malt tax it is, I think, expedient to deal with it in a large manner, I must consider what chance there is of fulfilling that condition in the present instance. We had an estimate by the Government of the loss to the revenue of a remission of one-fourth of the tax. I would put the amount of that remission at very little under £2,000,000, and, of course, I take the estimate of the Government without impugning it for a moment. Well, if that be the case—if we are to remit a fourth— we must lay our hands not merely upon that portion of the surplus which is to be applied to the remission of the sugar duties, but also upon that which was consecrated to the remission of the Income Tax too. But I do not understand that if a proposition of that kind was made it would receive any support. Well, then, with regard to what I would call the abstract question of preferring the remission of the sugar duties to the malt duty, even if we were to propose the remission of one-fourth of the latter—and, as I have said, that amount of remission would scarcely be of any avail— I should have to consider the comparative benefits arising from the remission of the duties upon sugar on the one side, and the duty upon malt to that amount on the other. Now, I wish to-night to decline that task, but this I will say—and I say it with great respect to any of my hon. Friends from whom I differ as to the course we take, though we have a common object—that if a Minister in this country comes forward and proposes a remission of duties upon sugar, it is most inexpedient and unwise, whatever our opinions may be as to the necessity of completely or

partially remitting the duties upon malt, to bring that question forward into competition and antagonism with the proposition for the reduction of the sugar duties, coming as that proposition does from a quarter so powerful and influential as that of the Government for the time being. So much for those two points, first as to the abolition of the duty upon malt, and secondly as to the expediency of applying the surplus, which the Chancellor of the Exchequer contemplates applying to sugar, in a proportionate manner to malt. But I come now to what I consider the most important point—one upon which it becomes this House to arrive at a grave and definite conclusion, and one which, in my opinion, ought to govern our conduct in this matter — namely, the engagements which, to my conviction, Parliament has entered into with the country on the question of remission of taxation. Now, I must call to the recollection of the House the circumstances under which these engagements were made. This country found itself involved in a war of considerable magnitude, and even of peril, and it was necessary to make great exertions. I shall say nothing about the origin of that war. I thought at the time, and I think so still, that it was an unnecessary war ; that if there had been sufficient discrimination in the first place and sufficient firmness in the second, that war might have been avoided. But this is quite certain—that whatever might have been the weakness or want of foresight of the Ministry, the moment the war was decided on, the country was unanimous, and the House of Commons was unanimous in supporting it. Well, the Finance Minister had to come forward with a statement then very unusual in the House of Commons—he had to come forward with a statement of the Ways and Means by which that war was to be conducted, and he told the House then that it was his duty and his wish to divide the increased burdens on the people as fairly as he could under the two heads of direct and indirect taxation. The increase of direct taxation it was very easy to indicate, and equally easy to foresee an increase, and ultimately an immense increase of our Income Tax. But the Minister told us that to obtain equivalent resources from our indirect taxation it was necessary to select those articles of general consumption which were in the greatest use ; and after due consideration, and putting the matter fairly and completely before the House, he fixed upon these ar-

Mr. Disraeli

ticles—first malt, secondly tea, and thirdly sugar. There was a complete understanding as to the sources by which this great war was to be conducted. It was conducted with varying fortune, and under varying Ministries. The increase of the Income Tax was at one moment between £9,000,000 and £10,000,000, and nearly an equal sum was raised from the three sources of indirect taxation. What happened? When the war was concluded it happened that the Act which levied between £9,000,000 and £10,000,000 of increased direct taxation was so drawn up that the Government would have the power for a year after the conclusion of the war to raise that large amount, although throughout the country it was clearly understood that upon the termination of the war that impost would cease. The feeling of discontent and indignation, or rather, I would say, of discontent and disappointment, throughout the country was so great that Parliament came to the determination at once to relieve the people of the £9,000,000 of direct taxation. By the mode in which the Act was drawn, at the conclusion of the war the increased malt tax ceased. But while Parliament interfered to relieve the country of direct taxation to the extent of nine or ten millions—prematurely as far as legislation was concerned—it immediately added that the war duties upon tea and sugar should be continued in order to relieve the strain upon the resources of the country, the war duty upon malt being absolutely relinquished. Very great considerations, far beyond mere considerations of finance, present themselves in questions of this kind. There are political considerations which this House ought not to forget. It fell to my lot—when there was a natural hesitation among men in office not to lose the nine or ten millions which, by the perhaps unintentional language of the statute, they might have engaged for the public service of another year—it became my duty to give notice of a Motion to ask the opinion of the House upon the subject; but public opinion out of doors was so strongly expressed that it became unnecessary to come to any conflict upon it. But at the time I based my argument for immediate relief upon this consideration—that when the country had shown such temper and high spirit, and had supported the Government in a great emergency, it was most important that any contract which the Government was supposed to have entered into with it should be kept in its spirit, and

upon that ground alone the country ought not to be disappointed of the relief which it expected from the remission of direct taxation, and upon the understanding of which it had borne heavy burdens with so much spirit and patriotism. It was upon high political considerations that the nine or ten millions of Income Tax was then immediately remitted, and not upon financial grounds. I say that, consistently with that view, hon. Gentlemen on this side—and I am quite willing to give credit for the same feeling to Gentlemen on the other side also — have always felt the political importance of terminating as soon as possible the war taxes, all the taxes specially connected with the Crimean struggle. If any great struggle were again to present itself, and an appeal to the people became necessary for a vast increase of direct taxation and heavy imposts upon the three great articles of public consumption, with what face could you appeal to them and expect the support of a high spirited and patriotic nation, if they could turn round and say, "In 1855, when the Sovereign was engaged in a dangerous war, you came to us with a financial programme, and induced us by certain representations to increase the direct and indirect taxes; but you have not complied with those terms, and you cannot expect us without a murmur to bear burdens which otherwise we would endeavour to bear?" It is said that the Chancellor of the Exchequer departed from the strict line of that policy when he proposed the repeal of the paper duty. I am not answerable for the Chancellor of the Exchequer. I never spoke upon this subject, without urging upon the House the necessity of relieving the country as soon as possible from these war taxes, not upon financial grounds, but from high political considerations; and when the Chancellor of the Exchequer brought forward his Motion upon the paper duty, it was with the sanction and assistance of myself and others that a Motion was made which proposed that we should remit the war duty upon tea, instead of repealing the duty upon paper; and I would at that time have also proposed the remission of the war duty upon sugar if circumstances had justified it. But the natural corollary to that proceeding—sanctioned, as I understood, by every Gentleman who sits around me — was that as soon possible, by getting rid of the war duty on sugar, we should terminate all those increased burdens which the Russian war had placed upon us. This is the position in which we are placed, and, therefore, it is not for me to enter into a discussion of the merits or demerits of a duty on malt. I think I have given in the course of my life tolerable proof of my sincerity upon that subject. We staked our existence as a Government upon carrying a measure which would have remitted one-half of the duty upon malt. That is not now the question before us. It is whether the House is not pledged, or feels itself pledged—I am myself pledged—by frequent votes, by more than financial considerations, by considerations of high policy, that it is our first duty to fulfil our engagements with the tax-paying people of the country, and to show that we are mindful of the engagements which by the Queen's Ministers we entered into in 1855; with the conviction that if we act with fairness and justice to them, if we appeal to them on a future occasion, on an equal struggle, and in an equal emergency, we shall be responded to in a spirit as firm and as patriotic. That must be our guiding principle to-night. I have not for one moment changed my opinion upon the malt tax. If the opportunity was a fair one—if a Motion had been brought forward under circumstances in which it could be fairly considered—if our engagements of honour and policy to the people of this country had been fulfilled, I should have been perfectly ready to give it my earnest and anxious consideration. I will say more. After all that has taken place as to remissions of indirect taxation of late, and after the frequent and almost complete changes which, with the exception of malt, have been made in the Excise laws, I say that in any future remission or modification of the scheme of indirect taxation the claim of malt must be brought forward, and will demand our earnest and serious attention. But what we have to do now is completely, and it may be severely, to fulfil the engagements which were entered into with the people of this country at the time of the Crimean war. When we have completed those engagements, if the country, as I hope it will, continues to be prosperous, when our resources are ample and abundant, then let us bring forward the claims of what may be called the last Excise duty, and in any future reduction of indirect taxation I will venture to say the article of malt cannot be passed over without notice. Those are the views which guide me upon the present occasion.

Mr. Disraeli

I regret that the hon. and gallant Member for West Sussex should have shaped his Motion in the manner he has, because I think the result will be calculated to give a false impression as to the feelings of this House upon the subject in which he is interested, and which he advocates with consistency and ability. I think it would have been better if the Budget of the Chancellor of the Exchequer having passed—a Budget which, I must say, has been significantly framed in accordance with the intimations which he has received from this side of the House, I think it would have been better if, after the Budget had passed, the question of the malt duty had been brought under the consideration of the House. We should then have been able to approach it without any of those difficulties which now necessarily present themselves, from what I regard as the solemn engagements of this House upon questions of finance. Then we might express an opinion without prejudice to those engagements, and I trust that when the measures of the Government have been passed, the opportunity will not be lost of bringing this question before the House in a more comprehensive and less objectionable shape.

MR. MORRITT: Sir, I do not wish to give a silent vote on this occasion; because, though this Motion was brought forward against my wish, and contrary to any feeling which I have with regard to the malt duty, yet I feel that we have a common cause; and, while I deprecate the manner in which the Motion has been brought forward, I should feel a cur if I did not vote for it. I shall, therefore, support the Motion of the hon. and gallant Member. If my hon. and gallant Friend is beaten—and we are told that he will be beaten by a large majority—it is my firm intention to bring forward the question in such a reasonable way that it shall not be beaten by a large majority. I am told by some hon. Members, "Oh, you are too early with your Motion;" while others again say, "You are too late." If you bring forward a Motion on the subject before the Budget it is said you are too early, as you cannot know what the Budget will be; and if you wait for the Budget it is said you are too late, for the Chancellor of the Exchequer has disposed of his surplus. I now give notice that I will be in the field at the earliest opportunity and with an abstract Resolution, which will pledge no one to any particular course. I shall so bring it forward that the House of Commons by its vote—

aye, every Member in it—will say that the time has come when, the duty on malt being left alone in its glory, must receive the same fate as other analogous duties which have been repealed or lessened. It ought to be done next year if there should be such a surplus as will enable us to do it. Why, I ask, should not the country have a large surplus next year? England has been working its way year by year under adverse circumstances to an increased surplus, and, thank God! England is so wealthy that she has borne with spirit her increase of taxation, and has proved that she can bear it. We are increasing in wealth, and are certain next year to have a surplus beyond even that of this year. We have flourished notwithstanding the infliction of the cotton famine. That is gone by. We have flourished under the infliction of constant and everlasting changes in our armaments and ships, and of every other expenditure of public money. I think there is a fair chance of a surplus next year. And supposing we have next year a surplus of £3,000,000, I would dispose of it thus: I would take off another penny in the pound of Income Tax — that would be £1,000,000—and I would devote the remainder to the reduction of the malt duty. I am not going to make a speech at this late hour. I am only sorry I was obliged to get up, and feel as if I was going to vote against my conscience. I tried all I could to induce my hon. Friend not to go on with his Motion, but as he has done so I shall back him.

Question put, "That the words proposed to be left out stand part of the Question."

The House *divided*:—Ayes 347; Noes 99: Majority 248.

AYES.

Acton, Sir J. D.
Adam, W. P.
Adeane, H. J.
Agar-Ellis, hon. L. G.F.
Angerstein, W.
Anson, hon. Major
Antrobus, E.
Ayrton, A. S.
Bagwell, J.
Baillie, H. J.
Baines, E.
Baring, H. B.
Baring, rt. hn. Sir F.T.
Baring, T.
Baring, T. G.
Barnes, T.
Bathurst, A. A.

Baxley, T.
Beaumont, S. A.
Beecroft, G. S.
Bellew, R. M.
Berkeley, hon. C. P. F.
Black, A.
Blake, J.
Blencowe, J. G.
Bonham-Carter, J.
Bouverie, hon. P. P.
Bright, J.
Briscoe, J. I.
Brown, J.
Browne, Lord J. T.
Bruce, H. A.
Bruce, Sir H. H.
Buchanan, W.

Buckley, General
Bulkeley, Sir R.
Buller, J. W.
Buller, Sir A. W.
Bury, Viscount
Butler, C. S.
Butt, I.
Buxton, C.
Caird, J.
Calthorpe, hon. F. H. W. G.
Cardwell, rt. hon. E.
Carnegie, hon. C.
Castlerosse, Viscount
Cavendish, Lord G.
Chapman, J.
Churchill, Lord A. S.
Clay, J.
Clifford, C. C.
Clive, G.
Coke, hon. Colonel
Cole, hon. H.
Cole, hon. J. L.
Colebrooke, Sir T. E.
Collier, Sir R. P.
Colthurst, Sir G. C.
Corry, rt. hon. H. L.
Cowper, rt. hon. W. F.
Cox, W.
Crawfurd, E. H. J.
Crawford, R. W.
Crossley, Sir F.
Cubitt, G.
Dalglish, R.
Dalkeith, Earl of
Davey, R.
Davie, Sir H. R. F.
Davie, Colonel F.
Dawson, R. P.
Denman, hon. G.
Dent, J. D.
Dillwyn, L. L.
Disraeli, rt. hon. B.
Divett, E.
Duff, M. E. G.
Duke, Sir J.
Dundas, F.
Dundas, rt. hon. Sir D.
Dunlop, A. M.
Dunne, M.
Egerton, Sir P. G.
Egerton, E. C.
Elcho, Lord
Enfield, Viscount
Estcourt, rt. hn. T.H.S.
Evans, T. W.
Ewart, W.
Ewart, J. C.
Ewing, H. E. Crum-
Farrer, J.
Fenwick, H.
Ferrand, W.
Foljambe, F. J. S.
Forster, C.
Forster, W. E.
Fortescue, hon. F. D.
Fortescue, C. S.
French, Colonel
Gard, R. S.
Getty, S. G.
Gibson, rt. hon. T. M.
Gilpin, C.
Gladstone, rt. hon. W.

Goldsmid, Sir F. H.
Goschen, G. J.
Gower, hon. F. L.
Gower, G. W. G. L.
Greenall, G.
Greene, J.
Greenwood, J.
Gregory, W. H.
Gregson, S.
Grenfell, H. R.
Gray, Captain
Grey, rt. hon. Sir G.
Grosvenor, Earl
Grosvenor, Lord R.
Gurney, S.
Hadfield, G.
Hamilton, Lord C.
Hamilton, Major
Hanbury, R.
Handley, J.
Hankey, T.
Hanmer, Sir J.
Hardcastle, J. A.
Hardy, G.
Hardy, J.
Hartington, Marq. of
Hervey, Lord A.
Hassard, M.
Hayter, rt. hn. Sir W.G.
Headlam, rt. hon. T. E.
Heathcote, Sir W.
Heathcote, hon. G. H.
Henderson, J.
Henley, rt. hon. J. W.
Henley, Lord
Hennessy, J. P.
Herbert, rt. hon. H. A.
Heygate, Sir F. W.
Hibbert, J. T.
Hodgkinson, G.
Hodgson, K. D.
Hood, Sir A. A.
Hornby, W. H.
Horsfall, T. B.
Horsman, rt. hon. E.
Howard, hon. C. W. G.
Howes, E.
Hubbard, J. G.
Hutt, rt. hon. W.
Ingham, R.
Jackson, W.
Jervoise, Sir J. C.
Johnstone, J. J. H.
Johnstone, Sir J.
Jolliffe, rt.hn.SirW.G.H.
Kekewich, S. T.
Kendall, N.
Kershaw, J.
Kinglake, A. W.
Kinglake, J. A.
Kingscote, Colonel
Kinnaird hon. A. F.
Knatchbull, W. F.
Knatchbull - Hugessen, E.
Lacon, Sir E.
Laird, J.
Layard, A. H.
Langton, W. H. G.
Lawson, W.
Leatham, E. A.
Leeke, Sir H.
Lefevre, G. J. S.

Lefroy, A.
Lee, W.
Legh, Major C.
Legh, W. J.
Lennox, Lord G. G.
Lennox, Lord H. G.
Lewis, H.
Liddell, hon. H. G.
Lindsay, W. S.
Locke, J.
Lopes, Sir M.
Lovaine, Lord
Lyall, G.
M'Cann, J.
M'Cormick, W.
MacEvoy, E.
Mackie, J.
Mackinnon, W. A. (Lyming.)
Mackinnon, W.A. (Rye)
Maguire, J. F.
Mainwaring, T.
Malins, R.
Manners, rt. hn. Lord J.
Marjoribanks, D. C.
Martin, P. W.
Martin, J.
Massey, W. N.
Matheson, A.
Matheson, Sir J.
Merry, J,
Mildmay, H. F.
Miller, W.
Mills, A.
Mills, J. B.
Monsell, rt. hon. W,
Montagu, Lord R.
Montgomery, Sir G.
Moor, H.
Morris, D.
Morrison, W.
Mowbray, rt. hon. J. R.
Mure, D.
Murray, W.
Neate, C.
Noel, hon. G. J.
Norris, J. T.
North, F.
Northcote, Sir S. H.
O'Conor Don, The
Ogilvy, Sir J.
O'Hagan, rt. hon. T.
O'Loghlen, Sir C. M.
O'Neill, E.
Onslow, G.
O'Reilly, M.W.
Osborne, R. B.
Owen, Sir H. O.
Padmore, R.
Paget, C.
Paget, Lord A.
Paget Lord C.
Pakington, rt. hn.Sir J.
Palmer, Sir R.
Palmerston, Viscount
Patten, Colonel W.
Paxton, Sir J.
Pease, H.
Peel, rt. hon. Sir R.
Peel, rt. hon. F.
Pender, J.
Pennant, hon. Colonel
Peto, Sir S. M.

Pilkington, J.
Pinney, Colonel
Pollard-Urquhart, W.
Ponsonby, hon. A.
Portman, hon. W. H. B.
Potter, E.
Powell, F. S.
Powell, J. J.
Powys-Lybbe, P. L.
Pryse, E. L.
Pritchard, J.
Proby, Lord
Pugh D.
Quinn, P.
Ramsden, Sir J. W.
Repton, G. W. J.
Ricardo, O.
Robartes, T. J. A.
Robertson, D.
Robertson, H.
Roebuck, J. A.
Russell, A.
Russell, F. W.
Russell, Sir W.
St. Aubyn, J.
Salomons, Mr. Ald.
Scholefield, W.
Scott, Sir W.
Scrope, G. P.
Seely, C.
Selwyn, C. J.
Seymour, H. D.
Seymour, W. D.
Seymour, A.
Shafto, R. D.
Shelley, Sir J. V.
Sheridan, R. B.
Smith, J. B.
Smith, M. T.
Smith, A.
Smith, M.
Smith, J. A.
Smyth, Colonel
Smollett, P. B.
Somes, J.
Stacpoole, W.
Staniland, M.
Stanley, Lord
Stanley, hon. W. O.
Stansfeld, J.
Steel, J.
Stuart, Colonel
Stuart, Lieut.-Col. W.
Sturt, Lieut.-Col. N.
Sykes, Colonel W. H.
Taylor, P. A.
Thompson, H. S.
Thornhill, W. P.
Tollemache, J.
Tracy, hon. C. R. D. H.
Traill, G.
Trefusis, hon. C, H. R.
Trelawny, Sir J. S.
Turner, J. A.
Turner, C.
Vandeleur, Colonel
Vane, Lord H.
Vansittart, W.
Verney, Sir H.
Vernon, H. F.
Villiers rt. hon. C. P.
Vivian, H. H.
Vyner, R. A.

Vyse, Colonel H.
Walpole, rt. hon. S. H.
Walter, J.
Warner, E.
Waterhouse, S.
Watkins, Colonel L.
Way, A. E.
Weguelin, T. M.
Western, S.
Westhead, J. P. B.
Whalley, G. H.
Whitbread, S.
White, J.
White, L.

Williams, W.
Willoughby Sir H.
Winnington, Sir T. E.
Wood, rt. hon. Sir C.
Woodd, B. T.
Woods, H.
Wrightson, W. B.
Wyld, J.
Wyvill, M.
Yorke, J. R.

TELLERS.
Brand, hon. H. B. W.
Dunbar, Sir William

NOES.

Adderley, rt. hon. C. B.
Alcock, T.
Bailey, C.
Barrow, W. H.
Bathurst, Colonel H.
Beach, W. W. B.
Bentinck, G. W. P.
Bentinck, G. C.
Benyon, R.
Beresford, rt. hon. W.
Bovill, W.
Bramston, T. W.
Bridges, Sir B. W.
Brooks, R.
Bruen, H.
Burghley, Lord
Burrell, Sir P.
Cartwright, Colonel
Cholmeley, Sir M. J.
Cobbold, J. C.
Curzon, Viscount
Dering, Sir E. C.
Dodson, J. G.
Du Cane, C.
Duncombe, hon. A.
Duncombe, hon. W. E.
Dunne, Colonel
Du Pre, C. G.
Dutton, hon. R. H.
Edwards, Colonel
Fane, Colonel J. W.
Fellowes, E.
Filmer, Sir E.
Fleming, T. W.
Floyer, J.
Forester, rt. hon. Gen.
Gallwey, Sir W. P.
George, J.
Gilpin, Colonel
Goddard, A. L.
Gore, J. R. O.
Gore, W. R. O.
Graham, Lord W.
Hartopp, E. B.
Harvey, R. B.
Henniker, Lord
Holmesdale, Viscount
Hopwood, J. T.
Humphery, W. H.
Hunt, G. W.
Ingestre, Viscount
Jermyn, Earl

Jervis, Captain
Jolliffe, H. H.
Kelly, Sir F.
Kerrison, Sir E. C.
King, J. K.
Knightley, R.
Knox, Colonel
Leader, N. P.
Leighton, Sir B.
Long, R. P.
Lytton, rt. hon. Sir G. E. L. B.
Mordaunt, Sir C.
Morritt, W. J. S.
Newdegate, C. N.
Newport, Viscount
North, Colonel
Packe, C. W.
Packe, Colonel
Papillon, P. O.
Parker, Major W.
Peacocke, G. M. W.
Peel, J.
Pevensey, Viscount
Phillips, G. L.
Ridley, Sir M. W.
Rolt, J.
Russell, H.
Sclater-Booth, G.
Sidney, T.
Smith, A.
Smith, S. G.
Stanhope, J. B.
Stracey, Sir H.
Stronge, J. M.
Sturt, H. G.
Sullivan, M.
Surtees, H. E.
Talbot, hon. W. C.
Thynne, Lord E.
Thynne, Lord H.
Tomline, G.
Treherne, M.
Walcott, Admiral
Watlington, J. W. H.
Williams, Colonel
Wyndham, hon. P.
Yorke, hon. E. T.

TELLERS.
Barttelot, Colonel
Cobbett, J. M.

Main Question put, and *agreed to.*

WAYS AND MEANS *considered* in Committee.

(In the Committee.)

Question again proposed.

"That, towards raising the Supply granted to Her Majesty, on and after the undermentioned dates, in lieu of the Duties of Customs now charged on the articles undermentioned, the following Duties of Customs shall be charged thereon, on importation into Great Britain or Ireland (that is to say):

On and after the fifth day of May, one thousand eight hundred and sixty-four—

Sugar—namely,

Candy, Brown or White, Refined Sugar, or Sugar rendered by any process equal in quality thereto the cwt.	£0 12 10

On and after the sixteenth day of April, one thousand eight hundred and sixty-four—

Sugar—namely,

White Clayed Sugar, or Sugar rendered by any process equal in quality to White Clayed, not being refined, or equal in quality to refined. . . . the cwt.	0 11 8
Yellow Muscovado and Brown Clayed Sugar, or Sugar rendered by any process equal in quality to Yellow Muscovado, or Brown Clayed, and not equal to White Clayed . . . the cwt.	0 10 6
Brown Muscovado Sugar, or Sugar rendered by any process equal in quality thereto, and not equal to Yellow Muscovado or Brown Clayed . . . the cwt.	0 9 4
Any other Sugar not equal in quality to Brown Muscovado. the cwt.	0 8 2
Cane Juice . . . the cwt.	0 6 7
Molasses . . . the cwt.	0 3 6
Almonds, paste of. . the lb.	0 0 1
Cherries, dried . . the lb.	0 0 1
Comfits, dry . . the lb.	0 0 1
Confectionery . . the lb.	0 0 1
Ginger, preserved. . the lb.	0 0 1
Marmalade . . . the lb.	0 0 1
Plums preserved in Sugar the lb.	0 0 1
Succades, including all fruits and vegetables preserved in Sugar, not otherwise enumerated the lb.	0 0 1."

—(*Mr. Chancellor of the Exchequer.*)

Motion, by leave, *withdrawn.*

Then on the Motion of *Mr. Chancellor of the Exchequer—*

(1.) *Resolved,*

That, towards raising the Supply granted to Her Majesty, on and after the undermentioned dates, in lieu of the Duties of Customs now charged on the articles undermentioned, the following Duties of Customs shall be charged there-

on, on importation into Great Britain or Ireland (that is to say):

On and after the fifth day of May, one thousand eight hundred and sixty-four—

Sugar—namely,

Candy, Brown or White, Refined Sugar, or Sugar, rendered by any process equal in quality thereto, and Manufactures of Refined Sugar . . : the cwt.	£0 12 10

On and after the sixteenth day of April, one thousand eight hundred and sixty-four—

Sugar—namely,

White Clayed Sugar, or Sugar rendered by any process equal in quality to White Clayed, not being refined, or equal in quality to refined . . . the cwt.	0 11 8
Yellow Muscovado and Brown Clayed Sugar, or Sugar rendered by any process equal in quality to Yellow Muscovado, or Brown Clayed, and not equal to White Clayed . . . the cwt.	0 10 6
Brown Muscovado Sugar, or Sugar rendered by any process equal in quality thereto, and not equal to Yellow Muscovado, or Brown Clayed . . . the cwt.	0 9 4
Any other Sugar not equal in quality to Brown Muscovado. the cwt.	0 8 2
Cane Juice . . . the cwt.	0 6 7
Molasses . . . the cwt.	0 3 6
Almonds, paste of . the lb.	0 0 1
Cherries, dried . the lb.	0 0 1
Comfits, dry . . the lb.	0 0 1
Confectionery, not otherwise enumerated . the lb.	0 0 1
Ginger, preserved. . the lb.	0 0 1
Marmalade . . . the lb.	0 0 1
Plums preserved in Sugar the lb.	0 0 1
Succades, including all fruits and vegetables preserved in Sugar, not otherwise enumerated the lb.	0 0 1

(2.) *Resolved,*

That, on and after the undermentioned dates, in lieu of the Drawbacks now allowed thereon, the following Drawbacks shall be paid and allowed on the undermentioned descriptions of Refined Sugar, on the exportation thereof to Foreign parts, or on removal to the Isle of Man for consumption there, or on deposit in any approved Warehouse, upon such terms and subject to such regulations as the Commissioners of Customs may direct, for delivery from such Warehouse as Ships' Stores only, or for the purpose of sweetening British Spirits in Bond (that is to say):

On and after the fifth day of May, one thousand eight hundred and sixty-four— .

Upon Refined Sugar in loaf, complete and whole, or lumps duly refined, having been perfectly clarified, and thoroughly dried in the stove, and being of an uniform whiteness throughout; and upon

2 M

such Sugar pounded, crushed, or broken in a warehouse approved by the Commissioners of Customs, such Sugar having been there first inspected by the Officers of Customs in lumps or loaves as if for immediate shipment, and then packed for exportation in the presence of such Officers, and at the expense of the exporter; and upon Candy . for every cwt. £0 12 10

Upon Refined Sugar unstoved, pounded, crushed, or broken, and not in any way inferior to the Export Standard Sample No. 1 approved by the Lords of the Treasury, and, which shall not contain more than five per centum moisture over and above what the same would contain if thoroughly dried in the stove . . for every cwt. 0 12 2

And on and after the twenty-first day of April, one thousand eight hundred and sixty-four—

Upon Sugar refined by the Centrifugal, or by any other process, and not in any way inferior to the Export Standard No. 3 approved by the Lords of the Treasury for every cwt. 0 12 10

Upon Bastard, or Refined Sugar unstoved, broken in pieces, or being ground, powdered, or crushed, not in any way inferior to the Export Standard Sample No. 2 approved by the Lords of the Treasury for every cwt. 0 10 10

Upon Bastard, or Refined Sugar unstoved, broken in pieces, or being ground, powdered, or crushed, not in any way inferior to the Export Standard Sample No. 4 approved by the Lords of the Treasury for every cwt. 0 9 6

Upon Bastard, or Refined Sugar being inferior in quality to the said Export Standard Sample No. 4 . . for every cwt. 0 8 2

(3.) *Resolved,*

That, towards the raising the Supply granted to Her Majesty, the Duties of Customs now charged on Tea shall continue to be levied and charged on and after the 1st day of August, 1864, until the 1st day of August, 1865, on importation into Great Britain or Ireland.

(4.) *Resolved,*

That, in lieu of the Duties of Customs now charged on the undermentioned Articles, on their importation into Great Britain or Ireland, the following Duties of Customs shall be charged (that is to say) :

Wheat, Barley, Oats, Rye, Pease, Beans, Maize, or Indian Corn, Buck Wheat, Bear or Bigg. the cwt. £0 0 3

(5.) *Resolved,*

That, towards raising the Supply granted to Her Majesty, there shall be charged, collected, and paid for one year, commencing on the 6th day of April, 1864, for and in respect of all Property, Profits, and Gains mentioned or described as chargeable in the Act passed in the 16th and 17th years of Her Majesty's reign, chapter 34, for granting to Her Majesty Duties on Profits arising from Property, Professions, Trades and Offices, the following Rates and Duties (that is to say) :

For every twenty shillings of the annual value or amount of all such Property, Profits, and Gains (except those chargeable under Schedule (B) of the said Act), the Rate or Duty of sixpence.

And for and in respect of the occupation of Lands, Tenements, Hereditaments, and Heritages chargeable under Schedule (B) of the said Act, for every twenty shillings of the annual value thereof,

In England, the Rate or Duty of three pence,

And in Scotland and Ireland respectively, the Rate or Duty of two pence farthing.

Subject to the provisions contained in section 3 of the Act 26 *Vict.* chapter 22, for the exemption of Persons whose whole Income from every source is under £100 a year, and relief of those whose Income is under £200 a year.

(6.) *Resolved,*

That, towards raising the Supply granted to Her Majesty, there shall be charged and paid on the Licences hereinafter mentioned, the following Duty of Excise in lieu of the Duty now payable thereon (that is to say) :

For and upon any Licence to be taken out yearly by any person to trade in or sell Coffee, Tea, Cocoa Nuts, Chocolate, or Pepper, in any house rated to the relief of the Poor, at a sum less than eight pounds per annum, and not being within the limits of a Municipal or Parliamentary Borough, the Duty of two shillings and sixpence.

(7.) *Resolved,*

That, towards raising the Supply granted to Her Majesty, there shall be charged and paid for and upon the several matters and things hereinafter mentioned, the following Stamp Duties, in lieu of the Stamp Duties now chargeable thereon respectively (that is to say) :

For and upon any Letter or Power of Attorney, Commission, Factory, Mandate, Voting Paper, or other Instrument in the nature thereof,

For the receipt of Dividends or Interest of any of the Government or Parliamentary Stocks or Funds, or of the Stocks, Funds, or Shares of or in any Joint Stock Company, or other Company or Society whose Stocks or Funds are divided into Shares, and transferable,

If the same shall be for the receipt of one payment only . . . £0 1 0

And if the same shall be for a continuous receipt, or for the receipt of more than one payment . £0 5 0

For the receipt of any sum of money, or any Cheque, Note, or Draft for any sum of money not exceeding £20 (except in the cases aforesaid), or any periodical payment (other than as aforesaid) not exceeding the annual sum of £10. . . 0 5 0

For the sole purpose of Voting, or appointing or nominating a Proxy to vote at any one Meeting of the Proprietors or Shareholders of any Joint Stock or other Company, or of the Members of any Society or Institution, or of the Contributors to the Funds thereof . . . 0 0 1

(8.) *Resolved,*

That, towards raising the Supply granted to Her Majesty, there shall be charged and paid for and upon the several matters and things hereinafter mentioned, the following Stamp Duties, in lieu of the Stamp Duties now chargeable thereon respectively (that is to say) :

For and upon any Donation or Presentation, by whomsoever made, of or to any Ecclesiastical Benefice, Dignity, or Promotion.

Also, for and upon any Collation by any Archbishop or Bishop, or by any other Ordinary or competent authority, to any Ecclesiastical Benefice, Dignity, or Promotion.

Also, for and upon any Institution granted by any Archbishop, Bishop, Chancellor, or other Ordinary, or by any Ecclesiastical Court, to any Ecclesiastical Benefice, Dignity, or Promotion proceeding upon the Petition of the Patron to be himself admitted and instituted, and not upon a presentation.

Also, for and upon any nomination by Her Majesty, Her Heirs or Successors, or by any other Patron, to any Perpetual Curacy.

Also, for and upon any Licence to hold a Perpetual Curacy not proceeding upon a nomination.

Where the net yearly value of any such Benefice, Dignity, Promotion, or Perpetual Curacy shall not amount to £50 . . . . Nil.

Where the same shall amount to £50 and not amount to £100 . . £1 0 0

Where the same shall amount to £100 and not amount to £150 . . 2 0 0

Where the same shall amount to £150 and not amount to £200 . . 3 0 0

Where the same shall amount to £200 and not amount to £250 . . 4 0 0

Where the same shall amount to £250 and not amount to £300 . . 5 0 0

And where such value shall amount to £300 or upwards . . . 7 0 0

And also, for every £100 thereof over and above the first £200, a further Duty of £5 0 0

(9.) *Resolved,*

That, for and upon any Licence to be taken out by a Hawker or Pedlar to travel and trade with more than one horse or other beast bearing or drawing burthen, there shall be charged and paid for every such horse or beast over and above one, the sum of four pounds in addition to the Duty now chargeable on a Licence to a Hawker and Pedlar to travel and trade with one such horse only.

(10.) *Resolved,*

That, towards raising the Supply granted to Her Majesty, the ad valorem Stamp Duties granted and made payable under the head of "Settlement" in the Schedule to the Act passed in the thirteenth and fourteenth years of Her Majesty's reign, chapter ninety-seven, shall be deemed to extend to and shall be chargeable upon or in respect of any definite and certain principal sum or sums of money of any denomination or currency, whether British, Foreign, or Colonial, and any definite and certain share or shares in the Stocks or Funds of any Foreign or Colonial Government, State, Corporation, or Company whatsoever, as well as upon or in respect of the Shares, Stocks, and Funds in the said Schedule mentioned.

And that where any principal sum of money secured or contracted for by, or which may become due or payable upon, any Bond, Debenture, Policy of Insurance, Covenant or Contract, shall be settled or agreed to be settled, or such Bond, Debenture, Policy, Covenant or Contract shall be settled or assigned or transferred by way of settlement, or shall be agreed so to be, then and in any of such cases the same shall be deemed to be a Settlement of such principal sum of money, and shall be chargeable with the said ad valorem Stamp Duties on the amount thereof accordingly.

And that where the subject of any Settlement chargeable with the said Duties shall be any share or shares in any such Stocks or Funds as aforesaid, or any sum or sums of money secured by any Foreign or Colonial Bond, Debenture, or other security, bearing a marketable value in the English Market, then the value of such share or shares, and of such Bond, Debenture, or other security respectively shall be ascertained and determined by the average selling price thereof on the day or on either of the ten days preceding the day of the date of the Deed or Instrument of Settlement; or if no sale shall have taken place within such ten days, then according to the average selling price thereof on the day of the last preceding sale, and the said ad valorem Duties shall be chargeable on such Settlement in respect of the value so ascertained and determined; and the value of any sum or sums of money expressed in coin of a Foreign or Colonial denomination or currency, shall be determined by the current rate of exchange on the day of the date of the Deed or Instrument of Settlement, and the said ad valorem Duties shall be chargeable in respect of the value so determined as last aforesaid

(11.) *Resolved,*

That, towards raising the Supply granted to Her Majesty, there shall be charged and paid the following Duties of Excise for and upon the Occasional Licences hereinafter mentioned (that is to say) :

For and upon every Occasional Licence to the Keeper of a Refreshment House, for each and every day for which such Licence shall be granted ...... Nil.

For and upon every Occasional Licence to retail Foreign Wine to be consumed at the place where sold, for each and every day for which the same shall be granted £0 1 0

For and upon every Occasional Licence to retail Beer to be consumed at the place where sold, for each and every day for which the same shall be granted 0 1 0

For and upon every Occasional Licence to deal in or sell Tobacco or Snuff, for each and every day for which the same shall be granted . . . 0 0 4

(12.) *Resolved,*

That it is expedient to amend the Laws relating to the Inland Revenue.

House *resumed.*

Resolutions to be reported *to-morrow;* Committee to sit again *to-morrow.*

PARTNERSHIP LAW AMENDMENT BILL.

Bill *considered* in Committee.

(In the Committee.)

On Motion of Mr. SCHOLEFIELD, *Resolved,* That the Chairman be directed to move the House, That leave be given to bring in a Bill to amend the Law of Partnership.

Resolution *reported.*

Bill *ordered* to be brought in by Mr. SCHOLE-FIELD, Mr. MURRAY, and Mr. STANSFELD.

Bill *presented,* and read 1°. [Bill 68.]

HIGH COURT AT BOMBAY BILL.

On a Motion of Sir CHARLES WOOD, Bill to confirm the appointment of Henry Pendock St. George Tucker, esquire, as one of the Judges of Her Majesty's High Court at Bombay, and to establish the validity of certain proceedings therein, *ordered* to be brought in by Sir CHARLES WOOD and Mr. Baring.

Bill *presented,* and read 1°. [Bill 67.]

House adjourned at a quarter after One o'clock.

HOUSE OF LORDS,

Friday, April 15, 1864.

MINUTES.]—PUBLIC BILL— *Third Reading*—Settled Estates Act Amendment* (No. 85); Charitable Assurances Enrolments* (No. 45), and *passed.*

LIMITED ENLISTMENT AND THE RESERVE FORCE.

MOTION FOR A RETURN.

EARL LUCAN, in rising to move for a Return of the Strength of the Reserve Force, said, it would be in the recollection of their Lordships that previous to the recess a noble Earl (Earl Desart) called the attention of the Government to the large number of men whose period of service in the army was about to expire, and who, it was to be apprehended, would not re-enlist. Having since then looked more thoroughly into the question, he (the Earl of Lucan) was of opinion that the apprehension of his noble Friend was well founded. He believed that a very large number of men were about to leave the service. In the year 1854, the first year of the war in the Crimea, as many as 33,000 recruits entered the army. Oddly enough, the military authorities, as he was informed, were unable to say what number of those men were still in the service; but it was calculated that about 10,000 men would take their discharge. He hoped it might be found to be an over-statement, but, at all events, the number would be very large; and it should be borne in mind that the same thing would happen next year. In 1855 as many as 29,600 men enlisted, and therefore it was to be presumed that next year 7,000 or 8,000 men would be entitled to their discharge; and it should be observed that many of the long service men, or those who had enlisted under the original law, would also be leaving the service. When it was remembered that we had now an army of above 210,000, a large portion of which was in India, and therefore subject to enormous casualties, the state of things would be admitted to be alarming. It was a question sufficient to create great anxiety, and he believed that such was the feeling of the military authorities, or they never would have resorted to the lowering of the standard, and a relaxation of the medical examination. Lowering the standard was a serious matter, for though a man of 5ft. 5in. was tall enough for a soldier, it was well known that men of that height had not the strength or muscular power of a man taller 5 ft. 6 in. or 5 ft. 7 in. And did not the relaxation of the medical examination imply that men were to be taken into this service of less robust and objectionable constitutions? The noble Earl the Minister for War assured the House, on a former occasion, that the question of the discharge of the men to whom he had referred was under his consideration, and that he hoped he should be able to adopt some course which would induce the men to continue in the service. But the noble Earl also added that it was not his intention to take any legislative action. Now, that was to him (the Earl of Lucan) a matter of extreme regret, and if possible of greater surprise; for he could not understand, if such evils were to be attributed to the Limited Enlistment Act, that the noble Earl should have so unhesitatingly and distinctly assured the House and the army that there was no intention to repeal or amend it. At all events, it was time that the House and the country should know thoroughly what the views of the noble Earl and the intentions of the Government were on this important subject. When the Act was passed seventeen years ago, the noble Earl (Earl Grey), who had charge of the Bill, stated that his main, if not his only, object was to create an army of reserve, which was indispensable for the safety of the country, and that the men of ten or twelve years' service were to form the army of reserve. No doubt the noble Earl indulged in the illusion that we were to have a sort of Prussian *landwehr*—some force which would add materially to the strength of the country; but he believed it would be found that instead of a *landwehr*, instead of a formidable army of reserve, we had some 300 or 400 men and no more, scattered over Ireland, Scotland, and England. At all events, whether the number were greater or not, he found, on referring to the Army Estimates, that the modest sum of £7,000 was asked for the pay of reserve forces. The whole thing was a failure, and if the noble Earl would allow him to give him advice, it would be to get rid of the reserve forces at once, and to get these 300 or 400 men to join the militia. It would appear that Lord Herbert, when Secretary for War, was not altogether satisfied with this Limited Enlistment Act; and accordingly in 1859 appointed a Commission, of which a noble Lord, a Member of the other House (Lord Hotham), was Chairman, and several officers of distinction were Members, to inquire into the subject. They devoted twelve months to the inquiry; at all events their Report was dated fifteen months after their appointment; and it was not until the summer of 1861 that

the Report was presented to Parliament, since which time, with the exception of some changes not of much moment, it has remained a dead letter. Lord Herbert's health unfortunately failed in the autumn of 1860, and in the spring of 1861 he resigned, and was succeeded by Sir George Lewis. That right hon. Baronet was perfectly new to the War Department and everything relating to the army, and he probably found quite enough to do without grappling with the *vexata quæstio* of recruitment. There can be no doubt that Lord Herbert's intention in having a Commission was thoroughly to sift the question, and that had he lived he would have taken some step towards disposing of the matter in some way or other. What was the Report of the Commissioners with regard to this Limited Enlistment Act? They said—

"When we consider the difficulties with which the recruiting service in this country has at all times to contend, and the increased demands upon it which the wants of that portion of Her Majesty's army stationed in India will create, we see no reason why enlistment for one period only should be allowed."

And they went on to say—

"And as we are led to believe that the certainty of a pension at the end of sixteen or eighteen years with a third good-conduct badge after thirteen years, would operate as an inducement to enlist for a longer period, we are disposed to recommend the expediency of so arranging the terms as to give the option of enlisting for sixteen years in the Infantry and eighteen in the Cavalry and Artillery, with a right, on termination of such period, to a pension, retaining, also, their good-conduct pay."

It was said that the Limited Enlistment Act would produce a better class of non-commissioned officers; but, if their Lordships would refer to the evidence, they would find the very contrary to be the result, for those men, anxiously waiting for their discharge, would not give themselves the trouble of qualifying themselves to be non-commissioned officers. It was also said that the effect of the Act would be to facilitate recruiting; this again has been a disappointment, as it was found that many men would not enlist because they could not depend upon being allowed to re-enlist. He had been told that the right of re-enlistment was not recognized by the War Office. If that were true, it was a breach of faith towards the soldier and towards Parliament, for a pledge had been given that men were to have a right within six months to re-enlist. Unless they were allowed to continue their services they could not entitle themselves to a pension; and all men, Irishmen in particular, attached more value to a pension than any other consideration. He believed that the great object of this unhappy Enlistment Act was to drive the men out of the army and save their pensions. Of that he had no doubt whatever. If economy were the object, could the Act be recommended on the score of economy, when these men are now at any price to be brought back to the army to earn the very pension which the Act was passed to save? He had heard that the men were now to be allowed £1 on re-enlistment, together with the full bounty and the recruit's kit; and instead of being allowed to re-enlist within six months, the time was to be extended to twelve months. How would that work? A man in India whose term had expired would come to England at the expense of the country; and, after remaining ten or eleven months, would take £1, the bounty, and the kit, and would re-enlist. At what expense to the country? There would be the cost of bringing the man from India, and sending his substitute to that country, at a frightful expense. And yet the Act had passed to get rid of these miserable pensions. In the discussion which had taken place lately in another place, the representative of the War Department asked that the Act might receive a further trial. Why it has received a trial of seventeen years; and it is to be further tried when all are alarmed at its monstrous effects. He had never heard in the army a favourable opinion of this Act. It may be said to have passed under the protest of the army, He would, however, allow that the late Duke of Wellington had voted for it. But how did he speak. He said that it was the duty of the Government to keep steadily in view the object of retaining old soldiers in the service during the whole time they were capable of rendering service—namely, until they reached the age of forty years. The Government could not do better than carry out the recommendations of the Commissioners; but his own opinion was, that the term of service ought not to be less than fifteen years for infantry, and sixteen for the cavalry and artillery. Power should be given to the men to re-engage, but former services should only be allowed to count towards pensions when they re-enlisted in their own corps. The noble Earl concluded by moving an Address for "Return of the Strength of the Reserve Force."

Earl Lucan

EARL DE GREY AND RIPON said, the subject was one of much importance, and he was not surprised that the noble Earl, from his connection with the army, should have brought the matter forward, or that he should have expressed the views to which he had given utterance, remembering that he had been an active and vigorous opponent of the Act of 1847 when it was before the House. Before discussing the wisdom or propriety of that Act, he would glance at the present military position of the country in relation to the number of men likely to be discharged during the present year; and he was happy to tell the noble Earl that he was greatly mistaken in the estimate which he had formed —of course without the advantage of official data. The noble Earl had spoken of 10,000 men as likely to take their discharge—but in giving that number he had fallen into the not unnatural mistake of setting down the number of men who were entitled to take their discharge as the number who would actually take their discharge. He had ascertained from the Horse Guards that 10,400 men at the outside would be entitled to take their discharge in the present year, but that only a portion of them would actually claim that privilege. The statistics on this head, unfortunately, were not as complete down to a recent date as was desirable; but his attention had been already directed to the matter, and, with the co-operation of the illustrious Duke at the head of the army, he hoped to effect an improvement in that respect. Up to the last quarter of 1860 an experience of three and a quarter years had been gained of the operation of the Act of 1847, and he found that in that time 7,335 men completed their term of service; 3,845 of that number re-engaged at once, and the remainder, 3,490, were discharged; 650 of these re-joined the army within the next six months, reducing the total of those who quitted the army to 2,840. Others, no doubt, enlisted again after the expiration of that six months; but he put these aside for the purposes of the calculation. Applying the same proportion to the 10,400 men who would this year be entitled to their discharge, and judging from the best information in the possession of the military authorities, it was expected that a loss to the service of about 4,000 men must be looked for in the present year. On the other hand, there could be no doubt that the Act had a very considerable effect in facilitating the recruiting for the army. The noble Earl passed very lightly over one portion of the subject, and attributed the diminution which had taken place in the death rate of the army to a long series of measures extending over several years. No doubt these were the causes of the salutary change; but among them, whatever the noble Earl might think of it, the Act of 1847 was certainly one. Taking the death rate for the years 1850, 1851, and 1852, it amounted to 29·7 per thousand; in 1860, 1861, and 1862 it had been reduced to 18·4 per thousand—showing a reduction equivalent upon the average numbers of the army to 2,200 men yearly. Had the old system continued in existence, it would have been necessary to replace those losses every year. Improvements in barracks, sanitary precautions, and other measures of a like nature had done much for the soldier, but most of these improvements were of a much more recent date than the Act of 1847, and, therefore, only entered partially into the calculation he had put before the House. He quite agreed with the noble Earl as to the value of maintaining in the army a due proportion of old soldiers; but he did not apprehend that it would be desirable to retain for long periods of service the whole of the men who enlisted. On the contrary, he believed that the views of those were sound who, in passing the Act, fully expected that a certain number of men would annually take their discharge. It was highly desirable to maintain the losses at something like an equable amount; but it was hard to do this when the enlistments at one time were much larger than at another. As we were now about to feel the effect of extensive enlistments during the Crimean war, he had felt it right to take some measure to encourage men to re-engage; and the noble Earl, instead of treating those measures as inadequate, as he had rather anticipated that he might do, spoke of them as involving a serious expenditure. One of the changes consisted in giving to a man when re-engaged a bounty of £1, in addition to the advantages held out by the existing regulations. A free kit must be given, if not to the soldier re-enlisting, to the recruit who took his place, and this £1 he looked upon as the value of the manufactured article over the raw material. The arrangement really involved no pecuniary loss to the public, because enlisting and recruiting expenses would involve as great

an outlay. It had been mentioned by the noble Earl that a soldier formerly had a right to engage after the lapse of six months, and carry on his former service. That was the rule up to 1854; in the beginning of 1855 that period of six months was extended to two years, and the arrangement was acted upon till 1861. His right hon. Friend the late Sir George Lewis then took a step, in which, with the utmost respect for his high authority, he thought he had gone too far. He reduced the period of two years to six months, he reduced the service from whole service to half, and he added the further condition that the man should have had a good conduct stripe at the period of his discharge. He thought that those changes went too far, and he, therefore, proposed to allow full service to a man who re-engaged within the period of one year, and he did not intend to make the actual possession of a good conduct stripe a matter of necessity. The man must have been a man of good conduct, but he might have forfeited his stripe just before his discharge, and still be a fit man to be re-enlisted. The noble Earl appeared to think that questions of the re-enlistment, as regarded individuals, were settled at the War Office. In this he was mistaken. Such questions were dealt with not at the War Office, but by the Adjutant General's Department. One of the consequences of the Act of 1847, and one that was foreseen when that Act passed, would be a considerable loss of men per year; but he was prepared to accept that consequence, and he thought that it would be unwise to attempt by the expenditure of considerable sums of money upon large bounties to attempt to escape it. Another charge made by the noble Earl was, that the difficulty of obtaining recruits had led to a reduction of the standard, and to a relaxation of the medical examination. It was true that, as recruiting was not going on so rapidly as might be desired, the illustrious Duke, the Commander-in-Chief, had reduced the standard to 5 feet 5 inches—it had been as low as 5 feet 4 inches—but the noble Earl was mistaken in supposing that there had been any relaxation of the medical examination. What had been done was to abolish the regulation which provided, that if a surgeon passed a recruit who was afterwards rejected for medical reasons, he should pay the expense of the subsequent examination. This charge on medical officers had given great dissatisfaction, and the reason of the proposed change was, that it was the opinion of the military authorities that the effect of this regulation was to cause the surgeons to reject many men who were perfectly fit to be admitted into the army. He now came to the Act itself, which had been so severely arraigned by the noble Earl. He could not agree with the noble Earl in thinking that the Act of 1847 had realized none of the anticipations which were formed when it was passed. The formation of a large army of reserve was not the main object of that Act; its object was to make the service more popular with the classes from whom recruits were principally obtained, and he could assure the House that that object had been attained. The Bill originally contained a proposition for the establishment of deferred pensions; but he believed that that was struck out while the measure was passing through Parliament. The present reserve force was not the creature of the Act of 1847. It was established by his noble Friend Lord Herbert in 1859, and although it had not answered the expectations which were formed at that time, the number of men of which it now consisted was not quite so small as the noble Earl supposed. According to the Returns which had been made, the number was not 300, but a little over 1,500. The formation of an adequate reserve was well worthy of attention, and was under his consideration. The real reason for the passing of the Act of 1847 was, that there was a reluctance on the part of a large portion of the population to enter the army for an unlimited period, and it was thought undesirable to take young men at the early age of eighteen, and make them enter into a military engagement for life. The present difficulty of obtaining recruits arose from the competition in the labour market. The position of the people of this country had greatly improved during the last few years, and that of the people of Ireland had materially changed. Formerly we got a large number of recruits from Ireland, but now we got very few, and we should not get more, but fewer recruits if we reverted to the old system of permanent enlistment. The noble Earl on the cross benches (Earl Grey) when he introduced the Bill alluded to the effect that it would have upon the mortality of the army, and the soundness of his anticipations was proved by the last Report of the Army Medical Department. According to that

Earl De Grey and Ripon

Report, the death rate of men in the army between the ages of twenty and twenty-four was 6·40 per 1,000, being less by two per 1,000 than the corresponding death rate among the civil population. Between the ages of twenty-five and twenty-nine the death rate in the army was 9·65 per 1,000; among the civil population, 9·21. Between thirty and thirty-four the death rate in the army was 11·97; among the civil population, 10·23. Between thirty-five and thirty-nine in the army, 12 and a small fraction; among the civil population, 11·63. At forty and upwards in the army, 23·61; among the civil population, 13·55. Thus between eighteen and twenty-eight, the ages to which the Limited Enlistment Act applied, the death rate in the army was at its lowest point, and was, on the average, somewhat less than that among the civil population. After those ages the rate rapidly increased, and more rapidly than the ordinary death rate of the country. With these facts before him, he saw no reason for saying that the Act of 1847, having regard to the principles upon which it was founded, had failed to attain the objects for which it was passed. He was perfectly ready to consider the matter in its various bearings, and to receive any suggestion with respect to it which the noble and gallant Earl, or any one else, might make with the view of amending the details of the existing Act. But, looking at the principle on which that Act was founded, and the results which it had achieved, he was bound to say that, in the opinion of the Government, that principle was sound, while the result had not occasioned disappointment.

THE EARL OF DALHOUSIE said, that as the person who had introduced the Limited Enlistment Act in the House of Commons, he must say, he felt, after the lapse of seventeen years, great satisfaction in listening to the speech of his noble Friend the Secretary for War, and hearing the testimony which he bore, with all the means of information to which he had access, to the fact that the objects of those by whom he had been commissioned to introduce the Bill had been accomplished. The reason why the Bill was brought in was simply that at the time it was not only found difficult to obtain recruits from the classes from which our officers wished to see them drawn, but that the service itself among the lower orders of the people of this country had become unpopular. Beyond that, Motions had been repeatedly made in the House of Commons for the amendment of the Enlistment Act, which at the time did not, as was generally supposed, extend merely to a period of twenty-one years, but to enlistment for life. Such a state of things it begun to be seen could not continue, and the measure which he had introduced to provide a remedy for it had the full concurrence of the late Duke of Wellington; without which, indeed, he would never have ventured to introduce it. The noble Duke, when he gave his assent to the measure, said that he had satisfied himself that its effect would be not to induce old soldiers to leave the army, but to increase the number of men and the popularity of the service. He thought it, he might add, a great advantage that the recruit during the period of the short leave of absence which he might have before he re-enlisted should have the benefit of seeing the difference between a military life and the hardships of manufacturing and agricultural occupations. He would thus have time to represent to the people of his district the good results which he had obtained from his service in the army; and if, after a time, a bounty were given him for all the recruits he might bring back with him to the service, a great stimulus would be given to enlistment. There were, he thought, very good reasons to be found why recruiting should at the present moment be somewhat slack in the dearth of labour. One of the main grounds, he was informed, why men in the Guards whose period of service was drawing to a close showed an unwillingness to re-enlist being, that as men who were trained and educated they were picked up by railways at a vastly increased rate of remuneration. The dearth of recruits in Ireland, also, from which we used to procure such large numbers of men, was, he thought, easily accounted for by the present condition of that country. These causes were, however, he believed, only temporary; but a great error would, he thought, be committed, if the present period of enlistment were extended to fifteen or seventeen years, and he was glad, therefore, that his noble Friend near him had arrived at a different conclusion on the subject from the noble Earl.

Motion *agreed to;* Return of the Strength of the Reserve Force, *agreed to.*

House adjourned at half past Six o'clock, to Monday next, half past Eleven o'clock.

HOUSE OF COMMONS,

Friday, April 15, 1864.

MINUTES.]— New Member Sworn — Edward Mathew Fenwick, esquire, *for* Lancaster Borough.
Select Committee — On Trade with Foreign Nations.
*Report—*On Barnstaple Election.
Supply—*considered in Committee**— Committee —R.P.

Ways and Means—*Resolutions*[April 14] *reported.*
Ways and Means—*considered in Committee.*
Public Bills—*Ordered—*Bridges (Ireland)*.
*First Reading—*Bridges (Ireland) * [Bill 70].
*Second Reading—*Copyright (No. 2) * [Bill 59]; Consolidated Fund (£15,000,000) *.
Referred to Select Committee — Copyright (No. 2) *.
*Considered as amended—*Registration of County Voters (Ireland)* [Bill 49]; Common Law Procedure (Ireland) Act (1853) Amendment *, and *re-committed.*

BOROUGH OF BELFAST.—QUESTION.

Sir HUGH CAIRNS moved that the Copy of the Report of the Commissioners appointed to inquire into the state of the affairs of the Borough of Belfast, with the Minutes of the Evidence, presented 24th February, 1859, be referred to the Committee on the Belfast Improvement (No. 2) Bill.

Mr. MAGUIRE said, he should oppose the Motion. The corporation of Belfast had been proved to have acted wrongly in the administration of the funds of that borough; and individuals belonging to that body had from time to time sought, by the aid of Parliament, to free themselves from the obligations which the Court of Chancery had imposed upon them. In 1857 they brought in a Bill which they were obliged to withdraw; and in 1858 another Bill which they brought in was rejected by a Select Committee. Subsequently, a Royal Commission was sent down to inquire into the matter. The charges preferred against the corporation before the Commission were, that it had kept the popular element out of the Council, and had closed the representation of the borough to all except those of its own way of thinking. The popular party, however, finding they could do nothing, ultimately withdrew from the inquiry; but the Report of the Royal Commission was nevertheless laid before Parliament. The case concerning the corporation was at present under trial; and it was sought to get the Report of an *ex parte* investigation laid before the Committee in order to prejudice those who were seeking an indemnity in the Court of Chancery. If the evidence taken before the Royal Commission were necessary to the Committee, the Chairman of the Committee would have been instructed to make the demand, but no such application had been authorised.

SIR HUGH CAIRNS said, he was surprised at the view taken of the question by the hon. Gentleman. When the matter of which he spoke was referred to the arbitration of the Colonial Secretary, it was agreed that the Report referred to should be taken as part of the materials on which the award should be made.

MR. BUTT affirmed that the Bill referred to was one intended to reverse a decree of the Court of Chancery, and urged the House to give the matter a careful consideration before agreeing to the Motion.

COLONEL WILSON PATTEN said, he wished to point out that the principle of producing before an existing Committee the evidence taken at a previous investigation was one usually followed. He saw o objection to the Motion.

Motion *agreed to.*

Ordered,

That the Copy of the Report of the Commissioners appointed to inquire into the state of the affairs of the borough of Belfast, with the Minutes of the Evidence [presented 24th February, 1859] be referred to the Committee on the Belfast Improvement (No. 2) Bill.—(*Sir Hugh Cairns.*)

LONDON MAIN TRUNK UNDERGROUND RAILWAY BILL,—INSTRUCTION.

MR. AYRTON moved—

"That it be an Instruction to the Committee on Group 1 of Railway Bills, if they think fit, to allow the promoters of the London Main Trunk Underground Railway Bill [ordered by the House not to be proceeded with in the present Session] to be heard upon Petition against the following Bills, with which such Bill would, if proceeded with, have been in competition—namely, Metropolitan Railway (Trinity Square Extension), East London Railway, Great Eastern Railway (Metropolitan Station and Railways), Metropolitan District Railways (No. 2), Metropolitan Grand Union Railway (No. 2); Provided that such Petition shall have been deposited within the time prescribed by the Standing Orders for depositing Petitions against Private Bills."

COLONEL WILSON PATTEN said, he should oppose the Motion. He wished to call attention to the recommendation of the Joint Committee of both Houses, that certain Bills should not be proceeded with during the present Session. The object

of that recommendation would be frustrated if every Bill rejected by it were allowed to come into competition with others.

MR. MASSEY said, he would remind the House that the Joint Committee only recommended the postponement of the Bill referred to, and not that the schemes involved in them were to be superseded by others which were recommended to be heard. If the promoters of these Bills were not to be heard before the Committees appointed to consider the more favoured schemes, they would be effectually superseded, and it would be useless for them to avail themselves of the privilege to proceed with their schemes at a future time. They did not ask for their schemes to be sanctioned now, but only to be heard against other schemes.

LORD JOHN MANNERS said, he hoped the applicants would be allowed to appear before the Committee, as their object was purely destructive and not constructive. He further hoped other parties might be emboldened to follow their example.

COLONEL WILSON PATTEN said, that after the observations of the hon. Member for Salford he should not press his objections.

Motion *agreed to.*

Ordered,

That it be an Instruction to the Committee on Group 1 of Railway Bills, if they think fit, to allow the Promoters of the London Main Trunk Underground Railway Bill [ordered by the House not to be proceeded with in the present Session] to be heard upon Petition against the following Bills, with which such Bill would, if proceeded with, have been in competition—namely, Metropolitan Railway (Trinity Square Extension), East London Railway, Great Eastern Railway (Metropolitan Station and Railways), Metropolitan District Railways (No. 2), Metropolitan Grand Union Railway (No. 2); Provided that such Petition shall have been deposited within the time prescribed by the Standing Orders for depositing Petitions against Private Bills.—(*Mr. Ayrton.*)

BARNSTAPLE ELECTION.

House informed, that the Committee had determined—

That Thomas Lloyd, esquire, is not duly elected a Burgess to serve in this present Parliament for the Borough of Barnstaple.

That Richard Bremridge, esquire, is duly elected, and ought to have been returned a Burgess to serve in this present Parliament for the Borough of Barnstaple.

And the said Determinations were ordered to be entered in the Journals of this House.

That the Committee had altered the Poll at such Election by striking off the names of John Gould King, William Henry Thomas, George

Smyth, Thomas Hooper, James Hooper, Thomas Lane Blackmore, Matthew Hutchinson, and Francis Hodge, as not having had a right to vote at such Election.

Also, of Richard Garnsey Adams, Francis Bowden, Henry Lewis, Edwin Ley, John Tinson Turner, Arthur Turner, Charles Hancock, and William Harris, it having been proved that they had received money for the purpose of influencing their Votes at such Election.

Also, of Benjamin Williams, Edmund Darke, Samuel Glyde, Richard Beneraft, Charles Snow, and William Verney Sanders, it having been proved that they have been guilty of Bribery at such Election.

House further informed, that the Committee had agreed to the following Resolutions :—

That Thomas Lloyd, esquire, was, by his agents, guilty of bribery at the last Election.

That it was proved to the Committee that Richard Garnsey Adams, Francis Bowden, Henry Lewis, Edwin Ley, John Tinson Turner, Arthur Turner, Charles Hancock, and William Harris had been bribed with the payment of the sum of five pounds respectively ; but that it was not proved that such bribery was committed with the knowledge and consent of the sitting Member.

That they have not reason to believe that corrupt practices have extensively prevailed at the said Election for Barnstaple.

Report to lie upon the table.

Clerk of the Crown to attend on *Monday* next to amend the Return.

Minutes of Evidence taken before the Committee to be laid before this House.

PENAL SERVITUDE ACTS AMENDMENT BILL.—QUESTION.

Mr. MAGUIRE said, he would beg to ask the Secretary of State for the Home Department, Whether he is aware of the fact that the operation of one of the provisions of the Penal Servitude Bill will be to abolish the Refuges for Female Convicts in Ireland ; and, if so, whether the Irish Government had been consulted upon the matter, and had approved or otherwise the abolition of said probationary institutions ?

Sir GEORGE GREY, in reply, said, it was not the intention of the Government, in preparing the Penal Servitude Bill, to interfere in any way with the practice which prevailed in Ireland of sending female convicts having tickets-of-leave to refuges, both Protestant and Roman Catholic, from which he believed very beneficial results had arisen. He had been in communication with the Irish Government on the subject, and he had given notice of an Amendment in Committee on the Penal Servitude Bill, which would effectually accomplish

the object which the hon. Member very properly had in view.

THE PROPOSED NEW MUSEUMS AT SOUTH KENSINGTON.—QUESTION.

Sir STAFFORD NORTHCOTE said, he wished to ask the First Commissioner of Works, What number of Plans have been sent in for the proposed New Museums at South Kensington, where and when he intends to exhibit them, and who are to be the Judges to decide upon them ?

Mr. COWPER said, in reply, that thirty-two sets of designs had been sent in by public competition, and those designs were now hanging up in the Royal Gallery, where they were accessible at any time to the Members of that House. The judges who would be appointed as a Committee to award the prizes would consist of five, and three of whom were architects of acknowledged reputation and experience, but not at that moment practising their profession. There would be also a painter, who was a professional man, and an amateur.

Mr. DILLWYN : What is the object of the Museum ?

Mr. COWPER said, the designs were for the plan of the new building that was to occupy one side of the front of the site which had been purchased at South Kensington, where the late Exhibition building stood, and which would afford space enough to receive the Natural History collection of the British Museum and a Museum of Patent Inventions, if it should be ultimately determined to place them in the building. The first thing would be, to get the designs for the new building as a preliminary step, and the use to which that building would be put would be a matter for further consideration. He apprehended that no steps would be taken which would prevent the hon. Gentleman, if he should think fit, in any form he might desire, bringing the subject under the attention of the House.

Mr. SOMERSET BEAUMONT said, he wished to know whether the judges were to be paid ?

Mr. AUGUSTUS SMITH would beg to inquire, by what authority all those plans were prepared ?

Mr. COWPER said, it was not usual to offer payment to gentlemen who were kind enough to assent to act as judges in such matters, and it would be going out of the ordinary course to press payment upon them. With regard to the other question, he thought it was his duty, as administering the affairs of the Board of Works, to endeavour to persuade the architects who were disposed to make designs to favour him with the exercise of their ingenuity and skill, and to prepare those designs for the consideration of Parliament.

MR. WALPOLE said, he wished to ask two questions relating to this matter. The one was, whether the Government propose to submit to the House their plans for the Natural History collection, and, if so, how soon; secondly, whether those plans will be submitted to the House before any steps are taken to provide a building for that collection?

MR. COWPER replied, that he was really unable to say at what particular period of time the matter would be brought before the House.

MR. BAILLIE COCHRANE said, he wished to ask the right hon. Gentleman what he intends to do with Burlington House?

MR. COWPER said, he believed that he would soon be able to lay on the table an estimate for erecting a National Gallery in the Garden of Burlington House, which was one-half only of the site.

TRIAL OF ARMSTRONG GUNS.
QUESTION.

MR. H. BERKELEY said, he rose to ask the Under Secretary of State for War, Whether, as the Armstrong breech-loading guns, constructed by Sir William Armstrong and now under trial at Shoeburyness, are made chiefly of solid blocks of mild steel (tempered in oil), and consequently totally different from the service guns which they are considered to represent; and whether it is the intention of the War Office to institute any and what trial of the Armstrong guns as at present employed in Her Majesty's service, it being evident, from Admiral Kuper's report, that some trial is urgently needed?

THE MARQUESS OF HARTINGTON said, he was afraid that he could scarcely, within the limits of a reply to a question, enter into a discussion of the points which the hon. Gentleman raised. He could only say that he would be very glad to enter more fully into the discussion of those points when they came to the gun Vote in the Army Estimates. He might, however, then state that the Armstrong guns now on trial at Shoeburyness were,

Mr. Cowper

with very trifling alteration, the same guns that were in the service. The guns in the service were constructed of barrels of steel strengthened by bands. That was the principle of the guns now at Shoeburyness. The object of the trial was to discover whether Mr. Whitworth or Sir William Armstrong could produce the best gun. As to whether it was the intention of the War Office to institute any trial of the service guns, he could only say that those guns were now undergoing a practical trial. A great many of them were now in possession of the army and the navy. Reports were received at the Horse Guards, and also quarterly Reports of the condition of the guns, stating any injury which they might have received during the practice.

MR. H. BERKELEY said, he wished to know, whether he was to understand that the Armstrong gun, which was to be tried, was not of homogeneous metal?

THE MARQUESS OF HARTINGTON: Only the barrel.

ASSIZE TOWN FOR THE WEST RIDING.
QUESTION.

COLONEL EDWARDS said, in the absence of his hon. and gallant Friend (Sir John Hay), he would beg to ask the Secretary of State for the Home Department, If he will lay upon the table of the House a Copy of the Letter from the Chairman of the West Riding Quarter Sessions, recently held at Pontefract, and of the Resolution passed there on the subject of the Assize Town for the West Riding of Yorkshire?

SIR GEORGE GREY replied that he had no objection to lay a Copy of the document in question on the table.

LABOURERS IN THE DOCKYARDS.
QUESTION.

SIR ARTHUR BULLER said, he wished to ask the Secretary to the Admiralty, Whether the Government intend doing anything towards the relief of the labourers in the several public Dockyards, who are at present paid at a rate considerably below the ordinary market value of labour?

LORD CLARENCE PAGET, in reply, said, the Government had no intention of increasing the pay of the labourers in the Royal Dockyards. The hon. Gentleman said they were paid at a rate considerably below the market value of their labour;

but he could only say the Admiralty had very numerous applications for the entry of labourers. It was, however, their intention to carry out—indeed, they were already carrying out—a limited system of building certain ships by piecework, as was recommended by the Committee on Dock-yards; and if the artificers used great exertions they would receive somewhat higher pay. The labourers would likewise participate in these advantages.

SIR JAMES ELPHINSTONE said, he wished to ask, whether the applications referred to by the noble Lord were not from men desiring to be put upon the fixed list of the Dockyard establishment, and whether there was not at present very serious difficulty in filling up the ranks of the hired men with persons of competent ability in the shipwright and other departments?

LORD CLARENCE PAGET said, there was no difficulty in filling up the vacancies with hired labourers.

UNDER SECRETARIES OF STATE.
QUESTION.

MR. DISRAELI: Sir, I wish to make an inquiry of Her Majesty's Government respecting the distribution of offices as at present arranged. The point is one of some gravity, and I trust I may be permitted to preface my Question with one or two remarks, which shall be confined strictly within the limits of an explanation of its purport. The matter to which I wish to call attention is the tenure of office by those Gentlemen who at present fill the post of Under Secretaries of State. The House is aware that the distribution of offices is, generally speaking, arranged by statute—by the Act familiarly known to every hon. Gentleman as the Act of Queen Anne, the 15th of *Geo.* II., and an Act of *Geo.* III., the celebrated Act of Mr. Burke when he introduced his economical reform. Then it was definitely arranged that two Secretaries of State might sit in the House of Commons, and two Under Secretaries. In very modern times, in the experience of all Gentlemen here—I think in 1855 or 1856—when a new Secretary of State was appointed, the Secretary of State for War, an Act was introduced which, referring to the previous state of the law on the subject, enacted that in future it should be legal for a third Secretary of State to sit in the House of Commons, and also a third Under Secretary.

Still more recently, when the President of the Board of Control became also a Secretary of State, in an India Act it was provided that it should be legal for a fourth Secretary of State to sit in the House of Commons, and also a fourth Under Secretary. Although it may not have occurred to them, the House upon reflection will become aware that, at the present moment, there are five Under Secretaries of State sitting in the House of Commons. The House will feel that this is a subject which unless it is capable of satisfactory explanation by the Government, is of a very grave character. It is grave in a constitutional point of view, but it may become still more grave in the consequences which may be entailed on the individual who, if my present view of the case be right, fills the office of that fifth Under Secretary of State. I have no wish at present to enter into any details. I wish to confine myself merely to making the question which I desire to put to the Government perfectly clear to the House. We shall have opportunities, if it be necessary, of entering into the discussion of the subject in a more convenient manner. But I cannot suppose that this point has not occurred to the consideration of Her Majesty's Ministers; and, therefore, I wish now to invite some explanation from the Government why their distribution of offices at present, as far as regards the Under Secretaries of State, should apparently be so opposed to the provisions of the statutes which exist on this subject.

VISCOUNT PALMERSTON: No change has recently taken place in regard to the distribution of Government Offices. It is the same now as it has been for a long time past. The question of the right hon. Gentleman is one which requires examination, and I am not prepared to discuss it off hand, no notice having been given of it.

MR. DISRAELI: My explanation of the reason why I did not give any notice of my intention to bring this question before the House is the same, I think, as that which has influenced the noble Lord in declining to consider it now. The fact is I was not before aware of the state of affairs in respect to this matter. But because I was not aware of that state of affairs that does not make the matter the less important. The noble Lord, I am sure, will agree with me that this is a question of great importance. And you, Sir (addressing Mr. Speaker), will say whether it may not be considered a question of privilege, and, being such, whether it may not be brought before you on the first opportunity.

THE HIGHWAY ACT.—DISCIPLINE IN PRISONS.—QUESTION.

Sir JOHN PAKINGTON said, he wished to ask the Secretary of State for the Home Department, What are his intentions in regard to two subjects which are now exciting great interest; whether he intends to introduce a Bill for the amendment of the Highway Act; and whether he will bring in the Bill he promised for the improvement of discipline in county and borough prisons?

Sir GEORGE GREY replied, that the Bill regarding highways was in print, and would be soon introduced. With regard to the other measure, he was waiting to receive the Report of medical men as to the dietary of borough prisons before he completed the provisions of the Bill.

SUPPLY.

Order for Committee read.

Motion made, and Question proposed, "That Mr. Speaker do now leave the Chair."

THE FOREIGN OFFICE AND THE BOARD OF TRADE.

SELECT COMMITTEE MOVED FOR.

Mr. W. E. FORSTER said, he rose to call the attention of the House to the arrangement between the Foreign Office and the Board of Trade in reference to trade with foreign nations, and to move for a Select Committee thereon. The first point that would suggest itself to any hon. Member reading the terms of his Motion would probably be that it was rather a serious thing to ask the Government for a Select Committee to inquire into the manner in which two of their Departments transacted their business. There were two precedents for such a course, however, to which he might refer—the one was the Select Committee which had been granted to inquire into the constitution of the Board of Admiralty, and the other a Motion by the hon. Member for Liverpool (Mr. Horsfall) two or three years ago, for inquiry into the constitution of the Board of Trade. That Motion was not, indeed, granted, but it was not opposed on the ground of being contrary to the practice of the House. He was quite aware that it

Mr. Disraeli

would require strong arguments to induce the House to grant a Select Committee in accordance with his Motion. He hoped, however, to show that a grievance existed and was felt strongly by the best informed of the commercial community. The merchants and manufacturers of the large towns, having the means of associated action through their Chambers of Commerce, had held a meeting at which the subject was discussed, and a brief but pithy memorial was drawn up and presented to the Secretary of State for Foreign Affairs. In that memorial nineteen principal towns were represented—including Birmingham, Bradford, Bristol, Coventry, Leeds, Nottingham, Newcastle, Sheffield, and most of the important commercial towns, except those in Lancashire. Although the Chambers of Commerce of Lancashire did not belong to this association, a deputation from the Manchester Chamber of Commerce which represented the whole of the cotton districts attended, and fully concurred in the representation. The memorial was to the following effect:

"That your memorialists understand that the arrangement between the Foreign Office and the Board of Trade is at present as follows:—That the Foreign Office takes action in commercial matters, solely in concert with the Board of Trade. That consequently communications from Her Majesty's Ministers and Consuls abroad on commercial matters are forwarded by the Foreign Office to the Board of Trade, in order that through such Board they may, if deemed desirable, be communicated to commercial men; and that, on the other hand, the suggestions of such commercial men for action by the Foreign Office in commercial matters are expected to be made to the Board of Trade. That while gratefully acknowledging the desire, both on the part of your Lordship, of the President of the Board of Trade, and of the staff of both offices, to promote the interests of commerce, your memorialists have found by experience that this double action tends to defeat the fulfilment of that desire. That the present movement throughout the Continent of Europe towards free trade, consequent on the reduction of its tariff by the French Government, makes it especially necessary that our Government should give constant and unremitting attention to all questions connected with foreign tariffs (especially to any changes that may be contemplated in them), and should be ready to take prompt action on information obtained, while at the same time it makes it especially undesirable that English manufacturers should find themselves compelled, by want of such prompt action, to make in Parliament or through the press such public expression of their wishes as tends to their defeat by alarming manufacturers abroad. That therefore your memorialists cannot but think that the interests of trade would be greatly promoted if commercial men in this country were put in immediate and direct communication with those who are responsible for the action of Government in commercial matters with foreign countries."

What was asked was a Select Committee to inquire whether means could not be found to put the trading interest of the country into immediate communication with that Department of the Government which conducted negotiations relating to trade with foreign nations. He had no doubt the members of the Chambers of Commerce would be able to prove their case if the Committee were granted. If the House would allow him he would point out very briefly how the present mode of administration was very likely to lead to the evils practically felt by the merchants and manufacturers throughout the country. The first thing was, that it required, as stated in the memorial, that there should be a concerted action between the two offices—the Board of Trade and the Foreign Office—before any representation relating to trade and commerce could be made abroad, or any negotiations conducted. In other words, it required that the two offices should be of the same mind. That occasioned great difficulty and caused great delay. Feebleness of action was also the result; frequently there was no action at all, or it was not resolved upon till so late that it had little or no weight. Another disadvantage was that the trading interest was forced by the theory of the arrangement to work upon the Foreign Office through the Board of Trade, and consequently it was almost an impossibility to obtain decisive action. The Foreign Office did the work; it made the representations and conducted the negotiations abroad, and it was best qualified to do so, because it received information from Her Majesty's consuls abroad, but the theory was, that the other part of the information — namely, that concerning the interests, objects, and wishes of commercial men at home should be received through the Board of Trade. That was a very inconvenient arrangement, and it would be much better if one office received the information from both quarters. As the Foreign Office did the whole work it should obtain the whole information. The theory was that if any question should be asked in that House with regard to negotiations abroad, instead of asking it of the Under Secretary, or, if they had the good fortune to have him among them, of the Secretary of State for Foreign Affairs, it was ad-

dressed to his right hon. Friend the President of the Board of Trade, who could not state in reply what he had done, but only what Earl Russell had done, but it would surely be much more satisfactory to the Members of the House, as well as to the country, if a reply could be given by the Minister who had conducted the matter. Then, again, commercial representations must depend on political representations and political negotiations; therefore it was desirable that the office which conducted political negotiations should feel itself responsible for the commercial negotiations, otherwise commerce would be sacrificed, as he feared it had been, to other questions more urgently brought before the Foreign Office. Under the present arrangement, moreover, there was a want of responsibility and a relief from responsibility. The Board of Trade was of very little use to the trading community in matters appertaining to foreign commerce, although possessing the greatest desire to serve the interests of trade, but it was of very considerable use to the Foreign Office by acting as a shield or buffer between them and any pressure which might be brought to bear upon them. These were some reasons why the present relations between the two offices were likely to be disadvantageous to trade; but the chief reason why, at the request of the very influential bodies to which he had alluded, he had been induced to take up the subject, was that, in consequence of the French Treaty, there had been such a movement towards free trade throughout Europe as made prompt action by the Government at this time especially desirable. Some hon. Gentlemen, indeed, supposed that the French Treaty was a reason why there should be slowness and inaction in this matter; but the trading community, on the other hand, thought it should rather beget watchful supervision on the part of the Minister who had the control of Foreign Affairs, with the view to the development of our foreign trade. It was difficult to find any question which was less of a party question, and he must candidly acknowledge the earnest desire not only of the present but also of the late and possible future occupants of the Treasury bench to further the interests of trade in every manner. But while making this acknowledgment he must state that some remarks he had made on a former occasion had been misapprehended by the right hon. Gentleman opposite the Member for Buckinghamshire, who appeared to suppose that merchants and manufacturers wished to return to the old system of reciprocity. But they had no such wish. They felt and knew, and were glad to feel and know, that the French Treaty had put an end to the possibility of reciprocity treaties on the part of England. They were prepared to abide every consequence of free trade. That was the almost unanimous feeling. But they did not think they were unreasonable in calling upon the Government to do all in its power to develop the principle of free trade in foreign countries, and in desiring that our agents abroad and our Ministers at home, while fully imbued with the principles of free trade, should be also sufficiently acquainted with the details of British commerce, and the wants of commercial men, that when an opportunity presented itself, the utmost should be made of it. They thought that the interests of commerce were of sufficient importance to warrant the political power of the country being exerted in asking in a perfectly respectful and friendly manner, from foreign countries these two things. First, that when a treaty was made between two foreign countries, England should be put in the position of the most favoured nation—a request that was perfectly reasonable; and next, that when any treaty of commerce or change of tariff was in contemplation in any foreign country, our Ministers should ask to be informed of such intended changes in order that they might be enabled to offer suggestions. It might be possible even in the most protectionist country to make suggestions so manifestly advantageous alike to the foreign nation and to the British producer, that it might be almost impossible to refuse to adopt them. But if those suggestions were not made at the time, they would be useless afterwards. He would mention to the House two or three instances in which the interests of English commerce had not been so well looked after as they might have been. The French treaty offered a great opportunity for developing our trade with foreign countries, but he feared that, to some extent, this opportunity had been lost. If the efforts of the hon. Member for Rochdale had been followed up in the same spirit in which he made them, that treaty would have been of more advantage to England than it had been. There was the old question of the Belgian tariff. When the treaty between that country and France was being negotiated, the Chamber of Commerce at Brad-

ford urged the Foreign Office to take some steps in the matter, and to make suggestions which might then have been successful, while the Belgian Government was uncommitted to its own manufacturers. The opportunity was, however, lost, and the consequence had been, he feared, that we had not so good a bargain as we might have had in respect to the Scheldt dues. Then in the case of Prussia, when the treaty between France and Prussia was under discussion, the Chambers of Commerce in this country made an earnest representation to the Foreign Office to send out some one to Berlin to watch the negotiation. After a delay, Mr. Mallet, of the Board of Trade, a highly qualified gentleman, who had co-operated with the hon. Member for Rochdale in making the French Treaty, was sent, but he was too late to do anything useful. He might as well not have gone at all, but if there had been but one office to consult, no doubt he would have been in time. The case was still stronger in regard to Italy. As soon as Italy became one nation it became necessary to establish one tariff for the whole country, and that tariff was decided upon after a treaty with France. He had frequently urged upon the Under Secretary of State the propriety of sending some one to Turin, who was well acquainted with English trade, that the unification of the tariff might be favourable to the interests of English manufacture. The answer always was that it would be of no use to send any one, as we must wait until France had made her bargain. But it was not necessary for us to be dragged after France. Although we had no reductions of tariff to offer, we might have been able to show to the Italian Government and to the men of commerce of that country, that there were many cases in which the tariff might be reduced without injury to any one. Mr. Mallet was at last sent out to Turin, but he was again too late. His presence was then more likely to do harm than good to the commerce of this country, and he (Mr. Forster), for one, was very anxious that he should come home again. In Russia the tariff was almost prohibitory. Upon his own goods, Orleans stuff, the present Russian duty was £26 per cwt. Hon. Members would appreciate the oppressive weight of that duty when they learnt that the 15 per cent *ad valorem* duty in France amounted to only £4 10s. per cwt. It was difficult to imagine a country where it was more the duty of the Government to care for the many consumers rather than the few manufacturers which Russia possessed. But even Russia was awakening to the impolicy of high tariffs, and last year it was stated that a reduction in the tariff had been made. Those reductions, however, did not assist English goods, and, according to the information he had obtained, the reason was obvious—they were adopted after being submitted to the French Ambassador. Our Ambassador ought to have been instructed to communicate with the Russian Government at the time, and he hoped the hon. Under Secretary would say whether any instructions had been given to the English Ambassador on the subject. His own opinion was that the departments were perfectly innocent of making any communication to him on that occasion. With respect to Austria, he would only say that it appeared to be the opinion both of the Board of Trade and of the Foreign Office that this was not a time to make any representations to Austria. The opinion of those engaged in the Austrian trade was quite different, especially as it was known that the Austrian Government had taken steps to obtain the opinion of the manufacturers of that kingdom. In reply to a memorial that had been presented, the Foreign Minister, after communication with the Board of Trade, said that this was not a right time to move in the matter. He would wish to know whether that reply was based upon political or upon commercial grounds. If it were based upon political reasons, he could only say that any political differences which existed would not be increased by appealing to the interest of both countries in the encouragement of mutual trade. It might be asked how it was that matters had got into their present condition. It was a general opinion among commercial men that our Ambassadors and our consuls abroad were in fault; but in that view he did not share. He believed that the fault really lay in the machinery of the two offices, rather than in any want of desire to do their duty on the part of our officers. Our Ministers abroad might have too little knowledge of commercial affairs, but he believed they were well disposed to assist commerce if they could. When representations upon commercial matters were sent by these gentlemen to the Foreign Office, that Office sent them to the Board of Trade, but those gentlemen looked to the Foreign Office for their promotion, and knew that they were not so likely to get it for exertions in matters which were considered by the Foreign Office to be not the business of that Office but Board of Trade business. It might be said that fault was attributable to commercial men for not bringing sufficient pressure upon the Government. Perhaps they did err in allowing the Government to lead too quiet a life; but for himself he must say he was weary of making representations to the Government. The difficulty that the commercial community experienced was in getting the two offices to work together. They had, first of all, to see that the Foreign Office was put in communication with the Board of Trade, and then to take care that the latter received the requisite information. This arrangement resulted in much delay and inaction, and when any failure occurred it was almost impossible to tell with whom lay the responsibility. It was the old story of Lord Chatham and Sir Richard Strachan over again. They all knew how in former days—

"The Earl of Chatham, with his sword drawn,
  Was waiting for Sir Richard Strachan;
Sir Richard, longing to be at 'em,
  Was waiting for the Earl of Chatham."

So it was now with the Foreign Office and the Board of Trade—

"The Earl Russell, with his pen made,
  Was waiting for the Board of Trade;
The Board of Trade, in helpless bustle,
  Was waiting for the Earl Russell."

What was complained of, in two words, was this, that while responsibility rested on one body, the power of action rested on another body. Their desire was that the office where the work was transacted should also bear the responsibility. The first objection to the alteration would in all probability come from the Board of Trade, and would, from its nature, carry with it some force. It would be said that the Board of Trade must not be made less powerful than it was, because it acted as the representative of the commercial interests; and that, if any change were made, it would be better to lodge the power as well as the responsibility in the hands of that body. That, of course, would be a question for the consideration of the Select Committee, if the Government would grant one. One thing, however, was certain. They could not have two sets of negotiations carried on at the same time. If his right hon. Friend the President of the Board of Trade cared about the influence of his office, he would remind him that a powerless responsibility carried with it no influence. Then came the question — if the work could not be given to the Board of Trade, why could not the responsibility be laid upon the Foreign Office? There was, however, one objection to this, which would proceed from the Foreign Office, and one which was very natural and hardly blamable. The state of things by which an office became relieved of responsibility was undoubtedly a very pleasant one, and one that the office so relieved would be loth to see changed. He did not believe that that objection would be expressed, but he was none the less convinced that it would be felt, though perhaps unconsciously. It might also be urged that the work of the Foreign Office was already so great that it could not be increased without injuring its efficiency; but he considered that no work was more legitimately within the province of that office than the furthering of our commercial interests with foreign nations. If any other subject received prior attention its claims ought indeed to be very great. He believed both his hon. Friend and the noble Lord at the head of the Foreign Office to be greatly mistaken if they imagined that they could escape this work by maintaining the existing arrangement. At present the commercial interest invariably applied to the Foreign Office, upon which was consequently entailed the additional labour of applying to the Board of Trade. He had already said that he believed they had missed the opportunity which the French Treaty had offered them, but they had now another opportunity of which they could avail themselves in consequence of the success of that treaty. The success of the Commercial Treaty with France had been wonderful, and he could not but believe that other nations, seeing that success, would enter into similar reductions of their tariffs, whereby their trade with England would be greatly increased. The French imports had increased in 1863 11 per cent as compared with 1861. In exports the manufactures showed an increase during the same period of 38 per cent, and the Customs had brought a larger amount to the revenue by 33 per cent. There was no part of the kingdom which had benefited from the French Treaty in a greater degree than the town he represented, and yet the French exports in woollen goods, the manufactures of which were supposed to be imperilled by the treaty, had increased by 54 per cent. That was

Mr. W. E. Forster

the result which all true free traders had anticipated, for it was one of their first principles that any loss experienced in one branch of manufacture would be compensated for by increased industry and energy in another. There was one reason for the alteration he proposed essentially English. The nation was, he believed, generally, but not universally, prosperous. They heard less about the Lancashire distress than they did some short time since, but the effects of that distress were still perceptible, and rendered necessary every exertion on the part of our Government to provide fresh markets for our manufactures, especially those connected with cotton. The inhabitants of Europe numbered 260,000,000, and our exports were above £50,000,000. Of that sum, France, with a population of 37,000,000, took a little above £9,000,000; Austria, with 35,000,000 inhabitants, about £780,000; and Russia, with a population of 74,000,000, little more than £2,000,000. Here then were countries civilized and interested in extending their trade with England, and every effort ought to be made to induce them to make alterations in their tariffs which would admit of such extension. He begged leave to move the appointment of a Select Committee to inquire into the arrangement between the Foreign Office and the Board of Trade in reference to our trade with Foreign nations.

Mr. HEYGATE seconded the Motion.

Amendment proposed,

To leave out from the word "That" to the end of the Question, in order to add the words "a Select Committee be appointed to inquire into the arrangement between the Foreign Office and the Board of Trade in reference to Trade with Foreign Nations,"—(*Mr. W. E. Forster,*)

—instead thereof.

Mr. LAYARD said, that he could not allow the subject touched upon by his hon. Friend to pass without observation, as it was one that was worthy of great attention. His hon. Friend had made it his study and possessed as much information upon it as any hon. Member of the House; in addition to which he believed that some resolutions passed by a deputation from a large number of Chambers of Commerce of the most considerable cities in the country, had a short time ago been confided to his care. Those resolutions, or rather memorials, had been somewhat largely circulated among the Members of the House. He had himself received one, and the value of the opinions expressed in it had been enhanced by the advocacy of his hon. Friend. The document had, however, been drawn up under an entire misapprehension as to facts, and the assertions which in it assumed the appearance of realities, were without any foundation whatever. The same thing might be asserted of much which had fallen from his hon. Friend. He did not for one moment mean to say that his hon. Friend had made any statements which he knew to be untrue, but he believed that his hon. Friend did not understand the relative positions of the Foreign Office and the Board of Trade. It was not unnatural that the Chambers of Commerce in this country should consider their interests as paramount to almost everything else in importance ; but it should be remembered that the duty of the Government was not to watch over one interest to the exclusion of all others, but that its aim should be the promotion of the general welfare of the community. He was the last man in the world to doubt the importance of our commercial relations. Our greatness and prosperity were, in his opinion, greatly dependent upon our commercial relations with other countries, and he could assure his hon. Friend that the Foreign Office was fully alive to that fact. His right hon. Friend near him (Mr. Milner Gibson) was one of the leaders of the free trade movement in this country, and therefore it was hardly necessary to say that neither the Foreign Office nor the Board of Trade were insensible to the representation of the commercial interests of the country. The position of our country was different from that of almost every other country in Europe. Some years ago, after a long and arduous struggle, the principles of free trade were accepted by the House. After we had carried out the reform of our own fiscal system, our attention was turned to the possibility of introducing the principles of free trade into our commercial relations with foreign countries. The first country to which the attention of the Foreign Office was turned was naturally France, with which, looking at the situation of the two nations, England ought to maintain the largest commercial relations. Commercial relations on the basis of free trade were proposed to the French Government, and, fortunately, at the head of the French Empire was a Sovereign of great liberality and intelligence, with Ministers who equally understood the advantages of the free trade system.

France itself was, however, by no means prepared for the introduction of anything like free trade; but, happily, the Commercial Treaty was carried through. He was not going to repeat the history of that treaty, but he would remind the House that the most eminent diplomatist in the employ of the Crown (Earl Cowley) represented the Foreign Office, and that the hon. Member for Rochdale (Mr. Cobden), than whom there could be no higher authority on commercial questions, acted as joint negotiator with Earl Cowley. The articles of the tariff were discussed one by one ; the hon. Member for Rochdale was able to make such amendments as, from his knowledge of the subject, he believed to be necessary, and the result was that a most satisfactory treaty was concluded. After the conclusion of the treaty a very different course was pursued by the two Governments. The wisest policy, in his opinion, was to do as the British Government had done, and give to all the world what they had given to France. But the French Government adopted another policy, reserving to themselves the right of negotiating with other countries upon the same terms as with ourselves, and they did not extend the provisions of the treaty to any other country. By following a different course England deprived herself of the means of making bargains with other countries, believing that those countries would in time be induced to follow her example, and that the increased prosperity of England and France, derived from that treaty, would have its effect in the course of time, would convince other nations of the vast advantages of free trade, and would lead them eventually to enter into more liberal commercial relations with us. He believed it was the opinion of the hon. Member for Rochdale, as it was the opinion of other men competent to judge, that after the conclusion of the Commercial Treaty with France it was not advisable to open negotiations for commercial treaties with other countries, that further tariff bargains were not advisable, and that it was better to leave free trade to carry its own conviction to the minds of foreign nations. It was impossible to make those nations understand as yet the importance and the advantage of free trade principles, and he believed that although many eminent statesmen did, there were very few countries in Europe, not even excepting France, which yet appreciated those advantages. It must be recollected that speeches were still made in this House by the hon. Member for West Norfolk among the rest, insisting that free trade had ruined some interests in England, and that the time must come for the re-imposition of protective duties. Whatever might be the value of those arguments they were repeated abroad; and the result was that when free trade arguments were used to foreign Governments, people were apt to say that, having lost our own tail, we wanted them now to cut off theirs; and the more our Chambers of Commerce urged these tariff reductions the more convinced were foreigners that we had some interested object in trying to induce them to adopt our system. The Foreign Office could only use diplomatic means in trying to bring about a better state of things. They could not go about to all the Prime Ministers in Europe with a blunderbuss, saying, "A commercial treaty, or your life!" All they could do was to lay before foreign nations the commercial prosperity of this country under free trade and the advantages which they would derive from a more liberal commercial policy. The Foreign Office must watch their opportunities, and the best moment for making representations must be a question for their consideration and for the consideration of those who represented us abroad. His hon. Friend complained of the British Government for following in the wake of France; but that instead of being a reproach, ought to be a cause of praise. It was the interest of England to get France to enter into commercial relations with other countries, because, until she did so, England had no *locus standi.* When a country made tariff reductions for the benefit of France, we could go to that country and say that the comity of nations entitled us to ask for similar reductions; that we had nothing to offer in return, but having given before all we had to give the same reductions ought to be made in our favour. This might be said, or there might be "a most favoured nation" clause, under which we could demand as a right what had been conceded to France; or if the treaty negotiated with France proved successful, we could point to the advantage gained by more liberal intercourse with her, and promise equal advantages from similar intercourse with ourselves. Thus, a treaty with France, or with any other nation, formed the strongest argument which could be urged in our own favour. The case of Belgium, which his hon. Friend had mentioned, was exactly in point. It

Mr. Layard

was a mistake to say that the Foreign Office had not entered into negotiations with Belgium, for as soon as they knew that the Belgian Government were about to negotiate a treaty with France, they communicated with that Government on the subject. But what was the answer given to them? Why, that Belgium could not negotiate with this country until she had finished her negotiations with France. The reason was obvious. France had something to give in return for tariff concessions, and what was said to England by foreign countries was, "If we reduce duties in your favour without any equivalent, we then cut ourselves off from asking for anything from France, since France would say, 'Why should we give you an equivalent for that which you have given to England for nothing?'" That was a fair argument, and one with which the Foreign Office were met.

Then, again, commercial questions were often so intimately mixed up with political questions that they could not separate the two. The fate of a Ministry might depend upon such a question. But Chambers of Commerce did not consider that, and did not take into account, and were often ignorant of, the political condition of the country with which they desired more liberal commercial relations. As in this country, a strong opposition to the Government of the day might exist. The Government might be willing to enter into negotiations, but the Opposition might dissent from that policy. Why, what would have been the result if, when the great struggle between free trade and protection was going on in England, a strong Power in Europe had been constantly pressing us to reduce our tariff? Such an attempt would have furnished a strong argument to the Opposition, and might have endangered the adoption of free trade. Something like that happened constantly on the Continent. It would not be prudent to give instances, but there were many statesmen in Europe who were convinced of the advantages of free trade, and who were yet either fettered by the existence of a strong Protectionist party, or by political considerations, from adopting free trade. As to the propriety of these constant solicitations from our Chambers of Commerce, there was a paragraph in a letter written by the hon. Member for Rochdale (Mr. Cobden), which was so wise and true that he would beg permission to quote it. The hon. Gentleman said—

" As a general rule, I should say that recommendations emanating publicly from our own commercial bodies must afford very disadvantageous grounds for the Foreign Office in attempting to move other Governments to reduce their tariffs. I can understand that our diplomatists abroad might, in a quiet way, by keeping Foreign Governments well informed of the benefits which a free trade policy has conferred not only on the prosperity of our people, but—what is still more precious to rulers—on the interests of the public revenue, induce them, from motives of self-interest, to follow our example. But from the moment that it is known that our diplomacy is set in motion by our Chambers of Commerce to urge a reduction in the tariffs of other countries, it places Foreign Governments, which are generally more enlightened and disinterested on economical questions than their people, in the disadvantageous position of appearing to move under foreign influence for the benefit of aliens, and thus the most seductive arguments are furnished to the Protectionists, who can appeal to the prejudices, and even the patriotism of the public, in defence of what they call the rights of native industry. I have, whenever an opportunity has offered, expressed these views to the members of our Chambers of Commerce."

With the opinions expressed in that letter he entirely agreed, and they were precisely the opinions on which the Foreign Office had acted, and, he hoped, would act. He would then turn to some of the facts mentioned by his hon. Friend. With regard to the Italian tariff, it was quite at variance with the facts to adduce that as an instance of want of attention on the part of the Foreign Office. The hon. Member said that if they had sent Mr. Mallet to Turin in good time he would have been able to obtain a reduction of the tariff. The hon. Member was entirely in the wrong. As soon as Her Majesty's Government were aware that the Italian Government were about to enter into commercial relations with France, they lost no time in communicating with the Government of Turin on the subject of the tariff; and he also wrote to several official persons there, pointing out that it would be of great advantage to Italy and the Italian Government to conclude a liberal commercial treaty with this country. In consequence of these representations, Signor Marliani, a member of the Italian Senate and a man of great knowledge and experience, was sent to this country, who, however, was bound by his instructions not to open any negotiations whatever until the French Treaty was settled. The reason for that was, that the Italian Government were afraid that France would avail herself of any concessions made to us, without giving any corresponding concessions on her own part. When the treaty with

France had been agreed to, then the Italian Government offered to make an arrangement with us, and Mr. Mallet was sent to Turin. Even then, however, the Italian Government refused to enter into the question of the tariff, or to do more than put us in the position of the most favoured nation. Her Majesty's Government in vain endeavoured to induce them to change their decision ; but the Italian Government said—

" We will give you the same privileges as we have given France ; but we will not make any further concession, because if we do the French Government would claim to have it extended to them, without giving us an equivalent."

He could not help thinking that the Italian Ministers did not quite understand the true principles of free trade, for they said they would not make any sacrifices. The English Government did not want them to make any sacrifice or to agree to any reduction which would not be mutually advantageous. In regard, for instance, to the duties on iron and coal, they believed that a reduction would be as much for the benefit of Italy as of England. The same proceeding had taken place in regard to Sweden as to Italy. The Swedes declined to enter into negotiations with us, until they completed their treaty with France. His hon. Friend complained that Her Majesty's Government were not earlier in the field in these cases, and that they did not insist upon being admitted to the negotiations. But how could the Government enforce admission ? If there was one subject more than another about which secrecy was scrupulously observed, it was the adjustment of a tariff, and it was, therefore, impossible for the Government to obtain the information to which his hon. Friend had referred. Then, in regard to Austria, the Government were constantly in communication with that country on commercial matters, but had received the usual answer, that they could not negotiate until they had settled their arrangements with the Zollverein. He believed, however, that there was a disposition on the part of Austria to enter into a more liberal course of commercial policy. On the subject of cured herrings, a question in which Scotland was very much interested, Her Majesty's Government had made repeated applications to Austria, but the same answer which he had mentioned had always been returned. It was an error to suppose that the treaty between Prussia, the Zollverein, and France would, as a matter of course, come into operation in 1865. A treaty had been under negotiation for some time, and Prussia, as the mandatory of the Zollverein, had arranged certain terms with France ; but in consequence of the Zollverein not having confirmed those terms, the agreement had not been ratified. Her Majesty's Government were in constant communication with Prussia, in reference to a commercial treaty, but the reply was, that nothing could be done till matters had been settled with France and the Zollverein. His hon. Friend had also spoken of Russia. There had been, he believed, some negotiations between Russia and Prussia—not between Russia and France; but he understood they were now at an end. Again, Her Majesty's Government had made repeated efforts, but without success, to enter into a commercial treaty with Spain. The policy of that country naturally depended very much on the Ministry and the Chambers, and they all knew how frequent were the changes which took place in that respect. There was an important question pending with Portugal in regard to a wine monopoly. Over and over again the Portuguese Government had promised to abolish the monopoly, and had once brought in a measure for that purpose; but when reminded that they had not fulfilled their engagement, the answer was, that it could not be carried out on account of the opposition of a large and influential party in the Chamber. It must be borne in mind that there were constitutional Governments in Europe, and the Chambers had to be consulted on these matters.

He then came to the subject of the Motion of his hon. Friend. The accusations of his hon. Friend with respect to the relations between the Foreign Office and the Board of Trade were not well founded. There was no divided responsibility at that time ; but there would be if the proposal of his hon. Friend were carried out, and in that case it would be impossible to conduct the business. Complaint was made that our agents abroad had no means of direct communication with the Board of Trade. [Mr. W. E. FORSTER said he did not make that complaint.] If not made by his hon. Friend the complaint was at least to be found in the memorial which he supported. It was impossible for agents abroad to have direct communication with the Board of Trade. If they had there would be a double machinery, and the agents would

receive instructions both from the Foreign Office and the Board of Trade, which might sometimes happen to be contradictory. He believed the division of labour and responsibility between the two offices was then just what it ought to be. All our agents were instructed to report on all matters occurring in the countries where they resided which were connected with trade and commerce to the Foreign Office. These reports were at once transmitted to the Board of Trade, who advised upon them, and the Foreign Office acted on the opinions thus given. The same thing happened with regard to the Colonial, Indian, or any other office. It was the duty of the Board of Trade, which had special knowledge and experience, to give its opinion on the subjects brought before it by the Foreign Office, and it was the duty of the latter to give effect to the views thus elicited. He wished to draw the attention of his hon. Friend to what had already been done. The Foreign Office had directed all the consuls to make periodical reports on the trade and commerce of the places in which they resided, and these Reports were first sent to the Board of Trade to be examined and digested, and were then printed and laid before Parliament. Moreover, the secretaries of embassies and legations were also required to make annual Reports of the commerce and finance of the countries to which they were accredited, taking, of course, more enlarged and comprehensive views ; and these Reports were also laid before the House, and had been received with favour by the country as containing valuable and important information. Again, since he entered the Foreign Office, he had caused instructions to be sent by circular to all our representatives abroad to communicate to the Department all alterations or notices of alterations connected with tariffs, navigation, or any question of trade and commerce in the countries where they were stationed. The consequence was that nothing was published in the local papers abroad, or in official papers connected with trade and finance, that was not at once communicated to the Government. Again, two years ago, when the cotton famine began, the Foreign Office sent instructions to all our representatives abroad to send home Reports as to the quantity of cotton raised or about to be cultivated in the countries where they resided. Those reports had been of great value, and many persons connected with the cotton associations in this country had told him that they had derived the greatest possible assistance from them. So also our policy in Japan and China was founded almost entirely upon our commercial interests. We had few political relations with either of those empires ; we were there because we wished to protect and extend our commerce. During the last few years we had entered into commercial treaties with France, Italy, Turkey, and other States. The question of rags had recently excited some interest in this country. Some time ago the Foreign Office sent circulars to all their representatives abroad, calling upon them to obtain information as to the possibility of a reduction of the duty on rags. Satisfactory assurances had been received from some countries. He was not at liberty to say from which, as every thing depended on secrecy in negotiation, but there was every reason to believe that in many countries in Europe the duty on rags would shortly be reduced. The Foreign Office took every opportunity to promote the commercial interests of the country, and he really believed the existing system was as good a one as could be well adopted, though he was willing to make any improvements in it which might be thought desirable. When the representatives of the Chambers of Commerce were assembled in London, he invited the hon. Member for Manchester, the hon. Member for Leeds, and others to discuss the whole question at the Foreign Office, with the view of seeing whether any such improvements could be made. His hon. Friends did not think fit to accept his offer, but if they had visited the Foreign Office he should have placed the whole system before them, and have paid every attention to their suggestions. Perhaps some slight departmental changes might be adopted with advantage, though he was not prepared to go even that length ; but he felt quite certain that any proposal to amalgamate the Board of Trade with the Foreign Office was altogether impracticable. It would be useless to attempt to introduce the machinery of the Board of Trade into the Foreign Office, and yet, if the Foreign Office was to be responsible for giving an opinion on commercial questions, it must be supplied with all the organization of the Board of Trade. At present the Board of Trade furnished the Foreign Office with the requisite information and

advice, and thus enabled it to carry on negotiations with foreign Governments. The functions of the two Departments were perfectly distinct, and it would be simply preposterous to lay upon the Foreign Minister, whose Department was the hardest worked Department of the State, the responsibility which rested with the President of the Board of Trade. The former was willing to be responsible for carrying out the instructions he received from the Board of Trade, but the latter must be responsible for those instructions themselves. His only desire was that our commerce should be extended as much as possible. He was, consequently, quite ready to give the Committee asked for, though he was afraid they would not get much from it.

LORD STANLEY said, he inferred from the words uttered by the hon. Gentleman that the House would not be put to the trouble of dividing. In the event of a division, he was in favour of the Motion of the hon. Member for Bradford (Mr. W. E. Forster), though, at the same time, he could not have supported it, had it involved any censure upon the conduct either of the Foreign Office or of the Board of Trade. Though the arrangement between the two Departments as to the conduct of business did not seem to be satisfactory, it was much easier to point out defects than to state the precise manner in which they ought to be remedied. But the hon. Member for Bradford asked only for an inquiry. He had made out a fair *primâ facie* case for investigation, and there could be no doubt that a strong feeling on the subject prevailed among the mercantile and manufacturing classes. Their complaint was, that although in the consular service we had an admirable agency for collecting facts connected with trade, yet when those facts were obtained no sufficient use was made of them, or else that the information did not arrive in time. If that statement were true—and its accuracy was a point upon which he did not wish to express any opinion—he should not be disposed to find fault with those who had the conduct of public affairs ; for he did not think it could be said that either the Foreign Secretary or the President of the Board of Trade was indifferent in the discharge of his duties. But if the Foreign Office had, as at present, the whole diplomacy of Europe upon its hands—if it had to undertake the settlement of the affairs of all the countries in Europe—it must follow as a necessary consequence that questions of trade would receive comparatively little notice. He held the opinion that the Foreign Office should undertake much less than at present, and that if it were to leave many questions in which we had no direct concern alone, in all probability the diplomacy of Europe would be managed, not worse, but better. Still, no one would deny that the Foreign Office was overworked. It was no exaggeration to say that within the last fifteen years, since the general introduction of telegraphic communication throughout Europe, the business of that office had more than doubled. That was not a temporary state of things, but one likely to last; and as coincidently with it there had been an immense increase of trade and extension of commercial relations among the different countries of the world, so, if European peace were preserved, there would be a still increasing trade, a constant growth of industry, and still more complicated commercial relations between different countries. He thought, therefore, that the manner in which the Foreign Office was able to deal with commercial questions might properly be investigated. It appeared to him that there were only two courses open for adoption. One was to give to the Foreign Secretary greater assistance within his office, by placing there, for the management of this special business, an official holding a higher position than that of a mere clerk. The other was indicated in some of the memorials of the Chambers of Commerce—namely, to transfer the commercial business bodily to the Board of Trade. To the latter course he entertained the most decided objection. He did not think the business could be managed in that way. There would be a complete separation between political and commercial negotiations, which frequently ran into one another, and there would be all the confusion of a double correspondence between different Departments of the Government at home and the same set of officials abroad. Members of the diplomatic service would be placed in subordination to a department from which they did not receive their appointments, from which they did not expect promotion, with which they had in other respects nothing to do, and to the good or bad opinion of which they must be comparatively indifferent. He thought the House must make up its mind that the business should remain in the Foreign Office. If so, the

Lord Stanley

responsibility must rest more completely than it did now upon the Foreign Minister. He was likewise of opinion that a great deal of good might be done by an inquiry into the organization of that heterogeneous Department the Board of Trade. The duties of that Department had been increased as new interests had arisen, and he was disposed to think that the President should hold a position of greater dignity in the official scale than he did at present. He had always thought that the Vice President, whose duties at present were not very obvious, should be placed more definitely in the position of an Under Secretary. If these things were to be done, the House must take the initiative. The reform of a department, however, would never originate in itself, because those who were most familiar with it had commonly been brought up under the system, and had come to regard it as necessary. But he would not dwell further upon that subject, because it was not included in the Motion before the House. The inquiry proposed by the hon. Member for Bradford would probably be attended with valuable results; at any rate, it would satisfy large and important interests that their claims and feelings had not been neglected.

MR. BAINES said, it was true that the Under Secretary of State had most courteously offered to receive a deputation from the Chambers of Commerce at the Foreign Office, and to give them every assistance. The deputation, accompanied by himself and the hon. Member for Manchester (Mr. Cobden), did go to the Foreign Office a few days after the invitation was given, and waited upon the Chief Secretary for Foreign Affairs, and also upon the President of the Board of Trade, and stated the view of the Associated Chambers upon those matters. He could confirm what had been said by the hon. Member for Bradford (Mr. W. E. Forster) as to the strong views entertained by the Chambers of Commerce on the subject, and their opinion was entitled to great weight, not only from the fact that they represented the mercantile communities of England, Scotland, and Ireland, but because they were frequently able to obtain from foreign merchants intelligence which was unknown to the Board of Trade. To give an illustration of how far the Department of the Board of Trade was behindhand in information, when the deputation waited upon the Board of Trade in February last, the President was asked whether he had seen a project which had been put forth by the Austrian Government for a new treaty with the Zollverein, and the right hon. Gentleman confessed that he had never seen or heard of it, though the schedule of the treaty had then been in the hands of the Chambers of Commerce for two months. He understood the hon. Member for Bradford did not intend to charge either the Board of Trade or the Foreign Office with neglect of duty, but simply to express an opinion that their duties were too heavy to enable them to give sufficient attention to an interest so vast as to be represented by a receipt of £450,000,000 per annum. Such an enormous interest might well claim to have a department or sub-department specially assigned to it.

Mr. BASS said, he was glad that the Government had consented to grant a Committee. In the French and Prussian Governments there was now a department in the Foreign Office which had charge of affairs of commerce exclusively, and he believed that a similar arrangement prevailed also in Russia. No one would question the ability with which the hon. Member for Rochdale (Mr. Cobden) had conducted the negotiations for the French Treaty, but there had not been uniformity of advantage, and great dissatisfaction was felt by many of his constituents, that the opportunity of altering tariffs in certain cases during the negotiations was lost. English subjects were only allowed to introduce some goods into France a year after the treaty was concluded, although France entered immediately upon her exports; there was still a suspense account, and for some years to come England would not be able to enter into fair competition with the French silk manufacturers. Considering the advantage that France derived from the treaty, and the enormous increase in her trade which it had produced, he believed that the Foreign Office might be well employed in inducing France to do away altogether with the suspense arrangement. The Under Secretary for Foreign Affairs had told them that the Government had done what they could in the case of Spain, but that their efforts had been totally unsuccessful. It would, he thought, have been only reasonable on the part of Spain, with the advantages she had derived from the French Treaty, to make some little concession to this country. Her commerce in wine with this country had doubled since the treaty was concluded, and the price of her wines had been increased 50 per cent, so that in point of fact the Spaniards were putting into their pockets very nearly the whole amount of the duty we had taken off. The wine growers of Spain were at the present moment enjoying an increase in the returns derived from their produce of from £800,000 to £1,000,000. He thought if the subject were fairly brought under the notice of the intelligent men who had now the commercial affairs of Spain in their hands, they would take a reasonable view of the matter. He was quite persuaded that if the Foreign Office devoted a small proportion of their efforts to the cultivation of trade which they now employed in writing despatches which almost smothered hon. Members when they received them, the country would derive double the benefit. It could not be doubted that if proper representations were pressed upon the Spanish Government we should have a more satisfactory condition of commerce with them. Portugal had derived great advantages from the treaty, but its tariff was prohibitory.

Mr. HENLEY said, that he too was glad to hear that the Government had agreed to the Committee. The importance of the subject could hardly be overrated, and he only regretted that the arguments of the Under Secretary of State seemed to him to be rather in opposition to the Committee which he had granted. The hon. Gentleman concluded his speech by telling the House that he had given the subject a great deal of consideration, and that, in his opinion, it was impossible that the business of the various Departments could be carried on in any other manner than it was at present. Having made that statement, the hon. Gentleman then said he agreed to the Motion. The principle of the matter was very simple and was one that applied to every transaction in this country. In every transaction of business in this country a man was never satisfied, when he wanted to get anything done, unless he could go direct to the persons who were to do it. When A was obliged to go to B to get C to do something, the work was multiplied, and was not done satisfactorily. He agreed with the noble Lord the Member for King's Lynn (Lord Stanley), that it was not very clear how there was to be an amendment; but, in his opinion, the present system was so palpably unsatisfactory that it was desirable there should be an inquiry to see whether some improvement could not be devised. He was not prepared to say whether the system could or could not be amended, but he was quite sure that the subject was one that ought to be looked into, and if it turned out that no remedy could be devised, at all events those great mercantile interests who entertained very strong opinions on the matter would have had their views heard and considered, and would, in consequence, feel much more satisfied than at present. He did not understand that the present Motion was made with any desire to blame the Foreign Office or the Board of Trade, but that the hon. Member desired to express the opinion, that if parties interested in commercial matters could get their views more directly brought before the persons who ultimately had to decide the case, it was possible that the work might be better done. According to the Under Secretary, the person interested went to the Board of Trade, which formed an opinion upon the case, and the duty of the Foreign Office was then merely to carry out the judgment of the Board of Trade. But it was possible that, though the judgment of the Board of Trade might have been right, and the duty of the Foreign Office rightly performed, the parties might say that the measure had failed through remissness in carrying it out; and in that case, where would the responsibility rest? He was of opinion that there would be a divided responsibility, and he believed such a system could not possibly answer as satisfactorily as one in which the duty was done by a single set of persons. He could not help thinking, that when the matter was carefully looked into, some arrangement might be made which would be more satisfactory to the commercial interests than the system at present existing. Nothing could be more objectionable than the present double system, and he hoped there would be a Committee to inquire whether it could not be amended.

Mr. NEWDEGATE said, that some years ago he had taken great interest in the collection of commercial statistics, which he was happy to say were now submitted to the House. It was at that period necessary that he should collect that information for himself, because when he commenced that task of calculation of the balance of Trade, the real value of the exports and imports of the country was not given, and he had to seek the information through his own channels. He (Mr. Newdegate) had also commenced the system for the adoption of which the coun-

Mr. Henley

try had to thank the noble Lord at the head of the Government—the system of requiring from our consuls information as to all changes, prospective and positive, in foreign tariffs—had not, when he commenced his labours, been carried out. Commercial men and Chambers of Commerce had derived great assistance from the system introduced by the noble Lord. It appeared to him that in the Board of Trade there was scarcely that distinct organization for information connected with the foreign commercial legislation which it was desirable to secure, and he thought the inquiries of the Government and of the proposed Committee might well be directed to the separation of the different functions of the Board of Trade and the allocation of distinct tasks to each sub-department when formed. He was afraid the commercial public would be in some degee disappointed with the results of the pending inquiry, for it could but indirectly facilitate negotiations with foreign countries as to commercial tariffs. One of the main objections he had taken to the Commercial Treaty with France in 1860 was, that under it the Emperor of the French was treated as the representative of all mankind, and the Under Secretary had explained to them to-night, when subsequently to that treaty the Government had approached foreign States, with a view to enter into commercial negotiations, England had been reminded that she was anything but mistress of the universe. It followed inevitably, from the conditions of the treaty, that England must come off second best. The energies of the Government ought to be directed towards liberating England from that position. The claims of England upon Spain and other countries ought not to rest on the reductions of duty which France might be inclined to make or refuse, but upon the commercial facilities and boons which the English nation had granted to those nations. Yet, under the treaty, there were stipulations on the importation into France of foreign including English goods. Thus if England obtained the most favoured nation clause, the most favoured nation being France, the clause contemplated the existence of many duties which England had abandoned, but which France retained, and the clause referred to some treaty in which these French import duties were considered as matters to be countervailed by equivalent duties, though these duties could not be imposed by England, owing to the terms of the French Treaty. He did not wish to say anything painful to the hon. Member for Rochdale (Mr. Cobden), as he believed he did the best he could under the circumstances in which he was placed by his antecedents; but the ruin month to month wrought on his (Mr. Newdegate's) constituents was painful to contemplate. The population depending on the silk trade in Warwickshire, in the district especially adjoining his own residence, had much decreased under the action of the French Treaty, and the district had been generally in a very depressed state; that population had much decreased, and between 1,600 and 1,700 empty houses were to be found. This made him the more anxious that the Government should make every exertion to induce the Government of France to hasten the period of the removal of the import duties on the introduction of silk goods and mixed goods. The Government might well say to France that she, having derived such enormous advantages from the treaty should, accelerate the period for the reduction of these duties, in recognition of the sufferings inflicted on our silk manufacturers. It had never appeared to him that the nations of the world would follow exactly in their footsteps. His conviction was that while France was deriving a great revenue from import duties and great benefits by her export trade, England might just as well have equivalent import duties, and yet share in that increase of revenue and extension of trade. That was his conviction. He had always thought that the French tariff was more wisely regulated than the tariff adopted by this country in 1860. He might be wrong, but he thought the present commercial state of France sanctioned that opinion. He hoped that the opinion of the House and of the country would become accommodated to those facts; and that it was their duty to hasten the period when the French duty on silk goods should be reduced. They had a right, he thought, to claim that reduction from France, because, while she had benefited largely by the treaty, some of our own interests—silk interests especially—had suffered grievous injury. There was another subject to which he wished to call the attention of the House. In the instructions given to our consuls there appeared to be some confusion. In many cases the business of consuls ought to be strictly limited to commercial objects. His question had

reference to a particular case. Six or seven years ago Mr. Plowden was sent out to Abyssinia as consul, and he should like to be informed as to what instructions that gentleman actually received. It was generally believed that the object of his mission was to open commercial relations with that country. It appeared that Mr. Plowden became mixed up with the internal politics of Abyssinia, and the result was that he was murdered. That was not an old story. He had a copy of the *Jewish Intelligencer*, a publication that was issued by some persons interested in the conversion of the Jews in Abyssinia, and he found that, at the present moment, our consul who succeeded Mr. Plowden had unfortunately mixed himself up with the politics of Abyssinia, and was a prisoner in the hands of the King. Those were two instances of the impolicy of allowing consuls commissioned for commercial purposes to mix themselves up with the politics of the countries in which they had to reside, and which were at best but in an imperfect state of civilisation. A distinction ought to be drawn between the functions of a consul sent merely for commercial purposes and those of a *chargé d'affaires*, because the person who might be competent for commercial purposes might be totally unfit for political negotiations. The instructions given to those persons ought to be so drawn up as to advance the purposes of trade, and to make them feel that they should keep clear of politics in the countries to which they were sent. It was unbecoming the dignity of this country that we should employ agents so incompetent as that one should fall a victim, and the next a captive, of the Government to which he was sent. He hoped to be assured that Captain Cameron had been liberated, and that in future such a limit would be put to the functions of any person sent to Abyssinia as would secure his personal safety, otherwise the dignity of the country would be endangered abroad, and the operations of commerce disturbed if not destroyed.

MR. MILNER GIBSON said, that as there was no objection on the part of the Government to grant the Committee, he did not know that it was necessary to prolong that debate, or to enter into a general discussion upon the mode in which commercial negotiations had been conducted between this country and foreign Governments. But he wished merely to notice some remarks made by the right hon. Gentleman the Member for Oxford-shire (Mr. Henley) on the immediate question before them. That right hon. Gentleman seemed to think that a divided responsibility now existed, and that it was very inconvenient that a person having business of a commercial kind to be transacted with a foreign Government should first of all be compelled to go to the Board of Trade, that then the Board of Trade should have to submit its views to the Foreign Office, and that the Foreign Office should afterwards make a representation to a foreign Government; or, in other words, that A had to communicate with B, and B had to communicate with C, in order that D might be induced to do something. That, certainly, appeared inconvenient, but the argument, if carried to its full extent, would make it necessary that they should have only one department for the general government of the country. There was nothing peculiar in the relations between the Foreign Office and the Board of Trade. Precisely the same relations existed between the Foreign Office and every other Department of the State. Questions of international law were constantly arising, and recently those questions had been of a most important character. Merchants whose property was in jeopardy, or whose ships had been captured under questionable circumstances, went to the Foreign Office, but the Foreign Office did not possess any knowledge which enabled it to make the fitting representation to the foreign Government, and it was obliged to refer the subject to the Law Officers of the Crown, and frequently to the Committee of Privy Council, consisting of the most eminent authorities in this country on questions of international law. When it had acquired the requisite knowledge, and received instruction from those who were competent to give it, the Foreign Office made the required representation to the foreign Government. The right hon. Member for Oxfordshire (Mr. Henley) to put the matter concisely—said that the knowledge was in the Board of Trade and the power in the Foreign Office, and thought the two things should be united in the same Department. If that were a sound principle, it applied to all the Departments in the State. When the House considered the matter calmly, it would be seen that there was really no divided responsibility. The Government, as a whole, was responsible for the conduct of foreign as of domestic affairs. The executive Government, as a whole,

Mr. Milner Gibson

was responsible to Parliament; and upon all branches of public business it was entitled to obtain the knowledge and advice necessary for carrying on that business with wisdom and safety. It would be inconsistent with the first principles of our system of Government to place a special responsibility for particular acts or a particular policy upon this or that department. The particular relation between the Foreign Office and the Board of Trade—namely, that the latter was a consulting department, and that the former made such representations to foreign Governments as after consultation might seem desirable, was in theory, he was inclined to think, a very good arrangement. From what he had observed, he believed that if they were to merge the Board of Trade in the Foreign Office, the commercial classes would be less likely to have an independent representation made to the Foreign Office of the merits of any commercial question when communications were going on between this country and foreign Governments. He believed it was of advantage that there should be an independent department, making representations on the purely commercial merits of the question, without reference to, and unbiassed by, the political or diplomatic negotiations that were proceeding. When the Foreign Office and the other Departments of the State were at least in entire possession of the impartial and strictly commercial aspect of the question, they could estimate it at its full value; and in the course of negotiation it was for them to consider whether the objects they had in view of a political nature conflicted materially with the commercial merits of the proposal, as explained after consultation with the Board of Trade. He thought the proposed Committee would be useful, because nobody for a moment contended that the internal arrangements of any of our offices were not susceptible of improvement. He could quite conceive that the mechanical part of the relations between the Foreign Office and the Board of Trade might, without interfering with principles, be made to work more smoothly and with greater advantage to commercial interests. Consequently, on that ground, and without admitting that there was divided responsibility, he saw no objection to the appointment of the proposed Committee. He thought that some hon. Gentlemen had over-estimated the power of this country to induce foreign nations which were hampered by protected interests to adopt more liberal tariffs. It was objected that this country went in the wake of France. Now, what had France been able to effect, though France was in a more advantageous position than this country to influence foreign Governments, to induce them to reduce their tariffs? Why, France went to foreign nations with a great bribe, being able to offer them those great reductions in her duties which she had already given to England; yet, after all, she had only been able to accomplish commercial treaties between two countries—Belgium and Italy. No doubt there were engagements between Prussia and France, but as the States of the Zollverein had not ratified them, they were not carried into effect as a treaty between France and the Zollverein, though they probably might be in 1865. France, then, had only concluded two treaties—one with Belgium and the other with Italy. But after France had concluded the treaty with Belgium, making those reductions in her tariff which Belgium now enjoyed, this country made a treaty with Belgium by which England obtained the "favoured nations clause" and thus came in for all the advantages which Belgium had granted to France. He did not believe that the English Government would have obtained that result if they had attempted to negotiate a treaty with Belgium single-handed; and it was with great difficulty it was obtained after all, on account of the fear felt by the protected interests of English competition. Not that the Belgian Government was not a most enlightened one; the difficulty was, that the Belgian manufacturers feared English competition. The Belgian manufacturers were not nearly so much afraid of French competition as of English competition; and he was convinced that the prestige enjoyed by England on the Continent, on account of her great manufacturing power and skill in producing articles at a cheap rate for the consumption of the masses, was the very thing which alarmed those foreign manufacturers, and made it more difficult for England than for France to induce foreign countries to reduce their tariffs. In fact, France, as matters now stood, was a better pioneer in the path of commercial freedom than England, and approached Belgium with offers which it was not within the power of this country to make. However, "the favoured nations clause," which the English Government

obtained from Belgium, was very advantageous, for the effect had been that the import duties on British manufactures into Belgium had been reduced from 40 and 30 per cent to 20 and 10 per cent. That, then, was the result of the policy pursued, however much criticised it might be; and any impartial man, considering the power of the protected interests, and the state of parties in Belgium, must admit that the effect accomplished was a great success. With respect to Italy, it had been said that the English Government were too late in the field, and allowed France to negotiate a successful treaty; whereas if they had been there in time they could have got the Italian Government to make their tariff more conformable with British interests and less exclusively in accordance with French interests. That was a mistaken view of the question. The basis of negotiation between France and Italy would not have allowed of England obtaining any advantage which she has not already obtained by the "favoured nations clause." The fact was that at the time of the negotiation all the duties in the Italian tariff, with some few exceptions, were lower than in the reformed French tariff, and therefore it was only in some few cases—in silks, he believed, and in one or two other articles—that Italy was asked to make any reduction in favour of France. The Italian tariff was already more liberal than the reformed French tariff; and France not making further reductions, the basis of negotiations did not admit at that time of those reductions in favour of England, which it was supposed would have been accomplished; and though Mr. Mallet, from the Board of Trade, went to Turin to do all he could, that gentleman observed that the Italian Government were little disposed to do more in the direction of commercial freedom than could possibly be helped. The Italian tariff had not heretofore been a high tariff; and, though there had been no change as affecting English productions, still the activity given to industry by other changes in Italy had occasioned a great increase of trade between England and that country. With regard to the Motion before the House, the Government regarded the proposal as manifesting a sincere desire on the part of his hon. Friend the Member for Bradford (Mr. W. E. Forster) to effect something practically useful, and they wished cordially to co-operate in such an object.

MR. COBDEN : Sir, as the Motion of my hon. Friend has been agreed to, there is little ground for prolonged discussion at the present moment, but I am anxious to say a few words to prevent any misapprehension here, and especially abroad, as to the scope of the proposed inquiry. It must be remembered that our manufacturers do not present themselves to this House at the present moment in the position of complainants as to the operation of the free trade policy carried out as we have carried it out in this country, irrespective of the action of other countries. The manufacturers do not come here asking the Government to forward their interests by promoting commercial treaties. The French Treaty arose from an accidental conjuncture of circumstances, and nothing of the kind can happen again. It so happened — opportunely happened — that we had considerable reforms of our tariff still to accomplish, which it would have been our interest to have effected, whether or not the French Government had simultaneously taken a large step in the same direction. But it so happened, fortunately, that the French Government was just in the disposition to make the first great step in the path of commercial freedom in that country. The two Governments were enabled with much more ease and advantage to perform these two operations together than they could have done separately. But it would have been equally their interest to have done it separately as by commercial treaty. Now, with regard to the argument that has been urged from time to time, that we have lost advantages by having carried out the principle of free trade so largely ourselves, without having first gone to other countries to induce them to go step by step with us, I venture to say there are not two opinions in the country amongst the mercantile and manufacturing population as to the gain we have made during the last twenty or twenty-two years by advancing without waiting for other countries to take any step with us in this policy. The immense increase in our commerce, as shown by the financial statement of my right hon. Friend the Chancellor of the Exchequer, has been the reward we have received for having anticipated other countries in the policy we have adopted. Now, having entered this caveat against any possible misrepresentation of the object of this Motion of my hon. Friend the Member for Bradford (Mr. W. E. Forster), I would ask whether,

Mr. Milner Gibson

without commercial treaties, or without any attempt publicly to agitate the question, it would not be possible for the Government of this free trade nation to diffuse those principles which have been so beneficial to us amongst other countries. I will give you an analogous case. I think in 1806 we abolished the slave trade. We did that by a municipal law as an act of humanity and justice. That was the result of a long and intense agitation, which deeply stirred the religious feeling and the national conscience in this country. We carried free trade after nearly as long, as anxious, and as intense an agitation. Did the Government remain passive with other countries after we had abolished the slave trade ? On the contrary, they made it the constant object of their diplomacy abroad to induce other countries to follow in the same enlightened and humane course. Almost the only ground on which I can look back to the Treaty of Vienna with satisfaction is, that it contains engagements, entered into at our instance by other countries, to abolish the slave trade. Our merchants and manufacturers think it would be a legitimate occupation of the Government of this free trade and commercial country if they would try to diffuse these principles in other countries. And how is that to be done ? This brings us to the question which my hon. Friend the Member for Bradford (Mr. W. E. Forster) has so very usefully raised. We have two Departments concerned in this matter; one is the Board of Trade, the other is the Foreign Office, situated on the two sides of Downing Street. Well, one of these Departments, during the last fifty years, has taken the most enlightened views upon questions of commerce, and has always been in advance of the community in its appreciation of our true interests with regard to commercial policy. I am speaking from my own knowledge when I say that that Department has constantly had within its walls gentlemen of the most enlightened views on that subject. But if we go to the other Office, it is no reproach to the Foreign Department to say that neither its Foreign Minister, nor its diplomatists, take charge of, or inform themselves on, commercial questions, because hitherto it has been considered that that Department has had no commercial objects in view in its negotiations. Well, now, my hon. Friend the Member for Bradford asks whether you cannot import into the Foreign Office some of the intelligence which rules in the Board of Trade. How that may be done, and how that spirit may be made to diffuse itself abroad, is a question that may fairly be considered in the Committee which is now to be appointed. I will not enlarge upon that subject further than by saying that there ought to be greater intelligence on the part of those who are engaged in the diplomatic service of this country upon these commercial questions; and in order to insure that, there must be a provision made henceforth (for it is too late to adopt it with reference to our present diplomatists) which will require a knowledge and appreciation of these commercial questions on the part of those engaged in our diplomatic service. We are a commercial and manufacturing people, and are so only considered abroad. We should be a third-rate people if we depended merely upon our agriculture. I desire that our interests, and that the spirit which rules in this country, should animate our diplomacy abroad. I think, for instance, that our diplomatists should be required not only to understand Adam Smith, the classic of free trade, but to be acquainted with the commercial policy of this country for the last twenty years. Let them read, for instance, the volume of speeches of my right hon. Friend the Chancellor of the Exchequer, lately published, and let them undergo an examination on the course of our commercial policy during the last twenty years. Let them know what has been done, not merely in the history of the past, but down to the present moment. Now, without publicly professing to be propagandists, without saying one word about it in public or in our despatches, if our diplomatic representatives knew that by exerting themselves in the cause of free trade abroad they would be as likely to get the decoration and rank of G.C.B. as if they had been successful in assisting at the ceremony of a dynastic treaty or some Court marriage, I think you would very soon find these young gentlemen begin to take an interest in commercial questions. Now, let us suppose a Minister living at St. Petersburg, where he has little to do, and where, of course, he has his secretaries and attachés, what might he not effect with a Government like that of Russia, if he were imbued with a free trade feeling, and were fully acquainted with free trade subjects. He would have every opportunity of converting the Government to his own views of free trade, by merely presenting clearly before them the facts of the case as

we have exhibited it for the last twenty years. Russia, like most other Governments, is in want of money, and the reform of their tariff in the direction in which we have been going for the last twenty years would be like the discovery of a gold mine at St. Petersburg. If we could only show other Governments that the reform of our tariff had increased the prosperity of the people, and the amount of our revenue, and that simultaneously we had progressed in skill and civilization, we need not ask them to reform their tariff in our interest; they would do so in their own interests. There is much ignorance about these subjects even in this House. An hon. Protectionist on an opposite bench, to whom I have listened for the last twenty years, has spoken to-day in the very terms which he used when I first entered this House. In order to present the facts of this case before foreign Governments I would suggest to the Board of Trade that as one means of instructing our diplomatists in commercial matters the Board of Trade should prepare a manual of our free trade policy, showing the progress of our legislation and its results, and should place that manual in the hands of those who represent us at foreign Courts. Let it be translated into the languages of those Courts, in order that it may be used as one of the means of converting them to our free trade principles, and let not those who belonged to the past generation of diplomatists imagine that it was a proposal to be treated with levity. This course is just what the commercial and manufacturing people of this country have a right to expect at the hands of any Government. And if the present Administration do not adopt a policy of this kind it will be adopted by a Government formed from the other side of the House. I do not ask for any discussions in this House, nor for any reports or blue-books. We have done more harm than good by discussing this question in this House in reference to our own interests. We have a vast and expensive machinery engaged in our diplomacy, and our manufacturing and trading community expect that our diplomatists shall devote some attention to our commercial interests abroad. Will anybody say that the employment of that machinery during the last few years has been satisfactory to this House or to the country? We have little mountains of blue-books on Schleswig-Holstein and does not everybody agree that they are unsatisfactory? Diplomacy has broken down in its own vocation, and the dynastic arrangements of Europe and the balance of power are questions which have ceased to engage the sympathies of the British public. In the interests of the Foreign Office, I exhort it to take a hint from my hon. Friend the Member for Bradford. By promoting the triumph of free trade principles, which can only be completely effected when they are adopted by other countries, our diplomatists will be laying the foundation for peaceful relations between the nations of the earth of a far more enduring nature than by anything they can achieve through the recognised arts of diplomacy.

Mr. BAZLEY observed, that the right hon. Gentleman the Member for Ashton-under-Lyne (Mr. Milner Gibson) had said that France must take the lead upon the Continent in reference to commercial treaties.

Mr. MILNER GIBSON begged to explain that what he had said was that France, not having given to other countries those advantages which she has given to us, it was inevitable that the negotiations should be commenced by France and other foreign nations.

Mr. BAZLEY: But the circumstances of our country were very different, and the manufacturers of England could not be fairly dealt with upon the basis of a treaty between France and other continental countries. The right hon. Gentleman seemed to think that our consuls should not be employed in negotiating commercial treaties; but for what better purpose did they keep up their consular and diplomatic establishments, at an expense of half-a-million sterling? Why should those gentlemen be kept in particular positions if they were not to perform duties which would be useful to the country? If foreign Governments were reminded of the advantages of free trade without there being any treaties, a great deal might be done. The vast amount of exports from the country required that more attention should be paid to the interests of commerce. During the last twenty years our imports and exports had quadrupled in amount, while our consular representation remained the same. He did not attribute any blame to the right hon. Gentleman the President of the Board of Trade, nor to the Under Secretary for Foreign Affairs, whom he had always found most courteous and attentive to any representations; but until our consular arrangements were amended, our com-

Mr. Cobden

mercial interests must suffer, and had, he contended, a perfect right to complain of the system by which they were bound.

Question, "That the words proposed to be left out stand part of the Question," put, and *negatived*.

Words *added*.

Main Question, as amended, put, and *agreed to*.

Ordered,

That a Select Committee be appointed to inquire into the arrangement between the Foreign Office and the Board of Trade in reference to Trade with Foreign Nations.—(*Mr. W. E. Forster*.)

SUPPLY—Order of the Day again read.

Motion made, and Question, "That this House will immediately resolve itself into a Committee of Supply," put, and *agreed to*.

Question proposed, "That Mr. Speaker do now leave the Chair."

INDICTABLE OFFENCES (IRELAND)
RETURNS MOVED FOR.

Mr. WHITESIDE said, he rose to ask for certain Returns of indictable offences committed in particular counties in Ireland, and laid before the Judges at the late assizes for Roscommon, Cavan, Longford, Limerick, and Westmeath. He did so with the object of eliciting an explanation of the causes for the prevalence of so large a proportion of undetected crime in those counties, and to ascertain what course the Government proposed to adopt to lessen the same. The assizes having now terminated the subject might properly be considered by the House, and if they could discover the causes of the defects in the administration of justice they might possibly suggest a remedy. The condition of Ireland had been described by the Attorney General for that country in very favourable terms, and the right hon. Gentleman had declared that no country in the world was so free from crime, and that although agrarian offences did occur, they were merely local, and left the normal condition of Ireland one of peace and order. The documents which he asked for were two in number. The first was a list of indictable offences and of persons indicted in the several counties named in his Motion. The second was a list the existence of which was not known to many hon. Members, and therefore he would describe it. When a Judge arrived in the town where the assizes were to be held, the principal officer of police was required to furnish him with a list of the offences which had been committed in the county since the previous assizes. It was not usual to make public those lists, although he did not know what reason there could be against doing so, but the reason for his asking for those lists was because they would give the real state of facts at the time of the last assizes in Ireland. He had he believed a correct extract from the calendar for one county—Roscommon, which he would take as an example. The list of offenders for trial was small, being seven in number. But the question was, did the calendar of offences show the real state of crime in that county? He could not, of course, give the official figures, but he had been supplied by a gentleman resident in the county of Roscommon with a statement which he believed to be correct, and from which he found that the number of offences committed for which the offenders had not been brought to trial was no less than eighty-seven, including eleven incendiary fires, five cases of maiming cattle, fifteen of writing threatening letters, seven of attacking dwelling houses, five attempts to upset railway trains, and fifteen aggravated assaults. He had also been favoured with another document bearing upon this subject. The number of applications at the last assizes for compensations for malicious injuries was fifteen or sixteen. Then came the question as to the provision made for the maintenance of the peace. As far as Roscommon was concerned, the state of things which he had described was by no means owing to a numerically inefficient police. The population of Roscommon was 157,000, and it had 412 members of the constabulary, while the county of Down, with a population of 300,000, had only 280 police. Upon those facts the learned Mr. Justice Christian made certain observations, and asked how it was that there were so many offences for which there were no prosecutions. The learned Judge said it could only be attributable to intimidation of the injured parties or to a general disinclination to assist justice, or to a deficiency of energy and skill on the part of the police. When the same learned Judge visited Galway he congratulated the grand jury upon the wholesome administration of the law in that county, as contrasted with others through which he had passed, and where he said there was not so much an absence of crime as a paralysis of justice. With respect to

the county of Cavan, he had not been able to get a list of the undetected crimes in that county. The next county was that of Limerick, in which crime was considerable, but the Returns showed that in the case of highway robberies (four in number), burglaries, arson, killing and mutilating cattle (six in number)—a very serious offence in an agricultural country—sending threatening letters (ten in number), not a single person had been made amenable to justice. The Judge thought it necessary to comment on such a remarkable state of things, and he stated in a neighbouring county that it was a matter of great gratification to him to find that the remarks which he thought it his duty to make upon the subject had received the concurrence and approval of so respectable a body as the grand jury of the county of Limerick. In the county of Westmeath the Lord Chief Justice informed the grand jury that the convictions, as compared with the offences, were infinitesimal, and he had scarcely left the assize town when an honest farmer was attacked by, he believed, a band of Ribbonmen, who beat him almost to death, and said that they would return next day and do the same to his father. With regard to Longford, which did not stand well in the matter, he would not trouble the House, nor with respect to Donegal, where the cases were principally connected with the policy of the Chancellor of the Exchequer, which had led to a great increase of crime; but the House would have an opportunity of expressing its opinion on that subject when he (Mr. Whiteside) submitted his Motion on the spirit duties. The right hon. Baronet the Chief Secretary for Ireland must allow him to say that it was not in his power to dispute the opinions of the five Judges. Of all things there ought to be certainty in the administration of the criminal law, because the whole peace of the country depended upon it, and in the counties to which he had referred there had been a complete failure of justice. It had been said that it was difficult to detect threatening letters. But let the Executive look sharply after the schoolmasters of the district. He had had occasion to deal with threatening letters, and had not found the difficulty quite insuperable. In one case a letter was sent threatening to shoot a respectable gentleman, in the county of Kildare, and the writer was now ruminating on the consequences in his transportation. When they looked to the facts which he had stated, they might be disposed to ask whether it was all the fault of the constabulary. He could not bring himself to believe so. He held in his hand a letter from a gentleman in one of the counties he had named, a magistrate of the highest respectability, and in it he was desired not to confine his attention merely to the police, but to ask what sort of men were the stipendiary magistrates, the age of the county Inspectors when they were appointed, how the whole administration of local justice was carried on, and what were the rules which governed the constabulary force. That gentleman said of the constabulary that he was informed they were instructed not to interfere with a crime that came under their notice unless they were absolutely on duty at the time, and that they were decidedly discouraged from what was called "officiously" exerting themselves to prevent the commission of offences. Was that the fact? [Sir ROBERT PEEL asked to see the letter, and the right hon. Gentleman handed it to him, though he stated it was a private one.] The real truth was that they had as moral, intelligent, and respectable a body of men as any in the world in the Irish constabulary; they were truthful witnesses, and in that capacity very fatal to the offender. But it was not persons that could march well or fight well that were wanted in Ireland; they had no one to fight with now; there were but few men in the counties, and every day was reducing the number. When he stated that fact on the second day of the Session he was contradicted, but it would be found that he was right. But he would ask the right hon. Baronet the Chief Secretary to the Lord Lieutenant, if a man were to put on his head a heavy helmet, then a belt round his waist, side arms, a big coat and other heavy accoutrements, and then he was to tell him, "There's a criminal, go and catch him," whether that man would be likely to do so? On one occasion, a very respectable gentleman, a Mr. Mauleverer, was murdered at one o'clock in the day, near the borders of the county of Louth. Some distance from the spot a police-officer, and a fine young man in the force, were accosted by a car-driver, who, he believed, was privy to the murder, and told that a gentleman had been killed on the road some distance off. They made the car-driver return to the spot, and found the body upon the road. He himself heard the constable describe what it was necessary to do. The officer remained with the body, but the

young man threw off his helmet, his coat, his belt, and then he pursued the murderers for three miles through the fields, came up with them, and they were arrested before they entered a house. It was not, then, a question of breaking up the force, for that would be the greatest loss to the country; but some reasonable change should be made in the details of its organization, with a view to the pursuit of criminals, and the detection of crime. But there was another matter. He was informed by country gentlemen in Ireland, who would not attack the Government, but do all in their power to support it, that attempts were made to deprive them of all authority over the police, to transfer it to the stipendiary magistrates, and to centralize the control. Nothing could be more injurious, as regarded the detection of crime. In Carlow the Lord Chief Justice found that every criminal had been detected, and he said that that must have arisen because the magistrates and police worked in harmony together. In the North of Ireland there was not so much crime, but that was chiefly owing to the fact that the people were in a more prosperous condition. He believed that what Mr. Justice Keogh had said in passing a severe sentence upon the young men detected in drilling was quite true, and from what he had heard in the House as well, it was evident that there was a very strong feeling in certain quarters of Ireland in favour of what was termed "nationality." There was no use in blinking the fact. The right hon. Baronet the Chief Secretary for Ireland, had described the country as being in a tranquil state. He might mention that on one occasion, when he was going to the college chapel in Dublin, he found himself in the midst of a very well-dressed assembly, so much so indeed that he at first believed that the gathering was in honour of a wedding. He made inquiries of a policeman, who informed him that it was the funeral of Mr. M'Manus, and that 7,000 young men had accompanied the body to the grave. He remembered that Mr. M'Manus was tried for high treason. It would be a great mistake to imagine that those young men who accompanied the funeral were either immoral or profligate. They were nothing of the kind. The right hon. Baronet would be told by them if they happened to meet him that there was not the slightest objection to him personally, but that the people would be very glad to get rid of him and his col-

Mr. Whiteside

leagues. The same feeling extended itself towards the Government ; but the fact that a feeling of discontent prevailed certainly would not justify the Government in making any attack upon the people. The House ought, however, to be on their guard, and not encourage theories which might prove destructive to the regular Government of the country. He moved

"For copies of the lists of all indictable offences laid before the Judges of Assizes at the late Assizes for the counties of Roscommon, Cavan, Longford, Limerick, and Westmeath ; and also for the names of the parties made amenable at the said assizes, and of the offences for which they were severally indicted, as appearing in the calendars of said counties ; and for an explanation of the causes why so large a proportion of undetected crime prevails in said counties, and what course the Government means to adopt in order to lessen the same."

He believed he was putting a very practical question in asking his right hon. Friend the Secretary for Ireland whether he had reflected upon the matter since he had last addressed the House upon the subject, and whether the Government had adopted, or was prepared to adopt, any plan which would have the effect of lessening the number of instances in which crime had taken place without leading to detection.

Amendment proposed,

To leave out from the word "That" to the end of the Question, in order to add the words "there be laid before this House, Copies of the Lists of all Indictable Offences laid before the Judges of Assize at the late Assizes for the counties of Roscommon, Cavan, Longford, Limerick, and Westmeath, and also for the names of the parties made amenable at said Assizes, and of the offences for which they were severally indicted, as appearing in the calendars of said counties,"— (*Mr. Whiteside*,)

—instead thereof.

SIR ROBERT PEEL said, he had given the subject much consideration since it had last been submitted to the attention of the House. He assured the right hon. Gentleman the Member for Dublin University (Mr. Whiteside) that the observations he made upon a former occasion were not intended to cast any slur upon the remarks of the Judges. His object on that occasion had been to show that the state of the country generally was not what it was sometimes described to be. Before, however, alluding to the subject, he wished to make one remark. They all knew that the right hon. Gentleman (Mr. Whiteside) was a very spirited and dashing speaker, and that when he made an assertion, which

probably in his own mind he was fully aware at the time was not literally true, he endeavoured to give it weight by stating that the assertion he had made had been erroneously corrected. Now, he would not allow the right hon. Gentleman to make any such statement concerning himself without correcting it. The right hon. Gentleman had stated on that occasion that 100,000 fighting men had left Ireland in the course of twelve months, and he had respectfully assured the right hon. Gentleman that such was not the case. He had acknowledged that 119,000 people had left Ireland, but he had also stated that 58,000 out of that number were women, and 12,000 children under twelve years of age. The severe correction which he on that occasion administered to the right hon. Gentleman he still maintained was well merited. The right hon. Gentleman might repeat that he had no right to correct him, but so long as he persisted in repeating his statement so long would he (Sir Robert Peel) continue to point out to the House and to the country that that statement was incorrect.

MR. WHITESIDE : I beg your pardon. What I stated was—

SIR ROBERT PEEL said, that the right hon. Gentleman would have an opportunity of referring to the subject afterwards. As regarded the Motion then before the House, the Government were quite ready to furnish the right hon. Gentleman with the copies he required. The right hon. Gentleman had also asked him if he could give any explanation as to the cause why so large a proportion of undetected crime prevailed in the country, and what course the Government intended to adopt in order to lessen the amount of undetected crime. The right hon. Gentleman had then gone *seriatim* through the counties of Roscommon, Cavan, Longford, Limerick, and Westmeath. He desired the attention of the House to the subject, because it was important for them, when learned Judges commented upon the amount of undetected crime, to know the difficulty under which they laboured respecting the detection of offenders. It was true, as the right hon. Gentleman had stated, that in the county of Roscommon the Judge had said, in March, that the total number of outrages since the previous assizes, a period of eight months, had been eighty-seven, and that out of that number the parties who were concerned in forty-seven of them were totally unknown. It was true that there had been eleven incendiary fires, five cases of killing cattle, one of demanding arms, and five of firing shots at night, without the perpetrators in any instance being discovered. It was also true that there had been fifteen cases of sending threatening notices, seven of injury to houses, and several attempts to upset trains, or cases in which stones had been thrown at them, without any person having been made amenable. Immediately that statement was made, he wrote to the county Inspector to ascertain the reason for the existence of such a state of things, and his answer was, that in thirty of those cases the injured parties had declined to lodge any information upon oath. How was it possible for the Government to compel injured parties to come forward and to lodge information against their will? There were thirty cases in which depositions were sworn but no individual offenders charged, and twenty-seven in which the offenders were sworn to, thus making up the total of eighty-seven. The right hon. Gentleman had also alluded to the county of Cavan. The Judge at the assizes held in that county in March last, had remarked that the return of offenders reported since the previous assizes showed fifty-four cases, in only sixteen of which had any person been arrested. Among the catalogue of offences in that county, he found that four incendiary fires remained undiscovered; that nine cases of housebreaking or burglary had occurred without more than two persons having been arrested, and that those two had been discharged; that there had been two cases of demanding or robbery of arms, two of administering unlawful oaths, and twelve of sending threatening letters. For the latter offence two persons were made amenable. He took the opportunity of making the same inquiry of the county Inspector in this instance as he had in the cases which had occurred in Roscommon. His reply was, that there had undoubtedly been four incendiary fires, but that in one case it did not appear to have been malicious, at least the landlord was of that opinion; in another that the owner said it was malicious and that he had £64 in the thatch, but that no one appeared to credit him; in the third case, the burning of a dwelling house and shop, it had since been ascertained to have been a wilful attempt to defraud creditors, and that the perpetrator was now being punished; in the fourth and last case, the fire, though reputed to have been a wilful one, was

Sir Robert Peel

now believed by the sub-Inspector of police and the public to have been accidental. In one of the cases of robbery of arms, the gun was stolen from the cabin of a caretaker while he was away at night. In the other a number of persons came to a house and carried away a gun. The owner and his family were examined before the magistrate, and swore they could not even give a description of any one of the party. That circumstance alone would give the House some idea of the difficulty they experienced in the due administration of justice. A party of men came in broad daylight without any disguise and took away a gun, and yet the parties aggrieved would not come forward and give evidence of the robbery. In cases of sending threatening letters, of which there were twelve, and one conviction, every one acknowledged the difficulty of bringing such offenders to justice. The remaining cases of undiscovered crime were principally assaults at public places or on the return home from fairs and markets by persons whom the injured parties swore they did not know. There were offences peculiar to some counties which were unknown in others—for instance, in Cavan there were threatening letters, which had generally something to do with the Ribbon system. Injuries to cattle and incendiary fires were also peculiar to that county. In the opinion of the county magistrates, however, Cavan had not been for several years past in a more peaceable state, and the Judges confirmed the statement that the constabulary enjoyed the respect of the magistracy and the public. The right hon. and learned Gentleman had told the House about the 7,000 persons who went to the funeral of Mr. M'Manus, in Dublin; but he had not stated that there was no breach of the peace committed. He did not know why it should fall to the province of the right hon. Gentleman to lower his country by raking up those cases and making the worst of a state of things which was not so bad as it seemed. Limerick had also been spoken of by the right hon. Gentleman, and there the learned Judge observed—

"I have been furnished by your county Inspector with his Report, containing a return of the amount of offences committed, and I am struck with suprise at the numbers set down for which no one has been made amenable, and others where the prosecutions had been altogether abandoned."

It was true that there were thirty-three cases brought before the Judge in which there were no informations, but in eight the injured persons declined to give any evidence, and in the remaining twenty-five the magistrates considered it either useless or injudicious to take informations, as they could implicate no one. That Report did not represent so bad a state of things in Limerick county as the right hon. Gentleman would have the House believe. It was true that in three or four counties the Judges did blame the constabulary for want of efficiency, as is evinced by the number of persons convicted; but in the remaining twenty-nine counties the Judges and the magistracy concurred in declaring that the state of those counties was satisfactory, and in speaking most favourably of the efficiency of the constabulary, that force which the right hon. Gentleman had ventured to criticize. He had spoken of their being armed with a helmet, with bayonets at their belts, as though a man could use his weapon there, and that they had as much on their backs as that table could carry. The constabulary had been organized for forty years as at present, and they were admitted to be the finest force in the world. The right hon. Gentleman had asked him whether he had turned his attention to this matter since last he had brought it before the House.

Mr. WHITESIDE: I never brought it before the House.

Sir ROBERT PEEL: Well, then, the right hon. Gentleman had ventured upon erroneous statements which he was obliged to correct. He had had drawn up for his own information the statements of the Judges of twenty-nine separate counties, and in every instance they had spoken favourably of the state of the country and of the constabulary. He would not weary the House by going through the whole of the charges, and would, therefore, only allude to the charge of Chief Justice Monaghan at Kerry, who said that he would not join in the cry that had been raised by his brethren, the other Judges, to run down the constabulary. The Chief Justice, on the contrary, expressed his belief that the police honourably and conscientiously discharged their duty. In twenty-eight other counties similar reports had been made by the Judges. So active and energetic had been the constabulary, indeed, within the last few years, that the annual Report of offences, arrests, &c., showed a decrease of offences last year compared with 1862 of more than 1,200. The right hon. Gentleman had spoken of the popula-

tion of Roscommon, Cavan, and Limerick and endeavoured to prove that a greater number of crimes were committed in the southern and western counties than in the north of Ireland. The population of Roscommon, Cavan, and Limerick was 483,979; the number of offences and arrests reported in the three counties for eight months was 227, and the number of arrests was 114. So that in those three counties there was one offence to every 2,132 persons during the eight months. The population of England and Wales, exclusive of the metropolis, was 17,263,857. The number of offences during eight months was 26,624, and the number of arrests was 15,871. In England and Wales, therefore, there was one offence for every 648 persons, while in Ireland there was only one offence to every 2,132 persons. The House could scarcely imagine the difficulty experienced by the authorities in Ireland in inducing persons to come forward and swear informations when offences had been committed. He had only that day received two remarkable statements respecting the unwillingness to assist the course of justice. He would read the report of the resident magistrate in Westmeath—

"County Westmeath, Kilbeggan, April 13.

"On Sunday night last, about eleven o'clock, James Casey, about twenty years of age, of Boston, county Westmeath, within two miles of Moate, was returning with four others from Ballycumber, in the King's County. Some talk about their respective fighting powers ended in one William Galvin's giving Casey a blow with a large stone held in his fist over the left temple. I saw him on Monday evening, and though perfectly sensible and collected he refuses to say one word about the affair, saying he knows nothing about it. [An hon. Member: That is a common case.] The information of Reynolds, who was of the party and present, clearly fixes it on William Galvin, who, he says, was provoked by Casey. We should have succeeded in arresting Galvin, who has got off, but that Casey's father, who sent for Dr. Mathews, at half past twelve a.m. on Monday morning, never called at the barrack, which was passed on the way to the doctor's, through whom, I understand, the police heard of the affair about noon of Monday last. William Galvin was at his usual employment up to that hour of that day, but did not return to it after dinner hour, for we were near him."

He would give another instance of the general unwillingness to assist the police from King's County—

"Parsonstown, April 11, 1864.

"I have to report that at ten o'clock a.m. on the 1st inst., two men, names unknown, went into a field in the above townland, where Michael Coughlan, his two brothers, and seven men (in the employment of Coughlan) were ploughing, and told Coughlan 'that he had no right to come there without first settling with John Doorley (the former tenant, who had been evicted from that farm in December last), and that if he did not settle with Doorley, that he, Doorley, would, if it was to go for three or five years, get a man to go into the field and shoot him.' Although there were nine men with Coughlan at the time, there was no effort whatever made on their part to arrest or even trace those men, nor did Coughlan report the matter to the police (although the barrack was within half a mile of the lands which they were ploughing) until the 8th inst. From the description Coughlan gave of the parties the constable at Rapemills at once arrested the parties I have named, whom I have no doubt (nor has Mr. Curran, R.M.) but that the two former were the two men who threatened Coughlan, but as he refused to identify them when brought before him on the 9th inst. they were discharged. The reason assigned for the outrage is that Coughlan refused compensation to Doorley for improvements done to the property."

He could have entered much more lengthily into the statements made by the right hon. Gentleman, but he felt that he had already trespassed upon the attention of the House. He was anxious, however, to disclaim any intention of having cast a slur upon learned Judges, one of whom was an intimate personal friend of his own. In what he had stated upon the occasion referred to he thought he was justified, because one of the Judges had, as he believed, made sweeping statements against the magistracy, although in twenty-nine other counties the most complete and thorough approval had been expressed from the judicial bench of the harmonious manner in which the magistracy and constabulary were acting together for the detection of crime. He trusted that the right hon. Gentleman would feel satisfied that he was always ready to pay immediate attention to any remarks from him upon matters properly within his province, and that his desire was that the Executive and magistrates should as far as possible act together in harmony upon all matters affecting the internal condition of the country. He only hoped that the favourable opinions which the Judges had been able to express in twenty-nine counties would, in the ensuing assizes, prove equally applicable to the other four. He was happy to say, that during the three years he had had the honour of being connected with the Government of Ireland, a vast improvement had manifested itself in the feelings and character of the people; and if irritating causes would only cease to agitate the people of that country, a corresponding advance would be observed in their social condition year by year, and the House might congratulate itself that

Sir Robert Peel

the state of crime in that country was rapidly and sensibly diminishing.

MR. WHITESIDE said, that in a former debate he had stated the number of fighting men who had emigrated from Ireland at 100,000 men. He afterwards applied to the proper quarter, and was told that he had stated the figures accurately.

MR. M'MAHON said, in his opinion, the Irish Members of that House ought to be thankful to the right hon. Gentleman the Member for the University of Dublin (Mr. Whiteside), for having brought that subject before the notice of the House. At the same time, he regretted that the debate was of a mere abstract character, and could be attended with no practical result. He would rather that the right hon. Gentleman had moved for a Committee to examine into the efficiency or inefficiency of the Irish police. If the right hon. Baronet the Chief Secretary for Ireland knew more about the country, he would not be so strenuous a supporter of the Irish police. That body, according to the judgment of most people, resembled more closely an army of occupation than a civil organization for the detection of crime. The Irish police were armed with swords, guns, and bayonets. They lived in barracks like fortresses, and did not mix with the people; thus they knew nothing of their character, and possessed none of the facilities which the English police force had for the detection of criminals. Every year, too, they were becoming more and more military. In the case of the English police, they lived among the people in their own houses, and knowing thoroughly all the various districts in which they lived, as well as the general character of the inhabitants, when a crime was committed they were in most cases able to pounce upon the criminal. Unfortunately, in Ireland, everything was managed in such a manner as to conduce to a job. In the case of a felony committed in England, the person who had been robbed gave information to the police, who generally succeeded in detecting the criminal. Then the person robbed employed his own attorney and barrister, and the offender was brought to speedy justice. In Ireland, on the contrary, a person was not allowed to vindicate the law by means of professional men of his own choice, and in consequence of the system upon which prosecutions were conducted juries would not convict. There certainly was a Crown prosecutor in Ireland, but he generally lived in Dublin, or the chief town of the county with which he was connected, and knew nothing and cared less about the details of those matters. He believed that it would be far better if the people were to employ their own attornies or law advisers. In every country where public prosecutors were part of the establishment there had been a gross failure of justice. He complained of the apathy of the public prosecutors, and expressed his opinion that until the system of conducting prosecutions in Ireland by the Crown prosecutors was abolished, justice would never be properly administered. He suggested that the right hon. Gentleman the Member for Dublin University (Mr. Whiteside) should move for a Committee to investigate the whole subject.

THE O'CONOR DON said, that as the county Roscommon, with which he was so intimately connected, and which he had the honour to represent in that House, had been so pointedly alluded to in the course of the present debate, he wished to make a few remarks. He was very desirous of ascertaining the true state of the facts connected with crime in Ireland ; but he greatly doubted whether the Return asked for by the right hon. and learned Gentleman (Mr. Whiteside), would give the information which he desired. The last list of crime in the county of Roscommon presented eighty-seven offences, but let not the House suppose that eighty-seven outrages had really taken place. In Judge Christian's charge, at the last assizes, he alluded to eleven incendiary fires as having been reported. Now, it should be remembered that there existed in Ireland a system under which compensation was granted for malicious injuries. Consequently there was a great temptation to induce persons to invent or exaggerate the character of offences. He found by a reference to the presentments made before the grand jury at the last assizes of Roscommon, that out of those eleven alleged incendiary fires there were only three instances in which compensation had been given. It was not, therefore, to be concluded that those eleven outrages had actually been committed. In three other instances the parties did not even swear informations, which proved the fact that they themselves did not believe that the fires were attributable to the deliberate designs of any person. When Judge Christian delivered his charge, in which he spoke of the disturbed and criminal state of Roscommon, he made inquiries into the nature of the offences

entered on the list, and although they were described with high-sounding names, in reality they turned out to be mere trifles. The first case was described as homicide ; but it turned out to be an accident. A carman who was driving home from Roscommon races accidentally knocked down a man, who died of the injuries which he received. The next was firing at the person, which turned out to be a joke. An old pensioner had a dispute with an old woman about a heap of manure, and he fetched a pistol loaded with powder, and snapped it at her. The next case was described as one of "burglary and robbery," which, it appeared, originated in the mistake of a bailiff, in serving a process in the wrong house after nightfall. There was a case of demanding arms, which turned out to be a hoax ; and there were said to have been fifteen cases of threatening letters in support of which there were no sworn informations. They presented no great feature of criminality. The detection of such a crime at the best of times was a great difficulty, and he thought it was a great injustice to the police to charge them with neglect in not discovering the writers. These offences differed very much in degree, in some cases the letters being sent out of mere foolishness and ignorance, without the slightest intention to carry out the threats ; and it was but just to the police to say that the discovery of their authors was a most difficult task. An analysis of the calendar showed how wrong it was to form conclusions by merely reading the headings of the charges. Allusion had been made to the efficiency of the English police, and it had been quoted as against the Irish police ; but he found, from a Return that had been published, that in fifteen of the English police districts, the proportion of arrests and convictions presented a worse case against them than had been made out against the Irish police.

LORD CLAUD HAMILTON observed, that the question of detection of crime in Ireland was not then before the House, but as it would have to be discussed he should reserve what he had to say about it till a future occasion. When the hon. Member for Roscommon (The O'Conor Don) sought to establish that only a small proportion of what he called incendiary fires were proved to be malicious, he merely proved that there existed extreme difficulty on the part of those persons who were the sufferers by those offences, in making clear the existence of malice in those cases. This was owing in some degree to the fact that they had to submit their claims to what might be regarded as in some degree an adverse tribunal. The number of serious charges also to which the hon. Gentleman alluded, such as homicide and burglary, as having been made against persons who were guilty of, comparatively speaking, much lighter offences, instead of being an argument in favour of the present system of prosecution in Ireland, plainly demonstrated that it required amendment. Into the larger question of the detection of crime he did not that evening propose to enter at any length; but as one who had experience as a magistrate for a period of twenty-nine years, he must protest against the absurd system of giving to the police in Ireland, who ought to be the main instruments in that detection, the military organization which they now received. It was impossible to expect that the police, who had been spoilt by military organization, could detect crime. It was their foolish military organization which made them useless as a detective police force. Had the right hon. Baronet the Chief Secretary for Ireland been in his place, he should have advised him to study gravely, and with filial reverence, the regulations which had been laid down by his illustrious father in reference to that body when they were called into existence, and from which of late there had been a serious departure. He would confer a great benefit on the people of Ireland if he would adopt those instructions, and have them carried out. He knew it would be said that to have an efficient force the men must be armed with the most efficient weapon. That was true, and that argument was used by the noble Lord at the head of the Government, and, owing to his influence and popularity, it seemed to satisfy the House on a former occasion; but he would venture to point out that, in discussing what was the most efficient weapon for a body of men, you must have reference to the duties those men have to perform. What, he would like to know, was the use of giving a policeman a rifle which would kill at 900 yards? Who ever heard of a member of the force taking a flying shot at a runaway pickpocket at that distance? Much better would it be to arm the men with the old carbine, which would carry only fifty or sixty yards, which was used as a weapon of defence and not of offence, which was light and handy, and which did not prevent

Lord Claud Hamilton

the police from giving effectual chase to a criminal. But, besides the rifle now in use, there was also the sword scabbard, which dangled about their legs, and rendered it almost impossible for them to be active in pursuit; while, being an expensive implement, and a stoppage being made from their pay for an injury done to it, they not unnaturally would prefer letting a man escape occasionally to running that risk. The consequence was that they dandled it like a baby rather than injure the precious weapon. The force, as a detective force, was a mockery. It would be far better to get rid of all that useless military organization and encourage the men to become good detectives, and thereby be able to trace criminals and to prevent crime. He believed the Irish police to have been a most excellent force until the military mania came over it. But worse than all was the fact that, owing to some secret instructions—and from whom they emanated he was not in the slightest degree aware, the police showed great reluctance to communicate with the local magistracy, standing aloof from them, and affecting a preference for the stipendiary magistrates of the district. Instead of the existence of a complete understanding between the resident country gentlemen and the police, it appeared that secret instructions were issued, and that the police were told to communicate only with the stipendiary magistrates. In illustration of the operation of that system he might mention that, on the occasion of the late assizes, when Mr. Justice Ball, a highly respected Judge, visited the county of Down to preside in the Crown Court, he, in speaking of the state of that county, expressed his regret at finding in it so lamentable a state of crime; and when his hon. and gallant Friend the Member for Down (Lieutenant Colonel Forde) who was foreman of the grand jury, assured his Lordship that he and his colleagues knew nothing about the crime of which he spoke, the answer was that the facts had been reported to him by the police; to which his hon. Friend replied that the police had not reported the crimes alluded to by his Lordship, to the resident magistrates and landlords of the county. Now, that was a state of things which ought not to be allowed to exist, and the Government would, he hoped, take the whole question into their serious consideration.

MR. O'REILLY said, he must deny that the amount of undetected crime could be estimated by a comparison of the number of offences alleged to have been committed with the number of persons brought to trial; because he was prepared to show that, in numerous instances, offences had been alleged where none had been committed. He had moved for a list of the outrages alleged to have been committed in Ireland, in order that it might be compared with the cases actually brought before the Judges of assize, and thus determine the actual amount of undetected crime. He would take three cases in the county of Longford and the county of Westmeath. In one of these there was a charge that a threatening notice had been served upon a particular gentleman, but the gentleman himself denied that any such notice had been served. In another case of a similar charge, after some inquiry, the person who had made it was threatened with a prosecution on the ground that he himself was the writer of the letter which he said had been sent to him. In the third, a copying book was found in the house of the person who made the charge, in which book there was a torn sheet corresponding with the one on which the threat was written. Again, with respect to incendiary fires, if the right hon. and learned Gentleman the Member for the University of Dublin (Mr. Whiteside) were a country gentleman he would know that many of the claims made on counties in respect of such alleged fires, were rejected by the grand juries. Out of eleven cases of alleged fires submitted to the grand jury of the county of Roscommon, only three were prosecuted. One gentleman, who in a more distant part of the country had alleged more than one case of malicious outrage as having been perpetrated against himself, came to reside at Swords, near Dublin, and made a similar accusation. He alleged that stones were constantly being thrown at his house. Policemen were sent to watch it, and whenever they were in the house no stones were thrown, but no sooner did they take their departure than the alleged attacks were again repeated. At length the police resorted to the expedient of hiding in a ditch, without the knowledge of the owner of the house, and having heard a volley of stones strike the buildings, they rushed out and found that the delinquent was the gentleman himself.

MR. BERNAL OSBORNE: Was the case referred to that of a clergyman?

MR. O'REILLY thought that the person in question was a clergyman. He hoped he had stated sufficient facts to show that a comparison of the number of alleged offences with the number of persons brought to trial would not show the amount of undetected crime in Ireland.

MR. BAGWELL said, that he must agree with most of the statements of the right hon. and learned Gentleman the Member for Dublin University (Mr. Whiteside). He believed the disinclination which at present existed among the Irish peasantry to give information against criminals was one of the effects of the police system, which did not afford protection to prosecutors. Not only had the magistrates and the grand juries no control over the police, but it was believed that their recommendation of a constable would prevent the man from getting promotion. The men composing the force were exceedingly fine men, but they had no inducement to exert themselves, as it was impossible for them, under the existing system, to improve their position in connection with the force.

MR. O'HAGAN (THE ATTORNEY GENERAL FOR IRELAND) wished to say a very few words before this discussion concluded, with reference to some observations which appeared to him to have unwarrantably dealt with the administration of criminal justice in Ireland. The general effect of the debate was very satisfactory, for it had dispelled delusion and done justice to public officers who had been assailed without sufficient reason. He did not think it necessary to go at length into the general question; but now, at the close of the debate, and after the testimony which had been given as to the condition of Ireland by so many representatives of large and important constituencies, he thought himself entirely justified in repeating the assertion he had made on a former occasion in that House, and to which his right hon. Friend the Member for the University of Dublin, adverted in the opening of his statement, that there was not at this moment in the world a people less tainted with vice or crime than the people of Ireland. His hon. and learned Friend the Member for Wexford had denounced the system of crown prosecutions in Ireland and urged the substitution of that which prevails in England. He confessed he did not admire the continual reiteration of the preference for all English institutions with which they were familiar in that House, and as to the matter in question he believed the Irish system to be incomparably superior to the English, and it was so considered by every man at the bar acquainted with their working and results. The Law Amendment Society and the Social Science Association were distinctly in favour of the establishment of a system of public prosecution, aiming to have justice fairly and calmly administered, without interest or passion in the prosecution or undue pressure on the accused. At the late meeting of the Social Science Association in Dublin, the venerable Lord Brougham expressed his high approval of the appointment of public prosecutors, and his desire that they should be appointed for England. As to the detection of crime, the Judges, whose opinions on such a subject should be received with extreme respect, had not pronounced the condemnation of the police. In three or four counties there had been complaints, but the learned Judge whose brilliant career in that House was so well remembered, Judge Keogh, whilst he lamented that some offences had not been discovered in Limerick, spoke in the highest praise of the police force, and his approval of it was echoed by the grand jury, who returned him their warm thanks for his address on the subject. Mr. Justice Fitzgerald, who had also held such a distinguished position in Parliament, had given it his equally emphatic approval; and many other Judges of the greatest eminence expressed the same opinion. In the vast majority of the counties of Ireland, at the last assizes, there was no objection taken, nor the slightest pretence for any, to the action of the constabulary, who were on all hands admitted to be a most intelligent, well conducted, and trustworthy body of men. Some difficulty they undoubtedly encountered, because in Ireland the people were not, as in this country, in perfect relations of amity with the law. Long years of partial and unjust legislation—laws not made in their interest or administered for their advantage had produced a deep impression on their minds. The traditions of the past were not forgotten. The brief quarter of a century which had elapsed since the tardy recognition of the principles of religious freedom and equal justice had not been sufficient to obliterate its painful memories. But a manifest improvement was taking place, and by persisting patiently in a firm and kindly course—by

Mr. O'Hagan

securing legal protection and fair play to all, the Government could induce the people to love the law and assist in its administration. He had been grossly misrepresented as having asserted that justice in Ireland was now satisfactorily dispensed to a contented community. He had never thought or said that the Irish community were content with their general condition, depressed and suffering as they were, but he had stated, as he believed, that they were more content than they had ever been with the manner in which prosecutions were directed, and with the conduct of the Judges and the tribunals. He lamented extremely—he thought it was a pity and a shame that there was still such a disposition amongst some Irishmen to exaggerate the criminality of their own country and lower it in the estimation of other lands, instead of boasting of the wonderful and unexampled purity and virtue which distinguished it, notwithstanding so many evil influences of poverty and temptation. In England, men were not found to throw discredit upon their poorer countrymen, although far larger masses of undetected crime existed there than in Ireland. Had they not heard of such terrible mysteries as the Road murder, the Waterloo Bridge murder, and the Haymarket murder? And were these things made the subject of attack by Englishmen on the authorities or the people of England? He had looked into the last volume of the English judicial statistics, and he found that whilst in a single year 13,289 crimes had been committed in the metropolis, only 5,444 persons had been apprehended; in the pleasure towns, as they were called, 940 crimes were committed, and 362 persons arrested; in the towns depending on agricultural districts, 472 crimes were committed, and 324 persons arrested; in the commercial ports, the crimes were 5,271, and the arrests 2,899; and in the seats of the cotton and linen manufacture, the crimes were 9,370, and the arrests 2,738. He believed that when the Irish judicial statistics, which he hoped to lay on the table of the House in the course of the Session, were compared with those of this rich and prosperous kingdom, the comparison would be found most favourable to Ireland as to the amount, the character, and the detection of crime. On the whole, he was satisfied that this discussion would be serviceable to the interests of truth, and not in any way detrimental to the character of the constabulary of Ireland.

VISCOUNT PALMERSTON begged to observe that there was a very important matter of deep public interest to be disposed of that night, the Report of the Committee of Ways and Means on the Sugar Duties. Very great commercial inconvenience would be experienced if the Report were not brought up that night, and it was then past ten o'clock. He therefore appealed to hon. Members to have the kindness to postpone their observations on the topic now before the House, and on any other subjects of which they might have given notice, to some other evening, as it would be a very great convenience to the public service.

MR. BERNAL OSBORNE expressed surprise that the noble Lord did not make this appeal before his own Attorney General for Ireland (Mr. O'Hagan) made his long and rather singular speech, in which he quite led the House away from the real subject. He was the last man to doubt the purity or impugn the morality of the Irish people; but the present was a question not of national morality, but of the organization of the police force. The Government of Ireland was framed on a vicious system, which had long been abandoned in England. It was a system copied from France. Everything in Ireland tended to Dublin, every question must be referred to the Castle. The only point on which Irish Gentlemen, who differed from one another on every other matter, were agreed was the utter inefficiency of the system of a military police. The constabulary were riflemen, but without the activity and discipline of soldiers. It had been said that they were a fine body of men, and that in one sense was true, for they were six feet in height. As a detective police, however, they were altogether useless, Irish gentlemen, whether magistrates, Judges, or grand jurors, all shared that opinion. Ireland might be pure and moral, but he doubted whether the Irish Government was so. Everything in the country was transferred to that sink of iniquity—the Castle. If such a Government were in existence in England the country would not go on for twenty-four hours. Irish gentlemen were reproached as absentees in this country, but what inducement had they to remain in Ireland? Their opinions were set aside, their services were declined; the Castle was everything, and except the Law Officers every official there was English. No Irishman was admitted to office; as Swift said, "The curse of Ireland was upon him." Hence it was that men illustrious for their ignorance of and inability to understand Ireland were preferred to Irishmen. As long as that system lasted, so long would crime remain undiminished, and the Irish Secretary and the Attorney General would talk about Irish purity and morality, neglecting the means of lessening crime and of placing the police on a better footing.

Question, "That the words proposed to be left out stand part of the Question," put, and *agreed to.*

COURTS OF JUSTICE.

QUESTION.

MR. ARTHUR MILLS said, he would beg to ask the First Commissioner of Works, Whether the Government have abandoned the intention of introducing any measure for the concentration of the Courts of Justice? The present suspense was extremely inconvenient to the profession and injurious to the owners of property on the site recommended by the Commission of 1859. He knew of one man of the latter class who a few years ago derived about £2,000 a year from his property, and who was now almost ruined by the proceedings of the Government in issuing notices year after year.

MR. COWPER said, the Government had not abandoned the project. It was at present under consideration, and he hoped shortly to be able to bring the matter before the House.

Main Question put, and *agreed to.*

SUPPLY.

SUPPLY *considered* in Committee.

House *resumed.*

Committee report Progress; to sit again on *Monday* next.

WAYS AND MEANS — THE SUGAR DUTIES.

Resolutions (April 14), *reported.*

Motion made, and Question proposed, "That the said Resolutions be now read a second time."

Mr. CRAWFORD rose, and said:* Sir, I have undertaken to invite the House to consider, this evening, the important question of the manner in which the sugar duties should be assessed, from a point of view very different from—very antagonistic to—that taken by the Chancellor of the Exchequer in submitting his financial statement to the House. I am not unaware of the responsibility which every Member incurs who seeks to interfere with the legislation proposed in the Budget of the Government; nor am I insensible to the boon which the Chancellor of the Exchequer has conferred upon the country, in the great remission of taxation which is involved in the relinquishment of 4s. per cwt. on all sugars imported into the United Kingdom. But, Sir, I have taken too active a part with those who disapprove of the manner in which the sugar duties are now levied, to accept the decision of the Government without inquiry and discussion. The question is a very important one. It affects the whole course of the sugar trade with our colonies, and with foreign parts. It relates to a trade which employs immense sums of money, and it involves, moreover, some of the most important principles of political economy. If I had had the good fortune to secure the attention of the House at an earlier period of the evening, I should have been tempted to answer some of the remarks which the Chancellor of the Exchequer made in the course of his financial statement the other evening. I should have been glad to refer to some of the authorities which he cited on that occasion, to notice some of the analogies which he quoted, and to examine some of the illustrations which he cited. But, Sir, I feel that at this late hour I should be unduly trespassing upon the indulgence of the House if I were not at once to go to the question at issue. That question may be briefly stated. For some time past the duties upon sugar have been levied upon the principle of a classification of the qualities, and the imposition of a differential rate of duty upon each quality. Those who object to that plan advocate the adoption of one uniform and fixed duty upon all sugars. The Chancellor of the Exchequer said, in the course of his financial statement—

"At present we have classified duties upon sugar—approved by many, a scandal and offence to many more. Now, I am not able to deny that a classified duty has been the growth of experience."

Again, further on, he said—

"I am not able to say that this system of classified duty has been condemned by experience."

It will be my duty to show, or, at least, to endeavour to show, that the statement of my right hon. Friend is founded in error, and that the system of classified duties is condemned by experience. The Chancellor of the Exchequer adopts, as what I may call the cardinal principle of his legislation, a suggestion thrown out in a memorial of the Manchester Chamber of Commerce, forwarded to him a few days before he submitted the Budget to the House. That suggestion was, that the duty should be levied upon the extractable crystallizable saccharine matter contained in sugar, so as, the Chancellor of the Exchequer told us, in an illustration he used, not to include the minor products of the refinery.

Now, the proposition I shall submit is, that the duty should be imposed upon the commodity as it is brought to the market for sale. My right hon. Friend illustrated his argument by the case of two cwts. of "jaggery" imported into this country from India; but I venture to say, with all due respect to him, that his illustration was not accurate. I assume that there are two parties principally and primarily interested in this question. The first of these is the consumer of sugar; the other is the Government, as guardians of the revenue of the country. The producer is interested in a less degree; and there is a fourth party, whose interests the classified system of duties protects, but who has, properly speaking, no *locus standi* before the House. That party is the refiner. He is the only party taken into account in the Indian case cited by the Chancellor of the Exchequer. The refiner holds in relation to sugar the position, if I may use the term, of an economical scavenger; his business is simply and solely to clean and purify the sugar brought to this country. Now, our argument is that the sugar brought to this country ought to come, and, but for the duties, would come in a condition fit for use. In the Indian case the only person damnified by a uniform duty would be the refiner. The consumer would be benefited because he would get his sugar cheaper. The revenue could not be injured, because the proposition of the Government is to charge the duty on the saccharine value only of the sugar; the producer would also be benefited; in short, all parties except the refiner would be benefited, and the refiner, I repeat, has really no *locus standi* before us, and no claim, economically speaking, to our consideration. But there is another point in connection with this case of "jaggery," to which I desire to draw the attention of the Chancellor of the Exchequer and of the House. My right hon. Friend supposes that these two cwts. of "jaggery" will, when refined, yield, without including the minor products of the refinery, one cwt. of sugar fit for consumption. Now, the cardinal principle of his proposition is that the crystallizable saccharine matter only is to be taxed. If, therefore, I sell to the refiner a quantity of this "jaggery," he pays me in the price a sum equivalent to the duty which I have paid upon the crystallizable saccharine matter only contained in the article; whereas, he gets out of the "jaggery," in addition to his refined produce, a large quantity of the minor residuary products—treacle and molasses—upon which no duty has been paid. In reference to this point, I may quote from a letter written to *The Times* a few days ago by a gentleman named Thomson, who has evidently had a good deal of experience, and who makes the following remark :—

"There is another reason of a practical kind which ought to tell in favour of low duties for inferior sugars, and it is this, they contain a great deal of treacle, which is quite uncrystallizable, and almost valueless in sugar-growing countries, but it is worth a good deal here."

Now, the refiner in the case supposed, having paid in the price the equivalent of the duty upon crystallizable saccharine matter only, gets a larger quantity of treacle or molasses, which he sells in the market, but upon which he has paid no duty, because the duty has been levied upon crystallizable saccharine matter only. But see, on the other hand, the position of the importer of treacle and molasses from abroad. Large quantities of molasses come from the West Indies, and under the proposition of the Chancellor of the Exchequer, the importer would be subjected to a duty of 3s. 6d. per cwt. in competition with the refiner, who has got his molasses altogether free of duty.

I have another remark to make with respect to "jaggery." My right hon. Friend assumed that it contains about 50 per cent of extractable saccharine matter. Now, I can inform the House that this "jaggery" sugar (and I could, if necessary, produce samples at this moment) contains fully as much as 70 or 75 per cent of crystallizable substance. It contains also from 10 to 15 per cent of what is termed in technical language "glucose;" that is, sugar that is not crystallizable in the form of treacle. As far, then, as my right hon. Friend's illustration from "jaggery" is concerned, it is clear that it is not to the extent which he assumed it to be, a fair case in point; and from the manner in which I have described the working of the duty, I think it will be evident, that if the principle is adopted of charging the duty in proportion to the extractable saccharine matter in sugar, it will do injustice to many members of the community.

I now pass to the proposition itself, which I have to submit to the House. I have stated that it is not possible for the officers of the Customs to ascertain by inspection the quantity of crystallizable saccharine matter contained in any sample of sugar; and I will undertake to show, from the evidence adduced before the Committee two years ago, that it is not practicable to do that which the Chancellor of the Exchequer asserts to be the basis of his proposition. I do not intend to occupy the time of the House by reciting the evidence taken before the Committee upon that particular point; but I hold in my hand extracts from the evidence given before that Committee by Sir Thomas Fremantle, which I think will suffice to show the House, that if the object is, as it is stated to be, to ascertain in an accurate manner what the amount of crystallizable saccharine matter in sugar is, it is not possible for the Custom House officer to do that by inspection in the ordinary way of business, to the satisfaction of the public. It is, of course, perfectly possible for the chemist to test and measure the separate quantities of the several constituents of sugar; but it cannot be done by practical men at the Custom House by ocular inspection ; and there is no other mode in which the operation of the Custom House can be carried on as regards sugar than the mere inspection and handling of sugars by the

Customs' officer. Sir Thomas Freemantle is asked—

"Is the comparison made entirely by the eye?"

And he says—

"There was a time when those questions of appeal were very numerous, and before we had adopted the practice of sending all sugars to one room to be assessed there, it was difficult to come to a decision; we then endeavoured to ascertain the saccharine qualities of the sugar by an instrument that was called the saccharometer."

I may here observe that subsequently Mr. Ogilvie, an officer of the Customs, stated to the Committee that the saccharometer was of no possible use. Sir Thomas Freemantle is further asked—

"Does not the judgment of the officers differ very much upon the same sugar?"

He answers—

"Yes; no doubt it is a very nice operation; I cannot say they could bring it to mathematical precision."

He is also asked—

"Their judgment is guided now entirely by the colour and the grain, is it not?"

He replies, "Yes." The House will see here that the Custom House officer does not in fact ascertain that which the Chancellor of the Exchequer says is the basis of his proposition, namely, the saccharine qualities of the sugar he has to assess. Sir Thomas Freemantle, in answer to a further question, stated—

"It is difficult to say how far the qualities of grain, and colour, and whiteness are indices of saccharine matter: if you consider them as the indices and exponents of saccharine matter, it becomes a mere question of saccharine matter altogether. I apprehend (he goes on to say), with respect to what are called grocers' sugars, and so forth, that the buyers purchase those sugars, and that those sugars have a value with reference to colour, irrespectively of their saccharine qualities."

So that here we see that colour and grain are taken into account to determine the value of the sugar. In fact, it was required by the Act of 1854, under which the duties upon sugar were levied, that you should adopt collectively the criteria of colour and grain, and the saccharine quality of the sugar. But my right hon. Friend now proposes to drop that which the Custom House authorities say it is necessary to keep before them as guides to a proper appraisement of value—namely, colour and grain, and to depend entirely

Mr. Crawford

upon the saccharine qualities of the sugar only. Mr. Fairrie, one of the largest sugar refiners in this country, stated, in his examination before the Committee—

"In consequence, I believe, of my representations, they (the Custom House officers) have been much more liberal than they were formerly; but still it is not a thing that the officers are able to judge of; they often lay the 12s. 8d. duty on melado, which is good for nothing, and let excellent quality pass at 10s. 4d. Not being refiners, they do not know exactly whether the melado is good or bad."

Here, then, is the evidence of one of the first refiners in London, who states that of that which is the principle of my right hon. Friend's proposition, the Custom House officers are unable to judge. Another important witness, Mr. Fryer, is asked by the Committee—

"You have assumed that a certain portion of each (sugar) is saccharine matter, and a certain portion is not?"

And he says—

"In this calculation I have not assumed that; I have simply taken a calculation in the *ad valorem* sense. I am quite able to show a similar calculation with respect to the saccharine matter, if desired, though I have not prepared such a statement; that is to say, I can produce a sugar that has paid the 13s. 10d. duty that contains 95 per cent of crystallizable saccharine matter."

So here we have a sugar containing 95 per cent of crystallizable saccharine matter, or 5 per cent less than absolutely pure sugar, admitted at the 13s. 10d. scale, while, if it were only 5 per cent better, it must come in at the highest duty of 18s. 4d. The other day a sample of sugar was passed through the Custom House at Liverpool at the 13s. 10d. duty, which was found on examination in London to contain 96 per cent of pure sugar; so that, if it had had in it only 4 per cent more of pure sugar, it would have been liable to the 18s. 4d. scale, as against the 13s. 4d. one, the difference arising from the difference in colour and grain.

I ask the House, then, to bear in mind that whereas the Chancellor of the Exchequer founds his proposal entirely on the principle of ascertaining the crystallizable saccharine matter in sugar, all experience shows us from day to day that in the assessment of these duties by the Custom House, other considerations, namely, colour and grain, must be kept in view. Now, a personal friend of my own, Mr. Guthrie, who appeared before the Committee, gave evidence to the same effect. He placed certain samples on the table, and when asked—

"Have you found that different rates of duty are sometimes assessed on exactly similar sugars?"

He answered—

"Yes; I have some samples here to show that; it happens sometimes, not only upon sugars of, you may say, exactly the same quality, but upon others. These are samples of Mauritius sugars. This one by the *Speedwell* is taxed at 13s. 10d. duty, and was sold at 37s.; here is one, per *Winterthur*, taxed at 12s. 8d., which was sold at 39s. 9d. on the same day and in the same sale."

That is to say, the sample that was taxed at a lower duty by 1s. 10d. than the other sold at 2s. 9d. more in the market. And why was that? Simply because of the colour and grain. There, again, the saccharine quality of the sugar was no index whatever of the market value of the article. I might proceed by quoting a good deal more of the evidence taken before the Committee, demonstrating more particularly how difficult, nay, how impossible it is for the Custom House officer to perform the function which the plan of the Government intrusts to him, and that he cannot, as experience has proved, satisfactorily appraise the correct value of sugars upon the saccharine principle. But there is another case which occurred not many days ago, to which I would especially desire to call the Chancellor of the Exchequer's attention. I believe it has already been brought to his notice. The firm in the City to which I have just referred, Messrs. Chalmers and Guthrie, imported some sugar from Natal. Of this sugar samples were drawn by the Custom House officers in the usual manner for the ascertainment of the duties to which it was liable. Those officers reported that the sugar was subject to a duty of 12s. 8d. The sugar was then put up for public sale, as it usually is in the City of London, with the duty marked in the catalogue for the guidance of the buyers, and it was sold subject to the 12s. 8d. duty. Two or three days later, however, intimation was sent from the Custom House to say that its officers had made a mistake—that they had looked at the sugar again, and found that the duty on it ought to be 13s. 10d. The sugar had, in the meantime, changed hands and been sold, as I have said, subject to the lower duty first fixed upon it; but the Custom House authorities insisted, nevertheless, on the duty fixed at the second inspection—namely, 13s. 10d., and determined that it should be made chargeable at that rate. A correspondence took place on the subject, and I will read one or two passages from it for the particular information of the Chancellor of the Exchequer. Mr. Ogilvie, in a note from the Custom House, dated March 22nd, 1864, wrote to Messrs. Chalmers and Guthrie, saying—

"Mr. Ogilvie presents his compliments to Messrs. Chalmers and Guthrie, and begs to inform them that having inspected the trade samples of sugar herewith returned, he finds that it is decidedly liable to the duty of 13s. 10d. per cwt. It appears from the inquiries he has made that the small sample by which the assessment was first made contained an undue proportion of the syrupy sugar, which misled the officers; but that soon after, having some reason to suppose they had made a mistake, they, as soon as they could, caused a second sample to be drawn, when they at once detected the error, and did their best to correct it, but, unfortunately, they were after the sale."

Mr. Ogilvie then goes on to represent that in cases where mistakes have been made in favour of the Crown, they have afterwards been set right, and the trade have received the benefit; but it must be remembered that in this particular instance the sugar had been sold subject to the lower duty. I know not whether that dispute has been settled yet; but I cite the case only to show that, even with all the experience of the Custom House officers, they are unable to tell accurately what rate of duty ought to be placed on a particular sugar. The case deserves the more notice because the sugar in question comes from Natal; and nothing can be more discouraging to the planters and merchants of that colony than to find such an extraordinary course of proceedings taken in the assessment of duty payable on their sugars. Then Mr. Ogilvie proceeds to make some remarks, which are valuable as showing the treatment which the trade sometimes meets with at the hands of the Custom House officials. He says—

"Of course, Mr. Ogilvie has no right to expect that parties should point out mistakes to their own detriment, though it is but justice to state that there are parties who have done so; but if a party knows that a mistake has been made, which was obvious in this case and prefers the chance of its passing unnoticed or undiscovered, and if afterwards those chances do not turn out so favourable as expected, there does not appear to be very strong grounds of complaint."

That is to say, Mr. Ogilvie takes upon himself to say that Messrs. Chalmers and Guthrie's firm were parties to a decided and deliberate fraud on the public. The object of these remarks has been to show that it is not possible for the Custom House officers under this classified system exactly to distinguish what amount of duty sugar ought to pay. I know there have been numerous instances of exactly the same parcels of sugar having been shipped from a colony to the ports of London and Liverpool at the same time, upon which after arrival two very different rates of duty have been assessed according to the judgment of the different officers who inspected them at the respective ports. I have known the same thing occur in London with the same shipment. I have known different rates imposed on the same sugar at different periods; nay, more, I have known the same sugar subjected to different rates according to the state of the weather, and according to any circumstances which may have influenced the Custom House officers at that particular time when the survey was made.

I cannot but think now, that I have shown the House that this system of classified duties is difficult and even unfair, and that it cannot be worked to the general satisfaction of the public. I can show also that the objections taken to the system of classified duties are not objections of recent date? I can show by reference to discussions which took place in this House, even as far back as 1845, when a differential duty was first proposed on raw sugar, that there were persons in this House who at that time objected to the system on the same grounds as we object to them at the present time.* On February 25th, 1845, Mr. Ricardo made a speech in this House strongly objecting to the differential duties then proposed for the first time; and I find that on the 14th March, 1845, Mr. Hume, who, I believe, was always regarded in this House as an economist of authority, moved an Amendment " that the duty on refined sugar should be reduced to the rate of duty charged on clayed sugar," considering the difference to be a premium or protective duty. He was supported by Mr. B. Hawes, and by the hon. Member for Birmingham (Mr. Bright). My hon. Friend the Member for Birmingham took exception, I am bound to say, to the plan of differential duties, not upon the point of protection, but because he anticipated great difficulty in assessing the duties on the classified system. It has been stated that there is no ground for the assertion that the differential duty is a protection to low

Mr. Crawford

sugar as against refined. I should like to quote a few words from a speech delivered in this House, in 1848, by my right hon. Friend the Secretary of State for India, who was then Chancellor of the Exchequer. I shall be able to show from his speech that he anticipated in 1848, when an additional grade of sugar was introduced in the sugar duties, that it would act as a protection to low sugars. The word " protection" occurs frequently in the speech of my right hon. Friend.

" There is another fault found with the Act of 1846, and that is also referred to in the Report of this Committee in the 10th Resolution—namely, as to the mode of levying the duty. It is said that the Act does not, in point of fact, give the protection it professes to give, that various sugars are subjected to one duty, and hence the whole of our colonial Muscovado sugar is exposed to the competition of the best brown clayed Havana. That is most clearly stated in the evidence of Mr. Greene. I will not trouble the House with quotations, but he states that there are differences of from 8s. to 9s. in value in the articles, and that what he wants is actual protection, whatever the amount may be which is given, and not a nominal protection as at present, which in many cases amounts to but 1s. or 2s., and in some cases to nothing at all. We propose, therefore, to introduce a new classification into the brown sugars, and to divide those sugars of foreign growth which at present come in under one duty with ' brown clayed' and ' Muscovado.'"

He then proceeds to show that this is done for the purpose of protecting the West Indian interest—

" If we are right in supposing that the greater part of the foreign sugar will come in at the higher rate of duty—if in fact the really formidable competition with colonial sugar is this description of foreign sugar—then we shall give a protection for a year higher than is now enjoyed by the West Indian proprietors."

In other passages of his speech my right hon. Friend goes on to propose to extend protection " in one way or the other." The word " protection" occurs very frequently in his speech.

My purpose is to show that the real object of establishing differential duties upon sugar was to protect certain interests, and that protection remains as the practical effect of differential duties. That effect is to protect low made sugar. I find that in July, 1848, when the subject was under discussion in this House, Mr. (now Sir) H. Barkly, now Governor of the Mauritius, objected to the differential duties, and proposed one uniform scale. In 1854 I find that when the late Mr. J. Wilson introduced the classified scheme—the one which is now in force practically—Mr. Ricardo made a speech in this House protesting, in the name of free trade, against these differential duties as being unequal and contrary to all the doctrines of true political economy. Mr. Ricardo was supported by the present President of the Board of Trade (Mr. Milner Gibson). The President of the Board of Trade asked then on what principle a difference had been made in the scale upon raw and fine sugars.

I have, then, the advantage of the opinion of the President of the Board of Trade in favour of the view of the sugar duties which I am now advocating. As to the effect of these duties on what we may term the interests of the producer, I will read an extract from a despatch of Governor Barkly then at Guiana, dated 10th of November, 1852, in which he forcibly points out the impediment which a system of differential duties places in the way of the improvement of sugar. In that despatch Sir H. Barkly says—

"The discouragement which the existing arrangement of duties offers to an improved system of manufacture will be best conceived from the following facts :—

"First. That the process of 'spoiling' sugar, when it seems better than would be likely to pass the lowest standard, is not of unfrequent occurrence on estates where the vacuum pan is used.

"Second. That a gentleman in charge of an estate on which vast expense has been incurred for steam clarifiers, bog and charcoal filters, vacuum pans, and pneumatic pumps, assured me that for a further trifling outlay of £100 he could, were it not for the *quasi*-prohibitive duty, ship the whole of his crop (1,000 tons) of a quality equal to refined sugar, though made *bonâ fide* by a single process from the raw material."

I have received a letter from that same gentleman, in which he goes into details as to the manner in which his sugar is made. I have no doubt whatever in the perfect integrity of his statement, that, with some little outlay for additional machinery, he could make the whole of his stock equal to refined sugar, had he not a motive in keeping the quality down in the protection which our classified system gives to low sugars. Governor Barkly, in his despatch, goes on to say—

"I venture most respectfully to conclude the observations which I have felt it my duty to make on a subject of so much importance to this colony in the words of a report addressed by the celebrated chemist Peligot to the French Colonial Minister in 1842 :— 'If colourless sugar cannot be produced from the cane (as was supposed a few years ago), if the molasses which impregnates and colours this sugar cannot be removed, if the production of colonial brown sugar must remain stationary as to quantity, if the quality cannot be improved, the excess of duty upon white sugar may to a certain extent be comprehended and

justified. But if, on the contrary, this colouration is the consequence of a bad mode of working, if it be demonstrated that the sugar which preexists in the cane is white, that it is obtained white when a part is not destroyed, that the proportion extracted is consequently as much greater as it is less coloured, what must be thought of a legislative measure which imposes upon that industry the exorbitant obligation of making small and bad products, and which places a barrier before one of the things which the laws should most respect—improvement !'"

The Despatch in question was submitted by the Colonial Office to the Board of Trade, and the Board of Trade made this Report upon it to the Colonial Office—

"In the present instance, my Lords are disposed to allow considerable weight to the arguments adduced by the Governor of Guiana ; and they would observe that the application of *ad valorem* duties on sugar appears to be in many respects less appropriate than to several other articles in regard to which it has been found expedient to abandon them. To impose a discriminating duty upon distinct kinds of a given produce, such as the produce of vineyards varying in richness, different qualities of tea or tobacco would appear to be a legitimate application of *ad valorem* duties ; but to strike with a superior duty one pound of sugar which, by a better mode of manufacture, contains more saccharine matter than another pound obtained from the same raw material, is to inflict direct discouragement upon improvement."

These are the words which I have introduced into the Resolution I have proposed, and I hope the House will be satisfied with their authority, for they are the words used by my right hon. Friend the present Secretary for the Colonies, who was then President of the Board of Trade. If these were the views he entertained then, I do not see how, in his present position, he can gainsay or deny the force of them. Now, if that was the view entertained by my right hon. Friend at that time, and giving him all credit for further enlightenment as years have passed by, I think it will be exceedingly difficult for him on the present occasion to unsay or to deny the force and truth of the language which he then used upon this subject. Other evidence was given before the Committee on the part of the producers in the West Indies, in the Mauritius, in India, and elsewhere, to show what was the effect produced upon their industry by these discriminating duties, and it was shown most conclusively that the object of the sugar-makers under the influence of those duties was always to degrade the manufacture of the article, so as to bring it just within any one of the different grades of duty here. Now, with regard to the question of the supply of sugar to the consumer, I wish most especially to call the attention of the Chancellor of the Exchequer to the figures I am about to read. He may not arrive at the same conclusion upon them as I do, and perhaps he has not examined so narrowly as I have the tables prepared by Mr. Messenger, of the Custom House, appended to the Report of the Committee. He will find from these tables that the consumption of sugar per head, from 1848 to 1854, showed an increase in quantity of not less than 9 lbs. The consumption per head in 1848 was 25 lbs., and in 1854 it was 34 lbs. Now, since 1854, in the nine years which have since elapsed, the progressive increase has been only 2 lbs. per head. That is, there has been an increase of consumption to the extent of 2 lbs. per head in the series of nine years, during which the differential duties have been in full force, against an increase in the previous seven years of 9 lbs. per head. Now, it is important to observe that during the first period the average duty paid was 12s. 3d. per cwt., and the average price 36s. 3d.; while in the second period the average duty paid was 13s. 5d., and the average price 40s. 4d. There has, therefore, been a very great increase in the price, but there has not been any great increase in the average amount of duty paid. I, therefore, attribute this arrest in the progress of consumption to some other cause than the duty. It is clear that the duty could have nothing to do with it. Now, let us consider to what cause this arrest in the progress of consumption is really due. The quantity of sugar which comes into this country has largely increased. It would naturally be supposed from that fact that the consumption also of sugar had greatly increased; but the fact was, that the quality had been gradually degraded and deteriorating under the influence of these duties. And when these sugars are refined and delivered to the consumer for use, they produce a much smaller quantity of sugar fit for the consumption of the population. That is the inference which I deduce from the arrest in the progress of consumption which is shown by the figures of Mr. Messenger. Now, as to the influence of these duties upon the supply of sugar, I would wish to refer to the estimate that was made by the late Sir Robert Peel, in the year 1845, when, for the first time, he proposed a scale of discriminating duties on sugars. Acting upon the information —the same information as that upon which

Mr. Crawford

the Chancellor of the Exchequer is now acting, that is, information from the Custom House—Sir Robert Peel assumed that the quantity of British plantation Muscovado not equal to white clayed consumed in this country in 1845 would be 160,000 tons, and the quantity of white clayed at 70,000 tons. No doubt the officers of Customs had good grounds for the information which they gave to the Chancellor of the Exchequer at that time; but what were the facts? Sir Robert Peel's estimate, based upon this information and reliance upon experience of the past year, was, that 160,000 tons of the lower quality would be received in this country, but the real quantity that did come in was 237,000 tons. Again, instead of 70,000 tons of white clayed, there were only 1,107 tons. In the same way upon foreign free labour sugar, Sir Robert Peel was told that he might rely upon receiving 5,000 tons of the lower quality, while the actual quantity received was 3,809 tons; and instead of receiving from those sources 15,000 tons of white clayed as he anticipated, we received only 54 tons. Now, what was the effect of all this upon the public exchequer? Why, it resulted in a deficiency of duty received, as far as the calculations for that year were concerned, of no less than £463,327. The deduction I make from these facts is this, that the effect of lowering the duty upon certain grades of sugar invariably is to offer a premium to the colonies to make worse sugar in order to bring it in under the lower scale of duty. I think it has been proved by the result of the calculations which I have made upon the figures before us. What said Mr. Wilson, in 1854, upon the same point? That gentleman, in recommending the House still further to increase the scale of differential duties in favour of the lower qualities of sugar, proposed to levy a duty of 12s. upon the great bulk of colonial sugar, and a duty of 11s. upon the lowest qualities. Mr. Wilson then said that—

"With regard to the lowest scale which would be charged with 11s. duty," (that corresponds with our 12s. 8d. duty at present,) " on sugars of a standard not equal to brown clayed, it was a very low standard, and therefore admitted only a very small quantity; last year he believed only 9,000 tons out of 390,000 tons consumed."

Now, let the House bear in mind that, in 1853, we imported 390,000 tons of sugar, of which, upon the authority of Mr. James Wilson, only 9,000 tons of the lowest quality came in under the 11s. duty. But look at 1863, when, out of a total consumption of 495,050 tons, no less than 298,000 tons were not equal to brown clayed. In 1853, only 9,000 tons out of 390,000 of this low sugar was imported, but, in 1863, the amount was 298,000 tons out of 495,000 tons, or something like 60 per cent of the total importation. Now, I would like the House to hear the opinion of a foreign writer — a writer in France — upon this subject. He will tell you what the people of France consider to be a true description of those low sugars, which come here purely to find occupation for and benefit to the refiners. This gentleman, M. Dureau, says—

"So that it may now be said on the banks of the Ganges, as well as in the West Indies, and in our own sugar factories of the North, the dregs, the fermentations, the leavings of molasses, are good enough for England."

That is an independent French opinion with reference to this proposition. Then again M. Dureau says—

"And thus it is that the English consumption is completely at the mercy of the refiners, from whom alone they can obtain the sugar they prefer; while, on the other hand, the planters of the West Indies, the Mauritius, and India, shackled by a barbarous legislation, and having no other outlet than the demands of the English refiner, take no pains to increase their produce, or to improve their implements, and are ten years behind the French planters."

That is indeed the fact. The sugar manufacture in Guadaloupe and Martinique, French colonies, is conducted upon methods far superior to those in practice in our colonies. I would like to quote to the House another French opinion upon this subject. It is a singular fact, that when the present Emperor Napoleon was in captivity at Ham, he considered among other things the question of the sugar duties, and he wrote a book about it. His object was to obtain an alteration of the French law.

There was then a system of French standards in France, but by subsequent changes those standards have been altered; and although in the conference which took place in Paris the other day it was stated that the Dutch, French, and English had agreed upon a uniform plan, (the Belgians alone dissenting, and taking the view which I venture to submit to the House), and although a *projet de loi* was brought into the French Chambers some months since, we have heard nothing about it

having passed into law. Public attention has, however, been directed to this subject, and one great writer, to whom we all in this country look with respect—M. Chevalliér—he protests against the change in the interests of the public of France. The public mind of France is against the change, and it has been brought to bear upon the French Government, and I have strong reasons for believing that the propositions of the English Commissioners at Paris will not be allowed to be carried into effect. But what did the Emperor Napoleon say of the differential duties? He said—

"It is evident that the obligation imposed upon the planter to send nothing but impure sugars to France, in order to preserve for that produce its greatest portable weight, is a law only fit for barbarians."

Those are the terms in which such a law as this is described by the French Emperor. There is one other passage in this book which I will trouble the House with reading. M. Dureau says—

"Never has England received a greater quantity of the worst sugars, and never has France received richer or finer.

That is during the period over which our differential scale of duties has extended. The French and Dutch beat our refiners out of the market. Every neutral market is closed against us, and open to the French and Dutch. Why is that? It is generally attributed to the system under which the drawbacks are regulated in France and Holland, and that may be true to a certain extent, but the real explanation is, that the foreign refiners have a better quality of sugar to refine from than we have. It will be seen, on referring to the Report of the Commissioners, that—

"The sugar refined in Holland is almost entirely the produce of Java, which is perhaps the best raw sugar in the world."

I take that to be undoubtedly one reason why the Dutch are able to beat us in neutral markets. Formerly, we used to export sugar to the Levant and to the Mediterranean ports, but that trade is gone now, and the French and Dutch beat us there. Those countries have a law which I wish to see introduced here—a law which gives them a supply of the best sugar, and by that advantage they are enabled to beat us in all neutral markets. M. Dureau tells us that—

"Since 1860, thanks to the suppression of the standards, France has become the market for the first sugars, both in colour and quality. Let the standard be re-established, and a contrary direction will be taken. France will receive those coarse sugars we have lost sight of—those sugars dripping with molasses, and losing as much as 10 per cent on their voyage, those sugars smelling of fermentation, smelling of burnt matter, reeking with the odour of bad manufacture; those bottoms, those greasy, clayey sugars, only fit for the refining pan, and which bear the indelible stamp of routine, want of care, or low cunning; for in order to escape from a higher duty, and to remain below what the English call the standard of colour, they will do what evil they please, and mix lamp-black, dirt, or ashes with the sugar. Such things have been, and will be again, and you call that encouraging manufacturers. For our part, we cannot see what the nation gains by such tricks and such frauds, which are not suitable to the present times, and are repugnant to the dignity of commerce and industry."

The terms which M. Dureau here employs are, I submit, most justly applicable to the system under which we, in this country, are condemned to suffer at present.

There is one other subject to which I wish to direct the attention of the House; that is, what is called the free trade argument. The Chancellor of the Exchequer said the other night that free trade was invoked by both parties in this dispute. The makers of low class sugar say that a uniform duty would operate as a protection in favour of the better class of sugars. The makers of the better kinds of sugar contend that a differential scale of duties acts as a protection in favour of low-class sugars. I take the bases of the argument to be this. You must go back to the raw material. The raw material is the sugar cane, and the juice which is expressed from it. That juice comes from the cane in a pure white liquid state. There are two kinds of manufacturers, the good and the bad. The good or the enterprising manufacturer possesses capital, command of labour and intelligence, and applies his machinery at once to the conversion of this liquid into marketable sugar. He makes sugar perfectly good and fit for the highest purposes of domestic use of this country. He sends it here, having expended 5s. or 10s. per cwt. in perfecting the quality, and making really good sugar, and immediately you take away his chance of profit by charging him an equivalent duty upon his product. Now, take the other case of the manufacturer who is not so good, who has not the means, or the intelligence, or the energy to apply himself to the production of a good kind of sugar. What does he do? He goes upon some old worn-out system, and in the conversion of this white syrup into sugar, he destroys it to a great extent, and converts a large portion of it

Mr. Crawford

into treacle. And you offer him a premium to do so. His goods come here not fit for use. Of the 295,000 tons which I referred to just now as being of this sort of sugar, not a pound is sold over the grocer's counter; the whole of it goes to the refiner. Will you tell me that can be done without great injury, in fact, a great robbery of the consumer?

I say that it is for the interest of the consumer that you should give encouragement to the production of fine sugar everywhere, whether in Cuba, in the Mauritius, or in Brazil. Your object ought to be to hold out every encouragement to planters to send good sugar fit for use to your markets, because you get it necessarily at a cheaper price than you can procure sugar for, of similar quality, from the refiner after he has had it in his hands to refine. I hold that to be the real argument in this matter. I will, for example, take the enterprising planter to be a planter in the Mauritius, and the man not so enterprising, generally speaking, to be a planter in the West Indies. I know that there are some estates in the West Indies where sugar is manufactured upon the highest and best processes. The West Indian planters generally complain that they have not the means or the power of going to such great expense as is necessary for the production of sugar of the best kind. And what are you asked to do? You are called upon to aid them by fiscal regulations, and to make good to the West Indian planters their deficiencies of energy, climate, labour, soil, and capital; and by the same process you are to deprive the manufacturers of sugar in other parts of the world of the just rewards of their labour and capital. In order to show that it is a protection, I have the words of a witness, Mr. Rennie, before the Commission, who was asked what in his opinion would be the effect of a uniform duty upon imports, and his reply was that he thought the immediate effect would be to put an end to the working of all estates producing the low kinds of sugar. That may be so, but it is no business of ours to legislate for the sugar producer of any particular country; we are legislating for consumers. What does Mr. Rennie then say? He says, "The West Indians are now struggling under a protection of 1s. 2d. per ton," and what does the Chancellor of the Exchequer propose now to do? He establishes a new grade of duty of 8s. 4d. with the same object, that of protecting the West Indian planters. Now, what has already been the effect of that proposal? Why, since this scheme has been promulgated, only eight days ago, instructions had been sent out to lower and degrade the sugar, so that it may come into this country under the new 8s. 4d. duty, so that we shall soon find, if this plan be adopted, a still larger proportion than 60 per cent of the sugar imported into this country of a character that will require the aid of the refiner before it can be made fit for use. To show the opinion of some persons in the retail trade as to the quality of the sugar which comes from the refiners, I beg leave to read a letter addressed to me a day or two since by a grocer and tea-dealer in the country, whose name I never heard of before, but whose letter I think will be instructive upon this question. He says—

"There seems to be one very important element overlooked in the sugar controversy among the confusion of fixed or graduated scales of duty, namely, that the process to which the imported sugars are submitted by the refiners of this country deprives them in a great degree if not altogether of their conservative qualities. This does not apply, of course, to the hard lump sugar, which is in every way unexceptionable, but to the remaining products—crushed lump, pieces and bastards."

The first, of course, is the sugar we use upon our tables, but the other kinds of sugar are extensively produced, and especially in the town of which my hon. Friend near me (Mr. Dunlop) is the representative, and those are the kinds of which this experienced grocer speaks. Pieces and bastards are not nice names, but they are well understood in the trade. This gentleman goes on to say—

"The first and second, though good in flavour and appearance, lack the sweetening properties of good raw sugar, and for preserving fruit, or wine-making, are almost worthless. The third named (bastards) are bad in taste, stinking in odour, spoiling everything coming in contact with them. Of these last named, because they are generally sold at a less price per pound than raw sugar, the poor people in the agricultural districts make their little keg or jar of elderberry wine."

And these are this gentleman's words—

"And the chances are that before Christmas it has become sour as vinegar. That is not the case with wine or preserves made from raw sugar, which will keep for many years."

That is the sugar which is brought into this country fit for use.

"Even the lollypop makers will not buy either of the three products named for their purposes, well knowing that disappointment is very likely to attend their operations. There is also another objection to the refiner's goods,—the quantity of water they contain not in chemical combination. Of course they are constantly losing this by evaporation, and we little know our losses in this respect."

That is, the refiners of this country, who refine these low descriptions of sugar—the stuff I have been describing—accommodatingly sell to the consumer a large quantity of water in their goods. But this gentleman goes on—

"The great bulk of the retail trade, who alone are brought into immediate contact with consumers, know by experience the facts as detailed in the foregoing letter. Upon our shoulders fall all the complaints of preserves that will not keep, and wine that turns sour; and we believe that a great deal of this state of things will be removed by a uniform duty on all kinds of soft sugar."

And he goes on to say that he believes the course I am advocating will meet with the approbation of the great body of the consumers of this country.

I will now refer to an article which appeared the other day in the *Economist* newspaper, to which the Chancellor of the Exchequer alluded in his speech. Now, I fully admit the authority of that paper. I believe there is no publication in the kingdom which has done more for the cause of free trade and for commerce generally than that paper founded as it was, and successfully conducted for so many years, by my late friend Mr. James Wilson. It is very well and ably conducted now, but I cannot but think that the opinions of the editor upon this subject lose somewhat of their authority from being as it were hereditary opinions. The *Economist* argues that the proper way to consider these duties is to consider that the "purification," as he terms it, of sugar is a process which ought to be carried on "inside" the Custom House. But I do not see how he draws that line. I say that in the interest of the consumer the object we should have in view is, that the commodity, one cwt. or one ton of sugar, should be subject to duty just as it comes to the customer, whereas now you say, "This sugar contains so much valuable substance, and you must pay so much duty." I think I have shown that the principle upon which that is done is really a discouragement to the introduction of good sugar, while it helps to introduce the worst kind of stuff at the lowest rate of duty. But the *Economist* remarks—

"It has been justly remarked that those more moderate advocates of a uniform duty who would have what they call one duty on 'refined' and one duty on 'unrefined' sugar, or one duty on 'liquid and another on 'ordinary' sugar, have put themselves in logic and upon principle out of court."

He goes on to say it is not at all material whether the saccharine substance is connected with solid matter and with liquid matter; whether it is in the state which the trade calls "refined," or in what it calls "unrefined," is entirely immaterial. And then the writer uses this strange expression—

"A uniform duty on liquid cane-juice, on the coarsest ' excrements ' of the sugar-cane, and also upon the nicest and most delicate product of the manufactory, is consistent and intelligible."

But to show that the *Economist*, great as its authority was, is not entitled to all the authority which was claimed for it, I will simply mention that the writer did not tell his readers that the "excrement" of sugar was merely the result of imperfect and wilfully bad manufacture of sugar at the place of its production. A writer in another paper of great ability and authority and influence on public opinion, the *Spectator*, made a similar statement, which is material, as showing the imperfect information of those who assume to instruct the public on these matters. He went into a long argument, ending in the designation of the extractable crystallized matter of sugar, proposed by the Chancellor of the Exchequer, as the sole subject-matter of the tax, as the "raw material."

These facts show the imperfect manner in which public writers, who set themselves to instruct the public, are really informed on these matters. There is an authority to whom I desire particularly to refer for one minute, Mr. Stuart Mill, and he, I am sure, will be listened to with respect in this House. He says that

"If a commodity is capable of being made by two different processes of manufacture, as is the case with sugar, it is for the interest of the consumer that that process should be adopted by which the best article will be produced at the lowest price ; and it is also for the interest of the producer, unless he is protected against competition, and the process most advantageous for the community at large, and which it will be most for the advantage both of the consumer and producer, is that which is least interfered with by Government."

He also says—

"That all Customs duties which operate as an encouragement to the home production of taxed articles are an eminently wasteful mode of raising revenue."

There is only one other point in connection with the free trade argument which I should like to mention. It has been argued that no system could be fairer

than that under which no duties at all are charged, and that that would be fairest to all parties. If there were no duties at all, the maker of refined sugar abroad could send his sugar to the market on equal terms with the maker of low or bad sugar. But if you have a system of differential duties, you immediately alter the case, and you put the maker of refined sugar in a positively disadvantageous position. This subject is one on which I should have liked to speak at much greater length, but I have had neither the opportunity nor the time of fulfilling that desire. I have been, therefore, obliged to leave unnoticed many matters which I should like to have spoken of. I can only hope that I have been successful in showing that the terms of my Motion are such as can be fairly accepted by the House. I contend that I have shown that it is not possible for the officers of the Custom House to ascertain by simple inspection the quantity of crystallizable matter in the raw material of sugar. I have also shown that to lay different duties on the produce obtained from the same raw material is unjust and unreasonable, because, according to the authority of the Secretary for the Colonies, it strikes a blow at all improvement. I think I have also shown, by reference to the figures connected with the supply, that the operation of the classified system of duties as at present existing is to exclude a large quantity of fine sugar from the market, and that the consumer and the revenue are therefore both injured by the system. Having discharged this duty, I have only to thank the House for the great indulgence it has shown to me, and whatever be the result of the Motion, I entertain a full and confident conviction in the integrity of the arguments I have used.

I conclude by moving the Resolution of which I have given notice.

MR. POTTER begged to second the Motion. He had served on the Committee which had been appointed two years ago on the subject, and had paid some attention to the facts of the case; while personally he had no personal interest in the matter, nor, as far as he knew, had any of his constituents, he begged to say that the conclusion to which he had come was that a single uniform duty was the most desirable. After subsequent communications with grocers and with consumers he still retained that opinion. The present duty was called an *ad valorem* duty—it was imposed upon the scale system; and the system was almost as bad as that which existed under the sliding scale for corn. Another strong objection was that the course was to fix by sight the value of the article and the consequent duty to be imposed; and the result was that as much as 50, 60, and even 90 per cent of real sugar had been admitted under the lowest duty. The right hon. Gentleman proposed to continue that system, though no doubt he reduced the distance between the scales; but, in his opinion, a fixed duty would yield a better revenue. The right hon. Gentlemen the Chancellor of the Exchequer had laid down the true principle in his financial statement, when he said—

"The proposition which I lay down, and which I invite the Committee to proceed on is that the form of our duty should be such as will least interfere with the natural course of trade, and be the least open to the charge of offering to the producer or manufacturer a premium on doing something different from that which he would do if there were no duty at all."

But if the right hon. Gentleman carried out his present intention it would be offering a direct premium to the refiner. The House would admit if they laid on indirect taxes great care should be taken that they were judiciously imposed, otherwise they would act oppressively on the consumer. The real duty of the Chancellor of the Exchequer was to obtain his revenue by the means which would effect the least injury to commerce, and he hoped that the House in legislating upon the sugar question would bear that principle in mind. He now came to the main point; how the proposed duty would affect the consumer. By an uniform duty the consumer would be benefited, as he would get sugar wherever he could, regardless of the duty, and the revenue would thereby receive no injury. There was no danger of a failure of the supply on the increased consumption which would be the result, as there were fifty sources of supply still to be opened up. The right hon. Gentleman, in support of his proposition, had sheltered himself under the name of the hon. Member for Rochdale (Mr. Cobden); but surely even the right hon. Gentleman would allow that that hon. Member was mistaken on some subjects. The right hon. Gentleman had quoted the petition of the Manchester Chamber of Commerce; but he would inform him that it was at his request that the words "saccharine crystallized matter" were introduced into that document. In the course of the

debate reference had been made to the *Economist* newspaper, but Mr. Wilson's 10 per cent protective duty in India would show the value that was to be attached to the free trade opinions advocated by that gentleman. He was certain that the Chancellor of the Exchequer would soon recoup himself for the proposed reduction, and he believed that in the course of three or four years that he would derive a revenue of £6,000,000 from the sugar duties, when he would in all probability propose a uniform tax of 6s. or 7s. per cwt.

Amendment proposed,

To leave out from the word "That" to the end of the Question, in order to add the words "it is not possible for the Officers of the Customs to ascertain by inspection the quantity of crystallizable saccharine matter contained in any sample of Sugar; and that a law, which seeks to effect such an object, is unjust to the producer, inasmuch as by striking with a superior Duty one pound of Sugar which by a better mode of manufacture contains more saccharine matter than another pound obtained from the same raw material, it inflicts direct discouragement on improvement; whilst at the same time it excludes large quantities of fine Sugars from the market, and thereby injures both consumers and the Revenue by limiting the supply,"—(*Mr. Crawford,*) —instead thereof.

MR. CARDWELL said, he had no desire to prolong the debate, as it was past midnight,·but as his hon. Friend the Member for the City of London (Mr. Crawford), who had advocated his Motion with so much ability, had referred to him in the most marked manner, and as he had acted as Chairman on the Committee to which the subject had been referred, he did not think that it would be respectful either to him or to the House if he were entirely silent. He trusted that his hon. Friend would excuse him if he used the greatest brevity in his remarks, and did not deal with the subject at the length which he should have devoted to it, but for the lateness of the hour. He should endeavour, in the few remarks he would make, to satisfy his hon. Friend that the three propositions into which his Resolution was divisible were not, either collectively or separately, worthy of the adoption of the House. The first of his hon. Friend's propositions was that it was impossible for the officers of the Customs to ascertain by inspection the quantity of saccharine matter contained in any sample of sugar. In answer to that he should appeal to the evidence before the Committee and to the practice of the trade throughout the world, in order to show that what his hon. Friend believed to be impossible was actually done, and could therefore be accomplished. The next was that a law which sought to effect such an object was unjust to the producer, inasmuch as by striking with a superior duty one pound of sugar which by a better mode of manufacture contained more saccharine matter than another pound obtained from the same raw material, it inflicted direct discouragement on improvement. His hon. Friend had done him the compliment of introducing these words as an extract from a letter of his written several years ago. He had no desire to alter those words as they stood in the original context, but he certainly disputed their meaning as rendered by the context in which his hon. Friend had placed them. The third proposition of his hon. Friend was, that the process suggested by the Government excluded large quantities of fine sugar from the market, thereby injuring both the consumer and the revenue by limiting the supply. He would show that, since the graduated scale had been adopted, the consumption had gone on increasing until it was larger than ever, and the object of the scale had been attained, because quantities of a class of sugar most valuable to the consumer in this kingdom had been imported—a class which, before the adoption of the scale, had been entirely excluded. If, then, those three propositions of his hon. Friend failed, the Resolution could not itself be worthy of the consideration of the House. With regard to his hon. Friend's first proposition he had before him the evidence of a most able witness, the friend and partner of the hon. Gentleman, who being asked whether there were any means of extracting the crystallizable saccharine matter, replied that there was a mode of ascertaining the quantity with perfect exactitude. [Mr. CRAWFORD: Yes, chemically.] He knew his hon. Friend would say that it could be done chemically but not commercially. He admitted the distinction; but how was the trade carried on? Sir Thomas Freemantle and other witnesses stated that there was at first much difficulty in working the graduated scale, but by practice it had been overcome. Appeals, at first frequent, were now very rare, showing that commercially as well as chemically, the Customs had a practical test to which they could resort. His hon. Friend's own witness, Mr. Guthrie, was asked whether

the Dutch system in which the standards ranged from six to twenty, interfered with the conduct of business, and replied, " No; it is found a convenient way to conduct the business." And his hon. Friend himself, in proposing Question 6,386, spoke of it as " the universal system recognized in all sugar-producing countries, in general use throughout the Continent of Europe." Every one knew that the trade was conducted by Dutch numbers, and if the trade could be commercially carried on by reference to fifteen standards, there was nothing to prevent the Custom House officers carrying into effect a scale consisting of a much smaller number of standards. The House was aware that there had been a Conference at Paris on this subject, at which the representatives of four countries were present. They went in three to one in favour of a uniform duty; they came out three to one in favour of a graduated duty. The representative of England was alone favourable to a graduated duty, but when they came out of the Conference the representatives of France and Holland were converted to the graduated duty, and the representative of Belgium alone adhered to the uniform scale. There was the most satisfactory reason for believing, both from argument and experience, that the difficulty of assessing a graduated duty on sugar was more imaginary than real. He now came to his hon. Friend's second proposition. His hon. Friend had read a letter from Governor Barkly. What happened in 1854 was the following :—Sir Henry Barkly, when Governor of Guiana, wrote home to the Government that the scale then about to come into operation would discourage the improvement of sugar. The matter was referred to the Board of Trade, in which Department he then had the honour to serve. The Board of Trade did not advise the Government to adopt Governor Barkly's recommendations, but suggested that inquiries should be made through all the colonies to see the bearing of the recommendation on other colonies, and also that inquiries should be made at home to ascertain the effect upon the revenue from the diminution of refining in this country. These questions were considered, and the result was that the Government decided against the views of his hon. Friend. The experience of ten years had since been obtained, and was it the fact that the adoption of the graduated scale had discouraged improvement? The testimony of all the

Mr. Cardwell

witnesses showed that never was more capital expended, and that never were more efforts made for the improvement of sugar than during the ten years of the graduated scale. His hon. Friend's third proposition was that the effect of the graduated system was to limit the supply. Now, he had before him the statistics of supply, and he found that during 1853, the last year of the old scale, the total supply of sugar was 7,487,000 cwt., while in 1861 it had risen to 9,180,000 cwts. The proportion of consumption per head on the population had risen in the same interval from 31 lb. per head to 35 lb. per head. His hon. Friend said that the graduated scale had diminished the supply, because it tended to exclude the white sugars. If the scale excluded any particular class of sugars, that was, however, not an objection to the principle of graduation, but only an objection to the figure in the scale that excluded that class. The Committee recommended that the scale should be altered so as to admit at lower relative rates of duty the white sugars which were now excluded, and also the inferior sugars, and those recommendations had been adopted by the Chancellor of the Exchequer in his present scale. The proposed graduated scale was, indeed, intended to allow those low sugars to come into the market, which would be excluded by an uniform duty. Large quantities of these sugars had been admitted, but still larger quantities had been excluded by the existing scale, which it was, therefore, desirable to alter. The Congress of Paris helped the House to understand how it happened that these white sugars went to France and Holland and did not come to England. If, for example, it appeared that there was a protective duty in other countries which operated to draw particular sugars to those countries, while England remained a free market, the imports of those sugars into England would naturally be small in comparison. He thought that these considerations showed that the Custom House officers could, in a commercial sense, satisfactorily deal with the standards now proposed —that a graduated scale did not discourage improvement — and that such a scale did not limit the supply, but would throw open the market to a large quantity of sugar that would otherwise be excluded. The Committee knew that sugar came into this country in different stages, as a raw material, partly manufactured, and completely manufactured; but it did not occur to

them to impose a tax equally on an article in all those various stages. Sugar came from countries differing in all the circumstances of soil and labour, rendering it for the advantage of one that it should be forwarded raw, and for the other that it should be sent to market in its most finished state. It did not occur to the Committee that they ought to give special encouragement to any of those. On his own part, and that of the majority of his Colleagues, he disavowed the view put forward by his hon. Friend, that they were appointed to give the utmost encouragement to good sugars. A tax on sugar being unfortunately necessary, their duty was to provide such a mode of levying the tax as would leave all producers in as relatively equal a position as they would have been had there been no tax at all. It did not occur to the Committee that the British refiner was a person of whom they ought to be peculiarly jealous, for under a system of perfectly free trade, raw cotton came from India to be manufactured in England, and copper was brought from the regions in which it was found to be smelted in Wales. It was calmly assumed by his hon. Friend, that a graduated scale was obviously at variance with the orthodox principles of free trade. Yet the graduated scale was first introduced by the Government of Sir Robert Peel—the Government that repealed the Corn Laws. It had been extended by the Government of 1854, under the auspices of the present Chancellor of the Exchequer and of the late Mr. James Wilson. After careful inquiry it had been confirmed by the Committee moved for by his hon. Friend, and of which he had himself the honour to be Chairman. It had since been ratified by the decision of the Conference at Paris. It had since received the approval of the hon. Member for Rochdale (Mr. Cobden), than whom on such a subject no one could speak with more weight or influence. But he had a far higher authority even than the hon. Member for Rochdale, or the Congress at Paris. His hon. Friend the Member for London, at the close of the Committee, moved certain Resolutions, in which he did not propose that the Committee should agree to the principle of a uniform rate, but, on the contrary, proposed two rates of 18s. 4d. for one class of sugars and 13s. 2d. for another. [Mr. CRAWFORD said, he had grown wiser since then.] He would endeavour to show that his hon. Friend had not even yet arrived at a sound conclusion. In the Committee he had proposed, in effect, that there should be a protective duty of 5s. 2d. in favour of one class of sugar, in spite of the declaration both by Mr. Nelson and the Customs authorities that the distinction between refined and unrefined sugar was not practical but obsolete. He now proposed an uniform scale, the manifest effect of which would be to protect the refiner in Madras against the refiner in England, and the importer of refined sugar from Madras against the importer and producer of raw sugar. How stood the question as regarded the lower classes of sugar ? In the discussion of the previous evening the hon. Member for Rochdale (Mr. Cobden) declared the principal objection to the malt tax to be that it gave to the producers a monopoly of the better article, to the exclusion of inferior articles from the market, and he proved his case by referring to the duty on hops as it affected those grown in Sussex and Kent. It was well known that various sugars contained widely different quantities of saccharine matter, some as much as 96 per cent, others only 50 per cent. The effect upon the lower classes of sugar of a system such as that proposed, would be not merely protective, but prohibitive. The Committee, satisfied of that, refused to adopt the plan of a double duty. His hon. Friend, having grown wiser by experience, as he affirmed, was now the advocate of a uniform or single duty, and in support of that proposition he quoted with great approval the writings of French authorities. It did not surprise him that French writers should think it for their interest to adopt that strain. For, if the French could import manufactured articles into the English market, at the same uniform rate that Englishmen paid upon the raw material, how long were manufactures of this class likely to continue in England ? It would be a fatal error to attempt to exclude any sugar from the English market. The object should be to bring into the market here every kind of sugar—high, medium, and low quality—that was produced in all the world. Accordingly, the Committee recommended that an uniform duty was unjust, that an exact *ad valorem* duty was impossible, and nothing remained but a graduated scale of duty. In that opinion he ventured to think the House would concur. The consumption in England had risen to between 35 and 40 lb. per head of the population, and he did not believe that in France it

Mr. Cardwell

had yet attained 15 lb. per head. Experience, authority, and analogy were all in favour of a graduated duty. He admitted that no principle should be inserted in our statute-book which was at variance with the strictest principles of free trade. But the true free trade doctrine was in favour of duties so proportioned to the value of the article that that article should come here with the same relative facility as if there had been no duty at all. An uniform duty, irrespective of value, was not free trade, but was, on the contrary, protection to some sugars and prohibition against others. There was an interest in the Mauritius, and behind other interests there was that of Cuba, which would benefit from an uniform scale. But the great interest of the producer in the British colonies and of the consumer in this country was on the side of a graduated duty, and he trusted, therefore, that the House would reject the Motion of his hon. Friend.

MR. J. B. SMITH begged to move the adjournment of the House. He thought that it was too late for them then to properly discuss his proposition that the duty should be imposed only for one year instead of three. The present question was one that ought to be brought on at a much earlier hour than it had been, in order to be properly discussed. There were several hon. Members who had not yet spoken who were desirous of expressing their opinions upon it. He trusted that the Chancellor of the Exchequer would promise to introduce the Bill at such a time of the evening as would allow of time fully to discuss a subject of that importance.

THE CHANCELLOR OF THE EXCHEQUER said, he thought that at that hour of the night (ten minutes to one o'clock) it was hardly to be expected that the House could then properly dispose of the question. In substance though not in spirit he considered the proposition of the hon. Member for the City of London (Mr. Crawford) perfectly fair. He hoped, however, the hon. Member would not prevent their proceeding with the business, and therefore he suggested that the discussion which the hon. Member desired relative to the period for which the proposed duties should be imposed might be more conveniently taken in Committee on the Bill, and he undertook that it should come on at an hour which would give hon. Members an opportunity of fully and fairly discussing the question.

MR. CRAWFORD begged to explain

that he had not at present, and never had, any personal interest in the manufacture of sugar, and that when his partner gave his evidence before the Select Committee neither he nor Mr. Nelson had any interest in the refinement of sugar in India.

Mr. CARDWELL said, that he had never intended to impute any personal motive to either the hon. Member for the City of London (Mr. Crawford), or to Mr. Nelson.

Question put, " That the words proposed to be left out stand part of the Question."

The House *divided :*—Ayes 133 ; Noes 17 : Majority 116.

AYES.

Adeane, H. J.
Agar-Ellis, hon. L. G. F.
Archdall, Captain M.
Ayrton, A. S.
Bagwell, J.
Barnes, T.
Barttelot, Colonel
Bathurst, A. A.
Bazley, T.
Beach, W. W. B.
Black, A.
Bramston, T. W.
Bridges, Sir B. W.
Bruce, H. A.
Bruce, Sir H. H.
Bruen, H.
Buckley, General
Bury, Viscount
Butt, I.
Calthorpe, hon. F. H. W. G.
Cardwell, rt. hon. E.
Castlerosse, Viscount
Clay, J.
Clive, Capt. hon. G. W.
Cobbett, J. M.
Colthurst, Sir G. C.
Cowper, rt. hon. W. F.
Dalglish, R.
Davey, R.
Dillwyn, L. L.
Duff, M. E. G.
Dunlop, A. M.
Dunne, Colonel
Evans, T. W.
Ewart, J. C.
Ewing, H. E. Crum-
Farquhar, Sir M.
Fenwick, H.
Floyer, J.
Forster, W. E.
Fortescue, C. S.
Gard, R. S.
George, J.
Gibson, rt. hon. T. M.
Gladstone, rt. hon. W.
Goddard, A. L.
Goldsmid, Sir F. H.
Gore, J. R. O.
Goschen, G. J.
Grenfell, H. R.
Gray, Captain

Grey, rt. hon. Sir G.
Grogan, Sir E.
Hanbury, R.
Hankey, T.
Hanmer, Sir J.
Hassard, M.
Hayter, rt. hn.Sir W. G.
Headlam, rt. hon. T. E.
Heathcote, Sir W.
Henderson, J.
Hennessy, J. P.
Hodgson, K. D.
Hornby, W. H.
Howard, hon. C. W. G.
Howes, E.
Hutt, rt. hon. W.
Kingscote, Colonel
Kinnaird, hon. A. F.
Knatchbull-Hugessen, E.
Layard, A. H.
Leader, N. P.
Lefevre, G. J. S.
Lewis, H.
Locke, J.
Mainwaring, T.
Malcolm, J. W.
Martin, P. W.
Matheson, Sir J.
Miller, W.
Mordaunt, Sir C.
Morris, D.
Morrison, W.
Mure, D.
Neate, C.
North, F.
Northcote, Sir S. H.
O'Brien, Sir P.
Ogilvy, Sir J.
O'Hagan, rt. hon. T.
O'Loghlen, Sir C. M.
Paget, C.
Paget, Lord A.
Paget, Lord C.
Palmer, Sir R.
Palmerston, Viscount
Peel, rt. hon. Sir R.
Peel, rt. hon. F.
Pilkington, J.
Powell, F. S.
Robertson, D.
Russell, A.

Russell, F. W.
Scholefield, W.
Selwyn, C. J.
Sheridan, R. B.
Smith, M. T.
Smollett, P. B.
Somes, J.
Stacpoole, W.
Stanhope, J. B.
Stewart, Sir M. R. S.
Stuart, Lieut.-Col. W.
Stronge, J. M.
Sullivan, M.
Taylor, P. A.
Thompson, H. S.
Thynne, Lord H.
Torrens, R.
Tracy, hon. C. R. D. H.

Turner, C.
Vandeleur, Colonel
Vane, Lord H.
Villiers, rt. hon. C. P.
Watkins, Colonel L.
Watlington, J. W. P.
Weguelin, T. M.
White, L.
Winnington, Sir T. E.
Wood, rt. hon. Sir C.
Wyld, J.
Wyndham, hon. P.
Wyvill, M.

TELLERS.

Brand, hon. H. B. W.
Dunbar Sir W.

NOES.

Bramley-Moore, J.
Buchanan, W.
Denman, hon. G.
Fitzwilliam, hn. C.W.W.
Greaves, E.
Greene, J.
Griffith, C. D.
Kekewich, S. T.
Lawson, W.
Leatham, E. A.
Lindsay, W. S.

Moffatt, G.
Repton, G. W. J.
Seymour, H. D.
Smith, J. B.
Whalley, G.
White, J.

TELLERS.

Crawford, R. W,
Potter, E.

Main Question put, and *agreed to.*

Resolutions read 2°, and *agreed to.*

Bill or Bills *ordered* to be brought in by Mr. MASSEY, Mr. CHANCELLOR of the EXCHEQUER, and Mr. PEEL.

WAYS AND MEANS.

Order for Committee read.

Motion made, and Question proposed, " That Mr. Speaker do now leave the Chair."

FIRE INSURANCE.—QUESTION.

Mr. THOMSON HANKEY asked, When it was proposed that the alteration in the Fire Insurance on Stock-in-Trade should take effect ?

The CHANCELLOR of the EXCHEQUER said that, as the 1st of July appeared to be an inconvenient day for the purpose, he should be happy to substitute for it the 24th of June. With the view of obviating another difficulty, he should propose that, in the case of all policies made after the Resolution on the subject should have been recorded, but before the new law took effect, the duty should be chargeable at the existing rate only to the 24th of June, and for the remainder of the period at the new rate. An apprehension, he might add, prevailed, that a new rate of policy on stock-in-trade would require a separate policy to be made in respect of all stock-in-trade; but the separate policy in the case of farming stock was required simply for statistical purposes, and there would be no need of a separate policy in the instances to which he referred. He also intended to propose a clause in the Bill to the effect, that where a policy did not distinguish the objects falling under the reduced duty, specifications might be made by endorsement upon it, so as to avoid the expense of a new one.

Motion *agreed to.*

WAYS AND MEANS *considered* in Committee.

(In the Committee.)
Resolved,

That, towards raising the Supply granted to Her Majesty, there shall be charged and paid for and upon every hundredweight, and so in proportion for any greater or less quantity than an hundredweight, of all Sugar which, on and after the sixteenth day of April, one thousand eight hundred and sixty-four, shall be used by any Brewer of Beer for sale in the brewing or making of Beer, the Excise Duty of three shillings and four pence.

House *resumed.*

Resolutions to be reported on *Monday* next; Committee to sit again on *Monday* next.

COMMON LAW PROCEDURE (IRELAND) ACT (1853) AMENDMENT BILL.

As amended, *considered:*—Notice taken, that two Clauses had been introduced by the Committee which were not relevant to the subject matter of the Bill:—Bill *recommitted*, in respect of the said two Clauses, and *reported*, with the said two Clauses struck out:—Bill to be read 3° on *Monday* next.

BRIDGES (IRELAND) BILL.

Bill to amend the Law relating to Grand Jury Presentments for County or County of the City Bridges in Ireland, *ordered* to be brought in by Mr. SULLIVAN, Mr. GREENE, and Mr. WALDRON.
Bill *presented*, and read 1°. [Bill 70.]

House adjourned at half after One o'clock, till Monday next.

HOUSE OF LORDS,

Monday, April 18, 1864.

MINUTES.]—PUBLIC BILLS—*Second Reading*— Union Relief Aid Acts Continuance * (No. 39); Land Drainage (Provisional Orders) * (No. 27). *Third Reading*—Vestry Cess Abolition (Ireland)* (No. 19), and *passed.*

The Chancellor of the Exchequer

ARTILLERY—MACKAY'S GUN.
OBSERVATIONS.

THE EARL OF DERBY: My Lords, on Tuesday last I took the liberty of privately directing the attention of the Secretary of State for War to what appeared to me a very remarkable report contained in a Liverpool paper of that date, of a trial that had taken place on the preceding day of a cannon new in construction. It seems to be founded upon a principle not only new in itself, but very much at variance with, and in opposition to that received and acted upon in such matters. Till now it has been a leading principle in gunnery that the windage shall be diminished as much as possible. In this new gun, on the contrary, the principle is to utilize the windage and make it serviceable to the purposes of the gun. The projectile used is a smooth cylindrical bolt fitting accurately the interior of the cannon. The cannon, however, is rifled, or rather spirally grooved; and the principle is that the gas having room to escape passes up the grooves and gives the bolt the rotatory motion essential to such a projectile. It is clear that if this principle can be established it will much reduce the necessity for heavy guns to give sufficient strength to bear the charge of powder, and it will also diminish the amount of recoil. It is stated that the initial velocity obtained at the trial the other day was remarkably high. The gun was manufactured at the well known Mersey Steel and Iron Works. It weighs nine tons, and has a bore of 8.12 inches. At the experimental trial the other day, it was fired with a charge of 30 lbs. of powder and a steel projectile weighing 167 lbs., at a range of 200 yards. The target was constructed to represent the side of the *Agincourt*, now constructing in Messrs. Laird's yard for the Government. It was 7 feet square, and consisted of an outer plate 5¼ inches thick, of rolled iron; next came 9 inches of teak, then an inner plate of iron three-fourths of an inch thick; then angle iron and ribbing, and finally, a backing up of timber balks and supports 18 inches thick. The bolt struck the target near the centre. It drilled a round hole through the plates of iron, shattered the inside of the woodwork into splinters, and not only passed through the whole thickness of the target, but was landed on the beach many yards beyond the target, carrying with it —and this was the remarkable point of the whole—a plug of iron it had drilled out of the plate in its progress. If this statement is correct it does appear to be a very extraordinary performance. What is remarkable is that the plug of iron and bolt were found near together, and the marks in the sand showed that the rotatory motion had been continued to the very last. The bolt itself was perfectly sound and entire, although the force of the impact had diminished its length and added to its breadth. This was the only shot fired—the target having been so completely deranged as to be unfit for further experiments—but it appears to have been a most remarkable success. I do not think anything was done to test the extent of range; but the principle is so new, and if it can be satisfactorily carried out, so important in every respect, and the success of the gun appears to have been so great, that I took the liberty the other day of calling the attention of the Secretary for War to it, and requested him to make some inquiry into the matter. I believe the noble Earl sent down an officer to examine and report upon the subject, and I would ask him now what report has been given, and whether it bears out to the full the details given in the newspapers? If it does, this gun, which is the invention of a Mr. Mackay, seems to me a very formidable rival to those of Sir William Armstrong and Mr. Whitworth.

EARL DE GREY AND RIPON said, he was very much obliged to the noble Earl for calling his attention to the statements concerning this gun, by which he received information a few hours earlier than they would otherwise have come under his notice. He had lost no time in sending an officer down to Liverpool to make inquiries as to the character of the gun and the results which had been obtained. The statements of the noble Earl were confirmed in regard to the main features of the gun by the report which he had received from the officer engaged in the investigation. The size and force of the projectile, the amount of the charge, and the general form of the gun, tallied with the description which had been given by the newspapers. There was some doubt as to the initial velocity, because the exact nature of the instrument used in testing it was not known. The instrument used in our trials is a foreign one of very delicate construction; of the one used in this case we know nothing, and, therefore, I do not know whether the results can be accurately compared. But, in the main features, the results as described by the noble Earl are correct. It might naturally be supposed that when windage could be turned to account, an advantage would be gained as to the weight of the gun, and the amount of the charge used. In these respects, however, there was scarcely any advantage on the part of the new gun over others which had obtained very similar results. The range at which the Mackay gun was tried was very short —only 200 yards; its weight was nine tons; and the charge of powder 30lb. At the same time, the results of the experiment were curious and interesting, and it would be desirable to make further inquiries. Their Lordships would however, perhaps, permit him to compare the results obtained by this gun with those of a few other experiments made by the Government with guns somewhat similar. A 150-pounder smooth-bore Armstrong gun was fired at 200 yards, with a cast-iron shot of 150lb., and a charge of 50lb., against a target representing a side of the *Minotaur*, and consisting of 5½ in. iron plate, backed by 9in. teak. Here the shot was cast-iron (that used with the Mackay gun being of steel) and, like all cast-iron shot, it broke up. The pieces were driven completely through the target, and the front portion of the plate which was struck was found 15 feet in the rear. The same gun, with the same shot and charge, was tried with the same results on another occasion. Then a Whitworth 120-pounder, with a steel shell of 151 lb., and a charge of 27lb., was fired at 800 yards range. The shell penetrated the plate and burst between the plate and the teak. On a second occasion the result was still more satisfactory. He would now compare this gun with the smooth-bored gun known by the name of the Duke of Somerset's gun, used with a lighter charge. That gun—a smooth-bored wrought-iron 100-pounder of six tons—was fired against the side of the *Monarch*, having a 5½in. plate, so that the thickness of the iron was precisely the same as in the target referred to by the noble Earl, but the backing was somewhat slighter. The distance at which the gun was fired was the same—namely, 200 yards; the shot weighed 115 lb., and the charge was 25lb.

THE EARL OF DERBY explained that he had stated that, in the experiment to which he alluded, behind the iron there was a backing of teak, then came another plate of iron, and behind that again thick timber.

EARL DE GREY AND RIPON said, he would read a description, which would explain the construction of the target used by Mr. Mackay. The target was about 7ft. square, formed of two 5½in. plates, each about 3ft. 6in. in breadth, laid horizontally. They were backed by 9 inches of teak, with an inner skin of iron ⅞in. thick, the whole secured by angle iron, and supported at the back by upright beams of timber, and struts 16 to 18 in. square at each end. All he wished to show was that they could not draw any decided conclusions from these experiments. The distance was short, but the result obtained by the smooth-bore gun seemed good. The matter was worth inquiring into, but he had not at present sufficient information to enable him to give a decided opinion as to the real merits of the gun.

THE EARL OF HARDWICKE said, that his noble Friend (the Earl of Derby), though not an artillerist, had been able to state his case with such clearness and accuracy, that anybody could perfectly understand it. The noble Duke opposite (the Duke of Somerset) was the inventor of a cannon, and he would, therefore, comprehend the importance of this discussion. The Channel squadron was now lying ready armed, manned, and equipped, ready for sea—ready to go to Denmark if required. There were on board the ships of this squadron many Armstrong guns, and he would venture to assert that they were useless. If one of these ships were to go into action to-morrow with these guns, and encounter a French ship, for example, in all probability she would be knocked to pieces in the smallest possible space of time, for her Armstrong artillery would be found worthless. He had been very much alarmed at reading the report of the performance of the Armstrong guns in the action at Kagosima. It appeared that the pivot gun on board the *Euryalus* became disabled after the discharge of thirty-five rounds, and the other guns in the squadron were disabled after firing from ten to thirteen rounds. The 40-pounders of the *Euryalus* became useless after ten rounds, and if that ship had been opposed by any vessel with the Whitworth gun or with a smooth-bored gun—one of the noble Duke's artillery—she would be knocked to pieces, and the

The Earl of Derby

result would be alarming to the country and disastrous to its honour. He asked what would be the feeling if any harm should happen to a British ship going into battle with these cannon, so well known to be worthless that the men disliked making use of them? The consequences to a ship having such an armament in an engagement would be so disastrous that the honour of the country would be at stake. He entreated the noble Duke not to delay twenty-four hours taking those guns out of the ships and replacing them, if he pleased, with his own invention.

THE DUKE OF SOMERSET said, he could not lay claim to the honour of being the inventor of the new gun; all he had done was what many other inventors had done, to take advantage of other people's ideas. Finding there was some difficulty about rifled guns he asked Sir William Armstrong whether he could not produce some smooth-bored iron gun, as he thought it might be useful to the navy during the time while scientific men were attempting to produce a rifled gun of the best description. The only condition he made was that it should be a strong gun, capable of standing a charge of 30 lbs. of power. When that gun was made, it turned out, though constructed only for a temporary purpose, a very good gun. The noble Earl was of opinion that the 100-pounder Armstrong guns, placed on board the ships of the Chinese squadron, were perfectly worthless. Against iron-plated ships they might not have sufficient power; but an officer, who had come back from China, gave him a very different account from that which the noble Earl had heard. That officer stated that some of the guns failed, but that in other instances they were admirable. The guns sent to China were made before the last improvements in the vent-pieces. The invention was very much improved now, and the gun was less likely to be damaged. There existed different opinions as to the best system of rifling, as to the number of grooves, and the amount of spiral twist or turn which should be adopted; and it would be most unwise to manufacture a great number of guns while those questions remained undecided. The Whitworth gun had one spiral in 20 diameters, the Armstrong one in 37 diameters; Messrs. Britten's one in 120 diameters, and Mr. Lynall Thomas's one in 25 diameters. Foreign rifled guns ranged from one in 25 to one in 40 diameters. He mentioned these things to show that there was no settled principle in respect to the rifling of cannon, and he should not be doing his duty if he ordered ordnance to be made to a great amount before this question was determined. He hoped in a few weeks they would be able to ascertain which was the best gun, as a regular course of experiments was now in progress.

THE EARL OF HARDWICKE said, he had put a vital question to the noble Earl which he had not answered. The fact was that they had on board their ships a description of gun which was ineffective. Those who were on board the Chinese squadron described the Armstrong gun as worthless. He maintained that the breech-loading gun would not answer. The report made with regard to the *Euryalus* was, that she had ten or twelve of these guns, not one of which lasted after thirteen discharges—the carriages breaking, or the vent-pieces becoming choked or being blown away, so that the guns were useless. At all events, the guns became wretchedly worthless by discharges in repeated succession, and after that he was bound to say let the navy be supplied with any description of gun rather than the Armstrong rifled breech-loader, which was not fit for naval service. They were spending public money lavishly upon experiments of which nobody knew the end, if they were to turn their attention to the small questions of how many turns were required, or what was to be the direction of a curve. He protested against risking the safety of our ships by putting on board of them worthless armaments.

THE DUKE OF SOMERSET observed, that though they might yet be far from perfection, the results obtained from the practice of the Armstrong guns were wonderful.

THE EARL OF MALMESBURY said, he had seen a letter from a civilian in Japan who stated that great disappointment was felt in the fleet about the action of the Armstrong guns. The only guns which might be said to have survived the action seemed to be the old 68-pounders. It was stated that on the first day of the action at Kagosima, when a heavy gale prevailed, and the ships were under fire, the men engaged in firing the Armstrong guns on the *Euryalus* between decks became alarmed at firing them. Next day, however, when the sea was calm and the weather fine, the sailors were said to have made good long shooting with the Armstrong guns.

THE EARL OF ELLENBOROUGH must say that what he had read in regard to the practice with the Armstrong guns in Japan had filled him with disappointment and alarm. If there were the slightest apprehension that the same misfortune would happen again, every Armstrong gun ought to be taken out of the ships. In war everything depended on time and on having the best instruments of war. Not a moment should be lost in placing these ships in an effective condition.

THE DUKE OF SOMERSET said, that the Admiralty had not lost a moment in sending out the plugs and materials for making these guns effective.

THE EARL OF ELLENBOROUGH said, that the noble Duke had got one good gun, and that if he would exert his own common sense in judging of these improvements, he would probably oftener be right than the scientific men.

COMMITTEE OF COUNCIL ON EDUCATION —RESIGNATION OF MR. LOWE.

EARL GRANVILLE: My Lords, I wish to call your Lordships' attention to a matter of considerable importance to myself, and in order to put myself in order I will finish by a formal Motion for the adjournment of the House. The Votes of the other House of Parliament are communicated to this House, and I will therefore read the Resolution to which that House came last week on the subject of the Reports of the Inspectors of Schools—

"That in the opinion of this House the mutilation of the Reports of Her Majesty's Inspectors of Schools, and the exclusion from them of statements and opinions adverse to the educational views entertained by the Committee of Council, while matter favourable to them is admitted, are violations of the understanding under which the appointment of the Inspectors was originally sanctioned by Parliament, and tend entirely to destroy the value of their Reports."

This Resolution appears somewhat unusual, and to be couched more in the sensational style than in the ordinary grave and guarded phraseology adopted in Parliamentary proceedings. With that, however, we have nothing to do; but what I do feel most strongly and deeply is the censure which has been cast upon the Department with which I am connected. It is a rule that no allusion shall be made to debates in the other House of Parliament. That is a good and a salutary rule, and one which it is most desirable should be observed. At the same time, it is so necessary to state that which I am about to say, that I will suppose that some similar Motion has been proposed in a distant country enjoying representative institutions, and that a debate took place on a Resolution of this character. I will do this as shortly as possible, and not with the view of answering the Motion, but for the purpose of explaining the position in which I stand in the matter. The Mover of the Resolution appears to have grounded it on certain alleged facts. He stated that the representative of the Education Department claims the right to expunge from the Inspectors' Reports all opinions differing from his own, and at the same time to retain all opinions agreeing with his own. He asked the House to believe him without proof, though proof he said he had, if challenged. He mentioned that certain passages were expunged from the Inspectors' Reports, and that if he had access to the Reports he could make out a much stronger case. The pith of the answer made by the Vice President of the Committee of Council on Education was, that the alleged facts were not true. In fact, he gave the most complete denial that it was possible to give. But, notwithstanding, the House divided; and by a majority of eight passed the Resolution which I have read. I have been informed—although I do not know it of my own knowledge—that while the Vice President was denying the allegations against him, proofs—not tendered to him for explanation, contradiction, or retractation, were, in the shape of either the original Reports or copies of Inspectors' Reports, privately handed round to Members of the House of Commons, with marks appended to certain paragraphs. That must have been done with the view of influencing their votes on the Resolution, when the question was really one of veracity on one side or the other. In a large office, with much routine business, the head of the office is officially responsible for everything, and that official responsibility ought not to be lessened in the slightest degree. But with regard to the particular matter which gave rise to this vote, I am not only officially but also morally and practically responsible for the proceedings which have taken place. And I will say further, that if I had been in the Vice President's place in the House of Commons on Tuesday last, and if the same accusation had been made against me, I should have made exactly the same

Earl Granville

statement. Your Lordships may well suppose that as soon as I heard of the circulation of this report, I called upon Mr. Lingen, the Secretary of the Committee of Education, to give some explanation of what had taken place, and to state whether it was possible that such a report should be in existence. It is one of the peculiarities of the Resolution of the other House that it complains of a breach of faith towards Parliament, and with regard to this Minute, on which action has taken place, I will venture to read it to the House. It is as follows:—

"Their Lordships having considered the instructions issued from time to time to Her Majesty's Inspectors of Schools for the preparation of their annual Reports, find the sum of those instructions to be that the Inspectors must confine themselves to the state of the schools under their inspection, and to practical suggestions for their improvement. If any Report in the judgment of their Lordships does not conform to this standard, it is to be returned to the Inspector for revision; and if, on its being again received from him, it appears to be open to the same objection, it is to be put aside as a document not proper to be printed at the public expense."

I will now read the explanation given by Mr. Lingen—

"Education Department, Council Office, Downing Street, London, April 18.

"My Lord—In answer to your Lordship's inquiries with regard to the alleged mutilation of the Reports of the Inspectors, I beg leave to submit the following statement:—From the earliest time of my connection with the Office it has always been the duty of some one officer to carry the Inspectors' Reports through the press, and the Secretary has discharged, permissively, a sort of editor's duty. Previously to 1858 this came to very little. A private note, or a personal communication, might pass, most frequently with a view to condensation. About that time, however, the increasing size of our volumes, and the wide range taken by some of our Reports, had become frequent matter of complaint at the Treasury, and had been noticed in Parliament. Fresh instructions were, therefore, issued in 1858 to reduce the length and confine the subject-matter of the Reports, and in 1859 the Vice President used to read the Reports himself in manuscript, and strike out from them, before they went to press, those passages which he regarded as not conformable to the instructions."

I may say here that I think such a course to be a perfectly right one. If properly done, it could not be open to a charge of mutilating. I should rather be inclined to look upon it as a pruning of extraneous and irrelevant matter.

"The Inspector, when he had his manuscript back with his proof, had an opportunity of seeing what had been struck out. The debates which occurred in Parliament about this time, appeared to me to leave the Committee of Council, at least in some degree, responsible for the exclusion of irrelevant matter from the Inspectors' Reports, and I, therefore, directed the officer who read them for the press to examine them with increased care. The mode in which he was to call my attention to anything requiring it was not fixed to any particular routine; he was at liberty either to speak to me with the Report, or to mark it at his discretion. The Report, at this stage of its progress to press, was treated like any other official paper. Such was the state of method throughout 1859, and I do not remember any particular change taking place in 1860, but one of the Reports printed in that year was objected to in Parliament as irrelevant, because it entered into a comparison of Protestant and Roman Cotholic countries in respect of chastity. This led to the Minute of the 31st of January, 1861 (the one now in force), being passed. For some time after this Minute the practice was to mark, or note, any passages in the Inspector's Reports which appeared to be irrelevant, or otherwise at variance with the Minute, and to return them so marked or noted to the Inspector for re-consideration, and this practice I did not consider to be inconsistent with the Minute; but as soon as it was brought prominently to Mr. Lowe's notice (which it was in consequence of certain of the Inspectors attempting to raise discussion on the marked or noted passages) Mr. Lowe ordered it to be discontinued, and directed that the Reports should for the future be returned to the Inspectors, when it was necessary to return them, without being marked at all. The date of this order was the 14th of February, 1862. Since that time the practice of marking or noting the Reports has, of course, been discontinued, and, if any later case has occurred, it must have arisen either from inadvertence, or for some special reason, which, if the marked or noted passage were shown to me, I have no doubt I should be able to explain. I conclude that it is some act or acts done in conformity with the practice above explained which is pointed to in the late Resolution of the House of Commons."

I think your Lordships will feel that Mr. Lowe was perfectly justified in the statements which he made in the House of Commons, and had I been so attacked my answer would have been conveyed in precisely similar terms. I may be allowed to say one word with regard to the policy of the Minute. I think it will be the general opinion that it is necessary for the central office to exercise some such check over the Reports which it receives from so large a body of Inspectors. The noble Marquess who preceded me in my office (the Marquess of Salisbury) and Mr. Adderley, the Vice President of the Committee of Council, exercised such a supervision; Sir George Grey exercises such a supervision over the Home Office Inspectors; and my noble Friend Earl de Grey will answer for himself and his predecessor, that such is the practice of the War Office; and I think that my noble Friend the First Lord of the Admiralty (the Duke of Somerset) will

bear me out in saying that the same supervision is exercised in the Admiralty. I very much doubt if there is any Department of Government where this principle has not only not been found advisable, but absolutely necessary. This being a well-understood principle, another question arises as to the correctness of the statement conveyed in the Resolution, that the practice of the Committee of Council is to expunge those passages which are unfavourable to its policy, while it retains those which express accordance with its arrangements. That statement I entirely deny. The marks upon the Reports sent back to the Inspectors were not the marks of the chief of the Office, but they were made by a clerk in attendance upon the Secretary, simply for the purpose of calling his attention to the passages so noted. I regret deeply the oversight by which the marks were allowed to remain on the Reports sent to the Inspectors, but I deny that they were sent back to them so marked because those passages were adverse to the policy of the Department. On the other hand it has been alleged that passages have been retained because they were considered favourable to that policy. Now I cannot help thinking that, considering the animus with which the attack was made, all the Reports which have appeared before Parliament must have been carefully sifted; and yet only one such case has been cited, and that is a passage giving the opinion of one of the Inspectors upon the system of certificated masters for the schools. As a proof that we are not influenced by the motives attributed to us, I may say that I remember four separate cases in which a request was made that opinions favourable to the policy of the Government should be omitted. Those opinions, as coming from some of the ablest of our Inspectors, would have carried great weight with them, and still could hardly have been considered as irrelevant under the Minute, but, as speaking so highly in favour of our policy, we thought it best to adopt the course I have mentioned. I think the statement I have now made will clearly and fairly dispose of the charge that we have garbled the Reports for our own purposes. I do not know whether your Lordships are aware of the number of Inspectors of schools. There are sixty in all, of whom twenty-two are laymen and thirty-eight clergymen. I believe that there is not in the service of Her Majesty, a body of men of greater ability and higher character. The offices are extremely sought after, and are filled by men of great ability. I have myself appointed twenty-eight, and in saying this I do not claim for myself the slightest credit for the manner in which I have exercised the power of making these appointments; I have merely endeavoured to follow the example set me by Lord Lansdowne and my predecessors. With the exception of one clergyman, whose treatment of educational subjects I had had an opportunity of observing, I do not think that I knew one of the persons I appointed, even by sight, at the time of their receiving their appointments from me. Even now I have no idea what the political opinions of those gentlemen may be. It has been said that if I had selected men bound to me by personal or political ties, they would have identified themselves more thoroughly with the working of the Office. This I utterly deny. I believe that the Inspectors are actuated, as a body, by a strong desire to discharge their duty, and the sincere wish to co-operate most cordially with the office to which they belong. It is true that during the very warm discussion which took place, not only in Parliament but also throughout the country, with reference to the Revised Code, there appeared some articles in the Reviews, showing certainly such an amount of knowledge regarding the details of the office as tended to imply that the information was obtained from some of the officials themselves. Not being thin-skinned I did not complain of this at the time, nor do I complain of it now; but I think I have a right to complain if any Inspector belonging to Her Majesty's service, and under the superintendence of the Committee of Council of Education, not only afforded elaborate information to Members of Parliament for the purpose of attacking the Department, but also actually furnished them with copies of papers belonging to the Council Office. I do think that I have a right to complain of that as a departure from that honourable discretion which I believe to be the characteristic of the civil service of this country. Not only do I complain of this conduct, but I believe it to be viewed with indignation by the whole of the other Inspectors. My Lords, I have endeavoured to show that this Minute is right in principle, and in harmony with the practice of other Government offices under different

Earl Granville

Administrations, and that our mode of carrying it out has been perfectly fair and honest. The condemnation of the Office, however, remains. The censure is one the import of which it is impossible for your Lordships not to see. Her Majesty's Government have considered the subject. They have thought that it is quite impossible that the House of Commons, having come to such a Resolution as this, hastily and upon imperfect knowledge, should refuse to inquire into the facts supposed to exist, and upon which the Resolution was founded. It appears to me that this is a just, right, and necessary course of Her Majesty's Government to take. I have not the slightest doubt, from the usual fairness of the House of Commons in matters of this sort, that the Committee will be granted without any difficulty and without any hesitation, and I am not afraid of the result of such an inquiry. Mr. Lowe has taken another course—he has resigned his office. He has resigned it on the ground that he could not sustain such a deliberate Vote of the House of Commons founded on what must have been a disbelief in his personal veracity, and that he could not remain under the weight of such a blow even until matters were more fully cleared up. My Lords, as a personal friend of Mr. Lowe, I may state that I have now been in political relationship with him for five years. I have remarked —what are generally acknowledged—his commanding intellect and his vast acquirements; and I may add that I have never been associated with any one who appeared to me to be more single-mindedly zealous for the advantage of the public service. As a private friend of Mr. Lowe, I cannot help appreciating the sensitive delicacy with which he has resented that which he considers an attack upon his personal honour; but I may be allowed to say further, that I regret the determination he has come to. I think it is a blow to the Government. I think it is a blow to the Department to which he belonged. The state of that Department as compared with what it was five years ago when Mr. Lowe entered into office is most satisfactory. The number of children in our schools has increased certainly by one-quarter, the schools have increased by between one-third and a quarter; I think that the number of certificated masters has been doubled, the number of Inspectors has necessarily been augmented; but notwithstanding the tendency of the Estimates to increase year by year they were last year brought down below the point at which they stood when he came into office, and that notwithstanding so much had been done for the improvement of the schools. I cannot help referring to the Revised Code. Whether that is a good or a bad measure is of course a matter of opinion. In my judgment it is an excellent one. I believe it has greatly increased the efficiency of the grants given by Parliament, and has established an economy which will do much to encourage Parliament to continue its grants for the promotion of the education of the lower classes of this country. By that Còde we have reduced the expenditure and have entirely set free all vested interests. If any improvements are needed, Parliament will be at perfect liberty to adopt them. The merit of the elaboration of that Code must be ascribed to the Secretary of the Committee of Council, Mr. Lingen. I believe that there are very few persons with ability, industry, and courage enough to grapple with what was a most difficult work. I believe that none could have attempted it but one who had had that daily experience of the administration of these Parliamentary grants which Mr. Lingen had had for several years. But the passing of the Code through the House of Commons —naturally representing as it did the considerable panic which existed, naturally reflecting the feelings of many intelligent and excellent persons who did not see the advantage which would be gained in the aggregate, but only the pressure and inconvenience which it inflicted in different directions — the passing of that work through the House of Commons was entirely owing to the patience and perseverance, to the singularly clear statements, and the great argumentative powers of Mr. Lowe. For these reasons, I deeply regret the course which he has taken in at once resigning. I have not the least doubt that the Committee will be granted by the House of Commons, and that the result of its inquiries will be favourable. I believe that it will be favourable to the principle which we have endeavoured to establish; but with reference to the personal character and personal veracity of Mr. Lowe I have not the slightest doubt in the world that the verdict of that Committee must be in his favour. I beg to apologize to the House for having trespassed on their attention for so long upon a personal and

somewhat egotistical matter; but I felt it necessary to make this explanation not only as a Member of the Government and of your Lordships' House, but because I have for some years been allowed to hold, however unworthily, a very prominent position in this House. I could not have held it, I could not continue to hold it, without the great support which I have received from my friends, and I must be allowed to say the considerable forbearance which I have met with from noble Lords on the opposite side of the House.

THE EARL OF DERBY: My Lords, no one can be surprised that under the circumstances the noble Earl should have taken the opportunity of making the statement which he has just concluded, and of entering into the details upon which he has given us. If I had had any idea that the noble Earl was about to enter upon the discussion of the debate which took place in the other House of Parliament, I would have endeavoured to make myself better acquainted than I am with the nature of that debate, of the allegations which were made against the Vice President of the Council, and of the answer which he gave to these allegations. With a great deal of what the noble Earl has said I entirely concur. It is in every Department absolutely necessary that a certain discretion should be left to its heads to strike out from the Reports made to them anything which appears to be irrelevant to the subject and which may lead to long disquisitions, and if not checked to the practice of each individual who makes a Report to the Government writing a pamphlet in support of his particular views. Therefore, my Lords, so far as any alteration or omission that may have been made in their Reports by the various Inspectors, I do not think that the Government is open to any censure if they insisted upon the Inspectors restricting their Reports to that which really bears upon the state of education and the condition of the schools, and refraining from matters of opinion. The charge, however, I understand to have been this—I hope the noble Earl will understand that I am not saying or suggesting that it was substantiated. I do not know upon what evidence or opinion it rests—the charge, as I understand, was that in a matter which has been made the subject of a great deal of controversy, and which appears to bear directly upon the efficiency of the system—I mean the question as to the comparative merits of certificated and uncertificated masters —expressions of opinion have been allowed to remain in these Reports strongly favourable to the superior claims of certificated masters; while, on the other hand, statements of an opposite character, statements tending to show that uncertificated masters were in many respects equal to certificated ones have been struck out. That I understand to have been the character of the charge made. Whether it is capable of being substantiated or not I do not know. Of this I am quite certain, that the noble Earl opposite—and I am sure that there is not one of your Lordships who will not concur in that description—I am certain that the noble Earl opposite would not, in anything which came under his personal superintendence, allow a Report to be placed either before the House of Commons or your Lordships, altered in such a manner as to convey a different impression from that which the reporter intended to convey, or to give undue bias or favour to the particular view which might be entertained by the Government on any subject. I have not the slightest means of knowing how these Reports have been dealt with, how the information was obtained, from whom the information came, or what, in point of fact, was the information upon which that Motion was made in the House of Commons, and carried by a small majority. It is not, it is true, very regular to refer to what takes place in the House of Commons; but, under the circumstances of the case, I am sure that the noble Earl's slight irregularity may be fairly justified and excused; and perhaps the noble Earl having originated the irregularity, I may be allowed to be guilty of an equal irregularity by stating what I am told has taken place this afternoon, and which may considerably modify the view that may be taken of the circumstances of the case. I am told that this evening the Vice President of the Council, having thought it necessary, in vindication of his own position, to resign the office which he held, has, after taking that step, made a very elaborate vindication of the course which he pursued and defence of his own conduct in office; and I am given to understand, that after hearing that explanation, the noble Lord who brought forward the charge (Lord Robert

The Earl of Derby

Cecil), and upon whose Motion the division took place, stated publicly that if what the right hon. Gentleman the Vice President of the Committee on Education had said to-night had been said in answer to the charge on a former occasion, he should have felt it his duty at once to abandon any attempt to press his Motion on the House. I understand that that has taken place to-night. I believe, also, that a Committee of the House of Commons is likely to be appointed for the purpose of investigating the facts of the case, and I think that is a very proper course to be pursued. I understand that although that proposition was made to Mr. Lowe it was one to which he did not think fit to accede, and insisted, perhaps from an over-scrupulous sense of duty, on resigning his office. I do not know that I can say anything further upon this subject, because I was not prepared, nor am I disposed, to enter into the merits of the Revised Code, or to renew discussions which occupied a good deal of our time on former occasions. I sincerely trust—and, from what the noble Earl says, I am inclined to hope and believe—that if an investigation is made into the circumstances it will prove that there has been no substantial mutilation of the Reports, and that the passages have been omitted, not out of favour or prejudice to one side or the other, but simply from a desire to bring these Reports within fair and reasonable limits, and to exclude from them everything which is not strictly within the limits of the duty of the Inspectors. What has been done I cannot pretend to say; but for the sake of the public service and of public men of all parties and all political views, I earnestly hope that the result of the inquiries of the Committee will be to clear the Council Office from any imputation of having improperly departed from their duty, or having tampered with these Reports.

EARL GREY said, there was one point in the statement of the noble Earl the President of the Council to which he wished briefly to refer. If he correctly understood his noble Friend, he said that there was reason to believe that the Motion which had been submitted to the House of Commons on the subject under discussion had been suggested or prompted by some person or persons in the employment of the Government. Now, that was a matter which, in his opinion, required carefully to be investigated by the Committee which it was proposed should be appointed; because he could conceive no more fatal blow to the interests of this country than that there should be any interference with that honourable understanding which, on the one hand, went the extent of implying that the Government should not use the power which it legally possessed of removing any public servant at the mere pleasure of the Crown, and without assigning any reason for so doing; and, on the other hand, that the civil servants were bound by the strictest principles of honour not to be guilty of the offence of entering upon anything like a secret or passive opposition to the course which the Government might deem it expedient to pursue. The Government of the country would not work a day if the political servants of the Crown did not receive the faithful and honourable support of those who acted under them, and we might eventually be reduced to that unfortunate state of things which existed in America, where when a change of Administration took place, all the civil servants were dismissed from the highest to the lowest. This was an unbounded source of corruption fatal to proper government. So far as our experience hitherto went, we had the advantage of maintaining a body of public servants who had been remarkable for their general order, knowledge, and zeal; and he, for one, felt surprised that any one in the service of the Crown could so far have forgotten his duty as to give any underhand support to the opponents of the Ministry of the day. He trusted that the investigation before the Committee would prove that no offence of that kind had been committed, and that, if it had, the guilty party might be at once removed from his situation.

House adjourned at a quarter past Six o'clock, till to-morrow, half-past Ten o'clock.

~~~~~~~

HOUSE OF COMMONS,

Monday, April 18, 1864.

MINUTES.]—New Writ Issued—For Merthyr Tydvil, v. Henry Austin Bruce, esquire, Vice President of the Committee of Privy Council on Education.

New Member Sworn — Richard Bremridge, esquire, *for* Barnstaple.
Select Committee—Scientific Institutions (Dublin), *nominated* (*List of the Committee*).
Ways and Means — *Resolution* [April 15] *reported* *.
Public Bills — *Second Reading* — High Court at Bombay * [Bill 67]; Bridges (Ireland) * [Bill 70].
Committee — Penal Servitude Acts Amendment; Consolidated Fund (£15,000,000) *.
Report — Penal Servitude Acts Amendment * [Bill 71]; Consolidated Fund (£15,000,000) *.
Considered as amended — Chain Cables and Anchors * [Bill 8], and *re-committed*.
Third Reading—Common Law Procedure (Ireland) Act (1853) Amendment * [Bill 43]; Registration of County Voters (Ireland) * [Bill 49].

BARNSTAPLE ELECTION.

The Clerk of the Crown attending, according to Order, amended the return for the Borough of Barnstaple.

MERTHYR TYDVIL WRIT.

Motion made, and Question proposed,

" That Mr. Speaker do issue his Warrant to the Clerk of the Crown to make out a New Writ for the electing of a Burgess to serve in this present Parliament for the Borough of Merthyr Tydvil, in the room of Henry Austin Bruce, esquire, who, since his election for the said Borough, hath accepted the Office of Vice President of the Committee of Privy Council on Education."—(*Mr. Brand.*)

SIR WILLIAM HEATHCOTE said, he did not wish to throw any unnecessary difficulty in the way of issuing the new writ, but the House should observe that the Motion now made was connected with a question of some importance, which had already been brought before them. As the question might arise, which of the five Under Secretaries had infringed the provisions of the Act regulating the number who could hold seats at one time, he would suggest whether it might not be expedient to adjourn the present debate for a day in order to give time for the consideration of the other and more important point. The Motion for a new writ assumed that Mr. Bruce was at present, or, at all events, had been till very recently, a Member of the House; but that was a question which stood for discussion to-night. He moved the adjournment of the debate.

Motion made, and Question proposed, " That the Debate be now adjourned."— (*Sir William Heathcote.*)

MR. HEADLAM said, he could not see any possible reason against issuing the writ. Assuming that Mr. Bruce could not sit as Under Secretary for the Home Department, at any rate he was Member for Merthyr Tydvil, and had now accepted office under the Crown. It was undoubtedly correct, under the circumstances, to move the issue of a writ for Merthyr Tydvil. Even if Mr. Bruce was not a Member of the House, it would be equally necessary to move a writ for Merthyr Tydvil, which could not be left without a representative.

MR. WHITESIDE said, the hon. and learned Gentleman (Mr. Headlam) had misunderstood the question under discussion. He had assumed that Mr. Bruce was a Member of the House, that he had accepted office under the Crown, and that consequently a writ ought to be issued. But the question raised by the hon. Member for the University of Oxford was, Whether Mr. Bruce had or had not been a Member of the House?

SIR DAVID DUNDAS believed that the right hon. Member for Buckinghamshire hit a blot when he directed attention to the fact that five Under Secretaries were occupying seats in the House. As far as he could see, the case was this. By the Act, only four Under Secretaries could sit in the House, therefore, as long as there were only four Under Secretaries sitting in the House everything was right; but if a fifth Under Secretary were appointed and sat in the House, he could not lawfully do so. Hence the person in default was the Under Secretary last appointed. That person was not Mr. Bruce, but Lord Hartington.

MR. HUNT said, "No" to the observation of the hon. and learned Baronet opposite, that the last Under Secretary appointed was the Marquess of Hartington. As a new Under Secretary for the Colonies had been made within the last few days in consequence of the resignation of the chief of that Department, he (Mr. Hunt) would suggest that the hon. Member for Louth (Mr. Chichester Fortescue) was the last Under Secretary appointed.

THE ATTORNEY GENERAL thought it was inconvenient that a discussion upon the more general Question of which notice had been given should be raised incidentally upon this Motion for a new writ. He was prepared to meet the arguments of hon. Gentlemen opposite when the proper

Sir William Heathcote

time came; but it was not necessary to do so now. One thing was perfectly clear, that if Mr. Bruce had been down to the present time a Member of the House—a fact of which there could be little doubt —his seat had became vacant by his acceptance of an office of profit under the Crown. Even if, as some hon. Gentleman opposite seemed to think, he was not a Member of the House, it was equally clear that a writ should be issued for Merthyr Tydvil. If the House postponed the issue of the writ until a full discussion should take place upon a controverted state of facts and of law, it would do a very unpractical thing. There was not the slightest ground for asserting that since the recent appointment of a Colonial Secretary any new appointment had been made to the office of Under Secretary. The division of Secretaries of State was not a thing recognized by law, which knew no Secretary for the Colonies, no Secretary for Foreign Affairs, no Secretary for the Home Department, and no Secretary for War, unless, indeed, in some exceptional cases the names of those Departments had crept into recent Acts of Parliament. When Mr. Bruce was appointed as Under Secretary, although he was appointed by the Principal Secretary of State, and not by the Crown, he became incumbent of the office, and had never since ceased to hold it, not having been since displaced by any act of the Secretary of State or of any other competent authority. Upon the whole, trusting that the House would not be led into a premature discussion, he thought they would not be placing themselves in the wrong if they agreed to the Motion for a new writ. He had only one thing more to say, though, perhaps, it was rather applicable to the more general question. In 1808, when some doubt was supposed to exist as to whether or not a third Under Secretary ought to sit in the House, Mr. Bagot, who had been appointed to the office, accepted the Chiltern Hundreds, and a new writ was issued on account of his having done so. That was a precedent applicable to a case of doubt; so that if any uncertainty hung about the effect of the acceptance of the office of Under Secretary, it was proper to reduce it to a certainty by the acceptance of another and a different office, which had the effect, at all events, of making the seat vacant.

MR. DISRAELI: I rise, Sir, to submit a Question of order. As far as I am concerned I am perfectly ready at this moment to argue the general Question of privilege, of which Question I have given notice. But still, I really think, in the absence of the First Minister, it would be inconvenient to discuss it now. I understand that the office which this gentleman has accepted is that of Vice President of the Committee of Privy Council on Education. We have no information that Mr. Bruce has been sworn in a Member of the Privy Council, and I believe that he cannot be considered as appointed until he has been so sworn. I trust that some explanation on this matter may be offered. I think it will be much better for the House not to move any of the writs until they have an opportunity of coming to a decision upon the general Question of privilege. It is a serious matter, and the Question must be brought within a brief space before the attention of the House. I hope, therefore, the Government will feel that the best course for them to pursue is not to enter into a desultory discussion, in which the merits of the case must be unsatisfactorily treated, and that it will be better for them to agree to the Amendment of the hon. Baronet the Member for the University, and allow the Motion of the Secretary to the Treasury to be postponed.

SIR GEORGE GREY said, he understood the proposition of the right hon. Gentleman to be, not that the debate should be postponed owing to any doubt that Mr. Bruce had vacated his seat, but merely that the issue of writ should be deferred till after he had had an opportunity that evening of bringing forward the Question of privilege to which he had referred the other night. He did not understand the right hon. Gentleman to ask for an adjournment till another day. There could be no objection to a postponement till the noble Lord at the head of the Government was in his place. With respect to the doubt as to the seat being vacant because Mr. Bruce has not been sworn a Member of the Privy Council, he believed there had been several instances in which a Gentleman had not been sworn as a Member of the Privy Council until the writ had been moved and the election determined. That was the case in regard to other offices, which were always held by Members of the Privy Council, such as those of the Judge Advocate and even of the Secretaries of State. In all those cases the writs were moved on the acceptance of office; and it was not till the writ had been moved, and generally not till after the Member was returned, that he was sworn as a Member of the Privy Council.

Motion, and Original Question, by leave, *withdrawn.*

ECCLESIASTICAL COMMISSION.
QUESTION.

MR. HENRY SEYMOUR said, he would beg to ask the Secretary of State for the Home Department, If the Government intend to introduce this Session any Bill relating to the Ecclesiastical Commission?

SIR GEORGE GREY, in reply, said he had communicated with the Ecclesiastical Commissioners on the subject of the Report of the Select Committee, and, with reference to those Resolutions of the Committee which related to matters of administration that did not necessarily involve a change in the law, the Report of the Ecclesiastical Commissioners was before the House. With regard to those Resolutions which did involve the necessity of a change in the law, the main Question, he believed, was the constitution of the Commission. Now, he was willing to admit, and he apprehended his hon. Friend would agree with him, that the constitution of the Commission was susceptible of improvement. At the same time, he was bound to say that, after a careful consideration, the recommendations of the Committee did not appear to him to suggest the best solution of that Question, or the best course to be taken with a view to the improvement of the constitution of the Commission. At present, therefore, he was not prepared to give notice of any Bill on the subject, but he hoped to be able to do so at a future time, though he could not say that it would be within the present Session. The subject was one of great difficulty, and required very careful consideration.

NATIONAL SCHOOLS (IRELAND).
QUESTION.

MR. O'REILLY said, he wished to ask the Chief Secretary for Ireland, When the Return relative to Religious Instruction in National Schools in Ireland, ordered last Session, and again early this Session, will be laid upon the table?

SIR ROBERT PEEL said, in reply, that the Returns for which the hon. Gentleman asked were very voluminous. They were received at the Castle on Saturday last, and would, he hoped, be presented in a few days.

CHINA—CAPTAIN GORDON AND THE FUTAI OF SHANGHAI.

QUESTION.

COLONEL SYKES said, he rose to ask the Under Secretary of State for Foreign Affairs, Whether any information has been received at the Foreign Office that Captain Gordon, of the Royal Engineers, who was in command of Chinese troops in the service of the Futai of Shanghai, has condoned the treachery of the Futai in putting to death the Taeping Princes at Soochow and plundering the city, and against which Captain Gordon himself, Major General Brown (commanding the British troops in China), and all the European Consuls at Shanghai had published an indignant protest ; whether he has consented to continue in the service of the Futai notwithstanding these indignant protests ?

MR. LAYARD said, he must beg to state that, as far as he was aware, Captain Gordon was not in the service of the Futai but of the Chinese Government. He understood that he was continuing in command of the troops which he had disciplined. He was not quite aware of his reasons for that, but he understood that his motive was that he was afraid that if these troops were disbanded great danger might ensue to the settlement of Shanghai.

MR. W. E. FORSTER said, he wished to know, whether the Government have received any information as to Captain Gordon having been engaged in the siege of a Chinese town ?

MR. LAYARD replied, that he was not aware of that fact, but he might add that accounts had been received that morning that Her Majesty's Minister at Pekin had made representations to the Chinese Government on the subject.

CORN RENTS.—QUESTION.

MR. HUBBARD said, he wished to ask the President of the Poor Law Board, Whether his attention has been directed to the decision in the Common Pleas on the 5th of February to the effect, " that lands

Mr. O'Reilly

charged with ' Corn Rents payable free of Rates' should be assessed at the full annual value, without making any deduction for the Corn Rent charge ;" whether the Board accept that decision as declaratory of the law, and will communicate it to such parishes as have asked for information ?

MR. C. P. VILLIERS said, in reply, that his attention had been directed to the decision in question, and, as a matter of course, the Poor Law Board had accepted it as declaratory of the law. If any parish or union, under entirely similar circumstances, applied to the Poor Law Board, they would be informed that that was the law as it stood on that point.

POLISH REFUGEES IN AUSTRIA.

QUESTION.

MR. YORKE said, he would beg to ask the First Lord of the Treasury, Whether there exists any extradition Treaty between Austria and Russia ; whether his attention has been called to an Order published by General Mensdorf, dated Lemberg, March 16, 1864, and to a similar Order published by General Meckl, dated Cracow, March 12, 1864, ordering all Polish Refugees to be immediately sent back across the frontier; and whether Her Majesty's Ambassador at Vienna has been or will be instructed to use the friendly influence of this country, in order to put a stop to such inhuman practices ?

VISCOUNT PALMERSTON : Sir, we are not aware of any treaty between Austria and Russia for the surrender of criminals. There may be some military arrangement about deserters that we do not know of. But when our Ambassador at Vienna reported to us that the state of siege and martial law had been proclaimed in Galicia, we were informed that any Russian subjects who were in Galicia and were provided with proper passports, were to be allowed to stay there if they showed that it was necessary for their private affairs that they should do so ; and those who had not done this were to be required to go to some other part of the Austrian dominions. But it did not appear by that edict that there was to be any surrender of such persons to the Russian Government.

MR. HENNESSY said, he would beg to ask the noble Lord, whether he will lay on the table the Despatches of Lord Bloomfield on the subject, including his Despatch enclosing the proclamation of General Meckl?

Viscount PALMERSTON : I will look into the Despatches, and see whether there is anything which, consistently with the public service, can be laid on the table. If so, it will be laid before the House.

GREENWICH HOSPITAL.

QUESTION.

Sir JOHN HAY said, he wished to ask the Secretary to the Admiralty, To lay on the table of the House a Copy of a Letter from Sir Richard Bromley, dated 9th April, and a Letter from the Governor of Greenwich Hospital, dated 11th April, on the proposed reforms at Greenwich Hospital. He also wished to know, when Sir Richard Bromley's Report on Greenwich Hospital will be produced?

Lord CLARENCE PAGET was understood to state that the first Report of Sir Richard Bromley on the proposed reforms at Greenwich Hospital, together with a letter from the Governor of Greenwich Hospital, were laid on the table of the House, but he did not think it advisable to lay the further communication received from Sir Richard Bromley on the subject upon the table, as it was only a rejoinder to the Report of the Commissioners.

MALTA HARBOUR—QUESTION.

Sir JOHN PAKINGTON said, he wished to ask the noble Lord the Secretary to the Admiralty, Whether, after the papers that have been laid upon the table, it is the intention of the Admiralty to persevere, and ask the House for a Vote of money towards the construction of the proposed docks at Malta, and, if so, when the Vote will come on?

Lord CLARENCE PAGET said, it was intended to ask for the Vote. He expected to bring the Vote on on Thursday next, but if not, early the following week. He would give notice when the Vote would come on.

DUTY ON CORN.—QUESTION.

Mr. CAIRD said, he would beg to ask Mr. Chancellor of the Exchequer, What are his intentions with reference to the Duty on low-priced Corn? It was a matter of great importance, and it would be satisfactory to the trade to know exactly what the right hon. Gentleman intends doing.

The CHANCELLOR of the EXCHEQUER stated, in reply, that he did not intend to propose to bring within the range of the foreign duty any grain not subject to duty before. He took that opportunity of giving notice that he proposed on Thursday, in Committee of Ways and Means, to move the Resolution relating to Fire Insurances.

UNITED STATES—THE MERSEY RAMS AND THE CONFEDERATE GOVERNMENT.—QUESTION.

Lord ROBERT CECIL said, he wished to ask a Question, which, at the interposition of the noble Lord at the head of the Government, he had postponed on Friday evening. He wished to know from the Attorney General, Whether he still considers a certain Report alleged to be signed by Mr. Mallory, on behalf of the Confederate Government, as a document of a character entirely unquestionable, as he on a former occasion had described it? He also wished to know whether the Government will lay on the table the Despatch of Mr. Seward with reference to that document?

The ATTORNEY GENERAL said, he had to thank the noble Lord for giving him the opportunity of assuring the House that when he referred to that document on a former occasion, and used the word " unquestionable," his meaning was simply this—that never having heard any suggestion that the document was not what it professed to be, and knowing that it had been placed in the hands of Lord Lyons by Mr. Seward, and sent on that authority by Lord Lyons to Her Majesty's Government, and that it had been referred to, as if substantially trustworthy, in a communication by Mr. Adams to Earl Russell; being ignorant also of the peculiar form in which such documents are presented to the Confederate Congress ; and also not being aware at the time that an opinion had been expressed by any person throwing doubt on the genuineness of the document, he, in his simplicity, did assume that the document was what it purported to be. Had it been so, emanating from the Confederate Government, it would undoubtedly have been as he had represented it, of unquestionable authority. His impression was, that the letter of Mr. Adams should be produced. [Mr. LAYARD : No, no ; the despatch of Lord Lyons.] He meant, that the despatch of Lord Lyons should be produced.

EDUCATION — REPORTS OF THE INSPECTORS OF SCHOOLS.
RESIGNATION OF MR. LOWE.

MR. LOWE : Sir, I have humbly to beg the House to interrupt the course of their proceedings for a few minutes this evening in order to allow me to make a personal explanation upon a matter which I little thought would have called for explanation at my hands. In order to make my meaning plain the shortest possible course is, perhaps, to read to the House a Minute of the Privy Council passed in January, 1861; because I shall have constantly to refer to that Minute in what I have to say, and I think it will facilitate the understanding of the House if I read it to them at once and without comment. The Minute is as follows :—

" Their Lordships, having considered the instructions issued from time to time to Her Majesty's Inspectors of Schools for the preparation of their annual Reports, find the sum of those instructions to be that the Inspectors must confine themselves to the state of the schools under their inspection and to practical suggestions for their improvement. If any Report, in the judgment of their Lordships, does not conform to this standard, it is to be returned to the Inspector for revision ; and if, on its being again received from him, it appears to be open to the same objection, it is to be put aside as a document not proper to be printed at the public expense."

That was the Minute of January, 1861. Last year the hon. Member for Bradford (Mr. W. E. Forster) called my attention to this Minute, and asked a question concerning it. I then explained very fully to the House the nature and object of the Minute ; and it was commented upon by the noble Lord the Member for Stamford (Lord Robert Cecil) in the course of the debate. On Tuesday last the noble Lord gave a Notice which I will read to the House—

" That in the opinion of this House, the mutilation of the Reports of Her Majesty's Inspectors of Schools, and the exclusion from them of statements and opinions adverse to the educational views entertained by the Committee of Council, while matters favourable to them is admitted, are violations of the understanding under which the appointment of the Inspectors was originally sanctioned by Parliament, and tend entirely to destroy the value of their Reports."

The noble Lord moved that Resolution on

The Attorney General

Tuesday last. The case of the noble Lord was a direct charge against myself personally, that in my official capacity as Vice President of the Council I had struck out passages from the Inspectors' Reports which were unfavourable to the Office, and he gave several instances of the kind of things I had struck out. A part of the noble Lord's case struck me at the time as a strange one. The noble Lord asked the House to believe him without asking him for proofs, but he said he could give proof, if challenged to do so, that the things cut out of the Reports were of that character. I did not know in the least to what the noble Lord referred in these statements, but I was anxious that the noble Lord should have the opportunity of giving the proof which he expressed himself ready to give if he were challenged to do so ; and therefore when it came to my turn on behalf of the Government to address the House, I took the only way I considered I could take in order to induce the noble Lord to produce that evidence, by denying in the most emphatic manner the assertions he had made on the faith of the evidence he said he could produce. I say there are only two ways in which it was possible for the Vice President of the Committee of Council to strike out passages of the Reports of Inspectors—the one would be, in direct violation of the Minute I have just read to the House, by the simple process of drawing his pen through them, and excluding them from the Report to be printed; the other would be, under the Minute I have read to the House, by sending back the Reports to the Inspectors with passages marked on them, so that they would very well understand if they did not amend these passages the Report would be laid aside as unfit for being printed. There are only those two ways of doing what the noble Lord seems to think we have done. One would have been in accordance with the Minute, and the other in violation of it. I denied them both. I denied that I struck passages out of those Reports, and I made use of this language, which clearly points to the other case—that is, of sending them back with passages marked—I said that the Department of Education does not point out any passages to which they object, but merely lays down a rule or principle upon which the Inspectors are to proceed, and leaves them to apply that rule or principle to their own Reports. Therefore, I think the House will agree with me that no contradiction could be more complete than that which I gave to the noble Lord's statement. And further, I gave that contradiction under as weighty sanction as man could speak under. I spoke as a Member of the House of Commons addressing this honourable House, I spoke as the official representative of a Department of the Government, and speaking on the part of that Government I spoke under a sanction fully as solemn as any oath which can be administered in a court of justice. The noble Lord had the privilege of a reply, and I did expect that in that reply the noble Lord would have produced the evidence which he said, if challenged, he was ready to produce. The noble Lord did not avail himself of the privilege of reply, and the House went to a division without any evidence whatever being given, having on the one side the assertions of the noble Lord, and his further assertion that he had evidence which he could produce, but which he did not produce, and on the other side my solemn and explicit denial. The House was pleased to vote by implication—not in very words, but by implication—that the Department of Education had mutilated these Reports, and had struck out passages from them hostile to their views, and therefore was open to censure. That, Sir, is a brief history of the proceedings of Tuesday night as far as relates to this Resolution. Now, Sir, under these circumstances it appeared to me that the course which I ought to adopt was an exceedingly simple one. The House having heard that declaration from me under the circumstances I have described, was pleased to resolve in flat contradiction to it. If the House had simply declared a want of confidence in me, I should of course have been bound at once to resign my office; but when the House did that which implied so much more than a mere want of confidence in my ability or fitness for office, it seemed to give me still less choice, and I felt it to be my duty at once to resign my office, and to bow to the decision of the House, and I have done so accordingly. But I beg the House to allow me, with all respect, to say that, while I fully admit their jurisdiction over all official persons, and their power to displace them from office, I would appeal to their calmer judgment, and request them to consider a little more the circumstances of the case. I have something more to say to which I earnestly beg the attention

of the House. I think if I were acting in a technical spirit, I might leave the matter here, as it does appear to me that—doubtless through inadvertence or misapprehension—the question coming suddenly before the House, was not fully argued, and that perhaps I had resented an attack upon myself with undue warmth; that for these and other reasons, it may be, the thing had been inconsiderately done. But I think it is only due to the House that I should not content myself with standing on a defensive or negative position, but that I ought to explain the whole matter, and what I believe to be the real meaning of the noble Lord's Resolution. The noble Lord let fall in the course of his speech, that the information which he had received was information which he had received from subordinates in my Office. Of course, if so, it was given by them in violation of their duty and fidelity to the Office. That fact was alleged by the noble Lord as a reason why he could not in the first instance produce the evidence. Now, supposing that the proof of which the noble Lord spoke had been produced, what would it have been? I think I am enabled to answer that question, and as I wish to make a full and fair disclosure, I will tell the House what I know. I was informed—and indeed my own eyes would have informed me were they able to inform me of anything occurring at any distance—I was informed, that during the course of the debate, certain gentlemen were engaged in handing about papers to be circulated among hon. Members. I have been since informed of the nature of those papers. I am informed—and the noble Lord can set me right if I am in error—that they consisted of documents purporting to be Reports, or copies of Reports, of certain Inspectors of the Privy Council, with marks placed against particular passages or sentences. Now, of course, I can easily understand, and I do not intend to blink the question, that the inference which it was intended should be drawn, and which must have been drawn, was that, while I in my place was declaring that the Privy Council always avoided marking passages in Reports to which they objected, here were instances where the Department had done so, and I was, therefore, contradicted by documents which appeared to be decisive. Sir, it is very difficult for a man to defend himself against evidence which he has never seen or heard.

of before an assembly the great mass of which had never seen or heard of it either. I would also say that probably there is no public Department of the country which may not be overthrown or discredited if its subordinate officials are base enough to communicate confidential documents, and if those documents are used not openly and in the face of day, are not placed before the official heads of that Department to explain them, but are used in a manner which gives them no opportunity of placing the true construction upon them. If the proofs to which the noble Lord, I presume, referred—if they had been placed before me—I should have been enabled to tell the House that the marks upon those documents ought never to have been placed there, and were not placed there with the knowledge of the heads of the Department. They were not placed there for the purpose of influencing—whatever they might have done—the Inspectors as to what passages should be omitted from their Reports; but they were placed there through a practice which ought to have been discontinued after the Minute of 1861 by a clerk in the Office whose business it was to read the Reports in order to call the attention of the Secretary to any particular passage in them which he judged to require consideration. It may not make much difference as to the impression produced upon the minds of the Inspectors, but it would have made all the difference in the world in the impression of the House or of those Members who saw these documents as to my veracity upon the subject of which I was speaking. I will now just state what has been my practice and the practice of the Office as to these Reports, and then I will conclude my remarks with thanks to the House for its kind indulgence. The fact is this—my predecessor in office, the right hon. Member for North Staffordshire (Mr. Adderley), got into some kind of trouble with the Inspectors by his endeavours to abridge or consolidate the Reports, using their own words, or to digest them under heads. He gave up that plan and substituted another. He did exactly that which the noble Lord has accused me of doing. He did cut out passages directly with his own hands from the Reports of the Inspectors, and reduced them to the formal shape which he thought proper. That was the practice of the right hon. Gentleman. Let the House clearly understand that I am not blaming him for it. I maintain

Mr. Lowe

that if he was to keep order and discipline in his Office it was his undoubted right and duty to exercise some control over these Reports, and I think he had a right, if so advised, to exercise that control in the manner that he did by striking out passages with his own hand. While this was the practice of the Office, it was delegated to a clerk to read the Reports, and he was in the habit of making marks against passages which appeared to him to require consideration, and then they were transmitted to the right hon. Gentleman, who dealt with them in the manner I have described. When I came into office, without at all questioning the right of the right hon. Gentleman to do what he had done, I declined to follow his example; for I was of opinion, and am so still, that the practice of striking out passages by the superiors of the Office was one very inconvenient and exposed to great drawbacks. It is very inconvenient, because the Inspectors may declare that the passages so struck out affect the meaning of other passages, and it is also inconvenient because it involves the head of the Department in what I should at all times deprecate—an angry controversy with his subordinates. Therefore, I did not act upon the principle of the right hon. Gentleman; and I can say with perfect truth that, having taxed my memory, and that of those with whom I have acted, and having searched the records of the Office, I have never, in any instance, struck out any passage from an Inspector's Report. There was a Report printed, as I mentioned the other night, which Report appeared to me to be a libel upon the Protestant religion, and calculated to stir up controversy between Her Majesty's Roman Catholic and Protestant subjects. My attention was called to the Report by an hon. Member of this House, and I felt it to be my duty to take some step to prevent such a scandal. After consultation with Lord Granville, and after the best consideration we could give, we issued the Minute which I have read to the House. The policy, principle, and nature of the Minute was this—that the Inspectors should be their own censors—that we should in no case point out what we deemed objectionable in their Reports, but that the Inspectors should be bound to make their Reports conform to the Minute of Council. We foresaw the difficulty that has arisen—if the Committee of the Council should commit itself to striking out passages, with whatever care or impartiality, they could not escape the imputation of striking out what was unfavourable and leaving in what was favourable. We foresaw it, and to avoid it we made this Minute. The system went on for two years, and I heard nothing more of it except that a Report was now and then brought before me by my private Secretary for my consideration. But on the 8th February, 1862, my private Secretary brought me a Report of one of our Inspectors which had been sent back for revision, accompanied by a letter which came into my hands, in which the Inspector said he had perused all the passages marked, and could find nothing in them that could be objected to. I was utterly astonished. I called for the Report, and then I found that the practice which had existed in the time of my predecessor in the Office, the right hon. Gentleman the Member for North Staffordshire (Mr. Adderley)—the practice of marking these Reports by the clerk — had most improperly been continued after the new Minute had come into effect. The House will probably ask me how I could have carried on this Minute for two years and not have been aware that these Reports were thus marked with marginal notes. The answer to that question is a very simple one. I am unable to read these Reports in manuscript—they are read to me by my private Secretary ; and the consequence is that I never saw one of these marks, and was not aware that anything was written on the margin until my attention was drawn to the fact by the letter from this Inspector which was brought to me. I then took immediate steps to put a stop to the practice. I gave orders that this kind of thing should never be done again, and pointed out that it was contrary to the whole intention and spirit of the Minute, that it entirely counteracted the object we had in view, and would expose us to all kinds of difficulties. In 1863, the same Inspector unfortunately had his Report returned to him, and he wrote back to ask that the passages to which the Committee of Council objected should be marked. I desired a letter to be written in answer to him to say that the Committee of Council could not undertake to mark any passages, that to do so would be contrary to the spirit of the Minute, and that he must himself discover, as well as he could, what there was in them

that militated against the Minute under which the Report ought to have been framed. And this was my practice in the matter. It was on the strength of these facts that I made the statement I did make in answer to the noble Lord, and I can only reiterate that what I said then was entirely true to the best of my knowledge and belief. One more thing I have to say, and that is, that my noble Friend and myself had received Reports—three of them, I remember—from very important and influential Inspectors, in which they spoke in terms of high commendation of the changes introduced under the name of "the Revised Code." Those passages were not of such a nature as would have justified us in sending back the Report, as they did not appear to us to violate the Minute that we had made. But we were very anxious that they should not appear, and we requested these gentlemen privately, not officially, to be good enough to expunge these passages from their Reports. All this I should have stated before, had these documents been brought before us. One word in justice to the noble Lord the Member for Stamford (Lord Robert Cecil). I do not know whether he circulated these documents, but I have no reason to doubt that whoever circulated them believed that these marks were impressed upon them by the orders of the heads of the Office of the Privy Council. I do not at all, therefore, say that they were conscious of the mischief they were doing. I only wish to point out the danger of departing from the ordinary principle of justice meted out to the poorest man in this country—that of never condemning him, more especially in the crushing manner in which I have been condemned, without at least giving him the opportunity of commenting upon the evidence on which the charge against him is based. Sir, I have little more to say. If there was any Gentleman who was anxious to drive me from the office I have held under Her Majesty's Government, his wishes are now fully gratified. I have disentangled this personal question, upon which my honour and much of the happiness of my future life depend, from any question of office. There is nothing now to be gained from any party or personal attack, and no one has now anything to gain by bolstering me up if I am wrong, or persecuting me if I am right. I beg the House, therefore, to take what I have said into their favourable consideration, and to weigh carefully the statement I have made to them. If it appears to them to be full and satisfactory—if it appears to them to bear upon it the evidence of truth—I shall be well satisfied. If it does not appear to them to bear that evidence, or if they think that any further statement or explanation is necessary, I entreat them to use in their wisdom those powers of inquiry with which they are vested, and to sift to the utmost every word I have uttered. Let them ransack our records, let them examine our clerks and secretary, let them examine me or any one else they please connected with the Office. If, on the other hand, they are satisfied that the statement I make is true and honest, then I ask them to do me justice.

LORD ROBERT CECIL: Sir, I can only begin by expressing my regret that the right hon. Gentleman should have taken the Resolution which I offered to the House and which was accepted by the House last Tuesday as directed personally against himself. The terms of the Resolution were directed against the Committee of Council. It was the practice of the Committee of Council which I desired to censure; and I did not venture to give any information, for I possessed none, as to whether it was the right hon. Gentleman or any other person who was guilty of the practice to which I referred. I think the House will have gathered from the statement of the right hon. Gentleman, that what I laid before them on Tuesday night was entirely supported by the facts. It was a fact that the Inspectors received back their Reports from the Committee of Council, in many cases with the passages marked, indicating that they were thought objectionable ; and it is the fact that whenever they declined to remove the passages so indicated their Reports were suppressed. The right hon. Gentleman has since informed us that that was done by a clerk in the office without his orders. But he must have been perfectly aware of this on Tuesday night. [Mr. LOWE: No.] Was he not? Then I can only regret that he was so little acquainted with the proceedings in his own office.

MR. LOWE: Of course I was aware that up to 1862 this had been done, because I did my best to stop it.

LORD ROBERT CECIL: If the right hon. Gentleman had told us on Tuesday night that he was perfectly aware that in

Mr. Lowe

previous years the Reports of the Inspectors had been sent back marked in that fashion —that Reports had been rejected from which passages so marked had not been removed, but that the practice was stopped, and the marks had not since been appended—if, I say, he had made that full and frank explanation, the result, both as regards himself and the House, I think, would have been very different. But he left us in absolute ignorance of the fact that there had been in the office any discussion with reference to the continued marking of these Reports. He did not inform us that the practice had ever obtained, or that he himself had ever taken any measures to stop it. The subject was first mooted at the beginning of last year. It originated, I believe, in a question put by the right hon. Gentleman the Member for Droitwich. At that time several Reports were missing, and we had reason to know that they had been marked in this way and sent back to the Inspectors. The right hon. Gentleman has always steadily refused to give any explanation on the subject. He has been constantly asked to lay these Reports on the table, and to give some pledge that the practice should be put a stop to. That pledge, however, he always steadily refused to give, and he also declined to place these Reports on the table. I ask any hon. Member whether he would not have drawn from this refusal an inference that the practice which existed before January, 1862, was going on still, and that the same agency was in operation for preventing this House from obtaining true and pure information that had been in operation before that time. Sir, I have no wish to prolong an angry controversy; but I am bound to say, with reference to my non-production of evidence, that my evidence was not the paper which I held in my hand The evidence which I had to produce, and which I would have produced if challenged to do so, was not papers but men. I should have asked for a Committee, I should have produced witnesses before that Committee, and I should have shown that Reports had been sent back marked in the way which I mentioned. One point more. The right hon. Gentleman has spoken in bitter terms of subordinates of public offices who communicate what they think to be abuses in their departments to Members of this House. I am quite sure that the House will not endorse this censure. I do not believe that in the service of the Crown any loyalty is due to heads of departments as against the House of Commons. The heads of departments and those departments themselves are alike subject to our jurisdiction; and if persons employed there see what they deem to be abuses they do no wrong in laying them before the representatives of the people.

I will end, if necessary, by moving the adjournment of the House, but I thought it due to myself, after the statement just addressed to the House, to say a few words on this subject. The reason why I referred to this evidence in terms which were purposely indistinct — and the hon. Member for Berkshire (Mr. Walter) took the same course — was because we were afraid of implicating these subordinates with their superiors, and because a recent instance led us to believe that the discipline of the Council Office was maintained with unusual rigour. On this ground it was mainly that I addressed the House. But I will only say now, that if the right hon. Gentleman had spoken the other night as fully and frankly as he has spoken to-night, I do not believe that the Motion would have been pressed to a division, or, if it had been, that the decision of the House would have been what it actually was. The hon. Member for Bradford (Mr. W. E. Foster) on Tuesday, challenged the right hon. Gentleman to contest our assertion by laying the impugned papers on the table, and that challenge was not accepted. Under those circumstances, I do not know what other course was open to us than to press the Motion to a division.

VISCOUNT PALMERSTON: Sir, nothing can be more painful than the discussion which has just taken place. If there be one thing more painful than another to a generous mind, it must be to see an honourable, able, and upright man defending himself before an Assembly like this, against a condemnation which he considers to have been passed upon him, but which he knows to be unjust and unfounded. Sir, the noble Lord who has just sat down has said that if he had been aware on Tuesday night of what my right hon. Friend has now stated, the result would have been different; but let me ask the noble Lord whether it did not occur to him, that when one makes a charge against another it might be well to ascertain by full inquiry whether that charge was just

and well-founded or not. The noble Lord stated, that as his remarks were made with respect to Reports sent back to Inspectors in 1862, he thought he had reason to conclude that the practice to which he objected was still continued. But the noble Lord having opportunities, which are well known to everybody, of ascertaining the real state of things from those who are concerned, I think it might have been as well if he had ascertained beforehand whether the practice which he called upon the House to condemn had or had not been continued since 1862. Having taken some part in the matter with respect to which my right hon. Friend has made his statement, I can only say that nothing could give more pain to myself and my Colleagues than losing the services of a man so eminently qualified to do good service to the public and his country, whether by the extensive range of his knowledge and the logical accuracy of his mind, or the soundness of his judgment and the uprightness of his character. I say it was a most painful thing to us to contemplate the loss of his services. When my right hon. Friend came to me immediately after the debate on Tuesday to state that he felt, after such a vote, he could not with honour to himself continue to hold the office which he then filled, I and my Colleagues—all of us—endeavoured to persuade him that that view was not a sound one. We said that it did not appear to us that the question at issue was one of veracity on his part ; that it related rather to the practice of a department. We felt that it would not be becoming, and would not be advisable according to the practice of Parliament, to ask the House to rescind the vote which it had come to after considerable discussion ; but it was our intention to propose to the House, what my right hon. Friend has just asked, that a Committee should be appointed to ascertain and inquire what was the manner in which the business was executed in the department concerned. It seemed to us that my right hon. Friend should have waited the issue of that inquiry, and we were convinced from what we knew that the result would bear out the assertion which he has made. No one has a right to judge the feelings of another in respect of questions which he considers to affect his personal honour, and therefore, after many days of unsuccessful endeavours to persuade my right hon. Friend to abide by the investigation and decision of the Committee, I was yesterday under the painful necessity of accepting his decided and peremptory resignation. Sir, I am sure that the House, having heard the statement which my right hon. Friend has made, will be of opinion that the vote the other evening was a hasty vote, not sufficiently considered; but the decision having been come to, I do not think it would be respectful to the House to ask them to reverse that decision. I think, however, it would be quite consistent with Parliamentary practice, and with the honour and character of the House, that they should agree to appoint a Committee to ascertain whether the impressions under which the majority voted on the occasion are or are not well-founded according to the practice of the department. I, therefore, intend on Thursday next to move for such a Committee, and I am quite sure that the noble Lord the Member for Stamford, after what he has said, will be prepared to agree to it. It is not my wish now to advert to the other topics which my right hon. Friend has announced his intention of bringing under the notice of the House, because I believe it was understood that they should remain over for discussion till a future opportunity.

MR. DISRAELI: Sir, this is the first time that I recollect that a Ministerial explanation has led to a debate. It is extremely irregular, but I will put myself in order if necessary by making a Motion. [*Cries of* "Order!"] When an appeal has been made to the opinion of the House by a right hon. Gentleman on a matter affecting his personal honour, I do not see how hon. Members on this side can be silent. At least, I wish to express my own opinion, and I have risen to say, for myself and hon. Gentlemen around me, that we take the statement of the right hon. Gentleman, as far as his personal honour is concerned, as perfectly satisfactory, and we estimate that honour after his explanation to-night as inviolate. I may say, as I am on my legs, that I hope this will close the discussion on the subject. I do not think that the observations made by my noble Friend (Lord Robert Cecil) at all called for the remarks of the noble Lord who has just spoken. My noble Friend's conduct in the matter has been perfectly straightforward. Notice of the Motion was given last year, and when the notice appeared on the paper this year the Government must have been fully aware of it;

Viscount Palmerston

but, for all that, I did not see those preparations made on that side of the House to support the right hon. Gentleman which I think his position in office and his eminent talents deserved. I have always opposed the right hon. Gentleman as to the principles on which his policy with regard to education has been carried on; but I have always borne, and I now bear, my testimony to his distinguished talent, the clearness of his intellect, and the vigour with which he has conducted the public business, and I only regret that so much talent has been lost to the public service, chiefly, as it appears to me, from the right hon. Gentleman in this, as in many other instances, not having been properly supported by his Colleagues.

MR. WALTER was about to address the House, when—

MR. SPEAKER: I wish to point out to the House that there is no Question before it. An opportunity of making a personal explanation is granted by the courtesy of the House; but it is not usual that such a matter should be concluded by a Motion, and made the subject of a general debate. I think the House will now agree with me, that all those who can be said to be personally concerned in this discussion have been heard by the House. [*Cries for* "Forster!"]

MR. WALTER: Sir, as I must consider myself one of the Members who took a prominent part in the discussion of Tuesday evening, and as I have not yet been heard, I wish, in consequence of what has fallen from my right hon. Friend, to make a very few remarks. I merely rise to say that, after the explanation which my right hon. Friend the late Vice President of the Committee of Council has given, I am sure the House will not think it necessary to adopt the course proposed by the noble Lord at the head of the Government. My own opinion is that, after that explanation, no Committee is required for making further inquiry into the subject. For myself, I wish to state in a very few words the position in which I conceive myself to stand. The House will recollect that when my noble Friend the Member for Stamford brought forward this subject, I was the Member who seconded the Motion. I had, therefore, no opportunity of replying to the speech of my right hon. Friend, and certainly I was not prepared for that unqualified denial which he then gave to the statements of my noble Friend and myself. On hearing my right hon. Friend that night, I felt convinced that there must be a mistake, and that my right hon. Friend could not have been cognizant of the facts which it was in the power of my noble Friend and myself to prove. I had in my possession at the time when I was addressing the House documents purporting to be a copy of one of these Reports which had been marked in the manner described by my noble Friend; and, after the explicit denial of my right hon. Friend, I think it my duty to put him in possession of all the information which I had then in my power to give. I regret extremely that my right hon. Friend should have felt it necessary to adopt the course of resigning his office, because it appears to me that that which he considered as a vote of censure on himself rested on an allegation which was either false or true. If it were false, it was in his power to place my noble Friend and myself in a very awkward position by showing that we had no grounds for making the statements which we did. If, on the other hand, the allegations proved to be true, it was in my right hon. Friend's power to give such an explanation as he has now given, which would have satisfied the House that he was in no degree responsible for the occurrence. I will not delay the House longer, but will merely express my regret that the vote at which we arrived the other evening has had such a result.

MR. W. E. FORSTER: I wish to make an explanation ["Order!"] with respect to the reasons which induced me, and, I think, forty or fifty other Gentlemen, to give the vote which we did the other night. ["Order!"] I wish to make this explanation in justice to the right hon. Gentleman also. I had no idea whatever that the Question under discussion was one affecting the personal veracity or the personal honour of the right hon. Gentleman. I regarded it as one which purely affected the policy of the department, and the course which those who differed from the department were obliged to take. Gentlemen in my district had been very much surprised that, in the Education Report, a Report of an Inspector in whom they had the greatest confidence did not appear. In consequence of that circumstance, the right hon. Baronet the Member for Droitwich asked why the Report in question was not produced, and the right hon. Gentleman (Mr. Lowe) was

asked to produce it. He refused to do so; and I was obliged to ask the right hon. Gentleman on what conditions in future he intended to produce the Reports of Inspectors. The right hon. Gentleman stated in reply that in future he intended to make the Inspectors their own censors, and added that he did not think those Reports should contain controversial opinions. I, and those who agreed with me, held that we ought to have those Reports without censorship. We then come to the question of the effect of those red marks; and I must in justice to myself and others say, that I never saw one of those Reports to which reference has been made before the debate; but I thought that sending back the Reports to the Inspectors in the way we have heard of, was virtual mutilation, as those gentlemen would know very well what such a proceeding meant. Therefore, I asked the right hon. Gentleman to produce the Report that we might see whether we were right or not. As he refused to do so, and justified his refusal on the ground that the Report of an Inspector ought not to contain anything against the chief of his department, I, and those who thought with me, felt bound to vote with the noble Lord. I regret, in common with the House, that the right hon. Gentleman should have thought that the vote was one which affected his personal honour, or anything but the policy of the department.

PRIVILEGE—UNDER SECRETARIES OF STATE.

MR. DISRAELI: Sir, it is now my duty, with a little more detail than I ventured to use the other night, to call the attention of the House to a Question of Privilege—arising out of the distribution of offices held by Members of Her Majesty's Government. The House will perceive that the Question is one of great gravity. Already it has led, in a constitutional sense, to considerable inconvenience, and it may, if neglected, produce results of a character so serious that it is difficult at this moment to adequately describe them. And, Sir, my opinion is, that the embarrassing and even dangerous position in which this House is placed in regard to the distribution of offices here—embarrassing certainly to the Ministry, and, as I shall show, dangerous to the House—had its origin in the way the present Government was formed when the noble Lord, the present Prime Minister, acceded to office. The House will remember that, at that time, a considerable number—I think I may say the majority—of the great offices of State, were represented in the House of Lords. I would not myself, Sir, lay down any inflexible rules, such as the laws of the Medes and Persians, with respect to the distribution, on the formation of a Ministry, of the offices of State between the two Houses of Parliament. On the whole, that must be left to the discretion of the person who undertakes the responsibility of forming an Administration. But there are considerations which I think, generally speaking, ought to guide the individual called on by the Sovereign to form a Government in regard to the distribution of offices. For example, I would venture to say that I think the heads of the two great Departments of public expenditure should find seats in the House of Commons. I do not think the due control of this House over the public expenditure can be sufficiently possessed under other circumstances; and if the control of the House is diminished in that respect, its authority in the estimation of the country will proportionately suffer. With respect to the Secretaries of State, I would say that the majority of them should have seats in the House of Commons — even a large majority of them, I would say, as was the case with the late Government. The House, upon reflection, will see that in this matter the Constitution has, in practice, adequately provided for the representation of the Ministry in the other House of Parliament. One Secretary of State must have a seat in the House of Lords—at least, he cannot sit here, and, therefore, he must find a seat in the House of Lords. The Lord Chancellor, one of the most eminent members of the Cabinet, and the head of the jurisprudence of the country, must have a seat in the other House; the Lord President of the Council must also be a Peer, as must also be the Lord Privy Seal. The Postmaster General is by statute prohibited from sitting in the House of Commons; and since the Reform Act—a measure which it was supposed would so greatly increase the influence and power of the popular branch of the Legislature—the Prime Minister, in the majority of cases, has found a seat in the House of Lords. Added to this, the chief offices of the Household, always held by Peers, have

Mr. Disraeli

sometimes been held by eminent statesmen, as by Lord Wellesley, for instance. I think no one can deny, therefore, that the Constitution has provided adequately for the representation of the Government in the House of Lords. And when we reflect on the manner in which the public business is divided between the two Houses —when we compare the labours of this House with those of the House of Lords —I think it is obvious that it is in this branch of the Legislature the great majority of offices should be represented. I recollect that, before the present Administration was formed—a few days—I believe hours—before the fate of their predecessors was decided — in a somewhat memorable speech, it was said that the Government in this country ought to be conducted by the educated section of the Liberal party. Well, Sir, I thought, at the time, that was a phrase more candid than felicitous; but though various interpretations were placed upon it by both sides of the House, I do not think any interpretation arrived at contemplated the conclusion which was subsequently accomplished—namely, that the great offices of State in the new Ministry were to be confided to the custody of half-a-dozen Peers of the realm. So far as we on this side of the House are concerned in the arrangement, if we took a party view of it, we should be sufficiently satisfied. I hardly know that any arrangement could tend more to the political degradation of the party opposite. When power was seized—I do not say in a spirit of rapacity, but certainly on that occasion without any unnecessary delicacy; when there were no great scruples as to the nature or the conduct of the Opposition; and when, subsequently, the country found that the great Liberal party were in office, and yet that in the opinion of the leaders of that great party there were not in that branch of the Legislature which had brought them into power men from whose ranks they could select persons fitted to administer the affairs of the country—I think that must have been regarded as a slur upon the vote of want of confidence which had just been passed upon their predecessors. But there is something dearer to both sides of the House than party triumph—namely, the character and authority of the House of Commons. In that we all share and all participate; and I am sure that every hon. Gentleman in this House feels really sorry when anything takes place that humiliates the character of this House, or places it in a position not calculated to preserve for it the confidence and support of the country. For my own part, believing that Parliamentary Government is practically impossible without two organised parties—that without them it would be the most contemptible and corrupt rule which could be devised—I always regret anything that may damage the just influence of either of the great parties in the State. Well, Sir, this question with respect to the distribution of offices has arisen because, in consequence of the plan on which the present Administration was formed, the principal offices of the State have necessarily been represented in this House by Under Secretaries, or by Members of the Administration bearing, perhaps, a different title, but holding similar rank. It was on more than one occasion, I believe, the intention of Gentlemen on both sides the House to advert to that condition of affairs as, on the whole, unsatisfactory, as tending to diminish the authority of this House, as calculated to greatly reduce its influence. I do not know that I should myself have interfered in the matter—though I intended to do so some weeks ago—had it not been for an expression of the noble Lord at the head of the Government, which opened my mind to the position that the House was fast coming to occupy. When I offered some quite legitimate criticisms upon the conduct of a Secretary of State who happens to sit in the House of Lords, the noble Lord, not in a hurried manner, but with a most premeditated phrase, taunted me with having attacked "an absent man." That opened my mind to what must be the consequence of our passing unnoticed the course which the Government had plainly adopted in the distribution of political offices ; and I saw clearly in what a situation Members of the Opposition would be placed who, bringing forward cases of importance or urging inquiries of interest, were always put in collision with gentlemen whose abilities we all recognize, who are frequently adequate to the offices they nominally hold, but who are obliged to encounter us upon questions which no one can properly treat who is not in the counsels of his Sovereign, who is ignorant of the motives and the policy really pursued by the Cabinet, and who cannot enter into those engagements and make those representations which the authority of Ministers of the Crown alone authorizes them to express. But on that occasion I refrained from bringing the sub-

ject under your notice, because there had been for a considerable time impending over us a probable reconstruction of the Government to a certain extent, occasioned by a cause which I am sure is regretted by hon. Gentlemen on both sides. At that time, it was daily expected that the Duke of Newcastle would quit public life, and it appeared to me that to bring forward the question of the distribution of offices at a moment when the Duke of Newcastle was still a Minister might lead to observations and discussions which, in reference to him, might have been painful. The Duke of Newcastle sat for a long time in this House, and on these benches. Perhaps, now that he has retired from public life, I may be permitted to say, I am sure in no glozing language, that, during twenty years of rather warm public life my relations of personal courtesy with the Duke of Newcastle have never terminated, and I think I may add that he withdraws with the reputation of a sedulous, able, and conscientious Minister. Well, the Duke of Newcastle quitted office, and then took place the reconstruction of the Ministry which was expected. It was not of so extensive a character as had been anticipated ; on the contrary, it was extremely partial—and the first thought on reflection was, that the subordinate members of the Government, who represented high offices of State in this House, were not materially reduced in number. We had to reconsider the question, and then it was suddenly discovered that the state of affairs which before we had thought practically injurious was, in fact, flagrantly illegal. The noble Lord asked me the other night how it was the thing never occurred to me before. I hardly know any subject more happy for a *tu quoque*, but I shall resist the temptation, great though it be. I remember reading somewhere of a Whig county Member, who, in the last century, questioned the right of Lord George Germain to sit in this House. Lord North asked Sir Joseph Mawbey, why he had not mooted the point before, seeing that Lord George had been sitting there for a year. "Why, to tell the truth," replied Sir Joseph Mawbey, "it never occurred to me." When the noble Lord with the blue riband made his inquiry nobody thought it was an answer to the point raised by Sir Joseph Mawbey, and so I am sure that to-night in discussing this Question, which is one of great gravity, we shall not be met by observations of that kind, but shall address our minds to the merits of the case, in order to ascertain clearly the position in which we are placed.

As the point to which I wish to call the attention of the House is to the offices held by the Under Secretaries of State, I wish at the outset to direct attention to the state of the law upon the question. It may appear a very arrogant thing that I, who am a layman, should presume even to make a statement, much less to draw an inference, upon a subject so technical and professional ; and I should, perhaps, have been daunted in this enterprize by the observations made by the Attorney General some time ago, when he told us incidentally, in order to give a cue to the House, that the subject is most refined and complicated. There are some men who have refined and complicated minds, and there is nothing they touch that, under their magical manipulation, does not quickly become refined and complicated. I would say to the Attorney General, whose talents I always admire, that I think he is a master in the art of refinement and complication. But, notwithstanding his statement, I venture to say that the question is really very simple; that any one who chooses to give his attention to it may understand it without being an Attorney General or a Queen's Counsel ; and that if I do not make it in a brief space as clear as crystal it will be from want of apprehension, or a deficiency in the powers of expression on my part, and not from any fault of the House or the subject. The tenure of office in this country is mainly regulated by statute, and it is principally regulated, as far as this House is concerned, by an Act passed in the reign of Queen Anne, with which I have no doubt hon. Gentlemen are all familiar, by name at least. A very remarkable Act is that famous Act of Queen Anne. About 1708 there was a strong Parliamentary opinion, if not a strong public opinion, that there were sufficient placemen in the House of Commons, and a Resolution was come to that the number should not be increased. An Act was accordingly passed, which—to give a general description of its main feature — enacted that henceforth any one who accepted any office of profit in the service of the Crown created after 1705— about three years before the passing of the Act—should thereby become incapable of being elected a Member of this House, or of sitting and voting here. The effect of that Act may be put briefly before the House. When the Act passed Queen Anne had two Secretaries of State and two Under Secretaries. Suppose the day

Mr. Disraeli

after Anne, as she had an undoubted right to do by her prerogative, had appointed a third Secretary of State, and, consequently, a third Under Secretary, both those offices would have been treated as new offices—offices, that is to say, created subsequently to 1705—and their holders would have been incapable of occupying seats in this House. Heavy penalties were attached to the violation of the statute ; but it is quite unnecessary to touch upon that matter now, because the question of penalties has nothing to do with this House. A very considerable time elapsed after 1708 before any fresh legislation took place affecting the seats of Members of this House—I think seventy years passed away. Great events, great disasters, had occurred during that long interval. We had lost our American colonies ; the country was in a state of distress and despondency ; and there arose, as always in England under such circumstances, a cry for administrative and economical reform. Mr. Burke, one of the greatest men who ever sat in this House, happened then to be a Minister of State ; and it fell to his lot to consider by what means the administration might be improved and economy effected. Mr. Burke therefore, in the year 1782, in the reign of George III., brought forward that great Bill, with which I am sure hon. Gentlemen are perfectly acquainted, his Bill for Economical Reform, and by that measure, among his other reductions and improvements, he abolished the third Secretary of State, who was the Secretary of State for the Colonies. England having lost her colonies, the administrative reformers of those days naturally thought, if reduction was desirable, that there was no necessity for a Colonial Secretary ; and in the Act of Mr. Burke the Colonial Secretaryship is abolished, and all those offices dependent upon it. The result of Mr. Burke's Bill was this—that two Secretaries of State were permitted to sit in the House of Commons, and two Under Secretaries. Sir, that was the state of affairs which prevailed, as far as the distribution of offices with reference to the House of Commons was concerned, for another seventy years, including the whole of the great Revolutionary War. Unquestionably during that period new Secretaries of State were created, who, of course, appointed Under Secretaries ; but they were appointed, all of them, solely by the prerogative of the Crown, not by statute, and none of them ever sat in the House of Commons. The hon. and learned Attorney General appealed to the case of Mr. Bagot. Now, that case would entirely substantiate, if necessary, the statement that I am making. Mr. Bagot was a Member of this House for Castle Rising, a borough which I suspect is now only to be found in schedule A. He was appointed Under Secretary of State for Foreign Affairs. There were two Under Secretaries then sitting in this House—one for the Colonial and the other for the Home Department. And what did Mr. Bagot do? He immediately accepted the Chiltern Hundreds; and the hon. and learned Attorney General endeavours to frame an argument on that, that he did not vacate his seat in consequence of accepting the office of an Under Secretary of State. Yet I apprehend it is a common course of Members of Parliament to accept the Chiltern Hundreds, even if they hold any other appointment than that to which the hon. and learned Gentleman referred. But I ought to remind the House that in Mr. Burke's Act of Economical Reform, which abolished the Secretaryship of State and the dependent offices, there is a special proviso—that in case hereafter any office for the same or for a similar purpose is created, then to all interpretations, intents, and purposes it is to be considered what is called "a new office—that is, an office subject to the provisions of the statute of Anne; and to the statute of Anne is attributable that distinction between old and new offices which once was very prevalent in political literature, and which may even now be found creeping into the statute book. All offices created before 1705 are "old;" all created subsequently to that date are "new" offices. Well, whatever refinement the Attorney General may found on the case of the retirement of Mr. Bagot from this House, I make him a present of it; for really it is not at all necessary to my argument, or to the clear case which we have before us. The hon. and learned Gentleman will not deny that the invariable practice of Parliament was that only two Secretaries of State and two Under Secretaries of State could sit in this House. That he will not contradict. And so it went on till we come to the times with which we are perfectly familiar, in which we were all actors, and which form part of our recent experience. Two Secretaries of State and two Under Secretaries, as I have stated, might legally sit in the House of Commons. Then occurred the Crimean war, with its military disasters, followed by a strong expression of public opinion that there ought to be a more effective organization of our military departments. Then the noble Lord, who ought to be familiar with this question, for he was then Prime Minister, recommended this House to sanction the appointment by Her Majesty of a new Secretary of State, who should be Secretary of State for the Department of War. For that purpose it was necessary in 1855 to bring in a Bill, which was afterwards passed into law. But now I request the House to mark this. Although there was not the slightest doubt from the language of Mr. Burke's Act that only two Secretaries of State could sit in this House—although that never was questioned for a moment — there had been doubts raised whether the terms of the Act of Economical Reform were sufficiently precise to touch the Under Secretaries; but the language was still so definite that it had never practically been infringed. There had been only two Under Secretaries of State in this House; but the lawyers knew of the doubts on the subject, and in the noble Lord's Bill —the Bill brought in by his Government, of course with his sanction, and, no doubt, with his intimate knowledge — it was thought advisable that the opportunity should be seized of removing all doubt on this point. If hon. Gentlemen refer to that Act they will find that a third Secretary of State is at once made, and there is a recital that, whereas doubts at some time have existed as to the number of Secretaries and Under Secretaries of State who might sit in the House of Commons—that was, doubtless, a reference to Mr. Burke's Bill—it is now decided that there shall be a new Secretary of State under this Act, and that three Secretaries and three Under Secretaries of State may sit in this House and "no more." I hope that, as far as I have gone, the House really will understand this case. We have now arrived at the period of the Crimean war. Well, the next great events in our history were the Indian mutiny and the expiration of the Company's charter, necessitating the bringing in of a new India Bill, which was to transfer to the immediate authority of the Crown the Government of those vast possessions. It fell to the lot of my noble Friend near me (Lord Stanley), then President of the Board of Control, to introduce that Act, and in deference to the Resolutions of this House upon which that Bill was founded, the office of President of the

Board of Control was converted into that of a Secretary of State for India, and with the power of appointing an Under Secretary of State instead of the two joint Secretaries of the Board of Control that previously existed. And by that Act four Secretaries of State became qualified to sit in this House, and four Under Secretaries of State. I believe there is no person in this House who will question the accuracy of that statement. There is no refinement here about the case of some half-forgotten gentleman who vacated his seat when made an Under Secretary of State in the reign of King George; but here you have the present state of the law, which depends on specific statutes, that you yourselves advised and passed, and that have been carried in consequence of your own Resolutions.

This then being, I venture to say, the unquestioned and unquestionable state of the law at this moment, expressed in the statutes before me, that in the House of Commons four Secretaries of State and four Under Secretaries may sit, and "no more," I must call the attention of the House to the strange fact that throughout this Session of Parliament at least five Under Secretaries of State have been sitting here. I have no doubt that on Friday night, if any discussion had occurred, it would have been necessary for me to mention in detail who those Gentlemen are. I feel sure that in the interval we have become sufficiently familiar with the subject. But, perhaps, on a question of this kind, it is expedient, both in the Resolutions which we may have to record, and in the statements which we may have to make, that we should make our case complete; and, therefore, I shall mention who are the five Under Secretaries of State who, during this Session, have been sitting in this House. There is the Under Secretary of State for the Colonies, the right hon. Member for the county of Louth (Mr. Chichester Fortescue); there is the hon. Gentleman the Under Secretary of State for India, the Member for Falmouth (Mr. T. G. Baring); there is the Under Secretary of State for Foreign Affairs, the hon. Member for Southwark (Mr. Layard); there has been, during this Session, the Under Secretary of State for the Home Department, late and still Member for Merthyr Tydvil (Mr. H. A. Bruce), whose fate we did not decide an hour ago; and lastly, there is the Under Secretary of State for the War Department, who is the Member, or who

Mr. Disraeli

supposes that he is the Member, for North Lancashire. The House will now, upon reflection, find that this is a question which it becomes themselves in the first instance to undertake. It is the duty of the House to see that its composition is complete and correct. It is of the utmost importance that no person should sit or vote in this House who is not qualified for the exercise of those functions. And, Sir, I do not think that I can place this matter, as to its importance and urgency, more completely before the House than by showing them how much may depend upon the materials of which this assembly is composed being of an authentic character. I have, on more than one occasion, reminded the House of the important historical events and the equally important laws which have been shaped and passed by slight majorities, and even by casting votes. I know that Gentlemen may in these days consider historical illustration to be of little value. I am not of that school. I do not believe that a popular assembly can maintain its authority unless it respects the example and experience of its predecessors. What makes the House of Commons so influential in contradistinction to the popular assemblies of other countries is this:—That when there is any great question of difficulty — of complication, as the Attorney General would call it—the country feels that we are not solving it merely by the present thought and existing intelligence of the Members of this House, but that we come down to its consideration fortified by precedent, and bringing to bear upon it the accumulated wisdom of the eminent men who have preceded us. I need not go far to show how important it is that we should be most strict in seeing that no one votes in this House who has not a right to do so. There is no subject, for example, more important than a question of a vote of confidence. When the two great parties of this country meet with contending principles and with opposite policies, and challenge the decision of the House of Commons, the issue, it may be said, is almost of an awful character—because the very tone and temper of the policy of the country depend upon the vote. In my time there has happened a struggle of this kind; and there are few in modern Parliamentary history more interesting or more important. It was the vote which brought Sir Robert Peel to the helm in 1841. Considering the character of that eminent man, considering the measures he carried or brought forward, considering the influence of his career upon parties and events in this House, no one can look upon that as an ordinary Parliamentary struggle. And yet Sir Robert Peel was made Minister of this country virtually by one vote. Supposing there had been one or two Under Secretaries of State on the Treasury bench when a vote of want of confidence had been brought forward, perhaps by Sir Robert Peel himself, they would not have had the same opinion as Sir Robert Peel; they would have had more confidence in themselves than in Sir Robert Peel, and they would naturally have voted accordingly. But what if after that discussion it had been discovered that these Under Secretaries had no right to vote that night? See, therefore, what considerable consequences may depend upon our taking care that this House is properly constituted. But I need not go so far. I will take the present Session as affording a most striking instance of the importance of our attention to this matter. Remember the division on the question of the Yeomanry. Her Majesty's Government thought it expedient to omit from the annual votes the sum necessary for calling out the Yeomanry. An hon. Friend of mine (Colonel Edwards) challenged by anticipation the propriety of that omission, and appealed to the House. The question was really not of that limited character to which, in the somewhat hurried discussion, an attempt was made to narrow it. Some looked upon it merely as a matter of reduction or the reverse. I am myself in favour of reduction. I see with the utmost satisfaction the reductions which the Government have made of late years, and I observe with equal satisfaction that the services of the country are not less efficient. But the question of the Yeomanry was of a peculiar character. Nothing seemed more inconsistent to me and to many others than that at a time when the country was expending so much money, thought, and energy in stimulating and maintaining the Volunteer institution—one of the most satisfactory events of our time—we should without thought deal a great blow and discouragement to our only considerable force of Volunteer cavalry. That was the view which we on this side of the House took of the matter, and I understand that was the view entertained, though not in this House yet in a place of considerable importance, by the noble Lord at the head of the Government. But what happened when the

division was called? We lost the policy which we believed to be sound, and which has since been adopted by the Government by one vote. The Motion was connected with the office of the Secretary of State for War, and upon it the Under Secretary of State for that Department, representing the policy of the Government, spoke with all the authority and influence which a person holding office must have on such a subject. But not only did he speak—he voted. We were defeated by one vote; and yet it turns out that at that very time the Under Secretary of State who took that influential and decided part upon the question had no more right to speak—had no more right to sit in this House—had no more right to vote than the stranger who at this moment is passing over Westminster Bridge. The House will agree, therefore, that this is a subject which is not to be neglected. I regret that it has been neglected so long. The noble Viscount seems to think it a surprising thing that I should not have called attention to this matter before. I consider myself that the House generally is, in some degree, at fault. I am perfectly ready to take my share of the blame, and even more. But ours has been a sin of omission ; but as regards the Government, theirs has been not only a sin of omission, but of commission. We have a right to expect from the Government, who have the distribution of patronage, that they should consider well how they distribute it. I say, with the greatest respect to the noble Lord at the head of the Government, that he is the individual to whom we look with confidence in such matters; and, perhaps, it is the unlimited confidence reposed in the noble Lord which has got the House into this scrape. It is not merely as the Chief Minister of the Crown that he sits on that bench—it is not merely to pass measures which he deems necessary to the welfare of the country—not merely to attend to the interests of his party that he sits there. He occupies a post second only in dignity and honour to that of Chief Minister of the Crown—that of leader of the House of Commons; and we have a right to expect from one who is the champion of our rights and privileges, and the trustee of our honour, whose first duty it is to see that the numbers of the House are complete, and if incomplete—are so only in consequence of the decision of the House itself—that he should take care that no one mixes in the deliberations and in the decisions of this House who is not justified by law in sitting here. I submit to the noble Lord, as the individual in this House who, if any one, is to be visited with its displeasure, that his own conduct rather requires explanation than that he should taunt those opposite to him, because they have discovered, however late, the critical position in which the House is placed.

I wish to suggest to the House a course which, I think, it ought to take. The position in which we find ourselves is one which deeply concerns the House. It is the duty of the House to set itself right without loss of time. We ought to do that in a manner which cannot be mistaken, which is becoming defined and decisive, but which, so far as expression of opinion is concerned, shall not in any way directly make any reflection upon the conduct of any Member of the House. I have no wish to shrink from the responsibility which every gentleman, to a certain extent, must have incurred by this unprecedented state of affairs; but, at the same time, it is absolutely necessary that we should take a constitutional course, and that having found the critical position in which we are placed, we should put on record the opinion of this House in a manner that cannot be mistaken, so that hereafter an Under Secretary of State shall not be appointed by a future Minister without due examination and reflection, and that there shall be a complete record of what has illegally been done, and of the remedy which the House of Commons proposed under the circumstances. It is with that feeling that I shall propose this Resolution, which I sincerely trust I may induce the House unanimously to adopt. It is in these words —

"Notice having been taken by a Member of this House that more than four Under Secretaries of State have been sitting and voting in this House at the same time during the present Session,— Resolved, that the provisions of the 21 & 22 *Vict.* c. 106, s. 4, have been violated, and that the Seat of the fifth Under Secretary of State has been and is thereby vacated."

Notice having been taken by a Member of this House, that more than four Under Secretaries of State have been sitting and voting in this House at the same time during the present Session:—

Motion made, and Question proposed,

" That the provisions of the Act 21 & 22 *Vict.* c. 106, s. 4, have been violated, and that the Seat of the fifth Under Secretary of State has been and is thereby vacated."—(*Mr. Disraeli.*)

VISCOUNT PALMERSTON : Sir, there are some things stated by the right hon.

Mr. Disraeli

Gentleman in which I entirely concur, and there are some things which afford a remarkable comment upon the progress of constitutional principles and government in this House. The right hon. Gentleman reminded us that whereas in the early part of the last century there was a jealousy in the House of Commons as to the sitting in it of persons holding high office in the State, now, on the contrary, by the great increase in the political power which by the progress of events this House has acquired, there is an opposite feeling, and desire that persons holding important offices in the State should—within certain limits at all events—have seats in this House, and sit face to face with, and be personally responsible to, the House of Commons. That does appear to me a significant commentary upon the great development of the power of this House between the period to which he referred and that in which we are now speaking. The right hon. Gentleman said that there ought to be in this House the full number of Secretaries of State which the law allows, namely, four; and he finds fault with those who framed the present Government for having put an undue proportion of the great officers of the Government in the House of Lords, and not a due proportion in this House. The right hon. Gentleman, I think, was speaking, when he said that, without having sufficiently attended to the circumstances of the case. When the present Government was formed it consisted of fifteen Cabinet Ministers, of whom ten were in this House and five only in the other House of Parliament. Four Secretaries of State were included in that number of ten. The chiefs of the War Department, the Foreign Office, the Home Office, and the India Office, were all Members of the House of Commons. Then came the unfortunate illness of Mr. Sidney Herbert, then Secretary for the War Department, which led to his removal to the House of Lords in the hope — which, unfortunately, proved vain—that by going to a House where less attendance was required, the afflicting disease which weighed upon him might be remedied or mitigated. Lord Herbert unfortunately fell a victim to that disease. When that occurred it gave the opportunity of bringing back the War Department to this House, in the person of Sir George Lewis; we therefore restored that Secretary of State who had been removed by the visitation of illness. Then, when my noble

Friend Lord Russell was removed to the House of Lords—the dignity of the peerage having been conferred upon him as a mark and reward of his long and distinguished services, and also from the circumstance that his health had suffered materially by his labours in the House of Commons—we had still three Secretaries of State in this House. Then Sir George Lewis was unhappily taken from us; and the peculiar circumstances connected with the interests of the army led to our placing that Department under the care of Lord De Grey, who had long been Under Secretary of that Department, and had acquired a knowledge of all the improvements which Lord Herbert had so successfully carried into effect, or had been anxious to carry into effect, during his lifetime. Well, but not only had we, when the Government was formed, ten Cabinet Ministers in this House, but among them was the person who held the office which I cannot pretend worthily to fill, which in the Government with which the right hon. Gentleman was connected was held by Lord Derby in the House of Peers; and, therefore, I maintain that if you compare the original distribution and progressive changes of Cabinet offices in the present Government with their original distribution in Lord Derby's Government, you will find that the House of Commons had its proper share of those Members who occupied important positions in the administration of the country. Well, I cannot undertake to go into those legal questions which the right hon. Gentleman dealt with, because I am unwilling to trespass on those grounds which my hon. and learned Friend the Attorney General, with so much greater knowledge and ability, and without complication, will very clearly explain to the right hon. Gentleman and the House. The right hon. Gentleman maintains that one of the five Under Secretaries must have vacated his seat—that question will be fully discussed by my hon. and learned Friend. But, Sir, I am quite ready to admit that we have unintentionally, and by oversight, done that which the law does not authorize. I must take blame to myself—because I quite agree with the right hon. Gentleman, that, holding the office I do, having to originate the different appointments, I ought, perhaps, to have inquired more deeply and minutely into the state of the law. I certainly was under the impression that we were doing that which the law authorized; that we might have five Under Secretaries in this

House. It turns out, however, on looking into the Act of Parliament, that we were wrong; and, therefore, I frankly admit that the right hon. Gentleman, or his learned Friend who, I believe, discovered the error, had a keener sight than we and the rest of the House possessed, But, at the same time, although I admit we were wrong—unintentionally wrong—the right hon. Gentleman and those who sit by him must share with us in the blame. Because, what is the natural occupation of an Opposition? What are they there for if not to find out when a mistake has been made by the Government? They are assigned by Providence to watch with keen eye the conduct of the Government they oppose—to trip them up even before they fall—at all events, if they stumble, mark their stumbling, and call upon them to set things right again. That is the peculiar function of the Opposition, if anything be wrong, or blameable, or liable to criticism in the conduct of the Government. I must say, therefore, we have a right to complain of the right hon. Gentleman and those who sit by him, that they have not previously announced that since April last year we have gone on in a course which they must have known—though they will not admit it—was wrong in point of law, and with reference to a law which they themselves brought in. They have laid a trap for us that I maintain is not fair in the course of a Parliamentary Opposition. But, I repeat, we candidly and frankly admit that we have done that which the law did not authorize us to do. I do not think that what the right hon. Gentleman proposes would be sufficient for the purpose; because, when a law has been broken, somebody must be liable to some penalty or other. Who is the person on whom the penalty would fall I am not prepared to say, nor what the penalty would be. I apprehend there is no penalty attached by the Act to either of the five Secretaries of State who, in excess of the law, has sat in the House; but where there is no penalty attached by the law it becomes a misdemeanour, and the person would be liable, of course, to the penalties of a misdemeanour. Well, my hon. and learned Friend will have to consider who the parties are who incur the penalty, and what we should propose as a measure of security to them, whoever they may be; and also, as a more effectual record than the proposal of the right hon. Gentleman, that a Bill of Indemnity should be brought in, which should record that the law has been violated, and by so recording, place, beyond all question, that nobody henceforward do the same thing. The illegal state of things has ceased, because, by the acceptance by my hon. Friend the Under Secretary for the Home Department of the office resigned, as I sincerely regret, by my right hon. Friend who was the Vice President of the Committee of Privy Council for Education, the hon. Member for Merthyr Tydvil has vacated office as Under Secretary of State, and there are now only four Under Secretaries in the House, which is the proper number. We are now, therefore, within the law, and I need hardly assure the House is is our intention to remain so. But we do not admit that part of the Resolution of the right hon. Gentleman which asserts that the seat of any of the five Under Secretaries is vacated. That is a question which my hon. and learned Friend will be more able to argue than I can. But that is our opinion; and, therefore, independently of the circumstance that we do not think the Resolution of the right hon. Gentleman covers the case as a Bill of Indemnity would, and because it makes an assertion we are not prepared to agree to, I hope the right hon. Gentleman will agree to a Bill of Indemnity; and if he is at all anxious on the subject, there should be a clause specially reserved for himself, in regard to any responsibility he may have himself incurred in the matter. However, we take all the responsibility on ourselves. We freely admit we ought to have looked more accurately, and it was my own indiscretion not to have looked more accurately into the matter. I certainly should have done so if I had entertained any doubt, and it was only because I thought we were within the law that the error was committed.

THE ATTORNEY GENERAL: Sir, it would have given me much pleasure to hear my right hon. and learned Friend the Member for Cambridge University (Mr. Walpole), (who had risen but sat down on there being a call for the Attorney General), before addressing the House on this subject, since I am sure we should all have derived benefit from any observations he might make; and I shall regret if, following me, he should make observations I shall not have the opportunity of answering. But I take it to be the wish of the House that I should

redeem the promise made by my noble Friend at the head of the Government, and I have no difficulty in doing so. The right hon. Gentleman (Mr. Disraeli) I think, attributed to me a statement which I do not recollect to have made, or, if I did; I used the expression in a different sense from that he placed upon it. He says that I represented this as a refined and complicated question, on which the House would have a difficulty in arriving at a clear understanding. But it will be necessary to correct several errors of no inconsiderable importance into which the right hon. Gentleman has fallen, with reference to the various Acts of Parliament bearing on this question. He started with a fundamental and radical error. He has misunderstood altogether the effect of the Act of Queen Anne, passed in 1707, which he supposes to have had the effect of making it impossible after that Act passed for more than three Secretaries of State, and three Under Secretaries, to sit in this House. That is an entire mistake of the right hon. Gentleman. The Act of Queen Anne had no operation whatever on the right of any Under Secretary to sit in this House; and in this consists the entire fallacy of his fundamental proposition. What the Act of Queen Anne said was this— that persons to be appointed to new offices created after 1705—not all new offices, but new offices under the Crown—should be ineligible and incapable of sitting or voting in Parliament. Now, nothing is more easy to demonstrate than that the office of Under Secretary of State is not an office created after that date; and the way in which we should deal with the point is by appealing to the practice of the House with regard to all persons who have held the office of Under Secretary since 1705. The right hon. Gentleman does not seem to have had his attention called to the fact that, although the clause absolutely disqualifying certain persons from seats in the House of Commons relates only to new offices, the clause which regulates the practice and law of the House as to persons vacating seats on the acceptance of office applies to old as well as to new offices held under the Crown. The 26th section is to the effect that if any person, being a Member of the House of Commons, should accept of any place of profit from the Crown, his election should be deemed void, and there should be a new election, as if in consequence of a vacancy by death; the Member in question being, however, capable of re-election, if not otherwise disqualified. Upon that clause rests the practice of Members when taking office in the Government resigning their seats and going down to their constituencies to ask for re-election. Consequently, if an Under Secretaryship of State is an office of profit accepted from the Crown, then each of the Under Secretaries, who accepted office from the date of the statute of Anne to the present time, ought thereupon to have vacated his seat:—but not one of them ever did so. I appeal to you, Sir, whether it is not the notorious and universal practice of the House that a Member, on accepting the office of Under Secretary of State, does not vacate his seat, and has not to be re-elected? Therefore, the uniform practice of the House, which is the best commentary on the meaning of the Act, proclaims distinctly that an Under Secretaryship of State is not an office of profit under the Crown, within the scope of the Act, whether created before or after the passing of the statute. What is the reason of that? The reason is to be found in the very language of the Act. It is that an Under Secretary of State is not appointed by the Crown, but is appointed, both in form and in substance, by the Secretary of State, and therefore his office is not an office held under or from the Crown. Thus the Act of Anne has no more to do with the matter than any other Act in the statute book. Then the right hon. Gentleman went on to say that there was an interval without change which lasted till we came to Mr. Burke's Bill for Economical Reform, in 1782. The right hon. Gentleman, however, either from taking a different view of the statute from mine, or from some other reason which it is not for me to divine, passed over an extremely material statute on this subject, passed in the fifteenth year of George II., 1742. For the purpose of further limiting and reducing the number of officers capable of sitting in this House, that Act provided that deputies and clerks in certain offices of the Government, including those of the Principal Secretaries of State, should not be capable of sitting in the House of Commons; but in order to make it perfectly clear that this was not intended to interfere with the eligibility of an Under Secretary of State to be a Member, there was a proviso that nothing in the Act should extend or apply to "the Under Secretaries to any of His Majesty's Principal Secretaries of State." Thus the rights of Under

Secretaries are distinctly preserved; they are not rendered ineligible, and they are not required to vacate their seats and to go to their constituents for re-election on accepting their offices. Next came Mr. Burke's Act; and there, again, the right hon. Gentleman contrived to make out his argument by putting into the Act what would have been very material if it were there, but what was not really there. It is true that the Act abolished, among other offices, the third, or Colonial Secretaryship, and declared that if any office thereby abolished were at any future time re-established, it should be reckoned a new office; but the Act did not say one word as to the Under Secretaryships. It left those offices as they were before. I need not remind the right hon. Gentleman that the division of the business of the Secretaries of State into departments is a matter which the law knows nothing about. On that point these Acts of Parliament are entirely silent, and no restriction is placed by them on the number of Under Secretaries whom the Secretaries may in their discretion think it necessary to appoint, nor on their capacity of sitting in Parliament. The only Acts which deal with that subject at all are that of 1855, when the fourth Secretary of State—the Secretary for War —was established, and that of 1858, on the appointment of an additional Secretary of State for India. In using the word "established," I do not mean that these Acts created the new Secretaryships. They recognised the power of the Crown to appoint as many Secretaries of State, and the power of the Secretaries of State to appoint as many Under Secretaries as might be deemed fit and proper; but they also limited the number as well of Under Secretaries, as of Secretaries, who might at one and the same time sit in the House of Commons. By the former Act it was provided that any three of Her Majesty's Principal Secretaries of State, and any three of the Under Secretaries, might sit and vote in the House of Commons at the same time, and that no more than that limited number should do so; and by the latter Act the number was raised to four Secretaries and four Under Secretaries. We ought to consider how the matter stands, not only in regard to the latest Act itself, but in comparison with the way in which Parliament has dealt with the capacity of the holders of particular offices for the functions of Members of this House. The Act does not specify that the Secretaries or Under Secretaries of certain Departments of Administration shall be entitled to sit in the House, but it only limits the maximum number of persons holding particular offices who shall at the same time be allowed to sit as Members. It is said that the Act has been violated, inasmuch as five Under Secretaries have been appointed, all of whom have sat and voted in this House at the same time. Now, I should be glad to know on which of the officers in question the Act throws the responsibility of violating the provision as to the number entitled to be Members at the same time. It is easy for the right hon. Gentleman to try to impose the responsibility on the person who last entered office, and to say what the Act certainly does not say, that he should be held on accepting office to have vacated his seat. But it is the sitting of five of these officers at one time, and not the sitting of one or other of them individually, which is the *corpus delicti.* I wish the House to see the absurd consequences that would follow if it could be maintained that you are to fasten upon any one of the five Under Secretaries and to say that he has vacated his seat. It may be that in this case you may be able to identify the order of time in which five persons holding office were appointed ; but it may happen that you may not always have the opportunity. Supposing that persons who are not Members of this House are appointed Under Secretaries during a dissolution, when, of course, no vacancy takes place. A general election follows — two, three, or more of those Gentlemen are simultaneously elected. Which of them has vacated his seat ? Of course, if Parliament had meant that a particular Member of this House should lose his status as such, it would not have left the law in a state which was open to such doubts. So, if two Under Secretaries simultaneously accepted office, the Act does not say that one or either of them, or all, shall vacate their seats. It only says that not more than a certain number shall sit in this House at one time. I promised that I would state what I found to be the language of other Acts of Parliament which bear upon this or analogous questions. I find that when Parliament intended to create ineligibility to sit in this House, it used language appropriate for that purpose. Thus in the 6 *Anne*, while in one clause it declares that a person who accepts any office shall always be incapable

of sitting or voting in Parliament, by a subsequent clause it says that if a person, being a Member of the House, accept any office, his election shall be declared void, and a new writ shall issue. There the process is marked out. A Member accepting office is incapable of sitting or of voting, the former election is declared void, and a new writ is issued. Exactly the same thing is done by the Act which prevents contractors from sitting in the House —the 22 *Geo.* III. There are other Acts which do not go on to say that the election shall be void and a new writ shall be issued ; but to mark the intention of Parliament persons holding particular offices were declared to be incapable of being elected or of sitting or voting in the House of Commons. Such is the 15 *Geo.* II., which says that the clerks in certain public offices shall not be capable of being elected or of sitting or voting in this House. Such is the Act passed in the 10th year of *Geo.* IV., excluding persons holding certain appointments under the East India Company; and even in the Indian Government Act itself, when it was intended to make the tenure of a particular office or the acceptance of it create a personal incapacity to sit as a Member of this House, it was enacted that the Members of the Council of India should not be capable of voting or sitting in Parliament. That incapacity is attached to the office and to the person of the holder of it. There is not a single Act intending such a thing in which it is not provided for. Now, I take it that if there be a well-settled principle of constitutional law, it is that you should never infer, without strong necessity, from the terms of an Act of Parliament, disabilities, incapacities, or penalties ; that you ought not to go beyond the language, if the object of the Act can be satisfied by adhering to it and keeping within it. It remains for me to endeavour to satisfy the House that there are upon the statute book sufficient reasons for holding, that we may give effect to these words, that not more than four Under Secretaries shall sit as Members of this House at the same time, without implying what the Act does not say, that some one or other of them, to be arbitrarily selected by the House, shall vacate his seat, which under other circumstances he would not do. The only Acts which contain at all similar words are those which show that the Legislature contemplated the possibility of a man retaining his status as a Member of this House,

The Attorney General

and yet being placed under a disability dependent upon variable circumstances, of voting and sitting. The Act of Charles II., well-known as the Oaths Act, is one in point. That Act has been rendered familiar to the House by the cases of Mr. O'Connell and of Mr. Salomons. It prescribes that no Member shall vote in the House of Commons, or sit there during a debate, until he shall have taken the oaths. A Member cannot sit upon these benches until he has complied with that requirement ; but his status as a Member remains unaffected, although his power of sitting and voting is in abeyance. That is the Act of which the language most nearly approaches the language of the statute we are considering ; and let not the House forget, that it is the earliest of all the statutes upon the subject. Exactly the same thing, in still more forcible terms, is done by the Act which excludes bankrupts from the House. When a Member becomes bankrupt, the Act says he shall remain during twelve months incapable of sitting or voting, unless the commission be superseded or his debts be paid in full ; and then, if at the end of twelve months certificate is made to the Speaker that he continued a bankrupt, the Act goes on to declare that his election shall become void, and a new writ shall issue. It is quite plain, therefore, that the Legislature recognizes a temporary incapacity of sitting and voting, as capable of being reconciled with the continuance of the status of a Member of Parliament. Upon what principle, then, are we to give to the same words in this Act affecting the Under Secretaries a different effect ? Every reason which induces Parliament to preserve the status of Members of this House in favour of persons who hesitate to take the oath, but who may do so at any time, and to afford to bankrupts a reasonable opportunity of ridding themselves of the incapacity, all these reasons apply *à fortiori* to the case of Under Secretaries. The public convenience may make it expedient to appoint a Member of this House. It may require some time to make arrangements, and in the meantime he ought not to resume his seat after appointment ; and thus the intention and the language of the Act of Parliament would be satisfied ; and but for some oversight, as in the present instance, arrangements would easily be made to limit the number of Under Secretaries in this House. There is nothing in the nature of such a case which makes it ne-

cessary that any particular individual should vacate his seat because there happened to be four persons already in the House holding similar appointments. It is to be presumed that when the attention of the Government is directed to the subject they will always take care to make the necessary arrangements. While the Legislature has carefully defined the maximum number of Under Secretaries who shall sit at the same time as Members of this House, it does not go on to say that the election of one or all shall be void if that number be exceeded, nor that any of them shall be incapable of voting or sitting ; so that I apprehend, upon all legal principles of construction, you cannot hold that any seat has become vacant ; although undoubtedly the Government is open to any censure which the House may think fit to pass upon them for not adverting to the terms of the recent Act of Parliament, which limited the number of Under Secretaries sitting in this House. When the attention of the Government was called to this subject no time was lost by them in making the necessary arrangements to comply with the terms of that Act of Parliament. Of course, the responsibility of that oversight rests with the Government ; but the very fact that hon. and right hon. Gentlemen opposite have not before discovered it, and that it escaped you, Sir, with all your vigilance, affords some explanation and excuse for the fact that the attention of the Government was not directed to it. I apprehend, therefore, that the House will not allow their notice of this matter to travel beyond the necessity of the case ; and that they will not declare that to be law which is not to be read in any Act of Parliament ; and which may, by comparing the language of the Act which governs this case with that of other Acts of a similar nature, be satisfied by taking a different course. I submit that, although the former part of the Resolution moved by the right hon. Gentleman is unquestionably true, and we cannot object that it should be placed upon record, yet the latter part of the Resolution declaring vacant the seat of—I suppose the right hon. Gentleman means the noble Lord the Member for North Lancashire, because he was the person last appointed—is entirely unwarranted by the Act of Parliament, is not supported by any legitimate or necessary inference arising from any of the former Acts, and is one, therefore, which it would not become this House to adopt.

Mr. WALPOLE : Sir, the latter observations of the hon. and learned Gentleman (the Attorney General) seem to imply that some censure is cast upon the Government by the terms of the Resolution, for an .error of conduct in having appointed a fifth Under Secretary. Now, I think the House will recollect that my right hon. Friend the Member for Bucks most carefully avoided casting any such imputations ; and, indeed, he stated in his speech to-night, that he was not going to cast any censure upon the Government ; nay more, he added that the whole House, and he himself as well as others, was to blame for not having noticed the illegality before. He adopted, in fact, the humorous observation of the old play as equally applicable to the noble Viscount and himself, "Brother, brother, we are both in the wrong." The only question now is, how are we to put ourselves right ; and this is a matter of grave importance—one that concerns the constitution of the House, and in reference to which we ought to take care to put upon record something to prevent a similar illegality or excess of authority from happening again. The noble Viscount seems to think that this could be done simply by a Bill of Indemnity ; but I take leave to doubt whether that is the way in which this House ever sets its records right. It has always taken care to put some resolution upon its Journals, declaring its opinion of a matter affecting the privileges of its Members, and its own constitution ; and the Motion of my right hon. Friend seems, therefore, to meet exactly the nature of the case. The observation of the Attorney General is that he concurs in the first part of the Motion, that there has been a violation of the Act of Parliament, and it is the latter part of the Motion to which he demurs. My hon. and learned Friend addressed to this Act of Parliament a very refined argument, but I do not think that that argument was sound. My hon. and learned Friend did not bear in mind two things, which if he had done he would have found the question to be plainer and clearer than he has represented it to be. The first thing I should have wished him to bear in mind was, that he should take the Act of Anne in conjunction with the Act of the present Queen ; and secondly, that the words of the Act of Anne, "shall be incapable of sitting and voting," are not more strong for vacating the seat than the words of the later statute "shall not sit and vote." The words are nearly synonymous, and

what construction you put upon one phrase you must put upon the other. Suppose that this blot had been hit the moment that the Under Secretary of State for War had been appointed to his office ; will anybody deny that a Member of this House might immediately have moved that a writ should be directed to the place represented by the fifth Under Secretary of State for the election of a new Member ? If you do not put that construction upon the Act of Parliament you would give to the Government the opportunity of creating offices without the checks imposed by the Legislature, and I cannot believe that the House would assent to a construction so contrary to its own independence and to all the privileges of Parliament. Now, what is the state of the law. In attempting to correct the speech of my right hon. Friend, I think the hon. and learned Gentleman himself fell into an inadvertence in reference to the statute of Anne. The two sections of that statute which relate to this subject are the 25th and the 26th ; the 25th relates to new offices, and the 26th to old offices. The 25th section prohibits any Member from taking any new office—that is, an office created since 1705—and declares that any person who shall have a new office under the Crown shall be incapable of being elected to this House, and of sitting and voting. The 26th section has not the word "new" office, and in order to give effect to that section you must interpret it as relating to "old" offices, otherwise you would repeal the 25th section, which immediately precedes it. When an old office is accepted, the Member is to vacate his seat, but he is eligible for re-election. As to new offices, on the contrary, the seat is to be vacated, and the person to be ineligible for re-election. This principle of vacating the seat runs through all the statute law ; and any statutes relating to Secretaries and Under Secretaries also, which give an exemption from the full operation of the statute of Anne, are only exemptions in the specified cases to which they extend. Then my hon. and learned Friend points to the statutes of George II., but that Act confirms my view, instead of giving weight to his argument. The statute of George II. was another disqualifying statute, for the very preamble and the very title of it make more persons ineligible than were ineligible before. That was the object of the statute ; but then a proviso is added which extends the exemption to any Under Secretary of a Secretary of State. I ask my hon. and learned Friend whether that would give exemption to any Under Secretary except one Under Secretary of each Secretary of State — would it give it to two? [The ATTORNEY GENERAL : I have no doubt whatever about it.] Will my hon. and learned Friend show me any authority for that? The proviso is to take them out of the ineligibility that rests upon them, and to give the benefit of the exemption to one Under Secretary of a Secretary of State, and not to two; or otherwise there could be a Power to create her officers without number, whilst the Legislature has taken good care that the number should be restricted. Pass we then to the statute of *Geo.* III. Now, that statute having done away with the third Secretary of State, says, in the strongest possible words, that the office of a third Secretary of State, under whatever name he is called, is to be considered as a new office; and what does that mean but that such office is to be considered a new office within the meaning of the statute of Anne. So that the third Secretary of State when he was appointed would receive his appointment as to a new office, and if there were three such officers in the House of Commons he would be rendered ineligible, and the Under Secretary would be in the same position. Then comes the Acts constituting the Secretary of State for War and the Secretary of State for India, giving the benefit of the exemption to these third and fourth Secretaries of State, but not to the fifth. Now, how does the Act deal with Under Secretaries? Why, in exactly the same words as it deals with the Secretaries themselves. The words are, that the four Secretaries of State may sit and vote as Members of the House of Commons, but that not more than four shall sit as such Members; and it is also said that not more than four Under Secretaries shall sit as members. If my hon. and learned Friend admits that these are disqualifying words as to the Secretary of State, how can he put a different construction upon identically the same words when applied to the Under Secretary. My hon. and learned Friend has quoted two Acts relating to Bankruptcy and to the admission of Baron Rothschild. The Bankruptcy Act is no doubt an enabling Act, giving to Members a limited time within which to obtain their certificates and sit again as Members of this House. By that Act it was provided, in the case of Members becoming bankrupts, that at the end of twelve months after the declaration of the bankruptcy the Speaker must be certified of the fact, and the election of such Members then became void unless the fiat were superseded or the creditors were paid in full. That being so, I ask my hon. and learned Friend to consider whether, supposing the law vacates the seat when a Member is declared incapable of sitting and voting, the law does not also vacate the seat when it says he shall not sit and vote? Could my hon. and learned Friend point out the distinction between those two propositions? If not, it appears to me that the case is established completely against him; and for the sake of the regularity of our proceedings, and in order to preserve the constitution of the House, as it was intended by the Legislature when it passed the law limiting the number of Members holding office to so many and no more, we have nothing to do but to declare at once not only that the law has been violated, but that the seat has been and is vacated; and then, I think, we shall set ourselves right. The question arises not only whether the noble Lord the Under Secretary for War has been guilty of a misdemeanour, for which, I understand, you purpose to bring in a Bill of Indemnity, but whether he has not also subjected himself to the penalty of £500. The Bill of Indemnity should extend to that and to everything. [The ATTORNEY GENERAL : The Bill will include all penalties.] Nevertheless, if the Under Secretary for War continues to sit here and vote without vacating his seat, the question may arise, whether he is not still guilty of a misdemeanour and still liable to penalties? My own belief is that that is a very doubtful point; and, if so, I cannot conceive why the Government should object to set forth the matter fully on the records of the House. The noble Lord the Under Secretary for War would then go to his constituents, and I hope he would soon be returned to the House; but in the meantime the House is bound to take notice that a Member has been sitting here who ought not to have sat here, and who might by his vote have decided some of the most important questions that come before us. If this is the proper construction of the Act of Parliament, we must take the consequence of our own inadvertence and set the matter right at once, or as nearly as we can; that is to say, we must now deal with the circumstance as it would have been dealt with if notice had been taken of it at the proper time; but for the House to adopt the proposition that a Member, holding an office which he cannot hold while he is Member, is to continue to sit and vote in the House as long as the Government and the Member himself may choose to hold such office, would be, I think, a course detrimental to the privileges and independence of the House, and therefore I shall support the Motion of my right hon. Friend.

SIR GEORGE GREY: It is very desirable that the House should come to some satisfactory decision on the matter involved in this discussion. We have heard the statements of the Attorney General and of the right hon. Gentleman opposite, and the Government have considered the question very fully since notice was taken of the circumstance which has given rise to the present debate. They have had high legal opinions, in addition to those of the Law Officers of the Crown, confirming the opinion of the Attorney General that the appointment of a fifth Under Secretary has not rendered his seat vacant, but there can be no doubt that an error has been committed by the fifth Under Secretary being in this House. Under the circumstances, I would suggest that we should avoid committing ourselves by any decision in this House, either to the proposition that the seat is actually vacant —for that may be wrong, and, if so, it is a serious constitutional error—or to the counter-proposition that it is not vacant. After what has passed in debate it appears to the Government to be the proper course that, in accordance with what has been done on former occasions, when a doubt arose whether the acceptance of an office involved the loss of a seat, a Select Committee should be appointed to report their opinion on the point. I will mention two instances when this course was adopted within my recollection. One was the case of Mr. Wynne, than whom there could not be a man with greater constitutional knowledge. Having accepted an office which seemingly involved the loss of his seat, he himself suggested the appointment of a Select Committee to consider the question. At a later period Mr. Daniel Whittle Harvey accepted an office which led to a doubt whether his seat was vacated, and the House, abstaining from committing itself to any declaration of opinion, referred the matter to the consideration of a Select Committee. I might refer to more cases of an analogous nature ; and I therefore think that, without committing ourselves to any opinion—for if we do we may be

Mr. Walpole

establishing a bad constitutional precedent —we should adopt the course of referring the matter to a Select Committee. Consequently, I propose, as an Amendment, that the latter part of the Motion of the right hon. Gentleman declaring that the seat is vacant should be omitted, and that there should be substituted instead thereof the words, " That a Select Committee be appointed to inquire whether the Under Secretary of State last appointed to that office has thereby vacated his seat." At the same time, the Bill of Indemnity may be proceeded with, because that is a distinct question. It will be proposed in general terms, exempting those who may have subjected themselves to penalties from those consequences, and it will also stand as a permanent Parliamentary record of the fact which has occurred, and thereby provide against its recurrence.

Amendment proposed,

To leave out from the words " violated, and that " to the end of the Question, in order to add the words " a Select Committee be appointed to inquire whether the Under Secretary of State who was last appointed to that office thereby vacated his Seat,"—(*Sir George Grey,*)

—instead thereof.

MR. DISRAELI: My opinion is that in questions of this kind it is highly desirable that the House should not arrive at a decision which might have the appearance of anything approaching to the character of a party proceeding. At the same time, I think that it is of great importance that the House should not act in a timid and hesitating manner. I have indicated the line that I think that the House ought to take, and I understand that the Government to a great extent adopt it. They acknowledge that there has been a violation of the law, and the only point they hesitate at is, whether it has vacated the seat of the Under Secretary of State who was last appointed. I should not object to refer that matter to a Select Committee in the way that has been suggested ; but there are one or two points upon which previously I think we ought to have a clear understanding with the Government. It should be clearly understood that the Bill of Indemnity should not be introduced before the Committee come to their decision, and I should like the House to have some understanding as to what is to be the conduct of this fifth Under Secretary of State. I was not indisposed to limit the inquiry to the fifth Under Secretary. But the noble Viscount the Prime Minister appeared to express a doubt whether the position of all the Under Secretaries was not affected? If there be any doubt I must say I do not think that these Gentlemen ought to take any part in the deliberations or decisions of the House until the question has been entirely settled by the Select Committee. Certainly, on the understanding that the Bill of Indemnity will not be introduced until the Committee comes to a decision upon this question, I shall look upon that as an arrangement which ought to be made. I think that an agreement of that kind should be entered into before the House is asked to assent to the Amendment of the right hon. Gentleman.

MR. AYRTON said, he was glad the Home Secretary had proposed the Amendment, because, although the question affected the privileges of the House to a great extent, it also affected the seat of an hon. Member, and the House ought not to pronounce an opinion upon the matter without duly investigating it, and giving the hon. Member affected by it an opportunity of being heard by counsel before the Committee. The speech of the right hon. Gentleman opposite, the Member for the University of Cambridge (Mr. Walpole), had raised many difficulties which did not occur to his mind before. The right hon. Gentleman said that the statutes spoke of the Secretaries and Under Secretaries in the same language. The effect of the construction put upon the statutes by the right hon. Gentleman might be not merely that the fifth Under Secretary must vacate his seat, but that all the Under Secretaries holding new offices might be equally subject to re-election. That was a reason why the House should proceed with great caution, because the later statutes did not declare that the new Under Secretaryships were not new offices. He doubted, after hearing the right hon. Gentleman, whether the reference to the Committee was quite large enough, and it might, therefore, be desirable that words should be added so that no doubt might arise herein.

SIR FITZROY KELLY said, he did not think any difficulty could arise on that point; but nevertheless the utmost possible care ought to be taken in the form of the reference to the Select Committee, as it appeared to him that the question involved one of the most formidable constitutional points that in his experience had ever arisen in the House. He thought that they ought to make the subject clear and specific, as

it related to the present constitution of the House in connection with the office of the Under Secretary for War. He was quite satisfied that the Committee would do full justice to the question.

VISCOUNT PALMERSTON: With reference to what has been said by the right hon. Gentleman about the Bill of Indemnity, I have no objection to postpone that until after the Committee has reported.

Question, "That the words proposed to be left out stand part of the Question," put, and *negatived*.

Words *added*.

Main Question, as amended, put, and *agreed to.*

Resolved,

That the provisions of the Act 21 & 22 *Vict.* c. 106, s. 4, have been violated, and that a Select Committee be appointed to inquire whether the Under Secretary of State who was last appointed to that office thereby vacated his Seat.

PENAL SERVITUDE ACTS AMENDMENT BILL—[BILL 23.]—COMMITTEE.

Order for Committee read.

Motion made, and Question proposed, "That Mr. Speaker do now leave the Chair."

MR. ADDERLEY rose to move, as an Amendment—

"That this House is of opinion that the system of discharge of prisoners from Penal Servitude on licence, without police supervision, should no longer be continued."

The right hon. Member said, that if he succeeded in inducing the House to adopt his Resolution, he thought it would effect the saving of much time and trouble to the Committee upon this most important question. The Resolution affirmed no more than what the House had already agreed to. If he collected the sense of the House rightly during the recent debates on this subject, it appeared to him that all shades of opinion were concentrated in the proposition he was about to submit. Those would agree in the proposition who took his view of the matter, that there ought to be no abbreviation of punishment, but that the sentence of the law, so far as its duration was concerned, should be carried out as pronounced by the Judge; and that all the advantages hoped for by the abbreviation of punishment were overbalanced by the indefiniteness which it brought on the penal law. He would rather trust to other processes of treatment for the moral effects which were required and desired in prison and under penal servitude than to the system of abbreviation of punishment. He would rather trust to discipline and salutary influence maintained over prisoners, and above all to the hope held out to a prisoner suffering penal servitude, that if he conducted himself well he might hope at the expiration of his sentence for the highest boon which an Englishman under such circumstances could possibly desire—namely, transportation out of the country, partly at the cost of benevolent and private societies and partly out of the rates of the locality to which the prisoner belonged. Those also would agree in the proposition who were represented by the hon. Member for Bedford (Mr. Whitbread), in the Amendment of which he had given notice, in favour of a remission of punishment, for good conduct, to the maximum limit of one-fourth of the original term. The supporters of such a proposition, from some fanciful notion of their own, appeared to see an advantage in hanging over the head of the prisoner so liberated the remainder of his punishment like the sword of Damocles, as a warning to himself and a beacon to others. They, however, were against licences, and therefore agreed in his proposition. Lastly, there were those who approved of the system of liberating prisoners on licence. But they also agreed that such licence should not be without supervision. What was the object of this Bill? It was simply to reduce into an Act of Parliament those conditions attached to tickets-of-leave which were at present vested in the discretion of the Secretary of State; under which discretionary power the Lord Lieutenant of Ireland had succeeded in realizing a successful police supervision in Ireland. In England these conditions were a dead letter; or the only effect was that greater facilities were given to ticket-of-leave men to commit crime than were possessed by any other class of offenders. The proposed Bill, if carried, would spoil the Irish system, and not benefit England, for it fell short of the conditions now actually enforced in Ireland, and did not impose such conditions as were required in England—yet both systems rested on the same bases—the Acts of 1853 and 1857. He thought it would be much better to assimilate the manner in which the system was carried out in the two countries by passing a Resolution by which the Secretary of State should be made to exercise the similar powers in England which had been exercised by the

Lord Lieutenant in Ireland. A Resolution would do as well as an Act, for the power existed which only needed to be exerted, and if it could not be done by Resolution it would not be done by Act of Parliament. What were the conditions provided in this Bill? First, it was enacted that the licence should be *ipso facto* forfeited if the holder should be convicted of any indictable offence. That was not a very stringent condition, seeing that any one who committed an indictable offence was liable to a punishment equal to such forfeiture. But then the unexpired term of his sentence was to be cumulative upon his new sentence. The same, however, might be done by larger punishments on second convictions. Then the holder of a licence who should fail or refuse to produce it when called upon by a magistrate or police officer, or shall break the conditions of his licence, was to be summarily punishable with three months imprisonment with or without hard labour. Then came a clause which empowered any police officer to apprehend without warrant any licence-holder whom he might suspect of having committed any offence, or of having broken any of the conditions of his licence. This was not so much a weak proposition, but rather a dangerous one, and yet one that, in efficiency for its purpose, fell short of the Irish system, where the ticket-holder must present himself once a month to the police, and if not, the police were authorized to apprehend him. There was something valid in that system, and anything that fell short of it would be wholly invalid. He protested against the provision in the Bill. A policeman might come up to him, and producing a photograph which he chose to think was something like him — and these photographs made all men alike villanous — ask him for his ticket; and though he might protest, the policeman might, on his not producing a ticket-of-leave, apprehend him and take him before a magistrate.

SIR GEORGE GREY said, there was nothing about a photograph in the Act. The policeman was empowered to apprehend a ticket-of-leave man on suspicion of having committed an offence, and demand his ticket.

MR. ADDERLEY said, he was aware there was nothing about photography in the Bill, but by police regulation that photographic resemblance was to be considered *prima facie* ground for suspicion; he objected to the mischievous and dangerous principle that was about to be introduced, of summary arrest on such suspicion. Besides, it would not meet the object in view, because ticket-holders would take care not to get within the scope of the active operations of the police. No man would remain within reach of his photograph. He had, however, no hope of his Amendment being adopted by the Government and allowed to modify the Bill. He should therefore support the Amendment of the hon. Member for Northampton. Sir Richard Mayne was the only person who at all recommended anything like supervision for England, and he doubted its possibility. Major General Cartwright had, however, offered to undertake to organize a supervision for England. He appeared to be a very sanguine man, and very much like one who would undertake at a moment's notice the conduct of the Channel fleet ; but he (Mr. Adderley) did not consider the House was justified in legislating upon such assurance as that. Sir Walter Crofton told them that the Irish system might be introduced into England, but he (Mr. Adderley) thought there was a great difference between the circumstances of the two countries. They had a much smaller number of convicts to do with in Ireland than were in England, and the police of the two countries were very different in constitution. The Irish were far more French in their ideas than the English. They looked more to the Government. The ticket-of-leave system was taken from Australia ; but there were two conditions attached to it in Australia that never would be submitted to in this country, namely, that a man should not leave a certain district, or be out after a certain hour of the night. It would be impossible to have a police force in this country that would be sufficiently strong for the efficient working of such a system. When the country was obliged to substitute penal servitude for transportation we adopted a most injudicious imitation of the terms of the old sentence. The Royal Commission reported last year that the increase of crime was to be attributed to two causes, the shortness of the terms of punishment and the inefficiency and inequality of the system. He thought they would much shorten their work if they were not to trouble themselves so much about the intricacies of punishment, and that they fell into a great error in constructing punishment to meet their own refined and philosophic views rather than the rough motives of the criminals with whom they had to deal. The main point should be to make the discipline more severe, more efficient for the deterrence from crime, and the punishment more strict and definite ; by which means they would have the best chance of diminishing the number of criminals now crowding the gaols of this country.

Amendment proposed,

To leave out from the word " That " to the end of the Question, in order to add the words " this House is of opinion that the system of discharge of prisoners from Penal Servitude on licence without police supervision should no longer be continued,"—(*Mr. Adderley,*)

—instead thereof.

Question proposed, " That the words proposed to be left out stand part of the Question."

Sir GEORGE GREY expressed a hope that the right hon. Gentleman would not oppose any obstacle to their proceeding with the Bill that evening. He did not understand the object of the right hon. Gentleman's Resolution as it had been explained that evening. He had at first imagined that the right hon. Gentleman wished the House to express an opinion to the effect that there ought to be strict police supervision over convicts who had been discharged from penal servitude with tickets-of-leave. At present, however, he appeared to wish the House to discountenance altogether the principles of granting tickets-of-leave. There had been a decided feeling in the House in favour of the Bill being read a second time, and he therefore hoped that the right hon. Gentleman would not expect them to go into a long discussion upon the principles of the Bill. He had no desire to enter into a comparison between the effects of the Bill in England and Ireland. If he did so he should be involved in a long discussion which would probably be attended with no good result. The object of the Bill was to enable the Government lawfully to do what it had hitherto not been possible to do in a legal manner — namely, to authorize the police to apprehend the holder of a ticket-of-leave upon suspicion of having broken its conditions, and to take him before a magistrate for the purpose of having the question adjudicated upon. The right hon. Gentleman had given expression to his views upon the Bill, and any further discussion on what he had stated would, in his opinion, be better postponed to the Committee.

MR. ADDERLEY said, he would withdraw his Amendment.

Amendment, by leave, *withdrawn*.
Main Question put, and *agreed to*.
Bill *considered* in Committee.

(In the Committee.)

Clause 1 *agreed to*.

Clause 2 (Length of Sentences of Penal Servitude).

MR. NEATE said, he did not think any ground had been made out for the severer treatment of criminals which it was proposed by this Bill to carry out. He proposed to move the omission of the second clause. The clause proposed to increase the minimum sentence of penal servitude from three years to five years—a change of which no notice was given in the Preamble, and without the attention of the Commission, on whose Report the measure was founded, having been directed to the subject. His objections to the change were first that it was too important an alteration of the penal laws to be made without sufficient notice, and next, that there was no such increase of crime as to justify the measure, notwithstanding the distress in Lancashire and other circumstances. That the number of criminals had increased was true enough, but that increase was sufficiently accounted for by the growth of our population, and by other circumstances. One cause of the increase of crime was the harsh treatment extended to tramps and vagrants in our workhouses; and therefore if we were to review our penal system we ought at the same time to review the Poor Law. One effect of increasing the period of penal servitude would probably be that Judges would frequently, in consequence of the severity, rather sentence to imprisonment for two years; and thus there would be an augmentation in the number of those who came under the system which now prevailed in the county gaol. The system pursued in county gaols was generally one of great severity. Magistrates generally made the arrangements for the management of convicts, and the law which required the sanction of the Secretary of State had become a dead letter. In illustration of what he meant, he referred to the severe arrangements recently made by the magistrates of Hampshire. He might add that he recollected his right hon. Friend the Member for Oxfordshire (Mr. Henley) saying, with respect to the system

Sir George Grey

of excessive severity which prevailed in different parts of the country twenty or thirty years ago, that men who had been subjected to it went home from prison without any apparent ailment and died. The comfort and luxuries of penal servitude had been made matter of common conversation, but it was a most foolish principle that the measures necessary for those who used expressions of defiance in reference to the punishment to which they were subjected, should be adopted as the measures necessary in all cases. In his own opinion no sufficient case had been made out for coupling with increased intensity of punishment increased duration; but he did not propose to press his Motion to a division.

SIR GEORGE GREY denied that it was in the power of magistrates to make what rules they pleased for the government of county gaols, without the sanction and approval of a superior authority. As to this clause, there was no point upon which the opinion of the Royal Commission was more decidedly expressed, or upon which those witnesses who were entitled to speak with authority on the subject, were more unanimous than that the minimum of penal servitude ought to be increased. He had stated, on a former occasion, to what extent the sentences of three and four years' penal servitude were passed, contrary to what was the intention of the Legislature when they sanctioned those short sentences. The Commission were fully justified in their recommendation that the term should be increased, upon the ground that there should be a substantial distinction between the sentence of penal servitude and the sentence of imprisonment; but the Bill did not go to the full length of the Report of the Commissioners, for their proposal was that the minimum should be seven years.

MR. BEACH said, the arrangement to which the right hon. Gentleman (Mr. Adderley) referred had not yet been reported to the Quarter Sessions, but when they were, they would be reported to the Home Secretary, in accordance with the law. So far from their being of extraordinary severity, they were a compromise between those who held extreme and those who held moderate opinions.

MR. HENLEY said, that in the old times of low diet, reports had certainly been made to the magistrates of his county that men occasionally went home out of prison in a weak state not fit for work, though he never recollected anything so strong being said as that men went home and died.

Mr. C. W. WYNN said, he wished to know what the probable operation of the alteration of the minimum of imprisonment from three years to five would be upon the number of prisoners to be received into county gaols, and what security the Home Secretary had that this new scale of punishment would be carried out any better than the old scale. According to the Judicial Statistics of 1862-3, of the number of persons convicted of offences for which they were liable to penal servitude for life, one-half had been sentenced to imprisonment; and of those who were liable to penal servitude for fourteen years, three quarters had been sentenced to imprisonment. Of 1,493 persons liable to penal servitude for life, only twenty-three were sentenced to it; and for 218, six months' imprisonment was deemed sufficient. Sentences for terms exceeding ten years were passed only on seventeen out of 4,499, who were liable to fourteen years penal servitude. As a county magistrate, he looked with some apprehension on the working of this second clause. The effect would be that something like three-fourths of those now sentenced to three years' penal servitude, instead of being sentenced hereafter to five years, would be sentenced to imprisonment. The consequence would be that the additional gaol accommodation for long sentences of imprisonment would be required to the extent of at least three-fourths.

Mr. BARROW asked how soon they might expect to have a penal discipline Bill by which they might judge of the probable effect of imprisonment upon prisoners in county gaols. He felt objection to the abridging of the discretion of Judges and Justices in giving sentences, because he thought it would extravagantly increase the number of prisoners in the county gaols. From his experience of our criminal law he felt a very strong objection to long imprisonments, believing them to be endured with a sullen endurance, and calculated to render criminals still more vicious.

Sir GEORGE GREY said, it was impossible for him to give an answer with confidence to the question of the hon. Gentleman opposite, because where the law, as it must necessarily do to a very great extent, left to the Judges a wide discretion as to the punishment to be awarded to particular crimes, it was impossible to say how the fifteen learned Judges would exercise it on the circuits. He believed the practical effect of the minimum term of punishment would not be of the character anticipated by the hon. Member. With regard to the question of prison discipline, that of course depended, in great measure, on the superintendence of local prisons was intrusted. With respect to the reforms of gaol administration, he should shortly introduce a Bill on the subject; but, of course, he could not enter on that subject now.

Mr. ADDERLEY thought, that by making the present minimum term of three years more severe — such as two years' imprisonment, and one year on public works—it would be a better introduction to liberty than a longer term of penal servitude.

Mr. HIBBERT said that, with the exception of the reduction in diet, he saw very little improvement in the present Bill over the old system.

Mr. EVANS said, that eighteen months' separate confinement was as much as most prisoners were able to bear, so that the proposal of the hon. Member opposite (Mr. Adderley) was not practical. He did not think that the effect of the lengthened minimum would be to choke the county gaols in the way that was supposed.

Clause *agreed to.*

Clause 3 (Punishment of Offences in Convict Prisons).

Colonel BARTTELOT suggested that, as the number of lashes which might be inflicted on a prisoner was not specified, the words " a number not exceeding fifty" should be introduced into the clause.

Sir GEORGE GREY said, that there would be power included in the Bill to inflict the present maximum number, which, he believed, was thirty lashes.

Clause *agreed to.*

Clause 4 (Forfeiture of Licence).

The O'CONOR DON said, that the schedule as it stood would prevent female convicts from being sent to refuges, as was now the custom in Ireland. A new clause, of which the right hon. Baronet had given notice, however, would meet that difficulty, and he would not press the Amendment which he had put upon the paper.

Sir GEORGE GREY said, that the system referred to by his hon. Friend was found to work extremely well, and he had therefore drawn a clause to prevent any interference with it.

Mr. J. J. POWELL (*Gloucester*) pointed out the hardship that might arise under this clause, which declared that a ticket-of-leave holder, on being convicted either by the verdict of a jury or upon his own confession of an indictable offence, should be liable to have his licence revoked, and to undergo the unexpired portion of his term of penal servitude in addition to the penalty for the new offence. The clause did not speak of any offence for which the person should have been indicted, but merely of an indictable offence. Now, it was an indictable offence to strike a man, and not the less so because it might be done under the greatest possible provocation—as, for example, where a man struck another for wantonly insulting his wife or his sister in the street. For the offence committed under such circumstances, a magistrate would, perhaps, only inflict a fine of 1s.; yet, if the offender happened to be a ticket-of-leave holder, under this clause he would have his licence revoked and be sent back to prison for the residue of the sentence.

Sir GEORGE GREY said that, no doubt, an extreme case might be put, however they might shape a Penal Servitude Act. The object was to make the law accord with what was the present practice, for a licence-holder on conviction for an indictable offence almost invariably had his licence revoked. If, however, the indictable offence committed was of so trivial a character as the hon. and learned Gentleman had described, the Judge might represent the facts to the Secretary of State, and there was nothing to prevent the prerogative of the Crown from being exercised so as to temper justice with mercy.

Mr. HUNT moved, at the end of the clause, to add the words—

" If any holder of a licence granted under the said Penal Servitude Acts, or any of them, who shall be at large in the United Kingdom, shall fail to report himself to the chief police station of the borough or district where he shall be on his arrival therein, and subsequently on the first day of each month, or shall change his locality without having previously notified the same to the police station to which he last reported himself, he shall be deemed guilty of a misdemeanour, and may be summarily convicted thereof, and his licence shall be forthwith forfeited by virtue of such conviction."

The words which he proposed to add embodied the rules laid down for the regulation of the police supervision in Ireland, where they had been in operation seven years. The question which he sought to raise, and on which he meant to take the

Sir George Grey

sense of the Committee, was whether the Irish system should be adopted in England. Two objections were urged against his proposition—the one that it was impracticable, and the other that it would prevent convicts from getting employment. Now, those two objections were incompatible with each other. If the proposal were really impracticable it could not prevent the convicts from getting employment, and even if it might prove a dead letter there could be no harm in trying it. Now, all those who said it was impracticable were merely theorists, whereas all those who said it was practicable based their opinion on actual experience. He would refer the Committee to the evidence given before the Royal Commission on the subject by Sir Walter Crofton, the head of the Irish Convict Prisons. Sir Walter stated that the public in Ireland generally approved of the system ; that employers were ready to engage these persons ; that he never heard of any complaints on the part of the public ; that the men obtained sufficient general employment, and that they went to the colonies if they had any difficulty in doing so. His own belief was that prisoners discharged on ticket-of-leave were not a class of persons who were exceedingly anxious to work hard for an honest livelihood, and that they would be induced to do so only by the adoption of such a system of supervision as his Amendment contemplated. Captain Whitty, Director of Convict Prisons in Ireland, stated in a memorandum that no instances had come to his knowledge of any evil or abuse having arisen from the supervision exercised in that country by the police, although the system had been six years in existence. He added that several discharged prisoners who left Ireland had returned there and registered themselves again for supervision. That showed that the well-disposed found the system beneficial rather than otherwise to their interests. It was said that, although the plan might work in the rural districts of Ireland, it could not be carried out in Dublin ; but experience did not support that objection. Mr. Organ voluntarily undertook to aid discharged licence-holders in obtaining work in Dublin, and where he had reason to fear that the men were relapsing into a dissolute life, he put himself in communication with the police in regard to them. His reports were made fortnightly, and were checked by the police, so that in Dublin a double system of supervision had been practised. It was said this system, though suited to Ireland, would not do for England ; but he did not see such a difference in the circumstances of the two countries as to warrant that conclusion.   As regarded protection to ticket-of-leave men, he believed the police in Ireland assisted them in getting work ; and in one instance, when a ticket-of-leave man was accused of a crime, the officer of the station where he was registered was enabled to prove an *alibi*.   Mr. Waddington had made an admission on this point very much against his own views, for he said if the supervision was carried out in London and not in the rest of the country they would drive the licence men out of London into the country.   But it was said the system had been tried in France, where it was obliged to be relaxed.   The French system, however, was very different from the Irish.   When a convict was released in France he was not allowed to choose the locality where he was going— the place was chosen for him ; even the villages and towns he should pass through to get to it were named, and after he got to work a letter was written to his employer warning him that the man was a convict. That was a very different system from what prevailed in Ireland.   There it was no part of the duty of the police to go to the employer and tell him that he had a ticket-of-leave man in his employ, or to tell the fact to his fellow-workmen.   The Inspector General of the Midland district in his last report urged strongly the introduction of the Irish system into this country, and said that in one month he could organise the machinery necessary to carry it out.

Amendment proposed,

At the end of the Clause, to add the words "if any holder of a licence granted under the said Penal Servitude Acts, or any of them, who shall be at large in the United Kingdom, shall fail to report himself to the chief police station of the borough or district where he shall be on his arrival therein, and subsequently on the first day of each month, or shall change his locality without having previously notified the same to the police station to which he last reported himself, he shall be deemed guilty of a misdemeanour, and may be summarily convicted thereof, and his licence shall be forthwith forfeited by virtue of such conviction."—(*Mr. Hunt.*)

SIR GEORGE GREY said, he did not think it would be expedient for the Committee to adopt the Amendment of the hon. Gentleman, which would establish a continuing supervision over all licence-holders from month to month.   The hon. Gentleman had not adverted to the essential difference between the police force in Ireland and in this country.   In Ireland there was an armed police of 13,000 men, who occupied barracks all over the country within a short distance of each other, while here the stations were much scattered, and policemen few, even in a large district.   The Royal Commission had reported against the proposal of the hon. Gentleman.   Substantially the same proposition had been made in the Royal Commission by the right hon. Gentleman the Member for the University of Cambridge (Mr. Walpole), and only two of the Royal Commissioners voted for it—namely the right hon. Gentleman himself, and the right hon. Member for Oxfordshire (Mr. Henley), eight other members of the Commission voting against it.   What was already required ?   That every licence-holder should in the first instance report himself to the chief of the police in the town or district where he should go on his discharge.   It had been found that it was the practice of convicts to return to the districts where they originally resided, and when once they had reported themselves on their arrival, the police would be able to keep an eye on them, especially as the gratuities would be paid through their hands.   If they attempted to do more than that, and to require that throughout the whole of the country every convict shall periodically report himself at the chief police-station of the borough or county in which he had taken up his residence, they would place an insuperable bar in the way of such men procuring honest employment.   Under such a system a convict's previous character would be published to all his associates ; and moreover, the very fact that he was obliged at certain intervals to leave home and visit a distant police-station, would in itself interfere with his chances of getting regular work.   He did not know whether the hon. Member who proposed the Amendment was favourable to the emigration of convicts.   [Mr. HUNT: I think emigration should be encouraged.] As the licence did not authorize emigration, the police would be bound to warn a convict who announced to them an intention of leaving the country that he would be committing an illegal act.   On these grounds he could not agree to the Amendment.

MR. BEACH supported the Amendment.   It was notorious that at present the conditions of the ticket-of-leave were not enforced. Convicts were left to the general superintendence which the police bestowed on all notorious criminal characters; but the difficulty was to know what man fell within that category. At present the police had no means of ascertaining the character of the convicts who entered their districts. It was all left to chance, and chance had been the bane of our criminal system. There was no communication between the police of different counties, or between the police of the counties and London. The police might, perhaps, recognize a man who returned to his original haunts; but criminals did not often return to the places from which they came—they sought a new district in which to carry on their depredations. How was their character to be known? There was an instance of a criminal mentioned by Mr. Recorder Hill, at Birmingham, who had been convicted eleven times. In March, 1850, he was sentenced at Maidstone to fifteen years' transportation for stealing a watch; but in January, 1857, or about six years and nine months after his previous sentence, he was sentenced to six years' penal servitude for stealing 15lb. of cheese; and when Mr. Hill was calling the attention of the grand jury to the case he was again under an indictment for felony. Mr. Hill felt that this was not right, for if the man had been discharged on the ground of merit, and had enjoyed the benefit of a well superintended supervision, he might have been saved from the commission of his subsequent crimes. Supervision was, in fact, the root and branch of the system, and it was a privilege due to the criminal population, each of whom must be guarded against himself lest he be led back into crimes which in his calmer moments he might wish to avoid. It was stated as an objection that it was difficult for such a class to obtain employment. But in Ireland, after the first time, employers were content to take them, and were even anxious to have them. One employer of labour in Dublin gave it as his opinion that, after an experiment of five years, they had given satisfaction, and the Inspector of the police in Dublin gave the same opinion. There was one instance of a man who, before he came under the instruction of Mr. Organ, was the terror of the neighbourhood in which he resided, and always slept with a blunderbuss under his head. He was sentenced for receiving stolen goods. This man was now leading a sober and settled life, and had a pig and

Mr. Beach

some fowls. Mr. Smith also gave it as his opinion that men under licence found it difficult to get employment, and that the great want of will to do well was the principal impediment, and that if the police were judicious their superintendence would not increase the difficulty of the well disposed to get employment. It was very right that there should be a sympathy with those who, having departed from the path of right, were discharged from prison; but this sympathy must not interfere with the well-being of society. He cordially supported the Amendment.

MR. MARSH said, that in Australia ticket-of-leave holders were preferred by employers because of the stringent supervision that was exercised over them. In those colonies convicts again offending were remitted to prison to complete their original sentence. That was no hardship, because, when a man was sentenced to four years' penal servitude, he ought to undergo the whole of the punishment, and any remission was a favour to him. The hon. Member who spoke last had referred to the sympathy that was felt for liberated thieves. He, also, felt some sympathy for them, but he felt more for those who were robbed. Unfortunately, the current of public sympathy had of late years run in favour of the thieves, and he was glad to think that the humbug was coming to an end.

MR. MOOR said, he should support the Amendment of the hon. Member for Northamptonshire (Mr. Hunt). He admitted that the subject was surrounded with difficulties; and, so long as transportation was kept in its present suspended state of animation, those difficulties must continue. The only way to meet the matter was to look it in the face. So long as the home-made criminals were turned out upon the country, they must make use of police supervision, for without it neither property would be safe, nor would there be a chance of reclamation for the convicts themselves. The supervision was recommended in the Report of the Royal Commissioners of last year, and he (Mr. Moor) regretted that the right hon. Baronet the Home Secretary did not read this paragraph instead of the one immediately succeeding it. The paragraph said that there would be much difficulty in securing efficient supervision on the part of the police, but that this object had now become of such extreme importance that it ought to be attempted. Again, Colonel Henderson, in writing to Mr.

Waddington, in September, 1863, recommended that strict police supervision should be exercised over the convicts on tickets-of-leave. There was no doubt that, to a certain extent, or for a certain time, the susceptibilities of the English people would be opposed to the strict supervision of the police. The right hon. Member for North Staffordshire (Mr. Adderley) said the case might occur in which a person having a resemblance to a notorious offender might be taken to a lock-up. Such little inconveniences might occasionally occur. In New South Wales the story was told of the Chief Justice being out late one evening, and not being well known to a new member of the police, was asked for his pass, and, not having it, was walked off to the station, and locked up until his friends could come and identify him. Such things the country must put up with. In France there was a regular supervision, which, according to the evidence laid before the Royal Commission, had led to a diminution in the number of crimes. He hoped the Amendment of the hon. Member for Northamptonshire would be successful, as it would be worth a trial ; and if the experiment did not succeed it could be abandoned afterwards. At any rate, it was a duty to make the experiment.

MR. EVANS remarked that the Irish system depended upon Mr. Organ, who was a man such as was seldom to be met with. He was sorry that he could not support the Amendment.

MR. HENRY SEYMOUR said, he believed it to be quite possible to establish in England the system adopted in Ireland, and Mr. Organ had stated that he would undertake to establish it if the Secretary of State would allow him to try. He hoped the Amendment would be carried, for he thought it would bring about an improvement in the police force. It was disgraceful that every reform had to be dragged from the Government through the aid of those who sat on the Opposition benches.

SIR JOHN PAKINGTON said, the Home Secretary had referred to a division which had taken place in the Commission upon a Motion of his right hon. Friend (Mr. Walpole). Had he (Sir John Pakington) been present upon that occasion he should certainly have supported that Motion. Speaking of the discharge of convicts under licence, the Commission said—

"We believe, on the contrary, that this system, coupled with a general prolongation of sentences of penal servitude, and arrangements for placing, convicts when so discharged under effective control and supervision, would afford the best prospect of giving to society a real protection against criminals without subjecting them to undue severity."

He would remind the right hon. Gentleman of this passage, and also of the fifth recommendation at the close of the Report—

"That those who may be unfit to go (to Western Australia), but may earn an abridgment of their punishment, and who may consequently be discharged at home under licence, should be placed under strict supervision till the expiration of the terms for which they were sentenced, and that the necessary powers should be given by law for rendering this supervision effectual."

The Commission distinctly laid down the principle that every man discharged under licence should be placed under supervision. It was very true that, by a division, a majority of the Commission recommended that, as in Dublin, licence-holders should be placed under the supervision of an officer in the Convict Department, assisted by the police. He dissented from that recommendation, believing that supervision exercised by the Convict Department would be very difficult and inconvenient. Nor could he assent to the proposal that discharged prisoners should be placed under the control of the Prisoners' Aid Society, for though he thought highly of that society as a voluntary institution, he thought it would be unwise to trust to it as an auxiliary of the State. The only safe mode of giving effect to the recommendation of the Royal Commission was by placing these men under the supervision of the police on the plan recommended by his right hon. Friend (Mr. Walpole), and now repeated in the Motion before the Committee. He earnestly hoped that the Committee would not allow the Home Secretary to fritter away the great principle now at stake. We had had enough of men discharged under licence without supervision. This system had caused well-founded dissatisfaction from one end of the kingdom to the other. He believed the best plan was to give men the chance of amendment by discharging them under licence, but he could only assent to that principle on condition that they were discharged under supervision. There should be either one thing or another. The Lord Chief Justice and his right hon. Friend (Mr. Henley) said, "Let us have fixed sentences entirely worked out, and no remission." His own feeling was that there should be remission accompanied by strict supervision, but that if no supervision was introduced there should be no remission.

MR. WHITBREAD thought it would be fatal to the prospects of convicts in this country obtaining honest employment on their discharge if they were bound to report themselves periodically to the police. Sir Richard Mayne, who said he was ready to undertake the supervision of these convicts, added that in doing so he could not prevent employers from knowing who they were. Whatever might be the case in Ireland, in this country, though employers were sometimes willing to employ licence-holders, workmen would turn them out if they knew the men were convicts. Moreover, he did not believe that the fact of a man's reporting himself once a month was any guarantee that, for the remainder of the month, he did not maintain himself by robbery. A man might report himself in London and be operating for the remainder of the month in Glasgow. Such reports offered no real security to society, while they would have the effect of driving these men out of honest employment.

MR. HENLEY said, he was against all licences at all, and thought that when you had got a thief the best way was to keep him to work out the full sentence passed upon him. Whether the sentence was one of six months' imprisonment or of six years' penal servitude, he saw no reason why there should be any remission. Being of opinion that the whole system of remission was a mistake, he was also of opinion that the mistake was not mended one bit by supervision, which was mere moonshine. Upon what was it founded? The hon. Member for Salisbury (Mr. Marsh) said, that in Australia employers of labour would sooner engage a thief than an honest man. Did he think that that was the case in England? Hardly. Mr. Organ, the great authority on this subject in Ireland, said he had great difficulty in getting employers of labour there to engage these men, and that, when this difficulty was overcome, it was necessary to keep the thing a secret from the workmen, who would otherwise have made the place too hot to hold them. With our police organisation, what chance was there that this could be kept a secret in England? Our workmen did not mind working with a man who had been transported, and who had served his term, for they had a strong

Sir John Pakington

sense of natural justice, and said, "The man broke the law, but he has suffered the consequences, and there is an end of it;" but the case would be quite different with ticket-of-leave men. In this country nobody liked tickets. The Nonconformists did not like to be ticketed, and if these unfortunate men were ticketed, no one would work with them, and the poor fellows would thus probably be driven into crime again. The compelling a man to report himself to the police would have a tendency to keep him out of honest employment, and make him a thief for the rest of his life; because a convicted man—and it was good that it was so—had enormous difficulties to contend with, and if those difficulties were increased, so were the chances of that man again becoming amenable to the law. The hon. Gentleman had given the House a lecture as to the course which public opinion had run in respect to this matter. There had been a good deal of getting rid of the gallows, and a good deal of getting rid of the "cat;" and for the last twelve years, during the period that the milder system had been at work, crime had, on the whole, decreased relatively to the population. As he was against licences and all supervision, he would vote with the Government on the present occasion. When he voted in the Commission he had merely voted against certain words standing part of the Question; that was to say, he voted against a stricter supervision than his right hon. Friend desired to have. He declined to sign the Report of the Commission, because the principle of "ticket-of-leave" ran through it, and he was dead against that system, for he thought that when a prisoner had served his term of punishment he should be let out a free man.

Question put, "That those words be there added."

The Committee *divided:* — Ayes 148; Noes 120: Majority 28.

LORD NAAS trusted that an addition would be made to the clause enabling the chief of the police to dispense with the periodical visits of the licence-holders if he were satisfied they were doing well. If no other Member did so, he would give notice of an Amendment to this effect on the Report.

MR. HUNT said, that there was nothing in his Amendment which need prevent the noble Lord's suggestion from being adopted. He imagined that the chief constable

would depute some constable to discharge
the duty of receiving these reports.

Clause, as amended, *agreed to.*

Remaining Clauses *agreed to.*

Schedule A.

Mr. HIBBERT moved to leave out
after "large" the words "in the United
Kingdom." One of the greatest services
that could be rendered to licence-holders
was to assist them in emigrating to the
colonies. The Discharged Prisoners' Aid
Society was willing to assist in this good
work, and his object in proposing this
Amendment was to enable the licence-
holders to emigrate legally.

Sir GEORGE GREY said, the proposed Amendment, if agreed to, would be
inconsistent with the power taken to revoke
a licence, which could only be done within
the United Kingdom, and he feared that it
would give rise to great dissatisfaction in
the colonies.

Amendment, by leave, *withdrawn.*

Schedule *agreed to.*

Mr. HUNT wished for some explanation
as to the course the right hon. Baronet
proposed to take with regard to the Amendment which he had induced the Committee
to adopt.

Sir GEORGE GREY said, it was his
intention to assist the hon. Gentleman in
giving effect to the decision of the Committee.

Sir GEORGE GREY then moved the
addition of a clause (Licences may be
granted in Form differing from that in
Schedule A).

Clause *agreed to,* and added to the Bill.

House *resumed.*

Bill *reported ;* as amended, to be considered on *Monday* next, and to be *printed.*
[Bill 71.]

ADMINISTRATION OF JUSTICE (IRELAND).
THE QUEEN v. DUIGAN AND OTHERS.
PAPERS MOVED FOR.

Captain ARCHDALL, in moving for
Returns connected with the administration
of justice in Ireland, said, that in expressing his opinion that things were not in a
satisfactory state in that country, he did
not wish to make any charge against the
right hon. Baronet the Chief Secretary to
the Lord Lieutenant. He believed that no
Gentleman who had ever filled that difficult
post had gone to Ireland with better in-

tentions than the right hon. Baronet. The
right hon. Baronet, however, had had to
fight single-handed, as he was surrounded
by men of different character. The conduct of Lord Carlisle had been described
by the hon. Member for Liskeard (Mr.
Osborne) in language which was certainly
strong, but not altogether inappropriate.

Motion made, and Question proposed,

"That there be laid before this House, Copies
of the Informations and of the Indictment in the
case of the Queen against Michael Duigan, Patrick Duigan, and Patrick Egan, tried at the
Summer Assizes 1862, at Mullingar, in the County
Westmeath, and of the Sentences passed upon
each of them.

"Of any Memorial or Memorials to the Lord
Lieutenant of Ireland, praying for the release of
the said prisoners.

"Of the Resolutions of the Grand Jury of the
County Westmeath, passed at the last Assizes,
remonstrating with the Lord Lieutenant upon the
liberation of the said prisoners, and of his Excellency's Reply thereto.

"And, of any other Correspondence which
may have taken place upon the subject."—(*Captain Archdall.*)

Sir ROBERT PEEL said, he did not
feel himself justified in according more
than the first and third portions of the hon.
Member's Motion. The men referred to
by the hon. Gentleman were sentenced to
two years' imprisonment, and the Lord
Lieutenant of Ireland thought fit, in the
exercise of his prerogative, to remit the last
three or four months of their sentences.
He did not think that the House should
call the prerogative into question. With
regard to the observations which had been
made by the hon. Member for Liskeard about
the Castle, if he had been in the House he
should not have allowed them to pass.

Mr. BAGWELL rose to order. The
hon. Member for Liskeard was not present.

Sir ROBERT PEEL would refer to
what had been said by the hon. Member
the mover of the Resolution. He had
thought fit to repeat the statement that the
Castle was a sink of iniquity. He held
that such language was unsuitable to the
House, and ought not to be used by hon.
Members. Had he been in the House at
the time the statement was originally made
he should have entered a strong protest
against it, and he felt certain that the
House would not endorse the opinion held
by the hon. Member for Liskeard.

Lord NAAS dissented from the opinion
of the right hon. Gentleman (Sir Robert
Peel), that the House had no right to ask
for the production of the memorials to the

Lord Lieutenant. The course that had been adopted by the Government in reference to these men had created great dissatisfaction throughout Ireland.

Captain ARCHDALL, in explanation, said, that he did not repeat the phrase made use of on a former occasion by the hon. Member for Liskeard. He said that the terms in which the Castle had been described were strong, but not inappropriate.

Motion, by leave, *withdrawn.*

Copies *ordered,*

"Of the Informations and of the Indictment in the case of the Queen against Michael Duigan, Patrick Duigan, and Patrick Egan, tried at the Summer Assizes 1862, at Mullingar, in the County Westmeath, and of the Sentences passed upon each of them.

"And, of the Resolutions of the Grand Jury of the County Westmeath, passed at the last Assizes, remonstrating with the Lord Lieutenant upon the liberation of the said prisoners, and of his Excellency's Reply thereto."—(*Captain Archdall.*)

GALWAY (WESTERN DISTRICTS).

PAPERS MOVED FOR.

Mr. GREGORY moved that there be laid before the House—

"Copy of the Report of Dr. Brodie, Poor Law Inspector in Ireland, dated the 21st day of November, 1861, on the condition of the Western Districts of Galway."

Sir ROBERT PEEL said, he was sorry to oppose the Motion of the hon. Gentleman. The Report, however, contained reflections upon the management of certain property, and he believed its production, after the lapse of three years, would not be fair to the parties concerned. It would only have the effect of raking up old sores without producing any good result.

Mr. GREGORY maintained that, as a public document, written by a public officer, and addressed to a public department, he was entitled to the production of the Report. It described the manner in which a property of enormous extent had been managed in the west of Ireland, by a large public company, during a time of unparalleled distress. His hon. Friend the Member for Mallow (Mr. Longfield) had given notice of his intention to bring forward a Motion upon the same subject. When the Motion of the hon. Member for Mallow came before the House, he should state the contents of the document, and if there was any inaccuracy in his representations of it, the blame must fall not upon him, but upon the person who communicated to him its contents, and who, at the same

Lord Naas

time, expressed the utmost indignation at the manner in which this great corporation, while it insisted upon its rights, fulfilled its duties. The right hon. Baronet knew to what he referred, and he also knew that what was told to him was not told in a confidential manner. If the right hon. Baronet refused to give this document he did it at the instigation of a Secretary of State who sat near him, and who was one of the directors of the corporation, the conduct of which was about to be impugned. If he went out alone he would divide the House to obtain this paper.

Sir GEORGE GREY said, that when his right hon. Friend consulted him as to the production of this Report, he said if any Parliamentary ground could be assigned by all means let it be produced, not alone but with all the correspondence connected with it. At the same time, he said that, as it related to events which occurred three years ago, and contained imputations upon the manager of the Law Life Institution, which were answered in a letter from that Society, he thought that unless some present ground could be shown, it would be unreasonable to go back three years and produce that correspondence. He was not then aware that there was any Motion relating to the Company pending. [Mr. Gregory: It was on the paper.] If the hon. Gentleman, instead of reserving his observations, had stated why he wanted the paper, he would have had no occasion to make the speech which he had just delivered. When the Report, the character of which his hon. Friend had, he thought, somewhat exaggerated, was sent to him, he wrote officially to the secretary of the Institution, and nothing would give him more satisfaction than that his letter and the reply should be laid before the House. He hoped that there would be no objection to the production of the Report together with the "Correspondence connected therewith."

Copy *ordered,*

"Of the Report of Dr. Brodie, Poor Law Inspector in Ireland, dated the 21st day of November, 1861, on the condition of the Western Districts of Galway, and the Correspondence connected therewith."—(*Mr. Gregory.*)

LISBURN ELECTION.

Mr. ADAIR moved—

"That the Minutes of the Proceedings of, and the Evidence taken before the Select Committee on the Lisburn Election Petitions should be printed"—

and expressed a hope that they would be placed in the hands of Members as soon as possible, because he understood that the hon. and learned Member for Youghal (Mr. Butt) had presented a petition from the petitioner in this case, which was to be taken into consideration on Thursday.

Mr. LYGON said, he did not intend to oppose the Motion of the hon. Member, but if he insisted upon bringing the proceedings of the Committee under the notice of the House and the consideration of the public, it was impossible that the House should consent to let the matter rest where it was. When the agent of the sitting Member withdrew from the Committee, he stated that he was convinced of the justice of his cause and could establish his case. It was impossible that a Committee should be allowed by an illegal act to come to an illusory conclusion, and defeat the object for which it was instituted. He regretted that the question had been mooted as it had been, because no useful object could be obtained, and injustice might be done to persons who could not defend themselves. He threw upon the Chairman of the Committee all the consequences which might follow the publication of the evidence.

Motion *agreed to.*

Ordered,

That the Minutes of the Proceedings of, and the Evidence taken before, the Select Committee on the Lisburn Election Petitions be printed.— (*Mr. Adair.*)

SCIENTIFIC INSTITUTIONS (DUBLIN)— NOMINATION OF COMMITTEE.

Mr. GREGORY having proposed that the following Members be Members of the Select Committee on Scientific Institutions (Dublin),—

Mr. WHITESIDE was proceeding to discuss the propriety of having two institutions—the Dublin Society and the Museum of Industry—situated within six minutes' walk of each other, when the professors were the same, the lecturers were the same, and the subjects were the same, when—

Mr. COGAN rose to order. The simple Question was the nomination of the Committee, and he submitted that it was not competent to the hon. and learned Gentleman to discuss the merits of the Question.

Mr. WHITESIDE submitted that he was quite in order, inasmuch as when the

subject was before the House on a previous occasion the understanding was that he might make any remarks which he thought necessary on the naming of the Committee.

Mr. SPEAKER said, it was perfectly true that the House had decided the Question that the Committee should be appointed, and under ordinary circumstances it would be desirable that the discussion should be confined to the names of the Members of whom it should be composed. He understood the right hon. Gentleman to object to some names, and to desire to propose others; it was impossible to prescribe the limits to which the argument of the hon. and learned Gentleman might extend in his endeavour to procure the substitution of one name for another.

Mr. WHITESIDE objected to the name of the hon. Member for Galway (Mr. Gregory), and proposed that the name of Mr. Lowe should be substituted.

Sir PATRICK O'BRIEN rose to order, stating that the only Question before the House was the nomination of Mr. Gregory as one of the Committee.

Mr. WHITESIDE said, the object of the hon. Gentleman opposite was to prevent him from stating the facts, but they had not the power of doing so. Sir Robert Kay having been made President of the College of Cork was also made President of the Dublin Society, obtaining two salaries. He could not help characterizing the whole thing as a complete job.

Mr. SPEAKER reminded the hon. and learned Gentleman that the main Question now was the nomination of the Committee.

Select Committee on Scientific Institutions (Dublin) *nominated :*—

Mr. Gregory, Lord Henry Lennox, Sir Robert Peel, Mr. Luke White, Mr. Lygon, Sir Colman O'Loghlen, Mr. Cogan, The O'Conor Don, Mr. O'Reilly, Mr. Dillwyn, Sir Edward Grogan, Mr. George, Mr. Leader, Mr. Lefroy, and Mr. Waldron:—Power to send for persons, papers, and records; Five to be the quorum.

Mr. ADDERLEY said, he should raise the Question in the Estimates, and move that the Vote be omitted.

Mr. GREGORY: In that case I shall move that the grant for the Royal Dublin Society be omitted.

House adjourned at a quarter after One o'clock.

HOUSE OF LORDS,

Tuesday, April 19, 1864.

MINUTES.]—PUBLIC BILLS—*First Reading—*
Registration of County Voters (Ireland)*
(No. 50) ; Common Law Procedure (Ireland)
Act (1853) Amendment * (No. 51).
Second Reading —· Land Securities Company ;
Improvement of Land Act 1864 (No. 36).
Committee—Union Relief Aid Acts Continuance *
(No. 39) ; Land Drainage (Provisional Orders)*
(No. 27).
Report — Punishment of Rape (No. 52) ; Union
Relief Aid Acts Continuance * (No. 39) ;
Land Drainage (Provisional Orders) * (No. 27).

DENMARK AND GERMANY—THE WAR.
BOMBARDMENT OF SONDERBORG.
QUESTION.

THE EARL OF MALMESBURY: I
wish to ask the noble Earl the Secretary
of State for Foreign Affairs, Whether he
has received any explanation from the
Prussian authorities with reference to the
bombardment of Sönderborg ? Every private letter I have seen, and every message,
confirm the original reports of what had
occurred and even tend to aggravate the
atrocity of the act. It is said that the
Prussians gave only a general notice,
which, in fact, was no notice at all ; and
that, contrary to the usages of civilized
nations, they did not give the twenty-four
hours' notice to non-combatants to leave
the town. The German papers put forward a statement that there were an arsenal and a place for the manufacture or
store of arms at Sönderborg, and that that
was the reason of the bombardment. That
may have been so ; but it is no reason for
not giving the usual notice. And further,
if it was deemed necessary to destroy the
arsenals, at least they need not have destroyed the town and the hospitals, which
last were destroyed in the earliest part of
the bombardment. The sick and wounded
had to be removed in the midst of the bombardment, and many perished in consequence. Such, at least, are the accounts
that we have received. And not only this,
but the shells which were used were not
fire shells, such as are used for tho purpose, but shells filled with the most terrible
missiles for the destruction of human life.
Now, my Lords, though I am opposed to
the intervention of useless despatches and
superfluous advice, still, in the present
instance, I do not know why that course
should not have been followed which is

common among the nations of Europe. I
think it is the duty of Her Majesty's Government to state in most positive terms
what the feeling of this country is respecting the conduct of the Prussian army—
feelings which are clearly expressed in the
sentiment that, although the Prussian
troops may have obtained a great victory
in Denmark, no success can wipe out the
stain which the Prussian army has inflicted
on its military reputation by their conduct
at Sönderborg. I wish to ask the noble
Earl whether he has received any reply
to the despatch which he dispatched to
Berlin asking an explanation of what has
occurred ?

EARL RUSSELL: In reply to the noble
Earl's Question, I have to state that I
desired Her Majesty's Ambassador at Berlin to ascertain the facts if possible. Our
Ambassador communicated privately with
the Prussian Minister, not being able to
go himself. No answer was given to the
inquiry. The Prussian Minister said he was
not well aware of the circumstances, and
that it was not usual for a neutral Power
to inquire as to the proceedings of belligerents. He promised, however, that if an
official inquiry were made he would give
an answer. I suppose the answer would
be merely that Her Majesty's Government
have no right to inquire in regard to the
proceedings of the belligerents, and I have
not directed any official communication to
be made in the matter. A statement has
appeared in the official, or, at least, semi-
official paper of Berlin, to the effect that
three weeks before the bombardment some
notice of it had been given. I can
not be surprised at the expression of
opinion by the noble Earl as to the conduct of the Prussian army in this matter.
I cannot apply any other terms to the
conduct of the Prussian army than those
which the noble Earl has applied. It
is astonishing that out of mere feelings
of humanity they should not have given
notice of what they were going to do,
in order that the women and children
might have been removed from the place
before the bombardment began. If it was
deemed a necessary operation of war, if
the Prussians imagined, as they said, that
the reserves of the Danish army were
placed there, and that the town contained
stores of arms and ammunition, it would
not at all have interfered with their carrying out the bombardment, if they had
given twenty-four hours' notice stating,
that for the future Sönderborg would be

reckoned part of the Danish fortifications, and that they would hold themselves at liberty to bombard it. The bad element of the affair is that the lives of innocent women and children and other non-combatants were sacrificed, through the inexcusable proceedings of the Prussian commander. Had any official explanation been given by the Prussian Government, it should have been laid upon the table ; but as the matter stands, this act must remain under the reprobation of civilized Europe.

DEPARTURE OF GENERAL GARIBALDI.
OBSERVATIONS.

THE EARL OF CLARENDON: My Lords, I wish to say a few words to your Lordships on a subject, concerning which it is due not only to the Emperor of the French, and to Her Majesty's Government, but, if I may take the liberty of saying so, to myself also, that there should be no misunderstanding. I refer to the reports respecting the departure of General Garibaldi, which have been very current in town this morning, and which have been embodied in an article in *The Morning Star*, from which I should like, with your Lordships' permission, to read an extract. A similar statement also appeared in *The Daily News. The Star* says—

"The story was in every mouth, and it would be idle to affect any reticence on the subject. People asserted that a pressure had been brought to bear by the French Government, and that the English Ministry, desirous to remove all cause of ill-feeling from the mind of an ally, had made a direct and personal appeal to Garibaldi to induce him to cut short his visit and leave the country. Any one who has time or inclination to read through the Paris correspondences of some foreign journals will find it often asserted of late that during Lord Clarendon's mission to Paris certain concessions were asked of the English Government, in the name of good feeling and cordial alliance. The rumour pervading London yesterday asserted that one of these concessions was to be made by inducing Garibaldi to cut short his visit, and leave England. We should be reluctant indeed to believe that any part of such a statement could be true. Nothing could be more ignoble on the part of either Government than such conduct as this report imputes. That the French Government could have had the weakness, the want of dignity, the want of common self-respect, to make such a request of our representative in Paris seems almost to surpass belief. That our Government could have condescended to listen to such a request, and to act upon it, ought to appear far less worthy of credit. Yet we have heard the statement vouched for as well founded by those whose authority removes any report sanctioned by them quite out of the range of the common every-day *canard*."

Now, my Lords, if there were any foundation for that report the strictures made on it would be well deserved; but I can assure your Lordships that neither directly nor indirectly from the Emperor of the French, or from any member of his Government, was any allusion made to me with respect to the cause of General Garibaldi's arrival in this country, or as to the probable duration of his stay here. I will not say that the subject was not mentioned, for it was adverted to by myself, and, describing the entry of General Garibaldi into London, and the enthusiasm with which he was received, I said that that enthusiasm was grounded on the circumstance of his having risen from the ranks of the people by the services he rendered to his country, and because he was brave and honest, and that similar scenes of enthusiasm would await him in whatever part of England he might visit. No one can be more unwilling than I am—because no one can be more aware than I am—of the inconvenience and impropriety of alluding to any communication with which I was honoured by the Emperor of the French ; but I think I am not betraying any confidence when I state that the Emperor said he fully understood and entirely believed how such qualities as those went home to the hearts of the English and commanded their admiration. No question was put to me on the subject by the Emperor of the French ; for he is too well acquainted with our Constitution and with the state of public opinion in this country to deem it necessary to make any inquiry that I must have considered as an affront. I had not heard the rumour, even, that Garibaldi was going to leave this country until this day, and I can say that the French Government has had no more to do with his departure than I have myself.

Before I sit down, I will simply refer to another matter, stated in this newspaper, with respect to myself and to the effect that during my mission to Paris certain concessions were asked of the English Government. I think that it will be satisfactory to your Lordships and to the country to know that no concessions were asked by the French Government or the English Government, by the one of the other. I found that there existed on the part of the Emperor of the French the same desire as on the part of Her Majesty's Government, that on all important questions which may arise there should be a combination of action between the two Governments and the two countries, as far as was possible, without compromise of the dignity or independence of either.

LAND SECURITIES COMPANY BILL.
SECOND READING.

THE DUKE OF MARLBOROUGH, in moving the second reading of this Bill, said, that the Land Securities Company was formed for making advances of money on real property to landowners or others for the purpose of making improvements on landed estates, or for effecting great public works, calculated to develop the value of the land. The company would be enabled to issue mortgage debentures, but not to any amount beyond the value of the securities they held.

Moved, That the Bill be now read 2ª.

LORD REDESDALE objected to the Motion, on the ground that this being a mere money-lending company, having no public object in view, it ought to be under the regulation of some general public law; so that all bodies having similar objects might be upon the same footing, and all know upon what principles to proceed. If several companies were to engage in the transactions which this company proposed to itself, the consequence would be that they would all be acting by private, not by public, rules. He did not see why any special privileges should be granted to this company, whether in regard to registration, stamps, or the power to pass their debentures from hand to hand like bank-notes without endorsement.

THE LORD CHANCELLOR said, he could not help thinking that the noble Lord had taken an erroneous view of this measure. The noble Lord appeared to think that it ought to be the subject of general legislation; but how could their Lordships legislate upon a matter until it had come into being? The noble Lord might as well have objected to the first Railway Bill that came before the House, and say that it ought not to pass until they had some general legislation on the subject of railways. The noble Lord also regarded this as a mere private speculation in regard to which there was no security. So far from objecting to this Bill, he looked upon it as the introduction of a series of measures which would greatly benefit the landed interest, by offering facilities for the raising of money and affording the means of ameliorating the position of the landowners. The Bill had passed a sifting investigation in the House of

The Earl of Clarendon

Commons, and it might be made the model for future measures of a similar kind. He trusted that the Bill would not be strangled in its present stage. If it passed a second reading, he should propose to refer it to a Select Committee.

LORD CRANWORTH said, that their Lordships were asked to give a second reading to a measure of which they knew nothing, but which the noble Lord (Lord Redesdale) who had had the opportunity of examining it, declared to be highly objectionable. If the Bill were to be debated and a division taken upon its second reading, their Lordships ought to have the same facilities as in the case of other measures, by having copies in their hands. It involved no disrespect to the noble Duke (the Duke of Marlborough) to say that no one could follow his statement conveniently. He suggested, and would move as an Amendment, that the second reading be postponed till that day week, to afford time for the Bill to be printed and circulated.

EARL GREY said, that copies of the Bill were upon the table, though they had not been circulated. He thought it very desirable that the Bill should be read a second time that evening and referred to a Select Committee — if possible to the same Committee as that which would investigate the measure originated by the noble and learned Lord upon the Woolsack —the Improvement of Land Act, 1864, which, if it was read a second time that evening, it was proposed should be referred to a Select Committee. The Bill now under consideration was one of great importance to the landed interest, and had it passed in the first instance he had no hesitation in declaring that it would have prevented particular companies from obtaining powers, many of which were very objectionable.

THE EARL OF MALMESBURY said, a difficulty might arise in the attempt to carry out the noble Earl's suggestion, owing to the fact that this was a Private, and the Bill of the noble Lord on the Woolsack a Public Bill. If the Bill were sent to its own Select Committee, this would not prevent the other Bill from proceeding *pari passu*. He thought legislation was highly desirable, for the restrictions placed by the Legislature upon the owners of land, in its effort to benefit them, had put them in the position of men in armour, whose panoply was impenetrable to club or steel, but who were so encumbered by their own defences that they could not move.

Amendment *moved*, to leave out ("now") and insert (" this Day Six Months.")— (*Lord Redesdale*.)

Earl GRANVILLE said, the measure, if carefully handled, was sure to become a model Bill. He thought it would be better to read it a second time, and to refer it, not to the ordinary Committee, but to a Committee composed of the same Peers as those who would consider the Public Bill which had been referred to.

The Duke of MARLBOROUGH, on the part of the promoters, said, he was willing to adopt the course proposed, and to consent that the Bill should be referred to a Select Committee.

Lord REDESDALE said, he was entirely in the hands of the House. He had merely done his duty in calling attention to a Bill involving a principle entirely novel. If properly dealt with in Committee, he did not see why the Bill should not be passed as one of a public character.

Lord CRANWORTH then withdrew his Amendment.

Motion (by leave of the House) *withdrawn :* then the original Motion *agreed to;* Bill read 2ª accordingly.

PUNISHMENT OF RAPE BILL.—[H. L.] (No. 22.) REPORT.

Amendment *reported* (according to Order).

The Earl of CARNARVON moved the omission of the proviso at the end of the first clause, so as to make it a special clause in the Bill, and moved to insert a clause placing in the hands of the Judge the discretionary power of whipping where the offender was convicted of an intent to commit the crime. Their Lordships would doubtless remember that in Committee on the Bill a change was introduced, rendering it compulsory on the Judges to award the punishment of whipping where a person was convicted of the crime. He was anxious to leave the discretion, as far as possible, in the hands of the Judge, especially as in other respects the Judge must have that discretion, and would move the Amendment of which he had given notice.

The Earl of HARROWBY said, the crime of committing rape was such a disgusting one, that, although it might generally be right to leave the amount of punishment to the discretion of the Judge, he would in cases of rape make whipping compulsory.

The LORD CHANCELLOR said, that

since this subject was last under discussion he had made some inquiries with the view of ascertaining whether making the infliction of the punishment of flogging compulsory would be more likely to produce greater certainty of punishment, or to augment the disinclination of juries to convict in cases of this sort. He found that in the year 1862, 135 cases of rape were tried, out of which there were eighty acquittals—an unusually large proportion. He had also consulted the Judges upon the subject, and although he had not obtained answers from all of them, the opinions of the majority of those from whom he had heard were in favour of annexing this punishment to the existing one, provided its imposition should be left to the discretion of the Judge. They admitted that it was a fitting punishment, but felt that in cases in which there was any uncertainty about the charge, if the punishment were made compulsory it would increase the disinclination of the jury to find a verdict of guilty. Under these circumstances he should be glad to see the punishment made discretionary rather than compulsory.

Lord WODEHOUSE thought that on the whole their Lordships would do wisely not to make the punishment compulsory. The other night he thought it would be desirable to make a distinction in the punishment for the committal of the crime and the attempt to commit; but now he was of opinion that it would be safer to leave the punishment in both cases to the discretion of the Judges.

Earl GREY pointed out that the effect of the Amendment proposed to-night, taken with the Amendment made on the previous debate, would be to render the punishment compulsory when the offence was committed, but discretionary when the offence was not committed.

The Earl of CARNARVON said, that so far as the Bill made the punishment compulsory that was not part of his Amendment. The Amendment simply went to make the punishment discretionary on the attempt to commit the crime.

The Earl of DERBY said, that the last time the Bill was before the House, the clause was amended to make the punishment compulsory in the case of a conviction for an actual committal of the offence. His noble Friend now sought to leave the discretion with the Judges in the cases of attempt to commit the crime.

Lord WODEHOUSE said, he would

2 T

rather see the clause restored to its former position, that the word "shall" should stand in the place of "may."

EARL GREY suggested that the House should now agree to the addition to the clause, and that on the next stage of the Bill the whole clause should be again considered, with a view of making the punishment of whipping discretionary and not compulsory in all cases.

Amendment *agreed to.*

Bill to be read 3ª on *Thursday*, the 28th instant, and to be *printed* as amended. (No. 52.)

IMPROVEMENT OF LAND ACT (1864) BILL—[BILL 36].—SECOND READING.

Order of the Day for the Second Reading read.

THE LORD CHANCELLOR, in moving the second reading of the Bill, said, it might be divided into two parts, the one of which embodied all the provisions which had been found most useful in the numerous Drainage Acts which had been already passed, and the purposes of which it was proposed by the Bill largely to extend. These Acts had hitherto applied only to the drainage of land, while it was clear that there were many other things equally important. The present Bill would, therefore, in the first place, facilitate the power both of borrowing money and applying it to the improvements for which it was meant to provide. The Bill was accompanied also by many greater securities than existed at present. The machinery was to be worked by the Inclosure Commissioners, and there was a safeguard introduced at the outset in the shape of the Report of an assistant Commissioner, to the effect that the proposed expenditure would tend to increase the annual value of the land to an extent more than equal to the interest of the money to be raised, the principle of the measure being that the land should be charged only with a terminable annuity in respect of the outlay. Thus, suppose the contemplated improvement was to be accomplished for £100,000, the Report of the assistant Commissioner must certify that the additional annual value of the land would exceed 5 per cent on the sum proposed to be expended. Then, after the work had been accomplished, and not till then, the Commissioners would deliver to the landowner a certificate entitling him to create a terminable annuity, charging the land with the repayment of the sum ex-

Lord Wodehouse

pended, with interest, the latter not to exceed 5 per cent, and the period to be not longer than twenty-five years. Other provisions in the Bill would enable a landowner to arrange with the tenants for an augmented rent in proportion to the improvements completed. A second and a more important division of the Bill was one which had its origin in the Report of the Committee which had been appointed last Session to inquire whether it was desirable that the power given to the landlords to charge their estates with terminable annuities, in order to raise money for drainage and building, should be so extended as to enable them to raise it on similar terms for the purpose of taking shares in railways passing through their properties. The conclusion at which the Committee arrived, was that it was quite possible to ascertain the augmented value to be derived by an estate from the construction of a railway through it, or so near it as to be readily accessible, at least with the same certainty as the improved value to be derived from drainage and building. It was, therefore, proposed by the Bill to apply the same machinery with regard to the construction of railways as the former part of it provided in the case of drainage and the other improvements enumerated. All that was necessary was that a Report should be obtained from the Assistant Commissioner, stating that the land would be benefited by the landowners' promoting the construction through it of a railway either in progress or about to be commenced, by subscribing or taking shares. Then he would be empowered to act as in the case of the other works to which he had alluded. The latter portion of the Bill conferring that power, was specially hedged in, however, by precautionary provisions. For instance, it was provided that the railway should be completed and opened for public use before any charge could be made upon the land, and then that the charge should be limited to the amount actually paid up. And it was specially set forth in order to facilitate the arrangements with the tenant, that the railway shares should be issued proportionately to the parties concerned; as, for example, if £2,000 were to be subscribed, and 2,000 shares issued, and the land was charged with a terminable annuity for twenty-five years of £100 a year, and suppose the tenant to have paid the augmented rate for three or four years, amounting to £200, he would be entitled to have an equal amount of certificates. The great object to be attained was the accuracy, certainty, and workability of the Bill; and as the subject required most careful consideration, if their Lordships would agree to read the Bill a second time, he should be prepared to move that it be referred to a Select Committee. Much yet required to be done to place the law in regard to tenants for life and tenants in remainder in a satisfactory condition. The result of the English system of the settlement of estates was that in a great many cases the successive possessors were never more than life tenants. The consequence of that state of things was, that these persons were deprived of the power to make such improvements as might be necessary from time to time to bring out the full value of their estates. It was only lately that a course of legislation had been entered on for the purposes of investing a tenant for life under proper control with the authority absolutely required for the successful management of the property. At the same time, while it was right that the tenant for life should be at liberty to make necessary improvements on the estates, it was a question whether the remainder-man should not have power to compel the tenant to perform that duty. For example, take the law as to waste. Actual or positive waste committed by a tenant for life exposes him to legal consequences; but that which was known to the law as permissive waste was a thing for which there was at present no remedy, and in regard to which the tenant in remainder had no redress against the tenant for life. Thus, the latter might allow buildings to fall into a mass of ruins, or let the land on such terms that the very marrow of the land might be extracted from it, and might leave it in this impoverished and desolate state to his successor, who would have no means of protection or redress. He hoped that the Select Committee would take care that, while the tenant for life obtained the advantages which the Bill proposed to give him, correlative duties should be imposed upon him. He had omitted previously to state that any person interested in land, and objecting to the exercise of the power of the Commissioners under this Bill, would have a summary and expeditious mode of appealing to the Court of Chancery.

Moved, That the Bill be now read 2ª.
—(*The Lord Chancellor.*)

LORD BERNERS was understood to express approbation of the Bill.

THE MARQUESS OF BATH said, the law on this subject was at present in a very confused state, and the noble and learned Lord deserved credit for having brought it before the House. The most objectionable feature of the Bill was, in his opinion, in regard to the borrowing powers.

Motion *agreed to*: Bill read 2ª accordingly; and *referred* to a Select Committee. And on *Thursday*, the 21st inst., the Lords following were named of the Committee:—

Ld. CHANCELLOR, Ld. PRESIDENT, Ld. PRIVY SEAL, D. MARLBOROUGH, M. BATH, E. DERBY, E. CARNARVON, E. MALMESBURY, E. ROMNEY, E. GREY, V. EVERSLEY, L. REDESDALE, L. PORTMAN, L. STANLEY of ALDERLEY, L. OVERSTONE, L. CRANWORTH, L. CHELMSFORD.

And on *Friday*, April 22nd—

The Earl of BANDON, The Viscount HUTCHINSON, and The Lord PONSONBY added to the Select Committee.

House adjourned at Seven o'clock, till To-morrow half past Ten o'clock.

HOUSE OF COMMONS,
Tuesday, April 19, 1864.

MINUTES.]—NEW MEMBER SWORN—Sir Thomas Bateson *for* Devizes.
SELECT COMMITTEE—On Taxation of Ireland, Mr. Monsell *discharged*, Sir George Colthurst *added*.
PUBLIC BILLS—*Ordered*—Promissory Notes and Bills of Exchange (Ireland) *.
First Reading—Charitable Assurances Enrolments [*Lords*] * [Bill 72]; Promissory Notes and Bills of Exchange (Ireland) * [Bill 74]; Customs and Inland Revenue * [Bill 73]; Promissory Notes and Bills of Exchange (Ireland) * [Bill 74].
Second Reading—Court of Chancery (Despatch of Business) [*Lords*] * [Bill 69].
Committee—High Court at Bombay * [Bill 67]; Bridges (Ireland) * [Bill 70]—R.P.
Report—High Court at Bombay * [Bill 67].
Third Reading—Consolidated Fund (£15,000,000).

FRANCE AND CAMBODIA.
QUESTION.

VISCOUNT ENFIELD: I wish, Sir, to ask the Under Secretary of State for Foreign Affairs, Whether it be true that a Treaty has been concluded between France and Cambodia (or that portion of Cambodia which is tributary to Siam), the provisions of which tend to an entire exclusion of all Foreigners from that country with the exception of the French; and, if so, whether Her Majesty's Government have taken, or intend to take, any steps to secure to British Subjects equal advantages with those obtained by France in that country?

MR. LAYARD: Sir, a treaty has been concluded between France and Cambodia; but I have not seen the treaty, and I am not able to state its provisions exactly. Still there is reason to believe that there are provisions in it which imply that exclusive privileges would be given to French subjects over those of other nations. The matter has been called to the attention of the French Government, and Her Majesty's Government have received an assurance from the French Minister of Foreign Affairs, that if there are provisions in the treaty which bear this interpretation, they have been inserted inadvertently; that it was the desire of the French Emperor that it should bear the most liberal interpretation, and that it should not grant any exclusive privileges. The French Government are willing to deal with all other nations in the matter of treaties with the greatest liberality, and that they should be carried out in the same spirit as treaties entered into by the British nation, namely, that the privileges extended to British subjects should be equally extended to all other nations.

BUILDINGS AT SOUTH KENSINGTON.

QUESTION.

MR. F. S. POWELL said, he would beg to ask the First Commissioner of Works, Whether he is prepared to lay upon the table of the House the Instructions according to which certain Architects have drawn Plans for Buildings at South Kensington, the use of which is stated by the First Commissioner to be matter for further consideration?

MR. COWPER said, there were no Instructions given.

PRIVILEGE—NEW WRIT FOR MERTHYR TYDVIL.

COLONEL FRENCH said, he wished to submit a Question to Mr. Speaker relating to Parliamentary usage and law. On the previous night a writ was moved for the borough of Merthyr Tydvil; and the ground alleged for that place being vacant was, that the hon. Member who represented it had accepted the office of Vice President

Viscount Enfield

of the Board of Education. Now, by the 19 & 20 *Vict.* c. 116, the choice of Her Majesty in appointing a Vice-President of the Board of Education was limited to members of the Privy Council; and the hon. Gentleman whose seat was declared to be vacant last night was not a member of the Privy Council. Under these circumstances he could not have accepted an office under the Crown, the House had no power to declare the seat vacant, and the course taken last night was therefore, he believed, totally irregular. The seat was not really vacant at the time, and he wished to call the attention of Mr. Speaker and the House to what had occurred.

THE ATTORNEY GENERAL said, that the subject to which the hon. and gallant Member had referred was one on which there could be no doubt whatever among those who were conversant with the law and practice of Parliament. The hon. and gallant Member who had just addressed the House had fallen into the mistake of confounding two things which were essentially distinct—the acceptance of an offer of an office, and the completion of the appointment. By the law the thing which caused a seat to be vacated was the acceptance of an offer of office; and what constituted such an acceptance had been repeatedly brought before the House. It had been determined over and over again that a vacancy, under the Act of Queen *Anne*, c. 7, attached on the earliest proof of the acceptance, whether by letter, word of mouth, the kissing of hands, or in any other manner, however informal; and that it was not necessary to wait for the complete appointment, but that then the writ might be issued and the election take place; and if afterwards the appointment were completed by warrant, letters patent, or in any other form, no new vacancy was thereby created, because such appointment was merely the sequel to the acceptance of the offer of office which had occasioned the original vacancy. The hon. and gallant Member referred to the Act of Parliament which told them under what circumstances and upon what qualifications a person might receive from the Crown the appointment of Vice President of the Privy Council for Education. That Act authorized Her Majesty under her Royal sign manual to appoint any person who was of her Privy Council to be during her pleasure Vice President of the Privy Council on Education. When, therefore, the investiture took place and the warrant passed under the sign manual, the person appointed must be of the Privy Council; but it was as much in Her Majesty's power to make any person a member of her Privy Council as to make him Vice President, and before his investiture in that office she could make him one of her Privy Councillors. Therefore, when Her Majesty authorized and offered that office to be made to a person, although not at the time a member of the Privy Council, she made an offer which it was in her power to carry into effect by completing everything that was necessary for the appointment. If the offer were accepted, it was an acceptance within the meaning of the general law, and it was most important that what the House had decided to be the general law should be strictly adhered to. What was the principle of the jealousy which Parliament had showed of placemen who were required to go down for re-election to their constituents, when the Act of Queen Anne was passed? Why, that from the moment when a man signified his acceptance of an office of profit in the gift of the Crown, he became of course subject to the influence which the Crown exercised over all persons so bound to it; and, therefore, it had been enacted that his mere acceptance, however informal, should cause his seat to be vacant. The House was aware that the Vice President of the Board of Trade was Vice President of the Committee of Her Majesty's Privy Council on Trade and Plantations. But when on the 9th of August, 1855, his right hon. Friend the present Member for Calne (Mr. Lowe) was appointed Vice President of the Board of Trade, a writ was issued for Kidderminster in the room of his right hon. Friend, who had accepted that office, although not then a Privy Councillor. A similar course was taken when a new writ was moved for Gateshead in the room of Mr. William Hutt, on his acceptance of the office of Vice President of the Board of Trade and Plantations, he not being then a member of the Privy Council. He believed it would be a departure from the law and the spirit of the Constitution well deserving the censure of the House, if in the case of any Member not a Privy Councillor accepting the office in question, a new writ were not at once issued. Therefore, the doubt suggested by the hon. and gallant Gentleman was not well founded, and the House need be under no alarm for having issued the writ, —on the contrary, it would have been a departure from law not to have issued it.

DEPARTURE OF GARIBALDI.
QUESTION.

MR. DARBY GRIFFITH: I desire to put a Question to the noble Lord at the head of the Government with respect to a matter on which it is fitting that the Government should have the opportunity of offering explanations that may take the place of the uncertain rumours now occupying the public mind. It is confidently stated that the reason of the termination —or rather of the interruption — of the visit of General Garibaldi to this country, unexpected as it is, and by no means confirmed by those who have had the opportunity of seeing the General this afternoon—it is confidently stated that the curtailment of the visit is due to a suggestion of the Government. And it is also inferred in the minds of some, that the suggestion of Her Majesty's Government is the result of a suggestion from other quarters. I therefore take this opportunity of putting a Question to the noble Lord on the subject, which, I have no doubt, he will be able to answer in a satisfactory manner, in order to put an end to rumours which will spread through Europe, and which would be extremely injurious to the character of any Government. I beg, then, to ask the noble Lord, Whether Her Majesty's Government have made any suggestion to General Garibaldi to induce him to curtail his visit to England?

VISCOUNT PALMERSTON: Sir, I have heard within a very short period the report which has suggested the Question of the hon. Member for Devizes. I have been told that it has been reported in different quarters in this town, that the termination earlier than was expected of the visit of General Garibaldi to this country is the result of some suggestion coming from Her Majesty's Government, and that that suggestion has been dictated by a communication received—there is no need for mincing the matter—from the Emperor of the French. All I can say is, that those who have spread or believed that report have done great injustice both to the Emperor of the French and to Her Majesty's Government. The Emperor of the French is, I am quite sure, too high-minded and of too generous a character to have made any such application to Her Majesty's Government, and I need not, I trust, say that any Government of this country receiving such a communication from any foreign Sovereign, tending to bear on purely domestic considerations, would have very civilly, no doubt, but, at the same time, very firmly resisted and repelled any such suggestion. But, Sir, with regard to the Emperor of the French, I am empowered to say by my noble Friend the Earl of Clarendon, who had some conversation with His Majesty on the reception given to General Garibaldi in this country, that, far from having looked on that reception with the slightest degree of jealousy—for which there could not be the least foundation, because there is nothing in that reception, of any kind, bearing on France or the French Government; it was simply an expression of the admiration of the people of this country for a great and distinguished man—I am authorized by my noble Friend to say that in that conversation the Emperor of the French, so far from expressing the slightest umbrage at what has taken place, said that he looked with admiration on the feelings which that reception expressed on the part of the British nation, and that it did them the highest honour. Well, Sir, the Government have had nothing to do with shaping General Garibaldi's arrangements—nothing whatever; but I am told that his visit is likely to be brought to a close earlier than it was at first intended, purely and entirely on the score of a regard for his health. Everybody must know that General Garibaldi, having received, I think, in August, 1862, a very severe wound, was confined to his bed or couch for well nigh twelve months after that period, and that he has not yet completely recovered the use of the limb which was then injured. The strongest man must, under those circumstances, have suffered materially in health from that long confinement; but General Garibaldi, it is well known, has lived a life of exposure, exertion, and fatigue that must have had an effect on his constitution. It is not, therefore, surprising that the General should be in a delicate and precarious state of health arising from these circumstances. The General's habits, too, are very different from the life he has had to lead since he has been in this country. In his island home in Caprera, free from deputations, free from levées, free from visits, free from all sorts of honour and attentions, which are accompanied by a considerable degree of exhaustion, he has been accustomed to go to bed at eight o'clock at night and get up at five. Well, when a person is in a feeble state of health, and suffering from the effects of a severe wound, to dine

Viscount Palmerston

at half past eight, and remain surrounded by admiring friends till between eleven and twelve at night, must have an effect on him; and, although I have not had the honour of seeing him as much as others, I can bear my testimony that his health has suffered in consequence of the exertions he has made. While, therefore, the earlier termination of his visits and his foregoing those honours which were awaiting him in every town in this country may be disappointing to those who admire him, I trust it may have the effect of preserving a life so valuable to his country. Vast multitudes of men, women, I might say children, in this country, desired an opportunity of seeing him, taking him by the hand, and doing him honour, but his most ardent admirers will feel that, in foregoing the pleasure of seeing him, they are contributing to the preservation of that life, health, and strength which everyone who admires Garibaldi must desire should continue unimpaired for the service of that country to which he has devoted himself.

DENMARK AND GERMANY—TREATY OF LONDON, 1852.—RESOLUTION.

MR. BERNAL OSBORNE : Whatever, Sir, may be the faults or shortcomings attributed to the House of Commons, I can hardly think it can be attributed to us amongst them that we are of an impatient or inquisitive turn of mind; for, though professing the greatest interest in the sanguinary contest now going on in the North of Europe, sympathizing and in many instances subscribing to the necessities of the Danes, in spite of five bulky volumes having been published, containing 1,215 despatches, no inquiry has been made into these bulky volumes, and no discussion has yet taken place upon the policy pursued by Her Majesty's Government. Whatever else then may be attributed to me, I do not think it can be said that I am acting in a premature manner in bringing this subject under the consideration of Parliament. In doing so I shall endeavour to avoid all the genealogical and all the other mystifications by which it has been endeavoured to sink this case of Schleswig-Holstein. I know it has been laid down on the highest authority in this House, that this case of Schleswig-Holstein is above the comprehension of the ordinary Parliamentary intellect. The mysteries of this Eleusis none but the favoured hierophants of the Cabinet can unravel or explain. On a recent occasion, one of the most skillful Members of the Cabinet, my right hon. Friend the Member for Ashton (Mr. Milner Gibson), declared to his constituents his utter inability to comprehend the points at issue between Denmark and her Duchies, and his resolution to leave these points to be elucidated by the German professors, and this at a time when the Cabinet of which he is a Member was consulting together as to the expediency of going to war with Germany. Let me hope the House of Commons will not follow the fatal example of my right hon. Friend the Member for Ashton, for, although the subject has been mystified by mediæval research and obscured by professorial explanations, it is simple in its origin and easy of comprehension. Had not diplomacy rushed in with the tyrant plea of expediency, the question would long ago have settled itself. When diplomacy stepped in and manufactured a succession, and also upset the rights of a people, then the question became almost inextricably confused. For to what is all this bloodshed, this confusion in the North of Europe—to what is it to be attributed? I am one of that, it may be small, but faithful, band which attributes all this confusion to that Treaty of London of the 8th of May, 1852, which was concocted by the noble Lord the present First Minister of the Crown, and was signed by another noble Lord, whom I consider not at all to blame for his signature, inasmuch as having but recently acceded to office, he could not be expected to have studied minutely a question of such intricacy. Be that as it may, the treaty was the concoction of one Government, and was signed by the Earl of Malmesbury as the Foreign Secretary of another. Now, let us see what were the provisions of that treaty. The provisions of that treaty trampled alike upon the rights of an ancient people, and also upon the rights of an hereditary Duke. The pretext for the treaty was, that it was to support the integrity of Denmark and that balance of power for which this country has paid so much and profited so little—the balance of power in Europe. What have been the effects of the treaty? Can anybody say that the Treaty of 1852 has settled the balance of power or maintained the integrity of Denmark? It has settled no point, and has satisfied no party. While Germany denied the legality, Denmark sedulously evaded all the stipulations in the agreements of 1851 and 1852, and

England is the only Power which, upon a strict examination of these blue-books, will be found pertinaciously adhering to and ready to go to war, mark you! for the maintenance of that treaty by which the people of the Duchies of Schleswig and Holstein are compelled to accept the supremacy of the Danish Monarch, which has no right or title to those Duchies.

The origin of that treaty is somewhat curious and recondite. I have no hesitation in saying, having taken some pains to look into the subject, that the noble Lord in making this treaty, in an unfortunate moment, and not exercising his usual sagacity, became the catspaw of the northern despot. For I shall show to the House most conclusively that England had no interest, no possible interest, for making this treaty, but that she became a tool in the hands of Russia to advance the ambitious designs of that despotic country. It will not be necessary for me to fatigue the House with the ancient history of this Question. I shall altogether pass over the questions so much insisted upon by the professors who have mystified my hon. Friend the right hon. Member for Ashton. I would remind the House that in 1448 Christian I. of Oldenburg succeeded to the Danish throne, and was elected ruler of the Duchies of Schleswig and Holstein in 1460. There was an old charter which he swore to maintain, and pledged himself that the two Duchies should remain for ever undivided. However people may dispute about the original title, all those who have studied this Question are agreed that the relations between Denmark and the Duchies were purely dynastic and of a personal character, much the same as the relations that formerly existed between this country and Hanover. It is necessary to remember that the local Governments of Schleswig and Holstein were conducted entirely apart from that of Denmark, and that since 1665 the succession to the Crown of Denmark was by females, but in the Duchies the succession was rigidly restricted to males. It is not necessary to go further into the ancient history of this Question, only always let the House bear in mind the nature of the succession. I will now take a skip from those almost antediluvian periods, and next will come to the year 1846. In that year Christian VIII. issued his famous letters patent. He, fearing the extinction of his dynasty, and dreading the separation of the Duchies from Denmark, issued letters patent which undertook to unite Denmark and the Duchies into one state, with a common constitution and a common succession. These unfortunate letters patent were the origin of all the subsequent conflicts of the unlucky Treaty of 1852, and of all the confusion that has since arisen. Upon these letters patent being issued, the Duchies appealed to the German Confederation, and some pressure having been applied, Christian VIII. recalled those letters patent, and not only recognized the rights to the succession of the Duchies, but—a most material point—he expressly recognized the union between Schleswig and Holstein. In the year 1846—let the House remember—he expressly recognized the union between Holstein and Schleswig. That state of thing endured for two years. In the year 1848 a democratic revolution broke out at Copenhagen, and the new King Frederick VII., who had succeeded to the throne of Denmark, was compelled to throw himself into the arms of what is called the Eider-Dane party, whose object was to let Holstein go, but to incorporate Schleswig into the Danish Kingdom. Thence arose the celebrated war of that year between Germany and Denmark. After a time Prussia, for whom I have nothing to say, but perhaps less for her conduct in 1848 than for that of 1864— Prussia interposed, and, after a conflict with Denmark, peace was established between those two Powers on the 2nd of July, 1850. But the Duchies, not being satisfied with the conduct of Prussia, and the engagements she had entered into affecting them, still held out, and at first with considerable success. But on the 25th of July, 1850, was fought the battle of Idstedt, in which the Danes routed the forces of the Duchies, and then Austria and Prussia stepped in, and they imposed a peace which was considered by the Duchies to be an ignominious peace. It is material to consider what were the terms of that peace. In the first place, Austria and Prussia took what was, in the eyes of the inhabitants of Schleswig-Holstein, the fatal step of giving up the political union of the Duchies—that political union which had been recognized for ages, and which had so recently as 1846 been explicitly guaranteed by Christian VIII. Denmark, on her side, gave up the incorporation of the Duchies, and gave solemn pledges never again to endeavour to incorporate Schleswig and Holstein with Denmark. She also guaranteed equal rights and pro-

Mr. Bernal Osborne

tection to the German and Danish nationalities, and granted to the Duchies separate legislation for their internal affairs. Those terms were to be submitted for the approval of representatives of each separate community. Need I tell the House that they never were submitted to the representatives of the States of Schleswig and Holstein ? Those, however, were the conditions of peace which were imposed upon the Duchies by Austria and Prussia.

I come next to the Correspondence which has been laid upon the table, and I hope I may be allowed some little latitude in dealing with it, although I will not quote overmuch ; but as it has been made the subject of accusation against me, that I have not read these blue-books, I must impress the House and the mind of the noble Lord by reading sundry passages, in order to convince them that I have studied the literature of Schleswig-Holstein with some attention. And, Sir, although it may appear an extraordinary complaint to make, that the mass of papers with which the House has been overwhelmed is insufficient, yet still I must say that I think we have not all the papers we should have before us. I regret that the correspondence upon this subject in 1848 and 1849 is not in possession of hon. Members, because most material information would be obtained from the Correspondence. In it would be found a note of the Chevalier Von Bunsen, dated May 18, 1848, in which he proposed to consult the feelings of the inhabitants of Schleswig, and first shadowed out the idea which was taken up by the noble Lord then the Foreign Secretary, but now the first Minister of the Crown—of separating the Duchy of Schleswig, drawing a line across it, and giving that portion north of the line to Denmark, and adding the portion south of the line to Holstein. What was the reply of the noble Lord then Foreign Secretary, and now First Minister ? If those papers were on the table the House would find that on the 19th of May, 1848, the noble Lord, improving upon the suggestion thrown out by the Chevalier Von Bunsen, made a proposal that the Duchies should be consulted, that a line should be drawn across Schleswig, and the portion of the Duchy north of the line should be given to Denmark, while the southern portion should be attached to Holstein. That was the proposal of the noble Lord, and I find it quite impossible to reconcile that proposal with his conduct now in 1864, when he is upholding quite dissimilar propositions. Not only that but on the 23rd of June, 1848, he followed it up by formal proposals to Prussia and Denmark upon the subject. That incident was the first interference of this country with respect to the affairs of the North of Europe. To come down, however, to the years between 1850 and 1853, it will be found that our first interference took place on February 19, 1850, —I beg the House to follow the date— when the noble Lord the present First Minister of the Crown, and then Foreign Secretary, wrote to Sir Henry Wynn, our Ambassador at Copenhagen. On that occasion the noble Lord, for the first time, impressed upon the Danish Government the advisability of settling the succession to the Crown, so as to insure the continuance of the Sovereignty of Denmark and of both Duchies in one person, and he goes on to suggest that the Duke of Oldenburg should be regarded as the successor to the reigning Sovereign. A great deal of correspondence took place upon this subject, but somehow or other after a time the name of the Duke of Oldenburg disappears from the scene, because, I believe, he was found to be obnoxious to the Emperor of Russia. The suggestion of the noble Lord, however, was not listened to. We then began protocolling. A protocol in diplomatic language is I believe a note of the Conferences which precede a treaty. On the 4th of July, 1850, was issued a protocol, called the protocol of London. There were present the plenipotentiaries of Austria, Denmark, France, Great Britain, Prussia, Russia, and Sweden and Norway. That protocol stated—

"Considering that the maintenance of the integrity of the Danish monarchy is bound up with the general interests of the balance of power in Europe, and is of high importance for the preservation of peace, it is unanimously resolved, at the invitation of His Majesty the King of Denmark, that the possessions at present under the Crown of Denmark should be maintained in their integrity; consequently they recognize the wisdom of the views which have determined the King of Denmark to regulate the order of succession and manner of facilitating the arrangements, and the means by which the integrity of the Danish monarchy shall remain intact."

That is the Protocol of London. "On the invitation of the King of Denmark," the plenipotentiaries of the different nations resolved to adopt a course recommended by that monarch, without at all taking into account the feelings of the people of the Duchies of Schleswig-Holstein, and without paying the slightest regard to their legal rights. Round the table which the noble Lord had characterized as the panacea of everything that would produce peace, they resolved to destroy and trample upon the liberties of the people of Schleswig-Holstein. A very remarkable circumstance took place with reference to the interference with the succession. The House will remember that in February, 1850, the noble Lord made his first suggestion concerning the order of succession, to select the son of the Duke of Oldenburg, he having no rights to succession. Something, too, was said about compensation, but he first of all in 1850 suggested this English meddling, or what I call this unhallowed proceeding of manufacturing Sovereigns without consulting the people. I find that on the 20th of March, 1851, the attention of the House was directed to our meddling policy, and that an hon. Member asked the following question:— " Whether there had been any negotiation as to the succession to the Crown of Denmark, or in respect to the succession in the Duchies?" The answer returned by the noble Lord (Viscount Palmerston) was a most extraordinary one, because the House will remember that it was the noble Lord himself who had proposed a successor to the Crown of Denmark. The noble Lord's reply was couched in the following terms:—

"A good deal had passed in regard to these points. But Her Majesty's Government had studiously and systematically held themselves aloof from taking any share in these negotiations. Her Majesty's Government had confined themselves strictly to the mediation which they undertook; which was a mediation for the purpose of bringing about a restoration of peace between Denmark and the Germanic Confederation."—[3 *Hansard*, cxv. 221.]

That was in 1851. I find that in 1864 Her Majesty's Government are still negotiating for the purpose of bringing about peace between Denmark and the Germanic Confederation, in spite of the Treaty of 1852. I think that the House is entitled to some explanation from the noble Lord. It is true that the question has remained for a long time in abeyance, because I well remember that when a noble Lord (Lord Robert Montagu) the Member for Huntingdonshire brought forward a Motion upon the subject, the whipper-in of the Government went to the Speaker and said, " Sir, there are not forty Members present," and the House vanished, and we heard no more of it. From that time to this not the slightest explanation has been given. I now come down in the history of protocols to the origin of the Treaty of 1852, and

I think it will somewhat surprise those Members of the House who have been in the habit of regarding the noble Lord as the emblem of the British lion, to find that the treaty emanated from the neighbourhood of Warsaw. On June 5, 1851, the Emperor of Russia, who began to feel rather uncomfortable as to this question of the succession in Denmark, arranged another protocol — a very quiet little affair—Russia and Denmark being the only parties connected with it. In this protocol the Duke of Oldenburg is, for the first time, not mentioned, but Prince Christian of Glucksburg is named by Russia as the eventual successor to the crown of Denmark, and also to the Duchies. I think the House ought to bear in mind that in naming Prince Christian of Glucksburg, who had no more hereditary right to the throne than the noble Lord himself, Russia passed over seventeen heirs, though not all of them in a direct line of succession, and that in endeavouring to carry out this protocol, which I shall afterwards show you she did, there remained only three lives between her and the succession, not only to the Crown of Denmark, but also to the Duchies. I think it will strike the House as an extraordinary circumstance, that a protocol which sought to effect such a policy was confirmed by the Treaty of London, on May the 8th, 1852. Sir, that treaty not only confirmed the protocol of Warsaw, and set aside the rightful succession to the Duchies of Schleswig-Holstein, but it never contemplated making any reference to the people whose interests were concerned, and it abstained altogether from referring the treaty to the Germanic Confederation, or asking their consent to the arrangement proposed by it. I shall have something curious to say about the history of the Germanic Confederation, which has been treated with so much slight in former years, and which is now so suddenly taken into the confidence of Her Majesty's Ministers. I find that on January 9, 1852, Earl Granville was so much struck with the injustice of the proposed treaty, that he insisted upon referring the question to the Germanic Confederation. In his despatch of that date, which, I think, the House ought to weigh very carefully, Earl Granville, writing to Sir Henry Wynn, says—

" Her Majesty's Government cannot but consider that in an arrangement affecting the succession to German as well as to Danish States, the acquiescence of the Germanic Confederation would

Mr. Bernal Osborne

be necessary before third parties could consider that arrangement as settled. You will urge these considerations upon the serious attention of the Danish Minister."

Sir Henry Wynn, in reply, on January 17, 1852, said—

" You have thrown the whole Court of Denmark into confusion."

And then he adds—

" It is my duty not to conceal from your Lordship the unfavourable effect of the proposition you have made. The Danish Minister came to me evidently harassed by a long previous discussion with his colleagues, and I had, therefore, more difficulty to satisfy him by expressing my opinion that he had given a false interpretation to your Lordship's despatch."

In a despatch from Berlin, on January 19, 1852, Mr. Howard, writing to Earl Granville, said that Baron Manteuffel did not consider a reference to the Germanic Diet to be requisite. That shows that Russia had set her face against this mode of settling the question. Earl Granville was evidently placed in an awkward position, and his reply to Sir Henry Wynn's despatch is a curious one—

" You were quite right in expressing the opinion that M. de Bluhme had given a false interpretation to my despatch. Her Majesty's Government do not require or expect that either the Diet or the Duke of Augustenburg should be made parties to the proposed arrangement as to the succession to the Crown of Denmark."

I believe that there never was a more extraordinary state of things. Here was the Foreign Secretary at one moment pressing on the consideration of Denmark the propriety of submitting the proposition to the Germanic Diet, and the second week afterwards, entirely abandoning the only interpretation that could be placed upon it, and characterizing it as false. The consequence was that the Treaty of 1852 has never to this day been recognized by the Diet, by whom it is considered to be, in fact, a nullity. I see my right hon. Friend the Member for Ashton (Mr. Milner Gibson) looking incredulous at this ; but if he will turn to these blue-books, and not leave this question to the German Professors, he will, with his ability, rise from the subject as well-informed respecting it as the noble Lord himself. I am afraid of becoming tedious ; but, with great humility, I say that this question of Schleswig-Holstein has never been discussed, and is totally misunderstood both in this House and in the country. What were the opinions of German statesmen upon this Treaty of 1852 ? On the 4th of February, 1851, in a remarkable memoir addressed by him to the King of Prussia, Count Von Usedom, a friend of the noble Lord's, writes as follows upon the proposed change of succession to the Crown of Denmark, before Prince Christian was nominated :—

"In attempting to break the legitimate succession in the Duchies, violently, and without a free renunciation on the part of those concerned, the dangerous principle of arbitrary power is installed in the place of existing rights, the seeds of future insurrections will be sown in favour of legitimacy. I pray your Majesty may at any risk keep free from establishing the principle of 'integrity not in existence, but intended to be artificially created.'"

These are words which I could have imagined the noble Lord using in his best days, whether speaking or writing. They do honour to this Prussian Minister, and I think they justly describe this attempt to palter with the rights of succession in Denmark. That was the opinion of Count Von Usedom in 1851. Again, on the 3rd of December, 1863, a remarkable speech was made in the Prussian Chamber by the son of a celebrated man, the Chevalier Von Bunsen, who lets the Chamber into the secret. He says—

"King Frederick William IV. long resisted the pressure of Russia, and of influences in the pay of Russia, urging him to sign the Treaty of 1852. I well remember my father's observation on that treaty :—'the first cannon-shot in Europe will annihilate this bungling piece of business.'"

This is the evidence of the son of the Prussian Minister. Have we not seen how accurately his father's prophecy has been fulfilled? Is it not patent, however you may try to hush it up, that this bungling piece of diplomacy has been rent asunder by a cannon shot? But this is not the only evidence I have to adduce. M. Von Beust, who is about to attend the Conference on behalf of the despised Germanic Confederation, in a speech made in the Saxon Chamber in 1863, corroborates the statement as to the pressure of Russia at that time on the minor Powers of Germany, and says that pressure was so great that they were obliged to recognize in some sort the Treaty of 1852. Perhaps I shall be told that the King of Denmark had a right to alter the succession to his Crown and to set aside the legitimate heirs to the Duchies. But I maintain, and I think I shall be supported in this by all who form any liberal party in this country, that the King of Denmark had no right to alter the succession of his own Crown ; that he had no right to call in the Powers of Europe to set aside the legitimate hereditary heirs of the Duchies ; and that he had no right,

and the noble Lord had no right, to call this a legal and proper mode of proceeding, as he does in these despatches. I was twitted the other night with having confounded the Treaty of 1852 with the engagements entered into by the Danes in 1851-2. I hope I shall set myself right on this occasion. Of course, there was a material distinction between the engagements of 1851-2 and the Treaty of 1852. In the first place, the engagements of 1851-2 were solely between Austria, Prussia, and Denmark ; while the treaty which provided for the succession was signed by all the great Powers. By the agreements of 1851-2 Denmark undertook that a common constitution should be provided for the whole monarchy ; that certain local rights should be guaranteed to the Duchies ; and that neither Holstein nor Schleswig should be incorporated with Denmark. To this day these engagements have never been carried out. Denmark has systematically evaded compliance with them ; and however we may sympathize, and very properly sympathize, with a small State which is fighting gallantly against great odds, we are at the same time bound to consider the justice of the case, and not to forget that the small State has availed herself of her weakness, and has for twelve years evaded compliance with the agreement she undertook to fulfil. And what has been her conduct in the Duchies? It has been marked by the most arbitrary and tyrannical pleas. In the first place she suppresses altogether the German language ; it is made penal for two or more householders to club together to maintain a German instructor for their families, and this prohibition is extended to females. Only three persons are allowed to sign a petition ; in fact, the most arbitrary powers are exercised over the German population of these Duchies. Do these statements rest upon mere German representation? Let the House turn to the remarkable Reports from Mr. Ward and Vice Consul Rainals, which have been laid on the table. Mr. Ward is one of our most active and intelligent Consuls, and it is certainly a great proof of fairness that, with the views which he enunciates, he should be retained at Hamburg, for he certainly writes with German sympathies. The date of Mr. Ward's despatch is the 28th of May, 1857, and he mentions an extraordinary fact— namely, that a town in the Duchies contributing £28,125 of taxes to the State is not allowed the convenience of a newspaper, even as a medium for advertisements—

"The town of Kiel has also no newspaper, except an insignificant sheet appearing three times a week, and carefully avoiding politics. The Duchy is, in fact, not allowed to have a press of its own, and is obliged to vent its complaints through the journals of other German States, as opportunities occur. The abolition of the censorship, proclaimed by the Royal ordinance of March, 1848, is merely nominal, for as every paper appearing without special permission, or containing objectionable matter, is immediately seized by the police, no man dares to publish anything without the previous approval of the Government functionaries; while in Denmark, on the contrary, since 1849 the press has enjoyed a very high degree of liberty, which it abuses often enough."

The liberty of the press is thus entirely suppressed in Holstein. Mr. Ward goes on to say—

"The feeling of all classes of the inhabitants of Holstein, from the nobility down to the common people (and I have had many opportunities of observing it), is equally strong against the partial and unjust system of government pursued by the Danes, and it is pretty certain that they will never rest satisfied until they have obtained guarantees for the protection of the German nationality within the monarchy, and for placing it on a footing of at least equality with the Danish race."

That is the position of Holstein. What takes place in Schleswig, which is the great bone of contention—Schleswig, which the Danes undertook should never be incorporated with Denmark and should have the same rights as other nationalities in Denmark? Mr. Ward adds—

"The practical grievances of that Duchy as regards its constitution, finances, administration, and exclusive employment of Danish functionaries, are in all respects the same as those of Holstein, with the addition of that most serious evil, the systematic forcing of the Danish language upon the German portion of the inhabitants."

In another passage he says—

"The Danish police in the Duchy is not only rigorous, but highly aggressive, in its treatment of the German inhabitants; consequently, it is not easy to see how the grievance of the language, or indeed any other grievance, is to be redressed so long as the corporate relations exist which have been forcibly established *de facto* between Schleswig and the kingdom."

And then he says—

"I submit, that what the great Powers have to consider is, not what the Danes are willing to agree to, but what they reasonably ought to agree to, considering the actual legal position of Holstein as a German State, the engagements entered into by the King with both Schleswig and Holstein, and the impossibility of making the people of those Duchies permanently submit to the exclusive rule of the Danish race."

That is a very strong report from Mr. Ward. But then the noble Lord will perhaps say Mr. Ward has German sympa-

thies. Will he say the same of our Consul at Copenhagen? It is evident that Mr. Rainals has Danish sympathies, and I do not complain of him for having them. The extract I am going to quote will be strong enough, I should think, even for the noble Lord—

"Most of the clergymen are Danes, and some of them, by the admission even of their own colleagues, are but imperfectly acquainted with the German language, in which, nevertheless, they have to deliver a sermon every alternate Sunday. With few exceptions, they appear abitrary in small matters, and consider their principal duty to be to force the Danish language upon their congregation, instead of propagating the Christian faith. In consequence they are generally more shunned and feared than respected and loved by their parishioners, and their churches are almost empty when Divine service is held in Danish, and indifferently attended when the service is German. I saw a few clergymen who made exceptions to the general rule. Their humane conduct was fully appreciated, and their churches were better attended, though the cause they were obliged to advocate was not more popular. I have, however, good reason to believe that such men run some risks of losing their appointments for want of 'zeal.'"

He goes on to say—

"That the espionage of the police and gendarmes is great, and that they annoy and irritate the population at large, I had evidence of during my journey, and afterwards personal proof of, so much so that I remained a week less in Angeln than I had intended, because I found I could not pursue my inquiries without fear of injuring others by making them suspected. The petty village officials I invariably discovered were chosen from among the few who are ready to serve as instruments of the Danish party, and the like persons almost exclusively held licences as carpenters, tailors, &c.; whereas, inns and public-houses were kept by opponents, as others did not apply for licences, knowing they would meet with no support from the public. I always sought these 'loyal' villagers, and found them, as a general rule, decorated with the Order of the Dannebrog; but, nevertheless, with few exceptions, they admitted, when alone with me, that forcing the Danish language on the people was unjust, and did not advance the Danish cause, but had rather a contrary effect. They said the clergymen were unpopular, not so much because they are Danes, as because they care less for the religious welfare of their congregations than for the progress of the Danish language and Danish institutions. These men invariably made me promise secrecy, lest they should lose their licence or their appointment."

I need not quote further, for I think I have shown conclusively from these Reports of Consul Ward and Consul Rainals that the Government of Denmark has been in the highest degree arbitrary and unconstitutional towards the people of these Duchies. [An hon. MEMBER: Mr. Rainals is a Vice Consul.] Well, I suppose he is not the worse for that. I believe he is a Dane also, but, Dane as he is, he cannot withstand the force of public conviction as to the arbitrary conduct of the Danish Government. You may say, "That was in 1861;" but what is the Report of Mr. Grosvenor, dated January 14, 1864— what are his accounts? I believe he is not a person who can be complained of as having German; sympathies; and in inclosure 713, sent by Sir Alexander Buchanan from Berlin, he says, after describing the unanimity of the townspeople in favour of the Duke of Augustenburg—

"Although the question may be settled at present, by the superior force of the great Powers, and Schleswig and Holstein be made to continue under the rule of Denmark, no satisfactory solution of the question will ever be obtained by this means, and the people of Schleswig, as well as those of Holstein, will never cease to endeavour to bring matters to a crisis, until they are freed entirely from the yoke of Denmark."

I will not go further with this diplomatic evidence, for we have it confirmed in the special correspondence of *The Times,* dated March 1, 1864, and coming from the "own correspondent" who writes such excellent letters, and gives us such a graphic account of what is going on in the Duchies. He states, he was surprised to find that even in the north of Schleswig the inhabitants were entirely opposed to Danish rule.

Well, Sir, I think that so far I have made out my case. I left the King of Denmark making peace with the Germanic Confederation; and now what has occurred since? On the 18th of November, 1863, Prince Christian of Glucksburg mounted the Danish throne as King Christian IX., and what was the first thing he did? Contrary to the express stipulations given twelve years before, he proclaimed the incorporation of Schleswig with the kingdom of Denmark. Well, Sir, that was a most extraordinary step to take, considering that over and over again Denmark had pledged herself never to incorporate Schleswig with Denmark. Nobody will dispute that the title of Christian IX. to the throne of Denmark is a good one, because it was submitted to the Parliament of Denmark Proper. It is true that the Parliament was dissolved three times before it could be got to consent to the change of succession; but on the third occasion, and after it had undergone some judicious manipulation, I believe it consented. But what possible title has Christian IX. to Schleswig-Holstein? The change in its succession to

those Duchies has never to this day been submitted to those Estates, and his claim to be rightful Sovereign of the Duchies I deny. I deny that he is Duke of Schleswig-Holstein. The Duke of Augustenburg has received very hard measure with the great Powers. I do not undertake to say, with the German professors, that the Duke of Augustenburg is the rightful heir to those Duchies; but a vast number of the people themselves say he is. The noble Lord says the Duke of Augustenburg has received compensation. The first idea of this compensation came from the noble Lord in the remarkable despatch of 1850. What was that compensation? It was nothing but an equivalent for his estates, which were seized by the Danish Government and confiscated at the instigation of the King. I believe the compensation amounted to one-half the value of those estates. But it is not necessary for my argument to show that he is the rightful Duke of Schleswig-Holstein. I only go the length of maintaining that Christian IX. cannot show his title to those Duchies. If the Duke of Augustenburg renounced his claim, he could only do so in the regular order of succession. What would be thought in this House if the Prince of Wales and all the male children of Her Majesty renounced their succession to the throne of Great Britain in favour of the Princess Royal, and if she renounced it in favour of the Prince of Prussia? That is exactly the case before us. Let us apply it to England, and ask could the female descendants of Her Majesty succeed to the throne under such circumstances? If the thing be wrong and illegal in itself, the agreement of five Powers cannot make it otherwise. Whatever may become of this act of secession, I do not think the House of Commons will affix its seal to an endeavour to force an unwelcome Prince upon an unwilling people without consulting the Estates. That is not a course which either a Liberal Government or that sham—that greater sham—the Liberal party, ought to consent to. I myself think that many hon. Gentlemen will be inclined to regret the settlement which was proposed by Earl Russell on the 24th of September, 1863, and for which the noble Earl was very much abused at the time, was not accepted by Denmark. If that settlement had been accepted, war never would have taken place, and Germany would have been perfectly willing to come to an agreement, and a settlement of the question; but

Denmark, with her usual obstinacy, and trading as usual on her weakness and on articles in her Ministerial papers, held out and would not consent. I, for one, grant from the beginning the excellent intentions of the noble Lord at the head of the Government ; but I regret that he has been so incessant in writing despatches, for it must be evident to every one who has waded through this desperate bog of papers in order to find the substratum on which our foreign policy may be supposed to be based, that by incessant meddling and interference this country has lost the ear of Europe ; that we are looked upon by the minor Powers as troublesome meddlers, and that the greater Powers regard us as an incorrigible bore. No one, after reading those papers, can help asking in his own mind whether they were intended to confuse or to instruct. I will not go through them at any length, because I think what has been so well typified in a despatch of the noble Earl the Foreign Secretary himself has really come to pass. I allude to the following passage, which is to be found in volume 4, 542, page 436. You must be particular in volume and page when making your quotations from these papers, or you will be told that you have not read them all ; and if I bore the House as much as the noble Earl bored Germany, it is in consequence of the noble Lord at the head of the Government telling me I had not read the papers. I will give him enough of them. Well, this passage is in a despatch of Earl Russell to Earl Cowley, dated December 28, 1863, and it is such good despatch-writing that I must commend it to the notice of the House—

"There can be no more ungrateful task than the labour of reading long and obscure despatches in which the meaning is concealed under a multitude of words."

I think the House will agree with that. But having read these papers with attention, it appears to me not a little remarkable that in another place Her Majesty's Government take great credit for their pacific policy. Let us see what that claim is founded on. I cannot help thinking that this House has not been treated with courtesy or candour in regard to the management of this question. I have a great respect for the noble Lord ; but I think he has been keeping bad company lately, and has been playing a double game with the House of Commons. In the Queen's Speech of the 4th of February in the present year, hon. Members will remember

Mr. Bernal Osborne

the following passage, which was alluded to by an hon. and gallant Gentleman the other evening :—

"Her Majesty has been unremitting in her endeavours to bring about a peaceful settlement of the differences which have arisen between Germany and Denmark, and to ward off the dangers which might follow from a beginning of warfare in the North of Europe."

What was Earl Russell doing on January 18, 1864 ? He was instructing Earl Cowley to inquire whether France would co-operate with England and Russia. The French Minister, with that remarkable simplicity which characterizes his class, professed not to know what our Ambassador meant by co-operation. Earl Cowley then let the cat out of the bag. He did not want, he said, to anticipate difficulties ; our people never do anticipate difficulties ; but he explained to the French Minister that co-operation with England in affording material assistance to Denmark meant a fleet—that, in fact, it meant war. So, then, while the Government told us on February 4 that they were unremitting in their endeavours to preserve peace, we have it proved that, a fortnight before, they were trying to get up a league with France for the purpose of going to war with Germany—to undertake that greatest of all madnesses—to uphold that balance of power of which we are so fond. They actually proposed to go to war with Germany, and if it had not been for the wise and prudent conduct of the French Government we might have been involved in war at this moment. What, under those circumstances, would have become of the splendid Budget presented to us the other night I really do not know, but I am satisfied that instead of a reduction of 1d. in the income tax we should have had an increase to 10 per cent, and a war likely to last many years. I think some explanation is due to the House of the discrepancy between the representations made to us in February and the overtures addressed to France in January. We are not safe from one moment to another so long as we permit Ministers to pursue so inconsistent and contradictory a course. If ever a nation, like an individual, can say " Save me from my friends," it is that unfortunate State of Denmark. We have been told that Denmark had no reason to rely upon England. I deny that altogether. The obstinacy of Denmark has proceeded from the hopes held out to her by Ministers in this House. Not long ago the Ministerial press in this country teemed with the names of the regiments which were to be sent to the aid of Denmark, and in one paper I actually saw the name of the Commander-in-Chief. Of course, those journals being read in Denmark, the foreign Ministers being more apt to rely upon them than upon the statements of our Government, Denmark naturally calculated upon direct assistance from England. But there was also a declaration made in this House. On July 23, 1863, on the third reading of the Appropriation Bill, when everybody was going out of town, the hon. Member for Horsham (Mr. Seymour Fitzgerald) drew attention to the relations between the Germanic Confederation and Denmark, and asked what was the policy of the Government ? The noble Lord at the head of the Government replied as follows :—

" We are convinced—I am convinced at least that if any violent attempt were made to overthrow or interfere with the independence of Denmark, those who made the attempt would find in the result that it would not be Denmark alone with which they would have to contend."—[3 *Hansard*, clxxii. 1252.]

I think that is pretty strong from the First Minister of the Crown. The noble Lord went on to say—

". . I do not myself anticipate any immediate danger, or, indeed, any of that remote danger which the hon. Gentleman seems to think imperils the peace of Europe, arising out of the Danish and Holstein question."

The noble Lord on that occasion gave a distinct promise to Denmark. If any man were to say to me, " I will stand by you ; you will not contend alone," I should most assuredly conclude that he gave me an express promise. That Denmark did take the words uttered by the noble Lord as a promise may be easily proved. The speech of the noble Lord was made at the end of July. In a despatch dated October 14, 1863, Sir Augustus Paget gives Earl Russell an account of a conversation with M. Hall, the Danish Minister. I shall read one passage—

" M. Hall, while admitting the gravity of existing circumstances, spoke nevertheless with considerable confidence as to the future. He said that Denmark had gone to the utmost lengths to meet the requirements of the Confederation ; that a free and independent position had been given to Holstein by the Patent of the 30th of March, and that the Danish Government had moreover declared that they were ready to negotiate with the Diet if there was anything in that Patent which withheld from the Holstein States aught that they had a right to claim. It was evident, therefore, that what the German Confederation was aiming at was not simply the position of Holstein

in the Monarchy, but had reference to other parts of His Danish Majesty's dominions which were not within the territory or competency of the Diet, and such demands the Danish Government and the Danish people were firmly determined to resist. His Excellency went on to observe, that although a war with Germany would undoubtedly be a misfortune now as at any time, the present moment was perhaps as favourable for Denmark and as unfavourable for Germany as any that would occur ; that it was impossible for Denmark to live under a continual menace of hostilities ; that Sweden was with her ; that the public feeling of England, France, and Europe in general was roused in favour of Denmark at this moment ; that there was a more complete comprehension of the rights of the question now than was, perhaps, to be hoped for at any future time ; in short, that there was a combination of circumstances highly advantageous to Denmark at the present time which might very likely never occur again. If, therefore, his Excellency continued, the question must be settled by an appeal to arms, it had better be so now ; and he felt convinced, he said, that Denmark and Sweden would not stand alone."

It will be seen that the Danish Minister used the very words of the noble Lord. Under all the circumstances it is not surprising, I think, that Denmark went to war thinking she would get direct material assistance from us. But there is more evidence of the effect produced by the statement of the noble Lord at the head of the Government. On February 11, 1864, the Danish Ambassador addressed a despatch to Earl Russell. He applied for the guarantee provided by the Treaty of 1720, which, he said, is still in full vigour ; but I need not follow him further upon that point, because the guarantee in question referred merely to certain portions of the Duchies, and because, too, as the matter has been referred to the Law Officers of the Crown, I am convinced we shall never hear another word about the Treaty of 1720. But M. Bille goes on to say—and it is curious as illustrating the reliance which, up to the last moment, the Danish Government placed on the aid of England—

" But the Danish Government need not look so far back in the past to gain the assurance that the active assistance of England will not fail them under the present circumstances. The Treaty of London, in contempt of which the German Powers are at the present moment invading a Danish country, is especially due to the invariable interest which England takes in the maintenance of the Danish Monarchy. And of all the great Powers, England has always been that which has endeavoured with most perseverance to remove the prospects of a collision. Recently, too, the Cabinet of London gave it to be understood at Frankfort that, in the case of an attack of Schleswig, Denmark would not be left alone in the contest. Germany has thought she could continue her course, and pay no attention to these words, but the Danish Government have not failed to see in them the expression of a determination which the British Government will put in execution with all the energy which characterizes the English nation."

"The invariable interest which England takes in the maintenance of the Danish Monarchy!" Unhappy Denmark! She now knows that England only requires to take an interest in a country to bring it to the verge of ruin. I can find no allusion elsewhere to the despatch to Frankfort mentioned by the Danish Minister. I am afraid the papers have been more than usually curtailed, and that that despatch is one of the elegant extracts to which I have referred. Talk of the mutilation of documents, I would suggest to the noble Lord the Member for Stamford (Lord Robert Cecil) that he should move the dismissal of the Under Secretary for Foreign Affairs for mutilating the despatches. If he were to do so I am sure the Under Secretary would meet with a juster fate than has been doled out to my right hon. Friend the Member for Calne (Mr. Lowe). Let me now show the extraordinary pertinacity with which the noble Lord at the head of the Government, after every other European Power had given up the Treaty of 1852, clung to his youngest child, the fruit of his diplomatic dalliance with Russia. That pertinacity is remarkable, and I might almost say that it is ridiculous. It seems that the people at Frankfort would not call the London Treaty a treaty at all, but only a "protocol," and that they would not call the new Sovereign of Denmark King Christian IX., but the "Protocol Prince." So Earl Russell took up his pen, and in a despatch dated December 22, 1863, directed Sir Alexander Malet, if anybody should have the impertinence in his presence to call the London Treaty a protocol and King Christian a protocol prince, to interrupt the speaker and not allow him to go on until he corrected his language. The same thing goes on with all the petty States of Germany. I fully expect to learn that one after another our Ministers have written to Lord Russell, "In accordance with your instructions I have had the honour to 'interrupt,'" and so on all round. Sir Alexander Malet—poor man —is placed in a most unfortunate position. After a brisk week of "interruptions" he writes on the 26th of December, 1863, to Earl Russell—and this, mind you, is the effect of our interference and the influence

Mr. Bernal Osborne

we get by it. It is only another of those "elegant extracts" to which I have alluded; and I must say I should certainly have liked to see what went before. It begins abruptly in this way—

"It will not be thought surprising in England that Her Majesty's Government exercise scarcely any influence in Germany as regards the dispute with Denmark. All publicists of Universities are engaged in demolishing the validity of the London Treaty."

It seems that on one occasion the noble Lord nearly drove a Foreign Minister mad. This is no joke, mind you. Mr. Gordon writes from Stuttgard on December 27, 1863. It is 557 in the blue-book. I hope the House will look at it for itself, for I never could have believed it unless I had read it myself. Mr. Gordon had been insisting on the treaty, and I am sure the poor baron was much to be pitied, and this is our Minister's account of his success—

"Baron Hugel said he might as well order an apartment in a lunatic asylum as counsel an adherence to the Treaty of 1852."

These are his literal words. Sir Henry Howard at Hanover does not quite drive his Minister mad, but he writes quite as despondingly. Hanover, you know, is one of those States which the noble Lord held fast to this treaty as long as possible. Hanover held to this treaty as long as she could, but at last on the 31st of December Sir Henry Howard writes, No. 596—and here goes their last hope—

"I regret to say that I have reason to apprehend that Count Platen is preparing to beat a retreat from the Treaty of London, 1852."

This is the end of all your despatches, and of your pertinacity in sticking to the treaty. All the German States cry in unison, "None of my child; it is a treaty and not a protocol;" and not one of them will give in their adhesion to that unfortunate instrument which we are endeavouring to patch up. But there is something more. France had been a signatary to this treaty. The noble Lord relies on France. The Earl of Clarendon has been sent to Paris, and we hear that in vulgar phrase he has "squared" it with the Emperor. We shall see. But what did the Emperor call the Treaty of 1852—the proudest treaty of the noble Lord's lifetime? The Emperor, in a letter well known to all the world, characterized it as "an impotent convention condemned by events." But there is another opinion still more curious. A noble Lord who was sent abroad as a plenipotentiary to preserve peace if possible (Lord Wodehouse), condemns altogether your policy in this matter and in regard to Poland, and he says he doubts altogether the expediency of such treaties. I am sure that the House—because an illegal treaty has been signed, taking away the rights of an ancient people—is not going to be led astray to sanction that treaty as the basis of this Conference. Has not this country paid enough already for the old superstition of maintaining the integrity of a kingdom and supporting the balance of power? All these treaties—whatsoever they may be, whether guaranteed or not—must give way to the "inexorable logic of facts." What has the noble Lord seen in the course of his career? He has seen Cracow occupied, Poland partitioned, Savoy and Nice annexed. He has seen the Treaty of Paris of 1815—by which this country solemnly guaranteed "with all her forces,"—that is the expression—that no descendant of Napoleon should ever sit upon the throne of France — treated as so much waste paper. He has lived to send over a plenipotentiary to beg the attendance of that proscribed Emperor at a Conference to settle the affairs of Europe, and he has lived, too, to declare in this House that that dynasty was necessary for the peace of Europe. Do not tell me then that the Treaty of 1852 is more sacred in the eyes of this House than the Treaty of 1815. We have got thus far—Düppel has been taken, numbers of gallant Danes have fallen — the horrors of war are raging worse than ever, and now we are to have the plenipotentiaries round the green table of which the noble Lord talks to settle the affair in Conference. I want to know the object of that Conference, because I think the House will be of opinion, that if the object of this Conference is merely to patch up the Treaty of 1852, it will be a failure. In fact the integrity and, what is better, the independence of Denmark can never be restored on the basis of that treaty. Considering the great mass of papers which the Government has been kind enough to give us, I am surprised that they have held back the replies of the Powers to the invitations to the Conference. I should have thought there was nothing so necessary to the information of this House as these replies of the Powers. The hon. Under Secretary, in a tone which I thought was more pert than complimentary, told the House the other night that it was not the intention of the Government to go on giving any

more papers. It was suggested to me—and it gave me a considerable fright—that it was evident from this that Her Majesty was going to dissolve Parliament. I hope it is not so; but, whatever the House does with the rest of my Motion, I hope that it will insist on that part of it which requires that the answers of the Powers to the invitations to attend the Conference shall be laid on the table.

Sir, I see with some surprise and some regret that the right hon. Gentleman opposite, a distinguished leader on the other side of the House, is going to move the Previous Question. I had hoped, with the strong opinions on this subject which I have heard him express, that his mind was made up entirely on this Danish question. Having put some questions to the Government, I think I am entitled to ask Her Majesty's Opposition, what is their foreign policy in this matter. If their foreign policy be merely, because the Earl of Malmesbury signed that Treaty of 1852, to patch that treaty up again; if they are prepared, like the noble Lord in another place, to make a league with France to enforce that treaty upon the reluctant Duchies, I say that no Government, whether it be taken from this side or the other side of the House, can hope for the confidence of the people which is prepared to plunge this country into a war for that purpose. In the absence of any declaration of policy on the other side of the House, the noble Lord may say in the words of Charles II. to his brother James, "No man will get rid of me to put you in my place." I do hope that hon. Gentlemen on the other side will tell us what their foreign policy will be. I hope they will tell us whether their foreign policy will be one not merely pacific in words, but one of non-intervention, and of refraining from this incessant meddling in affairs in which England has no interest, and from which she has no honour to gain. I have said so much, speaking in favour neither of Denmark nor Germany. We have heard much of sympathy with the Danes, and we have heard pleas for Germany. I have endeavoured to-night to speak entirely from an English point of view, and to represent to this country that England has no interest in maintaining what is called the balance of power in the North of Europe, nor in interfering with the affairs of another State. However content the taxpayers of this country may be to bear the burdens which have been entailed upon them by foreign statesmen and by old interferences in foreign affairs, I am well assured that they are not prepared at this time of day to have any new burdens cast upon them for the support of a worn-out diplomacy and an unjust attempt to meddle with the affairs of the North of Europe.

Motion made, and Question proposed,

"That it is both unjust and inexpedient to insist on the provisions of the Treaty of London, 1852, so far as they relate to the order of succession in the Duchies of Schleswig and Holstein, as a basis for the settlement of the Dano-German dispute."—(*Mr. Osborne.*)

MR. PEACOCKE said, he rose for the purpose of moving an Amendment slightly altered from the form in which it stood on the paper. Seeing that there were two other Amendments on the paper, the House was likely to have full opportunity of discussing the Question, he regretted he could not adhere to the course of the right hon. Gentleman who was about to move the Previous Question. If that motion was made and agreed to, the country would be under the impression that hon. Gentlemen on the Conservative side of the House had no policy, and that the House itself had no opinions on the question. He should like to know, whether the Amendment of the right hon. Member for Buckinghamshire had the assent of the gallant General the Member for Huntingdon, who some nights back promised the House and the country a speedy opportunity of discussing the matter. The "Previous Question" was an efficient mode of stifling discussion. Her Majesty's Government would have such a Motion with pleasure, as it would amount to a vote of confidence in the Government in a modified and diluted form. If they said they would not express any opinion as to what policy the Government pursued, it proved that they had no inconsiderable confidence in those who administered affairs; and he had no doubt that that was the spirit in which the Government would receive the proposition. He thought the House was called upon to express an opinion as to what policy ought to be pursued in the approaching Conferences; and he intended, therefore, to move, in order to give the House an opportunity of expressing an opinion upon it, the following Amendment—

"That in the opinion of this House it is the duty of Her Majesty's Government, at the approaching Conferences, while calling upon Denmark to fulfil the promises which she made to the two great German Powers in 1851-2, to maintain the provisions of the Treaty of London of 1852, so

Mr. Bernal Osborne

that the various States composing the Danish Monarchy may remain united under the same Sovereign."

The best defence of the Treaty of 1852 was to be found by a consideration of the difficulties which existed on the question as to who should succeed to the States of Denmark, supposing that monarchy to be broken up. As regarded the kingdom proper, the person who had the best claim to the throne was Prince Frederick of Hesse. That Prince gave up his rights in favour of his eldest sister, who, in turn, gave up hers in favour of her second sister; and the present King only sat in right of his wife. As to Schleswig there was a disputed succession. The Danes contended that it went with the kingdom; and the Holsteiners that it went with Holstein. Russia also claimed a portion of Schleswig. With respect to Holstein, Russia had the best claim to one portion, and a right to the rest was asserted by other claimants. Therefore, independently of the Treaty of 1852, what was the state of that question? Why, they had a disputed succession to Schleswig and to Holstein; and he held that the great Powers were perfectly justified in stepping in to remove such a fertile source of disorder and misunderstanding. Previous to 1848 the most intimate connection prevailed between Schleswig and Holstein. There was an administrative and judicial union between them, and they were governed by a Lord Lieutenant resident at Schleswig. When King Christian VIII. died, he was succeeded by Frederick VII., who, on ascending the throne in 1848, in accordance with the ideas of that time, gave a Constitution to the whole kingdom. That Constitution created a rebellion in Holstein. The people of Holstein invoked the aid of the Germans, and a Prussian army went to the assistance of the Schleswig-Holsteiners. After various successes Jutland was invaded, and so strongly was that invasion opposed by the great Powers, and notably by Russia, that Prussia was constrained to agree to the Treaty of Berlin. The terms of that treaty were, first, the *status quo ante bellum*, and secondly, that Denmark should apply to the Confederation for the pacification of Holstein. In consequence of that agreement an Austrian army entered Holstein, and then came the celebrated promises of 1851-2. By those promises Germany on her side gave up the administrative and judicial union between Schleswig and Holstein, and Denmark, on the other hand, undertook to bring forward no measure to incorporate, or tending to incorporate, Schleswig and Holstein. Disputes went on, and at last, by his celebrated despatch of September, 1862, Earl Russell attempted to settle the question. If the terms of that despatch had been accepted by Denmark in accordance with the promise of 1851-2, there would have been an end of that question. The proposal was agreed to by Germany, but rejected by the Eider-Dane party. So early as the spring of 1863, M. Hall declared that the maintenance of the common Constitution for the kingdom and for Schleswig was a question of life and death for Denmark. Instead of making any attempt to carry out the promises of 1851-2, King Frederick issued the patent of March, and Germany threatened Federal execution. Then came the Constitution of November, which Sir Augustus Paget condemned in the strongest manner. The execution was declared, Federal troops entered Holstein, and the Prince of Augustenburg was proclaimed. Austria and Prussia determined to take the matter out of the hands of the Diet, sent an army to occupy Schleswig, and summoned the Government of Denmark to suspend the November Constitution in forty-eight hours, and it was only after that period expired that Denmark evinced a disposition to yield. Count Rechberg said it was for the interest of Denmark that she should have to deal with Austria and Prussia and not with the Bund ; he said that if he allowed a Parliament to be assembled under the November Constitution to repeal that Constitution, he would be virtually acknowledging its validity, against which he protested. Great objections were urged against Austria and Prussia for not arresting the march of these armies, but Count Rechberg went on to ask who could guarantee that the Parliament of Copenhagen when called together would withdraw the November Constitution; and when he asked Lord Bloomfield whether England would guarantee it, that noble Lord observed the most discreet silence. It was a remarkable fact that the Parliament which was to have revoked the Constitution of November called on the King, in the strongest language, as its first act, not to weaken in any way the tie between Schleswig and the Kingdom. Up to the 1st of January last, Austria and Prussia were perpetually offering to go into Conferences and accept mediation; but after that day, when the Constitution of November came into operation, they said that they would no longer go into a Conference acknowledging the Treaty of 1852, while Denmark would not acknowledge her promises of 1851-2. Austria and Prussia then advanced beyond the Eider. The House had a right to complain of the conflicting tone of the English despatches. In one despatch Earl Russell disclaimed the responsibility of advising Denmark to resist; in another Lord Wodehouse told M. Hall that the English Cabinet would not take on themselves the responsibility of the determination at which the Danish Government might arrive. Again, Earl Russell said that Denmark might be aided; and Sir A. Paget told M. Hall that Denmark would, at all events, have a better chance of securing the assistance of the Powers by retiring beyond the limits of the Confederation. It was not surprising then that Bishop Monrad expressed to our Minister at Copenhagen his hopes that at least the English Government would abstain from urging negotiations or interfering with the policy which the Danish Government was then determined to pursue. Again, he found Earl Russell praising the great Powers for interfering. How, then, could he make war on them for the course they had taken ? The policy of Earl Russell was about to be crowned with a partial success. He presumed that noble Lord had two objects in view. The first was the pacification of Europe, and the second that these Conferences might last as long as the present Session. The latter result was a most likely one, but as to the former, he did not feel the same confidence. In the last volume of the despatches, Denmark positively declared she would never yield the incorporation of Schleswig with the kingdom until she was utterly exhausted. Now what was the position of the various Powers at the approaching Conference ? We find there England, Austria, and Russia sincerely desirous to maintain the integrity of Denmark ; next we had Prussia, the depth of whose policy nobody had fathomed; again we had France, avowing her adherence to the principle of nationalities; lastly we had Sweden, who alone, of all the Powers, had given the perfidious counsel, not to repeal the constitution of November, because she saw perfectly well that if Schleswig and Holstein gravitated towards Germany, Jutland and the Islands would gravitate towards Sweden; but he trusted that the Danish Government would see through the transparent hypocrisy of such perfidious counsels. What chance, then, was there of their arriving at peace with such conflicting elements? And if the principle of nationality was to be applied to Schleswig-Holstein, why should it not be applied elsewhere? If applied to Ireland, for instance, was it likely the Union would be maintained? He hoped the voice of England, in the approaching Conferences, would be raised strongly against the doctrine of nationalities. Using the language of peace and conciliation, and standing midway between conflicting interests, England, whilst urging on the one people that treaties must be respected as the landmarks of international policy, should equally impress upon the other that solemn promises and binding engagements must not be recklessly broken or lightly cast aside, but that they must be honourably observed and righteously fulfilled. He begged to move his Amendment.

Amendment proposed,

To leave out from the word "That" to the end of the Question, in order to add the words "in the opinion of this House, it is the duty of Her Majesty's Government at the approaching Conferences, whilst calling upon Denmark to fulfil the promises which she made to the two great German Powers in 1851-52, to maintain the provisions of the Treaty of London of 1852, so that the various States comprising the Danish Monarchy may remain united under the same Sovereign,"—(*Mr. Peacocke,*)

—instead thereof.

Question proposed "That the words proposed to be left out stand part of the Question."

MR. A. F. EGERTON said, he should support the Amendment, because he thought it a very proper one. The hon. Member for Liskeard (Mr. Osborne) appeared to have derived his arguments from German sources. Certainly he had taken entirely the German view of the subject. But the House should remember that there was the Danish view of the question, in support of which arguments of great weight might be adduced. The Amendment referred both to the course to be taken in the future and to that which had been taken by past diplomacy. So far as the policy of the noble Earl at the head of the Foreign Office was peace he entirely concurred with the object, and he did not think that any one who considered the subject would be of opinion that at any period of the dispute there had been a sufficient *casus belli* to justify this country entering

Mr. Peacocke

into the strife. The fault he found with the policy of the noble Lord was precisely the same as that found by the hon. Member for Liskeard. His desire for peace was very often doubtful in its expression. The Government never intended to go to war, but they seemed to wish to create an impression on the Continent that, under certain circumstances, England would go to war; taking very good care never to say what those circumstances were likely to be. In fact, the noble Lord used as strong language as he possibly could, without giving any settled clue to his intentions; and the German Powers might very well quote Shakespeare, and say of the noble Lord that he was letting "I dare not wait upon I would." Throughout the struggle no cause had arisen why we should mix ourselves up in the war. The Federal execution was a perfectly legal proceeding as far as Germany was concerned. There was no *casus belli* there. The Federal execution, however, was somewhat superseded by the Austrian and Prussian invasion. That course of invasion no Englishman approved of. Still they had a colourable right to invade Schleswig, their object being to make something more than a protest against what they conceived to be the wrongs done by Denmark to the Duchies. These wrongs were very considerable, and were brought to a point by the promulgation of the Constitution of November, 1863. It was true that the right of Austria and Prussia to invade Denmark was very harshly exercised. No time was given for the withdrawal of the constitution, although the Danes offered to do so. Still Austria and Prussia were in some respects the mandatories of the Diet, and were carrying out the wishes of the German people. There was no *casus belli* there. With respect to the course to be taken in future, he conceived the policy of the Government to be indicated in an extract he would venture to read from one of the despatches of Earl Russell to Sir Augustus Paget, in which he said—

"It will be for the neutral Powers to support the engagements of 1851-2 with the modifications adapted to present circumstances, and suggest such an organization of the monarchy as may lead to the permanence of the power and the strength of Denmark as an independent State.

If that was the policy to be pursued he entirely concurred in it. The hon. Member for Liskeard appeared to admit the doctrine of nationalities. That was a dangerous doctrine. How would it do to apply it to Europe ? France had a large German population ; England had a large Celtic population ; Austria had eight or ten different nationalities. It was, therefore, to be considered how far the doctrine should be applied to Schleswig-Holstein. If the election were carried on in Schleswig and Holstein there could be no doubt that the Duke of Augustenburg would be chosen. He, however, would deprecate such a course, because it would be conferring upon the Duchies a right to select their own Sovereign, which would be a virtual exclusion of Denmark from the Conference. It ought to be the English policy to keep a strong power in the Baltic in order to preserve the balance of Power. Denmark was the oldest Monarchy in Europe, and it would ill become them to adopt any course which would ·lead to its dismemberment. He hoped that the representatives of England in the Conference would do all in their power to retain the present boundaries and the independence of Denmark.

Mr. GRANT DUFF said, it seemed to him that as far as England was concerned, the whole pith and marrow of the controversy lay in the question whether the *casus fœderis* under the Treaty of London had or had not arisen. The first thing to consider was what were the stipulations of the treaty as affecting the signataries. He contended that they were to recognize the rights of succession of Prince Christian of Glucksburg to the whole of the Danish monarchy when that succession was created. The signataries had no power to create such rights in any part of the Danish monarchy. In order that these might be created, it was necessary that the regular constitutional machinery, which existed in various parts of that composite body called Denmark, should be put in motion. The late King, Frederick VII., understood that, and soon after the conclusion of the treaty he set to work to create a right of succession for Prince Christian of Glucksburg to Denmark Proper—that is, Jutland and the Islands. After some trouble, he carried his point, and, immediately after the breath was out of his body, it was the duty of the Powers which signed the Treaty of London to recognize Prince Christian's claim to the monarchy of Denmark Proper. Unfortunately, great difficulty arose in carrying out a similar policy with the two Duchies, and still more unfortunately death surprised Frederick VII. before he had been able to establish the right of Prince

Christian to succeed to the Duchies. It was no doubt painful to the noble Lord, whose scheme it was, and also to the noble Lord who signed the treaty, to find that their endeavours to settle this troublesome question had been in vain—*hinc illæ lacrymæ;* but those who agree with himself and the hon. Member for Liskeard could not doubt that the treaty had been a complete and ignominious failure. Even were that proposition doubtful, every one must admit that the Treaty of London was not a treaty of guarantee, and therefore we were not bound to assert its validity by force of arms. Those who had nothing to do with framing it were clearly at perfect liberty to declare that it was an impolitic treaty. That treaty marked the culminating point of the European reaction and also the culminating point of the influence of the Emperor Nicholas in Europe. If that work of English diplomatists had been as successful as they wished, England would have been committed to the task of imposing a monarch upon an unwilling people. He did not deny that the Treaty of London expressed on its face the good will of the great Powers who signed it to maintain the integrity of the Danish monarchy. He did not object to that integrity, but he could not see why its maintenance was of such extreme importance to this country. The only question which the House had to consider was, whether it would encourage the Government to go into the Conference merely in order to patch up the treaty—to gain a temporary diplomatic triumph, it might be, but entailing on Europe an inheritance of a third Schleswig-Holstein war ; or should the House encourage the Government to seek to obtain in the Conference what he considered to be the only reasonable and possible solution of the question—namely, to leave it in some form or other to the population of Schleswig and Holstein to decide who should be their ruler ? That might be done either by consulting the States of the respective Duchies, as he should prefer ; or by consulting the whole population, as France was supposed to desire should be done. There was no doubt that at last the question did resolve itself into a question of nationalities. With the cry of nationality he had but an imperfect sympathy, but if any people had a right to go mad upon that subject, surely it must be the inhabitants of the southern part of the Danish peninsula, among whom had been born the illustrious Niebuhr, who was the first man of any eminence who gave currency to the doctrine of nationality.

LORD ROBERT MONTAGU was not disposed to enter upon the ancient history of the question, but would confine himself to the blue-books which were before the House. There was one element of the Question which must be considered before a proper conclusion could be arrived at, and that element was the character of those persons who had been brought upon the scene—the *dramatis personæ*—as represented in the blue-books. In the first place, there was M. Hall, who was described as "inflexible," whose "determination was not to be shaken," who "pertinaciously resisted every friendly suggestion," who was "very little disposed to make concessions;" and yet, if some small concessions had at first been made, the present state of things would not have arisen; whenever a concession had been wrung from him, it came too late, and was accompanied by a taunt which spoiled its effect. Then there was the Eider-Dane party, which wished to separate Schleswig from Holstein and to incorporate Schleswig; and finally, to establish a Scandinavian kingdom, consisting of Sweden, Norway, and Denmark. Then came the German populations, who were in such a state of wild frenzy, that Austria and Prussia were hardly able to stem the torrent, while the smaller governments were obliged to yield to the pressure of the people. On June 20, 1861, Earl Russell wrote—

"The public mind of Germany has been roused and inflamed by a view of this question of the German Duchies, going far beyond the claims of the Diet of Frankfort. That view contemplates the re-annexation of Schleswig to Holstein, and the incorporation of Schleswig, as well as Holstein, in German territory. The parties who favour this view are closely connected with the 'active party in Europe.' . . . That active party is eager to promote changes in Germany, which . . . can only be brought about by civil war and revolution."

And Sir H. Howard wrote on December 21, 1863—

"There can be little doubt that the Schleswig-Holstein agitation was a revolutionary movement, got up by the party who are desirous of subverting the existing order of things."

The hon. Member for Liskeard had said that the stipulations upon which the Duchies had been given back by Austria and Prussia to Denmark after the events of 1848 were broken. But the hon. Member had forgotten that Austria and Prussia at that time desired that the King of Denmark should

Mr. Grant Duff

"rule as an absolute monarch;" and in that case what right had they to say that the question of the succession should be put to the vote? The facts of the case were as follows. In the eventful year of 1848, the Duchies desired annexation to Germany, and rose in rebellion for that end. Austria and Prussia then invaded that territory, nominally in the interest of the Duchies; when they had quelled the excitement, they handed them back to Denmark. But certain conditions were imposed on each party. Austria and Prussia stipulated that the King of Denmark should govern as an absolute monarch, and that "a concentrated direction of affairs was indispensable." The King of Denmark stipulated that Austria and Prussia should support his plans for the change of succession, and promised never to incorporate Schleswig. So early as the year 1851, the Prince of Glücksburg was designated as the future king, and the Duke of Augustenburg was deprived of his hereditary vote; and the German Diet approved of the King's Proclamation to that effect. He would now proceed to narrate the events which had recently occurred. The decree of the 30th of March, 1863, gave to the Holsteiners, as Sir A. Paget wrote, all that they could desire, if their only object was their legitimate interests and their real welfare. It, however, undoubtedly tended to the incorporation of Schleswig; it was part of the Eider-Danish policy. The present King protested against it. Bluhme, formerly minister for foreign affairs in Copenhagen, openly asserted that it broke "the engagement not to incorporate Schleswig." Sir A. Paget corroborated this opinion, and said, moreover, that M. Hall, by this act, threw down a gauntlet to Austria and Prussia, and precipitated the dreaded crisis of affairs. The four Powers, England, France, Russia, and Sweden, in 1861, had proposed this as a "provisional" arrangement; but M. Hall had then repudiated it, but promulgated it now when its effect could only be baneful. Then followed a great excitement throughout Germany. Meetings were held in all the great towns, and resolutions were passed at each town, so identical in their terms that they were evidently the production of the same hand. The objects aimed at in those resolutions were the abolition of the Treaty of 1852, and the repudiation of the engagements of 1851-2, so that the revolutionary status of 1848 might be brought back again ; and the central German Parliament of the Revolutionary Constitution again established. It was also desired to annex Schleswig and Holstein to Germany under Prince Frederick of Augustenburg. The active party in this affair was the National Verein ; the meetings were attended by the leaders of the Democratic party, who sought to bring about their object by civil war and revolution. In order to put an end to this excitement England, France Russia, and Sweden advised M. Hall that no opposition should be offered to the Federal Execution in Holstein, and that the decree of the 30th of March, 1863, should be withdrawn. M. Hall wrote that this " might easily be done ; but that Germany would not be satisfied." On this ground he refused to follow the advice, and was " inflexible" in his determination. At length, however, he was persuaded, with great difficulty, to make the arrangement provisional. M. de Bismark replied that this concession had come too late, and that Germany would not be satisfied because the decree had been " received with a storm of disapprobation in Germany." Bismark, however, allowed himself to be persuaded, and was about to yield, when a telegram arrived from Copenhagen, announcing that " Denmark would regard the execution in Holstein as an act of war." And our Minister at Berlin wrote home that " there was an end of all hopes of conciliation." In October, Austria and Prussia desired the mediation of England, and the German Diet promised to accept it. But M. Hall refused to propose mediation, and said that he " did not desire it." He was at length, however, brought to agree to it ; but he would not propose it, nor seem, in any way, to wish it. On the 14th of November, however, he made " another false move." The announcement by M. Hall, that the obnoxious Constitution of March, 1863, should come into force on the 1st of January, ended the whole of the negotiation for mediation. It " made mediation a mockery," as our Minister wrote. The next day came the death of the late King ; and on the 18th of November, Lord Bloomfield wrote to Earl Russell that Count Rechberg had stated that the event might have a favourable effect on the Holstein affair, as His Majesty's successor had always been desirous for the adoption of conciliatory measures ; but his Excellency " seemed apprehensive lest the ultra-Danish party at Copenhagen should

force the new King to abandon the principles which he had heretofore expressed." Then Mr. Jerningham wrote from Sweden that King Christian would have been obliged to leave Denmark if he had declined to sign the Constitution ; and consequently he was forced to take that step for fear of losing his throne. Mr. Ward wrote that the state of things in Copenhagen bore a strong resemblance to the condition of affairs in 1848, when the late King had been forced by a tumultuous assembly of people to identify himself with the party of Eider - Danes. After this the German Diet refused to allow the representative of Denmark to sit in that body, either for Schleswig or Holstein or Lauenburg. The Diet, unfortunately, was for forcing on an Execution, not as a mere legal act, but in the interest of the Prince of Augustenburg, so that the new King's authority might not be established. Count Manderström wrote that it was

" Not a question of the Patent now, but of separating Schleswig and Holstein for the benefit of the Prince of Augustenburg."

Then M. Hall appears on the scene again, and withdraws the decree of March, 1863, after first raising a frivolous question of etiquette. But he was told it was too late, because the question had gone by that; and besides, as the Constitution had been adopted, the Patent was nothing. Sir A. Paget thus related M. Hall's words—

" He (M. Hall) must confess it appeared that it would be now considered, by Germany, quite illusory to do so (to withdraw the Patent) ; because, since the passing of the Constitution, the Patent had become of very little importance."

It appeared from the despatches that " extraordinary means of agitation" were resorted to in Germany ; and professors of ultra-democratic opinions were foremost to uphold the rights of legitimacy in favour of the Prince of Augustenburg, whilst those of the most reactionary tendencies united with them in the same objects. He felt certain that whenever there was a combination between the tory and ultra-radical parties there must always be a loss of principle on both sides. The meetings held throughout all parts of Germany were of the most excited and democratic character. Incendiary articles were published in the newspapers calling on the people to revolt. Lord A. Loftus said the danger of revolution was imminent, and that the German Governments appeared powerless and unable to resist the popular will. They felt themselves placed, as it were, between two fires. On the one side was the danger of war abroad, and on the other that of revolution at home. Those assertions were borne out by the despatches of Lord Wodehouse and Count Rechberg. Lord Wodehouse wrote, December 12, 1863—

"M. de Bismark said, that the popular feeling throughout Germany was so violently excited . . . and the feeling in most of the minor States was so strong on the Schleswig-Holstein question, that the thrones of the Sovereigns of those States would be in danger if they attempted to oppose the wishes of the people."

And

"Count Rechberg said, he considered the smaller States to be acting under the direction of the National Verein, and to be rapidly passing into a state of democratic revolution."

The Diet of Germany and the smaller States did not desire peace ; they sought rather to provoke such a collision as would bring about a European war, in the hope of ultimately effecting the unity of Germany. With that view the Federal forces marched through Holstein with bands playing revolutionary tunes, and committed acts of revolution wherever they came. Austria and Prussia, on the other hand, endeavoured to establish a simple Federal Execution without the recognition of the claims of Prince Frederick of Augustenburg. In adopting that course the two great German Powers professed to be acting in the cause of peace, and endeavouring to check revolutionary tendencies and democratic influences. This was evident from the despatches of M. Bismark and Sir A. Buchanan. At all events, Austria and Prussia were then of opinion that the danger of war abroad was much preferable to that of revolution at home. Sir A. Buchanan wrote, November 28, 1863—

"To acknowledge the popular voice by adopting some half measure, seems (to the Prussian Government) to be the only safe course which is open to the Government ; and they maintain that an Execution in Holstein . . . would prevent any revolutionary movements in the Duchy. . . The danger of war abroad is preferable to the certainty of revolution at home."

Lord Bloomfield wrote, December 24—

"Count Rechberg said, one of the most important objects of Austria was to prevent revolution. . . . Both Governments feel intense alarm at the progress which the spirit of democratic revolution is making.

Prince Gortschakoff also held that this Execution would "check the designs of the revolutionary party." Austria and Prussia were ultimately successful in carrying a vote through the Diet of Frankfort in favour of simple execution, without the recognition of the claims of

Lord Robert Montagu

Prince Frederick of Augustenburg. The people of Germany became at once incensed against them, and did all they could to bring about a union of the smaller Governments, with a view of putting a pressure upon Austria and Prussia. Lord A. Loftus, in his despatch of January 26, 1864, stated that—

"The most violent language was held against the two great German Powers. The policy of Austria and Prussia was characterized as ' treason, to Germany. . . . No chance was now left to the minor German States, but that of accepting the thraldom of the two German Powers, or of civil war."

On February 16, he wrote that the Central Commission sitting in Frankfort

"Assumes a more and more authoritative tone, . . . and are now doing their best to excite to armed resistance against Austria and Prussia."

On February 15, Sir A. Malet wrote that there was nearly being a collision between the Prussians and the troops, under the Saxon General Hake. Things had now got to a very bad pitch. The minor States threatened revolutionary violence against the two German Powers. What did those two Governments do ? They said they did not care for the Diet—that it was nothing but a large assurance company—as bad as those described the other day by the Chancellor of the Exchequer ; that they did not mind the decrees of the Diet ; for that Federal decrees were either dilatory or unconstitutional ; and that they were determined to take the matter into their own hands. They thereupon marched their troops into Schleswig. The King of Denmark about this time desired to call together the Rigsraad, in order to abolish the obnoxious Constitution. M. Hall had taken care to dissolve the chamber that had existed, in order to increase the difficulty of repealing the Constitution. It was, therefore, necessary to call together a new Rigsraad, by virtue of that very law which the King intended to abolish by their means. M. Hall hereupon resigned. The day before he resigned Lord Wodehouse wrote a despatch from Copenhagen, dated December 25, in which he thus recorded M. Hall's words—

"The German Powers were, he knew, persuaded that it was useless to negotiate with any ministry of which he (M. Hall) was the head."

And Lord Bloomfield wrote, December 24, from Vienna—

"Count Rechberg said, that as long as M. Hall was at the head of the Danish Government, the chances of an arrangement as to Schleswig would be next to impossible."

Subsequently the troops of the two German Powers marched into Schleswig in order to anticipate the Federal forces. Lord Napier in a despatch from Russia, dated January 20, 1864, said—

"M. de Bismark has distinctly stated that the occupation of Schleswig by the forces of Austria and Prussia, is undertaken with a view to the maintenance of the Treaty of 1852, for the integrity of the Danish Monarchy."

And Lord Bloomfield wrote, January 28—

"The march of this large force could not be stopped. . . If they did halt on the Eider, the excitement produced thereby in Germany would become uncontrollable, and might lead to civil war."

This view was corroborated by Sir Alexander Malet, who wrote, February 2, from Frankfort—

"The agitation has been adroitly seized upon by the leaders of the National Verein and democratic party to create an organization, which will hereafter be used for other purposes, which are probably preparing more serious embarrassments for the Government of the Confederation than any which they have yet had to encounter since the year 1848."

It was in order to foil this attempt that Austria entered Schleswig. After the advance into Schleswig, Sir Alexander Malet wrote that Germany saw the unopposed advance of Austria and Prussia into Schleswig with "shame and bitterness," and appeals to the people to rise and constrain their Governments. This step, on the part of Austria and Prussia, raised the worst feelings in the minor States of Germany. That was clear from the fact stated by Sir Alexander Malet, that a very large meeting had been held at Hamburg, at which the National Verein had boldly advised a general rising of the people in order to overturn the thrones of their rulers. Two thousand agents of the National Verein were immediately sent into Schleswig and Holstein for the purpose of advocating the claims of the Prince Frederick of Augustenburg, after which a "system of terrorism prevailed." On the 19th of February Prussia entered Jutland, and matters became more and more complicated. Now, up to that time, if Earl Russell had interfered against Prussia and Austria, it was obvious that he would have interfered against the cause of order and Government, and in favour of anarchy and revolution. It was therefore impossible up to that stage for England to have gone to war on behalf of the Danes. For if his interference had been in favour of Denmark, the result would have been the weakening of the influence of Austria and Prussia; an influence which at that time was being exercised for the purpose of calming the revolutionary feeling which was so rife throughout Germany. A reaction, however, then took place. Lord A. Loftus stated that—

"The fear of the revolutionary party is becoming every day greater, and . . . is weakening the effervescence in favour of the Schleswig-Holstein cause. . . . The German Governments are beginning to pause and reflect on the dangers of a schism in Germany, which may eventually lead to the triumph of the democratic party, and the destruction of the minor Sovereignties."

Again, he wrote on March 1—

"A fear of the revolutionary party has lately produced a desire for a better understanding between the minor States of Germany and the two Great German Powers."

The minor States of Germany thought it prudent to pause in their onward movement in presence of the danger which threatened them—a danger which might lead to the destruction of the minor Sovereignties. Towards the end of March, Lord Russell wrote to say that it had been agreed to by all the great Powers that they should not go to war, inasmuch as they believed that such a step, instead of tending to produce peace, would only increase the embroilment in Europe. The chief difficulty at that time rested with Denmark, on account of the excitement caused at Copenhagen by the retreat from the Dannewerk. The Danish people had become greatly irritated at the belief that their country had been betrayed. The invectives uttered against His Majesty were loud and numerous. The people assembled in large crowds before the Royal palace and cried, "Death to the King!" and remained there "yelling and shouting the most seditious cries." That was the reason why the King of Denmark could not give a definite answer to Her Majesty's Government's invitation to join the Conference. This whole question was, in fact, an instance of the blindness of agitation. For it was not to be supposed, on the one hand, that Prussia would otherwise have consented to see her Constitution torn up, and allow the liberties of the people to be sacrificed, in order to relieve the Danish Duchies from a fictitious tyranny, and to enforce a hypothetical promise. And, on the other hand, there was the same want of rule in Denmark; the Danes also were swayed by an angry democratic faction; so that they refused good counsel through passion, and then made tardy concessions through weakness. No doubt a word from France might have concluded the strife. A breath from her would have fanned the flames of revolution; the word "Rhine" would have caused the sword to drop from Prussia's hand; a whisper of Venetia would have paralyzed the arm of Austria. The Emperor of France was the arbiter of the destinies of Europe. This was an expensive luxury; but not a glorious one, unless war was more glorious than peace. But there was as little doubt, also, that France had as difficult a card to play as Germany; for her finances were in a perilous condition; and she, too, was in imminent danger of the infection of revolution. As to Earl Russell, it seemed to him (Lord R. Montagu) that he could not have acted otherwise than he had done. If the noble Lord were to be blamed at all, he must be blamed for his over industry in the interests of peace. A charge might be brought against the Foreign Minister for his niggling in the matter, instead of taking a more decided course. For he had drilled foreign countries into the belief that they could despise our threats, and disregard our remonstrances. He seemed to have had no settled purpose; but whenever a suggestion had been made, he hastened to propose it; when a counter-proposition was offered, he as readily urged that; and when an objection was raised, he yielded at once. The noble Earl seemed to him (Lord R. Montagu) to resemble a good-natured female, who was trying to separate two angry combatants before a public-house. From her you hear repeated objurgations and reiterated supplications; from him you got a perplexing industry of voluminous despatches. He was devoting all his efforts to promote peace—

"Striving against his quiet all he can
To gain the title of a busy man;
And what is that, but one whose restless mind
Is made to tire himself and all mankind."

MR. CAVENDISH BENTINCK said, that after the able, comprehensive, and convincing speech of the hon. Member for Liskeard, he should not think it necessary to trouble the House with many details. He wished, however, to address a few words to Her Majesty's Government, with a view, if possible, of extracting from them a declaration of the principles upon which they acted when intervening in the affairs of foreign countries. He was desirous of asking them for some explanation of the strange inconsistency which was the characteristic of their foreign policy. There could be no doubt that in the month of

January last the Foreign Secretary wished to concert a league against the German States generally. The noble Earl had applied to France and Russia to assist him, and but for the good sense of the rulers of those empires he might have carried his purpose into effect. He ventured to say that if Germany had conducted herself selfishly or unfairly towards England, it might be retorted that England had conducted herself selfishly towards Germany. Now, what was the *casus belli* against Germany? Simply the alleged infraction of the Treaty of 1852. It appeared to him (Mr. Cavendish Bentinck) rather hard for the noble Earl, or any of his political friends, to object to the infraction of that treaty by Germany, for it was the opinion of many statesmen upon the Continent—an opinion, he must say, justified by circumstances—that the noble Lord and his Colleagues had done more in the last few years to destroy faith in treaties than any other statesmen who had governed in Europe during modern times. He would not go so far back as 1830, and allude to the violations of treaties which were then sanctioned, but would confine himself to what had taken place in the last three or four years, and more especially to two remarkable instances. Lord Russell charged the two great German Governments with violating the Treaty of 1852, and yet he was the Minister that allowed the Treaties of 1815 to be violated with impunity. Now, he (Mr. Cavendish Bentinck) would ask any jurist, or other person conversant with International Law, to compare those treaties together, and to say which was the most binding upon modern statesmen. He would venture to say that the Treaties of 1815 were infinitely more binding than that of 1852. His hon. Friend the Member for Liskeard had given many cogent reasons for the non-observance of this last treaty by the German Powers. Amongst others, it should be recollected that it wanted the respective assents of the German Diet, of the Estates, and of the Holstein Agnates. Those reasons might be considered valid or invalid, but he would say they, at all events, raised a question which was open to argument and discussion. It had been urged that the Treaties of 1815 were unfair, unjust, and inexpedient. But no jurist or person acquainted with the first principles of International Law would say that they were not valid. Remembering, however, how they had been violated, with

Lord Robert Montagu

the Foreign Secretary's assent, it was remarkable, under these circumstances, that he should insist on the strict fulfilment of the Treaty of 1852. But when the noble Earl inveighed so bitterly against the infraction of 1852, he (Mr. Cavendish Bentinck) would remind him of one or two cases that appeared to him to involve similar principles. The seizure of the Papal States in 1860 was one case. The Pope might not be considered a very popular Sovereign. Many persons in this country, even Members of that House, believed that to do the Pope a wrong was one of the highest services they could render. Nevertheless, every honourable-minded Englishman must maintain this principle—that the Pope had a right to the fulfilment of treaty obligations towards him as well as a Sovereign of any other religious denomination. But what happened in 1860 ? .The King of Sardinia wished to possess himself of the dominions of the Pope, if the French Emperor would but allow him. So, in September of that year, without any declaration of war—without any of those formalities which were recognized by all civilized nations, he ordered his troops to enter the Legations and Umbria, and to expel the Pope's troops. Within a fortnight of that occupation the Austrian Government addressed a strong circular to the great Powers of Europe protesting against that occupation, and asking for the co-operation of those Powers. Lord Russell in answer to the circular, justified the seizure of the Papal territory on the ground that the King of Sardinia had undertaken to be the chief of Italy, and it was his business to substitute a Government of order for one of oppression. But there was a still stronger case which occurred about the same time—the case of Naples. Now, he (Mr. Cavendish Bentinck) would not argue whether the acts of the King of Sardinia were right or wrong—expedient or otherwise. Indeed, for the sake of argument he was willing to admit that the state of affairs in those parts of Italy was bad, and that the Piedmontese invasions were desirable. But where was the legality of that policy ? The King of Sardinia, in like manner, wished to possess himself of the dominions of the King of Naples; but he did not dare to declare war or to fight for those dominions in a manly, straightforward manner. The King, thereupon, came to an agreement with General Garibaldi, and offered him material assistance if he would raise the standard of revolution in Sicily. Now, the noble Lord might have a high opinion of the veracity of General Garibaldi ; and if they were to believe General Garibaldi, Admiral Mundy had also afforded General Garibaldi material assistance, without which Garibaldi could not have succeeded in establishing himself in Sicily. It subsequently became a question whether Garibaldi should be allowed to transfer himself and his army to the continent of Italy. The French Government viewed this movement with great apprehension, lest it should lead to an attack upon Venetia, and ultimately to an European war. The French Government, therefore, made the strongest representations to the Government of England for a joint intervention to prevent General Garibaldi from proceeding from Sicily to Naples. In a despatch from M. Thouvenel to Earl Russell, dated in July, the former Minister stated that his Government did not think that France or England, with a due regard to their own dignity, could submit to be passive spectators of the advance into Naples of the revolutionary army, but that they ought to prevent General Garibaldi crossing the straits with an army of revolutionary followers, and effectually to interfere, so as to leave the question as one simply between the King of Naples and his own subjects. In the case of Naples Her Majesty's Government laid down for the second time that it was a question of the will of the population. Earl Russell wrote that the people of Naples should be left to themselves, whether to receive or reject Garibaldi. When that noble Earl said that people ought to be free and happy, and ought to be left to settle ·their own affairs and choose their rulers, did he reflect that he was introducing a new principle which might be turned against England at any time ? Indeed the case had happened, for in a despatch of the 19th of January Earl Cowley described his interview with M. Drouyn de Lhuys. The latter asked in what measure the proposed concert and co-operation were to be established, and then proceeded to say—

"We are not bound by any guarantee to maintain the stipulations of that Treaty of 1852. For instance, if we have to choose between its modification and the commencement of a war, uncertain in its duration and dubious as to its results, to speak frankly, we should prefer the former alternative ; and in saying this we are only following in the footsteps of Great Britain, who in 1859 thought it better to consent to the separation of Belgium from Holland than incur the risks of a war for the maintenance of the union, and who later (speaking of the Government then in power) would have preferred the continuation of the ancient order of things in Italy, guaranteed by proper liberties, but would not employ force for the purpose, both events having been in violation of existing treaties."

To that Earl Cowley replied—

"That the comparison would not hold good unless his Excellency could show that the same sentiments animated the Schleswig-Holsteiners as had been demonstrated by both the Belgians and the Italians. The Belgian revolution had been the work of the Belgians themselves; their desire to separate from Holland had been unmistakable. The aspirations of the Italians for unity had been the demonstration of a whole people, whereas there was every reason to believe that the present movement in the Duchies was mainly the result of foreign interference, and that the sentiment which generally pervaded the Duchies was not for separation from Denmark, but for the maintenance of close relations between themselves."

So that Earl Cowley maintained the extraordinary proposition, that if the will of the people had been against the treaty, the treaty would not have been binding. At first sight that reply, as published in the papers, looked very like the answer of a puzzled man, who had had a proposition put to him which he could not quite answer, and had given way to the impulse of his mind, and one would have thought that he would have been rebuked by the Home Government; but, so far from that, the Foreign Secretary, after stating that co-operation and concert meant the acting together of France, Russia, and Sweden in order to give, if necessary, material assistance to Denmark, stated that he considered Earl Cowley's answer to M. Drouyn de Lhuys as quite correct, and went on to add that in Belgium the people rose and got possession of the capital, whereas in Holstein the accession of the new King was peacefully accomplished, and it was not until the German troops encouraged revolutionary movements (just as if the case of Naples was not exactly in point), that the rural population showed any disaffection to the Government of the King. The noble Lord, therefore, bound himself to this — that if the people of Schleswig and Holstein had risen and made any stand whatever against the King, we should not be bound to the treaty. On the other hand, if the Prussians, or any other German Power, thought there was an under current of disaffection in the Duchies, and had engaged General Garibaldi, or any other adventurer, to go with a

Mr. Cavendish Bentinck

number of foreigners, dressed in red shirts and under a tricoloured flag, into Holstein, and if they had there defeated or made any stand against the Danish troops, and if Prussia, following the example of the King of Sardinia, had then supported the insurrection with an army — according to the precedents of the last four years—it would have been perfectly impossible for Her Majesty's Government to allege that the Treaty of 1852 was valid and of full force. He called, therefore, on Her Majesty's Government, especially now that the Conference was about to assemble, to give some distinct and intelligible statement of their policy with regard to the principle of non-intervention. If they stood to the propositions laid down in the despatches, he could not see how they could resist the Motion. If, on the other hand, they dissented from them, he hoped they would give to the House and the country their reasons for so doing. It had been said that England had been very much humiliated. He thought so. She had been humiliated, not only by the empty bombast and threats of the noble Lord the Foreign Secretary, but also by the want of any intelligible principles to guide her foreign policy, and he was almost prepared to agree with the remark that had been made in 1862 by a distinguished foreign Minister Count Apponyi, with regard to Earl Russell's policy—that the principles of his intervention were, indeed, elastic, for they seemed to take effect just as the interests of the Minister for the time being required. If he should not receive a satisfactory explanation of the policy of the Government on the points to which he had called attention, he should feel compelled to support the Motion of his hon. Friend.

Mr. BAILLIE COCHRANE said, that it would perhaps have been better if the Question had not been brought before the House on the eve of a Conference; but the Question having been introduced by his hon. Friend the Member for Liskeard, in a speech remarkable for eloquence and close reasoning, and the debate evidently promising to occupy the whole night, he was prepared to take part in it. His own opinion was that it was not so much a question of Schleswig, Holstein, and Denmark, which had been truly called a most complicated question, and one that, as his hon. Friend had said, had nearly driven one man mad, but he thought it very desirable that an opportunity should be taken of pointing out to the House and the country what really was the foreign policy of Her Majesty's Government. Having recently returned from the Continent, he was enabled to corroborate the statement of the hon. Member for Liskeard, that the moral influence of England had greatly deteriorated. Whatever the cause, since Earl Russell had been at the head of the Foreign Office the weight and consideration attending English opinion had diminished very much. That was a result that all must lament, and he would take the liberty of pointing out one or two circumstances which he thought had of late tended to a diminution of our influence abroad. In the first place, he wished to ask the hon. Gentleman the Under Secretary of State if he could explain in any way, by what principles his Department was guided, for in the cases of Poland, the Eastern Nationalities, and that of Denmark, they appeared to be altogether contradictory. It was not sufficient to say that the policy of Her Majesty's Government had prevented the country from becoming involved in war. The country demanded something further. We ought to abstain from meddling with other nations of Europe in such a manner as to lead them into war and misery. In the East the noble Earl's policy altogether differed from what it was in the West. At Constantinople he wore the turban, and in Italy the cap of liberty, except when he laid it aside, as in the case of Sir J. Hudson. The great evil of this policy was that it misled foreign countries, which were brought to ruin by the noble Earl's desire to write sentimental despatches. In the words of Sir Peter Teazle, " There is nothing so noble as a man of sentiment." He would not quote from the blue-books familiar passages about other countries " taking the responsibility" of interfering with Denmark, but there was a significant passage in a letter of the noble Earl to Lord Bloomfield, where he said that on a former occasion " he had spoken in the sense that Denmark would resist an occupation of Schleswig, and might be aided by Great Britain." Nothing could be more explicit than the manner in which Earl Russell, in the same despatch, dwelt upon the current of feeling in Parliament and in the nation as leading to active assistance of Denmark. Again, on the 4th of January, Sir A. Buchanan said to M. Bismark that if the Government of Germany invaded Schleswig unnecessarily they would be responsible for a war which might extend to the whole of Europe.

Independently of this, Earl Russell had laid down a general principle, which had had, and would exercise for a long time, a most injurious and misleading effect upon the Continent. The despatch of Earl Russell dated October 27, 1860, and addressed to Sir James Hudson, would, if carried out, lead to an active intervention in favour of Denmark. The noble Earl then quoted the eminent jurist Vattel, and said that when a people for good reason take up arms against an oppressor it was but an act of justice and generosity to assist brave men in defence of their liberties. If that principle were adopted, the Government were bound to assist the brave men who were then fighting in Denmark for their independence, for it was clearly the intention of the Austrians and Prussians to overrun Jutland as well as Schleswig. Earl Russell was responsible for the existing state of things. There was one despatch of Earl Russell on which everything turned, because the first excitement in Schleswig and Holstein arose from the noble Earl's despatch of the 24th of September, 1862. Nothing could be more touching than the reply of the Danish Government to that despatch. They declared that the acceptance of the noble Earl's propositions would lead to the destruction of constitutional life in Denmark, and would soon even imperil the existence of the Danish monarchy itself. The effect of the noble Earl's policy had been that Great Britain had not only sustained a great loss of influence on the Continent, but he had himself been subjected to the most severe abuse. When Earl Cowley, according to his instructions, applied to M. Drouyn de Lhuys, proposing that the French Government should join in active interference in the affairs of Denmark, M. Drouyn de Lhuys replied—

" The mode of proceeding suggested by his Lordship would be in a great measure analogous to the course pursued by Great Britain and France on the Polish question. He had no inclination to place France in the same position with regard to Germany as she had been placed in with regard to Russia. The formal notes addressed by the three Powers to Russia had received an answer which literally meant nothing, and the position in which those three great Powers were now placed was anything but dignified; and if England and France were to address such a reminder as that proposed to Austria, Prussia, and the German Confederation, they must be prepared to go further, and to adopt a course of action more in accordance with the dignity of two great Powers than they were now doing on the Polish question."

That reply showed the little confidence

which France placed in the policy of Earl Russell. The second interview, with regard to intervention, between Earl Cowley and M. Drouyn de Lhuys was almost amusing, because it proved the sort of dead lock to which the noble Earl's diplomacy had brought us. Earl Russell, on the 5th of January, 1864, sent a telegram to Earl Cowley, suggesting that the Confederated Powers should

"Stop all acts of hostility, if any are now being carried on, and be satisfied with the present state of military occupation in Holstein."

Earl Cowley's reply was as follows :—

"After listening to the proposal, M. Drouyn de Lhuys asked what was to be done should Germany refuse to suspend hostile operations ?"

The reply, in Earl Russell's words, was, that,

"If unsuccessful, each Power will be at liberty to pursue the course which its own honour and its own interests may seem to demand."

That was very like Bob Acres in *The Rivals.* Bob Acres said, if you call me coward it is nothing ; but call me poltroon —call me poltroon, and—I shall call you a very ill-bred man. The noble Lord said, "Remain as you are, and it is nothing; but cross the Eider—cross the Eider, and then you take a great responsibility on yourselves." Some of the statements of the hon. Gentleman who introduced the Motion were altogether untenable. For instance, he stated that Schleswig was never part of Denmark. Why, it was called South Jutland, and it had always been a portion of Denmark. As far as he remembered, however, Schleswig had always been a part of Denmark. From the most ancient times the Eider had been the boundary between Germany and Denmark. A French treaty, ratified by the King of France in 1720, gave a complete and regular guarantee on this point. The French King said—

"Having been informed that insurmountable difficulties have arisen as to the restitution to the Crown of Sweden of the island and principality of Rugen, of the fortress of Stralsund, and of the rest of Pomerania as far as the river Pehne, which are occupied by the Crown of Denmark, unless it should be assured of the possession of Schleswig, which His Britannic Majesty has already guaranteed, the most Christian King has thought it well, for these considerations, and on the representations of the Kings of Great Britain and of Denmark, to grant to that latter Crown, as he does by these presents, the guarantee of the Duchy of Schleswig, promising, in consideration of the above-stipulated restitutions, in the treaty signed this day at Stockholm by the plenipotentiaries of Sweden, to maintain the King of Den-

Mr. Baillie Cochrane

mark in the peaceable possession of the ducal part of the said Duchy."

Nothing could be more complete and regular than that guarantee, and the King of Denmark in consequence of it gave up possession of the island of Rugen, Stralsund, and Pomerania. If any further proof were wanting, it was to be found in the following declaration of the Prussian Plenipotentiary to the Diet in 1723 :—

"Upon the maintenance of the union between Holstein and Schleswig, the Federal Diet cannot exercise any imaginable influence, for this reason —that the Duchy of Schleswig does not belong to the German Federal territories, and consequently lies altogether beyond the influence of the Confederation."

The hon. Member was therefore, he submitted, in error in doubting the position of Schleswig in relation to Denmark. He regretted also to hear the manner in which the hon. Gentleman had spoken of the Danes, for the sympathy of the whole of Europe was enlisted on behalf of these poor people, who were fighting for their existence against such terrific odds. It was, indeed, somewhat ungenerous in the hon. Gentleman to attempt to weaken the influence of the Danes just when the Conference was about to assemble. There was something at once noble and affecting in the appeal which had been made by Denmark to Europe—

"Why," said this appeal, "does Denmark continue an apparently hopeless struggle ? Why does she not succumb to a superior force, and accept any peace she can obtain ? Surely there can be no dishonour in giving way before so many. Thus speak none of the high-minded and generous nations of Europe—none of those who, from far and near, from north, from south, from west, have shown a hearty sympathy for the struggling Danish people, which has raised its courage and imparted loftiness to its soul. But these questions may be asked by statesmen who stand coldly by and see a nation bleed to death in fighting for its rights, its independence ; by men who, totally dead to feeling for their own people, only seek to escape from the obligations they are bound in honour and by treaty to fulfil. To such men our answer is ready. As the matter now stands, Denmark cannot yield ; not only for her honour's sake, but because her existence as an independent nation is at stake."

That a Conference should be held at the present moment was like a consultation of doctors over a dying man. Schleswig was entirely overrun by the Germans, and they were Germanizing the whole Duchy, though Austria had promised that the integrity of Denmark should be respected. Would the noble Viscount at the head of the Government tell the House how long the Conference was to last, and what steps would be taken to stop the progress of military operations ? Earl Russell said he had been accused of unworthy motives, but he appealed to the commerce of the country and the danger of encountering 60,000,000 of people. He was not for a war policy. He was for keeping clear of war ; and he condemned this system of intervention—this giving of opinions unasked on every question of foreign politics —because he believed it was calculated to lead us into hostilities. He hoped that the foreign policy of the Government would soon be brought forward in a direct form, so that hon. Members might be able to express their opinion on the constant meddling and interference with other nations by the Foreign Secretary, on every possible occasion—a meddling without conciliation, and an interference without prevailing anywhere. If they were to have the Conference, which seemed to him so prejudicial to the interests of Denmark, he hoped the result would be such as to maintain the interests of Denmark and the honour and integrity of this country.

MR. NEWDEGATE said, that he hoped to be permitted to make a few comments on the speech of the hon. Member for Liskeard, who had condemned the pertinacity of the noble Lord at the head of the Government in adhering to the Treaty of 1852 as a guarantee for the independence of Denmark. He (Mr. Newdegate) was afraid, that the observations he was about to make might entail upon him the accusation of entertaining low and selfish motives. But he held that England never intervened with respect to foreign nations for an idea ; and it was his opinion that England had a deep interest in the maintenance of the independence of Denmark. He deprecated senseless interference with foreign nations as much as anyone ; but he could not forget that this country had very large commercial interests, and that it had always been her policy to defend them. With that view England maintained possession of Gibraltar on the extremity of the Spanish Peninsula. He had never heard any thinking man contest the propriety of England holding Gibraltar. It had always been conceded that the possession of Gibraltar was necessary to this country, in order to secure the free navigation of the Mediterranean ; and he believed that the independence of the Power which commanded the Sound, the mouths of the Elbe, and all the ports that were within the reach of Denmark, was the best gua-

rantee that we could have for the free navigation of the Baltic and for free access to these ports. In 1801 the maritime resources of Denmark had fallen under the influence of a first-rate Power, which was at that time hostile to us. The consequence was that England found it necessary to bombard Copenhagen and destroy the Danish fleet. In 1807 we were again obliged to take possession of the Danish fleet. He might be told that circumstances had changed since then ; but the relative geographical positions of countries had not changed — the map of Europe had not changed—and obviously, the independence of Denmark was, at least, quite as important for us at the present time as it was in 1801 and 1807. He held in his hand a Return of the quantity of British shipping which had passed the Sound, or had carried on the intercourse of this country with the other ports commanded by Denmark, during a period of three years. The total of British tonnage entered at and cleared from ports in the United Kingdom in the year 1860 was 24,689,000 ; in the year 1861, 26,595,000 ; and in 1862, 26,585,000. Of that tonnage there passed the Sound, or passed to and from the ports commanded by Denmark, in 1860, 25 per cent ; in 1861, 23 per cent; and in 1862 (the date of the last Return), 23 per cent. Since the commencement of the century, the changes made in our commercial system rendered the free navigation of the seas and ports commanded by Denmark still more important to us. England had to a great extent become dependent on foreigners for food. The total quantity of corn imported into Great Britain and Ireland in the three years he had named—1860-2, averaged 14,000,000 of quarters annually, and from 18 to 19 per cent of that corn passed through the Sound, or came from the ports within the command of Denmark. These were serious considerations, and matters of increasing importance ; and when he heard members of a peculiar school—he had almost said of the foreign Department of the House—sneering at the importance of maintaining the balance of power in Europe, sneering at our maintaining such posts as Gibraltar, and the independence of Denmark, which was in alliance with us, he could not help remembering with some astonishment that they were representatives of that portion of the population which depended chiefly upon our external commerce, and that they were sneering at our retention of those means upon our maintenance of which our credit depended, which was the very life-blood of their employment. It seemed an extraordinary policy on their part to sneer at the balance of power, to speak disparagingly of our means of defence, to raise their voices against the expenses necessary for the maintenance of our establishments, whilst they represented interests more directly dependent upon those establishments, and the protection they afforded to our shores and to our commerce than any other interest of the country. As the representative of a commercial constituency he should consider himself not only a madman, but as false to the interests of those whom he was sent to that House to represent, if he did anything to damage the credit of England. He regretted that the policy of Her Majesty's Government, in the matter of Denmark, had not been more decisive. It was obvious that a Power like England, always using strong language with an apparent fear of striking, must fall in the estimation of other nations. He did not, however, under-estimate the difficulties which the noble Lord at the head of the Government had to encounter with followers such as the hon. Member for Liskeard, with supporters who took every opportunity of threatening a domestic war, if a foreign war should become necessary. Encompassed as the noble Lord was by every difficulty—even in his Cabinet as he had been told—he (Mr. Newdegate) was not surprised at the policy of the Government; but he held it to be the duty of independent Members of that House to express the strong feelings of the people of England—that their interests and their honour both dictated that the Government should not hesitate in securing the independence of an ally so important in her position and in the proportions assigned to her in 1852 as Denmark. He was not urging war; but he deprecated that apparent fear of war which was sure eventually to lead to it; he deprecated that vacillating policy which brought into discredit the prestige of England, for on that prestige depended her credit, her safety, and the extension of her commerce. He should not have gone so far into detail, but it appeared to him that from the discussion some hon. Members had given an exaggerated weight of nationality. It was absurd to contemplate the idea of setting up another petty State. Holstein, by itself, was totally incapable of independence. Holstein might desire to be united to Germany, but that could not be said of the in-

Mr. Newdegate

habitants of Schleswig while they had an independent voice. He (Mr. Newdegate) could place no confidence in a mere *plebiscite*, extracted by the pressure of both military and civil power. Holstein, no doubt, desired separation ; but, on the other hand, Schleswig would wish to remain connected with Denmark, and it would be a most absurd policy on the part of England not to support that wish. He was decidedly adverse to the multiplication of petty States in Germany, for there were indications that such a multiplication would lead to a renewal of the petty wars which had disgraced the mediæval ages, and which, if renewed, would only terminate by being swept away through the predominance of some great military despotism. The object of the German democracy was an united Germany, with a strong fleet. English economists should bear that in mind, that in calculating the amount of naval force necessary for this country, it had always been usual to take into consideration what might be the united power of the other navies of the world. Another fleet would add another element to the calculation, and the establishment of a German fleet meant a permanent addition to our naval Estimates. In conclusion, he begged to state, that he felt fully the wisdom of the noble Lord in making earnest exertions for the independence of Denmark ; and, as an independent Member of that House, he should be happy to support the noble Lord in any means he might think necessary for effecting that object.

SIR HARRY VERNEY said, he was sure that the hon. Member for Liskeard was only anxious that the people of Schleswig and Holstein should have an opportunity of expressing their own free and unbiassed opinion as to the arrangements which were to be made, and he would desire that their feelings should be ascertained in the best way that could be devised. Probably, the best way would be by the convocation of an assembly *ad hoc* in each province, and withdraw all the troops until both assemblies had pronounced their opinion. He shared completely in the admiration of the courage and determination displayed by the Danes in their contest against overpowering odds. Never had there been a more remarkable instance of self-sacrifice than that exhibited by the Copenhagen regiment of infantry which had covered the retreat of the Danish army to Düppel. They owed, too, a deep debt of gratitude to the King of Denmark for the excellent education which he had bestowed on the Princess of Wales, which would render her as great a blessing in her mature age as she had been an object of admiration for her beauty in her youth. But the question was one of such deep importance to the welfare of Europe, that we must consider it independently of all considerations but those of truth and justice. It was said that the interests of the nations of Europe required that the entrance of the Sound should be in the hands of an independent Power; but it was likewise of importance to maintain that feeling of friendship and amity which had existed so long between this country and Germany. Twenty years ago there was a feeling of amity between Germans and Englishmen, but Englishmen were then regarded with hostility by Germans because they considered that our conduct in the matter of Schleswig-Holstein was unjust. The existing difficulties and the war in Schleswig might be traced to the conduct of the Eider-Dane party since the year 1848. Before that time there was no province more valuable to a kingdom than Schleswig and Holstein were to Denmark. He had never seen a people more calculated to excite sympathy and admiration, and any one who had read the interesting accounts of them given by *The Times* correspondent, must feel that they were not a people to be handed from one monarch to another without their own consent. Earl Russell over and over again had urged upon the Government of Denmark to fulfil their promises to Germany in. reference to Schleswig and Holstein, and not to give the German Powers a pretext for interference. But the Danish Government had taken a course directly contrary to his advice. By refusing justice to their subjects in the Duchies they had imposed on Germany the positive duty of interfering, and that really was the defence of Austria and Prussia. In 1851 the King of Denmark, as a member of the German Bund, called upon Germany to reinstate him in Holstein. The Bund assented; and Austria and Prussia, as mandatories of the Confederation, obliged the Schleswig-Holstein army to lay down their arms, at the same time engaging that they would obtain for the people of the Duchies the privileges to which they were entitled. The privileges which the King of Denmark then promised to concede were nothing extraordinary. They were only that he would equally protect both languages, and would make no attempt to incorporate Schleswig with the

kingdom of Denmark. The Germans complained that from the moment these promises were given they had been systematically violated, and the evidence of the blue-books established the truth of that assertion. M. Hall himself admitted to Sir Augustus Paget, that any attempt to incorporate Schleswig with the kingdom of Denmark would furnish a *casus belli* to Germany, and Sir A. Paget, Earl Russell, and Lord Wodehouse agreed that not only had such an attempt been made, but what was equivalent to that incorporation had been effected. If the noble Lord at the head of the Government had desired to prevent war, he should have said, not that if the Germans invaded Denmark she would not stand alone, but that if she obliged Germany to engage in war she would stand alone. What had induced Denmark to resist the performance of her promises was the belief that she would be supported by this country. That had produced all the evils and miseries of a dreadful war. He should like to know upon what authority Earl Russell made the assertion that the National Verein had sent 2,000 agents into Schleswig to induce the people to revolt. His belief was that the feeling in Schleswig as well as in Holstein was entirely in favour of independence, and that the movement to throw off the Danish yoke was entirely spontaneous, and needed no foreign emissaries to stimulate or originate it. No man desired more than he did the independence of Denmark; but if the aversion of the people of the Duchies was so strong as he believed it to be, he doubted whether their union with the monarchy would be a source of strength to that country. The Treaty of 1852 was solely for the advantage of Russia. It had been stated that seventeen lives had been swept out of the line of succession by the Treaty of 1852; another had since disappeared by the election of the new King of Greece. He believed that if the Treaty of 1852 was to remain in force there would be but three lives between the Imperial family of Russia and the Crown of Denmark, and he, therefore, looked with great satisfaction upon the despatch addressed by Earl Russell to Sir Alexander Malet, in which he assured the German Confederation that that treaty was not to be the basis of the Conference, but that the object of its deliberation was to be the restoration of peace in the North of Europe. All who desired the welfare of the present King of Denmark must regret that his first act as a

Sovereign was the signature of the Constitution of November. Only twenty-four hours before he had said to his brother that he would never forget that he had a million German subjects, and that nothing should induce him to sign it. Weakness in a king was worse than wickedness, and it was a lamentable want of strength which led him to give his assent to a measure which would alienate so large a number of his subjects. In conclusion, he might observe that one of the great objects which the Conference ought, in his opinion, to have in view, was to see justice done to the inhabitants of the Duchies. However, the existing difficulty might be patched up: if justice was not done to them, the seeds of future dissension would remain, and it was not for the British Parliament to do anything which might restrict their liberty.

MR. LIDDELL said, he fully concurred in the opinion which had been expressed by the hon. Member for North Warwickshire (Mr. Newdegate), that it was most desirable to maintain the integrity of Denmark. He regretted that the forms of the House precluded the hon. Member for Bridport from bringing forward his Amendment before the other had been disposed of, but he felt disposed to vote against the Amendment of his hon. Friend (Mr. Peacocke), because it asked the House to support the Government in maintaining the Treaty of 1852. As a Conservative Member of a constitutional House of Commons, he could not recognize the right of a constitutional Sovereign so far to step beyond the limits of the constitution as to violate the very condition of his sovereignty, and still less could he recognize the right of a democratic majority to tyrannize over, to stifle, and to suppress, the national rights of an independent people. In arguing this question of the Duchies, he begged to remind the Liberal party that they were treading on very tender ground. It had been said that we must not question the Treaty of 1852, because it now formed part of the public law of Europe. But, if it could be shown that the peace of Europe had been imperilled by the operation of that law, was it not, he would ask, time that it should form the subject of reconsideration? It was a law, he believed, which, in Parliamentary language, had been hastily framed and very inadequately discussed, and he desired to see it recommitted for the purpose of being amended. But be that as it might, the acts of Frederick VII. in 1851-2 were, he contended, a violation of the very conditions on which he held his sovereignty. What were the fundamental rights of those ancient Duchies? One was that they were to be regarded as independent States in their own right. The second was that they were indissolubly connected. The third was that males, and males only, had the right of succession. Two out of the three conditions were violated by the dishonest compromise of 1851, which led to the Treaty of 1852. That compromise was framed between the King of Denmark, as Duke of Holstein on the one hand, and the representatives of the German Confederation on the other. The conditions of the compromise were that Germany should give up the indissoluble union of the Duchies (the King of Denmark agreeing on his part to take no step towards the incorporation of Schleswig); and that offer was accepted, but it was a dishonest one on the part of the commissioners, because it violated one of the fundamental principles of the German Diet itself, that no state being a member of the Diet, could introduce or adopt any organic change except by constitutional means. Frederick VII., however, accepted the compromise, and coupled with the alteration of the law of succession, and the operation of those two circumstances had led to the war which was now being waged in the North of Europe. In arriving at a settlement of the question, the Government would not, he hoped, be too strict in their adherence to the terms of the Treaty of 1852, because that instrument had within it, he believed, the seeds of weakness to Denmark. Nor did he think that a fancied union, and a tyrannical rule, over a discontented people could ever be a source of strength to any nation. The rule of the democratic majority over the nationalities of the Duchy had been continued with increasing severity ever since the close of the great war in 1815. He knew well enough that the King of Denmark was an unwilling instrument and driven to what he did by his people, but he (Mr. Liddell) hoped that the voice of the House of Commons would be a warning to that people, and he hoped that that House would not justify the acts of the ultraparty in Copenhagen to whom he alluded. He hoped to see the union which had existed before 1846 restored, for he believed that such a restoration would be the best security for the integrity of the kingdom. In common with ninety-nine out of every hundred Englishmen he deplored this mis-

Sir Harry Verney

orable, this unnecessary war—he deplored it the more because he believed it to be an insincere war. He did not believe that the German Powers, in undertaking that war, were actuated either by motives of vengeance or even of hostility against the people whom they had gone to massacre. They were urged forward by the fear of revolution at home. Austria and Prussia knew, that unless they took the lead in that great German movement, revolution would be knocking at their own doors. They had therefore thrown aside their engagements, and sacrificed everything to what he could not help regarding as a most selfish feeling; but he trusted that the Conference that was about to assemble would remember that fact, and that they would not separate from their first meeting until they had found some means or other to stop this needless effusion of blood. Of course, they must all admire the valour and determination with which the Danes had defended themselves; but he blamed the obstinacy of the Danes. He had felt no sympathy with them up to the moment of the invasion of Schleswig. He even thought the Germans were justified in enforcing their claims on Denmark by a legal execution in Holstein, but from the moment they invaded Schleswig his sympathy, like that of ninety-nine out of every hundred Englishmen, was turned to the weaker side. It had been said that Denmark was not to be blamed, because she had made concessions. True, she had made concessions, but he could not help remembering that every successive concession had been made too late, and only under foreign pressure. Such had been the case with the constitution of October, 1855, with the Royal Decree of March, 1863, and the constitution of November last. In these respects he thought that Denmark had been to blame. He was about to give expression to an opinion which he was afraid would be unfavourably received in that House, and might possibly be regarded as foolish by the public. England was about to play at the Conference an up-hill game, and every possible method of conciliation would be wanted. He was at a loss to understand how our Government would be able to explain satisfactorily to Russia, Austria, and Prussia the very ill-timed visit which was now creating such a sensation in this country. [*Cries of* " Oh !"] He knew that that opinion would be unfavourably received, but it should be borne in mind that that distinguished man,

General Garibaldi, for whose private virtues he entertained the highest respect, represented in the eyes of the Northern Powers the principle of revolution. Foreigners could never be made to understand correctly the English people, and he could not help fearing that the cause which England had to plead in the presence of Powers flushed with success, and so possibly rendered more obstinate than ever in the assertion of what they believed to be their just rights, might be pleaded in vain. He had no great confidence in the success of the Conference. It was possible that Austria and Prussia, now that they had vindicated—to use a foolish phrase—their honour, lost in 1848, would be more reasonable and less violent in their demands; but he was afraid the chances of success were much more distant than the advocates of peace would desire to see them. Nevertheless, he trusted that means might be found to maintain the integrity of Denmark by that personal union which had existed before and which might, even under the altered circumstances of the moment, exist again.

MR. LAYARD said, he rose to address the House with great reluctance, for it appeared to him extraordinary, and not very desirable, that within a few hours of the time when a Conference was to meet to discuss questions of the greatest importance, those questions should be made the subject of debate in the House of Commons. He had no wish to curtail the privileges of the House. Every matter in which the Government were engaged was a fair subject of discussion in that place, but still he thought that when questions of such enormous importance were about to be considered by the assembled representatives of Europe, the present debate ought to have been avoided. The House must feel that he rose under great difficulties, inasmuch as, under other circumstances, he might be at liberty to say a great deal which on that occasion would be left unsaid, from a fear of prejudging matters that would shortly be deliberated upon elsewhere. He need hardly remind the House that the questions under consideration were of the greatest possible importance, to be discussed with calmness, and not treated with the rollicking rhetoric in which the hon. Member for Liskeard was so fond of indulging. [*Cries of* " Oh ! "] The hon. Gentleman had roundly rated almost every Member of the Government and it was only right that a reply should be made to his taunts and charges. He had said that the question in dispute between Germany and Denmark was so simple that he could in a few words explain it to the House ; that though it had driven German professors mad, he could make it plain and intelligible to the ordinary Parliamentary intellect. If the question were as light as the manner in which the hon. Gentleman had dealt with it, there would be little difficulty in explaining it to the satisfaction of the most ordinary intellect, but he had no hesitation in saying that the hon. Member had treated it altogether on false principles. He had talked with the greatest assurance, as if he alone could form a correct opinion upon the question of the succession to Denmark and the Duchies. [*Cries of* " Oh ! "] " Oh " was not an argument, and, perhaps, hon. Gentlemen would have the goodness, instead of interrupting him, to get up and answer his speech after he had made it. The right of succession involved considerations of the greatest difficulty, and had puzzled the most learned men in Germany. Whether the Estates of Schleswig and Holstein should have a voice in determining this right was also a question of no little intricacy, not to be treated in the light manner of the hon. Member for Liskeard, but to be calmly and gravely discussed. The Estates might have a right to be consulted, but the question was a most difficult one to decide, and Europe was divided upon it. Again, the hon. Member had spoken as if Schleswig and Holstein were one, and had for ever been united ; but that was another question, on which the opinion of Europe was divided, and he was afraid the *ipse dixit* of the hon. Gentleman would not settle it. Everything might be said to turn upon it, and it would shortly be made the subject of a solemn deliberation. The hon. Member had said that the German Diet had been treated with contumely, and that it ought to have been asked to become a party to the Treaty of 1852. Whether the assent of the Diet was necessary to changes in the succession in the States which were members of it, was a point in dispute among the German States themselves. Austria denied the right of the Diet to be consulted, and the same view was taken by other countries. The question, therefore, was not one which the hon. Member could hope to decide offhand, with the lively assurance belonging to him. But he would proceed to deal

Mr. Layard

with the speech of the hon. Gentleman point by point, showing how fallacious were his arguments and how baseless were his assertions. It was not necessary to go back to the early history of the Schleswig-Holstein question. After the events of 1848 the question assumed a new and distinct phase. It was well known that at that time, owing to events which had led to disturbances in Holstein, an interference took place on the part of the German Powers, including Austria and Prussia, who acted as mandatories of the Diet, which led to war with Denmark. The treaty which closed the war was negotiated under the auspices of the British Government, and peace was made upon certain terms. On the one hand, Denmark promised that no steps should be taken tending to incorporate Schleswig or Holstein with Denmark, and that certain rights should be secured to the populations of the Duchies; on the other, Austria and Prussia promised to agree to an arrangement for the settlement of the succession. His noble Friend at the head of the Government had been taunted, in not very elegant terms, with concocting that treaty, and also with being the cat's paw of Russia. He had really hoped that all that rubbish would have been thrown aside. The treaty was a thing that was wished for by all the great Powers of Europe. The papers opened with a despatch of the noble Lord which spoke of the arrangement of the succession, but which spoke of it as a question that had been long in agitation. Everybody knew that the great difficulty to be anticipated in respect to Denmark was, that if that question were not settled before the death of the late King it might give rise to war in Europe. We had no particular candidate. [Mr. BERNAL OSBORNE : The son of the Duke of Oldenburg.] The son of the Duke of Oldenburg and some others were mentioned ; but all we required was, that the succession of the then reigning monarch should be determined in the event of his dying without direct heirs. The Treaty of 1852 was concluded, a protocol recognizing its principle having been signed in 1850. The hon. Member had been very lively, as usual, about the difference between a treaty and a protocol ; but, although he appeared to know everything, he did not seem to know the difference between these two things. A protocol was a document which passed between plenipotentiaries, and was, indeed, binding on their respective States, but it was not a solemn instrument formally ratified by the sovereign like a treaty. The Treaty of 1852 was quite distinct from the Protocol of 1850, and whatever German philosophers might say, all who were not ignorant of the common forms of language knew the difference between the two things. The hon. Gentleman had insinuated that the treaty bound us as something like a guarantee. [Mr. BERNAL OSBORNE: No.] It merely bound us to recognize as the successor to the King of Denmark such a person as he might appoint—that was the Prince Christian of Schleswig-Holstein Glucksburg Sönderborg, and his issue by the Princess Louisa of Hesse. That was the simple article in the treaty which bound this country. Another special article of the treaty reserved the right of the Germanic Confederation as regarded Holstein—not the Duchy of Schleswig-Holstein, as the hon. Gentleman constantly repeated. The hon. Member said that though the Earl of Malmesbury signed the treaty he had nothing to do with it. That was not the case. On the contrary, the Earl of Malmesbury had a considerable share in its negotiation. He conducted the negotiation with much ability, and was justly proud of having brought about an arrangement of so much importance to the peace of Europe. He received several congratulatory despatches from foreign States on having concluded the treaty, and on the benefit which it had conferred on Europe. And who was it that had lauded that treaty? It was concluded by the great Powers, and afterwards communicated to the small German Powers, some of whom adhered to it, while others refused it their adhesion. Among those who adhered to it and praised it was Baron Beust, himself the leader of the opposition raised to it during the previous year. At page 232 of the papers, M. Beust would be found bearing his testimony to the gain to the peace of Europe from the conclusion of that treaty. Almost all the Powers looked upon it at the time as an excellent arrangement for the maintenance of peace. The hon. Member said it ought to have been communicated to the Diet. Now, he had reason to believe that Denmark was not opposed to the treaty being communicated to the Diet; but, on the contrary, desired that that should be done. Earl Granville proposed that it should be so communicated, but who opposed that? Why, Austria and Russia—and to some

extent Prussia also—on the ground that the Diet was not a body competent to deal with the question; that such instruments never were communicated to it, and that it would be giving it a power which it did not possess. Our Government was quite willing to communicate it to the Diet, and thought there was no reason why it should not be; but of course they respected the judgment of those Powers, who had the best right to form an opinion on the subject. The hon. Member said the States of Holstein and Schleswig ought to have been consulted. He had endeavoured to ascertain, if possible, what the attributes of those States were, and, although the hon. Gentleman thought that was an easy question, it really was not. The greatest confusion existed on that point. As he could understand it, the States of Schleswig and Holstein had no deliberative power whatever. They had merely local and provincial functions which were strictly limited, and no power over questions of that nature. The hon. Gentleman said it was otherwise; but therein he disagreed with some of the highest authorities. But the treaty did not settle the question of the succession at all. Count Rechberg, in a despatch given in the blue-books, disclaimed the doctrine that the treaty had settled that question, declaring that it only bound the signataries to recognize the course of succession which the King of Denmark by legal forms might bring about. A law regulating the succession was passed by the only representative body then existing in Denmark—the Rigsdag. That assembly was not, however, a Parliament, in our sense of a truly representative body. The Rigsdag — not the Rigsraag—the Rigsdag having had extraordinary powers given to it, had the subject of the law of succession submitted to it, and, after discussion, and having been twice dissolved, it agreed to alter it by repealing the *lex regia*. The alteration of the *lex regia* changed the order of succession in Denmark, and not the treaty. That Count Rechberg laid down as an undoubted fact. The step thus taken by the Danish Government was communicated in a proclamation to the Diet, and the Diet accepted that proclamation without ever objecting to it, thus virtually admitting the right of the King to change the succession. Moreover, it was contended that the States of Holstein themselves in 1853 had virtually thanked the King for what he had done in settling the succession, declaring that he had conferred a great benefit on the country. The Diet then were in full possession of the fact, but never protested against it; and the question of the succession was never raised in the Diet until within the last few months. Either that question was material or it was not; and, if material, it was extraordinary that the Diet should have overlooked it. The hon. Member said that by the proposal of his noble Friend's (Earl Russell) despatch of September, 1862, the question might have been settled, and then no war would have arisen; but that proposal did not in any way affect the question of succession. On the contrary, it admitted it. The hon. Gentleman had taunted Her Majesty's Government with having favoured one party in the quarrel; but, in fairness, he ought to have taken another view of the matter. So far from that being the case, Her Majesty's Government had incessantly, and to the last moment, urged Denmark to fulfil her promises. They had not denied for a moment that she had endeavoured to evade those promises and had not fulfilled them. But, on the other hand, he did not think that the great Powers had quite performed their promises but had violated them systematically by exciting constant disaffection and disorder in the Duchies. Again, it must be admitted that the engagements into which Denmark had entered, not by treaty but by protocols and despatches, the binding force of which he did not seek to weaken—were very difficult of fulfilment. Denmark virtually promised to give Schleswig and Holstein an equal representation in the common Parliament with Denmark itself. That would, in effect, have thrown the whole power into the hands of those Duchies. It was unfair, because it was not a representation according to population, but would have given the Duchies a preponderance over Denmark. But that ought to have been considered when the promises were made, and no doubt Denmark was bound as far as possible to carry out those promises. The Constitution of 1855, by which Denmark professed to fulfil her engagements, was abrogated upon the remonstrances of the Diet. Then came the unfortunate Patent of March, which was afterwards withdrawn; and next followed the November Constitution, which was a violation of the promises of Denmark as regarded Schleswig. There was scarcely a despatch sent to Denmark

in which the British Government did not insist that the engagements entered into had been violated, and did not urge the Danish Government to fulfil its promises. Such was the state of affairs when a new element was introduced by the sudden death of the late King, which brought into operation the law of succession. Reference had been made to the answers given last year by his noble Friend at the head of the Government to the hon. Member for Horsham (Mr. Seymour Fitzgerald), that, under certain circumstances, Denmark would not be allowed to stand alone. An interpretation had been given to that answer which was not warranted. [*Ironical cheers.*] Hon. Gentlemen opposite must not jump too hastily to a conclusion. One ought to try and be somewhat logical in the matter. What his noble Friend said was, that if the integrity of Denmark were threatened, Denmark would not be left alone. But under what circumstances was that answer given? It was before the death of the King, when Germany had no legitimate cause of complaint against Denmark. The question of the succession had not arisen. [Mr. PEACOCKE: It was after the Patent of March.] No doubt it was after the Patent of March, but the question of Schleswig had not arisen—it was then merely a question of Holstein. Had there been a wanton, causeless aggression on Denmark, he did not mean to say that the British Government would not have deemed it necessary to interfere. But that case had never arisen. The state of things contemplated in the answer of his noble Friend had never occurred. Well, the King died, and the British Government did all they could to induce Denmark to fulfil her promises. Most unfortunately a very strong party at Copenhagen drove the Government to pass the November Constitution, and only one thing was wanting to make it law—that was the signature of the King. Nobody ever accused His Majesty of anti-German tendencies. He had been throughout opposed to the very Constitution he was then required to confirm; but he felt it right now that he had ascended the throne to sign that Constitution. Her Majesty's Government were disposed at first to advise him not to sign the Constitution; but under the circumstances they afterwards thought, in presence of the strong feeling which existed, he had no alternative. Now, a state of things had previously arisen which justified the interference of the Diet in Holstein.

Mr. Layard

The Diet had already decreed execution, and it only remained to put the decree into effect. Some members of the Diet were inclined to convert the measure of execution, which was legal as against the Duke of Holstein as a member of the Confederation, into an occupation of the Duchy on international grounds. That proposal was negatived, however, and simple execution was ordered. The very act of the Diet in carrying out the execution was an admission of the right of the King who had succeeded under the new law of succession to be Duke of Holstein, because otherwise he could not have been treated as a member of the Confederation and execution decreed against him. Her Majesty's Government thought these proceedings too hasty, for in consequence of their representations and previous to the execution, the King of Denmark had already repealed the patent, and had made a promise to repeal the constitution. Thus, the King had gone even further than the Diet had a right to ask, because they were not entitled to demand a repeal of the Constitution, as Schleswig was not under the jurisdiction of the Diet. The execution was *de facto* converted into occupation. The troops of the Diet commenced by pulling down the arms of the King of Denmark and substituting German for Danish *employés*. The Duke of Augustenburg was allowed to enter the Duchies, and every encouragement was given to the German population to take part with the Pretender. Then the two great Powers of Germany appeared as the mandatories of the Diet, and as parties to the negotiation of 1851-2. They alleged that Denmark had broken her engagements by the attempt to incorporate Schleswig with Denmark, and gave forty-eight hours for the repeal of the constitution, threatening to march troops into Schleswig if the condition was not fulfilled within the time specified. The Danish Government being a constitutional Power, with Chambers to consult, it was impossible for it to accede to these terms. The British Government endeavoured to prevent the two Powers from carrying out their threat, but their representations were in vain. He could not but own that, in his opinion, M. Hall seemed to deserve the remarks which had been applied to him by hon. Members that evening, that his proceeding was certainly at variance with his desire to set Denmark right, in that he sent away the Chamber, for at that time the Chamber might have been induced to repeal the constitution. If that had been done, all pretence would have been removed for the invasion by the two German Powers. Her Majesty's Government, however, did their best to avert war. They had been taunted with supporting Denmark to a certain point, and then abandoning her. Such was not the case. The papers showed, and the Danish Minister had distinctly acknowledged to Earl Russell, that we had never promised more than moral support and sympathy. The British Government told that of Denmark plainly that they could give no material support. If they had promised support they would have given it. A great deal had been said about a despatch which had been sent to Earl Cowley. No doubt France and Russia were asked whether, in the event of any attempt being made to dismember the Danish Monarchy, they would co-operate with England to prevent such a proceeding. That situation had, however, never arisen. The Austrian and Prussian Governments, in consequence of the action taken by the British Government, distinctly declared that they had not in view the dismemberment of the Danish Monarchy, and that they adhered to the principle of the integrity of that kingdom. Well, then, would the British Government have been justified in going to war with Austria, Prussia, and the rest of Germany under such circumstances? Austria and Prussia might be behaving badly to a small Power, but as long as they maintained that they did not contemplate the dismemberment of Denmark, there was no ground for war. ["Oh!"] Did hon. Members opposite mean to say we ought to have gone to war? ["No!"] Then he must ask what they meant? That was always the way with the Opposition. When challenged on any point of policy they immediately backed out of it. He was satisfied, at any rate, that the country was with the Government in this matter, and that a war was not desired by the people. It was very easy to say that England had been degraded and humiliated. There was no humiliation in trying to preserve peace, even although their efforts had proved unavailing. In fact, they were bound when one proposal failed to make another. Her Majesty's Government were not intermeddling as had been said. ["Oh, oh!"] Would hon. Members get up and answer him, and not cry "Oh, oh?" The treaty was negotiated under our auspices. We were asked to mediate by the Diet, by Prussia, and by

Austria. If we had not complied with that invitation we should have been recreant to our principles. There was a great difference between intervention and mediation. The former implied the use of arms to force a people to accept a Government, or an arrangement to place a Government over a people. Mediation was a friendly attempt to reconcile differences and prevent war ; and it was a duty imposed on every civilized Government. Unfortunately, they had not been able to prevent the outbreak of war in Denmark, but they had been able to prevent that war from becoming a general, a great European war. It was entirely owing to the exertions of Her Majesty's Government, and the influence which they possessed in Europe, that the war had been prevented from extending over the whole Continent. That was his conviction ; the country believed so, too, and when the question came to be calmly considered, it would also be the opinion of the House. He would not follow the hon. Gentleman into the details of the question. Common decency prevented it. That was a House of debate, and he felt it would be wrong in him were he, humbly representing the Government, to express his opinion on questions of great gravity in which other Powers besides ourselves were deeply interested, when within twenty-four hours a Conference would assemble to consider them. The people of Schleswig-Holstein would be represented there ; if not adequately represented by the King of Denmark, by the Plenipotentiary of the Diet. The whole question would be heard and discussed, and, he repeated, it would be altogether unjustifiable and unprecedented if he ventured to express an opinion on its details. [*A laugh.*] He would not be driven by taunts or cheers to do so. He did not know that there was any other matter on which he need dwell. He believed no subject had ever been submitted to the consideration of the House involving so many and such difficult questions. It would be impossible for them to decide these questions in a hasty manner. The conduct which the Government had pursued was a just one. He believed the country was of the same opinion. They had endeavoured to keep the country out of a general war, and although the policy they had pursued had excited some feelings of animosity to England in Germany, yet he believed the German people were too moderate and calm not to see that Her Majesty's

Mr. Layard

Government had been influenced only by a desire to act justly. He made great allowance for the German population, but if his information was true, the feeling against this country was rapidly passing away. There was a much calmer feeling arising in Germany, and the German people, fairly considering the matter, could not fail to perceive that the conduct of the British Government had been just and moderate, intended to reconcile their differences and to respect their rights.

MR. DISRAELI : Sir, I wish to express to the House the reasons that have induced me to give notice of moving the Previous Question on the Motion of the hon. Member for Liskeard, in case, as I anticipate, I shall have an opportunity of so doing. And I am desirous on the part not merely of myself, but of many who sit on this side of the House, to take as early an opportunity in the discussion as I can for giving those reasons, because it has been said that proposing the Previous Question in this discussion implies a certain degree of confidence in the foreign policy of Her Majesty's Government. Now, Sir, as I am very much indisposed to gain any votes under false pretences, I beg to state that I have no confidence whatever in the foreign policy of Her Majesty's Government, and that I was animated in no degree by sentiments of that kind in giving a notice of this contingent character. Sir, I think the foreign policy of Her Majesty's Government, especially during the last twelve months, such as to occasion very just and grave anxiety and apprehension in this country. I think the course pursued with regard to the insurrection in Poland — a matter intimately connected with this affair of Denmark—the course pursued in that matter was one which certainly disentitled the Government to the confidence of this House. Sir, I have before referred to the total want of system which seems to characterize the management of our foreign affairs by the present Administration. I think the climax of mismanagement was reached in the conduct of the Government with respect to the Polish insurrection, and its diplomatic communications on that subject, both with France and Russia. The noble Lord, on a previous occasion when I expressed that opinion, said I was dissatisfied with the Government because they had not gone to war with Russia in the interests of Poland. Sir, although I may, and believe every one in this House must, feel that the partition of Poland was one of the most deplorable events in history, still I think that England going to war with Russia last year for Poland would have been an act of insanity—of insanity not less than going to war with Germany, which, it appears, Her Majesty's Government were quite prepared to do only a very few months ago. In conducting those negotiations we held out expectations to France, with respect to co-operating with France, in regard to the Polish insurrection which we were not justified in doing. We were not justified, because the course we apparently contemplated was one opposed to every principle of English policy, and one which no Ministry, I think, at any time was authorized to contemplate. The policy of France with regard to Poland is different from ours. We cannot blame France for that. We cannot say that France should have the same views on this question with ourselves; and when countries are on terms of intimate alliance and co-operation generally in the management of public affairs, and a different policy is pursued in matters of consequence, it is by friendly communications, sacrifices, and concessions that those misconceptions and misunderstandings which otherwise would occur are prevented. But Her Majesty's Government took a line with respect to the insurrection in Poland which anticipated all that the traditionary policy of France in regard to that country required, and then when France, encouraged by representations, by speeches in this House, by despatches in the regular course of diplomatic communications, and by extraordinary statements made by the Minister for Foreign Affairs on occasions made for the purpose—when France took a line and was prepared to follow a policy she sincerely believed perfectly consistent with her interests, we were under the necessity of suddenly drawing back and leaving France in a position which she herself candidly acknowledged was not one of dignity or self-respect in the eyes of Europe. I say we were not justified in taking that course; it was a very grave error—one of the gravest errors of modern times so to manage negotiations with Russia with respect to Poland, as to place a Power like France, in intimate terms of alliance and friendship with us, in such a position. I said we were not justified in taking that course, and the noble Lord the First Minister instantly replies, "Oh, you mean to say we ought to go to

war with Russia?" I say nothing of the kind. But I do say you committed one of the gravest errors statesmen could commit. The direct evil was great, but the indirect consequence on the position of Denmark is still graver, much more deplorable, and strictly to be traced to the conduct of Her Majesty's Government in their negotiations with respect to Poland. Now, this question of Denmark and the Duchies was most clearly, originally, a very small question. If you look to the size of the countries, the amount of population, and the resources that could be commanded by the States whose destiny was immediately at stake, it was impossible not to think that when a question of what may be called the police of Europe was raised, if there had been, which there was originally, a thorough understanding, a sincere similarity of opinion on the matter between England, France, and Russia—a rare circumstance that there should be a sincere and thorough similarity of opinion between three Powers of such paramount influence — it is impossible to suppose for a moment that the present deplorable state of things could have happened. But your influence you had destroyed by your previous conduct, and almost at the moment you quitted France and refused haughtily, even rudely, her proposition for a Congress, within forty-eight hours you were obliged, as it were, to appeal to her for assistance in the matter of Denmark and the Duchies, which has led to these serious results, to a bloody and destructive war, which has shaken the peace of Europe, and which even now may not be settled without a general state of hostilities. It may be said, and indeed it has been said, "If these are your views, why have you not brought this subject of the management of our foreign affairs under the consideration of the House?" Now, Sir, I think the answer to that is simple and satisfactory. The state of affairs which I have slightly sketched was a state of affairs existing before Parliament met. It was after the House was prorogued last year that the crowning absurdity of our negotiations with Russia was accomplished; it was during the recess that the estrangement of France arose, in consequence of our refusal to assent to a Congress; it was before Parliament met that the state of affairs with Denmark assumed its critical character. When Parliament met there was—I believe, and I have no object in concealing it—a general impression that the first duty of this House would be to consider the conduct of the Government in regard to our foreign relations, and we came here with a belief that, in the state of feeling existing in the country, and considering the alarming circumstances which attended the position of affairs on the Continent, the moment Parliament met those documents would be immediately placed upon the table of the House, which were the only foundation upon which, with any chance of success, a Motion could be based upon a subject of this kind. It is very well for the hon. Gentleman the Member for Liskeard (Mr. Bernal Osborne), concerning whose study of these papers I take a very different view from that taken by the noble Lord, for I think he has maturely considered them—it is very easy for the hon. Member, with no responsibility attaching to him, to get up and make a Motion with a very clever speech, and then to say to me and hon. Gentlemen sitting on these benches, "Why do you not come forward and declare your policy; and if you disapprove the policy of the Government, why do you not take the opinion of the House upon it?" But, Sir, at no time is a vote which really would amount to a vote of want of confidence to be lightly called for. It is not an act of mere courage, to be done without due consideration; and I maintain that, in the present position of parties, now nearly balanced, to bring forward a Motion impugning the foreign policy of Government, without at the same time taking every reasonable means of insuring success, would be an act of the greatest imprudence and of the most unjustifiable character.

In bringing forward a question of this kind there are two conditions of success which I hold to be absolutely necessary, and without which it is impossible to appeal to this House with any prospect of success. The first condition is that we should have before us all the Parliamentary documents which the House of Commons has a right to expect from the Government in explanation or vindication of its conduct. If I had given notice of a Motion challenging the policy of the Government as to Denmark, without having before us the information which we had a right to expect, the unanswerable argument of the Government would have been, "You, the House of Commons, are called upon to pronounce

upon a most important matter, and question the policy of Government while you have not the documents before you to enable you to come to any conclusion." We know well—and it is a fortunate thing it should be so—we know that there are Gentlemen on both sides of the House not holding extreme party views, who would not allow themselves to be influenced or to be brought to vote without full consideration; who would say that such an appeal could not be resisted, and consequently many Members who might perhaps have voted with us upon the merits of the question would probably vote against us. That being the first condition of success for such a Motion, how did we find ourselves situate as to the production of papers? We did assume that when Parliament met these papers would be immediately produced. There were no papers, although for weeks before Parliament met the whole country was talking of no other subject. It was not until nearly four weeks afterwards that what I may call the first batch—the first three parts of these papers—came into our possession. The explanations given by the Government upon the subject of the delay, are, I must say, to me most unsatisfactory. When the subject was first mooted in this House, the noble Lord at the head of the Government spoke in his usual manner, certainly implying that he intended to produce papers, and saying that they would be produced in due time. But the Secretary for Foreign Affairs in another place on the same evening, I think, said that no papers had been prepared, because it was not contemplated that any should be produced while negotiations were still going on. I say that the House of Commons for a considerable time was left without any knowledge of the course the Government were pursuing. It was nearly a month after they first met that these papers came into the hands of Members. Easter fell early, and just at the time when we had tolerably mastered these papers the Minister came forward and announced that negotiations were about to recommence with a considerable prospect of success.

Well, then, Sir, the second condition of success for a Motion of this kind is, that a Minister shall not be able to meet you with a statement that negotiations are going on; that by your Motion you would be interfering with them, and that you must accept the responsibility of what may follow. No person could bring forward a Motion impugning the foreign policy of a Government with any prospect of success, if the First Minister declares upon his authority that negotiations were going on. I say, then, that the two conditions of success for a Motion of this kind did not exist. We had various papers laid before us, but some of no ordinary importance—perhaps the most interesting papers—were not delivered to us until after Easter, so that we had not the opportunity of studying them during the holidays. When we met after Easter, and we had these papers in our hands, then we were told that the prospect of a Conference was almost a certainty. I took an opportunity at that time of expressing the little hope I had of any Conference without an armistice, because the incidents of one day would set aside the deliberations of the previous one. Still there was a possibility of a Conference, and we had to consider what was at stake. It was a question of great importance—no less than a question of peace or war—and although I admit that the feeling of the people of England has been one of great sympathy with the people of Denmark; although I think it is impossible not to admire the determined, even the heroic manner in which that people have defended their country, still, watching public opinion, naturally with some anxiety, I must say I am much mistaken if the predominant sentiment has not been from the first that peace should be preserved as long as it could be preserved consistently with the honour of the country. I say, then, that Gentlemen sitting on this side, strong as their feelings may have been, were not justified as patriotic men in bringing forward a vote of want of confidence—for it would have amounted to that—first, because they had no or insufficient information, and next, because they were told negotiations were about to commence.

It is impossible for any one not to have seen that for a considerable time the tendency of events has been that we should have a Conference certainly; and that probably, and now almost certainly, we should have a Conference with an armistice. The Conference is to meet to-morrow, and I shall not be surprised if an armistice is at once announced as the necessary consequence of events which I think disgraceful and deplorable, but which still are events of great magnitude, and which must exercise that influence upon human conduct and the situation of affairs that events of such magnitude usually do.

Well, we are on the eve of the Conference, and it is to meet in this city—in this parish—in the sound of that very bell which is now tolling; and this is the moment that we are asked to give an opinion—and what sort of opinion?—on the present state of affairs. The Motion of the hon. Member for Liskeard is not a censure of the general conduct of the Government—neither is the Amendment proposed by the hon. Member for Maldon, nor the Supplementary Amendment of the hon. Member for Bridgwater. They are all suggestions of bases for the Conference which is to meet to-morrow; and though I am the last person who would feel inclined to diminish the attributes and functions of the House of Commons, yet I do not think the House of Commons is exactly the place where the bases of a Conference should be devised. We have heard a great deal about sitting round a green table, but the Gentlemen sitting on these green benches are not exactly the persons to settle by commanding majorities in American style, with all their passions and Parliamentary conflicts, the bases of a Conference. On that ground I disapprove all these Motions and Amendments which are on the paper of the House. Then what is the course which we ought to adopt? My opinions on public affairs have been intimated pretty freely since Parliament met, though I have not felt justified in asking the House for a formal vote on the policy of the Government. Still, I reserve to myself the right to do so. The period of the Session is still early, and why, then, should we now be hurried to a decision? Weeks ago—before Easter—we were taunted because we did not ask the opinion of the House on the policy of the Government. All that has since occurred shows how prudent it was to allow them to develop their policy—if it may be so called —so that we might really understand what scheme they had, because it was most extraordinary that when Parliament met the Government seemed to have no policy. It is the fashion now to taunt the Opposition on the ground that they have no policy, but it would be a new function for us if we had one. We are the constitutional critics of public affairs; but the originators of measures and inventors of a policy, the individuals who come forward with their schemes and suggestions for public approbation, are not the Opposition, but the Ministers of the Crown, and we stand here to criticise the suggestions and schemes which they bring forward, and which are founded on knowledge which we cannot share, and inspired, no doubt, by the feeling of responsibility under which they act. My opinion, as far as I can orm one, on the conduct of the Government, with respect to their management of Danish affairs, is such as I have always expressed, and I have seen nothing to change it. So, with regard to the affairs f Poland, we have come to that deplorable position—for it is deplorable—which we have occupied for many months. As for the question of the Under Secretary for Foreign Affairs, "Are you for war or not?" I deny that that is the whole issue. I am not for war. I can contemplate with difficulty the combination of circumstances which can justify war in the present age unless the honour of the country is likely to suffer; but I can understand that things have been so mismanaged by Her Majesty's Government as to be brought into a position which, had they been managed with firmness, and at the same time with conciliation, they never would have occupied; and this system of Government—of always supposing that the Gordian knot can only be cut—is one which will some day drift us again into war, as it drifted us into the Crimean war. I have now given to the House the reasons, which I know are sincere, and which I trust are satisfactory, why we, with all our objections to the conduct of the Government in respect to foreign affairs, with respect to the affairs of Poland, and to the condition we are in by the estrangement of France, and with respect to the deplorable events in Denmark, have it not in our power, nevertheless, to bring forward a vote of want of confidence in the Government with those fair conditions of success which would counsel such a course in Parliament. Why, it would have been an act of absolute insanity to bring forward such a measure, had we placed it thereby in the power of the Government to say, "In the first place, you have not the information which would explain our conduct, or you are making this Motion at a time when we are about to carry on negotiations." I could not take the responsibility of bringing forward such a Motion at a moment like the present. I do not despair now that this Conference is about to assemble, but, on the contrary, I hope and believe that we shall speedily have the announcement of an armistice. I cannot, therefore, now take upon myself the responsibility of

Mr. Disraeli

challenging the Government of the Queen, and of throwing any additional obstacles in the way of the difficult task they have to accomplish. But, at the same time, I do not want our situation to be misunderstood, or our feelings to be misinterpreted. We reserve our right, as we have done from the first, to ask the House to give an opinion on the course of the Government with respect to its management of foreign affairs. I think that it is no arrogant step on our part if we presume to take the opportunity which we think the most advantageous and justifiable for that purpose. I think it is one of the first duties of those who are responsible for our party conflicts, not to fight the battle on the ground or at the time selected by our opponents. We think that we are ourselves the best judges of that question; but do not let the House suppose that in making the Motion of the Previous Question any degree of confidence is implied by us in the conduct of foreign affairs by the Ministers; and do not let the noble Lord at the head of the Government, or his Colleagues, suppose that we will not take the first fitting opportunity to ask the House to pronounce its judgment on their policy.

VISCOUNT PALMERSTON: I should have hoped that the right hon. Gentleman would have been sufficiently aware that we never could have fallen into the delusion that he would propose a vote of confidence in the Government. We do not expect that, for it is not in the nature of things, and the disclaimer on his part was by no means necessary to enlighten our minds. But if there had been any doubt on the subject, that which has just fallen from the right hon. Gentleman is calculated to dispel it. I did not, however, expect that, in a debate on Danish affairs, we should have been led back to discuss the question of Poland or that of the Congress. The right hon. Gentleman, greatly blaming our conduct throughout the whole of the transactions to which he referred, has omitted to explain what it is that we ought to have done. He blamed us for what we did, but omitted to state what he would have altered for the better. He has blamed the conduct we pursued in regard to Poland, but he has said that it would have been insanity for the English Government to go to war with Russia in respect to the affairs of Poland. Then, what other course would he have had us take? Are we to infer that, while on the one hand he thought war insanity, on the other he thought silence proper? But was it possible for the British Government to be silent in respect to the affairs of Poland? Hardly a fortnight passed last year without some question or Motion on the part of hon. Members, especially those sitting on the other side, urging Her Majesty's Government to take steps to remonstrate with the Russian Government on what was justly deemed the violation of the engagements of the Treaty of Vienna with regard to Poland. We were urged not simply to express our own opinion, but that of this House and the country, and we were urged too, not to express the English opinion only, but to endeavour to collect in a body the opinion of all the Powers of Europe, in order that the collective voice of Europe might sway the Government of Russia, and induce them to do that which it was justly contended they were bound to do by the engagements they had entered into. Therefore I say that the steps which we took with regard to Poland, were steps urged on us by the opinion of this House and of the country, and we should have been liable to censure if we had not done that which the unanimous opinion of the House and the country imperatively called on us to do. Consequently, the right hon. Gentleman having only blamed what we did, and having omitted to say what we ought to have done, we are entitled to say that our conduct with respect to Poland does not deserve the censure he has passed on it, and that there was no other course which we could pursue even according to the sentiments he has expressed. Diplomatic action was strongly forced upon us. We were repeatedly told to go to Russia with the opinions of all Europe. We did go and we failed, but that was not our fault, and we are not blameable for it. But, when the right hon. Gentleman says we lured France into a position of humiliation, I utterly deny the allegation. There was no humiliation to France. France, like Spain, like Austria, like Prussia, joined with us in urging upon the Government of Russia to fulfil the obligations of the Treaty of Vienna. Russia, admitting those obligations, and not saying, as she did before, that the conquest of Poland in 1832 emancipated her from the obligations of the Treaty of 1815, declared that she would perform them when peace and tranquillity was restored to Poland. And therefore I say we gained a point, although it was, perhaps, a small one, and there was no humiliation suffered by any of the Powers concerned—by this country, by France, by Austria, or by any other State; and I say further that that which we did was in harmony with the wishes of this House and of the country, and that France, so far from being humiliated, may look back upon the result with a feeling of satisfaction that her exertions have not been thrown away.

Then, again, we are brought back by the right hon. Gentleman to the discussion of the Congress. But, when that question was discussed in this House, we gave reasons which we thought unanswerable for not acceding to it; but as to giving a "rude" answer, I entirely deny that there was anything which could merit that epithet, although we gave in a plain and straightforward manner the reasons why we thought that Congress would lead to no useful result. So much for that which is past and gone. Now, Sir, the right hon. Gentleman has at considerable length stated the reasons why he and those who act with him have not thought fit upon those Danish affairs to call upon the House to pronounce an opinion on the policy of Her Majesty's Government. In all sincerity, I think the right hon. Gentleman has made out a very sufficient case for the satisfaction of his own party. For I admit there has not been a moment since the meeting of Parliament at which, consistently with Parliamentary practice and the real interests of the question, he could properly have called upon the House to express an opinion upon the transactions which were going on. It was no fault of ours that that could not be done. We produced the papers as soon as they were ready—we gave them by instalments from time to time up to the last moment; but the transactions to which they relate were going on from week to week and from month to month, and therefore there was no moment at which we could have given all the papers which had passed up to that time. We could only give them by instalments, and the right hon. Gentleman was quite right in saying that, the papers being always in arrear, he could have been always met by the assertion that circumstances had changed since the period up to which the papers were given, that the negotiations were still going on, and that discussion might prejudice the transactions which were then in progress. But the right hon. Gentleman gave two reasons why he could not hope for success, and I quite admit the weight and justice of those reasons. But might I presume to suggest a third, which is that the opinion of the country and of the House upon the subject of these negotiations was such that I do not think he could have hoped for success in any such Motion? This is a question upon which he and I naturally entertain a difference of opinion. I think, however, the right hon. Gentleman in the course which he has pursued or means to pursue this evening is acting very judiciously. For the reasons stated by my hon. Friend (Mr. Layard), it is exceedingly difficult for a Member of the Government upon the eve of a Conference at which the representatives of different Powers will meet to discuss an event of great and European importance—it is difficult, nay impossible, for a Member of the Government to speak without the greatest reserve upon matters which are to be subjects of discussion and deliberation in that Conference. Anything which might be said bearing upon matters which are to be made the subject of discussion would be liable to do injury either one way or the other—either by implying admissions which we ought not to make, or by laying down conditions which it might not be expedient to urge, and therefore I am precluded by the position in which I stand from following the hon. Member for Liskeard into the long and elaborate statement which he made in connection with the Danish question and the Treaty of 1852. All I can say is to repeat what my hon. Friend the Under Secretary insisted on—namely, that perpetual confusion arises from not realising and bearing in mind the distinction between a protocol and a treaty, a protocol being simply an engagement between plenipotentiaries which may be disavowed by the Government, and a treaty being a document not only signed by plenipotentiaries, but ratified by the hand of the Sovereign, and therefore binding upon the State whose Sovereign has concluded and ratified the engagement. The Treaty of 1852 is a document of that description, and my noble Friend at the head of the Foreign Office is perfectly justified in saying, that when any person talks of the Treaty of 1852 as an instrument of no effect, he is wrong, because it is a treaty to the observance and execution of which every Sovereign who ratified it is bound. Well, Sir, all the Powers who were parties to that treaty, and whose plenipotentiaries are to meet to-morrow, acknowledge its validity and obligation, and therefore the case which was contemplated by the questions and answers to which allusion has been

Viscount Palmerston

made as a case of intended dismemberment of the Danish monarchy has not arisen, and cannot arise as long as the Powers who are parties to the Treaty of 1852 maintain that which I hold they are bound in honour to maintain—namely, the engagements to which they pledged themselves by that treaty. As for the share which fell to my lot in the negotiation of that treaty, I am proud of it; but the merit of having finally concluded it belongs to the Government of the Earl of Derby, and to the Foreign Secretary of that day, the Earl of Malmesbury, who signed it, and brought it to its completion. Therefore, the merit, if merit there be, is to be divided between us, and of the blame, if there be any, the right hon. Gentleman must consent to take his share. As I have said before, I think that the course which the right hon. Gentleman proposes to adopt on the present occasion is the right one. I think that upon the eve of the meeting of a Conference of the different Powers who signed the Treaty of 1852, for the purpose of endeavouring to restore peace, and of establishing at the outset, as I hope, an armistice, if there were to be any strong expression of opinion on the part of this House, it would tend prejudicially to effect the result of the negotiations which are about to take place. I therefore concur with the right hon. Gentleman in thinking that the course which this House would most wisely adopt would be to agree with him in his Motion of the Previous Question. I will myself cordially be his follower on the present occasion. I will give him that confidence in this instance which he refuses to give to me, and I will most willingly follow him into the lobby on the Previous Question.

MR. KINGLAKE said, it was with the greatest reluctance that he rose on that occasion after the leaders of the House on either side had spoken; but as he had an Amendment on the paper, he thought it his duty to address a few words to the House. The noble Lord who had just sat down had stated that the near approach of the Conference forced upon him so great a reserve that anything like free discussion on his part was all but impossible. But the Amendment which he (Mr. Kinglake) had put upon the paper was in the interest of that very reserve. It was founded on the fact that the noble Lord a few days ago, well knowing that the Conference was about to meet, came down to the House and prejudged the question by asserting that the King of Denmark was to be deemed the lawful Sovereign of the people of the Duchies. So much, therefore, for that Ministerial reserve of which the noble Lord would make so great account. The noble Lord had thought it necessary for the third or fourth time to explain the difference between a protocol and a treaty; just as if his hon. Friend (Mr. Osborne), who had shown so intimate a knowledge of the whole question, did not know the one from the other. But the noble Lord entirely misunderstood the cause of the use of the phrase "protocol of London" on the Continent. It was not that the Germans did not know the difference between a protocol and a treaty; they knew it very well, but the indignant people intentionally went back to the origin of those proceedings, and called it the hateful protocol of London, because it was hateful to them. To that very day the Treaty of 1852 had not received the assent of the German Confederation. He entirely agreed with the opinion expressed by the hon. Under Secretary of State that there was no justification for a war in the matter against Germany; and he compared that opinion very gladly with the invitation which, towards the end of January, was addressed to France, Spain, and Russia, to join in a league for resisting, if necessary, the invasion of Schleswig. That proposal failed, partly because it encountered the refusal of the French Government; and, when Parliament met, the feeling of the House of Commons was sufficiently shown to make it certain that England would not go to war in any such cause. It was true that in the progress of the negotiation there was seemingly an approach towards war. And now that we knew there was to be no war, the country was undoubtedly open to the taunt of its enemies, that while England had acknowledged in many ways that she was bound in honour to go to war for Denmark, she, in fact, had not done so. That was a wrong conclusion gratuitously arrived at, but it was one full of danger, for the people of England would not long endure to have it imputed to them that they were enjoying a dishonourable peace. In his opinion, it was not a dishonourable peace, and war would have have been unjustifiable under the circumstances. But it was of the greatest importance for the honour of England to show that the peace which we were enjoying was not a peace arrived at for the sake of retaining the magnificent state of things indicated in the Budget; that

it was not a peace to which we clung for any base purpose, but that we held to peace simply because war would have been impolitic and unjust. A moment's thought would show us that the position of England in this matter was not so dishonourable as the enemies of the country represented. When a weak Power was leaning on a strong one in the expectation of assistance, the former did not immediately plunge into war, but proposed terms of a moderate kind which might be acceptable to the smaller Power, and which its opponent might also be persuaded to accept. Well, that was what England did. She succeeded in obtaining the assent of Austria and Prussia to certain terms, but Denmark refused them. No doubt, Denmark had a perfect right to refuse them, but that refusal surely absolved England from responsibility. On the first day of the Session he had pointed out that neither the Earl of Malmesbury nor any of those who were parties to that treaty could have framed it on such a plan as that the consent of the Estates of Holstein and Schleswig should be excluded. He never supposed that any English statesman would deliberately set his hand to a treaty which was to infringe the liberty of a constitutional country. But, since then, papers have been laid before Parliament which explained in the frankest way what were the views of those who commenced the negotiations in 1850, and who brought them to a close in 1852. In 1850 the noble Lord was inviting the Powers of Europe to a Conference. Did he then pretend that by a treaty of the kind the rights of persons in the country dealt with were to be superseded? Not at all; and that was a view which extricated the noble Lord from much of what was said by his hon. Friend (Mr. Osborne). The noble Lord thought that all the internal arrangements necessary for giving effect to his scheme should be made in Denmark and the Duchies, and that then Europe should give its sanction to the arrangement so made. The noble Lord then wrote that it was not professed that the Conference of London should interfere with the arrangements which the King of Denmark should make in the order of succession, but that the parties to the protocol should approve these arrangements when and after they should have been made. In other despatches the noble Lord used language which was equally clear; and again, in a statement drawn up on the eve of the treaty by Baron Brunnow, who was propelling these arrangements, he distinctly said that the Chambers would be crushed. That being the intention of those who were acting at the time, and it being obviously consistent with what the statesmen of a constitutional country must have intended, he could not help thinking, that when the matter came to be properly understood, the Government would see the necessity, not of asking these Estates to choose a Government, but of requiring that they should be consulted before the change of succession took place. The answer of the Foreign Secretary to that question seemed a most curious one. The reason for not appealing to those Estates was, he said, that they came into existence after 1815, and that, therefore, as he explained it, they had no attribute to alter the law of succession. But, surely, it was unnecessary to go back to a period anterior to 1815 in order to find a right to be consulted upon changes of the kind. It really seemed to him that the course pursued was one which involved a misinterpretation of the treaty, a contempt for that principle of nationality which in other cases we had taken so much to heart, and for that principle of non-intervention which was never so well applied as when it was directed to prohibit interference in the affairs of foreign States. It was a course besides which put us in antagonism to nations of Europe who were our natural allies, and all that was done not to avert a war, but to prevent the restoration of peace.

Colonel WILSON PATTEN said, that before the Question was put he wished to know how they were to vote. There were two Amendments before the House as well as the Motion of the hon. Member for Liskeard. Now he intended to vote for the Previous Question, but what he wished to know was, whether in order to do so they must not first vote against the Motion of the hon. Member for Maldon, and then, as it were, for the Motion of the hon. Member for Liskeard, and afterwards, when the original Motion was put, to vote in favour of the Previous Question.

Mr. BERNAL OSBORNE: I think I shall simplify the Question very much by saying that I am so satisfied with the discussion which has taken place, so satisfied with the reserve which has been displayed by the Under Secretary for Foreign Affairs, who has come out to-night in a new character as the representative of decency and delicacy, so satisfied with the reserve of the noble Lord, and above all, so convinced that this Treaty of 1852 is a dead letter,

Mr. *Kinglake*

which will never patch up the so-called integrity of Denmark, that I shall be content to be adjudged by the events of the Conference. I will therefore simplify matters by saying that on this occasion, like the noble Lord, I shall also be a follower of the right hon. Gentleman (Mr. Disraeli). [*Cries of* "No, no!"]

Mr. PEACOCKE said, he wished to ask how the question really stood. As he understood it, the hon. Gentleman the Member for Liskeard did not press his Motion, and consequently his (Mr. Peacocke's) Motion was gone.

Mr. BERNAL OSBORNE: I beg to withdraw my Motion. ["No, no!"]

Mr. SPEAKER: Does the hon. Member propose to withdraw his Amendment?

Mr. PEACOCKE: On the understanding that the Original Motion be withdrawn.

Amendment, by leave, withdrawn.

Original Question again proposed.

Mr. SPEAKER said, that the Amendment had been withdrawn by the consent of the House; but as the House did not consent to the withdrawal of the Original Motion, the right hon. Gentleman (Mr. Disraeli) would have an opportunity of moving the Previous Question.

Mr. DISRAELI: I beg to move the Previous Question.

Whereupon Previous Question, "That that Question be now put,—(Mr. Disraeli) —put, and negatived.

COURT OF CHANCERY (IRELAND) BILL.

LEAVE.

Mr. O'HAGAN (THE ATTORNEY GENERAL FOR IRELAND) said, he rose to move for leave to bring in a Bill to alter the constitution and amend the practice and course of proceeding in the High Court of Chancery in Ireland. Owing, however, to the lateness of the hour, he would reserve any remarks he might have to make until the second reading of the Bill.

Motion made, and Question proposed,

"That leave be given to bring in a Bill to alter the constitution and amend the practice and course of proceeding in the High Court of Chancery in Ireland."—(*Mr. Attorney General for Ireland.*)

Mr. WHITESIDE said, he must protest against the Bill being brought in without any statement of the places which it purposed abolishing, and, above all, of the places which it would create.

Mr. SCULLY said, he was of opinion that the second reading would be the fitting opportunity for the discussion of the details of the Bill.

Mr. O'HAGAN was ready to make the statement at once if it was wished. The object of the Bill was to assimilate the Chancery practice according to the recommendations of the Royal Commission, whose Report was laid on the table of the House last Session. He thought the more convenient course would be to print the Bill, and make the statement at the second reading.

Mr. HENNESSY said, that hon. Members had not yet had time to read the Report of the Royal Commission; and he therefore begged to move the adjournment of the debate.

Motion made, and Question proposed, "That the Debate be now adjourned." —(*Mr. Hennessy.*)

Sir JOHN SHELLEY said, he thought that it would be more convenient to allow the Bill to be introduced and printed before a statement was made.

Lord NAAS observed, that hon. Members on his side of the House had no wish to obstruct the public business, but the Bill was one of enormous importance, and the House ought to be informed of the reasons which induced the Government to propose it.

Sir ROBERT PEEL said, his right hon. and learned Friend the Attorney General for Ireland was quite prepared to make his statement; and, as it would only occupy about an hour, he hoped his hon. Friends on the other side would not prevent him from making it at that early hour (ten minutes past twelve o'clock), seeing that a Session or two ago Irish Bills were frequently introduced at one or two in the morning.

Mr. WHITESIDE remarked that he had introduced several Irish Bills, but he had never ventured to introduce a Bill of such importance as the present one without a word of discussion.

Mr. MALINS said, he thought that the Government ought not to persevere in introducing the measure without a statement when there was such a strong party in the House against their adopting such a course.

The ATTORNEY GENERAL submitted that, as the Bill was introduced for the purpose of carrying out the recommendations of a Royal Commission, it was not necessary to make a detailed statement on the Motion for the first reading.

Lord CLAUD HAMILTON said, he was of opinion that Irish Bills of importance ought not to be brought in without that full and clear explanation which was invariably given in the case of English measures.

The CHANCELLOR OF THE EXCHEQUER said, it was a very common practice on both sides of the House, and served the purposes of general convenience, to allow the introduction of a Bill, and to explain its details at a subsequent stage.

Mr. GEORGE said, the Bill involved matters of very considerable importance, and had reference to the abolishment and creation of offices. He thought it was due both to the House and to the public that some explanation should be offered on the introduction of the Bill.

Mr. CRAUFURD said, that the course proposed by the Government was often pursued with reference to Scotch Bills.

Viscount PALMERSTON said, that no Irish Member could be ignorant of the objects and arrangement proposed by the Bill. He therefore trusted that the discussion of the details would be postponed until the second reading.

Mr. SEYMOUR FITZGERALD said, that the uniform practice was that Bills were not brought in without explanation, when hon. Members declared that the public interests required such explanation.

Sir JAMES FERGUSSON thought they had a right to insist upon explanations being given before the Bill was proceeded with.

Question put.

The House *divided*:—Ayes 28; Noes 57: Majority 29.

Original Question again proposed.

Mr. WHITESIDE said, that those entrusted with the business of the country were not taking a wise course in endeavouring to force laws upon Ireland, the nature of which they would not state.

Colonel DUNNE moved the adjournment of the House.

Mr. O'HAGAN said, he must protest against the assumption that he had acted disrespectfully towards the House, whose convenience he endeavoured to consult. After what had occurred, and the feeling which had been shown, he should certainly not press the measure that evening.

Motion, by leave, *withdrawn*.

PROMISSORY NOTES AND BILLS OF EXCHANGE (IRELAND) BILL.

Bill to remove certain restrictions on the negotiation of Promissory Notes and Bills of Exchange under a limited sum in Ireland, *ordered* to be brought in by Sir COLMAN O'LOGHLEN and Captain STACPOOLE.
Bill *presented*, and read 1°. [Bill 74.]

CUSTOMS AND INLAND REVENUE BILL.

Bill to grant certain Duties of Customs and Inland Revenue, *presented*, and read 1°. [Bill 73.]

House adjourned at a quarter after One o'clock.

~~~~~~~~

HOUSE OF COMMONS,

Wednesday, April 20, 1864.

MINUTES.] — SELECT COMMITTEE — On Dockyards, Mr. Stansfeld, Captain Talbot, *added*; on Taxation of Ireland, Lord Stanley *discharged*, Mr. Banks Stanhope *added*.
PUBLIC BILLS—*Ordered*—Oyster Fisheries (Ireland)°.
First Reading — Oyster Fisheries (Ireland)° [Bill 75].
Second Reading — Grand Juries (Ireland) [Bill 35]; Chief Rents (Ireland) [Bill 52].
Committee—Bridges (Ireland)° [Bill 70]—R.P.

GRAND JURIES (IRELAND) BILL.

[BILL 35.] SECOND READING.

Order for Second Reading read.

MR. BLAKE said, he begged to move the second reading of the Bill, the main principles of which consisted in the separation of the criminal from the fiscal business of counties, leaving the first to be discharged, as hitherto, by the grand jury summoned by the sheriff, and transferring the latter to county and baronial Boards of an elective and representative character, consisting of an equal number of members severally appointed by the magistracy and ratepayers. Although the Bill had not the merit of originality, still for that very reason it recommended itself for their adoption—as measures of nearly a similar character had been introduced, not only by distinguished private Members, but by Ministers of the Crown, one of whom, the Secretary of State for the Home Department, he was glad to see in his place, as he and Sir William Somerville, when Chief Secretary for Ireland, had introduced so good a Bill that he (Mr. Blake) had adopted several of the best clauses. Numerous petitions from Ireland in former years had prayed for the reform which he sought to effect, and the Royal Commission, appointed in 1842, to inquire into the subject, had made suggestions which he had adopted. There was one most important principle omitted from the Bill—that of relieving the occupier from a portion of the rate now entirely borne by him. There could not be a final and just settlement of the question until that was done, but no provision was made for it in the Bill, for the simple reason that with an Irish representation, consisting of three-fourths landlords, unpledged to support such a proposal, it was hopeless to attempt to carry it under existing circumstances — it should be left to other times, and, perhaps, to other men, to accomplish that reform; but it should be quite understood that neither he nor his hon. Friends for a moment surrendered the principle, as he believed there were far greater grievances which the Irish tenant had to complain of than being obliged to pay all the rate. Landlords would, no doubt, assert that practically they paid it, as they let their land subject to the rate, which, if they had to pay, they would add to the rent. But he believed that, practically, the tenant gets the land not a shilling less because he pays the rate; and, once in possession, it was really the interest of the landlord to allow as much baronial rate to be heaped on him as possible, as thereby his property was improved by the outlay for bridges, roads, and other permanent works, of which the tenant, from the system of land tenure in Ireland, may be said to have only temporary advantages, whilst the landlord got an increased rent for his ground, rendered of more value by the outlay on county and baronial works near it, for which the tenant had borne the cost. The large increase in the grand jury rate, now nearly double what it was formerly, and amounting to over a million a year, proved its uncertain nature and tendency to increase, notwithstanding the transfer of the charge for police to the Consolidated Fund, the depressed condition of the country, and the less wear and tear of the public roads consequent on the increase of railroads, which must absorb much of the traffic which used to pass over the former. It was a strange anomaly that those who contributed most to the rates had no control over their expenditure; and down to 1836 no matter how profligate the waste of the public money might be, the ratepayers had no means of knowing who were parties to it, as the grand jury sat with closed doors, and were bound by the same oath of secrecy regarding fiscal as criminal matters. In that year, however, a great change for the better took place. An Act was passed giving publicity to the proceedings, and an attempt was made to introduce something of representation into the system, but which practically proved nugatory. The sheriff was obliged to summon a person on the grand panel from each barony; but it was open to him to summon those whom he knew would not attend (of which there were many instances), and having fulfilled the law, could form the jury just as he pleased, whenever he had any object to accomplish. Presentment sessions were appointed, when a certain number of cesspayers were associated with magistrates; but these were the nominees not of those whom they were supposed to represent, but of those whom they were to control, as the plan adopted was for the cess collector of each barony to send in the names to the grand jury of 100 of the highest ratepayers, and from these were selected double the required number usually drawn by the grand juror from the barony, and those to serve were then drawn from a hat at the next presentment sessions. It is only natural to suppose that the grand juror selected those who would be most likely to obey his behests, and even if they were the most independent men imaginable they could be, as, indeed, they sometimes were, outvoted by the magistracy who could attend from all parts of the county. True, there was an appeal to the grand jury, but that was only an appeal to the same body, and as to protesting before the Judge of assize he would be a rash ratepayer who would resort to it, as, besides having to bear all the expense, he would run the risk of incurring the vengeance of some one of the grand jury, probably his landlord, and might be quite sure he would never enjoy the dignity again of sitting as an associated ratepayer with the justices from whom he had presumed to dissent. Some idea might be formed of the pliant instruments who were nominated as associated ratepayers, when, according to the Report of the Royal Commissioners of 1842, in the county of Kerry, persons little above the class of labourers were nominated to sit with the magistrates, who could not speak English, and deaf and blind persons were appointed in other places. The whole affair, therefore, became a farce, and was well described in

the concluding part of the Report of the Royal Commissioners of 1842:—

"The intent of the Legislature in establishing presentment sessions seems to have been to give to the ratepayers such a representation thereat as would enable them to prevent improper or improvident presentments; but the law is not effectual for its purpose. Magistrates may, and when a particular object is to be carried, not unfrequently do, attend the presentment sessions of baronies where they have no property, and outvote those who have. Then, as to the associated ratepayers, they are not chosen by the ratepayers at large, but are taken by lot from the reduced lists made by the grand jury in the way already described. They are, therefore, nominees, not of the class they are to represent, but of the class they are to control. The lot, too, may fall upon the most unfit, which is of itself a serious fault in the system, and the uncertainty in which the ratepayers named by the grand jury are left until the day of the presentment sessions, as to the particular individuals who may be drawn to serve, is obviously calculated to prevent a regular attendance.

"(Signed) J. BLAKE, Chief Remembrancer, JOHN YOUNG, Bart, BARON GREENE, WM. SOMERVILLE, Bart., JOHN L. O'FERRALL."

He would read for them a small portion of the evidence on which that Report was founded, and would select the opinions of men who were neither radical reformers or having revolutionary ideas, but noblemen and gentlemen of aristocratic position, and having a large stake in the country, but who were impressed with the necessity of reform, and willing to make just concessions. (Mr. Blake here read several extracts from the evidence of Lord Clancarty, the hon. Admiral Trench, Sir Richard Musgrave, Sir Richard Kane, Mr. Kincaid, agent to Lord Palmerston, Mr. Hancock, agent to Lord Lurgan, in favour of the division of the rate between landlord and tenant, and a representation from the latter by election, and also an extract from a speech of Mr. Butt's in 1861, showing the various Bills that had been introduced by Government and private Members to amend the system which had fallen through, and proceeded)—twenty-one years had passed since the Report of the Commissioners, and not one of their suggestions had been carried out. Bills containing some excellent provisions had been introduced, amongst them, Sir William Somerville's and Sir Denham Norreys's, the latter going far to remedy the evils complained of, including the division of the rate, and was such a reform that it would have produced much good, but his zeal and ability proved fruitless. Chief Secretaries promised everything if the hon. Members would only postpone the matter, but did nothing. Two years ago he had brought the subject under the notice of the present Chief Secretary. The right hon. Baronet had promised to consider the subject during the recess, and, without having given an absolute undertaking, had certainly led him to hope that legislation would have followed, but there was no sign of it; therefore he had put together the Bill now before the House as something of a suggestive character for the Government. He was sure there were many defects in it, as he was not accustomed to draw Bills. His hon. Friend the Member for Wexford had aided him so far as his numerous occupations permitted him, and they only intended the Bill as an embodiment of principles, leaving details of working them out to be supplied if it went into Committee. It provided for appointment of the county and baronial Boards, rotation of Members, mode of election, and giving to these bodies the character of county corporations, which would be an improvement on their present transitory character, in consequence of which many works taken up by one grand jury were left unfinished, as there was no provision enabling them to meet between one assize and another, no matter how great the necessity. Rank and property were given their legitimate weight, by allowing half of each Board to be appointed by the magistracy, and peers, hitherto excluded, were rendered eligible for both. Under no circumstances could the democratic element preponderate, whatever chance there might be for the aristocratic to be in the ascendant. As, besides, half of each body being sent in by the magistrates, no doubt many of the gentry would be selected by the ratepayers to represent them. The 25th clause conferred on county and baronial Boards all the powers of the Land Drainage Act of last year. He had inserted it at the instance of one of the first men in Ireland, as occupying the foremost commercial position, and having done much to develop the enterprise and progress of the country, and whose opinion on any subject for the benefit of Ireland deserved the utmost weight. He could do no better than quote the very words of the gentleman he alluded to :—

"Your favour of the 15th has found me here. I cannot go into the defence of the drainage so fully as if I were at home, but I think it will be evident that in all countries there are systems of arterial drainage that in some cases will require to traverse large sections of the county, and that, like roads, will require to come before dis-

Mr. Blake

tinct interests, which will require the combined legislation of the county—for instance, a branch road may run through only three or four properties, but if you have to lead water either to the coast or the main river, it may require an arterial outlet as far as from Tramore to Waterford, in which case more than one of your county divisions will be interested; besides, it may be a question for electing a member to the county Board if he will advocate the arterial drainage. It will also afford an opportunity at its meeting for pressing the necessity for such in certain localities if it is made one of the powers and duties of the county Board, and private proprietors will bow to its decisions of the necessity for such when wanted, when they may otherwise decline to entertain its consideration. In fact, I think it will be one of the most useful functions of the Board, and funds would be more secure in their hands, and having the official engineer of the county under their control, they are in a better position to obtain practical advice than others. I hope you will be able to make a good case, though you may not succeed this time."

Clause 26 gave County Boards the power of appointing an equal number of representatives on the Boards of Lunatic Asylums with those nominated by the Lord Lieutenant, which, he believed, would be as just as it would be desirable. Though these institutions were wholly supported out of county rates, grand juries had no power over them beyond visiting them at each assizes. The Lord Lieutenant, having no local knowledge generally speaking, had, he believed, to rely in a great measure on the suggestions of the inspectors as to the persons to be appointed. He had reason to think that many members of the different Boards owed their seats to that source, the policy of which he very much doubted, as governors ought to be wholly independent of those officers. Indeed, he had found great difficulty in his efforts to have beneficial changes introduced into the system of moral treatment of lunatics in Ireland when matters did not accord with the views of the inspectors, the governors usually deferring to them when they ought to act for themselves. Such were the leading features of the Bill which he had the honour to submit for the consideration of the House, and trusted they would allow it to go into Committee. An hon. and gallant Member had proposed its rejection, on what grounds he was at a loss to conceive, as he believed the hon. Member was a man of enlightened and progressive views, and not opposed to making just concessions to popular wishes. Surely the order to which he belonged had ample safeguards in the Bill to protect their legitimate privileges, and he would ask the hon. Member, as a grand juror, would not his position be a more independent and satisfactory one if he owed it to his brother magistrates, or fellow ratepayers, than to the favour of the high sheriff himself, a nominee of the Government'; and he would further ask what reasonable objection could there be to allowing the ratepayers to appoint their own representatives, and to provide that they should not, on particular occasions, be utterly overborne by magistrates having no property in connection with their barony. He respectfully asked them to reverse a system founded on laws opposed to the whole system of modern legislation. The grand jury laws, as they stood at present, were, as was justly remarked, a last relic of the rude and lawless times when they were called into existence. What the precise time that a court formed for purposes of criminal judicature assumed the fiscal powers so foreign to its character, was more a matter of antiquarian interest than practical import; but it was certain that it must have been when the want of education amongst the great mass of the people disqualified them from taking that share in the management of their own affairs for which they were now fitted, and when also the ascendancy of the law, not being perfectly established, local duties were but little regarded, and local duties not properly understood. At such a time there may have been a justification, which did not now exist, for a court of criminal adjudicature taking on itself the duty of presenting for the repairs of roads and other fiscal powers, in addition to that which devolved on it, of indicting and prosecuting those who neglected the proper maintenance of the public highways. At this hour, however, it was as unjust as it was absurd and unconstitutional to continue a system which could not fail to be a source of continued dissatisfaction—exacting, as it did, a million a year from the occupier without his consent, and expending it without his approval. There was no system so bad, said a writer on the subject, for the performance of public duties, than that which confers nominal without real responsibility — and which professed to create representation, whilst the representative power was practically withheld. In the absence of this practical reality, the cesspayers felt they had no real powers, and thus the odium of increasing taxation was thrown on the grand jurors, no matter how zealously and honestly they discharged their duties.

They ought, therefore, to be glad for their own sakes to see the representative principle extended to county fiscal administration; it was the true one as regarded taxation, and there seemed no more reason why it would not be adopted in Irish county affairs than in the raising and disbursement of the finances of the Empire by the Commons, or, to go a little lower, as occurred under the Poor Laws and municipal affairs —some civic authorities having now taken the whole of the fiscal affairs of their towns into their own hands. He earnestly appealed to the hon. Baronet to realize the hopes which were entertained, that he would make a real effort to settle this important question satisfactorily. It was a remark of the illustrious man whose name he bore, that he never knew a Session of Parliament without the introduction of an Irish Grand Jury Bill, which usually fell through at the first stage; a good proof of how even in his time there existed a strong desire on the subject, which Parliament trifled with. Quite as much feeling on the subject existed now. Petitions had been sent until the people had been tired out sending them. A Grand Jury Reform Association had sat in Dublin for a long time and did good service in getting up an agitation, and published an able and interesting pamphlet on the question, but ceased its labours when it found Parliament would do nothing. The Chief Secretary had favourably identified himself with one of the most useful measures which had been passed for Ireland for many years—the Fishery Bill of last Session. Grand Jury Reform was equally worthy of his attention. He professed to love English institutions; let him, then, extend to Ireland the good old Saxon principle of local self-government and the right to manage their own affairs. By doing so he would foster habits of self-reliance and independence, and promote feelings of confidence between the different classes, and county burdens would then be more cheerfully borne when the people would have extended to them that great maxim of the British constitution which said "there shall be no taxation without representation."

Motion made, and Question proposed, "That the Bill be now read a second time."—(*Mr. Blake.*)

MR. DAWSON said, he did not think the Bill afforded any prospect of wholesome legislation, and would therefore move that it be read a second time that day six months. It had upon the face of it many sins, both of omission and commission. It abolished, as far as fiscal matters went, an old and time-honoured tribunal, which had for centuries transacted, with economy and impartiality, both the fiscal and criminal business of the counties; and yet so carelessly had the Bill been drawn, that it contained no provision for regulating the manner in which the public works of counties were to be carried out. A long experience of the working of the present system in his own county enabled him with pleasure to bear his testimony to the capacity for business and the high sense of honour which invariably had characterized the members of the grand jury. The Bill amounted to nothing less than a thorough demolition of that system; and although he was not opposed to some alteration in it by which a more independent position might be given to the associated cesspayers and their number increased, yet he maintained that any such changes ought to be proposed on the authority of the Government, to whom the responsibility of such a proceeding would properly belong. Hasty and sweeping legislation on such a question was seriously to be deprecated, and the people of Ireland had a right to complain that the measure had not been introduced and printed on an earlier day. The grand juries had had no opportunity of considering it in their corporate capacity.

Amendment proposed, to leave out the word "now," and at the end of the Question to add the words "upon this day six months."—(*Mr. Dawson*).

Mr. BAGWELL said, he had never joined in any cry that the gentlemen of Ireland had not with the utmost ability and integrity of purpose fulfilled their duties as grand jurors. But there were two main points in the proposition before the House, the one social and the other fiscal. Socially nothing could be more beneficial to Ireland than bringing together the magistrates and the occupiers of land. That had been found to be of the greatest use in the administration of the Poor Law. When gentlemen of high position and the ratepayers came together for public purposes, it was found on the one hand that the latter were not quite so ignorant as was supposed, and that the former were neither so selfish nor so inconsiderate as had been alleged against them. But he had always objected to

Mr. Dawson

the county cess being divided between the landlord and the tenant as calculated to disarrange their mutual relations. He thought it a mere matter of justice to hand over the arrangements as to the making of roads to the ratepayers and magistrates. The valuation of Ireland in 1862 was £12,567,494. In 1862 the grand jury assessment for the whole of Ireland was £1,808,828, or in round numbers about one-twelfth. The poor rates were £516,759. Seeing that so large an amount administered by the grand jury was paid by occupiers, they ought to have some control in the matter. In the case of the Poor Law there were elective guardians, though tenants only paid half of the rate. How much more ought they to have a control where they paid the whole of an assessment. The proposer of the Bill had stated that he regarded it as valuable only as laying down a principle, and if it were allowed to go into Committee he should be ready to accept any Amendment that would carry out that principle. He was afraid, however, much support would not be given to the Bill on the other side of the House. He hoped, if the right hon. Baronet the Chief Secretary for Ireland opposed the Bill, he would give some promise of introducing a measure on this subject himself.

Mr. POLLARD-URQUHART said, that whatever the faults of omission or commission the Bill possessed, it should be allowed to go into Committee where they could be remedied. He believed that the magistrates and landlords in Ireland discharged their duties on the grand juries with integrity; but, he asked, whether the time had not arrived when something should be done to associate the cesspayers, farmers, and others in the administration of the cess. The experiment of elective guardians had been tried for the last seventeen years in the administration of the Poor Law; and it was stated before the Poor Law Committee of 1861, that the effect had been to remove many prejudices. He hoped the Government would allow the Bill to be read a second time.

Mr. MAGUIRE said, that considering the admissions he had made, he did not think that there was any extraordinary difference of opinion between the hon. Member for Londonderry (Mr. Dawson) and his hon. Friend who had brought in the Bill on the subject of it. It was a matter of little consequence whether the party with which he acted received support from the occupants of the benches on his side or the Ministerial side of the House. The Irish Members made no covenant or bargain with any party. They were as independent of either as either was independent of them. Hon. Gentlemen were returned to that House to represent the nation at large, and to regulate the fiscal affairs of the kingdom up to £70,000,000. Why should not this principle of representation be applied to the regulation of the money of the taxpayers of counties ? The fiscal powers had been already taken away from the grand juries in various localities —such, for example, as Dublin and Cork —and with the most useful results. If it worked well in the cities why should not the principle be extended generally throughout the country ? His hon. Friend wished to put the elective cesspayers and the elected magistrates upon the same footing. He could mention cases in which five or six rated associated cesspayers sitting at presentment sessions were swamped in their votes by magistrates living some thirty, forty, or fifty miles distant from the barony, who trooped in for the purpose of carrying—he would not say a job—but the particular object which they had in view. It should be recollected that the owner had a permanent interest in the expenditure of public money for the improvement of his property, whilst the interest of the tenant was but temporary. Nevertheless, those improvements were not effected with the money of the landlord, but with the money of the tenant, who paid the entire rates. The country gentlemen of Ireland ought to be the first to propose such a change as would give confidence in those who had none at present in the existing system. He wished his hon. Friend had gone farther, because he considered it was unfair that the landlord should be free from this charge. It ought to be divided between the landlord and the occupier, as was the case with the poor rate. The landlord and the occupier had to divide the charge of a pauper ; but when he became a lunatic then the whole charge was thrown on the occupier. That was unfair, and he challenged the landlord interest to give a good reason for the continuance of that principle. His hon. Friend (Mr. Blake) had omitted from the Bill what he should like to see established—namely, an equal division of the rate between landlord and occupier. But this was a landlord's Parliament, and there had not been sufficient agitation upon the subject to compel landlords to pledge

themselves that there should be an equitable division of this burden, and until that pressure was put upon them it would be difficult for any one to expect to carry such a proposition. But his hon. Friend did not abandon the hope. The boards of guardians fairly represented all classes of the community, because those who paid the rates elected to a certain extent those who had to administer the law and expend the money. The same principle ought to be applied to the county cess, because they were at present the nominees of the sheriffs, who were the nominees of the Crown, and who were able to perpetrate any job. The present machinery was certainly not such as could be defended. Taxation and representation in this matter ought to go hand in hand. His hon. Friend did not expect to be able to carry the Bill, but he did hope to have the principle affirmed by a second reading, in which case it was desirable that the Government should undertake to deal with the subject, and by their influence obtain the passing of a satisfactory measure.

LORD JOHN BROWNE said, he would assent to the second reading, though he could not support the Bill as it stood. He believed the existing grand jury system to be a very bad one, and that it would have been long ago abolished but for the circumstance that it had been well administered. The grand jury was arbitrarily chosen by the sheriff, who was himself arbitrarily chosen by the Judge of assize. They were supposed to be representatives of the largest properties in Ireland, but this was by no means always the case. They were called together twice a year, and in a couple of days were required to go through a quantity of business, requiring twice as large a portion of time. One most important clause in the existing law was so absurdly worded that it bore a different interpretation in different counties. Again, at present there was a risk of loss from defalcations of the High Constables who received the county cess, and if those losses had not been frequent it was attributable to the care taken by the grand juries in the selection of persons to fill the office of High Constable. He would. desire to see Baronial Boards appointed, but he should object to the formation of County Boards as proposed by this Bill. Sir William Somerville introduced a Bill in 1849 which he much preferred to this. It was, however, impossible to expect that the Bill could pass this Session, and he trusted that the subject would engage the attention of the Government, and that they would introduce a measure next year, as it was beyond the power of any private Member satisfactorily to deal with it.

LORD NAAS said, he was pleased to find that the Bill had been discussed in so calm and moderate a tone; but he could not but think that the case against the present law had utterly broken down. The supporters of the Bill had failed to show that there had been any want of economy or any jobbing or neglect of duty. If there was any dissatisfaction in Ireland with respect to the working of the grand jury law, all he could say was that it had been kept a profound secret until now. If, then, no case had been made out against the administration of the present law, and no dissatisfaction existed with regard to its working, he thought the House should be very careful before it sanctioned so radical and complete a change as that proposed by the hon. Member for Waterford (Mr. Blake). It had been stated that great dissatisfaction existed amongst the ratepayers and occupiers as to the working of the grand jury system; but if such dissatisfaction existed it was kept a profound secret. No case having been made out for the proposed change, the House ought to be very careful before it rejected a system which had worked well for the purpose of introducing another, the working of which was very problematical. There was one point which had not been so prominently put forward, but which was at the root of the whole affair—and that was a certain amount of dissatisfaction as to the incidence of the taxation prevailing in counties, and it was clear from the speeches of the hon. Members for Waterford (Mr. Blake) and Dungarvan (Mr. Maguire) that their object was to get rid of the present mode of levying county cess, and assimilating it to the mode of levying the poor rate. Now a change of that kind would amount to nothing less than confiscation, as far as it went. The enormous amount of property which had of late years changed hands had been purchased under the existing law by which one half the county cess was paid by the occupier, and he could not believe that the House would consent to inflict on the owners such an injustice as to remove the charge from the occupier and place the whole payment on the landowner. So far from any charge of want of economy having been brought against the grand jury system, he believed

Lord John Browne

it was generally admitted that the greatest economy was practised, and that with respect to roads the charge as compared with England was immensely in favour of Ireland, and as to the public buildings they were only too good. There was, however, one real grievance which the ratepayers had—that was as to the superintendence of lunatic asylums—but he was surprised that that should have been made a subject of complaint by certain hon. Members. For when he (Lord Naas) was Chief Secretary he brought in a Bill to remedy this very grievance, and proposed to give to local bodies the power to watch over these asylums; but the very Members who now complained preferred to leave the control in the hands of the Government Inspectors, opposed his Bill and it did not pass. He hoped that those hon. Members who now complained of the grievance would give their support to his Bill, should it be re-introduced. All the real objections to the present grand jury system related to minor matters, which could be easily amended without entirely destroying the system. Defalcations by High Constables were rare, and loss from that cause was still more rare, owing to the great care exercised by the grand juries in the acceptance of sureties. The hon. Member for Dungarvan had drawn a contrast between the way in which corporations and grand juries managed matters; but without saying anything disrespectful of corporations, he might say that the reports of their proceedings which appeared in the newspapers tended to amuse rather than edify. He looked upon the principle of the Bill as tending to abolish the grand jury system of Ireland, for the election or non-election by ratepayers was not its main principle; and considering that no other body could be found to represent so accurately the wants of the ratepayers, and that the present system had worked well, he could not consent to a change which must tend to oppress the poorer ratepayers.

MR. HERBERT said, he had been so pointedly referred to by the hon. Gentleman the Member for Waterford, in introducing the second reading of the Bill, that he felt called upon to say a few words. The hon. Gentleman had appealed to him for his support, on the ground that he had brought in a Bill the object of which was similar to that of the Bill now before the House, and that in so doing he had admitted the existence of many anomalies and abuses in the grand jury system. He spoke in the presence of many who had heard what he said in the debate referred to, and they would bear him out when he said that though he had admitted certain anomalies and abuses to exist in the grand jury system, he had stated that he never would be a party to any Bill which proposed to destroy entirely the grand jury system of Ireland. The present Bill professed to be a Bill to amend the law relating to grand juries, and had it really been so he would have supported it ; but the real tendency of the measure was to abolish the grand jury system altogether, and was far different from a Bill for the mere correction of abuses which he had advocated on the occasion alluded to by the hon. Member for Waterford. What he complained of was the election of the baronial cesspayers by the grand jury instead of their nomination by that body, and the power that the magistrates possessed of coming out of their own districts in order to make particular presentments which would not be passed by the local magistrates. The whole of the taxation of the country over which there could be any control did and must always originate with the cesspayers, so that on financial grounds the sweeping measure proposed by the hon. Member for Waterford was not required. An instance had been mentioned of the appointment of a cesspayer who could not speak English ; but he simply regarded that circumstance as a favourable sample of the equitable working of the present arrangement. It reminded him of something that occurred on the occasion of a visit from one of the former Lord Lieutenants of Ireland to the part of the country in which he resided. One of the inhabitants, who did not understand English, came down from the hills and presented the lady, the wife of the Lord Lieutenant, with a bottle of whisky. She refused the present but offered him some money, which he received without making any acknowledgment. The lady asked the boatman if the man understood English, to which the boatman replied, "He understands what sort of English." In the same way the duties which would demand the attention of the cesspayer were such as he would find no difficulty under any circumstances in comprehending. He had listened carefully to the speeches of the hon. Members who had supported this Bill, but he found that not one of the practical difficulties of which they complained

would be removed by it. The Bill left all the imperfections and anomalies of the existing system wholly uncorrected. Because the Bill failed to remedy any of the evils against which he had over and over again protested, and to remove which he had himself endeavoured to provide a legislative remedy, he felt himself compelled to vote against the second reading.

Mr. M'MAHON said, he trusted that the Secretary for Ireland would decline to take the advice of the two ex-Secretaries for Ireland who had addressed the House, but would give all his assistance in furtherance of the present measure. He had himself presented numerous petitions which showed how great was the dissatisfaction existing in Ireland with the operation of the grand jury system ; and how great the evil was might be gathered from the manner in which the grand jury cess had been continuously increasing from the commencement of the present century. In 1800 the county cess was £400,000 ; in 1815 it was £819,000 ; it 1835 it was £945,000 ; in 1840 it was £1,268,000 ; and in 1845 it was £1,159,000. In 1846 Sir Robert Peel, on the repeal of the Corn Laws, relieved Ireland of between £500,000 and £600,000 per annum for the expense of the police, and threw it on the Consolidated Fund ; but the result was that instead of the cess falling by that amount it was, in 1850, £1,037,000 ; in 1859 it was £1,059,000 ; and in 1862 it was £1,088,000, which was an enormous sum ; and he defied any one to account for that increase except from the indifference of the grand juries to that economy which they would practise if they had to pay the whole of the rates themselves, or from the people having nothing to do with its administration. He complained of the indifference of English Members to Irish affairs. They had a great many Motions proposed for assimilating the laws of the two countries, but the English Members did not give them their support. The expenditure by the grand juries of Ireland was so great that it exceeded those of the kingdom of Denmark, of Switzerland, of Norway, and of Greece. The Bill only asked that the Irish people might be placed on an equality with England in respect to the principles of self-government. He hoped the Bill would be read a second time.

SIR ROBERT PEEL said, it was impossible that the Government could affirm the principle of the Bill, striking as it did at the root of the grand jury system of Ireland. One of its principal provisions being to abolish grand juries and to establish county boards in their place. For twenty-eight years the whole of the fiscal duties of the country had been administered with great advantage by united bodies of magistrates and cesspayers, and he did not think it desirable that that form of government should be altered. The hon. Gentleman the Member for Waterford in introducing his Bill had asserted that he only proposed to carry out a principle which had been acknowledged in former Bills; but that assertion, he would respectfully submit, was not well founded. The Bills referred to by the hon. Gentleman, though proposing certain Amendments in the grand jury system, had none of them aimed at its abolition. Now, if the time-honoured system of grand juries had worked well, it ought not to be given up for the sake of a system confessedly crude and ill-digested. His hon. Friend had said that though there was no sign of an agitation on this subject in Ireland, it could be got up; but would it not be better for the House to wait and see what were the views of the country gentlemen and of the people on that matter? His hon. Friend complained of the amount of taxation under the grand jury system; but that taxation was incurred principally in the useful work of making and maintaining roads. Within a period of a very few years, 23,000 miles of new roads had been made in Ireland, and out of a sum of £1,080,000, for which the Irish grand juries had presented in the year 1862, over £600,000 was for roads. Hon. Members asked the Government to undertake the preparation of a Bill on this subject; but if they did so at this period of the Session, it could not be considered by the Irish country gentlemen till the July assizes. He had, however, to inform the House that the Government had considered the subject with great attention during the last vacation, but had thought it better, now that they had the advantage of the services of the Attorney General for Ireland in the House, to proceed in the first instance with important law Bills, which had been in abeyance for two years, rather than occupy the time of the present Session with a scheme which would, at all events, require much more consideration than could be given to it before the recess. They would, however, be prepared to deal with the subject early next Session.

Sir Robert Peel

MR. M‘EVOY said, he had no objection to grand juries, but he thought that when men paid taxes they ought to have some control over their expenditure. It was on that ground he supported the second reading of the Bill.

CAPTAIN STACPOOLE said, that the only alteration required in the grand jury law was that of a division in the payment of the county rates between the landlords and the tenants; and that no magistrate should be allowed to vote in any barony in which he did not possess property; and that the ratepayers should be permitted to share in the suffrage with the magistrates.

CAPTAIN ARCHDALL said, if this Bill were what it professed to be—namely, one to amend the grand jury system in Ireland—he should vote for it; but it appeared to him that it was not such a Bill, and, therefore, he could not support it. He was glad to hear the Secretary for Ireland state that the Government had considered the subject, and if the right hon. Gentleman should not be in office next year, he hoped he would be in the House to support the measure to which he had shortly referred.

MR. BLAKE, in reply, stated that he had no alternative but to proceed with the Bill, as it appeared to him that the measure foreshadowed by the Secretary for Ireland would not go far enough.

COLONEL FRENCH said, that the present grand jury system was on the whole economical and most efficiently conducted, and he could not support the changes proposed by this Bill.

MR. MONSELL recommended the hon. Member for Waterford not to go to a division, as it would be impossible to pass a Bill this Session. He was, however, of opinion, that in the case of the county cess, the same incidence of taxation as that which now prevailed in respect of poor rate ought to be adopted. An arrangement to that effect might be made in all future contracts between landlord and tenant.

MR. COGAN suggested that the Bill should not be pressed to a division, otherwise the cause of grand jury reform would be retarded, as many who wished reforms in the grand jury system must oppose the Bill. He had not much faith in the promise made from the Treasury bench; and thought that a reform in the grand juries would be more likely to be effected if there was a change in the occupants of that bench.

MR. BUTT said, the question at issue was whether the members of the grand jury were to be nominees of the high sheriff, or to be elected by the people. He would support the Motion for the second reading.

Question put, "That the word 'now' stand part of the Question."

The House *divided* :—Ayes 27 ; Noes 150: Majority 123.

Words *added.*

Main Question, as amended, put, and *agreed to.*

Bill *put off* for six months.

FORFEITURE OF LANDS AND GOODS BILL—[BILL 21.]—SECOND READING.

Order for Second Reading read.

Moved, "That the Bill be now read a second time."—(*Mr. Charles Forster.*)

THE ATTORNEY GENERAL said, this was a Bill requiring much consideration in order to see whether amendments in the law could be introduced with advantage. The measure was one which, in its present form, could not be accepted without further inquiry, and he therefore asked the hon. Member who had charge of it to postpone the second reading.

MR. CHARLES FORSTER said, that having already once postponed this Bill to meet the convenience of the Government, he had not expected to be called upon to postpone it again. However, at that late period of the afternoon, he had no alternative but to accede to the suggestion which had been made.

Second Reading *deferred* till *Wednesday,* 15th June.

CHIEF RENTS (IRELAND) BILL—(*Lords.*)
[BILL 52.] SECOND READING.

Order for Second Reading read.

MR. LONGFIELD, in moving the second reading of the Bill, said, that it was purely permissive in its nature, and its object was to facilitate redemption of chief rents by enabling tenants to make arrangements for that purpose. There were several provisions in the Bill which would effectually secure the interests of the remainder-man, and guard him against fraud. The measure was passed last Session by the House of Lords, but it was found to be too late in the Session to proceed with it in that House. He (Mr. Longfield) introduced the Bill in that House immediately at the commencement of the present Session ; but the Earl of Donoughmore, having happily recovered from his recent illness he (Mr. Longfield) thought it better that that noble Earl should introduce it first in the House of Lords. He therefore obtained leave to withdraw the Bill, and under the auspices of the noble Earl it was re-introduced into the House of Lords, by whom it had been passed and sent down. Having gone through all its stages in the other House, and received its approbation on two successive years, he trusted that the House of Commons, feeling satisfied that the Upper House had carefully considered all its details, would assent to its second reading.

Motion made, and Question proposed, "That the Bill be now read a second time."—(*Mr. Longfield.*)

MR. WHITESIDE said, he should be sorry to oppose any measure introduced by his hon. and learned Friend; but it appeared to him that the provisions of the present Bill were not reasonable, and if adopted without considerable alteration might result in grave consequences. According to this Bill the limited owner of an estate—that was, a tenant for life—would be at liberty to effect an arrangement with the owner of the rent by which the rights of the incumbrancer might be ousted for ever. Now he (Mr. Whiteside) could well conceive the existence of a collusive understanding between those two parties to effect an arrangement of that kind, with the object of destroying the rights of all other parties interested in the property. His hon. and learned Friend, in asking the assent of that House to this measure, thought it was a strong argument in its favour that it had been approved of by the House of Lords; no doubt a decision of the House of Lords was entitled to great respect, but he (Mr. Whiteside) submitted that the Members of the House of Commons were as capable of looking after the rights of property as their Lordships' House. The only safeguard in the Bill against fraud was that the assent of a Judge of the Landed Estates Court was required before the purchase was completed. But the learned Judge would not be compelled to look into the title in case the two contracting parties declared themselves perfectly satisfied with the arrangement. That, in effect, was no protection against a collusive sale and purchase to defraud incumbrancers. The principle was a novel one, and the Bill itself an important one. It occurred to him (Mr. Whiteside), in reference to such a measure as this, that it was most desirable to have the opinions of the Law Officers of the Crown. Indeed, he thought that all Bills dealing with property ought to be introduced under the sanction of the Government. He would suggest that the learned Attorney and Solicitor General and the Attorney General for Ireland should look carefully into the provisions of this Bill, and should tell the House whether they thought that property of this kind ought to be disposed of in the way proposed. He should not like to oppose the measure of his hon. and learned Friend; nevertheless, he thought that it ought to stand over for further consideration.

MR. O'HAGAN (THE ATTORNEY GENERAL FOR IRELAND) said, it appeared to him that the principle of the Bill was not open to objection. The details of the measure, however, he thought, required the most careful consideration. He was of opinion that much more protection against fraud than that contained in the Bill was necessary. It would be absolutely necessary to provide that if the title for rent should fail the land should cease to be burdened —that if there be a failure on the one side there should be also a failure on the other. He would not oppose the second reading; but he thought the provisions required a great deal of careful deliberation in Committee before the measure was made law.

MR. GEORGE said, he observed that the Bill was confined altogether to Ireland. He thought that if it were good for one part of the United Kingdom it ought to be good for another, and should therefore be extended to England. He saw no provision in the Bill for giving notice to the incumbrancer, which was in his mind a great defect in the measure. He was unwilling to vote against the second reading, but it appeared to him to be open to many objections in its details, and he thought it should be referred to a Select Committee, to see if any further safeguard could be provided for the interests of third parties. He thought the Bill an extremely unsafe one, and he doubted if they read it a second time whether they would be able to effectually amend it in Committee.

SIR EDWARD GROGAN considered the Bill unnecessary, save in very exceptional cases. The present law provided

Mr. Whiteside

ample means for the sale of all settled estates where such sales were considered advisable. The principle of the Bill was both dangerous and mischievous, and ought not to be further proceeded with. He objected to the Bill being confined to Ireland, because if it was good for Ireland it was good also for England. He moved the second reading of the Bill that day six months.

COLONEL DUNNE seconded the Motion. If the Bill was read a second time he should move in Committee that its provisions be extended to England; by that means they would obtain a sure test of the value of the Bill, and if approved for England he thought Irish Members might assent to it.

Amendment proposed, to leave out the word "now," and at the end of the Question to add the words "upon this day six months."—(*Sir Edward Grogan.*)

Question proposed, "That the word 'now' stand part of the Question."

MR. HASSARD said, there was a very analogous measure for England—the Enfranchisement of Land Act. He did not think the Bill was perfect in its details, or that its scope was hardly large enough. It should be extended to corporate bodies. There were plenty of materials in it to be moulded into a good and useful measure, and he hoped, therefore, it would not be thrown out on the second reading.

MR. BUTT said, he approved of the principle of the Bill, though no doubt it was open to some objections in detail, which might easily be remedied in Committee.

MR. WHITESIDE suggested, that the Amendment should be withdrawn, on the understanding that the Law Officers would consider the machinery proposed and the propriety of extending the Bill to England.

MR. LONGFIELD said, he should be happy to accept any Amendment the Committee might think proper to adopt. His only object was to make the Bill useful and efficient.

Amendment, by leave, *withdrawn.*

Main Question put, and *agreed to.*

Bill read 2°, and *committed* for *Wednesday,* 4th May.

OYSTER FISHERIES (IRELAND) BILL.

On Motion of Mr. M'MAHON, Bill to amend the Law relating to Oyster Fisheries in Ireland, ordered to be brought in by Mr. M'Mahon and Mr. Blake.

Bill *presented*, and read 1°. [Bill 75.]

House adjourned at seven minutes before Six o'clock.

~~~~~~~

HOUSE OF LORDS,

Thursday, April 21, 1864.

MINUTES.]— *Sat First in Parliament*—The Viscount Sidmouth, after the death of his Father.

Public Bills — *First Reading* — Consolidated Fund (£15,000,000)* (No. 54); Mortgage Debentures, H.L. * (No. 55).

Second Reading—Joint Stock Companies (Foreign Countries)* (No. 45); Scotch Episcopal Fund * (No. 123).

Select Committee — Improvement of Land Act 1864 [H.L.] (No. 36), *nominated* (see p. 1278).

Third Reading — Union Relief Aid Acts Continuance * (No. 39); Land Drainage (Provisional Orders)* (No. 27).

PRIVATE BILLS.

Ordered,

That no Private Bill brought from the House of Commons shall be read a Second Time after *Thursday*, the 30*th Day of June next*.

That no Bill confirming any Provisional Order of the Board of Health, or authorizing any Inclosure of Lands under Special Report of the Inclosure Commissioners for England and Wales, or for confirming any Scheme of the Charity Commissioners for England and Wales, shall be read a Second Time after *Thursday*, the 30*th Day of June next*.

That when a Bill shall have passed this House with Amendments, these Orders shall not apply to any new Bill sent up from the House of Commons which the Chairman of Committees shall report to the House is substantially the same as the Bill so amended.—(*The Chairman of Committees*.)

LAND TRANSFER ACT.

OBSERVATIONS.

Lord CHELMSFORD rose to call attention to the Returns which had been made to the House under the Land Transfer Act (*Parl. Paper*, No. 23). He had moved for these Returns because he wished to know how far the operation of the Act had realized the high expectations which it had excited when it was passed, and to what extent persons for whose benefit it was intended had availed themselves of its proposed advantages. Their Lordships were aware that, for a long time, there had been a great desire for the introduction of some scheme which would simplify titles to landed property, and facilitate its transfer. Various attempts had been made from time to time to legislate on the subject, and at last, in 1853, their Lordships passed a Bill · which was sent down to the House of Commons and referred to a Select Committee. That Committee recommended that a Royal Commission should be appointed to inquire into the whole subject. Accordingly, in 1854, a Commission was appointed for the purpose of inquiring into the registration of titles to land, with reference to its sale and transfer. That Commission was composed of persons who were eminently qualified to form a correct judgment on the subject. The Chairman was his right hon. Friend Mr. Walpole, and his noble and learned Friend on the Woolsack, the right hon. Gentleman the Member for Kidderminster (Mr. Lowe), and other gentlemen of great legal experience were members of the Commission. That Commission examined a great number of witnesses, and obtained information in answer to a circular from all parts of the kingdom, and in 1857 they presented a very able and elaborate Report. He would not enter into the details of that Report; it would be sufficient to say that the Commission rejected the idea of a registration of assurances, but strongly recommended that a measure should be passed for the registration of titles. To show the extravagant expectations that were then formed, it would be sufficient to say that one of the great objections felt to the adoption of a measure for the registration of assurances as distinct from a registration of titles was the enormous accumulation of deeds which was likely to take place—it being calculated that no less than 300,000 deeds would be the annual average amount which would be registered. The registration then proposed was of a very simple character, and related only to fee-simple titles, and leases of a certain term with a distinct register of charges and incumbrances. In the consideration of this subject it was necessary to bear in mind that there were two parts perfectly distinct, though often blended; one as to the declaration, the other as to the registration of title. There might be a declaration of title without registration, and there might be a registration without a declaration of title. No one was better acquainted with that distinction than his noble and learned Friend opposite (Lord Cranworth), who, when he occupied the Woolsack in 1858, introduced a Bill to facilitate the declaration of title

(Transfer of Land Bill). The Bill passed that House, and was sent down to the House of Commons. That was the state of affairs when a change of Government took place, and his noble Friend behind him (the Earl of Derby) succeeded to office. There was a very general desire for a measure of this description, and an able Report on the subject as a guide, and the Government of his noble Friend accordingly thought it their duty to introduce one. An hon. and learned Friend of his (Sir Hugh Cairns), then Solicitor General, was intrusted with the duty of introducing the measure into the House of Commons, and it must be admitted that it could not have been in better hands. He founded himself almost entirely upon the Report—in one respect he departed from it. The Commissioners had adverted to the suggestion of establishing a Lords' Tribunal and had rejected it. His hon. and learned Friend struck with the success of the Incumbered Estates Court in Ireland proposed to create a separate court for the purpose of a judicial declaration of titles. He embodied the measure in two Bills, one for the declaration of titles, the other for a registry founded entirely upon the system proposed by the Commission. In this respect the measure had an advantage over the Land Transfer Act, because you might have stopped short and been contented with the establishment of title; but in the Act the ascertainment of title is only a preliminary to registration, and having once begun you must go on or lose your outlay. The Bills were received with great approbation. My noble and learned Friend on the Woolsack, then a Member of the House of Commons, said,

"In all its stages the measure will receive the most cordial support from my hands, and I trust that so great a measure of legal reform, and one so well calculated to confer advantage upon the community, will be successfully carried through both Houses during the present Session."

And the right hon. Member for Kidderminster, Mr. Lowe, who was upon the Commission, said—

"The introduction of this measure reflects the highest credit upon the Government."

The measure thus favourably introduced was, however, dropped, in consequence of the change of Government. It was not likely that a measure to which the attention of my noble and learned Friend had been so long directed would be allowed to sleep after he received the great seal. His opinions, as he told us,

Lord Chelmsford

had undergone considerable fluctuation upon the subject. On introducing the Bill, he said—

"In 1853 a Bill for the Registration of Deeds passed your Lordships' House. It came down to the other House, and I felt that, individually, I could not take any part in support of that measure. The measure was referred to a Select Committee, and I had the honour of bringing before that Committee the plan which I had then formed for the Registration of Titles. But that plan consisted merely of this—the putting of certain names upon the Registry, as if they were the absolute owners of the fee simple of the estate, and letting all persons who had partial interests in the property depend for their security upon the system of caveats and checks. I have always felt that that was a very imperfect mode of proceeding."

Of course, the word "always" must be a mistake for "since," for my noble and learned Friend signed the Report of the Commission which recommended this very plan. However, it was clear that the mind of my noble and learned Friend was not (to use the phrase of the day) running in a groove on this subject, and that the public was likely to have the result of his matured and deliberate opinion. The Government were, therefore justified in holding out expectations in the Speech from the Throne, that measures for the improvement of the law would be laid before Parliament, and among them will be a Bill for rendering the title to land more simple and its transfer more easy. What the other measures were he had been unable to discover. They were probably like the words "and Company" in the name of a firm, which are frequently used when it consists merely of an individual, or like the predictions in *Moore's Almanac*, which can be made to fit any future event. However, it was evident that it was to be the great work of the Session, and that the Government meant to found political capital upon it. My noble and learned Friend said, on introducing the Bill, "that a measure more important to the landed interest had never been introduced into Parliament."

The Bill was referred to a Select Committee, with two other Bills introduced by Lord Cranworth, and the two Bills of Sir Hugh Cairns, which were laid upon the table for reference to the same Committee. In the Committee, Sir Hugh Cairns' Bills were speedily disposed of. The principal objection to them was the expense which would be occasioned by the creation of a new court. Upon this, he (Lord Chelmsford) said that if expense were the objection, he should prefer Lord Cranworth's Bill to the Lord Chancellor's, whose registrar was only a judge under another name. It is curious that this very remark was made by the Attorney General when the Bill was in the other House, and who, in answer to an objection by Sir Hugh Cairns to entrusting the great power of giving an indefeasible title to a registrar said—

"Except that the officer was to be called a registrar and was not to have so large a salary as a judge, he saw no difference between him and a judge."

But the Lord Chancellor's and Lord Cranworth's Bills went through the Committee, passed the House of Commons and became law; and the Session closed with a triumphant note of congratulation upon the event, the Royal Speech containing this passage—

"The Act for rendering more easy the transfer of land will add to the value of real property, will make titles more simple and secure, and will diminish the expense attending purchases and sales."

The noble and learned Lord's Bill having passed into law, it became necessary to establish the machinery for carrying it into operation. A principal registrar was appointed at a salary of £2,500 a year; an assistant registrar at £1,500 a year; a chief clerk at £400, and a second clerk at £200 a year. He would admit that this was a moderate staff for the business that was expected to flow in. The selection of the principal registrar did infinite credit to his noble and learned Friend on the Woolsack. It was not a selection from party motives, for the learned Gentleman in question, when a Member of the House of Commons, was an opponent of the Government. There could be no doubt that the registrar was selected for his fitness, and was eminently qualified for his office if there were any duties to perform. He was exceedingly desirous in the last Session to know what business had been transacted, and obtained a Return in February, 1863, which stated that there had been several applications for registry, but that no single estate had then been registered. It might have been said that the measure at that time had not had a fair trial, and he, therefore, forbore to make any observations upon the working of the Act. In March of the present year, when it might be supposed that time had been given for the Act to come into full working operation, he moved for another Return. He found that since the passing of the Act there had been sixty-five applications in all, of which eleven had been withdrawn. Only nine titles had been registered; but there were two others ready to be entered on the register, so that eleven might be taken as the total number placed upon the register. There were forty-six applications still to be decided on. The value of the property — as far as could be ascertained — was £1,500,000; and there were nineteen applications in respect of estates, the value of which was not yet known. The information as to acreage was also incomplete; but it appeared that there were not more than 4,787 acres. [The Lord Chancellor: Those are the pending applications.] He thanked the noble and learned Lord for the information, but he was, of course, obliged to confine himself to the facts disclosed by the Return. He believed that the description of the property to which the applications applied, would be found to justify the expectations entertained by a noble Lord who was a member of the Committee on the Bill, that the measure would be principally beneficial to those who possessed building land in the neighbourhood of towns which they were desirous of selling in lots. But the worst part of the story was still to come. The expectations which had been held out that 300,000 deeds would be registered annually, of course, made every one believe that such an establishment would be self-supporting. But he regretted to say that those anticipations had been utterly disappointed. What did their Lordships suppose was the amount of fees which had been received from the passing of the Act down to the 1st of March last? £180. He was unable to say what the other forty-six applications, if carried out, were likely to produce, but he was afraid their Lordships could hardly expect that they would yield sufficient to cover the expenses of the present year, much less of that which had already passed. The measure itself, bearing in mind the great expectations excited in reference to it, and the fact that it was considered the great political achievement of Her Majesty's Government in the year 1862, must be pronounced, he regretted to say, a complete failure. He had no doubt that the mind of the noble and learned Lord by whom it was framed, having been directed to the subject, he would be able to assign some reason why the measure had not found that favour with the public which was anticipated. To him it seemed that the public had deceived themselves. They thought they wanted a measure of the kind, and when it was offered they found they were mistaken. Its provisions in some degree departed from the recommendations of the Commission of which the noble and learned Lord was a Member; because, disguise it how they might, the Bill was not one for the registration of title — in its results it was an Act for the registry of deeds. As such its principle had been strongly objected to on all sides, and by no one more strongly than the Members of that Commission of which the noble and learned Lord was a Member. He had been anxious to produce these facts before their Lordships, in order that if there were any defects in a measure which seemed to be so ardently desired, which for many years had been so perseveringly called for, and which yet had entailed a charge upon the revenues of the country, without affording any corresponding benefit, that Act might be amended and brought more into accordance with the public requirements, so that ultimately a measure might be passed productive of those effects which had been so sanguinely anticipated.

[The speech of the noble and learned Lord was in great part inaudible, owing to the bustle and distraction occasioned by the presence of General Garibaldi.]

THE LORD CHANCELLOR : My Lords, I may say with very great sincerity that I am obliged to my noble and learned Friend for having called your Lordships' attention to this subject. I may say that he has done so with my entire consent and concurrence; for when there is an institution of this kind in existence, particularly a newly-established one, it is right and fitting that its progress should be brought before Parliament. I have not the least complaint to make of any of the observations of my noble and learned Friend, although to some of his representations I shall feel it right to reply. I am not at all sore at the criticism he has applied to this Act. But, with regard to the expectations raised in 1862 and to the expenditure which the Act has entailed, I have this consolation that had the measure introduced in 1859, under the auspices of my noble and learned Friend, been passed instead, it would have caused an expenditure at least double in amount. My noble and learned Friend, therefore, judging

Lord Chelmsford

from the importance which he attaches to considerations of expense, must have reason to rejoice that the Bill to which I refer was not passed into law. I may, perhaps, set my noble and learned Friend right upon one point. It is perfectly true that in the Report made by the Commission in 1857 I concurred with the majority of my Colleagues in recommending the system of registration which was afterwards embodied in the Bill introduced under the auspices of the Government of the noble Earl (the Earl of Derby) in 1859. But had my noble and learned Friend examined into the question, he would have found that I then entertained views identical with those which were finally embodied in the Bill I afterwards originated; but I thought it right not to imperil the Report at the time by insisting on those opposite views. When Lord Derby's Government brought in a Bill in 1859, I thought it becoming and right to give it a steadfast support, and, had the Government continued long enough in office to carry that measure, I should never have set up in opposition to it any proposal of my own. But when the Government of their successors was formed, and I had the opportunity of dealing with the subject, I undoubtedly reverted to the opinions which I had originally entertained. My noble and learned Friend was in error on another point. Before the Committee to which your Lordships thought it right to refer the various measures brought forward on this subject in 1862, the Bill produced under the auspices of my noble and learned Friend was rejected, not on the grounds of expense, but because the principle upon which it proceeded was the creation of an artificial ownership for the purpose of registration. The question put to the Committee was, whether they would approve registration being based upon a footing of an artificial kind created for the purpose, and not being the real title, or whether they would desire to have a registry that should be a perfect mirror in its faithful reflection of the actual existing ownership. I believe the Committee were almost unanimous in the conclusion which they came to, that if they were to establish a registry, that registry ought to proceed upon the basis of actual and not fictitious ownership. And it was on that ground, being in conformity with the opinions which I have always entertained, that the Bill of 1859 was postponed, and a preference given to the measure eventually passed into law. But I repeat that had the question arisen under the Government of the noble Earl (the Earl of Derby), I should have persevered in giving to the Bill emanating from his Government my most hearty support. Passing over this personal matter, I am very desirous of giving to your Lordships' an exact statement of the present condition of the system, its promises for the future, and of the reasonable grounds which exist for expecting that it will eventually succeed. The apprehensions which have been expressed in consequence of the small modicum of success hitherto attained are, I think, unfounded; particularly when we refer to the history of the early stages of measures now of acknowledged and general utility. Of measures passed by the Legislature in modern times, I believe none have been more useful, none more resorted to, than the Copyhold Enfranchisement Act, passed in 1841. How many instances of applications were there under that Act the first year after it was passed? One. In the next year there were twelve; in the next, twenty-nine; in the next, forty-nine—so slow was its progress; but in the year 1861, twenty years after the passing of the measure, its utility was so generally recognized that the applications under it were no less than 786. The Act authorizing the making of exchanges under the powers of the Inclosure Commissioners was passed in the year 1845. In the first year there were only ten cases under it; in the second year, twelve cases; in the third, thirty-nine; but, in the year 1862, seventeen years after the Act passed, there were no less than 246 cases. These instances show the slowness with which the utility of institutions of this kind is recognized, and with which they are adopted. Let the House contrast with them the facts as to this measure of 1862. My noble and learned Friend has twitted me with not having that vast amount of business that I anticipated. Will he permit me to remind him that the Bill for the registration of assurances was compulsory; but Parliament refused to make this measure compulsory, and I was obliged to adopt the voluntary principle, and leave parties to find out its utility for themselves; and, when they had found it out, to get over the opposition of their solicitors in order to get their titles [registered under this Act. The measure did not come into operation until the end of October, 1862.

The orders putting it into operation were signed by me on the 15th of October, 1862, and we then had to issue a general notice that the Act had come into force. From that time until the 1st of March in the present year—the date to which the Return comes down—there have elapsed only sixteen months. In those sixteen months, notwithstanding the most determined opposition on the part of the great body of solicitors throughout the country, there have been brought into this Office very nearly two millions worth of property. Is that a failure? Contrast it with the instances which I have given, and tell me whether it is not in truth great evidence of success in an institution of this character. In addition to the Return now before the House, I have this morning received from the chief registrar a letter, which tells me that since the 1st of March there have been additional applications, comprising between 1,700 and 1,800 acres of land, and including property exceeding £130,000 in value. Now, what have been the obstacles to a general registration of titles? They are such as your Lordships will most readily understand and appreciate. The mode of remunerating solicitors in this country is unfortunately very bad and very erroneous in principle. The solicitor is paid according to those erroneous principles upon which the Legislature acted in former days, when it appointed a tariff of wages for artisans and different persons employed in trade and other occupations. He has prescribed for him by the Legislature the charges which he shall make, and, unfortunately, those charges are calculated according to the length and repetition of his deeds. He is obliged to make everything as long as he reasonably can, and he is obliged to continue a system of the greatest complexity and of minute involution of facts and circumstances, because there is no other mode by which he can obtain his bread. These are the reasons why — though I readily bear testimony to the honourable conduct and feelings of the great body of solicitors—it is utterly impossible to expect that they can adopt any other course than that of opposing an institution of this kind, that will actually take the bread out of their mouths, and deprive them of the chance of getting any fair remuneration for their skill. The best informed among them have said with great justice, "The law, as it now stands, rewards us for prolixity and fines us for brevity." That is an exact representation of the law. Accordingly I have made another attempt to make the Act work by preparing a Bill enabling the Lord Chancellor, with the aid of the other Judges, to establish a system of remuneration of solicitors upon an *ad valorem* principle; and I earnestly desired and trusted that the solicitors would give me their assistance and enable me to introduce a practice which would render this system of conveyance of property compatible with the liberal and fair remuneration of solicitors. I am sorry to say that I have not received the assistance which would have enabled me to accomplish that object. I hope next week to make a new attempt to do so by introducing a Bill which I trust your Lordships' will receive, and which will, by the authority of the Legislature, alter the law upon the subject of the remuneration of solicitors. Allow me for a moment to point out to you how plainly the solicitors threatened that they would join in a body, upon the principle of self-preservation, to oppose the system which I was introducing. I will take only one or two extracts. A paper was presented to this House by the Metropolitan and Provincial Law Association, in which they say this—

" It will be impossible to establish any new system of transfer of land until it has been made the interest of the profession of solicitors to support such change."

That was telling the truth openly and fairly, and that has been the reason why this plan has been kept from the knowledge of the people, and why, whenever any landowner has asked his solicitor, " Why cannot I put my title upon the land register, and then I can go into the market with a piece of parchment showing exactly my interest in the estate and the estate itself, and all these masses of dirty, musty parchment may be sent to the fire ?" The answer has been, in the great majority of cases, " You will incur I know not what danger "—and all sorts of legal hobgoblins have been conjured up to frighten the questioner from resorting to this office. I appeal to your Lordships. Does any one of you know anything about your title to your estates ? Is there not dwelling upon every estate, or rather sitting upon the shoulders of every landed proprietor, a solicitor who guides him in all things, controls him in all things? Can he ever shake off that Old Man of the Sea ? Why, my Lords, it is impossible. Talk of a priest-ridden country—there may be such things

The Lord Chancellor

—but that we are a lawyer-ridden country with regard to the condition of real property is a truth beyond the possibility of denial by any one who is conversant with the subject. What has thrown light upon every subject of knowledge ? It has been the introduction of printing. Why has not printing been introduced into legal deeds ? Why is it that you have presented to you a mass of parchment so repulsive in its character, so utterly forbidding in its condition, its language, and even in the style of its writing, that you surrender up yourselves in despair ? You do not know what you are signing. It may be a consignment of your property to some condition of things from which you can never extricate it; but you blindly accept it. All other mysteries have been unfolded, but this thing which comes home to you all is still a sealed book. The Scripture declaration is verified to the letter. " The lawyers keep the key of knowledge to themselves, and load men with grievous burdens heavy to bear." I have in my hand for your Lordships' inspection one of the new deeds—a Certificate of Title under this Act. It is a piece of parchment written on one side only, and is the result of the investigation of an abstract of title extending over 150 sheets — there is an accurate map of the property—there is the accurate result of the title, and there is a copy of the entry on the register, and according to the Act the owner of this property will, when he wants to sell it, have nothing to do but to carry this document to the auctioneer, and the purchaser will have nothing to do but to see that the document corresponds with the entry in the book of register; and then, instead of entering into an investigation lasting for six months, or perhaps for two or three years, he can go to the registry, ascertain the fact, and, upon the payment of 5s. or 6s. beyond the price of the moderate stamp imposed by the Government, he has his name entered upon the book, and has given to him a document corresponding with this, and the estate is conveyed to him for ever with an indefeasible title. If the owner of land with this kind of title wants money he has nothing to do but to hand over this document to the lender with a corresponding statement, which may be secured at the cost of half-a-crown. This he may do by way of mortgage; but if he simply requires a loan, without mortgage, he has simply to go to his bankers with the document, and to say to him,

"Will you lend me £5,000 or £10,000?" He can then deposit it with the banker by way of collateral security to his personal credit, and his banker would receive it with the most perfect confidence, because, while the document is in his hands, there can be no possible dealing with the land, and the document itself proves the indefeasible title of the landowner. I am happy to be able to add that, by the great assistance which I have received from the Inclosure Commissioners, I have, in bringing out this scheme of registration, obtained the invaluable services of Colonel Leach, one of the officers engaged on the Commission, and we have been enabled to adopt a system of mapping which gives the most accurate delineation of the area and boundaries of the land to which the certificate of title refer, in such a manner that the document carries with it the most conclusive evidence of everything which it is important to know with regard to the subject matter, and which may be delineated at an expense not exceeding £5. I have here a letter from a gentleman who, hearing that this discussion was about to take place, writes to me to say that having some time ago purchased forty-two acres of valuable land, for which he gave £4,000, he was desirous of having his title placed upon the register. He applied to his solicitor with that object, but his solicitor expressed his indisposition to be a party to the transaction, saying that it was against the spirit and the law of his caste. The consequence was that the gentleman himself went and got the title registered. He has furnished me with the details of the whole amount he had had to pay for the registration of his title to the land which was likely to be sold for building purposes, and the whole expense of putting his title upon the register, and emancipating the land and its owners for ever from all parchments and mystification was £29 7s. 1d. These are proofs that this, after all, has not been an ill-considered measure; and I may, perhaps, without being open to the charge of vanity, be allowed to say that having given many years' anxious attention to the subject, and having framed this Bill, every word of which I drew with my own hand, I look upon it as matter of great satisfaction to be able to state that there has not been found a single difficulty in the working of the measure. It is undoubtedly true that your Lordships' and the other House of Parliament in dealing with it, very wisely and very prudently inserted several precautionary provisions—especially in reference to public notices — and these necessitated certain preliminary proceedings, which, of course, produced delay, and in some degree generated expense. But what, after all, does the delay of a month or two amount to when the land is placed in a position in which it can be carried into the market with perfect security, thus enabling a man to complete his contract within a week or two, without any doubt as to the money, and without the vexation of having over and over again visits from a solicitor; while under the present system he would probably have to wait for months, and perhaps for years, before the matter could be brought to a satisfactory conclusion? These, my Lords, are the great objects which I desired to carry into effect. My noble and learned Friend (Lord Chelmsford) taunts us a little with having spoken somewhat too triumphantly of the measure in the Speech from the Throne; but I must say that the language of that Speech, in which I had some little concern, is as little triumphant, in my opinion, and as moderate as it can possibly be. The passage which my noble and learned Friend alludes to simply expresses a hope that the measure would be productive of general utility; and I can scarcely imagine that my noble and learned Friend will continue to be of opinion that in saying so we were going too far. I may add that I thank my noble and learned Friend for having given me an opportunity of making this statement. I beg of your Lordships to bear in mind how great is the infliction in the shape of taxation on the landed interests, owing to the state of the law, which it is the object of the Bill to do away with. You could not grant a lease, you could not sell a bit of land, you could not make a charge or a settlement, without having to go through operations so laborious and expensive, that the most ordinary acts connected with real property involved you in a bill of £100 or £150 or more. Let any noble Lord run up in his memory the sums he has paid to his solicitor from year to year, and then he will be in a better position to perceive how important is the change. And was all the perplexity and confusion—the solicitor alone was familiar with the title to his estate, and an enormous amount of expense and burden was the consequence—was all this necessary? By no means. All that is wanted is this —that the title should be examined; that the result of the examination should be duly recorded, and the record continued in a simple manner, so as to prevent the intricacy—frequently the inaccuracy—which was the result of the law as it stood; then the titles to real estate will become transparent and clear and certain, precisely in the same manner as the title to stock in the funds, to railway stock, ships, or any other analogous form of property. That this measure has been a failure I entirely deny. That it will be a failure is a thing which I venture humbly to anticipate as impossible. I have had the good fortune to assist in the passing of some measures of legal reform, and of originating others; but if there is one measure on which I could put my finger with the hope of being hereafter remembered, it will undoubtedly be this Bill, when its utility and the relief which it is calculated to give to the owners of landed property shall have been fully developed. I will further only trouble your Lordships with one or two instances of the slow progress made in the case of the solicitors. I hold in my hand an article from a well-conducted journal which concludes with the following sentence adverting to the mode of remunerating solicitors:—

" This must be borne in mind when the scale of costs comes to be settled. If it be not, it will be so much the worse for the chances of this new legal department, so far as the amount of its business is concerned."

That is a prophecy which those who made it had the means in their own hands of fulfilling, and which they have certainly not failed to some extent to carry into effect. These are the occasions of the slow progress of the measure; but I do not think your Lordships will be disposed to regard that progress as very slow when you take into account the great confusion which the Bill was introduced to remove. There are many other circumstances connected with the subject which I should be glad to lay before the House, but I feel that I have already trespassed too long upon its attention. I am very thankful—and I speak with the greatest sincerity—to my noble and learned Friend for having brought this matter forward, and I trust he will concur with me hereafter in—if I may use a familiar expression—saying a good word of the Bill, which I assure him I introduced in the earnest but humble

The Lord Chancellor

expectation that it would prove to be of the greatest possible service to the landed interests of the country.

LORD CRANWORTH said, they all had the same object in view in the various alterations which they had suggested; and he hoped that they would all rejoice as the present measure became more and more successful. He must say he thought it scarcely fair to describe this measure, which had only been in existence sixteen months, and which had had great difficulties to encounter, as a failure. If his noble and learned Friend (the Lord Chancellor) could succeed in framing any measure to institute a more rational mode of remunerating solicitors, it would be worth all the Bills upon this subject; but he must express very great doubt whether such a measure was possible. An *ad valorem* remuneration had been talked of; but to that there was the greatest objection, for it would give to the rich a monopoly.

THE DUKE OF MONTROSE said, that some years since an alteration had been made in the law of Scotland, with the view of shortening documents of title. As feudal superior of certain lands in Scotland, he had been called upon to sign many charters which were of great length and full of recapitulations. When the alteration of the law took place, he had a charter brought to him to sign, which only consisted of half a page instead of thirty pages. He was sorry to say that he had never signed but that one short charter, for the lawyers persuaded their clients that it was much safer to have everything recapitulated. This showed how hard it was to bring about a change of this sort. As to registration of titles, he must say that that worked remarkably well in Scotland.

LORD OVERSTONE said, he had heard with great satisfaction the statement of the noble and learned Lord on the Woolsack. He was sure that if the noble and learned Lord would allow the document which he had read (the Certificate of Title under the Act) to be printed and circulated, it would produce a great effect on the public mind, and would do more than anything else to make the measure intelligible to the public.

THE LORD CHANCELLOR said, he should have great pleasure in directing the document to be printed. It must be understood that it was an exact transcript from the register of an existing estate—

tho names, of course, being omitted, and it represented the abstract of a title extending over 150 sheets.

DENMARK AND GERMANY.
THE CONFERENCE.—QUESTION.

THE EARL OF CARNARVON : My Lords, before your Lordships adjourn, I wish to ask the noble Earl the Secretary for Foreign Affairs a Question, of which I have given him notice. Your Lordships are aware that the meeting of the Conference was fixed for yesterday, and you are aware, perhaps, that owing to the absence of the representative of the minor German States, the representatives of Austria and Prussia did not attend. Consequently, one day was lost, and one day at such a moment is of great importance. I understand that the Conference is postponed until next Monday, and your Lordships will bear in mind that this is not the first postponement. The Conference was originally fixed for the 12th, and then postponed until the 20th; now, again, it is postponed till Monday. It was distinctly understood that one of the first steps of the Conference would be to require a suspension of hostilities between the belligerents; but I am sorry to say that there are reasons which it may be very easy to understand, which may induce Austria, and especially Prussia, not to desire an armistice. I wish to ask the noble Earl whether, in the event of a further postponement, any steps will be taken at once to secure such an armistice, as will entirely prevent an indefinite postponement of the Conference combined with a continuation of hostilities against Denmark. I have seen it stated that it is the intention of the Prussians to despatch the troops which have been in the intrenchments of Duppel to invade Jutland; and I have heard also, though I hope this is not on good authority, though it has appeared in some of the German newspapers, that this occupation is for the purpose of making Denmark pay the expenses of the war. Under the circumstances, it is most desirable to know what probability there is of an armistice being agreed to.

EARL RUSSELL : With regard to the meeting of the Conference, I have to state that the German Diet having been requested to appoint a plenipotentiary, they appointed Baron von Beust, who holds the different offices of President of the Council, Home Minister, and Foreign Minister, in Saxony. It was necessary for him to make arrangements for the discharge of the business of these offices during his absence from Dresden, and consequently it was found that he would not be here till Monday. When the Conference met here yesterday, it was found that the Austrian and Prussian Ministers had strict injunctions not to attend the Conference until the representative of the Federal Diet was present. Into the noble Earl's question, in reference to the armistice, I must decline to enter; but I may say, perhaps, that when the Conference meets, as I trust it will on Monday, it will, no doubt, take all these matters into its serious consideration. It is obvious, however, that there can be little hope of any successful termination being arrived at, if Members of both Houses daily put questions as to what the Ministers of the Crown will do in certain cases.

THE EARL OF MALMESBURY : Under the circumstances which are about to take place—I say about to take place, because the Conference only stands adjourned—I entirely approve the noble Earl's discretion. I think he is quite right; but, for my own part, I hope the noble Earl and the Government will be on their guard against a repetition of these postponements. It is impossible not to see the probable consequence of these postponements. It is evident that certain parties may make use of these postponements to come before the Conference in a better position than that which they occupy at the present moment. Therefore, I trust that the Government and the noble Lord will apply their best attention to noting accurately the excuses which may be made in the event of any further postponement being attempted. In the present instance, looking to the distance to be travelled, and generally the course taken by the gentlemen to whom the noble Earl has alluded, I cannot help being extremely suspicious as to the validity of his excuse.

LORD STRATFORD DE REDCLIFFE : My Lords, I am glad to observe that both sides of the House acknowledge the propriety of, as far as possible, avoiding discussion in the present circumstances of the case. I have no reason to doubt that the noble Earl the Foreign Secretary has already had in his mind the observations made by the noble Lord opposite. At the same time, it appears to me that very great value ought to be attached to what has fallen from my noble Friend. It is a satisfaction to those in a position to observe what is passing, that the attention of both sides of the House is directed to the course pursued by some of the Powers. There are circumstances connected with the progress of affairs which appear to me to justify a close observation of the proceedings of Austria and Prussia. It is impossible for any one to read the accounts which have transpired of what has taken place with regard to Sönderborg—the continuance of hostilities in a cruel and murderous spirit, and the apparent intention of extending hostilities to all the principal fortresses of Denmark and throughout Jutland—without recognizing the very great importance that attaches to the disposition shown in the beginning of the Conference. As it is, I can only hope that its progress may be accelerated, and that it may have a happy ending.

EARL RUSSELL : The noble Earl was no doubt justified in asking a question as to when the Conference is to meet. In regard to the other observations which have been made, it is, however, only just to all parties to remember, that when Austria and Prussia had expressed their willingness to enter into the Conference, the Court of Denmark desired that I would not press for an immediate answer to my invitation, because great excitement then prevailed at Copenhagen, and it was desirable to wait till the matter could be more calmly and coolly considered. Consequently, I did not press for an answer at the time; and on communicating the reason of the delay to the Courts of Berlin and Vienna no objection was raised.

MORTGAGE DEBENTURES BILL.

A Bill to enable certain Companies to issue Mortgage Debentures, and for the greater Security of the Holders of such Debentures—Was *presented* by The Lord REDESDALE; and read 1ª. (No. 55.)

House adjourned at Seven o' clock, till To-morrow half past Ten o' clock.

HOUSE OF COMMONS,

Thursday, April 21, 1864.

MINUTES.]— NEW MEMBER SWORN — Hugh Culling Eardley Childers, esquire, *for* Pontefract.

SELECT COMMITTEE—On Seat of Under Secretary of State *nominated* (see p. 1481); on Bankruptcy Act *nominated* (see p. 1482).

Lord Stratford de Redcliffe

SUPPLY —*considered in Committee* — *Committee* —R.P.

WAYS AND MEANS—*considered in Committee.*

PUBLIC BILLS—*Ordered*—County Bridges *.

First Reading—County Bridges * [Bill 77].

Second Reading—Charitable Assurances Enrolments (*Lords*) * [Bill 72].

Select Committee — On Government Annuities [Bill 11] *nominated* (see p. 1473); on Judgments Law Amendment * [Bill 72] *nominated* (see p. 1482).

Committee — Court of Justiciary (Scotland)* [Bill 31]; Fish Teinds (Scotland)* [Bill 45]; Summary Procedure (Scotland) * [Bill 32]; Bridges (Ireland) * [Bill 70] [No Report].

Report—Court of Justiciary (Scotland)* [Bill 31]; Fish Teinds (Scotland) * [Bill 45]; Summary Procedure (Scotland) * [Bill 76], and *re-committed.*

Third Reading—High Court at Bombay * [Bill 67].

NEW LAW COURTS.—QUESTION.

MR. SELWYN said, he would beg to ask the First Commissioner of Works, Whether Her Majesty's Government intend to accept the offer made by the Society of Lincoln's Inn in 1859, and since repeated—namely, either to give the ground necessary for the erection of Courts for the Vice Chancellors, or to build such Courts at the expense of the Society upon receiving, for a term of years, £4 per cent per annum on the actual outlay on the buildings from the Suitors' Fund, but without any charge upon or guarantee from the National Exchequer ?

SIR FITZROY KELLY said, he wished to ask whether, in case the Government contemplate any measure such as his hon. and learned Friend had alluded to, it was part of the scheme they had in view that one large building should comprise all the Law Courts ?

MR. COWPER said, in reply, that the proposal made in 1859 for erecting Vice Chancellors' Courts within the precincts of Lincoln's Inn was more for the benefit of the Inn than that of the public, as it would no doubt have enhanced the value of chambers there. It would not be so much for the advantage of suitors at large or the entire legal profession as the scheme proposed by the Commissioners for the concentration of all the Courts of Law and Equity and their offices in one building. It was, he believed, on this ground that the offer was refused by Lord Derby's Government at the time it was made, and it was on the same ground that the present Government could not avail themselves of the proposal of the Society of Lincoln's Inn. The scheme now in the contemplation of the Government had for its main feature, in accordance with the recommendation of the Commissioners, the bringing together of all the Courts and their offices under one roof, or in immediate contiguity to each other.

SIR FITZROY KELLY said, he wished to know when the scheme would be brought forward ?

MR. COWPER said, he believed it would be brought forward soon.

WEST INDIA MAILS.
QUESTION.

MR. CAVE said, he wished to ask the Secretary to the Treasury, Whether the West India Colonies have been called upon by the Treasury to contribute the sum of £37,554 for the present year towards the subsidy to the Royal Mail Steam Packet Company ; and, if so, whether the consent of those Colonies had been previously obtained ; and, whether he will lay upon the table of the House the copy of a letter from himself to Sir Frederick Rogers, together with the copy of a letter from the Postmaster General enclosed therein, on the subject ?

MR. PEEL, in reply, said, the Home Government two years ago had given notice to the Governments of the West India Colonies that from the present year, when the new contract would commence, they would apply to those Colonies that principle of half contribution for the cost of the Mail Service which was already in operation in respect to the Australian and other Colonies. The loss upon the West India Mail Service had been much reduced under the new contract, but it still amounted to a considerable sum — about £115,000. They had ascertained how much of that sum was due to the West India part of the service, and how much to the Mexico and Pacific part. This country would bear the whole loss on the Mexico and Pacific branch, but as regarded the West India branch, it was thought fair that the West India Colonies should bear a share of the loss upon it. Of course, it rested with those Colonies entirely whether they would give or withhold their consent to the arrangement, but that consent was necessary to their participating in the benefits of that service.

PAROCHIAL ASSESSMENT COMMITTEES.—QUESTION.

MR. SUTTON WESTERN said, he would beg to ask the President of the Poor Law Board, Whether any steps have been taken to enable Parochial Assessment Committees to appear by Counsel or otherwise for the purpose of defending their decisions before Petty or Quarter Sessions, and to provide means for meeting the expenses attending such defence ?

MR. C. P. VILLIERS said, in reply, that, as the Law now stood, if there was an Appeal against the valuation of a parish by the Assessment Committee, the Guardians could appear as respondents to that Appeal, and charge their costs, in case of failure, on the common fund; but it appeared that if the overseers made a rate upon the valuation so made by the Assessment Committee, and there was an Appeal against the rate, there was no provision for either the Committee or the Guardians to appear in defence of their valuation. This was considered a serious defect in the Act, and many representations of the injustice which this occasioned had reached the Poor Law Board. He had, therefore, determined to introduce a Bill to amend the Act in that respect, and he would do so in time for it to become law before the July Sessions.

MR. ALDERMAN SALOMONS said, he would beg to ask the President of the Poor Law Board if he intends to propose any Amendment of the Union Assessment Act during the present Session, and particularly if he intends so to alter that Act as to make it compulsory on parties to appeal to the Assessment Committee before appealing to the Justices in Quarter Sessions ?

MR. C. P. VILLIERS said, he had already stated that he would introduce an Amendment in the Union Assessment Act. He thought the provision which his hon. Friend suggested was very useful, and would take care that it was not overlooked in the Bill.

DEPARTURE OF GENERAL GARIBALDI.
QUESTION.

MR. KINNAIRD : Sir, a rumour has been prevalent within the last few days, and it has also appeared in the public press, that a Member of Her Majesty's Government and a Cabinet Minister has been instrumental in inducing the departure of General Garibaldi in deference to the French Government. In order to avert any misunderstanding on the subject, I wish to ask the right hon. Gentleman the Chancellor of the Exchequer, Whether there is any truth in that rumour ?

THE CHANCELLOR OF THE EXCHE-QUER: Sir, as far as I am concerned, I am obliged to my hon. Friend for putting this Question to me, because, undoubtedly, mysterious statements have appeared in the public journals. The subject is one in which the people of England take a very lively interest, and I do not think there is anything which they so much dislike as the appearance of mystery in anything when public matters and public men are concerned. With the permission of the House, therefore, I will shortly state my share in the proceeding which has given rise to these incorrect and even absurd rumours. Sir, on Sunday last, the Duke of Sutherland communicated to me that he and other friends of General Garibaldi were beginning to entertain considerable apprehensions in regard to the state of his health, and that a very eminent medical man, indeed one of the first names in the profession, who had visited him, Mr. Ferguson—

MR. SCULLY: Sir, I rise to order. I am kept very strictly to the Question in this House, and am not allowed to make the slightest statement of any sort that is the least irrelevant; and I say that in answering questions the right hon. Gentleman ought not to make use of irrelevant statements.

MR. SPEAKER: A Question having been addressed to the Chancellor of the Exchequer, there is nothing at all out of order in his replying to it.

THE CHANCELLOR OF THE EXCHE-QUER: The Duke stated to me that General Garibaldi's friends were beginning to entertain very serious apprehensions as to the effect of his protracted labours and his meditated excursion to the provinces on his health, and he requested me to come to Stafford House about nine o'clock in the evening for the purpose of consider-ing whether any advice should be tendered to the General on the subject. I considered, certainly, that the Duke of Sutherland, by the course which he had pursued in regard to General Garibaldi, had not only been exercising a princely hospitality, but really had been rendering a great public service; and I felt it to be my duty—I felt that it became me—if he thought it advisable to consult me in that matter, to comply with his wish. I went to Stafford House accordingly, and I found there that considerable apprehension prevailed on the subject; that General Garibaldi had already accepted, conditionally,

invitations to visit about thirty towns in the country; that the list was one which was rapidly growing from day to day; and that there was an explicit declaration of Mr. Fergusson to the effect, that it was quite impossible that the General's strength could stand the exhaustion incident to these continual public demonstrations—demonstrations which are the more fatigu-ing in proportion as they are ardent and affectionate. Well, the noble Duke, Lord Shaftesbury, Colonel Peard, General Eber, and one or two other friends of General Garibaldi, consulted together upon this matter, and we all came to the conclusion that it was our duty to advise General Garibaldi to contract very greatly the circle of his provincial excursions, and not to contract it only but likewise to fix it absolutely before leaving London, in order that it might not be capable of being afterwards extended and enlarged by the new applications which were coming in. That was made known to General Garibaldi in the first instance by two of his friends; and afterwards I was requested and did undertake to tell the General what my opinion was on the subject. I ventured to represent to him—what most of us on an inferior scale might give some opinion upon—that it was scarcely possible he could go through such labours without great injury to his health, and I also ventured to add that the people of England held that to be an object of great value, not only to his own country but to the world. I represented it as his duty to consider what would be the effect on his health of the engagements which he had made or appeared to have made, and what he might be called on to make in addition to those already contracted. I ventured also to say that there was some risk lest the magnificent national reception which had been given to him in the great metropolis of this country, and which really formed an historical event, should not gain, but even lose, some of its real dignity from being frequently repeated elsewhere. That was the whole substance of my communi-cation to General Garibaldi, the upshot of it being a very strong and urgent repre-sentation to the effect, that we prayed him to consider whether he ought not to contract greatly the circle of his tour, and fix it absolutely before leaving London. General Garibaldi heard me with great patience, and then proceeded to state that, in his opinion, there was great force in what I had stated, but that there would be very great difficulty in drawing distinctions between the wish of one town and the wish of another, and that he considered the purpose of his journey was already at an end. He said he had come to England, not with the view of obtaining honours to himself, which the people in any town might be disposed to pay, but with a view to render his thanks and acknowledgments to the Government and people of England for what he considered they had done for his country. He said that it appeared to him that, in visiting London, which is the metropolis, he visited the entire nation, and consequently, as he had so visited the nation, the purpose of his visit being accomplished, he felt himself at perfect liberty to withdraw the promises he had given conditionally; and he thought the best plan would be to decline visiting the provinces at the present moment. He stated also that he hoped at a future time he should be able to come back to England and indulge the wishes of his old friends by seeing them in a less formal manner than it was now possible for him to effect that object. That was the substance of the conversation which passed. I need hardly say that I have omitted nothing whatever that is material to the point, and that only the very busy and active imaginations of people having nothing to do, going from club to club inquiring for some new thing, could have given rise to the belief that political motives had been imported into this transaction. Perhaps it is hardly material to the question, but it was within my knowledge even at the time of the conversation, both through an official and unofficial channel, that so far from there being any truth in the ridiculous story of umbrage being taken on the other side of the water at the reception of General Garibaldi, the feelings of the Emperor of the French upon that point were entirely such as my noble Friend at the head of the Government described the other night. A little truth is often the means of introducing a great deal of error, and the accidental circumstance of my having been called upon, whether with reason or without reason, to advise in the matter of General Garibaldi's health, has been made the occasion of stories which are entirely destitute of the slightest shadow of foundation.

Sir HARRY VERNEY: May I be allowed to say one word? ["Order!"]

Mr. SCULLY wished to put a question to the Chancellor of the Exchequer relative to the reply he had just given to the hon.

Member for Perth—whether, in the course of the conversation he had with General Garibaldi, he stated to him that the feeling of the metropolis of England represented the feeling of the people of Ireland on this subject; and did he recommend him not to go to Ireland?

The CHANCELLOR of the EXCHEQUER: In the conversation referred to, I made no statement whatever with respect to the population of Ireland; and with respect to the population of England, I left it to General Garibaldi to judge of their feelings by what he saw.

LISBURN ELECTION.
SELECT COMMITTEE MOVED FOR.

Petitions of Russell Kennedy, and Bryson Pelan, and Jonathan Joseph Richardson, *considered.*

Mr. BUTT who had given notice, on consideration of the Petitions of R. Kennedy and B. Pelan, and J. J. Richardson, to move, That the Select Committee on the Lisburn Election Petitions do re-assemble and report upon the matter referred to them by the House, said, whatever opinion might be entertained with reference to the course the House ought to take in this matter, he thought everybody would admit that it was a question of great importance as affecting the privileges of that House and the practice of Election Committees. The Petitioner, Mr. Richardson, was formerly a Member of that House. He was a candidate at the last election for Lisburn, and had presented a petition against the return. He had attended the Committee at a very great expense; and he now complained that, after eleven days had been spent in the inquiry, he was in a worse position than when the inquiry commenced. He considered that having presented a Petition he had a right to have it heard and decided, and that he could not be deprived of that right except through some fault of his own, or some defect in the rules, regulations, and proceedings of that House. He had complied with every rule and regulation, and he asked the House to find some means of remedying the injustice he had suffered. The hon. and learned Gentlemen then stated the facts connected with the lapse of the Committee by the illness and absence of Mr. Stirling, the Act of Parliament in relation to Election Committees not having provided for the case which actually occurred. The provisions were not, as had been asserted, new.

They were contained in the Grenville Act of 1779. At that time the House sat at nine o'clock in the morning, and the Committees sat in the evening, so that the meetings of the Committees were subsequent to the sittings of the House. The clause, which had a meaning in 1770, had been copied into every subsequent Act, although the altered circumstances of the case, the meetings of the Committees now preceding instead of following the sittings of the House, rendered it utterly inapplicable. In the present case the Committee acted in the spirit, though not in the letter of the statute, by adjourning over the day when they could have taken the Orders of the House. All that the Committee had since decided was that they had lapsed their powers by adjourning to the wrong day. Every one would admit that there had been a grievous failure of justice. He had no right to assume what would have been the result of the deliberations of the Committee; but the House was in this position, that it contained a Member whose seat was impeached for bribery, and, unless the House devised a remedy, the electors of Lisburn might say that they were misrepresented in that House. And was this the result of all our detailed legislation on the subject? He believed that justice might still be done. In 1848, some difficulty arose relative to proceedings connected with an election petition; and an Act of Parliament, introduced by the right hon. Member for Cambridge University, was passed to provide a remedy for the inadvertence. Another course might be pursued. The Acts of Parliament regulating election petitions had nothing to do with the limitation as to time. This depended entirely on the Sessional Order of the House, and by special direction the Order might be suspended, and a new mode of proceeding directed by the House. There were two precedents of this on the books; one in 1831, when such a proceeding was resorted to, to provide a remedy for a delay in presenting a petition caused by a great storm of snow. It had frequently been said that the jurisdiction of Election Committees was entirely derived from statute. This he denied. By the ancient law of Parliament the House had a right to decide on the mode of trying election petitions. In olden time, the practice had been to refer them for trial before Committees; after this the number of petitions became so great that this mode of proceeding was abandoned,

Mr. Butt

and the petitions were tried by Speaker Onslow at the bar of the House. It was a well known principle of law that power could not be taken away, except by express words of legislation. It followed, then, that wherever Acts of Parliament did not regulate the proceedings of Election Committees the House had power to supply the deficiency. The House had power to make orders for anything not provided for by the statute. Had the Lisburn Election Committee chosen to go on the next day their proceedings could not have been set aside, as was shown in the St. Alban's case, where Edwards was even committed to prison on proceedings subsequent to an irregular adjournment. The circumstances of the earlier sittings of the St. Alban's Committee were precisely similar in this— that neither the petitioner nor the sitting Member offered any objection to the constitution of the Committee after its adjournment; and though, on the presentation of the Report, the objection was urged by a Member of the House, the Report was nevertheless received, and an Act of Parliament was passed taking away the franchise of the borough. The words of the Act were, "The Committee shall try." Was, then, the express purpose of the Act to be set aside merely because the Committee did not sit *de die in diem?* Was the Act most obeyed by calling on the Committee to re-assemble, or by paying pharisaical attention to minute matters? The question was not to be determined by passion or party feeling ["Move."]

Motion made, and Question proposed,

"That a Select Committee be appointed to inquire into the matters contained in the Petition of Jonathan Joseph Richardson, which was presented on the 18th day of this instant April, and to report their opinion thereon."—*(Mr. Butt.)*

MR. HUNT said, that the House had been more occupied that evening with the inhabitants of Caprera than with the events of the Lisburn Election Petition, and therefore it had been quite impossible for him, under the circumstances of the evening, (the hon. Member alluded to the presence of General Garibaldi in the seats under the gallery of the House,) to follow the whole of the arguments of the hon. and learned Gentleman who had just sat down; and, therefore, in the remarks which he was about to make, he had to beg the pardon of the House if he neglected to reply to all the learned Member's arguments. He wished to call the attention of the House to what occurred after the recess. A debate arose, and the Secretary for the Home Department proposed an adjournment to the following day. Not one lawyer attempted to take exception to the position which he (Mr. Hunt) had laid down, that the Committee were dead as a Committee, and had no power to proceed further. The Attorney General recommended the House to give no advice, but to leave the Committee to flounder in the mud as they liked, and to get out of it in the best way they could. On the following day the four Gentlemen met again, and came to a determination that they were no longer legally able to proceed. These Gentlemen sat as a kind of coroner's inquest on themselves, and, no doubt, struggled hard to bring in an open verdict; but the force of circumstances and the legal advice which they received compelled them to return a verdict of *felo de se*. The hon. and learned Gentleman (Mr. Butt) asked the House to afford the petitioners some redress ; but he had omitted to state one important fact—namely, that it was upon the advice of the counsel for the petitioners that the Committee took the step which led to their dissolution. But for that advice the Committee would have adjourned until the 4th instead of the 5th. When the counsel for the petitioners had led them into this error they certainly had no claim upon the House for redress. The hon. and learned Gentleman seemed to be of opinion that the House had some jurisdiction in the matter of elections independently of the Act under which the proceedings took place. Now, he (Mr. Hunt) ventured to dispute that proposition, and contended that the House was tied down by the Act, and could not go a step beyond it. The second section enacted that every petition presented within the proper time should be deemed an election petition, and then went on to provide how it should be dealt with. It provided that the Committee should determine by a majority of votes, whether the sitting Member was duly elected, or what other person was duly elected; or whether it was a void election, &c.; which determination should be final; and the House, on being informed thereof, was directed to order the Report of the Committee to be entered on the Journals, and the House gave directions for altering the return, or issuing a new writ, &c. All, therefore, that the House had to do was to carry the determination of the Committee into execution. The House, no doubt, had the power to direct any four Members to report on any matter referred to them ; but he would venture to say that if any Report was made by the four Gentlemen who sat on the Election Committee, such Report would not be within the terms of the Act, and would have no force or validity. The sitting Member might treat that Report as waste paper, and the House would have no jurisdiction in the matter, so far as to affect the seat. He did not see for what object a Select Committee could be appointed. If there was any probability of a Committee finding its way through this slough of despond, by all means let the hon. and learned Gentleman have it ; but it would be much better for him to withdraw his Motion, and turn his attention to the improvement of the law respecting election matters, where it was very much needed.

THE ATTORNEY GENERAL said, he agreed in much that had fallen from the hon. Gentleman opposite, and was glad to find that his hon. and learned Friend the Member for Youghal did not ask the House to assent to the terms of the Motion as it originally stood, but was prepared to submit it to the House in a modified form. It would be a dangerous precedent if the House were to take upon itself the introduction, by its own authority, of any Amendment in the course of procedure under the Election Petitions Act. The Cheltenham case, which occurred in 1848, appeared to tell against the Motion of his hon. and learned Friend. In that case an error was discovered in the preparation of the usual recognisances ; but it turned out that there were seven or eight other cases in which similar errors had been committed, and, on petitions being presented by the sitting Members, the right hon. Gentleman the Member for the University of Cambridge moved the appointment of a Select Committee much in the form of that now proposed. That certainly was a precedent so far; but what was the bearing of their Report, and what was the practical result? The Committee reported that it might be desirable to relieve the petitioners by legislation. The error in the Cheltenham case had occurred in seven or eight cases; and it was corrected, by legislation, before the inquiry, in any of these cases, had begun; but in the present case only one individual was concerned; the inquiry also was at an end ; and if the Motion before the House were agreed to, it would be impossible to avoid the suspicion of being actuated by party or political motives, and of a desire to legislate against one single individual. Under these circumstances, the Government could not undertake the responsibility of advising the House to legislate on this particular case, or to enter upon an inquiry with a view to such legislation. There was another course which might have been worthy of the consideration of the House, and that was whether advantage might not be taken of the Motion to appoint a Committee to consider the expediency of making provision in future for errors in point of form or irregularity of proceeding on the part of Election Committees. But there was a Bill now before the House for the amendment of the law relating to Elections, introduced by the hon. Member for Northamptonshire (Mr. Hunt) ; and, perhaps, it might be desirable to refer both these matters to a Committee. Under all the circumstances, he did not think it would be advisable to agree to the appointment of the Committee proposed by his hon. and learned Friend.

MR. BUTT said, he would withdraw his Motion after the statement of the Attorney General.

Question put, and *negatived.*

WAYS AND MEANS.
Order for Committee read.

THE CHANCELLOR OF THE EXCHEQUER : Sir, notices having been given of Motions on the subject of Fire Insurance duty, I wish to make a short statement before you leave the chair ; because, in point of fact, one of these Notices relates not so much to Fire Insurance as to the general principles on which the financial statement should be submitted and disposed of by the House. There are two Motions which are to be submitted to the House—one by the hon. Baronet the Member for Evesham (Sir Henry Willoughby), which, as it stands on the paper, does not, I believe, disclose the nature of his object ; but he has been good enough to explain his object to me, and I will explain it to the House, in order to draw the distinction between the Motion of the hon. Baronet and that of which notice has been given by the hon. Member for Dudley (Mr. H. B. Sheridan). As I understand, the hon. Member for Evesham does not propose to interfere with the financial arrangements of the Government ; but he questions the judgment and discretion of the manner in which the Government, being

The Attorney General

only able to give a limited relief in respect of duty paid on Fire Insurances, give that relief by reducing the duty paid by stock in trade instead of that paid by property. We propose to give the relief to stock in trade ; the hon. Baronet proposes to give it to houses, buildings, and furniture. He therefore raises a simple question. He will argue that my proposal is bad. I will take the liberty of submitting that his is bad also ; but whenever it is before the Committee of Ways and Means, the Committee will be able to dispose of it without disturbing any financial principle, or placing the Government in the position of not being able to defer to the wishes of the Committee in whichever direction that wish may be. But the hon. Member for Dudley gives notice of a Motion of a different character. He says that the reduction of the Fire Duty in the manner proposed by me is not the mode of reduction contemplated by the Resolution of the House passed last Session on this subject, and that a uniform reduction of 1*s.* per cent on all descriptions of property liable to the said duty would be more acceptable to the country. I believe that there is some difficulty attaching to that Resolution in the pointed manner in which it alludes to a Resolution to be proposed in Ways and Means ; but that is immaterial, because it can be cured ; but the object of the hon. Gentleman is to pledge the House before going into Committee to make a general reduction on both property and stock in trade, and he fixes that reduction at 1*s.* per cent. Now, with respect to the Motion of the hon. Gentleman I wish to remind the House of our financial position ; because they will do me the justice to recollect that in the midst of a long statement—or rather near the close of a long statement—when I was naturally unwilling to burden the House with long details, I, notwithstanding, stated that the proposal which we made in respect of Fire Insurance, limited as it was, was not one which we made so much on our own judgment in regard to what should be done, as out of our desire to go to the extreme of our limits, to meet a wish which we believed to prevail extensively in the House. That is material for the House to recollect, because it is the last feather that breaks the back of the horse or the camel, and the Government, which goes to the extreme of what it can in financial reduction, is not in a position to go quite as far as is proposed in this instance. Now, I stated to the House that we presented an estimate of revenue and expenditure which, without making any reductions, showed a surplus of £2,570,000; but, with respect to that surplus, it is right I should remind the House that half a million of our revenue is not dependent on resources within our reach, but, in fact, on a portion of the taxation of China, and is liable to be affected by any incidents tending to disturbance in that empire. I believe that if it is in the power of China she will pay, and I believe it is probable that it will be in her power; but that portion of our revenue must be regarded as an element of weakness in the Estimate for the year. It will be recollected, also, that I said it might be argued that we ought to provide in the Estimates of the current year for the second portion of the payment in redemption of the Scheldt dues. The sum that would be required for the purpose is £176,000. The way we propose to proceed with our surplus of £2,570,000 was this:— We began with £1,330,000 for the reduction in the Sugar Duties; and then came £800,000 for reduction in the Income Tax; making a sum of £2,130,000, and leaving still a surplus of £440,000. Against that surplus of £440,000, as I stated before, it is quite arguable that the second portion of the Scheldt redemption money should be charged; and the amount remaining of the surplus was not such as we considered it unreasonable to ask the House to leave in our hands, because it was not unlikely that between the month of April and the close of the Session fresh demands of one kind or another might be made on the public purse. And even since the 7th of April, when I made the financial statement, a new demand has arisen—though I cannot state the amount—to affect the limited balance as I then stated it to the House. Still, with this surplus of £440,000 as we felt that we might be justified in carrying over the Scheldt redemption money to a future year in case of need, we did attempt to meet the wishes of the House by offering them a reduction of the Fire Insurance duty, as regards property limited in amount, but, as we thought, sufficient, considering all the circumstances of the case. That reduction involves a loss to the revenue of £192,000, which, with the small loss by the reduction of the licence duty for the sale of tea, reduces our surplus to £238,000; and, as I have observed, that has been reduced since by a new demand on the Government, of a kind which it was not open to us to reject. Without taking into account the £176,000 which a rigorous financier might argue we ought not to postpone for a future year, the upshot of all this is, that the Government is not in a position to go further and dispose of more revenue, having reduced the surplus to the minimum amount of the sum I stated on a former evening, which sum has sunk since then. Under these circumstances, it is proposed, in lieu of a reduction of 1s. 6d. upon stock in trade, that we should make a less effective reduction—or, in other words, a reduction less likely to produce reproductive action —a reduction, namely, of 1s. upon all descriptions of property insured against fire. I know there is an opinion that house property and furniture would be quite as likely to become the subjects of increased insurance, in the event of a reduction of duty, as stock in trade, or even more so. I dispute that; I think it contrary to experience; but, at any rate, it will hardly be alleged that a reduction of 1s. upon all kinds of property would produce as large a percentage increase as a reduction of 1s. 6d. upon stock in trade alone. It is quite idle to reduce a duty of this sort by small driblets. On the first night of the discussion it was proposed to make a reduction of 6d. over all. If the House wishes to make a distinct present of so much money to those who insure, without any view to extension of insurance, I cannot conceive a better scheme for that purpose than spreading a sixpenny reduction over the whole mass of property now insured against fire. I am bound to say that I have always agreed with the hon. Member for Dudley, that if there is to be a reduction at all it ought to be a large one; and I am bound, in justice to the hon. Member, to say that, although he now proposes a reduction of 1s. the reduction which he formerly proposed—not last year but previously—as a proper terminus to arrive at was a reduction from 3s. to 1s. In that opinion he was right. I wish I could have proposed such a reduction upon stock in trade. It was not in my power to do so with a due regard to financial considerations; but a reduction of one half of the duty is the very smallest which I would recommend to the House. It is not my intention to go into the details of the Fire Insurance question. I admit it may fairly be said that the rate of premium upon property is much lower than that upon stock in trade, and that consequently the rate of duty in proportion to the premium is much higher. In that sense and to that degree the hon. Member for Evesham (Sir H. Willoughby) may argue rightly enough that we might expect recovery upon property; but against that I place, what is of more consequence, the slackness of recovery upon property, and the rapidity of recovery upon stock in trade. But that is not the point. I have spoken of the reproductive element, and I will explain to the House how we stand. The effect of a reduction of 1s. upon all kinds of property would be about the following:—I take the revenue from the Fire Insurance duty at £1,700,000. One shilling off the 3s. amounts to £566,000. I allow 6 per cent for recovery against a reduction of 1s., as I should be disposed to allow 10 per cent against a reduction of 1s. 6d., and 15 per cent against a reduction of 2s. A recovery of 6 per cent upon a reduction of 1s. would mitigate the loss by £34,000, leaving a loss of £532,000. That would be the real amount of revenue surrendered; but as the reduction only takes effect for nine months out of the twelve of the present year, the effect would be a total loss during the financial year of something over £400,000. Now, inasmuch as I am not able at present, even without taking any account of the Scheldt dues, to place my surplus at more than £200,000, the addition to the £192,000 of loss which I anticipate from the reduction of duty upon stock in trade of a sum exceeding £200,000 absolutely sweeps away the whole of that surplus and something more, and makes it entirely impossible for the Government to persevere with the proposals they have submitted to the House. If the House thinks it is better to leave the question alone than merely to deal with stock in trade, that is matter for argument. As Chancellor of the Exchequer, although I might regret that a boon should be withheld, I should have consolation in the greater security of my position. If the House thinks it is wiser and fairer to reduce upon property than to reduce upon stock in trade, I shall argue against the proposition; though I admit that if you do not extend the area of your reduction, you do not break in on the elementary principles of finance. But it is impossible for us, with any regard to our own duty, after the course we have taken and the manner in which we have stretched our proposals, with a view to meet the presumed wishes of the House, entirely to sweep away that most moderate — that

The Chancellor of the Exchequer

even less than moderate—surplus, which experience, propriety, and almost decency require us to preserve. There may be cases in which the Government may commence the financial year without a surplus. Supposing, for example, you find yourselves, as we found ourselves at the beginning of the financial year 1862-3, with the estimated produce of the taxes exactly balancing the estimated charge of the country. At that period, I stated to the House, on the part of the Government, and the House concurred in the view, that it would not be wise to impose a tax for the purpose of creating a surplus; but that was with special reference, not only to the circumstance that if we were to have a surplus it must be got by means of a new tax—which is a very different thing from parting with an old one—but likewise to the fact that the menacing state of Lancashire rendered it impossible to form an estimate of what the wants of the country might be, and that, therefore, it would be better to wait to obtain the benefit of experience, and to do, when the proper time arrived, what experience might seem to suggest. But I hope the House will not ask us, under existing circumstances, to adopt a proposal which I believe to be unexampled in the history of Parliament—namely, when the Government have proposed a provision for the services of the year extremely moderate in its character —perhaps too moderate—perhaps open to criticism on that score, but at any rate, not extensive as regards the amount of funds which they ask the House to leave in their hands — that, with the view of meeting, not an urgent or immediate, but a general public purpose connected with the reduction and improvement of a particular tax, the whole of the surplus should be swept away and the Exchequer left to provide for new public demands without any possible means of making such provision. At the time when the Government determined upon their financial proposals, they entertained a hope that those proposals would be substantially acceptable to the House. It was with a view to make them acceptable that they extended them in the direction I have named by including the element of Fire Insurance. They have been so far acceptable that the right hon. Gentleman the Member for Bucks has claimed their authorship. I am not going into any dispute about that. We are too well satisfied with being able to obtain assent and approval, independently of distinctions of party, in matters in which all have a common interest, to encumber the discussion or retard the progress of our measures with any question as to who is entitled to the credit of the parentage. But I venture respectfully to put it to the House that we have framed our entire plan for the year in a spirit of concession—in a spirit of respect to the wishes of the House, even where they went beyond our own views, so far as considerations of imperative public policy would permit us to proceed in that direction ; and I rely upon the fairness and kindness of the House not to depart from its old well-understood rules in financial proceedings, by taking out of the hands of the executive Government the whole remainder, and something more, of that very modest sum which they ask the House to leave with them in order to meet the casual exigencies of the year. Do not let the House be misled into exaggerated anticipations concerning the revenue of the coming year, from the fact that the revenue last year exhibited a large surplus over the estimate formed at the commencement of the year. The correspondence of estimates of revenue with their results is a matter beyond the control of any Parliament or of any Government. If it be true that last year the revenue yielded £2,000,000 more than the estimate made at the beginning of the year, it is also true that in 1860-1 the revenue yielded as nearly as possible £2,000,000 less. Perhaps you may say that is owing to some difference in the principles upon which the Estimates are made. There is no such difference at all. It is owing to the circumstances of the trade and industry of the country; it is owing, above all, to that great circumstance of a good or bad harvest, which at once powerfully acts upon the receipt of revenue. What does a good harvest mean ? When we have a good harvest it means, first of all, that £20,000,000, £30,000,000, or £40,000,000 of agricultural wealth are put into the hands of agricultural producers which in the case of a bad harvest would not have been there. It means, in the second place, that moderate prices rule throughout the country for all the articles of first necessity, and that the money saved upon those articles is spent, in great part, upon duty-paid commodities. That was the reason why the revenue of last year was so good, and the revenue of the last part of the year better than the revenue of the first part. At the commencement of the year we

were not enjoying the benefits of a very good harvest, whereas, for the last few months of the year, we had been enjoying those benefits in full. But it is impossible to guarantee these Estimates of revenue. I venture to say, comparing the estimates of 1860-1 with the present Estimates, that those for 1860-1 were simply the Estimates of the official advisers of the Chancellor of the Exchequer, adopted without minute examination, and without the slightest change. Now, I do not scruple to say that in the present year, partly with regard to the due position of the Government, and partly from a desire to find the funds with which to meet the wishes of the House, I did make a minute examination of the Estimates both of the Customs and the Board of Inland Revenue, in concert with the able gentlemen at the head of those departments, and we did make certain additions to them which, of course, swell the amount of the estimated surplus. If the House distrusts these Estimates, or thinks that there are funds available for the remission of taxes which the Finance Minister is unduly holding back, then the House has it in its power to appoint a Committee to consider the Estimates, and say whether, in the opinion of competent judges, additions can or cannot be made to them. But in the absence of such an inquiry as that I must stand upon these Estimates, and I apprehend the House will stand upon them also. It is impossible to conceive of a practice more dangerous than for the House, upon mere vague general allegations, resting upon no distinct authority, that the country is going to be prosperous —as if we could foresee what the harvest will be at the end of August or in September—to say that we may proceed to remit taxes from sources on which, in the present state of affairs, we are not able safely to reckon. I am not now disputing so much the question of the Fire Insurance duty as pointing out that this is a proposal interfering with an elementary and cardinal principle of finance, which, as far as I know, is always respected by the House— namely, the principle that where the executive Government has on its own responsibility computed the provision required for the services of the year, with a very narrow margin and moderate surplus for unforeseen exigencies, that surplus should be accorded to them, it being impossible for them, without an entire violation of their duty, to acquiesce in the absorption of funds which it is absolutely necessary to retain in order to meet the probable wants of the country. I beg, Sir, to move that you now leave the Chair.

Motion made, and Question proposed, "That Mr. Speaker do now leave the Chair."—(*The Chancellor of the Exchequer.*)

Mr. H. B. SHERIDAN said, he did not dispute the accuracy of many of the right hon. Gentleman's figures, but he differed considerably from his conclusions. He accepted the construction which the right hon. Gentleman had put upon his Resolution—namely, that, instead of a reduction of 1*s.* 6*d.* in the Fire Insurance duty on stock in trade, which the right hon. Gentleman proposed, there should be a uniform reduction of 1*s.* on all descriptions of property without any exception. Of course, farming stock, being now exempt, did not come within the range of his Resolution. He had consulted experienced practical men, and had received various communications from the country—among others one from the Chamber of Commerce of Birmingham, one of the most enlightened bodies of merchants in the kingdom—all pointing in the same direction as that indicated by his Motion; and they had the evidence of the Insurance Offices, that it would be impossible to carry out the proposal of the right hon. Gentleman without considerable expense, which would render the benefit little more, if more, than the proposed benefit which his proposed reduction of 1*s.* involved, and they would, he believed, themselves gratefully accept the alteration which he now suggested in that proposition. The Resolution he had to submit to the House did not involve an encroachment on the financial arrangements of the Budget. It did not take away the surplus which the right hon. Gentleman said he had in hand. As the right hon. Gentleman had stated, £1,700,000 was the revenue derived from the Fire Insurance duty. One third of that amount, as the right hon. Gentleman estimated, was obtained from stock in trade, or £566,000. The right hon. Gentleman proposed to remit one-half of that sum, or £283,000, by reducing the duty from 3*s.* to 1*s.* 6*d.* on stock in trade only. From that sum, however, the right hon. Gentleman deducted £70,000, being the amount of the fourth quarter, which he would not receive. That reduced the amount to £213,000. Then 10 per cent must be deducted for the increase anticipated by the

The Chancellor of the Exchequer

right hon. Gentleman upon his reduction of the duty, or £21,000, which brought the loss down to £192,000. Turning next to the plan involved in his own Resolution, the figures would stand thus :—£1,700,000 was the amount of the revenue from the 3*s.* duty now levied ; one-third of that was £566,000 ; and he proposed to reduce the 3*s.* duty by 1*s.*, or one-third, on all descriptions of property. From the £566,000 they must deduct £142,000 for the fourth quarter. Thus they had £424,000, and not £500,000, as the amount represented by the demand which his Resolution made. How was that to be provided ? First, there was the natural increase of the duty, £50,000. Then there was the further increase of 10 per cent, which the right hon. Gentleman anticipated from the reduced tax. Proceeding on the same principle of calculation, he argued that his plan of reduction would be followed by an increase of 10 per cent of the £424,000. That 10 per cent made £42,000, and £50,000 represented the natural increase of the duty. Then the right hon. Gentleman had not taken into his calculation the discount allowed to the Insurance Offices for the collection of the revenue, amounting to £21,000. That gave £330,000, or nearly that sum, to meet the £424,000. Then there were the unappropriated balances of the Exchequer, which, after the deductions to which the right hon. Gentleman had referred, still left £238,000. Thus nearly £100,000 would be the amount remaining in hand, should the House be pleased to adopt his proposal instead of that of the Chancellor of the Exchequer. But the right hon. Gentleman said they had no right to reckon on an increasing revenue in the ensuing year, although he had estimated it at something like half a million less than it was last year. Now, the House could not shut its eyes to the fact that last year every branch of the revenue increased, while nearly every branch of the expenditure diminished ; and there was now a large surplus with which the right hon. Gentleman had dealt ably in every way except in respect to Fire Insurance. However, he would not depend on that argument, but on the argument that the right hon. Gentleman had enough for the purpose of satisfying the object of his Motion. But, even if the right hon. Gentleman had not enough, that was not his fault or the fault of the House. By two Resolutions passed in succeeding years, the House had called on the right hon. Gentleman to make provision for the reduction of the duty. Now, his Resolution would not take the whole even of the unappropriated balance in the hands of the right hon. Gentleman, and, therefore, no embarrassment could ensue from its adoption. It was enough for him to show that there was sufficient money to provide for that uniform reduction of this duty which the country required, and which the House had declared should be carried out. The House leaned on the anticipated surplus and the probable prosperity of the country for any wants that might arise. But to say that this balance should not be applied as the House had said it ought to be applied, would be using the House in a manner he should not have anticipated. The right hon. Gentleman had based his calculations on the assumption that two-thirds of this duty were derived from the insurance of property and one-third from stock in- trade. The right hon. Gentleman admitted that this was conjecture, and it must be so—he did not know where he could possibly get figures to enable him to arrive at such a calculation. It was true, he might have obtained information from Insurance Offices, but he had not said that he had so obtained it, and he was not aware that Insurance Offices could give him such information. They had no index or handy-book which would supply it. The right hon. Gentleman had not told the House that, from the experience of the whole of the Insurance Offices, he had been enabled to arrive at an equitable average. He could not help reminding the right hon. Gentleman that, in the strongest manner, he had himself condemned the use of figures that could not be substantiated. What, then, was the basis of his argument? Fire Offices could not supply the figures, for another good reason. They had been holding meetings, and expressing the difficulties they had in understanding the words "stock in trade." If the right hon. Gentleman had not heard of these meetings, he probably would. If he had not received a communication from the Secretary of the "Sun," he no doubt would. Out of a million and a half of policies issued, one-third might possibly contain items only of stock in trade; but that was a very different result from saying that one-third of this duty was received on stock in trade. If the traders in insurance were not themselves agreed as to what the term "stock in trade" might affect or include, how could they possibly give the Chancellor of the Exchequer the calculations on which he rested? But these were not the only parties who had difficulty in understanding the meaning of "stock in trade." He had received, and no doubt others had received, many communications on this subject. Insurance Offices were in great perplexity, and the right hon. Gentleman would have many questions put to him—whether, for instance, the handsome plate-glass fronts, fittings, and ornamental work of shops, were utensils or stock in trade; whether the horses and vans employed by Pickford were stock in trade, or utensils of trade. Houses built for the purpose of selling were stock in trade—would they be excluded? The mills at Bradford and other places must be utensils of trade. Merchants might say that their ships were either stock or utensils of trade. Certainly all the fittings of those ships, their luxurious accommodations, their plate-glass, their linen, their wines, would be stock in trade. The stock of innkeepers and hotel-keepers, with the whole property in their houses, must be stock in trade. But what would the right hon. Gentleman say to the rolling stock of railways and their stations? Surely these must be stock in trade or utensils? The right hon. Gentleman had raised a distinction as to machinery used for the purpose of manufacture and machinery used for the purpose of trade. These formed two distinct items in his calculation. Who was to decide between them? A thousand-and-one other objections would naturally suggest themselves to persons who understood this question; and endless difficulties, vexations, and perplexities would be occasioned. The proposition of the right hon. Gentleman was impracticable; or, if at all practicable, it would end in litigation and annoyance. Such being the conditions attaching to the proposal, what were the reasons which had induced the right hon. Gentleman to make this distinction? There must be some substantial reason to induce the right hon. Gentleman to propose that the House should consent to alter the Resolution they passed only a year ago. What were the reasons which had induced him to wade into the by-paths of this question, that could only end in doubt and perplexity, when the open road lay before him in the Resolution of the House? The right hon. Gentleman gave two reasons. The first was that there was the greatest possible difference of opinion as to the self-recovering power of the Fire Insurance duty. He should like to know where he found those opinions. Whose opinions were they to which he referred ? Who was it that said there was doubt as to the recovering power of this duty ? The right hon. Gentleman had not adduced any authority on the subject. The right hon. Gentleman had not produced a single authority in support of his view. The more correct way of putting the case would be, that the opinions of writers on the subject were all the other way—they were all unanimous in their conclusions with regard to the reproducing power of this duty. M'Culloch, Porter, Newmarch, Samuel Brown, all the practical men on the question, and those who felt the pulse of the people in regard to it, combined in opinion that a moderate reduction of the duty would be followed by a replacement of revenue. But the public pointed to a reduction of 2s. per cent in the duty, and that, he had no doubt, would be ultimately effected. Stock in trade was insured nearly to its limits, whereas it was calculated that 80 per cent of houses and furniture were yet to be insured. The only person who appeared to entertain the opinion of the Chancellor of the Exchequer on this point was Mr. Coode, the counsel for the Exchequer, to whom the right hon. Gentleman so largely referred last year. It would be desirable to know what were the authorities upon which the right hon. Gentleman justified his conclusions. The next argument of the Chancellor of the Exchequer was that taxes on trade and industry replaced themselves more easily and more rapidly than taxes upon property, and the illustration given by the right hon. Gentleman was very amusing. He gave the instance of the assessed taxes. Was it possible that the House could be brought to accept such an illustration ? The assessed taxes were compulsory taxes, levied upon all ascertained property of certain kinds, and it was perfectly monstrous to suppose that duties which were compulsory, with penalties attaching to attempted evasions of them, could be likened to a voluntary tax which might be paid or not, without any liability to penalties. There was no analogy between the two cases. If the assessed taxes were reduced to any slight extent, what expectation could there be of an increase of revenue from that source ? No one would in consequence set up another carriage, or keep another dog, or wear more

hair powder. And yet the right hon. Gentleman told the House that because the assessed taxes would not maintain themselves or increase after reductions in the rates of duties, therefore the income from Fire Insurances would equally fail to recover or increase after reduction. That, too, was assuming that the duty upon Fire Insurances was a tax upon property. He disputed that view. He denied that it was a tax upon property as much as it was a tax upon income. A person with an income of £500 a year, and insuring for £3,000, would, if the duty upon insurances were removed, save 2d. in £1, and a person with £250 a year income, insuring for £1,500, would save an equal amount. It was in such cases an income tax, but it certainly could not be called a tax upon property. The House had come to a Resolution upon this subject so long ago that he hardly liked now to trespass upon their time to show how incorrect was the description of the tax given by the Chancellor of the Exchequer, but he would just give one illustration to show its real nature. He would take a street with houses of equal value and furniture of similar amount on either side. The inhabitants of the houses on one side might insure, and then they would pay the tax ; but the inhabitants of the houses on the other side might decline to insure, and then they would pay no tax. That illustration would prove that the tax was not a tax upon property, but upon the act of insuring. How, then, could the right hon. Gentleman call it a tax upon property, and draw a parallel between it and the assessed taxes, and then call upon the House to come to a conclusion based upon such an assumption ? He could not understand why a distinction was to be made in favour of stock in trade. The right hon. Gentleman's figures were hardly reliable, his reasons were erroneous, and the parallel he drew between the assessed taxes and the tax on Fire Insurance would not hold. Was it possible that the right hon. Gentleman had remembered that those who had pressed upon him hardest for a remission of the duty were the dwellers in houses, the masses, the millions of the people, whom he now passed over by the distinction he made, the middle classes, the workmen with their small stocks of furniture and tools, whom he chose to style property-holders ? Did he wish to tell those classes that they had been too urgent in their demands, had pressed too hardly upon the Government for the re-mission of this tax, and therefore he took this opportunity of saying to them, "You must stand by and let others be served first?" It was difficult to believe that such could be the right hon. Gentleman's meaning, but some such idea would pre-sent itself to the minds of those who would be excluded from all benefit of the proposed reduction. It was possible that the right hon. Gentleman might have a better argument on the last point which he had put forth, as to the exemption of farming stock. The Chancellor of the Exchequer naturally was shocked at that exemption, and had not hesitated to ex-press the indignation he felt at it. The right hon. Gentleman said, "There is something very invidious on the present exemption of farming stock. That ex-emption was unfairly granted." He (Mr. Sheridan), quite agreed that the distinc-tion was invidious and unfair, and he had been anxious to discover how the right hon. Gentleman proposed to re-medy it. The right hon. Gentleman told them he proposed to mitigate that exemp-tion by a reduction of one-half the duty upon Fire Insurance upon stock in trade. That was a proceeding which it was diffi-cult to understand. An exemption was condemned, and the cure proposed was the creation of another and a similar wrong. Thus two wrongs were supposed to make right; but that was a novel way of legis-lating upon a vexed question. What did the public out of doors think of that pro-position? There had been at first a feel-ing among the public that the exemption of farming stock was due to the fact that the farmers had so many friends in that House; but that feeling died out when it was found that the best friends to the general reduction of the tax were the country Gentlemen and the owners of land, who, to their credit, had, without regard to party views, always been the most earnest supporters of a universally reme-dial measure. Now, however, it was pro-posed to establish another exemption that was equally as objectionable as the former. The result would be confusion worse con-founded, more ill blood created, and the existing wrong to the great body of the public heightened, and that was called a mitigation of the first exemption. Of course, the people out of doors grumbled at that; they were not worthy of a Chan-cellor of the Exchequer who looked after their interests in that way. But the fact

was that there was a great disinclination among the public to receive this proposi-tion as a boon. It was impossible to find in the reasons which had been assigned any excuse, he might even say any apo-logy, for the proposition now made by the Chancellor of the Exchequer. The right hon. Gentleman told them it was in defer-ence to the formal indication of the opinions of the House that the Govern-ment had thought it their duty to deal with this tax, although they were not pre-pared to make a reduction of any great extent. But the House knew, before it passed its Resolution, that the Chancellor of the Exchequer was not prepared with an immediate and large reduction. The proposal that he (Mr. Sheridan) had made to the House was a reduction of 1s. in the duty on all insurances all round, and after two or three years a further reduction of another 1s. The right hon. Gentleman accepted that Resolution as an instruction to the Government, but it was possible that he had not understood fully the effect of that Resolution, and had mistaken the meaning of the House in passing it. The right hon. Gentleman had told them what his object was without the slightest at-tempt at concealment. He hoped that the House would not allow itself to be trifled with, but that it would support his Reso-lution, which involved a general reduction of the Fire Insurance duty, instead of the reduction of a particular portion. The House should at once show the right hon. Gentleman that its Resolutions must for the future be binding, and that it was not prepared in every instance to be implicitly guided by the right hon. Gentleman. Was the House to have no opportunity of giving force to its views and to those of its con-stituents? The petitions which had been presented upon this subject did not origi-nate from a portion of the people, but were participated in by the bulk of the community. The hon. Gentleman con-cluded by moving his Resolution.

MR. HADFIELD, in seconding the Amendment, said, he was convinced that the revenue would suffer considerably if the present mode of taxation were adhered to. One of the railway companies, paying £1,000 a year for Fire Insurance, of which sum two-thirds was on account of the duty, had determined to insure themselves, and the consequence was that the revenue had suffered severely from the exorbitant amount of the rate. This example was also being followed by other railway companies.

Amendment proposed,

To leave out from the word "That" to the end of the Question, in order to add the words "in the opinion of this House, such a reduction of the Fire Insurance Duty as that contemplated by the Resolution of the House passed last Session would be best effected by an uniform reduction of one shilling per cent on all descriptions of property liable to the said Duty,"—(*Mr. Henry B. Sheridan,*)

—instead thereof.

THE CHANCELLOR OF THE EXCHEQUER said, he would endeavour to curtail his remarks as far as possible, and he should therefore begin by throwing aside all the arguments connected with the hon. Gentleman's interpretation of his motives, which really had nothing whatever to do with the subject under the consideration of the House. He would also draw a distinction between those of his arguments which were relevant and those which were not. The argument employed by the seconder of the Amendment (Mr. Hadfield) though they might apply to the Resolution of the hon. Member for Evesham, were not relevant to the question, which was purely a financial one. He need not dwell upon what the hon. Gentleman had said about the absence of any authorities on his part. The hon. Gentleman had, however, in his arguments put entirely aside the testimony of all those who had been responsible during a long series of years for the proper conduct and management of the revenue of the country, and of all those whose duty it was to have formed a responsible opinion upon the subject. It was not, however, necessary to dwell further upon that portion of the question. The hon. Gentleman had asked him where he had obtained his estimate. He did not think that it was at all necessary to give an answer to that question; but he would state that he had obtained it by requesting the persons connected with the Board of Inland Revenue to wait on the largest and best of the Insurance Companies, and he believed that that estimate was the best that could be arrived at. The hon. Gentleman was wrong in supposing that there was any greater difficulty in determining stock in trade than there was in defining farm stock. The hon. Gentleman had made two statements. One was, that he did not wish to take away the means he (the Chancellor of the Exchequer) had, and that his Amendment would leave him sufficient means for the public service; and

the second was, that if he had not sufficient means it was his own fault. Now, he would confine himself to those two statements. What did the hon. Gentleman mean by saying that it was his fault if there were any insufficiency in the revenue after the reduction of the tax as proposed by the Amendment? His meaning was that Her Majesty's Government had been wrong in proposing the reduction of the Income Tax from 7*d.* to 6*d.* The meaning of the hon. Gentleman was that they should have reserved that sum, and have applied it to a more liberal reduction of the Fire Insurance duty instead. There were undoubtedly arguments for each course, but he believed the preponderance to be against the plan proposed by the hon. Gentleman. The hon. Gentleman to be honest, ought not, however, to have moved a Resolution which would have the effect of leaving him with a financial deficit—he should rather have proposed a Resolution blaming Her Majesty's Government for their proposed reduction of the Income Tax, and, at the same time, suggesting as a substitute the reduction of the Fire Insurance duty to 1*s.* The hon. Gentleman had said that the fault was his if he had not the money; but where did the hon. Gentleman expect him to find it? He had already stated on the part of the Government that sugar had the first claims on the surplus, and that the Income Tax ranked next in importance. The hon. Gentleman must either agree to those propositions or dissent from them. If he did coincide in the views expressed in them, it was useless to talk about a further reduction of the Fire Insurance duty at the present moment. It was really surprising to see how the hon. Gentleman had dealt with his figures. If the hon. Gentleman could also give him the power of counting his money twice over he would undertake to repeal the Fire Insurance duty to-morrow. He had stated that the hon. Gentleman proposed to deprive him of a trifle over £400,000; but the hon. Gentleman had charged him with omitting to take into consideration the natural increase of the revenue. He had, of course, made the omission, because the increase had already been once provided for—it was taken into account when the estimate was made. The hon. Gentleman had said that he would obtain £21,000 more by means of the discount, but that discount had already disappeared in the reduction. The discount was chargeable equally on the

Mr. Hadfield

whole of the £1,700,000, and, whether they deducted it upon a larger or upon a smaller sum, the proportion of discount would disappear with it; and, therefore, in point of fact, with the exception of some £5,000 or £10,000, in which his statement as to the reproductive powers of the tax differed from that of the hon. Gentleman's, the case would stand precisely as he had at first stated it to the House. If the proposal of the Government was a bad one, let the House reject it; and if they thought the proposal of the hon. Member for Evesham a better one, let them take that: but the hon. Member for Dudley proposed to take away every rag and shred of the surplus which, in deference to the wishes of the House, he proposed to hold, and would land him in all probability in financial bankruptcy. If the proposal of the Government could be improved, let that improvement by all means be made; but they should on no account permit that improvement or pretext of improvement to be the ground for violating those wider principles which were essential for the welfare of the community, and for the maintenance of the public credit.

MR. HUBBARD rose amid loud cries of "divide." The hon. Member said that he would not detain the House more than a quarter of an hour—[*Great laughter— whereon the hon. Gentleman sat down.*]

MR. DISRAELI: Sir, I will not speak for a quarter of an hour, but only for two minutes. I wish merely to explain the vote I shall give. I think that the principle laid down in the Amendment, as distinguished from the proposition of the Government, is the right principle. I have, first of all, to consider the Resolution which the House has arrived at, and then to consider the difficulties in the way of taxing stock in trade—a consideration which weighs much with me, though the Chancellor of the Exchequer holds it light. At the same time, I entirely agree with the right hon. Gentleman that, after the financial statement which he made to the House, no alteration ought to be made in that arrangement, and that we ought to confine ourselves to appropriating the sum understood to be at our disposal, in the manner best calculated to carry out the views adopted by the House. Therefore, though I shall vote for the Amendment of the hon. Gentleman, I shall, in case that is carried, move, when it becomes a substantive Motion, the omission of the words, "1s. per cent," and then it will run—

"That in the opinion of this House the reduction of the Fire Duty in the manner proposed by the Chancellor of the Exchequer is not the mode contemplated by the* Resolution of the House passed last Session on this subject, and that the uniform reduction of duty on all descriptions of property liable to the said duty will be more acceptable."

MR. T. BARING said, that he should vote against the Resolution, because he was against the sacrifice of revenue.

SIR HENRY WILLOUGHBY also felt bound to vote against the Amendment, as he did not think it proper, after the House had accepted the main principles of the Budget—the reduction of the sugar duties and the reduction of the Income Tax—now to introduce any Motion destroying the surplus altogether.

SIR STAFFORD NORTHCOTE explained that his right hon. Friend the Member for Buckinghamshire did not propose to interfere with the surplus; but, thinking the proposal of the Chancellor of the Exchequer with respect to the Fire Insurance duty not satisfactory to the country, intended, in case the Amendment became a substantive Motion, to move the omission from it of those words which, according to the Chancellor of the Exchequer's calculations, involved a sacrifice of revenue.

Question put, "That the words proposed to be left out stand part of the Question."

The House *divided* :—Ayes 170; Noes 117 : Majority 53.

Main Question put, and *agreed to.*

WAYS AND MEANS.

WAYS AND MEANS *considered* in Committee.

(In the Committee.)

Motion made, and Question proposed.

"That, in lieu of the yearly per-centage Duty now chargeable for or in respect of any Insurance from loss or damage by Fire only, which shall be made or renewed on or after the 25th day of June, 1864, of or upon any Goods, Wares, or Merchandise, being stock in trade, or of or upon any Machinery, Fixtures, Implements, or Utensils used for the purpose of any manufacture or trade, there shall be charged and paid yearly a Duty at and after the rate of one shilling and sixpence per annum for every £100 insured; and when any such Insurance as aforesaid shall be made or renewed at any time between the 22nd day of April, 1864, and the said 25th day of June, for any period of time extending beyond the said last mentioned day, there shall be charged and paid for and in respect of the time intervening between the making or renewing of the said Insurance and the said 25th day of June, the yearly per-centage Duty at and after the rate chargeable on the said 22nd day of April, and for and in respect of any subsequent period, including the said 25th day of June, the rate of Duty chargeable according to this Resolution; and no Return or allowance of Duty, except at and after the last-mentioned rate, shall be made in respect of time unexpired, or otherwise, on any such Insurance as aforesaid which shall have been made or renewed before the said 22nd day of April, 1864."—(*Mr. Chancellor of the Exchequer.*)

SIR HENRY WILLOUGHBY moved an Amendment, in the fourth line, after the word "any," to leave out the words "goods, wares, or merchandise, being stock in trade, or of or upon any machinery, implements, fixtures, or utensils used for the purpose of any manufacture or trade," and to insert "houses and buildings." Her Majesty's Government had determined to touch the Fire Insurance duties, whether wisely or not he could not say; but that being so, it appeared to him to be of great importance that they should correctly understand what class of property it was the partial remission of the duty was intended to benefit. The right hon. Gentleman had selected "stock in trade," and since the announcement was made, he (Sir Henry Willoughby) with others, had received communications from various Insurance Offices which went to show that the difficulties attending the proposed alteration would be very great. Setting aside the difficulty that would arise in defining what "stock in trade" was, he thought that that was the last class of property on which a remission ought to be made, seeing that an insurance for £1,000 would, in the course of a year, cover many thousand pounds worth of property. But the main argument upon which he asked for the support of the Committee to his Amendment was that stock in trade ought not to be benefited at the expense of houses and buildings. No species of taxation was so much harassed by taxation as houses and buildings; for besides what it had to bear towards the general taxation of the country, it bore in an especial manner the burden of local taxation, amounting to no less than from £19,000,000 to £20,000,000 annually. It was a perfect truth that real property paid one-half, and houses and buildings nearly four-tenths of the taxation of the country, and it was also as true that stock in trade did not pay a shilling. Then, again, in considering how the revenue might best recover from any reduction, the largest margin of uninsured property consisted of houses and buildings. How, therefore, stock in trade could be selected in preference to houses and buildings, he was at a loss to conceive. For the sake

of justice, therefore, he should press his Amendment. He should not enter into the financial part of the question, because he was not prepared to throw Her Majesty's Government into a financial difficulty, not because it was impolitic, but that it would be most unfair to do so at that stage of their finance; but he trusted, if in the opinion of the Committee it was considered fairer to relieve houses and buildings than stock in trade, the right hon. Gentleman would have no difficulty in re-arranging the financial position of the question.

Amendment proposed,

In the fourth line, after the first word "any," to leave out the words "Goods, Wares, or Merchandise, being stock in trade, or of or upon any Machinery, Implements, Fixtures, or Utensils used for the purpose of any manufacture or trade," in order to insert the words "Houses or Buildings,"—(*Sir Henry Willoughby,*)

—instead thereof.

THE CHANCELLOR OF THE EXCHEQUER said, that as he had dealt with the very points which had been raised by the hon. Baronet in his reply to the hon. Member for Dudley, it would not be necessary for him to go into the subject again at any length. He must divide what he had to say into two parts—one, the financial, the other the general merits of the question. With regard to the financial part of the question he quite understood the fundamental principle of the hon. Gentleman's Amendment—namely, that he was not disposed to wrench anything from the Government, but that what he wanted was what he considered a better division of the surplus. Now, his (the Chancellor of the Exchequer's) proposition was that a sum of between £190,000 and £200,000 should be given by way of relief with respect to Fire Insurance in the present year. The hon. Baronet, however, proposed to insert certain words in a Resolution which spoke of a reduction of duty by one-half. If, therefore, the proposal of the hon. Baronet was carried, it would have to be adjusted to the state of the finances. There were two ways by which that adjustment might be effected—the one by a postponement of the remission, the other by a reduction in its amount. He (the Chancellor of the Exchequer) proposed to take only three-fourths off the remission off the shoulders of the present year, so that the full force of it would not be felt until next year. But if he was to retain the 1s. 6d. rate, and apply it to twice the number of subjects, then the postponement must be of a different character, for it would not be possible to commence the reduction until the beginning of next year. And what character would that proceeding affix to the vote that night? It would be said that, wishing to do a popular thing by their constituents, and not having the money to do it out of the resources of the present year, which alone were properly at their disposal, they voted a reduction of taxation and got credit for it, but postponed it to the following year. That, he thought, was an objectionable course to pursue, although there were instances where they had been obliged to do it; such, for instance, as the tea duties; but he knew of no instance where the House had adopted a course of voting the abolition or partial repeal of a tax by throwing almost the entire burden of it upon the next year. If the hon. Baronet's Motion was carried, the only other mode of adjustment was by halving the remission, and instead of giving 1s. 6d. upon stock in trade to give 9d. upon houses and buildings. Ought that proposal to be adopted or not? The hon. Member for Dudley quoted the Insurance Offices, and correctly quoted them, as greatly preferring a uniform rate. No doubt they would, as it would simplify matters. There would be a certain amount of labour in looking over the accounts with a view to fixing some at 3s. and some at 1s. 6d. But the Companies had been well paid hitherto. But as far as the authority of the Companies was concerned they were in favour of a uniform duty, and consequently the proposals both of the hon. Baronet and himself fell foul of those Companies. But the hon. Baronet had raised an objection about the definition of stock in trade and the difficulty of distinguishing between landlords' fixtures and tenants' fixtures. But difficulties of that kind would operate plainly as much under the hon. Baronet's plan as under his. Under his (the Chancellor of the Exchequer's) proposal everybody would be trying to show that he was a trader, and that his house and furniture were stock in trade, while under the proposal of the hon. Baronet everybody would try to prove that he was not a trader. The hon. Baronet stated that nothing was so much burdened as houses and buildings. He (the Chancellor of the Exchequer) was not quite so sure of that. He heard the hon. Member for Sheffield (Mr. Hadfield) cheer the statement when made by the hon. Baronet—but what was the hon. Member's opinion about the succession duty? Did he think it more severe than the legacy duty and the probate duty? And yet house property was taken out of the probate and legacy duty and placed under the succession duty, which

was a large concession. Was it true that nothing had been done of late years for the relief of houses and buildings? The brick duty had disappeared. An enormous differential duty on timber had given place to what was called a nominal rate of duty, but which he would admit it was extremely desirable to abolish. Even in the present Session houses and buildings were relieved by the financial proposal of the Government. He doubted whether there was any class in the whole country, except professional men, to whom the reduction of the Income Tax was so great a boon as to owners of houses and buildings, for there was no class on which it operated with such severity, especially the owners of inferior houses, inasmuch as the Income Tax was paid upon the gross rental, 25 per cent of which was often expended in repairs. The question was between a reduction of 1s. 6d. on stock in trade and 9d. on houses and buildings. Now, if the House touched a tax of this kind it ought to make a liberal reduction; it was better to give a telling reduction on a small part than a reduction that would not be appreciated on a small part. The hon. Baronet said that in the case of stock in trade that property was fully insured, while houses and buildings were insured only in part. But his (the Chancellor of the Exchequer's) inquiries by no means satisfied him that there was a greater margin uncovered by fire insurance in the case of houses and buildings as compared with stock in trade. He believed that, on the contrary, there was rather less. No doubt, in certain trades and certain descriptions of trades the stock was not fully insured; but generally speaking the very large traders were fully insured. When a fire came on the large traders it spared very little. In the case of houses there was something left worth saving; and so with regard to furniture; a great deal of it was generally carried out. In these latter cases people did not insure to the full. He could only ascertain whether buildings were insured or not in about half the cases of fires in the metropolitan district; but according to the best information he could get from the Insurance Offices and the Fire Brigade, the number of fires in 1863 was 1,746 of houses and buildings. Of these there were known to be insured 682, and known to be uninsured only seventy-three. That was a very small margin. In the case of the contents of houses and buildings there were known to be insured 963, and known to be uninsured 517, which left a considerable margin of uninsured stock in trade. As to the unknown cases, according to the best estimate about one-half were found to be insured. Suppose the other half to be all uninsured, the effect would be that 500 would have to be added to the 682 insured buildings, bringing the number up to 1,182; and adding the same number to the uninsured buildings, they would then stand at 573. With respect to the margin in the case of stock in trade, the largest traders and the best trades were commonly fully insured; the smaller traders, according to his information, were deterred from insuring by the amount of the duty. He could not concur in the opinion of the hon. Baronet that real property was unfairly dealt with in this country. The system of taxation in this country bore quite as hardly as it ought to do on the consumer and the lower class of the population. His hon. Friend the Member for Bradford (Mr. W. E. Forster) came to him in presence of the representatives of the Associated Chamber of Commerce. He said that within his own knowledge the deficiency of insurances in manufactures was so great that he was convinced a reduction of 1s. would pay itself within three or four years. He (the Chancellor of the Exchequer) would not go so far as that, but the case in favour of this class of reduction was very strong. A great deal had been said about removing the charges on trade. He (the Chancellor of the Exchequer) desired to remove the charges from trade; but he denied that taking a tax off trade was a concession to the poorer classes. Taking a tax off trade was removing an obstacle from the channel between the producer and the consumer. The object was to make trade unshackled, and relieving trade was not relieving a class, but it was relieving all those who consumed the articles from which the tax was removed. Suppose the Government laid a tax of 1d. on every transaction of trade in London — would that be a tax which the trader and not the consumer would pay? With the exception of a tax on receipts and bills of exchange, he did not know that there was a single tax on trade remaining. If the House concurred in the view which he had just submitted, he thought they would do well to vote for his Resolution. He thought a reduction of 1s. 6d. preferable to one of 9d.; but he did not stand on that alone. He stood more on the proposition that reducing the duty on houses and buildings would be a relief to a class, while a reduction of the

duty on stock in trade was not a relief to a class but to the general community who were the consumers of articles of trade and manufacture, that community including among its members the owners of houses and buildings. He waived at once all objections of a financial class, except that he thought his measure would prove greatly more reproductive than that proposed by the hon. Baronet.

SIR FRANCIS GOLDSMID said, he could not concur with the Chancellor of the Exchequer that the reduction which the right hon. Gentleman proposed was the one most likely to be reproductive. He supported the proposition of the hon. Baronet the Member for Evesham, not because he wished to favour the owners of houses and buildings, but for this reason— that, as far as one could learn, the rate of insurance on stock in trade was considerably higher than that on other matters. What was the conclusion from that? Not the one which the Chancellor of the Exchequer had attempted to draw from it— namely, that because persons could hardly afford to pay 6s., therefore they could not afford to pay 7s. 6d.—it would be much more natural to conclude that though a man might pay 1s. 6d., he might not be in a position to pay 4s. 6d. If, as in the case of stock in trade, a man paid the Insurance Office 9s. or 10s., it did not matter so much to him whether he paid the State 3s. or 1s. 6d. In the one case the ratio of reduction to the whole cost of insurance was very large; in the other almost inconsiderable, and reduction of duty on any article must be the greatest boon to the person who paid lowest for that article.

MR. HUBBARD said, he could not but imagine that if his right hon. Friend the Chancellor of the Exchequer had been as anxious to carry out the wishes of the House, pronounced on two occasions, as he had been to evade them, the first reduction he would have announced in his Budget would have been one of 1s. 6d. on all the duty paid for Fire Insurance. The reduction in the Income Tax was one very acceptable to the House, but it was not one for which they had specifically asked. The reduction of the sugar duties was also acceptable to the House, but the House had not asked for any exact amount of reduction on these duties. However, when they came to that duty of which the House had asked specifically for a general reduction, his right hon. Friend presented them with nothing but "a delusion and a snare." The expectation of a large increase in the insurances of stock in trade was a "delusion," and the invitation to the House to stake on the event of that increase the reduction of duty on the insurance of houses, was a "snare." The rate of insurance on stock in trade in London varied from 4s. in the best dock warehouses to 21s. in warehouses throughout the town. Take the medium, and it would at once be seen how unimportant was the duty now charged by the Government, comparatively with the premium of insurance on stock in trade as contrasted with houses. Besides, it should be borne in mind that whatever was spent in the insurance of stock in trade was but one element in the price to the consumer. The trader did not abstain from insuring his stock, because he knew that whatever the sum it might cost him to do so, his customers had ultimately to pay the amount. But it was not so with the owners of houses and buildings. The fact of having to pay 3s. duty on a payment of 1s. 6d. to the Insurance Office was a greater bar to insurance than the fact of having to pay a similar amount of duty on a payment of 21s. to the office. He thought that the simplicity of a general reduction strongly recommended such a measure. The Chancellor of the Exchequer had said that the insurance tax was a tax on property. Therefore did he (Mr. Hubbard) regard it as objectionable; because a property tax should be applicable to all houses, and the insurance tax was applicable only to the houses that were insured. The houses insured were not the houses of the rich—the rich could afford not to insure. It was of no consequence to the rich to insure. With extensive property the rich found it cheaper not to insure, or, in other words, like the large shipowners, to become their own insurers. He had been informed, within the last few days, of a nobleman who had cancelled no less than eighty-one policies on his houses and buildings in one county, on the ground that he would not pay to Government, in the shape of insurance duty, what the Chancellor of the Exchequer admitted was in reality a second property tax. The other day, the right hon. Gentleman sought to equalise a burden which bore upon clergymen. Now, he (Mr. Hubbard) had received a letter from the perpetual curate of a church which depended entirely upon pew rents, out of which the whole expenses of the church had to be defrayed. In his case, the duty paid to the Government upon the insurance of the church amounted to no

less than 2 per cent on the net receipts, being practically an additional Income Tax to that amount. There were other cases in which the magnitude of the tax was so much felt that the churchwardens refused to spend money belonging to the congregation upon insuring at all. As the result of a personal experience of nearly forty years, he declared that nothing could be more delusive than the propositions of the Chancellor of the Exchequer. He would infinitely rather see the question of Fire Insurance passed by altogether this Session, than see the House fall into the trap laid for it, of agreeing that the realisation of the object, which, in two successive years, had been affirmed by increasing majorities should depend upon the occurrence of an impossible condition. The right hon. Gentleman, he thought, had been highly favoured by the arrival of the dinner hour, which had carried away many Members who would have taken part in the debate. He should be glad if the House were to refuse the proposition of the right hon. Gentleman. He should infinitely prefer either to leave things alone, or that the remission should apply to all property alike, so far as the means at the disposal of the Government permitted. He did most earnestly protest against accepting the Government proposition with all its prospective bearings, and he regretted that the Government had not carried out more effectively for public benefit the principle twice approved by the House in successive years by increasing majorities.

Sir FRANCIS CROSSLEY said, he approved of the Budget as a whole, and, on that principle, he had voted that evening with the majority, though, if he had looked to the question of Fire Insurance alone, he should have taken a different course. He regarded the question of Fire Insurance as the weak part of the Budget, otherwise a very good one; and regretted that, having dealt satisfactorily with the two great questions of the Sugar Duties and the Income Tax, the right hon. Gentleman should have touched the subject of insurance, not having a sufficiently large balance to do so with good effect. To reduce the tax generally from 3s. to 1s., would have been a substantial boon; but to reduce it from 3s. to 1s. 6d. upon a single branch was altogether unsatisfactory. He had been surprised to hear the right hon. Gentleman lay such stress upon arguments as to the increase which might be expected upon insurances of stock in trade.

The great factories and warehouses from their enormous value were insured almost as a matter of necessity now; but the owner of a private house having to pay the Government 3s. for every 1s. 6d. of insurance, very often thought that the cheapest thing he could do was to be his own insurer. In the division which had just taken place he had supported the right hon. Gentleman, and should support him again, because he regarded the Budget as a whole; but, with regard to the particular question of insurance duties, he believed that the Chancellor of the Exchequer was in error. His proposal would produce immense complication of accounts, and would not, he hoped, be regarded in anywise as a settlement.

MR. H. B. SHERIDAN did not think that the cause of the Fire Insurance duties would be helped on by a division being taken then. He thought it would be better for the hon. Baronet to leave the matter as it stood. The principle of reduction had been admitted, and next year with renewed agitation they might hope for a more substantial remission.

SIR HENRY WILLOUGHBY said, he would not press his Motion to a division.

MR. HUBBARD wished to renew his solemn protest against this measure, which he deemed to be of a most delusive character.

Question, " That the words proposed to be left out stand part of the proposed Resolution," put, and *agreed to.*

Main Question put, and *agreed to.*

Resolved,

That, in lieu of the yearly per-centage Duty now chargeable for or in respect of any Insurance from loss or damage by Fire only, which shall be made or renewed on or after the 25th day of June, 1864, or of or upon any Goods, Wares, or Merchandise, being stock in trade, or of or upon any Machinery, Fixtures, Implements, or Utensils used for the purpose of any manufacture or trade, there shall be charged and paid yearly a Duty at and after the rate of one shilling and sixpence per annum for every £100 insured; and when any such Insurance as aforesaid shall be made or renewed at any time between the 22nd day of April, 1864, and the said 25th day of June, for any period of time extending beyond the said last-mentioned day, there shall be charged and paid for and in respect of the time intervening between the making or renewing of the said Insurance and the said 25th day of June, the yearly per-centage Duty at and after the rate chargeable on the said 22nd day of April, and for and in respect of any subsequent period, including the said 25th day of June, the rate of Duty chargeable according to this Resolution; and no return or allowance of Duty, except at and after the last-mentioned rate,

Sir Francis Crossley

shall be made in respect of time unexpired, or otherwise, on any such Insurance as aforesaid, which shall have been made or renewed before the said 22nd day of April, 1864.

House *resumed.*

Resolutions to be reported *To-morrow.*

Committee to sit again *To-morrow.*

SUPPLY.

Order for Committee read.

Motion made, and Question proposed, " That Mr. Speaker do now leave the Chair."

SCHOOL OF NAVAL ARCHITECTURE.
QUESTION.

MR. AUGUSTUS SMITH said, he wished to ask the noble Lord the Secretary of the Admiralty, On what footing it was intended to establish the School of Naval Architecture, for which the House had voted a small sum of money? He was anxious for this information, in order that the House might not be surprised into a large and costly scheme without knowing what it was about. When the subject was last under discussion, almost every one deprecated the establishment of the School at Kensington. There were already in our dockyards the *nuclei* of schools of naval architecture, which to a certain extent had answered their objects, and had done a great deal of good. He desired to know how the private pupils who, it was said, were to be received into this School, were to be treated during the six months when the students were to be transferred to the dockyards; but, above all, he was anxious to learn whether this subject had been thoroughly investigated by the Treasury, or whether the whole matter had been left to the Admiralty?

CORK HARBOUR.—QUESTION.

MR. MAGUIRE wished to know, Whether the Select Committee on Dockyards had consented to take evidence as to the capability of the harbour of Cork, and the expediency of establishing a naval dockyard in it?

CLAIMS OF MR. JOHN CLARE, JUN.
SELECT COMMITTEE MOVED FOR.

COLONEL DICKSON, in rising to move for a Select Committee to inquire into the claims of Mr. John Clare, jun., on the Government for compensation for Inventions and Designs supplied to the Admiralty in connection with Iron Ship Building and the construction of Gun Boats, said, he must ask from the House more than an ordinary share of indulgence in bringing the subject forward. He feared, on the one hand, that his client might suffer from him, and be from his client; because, as to the last, in this case it was supposed that a great demand had been made; and when a great or disproportionate demand was made for compensation a prejudice was created. But, on consideration, he believed the House would think that Mr. Clare was deserving of sympathy and assistance. Mr. Clare had suffered great injustice and oppression, and that would be regarded as some condonation for the eccentricities he had displayed. He (Colonel Dickson) intended no attack on the present Board of Admiralty by this Motion, for Mr. Clare had been the victim of injustice to Boards of Admiralty composed of different parties in the House. Mr. Clare was a young man of the most respectable position, possessed of great talents and ingenuity. In 1847 he had his attention first drawn to the subject of iron shipbuilding, and the necessity of substituting iron for wood in those great sea defences in which this country had always felt a pride. It was in 1853 that his correspondence with the Board of Admiralty first began. The House would remember that this was a most interesting period in our naval history, when we were commencing a struggle with a powerful nation of which no one could foretell the end, and when it became necessary that there should be a total re-arrangement of our naval forces. The first letter of Mr. Clare was in December, 1853, and was addressed to Mr. Bernal Osborne, then Secretary to the Admiralty, in which he sketched the nature of his invention, and sought the attention of the Admiralty to it. A correspondence took place with various Boards of Admiralty—as well during the administration of those who sat on his own side of the House, as while the party opposite were in power. The reply of the Admiralty to Mr. Clare's application was to the effect that, if "Mr. Clare had anything new to suggest as to the mode of constructing gunboats, and would forward it to the Admiralty, it would be considered." He did forward his ideas to the Admiralty; but for some time heard no more of the matter. In 1855 he addressed Sir Charles Wood then at the Admiralty, pointing out the futility of employing the then description of gun-

boats against the Russian batteries. And here he (Colonel Dickson) should like to know what had become of those gunboats which Mr. Clare had denounced. But then followed a letter from his right hon. Friend Mr. Corry, when his right hon. Friend Sir John Pakington was at the Admiralty; and in that letter in reply to Mr. Clare, the singular answer was returned that the Board of Admiralty limited applications to their own officers and to those who were in a position to build the vessels, and that therefore they could not comply with Mr. Clare's request, but would be willing to receive any suggestion on the subject. So that in order for the Admiralty to avail themselves of an invention, it was a necessary condition that a man should either be able to build a ship or have a large balance at his banker's. The correspondence with the Admiralty went on for six years. The plans and models of Mr. Clare were placed in the hands of the Admiralty in 1854 and 1855; they were in Sir Baldwin Walker's office in 1857, and the *Warrior* was not built till 1859. The *Warrior*, let it be remembered, was built entirely on Mr. Clare's plan—a plan on which no ship had been ever built before, and to the invention of which that gentleman was wholly and solely entitled to lay claim. He (Colonel Dickson) should be told that this case had been tried in a court of law, and that, therefore, Mr. Clare had no claim on the sympathy of the House. Now, he in no way intended to make the House of Commons a court of appeal from a court of law, and far be it from him to impugn a court of justice like the Court of Queen's Bench; but this he would say, that with the usual fatality that had attended all Mr. Clare's attempts to get justice done him, his case was most wretchedly put into the hands of counsel, evidence which should have been brought forward was not brought forward, and the evidence on the part of the Government was the evidence of partisans, almost all of them, being officially connected with the Admiralty. If a Committee were granted, almost every part of that evidence could be contradicted. He would refer to the not unimportant evidence of Sir Charles Fox. That witness, in speaking of the ship constructed in the yard of Messrs. Laird, of Birkenhead, in 1852, and in which Mr. Macgregor Laird went out to the west coast of Africa, deposed that she had her longitudinal and vertical framework on the principle now claimed by Mr. Clare; but Mr. Morrison, in the employ of Messrs. Laird, who had witnessed the building of the ship from first to last, and who ought to have been examined but was not, declared he was in a position to give a flat contradiction to the evidence of Sir Charles Fox on this point. In fact, it was well known that before the *Warrior* no ship had been built with longitudinal framework. In the same way a gentleman who was subpœnaed from the Admiralty sent a medical certificate stating that he was too unwell to appear, though it was known that he was in town, and at the Admiralty that very day. No doubt the demands that were made by Mr. Clare were extravagant, and his manner of supporting them eccentric, and this might have had an effect upon the Judge, whose summing up was more like the impassioned argument of an interested counsel than the calm deliberation of an impartial Judge. The jury arrived at an adverse verdict, finding that the patent was not infringed, and secondly, that the specification did not show longitudinal and vertical framework separate from the plates—which he (Colonel Dickson) contended it did. But he (Colonel Dickson) would ask, if Mr. Clare did not design the *Warrior* who did? She was not built until 1859, and she was the first ship built upon the principle of longitudinal framing. Had anybody claimed that invention? Nobody but the officials of the Admiralty. Where did Mr. Eady, Mr. Ward, and Sir Baldwin Walker, obtain their ideas about the *Warrior?* Mr. Clare's plans and specifications were at the Admiralty for six years, and it was not until 1859 that the first ship, the *Warrior*, was built embracing the novelty which they contained. Sir Baldwin Walker and the other officials had been confined all their lives within the Admiralty routine, addicted to the building of wooden vessels, and where then could they have got their ideas of iron shipbuilding? Considering that Mr. Clare's plans had been at the Admiralty all this time, and that a correspondence had been going on which must have drawn the attention of everybody at the Admiralty to the subject, it was pretty palpable that their plans for the *Warrior* must have been founded on hints at least drawn from Mr. Clare's invention. He (Colonel Dickson) believed that Captain Cowper Coles had taken a great many of his ideas from Mr. Clare's invention, and Captain Cowper Coles had received for his

remuneration captain's pay, £600; three guineas a day, £1,149; expenses of travelling, £470; and interest on £5,000 at 5 per cent, £250; with £100 for every cupola he made for fourteen years. Captain Cowper Coles, however, had rather higher connections than Mr. Clare. He (Colonel Dickson) would appeal to the noble Lord at the head of the Government, who, he believed, entertained pretty much the same sentiments on the subject of Mr. Clare's claims, and the manner in which he had been treated, that he (Colonel Dickson) did, to use his influence with the House in behalf of justice to Mr. Clare; and he appealed to the noble Lord the Secretary to the Admiralty to throw off the trammels of red tape, and, like the generous sailor that he was, to take a similar course; and lastly, he appealed to the House, whose duty it was to protect the interest of every subject of the realm.

Amendment proposed,

To leave out from the word " That " to the end of the Question, in order to add the words " a Select Committee be appointed to inquire into the Claims of Mr. John Clare, junior, on the Government for compensation for Inventions and Designs supplied to the Admiralty in connection with Iron Ship Building and the Construction of Gun Boats,"—(*Colonel Dickson,*)

—instead thereof.

Lord CLARENCE PAGET stated, in reply to the question of the hon. Member for Dungarvan (Mr. Maguire), that the case of Cork came within the order of reference to the Committee now sitting on the subject of dockyards, and would receive fair and full consideration.

In answer to the question of the hon. Member for Truro (Mr. A. Smith), he said the Government could not undertake to publish the paper of Sir Snow Harris on the School of Naval Architecture. If they were to do so they would have in fairness to publish all the papers which had been written on the same subject, including the very able and interesting one from the pen of the noble Lord the Member for Huntingdon (Lord R. Montagu). The better way would be for Sir Snow Harris to print his essay at his own expense, and send a copy to the hon. Member for Truro. Although it had been determined to establish a School of Naval Architecture in London, the hon. Member wanted the House to rescind its vote, so that naval architects might be educated in the provinces. Now, we had already got good dockyard schools, but the education given in them was not of that high order which naval architects required; and London had been chosen as the site of the new schools, because there eminent lecturers and professors could be obtained with the greatest facility. He was persuaded the public would have reason to be satisfied with the course the Government had taken. The hon. Member had asked what was to become of the youths in the summer when they went round the dockyards to learn their practical duties. They would have a certain allowance per head for their personal expenditure, and whether they got it in London or at the dockyards, would make no difference in the matter of cost. So far as he could ascertain, the School of Naval Architecture would not cost more than £4,000 a year, and, indeed, some thought it would become self-supporting, though he himself was not quite so sanguine as that.

There was one passage in the speech of the hon. and gallant Member for Limerick (Colonel Dickson) with respect to the case of Mr. Clare, in which he cordially concurred—that the House of Commons should not be turned into a court of appeal from the ordinary tribunals. He had heard with great regret the remark of the hon. and gallant Colonel—that the summing up of the Lord Chief Justice was more like the impassioned speech of an advocate, than the calm judicial charge of a Judge. The Solicitor General who was employed in the trial in the Court of Queen's Bench, would be able to give a different version of the summing up; but he might be allowed to say that, in the opinion of all, the Lord Chief Justice was one of the most able and upright Judges who ever adorned the Bench. Another accusation made by the hon. and gallant Gentleman was that nearly all the witnesses were Government officials. Could Sir Charles Fox be considered a Government official? Mr. Samuda was a private shipbuilder. [Colonel Dickson: He has held Government contracts.] He admitted that Mr. Samuda, like many other private traders, had held Government contracts; but surely nobody would say that an eminent shipbuilder would give evidence contrary to what he conscientiously believed, merely because he occasionally took a Government contract. He could not say at that moment whether Mr. Eady was at the Admiralty when he was represented to be too unwell to attend the trial, but he should think it exceedingly improbable. Did the hon. and gallant Gentleman think the jury had been packed?

Colonel DICKSON explained that nobody could speak in higher terms than he had done of the Chief Justice and the jury who tried the case.

Lord CLARENCE PAGET had only quoted the hon. and gallant Member's words, but was glad if they had not been intended to have the meaning he had supposed. He believed that Mr. Clare had had as fair a trial as ever took place in this country. The trial lasted five days, and it was conducted with the greatest patience by the Judge and jury, and the decision was that the Admiralty had not infringed any of Mr. Clare's patents. If the accusations made against the witnesses were founded on fact, the courts were open to Mr. Clare to prosecute them. Having some knowledge of matters connected with the construction of these ships, he (Lord Clarence Paget) had done his best to look into this subject, but he could not for the life of him see that any patent of Mr. Clare's had been infringed in the *Warrior*, or any other of Her Majesty's ships. That was not the only case of the kind. Mr. Chalmers said that the Admiralty had pirated his invention. It was impossible to state that in some of the details of a ship's construction there might not be some similarity to the inventions of various persons; but, after the decision which a court of law had duly pronounced on Mr. Clare's claims, he trusted that the House would not now consent to re-open the case.

The SOLICITOR GENERAL said, that he was counsel for the Admiralty in Mr. Clare's case, and he would take upon himself the responsibility, which was shared by the Law Officers of the Crown, in advising the Admiralty to resist the petition, for a claim more unfounded and preposterous, he would venture to say, was never brought into a court of justice. Mr. Clare's first demand was in respect of an alleged contract with the Admiralty, upon the terms of his having a percentage upon all the ships built, amounting to £200,000. Then he further claimed some £400,000 or £500,000 for a supposed infringement of his patent. The case came on to be tried, and the evidence in support of the claim consisted of about 100 letters written by him to the Admiralty, to which he believed only two replies were sent, the substance of them being this:—" Sir, we have considered your application, and cannot comply with it; and you cannot be employed." There was no pretence, on Mr. Clare's own showing, of there having been any contract. The rest of the case, as to the infringement of the patent, was equally groundless. Mr. Clare never built a ship, and never laid down the lines of one. The supposed patent contained nothing new, and there was no pretence for saying that it had been infringed in the case of the *Warrior*. The case was tried before the Lord Chief Justice and a special jury. The hon. and gallant Member for Limerick (Colonel Dickson) had said, that the Lord Chief Justice had summed up the case not as a Judge, but as an advocate. That was a serious imputation, which ought not to be made lightly or loosely. He asserted that the imputation was wholly unfounded, and ought never to have been made. The Lord Chief Justice summed up in a perfectly impartial and judicial manner. The jury did not hesitate; they found that Mr. Clare had no case, and no pretence of a case. That an eminent shipbuilder's evidence was not to be trusted because he had once held a Government contract was an imputation that no counsel would venture to make in a court of justice, and which never ought to have been made in that House. No case was ever more fairly tried. A Motion was afterwards made before the full court, and they entirely concurred in the summing up of the Judge. He trusted the House would not re-open the Question, that they would be satisfied with the results of the trial, and not interfere with the action of courts of justice.

Mr. DENMAN said, he had been appealed to on that subject by Mr. Clare, one of whose counsel he had been at the trial which had been referred to: he had, however, declined to take any part in the present discussion, or to vote on the Question before the House, thinking that to abstain from doing so became a Member who had been professionally engaged in the case. If he were to declare his opinion in Mr. Clare's favour, it might be said that he was speaking as an advocate; and if he gave an opinion against the claim, it might be objected that he had made use of some confidence or trust reposed in him, to the prejudice of the interests of the person by whom he had been engaged as counsel.

Mr. HENNESSY said, that whereas the Solicitor General had stated that Mr. Clare received but two letters from the

Admiralty, and those only stating that they could not consider his plans, he now held in his hand seven letters from the Board of Admiralty to that gentleman. One of them, dated June 22, 1855, was from the Secretary to the Admiralty, telling Mr. Clare that if he had anything new to suggest, and forwarded it to that office, it would be considered. Mr. Clare accordingly sent in his plans, and a letter describing them. That was surely consistent with the statement they had heard. He fully agreed in what had been said about the high and impartial character of the Lord Chief Justice; but in a passage of his summing up the learned Judge observed—

" Mr. Clare was evidently a disappointed man. He was disappointed at not having his plans and specifications adopted by the Admiralty. He had impressed upon the Admiralty the great importance of the subject of Iron Shipbuilding, and it was not till some years afterwards that it was taken up."

When the history of this great change in our naval architecture came to be written, it would have to be said that Mr. Clare impressed the subject on the Admiralty, but the Admiralty refused to take it up; that they had afterwards adopted his plan, and that Mr. Clare appealed to them in vain. He trusted that Mr. Clare would not appeal to that House in vain. This was no technical question as to the specification. He trusted that the Committee would be granted to Mr. Clare.

Mr. H. BAILLIE said, that that discussion only supplied another proof, if an additional proof were wanting, of the great necessity for a change in our patent law, for as matters now stood it seemed almost impossible for the Admiralty to adopt any improvement without some inventor stepping in and claiming a patent right in it. In that case a court of justice had decided in favour of the Admiralty and against Mr. Clare, and the Admiralty had now nothing to do with the question.

Sir JOHN PAKINGTON said, he felt bound to state, though with every wish to do justice to this unfortunate man—for he believed that he might speak of him in those terms—that the House would make a great mistake if, after the decision of a court of justice, they would pass this Vote. His hon. and gallant Friend had repeated the allegation that Mr. Clare was the first inventor of armour-plated ships, and that the *Warrior* was built upon his plans. There never was any allegation more unfounded. It was said that the Board of Admiralty were only willing to listen to men of capital. Now, the fact was, that when the question of armour-plated vessels arose, the Admiralty felt it their duty to call upon the most eminent shipbuilders, both in England and Scotland, and invite them to offer suggestions upon iron-plated ships. He declared that Mr. Clare had nothing to do with the merits of the construction of the *Warrior* vessel. He regretted that Mr. Clare should think that he was treated with injustice by any Department of the Government. Last year he (Sir John Pakington) was anxious to know whether Mr. Clare had any grounds for so thinking; and as he met him accidentally in the lobby of the House he asked him to withdraw with him. He heard all he had to say, and after he had done so tried to enter into conversation with him, but he found it impossible in consequence of the state of excitement in which Mr. Clare was. The hon. and learned Solicitor General who saw Mr. Clare in the court of justice, must have had experience of this excitement. With regard to the proposed School of Naval Architecture, he (Sir John Pakington) might say that he had long had the pleasure of an acquaintance with Sir William Snow Harris, and felt for him a great respect; but feared that that gentleman had fallen into a serious error in his paper, as he seemed to think that this School had originated with the Board of Admiralty. He (Sir John Pakington), while anxious to do full justice to the support which the proposal received from the Admiralty, must say that the first suggestion to found the school came from the Institute of Naval Architects. Perhaps it might be some satisfaction to the hon. Member for Truro (Mr. Smith)—after the refusal of the noble Lord to print the paper at the public expense—to state that the most eminent naval architects were of opinion that this arrangement to place the School in the metropolis, in order that they might have the benefit of superior teachers, afforded the best prospect of bringing the experiment to a successful issue.

Question, "That the words proposed to be left out stand part of the Question," put, and *agreed to.*

THE CHANNEL FLEET.—QUESTION.

SIR JOHN PAKINGTON said, he wished to put the Questions to the noble Lord the Secretary of the Admiralty of which he had given notice. The first Question referred to the present state of the Channel fleet. The information which he had received led him to infer that this fleet was not in the state of efficiency in which it ought to be. He wished to know from the noble Lord, whether he could furnish such information as would remove this impression; and if it was desirable that, under existing circumstances, the Channel fleet should remain for so long a period in the Portland Roads? The Channel fleet returned in the month of March, after a cruise of three months in the Atlantic, and it had not been sent to any arsenal for the purpose of having the necessary repairs effected to place it in a state of efficiency. He had heard many suggestions, and some of them from high quarters, during the debates in both Houses on the Danish Question, that looking to the war now carried on in the North of Europe, it would be desirable that the fleet should be in a condition to be sent off on a short notice to perform any duties which it might be called upon to perform. He therefore thought he was justified in calling attention to the subject. The information he had received was this:—When the Channel fleet came to Portland after the cruise, it wanted provisions and coals; but neither were to be had. At first the Admiral applied for 900 tons of coals, and was told that there were only 50 at hand, and that it would take three weeks to obtain a further supply from Cardiff. A week elapsed before they obtained their provisions; and after a lapse of three weeks only 280 tons of coal had been supplied. He was also informed that it was impossible to carry out the required repairs, owing to the disadvantages of the anchorage at Portland. The fleet was last repaired in December; and as a portion of it was iron-clad, it was notorious that these became very foul after a time at sea. They had been out on a cruise in the Atlantic, and it would be remembered they had gone as far as Madeira at a time that it was supposed they would be ordered home. They were then likely to require repairs. The fleet were now at Portland, and might be ordered to foreign service on short notice; but, in the present condition of many of the ships, it would be impossible for them to go until they had been docked for repairs. Until they had been docked, it would be impossible to send them on this service. This would require a considerable time, for he was sorry to say that the dock accommodation was so limited that they could only go into dock one after another. He did not know whether his noble Friend would be able to contradict the reports he had heard, but he thought the House ought to be informed whether the detention of these ships so long at Portland was consistent with that efficiency which was so essential to the navy. The other Question which he wished to ask was founded on a statement given by the noble Lord in reply to the right hon. Gentleman the Member for Tyrone (Mr. Corry) on a former evening. His right hon. Friend drew attention to the unsatisfactory state of the reserves in the home ports, and the noble Lord, with a candour which was more creditable to himself than to the Admiralty, admitted that the reserve fleet was not in a satisfactory condition. He (Sir John Pakington) wished to know how far steps had been taken to remedy this state of things. Was the House to infer from the noble Lord's admission that the Admiralty had determined to neglect the wooden fleet? This was a serious matter. He believed that the time had not yet come when the wooden ships of England could be neglected. At this time they had not sufficient iron armour vessels to carry on a maritime war, and must depend on their wooden ships to protect their commerce and possessions in all parts of the world; it would, then, be a great mistake to allow them to fall into a state of decay. He would be glad to hear that the Admiralty intended to maintain them in a state of efficiency, so that they should be ready for any service they might be called to perform. He would then ask the noble Lord as to the state of the Channel fleet, and the vessels in the home ports.

LORD CLARENCE PAGET said, he wished the right hon. Baronet had put his Question upon the paper in more specific terms, as he was not prepared to state offhand what quantity of coals or provisions would be required to be taken on board the ships forming the Channel squadron. All he could say was that the squadron was ordered to be ready for sea, fully provided with coals and stores, by the 15th of the present month. It was known that probably some of the ships might be sent north, and by the 15th of April it was expected the ice would be broken up in the Baltic. Those ships were all ready, but how long they had been engaged in

Sir John Pakington

taking on board provisions and coals he could not say, but he believed there had been no delay, although the question of the right hon. Baronet would induce him to make closer inquiries into that question. With respect to the state of our iron-ships he could not state the last date of docking, but he did not believe that their bottoms could be in such a state as to render them unfit for service. There was no doubt that iron bottomed-ships did require constant docking, and that constituted their chief defect. For that reason the Admiralty were giving their best attention to the subject of providing increased dock accommodation. With respect to our ships in the reserve, he had already stated that they were not in the condition in which he could desire to see them; but he had proposed a large labour vote to enable them to be placed in a better condition. He would, however, remind the right hon. Baronet that, while the reserve during his tenure of office consisted only of four line-of-battle ships, three frigates, and three sloops, the reserve at present included three armourplated ships, two line-of-battle ships, three frigates, two corvettes, and three sloops. The reserve, therefore, had not deteriorated. [Sir JOHN PAKINGTON: Are they fit for service?] They are fit for service now; and I hope next year will be in a still more satisfactory state.

MR. CORRY said, the noble Lord, in moving the Navy Estimates, had said that it was intended to pay off sixty-four ships in the course of the year, and therefore it would be necessary to have a large labour Vote to enable the Admiralty to replace them. That Vote, therefore, would not tend to increase the efficiency of the reserve. The Admiralty ought to place the ships paid off on the steam reserve, and have the ships forming the naval reserve ready for sea whenever their services might be required. One part of the service ought not to be neglected because attention was directed to another. The whole reserve ought to be kept in a state of efficiency. The comparison which the noble Lord had made between the reserve at the present time, and that which existed during the time when the right hon. Baronet the Member for Droitwich was in office, was not exactly correct, as the Government of 1859 had not had the advantage of five years' tenure of office to re-organize the navy. The right hon. Baronet at that time asked for a Vote to increase the number of artificers in order to bring the reserve up to a proper condition.

Main Question put, and *agreed to*.

SUPPLY.

SUPPLY *considered* in Committee.

CAPTAIN TALBOT reminded the noble Lord the Secretary to the Admiralty of his promise not to proceed with the Malta Dock Vote after ten, it being now half-past that hour.

MR. WYKEHAM MARTIN, who had a notice on the paper concerning the spinning machinery at Chatham, expressed a hope that the Government would fix another night for that Vote, when it could come on early. He had been about twelve hours in the House that day, and he would possibly be as long to-morrow, so that if the question came on late at night he would be almost physically incapable of making his Motion.

LORD CLARENCE PAGET agreed to postpone the Estimates till Monday.

SIR JOHN PAKINGTON hoped the Malta Dock Vote would be fixed for a night when Members could know with some certainty that it would come on.

VISCOUNT PALMERSTON said, his noble Friend was quite ready to proceed with it at once. It was the preliminary discussions which took up so much time.

LORD JOHN MANNERS said, it would be a breach of faith to go on with the Vote now, as many Members had left the House under the impression that it would not come on.

SIR GEORGE GREY said, the Navy Estimates would be placed first on the paper for Monday, and he hoped no Motions would be interposed to prevent them from going into Committee at once.

House *resumed*. Committee report Progress; to sit again *To-morrow*.

GOVERNMENT ANNUITIES BILL.

[BILL 11.] NOMINATION OF COMMITTEE.

THE CHANCELLOR OF THE EXCHEQUER moved that the following Members be Members of the Select Committee on the Government Annuities Bill:—

"The CHANCELLOR of the EXCHEQUER, Mr. SOTHERON ESTCOURT, Mr. MILNER GIBSON, Mr. HENLEY, SIr MINTO FARQUHAR, Sir STAFFORD NORTHCOTE, Mr. HORSFALL, Mr. GOSCHEN, Mr. CHARLES TURNER, Mr. HERBERT, Mr. HUBBARD, Mr. HENRY B. SHERIDAN, Mr. AYRTON, Mr. HODGKINSON, and Mr. PAGET.

Motion *agreed to*.

SIR MINTO FARQUHAR said, it was rather remarkable that a Bill of such importance should be sent to a Committee and at the same time that an objection should be made to taking any evidence. He always understood that when a measure was sent to a Committee it was for them to decide whether they would hear evidence. His right hon. Friend supposed that he wished that witnesses should be called for the express purpose of defeating the Bill. That was not his object. What he wanted was that the Bill should be thoroughly investigated, that the Committee should see how the machinery was to be worked, and above all should hear some persons connected with Friendly Societies, so as to ascertain why they objected to the Bill, where the shoe pinched them, and how they carried on the sort of business which would be transacted by the Government if the Bill passed. He had not the least intention of entering into the insolvency or solvency of these societies, because the inquiry then would be interminable, and the Bill would, as his right hon. Friend said, be "hung up." All he desired was, that the Committee should understand thoroughly the nature of the Bill, and in order that they might do this he now begged to move that they should have power to send for persons, papers, and records.

Motion made, and Question proposed, "That the Committee have power to send for persons, papers, and records."—(*Sir Minto Farquhar.*)

THE CHANCELLOR OF THE EXCHEQUER said, he did not desire to impute anything to the hon. Baronet that he had disclaimed, but the intention and the effect of his Motion were two different things; the effect—though he was sure he did not intend it—would be to put off the passing of the Bill for the present Session. His hon. Friend wanted the House to understand the machinery of the Bill and the bearing of its clauses, and to examine the promoters of the Bill as to its probable effect upon Friendly Societies. But his hon. Friend was mistaken in supposing that they could examine the bearing of the Bill and its effect upon Friendly Societies without involving these consequences. The societies would be entitled to show whatever injury might result to them from the measure, and in that way it would be impossible to escape examining how far their own rules and constitution were sound. But there was another broad distinction

3 B

between a Committee of that kind and such a Committee as was suggested by the right hon. Gentleman the Member for Wiltshire (Mr. Sotheron Estcourt), to which the Government had acceded. The hon. Gentleman wanted to examine the real promoters of the Bill. But who were the real promoters? The Government. Sir Alexander Spearman and Mr. Scudamore were the persons with whom they took counsel, but they were not the promoters of the Bill. They might as well ask for such a Committee on Monday next to inquire into the Taxes Bill and examine Sir Thomas Freemantle. Sir Alexander Spearman and Mr. Scudamore were not the promoters of this Bill, but the assistants of the Government, and it would be an injustice to them and a flinching from responsibility by the Government, if they allowed the Bill to depend upon the examination and cross-examination of these witnesses. The meaning of such a Committee as he (the Chancellor of the Exchequer) was prepared to send the Bill to was simply this — to enable the Members of it to have more free and familiar communication with the responsible author of the Bill, of cross-examining him more fully, and ascertaining more precisely with what views the Government proposed it than could be done in that House. The House would see there was the greatest difference between a Committee of that kind and a Committee taking general evidence. Let it be shown that a great deal of injury would result to Friendly Societies, and did his hon. Friend mean to say that if independent Assurance Societies came forward and alleged that they also were liable to be injured by the Bill they could be excluded? His hon. Friend would see it would be totally impossible to draw the line which he supposed. He quite agreed with his hon. Friend that the Bill ought to be thoroughly understood. But there were three securities for that. First, there was the responsibility of the Government; secondly, bringing to bear all the intelligence and knowledge of the Select Committee upon it, and afterwards subjecting it to a Committee of that House; and thirdly, and most important of all, giving time to the country to consider it fully after it had come from the Select Committee and had passed the Committee of the Whole House. His hon. Friend might say it was an invidious thing not to hear witnesses — it was like shutting out the daylight. He (the Chancellor of the Exchequer) was responsible for the Bill, in a

sense in which no other Member of the Government was responsible, and did his hon. Friend think it would be possible for him, with all the other duties which he had to perform, to go into such an inquiry as his hon. Friend proposed? He could not do it unless he resigned his office for the purpose. He wished it to be distinctly understood that the Motion of his hon. Friend came simply to this—whether the Bill was to be allowed to go forward during the present Session. If his hon. Friend thought fit to propose such a Motion, it was open to him to do so; but it was his (the Chancellor of the Exchequer's) duty to represent that the effect of such an inquiry as that recommended by the hon. Gentleman, would be to block up the Bill in Committee upstairs until a period when it would be totally impossible to give the country time to consider it so that it might be passed this Session. This Bill had been largely, carefully, and minutely considered in its principle, and the effect had been, that all those who had acted spontaneously upon their own judgment had largely petitioned in its favour. That very day he had received a statement from the whole body of the Life Assurance Societies of Scotland, in which they expressed their approval of the Bill. They thought Parliament must deal with the question how far Government was capable of interfering in a matter of this kind; but if Government could properly undertake it, they believed it would be beneficial to the country. He objected to examining Sir Alexander Spearman and Mr. Scudamore, but they might examine himself. It was impossible to have a Bill of that kind, involving important financial results, without having a responsible Minister of the Crown ready to answer for it. He had already suggested what would be the best possible mode of proceeding—namely, to have the machinery of the Bill, such as it was, laid upon the table of both Houses, subject to be interrupted by an Address from either House, and until it had lain there for a sufficient time it would be totally inoperative. But as for inquiring into the position of other societies, that, though his hon. Friend did not intend it, was merely losing time, and would lead to the indefinite postponement of the Bill.

Mr. SOTHERON ESTCOURT said, he imagined that this Committee would not be bound by any other rules than those which regulated the proceedings of every other Committee. It would be better to go upstairs to enter upon the clauses, and then, if they required evidence on any point, it would be competent for them to come to the House, and through their Chairman to propose a Resolution similar to that of his hon. Friend. He was able to speak with some authority on this point, because he was Chairman of a Committee to which was referred a Bill in 1850 on this very subject of Friendly Societies, and which was the first instance of a Committee upon a Bill which obtained leave of the House to take evidence. When the Committee entered upon the first clause, it was evident they required further information. He asked the late Speaker whether it was competent to obtain the means of gaining that information on Motion. The matter was considered, and leave was given by the House. His hon. Friend (Sir Minto Farquhar) had, he believed, persevered with his Motion, because something fell from the Chancellor of the Exchequer which implied an understanding that the Committee should abstain from exercising the power enjoyed by all other Committees, and that there was to be something like a promise or engagement that the Committee should not call for evidence. His hon. Friend had, therefore, very properly raised this question. The House had thought proper to appoint this Committee, and, no doubt, intrusted it with the same independence and control over its proceedings as was possessed by other Select Committees, and with that understanding he should recommend his hon. Friend to withdraw his Motion. On the other hand, he hoped he would not do so unless they had a distinct understanding that when they got into Committee, and it should be the pleasure of the Committee to require evidence, nothing that had hitherto passed, or which should pass, would prevent the Chairman from coming down and making the same Motion. The Committee would have to inquire into three points—first, whether it would be possible by any machinery to carry out the right hon. Gentleman's intentions in proposing this Bill; secondly, in what manner that machinery would be likely to affect similar institutions; and thirdly, as to the risk that the Government would run in undertaking the operations sketched out by the Bill. If the right hon. Gentleman had made up his mind that the Committee should not take evidence, he hoped he would say so distinctly, because in that case it would be useless to go into Committee at all. For himself, he could

say he was honestly determined to facilitate the passing of the Bill, if he had fair means of satisfying himself on these three points. Suppose they went into Committee, and he wished to know Mr. Tidd Pratt's opinion on these three points, if the Committee were of opinion that his wish was unreasonable, they would negative the Motion, and he should submit. But suppose the Committee agreed with him — were they to be stopped by the Chancellor of the Exchequer telling them he had only allowed the Committee to be appointed on the understanding that they should not take evidence? The character of the Gentlemen named upon the Committee ought to go for something. He had served on many Committees, and he had never heard that a desire to hear evidence implied any degradation or disparagement of the Member who moved for the Committee. He trusted that his hon. Friend would withdraw his Motion, on the understanding that the determination to hear or not to hear evidence was to rest with the Committee and nowhere else.

MR. THOMSON HANKEY said, he hoped the Motion would not be withdrawn except on the distinct understanding to the effect stated by the last speaker. The Chancellor of the Exchequer said he took upon himself the responsibility of the Bill, and suggested that he alone should be examined. This was not satisfactory. The Bill consisted of two clauses, one of which was accepted, the other objected to. An investigation of the subject was asked for; but were the Committee to investigate with their hands tied, and if we are told that they were not to examine into the only point which was important, he thought there ought not to have a been Select Committee at all. The only question was whether the business was to be undertaken by an already overworked Department of the Government — the Post Office. He did not object to giving the facilities for insurance to the poor people, but he doubted whether Life Assurance was what they wanted. What they wanted was security, not for a provision in case of death, but in case of sickness. A Select Committee had been appointed to examine into the question—let them examine whether the provisions of the Bill were expedient, but unless the Committee had full power to call witnesses they would never have the question satisfactorily answered.

SIR MINTO FARQUHAR was willing to withdraw his Motion, but only on the distinct understanding that the Committee should have full independence, and be able to call for any evidence they might want.

THE CHANCELLOR OF THE EXCHEQUER said, he was willing to afford every information that should be given with respect to the clauses, and he thought that information might be afforded by those who assisted the responsible Ministers; but that was altogether different from taking general evidence on the principle and bearing of the Bill. He entirely must decline to hold out any expectations that the Government would be parties to examining into the effect of this Bill on Friendly Societies.

MR. AYRTON observed, that as the Chancellor of the Exchequer had not given the pledge that he had been asked to give —namely, that the Committee should go upstairs unfettered, to decide for themselves whether they should have evidence or not, it was obvious that there must be some concealed meaning in his refusal to consent to that arrangement. It was inconsistent with usage, and with the respect due to the House, to say that a Committee on a Bill should not receive any information which they might think it necessary to ask for.

MR. ROEBUCK thought, that as the Committee would have power to direct their Chairman to come down and ask for leave to take evidence, it was merely fighting with a shadow to contend for the permission of the Chancellor of the Exchequer for the examination of witnesses.

LORD JOHN MANNERS understood the declaration of the Chancellor of the Exchequer to mean this—that if the Committee thought they ought to call witnesses, the Chancellor of the Exchequer, with the force of the Government at his back, would oppose the Motion. He understood that the Chancellor of the Exchequer was not unwilling that they should have information, but that he himself was willing to give all the information that could be required. If he (Lord John Manners) were a Member of the Committee, he should say, "We have heard sufficient information from that quarter; we desire to hear other statements." If the House received no further explanations of a more satisfactory character, he saw no other course than to support the Motion of his hon. Friend.

MR. MILNER GIBSON would remind

Sir Minto Farquhar

the House that to take independent evidence on the whole merits of the question, and on the bearing of the Bill on Friendly Societies, would be quite a different thing from receiving information on the clauses. An inquiry such as the former, in the case of a Bill, the principle of which had been affirmed by a second reading, would be against all precedent, and would be fatal to the Bill.

MR. WHITESIDE said, the Chancellor of the Exchequer seemed to say, "I will answer questions as I think fit, and if you are not satisfied you must be an incorrigible Committee; but if you ask for independent evidence, then your proposal is so unparliamentary that we cannot hold out any hope of its being adopted." Why should he not have said at once, "You shall only have such evidence as I like on the clauses of the Bill?"

MR. HUSSEY VIVIAN was sure that the Chancellor of the Exchequer had no fear for the Bill on its merits. What he feared, and properly feared, was that a general inquiry into the principle and bearings of the Bill, and an examination of the officers of the various Friendly Societies, would consume so much time that the measure would be shelved.

VISCOUNT PALMERSTON : The question has really been put upon its true footing, and I wish the House to understand what it is we are going to vote on. It is whether this Bill shall be thrown over entirely. ["No!" "Cheers!"] That this was the real effect of the Motion must be evident to any one who reflects for an instant—because what is the object of the proposed inquiry? The Chancellor of the Exchequer has explained that it necessarily involves our going into the affairs of all those who wish to prevent the Bill passing into law. ["No!" "Hear, hear!"] It would be much more fair to vote that the Bill should be read this day six months, and the effect would be the same. ["No!" "Hear, hear!"] Let the House understand that what is now proposed is not to obtain information. It is not Parliamentary to impute motives, but let me say that the Motion, if carried, would render it perfectly impossible for the Bill to pass this Session.

SIR WILLIAM JOLLIFFE said, the House had before it two conflicting statements. At one side it was urged that the Motion, if carried, would defeat the measure; at the other they had the positive declaration of Gentlemen supporting it that they entertained no such intention. Between two interpretations so diametrically opposed the House must be left to decide. He confessed himself unable to see the purpose of the Committee if they were to be bound by every statement of the Chancellor of the Exchequer, however dark, and were to make no attempts at elucidation.

The CHANCELLOR of the EXCHEQUER explained that so far from desiring that his voice should be the only voice to be heard before the Committee, he had expressly intimated that they might ask for further information; but he said that the responsibility for the measure must rest with the Government and the Government only. He desired to give the Committee every information, and for that purpose would lay before them explanations and conversations of the official advisers of the Government.

Mr. BUCHANAN thought the Committee ought to be placed in a position to express some opinion, and not merely to return the Bill as sent to them.

Question put.

The House *divided*: — Ayes 104; Noes 127: Majority 23.

Five to be the quorum.

SEAT OF UNDER SECRETARY OF STATE.
NOMINATION OF COMMITTEE.

On Motion of *Sir George Grey*, Select Committee on Seat of Under Secretary of State *nominated* :—

Sir GEORGE GREY, Mr. DISRAELI, Mr. WALPOLE, Mr. ATTORNEY GENERAL, Sir HUGH CAIRNS, The LORD ADVOCATE, Mr. GATHORNE HARDY, Mr. ATTORNEY GENERAL for IRELAND, Sir WILLIAM HEATHCOTE, Mr. MASSEY, Lord ROBERT CECIL, Mr. BRIGHT, Mr. Serjeant KINGLAKE, Mr. HUNT, and Mr. DODSON :—Power to send for persons, papers, and records ; Five to be the quorum.

LAW LIFE SOCIETY.—RETURN MOVED FOR.

Mr. GREGORY moved for a Return of all Civil Bill Ejectments entered at the suit of the Law Life Society before the Chairman of Quarter Sessions of the County of Mayo and the county of Galway, from Hilary Quarter Sessions, 1850, up to the present time, distinguishing the ejectments of each year.

Mr. HODGKINSON said, that as a director of this Society, he should offer no opposition to any inquiry into the management of its property in Ireland ; but as the Society did not acquire the property in question till 1852, he suggested that that date should be substituted for 1850 ; and as their Civil Bill ejectments were almost without exception merely proceedings for the recovery of rent, and were not followed by evictions, he proposed that the Return should also show the number of evictions which had taken place upon these ejectments.

Mr. GREGORY disclaimed any intention to take an unfair advantage of this Society, and would accept the hon. Member's first Amendment ; but he could not assent to the second, because there were no means of ascertaining how many evictions had taken place.

Motion amended, and *agreed to*.

Return *ordered*,

" Of all Civil Bill Ejectments entered at the suit of the Law Life Society before the Chairman of Quarter Sessions of the county of Mayo and the county of Galway, from Hilary Quarter Sessions 1852, up to the present time, distinguishing the ejectments of each year."—(*Mr. Gregory.*)

BANKRUPTCY ACT.—NOMINATION OF COMMITTEE.

Mr. MOFFATT, Mr. ATTORNEY GENERAL, Mr. GEORGE CARR GLYN, Mr. MURRAY, Mr. MALINS, Mr. WEGUELIN, Mr. HUBBARD, Mr. GATHORNE HARDY, Mr. DUNLOP, Mr. LOWE, and Mr. HASSARD, nominated Members of the Select Committee on the Bankruptcy Act.

Motion made, and Question proposed, " That the Lord Advocate be one other Member of the said Committee."

Debate arising,

Debate *adjourned* till *this day*.

JUDGMENTS, &C., LAW AMENDMENT BILL.
NOMINATION OF COMMITTEE.

Select Committee on Judgments, &c., Law Amendment Bill *nominated* :—

Mr. HADFIELD, Mr. ATTORNEY GENERAL, Mr. SELWYN, Mr. HANKEY, Mr. Alderman SALOMONS, Mr. HENLEY, Mr. M'MAHON, Mr. JOHN JOSEPH POWELL, Mr. LOCKE KING, Mr. JOSEPH EWART, Mr. HUMBERSTON, Mr. HODGKINSON, Mr. STEEL, Mr. MURRAY, and Mr. REMINGTON MILLS :—Power to send for persons, papers, and records ; Five to be the quorum.

House adjourned at one o'clock.

HOUSE OF LORDS,

Friday, April 22, 1864.

MINUTES.]—PUBLIC BILLS — *First Reading*—
High Court at Bombay * (No. 57); Sentences
of Death [N.L.] (No. 58).
Second Reading — The Consolidated Fund
(£15,000,000) * (No. 54).
Select Committee—On Improvement of Land Act,
1864, The Earl of Bandon, The Viscount
Hutchinson, and The Lord Ponsonby *added*.

SENTENCES OF DEATH BILL.

BILL PRESENTED.   FIRST READING.

THE EARL OF ELLENBOROUGH *presented* a Bill to regulate the Mode of
Proceeding in Cases of Sentences of Death.
The noble Earl said that recent events
had shown it to be most desirable, that
the law relating to the infliction of capital
punishment should be placed upon a more
satisfactory basis.   It seemed to him to
be necessary that the greatest weight
and authority should be given to the
ultimate decision as to the carrying out
the sentence, whatever the sentence might
be.   It seemed most inexpedient that the
final decision in cases of so much importance should be cast upon the sole responsibility of the Home Secretary, and that
where the life of any man was concerned
it should depend upon the peculiar views
or temperament of any particular man.
In endeavouring to put an end to the evils
of the present practice, and to establish
more confidence than was now placed in
the decision finally arrived at, he had only
to recall his own experience; and though
the course he had to propose to their Lordships had not much of the merit yet it
had not the inconvenience of novelty.
Looking back to his own official experience, extending back a period of more
than thirty-five years, he remembered
when the Recorder of the City of London
presented his report of the capital cases
for the decision of Government   In these
cases all the principal Members of the
Government, with the addition of the
Lord Chief Justice of the King's Bench,
were summoned to attend the King, who
presided on the occasion, and took part in
the discussion.   He knew that his late
Majesty George the Fourth regarded this
duty as one of the most important that
he had to discharge.   He had no recollection that in those days, under any circumstances, distrust was manifested concerning
the decisions arrived at.   On the contrary,
they appeared to give general satisfaction.
This course of proceeding continued until
the accession of Her present Majesty.   It
was then deemed advisable—and he did
not dispute the expediency—that a youthful female sovereign should not be present
to adjudicate concerning certain crimes
then capitally punishable.   He remembered sitting beside the Duke of Wellington when a Bill giving effect to those
views was introduced into that House,
and though the noble Duke admitted the
necessity of the alteration at the commencement of a female reign, yet he
deeply regretted the necessity for a change
in the course of procedure which had
existed for so many years.   The penalty
of death no longer attached to certain of
these crimes, which it was then deemed
improper to bring under the notice of a
youthful Queen, and that reason for the
new system therefore no longer existed.
At the same time, he did not propose to
place any additional burden on Her Majesty; but, recollecting the value of the
solemn proceeding of the Sovereign in
Council with regard to decisions or sentences of death, he thought it desirable
that it should be revived, with the condition that the presence of the Sovereign
should not be insisted upon.   His Bill
therefore proposed that the final decision
upon cases where the life of a subject
was concerned should rest with a body
of persons selected from the Privy Council, together with the Chief Justice of
the Queen's Bench, and not as at present with the Home Secretary alone.
The Bill, therefore, to some extent, proceeded upon a revival of the ancient
practice to which he had referred.   If the
principle of the Bill met with approval,
he trusted the Government would adopt it,
for he felt it was more appropriate that
the responsibility of such a measure should
rest on them than on an individual peer.
If, on the other hand, the Government
would not accept the Bill, he hoped that
at the earliest opportunity they would
submit some proposal of their own on the
subject, better than that he now tendered.
He was satisfied that the practice of the
law ought to be amended, so that the
utmost authority and weight should attach
to decisions in regard to capital sentences,
and that the whole responsibility should
not be thrown on the Home Secretary
alone.   Unless the country was made to
understand that entire confidence could be
placed in the decisions on these questions,

there would be some danger of our being forced to abandon a punishment which he believed to be necessary to the interests of society.

Bill read 1ª; and to be printed. (No. 58).

ENGLISH AND IRISH COURTS OF COMMON LAW AND CHANCERY COMMISSION.—OBSERVATIONS.

QUESTION.

THE MARQUESS OF CLANRICARDE rose to call Attention to the First Report of the Commissioners of Inquiry into the English and Irish Courts of Common Law and Chancery ; and to ask, Whether the Government intend to introduce Bills in accordance with the Recommendations of that Report during the present Session of Parliament : also, whether a further Report of the Commissioners is likely to be presented soon : and when we may expect to have the Irish Judicial Statistics? The noble Marquess said, their Lordships were aware that notice was given last year by his right hon. and learned Friend the Attorney General for Ireland of a Bill to carry out the recommendations of the Commissioners with respect to the Common Law Courts in Ireland. It was subsequently withdrawn ; but he had no doubt it would be carried through this Session, and that a similar course would be taken with respect to the Irish Courts of Chancery. The Report to which he referred had been considerably misrepresented in Ireland, and so had the objects of the Motion which he had made on the subject, and therefore he wished to address a few words to the House in explanation. It had caused him no regret to find that the Commissioners recommended that there should be no diminution in the number of the Irish Judges. He was, however, astonished at the great importance attached to that part of the Report by a certain portion of the Irish Bar, for he attached but very little to it himself. He did not care whether the number of the Judges was to be twelve, fifteen, or twenty-five, but he did care for the saving of the money of the suitors, and for the improvement in the practice of the Courts of Law of the United Kingdom. It was not because the Report contained anything new or original that he considered it valuable. Indeed, one of its great merits was, that it recommended nothing which had not been approved by former Commissions and by the highest authorities that had inquired into the subject. One of his complaints had been that the alterations which had been introduced in the Irish Courts were founded upon the opinion—he might call it the crotchet—of an individual ; whereas in England an entirely different course was taken, and the Reforms there introduced were the result of ample inquiry. The Commissioners appointed in 1851 in England reported—

"It seems to us that the combination of the writ and declaration together would lead to greater expense than is at present incurred. It would render a declaration necessary in every case, while we have seen in one-half the actions actually commenced no declaration is prepared or required."

And yet in the teeth of that Report a Bill was introduced in 1853 and an Act passed which made summons and plaint combined the foundation of every action at common law in Ireland. Their Lordships would not be surprised to hear that one of the strongest recommendations of the Commissioners was that the provisions of the law in England on that point should be extended to Ireland. All the changes which they recommended had the character of assimilating the laws of the two countries, the changes which had been recognized in this country as improvements being recommended to be extended to Ireland, while a few alterations in English practice in accordance with the practice in Ireland were suggested, especially in some minute details where the Irish practice was beneficial. The case with regard to the Courts of Chancery was infinitely stronger. The Commissioners said at page 23—

"In November, 1854, a Commission was issued to inquire into the Irish Incumbered Estates Court, and whether its powers should be transferred to the Court of Chancery, and by their Report the Commissioners recommended that the office of Master in Chancery in Ireland should be abolished, one Master being retained for the management of the business of receivers and for auditing certain public accounts under statutes provided for that duty. They also stated their opinion that it would be for the interest of the public and of the profession that the practice of the English and Irish Courts of Chancery should be assimilated as closely as circumstances would permit, so that the decisions of each should be applicable to both, and thus tend to establish a uniform system of equity in the two countries. We have come to a unanimous resolution in favour of this assimilation. We think it is of paramount importance to restore and preserve as far as possible an uniformity of system in the equity jurisprudence of the two countries."

Again, at page 24, on the general question of assimilation of equity practice and procedure, and the changes connected with it, they said—

"We are of opinion that the practice and procedure of the Court of Chancery of England are generally to be preferred to the practice and procedure of the Court of Chancery in Ireland."

The Lord Chancellor of Ireland now was the Lord Chancellor of Ireland ten years ago when the Report of the Commission of 1854 was drawn up, and one of the names signed to it was Chancellor Brady. He hoped, therefore, he should receive an assurance that in the present case the Report of the Commissioners would not be allowed to remain a dead letter. The Master of the Rolls, one of the highest authorities upon the matter in Ireland, was the only person that made any objection whatever. The Commissioners said—

"The Master of the Rolls in Ireland, in the paper which he submitted to us, indicates only one objection to his undertaking the carrying out of the share of a new system of Chancery practice which would, under our recommendations, devolve on any new holder of that office. He objects to work out the arrears of business now in the office of any of the Masters."

Their Lordships were aware that it had been shown that the Chancery business in Ireland was not one-fifteenth of the business in England, and yet so full of arrears was the Court that the Master of the Rolls suggested the great difficulty of altering the system to be the working out of the arrears. The noble Marquess concluded by putting his Question.

EARL GRANVILLE said, he was glad to hear the noble Marquess speak in such high terms of the Report of the Commissioners, because the measure proposed by the Government had for its object to carry out the recommendations embodied in that Report, and he rather thought the Attorney General for Ireland had already given notice in the other House of his intention to bring in the Bill. With regard to the Judicial Statistics, part of the Return had been already made; but this being the first year of their preparation, there had been some delay with regard to some portions of them. Those received, however, had been arranged and digested, and there was hardly any doubt that they would be published about the middle of June, very nearly at the same time that the English Judicial Statistics appeared.

The Marquess of Clanricarde

METROPOLITAN RAILWAYS.— WORKING CLASS TRAINS.
RESOLUTION.

THE EARL OF DERBY said, the attention of their Lordships had been so often called by himself and others to the great amount of distress and suffering entailed upon the middle and lower classes of the metropolis by the extensive displacements consequent on public improvements and railway enterprise, that in introducing the Motion of which he had given notice he should only think it necessary to trouble their Lordships with very few observations. A further inducement to brevity presented itself, as from communications held with the noble Lord the Postmaster General on the part of the Board of Trade, and the noble Lord the Chairman of Committees, he believed they both concurred in the appropriateness of the remedy he proposed to apply. There were certain classes of the metropolis who suffered peculiarly from these displacements, to whom nevertheless no compensation could be given. Small tradesmen and shopkeepers, for instance, being removed from the positions they had long occupied, were frequently unable to find in the neighbourhood any place suitable for the purposes of their business, and were, therefore, obliged to break up their connection and sacrifice their trade prospects. Workmen and artisans, again, were dependent for their daily bread upon proximity to the scene of their labours; and in taking steps to diminish the inconvenience under which they laboured it might even be possible to extend to them some other advantages. In these days nearness did not depend merely upon distance between one place and another; the time occupied in the transit and the convenience of the journey entered largely into the calculation. On a recent occasion he had presented a petition from one of the large parishes of London, praying that all new Railway Companies should be compelled to make provision for the labouring people who were displaced by the removal of their houses for the construction of the railways; and for this purpose they prayed the House to pass a measure causing all railways having termini in London to run at least one train morning and evening, bringing persons into town in time for their work, and taking them back again upon its completion at such rates as would enable them to live in the country and yet to attend to their work in town. The expenses of such a journey would be repaid to the working classes by the difference between the cost of lodgings in the country and in town; their families would enjoy the almost inestimable advantage of pure air contrasted with that which they had to breathe in crowded rooms in London, and workmen themselves would at any rate be able to sleep out of town and to spend Sunday and a good portion of Saturday there, a boon which the better classes so greatly enjoyed. Inconveniences were inseparable from suburban residence, but in this case he believed they would be more than balanced by the advantages attendant on the plan. On a former occasion he mentioned to their Lordships that the London, Chatham, and Dover Railway— a line which seemed to run from everywhere to anywhere — had voluntarily adopted the principle embodied in his Motion, and had consented to a clause pledging themselves to run trains morning and evening at no higher charge than 1s. per week, being at the rate of 1d. per journey. He was not then aware that a direct precedent existed for the plan he was about to submit; and, as it was rather difficult to lay down precise rules on such a subject in a Resolution of a general character, he proposed to refer, by way of example, to the Act passed in 1861, in which the principle was recognized. That Act had reference to the North London Railway, and was entitled the 24 & 25 *Vict.* c. 196, s. 45. The Companies were at all times after the passing of the Act, Sundays, Christmas Days, and Good Fridays alone excepted, to run a train every morning and evening between Liverpool Street and Kingsland, not later than seven a.m., or earlier than six p.m., at such hours as might prove most convenient to the working classes, and at prices not exceeding one penny per passage for each journey. And the Act very judiciously provided that, in case of any complaint being made of the want of proper facilities, the Board of Trade from time to time should have power to fix and regulate the hours of starting. There was a further provision, which was only a matter of justice to the railway company, and if for a continuous period of a certain duration the railway authorities should be able to show that less than 100 passengers on an average had been conveyed by such trains, the company, on proof of that fact to the satisfaction of the Board, might obtain their assent to discontinue the trains; but the Board were to be at liberty to order their resumption whenever they thought proper. Such a clause as that introduced into every Metropolitan Railway Bill would accomplish the object which he had in view. He, therefore, asked the House to pass a Sessional Order requiring that it should be an instruction to the Committee on every Bill providing for the construction of any new railway within the metropolis; and this their Lordships would see applied as well to the extensions of existing railways as to novel undertakings, to insert in the Bill provisions analogous to those contained in the North London Railway Act, 24 & 25 *Vict.* c. 196, s. 45, for the purpose of securing to the labouring classes a cheap transit to and from their labour by a morning and evening train, with such modifications as may appear to be required by the circumstances of each case. That Resolution laid down a principle which should guide the Committee, and the Committee would be able to specify within what limits, and to what distances, it would be for the public convenience that the regulations affecting these trains should extend. He hoped that in the end this proposal would not prove disadvantageous to the railway companies; but even if it entailed upon them some degree of loss, the sacrifice was not too great to require at their hands, seeing what immense sacrifices had been imposed for their convenience upon large classes in the metropolis having no power to protect themselves. The noble Earl concluded by moving a Resolution.

Resolved,

That it be an Instruction to the Committee on every Railway Bill providing for the Construction of any new Railway within the Metropolis to insert in the Bill Provisions analogous to those contained in the North London Railway Act, 24 & 25 *Vict.* c. 196, s. 45, for the Purpose of securing to the Labouring Classes a cheap Transit to and from their Labour by a Morning and Evening Train, with such Modifications as may appear to be required by the Circumstances of each Case.— (*The Earl of Derby.*)

LORD STANLEY OF ALDERLEY said, that when the intention of the noble Earl was made known to him, he communicated with the Board of Trade, and was informed that they had no objection to the proposal. He thought it very desirable that the principle should be made to apply to extensions of existing lines, as well as to new lines coming into the metropolis, otherwise it would be practically inoperative, inasmuch as he thought it very improbable that many new lines would seek for power to enter London. It was extremely important that these provisions should be placed under the supervision of the Board of Trade, both in regard to the hours of the trains and the power to discontinue them under certain circumstances. He had heard that the inconvenience represented by the noble Earl had been felt to some extent in Paris, and that provision had been made for securing to the labouring class the means of cheap access to the city, and had been found to work exceedingly well.

THE EARL OF ELLENBOROUGH said, that the working man usually began his day's work at six, and it would be necessary the train should run at an hour which would enable him to be at his work at the usual time.

THE EARL OF DERBY said, it would be better to leave the regulation of the hours to the Board of Trade.

EARL GREY thought that the arrangement ought to be carried into effect on metropolitan lines, even if they did not come to Parliament for an extension of powers.

THE EARL OF SHAFTESBURY agreed as to the desirability of the morning and evening trains proposed by the noble Earl, but the great difficulty they had to contend with in the matter was in providing residences. At present, there were no residences suited to this class of the community in close proximity to railway stations, but the Society for Improving the Dwellings of the Labouring Classes had under their consideration plans for building large blocks of model houses suited to their wants. The difficulty was not so much in the cost of the land or the erection of the houses, as in the objection raised by the labouring people themselves. Their Lordships knew that the metropolis was grievously over-crowded, and he could not see how the evil was to be effectually encountered. There was an immigration of 60,000 into London every year, which largely increased the evil. When the more provident families now living in the metropolis were asked whether they would like to reside in these model buildings out of town, they objected, for this reason—that some members of their families went out as charwomen, and others to nurse the children of persons superior in position to themselves; if, however, they went down the line to live in these houses, they would all be on the same level, and they would

Lord Stanley of Alderley

lose many opportunities of making up their wages which they now enjoyed. These were the objections raised by almost every woman in the humbler ranks to whom he had spoken on this subject. It was, however, most desirable that the present experiment should be made. The 60,000 persons who immigrated into London had not yet formed the connections which those long resident in the metropolis had made, and it would be a great inducement to them to stop at some of these villages on the line of railway if they could find good house accommodation and railway facilities for going to and from their work. It would be necessary, he thought, to have two morning and two evening trains. A working man might be too late for his morning train, and if there were no chance of getting another, he would not be able to get to his day's work, and would lose his day's wages. The experiment was very well worth trying, and he trusted that all who could help in providing good house accommodation, either in single houses or blocks of houses, would come forward and assist in the work.

Motion *agreed to.*

RETIREMENT OF NAVAL CAPTAINS.
OBSERVATIONS.

LORD CHELMSFORD rose to call the attention of the First Lord of the Admiralty to the Effect of the Order in Council of the 1st of August, 1860, upon those Naval Captains who did not become Applicants for the Retirements offered by the Orders in Council of the 1st of September, 1846, and 25th of June, 1851. He was desirous of calling public attention to what he considered an act of great injustice inflicted by the Admiralty upon these naval officers, to whom all redress had been refused. He was glad to hear from a right hon. Friend of his fully acquainted with the subject, that it was likely to come under the notice of the other House of Parliament in the course of a few days. Captains on half-pay were entitled to different rates of pay, according to their standing on the List — the first seventy received 14*s.* 6*d.* a day, the next hundred, 12*s.* 6*d.* a day, and the remainder 10*s.* 6*d.* a day. Inducements from time to time were held out to officers to retire, and with this object the Orders in Council of 1846 and 1851 were passed. The Order in Council of 1846 offered to those who received 12*s.* 6*d.* and

10s. 6d., an addition of 7s. 6d. to their pay on retiring, thus making up their incomes to 18s. and 20s. a day respectively. They were to advance to the rank of Rear Admiral, as though they were on active service, but they would be placed on a retired list, which was to consist of one hundred, the first twenty-five of whom would receive 25s. a day, but none of the others were to advance to that amount until the list was reduced below twenty-five. These Orders in Council left it optional to the captains whether they would accept the retirement, or remain on the active list. Several officers refused the retirement of 1851, and preferred remaining on the active list. They had a perfect right to choose for themselves, and by the exercise of their choice they acquired a vested right to advance ultimately to the rank of Reserved Rear Admiral, with a pay of 25s. a day. Under these circumstances, in the year 1860 a new Order in Council was issued, providing for the retirement of officers, giving them no option, but making it compulsory that all officers who had not served the proper time in their rank, and had arrived at the age of sixty, should be placed upon the retired list with half-pay, which would never exceed 20s. a day. That was a gross injustice, and a direct interference with the vested rights of the officers who had made their choice, and were entitled to receive all the advantages which had been promised to them. Under this Order in Council, nine of the captains who refused to accept retirement in 1851 had been forced upon this retired list. Their Lordships would naturally be anxious to hear what arguments were put forward to justify so arbitrary an act, and fortunately they had an opportunity of becoming acquainted with them. The noble Duke the First Lord of the Admiralty was examined on this subject by the Select Committee for inquiring into Naval Promotion and Retirement, and he said—

"The officers have benefited by the reductions. They have gained promotion by them, and obtained advantages from them quite unexpected when they entered the service." "For instance," said the noble Duke, "when any future measure touches them, they seem to forget all the advantages gained by former retirements and say that any new arrangement is a breach of faith with them."

That was not an argument, but rather a statement of the very ground of complaint. These officers had refused to accept the retirement upon the view which

they took of their position and of the advantages which they were offered, and no one had any right to deprive them of a right which was vested in them by their choice. The private secretary of the noble Duke, who was examined by the same Commitee, said, that he did not believe that any officer had been damaged by the order—

"The officers who refused the 18s. a day, and have been forced to retire, received 2s. a day additional, making 20s., and in several instances officers have preferred the retirement of 1860 to that of 1851."

He admitted, however, that they were deprived of the prospective advance to 25s.; nor was it surprising that some officers—those, for instance, who were low down on the list, and above the age of sixty—should prefer this scheme of retirement to that of 1851, because it would advance them to a position on the list at which they would otherwise never have arrived. When this subject was mentioned in another place, the noble Lord the Secretary of the Admiralty stated that the case of these officers had been considered by the Committee to which he had already referred, and that the conclusion arrived at was that they had no grievance to complain of. The noble Lord must have made this statement under an entire misapprehension. The subject of pay and allowances was never considered by that Committee, and in their Report they stated that—

"All that your Committee have ventured to do is to decide, so far as the limited nature of the inquiry would admit, what, irrespective of financial considerations, would be most conducive to the public service with regard to numbers, promotion, and retirement."

He said that the Admiralty might as well have taken from the officers who accepted the retirement of 1851 the right to receive 25s. a day as have deprived those officers who chose to remain upon the active list of their right to advance to the rank of Rear Admirals on the reserved list with 25s. a day. He believed that nothing had ever created greater dissatisfaction and alarm among naval officers than had this Order in Council, which they felt had deprived them of all security as to their positions, or as to the pay which they enjoyed; and, therefore, he had thought it his duty to bring the subject under the notice of the noble Duke and of their Lordships.

THE DUKE OF SOMERSET said, that as this question involved a great many details, and was very difficult of explanation, it could be better discussed before a Committee, in which questions and answers might elicit the facts of the case, than in their Lordships' House, and it had had the advantage of such a discussion. It was the subject of inquiry by the Committee to which the noble Lord had referred, and he was satisfied that the majority of that Committee were convinced that no great injustice had been done to these officers. The noble and learned Lord said that an injustice had been done to these men, and that faith had been broken with them. To ascertain whether there had been a breach of faith, their Lordships must look at the engagement which was made with these officers when they entered the service and the position which they then occupied. When these officers who were now complaining entered the service, they had no claim to any Order in Council. The Orders of 1847 and 1851 were Orders made for the general good of the service. The Orders in Council were the gratuitous gift of the Crown for the benefit of the service; but no officer entering the service before they had passed had a right to say an Order in Council to a certain effect shall be issued; and no injustice, therefore, would have been done to them if no Order had been made either in 1847 or 1851. And where, he would ask, in the event of no Order in Council having been issued in the year 1847, would those captains stand? The senior captain who complained was then at the bottom of the list; the list of captains, instead of 570, was 730. And what was the rate of promotion? It then took a captain to rise from the bottom to the top of the list thirty-seven years on an average; and those captains, therefore, who were at the bottom could not reasonably look forward to having their names placed on the flag list before the expiration of that period. That was their position and they knew how they were situated. Assuming, under those circumstances, that no Order in Council had been issued in 1847, 1851, or 1860, those officers would not yet have reached the 14s. 6d. list, and would now be in the receipt of only 12s. 6d. a day, and for fourteen years more would be in the same position. Was he wrong, then, when he had stated before the Committee that the measure of 1847 had been to them a great advantage? Not one of those men, whose case is now specially brought forward, he

The Duke of Somerset

might add, was in a position to take advantage of the Order in Council of 1847, because he must have been fifty-five years of age and must have served twenty years on the list of captains; while those very men who complained had not yet been twenty years on that list. He should next refer to the Order of 1851, which said that captains above fifty-five years of age, and who had been ten years on the list of captains, might be eligible for retirement, and would receive a certain rate of retiring allowance. When, however, the Admiralty again considered this subject in the year 1860, they had to take into account what was the condition of the Admiralty list. We had then passed through fifty years without a naval war. We had now 327 Admirals, and the question was naturally asked in the country how many Admirals are required for the navy. It could do very well with from twenty to thirty; but the taxpayers were called upon to pay for 242 Admirals, and were we to go on adding to the Admirals' list? — for that was the real question. For his own part, he must confess that, even for the interests of the navy itself, he thought that great caution should be used in adding to the list of Admirals, otherwise there would probably be a re-action against the whole system. The senior of the captains in question, he might add, had served as a lieutenant for six years, and as a commander for nine years and nine months, and for that service he had been paid as a captain for a long time, while he claimed to be for ever after paid as an Admiral. The commanders' list, he might further observe, when he came to the Admiralty stood at 500, and it had been reduced to 450, a step which created more rapid promotion to the great benefit of the service. He, therefore, contended, that without the Orders in Council, which constituted no part of the engagements of the Admiralty, the senior captain whose cause the noble and learned Lord advocated, would have stood in a worse position than that in which he was now placed.

The EARL OF HARDWICKE said, that the case was not without difficulties, but it might be understood exclusively of the list altogether. A certain number of officers on the post captain's list had been assured by the Orders in Council that they might accept their retirement or not, as they thought fit, on 25s. a day, with the rank of Rear Admiral; but that it was left to their own option whether they should accept the proposal or not. The great injustice perpetrated was the Order of 1860, which expelled these officers from the list and gave them only 18s. and 20s. a day. If they had known in 1851, that such an Order as this was to be issued in 1860 they would, undoubtedly, have accepted the offer then made to them. The noble Duke asked, what was the moral understanding with officers who enter the service? He (the Earl of Hardwicke) answered that the moral understanding with officers was, undoubtedly, the state of the law of the service of the day, whatever that might be; and the great hardship of the profession was the uncertainty as to the different Orders which might be issued. This was the kind of policy which would take away all inducement to enter the navy, and would certainly, in the end, alienate the gentry of the country from it. But, after all the heartburnings and dissatisfaction which had been created, and after loading the country with a great additional outlay, the Admiralty had not yet succeeded in obtaining an active list of entirely able-bodied men perfectly fit to serve the country. The noble Duke, by some extraordinary oversight, had not touched on the strong point of his case; and as the case stood at present, and as he had defended it, an act of the grossest injustice had been perpetrated. There were upon the list referred to by the noble and learned Lord, only fifteen officers altogether, and to give those men what they were morally entitled to, would cost the country only £1,293 a year.

THE EARL OF DERBY said, that having listened with considerable interest to the speeches which had been made, it appeared to him that there was one very important point upon which the noble Duke had not answered his noble and learned Friend. The noble Duke had argued that there was great advantage to the service from the Orders in Council of 1847 and 1851, and there was no doubt that by these Orders almost all the officers in the service had gained considerable advantage in more rapid promotion and in the clearing of the list. But the question was, whether the Order in Council of 1860 did not do away with the option which had been given to officers by the Order in Council of 1851. Now that Order gave to the officers the option of either receiving an immediate increase of pay, or, on the other hand, prospective advantages if they remained at the lower rate. From 1851 to 1860 they received the diminished rate of pay instead of the higher rate that they would have had; they took the alternative; on the footing of the Order in Council they consented to remain on the lower rate until the time when they would succeed to higher rank, on the distinct understanding that they would receive the progressive increase of pay to which they would but for this Order have been entitled. The hardship of these officers was that they were left at a low rate of pay for a series of years, and that by the Order in Council of 1860, they were deprived of the advantages that had been held out to them by the Order of 1851. He defied the noble Duke, if he could not contradict these facts, to say that there had not been a gross breach of faith committed in reference to those officers who had consented to receive the reduced rate in order to get the prospective increase of rank and pay.

THE DUKE OF SOMERSET said, he could not at all agree with the view of the noble Earl. Arrangements had been made in 1851.

THE EARL OF DERBY: Were they proposed as conditions of a bargain between the officers and the Government?

THE DUKE OF SOMERSET: No, they declined to take it. They said they would remain where they were. With the men who accepted the terms there was a bargain, but with the men who refused them there was no bargain. If there was a bargain with these particular officers, then there was a bargain with every commander and lieutenant in the navy.

LORD CHELMSFORD said, that it was perfectly clear that under the Order in Council of 1851 certain captains on the list were offered retirement upon a certain amount of pay, and that Order in Council left it entirely optional to officers upon the active list to accept that retirement or not. Certain of the officers, in view of the advantages that the Order in Council held out, accepted the retirement, and, as the noble Duke said, entered into a bargain. Certain other officers upon the active list preferred to remain there, and did not accept retirement, and therefore, in a certain sense, did not enter into any bargain. Remaining upon the active list upon a lower rate than they would have had if they had retired, they would advance in due course until they became reserved Rear Admirals, when they would receive 25s. a day. The noble Duke would not deny that they had an undoubted right to choose for themselves whether they would retire or would remain upon the active list with the prospective advantages. Having remained upon the active list they received between 1851 and 1860 the old rate, instead of having had 7*s.* 6*d.* added to their pay in the former year, hoping that they would in time advance to 25*s.* a day as being on the reserved list of Rear Admirals. He asked whether they had not a vested right to do as they had done; and whether the Order in Council did not deprive them of the rights which they had expected to enjoy, because, instead of advancing to 25*s.* a day, that Order forcibly put them upon the retired list, and the maximum of their pay was 20*s.* a day. The question was, whether these officers had in 1860 a vested right to remain on the active list and to advance till they became Rear Admirals upon the retired list, for if they had that right then the Order in Council of 1860 was arbitrary and unjust.

THE EARL OF HARROWBY said, the case of these officers seemed to be a very hard one, and would, in his opinion, have met with different treatment in a court of justice from that which it had received at the hands of the Admiralty. In private life, if a person had made such a bargain he would have been bound to carry it out.

THE DUKE OF SOMERSET said, that the officers who did not choose to accept the terms offered in 1851 remained on the active list subject to any Order in Council which might be made afterwards, and had no right to complain because the arrangement did not turn out to be as advantageous as they had expected.

House adjourned at Seven o'clock, to Monday next, half past Eleven o'clock.

~~~~~~

HOUSE OF COMMONS,

Friday, April 22, 1864.

MINUTES.]—NEW MEMBER SWORN—Sir Robert Anstruther, baronet, *for* Fifeshire.
SELECT COMMITTEE—On Seat of Under Secretary of State, *First Report* (No. 226).

INDIA—TERRITORY OF DHAR.

QUESTION.

LORD STANLEY said, he wished to ask the Secretary of State for India, Whe-
Lord Chelmsford

ther the territory of Dhar, confiscated during the war of 1857-8, and promised to be restored to its native ruler, has been so restored; and, if not, when the cession will take effect?

SIR CHARLES WOOD was understood to say, that it was stipulated that the territory of Dhar should be restored to its Rajah when he became eighteen years of age; but on his arriving at that age it was found that his physical and moral health was such as to render him quite incapable of discharging the duties of Government. Since that time he had very much improved, and although the whole administration of the country was not placed in his hands, by far the greatest portion of the business was carried on by himself and his Minister.

INDIA—BURNING THE DEAD.

QUESTION.

LORD STANLEY said, he had seen it stated in the Indian newspapers that an order had been issued by the Lieutenant Governor of Bengal prohibiting the immemorial native custom connected with the native religion of burning the dead on the banks of the Hooghly. He wished, therefore, to ask the Secretary of State for India, Whether it is true that the Government of Bengal has issued an order prohibiting the burning of dead bodies on the banks of the Hooghly river; whether the terms of that order, and the reasons on which it is based, have been made known to him; and, if so, whether there is any objection to make them public?

SIR CHARLES WOOD said, in reply, that no despatches had been received from India on that subject, and the only information he possessed was derived from private sources. The cholera had been exceedingly prevalent at Calcutta lately, and the greatest possible alarm had been created there in consequence. The state of the city was very bad, and the subject had been taken into consideration by the authorities with a view to remedy the evils complained of, and see what was to be done to check the spread of the disease. An order was subsequently issued to prevent the throwing of dead bodies into the Hooghly. Anything more disgusting and more calculated to generate disease than the dead bodies floating up and down that river could hardly be imagined, and it was thought most desirable to prevent that practice. With regard to the burning of dead bodies, he did not believe that any order on that subject had been issued; but there was, he thought, a proposal that means should be provided for the burning of dead bodies at a short distance from Calcutta. He had reason, however, to know that, if the objections to it were as strong as was represented by some persons, that proposal would not be persevered with.

LIGHTHOUSE AT HOLYHEAD.
QUESTION.

MR. STANLEY said, he wished to ask the President of the Board of Trade, If instructions have been given to remove the Light Ship at Holyhead, and erect a Lighthouse on the structure of the Northern Breakwater?

MR. MILNER GIBSON said, that instructions of that nature had been given.

REPORTS OF FACTORY INSPECTORS.
QUESTION.

MR. F. S. POWELL said, he would beg to ask the Secretary of State for the Home Department, Whether the Reports of Factory Inspectors, as printed and circulated, are copies of those originally sent in by the Inspectors; if not, what are the regulations under which revision or alteration of those Reports is conducted?

SIR GEORGE GREY, in reply, said, the Reports of the Factory Inspectors, as printed and circulated for some years past, were copies of those originally sent in by the Inspectors. The last Instructions issued on the subject were issued nearly nine years ago, when a letter was written to the Inspectors, pointing out to them that their efficiency depending on their Reports being calmly and impartially written, it would be better that they should avoid commenting on the decisions of magistrates, and also on what took place at public meetings at which their conduct was impugned. At the same time, the Inspectors were told that if they thought a defence of their conduct in any case was necessary, they might address a letter to the Secretary of State, and, if requisite, publicity would be given to it. Since those instructions were issued he did not think that he had had any reason to complain of any Report of a Factory Inspector.

MR. F. S. POWELL said, he wished to know whether the right hon. Gentleman will lay those Instructions on the table?

SIR GEORGE GREY said, he did not think that that would be desirable, but he would look at them and see whether it could properly be done.

THE BRADFORD RESERVOIRS.
QUESTION.

MR. FERRAND said, he rose to ask the Secretary of State for the Home Department, If Mr. Rawlinson, the Government engineer, has sent in his Report on the Bradford Reservoirs; and, if not, when he will do so?

SIR GEORGE GREY said, he believed that Mr. Rawlinson was incurring no unnecessary delay in preparing his Report, which he wished to make as complete as possible on all points.

FORTIFICATIONS — DEFENCE OF THE BRISTOL CHANNEL.—QUESTION.

MR. NEWDEGATE said, he would beg to ask the First Lord of the Treasury, What arrangements for the defence of the Bristol Channel have been made?

VISCOUNT PALMERSTON replied, that his noble Friend at the head of the War Department had made arrangements for the purchase of sites at Portishead, with a view to the erection of batteries for the defence of the south side of that channel. There were two Holmes called the Steep and the Flat Holmes in that vicinity, and also another point, he thought, on the north side. Surveys were being made, and steps would be taken in order to obtain sites at those places in the event of batteries being required there.

FORTIFICATIONS—THE SPITHEAD FORTS.—QUESTION.

MR. BERNAL OSBORNE said, he would beg to ask the noble Lord, Whether Her Majesty's Government intend to proceed with the Spithead Forts according to the original plans; or whether they have not altogether abandoned the idea of a fort on the Horseshoe Sands?

VISCOUNT PALMERSTON said, he rather thought they had abandoned the Sturbridge Fort.

MR. BERNAL OSBORNE: The Sturbridge and Horseshoe Forts?

VISCOUNT PALMERSTON: No, not both; only that of Sturbridge, in consequence of the foundations being bad.

MR. BERNAL OSBORNE: Then you do not intend to continue the plan?

Viscount PALMERSTON: No, certainly not, when we cannot get good foundations. The Sturbridge Fort will not be proceeded with.

BALLAST HEAVERS' OFFICE.
QUESTION.

LORD JOHN MANNERS said, he wished to ask the Vice President of the Board of Trade, What alterations, if any, are intended to be made under the provisions of the Thames Conservancy Bill in the regulations now in force respecting the Ballast Heavers' Office?

MR. HUTT replied, that there was no intention whatever of interfering with the regulations of the Ballast Heavers' Office. On the contrary, he was very anxious to retain the regulations of that Office in their present position. Under the provisions of the Bill, considerable powers were transferred from the Trinity House to the Thames Conservancy Board, and he believed that the Conservancy Board would not only maintain the Ballast Heavers' Office, but would act in the same spirit of kindness and consideration towards a hard-working and deserving body of men as the Trinity House had done.

IRELAND—BREHON LAWS.
QUESTION.

MR. M'MAHON said, he rose to ask the Chief Secretary for Ireland, When the Brehon Laws, now in course of arrangement and translation, will be published?

SIR ROBERT PEEL said, in reply, that he had received a letter from the Secretary of the Commission, stating that one volume was in the press and would be published forthwith. The rest would be got ready as speedily as possible.

DUTY ON RAGS (ITALY).
QUESTION.

MR. BLACK said, he wished to ask the President of the Board of Trade, as the Duty on rags continued to be charged at Leghorn up to the 14th of this month, Whether he understands that the Duty is abolished by the Italian Government, or that there is an agreement that it is to be abolished, and when?

MR. MILNER GIBSON replied, that he did not understand from the information Her Majesty's Government had received, that the Italian Government had abolished the export duty on rags. Misapprehension had arisen on that subject,

Mr. Bernal Osborne

in consequence of the treaty between France and Italy being rather ambiguous on that question. If France had obtained from Italy a free export of rags, of course England would have been entitled, under the favoured nation clause, to the same privilege, but at present they were not informed that the Italian Government had made any change in the system which was in force before the conclusion of the treaty with France.

UNITED STATES—OUTRAGE ON A BRITISH SUBJECT.—QUESTION.

LORD ROBERT CECIL said, he would beg to put a question to the Under Secretary of State for Foreign Affairs with respect to the outrage committed on a British subject, of which a report had recently appeared in the public papers. The outrage took place on the coast of North America. It was alleged that a lieutenant of Marines, serving on board an American ship, had wounded a British subject who had been taken on board a blockade runner, and under circumstances of some aggravation. The result was, that the British subject had been maimed for life. The question he had to ask was, Whether they had received at the Foreign Office any information respecting that case, and whether any communication had been addressed to the American Government on the subject?

MR. LAYARD, in reply, said, Her Majesty's Government had received information on the subject which very nearly agreed with the information that had been published in the newspapers. Her Majesty's Government had demanded redress from the Government of the United States, and a correspondence had been going on for some time between the two Governments on the subject.

CASE OF CAPTAIN MELVILLE WHITE.
QUESTION.

COLONEL FRENCH said, he wished to ask, Whether the Foreign Office have received the award of the Senate of Hamburg in the case of Captain Melville White, and whether they are prepared to lay it on the table of the House?

MR. LAYARD said, in reply, that a despatch from the *Chargé d'Affaires* at Hamburg had been received, stating that the Senate had given their award, and it was, he regretted to say, unfavourable to Captain Melville White. If that gentleman had not yet received a copy of the award he might expect to receive it every day.

SUPPLY.

Order for Committee read.

Motion made, and Question proposed, "That Mr. Speaker do now leave the Chair."

CIVIL WAR IN CHINA.

RESOLUTION.

MR. LIDDELL: Sir, it is necessary, before I proceed to make the Motion which stands in my name, to explain to the House that, in consequence of some mistake, the Notice which I originally gave upon the subject does not appear in the form in which I first gave it. My Notice was to the effect, that I would call the attention of the House to the disbandment of the Anglo-Chinese force under the command of Captain Sherard Osborn, and I coupled with it the Motion which is on the paper, and which I shall end by moving—

"That in the opinion of this House further interference on the part of this country in the civil war in China is impolitic and unnecessary."

In proceeding to discharge that task I must throw myself upon the indulgence of the House, because it will be necessary for me to occupy some time, and refer to many details. I cannot, however, promise the House, in the present state of excitement on foreign affairs, a discussion presenting so many stirring and interesting incidents as are now of daily occurrence in the quarrel between Germany and Denmark; but the House may rest assured that there is no question with which the material interests of England are more closely associated, or in which the honour and dignity of the country are more deeply involved, than the one which I am now about to raise. It may be objected to the Motion that it has reference to bygone events, and that the interest attaching to it has ceased to exist; I would urge in reply, that although undoubtedly the piece has been played out, and the curtain may be said to have fallen on the performance, the actors still remain on the stage; and it is incumbent on Parliament to express an opinion as to the manner in which they have played their respective parts. I am anxious, also, in bringing this question forward, that while I refer to the events of the past, the future should not be lost sight of, for upon our future policy in China much depends. We have

a very large stake in that country, and our position there is a very peculiar one, and it depends entirely upon our future policy whether we shall secure or imperil that stake, and whether we shall render our commercial relations beneficial alike to England and to China. The history of the Anglo-Chinese expedition is a very simple one, and I will endeavour to pass over it as quickly as possible; but I must refer to the circumstances under which it left and returned to this country. The first idea of forming a European force for the service of the Emperor of China appears to have originated in an interview which took place between Mr. Hart, then Acting Inspector General of Her Majesty's Customs in China (Mr. Lay, the Inspector General, being at that time on sick leave in England), and Prince Kung the representative of the Emperor. That interview took place so far back as the autumn of 1861, and the objects to be obtained by the formation of this force, which was to consist of powerful vessels well armed and manned, and to be under the command of an English officer of experience, were mainly two. The one was the re-establishment of the Imperial authority upon the Yang-tse-Kiang River, and the other the suppression of piracy and smuggling in the Chinese waters, which duty the Chinese navy was altogether incompetent to perform from the fact of their crews being mostly pirates themselves. Well, Sir, Mr. Lay being in this country on sick leave, was selected by Mr. Hart as a fit and proper agent to carry out the purchase of those vessels and to make the necessary arrangements for fitting out the fleet and manning it. The Custom Houses in China contributed their quota in due proportions towards this very large outlay, and the money was forwarded to Mr. Lay. The first document to which I shall refer is a copy of Prince Kung's instructions conveyed in a letter through Mr. Hart to Mr. Lay in England, in which the Prince stated that he transferred the management of this affair to the hands of the Inspector General, who was instructed to purchase vessels, guns, gunpowder, coals, and other miscellaneous articles required for the use of the ships, to engage officers, seamen, and gunners for the service; and, in fact, to make all necessary arrangements for the formation of the fleet. In consequence of the receipt of that letter Mr. Lay proceeded, as the agent of the Chinese Government, to purchase the vessels and make all necessary arrangements. He at once placed himself in communication with Captain Sherard Osborn, an officer who had had considerable experience in China, who possessed the confidence and the respect of Her Majesty's Government, and who was chosen to command the fleet. The next document to which I must call the attention of the House is a copy of an agreement made between Mr. Lay and Captain Osborn in reference to the command he was about to take in the Chinese waters. The name of the Emperor of China, or his representative, does not appear in that agreement. So far from it, this copy of the agreement was altogether ignored by Prince Kung, who, in fact, never acknowledged the receipt of it. When I read the document in question, the House will not be surprised that it was so ignored. The following conditions embody one mutual understanding :—

" 1. Osborn agrees to take the command of the European Chinese navy for a period of four years, and stipulates that there shall be no other European naval Commander-in-Chief. 2. Osborn, as Commander-in-Chief, is to have entire control over all vessels of European construction, as well as native vessels manned with Europeans, that may be in the employ of the Emperor of China, or, under his authority, of the native guilds. 3. Lay will procure from the Emperor such an authority as may be necessary to cover Osborn's acts as the Commander-in-Chief of the European Chinese navy. 4. Osborn undertakes to act upon all orders of the Emperor which may be conveyed direct to Lay ; and Osborn engages not to attend to any orders conveyed through any other channel. 5. Lay, upon his part, engages to refuse to be the medium of any orders of the reasonableness of which he is not satisfied. 6. Osborn will appoint all officers and men on board the vessels of the force, subject, however, to the approval of Lay, as the representative of the Emperor."—*Correspondence*, China, No. 2 (1864), p. 7.

I see the House is as much surprised as I was, when I first read those clauses, which conclude thus—

" The conditions of this understanding, the terms of the formal agreement, and the printed instructions, shall be formally ratified by the Emperor at Pekin before Osborn shall be called upon to act with the force under his command."

I want the House to bear those words in mind. What is the meaning of those words? and what would have been their effect if they had been carried out? The meaning of those words is simply that the absolute and complete control of the whole of the naval operations in China was to be vested in Mr. Lay. And what was the instrument by which that control was to be exercised? An instrument omnipotent for

Mr. Liddell

its purposes, an English fleet armed with all the appliances of modern warfare, manned by the *élite* of the English navy, and commanded by one of the best officers in Her Majesty's service. And what would have been the effect of carrying out the instructions of Mr. Lay, of the nature of which he was in all cases to be the sole judge? Why, that every port and estuary and river in China would have been absolutely at the mercy of the Anglo-Chinese fleet, the whole commerce of China would have been under his absolute control. I say, without fear of contradiction, that such gigantic power, so great an extent of authority, was more than it was safe to intrust to the hands of any two private individuals practically irresponsible—that the possession of such an authority was incompatible with the existence of any legitimate authority in China. Mr. Lay, it will be remembered, in his capacity of Inspector General of Customs, had the whole of the receipts of the Customs revenue in China at his disposal, and I think he was placed in a position of no ordinary trust and responsibility. Can we wonder that Prince Kung ignored the receipt of that agreement? Can we blame him for refusing to accept any such terms? I always liked that old precept which enjoins us " to do as we would be done by." I think the application of the *argumentum ad hominem* is very useful in certain cases in which self is concerned. It tends to remove from the mind the prejudices we are apt to entertain when discussing the affairs of others in which we are interested. Suppose, then, that one day a distinguished stranger were to present himself in this country, and having claimed an interview with the noble Viscount at the head of Her Majesty's Government were to say to him, " My Lord, your naval affairs, your Board of Admiralty, are infamously mismanaged, your Chancellor of the Exchequer knows nothing about his duties, and the revenues of this great Empire are squandered." There may be some hon. Gentlemen both in the House and out of it who think that the illustrious stranger would have some grounds for making such a statement. Suppose he were to add, " Give me the control of your Admiralty department, place your revenue in my hands, and I will set everything right, but I will not act in concert with yourself or with any one of your colleagues. I will have nothing to do with any Member of the Government. I will receive my orders direct from the mouth of Her Majesty, and Her Majesty alone; and in every case I will be the judge of what those orders are to be." Suppose all this to take place, and the House will have a correct description of the post that Mr. Lay was to occupy in China. If the noble Lord were to listen to any such communication from the distinguished foreigner, I should say he would signally fail in his duty to Her Gracious Majesty and to the country; and I think that if Prince Kung had listened to the agreement between Mr. Lay and Mr. Osborn he would have been a traitor to China and to the Emperor. But he altogether ignored the document; he never acknowledged the receipt of it; and I think the House will agree with me that he was perfectly justified in this course of conduct. Such was the agreement made between Mr. Lay and Captain Osborn. The fleet under Captain Osborn appears to have arrived in China about the end of August, or the beginning of September. On his arrival Captain Osborn found a pressing letter awaiting him from Mr. Lay, urging him to proceed at once to Pekin to meet him there. On the way from Shanghai to Pekin Captain Osborn appears to have seen that some alteration in the state of affairs had taken place; that all was not going so smoothly as he had been led to expect. In fact, while he was at Shanghai attempts had been made to tamper with some of his crew, and by the offer of increased wages to induce them to take service elsewhere. He received from Mr. Lay a letter of instructions from Prince Kung; and I think the first clause of it will place the House in possession of the difference between the intentions of the Chinese and those of Mr. Lay. The first clause of those instructions is to the following effect:—

"It has been settled that the post of Chinese commander-in-chief of the steam fleet now purchased, shall be filled by the high officer selected by the Chinese Government, and that Captain Osborn, C.B., a British subject, shall be assistant commander-in-chief for a period of four years. The affairs of the fleet are to be managed by the said commanders-in-chief in a friendly spirit of co-operation. While Captain Osborn assists the Chinese Government in command of the fleet, he will take the instructions of the governors-general and governors as to the employment or distribution of the force. In all operations he is always to confer personally with those officers before either undertaking or staying these, and is to accept the Chinese decision as final."

That is the substance of the instructions

sent to Captain Osborn on his arrival in China, from Prince Kung.

"3. Captain Osborn will receive his commission from the Foreign Board defining his powers."—*Correspondence*, 1864 (No. 2), p. 9.

Captain Osborn at once saw that were he to accept service on those terms he would be placed under the control and order not of the Emperor of China, not of the authorities he went to serve, but of the local governors, the local mandarins, and governors of provinces, and, in fact, of any persons who might be in command when his services might be required. He felt that to accept service on those terms would be either to ensure the failure of the operations or to engage himself and those under his command in operations, perhaps disgraceful, and certainly not likely to be agreeable to Englishmen. He found that, instead of having the supreme command, he was merely to be employed as an assistant, and that he would be under the rule of the local authorities, and not of the central Chinese Government whom he went out to serve. He refused to accept service on any such terms, and I think he was perfectly right. I think that Captain Osborn throughout the whole of that transaction behaved like a man of honour, and in a manner worthy of an English sailor. His conduct was straightforward and sagacious, but I think that he was deluded by Mr. Lay. I do not say intentionally deluded, but nobody can have read, as I have read, the whole of the transactions, without being convinced that Mr. Lay had exceeded his authority, that he persuaded Captain Osborn, the Government, and himself, that he possessed authority which it was never the intention of the Chinese Government to confer upon him, and which was incompatible with his position—albeit a foreigner, in the service of the Chinese Government, a position with which no foreigner ought to be intrusted in any country. I will not, however, further trouble the House with my own opinions on the subject, but I ask them to follow me while I give them the opinion of our Ambassador, Sir Frederick Bruce, on the matter. The following was the language of Sir Frederick Bruce, when describing the failure of this great expedition:—

"Mr. Lay mistook his position, and overrated his influence when he resolved on starting his flotilla, without having previously ascertained that the terms agreed upon by Captain Osborn would be accepted. It was not till Mr. Lay arrived in China in the spring, that the Chinese Government had any information as to the composition of the force or the cost of its maintenance. They looked upon him merely as an agent to purchase ships, and to engage men to man them. Having exceeded his authority, they attributed his conduct to personal motives, and their confidence in the good faith of foreign nations had been very much shaken."

Such was the opinion of Sir Frederick Bruce. But it is fair to the Chinese Government to state what they have done with regard to Mr. Lay. Had he not been an English subject, on his exceeding his authority in purchasing ships that were not those required, and in squandering money at his disposal, he might have paid the penalty with the loss of his life or liberty. But the Chinese Government allowed him £2,000 a month for his establishment in Pekin; £8,000 a year salary, to March next; and presented him with a gratuity of £2,000 on leaving their service. The Chinese Government, therefore, cannot be charged with behaving to Mr. Lay either illiberally or harshly. I say then, that, in a great measure, I attribute the blame of all this failure of a great scheme to Mr. Lay for having mistaken his post and exceeded his authority. I will now trace the connection of Her Majesty's Government with all these matters. When Mr. Lay first applied for permission to enlist men and equip vessels for the service of the Emperor of China, grave legal objections presented themselves. The Foreign Enlistment Act stared the Government in the face; and the noble Earl at the head of the Foreign Office was rather alarmed about a certain Neutrality Act of Sir John Bowring. At the Admiralty Office, the Colonial Office, the Home Office, the Foreign Office, they were all in a state of ferment. The Home Secretary described the application of Mr. Lay as an unusual demand; Earl Russell was alarmed at the neutrality ordinance of 1855, which made interference in the Civil War a misdemeanor punishable by two years' imprisonment and a fine. At the Colonial Office, Earl Russell was informed that the ordinance had ceased to exist in 1858. To my utter astonishment, however, I heard the other day of the trial at Shanghai of a man of the name of George White who had captured a prize in Chinese waters. He was indicted before the consular court on two counts, the one for piracy, of which he was found guilty and sentenced, and the other for a breach of the Hong Kong ordinance of 1855. He was found guilty, and sentenced to two years' im-

Mr. Liddell

prisonment on the second count. The unfortunate man had since died. The noble Duke at the head of the Colonial Office distinctly informed the noble Earl at the head of the Foreign Office that that ordinance had ceased to exist in 1858. It appears, however, that it is still in operation. Another difficulty was the Foreign Enlistment Act. The Law Officers of the Crown were consulted; a great conflict of opinion took place among the heads of the various departments, but it was ultimately smoothed away. Two Orders in Council were passed, the one dated August 30, 1862, which had reference strictly to Mr. Lay, Captain Osborn, and other officers; the other, dated January 9, 1863, and applying to the whole army and navy of England, for every officer in the army and navy was invited to take service under the Emperor of China. The issuing of those Orders in Council confirms me in the belief that this was the crowning act of a policy which had for its object the creation of a British protectorate in China. All this was done without any application to Parliament. It might not have been known to Parliament but for the questions which were from time to time asked by certain hon. Members. Such were the measures taken by Her Majesty's Government to forward the gigantic scheme for the formation of an Anglo-Chinese fleet. Mr. Lay speaks of the great power and responsibility conferred by the Order in Council; and Captain Osborn says, "If I accept the position I shall be acting contrary to the spirit of the Order in Council, and to the wishes of Her Majesty's Government." I there trace the intention of the Government. What they desired was a dictatorship in the person of Mr. Lay, supported by a fleet under the command of Captain Osborn. Now I say that the Government, in the part they took in this matter—inasmuch as they sold some of the ships to the Chinese—set aside the laws of the country to facilitate the formation of this fleet and to enable persons to take service under the Emperor of China. I say that Her Majesty's Government would have been responsible for the success or the failure of the enterprise; and I will tell the House what the opinion of their Ambassador, Sir Frederick Bruce, is on that important point. It is perfectly clear to my mind that this scheme never received the sanction or approval of Sir Frederick Bruce. Sir Frederick says, in page 24 of the Correspondence—

" Had the Chinese voluntarily accepted the squadron, the onus of the difficulties it would have encountered would have rested on the Chinese Government; but the burden would have been thrown on Her Majesty's Government by the Chinese, and with justice, had it appeared that this flotilla, exclusively British in its character, directed by British officers and agents, and imposed by British pressure, was acting under a Chinese flag, which the Chinese Government, contrary to its wishes, had been compelled to hoist on board the ships."—*Page* 24.

Had Captain Osborn, in the discharge of his duty, come into conflict with a foreign nation, and the subjects of that nation had applied for protection to their respective Governments, there must have been great complication and embarrassment for which Her Majesty's Government would have been responsible. Had the enterprise failed, and our countrymen been placed in a perilous position through the perfidy of the Chinese, does any hon. Member believe that the matter would have ended there? The English people would have demanded more men and more ships for China, and the demand would have been irresistible, whoever might have been the occupants of the Treasury benches. I wish only to quote one more passage, which has special reference to Her Majesty's Government. Sir Frederick concludes by saying—

" If it was considered necessary that the flotilla should be taken out of the hands of the Government who paid for it, and the exclusive control over its operations vested in its foreign commander and the foreign agent employed in procuring it, these conditions, of so singular a nature, ought to have been submitted and agreed to before the vessels were allowed to sail for China."—*Page* 24.

A harder hit, a more just rebuke, was never administered to a Government at home by a minister abroad. That passage contains the very pith and gist of the complaint I make against the Government. I complain of the Government that they trusted to the *ipse dixit* of Mr. Lay as proof positive of the authority he claimed to possess, but which, in fact, was never conferred upon him. They ignored their own ambassador while trusting to the amateur diplomacy of Mr. Lay in this most important matter, and rendered themselves responsible for obligations of which they could not possibly see either the end or the extent. They allowed that fleet to leave the country, perfectly ignorant of the real extent of the authority by which it had been formed. Such is the history of the Anglo-Chinese expedition. I leave my plain, unvarnished tale in the hands of the House, for hon. Members to draw their conclusions from it. And now I proceed to ask the House permission to make one or two observations upon these general facts. Although I do not think the failure of this great scheme very creditable to the promoters of it, I think the Government ought to be congratulated on that failure. I have heard of great successes being described as " untoward events;" and this great failure deserves to be described as an auspicious event. I think all the parties concerned in it have had a great escape. The Emperor of China has had a great escape from an *imperium in imperio*, which it was the intention of Mr. Lay, with the sanction and approval of Her Majesty's Government, to establish at Pekin, his own capital. Captain Osborn has had a great escape, thanks to his own sagacity and foresight, and straightforward course, from becoming involved in disaster or certain failure. I think Her Majesty's Government has had the greatest escape of all from the embarrassments of the position in which they would have been inextricably involved. Mr. Lay has been dismissed by the Emperor of China; Captain Osborn has returned home, and the fleet has been dispersed. But there is more in the dismissal of Mr. Lay, there is more in the rejection of the service by Captain Osborn than meets the public eye. I cannot help thinking that whilst the Emperor of China has engaged these men to fight his battles, the representatives of foreign Powers have got round the Chinese Government, and have whispered in their ears some words like these—I can imagine them to have said, " England is a selfish Power—England does nothing except it be to promote her own interests—take care how you give England any hold upon China." Of course, we Members of this House know nothing of Cabinet intrigues and secrets, but we know perfectly well that Russia's pet project has been to extend her empire in the East; that France likes to play the first fiddle wherever she may be; we know that America, whose policy in the East I admire because it is conciliatory and pacific, is perfectly insane in her jealousy of England; and I never will believe that the representatives of any of those Powers will sit still at Pekin with their arms folded and see English supremacy paramount in China. I believe that if Mr. Lay had succeeded in establishing himself in the position which he wished to occupy with the customs revenues in his pocket, that would have been the first step, and a very long one, towards establishing English supremacy in China. I have heard it said that the rejection of the services of Mr. Lay and Captain Osborn, and of the fleet, are signs of a retrogressive policy on the part of China. This is the language of what I call the protectorate party in this country. They have able men among them, and have open to them means of expressing their opinions and of guiding public opinion in England which few men possess, and I can imagine that they feel disappointed at the failure of their hopes and expectations. They thought of regenerating China by European influence and means, and feel somewhat annoyed at their want of success; but so far from looking upon this as a sign of retrogression, I regard it as a healthy symptom of Chinese vitality. It seems to me that this rejection of foreign interference is a proof that the Chinese nation is awakening to a sense of its own degradation, for there is nothing so degrading to a nation as to ask for aid in the internal management of its affairs. There is a very able man in China at this time—the Tsing-Kwo-Fan, governor of the two Kiang provinces, whose influence is paramount, and he is conducting certain siege operations before Nankin with much ability and with great probability of success. And I venture to predict, that unless we confine ourselves strictly to peaceful trading operations, unless we abstain from interference in the internal affairs of China, unless we insist upon a strict fulfilment of treaty obligations, and that only, we shall experience considerable trouble in our dealings with China. I now come to the Motion before the House, and I will ask the House to say that foreign interference in the civil war of China is impolitic and unnecessary. I expect to be told that the Government have not interfered. Now by interference I mean the system initiated by Admiral Hope and General Stavely—that was so especially followed up by Captain Dew, and which has continued ever since—the system of affording aid to the Imperial cause in China. That material aid has been afforded in two ways—in an indirect and in a direct way. I mean by an indirect way that Her Majesty's forces in China have been employed as an army of reserve to assist and support the Chinese army. Towns have been garrisoned, positions have been occupied, siege guns have been

Mr. Liddell

lent, and ammunition to any extent has been afforded to the Chinese forces. Now, this question of supplies is a very serious one. It touches one of the highest constitutional functions of this House. We have been engaged lately in voting supplies for the army and navy, and we are bound to ask for whose service these supplies were voted. Were they voted for the service of the Queen, or for the service of the Emperor of China? I have found a curious document on this subject which I will read to this House. It is a statement made by the lieutenant commanding the *Harrier* at Ningpo in May last— and he says—

"Great efforts have been made and assistance afforded by Her Majesty's Government in this neighbourhood, both as to supplies of munitions of war, drilling troops, and otherwise, but I am afraid without effect. The last supply of munitions brought by me from Shanghai and handed over to the Taoutae, by Captain Dew—namely, 1,000 Tower muskets, 100,000 rounds of ball cartridge, besides guns and other stores—I ascertained, too late to remonstrate, have been handed over to the Taoutae and his undisciplined troops, which is almost throwing them away."

This is a statement made by an officer in Her Majesty's navy. If this conduct has been pursued in one case, I believe it has been pursued in many others, and that an unlimited amount of guns, stores, and ammunition has been furnished to the Chinese troops for the purpose of enabling them to carry on the war. This is what I call interfering in an indirect way. Last year we heard a good deal about the intentions of the Government to protect the treaty ports, and the district thirty miles round, and especially Shanghai. Now, I want to know what we are to understand by a protection of "thirty miles round." I should have thought the difficulty of protecting a settlement was quite sufficient for any nation to undertake; and I cannot but think that if we are to hold against all comers a radius of thirty miles, it amounts to a military occupation of the country. Let us be told whether that be the effect or not. If it be, the House must consider how this Quixotic undertaking is to be carried out; for I do not see how it can be done except by the employment of a large military force. It appears to me that we should have some explanation on the subject, for I find among the Parliamentary papers that have been recently laid before the House the following statement made by the Chamber of Commerce of Hong Kong to Earl Russell:—

"The great majority of the respectable commercial classes (foreign) in this country strongly disapprove of the present action of our authorities; and many persons, even who at an earlier period gave all their influence in opposition to the maintenance of neutrality, have seen reason materially to modify their opinion. The commercial body, for the most part, have no faith whatever in the regeneration of China by such foreign aid as is now afforded; nor do they believe that hearty co-operation in introducing the foreign element into the various branches of the Chinese public service can be expected from any native officials, beyond, perhaps, the few men at Pekin within the personal influence of the foreign ministers. . . . . It may not be too late to withdraw from Shanghai with either safety or honour, but there can be no difficulty in restraining the energy of our military chiefs within the defined thirty mile radius round that city and settlement; and the extension of the system of protected areas round the other treaty ports would, in the general opinion of foreign residents in China, be a most serious mistake, and one much to be deprecated."

This is signed by the President of the Chamber of Commerce at Hong Kong. [An hon. Member: What is the date?] The date is October 22, 1863, and the statement is addressed to Earl Russell. After this I hope we shall not hear the argument used that this extraordinary policy has been adopted for the protection of trade. I maintain that our trade has never been attacked, and I challenge the hon. Gentleman the Under Secretary for Foreign Affairs (Mr. Layard), to point out one instance in which the property or persons of British subjects have been injured by the Taepings. There may possibly have been an isolated case of a cargo of tea being detained, but there has been nothing in the shape of systematic robbery or injury to British persons or property; and the difficulties to which our trade has been exposed at the hands of the Imperialists has been far greater than ever they have been at the hands of the Taepings. With reference to the occupation of the thirty mile radius, Sir Frederick Bruce says—

"It was reluctantly, and in deference to the naval and military authorities, that he assumed the responsibility of defending the thirty mile radius."

Now I submit that naval and military authorities are not the best judges in such cases. They are men of action and fond of creating work. It is natural—it is professional. They are not the best judges of policy. I have given the House the opinion of merchants upon this question. I have also given the opinion of our Ambassador. I have said that the aid afforded was of two kinds. I have described the indirect aid afforded by garrisoning towns

and by similar movements. But I may remind the House that the aid given has not been limited to the thirty mile radius; for two of the towns, which had been garrisoned under the immediate superintendence of General Brown, were at a distance of sixty miles from Shanghai. As an excuse for our officers I must say that the instructions issued have been so complicated and difficult to understand, that I do not wonder that being unable to make out their meaning they should disregard them altogether. There are, for example, two distinct sets of orders respecting officers taking service in China. The officers on half-pay are allowed to take service where and in what manner they like. There is another class of officers taken temporarily from their regiments to discipline the Chinese. They keep their full pay, but they are forbidden to act with the Chinese troops or in the field, so that if an English officer be drilling a body of the Chinese at a barrack or station, and that station be attacked, he is not allowed to lead his men to repel the attack. I undertake to say that these shilly-shally orders must very much hamper our officers, frustrate their operations, and, in some cases, induce them to disobey their instructions altogether. These indefinite orders, and this lax system, must be both detrimental to discipline and demoralizing to themselves. I will now explain to the House what I mean by direct aid. This has been afforded to the Imperialists under Orders in Council, enabling English officers to serve under the Chinese authorities. I may remark that the Order in Council, authorizing British subjects to enlist, has been lately cancelled. I have every desire to speak with the greatest respect of Major Gordon. I particularly wish to ask some questions relating to that officer. I want to know in whose service he is—whether he is in the service of the Emperor of China, or in the service of the Local Governor of the Province of Kiangsu. I find, on the authority of Captain Osborn, that Major Gordon holds no commission from the Emperor of China at all. Is this the case? The question is a very serious one; for to carry on hostilities in a country without the authority of the Sovereign is not war, but murder. Unless he holds a commission from the Emperor of China, the House must form its own conclusion as to what Major Gordon has been doing for so many months. I find, in confirmation of this view, that another officer (Major Cook) commands another contingent at Ningpo, concerning whom Commander Bosanquet lets fall a remarkable expression—namely, "that the sooner he obtained a commission from Pekin the better." I draw the inference that he does not hold a commission at present. I wish the House to listen to the opinion of Sir Frederick Bruce respecting the employment of these officers. He says that the course which we have adopted in giving the Chinese this assistance has been attended with serious embarrassment, arising from jealousies among the different nationalities represented in China, and that the most effectual means of assisting the Chinese is to throw them entirely on their own resources. I now come to a painful part of my task. I ask these two questions. Who are the men with whom, through this remarkable and unprecedented policy, you have associated your officers, and what have been the consequences of so associating them? Captain Osborn thus describes the character of the men in whose service one of them is employed—

"Futai Le is as unprincipled as all Chinese officials; he is squandering the revenue of the province, and is in league with unprincipled traders at Shanghai."

That is a class of men with whom you have associated your officers. And what is the species of war in which you have allowed them to engage? Of all the wars from which a civilized country and a foreign country ought more especially to abstain, a civil war stands foremost. Civil war lets loose the worst elements of society, and arouses the worst and fiercest passions of mankind. In civil war, humanity, justice, right and law are all forgotten. There is an old saying, but a true one, that no man can touch pitch and not be defiled. The result of our policy has been that the names and persons of English officers have been identified with transactions, with scenes, and with deeds, at which English humanity and English honour alike revolt. We have heard something of the siege of Soochow; we have heard an Order in Council cancelled, to punish the Chinese for the murder of 30,000 persons, carried on for a period of twenty days; we have heard the noble Lord at the head of the Government express his regret at the act of perfidy by which the rebel chiefs fell victims to treachery; we must remember that the night preceding the capture of that town,

Mr. Liddell

Major Gordon, with one of the rebel chiefs, concerted a scheme by which the gates were handed over; and we must remember that Major Gordon with his disciplined troops left the town at a critical moment. I do not blame him for what occurred, for his troops being bribed, in all likelihood he was perfectly powerless. But his name is unhappily associated with the perpetrators of these deeds, and I believe that our unhappy connection with the unhallowed proceeding is a retribution upon England for the absence of principle and the abandonment of pledges which for a long time have unfortunately marked our policy in China. I have another miserable event to notice before I sit down. There is in this blue-book an account given of an execution of certain prisoners of war by the Chinese Imperial troops. It is recorded in the papers for which I moved myself, and therefore I am the more justified in referring to it. I will give the simple statement of an eye-witness who saw the transaction. Eight prisoners of war, naked, tied to stakes, were tortured and mutilated, exposed from midday till five o'clock in the afternoon, and afterwards decapitated with a blunt sword. This was witnessed by several officers in Her Majesty's service, and the fact was brought to the notice of the noble Lord at the head of the Foreign Office by the Bishop of Victoria. The noble Lord, of course, ordered a full inquiry into the truth of the statement, and Sir Frederick Bruce says—

"I am inclined to believe that the punishment of death of a slow description has been exceptionally awarded in this instance; and I shall do my best to put a stop to the infliction of this barbarous punishment—though we have to contend with this difficulty, that it has the sanction of the law."

Now, Sir, I am not going to waste the time of the House in any vague declamation upon the horrors of these things. I want the people of England and the House of Commons to know that this is the law of China, and that these are the modes of punishment resorted to by the Chinese soldiery, alongside whom our countrymen are fighting. An Order in Council has been cancelled, we are told, but that will not cancel the memory of these proceedings. The noble lord at the head of the Government has expressed regret at—alas! too late—the horrors of Soochow having taken place; but that will go very little way to remove from the minds of Englishmen the indignation and disgust which the recital of these atrocities has produced. I have alluded to the circumstance of the capture of Soochow for these reasons. Since the debate occurred in this House, two remarkable events have transpired: the Footai, the hero of Soochow, has been held up to public esteem, and has received honour and decorations at the hands of his Sovereign for the part he played in the capture of that place; and, what is still more extraordinary, Major Gordon has returned to the service of the Footai. Now, I wish to ask the Government whether Major Gordon's return to that service has received their sanction. Are we to encourage China in such practices as I have very faintly described, and by the presence of our officers to identify ourselves with the disgrace? What is the government that we are supporting so warmly in China? The Manchou dynasty is a foreign dynasty; it is hated by the people over whom it rules. It was founded some 200 years ago in massacre and violence, and it has been maintained ever since by extortion. Now, does the House know what the system of the public service is in China? Persons selected for the service of the Government are chosen in the first instance by public competition; but the young man whose relatives pay the highest premium is ordinarily the successful candidate. The official salaries are miserably small, and they are absolutely encouraged by the system to eke them out by the sale of justice and the oppression of the people. It is a system of extortion from the highest personage to the lowest. Every official carries out this system in his own department, and thus they amass sums of money, by which they purchase promotion to higher offices, and they at last retire on their ill-gotten gains to spend their old age in debauchery and sensuality. That is no highly-coloured picture, I believe, of the system of public employment in China. Now, can anybody wonder that, under such a system as this, anarchy prevails? Does anybody believe that whatever the amount of military force or foreign aid, there will not be rebellion against a Government which maintains such a system? It is said that the rebellion is on its last legs; but although it may be trampled out, does anyone believe that the Chinese Government can be stable so long as the system of administration exists that I have described. There are elements of anarchy existing in that country, which may at any moment burst into a flame.

Even supposing the Taepings are ejected from their strongholds, the great producing districts of China—the tea and silk districts—are in their hands. They will spread themselves in all probability like a destroying flood over these districts, and they will burn and ravage them as they retreat, and defy the efforts of anyone to prevent them. While these districts have been in their possession, the supplies of silk have been punctual; they have not been interrupted; they have been gradually increasing. We have turned the minds of the Taepings against ourselves. They know perfectly well that if they are ejected from their strongholds it will be by material aid afforded by England to the Imperial forces. They say we have broken our pledge, and that they have fulfilled their obligations to us. It is not improbable that, when deprived of their strong places, they may spread themselves over the tea and silk districts, burning and destroying wherever they go; and, if so, we shall only have our own policy to blame. Now, Sir, I come to the Motion itself before the House. I ask the House to declare that further interference in the war in China is impolitic and unnecessary. I have endeavoured—very inadequately I know—to show that it is impolitic and unnecessary. It is impolitic for the various reasons I have stated, and it is unnecessary because our trade has never been attacked. What I want the House to say is simply this, "We want to trade with China, and China wants to trade with us. If you diplomatists, envoys, and political agents will leave us alone, that trade will go on smoothly and satisfactorily." Now, Sir, I say that the present moment is a turning point in Chinese affairs.

"There is a tide in the affairs of men
Which, taken at the flood, leads on to fortune."

It is the turning-point, because China, having rejected the service of the fleet and the dictatorship of Mr. Lay, having rejected foreign assistance, the Government are enabled to recede from the very difficult and dangerous position they have assumed in China without any appearance of fear, without any sacrifice of prestige (if that word can be applied to any honours we have gained in China), and without any appearance of weakness; and I do implore the House of Commons to make that its policy. I have not asked the House to pass a vote of censure on the Government to-night, though I think—

and I will not blink my opinion—that the policy of the Government has been erroneous in many material respects. I ask the House, by its vote, simply to join with me in dissuading the Government from a further continuance in a course of policy which I believe is unprecedented in the past, and which I trust will find no imitation in the future.

Amendment proposed,

To leave out from the word "That" to the end of the Question, in order to add the words "in the opinion of this House, further interference on the part of this Country in the Civil War in China is impolitic and unnecessary,"—(*Mr. Liddell,*)

—instead thereof.

Question proposed, "That the words proposed to be left out stand part of the Question."

Mr. LAYARD said, that the hon. Member for south Northumberland (Mr. Liddell) had on more than one occasion brought the question of China before the House, and he had done so with considerable ability. He would willingly admit that the opinions of the hon. Member, in consequence of the close study he had given to the subject, well deserved the consideration of the House. The hon. Member had to-night concluded his speech with a Motion, and it was only right that the House should at once be informed of the course which the Government intended to pursue with respect to that Resolution. The forms and rules of the House precluded him from moving the Previous Question, but the Government would support the Motion for going into Committee of Supply, to which the Resolution of the hon. Member might be regarded as an Amendment. They would do so because, whatever the words of the Resolution might be, the intention of the hon. Member, as explained in his speech, was that the policy hitherto pursued by the Government should be reversed, and that a course entirely different should be adopted in its stead. He thought he should be able to show that if such a Motion as that were carried, and a report of the debates of that House went out to China, the effect might be so disastrous that he believed no Government and no House of Commons would take on itself the responsibility of passing such a Resolution. He would now call attention to our position in China. The question was one of enormous importance, and the interests at stake were of vast magnitude.

Mr. Liddell

He knew that in that matter some persons were of opinion that Her Majesty's Government were something like the ogres read of in children's books, who had no other object than to scatter misery and destruction in all directions; and he must say he had read with surprise a speech made to his constituents in the autumn by the hon. Member for Bradford (Mr. W. E. Forster), in which brutality such as made his blood run cold was laid to the charge of the Government, making him almost begin to think that they were as bad as the Taepings. But he appealed to the hon. Gentleman to discuss that subject with him fairly and calmly—to lay aside all the accusations of wilful atrocity, which he had accumulated on the heads of the Ministry, and to look on the question merely as one of policy. The only desire of the Government was that British interests in China should be maintained, and maintained in a manner consistent with right and honour. Many years ago our commerce with China was entirely in the hands of the East India Company. Then those persons who carried on that commerce were under a certain control, their operations were restricted to one port, the trade was limited, and there was no difficulty in dealing with the Chinese Government. That system of monopoly, however, was abolished, the trade was thrown open, and the result was that a large number of adventurers rushed to the East, over whom no control could be exerted. The consequence was that this country was involved in several long and costly wars with China. There ensued, indeed, almost a chronic state of war on our part with China. That position of affairs was brought to an end by the celebrated Treaty of Tien-tsin, or Pekin — the most important instrument ever concluded by this country with any Eastern nation. It completely changed our relations with China. Previously our intercourse had been confined almost entirely to communication with the provincial authorities. When we gained a victory the Central Government was led to believe we were beaten; when we exacted an indemnity, it was told that "the barbarians" had been bribed. But when that treaty was made, we and other European nations were enabled to have a Minister resident at Pekin, and direct relations were opened with the Chinese Central Government. Anybody who read the papers lately laid on the table of the House would be struck with the change that had taken place in that respect. Instead of the former chronic state of war, we were in a state of peace with China such as had been utterly unknown before. We were never more free from war with that country than at the present moment; and the precise relations he had always wished to see established when he sat below the gangway were now carried on, which the hon. Members for Rochdale (Mr. Cobden) and Bradford (Mr. W. E. Forster), ought also to desire to see established—relations which instead of leading us into wars through mere local quarrels, put a stop to wars by placing us in direct diplomatic intercourse with the seat of Government. If we now had any grievances to complain of, instead of hostilities being at once commenced against some local authority, a correspondence passed between Sir Frederick Bruce and Prince Kung, which was carried on almost in the same way as a correspondence between two European Courts. In fact, we treated China almost for the first time as a civilized Government. The Chinese Government itself had now began to see the value and importance of these international communications. He was amused the other day to find that an order was given by Prince Kung for the translation into Chinese of a work on international law, for the use of the Chinese Foreign Office and the benefit of its young diplomatists. That marked an extraordinary change in the relations of Western nations with China, and the rise of a state of things which he had long been anxious to see, because it gave the only hope of maintaining peace with that country. If a tithe of the questions now arising in China had arisen fifteen years ago, they would have produced war upon war with her, whereas they were all settled now by diplomacy. Our great difficulty had been to restrain our consuls and different officials at the ports of that country. He did not wish to cast blame on those gentlemen, who possessed great ability and experience in the public service; but they had been brought up in the old school, and had been in the habit, if they had a grievance, to insist at once on redress, sometimes without a good cause, and without a reference to head-quarters. Sir Frederick Bruce had, however, restrained the consuls in many instances, requiring them to communicate with him, in order that he might make representations, where that course was necessary, to the Court of Pekin. After the Treaty of Tien-tsin

various ports were opened for commerce in China. But it must be remembered that China was in an exceptional position. He did not think that that put her out of the pale of law, or justified them in treating her differently from any other nation; but, after all, they had to deal with an Eastern people, with different laws and a different civilization from our own. The hon. Member said, as was true, that their modes of punishment were barbarous, and such as we could not submit to—that we could not allow British subjects to be cut in two or exposed to torture. Now, a large number of Englishmen and other Europeans had resorted to the treaty ports. These persons had a certain right to the protection of their own country, and claimed to be under its laws rather than under the barbarous laws of China. These claims were to a great extent justified. Out of them arose what was called the extra-territorial jurisdiction in China—that was to say, each of the ports had a settlement beyond the Chinese quarter, in which Europeans lived, and were subject only to the law of their own country, administered by the consuls. Thus sprang up a number of these almost independent settlements; and that system, together with the humiliation which the Chinese Government underwent by wars and by the taking of Pekin, greatly weakened the central authority, and rebellions broke out. One important rebellion was that of the Taepings. He could scarcely call that a civil war. The Taepings were admitted to be a horde of mere marauders by everybody but the hon. and gallant Member for Aberdeen. [Colonel SYKES: No!] Merchants, missionaries, soldiers, sailors, our own consular and diplomatic agents, all parties were agreed as to the fact that the Taepings had no form of government, that they did not aim at establishing any kind of administration, but were a mere set of plunderers, spreading ruin and devastation everywhere they went. There was not a doubt as to that. Having, at last, overrun a large portion of the central provinces, the Taepings came down to the neighbourhood of Shanghai. It was all very well for gentlemen resident at Hong Kong, under the protection of the British fleet and British troops, to pretend to dictate the policy which the Government ought to pursue in regard to Shanghai—a very different place from Hong Kong. But let him quote to the House the opinion expressed by the British subjects living at Shanghai itself on that point. [An hon. MEMBER: How long ago?] He thought it was three years ago. That opinion appeared in a blue-book, laid on the table, he believed, in 1862, and, although it had been cited before, yet so entire a misunderstanding seemed to exist on the subject, that he hoped he might be allowed to read it to the House again. When the Taepings approached the neighbourhood of Shanghai, our merchants there were in the greatest alarm, and the Chamber of Commerce met and passed a series of resolutions. [The hon. Member then proceeded to read the resolutions in question, which declared that the meeting felt strongly the advisability of our Government sending a regular force to protect the residents of the settlement, and prevent the recurrence of panics utterly destructive of trade; that the understood policy of Her Majesty's Government to defend the settlement and city of Shanghai from the rebels had led to a vast accumulation of population and wealth there; that that accumulation of wealth offered a greater temptation to the Taepings to go and plunder the place, more especially after what had happened at Hankow, the rebels being also flushed with the capture of Ningpo; and that the meeting cordially agreed that a considerable permanent addition ought rapidly to be made in the force of troops sent there.] Suppose they had allowed the Taepings to enter Shanghai, the place would have been sacked, trade would have been utterly destroyed, a terrible massacre would have taken place, and the whole Chinese population would have fled. [Colonel SYKES: No!] He would show that presently. But let him ask the House if the Government, notwithstanding the representations of the Chamber of Commerce of Shanghai, of our consuls, of our military and naval authorities, missionaries, and others, had allowed the Taepings to enter Shanghai, and its commerce had been destroyed, what would have been the opinion of the House and the country of the conduct of Her Majesty's Government? One of three things had to be done; to leave the defence of Shanghai in the hands of the Chinese themselves, to defend it with our own troops, or to assist the Chinese by allowing English officers to command and discipline their forces. The Government had to choose one of these three modes of action. To have left Shanghai in the hands of the Chinese

Mr. Layard

would have been virtually to abandon it to the Taepings. Had we taken on ourselves the defence of Shanghai we should have had to maintain an English army in the place, and would not the House have complained had the Government sent more troops there? They took the third course. It was by far the cheapest and most advantageous. They had reduced their troops there to the minimum, and they had encouraged not English officers only, but foreign officers also, to take service under the Chinese, to endeavour to organize and discipline the Chinese troops so as to enable them to defend Shanghai. That was, he contended, a most reasonable policy, and one which was least likely to involve this country either in expense or in embarrassing relations with China. It now became a military question how Shanghai should be defended. It was discussed by Admiral Hope, Brigadier Stavely, and others. It was thought necessary that with regard to Shanghai, but not with regard to all the treaty ports as it had been erroneously alleged, there should be a thirty miles' radius, and instructions, which would be found in the blue-book, were given that British officers should not go beyond that radius. In some instances that radius had been exceeded. In one case General Brown thought it necessary to exceed the thirty miles' radius in order to prevent Shanghai falling into the hands of the rebels. He wrote to this country and gave his reasons, and what did the Government do? They thought the case entirely exceptional, and, in accepting his explanation, they adhered to their orders that the thirty miles' radius should not be exceeded. The instructions were particularly clear. What the Government said was —Officers on half-pay might take service with the Chinese Government, and go beyond the thirty miles' radius; but so long as men were in the service of Her Majesty they should not in any case exceed the thirty miles' radius. No conflicting instructions were given. In order to allow British subjects to take service under the Chinese, Orders in Council were issued. They were issued after mature deliberation, and after taking the advice of Sir Frederick Bruce and the commanding officers, and communicating with other Powers, we decided to allow English officers, men of character and skill, to take charge of the Chinese troops, with the view of enabling them to defend the treaty ports and of exercising some restraint over them, and thus preventing those horrors which it was the custom of Chinese troops, when under the command of Chinese officers, to commit. No doubt there was some inconvenience in allowing British officers to take service under the Chinese Government. That was fully taken into consideration, but it was considered better to encounter that inconvenience, and have the Chinese army well disciplined, than allow that army to be broken up, and let Shanghai fall into the hands of the Taepings. Major Gordon was a very distinguished officer, a man of great ability, and the accounts of what he had done in China were highly creditable to him. He enjoyed the high opinion of Sir Frederick Bruce, not only as a man of ability and skill, but of humanity. He would not go over the history of Soochow. No doubt it was a very horrible case. His noble Friend at the head of the Government had, on a former occasion, condemned it in appropriate terms. In fact, every one who had spoken on the subject had done so. He was not there to justify it. But he must warn the House against exaggerating these things. They had had a recent instance in Japan connected with the bombardment of Kagosima. He was not going to justify the Footai; but the 20,000 said to have been massacred in Soochow proved entirely a myth. The English papers published in China were not remarkable for diminishing the horrors of any event they might have to describe. The first account of this alleged massacre appeared in the Chinese papers, and the *China Mail*, of January 1, within a week after that account had appeared, published the following :—

"Since we wrote last week upon the fall of Soochow further accounts tend to show that the slaughter of the besieged was not carried out to the extent which was on all hands expected. Indeed, from what we can learn, there was little more, comparatively speaking, than a show of bloodshed sufficient to stamp Ching's troops with the character of conquerors. It is not unworthy of notice with regard to the Imperial troops under the Footai that, notwithstanding the number of 'eye witnesses' by which they were constantly surrounded, and the demand which existed in the news market, if we may so speak, for reports about Imperial cruelty, 'sanguinary atrocities,' and so on, no instance of cruelty except that at Taitsan was ever adduced against them ; and in that case the Chinese commander was remonstrated with. . . . . The Footai in the hour of victory certainly forgot himself, and disgracefully broke faith with Major Gordon, but the indiscriminate slaughter of old and young at

first vaguely reported does not prove to have followed as we confess to have expected. There is reason to believe that foreign influence went far to restrain the barbarities of the Imperial troops, and therefore it is advisable that foreign assistance should not too hastily be withdrawn."

The hon. Member had asked what Major Gordon's position was. He continued to act under the Footai, and he must say he did perfectly right. The reasons he gave for doing so entitled him to the highest credit, and justified the good opinion entertained of him by those who knew him. He had remonstrated and protested against the conduct of the Footai, but he felt that if he had, thinking only of his own reputation, and acting upon the first impulse of indignation at the act of treachery that had been committed by his aid, thrown up his command, the troops to a man would have gone over to the Taepings, the Chinese would have been defeated, Shanghai would have been sacked, and an enormous amount of British property would have been destroyed. He determined, therefore, to sacrifice his own feelings rather than sacrifice the interests of his country. He thought that Captain Gordon was quite right in the view he took. The hon. Member had asked what was the position which Captain Gordon now occupied. The answer was that Captain Gordon was no longer in the service of the Chinese Government; because, when Her Majesty's Government learnt the disgraceful act of treachery that had been committed, they immediately repealed the Order in Council which gave permission to British officers to take service under the Chinese Government. His hon. Friend had accused Her Majesty's Government of not only giving the Chinese Government the assistance of British officers, but also of supplying them with arms and ammunition. The fact was that some old stores had been supplied to the Chinese Government, and had been paid for, except a trifling balance, so that there had been no loss to the country on that account. The hon. Member had dwelt at considerable length upon the circumstances attending the expedition of Captain Osborn and his flotilla, but there really was very little in the statement he had made. The British Government had nothing to do with the flotilla, and were not in any way answerable for it; and after the passage which his hon. Friend had quoted from Sir Frederick Bruce's despatch, disclaiming all interference in the matter, and avowing a conviction that the Government at home had not made themselves responsible for the proceedings of the flotilla, it was surprising that any attempt to mix up the British Government in the affair should be persevered in. The real history was that Mr. Lay came to this country stating that he had authority from the Chinese Government, and it was not the business of the British Government to inquire into the nature of the authority. If they had inquired into that and then had said nothing, they would have been told that they had acquiesced in those instructions, and had virtually approved them; but they abstained from all interference. They knew that in the Chinese seas and rivers there were swarms of pirates, which it was for the interest of British commerce should be got rid of; and it appeared that the Chinese Government, instead of relying as heretofore upon the British squadron for that purpose, had determined to obtain a fleet of their own to carry out that object. If they had been able to effect that object, it would have been a great advantage to this country, as it would have relieved our ships from the task of suppressing piracy in the Chinese waters, and the fact that Captain Osborn was to command the squadron was a guarantee that the purpose intended would be attained. Accordingly, Captain Osborn did go out, but when he got to Pekin he found that Mr. Lay had exceeded his instructions and had gone beyond the authority he had received, directly or indirectly, from the Chinese Government. What did Sir Frederick Bruce do then? No one could have behaved with more straightforward candour or with greater impartiality than Sir Frederick Bruce. He determined not to interfere personally in the matter, but requested the United States Minister to settle the question, and to communicate with the Chinese Government. The result was that the negotiations thus carried on were brought to a conclusion without any jealousy having arisen between the English and Chinese Governments. The Chinese Government behaved with great liberality to Captain Osborn and Mr. Lay, but refused to accept the flotilla upon the terms proposed to them, and the ships were sent home to be sold. There was nothing in the whole of these transactions to warrant any condemnation of Her Majesty's Government for the part they had taken, but, on the contrary, Mr. Burlinghame, the United States Minister, spoke in his despatches in the highest

Mr. Layard

terms of the course that had been pursued. Nothing could be more conducive to the maintenance of friendly relations with the Chinese Government, and a good understanding with the representatives of other Powers in China, than the conduct of Sir Frederick Bruce. In one of his despatches Sir Frederick Bruce wrote—

"The belief that I, as British Minister, would respect the rights of the Chinese, and that I would not force the flotilla upon them from selfish political considerations, induced my colleagues to abstain from interfering while the question was under discussion, and thereby secured for the flotilla a deliberate and unfettered consideration on the part of the Chinese Government; and I am certain that this course was more favourable to the success of the scheme, had success been possible, than any other that could have been adopted. It appeared to me, also, that I should not have been justified in taking a more active part, for I had reason to believe that your Lordship had no cognizance of the undertaking of so novel a character entered into by Mr. Lay with Captain Osborn; and the absence of instructions was to me a significant proof that Her Majesty's Government had no intention of being a party to, or responsible for, the arrangements under which the operations of the flotilla were to be conducted."

Nothing could be plainer than these words. The hon. Member had talked about the Government intending to assume a protectorate of China, but the suggestion was really so absurd that it was almost impossible to reply to it in sober seriousness. To talk about intrigues on the part of the British Cabinet to obtain the exclusive control of the Chinese empire was unintelligible, because even if such intrigues could be contemplated they must fail, as the representatives in China of France, Russia, the United States, and other Powers, would exercise a vigilant control to defeat them. Upon that subject, however, he must say a few words more. He had seen an article in a China newspaper alleging that this expedition was a speculation on the part of the British Government, and that Sir Frederick Bruce had endeavoured to force it upon the Chinese Government, who were so indignant that for a whole year Sir Frederick Bruce was not permitted to enter the presence of Prince Kung. Such statements were too ridiculous to need contradiction. But when gentlemen who claimed to be authorities on these subjects signed their names to communications made to the newspapers their statements might require some notice. There was a gentleman not unknown to the world, a professor at Oxford, Mr. Goldwin Smith, who, in a letter to a newspaper, used the following expression:—

" In the case of China a step has been gained, though at the expense of a great dishonour to the nation. The Chinese have detected and frustrated the design of our Government in sending out mercenaries, ostensibly to serve the Emperor of China, but with secret instructions to seize the supreme command. This great England of ours has been placed by her rulers before the world in the position of a pickpocket caught with his hand on a handkerchief, and exposed to the jeerings of the crowd. But the filibustering policy has received a serious check, and the Order in Council inciting British soldiers and seamen in the name of their Sovereign to sell themselves as mercenaries to a barbarian Prince has been withdrawn."

If Mr. Goldwin Smith by a reckless disregard for truth had not reduced his authority to the lowest level, it would be necessary to answer such a statement, coming from a professor of history; but did any hon. Gentleman believe that Captain Osborn went out to China with secret instructions to seize upon the country and to obtain a complete control over it? He was sure that if the hon. Member sat upon the Treasury bench and he were to make such a statement, the impression created would be that the person who uttered it was a fit subject for confinement in Hanwell Asylum. But the truth was that Captain Osborn was in a position to make his own terms, but in a manner becoming a gentleman and a British officer, he abandoned the undertaking, which might have been a source of great profit to himself, and returned to this country. Could any one say that Captain Osborn's conduct had been that of a buccaneer or a filibuster? With regard to Mr. Lay, he did not wish to say anything unfavourable, but he believed that Sir Frederick Bruce was correct in saying that Mr. Lay had exceeded his instructions, and had misunderstood his position. Mr. Lay was a man of great capacity, of large views, and extensive schemes, who had rendered most eminent services to China. His efforts in the revenue department had been exceedingly successful; but, in the present instance, it must be admitted that he had made a mistake. But in that mistake he did not receive the support of the British Minister, and he actually complained that he had not received that support. The policy of the Government had been to avoid all interference in the civil war, if such it could be called, that was going on in China, so long as the combatants did not approach the treaty ports. If the order of the Government had been disobeyed, and our officers had gone beyond the thirty miles radius, it was through

misconception or from special causes, but the Government had never authorized such expeditions. His hon. Friend had not been quite correct in his statements as regards the increase of the silk trade in the districts occupied by the Taepings, because the silk trade had actually fallen off considerably for the last three years, though our trade had increased in almost every other branch to an enormous extent. In Shanghai, in 1845, the imports and exports connected with the British and foreign trade amounted to £2,571,033; in 1850, £7,449,360; 1853, £11,217,420; 1856, £17,911,280; 1860, £23,589,417; 1861, £25,961,019; 1862, £37,531,359. The tonnage of vessels at Shanghai in 1861, inwards and outwards, was 827,000, while in 1862 it had increased to 1,447,000. The results of the general trade at some of the principal ports in China was exhibited in the following figures, representing the imports and exports: — Canton, £6,473,261; Amoy, £1,056,510; Swatow, £1,988,043; Foochowfoo, £5,365,425; Hankow, £6,189,952 (showing an increase of £3,011,482 over previous year); Shanghai, £58,604,550. In addition to these amounts, there had been considerable trade at Tien-tsin and at the other open ports, of which the particulars had not been given. Their imports and exports, however, amounted to £2,341,589; making a grand total, in the general commercial movements of those ports, of £60,946,139. He was afraid lest the statistics might prove wearisome to the House, but they were necessary for the purpose of showing that the policy of the Government had been successful and justifiable, and he was certain that there was not a respectable merchant in China who would not have protested against a reversal of that policy. Sir Frederick Bruce, on the 30th of April, 1863, speaking of Shanghai, said—

" The growth of Shanghai is wonderful; its population is estimated at 1,500,000, and it bids fair to become soon the most important city of the East. The Chinese flock to it on account of the security it enjoys, and the silk manufacture, which was destroyed by the Taeping occupation of Soochow and Hangchow, is taking root at Shanghai. It is a subject of great satisfaction to me that our resolution to save Shanghai from the destruction that menaced it at the hands of the Taeping hordes has not only been productive of great benefit to trade, but has afforded a safe asylum and an escape from ruin to so large a body of the industrious and respectable native population."—*Correspondence* (No. 3) (1864), p. 93.

He believed, therefore, that Her Majesty's Government might fairly take credit for the policy it had pursued with regard to Shanghai. The policy of the United States had been held up for admiration, and recommended to Her Majesty's Government for imitation. He thought it quite fair that our policy should be judged by that of other nations. He would, therefore, read a despatch from Mr. Burlinghame, which would enable the House to see for themselves what the opinion of the American Minister was upon that policy—

" Mr. Burlinghame to Mr. Seward.
" Legation of the United States, Pekin,
" June 20, 1863.

" In despatch No. 18, of June 2, 1862, I had the honour to write ' if the treaty Powers could agree among themselves to the neutrality of China and together secure order in the treaty ports, and give their moral support to that party in China in favour of order, the interests of humanity would be subserved.' Upon my arrival at Pekin, I at once elaborated my views, and found, on comparing them with those held by the representatives of England and Russia, that they were in accord with theirs. After mature deliberation, we determined to consult and co-operate upon all questions. : . . . . In all our conversations Sir Frederick Bruce, with great force, urged the adoption of a co-operative policy in China, and as the representative of the largest trading power here said he was willing to lead in a liberal direction. Indeed, so striking were his views, and so in contrast to what had hitherto been the English policy, and so in accordance were they with the policy strongly urged by me before I came to Pekin, that I expressed a warm desire that he would present them to his Government that they might become the basis of our future co-operation. . . . . Upon this frank avowal of the policy of England, it would be impossible to refuse co-operation. The Russian Minister and myself both concurred in the view that the position of Sir Frederick was just what we desired, and we hailed with delight its avowal. The French Minister, M. Berthemy, agrees with us. Being a broad and experienced statesman, he at once saw the advantages which would flow from the casting down of all jealousies, and by a co-operation on every material question in China. . . . . The policy upon which we are agreed is briefly this—that while we claim our treaty right to buy and sell and hire in the treaty ports, subject in respect to our rights of property and person, to the jurisdiction of our own Governments, we will not ask for nor take concessions of territory in the treaty ports, or in any way interfere with the jurisdiction of the Chinese Government over its own people, nor ever menace the territorial integrity of the Chinese Empire. That we will not take part in the internal struggles in China beyond what is necessary to maintain our treaty rights. That the latter we will unitedly sustain against all who may violate them. To this end we are now clear in the policy of defending the treaty ports against the Taepings, or rebels, but in such a way as not to make war upon

Mr. Layard

that considerable body of the Chinese people by following them into the interior of their country. In this connection, while we feel desirous, from what we know of it, to have the rebellion put down, still we have begun to question the policy of lending Government officers to lead the Chinese in the field, for fear of complications among ourselves, growing out of the relative number to be employed, &c. That while we wish to give our moral support to the Government, at the present time the power in the country which seems disposed to maintain order and our treaty rights, we should prefer that it would organize its own people, as far as possible, for its own defence, taking only foreigners for instruction in the arts of peace and war, and these, as far as possible, from the smaller treaty Powers. To maintain the revenue laws of the Government, to relieve the treaty Powers from the burdens attending the suppression of piracy along the coast, the Chinese Government has been persuaded to purchase several war steamers, and to man them temporarily with foreigners. This fleet is coming out under the command of Sherard Osborn, and is manned chiefly by English sailors, with the understanding that it is a temporary arrangement. . . . . While Sir Frederick Bruce shall remain, or while the policy now agreed upon shall be maintained, no harm can come from it. That the indemnity may be collected and accounted for, and that the Chinese Government may have a fund to maintain a national force, organized upon European principles; that the local authorities may be checked in their corrupt practices, and a uniform system for the collection of the revenue maintained, it is agreed on all hands that the present foreign Custom House system is the best as yet devised, and as it has been administered by Mr. Lay entitled to our support. Indeed, it is alone through such instrumentalities that we can hope to advance the cause of civilization in China."

That was the policy which the English Government had uniformly adopted with reference to China, and it was the policy they were now called upon to reverse. [An hon. MEMBER: No, no!] Hon. Members might say "No," but surely the Government were the best judges and exponents of what their policy was. The hon. Member was mistaken in imagining that the jealousy he had described as being entertained by the representatives of other Powers of the policy of this country really existed in China. It was not true that the merchants in that country were adverse to the policy we had adopted. Mr. Mickie, one of the partners in the well-known firm of Lindsay and Co., a short time since journeyed from Shanghai to England, through China and Russia. Would any Member have ventured ten years ago to predict the possibility of such a journey? The fact, also, that telegraphic communication had been established spoke volumes in favour of the policy of Her Majesty's Government—a policy which he believed would be regarded with favour by every well-wisher of China. When he heard that Mr. Mickie was in this country, he submitted a series of questions to him, and this is what he said in reply—

" I have no reason to think that if the Taepings had taken possession of the treaty ports they would have established order and good government, respected our treaties, or protected our trade. My whole knowledge of the Taepings leads me to an opposite conclusion."

His hon. Friend the Member for Aberdeen (Colonel Sykes) had no personal knowledge of the Taepings, and he hoped he never would.

" Even if they had the will, I esteem them incapable of organizing a civil Government. They have held Nankin for eleven years, with little or no molestation for several years; but it is still only a fortified camp, absolutely without trade or population. The interior of the city is a desert. Having had the privilege of accompanying Admiral Hope in his expedition up the Yang-tze-kiang in 1861, I became acquainted with his views regarding the Taepings. He endeavoured to establish friendly relations with them, and in March, 1861, obtained permission for Lieutenant Colonel Wolsley, Vice Consul Hughes, Rev. Mr. Muirhead, and myself to reside in Nankin for a week, in order to become acquainted with the Taeping chiefs. Colonel Wolsley reported his impressions in his interesting *Narrative of the China War* in 1860. The impressions of Mr. Hughes and myself, and I think also of Mr. Muirhead, are reported in the Parliamentary blue-book of 1861. During the whole of that year Admiral Hope was indefatigable in his endeavours to keep on good terms with the Taepings, and in December he again paid a visit to Nankin, accompanied by Sir Harry Parkes, to remonstrate with the chiefs for the violations of agreements of which they had been guilty. In the same month the treaty port of Ningpo was captured by the Taepings, and I know, by personal conference with Admiral Hope, that up to that time he had not abandoned the idea of giving the Taepings a fair chance of showing their ability and disposition to establish an administration under which it would have been possible to carry on trade. How these experiments failed is well known, and it is a significant fact that Sir James Hope, the last friend the Taepings had among British officers, with the exception of one of our Consuls, who years ago committed himself to Taeping advocacy on theoretical grounds, should have been the first officer who took the responsibility of leading a British force to the field against them, which he did with energy and determination in the spring of 1862."

Now Admiral Hope was a man of the most enlarged and liberal views; he was a most humane man—had no prejudice against the Taepings; and yet he was obliged to give up the Taeping cause and was the first to lead an army against them.

" The course pursued by Sir James Hope towards the Taepings ought to be a convincing proof to impartial minds of the impracticability of maintaining relations with the rebels in China. I need not say that my own opinion on the subject is very strong, and has been for the last five years. I am not aware of any influential firms who were in favour of allowing the Taepings to take possession of any treaty ports, although, no doubt, many were pleased to see Admiral Hope's experiment tried at Nankin and Ningpo. Nor am I aware that any influential firms entered into commercial relations with the Taepings. The agents of European firms who have been engaged in the transport of produce to and from the interior have, no doubt, come into contact with Taeping troops, and have had to negotiate with them for the passage of goods. A certain class of traders have carried on an extensive and lucrative trade with the Taepings in munitions of war. This traffic is considered disreputable. Munitions of war can only be entered by smuggling and making false declarations — for example, gunpowder has been passed through the Custom House under the name of Bibles, and rifles and bayonets under the name of umbrellas; and to disarm the suspicions of the Custom House officers these packages have occasionally purported to be consigned to missionaries and others. For the sake of accuracy I should also mention that some business has been done with the Taepings in opium and cotton goods, and that they have at times had tea and silk to sell, which has either been seized by them or abandoned in terror by the owners. The British merchants most largely connected with China are in favour of the British Government giving such assistance to the Chinese Government as will enable them to keep the Taepings out of the treaty ports; nor do I think there is any difference of opinion as to the advisability of pushing our assistance to the ultimate crushing of the rebellion. The *modus operandi* may have been questioned, and I know some merchants have considered that the Government might with advantage have gone a step further than it has done. But all feel and acknowledge the difficulty and delicacy of the position. The suppression of the rebellion would be deemed an inestimable blessing by all—natives and foreigners; and if peace again reigns in China the means of access we now possess to the interior of the country, and the amount of European enterprise that is in readiness to be let loose, would inaugurate an era of commercial expansion that would be without parallel in history. I do not think there are any merchants of influence in China who would like to see the Government withdraw all assistance from the Chinese, for that would cause anarchy. The great majority, however, have been in favour of the plan pursued, as being the most economical to this country and the soundest in policy, not compromising the British Government more than necessary, and teaching the Chinese to help themselves. It would be disastrous to British trade in China to withdraw from relations with the Chinese Government, and disastrous alike to the Chinese Government and people. It would be a breach of faith with all the merchants and others who have invested large sums in China on the faith of treaties and permanent relations with China. The employment of officers of rank and character has, moreover, done more than anything else to check the rise of that dangerous class of military adventurers in China. The Chinese Government will certainly employ foreigners of some sort, and. in the absence of anything better they will accept men of the worst characters. Our commerce with China has increased, and is increasing, under the policy at present pursued by our Government. I doubt if it would have improved more under any other policy. That our trade has increased at all under the incubus of the rebellion, I take to be an earnest of what it may grow to when that incubus is removed."

He took that reply to be the most remarkable and complete testimony that could be given of the success of the policy pursued by Her Majesty's Government coming as it did from the representative of one of the most eminent firms engaged in the China trade. But the Government were now asked to reverse that policy. Well, then, what policy was to be put in its place? They had heard lately that it was not for the Opposition to suggest a policy. It was very easy to criticize and protest; but if the Government had done wrong, they who said so were bound to point it out, and show how they could set themselves right. But he had not heard any suggestions of that kind. The opponents of the policy pursued by the Government in China would not, he presumed, admit the Taepings into the treaty ports; would they ask the Government to do so? He had heard that the hon. Member for Rochdale (Mr. Cobden) said we ought to withdraw from China altogether, establishing ourselves in islands along the coast, or establishing trading factories, and allowing our people to trade at certain fixed stations. He had asked a member of one of the largest Chinese firms if that policy were possible, and what would be the result, and that gentleman replied that the merchants would at once invest £100,000 in well armed steamers, which would engage in smuggling, and would carry on their trade by force. A paper has been actually established at Shanghai, called the *Chinese Recorder*, and paid in order to advocate the policy that each merchant should be allowed to make his own arrangements with the Chinese authority on the spot, and should only pay such duties as the latter agreed to take—he having, of course, been bribed—and that there should be no diplomatic relations between this country and China. He would not trouble the House to read the answer which had been published in the *China Mail*; it was to be found in the blue-book; but that answer was so complete that it led, he believed, to the suppression of the *Chinese Recorder*.

Mr. Layard

The *China Mail* showed that that policy would lead to a system of buccaneering along the coast, that the large firms would purchase vessels of the kind required, that the very small firms would fail, and that the result would be to involve us in a war with China. No Gentleman in that House would recommend such a course of action, or say that we ought to reverse a policy which, like all other things, had faults, but which on the whole had been attended with the most striking success. He had shown how the most marvellous superstructure of trade had been raised upon that policy —a general trade amounting to something like £60,000,000, most of which was carried on by British subjects. Another policy might be successful; but it might also fail to succeed; and no Government would take upon itself the responsibility of reversing their system merely upon a theory brought forward by an hon. Member who could not have materials at hand to form a correct judgment. The policy of Her Majesty's Government had been approved by merchants in the East; it had been approved by missionaries, by naval and military authorities, by Sir Frederick Bruce, and by Mr. Burlinghame, and he trusted it would receive the approval of the House. If it had been in his power he would have moved the Previous Question, but as he was not able to do so, he thought the best way of meeting the Motion of the hon. Member, since he could not agree to it, was to conclude by moving that Mr. Speaker do leave the Chair.

MR. W. E. FORSTER said, that in his opinion the hon. Member the Under Secretary for Foreign Affairs (Mr. Layard), had not met this question at all. There was no one who thought we ought to withdraw protection from our trade in China. The Question before the House was whether they should sanction the interference of the Government in the civil war in China for the purpose of putting down the rebellion? His complaint was that the policy of the Government was not a fair policy as regarded that House. In the debate of last year a question was raised whether Her Majesty's Government intended to interfere for the purpose of putting down the rebellion, and reference was made to the movements of the flotilla. The hon. Under Secretary for Foreign Affairs, however, met that question by observing that Her Majesty's Government had done no more in China than they had done for Russia and Turkey. He contended that the steps taken by this country in respect to China constituted as complete a breach of the principle of neutrality as had ever been committed by any nation. We departed from our professed principles of neutrality in the beginning of 1862. Up to that period Sir Frederick Bruce in his despatches expressed the opinion that any interference on behalf of the Chinese Government would be as impolitic as a war for conquest would be hopeless. Subsequently a change came over his mind when he observed the successes of the disciplined Chinese force under the direction of Mr. Warde. Sir Frederick Bruce then wrote to express his hopes in the success of the Chinese Government. In consequence of the receipt of that letter, Earl Russell wrote back to Sir Frederick Bruce, saying that the rational course for us to pursue was to defend our own trade. He agreed in that. The noble Earl went on to add, "to protect the treaty forts." He thought that that might be open to doubt, but that was not the question now. And, continued the noble Earl, "to encourage the Chinese Government to raise such a force as would be sufficient to overcome the rebels, and to reduce them to subjection." Now, that was what the Under Secretary for Foreign Affairs called following the principles of neutrality. The noble Earl went on to say, "Should this plan fail, grave questions may arise, which it is not necessary to enter upon now." He thought that this plan had failed, and that graver questions had arisen. The hon. Member the Under Secretary wrote a letter to the Admiralty and a similar one to the War Office, in which he said he was directed by Earl Russell to transmit copies of despatches relative to the measures to be taken against the Taepings, and which had been approved of by Her Majesty's Government; and that was what was called neutrality. The noble Earl even went so far as to express a hope that a disciplined force would be sent out to China to co-operate with the Imperialist troops. [Mr. LAYARD: Hear, hear!] He hoped that as the hon. Under Secretary had sanctioned the suggestion, that some work upon international law should be translated into Chinese for the benefit of the Chinese Government, that he would send out a volume of international law, with his version of the word "neutrality" for their benefit.

Her Majesty's Government had sanctioned the principle of our officers enlisting in the service of the Chinese Government, and they had enabled the Imperial Government thus to obtain arms and ammunition which they could not otherwise have procured. But the hon. Under Secretary said that we had nothing to do with this Anglo-Chinese force, which was led by our own officers. What did the blue-book say? General Brown stated that after the death of General Burgevine he had appointed Captain Holland in temporary command of those forces. His hon. Friend said that we had nothing at all to do with, nor were we responsible for, the acts of those men. But we had always that respect for British officers, that when we found them in a difficulty we felt ourselves bound to get them out of it. They had got into such a position in Soochow in consequence of the Chinese General forgetting himself, as his hon. Friend called it, and committing the most barbarous slaughter. And what followed? Why, at a meeting held at the British consulate in China, and at which all the consuls attended, General Brown made a speech, telling all the European officers that Major Gordon was so connected with him as a British officer, that he could not do less than give him his best support. Now, it was impossible in time of war to give material assistance, and the use of British officers and skill, without being responsible. They could not carry on war without suffering the consequences. That policy was tried as regarded the flotilla. When this question was raised, the hon. Member stated that that naval force was intended to put down piracy, and for that object almost alone. He would remark upon the words "almost alone." Before that time a memorandum had been sent by Mr. Lay to Earl Russell, describing what were the real objects of that flotilla. Mr. Lay said that they were twofold: the first and most prominent was to establish the Imperial authority upon the Yang-tse, and commercial security upon the inner waters. Now, that was the precise sort of intervention which we ought not to have been party to. That was the first object. The next object was stated to be to suppress piracy between the open ports. It was evident from this memorandum, that the first and foremost object of the flotilla was to re-establish the Imperial authority over the rebels. He would say, in addition to that, that his hon. Friend ought to have been aware of the conditions entered into between Mr. Lay and Captain Osborn. He contended that Her Majesty's Government ought not to have allowed such a breach of neutrality, such a violation of the Foreign Enlistment Act, as was involved in the sailing of a flotilla from England for the avowed purpose of putting down an extensive rebellion, without being aware of all the conditions laid down by a distinguished officer of their own service, whom they had allowed to go out to China in command of this flotilla. That officer even went out with the blessing given him by the Chancellor of the Exchequer at a meeting of the Royal Geographical Society. His hon. Friend said it was unfair to charge the Government with the design of making Mr. Lay a dictator of China. He charged them with great negligence in not making themselves aware of that which they ought to have known must have been the result. If Captain Osborn and Mr. Lay had agreed to carry out that memorandum, he should like to know what other result could be looked for than that Mr. Lay would become the dictator of China. Prince Kung did not suppose that the flotilla had come out to China for the purpose of putting down piracy alone. It was evident that that Prince looked forward to the flotilla as a means of sweeping away the rebellion. Now, an English fleet, commanded by an English officer and manned by British sailors, could not make themselves masters of China without the English Government being from first to last responsible? It was not a question whether we should remain in the treaty ports, it was a question whether we should interfere in this war. He did not wish to use a harsh expression, but he thought that the word "filibustering" might be appropriately applied to such interference. He did not apply that epithet to Captain Osborn, whose conduct had been most noble and honourable throughout. He resisted great temptations, and by his honest and noble conduct he saved the country from the consequences of a false position, in spite of the Government which had sent him out, and such a result they would have rued for years to come. The Government were aware of the theory upon which this affair was conducted. How did Mr. Lay conclude the memorandum which he had sent to Earl Russell? He ended that memorandum by saying that it would in no way compromise Her

Mr. W. E. Forster

Majesty's Government, while it possessed at the same time all the advantages without the inconveniences of war. He submitted that they could not have the advantages without the inconveniences of war. If they attempted to give material assistance to any Power, they must be prepared to take all the consequences following such an act. They now wanted to know whether this policy was or was not to go on. The time had come when graver questions had occurred. The policy of Her Majesty's Government had failed; it failed in the case of Major Gordon and in that of Captain Osborn, when he found he could not put himself in communication with the central authority. Therefore he wanted to know whether the Government would go on with this system of intervention and of making private war? They were not now deciding whether they would withdraw from Shanghai or not. His hon. Friend said that there had been no interference in the civil war, except so far as to protect Shanghai. He asked whether Soochow was taken in order to protect Shanghai? It could not possibly have been taken except by the assistance of those officers who were sent out to China, in violation of our professed neutrality. It could not have been taken, except by those officers, for whom General Brown said he made himself responsible, and over whom General Brown had appointed a commander. His hon. Friend quoted the American minister's despatch of the 20th June last year, in support of his view. But there was a long despatch from Mr. Burlinghame, of the 23rd June, in which he stated that the encouragement of foreigners to take part in the war in China was a policy of the grossest injustice to the Chinese, and such as would be likely to cause dangerous complications amongst the Europeans. It was clear from this despatch that Mr. Burlinghame saw the danger of the policy of interference, and, therefore, instead of quoting him in favour of the view taken by the hon. Member, he was an authority totally opposed to it. He granted them that there might be an argument made for the conquest of China. They might be tempted thereto by ambition or interest—but there might, perhaps, be a stronger motive than either actuating Her Majesty's Government. He thought it was impossible, looking back to our connection with that country, not to see that we were possibly in a great measure the cause of the anarchy which at present existed in China. He thought that the noble Lord at the head of the Government could not look back to our relations with China— to the horrible accounts of war and the ravages caused by war — without feeling some regret that the policy which he had so energetically pursued had very possibly been the means of weakening the authority of the Central Government in China, and of causing the rebellions that took place in consequence. Having done that harm to the Chinese people, the noble Lord might well think he ought now to use all his efforts towards the restoration of order. If he could do that, even with some cost of British blood and life, he might say that it was his urgent duty to do so. But this was too great a business for us to undertake. We could not take China upon our backs. The hon. Member said that, as regarded China, we were in a better position now than we were before. It was true that we were at peace with the Chinese Government, but we were not at peace with the Chinese people. No Government could face the country with the idea of making a conquest of China. Then, he said, that the question must be conquest or non-intervention. They could not choose between the two. If they sought to gain the advantages without the inconveniences of war, the result would be they would have all the evils of a distant war, whilst they would be deluding and misleading their own people.

Mr. FERRAND said, he agreed with the hon. Member for Bradford (Mr. W. E. Forster) that the noble Lord at the head of the Government must experience some pain at what had taken place that night, when he considered how he himself must be identified with the policy which we had pursued towards China since 1832. He had heard the noble Lord protest, in eloquent and indignant language, against the atrocities perpetrated in Europe by military despotism; but he (Mr. Ferrand) doubted whether in the whole of Europe, during the last twenty-five years, atrocities had been perpetrated by any European authority to equal those which had been perpetrated in China under the government and instigation of the noble Lord. Atrocities had been perpetrated in the East which neither the British Government nor any other Government would dare to perpetrate in Europe. The noble Lord not long ago denounced the atrocities perpetrated in Poland, and the

Foreign Minister declared in another place that the Almighty would not suffer these atrocities to pass unpunished. But the time had now arrived for the House of Commons and this country to inquire whether the atrocities perpetrated in Poland by Russian authorities, or in Denmark by Prussia and Austria, had been equalled by the atrocities perpetrated in China by the British army. We had heard a great deal about the bombardment of Sönderborg, but Her Majesty's Government had acted in a far worse manner in China. He thought it was in 1837 that the Earl of Carlisle, then the representative of the West Riding, at a meeting at Leeds, boasted that the Whigs in 1833 had opened the trade of China without shedding one drop of blood. From 1834 to 1839 the noble Viscount himself tacitly encouraged the opium trade in China, which led to a state of chronic war, lasting up to the present time. From 1834, at which time the noble Lord commenced the persecution of the Chinese Government, for the purpose of forcing them into a war, our policy towards China had been unjust, cruel, and dishonourable. The Whigs and the noble Viscount himself were answerable to this country for the present state of affairs in China. The Conservatives, both in opposition and in office, had opposed their policy, and warned them of its fatal results, but in vain. The noble Viscount and his Government were frequently implored to treat the Chinese with mercy and consideration. Our navy and army were repeatedly engaged in bloody wars in China —wars from which many of our officers had shrunk, and in describing which even our private soldiers, in their letters written home, said they felt disgraced and degraded for having taken such a part against the Chinese. In spite of the advice of the most eminent statesmen of the day they had gone headstrong into that policy, and had brought England into disgrace. In 1840, when a debate took place on the policy of Her Majesty's Government, and more especially on the conduct of the noble Lord at the head of the Government, Sir James Hogg, a man who had lived for many years in the East, and who was thoroughly acquainted with China, expressed his fears that the confidence of the population of China would be shaken in the government of that country, and that the most disastrous consequences would result. The late Sir Robert Peel foretold that state of things which the hon. Member for North

Northumberland had described that evening, though the Under Secretary for Foreign Affairs had ridiculed the statement. The policy of the noble Lord in China had been condemned, not only by hon. Members on both sides of the House, but it was disapproved of by the country generally. The late Sir Robert Peel prayed to God to avert from China the calamities that would fall upon it from our policy, and turn from this country those evils which, by the neglect and incapacity of our rulers, it had most righteously deserved. But it had not been as the right hon. Baronet wished. The right hon. Gentleman, the present Chancellor of the Exchequer, also in the course of a speech delivered by him in condemnation of the noble Lord's conduct towards China, had charged him with having waged a most unjust and iniquitous war in that country. As the Under Secretary for Foreign Affairs had attempted to gloss over our conduct in China with reference to these wars, he should like to give a brief sketch of some of our warlike proceedings in that country, and he pledged himself to prove that, however cruel Russia had acted towards Poland, and however cruel Prussia and Austria had acted within the last few months towards Denmark, that our conduct as a nation, under the direction and guidance of the noble Lord, had been ten times worse in China.

Notice taken, that 40 Members were not present; House counted, and 40 Members not being present,

House adjourned at a quarter after Eight o'clock till Monday next.

HOUSE OF LORDS,

Monday, April 25, 1864.

MINUTES.]—PUBLIC BILLS—*Second Reading*—Warehousing of British Spirits * (No. 46).
Select Committee — On Insane Prisoners Act Amendment, *nominated* (see p. 3).
Third Reading — The Consolidated Fund (£15,000,000) *, and *passed*.

Their Lordships met; and having gone through the business on the paper, without debate,

House adjourned at half past Five o'clock, till To-morrow, half past Ten o'clock.

Mr. Ferrand

HOUSE OF COMMONS,

Monday, April 25, 1864.

MINUTES.] — SELECT COMMITTEE — On Bankruptcy Act, *nominated* (see p. 1482).
WAYS AND MEANS—*Resolution* [April 21] *reported*.
PUBLIC BILLS — *Ordered* — Court of Chancery (Ireland).
First Reading—Court of Chancery (Ireland) * [Bill 78].
Second Reading — Customs and Inland Revenue [Bill 73]; Thames Conservancy [Bill 60]; Partnership Law Amendment [Bill 68].
Committed to Select Committee—Thames Conservancy.
Committee—Civil Bill Courts (Ireland) *re-committed* [Bill 79]; Court of Chancery (Despatch of Business) (*Lords*) * [Bill 69]; Charitable Assurances Enrolments (*Lords*) * [Bill 72].
Report—Civil Bill Courts (Ireland) *; Court of Chancery (Despatch of Business) *; Charitable Assurances Enrolments (*Lords*) *.
Withdrawn— Penal Servitude Acts Consolidation * [Bill 23].

ADMIRALTY COURT (IRELAND).

QUESTION.

MR. MAGUIRE said, he wished to ask Mr. Attorney General for Ireland, Whether the Report of the Royal Commissioners with respect to the Irish Admiralty Court has been received by the Government; and, if so, when the promised Bill for the re-constitution of that Court will be introduced?

MR. O'HAGAN said, in reply, that the Report of the Commissioners had not yet been laid before the Government, but there had been a final meeting of the Commissioners, and he hoped their Report would be such an one as might be acted upon.

MAIL PACKET CONTRACTS—THE WEST INDIA COLONIES.—QUESTION.

MR. CAVE said, he wished to ask the Secretary to the Treasury, Whether he will lay upon the table, in order to complete the Papers already promised, the communication stated by him to have been sent from the Treasury to the West India Colonies two years ago, apprising them that they would be called upon to contribute to the new Mail Packet Contract, as well as any Replies received from them thereto; and whether similar notices were sent to those Foreign Countries and Colonies whose Mails are conveyed under the same Contract?

MR. PEEL was understood to state that he had no objection to the production of any papers on the subject which might be required.

GENERAL GARIBALDI — MEETING ON PRIMROSE HILL.—QUESTION.

MR. HARVEY LEWIS said, he wished to put a question, of which he had given notice, to the Secretary of State for the Home Department with reference to a meeting held on Primrose Hill on Saturday last, which had been dispersed in a very summary manner. He wished to know, Whether the right hon. Baronet had given any and what instructions to the Police to disperse the meeting over which Mr. Edmund Beales presided ; and, if he had not given such instructions, whether he has inquired into the circumstances, and will state the result of his inquiries to the House ?

SIR GEORGE GREY said, he had to state, in answer to the Question of his hon. Friend, that neither he nor any Member of the Government, nor the Commissioner of Police, had given any special instructions to the Police to interfere with the meeting held on Primrose Hill on Saturday. Indeed, he never heard of such a meeting being held there till yesterday morning, but the facts he had ascertained to be these :—The First Commissioner of Works had given his sanction to the holding of a meeting in connection with the Shakspeare Commemoration, for planting a tree on Primrose Hill, and at his suggestion the Commissioner of Police had made arrangements for the attendance of a certain number of Police to prevent obstructions and preserve order. After planting the tree, a person was moved into the chair, and another got upon a bench to address the meeting on a different subject; on which an Inspector of Police went up to him and requested to be allowed to speak to him. The person came down, when the Inspector told him he could not be allowed to hold the meeting there. A short conference took place. There was no violence whatever ; the people quietly dispersed, and the meeting was adjourned till another time and place. He ought to state that, owing to the scenes which some time since had taken place owing to meetings held in Hyde Park, a notice was issued forbidding all assemblages of persons in any of the Parks for the purpose of delivering speeches or discussing exciting topics leading to disorder, such meetings being wholly incon-sistent with the object for which the Parks were thrown open to the public. The Inspector of Police, therefore, acted on no special instructions, but may have thought he was acting in the spirit of that notice when he requested the meeting to disperse. There was not the slightest appearance of tumult or disorder; and although, under the circumstances, it might have been as well to have allowed the meeting to have continued, yet the Inspector may have supposed he acted under general instructions in not allowing the meeting to be held without special authority.

GENERAL GARIBALDI AND ADMIRAL MUNDY.—EXPLANATION.

MR. CAVENDISH BENTINCK said, he rose to make a personal explanation. In the observations which fell from him the other night on the Motion of the hon. Member for Liskeard (Mr. Bernal Osborne) he made a statement which might possibly do injustice to a distinguished and gallant officer, Admiral Mundy. On that occasion he stated that if General Garibaldi was to be believed his success in Sicily was owing to the material assistance which he received from Admiral Mundy. That was stated in the newspaper report, and it was a fair illustration of the argument that ho used. However, as he had since ascertained that there was not a syllable of truth in the assertion of General Garibaldi, it was only right that he should state his sincere conviction that Admiral Mundy neither directly or indirectly interfered so as to commit a breach of neutrality, and that when ho received General Garibaldi on board his flag ship in the harbour of Palermo, he did so at the request of General Lanza, the royalist commander. Afterwards Admiral Mundy made prisoners of the Garibaldian pirates who had seized the British ship *Orwell*, and sent them to Malta, where they were released most illegally by the authorities there.

WAYS AND MEANS.

Resolution [April 21] *reported.*

SIR JOHN PAKINGTON said, he rose to put a Question—

MR. SPEAKER said that, according to the rules of the House, the Question must refer directly to the Resolution itself.

SIR JOHN PAKINGTON said, he proposed to make some observations with reference to Supply.

MR. ROEBUCK said, he wished to know what the Resolution was about. He had not been able to hear a word of it as read, and he did not think any other Member had been able to collect its purport.

MR. SPEAKER read the Resolution—

" That, in lieu of the yearly per-centage Duty now chargeable for or in respect of any Insurance from loss or damage by Fire only, which shall be made or renewed on or after the 25th day of June, 1864, of or upon any Goods, Wares, or Merchandise, being stock in trade, or of or upon any Machinery, Fixtures, Implements, or Utensils used for the purpose of any manufacture or trade, there shall be charged and paid yearly a Duty at and after the rate of one shilling and sixpence per annum for every £100 insured ; and when any such Insurance as aforesaid shall be made or renewed at any time between the 22nd day of April, 1864, and the said 25th day of June, for any period of time extending beyond the said last-mentioned day, there shall be charged and paid for and in respect of the time intervening between the making or renewing of the said Insurance and the said 25th day of June, the yearly per-centage Duty at and after the rate chargeable on the said 22nd day of April, and for and in respect of any subsequent period, including the said 25th day of June, the rate of Duty chargeable according to this Resolution ; and no return or allowance of Duty, except at and after the last-mentioned rate, shall be made in respect of time unexpired, or otherwise, on any such Insurance as aforesaid, which shall have been made or renewed before the said 22nd day of April, 1864."

LORD ROBERT CECIL said, he wished the right hon. Gentleman would have the goodness to state what was the precise rule of the House to which he referred when he informed the hon. Baronet that ho must confine himself to the Question that the Resolution be agreed to. It would be convenient to know whether they could not discuss grievances before they voted the money.

MR. SPEAKER : In order that every opportunity might be afforded to hon. Gentlemen to speak on the subject, I delayed in rather an unusual manner in putting the Question. The rule of the House is this:— On the Report of Supply, the Question is, " That this Resolution be read a first time." Then, " That it be read a second time." When the Question is put that the Resolution be read a second time, it is open to any hon. Member to make any observations he may think necessary. I do not know if any hon. Member observed it, but I rather paused in putting the Question that the Resolution bo read a second time. No hon. Member rising to make any observations, the rule of the House is, that when the Resolution is read a second time, and tho Question is that the House do agree

Sir John Pakington

to the said Resolution, no observations may be made of a general nature, but they must refer to the Resolution under discussion.

Resolution *agreed to.*

CUSTOMS AND INLAND REVENUE BILL.

[BILL 73.] SECOND READING.

Order for Second Reading read.

THE CHANCELLOR OF THE EXCHEQUER said, he rose to move that this Bill be read a second time. He would take that opportunity of giving the information sought the other evening by the hon. Baronet the Member for Ayrshire (Sir James Fergusson), with regard to the estimated value of the new assessment for Income Tax. The hon. Baronet was under the impression that no allowance was made for that new assessment ; but that was not so. The new assessment under Schedules A and B, which took place in 1857, exhibited an increase of £12,000,000 over that for 1856 in the amount of property and profits charged to duty ; the new assessment for 1861 exhibited an increase of £9,000,000 over that for 1860. It might fairly be presumed, therefore, that a new assessment for 1864 would result in an increase of at least £9,000,000 under those schedules over those for 1863, which at the rate of 6d. per pound would produce £210,000 on the year's assessment, and in the financial year 1864-5 about £140,000. To the increase under Schedules A and B was to be added the improvement that might be reckoned upon under Schedule D; and as the assessment for 1862 over that for 1861 at like rates showed an increase of £100,000, and the assessment for 1863 over that for 1862, corrected to 7d., an increase of £110,000, it had been assumed that the profits of trade in the assessment for 1864 would yield a further increase of £90,000, which would produce in the financial year 1864-5 about £50,000. The total estimated produce of the new assessment for 1864 was, therefore, £190,000. In Committee upon the Bill he should move to insert the Resolution which had been agreed to by the House relating to Fire Insurances, and he should also move to insert certain clauses referring to Fire Insurances which he would lay upon the table that evening. He should also move in the licences to be granted to the sellers of tea to strike out altogether the words, " and not being within the limits of any municipal or parliamentary borough." In accordance with a suggestion from some other hon. Members, he would also move to enlarge the words to describe the bodies at whose meetings proxies might be used. He also intended to move a formal clause relating to a standard of sugar. The hon. and learned Member for Wallingford had called his attention to a point connected with the stamp duties upon policies of insurance under settlement, and he had made a provision which he thought was a liberal one. In cases where the payment of the premiums upon a policy of insurance was secured by a covenant on the settlement, then the sum secured would be taken to be the property liable to the stamp duty.

Moved, "That the Bill be now read a second time." — (*Mr. Chancellor of the Exchequer.*)

MR. MALINS said, he thought that upon the last point which he mentioned the Chancellor of the Exchequer might very properly make a further concession. It was a common thing for a husband to make a marriage settlement, a policy of insurance upon his life being the subject of the settlement. Supposing the case of a policy of insurance of £10,000 being so settled, upon which only one premium, amounting perhaps to £100, had been paid, it would be a hardship to call upon the settler to pay an *ad valorem* upon the whole amount as though it were £10,000 in money or Consols. The concession offered by the Chancellor of the Exchequer would be but a little relief, as in nearly all marriage settlements conveying policies of insurance there were covenants to pay the premiums. It was generally felt that it was a hardship to enforce the *ad valorem* duty in cases of policies of insurance, and he therefore hoped that if he gave notice of a Motion to omit the words "policies of assurance" from the clause he should have the support of the right hon. Gentleman.

THE ATTORNEY GENERAL said, that as the law stood, if a settlement contained a provision that after the death of the settler a given sum of money should be paid to a certain person, and if the sum of money so covenanted to be paid was settled, then it paid the stamp duty upon the amount settled. If in order to insure the payment of the sum by the Insurance Office a covenant to pay the premiums was inserted in the settlement, there was no difference in principle between the two cases.

SIR WILLIAM JOLLIFFE said, there was another important subject to which he wished to call the attention of the Chancellor of the Exchequer, namely—licences for the sale of intoxicating liquors. Of late years legislation upon that subject appeared to have diverged further and further from the principles which had been laid down by Committees which had considered the question. In 1850, twenty years after the passing of the Beer Bill of 1830, a Committee of the House of Lords, after an elaborate inquiry, recommended that beer licences and spirit licences should, as was formerly the case, be included in one form of licence. In 1854 a Committee of the House of Commons made a similar recommendation, and added that licences should be granted by the magistrates. All recent legislation had been in a diametrically opposite direction, and year by year had tended to put licences under the Excise, while the influence of the magistrates was becoming less and less; and in the Bill before them provision was made for occasional licences which were to be granted by the Excise authorities quite independent of the magistrates. From his own experience he could speak of a practice which especially prevailed in the counties adjoining the metropolis. When the beer licence was obtained the house for which it was granted was fitted up as a gin palace in a most expensive manner. That expense was incurred not solely for the purpose of attracting custom, but also with a view to influence the magistrates when applied to for a spirit licence by an appeal to the excellent accommodation provided. Those houses were usually built by brewers and distillers, who spared no expense to obtain the licence, which would be of much benefit to them, as when a licence was granted the rent was immediately enhanced. If that system were to continue it would be as well to consider whether the State might not derive some advantage from it, and, therefore, he would submit to the Chancellor of the Exchequer whether he could not deal with the whole subject of licences upon the consumption of intoxicating liquors, and establish a uniform licence whereby the State would be a gainer.

SIR GEORGE GREY was understood to say that the Bill merely recognised the existing licences, giving the owner power under certain restrictions of having occasional licences. But the points raised by the hon. Gentleman could be discussed with more advantage in Committee.

SIR MINTO FARQUHAR said, he thought that the stamp duty on marriage settlements ought not to be charged at the same rate upon realized property, and which would accrue from a Life Insurance policy.

MR. THOMSON HANKEY said, he had understood the right hon. Gentleman the Chancellor of the Exchequer to say, that there would be no extra duty imposed by the Bill under the consideration of the House. He found, however, that on orders of all kinds for receiving money, stocks, shares, or any property partaking of the character of stocks, there was to be a duty of 5s. He did not object to such a proposal, but merely called the attention of the right hon. Gentleman to it. At present he believed it was the practice with dock companies, some railways, and a great many public companies, to issue merely written letters authorizing parties to receive dividends on stocks. He believed that the arrangement proposed by the Bill would be fair, but he thought that the matter was hardly understood by the public.

SIR JAMES FERGUSSON said, he would remind the right hon. Gentleman that he had not carried out his promise, that under Schedules A and B the assessment was to be made by Inland Revenue officers, instead of by the local assessors. He thought that the burdens of the Income Tax would be considerably mitigated if the Government availed themselves of the services of the local assessors, instead of permitting the Inland Revenue officers to do the work.

THE CHANCELLOR OF THE EXCHEQUER said, he could not speak again, but he believed that he should be able to satisfy the hon. Baronet at a future stage of the Bill.

Motion *agreed to*.

Bill read 2° accordingly, and *committed* for *Thursday*.

CIVIL BILLS COURT (IRELAND) BILL.

[BILL 79]—(*re-committed*)—COMMITTEE.

Bill *considered* in Committee.

(In the Committee.)

MR. O'HAGAN (THE ATTORNEY GENERAL FOR IRELAND) explained the nature of some changes that had been made in the Bill. They had intended to make the Sub Sheriffs the officers of the court, but on consulting with the grand juries it was considered by them and by the High She-

Sir George Grey

riffs themselves that the duties should be performed by the High Sheriffs. They had altered the Bill, therefore, in that respect.

Clauses 1 and 2 *agreed to*.

Clause 3 (Interpretation of Terms).

MR. TORRENS proposed to insert words for the purpose of re-constituting the Civil Bill Court in Carrickfergus.

MR. O'HAGAN said, there was no necessity for the Amendment, because the Lord Lieutenant had already the power under the Civil Bill Act, 15 *Vict.* c. 57, of re-constituting the court of Carrickfergus.

MR. TORRENS said, that he would withdraw his Amendment, on the understanding that the right hon. and learned Gentleman would represent to the Lord Lieutenant the hardship of the case of Carrickfergus.

Amendment, by leave, *withdrawn*.

Clause *agreed to*.

Clauses 4 to 36 *agreed to*.

Clause 37 (Power to refer Matters of Account).

MR. SCULLY said, he objected to the power proposed by the clause to be given to County Court Judges to force arbitration upon suitors. He should move the omission of the clause.

Clause *withdrawn*.

Remaining clauses *agreed to* :—Schedules *agreed to*.

MR. LONGFIELD moved, after Clause 5, to insert the following clause :—

> The chairman shall have power to fine any of the bailiffs appointed to execute civil bill decrees for neglect or misconduct in a sum not exceeding five pounds, to be levied by distress on his goods and chattels.

—*agreed to*.

MR. BUTT moved, after Clause 8, to insert the following clause :—

> (Sheriff may issue a special warrant.)
> Provided always, That if at any time the sheriff shall in his discretion think fit that in any case any other person or persons besides the ordinary bailiff should be employed in the execution of any civil bill decree, then and in that case it shall be lawful for the sheriff, in addition to the warrant added to the civil bill decree, to issue under his hand and seal a special warrant addressed to any person or persons whom the sheriff may see fit to nominate, and inserting in such warrant the substance of the decree, and every such warrant shall be a sufficient authority to the persons named therein to proceed in the execution of such decree, and the sheriff shall be responsible for all the acts of such persons in the same manner as

if they had been bailiffs duly appointed under this Act; and in case such special warrant shall have been issued at the request of the plaintiff or his attorney, the sheriff shall be entitled to demand and receive for every such warrant the sum of one pound, to be paid by the plaintiff or his attorney requiring the same, in addition to any fees to which he would be entitled under this Act.

MR. O'HAGAN said, he could not accept the clause, which he thought would be a departure from the principle of the Bill.

Clause *negatived.*

SIR COLMAN O'LOGHLEN moved, after Clause 25, to insert the following clause :—

(Interest in land not to be sold under civil bill execution.)

It shall not be lawful to seize or sell under any civil bill execution any term for years, or any estate or interest in lands.

MR. M'MAHON said, he did not see why, on the matter referred to, power should not be given to sell chattel interests under a Civil Bill execution.

Clause *agreed to.*

MR. LONGFIELD said, he wished to propose a clause that all actions against the sheriff should be laid in the county for which such sheriff was appointed, and that the defendant might plead the general issue.

SIR COLMAN O'LOGHLEN said, he would not object to the clause if some Amendments were made upon it.

MR. M'MAHON said, he should oppose the clause. It was notorious that in Ireland it was the practice of the country for the sheriffs to pack the juries; and it would be monstrous to give those officers the privilege of having actions brought against them for wrong done to be tried in their own counties.

MR. BUTT said, that because he desired to see the law assimilated in the two countries, he would support the clause with the restrictions proposed by the hon. Member for Clare. He denied that jury-packing was the practice in Ireland. He would, however, propose the omission of that part of the clause which limited the costs of a plaintiff recovering under £20.

Clause *withdrawn.*

(Cases above £20 removable by *certiorari.*)

MR. BUTT said, he would move the insertion of £20. Many cases involving important principles and issues occurred in which the money claim was not greater

than £20, and there ought to be a power of removing them to a superior court.

MR. GEORGE said, he thought the clause most objectionable. He regarded it as an endeavour, by a side wind, to limit the jurisdiction of the Civil Bill Courts. If there were to be a *certiorari* clause, let it be a general one.

MR. M'MAHON said, he should support the clause, as the power given by it was only available under the discretion of a Judge.

SIR COLMAN O'LOGHLEN said, he thought the clause too important to be decided without fuller discussion than could be then given to it; but it did not really belong to the objects of the present Bill, which were chiefly to regulate the execution of Civil Bill process.

MR. O'HAGAN said, the clause was quite novel, and beyond the scope of the Bill.

Clause *withdrawn.*

House *resumed.*

Bill *reported;* as amended, to be considered on *Thursday.*

THAMES CONSERVANCY BILL.—[BILL 60.]

SECOND READING.

Order for Second Reading read.

Moved, "That the Bill be now read a second time."—(*Mr. Hutt.*)

MR. LOCKE said, he did not rise to oppose the Bill, but to say that he had expected some statement would have been made with regard to the provisions of the measure, that those persons who were deeply interested in it might know what they were to expect either for their benefit or injury. He believed that some of the clauses, though only those who were *au fait* in those matters could understand their scope and object, would directly destroy the rights of that excellent class of men the Thames watermen. At present, it was necessary that one of that body should be on every barge that went up or down the river. He apprehended that the Bill would take away the privileges of that body, but as the House usually dealt circumspectly with vested interests, he hoped that his right hon. Friend would agree to refer the Bill to a Select Committee. He thought that the watermen were entitled to as much consideration as the proctors, who had compensation awarded to them; and he wished to know whether the Bill would be sent to a

Select Committee, before which the rights of all parties could be gone into?

MR. HUTT observed, that the Bill was one of that description which was known by the term hybrid—that is, it partook of the nature both of a public and also of a private measure. The general course with regard to such Bills, was to send them to a Select Committee, and all parties who supposed themselves aggrieved, or who desired Amendments in the measure, might offer evidence, and be heard by counsel. Subsequently, the clauses would be again considered in a Committee of the Whole House, and every possible care would thus be taken to remedy any grievance which might be thought to exist.

MR. ALDERMAN ROSE said, he wished to draw attention to the fact that the corporation of London was very much interested in the Bill. The Conservancy Act had its origin in a protracted dispute between the corporation and the Crown regarding the right to the bed and soil of the Thames. That dispute was terminated by a compromise, and between £6,000 and £7,000 was paid to the Crown solicitor as part of the arrangement. He, therefore, thought it hard that only seven years after a compromise had been come to upon the subject, they were called upon again to consider the construction of the Conservancy Board. He must also say, that he concurred in the remarks of the hon. Member (Mr. Locke) in reference to the watermen, whom he should be sorry to see suffer by any change; but as they were assured by the right hon. Gentleman that all interests should be fully considered, he should not, at that stage, offer any opposition to the measure.

Motion *agreed to.*

Bill read 2°, and *committed* to a Select Committee.

PARTNERSHIP LAW AMENDMENT BILL.
[BILL 68.]   SECOND READING.

Order for Second Reading read.

MR. SCHOLEFIELD, in moving the second reading of this Bill, said, its principle was identical with that of the Bill which he brought forward in the previous year, which was referred to a Select Committee, but was sent up to the House of Lords at too late a period of the year to allow of its passing into law. The difficulty which the Bill was intended to remove was this—If a capitalist wished to lend money to a

Mr. Locke

private partnership he must do so either at a fixed rate of interest or by becoming a partner and thereby risking his entire property. That risk was so great that few persons were willing to incur it. The Bill therefore proposed that capitalists should in future be at liberty to join as what was called limited partners in any general partnership, on condition that, in a public register to be kept for that purpose, the sum he advanced, the time for which he advanced it, and other particulars, should be stated. In his opinion the Bill was emphatically a creditors' measure, for at present a loan to a partnership was a secret transaction. A firm might receive credit for ample capital, but if they became bankrupt it was often found that the capital had been borrowed, and that the lender had swept away the greater part of the available assets. Under the Bill, however, such a state of things would be impossible, as the capitalist who lent his money under it would practically inform the public of the conditions of the advance. Again, the Bill did not in the slightest interfere with the present law of partnership *qua* those who were held out to the public as being partners. The only persons who would be limited to the amount which they had put down were those who had no contract with the creditors, and whom the creditors did not know, excepting as far as they appeared on the registry for the amount for which they were liable. The Bill was not a new one. The principle of the measure had been recommended in the Report of a Committee in 1851, and had been affirmed in a Resolution brought forward in 1854 by the hon. and learned Solicitor General. Under those circumstances, he hoped the House would read the Bill a second time.

Motion made, and Question proposed, "That the Bill be now read a second time."—(*Mr. Scholefield.*)

MR. HUBBARD said, he hoped that his hon. Friend (Mr. Scholefield) would not think he impugned his motives in bringing forward the Bill, or that he wished to oppose all improvements in commercial legislation, because he felt obliged to move, as an Amendment, that it be read a second time that day six months. This Bill was not identical with any of the measures on the same subject which had been before presented to the House; nor was it entitled to the support which previous Bills had received from the great commercial bodies whose opinions were of much weight. The former Bill had received the support of many Chambers of Commerce, but those bodies were opposed to the Bill before the House. The Mercantile Law Society of London was composed of men who were admirably well-informed upon these subjects; and in remarks put forward by that association it was stated, that if a clerk or workman had an engagement with his master, by which in addition to his salary he was to receive a percentage on profits, there was no partnership; but if he was entirely paid by percentage that would constitute him a partner. From that statement it appeared that the difficulty which was intended to be provided for by the second section of the Bill might be altogether removed by payment being made in the shape of both salary and percentage. The strongest argument put forward in support of the Bill was that illustrated by the case of a young man exceedingly well disposed, intelligent, and industrious, but wanting capital. It was supposed that such a young man had a friend who would assist him, but who demurred to a low rate of interest, because the compensation would be insufficient, and who was afraid of imposing a high rate, from the fear that his debtor might not be able to pay it. But it must be remembered that, in reality, capital produced nothing but interest, and that the capitalist had no right to demand more on his advance of capital than the stipulated rate of interest, which rate of interest varied in proportion to the risk. If they granted to the capitalist more power to reap indefinite profits, they had no right to limit his responsibility. To upset that theory seemed utterly contrary to the whole nature of commercial equity and justice. He ventured to urge the rejection of the Bill in the interest of the creditor. Let the partnership be registered ever so carefully, practically not one man in ten would be able to keep himself *au fait* in the varying circumstances to which that partnership might be exposed. The object of these partnerships would be not to do business with the capital which they might acquire by these arrangements, but to do business on as extended a system of credit as possible. Only that morning a case had appeared in the papers, in which a shipowner who had commenced business on borrowed money had failed for forty times the extreme amount of his capital. If that was possible under the present

system, what might not be done under the Bill? At present a person who lent money had his option. He might either go in as a capitalist and be content with a fixed interest; or he might go in as a trader with unlimited profits. If he chose the latter it was only right that his responsibility should also be unlimited. In what was now proposed by the Bill the interesting young man they had heard so much of vanished, and in his room they were asked to allow a capitalist to set up a man of straw as his creature and his agent. He would put into his hands a certain sum, but the business would be administered under his own eye, and he might obtain unlimited credit. It was doubtless very true that no one would trust him beyond a certain amount, but then he might obtain credit to that amount from each of forty persons. If the concern answered, the capitalist would pocket the profit; if it failed he would snap his fingers at the creditors, and walk out of the affair with impunity, beyond the loss of the sum he had invested. Such a system as the House was asked to institute would demoralize the trade of England. The scheme had been supported by reference to French and American experience. But the Committee of the Law Amendment Society distinctly stated that they did not desire to see partnerships established in this country on the same regulations as the partnerships *en commandite* in France, and the special partnerships in America. They objected to the *commandite* system because it did not secure the actual payment of the capital agreed to be subscribed. The registry simply represented a promise to pay a certain amount of capital; there was no security for its actually being paid down. The Bill, in the same way, stated that a partnership should be constituted, not with reference to the money paid down, but with reference to the sum promised to be paid. The Committee also state that in France and America the capitalist was prohibited from interfering in the management of the business, even in the most trifling questions; but there was no such prohibition in the Bill. Therefore the argument in favour of the Bill drawn from foreign examples entirely failed. The object sought to be attained by the Bill could be obtained in a much less objectionable manner. Why should not a capitalist be permitted to make advances upon a bonded loan, certified and registered, for a certain period at a rate of interest sufficient to satisfy him, and under arrangements which would give his agent command of money for a certain time, securing him all the advantages which the Bill proposed to provide, but avoiding all the temptations to fraud and mismanagement? He was anxious to know for what reason Scotland was by the last clause exempted from the operation of this Bill. No doubt, the acute and sensible commercial men on the other side of the Tweed objected to having that mischievous principle introduced into their mode of doing business; and to avert their opposition this limitation had been consented to. If the Bill were good for England it was good for Scotland, but, believing it to be good for neither country, he should move that it be read a second time that day six months.

Amendment proposed, to leave out the word "now," and at the end of the Question to add the words "upon this day six months."—(*Mr. Hubbard.*)

MR. MALINS said, it was impossible not to see that the speech of the hon. Member for Buckingham was in favour of unlimited liability, but he thought the House would consider it was impossible for them to retrace their steps and adopt the principle which the hon. Gentleman advocated. Limited liability was a principle firmly established in the minds of commercial men, and it was being acted upon every day to a surprising extent. Joint-stock companies and banks were being carried on upon that principle, and experience showed that great commercial concerns could not be carried on so well by individuals as by companies, because, among other reasons, they were subject to changes in consequence of deaths, which tended to interfere with their prosperity. What the Bill under these circumstances proposed to do was to extend the benefit of the limited liability principle to establishments comprising a smaller number of partners than legally constituted a company. That, however, the hon. Member for Buckingham contended was a course opposed to all commercial morality, but why it should be so, he, for one, could not understand. It was to the advantage of the public that young men who possessed skill and ability, though they might not have capital, should be able to enter into business; and his hon. Friend the Member for Birmingham desired to confer facilities for that purpose. But by the law, as it stood, a man of capital could not assist a

Mr. Hubbard

deserving youth without becoming liable to his last farthing if he participated in the profits. If he lent the money on bond the consequence was that if the person he assisted failed he came into competition with the creditors, and had his dividend. By the Bill it would be different. The lender of the money would only be liable to the extent of the money he had advanced, or had promised to advance, and he did not come in as a competitor with the creditors. In those cases in which the principle of limited liability at present operated any one might ascertain from a public record who the members of a particular firm were, what was the amount of their capital, and how much of it was paid up; and it was a person's own fault if he did not take the proper precautions before investing his property in such hands. What, then, he should like to know, was the harm of proposing, as the hon. Member for Birmingham did, that A might carry on a business in the name of A and B, provided he gave notice that the person with whom he was in partnership was not a general partner? Could the creditor who gave credit to a concern complain when he was informed by a document to which he might refer, that the non-acting partner's was a limited liability only? It was well known in the case of even the best-conducted private banks that the partners put no capital in them — the capital being supplied by the deposits of the public; but it was also true that everything the principals possessed was at stake under the unlimited liability system. Under this Bill, if a man were a trader, and got another to join him with £10,000, of which £3,000 was paid up, and the remaining £7,000 liable to be called for as it was required, what objection, he should like to know, could the public have to a partnership of that description? In the event of a failure, how would the public suffer? The Bill provided that in that event the limited partner should pay up in favour of the creditor the difference between the sum he had paid and that which he had agreed to pay; so that, instead of anything being taken away from the creditors, they would have the advantage of a fund to which to resort. He recollected well having fought battles on the subject with eminent commercial men, such, for example, as Mr. Alexander Hartie, and the principle for which he contended had, he was glad to say, triumphed; nor could he conceive why it should stop short with companies consisting of seven members and not be made applicable to partnerships of two or three persons when hedged round, as in the case of the present Bill, by proper safeguards. The Bill, notwithstanding the opposition it met with during the last year in the Select Committee from the hon. Member for Huntingdon, was read a third time, and was not sent to the Lords because it was too late in the Session. It was not surprising to find that those who had flourished under a particular system should be opposed to any alteration, and that those eminently successful commercial men, whom the hon. Member for Buckingham so well represented, who had experience of establishments flourishing on the principle of unlimited liability, were slow to believe that any other system could be successful; but when his hon. Friend gave as an instance of the disadvantages of the opposite system the case of a gentleman who commenced trade without a penny, and lost forty times his capital, he was scarcely dealing fairly with the question. The man who had succeeded in inducing others to trust him to so large an extent was clearly no fool. He must, in short, have been a man of some capacity; and how much better would it be if, under the operation of such a measure as that under discussion, he had been enabled to go to a capitalist and say, "I have a knowledge of shipping, I know how to buy and sell, and if you supply me with £10,000 I think I can make a certain profit." Having that money, the gentleman in question, instead of causing the public to suffer, and losing forty times his capital, might have doubled it and been a successful man. If the Bill was imperfect in its details, its imperfections might be remedied in Committee. Its principle followed from that which had already been established in regard to limited liability companies; and, as he thought that it would remove an existing evil, he should give it his most strenuous support.

Mr. KIRKMAN HODGSON said, that he could see no objection to the principle of the Bill. If under its operation persons obtained credit to which they were not entitled, it could only be in consequence of want of prudence on the part of those who trusted them. The great evil of commerce at the present moment was that men gave credit to others without inquiring what was their property, or what right they had to be trusted. The hon. Member for Buckingham seemed to object to the Bill because it would compel persons to inquire what were the means of those to whom they gave credit; and he proposed as a remedy the advance of money at a high fixed rate of interest. But the Bill was intended for the benefit of persons who had acquired a character for prudence, and nothing could more clearly show that a man was unworthy of such a character than that, knowing the uncertainties of business, he should consent to pay a high fixed rate of interest, whether he made it or not. He could see no difficulty in the way of the adoption of the principle of the Bill. It had been admitted with regard to large matters; why should it not be extended to small ones? In his opinion legislation upon the subject had commenced at the wrong end. This was where it should have begun. Old houses generally came to grief either by the partners adhering to old-fashioned modes of doing business, or by their retaining the management after they had lost the energy and enterprize which were essential to the success of all commercial concerns. A business could not stand still, it must either go backward or forward; and nothing could be more justifiable than that persons who had made their fortunes, but were anxious to keep up the name of the old house, should leave some portion of their property in the business under the management of young, energetic, and prudent men in whom they might have confidence. So far from the Bill injuring the tone of commercial morality, he believed that it would elevate it. It would give greater freedom to contract, which meant greater freedom to industry, and would confer upon honest, deserving, and excellent men opportunities of reaping the fruits of their industry which they had not hitherto enjoyed.

Sir GEORGE BOWYER said, the speech of his hon. Friend the Member for Buckingham (Mr. Hubbard), seemed to be based on the principle that where there was unlimited profit there should be unlimited liability; but he was sure the House would say it was too late to go on a principle which had already received a negative by the decision of Parliament. Again, the hon. Member appeared to think that the Bill introduced a new principle destructive to the sound doctrines of commercial law and commercial morality. It was no new principle at all. It was a principle more than 2,000 years old; and they would find embodied in the civil law every possible variation and modification of the law of unlimited liability. If the question came to a division, ho should certainly vote for the Bill.

Mr. GREGSON said, he wished to point out that while under the measure there was to be a limit to the extent to which the non-active partner was to be liable, there was no limit as to the number of persons from whom credit might be obtained upon the strength of the sum which he advanced. Therefore, if a capitalist put £10,000 into a concern, and one man gave credit to the amount of £10,000 on the faith of the capital of £10,000 subscribed under the Act, a dozen other persons might do the same thing, and then where was the security for the creditor? In railways there was a limit on both sides; under the Bill there was not. He thought the hon. Gentleman might as well have gone a little further, and have applied the principle of limited liability to one as well as to two persons.

Mr. ALDERMAN SALOMONS said, he thought that the Bill would supply a great public want, which was finding its expression in the creation of credit companies. In times of peace there was an extension of enterprise, and this rendered fresh capital necessary. It had been said, if the principle of limited liability was to be carried so far, any one man should be able to limit his responsibility; but he took it that the very principle of the Bill was, that the man actually carrying on trade should be liable to his last shilling, but that those persons who should be registered as partners, simply contributing capital, should be responsible only to the amount for which they were registered. The Bill had been described as a capitalists' measure. He contended, on the other hand, that it was a trader's measure. It would enable honest industrious tradesmen to procure the capital which at present was beyond their reach, and would assimilate the law of England in that respect to the laws existing in every other country in Europe. He saw no reason why in this commercial country, where we had free trade in so many things, there should not be free trade in capital, provided the party who contracted the debt was held responsible for it.

Mr. BUCHANAN said, he held that the previous adoption of the principle of limited liability in favour of certain companies could not be advanced in support of the measure, as it extended the principle so far as virtually to create a new one. The statement that the question was vir-

Sir George Bowyer

tually settled last year required this commentary, that the Select Committee refused to take any evidence, although the requisite powers had been conferred. There was no record of their opinions, which, he might state, were utterly at variance upon every point submitted to them, and the Bill might just as well never have gone upstairs at all. He would, therefore, propose that, in deference to the opinion of those commercial bodies who best understood what was suited for commercial interests, the measure should now be referred to a Select Committee, with the understanding that they would reconsider the whole question. In some respects the present Bill differed from that of last year—for instance, its application was not extended to Scotland. Of such an omission he did not approve, for if the measure were approved by the House, what was good for England would be equally good for Scotland. On the other hand, he was glad to perceive that there were some important improvements in the management clauses. ["Divide!"] He saw that the feeling of the House was against him, and therefore he would abstain from further protest against the measures.

Mr. SCHOLEFIELD said, he wished to explain that the Bill had been delivered to him in its then shape, and that he had only been able to read its principal clauses. He should be very glad to extend its operation to Scotland.

Question, "That the word 'now' stand part of the Question," put, and *agreed to.*

Main Question put, and *agreed to.*

Bill read 2°, and *committed* for *Monday* next.

BANKRUPTCY ACT — NOMINATION OF COMMITTEE.
ADJOURNED DEBATE.

Order read, for resuming Adjourned Debate on Question [21st April], "That The Lord Advocate be one other Member of the said Committee."

Question again proposed.

Debate *resumed.*

THE LORD ADVOCATE said, that with reference to what had passed on a previous night, he wished to explain that, in answer to an application from the hon. Member for Honiton, he had stated that he took a great interest in the subject of bankruptcy, but that, if nominated on the

Committee he could not promise to give an assiduous attendance. Understanding subsequently that the hon. Member for Sheffield was anxious to serve, he said he had no desire to stand in his way, but that having undertaken to act himself he could not withdraw without the consent of the hon. Member for Honiton, who had induced him to do so. He would leave the matter entirely in the hands of the House.

Question put, and *agreed to.*

MR. LOCKE said, he would move that the name of the hon. and learned Member for Sheffield (Mr. Roebuck), be also added.

MR. MOFFATT said, he apprehended that it would be necessary, in the first instance, to move that the number of the Committee be enlarged to sixteen.

MR. WHITESIDE expressed a desire that the name of the hon. Member for the City of Dublin (Mr. Vance) might be added to the Committee.

MR. HASSARD said, that he would be glad to make way for the hon. Member, he himself being engaged upon another Committee.

MR. SPEAKER held that notice of the alteration must be given.

Mr. GOSCHEN, Mr. CAVE, and Mr. CRUM-EWING nominated other Members of the said Committee:—Power to send for persons, papers, and records; Five to be the quorum.

And, on April 26, Mr. ROEBUCK and Mr. VANCE *added,* and Mr. HASSARD *discharged.*

COURT OF CHANCERY (IRELAND) BILL

LEAVE.　FIRST READING.

MR. O'HAGAN (THE ATTORNEY GENERAL FOR IRELAND): Mr. Speaker, Sir, in moving for leave to introduce a Bill to alter the constitution and amend the practice and course of proceeding of the High Court of Chancery in Ireland, I have to crave the indulgence of the House while I state the circumstances under which the Bill was framed, and refer, as briefly as I can, to some of the details of the measure. And it will be convenient in the first place, with a view to understanding the necessity that exists for this measure, that I should state something of the circumstances which have produced in the system of Equity practice and procedure in the two countries a divergence of a very remarkable and, I think, a very unfortunate character. It is matter of common notoriety that, for a lengthened period, great dissatisfaction pre-

vailed in this country, arising from the delay and expense attending proceedings in the Court of Chancery. That dissatisfaction continued for years; it culminated to a very great extent in the time of Lord Eldon; and in the year 1825 a Commission was appointed for the purpose of considering the amendments that should be made in the Equity proceedings in England. That Commission was followed by a Report in the year 1829, and upon that Report reforms in the Court of Chancery in this country were subsequently founded. The Act of 3 & 4 *Will.* IV. c. 94 extended the powers of the Chancellor and Vice Chancellor and of the Master of the Rolls to make General Orders for the regulation of the Courts of Equity in England; and, accordingly, in the years 1833, 1841, and 1845, Lord Brougham, Lord Cottenham, and Lord Lyndhurst framed orders which, to a great extent, carried out the reforms of the Court of Chancery, which were recommended by the Commissioners. But it is important to observe that they were not extended, nor was the statute under which they were made extended at all to Ireland. These General Orders were not, however, in their operation considered sufficient for the purpose for which they were framed, and in the year 1850 a Royal Commission was issued to consider further reforms in the Courts of Equity. In the same year, 1850, an Act was passed—Lord Justice Turner's Act—the 13 & 14 *Vict.* c. 35. It was entitled an Act to diminish the expense and delay of proceedings in the High Court of Chancery in England; and by it very important Amendments were effected in the Equity system in this country. The Commission of 1850 continued to sit for a considerable period. It made three very important Reports, and upon these Reports Parliament immediately acted in the two statutes, the 15 & 16 *Vict.* c. 80, and another of the same year—the 15 & 16 *Vict.* c. 86. By the first of these statutes, the Masters in Chancery in England were abolished, and Vice Chancellors were added to those who before existed, with chief clerks, taking the place in certain instances and for certain purposes of the Masters, who ceased to exist. The second statute was aimed to amend the practice and procedure of the Courts of Equity in this country; and under it general orders of the Court have continued from time to time to be made, by very able Judges, and have carried forward Chancery reform in England to a very considerable extent indeed. It is, I am sorry to say, otherwise in Ireland. In Ireland, the Equity system was identical at its introduction with the Equity system in England, and it continued to be identical with it for hundreds of years. In point of fact, it continued to be identical with it substantially up to the year 1850, because, although there was no Commission leading to legislation for the Irish Court, an Act was passed in the 4 & 5 *Will.* IV., which gave to the Chancellor of Ireland and to the Master of the Rolls in Ireland, powers to make general orders for the regulation of the practice in the Court of Chancery in Ireland, and general orders under the provisions of this Act were made by Lord Plunket and by Lord St. Leonards, in the years 1834 and 1843, with the object and with the effect of identifying, as far as possible, the system in England with the system in Ireland. So it continued until the year 1850; but in that year a complete divergence of the systems began to be established. In that year a totally new system of practice and procedure was introduced in Ireland, by an Act called the Irish Chancery Regulation Act, 13 & 14 *Vict.* c. 89. It is important for the House to observe that that Act was not introduced by, and was not founded upon, the recommendation of any Royal Commission, or the Report of any Committee, or any preparatory inquiry such as that upon which, so far as England was concerned, all measures of the kind proceeded. That Act was passed, as I have said, in the year 1850, and it altered the practice of the Court of Chancery in Ireland to a very great extent. It abolished the old system of Bill and Answer, and established a system of Cause Petitions, giving to Ireland a course of procedure which, I believe, and I think I shall prove before I go much further, has not worked satisfactorily. That system has not been satisfactory either to the practitioners or to the suitors of the Court ; and however well designed, and however in some respects accompanied with substantial benefits, it has created considerable abuses. It has resulted in the multiplication of affidavit upon affidavit ; there is under it no machinery for joining issue, or eliminating the issue from the pleadings, and the result has been exceedingly injurious in Ireland. The Act also vested a new jurisdiction in the Masters of the Court. It created what has been called the Fifteenth Section Petition. It threw into the Masters' offices mortgage causes, testamentary causes, foreclosure causes, and various others, with an enumeration of which I need not trouble the House. So matters went on until, in the year 1854—the Incumbered Estates Court having been established some years before, and having become a very important institution, indeed, in Ireland—a Royal Commission was appointed for the purpose of inquiring into the working of that Court. Upon that Commission, some of the most distinguished men in England and in Ireland took their places. From Ireland we had the present Lord Chancellor of Ireland; we had the Lord Justice of Appeal, Mr. Blackburne ; we had Chief Justice Monahan ; Mr. Justice Fitzgerald, whose name is honourably known in this House; Judge Longfield, a very distinguished Judge of the Landed Estates Court; and Mr. Brewster, to whose eminence at the bar I need not refer. Upon the English side there were the present Lord Chancellor, then Sir Richard Bethel ; Sir John Romilly, Master of the Rolls ; and the hon. and learned Member for Belfast, Sir Hugh Cairns. It was a very strong Commission, and the character of its Members, and the knowledge and experience they possessed, entitled their recommendations to the highest consideration. Well, that Commission recommended an assimilation of the system of Equity in England and in Ireland. Nothing, however, was done, and nothing has been done up to the present time upon the recommendations of that Commission. The Lord Chancellor and the Master of the Rolls in Ireland had very large powers for the making of rules and orders — general rules and general orders—very large powers indeed. These powers were extended by the statute which passed subsequently to the year 1850; but I am sorry to say that, from peculiar circumstances, those powers have not been acted upon. Differences of opinion between the learned Judges of the Court prevented action upon those powers—and the result has been, that they have not been used for the purpose of the assimilation of the systems of the two countries—or, very much, for any other purpose. The Commission to which I shall now immediately refer was appointed owing to representations made as to the unsatisfactory state of things which existed ; and that Commission, I may state, before I communicate to the House its nature and constitution, has found that, at this moment, the practice and procedure of the two countries, originally similar, have by the effect of ·   ·tion become

Mr. O'Hagan

almost entirely different. I need not say that that is a condition of things which is very much to be regretted. It is very much to be regretted that the principles of our law being identical, that the system of our jurisprudence, so far as England and Ireland are concerned, being the same—there should be, in practice and in procedure, almost an absolute difference; a difference which results in great inconvenience to the profession, at all events so far as Ireland is concerned, by preventing the attainment of the advantage to be had from the authoritative decisions of the Courts on common principles. And further, in a united kingdom it certainly is a desirable thing that the practice and procedure of the respective Courts should be identical. Well, it was in the position of matters which I have described, that in the year 1862 a new Commission was appointed. That Commission had upon it several of the distinguished persons whose names I have mentioned in connection with the Commission of the year 1854. Others were added to them. I shall mention the names of the Commissioners, and the value of their recommendations will be at once patent to the House. Upon it sat the Master of the Rolls in England Sir John Romilly, Vice Chancellor Sir William Page Wood, my hon. and learned Friend the present Attorney General, the late Attorney General Sir William Atherton, the hon. and learned Member for Belfast, Sir Hugh Cairns, Mr. Justice Willes, and two gentlemen who were very well acquainted with the practice and procedure of the Courts here—Mr. Gifford and Mr. Follett. The Irish Members of the Commission were the Lord Justice of Appeal, known in this House as a man who during his life has maintained a position of the highest eminence, who has passed through the great offices of the law with the greatest distinction, who has been successively Attorney General, Master of the Rolls, Lord Chief Justice of the Queen's Bench, Lord Chancellor of Ireland, and is now Lord Justice of Appeal. With him were associated my right hon. Friend (Mr. Napier), who was late Lord Chancellor of Ireland, and whose high position is also well known in this House; Mr. Brewster, of whom I have spoken before as a man of great eminence at the Irish bar; Chief Justice Monahan, who is certainly one of the most distinguished men on the Common Law Bench in either country; Baron

Hughes, who was specially qualified to judge of every question relating to the Courts of Equity; my colleague, myself, and Mr. Orpen, who represented the Incorporated Society of Solicitors and Attorneys in Ireland. I need not say that a Commission more entitled to public respect and deference in any recommendation which it might make, could not by possibility have been arrayed by the Royal Authority. The Commission was issued for the purpose, as stated in its Report, of inquiring into the following matters, with a view to reduce costs to suitors and the expenditure of the public money, and to assimilate, so far as may be practicable, the administration of Justice in England and Ireland :—

1. "The constitution, establishment, practice, procedure, and fees of the Superior Courts of Common Law in Ireland.

2. The differences between the constitution and the forms of practice, procedure, and fees of the Courts of Chancery of England and of Ireland."

That was the scope of the Commission; and I may state that, when the Commissioners assembled, they took the best means possible of securing the fullest and most reliable information which the profession could afford. They had that information collected, both as to the law and equity, by lawyers thoroughly acquainted with the subject, and furnished to them in Reports, showing the differences which existed upon the one side and upon the other. They appealed, not only to the members of the bar but to the members of the kindred profession of solicitors, and they received answers to elaborate queries upon all points connected with the management of the Courts of Equity in Ireland. And having done so, they stated their conclusions in the Report which I have before me, and which I had the honour to lay upon the table of the House on the last day of the last Session in these terms —

"On the general question of assimilation of Equity practice and procedure, and the changes connected with it, we are of opinion—

1. That it is expedient that the system of practice and procedure of the Courts of Chancery of England and of Ireland should be assimilated as far as practicable.

2. That the practice and procedure of the Court of Chancery of England are generally to be preferred to the practice and procedure of the Court of Chancery of Ireland.

3. That demurrers should be allowed for want of equity or for multifariousness only.

4. That the Irish rule of not requiring an attachment, and a return of *non est inventus*, in order to obtain a sequestration, should be extended to England.

Our recommendations as to the changes in the constitution and fees of the Court of Chancery of Ireland, rendered necessary by the adoption of assimilation, are as follows :—

We are of opinion—

1. That the office of Master in Chancery in Ireland, other than that of the Receiver Master, should be abolished.

2. That the existing Master should be retained so long as it may be found necessary that they may, as far as practicable, complete the business pending before them.

3. That, having regard to the special statutable duties now discharged by the Receiver Master, that office should be retained.

4. That the Master of the Rolls, with one Vice Chancellor, having each one chief clerk and two assistant clerks in addition to the Lord Chancellor and Lord Justice of Appeal, will be sufficient to dispose of the Equity business in Ireland.

That it is desirable that power be given to the Lord Chancellor, with the advice and consent of the Master of the Rolls and Vice Chancellor in Ireland, or one of them, by order under their hands, to appoint an additional chief clerk or assistant clerks to the Master of the Rolls and Vice Chancellor, or either of them.

That power should be given to the Lord Chancellor of Ireland, with the advice and consent of the Lord Justice of Appeal, Master of the Rolls, and the Vice Chancellor in Ireland, or any two of them, to regulate the fees to be paid, so far as it shall be necessary to make any changes in the same in consequence of the alterations produced in Equity practice and procedure by carrying into effect the preceding recommendations."

These are the recommendations of the Commissioners. They specify some particulars in which, owing to the peculiar circumstances of the country, the present system ought not to be changed, and they make a great many other recommendations ; and, upon these recommendations, the Bill which I now introduce to the House has been based and framed. I can assure the House that, so far as I am able to judge, the Bill faithfully and carefully carries out the conclusions of the Commission and of the antecedent Commission of 1854; and that being so, I think I need not add that it has, at all events *primâ facie,* a very strong title to the consideration of Parliament. The Bill may be said to be divided into five parts : the first of these regards the appointment of a Vice Chancellor and Chief Clerks in Ireland ; the second relates to the abolition of the Masters, three of the four Masters who at present exist in that country ; the third division relates to the process and practice of the Court of Chancery in Ireland ; the fourth concerns stamps and fees payable in that Court; and the fifth relates to some miscellaneous matters of no great consequence, except in one respect—namely, as

Mr. O'Hagan

it touches unclaimed dividends. That Bill I may say in the inception is, with the necessary modifications which the Report suggests, a consolidation of the three great English statutes, the 13 & 14 *Vict.* c. 35, the 15 & 16 *Vict.* c. 80, and the 15 and 16 *Vict.* c. 86. The first division of the Bill, relating to the appointment of a Vice Chancellor and chief clerks, is founded upon a principle on which the Commission in England acted, and on which the Commission for Ireland has been disposed to act, and it is this : that it is of great importance in disposing of an Equity cause, that a single judicial mind should apply itself to the case from the beginning to the end ; that in one judicial mind there should be complete control over the cause ; that it ought not at one stage to be tossed into the Master's office, and at another tossed back again ; one man thinking of this part of the cause, and another of that—but that the whole of the proceedings should be homogeneous ; that there should be harmony throughout, and that in that way the proceedings of the Court might be made more beneficial. That being so, it has been considered by the Commissioners that there should be a Vice Chancellor appointed for Ireland, and that the disposal of the entire business should be committed to the Lord Chancellor, the Vice Chancellor, and the Master of the Rolls. The Masters being abolished, two chief clerks will be required, a chief clerk for the Master of the Rolls, and a chief clerk for the Vice Chancellor ; and it has been considered right and proper in that, as in other particulars, to follow the precedent set in England, and to provide that these two chief clerks shall be members of the profession of Solicitors, or be taken from the Examiners of the Masters who will be abolished. So far for the first part of the Bill. Then, as to the second, the abolition of the Masters. I believe no one who knows anything of legal affairs in Ireland will have a doubt that the Masters now in existence are able and conscientious men. I believe there is not one of them who would not hold his place with honour in any Court in the world; but, at the same time, the nature of the proceedings in these Courts has not been very satisfactory to the public. It has been considered, at all events, that they are not satisfactory—not from the Masters not doing their duty, but because the system which they had to administer was not satisfactory. Let me in this matter not be misunderstood. I am not making any imputation whatever upon the Masters. Quite the contrary; but as in England the machinery of Masters was not considered· in reference to the appointment of the Vice Chancellor and chief clerks the best for the performance of the duty to be done, so in Ireland the same objection to the system has been started, and has been yielded to. There are, as the House may be aware, four Masters in Ireland. It is proposed by the Bill to abolish three of the four. The fourth Master is what is called a Receiver Master. He has peculiar duties to discharge—duties which could not be well discharged either by a Judge in the Courts of Equity, or by either of the chief clerks. He has to do with the accounts of guardians, of minors, and lunatics, and with the accounts of receivers over estates. He has also very extensive duties to perform in auditing the accounts of treasurers of grand juries in Ireland—and the county rate with which he has to deal amounts to something like a million sterling a year. He has also to audit the accounts of the collector general of taxes in Dublin— whose collection amounts to £190,000 a year, and it has accordingly been thought desirable and necessary that he should continue to discharge his peculiar duties when the other Masters have ceased to act. And I may say that even in that particular there has been no want of attention to the principle of assimilation recommended by the Commissioners, because while here in England the Masters generally were abolished, the Master in Lunacy continued to act, —and he continues to act with less extensive powers and less important duties than the Receiver Master will have to discharge in Ireland. While the Masters, according to the recommendation of the Commissioners, are to be abolished, it has been thought right and proper that the Cause Petitions presented under the fifteenth section to which I have referred, and which are now in their offices, shall be disposed of by themselves. The Master of the Rolls in Ireland, a very eminent Judge as we all know, and a man to whose opinion upon any subject great respect must be paid, protested against the transfer of that business to the Court, which will subsist upon the extinction of the Masters ; and not only was deference paid to his opinion, but it was con-

sidered that the mixing up of the old principle and the new would be attended with great difficulty and complication, and it was thought better that the old business in these offices should be disposed of by the Masters, and that the new business should be disposed of by the new Court. Again, in that instance, the English precedent has been followed, for the Masters here continued, in order to wind up their business, for a considerable time after the Act by which they were finally abolished had passed. I should state that, as to the appointment of a Vice Chancellor, and as to the abolition of the Masters and the creation of chief clerks, the opinion of the Commissioners was unanimous. And, indeed, I am not aware that there is any difference of opinion upon that subject, in either branch of the profession, or in the mind of the public. I will now go on to refer to the offices which it is proposed to create under this Bill, and the offices which it will abolish. I heard the other night some reference to this matter. Some anxiety was expressed to find out what offices were to be created and what offices were to be destroyed. And some allusion was also made which, I confess, I did not understand, to the intervention of the Treasury in this matter. I did not think at the time, nor do I now think, that the observation was called for, considering who the Commissioners were, upon whose authority and recommendation the measure is to be carried out. Now, I have to inform the House that by the Bill, following the recommendation of the Commissioners, the entire existing staff is to continue to be employed, that it is designed that there shall be no new offices created, none whatever—except the office of Vice Chancellor and the office of the two chief clerks — and that the officers, who at present do duty in the Master's offices, shall not be superannuated, but that, in so far as they are capable of doing duty at all, they are not to be relieved from duty, but shall be compelled to do in new offices work which will entitle them fairly to the salary they receive. The Assistant Registrars and Junior Clerks necessary in the new Court will be all taken from the old staff. So far as that staff is concerned, to some small extent there may be a want of employment for a very few men, but it is recommended by the Commissioners that, in order that the public may not be burdened with any expense for which they do not receive the fullest compensation, those persons who may have time at their disposal are to be employed in arranging the records of the Master's offices, a duty which it is most important for the country should be done. [Mr. WHITESIDE: What about the chief clerks?] The chief clerks are to be taken from the profession of solicitors, or from the Examiners to the Masters; and I may inform my right hon. Friend that the appointments are, so far as I remember, to rest with the Judge of the Court—with the Lord Chancellor and the Vice Chancellor; and it is only right, and fair, and proper, that those who have the burden and responsibility of most important and onerous duties, under the new system, should have the appointment of those upon whom they must rely—whom they must trust—nay more, whom they must train to do their duty. Now, I must state further, that I believe it will appear very clearly, when the details of this measure are considered, that the ultimate result of the passing of the Bill will be, not the casting of a bduren upon the Treasury, not the creation of additional expense, but that at least some £4,000 or £5,000 a year will be saved by a reform of the greatest possible value. So far with regard to the first and second parts of the Bill. The third, as I have stated, relates to the practice and procedure of the Court, and the important portion of that third part unquestionably is this, that it abolishes the Irish Chancery Regulation Act, so far as that Act governs the procedure of the Court. An imposing array of testimony has been accumulated by the Commissioners upon that subject, and is presented by them. That evidence, if I could venture to trouble the House with it, but I shall not, would, I think, abundantly satisfy it, that a more wise proceeding than that which is proposed by the Bill could not well be conceived. In the 23rd page of their Report, the Commissioners say this—

"The procedure introduced into Ireland by the Chancery Regulation Act of 1850, of petition, answering affidavit, and affidavits by way of evidence without proper limits to the filing of such affidavits, has not, in our opinion, worked satisfactorily.

"The references to Masters are attended with all the disadvantages which led to the abolition of the office of Master in England.

"The jurisdiction under the fifteenth section of the Irish Chancery Regulation Act of 1850, has generally failed in the objects for which it was intended, and has not been attended with the advantages experienced under the English system, based upon the recommendations of the English Chancery Commissioners of 1850. There are,

Mr. O'Hagan

however, some portions of the Irish procedure which we recommend to be retained."

That opinion of the Commissioners—that judgment of the Commissioners—is founded upon the evidence of the ablest men connected with the bar and the Chancery Bench in Ireland. Master Brooke, who is a gentleman of the greatest ability, experience, and conscientiousness, in his answer to the Commissioners wrote thus—

"Our greatest want has been the deficiency of information for the practitioner's guidance, and the most valuable of all reforms would be the adoption of the practice of the English Court of Chancery, with its precise rules and printed decisions. Since 1850 we have been like travellers without a chart. The Act of that year, sec. 17, empowered the Master, without reference to any rule or course of practice of the Court, save as by the Act provided, to regulate the course of proceedings as he might think expedient for rendering the same speedy and inexpensive, so far as justice would admit. So vast a power exercised by five Judges, whose decisions are not reported, nor even known in the other Masters' offices, though hitherto exercised, I believe, with great caution and moderation, cannot but have led to much diversity of practice and caused great perplexity, of which both counsel and solicitors frequently and justly complain. The obvious remedy is to bring us under the control of English authorities, which are accessible to all; and if there be any particulars in which our system is superior to the English, we would gladly surrender the advantage, if we could thereby obtain the benefit of fixed and known rules of procedure."

And Mr. Serjeant Sullivan, a very distinguished member of the Irish bar, speaks in these terms—

"In my opinion, the working of the present system of proceeding by general cause petition and affidavits in Ireland, has been unsatisfactory. For a considerable period after the introduction of the system the utmost confusion and the loosest practice prevailed, and these continued long subsequently to the time at which they should have ceased, if they were to be regarded simply as the natural or unavoidable consequences of a new state of things; in fact, they have not yet been entirely removed, and they seem to me to exist as incident to the present system of Equity procedure."

And Mr. Warren, whose name is also extremely well known at the Irish bar, and not the less honourably known by his connection with one who in his day and generation held a foremost place amongst the ablest lawyers in the empire, says—

"Under the system which has obtained in the Equity Court of Ireland, since the passing of the Chancery Regulation Act, 1850, many useless technicalities have been abolished, and the costs of suits as regards pleadings and some other items of expense, have been diminished. These improvements have been effected, either by a limited application of the Irish statute, or (as in England) by reforms of the old practice. But, in fact, the new system has altogether superseded the old practice, an effect which I cannot think the Chancery Regulation Act was intended to produce (Glascock v. Ross,· 1 Irish Ch. Rep., 55), and which, in my opinion, even in the Courts of the Lord Chancellor and the Master of the Rolls, has not been beneficial. The loose nature of the cause, petition, and respondent's affidavit (to which the name of pleadings has been denied), has promoted vagueness of statements on the part of professional gentlemen, and of testimony on the part of witnesses, has thrown an undue measure of responsibility on the discretion of Judges, and has tended to make results uncertain. I think speculative litigation has been encouraged by the present system, and has increased since 1850.

" I entertain and desire respectfully to express the strongest opinion, that the change of procedure in the Irish Equity Courts which would be most beneficial to all parties interested, to the Judges, and to the bar, to solicitors and suitors, would be the simple substitution for it of the system of the English Equity Courts. If the English system were inferior to that of Ireland, I think compensation would be found in the advantages of uniformity in the administration of the same law in all the Courts of the United Kingdom, and in the aids which Judges and lawyers would derive from reported decisions on the rules of a common system. But if, as I think, the English system on the whole, and in almost all its details, is superior to that of Ireland, the principles of public policy and justice to this country seem to call for the substitution which I have presumed to suggest." ,

And Mr. Law — (I shall not trouble the House with any other extracts from this voluminous evidence) —Mr. Law, a friend of my own and a very able man, says—

" I think the present system of proceeding by cause petition and affidavits, in the Courts of the Lord Chancellor and Master of the Rolls in Ireland, under the Chancery Regulation Act of 1850, works unsatisfactorily in several respects. Thus, without noticing mere details, our procedure is, in my mind,· highly objectionable in its combination, or rather confusion of pleading and evidence in the same document ; in the indefinite allowance of alternate statements, instead of having fixed times for closing, first the pleadings and then the evidence ; in the practical admission of hearsay, and other illegal evidence in affidavits; and in the absence of any efficient check on the manifest tendency to mis-statement and suppression of material facts.

"As to ' the other parts of the practice and procedure of the Court of Chancery in Ireland, under the Irish Chancery Regulation Act of 1850,' besides those already observed upon, they are of comparatively small importance. In themselves they are, perhaps, for the most part, unobjectionable ; but I would earnestly recommend that the system of procedure, as a whole, should be made identical with that of the English Courts of Chancery. There is nothing whatever to justify the maintenance of a distinct and different system here. Without insisting on the truth, that all needless

distinctions between the two countries are mischievous in many other ways, I would submit, that even if our system of procedure were in itself as good as the English, it must be less satisfactory and efficient by the mere fact of its being different ; for we are thus deprived of all the assistance which the English reports and text-books would otherwise afford us, and this is much more than enough to counterbalance any small merits our system may be supposed to possess. But, in truth, the English system of Chancery procedure appears to me to be, in all important points, greatly superior to ours ; and, therefore, I would gladly see it entirely adopted here, and wait for such improvements in the common system as the experience of both countries may from time to time suggest."

These are the opinions certainly of very eminent persons at the Irish bar, and they go with the other opinions in this report, which is, I presume, in the hands of hon. Members, to sustain the finding of the Commissioners in favour of the assimilation of the practice and procedure of the Courts of Equity in the two countries. Well, the Bill which I now lay upon the table of the House, is in all its parts framed to carry out the recommendation of the Commissioners, as to the system of printing Bills which prevails in this country, as to the duty of the Vice Chancellors and the chief clerks, and as to a multitude of other matters, which, of course, I shall not now trouble the House with. The details of the measure are very large indeed ; the number of clauses in the Bill is very numerous, but the principal objects which it has in view are those to which I have already referred. It, in fact, contains some eighty or ninety clauses, taken, I may say, in terms from the English Bills; and if the House shall see fit to adopt the measure, the English system substantially, and in all its parts, will be transferred to Ireland. Well, that being so, the system of Cause Petitions will cease; we will have, of necessity, to modify the system so as to bring into operation the general orders which exist in this country. I think there are only two matters as to which the Commissioners think that there ought to be a difference—not a difference exactly—but in which they think that the English system ought not to be introduced. They do not think that the system of pleas ought to be established in Ireland. They think, further, that the demurrer which has been abolished in Ireland, but exists in England, should be re-established in Ireland upon certain conditions. The Commissioners were of opinion that a demurrer for multifariousness, or for want of equity, might be a useful thing ; and the Bill proposes to make that change. When I come to introduce another Bill, I will show you how very candidly and how very liberally the Commissioners have acted—how willing they have been to consider the question of assimilation, not in a narrow spirit, nor merely with a view to take that which exists here and apply it in Ireland, because it exists here and not there, but that they have considered carefully, and fully, and substantially what is good here and there, and have been willing and anxious to act with generous reciprocity ; to take for England that which was good in Ireland, and to give to Ireland that which was good in England. So far I have gone—and as fully as I could at this hour of the night—through three parts of the Bill. The fourth part relates, as I have already stated, to fees and stamps— a very important though a very dry part of the subject. It is important, not only to the revenue, but for the proper management of the affairs of the Court. Very proper arrangements have been made in this respect in England, but in Ireland, unfortunately, the condition of things is not satisfactory.

As the matter stands at present in the Court of Chancery in Ireland, there are not less than four separate systems of fees and stamps all existing together. The fees, which were formerly paid to the Masters in Chancery, were converted by a statute of *Geo.* IV. into Chancery Fund stamps, and they are so carried to the general taxation of the country. Formerly the Lord Chancellor had fees, and the fees are still collected in cash and accounted for to the Exchequer. The fees paid to the Deputy Keeper of the Rolls are paid in cash, and are also accounted for to the Exchequer; the Lord Chancellor's secretary also receives fees in cash, and those fees are accounted for to the Suitors Fee Fund. There are still some officers of the Court of Chancery in Ireland, I am sorry to say, who are paid by fees—a system quite contrary to modern notions. By the Bill which I now ask leave to introduce, it is provided that in future no officer shall be paid by fees, and that all fees shall be received in stamps. The fifth part of the Bill, to which I have adverted, relates to some miscellaneous items to which I need not refer, except as to one of them. In the Court of Chancery in Ireland there are very many sums of small amount which have been unappropriated and unclaimed ; and while in England such sums, unclaimed for

Mr. O'Hagan

fifteen years, are allocated to the Suitors Fee Fund, in Ireland there is no power to allocate them at all. There are 163,820 accounts of this description, and the sums represented by these accounts amount to £74,632 4s. 5d. cash, and £43,198 17s. 5d. stock. The Bill, following the English precedent, provides that this large sum, and all other sums, after the lapse of a period of fifteen years shall be carried to the credit of the Suitors Fee Fund, and applied as they are applied in England. Such is the scope of the Bill which I now submit to the House, and I shall only add, that there is not a clause of the entire Bill, that there is not a line of it, which is not covered and sustained by the finding of some one of the English Commission to which I have referred. These Commissions were of the highest order, and statutes were founded upon their Reports ; but, principally, the Bill is founded upon the recommendation of the two Commissions for Ireland, of the great authority of which I have already spoken. Taking this into account, taking into account that the men who conducted the inquiry were of the highest eminence upon the one side and upon the other ; the English Commissioners represented by such persons as the Master of the Rolls, the present Attorney General, and Sir Hugh Cairns ; and the Irish Commissioners by such men as Lord Chief Justice Monahan and Ex-Chancellor Napier ; and that the recommendations in their Report are supported by the opinions of the oldest men in the profession of solicitors, men thoroughly and intimately acquainted with the working and management of the two systems ; taking also into account that their recommendations are backed up by the earnest prayer of the bar of Ireland, I cannot but think that a Bill which is intended to give effect to those recommendations is entitled to the favourable consideration of this House. I beg, Sir, to move for leave to introduce the Bill.

Motion made, and Question proposed,

" That leave be given to bring in a Bill to alter the constitution and amend the practice and course of proceeding in the High Court of Chancery in Ireland." — (*Mr. Attorney General for Ireland.*)

Mr. WHITESIDE said, he thought it must be admitted that the Irish Administration were at last approaching subjects of some importance. The Civil Bill Act had been amended that evening, and the House was then asked to plunge into Chancery ;

and, although the question appeared un-inviting, he must own that his right hon. and learned Friend had given them a clear and able statement. Even poets had been known to write on a suit in Chancery. His right hon. and learned Friend had referred to what was done in regard to Chancery reform twenty years ago ; but what had been accomplished in that respect had been accomplished by the House of Commons, whose labours his right hon. and learned Friend had entirely overlooked, and which labours the Commission had also strangely forgotten. His right hon. and learned Friend had complained that the attention of Chancery reformers had long been be-stowed almost entirely upon England, and that nothing effectual was done in Ireland till 1850. But what was done in that year, and who did it ? Sir John Romilly, then a Member of that House, desiring to improve the administration of justice in Ireland, passed an Act of Parliament which it was the purpose of the ruthless destroyer now to overturn. That was called the Chan-cery Regulation Act, and its author acted in some respects with common sense. In looking at the Court of Chancery, he found gentlemen there who had almost as good a right to be Superior Judges as some who had reached that rank, and he thought he would avail himself of the staff then existing. To the suitor he gave the choice of suing by bill, which it was now sought to restore, or by cause petition, which, as the cheaper and shorter method of the two, was preferred by the whole Irish community ever since, but which was, nevertheless, now to be abo-lished. That act of Sir John Romilly had been most successful. But how did Sir John Romilly deal with the Irish Masters ? Because it might be thought that these gentlemen were gouty old men of eighty, as in England, whereas they were as full of vigour and animation when Sir John Romilly undertook the matter as any Judge in either kingdom. Sir John Romilly kept them in office and succeeded in saving £15,000 a year for fifteen years ; for which he deserved a vote of censure from his right hon. and learned Friend ; for, according to the argument of his right hon. and learned Friend, he ought to have abolished the Masters fifteen years ago. There were at present four of them, re-ceiving, with their staff, £4,000 per annum, and if their offices were abolished, what could be more agreeable for them than to draw liberal pensions from that old friend, the Consolidated Fund? Sir John Romilly

gave them jurisdiction over various impor-tant matters, and his right hon. and learned Friend had forgotten to point out what evils had resulted from that legislation. There never were four gentlemen who, ever since that complete jurisdiction was conferred on them, had more faithfully and efficiently discharged their duties. They had decided ten cases for every case decided by the Lord Chancellor, and he challenged his right hon. and learned Friend to show how many of their decrees had been re-versed. He had taken the trouble to in-quire, and he found that the proportion was not 3 per cent. What was to be the expense of the new system? That was the vital part of the Bill. The rest was all "leather and prunella." He would state to the House what they were to get. The whole business confided to the Masters was now done by four gen-tlemen and their staff at an expense not exceeding £14,000 a year. The present staff were all to be paid off handsomely and sent on their travels either to England or to Rome to revive their classical recollec-tions. It was proposed that the Master of the Rolls and the Vice Chancellor should have each one chief clerk and two assistant clerks, but then came this clause, which was to be regarded with infinite attention—

"Power, however, should be given to the Lord Chancellor, with the advice and consent of the Master of the Rolls and Vice Chancellor, or one of them, by order under their hands, to appoint an additional chief clerk or assistant clerk to the Master of the Rolls and Vice Chancellor, or either of them."

The salary of the Vice Chancellor would be £4,000 a year. The salary of his first clerk, he heard it whispered, would be £1,500 ; of his second, £800 ; and the third, £600. The Master of the Rolls would have the same. That would make the sum £9,800. But then the staff might be doubled should that be thought necessary. That was done because it was known it would be necessary. From his knowledge of the habits of his country, he would say his impression was that the staff would be doubled forthwith. The staff would then cost £15,400. A noble Marquess in another place, whose talents he admired, and whose anxiety to econo-mize was undoubted, had laid it down that economy was to be practised above all things ; and the total of the economical advantages of the proposed arrangement stood thus, that whereas the work was now done for £12,000 a year, it would under the Bill be done for £27,000. He admitted that in these days of liberality, when the country was suffering, £27,000 a year was a very moderate allowance to be given for the promotion of justice; but it raised the question, Was that a work of utility and necessity? If so, he would join heartily with his right hon. and learned Friend in passing the Bill; but it must be understood before they passed it. He would show the condition in which the question came before the House. His right hon. and learned Friend mentioned the Incumbered Estates Court, and he said truly a Commission was issued to consider, in regard to the continuance of that Court, what was to be done. There was a report that two Vice Chancellors should be appointed, and that the Incumbered Estates Court would be thrown into Chancery. Now, the late Sir Robert Peel founded the Court, but he did not put it into Chancery; on the contrary, he took it out of Chancery. However, when that announcement got abroad, consternation took possession of the House. That recommendation was objected to; but his right hon. and learned Friend, who was, probably, not aware of what took place on that important occasion, made no reference to an important Committee. He quoted the appointment of the Commission; but why pause there? They sometimes had upon Irish questions a Commission to overturn a Committee, and then a Committee to upset a Commission. Public opinion was alarmed, and as soon as Mr. Justice Fitzgerald proposed his Bill to carry out the proposed alterations, and he (Mr. Whiteside) proposed his for the Amendment of the procedure of the Court of Chancery, it was said this Government Commission would never do; they must not give way to a lawyer's Commission; the House must have a Committee of their own. But not a word was said of that by his right hon. and learned Friend. He never noticed the elaborate, able, instructive Report which that Committee had made, founded on the evidence given before them, not upon questions cut and dry, young gentlemen sending in their essays in reply, and telling the Commissioners in reply what occurred in the reign of King John. The Committee consisted of whom? Of the best men they could get—of the late Sir James Graham, of the right hon. Member for Oxfordshire, of the late right hon. Member for Coventry, Mr. E. Ellice, of the right hon. Member for the University of Cambridge, of

Mr. Whiteside

Sir E. Perry, of the Member for Horsham, of the late Chief Secretary to the Lord Lieutenant of Ireland (Mr. Herbert), and several other eminent persons. How did they proceed? The Commission on whose Report they were now called upon to act and the Report of the Committee were in direct opposition. They must, therefore, choose between them. The Committee made a Report, founded upon evidence, filling 400 pages. His right hon. and learned Friend had made no observation upon it. He never referred to the fact that the whole subject had been probed and sifted to the very bottom by the members of that Committee. Never had a body of men, not interested in the question, and not connected with Ireland, devoted more time, ability, knowledge, and capacity in dealing with this subject than the members of that Committee. Whom did they examine? They said the witnesses should be few, but that one should be able to give the sense of a score. They examined the Master of the Rolls in England, because he was the author of the original Incumbered Estates Act and the Chancery Regulation Act; they examined the Master of the Rolls in Ireland, the Judges of the Incumbered Estates Court, two Masters in Chancery, and they summoned the Incorporated Society of Solicitors to send one or two to tell their opinions on the whole matter. His Bill was thrown over, and, although at the time he was dissatisfied, his regret had since diminished. The proposition then made was to take three of the Masters (not altering the salaries) and to call them Vice Chancellors. To that the Committee was directly opposed, because it was shown by the witnesses that nothing could be more satisfactory than the manner in which the Masters disposed of the business under Sir John Romilly's Bill, and the Committee, therefore, rather desired to see their humbler title preserved and their jurisdiction increased. The reason as given in evidence was, that business could be done quickly and efficaciously before a Master, while a Vice Chancellor would be unapproachable, to use the words of a solicitor who was examined. But then came a point not entirely to be lost sight of: the costs to the suitors, which he was afraid would be largely increased. Up to that time, although the Master had power to get in money, he had no power to pay it out. The Committee did not see any reason why complete jurisdiction should not be given. The recommendations of the Committee were that a tribunal should exist in which unencumbered properties could be disposed of. They also held that Masters in ordinary should have in a large class of cases original jurisdiction. The Report of the Commissioners was opposed to that view. The next recommendation of the Committee was that the Lord Chancellor and the Master of the Rolls should make general orders and give power to the Masters to obtain the assistance of scientific persons, to enable such Court to decide the matters in issue. At present the only persons who disposed of matters without reference were the Masters, and yet they were to be abolished, while it was contemplated to establish a reference to chief clerks, or a kind of inferior Masters, to do what the present Masters who had been well trained to the work did perfectly. It was extraordinary to hear stated as a reason why the orders which, if made, would have obviated the necessity for the Bill—that those orders had not been made because there was a difference of opinion among the Judges. No words could be more distinct than those which gave the power of making general orders and of distributing the business; and if those powers had been properly exercised there would have been no necessity for applying again to Parliament, as he had no idea of the Judges declining to exercise powers conferred upon them for the benefit of the suitor. It was clear that what could be done in England could in point of economy, simplicity, and expedition be equally well done in Ireland. If the Master of the Rolls had been asked courteously he would have told them his opinion in one moment. The number of references during the past year made by the Master of the Rolls was very small ; that learned individual was careful to make as few references as possible. The Bill recommended by the Committee was introduced to carry out the object of enabling the Masters to deal with monies in court. If the Master of the Rolls had been asked what staff he would require to carry on the work in his own court without reference, he would have replied that all the powers needed to reform the court would be the exercise of the powers conferred by the statute, and giving to the Master of the Rolls the aid of such chief clerks as he might require, capable of carrying out the objects specified in the Report of the Committee. It was not within the power of the Committee to frame rules, and the reason why more specific provision had not been made

in the Act of Parliament was, that the House considered it unadvisable to incorporate general orders in a statute. In looking over the evidence of the Master of the Rolls before the Commission, he (Mr. Whiteside) observed that he stated that the carrying out of certain objects alluded to might have been accomplished by general orders, but if such orders had not been made it was not the fault of Parliament. The right hon. and learned Gentleman referred in support of his plan to the evidence of the profession, but it was a curious fact that the professional evidence was equally balanced on either side. Promotion was now so rapid that there was no knowing how soon his right hon. and learned Friend might have a successor in that House, and there might be proposals for the creation of a second Vice Chancellor and a second chief clerk to take the place of the Masters. What was the evidence upon the point ? Mr. Pilkington, a very sensible gentleman in the profession, said—

" In my opinion the working of the jurisdiction which the Masters exercise in Ireland, under the 15th section of the Irish Chancery Regulation Act, is satisfactory."

Mr. William Smith, who was said to have more practice in the court than any other junior, said the result of his experience of the working of the jurisdiction which the Masters exercised was strongly in its favour ; and so said two other juniors. The Incorporated Society of Solicitors declared that in its general bearings the Irish Chancery Regulation Act had worked well for the public, and that there had been a great saving of expense, particularly in suits for the administration of real estates. The body of solicitors in Belfast stated that

" The system of proceeding by cause petitions and affidavits in the courts of the Lord Chancellor and the Master of the Rolls, as affected by the Irish Chancery Regulation Act, is a vast improvement upon the present system, though capable of being still further modified."

He admitted that amendment was necessary, but had no hesitation in saying that the Attorney General might suggest all that was required without either commission or statute. If the Attorney General had bestowed only two hours in drawing up a code of rules which would apply to the existing machinery, adding any improvement that might be found in the English system, the result might have been satisfactory ; but instead of that the proposal was to substitute an inferior system for one that had worked well in all respects. When the Report of the Committee was made there were four Masters, but subsequently one died, and the vacancy was not filled up. If one of the three retired, of which there was a hint in the Report of the Commission, they might try whether the work could not be done with two. The simple way to economize was not to fill up vacancies and not to create new places. When the Bill came on for a second reading he would appeal to the English Members to say whether the system of chief clerks had been successful. If some difficult cases had got before the Irish Masters, that was because no order was made for the distribution of the business, and, certainly, nobody could pretend that the decisions of the Masters were not sound. Did the right hon. Gentleman really adhere to his opinion that the examiners of the Masters would be fit persons for chief clerks under the new system? He had been informed that the Master of the Rolls in this country and the Vice Chancellors got the most experienced and able men they could find to discharge the important duties of that office. The question of expense was a most important one, and he trusted the House would look carefully at the proposed table of fees, in order to ascertain whether the costs of a suit, which were not now extravagant, might not be magnified instead of being diminished. He hoped the second reading would be put off till a distant day, so that the opinion of the public and the profession might be expressed upon the principle and details of the Bill.

SIR PATRICK O'BRIEN said, it was hardly fair of the right hon. and learned Gentleman (Mr. Whiteside) to oppose the introduction of a Bill founded upon the Report of a Commission. He was also surprised at some of his observations, especially with reference to the Incumbered Estates question. The right hon. and learned Gentleman had always been ready to appoint his own friends to offices when he had the opportunity, and he (Sir Patrick O'Brien) did not blame him for doing so; but he was astonished to see him, the head of the legal profession in Ireland, come down here and oppose the introduction of a measure of the kind before them upon such grounds as he had given.

MR. WHITESIDE explained that he had brought in the Bill to limit the Judges in the Incumbered Estates Court of Ireland to two, but was forced to allow three Judges to continue.

Mr. Whiteside

MR. SCULLY said, he thought that the right hon. and learned Gentleman should have permitted the Bill to be printed before entering into a discussion upon its merits. At the same time, he should be happy to give the right hon. and learned Gentleman any assistance in his power to oppose the perpetration of any job, or the addition of any new burdens to the Consolidated Fund. He (Mr. Scully) would be glad to avail himself of the present staff, and to make one of the Masters a Vice Chancellor; for that gentleman had no more right to be pensioned off than any clerk in the office. It might be that the Irish Vice Chancellor would be unapproachable; certainly the English was such. It was true that the Irish Judges were the aristocracy of Dublin, while the English Judges were scarcely of the middle classes of England. He believed the right hon. and learned Gentleman to be mistaken in his estimate of the speed with which business was transacted in the Master's Office. The right hon. and learned Gentleman would find it rather difficult to extricate himself if he were unfortunate enough ever to become involved in legal proceedings in the Master's Office. A system of great delay existed, especially in connection with suits for the sale of property. Under the old method, suits had lasted thirty, sixty, and even eighty years, and though that state of things had been improved, he was sorry to say that of late years there had been a tendency to relapse. The affairs of Mr. John Sadleir, as a case in point, were not set free for nine years. It was necessary that some of the existing evils should be removed, but the Lord Chancellor and the Master of the Rolls could not agree in framing the necessary rules, and for that reason he approved of the Bill, because it would make the necessary changes effectual by Act of Parliament.

MR. VANCE said, he saw no necessity for the violent changes proposed in the Bill. It could not be defended on the ground of economy, for it would pay off the present officers only for the purpose of creating others. Neither the Lord Chancellor nor the Dublin Chamber of Commerce approved the measure, and the Report of the Commission on which it was based was more than counterbalanced by the Report of the very able Committee, which came to quite a different conclusion. There was great alarm and dissatisfaction among his constituents as to these continual changes in the administration of the law and removal of officials. There was no ground of complaint against cause petitions, which, in his own experience, were cheap and expeditious. The great objection to the Bill was that it did not utilize the present officials, as was done in the case of the English Bankruptcy Act. He hoped the Attorney General would give ample time for the consideration of the measure, which, if read a second time, it would be well to send to a Select Committee.

MR. GEORGE said, he should offer no factious opposition to the bringing in of the Bill, but he had to remark that what had occurred that night was a sufficient justification of the course taken by his right hon. and learned Friend and others in preventing the introduction of the Bill on a former occasion without any statement. When the Reports of the Committee and of the Commission came to be examined, there would, he thought, be found reasons for doubting whether the Bill would become the law of the land. He hoped the second reading would not be taken till after Whitsuntide.

MR. HENNESSY desired the Attorney General to state distinctly whether he would agree to postpone the next stage of the Bill till after Whitsuntide. It was not right that these important measures should be brought on so late at night, when there were not half a dozen Members present, when the Ministers had all retired, and even the Chief Secretary had gone to bed. If the right hon. and learned Gentleman would not give him an answer, he knew what would happen.

Motion made, and Question put, "That the Debate be now adjourned."—(*Mr. Hennessy.*)

MR. O'HAGAN said, he thought the manner in which the Question had been put to him quite unjustifiable. He was quite willing to allow reasonable time for considering the Bill—say a fortnight or so—but hoped it would be read a second time before Whitsuntide.

MR. WHITESIDE suggested that it would be better to postpone it till after that period.

MR. BUTT said, that to delay the Bill so long would be to lose it.

Motion, by leave, *withdrawn.*

Original Question put, and *agreed to.*

Bill *ordered* to be brought in by Mr. ATTORNEY GENERAL for IRELAND, Sir ROBERT PEEL, and Sir GEORGE GREY.

Bill *presented*, and read 1°. [Bill 78.]

SEAT OF UNDER SECRETARY OF STATE.

Ordered,

That the Marquess of Hartington be at liberty to appear, by his Counsel and Agents, before the Select Committee appointed to inquire whether the Under Secretary of State who was last appointed to that office thereby vacated his Seat.

House adjourned at One o'clock.

HOUSE OF LORDS,

Tuesday, April 26, 1864.

MINUTES.]—PUBLIC BILLS—*First Reading*—Prevention of Trespasses (Scotland) [H.L.]* (No. 60).
Second Reading—Mortgage Debentures [H.L.], and referred to Select Committee on Improvement of Land Act, 1864, (No. 99).
Committee — Joint Stock Companies (Foreign Countries) [H.L.]*.
Report—Joint Stock Companies (Foreign Countries)*.
Third Reading—Warehousing of British Spirits * (No. 54), and *passed.*

MORTGAGE DEBENTURES BILL.—[H. L.] [No. 99.]   SECOND READING.

Order of the Day for the Second Reading read.

LORD REDESDALE *moved* the second reading of this Bill, which was a substitute, in the shape of a Public Bill, for the Private Bill—the Land Transfer and Mortgage Bill—which was discussed in their Lordships' House some days ago, and with respect to which some of their Lordships had expressed an opinion that the subject was one of too much importance to be dealt with by a Private Bill. He did not pretend that the present Bill was perfect. If it were now read a second time, however, he proposed that it should be referred to the Select Committee to which the Bill of the Lord Chancellor on the same matter—the Land Securities Bill—had been referred.

Moved, That the Bill be now read 2ª.

THE DUKE OF MARLBOROUGH said, this Bill required very careful consideration. It gave power to trustees to lend money upon debentures, secured upon real property, and he was afraid it would be taken advantage of by Companies engaged in various speculative kinds of business, and that the result would be to damage the debenture system, which, within proper limits, was very useful.

LORD TAUNTON conceived the whole subject to be one of the greatest importance, and he believed that legislation with respect to it by means of a Public rather than by a Private Bill would cause the matter to receive greater consideration.

LORD REDESDALE observed, in regard to the objection that speculative companies of various kinds might obtain privileges under the Bill, that one subject for the consideration of the Select Committee would be to define the character of the companies to which these powers should be confided.

Motion *agreed to :* Bill read 2ª accordingly, and *referred* to the Select Committee on the Improvement of Land Act, 1864, Bill.

UNITED STATES—THE LAW OF PRIZE.

LORD CHELMSFORD, in rising to call the attention of the House to the statement of the views of Her Majesty's Government as to the mode of dealing with Prizes brought by the belligerent Powers of America within the dominions of Her Majesty, contained in the Correspondence respecting the *Tuscaloosa*, which has been presented to the House, said, that the subject was of such great importance that he would not apologize for submitting it to the attention of their Lordships. In the deplorable war which had been so long raging on the other side of the Atlantic, both belligerents had shown themselves so extremely sensitive as to the conduct of this country, that it was necessary for the Government to be extremely careful not to exceed the strict limit of neutral rights and obligations, and to do nothing not strictly in conformity with the principles of international law. In the papers laid on the table of the House under the title of " Correspondence respecting the *Tuscaloosa*," he found some instructions issued by the Government with respect to the mode of dealing with prizes brought by the belligerents into ports belonging to this country, which appeared to him so much at variance with principle and policy, and which, if acted upon, seemed so likely to lead to unpleasant consequences, that he felt bound to present to their Lordships his views on the matter, for their Lordships' careful consideration, or necessary correction. At the commence-

The Duke of Marlborough

ment of the present unhappy war in America, Her Majesty was advised to issue a proclamation interdicting the armed ships of both contending parties from coming with their prizes into the ports, harbours, and roadsteads of the United Kingdom, or of any of the British Colonies and Possessions. This he thought a wise precaution and perfectly consistent with our neutral character. The writers on International Law laid it down that, although it was not a violation of neutrality for a belligerent to bring her prizes into a neutral port, and even to dispose of them there, yet they all added that the neutral might refuse that privilege provided the refusal extended to both parties. No fault, therefore, was to be found with the proclamation, and the only consideration was as to the proper course of proceeding in case the prohibition should be disregarded. The *Tuscaloosa* was originally a Federal vessel named the *Conrad*. On the 21st of June last, she was off the coast of Brazil with a cargo of wool, and was there captured by the well-known Confederate cruiser, the *Alabama*. The captors put some guns on board, placed in her a lieutenant of the Confederate navy, and ten men, and changing her name to the *Tuscaloosa*, employed her as a tender of the *Alabama*. The two vessels were in company at the Cape of Good Hope in the beginning of August, and Captain Semmes ordered the *Tuscaloosa* to Simon's Bay for the purpose of obtaining provisions, and undergoing some slight repairs. She arrived off Simon's Bay on the 7th of August. The Admiral upon the station, Sir Baldwin Walker, who had heard something of the previous history of the *Tuscaloosa*, doubted whether she could properly be considered as the tender of the *Alabama*—whether she did not retain her previous character of an uncondemned prize, and, therefore, whether she could be admitted under the terms of Her Majesty's Proclamation. He wrote to Governor Wodehouse, and requested that he would take the opinion of the Law Officers of the Colony on the subject. The Governor accordingly consulted the Attorney General at the Cape, who founding his opinion upon passages of International Law which were to be found in *Wheaton*, and which were printed in the papers, and also upon a despatch from Earl Russell, of the 31st of January, 1862, gave it as his opinion that, by reason of the vessel having been armed by the captors, and having had a lieutenant and crew put on board, the *Tuscaloosa* had been "set forth" as a vessel of war, and might be permitted to enter the bay. A communication to that effect was made to Sir Baldwin Walker, who was not quite satisfied with the opinion of the Attorney General ; but, of course, he yielded, and the *Tuscaloosa* anchored in Simon's Bay on the 8th of August, and remained there till the 15th. While she was lying at anchor there, the American Consul claimed that she should be retained on behalf of the original owners, and that claim had such an important bearing on the instructions which he should bring under the consideration of their Lordships, that he begged their special attention to it. Having mentioned that the *Tuscaloosa's* true name was the *Conrad*, and that she had never been condemned as prize by any lawfully constituted Admiralty Court, he proceeded to say—

" I am well aware that your Government has conceded to the so-called Confederate States the rights of belligerents, and is thereby bound to respect Captain Semmes' commission ; but having refused to recognize the ' Confederacy' as a nation, and having excluded his captures from all the ports of the British Empire, the captures necessarily revert to their real owners, and are forfeited by Captain Semmes as soon as they enter a British port."—*Correspondence*, No. 6 (1864), p. 11.

Now, the Governor, with his Attorney General, seemed to have taken a more correct view of International Law than Her Majesty's Government, for in reply to the American Consul, he says—

" The Governor is not aware, nor do you refer him to the provisions of International Law by which captured vessels, as soon as they enter our neutral ports, revert to their real owners, and are forfeited by their captors. But his Excellency believes that the claims of contending parties to vessels captured can only be determined in the first instance by the courts of the captor's country."—*Correspondence*, No. 6 (1864), p. 12.

The American Consul was not satisfied with that reply, and wrote another letter repeating his claim, and repeating it in the most extraordinary manner. He said —

" The *Tuscaloosa* being a prize, was forbidden to enter Simon's Bay by the Queen's Proclamation, and should have been ordered off at once, but she was not so ordered. Granting that Her Majesty's Proclamation affirmed the right of Captain Semmes as a 'belligerent' to take and to hold prizes on the high seas, it just as emphatically denied his right to hold them in British ports. Now, if he could not hold them in Simon's Bay, who else could hold them except those whose right to hold them was antecedent to his—that is, the owners !"—p. 12.

He (Lord Chelmsford) would have said that that claim was as extravagant as the reasoning was illogical, if he had not been checked by finding that it had been sanctioned by Her Majesty's Government apparently on the advice of the Law Officers of the Crown. The Governor sent a despatch upon the subject to the Secretary for the Colonies :—and he could not refer to the noble Duke who lately held the seals of the Colonial Office without expressing his deep and sincere regret that the country should be deprived, he feared, not for a time only of his long tried and eminent services. In that despatch Governor Wodehouse says—

" An important question has arisen in connection with the *Alabama*, on which it is very desirable that I should, as soon as practicable, be made acquainted with the views of Her Majesty's Government. Captain Semmes had mentioned, after his arrival in port, that he had left outside one of his prizes previously taken, the *Tuscaloosa*, which he had equipped and fitted as a tender, and had ordered to meet him in Simon's Bay, as she also stood in need of supplies. When this became known to the Naval Commander-in-Chief, he requested me to furnish him with a legal opinion ; and whether this vessel could be held to be a ship of war before she had been formally condemned in a Prize Court ; or whether she must not be held to be still a prize, and, as such, prohibited from entering our ports. The Acting Attorney General, founding his opinion on Earl Russell's despatch to your Grace of the 31st of January, 1862, and on Wheaton's *International Law*, stated in substance that it was open to Captain Semmes to convert this vessel into a ship of war, and that she ought to be admitted into our ports on that footing."—*Correspondence*, No. 6 (1864), p. 5.

It was in reply to that despatch that the answer was sent by Her Majesty's Government, to which he was about to direct their Lordships' attention, and he could not help thinking that the instructions conveyed in it were the result of Federal pressure. He ought not to make that assertion without proof ; but he thought he was in a position to prove it, and it would be for their Lordships to say how far he was successful. During the time in which the proceedings to which he had referred were going on, a very active correspondence was being prosecuted between the noble Earl the Foreign Secretary and the American Minister, upon the subject of what Mr. Adams called " the depredations " of the *Alabama*, and the claims of American citizens to be indemnified for the losses which they had sustained by the capture of their vessels by the *Alabama*. Those claims the noble Earl of course repudiated ; but Mr. Adams mentioned many causes of complaint, and amongst them he sent to the noble Earl the extraordinary claim of the American

Consul at the Cape, to which he (Lord Chelmsford) had directed their Lordships' attention. In the papers No. 1, North America, the Correspondence respecting the *Alabama*, their Lordships would find a despatch of the noble Earl, of the 29th of October, just six days before the despatch of the 4th of November, in which the instructions to the Governor were contained. The noble Earl mentioned various matters of complaint under three different heads, and among others the case of the *Tuscaloosa*, and how it had been dealt with by the authorities at the Cape. He said—

"As regards the *Tuscaloosa*, although Her Majesty's Government would have approved the British authorities at the Cape if they had adopted towards that vessel a course different from that which was adopted, yet the question as to the manner in which a vessel under such circumstances should, according to the tenour of Her Majesty's Orders, be dealt with, was one not altogether free from uncertainty. Nevertheless, instructions will be sent to the British authorities at the Cape for their guidance in the event of a similar case occurring hereafter, and Her Majesty's Government hope that under those instructions nothing will for the future happen to admit of a question being raised as to Her Majesty's Orders having been strictly carried out."—*Correspondence*, No. 1 (1864), p. 43.

Thus, then, on the 29th of October, after a rather menacing correspondence on the part of the American Minister, Her Majesty's Government promised that instructions should be issued, and they were issued six days afterwards, sanctioning and adopting the extraordinary claims made by the American Minister. The noble Duke gave the following instructions:—

"With regard to the vessel called the *Tuscaloosa*, I am advised that this vessel did not lose the character of a prize captured by the *Alabama* merely because she was, at the time of her being brought within British waters, armed with two small rifled guns, in charge of an officer, and manned with a crew of ten men from the *Alabama*, and used as a tender to that vessel, under the authority of Captain Semmes. It would appear that the *Tuscaloosa* is a bark of 500 tons, captured by the *Alabama* off the coast of Brazil, on the 21st of June last, and brought into Simon's Bay on or before the 7th of August, with her original cargo of wool (itself, as well as the vessel, prize) still on board, and with nothing to give her a warlike character (so far as is stated in the papers before me) except the circumstances already noticed. Whether, in the case of a vessel duly commissioned as a ship of war, after being made prize by a belligerent Government, without being first brought *infra præsidia* or condemned by a Court of Prize, the character of prize, within the meaning of Her Majesty's Orders, would or would not be merged in that of a national ship of

Lord Chelmsford

war, I am not called upon to explain. It is enough to say that the citation from Mr. Wheaton's book by your Attorney General does not appear to me to have any direct bearing upon the question."—*Correspondence*, No. 6 (1864), p. 18.

And then the noble Duke concluded as follows:—

"The question remains what course ought to have been taken by the authorities of the Cape—1st, in order to ascertain whether this vessel was, as alleged by the United States Consul, an uncondemned prize, brought within British waters in violation of Her Majesty's neutrality; and 2nd, what ought to have been done if such had appeared to be really the fact. I think that the allegations of the United States Consul ought to have been brought to the knowledge of Captain Semmes while the *Tuscaloosa* was still within British waters, and that he should have been requested to state whether he did or did not admit the facts to be as alleged. He should also have been called upon (unless the facts were admitted) to produce the *Tuscaloosa's* papers. If the result of these inquiries had been to prove that the vessel was really an uncondemned prize, brought into British waters in violation of Her Majesty's Orders, made for the purpose of maintaining her neutrality, I consider that the mode of proceeding in such circumstances most consistent with Her Majesty's dignity, and most proper for the vindication of her territorial rights, would have been to prohibit the exercise of any further control over the *Tuscaloosa* by her captors, and to retain that vessel under Her Majesty's control and jurisdiction until properly reclaimed by her original owners."—p. 19.

These were the views of Her Majesty's Government; and the despatch having been sent to the Governor, he found himself in a situation of great embarrassment. He required further explanation with respect to the mode in which he was to act, and he wrote on the 19th of December as follows:—

"I think it right to take advantage of the first opportunity for representing to your Grace the state of uncertainty in which I am placed by the receipt of this communication, and for soliciting such further explanations as may prevent my again falling into error on these matters."

He added—

"Your Grace intimates that the citation from *Wheaton* by the Acting Attorney General does not appear to have any direct bearing upon the question. You will assuredly believe that it is not from any want of respect for your opinion, but solely from a desire to avoid future error, that I confess my inability to understand this intimation, or in the absence of instructions on that head, to see in what direction I am to look for the law bearing on the subject. The paragraph cited made no distinction between a vessel with cargo and a vessel without cargo; and your Grace leaves me in ignorance whether her character would have been changed if Captain Semmes had got rid of the cargo before claiming for her admission as a ship of war. Certainly, acts had been done by him which, according to *Wheaton*, constituted a 'setting forth as a vessel of war.'"—*Correspondence*, No. 6 (1864), p. 19.

To add to his embarrassments, the *Tuscaloosa*, after an absence of four months, returned on the 26th of December to Simon's Bay. Admiral Sir Baldwin Walker wrote to the Governor stating the course which in his opinion ought to be pursued—

"As it appears that this vessel, the *Tuscaloosa*, late Federal ship *Conrad*, is an uncondemned prize, brought into British waters in violation of Her Majesty's orders, made for the purpose of maintaining her neutrality, I therefore consider that she ought to be detained with the view of her being reclaimed by her original owners, in accordance with the opinion of the Law Officers of the Crown, forwarded for my guidance, the copy of which I have already transmitted to you."—p. 21.

He could not pass over the extraordinary departure from the usual course which this letter disclosed. They had been told in that House over and over again, that the opinions of the Law Officers of the Crown were confidential, and the Government had repeatedly refused to lay them upon the table. The noble Earl (Earl Russell), when asked in the House when it was that the Attorney General had changed his opinion on the subject of the steam rams, said—

"I consider the opinion of the Attorney General to be a privileged communication, and I decline to answer the question."

Yet it now appeared that these confidential communications were sent out as instructions to Admiral Sir Baldwin Walker, and by him communicated to the captains of the fleet. If they obtain such publicity as that, he (Lord Chelmsford) could see no reason for withholding them from the House of Lords or the House of Commons. The Governor of the colony agreed with Sir Baldwin Walker that, in conformity with the instructions furnished by the Government on the 4th of November, the vessel ought to be detained for the purpose of being delivered up to her original owners; and, accordingly, she was seized by the colonial authorities. The Governor offered her to the United States Consul, who most fortunately appeared to have some scruples about receiving her. The Consul said—

"I can institute a proceeding *in rem* where the rights of property of fellow-citizens are concerned, without a special procuration from those for whose benefit I act, but cannot receive actual restitution of the *res*, in controversy without a special authority."

If the Consul had not had these scruples, there would have been a little bill to pay at the present moment to the captors. The stores and ammunition were taken out and deposited in the dockyard, but not without an indignant protest on the part of the Lieutenant of the Confederate Navy who was in command of the *Tuscaloosa*. He said—

"In August last the *Tuscaloosa* arrived in Simon's Bay. She was not only recognized in the character which she lawfully claimed and still claims to be—namely, a commissioned ship of war belonging to a belligerent Power, but was allowed to remain in the harbour for the period of seven days, taking in supplies and effecting repairs with the full knowledge and sanction of the authorities. No intimation was given that she was regarded merely in the light of an ordinary prize, or that she was considered to be violating the laws of neutrality. Nor, when she notoriously left for a cruise on active service, was any intimation whatever conveyed that on her return to the port of a friendly Power, where she had been received as a man-of-war, she would be regarded as a prize, as a violator of the Queen's Proclamation of neutrality, and consequently liable to seizure. Misled by the conduct of Her Majesty's Government, I returned to Simon's Bay on the 26th inst., in very urgent want of repairs and supplies; to my surprise the *Tuscaloosa* is now no longer considered as a man-of-war, and she has, by your orders, as I learn, been seized for the purpose of being handed over to the person who claims her on behalf of her late owners. The character of the vessel—namely, that of a lawful commissioned man-of-war of the Confederate States of America—has not been altered since her first arrival in Simon's Bay, and she, having been once fully recognized by the British authorities in command in this colony, and no notice or warning of change of opinion or of friendly feeling having been communicated by public notification or otherwise, I was entitled to expect to be again permitted to enter Simon's Bay without molestation. In perfect good faith I returned to Simon's Bay for mere necessaries, and in all honour and good faith in return I should, on change of opinion or of policy on the part of the British authorities, have been desired to leave the port again. But, by the course of proceedings taken, I have been (supposing the view now taken by your Excellency's Government to be correct) first misled and next entrapped. My position and the character of my ship will most certainly be vindicated by my Government. I am powerless to resist the affront offered to the Confederate States of America by your Excellency's conduct and proceedings."—*Correspondence*, No. 6 (1864), p. 23.

In due course the Governor communicated to the Secretary of State for Colonial Affairs the seizure of the *Tuscaloosa*. In a despatch, dated the 11th of January, he said—

"I very much regret having to acquaint your Grace that the Confederate prize vessel the *Tuscaloosa* has again entered Simon's Bay, and that the naval Commander-in-Chief and myself have come to the conclusion that, in obedience to the orders transmitted to his Excellency by the Admiralty, and to me by your Grace's despatch of the 4th November last, it was our duty to take possession of the vessel, and to hold her until properly claimed by her original owners. The Admiral, therefore, sent an officer with a party of men from the flagship to take charge of her, and to deliver to her commander a letter in explanation of the act. Copies of his protest, addressed to me, and of my reply, are enclosed. He not unnaturally complains of having been now seized after he had, on the previous occasion, been recognised as a ship of war. But this is manifestly nothing more than the inevitable result of the overruling by Her Majesty's Government of the conclusion arrived at on the previous occasion by its subordinate officer."—*Correspondence*, No. 6 (1864), p. 25.

By a despatch, dated the 4th of March, the Governor was directed by the noble Duke the Secretary of State to deliver back the *Tuscaloosa* to the lieutenant who commanded her, the reasons for so doing being promised to be communicated to him in a subsequent despatch. Now, the instructions sent out on the 4th of November were either right or wrong. If they were wrong, Her Majesty's Government ought not to have been satisfied by merely ordering that the vessel should be restored —they need have felt no humiliation in admitting their error and making an apology, and it would further have been a generous act to which the Confederates are entirely unaccustomed. If the instructions were right, let their Lordships see the position in which the Government placed itself by the order to deliver back the vessel. By the seizure of the vessel under the instructions, the original owners had been remitted to their rights, and the Government ought not to have ordered her to be given back to the Confederates without the consent of the owners. The fact was, Her Majesty's Government did not like to admit they were wrong, and could not assert that they were right; and, therefore, in the despatch communicating the reasons why the *Tuscaloosa* was to be restored, they took a course which was always an indication of weakness — they made the *Tuscaloosa* a special case. The announcement was conveyed in these terms—

"I have now to explain that this decision was not founded on any general principle respecting the treatment of prizes captured by the cruisers of either belligerent, but on the peculiar circumstances of the case. The *Tuscaloosa* was allowed to enter the port of Cape Town and to depart, the instructions of the 4th of November not having arrived at the Cape before her departure. The captain of the *Alabama* was thus entitled to assume that he might equally bring her a second

Lord Chelmsford

time into the same harbour, and it becomes unnecessary to discuss whether, on her return to the Cape, the *Tuscaloosa* still retained the character of a prize, or whether she had lost that character and had assumed that of an armed tender to the *Alabama;* and whether that new character, if properly established and admitted, would have entitled her to the same privilege of admission which might be accorded to her captor, the *Alabama*."—*Correspondence*, No. 6 (1864), p. 31.

So ended the history of the *Tuscaloosa.* That the Government were wrong in seizing that vessel, and that they were right in restoring her, he was willing to concede; and if that were an individual case in which no general principle was involved, he should dismiss it without any further observations. But the instructions issued on the 4th of November had never to his knowledge been recalled, their impropriety had never been acknowledged; and, therefore, he desired to point out what in his view formed the error and illegality of those instructions. He said — and he challenged contradiction of the statement —that no writer on International Law had laid down the doctrine that a neutral which had prevented a belligerent from bringing prizes into her ports had any right whatever, if that prohibition was disregarded, to seize the prize and to restore her to her original owners. All that the neutral had a right to do in such a case was to order the vessel away; and, if she refused to go, the neutral might use force for the purpose of urging her departure. By the rules of International Law the moment a capture takes place the property, as between belligerents, is vested in the captors, and therefore a neutral dealing with the property in the way proposed by Her Majesty's Government would be taking the property of one of the belligerents and giving it to the other. A neutral has no right whatever to enter into the consideration of the validity of prizes brought into its waters. The capture may have been invalid and illegal, but the neutral has no right to raise the question. There were only certain cases in which the neutral might and ought to inquire, and those were exceptions very strongly establishing the rule. Where a vessel is seized by a belligerent within neutral waters, a violation of neutrality takes place, and it is not only the right, but the duty, of the neutral to restore the vessel to its original owners, because the captures are illegal and void, and there never was a moment at which the vessel was legally a prize. But that rule certainly could not be made to apply to the case of the *Tuscaloosa*, which, after a lapse of six months from the time of her capture, came into neutral waters. So it is held that a neutral may exercise the authority of seizing prizes brought into its waters, and of returning them where the property of its subjects has been illegally captured and afterwards brought into its ports: the extraordinary reason upon which his right is founded being, that it is a compensation for the asylum afforded. But he repeated that no authority was to be found for the proposition that neutrals were entitled to deal with prizes brought into their waters in the manner in which Her Majesty's Government had dealt with the *Tuscaloosa*. It would, no doubt, be urged by the Government, that the bringing of a prize into neutral waters, contrary to the prohibition contained in the Proclamation, was a violation of neutrality. But with this view, taking the plain meaning of the words "violation of neutrality," he could not agree. He contended that the instructions issued by Her Majesty's Government were wholly improper and illegal. He presumed, they had not been confined to the Governor of the Cape of Good Hope, but had been sent round to all our colonial possessions. At the very moment when he was addressing their Lordships, it might be that prizes had been seized in some of our colonies and delivered up by the different local Governors either to the Confederates or the Federals. If the prize improperly seized under the instructions of the Government belonged to the Federals, he could anticipate fully what would happen: strong remonstrances and high toned menaces on one side, submission, apology, restoration, and, perhaps, compensation, on the other. Should the prize taken be from the Confederates, the remonstrances might be equally loud, but they would not be so much regarded. Restoration, as shown by the present case, might be necessary; but it would be restoration unaccompanied by any apology— it would be mere restoration, and nothing more. Whichever alternative happened, the position of the British nation would not be very dignified. He trusted that, in the reply about to be made by Her Majesty's Government, he should hear either that the propositions which he had ventured to lay down were capable of refutation, or that the instructions issued by the Government had been recalled, or were about to be recalled. In either event, he

should feel that he had not provoked the discussion in vain.

EARL RUSSELL: My Lord, the noble and learned Lord has, no doubt, brought a very serious question under your Lordships' consideration. At the same time it must be recollected, that all these applications of the principles of international law to the contest between the Federals and so-styled Confederate States have to be made under very exceptional circumstances. It has been usual for a Power carrying on war upon the seas to possess ports of its own in which vessels are built, equipped, and fitted, and from which they issue, to which they bring their prizes, and in which those prizes, when brought before a court, are either condemned or restored. But it so happens that in this conflict the Confederate States have no ports except those of the Mersey and the Clyde, from which they fit out ships to cruise against the Federals; and having no ports to which to bring their prizes, they are obliged to burn them upon the high seas. It is natural, under these circumstances, that the Confederate officers and Confederate authorities should somewhat resent the Orders of Her Majesty, of which the noble and learned Lord was pleased to approve, and should endeavour to evade their operation. These Orders, as your Lordships are aware, were that no prizes made by either belligerent should be brought into the ports of the United Kingdom or of Her Majesty's possessions abroad. It thus became very difficult for the Confederates to determine what they should do with their prizes. The *Tuscaloosa*, so called, was brought into a port of the Cape of Good Hope. The noble and learned Lord passed over with little more than a depreciatory notice the Reports of the naval officers upon that station. For my part, I have found that the officers of Her Majesty's naval service, being bound to apply the law of nations according to the rules with which they are furnished, and the books which they have in their possession, have, generally speaking, applied them with remarkable sense and discretion, and in a spirit of equal firmness and moderation, showing themselves disposed always to maintain the rights of the British Crown and the honour of the British flag, but at the same time to do nothing for the purpose of irritation or mere vexatious interference. Such has been the conduct of Sir Alexander

Milne, who has for four years directed the operations of Her Majesty's forces on the coast of America, in such a manner as, while securing the approbation of his own Government, to conciliate the regard of all with whom he has had to deal, and particularly of the Government of the United States. And such, I will venture to say, was the conduct of Sir Baldwin Walker. Now what had he to consider in this case? It struck Sir Baldwin Walker, as, I think, it would have struck any one else, that if Confederate ships of war were to be allowed to send in prizes with their cargo on board, and by putting one or two guns and a Confederate officer on board to call them ships of war, the policy of Her Majesty's Government would be defeated, and Her Majesty's Proclamation would become null and void. They would send in their prizes with a couple of guns and an officer, who, having sold first the cargo and then the vessel, would return to his ship; and this process might be repeated with any number of prizes. Thus Her Majesty's neutrality would become a mere name. Sir Baldwin Walker has expressed this in some passages to which the noble and learned Lord did not refer, but which I will read to your Lordships. In his letter of the 19th of August he says—

" On the 8th of August the tender *Tuscaloosa,* a sailing bark, arrived in Simon's Bay, and the boarding officer having reported to me that her original cargo of wool was still on board, I felt that there were grounds for doubting her real character, and again called the Governor's attention to this circumstance. My letter and his reply are annexed. And I would here beg to submit to their Lordships' notice, that this power of a captain of a ship of war to constitute every prize he may take a ' tender' appears to me likely to lead to abuse and evasion of the laws of strict neutrality, by being used as a means for bringing prizes into neutral ports for disposal of their cargoes, and secret arrangements—which arrangements, it must be seen, could afterwards be easily carried out at isolated places."—*Correspondence,* No. 6 (1864), p. 1.

And in another letter—

" The admission of this vessel into port will, I fear, open the door for numbers of vessels captured under similar circumstances being denominated tenders, with a view to avoid the prohibition contained in the Queen's instructions; and I would observe that the vessel *Sea Bride,* captured by the *Alabama* off Table Bay a few days since, or all other prizes, might be in like manner styled tenders, making the prohibition entirely null and void."—p. 3.

With reference to that the noble and learned Lord expressed no opinion. He did not tell us whether, under the law of

Earl Russell

nations, it is permissible for the captain of a man-of-war to make any number of his prizes into tenders or vessels of war, and send them into neutral ports, and thus evade a proclamation of neutrality. Sir Baldwin Walker further says—

" Now, this vessel has her original cargo of wool still on board, which cannot be required for warlike purposes, and her armament and the number of her crew are quite insufficient for any services other than those of slight defence. Viewing all the circumstances of the case, they afford room for the supposition that the vessel is styled a ' tender,' with the object of avoiding the prohibition against her entrance as a prize into our ports, where, if the captors wished, arrangements could be made for. the disposal of her valuable cargo, the transshipment of which, your Excellency will not fail to see, might be readily effected on any part of the coast beyond the limits of this colony."—p. 3.

The question was, whether it was to be permitted that prizes should be sent into our ports under the disguise of being vessels of war, and thus Her Majesty's Proclamation should be entirely defeated. The Attorney General of the colony thought this was perfectly permissible, and that it could not be avoided or counteracted in any way, and in support of that opinion he quoted a paragraph of *Wheaton.* The Law Officers in this country are of opinion that that paragraph does not apply, because it was written with reference to a different subject, namely, the Prize Acts. In that paragraph it is said—and very truly and justly said—that although in certain cases merchant ships which have been recaptured must be restored to their owners, yet when a vessel has taken the character of a man-of-war, if the captain of a British man-of-war has to fight such a vessel, and has to use his warlike forces to capture her, she then loses the character of a merchant ship, and the naval officers are fairly entitled to consider her as a prize. That principle does not seem to apply to the present case. This, then, was the case with which the Government had to deal, having the opinion of the Attorney General of the colony on the one side, and that of Sir Baldwin Walker on the other. The opinion of Sir Baldwin Walker is clearly the opinion of common sense, and the Law Officers say that it is well founded in law, and that it is not permissible to put a few guns into a prize, retaining her cargo on board, and send her into a neutral port to sell it. My noble Friend (the Duke of Newcastle) who, with the noble and learned Lord, I regret, has been compelled by ill-health to resign his office, or we should have heard him vindicate his own despatch—my noble Friend the late Secretary for the Colonies followed the opinion of the Law Officers. Their opinion was that this vessel, not being, in fact, a vessel of war, but being a prize, ought not to have been admitted to the Cape as a vessel of war. But it then became a question—and a very serious question I admit it to be—whether she ought to have been warned off in the first instance, or whether she should be taken possession of and restored to her owners? The noble and learned Lord seemed at first to say that there was no such thing as taking possession of the prize of a belligerent; that when it once became a prize it was out of the power and jurisdiction of the authorities of another country; but he afterwards very properly and justly said that there were certain cases in which the courts have held, and authorities have concurred with them, that vessels can be restored to their owners if they are not properly prizes, and he avoided the contradiction into which he had fallen by saying that in that case they never had been prizes. That, however, does not get over the contradiction of the general *dictum* which he had laid down; because it is certainly true that there are cases decided by the Courts of the United States in which vessels have come in as vessels of war, and, nevertheless, the Courts have, after argument, ordered them to be restored to their owners, and they have been so restored. Undoubtedly the ground of their being restored has been that the vessel which took them had been originally fitted out and manned by the United States themselves, and, therefore, they were bound to restore those vessels and their cargoes to the owners. But, whatever the ground may be, it is quite clear that there are cases in which according to principles which the United States admit the vessels ought to be restored, and here is a passage from *Wheaton* on the subject. He says—

" In such cases the judicial tribunals of the neutral State have authority to determine the validity of the capture thus made, and to vindicate its neutrality by restoring the property of its own subjects, or of other States at amity with the original owners."

Therefore, there are cases in which a vessel may be considered as a prize unlawfully taken, and it may be restored to the owners. The Duke of Newcastle at the end of his despatch said that the real character of the *Tuscaloosa* ought to have been inquired into, that Captain Semmes should have been called upon to produce her papers, and he concluded—

" If the result of these inquiries had been to prove that the vessel was really an uncondemned prize, brought into British waters in violation of Her Majesty's orders made for the purpose of maintaining her neutrality, I consider that the mode of proceeding in such circumstances most consistent with Her Majesty's dignity and most proper for the vindication of her territorial rights would have been to prohibit the exercise of any further control over the *Tuscaloosa* by the captors, and to retain that vessel under Her Majesty's control and jurisdiction until properly reclaimed by her original owners."—*See* p. 19.

Now, I must say, as the general tenour of the despatch is founded on the opinion of the Law Officers of the Crown, that the Duke of Newcastle, in this instance, as I would have done in his place, went somewhat beyond that opinion. The Law Officers said, " it is worthy of serious consideration," meaning that it was a point evidently deserving of being maturely weighed. The Duke of Newcastle, however, clearly saw that it was a point which he must decide for the time, and that his instructions to the Governor must be explicit. I am at the same time ready to admit that this is a question which turns on a nice point of International Law, arising under circumstances which are quite new, owing to the fact that the Confederate States have no port to which they can send their prizes. The point, therefore, is open to further consideration, whether the proper treatment of such vessels should not be to warn them off rather than to allow them to remain in port. But to say that the question can be decided only in the courts of the captors is, I think, altogether an error. It is impossible to say, " Here is a vessel with a cargo evidently a prize; but no action shall be taken with regard to that vessel until some prize court at Richmond or Charleston shall have pronounced an opinion." The Law Officers of the Crown held—and most rightly—that these are questions to be decided in Her Majesty's courts and not in the courts of the captors. The noble and learned Lord ended by saying, that if this had happened in the case of a vessel captured by the Federals there would have been strong and angry remonstrances on their part, and we should have made an ample apology. Now, in my opinion, we have heard enough of this kind of allegation. If the noble and learned Lord alluded to the course Her Majesty's Government took with respect to the *Trent*, in which our honour was at stake, and we acted so mean a part and played so truckling a part that the Americans had it all their own way, and kept their prisoners; and if the other day, when an American vessel committed a breach of neutrality in British waters, and Her Majesty's Government were satisfied to allow that violation to take place and did not ask for an apology, then the remarks might be true. But I must tell the noble and learned Lord that there have been many cases pending in which very loud complaints were made in this House when the question was not decided; but immediately there has been any concession to justice on the part of the United States, the noble Lords opposite are so mortified that the British Government should have justice done them by the American Government, and so mortified with the United States for doing them that justice, that there is a total silence on their part. We were told early in the Session, that the case of the *Saxon* was a violation of neutrality, and that a murder had been committed, and that the officer ought to be tried. The case was brought before the United States Court; the *Saxon* was given up, and the further question with regard to damages was pending; but in the main, justice has been done to the owner. Then a complaint was made that the accused ought not to be tried by a court martial; it was pointed out that in the way in which the accusation was drawn a fair trial could not take place. The United States Government agreed to amend the indictment, and the question is still under consideration. I really think when this is done, it would be but decent on the part of noble Lords opposite to admit that the United States Government were ready to do justice when a fair case was pointed out to them. But I own that in all these cases Her Majesty's Government ought not to take one side or the other; and that we ought not to be, as the noble Lords opposite are, animated by any partiality to the Federal or Confederate States, but ought to do justice between both.

Lord KINGSDOWN said, that two entirely distinct questions had been raised in the despatches of Sir Baldwin Walker —one whether in point of law the prize ship had been converted from a prize into a ship of war—the other supposing her to remain a prize, what ought to be done with her? With the first question their Lordships at present were not concerned; the other—if it were a question at all—

Earl Russell

was one of the most important that had arisen out of the application of the principles of International Law. The proposition of Sir Baldwin Walker was, that a prize remained the property of the original owners until it had been condemned in a court of legal competency—namely, a Prize Court; and that any one into whose hands it might afterwards come must hold it for the original owners. That, so far as he (Lord Kingsdown) understood, was also the view taken by the Government. Now, it was a great relief to him to hear that the Duke of Newcastle, in his despatch on the subject, had gone beyond the opinion of the Law Officers of the Crown. It was not the first time that he (Lord Kingsdown) had expressed his high opinion of those distinguished persons, and it was in a great measure owing to this opinion that he and noble Lords who sat on the same side of the House had abstained from interfering in those nice questions and angry discussions which had arisen between Her Majesty's Government and the Government of the United States. The attacks which had been made on the Government policy had proceeded not from that side of the House but from the other. He (Lord Kingsdown) must say that a grave mistake had been fallen into on this occasion. It was very unfortunate that the copy of *Wheaton* which had been referred to was an old edition in which the passage was found that the despatch quoted; but in a later edition of *Wheaton* the doctrine was more fully stated and explained. The rule requiring the condemnation in a Prize Court in order to change the property had nothing to do with the rights as between belligerents. When one belligerent had captured and taken possession of the vessel of another, it became his property as if he were the original owner, as completely as if it had been condemned by all the Prize Courts in Europe. The law upon this subject was very clearly and accurately stated by Dr. Twiss in his recent *Treatise on the Law of Nations*, vol. ii. p. 330. He states distinctly that the personal obligation of a captor to bring his captures into port for inquiry and adjudication is founded on the instructions that he has received from his own Government; that this rule is for the benefit of neutrals and not of belligerents who have no *locus standi* in a Prize Court, and cannot claim a right that their property, upon capture by a belligerent, should be taken into port for adjudication ; that capture alone divests an enemy of his property *jure belli.* Let their Lordships observe what had been done in the present case. Her Majesty had forbidden armed vessels, with their prizes, to come into her ports. According to law, if a ship of war with her prize entered a British port, she could be ordered away, but in what way did the British Government obtain the right to take possession of this ship? They might have sent her away upon the ground that she had come in contrary to the Orders in Council; but how did she become liable to seizure and confiscation by the British Government? Even supposing it could be said that the violation of the municipal laws of Great Britain entitled the British Government to seize her and confiscate her to the Crown, their Lordships would observe that the conduct pursued by our authorities was based upon an entirely different ground. Their argument was that the *Tuscaloosa* having come under their control, they were bound by law to restore her to her original owner. But, beyond all doubt, the original owner had lost his property, for the ship had never been re-captured. If the Governor had seized the ship for violation of our municipal laws, we were entitled to confiscate it, which he entirely denied. The original owner would have had no possible claim, unless the Queen had thought fit to make a present to him. The cases in which, and the purposes for which, adjudication was required were very distinctly stated by Dr. Twiss in a passage of his work at page 340—

" Every capture of a vessel is complete as between the belligerents when the surrender has taken place, and the *spes recuperandi* is gone; but as between the original owner of the vessel and a third party in respect of the *jus postliminii*, if the vessel should be re-captured, or as between the captor of the vessel and a third party in respect of the right of the former to dispose of the vessel in favour of the latter by way of sale, positive rules have been introduced, partly from equity to extend the *jus postliminii* in favour of the original owner, partly from policy to prevent any irregular conversion of property before it has been ascertained to have been lawfully acquired *jure belli.*"

The Confederate States could not obtain adjudication in their own Courts, for by reason of what was recognized by Europe as the blockade they had no means of carrying their vessels in safety into their own ports. Under such circumstances, Lord Stowell had, in the case of the *Felicity,* laid it down that it was not only the right but the duty of a belligerent to destroy the enemy's property. He said that, in such a case—

" Nothing is left to the belligerent vessel but to destroy the vessel which she has taken, for she cannot consistently with her general duty to her own country, or, indeed, under its express injunctions, permit enemy's property to sail away unmolested. If it should be impossible to bring her in, her next duty is to destroy enemy's property."

He did not blame the officers of the Cape. It was not to be expected that they could be familiar with the law upon such subjects. But it was necessary to point out the mistake which had been made, as we might otherwise be involved in serious difficulties. Fortunately in this case the American consul had disclaimed any interference with the ship. If the Government had held it, and a claimant had come forward, how was the right to be determined? What Courts had any jurisdiction? He was satisfied that the opinions of the Law Officers had been misunderstood; and for his part he should not be unwilling to leave it to them to say, whether the law, as it had been laid down in the despatch by the Government, could be maintained?

THE LORD CHANCELLOR: My Lords, I am always unwilling, in a matter of this kind, to take part in the debate, because no noble and learned Lord who is in the habit of sitting here on appeals can feel certain that some question on which he gives his opinion in the House in his deliberative character may not come before him in his judicial capacity, when he may be considerably embarrassed by his speech. It is in that spirit of caution that I rise now, because my noble and learned Friend who has just spoken (Lord Kingsdown) has expressed opinions which, if they went forth to the world on his authority and in no respect questioned or modified, might be received as doctrines which had commanded the assent of your Lordships. I should have been glad if my noble and learned Friend had examined the cases which have been cited, instead of being content with the language of the text written. Let me beg him to observe the case of the *Actæon.* [Lord KINGS-DOWN: It was the *Endymion* I referred to.] Then that is a still stronger case. Sir William Scott says—

" There was no doubt that the *Endymion* had a full right to inflict that (that is, the burning of the vessel) if any grave call of public service required it. Regularly a captor is bound by the law of his own country, conforming to the general law of nations, to bring in for adjudication, in order that it may be ascertained whether it be enemy's property; and that mistakes may not be committed by captors in the eager pursuit of gain, by which injustice may be done to neutral subjects, and national quarrels produced with the foreign States to which they belong."

Thus, the very case on which my noble and learned Friend rested his argument would, if he had examined it, have led him to the conclusion that the old rule by which the object seized became at once the property of the captor has been qualified by the more merciful usage of civilized nations, and that there is an obligation to obtain condemnation; and Sir William Scott distinctly explains that this law has been established in order to place some control upon captors, that, in pursuit of gain, they might not be led to commit injustice. The case of the *Endymion* was this:—She was on a cruise in search of the American frigate *President*, and in the course of her cruise she captured an American merchantman. She was, however, so confined by her instructions to continue cruising that she could not bring her prize into court, but burnt it at sea. Afterwards a claim was brought by the owner of the prize for damages in consequence of its destruction, and Sir William Scott held that the captor was excused from the obligation of bringing in the prize for adjudication by reason of the express and stringent nature of his instructions, which did not allow him to quit the sea. But there is not only that opinion. My noble and learned Friend will find that Lord Mansfield, the greatest authority in English law, held the same view. I would also direct his attention to the remarks which Lord Stowell made in the case of the *Flad Oyen*. [1 *Robinson*, page 135.] It was the case of a ship taken by a French privateer, and carried into a port in Norway, where she underwent a sort of process which terminated in a sentence of condemnation pronounced by the French Consul. It was therefore a case of capture by a belligerent. Lord Stowell, in that case, said—

" But another question has arisen in this case upon which a great deal of argument has been employed—namely, whether the sentence of condemnation which was pronounced by the French Consuls is of such legal authority as to transfer the vessel, supposing the purchase to have been *bond fide* made ? . . . It has frequently been said that it is the peculiar doctrine of the law of England to require a sentence of condemnation as necessary to transfer the property of prize; and that, according to the practice of some nations, twenty-four hours, and, according to the practice of others, the bringing *infra prœsidia* is authority enough to convert the prize. I take that to be

The Lord Chancellor

not quite correct; for I apprehend that, by the general practice of the law of nations, a sentence of condemnation is at present deemed generally necessary, and that a neutral purchaser in Europe, during war, does look to the legal sentence of condemnation as one of the title deeds of the ship, if he buys a prize vessel. I believe there is no instance in which a man, having purchased a prize vessel of a belligerent, has thought himself quite secure in making that purchase, merely because the ship has been in the enemy's possession twenty-four hours, or carried *infra prœsidia*."

Without saying that there may not be contradictory passages found in a great variety of writers, I think the passages I have quoted are sufficient to show that property is not, as a rule, transferred by the mere fact of capture; and the reason why the old rule has thus been qualified by the general practice of nations is, as stated by Sir William Scott, the necessity of putting some limitation on the act of the captor. Nothing in the world can illustrate that so strongly as the case of the *Endymion*, which has been referred to where the captor was not held to be justified in destroying his prize, except by reason of the urgency of the service on which he was engaged, because otherwise he would have been held to be under an obligation to bring the ship to a court for adjudication. Hence this question is, in the language of the Law Officers, "worthy of very serious consideration." There may be no instance precisely parallel, but, at the same time, the Law Officers were perfectly justified in the opinion they gave, that the matter required serious consideration. Serious consideration has been given to it, and the result will be embodied in clear and definite instructions, which will be generally circulated throughout all our colonial possessions. The only point in which the despatch in question is open to challenge is, that it speaks of the course taken as being deemed the best, instead of saying that the question deserved " very serious consideration;" but it should be borne in mind that the despatch was written in regard to a past transaction, and that it did not lay down a rule, but merely described the application which had already been made of one.

THE EARL OF HARDWICKE said, he had looked carefully through the history of the American war, and he had found a case which occurred to him to bear precisely upon the one under discussion, with this exception, that the captor was not a neutral, but a belligerent. The case was this : a United States frigate, on the 14th of March, 1813, having previously captured the *Nottingham*, and taken £11,000 in specie out of her, proceeded to cruise on the coast of Chili, and during that cruise she captured twelve whalers; but did she send them to the United States for adjudication? She did not, for they were all re-captured by the English. But there was one of them that fitted this case, and that was the case of the *Georgina*. Captain Porter, thinking her a useful vessel, armed her with sixteen guns and put a crew on board of her, and in that condition she was captured. She had never been condemned in any of the United States Prize Courts, but on her being re-captured by one of our ships she was brought into our Prize Courts; and after an elaborate argument, which he had no doubt the present noble and learned Lord on the Woolsack would respect, Sir William Scott gave judgment in favour of her original captors, and she was accordingly handed over.

Lord CHELMSFORD, in reply, said, he had understood the noble and learned Lord on the Woolsack to say there had been a modification of the instructions, and, if so, he thought their Lordships had a right to know in what respect they had been modified.

The LORD CHANCELLOR explained he was sorry he had been misunderstood. What he said was, that new instructions were under consideration with a view of being sent out.

House adjourned at half past Seven o'clock, to Thursday next, half past Ten o'clock.

HOUSE OF COMMONS,

Tuesday, April 26, 1864.

MINUTES.]—Select Committee—On Standing Orders (Parliamentary Deposits) *appointed*; Sewage (Metropolis, &c.) *appointed* *; Trade with Foreign Nations *nominated* *; Bankruptcy Act, Mr. Roebuck *added*, Mr. Hassard *discharged*, Mr. Vance *added*.
Public Bills — *Ordered* — Writs Registration (Scotland) * ; Local Government Supplemental *.
First Reading — Local Government Supplemental * [Bill 80].
Select Committee—On Judgments Law Amendment *, Mr. R. Mills *discharged*, Mr. Malins *added*; Copyright (No. 2) * [Bill 59], *nominated*.

Considered as amended — Court of Chancery (Despatch of Business) * [Bill 69] (*Lords*); Fish Teinds (Scotland) * [Bill 45].
Third Reading— Charitable Assurances Enrolments * [Bill 72] (*Lords*).

COPYRIGHT (NO. 2) BILL.

Select Committee on the Copyright (No. 2) Bill *nominated* :—

Mr. Black, Mr. Massey, Mr. Walpole, Mr. Dunlop, Sir William Heathcote, Mr. Grant Duff, Mr. Cave, Earl Grosvenor, Mr. Maguire, Mr. Arthur Mills, Mr. Neate, Mr. Walter, Mr. Pollard-Urquhart, Mr. Lowe, and Mr. Whiteside :—Five to be the quorum.

TRADE WITH FOREIGN NATIONS.

Select Committee on Trade with Foreign Nations *nominated* :—

Mr. William Edward Forster, Mr. Milner Gibson, Mr. Henley, Mr. Cobden, Mr. Layard, Mr. Seymour FitzGerald, Sir Stafford Northcote, Sir Minto Farquhar, Mr. Charles Turner, Mr. Baxley, Mr. Somerset Beaumont, Mr. Gregory, Mr. Kinnaird, Mr. Butler-Johnstone, and Mr. Pender :—Power to send for persons, papers, and records ; Five to be the quorum.

JUDGMENTS, &c., LAW AMENDMENT BILL.

Ordered, That Mr. Remington Mills be discharged from further attendance on the Select Committee on the Judgments, &c., Law Amendment Bill:—Mr. Malins added to the Committee.

BANKRUPTCY ACT.

Ordered, That the Select Committee on the Bankruptcy Act do consist of sixteen Members: — Mr. Roebuck added to the Committee.

Ordered, That Mr. Hassard be discharged from further attendance on the Select Committee on the Bankruptcy Act: —Mr. Vance added to the Committee.

STANDING ORDERS (PARLIAMENTARY DEPOSITS).

SELECT COMMITTEE MOVED FOR.

Mr. SCOURFIELD said, he rose to call the attention of the House to the Report of the Select Committee on Standing Orders of the 8th of March, 1864, in the case of the Sheffield, Chesterfield, and Staffordshire Railway Bill, and to move—

" That a Select Committee be appointed to inquire into the operation of the Standing Orders of this House, and of the Act 9 & 10 *Vict.* c. 20, which regulate the depositing of money, or of public securities, with the Courts of Chancery in England and Ireland, and the Court of Exchequer in Scotland, in respect of works and undertakings requiring the authority of Parliament by Private Bills.

The Select Committee, of which he had the honour to be chairman, had reported that there had been, in the case of the railway brought under their consideration, a clear evasion of the conditions laid down by Standing Orders of the House in regard to the deposit of money with the Accountant General. The Committee stated that the deposit for the occasion was borrowed from other parties wholly unconnected with the undertaking, and that, in order to secure the transfer of the stock, the promoters were constrained to hand over the control of the Bill to those parties. It was, however, only fair to the parties engaged in the transaction to say that they considered they had only followed an example which others had set, and that the only difference between this case and others was that it had been found out. There could be no doubt that this practice, which very generally prevailed, set aside the proper necessary restrictions imposed by Parliament on Railway Bills, and this being the first case in which it had come officially to the knowledge of the Committee, they in consequence considered it of so important a nature as to require the attention of the House. It was highly desirable that the House should express their opinion upon the practice, and at once condemn it, unless they wished to establish it as a precedent to be followed hereafter by other Companies. In this particular case the fact was made out to the satisfaction of the Committee; and the hon. Member for the University of Cambridge (Mr. Selwyn) was in possession of documents relating to another case, but showing how, and under what circumstances, a deposit of stock was usually made. There were various reasons why they should not allow the existing restrictions on the introduction of Private Bills to be relaxed. The object of Parliament in requiring the deposit was to have something like an assurance that a Company started with sufficient capital for their project, but from what was revealed to the Committee, it appeared that this particular Company started with a debt, namely, that due upon the deposit. Again Railway Companies had large powers granted to them, and in London especially they interfered with the comfort and threatened to take away the livelihood of many persons. The time of the House ought not to be unnecessarily occupied by a multitude of Bills which had

Mr. Scourfield

not in their first initiation complied with the conditions laid down by Parliament. He desired, therefore, to see the existing securities on the subject enforced, so as to prevent the substitution of a species of legerdemain for the faithful performance of a legitimate obligation. He, therefore, hoped the House would consider the subject was a proper one for inquiry.

Mr. MILNER GIBSON said, he had no objection to offer to the Motion.

Mr. RICHARD HODGSON said, he did not oppose the Motion, but he would suggest that something should be done to facilitate the withdrawal of the deposits from the office of the Accountant General in Chancery, and also to lessen the expenses attending it.

Mr. SELWYN said, that the Standing Orders of the House had been so systematically and continuously evaded that they had been rendered ridiculous. Without mentioning names, he would read one of the documents referred to by the hon. Member, and if necessary he would place it in the hands of the Speaker or the officers of the House. It was an agreement entered into by the promoters of a company, and was to the following effect: —That, in consideration of certain other parties having advanced a deposit of £10,400 to the Accountant General of the Court of Chancery in the names of A, B, as the Parliamentary deposit of the Railway Company, the promoters undertook that, unless the amount was repaid before the Bill was read the third time in the House of Lords, they would withdraw the Bill and do all that was necessary to enable the parties who advanced the deposit to obtain its repayment. The solicitor of the company and the Parliamentary agent also entered into agreements, by which they undertook, in pursuance of instructions from the Board, that the Bill should not be read a third time in the House of Lords unless the sum deposited was previously paid or satisfactorily secured to the bank who advanced it. Therefore the orders of the House, which obliged the promoters to give a guarantee that they were in a position to carry their undertaking to a successful issue, resulted in their putting themselves entirely in the hands of other parties, who might be called the fourth estate of the realm, as they had the power to set aside the authority of Parliament; for although Committees of both Houses might have determined that the scheme was for the public advantage, and the Bill might have arrived at its final stage, it could not pass into law except at the pleasure of this banking company. He would not then discuss the matter, but he could not refrain from reminding the House that the real interests of landowners, shareholders, and the public were deeply concerned in the matter, and he would express a hope that so long as they retained the Standing Orders they would take care they were adequate and effectual for the purposes for which they were designed.

Mr. HADFIELD said, he wished to point out that the practice referred to seriously affected owners and occupiers of property through which projected lines of railway were to pass. Notices were given to owners and occupiers in all directions, without the slightest real responsibility on the part of the promoters. He was not only of opinion that the responsibility of promoters of undertakings should in all cases be reliable, but that owners of property ought not to be called on to pay fees in defending their property against projectors.

Motion *agreed to.*

Select Committee *appointed,*

"To inquire into the operation of the Standing Orders of this House, and of the Act 9 & 10 Vict. c. 20, which regulate the depositing of money, or of public securities, with the Courts of Chancery in England and Ireland, and the Court of Exchequer in Scotland, in respect of works and undertakings requiring the authority of Parliament by Private Bills."—(*Mr. Scourfield.*)

And, on April 29, Committee *nominated* as follows :—

Mr. SCOURFIELD, Mr. MILNER GIBSON, Mr. MASSEY, Lord HOTHAM, Colonel WILSON PATTEN, Mr. SOTHERON ESTCOURT, Mr. EDWARD EGERTON, Colonel FRENCH, Mr. ADAIR, Mr. HEYGATE, Mr. SELWYN, Mr. KIRKMAN HODGSON, Mr. CRAWFORD, Mr. WESTHEAD, and Mr. TITE :—Power to send for persons, papers, and records ; Five to be the quorum.

RAILWAY BILLS.—RESOLUTIONS.

Mr. RICHARD HODGSON said, he rose to move that certain clauses relative to companies entering into traffic agreements, and to companies owning or working railways and steamboats, be referred to the general Committee on Railway and Canal Bills, with an Instruction to the Committee that they Report to the House their opinion whether the said Clauses, with such Amendments as may be proposed by the Committee, may with advantage be inserted in all Bills con-

taining powers to companies to "enter into traffic agreements" or to "work railways and steamboats" respectively. His object was to secure—first, due publicity to all traffic agreements between these companies; and secondly, that where those agreements seemed to create any monopoly, other railway companies and other persons affected thereby might have an opportunity of entering into similar agreements. A Committee on private business sat during the last Session, and a Bill was introduced by the right hon. Gentleman the President of the Board of Trade, which contained some clauses of the nature to which his Resolution pointed; but they fell short of his object. He proposed to go a little further, and not only to give notoriety to these agreements, but to enable parties affected by them to appear before the Board of Trade and state their objections, and also to enable others to enter into similar agreements. He proposed that the clauses should be referred to the general Committee upon Canal and Railway Bills, which was composed of the Chairmen of those Committees which had to consider the different Railway Bills. These Committees would be enabled to insert in the different Bills such clauses as would at once protect the public and prevent any one company from having a monopoly as against another. To show to the House what these traffic agreements were, he might mention that there was at present a Bill before Parliament to give increased facilities for making agreements between railway companies and steamboat companies, by which the London and North-Western Company took powers to make agreements with eight railway companies in Ireland and with two steamboat companies for the division and conduct of traffic. It was unsafe to give such powers without due deliberation. The first of his clauses was one relative to companies entering into traffic arrangements. It provided that the powers to enter into traffic arrangements under the Act should be subject to certain regulations. Of these the first regulation was that traffic arrangements should be made by written agreement, and that notice, in a form approved by the Board of Trade, should be given by advertisement; the second was, that such agreement should not have any operation till approved of by the Board of Trade; the third, that the agreement should be printed at the expense of the parties thereto, and deposited with the Board of Trade; the fourth, that such agreement should be open to inspection; the fifth, provided that a competitive company should be entitled to the benefits of an agreement made with a competitor; and the sixth stipulated that, in case of a dispute as to whether a particular route was competitive, the same should be decided by the Board of Trade, and fixed the penalty for non-compliance with the Board of Trade's decision at £100 a day. The second of the two clauses was one relative to companies owning or working railways and steamboats, and regulated fares and charges for passengers carried by land and sea. The hon. Gentleman concluded by moving that Clause 1 be referred to the general Committee on Railway and Canal Bills.

Mr. MILNER GIBSON said, he thought it rather an unusual course to refer these clauses to the consideration of the general Committee on Railway and Canal Bills. It would certainly be better in matters of the kind that a Bill should be brought in containing the various clauses it was thought desirable to introduce in certain clauses of private Bills; but, although that was also the opinion of his hon. Friend the Chairman of Ways and Means, he did not wish to object to the course taken by his hon. Friend. Three or four of the Regulations were inserted in the Railway Clauses Bill, which passed last Session, and there was no objection to refer the whole of them to a body so well qualified to consider the subject, as the general Committee on Railway and Canal Bills.

Sir JAMES FERGUSSON said, he hoped it would be understood that in assenting to this course being adopted, the House did not express any opinion as to the clauses themselves.

Motion *agreed to.*

Ordered,

That the Clauses be referred to the General Committee on Railway and Canal Bills; and that it be an Instruction to the Committee that they do report to the House their opinion whether the said Clauses (with such Amendments as may be proposed by the Committee), may with advantage be inserted in all Bills containing powers to Companies to "enter into Traffic Agreements," or to "work Railways and Steamboats," respectively.

NATIONAL PORTRAIT GALLERY.

QUESTION.

Mr. CAVENDISH BENTINCK said, he wished to ask the Secretary to the Treasury, Whether a portrait of Arch-

Mr. Richard Hodgson

bishop Laud, attributed to Vandyke, has been lately purchased by the Trustees of the Portrait Gallery for the sum of £75; and, if so, whether as an original work or as copy after the master; and, whether it is the intention of Her Majesty's Government to remove the Portrait Gallery to any other and what locality?

The CHANCELLOR of the EXCHEQUER said, in reply, that the portrait of Archbishop Laud referred to had been purchased by the Trustees of the National Portrait Gallery for the sum of 72 guineas. It had not been purchased upon the ground of its being ascribed to Vandyke. There were two views taken of that question by gentlemen who were most competent to form a judgment—one view being that it was an original picture of the school of Vandyke, and the other that it was a copy of an original by Vandyke. The Trustees, however, were not ashamed of their purchase, as they believed it to be a valuable picture which had been obtained at a cheap rate. There was some difference of opinion as to what would be the value of the picture if it were an original Vandyke, some excellent authorities putting it at £1,000, while no estimate was under £300. With respect to the removal of the National Portrait Gallery, he had at present no announcement to make; but the Government would declare their intentions at or before the time when they invited the attention of the House to the subject of buildings and the arrangements connected with buildings of that class contained in the Miscellaneous Estimates.

ARMY—ARMSTRONG GUNS AT
KAGOSIMA.—QUESTION.

Mr. HANBURY TRACY said, he wished to ask the Secretary to the Admiralty, Whether the attention of the Admiralty has been drawn to the failure of the old pattern vent-pieces of the 40-pounder Armstrong Guns in the action off Kagosima; and whether the Admiralty intend to withdraw from the service all the old pattern vent-pieces of the 40-pounder Gun, substituting the present pattern authorized as long ago as May, 1862, and adapting the earlier Guns for the present vent-pieces?

Lord CLARENCE PAGET, in reply, said, the attention of the Admiralty had been called to the defects in the vent-pieces, not only of the 40-pounders but

also of the 110-pounder Armstrong, and
to the inconveniences arising from the old
pattern fitments of these guns. He trusted
that steps would shortly be taken to place
them in a more satisfactory condition.

DENMARK AND GERMANY—THE DANISH BLOCKADE IN THE BALTIC.
QUESTION.

MR. SOMERSET BEAUMONT said,
he wished to ask the Under Secretary of
State for Foreign Affairs, Whether the
Blockade proclaimed by the Danish Government against certain ports in the
Baltic will be raised in the event of an
armistice being agreed to by the Powers
met in Conference?

MR. LAYARD: I am, Sir, quite unable to give a reply to the Question of the
hon. Gentleman. It must depend on any
arrangement that may be made at the
Conference.

GOLD IN TASMANIA.
QUESTION.

MR. ROGERS said, he would beg to
ask the Secretary of State for the Colonies,
Whether, in case of the discovery of a
Goldfield in Tasmania, the Grant Licences
for procuring Gold will be regulated in
the same way as has heretofore been done
in the other Australian Colonies; and
whether there is any objection to printing
the Report of Mr. Gould, the Government
Geologist, which is referred to in the last
Report of the Governor of Tasmania, of
August 21, 1862, p. 77?

MR. CARDWELL replied that there
would be no objection to lay the Report
on the table. With regard to the other
Question, that would depend on the view
the Legislature of Tasmania might take
on the matter and the regulations they
might make.

THE WAR IN NEW ZEALAND.
PAPERS MOVED FOR.

MR. ARTHUR MILLS said, he rose to
call the attention of the House to the War
now going on in New Zealand, and to
move an Address to the Crown praying
that all Correspondence that had taken
place between Governor Sir George Grey
and the Colonial Office relating to the
policy of confiscation which had been
adopted by the New Zealand Legislature,
might be laid before Parliament. The

subject was one of the greatest importance, even if only regarded in its bearings
on Imperial finance, for although there
was a comfortable feeling out of doors
that the war would not cost more than
£300,000 or £400,000, there was good
reason to believe that the expenses during the present year to be borne by the
British taxpayer towards the maintenance of the war could not be less than
£1,000,000. It was not, however, on the
ground of finance that he brought the subject forward, as the matter had become
far more important than any mere question of finance. The Local Legislature had
sent home acts of such a character that
they must have a tendency to prolong the
war indefinitely, and, therefore, he thought
the time had come when the intervention
of Parliament was imperatively called for.
He would not ask the House to wade
through that sea of unpronounceable
names and unintelligible distinctions which
lay between the discussion and the solution of all problems affecting the colony
of New Zealand. He did not ask them
to express an opinion whether the Treaty
of Waitangi, or any other treaty between
civilized and barbarous nations, was wise or
foolish. He did not mean to criticize the
policy of the successive Governors, he knew
that the difficulties which those Governors
had to contend against were enormous, and
fairly exempted them in their absence
from the hostile criticism of Parliament.
Nor did he propose to enter on the comparative merits of the administration of
Sir George Grey and Governor Browne.
The simple issue which he ventured to
lay before the House was what, under the
circumstances, was the duty of Imperial
England. It appeared to him to be quite
unnecessary to enter into a review at any
length of the past policy of this country
towards the colony. We had held New
Zealand for rather more than a quarter
of a century, which period divided itself
into two parts—the time before and the
period after the concession to the colony
of representative institutions in 1852. The
former period might be described as one
of incessant Native war and wrangling
between land companies, missionaries, officials, and Natives, whose conflicting views
had been sufficiently represented before
Committees of that House. Those wrang-
lings ended in the grant of representative
institutions to the colony, which was par-
celled out into provinces, while the Natives
were practically excluded from any repre-

sentation in the Local Parliament. Two years after the passing of the Constitution Act, "responsible Government" was engrafted on the new institutions, which were found to involve the blessings of a perpetual scramble for patronage and the privilege of worrying the representatives of the Crown. Since 1852 their time had been employed in wrangling of a very different character. In the intervals of the Native war, disputes had arisen between the representatives of the Crown and the colony, which had ended at last in the absolute concession of the entire control over Native affairs to the Local Administration. The last news from the colony showed that the Local Legislature had freely exercised the powers committed to them by the Imperial Government. They had passed two Acts, the first of which had been well described as an Act for the confiscation of 5,000,000 acres of Native land on suspicion of treason, giving to innocent persons a right to compensation on establishing their innocence. The other of those Acts empowered the Governor to suspend altogether the operation of the ordinary Courts of Law, and to detain in prison or otherwise punish all those who had committed treason, or who were suspected of that offence, and to authorize their trial by regular or militia officers. The powers conferred by the Act were of the most arbitrary character, and, as he believed, almost unprecedented in the annals of legislation. He understood that both these Acts were at that moment in operation in New Zealand, and he believed, therefore, that the House would concur with him in the opinion that the question should be considered without delay. It might be said that, in dealing with New Zealand, England was beset with a peculiar difficulty in having to send troops at the present moment to vindicate a policy over which she really had no control. He knew that there were some who were in the habit of disposing of all questions of this kind in a very summary manner. In their opinion, the Maori race was already doomed, and they held that the sooner they were exterminated the better it would be, both for themselves and mankind generally, and that every contrivance to prolong their existence would only add to their misery. He trusted, however, that in that House such views would not be entertained. There might be those who believed that the extermination of Native races, either by force or fraud, had been,

and would be, the inevitable result of Anglo-Saxon civilization, but he trusted that there were none in that House who would be willing by any act of theirs to bring about this result. What was the offence of the Natives? It was said, not only that they were murderers, but that they had established a treasonable form of Government, and that they must now be punished as traitors. That was what might be called the colonial view of the question. Now, he was not appearing as the advocate of the Natives; he wished only to present to the House a fair and impartial view of the case, though the Maories seemed now to be unfashionable, and to be forsaken alike by bishops, missionaries, and all their former patrons. The main charge against them was their origination of what was called the "King movement." Now, during the twenty-five years Great Britain had held New Zealand, though the Colonial Legislature had been very careful to facilitate the acquisition of Native land by the settlers, there had been a by no means commensurate desire to establish law and order throughout the Native districts. On that point he might quote Governor Gore Browne, who said—

"Some of the most populous districts, such as Hokianga and Kaipara, have no magistrates resident among them; and many others, such as Taupo, the Ngatiruanui, Taranaki, and others, and the country round the East Cape, have never been visited by an officer of Government. The residents in these districts have never felt that they are the subjects of the Queen of England, and have little reason to think that the Government of the colony cares about their welfare."

His (Mr. Mills's) case was this, that having been neglected by the Government, who ought to have established law and order in their districts, the Natives had been tempted, whether wisely or foolishly he did not say, to extemporize a rough system of government which might be construed into treason, but which was never intended as treason by the Maories themselves. If he quoted, in support of this opinion, high authorities in New Zealand, such as Bishop Selwyn or Sir W. Martin, it would perhaps be said, that he was appealing to the testimony of partisans; but it so happened, that the important witnesses to whom he alluded were corroborated in their evidence on this question by one of our ablest colonial governors wholly unconnected with New Zealand. Sir W. Denison, in a document to be found among the Parliamentary papers, expressed the decided opinion that the King movement was in the right direction. Sir W. Denison said, on this point—

"You have now, as a fact, the establishment of something analogous to a general government among the Maories—a recognition, on their part, of the necessity of some paramount authority. This is a step in the right direction; do not ignore it. Do not, on the ground that some evil may possibly spring from it, make the Natives suspicious of your motive by opposing it, but avail yourself of the opportunity to introduce some more of the elements of good government among them. Suggest to them the necessity of defining and limiting the power of the person who has been elected as the Chief or King (I should not quarrel with the name), of establishing some system of legislation, simple, of course, at first, but capable of being modified and improved; but do not attempt to introduce the complicated arrangements suited to a civilized and educated people; recognize publicly and openly the Maories, not merely as individual subjects of the Queen, but as a race—a body whose interests you are bound to respect and promote; and then give to that body the means of deciding what their interests are, and of submitting them, in a proper form, for your consideration."

Chief Justice Martin and other distinguished men in the colony had given expression to a like opinion. There was one other point which offered, at least, some extenuation of the conduct of that unhappy race. On their behalf it might be said that they had witnessed, on the part of those sent to govern them, acts of a conflicting character, and that might have caused an inference in their minds that we were wrong and they were right. For instance, with regard to the purchase of land. He would not go into the old question of the Waitara Block, and say whether Sir George Grey or Governor Browne was right; but within three short years the Natives witnessed conflicting acts, done in the name of the Queen and Government of England, which must inevitably have induced a belief in the Native mind, with regard to the Government, of imbecility and vacillation. On the 5th of March, 1860, forcible possession was taken of the Waitara block of land, under the orders of Governor Gore Browne. On the other hand, on the 11th of June, 1863, Sir George Grey issued the following proclamation:—

"Whereas an engagement for the purchase of a certain tract of land at the Waitara, commonly known as Teira's block, was entered into by the Government of New Zealand in the year 1859, but the said purchase has never been completed; and whereas circumstances connected with the said purchase, unknown to the Government at the time of the sale of the land, have lately transpired, which make it advisable that the said purchase should not be proceeded with; now, therefore, the Governor, with the advice and consent of the Executive Council, doth hereby declare that the purchase of the said block of land is abandoned, and all claim to the same on the part of the Government is henceforth renounced."

Thus, in three years, a policy which was solemnly adopted was with equal solemnity cancelled. He would not discuss the question which of these acts was right and which was wrong; but at any rate he thought it would be a monstrous thing to treat as waste paper a treaty solemnly entered into twenty-five years ago with the Natives on the ground that they were guilty of treason, when they had probably been urged into acts of insubordination by vacillation of that kind. Perhaps such vacillation was no absolute justification of their conduct; but, looking at the conflicting course taken respecting them, they might fairly suppose that they were only enforcing just claims, and had done nothing worthy of martial law, confiscation, and extermination. The Queen of England had guaranteed to the Natives the full, exclusive, and undisturbed possession of their lands, so long as they accepted allegiance to her Crown; and he believed that no unprovoked act of the Maories had put them out of the pale of that treaty. When the rights and obligations involved in the treaty were formally considered in 1842 by a Committee of that House, a Resolution was moved by the right hon. Gentleman opposite, now Secretary of State for the Colonies, to the effect that the Treaty of Waitangi is binding in conscience and in policy on the British Government, that it was impossible to limit the construction of the treaty to the ground actually cultivated by the Natives; and that any attempt to carry out such a construction of the treaty must alienate the Natives and lead to conflicts of a sanguinary character. He had no wish to anticipate any change of policy or of opinion on the part of the Secretary of State. He only referred to the Resolution to show that the right hon. Gentleman was not one of those who entertained the view that the extermination of Native races was a necessary condition of civilization, or that bargains which they had made with us at our own solicitations were to be treated by us as null and void whenever it might suit our convenience to repudiate them. He knew very well that it was in vain for him to appeal to those whose fortunes were to be built upon the ruins of the Maori race, on any antiquated grounds of right and wrong. It would, indeed, be over sanguine to expect that the merchants of Auckland, who were now receiving from £1,000 to £1,500 a day out of the commissariat expenditure, would look with much respect upon the Treaty of Waitangi, or consider it binding on their part. He would venture nevertheless to appeal to them on the very lowest ground—that of self-interest—and would read a short extract from the speech of Dr. Pollen, a Member of the New Zealand Legislature, when the Confiscation Acts were discussed, in order to show the views entertained by some of the most experienced and intelligent men in the colony—

"Successful settlement meant peaceful settlement, but not many furrows would be turned in Waikato, if the ploughman must take his life in his hand into the field, and work with his rifle and cross-belts slung upon his shoulders. If any attempt at such wholesale confiscation as appears to be contemplated were made, the effect would be to increase the exasperation already existing in the Native mind, and it would need for its success the extermination of the race. The soundness of the financial policy of confiscation may be tested by a very simple calculation, the elements of which are at hand. We could determine, approximately at least, the cost of the work of extermination; we may be said to have been at war for three years; we have spent, including the Imperial charges, perhaps £5,000,000 during that period; we have killed 150 or 200 Natives. How much, at that rate, will it cost to kill 10,000? This policy of confiscation is immoral, and cannot be made profitable financially; unfortunately, it is a popular policy; but in that Council, when hon. Gentlemen were safe from the storms of the hustings, calm and dispassionate consideration might at least be expected to be given to such a subject as this. He had, however, ceased to hope for that at present, and when he remembered how, upon a recent occasion, when a question affecting the life, the liberty, and the property of the people was under consideration, the expression of honest indignation had been met, he could not expect that anything he could then say would arrest or alter the downward current of events. He (Dr. Pollen) had hopes, however, that the statesmen of England would stand between them and the Natives, and, if need be, prevent the wrong which might be inflicted under the powers which this Bill proposes to give. He had hopes, also, that the administration of the law would be better than the law itself; and that, in carrying it out, the gentlemen who were charged with a trust so important would forget that a particular course was popular, and would be guided only by the dictates of justice, good faith, and public honour."

He assured the House that his object was not to make an *ex parte* statement. He believed that there was an unhappy but very small section of the Maories disaffected towards this country; but out of 50,000 of a Native population it would be

an exaggeration to say that one-tenth were mixed up with those Acts which those local Bills were intended to punish. He put it to the House that it would be very cruel as well as impolitic to sanction a war of extermination. He put that to them not only on the higher ground of right and wrong or of treaty rights, but on the lowest ground—that of self-interest. It might be said, perhaps, that the lands to which the confiscation would apply were held in common, and that it would be impossible to adopt any measure of that character without punishing the innocent as well as the guilty. That was true, but by a wholesale confiscation they would punish even those who had used all their influence to prevent the acts of which we complained. The question which he raised was this: whether the aggravation to which the Natives had been exposed—whether our inconsistent policy had not been such as to afford some extenuation, and lead Parliament to pause before it sanctioned such an awful expenditure of blood and money as would take place if the war of extermination was carried *à l'outrance*, and the Natives were driven to fight for their hearths and homes, which certainly they would do to the last man and the last cartridge. He believed that there were at present 12,000 Imperial troops in New Zealand, a naval brigade was on land there, and we had three or four ships of war in the harbours; and he contended that, if the colonists wanted a policy of extermination to be indefinitely carried on against the Natives, that ought not to be done at the expense of the British taxpayer. We ought not to be deceived by rose-tinted despatches, telling us constantly that the war was coming to an end. In his opinion, the consequence of such a policy as that which we were asked to adopt would be not only ruinous to the colony, but highly injurious to Imperial interests. He submitted that there were only two courses open to the Government—either to disallow those Acts altogether, or to throw upon the Local Legislature the entire responsibility of the course it was taking. He did not, however, wish to dictate what course the Government ought to take, feeling confident that the honour of England and the interests of the Colonial Empire would be safe in their hands if they adopted a temperate, firm, and decided policy. If they adopted such a policy he believed they would not only meet with the support of the House of Commons, but the general approval of the country. In conclusion, he begged to move an Address for all Correspondence that had taken place between Governor Sir George Grey and the Colonial Office relating to the policy of confiscation which had been adopted by the New Zealand Legislature.

MR. BUXTON said, he rose to second the Motion. No one who had paid attention to the subject would think that his hon. Friend had exaggerated its importance. It was a matter of life and death to the great Maori race in New Zealand, and it was also one of great moment in a financial point. If the policy of confiscation was proceeded with, he thought his hon. Friend had under-estimated the pecuniary cost to this country. That cost would be at least £1,000,000 a year, and perhaps more. It was essential to keep in view the very words of the Treaty of Waitangi, which was the sole title by which we could lay claim to sovereignty over the Natives of New Zealand. The terms of the treaty were these—

" The Queen of England confirms and guarantees to the chiefs and tribes of New Zealand, and to the respective families and individuals thereof, the full, extensive, and undisturbed possession of their lands, estates, forests, fisheries, and other properties which they may collectively and individually possess, so long as it is their wish and desire to retain the same in their possession."

And Dr. Pollen informed the Legislative Council that he had been present when the treaty was proposed, and had himself heard Her Majesty's representative pledge the faith of the Queen and of the British people to the due observance of this treaty, giving, upon the honour of an English gentleman, the broadest interpretation of the words in which that treaty was couched. And let no one fancy that that was a matter of trifling import. The Natives clung to their possession of the land with intense tenacity. Our own feeling of ownership over land was not stronger than theirs. In fact, our greatest difficulties in New Zealand had arisen from the complicated tenures under which they held their land, and the tight grasp they kept upon it. The Act to which his hon. Friend had called attention had been greatly misrepresented. It had been spoken of as an Act for enabling the Government to obtain land for military posts with a view to the defence of Auckland. There was not a word in the preamble or clauses referring to military posts. The Act was entitled "an Act to enable the Governor to establish settlements for colonization." It said nothing at all about military posts. Its title, its preamble, and its clauses related solely to the introduction of settlers and the creation of settlements. Again, the Act had been misrepresented on a more important point. It had been spoken of as one for seizing the land of the Natives who had rebelled against the Queen. It was no such thing. What it proposed was to seize not the land of those Natives who had taken up arms, but the whole land occupied by any Natives whatever in the whole Northern Island of New Zealand. An exception, indeed, was made in those few cases where Crown certificates of title and grants had been previously given. All the land of all the Natives was to be seized. The only difference was that those Natives who had not in any kind of way had anything to do with the war were to be allowed compensation for the land taken from them, if they could get it, in courts established by the colonial authorities. From the statement made in the Colonial Treasurer's speech, on the second reading of the Loan Bill, they learnt that the total area of land, the Native title to which it was thus proposed to extinguish thus summarily, amounted to eight millions and a half of acres, one-half of which was available for settlement. One merit certainly could not be denied to the Act. A more straightforward scheme never was known. It was always well, if possible, to put one's self in the place of those whose conduct was being canvassed, so as to see the thing from their point of view; and nothing could be more easy than to do so in this case. The case was simply this: —A observed that Z possessed a valuable property. A had reason to believe that a third party M would, at his own expense, take that property from Z, and give it to A. What could be more natural than that A should think this was the most just, right, expedient, and politic thing that could possibly be done? On the one hand, there were the settlers, hungering and thirsting for land, and on the other side there were millions of acres of land owned by those of whom it had unhappily become usual to speak of as "damned niggers;" and a third party appeared on the scene in the shape of the mother country, who probably could be cajoled and blinded into laying out a few millions of money, and risking the lives of a few thousands of soldiers, in order to effect—let them not call it a robbery, but a transfer of the property. That was a plain but as he believed a true account of the feeling from which the proposal had sprung. The appetite of settlers for land amounted to nothing less than a passion. As Governor Browne wrote to the Duke of Newcastle in 1857, "The Europeans covet these lands, and are determined to enter in and possess them, *rectè si possint, si non, quocunque modo.*" And that hunger after land had become inflamed beyond all self-control by the furious hatred of the Natives, engendered by the war that had of late been raging. His only surprise was that so many gentlemen should have had the moral courage and humanity to protest against the passage of that Bill through the Legislative Council. He was strongly confirmed, however, in the view that his hon. Friend (Mr. Mills) and himself took of that matter, from finding that, even amid all the excitement of the time, men like the Hon. Mr. Swainson, the Hon. Dr. Pollen, Mr. Stokes, and others, stood out so manfully against that scheme, and that it was condemned by one so profoundly versed in New Zealand affairs as the late commissioner of the Waikato district, Mr. Gorst. Well, now, let them examine candidly what amount of justification could be alleged for that measure. It must be remembered that our position as regards the Natives of New Zealand was of a most peculiar kind. He was not one of those who thought very highly of rights conferred by conquest, but we had never conquered them. We had never, and we did not now, put forward any claim whatever to dominion derived from conquest. We had dealt with them as an independent people, who, of their own accord, upon certain stipulations, had entered into an agreement to accept the Queen of England as their sovereign. We had no right whatever over them, except that which that Treaty of Waitangi conferred. But what, after all, was the nature of that agreement, and how was it obtained? We had to obtain the consent of the chiefs of the different tribes. Now, in the first place, it appears that they had not the least idea that, in agreeing to place New Zealand under the sceptre of the Queen, they were sacrificing or endangering their own national rights or independence. Then, too, the ridiculous way in which they were got to acquiesce in our proposals

showed how absurd it would be to affect to regard the breach of the agreement on their side as being a flagrant crime, an act of treason, an act which could only be punished worthily by the confiscation of their land, and the consequent extermination of their race. Moreover, the treaty was entered into twenty-five years ago, between the first Governor of New Zealand and the chiefs of a certain tribe. It was then hawked about the country, and any chief who could be got to sign it was rewarded by the British Government with a blanket. The only treaty which that resembled was that made between a recruiting sergeant and a drunken recruit. Just as the sergeant gave him a shilling and made him a soldier, so we gave these poor chiefs a blanket each, and then we turned round upon the whole Native race, and said that they were bound, then, to submit with absolute obedience to our rule, and that if they resisted it, then they might be punished for that terrible breach of faith, for that crime of treason, by being driven from the lands which they and their fathers had kept for ages. That, however, vastly understated the case. He was willing to admit that in receiving those blankets and signing the treaty, the chiefs did involve the tribes over which they had authority, in a responsibility surrounded with such tremendous pains and penalties. But the tribes which occupied the greater part of the rich plains of Waikato, which it was proposed to confiscate, had never got them. They never signed the treaty. It was true that six old men in Waikato did take their blankets, and did sign the agreement. But the two principal chiefs of Waikato refused to sign, and the son of one of them, William Thomson, who took a very leading part in this war, put forward what Mr. Gorst justly calls this unanswerable argument—namely, that neither his father nor himself nor any of his people ever agreed to this cession to the Queen. In reality, we had no claim of any sort or kind upon which, with the faintest show of legality, we could accuse them of treason. There are two parties to a bargain. But what were the stipulations by which we bound ourselves in order to induce them to accept that treaty? That Treaty of Waitangi pledged the Queen's faith and the Queen's honour to the Natives of New Zealand, that all the rights and privileges of British subjects should be imparted to them. Again, it declared that they should be secured in the enjoyment of peace and good order, and that a settled form of civil Government should be established among them. He (Mr. Buxton) stood there to assert that our part of that treaty had been left utterly unfulfilled. We had not imparted to the Natives the rights and privileges of British subjects. We had not secured to them the enjoyment of peace and good order. We had not established among them a settled form of civil Government. The plain matter of fact was that the European authorities in New Zealand had refrained from any interference with the Natives at all. That might have been wise, he was inclined to think it was wise. It might have been wrong. Men of a thousand times higher authority on that point than his assured them that it had been wrong; but, whether right or wrong, we had acted upon the principle of minding our own business and leaving the Natives to mind theirs; and if they had possessed any political or social organization, then, without any question, this would have been fair towards them and politic as regarded ourselves; but unhappily, there was no such political organization, and the consequence was they had been living in a state of anarchy. Internecine warfare had been chronic among them, filling the country with ruin and bloodshed. Plunder, murder, and slaughter had gone on, and still we had not ventured to interfere. So far from establishing any kind of civil government among them, as we had undertaken to do, we did scarcely anything for them at all beyond at intervals passing excellent minutes which never were carried out, and a scheme was at one time arranged for giving them municipal institutions; but nothing was done. A scheme was arranged for training English functionaries for obtaining authority among them; but nothing was done. A scheme was arranged for appointing magistrates among them, and at last a few Natives were appointed, under the name of assessors, to carry out a kind of rude justice among them. But a more ridiculous caricature of justice was probably never heard of than that which resulted from this seemingly beneficent plan. There was much talk of appointing inspectors of the schools set on foot by the missionaries. The whole scheme was beautifully arranged, only nothing was done. The Natives finding that they were being demoralized and ruined by the sale of spirits among them, proposed a plan to the Government for the

suppression of that traffic. An admirable minute was drawn up for carrying out the wishes of the Natives; only nothing was done. And while there was that absolute paralysis of all civil government among them, we refused what the Bishop and other leading Europeans earnestly advocated—namely, that we should treat the Maories as fellow subjects of the settlers, and let them be represented in some way in the House of Assembly. He (Mr. Buxton) said, then, that in the first place the treaty was in its nature so invalid as scarcely to confer even a shadow of sovereignty upon us. But, secondly, had it been ever so valid in itself, we had so utterly neglected to perform our part of the bargain, that it would be outrageous for us to inflict tremendous penalties upon them if they at length refused to perform their part. With regard to the origin of that so-called rebellion, they would find that the Natives had not, in fact, been seeking to shake off the sovereignty of the Queen, or to drive the English out of the island. They would remember that what originally kindled the strife was that Colonel Browne sent soldiers to enforce the sale of the land at Waitara. Well, three years after that most unfortunate transaction, it was discovered that Wiremu Kingi had a real right to forbid this land to be sold, and Sir George Grey had actually to acknowledge in a proclamation that we had been wrong, and to annul the sale; but, unhappily, the mischief had been done, and our conduct on that and other occasions naturally created great alarm in the Native mind with regard to the possession of their land. But, undoubtedly, what led to the rupture was that which was generally called in New Zealand the "King movement," the determination on the part of the Natives to set up a king for themselves. He said a part of the Natives, for they must not forget that a very large portion of them deprecated the scheme, and either stood aloof or were driven into supporting it much against their will. Now, of course, to English ears, the proposal on the part of the Natives to set up a king of their own sounded like flat treason. But the plain truth was that all those most versed in the affairs of New Zealand, such men as Sir William Martin, Sir George Grey, the Duke of Newcastle, Sir William Denison, and others, assured them that the King movement was not in the least degree intended by the Natives as a rebellion against our rule, or as an attempt to drive us out of their island. They were assured by the highest authorities that what led the Natives to set up a king of their own was the profound feeling they had that we were threatening their possession of their land, and also that they were being ruined by the anarchy and chronic war prevailing among them, owing to our abnegation of the functions of government. It was somewhat touching to see what Wiremu Tamihana wrote to Colonel Browne with regard to the King movement. He describes the effort he and others had made to put a stop to the chronic state of warfare between the tribes. He went on to state that his efforts had failed, "for" said he—

"The river of blood has not yet stopped. The missionaries behaved bravely, and so did I; but the flow of blood did not cease. I, therefore, sought for some plan to make it cease. I considered how this blood might be made to diminish in the island."

And he went on to say that he consulted the Bible on the subject, and that various texts in the Pentateuch and Samuel, as he thought, and as he had persuaded his brethren, pointed out that the true remedy would be that they should set up a king over them. And he told Colonel Browne that on that king being set up the shedding of blood at once ceased. "What I say is," he added, "the blood of the Maories has ceased." Nothing, then, could be more absurd as well as cruel than for us to pretend that the mere use of the word king, with such a wholly different intention from that which in Europe it would have had, constituted the uprising of the Natives into an act of treason against the Queen. He affirmed, then, that there was nothing in the origin of that war that could justify them in dealing with the Natives as with traitors and rebels to the Crown. Nor could it, with the least fairness, be said that their mode of conducting the war had been such as to put them beyond the pale of law, justice, and humanity. It would be easy to imagine a war levied by semi-savages against their masters, which might have been made so bloody, so terrible, with massacre and conflagration, that scarcely any vengeance could be too heavy to inflict. Had that been so in that case? On the contrary, he did not hesitate to affirm that, upon the whole, the conduct of this war on the part of the Maories had been distinguished for humanity and self-control which they displayed. No doubt, one of the acts which, last year led to the renewal of the war at

Mr. Buxton

Waikato was the massacre of an English escort by the Natives. That was a shocking event; but it would be mere folly to regard it as a cold-blooded murder. The Waikatos had distinctly warned us that they would not allow the military road to be pushed on into their territory, into which we had no right to carry it. They said that they quite appreciated the value, in other respects, of such a road, but that they knew that the object of making the road was in order that what they called "that strange cart, the cart of terror,"— that was to say, the gun-carriage—might be brought against them. They fully warned us that they should regard its continuation as an act of war, and when the Governor persisted, they regarded it as a fair act of war to attack the soldiers who were employed in carrying it on. It would be mere folly to confuse this with an ordinary massacre. The Natives had not an idea that it could be regarded otherwise than as a legitimate act of war. Afterwards, two settlers, a man and a boy, were murdered, and a few others had also, he lamented to say, fallen victims; but, in spite of those incidents, the work apparently of a few excited individuals, he ventured to maintain that the Natives had acted upon the whole with remarkable humanity and good faith. Mr. Gorst, who was at that time a commissioner of the disturbed district, told them, in his most interesting book, which had just come out, that although the presence of an official among them was extremely distasteful, still, he said, even when they broke into open insurrection, not only were all Europeans living among them spared, but he said—

"Not a cow, nor a pig, nor a horse, nor any kind of property, was taken from us; our houses, our furniture, and all goods which could not be removed, four months after the war had begun, were still remaining as we left them, untouched and unharmed."

The Natives took up arms under what they conceived to be great provocation. They looked upon it as a defensive war, and he denied that they had conducted it with such cruelty as to justify us in inflicting upon them a tremendous penalty. And now as to the policy of that proposal. Let him again remind the House of what was stated last November in the Legislative Council, and which had been already quoted by the hon. Gentleman—namely, that the present war had cost £5,000,000, and only from 150 to 200 Natives had been killed. And yet England was coolly asked to drive all the Natives of North New Zealand off their lands, and plant settlers there instead, whom of course we must protect. Why, that plain of Waikato, which was the great prize in view, was surrounded by mountains with boundless forests and swamps and thickets of grass and fern, affording one of the best positions in the world for a defensive guerilla war. A few days' labour was enough to supply the Natives with potatoes and maize enough for a whole year, pumpkins and melons were in abundance, pigs abounded everywhere; in short, there was no reason whatever why Native bands should not keep up for 100 years an incessant warfare against those who had seized their property, and fill the land with murder and ruin. Such were the solemn warnings uttered by those who had themselves lived in Waikato, and of those warnings he trusted that they would take heed. In short, it was open to them to take the one or the other of two courses. They might treat the Maori as "damned" niggers—to use the common phrase—who were to be plundered and killed off as soon as might be; or they might endeavour to win them by good faith and justice; they might treat them with scrupulous regard for their rights, with respect for their feelings, with a sense of their high qualities. He felt no doubt that the right hon. Gentleman the Secretary of State for the Colonies would be an advocate, as the Duke of Newcastle had been, of that wiser course; and he felt sure that not merely every statesman but every Gentleman in that House would give him cordial support in carrying out that policy.

Motion made and Question proposed,

"That an humble Address be presented to Her Majesty for ' Copy of all Correspondence that has taken place between Governor Sir George Grey and the Colonial Office relating to the policy of confiscation which has been adopted by the New Zealand Legislature.'"—(*Mr. Arthur Mills.*)

Mr. CARDWELL, who was indistinctly heard, said—I have, of course, no objection to the Motion of my hon. Friend, which is one for papers on a subject of great interest and importance, on which I entirely agree with him that it is most desirable for the interest of the Natives of New Zealand that the British Parliament should be fully informed. My hon. Friend has done me the honour to refer to the part I took twenty years ago with regard to the Treaty of Waitangi, which is the origin of our possession of New Zealand and the

rights of sovereignty which we exercise in the colony. I have not the least desire to alter or modify any opinions I expressed at that time, or to adopt any policy that is indifferent to Native interests or regardless of their welfare, or which did not at that time appear consistent with reason or humanity. This question refers entirely to the Northern Island of New Zealand, not to that island colonized by a large body of English settlers, but to an island consisting of many millions of acres of land, most of it wild and desert, and containing a population of only 100,000, equally divided between the European and Native races. My hon. Friend said this may justly be described as a question of great difficulty in regard to the mode in which it should be dealt with. The people with whom we have to deal are the most remarkable people with whom our colonial enterprise has ever brought us into contact. Originally cannibals, in a short time they became Christians, and manifested a greater aptitude to receive the blessings of Christian truth and religion than any other race. They are a highly poetical people. At the time of concluding the Treaty of Waitangi, a chief made use of this memorable expression, "I understand it; the shadow goes to Queen Victoria, the substance remains with us." Again, in the blue-book which has been laid on the table, Sir George Grey reports language used by Wirimu Kingi as no less remarkable. I will venture to read it to the House. Speaking of that block of land which was the foundation of the former war, he said—

"At Mokau is the boundary of the land for our own selves. These are the lands which will not be given up by us to the hands of you and the Governor, lest we become like the birds of the sea which are resting on a rock. When the tide flows, that rock is covered by the sea. The birds fly away, because there is no resting place for them.

This language is highly characteristic of the people. In some respects they resemble children rather than men, and I entirely accede to the proposition laid down, that if they therefore require greater measures of control to reduce them to good order and obedience, they also deserve to be treated with the greatest consideration and forbearance. On the other hand, Parliament has thought proper to establish not only in the Southern Island, but also in the Northern Island, free institutions, to be exercised by the European race; and only two years ago, when my noble Friend applied to Parliament for greater power intended for the institution of a Native Council and the protection of the Native race, those powers were not granted, and finally the whole power and management of the Natives were given to the Colonial Government of New Zealand. I do not refer to that for the purpose of expressing any regret, because I am bound to say that in my judgment, when you have an European race equal in numbers to the Native race—when you have the European race constantly increasing and every tendency at work to diminish the number of the Native race, it is as certain as that the tide will rise and fall that the energy and power of the European will acquire pre-eminence and superiority. It is for you to moderate and direct the dominant spirit, but in vain will you deny to the Englishman that which is the natural prerogative of his race. Well, but you have established that Government, and when my noble Friend endeavoured to obtain additional powers for the protection of the Native race, it was the indisposition of this House to entertain that subject which disappointed and frustrated his efforts. I was disappointed to hear the hon. Gentleman describe local government as a scramble for patronage. Local government, I acknowledge, has its faults; but we have established local government, and that is one question with which we have to deal. You have a highly imaginative people, peculiarly sensitive on the question of land, and you have a local Legislature in which they have no voice, and to which the Imperial Parliament has given very large and comprehensive powers.

Reference has been made to the origin of the present war, and the names of Governor Browne and Sir George Grey have been introduced. I may say I have the honour of Governor Browne's personal acquaintance. I believe a more upright and honourable man never served the public. I happened, before he left this country, to have some conversation with him on the subject of the Treaty of Waitangi. I know he went to New Zealand animated by the most earnest desire by every means in his power to protect the Native race and promote their interests; and the very words which my hon. Friend has quoted from Governor Bowne—*rem si possis rectè, si non quocunque modo, rem*, as applied by him to the European settlers, are the strongest proof of his determination to resist their usurpation of the Natives' lands. My hon. Friend who seconded the Motion has referred to Sir George Grey in terms of

Mr. Cardwell

honour, which I thoroughly believe he justly deserves. Well, what is the history of Governor Grey's connection with New Zealand? He went there when the Taranaki war broke out; he went there, not by way of promotion, but at great inconvenience and sacrifice to himself to rescue New Zealand a second time from difficulty. He went there because he knew the people, and because the Government at home considered he was singularly able to rescue the colony from the difficulties in which it was involved. Did he go there to provoke a conflict with the Natives on the subject of land? He went there in a spirit of conciliation. He made a long journey, of which an interesting account is given in the blue-book, into the very heart of the country inhabited by the Natives who were in rebellion against us. Those Natives said to him, "Welcome, our old friend; welcome, our father; welcome, parent of the people; if you had been here this war never would have taken place." He then commenced that policy of conciliation which is sometimes known as the policy of 1861, and sometimes as Sir George Grey's policy. I mention this to show that this war which we now regret, and with the difficulties arising from which we have now to deal, did not originate in any determination on the part of the Government of New Zealand to force a conflict upon the Natives for the purpose of obtaining their lands for the use of the settlers. It is upon record that Governor Browne desired to avoid that mischief, and upon the admission of the hon. Member opposite Sir G. Grey had the same object. Let me assure my hon. Friend that neither is the war to be attributed to the King movement. Sir George Grey told the Natives at the interview I have mentioned, that the King movement by itself should never be a cause of war. It has not been a cause of war; it has not been the cause of the present war, and no war would have been entered upon by Sir George Grey solely on account of the King movement. Not only was it no part of Sir George Grey's policy to renew the war for the Waitara purchase, but having received new and unexpected information upon the original merits of that purchase, he resolved at once to abandon the European claim, and that renunciation he had to carry into effect under very difficult circumstances. But in the meantime there occurred that lamentable outbreak which has been palliated to-night. We must, indeed, remember the position of the Natives, but something is also due to the victims of the slaughter, in which two officers and several men were shot down, and, in the words of Sir George Grey, "at a single volley all of them but one or two were killed or mortally wounded, and the wounded were brutally cut about the head with tomahawks." From that dates the origin of the present war, because it appears that that was not a solitary outrage, but was the result of a combination which had taken place between some of the leaders of those tribes for the purpose of levying a general war against the European race. That determination is described by Sir George Grey in these words—

"A very serious state of things has arisen in the Northern Island of New Zealand, and there is great reason to apprehend that a general rising of the Native population may shortly take place, for the purpose of making a simultaneous attack upon the several centres of European population, with a view to the total expulsion of the white race from this island. I am quite satisfied that such a plot has been formed by a large number of influential Natives, as also that they are now busily engaged in trying to carry it into effect. I still hope that they will fail in conducting it on such a large scale as they propose, but I believe the danger to be of a very serious and alarming kind, which may lead to a vast destruction of life and property."

Then it was that Sir George Grey wrote to the Home Government for an addition to his forces of 3,000 men, which was immediately complied with. With the circumstances of the war I need not trouble the House, but I will refer to the language of the Governor, who had exhausted every measure of conciliation, and to whom my hon. Friend has referred as a Governor whom we ought to support because of his regard for the interests of the Natives and his tenderness for their feelings. On July 4, the Governor wrote—

"It has now been clearly proved that some of the chiefs of Waikato ordered the recent murders at Taranaki, and that, being thus responsible for them, they have determined to support the people who carried out the orders which they issued. For this purpose they are quite prepared to attack this populous district, and even to commit similar murders here. I have, however, arranged with the lieutenant general a plan of operations which will, I trust, not only effectually protect the Auckland district and its inhabitants from the dangers which threaten at this moment, but will also have the effect of placing this part of New Zealand in a state of permanent security."

He afterwards says—

"The colony is in great danger, and no permanent peace can now be hoped for until the Waikato and the Taranaki tribes are completely subdued."

This war has since gone on until now.

As has been truly stated, there are more than 10,000 of the Queen's troops in the colony, whilst there are also in arms against the Natives nearly 10,000 colonial militia and volunteers. The war has justly been described as a war which is very costly to the people of this country, but that evil, great as it is, seems to be one of the least evils attaching to a sanguinary and protracted contest. It is, then, our duty to consider by what methods we are most likely to be able to effect a permanent pacification of New Zealand. Sir George Grey has made these suggestions. He says that in order to put an end to this war, and to prevent the necessity in future of calling upon the army and navy of Great Britain to take part in other contests in New Zealand—

"I can devise no other plan by which both of these ends can be obtained than—1st, by providing for the permanent peace of the country by locating large bodies of European settlers, strong enough to defend themselves, in those natural positions in this province which will give us the entire command of it ; and 2ndly, by taking the land on which this European population is to be settled from those tribes who have been guilty of those outrages detailed in my various despatches. A punishment of this nature will deter other tribes from committing similar acts, while their own countrymen will generally admit that the punishment is a fair and just one, which the Waikato chiefs have well deserved."

I have stated to the House exactly what were the original proposals of Sir George Grey. Those proposals were received by my noble Friend, and were adopted upon terms of great caution and reserve, and with many suggestions of the difficulties that might arise if they were not very carefully carried into effect. In October last, Sir George Grey assembled the New Zealand Parliament, in order to give effect to this policy, and the speech which he addressed to them upon opening the Session will be found in the blue-book. That Parliament passed the Acts to which reference has been made, and which I am not going to defend. Neither am I going to say that those Acts ought to be left to pass into operation unrestrained, nor will I say that the language of those Acts is not open to the objections which have been taken to it. I am not going to contend that the language is such as to make the necessary distinction between the innocent and the guilty, or between the more guilty and the less guilty. On the contrary, the language of the particular Act most objected to is wide and sweeping, and would enable the Governor in Council to extend his confiscating powers over all the lands of the Natives. I believe, indeed, that it would extend not only to all loyal and disloyal Natives, but there are cases in which it would extend to Europeans themselves. If that be the case, the question is, what course ought the Government to pursue on receiving these Acts? Should we disallow them? There are many serious objections to that course. You have not only given to the colonists the right to govern the Native population of New Zealand, but you have imposed upon them as a duty the carrying out of that power. Are you now prepared to turn round on the first occasion when that power has been exercised, and to say, in the name of this great model of popular institutions, "We intended you to govern the country, but only according to limitations and rules which we should lay down?" There is another and more serious objection, however, to the adoption of this course. This law has not been reserved by the Governor for the signification of the Queen's pleasure upon it, and it is, therefore, at this moment, in actual operation. The 4,000 settlers who, on Sir George Grey's advice and suggestion, had been invited to take part in the military operations in New Zealand, may at this moment be enjoying the reward of their services under this Act. It is quite probable that at this moment, by the success of our arms, peace may have been restored. Who can foresee the consequences which may arise if the intelligence of the disallowance of this Act were to reach New Zealand under the present circumstances? Who can insure us from the anarchy which may possibly be the result, an anarchy far more mischievous to the Natives and Europeans than the worst form of Government would be? I do not think, then, under such circumstances, it is wise or politic to disallow the Act. What is the next course that is open to us? It is in the power of the British Government, by instructions to their Governor, to restrain and prescribe the operation of this statute within the limits dictated by justice and equity. That course we have already pursued. We have put the Governor in possession of our views, and what we believe to be the views of Parliament, with respect to the crisis now taking place in New Zealand—a crisis which, I trust, may through the skill of our general, the courage of our troops, and the wisdom

Mr. Cardwell

of our Governor, result in the perfect restoration of peace. These instructions have been dictated by the Government in the desire to promote the interest of the Native as well as the European population, to vindicate the Sovereignty of the Queen, and to enable the authorities in New Zealand to extend as far as possible to all classes the protection which results from strict order and established government. We also wish to assert the right of the mother country, which has sent out 10,000 men for the protection of the colonists in New Zealand, and which has given them a most distinguished general and a most able governor, to make her voice heard above all others in this crisis of affairs. We desire to sustain the personal authority of a governor who is distinguished for the vigour of his administration. We have accepted the principles upon which he has acted, the chastisement of the guilty Natives, the exaction of a reasonable indemnity for the expenses incurred by the war, and a moderate security for the settlement and future protection of the colony. We have also insisted that the punishment shall not be too severe, and that a distinction shall be drawn not only between the guilty and the innocent, but also between those who are the real contrivers and authors of the war and those who from less culpable motives may have been drawn into it after its commencement. Our desire is not to inflict such a punishment as shall drive the guilty to despair, while it must at the same time be severe enough to confirm the loyalty of those of the Native race who have remained true to us, and to assure to them safety and security. To effect this we propose that a cession of territory be one of the terms of pacification when the Queen's clemency is extended to those who have been in arms. Some maintain that the Natives should be treated as rebellious subjects, and others as belligerents, but it appears to me that the principles of justice and equity must rise above these legal distinctions, and that we cannot treat them entirely as rebellious subjects, but must extend to them greater lenity. We have also prescribed that no confiscation shall take place without the personal concurrence of the Governor, Sir George Grey; that there shall be an open commission for the purpose of investigating into cases in which it is intended to confiscate; and that where, owing to the misfortune which arises in cases of tribal tenure, where the majority of the tribe go to war, and where it would be impossible to do strict justice, compensation should be provided for every person who unjustly suffers; and finally, we have directed that when just chastisement has been inflicted, a measure should be brought before the Legislature of New Zealand for the purpose of abolishing the powers conferred by this Act, so that the loyal may know that they have nothing to fear, and the guilty may feel that no further punishment will be inflicted on them. When this is accomplished we have instructed the Governor to proclaim a general amnesty, excepting only those who have been guilty of heinous crimes, such as the slaughter of unoffending persons in cold blood; crimes which in times of peace would draw upon the offender the utmost rigour of the law, and which cannot be palliated by any circumstances which arise during war. That these offences may not be capriciously multiplied, or any trap laid for the entanglement of innocent persons, we have desired that at the time of the amnesty the charges may be distinctly specified and made known. Reference has been made by my hon. Friend to the vast expense incurred by this country in conducting the war. Hitherto the arrangement between this country and New Zealand has been that only nominal contribution has been made by the colonists towards the support of the forces employed for their defence; but hereafter, when the policy of the New Zealanders chances to entail a war, and when she applies for assistance to the mother country, substantial and not nominal contributions will be exacted from the colonial resources. A proposal has been made in one of these Bills to contract a large loan for the service of New Zealand. It is probably known to the House that the proposal was to obtain the loan upon the guarantee of the British Parliament, but we have conveyed to the Governor our opinion that that guarantee would, in all probability, not be granted. It will, however, be my duty at some future time, within narrower limits, to make some such proposal to the House, in accordance with the known pledge of last year, and the subject will, of course, then come on for consideration. In conclusion, I think that, while we are considerate of the feelings of the Natives, we ought at the same time to entertain some consideration for those who, of the same race as ourselves and settled in that distant part of the world, live

in apprehension for the safety of their families and themselves, and in constant fear of massacres and the destruction of their property. I have had the advantage of conferring with one of the New Zealand Ministry at present in this country, and his language to me—and I am sure it is the genuine expression of his mind—is the language of a man who is sincerely desirous of the pacification of the country upon just and equitable terms, and who will not be a party to any attempt at forcing Sir George Grey into any policy of inequitable and wholesale confiscation.

LORD ROBERT CECIL said, he would wish to describe in no other language than that used by the right hon. Gentleman his estimate of the measures, passed by the New Zealand Legislature. That language was highly creditable to the right hon. Gentleman, but he confessed he should have listened with much greater satisfaction to the right hon. Gentleman if he had stated that the atrocious Bill passed by that Legislature was to be disallowed by the Crown. As to the plan proposed, he feared it was cumbrous and might fail to attain the object desired. There were two objections to it. One of the great evils of confiscating all the land of the Natives, the innocent as well as the guilty, was that the difficulty of pacification was increased a hundredfold by reinforcing the enemy with tribes which were then, perhaps, doubtful or wavering in their allegiance. As he understood, there was no intention of proclaiming that this Act should be limited.

MR. CARDWELL: I stated that we have desired that a Bill should be immediately introduced into the Assembly of New Zealand for putting an end within a limited time to the whole powers of the Act.

LORD ROBERT CECIL said, he had understood the right hon. Gentleman to say that the Bill would be introduced as soon as the war was terminated.

MR. CARDWELL: I am speaking upon a certain hypothesis which may not turn out true—namely, that the war is at an end before this time. The last accounts lead us to believe that the war in all probability is concluded by this time.

LORD ROBERT CECIL: But suppose the war to continue, and the Natives to know that the Act had been sanctioned by the Queen, and that they had no further security for the possession of their land, they would have reason to say that the Treaty of Waitangi had been violated, and they might come to the conclusion that it was safer to plunge into rebellion, and take their last chance of throwing off the stranger who was trying to rob them of their land. There ought to be some pledge that the provisions which the Bill contained for depriving the innocent of their land would never be practically carried out. There was still another danger. He concurred in the eulogies which the right hon. Gentleman had passed upon the tact, the temper, and the ability of Sir George Grey; but if the war went on and Sir George Grey ceased to be governor, his successor, who would possess under the Act all the powers lodged in Sir George Grey, might be a man open to popular pressure in the colony. They knew from Sir George Grey how heavy the pressure was upon him to obtain the Native land for the settlers. It was something like weakness on the part of Governor Browne which had brought on the horrible war that was then raging. And they ought not to trust to the expectation that every Governor of New Zealand would act with the wisdom and justice which Sir George Grey had shown. His fear, therefore, was that when the present Governor left the colony, and while the Act was still in operation, they would hear that his successor had yielded to popular pressure, that land belonging to some powerful tribe had been seized without a show of justice, and that the colony was plunged anew into the horrors of war. Some protection should be afforded against that. Otherwise, he thought the speech of the right hon. Gentleman had been exceedingly satisfactory; and though some might have desired that measures of a stronger character should have been adopted, the New Zealand Assembly would probably accept the rebuke which was implied in the observations of the right hon. Gentleman, and would understand that England would not endure that the name of English Sovereigns should be dishonoured, and that treaties solemnly entered into should be set aside by an inferior Legislature. The right hon. Gentleman talked of procuring the introduction of a Bill into the Assembly. But what security had he that it would pass? At present he had such a security, because he might threaten to withdraw the soldiers if it did not pass. But he would lose that security after the war was over, and might then find that, though he could prevent new

Lord Robert Cecil

legislation, the Bill which had been passed would not be withdrawn. These were objections which occurred to him at the moment. He had confidence in the purity of the intentions of the right hon. Gentleman and in the zeal with which he was administering his office; and it was to be hoped that the right hon. Gentleman would take every security in his power for the adoption of the measures he had sketched out that evening.

Sir JOHN TRELAWNY said, that the state of New Zealand might well cause anxiety, for, in his opinion, if we were at war with the United States, the first thing the American Government would do would be to send a force to New Zealand and raise a rebellion there. He did not think the way in which Governor Browne had been spoken of that night was altogether just. The seizure of the Waitara block had been defended at the time by the Government, though now Governor Browne's policy had been rescinded. But Governor Browne had been entirely whitewashed by the Government, and he could not, therefore, absolve the Government from responsibility for the bloodshed and the expenditure which had taken place in New Zealand. As to the suggested guarantee, he considered that a solemn and serious matter. He had protested against that which was granted for £500,000, and in the Committee which had sat upon the subject several Members were completely deceived by the plausible statements which were then offered in evidence by persons who had come from New Zealand to obtain the guarantee. A Return for which he had moved on the subject would show that clearly, and he would now ask the right hon. Gentleman (Mr. Henley) how he came to be so easily led into inducing the House to give a guarantee upon evidence which turned out to be untrue.

Lord ALFRED CHURCHILL said, he was much gratified to hear the assurance which the right hon. Gentleman had given with respect to the future government of New Zealand. He had no doubt that if the line of policy enunciated by the right hon. Gentleman should be carried out under the able administration of Sir George Grey, it would conduce very much to the consolidation and strengthening of the Imperial Government in that country. It was difficult to come at the origin of the "King movement," but it was, he believed, to be partly attributed to the desire of the Natives for the establishment of law and order amongst themselves. They had no means of bringing to justice those who committed crime, and they wished to have the means of punishing criminals in imitation of the system adopted for the purpose by Europeans. It was natural that the colonists, seeing the land of the Natives running to wreck and ruin, should desire to possess and cultivate it, and he believed that when the Natives were satisfied that a fair price would be paid to them, their natural desire for gain would induce them to clear the land from rough timber and sell it to the Europeans. The Government got the land from the Natives at half-a-crown an acre, and it was immediately put up at 10s. an acre. Now, the Natives were what the Americans call 'cute, and they did not understand how land sold for 2s. 6d. an acre should·be immediately sold for 10s. an acre. The Government, however, had made surveys, and had been at some expense in bringing emigrants, who wanted more land. He rejoiced to hear that the law for the confiscation of land was not to be carried out in its integrity; but, even if the war were to end to-morrow, it was absolutely necessary that a considerable number of soldiers should remain in the country to prevent any outbreak that might subsequently arise. He denied that there was any general desire on the part of the colonists to exterminate the Natives. As an instance of the friendliness of the colonists to the Natives he might mention, that last year one of the most distinguished Members of the Legislature of New Zealand proposed that Native members should sit side by side with European members in that assembly, and that that proposal very nearly succeeded. He was glad to hear the policy enunciated by the right hon. Gentleman.

MR. CHICHESTER FORTESCUE observed, that he wished to add a few words to what had been stated by his right hon. Friend. It had been his lot to follow very closely the disturbances in New Zealand, and, notwithstanding what had been said by the hon. Baronet (Sir John Trelawny) that evening, he still adhered to the views which, on more than one occasion, he had stated to the House. At the same time he deplored as much as any man could the unfortunate transactions to which the hon. Baronet had alluded, and admitted that great misfortunes had followed from them; but Governor Browne was a man of the greatest humanity, and certainly was not intentionally harsh or unjust towards the Native race. The measures he had taken against an obstinate chief, of the name of William King, were in themselves justifiable. That chief not only put himself in opposition to the Government of this country, but affected to dictate to other Natives what line of conduct they should pursue in the selling of their own lands, and had attempted to raise himself to the position of dictator over those whom he had no right to control. He believed, therefore, that there was nothing unjust in Governor Browne's conduct towards that person or towards the Natives generally, though it might have been deficient in policy. With respect to the present war, it was satisfactory to know that the turbulent and hostile tribes, however gallant an enemy they might be, were a decided minority of the Native tribes. He could assure the House that some of the ideas on the subject of the hostilities in New Zealand put forward by able pens through the press, and which had found moderate expression in that House, were totally opposed to the facts. He thought, however, that there were hardly two opinions with respect to the justice and necessity of the present war. It was well known that, from the time he arrived in New Zealand, Sir George Grey devoted all his energies to avert the necessity of the renewal of war, and to pacify the Natives. He had done his best to introduce into Native districts those simple forms of government, and provisions for law and order, which it was alleged formed one great cause of their discontent, and had led to their futile attempt at establishing a Government of their own. Sir George Grey, after noble efforts, carried on for many months, had at last been driven to the conclusion that nothing was left but to vindicate, by means of the forces placed at his disposal by this country, the authority of the law and the sovereignty of the Queen, and to bring the misguided Natives to a sense of their position in defying the power of this country. With respect to the Act of the Colonial Legislature, about which so much alarm had been expressed, and of which the noble Lord opposite (Lord R. Cecil) had expressed a fear that the evil consequences would not be averted by the instructions which went out by mail that night to New Zealand, however violent that Act might be, much might be said in extenuation and in excuse of the Legislature of the colony.

They were not sitting calmly like the House of Commons discussing matters of distant interest. They formed almost the only able-bodied men in the northern part of the North Island, who were engaged in peaceful pursuits at a time when the whole population were in arms against a formidable and sanguinary insurrection. The noble Lord, if he would look a little closer into the matter, would probably see that the instructions described by his right hon. Friend would prove adequate to the occasion. The noble Lord complained of the Natives being treated like foreign enemies. They were treated so for their own good, as they were in fact regarded not as rebels but as enemies, entitled to all the rights of belligerents. When taken prisoners they were treated with the utmost kindness and humanity, and no more life was taken than was absolutely necessary to take in the field. But although for the sake of humanity we had treated the Natives as foreign enemies, and not as revolted subjects, yet they were legally British subjects. If we had chosen to treat them wholly as foreign enemies, on their subjugation it would have been easy for the Governor and General-in-Chief to deprive them of a large portion of their territory, but, as we were treating them as British subjects, legislation was necessary in order to deal with them satisfactorily. He had seen nothing in the language of the New Zealand Ministers or Members of Parliament, which led him to suspect that they intended to make a tyrannical use of the powers of this Act. It would be an insult, too, to Sir George Grey—always a warm friend of the Native—to suppose that in the strong position in which he found himself, and armed with the instructions he was about to receive, he would not control every step to be taken under the Act, and take care that its operation was not carried to any unjust length. The effect of the instructions would be, that when the tribes in arms should submit, and when the Governor and General commanding came to dictate terms to them on their submission, the Governor would announce to them that as part of these terms the surrender of a certain portion of their lands for the purposes described would be required from them. The Natives would be informed at once that a certain portion of their lands would be taken from them, and afterwards they would be restored to all the privileges which they obtained under the Treaty of

Mr. Chichester Fortescue

Waitangi. With regard to a part of the Act which had been greatly blamed—that which gave power to take lands from those Natives even who were not implicated in the war—it must be borne in mind that the tenure of land in New Zealand was so complicated that not an acre of land could be taken if the assent of every single joint owner were required. The joint owners of the lands not implicated in the rebellion would receive fair compensation for their interest in the land by the verdict of a court appointed by the Governor himself. He believed that these terms of peace would be the only means of really punishing the guilty and preventing them from rushing to arms again. Under the instructions which Sir George Grey would receive, there was reason to hope that he would be able to prevent future wars, and enable the two races to live side by side in peace and prosperity.

SIR JOHN PAKINGTON said, he could not allow the discussion to close without expressing his satisfaction, both to the Colonial Secretary, for his clear and able statement, and to his hon. Friend (Mr. A. Mills), for having raised the Question. The recent events in New Zealand were the firstfruits of the change of policy by which the Local Legislature had been enabled to deal with the affairs of the Natives. In the Constitution Act of New Zealand, Native affairs were reserved for the Home Government; and it was impossible not to feel some anxiety as to the transference of those affairs to the colony, when they found that it had led to the passing of Acts of so doubtful a character as those they were now discussing. He was rather disposed to agree with his noble Friend (Lord R. Cecil), who expressed his regret that Her Majesty's Government did not propose to disallow these acts, though he was bound to admit that the fact of the Governor not having reserved them for consideration had much increased the difficulty of taking that course. The whole state of affairs in New Zealand was embarrassing and difficult, and if these acts of confiscation were to be carried out to their full extent, the difficulties of the Government would be greatly increased. He had, however, every reason to trust in the wisdom and moderation of Sir George Grey, and hoped that the agreeable prospects held out by the right hon. Gentleman opposite would be realised.

MR. SELWYN said, that the speech of

the right hon. Gentleman the Secretary for the Colonies was so temperate and so satisfactory that he would not have said a single word but for the speech of the hon. Under Secretary, which he feared would in some respect mar the effect of the observations of his superior. What he found fault with was, that the hon. Gentleman stated that he adhered to the statements made by him in this House in 1861, although those statements had since been proved to be mistaken, and had been repudiated by Governor Sir George Grey and by the responsible advisers of the Governor. He believed—and subsequent events had shown—that if the recommendations made in 1861 by the Church Missionary Society, and urged by himself, had been adopted, the recent war in New Zealand might have been prevented. He felt satisfied that there was no real antagonism between the Natives and the colonists. The prosperity of one race was intimately connected with that of the other. They might occupy New Zealand with their troops, and make it another Algeria, but that would not be for the benefit either of the colonists or the Natives, and still less of the mother country. He believed the Natives never had a better friend than Governor Browne. No one in dealing with the Natives ever laid down wiser or better rules of conduct. Unfortunately for the colonists, and for this country, the wise counsels of Governor Browne were overruled by the rapacity of certain persons, who were determined to possess particular portions of land. When the question was last before the House, the friends of New Zealand had two difficulties to contend against, both of which were now removed. The first was the indifference of the Legislature and the country. Considering the expenditure of blood and treasure which had taken place in New Zealand, and considering that the question of calling out the Yeomanry of England depended, according to the noble Lord at the head of the Government, on the result of the war in New Zealand, the indifference with which the question was formerly regarded might now be considered at an end. The second difficulty, which they encountered at every stage of their proceedings, was some disputed question of fact. The last time the question was before the House, he had to meet many of the statements of the Under Secretary of the Colonies with a simple denial. He did not expect that the House would receive the assertion of an independent Member of that House in preference to that of a Minister of the Crown; but let the House now refer to that debate, and to the subsequent despatches of Governor Sir George Grey, and say which was right, and whether the right hon. Gentleman was justified in saying that he adhered to every statement which he then made. He would let bygones be bygones, but he concurred with those who recommended that a treaty which had been deliberately entered into on behalf of Her Majesty, and which had been acted upon by the people of New Zealand when they were strong and the colonists were weak, should be still observed. For a period of twenty years the New Zealanders could have swept the whole military of the country and the colonists into the sea, and they were only restrained from doing so by the representations of the missionaries and others that the faith of England was inviolable. It was not by mistake on either side that the treaty was entered into. On the 18th of June, 1845, when the Earl of Derby was Secretary for the Colonies, he felt it necessary to repudiate with the utmost possible earnestness the doctrine maintained by some, that the treaty which they had entered into was to be considered a mere blind to amuse and deceive a set of ignorant savages; and in the name of the Queen he utterly denied that any treaty could have been conceived in a spirit so disingenuous or for purposes so unworthy. The terms of that treaty were drawn up with a kind of prescience of what was to follow, for it was stipulated that not only their individual, but their collective possessions were to be guaranteed to the Natives by Her Majesty as long as it was their wish and desire to hold the same. He would recommend, therefore, as the Church Missionary Society had done, that we should repeat the declaration made in 1845 by the Earl of Derby. Circumstances made that declaration more necessary now than it was then; and when, in 1861, he (Mr. Selwyn) urged the expediency and necessity of repeating it, the Under Secretary for the Colonies said, "I did not mean to decline that." But he would ask the hon. Gentleman and Government if they had ever in fact complied with that suggestion, or repeated the Earl of Derby's declaration? If they had done so, the present war would not have broken out. The war had been brought on partly by an accident and partly by the course pursued by the Government. Sir George Grey, with great generosity, had taken upon himself the blame of not issuing the proclamation sooner, but he had scarcely done justice to himself. It was the difficulty imposed by Her Majesty's Government in persisting in the error which had been clearly demonstrated, which fortified the position of the colonial advisers of Sir George Grey, and made it no easy matter for him to issue the proclamation. But had it been issued a few days sooner the outbreak would never have taken place. He should have thought, when a proposition was referred to in that House, and when a Member of Her Majesty's Government got up and said, "We do not decline that;" he would have meant, "We intend to do it." He had no desire to revive former discussions, to impute blame, or to boast of empty triumphs if Her Majesty's Government would do what was right now. He quite accepted the policy indicated in the speech of the right hon. Gentleman the Secretary of State, and if sincerely carried into effect it would go far to put an end to this unfortunate war. There never had been a difference of opinion among Englishmen upon the point that the Queen's supremacy must be before all things maintained; and there never was any difference of opinion on the point amongst Englishmen, that every armed insurrection against that supremacy must be put down. But let it not be said that when they entered into a treaty, and the Natives were the stronger, they obeyed it; but when England was the stronger she broke it. In conclusion, he would observe that in former times in the colony they had been rapacious and hasty; at home they had been indifferent and careless. Let them now be wise, and amend; and as they had been unjust before let them be merciful now.

Mr. ARTHUR MILLS briefly replied, stating he had by no means altered his opinion as to the value of local self-government of the colonies, and that he did not cast any imputations on the governors, the peculiar difficulties in which they were placed being the excuse for the errors which they might have committed.

Motion *agreed to.*

Address for

"Copy of all Correspondence that has taken place between Governor Sir George Grey and the Colonial Office relating to the policy of Confiscation which has been adopted by the New Zealand Legislature."—(*Mr. Arthur Mills.*)

Mr. Selwyn

HARBOURS OF REFUGE.

RESOLUTION.

MR. LINDSAY said, he rose to move a Resolution on the necessity for the construction of harbours of refuge, and in so doing he would say that he wished to alter the terms from the Resolution as it stood originally on the paper, so that it would now run thus:—"That, in the opinion of this House, Her Majesty's Government should now adopt measures for the construction of Harbours of Refuge on the coasts of Great Britain and Ireland, recommended by a Committee of the House in 1858, by a Royal Commission in 1859, and by a Resolution of this House in 1860." What he wished to point out was this, that two Committees of that House and a Royal Commission had recommended that harbours of refuge should be constructed, and that recommendation had been confirmed by a Resolution of that House. He had no desire to point out to the Government the method in which they should carry out the recommendations, but he did hope they would take such steps as they might judge best for constructing those harbours of refuge which had been so frequently and so strongly recommended. The hon. Baronet the Member for Stamford (Sir Stafford Northcote) had put a notice upon the paper by which he proposed to add certain words to the Resolution, and he (Mr. Lindsay) had altered its terms in the hope that the hon. Baronet would not think it necessary to move the addition. He did not believe that the hon. Baronet was opposed to the construction of those harbours, but that, considering the position which he then occupied in that House, and the higher position which he was likely to occupy, and deservedly so, he was no doubt frightened at the very large claim that might be made upon him by-and-by for the construction of harbours of refuge. He was therefore not surprised, under the circumstances, that the hon. Gentleman should have thought of adding the words standing upon the paper to the Motion of which he had given notice. But that Motion only called upon the Government to carry out the repeated recommendations in favour of harbours of refuge, leaving them free to determine what measures were best for that purpose. In connection with the subject it was impossible to pass over a paper from the Board of Trade which had been laid upon the table of the House.

Somehow or other a copy had not been sent to him, but he bought one in the Vote Office, and he had read it with great care and considerable surprise. The document was meant to guide the opinion of Members of the House, and to answer the deliberate Resolution of the Committee, of the Commission, and the Vote of the House; and when a document of that kind was laid before the House, it ought to be correct as to its facts; it ought to lay before them statements which no one could doubt; but he was sorry to say that this document was calculated to lead hon. Members astray. For his part, he thought the deliberate convictions of Parliamentary Committees and Royal Commissions, formed upon full information, and backed by the vote of a majority in a full House, were entitled to more respect than a document concocted at the Board of Trade by any gentleman, however competent. In dealing with this question he desired, first, to consider the necessity for harbours of refuge; secondly, the cost; thirdly, the amount of life and property that would be saved by their construction. The paper to which he alluded dealt with two of these points—it admitted all the startling facts forming the true recommendation of harbours of refuge—namely, the fearful losses of life and property along the coast; but it opened with the expression of doubts whether these harbours could be constructed for the sums named by the Commission. Now, who were the persons against whom that single gentleman at the Board of Trade set up his opinion? Admiral Hope, a gentleman of great abilities and shrewd common sense; Admiral Washington, the late hydrographer to the Admiralty, a man well fitted to give an opinion on the matter, whose loss was still deplored; Captain Veitch, of the Royal Artillery, and for some time attached to the Board of Trade; Mr. John Coode, an eminent civil engineer with considerable experience in the construction of breakwaters; and his hon. and gallant Friend (Sir Frederic Smith), than whom no one was more competent to form a sound opinion. He himself was also a Member of the Commission; but, without bringing his own name into controversy, he asked, might not the view of these five gentlemen be adopted against that of an unseen clerk of the Board of Trade? The document in question contended that the original Estimates as to harbours of refuge already existing had been exceeded.

No doubt such had been the case with harbours of a military character, like Dover and Alderney, and also at Holyhead, which had been altered, for naval or postal purposes, by every successive Board of Admiralty. The only two pure harbours of refuge, Kingstown and Portland, were the only two which had been kept within their limits. Kingstown cost less than the original Estimate, and the same might be said of Portland, if the expenditure made with a view of turning it into a naval harbour were deducted. In the paper emanating from the Board of Trade every vessel was struck out of the account which was not lost in a gale of wind. An attempt was made to measure the strength of gales, and it was contended that because in one, of which the violence was indicated by the figure 9, a vessel could carry close reefed topsails, she would have no right to seek a harbour of refuge, and, therefore, if lost ought not to be counted among those which might have been saved by such means. But by what process was the strength of the wind arrived at? It was often blowing only a stiff breeze on shore when the sailor outside knew that a hurricane was raging. In the same way the paper eliminated all collisions from the account. But the fact was notorious that collisions were frequent among the vessels which particular winds kept crowding under Flamborough Head. It also eliminated all vessels which foundered at sea. Why the foundering of many of those vessels was directly attributable to the want of a harbour of refuge. In the absence of such a haven vessels caught by a gale from the E.S.E. at Flamborough Head had no shelter on that iron-bound coast, but had to run to the Frith of Forth, and many of them foundered on the way. The Board of Trade, however, took no notice of them, which ought to have been done when they put forth a document for the purpose of guiding the judgment of the House on a great question of national policy affecting the interests of a class of men on whom we all depended, especially in the hour of need —he meant the seamen of England. Another deduction was made on account of losses attributable to bad seamanship. Bad seamanship! Did they not know that the coasting trade trained the best seamen that England had ever possessed, and how could the author of this document judge whether or not a vessel had been lost by bad seamanship when the crew had all perished?

He would not trouble the House further with the document, but would pass on to the real facts of the case. The question first attracted public attention in 1852. In 1857 a Committee was appointed to inquire into it, of which the late Mr. James Wilson was chairman. That Committee sat for two years, and examined a great number of witnesses, all of whom agreed as to the necessity of these harbours. In 1852 the entries inwards and outwards in the foreign and coasting trade of vessels with cargo represented 39,000,000 tons; and the Committee, in order to ascertain the loss, took the average between the years 1832 and 1852. They found that there were upon an average 5,128 casualties per annum to sea-going vessels, many of which were totally wrecked, and that every five years 4,184 lives, exclusive of fishermen, were sacrificed. The amount of property annually lost was £1,500,000. This state of things was most appalling. The Committee reported that they could not "too earnestly press upon the House the necessity of these works being undertaken at as early a period as possible, and placed under some system which will secure their steady and speedy progress;" and further, that, considering the commercial and political non-security of the country, and the enormous loss of life and property at sea to which the nation was exposed from the unprotected state of the coast, there was no one object to which the public money could be more usefully and properly employed, having regard to the future prosperity of the nation. In 1858, Mr. Wilson, who was chairman of the Committee, moved for a Commission to make further inquiry upon the coasts, and to point out the sites at which harbours ought to be constructed. The Motion was assented to by the right hon. Baronet the Member for Droitwich, who was then First Lord of the Admiralty, and the Commission to which he had already referred was appointed. That Commission heard much evidence at a great variety of places, and unanimously confirmed the opinion of the Committee that harbours of refuge were necessary. In their visit to the coast the Commissioners found all seafaring men anxious that these harbours should be constructed, but many large shipowners, whose vessels were seldom upon the coast, were unwilling to be taxed in the shape of a passing toll to carry out the object. They found also in many places, especially in the cast of

Mr. Lindsay

Scotland, that every witness considered his particular town the most suitable place for a harbour; and his hon. Friend the Member for the Montrose Boroughs actually recommended a grant of public money to the harbour of Arbroath, the whole of the entrance to which was surrounded with sunken rocks. After giving the subject a very full and impartial consideration, the Commissioners made their Report. The document to which he had already referred stated that they had recommended grants of money to the extent of £4,000,000; but that was not correct. For the purely national harbours they recommended grants to the extent of £1,340,000, and they also recommended that grants should be made to other places for smaller amounts, on condition that those who were locally interested should contribute equal, or, in some cases, larger amounts. They said they should not recommend passing tolls for the purpose of erecting harbours, because those tolls had long since been condemned by the House of Commons; but it was urged that the parties who would be gainers by the harbours should tax themselves, and by so doing benefit the public at large, before the public were called upon to contribute a shilling. The public, too, would profit by their construction, because these harbours of refuge could be made of the greatest service to our navy in the event of a European war. The question had, however, been asked—could they be constructed for the sum specified in the Report of the Commission? Now, the Members of the Commission were competent to form an opinion on the subject, and in addition they had examined all the most eminent civil engineers on the subject. He would not say that the work could be done for the sum named in the Report of the Royal Commissioners if the Government in office were to "meddle and muddle" the matter; but if tenders were issued on the following day for a plan as laid down by the Commission, he would undertake to assert that responsible contractors willing to accomplish the work for the amount set forth in the Report might readily be found. It need not cost even the amount named by the Commissioners, for what better employment for our convicts could we have than to send them down, for example, to Filey, where they would enable us to construct a harbour of refuge at a much smaller expense? It was not merely, he might add, in the opinion of the Commission that harbours of refuge were necessary on our coasts. His right hon. Friend the President of the Board of Trade and the noble Lord at the head of the Government had also borne testimony to the expediency of those harbours in the strongest possible manner. And if they were required in 1852, how much more were they required at the present day, when there was an increase since then in the entrances and clearances of our tonnage of 18,000,000 ? He might further observe that during the last five years for which we had Returns, there had been 6,941 casualties on our shores, including a vast number of total wrecks. Upwards of 4,000 lives had during that time been sacrificed. Again, taking the year 1862, he found that there had been 1,418 casualties, with a tonnage of 326,000, and crews amounting to 14,714 men. The estimated value of the ships wrecked, together with their cargoes, was, during that year, not less than £6,000,000. If out of that amount £3,500,000 were saved, there would still remain an annual loss to the extent of £2,500,000. Then came the question, what amount of life and property would be likely to be rescued by the construction of harbours of refuge? The paper from the Board of Trade stated that, on the north-east coast, in the severe gale of the 4th of January, 1857, sixty-five vessels and eighty-six lives had been lost, but by the system of elimination to which he alluded they had reduced the number of lives which would probably have been saved if there had been a harbour of refuge on the coast to half of the number which actually perished. Now, if one-half of the lives would have been saved, one-half of the property would have been saved also ; and in a valuable pamphlet which, no doubt, most hon. Members had seen, and which had been written by a gentleman who resided on the coast for twenty years, and who took up the matter as a philanthropist, would be found an analysis of the Board of Trade Returns, which showed that in the gale in question there were ten vessels lost and fifty-six lives of which the Department had no account. But let him suppose, taking the lowest estimate, that the construction of harbours would save only one-sixth of the property and one-sixth of the lives which were annually lost on all parts of our coast. What he asked from the House was £134,000 per annum for

the next ten years; or, if the parties locally interested raised the £1,600,000 he had named, the full extent of the demand on the House for the next ten years for the construction of all these harbours would be £236,000. Now, taking the saving of property that would ensue at £400,000, or about one-sixth of the entire loss (£2,500,000), they would thus have the harbours made for nothing, with a saving to the nation in the one case of £266,000, and, in the other, of £164,000 annually. They would recoup themselves for all their outlay and have a considerable sum over; in addition to which they would have the satisfaction of saving the lives of those hardy mariners whom they could so ill spare. He had, he was afraid, trespassed too long on the patience of the House. But he had felt as an old sailor, who had been brought up among the hardy men to whom he had referred, that it was incumbent on him to make another appeal to the House on their behalf, and he would now leave his Motion in the hands of the House, confidently hoping that his appeal would not be made in vain. The hon. Gentleman concluded by moving the Resolution.

MR. CAVE, in seconding the Motion, declared his opinion that the hon. Member for Sunderland (Mr. Lindsay), and the gallant Officer the Member for Chatham (Sir Frederic Smith), deserved great credit for the perseverance with which they had kept this Question before the House. The Reports of the Committee and the Commission both appeared to have been strangely ignored and neglected; but as the representative of a commercial port, the vessels belonging to which were constantly braving the perils so well described by his hon. Friend, and too many swelling the wreck chart to which he had alluded, he felt that the importance of the subject before them could not be overrated. He differed also from the Board of Trade Report quoted by his hon. Friend, not only in the points he had mentioned, but in those which stated that these harbours of refuge would be of such pecuniary advantage to shipowners that they ought to be paid for by passing tolls. Shipowners were generally covered by insurance, charged practically on freight, and it was doubtful whether the premiums would be affected by the formation of harbours. Underwriters and consignees might possibly be to some extent interested, if it were true that property to the extent of

£2,000,000 was lost annually on our shores, but especially the seamen themselves, the widows and orphans of shipwrecked mariners—no small number, when it was remembered that 1,000 lives were annually lost. And those ratepayers were deeply concerned whose burdens were augmented by so many helpless creatures left without means of subsistence. Still less weight was due to the argument that ships were often wrecked on a coast abounding with harbours, and that fewer ships than might be supposed were lost on that part of a coast which was notoriously deficient. With respect to the first, no one expected that any measure would make navigation a safe and easy calling. With respect to the second, the number of ships absolutely stranded on an inhospitable coast was no measure of those which were lost because the coast was harbourless, or which might have been saved had a port been under their lee. Many a vessel was wrecked on the Shetlands for want of harbours in Yorkshire. The actual loss might take place hundreds of miles from the cause of it. Hon. Members would clearly perceive this by listening to a few words of Robert Stevenson upon a kindred subject — not the lamented Robert Stephenson, lately a Member of that House, but the architect of the Bell Rock Lighthouse. Robert Stevenson wrote thus—

"In 1799 a three days' gale from the S.E. drove from their moorings in the Downs and Yarmouth Roads, and from their southward courses, a large fleet of vessels. Borne north by the gale, these ships might easily have reached the anchorage of the Frith of Firth, for which the wind was fair, but night came on, and fearing the Bell Rock, these ill-fated navigators resolved to keep to sea and thus escape its dangers, but driven before the storm they were wrecked, about seventy, on the eastern shores of Scotland, where, sad to tell, many of their crews perished."

The objection of expense was more deserving of consideration. The House, which vibrated between parsimony and extravagance, was now in an economical mood, and he must be a bold man who would put a large extra charge upon the Estimates. He was as glad as his hon. Friend to find the hon. Baronet so careful of these finances, over which he hoped, with him, that he would some day have more control. Yet they had endangered shipping by making an artificial shoal at an enormous cost in Alderney. The engineers were now destroying in Corfu, at great expense, works which he had seen

Mr. Cave

them a year ago constructing at a still greater. In the neighbourhood of Portsmouth, the Government was busy altering the face of nature—*Diruit, ædificat, mutat quadrata rotundis* — and was spending millions in works which a succeeding generation of engineers would probably point to as examples to be avoided. But it seemed really that the most economical way of carrying out such works was that recommended by his hon. Friend. Friend, which might not only be of great benefit to the marine of this and other countries, but might solve a difficulty which threatened to be more pressing than ever—namely, what we were to do with our convicts. In corroboration of his hon. Friend's opinion, he might read what Captain (now Sir Walter) Crofton, then Director of Irish Prisons, wrote in 1858, on intermediate prisons. His words were—

"On reference to the Report of the Committee on Harbours of Refuge made at the close of last Session, it will be observed how numerous and pressing are the calls for different works on our coasts, varying from £800,000 to £20,000 in estimated value. It will be quite evident, then, how convenient would be the application of special convict labour for these purposes, provided it could be economically located on the site of the works by means of moveable iron buildings. Those used in Ireland for this purpose accommodate fifty men and three officers in each at a cost of about £330. The fifty men are in association like soldiers in a barrack. Cellular accommodation would much increase the expenditure, and is not to be desired. With prisoners whose merit and industrial exertion during detention have placed them in the intermediate stage before release, this system has been found reformatory and economical, the association operating as a further test by which we may induce the public to employ the criminal. If we cannot control them in association after our long course of discipline and training, we cannot expect the community will have much confidence in their future well doing. It is by the use of economically constructed moveable buildings that the labour of convicts can be made of greater utility to the State."

There was the task, and there were the means of performing it, and he hoped the Government would have energy and determination enough to undertake a work of such vast importance not only to the whole maritime population, but to the country at large.

Motion made, and Question proposed,

"That, in the opinion of this House, Her Majesty's Government should now adopt measures for the construction of Harbours of Refuge on the coast of Great Britain and Ireland, recommended by a Committee of this House in 1858, by a Royal Commission in 1859, and by a Resolution of this House in 1860."—(*Mr. Lindsay.*)

SIR STAFFORD NORTHCOTE said, he would detain the House only a very few minutes in explaining the Amendment he had put on the paper to the Motion of the hon. Member for Sunderland; and he must claim their indulgence for the few remarks he should make, because he felt he rose at a great disadvantage after a speech so full of feeling and knowledge as that with which the hon. Gentleman had just favoured the House. He could not possibly attempt to put anything he might have to say in comparison with what fell from the hon. Member, for, on the one hand, he had not the advantage of being able to speak with authority on the subject, and, on the other hand, he could not appeal to the feelings of the House, because he was there to plead the cause of the British taxpayer, who certainly did not excite the same feelings as our brave British sailors were so justly entitled to raise. But he thought it well for the House to consider, before they came to a vote on the question, what their real position was in regard to it. They ought to consider whether a constitutional question was not involved in the course which had been taken, and which it was now proposed they should take with regard to the matter. The proceedings which the House had taken of late years with regard to harbours of refuge should not be forgotten. For a good number of years (probably for twenty or twenty-five years) the question had engaged public interest. There had been discussions as to the mode in which they could provide against the dangers of wreck, and various plans for the establishment of harbours of refuge had been from time to time considered, until at length in 1857 a very remarkable and unusual course was taken by the Government of the day in moving for a Select Committee of that House to consider the question of the policy of making public grants towards harbours of refuge. That Committee was appointed not on the Motion of any private Member on either side of the House; but it was actually originated by a Member of the Government, and by a Member peculiarly interested in looking after expenditure. It was not proposed by the Admiralty or Board of Trade, but by the Secretary of the Treasury. Mr. Wilson, representing the former Government of the noble Lord (Viscount Palmerston), proposed, in order to solve the difficult question they had to consider, that a Select Committee should be appointed, not to inquire whether harbours of refuge were good or bad things, or where they should be placed if it was thought desirable they should be constructed, but "to inquire into the policy of making further grants of public money for the improvement and extension of harbours of refuge." That Committee was appointed with considerable solemnity. It did not appear to have been introduced by Mr. Wilson in any speech, but when the nomination of the Committee was in question, the hon. Member for St. Andrew's (Mr. E. Ellice) made a suggestion that the Members should be appointed not in the usual way by the House, but by the Committee of Selection. That course, however, was not taken. The Committee at first consisted of sixteen Members; it was afterwards raised to twenty-two. It sat for two Sessions, and finally reported in June, 1858. The inquiry, conducted by the Committee, divided itself into two branches—first, whether it was desirable that harbours of refuge should be established; and secondly, where and at what cost they should be made. On the first branch of inquiry the Committee appeared to have taken a good deal of evidence, and after ascertaining in what parts of England or Scotland there should be harbours of refuge, if anywhere, and after estimating the expense, they proceeded to suggest the appointment of a Royal Commission, where men of professional skill might thoroughly investigate the question of cost and the exact locality where the harbours should be placed. But upon the second and the main point of inquiry—namely, the policy of making further grants of public money, and the mode in which these harbours, if made, should be paid for, they came to the conclusion that harbours should be made by advances of public money, the interest of which was to be paid in a considerable proportion by a charge upon the shipping interest. That recommendation was important, because it had a material bearing upon subsequent proceedings. It was because that part of the recommendations of the Committee had been lost sight of that they were now left in exactly the same position, with regard to these questions, as they were in the days of the late Mr. Wilson, before the appointment of the Committee. Upon that point he would read to the House the 18th paragraph of the Committee's Report—

"The conclusion at which your Committee has arrived, therefore, is that a charge not exceeding in any case 1*d*. per ton may fairly be made upon all ships entering into or clearing from ports in the United Kingdom, which ships in the ordinary course of their voyages would pass the harbours to be constructed; and that, whatever rate is fixed upon at first, it shall be reduced from time to time, so as not to exceed a total sum which shall be equivalent to three-fourths of the interest, which should be computed at the rate of 3 per cent, and of the cost of maintenance. Your Committee feels more confidence in recommending this principle for adoption, because it is one so manifestly fair to the rest of the community, that no such objection can be taken to it as would be likely to interfere with the speedy construction of these important works; whereas, it would have much less confidence in that object being attained if the charge were proposed to be defrayed from the Consolidated Fund; against which objections might, with every appearance of justice, be raised by those not interested in shipping or seaport communities. Your Committee is aware that it would require great care to carry out the principle in all its details, but it is of opinion that this duty may fairly be left to Her Majesty's Government."

The House would observe that the Committee distinctly left it to Her Majesty's Government to adjust the mode of repayment. Mr. Wilson, in his draft Report, had proposed that the question should be left to the Royal Commission, whose appointment the Committee had recommended; but the Committee, by a majority of two, decided that it should be left to the Government. He wished to call the attention of the House to the constitutional question involved in this matter. If they wished to exercise economy and a control over the expenditure of the country, they must adhere to the principle of throwing upon the Government the responsibility of originating expenditure, while they retained to themselves the duty and the power of controlling and checking the proposals of the Government. They ought also to look with jealousy upon proposals for expenditure issuing from the representatives of particular interests, or even from what were called the representatives of humanity, because such proposals were not made under the pressure of responsibility as the propositions of the Government were made. He was bound to say, with all respect for the late Mr. Wilson, that the appointment in the first instance of the Select Committee was an imprudent step, which the House should be careful to avoid repeating. But let the House consider how the matter stood after the Committee had reported. They re-

Sir Stafford Northcote

ported, first, that harbours of refuge would be of use for the saving of life and property, and next, that estimating the cost at £2,000,000, three-fourths of the cost should be refunded by a charge on the shipping interest, and that the remainder should be defrayed from the Consolidated Fund, in consideration of the saving of life and of the services which might be rendered to the naval forces of the country. They also recommended that a Royal Commission should be appointed to complete the work of selecting the sites for the harbours, and, in compliance with an address from the House in accordance with that recommendation, his right hon. Friend near him (Sir John Pakington), who was then First Lord of the Admiralty, advised Her Majesty to appoint a Royal Commission. Upon the proceedings of that Commission he had nothing to say, except in praise of the spirit in which they performed their labours. He did not dispute their plans nor question their estimates, although it was a difficult thing to place entire reliance upon estimates so framed. But, without challenging the sufficiency of their estimates, he would draw attention to the fact, that the Royal Commissioners threw aside the recommendation of the Committee that a considerable portion of the expense of these harbours should be defrayed in some way by a charge upon shipping, and recommended that it should be borne partly by local contributions, but chiefly by the Consolidated Fund. It was this conflict of principle between the recommendations of the Committee and of the Commission, which he believed to be at the bottom of all the difficulty of the case. He had, therefore, placed upon the paper notice of a Motion to add certain words to the Resolution of the hon. Gentleman, with a view of recalling the attention of the House to the recommendations of their own Committee. It was true that he had proposed his Amendment under circumstances somewhat different from those in which they found themselves placed at present, because there had been a change in the wording of the Motion; but, reading the Motion as it stood now, he found it difficult exactly to understand it. In fact, he thought it might be said in legal phrase, that the Resolution proposed was void for uncertainty. The Resolution proposed—

"That, in the opinion of that House, Her Majesty's Government should now adopt measures for the construction of harbours of refuge on the coasts of Great Britain and Ireland, recommended by a Committee of the House in 1858, by a Royal Commission in 1859, and by a Resolution of the House in 1860."

But was it the recommendations of the Committee or those of the Commission that it was proposed to the House to enforce? The two inquiries differed in their results; but, as the Resolution of the House in 1860 was in favour of the Report of the Commissioners, he presumed the conclusions of the Royal Commission were those intended to be favoured by the present Resolution. As the Motion, if carried in that sense, would tend to throw upon the Consolidated Fund a considerable burden, and as he was anxious, as far as possible, to protect that fund from improper charges, he had given notice of his Amendment; but as to whether he should press it to a division or not he should leave it to the House to decide. But he did hope and trust that the House would not fetter the Government by any Resolution of the kind proposed by the hon. Member, unless they were prepared to indicate some mode by which payment should be made. The hon. Member for Shoreham (Mr. Cave) appeared to cast a doubt upon the propriety of levying a charge upon shipping for the purpose. There could be nothing inappropriate in laying a charge of some kind upon the shipping, because the principle of taxing the interest which would derive the most benefit was a fair one. He could not understand the argument which was occasionally employed, that no special interest should be subjected to taxation for such an object, because the general interest was also benefited. It was perfectly possible, if they traced the matter thoroughly, that the benefit would not ultimately fall upon the interest taxed, although that interest might at first be benefited; but, in the same way, any charge which might be laid on the shipping, though it would at first be borne by the shipping interest, would ultimately be diffused throughout the country. What was true of the benefit must also hold good of the burden. The foreign shipowners, too, ought not to be exempt from the payment of this tax, as they would also derive benefit from the establishment of harbours of refuge; but the plan of the Royal Commissioners would let them off altogether, and would throw the whole burden on the British taxpayers. What he desired to do was, to raise the question of principle and to secure that those who received the greater

part of the benefit should bear the chief burden of the charge.

Amendment proposed,

At the end of the Question, to add the words "and should make provision for wholly or in part defraying the expense of such Harbours as it may be thought right to construct, by means of tolls upon shipping, as recommended by the Committee of this House."—(*Sir Stafford Northcote.*)

Question proposed, "That those words be there added."

MR. BLAKE felt bound to say something in support of the Motion of the hon. Member for Sunderland, from the circumstance of residing near one of the proposed harbours of refuge, and having personal knowledge of the advantages which would result to the shipping interest from its formation. He had some reluctance, however, in doing so, fearing it might be supposed that he was advocating the matter for the interests of his constituents. He could say, with truth, the advantages they would derive would not be very much, as Waterford harbour was deep enough for their purposes. He quite concurred with his hon. Friend in taking exception to many portions of the document lately issued by the Board of Trade, with a view of showing that the construction of the refuges recommended by the Royal Commission would not be as useful as was supposed. At page 12 the following passage occurred:—

"There is no doubt whatever that the greater portion of the vessels lost are coasters of small value, and comparatively ill found."

Again, at page 15—

"That it is not generally the good and well found ships which are lost for want of harbours of refuge."

Now, to refute that very erroneous statement, he had only to refer to the document itself; and as other hon. Members, he supposed, would call attention to the misstatement as regarded their own part of the coast, he would confine himself altogether to the wrecks along that part of the coast of Ireland, which a refuge at Waterford would have been likely, to a great extent, to have prevented. In the 10 years (between 1850 and 1860) there were 42 vessels wrecked along the coast between Wicklow Head and Waterford, representing 16,628 tons register, and with the vessels perished 673 human beings. Although the Board of Trade Report would lead to the supposition that it was only small coal vessels that were lost, he could only find three colliers amongst them, the greater number being large vessels, well found and manned; seven of them were over 1,000 tons, burden; one, the *Columbus*, 1,849 tons; the *Racer*, 1,669; the *Pomona*, 1,500; the *Adriatic*, 1,327; and numerous others from 300 to 800 tons. Since that list has been made out other magnificent ships had been lost close to Waterford, two of which only he would mention— the *Tiger*, worth £13,000, and her cargo £11,000; and the *Angelina*, ship and cargo worth £8,000. No doubt, some of the 42 vessels wrecked between 1850 and 1860 could not have been saved, even if there had been a refuge at Waterford; but it was not going too far to assume that many of them would have been preserved, and several lives as well, if they could have taken shelter within the harbour. None of the wrecked vessels were bound to Waterford. There was a curious table in the Report, intended to prove that the greater number of vessels wrecked near the sites of the proposed refuges could not have been saved even if they existed. How they were able to prove that he was utterly at a loss to understand, as it did not follow that because a vessel went ashore at some distance from the place recommended for a refuge, that she would not have made for it if the captain thought he could have entered with safety. It was really melancholy to think that much of the deplorable casualties he had detailed might have been averted for such a paltry outlay as £50,000. No doubt, more could be accomplished for the requisite amount in Waterford than in any other part of the kingdom; but if all that the hon. Mover of the Resolution had stated could be accomplished for £2,000,000, it was a great reproach to the House of Commons if they hesitated a moment about it. Probably it would be said that night, as it had been on a former occasion, that owners of vessels could protect themselves by insurance; but, knowing something of commercial matters, he could assure the House that the profits on freights were, and had been for a long time, so low, that few owners could afford fully to insure themselves; and even supposing they did so, and underwriters had to bear the loss, still would not so much of the capital of the country be lost? Besides getting the mere value, or even the margin of profit over, allowed on ships and cargo insured would not always compensate the

Mr. Blake

owners for the inconvenience they might suffer in their business. A ship might take a long time to replace; and there were certain descriptions of goods not always easy to be had, and for the want of which, at particular times, the community might suffer, as in the instance of cotton or corn. A great saving would also be probably effected by merchants if the harbours of refuge were made, by the diminution of risk, and consequently reductions in the rates of marine insurance. There was, however, one species of loss which, as the noble Lord at the head of the Government admitted on the last occasion that this subject was brought forward, that no insurance could guard against or compensate for—that of the gallant fellows who perished with the wrecked vessels, and who some years amounted to the fearful number of 1,500, the average loss of human life along the coast on each side of Waterford harbour for the last ten years being nearly seventy per annum. Now, if there was no other motive than the preservation of these poor men for their country and families, the entire of the outlay, even if it amounted to £4,000,000, would be well expended. There was another point he wished to touch on, which certainly ought to influence the Government and House considerably in the vote they would give that night. Iron-clad vessels were now superseding the old timber men-of-war, and whatever superiority the former might have in resisting shot and shell better, they certainly were inferior to the latter in sea-going qualities, and in a storm were infinitely more helpless and likely to be driven on shore. Now, let them suppose the *Warrior* or *Prince Consort* caught in a storm, with the wind in shore, somewhere along the coast he had been describing, between Kingstown and Cork, the chances were that vessels and crew would go to the bottom, or be dashed on the rocks. Each of these vessels, besides their equipment, cost the country fully £500,000, and took a long time to build, and at a particular time might place the country in a very serious difficulty to replace. How deep, but how unavailing then would be the regret that a miserable short-sighted economy to save the comparatively trifling sum of £50,000, had led to such a disaster. He had no hesitation in saying that there never was an occasion when a due regard for the protection of the most valuable part of the Royal Navy, the requirements of commerce, and the interests of humanity more strongly claimed the vote of the House than the present one; and he trusted if, as on a former occasion, that his hon. Friend obtained a majority, the Government would not again venture to treat with indifference the wishes of the people, expressed through their representatives.

MR. PEASE said, it would be out of place in him to follow the hon. Member for Stamford (Sir Stafford Northcote) into the various questions he had raised. He had understood the hon. Baronet however to say, that the measure had originated with the Government. There was no doubt that it ought to have so originated; but, unfortunately, it had not done so, nor had it even received their approbation. It was stated that harbours of refuge were essentially necessary in the case of any war in which we might be engaged. Why, then, were they not put upon the same footing as the fortifications, and why was not the money provided in the same way? But the House ought not to consider that as purely a money question. Where the incidence of taxation fell was immaterial. The nation would get a valuable return for its expenditure. Every year our able-bodied seamen were being lost by the score. We were losing in money value at the rate of more than a million per annum. And the President of the Board of Trade, before he frittered away these facts, ought to remember the duty which we owed to the poor fellows who manned our ships, and the great loss both of life and money which now took place for the want of these harbours.

MR. RICHARD HODGSON said, he rose to ask the hon. Baronet (Sir S. Northcote) not to press his Motion to a division. It was desirable that the House should vote upon the main Question, whether or not the Government should carry out, by such measures as they thought fit to adopt, the recommendations of the Committee or the Commission. He regretted to find the principle of passing tolls supported by the hon. Baronet, for that system had been discarded by the Government and the Legislature, and would, he hoped, never be renewed. The taxpayers at large were not asked solely to provide these harbours, for a large proportion of the cost was to come out of the pockets of the shipowners and merchants at the ports at which the expenditure was to take place. The Chancellor of the Exchequer had himself been a witness to the improvements car-

ried out in the Tyne by means of dues paid by the shipowners there, and the proposed grant of £250,000 was well earned by the expenditure which had taken place in the Tyne, for the benefit of the whole country as well as for that of the district.

MR. BAXTER said, that seeing the pressure brought to bear upon the Government, he felt it his duty, on behalf of the taxpayers of the country, to state his views upon this question. He was surprised to find that his hon. Friend asked the House to commit themselves to the recommendations both of the Committee and of the Commission, for, as the hon. Baronet had pointed out, these recommendations were not consistent with each other. The constitutional question was also one of high importance, for instead of the House of Commons checking the Government they had been initiating expenditure, and forcing it upon the Government against their wishes. As to the cost of the proposed works, he doubted whether it was possible to carry them out at anything like the sums estimated. His hon. Friend said the Commission had examined gentlemen of experience on the point, but in speaking of the Tyne, the Report itself said that the magnitude of the works contemplated there, and their novel character, rendered them to a great extent experimental. So that the Commissioners admitted the uncertainty of the outlay in that instance. In noticing the construction of the Committee, the hon. Baronet had omitted to state that it was composed chiefly of representatives of counties interested in the expenditure of the public money. In the Report of the Committee the expenditure at Carlingford and Waterford was set down at £20,000 each; but the Royal Commission contemplated an expenditure of £75,000 at Carlingford and £50,000 at Waterford, so that the House was preparing to legislate in the dark without knowing what the real cost of these works would be. The experience of Holyhead, where the original estimate had been greatly exceeded, might be a guide to them on the point. The works at Portland were estimated to cost £584,000, but £896,000 had already been expended on them, and the estimate now before the House was £932,000. The truth was that if the House began the proposed expenditure of £4,000,000 or £5,000,000, they might be thankful if they got off for less than £10,000,000. He objected altogether to some of the recommendations of the Commissioners, who took great credit to themselves for not asking the House to vote the whole of the money, but recommending that some part should be raised in the localities. They proposed, for example, that the public should give £125,000 to Wick, provided an equal sum were raised on the spot. Why, the people of Wick might as well be asked to pay off the National Debt. Reference had been made to Dundee, but all the captains trading between that port and the Baltic gave evidence that no harbour of refuge was required on the north-east coast of Scotland. One master trading between Scotland and London stated that more ships were lost in running for harbours of refuge than in remaining out at sea, and in that opinion he concurred. The great cause of the loss of life in the North of England was not the want of harbours of refuge, but the state of the vessels themselves. If the ships were better found, better manned, and better commanded, there would be fewer wrecks on our coasts. If he thought that any considerable amount of life and property would be saved by the proposition before the House, he should gladly vote for it, but it was because he did not believe that the erection of six or seven harbours of refuge would have much effect, that he hoped the Government would not sanction the expenditure.

Sir JOHN PAKINGTON said, he hoped the House would not accept the advice of the hon. Member for Montrose, who, indeed, could hardly expect them to be influenced by the opinion he had expressed in opposition to the weight of evidence in favour of the Motion of the hon. Member for Sunderland. The terms of the Resolution had been criticized rather severely, but whether they were open to criticism or not, he did not believe there was a man in the House who did not perfectly understand what the hon. Member for Sunderland meant. He thought the hon. Member was entitled to great credit for the perseverance with which he had followed up the question from Session to Session. The present state of the question did not reflect honour either upon the Government or upon the House. If the Government agreed with the hon. Member for Montrose—if they rejected all the evidence that had been collected—if they thought harbours of refuge were valueless and not worth the cost, let them frankly say so, and the House would un-

Mr. Baxter

derstand the position which they took; but, on the other hand, if they were not prepared to go so far, they must acknowledge that something should be done in the direction indicated by the hon. Member for Sunderland. There was an overwhelming weight of evidence in favour of harbours of refuge. First of all, there was the Report of a Committee appointed by the Government themselves, and presided over by the late Mr. Wilson; then, there was the Report of a Royal Commission; and lastly, there was the Resolution moved by the hon. Member for Sunderland in 1860 and adopted by the House. Here was a combination of opinion which no Government was at liberty to disregard. What, then, had the Government really done? They had taken the extraordinary course of laying before the House a memorandum from the Board of Trade. The hon. Member for Sunderland had dealt too mildly with that document. As an answer to the two Reports and the Resolution he had mentioned he could hardly treat it with gravity, and he wanted to know who wrote it, for it bore no name. It was written in 1861, but it did not see the light till 1864. The President of the Board of Trade was well acquainted with nautical matters; he had been a good deal at sea, and to that circumstance might be attributed the fact of his having suppressed this peculiar memorandum for three years. Admiral Sullivan, the only man connected with the Board of Trade to whose opinion on the subject he should be inclined to attach much weight, could not be the author of the memorandum, for he was one of the Royal Commissioners and joined with his colleagues in reporting in favour of harbours of refuge. One of the arguments urged by the writer was, that a considerable number of the shipowners were not disposed to submit to a tax upon shipping for the support of harbours of refuge. Now, with all respect to so respectable a body of men as the shipowners, they were not the men to whose opinion he should attach most weight in this matter. The hon. Member for Shoreham (Mr. Cave) had glanced at the reason. The wealthiest and most influential of them insured their ships, which were generally well found, and rather than submit to additional taxation were inclined to run all the chances of the sea. But there was another class whose opinion was entitled to more consideration

—the captains and crews of the ships; and the evidence of all the captains who had been examined was all in favour of harbours of refuge. Another argument used in the document was, that these harbours of refuge would be of value only to the smallest and most worthless of our ships and coasters. He thought that was a very unsound opinion. The Report further stated, that of a total of 1,654 lives lost by shipwreck, in one year 926 were lost in three fine ships. Now, one of those ships was the *Pomona*, and the hon. Member for Waterford had told the House that if there had been a harbour of refuge at that port she would not have been lost. Another was the *Royal Charter*, which he believed had fallen a victim to the fatal ambition of making rapid voyages. She was lost after she had passed Holyhead harbour, on her way to Liverpool, and had she taken advantage of the harbour, he believed she would have been saved. The Report likewise stated, that if from the casualties from stress of weather they deducted those caused by ships foundering at sea, very few of the whole number would have been saved by harbours of refuge. Without meaning any offence to his Irish Friends, he must express his opinion that some Irishman had a hand in drawing up the Report, for it was self-evident that if a ship was in harbour she could not founder at sea. One of the last paragraphs in the Report stated that the existing harbours of refuge were always crowded in gales of wind, and that, if additional harbours of refuge were formed, vessels unable to face a gale would use them, instead of running back to their own port, or seeking a more distant anchorage. He might ask what vessels were able to face some of the gales experienced in our channels at times. But on the fact so stated the comment in the Report was —"This is a very different thing from saving vessels from wreck." He could only account for such a Report on the supposition that it was written by some gentleman who might be very conversant with the details of the Board of Trade, but who knew nothing about shipping or harbours of refuge or gales of wind. It was impossible such a Report could be accepted as against the Report of a Royal Commission and the deliberate Votes of the House. He presumed that the Government looked upon it merely as a money question—as a question how they were to pay the cost of constructing those harbours of refuge; and he thought his hon. Friend the Member for Sunderland had taken a perfectly legitimate course in bringing forward the subject and calling on Her Majesty's Government to state how they intended to deal with it. His hon. Friend near him had thrown out a suggestion in conformity with the spirit of the Report of Mr. Wilson's Committee —that a portion of the expense of those harbours should be borne by the shipping interests. He did not see any objection to that proposition. Whether the Amendment would be added to the Motion he did not know, but he should feel bound to give his vote substantially with the Motion. At all events, he hoped the persevering efforts of the hon. Member for Sunderland would be crowned with success before long, and that the shipping interests of this country might at no distant day have those harbours, of the great advantage of which, in the saving of lives, he had not. the smallest doubt.

MR. MILNER GIBSON said, the right hon. Baronet who had just sat down had informed the House that the Resolution which they were invited to consider was perfectly clear, and that he thought there was no one in the House who did not understand its meaning. [Sir JOHN PAKINGTON: The object of the hon. Member.] He thought the right hon. Baronet had said the "Motion," because he had said distinctly that he understood what the meaning of the Motion was. But the hon. Baronet the Member for Stamford had said he thought the Resolution was vague and uncertain, and that therefore it ought not to be supported, because hon. Gentlemen supporting it would not know for what they were voting. He (Mr. M. Gibson) agreed with the hon. Member for Stamford. And unless they were to be indifferent to the wording of their Resolutions—unless they were to be contented with transacting their business in a slip-slop manner, and to vote for any form of words which it might please any particular Member to submit if they guessed the object — they were called upon to look carefully to the meaning and wording of any Motions that were submitted for their approval. The right hon. Baronet (Sir John Pakington) strongly relied on the fact, that a Resolution was passed by the House in 1860, on the Motion of the hon. Member for Sunderland, calling on the Government to carry into effect the recommendations of the Royal Commission on Harbours of Refuge. A Member, also, who could introduce a proposal to the House with the statement that a similar proposal had already received their approval, came before them under very advantageous circumstances; but it was to be borne in mind that on the 6th of May, 1862, a Resolution on the subject was submitted to the House in these words—

"That in the opinion of this House it is the duty of Her Majesty's Government to adopt measures to carry into effect the Resolution of the House passed on the 19th of June, 1860, in regard to harbours of refuge."

A division was taken; and the Ayes were 77, the Noes 115; so that in May, 1862, the House voted the very reverse of the Resolution which had been voted in June, 1860. He therefore contended that they came to the present discussion practically unrestricted by any Resolution of the House. Setting aside the Resolution of 1860, they were asked to do two things —to give effect to the recommendations of the Select Committee of 1858, and also to those of the Royal Commission of 1859. As had, however, been pointed out by the hon. Member for Stamford, these two recommendations were essentially different from each other. The Committee proposed that harbours of refuge should be made only on condition that three-fourths of the cost of construction and maintenance should be provided by the shipping interest for whose benefit it was contended they were constructed. On the other hand, the Commission were of opinion that passing tolls as charges upon shipping were to be utterly condemned, and they proposed that large votes of public money should be provided and aided by local subsidies from the different towns and places where the harbours were to be constructed. Again, the harbours proposed were different, and varied in number in each case. Therefore, whatever might be the view with respect to harbours of refuge, it was impossible to place the Resolution before them on their minutes. The right hon. Gentleman the Member for Droitwich had stated that Admiral Sullivan, a distinguished officer of great experience and knowledge, connected with the Board of Trade, was a member of the Commission. The right hon. Gentleman the Member for Droitwich had forgotten to tell the House that Admiral Sullivan did not entirely agree to the Report of the Commission, not because he was an enemy to harbours

Mr. Milner Gibson

of refuge, but because he regarded it as a *sine quâ non* that such works should be supported to a great extent by the shipping interest. The right hon. Gentleman had commented severely on the memorandum of the Board of Trade. He held himself responsible for the document as emanating from his Department. There might be errors in it, for they would creep into public papers in spite of all precautions. He could say that if there were any they were not intentional; but he would like to see some of them distinctly pointed out, for that had not yet been done. The table showing the number of vessels that might have been saved by the proposed harbours of refuge had been carefully examined by Admiral Sullivan and Captain Walker, in order that through their professional criticism it might be rendered as accurate as possible. He agreed with the right hon. Member for Droitwich, that the Members of the Commission were most competent to deal with the question referred to them; but they went far beyond the scope of the inquiry which they were asked to undertake. They were commissioned to give a professional opinion as to the best sites for harbours of refuge, on particular parts of the coast; but it was no part of their duty to discuss the mode in which funds should be raised, or to apportion the burdens to be borne respectively by the State and by the local public. His hon. Friend the Member for Montrose (Mr. Baxter), said that the Select Committee was mainly composed of gentlemen interested in particular ports, and favourable to public grants for the benefit of these localities. Upon that point he was not informed, but he had no doubt that they did not call witnesses unfavourable to their views. They could not, however, induce a single shipowner to express an opinion on behalf of harbours of refuge if their construction would cost him a penny; but they got mariners to come forward and say that under certain circumstances harbours of refuge would be a benefit — only they could not agree as to the sites. The Commission consisted of Admiral Hope, Sir Frederic Smith, Admiral Sullivan, Admiral Washington, Captain Veitch, Mr. Coode, and Mr. W. S. Lindsay; but of that number only Admiral Hope and Mr. Lindsay were unconnected with the Select Committee, all the rest having been either members of it or having given evidence before it. His confidence in the

Commissioners had been in some degree shaken, because they had recommended an impracticable plan. They recommended a total expenditure of £4,015,000. Of that, £2,390,000 was to come out of the Consolidated Fund without repayment, and the remainder £1,625,000 to be advanced from local sources; but they were not entitled to express an opinion that, of the total amount to be expended on harbours of refuge, £1,625,000 could be obtained from local sources, because there was no evidence that the money would be forthcoming. The hon. Member for Montrose had remarked that it was quite out of the question to expect Wick to contribute £125,000, nor could Peterhead furnish as much as £200,000. On the Tyne £750,000 was to be supplied locally and £250,000 by the State. He knew well the enterprise and great capital that could be brought to bear in the Tyne, but he could not believe that such a sum as £750,000 would be supplied for this purpose by local contributions. With respect to Hartlepool, the Commissioners proposed that the Government should spend £500,000, and the place £500,000; but the hon. Member for Sheffield, who knew something of the affairs of that place, could tell what chance there was of £500,000 ever being obtained from the locality for the purpose. In 1854 Hartlepool obtained an Act to construct works with £50,000 to be raised on the security of the tolls, but though Mr. Ward Jackson, a most energetic man, had made two attempts, the money had not been raised. It was therefore absurd to expect that £500,000 would be raised in the place. The extraordinary proposals made by the Commissioners were calculated to shake one's confidence in those gentlemen. There was not the least chance of these large sums being provided by the different localities; but he had no doubt that if the Commissioners had kept themselves within the scope of their inquiry, and had only applied their minds to indicate the sites where harbours should be erected, they might have given advice well worthy to be followed by that House. With respect to passing tolls, the shipping interest had insuperable objections to making all shipping pay for harbours from which only inferior vessels would derive a benefit. It would be making good ships pay for bad if the former were obliged to contribute towards harbours for ill-found vessels, and the proposition, therefore, appeared to be wholly wrong in principle.

He did not object to the principle of tolls with the condition that the tolls should only be paid by those who derived benefit from and used the harbours—in the same way as they were paid for a light or buoy by ships which were aided in their navigation thereby; but one of the witnesses before the Commission expressed his opinion, that passing tolls would be universally opposed by all the shipowners in the kingdom; and another witness, Mr. Alcock, from Sunderland, stated that passing tolls would be most strenuously objected to. Therefore he must take it for granted that there was no chance of supporting these harbours of refuge by passing tolls, nor of obtaining money for them by local contributions; and the matter resolved itself into the plain and naked truth that, if the harbours of refuge recommended by the Commissioners were to be constructed, the House must be prepared to vote the cost of them —£4,000,000. The Commissioners suggested that the work should be carried on by an annual expenditure of not less than £250,000. In that respect he conceived the advice of the Commissioners to be wise, for he had heard it stated by most competent authorities that there could be no worse policy than too much delay in carrying to completion works connected with the sea, such as breakwaters and piers, as heavy gales and seas did them great damage when in a half-finished state. It was, therefore, bad economy not to carry on these works in the most vigorous manner; but he doubted whether the large sum of £250,000 a year would be sufficient. They would be shutting their eyes to all experience in regard to works of that description if they were to hope that in that particular case the estimates would not be exceeded. In respect to works executed in deep water, and exposed to the shock of heavy gales and seas, the most experienced engineers could not say what they could be accomplished for, and, therefore, the House must be prepared, if it entered upon the construction of these harbours, to incur a larger expenditure than £4,000,000 The House was asked to tax the people of this country to confer a benefit on shipowners, so that their ships and cargoes might be protected. Now, the shipowners were carriers by water and competed with the railway carriers by land, and the House would be giving the former a peculiar advantage over the latter if it voted money in order to render coast navigation more easy and the necessity of only sending well found ships on coasting voyages less urgent. He had heard of a part of the country where there was a class of vessels called "summer vessels," which never ventured out in the fall of the year or winter months, because they could not encounter the gales then occurring; but in summer they obtain a trade and a profit, the shipowners, in fact, running the risk of sending ill-found ships to sea during the fine season. It was just the same sort of thing as people going into doubtful speculations for a large interest with a chance of losing their capital. He contended, then, that what was asked for by the present Motion was, that the country should pay to make that operation more easy, and then the particular class of ships for which these harbours were intended were likely to be even less seaworthy than at present. He was not now speaking of the long sea-voyage ships, but of the small coasters. The Returns presented by the Board of Trade had been criticized and complained of, but he was surprised to hear it stated that that Board was wrong in excluding from the Returns casualties arising from collisions. Why, the fact was that those collisions arose from some misunderstanding or neglect of the rule of the road when vessels met each other, and the question of harbours of refuge had nothing to do with such cases. He undertook to say that the Returns would have been most fallacious unless the cases of collision had been eliminated from them; and the elimination had been performed under the careful scrutiny of Admiral Sullivan and Captain Walker. With respect to the number of ships likely to be saved by these harbours of refuge, he disagreed with the right hon. Member for Droitwich, who instanced the case of the *Royal Charter*, which had passed Holyhead, so that it appeared that the contiguity of a harbour of refuge did not prevent the loss of the ship and the loss of life. Then with respect to the case of vessels foundering at sea. Colliers sometimes sprung a leak suddenly and foundered, and could not be saved even if a harbour of refuge were near them. He would with permission refer to the Board of Trade Returns, from which it appeared that on the east coast some of the ships lost were 30, 50, and even 90 years old, which foundered at a considerable distance from the coast. Thus, in 1862,

Mr. Milner Gibson

the *Sarah*, 50 years old, was lost off Whitby; the *Saratoga*, 30 years old, was lost 25 miles east of Sunderland; the *Duke of Buccleugh*, 33 years old, was lost in Robin Hood's Bay; the *Robert and Margaret*, 99 years old, foundered 35 miles E. by S.E. of the new Sand Light Ship; the *Fidelity*, 68 years old, foundered with all hands, somewhere between Shields and London. Many of this class of vessels were lost, and if there had been a harbour of refuge every five miles they could not have been saved. The number of lives lost during 1863 was 608. Of that number one half were lost during the gales of December, which were from the westward. Of the lives lost in the gales of December, nearly 200 were lost on the East coast; and it was a remarkable fact that, during these gales, harbours of refuge on that coast, would have been of no advantage, for all the vessels were blown off the coast, and the lives were lost in the North Sea or on the Dutch coast. The number lost during the gales in January 1864 was 148, and it was a curious fact that they were lost during gales from the westward. He could give a number of cases of ships being lost with every soul on board, but going through the cases with the most critical examination, it was impossible to say that the harbours of refuge which had been projected would have been of any use. The test applied by the Commission for the expediency of a harbour of refuge was the number of lives lost upon a line of coast, but they did not appear in their recommendations to have acted entirely on that test. The Returns for the last thirteen years showed an annual average loss of fifty-two lives between the Fern Islands and Flamborough Head, and in the same time eighty-seven lives between Flamborough Head and the North Foreland, and yet the Commission did not propose a single harbour of refuge from Flamborough Head to the North Foreland. The greatest loss of life on the whole coast of the United Kingdom was in the Quadrilateral, if he might so call it, which would be formed by drawing a line from the Skerries to Lambay Island, and from Fair Head to the Mull of Cantire, and yet some of the finest natural harbours—Lamlash Bay and others —were situated within these limits. Certainly his hon. Friend the Member for Sunderland had not been very liberal in his proposal for the expenditure of public money in Ireland. All he had proposed was some thousands for dredging the entrance to the harbours of Carlingford and Waterford. His chief anxiety seemed to be the coast from Fern Islands to Flamborough Head, which was by no means the most dangerous part of the coast. There was an open sea there, but between Flamborough Head and the North Foreland vessels had to contend with outlying sands, which made it always more difficult for them to lie to. Why then was it that all the money was to be expended between Flamborough Head and the Fern Islands, when the loss of life was not so great as in other parts of England? From Start Point to the Land's End there had been thirty-six lives lost in one year—and the annual average loss is 38 a year; but within those limits there were the fine harbours of Falmouth and Plymouth, proving that the loss of life had to do with something else than the non-existence of harbours of refuge. It was a consideration of some weight when they found this annual loss of ships and life along a coast provided with fine natural harbours. He begged now to call the attention of hon. Members to the point upon which they would actually vote. It was not as to the selection of a few particular places upon which £4,000,000 was to be spent, but it was as to the commencement of what the Commissioners called "the carrying out of a national policy." The Commissioners reported that what they recommended was a "basis" upon which was to be erected some superstructure to be called a "national policy," the steady prosecution of which could not fail ultimately to produce beneficial results. And they went on to say that every harbour was useful for life and refuge purposes to the extent in which it possessed freedom of access and good shelter, and so far had claims upon the public money. But why was the House of Commons to raise up ports at the public expense in opposition to ports maintained by private enterprise? If once hon. Members were to come, at the instance of their constituents, and ask the Chancellor of the Exchequer to give money from the Consolidated Fund in that reckless way, it would be a proceeding dangerous to the finances of the country and to the independence of that House. If public money was to be granted to particular places, the support hon. Members would receive would depend upon the amount of public money they could obtain. Nothing excited greater jealousy than to find that one port was getting large sums of public money, when perhaps a neighbouring one was struggling with great difficulties to maintain its own prosperity unaided. He had gone through the evidence given before the Commission with respect to the ports in the east of Scotland and the north-east of England, and the result was this, that the several witnesses advocated their own ports in preference to all others, and if their own ports were not suitable they doubted the necessity for any harbours of refuge at all. The people of Wick were of opinion that Wick was the best place that could be selected, and that natural harbours of refuge were of no use at all. The people of Peterhead thought that Peterhead was better than Wick; and the people of Fraserburgh, that Fraserburgh was better than either Wick or Peterhead. At Aberdeen a harbour was not wanted, but the witnesses from that city thought that if money was to be spent at all then Aberdeen was the best place. At Dundee a harbour of refuge was not needed, and the witnesses from that place were of opinion that one was not needed either at Wick, Peterhead, Fraserburgh, or Aberdeen. And so on the north-east coast of England, at Filey, Hartlepool was considered the wrong place; and Hartlepool at Filey. At Redcar people considered their place preferable to Hartlepool and better than Filey; and at Whitby, that Whitby was better than Filey, Hartlepool, or Redcar. Then, at Scarborough, that place was considered the best of all. He quoted these things to show how difficult it was to get rid of local jealousies when it came to be a question of expenditure of public money. There was one recommendation which both the Commission and the Committee emphatically made, and that was as to the policy of assisting harbours to improve themselves by loans of public money at a moderate rate of interest, thus enabling the Government to co-operate with private enterprise. The Commission reported that there were many tidal and other harbours on various parts of the coast which were susceptible of great improvements, exclusive of those to which grants should be made; and that the improvement of existing harbours would in many instances do more for the preservation of life and property than the expenditure of an equal sum applied to only one harbour. Great loss of life and a very great proportion of wrecks occurred from the collection of ships around tidal estuaries which they could not enter, and where they were obliged to remain during long winter nights. It was obvious, therefore, that to render tidal harbours accessible at all times, and, under all circumstances, would be much more effectual for the preservation of life and property than to place one or two life harbours on parts of the coast, at a distance from ports or tidal harbours; because if the ship did not happen to be exactly in the right position when the gale took her, the life harbour was of no use. He thought it, therefore, a wise recommendation that they should co-operate in the improvement of existing harbours. Well, the Government did co-operate. They brought in a Bill nearly in conformity with the advice of the Commission and the Committee, to enable Harbour Commissioners to raise loans at 3¼ interest, to be repaid in fifty years. Although that Bill passed only two years ago, it had been very extensively used, for they had already granted no less a sum than £863,500, either promised or actually paid, and they had under consideration further applications for sums amounting to something like £250,000. The policy, then, of assisting harbour authorities to improve their own harbours and of co-operating with private enterprise, had been successful; and he thought it a far wiser policy and more consonant with the genius of the people than to make presents of money pell-mell for the construction of life harbours on particular parts of the coast. There had been advanced to the Tyne £100,000, and to the Wear £150,000; to Wick £60,000, and £20,000 more was under consideration. The people of Wick instead of waiting from year to year for the success of the Motion of the hon. Member for Sunderland had put their shoulders to the wheel and had provided works which he believed would be very valuable to the fisheries of that town. The Tees had obtained £30,000; Carrickfergus, £5,000; the Isle of Man, £45,000; Belfast, £100,000, and so on. It was a mistake, therefore, to say that nothing had been done. The Government were not insensible to the public feeling on this matter, and it was their desire to do all that was right in policy and just to the taxpayer in the attempt to save life and property. In other directions a great deal had been done. A Select Committee on Shipwrecks sat in 1836, and another in 1843. Another Committee, known as the Harbour of Refuge Committee, sat in 1858.

Many of the recommendations of these Committees had been carried into effect. The Committees of 1836 and 1843 attributed the occurrence of many wrecks to the incompetence of masters, mates, and engineers, and Parliament had provided for their examination, and required from them certificates of competency or service. Courts of inquiry had been instituted for the express purpose of inquiring into the causes of wrecks. Some inquiry took place in the case of every wreck, although no formal court was held, except in the case of the more important wrecks. Parliament had taken measures for improving the discipline of the merchant service, and for the survey of passenger ships, which were obliged to carry one lifeboat at least. The number of lifeboats stationed on the coasts of the United Kingdom had largely increased, and they had been subsidized and improved. In 1856 there were 124 inefficient lifeboats; in 1864, 180 efficient lifeboats, 150 of which were subsidized out of the Mercantile Marine Fund. In 1856 there were 198 inefficient sets of mortar and rocket apparatus; in 1863 there were 240 efficient sets on the coasts, entirely supported by the Government. There were 164 lifebelt stations on the coasts, at which were placed 663 lifebelts. Regulations had been agreed to for making the rule of the road at sea uniform among ships of all nations, with the view of preventing collisions. The Government had during the last eight years given not less than £40,000 out of the Mercantile Marine Fund towards defraying the expenses of lifeboats and mortar and rocket establishments, &c., and in the shape of rewards and encouragements for the saving of life. All this proved that the State had not been unmindful of the importance of saving life, and he trusted, with all respect for the House, that it would not urge the Government to go too far in this direction. He should very much dislike to see Englishmen submitting to a number of petty regulations even in regard to the saving of life and property. The principle on which much of the greatness of this country was based was that of self-reliance: and the more regulations that were made, and the more interference that took place with seamen and shipowners, the greater the tendency to lessen the principle of self-reliance. He would not go into the opposite extreme, and say that there should be no regulations; but, seeing the tendency of

Mr. Milner Gibson

legislation of late years, he should be sorry to see Parliament going too far in relieving Englishmen from the necessity of exercising that vigilance which was, after all, the best protection for life and property. It had been stated that there had been a gradual increase in the loss of life from ships of the United Kingdom; but if they were to eliminate carefully from the Returns all the cases in which harbours of refuge would have been of no service, he believed it would be found that the numbers had not increased, but that there had been a gradual decrease. In 1853 the number of our vessels was 35,310; the whole number of sailors was 253,896, and the number of lives lost was 689. In 1862 the vessels had increased to 39,427, the sailors to 304,171; while the lives lost were 690. So that the number of sailors having increased very largely, it might have been supposed there would have been a proportionate increase in the number lost, but that was not the case. He believed that the House would mislead itself, as well as others, if it agreed to the Resolution of the hon. Member for Sunderland.

MR. HENLEY said, that the right hon. Gentleman had made a very curious statement, the last portion of which did not appear to bear on the subject. He had urged on the shipping interest the necessity of being self-reliant, and yet he had given the House a long list of enactments passed for the regulation of the shipping interest. He should like to know whether the right hon. Gentleman's statement as to the loss of life referred to the losses all over the world, or on the coasts of England only. The right hon. Gentleman gave the House the number of British ships all over the world, but the wreck Return was, he feared, the list of the vessels lost on the coast of the United Kingdom. The effect of that legislation had been, he said, very beneficial, yet the right hon. Gentleman hoped it would not be carried too far, and that the shipping interest would not cease to be self-reliant. The Legislature had been particularly kind to the shipping interest during the last thirty years, and that interest was getting every day more and more into leading-strings. They had got a Return, extending over thirteen years, of the success of this "meddling and muddling"—to use a favourite phrase. The recent wreck Return stated that in 1852 of the whole number of British vessels one vessel came to grief in every 209 voyages, by collision or other accident. In 1862 the number increased to one in 138. That was a very ugly increase. Whether the legislation which the right hon. Gentleman had magnified as so beneficial had anything to do with it he did not know, but that was the fact, and it was a very awkward one. The right hon. Gentleman rather led the House to believe that the majority of the vessels wrecked were old and worn-out coasting vessels. There could not be many of these which were 100 years old, and if there were they must be the very last of their race. But, according to the wreck Returns, it appeared that of sailing vessels engaged upon coasting voyages one in every 130 came to grief, while the proportion of oversea vessels was one in 137. It must be remembered that the wreck Returns only dealt with wrecks upon or close to the coast of England, and that oversea vessels only entered within these limits at the close of their voyage. The difference, therefore, was not as great as might be expected. They were, however, disagreeable figures, and showed that with all our legislation, and our teaching the people to be self-reliant, in thirteen years the wrecks had increased from one in 209 to one in 138. And if they followed it still further down they would find that from 1857 (and he was speaking from recollection) to the present time the increase in wrecks was no less than 30 per cent. That was a disagreeable state of things to meet. These remarks diverged somewhat from the subject before the House, but he was induced to make them, because the right hon. Gentleman had laid so much stress on these matters. Upon the general question he agreed with what had fallen from the hon. Baronet the Member for Stamford. As far as evidence went, there was a great weight of authority in favour of harbours of refuge, but his own expectations were not too sanguine. He did not, however, propose to set his opinion against the professional men who had given evidence upon the subject; but he did not believe the success would be so great as was anticipated. There was also a great difference of opinion where these harbours of refuge should be put, and it was upon that ground also that he supported the hon. Baronet. Of this they might be certain, that persons who were called upon to spend so much money locally, in order to obtain the assistance of Government, would ventilate the matter thoroughly, and take means to have the expenditure made, if it was made, at the right time and in the right way. Another reason for voting in favour of the proposition of the hon. Member for Stamford was, that no one could make out from the Resolution of the hon. Member for Sunderland whether he intended the whole of the money to come from the Consolidated Fund, or partly from that source and partly from others, for on that point the Report of the Royal Commission and the Report of the Committee were absolutely at variance. The Resolution took them both in, and, therefore, so far as he saw, it was not clear from whence the money was to come. He should oppose the Motion.

Sir FREDERIC SMITH said, that as a member, both of the Committee and Commission, he stood forward to defend the Estimate which had been attacked by the right hon. Gentleman the President of the Board of Trade. The details had been repeatedly gone into, and after the sittings of the Committee had closed, the professional members remained for several weeks going over the Estimates in the most minute and cautious manner. There was not one of those gentlemen who would not pledge his reputation for the sufficiency of the amount, and a strong argument in confirmation of the Estimate was afforded by the fact that one of the most extensive contractors, a gentleman who had been engaged by the Government upon works at Portland, at Holyhead, and at Anglesea, had expressed in writing his willingness to carry out the works proposed, in accordance with the plans, and at the rate of remuneration specified in the Report. The right hon. Gentleman attacked the Committee for having exceeded their duty in stating how the funds were to be raised, but having ascertained that there existed on the part of the shipowners an insurmountable aversion to the method previously contemplated, it was only their duty to acquaint the House and the Government frankly with the fact. The harbours had been divided into two classes—those for the preservation of life and those for commercial purposes. The former they proposed to construct at the public expense; in the formation of the latter to assist in a stipulated proportion. Was not that plan a fair and just one? If the local contributions were withheld, the country would only have to pay £1,500,000 instead of £4,000,000; if, on the contrary, local contributions were given, the country would reap the advantage in vastly im-

Mr. Henley

proved harbour accommodation. Was it politic, was it wise, to continue year after year throwing away the national capital, refusing to make any effort to diminish these losses? The Government, he maintained, would be culpable if, having thrown over the Motion by a majority, they did not come forward themselves with a proposition. The opinions of Admiral Sullivan and Captain Walker had been referred to; but why had not the right hon. Gentleman brought forward Returns properly signed by them? These Returns were disavowed by the Department that made them. Although the witnesses differed, the Commissioners did what they went down for, with the view of avoiding being led away by local jealousies; they set the evidence of one witness against another, and then formed an opinion. If there was any place at which a harbour of refuge was wanted, it was on the East coast. It was said that the vessels were badly found and insufficiently manned; but was the poverty of the trade any reason why the sailor, who was compelled to go into it in order that he might earn his bread, should not be protected? The right hon. Gentleman said that the Commissioners exceeded their duty when they gave an opinion upon commercial questions; but the hon. Member for Sunderland was placed upon the Commission to represent commercial interests; and no man could have taken more pains than he did to investigate every portion of this question. He deserved well of his country, and of the profession of which he was an honour, for the part which he had taken with regard to it.

Sir JAMES ELPHINSTONE said, the blue-book from which the right hon. Gentleman had quoted was not circulated amongst Members of the House; it was a paper prepared in the office of the right hon. Gentleman. He had quoted from it partially. He found on reference to it that, out of twenty-nine shipwrecks, twenty-two would have been saved by harbours of refuge. In the next page he found that, out of twenty-six cases of shipwreck, nineteen might have been saved by harbours of refuge. With reference to that point, from his knowledge of groping in the Channel, there was no place where a harbour of refuge was so much required as at Start Point.

Mr. MAGUIRE said, that he had never heard anyone deal more lightly and pleasantly with tales of disaster and distress than had the President of the Board of Trade, but the right hon. Gentleman had not destroyed the effect which was produced by the touching and affecting speech of the hon. Member for Sunderland. However much Englishmen or Scotchmen might differ as to the proper sites for harbours of refuge on the coasts of their respective countries, no representative of Ireland would dispute the claims of Carlingford. The present condition of that harbour was a cause of disaster, not only to local but to national shipping, and so small were the resources of the people that they could neither advance money nor pay the interest of an advance from the Government for its improvement. When the House was so extravagant as it was with respect to forts and ships, when it squandered so much money upon art, and was so reckless in regard to other expenditure, it ought to think of the poor sailors in the midnight storm, and carry out a policy at once of generosity and humanity.

MR. SOMES was understood to mention the case of a wrecked vessel, which would have been saved had one of the harbours of refuge recommended by the Committees been constructed. He had a suspicion that the Return of wrecks and casualties for 1862 had undergone some manipulation.

MR. LINDSAY, in reply, said, he had to complain of some of the statements which had been made by the representative of the Board of Trade. The sum and substance of the right hon. Member's speech was, that harbours of refuge were neither necessary nor desirable. Against this, there were the Report of two Committees, the Report of the Royal Commission, the Resolution of the House, the speech on a former occasion of the right hon. Gentleman himself, and the speech of the noble Viscount at the head of the Government. What he (Mr. Lindsay) asked the House to say was, that the harbours of refuge should be constructed; and he asked the Government to carry out the recommendations, leaving it to them to provide the necessary funds in their own way.

THE CHANCELLOR OF THE EXCHEQUER said, that as the Amendment of his hon. Friend the Member for Stamford was about to be put, he wished to explain the vote which the Government would feel it their duty to give. They concurred very much in what had fallen from his hon. Friend and the right hon. Gentleman the Member for Oxfordshire, to the effect that

of the two alternatives for raising the money—namely, out of the Consolidated Fund, or by means of passing tolls—the latter was the more just. [Sir STAFFORD NORTHCOTE: I did not say passing tolls.] Well, passing tolls or some other method of that description; but while that was the view of the Government, they could not vote for adding the words of his hon. Friend to the Resolution, because if they were to do so they would be pledging themselves to some plan, to the adoption of which they did not see their way.

Question put, the House *divided:*—Ayes 39; Noes 191: Majority 152.

Main Question put, the House *divided:*—Ayes 84; Noes 142: Majority 58.

SEWAGE (METROPOLIS), &c.
SELECT COMMITTEE MOVED FOR.

LORD ROBERT MONTAGU said, he rose to move that a Select Committee be appointed to inquire into any plans for dealing with the Sewage of the Metropolis and other large Towns, with a view to its utilization for agricultural purposes. He did not desire to enter into the commercial value of sewage. All he wished was the Committee should consider the plans which had been laid before the Metropolitan Board of Works for transporting sewage from London and other large towns to the country. It was very desirable to know how the engineering difficulties could be overcome, in order to the utilization of sewage. The Government were favourable to the Committee, the Metropolitan Board were most desirous that it should be appointed, and the ratepayers were also anxious that an inquiry should take place, in order to their relief, if possible, from a portion of the burden of local taxation. The Lord Mayor and Sheriffs had appeared at the Bar of the House, and petitioned in favour of the appointment of the Committee.

SIR FREDERIC SMITH seconded the Motion.

SIR JOSEPH PAXTON said, he did not consider that any good could arise from the Committee. Already a Committee had sat on the subject, and had produced a large blue-book which no one had read. He thought it would be better to leave the matter in the hands of the Metropolitan Board of Works and the authorities of the different towns throughout the country.

MR. T. J. MILLER said, he should

support the appointment of the Committee, on the ground that the Metropolitan Board of Works could not otherwise ascertain which of the many plans that had been submitted to them was the best for dealing with the sewage of the metropolis, which was estimated in value at a million sterling — more than the amount of rates levied by the Board.

Mr. CAIRD said, he thought the Government ought to have dealt with the subject, in pursuance of the Report of the Committee of 1862. But if the noble Lord succeeded in his object he would perform a good work.

Motion *agreed to.*

Select Committee *appointed,*

" To inquire into any plans for dealing with the Sewage of the Metropolis and other large Towns, with a view to its utilisation to agricultural purposes."—(*Lord Robert Montagu.*)

On April 29, Committee *nominated as* follows:—

Mr. COWPER, Mr. WALPOLE, Mr. BRIGHT, Mr. ADDERLEY, Sir WILLIAM RUSSELL, Sir Frederic SMITH, Lord FERMOY, Sir JOSEPH PAXTON, Mr. CAIRD, Mr. TITE, Mr. LEADER, Mr. HIBBERT, Mr. SCLATER-BOOTH, Dr. BRADY, and Lord ROBERT MONTAGU:—Power to send for persons, papers, and records : five to be the quorum.

And, on May 11, Mr. NORTH and Mr. FERRAND *added.*

GARIBALDI MEETING AT PRIMROSE HILL.—PAPERS MOVED FOR.

Mr. TAYLOR said, that in consequence of discrepancies between the statement made by the right hon. Gentleman the Home Secretary as to what occurred last Saturday at the meeting on Primrose Hill, and what had been represented to him by persons who were present at that meeting, he thought it would be for the benefit of the public that the real facts should be known, and therefore he would move for an Address for a Copy of the Report of the Superintendent or Inspector in command of the Police employed at Primrose Hill on Saturday last, together with any Instructions that were issued to the Police upon that occasion.

Motion *agreed to.*—Address for

" Copy of the Reports of the Superintendent and Inspector in command of the Police employed at Primrose Hill on Saturday, the 23rd day of April, 1864 ; and of the Instructions to the Police ordered to be on duty on the occasion of the Meeting held there on that day."—(*Mr. Taylor.*)

House adjourned at half after One o'clock.

Mr. T. J. Miller.

HOUSE OF COMMONS,

Wednesday, April 27, 1864.

MINUTES.]— NEW MEMBER SWORN — Right Hon. Henry Austin Bruce *for* Merthyr Tydvil.
Resolution—Standing Orders [April 26] *reported.*
PUBLIC BILLS — *First Reading* — Valuation of Lands and Heritages (Scotland) Act Amendment * [Bill 81].
Third Reading—Fish Teinds (Scotland) * [Bill 45], and *passed.*
Report—Seat of Under Secretary of State * [Second Report].

CHURCH RATES COMMUTATION BILL.

[BILL 8.]   SECOND READING.

Order of the Day for the Second Reading read.

Mr. HADFIELD begged to call the attention of the House to a violation of its Standing Orders by the manner in which this Bill had been introduced and was now proceeded with. By those Orders no Bill imposing any charge upon the people could be introduced until the House, in a Committee of the Whole House, had passed a Resolution, on which the Bill imposing the tax was founded. That was a very salutary regulation and was designed for the protection of Her Majesty's subjects : but in the case of this Bill it had not been observed. The Bill was introduced on the 9th of February—or rather at one o'clock on the morning of the 10th—without the preliminary formality of a Committee of the Whole House : and from the Reports of the proceedings in the ordinary channels, there did not appear to have been any observations made, and, therefore, it came upon the House by surprise. The clauses of the Bill were remarkably extensive. They affected all owners of real property in England, and he was not sure whether they would not extend to Ireland. These clauses provided that church rates in respect of occupation should cease, and that all real property should be subject to an annual charge of 2*d.* in the pound. The income arising from the change would, he understood, amount to £934,022 per annum, which at thirty years purchase would represent a capital sum, which the hon. Member for Warwickshire had sought to raise, of £28,020,660. The 15th clause of the Bill proposed that the charge, which now fell upon occupiers, should be transferred to the owners of real property, who would thus be subjected to a new impost. It had been ruled in reference to the Irish Church

Temporalities Bill, which affected bene-fices in Ireland, that the Bill should have been founded on a Resolution, and the Bill was ordered to be withdrawn accord-ingly. As the Bill had been introduced without the proper formalities, he sub-mitted that the Order for the Second Reading should be discharged, and that the Bill should be withdrawn.

MR. SPEAKER: The rule of the House is this — that Bills which directly impose a State charge upon the people must origi-nate in a Committee of the Whole House. But the rule has been held not to apply to Bills authorizing the levy of rates or charges for local purposes by local autho-rities. The question is under which head should this Bill for the commutation of church rates be classed. In my opinion it would be most in accordance with the spirit of the general rule of the House, and with the course of precedents, that it should be placed in the second class. The hon. Member urges that by the 15th clause a new tax is imposed on the owners of property to which they have not been hitherto liable. But so in the Tithe Com-mutation Act, the 6 & 7 *Will.* IV. c. 71, the tithe payable by the occupier was made a charge upon the land. The Bill was brought in without having been first considered in a Committee. Then came the Metropolis Police Act, the 10 *Geo.* IV. c. 44, which shows that a Bill enacting that local rates are to be imposed by local authority does not require a preliminary Committee. That Act empowered over-seers in every parish within the metropo-litan district to levy a police rate not to exceed 8*d.* in the pound, and it was brought in without a Committee. In 1839, the Prisons (Scotland) Bill provided for the erection of a general prison, the cost of which was to be defrayed by the several counties according to the number of prisoners, and the amount was to be levied by assessment. That Bill was brought in without a preliminary Com-mittee. In my opinion there has been nothing irregular in the introduction of the present Bill, and I think the House may properly proceed to consider it on its merits.

MR. NEWDEGATE *: Mr. Speaker— Before proceeding to move the second reading of this Bill, perhaps I may be allowed to say a few words with regard to the point of order which has been raised by the hon. Member for Sheffield. I beg to state, that I have acted entirely in de-ference to your authority, Sir, in reference to the mode in which the Bill has been introduced. For two successive Sessions I have sought and obtained the advice which you are ever ready to offer to every Member of the House. For two succes-sive Sessions you informed me, that I ought not to move for a Committee of the whole House, in order to introduce this Bill, because my doing so would give the Bill a character which would be inconsis-tent with its purport, since it does not impose a general charge or tax. The hon. Member for Sheffield will, I trust, allow me to assure him that, so far from having avoided giving due notice of the introduc-tion of this Bill, I last Session gave notice of my intention to re-introduce it this Session; that I repeated that notice in the present Session, and that it was only the accident of my being called on to move the first reading late at night, that I was prevented from stating the objects of the Bill to the House at that time, and was compelled to defer doing so until the second reading. With respect to the amount of property affected and the amount of charge to be created, which has been adverted to by the hon. Member for Shef-field in enforcing his objections on the point of order, I will only say at present, that the amount of the charge actually imposed will not be much more than one-third of the sum which he has stated. Having made these observations, I will now move the second reading of the Bill. I postponed this Motion from the day for which it was first appointed, because I found that on that day His Royal High-ness the Prince of Wales was to hold a Levee for the first time on behalf of Her Majesty. I have given notice of Amend-ments, which propose that the period should be extended for one year; and, if the Bill goes into Committee, I shall pro-pose to amend it in this respect, as also in the amount of purchase-money for com-mutation of the charge to be substituted for church rates, which should be calcu-lated at twenty-seven years instead of thirty years' purchase. I expected to have seen a notice of these Amendments on the paper this morning; but I con-clude that those who have charge of the printing of the House thought that the printing of these Amendments should be postponed until a subsequent stage. I wish now to state the reasons for my having retained this Bill very much in the form in which I introduced it last Session, notwithstanding the decision of the House, that the Bill would not then be proceeded with. My reason is, that for several years I proceeded by Resolution, and I found that throughout the country and in this House the impression widely prevailed, that these Resolutions were merely a form of opposition to the Church Rate Abolition Bill, and that they did not contain the germs of practical legislation ; I was also told that the scheme of commutation which they suggested was totally unworkable. Now I should have been very glad had some hon. Member, like the right hon. Gentleman the Member for Wiltshire, introduced this Bill, for it is consistent with the views which the right hon. Gentleman has expressed ; it is also in accordance with the Bill which was introduced on behalf of the Government of Lord Derby, by the right hon. Gentleman the Member for the University of Cambridge ; but it differs from that Bill in this respect—that Bill contemplated not only the commutation of church rates in the manner which the Bill before the House suggests, but it also contemplated a system of exemptions to be claimed by individuals, which seemed to me inconsistent with the general principle of the measure, and to which the objections are so grave, that they have been held to be fatal by both sides of the House. I hope the House will not think me presumptuous, because I persevere with this measure. I do not think it would have been respectful to the House had I laid upon the table a curt proposal, stating the bare object without proof, that I have sought from others more competent than myself, the means of giving effect to that proposal by law in a manner consistent with the local organization of parishes and of counties, consistent with the practice which prevails in the collection of the poor and county rates, and consistent with the character of the Church of England, but avoiding the interference of the Ecclesiastical authorities in the collection of the charge which I would substitute for church rate — an interference which has been condemned by Dr. Lushington and by all the authorities, whose experience is the most extensive on this subject, and condemned also by the Committee of the House of Lords which sat upon the question of church rates in the year 1861.

Sir, I wish the House to understand that I am not presumptuous enough to hope that it will accept this Bill unaltered at my hands, or without examination. The Bill is not of my framing. It has been

Mr. Newdegate

framed by far abler men than myself ; but my object now is to ask the House to allow the Bill to be read a second time, in order that it may be referred to a Select Committee. Thus far my proposal is in the sense of the hon. Member for Sheffield. My desire is that a Committee should examine the provisions of the Bill, for the purpose of ascertaining how far they are, as they stand, in accordance with the purposes and the wishes of the House, and for deciding which of these provisions should be retained and which of them should be rejected. If the House should be of opinion, as was expressed in the debate of last Session, that the machinery of the Bill is cumbrous and intricate, the measure is so framed as to admit of ready curtailment or alteration ; not that I believe that a Select Committee of this House would have much difficulty in dissecting the most intricate composition that ever assumed the form of a Bill ; but this Bill has been so drawn that, if any of its proposals with reference to the creation of the Depository which the Bill would form in the hands of the Governors of Queen Anne's Bounty, for the safe keeping of the charge or of the surplus arising from the charge which the measure would create, were unnecessary. If the Committee were of opinion that the appeal to the Lords Justices proposed by the Bill would be superfluous, such provisions might be expunged without interfering with the principle of the Bill ; that principle being, that whereas church rate has been for centuries a charge upon the occupiers of land and of real property in respect of their occupancy, a charge which is anterior to rent, which appropriates a portion of the gross proceeds of property, to this the inhabitants of every parish are entitled, as absolutely, if not more absolutely than the owner of the property is entitled to his rent. That the parishioners have been entitled from Saxon times to this portion of the gross value for the purpose of maintaining the fabric and services of their Church, is a fact attested by the highest authority. The Bill proposes, that this fact should be acknowledged, and that the law, so far as the average of the church rate, that is 2*d.* in the pound of the annual value, should declare that amount to be a charge directly binding upon property, and that the occupiers of such property should have the power of deducting this amount from their rent, a power similar to that which they possess, and for twenty years have exercised, under the provisions of the Income and Property Tax Acts. Thus the object of the Bill is to secure the right of the inhabitants to that portion of the gross value of property to which they have ever been entitled for the purposes of church rate: I say " ever," for their right extends beyond legal memory. The object of the Bill is to secure to them this right and this property, and at the same time to relieve the whole community, to relieve all the Nonconformists, to relieve the whole occupying class from that personal liability which has given rise to the objections against church rates, that have created so much division in this country now for more than thirty years. [Mr. HADFIELD : Hear, hear !] Let me appeal to the hon. Member for Sheffield. My object, I repeat, is to meet the conscientious scruples, to meet the legitimate objections, which are raised by the Nonconformist body against their being expected to contribute personally one penny towards the maintenance of the Established Church. Sir, the process which I propose is the same as has been adopted with respect to tithes in England and in Ireland ; the consequence of the change in the case of tithes being that, whereas the collection of tithes used to be the occasion of disgraceful scenes in many parts of either country, of religious feuds and political differences, the provision for the maintenance of the clergy is now collected from the owners of real property without a murmur and with the deepest satisfaction. And I ask the House is it not, after thirty years of strife, an object worthy of their consideration, whether by sending this Bill to a Select Committee provisions may not be framed, which may afford the same elements of peace between fellow Christians and Protestants in the case of this matter of church rates, as in the case of tithes, in the respect of the collection of which a happy peace has been secured that has existed now for more than thirty years ? That, Sir, is the object of this Bill. I know that there are opponents to it. In the first place I am opposed by the ultra advocates of extreme nonconformity. But why ? Because if this Bill were to pass into a law, they would be deprived of all fair excuse for enlisting other Protestant Dissenters in wholesale attacks upon the Church of England ; attacks which, but for this pressure, large bodies of Nonconformists to the discipline of the Church of Eng-

land would never engage in. But I am opposed also in another quarter. I am opposed by the extreme high Churchman, who is unwilling that the Church should relax one tittle of that dominant right, which she possesses as he thinks, of taxing through church rate, personally and individually, every inhabitant of this country for the maintenance of the fabric of the Church. Sir, I am opposed to the extreme spirit of Nonconformity, which, after having troubled Queen Elizabeth during her reign, the period of the accomplishment of the Reformation, was equally unruly under James I., and struggled under Cromwell in the Long Parliament, which it drove into excesses. That spirit of Nonconformity I cannot hope to reconcile. I am opposed also to those who would, as Churchmen, ignore the fact that one-fourth of the population at least no longer accepts the doctrines and the discipline of the Church of England ; who would ignore the fact that in this very diocese, as has been stated by the Bishop of London but the other day, that there are a million of people, certainly more than 900,000, for whom, neither by the Church, nor by Nonconformity, nor by Roman Catholicism, has any spiritual provision whatever been made ; nearly a million of persons for whom there is no pastoral care ; for whom there is no space in any places of worship within reasonable distance from their residences. And I would say to my brother Churchmen, do not hold out or cling to the vain hope that the Church will ever again be able to inflict such an injustice as that of levying church rates upon that million of people so long as her ministrations are inaccessible to them, that is, until spiritual necessities have been supplied ; for to attempt this would be contrary to the very essence and principle of the law of church rate from the beginning ; because church rate ever was a local charge, which entitled the ratepayer to a direct return in the means of divine worship, in spiritual advice, and in church accommodation. As one of the representatives of Birmingham, I am in a position to assure the House, that it was from the total deficiency of church accommodation within that town, that the sense of injustice sprang up in former years which led to those contests against church rates, which have ultimately extended so far as to have exempted the property in many large towns for several years past from all contributions for the purposes of church rate. The intention of the law was that the owners of property should provide church accommodation, and that then the inhabitants should aid them by church rates in maintaining that accommodation; but the fact that large populations are left without church accommodation condemns the application of the law of church rate in localities where such a sad deficiency of church accommodation and of spiritual ministration exists, as is the case in the diocese of which the great metropolis forms a part, according to the showing of the respected bishop of this diocese. Then, if there is this sad deficiency of spiritual provision, if there is this amount of spiritual destitution, if there are nearly a million of people within the diocese for whom no accommodation in church or chapel is provided, for whom no spiritual provision is made either by the National Church or by the Nonconformists; if it is true that the estimate which has been submitted to the Bishop of London is correct, that no less than £6,000,000 would be required to supply the deficiency in this one diocese alone, I do appeal to the representatives of the Nonconformists in this House—I appeal to the hon. Members who are particularly attached to the Church of England in this House, whether the House has not done wisely in refusing to deprive the parishioners of this country generally of the amount of church rates which remain; since it is a known fact that if the cost of the maintenance of the churches throughout England and of their services, hitherto provided by church rates, were to be cast upon voluntary contributions, the sum so required and obtained will be deducted from the fund to which the Bishop of London and other Bishops look, in order to provide a remedy for this enormous amount of spiritual destitution, an evil that I must say has with truth been lately represented at Rome by one who has left the Church of England to become a Roman priest, as a disgrace to this Christian and highly civilised country. Sir, I cannot believe that the House will be induced to withdraw from the parishioners of this country this right to this portion of the real value of its property. I am confident that Parliament would not yield, that the House of Commons would not be induced to do so great an injustice, to be guilty of so gross an act of impolicy—an injustice, remember, not to the clergy, but to the inhabit-

Mr. Newdegate

ants of every parish in England. For church rate is a lay property. It belongs to the laity; it does not belong to the clergy. The whole organization by which it is administered proves that fact; for church rate cannot be collected or expended unless by the direct authority and sanction of the laity, convened in vestry through their representatives the churchwardens. It is a property belonging to the laity of the Church of England, then, that I seek to commute and to establish in a form that shall be inoffensive to the consciences of those who object to contribute personally to the support of any form of religion but their own. I really am unwilling to detain the House, but I have been asked by some hon. Members who are attached to the Church of England, "Why do you persevere? The Church Rate Abolition Bill has ceased to be proposed, and we, the representatives of the Church, are therefore in a better position; why persevere?" Sir, my answer to that is a very simple one, and I think I cannot give it better than in the words of one, whom I believe every Member on this side of the House respects. Just thirty years ago the Government of Lord Grey proposed a measure for the appropriation of a certain amount of direct taxation, some £250,000 from the land tax and certain Church property, in lieu of church rates. A debate ensued, and in the course of that debate, the late Sir Robert Inglis used language something like that of those who say to me, "There is no Church Rate Abolition Bill in the agitation: why do you proceed with this Bill?" What was the answer given by Lord Stanley, then Chief Secretary for Ireland, the organ of the Government, who were attempting to improve the law? Lord Stanley said—

"But his hon. Friend had not stated in how many instances opposition had been put down for a time in order to be renewed at a future opportunity, should no proposition be brought forward by the executive and submitted to Parliament for the relief of Dissenters, and all parties upon whom that burden might unjustly press. His hon. Friend forgot to tell them how many hundred parishes there were waiting to follow the example of those which had successfully resisted, should the decision of the Legislature give them no hope of relief."

I appeal, Sir, to those who have been for a lengthened period Members of this House, whether the expectation thus expressed by Lord Derby has not been amply fulfilled; whether the last thirty years have not been marked by religious agitation, by a slumbering discontent, or by open attacks upon church rates? And I ask those who would have me desist, "Do you desire to see another thirty years of strife among fellow Christians and Protestants upon the subject of church rates, when, as I humbly believe, and as men far better informed than I am—men most fully competent to understand the question, are confident that the means of securing peace are ready to your hand?" Why, Sir, the same statesman who gave the advice which I have quoted thirty years ago, repeated it but three years since. In the Committee of the House of Lords upon Church Rates, which sat in 1861, Lord Derby proposed and carried this Resolution—

"That the principle of assessing the owner instead of the occupier to the church rate, is well deserving the serious consideration of Parliament in any future legislation on this subject."

Sir, it is in accordance with that wise opinion enunciated by Lord Derby that this Bill has been framed; for in that Resolution is embodied the very principle of the Bill, except that the Resolution contemplates continuing the charge in the form of a rate. The example of Scotland has warned me that the personal liability which a rate imposes must be abandoned, if peace is ever to be secured in this matter. For, in Scotland, the charge which provides for the fabrics of the Kirk, and for the support of her Ministers, and I believe for Schools, is almost, without exception, levied through the heritors upon real property. It is not a personal charge: it is a charge upon property. Now, in England, we have no persons in the position of heritors. Had there been such persons, representing property in this country, such as the heritors in Scotland, I should have been willing to leave the assessment to them as the representatives of property. That, however, is not the case in this country. In many parishes there is only one owner; in some there may be two, and in others three. In many cases the owners are not resident; and in others again they are not Members of the Church of England. It would not be wise or safe, therefore, that the House should commit to the hands of these individuals the assessment for maintaining the fabric and the services of the Church. Indeed, it would be unjust to the inhabitants to do so; because by this process you would annul the functions of the vestry; you would annul the voice of the congregation and inhabitants of the parish with regard to the arrangements of their own Church; you would inflict upon the congregations of the Church of England an incapacity to which no other denomination of Christians is willing to submit. It would be unjust to allow the occupiers alone to tax the owners. I therefore wish to substitute a poundage of fixed amount, the collection of which should be made with the poor and county rates; and further, that the sum collected should be transferred through the Clerks of the Peace to a depository, to be drawn thence by the inhabitants in vestry assembled, for the purpose of being applied at their discretion within the limits prescribed by the law for the purposes of church rates. My proposal is, that the collection should be entirely by a civil process. And the Bill will attain this great object, which is recommended by the Committee of the House of Lords; so that whilst the collection and the means of recovery will be by purely civil process, the whole administration of the charge for the purposes of church rate will be Ecclesiastical in the sense of the Church of England, which has ever recognised the ecclesiastical rights and functions of the laity in all matters contemplated or provided for by the law of church rate. Thus, although the Bill proposes a change, it does not propose a novelty. Throughout, the framers of the measure have sought to create no new machinery, but to effect a gradual change through existing agencies, so that within a reasonable period we may hope for that peace upon the question of church rates which has been so effectually achieved in the matter of tithe, both in England and Ireland. We, English Protestants and Members of the Church, desire to have the privileges secured to us similar to those which are secured to the Members and Laity of the Church of Scotland, and which have been so for some hundreds of years. These, Sir, are the objects of the Bill. But let not the House imagine that I have any coxcombical attachment to its provisions. I am not so presumptuous; but I may mention that I have transmitted copies of this Bill, or a statement of its object, to a great number of the clergy of the Church of England, to every Clerk of the Peace in England and Wales, to every Board of Guardians and to all the principal Denominations of Dissenters. The result of this labour, which I thought was due to the House before I presumed to lay upon the table this measure for their consideration, is, that I find a general concurrence of opinion among moderate men in favour of the principle of the Bill; though I admit fully that I have received statements of objections to several parts of its machinery; objections some of them based no doubt upon valid grounds, whilst some were contradictory to each other, and therefore claim a solution at the hands of a Committee of this House. I hope the House will allow me very shortly to refer to some authorities in confirmation of the position that church rate in its average amount is a charge upon property. I will simply cite by name the authorities which I have quoted in former years. These include the names of the late Sir Robert Inglis and Mr. Whittle Harvey, who in the debate of 1834 asserted that church rate is a charge upon property. I have quoted the Poor Law Commissioners in their Report of 1843 in support of this fact; I have quoted the authority of the late Sir Robert Peel; I might have quoted the authority of the late Sir James Graham; I have quoted the authority of Mr. Goulbourne, and that of Earl Russell; and I might refer to the evidence which was given before the Select Committee of the House of Lords in 1861, by Mr. Coode, who of all the public officers now living is perhaps the person best qualified to give information to Parliament upon this subject: nothing can be more conclusive than the proofs which he adduced that church rate in its average amount ever has been and still is a charge upon the real property of each parish. Let me also for one moment advert to that which has fallen from the hon. Member for Sheffield. The hon. Member stated that the amount of this charge levied under this Bill would be not less than £900,000 annually; during the debate of last year another hon. Member stated the amount at £700,000 annually. Well, Sir, I have felt bound to obtain an estimate of the amount, and I find that, instead of £900,000 a year, or even of £700,000 a year, the amount that would be directly levied by this Bill, as far as I was able to calculate two years ago (and I had the kind assistance of Sir George Lewis, when he filled the office of Secretary of State for the Home Department) would amount to £318,000 a year. The fact is that considerable misapprehension prevails upon the subject;

Mr. Newdegate

and let me give this explanation to the hon. Member for Sheffield. In a note appended by the Home Office to a Return for which I moved (No. 7, 1859) he will find this statement—

"Remarks preliminary to the Return of church rates," ordered to be printed February 3, 1859 :— "The question under the head of 'amount rated to the relief of the poor' has in very many cases been incorrectly answered, the amount of the rating or poundage being given instead of the rateable value of property upon which assessment is made. From a Return made to Parliament in 1852 (No. 539) it appears that the total amount rated to the poor rates in England and Wales was £67,700,153 13s. 7d.; but this includes the glebe and tithe land, which, though liable to the poor rate is exempt from church rate, and the difference in amount is considerable, varying from 7 to 27 per cent, and even higher."

As much as 20 per cent of real property is thus exempt either as tithe or glebe land, and this the hon. Member for Sheffield has overlooked. But the exemptions under this Bill are not limited to that extent. The Bill proposes that no property, upon which church rate has not been levied within seven years, shall be affected by the charge created by the Bill; that no property in any parish where a church rate has been rejected on three successive polls, or where no church rate has been levied for seven years, shall be touched by the charge, unless two-thirds of the inhabitants shall sign a Memorial to the Quarter Sessions, reclaiming for themselves their inalienable right to the portion of that real property which has, from time immemorial, by the Common Law as declared by the Judges, been treated as liable to a charge for the maintenance of the fabric and the services of the Church. I hope the House will forgive me for having made this explanation in order to show that the proposal I make is not of the exaggerated character that the hon. Member for Sheffield supposes, for the amount levied in the first instance will not much, if at all, exceed the amount levied up to this day for the purposes of church rate; because, though it appears by the Returns that this amount is £260,000, the Returns of church rate are avowedly imperfect, and the nearest amount at which I have been able to arrive, and I have made careful inquiries on the subject, is, that church rate is worth to the parishioners in the aggregate for England and Wales about £300,000 a year. This Bill, therefore, if the House sanctioned it, would create a charge equivalent to the amount which the parishes now actually receive and possess in the form of church rate. I was unwilling to detain the House, but, as the hon. Member for Sheffield complains that when I introduced this Bill I did not fully explain its provisions, perhaps the House will allow me to lay before them a rapid summary of those provisions; and, in so doing, I beg the House to consider that I ask no hon. Member to pledge himself to the details of the Bill, or to the Bill itself, except as it may be approved by a Select Committee. The objects of the Bill, then, are—

1. To remove all personal liability in respect of church rate.

2. To acknowledge and confirm the right of the parishioners to that portion of the gross value of real property in each parish, which, being beyond the rent paid to the landlords, has always been reserved for church rate.

3. To exempt all parishes in which no church rate has been levied for seven years, or in which a church rate has been rejected on three successive polls, from the charge on real property, reserved by the Bill elsewhere to the use of the parishioners.

4. To give to two-thirds of the ratepayers of parishes, exempt as above, power to claim that the exemption shall cease, and thus to bring their parish within the charge.

5. To provide for the eventual commutation of the charge, thus substituted for church rate, into an endowment for each parish, the proceeds of which shall be applicable to the purposes of church rate.

6. To provide that the charge substituted for church rate shall cease on the creation of such an endowment.

The machinery by which the Bill proposes to attain these objects is—

1. To render the whole process for levying the charge, local and civil, analogous to and combined with that for collecting the poor and county rates.

2. To create a Depository, in which the proceeds of the charge thus levied may be safely kept, and whence it may be easily drawn by the representatives of each parish, as required for annual or occasional purposes.

3. To provide that any surplus of the charge remaining to the account of any parish in the above Depository, shall accumulate to the credit of such parish for the purpose of forming an endowment.

4. To render this Depository ecclesiastical in the sense of the Church of England, which combines the clerical with the lay element, both regulated by legal knowledge.

5. To provide that the money thus rendered available be appropriated by an agency, ecclesiastical in the sense of the Church of England.

6. To revive and strengthen the parochial system of the Church of England by conferring upon the incumbents and churchwardens of each parish corporate powers (analogous to those which they possess in the case of Church of England Schools) for receiving the charge, and for holding benefactions or endowments for the purposes of church rate, subject to the legitimate control of the vestries.

Sir, throughout this Bill it has been the object of its framers to retain to the parishioners, to the inhabitants of the parishes in this country, to retain to the congregations of the Church of England, that liberty to control the mode in which the fabrics of their churches shall be maintained, and the mode in which services therein shall be conducted within the limits of the law, which is incident as a first element of freedom to every other denomination of Christians in this country. During the last Session of Parliament, I am aware that one of the leading organs of public opinion appeared to have had a dream that I desire to confer some arbitrary power upon the Church. Sir, I am one of those who would secure freedom by law. I am ready by law to resist intolerance and tyranny of every kind. I am attached to the law because I believe the law, when rightly framed—and, thank God! the principles of English legislation are such that it is difficult to make bad laws—affords the only real security for freedom, as contra-distinguished from vesting in any living human being a capricious discretion, which he may exercise according to the whim and fancy of the moment tyrannically upon his fellow countrymen and neighbours. That, Sir, is the reason why I wish to see the law maintained; the law improved ; the law rendered charitable in the case of Nonconformists, who conscientiously object to any particular charge; the law rendered just in the case of populations which are deficient of or are left altogether without spiritual provision by the Church or other denominations. Such, then, are are the objects of this Bill. I trust it is framed in the true spirit of Christian charity, not of vague sympathy, but in the spirit of that Christian charity, which makes allowances for feelings which we may deem the errors and weaknesses of our neighbours, which would deprive the members of the Church of England of some power of personal taxation, provided the objects for which that power of taxing personally was granted, can otherwise be accomplished. On such terms it would be both right and wise to act with deference to the feelings of our neighbours and fellow citizens by abandoning a power which they deem offensive, which has been the source of division and discord between Christians — Churchmen and Protestant Dissenters—amongst whom there ought to prevail that catholicity of spirit which is best expressed in the Divine command,

" Do unto your neighbour as you would he should do unto you ; " for in thus doing we fulfil the behest of the beneficent Creator of us all.

Motion made, and Question proposed, " That the Bill be now read a second time."—(*Mr. Newdegate.*)

Sir CHARLES DOUGLAS thought that the reasons which he should give in favour of reading the Bill that day six months would receive the support of a large majority of the House. With the highest respect for the ability and honesty of the hon. Member for North Warwickshire, he believed that the opinion of the majority was that the best course to be taken at present was to decline dealing with the question in the present Parliament. Those who supported the abolition of church rates might regret the position in which the question had been placed, but they were prepared to accept the situation. For his own part, he deeply regretted that position, for it was certain to be warmly discussed with the violence of party spirit upon the hustings in the country at the next general election, and it would be far better if it could have been settled before that election took place. Giving the hon. Member for North Warwickshire all credit for consistency, and an earnest desire to carry out what he believed to be a measure of relief, it was to be regretted that it was not in the power of the Members on that side of the House to accept any such measure as that now proposed. He believed it was the wish of the hon. Member for North Warwickshire—as it certainly was his own—that perfect freedom should be given to Dissenters ; and it was manifest that so long as the question was discussed without the introduction of party feeling, and while reason alone was brought to bear upon it, the chance of a settlement was becoming more and more probable, as the majorities in favour of the abolition of church rates were continually increasing ; and it was only when the influence of party was brought to bear on the opposite side, which could not on this, that those majorities ceased. The leader of the party opposite had stated that if the House could be brought to rescind the Resolution in favour of abolition, he hoped to find the means of obtaining a final and satisfactory settlement of the question. Unfortunately it had not been possible to form a Government which was

Mr. Newdegate

united upon the question of church rates; and while it was made a party question on the other side of the House, there was a want of that combined action on the Ministerial side which was required to bring the matter to a final conclusion. The Bill, or one similar in its principles, which was brought forward last year, did not obtain the support of the right hon. Gentleman's own friends; and the absence upon the present occasion of the right hon. Gentleman the leader on that side, and of his friends, was a proof that they did not incline favourably to this measure as a solution of the vexed question. In his opinion, if the great party who had defeated the measure for the abolition of church rates were unable or unwilling to settle the question, the course for the advocates of abolition to support was not to attempt in this Parliament any legislation on the subject. They accepted the situation, and would go to the hustings on this question at the end of the present Parliament. He hoped that the Government which should be in power when the new Parliament was sitting would then take up the subject, as he thought it was one which properly belonged to the Government to deal with. In his opinion, however, the question of church rates could be settled in no other way than total abolition, and, therefore, without attempting to discuss the nature of the Bill, he should simply move that it be read a second time on that day six months.

Viscount ENFIELD seconded the Amendment.

Amendment proposed, to leave out the word " now," and at the end of the Question to add the words " upon this day six months."—(*Sir Charles Douglas.*)

Mr. SALT said, he would vote for the second reading of the Bill, because he was favourable to any reasonable attempt to settle this difficult question; but was not prepared to say that he should support the Bill in its future stages. The Bill proposed to introduce two material alterations in the law respecting church rates. In the first place, it proposed to remove the liability from the parishioners to the landowners. Whatever difficulties might exist, still from time immemorial the general character of the law was that of a law to compel parishioners to perform their duty of repairing the Church, and he should feel some hesitation in supporting any principle that would limit that duty. The second alteration proposed in the Bill was one of more importance. The character of the rate was essentially local; it was a matter of local privilege, of local duty, and of local action in every respect. He could not help thinking that the provisions of the Bill which had reference to the operation of Queen Anne's Bounty were very unnecessary, cumbrous, and inconvenient. Still he admitted the urgent necessity for legislation. Some of the difficulties of the question might be removed; but there were others which in his opinion were insuperable. Church rates had their origin centuries ago, in times when society and manners were very different to what they are now. It was a very rude piece of legislation, and required to be polished and suited to the habits and opinions of modern times. He therefore desired to see some prudent and well-considered legislation on the subject. But whenever any proposition for legislation had been made, it had been rejected by the representatives of the Dissenters in the House almost with scorn. A more particular difficulty was that of calling on Dissenters to pay church rates. He had considered this question carefully, and he had always come to the conclusion that justice and argument were against the Dissenters; but still he had always felt some dissatisfaction at such a conclusion. Then there was another point of great importance, which he had never heard brought forward in the House, and seldom mentioned out of doors. He must confess he could not see the justice of calling on parishioners to pay a rate for the maintenance of a building, which was public property and for general use, but from which they themselves were excluded, and in which there was not room for the performance of the sacred functions for which the building existed. Where the poor were not admitted, or where the parishioners could not get seats, it was hardly fair that church rates should be levied at all. That was a question which had never been prominently before the House. That was a question which must be dealt with after more experience and at a future time. In legislating upon this subject the great point to keep in view was, that it was purely a local question, and that it had gained an importance that was not essential to it, and which really did not belong to it. It was a matter of local difficulty and of local amendment;

but from the peculiar circumstances attending it and the position of the parties, it had become the battle-ground of party in that House and an Imperial question. Were they, however, to bring the question back to its natural limits and position, he thought it would not be a hard task to find remedies for most of the evils which were at present complained of. He reminded the House that the question must be considered purely in its local character, and in a local point of view there were four matters greatly requiring attention, namely: the present system of ecclesiastical jurisdiction; the position of district churches; the especial purposes for which a church rate might be levied; and another point still more important, that a new rate could not, as the law now stands, be levied unless the whole of the previous rate had been levied from every inhabitant liable to the rate. He thought that if that rule was to be done away with it would enable parishes to relieve Dissenters and others from the impost. If, therefore, these four propositions could be carried out, and the question dealt with in a local rather than in an Imperial point of view, it would set the matter at rest, for the present at least. Taking a more general view of the subject he would remark, that appeals had often been made in that House for concession to certain parties; but he thought "concession" was a wrong term; concession must be mutual, or if made wholly by one party must be regarded as admissions of defeat. Now, he did not see that either party was prepared to own itself vanquished, and there was no chance of their mutually agreeing upon the subject; therefore he wished that the term used had been, not "concession," but "conciliation." Men might be conciliatory in tone, in manner, in expression, even in thought; and he believed that many men, sitting on different sides of the House, and holding different opinions, yet started honestly and sincerely from the same basis and with the same object, namely, the promotion of the moral and religious welfare of the people. There was another side of the question. It had been said that there was a Church party growing up in that House and the country; but if that was so, it must have been created not by its own action or have grown up by its own merit, but from the action and the policy of the opponents of church rates. What, therefore, he asked, must be the policy and position of such a party? They had been year by year, Session after Session, forced back into a position which he believed to be almost unassailable and almost impregnable. They had become the advocates of a moderate reform, as opposed to a measure which had been described by a high authority to be almost revolutionary. They had become the advocates of nearly every landed proprietor in the country. They appeared as the protectors of the local rights and privileges of between 6,000 and 8,000 parishes. They had become the professed defenders of the English Church — a church which, with all its faults, with its sad want of the power of expansion and of adaptation, was yet the noblest, the purest, the most effective church system which ever existed in any country in the world, and which was most closely bound up with the liberties and the institutions of the country. That, he believed, was a policy and a position of which no party need be ashamed, and to such a party no man need be ashamed to attach himself.

Mr. ALDERMAN ROSE said, that if he had entertained any doubt as to the vote he ought to give upon the present occasion, it would have been removed by the speech of the hon. Baronet who moved the Amendment (Sir Charles Douglas). The hon. Baronet had told them that he and his friends were content to let this question remain as it was during the continuance of the present Parliament, which had determined to maintain church rates, but that they intended to resort to a general agitation at the hustings at the next General election. He (Mr. Alderman Rose) would, therefore, vote for the second reading, in order that this question might, if possible, be settled before the threatened agitation could arise. The policy of those Gentlemen was quite intelligible. It was a policy whereby a minority, by a system of complete organization, could exercise a terrorism over the country in order to coerce the majority to accept their views. He was not quite sure that the agitation would result according to the expectations of those who promoted it, but he deprecated it as injurious alike to the Church and to Dissenters. He should support the second reading of the Bill, and thought it would be very unwise to reject a settlement of this question when an opportunity presented itself.

LORD FERMOY said, he could see nothing in the Bill which would give him

Mr. Salt

the smallest hope of any compromise being come to upon fair and reasonable terms, and, therefore, he could not support the second reading, even with the view of sending the Bill to a Select Committee. So far as he understood the Bill, he thought it would make bad worse. The hon. Gentleman simply proposed to remove the payment from the occupier to the landlord.

Mr. NEWDEGATE: From the person to the property.

LORD FERMOY: That was the same thing in other words, and the result was, the landlord would put the charge on the tenant in the shape of rent, and the tenant would still have to pay to support a Church in which he did not believe. The hon. Member for North Warwickshire said it was a lay question—then let them settle it on the principle of lay justice, and not refuse to let the members of the Established Church bear the onus of supporting their own Church. There was no principle of reason or of justice on which they could call on a man to support a religion which he did not believe; and if the members of the Established Church were in the majority, why did they fear to leave them to support their own church? He believed that, under the voluntary principle, the Church would be better supported, and he moreover believed that those were its enemies who endeavoured to force on Dissenters these church rates. There had been no compromise proposed by the other side. The fact that there was but one solution to the difficulty, and that was by abolishing church rates altogether and relying upon the voluntary system, by which already so many new churches had been built and endowed. This was the only step that would allay agitation in the country, and would make people better friends and better neighbours, and establish the Church on a more solid and a safer foundation.

Mr. R. P. LONG said, he was astonished to hear the noble Lord say that no compromise had been offered on this question. Did the noble Lord forget that, when Lord Derby was in office, the right hon. Member for Cambridge University proposed a Bill that was a compromise? He did not say a word as to the merits of that Bill, but he ventured to remind the noble Lord that that measure was brought forward as a compromise by the right hon. Gentleman, who in that Government occupied a position which was much more creditably filled then than it was at this moment in the present Government; for when a question of so much importance as this was under discussion, they had a right to expect to find the Secretary for the Home Department in his place. He would also remind the noble Lord that the right hon. Member for Wiltshire (Mr. Sotheron Estcourt), when in office, also introduced a measure which was a compromise; and they had now before them the Bill of the hon. Member for North Warwickshire, the object of which was to allay the animosities which had existed on this subject for thirty years. All those propositions were honest attempts to meet the objections of the Dissenters; but the present Government had not the courage to bring forward any measure of its own, nor even to father the proposition of the hon. Baronet the Member for Tavistock (Sir John Trelawny), although a continued delay in the settlement of this question was a positive disgrace to the House. He was content to accept this Bill as the basis of a settlement, and as such would give it his support.

MR. LOCKE said, the hon. Member asked why did not the Government come forward with a Bill? Well, why not? There was only one way of settling that matter; and the country had come to the conclusion to which the House must also come, that that only way was by the abolition of church rates. Some Members of the Government might have a misgiving as to the desirability of that course, and therefore as a Government they did not bring forward a measure for the purpose. But the matter had been discussed over and over again, all compromises had been met by a negative, and there was but one solution of the difficulty. If the hon. Gentleman who had introduced this Bill did not represent North Warwickshire he should have thought that he had framed his Bill on an Irish Bill introduced the other day with reference to the Game Laws, which transferred the privilege—or the burden, whichever it was—of prosecuting poachers, from the tenant to the landowner. The present Bill amounted to this, that instead of the occupier paying church rates, the landlord should pay them, without reference to whether he belonged to the Church of England or was a Dissenter, and the landlord would of course put the church rate on to the rent of the occupier. Then what the better would he be for the compromise? He said he did not like to pay a rate for the sup-

port of a church to which he did not belong; but he would be obliged to pay if this Bill were passed. He really believed that in North Warwickshire there might be found a landowner who was a Dissenter, and in what position would the hon. Member place this constituent if he passed this Bill? The hon. Baronet the Member for Tavistock (Sir John Trelawny) had given up the church rate question in despair. The hon. Member opposite (Mr. Long) asked the Government to bring in a Bill to settle the question; but when such a measure was brought forward by the hon. Baronet the Member for Tavistock, the hon. Member opposite and his party had always opposed it. Next year there would be a new Parliament, the opinion of the country would be taken on the question of church rates, and then would be the time to re-introduce the Bill of the hon. Baronet. It was useless to bring in the Bill till the sense of the people had been taken with respect to it. Why, then, did the hon. Member for North Warwickshire on the present occasion bring in this wretched measure. It was a farce. It was not a compromise. The Bill of the right hon. Member for the University of Cambridge was a compromise, but it was opposed on his own side of the House, and it fell to the ground. That Bill was a compromise. The present measure merely made this alteration —that a man who had previously paid his church rates in half-crowns should in future pay it in shillings. He would like to ask the Speaker whether, looking at the title and preamble of the Bill, it was competent to the House to pass one clause only—that was the 38th. The clause proposed to enact that after a particular day all church rates should be abolished, but he supposed it would not be in accordance with the preamble to omit all the other clauses, and then pass the Bill containing that clause only. He certainly coincided with the Bill to that extent, and he would give the second reading his support, on the understanding that they might exercise that power in Committee.

LORD JOHN MANNERS said, he was sure that the House could not but be sensible of the pains and unwearied assiduity bestowed on the Bill by the hon. Member for North Warwickshire: but it seemed to him that the hon. Gentleman who had just sat down seemed to be a kind of Parliamentary Rip Van Winkle, who had been in a state of coma on the church rate question for the last two years. The hon. and learned Member said that nothing short of total abolition of church rates would satisfy the House. The hon. and learned Member must either have absented himself from the church rate debates during that period, or his memory failed him. The Bill of the hon. Member for Tavistock (Sir John Trelawny) which had formerly been passed by large majorities, had been defeated on the last two occasions, and for two years the House had refused to vote the abolition of church rates. [Mr. Locke: I know that.] Then he had the greater difficulty in reconciling the hon. Member's opinion to his knowledge. The hon. Member for Banbury (Sir Charles Douglas) was of opinion that the House having given its assent to the principle of total abolition, and then said that the abolition ought not to take place, was incapable in this the fifth year of its existence to settle this church rate question, and that the public discussion of this intricate and difficult question ought to be remitted to the hustings and to another Parliament; and the hon. Member for Southampton (Mr. Alderman Rose) appeared to be so alarmed at that prospect, that he was prepared to vote for this measure. But he (Lord John Manners) had no fear of the question being discussed at a general election ; for he believed that the change in the votes of the House of Commons was in accordance with a change which had come over the country at large. It was clear this Bill did not satisfy the opponents of church rates; but were the supporters of church rates in its favour? Never since he had had the honour of a seat in that House had a more desirable period existed for the discussion of the church rate question. The great synod of the Church was sitting. There was not only this great Church Congress, there was every rural deanery in the country assembled ; the churchwardens were brought together, and their opinions pretty nearly represented the laity of the country. But had any of these bodies pronounced in favour of this measure ? He asked his hon. Friend the Member for North Warwickshire, had he any hope that this measure would really satisfy the Church feelings of the country ? He (Lord John Manners) did not believe it would. While he recognized in much of what his hon. Friend had said sentiments in which he fully agreed, and gave him

Lord John Manners

credit for the pains he had taken and the assiduity he had displayed, he could not think that the measure was one really calculated or in the least degree likely to settle the question. Therefore he would counsel his hon. Friend to rest satisfied with having, in the course of a full and exhaustive speech, directed the attention of the country to his scheme, and to withdraw the Bill.

SIR CHARLES WOOD said, that his right hon. Friend (Sir George Grey) was engaged in an important Committee which was sitting upstairs on a question which concerned the constitution of the House, and therefore there was no dereliction of public duty on his part in not being present in the House on the present occasion. He entirely concurred in every encomium that had been bestowed upon the trouble which the hon. Member who had brought in the Bill had taken in reference to the question of church rates; but with regard to the Bill itself he could not agree with it. He believed it to be open to the objection which was urged against a similar measure last Session by his right hon. Friend the Secretary for the Home Department — namely, that it would be ineffectual in attaining a settlement of the question. He was fully persuaded that it would be better if they did not pursue the discussion on the subject during the present Parliament, or, at all events, during the present Session. It was a subject which the country ought fully to consider, and it would, no doubt, as the hon. Gentleman had said, be dwelt upon at the hustings. He thought the wisest course was to avoid the use of irritating language on the subject, and that the hon. Gentleman would do well to adopt the suggestion of the noble Lord.

SIR JAMES FERGUSSON said, that the speech of the right hon. Baronet (Sir Charles Wood) held out little prospect of the solution of a question which had occasioned the most violent contests on a matter which ought not to be made the arena of party contest. The right hon. Baronet suggested that it would be better to allow the question to rest for the present. That course might suit those who wished to have a fertile field for discussion on the hustings kept open. But this was a question which entered so closely into the comprehension and daily life of every parish, that it was most unfortunate that the question of attachment to the national Church should be canvassed and agitated in support of what was after all but a miserably small question. If a plan could be devised which would intrust the maintenance of the national Church to the property of the country, he should consider it a most wholesome settlement of the question. He had watched the working of a similar system in Scotland. In that country the ecclesiastical difficulties were greater than in England, and the gentry to a great extent did not belong to the national Church. Under such circumstances, it might naturally be imagined that difficulties would arise in the erection and repair of churches; but such was not the case; and he did not recollect an instance in which it had been found necessary to put the law in force to carry those objects into effect. This was a proof of the good working of the system which his hon. Friend wanted to introduce; and unless the noble Lord (Lord John Manners) or the Government were prepared to propose a better scheme, he trusted the House would allow the Bill to be read a second time, in order that its provisions might be fully considered.

Question put, "That the word 'now' stand part of the Question."

The House *divided:*—Ayes 60 ; Noes 160 : Majority 100.

Words *added.*

Main Question, as amended, put, and *agreed to.*

Second Reading *put off* for six months.

AYES.

Archdall, Captain M.	Grogan, Sir E.
Beecroft, G. S.	Haliburton, T. C.
Bentinck, G. W. P.	Hamilton, Lord C.
Bentinck, G. C.	Harvey, R. B.
Beresford, rt. hon. W.	Hay, Sir J. C. D.
Bremridge, R.	Hesketh, Sir T. G.
Bridges, Sir B. W.	Hornby, W. H.
Bruce, Major C.	Hume, W. W. F.
Bruce, Sir H. H.	Jones, D.
Butt, I.	Knightley, R.
Cargill, W. W.	Langton, W. G.
Cartwright, Colonel	Leslie, W.
Cole, hon. H.	Long, R. P.
Cole, hon. J. L.	Lopes, Sir M.
Copeland, Mr. Ald.	Lyall, G.
Du Cane, C.	Miller, T. J.
Duncombe, hon. A.	Morritt, W. J. S.
Du Pre, C. G.	Pakenham, Colonel
Fellowes, E.	Rose, W. A.
Fergusson, Sir J.	Salt, T.
Finlay, A. S.	Scourfield, J. H.
Forde, Colonel	Selwyn, C. J.
Galway, Viscount	Smith, A.
Gard, R. S.	Smollett, P. B.
Goddard, A. L.	Somes, J.
Gore, J. R. O.	Stracey, Sir H.
Grey de Wilton, Visct.	Surtees, H. E.

Tottenham, Lt.-Col.C.G.	Whiteside, rt. hon. J.
Treherne, M.	
Vyse, Colonel H.	TELLERS.
Walcott, Admiral	Newdegate, C. N.
Way, A. E.	Montagu, Lord R.

NOES.

Adair, H. E.	Gibson, rt. hon. T. M.
Adam, W. P.	Gilpin, C.
Agnew, Sir A.	Gladstone, rt. hon. W.
Alcock, T.	Goldsmid, Sir F. H.
Angerstein, W.	Gore, W. R. O.
Anson, hon. Major	Gower, hon. F. L.
Anstruther, Sir R.	Greene, J.
Ayrton, A. S.	Greenwood, J.
Aytoun, R. C.	Gurney, S.
Bagwell, J.	Hadfield, G.
Barnes, T.	Hanbury, R.
Bass, M. T.	Hankey, T.
Baxter, W. E.	Hardcastle, J. A.
Bazley, T.	Hartopp, E. B.
Beach, W. W. B.	Hayter, rt. hn. Sir W.G.
Berkeley, hon. Col. F.	Henderson, J.
W. F.	Henley, Lord
Berkeley, hon. C. P. F.	Heygate, Sir F. W.
Biddulph, Colonel	Hibbert, J. T.
Black, A.	Hodgson, K. D.
Blencowe, J. G.	Hopwood, J. T.
Bond, J. W. M'G.	Horsman, rt. hon. E.
Bouverie, hon. P. P.	Humphery, W. H.
Brand, hon. H.	Hutt, rt. hon. W.
Briscoe, J. I.	Jackson, W.
Buchanan, W.	Jervoise, Sir J. C.
Buller, Sir A. W.	King, hon. P. J. L.
Butler, C. S.	Kinglake, A. W.
Buxton, C.	Kingscote, Colonel
Carnegie, hon. C.	Knatchbull - Hugessen,
Clifford, C. C.	E
Clifton, Sir R. J.	Langton, W. H. G.
Clive, G.	Lawson, W.
Cobden, R.	Leatham, E. A.
Cochrane, A. D. R. W.B.	Lefevre, G. J. S.
Cogan, W. H. F.	Lee, W.
Coke, hon. Colonel	Lennox, Lord G. G.
Colebrooke, Sir T. E.	Lewis, H.
Collins, T.	Lindsay, W. S.
Colthurst, Sir G. C.	Locke, J.
Cox, W.	M'Cann, J.
Craufurd, E. H. J.	Mackinnon, W.A. (Rye)
Dalglish, R.	Maguire, J. F.
Damer, S. D.	Manners, rt. hn. Lord J.
Davey, R.	Marsh, M. H.
Dawson, R. P.	Martin, J.
Dent, J. D.	Mildmay, H. F.
Dering, Sir E. C.	Morris, D.
Duff, R. W.	Morrison, W.
Dunbar, Sir W.	Neate, C.
Dunlop, A. M.	O'Conor Don, The
Egerton, Sir P. G.	Paget, C.
Elcho, Lord	Paxton, Sir J.
Evans, T. W.	Pease, H.
Ewart, W.	Peel, rt. hon. Sir R.
Ewart, J. C.	Pender, J.
Ewing, H. E. Crum-	Pilkington, J.
Fenwick, E. M.	Pollard-Urquhart, W.
Fermoy, Lord	Potter, E.
Ferrand, W.	Powell, W. T. R.
Finch, C. Wynne-	Powell, J. J.
Fitzwilliam, hn. C.W.W.	Price, R. G.
Fleming, T. W.	Pryse, E. L.
Foljambe, F. J. S.	Ramsden, Sir J. W.
Forster, C.	Ricardo, O.
Gaskell, J. M.	Robartes, T. J. A.

Robertson, D.
Robertson, H.
Roebuck, J. A.
Rogers, J. J.
Russell, A.
St. Aubyn, J.
Sclater-Booth, G.
Seymour, A.
Smith, J. B.
Stacpoole, W.
Taylor, P. A.
Tollemache, hon. F. J.
Tracy, hon. C. R. D. H.
Tynte, Colonel K.
Verney, Sir H.
Vivian, H. H.
Vyner, R. A.

Waldron, L.
Walter, J.
Warner, E.
Waterhouse, S.
Watkins, Colonel L.
White, J.
White, hon. L.
Wickham, H. W.
Williams, W.
Wood, rt. hon. Sir C.
Woods, H.
Wynn, C. W. W.

TELLERS.

Douglas, Sir C.
Enfield, Viscount

BANK NOTES (SCOTLAND) BILL.
[BILL 53.]   SECOND READING.

Order for Second Reading read.

SIR JOHN HAY, in moving the second reading of the Bill, said, he would not delay the House long in explaining its object, which was a very simple one. The House was aware that by the Bank Act of 1844-5 the Scotch banks then existing (twenty-three in number) were permitted to resort to a fixed issue as against their credit; and, in addition to the issue of notes so granted against their credit, they were further allowed to issue notes as against the amount of gold which they might have from time to time in their coffers. This issue was totally independent of the fixed issue, and could not be changed save by the action of the Legislature. Since that time, several of those banks had either joined together or had completely passed away. The Western Bank of Scotland, for instance, had completely disappeared from public business. But the issue of notes by the Scotch banks had not consequently diminished, because the gold having increased, and the issue of notes being dependent on the amount of bullion in the bank coffers, the issue has not diminished to any very great extent. This Bill did not in any way apply for a fixed issue as against credit for new banks which might in future be established. The commercial necessities of Scotland required, however, an extension of the banking system, which had been curtailed, while the commercial transactions of the country had considerably increased. The simple proposal of the Bill was that any person or persons carrying on the business of banking in Scotland should have power at any time to issue notes as against the gold they might have in their coffers. His sole reason for proposing this measure to the

House was the fact that it was all but impossible for any banking house in Scotland to carry on business with advantage to the commercial interests of the country if they had not the power of issuing notes. All business persons in Scotland preferred as a rule to receive the £1 note to the sovereign, and all commercial business was, in fact, carried on through the medium of notes of that description. It might be said that any bank establishing itself in Scotland could avail itself of the notes of the existing banks. But the gold must be in the cellars of the particular bank accommodating, and this would be equivalent to refusing to any new bank the custody of their customers' money. He did not at all interfere with the right of the fixed issue; what he desired was, that any bank should have the power to issue notes against gold.

Motion made, and Question proposed, "That the Bill be now read a second time."

MR. BLACK: Sir, this Bill is certainly rather remarkable. For two reasons it is remarkable—first, for what it says; and secondly, for what it does not say. By this measure we are told that the Act of the 8 & 9 *Vict.* was passed with the view of regulating the monetary system of the United Kingdom. The Bill then says that by that Act provisions were made for limiting the amount of issue of bank notes in Scotland; as if it were only in Scotland that the issue of these notes was limited. The Bill further says, that the population, trade, and banking requirements have considerably increased of late years in Scotland. This is equivalent to saying that all these things have taken place in Scotland while they have not done so elsewhere. Now we may, I think, reasonably suppose that population and commerce have increased in England, at all events, as much as in Scotland. The whole object of this Bill may be said to be contained in its third clause, which in effect says: "It shall be lawful for any company carrying on banking business to make an addition to their own bank notes in Scotland." The real meaning of the clause is this: that means must be taken to procure a greater issue of paper money in Scotland. Sir, the monetary system for the United Kingdom was settled in a wise and intelligible manner in 1844-5, and under that general system the trade and commerce of the whole kingdom have greatly increased. We enjoy the very greatest prosperity under that system. But this Bill proposes that any seven men may join together for banking purposes, and may manufacture and issue bank notes. Doubtless, it is stated that those persons must have bullion to meet these notes; but have we not had ample experience that a number of unprincipled men, in spite of all precautions in the way of checks and regulations, have before now conspired together to commit frauds which they may do on a gigantic scale, under the pretence of banking or other commercial pursuits? Now, what will this Bill lead to if we pass it? I am convinced it will inevitably lead to greater frauds and failures than we have as yet experienced. But that is not the main point. The main question is whether you are really willing to alter or in any way to interfere with the monetary system of the kingdom? whether you desire to alter the law as regards only one particular section, or as it relates to the whole? I appeal to the House, is it right to alter the law for Scotland in this respect, and not for the other parts of the United Kingdom? I should like to know whether the people of Scotland have so managed or mismanaged the business of their banks as to reduce the value of the currency; or have they injuriously affected the general prosperity of the kingdom by the improper manner in which they have conducted their business? But if, as I believe it will be admitted, there is not the slightest reason for casting a doubt upon the security or solvency of their commercial establishments generally, or for finding fault with the manner in which they as a rule conduct their business, does the House think it would be wise to interfere with their banking system? Sir, I consider that this frequent meddling with the commercial institutions of Scotland is not only undesirable, but is absolutely injurious to the general interest of the country. If we are at all dissatisfied with the working of the statute passed by Parliament in 1844-5—a statute the provisions of which, I think, were so admirably constructed as to be of great benefit to the public at large—if, notwithstanding, we are still displeased with the machinery of that statute, and if we deem that some modification of it would be desirable, let us, instead of the fragmentary interference that is now proposed, apply our legislation to the whole kingdom, and not to any

particular part of it. Since 1845, thirty-six banks in England have failed to meet their engagements, and caused fearful misery in the districts in which they were established; but, I am proud to say, that not one pound has been lost by the public out of all the millions they have intrusted to the different banks of Scotland, and every one of their notes have been paid as regularly as presented. It is quite true that two banks did fail; but the public did not suffer. The sufferers were the proprietors of the banks themselves. It is now stated that we ought to have free trade in banking. Now, what does free trade in banking mean? The proposition involved in this Bill is that there ought to be free trade in banking, and issuing paper money in Scotland, because certain parties in that part of the kingdom are empowered to issue bank notes. But if you limit the power to three millions of the population, I ask if you can call that free trade? You have in England 20,000,000 of people, and 6,000,000 in Ireland, and I therefore ask if it would be free trade to limit the powers now sought to be obtained to 3,000,000 in Scotland. If your object is free trade, it is necessary that you should apply it to the whole of the United Kingdom. The population of London is about as large as that of the whole of Scotland; while it possesses a much larger amount of property. Then why should you not introduce the same system into London? The banks of London ought to have free trade as well as those in Scotland; and, if that is to be the principle, I contend that its adoption would subvert the whole system which was settled some years ago. What is the cause of all this agitation? We are told that poor old Scotland has lost no less than £300,000 in lapsed capital—as if a box containing 300,000 sovereigns had slipped overboard into the deep sea—and that there has been such a contraction of the currency in consequence that legislation upon the subject is now absolutely necessary. Now the fact is, that the whole thing is moonshine. There has not been one single sovereign lost, and there has not been the contraction of one single shilling of currency in consequence of this lapse. When people come here and relate this lamentable story with regard to our unhappy country, it is quite clear that there is something behind which does not appear above-board. I am uncharitable enough to suspect so, at any rate. In my opinion this is merely an attempt to accomplish by a side-wind, by a public Bill, that which never would have been obtained by private legislation. With regard to free trade in banking we have the lessons of experience. Free trade in banking did once exist in this country. Before the year 1800 there were 280 country banks in existence; but they increased so rapidly that in 1813 they amounted to 900. During the years 1814-15-16 no less than 240 of these banks stopped payment, spreading ruin around them; and during the time of these excessive issues the depreciation of bank paper was rapid and unbroken, sinking from 2½ to 25 per cent. I do not think it would be desirable to return to those glorious days of banking. Some people tell us that the existing banks of issue possess a monopoly. This is a favourite expression; but I must be permitted to say that free trade in banking is at present complete. Any man might commence the business of banking to-morrow if he chose. But what they really want is, free trade in coining — that is, of coining paper into money. It appears to me that that would be a most dangerous licence, because if free trade in that sense were established, the consequences would be disastrous. It is alleged that certain Scotch banks have a monopoly. Now, I am quite prepared to admit that if a monopoly existed it would be a very bad thing; but I contend that there is abundance of competition at the present moment. I have in my hands a Return showing the number of banks in Scotland, England, and Ireland, with the different populations and value of property, and I can show the House how many individuals there are to a bank in each of the three countries. The number of banking offices in England is 1,406, in Scotland, 635, and in Ireland 220. The population of England is 20,066,224, the number of the banks 1,406, and that gives one bank to every 14,271 of the population. In Ireland, the population is 6,764,543, the number of banks is 220, giving a bank to every 26,202 of the population. In Scotland, the population is 3,062,294, and yet it has no less than 635 banks, giving one bank to every 4,822 of the population. In whatever mode you apply a test, the result is the same. Take the income tax. The amount assessed to that tax in England is £262,000,000, and with 1,406 banks we have a bank for every £200,000. In Scot-

Mr. Black

land, the amount assessed to income tax is £30,000,000, which gives one bank for every £47,244. In Ireland the amount assessed to the income tax is £23,000,000, and this gives one bank for every £104,545. The principal banks in Scotland have branches all through the country, so that even in small parishes with a thousand inhabitants you will find a banking establishment. A few years ago I happened to be in Buxton, and although possessing a population of upwards of 2,000, when I enquired for a bank I was unable to find one. In Scotland, the circumstances are very different. In Inverary, with scarcely 1,000 inhabitants, there are two banks. I cannot help thinking, therefore, that the outcry about the want of banks and of circulation in Scotland is altogether moonshine. I say there is no want of circulation. If any man who complains of our banks will give us good security, I will engage that he shall have as much paper money as he likes. We will supply him with the money if he will give us the security; but if he wants a large loan upon a doubtful security, and wishes to keep the money lent to him a great deal longer than is consistent with good banking principles, then I must confess that the transaction is one of which we do not approve, and I am afraid he will not be accommodated. No doubt if abundant accommodation could be procured by the manufacture of an old shirt-sleeve into thousands of pounds, it might be very convenient for the speculator, but disastrous to the country. I maintain that the people of Scotland are perfectly satisfied with their banks; so much so, indeed, that they prefer the Scotch bank note to the gold; and, at the same time, the country is continually prospering under this system. If you are going to change it, I contend that you cannot with propriety accomplish your object unless you are prepared to deal with the whole monetary system of the kingdom. I want to know why Scotland should be always held up as if there were something rotten in that state; whereas I believe that our banking establishments especially are thoroughly sound, and I believe I should be able to show that not only are our operations simple and advantageous, but that they are better than those carried on in any other part of the kingdom. I beg to move, as an Amendment, that the Bill be read a second time this day six months.

Mr. DALGLISH seconded the Amendment.

Amendment proposed, to leave out the word "now," and at the end of the Question to add the words "upon this day six months."—(*Mr. Black.*)

Question proposed, "That the word 'now' stand part of the Question."

Mr. FINLAY: As my name appears on the back of this Bill, perhaps I may be allowed to state my reasons for supporting the second reading. I do not approve of all the details of the Bill; I merely approve of its principle, which I consider is the establishment of free competition in banking. In Scotland the existing banks have an exclusive privilege of issue. I do not say that those banks have used that exclusive privilege oppressively. They did not ask for that privilege — it was forced upon them—and, upon the whole, they have used it fairly. But still it is found by experience that exclusive privileges of any kind are contrary to the interests of the public. My hon. Friend the Member for Edinburgh (Mr. Black) states that there is plenty of free trade in banking. But let me remind him that, until all banks are placed on an equal footing, there can be no such thing as free competition. If one bank has a privilege over another it necessarily has an advantage over that bank to the extent of that privilege. If he desires to place the whole of them on the same level he must give to all the right of issuing notes, or else enact that none of them shall have that right. In either case the result is the same, they would be on the same footing. If Parliament gives to none of them the privilege of issuing notes, then they must return to a metallic currency, or have notes issued by the State. There are insuperable objections, as every practical man knows, to a return to a metallic currency, not only on account of the expense, but also on account of the impossibility of at all times procuring the necessary coin to meet the exigencies of trade. It is hardly necessary, therefore, to say anything upon that subject, because I imagine no one in this House will advocate the adoption of a system of pure metallic currency. I am aware that the plan of having notes issued by the State is popular with some persons; but the more one considers the subject, the more insuperable do the obstacles to the working out of that principle appear.

I should, in the first place, like to ask the supporters of that proposal who are to issue these notes and to keep them in circulation? The State, it is evident, cannot do it. It can only be done by those who have to make frequent payments to a large amount. If this circulation is to be kept up by the banks, who are to guarantee the notes? If the State guarantee the payment of the notes, then the State undertakes the duty of a trader without a trader's profit. But if the banks are to be responsible for the payment of the notes, then the public are in the same state as they were before, and have no additional security. Besides, there are constitutional objections to such a measure. At present it is not necessary that I should go at length into that part of the question; but I am anxious to quote a statement of Lord Monteagle's, which is contained in the Appendix to the Report of the Commission of 1858. He says—

"Let us not deceive ourselves into a belief that our free Government would afford us any protection whatever about the probable abuse of such a power. . . . I venture to suggest that a free Government might furnish the most active and dangerous agency for forcing on the Treasury to rash and fatal resolves if it should unadvisedly undertake the functions of a bank of issue. I believe a Government in such a position would be driven onward to the very measure which wisdom and experience would most strongly deprecate and condemn."

Sir Robert Peel himself was in favour of free trade in banking. In 1844, he said—

"The principle of competition, though unsafe in our opinion when applied to issue, ought, we think, to govern the business of banking."

My hon. Friend the Member for Edinburgh stated that free banking in England had been attended with very bad results. He said that about 200 banks had failed in the course of three years. But free banking was not the cause of that lamentable overthrow of English banks. What was the position of English banks at that time? Six partners only were allowed to each bank. It was, in point of fact, a system which necessarily created weak banks, for it enabled persons with very little capital to issue notes to a great extent, and prevented the formation of powerful banks with large paid up capitals. You cannot call such a system a system of free banking. I should prefer taking a better example—one which we fully understand in Scotland. Let us go back to the old banking system in Scotland before it was

1735   *Bank Notes*   **{COMMONS}**   *(Scotland) Bill.*   **1736**

destroyed by Sir Robert Peel's Act of 1845. What was the Report of the Committee appointed to investigate the working of that system in 1826? I would beg to remind the House that the Committee was one hostile to the Scotch system of banking. I will read an extract from their Report. They say—

"The Committee are unwilling, without stronger proof of necessity, to incur the risk of deranging from any cause whatever a system admirably calculated in their opinion to economise the use of capital, to create and cherish a spirit of useful enterprise, and even to promote the moral habits of the people by the direct inducements which it holds out to the maintenance of a character for industry, integrity, and prudence."

Such was the old Scotch system of banking before Sir Robert Peel interfered with it by the Act of 1845. They go on to say—

"During the civil commotion of the last century, in the rebellion of 1715 and 1745, the confidence in paper securities in Scotland was not shaken. The Scotch banks maintained their stability, and were not called upon for any extraordinary issue of gold in exchange for their notes during the shocks to which mercantile credit was exposed in this country in the years 1793, 1797, and, more recently, in 1825. It cannot be assumed, therefore, that a circulation of specie is necessary in Scotland for the purpose of guarding against the effects of sudden panic. . . . . So far as the interests of the Bank of England are concerned, it will be seen that the directors of that Bank, who were examined before your Committee, urge no objection to the continuance of the present system in Scotland, provided that the paper circulation in Scotland can be effectually retained within the limits of that country."

Sir Robert Peel did not contradict that statement when he introduced the Bank Act in 1845, nor did he deny that the Scotch system was an admirable system. But what were his objections to that system? I think it is necessary that the House should know exactly what his remarks were; and, not to weaken this argument, I will read the remarks which he then made. He said—

"The security of the system which prevails in Scotland rests in the amount of gold in England, and it is this which enables Scotland to dispense with the amount of bullion in proportion to its circulation, which, and not the solvency of the banks, ought to be the foundation of the promissory notes. I am not surprised that Scotland should wish to be exempt from this—I am not surprised that Ireland should wish the same ; and I do not say that it may not be possible, by taking the whole expense of maintaining a gold currency upon this part of the empire, that another system may not succeed in other parts ; but I do say that it is just that the burden should be borne in equal proportions by all parts of the empire."— [3 *Hansard*, lxxxi. 147.]

Mr. Finlay

I quite admit the force of his assertion, that the stability of the issue of the banks ought to depend upon the gold that the bank holds. But the question arises, who is to determine the amount of gold required? It seems to me that the bank directors should not only know, but should always be careful to provide that the bank under their charge should at all times be in a position to pay its own promissory notes in gold? We know, from the experience of a great many years, that Scotch banks founded on that principle never failed to meet their engagements. The reason that induced Sir Robert Peel to alter the Scotch system was simply this. He believed, and asserted, that the stability of the Scotch system depended upon the amount of bullion in England, and he thought it was unfair to put England to the whole expense of maintaining a gold currency for Scotland. That was the ground of his opposition to the old system of banking in Scotland, and at first sight it is a plausible objection ; but when we subject it to a close examination, it does not appear deserving of much weight. I deny, in the first place, that the Scotch banks are responsible for the expense of maintaining the gold necessary to be kept in London. London is the centre of all the pecuniary operations not only of England, but of the whole world, and as it obtains all the emoluments incident to that position, it would be unfair for it to shirk the responsibilities. One of the responsibilities of a banker is to provide sufficient cash to pay his balances. The Scotch mercantile community hold large balances in London, and why should they not have the right of withdrawing those balances when it suits them? France and America withdraw their balances whenever they desire to do so; and if the Bank of England is sometimes called upon to pay gold at a moment when it may not be convenient, it is no fault of the Scotch system. The law which imposes that obligation on the Bank of England was not made by the Scotch people. On the contrary, the Bank of England undertook the duty voluntarily, and is it relieved in any way from that inconvenient obligation by the Bank Act of 1845? I believe quite the reverse. Since that Act passed, there can be no doubt that the demand upon the Bank of England for gold for the Scotch banks has greatly increased. The fact is, that the stability of the Scotch system does not depend on the gold in England at all. At least, it did not previous to the year 1845. It was maintained for 150 years without any support from the gold in the Bank of England. As a remarkable proof of that fact, I may mention what occurred on the suspension of cash payments in 1797. Cash payments were suspended in England for twenty-five years, and during that time the whole of the Scotch banks paid their notes in gold on demand. Cash payments were never suspended in Scotland, and how could they then depend on England for gold? England could not have supplied the gold if Scotland had required it. If we could find out the quantity of gold transmitted to Scotland previous to 1845 and since that year, we should discover that the amount has very much increased during the latter period. Sir Robert Peel, in order to get rid of an imaginary evil, introduced a much greater one, for there never had been any great demand for gold from the Scotch banks on the Bank of England previous to 1845. What was the evidence in reference to the interests of the Bank of England before the Committee of 1826? The Directors of the Bank, when examined before the Committee, urged no objection to the continuance of the then existing system in Scotland. Mr. Richards, the Governor of the Bank of England, was asked—

"Do you think the existence of a paper currency in Scotland at the time there was a gold currency in England might lead to any inconvenient demand upon the Bank of England for gold for Scotland."

His answer was—

"Scotland could not reach the gold of the Bank of England by getting possession of the paper of the Bank of England. She could only do that by discounting bills through her agents in London, or by the sale of stock or any public securities that she might hold; but, by her own paper, she could not touch us."

It is undoubtedly the fact that, if there were no bank notes in Scotland at all, and nothing but sovereigns, the Scotch people could withdraw their balances from London in gold quite as easily as they do now. It is quite a mistake to suppose that the issue of bank notes is the cause of the withdrawal of gold from the Bank of England; and that perfect freedom in the issue of promissory notes, such as existed in Scotland previous to 1845, can imperil the solvency of the Bank of Eng-

land. I trust that the Chancellor of the Exchequer will turn his powerful and logical mind to the question, and that having been instrumental in removing many restrictions to free trade, he will support freedom in banking. I hope he will feel it not inconsistent with his duty to consider the subject with that spirit of fairness, and with that ability, which characterize him ; and, in that case, I have no doubt that before long we shall have a very great and beneficial reform in our monetary system.

THE CHANCELLOR OF THE EXCHEQUER : 'Sir, in answer to the appeal which has been made to me by my hon. Friend (Mr. Finlay), I am bound to say that I cannot respond to it in a favourable manner, if it implies that I shall vote for the present reading of this Bill. On the contrary, I intend to support the Motion made by my hon. Friend the hon. Member for Edinburgh. The grounds upon which I shall give that vote are not grounds connected with inveterate hostility to the principle upon which the measure rests; on the contrary, I think that the principle of the extension of issues against gold is one that, under favourable circumstances, might fairly form the subject of consideration by Parliament. I think the hon. Baronet (Sir John Hay) who has brought in this Bill is entitled to claim certain admission at our hands. It is not *primâ facie* unreasonable or incredible that there may be a demand for an augmentation of issue in Scotland. At the same time, that demand for augmentation for issue may be founded not so much upon the proof that the issues of Scotland are deficient in quantity, as upon the connection which, owing to the habits and ideas of the people, is found to exist there between issue of notes and the business of banking. I do not believe that a sounder principle was ever enunciated by Sir Robert Peel than that which has been quoted to-night, when he said that in his judgment issue ought to be subject to strict regulation by the State; whereas the business of banking ought to be made as free as any other business, and ought to depend entirely upon the principle of competition. But in Scotland there appears undoubtedly to exist a feeling in regard to the nature of the circulating medium which they are accustomed to use, and which lies at the foundation of this Bill. It cannot be said that in principle there is anything dangerous or unsound in issue against gold. The question which would at first sight suggest itself to those who might be disposed to criticise the proposal would be, where could be the economy of a system of issuing paper against gold? It is well known that there is a very considerable economy in an issue of that description. But I will state to the House why, looking to all the circumstances of the case, I think it is impossible to accede to the demand for the second reading of this Bill. In the first place, I think that the parallel and analogy which the hon. Baronet drew between the law now existing in behalf of the old Scotch banks and the case of the new banks are fallacious. The existing provisions which authorise the old Scotch banks that existed before 1845 to issue notes against gold, are not to be considered as founded upon any permanent principle. They are part of a set of provisions adopted by Sir Robert Peel as being well calculated for the circumstances of the time, and suitable upon the whole to further the general principles of policy of which he desired to secure the introduction and the permanent and solid extension in the country. That being the case, it would be a most hasty and precipitate inference to select from among them provisions adopted upon grounds more or less of a transient and temporary character, and make them without further consideration the basis of any extended system. We are not justified in arguing that, because in the Act of 1845 we find power given to the existing Scotch banks to issue notes against gold, we may without consideration extend the exercise of that power to any other banks that may seek to do business in Scotland. The truth is that when we come to consider a permanent system with regard to the issue of notes against gold, it will not be enough to say, as is stated in this Bill, that any bank that is so minded may issue promissory notes to the extent to which it shall be proved to have gold in its possession; because, although it may have the gold, the question immediately arises—in what way is that gold appropriated so as to become a basis of security to the paper issue? It is impossible to avoid that question if we are to consider any permanent system of that kind. Here, of course, I might be met by an *argumentum ad hominem.* It may be argued that I have presented to the House a Bill which proposes to deal with a certain

The Chancellor of the Exchequer

portion of what is called lapsed issue, and to authorize the resumption of that issue, without making any provision for its security. Undoubtedly, that so far is true; but this has been proposed with reference to a particular part of the old Scotch banking system, because we think we may truly rely on the general condition of the Scotch banking system as a sufficient security for a limited arrangement of that kind. And I am not sure that we are justified in arguing from that Bill as if it had been accepted by the House. For, on the one hand, it is a Bill which, if I may judge from the notices that have been given, is not likely to meet with unanimous acceptance; and, on the other hand, it is a Bill which, as I have stated from the first, aimed at nothing but an arrangement for temporary convenience. It does not attempt to lay down any new principle to govern banking in Scotland. It is not a Bill of that character; and it is a measure which I would not think it right to press forward in the face of any considerable difference of opinion. But it stands widely distinct from such a measure as that which we are now discussing, which enters into a much deeper question, and which we can evidently see is permanent in its application, and is capable of wide and general extension; and I would therefore suggest to the hon. Baronet, that if the time has really come when we can fairly deal with the subject of banking in Scotland, and authorize the extension of issues of promissory notes against gold, it would be necessary for us to devise, in addition to the provisions that he has inserted in his Bill, a set of very important collateral provisions. It is quite evident that gold itself will not form directly a security for the notes. It is also quite evident that the gold could not be held on general grounds to form indirectly a guarantee for the solvency of the banks. If that be so —if we could not make sure by those provisions, either directly or indirectly, that those of which we are authorizing the issue would be worthy of the confidence of the public—I think it is quite plain that we must resort to other provisions, and that those other provisions would require to be made the subject of careful consideration. It is not possible, in point of fact, to avoid seeing that the Bill of the hon. Baronet, although it appears to be comparatively limited in the direct scope of its clauses, entails and draws after it the consideration of a very extensive question—because, as I have just said, if you authorize the issue of notes against gold in Scotland, we must have a carefully constructed system of collateral provisions; but if we proceed to establish such a system of provisions, it is clear that we must take into our consideration the position of the old banks. When the time comes to establish such provisions for authorizing the issue of notes against gold, that will evidently be the time for considering the provisions of the present law, which authorizes the issue by the old banks of notes against gold. I take it that the legislation of 1844-5 proceeded on the general principle of the confidence which the Legislature reposed in the old banks of Scotland—a degree of confidence which it would not be safe to assume with respect to new banks; but I do not consider it possible for Parliament to construct this new system for the issue of notes against gold in respect of new banks, without considering the question whether the provisions of the law regarding the issue of notes against gold by the old banks do not also require consideration and revision. If that be so, it is plain that the Bill of the hon. Baronet entails and necessitates a full consideration of the entire banking system of Scotland. I am speaking with no adverse prepossession. I should be very sorry, upon merely selfish grounds, to take any step which would arouse the angry shade of Malachi Malagrowther. I should be sorry if any man occupying the position which I have the honour to hold should, within any period to which we can reasonably look forward, feel disposed to raise the question in an adverse sense of the small note currency of Scotland. If that system be effectually limited and guarded, I think it may be made as safe as any other; but I should be misunderstood if it were supposed that I intended to imply that rules which are good for this country are without modification or alteration equally good for Scotland. On the contrary, I hold that the circumstances of Scotland, and the customs and usages of that country, are to be taken into our view, as well as the state of the Scotch law, before we can argue that what we do for England the same should be done for Scotland. Having thus guarded myself against being supposed to contemplate the application of a new system of uniformity with respect to the currency of the three king-

doms, I must nevertheless say, that I do not think the House could, with wisdom or safety, proceed to the consideration of the general subject of banking and currency for Scotland until it has fully considered the state of the law on this subject in respect to this country. It is quite clear that London—which is the centre of the monetary operations of the world—and being at the head of the whole monetary system of England, we must regard England as *à fortiori* the centre of the whole monetary and banking system of the United Kingdom. I consider it essential, before we proceed to consider any new proposal involving that principle with respect to Scotland, that we inquire whether our legislation for England has been brought into a state which expresses and corresponds with the permanent view of Parliament. My answer to that question is, that our legislation for England has not yet been brought to that state. However, it is far from my desire to say one word that can be construed into a disparagement of the legislation of 1844. Whether it be approved of or disapproved of, I have no hesitation in saying that in my opinion essential service has been conferred upon the country by that legislation so far as all fundamental principles are concerned. But the Act of 1844, besides its permanent and fundamental principles, contained many provisions that were partial, temporary, and provincial. It left the right of issue, other than those of the Bank of England, in such a state as to require re-consideration at the hands of Parliament at some future period. That being the case, the question arises and offers itself to the minds of all who have considered the subject of this measure, whether we can be ripe for legislation founded on this new principle for Scotland before we have considered and arrived at a definite conclusion with respect to the state of currency legislation in England. I do not hesitate to say, from various circumstances, that I think the time is approaching when the attention of Parliament ought to be given to several matters connected with the provisions of the Act of 1844; and on this account, I would venture to express a hope for the assent of the hon. Baronet to my main proposition, that we are not yet ripe for entertaining his view. If he asks when there will be a commencement of the general legislation which I have indicated, I can only say that I make the admission that circumstances have ripened in a considerable degree for such legislation, and that when we see a fitting opportunity for introducing the question to the notice of Parliament, we shall feel it our bounden duty to lose no time in doing so. But if the Government were to introduce a general measure, their first proceeding must be to endeavour to ascertain the opinion of Parliament with respect to the banking system of England; and it is quite clear that it could not be possible to adopt such a process as that, and likewise approach the consideration of the important conclusions that might be arrived at in the course of the present Session. I therefore feel obliged to vote against the present Bill; but I hope the House will not think that that vote implies an intention to proceed to immediate legislation on the subject, because it could not be possible for us to do justice to it under present circumstances. I have not professed any indiscriminate hostility to the principle of the Bill of the hon. Baronet, which, so far as I can gather, appears to be a correct one, and I cannot say that the *status quo* should be permanently maintained. On the contrary, my opinion is that from the state of the law of issue in England and the restrictions upon banking which the present law imposes in consequence of the possession of exclusive privileges by certain banking establishments, the time must come when it will be necessary for the Government to propose the adoption of some well-considered scheme for the further development and advancement of several of the provisions of the Acts of 1844 and 1845.

Mr. DUNLOP said, he had heard with much gratification the disavowal by the Chancellor of the Exchequer of any feeling of general hostility to the principle of the Bill, as well as his admission that Scotland stands in a peculiar position in consequence of the peculiar prejudices which in Scotland make the right of issuing notes essential to the establishment of a bank. When his hon. Friend the Member for Edinburgh (Mr. Black) talked of 800 banks, he ought to have said 800 offices, for the number of banks did not exceed thirteen in the whole country; and so long as the right of issue is confined to those banks, there must be a practical prohibition upon the establishment of any new bank. It was, in fact, a monopoly enjoyed by the bank of which the hon. Member was a governor, and a dozen others, of

The Chancellor of the Exchequer

so regulating the terms upon which they will make advances to the community as to make the largest possible profit for themselves. It was to give the right of issue against gold to any new bank that might be established, and so to put an end to the present monopoly, that this Bill was supported. The right hon. Gentleman the Chancellor of the Exchequer said, that the provisions of the Acts of 1844-5 were temporary, and had reference to the peculiar circumstances of the then existing banks; but these banks had a privilege of issue which went far beyond what was asked for by this Bill. They had a right of issue to the extent of the average of their issue in 1845 without any security whatever. They also had a right to issue against gold over and above the amount of the issue under the statute. So far from the issues of banks established under this Bill being placed in a weaker position than the old banks, they would rest on a much stronger foundation, inasmuch as the old banks had a large issue that was altogether unsecured, whilst the new banks would provide ample security for all their issue, whatever the amount might be. The Bill did not propose to interfere with the monetary system at all. It simply allowed the extension of a privilege which was now enjoyed by the existing banks, but on a more permanent footing, because it required that the new banks should have gold to the full extent of the issue of their notes, whilst the existing banks were only required to possess gold for their issue over and above the amounts which they were authorized to issue by the Act. This Bill could in no respect prevent the introduction of a general measure on the subject of banking.

Sir EDWARD COLEBROOKE said, he admitted that this Bill proposed legislation of a somewhat exceptional character; but, after the speech of the Chancellor of the Exchequer, no doubt can be entertained as to the justice of the principle on which it was founded. The right hon. Gentleman had not said one word in defence of the monopoly of the present banks; on the contrary, he confessed that there existed a practical evil, because the present system rendered it impossible for a new bank to be established in Scotland without the power of issue. The principle of the Bill was strictly in accordance with the Act of 1845, by which the Scotch banks had a power of issue conferred upon them which no bank in England was allowed to enjoy. They were permitted to exercise that privilege so far as their issues had extended; but if they exceeded that, it was provided that gold should be deposited against any further issue. The question is, why should that privilege be confined to a small number of banks? He contended with the hon. Baronet (Sir John Hay) that a privilege of that kind ought to be common to all banks, without restriction. He had no desire to reverse the legislation of 1844-5 —so far from it, he desired to support it. But when that Act was applied to Scotland it was upon a different principle from that which was applied to England. The Acts applicable to England were consistent in themselves, and there was an absolute restriction upon all new issues on the part of the country banks. That legislation provided for the extension of the banking and currency of the country, and the principle upon which it was applied by Sir Robert Peel was justly quoted by the hon. Member for Argyleshire (Mr. Finlay) that, while drawing a distinction between the power of issue and of banking, he wished to make banking free. Sir Robert Peel said—

" Our general rule is to draw a distinction between the privilege of Issue and the conduct of ordinary banking business. We think they stand on an entirely different footing. We think that the privilege of Issue is one which may be fairly and justly controlled by the State; and that the banking business, as distinguished from Issue, is a matter in respect to which there cannot be too unlimited and unrestricted a competition. The principle of competition, though unsafe in our opinion when applied to issue, ought, we think, to govern the business of banking."—[3 *Hansard,* lxxiv. 743.]

In Scotland, however, the Act of 1845 had operated as a positive bar to the establishment of new banks, and when banks had failed, their business and the profits arising therefrom had been divided amongst the old banks, which were now reduced to thirteen. Of course, concurrently with this, these establishments had considerably extended their branches and operations, and enjoy very great advantages. In a paper on the laws of currency in Scotland, by Mr. Gilbart, whose opinions on the subject were entitled to the greatest weight, and which was read before the British Association at Glasgow in the year 1856, ten years after Sir Robert Peel's measure had been in operation, there was this passage—

" The Act of 1845 has produced several practical effects in the management of the banks of Scotland. Had not the Act of 1845 been passed, it is probable that new banks of Issue would have been framed in Scotland during the speculations of the year 1846, and there might have been great competition between the old and the new banks. There is now among the banks a less spirit of competition than formerly. There are fewer attempts to attract customers by the offer of increased accommodation. There is a less disposition to grant cash credits, and less anxiety to obtain those accounts that put into circulation a large amount of notes. Some advances too have been made upon banking charges. The banks have attempted to reimburse themselves for the increased expense of keeping gold by charging a commission upon the amount of the cash credits, and upon payments made in London, thus confirming the doctrine that statesmen are slow to learn that restrictions on banks are a tax on the public."

He protested against leaving the question for an indefinite period in its present state, or until it should please the English Members of this House to agree to a change in respect of their own system. He looked upon the system in Scotland as an exceptional system, to which a special remedy can be applied if the Government and the House thought proper, without prejudice to the consideration of the entire subject of banking as it affected the United Kingdom. If, however, the general question must be entered upon in the first instance, he trusted that it would be done with the least possible delay.

Mr. KIRKMAN HODGSON said, that the principles of the Act of 1844 were correct, and ought to be made permanent. It had effected all that it was intended to effect—the convertibility of the bank note; and if it had not averted panics it was not intended for that purpose, which, indeed, was beyond the reach of legislation. The time was not far distant when the restrictions and privileges conferred by the Acts of 1844-5 would have to be re-considered; and when the time did come, he was of opinion that the English question ought, following the precedent of 1844, to precede the Scotch question. As to the Bill now before the House, if the hon. Baronet the Member for Wakefield persisted in his Motion, he should feel obliged to vote for the Amendment of the hon. Member for Edinburgh; but he hoped the hon. Baronet would consent to withdraw his Motion, and that the hon. Member for Edinburgh would also withdraw his Amendment, upon the understanding that the consideration of the question is only deferred for consideration and settlement, and that the Government will be shortly prepared to introduce a measure upon the subject.

Mr. CRUM-EWING addressed the House, but the hon. Member was very imperfectly heard.

Mr. BUCHANAN: Sir, as I represent a large commercial constituency, I must say that I have heard with some pleasure the statement of the right hon. Gentleman the Chancellor of the Exchequer, to the effect that he is prepared, on a future occasion, to take the whole question into consideration. I can assure the right hon. Gentleman that the opinions entertained by very many persons of the operation of the Act of 1844 are very different from those expressed by hon. Members who have addressed the House this evening. Sir Robert Peel when he introduced his Bill said, that his purpose was to give something like stability and certainty to the value of money; and I put it to the right hon. Gentleman whether that has been the result produced? Are we not at the present time exposed to perpetual vacillations in the value of money? I will not, however, enter into that question. Various and conflicting opinions as to how any Bill, which the right hon. Gentleman might introduce, would work, would no doubt be entertained. I am anxious to learn whether there would be a probability of our having a Report from any Committee to whom that Bill might be referred in a moderate space of time, and also whether that Report would likely be of such a nature as to satisfy the House. I cannot, for my part, see why we should defer legislation upon this question for an indefinite period, and I wish to remind the right hon. Gentleman the Chancellor of the Exchequer, that the main grievance of which we complain has not yet been brought forward. Issue and deposit banks are mixed up together, not only in the minds of the Scotch people, but as a consequence of existing legislation. The evil is, that there is no competition in banks of deposit, and that the trade of banking is unnecessarily narrowed. I think I could from papers in my hand supply the House with information which it is hardly prepared to receive. Is the House aware of the change which has taken place since the Act of 1845 was passed? We had twenty-four banks in Scotland in 1844. At present they are reduced to thirteen. We had shareholders in these banks holding £12,000,000 stock in 1844, and now we have only £9,000,000 of banking capital.

Mr. Kirkman Hodgson

And, in point of fact, although we have at present thirteen banks, only eight of them are of any consequence or extent. If any hon. Member will look at the schedule of the Bill introduced by the Chancellor of the Exchequer, he will see that the authorized issue of five out of the thirteen banks is so small as to be scarcely worth consideration. One of them is limited to £33,000, another to £42,000, while the average of the authorized issue of the five is £55,000. The remaining eight banks have an authorized issue of £2,476,000. Therefore, there are only eight real banks in Scotland for the purpose of bank accommodation, which, in my opinion, is quite inadequate. Nor is that the worst of it, for I am prepared to show that nearly all those banks are in Edinburgh. I do not object to their being located there, any more than I should to their being in Glasgow, except in so far as it gives them facilities for acquiring a monopoly which they would not otherwise have. Of these eight banks five are essentially Edinburgh establishments—one belongs partly to Edinburgh and partly to Glasgow, only one is a Glasgow establishment, and one belongs to the north of Scotland. There are thus five banks which are exclusively to Edinburgh, and you can easily see how they could work together if they felt so disposed. One or two will rule the rest; and as the managers are constantly meeting together, it is easy to see how small a number would pull the strings of this large banking machine. But that is not the worst of it. The Act of 1845 seems to contemplate the amalgamation of banks. So far from there being anything to prevent it, there is a clause inserted in the Act of 1845 facilitating such arrangements; so that, instead of there being eight banks, it is possible that there may soon be only half that number, and that we shall find a monopoly so far completed that one or two banks may control the whole banking and monetary system of Scotland. It appears to me that it is no argument to the objection as to the small number of banks of issue to say that there are numerous branches in different parts of Scotland. No doubt great practical conveniences and advantages have arisen from the establishment of those branches —no one can deny that; but, on the other hand, the machinery of those branch banks has tended to establish a monopoly. These bank agencies have worked so successfully that whereas, in 1843, £30,000,000 represented the amount of deposits in Scotland, there are now £60,000,000 of deposits. All this immense sum is under the control of one or two men in Edinburgh. I do not think that that is a position of affairs which we should be desirous of continuing. We have cast off the trammels of monopoly in other respects, and I think if the question were fairly put to the House, there are few who would say that the whole banking business of Scotland should be under the control of one or two men in the capital. The evil is so great that it ought not to be allowed longer to exist, and I shall be happy to hear when the Chancellor of the Exchequer is prepared to deal with the subject. I am not prepared to say that this Bill is one which in all its provisions I would be willing to adopt; but its main feature is to extend a principle which has already been introduced. Against gold there may be any extent of issue, and I cannot see what objection there can be made to the extension of that principle. As there may be much discussion of doubtful principles, and long delay, before we can arrive at a conclusion upon any Bill of the Chancellor of the Exchequer, I think we are justified in dividing in favour of the second reading of this Bill.

MR. KINNAIRD said, he thought it would be wise on the part of the hon. Baronet opposite not to press his Bill at the present moment, and that it would be better that they should first dispose of the measure introduced by the Chancellor of the Exchequer. As a Member for Scotland, he must express his surprise at the attack which had been made on the Scotch system of banking—though he thought that the speech of the hon. Member had, in a great measure, answered itself; for he had admitted that the amount of deposits in the Scotch banks had increased from £30,000,000 to £60,000,000 since the passing of the Act of 1845. In point of fact, at that moment, there was hardly a Highland village that had not adequate banking accommodation. It could hardly be called a monopoly when all those banking agencies were in competition with each other. In his opinion the existing system gave ample banking accommodation to the people of Scotland; and he believed that the Scotch people themselves were exceedingly attached to the system as it at present existed. He greatly doubted the policy of the present Bill, and

should certainly vote against the second reading. The speech of the Chancellor of the Exchequer had given great satisfaction to the people of Scotland; at all events, it showed that he had no objection to the introduction of improvements, though before introducing changes having that object in view, he was desirous that they should be well and carefully sifted.

MR. GOSCHEN said, that the value of money could not be fixed by Act of Parliament, any more than the value of any other commodity. The Act of 1844 had conferred great benefits on the country, and the occasions on which it was supposed by some persons to have broken down were scarcely cases in point. It was not at the instance of the Bank of England that the Act had been suspended, but at the instance of the public, who demanded greater accommodation than the law allowed the Bank to give. He hoped that in any legislative alteration the great principle of the Act of 1844 would be upheld.

MR. H. BAILLIE: Sir I agree with the hon. Member for Perth (Mr. Kinnaird), that it would be an absurdity to call the banking system of Scotland a monopoly, for although banks for issuing paper are restricted, all of them have large establishments with branches in almost every village in Scotland. There is scarcely a village in Scotland with a thousand inhabitants that has not a branch bank. At present there was no limitation to the establishment of banks in Scotland, except this—that it must be on the express understanding that they have no permission to issue paper. The Bill of my hon. Friend, if I rightly understand it, proposes to repeal the Bank Act of 1845, and establish virtually an unlimited paper currency in Scotland. It is true that the banks to be established could only issue paper upon retaining the same amount of gold in their coffers; but this is not affording to the public any security for the value of the notes. Suppose a bank is established which issues notes to the value of £100,000, and that it retains 100,000 sovereigns as reserve—that I take to be the proposal of my hon. and gallant Friend — but the 100,000 sovereigns would be no security for the notes, because the bank might have £1,000,000 of deposits, and if there should be a run on the bank the depositors would get possession of the gold, and the burden of the notes would be left without security. That would be the natural operation of allowing an unlimited amount of paper issue if you were obliged to retain gold to meet it. On the whole, I do not think that the House is likely to agree to a proposition for repealing the Bank Act of 1844. I believe it to have been perfectly successful, and I should be sorry to give my support to any Bill which in my opinion is calculated to impair it.

MR. BLACK: Sir, I wish to say that, after the discussion which has now taken place, in the event of the hon. Member opposite (Sir John Hay) being desirous of withdrawing his proposal, I shall not press the Amendment which I have moved.

SIR JOHN HAY: I wish to say a few words in explanation. After what has fallen from the Chancellor of the Exchequer, I think it would be wrong on my part to intercept the course of policy which he has indicated. I trust that at an early period he will endeavour to amend those parts of the Act of 1844 which press unduly on commerce. I do not accept the interpretation which the hon. Member for Inverness (Mr. H. Baillie), has placed upon the Bill; but throughout the debate, it seems to me that a fallacy has prevailed in the minds of some of the hon. Members who have addressed the House. They seem to think that a Bank of England note is a legal tender in Scotland. Such is not the case. It is there deprived of the character of a legal tender, which in England is a guarantee of its value. On the understanding that the Chancellor of the Exchequer intends soon to legislate upon this subject, gathering from his statement that his views coincide very much with mine, feeling that on this occasion I have obtained from him everything but his vote, and on the understanding also that the hon. Member for Edinburgh will withdraw his Amendment, I am prepared to withdraw the Bill.

THE CHANCELLOR OF THE EXCHEQUER: The understanding of the hon. Baronet is rather large. That I will very soon introduce a Bill is more than I can undertake; and I do not think that the remarks I made justify the hon. Gentleman in placing that construction upon my language. What I said was that the whole question requires careful consideration with a view of introducing Amendments into the present system, and that

Mr. H. Baillie

at some subsequent period I shall be prepared to enter on the subject.

Amendment, and Motion, by leave, *withdrawn.*

Bill *withdrawn.*

TRESPASS (IRELAND) BILL—[BILL 13.]
COMMITTEE.

Order for Committee read.
Bill *considered* in Committee.

(In the Committee.)

CAPTAIN ARCHDALL said, he had to bring under the notice of the Committee what appeared to him to be a breach of privilege. It would be in the recollection of hon. Members that during the discussion on the second reading of this Bill he stated that in Ireland the Sub-Inspector of police was sometimes a poacher. That statement had given great offence to the Irish police, and a violent and abusive article directed against him had appeared in a Dublin newspaper. The editor of that newspaper had also admitted into its columns a letter signed "Sub-Inspector," in which it was stated he (Captain Archdall) had sheltered himself under his privileges as a Member of Parliament, and stated what was a gross calumny and an unfounded slander, and what he would not have dared to utter out of that House. The Irish Members generally were included in the charge made by "Sub-Inspector;" for the letter stated that there was not one of them who would get up and defend the constabulary against the calumny. Now, when he made his former statement he did so on circumstances which were within his own personal knowledge, and also with the conviction that he could be corroborated by other hon. Members. A Sub-Inspector, quartered in a village on his own property, had made raids on his shooting ground. He was annoyed at this conduct, and remonstrated with the gentleman; but he neither summoned him before the magistrates nor reported him to the Inspector General, fearing that his dismissal from the force would be the result if he adopted the latter course. He, however, found that he had been mistaken in that supposition; for by the code of instructions issued to the police by Sir Henry Brownrigg, the Inspector General, he perceived that the Sub-Inspectors were allowed to shoot, fish, and hunt. The hon. Member for Galway (Mr. Gregory) some time ago invited a party of friends to shoot over his property; but an Inspector of police was beforehand with him, and when the hon. Member and his friends arrived there was nothing for them to shoot at. In the county of Donegal, Inspector Hill and Sub-Inspector Scully were warned off from fishing without permission in a river belonging to the Earl of Leitrim. Last year, at the Mohill Petty Sessions, a Sub-Inspector was fined in four instances in the mitigated penalty of £5 for using guns and dogs without a licence. The resident magistrate, Mr. Triston, who was on the bench, seemed to have acted as counsel for the Sub-Inspector, and threw every difficulty in the way of a conviction. It was not until after reference had been made for the opinion of the Law Officers of the Crown, the Revenue Department was able to carry out the punishment. He did not wish in the slightest degree to detract from the accomplishments of the Inspectors and Sub-Inspectors of the Irish constabulary. In light literature, the dead languages, and metaphysics they were not inferior to any hon. Gentleman in that House; and to see them in full dress reminded one of the 10th Hussars in the early days of George IV.; but he did not approve the manner in which they were organized; and he looked upon the appointment of Sir Henry Brownrigg as an unfortunate one.

Sir ROBERT PEEL said, he could not have expected that his hon. and gallant Friend would have made this attack upon the Irish constabulary without giving him notice of the particular cases to which he intended to refer. Had he done so he (Sir Robert Peel) would have been prepared to meet him; but though the topic which he has introduced has nothing to do with the subject which we are in Committee to consider, I cannot allow his reference to the Inspector General to pass without observing that the Irish constabulary is in a high state of efficiency, and that Sir Henry Brownrigg, who was appointed by Lord Eglinton, has received the thanks of successive Governments in Ireland. I believe the hon. and gallant Gentleman has referred to the estate of my hon. Friend the Member for Galway (Mr. Gregory) in connection with some little partridge shooting. I would ask the hon. and gallant Gentleman whether that was a very grave offence in that wild part of the country? Why, have we not all been accustomed, when the fancy took us, to sport, perhaps, a little unlawfully?

I have no hesitation in saying that when I was a boy at school I frequently poached. We all recollect hearing of the famous statesman who, when at Eton, poached on the manor of George III. And, Sir, are we not at this instant celebrating the tercentenary festival of Shakespeare, who was himself a poacher? I protest against those general charges being made on the Irish constabulary because a constable or sub-constable who has nothing else to do kills a snipe or a partridge. If the hon. and gallant Gentleman would bring forward this matter as a substantive Motion, he had no doubt he should be able to encounter him on the merits.

Mr. BAGWELL said, he hoped the House would not sanction any extension of the Game Laws in Ireland, and that was the object of this Bill. He was quite sure an attempt to do such a thing in England at the fag end of a Wednesday sitting would cause a revolution. ["Hear!"] It was all very well for hon. Members to laugh, but less things had caused a revolution. He was opposed to the Bill, and so convinced was he that it was radically wrong, that he moved that the Chairman leave the chair.

Mr. LONGFIELD said, that the Bill did not deserve the sweeping reprobation of the hon. Member for Clonmel. It proposed to do nothing more in Ireland than what had been done for the last forty years in this country. The simple object of the Bill was to enable the landlord in whom the property in the game on his estate was vested to prosecute in case of trespass, instead of throwing that duty on the occupying tenant.

Mr. M'CANN contended that the hon. and learned Gentleman was misleading the Committee by stating that that was the sole object of the Bill. The fact was that it was nothing more nor less than a proposal to introduce into Ireland the English Game Law.

Sir ROBERT PEEL said, the Game Law in Ireland was more oppressive than the Game Law in England. At present fines for poaching were inflicted to the extent of £10; this Bill would make the maximum penalty £2 only. The measure, so far as the purpose to which it was directed was concerned, would make the law less oppressive and more effective.

Mr. MAGUIRE said, he could see no reason why the law in Ireland should be changed in the manner proposed by this Bill. Reading daily in the papers the mischief that arose in England from the Game Laws, he was by no means anxious to see those laws introduced into Ireland.

MR. FERRAND said, game could not be preserved by legislation, but only by a good feeling between landlord and tenant. He supported the Bill.

MR. BUTT said, it was impossible to conceive a Bill framed in a more oppressive spirit than the measure now under consideration. Whilst in England the magistrates had the power of mitigating the penalty, in Ireland the magistrates would be obliged to impose a penalty of £1, and if the penalty should not be paid the offender must be committed for two months.

MR. W. ORMSBY GORE said, he was prepared to make the penalty the same as that in the English Bill.

MR. O'REILLY objected to the Bill, which not only introduced a new class of offences, but imposed a high and excessive standard of penalties. It was his intention to oppose the Bill at every stage.

And it being now Six of the clock,

House *resumed*.

Committee report Progress; to sit again *To-morrow.*

VALUATION OF LANDS AND HERITAGES (SCOTLAND) ACT AMENDMENT BILL.

On Motion of *Mr. Dunlop*, Bill to amend the Act for the Valuation of Lands and Heritages in Scotland, *ordered* to be brought in by Mr. DUNLOP, Sir JAMES FERGUSSON, and Mr. BAXTER.

Bill *presented*, and read 1°. [Bill 81.]

SEAT OF UNDER SECRETARY OF STATE.

Second Report *brought up*, and read, as follows:—

The Select Committee appointed to inquire whether the Under Secretary of State who was last appointed to that Office thereby vacated his Seat, have further considered the matters to them referred, and have come to the following Resolution, which they have agreed to report to the House:—

That the Seat of the Under Secretary of State last appointed is not vacated.

Report to lie upon the Table, and to be *printed.* (No. 244.)

House adjourned at ten minutes before Six o'clock.

HOUSE OF LORDS,

Thursday, April 28, 1864.

MINUTES.]—PUBLIC BILLS—*First Reading*—Fish Teinds (Scotland)* (No. 62).
Second Reading—Regius Professorship of Greek (Oxford) (No. 44); Registration of County Voters (Ireland)* (No. 50).
Third Reading—Punishment of Rape (No. 52); Joint Stock Companies (Foreign Countries)* (No. 45), and *passed.*
Royal Assents—Consolidated Fund (£15,000,000) [27 Vict. c. 11];
Bills of Exchange and Promissory Notes (Ireland) [27 Vict. c. 7];
Conveyancers, &c. (Ireland) [27 Vict. c. 8.]
Malt for Animals [27 Vict. c. 9];
Union Relief Aid Acts Continuance [27 Vict. c. 10];
Warehousing of British Spirits [27 Vict. c. 12].

SEAT OF GOVERNMENT IN INDIA.

QUESTION.

THE EARL OF ELLENBOROUGH said, the Department of the Colonies having been transferred from the noble Duke (the Duke of Newcastle) who had for a considerable time discharged the duties of Secretary of State with great efficiency and ability, he wished to put some Questions regarding India to the noble Lord opposite, the newly appointed Under Secretary for the Colonial Department (Lord Wodehouse). The first Question he wished to ask related to the seat of Government in India. The most contradictory reports appeared in the public newspapers on the subject. One of those reports declared that the seat of Government was to be removed from Calcutta to the Upper Provinces; whilst another report was that a despatch had been received by the Governor General from the Secretary of State directing that no change should take place. He wished to ask the noble Lord, Whether either of those reports were true; and, if so, which of them?

LORD WODEHOUSE: The answer which I have to give is this—that no opinion had been expressed by the right hon. Gentleman the Secretary for India with regard to the removal of the seat of Government. The matter was, no doubt, an important one, but no decision had been come to on the subject.

THE EARL OF ELLENBOROUGH said, it would probably aid the Secretary of State in coming to a decision on the subject, to know that the late Duke of Wellington had more than once expressed to him (the Earl of Ellenborough) his decided opinion that the Government of India, depending for its support upon our maritime power, should be in a position to maintain always certain and free communication with that power; and that the seat of Government in India should be in a place unattackable by land or by sea, as it is now.

DISPOSAL OF THE NATIVE DEAD.
QUESTION.

THE EARL OF ELLENBOROUGH said, he had another Question to put to the noble Lord relating to a matter of rather recent occurrence in India. He wished to know, Whether it was the intention of the Bengal Government to interfere with the custom of the Natives in disposing of their dead by throwing them into the Hooghly; and, if so, whether that order had been communicated to the Governor General previous to its promulgation?

LORD WODEHOUSE was understood to state, that no official information had been received at the India Office, but the Secretary of State had heard that the order of the Bengal Government prohibiting the throwing of dead bodies into the river Hooghly was issued with the sanction of the Governor General. His right hon. Friend had also heard that the order for removing the burning-place to a greater distance from Calcutta was not published with the previous sanction of the Governor General, but was issued by the Governor of Bengal upon his own responsibility.

THE EARL OF ELLENBOROUGH said, he could not but regret that, before the order was issued prohibiting the throwing of the dead bodies into the river, some arrangements had not been made to enable the Natives to dispose of those bodies by burning, and thereby to have avoided any ground for a disturbance of the peace of the country; and that the order for removing the burning places, a matter so deeply affecting the feelings of the people, should have been published without the previous sanction of the Governor General residing within a few hundred yards of the Governor of Bengal.

PUNISHMENT OF RAPE BILL—[BILL 52.]
THIRD READING.

Bill read 3ª (according to Order).

LORD WODEHOUSE said, on a former occasion, he had given notice of an Amendment which he intended to move on the third reading. The punishment of flogging might be very appropriate in many cases of rape, but was not necessarily so in all, and the object of his Amendment was to render it discretionary, and not compulsory, on the Judges to order the infliction of flogging in addition to the other punishment in cases of conviction. This would be effected by striking out the word "shall" from the first clause, and restoring the word "may" as it stood in the original Bill.

Amendment *moved*, to reinstate the word ("may") in lieu of the word ("shall").

LORD WENSLEYDALE opposed the Amendment upon the ground, that if the punishment of flogging were to be inflicted at all for the crime, that sentence should be made compulsory.

THE LORD CHANCELLOR said, that it was necessary to consider what would be the effect of a particular kind of punishment, not only as deterring from crime, but as influencing a jury in convicting a prisoner. Now, however much the Judges might differ as to the propriety of inflicting the punishment of whipping at all in the cases to which the Bill referred, they were, he believed, unanimous in holding that, if authorised, a discretionary power should be given to Judges to inflict it. If it were made compulsory it would tend to produce a greater disinclination in juries to convict than existed at present. He had previously received the opinions of the Judges of the Common Pleas and Exchequer in that sense; and he had since learned the unanimous opinion of the Judges of the Queen's Bench, to the same effect, through a letter from the Lord Chief Justice. That learned Judge stated it to be his persuasion that the reluctance and hesitation of juries to convict did not arise from any want of a proper abhorrence of the offence, but from the frequency of cases in which this charge was made either without any foundation, or where the woman turned round upon the man to whom she had given encouragement. Hence the Judges thought that to make flogging compulsory would have the effect of increasing the disinclination of juries to convict, and that it would be better to make it discretionary.

THE MARQUESS OF WESTMEATH said, after what he had heard he should be unwilling to do anything that would be likely to endanger the result of trials of this character. He would therefore assent to the Amendment.

EARL GREY said, that the arguments contained in the letter of the Lord Chief Justice did not bear out the conclusion which it announced. He had no doubt that charges of rape were frequently made without just grounds. No man, however, ought to be convicted unless there was a reasonable certainty of his guilt; and in such a case he did not see why a jury should be indisposed to convict merely because the consequent punishment would be a flogging. In his opinion the sort of punishment which was inflicted on an animal was exceedingly fit and appropriate as the penalty of so brutal a crime.

On Question, their Lordships *divided*: Contents, 55; Not-Contents, 20; Majority, 35.

Resolved in the *Affirmative*.

THE MARQUESS OF WESTMEATH, in moving that the Bill do pass, expressed his opinion that it was most injudicious ever to have taken away the capital punishment for offences of this sort where more than one person was concerned.

Bill *passed*, and sent to the Commons.

CONTENTS.

Westbury, L. (*L. Chancellor*).

Devonshire, D.
Somerset, D.

Bath, M.
Bristol, M.
Westmeath, M.

Albemarle, E.
Bandon, E.
Bantry, E.
Carnarvon, E.
Cathcart, E.
Clarendon, E.
De Grey, E.
Ducie, E.
Effingham, E.
Hardwicke, E.
Home, E.
Lucan, E. [*Teller.*]
Romney, E.
Saint Germans, E.
Stanhope, E.
Stradbroke, E.
Verulam, E.
Wicklow, E.

Eversley, V.
Hardinge, V.
Leinster, V. (*D. Leinster*).
Sydney, V.

St. Asaph, Bp.

Annaly, L.
Aveland, L.
Belper, L.
Boyle, L. (*E. Cork and Orrery*).
Carew, L.
Chelmsford, L.
Chesham, L.
Clandeboye, L. (*L. Dufferin and Claneboye*).
Cranworth, L.
Dacre, L.
Dartrey, L. (*L. Cremorne*).
Foley, L.
Houghton, L.
Lismore, L. (*V. Lismore*).
Methuen, L.
Monson, L.
Overstone, L.
Ponsonby, L. (*E. Bessborough*).
Rivers, L.
Rosebery, L. (*E. Rosebery*).
Saltersford, L. (*E. Courtown*).
Skene, L. (*E. Fife*).
Somerhill, L. (*M. Clanricarde*).
Stanley of Alderley, L.
Taunton, L.
Wodehouse, L. [*Teller.*]

The Marquess of Westmeath

Marlborough, D.

Derby, E.
Ellenborough, E.
Grey, E. [*Teller.*]
Harrowby, E.

Hawarden, V.

Churston, L.
Colville of Culross, L.
Congleton, L.
Dunsany, L.
Harris, L.

Hunsdon, L. (*V. Falkland*).
Inchiquin, L.
Lyttelton, L.
Lyveden, L.
Silchester, L. (*E. Longford*).
Sundridge, L. (*D. Argyll*).
Tredegar, L.
Wensleydale, L. [*Teller.*]
Wynford, L.

REGIUS PROFESSORSHIP OF GREEK (OXFORD) BILL.

[BILL 44.] SECOND READING.

Order of the Day for the Second Reading read.

Moved, That the Bill be now read 2ª.— (*The Lord Chancellor.*)

THE EARL OF DERBY said, that in some respects the Bill was likely to attain a good object, and he was informed that, upon the whole, the University of Oxford were desirous to see the measure passed. But while he did not intend to offer any decided objection to the second reading, the Bill seemed to him to be open to some serious objections. The chief of these was, that by the operation of this Bill it would become necessary that the Professor of Greek should be a clergyman; and although, undoubtedly, there were among the clergymen as well qualified as any others for the duties of the Professorship, yet these duties were not such as appertained exclusively to clergymen, or for which they were peculiarly adapted. If such a Bill had been in operation some years ago in the sister University, the result would have been that Professor Porson would have been disqualified from occupying the office of Greek Professor there. The present Professor of Greek at Oxford was a man of extreme ability, who had laboured most zealously in the duties of the Professorship, and it was needless to say that the wretched stipend of £40 a year was totally inadequate to remunerate a man who was both a gentleman and a scholar. But then came the difficulty of assigning an endowment for the Professorship out of the revenues of the Church, thereby rendering it necessary to select a clergyman for this office.

THE LORD CHANCELLOR said, the Crown appointed to the Regius Professorship of Greek.

THE EARL OF DERBY said, he was quite aware of that, and it was one of the chief points of objection. The chief merit of this Bill was that it was likely to put an end to the unhappy controversy that existed in the University on the subject of the remuneration of the Greek Professor. The members of the University had been actuated by two motives in not granting an augmentation of the salary; first, that such a course would be looked upon as a tacit approval of the sentiments put forth by the present Regius Professor, to which the majority of the University were opposed; and, in the second place, they objected to endow out of the University funds a Professorship with respect to which they exercised no choice, the appointment being in the Crown. The noble and learned Lord met one part of this difficulty by proposing to assign to the Professorship as an endowment one of the canonries in the gift of the Crown. But this carried with it the necessity that the Regius Professor of Greek shall always be a clergyman. This he (the Earl of Derby) objected to, not only because of their limitation, but because it would still further increase the number of canonries to which special duties elsewhere than in their cathedrals were attached. Such was the case at Gloucester, at Norwich, and at Rochester. At Gloucester, where the number of canonries was now four, one of them was attached to the Mastership of Pembroke College, Oxford; at Norwich two canons had separate duties assigned to them; and at Rochester three had duties assigned to them separate from those connected with the cathedral. He confessed he had great doubt whether this was a proper mode of legislation. No doubt, if the noble and learned Lord should hold office until the canonry should fall vacant, it would be quite competent to him to endow the Greek Professorship with it; but he could not help thinking that such a course was open to grave objections. At the same time, with the feeling in the University that it was most desirable to get rid of the anomaly of a Professorship founded by the Crown and endowed by the University, he should not take upon himself the responsibility of asking their Lordships to reject the Bill on the second reading.

THE EARL OF ELLENBOROUGH said, he quite agreed with his noble Friend in all the objections which he had stated against this measure, but there were others of a very serious kind to which the noble

Earl had not adverted. He could not consent to take away one of the very few rewards which were left for hard-working clergymen, and apply it to secular purposes. He was aware that this had been done in other cases, but the precedent was bad, and it was better to make a good precedent than follow a bad one. What was the use of teaching critical Greek? He would much rather at all times, but more especially at present, when clergymen were called to defend the very foundation of the Christian faith, that they would apply themselves to theology than to the peculiarities of Greek literature. He objected, therefore, to force, as it were, a clergyman upon that Professorship. He would not enter into the peculiar opinions which Professor Jowett might entertain. Those opinions were not sufficient grounds for refusing to give him an adequate remuneration. He wished the Professor had a remuneration adequate to his great abilities and knowledge, and doubtless he ought to have it. But knowing what Professor Jowett's opinions were, and that they were contrary to those of the vast majority of the members of the Church of England, he could not consent by Act of Parliament to allow to devolve upon that gentleman a piece of preferment belonging to the Church of England. It would be done knowingly — indirectly, indeed, but still knowingly — and that he did not think right. It was the duty of Government and of Parliament, whenever Parliament was called upon to act, to preserve the whole patronage of the Church of England for the benefit of those who were unmistakably and wholly members of that Church, and who agreed with the vast majority of those who professed its doctrine.

THE LORD CHANCELLOR said, he could not conceal his regret that the noble Earl who had just spoken, and to whom their Lordships always listened with so much pleasure and even instruction, had, on the present occasion, departed—in his humble judgment—from the usages which ordinarily governed that House. There was nothing in the world which he deprecated more than that theological controversy should be introduced into a discussion of that kind. He had carefully abstained from doing so on introducing the Bill, and the noble Earl (the Earl of Derby) who had most properly drawn attention to the difficulties inherent in the nature of the case, had not only abstained from theological discussions, but had given this cheering assurance that, upon the whole, the measure was satisfactory to the great body of the University, and had been accepted by them in the spirit in which it was offered, as the best remedy under the circumstances which could be devised, and one calculated to prevent the recurrence of the painful scenes they had lately witnessed. The noble Earl (the Earl of Ellenborough) said that one of the rewards of Churchmen would be taken from the Church and given to a secular purpose, and then he talked of critical Greek not being necessary for a clergyman. Did the noble Earl mean to contend that the most acute critical knowledge of Greek was not of the greatest importance—was not essential for clergymen, even for the purpose of defending the very foundations of the Faith? Did the noble Earl mean that the highest critical knowledge of Greek was not necessary in a University where the great majority of the students were destined for the Church? He (the Lord Chancellor) must offer the strongest possible opposition to such a doctrine, and protest against its being accepted for one moment. Well, then, what better purpose could the canonry be given for? He came now to the more important objections of the noble Earl the Chancellor of the University (the Earl of Derby). And first with regard to the supposed exclusion of a layman from the Professorship. It was perfectly true that this Bill did not provide for the alternative of appointing a layman to the Greek chair, if such a person should be selected on account of his peculiar endowments. But suppose there should be at Oxford a layman as eminent for his knowledge of Greek as Professor Porson of Cambridge, the Crown would say to the University, "It is our desire to appoint that man, but inasmuch as the canonry cannot be applied to his sustentation, will the University consent for this particular occasion to make provision for him?" He could not suppose for a moment that the University would be slow in making provision for a case which would happen in the proportion of about one to ninety-nine out of 100. There had not been a single lay Professor—he spoke under correction, but such was the result of his inquiries—in the chair of Greek from the time of its first institution to the present day. Therefore, this Bill had the merit of providing for a state of thing which, judging from past experience, from the present condition of affairs, and from the expectation of the

The Lord Chancellor

future, was most likely to occur; and if a case should arise which the Bill did not provide for, he had no doubt that the University would make the necessary provision. Their Lordships would remember that the University of Oxford had received certain pecuniary exemptions on the understanding that it would make proper provision for its Professors. First of all it enjoyed an exemption from stamp duties on its degrees; it was also exempted from the patent of the Queen's Printer— a benefit amounting in value, as he was informed, to £12,000 or £14,000 a year. In addition to that, by the late Oxford University Act, colleges were enabled by the suppression of some of their scholarships and otherwise to make provision for the public Professors. Now, he was perfectly ready to attach to this Bill a proviso of this character—that whenever the University or any college would make a permanent endowment for the chair of Greek to the amount of £600 per annum, the canonry which he proposed to attach to the chair would be placed at the disposal of the University, if the endowment was made by the University; or of the college, if the endowment was made by the college. If, then, the objection was real—he did not mean on the part of the noble Earl, for the noble Earl was incapable of making any objection which he did not believe to be real— let the University meet the Bill by the provision which he had suggested, and he would most readily introduce a clause to the effect that the endowment should be the price of the canonry, and that the canonry should be placed in the gift of the University. The difficulty which had occurred in this case had not been raised during the passing of the Act 3 & 4 *Vict.*, by which it was provided that as soon as might be convenient two canonries in the cathedral church of Ely should be permanently annexed to the Regius Professorship of Hebrew and Greek respectively in the University of Cambridge. No objection was then raised on the ground that the Professor of Greek at Cambridge might be a layman; but now it was said that another Porson might arise, and that the effect of this Bill would be to compel the Government to give the chair of Greek to a clergyman. Although he would admit that the effect of the Bill would be greatly to influence the election of a clergyman, yet it did not by any means render it indispensable that a clergyman should receive the appointment The Legislature had provided that no person should be capable of receiving the appointment of dean, archdeacon, or canon until he should have been a certain time in complete orders, except in the case of a canonry annexed to a professorship or the headship of a college. The Regius Professorship of Greek at Cambridge was provided for by a canonry, and why not the Regius Professor of Greek at Oxford? The Professor of Ecclesiastical History need not be a clergyman, yet he was provided for by a canonry. The Regius Professor of Hebrew need not be a clergyman, yet he was provided for by a canonry in both Universities, and only by a canonry. He trusted that their Lordships would share in the sympathy felt for the eminent person who now displayed so much ability, zeal, and energy in the discharge of his duties, and who was by none more admired and beloved than by the youth of the University. He hoped that their Lordships would have no difficulty in acceding to the second reading, and that the effect of the Bill would not be marred by a division. When their Lordships went into Committee he would propose some Amendments which would, he trusted, obviate some of the objections to which the measure might appear to be fairly open.

THE EARL OF HARROWBY said, that having had the honour of being one of the Oxford University Commissioners, he might be allowed to say a few words on this subject. In other cases the Commissioners were able to offer the Colleges a share in the patronage; but in the case of the Regius Professorship of Greek the difficulty was twofold. The first was one of a personal character, and arose from an unwillingness on the part of the colleges to identify themselves with the opinions of the gentleman in question. The Commissioners, in the next place, had no power to give the Colleges any share in the appointment, which was vested in the Crown. They were obliged, therefore, to leave their work imperfect in this respect. It appeared that the Regius Professor of Greek at Cambridge was provided for by a canonry, and he did not see why an objection should be felt to do that at Oxford which was already done in Cambridge. He believed that a canonry was just the appropriate reward for learned men in the Church, and there could hardly be a better application of it than to attach it to an office which must be held by an eminent scholar. He thought that no practical difficulty would arise from the Professor's

absence, and that he might without inconvenience reside for three months in the year at his canonry. He considered that it was a very graceful act on the part of the Government to give up a valuable piece of patronage for an object so praiseworthy in itself, and which it was hoped would have the effect of allaying much of the dissension that had arisen in the University on this matter.

EARL GREY could not say that either the noble and learned Lord on the Woolsack or the noble Earl who had just sat down (the Earl of Harrowby) had in his opinion given any satisfactory answer to the objections that had been raised to this Bill. It was very desirable that nothing should be done to restrict education to clergymen alone. He had no objection to see a clergyman fill the chair of Greek if he were properly qualified, but he could not think it desirable that so important an appointment should be practically confined to one profession. The Lord Chancellor had expressed his belief that if a layman—another Porson—were appointed to the chair, the University would make an adequate provision for him; but it was a curious recommendation of the Act that it must be set aside whenever the Crown appointed a layman to fill the chair. He could not think it would become the dignity of Parliament to pass a measure which would have to depend for its fulfilment on the course to be pursued by the University; and, in his opinion, if they interfered at all in the matter, their legislation ought to be of a complete and final character. The noble and learned Lord had shown that the Legislature had done in the case of Cambridge what it was now asked to do for the same chair at Oxford. But because they had made a mistake with respect to Cambridge, was it wise to repeat it at Oxford? He thought it a valid objection that it withdrew so valuable a piece of Church preferment from the rewards of purely clerical service. In the metropolis there were many devoted clergymen who had toiled for the greater portion of their lives in populous parishes upon scanty stipends. After a time it was frequently found that the health of these clergymen broke down, and a canonry would afford a well merited retreat in their advanced years. He confessed that he was not reconciled to the measure by the Amendments which the noble and learned Lord proposed to introduce. He should view with strong objections any arrangement under which the canonry would cease to be attached to the Professorship, and the patronage given to the University, in return for a suitable endowment for the Professor of Greek to be provided by that body. He did not think the University a proper body to exercise the patronage of the canonries of the Church; and, if Parliament having full power to legislate directly on the subject, refrained from exercising its authority in a straightforward manner, the attempt to bribe the University to fix an endowment upon the Greek Professorship would be utterly unbecoming. At the same time, he concurred with the noble and learned Lord in regretting that in discussions upon this subject reference had been made to the religious opinions of the Professor; it would have been far better for the question to be considered totally irrespective of the views imputed to that very distinguished scholar, and his own opinion had certainly been formed free from any such influences. He could not think it creditable to the University of Oxford that they should upon such grounds have refused an adequate remuneration to the holder of the office.

THE EARL OF CARNARVON said, that the opinion of the University of Oxford, especially when backed by that of his noble Friend (the Earl of Derby), must carry very great weight, and he should certainly rejoice at the carrying of any measure which would tend to allay the unfortunate antagonism and irritation existing in that University, in reference to the remuneration of this Professorship. Any fair compromise would be hailed, he was sure, by those who loved the University. But after what had passed, both in that House and out of doors, he felt that objections were capable of being urged to the Bill, and he could not divest himself of the impression that the proposal was most unfortunate which virtually required that the Regius Professor of Greek should henceforward be a clergyman; for it could not be reasonably expected that any but a clergyman would be appointed when in one case there was to be an income provided for him, and in the other none at all. He thought also that it would be an unfortunate thing in the present state of the Church to withdraw from her ministers one of the few remaining prizes and emoluments fairly applicable to the rewarding of long services or great ability; but he thought it beneath the dignity of the

Earl Grey

Crown to bargain with the University of Oxford as to the terms on which she should remunerate the Professor of Greek; and, in fact, the proposal was hardly fair to the Professor himself; for with the limited number of canons to which the cathedral of Rochester had been reduced, he thought that a continuous residence at Oxford would be found imcompatible with the performance of the ecclesiastical duties, or *vice versâ*. He would also add that it appeared to him highly improper that Parliament should legislate upon the assumption, that if a distinguished layman should hereafter be appointed to the Professorship, the University might, in the exercise of their discretion, remunerate him from their own funds.

THE BISHOP OF LONDON said, when the Oxford University Commission was in existence several years ago, it appeared that the endowment of this Professorship of Greek was made out of an estate or estates belonging to Christ Church College. The endowment was £40 a year, but the real value of the estate must now be some £600 a year. The natural impression of the Members of the Commission was that the Professor ought to receive the real and not what had once been the nominal value of the estates out of which he was paid. But it was afterwards urged, on behalf of Christ Church, that legislation had diverted the funds of Christ Church from their original channel by compelling them to make provision for two other Professorships. As legislation had caused the difficulty, it ought to remedy it. In the meantime, however, a great hardship had been inflicted upon the Professor of Greek. He appreciated the full force of the objection that this Bill would practically restrict the appointments to this Professorship to clergymen; but the evil would not practically be very great, for he was happy to know that by far the greater part of our eminent Greek scholars had been clergymen of the Established Church, and there was no reason to apprehend that in future there would be any difficulty in finding men properly qualified among that body to discharge the duties of the Greek Professorship. It was true that under the Bill another class of ecclesiastics would be prevented from receiving appointments to one of those canonries; and no one could feel more strongly than he did the desirableness of reserving such preferments for clergymen who had passed their lives in the discharge of laborious parochial duties. But this was only one of a number of canonries, and he should be glad to be assured that none of them would ever be worse disposed of than by attaching it to an office whose holder must be one of the most eminent Greek scholars in the country. He could not, besides, help remembering that the scheme for the reform of the University of Oxford, which had been conceived in 1850, could not be completed in one of its most important features, while the Greek Professorship remained unprovided and without any adequate remuneration.

The Duke of MARLBOROUGH said, in addition to the objections on account of theological opinions which had been felt against the endowment of this chair, there was felt one in many minds on the ground that while the endowment was to come from the University, the patronage of the Professorship remained vested in the Crown. He could hardly sympathize with the remarks which had been made by the right rev. Prelate as to the large number of canonries which now existed. Those preferments had lately been considerably reduced, both in amount and in number. There were now only thirty-five or forty left, and he thought that these rewards of the clergy ought to be further diminished, either in number or value. As a solution to the difficulty which this Bill was intended to meet, he suggested that the Government should advise Her Majesty to surrender the patronage of the Professorship to the University, in which case he had no doubt that the University would be induced to provide an endowment. If their Lordships divided upon this question, he should support the objections of the noble Earl below him (the Earl of Ellenborough).

The Earl of DERBY said, he had not very recently been to the University, but he had sent down a copy of the Bill. He did not believe that the question had been deliberated on up to this time by the University; but though he did not wish to commit the University in the matter, he might say that he had heard that the Bill was likely to be accepted. After all that was said on the subject he still adhered to his former position; but he would not take upon himself the absolute rejection of the Bill on its second reading. At the same time he hoped that the objections which had been offered would be well considered before the Committee was appointed, and that ample time would be given to the University and those who took a deep interest in the subject to consider the Amendments, which he hoped would be printed and distributed before the Bill went into Committee. If their Lordships should divide upon the question of the second reading, he was very unwilling to support the Bill as it stood; but if the question was, whether the Bill be summarily rejected, or be allowed to proceed to the second reading, he should feel himself obliged to support the second reading.

Motion *agreed to :* Bill read 2ª accordingly, and *committed* to a Committee of the Whole House.

House adjourned at a quarter before
Seven o'clock, till To-morrow,
half past Ten o'clock.

HOUSE OF COMMONS,

Thursday, April 28, 1864.

MINUTES.]—Supply—*considered in Committee* —Committee, R.P.
Public Bills — *Ordered* — Union Assessment Committee Act Amendment*.
First Reading—Union Assessment Committee Act Amendment* [Bill 83].
Second Reading—Local Government Supplemental* [Bill 80]; Promissory Notes and Bills of Exchange (Ireland)* [Bill 74].
Select Committee—On Cattle Disease Prevention and Cattle, &c., Importation, Mr. Bruce *added*.
Committee — Customs and Inland Revenue* [Bill 82].
Report—Customs and Inland Revenue*.
Third Reading—Court of Chancery (Despatch of Business)* [Bill 69] (*Lords*), and *passed*.
Withdrawn — Landed Property Improvement (Ireland) Act Amendment* [Bill 2].

INDIA—ARMY MEDICAL OFFICERS.

QUESTION.

Colonel SYKES said, he would beg to ask the Secretary of State for India for an explanation of a "Head Quarter" Circular, addressed to "British" Army Medical Officers in India, calling for volunteers for the "New Line Corps and Brigades of Royal Artillery."

Sir CHARLES WOOD was understood to say that he had received no such order, and was not aware of its existence.

CANADA—DUTY ON MANUFACTURED GOODS.—QUESTION.

Mr. AYTOUN said, he would beg to ask the Secretary of State for the Colonies, Whether he is in possession of such information as would enable him to lay upon the table of the House Returns of the number of persons employed in Canada in manufacturing such descriptions of goods as are charged with duty on entering that country ; and, if so, whether he has any objection to do so ? And if any efforts have at any time been made to induce the Canadian Government to remove or reduce the duties charged upon British goods entering Canada ; and, if so, whether he has any objection to lay upon the table of the House copies of any Correspondence which may have taken place upon this subject ?

Mr. CARDWELL, in reply, said, he was ready to lay the Correspondence on the table if his hon. Friend would move for it. With reference to the first part of the Question, he had not in his possession any information to enable him to make the Returns.

STATUE OF RICHARD CŒUR DE LION.
QUESTION.

Mr. THOMSON HANKEY said, he wished to ask the First Commissioner of Works, Why the bas-reliefs intended to be placed on the base of the statue of Richard Cœur de Lion in Palace Yard have not been so placed ; and whether he will communicate with Baron Marochetti, and have them done at an early period ?

Mr. COWPER replied, that the sculptor had been asked to furnish designs, but the matter was still under consideration.

WEIGHTS AND MEASURES.
QUESTION.

Mr. LOCKE said, he wished to ask the President of the Board of Trade, Whether any communications have been received by Her Majesty's Government from the Astronomer Royal and Comptroller General of the Exchequer as to the urgent necessity for an adjustment and re-verification of the Exchequer standards of Weight and Measure; and, if so, the date thereof ; whether any steps have been taken for effecting such adjustment and re-verification ; and, if so, when the same will be completed; whether any representations have been made with a view of relaxing the Law against tradesmen for small deviations in their Weights and Measures until the standards have been ad-

Mr. Aytoun

justed and re-verified ; and whether it is the intention of Her Majesty's Government to submit any Bill to Parliament this Session, in reference to the present state of the Law relating to Weights and Measures ?

Mr. MILNER GIBSON said, in reply, that a communication had been received from the Astronomer Royal to the Comptroller General of the Exchequer, dated February 1, 1859. It had been transmitted to the Secretary of State for the Home Department, with a letter from the Comptroller General, dated February 9, 1859. It would be found printed and appended to the Report of the Committee on Weights and Measures in 1862. Since that time the Report of the Astronomer Royal to the Treasury, dated March 30, 1864, as Chairman of the Standard Committee, lately revived by the Treasury for the examination of the national standards, had been received, transmitting a Resolution of the Committee of March 16, 1864, with reference to the re-verification of the Exchequer standards—

"That the Committee entirely recognize the importance of this subject, and the necessity for again urging it on the attention of the Government."

No official instructions had yet been issued for effecting that object, the subject being still under the consideration of the Treasury. Two letters addressed to the President of the Board of Trade by Mr. James Hayman, as secretary of the Society for Promoting the Interests of the Trading Community, dated respectively July 10, 1863, and September 26, 1863, had been received ; but, as at present advised, it did not seem necessary that any Bill should be brought in to alter the law imposing penalties for small deviations in weights and measures.

ROYAL COURT OF JERSEY.
QUESTION.

Mr. SCLATER-BOOTH said, he would beg to ask the Secretary of State for the Home Department, Whether he has any objection to produce the Correspondence between himself and the Lieutenant Governor of Jersey, relative to proposed alterations in the constitution of the Royal Court in that Island ?

Sir GEORGE GREY, in reply, said, there would be no objection to produce the Correspondence, which would be in continuation of that produced last Session.

PATENT LAW COMMISSION.
QUESTION.

Mr. DILLWYN said, he would beg to ask the Secretary of State for the Home Department, When the Patent Law Commission will make their Report ?

Lord STANLEY said, as he was Chairman of the Commission, he would answer the Question. He hoped to have the Report ready about Whitsuntide. It would have been ready before now, but it had been delayed through the necessity of sending communications to the Chambers of Commerce and other public bodies who had to make their Returns, some of which had not yet been received.

SHEFFIELD AND BRADFORD RESERVOIRS.—QUESTION.

Mr. FERRAND said, he rose to ask the Secretary of State for the Home Department, Whether Mr. Rawlinson has sent in his Report on the state of the Sheffield Reservoirs ; if so, whether he will lay it upon the table of the House ; if he has yet sent in his Report on the Bradford Reservoirs ; and if he has been engaged in inspecting any other than the Sheffield and Bradford Reservoirs under the authority of the Home Office ?

Sir GEORGE GREY, in reply, said, Mr. Rawlinson had not yet sent in his Report on the state of the Reservoirs. He had been very much engaged in Lancashire. He was sure the hon. Gentleman wished the Report when sent in should be complete. But Mr. Rawlinson had assured him, a few days ago, that he had been preparing his report, in communication with Mr. Beardmore, with regard to the Sheffield Reservoir, Mr. Beardmore being associated with him in that examination. He had also promised to furnish Reports on the Bradford Reservoir, and had inspected two other Reservoirs, one near Dewsbury, and the other at Burnley, in Lancashire. That was a Reservoir erected out of money raised under the Public Works Act. He said in regard to all the Reservoirs that were considered unsafe the water had been drawn off, and an assurance given that they would not be again filled until they had been examined by a competent civil engineer, so that there was no local danger now.

Mr. FERRAND : Was not the same assurance given two years ago by the Mayor of Bradford ?

Sir GEORGE GREY said, an assurance was given that the water should be drawn off when repairs were going on.

CHINA—TRIAL OF GEORGE WHITE AT SHANGHAI.—QUESTION.

Mr. LIDDELL said, he wished to ask, Whether the attention of the Law Officers of the Crown has been directed to the Report of a recent Trial before the Consular Court at Shanghai, at which a man named George White, charged as an accomplice in the capture of the *Firefly* steamer, was convicted and sentenced for a breach of the Hong Kong Neutrality Ordinance, No. 1, of 1855 ; and further, to a statement made on July 1, 1862, by the Duke of Newcastle, then Colonial Secretary, for the information of Earl Russell, to the effect that there is no Ordinance then in force enjoining the observance of neutrality by Her Majesty's subjects between the contending parties in China ; and, if so, whether that statement of the Duke of Newcastle was correct or incorrect ; and, if correct, whether the conviction of the said George White can be held to have been a legal conviction ?

The ATTORNEY GENERAL, in reply, said, with reference to the first part of the Question, he had received no authentic information on the subject, and it was therefore impossible that the attention of the Law Officers of the Crown could have been directed to it. He knew nothing whatever of the facts, and could give the hon. Gentleman no information on the subject. With regard to the other part of the Question, he had only to say that the statement made on the 1st of July, 1862, was this, that the first section of a Hong Kong Ordinance containing several sections had lapsed, which first section contained several provisions on the subject of neutrality—namely, for the punishment of all persons who might be engaged in war service in opposition to the Chinese Government, and some other things then mentioned. But the Duke of Newcastle also stated that other sections of the same Ordinance—3 to 8—had been renewed and made perpetual by an Ordinance made in 1857. These sections provided for the punishment of persons who were concerned on board armed vessels carrying the Chinese flag in the waters of the colony ; and also for the punishment of persons who might sell guns or munitions of war in the colony without a permissive licence. Those were still in force ; and, for anything he knew to the contrary, it might be under them that this conviction took place.

UNITED STATES—CONFERENCE ON AMERICAN AFFAIRS.—QUESTION.

Mr. HOPWOOD said, he would beg to ask the Secretary of State for the Home Department, in the absence of the First Lord of the Treasury, If he would be willing to propose a Conference on American Affairs ?

Sir GEORGE GREY : Sir, Her Majesty's Government have no intention whatever of proposing a Conference upon American affairs. If the hon. Gentleman means a Conference, comprising representatives from all the European Governments, I can see no ground that has been laid for such a proposal, to which it is quite certain the Government of the United States would not agree.

TENURE AND IMPROVEMENT OF LAND ACT (IRELAND).—QUESTION.

Mr. VANCE said, he wished, in the absence of his hon. Friend (Mr. Darby Griffith), to ask the Chief Secretary for Ireland, When the Return moved for as to the operation of the Tenure and Improvement of Land Act (Ireland) will be laid upon the table ?

Sir ROBERT PEEL replied, that the officials employed under it were not Government officers. They had been invited to give a Return, and he believed it would shortly be on the table.

THE FACTORY ACT—CHILDREN IN PAPER TUBE FACTORIES.—QUESTION.

Mr. FERRAND said, he wished to ask the Secretary of State for the Home Department, Whether it is intended to include Paper Tube Manufactories in the Factory Acts Extension Bill; if not, whether he will direct the Commissioners to inquire into the Working of the Children in these Factories ?

Sir GEORGE GREY said, in reply, that paper tube manufactories were not included in the Bill referred to, because they had not yet been reported upon by the Commissioners; but he was told the Commissioners expected to include them in their next Report.

NATIONAL GALLERY.—QUESTION.

Mr. HEYGATE said, he would beg to ask the First Commissioner of Works, Whether the scheme for erecting a new National Gallery at the rear of Burlington House, and which was last year stated by the First Commissioner of Works to "have been for a considerable time under the consideration of the Government," has yet been approved ; and, if not, to what national purposes it is proposed to devote the Estate purchased for the Nation in 1854, at a cost of £140,000, and now occupied by Burlington House and Gardens ?

Mr. COWPER, in reply, said, Her Majesty's Government had determined on proposing to Parliament a Vote in the Estimates for erecting a National Gallery on the vacant ground in the rear of Burlington House, and the Estimate was now being prepared, and would shortly be laid on the table of the House.

BUSINESS OF THE HOUSE.—QUESTION.

General PEEL said, he wished to inquire, when the Army Estimates would be taken ?

The Marquess of HARTINGTON said in reply, that in the present state of public business, it was impossible to name any day. He understood that it was intended to proceed with the remaining Navy Estimates before resuming the discussion of the Army Estimates.

Mr. J. B. SMITH said he would beg to ask whether the Land Revenue Bill will be taken at a late hour ? The Chancellor of the Exchequer had given notice of a new clause affecting the standards of sugar. Does the right hon. Gentleman intend to make a statement of the changes he proposes ?

The CHANCELLOR of the EXCHEQUER said, he should bring on the Inland Revenue Bill that evening, however late the hour might be. There were a number of alterations, chiefly of a formal character, to be made ; and there were also the provisions to which the House had agreed to be inserted in the Bill. He wished to introduce those alterations, and then to reprint the Bill. He was not aware that there was any point upon which it was likely there would be much discussion, unless it were the question which the hon. Gentleman himself intended to raise. If the Bill passed through Committee that night, he should not ask the hon. Gentleman to discuss that question under pressure of time, but would undertake that a thoroughly convenient hour for that discussion should be given upon an early night.

The Attorney General

Sir JOHN PAKINGTON said, he wished to ask with reference to the Resolution as to Inspectors of Schools mentioned last night, if the Government will lay the Resolution on the table to-day or to-morrow, previous to its discussion on Monday.

Sir GEORGE GREY, in reply, stated, that what was said yesterday was that notice would be given of the Resolution on Monday, not that it would be then discussed.

Sir HENRY WILLOUGHBY said, he wished to know what opportunity there will be for discussion, if any point arises on the Navy Estimates.

The CHANCELLOR of the EXCHEQUER said, he was not aware that any discussion was likely to take place, except on the point suggested by the hon. Member for Wallingford (Mr. Malins), and that was a very narrow point, and might be settled in a few minutes.

Mr. FERRAND: If these Estimates were not proceeded with to-night, would they be taken to-morrow night?

Sir GEORGE GREY: An arrangement on the subject could be made when they saw how they progressed to-night.

SUPPLY.

Order for Committee read.

Motion made, and Question proposed, "That Mr. Speaker do now · leave the Chair."

UNITED STATES—SEIZURE OF THE "TUSCALOOSA."

RESOLUTION.

Mr. PEACOCKE rose to call attention to the subject of which he had given notice, and thought, when the House was made acquainted with the facts, that they would agree with him that it was one of the most bungling transactions that any Government was ever engaged in. It would appear that the Confederate vessel of war the *Alabama*, under the command of Captain Semmes, captured off the coast of Brazil a Federal bark, the *Conrad*, which he armed and converted into a tender to the *Alabama*, under the Confederate flag. Some weeks afterwards Captain Semmes had occasion to proceed to the vicinity of the Cape, accompanied by the tender, then called the *Tuscaloosa*, and he informed the authorities at the Cape that his vessel needed some repairs,

and that the *Tuscaloosa* was a tender to his ship cruising off the coast. When that information reached the authorities at the Cape, there began a correspondence to which he should have to call attention. In the first place, he must observe that a valuable and esteemed friend—no less a person than Sir Baldwin Walker—was the Admiral on the station, and it would be a consolation to that gallant officer's admirers to know that although so distant from this country, he still displayed the same amount of party zeal which had distinguished him at home. Sir Baldwin Walker immediately wrote to the Governor of the Cape to know how the *Tuscaloosa* was to be treated; and he was informed that in the opinion of the Attorney General of the Colony that vessel must be regarded as a tender and not as a prize. But Sir Baldwin Walker was not satisfied with this opinion of the Attorney General —he returned to the charge, and again asked the Governor how the vessel should be treated and then he was referred to *Wheaton*, to show that if certain conditions were complied with—that if the vessel had a commission of war, or was in the command of an officer of the Confederate navy —she must be treated as a tender and not as a prize. That reply reduced Sir Baldwin Walker to submission, but not to silence. He was determined that if the Attorney General had the best of it at the Cape, he would have the best of it at home; so he wrote home at once to the Admiralty a despatch, in which he said—

"I would here beg to submit to their Lordships' notice that the power of a captain of a ship of war to constitute every prize he may make a 'tender,' appears likely to me to lead to abuse and evasion of the laws of strict neutrality, by being used as a means of bringing prizes into neutral ports, for disposal of their cargoes and secret arrangements."—*Correspondence, North America,* No. 6 (1864), p. 1.

Now, what was this opinion of Sir Baldwin Walker but an imputation upon that of the Attorney General; nor was it consoling to think, when so many delicate and difficult questions were likely to arise there, that we had a second Commodore Wilkes commanding at that station. These facts were duly reported by Sir Philip Wodehouse to the Duke of Newcastle, who also forwarded the claim which had been made by the United States Consul at the Cape, that the *Tuscaloosa* should be given up. He would read to the House the grounds upon which the claim was made by Mr. Graham—

" I am well aware that your Government has conceded to the so-called Confederate States the rights of belligerents, and is thereby bound to respect Captain Semmes's commission ; but having refused to recognize the ' Confederacy' as a nation, and having excluded his captures from all the ports of the British Empire, the captures necessarily revert to their real owners, and are forfeited by Captain Semmes as soon as they enter a British port."—*Correspondence*, No. 6 (1864), p. 11.

Now, as Her Majesty's Government had thought fit to endorse that claim, he would ask whether Her Majesty's Government acquiesced in the reasons which were urged in its favour. Meanwhile, Mr. Adams had not been idle. He brought a good deal of pressure to bear upon Lord John Russell, who wrote a despatch in compliance with his demand.

Now, the House would observe that there was at least one pleasing feature in the despatch, because it showed that there was at all events one country to which Her Majesty's Secretary for Foreign Affairs could be courteous or even submissive. He could picture to himself the surprise with which the Ambassadors of Russia, Austria, Prussia, and even France would have received a despatch couched in such language; and he would venture to assert that if such a despatch were addressed to any of the smaller Powers of Europe, such as Portugal or Greece, the document would be looked upon as a hoax, and the signature as a forgery. These were not mere idle words upon the part of Earl Russell—the promise was fulfilled to the letter; and in consequence of this promise a despatch was sent out from the Colonial Office to Sir Philip Wodehouse, the Governor of the Cape, which was one of the most extraordinary documents he had ever read. He believed he was stating an undoubted fact when he asserted that, although the despatch was signed by the Duke of Newcastle, it was no more that nobleman's than it was his own, the Colonial Office acting merely as an official channel for the transmission of the despatch from the Foreign Office. He would begin by calling attention to the 7th paragraph—

" Whether, in the case of a vessel duly commissioned as a ship of war, after being made prize by a belligerent Government, without being first brought *infra præsidia*, or condemned by a Court of Prize, the character of prize, within the meaning of Her Majesty's Orders, would or would not be merged in that of a national ship of war, I am not called upon to explain."

He called upon to explain ! Why, this is precisely one of those questions upon which

Mr. Peacocke

it was his duty to give the most clear and positive instructions. The despatch went on to say—

" I think it right to observe that the third reason alleged by the Attorney General for his opinion assumes (though the fact had not been made the subject of an inquiry) that ' no means existed for determining whether the ship had or had not been judicially condemned in a Court of competent jurisdiction ;' and the proposition that, ' *admitting her to have been captured by a ship of war of the Confederate States*, she was entitled to refer Her Majesty's Government, in case of any dispute, to the Court of her States, in order to satisfy it as to her real character.' This assumption, however, is not consistent with Her Majesty's undoubted right to determine within her own territory, whether her own orders, made in vindication of her own neutrality, had been violated or not."

The Attorney General's opinion was not given at length; but he (Mr. Peacocke) would show, in a case he should quote, that the part of it which was found fault with was exactly in accordance with the law as laid down in the Courts. As regards the concluding part of the despatch, it might be nothing more than a harmless platitude; but it might mean a good deal more; it might mean that we were to look behind the flag and the commission of a vessel of war, and he would presently show that such was the spirit in which those instructions were understood and carried out. The cream and gist of the despatch lay in the concluding paragraph—

" I think that the 'allegations of the United States Consul ought to have been brought to the knowledge of Captain Semmes while the *Tuscaloosa* was still within British waters, and that he should have been requested to state whether he did or did not admit the facts to be as alleged. He should also have been called upon (unless the facts were admitted) to produce the *Tuscaloosa's* papers. If the result of these inquiries had been to prove that the vessel was really an uncondemned prize, brought into British waters in violation of Her Majesty's Orders, made for the purpose of maintaining her neutrality, I consider that the mode of proceeding in such circumstances, most consistent with Her Majesty's dignity and most proper for the vindication of her territorial rights, would have been to prohibit the exercise of any further control over the *Tuscaloosa* by her captors, and to retain that vessel under Her Majesty's control and jurisdiction until properly reclaimed by her original owners."— *Correspondence*, No. 6 (1864), pp. 18, 19.

Now, he did not believe that there was any learned Gentleman in that House who would rise in his place and defend the legality of those instructions. Let there be no mistake upon the point. He asked the hon. and learned Member for Richmond (the Attorney General) if he was prepared to stake his professional reputation in defence of those instructions, for it was a well known principle of International Law that, as between two belligerents, the property of one belligerent, when seized by another, became the property of the captor, and that the claim of the original owner was entirely and absolutely extinguished; and therefore it would have been just as much within the principles of International Law if our Government had ordered our Governor at the Cape to seize the vessel and hand it over to the Emperor of Russia as to hand the vessel over to the original owner. But he had the satisfaction of finding that whereas, in a previous paragraph, the Colonial Secretary stated that he was advised in the last paragraph the writer only " thought ;" and putting this in connection with what he had heard in another place, he believed that these instructions were not issued in accordance with the advice of the Law Officers of the Crown, but simply and solely upon the responsibility of Her Majesty's Government. He regarded them simply as a weak and illegal concession by Lord Russell to the demands of Mr. Adams. Sir Philip Wodehouse replied—

"Your Grace intimates that the citation from this authority by the Acting Attorney General does not appear to have any direct bearing upon the question. You will assuredly believe that it is not from any want of respect for your opinion, but solely from a desire to avoid future error, that I confess my inability to understand this intimation ; or, in the absence of instructions on that head, to see in what direction I am to look for the law bearing on this subject. The paragraph cited made no distinction between a vessel with cargo and a vessel without cargo ; and your Grace leaves me in ignorance whether her character would have been changed if Captain Semmes had got rid of the cargo before claiming for her admission as a ship of war. Certainly, acts have been done by him, which, according to *Wheaton*, constituted a 'setting forth as a vessel of war.' Your Grace likewise states, ' Whether in the case of a vessel duly commissioned as a ship of war, after being made prize by a belligerent Government, without being first brought *infra præsidia*, or condemned by a Court of Prize, the character of prize, within the meaning of Her Majesty's orders, would or would not be merged in a national ship of war, I am not called upon to explain.' I feel myself forced to ask for further advice on this point, on which it is quite possible I may be called upon to take an active part. I have already, in error apparently, admitted a Confederate prize as a ship of war. The chief authority on International Law in which it is in my power to refer is *Wheaton*, who apparently draws no distinction between ships of war and other ships when found in the position of prizes, and I wish your Grace to be aware that within the last few days the commander of a United States ship of war observed to me, that if it were his good fortune to capture the *Alabama* he should convert her into a Federal cruiser. I trust your Grace will see how desirable it is that I should be fully informed of the views of Her Majesty's Government on these points, and that I shall be favoured with a reply to this despatch at your earliest convenience." — *Correspondence*, No. 6 (1864), p. 20.

He had only to add that his Grace had not considered it "desirable" to furnish Sir Philip Wodehouse with the information he required, nor to reply to him at his earliest convenience ; for (the House would hardly believe it) no answer had been sent up to the present time, or at all events there was no reply included in the papers before the House. The *Tuscaloosa* sailed from the Cape and returned, after a cruise of some weeks' duration. She had before been treated as a vessel of war, and expected to be so treated again ; but on her return she was captured by Sir Baldwin Walker, who thus reported the circumstance. On the return of the *Tuscaloosa* to the Cape they found their old friend Admiral Sir Baldwin Walker writing—

"As it appears that this vessel, the *Tuscaloosa*, late Federal ship *Conrad*, is an uncondemned prize, brought into British waters in violation of Her Majesty's orders made for the purpose of maintaining her neutrality, I therefore consider that she ought to be detained, with the view of her being reclaimed by her original owners, in accordance with the opinion of the Law Officers of the Crown forwarded for my guidance, the copy of which I have already transmitted to you."—p. 21.

He believed that when the hon. and learned Member for Richmond rose to address the House, he would not defend the course of transmitting the opinion of the Law Officers for the guidance of the Colonial authorities, but observe a discreet silence upon the point. When he (Mr. Peacocke) asked the noble Lord at the head of the Government to produce the opinion of the Law Officers, the noble Lord replied that it was not the custom to lay on the table the opinions of the Law Officers, and that those opinions were confidential and were intended only for the guidance of the Government, upon which they could act or not as they pleased. He concurred with this statement ; but why, then, was not the opinion of the Law Officers embodied in a despatch ; and why was not that despatch sent to the authorities at the Cape for their information and guidance ? A very bad habit had grown up of late upon the part of many Ministers, and more especially on the part of Lord Russell, of stating, whenever a point of International

Law arose, that he had taken the opinion of the Law Officers ; and, as this opinion could not be produced, the jurisdiction of the House was thereby fettered, and they were unable to discuss satisfactorily a question of policy. Responsibility was thus shuffled off, if even the paper was ultimately laid on the table. Matters were not very much improved, for, even in that case, Ministerial responsibility would be very much shuffled off and evaded. Take the present case for instance. Who were responsible ? The authorities at the Cape were not responsible, for they had only acted on a fair interpretation of the opinion forwarded to them for their guidance. The Ministry were hardly responsible, for they had been little more than the official channel for sending the opinion of the Law Officers to the Cape. And lastly, the Law Officers could not be regarded as responsible, because, in the language of Lord Palmerston, they had only given a confidential opinion to the Ministry. He hoped that the noble Lord, who seemed to be alive to the unconstitutional nature of the practice, would at once put a stop to it on the part of his Colleagues and subordinates. Though they had not got the opinion of the Law Officers, the House might arrive at some approximate idea of what that opinion was from the answers given to questions which Sir Baldwin Walker, in accordance with instructions, put to the commander of the *Tuscaloosa*. From this it appeared that the vessel was sailing under the Confederate flag ; that her commander was Lieutenant Low ; that she had on board four officers and twenty men ; that she had three small brass guns — two rifled 12-pounders, and a smooth-bore ; that she was cruising and had put into the Cape for repairs and supplies ; that her commander had a commission from Captain Semmes ; that the other officers also had commissions signed by him, and that she had no cargo on board. This showed that the opinion of the Law Officers of the Crown did not turn upon the nature of the cargo. Now, what was the law upon this question ? Wheaton said that the jurisdiction of the National Courts of the captor to determine the validity of captures made in war under the authority of the Government was conclusive of the judicial authority of every other country, with two exceptions only—1, when the capture was made within the territorial limits of a neutral State ; and 2, when it was made by armed vessels fitted out with-

Mr. Peacocke

in the neutral territory. Neither of these exceptions applied here. In the case of the *Exchange*, an American vessel seized by the French, and armed by them, and which afterwards entered under the French flag the Port of Philadelphia, where she was attached, Chief Justice Marshal said—

"It seems, then, to the Court to be a principle of public law that ships of war entering the port of a friendly Power open for their reception are to be considered as exempted by the consent of that Power from its jurisdiction. . . . . The arguments in favour of this opinion have been drawn from the general inability of the judicial power to enforce its decisions in cases of this description, from the consideration that the sovereign power of the nation is alone competent to avenge wrongs committed by a Sovereign ; that the questions to which such wrongs give birth are rather questions of policy than of law, that they are for diplomatic rather than legal discussion."

In other words, if the English Government had wished to raise any question in this case, they should have raised it at Richmond and not at the Cape. In the case of the *Santissima Trinidad*, Chief Justice Story said—

"Nor will the Courts of a foreign country inquire into the means by which the title to property has been acquired. It would be to exert the right of examining the validity of the acts of the foreign Sovereign, and to sit in judgment upon them in cases where he has not conceded the jurisdiction, and where it would be inconsistent with his own supremacy. The commission, therefore, of a public ship when duly authenticated, so far at least as foreign Courts are concerned, imparts absolute verity, and the title is not examinable. The property must be taken to be duly acquired, and cannot be controverted."

These opinions established the fact, that if there was a commission you could not look beyond it ; and the only question remaining, therefore, was whether Captain Semmes had any right to grant this commission. In the case of the *Ceylon*, which was an English East Indiaman, captured by some French frigates, supplied with carronades and a crew of seventy men, and which then cruised under the command of a lieutenant, with a commission from a commodore, Sir William Scott, afterwards Lord Stowell, said—

"I hold it to be unnecessary that she should have been regularly commissioned ; it is enough that she was employed in the public military service of the enemy by those who had competent authority so to employ her."

Sir William Scott then quoted the case of the *Castor*, which ship was not carried into port, and added—

"There was no regular commission, for it is not in the power of the Admiral to grant a regular commission ; he has only an inchoate authority for such a purpose, and his acts necessarily require confirmation. Yet in that case it was held that the ship, though commissioned by the Admiral alone, was sufficiently clothed with the character of a vessel of war. . . . We know extremely well that in remote parts of the world where the domestic authority cannot be immediately resorted to, the commanders are of necessity vested with larger powers than are usually intrusted to them when employed on European stations. I think this vessel was sufficiently commissioned by the French commander on the station. This *lieutenant de vaisseau* and seventy men were put on board by his order in the first instance, subject undoubtedly to the approbation of the French Minister of Marine ; but can I doubt that this appointment would have been confirmed by the constituted authorities at home in the present situation of the French navy."

Could the Government doubt that the commission granted by Captain Semmes would have been duly confirmed by the authorities of Richmond. Another case, that of the *Georgiana*, was stronger still, and seemed to be exactly on all fours with the present. The *Georgiana* was a British whaler, captured by the American frigate *Essex*. The American captain, without taking his prize into port or taking out the cargo, supplied her with ten additional guns and sixty men, and employed her, under one of his lieutenants, to cruise against British vessels. The force with which she had been supplied was subsequently reduced, and when she was taken she had only four guns and fifteen men on board. In that case Sir William Scott held that she was sufficiently set forth for war, and that a commander of a single vessel had the same authority to grant a commission as a commodore. It seemed to him that, unless the Law Officers could override this decision by Lord Stowell, it was decisive of the question. It had been commonly our practice to commission vessels captured from an enemy; it is repeatedly referred to in *James's Naval History*; and this practice was so commonly received that the American captain at the Cape told the authorities there that if he captured the *Alabama* he would turn her into a Federal cruiser. It was a curious fact that the Government had taken no notice of these despatches until March 4, and the dates coincided exactly with the time when this subject was taken up by the House. When pressed on the subject, and asked if the vessel had been seized, the Government took the matter into consideration and came to a hasty conclusion to write to the Governor and say that they would give up the vessel; but they took a week to wrangle among themselves as to the reasons which

should be assigned for that conclusion. At last, in a despatch of March 10, (the Duke of Newcastle to Sir Philip Wodehouse,) they assigned these special reasons—

" I have now to explain that this decision was not founded on any general principle respecting the treatment of prizes captured by the cruisers of either belligerent, but on the peculiar circumstances of the case. The *Tuscaloosa* was allowed to enter the port of Cape Town and to depart, the instructions of the 4th of November not having arrived at the Cape before her departure. The captain of the *Alabama* was thus entitled to assume that he might equally bring her a second time into the same harbour, and it becomes unnecessary to discuss whether, on her return to the Cape, the *Tuscaloosa* still retained the character of a prize, or whether she had lost that character, and had assumed that of an armed tender to the *Alabama*, and whether that new character, if properly established and admitted, would have entitled her to the same privilege of admission which might be accorded to her captor, the *Alabama*. Her Majesty's Government have, therefore, come to the opinion, founded on the special circumstances of this particular case, that the *Tuscaloosa* ought to be released, with a warning, however, to the captain of the *Alabama*, that the ships of war of the belligerents are not to be allowed to bring prizes into British ports, and that it rests with Her Majesty's Government to decide to what vessels that character belongs." —p. 31.

Now, in all this, there was not a single word in answer to the request of Sir Philip Wodehouse, to have some requisite instructions given him how he was to act, and not one word as to the damages which had been incurred. What were the leading characteristics of the despatch ? They were uncertainty, uncertainty, uncertainty. Her Majesty's Government declined to discuss the point whether the *Tuscaloosa* still retained her original character of a prize. They preferred shifting the responsibility from their own shoulders to those of the Governor of the Cape—ready to condemn him if he was wrong, equally ready to condemn him if he was right. They gave him to understand that the *Tuscaloosa* was a prize, was seized as a prize, and that she was released because she had not before been treated as a vessel of war. But they did not lay down one of these propositions distinctly, and the Governor could only arrive at this conclusion by implication. It was true that in this despatch the Duke of Newcastle stated that the *Tuscaloosa* had been released for special reasons, but the Governor could only judge what those reasons were by implication. Now, he would ask, was this a fair and straightforward manner of dealing with a servant of the Crown ? Was it not, on the other hand, acting in a most cowardly and impolitic manner? If the servants of the Crown were to observe the law, they ought to have clear and definite instructions; but if the Government wished to embroil the country with foreign Powers, the best way was to take the opposite course, to act as they had done, to harass them with contrary instructions, to involve them in legal subtleties which they themselves refused to solve, and to embarrass them with diplomatic difficulties which they refused to explain. If everything else was misty and uncertain, one thing, at all events, was sure, and that was that the instructions of November remained unrepealed, and were virtually re-affirmed; and he now called upon the House to demand their immediate repeal. As long as they continued in force what was our position? If we enforced them against the South we must also enforce them against the North. A Federal captain had given notice that if he captured one of the Confederate vessels he would turn her into a cruiser. If we were to seize that vessel and give her up to the Confederates, would the Federal Government tolerate such treatment? If we applied these instructions against a strong Power we should plunge the country into war. If we applied them against a weak Power we should cover the country with unutterable shame. In the interests of peace, he called upon the House to pass a Resolution for the revocation of those instructions, which, so long as they remained in force and unrepealed, were to this country a standing source at once of danger and disgrace.

Amendment proposed,

To leave out from the word "That" to the end of the Question, in order to add the words "the instructions contained in the Despatch of the Duke of Newcastle to Sir P. Wodehouse, dated the 4th day of November, 1863, and which remain still unrevoked, are at variance with the principles of International Law,"—(*Mr. Peacocke,*) —instead thereof.

Question proposed "That the words proposed to be left out stand part of the Question."

THE SOLICITOR GENERAL said, the hon. Member who had moved the Resolution (Mr. Peacocke) did not ask the opinion of the House on a question of policy, but asked their judgment on a pure question of International Law. He did not specify any objection he had to the despatch of the Duke of Newcastle, but

Mr. Peacocke

left his objection to be gathered from the tenor of his speech. In replying to the hon. Member, he was far from denying the perfect right and the competence of the House to entertain questions of International Law; but all would agree that if the House were to entertain such questions they should approach them in a judicial spirit, apart from any sympathies or antipathies that might be entertained. Questions of International Law were not questions of a party character. And it appeared to him that the House ought to well consider before, by a solemn Resolution, they affirmed or denied any principle of International Law. It was not a usual course for the House to adopt. We should remember that we were now neutrals and looked upon questions of International Law from a neutral point of view. But the time might come, and might not be far distant, when we might again be belligerents and have to exercise belligerent rights; and when we exercised them it might happen that other neutral nations might turn any decision at which this House might arrive against us. It was right, therefore, to consider well before we furnished them with a weapon forged by ourselves and which might be turned against us. Nothing could be quoted with such crushing effect as a Resolution which the House had gone out of the way to adopt. The first question to be determined in this case was this—was the *Tuscaloosa* when she came into Simon's Bay still a prize, or had she lost the character of a prize and assumed the new character of a vessel of war? There was no dispute about this—that she was a prize—that she had not been taken into any port of the Confederate States to be adjudicated upon and condemned, and that she was brought into the neutral harbour of Simon's Bay. Now, had she been *bonâ fide* converted from a merchant ship into a vessel of war in the Confederate service — had she been *bonâ fide* converted? That was the real question. International Law, like all other laws, distinguished between real transactions and mere pretences. If in one of our Courts it appeared that a trader had passed his property by a bill of sale to a friend, even though all the formalities had been adopted, the Court would inquire as to whether the transaction was real or was merely a pretence — whether the trader really meant to convey his property or merely intended to deceive his creditors.

There was no rule of International Law which required us to bandage our eyes so as not to see the reality of a transaction. The question here was, whether the conversion of this trader into a man-of-war was a reality or a mere sham for the purpose of evading the Queen's orders. He thought the evidence would show beyond doubt that the conversion into a man-of-war was a mere pretence. What would be the consequences of adopting the opposite doctrine? Was it to be asserted that, upon either a Federal or a Confederate captain bringing a prize into one of our ports, choosing to say, "This is a vessel of war," we had not the right to inquire whether that statement was true or false? If this were so, what would be the use of the Queen's orders? They might be set at naught, vessels might be brought into a port with two or three guns, or a flag to conceal their true character, in defiance of the Queen's orders, and the effect of those orders would be rendered null and void. Now, what were the facts as to the *Tuscaloosa*? Upon this point he could not help expressing his surprise and astonishment at the terms in which the hon. gentleman had spoken of so distinguished an officer as Sir Baldwin Walker. His case could not be very strong if it required to be supported by such unfounded and ungenerous attacks. What difference on earth could it make personally to Sir Baldwin Walker whether this was a vessel of war or not? But certainly if there was any man who knew the difference between a merchantman and a vessel of war it was Sir Baldwin Walker, and the opinion of Sir Baldwin Walker was conclusive. It appeared that Captain Semmes mentioned, after his arrival at the port, that he had left outside one of his prizes previously taken, the *Tuscaloosa*, which he had equipped and fitted as a tender, and had ordered her to meet him in Simon's Bay, and said that she was a vessel of the Confederate navy. That was the communication which he made to the Governor. There was not one single word said as to any real or supposed commission. The Attorney General of the colony thought upon that statement that it was not necessary to prevent her from coming into the port, and it was not necessary to determine whether that gentleman was right or wrong in that view of the case, and indeed it had never been the intention of the Law Officers of the Crown, or of the Government, to impute the slightest blame to the Attorney General or the Governor; so far from it, in the last despatch of the Duke of Newcastle, he disclaimed any imputation whatever on any of the colonial authorities. The Government differed from his second, if not from his first opinion, but it would be highly improper if they had attempted to blame him for the conclusion at which he had arrived on a difficult question, which might well be argued for several days, as in a late well known case, before four learned Judges, who in the end might be divided in opinion. The report of Sir Baldwin Walker upon the state of the vessel was perfectly conclusive as to her real character. Sir Baldwin, in his letter of the 8th of August, said—

" The vessel in question, now called the *Tusca-loosa*, arrived here this evening, and the boarding officer from my flagship obtained the following information :—That she is a bark of 500 tons, with two small rifled 12-pounder guns and ten men, and was captured by the *Alabama* on the 21st of June last, off the coast of Brazil ; cargo of wool still on board."—*Correspondence*, No. 6 (1864), p. 31.

These guns, it appeared, were guns which had been taken from another prize ; they were no portion of the *Alabama's* armament. Sir Baldwin Walker then went on to say—

" The admission of this vessel into port will, I fear, open the door for numbers of vessels captured under similar circumstances being denominated tenders, with a view to avoid the prohibition contained in the Queen's instructions ; and I would observe that the vessel *Sea Bride*, captured by the *Alabama* off Table Bay a few days since, or all other prizes, might be in like manner styled tenders, making the prohibition entirely null and void. I apprehend that, to bring a captured vessel under the denomination of a vessel of war, she must be fitted for warlike purposes, and not merely have a few men and two small guns put on board her (in fact nothing but a prize crew) in order to disguise her real character as a prize. Now this vessel has her original cargo of wool still on board, which cannot be required for warlike purposes, and her armament and the number of her crew are quite insufficient for any services other than those of slight defence. Viewing all the circumstances of the case, they afford room for the supposition that the vessel is styled a 'tender' with the object of avoiding the prohibition against her entrance as a prize into our ports, where, if the captors wished, arrangements could be made for the disposal of her valuable cargo, the transhipment of which, your Excellency will not fail to see, might be readily effected on any part of the coast beyond the limits of this colony."—p. 3.

He would now call the attention of the House to the statement of Mr. Graham, the United States Consul, which showed that the fears of Sir Baldwin Walker were not unfounded. This gentleman said—

" The *Tuscaloosa* remained in Simon's Bay seven days with her original cargo of skins and wool on board. This cargo, I am informed by those who claim to know, has been purchased by merchants in Cape Town ; and if it should be landed here directly from the prize, or be transferred to other vessels at some secluded harbour on the coast beyond this colony, and brought from thence here, the infringement of neutrality will be so palpable and flagrant that Her Majesty's Government will probably satisfy the claims of the owners gracefully and at once, and thus remove all cause of complaint. In so doing it will have to disavow and repudiate the acts of its executive agents here—a result I have done all in my power to prevent."—*Correspondence*, No. 6 (1864), p. 12.

Now, he thought the House would be of opinion that the American Consul's information was very correct, for something more was known of this transaction. The case of the *Saxon* had been brought before the House a short time since, and it was known what had become of the cargo of the *Tuscaloosa.* The cargo of the *Tuscaloosa* actually was deposited at a place just outside the limits of the colony called Angra Pequena, and the *Saxon* was sent from Cape Town to fetch it. No man could doubt for a moment that the arrangement was made while the *Tuscaloosa* was at Simon's Bay, and the object of this disguise, this sham, this imposture, was to make that arrangement. That was the real transaction. The Government were of opinion that, under the circumstances, the vessel did not lose her character as a prize, and that she had not obtained the character of a vessel of war. They were also of opinion that the passage from *Wheaton*, which the Colonial Attorney General had fired at the Admiral, to which that gallant officer reluctantly succumbed, did not apply. The Admiral stood out, but the Attorney General and *Wheaton* compelled him to surrender. The passage cited by the Attorney General referred entirely to the construction of the words of a municipal statute, which this country and the United States, in pretty nearly the same words, were in the habit of passing at the breaking out of a war, for the simple object of regulating the distribution of prize money. It was to the effect that if a merchant vessel were captured by the enemy, and if subsequently she were recaptured by one of our own vessels, then, if she had been "set forth as a vessel of war," her proceeds would go to her captors ; but if she retained her original character of a merchant vessel, then she would revert to her original owners, paying salvage. That was the sole object of the

* *The Solicitor General*

statute, and it had no reference whatever to International Law. The House would see, therefore, that the question which arose in this case could not possibly arise under that statute, because the enemy could have no object in colourably and ostensibly "setting forth" a vessel as a vessel of war ; for it was no matter to him, if she were recaptured, to whom her proceeds would go. No doubt it was easy for any one reading only the passage by itself, without referring to the authorities, to be misled by it. This was what *Wheaton* said—

" Thus it has been settled that where a ship was originally armed for the slave trade, and after capture an additional number of men were put on board, but there was no commission of war and no additional arming, it was not a setting forth as a vessel of war under the Act. But a commission of war is decisive if there be guns on board, and where the vessel after the capture has been fitted out as a privateer it is conclusive against her, although, when re-captured, she is navigating as a mere merchant ship."

The hon. Gentleman said it did not signify how many guns there were. He (the Solicitor General) had taken the trouble to ascertain on what authority that rested, and he found it to be the case of the *Ceylon*, in the 1st volume of *Dodson's Reports.* Here were the words of Lord Stowell's judgment—

" She had on board twenty-six guns, 110 men, with arms and ammunition of every description in sufficient quantities for offensive and defensive operations. . . She sustained an engagement with British ships, and assisted in the destruction of the *Sirius* and *Magicienne*, and in the capture of two English frigates. Here, then, was an operation, not merely defensive, but an actual offensive attack, terminating in the destruction of the British blockading squadron. I cannot doubt that under these circumstances the ship was sufficiently ' set out for war.' "

He ventured to think that if Lord Stowell had had the case of the *Tuscaloosa* before him, and had to determine the question whether she was " set out" as a ship of war, he would, unquestionably, have said that she was not sufficiently set out for war. She was armed with two guns only; she had only ten men—hardly enough for navigating her, to say nothing of fighting ; and she had her cargo on board, which made her almost unavailable for fighting purposes. She had not been employed for any hostile operations ; and further, Admiral Walker said, after inspecting her, that in his judgment she was not capable of attack or defence. His words were, "except of very slight defence." Now, even if all the cases cited did apply—if the statute did apply—which he had shown that it did not, still, he ventured to say there was no case of " setting forth for war " that would not exclude the *Tuscaloosa*. It therefore appeared to him perfectly clear that Admiral Walker was right in his view of that vessel not having lost her character of prize, and that unquestionably she ought not to be admitted as a man of war. This led him to the despatch sent to the authorities at the Cape that had been objected to by the hon. Gentleman. The Motion of the hon. Gentleman would appear to intimate that every proposition of International Law contained in that despatch was wrong, although he understood him to limit that by his speech. Now he (the Solicitor General) undertook to show that it was strictly in accordance with the principles of International Law. After referring to the *Sea Bride* the despatch said—

"With respect to the *Alabama* herself, it is clear that neither you nor any other authority at the Cape could exercise any jurisdiction over her ; and that, whatever may have been her previous history, you were bound to treat her as a ship of war belonging to a belligerent Power."—p. 18.

He apprehended that hon. Gentlemen opposite would admit that that was right. Then came this passage—

"With regard to the vessel called the *Tuscaloosa*, I am advised that this vessel did not lose the character of a prize captured by the *Alabama*, merely because she was, at the time of her being brought within British waters, armed with two small rifled guns, in charge of an officer and manned with a crew of ten men from the *Alabama*, and used as a tender to that vessel under the authority of Captain Semmes."—*Correspondence*, No. 6 (1864), p. 18.

The hon. Gentleman had imported into the case the state in which the vessel was when she returned at another time ; but the real question was as to her state at the time when she first entered Simon's Bay. His Grace's despatch went on to say—

" It would appear that the *Tuscaloosa* is a bark of 500 tons, captured by the *Alabama* off the coast of Brazil on the 21st of June last, and brought into Simon's Bay on or before the 7th of August, with her original cargo of wool (itself, as well as the vessel, prize) still on board, and with nothing to give her a warlike character (so far as is stated in the papers before me), except the circumstances already noticed. Whether, in the case of a vessel duly commissioned as a ship of war, after being made prize by a belligerent Government, without being first brought *infra præsidia* or condemned by a Court of Prize, the character of prize, within the meaning of Her Majesty's orders, would or would not be merged in that of a national ship of war, I am not called upon to explain. It is enough to say that the citation from Mr. Wheaton's book by your Attorney General does not appear

to me to have any direct bearing upon the question."—*Correspondence*, No. 6 (1864), p. 18.

That was perfectly correct, for the question there was a question of fact, whether she was actually turned into a public vessel of war. It was clear that she was not, and therefore the question did not arise of what would have been done if she had been. The Duke of Newcastle very properly eliminated points of difficulty which it was thus unnecessary to consider. The despatch continued—

" Connected with this subject is the question as to the cargoes of captured vessels which is alluded to at the end of your despatch. On this point I have to instruct you that Her Majesty's orders apply as much to prize cargoes of every kind which may be brought by any armed ships or privateers of either belligerent into British waters as to the captured vessels themselves. They do not, however, apply to any articles which may have formed part of any such cargoes, if brought within British jurisdiction, not by armed ships or privateers of either belligerent, but by other persons who may have acquired or may claim property in them by reason of any dealings with the captors. I think it right to observe that the third reason alleged by the Attorney General for his opinion assumes (though the fact had not been made the subject of any inquiry) that ' no means existed for determining whether the ship had or had not been judicially condemned in a court of competent jurisdiction ;' and the proposition that, ' admitting her to have been captured by a ship of war of the Confederate States, she was entitled to refer Her Majesty's Government, in case of any dispute, to the Court of her States, in order to satisfy it as to her real character.' This assumption, however, is not consistent with Her Majesty's undoubted right to determine within her own territory, whether her own orders, made in vindication of her own neutrality, have been violated or not."—p. 18.

He apprehended that the assertion of that proposition was necessary to the maintenance of any independent sovereignty. Was it to be contended that, when Her Majesty issued an order, directing that prizes should not be brought into her ports, if a Federal or a Confederate brought in a prize and said, "Oh ! this is a vessel of war," Her Majesty was not to determine the question ? It was an admitted fact that the vessel had not been condemned or taken before any court of competent jurisdiction by the captor. The hon. Member had referred to the case of *Santissima Trinidad ;* but if he had examined it he would have found that it affirmed, beyond all question, the doctrine for which he (the Solicitor General) was now contending ; because in that case the United States took upon themselves to determine whether a prize brought into their ports should or should not be restored to the original owners. And they did determine that question in their own courts. Ordinarily, the determination of the question of prize or no prize was for the court of the captor; but the United States, where the prize was brought into their ports in violation of their neutrality, claimed to determine, and did determine, that question. Therefore the case cited by the hon. Gentleman was entirely fatal to his argument. He now came to the latter part of the despatch, which was in these terms—

" The question remains what course ought to have been taken by the authorities of the Cape—1, In order to ascertain whether this vessel was, as alleged by the United States Consul, an uncondemned prize brought within British waters in violation of Her Majesty's neutrality; and 2, What ought to have been done if such had appeared to be really the fact? I think that the allegations of the United States Consul ought to have been brought to the knowledge of Captain Semmes while the *Tuscaloosa* was still within British waters, and that he should have been requested to state whether he did or did not admit the facts to be as alleged. He should also have been called upon (unless the facts were admitted) to produce the *Tuscaloosa's* papers. If the result of these inquiries had been to prove that the vessel was really an uncondemned prize, brought into British waters in violation of Her Majesty's orders made for the purpose of maintaining her neutrality, I consider that the mode of proceeding in such circumstances, most consistent with Her Majesty's dignity and most proper for the vindication of her territorial rights, would have been to prohibit the exercise of any further control over the *Tuscaloosa* by the captors, and to retain that vessel under Her Majesty's control and jurisdiction until properly reclaimed by her original owners."—p. 18.

On that subject he would deal quite frankly with the House. He would admit, on the part of Her Majesty's Government, that upon re-consideration, they thought these instructions were not as full and explicit as they ought to have been—that was to say, as they should and would have been if meant to be used as a guide for colonial Governors throughout the empire. But he would be allowed to observe that that despatch was not in the nature of a circular or order issued to the Governors of colonies throughout the empire. It was merely a comment of the Duke of Newcastle on that particular transaction after it had passed, and when he had no reason to suppose that the *Tuscaloosa* would return. If it had occurred to his Grace as probable that she would return (and he would hardly be blamed for not foreseeing what, after all, was a remote possibility), the despatch would have contained some

further instructions—such instructions as were subsequently given to the effect that, inasmuch as the *Tuscaloosa* was, rightly or wrongly, treated as a vessel of war after she came into their ports, and after her real character was ascertained, she should have been warned off. If it had occurred to the Duke of Newcastle, provision might have been made in the despatch for possible circumstances, and, undoubtedly, some fuller instructions would have been advisable to the effect that a vessel of war bringing with her a prize should be prohibited from entering our ports, or if she entered, be immediately warned to depart. He might inform the House that this subject had received the serious consideration of the Government, and instructions were about to be sent by way of a circular to the colonial Governors of this country. These instructions were, in fact, drawn up, though they had not yet been sent off. Ample and detailed instructions would be given, which would hereafter leave no difficulty to colonial Governors and Law Officers. He was at liberty to say that those instructions would in a very short time be laid on the table. The House would, therefore, see that this was an isolated case, and not likely to be drawn into a precedent. But having said thus much, he now proceeded to the question raised by the hon. Gentleman, whether this despatch asserted doctrines at variance with the principles of International Law. He contended that, it did not. He had frankly admitted that more full instructions were desirable, and would be sent; but that the despatch enunciated any false principle of International Law he entirely denied. What was the principle of International Law on this subject? He apprehended that the governing principle of International Law applicable to such cases as this was that the territory of a neutral was inviolate—that a neutral had the right to possess its territory entirely free from all hostile operations, direct or indirect, and if it pleased, from the presence of either belligerent. A neutral had a right to say to both belligerents—*procul este profani.* Her Majesty had not gone the length she might have done, of preventing the entrance into her ports of armed vessels of either belligerent; but she had strictly prohibited armed vessels bringing their prizes within her ports. He was now dealing with the question of International Law, and the hypothesis was this—a prize was brought in in violation of the Queen's orders, and of her neutrality: and he said if a prize was brought iu in defiance of the Queen's orders, the captain was guilty at once of a violation of International Law and of the Queen's neutrality. Under these circumstances, it was for the Queen to determine in what manner she should think fit to vindicate her neutrality; and if she chose to vindicate her neutrality by detaining the prize, in order that the claimant might have the opportunity, which the United States Consul desired, of instituting proceedings, or that other inquiry she thought fit might be made, she had a right to do so; and further, if she did exercise that power, he maintained that the captain of the offending vessel who brought the prize in in contravention of the Queen's orders being himself an offender against International Law and a wrong-doer, had no *locus standi* on the ground of International Law, to complain of any measures Her Majesty might think proper to take for the vindication of that neutrality which he had violated. That was the principle of International Law applicable to this case. The Queen had a perfect right to restore the vessel to her original owner. There was abundant authority for that doctrine. He repeated it. The principle was that neutrality had been violated, and it was for the neutral whose neutrality was violated to determine the manner in which that neutrality should be vindicated. Suppose a vessel captured within neutral waters —in our waters—and subsequently brought back as a prize, had the Queen, aye or no, the power of restoring her to her original owner? The right hon. Gentleman who was about to follow him must deal with that question. All authority was in favour of the right. *Wheaton*, who has been so much referred to, had this passage—

"Where the capture of enemy's property is made within neutral territory, or by armaments unlawfully fitted out within the same, it is the right as well as the duty of the neutral State, when the property thus taken comes into its possession, to restore it to the original owners."

What was the principle on which a vessel taken in neutral waters was restored? Be it remembered that as between belligerents the capture of a vessel in neutral waters was perfectly good. The principle was that when neutrality had been violated, it was for the neutral to determine in what manner he should vindicate his neutrality. The United States had acted on that principle for upwards of seventy years. The same principle applied to cases of the restoration of prizes made by armaments unlawfully fitted out within the territories of neutrals. That had been done again and again. Why? Because their neutrality had been violated. It was true that there had been no case decided in the United States in precisely the same circumstances, and why? Because the circumstances had never existed. The United States had not issued, like Her Majesty, orders prohibiting prizes coming into their ports, and therefore a breach of neutrality of that species had not occurred; but there could be no doubt, if it had occurred, the United States would have acted accordingly. This principle and practice were entirely applicable to this case, which was, no doubt, novel in its circumstances; the principle, however, was identical. He therefore called on the House most emphatically not to approve the Resolution of the hon. Gentleman, which went the full length of declaring that *Wheaton* was wrong and the whole course of the United States for seventy years, of which we had enjoyed the benefit, had also been wrong. If these authorities were to be upset, it should be not by one night's discussion in that House, but by the judicial decision of a competent Court of Law. He ventured to point out to the House the great danger of adopting such a Resolution as that of the hon. Gentleman. Such a course might be very inconvenient to this country, as he would show. We believed that our maritime strength was such that with whatever Power we might happen to be at war we should always be able to blockade his ports to prevent the issue of vessels of war and the entrance of prizes taken from us. But suppose that the enemy resorted to American ports, and fitted out *Alabamas* from them, and took their prizes into the American ports? What should we do? We should claim that those prizes be restored to us. But how could we do that if this Resolution were passed? We should be met with the reply, "You have passed a Resolution which, in fact, avers that, however much, and in whatever manner, the neutrality of a State has been violated, the State has no jurisdiction to restore prizes." In that way we might find this Resolution, to the last degree, inconvenient to ourselves. Upon those grounds, and thanking the House for the patience with which they had listened to him upon what was chiefly a technical subject, he trusted that the House would not affirm a Resolution which was not necessary, which could not be useful, which could have no practical effect, and which might hereafter be attended with serious inconvenience to ourselves.

MR. WHITESIDE : Sir, the hon. and learned Gentleman said, at the outset of his able speech, that there was no question of policy involved in this discussion. I beg leave to deny that proposition. There is the policy which led to instructions so legal and so perfect that we are told by the hon. and learned Gentleman that they are about to be immediately modified or repealed. I say there are involved in this debate questions of policy and law, of a very interesting character. I agree with the hon. and learned Gentleman that these questions should be discussed in a manner commensurate with their importance. When I first read those papers I asked myself how it happened that such extraordinary despatches should have emanated from any Department of the Government. I answered myself by saying, "The authorities ruling at the Foreign Office at that moment thought the war was going against the South, and that it was extremely likely the North would be successful." I called to mind the speech at Blairgowrie ; and although I remembered the more statesmanlike speech of the Chancellor of the Exchequer at Newcastle — that Jefferson Davis, as he called him, had not only made an army and a navy but had made a nation —yet I saw that one was later in date than the other. I accept the declaration of the Solicitor General that we ought to preserve strict neutrality. But we complain that the law of neutrality has been improperly violated in this matter, that the transaction is indefensible, and I am satisfied that the hon. and learned Gentleman, and his learned Colleague the Attorney General, have advised the Crown that it is indefensible, and that they have corrected the very instructions of this despatch, which the Solicitor General employed a good portion of his speech to prove were so perfect as not to need correction. The facts of the case are very simple. I heard with surprise the hon. and learned Gentleman, several times in the course of his speech, talk of "shams" as well as realities. There are no "shams" in the case of the *Tuscaloosa*—it was a painful reality as my hon. and learned Friend would admit. That vessel was originally called the *Conrad*, under which name she had been a merchant vessel. It is important to bear

The Solicitor General

in mind the real facts when we find astute lawyers raising questions which do not arise, supposing facts which do not exist, upon which they construct a visionary argument, and call upon the House to decide, not upon the facts before us, but upon other matters imagined by the learned Gentleman who addresses us. It seems to me that now it is the Admirals who decide the law and the lawyers who decide upon naval tactics ; because, as the case stands, Admiral Walker has overruled the Attorney General, and I understand the Law Officers at home have sent out instructions to the naval captains, telling them how they are to behave. It was not by acting upon such instructions that Nelson won the Nile and Trafalgar. I will not say anything about the Duke of Newcastle in relation to this despatch, because I agree with my hon. Friend that there are traces of another hand being engaged upon it— a hand with which we are painfully acquainted. Now, it is agreed that the *Tuscaloosa*, while called the *Conrad*, formerly belonged to the Federal States. The vessel was captured by the Confederates off the coast of Brazil on the 21st of June with a cargo of wool on board. I ask my hon. and learned Friend and the House what was on that day the law arising out of those facts. When the ship of one belligerent strikes its flag to a ship of the other belligerent, what is the result that arises ? Does not the ship which yields belong to the captor ; or can it by any ingenious argument be made to belong to somebody else ? The captor may burn or destroy the vessel, or not, according as the interests of his country might suggest. That has been done, and Lord Stowell says the captor has a right to do so when he is so instructed. It is really ridiculous to argue, then, as though there were any nation which had more frequently asserted that right than ourselves. Surely you are not going to apply a different law to tho Confederate States from what our own Admirals act upon, and then plume yourselves upon your strict neutrality, and your strong sense of justice ? I say that the ownership of the property was changed by the fact of the capture. I deny that any judgment or adjudication was necessary. If a man on board a captured ship disputed the right of the captor, his answer would be, " Do not make a noise, or I will shoot you." The object—the horrible object— of war is to cripple the commerce and to damage the power of the country with which you are at war, and not to indulge in the interchange of polite compliments. We have acknowledged to be a belligerent that Power which the Chancellor of the Exchequer has described as a Nation—a Power which is now commencing her fourth campaign in vindication of her independence ; she is entitled to all the rights of a belligerent ; and having by the exercise of such rights captured the *Conrad* on the 21st of June, the property in that vessel passed at once to Captain Semmes without any necessity for adjudication or condemnation. The captain of the *Alabama* then put on board two guns and ten men, under a lieutenant, and changed her name to the *Tuscaloosa.* The next question is, whether the officer in command of the *Alabama* was lawfully commissioned by the Confederate States ? That has been clearly admitted by the Duke of Newcastle, who says that his authority as commander of a vessel belonging to a belligerent Power is not open to dispute. The next question is, had Captain Semmes power to grant a commission to the person he placed in command of the *Tuscaloosa?* Is that denied by the Law Officers of the Crown? The words of Lord Stowell in a similar case were, that it was only necessary to see that the officer put in command had even the semblance of authority, and we ought not to inquire at length into the nature of the commission. We will see how the matter stands when we come to the statement of Sir Baldwin Walker, as we find that all he says is to be adopted, and everything said by everybody else at the Cape is to be rejected. Our practice is, that a commission granted by the Admiral or captain abroad is subject to the approval of the Admiralty at home ; but Lord Stowell decided that the commander of a single ship might grant a commission; and thus the commander of the *Alabama* would have full authority to do so. I say that you cannot go behind the Commission according to the decisions of our own Courts, nor by the reason of the thing; nor can you inquire whether the ship is something different from what she appears to be. I say the effect of the commission in this case was to change the character of the captured ship and to make her a vessel of war, employed by a lawfully appointed commander in the Confederate navy. She was a ship in the lawful employment of a belligerent Power, having the right to burn, sink, destroy, or capture the ships and property of an enemy with whom that

Power was at war. We find that the *Alabama* and *Tuscaloosa* remained some time in company. The talk about the wool is a mere device of no value — of no more value than it would have been if the whaler captured by the Americans during the last war had had a cargo of whales on board. It was decided by Sir William Scott that the fact of the American officer having put some guns on board the whaler had changed it into a ship of war, and it became the prize of the officer who took it. The *Alabama* and *Tuscaloosa* continued in company until the 6th of August. It is, as the Solicitor General said, quite true that the Cape of Good Hope is a neutral port ; but, then, this vessel must be regarded either as a prize or as a ship of war; and if it was a prize, the conduct of the framers of these instructions is indefensible, while, if it was a ship of war, the course which they took is quite inexcusable. Now, I admit that there was a proclamation of the Queen that forbids the captor to bring a prize into the Cape ; but there remains the question, what was to be done in the present instance ? The course which was taken, notwithstanding what has fallen from the Solicitor General, will, I would venture to say, never again be repeated by this or any other Government. Be that, however, as it may, the proclamation was very important. It was perfectly well known to the commander of the *Alabama*, who is described by Sir Baldwin Walker— (banished at a particular crisis from the country to appear in a superior position at the Cape) as a courteous and gentlemanly person. Captain Semmes, it seems, applied for leave to procure some fresh water and provisions, and repairs, and announced that he had outside the harbour his tender called the *Tuscaloosa.* [*A laugh.*] His hon. and learned Friend the Attorney General appeared quite amused ; but it appeared to him (Mr. Whiteside) a very proper course to pursue ; and here I may observe that it is somewhat remarkable that, if an official or a clerk at a distant station acts illegally, rashly, or unscrupulously, he is sure to be defended by the noble Viscount at the head of the Government ; while, if he acts with ability and discretion, he is certain to be thrown overboard. We all remember the declaration of the noble Viscount about the judgment and discretion displayed in the well known case of the lorcha *Arrow;* but passing by that point, it would seem that Admiral Walker undertook to decide the law in this matter. Now, although I have the greatest respect for seafaring men, yet I deny that their authority is in such cases so satisfactory as that of the Attorney General. Now, there is an Attorney General at the Cape—Mr. Porter—than whom, if he be the man I knew in former times, you could have no better educated person. [An hon. MEMBER: Mr. Stevenson is the acting Attorney.] Well, that did not matter; the Attorney General gave his opinion, but the Government set it aside. The Solicitor General has used the term sham, and repeated the expression. He compared the case to mere cases of roguishness that occurred in Westminster Hall. The captain of the *Alabama* was asked how long he wished to remain, how many days, and what was the list of articles he required. All these particulars were furnished. During that time was there a particle of evidence to show that he sought to sell the wool; and what was the use of the Solicitor General saying that he meant to do that which he did not, and that the fact asserted was to be taken for granted. He remained there as he ought to remain; got his provisions ; the *Tuscaloosa* got the repairs she wanted ; Admiral Walker was overruled, and the two vessels left, I believe, in about seven days. I beg now to call the attention of the House to what was said by another able lawyer, the Consul of the United States at the Cape. Before the ships left, he applied to the Governor to seize the vessel. " I cannot," said the Governor. " I tell you what we will do then," answered the Consul ; " the moment we take the *Alabama* we will do everything this captain has done with the *Tuscaloosa ;* we will turn it into a ship to be used against the Confederates." " Quite fair," added the Governor ; "I cannot prevent you from doing so any more than I can prevent this gentleman from turning the *Tuscaloosa* into a tender to the *Alabama,* and putting a lieutenant on board." " But," replied the Consul, " if you do not seize the vessel, you ought at once to order her to depart from this port." Here the Consul suggested the right course to adopt if there had been a violation of the law and the proclamation of neutrality. Now, I do not find a single thing to complain of in this Correspondence. I do not at all complain of Sir Baldwin Walker for having laid his doubts before the Governor ; and it will, I think, be time enough for the Solicitor Gene-

Mr. Whiteside

ral, when every ship taken is converted into a tender to lay down his maxims with as much solemnity as he has done to-night. No candid man can, in my opinion, underrate the fact that the lieutenant on board the ship had a legal commission at the outset. And what happened next? The proceedings at the Cape were, together with the opinion of Sir Baldwin Walker, sent to the Government in this country. The affair so far as the Cape of Good Hope was concerned was at an end, and the vessels departed unmolested. The subordinate officials at the Cape performed their duty faithfully, conducted the inquiry honourably, and acted with the strictest propriety, and without the least deviation from the laws of neutrality. And here I may observe, that we had in the North American Correspondence a despatch which gives us a key to the course pursued by Earl Russell. Mr. Adams having had the case laid before him by the American Consul at the Cape, pressed the noble Earl to do something in reference to this ship. The despatch of the 29th of October shows pretty clearly what led to the issuing of the instructions of the 4th of November. As to those instructions, they were told that nothing occurred prior to the 4th of November of any consequence. But with all deference to my hon. and learned Friend a very important matter occurred in the interval. The *Alabama* visited the Cape again. On the 17th of September there is a despatch from Sir Baldwin Walker, who had misgivings about the ship. This document was in your possession early in October, and it proves that the Commander had made explanations to the gallant Admiral in reference to what had been done. On the 17th of September Sir Baldwin Walker writes—

" Captain Semmes frankly explained that the prize *Sea Bride*, in the first place, had put into Saldanha Bay through stress of weather, and on being joined there by the *Tuscaloosa*, both vessels proceeded to Angra Pequena, on the West Coast of Africa, where he subsequently joined them in the *Alabama*, and there sold the *Sea Bride* and her cargo to an English subject who resides at Cape Town. The *Tuscaloosa* had landed some wool at Angra Pequena and received ballast, but, he states, is still in commission as a tender. I have no reason to doubt Captain Semmes' explanation ; he seems to be fully alive to the instructions of Her Majesty's Government, and appears to be most anxious not to commit any breach of neutrality."— *Correspondence*, No. 6 (1864), p. 17.

Thus the matter stands — the wool was not sold at the Cape, but was disposed of long afterwards in Africa; Captain Semmes returned to the Cape in September, and gave an explanation of everything connected with the *Tuscaloosa* to Sir Baldwin Walker, who wrote home that he was entirely satisfied with that explanation, part of which was that the *Tuscaloosa* was still in commission as a tender to a Confederate ship of war. It was with these facts before him, and advised by the lawyers whom I see opposite, or rather, I suspect, not advised by them, that somebody at home sat down and contrived the despatch to which I must now call attention. The Solicitor General asks what complaints we have to make. I complain of almost everything in the conduct of the case, whether as matter of fact or of law. After Sir Baldwin Walker had written home, stating that he was satisfied with the explanation of Captain Semmes respecting the *Tuscaloosa*, the following despatch was sent out from Downing Street:—

"With regard to the vessel called the *Tuscaloosa*, I am advised that this vessel did not lose the character of a prize captured by the *Alabama*, merely because she was, at the time of her being brought within British waters, armed with two small rifled guns, in charge of an officer and manned with a crew of ten men from the *Alabama*, and used as a tender to that vessel under the authority of Captain Semmes."—p. 18.

Let me here remark that the question whether she was or was not that thing had been investigated at the Cape. The despatch of the Governor is explicit on the matter; the decision of the Law Officers is clear; the opinion of Sir Baldwin Walker is conclusive; yet with all those things before him the Colonial Secretary disputes a fact that had been inquired into in the only place where it could be investigated. He then proceeds to lay down this most extraordinary doctrine—

"Whether, in the case of a vessel duly commissioned as a ship of war, after being made prize by a belligerent Government, without being first brought *infra præsidia* or condemned by a Court of Prize, the character of a prize, within the meaning of Her Majesty's orders, would or would not be merged in that of a national ship of war, I am not called upon to explain."—p. 18.

Not called upon to explain? The Colonial Office might as well be shut up at once. It was its business to explain. The distracted Governor at the Cape says, "Tell me what to do." "No," replies the Colonial Secretary, "I scorn to enlighten you, I will leave you in your difficulties, but, at the same time, I will reverse your decision;" and the ground alleged is that most exquisite one by the Solicitor General,

"We do not believe any such case will occur again. We do not believe it could." They never wish to hear the name of the *Tuscaloosa* again, and while they invent a doctrine theoretically, it is not to be put in force practically. Surely, says the Solicitor General, the Duke of Newcastle could not suppose that the *Tuscaloosa* would return. Alas for the Duke! she did come back, for at the end of five months the same ship upon which an inquiry had been held, and the explanation respecting which given by Captain Semmes had been considered satisfactory, sailed one fine morning into the Cape. "Oh!" cried Sir Baldwin Walker, "here she is again. Do not breathe a word to the Attorney General, but seize the ship." The Governor says there is no ground for seizing her; she has no wool on board. "We are to seize her," replies Sir Baldwin Walker, "in accordance with the general principles of International Law, which do not apply to the case; we are to suppose she was in neutral waters when she was not so; we are to suppose she had English property on board, when she had no English property on board; we are to suppose that she was re-captured, when she was not re-captured; we are to suppose every thing we cannot suppose, and, after exhausting our imaginations by inventing impossible cases, we are to obey the Duke." During her absence the *Tuscaloosa* had been cruising in the service of a belligerent Power, under the Confederate flag, with a commission from a lawfully constituted officer, and she was seized because five months before she had wool on board, which she did not sell. "It is not possible," cried her astonished commander, "that you have seized my ship. Why have you done so?" They were very delicate about giving him the information he sought for, but eventually they told him they had been directed to act as they had done against their own judgments, and that they had no discretion but to obey orders, and I must do our authorities at the Cape the justice to say that it was impossible to understand their instructions. The officer in command of the *Tuscaloosa*, when his vessel was seized, sat down and wrote words which, I think, no Englishman can read without a blush. I felt ashamed when I read them. Lieutenant Low, writing from Simon's Bay to Sir Philip Wodehouse, on the 28th December, 1863, said—

"In August last the *Tuscaloosa* arrived in Simon's Bay. She was not only recognized in the character which she lawfully claimed and still claims to be—namely, a commissioned ship of war belonging to a belligerent Power, but was allowed to remain in the harbour for the period of seven days, taking in supplies, and effecting repairs with the full knowledge and sanction of the authorities. No intimation was given that she was regarded merely in the light of an ordinary prize, or that she was considered to be violating the laws of neutrality. Nor, when she notoriously left for a cruise on active service, was any intimation whatever conveyed that on her return to the port of a friendly Power, where she had been received as a man-of-war, she would be regarded as a prize, as a violator of the Queen's proclamation of neutrality, and consequently liable to seizure. Misled by the conduct of Her Majesty's Government, I returned to Simon's Bay on the 26th inst. in very urgent want of repairs and supplies; to my surprise I find the *Tuscaloosa* is now no longer considered as a man-of-war, and she has by your orders, as I learn, been seized for the purpose of being handed over to the person who claims her on behalf of her late owners. The character of the vessel—namely, that of a lawful commissioned man-of-war of the Confederate States of America, has not been altered since her first arrival in Simon's Bay, and she, having been once fully recognized by the British authorities in command in this colony, and no notice or warning of change of opinion or of friendly feeling having been communicated by public notification or otherwise, I was entitled to expect to be again permitted to enter Simon's Bay without molestation. In perfect good faith I returned to Simon's Bay for mere necessaries, and in all honour and good faith in return I should, on change of opinion or of policy on the part of the British authorities, have been desired to leave the port again. But by the course of proceedings taken I have been (supposing the view now taken by your Excellency's Government to be correct) first misled and next entrapped."—*Correspondence,* No. 6 (1864), p. 23.

That is the statement of Lieutenant Low. Is it not strictly true? Was he not first misled and then entrapped? All the answer the Governor at the Cape could make was, that he could not help it. I have referred to the despatch of the 4th of November from Downing Street, and to the ingenious argument which the Solicitor General founded upon it. He asks what would be the case of a vessel taken in neutral waters? Why, the law applicable to a clear violation of neutrality would be enforced. But the present case is one wholly different. The *Tuscaloosa* could not lawfully be seized either as a ship of war or as a prize. It is admitted on all sides that, if a ship of war, she could not be touched, while, if a prize, she could be sent away for violating the Royal proclamation. Our authorities could have warned her off, but they had no authority to pursue any other course, and all the ingenuity of the Solicitor General has been employed simply to conjure up some fanciful case, which has

Mr. Whiteside

nothing to do with the subject of our present discussion. How were they to find the owner, and how was a question of the kind to be properly investigated? The invariable course adopted was, therefore, to warn such a vessel not to enter a port, or, if it had already entered, to order it to quit. The latter part of the despatch of the 4th of November—which my hon. and learned Friend read in a gentle tone, and said required amplifying and explaining —which is perfectly true—and adding to, which is not only correct, but will be done, said, "You are to keep the *Tuscaloosa,* if she comes in again, until properly reclaimed by her owners." Such an instruction was indefensible, and the plea that it applied only to a particular ship, and to a particular harbour, could not possibly be upheld in fair argument. To make the thing more completely ridiculous, the advice of the Law Officers of the Crown was taken, and another despatch was written, instructing the Governor to give back the vessel, which, according to the opinion of the Solicitor General, had been rightly seized. Whether you admit my hon. and learned Friend's argument or not, they cannot but confess that the conduct pursued was highly inconsistent. The whole thing proves that the course adopted was a wrong one, and that the statement of the captain, when he said he had been deceived and entrapped, is perfectly correct. The case is not at all improved from the manner in which this restoration was effected. It was not pretended that the restoration was made because any unwise or unsound principle had been laid down, but simply because of certain facts which had occurred in connection with this particular vessel. I deny that the ship could be termed a prize under any circumstances, acting as she had done, in the belief of Sir Baldwin Walker and every one at the Cape, for six or seven months as a tender to a man-of-war under a lawful commission. This is a case, I submit, in which the House ought to affirm the Resolution of the hon. Member for Maldon, by way of taking care that in future the principles of International Law shall not be violated, and in order to declare that the doctrine of neu' ality shall be observed towards all nations — towards the South and towards the North—towards Germany and towards Denmark—with impartiality, consistency, and justice.

Mr. J. J. POWELL (*Gloucester*) said, it seemed to him that the right hon. Gentleman who had just sat down had concealed behind the exuberant foliage of his speech the barrenness of his answer to the facts and arguments brought forward by his hon. and learned Friend the Solicitor General. He presumed that those who had listened attentively to the speech of the right hon. Gentleman would regard, as the most powerful portion of it, that which impugned what the Government had never concealed to be a mistake — namely, the seizure of the *Tuscaloosa* on her return to Simon's Bay. The hon. and learned Gentleman contended first of all that when the vessel arrived at that port she was duly commissioned, and that we had no right to seize or deal with her. He would ask the right hon. Gentleman what authority there was beyond his own statement for the assertion that the *Tuscaloosa*, when she first entered Simon's Bay, had on board any commission whatever? Captain Semmes, who must have known whether such was the case, had not said a single word about it. The Government conceded that if she had been a commissioned vessel, and *bonâ fide* a tender to the *Alabama*, she would have had as much right to be there as the *Alabama* herself; but as far as the facts were known to the House and to the country, they all went to show that she was only colourably a tender, and that she was then without any commission. When she first came into Simon's Bay she had her cargo on board, and only two small swivel guns and ten men. He did not profess to know much about naval matters, but he believed that there were few vessels which now traversed the ocean without having a few such arms on board. Every fact, therefore, which had come to their knowledge proved that the *Tuscaloosa* remained then what she originally had been — a merchantman and a prize. He had read these papers with the greatest attention, and with the greatest respect for the Gentlemen who had penned them, and he rejoiced to find that the national interests were so well looked after by our officers at the Cape. He ventured to think that if any mistake had been made in the first instance it was to be attributed to the acting Attorney General at the Cape, and not to the Governor, or any one else. Sir Baldwin Walker said—

"On the 8th of August the tender *Tuscaloosa*, a sailing bark, arrived in Simon's Bay, and the boarding officer having reported to me that her original cargo of wool was still on board, I felt that there were grounds for doubting her real character, and again called the Governor's attention to this circumstance. My letter and his reply are annexed. And I would here beg to submit to their Lordships' notice, that this power of a captain of a ship of war to constitute every prize he may take a 'tender,' appears to me to be likely to lead to abuse and evasion of the laws of strict neutrality, by being used as a means for bringing prizes into neutral ports for disposal of their cargoes, and secret arrangements—which arrangements, it must be seen, could afterwards be easily carried out at isolated places."—*Correspondence*, No. 6 (1864), p. 1.

He maintained that the view taken by Sir Baldwin Walker was a very sensible one. The Attorney General, however, naturally enough had recourse to *Wheaton*, but interpreted his rules according to the letter instead of the spirit, and gave his opinion on a technical rather than on any broad ground. The vessel was accordingly allowed to leave. Then came the despatch of the Duke of Newcastle, about which so much had been said. Having received the decision of the Secretary of State, Sir Baldwin Walker and the Governor, of course, had no other course left them but to seize the vessel. The hon. and learned Gentleman opposite had challenged both the facts and the law in the Duke of Newcastle's despatch; but he (Mr. Powell) maintained that the facts were correct and law sound. This was a case, it should be remembered, where, if there was no authority for the law laid down, it was equally impossible to cite any authority against it; and, in his opinion, it would be better for the House, instead of attempting to decide a question with which it was really incompetent to grapple, to wait until it had been disposed of by a proper tribunal. He begged the House to observe that the despatch did not assert any general principles of law, but was limited to the specific case under consideration.

"With regard," wrote the Duke, "to the *Tuscaloosa*, I am advised that this vessel did not lose the character of a prize captured by the *Alabama* merely because she was, at the time of her being brought within British waters, armed with two small rifled guns, in charge of an officer and manned with a crew of ten men from the *Alabama*, and used as a tender to that vessel under the authority of Captain Semmes."—*Correspondence*, No. 6 (1864,) p. 18.

The Duke of Newcastle assumed the facts to be as he stated them, and was justified in doing so from the information he had received. No one could doubt for a moment that if the vessel was armed, not *bonâ fide*, but merely for the purpose of evasion, she did not thereby lose the character of a prize.   Then the Duke of Newcastle went on to say—

"I think that the allegations of the United States Consul ought to have been brought to the knowledge of Captain Semmes while the *Tuscaloosa* was still within British waters, and that he should have been requested to state whether he did or did not admit the facts to be as alleged.   He should also have been called upon (unless the facts were admitted) to produce the *Tuscaloosa's* papers.   If the result of these inquiries had been to prove that the vessel was really an uncondemned prize, brought into British waters in violation of Her Majesty's orders made for the purpose of maintaining her neutrality, I consider that the mode of proceeding in such circumstances most consistent with Her Majesty's dignity, and most proper for the vindication of her territorial rights, would have been to prohibit the exercise of any further control over the *Tuscaloosa* by the captors, and to retain that vessel under Her Majesty's control and jurisdiction until properly reclaimed by her original owners." —*Correspondence*, No. 6 (1864), p. 19.

He would not enter into the question whether a correct interpretation of International Law was given in the concluding portion of the despatch, which said that the vessel ought to be retained until properly reclaimed by her original owners. That was a point quite beside the main and substantial question at issue, which was —not what was to be done with the vessel after she had been detained and forfeited —but whether the authorities at the Cape had the right to detain and forfeit her at all.   He would not say that a vessel under such circumstances ought not to be given up to her original owner; but he was disposed to think that the forfeiture would enure to the benefit of the Crown, and that the original owner would have little or no right to reclaim the ship.   Putting that question, however, aside as immaterial to the main issue, he submitted that all the principles of law were in favour of the assertion that, under such circumstances, the Crown had a right to detain the vessel. At the commencement of the war Her Majesty had issued a proclamation forbidding both belligerents alike to bring prizes into our ports.   That Captain Semmes was acquainted with that proclamation, was proved by some of the facts in this very case.   It was significant that Captain Semmes did not bring in the tender with him in the first instance.   He left her outside, but mentioned in port where she was. Thus he ascertained whether there would be any objection to the tender being brought in.   The authorities at the Cape naturally assumed that Captain Semmes was speaking the truth, and that the tender to which

Mr. J. J. Powell

he referred really was a vessel answering to that description, and not one merely fitted up for purposes of evasion.   Consequently, they offered no opposition to her coming in. As soon, however, as they discovered the truth of the matter—that the *Tuscaloosa* was not properly a tender, but was only disguised as one—they ought to have done as the Duke of Newcastle pointed out— prohibited the exercise of any further control over her by the captors, and retained her under Her Majesty's jurisdiction.   All vessels entered foreign ports only by the courtesy and permission of the Sovereign of the country, who had an undoubted right, especially in time of war, to prescribe the conditions under which ships should be admitted.   Any vessel which disregarded or violated the limitations thus imposed offered an insult to the Sovereign, and rendered herself liable to punishment accordingly. Could any one doubt that if Captain Semmes had brought the *Tuscaloosa* as a prize into Simon's Bay, and had persisted in entering after having been warned to desist, Admiral Sir Baldwin Walker would have been justified in opening fire and even sinking both the *Alabama* and the *Tuscaloosa ?*   Well, then, if he would have been entitled to sink her when force was used, surely he had a right to seize and detain her when fraud, the substitute for force, was resorted to.   The hon. and learned Gentleman had blended together two things which were totally distinct—the arrival of the *Tuscaloosa* on the first and on the second occasion.   "How inconsistent," it was said, "is the Duke of Newcastle.   The first time the vessel comes in he says you ought to keep her, and when she returns again and is seized he orders her to be let go directly."   The right hon. Gentleman well knew, however, that in the interval between the two visits a great change had occurred in the circumstances of the case—such a change as made what was wrong in the first instance right in the second.   The second time the vessel appeared, whether or not she had a formal commission from Captain Semmes or the Confederate Admiralty, she was a duly commissioned vessel within the case of the *Ceylon*, which had been cited.   She had got rid of her cargo; she had mounted several guns, instead of two; she was manned not by ten, but by twenty men.   In fact, she had become a vessel of war. Where a vessel had become beyond all question the property of the captor, the conduct of the captor might, nevertheless, be such as warranted the forfeiture of the vessel. As to this there was no doubt, and if you wanted an instance of misconduct which justified forfeiture, it was certainly supplied by the entrance of a belligerent vessel into a neutral port in defiance of the proclamation of the neutral Government. He wanted to know what, after they had spent the night in discussing this question, the issue was to be? Of course, the House had a right to discuss abstract questions of law if they thought fit, but in doing so they were, in his opinion, travelling beyond their proper functions. What good would result from any discussion of the House on this question? Their decision was just as likely to be wrong as right; but whatever it was, would the Government venture to advise Her Majesty upon the strength of it? Would the Judges even take judicial notice of it should any case arising out of it come to be tried before them? Certainly not. Instead of applying itself to its proper business, which was legislation, the regulation of finance, the amending of grievances, and the material and political welfare of the nation, this House became something like a Discussion Hall when it debated abstract questions of law, a decision upon which could answer no good purpose whatever. He submitted that it was most inconvenient for the House to debate such questions; still more to attempt to decide them. He therefore hoped they would not come to any decision on this question; but if they did decide, he hoped the decision would be based on those sound principles of International Law which had been laid down by the Solicitor General, and which he also had humbly attempted to enforce.

Sir JAMES ELPHINSTONE said, that in his opinion it was clear that the *Tuscaloosa*, on her second visit to Simon's Bay, had all the appearance of a vessel of war. She had increased her crew to twenty-five officers and men, and was fitted with all the necessary instruments for the navigation of a large ship. Her armament was such as would have enabled her to capture easily any unarmed merchant vessel—in fact, she was a man-of-war of a most formidable character. Acting on the advice to detain the vessel till claimed by her proper owners, Sir Philip Wodehouse offered the ship to the American Consul, who, however, declined to have anything to do with her. Some stress had been laid upon the fact that on the first occasion when she entered Simon's Bay she had a cargo on board, and it was argued that this fact invalidated her pretensions to be considered a vessel of war. Upon this head, however, he begged to call attention to what took place in the Pacific in 1813. In that year the American Commodore Porter of the *Essex*, having captured twelve British whaling ships fitted out two of them as cruisers, after re-christening them the *Essex Junior* and the *Georgiana*, sent them to cruise on the coast of Chili. Both these vessels were re-captured by the British—the *Essex* and the *Essex Junior* off the harbour of Valparaiso by the *Phœbe*, and the *Georgiana* on her way to the United States by the *Barossa*. She had then on board an armament of fifteen guns and forty men, and a valuable cargo of oil and spermaceti. The owner of the *Georgiana* claimed to have her restored. Now, here was a case of an armed vessel loaded with property which had confessedly belonged to the former owners of the ship; but the Prize Court held that she was a national ship, and that being the prize of the captors the property found on board no longer belonged to the former owners. The case of the *Georgiana* seemed to be upon all fours with that of the *Tuscaloosa;* she was an armed ship, confessedly loaded with a cargo which belonged to her original owners, yet a Prize Court held that she belonged to her captors. It had been asked what was the licence under which the *Tuscaloosa* sailed? And the reply was that her licence was the commission of the officer who had charge of her; a commission which rendered him perfectly qualified to command her as a ship of war. It was quite clear that the Government did not intend to uphold the order by which the ship was seized. But there remained the question, who was to assess the damage which had been done to the Confederate States by the *Tuscaloosa* having been detained at the Cape, her cruise having been spoiled by the intervention of Her Majesty's Government. It appeared to him that throughout the whole dealing of Her Majesty's Government with the Confederate States they had been actuated more by a spirit of hostility than of neutrality. We had acknowledged the Confederate States as belligerents, but we would not acknowledge that they could have a Government to direct their movements; and the consequence was that we had not been able to communicate with them upon any of the questions of International Law which had arisen between us,

He must repeat that it would be a flagrant breach of justice if Her Majesty's Government did not compensate the Confederate States for the detention of the *Tuscaloosa*, which had rendered her cruise abortive.

MR. SHAW LEFEVRE said, the Question before the House was one of great difficulty, and much better fitted for discussion in a Court of Law than in the House of Commons; but, at all events, it ought to be treated by hon. Members in a spirit of neutrality. There appeared to him to be two questions involved— first, what course should have been adopted in reference to the *Tuscaloosa* when she went into Simon's Bay for the first time; and second, what course should be adopted in reference to prizes which might in future come into our ports. After a careful reading of the despatches—particularly those of Sir Baldwin Walker—he could come to no other conclusion than that arrived at by the Duke of Newcastle, that the *Tuscaloosa* should, on her first visit, have been detained and handed over to the original owners. He thought that it had been conclusively shown that the *Tuscaloosa* had not at that time lost her character as a prize, but that her captors had to some extent given her the character of a vessel of war, for the fraudulent purpose of enabling her to evade the Queen's Proclamation so to come into our ports ostensibly as a vessel of war, but really for the purpose of disposing of her cargo and equipping her as a vessel of war. Subsequent events showed what the intention of her captors had been, as they had disposed of her cargo, and had added to her equipment, doubtless at Simon's Bay, thus effecting the very purpose which it was the object of the Proclamation to prevent. A precisely similar case had not before arisen, and, therefore, they could only treat it by analogy; and, perhaps, the closest analogy was that of prizes brought into the ports of a neutral by ships which had been illegally equipped as vessels of war in violation of the laws of the neutral. The earliest cases of this kind arose in 1793, in America, where prizes had been brought in captured by French privateers illegally equipped in American ports. Washington was in doubt as to what course should be adopted with respect to these prizes which England demanded to have restored to her; and the question was referred to the Judges, who refused to enter upon the question on the ground that they had no jurisdiction, and

Sir James Elphinstone

that the question was one for the determination of the Executive. Washington was therefore obliged to take the case in his own hands; he directed the prizes to be restored to their original owners, and afterwards introduced the Foreign Enlistment Act, which not only settled the law as to the equipment of vessels of war in their ports, but also gave power to the Courts of Law to determine questions arising upon prizes coming into their ports. Our own Foreign Enlistment Act, though mainly taken from the American Act, contained no clause similar to this last. It was, he thought, most desirable that our Courts of Law also should have cognizance of such cases. Reasoning from what had occurred in those cases, we ought at first to have handed over the *Tuscaloosa* to her original owners, on the ground that there had been a violation of our neutrality by the *Tuscaloosa* in coming into Simon's Bay. There was also another ground upon which this should have been done—a ground not raised by the Government, nor alluded to in the Duke of Newcastle's despatch, but one which could not have escaped the notice of our Law Officers—and that was that the *Tuscaloosa* was prize to a vessel which had been equipped in our ports in violation of our neutrality. There was no International Law which was more clearly laid down than this—that a prize taken by a vessel equipped in violation of the neutrality of another country, if brought into the port of that country, should be restored to its original owners. Without entering into questions as to the meaning of the Foreign Enlistment Act, he apprehended there could be no doubt that the *Alabama* had been equipped and manned in violation of our neutrality. The question also arose whether vessels like the *Alabama* were justified in burning their prizes upon the sea without attempting to send them into port for condemnation. In the days of Grotius, no doubt, a vessel within twenty-four hours of her capture became the absolute property of her captors; but considerable alteration in the law, and especially in the law of England, had taken place since that time. Sir William Scott in his well known letter for the information of Prize Courts in America, said that before a ship could be disposed of by her captors, there must be a judicial proceeding, and a condemnation of the prize; and in the instructions to our commanders of vessels of war, and in the letters of marque to privateers, it was laid down that when vessels were captured they were to be taken into a court for condemnation; and there were no instructions which warranted their being burnt as soon as seized. This showed that a great change had taken place, and it could not now be considered a usage sanctioned by International Law to burn and destroy private property at sea, and consequently, in the consideration of this question, the *Alabama's* constant practice of burning her prizes ought to be borne in mind. No doubt it might be said that as between belligerents there was no law upon the matter; but, still, whenever a neutral had the power to interfere to put a stop to such a practice, was it not her duty to do so? Had a country which had no ports into which it could send its ships, a right to have cruisers upon the sea capturing and destroying vessels? He thought not, and he was glad to observe that so great an authority as the Lord Chancellor had expressed the opinion that such practice could not be considered as altogether according to the usage of modern warfare.

[Notice taken, that 40 Members were not present;

House counted, and 40 Members being found present,]

Mr. SHAW LEFEVRE: With respect to the course to be adopted in future towards prizes brought into our ports, it was hardly safe to say that all prizes which came into ports belonging to Her Majesty should be handed over to their original owners, for ships with prizes intended to be submitted to the adjudication of a Prize Court might be obliged by stress of weather, or for want of provisions, to enter those ports. In such cases the prizes should not be handed over to the owners, unless the vessels which captured them had been equipped in British ports, in violation of the Queen's proclamation of neutrality. But in all cases where there was reason to believe that they came in for other purposes than that of going to the ports of their captors for condemnation, he thought they should be detained or restored to their original owners. In common with many other hon. Members, he sympathised with the gallantry of the Confederates, though he had no sympathy with their cause; but he must say that he had also no sympathy for them in respect of vessels like the *Alabama*, which were equipped, not for fighting, but for lighting bonfires upon the sea by burning private property; and he thought that if Her Majesty's Government could put a stop to such a practice, it became them to do so. They might do much towards effecting this by prohibiting all access to our ports to vessels which were given to this practice, and by detaining their prizes on whatever pretence they came into our ports. By all means in your power, he would say, *Prohibe infandos a navibus ignes.*

Sir JOHN HAY said, he should not have risen to take part in the discussion but for one observation made by the hon. and learned Member for Reading (Mr. Shaw Lefevre), but before he did so he must say that Her Majesty's Government did not deserve any great credit for attempting again a count out after the very disgraceful manœuvre the other night on the China debate. It was a very easy, and, no doubt, convenient mode of getting rid of a disagreeable question—when they found that the feeling of the House was setting strongly against them, to get one of their supporters to move the count out of the House; but he thought that some quieter mode of getting rid of the discussion would have been more consonant with their dignity than resorting to this flagrant abuse of one of the privileges of that House. Having made those remarks, he must say that the hon. and learned Member for Reading had advanced some doctrines which he, as a naval officer, must pronounce altogether heretical. He must remind the hon. and learned Member that there was a wise distinction between a privateer and a tender. A tender carried with her all the powers and character of the ship from which she receives her commission, and, therefore, the *Tuscaloosa* derived her power to navigate the ocean and carry on war entirely from the commission which was borne by the captain of the *Alabama*. It might be that Captain Semmes was not, in the opinion of the House, the captain of a man-of-war, and in that case the hon. and learned Gentleman's argument might hold good; but Her Majesty's Government had acknowledged, through their officers, the commission of the *Alabama*. He was recognized for the purposes of war as the captain of a man-of-war navigating the ocean, and he communicated to the captain of his tender the same full power and authority he exercised as a captain of the Confederate navy, and, therefore, the argument which the hon. and learned Member based upon the supposition that the *Tuscaloosa* was merely a privateer, entirely fell to the ground. It was quite a new doctrine to him that Her Majesty's ships, or the ships of any other Power when at war, were not to sink, burn, or destroy the vessels of the other belligerent Power. As to its policy he would not then inquire ; but there could be no doubt that if war was to be carried to anything like a successful issue, no naval officer would consent to be bound to hamper himself with a number of prizes which must necessarily reduce the number of his crew, which he required for the purposes of fighting his ship. In such a case it was the duty of every naval officer not to respect the feelings or interests of those who belonged to the captured ships, or the advantages which might accrue to himself and crew by retaining those prizes, and bringing them into port to be condemned by a Prize Court, but to sink, burn, and destroy them on all occasions when the public service demanded it. Speaking for those officers on foreign stations who had been the victims of the extraordinary and ambiguous despatches of the Government, he trusted they would be more explicit for the future, and not seek thereby, as had been the case in this instance, to shirk the responsibility, and cast it upon their officers. He could assure the House that naval officers endeavoured to discharge their duty, in spite of the mistaken opinions of the hon. and learned Member for Reading and others in that House, who thought it their duty to state such heresies at home.

Mr. NEATE said, that although the proposal to count out the House had proceeded from that side of the House, there was no reason to impute it to the Government. Of those who rushed in to make the House a large majority belonged to the Government side, and all through the debate there had been two Members on the Government side to one on the other. He thought there would not be much difference of opinion that the *Tuscaloosa* ought to have been detained at the outset if the Duke of Newcastle's despatch had arrived earlier. When the *Tuscaloosa* was first brought into Simon's Bay she was brought in in fraudulent violation of our neutrality. She was a ship of 500 tons, and she was brought into the bay commissioned as a vessel of war, with ten men on board. He would ask the hon. and gallant Gentleman (Sir John Hay) if he had the honour and responsibility of commanding Her Majesty's fleet, whether he would send such a ship to sea with less than 100 men ? But it had been said

Sir John Hay

that upon her return she was, to all intents and purposes, a vessel of war. But what was her state then ? Why, she had twenty men and three guns on board, 100 cartridges, six 12-pounder shot, and twelve revolver pistols. Sir Baldwin Walker said he had learnt since the departure of the *Alabama* and her so-called tender, that overtures were made to some parties in Cape Town to purchase the *Tuscaloosa's* cargo of wool. Would the hon. and gallant Gentleman opposite think a transaction of that kind the business of a vessel of war ? He was not entirely satisfied with the vague and general language at the end of the Duke of Newcastle's despatch ; it would have been desirable that there should have been a little more precision. But they had been told that that defect had been remedied, and therefore he submitted that no injustice had been done.

Mr. MONTAGUE SMITH said, he agreed with his hon. and learned Friend the Solicitor General that, in dealing with questions of this kind, the House should approach them in something like a judicial spirit. He also agreed with him that there was some inconvenience in the House of Commons taking up questions of International Law ; but it had always been the practice both of that and the other House of Parliament to express an opinion upon such questions. And when the Solicitor General expressed a hope that the votes of hon. Members would be given that evening without any party spirit he entirely sympathized with him ; but he ventured to say that in that case his hon. and learned Friend himself must vote in favour of the Resolution. His hon. and learned Friend had made a most gallant defence of the instructions sent out, probably by his own advice, to the colony. He (Mr. M. Smith) was quite willing to admit the difficulty, which none but a lawyer could properly appreciate, in which the Law Officers of the Crown would feel themselves placed in such a case. They would have to apply principles not to be found in the ordinary current of authorities, but in books of international jurisprudence, which required some research, and to apply them to cases presenting circumstances of novelty and difficulty. But when he was asked to express an opinion upon the despatch of the Duke of Newcastle, and when his hon. and learned Friend the Solicitor General in such bold and defiant language laid it down that nothing in that despatch could be said to be wrong in point of law, in that case a duty was cast on hon. and learned Members on his (Mr. M. Smith's) side of the House to state what opinion they had formed on the subject. Now, there were three points in the question before the House, in which he felt bound to state his opinion that the Government had gone wrong. The first point was whether the *Tuscaloosa*, when she first came into Simon's Bay, ought to have been treated as a prize, or as a ship of war commissioned by Confederate authority. The Government decided that she was to be treated as a prize and not as a ship of war, and he thought in that decision the Government were wrong. The second point was whether, supposing she were a prize, the Admiral on the station was entitled to detain her for the purpose of having her handed over to her original owners. The Home Government thought that she should have been detained until claimed by the original owners. That decision appeared to him (Mr. M. Smith) to be utterly erroneous in point of law, and to be a clear misconception of all the authorities upon International Law. The third point was whether, when the *Tuscaloosa* came in the second time and was seized, and when the Home Government felt it necessary that she should be restored to those from whom they had taken her, they acted rightly or not. He thought that even in this last case the Government had mistaken their course, for they had not the courage and right feeling to order her to be restored upon the proper grounds, but they put the restoration upon the narrow, mistaken ground, that because she had been once in the bay and had been allowed to sail she ought to be restored. The two former errors were mistakes in point of law, the latter was a mistake in point of policy, and was, perhaps, the most serious of all, because the Government, more than their Law Officers, were responsible for it. With reference to the first question, whether the *Tuscaloosa* ought in the first instance to have been treated simply as a prize brought in in contravention of the proclamation, or as a ship of war, he agreed with his hon. and learned Friend to a certain extent that it was a question of fact, and that to some extent the *bona fides* of the conversion might have been inquired into. It was clear if a ship were brought in without any of the insignia of a vessel of war, those who had to exercise the Queen's authority might take it upon themselves to say, "This is in clear contravention of the Queen's proclamation—it is a mere deception intended to be practised upon us." But on this question the colonial authorities appeared to have formed a correct opinion both on the facts and the law. The question was, whether the *Tuscaloosa* was a ship of war or a tender, and as such entitled to the privileges of a ship of war; or whether she went in to deliver her cargo and make a profit to the captors? He thought that any one who read the papers that had been laid before the House on this subject without party spirit must come to the conclusion that the *Tuscaloosa* had been made a *bonâ fide* tender to the *Alabama*, and therefore was as much a ship of war as the *Alabama* herself. One great test of a ship of war was, had she a commission? The Duke of Newcastle, in his despatch, omitted altogether the circumstance that she had been commissioned by the Commander of the *Alabama*. There could, however, be no doubt that the fact was known to Sir Baldwin Walker, for he wrote to the Governor on the 7th of August, saying—

" Captain Forsyth has informed me that the *Alabama* has a tender outside captured by Captain Semmes on the coast of America, and commissioned by one of the *Alabama's* lieutenants."

From beginning to end, the fallacy that ran through the Correspondence and influenced the decision of the Government was that, because the *Tuscaloosa* was not condemned as a prize she was not to be treated as a ship of war. This was in the minds of the American Consul, of the legal advisers of the Crown, and of the Duke of Newcastle. Was she then a tender? Why, Sir Baldwin Walker himself said she was; it is true she had a small crew, but a tender to a man-of-war did not carry as many men as the man-of-war herself—she was simply what her name indicated her to be, an attendant upon a man-of-war. Could there be any doubt that the *Alabama* was a ship of war? and was the Solicitor General entitled to say that it was a mere sham to take the *Tuscaloosa* into Simon's Bay as her tender? On what ground did the American Consul desire that she should be detained? Why, on the very ground that she was a warlike vessel. On the 10th of August he wrote—

" An armed vessel, named the *Tuscaloosa*, claiming to act under the authority of the so-called Confederate States, entered Simon's Bay on Saturday, the 8th inst. That vessel was formerly owned by citizens of the United States, and while engaged in lawful commerce was captured as a prize by the *Alabama*. She was consequently fitted out with arms by the *Alabama* to prey upon the commerce of the United States, and now, without having been condemned as a prize by any Admiralty Court of any recognized Government, she is permitted to enter a neutral port in violation of the Queen's Proclamation, with her original cargo on board. Against this proceeding I hereby most emphatically protest, and I claim that the vessel ought to be given up to her lawful owners."

What stronger evidence could there be that she was a vessel of war than this statement of the American Consul? And as to the argument that the vessel had not been condemned by any Prize Court, and therefore remained the property of her original owners—that could not be admitted for a moment. No doubt, as between neutrals, according to some modern authorities, the property was not changed by the capture for all purposes; but as regarded belligerents themselves, when the capture was complete, the dominion and property passed to the captors. The fact that the *Tuscaloosa* had a commission was, to a great extent, decisive of her character as a public ship of war. The case of the *Georgiana*, decided by Lord Stowell, was almost exactly similar to that of the *Tuscaloosa*, and both the American and English lawyers bowed to the authority of that learned Judge. Lord Stowell said—

"It has been usual for the Court to look in the first place for the commission of war, because where that is found nothing more is wanted."

In answer to the argument that it was the case of a commission from an officer of a single ship, Lord Stowell said—

"Take it to be as stated, that it is the act of an officer commanding one ship only, the distinction does not appear to me to be very material. When it has been held that the commander of two or three ships may sufficiently ' set forth to war,' it is not going much further to say that the commander of a single ship may possess the same authority."

He had not heard it asserted that the commission given to the *Tuscaloosa* was not a real commission, nor was it disputed that the captain of the *Alabama* was competent to give such a commission. Having, as he (Mr. M. Smith) hoped, established the fact that she was a ship of war—then came the question, how she ought to have been dealt with? It was no answer to say that the Confederate States had not been recognized, because the Government of this country had conceded to the Confederate States belligerent rights. There could be

Mr. Montague Smith

no degrees in belligerent rights, for once given to a State they were possessed by it fully and entirely. They were bound to have treated the *Tuscaloosa* not as a prize, but as a ship of war of the Confederate States. As he had already said, considerable allowance must be made for the difficulties under which the Law Officers laboured; but this was a question of fact, and there was ample evidence on which they could have grounded their opinion ; and upon a question of International Law the Governors of their colonies were entitled to be heard, and their opinions were entitled to some respect. In this case, too, the Colonial Governor acted on the advice of his Law Officers ; and he ventured to say that in this case the colonial Law Officers were right ; and, therefore, he thought his hon. and learned Friend the Solicitor General assumed an amount of dignity to which he was not entitled when, with great condescension, he said the Law Officers here did not throw blame on the Law Officers of the colony. In fact, the Law Officers of the colony had been right throughout, and the Duke of Newcastle's despatch was wrong throughout. Then, supposing the ship was a prize, how was she to be dealt with? He (Mr. M. Smith) held that the Government had no right to detain her, and to hand her over to the Federal Government, or to her original owner. His hon. and learned Friend was determined to support the despatch throughout, but he confessed he was rather surprised at his hon. and learned Friend saying there was nothing wrong in the despatch, except that it was not sufficiently explicit. That might be a convenient mode of getting rid of a despatch that was wrong in point of law, but he should have thought that that was the last thing for which this despatch could be found fault with. It seemed to him so explicit that no one could mistake it. It was so explicit that the Governor felt bound to act upon it, and did act upon it, against his own convictions. Like a former memorable despatch of the noble Duke, it was too peremptory—it left no discretion to the Governor as to what he was to do with the vessel, supposing she were a prize; indeed, nothing could be more explicit or more to the point, and the Admiral acted on it most effectually by turning her own crew out of the *Tuscaloosa*, and placing a crew of British man-of-war's men on board. His hon. and learned Friend contended that a right view of International Law had been taken, but he must say he thought differently—it seemed to him entirely novel and fraught with the most dangerous consequences ; because, if Governors of our colonies were to act on the law laid down by the Colonial Office in this case, we should be in danger of war every day of our lives. His hon. and learned Friend had adverted to what had occurred in another place. In the debate so referred to, a noble Lord high in office and particularly interested in this transaction observed that the despatches written by the Duke of Newcastle went beyond what the Law Officers advised, and that the Law Officers entertained serious doubts.

THE ATTORNEY GENERAL : Earl Russell said the Law Officers declared that it was a matter for serious consideration.

MR. MONTAGUE SMITH said, he quite accepted the interpretation that it was " a matter for serious consideration ;" but the Solicitor General went much further than this, and treated the question as beyond doubt, and that all that had been done was perfectly right. Surrounded as they were by eminent politicians, he could not help thinking that the law of his hon. and learned Friends was somewhat warped by the politics and exigencies of the moment. Away from their present associations, it was impossible to have two better opinions; but, unconsciously to themselves, no doubt, their views had been distorted by their position. His hon. and learned Friend had referred to instances in which a neutral Power was entitled to seize a ship in the hands of a belligerent when brought into its own ports ; but in the authorities from which those instances were drawn, including the excellent treatise of the Queen's Advocate on "International Law," he must have seen that they were all exceptions, founded on the fact that the original capture was bad in law. There was no authority justifying the neutral Power in manning the prize from one of its own ships of war in such a case ; and had the Confederates been a strong Power, no doubt they would have resented that proceeding as an act of war. If the same step had been taken with a nation able to enforce its own views on international usage, he believed the " serious doubts" of the Law Officers would still have remained. What was such an act, in effect, but making the Queen a re-captor for the Federal Government ? In explanation of the instructions sent out to the Cape, altering the decision of the colonial authorities, both as to the law

and the facts, and giving explicit and arbitrary instructions for the future, his hon. and learned Friend urged that it was not then foreseen that the *Tuscaloosa* would return. If not, then these instructions were a mere waste of harmless powder. But, unfortunately, the *Tuscaloosa* did come again, and was seized. His hon. and learned Friend could not have been as confident then as he was now ; because no one could read the despatches which were subsequently written, without seeing, that when it became known that their instructions had been acted on, and the *Tuscaloosa*, in fact, detained, the Government were in a great fright and endeavoured to recall what they had done. The colonial authorities were then told to restore the ship ; and when they inquired the grounds for so doing were supplied with very scanty information, and left utterly without guide for their future action. The vessel in truth was to be let go because it was not expedient to keep her. But she was detained for her original owner ; how then, to be consistent, could the Government let her go without his consent ? It would have been more generous to the colonial authorities to have said that they were right in their original opinion, and therefore the ship must be released ; and it would have been more generous to the Confederate States if her liberation had been accompanied by some expression of regret for what had occurred. Such an act from a strong Power to a weak one could not have been mistaken, and might have been gracefully rendered. He thought it unfortunate that Lieutenant Low should have cause to make use of such strong expressions as that he had been " misled " and " entrapped." He admitted that there were difficulties in maintaining a strict and impartial neutrality ; but the House and the country had a right to expect that our neutrality, more especially in a contest between a weak country and a strong one, should, if rigid, be at the same time impartial.

MR. DENMAN said, that if the discussion of questions of this sort in that House was attended with inconveniences, still greater were those which would arise from rash votes upon questions of great international importance. He hoped that, in the present instance, no vote would be come to upon the Resolution before the House, because either its adoption or rejection could not fail to be productive of mischief. If it was carried, there would be danger, not only that it might be quoted against us at some future time, but that a wrangle would take place between our own and some foreign Government as to what it was that the House had affirmed. If it was rejected, it was certain that on some future occasion either our own or a foreign Government would appeal to it as affirming positively as good and legal every word which was contained in the despatch of the Duke of Newcastle. He, therefore, trusted that the Resolution would be withdrawn. Passing to the subject of this Correspondence, he apprehended that nothing could be clearer than that the question as to whether the *Tuscaloosa* was a prize or a ship of war was not a pure unadulterated question of law, but a question of law so entirely depending upon facts that you could not have any better judge in such a matter than a naval officer like Sir Baldwin Walker, who had seen the vessel on the spot, and who understood her character, her equipment, and all about her. The evidence of experts was constantly admitted in our courts of law, and in this instance there was no better authority than—there was, in fact, no competent authority except—Sir Baldwin Walker. And was there any authority to the contrary? Not a bit. Even the hon. and learned Gentleman the Member for Truro (Mr. Montague Smith) had abstained from saying that he did not accept the authority of Sir Baldwin Walker. [Mr. MONTAGUE SMITH: I said distinctly that I thought she was a ship of war.] He was aware that it was his hon. and learned Friend's opinion that she was a ship of war; but that opinion was held entirely against Sir Baldwin Walker's better judgment. All those who had in this debate opposed the view taken by Sir Baldwin Walker had relied upon passages culled from text books and upon decisions by Lord Stowell and others ; but those decisions, as presented by the hon. Gentlemen themselves, did not make out the proposition that the mere existence of the commission was enough to make the vessel a ship of war, and that you were not to look behind that commission, and go into other facts, and examine whether the vessel really was a ship of war or an uncondemned prize. On the contrary, in the case of the *Georgiana*, his hon. and learned Friend quoted words which showed clearly that the judgment of the Court was not founded upon the mere fact that there had been a commission, but upon other facts which were of great importance. [" No, no !"] The hon. and learned

Mr. Denman

Member for Truro cited the strongest case, that of the *Ceylon*, which had been quoted in the course of the debate as to the power of a captain to commission another ship as a tender; but even there the words were that the officer who received the commission might set the vessel forth as a ship of war; and there was nothing in the decisions which established that where there was nothing but a commission and an officer put on board the vessel you were in, the presence of all facts and in spite of all arguments to the contrary, to consider the vessel a ship of war. In the case of the *Georgiana* there had, as stated by the hon. Member for Maldon (Mr. Peacocke), been put on board ten additional guns and a fighting crew of sixty men, and Lord Stowell decided that the officer had sufficiently " set her forth for war." Now, in the case of the *Tuscaloosa*, Admiral Walker in effect said: " I, who am a naval officer and who know what a ship of war and also what a tender is, am perfectly certain that this vessel was not a ship of war, but a merchant vessel, with her cargo on board." That, he contended, was a statement worth a hundred opinions of legal Gentlemen in that House who took a contrary view, who could not have the same knowledge of the character of a ship, and who, moreover, had never set eyes upon this ship. But the truth was, that questions of International Law were perpetually arising upon which no decision had been previously given, and this case of the *Tuscaloosa* was an exceptional case. Was there to be found among the records of past cases any case standing on all fours with this? In such a case what were they to do? They could only look to analogy and reason, and submit to be governed by those two principles ; nor was it possible, he thought, to deny that the analogy drawn by his hon. and learned Friend the Solicitor General was a good one. The real principle involved in the question was, that the neutrality of this country had been violated, and that the parties by whom it had been violated had no right to turn round and demand restitution for the results of their own wrong. That was a true principle, which would be admitted by all. With regard to Captain Semmes, it was stated that he had pledged his own truth to the fact that this ship was a tender, and that the British authorities ought to have accepted his statement as a verity. Sir Baldwin Walker had no doubt said that he saw no reason to dispute the accuracy of Captain Semmes' statement. Now, a considerable fallacy lay concealed under this argument. Captain Semmes was a commissioned officer of the Confederate States. It was his duty, if he found the British Government willing to let him treat this vessel as a tender, to run the gauntlet through all our arrangements. But Captain Semmes had really no authority for calling this vessel a tender. He (Mr. Denman) did not mean to impute anything dishonourable to Captain Semmes in the conduct he had pursued. There was little doubt but that Captain Semmes thought that by putting a commissioned officer on board and by calling the vessel a tender, he actually made her what he called her ; but then he had done an act which was no less an evasion of our neutrality. The Attorney General at the Cape, he might add, in giving his opinion on the matter, had cited a passage from *Wheaton*, which was not applicable to the case ; but the Governor had, nevertheless, done quite right in acting on that opinion ; while, with respect to that portion of the despatch of the Duke of Newcastle which had been complained of, it was quite clear that it was not the result of the deliberation of the Law Officers of the Crown, but had been added in the urgency of the moment by the Duke himself. If that were so, the House would, he thought, hardly deem it desirable that when the subject was said to be under the consideration of the Law Officers of the Crown, they should bind themselves and the country in all future wars to the statement that the particular part of the despatch to which he referred was at variance with the principles of International Law. With respect to the third point raised by the hon. and learned Member for Truro, he maintained that, as gentlemen and as Englishmen, the heads of the Colonial Office could not have acted otherwise than they did after receiving intimation that the *Tuscaloosa* had been detained. The letter of Mr. Low, the officer in command of the vessel when Captain Semmes was absent, had been quoted to the House. The writer spoke of having been " entrapped." When the ship went away the first time she had the wool and the skins on board, and the two small guns which Admiral Walker said it was ridiculous to call an armament. She went away as a regular uncondemned prize. When she returned again she certainly had more the appearance of the tender of a man-of-war ; and, therefore, if they were not en-

titled to stop her on the first occasion, she had a right to consider that she would not be stopped on the second. Whatever, therefore, their opinion might have been as to the right of detaining her on the first occasion, it would have been a wrong thing, and, he would add, a shabby thing, for the Colonial Office to detain her on the second occasion. However, she was then seized, owing to a misconception of his instructions on the part of Sir Philip Wodehouse. The despatch of the 4th November never told him that he was to shut his eyes to altered circumstances and act in a blindfold manner. There was to him something like the exhibition of a little pique in the letter of Sir Philip Wodehouse, stating that the commander of the *Tuscaloosa* not unnaturally complained of her having been seized after being recognized on the previous occasion as a ship of war ; but that that was manifestly nothing more than the inevitable result of the overruling by the Home Government of the decision of a subordinate officer. He thought it was rather the natural result of Sir Philip Wodehouse's not having — as he did on the first occasion — consulted his Attorney General, who would most probably have told him that he was estopped from detaining the vessel. The Home Government then sent out another despatch cancelling the detention. The hon. Member for Maldon (Mr. Peacocke) had complained that this despatch assigned no special reasons for that course being taken. To him (Mr. Denman) it seemed that the reasons assigned were very special. It was stated that the decision taken was not founded on any general principle, but on the peculiar circumstances of the case, among which one was, that she had been called the tender of a ship of war, when really she was merely an uncondemned prize; nevertheless, she had been allowed to enter and to depart from the Cape, by which her commander might naturally have thought that he could go there again. The Government, therefore, came to the conclusion that she ought to be released, with a fair warning to her commander and to the captain of the *Alabama*, that ships of war could not be permitted to bring their prizes into British ports, and that it rested with Her Majesty's Government to decide to what vessels that character belonged. The despatch concluded by expressly disclaiming, in kind and courteous terms, the intention to censure, in any degree, the course pursued by Sir Philip

Wodehouse on a question of difficulty and doubt. Now that the Duke of Newcastle had retired from office, he thought it was as ungracious as it was unnecessary and improper, and even mischievous, for the House to put on record a Resolution which would be quoted against them as meaning something which it did not mean; and, for the sake of the country, for the sake of that which they would all allow Her Majesty's Government desired in spirit to preserve—namely, an honourable neutrality in our relations with America, he trusted that his hon. Friend would not force the House to a vote on that occasion.

Mr. BOVILL said, he concurred in thinking that a vote on this subject might lead to a mischievous result if it should affirm a principle of International Law which was not correct. The country had been placed in a state of humiliation by the seizure of a vessel belonging to a weak State, and our being afterwards obliged to surrender the vessel so seized; and whilst the instructions which had been given remained unrepealed, what had occurred might occur again, and subject us to further humiliation. While the instructions of the 4th November, issued to the Governors of the Colonies, remained uncancelled and unaltered, other cases might occur which would be equally mischievous; and although he quite agreed that that House was not a proper tribunal for the discussion of questions of International Law, yet the attention of Parliament must be called to the subject, and an attempt made to put the matter upon a proper footing. In cases of this kind there was always a difficulty in ascertaining the precise facts to which the law was to be applied; and a dispute had arisen as to the true character of the *Tuscaloosa*. She was originally a Federal merchant vessel, and was captured by the Confederate vessel of war, the *Alabama*. On her capture, an officer of the Confederate navy was placed on board with a complement of men from the *Alabama*, and from that time she had been continuously employed in the service of the Confederate States. The only ground on which the American Consul claimed the restitution of the vessel was, that having been fitted out as a vessel of war and a tender of the *Alabama*, she was allowed to enter a neutral port, not having been condemned as a prize in any Admiralty Court. The character of the vessel, however, was placed beyond all dispute by the demand

Mr. Denman

made by Mr. Graham on Sir Philip Wodehouse, wherein he stated that she was subsequently fitted out with arms by the *Alabama* " to prey on the commerce of the United States." Every person capable of forming an opinion arrived at that conclusion. Sir Baldwin Walker saw the vessel, and communicated with her commander, and he came to the conclusion that she ought to be treated as a vessel of war. If hon. Members would refer to the correspondence they would see that an officer and ten men of the crew of the *Alabama* were put on board, and it was admitted that she had been fitted out " to prey on the commerce of the United States." The conclusion come to by Sir Philip Wodehouse, by the acting Attorney General at the Cape, and by the Consul of the United States, was that the vessel was fitted out for that purpose. If all parties came to the same conclusion, how was it that the Duke of Newcastle was entitled to consider the vessel to possess a character which all admitted she had not—the character of a merchant vessel? But all were overruled, and notwithstanding that every one said that this was to be considered a vessel of war, his hon. and learned Friend the Solicitor General said that to consider this as a vessel of war was a mere sham. The only allegation of weight on the other side was that she had a cargo of wool on board; but it never could be made a question, in the face of the papers, whether she was a vessel of war or not. He would challenge his hon. and learned Friend the Attorney General to say that she had not this character simply because she had not been condemned as a prize. It would be a most serious thing if the House should be called on, upon the authority of the Law Officers of the Crown, to affirm the correctness of the instructions sent out by the Duke of Newcastle, and within a few days afterwards to find on the table amended instructions on which all colonial officers were in future to act. But the misfortune was that those instructions being sent out on the 4th of November, a despatch of the 10th of March of the present year placed the release of the vessel on entirely different grounds. To this hour no alteration had been made in the instructions, and if another merchant vessel which had been taken as a prize, fitted out by the Confederate States, and placed in charge of an officer of their navy found its way to Simon's Bay, what course would Sir Baldwin Walker take with regard to it? The instructions of the 4th of November remained uncancelled, and he would only have one course to pursue. He had no alternative but to act on those instructions. He acted on them, and seized a vessel of war. Could anything be more humiliating? Instructions went out; contrary to the opinion of the officers of the colony, they were acted on; and when the Government could not retain their position, they were glad to put forward some excuse for giving up the vessel by admitting that the captain had been misled and entrapped. Hence the necessity for the House taking notice of the subject. If the vessel was not of the character which had been supposed, then she was a vessel of war. It was not necessary to be a vessel of war that she should be equipped as a large vessel would be. Even a launch, under the command of a midshipman, detailed for a cutting-out expedition, was a vessel of war. But even supposing that she could be treated in any other character, then she must be a prize. Then she was a prize, taken lawfully, and the property in her had passed to the captors, and no adjudication was necessary. The Solicitor General said that the vessel passing through neutral waters became liable to seizure, and to be handed over to the original owners. He (Mr. Bovill) maintained there could be no more false proposition, and he should be surprised indeed if it were put forth by the Attorney General. The country had a right to expect a clear statement of the law, because they were told that the subject had been under the serious consideration of the Government. The Solicitor General had referred to captures in neutral waters. Everybody knew that such captures were illegal'if the neutral State interposed; but in the case of a captured vessel passing within neutral territory, there was no power to restore the property to persons who had ceased to be the owners by the law of nations. He would not enter further into the argument, but he thought it would have been better if more candour had been shown. It had been admitted that the instructions issued had gone beyond what had been sanctioned by the Law Officers of the Crown, and he trusted that, in future, instructions of a different character would be issued.

THE ATTORNEY GENERAL: Sir, there are two principal questions as to which, if I rightly understand the Motion of the hon. Gentleman opposite, it is intended by this vote to ask the House to pronounce, that this despatch contains doctrines at variance with the principles of International Law. At all events, in the course of the debate, two questions have been raised and discussed on one side or the other. The first proposition laid down in the despatch is, that the vessel called the *Tuscaloosa* did not lose the character of a prize captured by the *Alabama*, merely because she was at the time of being brought into British waters armed with two small rifled guns, in charge of an officer, and manned with a crew of ten men from the *Alabama*, and used as a tender to that vessel, under the authority of Captain Semmes, having nothing to give her a warlike character except those circumstances. The first question is, whether that proposition is contrary to the principles of International Law. The second question is, whether the final proposition in the despatch is of that character. I must express my unfeigned surprise at the manner in which the hon. and learned Member for Guildford (Mr. Bovill) has dealt with the facts bearing upon the first of these two propositions. I had hoped that all who took part in this debate would confine themselves to the real facts, and there was no Member from whom I should less have expected a miscarriage in that respect than from my hon. and learned Friend. But when my hon. and learned Friend gravely rises and gravely tells the House that every authority at the Cape—Sir Baldwin Walker as well as others — had agreed in pronouncing this vessel to be a ship of war, and entitled to be recognized in that character, I am placed in the dilemma of supposing either that he has not read the papers, or that—which, of course, I do not suppose—having read them he meant to misrepresent them. ["Oh!"] The House shall judge whether I have reason for saying so; and I must also correct an error into which, I am sure by accident and involuntarily, my hon. and learned Friend the Member for Truro (Mr. Montague Smith) has fallen. He said in the course of his able speech—to which I listened with much attention — that Sir Baldwin Walker had expressed an opinion that this ship was duly commissioned as a ship of war. I will show the House that a more complete mistake could not be made. What are the facts? In the first place, the letter to which the hon. Member for Truro referred does, indeed, use the word "commission," which is the source of his mistake; but how do the subsequent papers correct the erroneous ideas suggested by its use? Under the date of the 7th of August, Sir Baldwin Walker, writing to the Governor of the Cape, says—

"Captain Forsyth having informed me that the *Alabama* has a tender outside captured by Captain Semmes on the coast of America, and commissioned by one of the *Alabama's* lieutenants."

["Hear, hear!"] The hon. and gallant Gentleman opposite (Sir John Hay) may have a better idea of these words than myself, but it seems to be that of one of the lieutenants of the *Alabama* granting a commission. ["Oh!"] I can only say that it appeared ultimately that there was no commission in the proper sense of the word. I read the words as set down by Sir Baldwin Walker, "commissioned by one of the *Alabama's* lieutenants," and I defy anybody to define from them what sort of commission this represents. ["Oh!"]

SIR JOHN HAY said, that having been personally alluded to by the hon. and learned Gentleman, he wished to remark that when it was said that a captain at Portsmouth had commissioned one of Her Majesty's ships, it did not mean that he had conferred that commission upon himself.

THE ATTORNEY GENERAL: The hon. and gallant Gentleman interprets those words as equivalent to "under the command of one of the *Alabama's* lieutenants." I believe that is so, and the sequel shows that when the matter came to be more carefully considered, the element of a commission was eliminated, and there is nothing to be founded on that consideration. In the first place, Sir Baldwin Walker having requested the opinion of the Colonial Law Officers, obtained that opinion, and the House will observe the important consequences which followed from it, as expressed in Sir Philip Wodehouse's letter of the 8th of August to Sir Baldwin Walker, enclosing the opinion of the acting Attorney General—

"I shall take care to submit this question to Her Majesty's Government by the next mail, but in the meantime I conclude that your Excellency will be prepared to act upon the opinion of the Attorney General in respect to any vessels which may enter these ports in the character of prizes converted into ships of war by the officers of the navy of the Confederate States."—*Correspondence,* No. 6 (1864), p. 3.

I confess that was a somewhat alarming proposition, as it would suggest to the officers of the Confederate States navy a

The Attorney General

very simple and easy mode of escaping the provisions of Her Majesty respecting the bringing prizes into her ports by putting them into the position of the *Tuscaloosa,* and calling them ships of war, and introducing them into our ports as acknowledged in that character. Sir Philip Wodehouse treated that as a conclusion which naturally followed from the opinion of the Colonial Attorney General; and he said that he should take care to submit the question to Her Majesty's Government. But what was the effect of that opinion upon the mind of Sir Baldwin Walker, who has been treated by my hon. and learned Friend as among those who have pronounced this vessel to be a ship of war? Sir Baldwin Walker having, for the first time, through his own officer, obtained true information of the real facts, wrote on the 16th of August to this effect—

"The vessel in question, now called the *Tuscaloosa,* arrived here this evening, and the boarding officer from my flagship obtained the following information:—That she is a bark of 500 tons, with two small rifled 12-pounder guns and ten men, and was captured by the *Alabama* on the 21st of June last, off the coast of Brazil; cargo of wool still on board. The admission of this vessel into port will, I fear, open the door for a number of vessels captured under similar circumstances being denominated tenders, with a view to avoid the prohibition contained in the Queen's instructions; and I would observe that the vessel *Sea Bride,* captured by the *Alabama* off Table Bay a few days since, or all other prizes, might be in like manner styled tenders, making the prohibition entirely null and void. I apprehend that to bring a captured vessel under the denomination of a vessel of war she must be fitted for warlike purposes, and not merely have a few men and two small guns put on board her (in fact, nothing but a prize crew) in order to disguise her real character as a prize."—*Correspondence,* No. 6 (1864), p. 3.

My hon. and learned Friend must have overlooked that despatch. Then what does Sir Baldwin add?—

"Now this vessel has her original cargo of wool still on board, which cannot be required for warlike purposes, and her armament and the number of her crew are quite insufficient for any services other than those of slight defence. Viewing all the circumstances of the case, they afford room for the supposition that the vessel is styled a 'tender' with the object of avoiding the prohibition against her entrance as a prize into our ports, where, if the captors wished, arrangements could be made for the disposal of her valuable cargo, the transhipment of which, your Excellency will not fail to see, might be readily effected on any part of the coast beyond the limits of this colony. My sole object in calling your Excellency's attention to the case is to avoid any breach of strict neutrality."—*Correspondence,* No. 6 (1864), p. 3.

It is not upon the papers, but we know, as a matter of fact, that what Sir Baldwin Walker apprehended about the cargo actually happened. We know that when the *Tuscaloosa* left the Cape she went to Angra Pequena, and deposited her cargo of wool and skins on the rocks of an island, having previously, while in the waters of the Cape, made such an arrangement that she was followed by the colonial ship *Saxon*, which took in the cargo for the purpose of disposing of it for Captain Semmes in the Cape Colony—an enterprise which unhappily resulted in loss of life, and in the capture of the *Saxon* by the *Vanderbilt*. The real question is, whether that is not a mischief of the most serious character, which, if permitted, would place it within the power of any captain of the Federal or Confederate navy by an easy *ruse* to set at nought and violate and trample under foot, with contempt, the order made by the British Crown for the preservation of British neutrality. If any opinion can be more strongly expressed than another it is that of Sir Baldwin Walker, and I agree with my hon. and learned Friend the Member for Tiverton (Mr. Denman) that this matter of fact is one of which Sir Baldwin Walker was a far better judge than all the lawyers in the world. It was his conclusion, from the ascertained facts concerning the *Tuscaloosa*, that the character assumed of a ship of war was not real but feigned, and that to recognize it would have the effect of enabling anybody to laugh at Her Majesty and set her prohibitions within her own territory at defiance. What was the result? So much impressed was Sir Philip Wodehouse with the force of these observations, and with the authority from which they proceeded, that he thought it necessary to refer the question once again to the acting Attorney General of the colony. I wish to speak with the utmost respect of the colonial Attorney General. I have had more opportunity than the House would have, from the simple perusal of these papers, of knowing that he is a most able, upright, and excellent public servant. He exercised his judgment to the best of his ability upon the question put before him. If he was in error—and it is not for me to do more than submit my view upon that point to the House—he is not to be blamed for it, for it was one into which he fell because he was called upon to determine a most difficult question under circumstances which precluded him from having full and accurate information. The House will understand, therefore, that not a word I say is intended otherwise than most respectfully towards that learned person. I believe his first opinion was based upon an assumption of facts which, if correct, would probably have justified it; but I must take the liberty respectfully of saying, that the propositions contained in his second opinion, which was given on the 10th of August, 1863, are propositions which, I think, are most dangerous and erroneous. He was evidently misled by the error of supposing that the passage he had referred to in *Wheaton* was applicable to this case. Of course, you may reason by analogy from one thing to another, but I shall show that the passage in *Wheaton* cited by the colonial Attorney General and the authorities referred to in this debate are quite beside the mark, relating to a subject of an entirely different character. What were the conclusions drawn by the colonial Attorney General from those authorities? They are stated in a despatch of the Governor, dated August 10—

" The information given respecting the actual condition of the *Tuscaloosa* is somewhat defective; but, referring to the extract from *Wheaton* transmitted in my last letter, the Attorney General is of opinion that if the vessel received the two guns from the *Alabama*, or other confederate vessel of war, or if the person in command of her has a commission of war, or if she be commanded by an officer of the Confederate navy, in any of these cases there will be a sufficient setting forth as a vessel of war to justifying her being held to be a ship of war."—*Correspondence*, No. 6 (1864), p. 4.

So that the Colonial Attorney General was of opinion that though the *Tuscaloosa* should have no commission, though she should not even have an officer of the Confederate navy on board, yet if her two guns had been received from the *Alabama*, that was a good reason for calling her a ship of war. He was also of opinion that though she should have no commission and no guns, yet if she were commanded by a Confederate officer that was enough. I am bound to say that I think his opinion was founded upon a complete misconception of the law. The authorities to which he referred—although I admit he discharged his duty to the best of his ability and judgment—misled him, because he read them in a text-book, was not able to make himself acquainted with the cases on which the passages he cited were founded, and did not observe how special and limited was their bearing upon the question before him. Let the House mark what was the result.

The Governor, who of course thought it his duty to act upon the opinion of the Attorney General, communicated that opinion to Sir Baldwin Walker. Sir Baldwin did not change his own original opinion, but of course he had to apply the law of the Attorney General to the facts of the case. Accordingly, on the 11th of August, he writes—

"I have the honour to acknowledge the receipt of your Excellency's letter, dated yesterday, respecting the Confederate bark *Tuscaloosa* now in this bay. As there are two guns on board, and an officer of the *Alabama* in charge of her, the vessel appears to come within the meaning of the cases cited in your above-mentioned communication."—p. 4.

There were three cases put—first, guns put on board by a Confederate vessel; second, a commission; third, an officer of the Confederate navy in command; and Sir Baldwin Walker finds that the first condition is fulfilled, and the third, but not the second. To make it more clear it is distinctly so stated in the despatch of Sir Philip Wodehouse, dated August 19. I ask the attention of those, who wish to see how serious a question the Government had to consider and determine, to the whole of that despatch, because it shows that with all the courtesy, address, and gallantry which would no doubt distinguish officers in command of ships of the Confederate, or, I should hope, any other navy, yet if you give them an inch they will take an ell, and that the effect of any relaxation of your laws and rules of neutrality may be such, that you will soon be entangled in questions of a character which, if you permit them to arise, will embarrass you in a manner which it is the interest as well as the duty of this country to avoid. No one can accuse Sir Philip Wodehouse of any prejudice against Captain Semmes, or any partiality against the *Alabama*. I believe him to be impartial, fair, and just. But what are the doings of the *Alabama* in the Cape waters recited by Sir Philip Wodehouse himself? He says—

"The *Alabama* leaving her prize outside, anchored in the bay at 3.50 p.m., when Captain Semmes wrote to me that he wanted supplies and repairs, as well as permission to land thirty-three prisoners. After communicating with the United States Consul, I authorized the latter, and called upon him to ascertain the nature and extent of his wants, that I might be enabled to judge of the time he ought to remain in the port. The same afternoon he promised to send the next morning a list of the stores needed, and announced his intention of proceeding with all despatch to Simon's Bay to effect his repairs there. The next morning (August 6) the paymaster called on

The Attorney General

me with the merchant who was to furnish the supplies, and I granted him leave to stay till noon of the 7th. On the morning of the 8th Captain Forsyth, of the *Valorous*, and the port captain, by my desire, pressed on Captain Semmes the necessity for his leaving the port without any unnecessary delay; when he pleaded the continued heavy sea and the absence of his cooking apparatus, which had been sent on shore for repairs and had not been returned by the tradesman at the time appointed, and intimated his own anxiety to get away. Between 6 and 7 a.m. on Sunday, the 9th, he sailed, and on his way to Simon's Bay captured another vessel, but on finding that she was in neutral waters, immediately released her."—*Correspondence*, No. 6 (1864), p. 5.

It was quite right to release her, and it was also necessary. But see the state of things you have got here. Captain Semmes gets an enlargement of time, and when he leaves he captures a vessel in neutral waters. These are circumstances which ought to warn every one of the importance and necessity of observing strictly the rules made for the preservation of neutrality. Further on, in the same despatch, Sir Philip Wodehouse says—

"An important question has arisen in connection with the *Alabama*, on which it is very desirable that I should, as soon as practicable, be made acquainted with the views of Her Majesty's Government. Captain Semmes had mentioned, after his arrival in port, that he had left outside one of his prizes previously taken, the *Tuscaloosa*, which he had equipped and fitted as a tender, and had ordered to meet him in Simon's Bay, as she also stood in need of supplies. When this became known to the Naval Commander-in-Chief, he requested me to furnish him with a legal opinion; and whether this vessel could be held to be a ship of war before she had been formally condemned in a Prize Court; or whether she must not be held to be still a prize, and as such prohibited from entering our ports. The acting Attorney General, founding his opinion on Earl Russell's despatch to your Grace of the 31st January, 1862, and on *Wheaton's International Law*, stated in substance that it was open to Captain Semmes to convert this vessel into a ship of war, and that she ought to be admitted into our ports on that footing. On the 8th of August the vessel entered Simon's Bay, and the Admiral wrote that she had two small rifled guns with a crew of ten men, and that her cargo of wool was still on board. He was still doubtful of the propriety of admitting her. On the 10th of August, after further consultation with the acting Attorney General, I informed Sir Baldwin Walker that if the guns had been put on board by the *Alabama*, or if she had a commission of war, or if she were commanded by an officer of the Confederate Navy, there must be held to be a sufficient setting forth as a vessel of war to justify her admission into port in that character. The Admiral replied in the affirmative, on the first and last points, and she was admitted."—*Ibid.*

Sir Baldwin Walker replied in the affirmative as to the guns and as to the officer, but not—and let the House and the hon. and learned Member for Guildford take notice — not as to the commission. My hon. and learned Friend the Member for Truro (Mr. Montague Smith) will see that his inference from the use of the word "commission" in the first letter of Sir Baldwin Walker, written before the facts were ascertained, falls to the ground when we know that the facts when they were ascertained were found to meet the first and last points laid down by the Attorney General, but not the second. One thing is quite clear, that no commission belonging to the *Tuscaloosa* was at that time exhibited.

And now I wish the House to do me the favour to turn for a moment to the error into which the Acting Attorney General, not at all unnaturally, fell—an error in which he has been followed by several speakers in the debate this evening—when he took the "setting forth" the vessel for war as being a criterion for deciding the question which arose under the Queen's neutrality orders. The authorities on that subject, to which he referred, are authorities on the construction of particular words in the English Prize Acts, and in some similar American statutes. These statutes provided, that if in a war in which we were belligerents one of our ships were taken by the enemy, on being re-taken at a later time it should be restored to the original owner, except in cases where the vessel, after her capture, had been "set forth" or employed for purposes of war. We had all the dangers and perils of war to encounter in capturing a ship once employed in fighting against us, and it was therefore but fair that the reward of that danger and peril should also fall to the lot of the re-captors, and that the title of the original owner should not in that case be recognized. The title of the original owner is, however, recognized by these statutes in many cases where it would have been entirely forfeited by International Law; it is recognized by them, even after a regular sentence of condemnation has been pronounced. The rule thus laid down to govern cases of re-capture by a belligerent Power, has nothing to do with the question, whether a neutral Power not at war shall in one way or another vindicate its neutrality when that neutrality has been violated. The Prize Acts have no force in reference to the subject with which you are dealing. This view was taken by Mr. Justice Story, no mean

authority, in a similar case which has been decided by him. I refer to the case of the *Nereyda*, a Spanish ship of war, taken by a privateer which had been fitted out in the United States for the service of the Venezuelan Government contrary to the Foreign Enlistment Act of the United States. The *Nereyda*, after her capture, was herself regularly commissioned and set forth as a privateer, in the service of the Venezuelan Government. If re-taken by a Spanish vessel (and supposing the Spanish law as to restitution in cases of re-capture to be similar to our own) she would have been condemned as prize to the re-captors, and would not have been liable to be restored to her original owners. But, nevertheless, Judge Story adjudged her original character of a prize taken from Spain not to be obliterated by her subsequent employment for warlike purposes, when the question was, what was to be done with her on her being brought within the waters of the United States; and he ordered her to be restored to her original Spanish owners on the ground, that the ship which took her was fitted out in violation of the laws of the United States. That case went much beyond the present. We were bound, in the present case, to guard ourselves against admitting what I believe to be a very dangerous doctrine—namely, that we should allow any concealment of the character of the prize to be the means of enabling the captor to take the vessel beyond the reach of Her Majesty's neutrality Orders. Such a principle would find no authority in International Law. No Sovereign would be mindful of his dignity if he allowed his authority to be set at naught by the captor of a ship merely going through certain forms. It is as competent for a Sovereign to prohibit or limit the entry even of public ships of war within his territory as to prohibit the entry of prizes. The principles of International Law would fully vindicate a Sovereign in the exertion of such authority. The methods for effecting this object are within his discretion; though, at the same time, he ought not to use harsher means than the exigencies of the case demand. It appears to me, therefore, that this portion of the despatch is not only well justified, but that this country would have been unmindful of its dignity, and its neutrality orders might have been absolutely set at defiance, if it had arrived at a different conclusion, taking the facts as they were reported. When the *Tuscaloosa* came back the second time there was something resembling an equipment, and something resembling a commission, and therefore questions of a totally different character then arose as compared with those which her first visit gave rise to. The question, however, before the House is not the determination of her character upon the occasion of her second visit. We must take the facts as they stood upon the 4th of November, and as they were reported to the Government.

And now I come to the second branch of the case, and that is, the suggestion of what should be done if the result of the inquiries proved that the vessel was really an uncondemned prize brought into British waters in violation of Her Majesty's orders made for the purpose of maintaining her neutrality. The words employed by the Duke of Newcastle are—

"I consider that the mode of proceeding in such circumstances most consistent with Her Majesty's dignity, and most proper for the vindication of her territorial rights, would have been to prohibit the exercise of any further control over the *Tuscaloosa* by the captors, and to retain that vessel under Her Majesty's control and jurisdiction, until properly reclaimed by her original owners."—p. 19.

Now, I have not the least wish to avoid any portion of the responsibility for that passage. It is true, as was stated in another place, that the Law Officers of the Crown had suggested that which is expressed in the words I have read as matter for serious consideration. Undoubtedly if the despatch had been submitted to them, it is probable that they might have proposed some qualifications, or some supplement to it, and it would not have been entirely in accordance with their intentions that it should go out in a form so short and little developed as that in which it now appears. Of course the House will understand that I would not have said so much, if it had not been for the statement made in another place, that the despatch went beyond what was stated by the Law Officers of the Crown. We are bound to accept the full responsibility for the passage as it stands, because, with the exception that the matter was mentioned by us as worthy of serious consideration and not with a view to its immediate settlement in those precise terms, the very words are those in which it was suggested for consideration by the Law Officers. The Duke of Newcastle might naturally suppose that the Law Officers intended thereby to intimate the opinion which he adopted, and they would

not have intimated what they did had they not thought the principle involved sound. If blame be due anywhere, it is to us, and I am ready to take upon myself a principal share of it. At the same time, although the question is an open one, and there may be differences of opinion as to whether or not, under such circumstances as those of the *Tuscaloosa*, it would be an extreme exercise of Her Majesty's powers to retain a prize for the purpose of restoring her to the original owner, I am prepared to maintain with confidence that no principle inconsistent with International Law is expressed in any part of this passage. The case assumed is that either of a wilful violation or fraudulent evasion of the Orders issued by the British Crown for the maintenance of our neutrality, that violation or evasion taking place within the territory of Great Britain. That is the state of facts which raises the principle involved. The rest is merely a question of discretion and moderation in carrying out the principle. Can it be said that a neutral Sovereign has not a right to make orders for the preservation of his own neutrality, or that any foreign Power whatever violating these orders, provided it be done wilfully or fraudulently, is protected to any extent by International Law within the neutral territory, or has any right to complain on the ground of International Law of any means which the neutral Sovereign may see fit to adopt for the assertion of his territorial rights? By the mere fact of coming into neutral territory in spite of the prohibition, a foreign Power places itself in the position of an outlaw against the rights of nations; and it is a mere question of practical discretion, judgment, and moderation, what is the proper way of vindicating the offended dignity of the neutral Sovereign? We have had no answer to what was stated by the Solicitor General as to the principle upon which neutral Governments have hitherto acted, when their neutrality had been violated under circumstances at all of a parallel character to those of the present case. Reference has been made to the case of prizes taken within neutral jurisdiction, as if that case depended upon some different principle; but there is some confusion on this point. If there is one proposition more clear than another in International Law it is, that in such a case the wrong is against the neutral alone. At the engagement off Lagos, in the time of Lord Chatham's Ministry, our navy captured a number of ships in Portuguese waters. Lord Chatham said to our Minister, "Make any apology you please, say anything you like to satisfy the dignity of the King of Portugal, but give back not one of the ships." Thus we see the principle laid down that between belligerent and belligerent a prize is a good prize, provided the neutral does not interfere to vindicate his own neutrality. It is usual for the neutral who has interfered under such circumstances to restore the prize to the original owner, but the latter has no right to claim it from the neutral as a man can claim his property in a court of law. The object of the proceeding being to vindicate the territorial rights and guard the neutrality of the Sovereign, he does not, of course, want to make money out of the transaction, and therefore restores the prize to the original owner. The considerations which suggest the determination to vindicate the neutrality of the Sovereign suggest the propriety of the neutral restoring the prize taken from the captors to the original owners. No one disputes that, as between belligerent and belligerent, there are no rights in such a case ; the capture is good, provided the neutral does not interfere to vindicate his sovereignty; but where the neutral does interfere to seize the prize, the invariable practice is to restore the property to its original owners. I quite admit that the United States Consul was all at sea about the matter. He seems to have thought that, until there was a condemnation in a Prize Court, or something else done, the original owner, in a neutral territory, would, as a mere matter of course, be entitled to the restoration of his property. There is no foundation for that idea. If Her Majesty's Government had not been pleased to issue orders that prizes should not be brought into British ports, it would have been competent to bring them in, and no demand for the restoration of any prize by the original owner could have been listened to.

I must now remind the House of a still more recent doctrine as to the restoration of prizes, the origin of which may be said to be due in a great measure to ourselves, and which has been laid down and recognized in the United States. I refer to the case where, although the prize itself has been captured at sea far from the jurisdiction of the neutral Sovereign, yet it has been taken by a ship which has violated by equipment or fitting out the territorial rights of the neutral Power, into whose ports it is afterwards brought, and is consequently supposed to come in with the taint of a violation of neutrality attaching to it. Under these circumstances it has been held, that the neutral Sovereign has a right to retain the prize, with a view to restore it to the original owner. In 1793, when certain privateers were fitted out by the French in the ports of the United States, if not with the connivance of, at least without being prevented by, the Government of the States, Mr. Hammond, the English Minister, urged them not only to repress those privateers for the future, but to restore every prize which they had brought into the ports of the United States. What was the course taken by the United States Government on that occasion ? They took a course which has been the foundation of the doctrine acted upon by them ever since. They determined at once to accede to that part of the demand which was directed against the future preparing of privateers in their ports, and communicated that decision on the 5th of June to M. Génét, the French Minister. At the same time, they refused peremptorily to restore the prizes already brought in by those privateers, because they had been fitted out, they said, with the knowledge and permission of the Government. The French, however, continued to fit out more privateers, and the American Government, after again considering the matter, on the 25th of June, 1793, determined that all prizes brought in by privateers fitted out after a certain date should be detained in the custody of the Consuls of the ports " until the Government of the United States should be able to inquire into and decide on the facts." Subsequently the President, on the 12th of July, announced his resolution to refer the questions concerning prizes " to persons learned in the laws," and requested that certain vessels enumerated in the letter should not depart " until his ultimate determination should be made known." Again, on the 7th of August, the President, through his Secretary, informed M. Génét that he had determined to restore all such prizes brought into American ports by privateers fitted out in their ports. When the treaty was made in 1794-5, there was an article by which the United States bound themselves to make compensation to this country for all prizes which might be brought into their ports by privateers fitted out in their territory after the 5th of June, and the restitution of which had not been effected. That is the origin of the doctrine, and it shows that all these cases proceed upon the principle that where there has been a violation of neutrality the neutral Government has, within its own territory, the right to determine how that violation shall be redressed, as regards all prizes brought within its jurisdiction. The principle upon which the American Government acted in establishing this doctrine—the principle upon which all Governments act with respect to the restitution of prizes taken within their territorial limits—is applicable here, subject only to the question, whether in the particular circumstances it is necessary to resort to that mode of vindicating the honour and dignity of the Sovereign? I can refer to an older precedent even more directly in point than those that have been given. In 1658 the States General of Holland had occasion to issue ordinances for the purpose of preventing the entrance into their ports of ships of war bringing prizes. It had been usual to allow the free access of such ships with their prizes; but these ordinances were issued, and in some parts they go far beyond anything which is suggested by the Duke of Newcastle in his despatch. The first ordinance, issued on the 9th of August, 1658, prohibited the captors of prizes brought into the ports of Holland, even under stress of weather, from disposing of anything on board, and they were put under strict watch and ward. In the ordinance of November 7, 1658, there was a further prohibition against bringing the vessel into the harbour; it could only be brought into the Zee-gaten, where it was safe from danger; and if any one acted otherwise, the prize, as if it had not been captured, was to be restored to him from whom it had been taken, the captor was to be detained, and, after due inquiry, his ship was to be forfeited and sold. These ordinances were, indeed, disapproved by Bynkershoek, who advocated the practice of allowing all belligerents to bring in their prizes; and they certainly went a great deal further than Her Majesty's Government could ever be advised to go. It is quite plain, however, that the States General had no doubt about their right to enforce these prohibitions, by the threatened restitution of prizes and even by stronger measures. Then I say that the principle cannot possibly be shown to be against International Law. Whether or no persons may come to the conclusion that, under certain circumstances, a less strong course would be sufficient is another question. But the question before the House

The Attorney General

now is, whether the principle laid down in the despatch is against International Law; and I say that it is justified by every precedent which can be cited on the subject. It does not follow from this proposition either that all uncondemned prizes are to be restored, or that the original owner has a right to claim their restitution. The neutral Sovereign restores them, when they are restored, in vindication of his own dignity and authority, and the violation of neutrality is the indispensable condition of calling this principle into play at all. It is on this principle that the despatch was written, and there is nothing in it contrary to the principle of International Law. Reference is made to the absence of a sentence of condemnation, not under the notion that every uncondemned prize should be restored where there is no violation of neutrality; but because the fact of a condemnation in a Prize Court may be a reason for not treating the vessel as still having the character of a prize. In the case before Mr. Justice Story, it was attempted to be proved that a condemnation had taken place; and he seems, undoubtedly, to have entertained the opinion that, if it had been shown that the ship had been regularly condemned, there would have been an end of the question. I think I have now said all that is necessary to meet the Motion of the hon. Gentleman, and to prove that no principle is here laid down at variance with International Law, and that within her own territory Her Majesty is absolutely sovereign and supreme; that she has a right to prohibit the entrance of any foreign ships which she pleases, prizes or no prizes; and that, if her prohibition be disregarded, she is the competent and the only judge of the measures which ought to be taken for the vindication of her authority. That is the principle of the despatch, and it cannot be shown that such an offender against International Law, as a belligerent who disregards such orders, is entitled to complain of the measures taken to vindicate the rights of the territorial Sovereign. Whether milder measures would have been sufficient in any particular case is fair matter for consideration and controversy. The Government is not bound by what has passed, and is as much at liberty now as before the despatch was written to consider the question, and either to recede from or adhere to the course indicated, as they may think proper. Although I have no doubt that Sir Philip Wodehouse acted in the most loyal manner, with the most sincere and upright intention to follow his instructions, I think with the hon. and learned Member for Tiverton (Mr. Denman) that, if he had construed his instructions differently, he would have been well borne out. For what do his instructions say?—

"If the result of these inquiries had been to prove that the vessel was really an uncondemned prize, brought into British waters in violation of Her Majesty's orders made for the purpose of maintaining her neutrality, I consider that the mode of proceeding in such circumstances, most consistent with Her Majesty's dignity, and most proper for the vindication of her territorial rights, would have been to prohibit the exercise of any further control over the *Tuscaloosa* by the captors, and to retain that vessel under Her Majesty's control and jurisdiction until properly reclaimed by her original owners."—p. 19.

But when the ship had been recognized by the authorities of the colony as a public ship of war on a former occasion, of course her commander had a right to assume that on a subsequent occasion, even if her claim to that title were no better than before, she would be received in the same character. As soon as the news that the *Tuscaloosa* had been detained arrived here, Her Majesty's Government felt not only deep regret, but a stronger feeling, and had no doubt that she ought to be released. She was released, and for doing this on the ground that good faith and honour required us to do so we have been taunted. Why, when good faith and honour are in question, will any one say that you ought not to put those grounds first and foremost? If this ship had come into the port with fewer men and with fewer guns on board, and with the character of a vessel of war less strongly impressed upon her, still these grounds of honour and good faith would have made it absolutely necessary under the circumstances not to take advantage of that state of things, but at once to release her. The only becoming course for the Government to take, therefore, was to recognize immediately the justice of Lieutenant Low's reclamations, founded upon the fact that the ship had been at first received without question—to treat her as coming in under a virtual safe-conduct, and to say that the instructions sent to the Cape had been misconstrued. I regret that this should have occurred, but no other course could properly have been taken by the Government. Well, then, is the House to affirm the Resolution of the hon. Member, that the principles laid down in the despatch are contrary to International Law? I say that if the House affirms any such thing it will be affirming that which will be derogatory to the supremacy and the sovereignty of the Queen; it will be affirming that there are Powers in time of war which have a right to set at nought, either by device and fraud or otherwise, the orders of the territorial Sovereign, not only upon the high seas but within the territory of that Sovereign; it will be affirming that belligerents may violate that territory, and at the same time claim the benefit of International Law against any measures taken in vindication of the authority of the territorial Sovereign. I hope the House by its vote will protest against such a doctrine. The question is, not whether this was the wisest, the most moderate, the most proper course; a point on which opinions may differ, though some credit should be given to the sincere desire of the Minister who wrote this despatch to be strictly impartial and fair in carrying out a sound principle. Even if the House thinks that the orders given went upon too extreme an application of the principle, still it must appreciate the purpose and intention of the Minister—namely, to enforce the authority of his Sovereign within her own territories, and to maintain that neutrality to which this country stood pledged towards both parties in the present unhappy war.

Sɪʀ HUGH CAIRNS: Sir, I am glad the Attorney General has told us that our business was not to affirm the wisdom of the conduct of the Government in these transactions. I believe if that had been the proposition before the House, not even the Attorney General, who has been as bold as most men to-night—not even the Solicitor General, who was not quite so bold as the Attorney General—not a single Member—would have ventured to say that the transactions which are detailed in these papers have been characterized by the attribute of wisdom. But before we go to a division, I want the House to understand what is the question on which we are going to divide, for I think the Attorney General has mistaken the question. I venture to think that the discussion has ranged over two questions which are of a very different nature. The first is—What was done to the *Tuscaloosa*, and was she a ship of war or not? The other, the one raised by the Motion of my hon. Friend the Member for Maldon (Mr. Peacocke) is

—What are the instructions given to our agents as to what is to be done in future ? Now, on the *Tuscaloosa* and her character I shall say a very few words. It has been stated by the Attorney General, and by the Solicitor General also, that the circumstances connected with this vessel when she first came to the Cape were of a very suspicious character. Now, I will make an admission to the Government. I think those circumstances were very suspicious. I think that was eminently a case in which the Colonial Government was bound to consider what was really the character of the *Tuscaloosa*, and whether she was in reality a prize when she was passed off as a vessel of war. But I think no better opinion could have been had on that point than the opinion of the American Consul. He of all men was interested in making the best case he could against the vessel, and I will take his statement concerning her when she came into the harbour and before the Attorney General was consulted. I find, on the 10th of August, the United States Consul writing to Governor Wodehouse in these terms —

"An armed vessel, named the *Tuscaloosa*, claiming to act under the authority of the so-called Confederate States, entered Simon's Bay on Saturday, the 8th instant. That vessel was formerly owned by citizens of the United States, and while engaged in lawful commerce was captured as a prize by the *Alabama*. She was subsequently fitted out with arms by the *Alabama* to prey upon the commerce of the United States."—*Correspondence*, No. 6 (1864), p. 11.

The United States Consul says she came in as a man-of-war, to do the business of a man-of-war, and prey on the commerce of the United States. Now, what is the use of splitting hairs on the number of guns she had on board or the number of men, when the only person put in Motion at all was the United States Consul, and that is his judgment as to the character of the vessel ? I must also set the Attorney General right with respect to a grave mistake. He says the commission of the ship was moonshine—there was no commission at all — nobody supposed there was any commission. I should like to know whether Sir Baldwin Walker, or any other person on the part of the Government, asked for her commission. Did any one say, "As you are equipped for warfare, have you a commission from the belligerent Government you represent ?" That was the natural course to take. We must remember that, of course, the officer in command could not volunteer that in-

Sir Hugh Cairns

formation, because there never was a word said to him on the subject, though this controversy was going on between Sir Baldwin Walker and Sir Philip Wodehouse, and the only person not acquainted with the subject of the controversy was the person who could have given the necessary information. But what took place when she came back ? Why, then it occurred to the authorities to ask whether she had a commission or not; and a number of very proper questions were framed by Sir Baldwin Walker to be put to the commander, and among them was this, "What papers are on board to constitute her as the Confederate bark *Tuscaloosa ?*" To which the commander's reply was, "The commission of the Lieutenant commanding the *Tuscaloosa*, from Captain Semmes. The officers also have commissions to their ship from him." It thus appears that as to her papers the vessel was regular, and that the necessary ingredient which the Attorney General said was wanting was not wanting at all, and the moment it was asked for it was produced. When they did not know whether she had a commission they let her alone, but the moment she produced her commission they seized her. I shall now state the objection I have to what the Duke of Newcastle did when information was sought from the Home Government by our agents at the Cape. When I say the Duke of Newcastle, I do not mean to throw the responsibility on him, because the reports and despatches sent out by him were the embodiment of the deliberate opinion of the Government. The Government knew that the difficulty experienced by our colonial agents arose from the fact that the *Tuscaloosa* had been a prize, but had come into the harbour under the appearance of being a man-of-war, and that what they wanted to know was whether her character as a man-of-war merged the character she had as a prize. That was a very plain question. What was the reply given to it by the Duke of Newcastle, writing for the Government ?

"Whether in the case of a vessel duly commissioned as a ship of war, after being made prize by a belligerent Government, without being first brought *infra præsidia* or condemned by a Court of Prize, the character of a prize, within the meaning of Her Majesty's orders, would or would not be merged in that of a national ship of war, I am not called upon to explain. It is enough to say that the citation from Mr. Wheaton's book by your Attorney General does not appear to me to have any direct bearing upon the question."—*Correspondence*, No. 6 (1864), p. 16.

The Colonial Ministers having pressed Her Majesty's Government to give them their views on that and other very important questions, the despatch in reply commences—

"I will now proceed to convey to you the views of Her Majesty's Government on these questions."

And then proceeds, in the passage which I have just quoted, to state that on the first of these questions the Government did not consider themselves bound to give any information at all. Well, on the second visit of the *Tuscaloosa* she was seized by the authorities in the Cape, and when the Home Government heard of her seizure they gave orders for her release. I agree with the Attorney General in thinking that that was the best thing that could be done under the circumstances. But observe the ungracious way in which that was done. In a letter of the 10th of March the Duke of Newcastle says—

"Her Majesty's Government have, therefore, come to the opinion, founded on the special circumstances of this particular case, that the *Tuscaloosa* ought to be released, with a warning, however, to the captain of the *Alabama*, that the ships of war of the belligerents are not to be allowed to bring prizes into British ports, and that it rests with Her Majesty's Government to decide to what vessels that character belongs."— *Correspondence*, No. 6 (1864), p. 31.

Her Majesty's Government had decided that the *Tuscaloosa* was a ship of war. Her Majesty's Government had not blamed or reprimanded Sir Baldwin Walker for the view he had taken, and the Attorney General has told us, that, as she had been allowed to depart after her first visit, it would have been a gross violation of faith to keep her when came the second time. Accordingly she was ordered to be released ; but as she had been detained for some time the duty of the Government was to have made an apology—to have said, "We are sorry for what has occurred; it occurred under a misapprehension ; you shall have your ship back, and for any loss you may have sustained you shall be indemnified." The Government say that they wish to maintain strict neutrality ; but I want to know whether they do so. Will any Member of the Government stand up and say, that if a ship of ours had been seized by another Power, as they seized the *Tuscaloosa*, would they have been content with a despatch stating that it was a mistake, and with the restoration of the ship without apology? You act so with a people with whom you think you can deal in that way with safety; but would you have acted so with the United States ? Was that the course you took with the United States when you found that they had been guilty of a gross violation of our neutrality with respect to enlistment on the coast of Ireland ? This may be the vaunted neutrality of the Government, but it in no wise deserves the name, because it consists in doing all the mischief you can to one belligerent so long as you think it is safe to do it, and, when you find you can no longer do it with safety, in ungraciously, churlishly, and without apology, restoring the property you are afraid any longer to keep.

I now pass from the matter connected with the *Tuscaloosa*, and come to the more important point to which the Motion of the hon. Member for Maldon refers— namely, that the instructions contained in the Duke of Newcastle's despatch of the 4th of November, 1863, which still remains unrevoked, are at variance with the principles of International Law. This has nothing to do with the case of the *Tuscaloosa*, for that is past and gone, and the question is, whether those instructions, issued for the future, may not land you any morning in a war, not only with one of the belligerent Powers, but with the neutral Powers of Europe ? I thought from what had passed a few evenings ago in another place, that we might have been relieved from discussing this question. I did not understand the Foreign Secretary to have justified for one moment, in point of International Law, the correctness of the Duke of Newcastle's instructions with respect to the future. On the contrary, I understand him to have said that he agreed in thinking that the despatch went somewhat too far ;—considering the noble Lord's capacity for putting everything into a despatch which ought not to be there, that was saying a good deal ;—and he said that the question whether prizes should be seized and detained was one deserving serious consideration. If the despatch had contained those words it would have been the climax of the despatch, for in the first part it would refuse to give the information asked for in one point ; and on the other point it would have stated that the question was one deserving serious consideration. However, to-night we have had a view presented to the House, which makes it incumbent for the House to deal with the question. If the Law Officers of the Crown had followed the course taken by the Foreign Secretary, " we do not justify the instructions in that despatch, and are proceeding to take measures to revoke them," we might have been relieved from the present discussion ; but to-night, in the boldest and strongest language, the Attorney General and the Solicitor General have been heard to affirm every word of the instructions, and to contend that they are consistent with International Law. What is the order of Her Majesty which is said to have been violated ? It is this (it will be found in one of the papers before the House) :—Lord Russell, writing to the Lords of the Admiralty, says that Her Majesty is desirous of preserving strict neutrality; and with a view to carry that intention into effect, it is proposed to interdict the armed ships and privateers of both parties from bringing prizes into the ports, harbours, and roadsteads of the United Kingdom and colonies ; therefore, the Government desire to issue instructions to naval and other authorities accordingly. That is the only intimation given ; and if the matter rests there, I contend, with perfect confidence, that it would have been a gross violation of good faith and International Law for the Government to give instructions to their officers without notice to the officers of either of the belligerents —that, if a prize came into a harbour belonging to the Queen, they were to seize it, divest it from the persons who brought it in, and restore it to the original owner —there is no good faith in that. But the matter does not rest there. I will ask the House to get rid of the question altogether as relating to the Confederates, because some Gentlemen have strong views with regard to them ; but suppose a vessel belonging to the United States captured a prize at sea, and found it convenient to bring it into one of our colonial harbours, I want to know what course would be taken. I can understand that our officials in the colonies might desire the prize to be taken away, might prevent the prize having communication with the shore, and might use force, if necessary, to make the prize leave the harbour and go out to open sea; but do you suppose that if our naval forces at one of our colonies were to attempt to capture the prize and give it over to the Confederates, that the United States would for one moment tolerate such conduct ? It would be as clear a *casus belli* as any step that could be taken. The Attorney General asks if a belligerent ought not to bear

Sir Hugh Cairns

the blame if he violates an order of which he has notice ? Take the case of a Power not a belligerent. Suppose the Northern States of America captured a French ship, thinking her a proper prize, and carried it into one of our harbours. The Governor, acting on your instructions, seizes the prize and hands it over to the French owner. But he will not come to you at all ; he will go to the court of the capturing Power—the Prize Court of the United States—and say, " Where is my ship ? Restore it to me with costs and damages." The French owner goes to the American Court and says, " Bring in my ship, in order that I may have it restored and get my costs and damages." " No," says the captor, " we havn't got it ; the English Government took it from us—very likely they are keeping it for you at the Cape of Good Hope." To the Cape of Good Hope then goes the French owner and makes his demand. " Oh yes !" says the Colonial Governor, " We've got it all right ; here it is, you are quite welcome to it." " Well, but," says the French owner, " what about my costs and damages, my ship has been rotting, she has lost a voyage, and the damages I want are a great deal more than the value of the ship ;" I want to know whether the Government are going to undertake to pay costs and damages in such cases. This is not the case of a belligerent ; it is the case of the French Government; and will you tell the French Government that you will not pay costs and damages, that they may be thankful to get back the ship, although you have deprived them of the advantage which International Law gave them of going to the court of the captor and getting costs and damages there ? Does the Attorney General mean to say that is International Law—that there is any precedent for such doctrine ? If we are to have any more argument to-night, I shall be glad to hear whether the Government can controvert that clear proposition ? I should like to know how Government are prepared to deal with cases of this kind ? I venture to say that it is as clear as any proposition of International Law, that in such a case you are injuring not the belligerent but a co-neutral power. What is the sole fragment of authority for the doctrine which the Attorney and Solicitor Generals have propounded in the House of Commons to-night ? I was very much surprised to hear this authority first put forward by the

Solicitor General in a very solemn manner, and repeated afterwards by the Attorney General. Says the Solicitor General, it is not a new doctrine—it is quite old and common; it depends upon the simplest and clearest principles, because it is a plain doctrine of International Law, that if a prize is taken in neutral waters the neutral steps in, takes the prize, and restores it to the owner. Moreover, he said, the same thing happens when a prize is taken on the high seas by a ship fitted out in the neutral jurisdiction -- whenever the prize comes within the jurisdiction of the neutral, the neutral may seize and hold it for the owner. And say the Attorney and Solicitor General, the ground of this is that your neutrality has been violated, and whenever your neutrality has been violated you may go at once and seize any prize which comes into your possession. I was very much amused at an observation of the Attorney General in reference to his fellow Attorney at the Cape, which he might perhaps have rather more justly applied to the Solicitor General. My hon. and learned Friend said, that the Colonial Attorney General when he quoted *Wheaton*—which was a text-book — did not perceive the special and limited application of what he was quoting. I venture to recommend that observation to the Solicitor General. It is a dangerous thing to quote elementary writers unless you cite the whole of what they say on a particular subject. If the Solicitor General had looked a little closer at this part of *Wheaton* he would have seen there a most material statement, which would have relieved him from much of the obscurity into which he has fallen. *Wheaton* says—

" The jurisdiction of the national courts of the captors to determine the validity of captures made under the authority of their Government is exclusive of the judicial authority of every other country, with two exceptions only."

Which two exceptions are the cases mentioned by the Solicitor General, and which, being two exceptions only, negative the idea of there being any other exceptions. The first is where a capture has been made within the territorial limits of the neutral, and the second where it has been made by an armed vessel fitted out within the neutral jurisdiction. *Wheaton* then goes on to say that Louis XIV. did make an *ordonnance* in 1681, by which he attempted to extend the rule; but it was always considered unsound International Law, and had never been acted on. This is not a mere question of words. No Power has got the right to take a prize by the strong hand and restore it by the strong hand. What your right is, is to set up an Admiralty jurisdiction to determine the question of rightful capture. These questions are not to be determined by a Colonial Secretary, but by a Court duly founded for the purpose; and no International Law has said that you may have a Prize Court unless in those two excepted cases; and if you go beyond those cases you go beyond the limits and violate International Law. The Attorney General was driven by despair to rely on an ordinance of Holland 200 years old, which, so far as we know, has never been acted on, and which, if it were acted on, would prove immensely too much; in fact so much, that I do not suppose the Attorney General would rely on it for a moment. It was a municipal ordinance passed to this effect, that if a ship of war and a prize came into a certain part of their canals, not only the prize should be seized, but the ship of war also, and everybody on board put in prison. Is that the view of International Law taken by the Government? These are the only authorities which the Government can produce. Mr. Wheaton, into whom the Solicitor General has only cursorily looked, when he is properly understood, limits interference expressly to two exceptional cases; and as for the Dutch ordinance, I make the Attorney General a present of that with all my heart. If the Government had told us here as was declared in another place, that they were not prepared to contend for such propositions of International Law, then we should have no more to say; but here they contend that these propositions are right; and I say it is the duty of this House to take the matter up. The Government, we are told, are considering the matter, but they are considering it with the idea that they have got a right to seize these prizes. It is an affair which demands the attention of the House of Commons, for some morning we may wake up and find a conflict arisen in some one of our colonies, in which we shall have the mortification of having to admit that we are altogether in the wrong. I appeal, therefore, to the House of Commons to affirm the proposition contained in the Motion of my hon. Friend, that the instructions given by the Duke of Newcastle to Governor Wodehouse, which remain still unrevoked, are at variance with the principles of International Law.

Question put.

The House divided :—Ayes 219 ; Noes 185 : Majority 34.

Main Question put, and agreed to.

SUPPLY.

SUPPLY considered in Committee.

House resumed.

Committee report Progress ; to sit again this day.

CUSTOMS AND INLAND REVENUE BILL—[BILL 73.]—COMMITTEE.

Order for Committee read.

Bill considered in Committee.

(In the Committee.)

Clause 1 agreed to.

Clause 2 (Provisions of former Act to apply to this Act).

MR. CRAWFORD moved the addition of a proviso reserving the right of the Corporation of the City of London, the fellowship porters, and other corporate bodies, to charge for the weighing of all grains rates equivalent to the present charges for the measuring of such grains.

MR. AYRTON said, he was astonished that the Chancellor of the Exchequer should assent to a clause of this kind being smuggled into this Bill. It was an attempt to revive a duty that had formally been condemned by Committees of the House. The City did nothing for the money it received for measuring grain, and hitherto it never had the power to weigh grain. Already Committees of the House had reported against the City being allowed to retain these rights. The proposition was most extravagant, and he called upon the Committee to negative the proviso.

MR. ALDERMAN SIDNEY said, the merchants of London were satisfied with the existing state of things, and the question did not so much affect the privileges of the City, as the means of livelihood of 1,500 or 1,600 fellowship porters, who were of great service to the trading community.

SIR JOHN SHELLEY advised the Chancellor of the Exchequer not to mix himself up with what was likely to be a very pretty quarrel between the City and the rest of the metropolis. He rejoiced to find that grain was in future to be sold by weight. He thought the Chancellor of the Exchequer would do well to omit the

Sir Hugh Cairns

clause, for if it passed, the deputy corn meters would be entitled to compensation.

MR. NORRIS said, the metage of corn established by immemorial custom, and confirmed by charter of James I., was instituted for the purpose of enforcing justice between vendor and purchaser, and, as at present carried out, gave satisfaction. The matter was of sufficient importance to justify the moderate favour conferred by the clause.

MR. LOCKE believed the City of London received £13,000 a year for the metage of corn, after paying for the metage. The meters paid for their offices, and were entitled to protection.

THE CHANCELLOR OF THE EXCHEQUER said, that he disclaimed any interference with the Corporation of London, except by separate and direct legislation ; but if hon. Members desired to introduce a clause to preserve existing interests, he did not know that he should object to it, but he thought it should not be done in a Bill affecting the general interests of the revenue. They should make the proposition by a Bill on another day.

MR. CRAWFORD consented to withdraw the proviso, at the same time announcing that he should adopt such other measures as might seem most desirable for the protection of the interests of his constituents.

Clause agreed to.

Remaining clauses agreed to.

Schedule C.

MR. HENNESSY moved, by way of Amendment, the omission of that portion of it, under the operation of which a sailor might be charged a fee of £1 for a letter of attorney for the purpose of having his wages amounting to £10 drawn. That, he contended, was a provision which operated oppressively, seeing that an hon. Member of that House might draw out of the funds £10,000 under the operation of the same Schedule for a sum of 5s.

THE CHANCELLOR OF THE EXCHEQUER hoped that, as no notice had been given of the Amendment, the hon. Gentleman would consent to raise the Question on the Report.

MR. HENNESSY said, he would comply with that suggestion.

Amendment withdrawn.

MR. COX gave notice that, on the bringing up of the Report, he would move that the property in possession of pawnbrokers, and the carriages and horses of jobmasters should be deemed stock in trade.

THE CHANCELLOR OF THE EXCHEQUER approved the proposition as respected pawnbrokers, and moved the insertion of words to that effect; which was agreed to.

House *resumed*.

Bill *reported*, as amended; to be considered on *Monday* next, and to be *printed*. [Bill 82.]

UNION ASSESSMENT COMMITTEE ACT AMENDMENT BILL.

On Motion of *Mr. Villiers*, Bill to amend the Union Assessment Committee Act, *ordered* to be brought in by Mr. VILLIERS and Mr. GILPIN. Bill *presented*, and read 1°. [Bill 83.]

House adjourned at Two o'clock.

HOUSE OF LORDS,

Friday, April 29, 1864.

MINUTES.]—PUBLIC BILL—*Second Reading*—High Court at Bombay * (No. 57).

POSTPONEMENT OF MOTIONS. NOTICE OF MOTION ON POLAND.

THE EARL OF DERBY said, he desired to call attention to a matter which appeared to him to be of some importance as regarded their Lordships' convenience. A noble Lord opposite (Lord Campbell), whom he saw in his place, had given notice of his intention on three successive Mondays to bring before their Lordships a very important question relating to the condition of Poland. On three successive Fridays, when it was impossible for any other Notice to be placed on the paper, the noble Lord had announced his intention—not in the House—to postpone his Motion for another week. Now, as there were only two days in the week on which Notices of Motion took precedence of Orders of the Day, it was very inconvenient that other noble Lords should be prevented from putting Notices on the paper by the fact of the noble Lord opposite having a Notice of Motion there, which might lead to a lengthened discussion. He understood that the noble Lord had again postponed his Motion, he did not know till when, but probably till the following Monday. For his own part, he had no personal

interest in the matter, because he had no intention of taking a part in the expected discussion; but he thought that this practice of putting Notices on the paper week after week, and then postponing them at the very last moment, was one both unusual and inconvenient. He therefore begged to ask the noble Lord, whether it was his intention to bring forward his Motion on the day for which he had now fixed it?

LORD CAMPBELL said, the specific ground on which he had postponed the notice till next Monday was, that a debate upon the subject was expected in a few days in the other House of Parliament, which he deemed it better to follow than precede, because it might elicit facts important to be brought under the notice of their Lordships before they entered on the Question. He should proceed upon the 9th of May, unless the business or convenience of the House prevented him from doing so. With regard to the notice having already been postponed, he (Lord Campbell) could not enter into any explanation of the circumstances without going into matters which were to some extent personal and private. By taking such a course, he should stand too long between the noble Earl and the large number who were there to hear him on the interesting Question of the Steam Rams.

THE STEAM RAMS IN THE MERSEY.
ADDRESS FOR CORRESPONDENCE.

THE EARL OF DERBY, who had given notice "to call attention to the published Correspondence between Her Majesty's Government and Mr. Laird as to the Steam Rams," said: My Lords, early in the present Session, I asked the noble Earl the Foreign Secretary, Whether he would lay on the table a Correspondence which had taken place between her Majesty's Government and that of the United States —perhaps I might borrow the noble Earl's own phraseology, and say the "so-styled United States,"—in regard to various matters of deep interest, and, among others, the construction of Steam Rams in the Mersey, alleged to be intended for the Confederate States? The noble Earl informed me that there were objections to producing that Correspondence, inasmuch as it might prejudice a legal question that would shortly come on for decision. I yielded, I must confess, rather to the authority of the noble Earl's position than to his arguments. Soon after, however, a

Motion being made for the production of the same papers in the House of Commons, they were granted without hesitation by Her Majesty's Government. I then called on the noble Earl to explain the apparent diversity of opinion between himself and his colleagues on the subject of this Correspondence; and I was told that the objection for giving the papers was not his, but the Attorney General's ; and that the Attorney General had since seen that his first impression was erroneous, and that mischief at least would not be done to the extent he had apprehended from the production of the papers. Now I beg to enter my protest against that doctrine altogether. We have here nothing to do with the Attorney General. Those who are responsible for the production or withholding of documents connected with the public service are not the Law Officers, whom, however, it is quite right that the Government should consult, but the Ministers of the Crown themselves. It is by no means a satisfactory answer to us, that the Attorney General has changed his mind on a point which rests within the discretion of the Government and not of the Attorney General. Shortly afterwards a Motion was made in the House of Commons for the production of another Correspondence—that between the Government and Messrs. Laird on the subject of the Steam Rams. The question was argued very ably in the House of Commons, and was finally rejected by a majority not very large, but perhaps as large as Her Majesty's Government usually deem sufficient—a majority of twenty-five. The refusal of the papers was based on the ground that their production would be prejudicial to the public service. As in the former case the first class of papers had been laid before Congress, and therefore was open to the examination of any one ; so in the second case the whole of the papers are in the possession of one of the parties, by whom they have been published. I hold the Correspondence in my hand. I can assure your Lordships it is quite genuine ; it is neither intercepted nor forged ; it is entire, and has not been garbled or mutilated. It is the whole Correspondence between the two parties ; consequently, if I now move for the formal production of that Correspondence, I must confess that the answer which the noble Earl may give is a matter of comparative indifference, because I make my Motion for the purpose of commenting on the papers as I go on, having them in my

The Earl of Derby

hand, and being able to compare them with the documents laid on the table of the House, by which a very considerable amount of light is thrown upon what hitherto has been a very partial disclosure of facts.

I am afraid, my Lords, in bringing this Question before you, that it will be necessary to trespass on your patience for a considerable time, and that I shall have to do that which I know is most distasteful to your Lordships—to call your attention to a number of quotations from the printed documents. I beg your Lordships' attention to what I consider of no less importance — the several dates to which I shall refer as illustrating this Correspondence. At the outset I must express the conviction, in which I believe I am not at all singular, that this Correspondence discloses, on the part of the Messrs. Laird, the most unlimited frankness and openness, the most complete desire to meet the reasonable and even the unreasonable demands of the Government, a perfect alacrity to satisfy the Government on every point on which they are asked to give an explanation, an entire absence of all concealment, and a very ready, if not cheerful, submission to consequences which they must have felt to be very hard. On the other hand, I have come to the painful conclusion that, on the part of the Government, the Correspondence has been of a character most unusual, most vexatious, most arbitrary, and I will even go the length to say illegal. Who are the gentlemen with whom the Correspondence has been carried on ? They are young men now conducting one of the most extensive shipbuilding establishments in the country—a firm of the highest possible reputation, and personally of unimpeachable integrity and character. As to their works, I may mention that at this moment they are engaged in building for Her Majesty's service a most powerful iron-plated steam frigate. The father of these young men for many years conducted the same business, and during that time constructed numerous vessels for our own and other Governments. Unfortunately for him, perhaps, he entertained strong Conservative opinions. Perhaps more unfortunately still, it was his desire to have an opportunity of giving effect to those opinions by obtaining a seat in Parliament ; and most unfortunate of all, having, for the purpose of entering Parliament, transferred his business to his sons in order to divest himself from any objection of being a "contractor." Such was the respect and esteem in which he was held by his neighbours that he was elected the first representative of the newly-constituted and important borough of Birkenhead, in opposition to a gentleman of great local influence, and a strong supporter of Her Majesty's Government. These are the gentlemen with whom and against whom this Correspondence has been carried on.

My Lords, it is not necessary for me to call attention to any document in the Correspondence earlier than the 1st of September, except to point out that, as far back as the 7th of August, the United States Consul at Liverpool informed Mr. Adams that one of the rams had her masts up, her boilers and machinery in, and might be got ready for sea in a week's time. On the 3rd of September the same Consul wrote to Mr. Adams that the ram was taking coal on board, and that she might go to sea at any time, if not detained. Mr. Adams, of course, accepted the report of his Consul, and made various representations on the subject to the noble Earl opposite, on the 11th, 16th, and 25th of July, and again on the 14th of August. To none of these does the noble Earl appear to have given any answer till the 1st of September. During the whole of that interval he was carefully, elaborately investigating the matter, and endeavouring to ascertain whether there was a scrap of evidence which would justify him in detaining the vessel. On the 1st September the noble Earl then came to the following conclusions :—

"Whatever suspicion may be entertained by the United States Consul at Liverpool as to the ultimate destination of these vessels, the fact remains that M. Bravay, a French merchant residing at Paris, who is represented to be the person upon whose orders these ships have been built, has personally appeared, and has acted in that character at Liverpool. There is no legal evidence against M. Bravay's claim, nor anything to affect him with any illegal act or purpose; and the responsible agent of the Customs at Liverpool affirms his belief that these vessels have not been built for the Confederates. Under these circumstances, and having regard to the entire insufficiency of the depositions to prove any infraction of the law, Her Majesty's Government are advised that they cannot interfere in any way with these vessels. . . But I am sure you will be disposed, in justice to Her Majesty's Government, to admit that in the absence of all evidence, upon mere hearsay, surmise, conversation, and conjecture, Her Majesty's Government could not properly direct a prosecution or action under the Foreign Enlistment Act. A court of justice would never condemn in the absence of evidence, and the Government would be justly blamed for acting in defiance of the principles of law and justice long recognised and established in this country."

Mr. Adams on the 3rd of September wrote a more pressing letter, which appears not to have reached the Foreign Office till the 4th. On the 4th of September, the noble Earl informed Mr. Adams that these matters were under the consideration of the Government. Some discussion has already taken place as to the time when the directions were issued, and how far they were or not to be attributed to the representations, couched in strong language, of Mr. Adams; and I can only account for the singular involution of dates about this period by imagining that the noble Earl about that time assumed a sort of double character, and that his mythical and epistolatory form was in Downing Street, but that his physical and bodily part was, during the whole of September, in Scotland, where he was delighting and astonishing the world in general, and, not the least, his own political supporters, by making some astonishing revelations respecting the foreign and domestic policy of the Government to the inhabitants of Dundee and Blairgowrie. I do not trace the noble Earl's precise migration, but that he was present in Scotland previous to the 9th is clear, because on that day he harangued the people of Dundee; and that he had not departed on the 26th is clear, for on that day he was displaying his oratorical powers to the admiration of an audience at Blairgowrie. But during the month of September he seems to have been in bodily presence in Scotland, and carrying on a correspondence by proxy from Downing Street, which may certainly account for some little confusion of dates. The noble Earl must I think, however, have been misunderstood — certainly he was understood—to have stated that the letters of Mr. Adams could have had no influence upon him, because the decision to detain the vessels was taken so early as September 3, while Mr. Adams only wrote on the 3rd, his letter being received on the 4th, and the subsequent and stronger letter was only received on the 5th. I think that must be a mistake, because I find it mentioned in the Correspondence—

"That the determination to detain the rams was not come to until September 5, on which day the second letter of Mr. Adams was written."

That is not a point of much importance, because I will admit to the noble Earl that in all probability the last letter had no influence upon the determination of the

Government. But on the 5th September there is a letter from Mr. Layard, M.P., to Mr. Stewart —

"We have given orders to-day to the Commissioner of Customs at Liverpool to prevent the two iron-clads leaving the Mersey. These orders had scarcely been sent when we received the note from Mr. Adams, of which I send you a copy. Mr. Adams is not yet aware that orders have been given to stop the vessels; you may inform Mr. Seward confidentially of the fact."

This seems a most extraordinary conclusion; though the decision was come to on the 5th of September, no communication of it appears to have been made to Mr. Adams, to whom it was most important to have the earliest information, until the 8th, though his Government was confidentially informed by a despatch on the 5th that that decision had been come to. I think it unfortunate that that delay should have taken place, because if a communication of it had been made to Mr. Adams on the 5th, it might have induced him very considerably to modify the language of the despatch which on that day he addressed to Her Majesty's Government. Now comes a matter which appears to me still more extraordinary. On the 8th Mr. Adams has a communication addressed to him from Her Majesty's Government, stating that the iron-clads would not be allowed to leave Liverpool. On the 9th he acknowledges the receipt of that communication, and states the pleasure he shall feel in transmitting a copy for the information of his Government. One would have thought that the matter was closed there; or at all events that, by private communications, any further unpleasant correspondence might have been rendered unnecessary; but the noble Earl's epistolary *penchant* was too strong for him, and although the matter was settled to the entire satisfaction of Mr. Adams, he cannot resist the opportunity of entering into a critical discussion on the 11th of the despatch dated on the 5th. This correspondence leads to a rejoinder, this rejoinder leads to a further answer, after which a correspondence of considerable warmth seems to have taken place, which was not concluded till October. Now, I think Mr. Adams was hardly dealt with in not having had the communication of the determination of the Government made to him earlier. But there is another party who were still more hardly dealt with—the Messrs. Laird—who had no information given them of the determination to detain the vessels until the letter dated the 9th; and meantime a correspondence had been

The Earl of Derby

going on, the Messrs. Laird being in utter ignorance of the facts of the case. I cannot but confess the hope that the noble Earl will inform us what were the circumstances which so materially influenced the views of the Government. I can only say that it is a most unfortunate circumstance that, having waited patiently for six weeks, and having determined that there was no ground for proceeding against the builders of those vessels, they should, forty-eight hours afterwards, have received such a flood of information as to justify them in coming to such a contrary conclusion. I assume, of course, that they did receive such information; but it is an unfortunate coincidence that they did not receive it rather sooner, or that they did not communicate it at once. It appears from the Correspondence that on September 4 Messrs. Laird wrote to Mr. Price Edwards, the Collector of Customs at Liverpool —

"As the many rumours afloat in respect to the two iron steam rams built by us, and now lying in our dock, have induced frequent and unusual visits of Mr. Morgan, the Surveyor of Customs, to our works, we are desirous of saving you any further unnecessary trouble about these vessels by giving you our promise that they shall not leave the port without your having a week's notice of our intention to deliver them over to the owners, and we shall inform the owners of this engagement on our part. We may add that the first vessel will not be ready for a month, and the second for six or seven weeks from this date."

In the meantime the Collector of Customs thanks Messrs. Laird for the communication, which, he feels certain, will be highly satisfactory to the Board of Customs. And I here take the opportunity of saying that throughout the whole of this Correspondence all those who had to deal with these gentlemen—the authorities of the Customs, Captain Inglefield, Admiral Dacres—one and all express in the strongest language their entire and absolute reliance on the good faith of the Messrs. Laird. Messrs. Laird, against whom no suspicion of bad faith can be entertained, on the 4th of September promise to give a week's notice of their intention to deliver the two iron steam rams to the owners. But on September 4 the noble Earl, well aware that these vessels are the property of the shipbuilder, writes to say that he has been

"Led to understand that you have intimated, that while you were not in a position to volunteer information respecting the iron-clad vessels, lately launched and now being fitted out at your yard, you would readily furnish information upon an official application, in writing, being made to you for it. Under these circumstances, Lord Russell has instructed me to request you to inform him, with as little delay as possible, on whose account, and with what destination these vessels have been built."

On September 1st, the noble Earl had told the American Minister that he had sufficient information. Why, then, should he ask for further information on the 4th? Messrs. Laird were not inclined to withhold anything; the character of the vessels was known, and hundreds of people had had the opportunity of inspecting them. On the 5th of September, Messrs. Laird, in reply to the communication from the Foreign Office, wrote —

"That, although it is not usual for shipbuilders to declare the names of parties for whom they are building vessels until the vessels are completed and the owners have taken possession, yet, in this particular case, in consequence of the many rumours afloat, coupled with the repeated visits of Mr. Morgan, the Surveyor of Customs, to our works, we thought it right to ask permission of the parties on whose account we are building the vessels to give their names to the English Government, in the event of such information being asked for officially in writing. They at once granted us the permission we sought for. We therefore beg to inform you that the firm on whose account we are building the vessels is A. Bravay and Co., and that their address is No. 6. Rue de Londres, Paris, and that our engagement is to deliver the vessels to them in the port of Liverpool when they are completed according to our contract. The time in which we expect to have the first vessel so completed is not less than one month from this date, and the second not less than six or seven weeks from this date."

Now, my Lords, when I read this Correspondence it occurred to me that possibly it might be said that the arrangement to deliver the vessels in the port of Liverpool might appear a questionable matter, and I asked whether that was the usual arrangement? I was informed by Mr. Laird, the father of the Messrs. Laird, that he had built fifty vessels for the English, Indian, and foreign Governments, and that invariably his contract was, unless when a different stipulation was expressly made, to deliver the vessels in the port of Liverpool. Therefore, there was nothing unusual in that form of contract. Not satisfied with having received that information from Messrs. Laird, Her Majesty's Government directed Mr. Hoares, the naval attaché to the Embassy at Paris, to wait on M. Bravay. He did so accordingly and they showed him the whole of the documents connected with the transaction, and allowed him to inspect the books and examine the papers. The naval attaché expressed himself perfectly satisfied with

the *bond fide* ownership of the vessels by M. Bravay, and so reported to Her Majesty's Government. So satisfied were Her Majesty's Government on this point that, at the close of the month of November, they directed the attaché to treat with M. Bravay for the purchase of the vessels. In this state matters remained, except that on the 8th of September Messrs. Laird wrote to the Collector of Customs at Liverpool, stating—

"We think it right to inform you that it is our intention to take one of the iron-clads—the *El Tousson*—from our graving dock for a trial trip on Monday next, within the usual limits of such trial trips ; and you may rely on our bringing the vessel into the Birkenhead float when the trial is finished, it being our intention to complete the vessel in the Birkenhead float. This trial is necessary to test the machinery and other parts, but will not alter the time previously stated for the completion of the vessel."

This was at a time when Her Majesty's Government had already come to the conclusion to seize the vessels, and before Messrs. Laird were aware of that determination. Messrs. Laird received the information on the following day, that the Collector of Customs at Liverpool could not allow the trial trip to take place without the leave of Her Majesty's Government. That was on the 11th ; but on the 17th the Collector of Customs at Liverpool received a communication for Messrs. Laird conveying the sanction of Her Majesty's Government for the trial trip in these words—

"The Lords Commissioners of Her Majesty's Treasury will allow the trial trip to be made by the vessel referred to in your letter of the 18th inst., relying upon the honourable engagement which has been given by you that the ship shall, after the usual trial trip, be brought back again to Liverpool, and shall not leave that port without a week's notice to Her Majesty's Government of the intention to send her away."

But, in the meantime, a letter had been already received by Messrs. Laird from the Secretary to the Treasury informing them that—

"The two iron-clad steamers now in course of completion in your dock at Birkenhead are not to be permitted to leave the Mersey until satisfactory evidence can be given of their destination, or at least until the inquiries which are now being prosecuted with a view to obtain such evidence shall have been brought to a conclusion."

My Lords, I must pause here for a single moment, because I consider this a matter of the greatest possible importance. I hold —and I think it cannot be denied—that no one in this House, whether lawyer or layman, can maintain that the instruction to detain the vessels in the Mersey until Her Majesty's Government should obtain satisfactory evidence of their intended destination, or until the inquiries which were being prosecuted to obtain such evidence should be brought to a conclusion, was not a proceeding utterly unwarranted by law, and one for which there was not the slightest justification. I could understand the seizure of those vessels with sufficient evidence of whatever cause assigned, whether or not under a charge of having violated the Foreign Enlistment Act, because such a seizure would involve the necessity of ultimately coming to trial, and would give the parties accused an opportunity of coming forward to vindicate their conduct ; but detention until such time as Her Majesty's Government were satisfied of the guilt or innocence of the owners appears to me inconsistent with the first principles of English law and justice. You are not to call upon a person to prove his innocence ; you are to prove his guilt, and not throw upon the defence the *onus* of showing that he was not engaged in anything illegal. What was the natural reply of the Messrs. Laird ? It was, in effect, this : — " We have given you the name of the owner, and forwarded a copy of your letter to Messrs. Bravay. As to what Messrs. Bravay are going to do with the vessels when they have received them it is not for us to inquire." I submit that was a very proper answer ; but to say that you will detain the vessels in the Mersey until you have made inquiries, no matter what time it may take you, whether nine, ten, or twelve months — in fact, nobody knows how long—is to my mind a proceeding not consonant with law or justice. And the Attorney General was obliged to admit that that was a course taken upon the responsibility of Her Majesty's Government, for the purpose of preventing and anticipating an evasion of the law. "Well, then," said my hon. and learned Friend Sir Hugh Cairns, "the answer on the part of Her Majesty's Government is, " We have violated the law for the purpose of vindicating the law.'" It is impossible to put the matter more tersely and more distinctly, and I venture to say that no lawyer in this House will take upon himself to say that Her Majesty's Government were justified in detaining the vessels without cause shown and for an indefinite period. Well, on the 17th of September, as I have already said, permission was given to go on the trial trip, which hardly

The Earl of Derby

extended beyond the limits of the port of Liverpool, and was not outside the light ship at the mouth of the harbour ; but if Messrs. Laird had any sinister intention they would have had no difficulty in going out, with the full permission of Her Majesty's Government, and evading the law. But a change came over the spirit of the dream of the noble Earl very rapidly, almost as rapidly as the sudden influx of evidence which took place between the 1st and 3rd of September; for on the 19th, two days after the sanction for the trial trip had been received, the Messrs. Laird were informed by the Secretary to the Treasury as follows :—

"I am now commanded by the Lords Commissioners of Her Majesty's Treasury to inform you, that since that permission was given circumstances have come to the knowledge of Her Majesty's Government which give rise to apprehension that an attempt may be made to seize the vessel in question while on her trial trip. I am to state to you explicitly that Her Majesty's Government are convinced that it is your intention, as far as it is in your power, to fulfil honourably the engagement into which you have entered ; and that if any such attempt were made, it would be entirely without the privity of your firm, in whose good faith they place perfect confidence. Inasmuch, however, as such an occurrence, in whatever method it may be brought about, would be contrary to the determination expressed by Her Majesty's Government that the iron-clad vessels should be prevented leaving the port of Liverpool until satisfactory evidence may be given as to their destination, I am to state to you that this Board feel it their duty to apprise you that they cannot permit the trial trip except under provision against any forcible abduction of the vessels."

Was that forcible abduction to take place by a sudden rising of any portion of the crew who were to be put on board by Messrs. Laird, by their own hands, men who had been in their employ for years; or was it to be effected by any other vessels at the mouth of the Mersey making an attack upon this powerful ram, seizing her and carrying her off to sea ? And what was the time selected for such an attempt? It was the time of all others, when the whole Channel Fleet was in the Mersey ; when an unusually large population was crowding the river, who must have been witnesses, and could not be passive witnesses of any such attempt. I happen to recollect the fact, because I had on Saturday, the 19th, the pleasure of receiving at Knowsley most of the officers of the squadron, and Admiral Dacres was to do me the honour of remaining with me over the Sunday, in the hope of spending a quiet day. But he was lamentably disappointed; for over came a messenger, post haste, to say that there was not a moment to lose, for that he was charged by Her Majesty's Government to take measures for preventing the escape of the steam rams. The gallant Admiral went over to Liverpool, and the first persons he called on were the Messrs. Laird, who acted towards him with the greatest possible openness and candour. I will not say what were the expressions of the gallant Admiral upon his return to Knowsley; but it occurred to me then, and it occurs to me now, that the gallant Admiral was sent on a fool's errand. But did the Messrs. Laird make any remonstrance? Not at all. On the 21st of September the Messrs. Laird wrote to the Government—

"We have the honour to reply to your letter of the 19th inst. (received and acknowledged yesterday), informing us that circumstances have come to the knowledge of Her Majesty's Government, giving rise to an apprehension that an attempt may be made to seize our iron-clad steam vessel on her trial trip, and stating that authority had been given to Admiral Dacres to place, with our concurrence, a sufficient force of seamen and marines on board her to defeat any such attempt. We are not ourselves aware of any circumstance to induce us to entertain any such apprehension, but we beg to thank Her Majesty's Government for the protection thus placed at our disposal, of which we shall gladly avail ourselves. Owing, however, to what you have brought under our notice, and the incomplete state of the vessel, and also the present crowded state of the river Mersey, it will be desirable to defer the trial trip for some days; and, in the meantime, we trust that Her Majesty's Government will be able to obtain further information as to any project that may exist to deprive us of our property."

We see now the conditions upon which, on the 21st of September, Her Majesty's Government were prepared to allow the trial trip; and they were prepared to allow it so late as the 24th of September, because the Government then informed Mr. Adams that they had given permission under those engagements and with those precautions which have been described to make the trial trip. I hope your Lordships will bear these dates in mind, as they throw light upon the grounds upon which Her Majesty's Government took the very extraordinary steps of which I complain. On the 7th of October a further communication was made to Messrs. Laird in these terms—

"Referring to your ready acceptance of the offer of Her Majesty's Government to prevent any attempt at the forcible abduction of your property, the iron-clad vessel now nearly completed at Birkenhead, and understanding that the trial trip which has been the subject of former correspondence has been abandoned, I am directed by the Lords Commissioners of Her Majesty's Treasury to acquaint you that, from information which has been received, it has become necessary to take additional means for preventing any such attempt."

On what grounds it is assumed that the trial trip was abandoned I do not know. It is because it was stated by the Messrs. Laird that it was desirable to postpone it until Her Majesty's Government should obtain further information as to the dangerous plot against their property? But what were the additional means for guarding against these supposed enemies—these anonymous depredators?

"Their Lordships have therefore given instructions that a Custom House officer should be placed on board that vessel, with full authority to seize her on behalf of the Crown, in the event of any attempt being made to remove her from the float or dock where she is at present, unless under further directions from their Lordships; and likewise to obtain from the officer in command of Her Majesty's ship *Majestic* any protection which may become necessary to support him in the execution of this duty. My Lords request you to understand that these precautions are taken, not from any distrust of your intention to fulfil your engagement of giving a week's notice before the removal of the vessel, nor with the view of interfering in any way with your workmen in the completion of her, but exclusively for the purpose of preventing an attempt which may be made by other parties to nullify your engagement."

Still no objection on the part of Messrs. Laird, for they say in reply—

"We have given the necessary order for admission to the vessel (called by us the *El Tousson*) to Mr. Morgan, the Surveyor of Customs."

Well, Mr. Morgan thanks the Messrs. Laird, and acknowledges their frankness and openness throughout the whole business. And now what was the position of this injured vessel at this time? It was lying in the Great Float of Birkenhead, under the protection of the dock authorities, the police, among a number of other vessels; it could not be removed without forcing open the entrance gates of the dock, a measure not easy at any time, and only possible at certain times of the tides, and consequently the attack must be very summary—a *coup de main*, in fact—by which the Custom House officers, the authorities of the dock, the harbour-masters, were to be suddenly overwhelmed by an inroad which should force open the docks, lay hold of the ship, carry her out to sea; and all that time the ship was incapable of moving because she had neither fuel on board nor her steam up. That was the danger apprehended, and against which it was thought the placing of a Custom House officer on board was an effectual provision. My Lords, the Custom House officer might seize the vessel; but if the danger apprehended were a real one, he would stand a very good chance of being seized himself, and he would be very fortunate if he were allowed to go on shore. But if danger really existed, there were very simple precautions that might have been taken. The authorities might have detached the screw, might have taken off the rudder, or might have displaced some portion of the machinery, so as to render it impossible for any force to have removed the vessel suddenly. Could anything be more ridiculous than the apprehension of the seizure of such a vessel in its incomplete state in the middle of the port of Liverpool? But this was not enough. On the 9th of October, Messrs. Laird wrote to the Treasury as follows:—

"We have received this day a letter from Mr. Morgan, the Surveyor of Customs, giving us notice that, by direction of the hon. Commissioners of Customs, he has this day seized the iron-clad vessel now lying in the Great Float at Birkenhead. Since the receipt of your letter of the 7th inst. no attempt has been made to remove the vessel from her moorings at the quay in the Great Float, and we are therefore at a loss to understand this apparent deviation from the decision of their Lordships, as expressed in their letter of the 7th, above referred to. But we consider this has been done not with any distrust of our intentions to fulfil our engagement of giving a week's notice of our intention to remove the vessel, nor with the view of interfering in any way with the workmen in the completion of her, but exclusively for the purpose of preventing an attempt which may be made by other parties to nullify our engagement. Although we are not aware of any circumstances to induce us to entertain any apprehension of any attempt being made to deprive us of our property by force, we gladly avail ourselves of any protection Her Majesty's Government may think necessary for its security. The vessel is still far from being ready for sea, and the work has been so much retarded by the excessively wet weather, that it will be some weeks before she is finally completed."

Not satisfied with what they had done, the Government, on the 9th of October, wrote to say—

"In consequence of information that has been received by Her Majesty's Government as to the probability of a forcible abduction of one or both of the iron-clad vessels in course of completion in the Float at Birkenhead, their Lordships have felt it their duty to order the seizure of both these vessels, and have issued the necessary directions to the Commissioners of Customs accordingly."

The Messrs. Laird replied—

The Earl of Derby

"We have made the fullest inquiry, and have not been able to ascertain any circumstance to induce us to apprehend the probability of a forcible abduction of one or both of the iron-clad vessels in course of completion by us at Birkenhead—one, the *El Tousson*, in the Great Float, the public dock, and the other, the *El Monassia*, in our own dock, on our own premises. Both vessels are incomplete, and unfit for seagoing; the second vessel has not even got masts or funnel in, and both are in the sole charge of our own people. We believe, further, that if any such project as the forcible abduction of these vessels had ever been thought of, it could not successfully have been carried out in the port of Liverpool. Their Lordships have so often assured us that they are convinced that it is our intention, so far as in our power lies, to fulfil honourably the engagement which we have entered into with Her Majesty's Government, that we have deferred making any formal protest against the seizure of these vessels, or the arbitrary and extraordinary measures that have been carried out in placing an armed force in charge. We can only suppose that their Lordships have been induced to act as they have done by some information, which will be found, on further investigation, to have been entirely erroneous or greatly exaggerated, and that they will, on the termination of the inquiries they have set on foot to investigate the case, feel justified in removing the vexatious restrictions they have placed upon our property, which have already caused, and are still causing us an amount of loss and annoyance not easily estimated."

What was the position of this second vessel? She was a mere hulk, without masts, funnel, or steering apparatus. She was lying, not in the floating dock, but in the private yard of the Messrs. Laird, which was secured by a caisson that blocked up the entrance. This could only be removed so as to allow of the launching of the vessel within an hour or so of high water, and which could not be removed even then at low neap tides. The vessel, further, could not be floated out of the dock unless the sluices were opened, the keys of which were in Messrs. Lairds' own custody, or in that of their chief superintendent. This was the state of things up to October 9.

I will now ask your Lordships to bear with me—although I feel I am detaining you at undue length—while I endeavour to connect by means of the Parliamentary papers the extraordinary steps taken by Her Majesty's Government on the 19th of September, and again on the 7th and 9th of March. Here is a despatch from Mr. Adams, dated the 24th of September, which will cast some light on the circumstances that threw the Government into this state of panic. Mr. Adams says—

"I am credibly informed that seventy or more of the men belonging to the insurgent vessel the *Florida*, formerly the *Oreto*, nearly all of them

British subjects, have been sent over from Brest, and are now in Liverpool. They were provided with a letter to the person acting on behalf of the insurgents at Liverpool, a copy of which is herewith transmitted. I need not point out to your Lordship the fact, that the last sentence implies habitual action in direct violation of the law of the realm; such, indeed, as if committed by any agent of the United States, would be likely to attract the immediate notice of Her Majesty's Government. It corroborates all the evidence heretofore presented by me on the same subject. I have further reason to believe that under this sentence is intended a transfer of many of these men to one of the iron-clad war vessels now in preparation at Liverpool with intent to carry on war against the United States. It is known to me that the intention to despatch that vessel is not yet abandoned by the parties concerned in the enterprise."

That letter was received on the 26th of September at the Foreign Office, but not by the noble Earl, who was then in Scotland, addressing the people of Blairgowrie. It was answered by the Foreign Office on the 30th of September, probably by the desire of the noble Earl, as follows:—

" I have the honour to acknowledge the receipt of your letter of the 24th inst., calling my attention to the arrival at Liverpool of a large party of men belonging to the Confederate steamer *Florida*; and I have to acquaint you that I lost no time in communicating to the Secretary of State for the Home Department copies of your letter and of its enclosures. I have to add, however, that the attention of Her Majesty's Government had been, some days previously to the receipt of your letter, attracted by paragraphs in the public papers to the arrival of these men, and that inquiries were at once set on foot, and that the course which can be taken in regard to them is under the serious consideration of Her Majesty's Government."

Now, some days before the 24th—that is to say, on the 19th of September—the Government retracted the permission they had given to Messrs. Laird on the 14th to make a trial trip, and which permission was received by the Messrs. Laird on the 17th of September. On the 25th of September, Mr. Adams was informed that permission to make a trial trip had been given to Messrs. Laird. On the 26th, a letter was received from Mr. Adams, which I have read to your Lordships, announcing the arrival of the seventy men of the *Florida*, and the rumour that they had formed a plan for carrying off the iron-clad. That letter was answered on the 30th of September, when the Government stated that their attention had been for some days attracted to the subject; and on the 7th of October, the further step was taken of seizing these vessels in the dock and works of Messrs. Laird. A comparison of these dates will show that there is some connection between the alarming information conveyed in Mr. Adams's letter and the steps taken against Messrs. Laird. I must admit that the alarm of the Government appears to have been genuine, because, when the Channel Fleet left Liverpool on the 24th or 25th, the Government thought the danger so great that they considered it necessary not only to leave the *Majestic* in the Mersey, but also the *Liverpool* and a gunboat, to watch this steam ram. And when it was proposed to withdraw the *Liverpool*, so serious was the danger and so imminent the probable catastrophe, that the Government, on the 23rd of October, despatched to Liverpool, in an incomplete state, one of the first iron-clads in the service, which was within an ace of foundering in the Channel. That vessel, accordingly, did not reach the port of Liverpool, and did not contribute to the safety of that port. What were the facts in regard to these seventy men from the *Florida*, who were to carry away this vessel by main force, to cause an insurrection in Liverpool, and overbear all law and order there? The noble Earl will say that he was bound to take measures to prevent the possibility of such an occurrence. But does he know the circumstances connected with the cruise of the *Florida*? Because I think, if your Lordships will allow me, I can throw a little light upon it. It is true that sixty or seventy men of the *Florida* did arrive in Liverpool, and that they were dispatched with a letter from Captain Maffit, commander of the *Florida*, to Captain Bullock, the Confederate agent at Liverpool. But they arrived, not as an organised body of men in the Confederate service, not having their officers with them, but simply as discharged seamen, with their discharge papers in their pockets, and with their accounts and notes giving them a title to receive the wages they had earned according to length of service. They had left the ship at Brest, they had been refused leave to go on shore before their discharge, and they came to Liverpool to obtain payment of their wages. Captain Bullock was not then in Liverpool, but before the 17th of September they went to a firm which they thought had authority to pay them. This firm demurred as to their liability and disputed the claim; and these dreadful depredators, conspirators, and incendiaries, who in their mad love for the Confederates were about to venture upon a deed of unparalleled audacity—where did they go to? Why, to the United States Consul. Upon the refusal to pay their wages they proceeded to the United States Consul, showed him their claims, placed themselves in his hands, and entreated him to procure for them the money unjustly withheld. This was just before the 17th; and who is supposed to have put those paragraphs into the papers which attracted the attention of Her Majesty's Government? Why, of course, the United States Consul. He obtained this information, and thinking it much too good to be lost, sent off and frightened the Government into preventing the trial trip of the vessels. And what did the United States Consul do with the seamen? He recommended them to his own attorney. He sent them to a very respectable attorney—Mr. Carr, of Capel Street, if the noble Lord wants to know who he is. On the 17th of September, this gentleman made a formal demand on the firm in question for the money due to the men. On the 23rd of September, a second demand was made, accompanied by an intimation that the men had been with the United States Consul, and on the 25th the attorney served five writs on the parties in order to enforce payment. The liability was disputed; but upon a conference between the attorneys for the parties respectively, and after communicating with France, the money was paid. Some of the sailors had received their pay previously, but the whole of them, fifty-five in number, were paid on the 13th of October, with the exception of a few, who, being tired of waiting, had already engaged in other ships. On receipt of their money, and on procuring employment, they went away, declaring one thing—that no power on earth should induce them to re-enter the Confederate service, where they had been so scurvily treated. These are the men whose arrival in Liverpool put the noble Earl and the Government entirely off their balance, and led them to take such extraordinary precautions against dangers which never existed, and which I should have thought would never have been entertained seriously by any Government in its sound senses. After the events I have just stated took place, Messrs. Laird renewed their application for permission to hold the long-delayed trial trip, subject to the conditions originally agreed upon, of having sufficient guard placed on board the vessel. On the 24th of October, the Lords Commissioners of Her Majesty's Treasury stated that, after duly

weighing all the circumstances of the case, they were unable to consent to the trial trip of the *El Tousson*, neither could they allow the removal of the armed force which was stationed for the purpose of upholding the Custom House officer in possession of the vessel. Messrs. Laird explained that they did not wish to dispense with the presence of an armed force if the Government still thought it necessary; but they respectfully renewed their application to make the trial trip in the course of the next week, or within any suitable time. The only answer to that was the following:—

"Gentlemen,—In reply to your letter of the 24th instant, I am commanded by the Lords Commissioners of Her Majesty's Treasury to acquaint you that they are unable to comply with your request to make a trial trip of the *El Tousson*, one of the iron-clad vessels fitting in your yard in Birkenhead, in the course of this week, or within any other suitable time."

Then we come to a fresh step in these proceedings, not perhaps illegal, but involving further injury to those gentlemen. On the 27th of October, the Collector of Customs at Liverpool wrote to Messrs. Laird, saying—

"Gentlemen,—I hereby beg to inform you that your two cupola vessels are now detained, under the 223rd section of the Customs Consolidated Act, the ground of detention being a violation of the Foreign Enlistment Act: and I take leave further to state, that the officers in charge have received directions to remove your workmen at once from on board the ships."

Not only were directions given to seize the vessels for this alleged breach of the Foreign Enlistment Act, but so strong were the apprehensions entertained that these two unfinished vessels might be carried away by force, that the most extraordinary order, as it appears to me, was given—that the vessels should be taken out of the docks, where they were in perfect safety, and moved out into the estuary, where no protection whatever existed, except that they were under the guns of Her Majesty's ship. Messrs. Laird wrote to the Foreign Office, saying—

"Captain Inglefield informs us that his orders are to take the two iron-clads into the river Mersey. We protest against the probable destruction of our property in having ships (one of which is a mere hulk without masts, funnel, or steering gear) taken out of docks, where they are now in safety, and moored in the river at this inclement season of the year, and we trust that the orders sent to Captain Inglefield will be reconsidered."

To this protest the following reply was sent by telegraph from the Treasury:—

"Captain Inglefield will, no doubt, in his dispositions regarding the iron-clad vessels, take every proper precaution for the preservation of the property. The orders have been well considered, and cannot be revoked or altered."

I may say, in passing, that Captain Inglefield, in the discharge of his very painful and embarrassing duty, certainly appears to have conducted himself with the most perfect courtesy, in the most gentlemanlike manner, and without the slightest feeling against the parties towards whom he must have known that his orders were compelling him to act very harshly. On the other hand, Captain Inglefield bears positive testimony to the ready and cheerful compliance of the Messrs. Laird with all his requirements, and to the facilities which they afforded him in every way in carrying his orders into effect. Indeed, so far did he rely on the entire readiness of the Messrs. Laird to meet his wishes, that actually, when, contrary to their protest, he was about to take the vessels out of dock and moor them in the river, he applied to them for the loan of an anchor and cable to enable him to moor the vessels in safety, which otherwise he could not do. This was a stretch of politeness even beyond the Messrs. Laird, and they accordingly wrote to say, that although they should offer no obstruction to the course proposed, upon Her Majesty's Government would rest the whole responsibility of that course, as they were not going to make themselves parties to an act of which they entirely disapproved, and against which they had strongly protested. With regard to the process of getting the vessels out of dock, the difficulties were such that it was a considerable time before Captain Inglefield could get a favourable opportunity of raising the caisson and moving them out ; and, for the greater security of the vessels, an order was made and assented to by the Messrs. Laird, that whenever it was proposed to raise ·the caisson, twenty-four hours' notice should be given and permission obtained. Looking at all these transactions, it is impossible to say that submission to arbitrary demands could be carried further, or greater willingness to meet the Government in a fair spirit shown than was exhibited by the Messrs. Laird. On the 29th of October, Messrs. Laird thought it time to protest energetically, going in detail through all the circumstances of which they complained, and they concluded by saying—

"We made no objection to these means, provided by the Government for our protection, though we were then, and still are, unable to discover any grounds whatever for these precautionary measures, and we are satisfied that Her Majesty's Government have lent too credulous an ear to the inventions of designing persons. But when Her Majesty's Government, without giving us any information to show us that they have any just grounds for doing so, proceed to seize our ships and turn off our workmen, and threaten to remove a helpless hulk from a place of safety into the open roadstead of the Mersey, we feel it our duty to enter our indignant protest against proceedings so illegal and so unconstitutional. We have dealt candidly and openly with Her Majesty's Government. We have, with the owners' permission, given the names of the owners, and we believe we have a perfect legal right to build ships for a French subject without requiring from him a disclosure of his object in having such vessels constructed. It forms no part of our duty to interfere in any way with his affairs, and we shall not do so. We need hardly say that we hold ·the Government responsible to us for the large pecuniary loss we shall sustain by these arbitrary proceedings."

That remonstrance was addressed to the Admiralty, the Foreign Office, and the Treasury. The Admiralty forwarded the despatch to the Foreign Office, the Foreign Office forwarded both despatches to the Treasury, and the Treasury took no action whatever upon them. On the 7th December, Messrs. Laird wrote—

"My Lord,—We beg to call your attention to the present condition of the two steam vessels, the *El Tousson* and the *El Monassia*, which have been removed by Captain Inglefield from dock into the river Mersey. On Thursday last, it blew a very heavy gale of wind here, and several large vessels, one of them a large steamer, were driven from their moorings within the estuary. We understand that no steps are as yet taken to bring the rights of the Crown before a jury, and in the meantime the vessels are exposed to great risk. It is a matter of serious importance to us, as in case the vessels should be lost or burned in the Mersey before we can deliver them to the owners, we shall be thereby prevented from completing our contract. Our attention is more immediately called to this subject by the fact that one of the fire policies of the *El Monassia* expires to-day, and we are in doubt what, under the circumstances, we ought to do. It is evident that the vessels ought to be insured, both against sea-risk and fire, and we shall be glad to know whether Her Majesty's Government have taken these precautions for the security of the property, and if not, whether they intend to do so. We may further state that we trust the Government have given strict orders that proper precautions are taken for the preservation of the property from the injury and deterioration it is liable to from exposure to the damp and wet at this inclement season."

On the 18th of December, the policy referred to having expired on the 7th, the Treasury condescended to inform the Messrs. Laird—

"Gentlemen,—With further reference to your letter of the 7th instant, respecting the present condition of the two steam vessels, *El Tousson* and *El Monassia*, I am desired by the Lords Commissioners of Her Majesty's Treasury to acquaint you, that it is the intention of Her Majesty's Government that the existing insurances on these vessels should be kept up or renewed, *ad interim*, at the cost of the public, and in the name of some person on Her Majesty's behalf, who, if you will agree to repay the cost of such insurance in the event of the property in the vessels being hereafter adjudged to you, may be constituted a trustee for the policy of Her Majesty, or for such person or persons as may hereafter be adjudged to be the owner or owners of the vessels, according to the result of the proceedings which may be taken for the purpose of deciding on the validity of the seizures. As regards the precautions to be taken for preserving the vessels from injury by weather, my Lords are satisfied that every possible precaution has been already taken, and will continue to be taken, by the naval officer in command at Liverpool, and that no deterioration of any kind need be anticipated."

The Messrs. Laird had very naturally refused to comply with the condition which was thus demanded of them, and they stated their objection to it in the following communication of the 22nd of December :—

" To the Secretary to the Treasury.

" Sir,—We have the honour to acknowledge the receipt of your letter of the 18th instant, stating that it is the intention of Her Majesty's Government to keep up and renew, *ad interim*, the insurances of the *El Tousson* and *El Monassia*, at the cost of the public, provided we will agree to repay the cost of such insurances in the event of the property in the vessels being hereafter adjudged to us, according to the result of the proceedings which may be taken for the purpose of deciding on the validity of the seizures. In reply we beg respectfully to submit to you that the condition we are asked to agree to is not reasonable. For, not only do the vessels incur marine risk by being exposed in the estuary of the Mersey, which risk would not have arisen if the vessels had remained in the docks, but the time has expired during which they would have been in our possession at all. If they had remained in dock no marine insurance would have been necessary; and if they had not been seized they would, ere this, have been delivered to the purchasers. Under these circumstances we respectfully submit that the vessels should be insured, and kept insured, at the public cost, without any such condition being imposed on us. We beg to inform you that another policy against fire for £20,500 expires on the 24th inst."

A postscript to the same letter mentioned the fact that two further policies against fire, one for £14,000 and another for £5,000, also expired on the 24th inst. One would have thought this a pressing matter, deserving of early consideration on the part of the Treasury. But on the 30th of December, Messrs. Laird write again to draw attention to their letter of the 22nd, and still no answer is returned. On the 9th of January they write again to the same effect, the policies having expired in the meantime; and ultimately, on the 20th of January, a response is vouchsafed from the Treasury, saying that Her Majesty's Government would do what from the first they were bound to have done—namely, provide in the manner they might consider requisite against the risks from fire and other damages to the iron-clad vessels while they remained in possession of Her Majesty's Government.

My Lords, I pass now to another transaction. On the 12th of January, no answer having been given with regard to the insurance, and no steps having been taken to bring the question to trial, Messrs. Laird wrote again, making the following proposals to the Government :—

" That the vessels should be moved into the Birkenhead public docks, and placed at the top end of the Great Float, about a mile from the entrance, the Government retaining possession by an armed force, or otherwise, as they may think requisite, so that we may be able to complete our contract, which we are desirous of doing, although the value of the additional fittings which we should put on board would be very considerable."

I think it will be apparent that it indicates no consciousness of guilt on the part of Messrs. Laird, that they were willing to go to much further expense upon vessels which had been seized by and were in the possession of the Government. They put the case very fairly—

" In the event of the Government proving their right to retain the vessels, they will, if our proposal be agreed to, be in a much more perfect state. On the other hand, should the Government not succeed, the vessels will be sooner ready for delivery by us to the owners, and consequently any claim for damages against the Government would be reduced."

Could there be a more reasonable proposal than that the vessels should be taken to the top end of the Great Float, a mile from the entrance, under the charge of an armed force, and that Messrs. Laird should be allowed to complete the vessels, thus adding to the security which the Government possessed ? What was the answer ?

" Gentlemen,—In reply to your letter of the 12th inst., proposing that the *El Tousson* and *El Monassia* should be placed in the Birkenhead docks, and there completed, I am commanded by the Lords Commissioners of the Treasury to inform you that their Lordships regret that they are unable to comply with your request."

No reason assigned ! no objections taken ! but a mere absolute refusal to permit the owners to do that which if they had been allowed to do it would have been materially to the advantage of the Government. My

The Earl of Derby

noble and gallant Friend behind me (the Earl of Hardwicke) says, " I cannot understand that." I am not surprised at this difficulty. It was a self-stultifying policy on the part of the Government. On the 25th of January, Messrs. Laird say—

" In the meantime, we beg to call the attention of the Lords of the Treasury to the fact that, though it is now several months since the vessels were seized, yet no steps have as yet been taken to bring the matter to a legal decision, although our attorneys have repeatedly pressed this course on the Law Advisers of the Crown."

That remonstrance met with the same plain refusal. Again, on the 3rd of February, these unfortunate owners, who had been kept out of their property for four months, say—

" We beg, however, to call your attention to the fact, that no information has yet been afforded to us in reply to our repeated requests to know when the legal proceedings in the Court of Exchequer will be brought to trial before a jury. We are informed by our legal advisers that they have repeatedly pressed this matter on the attention of the Law Officers of the Crown, but are unable to obtain any satisfactory information, although the case might have been brought to trial in November last, or in January last. We therefore feel ourselves entitled to urge upon Her Majesty's Government the propriety of their at once informing us as to the time when they propose to bring this matter to trial."

In answer to that communication they at last, on the 8th of February, received this letter from the Secretary of the Treasury—

" Gentlemen,—In reply to your letter of the 3rd inst., I am commanded by the Lords Commissioners of Her Majesty's Treasury to acquaint you that they are informed that an ' information,' in the case of the iron-clad vessels built by you, and now under seizure by Her Majesty's Government, will be filed in a few days, and that it may be necessary to send a commission abroad for the purpose of collecting evidence."

To send a commission abroad for the purpose of collecting evidence on the 8th of February! Why, four months before the Government had actually seized those vessels on a charge of violating the Foreign Enlistment Act, and a month before that they had illegally detained them upon no evidence or information whatever; and at the end of four months they inform the owners of these vessels, which had been lying through the whole winter unprotected in the open estuary of the Mersey, whereby they had been prevented from completing their contract, that they are about to send out a commission for the purpose of obtaining evidence.

The last part of the subject with which I shall have to trouble your Lordships is the circumstances which led to the writing of that letter of the 8th of February. We have seen that for four months Messrs. Laird had been constantly persevering and vainly pressing Her Majesty's Government to bring this case to trial. They had done so unsuccessfully until a few days after the meeting of Parliament ; and my firm belief is that no information would have been filed up to this hour if it had not been for two circumstances—one, that Parliament was meeting on the 4th or 5th of February, and some very inconvenient questions were likely to be put ; and the other, the transaction to which I am about to refer, and which, I think, is one of the most extraordinary that ever occurred in the history of diplomacy. On the 19th of January, Mr. Adams writes—

" I have the honour to submit to your consideration a copy of what purports to be the annual report of Mr. S. R. Mallory, the person who is known to be officiating at Richmond as director of the naval operations of the insurgents in the United States. Although this paper has been received only in the form here presented, I entertain little doubt that in substance it may be relied upon as authentic."

I must do Mr. Adams the justice to say, that nothing can be more artful and ingenious than the way in which he gradually arrives at perfect certainty and absolute proof. First, he says, " what purports to be the annual report of Mr. S. R. Mallory ;" in the next place he entertains " little doubt that in substance it may be relied upon as authentic ;" and then, having once assumed this, he proceeds to point out all the serious consequences which would result from it, and continues—

" In laying this information before your Lordships, I am directed to convey the opinion of my Government that the proof thus furnished is sufficient to remove all doubt that may yet be lingering over the objects, character, and designs of the builders of the steam rams now under detention in the ports of this kingdom, upon the strength of former representations which I have had the honour to make to Her Majesty's Government."

Allow me to say in passing that, although the noble Earl opposite expressed great reluctance to produce any portion of the Correspondence which might prejudice the course of justice, or unduly affect the trial which is about to take place, that tender feeling for anything which might warp the views of Her Majesty's Judges did not extend to anything which would have an injurious influence upon the case of M. Bravay or the Messrs. Laird, because he made no difficulty about laying before Parliament that which purported to be the confession of the Naval Secretary of State of the Confederate States that these vessels had been built in Liverpool for the Confederate Government. Lord Lyons had shortly before communicated to the noble Earl a similar document. In the first instance he said—

"I have the honour to transmit to your Lordships an extract from the Washington newspaper *Star* of the 19th inst., containing what purports to be parts of a report of the Secretaries of the so-called Confederate Treasury and Navy. . . . The Secretary gives, moreover, particulars respecting contracts for building iron-clad vessels for the Confederate service in England and France, and respecting the use to which those vessels were to be put."

A week afterwards, having had time to obtain more full and perfect information, Lord Lyons says—

"My Lord,—I have the honour to enclose an extract from the *New York Times* newspaper of yesterday, containing a complete copy of the report of the Secretary of the so-called Confederate Navy."

Mr. Adams only speaks of what purports to be a report, but he encloses it to the noble Earl. The noble Earl at once jumps at it. I think he will find that, to use Captain Semmes' expression, he had been "misled and entrapped," and writes to this effect—

"Her Majesty's Government have had under their consideration the representations contained in your letter of the 19th ultimo, with regard to the alleged use of British territory for belligerent purposes by the Government of the so-styled Confederate States as shown in the Report of the Confederate Secretary of the Navy, Mr. Mallory, of which you enclosed a copy."

The noble Earl is delighted to find that the document bears irrefragable proof of the cordiality and sincerity with which the duties of neutrality have been fulfilled, and goes on—

"And I have now to state to you that this document appears to Her Majesty's Government to contain the strongest proof, if any were wanted, that they have endeavoured in good faith to observe strictly and impartially, under circumstances of no small difficulty, the obligations of neutrality which they have undertaken, and that the practical effect of their doing so has been advantageous in no slight degree to the more powerful of the two belligerents—namely, the United States. What is termed in Mr. Mallory's Report 'the unfriendly construction of Her Majesty's Laws' is therein made matter of grave complaint against England by the Government of the so-styled Confederate States, while to the same cause is ascribed the fact that those States have been prevented from obtaining the services of the greater part of a formidable war fleet which they had desired to create. Her Majesty's Government are fully sensible of the nature and importance of the admissions made in Mr. Mallory's report of the endeavours of the Government of the so-styled Confederate States, by their agents in

this country and in Canada, to violate in various ways Her Majesty's neutrality. Her Majesty's Government have already taken steps to make that Government aware that such proceedings cannot be tolerated, and Her Majesty's Government will not fail to give to these admissions, to which you have invited their attention, the consideration which they undoubtedly deserve."

As soon as this paper was made public, all those persons who were best acquainted with the character of official documents in the United and Confederate States at once pronounced it to be a forgery—and not only a forgery, but a clumsy forgery—though it did take in Her Majesty's Government and Her Majesty's Attorney General. It was clear to any one who knew the character of these reports, that it was a clumsy forgery, because in the first place it was addressed, not to the President, as was invariably the custom, but, of all people in the world, to the Speaker of the House of Representatives. In the next place it stated, that no less than five rams had been ordered in England, whereas all that were ever heard of and assumed to be for the Confederate States were these two. Again, it entered into no detail whatever with regard to the internal management of the Naval department, which, practically speaking, was the main object of the reports of the Secretary of the Navy; and lastly, it gave information, as from the President, that these rams had been ordered by persons sent from Richmond in the early part of the year 1863. If that was so, the expedition displayed in their construction must have been something surprising and unheard of, because they were represented by the Consul to be ready for sailing in the month of August ; and if the agents sent from Richmond in the early part of the year arrived in England, looked about them, gave their orders, had them executed, and got the vessels launched and ready for sailing in the month of August; it is the most astounding fact in shipbuilding that I ever heard of. From all these circumstances the alleged report was pronounced by gentlemen well acquainted with the subject to be a clumsy forgery. The noble Earl, on the 11th February, having received this information, was quite jubilant at the clear, indisputable, and unexpected proof which was thus furnished of the object with which these rams were being built, and at the certainty of obtaining a conviction. Had it not been for the production of this document, I do not believe that even, although Parliament had met, the information would have been filed immediately after the 8th of February. When this information arrived, not only was the noble Earl jubilant, but the Attorney General was jubilant too. The Attorney General in a discussion on the subject assumed it to be indisputable that the Government had in their possession facts and evidence which could leave no doubt whatever as between them and the Confederate Government that the vessels in question were being built for the use of the latter. The information, I may add, was filed on the 19th of January, and, after carefully examining the evidence, it was determined on the 8th of October to issue a commission to search for additional evidence in Egypt, and in the meantime this document was brought forward to substantiate a case for the detention of the Confederate Rams. It may be only a coincidence, but it is a very curious coincidence, that the date of the intention of the Government to file this information is to a day precisely the same as the date of the despatch to which I have already referred, in which the noble Earl stated that steps had already been taken for the purpose of remonstrating with the Confederate Government, and preventing, as far as possible, such outrages against the law. The noble Earl issued orders, on the strength of the document to which I have been alluding, to Mr. Crawford, to proceed from the Havannah on a mission to remonstrate with the Confederates on the atrocious violation of the law of neutrality of which they had been guilty. It was, however, I think fortunate for the noble Earl, and more fortunate for Mr. Crawford, that he was not allowed to land, and that he was not permitted to make those remonstrances which I am mischievous enough, for my own part, to wish that he had been permitted to make.

I wish to add a few words more before I release your Lordships from the lengthened observations which I have felt it my duty to inflict upon you. I cannot consent to pass this matter over in the light and frivolous manner in which the noble Earl on a former occasion introduced it to your notice. At the close of a discussion in this House not long ago, on our relations with America, the noble Earl at the close of his speech dropped out, in the quietest and gentlest tone, as if the point to which I am now particularly referring had no possible significance, the fact of his having discovered that this document was not a genuine document, but a hoax practised on the President by some gentleman at

New York, and that it did not furnish the slightest ground for remonstrating with the Confederate Government. I certainly should have expected that the foreign Minister of this country would not have treated the transaction in so light a tone, and should see in it no peril to the proper maintenance of diplomatic relations between different States. It is, in my opinion, no trifle that a document should be forged, and that it should be transmitted by the British Minister at Washington to the Secretary of State at home, and by the Federal Secretary to the Representative of the United States in London, and made by him the ground of serious remonstrance with Her Majesty's Government, without the strictest and most rigid investigation being made to ascertain that there did not exist the slightest doubt of its genuineness. I cannot acquit even Lord Lyons of having displayed some credulity in this matter, because, being at Washington, and seeing the document in the newspapers, first in a garbled state and afterwards in full, and being aware that the Richmond papers came constantly into Washington, and that no Southern papers had any account of it, I cannot conceive how he could have imagined it to be correct. Mr. Adams, no doubt, was acting under instructions from his Government in making representations on the subject to Her Majesty's Government ; but that Mr. Seward, from whom those instructions emanated, could entertain any doubt as to the genuineness of the document, and should have deemed himself, as Secretary of State, justified on the faith of a paragraph in a newspaper in addressing friendly remonstrances of a most serious character to a foreign State, without giving himself the trouble of finding out that which he might so easily have discovered, seems to me, I confess, somewhat extraordinary. I do not go so far as some, and attribute to Mr. Seward himself the authorship of this document. It first made its appearance in *The Star of Washington*, a very obscure paper, and being by that means transmitted to New York it appeared at full length in the *New York Times*, which is notoriously the organ of Mr. Seward himself. It was on the authority of that paper, at all events, Mr. Seward transmitted the document with his remonstrances to the British Government ; and he certainly could have no difficulty in sending to the editor of the paper and requesting to know where the document had been obtained, what was the authority for it, and who had given it circulation in his journal. The paper, in short, is under the control of Mr. Seward, and to say that he could not have obtained the information to which I refer is absurd. There is, therefore, no excuse for his conduct in sending over here the representations which he made founded on a newspaper paragraph. I may, however, say, to the credit of one portion, at all events, of the United States press, that the *Philadelphia Age,* which I hold in my hand, deals with this transaction as I trust any Englishman would be disposed to do. It says—

"We have always regarded Mr. Adams as a man of honour, but we have not, and never had, a good opinion of Mr. Seward."

It adds—

"There is no excuse for thus counterfeiting history."

And it asks the question—

"What will English or French statesmen say of a man who, if innocent, seems willing to be gulled, and is ready, by any means, to obtain some temporary or paltry result ?" "What," it goes on to say, "could be easier than to ascertain the genuineness of the Mallory report ? But the person most to be pitied in connection with this grim joke is poor Lord Lyons. We trust for the credit of the Government this most impudent fraud will be explained. . . . In diplomacy truth is a good deal better weapon than falsehood."

I thought it but right to bring these statements under your Lordships' notice, to show the light in which the matter is viewed by some persons in America ; and I must express my disappointment that not even the last despatch from Lord Lyons contains any expression of feeling with respect to the discreditable trick which was played on him. We do not even know up to the present moment whether any apology has been made to Her Majesty's Government for, to say the least of it, the credulity with which Mr. Adams and Mr. Seward have laid themselves open to be charged. I have mentioned this subject because it is, in my opinion, one of deep importance, and because I look upon it as being closely connected with the papers which I have brought under the notice of the House ; the delay in taking final proceedings in the case of the steam rams, and the period at which it was determined that those proceedings should be taken. I have, I may say, in conclusion, brought forward this subject, not for the purpose of protecting the Messrs. Laird against any consequences to which they may be fairly liable, or entering into the question whether

The Earl of Derby

they have or have not been guilty of a violation of the provisions of the Foreign Enlistment Act. All I desire is, that justice may be done ; I have no wish that persons should be permitted to violate the law with impunity. I hope the noble Earl will continue in the same course which, he says, he has always adopted, of dealing with all parties with the utmost impartiality. I am anxious to see an equitable neutrality preserved between those who are engaged in the unhappy conflict raging on the other side of the Atlantic. But, while I entertain these views, I do not like to find legal proceedings unjustly and unnecessarily delayed, and I am desirous of seeing all Her Majesty's subjects enjoying the full benefit of that protection which the laws of the country were framed to confer. The noble Earl concluded by *moving—*

"That an humble Address be presented to Her Majesty for Copy of Correspondence between Her Majesty's Government and Messrs. Laird with respect to Steam Rams."

EARL RUSSELL : My Lords, the noble Earl has not deemed it to be inconsistent with his duty to bring under your Lordships' notice, and to pass under minute review, a case which, within a month from this time, is to be tried in our Courts of Law ; and this he has done in favour of one party, and that party the one against whom the accusation is brought. I do not say that there may not be instances of oppression so aggravated that it may be right to bring before the House of Lords— the great tribunal of ultimate appeal from those Courts—the preliminary proceedings connected with those cases. Such a course may be necessary in a case of notorious injustice ; but I submit the noble Earl has made out no such case. He has for nearly two hours engaged the attention of your Lordships ; but I venture to say he has shown no case of illegality or oppression. In treating this question, I must, in defence of the Government, make two observations to which I request the assent of your Lordships. The first is, that your Lordships are desirous of maintaining relations of amity with the United States of America — a great, a powerful, a free State, with which, for nearly eighty years, with the exception of the short interval from 1812 to 1815, we have held relations of peace, and with which it is our interest, our desire, and our duty, if possible, to maintain those relations. I am not, I hope, asking too much when I ask your Lordships to assent to that postulate. The next remark I have to make is that the Messrs. Laird, whatever may be their politics—a point with which I have nothing to do—have no right to go to war with any Power in friendly relations with Her Majesty. The power of going to war is one of the prerogatives of the Crown, and it is not a privilege of the Messrs. Laird, however respectable they may be as shipbuilders. Yet, I have no hesitation in saying that the Messrs. Laird had it in their power to commit this country in hostilities with the United States of America, and it was nothing but the vigilance of the Government—what the noble Earl describes as their over-vigilance—which prevented those respectable gentlemen from involving this country in war with the Northern States. In arguing this question, I must state many things which the noble Earl, in his long and able speech, has entirely omitted; and the first of those matters is the existence of the Foreign Enlistment Act. That Act, as your Lordships are aware, was passed in circumstances not very dissimilar to the present, when Spain was at war with her colonies, when this country had acknowledged the belligerent rights of those colonies, and when those colonies were endeavouing to procure aid from England in the shape of regiments, officers, and ships fitted out for warlike purposes. In order to counteract the mischief which those attempts, if successful, might produce, the Government of the day proposed to Parliament, and carried a Bill, which is now the law of the land, and is known by the name of the Foreign Enlistment Act. The preamble of that Act states as follows :—

" Whereas the enlistment or engagement of His Majesty's subjects to serve in war on foreign service without His Majesty's licence, and the fitting out and equipping and arming of vessels by His Majesty's subjects for warlike operations on or against the dominions or territories of a foreign Prince may be prejudicial to and tend to endanger the peace and welfare of this kingdom."

I venture to submit there can hardly be a greater crime in its effects than to do acts which endanger the peace and welfare of this country ; in other words, which tend to put us into a state of war with a foreign country with which we are at amity, and which would bring upon us all the calamities which war never fails to produce. But I shall give your Lordships a more full description of the Foreign Enlistment Act, not taken from an authority favourable to the Government, but expressed in the language of a learned and able counsel, who is arguing against our application of the Act, and whose authority will hardly be disputed on the other side. Sir Hugh Cairns says—

" The intention of the Act of Parliament was this, and this only, to prevent warlike expeditions leaving the ports of this country at a time when this country was neuter, issuing from the ports of this country in a shape and form in which they could do injury to either belligerent, and thereby enable one or other of the belligerents to come to this country and say, ' Look at your port of Plymouth ; there sailed out of that port on a certain day a ship fully armed, ready to capture any ship she might meet with. Your ports are being used as places of safety and shelter ; armed vessels can sail out, or transports or storeships can sail out, prepared to do all the mischief in war which a transport or storeship, or an armed vessel can do.' The belligerent Government would say, ' Observe the consequences ; we cannot pursue these vessels into your ports ; we cannot go into your ports to take out a privateer, and yet you allow a privateer to go armed from your ports at the same time that we cannot enter your ports. to destroy that vessel.' I apprehend that that was a very intelligible and clear principle, if we find that that was the principle which was proceeded on."

My Lords, that statement falls somewhat short of the case, because it speaks of vessels fully armed and going out on warlike expeditions ; but it does not mention the arming, furnishing, and fitting out of ships, which is likewise forbidden by the Foreign Enlistment Act. Before proceeding further, I must state to your Lordships that which is perfectly notorious. Much of it has already been proved in courts of law ; and if other parts were not allowed to be proved in the *Alexandra* case, they are well known, and, indeed, have obtained a notoriety so great that they can no longer be concealed. I mean that the Confederate States of America—naturally enough, and not to be wondered at in an arduous attempt to establish independence —have sent agents to this country and to France, but more especially to this country, and that those agents were furnished with the means to have ships built here in order that such expeditions as Sir Hugh Cairns refers to, and as are forbidden by our own law, should be undertaken against the United States—a Power with which we are at peace. This was proved in the case of the *Alexandra*. It was there shown that there was an office in Liverpool and a firm there by which all these transactions were carried on. The learned Judge prevented evidence being given as to what was the particular business transacted, but it was proved that a certain Captain Bullock, to whom the noble Earl has himself referred, was the chief agent of the Confederate States at Liverpool, that he drew draughts for the payment of those persons who were serving the Confederate States, that he appointed an individual paymaster of the ship, afterwards called the *Alabama;* and that, in short, he took upon himself all the functions of a regularly authorized agent of a foreign Power. I do not express any surprise at that, for it is not wonderful that the Confederate States, desirous to establish independence, and while they were engaged in a perilous war for that purpose, should endeavour by every means to hurt their enemies ; but what I do feel surprise at— what I do feel regret at—is that the provisions of the Foreign Enlistment Act forbidding them to do any act against neutrality and the laws of nations having been brought to the knowledge of all Her Majesty's subjects by proclamation, any of them should engage in these undertakings, contrary to their duty to the Crown, entirely forgetting their obligations to their own country, and careless whether or not they put us in a state of war with the United States. Such appear to me to have been the character of the transactions in which those respectable gentlemen the Messrs. Laird, the Messrs. Miller, the Messrs. Fraser, and others engaged. They have done everything in their power, by fitting out ships, by engaging in contracts for supplying vessels of war to the other belligerent, to give the United States a just cause of war against this country. What I have endeavoured to avert—what I have been apprehensive of—is giving the United States just cause for war. It may be that, filled with unfounded suspicions, or animated by unjust animosities, they may make war against this country. That may befall us or any other country ; and, if it does, we must bear it—we must return blow by blow, and carry ourselves through the war as well as we can. But what, I confess, I do dread is, that we should commit such acts that the United States Government can say truly, " You, professing to be neutral, are, in fact, at war with this country, and are carrying on hostilities against us under the guise of friendship and peace." The only thing with which I should be disposed to reproach myself in the present case is the degree of credulity with which I received the assurances that were made that the

Earl Russell

iron-clads were not intended for the Confederate States. The Collector of Customs at Liverpool, Mr. Edwards, said he believed it never was intended to use them for that purpose. The Law Officers, on his authority, took the same view. I was at first disposed to share that opinion ; but evidence was poured in on me which there was no resisting, and I am convinced that the vessels were originally built for the Confederate States. These vessels are of themselves vessels of war. There is no need to discuss how much they are equipped or armed, or how far those various things have been done which the learned Chief Baron in the Court of Exchequer proved out of *Webster's Dictionary.* All meant the same thing. These iron-clads have the build and construction of vessels of war which could be used to destroy the ships of the United States engaged in blockading the Southern ports. It was necessary for me to make inquiries as to the party for whom these vessels were built. We became aware that the Confederates had got builders both in the Mersey and the Clyde to lend themselves to their projects. Only the other day my learned Friend the Lord Advocate of Scotland prosecuted a firm on the Clyde for being engaged in such transactions, and after a time the defendants pleaded guilty to one of the counts of the indictment, which charged them with attempting to furnish a vessel of war, with the view of making war on behalf of the Confederate States against the United States. With regard to the iron-clads in the Mersey the noble Earl complains that they were stopped, and that they were in the first place detained before they were seized. For the part I took in concert with my noble Friend at the head of the Government in directing that the vessels should be detained, I can only say I am not sorry. I do not regret it in the least. On the contrary, I believe that I took a course which was consistent with the peace of the country, which was necessary for the peace of the country, and which was in favour of all the commercial and political relations which we maintain with other nations. Only suppose that instead of Foreign Secretary I had been Home Secretary, and that I had information, on which I could rely, that a treasonable plot was about to break forth—that parties meditating high treason were on the eve of completing their bad designs against the internal peace and welfare of the kingdom. Under such circumstances, I should have no hesitation for a moment in desiring that these parties should be detained. It might be that the information proved wrong; but if I felt I had reason to believe it, it would be my duty as Secretary of State to take the responsibility of directing the apprehension of the parties. There are great powers belonging to a Secretary of State. There was, as I conceived, an attempt being made against the peace and welfare of the kingdom in its foreign relations, and I was as much bound to take the same precautions in that case as the Home Secretary is bound to do when the domestic peace and welfare of the country are menaced. Of course, I am not going to tell the noble Earl what was the information which I received. I am not going to detail to him the evidence on which we acted, in order that answers may be given to our allegations in a court of justice. It is clear that those who were engaged in this affair laid their plans very artfully and cunningly; and it was necessary on our part to meet the allegations they made. First, it was said that the iron-clads were intended for the French. The Collector of Customs was quite convinced that they had been ordered either for the Emperor of the French or for M. Bravay, who was supposed to be entitled by the law of France to go to war against any Power he chose to select. That turned out to be an utter falsehood. Next the names of *El Tousson* and *El Monassia* were bestowed on the vessels, in order to support the allegation that they were intended for Egypt, the late Pasha having contracted for them. That story turned out to be equally untrue. But, of course, it was necessary for us to make inquiries, in order to be able to answer the various allegations which were made as to the object of the vessels.

THE EARL OF DERBY: As far as I am informed, the builders of the vessels never made any of those allegations. The only allegation they made was that the contract was given by M. Bravay.

EARL RUSSELL: It does not much signify whether it was M. Bravay or Messrs. Laird who made the allegations. What the Government have to prove, and what I believe we shall be able to prove, is that the iron-clads were built for the use of the Confederate States, and consequently it has been necessary to disprove the various stories which were invented as to the destination of the vessels. The noble Earl seems to think that the prevention of this expedition from sailing is a matter calculated to excite great displeasure in this House and great disapprobation. But let me first say that if the several steam rams had gone forth from this country, two now, two on another occasion, and several following, and had destroyed the ships which were blockading the ports of the Southern States, what man would venture to say we were not making war against the United States; that the very evil which the Foreign Enlistment Act was meant to prevent had not occurred; and that under the name of neutrality we had not committed offensive war against those with whom we were ostensibly at peace? Let me ask your Lordships, was there no reason to suspect the Messrs. Laird? Were they persons so entirely innocent of any transactions of this kind that we were bound to believe every allegation which they made? Were we to accept at once, without hesitation, their assertion that the iron-clads were not intended for the purposes which we supposed? We were aware of the case of another vessel, built and partly equipped in the Mersey by these same Messrs. Laird, which had gone out from the docks in the Mersey, and had committed, as she was now committing, hostilities against the vessels of the United States. The United States Government had no reason to complain of us in that respect, because we took all the precaution that we could. We collected evidence, but it was not till it was complete that we felt ourselves justified in giving orders for the seizure of the vessel. These orders, however, were evaded. I can tell your Lordships from a trustworthy source how they were evaded. I have here a remarkable pamphlet, entitled *Our Cruise in the Confederate War Steamer Alabama*, and said to be written by an officer who was on board of her. The narrative is written, not with the caution of a lawyer, but with the frankness of a sailor. [The Earl of DERBY: I suppose, of course, it is genuine?] Perhaps, we may be deceived here as we were before in regard to the report. I understand, however, that this pamphlet is genuine. It is published at the Cape of Good Hope. The writer says—

"After the outbreak of the war the immense naval superiority of the North gave them considerable advantages over the South, who, lacking convenience and material, were not able to build vessels with sufficient despatch, and the Confederate States Government sent over Captain J. D. Bullock to England for the purpose of purchasing a war steamer. Accordingly, the No. 290 was built and intended for a Confederate vessel of war. The No. 290 was launched from the building yard of Messrs. Laird, of Birkenhead. . . . . At 9.15 a.m. of the 29th of July, 1862, we weighed anchor and proceeded slowly down the Mersey, anchoring in Moelfra Bay—having on board relatives and friends of the builders, both ladies and gentlemen. Our ostensible object in sailing was to go 'on a trial trip,' and the presence of the ladies and gentlemen gave a certain colour to the report. In the evening we transferred our visitors to a steam-tug. Our unceremonious departure was owing to the fact of news being received to the effect that the Customs authorities had orders to board and detain us that morning."

That was the fact. However the owner came to be informed of it it is impossible for me to say, and there certainly seems to have been treachery on the part of some one furnishing the information. In what character did the vessel go out? Did she go out as a man of war completely equipped? No; she went out seemingly on a trial trip, with ladies and gentlemen on board, for the purpose of deception, those ladies and gentlemen being the friends and relatives of the builders. And yet the noble Earl speaks for an hour of the enormous cruelty and oppression of my suspecting a vessel built by the Messrs. Laird, which was clearly intended for war, and could act with great effect on any enemy it might encounter. But here is another rather strange circumstance. On the 8th of September, Messrs. Laird said that they wanted to have a trial trip for the next Monday. Mr. Laird said that he must have it without delay, and I gave my consent. That was on the 8th or 9th of September; and yet, on the 21st of September, Messrs. Laird declined the offer of a trial trip at that time, saying that the vessel was not sufficiently ready to make a trial—that she was not ready on the 21st for a trial trip for which they had urgently pressed on the 8th. Then I am supposed by the noble Earl to be the most arbitrary person ·in the world, because I will not believe all these assertions; that although the *Alabama* escaped detention by going out to sea on pretence of a trial trip, I should be suspicious with regard to the *El Tousson* and another vessel, and not allow them to leave port on a similar pretence. I do not mean to go through all that correspondence which the noble Earl so laboriously followed out; I shall only give my general allegation that my suspi-

Earl Russell

cious with regard to these vessels were roused; that Captain Inglefield, on whose discretion entire reliance can be placed, was consulted on every step that was taken; and if any of the precautions adopted had been omitted, the vessel might have been taken away. In that case, many of those men whom the noble Earl said are in want of employment—as no doubt they may be in consequence of this plan being defeated—would have formed the crew of the vessel, and that vessel would have been directed against the ships of the United States. Therefore this was a case in which the Foreign Enlistment Act was clearly about to be violated, and it was my duty to take care that the matter should be brought into the courts of this country. I might have made a mistake, as it might happen that a policeman in the street, apprehending a man whom he sees quitting a house at three or four o'clock in the morning with a sack full of plate, might make a mistake, because it might turn out, singularly enough, that the man seized was the master of the house, who desired to go out for a walk at that early hour with a sack of plate on his back. That would be a singular occurrence, certainly; but no one would blame the policeman for having stopped the man. That was the sort of case which we had to consider. It may turn out that this vessel was built for M. Bravay, because of some desire of his to make war on his own account against some State in the world; or he may think that he ought to take part in the present war in America. However, as I have said, I will not go into particular facts; I believe it will be seen, when this question comes on for trial, that there were reasons which justified the Government in the course they pursued. At all events, the reverse of the course pursued · might have been very serious. If the suspicions of the Government with regard to these vessels turn out to be correct, there would have been the greatest inconvenience having allowed them to go out, as that circumstance would have tended to create unpleasant relations if not hostilities between the United States and this country. This Act was so far in my custody that I considered myself bound to see it carried into effect; and I think the noble Earl and the public will admit that I was bound, if it appeared to me to be a case in which the parties were infringing the Foreign Enlistment Act, that I should take steps in order to bring these vessels and their agents before a court of justice.

The learned Judge who tried the case of the *Alexandra* stated as a point of history, that the object of the Act was to prevent two belligerents from building ships in the same port and coming into collision in that port. That is not a correct history of the Act. On the contrary, it was passed, as Sir Hugh Cairns correctly said on the trial, for the purpose of preventing this country being involved by the acts of our subjects against the views of the Crown in hostilities with another country. And here, having stated what was the course which I took, let me again say that I think we are bound — more especially in this case where there is a conflict between two parties on the continent of the United States of America—to preserve our neutrality and to remain at peace with both. Great issues are there under decision; and no issue can be greater than the question of what is to become of the four millions of the negro race who have been hitherto retained as slaves in the United States. I, for my part, have never been able to feel much sympathy with either of the contending republics—the United States or the Confederate States. I saw that on one side there was a declaration in favour of the perpetuity of slavery; on the other side there seemed no measures taken even to undo that unholy compact contained in the constitution of the United States, by which a slave brought into a free State, however much he may have suffered in endeavouring to fly to that free State, is again restored to his master. It is to be hoped that this contest, with whatever calamities it may have been accompanied — with whatever slaughter may have been committed in their battles—with what fields that have been subject to devastation, and industry interrupted—that Providence has in store some reward for those services which are engaged in an issue that will place those four millions of the black race in a condition of freedom that may hereafter lead to their prosperity and the enjoyment of that liberty which the United States themselves have proclaimed as the most sacred principle of the constitution. But it must be left to these contending Powers to work out this great problem, and I, for my part, should think it was the greatest misfortune that could befal this country, if we were obliged by any paramount considerations to take part in the contest. Our policy is to remain neutral. I believe that Providence will work out her own ends, for

> "There is a divinity that shapes our ends,
> Rough-hew them as we may;"

and that the result of this contest, the beginning of which we all deplore, and the continuance of which we all regret, will be, that that stain—that that crime—that detestable state of slavery, may be for ever abolished from among civilized nations.

Lord CHELMSFORD said, he agreed with the noble Earl (Earl Russell), that it was most desirable that we should preserve amicable relations with the United States, and also that neither Messrs. Laird nor any other person should be allowed to levy war upon a nation with which we were at peace; but he did not think the noble Earl justified in assuming that the Messrs. Laird were levying war, as that was the very question which was to be tried. Strongly as the noble Earl had asserted that the Messrs. Laird were levying war, he (Lord Chelmsford) was entitled as strongly to deny it. The noble Earl adverted to the conduct of Captain Bullock, concerning whom he said that he had strong proof that he had been connected with the fitting out of the *Alabama*. But if the noble Earl had that proof, he knew very well that, under the Foreign Enlistment Act, a person engaged in fitting out vessels of war for a belligerent without licence from Her Majesty was guilty of a misdemeanour—why, then, had there not been an indictment against Captain Bullock? Why had not Captain Bullock, Messrs. Laird, or any other person so engaged, been called to account for their illegal conduct? The noble Earl also said that he was perfectly justified in not trusting the Messrs. Laird. But that was not always the opinion of Her Majesty's Government, because in the Correspondence to which his noble Friend (the Earl of Derby) had called attention, it would be recollected that Her Majesty's Government had expressed, in the most explicit terms, their confidence in Messrs. Laird's honourable conduct. They say, in their letter of the 19th September—

"I am to state to you explicitly that Her Majesty's Government are convinced that it is your intention, as far as it is in your power, to fulfil honourably the engagement into which you have entered, and that if any such attempt were made it would be entirely without the privity of your firm, in whose good faith they place perfect confidence."

And again, Captain Inglefield stated—

"I consider that your proposals that the keys whereby these sluices are worked should be removed from the place they are at present kept to another of greater security, under your personal care, is deserving of my thanks, and is again suggestive of the good faith which has marked your transactions with me in this unpleasant matter."

The noble Earl had said that he considered it right to prevent the trial trip of these vessels, because it was extremely probable that they might be seized by force and taken out of the possession of the Government. But the noble Earl had entirely forgotten that he had desired that a number of seamen and marines should be placed on board to prevent her forcible seizure, to which Messrs. Laird had assented; and how, under such circumstances, the noble Earl could have believed such an attempt likely to be made, he (Lord Chelmsford) was utterly at a loss to understand. He denied that the object of his noble Friend's Motion was to obtain a sort of Bow Street inquiry—a preliminary examination into the guilt or innocence of the Messrs. Laird. He had done no such thing; for he had confined himself partly to the Correspondence that had been laid upon the table of the House, and partly to that Correspondence to which his Motion was directed. It must be apparent to all that the excuse made by the Government against producing the Correspondence, on the ground that it would prejudice the pending trial, was utterly without foundation. Either the facts contained in it were admissible in evidence, or they were not. If they were not admissible, no prejudice whatever could be created ; and if they were admissible, then there was no doubt whatever that Messrs. Laird's counsel, being properly instructed, would extract from the witnesses on the part of the Crown all those facts to which his noble Friend had called attention, and show from them the detention without seizure, and all that had been done from that time up to the present.

He intended to confine his remarks to the simple view of the case, that the detention of the vessels was an illegal act, and that it was done in consequence of the pressure that was brought to bear upon them. The first letter which introduced the subject to the notice of the noble Earl (Earl Russell) was dated 11th July, 1863, in which Mr. Adams complained of the determined perseverance of persons at Liverpool, the agents of the so-called Confederate States, to obtain vessels for the purpose of committing hostilities, and that it had formed the subject of his remonstrances almost ever since he had been in

Lord Chelmsford

this country; and he drew the noble Earl's attention to the latest evidence of hostility—namely, the construction of a steam-vessel of war of the most formidable kind. With that letter he sent numerous depositions to prove that this vessel was constructed for an illegal purpose. On the 1st of September the noble Earl wrote a letter to Mr. Adams, which appeared to him to be of great importance, because it showed what was the evidence upon which the noble Earl acted, and which led up to the 5th September, when Her Majesty's Government illegally, as he contended, detained the ship. The noble Earl in that letter said—

"But I am sure you will be disposed, in justice to Her Majesty's Government, to admit that, in the absence of all evidence, upon mere hearsay, surmise, conversation, and conjecture, Her Majesty's Government could not properly direct a prosecution or action under the Foreign Enlistment Act."

Now these expressions were used at the time when the depositions had been furnished by Mr. Adams, consisting of nothing but hearsay, conjecture, surmise, conversation. On the 3rd September, Mr. Adams forwarded further depositions to the noble Earl, accompanied with a very strong remonstrance, in which he said—

"At the same time I feel it my painful duty to make known to your Lordship, that in some respects it has fallen short in expressing the earnestness with which I have been in the interval directed to describe the grave nature of the situation in which both countries must be placed in the event of an act of aggression committed against the Government and people of the United States by either of these formidable vessels."

Their Lordships had an opportunity of ascertaining the American Minister's opinion of the value of the additional evidence, by referring to the despatch of Mr. Adams to Mr. Seward of the 3rd September, 1863, in which he said he thought it was the wisest course to make a remonstrance; and for that purpose he had taken advantage of some additional depositions "of no great additional weight." Up to the 3rd of September there was no evidence to warrant any interference with the vessels ; but on the 5th September a rather extraordinary letter was written by Mr. Adams. After pointing out that one of the iron-clad war vessels was on the point of departure from this kingdom on its hostile errand against the United States, Mr. Adams said this was war, no matter what theory of neutrality was adopted. He added that it was impossible that any nation retaining a proper degree of self-respect could tamely submit to a continuance of relations, so utterly deficient in reciprocity. This was a very strong remonstrance. Well, on the 5th of September, orders were issued to prevent these iron-clads leaving the Mersey. But there were some very curious circumstances connected with this case. On the 5th September, Mr. Layard was most anxious to show that the orders were given before the threatening despatch was received, and he wrote to Mr. Stewart as follows—

"We have given orders to-day to the Commissioners of Customs at Liverpool to prevent the two iron-clads leaving the Mersey. These orders had scarcely been sent when we received the note from Mr. Adams, of which I send you a copy. Mr. Adams is not yet aware that orders have been given to stop the vessels. You may inform Mr. Seward confidentially of the fact."

And the noble Earl also wrote, on the 8th September, to Mr. Adams, as follows:—

"Lord Russell presents his compliments to Mr. Adams, and has the honour to inform him that instructions have been issued which will prevent the departure of the two iron-clad vessels from Liverpool."

On these papers, however, there was no proof that the instructions were given to the officer at Liverpool to detain those vessels till the 9th September. The noble Earl thought it was right to answer the letter of the 5th September on the 11th. He then wrote rather a strong letter to the following effect:—

"Her Majesty's Government have for the most part succeeded in this impartial course. If they have been unable to prevent some violations of neutrality on the part of the Queen's subjects, the cause has been that Great Britain is a country which is governed by definite laws, and is not subject to arbitrary will. But law, as you are well aware, is enforced here, as in the United States, by independent courts of justice, which will not admit assertion for proof, not conjecture for certainty. . . . I have to add that instructions have been issued for preventing the departure of the iron-clad vessels in question from Liverpool until satisfactory evidence can be given as to their destination, or, at all events, until the inquiries which are now being prosecuted with a view to obtain such evidence shall have been brought to a conclusion."

It was to this part of the case to which he (Lord Chelmsford) wished to draw particular attention, because he said that the noble Earl had no right to issue the orders for the detention of these vessels at all, much less their detention, "until satisfactory evidence was given as to "their destination." It was not, as his noble Friend had observed, that Government would detain the vessel, until it obtained information as to its destination, but until evidence was given by the parties themselves as to

its destination. First, then, the Government committed the illegal act of seizing the vessel, and next of throwing upon the parties who were charged with a criminal act the onus of showing their innocence. He apprehended from what the noble Earl had said, that he was not at all prepared to defend the legality of the act of detaining the vessels, as he said he had no right to do it; but that the Government did it on their own responsibility—and that he observed was also the language of the Attorney General. He said they knew that in ordinary criminal cases the parties went before a magistrate; information was taken to justify a committal, and the prisoner remanded from time to time. That course could not be adopted in the case of the seizure of vessels of this description; the law gave no means of that nature; and on their own responsibility they had acted to prevent a repetition of what took place in the case of the *Alabama* with reference to these ships until the Government was satisfied for commercial purposes. It was also necessary to consider whether the Government were acting under International Law or the Foreign Enlistment Act; and he could not do better on that point than quote the words of the noble Earl himself, in his letter to Mr. Adams, of the 11th September, where he said—

"I deem it right, however, to observe that the question at issue between yourself and Her Majesty's Government relates to two separate and distinct matters—the general international duties of neutrality and the municipal law of the United Kingdom. With regard to the general duties of a neutral according to International Law, the true doctrine has been laid down repeatedly by Presidents and Judges of eminence of the United States, and that doctrine is, that a neutral may sell to either or both of two belligerent parties any implements or munitions of war which such belligerents may wish to purchase from the subjects of the neutral, and it is difficult to find a reason why a ship that is to be used for warlike purposes is more an instrument or implement of war than cannon, muskets, swords, bayonets, gunpowder, and projectiles to be fired from cannon and muskets."

It was clear that at that moment the noble Earl was intending to proceed under the Foreign Enlistment Act; and it was clear that under that Act the Government had no right to act as they did. It was also clear that supposing they had no evidence of the vessel being fitted and equipped for the purpose of serving in the Confederate navy, the only course open to them was to hold their hands until they had sufficient evidence to justify the seizure of the vessel. Because the House would observe that the seizure of the vessel was the commencement of the proceedings, and it was unlawful to detain the vessel for the purpose of prosecuting inquiries to see if evidence could be obtained, or till the parties could prove their innocence ; therefore the detention of the vessels from the 5th or 8th September to the 9th of October was an illegal act. The American Minister had succeeded in leading the noble Earl into the detention of the vessels ; but he was not satisfied with that, but on September 16th wrote another strong letter to the noble Earl, in which he said—

"You are pleased to observe that Her Majesty's Government hopes my Government may take a calmer and more dispassionate view of the matters involved in that discussion than seems to be inferred from my note. If in that note I should have unfortunately led Her Majesty's Government to any inference of the kind, I can only assure your Lordship that the fault must be exclusively mine. At the same time, I feel it my duty not to disguise from you the very grave sense it entertains of the danger that Her Majesty's kingdom may be freely used by the enemies of the United States, in conjunction with numerous ill-disposed subjects of her own, to carry on a war against them in manner and spirit wholly at variance with the rules of neutrality which Her Majesty's Government has prescribed for itself in the present contest, as well as with the stronger obligations of amity and good-will imposed by solemn treaties long since entered into between the parties."

He also states—

"I respectfully submit that the interests of two nations are of too much magnitude to be measured by the infinitesimal scale of the testimony permissible before a jury and the common law courts."

It was curious that this letter and one connected with the *Alabama* were both written on the 16th of September and received by the noble Earl on the 18th, the very day before that upon which the permission previously granted to take these vessels out of dock for their trial trip was withdrawn ; and the inference was not an unfair one that these letters, coupled with all the circumstances affecting the *Florida*, had exercised some influence upon the course taken by the Government. There was another letter written on the 17th of September, in which Mr. Adams, addressing the noble Earl, expressed regret that he should have adduced the evidence of Messrs. Laird in support of his own despatches, the statements of one of those gentlemen in Parliament regarding others not being such as to exact implicit credence for any assertions regarding his own affairs.

Lord Chelmsford

That letter arriving with the others at a time when the mind of the Government was agitated—the American Minister, indeed, seeming to impute that it was in a state almost of paralysis—Ministers found it necessary to interpose in the case of the Messrs. Laird. It might be a mere coincidence, but it certainly was an extraordinary fact that throughout the whole of these transactions, whenever a step was taken affecting the members of that firm, there had always been a previous letter from the American Minister, having the appearance, at any rate, of urging on the Government. He maintained that the delay which had taken place in the institution of proceedings was not a fair and proper course to adopt. The seizure of the vessels on the 9th of October was virtually the commencement of proceedings, and had proper diligence been used, the commission might already have returned from Egypt. In the two Terms, Michaelmas and Hilary, which had since elapsed, the proceedings might have been closed, and a trial at bar, if a trial at bar were necessary, have taken place. His noble Friend had shown that the conduct of the Government, from beginning to end, had been most unjust, oppressive, and arbitrary; and that, yielding to the pressure of the American Minister, they had stretched the law far beyond its proper limits. The Motion of his noble Friend had not in the slightest degree affected or prejudiced the trial which was to take place in the Court of Exchequer. But where injustice and oppression had been practised by the Government, it was the duty of Members of Parliament, both in that and the other House, to bring forward the facts, in order that these might be fully and publicly known.

THE DUKE OF ARGYLL said, he had listened to the debate with some surprise. In the discussion which took place a few evenings ago regarding the *Tuscaloosa*, the noble and learned Lord on the Woolsack expressed the regret with which he was led to express any opinion upon any legal questions which might afterwards become the subject of judicial decisions in that House, and that evening his noble and learned Friend had apprised him distinctly that he would not take any part in the discussion. The case of the *Tuscaloosa* had been decided by the action of the Government, and it was scarcely possible that it could come in any shape under the judicial consideration of their Lordships'

House. But the present question was still in issue ; it might come up by way of appeal from the Courts below, and the noble and learned Lord who had last spoken might be one of the judges of the legality or illegality of the conduct of the Government. He regretted that the noble and learned Lord should so have expressed himself in debate as to show that he had prejudged the question, and that he viewed it somewhat under a political aspect. He regretted to detain the House at such an ungenial hour, but when the Government had been bitterly attacked, and when the noble and learned Lord upon the Woolsack —owing to scruples which were not shared by the noble and learned Lord opposite— had withdrawn from the debate, it was only natural that a Member of that Government should rise in its defence. The noble Earl who introduced the debate laid great stress upon the perfect frankness and openness of the Messrs. Laird ; but, for his part, he (the Duke of Argyll) had never known conduct less frank or open. In accordance with a verbal intimation previously given to the Government, that the Messrs. Laird, though unable to volunteer information, would willingly supply it if questions were asked by the Government, 'Earl Russell wrote the letter already quoted, asking on whose account and for what destination the vessels were being built. Messrs. Laird did not explain that this answer would refer to one of these questions only, and that they must refuse to answer the other; but they sent back a letter purporting to be a reply to the whole; and in this they begged to inform the Government that the name of the firm on whose account they were building was the Messrs. Bravay. He maintained that this was an evasion, and an intentional evasion, of the real and important question put by the Government. Messrs. Laird knew well enough that what the Government desired to ascertain was, whether these vessels had been built under contract for the Confederate Government, and not whether, by any collusive transaction with third parties, they had tried to divest themselves of their responsibility. Messrs. Laird might have refused to answer the questions put to them, or to give any information ; no one could blame them for being careful or secret if they thought it necessary to be so ; but they certainly were not entitled to that credit for candour and openness which was claimed for them by the noble Earl. He contended that they had not

acted in accordance with their duty to the Crown, and with what other subjects of the Crown in similar circumstances had felt to be their duty. A vessel much of the same character as the *Alabama* was building upon the Clyde, and, acting under instructions from the Government, a close watch was set — latterly, he believed, a gunboat had been anchored alongside— and when the vessel approached completion his noble Friend thought it right to address to the builders the same questions which he had put to the Messrs. Laird. They replied immediately that it was perfectly true the vessel had been built for the Confederate Government ; but that as soon as it appeared that by so doing a violation of the law was committed, the contract had been broken and the vessel was now at the disposal of Her Majesty's Government. That was a case in which the builders had acted with perfect frankness ; and an arrangement had been come to under which, while a verdict would be entered for the Crown, the vessel would be freed, subject to certain bonds and restrictions preventing it from falling into the hands of the Confederates. He confessed that he could not understand the tone in which this question had been debated by noble Lords opposite. He could understand a certain amount of sympathy with Messrs. Laird, and of irritation and dislike against the American Government, which had been manifested on more than one occasion ; but what he could not understand was, that noble Lords opposite should forget that this was not a mere question of a municipal statute, but that there was a great question of International Law and international obligation lying under it; and that if they were called to office it would be their duty to protect the neutrality of the Crown against the dangerous attempts of belligerent Governments to make them parties to the war. The noble and learned Lord had treated the question as one with which International Law had nothing to do, and had quoted some words of the noble Earl the Foreign Secretary, to prove that that was so. The language of his noble Friend proved nothing of the sort. The Foreign Enlistment Act was a municipal statute, enabling the Government to fulfil its international obligations ; but he did not believe that the provisions of that statute entirely limited the action of, the Government upon such questions. Take the famous case of 1793. In that year, vessels of a formidable character were being built and armed in the ports of the United States. Mr. Hammond was instructed to remonstrate with Washington, then President, and Mr. Jefferson; and although the Americans had at that time no Foreign Enlistment Act, yet, after a celebrated correspondence, they seized the vessels under the obligations of international neutrality. In the year 1793, the United States Government had acted towards us precisely as his noble Friend had recently acted towards them. He entreated noble Lords opposite to put aside party feelings, and to remember the immense national importance of this question. For many centuries England had been almost uniformly a belligerent Power, and she had raised for herself and other belligerents a great system of belligerent law, which told very severely against neutrals. We were now almost for the first time neutral in a great maritime contest, and some of our subjects had been wincing and were still wincing under the operation of those rules which we had formerly applied to others. He believed, however, that with the good sense and spirit of fairness which characterized the people of this country, they perceived that it was our duty and interest to submit to the application to ourselves of every one of the rules which we had before enforced against others; and he trusted that now we were neutral we should not pursue the suicidal policy of encouraging or permitting other nations to fit out vessels of war in our ports—a policy which would have the double effect of endangering our neutrality and seriously impairing our power as a belligerent if we should ever again be compelled to engage in war. When it was alleged in the Court of Exchequer that Messrs. Laird had evaded the law, Sir Hugh Cairns said that that was all he cared for, because if they had evaded the law they could not be guilty under it; but we could not get rid of international obligations by quibbles like that, and it was the duty as well as the interest of public men of all parties to do their best to encourage a high tone of morality among the commercial classes as to those obligations. When, during the Crimean war, a charge which turned out to be unfounded was made at the instance of our Government—that a vessel which was building in New York was intended to be employed in warlike operations against this country, the Chamber of Commerce of that city adopted a series of resolutions

The Duke of Argyll

in which they described the charge as a disgraceful impeachment, which ought not to be made lightly or without serious inquiry. He should like to hear Messrs. Laird treat this matter in a similar spirit. He should like to hear them say that they thought such a charge an impeachment of their honour, and declare that they had never entered into any contract with the Confederate Government to build vessels to be employed in this war. Much had been said about the yielding to the demand of Mr. Adams, the American Minister. He (the Duke of Argyll) contended that it was our duty, in obedience to International Law, to attend to the representation of Mr. Adams. It was as much for the interest of the commercial community as of the Government that the principles of International Law should be strictly adhered to; and that this was felt to be so by merchants themselves was proved by the fact that a petition had been presented in favour of the improvement and strengthening of the Foreign Enlistment Act, which was signed by thirty-seven of the largest and most respectable mercantile firms in the town of Liverpool. It was pre-eminently for the advantage of England to maintain those principles, and he therefore hoped that nothing would be done to weaken or endanger them. Under these circumstances, the course which had been pursued by his noble Friend near him and his Colleagues was, he contended, in accordance with the solemn obligations imposed on them as Ministers of the Crown, and they deserved the thanks of the country for the manner in which they had equally upheld the principles of International Law and vindicated the honour of the country.

THE EARL OF DERBY said, after so long a discussion, he was unwilling to offer any observations in reply. Certainly the temptation to do so was not increased by the present state of the House. He had formally moved for the production of those papers merely for the purpose of enabling himself to bring forward all the material facts connected with the case, and to show that Her Majesty's Government had performed their indisputable duty with unnecessary harshness and severity, and not according to the terms of the law, but rather in a manner evading the law. Not having heard anything from the noble Earl or the noble Duke opposite to controvert that statement, he (the Earl of Derby) was perfectly satisfied with having thus performed his duty. If he did not desire to continue the discussion in the present state of the House, he was still less desirous of pressing his Motion to a division, looking at the overwhelming majority that would meet him from the Ministerial bench. He had made the Motion for the production of papers which he had already possession of. His object was, therefore, achieved, and he was utterly indifferent whether the noble Earl consented to produce them or not.

EARL RUSSELL said, he would rather not produce the Correspondence, seeing that it had been refused in the other House of Parliament.

Motion (by Leave of the House) *withdrawn.*

House adjourned at a quarter before Nine o'clock, to Monday next, half past Eleven o'clock.

~~~~~~~~

HOUSE OF COMMONS,

Friday, April 29, 1864.

MINUTES.]—SELECT COMMITTEE— On Sewage (Metropolis, &c.), *nominated* * (see p. 1699) ; On Standing Orders (Parliamentary Deposits), *nominated* * (see p. 1621) ; Turnpike Trusts *, Mr. T. G. Baring *added* (see March 8); On Case of Mr. Bewicke, *appointed.*
SUPPLY—*considered in Committee*—Committee.—
R.P.
PUBLIC BILLS—*Ordered*—Under Secretaries Indemnity *; Superior Courts of Common Law (Ireland) *.
First Reading—Writs Registration (Scotland) * [Bill 84]; Under Secretaries Indemnity * [Bill 85]; Superior Courts of Common Law (Ireland) * [Bill 86].
Select Committee — On Thames Conservancy *nominated* *.
Considered as amended—Penal Servitude Acts Amendment * [Bill 23]; Civil Bill Courts (Ireland) * [Bill 79].

PROCEEDS OF UNCLAIMED WRECK.

QUESTION.

MR. ROGERS said, he wished to ask the President of the Board of Trade, By what authority the proceeds of unclaimed wreck, to which the right of private owners had been acknowledged by the Crown, have been retained by the receivers since such acknowledgment of claim?

MR. MILNER GIBSON, in reply, said, he had obtained information on the subject to which the Question of the hon. Gentleman referred. Under the Merchant Ship-

ping Act, wreck was delivered over to the persons who made a *primâ facie* title to it; but if adverse claims were put in, the proceeds of the wreck were held by the receiver until the question of title was decided, because it formed no part of the duty of the Board of Trade to settle any question of disputed title. The question of the hon. Gentleman pointed to a dispute between the Duchy of Cornwall and certain Cornish proprietors : so long as the matter was in dispute, the Board of Trade would hold their hand, and only deliver the proceeds to those legally entitled to receive them. The Board of Trade had no authority but to deliver the proceeds to the party having the title to receive them—it was not for them to settle the title.

RULE OF THE HOUSE—QUESTIONS TO PRIVATE MEMBERS.—QUESTION.

CAPTAIN ARCHDALL said, he rose to ask the hon. Member for Galway (Mr. Gregory). If it is true, as has been stated, that a Sub Inspector of Police, attended by men of the force under his command, trespassed and shot game on the estates of the hon. Member, without permission or authority ; and that he refused to desist or to leave the lands, when warned off by the tenants.

SIR COLMAN O'LOGHLEN rose to order. He wished to know, whether it was consistent with the rules and orders of the House that such a Question as the hon. and gallant Gentleman had placed on the paper should be asked of any private Member?

MR. SPEAKER: The rule of the House with respect to asking questions of a private Member is that any question may be put relating to any Bill, Motion, or other public matter connected with the business of the House in which such Member may be concerned. If the hon. Gentleman is prepared to show that the Question he is about to ask comes within these limits he may put it ; otherwise he may take the opportunity in debate of referring to the matter, but he cannot put it in the shape of a question.

CAPTAIN ARCHDALL said, he would bring up the matter in another form.

DENMARK AND GERMANY—THE CONFERENCE.—QUESTION.

MR. DISRAELI : I wish, Sir, to put a Question to Her Majesty's Government with respect to the Conference. The House is aware that the Conference met on Monday last. It is adjourned ; and I wish to know from Her Majesty's Government, Whether on Monday it adjourned to any particular day, and whether they can inform us when the Conference will re-assemble?

SIR GEORGE GREY: I am not able to say on what day the Conference will re-assemble. They have not adjourned *sine die*, but to an early day. I do not, however, know that the day is fixed.

MR. HORSMAN: May I venture to ask the Government whether they can state to the House what is the cause of the adjournment of the Conference?

SIR GEORGE GREY: I am not prepared at this moment to state.

SUPPLY.

Order for Committee read.

Motion made, and Question proposed, "That Mr. Speaker do now leave the Chair."

SALMON FISHERIES ACT.

QUESTION.

MR. PERCY WYNDHAM said, he rose to ask the Secretary of State for the Home Department, If it is the intention of Her Majesty's Government to bring in a Bill this Session to amend the Salmon Fisheries Act (1861)? The Report of the Inspectors had for some time been in the hands of hon. Members. It contained information from every part of the kingdom, and suggested the Amendments required in the present Act. One of those recommendations was that powers should be given to raise a fund for the protection of the rivers from poachers, and to secure the carrying out of the Salmon Fisheries Act. In certain places the Act was notoriously a dead letter, and it was certain that persons could be found everywhere who would break the law if they could do so with impunity. There were at the present moment many associations for the protection of salmon rivers, but they had spent every farthing they had obtained by private subscription, and they must certainly collapse unless other funds were forthcoming. In the case of the Fowey, in South Wales, after working with considerable success, the association had been compelled to give up and abandon the fruits of their labours to the poachers; he knew of poachers that had made £40 or £50 a year by the fish they took. The Inspectors were unanimous that powers should be given to raise funds, and almost unanimous as to the best means of

Mr. Disraeli

doing so—namely, by assimilating the law of England to that of Ireland poaching might be, to a large extent, prevented. In 1848 an assessment Act was passed for Ireland, and the country was divided into districts, containing one or more rivers, and power was given to charge a duty on every engine or rod used for taking salmon, the duty varying according to the destructiveness of the engine employed. The benefit of that system might be seen by a comparison of the two rivers, the Shannon and the Severn; both drained an area of about 4,500 square miles in extent, and possessed equal natural advantages for the production of fish. On the Shannon the sum received was £1,339 annually, which was expended for the protection and improvement of the fishery. In the case of the Severn, only £138 was last year raised for the same purpose by voluntary subscriptions, and that to a great extent from persons who were not individually interested. He hoped the Government would bring in a Bill this Session for the purpose of assimilating the law of England to that of Ireland on that subject, with the view to remedy the present state of things which was productive of serious injury. It might be urged that it was very strange that the proprietors of the Fisheries did not combine together for the purpose of protecting the rivers, but he assured hon. Members that it was quite impossible to carry out objects of this kind by voluntary efforts; they might as well attempt to collect the metropolitan water rate on voluntary principle. The only way to meet the evil was to compel those persons who fished for profit or pleasure to contribute towards the preserving of the rivers. That might be done by the assessment of a small rate, and he was sure that the poorest man engaged in the Fisheries would not object to pay 10s. for a licence in order to provide for the protection of the river against poachers. He did not now refer to the injury done to the Fisheries by the pollution of rivers, as that was a subject of such great importance that it should be dealt with in a separate measure?

MR. T. G. BARING said, the answers to the queries which were issued by the Fishery Inspectors showed a very great unanimity of opinion, that some method of collecting a fund for the protection of the Fisheries was necessary and should be established by law. The hon. Gentleman the Member for West Cumberland (Mr. Percy Wyndham) had, he thought, stated fairly the principle on which such a rate should be levied when he said, that those persons who derived profit or pleasure from fishing should be called upon to pay for protecting the Fisheries. The question, however, was one of some intricacy, and it required great care to put into a legislative form a provision for enforcing the collection of revenue by means of licences, and more especially for arranging the assessment of different interests in a river for the purpose of levying a rate. Both those matters were under consideration, and the right hon. Baronet the Secretary of State for the Home Department (Sir George Grey) was in communication with the Fishery Inspectors, and with the assistance of his right hon. Friend the Member for Merthyr Tydvil (Mr. H. A. Bruce), who had paid great attention to the subject, he hoped it might be in the power of the Government to introduce some measure in the course of the present Session which might to some extent at any rate meet the wishes of those persons who were interested in the Fisheries. He could not give a pledge on the part of the Government that any measure would be introduced in time for it to be passed this Session. All he could say was that further attention would be given to the subject.

CASE OF MR. BEWICKE.—COMMITTEE MOVED FOR.

MR. H. BERKELEY said, he rose to call the attention of the House to the case of Mr. W. Bewicke, of Threepwood Hall, in the county of Northumberland. He trusted the House, when they considered the nature of the subject, would excuse him for bringing it forward a second time. When he last brought this subject before the House, there were forty-six hon. Members present, of whom, deducting four tellers, twenty-two voted against his Motion, and twenty voted in its favour. But the hon. Member for Shoreham (Mr. Cave) by mistake went into the Government lobby, but for which accident the numbers would have been equal, and the result would have been decided by the casting vote of the Speaker. He would not presume to inquire how that right hon. Gentleman would have voted, but from his known character as a friend of the oppressed, he was confident that his Motion would have been carried. After the division he received many communications expressive of regret that his Motion had been unsuccessful,

and the press generally took up the subject in a fair and generous manner. He was, therefore, induced a second time to trouble the House with the story of Mr. Bewicke's wrongs. Mr. Bewicke was a man of respectable position, of independent fortune, and of an ancient family, which had been in the armigery of the county of Northumberland for 800 years. He got into a lawsuit, but, for some reason or other, he refused to pay the costs, and allowed the sheriff to levy for them. It became important to consider who were the men employed by the Sheriff of Northumberland. Although it was quite proper that strict inquiries should be made into the character of men seeking to enter the police force, yet it was still more necessary to be particular in selecting persons to serve as sheriff's officers, because, while the policeman had to deal with crime, the sheriff's officer had to deal with misfortune. In that case, the chief officer employed to levy was a man named Stainthorpe, who, he found, from recent intelligence, had been discharged for embezzlement. That man had been convicted before the Hexham magistrates for beating his wife, had been fined and bound over to keep the peace. He had been several times summoned for assaults, and upon another occasion for deserting his wife and family. Such were the antecedents of one of the men employed to carry out the law. The second officer was a person of the name of John Dodd. That gentleman had been sentenced in 1852 to seven years' transportation for perjury, and he was at the time of that transaction out upon a ticket-of-leave. [Sir GEORGE GREY: That was nine years after, in 1861.] That man was then at large upon a ticket-of-leave, and he was employed to assert the majesty of the law. He had also been convicted of poaching and other offences, and altogether he was a very pleasing character. The third man employed was named Hutchinson, against whom were recorded four convictions for assaults, as well as two other convictions for felony. Dagliah, the fourth man, was an extremely bad character, and had been brought up for assaults and poaching times without number. There might be some hon. Members in the House who looked with great leniency upon poaching, but for himself he had always found poaching and graver offences went hand in hand. These men proceeded to Threepwood Hall to arrest Mr. Bewicke, who, it seemed, had been prepared to pay the debt, which amounted to something like £49. When he observed the banditti approaching, he was somewhat startled; he thought it would be best to pay the money to prevent them from robbing his house. The chief of the party proceeded with great nonchalance to pull out pistols and to distribute them among his followers. Thereupon Mr. Bewicke went into his house, produced his revolver, and said, "the fact is, if this is your sort of game you shall not play it with impunity." He said "I will not admit such a set of blackguards into my house, for you will pillage it." They then waxed somewhat more civil. He went into his house and barricaded it, there being carts and cart horses which he permitted them to take in execution. The sheriff's officer departed, leaving the other four worthies outside. It had since come out that when the men were approaching the house they halted and resolved themselves into a sort of committee of supply, and held a council as to how they should proceed when they got into the house. The sheriff's officer said they showed great ignorance; that they knew nothing of their profession, as it was always a settled thing to go at once to the wine cellar. Well, it was settled *nemine contradicente* that that should be their mode of proceeding. During the night, probably finding themselves chilly, they sent to Mr. Bewicke begging for provisions, and being an open hearted Englishman he sent some out to them. The next morning. Mr. Bewicke, having occasion to discharge his pistol, called out to the men down below to get out of the way, as he was going to fire. They called out, "All right," and then he discharged the weapon. Thereupon they said, "Now we have got him," and they went to a magistrate and laid an information against Mr. Bewicke for obstructing them in the execution of their duty, and firing at them with intent to do them some bodily harm. Dodd brought a bullet in his waistcoat, which another of the villains was to find and did find. The characters of all the men were perfectly well known to the magistrates; but in spite of this, Mr. Bewicke was committed for trial, bail to the amount of £2,000 being accepted for his appearance. Mr. Bewicke, who regarded the turn affairs had taken as being merely an exhibition of ill-feeling on the part of the magistrates, employed no counsel to defend him, believing that the characters of the

Mr. H. Berkeley

men alone would be sufficient to repel so monstrous and absurd a charge. He was, however, found guilty and sentenced to four years penal servitude. In prison Mr. Bewicke might have remained until now—or he would not say that Mr. Bewicke would have remained until the present time, because he was nearly dead when he was released. It happened that he had a faithful and very clever housekeeper, a Mrs. Lodge. She had been examined at the trial, but her feelings overcame her and she broke down. Afterwards, however, she collected a large mass of evidence; and she went straight to Mr. Serjeant Shee, who received her kindly, and since counsel cannot look at a case in the first instance, gave her a note to Mr. Ivimey, of Staple Inn. Mr. Ivimey looked to the proof, found it to be valid, went down into the country, arrested the four men, and brought them to trial. John Dodd was sentenced to two years' hard labour for the part he took with reference to the bullet, Daglish was sentenced to one year's imprisonment in Morpeth gaol for perjury, and Hutchinson was sentenced to four years' penal servitude. This last villain had been a perjurer from the commencement; had come out of prison on a ticket-of-leave, had perjured himself on the trial of Mr. Bewicke, had perjured himself for his companions, and when he came to be tried himself pleaded guilty. It was not for him to question the decision of the Judges, but Mr. Justice Mellor let this rascal off from the severer part of the punishment on account of his having pleaded guilty. It was not necessary for him to dwell upon that point, but it struck him as being rather an extraordinary one. Stainthorpe, who, as he himself expressed it, had had so much of prison that he did not want any more, turned Queen's evidence. Would it be believed that Dodd, instead of being allowed to pass his full term in prison, was permitted to go at large at the expiration of sixteen months on a ticket-of-leave. What must have been the feelings of Mr. Bewicke during his dreary imprisonment of twelve months? A man born and educated as a gentleman, having ancestors to look back to, and desirous of not dishonouring them, must have suffered most acutely. A fine, robust, powerful man when he went to prison, he came out broken in constitution and in heart. He was liberated on the authority of a most objectionable document, granting him Her Majesty's pardon.

Could innocence be pardoned? Could a man be pardoned for being innocent? If it were necessary to keep to forms, and if the word "pardon" must be employed in the warrant, then the "pardon" should be granted to the Judge and jury who had made the blunder. But this was not the end of Mr. Bewicke's troubles. The trustees of Greenwich Hospital, it appears, are Lords of the manor of Langley, on which Mr. Bewicke's property is situated, it having been granted to them by the Crown on the attainder of the Earl of Derwentwater. On Mr. Bewicke's conviction, they came down, and at one fell swoop seized everything in the house. Away went the family pictures; away went the timber; away went the plate, that had been in the family for years; away went the library, Mr. Bewicke's chief solace. There was one little room which the ruffians employed did not touch; it was the room of the housekeeper —Mrs. Lodge. She was a widow, and when she came to live at Mr. Bewicke's she asked permission to bring some of her furniture to increase the comfort of her own room. That was accorded to her, and the sheriff's officer, with good feeling, said he did not desire to take her furniture. The chief officer went away, but that same evening the rest of the men broke into the room, took Mrs. Lodge's bed from under her, and left her to lie upon the floor. Mr. Bewicke returned, and found bare walls and discomfort where all had been comfort; but the circumstance which hurt him more than anything else — and that showed the good feeling of the man—was the treatment received by Mrs. Lodge. Mr. Bewicke determined to proceed against the Commissioners of Greenwich Hospital, but when the case was laid before counsel, the opinion given was, that he was not capable of bringing the action, being a felon when the furniture was seized. Thus a pardon did not remove the stain of felony from even an innocent man. Such was one of the beautiful anomalies of the existing law. It was not for him to point out the remedy for such a state of things, but the hon. and learned Member for East Suffolk (Sir Fitzroy Kelly), who was, unfortunately, absent, had taken up this matter strongly, and was of opinion that there should be a Court of Appeal. Such, then, was the end of the tragedy, for he might almost call it a tragedy. Mr. Bewicke's law expenses amounted to between £2,000 and £3,000, and the loss consequent upon the forced sale of his furniture was fully 80 per cent. Among this furniture, much of which was quite new, was a marble tessellated and antique table, which he had obtained from Italy, and for which he gave 100 guineas. This was sold for £17, and it was afterwards offered to Mr. Bewicke as a favour for £37. A grand piano by Broadwood, in excellent order, sold for £20. A pony sold for £14, and was offered back to Mr. Bewicke for £25. He had a great many valuable books, especially in French literature. He had the whole works of Voltaire, Racine, Molière, and Corneille, and down in that part of the country those books fetched little more than the price of waste paper — they were in all probability destined to become wrappers for tobacco and cheese. He appealed, then, to the House to take the hard case he had again stated into consideration. He could not, for his life, understand what answer the Attorney General would make, though it would, no doubt, be very ingenious. Perhaps he would say that if there were one Bewicke with such a case, there might be twenty. He would answer that as long as the Legislature thought proper to keep the law in its present state, it was their duty to satisfy every one of these cases. The House might compensate Mr. Bewicke for his furniture, they might give him a *quid pro quo* for that which he had lost, but how were they to compensate him for his sufferings? How were they to compensate a man of honour and a gentleman for having been herded with the lowest felons, and subjected to every indignity to which the most wretched criminal could be subjected? Let them ask Mr. Bewicke which he would rather do—meet death or undergo another year of penal servitude, and he would tell them to be merciful, and to give him death. As far inferior as was bodily suffering to mental anguish, so to a man of honour a crushed reputation far exceeded the agony of death. It was to compensate Mr. Bewicke, then, that he appealed to an assembly formed of 600 Gentlemen, the first assembly in the world; and he did not believe that he should ask in vain, or that little Home Office scruples, or the quirks of the legal profession, would prevent that compensation being granted.

Amendment proposed,

To leave out from the word " That " to the end of the Question, in order to add the words " this House will, upon Monday next, resolve itself into a Committee, to consider of an Address to Her Majesty, praying that Her Majesty will be graciously pleased to direct adequate compensation to be made to William Bewicke, of Threepwood Hall, in the county of Northumberland, for the pain, degradation, anguish of mind, and consequent ill-health, he has suffered, in being confined for twelve months in a prison as a felon, on a charge since proved to be false ; for the confiscation of his goods, chattels, family pictures, plate, and library, thus inflicting upon him an irreparable injury ; also for the heavy pecuniary loss he has suffered in prosecuting and bringing to justice the persons who had conspired against him, such having been the only means by which eventually he was enabled to establish his innocence ; and that this House is prepared to assure Her Majesty that it will make good the same,"—(*Mr. Henry Berkeley*,)

—instead thereof.

SIR GEORGE GREY said, he was aware of the disadvantage under which he laboured in objecting to a Motion of that nature, in a case which was undoubtedly calculated to excite the sympathy of the House, and to which, were he to be guided only by personal feelings, he should be very glad to assent. In the discharge of his duty, he should be compelled to ask the House seriously to consider the question raised by the Motion, and to hesitate before they committed themselves to a principle which must have a much wider application than to the particular case before them, and which, in fact, involved an entire alteration of the law. He did not mean to prejudge the consideration of the particular question, if it were brought properly before the House ; but it would be his duty to point out the results which, in his opinion, would follow from the adoption of the Motion in its present form. With regard to the facts of the case, he had heard for the first time some of the details in the picturesque narrative of his hon. Friend, but there was no difficulty in gathering an outline of the case, and that he took from Mr. Bewicke's petition, presented during the last Session. In 1861, Mr. Bewicke was defendant in an action in which the verdict was against him, and as he refused to pay the costs, the sheriff of Northumberland by his officers proceeded to levy them. He was not about to defend the character of the sheriff's officers, but he thought the hon. Member for Bristol (Mr. H. Berkeley) must be mistaken in his statement that one of those men, who was afterwards convicted of perjury and sentenced to two years' penal servitude, was discharged with a ticket-of-leave after only sixteen months of his sentence had expired. He could not understand how that had happened unless

Mr. H. Berkeley

it was upon the recommendation of the visiting justices of the gaol, on the ground of danger to life from further imprisonment. If the visiting justices stated that longer confinement would endanger the life of a prisoner, and their statement was supported by medical testimony, then the sentence of imprisonment was not converted into a capital sentence, as would be the case if the prisoner were longer confined, and he was released. He did not know whether that had been the case in the present instance, but he would make inquiry as to the facts. Mr. Bewicke resisted the execution of the process, and was charged with the very serious offence of shooting with intent to do some grievous bodily harm. He was committed for trial by magistrates residing in his own neighbourhood, with regard to whom the hon. Member for Bristol (Mr. H. Berkeley) might have spared the imputation that they acted upon feelings of personal dislike for Mr. Bewicke. With regard to one of these gentlemen, who had served the office of High Sheriff, he believed him to be utterly incapable of having been actuated by any other feeling than that of a desire to discharge his duty ; and he presumed the same might be said of the other though he was not personally known to him. Mr. Bewicke was committed for trial, and the case came on before Mr. Justice Keating at the Spring Assizes for 1861. Mr. Bewicke, unfortunately for himself, employed neither attorney nor counsel, but conducted his own defence. The case was tried with great patience and forbearance by the learned Judge, for there was public testimony to this, and the jury found Mr. Bewicke guilty—a verdict in which the learned Judge, upon the evidence given, entirely concurred—though it was known that the character of the witnesses was not the best. The Judge did not pass sentence instantly, but communicated with Mr. Justice Hill, who was on circuit with him, and than whom there was no more learned or able Judge upon the Bench. The facts were considered by those two Judges, and next day Mr. Bewicke was sentenced to four years' penal servitude— a sentence which both Judges were of opinion was demanded under the circumstances of the case. A petition was subsequently presented to the Home Office on behalf of Mr. Bewicke, and it was referred to the Judge who had tried the case ; but, notwithstanding the statements made on behalf of Mr. Bewicke, that learned Judge and Mr. Justice Hill, with whom he conferred, were of opinion there was no reason to doubt that the verdict was a right one. He had understood his hon. Friend to suggest that a pardon ought to be granted to the Judge and the jury to free them from their guilt in the transaction ; but he could not think that any blame whatever was attributable to either the Judge or the jury. Well, then, they came to the year 1862, when Mr. Bewicke was enabled to bring forward evidence to show that those who had deposed to the important fact in the case— namely, whether the gun was loaded or not—had committed perjury. Those persons was prosecuted and a conviction was obtained against them. When the conviction was obtained a free pardon was at once granted to Mr. Bewicke. A wrong had been done him undoubtedly, but that was the only way it could be redressed— by means of a free pardon. Bills to establish a Court of Appeal had been brought forward from time to time ; but he had never heard it proposed that the time of appeal and of application for a new trial should be indefinite. In the present case the Judge was perfectly satisfied with the verdict, and it was not till nearly a year after the trial the evidence was discovered which proved the perjury. He did not think that hon. Gentlemen would propose that a power of appeal extending over so long a period should be given in criminal cases. A free pardon, therefore, was the only form by which the wrong committed on a prisoner in such a case could be redressed. But his hon. Friend complained that as soon as Mr. Bewicke was convicted the Commissioners of Greenwich Hospital, as grantees of the Crown, became possessed of his property, stripped his house of all it possessed, and took away his furniture. He spoke from information communicated to him from a source which he could not doubt, when he said that the Commissioners of Greenwich Hospital had been most anxious that not a particle of the furniture should be removed from the house. They had made repeated attempts by communications with members of his family to make arrangements by which the property might remain in the house until Mr. Bewicke himself was set free ; but all those attempts having failed, as Trustees for a Public Charity, they were bound to advertise the property for sale. It was sold, with the exception of some of the pictures, and the whole proceeds of the sale, minus £30 for expenses, and the

unsold pictures were handed over to him when he was discharged on the free pardon. Those being the facts of the case, his hon. Friend asked for compensation for Mr. Bewicke on three grounds—first, " for the pain, degradation, anguish of mind, and consequent ill-health he had suffered in being confined for twelve months in a prison as a felon on a charge since proved to be false." That demand appeared to him to raise the important question, whether in every case in which a person had been convicted of crime, and was afterwards proved to be innocent of that crime, though the conviction might have taken place not through any defect in the law, or in the administration of the law, but from the inherent defect of human testimony, compensation was to be given to the sufferer out of the public funds. No doubt the case of Mr. Bewicke was one calculated to call forth the sympathy of the House ; but he was sure the House would not agree on a Motion to give him compensation, unless they were prepared to give it to every person, however humble, who might be convicted and imprisoned, and whose innocence might afterwards be proved. Those cases, happily, were not very numerous ; but his experience informed him that they were not very rare. Cases occurred of mistaken identity, in which the evidence had been honestly given, but in which there had been an unintentional mistake as to identity. In these cases, when the mistake was discovered, no compensation was given, even although the innocent person had suffered imprisonment. Then there were other cases in which convictions had taken place in consequence of wilfully false swearing. Some time ago the chaplain of a large county gaol in the neighbourhood of London was charged with a very serious offence, and convicted on the evidence of two girls. He lost his situation as chaplain of the gaol, and suffered imprisonment. After a considerable time he was able to convict the witnesses of perjury, and, of course, he was discharged from prison ; but no compensation was asked for him, though he must have suffered very much from the charge and the conviction, the more particularly as he was a clergyman. He believed that gentleman's friends raised a subscription for him, but no claim was made on the public for compensation, though the case was a stronger one than that now before the House. He wanted to know how compensation of this kind was to be measured

—how the suffering in mind and body was to be estimated? There was one circumstance in this case which it appeared to him did not tell in favour of Mr. Bewicke's claim. That gentleman had defended himself, and had employed no lawyer or counsel. Were persons who acted in that way to come to Parliament and ask for compensation if they were convicted on the evidence of witnesses for the prosecution? He believed himself it was highly probable that those witnesses whose evidence had convicted Mr. Bewicke would have broken down under the searching cross-examination of counsel. Passing from the first ground on which compensation was asked for Mr. Bewicke, he would take the third before the second. The third ground was "for the heavy pecuniary loss he had suffered in prosecuting and bringing to justice the persons who had conspired against him, such having been the only means by which eventually he was able to establish his innocence." If the House agreed to the present Motion, was it to be understood that they were prepared to grant compensation, not only to Mr. Bewicke, but to all other persons who might be obliged to undertake a prosecution in order to prove their innocence. Were they prepared to pay the expense of all such prosecutions out of the public purse? If so, that ought to be clearly understood. The second ground of compensation, which he was taking last, was really the main ground—namely, "the confiscation of his goods, chattels, family pictures, plate, and library." He was bound to say he thought that claim stood in a different position from the two others. A Bill had been brought in by his hon. and learned Friend the Member for Walsall (Mr. Charles Foster), to abolish the law by which the property of felons went to the Crown. That subject, in his opinion, deserved attention; but it was one on which hasty legislation would be very unadvisable, and therefore he thought his hon. and learned Friend had done well to give time for its further consideration. If it were true, as Mr. Bewicke appeared to think, that his property was sold for far less than its value, then he might have some claim on the consideration of the House, and he should have no objection to a Committee to inquire into those special circumstances of the case. He believed that such an inquiry would show that the conduct of the Commissioners of Greenwich Hospital towards the family of Mr. Bewicke had been marked by great kindness and consider-

Sir George Grey

ation, and it would enable the House at the same time to say whether there were any special circumstances in the case which would justify them in deciding that Mr. Bewicke was entitled to compensation in that respect. The House would take the course which it thought best under the circumstances, but he had felt himself compelled to point out the inexpediency of introducing any new principle of law founded on a particular instance without a deliberate inquiry. The form in which the hon. Member for Bristol (Mr. H. Berkeley), had made his Motion prevented him from moving his Amendment, but if the hon. Gentleman was disposed to accept the suggestion he had made, and would on a future occasion move for a Committee to inquire into so much of the petition as referred to his loss by the sale of his property, he should not offer any objection.

Lord JOHN MANNERS said, he was not aware what course the hon. Member for Bristol (Mr. H. Berkeley) meant to pursue, but, if he might offer a word of advice, he should counsel him not to close with the offer of the right hon. Baronet. The whole argument of the right hon. Baronet was simply, that the House of Commons was not to perform one act of justice, lest it should be called upon at some future time to do another. The illustration which he had used to prove the soundness of his advice to the House proved its unsoundness. He cited the case of a clergyman who was convicted unjustly, and who never made any claim on the Crown for compensation. That showed that if the House did justice in the present case it did not follow that it would be called on to do justice in every other similar case which might happen. Whether it were in respect to a gentleman of birth and education equal to themselves, as Mr. Bewicke was said to be, or in the case of the humblest member of society, he hoped the House would never hesitate to do such an act of justice as the hon. Gentleman now called on them to perform. The right hon. Baronet said that, though he might have no objection to change the law, as long as it remained unchanged he objected to justice being done in exceptional cases; but so long as the Government, who were chiefly responsible for the existing state of the law, were contented with that state of the law, and permitted those exceptional acts of injustice to be perpetrated, it was to that House the sufferers must appeal. The right hon. Baronet had not referred to the case of

Mr. Barber, which was a precedent for the course they were now asked to take. It could not be said that any great evil had followed from the act of justice which the House of Commons then performed. The right hon. Baronet's own statement showed that those cases occurred very rarely, and he hoped the House of Commons would not be frightened by the terrible unknown consequences which the right hon. Baronet had conjured up from the performance of an act of justice, whether it were to a well-born, educated man, or to the humblest member of society.

Mr. INGHAM said, that being well acquainted with the unfortunate gentleman who was the subject of the present Motion, he trusted the House would allow him to make a few remarks which would generally confirm the statement of the hon. Member for Bristol (Mr. H. Berkeley). When he first heard of the charge from the High Sheriff of the county, he was under the impression that it was merely an ordinary charge of a trifling breach of the peace, violent language, or something of that sort. To his surprise he found he was charged with wilfully firing at the sheriff's officer with a felonious intent. He went to see him, and could scarcely bring him to realize the gravity of the position in which he was placed. In fact, Mr. Bewicke treated the charge from the first as a monstrous one; he could not be persuaded to attach any importance to it. So fully was the evil character of these men known, that he fully expected that when the charge was examined in court it would explode of itself. He could hardly describe the consternation and dismay created in the north of England when Mr. Bewicke was convicted. A large number of memorials were forwarded to him from almost every parish in the neighbourhood, signed by thousands of persons, which he laid before the right hon. Baronet the Home Secretary. Of course, the Home Office could not act until some new facts were laid before it, and though the men on whose evidence Mr. Bewicke was convicted had been heard afterwards to express their disappointment at not getting the compensation, or hush money, they wanted, yet it was some time before any trustworthy, credible witnesses could be procured, whose evidence proved that the charge was provoked by the cupidity of those perjured witnesses.

Mr. LIDDELL said, he felt bound to make a few remarks on this matter, as in some respects the character of his fellow magistrates had been impugned. He must express, with all his heart, his thanks to the hon. Gentleman the Member for Bristol (Mr. H. Berkeley), who had, in so feeling and able a manner, brought this melancholy case before the House; and he was also bound to thank the House for the way in which it had received the hon. Member's statement. When precedents were spoken of, he must say he believed that such a case of hardship as the present was quite unprecedented, and would probably never occur again. It was, he thought, a case alike discreditable to English law and practice, and the sooner the House set about finding a remedy for such legal anomalies the better. He desired, however, to say that one of the magistrates who, he believed, acted on the bench on that occasion was Mr. Errington, whom he had the pleasure of knowing as one of the most active and able members of the bench, and a gentleman who was held in the highest estimation in the district. He must have been misinformed as to the real facts, or he never would have allowed the character of those rascals, who acted as assistants to the sheriff's officer, to pass without inquiry. It was to be regretted that Mr. Bewicke had undertaken to defend himself at the assizes, instead of obtaining professional assistance; but that was only an additional proof that he was conscious of his own innocence. He trusted that the hon. Member for Bristol (Mr. H. Berkeley) would not accede to the proposition of the Government, but would take the sense of the House on his Motion.

THE ATTORNEY GENERAL said, it would, no doubt, be far more agreeable to the House to support a Motion of that kind, if convinced that it was right, than it would be to oppose it; but persons who stood in his position were bound to take care that the House should, as far as possible, be made thoroughly aware of the true nature and probable consequences of the Resolution it was asked to adopt. The Question was one which emphatically belonged to the House; and the Government could have no object except that if the House thought fit to affirm the Resolution it should clearly understand the principle involved, and the serious pecuniary charge which might possibly be placed upon the nation. The hon. Gentleman the Member for South Northumberland (Mr. Liddell) described that case as discreditable to

English law and practice, and as resulting from legal anomalies. If they considered the different steps of the transaction, it would be difficult to say what part of the case was discreditable to the law or could be held justly chargeable to its administration. In every country in the world where justice was administered, if persons came before the competent authorities and laid informations upon oath of offences said to have been committed against the law, it was the bounden duty of the magistrates to receive those informations, and deal with them according to the evidence adduced and the principles of law applicable to the case. The criminal law had been brought into operation before the Hexham bench in the usual manner; and it would surely not be said that the magistrates, having the means of knowing that no credit ought to be attached to the evidence given before them, nevertheless proceeded to require very heavy recognizances for the appearance of that unfortunate gentleman Mr. Bewicke to take his trial. The magistrates had discharged their duty with perfect honesty; and there being nothing before them at the time to discredit the evidence, they could not do otherwise than act upon it. What possible amendment of the law could alter that state of things? Nothing could be more disagreeable to him than to have to remind the House that the indiscretion and want of judgment which that unfortunate gentleman displayed had placed him in a most false position. He originally refused to pay the costs recovered in an action against him, and legal process was employed to enforce their payment. Unfortunately, his indiscretion did not stop there. As if to supply to malicious persons a link that might be wanting in the chain of evidence against him, he fired off a pistol, and that the pistol was actually fired there could be no doubt. The trial took place before a jury and before Judges of the highest impartiality; but, unhappily, Mr. Bewicke treated the charge with contempt. No man in the kingdom was entitled to treat such a criminal charge with neglect, or to leave that to be done after his conviction which ought to have been done before it. That, however, was the course taken by Mr. Bewicke. He omitted to retain an attorney or counsel for his defence. [An hon. MEMBER: He did quite right.] He could not think that any Gentleman whom he now addressed would, if placed in a similar position, not have felt it his bounden duty to prepare for his trial

on so serious a charge, and employ those indispensable adjuncts of justice—attorneys and counsel. They must all lament what had happened in this case, and sympathize with Mr. Bewicke's misfortune; but when a Motion like the present was proposed, the House could not overlook the indiscretion and the negligence which that gentleman had shown after solemn warning. Was the jury to blame? Were they to know by intuition that the witnesses were perjured, and had convictions recorded against them? Was it the duty of the Judge or jury to supply evidence out of their own imagination? That evidence ought to have been brought forward by the diligence of the person accused. There had been no defect in the administration of justice. The Judge and jury were satisfied; and it was only some time afterwards that steps were taken to discover those facts, which due diligence should have discovered before. What was the charge against the law? That when this gentleman had been convicted the law could not assume his innocence till he had prosecuted these parties for perjury by evidence which ought to have been produced by him at his own trial; and the country was now asked to repay the expenses of that prosecution for perjury in consequence of his own neglect to take the proper means of defending himself in the first instance. The next charge against the law was that Her Majesty had granted this unfortunate gentleman a free pardon. But a solemn sentence could not be treated as a nullity merely because a conviction had proceeded on false evidence, for which the law was not responsible, and which did not appear in the course of the trial. If this Resolution were affirmed, except so far as it had been assented to by his right hon. Friend the Secretary of State for the Home Department, the House would be asserting the principle, that wherever false evidence in the due administration of the law had resulted in procuring a conviction which afterwards turned out to be erroneous they would make compensation, although the neglect of the person who was the sufferer had contributed in a very great and important degree to that result. In that particular case they were all satisfied of the innocence of Mr. Bewicke. The circumstances were remarkable which established his innocence. But if the House agreed to the present Motion, would it not afford a general encouragement to convicted per-

The Attorney General

sons of all degrees to speculate on the means of throwing doubt on the justice of their convictions, relying on Parliament afterwards indemnifying them for their sufferings? It was not very easy to see to what extent such demands on the public would go. If the House was determined still to assent to the Motion, he hoped they would do so on some ground which might hereafter be referred to as exceptional. The only point he could find of that nature in this case was, that the persons out of whose perjured accusations this series of misfortunes originally arose were persons in a certain sense denominated officers of the law, but not officers of the public administrative law of the land. They were officers of the sheriff, selected by him, and for whose acts the sheriff was civilly responsible. If anyone ought to pay this gentleman's expenses it was the sheriff. He hoped if a Committee were appointed they would take care to state the grounds on which they proceeded, and that, at least, the nation would be saved from the consequences of other demands of a similar character.

SIR HENRY WILLOUGHBY said, there could be no doubt that the case of Mr. Bewicke not only demanded but had the sympathy of the House. The only question was as to the best mode of doing him justice. He understood the right hon. Baronet was willing to refer the question of the forfeiture of the goods to a Committee of Inquiry. That being so, why not add to that inquiry the best means of doing justice to Mr. Bewicke. It would be difficult to adopt the Motion as it now stood, but he certainly considered that some inquiry was necessary.

MR. SOMERSET BEAUMONT observed, that the great fault which, according to the Attorney General, the unfortunate gentleman had committed was, that he neglected to retain the services of counsel. No doubt that was a grave error in the estimation of those hon. Members who belonged to the Bar, but in the present case it had arisen from the entire consciousness of innocence. Besides, Mr. Bewicke possessed considerable abilities, and he thought he should have no difficulty in establishing his innocence. The Attorney General had said this was a question more for the House than the Government to consider, he therefore hoped he might appeal to his hon. and learned Friend and his Colleagues, as Members of the House, so to record their votes that justice might be done.

SIR GEORGE GREY stated, with reference to what had fallen from the hon. Baronet the Member for Evesham (Sir Henry Willoughby), that he proposed that the petition of Mr. Bewicke should be referred to a Select Committee, so far as it related to the sale and disposal of his property.

MR. GATHORNE HARDY said, he was not able to give a silent vote on the Motion before the House, because it might go further than many hon. Gentlemen supposed. It was most important that the House of Commons should not constitute itself a tribunal to decide on *ex parte* statements without a full and adequate inquiry. There was the case of Mr. Barber. An inquiry was instituted, a careful investigation was made by a Committee, and upon the Report of that Committee and the evidence it obtained the House came to a decision. But now, what they were called upon to do was, in a most unreasonable manner to judge, under the heat and indignation which they all felt (and he must say that he had the deepest sympathy with the story of the wrongs of Mr. Bewicke), as to the compensation due to that gentleman upon grounds which they did not thoroughly understand. He must urge upon the hon. Gentleman opposite to consent to the appointment of a Committee to inquire into the whole petition, in order to see whether the circumstances of the case were not so exceptional as to justify the House in going out of its way to deal with it in a manner different from that in which it had dealt with former cases. The House wished to see justice done, but let them act with deliberation, and not with too great haste. Let the Committee be appointed, and if the Government agreed to that course he could never consent to vote for the Resolution before the House.

MR. MALINS said, it was the universal opinion that the sufferings of Mr. Bewicke were such as to entitle him to compensation. The right hon. Baronet (Sir George Grey) had consented to refer part of the petition to a Committee—that part having reference to compensation with respect to the loss of his furniture. He quite agreed with his hon. Friend the Member for Leominster (Mr. Hardy) that the reference ought to be general; that the whole petition should be referred to a Select Committee, who should be desired to report upon all the allegations, and say whether Mr. Bewicke was entitled to any and what compensation. The substance of the whole case ought to be referred.

THE CHANCELLOR OF THE EXCHEQUER: My right hon. Friend has explained that it is impossible for the Government to assent to a Resolution which, like the one before us, pledges the House, as we consider and construe it, to this principle—that whenever pain, degradation, and anguish of mind arise out of an erroneous conviction, quite irrespective of loss of a tangible kind, the case should be made the subject of an application to Parliament for pecuniary compensation. The hon. Member for Leominster (Mr. Hardy) opposite, and the hon. and learned Gentleman (Mr. Malins) who followed him, have made a proposition which we feel ourselves able to assent to. I do not deny, and my right hon. Friend has not denied, that there are contained in the petition allegations which may be made the subject of inquiry. The best mode of proceeding will be to agree that the petition should be referred to a Select Committee, and the Government assent to it on the understanding that the Resolution is withdrawn.

MR. H. BERKELEY: I should like to understand distinctly whether the whole merits of the case are to be referred to a Committee. I confess I have a sort of compunction in agreeing to the suggestion, because we do not always know that the formation of a Committee is one on which we can depend. However, I am in the hands of the House, and if they consider I ought to agree to this proposal, I will do so.

SIR JOHN TROLLOPE said, he was a Member of the Committee in Mr. Barber's case. The whole petition was referred to them to report as they thought fit.

MR. HORSMAN: I understand my hon. Friend is invited to follow the precedent set in the case of Mr. Barber. A Committee was appointed to inquire into the circumstances; they made a Report; upon that Report the House took action, and awarded compensation.

SIR GEORGE GREY: What we agree to is the appointment of a Committee, to whom the petition [MR. DISRAELI: What petition?] shall be referred, with a direction to report their opinion to the House. It is impossible to pledge the House to act upon the Report of the Committee.

MR. DISRAELI: I wish to remind the House that there is a great difference between the case of Mr. Barber and the case of Mr. Bewicke. Mr. Barber had not convicted any person of perjury against him. The case of Mr. Bewicke is the case of an individual who has found that those who were the origin and cause of the infamous injustice he has experienced were perjurers. The case of Mr. Barber required great investigation, because in it were involved circumstances of a suspicious character; but in this case the whole facts are before us; nobody doubts them. Then, again, we are told about a petition being referred to a Committee. We know of no petition for our consideration to-night; and how can we agree to refer a petition to a Committee when it is a document with which we are not acquainted? Besides, we are not sure that the petition is wide enough to bring the whole facts of the case before the Committee. With regard to the case itself, there has been a great objection made against Mr. Bewicke that he was indiscreet, because he did not avail himself of the assistance of the members of the long robe and the other learned branch of the profession. It has been very well said by one of his neighbours, that he had great confidence in his own abilities (which, I believe, are not inconsiderable); but we are not to treat it as a great offence because an individual on his trial does not retain counsel. Then we are told that no one can question the conduct of the Judge. Well, the Judge might have cross-examined these men; and if a man like the present Lord Chief Justice of England had been Judge in this case, he would soon have found out the character of the witnesses. Or the Judge might have appointed counsel to watch the case for Mr. Bewicke. This is a case of infamous oppression. I do not remember any case like it. The argument of the right hon. Baronet the Secretary of State for the Home Department, and the argument of the hon. and learned Attorney General, is most inconsistent. They say, "We admit the sufferings of Mr. Bewicke and the injustice which he has experienced; but if you agree to this Resolution you establish a precedent dangerous in its consequences, and the claims which will be pressed on the consideration of the House will be so numerous that they will weigh seriously upon the Exchequer." Then they immediately say, "The case is rare; it never happened before; and it may never happen again." How can they reconcile these two statements? The fact is, that instances of this kind must be decided upon their merits, and there is no gene-

Mr. Malins

ral principle which can be applied. The case of Mr. Bewicke is before us; the facts are known; no investigation is required. It is one of unparalleled oppression, and exactly one with which we can deal. As to the petition which we are asked to refer to the Committee, I myself know nothing about it; and my advice to the hon. Member for Bristol (Mr. H. Berkeley) is to stand upon the Motion which he has placed before us, and take the opinion of the House.

MR. H. BERKELEY: There is no petition before the House. Under the circumstances, feeling that the sentiment of the House is with me, I hold it to be my duty, after the best consideration, to proceed to a division.

Question put, "That the words proposed to be left out stand part of the Question."

The House *divided* :—Ayes 118 ; Noes 120 : Majority 2.

Question proposed,

"That the words, 'this House will, upon Monday next, resolve itself into a Committee, to consider of an Address to Her Majesty, praying that Her Majesty will be graciously pleased to direct adequate compensation to be made to William Bewicke, of Threepwood Hall, in the county of Northumberland, for the pain, degradation, anguish of mind, and consequent ill-health, he has suffered, in being confined for twelve months in a prison as a felon, on a charge since proved to be false ; for the confiscation of his goods, chattels, family pictures, plate, and library, thus inflicting upon him an irreparable injury; also for the heavy pecuniary loss he has suffered in prosecuting and bringing to justice the persons who had conspired against him, such having been the only means by which eventually he was enabled to establish his innocence ; and that this House is prepared to assure Her Majesty that it will make good the same,' be added,"

—instead thereof.

Amendment proposed,

To the said proposed Amendment, by leaving out from the words "this House" to the end of the said proposed Amendment, in order to add the words "is of opinion that a Select Committee should be appointed, to consider a Petition presented to this House by Mr. William Bewicke, of Threepwood Hall, in the county of Northumberland, on the 28th day of April, 1863, and to report its opinion to the House as to whether Mr. Bewicke is entitled to any and what compensation,"—(*Sir George Grey,*)

—instead thereof.

MR. DISRAELI : I look upon this merely as a proposition to rescind the vote which the House has just come to. Therefore it is unnecessary to revive the discussion which has just terminated, and the best thing to be done is at once to go to a vote.

MR. H. BERKELEY : I cannot accept the proposal, which appears to me to be an attempt to upset the vote, and to be indecent and unparliamentary.

SIR GEORGE GREY : I am sure the Amendment is not unparliamentary. I ask you, Sir, whether I am in order in moving the Amendment ?

MR. HORSMAN : I think the course which the Government is taking is very unusual. It is taking the House by surprise, and putting it in an unfair position. Who knows anything about this petition ? It was not presented during the present Session, and therefore it was presented before many hon. Members were elected who have now a seat. We have never seen it, and yet we are asked to rescind a vote which we have just come to, upon a Motion that has been made, by referring to the consideration of a Committee a document which we know nothing about. We do not know whether the allegations in the petition were the case as stated by the mover of the Resolution. There is this difference between the case which has been referred to and that of Mr. Bewicke. Here the facts are universally accepted. The statements of my hon. Friend the Member for Bristol (Mr. H. Berkeley) are not disputed by the Government. It is quite evident that Mr. Bewicke has been treated unjustly, and we are very much aggravating that injustice by the course proposed.

THE CHANCELLOR OF THE EXCHEQUER said, that it was evidently not within the knowledge of his right hon. Friend the Member for Stroud (Mr. Horsman) that the petition referred to had formed the subject of a division as well as of a debate, and that the House had recorded its opinion upon the question whether the grievances suffered by Mr. Bewicke, as set forth in this petition, were such as to entitle him to the consideration of Her Majesty's Government. The right hon. Gentleman had complained of the course adopted by his right hon. Friend the Secretary of State for the Home Department (Sir George Grey). The House had just divided on the Question, in which only one of the alternatives before it was presented. His right hon. Friend had met the difficulty at the first possible moment by proposing a substantive Motion, and the House had now before it in precise terms each of the two propositions between which it had to choose.

MR. HUNT said, the right hon. Member for Stroud (Mr. Horsman) said the Amendment took the House by surprise. But he (Mr. Hunt) thought the division had taken the House by surprise. His hon. Friend the Member for Leominster (Mr. Hardy) made a suggestion to the Government which the Chancellor of the Exchequer accepted on their part. It was put to the hon. Member for Bristol (Mr. H. Berkeley) whether he would accept it, and the hon. Member said he accepted it. He believed that many hon. Members had left the House on the understanding that the matter had been arranged. He thought no complaint could be made against the Government.

Mr. WHITESIDE said, he understood this proposition to be an attempt to negative the vote which had just been taken. He understood the House had affirmed by their vote that Mr. Bewicke was entitled to compensation ; and the proposition now was to refer it to a Committee to say whether he was to receive anything or nothing. No attentive listener could have misunderstood the Question; but the complaint was that they had not decided upon a petition which was not before them. That was not the first, or second, or third time that compensation had been given to an aggrieved man whom the law left with no appeal, and against whom the accusations were false.

Mr. SOMERSET BEAUMONT was of opinion that the proposals of the Government completely met the justice of the case.

Question put, " That the words proposed to be left out stand part of the said proposed Amendment."

The House *divided :—*Ayes 100; Noes 148 : Majority 48.

Question,

" That the words 'is of opinion that a Select Committee should be appointed, to consider a Petition presented to this House by Mr. William Bewicke, of Threepwood Hall, in the county of Northumberland, on the 28th day of April, 1863, and to report its opinion to the House as to whether Mr. Bewicke is entitled to any and what compensation,' be added,"

—instead thereof, put, and *agreed to.*

Main Question, as amended, put, and *agreed to.*

Ordered,

That a Select Committee be appointed, to consider a Petition presented to this House by Mr. William Bewicke, of Threepwood Hall, in the county of Northumberland, on the 28th day of April, 1863, and to report its opinion to the House, as to whether Mr. Bewicke is entitled to any and what compensation.—(*Sir George Grey.*)

Mr. *Hunt.*

On May 6, Committee *nominated as* follows :—

Sir FRANCIS BARING, Sir JOHN TROLLOPE, Mr. SOLICITOR GENERAL, Mr. EDWARD PLEYDELL BOUVERIE, Mr. HENRY BERKELEY, Colonel DUNNE, Sir DAVID DUNDAS, Mr. LIDDELL, Viscount ENFIELD, Mr. GATHORNE HARDY, Sir GEORGE COLTHURST, Mr. CAVENDISH BENTINCK, Mr. HUNT, Mr. SCOURFIELD, and Mr. BAILLIE COCHRANE :—Power to send for persons, papers, and records; Five to be the quorum.

And, on May 26, Colonel DUNNE *discharged* and Lord JOHN MANNERS *added.*

Moved, " That this House do immediately resolve itself in the Committee of Supply.

Motion *agreed to.*

Motion made and Question proposed, " That Mr. Speaker do now leave the Chair."

CHIMNEY SWEEPERS.—QUESTION.

Mr. DIGBY SEYMOUR said, he rose to call attention to the extensive employment of Climbing Boys in sweeping Chimneys, and the systematic violation of the " Act for the Regulation of Chimney Sweepers and Chimneys" (3 & 4 *Vict.* c. 85); and to ask the Secretary of State for the Home Department, Whether it is the intention of Her Majesty's Government to introduce any Bill during the present Session founded on the recommendations of the Children's Employment Commission (1862)?

Mr. HUNT said, he rose to Order. He wished for the opinion of the right hon. Gentleman as to whether the fact of an Amendment having been already carried to the Motion for going into Supply the House must not proceed to the Order which came next after Supply.

Mr. SPEAKER said, that an Amendment had been proposed to the Motion that the Speaker do now leave the Chair, and had been carried. It had been for some years the practice of the House, under such circumstances, for the Minister to move that the House should immediately resolve itself into a Committee of Supply, and that the Speaker should leave the Chair. Such a Motion had been made, and the business of the evening might thus proceed without interruption.

Mr. DIGBY SEYMOUR said, his attention had been directed to the subject to which his question related by an article in *Good Words,* the statements in which induced him to make personal inquiries in quarters where the best information was accessible. The result of these inquiries had been to satisfy his own mind that the humane and benevolent intentions of past legislation were to a very large extent frustrated, and that the practice of employing boys to sweep chimneys had been extensively re-introduced. In London, perhaps, the statute was not evaded to the same extent as in the provinces, but there could be no doubt that the number of boys secretly employed was on the increase. From 1788 till 1840 the House had passed various measures for protecting children against that barbarous employment. The last Act which they had passed being practically a dead letter, it was incumbent on them to pass an amending Act, or adopt some other course to stop the growing evil. In the metropolis and some other towns boys were employed, but only clandestinely. The practice of employing boys was increasing in London. In Marylebone alone eleven boys were employed, and only one of them by his father. The West End capitalists ought to blush at that fact, that it was chiefly in their centre of fashion and capital—in that part of the metropolis where Members of the Legislature chiefly resided — encouragement was given to a violation of the Act. A man named Muggeridge, who had been a chimney sweeper for forty-three years, had stated in evidence given by him on the subject, that those who made the law broke it, and that the owners of houses in Piccadilly, and other parts of the West End, required the services of climbing boys because they would not have their chimneys altered to suit the machines. At Manchester there were twenty climbing boys ; and it was believed that if anything were to happen to a gentleman in that city who looked after the master sweeps, the number would soon be increased to sixty. It was stated that these boys were often sold for a pound. The comparative slightness and suppleness of the female form had caused even girls to be immolated by their own parents, when these latter, to use the expression of St. Paul, were " without natural affections." At Birmingham, notwithstanding the expenditure of £500 by a local society, twenty-two climbing boys were now employed, that number having increased from fourteen in the year 1861. It appeared from a case reported in the *Cheshire News* that a master sweep was charged with an attempt to force a boy to go up a chimney which had been on fire, and in which the fire was scarcely extinguished. Yet for such barbarous conduct the magistrates only imposed a fine of £3

to one fund, and £3 to another. According to the Report of a local association there were in Birmingham fourteen boys employed, two being under twelve years of age, two under ten, one under nine, and one only seven years old. In 1863 the same association reported that twenty-two children of tender age were employed in Birmingham as climbing boys. In Nottingham, according to the evidence of a chimney-sweeper, the law against climbing boys was a dead letter. The coroner, Mr. Brown, had given evidence of having held inquests on two boys who had died from injuries they had received in their attempts to go up a chimney. In Staleybridge it was found that boys were plied with beer, and that two boys had swept seventy-eight chimneys in two days. In a prosecution at the latter place the prisoner said to one of the sitting magistrates, " You know my boy sweeps your chimneys." At Wolverhampton, according to the evidence, the system was encouraged by the local officials, and the Act of Parliament was a dead letter, for the chimneys of the Town Hall were swept by boys. At Sheffield twenty-two, in Chester fourteen, and in Newcastle ten climbing boys were employed ; and at Walthamstow the flue of the parish church had to be swept by a boy, who, owing to its peculiar formation, had to go into it head downwards. The barbarous practice was on the increase; and at Buckingham, in particular, it was reported that boys were preferred by most of the tradespeople, the gentry, and particularly by one of the Members for the town, though the other Member had used all the appliances of the law to put down the system. A master sweep at Nottingham described the manner in which the limbs of the poor children were hardened for their work. They were rubbed with the strongest brine, the master compelling them, by coaxing or by blows, to submit to the process a little longer. When the little sufferers first went out to work they returned with their flesh bruised and bleeding ; but their wounds were again rubbed with the brine. Some children did not become hardened for years ; and it was stated that four or four years and a half was a very good age to begin with them. By that fearful training their bodies were deformed and their backs often covered all over with sores. The " sooty cancer " also prevailed among these children, who had to sleep nine and twelve in a bed in the most fetid atmosphere. The abominations of negro slavery in South Carolina were surpassed by the daily miseries to which these defenceless young creatures were exposed. Mr. Ellis, a magistrate at Leicester, said it had been most painful to him to find that there was a regular system established in this country for the hire and sale of children for the purpose of carrying on that illegal and cruel occupation. What was the cause of that state of things? There was an extraordinary and inexplicable apathy on the part of the judicial bench to enforce the law in many places. It might be that there was some mysterious influence at work, or that magistrates sometimes thought their own houses were so built that it might be necessary for them to employ these boys; or, again, it might be that they had a distrust of informers, by whom cases of that kind were frequently brought forward. But in many cases, though the evidence was overwhelming, the magistrates hesitated to impose even a small fine. Perhaps, also, the law itself was defective. It was a remarkable fact that in Scotland no trace of the evil which existed in England could be found. That resulted most probably from the fact, that in Scotland there were superadded to the provisions of the Act 3 & 4 *Vict.*, certain local municipal regulations empowering the police to interfere, and no person could act as a master sweep in Glasgow or Edinburgh unless he had a licence, which might be forfeited by misconduct. The Commissioners thought that great benefit would arise from the introduction into England of that system of licensing. In conclusion, he earnestly hoped that the Government would promise to adopt the recommendations of the Commissioners, or at least to take some steps for rendering the present law more effectual, and thereby remedy a great and growing evil, which was a reproach to the 19th century and a scandal to our common Christianity.

SIR GEORGE GREY said, he regretted to say that the Report of the Commission, and the evidence on which it was founded, fully sustained the statement of the hon. and learned Gentleman, that there were very extensive violations of the law which prohibited the employment of climbing boys in the sweeping of chimneys. He would not go into the question in the then state of the House, and for this additional reason —the attention of the Government had for some time been directed to the Report; but a noble Friend of his (Lord Shaftesbury), at whose instance the Commission

Mr. Digby Seymour

was issued, had expressed his wish and intention elsewhere to bring in a Bill on the subject. That noble Lord had been good enough to place himself in communication with the Home Office, and they were giving him all the assistance they could. As the subject, then, would come before Parliament soon, he hoped its discussion would be postponed till that period.

PENSIONS TO GOVERNORS OF COLONIES.

OBSERVATIONS.

MR. BAILLIE COCHRANE said, he felt great reluctance in the then state of the House to introduce a question of very considerable importance, but he was anxious that the case of a most distinguished body of gentlemen should be put fairly before Parliament and the country. They had had a discussion that night as to the injustice which had been done in an individual case, but the case he had to submit was one of injustice to a large class of most distinguished gentlemen. It was a case of justice to Governors of Colonies, but it also involved the best interests of the colonial service generally. For the last half century great attention had been paid to the case of pensions and superannuation allowances to meritorious officers. Several Committees had sat on the question from time to time. Of these the most important was appointed in 1856 and reported in 1857. In 1859 the present system was introduced, by which superannuation allowances were given out of the Consolidated Fund to all who had served the Government in civil employments; but Governors of Colonies were excluded from participation in the benefits, in the face of the new regulations for the diplomatic service. In the case of the diplomatic service the necessity of paying their officers and giving retiring allowances had been accepted. It was decided that an attaché should begin to count his time after three or four years' service, and the system of retiring allowances to begin after fifteen years' service was carried out to a much greater extent than formerly. It seemed extraordinary that only one class of public servants were excepted from the privilege of superannuation allowances or retiring pensions, that class being gentlemen of the highest consideration, who had filled offices of the highest responsibility in the State. They were more important than attachés, because they represented the person of the Sovereign. He believed the circumstance had arisen altogether from an oversight or misapprehension. It was never intended to leave them out; but the fact was they did not exactly come under the Superannuation Act of the 22 *Vict.* They were apt to speak of a Colonial Governor as if, when a gentleman took the situation of the Governor of a colony, he adopted the colony altogether and broke off entirely from the mother country. But there was no such thing as a Colonial Governor; he was the Governor of a colony, not a colonial Governor; he was the officer of the Home Government, and in constant intercourse with them. A colonial Judge or secretary was connected with the colony, and received his instructions, as it were, from the colony; but the Governor received his instructions from home, and if not paid in the colony he would, in the last resort, come to the Home Government for his salary. They had forty-five colonies. In twenty-four of these the Governors were paid by the Home Government. Ten were paid indirectly by arrangements made with the colonies, the Home Government having sacrificed certain sums of money or land which they possessed when they gave responsible government to the colony—as in the case of Jamaica, where they gave up a claim of £200,000, on condition that the colony paid the Governor. In other cases they had thrown on the colonies the responsibility and charge of paying the Governor's salary. Was that a case in which when a man returned home they should refuse to give him the same privileges and retirement which had been given to other distinguished servants of the Crown? In Geelong and other Australian colonies a system of superannuation had been adopted, and the only persons who were omitted from its benefits were the Governors of the colony. He was quite certain that no eminent statesman who had filled the office of Secretary for the Colonies—whether his right hon. Friend below (Sir John Pakington), the Duke of Newcastle, or his right hon. Friend who had just entered on that important post—would desire to act unjustly; but the case he had to submit was a very grievous one. Formerly these appointments were very frequently conferred on officers of the army and navy, who while employed abroad moved on in the service, and received other appointments, perhaps, when they came home; but then there were not more than four or five colonies where the Governors were officers in either service. Then there was no branch in which there had been

such great reductions. In nearly every colony the salary of the Governor had been reduced. He remembered that a relative of his who was formerly Governor of Newfoundland received a salary of £5,000 a year, with everything found; it was reduced to £2,000. In Jamaica and Mauritius the salary was also reduced, and the whole amount was scarcely sufficient to enable the Governor adequately to fill his post. Nothing could be saved. It was said these gentlemen should insure their lives for the benefit of their families. But they only held office for six years; they might be recalled, and the policies would lapse. No system could be more unsatisfactory than that of underpaying the public servants, and no one could deny that it was great injustice that gentlemen of great ability, who had served their country for many years in distant colonies, might be brought home to starve—not a sixpence of pension being allowed to them. If a retired Governor had no resources of his own such might be his fate, although he had been the faithful representative of his Sovereign for twenty or thirty years. The practice of other countries was vastly different. In France not only were all public servants entitled to pensions, but their widows also, and their children, if orphans, were maintained at the public expense. The same system prevailed in Austria, and England was the only country where such injudicious economy was practised. Military and naval officers serving abroad were entitled to pensions, and to count the time they might have spent in the civil service, thus giving them an advantage which civil Governors did not enjoy. In a pamphlet written by Sir Edmund Head there was a passage which gave a painful description of the present system. Sir Edmund Head said—

" In short, my deliberate opinion about colonial service is this :—The public, in this department, is the worst master a man worth anything can have. Under the present system there is no career, properly so called, and an able man who devotes himself to the colonies makes a great and serious mistake. It may be, in many cases, that a man cannot help himself; but I speak of those who have an opportunity of advisedly selecting their line of life. It is not a comfortable reflection, after spending the best part of one's life in the public service, to find that the provision thought equitable in other cases is denied specially in yours. Whether a man can or cannot do without it, there must be a certain bitterness of feeling generated by the contrast."

He was sure the House would concur in

the opinion thus expressed. It was certain that such an unfortunate state of things must have arisen from mistake, and from the facts not having been made known to Parliament and to the country. If the Chancellor of the Exchequer had been present, he being thoroughly acquainted with colonial matters, that right hon. Gentleman would not put forward upon the occasion any financial consideration to oppose an act of justice, and especially when the sacrifice demanded was really inconsiderable. When it was remembered that putting aside India, our colonies represent an extent of country twenty times larger than Great Britain and Ireland, with exports and imports continually increasing, having reached in the last year above £100,000,000, and a continually growing population, it could not be denied that it was most important to have men of character and ability to represent the Sovereign in those colonies. And what had these men to submit to? It would be invidious to mention names, but there were gentlemen who had spent forty years of their lives in various climates as servants of the Crown, and who were unemployed without a sixpence of retiring allowance. The service was not one in which were employed mere ordinary men whom it was desired to get out of the country, but it was a service which had been adorned by the most eminent names, such as Elgin, Sydenham, Denham, Normanby, Grey, Hamilton, and others. If the country availed itself of the services of such men it should pay them properly; but, as the matter stood, a Governor who had no private resources, and had saved nothing from his very limited salary, might come home to live and die in a garret, with a feeling of regret that he had ever entered the service of the country. It would be no answer to say that there was no difficulty in obtaining men to fill the posts under the present arrangements. That might be so, but it was no argument for not dealing justly with them. He regretted that he had not been able to state these facts in a fuller House, but he had felt it to be his duty to state them, in order to enable the right hon. Gentleman opposite to express an opinion upon them, because it would give confidence to the gentlemen whose position he had described; and, at all events, he had laid the foundation for a consideration of the subject under more fortunate circumstances, and in a more adequate manner. When the facts were duly considered, he had no doubt that the

decision of the House would be worthy of the dignity of the Crown, and in support of the interests of the colonial service.

Mr. CARDWELL said, that when he had the honour of succeeding to the Colonial Office he found that his noble Friend who had preceded him in that Office had taken a deep interest in the question. A departmental letter had recently been sent to the Treasury, containing, in general terms, the same arguments which had been adduced by the hon. Member who had just spoken. Owing partly to the illness of his noble Friend, which all would regret, no answer had been received. The subject had been under his own consideration, and he had been in communication with the Chancellor of the Exchequer respecting it. In all such communications the Departments at first adopted different views. Those who stood in his position adopted much the same view as the hon. Member for Honiton, while it was the necessary duty of the guardians of the public purse to examine most minutely all the arguments that were advanced in favour of any increase in expenditure. He could only say that the subject had received the most careful consideration of his Department, and it was receiving the most earnest attention of the Treasury Department. He was not prepared to announce that it was in such a state as that the decision of Government could be given upon it; but he hoped before long to be able to make a statement respecting it. Meanwhile, he thought his hon. Friend would agree that it was not desirable that he (Mr. Cardwell) should enter into any discussion of the arguments either for or against the proposed change.

Sir JOHN PAKINGTON said, he would have been very well content to receive the answer which the right hon. Gentleman had just given, if that had been the first occasion upon which a similar reply had been given to the House, and he would be very well content to receive it then as the expression of feeling of the right hon. Gentleman himself. It showed, however, that the Motion of his hon. Friend had been very well timed. The noble Duke, whose illness they all regretted, had, he believed, been sincerely anxious to deal with the question according to its merits, but the real objection, as he had heard for a long time, came from the present Chancellor of the Exchequer. He regarded the existing state of the question as nothing more or less than a national scandal. Sir Edmund

Mr. *Baillie Cochrane*

Head, who every one would acknowledge to be an able, honourable, and distinguished public servant, had stated his deliberate opinion that the Colonial branch was the worst Department of the public service, and that an able man devoting himself to that portion of the service made a serious mistake. The high spirit of English gentlemen would lead them to go wherever the Queen sent them, and spend their salaries to the last sixpence. But that was not the footing on which the question should stand. It was both impolitic and unjust to continue the existing system, and when he had the honour of holding the seals of the Colonial Office he endeavoured to commence a change in the case of Sir Charles Grey, the Governor of Jamaica. The question was one of most pressing public policy. He hoped that the time would come when the right hon. Gentleman opposite (Mr. Cardwell) would be able to give the House a more satisfactory answer.

MR. MALINS said, he rose to express his great satisfaction at the observations which had fallen from the right hon. Gentleman the Colonial Secretary, because he knew the right hon. Gentleman was one of those persons who never made professions without an endeavour to give them effect. It so happened that he was acquainted with several gentlemen who had been colonial Governors, and no position could be more painful, or more disgraceful to the country, than to see gentlemen who at one time represented the Queen abroad, obliged to live, he would not say in garrets, but in obscure lodgings in obscure streets in London. That was a most unfortunate state of things. A distinction had been drawn between · the diplomatic and the colonial service ; but he should like to know why gentlemen connected with the Colonial Department were not equally entitled to pensions with those in the Diplomatic Department. The Colonial Governors, he believed, did not amount to more than fifty ; and certainly the amount required would not exceed £10,000 or £15,000 a year. He was satisfied that the right hon. Gentleman would do his best to carry out his promise. The question was too important to be burked, and he regretted that the Chancellor of the Exchequer had not been present to hear the discussion. Daylight having been once let in upon the question, he felt satisfied that the discussion would lead to a valuable result.

LORD JOHN MANNERS said, he sincerely trusted that the indication which they had heard of the intentions of the Colonial Office would be verified by the result. He felt, however, that the few observations which fell from his right hon. Friend, showed the great difficulties which surrounded his path. He could not divest his mind of the remembrance of the debate which had taken place on the previous evening, when they had under discussion a subject of national and great political importance. A part of the question was the divergence of opinion between an Admiral upon a station and the Governor of a Colony. That Admiral, distinguished in his profession, had a future course of emolument, distinction, and promotion open to him on his return home, while the Governor, by whose decision the Admiral was guided, on returning, would be allowed to remain an unknown and unrecognized public servant. Was it politic, could it pay, to engage men to fill the office of Colonial Governor, in which they might have to determine questions of peace and war, and then, when they came home, having, perhaps, earned the respect and gratitude of their fellow countrymen abroad, condemn them probably to obscurity and poverty for the rest of their days ? The time was come for the serious consideration of the question, and he trusted that the House would press upon Members of the Government, who were, perhaps, adverse to the proposal just made with so much ability by his hon. Friend, the duty and the necessity of some change in the present system.

THE PATENT OFFICE.—OBSERVATIONS.

MR. DILLWYN said, he rose to call attention to the insufficiency and inconvenience of the temporary Museum for Inventions at South Kensington, and the Patent Office in Southampton Buildings, and to the expediency of uniting the Museum of Inventions and the Patent Office under one building, and at a convenient distance from the law courts. On two former occasions when he had the Motion on the paper the House was counted out. He therefore had no alternative but to bring it forward even in the then thin state of the House. The Patent Office in Southampton Buildings, Chancery Lane, contained the specifications of patents and a valuable collection of books. It was near the law courts, and as far as site was concerned, was well enough adapted to its purpose. Several years ago the patented and other inventions which had come into the possession of the institution in Southampton Buildings were removed to South Kensington for exhibition at the request of the authorities. Though the exhibition was attended by some success, it did not prove very attractive, for the authorities at South Kensington devoted their energies rather to giving amusement than real practical instruction.

Notice taken that forty Members were not present, House counted, and more than forty Members being present,

MR. DILLWYN resumed his statement. In 1859 a proposal was made that the inventions should be transferred from the South Kensington institution to a building to be erected on a piece of ground in the same neighbourhood. Desiring that they should be exhibited at some place near the centre of the metropolis, and knowing the grasping disposition of the authorities at South Kensington, he took exception to the estimate for the new building, as he feared that if once located there they would probably be permanently retained there. The Government told him, in reply to his remarks, that they had considered the question of site and had determined that the new building at South Kensington should be regarded as a temporary erection. Eventually the vote passed on that distinct understanding. After some time the inventions were transferred to it. They still remained there, and a large number of fresh models had been added to the collection, which now formed the nucleus of a very valuable museum. But the authorities at South Kensington were quite unable to exhibit the inventions to advantage. The models were crowded higgledy-piggledy together at a great distance from the law courts, which prevented the possessors of inventions from sending them for exhibition, and so the museum was at a complete standstill. Matters were even worse in Southampton Buildings, where the books and specifications were stowed away in narrow inconvenient cells and passages, in the latter of which they were not sufficiently protected from the weather. The Government appeared to be quite alive to the necessity of doing something in the matter; but he was rather afraid they were proceeding too fast. It was a subject upon which the opinion of the House certainly ought to be taken. There was something very curious in the absorbing powers of Brompton for museums. The Members of

Mr. Dillwyn

the Government seemed to have taken a new oath of allegiance which bound them to Brompton. He knew several who used to speak rather disparagingly of the South Kensington concerns when independent Members, but who became thorough and devoted supporters of them as soon as they took their seats on the Treasury Bench. He hoped that the Patent Library would not be transferred thither. It ought to be placed in the vicinity of the law courts, where patent agents and others interested in these matters chiefly congregated. Then again, the utility of the Patent Museum would very much depend on its being in the neighbourhood of the library, so that persons might inspect the models when they had consulted the specifications and books. It would be very hard on manufacturers, mechanics, inventors, and others of the kind, to compel them to go all the way to Brompton in order to visit the library and museum. He was surprised at the extent and magnificence of the buildings proposed to be erected according to the exhibited plans. If sanctioned, they would involve a vast amount of expenditure, and he could not help suspecting that they formed only an instalment of an undertaking of much wider scope. It was rather significant that one of the plans was labelled "Acropolis of Art," that was not a title which could apply either to a Patent Museum or a Gallery of Natural History, and he thought if carried out it might be more properly called a Necropolis of the Chancellor of the Exchequer's surplus revenue. The Government found it necessary to provide attractions to induce people to visit the building at Kensington, and wines and spirits, cold luncheons and lobster-salads were to be obtained there. It would no doubt be said that it was difficult to obtain a site elsewhere; but Chancery Lane would be a much better spot, and he believed there was available space in the locality. A scheme had once been put forward by a private company for building a museum in Southampton Buildings, and it would have been handed over to the Government when completed. He earnestly hoped the Government would consider their decision.

MR. GREGORY said, he thought the hon. Member had done well in calling attention to the matter. He wished to know whether the First Commissioner of Works had had any communication with the Patent Commissioners on the subject of the future Patent Museum, and whether they agreed that it should be located at Kensington; because, if so, he should be curious to know what had induced them, within the short period of two years, to change the opinion they expressed in favour of the Patent Office, library, and museum being placed, not merely in close contiguity to each other, if not under one roof, but also in close proximity to the class of persons such as barristers, mechanical engineers, skilled workmen, solicitors, and patent agents, who were most interested in the use of them. He, therefore, asked whether the Patent Commissioners were now willing, in spite of their Report, to dissociate the museum from the library and office ; and whether they considered Kensington to be a central situation, such as is considered indispensable in the Report ? He calculated that there must now be about £240,000 derived from patent funds, and which should be applicable for patent purposes, and he thought that sum would be sufficient to buy ground in a region proper for patent purposes, and to build on it. In the temporary structure at Kensington there were 909 models, but of these only 108 belonged to the owners of patents. The rest were models which had been lent to the superintendent of specifications, and might be taken away at any time. He was afraid, therefore, that the Government might be miscalculating, and might erect a very large building and have only 108 models to put in it. The House had been asked last year by the Prime Minister, whether they would grudge the Government three acres for this purpose, while the Americans had eleven acres. But he ventured to say that there was no building in the world which contained such rubbish as that which contained the models at Washington. The most interesting model in the collection was one of the famous ballot-box with a false bottom, which was used at San Francisco. The persons appointed to be the judges of the building which the First Commissioner of Works proposed to erect were three architects, one amateur, and one painter. In the case of the British Museum and that of the new building at Kensington the proper persons had not been consulted. If the gentleman who had charge of the mediæval collection had been consulted, when the large northern court at Kensington was constructed, a huge glass-house with excessive light in the main portion of the structure would not have been the result. Objects of the slightest delicacy had to be placed in the arcades where they could not be seen — places which were nothing but the abodes of Nox and Erebus. He trusted, therefore, if these new Museums were to be made, that no final decision would be arrived at without the persons who were intrusted with the care of the collections to be exhibited being consulted as to the suitability of the galleries.

MR. COWPER said, he quite admitted the importance of the subject under discussion, as no one could doubt that the Patent Office was unfit for its purpose. It was placed in Chancery Lane in 1853, and the building there was at that time sufficient for the wants of the office and the library, but the library had increased so rapidly that it had outgrown the space allotted to it. The necessity, therefore, for increased accommodation had pressed upon the Government and upon the Commissioners; but, for the convenience of persons engaged in legal proceedings, the Patent Office must be in the neighbourhood of the Courts. It was exceedingly difficult to find accommodation for the purpose in that part of the town; but there was a building which appeared to be suitable. Last year, when they were asked the purposes for which they wanted to purchase the site of the Exhibition building at Kensington, they mentioned the Patent Museum and the Collection of Natural History, for it was not possible to find sufficient accommodation for the models in the same building with the office. The House had thought proper not to agree to the proposition of purchasing the Exhibition building itself, and therefore he felt bound to turn his attention to the erection of a new structure, and with that view he had invited competition for a design for one which would hold the patent models and the Natural History collection of the British Museum, and which would harmonize with other buildings that might subsequently be erected for purposes of science and art. South Kensington, to which the hon. Member for Swansea seemed to have such an objection, would be equally and even more convenient for the working men of the metropolis and of the country at large than Chancery Lane. It had never entered into the mind of any one to remove the library from the office, but the Museum was not an essential part of either one or the other. A model was not a part of a legal description of a patent, which consisted altogether in the verbal description and engravings. A great number of the models in the Museum were not models of patents, and it was very desirable that these models of mechanical inventions should be placed in those spots to which the working classes were in the habit of resorting for that kind of amusement and instruction. The Commissioners were of opinion that the Museum ought to be an historical and educational institution, for the benefit of the skilled workmen in the various factories of the kingdom. At present, they calculated that about half an acre would be required, but as the number of models was certain to increase rapidly, provision ought to be made for the future extension of the Museum. In the plans, half an acre had been provided, or 23,000 square feet, on two stories, independent of future requirement. It would be impossible to provide space sufficient for present and future requirements in close contiguity to the office, and he, therefore, thought it desirable that the vacant space at South Kensington should be employed as the receptacle for the interesting models which it was certain would be congregated there. The hon. Gentleman the Member for Galway had asked whether the Commissioners had approved the proposed site of the Museum. He could not point to any particular statement of theirs to that effect, but he gathered from the general terms of their Report that they wished to see an ample space provided for the Museum, and that they did not attach importance to its being under the same roof as the office. Former Commissioners had recommended that the Museum should be placed at South Kensington. The Government had not lost sight of the matter, and when their plan was matured and brought before the House, he did not think it would meet with the opposition which the hon. Gentleman anticipated.

COLONEL BARTTELOT said, he wished to correct an erroneous impression which the right hon. Gentleman seemed to be under—namely, that the House last year consented that the Patent Museum and other collections should be placed at South Kensington. They did no such thing. All that the House did was to affirm by one vote that the land should be purchased, and by another that the buildings upon it should be pulled down. He believed South Kensington was a great deal too far out of London to have the Museum, or any other collections removed there.

MR. AUGUSTUS SMITH said, he thought that looking to the responsible position of the right hon. Gentleman, he ought to have consulted the Patent Commissioners. It had so happened, however, that the Commissioners had already given an opinion which was to be found in a paragraph a little below one to which the right hon. Gentleman had referred. It was hardly ingenuous to overlook that paragraph. And who were the Commissioners? They were such eminent men as the Lord Chancellor, Sir J. Romilly, Sir William Atherton, the late Attorney General, and Sir Roundell Palmer; and yet, without consulting them, the right hon. Gentleman had determined upon a particular plan, and then said he should be very much surprised if they should object to it, merely because they had incidentally remarked on one occasion that the most important consideration in connection with the erection of the necessary buildings was the spot to be selected, and that the readers being a class of scientific persons, it was obvious they should be enabled to read the books and examine the models and machines, and consequently that the Patent Office, the library, and the Museum should be under the same roof, or in close proximity. Could not the right hon. Gentleman take the trouble to read the Report? Before the First Commissioner of Works advertised for enormous plans for a special purpose, that House ought to be consulted. The right hon. Gentleman could not appropriate money belonging to the Patent Office to other purposes. It should be recollected that the plans and designs which the right hon. Gentleman called for must cost something, and was it right that they should be involved in that expense without the consent of the House? Unless the purposes for which the buildings were to be erected were clearly defined, it was impossible that proper designs could be got. He was quite dissatisfied with the explanation of the right hon. Gentleman. He supposed they should hear no more of those Estimates until the House was about to be prorogued, and then next year they would be obliged to follow up the plans to which Parliament would be said to have given its assent.

MR. AYRTON said, the position in which the Question had been left by the explanation of the right hon. Gentleman was most ambiguous and unsatisfactory. He was not acting in concert with the Commissioners of Patents, and the whole responsibility, therefore, was cast upon the

Mr. Cowper

House. If the right hon. Gentleman proceeded without due regard to the objects of the Commissioners, the money available for the Museum would be entirely lost to the public, and it would be necessary to pay for the buildings out of the Consolidated Fund. He hoped, then, that his hon. Friend who had brought the subject forward would not lose sight of it, but would press for a Select Committee, so that when the House should be called upon to vote it would have ample information. Unless that were done, they would have no information except what the right hon. Gentleman chose to give.

MR. SPEAKER put the Question— " That I leave the Chair ; " and having declared it carried left the Chair.

Motion *agreed to.*

SUPPLY.

SUPPLY *considered* in Committee.

Mr. HUTT in the Chair.

(In the Committee.)

PRIVILEGE.

MR. BERNAL OSBORNE: Sir, I protest against the Chair being vacated in this way. It is a gross breach of the common courtesy due to the House. My hon. Friend the Member for Buckingham (Sir Harry Verney) got up to address the House and yet Mr. Speaker left the Chair. In all the course of my Parliamentary experience, I never saw anything like that done before. I put it to the House if this can be permitted. It appears to me that we are to be treated like the Conference, and be adjourned *sine die.* I move that the Chairman report Progress and ask leave to sit again.

SIR GEORGE GREY: I think that any observation of this kind ought to be made when the Speaker is in the Chair.

MR. BERNAL OSBORNE : Why, the Speaker ran away !

SIR GEORGE GREY : I heard the Speaker put the Question. The Motion which the hon. Member has made I had already made, for I had moved that you, Sir, report Progress and ask leave to sit again.

SIR HARRY VERNEY : As soon as the last speaker had finished his address, I rose, and before the Speaker left the Chair I got up and addressed him.

MR. AYRTON : I think it very inconvenient to report Progress ; the proceedings which have taken place must be reversed. There is no doubt that the hon. Baronet was on his legs when the Question was put. There can be no doubt that any erroneous proceeding can be reversed.

SIR GEORGE GREY : The proceedings cannot be reversed. The course will be for the hon. Member now in the Chair to leave the Chair.

MR. AYRTON : I beg your pardon ; we can request the Speaker to return.

LORD ROBERT MONTAGU said, he could answer for it that the Speaker had put the Question and said, the " Ayes have it." The hon. Member for Buckingham then rose, and the Speaker said he had already put the Question.

Motion *agreed to.*

House *resumed.*

Committee report Progress ; to sit again on Monday next.

SIR HARRY VERNEY : Sir, I move the adjournment of the House.

MR. SPEAKER : The hon. Baronet can address the House on a Question of order without moving the adjournment.

SIR HARRY VERNEY : Sir, I wish to address you on a point of order. I beg to state that the name of a Member (Mr. Black) was on the paper before mine. I waited, expecting his name to be called. I thought I had risen to address you before you left the Chair. If you say otherwise, I bow to your decision, but I hope that I may be allowed to proceed with my Motion.

MR. BERNAL OSBORNE : I second the Motion for adjournment. [" Order, order ! "] I maintain that this is a Question affecting the privileges of this House ; and, without making any pointed allusion to you, I must say that I did not hear you, Sir, put the Question. A noble Lord on the other side (Lord R. Montagu) said he did hear it ; but he was sitting in close proximity to the Chair. I was not favoured with that private and confidential communication. My hon. Friend below me rose before you left the Chair. [*Cries of* " No!"] We on this bench are certainly gifted with eyes and ears as well as the more favoured inhabitants of that lower region, and I say the hon. Member rose before you left the Chair. If you put the Question, it was put so indistinctly and so hurriedly that no Member on this bench heard it ; but I maintain it, contrary to the Under Secretary of State for Foreign Affairs, that we did not hear the Question. I cannot help thinking that independent Members are hardly treated, and in their name I protest against this sharp practice.

3 R 2

MR. HUMBERSTON : Sir, it so happened that when the Question was put I was standing behind the chair of the Sergeant at Arms ; and it seemed to me that that Gentleman rose to advance towards the mace before the hon. Baronet rose from his seat.

SIR GEORGE GREY said, that his hon. Friend (Mr. Black) had given notice of his intention to move an Amendment on going into Supply, and his hon. Friend (Sir Harry Verney) had evidently waited for the hon. Member for Edinburgh to be called upon. But the right hon. Gentleman had not called upon the hon. Member for Edinburgh, nor was it necessary or usual for him to do so. For himself, he must say that he distinctly heard the Question put, and he believed that the right hon. Gentleman left the Chair before the hon. Baronet rose. What had occurred was explained by the fact that his hon. Friend (Sir Harry Verney) had waited for the hon. Member for Edinburgh, who was before him, and who did not rise. He thought that no blame whatever attached to the Speaker, whose conduct was always marked by the most perfect impartiality.

MR. CARNEGIE : Sir, I was farther off than the hon. Member for Liskeard (Mr. Osborne) ; and though I do not deny that the hon. Member has eyes and ears, I also claim the privilege to have eyes and ears, and I think it is only due to you, Sir, to state that I heard you put the Question before the hon. Member rose.

MR. DILLWYN : As it is a matter of evidence in some respect, I may give the evidence of my senses. I was sitting here very near my hon. Friend the Member for Liskeard, and I did not hear the Question put by the Chair. I can confidently assert that my hon. Friend rose before the Speaker left the Chair, because when my hon. Friend rose I could not see the right hon. Gentleman in the Chair for my hon. Friend.

MR. AYRTON said, he had heard the Question put, but he did not hear it carried. He heard the Ayes but not the Noes. He suggested that there might be some confusion as to what was meant by putting the Question. He had very clearly heard the Speaker put the Question, "That I do now leave the Chair." At that moment the hon. Baronet rose. He did not hear the rest of the Question put, "You that are of that opinion say aye, &c." In his opinion the hon. Baronet had risen before the complete form had been gone through.

Mr. Bernal Osborne

MR. WYKEHAM MARTIN said, he had distinctly heard the whole of the Question.

LORD ROBERT MONTAGU : I heard the Question, and if those hon. Gentlemen opposite did not hear it, perhaps that is due to the somniferous state into which they had been brought by the speeches which had been previously made.

MR. SPEAKER : I am sorry that any misunderstanding or misapprehension should have arisen on the part of any hon. Members as to the course that was pursued. At the same time, I cannot admit for a moment that there was anything in that course which was not strictly in accordance with the exact rules of the House. With no hurry, I rose and put the Question that I should leave the Chair. No hon. Gentleman rose, and I declared the Question carried. I can now understand why the hon. Baronet the Member for Buckingham did not rise—because he says he thought I should call on the Gentleman who stood before him on the list. Now, the House is aware that unless an hon. Member rises to move an Amendment I do not call upon him. If any Gentleman wishes to move an Amendment it is for him to rise, and then I call upon him to proceed. On this occasion I put the Question, "That I do now leave the Chair." No one rose, and I then said, " As many as are of that opinion say aye ; of the contrary opinion, no ; I think the ayes have it." I then turned to leave the Chair, and the hon. Member for Buckingham rose in his place. It is perfectly true that the hon. Member rose in his place before I left the Chair, but not before I put the Question. That is an exact statement of the case, and I regret that any hon. Member who was paying any attention to the business of the House should have arrived at a different conclusion.

MR. KINGLAKE said, that as he was sitting [" Order, Order !"]

SIR GEORGE GREY said, the hon. and learned Member had a right to speak on the point of order.

MR. BERNAL OSBORNE declared that his learned Friend was in order.

MR. KINGLAKE said, that as he was sitting in exactly the same latitude as his hon. Friend (Sir Harry Verney), he could judge what it was possible for him to hear. In the state of the House at the moment a whisper almost might have been heard in the distance, and yet he had not heard the Question put in such a manner that it would have been possible for him to say "No" to the Question that the Speaker do leave the Chair.

PENAL SERVITUDE ACTS AMENDMENT BILL—[BILL 23]—CONSIDERATION.

Bill, as amended, *considered.*

MR. WHITBREAD said, that in moving the clause of which he had given notice, he had no wish to interfere with what was called the Irish system, but he should pause before introducing it in its integrity into this country, and certainly should not be willing to adopt one portion only, and that the most objectionable part of that system. According to Sir Walter Crofton's view, expressed in a letter to *The Times* after the debate the other evening, what was needed in this country was a department of supervision, an argument which he thought would not be very consolatory to Gentlemen already complaining of the growth of the Estimates. But if supervision was introduced, he thought it would become absolutely necessary to provide the convicts with situations after they were discharged. This, except by voluntary effort, would be highly objectionable, but what alternative would there be if by interference with convicts in possession of tickets-of-leave they were debarred from competing freely with others in the labour market? A Return relating to the re-committal of persons discharged from the intermediate prisons for the years 1856-62 showed at first sight a very startling result — namely, that they did not amount to more than 7 per cent. But if the cases of persons who were stated in the Returns from Ireland to have gone abroad were eliminated from the list, and the Return compared year by year, it would be found that the re-committals began with less than 1 per cent in 1856, and, after steadily increasing, ended with more than 100 per cent in 1862. The right hon. Gentleman the Home Secretary, he feared, had been guilty of a piece of refined cruelty in compelling the man to retain his ticket-of-leave and in creating a new offence if he laid it aside. A navvy, unlike a statesman, had no bureau or pigeonholes to keep his papers in, and yet he might just as well be found with his neighbour's gold watch in his pocket as with his ticket-of-leave. The question of emigration, too, was one of some importance. We had hitherto had no serious representations either from our colonies or from foreign countries as to ticket-of-leave

men going there, but there was no doubt that a great many of them went abroad, and they did so upon a gratuity of money voted by Parliament. If exception was taken to that, we could neither assert that they went as free men, nor deny that they were enabled to do so by money provided by the State. He therefore thought that it would be desirable to adopt such a provision as he proposed, under which, when a man came out of prison, he would be absolutely free and at liberty to go to any part of the world. The last part of his clause provided that if, during the period of sentence which had been remitted, a man committed any offence for which he was summarily committed to prison for three months, or convicted upon indictment, he should return to prison and complete the term of his sentence. To this provision it had been objected that it was too sweeping, and that it would interfere with the Royal prerogative, but he did not think that either of those objections was well founded. If a man committed an offence within a short time after his discharge, it showed that he was not a proper subject for a remission of any part of his punishment; and, as the Act was to be read with those of 1853 and 1857, the words in the former of these Acts which saved the Royal prerogative would apply also to this measure. The proposal was founded upon the broad principle that it was the duty of the State to punish convicts, but that after their discharge it ought neither to debar them from employment or to provide it for them, and he hoped that it would receive the sanction of the House. The hon. Gentleman concluded by moving the following clause:—

"It shall be lawful for Her Majesty, by an order in writing under the hand and seal of one of Her Majesty's Principal Secretaries of State, to grant to any person sentenced to penal servitude after the passing of this Act a remission of such portion of his sentence, not exceeding one fourth part, as to Her Majesty shall seem fit, provided that if any person to whom such remission has been granted shall, before the time at which his original sentence would have expired, be convicted either by the verdict of a jury, or upon his own confession, of an indictable offence, or upon summary conviction of an offence punishable with imprisonment for three months or for a longer period, he shall, after undergoing the period of imprisonment to which he may be sentenced for such offence, further undergo a term of penal servitude equal to the portion of his original sentence so remitted to him; and shall, for the purpose of his undergoing such last-mentioned punishment, be removed from the prison of any county, borough, or place in which they may be confined, to any prison in which convicts under sentence of penal servitude may lawfully be confined, by warrant under the hand and seal of any justice of the peace of the said county, borough, or place, and shall be liable to be there dealt with in all respects as if such term of penal servitude had formed part of his original sentence."

Clause (Application of Acts to Licence,) —(*Mr. Whitbread,*)— *brought up,* and read 1°.

Motion made, and Question proposed, "That the Clause be now read a second time."

MR. CAVE said, that his hon. Friend appeared to desire remission of sentences without subsequent supervision. He confessed he would himself rather have remission without supervision than none at all. If probation was valuable, especially when carried out by means of intermediate prisons, he should be sorry to lose it. The ticket-of-leave system failed, not so much in consequence of want of supervision, as because the probation was really worthless. The prisoners were, in fact, discharged before their time because the gaols were overcrowded. But if remission of sentence without supervision were resolved upon, there would be the inconvenience of having different regulations for England and Ireland; and besides this, there would be a feeling of insecurity, which he thought the public would not tolerate. Independently of this, supervision was advisable on these two grounds: — In the first place, the clever rogue would frequently work himself out of prison sooner than the really penitent man. He would have sufficient control over himself to go through the whole probation, but that self-control would not last beyond the prison. Once out, he would be a dangerous character, a corrrupter of the young, and the sooner he was brought back the better. It was cheaper for society to keep such a man in prison than out of it. He quite agreed with a remark of Lord Dudley, at Worcester, though not with his conclusion. " When they gave prisoners a fair trial, and found that all that had been done had been thrown away, the least they could do would be to render them incapable of doing any further harm for some time." The Prisoners' Aid Society would be useless in such a case, even if Government ought to intrust so important a part of their system to anything so uncertain, transient, and irresponsible as voluntary agency. There was no force in the objection to the espionage of

Mr. Whitbread

the police. The police now kept a watch over thieves, companions of thieves, and suspicious charactérs of all kinds, except those which have given so much ground for suspicion, as convicts on licence. He thought the supervision should be intrusted to the police, or to Government agents, backed by the police (as in Dublin, and, he believed, once in Scotland), which was much the same thing. The plan proposed might not be the best. It might be that a single report to the police on each change of residence might be sufficient, with the understanding that a conviction for an offence in a place where the licence-holder had not reported himself would be more severely punished. But, in the second place, supervision would be useful to the reclaimed convict. The police would be of great assistance to him in obtaining work, if they had proper instructions; and if any hon. Member doubted the wish of many of these poor people to lead an honest life, let him go to the Refuge, established by Captain Shepherd just outside Wakefield Gaol, and he would there see men patiently labouring for the hardest fare and roughest shelter, determined to bear anything rather than return to crime. At the same time, he was not of opinion that a large number of licence-holders would find it easy to obtain employment here; he thought their future career would generally be more hopeful out of England, and here the Discharged Prisoners' Aid Society would find its proper work. A man leaving the country partly by means of his own gratuity would give better securities for his future good conduct than if sent at the expense of the State. His mind would be enlisted in his own reformation, and he would work with, and not against us. Fault had been found with the Irish Returns, on account of the large emigration. He thought that was the greatest success of the system. And though no doubt the Irish were more migratory, the English could scarcely be said to be unduly wedded to the soil. In Sweden, where he had once been, the scarcity of workmen was so great that prisoners were in some instances farmed out to contractors on public roads and other works. Yet the disinclination of the people to employ discharged prisoners was so extreme, that the clergy were in the habit of inculcating from the pulpit the duty of giving these poor men a chance of earning a living, as a work of Christian charity. If, then, their difficulty was so great in a thinly peopled country, how much greater must it be in England where every kind of employment was already over-filled. He hoped honest men would always be preferred; he should be sorry to see a stainless character lose its value; therefore, he looked for a solution of this difficulty beyond our own shores. He would be sorry to speak confidently; the subject was a very embarrassing one; the fluctuations of crime depended very much upon external causes mostly beyond our control; but he thought the experiment worth trying, and he was not without hope that it would in time make some impression upon the regular professional crime of this country.

SIR GEORGE GREY said, he thought the House had expressed a very decided opinion that remission should not be conditional, and that a ticket-of-leave should be given subject to regular supervision. He believed the effect of the supervision as proposed would be, that the greater number of these ticket-of-leave-holders would be driven out of the country. What the effect would be in the colonies he did not know, but, at all events, we should have the benefit of their leaving the kingdom. He hoped his hon. Friend would not press the Question at this moment.

MR. POLLARD-URQUHART said, he thought it highly desirable that some supervision should be exercised upon the ticket-of-leave man in order to see that he did not associate with criminal characters. It was very often difficult to find superior labourers in England, whilst it was not so frequently the case in Ireland. He thought that the isolation of the ticket-of-leave man was, to a great extent, asserted by the Bill of the right hon. Gentleman. He, nevertheless, thought the Bill would be better without the clause now proposed.

MR. COGAN said, that the Irish system had not prevented the convict from getting employment in Ireland. He trusted the hon. Member would withdraw the clause.

MR. WHITBREAD said, he would withdraw the clause.

Motion, by leave, *withdrawn.*

Clause *withdrawn.*

MR. HUNT said, he would propose several Amendments in Clause 4, which would make the clause stand thus—

" If any holder of a licence granted under the said Penal Servitude Acts, or any of them, who shall be at large in the United Kingdom shall, unless prevented by illness or other unavoidable cause, fail to report himself personally to the chief police station of the borough, or police sta-

tion to which he may go within three days after his arrival therein, and subsequently once in each month, at such time and place, in such manner, and to such person as the chief officer of such station shall appoint, or shall change his residence without having previously notified the same to the police station to which he last reported himself, he shall be deemed guilty of a misdemeanour, and may be summarily convicted thereof, and his licence shall be forthwith forfeited by virtue of such conviction, but he shall not be liable to any other punishment by virtue of such conviction."

Clause, as amended, *agreed to.*

Bill to be read 3° on Monday next.

CIVIL BILL COURTS (IRELAND) BILL.
[BILL 79] CONSIDERATION.

Bill, as amended, *considered.*

Clause (Judge of Assize may state case for opinion of Superior Courts,) — (*Sir Colman O'Loghlen,*) — *brought up,* and read 1°; 2°; amended, and *added.*

Other Clauses *added.*

Another Clause (Judges to make Rules,) —(*Sir Colman O'Loghlen,*)—*brought up,* and read 1°; 2°; amended, and *added.*

Other Clauses *added.*

Another Clause (Claims as to Goods taken in execution under a Decree to be adjudicated in the Civil Bill Court only,) —(*Mr. Longfield,*)—*brought up,* and read 1°.

Motion made, and Question proposed, " That the Clause be now read a second time."

Motion, by leave, *withdrawn.*

Clause *withdrawn.*

Another Clause *added.*

Amendments made.

MR. TORRENS proposed to add the following proviso to Clause 25 :—

" Provided, that in every case where the Civil Bill Court for any county of a city, or county of a town, shall be held in the adjoining county at large, the under sheriff of such county of a city, or county of a town, shall only be required to attend the sittings of such court, and provide such bailiffs as aforesaid, while the business arising within such county of a city, or county of a town, is being transacted ; and the chairman is required to provide, making such general rules as aforesaid, for the due and orderly hearing and transacting of such business successively, at one particular time during such sittings."

Question proposed, " That those words be there added."

MR. O'HAGAN said, he hoped that the hon. Member would not press his Amendment, as he believed that the object which the hon. Member had in view would be as well effected by the Bill as it stood as by the introduction of the words contained in his Amendment.

MR. TORRENS said, upon that understanding he would withdraw his Amendment.

Amendment, by leave, *withdrawn.*

Other Amendments made.

Bill to be read 3° on *Monday* next.

SUPERIOR COURTS OF COMMON
LAW (IRELAND) BILL.
LEAVE. FIRST READING.

MR. O'HAGAN (THE ATTORNEY GENERAL FOR IRELAND): Sir, in moving for leave to bring in a Bill to amend the process, practice, and mode of pleading in the Superior Courts of Common Law at Dublin, I shall very briefly call the attention of the House to the circumstances under which the measure has originated, the necessity which appears to me to justify it, and the objects it attempts to accomplish. The lateness of the hour induces me to postpone very many of the observations I had meant to make, especially as I shall have ample opportunity to discuss the provisions of the Bill in its future stages ; but it is desirable that I should put before the House and the country, in the fewest possible words, some representation of the state of things, which seems to me to commend to their approval a scheme of legal reform of such importance and extent as I shall show this to be. The same diversity which has prevailed between England and Ireland in the course of administrative and legislative dealings with the Courts of Equity, has equally affected the Courts of Law in the respective countries. I have already had occasion to explain historically to the House how the Equity Courts have been dealt with, and it is necessary that I should offer some similar explanations as to the Courts of Law. In England there has been a series of reforms, commencing in the year 1827, and progressing continuously down to the year 1860, when the last legislative measure on the subject was framed. The real reform of the Courts of Law in England dates from the great speech of Lord Brougham in 1827. Up to that time nothing was done substantially to rectify the errors which undoubtedly prevailed in the Courts of Common Law in England ; but that

Mr. O'Hagan

memorable oration so wrought upon opinion by its power and eloquence, that a Royal Commission was issued in 1828, to inquire into their condition. It was composed of very distinguished men. It laboured long and earnestly, and its fruits are to be found in six excellent Reports, and in the Uniformity of Process Act, the 2 & 3 *Will.* IV. c. 39, and in the further Act the 3 & 4 *Will.* IV. c. 42. These were most wise and valuable measures, but I am sorry to say that all the proceedings that were then instituted and carried on deliberately and usefully in reference to law reform, were confined to England, and had no application whatever to Ireland. Neither the Commission to which I have referred, nor the legislation which it produced, had any application to her legal institutions. In the year 1834, the English Judges, acting on the powers with which they were invested by the new statutes, adopted new rules of pleading, which, I may say, largely revolutionized the English system. Those rules, also, had no application to Ireland, and for seventeen years her pleading and practice remained unchanged at the point at which they had been before the Commission of 1828 was thought of. The English reforms—great as they were—were in the course of time deemed insufficient, and in 1850—the rules having continued to operate from 1834— this House felt that it was necessary to have further changes in England. Accordingly, in that year, 1850, a new Commission was issued for the purpose of extending legal reform. It was constituted of the very ablest men connected with the law in this country, but from its operation, also, Ireland was wholly excluded. That Commission sat for a very considerable period, and it produced three admirable Reports. It continued to work and watch the development of the existing system, and, on its Reports, Parliament adopted measures in 1851, 1853, and 1860. During the whole of that long period, from 1850 to 1860, the Commissioners continued from time to time to sit, and from time to time to suggest those measures which were most desirable and important for the improvement of the law in England. The result was the three Common Law Procedure Acts, the 15 & 16 *Vict.* c. 76, the 17 & 18 *Vict.* c. 15, and 23 & 24 *Vict.* c. 124—measures most carefully prepared, and of the most useful character—which now regulate the Law Courts of England. But not one of these

Acts was applied to Ireland. This has been the course of English reform, continuous and careful, deliberate and cautious, every step guarded and guided by the soundest judgment and the largest experience which the country could supply, and sustained throughout by the solemn finding of Commissions of the highest authority. Surely Ireland has some reason to complain that these great advantages have so far been denied her. Not one Commission has considered the defects of her judicial system, not one alteration in it has been based on inquiries such as have insured safety and efficiency to legal changes in England. From the time of King John—for nearly six hundred years after the first introduction of the Common Law of England, down to the year 1834—the law of Ireland and England, and the practice and pleading in the Courts in Ireland and England continued to be the same. Poyning's Act in the reign of Henry VII. extended to Ireland the whole Statute Law of England then existing ; and in 1782, Yelverton's Act, passed by the Irish Parliament, in the same way extended to Ireland the Statute Law of England up to that period. The existence of separate Legislatures, the distinct circumstances of the two countries, and other differences, created some divergence in the English and Irish procedure, but it remained substantially the same until the period of the Union ; and it is very remarkable that not until thirty years after that Union had been effected, did the strange diversity which is now established begin to have existence. Such a diversity had been pronounced by Yelverton's Act in 1782, to be inconsistent with the true interests of the people of Great Britain and Ireland ; yet it commenced fifty years after, in a condition of circumstances which ought to have made it impossible. The Commissioners of 1862, to whom I shall refer just now, in their Report, have stated their view of the different course of proceedings in the two countries, and the fact that for seventeen years the reforms that had been in operation in England did not apply to Ireland. Only in 1850, when a new Commission was granted for England, some of the English changes, after the lapse of seventeen years, were applied to Ireland by the Irish Process and Practice Act, 13 & 14 *Vict.* c. 18. But this created a very partial assimilation, and the differences of the two systems were made more pronounced and absolute by the English Act of 1852, which did not apply to Ireland. Then came the Irish Common Law Procedure Act of 1853, which established a new mode of pleading and practice, and rendered those differences still more pronounced and absolute. It was the work of my right hon. Friend the Member for the University of Dublin, who sits opposite to me. The Act was introduced upon his responsibility, and with an anxious desire, no doubt, to advance the interest of the country, and to improve the condition of the law. It was designed with the best intention—to simplify procedure, to destroy technicalities, and to save expense, to avoid the complication of pleadings, and to reduce the whole, as far as possible, to a plain and simple system. It abolished the general issue, it not only abolished the general issue but the various forms of actions ; it destroyed altogether the ancient distinctions between actions in the Courts of Common Law, and more than that, it destroyed the ancient system of pleading by which the pleaders on the one side, and on the other between them eliminated the issue which was to come before the Judge and jury, and upon which were to be determined the merits of the case. The result of that Act was this, that a complete distinction was established between the practice and pleading of the Courts of Law in the two countries. I do not say it without respect for my right hon. Friend, but the fact is, that his Act was preceded by no inquiry ; it was not authorized, as were all the reforms of England, by the deliberate and cautious judgment of a responsible Commission ; it adopted new principles, it ventured on untried experiments, and the result has not been satisfactory as the evidence I shall lay before the House will abundantly demonstrate. It was passed upon the responsibility of the very learned and able persons by whom it was framed, and one of whom was the ex-Lord Chancellor of Ireland. [Mr. WHITE-SIDE : He had nothing to do with it.] Then I am mistaken in that. At all events, he was in the House at the time. No doubt my right hon. Friend, with a natural affection for his own creation, has given testimony in its favour; but that testimony is encountered and overborne by the general sentiment of the Bar of Ireland, and the Bill which I now ask leave to introduce condemning its peculiar provisions is in·

full accordance with that sentiment. The measure of my right hon. Friend carried further than ever the divergence between the English and Irish systems. And another Irish Common Law Procedure Act—that of 1856—though mainly founded on the English Act of 1854, left these great distinctions substantially undisturbed. The systems of the two countries are at this moment founded on different principles, and have different machinery and inconsistent aims. In this state of things the Royal Commission of 1862 was issued, to inquire, amongst other things, into the constitution, establishment, practice, procedure, and fees of the Superior Courts of Common Law in Ireland, with a view to reduce costs and expenditure, and to assimilate, as far as might be practicable, the administration of justice in England and Ireland. I have already stated to the House how that Commission was constituted, and I need not advert to it again, further than to say that the very ablest and most distinguished lawyers of the two countries took part in its deliberations, and unanimously adopted the conclusions at which it arrived. It sought the assistance of the leading members of the legal profession, and, after the fullest consideration, it reported upon the system which was introduced in the way I have described, in 1853, in these terms—

" We have carefully considered the working of the system of pleading and practice introduced into Ireland by the Irish Common Law Procedure Act of 1853, and find that it has not been satisfactory, nor has it been attended with such advantage as would justify a continuance of a diversity of practice between the two countries. And we have come to a unanimous resolution, that the system of practice and procedure of the Courts of Common Law of England and Ireland should, as far as practicable, be assimilated. In adopting this resolution, we feel that we are only, in effect, restoring that substantial uniformity which existed in course and practice of the Superior Courts of Common Law in both countries, from the reign of King John to that of King William the Fourth."

This is a very clear and distinct finding of the Commission, and it is perfectly supported by the evidence they have collected from the most able and experienced members of the Irish Bar. I have marked a number of passages from that evidence for the consideration of the House, but at this hour I can venture to produce only a few of them. I should state, however, that the whole of the evidence, with the exception of that of my right hon. Friend, who, as I said before, is naturally attached to the

Mr. O'Hagan

system of which he was the author, and of that of one or two others, the whole of the evidence was in favour of assimilating the Irish and English systems of pleading and practice, and of the system of issues and of pleading generally introduced by this Bill. I shall first read a passage from the evidence of a very distinguished lawyer — Master FitzGibbon—a man of great capacity and integrity and of very large business while at the Bar in the Common Law Courts of Ireland. He says—

" The law of pleading in civil suits had been settled in the course of centuries by Judges of the greatest learning and ability, instructed by experience and assisted by able lawyers, in repeated discussions of every important principle—the only way in which such a law could or can be made reasonably perfect. A fabric had been thus erected which had long been the boast of English jurists and English Judges. The erection of it was the work of the judicial wisdom of ages. Its destruction was a summary act of legislative power. The substitute for it is the hasty fabrication of empiricism. The framers of the Irish Procedure Act assumed that all established forms were either absurd or mischievous, and that the abolition of them was the first great step towards the simplification of law. Forms and fictions which had been for centuries established, which had been approved of by sage writers and jurists, and had been jealously guarded by the wisest of our Judges, suddenly became the subject of sarcasm and ridicule. The abuse of them became a road to popularity, and the abolition of them was so loudly applauded by the multitude, who did not understand their utility, that the few who did were abashed, and no one raised a voice in support of them. If it were possible to read the mass of absurdity, of falsehood, and of inconsistency which the last eight years have placed on the files of the Irish Courts in the shape of so-called truthful and simple pleadings, and if it were possible to narrate the series of forensic discussions to which these shapeless pleadings gave rise, at the expense of suitors for justice, if the censures from time to time expressed by able Judges upon the mischievous novelties by which the administration of the law was clogged and impeded, could be recalled and repeated, we should be astonished at the apathy of the public and its rulers, by which this evil has been so long tolerated."

This is the opinion of Mr. Serjeant Sullivan —

" The result of my experience of the working of the present system of common law pleading in Ireland is that such system has been, on the whole, extremely unsatisfactory. It has brought about a most involved and perplexing system of making up records for trial, and of sending questions to juries, and it has led to very great and unnecessary expense."

My hon. and learned Friend the Member for Clare who will, no doubt, speak for himself in the course of the discussion on this Bill at a future stage in its progress through the House, says—

" The existing system of common law pleading in Ireland does not, in my opinion, work well ; and I consider it calculated seriously to embarrass parties in the assertion of their rights, and to be attended with unnecessary prolixity and expense."

A similar opinion is given by Mr. J. T. Ball, a very eminent Queen's Counsel in Ireland. He says —

" I have to express my opinion that uniformity of practice and procedure in the English and Irish legal tribunals is attended with such advantages, that to the attainment of this object all minor details must give way. For this reason, even if the Irish system had been superior, I yet should have been favourable to the adoption of the English ; but, so far as I have had opportunity to compare the two systems, I consider that the English ought to be preferred. My experience has been that a loose and uncertain mode of pleading prevails under the Irish system ; that in actions of tort, the want of the general issue, or some equivalent plea, entails such difficulties upon the pleader as to impede the proper defence of his client ; that the ascertainment of the issue to be tried before the evidence has been heard, embarrasses both Judge and jury in the discharge of their duties at the trial ; and that the abolition of local venues, and the permission to plaintiffs, by choosing their own place of trial, to withdraw the case from the neighbourhood where the character of the parties and their witnesses is known, has tended to increase expense, encourage speculative actions, and make the result uncertain."

Mr. J. K. Lowry, one of Her Majesty's Counsel, gives this pithy judgment—

" The result of my experience, and my opinion of the present system of common law pleading and practice in Ireland is, that nothing can be worse. The change in the present system of pleading and practice in the Common Law Courts of Ireland that I would suggest is to assimilate it, in every respect, to the English system."

There is a very large body of testimony to the same effect which I had intended to lay before the House, but the extracts I have read may suffice as specimens of the general sentiments of, I may say, all the lawyers who have been examined before the Commission, upon whose evidence their Report was founded. They go on in that Report, which has received the highest approval from the most competent persons, to state in detail the changes which they recommend. Amongst others, they desire to have the use of the general issue restored, under the restrictions which have been introduced in England ; the Irish mode of raising issues, in fact, assimilated to the English, and the English system of writ and declaration substituted for that of the summons and plaint. They recommend that the distinction between actions in the Courts of Law shall not be ignored, and that the issue to be tried shall not be settled by the Judges, as it now is, a system which has been found productive of inconvenience and confusion. There are other recommendations to which I shall not now call attention. It is impossible at this hour, and would be useless, to bring them all under the notice of the House, but I ought to observe that the Commission, which had upon it an equal number of gentlemen of either country, has dealt with the matter in the fairest and most liberal spirit of honest reciprocity. It has not recommended assimilation merely because it is assimilation. Looking to the real merits of the conflicting systems, it has laboured to adopt from each what in each is useful and desirable—to give to England what is good in the Irish system—and to Ireland what is good in the English system—and to identify them beneficially by raising both to the level of a common advantage. Thus I find, that in fifteen important matters of practice and procedure, it is recommended that the course of the Irish Courts shall hereafter be adopted by the English, and in eight as important matters, that the course of the English Courts shall hereafter be followed in Ireland. In a few peculiar instances, Ireland is to retain her peculiar practice, as with respect to the rotation of writs, the Consolidated Nisi Prius Court, the speeding of Writs of Inquiry, and the arguing of Bills o. Exceptions, in which the actual circumstances of the profession and of the country make that practice more convenient for the time. Then there are general improvements suggested as applicable to both countries, and fit to be adopted simultaneously by each. The Crown Office of the Queen's Bench in Ireland is the subject of a separate finding, and it is suggested that the Crown practice in Ireland, at present somewhat uncertain and obscure, shall be assimilated to the Crown practice of England, and shall be made public and patent to all the world. These are, in very general terms, the recommendations of the Commissioners ; and to carry them into effect, so far as Ireland is concerned, is the object of this Bill. It has been laboriously and carefully prepared. It endeavours to give operation to all the Commissioners have advised, and for the purpose of accomplishing a wise, discriminating, and judicious assimilation, it, to a large extent, consolidates the provisions of the English statutes which have been originated by the English

Commissioners, and adopted by the Legislature. The Bill has been prepared in such a way that hon. Members by looking at the margin will be able at once to refer to the corresponding sections of the English statutes; and they will find that there is no portion of it that has not the sanction of great authority, and very few of its provisions that are not commended to adoption by a sound and large experience of their successful working. If it be accepted by the House, it will establish in England and Ireland a homogeneous and consistent scheme of pleading and practice, to the great advantage of the professions in both countries, while it will enable both to afford to each other the benefits of their mutual intelligence, experience, and authority—and to the advantage also of the Community and the State. For the first time a comprehensive system is offered to Ireland—the issue of full inquiry and authoritative decision—and I trust it will be accepted by the House as possessing the sanction of the successive Commissioners whose labours Parliament has already made the basis of salutary legislation, as invited and approved by the opinion of the Irish Bar, and faithfully embodying the proposals unanimously submitted to the Sovereign, after anxious inquiry and long consideration, by many of the most eminent Englishmen and Irishmen who, at this day, adorn the profession of the law. I beg, Sir, to move for leave to introduce the Bill.

MR. WHITESIDE said, he would not object to the introduction of the Bill, but unless coerced by the votes of the House he would never consent to the retrograde propositions it contained. There was a general opinion in the profession that the present system of pleading worked well. It facilitated the despatch of business in the Courts, and gave entire satisfaction to all parties. He believed the Bill would be the introduction of a system of litigation, delay, and expense such as his right hon. Friend did not anticipate. He hoped that the second reading of such a revolutionary Bill would not be taken for a month.

Motion *agreed to.*

Bill to amend the process, practice, and mode of pleading in the Superior Courts of Common Law at Dublin, *ordered* to be brought in by Mr. ATTORNEY GENERAL FOR IRELAND and Sir ROBERT PEEL.

Bill *presented*, and read 1°. [Bill 86.]

House adjourned at a quarter after One o'clock, till Monday next.

Mr. O'Hagan

HOUSE OF LORDS,

Monday, May 2, 1864.

MINUTES.]—PUBLIC BILL—*Committee*—High Court at Bombay* (No. 57).

Their Lordships met; and having gone through the business on the paper, without debate,

House adjourned at half past Five o'clock, till To-morrow, a quarter before Five o'clock.

HOUSE OF COMMONS,

Monday, May 2, 1864.

MINUTES.]—SUPPLY—*considered in Committee*—NAVY ESTIMATES.
PUBLIC BILLS—*Ordered*—Rivers Pollution (Scotland)*; Admiralty Lands and Works*; Administration of Trusts (Scotland)*.
First Reading—Joint Stock Companies (Foreign Countries) [*Lords*]* [Bill 87]; Admiralty Lands and Works* [Bill 88].
Committee—Promissory Notes and Bills of Exchange (Ireland)* [Bill 38].
Report—Promissory Notes and Bills of Exchange (Ireland)* [Bill 38].
Considered as amended — Customs and Inland Revenue [Bill 82].
Third Reading—Penal Servitude Acts Amendment* [Bill 23]; Civil Bill Courts (Ireland)* [Bill 79], and *passed*.

LANDLORD AND TENANT (IRELAND).

QUESTION.

MR. MAGUIRE said, he rose to ask Mr. Attorney General for Ireland, Whether it is the intention of the Government to propose any measure to the House during the present Session, with a view to establish more equitable relations between Landlord and Tenant than exist at present in Ireland, and to induce increased exertion on the part of the Tenant by securing to him the results of his outlay and industry?

SIR ROBERT PEEL, in reply, said, it was not the intention of the Government to introduce any measure of the nature alluded to by the hon. Gentleman.

POST OFFICE—SATURDAY HALF HOLIDAY—QUESTION.

MR. O'REILLY said, he wished to ask the Secretary to the Treasury, Whether any inconvenience has been felt, or any extra expense by the employment of additional clerks incurred, in consequence of the officials of the Money Order Office, and other departments of the Post Office, having the advantage of the Saturday half-holiday?

MR. PEEL said, in reply, that he understood from the Post Office authorities that no inconvenience had been sustained, or extra expense incurred, by the Saturday half-holiday.

BANK NOTES (SCOTLAND) BILL.
QUESTION.

MR. BAXTER said, he would beg to ask Mr. Chancellor of the Exchequer, Whether, after the expression of opinion in the debate on the Bank Notes (Scotland) Bill, he means to proceed with the Bank Acts Bill for Scotland?

THE CHANCELLOR OF THE EXCHEQUER replied, that during the recent discussion, a general opinion had been expressed on the part of the representatives of Scotland, that it would be better not to deal partially with any isolated point belonging to the currency or banking; and as no great public interest was involved in going forward with a Bill of so limited a scope, he would defer to that feeling, and not ask the House to proceed further with the Bill.

VACCINATION OF SHEEP.
QUESTION.

SIR JERVOISE JERVOISE said, he wished to ask the Vice President of the Committee of Council of Education, When the results of the experiments in vaccinating sheep, begun in 1862, concluded in 1863, and the Report of which was promised by Easter, 1864, will be laid before Parliament?

MR. H. A. BRUCE replied, that the experiments with reference to the vaccination of sheep were concluded at Michaelmas last. At the commencement of the present year, the gentlemen who had charge of those experiments were asked for their Report, and they undertook that it should be ready by Easter. They were not officers in his department, and all that they could do was to urge upon them to be expeditious. That Report had not been presented, but he might state the general effect of it was within the knowledge of his (Mr. Bruce's) department. It had been found that sheep were very imperfectly suscep-

tible of vaccination, and that the vaccination so taken afforded no real security against the sheep taking small pox.

LAW OF HYPOTHEC.
QUESTION.

MR. CARNEGIE said, he wished to ask the Lord Advocate, Whether it is the intention of the Government to appoint a Royal Commission to inquire into the nature and working of the Law of Hypothec as regards agricultural subjects in Scotland?

THE LORD ADVOCATE said, in reply, that it was the intention of the Government to appoint a Royal Commission to inquire into the nature and working of the Law of Hypothec in Scotland.

MR. CARNEGIE then said that he should not proceed with the Motion upon the subject which stood upon the paper for to-morrow.

UNITED STATES—THE FORGED DESPATCH.—QUESTION.

SIR JAMES ELPHINSTONE said, he wished to ask the Under Secretary of State for Foreign Affairs, Whether Her Majesty's Government have expressed any opinion on the circumstances of Mr. Seward having presented a document to Lord Lyons on the 22nd of December last, which, on the 19th of March, he "felt bound" to tell him he had "just discovered" to be "a forgery;" and whether Her Majesty's Government communicated with the agents of the Confederate States in Europe on the subject, or with the Government of the Confederate States at Richmond, and with what result. He also wished to know, whether Mr. Seward had been called upon to name the gentleman who was the author of the report?

MR. LAYARD said, Her Majesty's Government had not expressed any opinion upon the communications from Mr. Seward. As the hon. Member was aware, there was no agent of the Confederate States in this country to whom questions could be addressed, and it was not usual to address questions to the agent of a Government which was not recognized. Every endeavour was made by the Government to ascertain whether the document referred to was genuine. As soon however as it was found that the document was a forgery, that fact was stated by the noble Lord (Earl Russell) in another place.

SIR JAMES ELPHINSTONE said, he wished to know whether an agent had not been despatched from the Havannah to the Confederate States, in order to communicate with the Government at Richmond, and whether that agent was not refused permission to pass through the blockading squadron?

MR. LAYARD: That is so. He was not permitted to pass through the blockade.

SIR JAMES ELPHINSTONE said, he also wished to know whether the circumstance of an agent being accredited by Her Majesty's Government and sent to communicate with the Confederate States Government did not amount to an acknowledgment of the Executive power of the Confederate States?

THE CHANNEL FLEET.—QUESTION.

SIR JOHN PAKINGTON: I beg, Sir, to ask my noble Friend the Secretary of the Admiralty, Whether it is true that the Channel fleet has been moved from Portland to the Downs; and, if not, whether they are under orders to proceed thither? I wish next to ask, whether the noble Lord is in a position to say that the ships constituting the Channel fleet have been completed with respect to their coals, provisions, and other stores? I also beg to ask the noble Lord whether the large iron ships of the Channel fleet have been into dock since their return from their winter cruise in the Atlantic?

LORD CLARENCE PAGET: Sir, the Channel squadron are in the Downs. They are very nearly complete, and they are perfectly ready to proceed to any part of the world at twenty-four hours' notice. The iron ships have not been docked since their winter cruise; but the *Warrior* was docked on the 12th of November, the *Black Prince* on the 22nd of October, the *Prince Consort* on the 11th of November, the *Hector* on the 12th of January, and the *Defence* on the 10th of October.

THE AUSTRIAN FLEET.—QUESTION.

LORD ROBERT CECIL: In connection with the Question just put by my right hon. Friend (Sir John Pakington), I beg to ask, Whether any information has been received with respect to the movements of the Austrian fleet which has moved northwards; whether it is known that any kind of guarantee or pledge has been given that it shall not go beyond the North Sea; or

Mr. Layard

if not, whether there will be any opposition to its entering the Baltic?

MR. LAYARD: If the noble Lord will put the Question on the paper I will answer it to-morrow.

SEATS OF UNDER SECRETARIES.
QUESTION.

MR. WALPOLE said, he wished to ask a Question respecting the subject which had been referred to a Select Committee —the seats of the Under Secretaries. The House was aware that the Committee had made a Report, but that there had been great differences of opinion. He wished to know, Whether the Government intend to propose any legislation upon the subject?

SIR GEORGE GREY, in reply, said, the general opinion seemed to be that there was a great difficulty as to the construction of the Act of Parliament, and therefore the Government did intend to introduce a Bill to amend it.

CUSTOMS AND INLAND REVENUE BILL.
[BILL 82.] CONSIDERATION.

Bill, as amended, *considered.*

MR. J. B. SMITH, who had given notice to move, "That the duties on sugar be continued in force for one year only," rose to make the Motion—when

MR. SPEAKER said, that the Amendment, if carried, would have the effect of stopping the Bill—a result which he believed was not within the contemplation of the hon. Member.

THE CHANCELLOR OF THE EXCHEQUER said, that the hon. Member could move the insertion of his restriction on the consideration of Schedule D.

SIR HENRY WILLOUGHBY asked what effect this Bill would have upon the stamp duties? It was important that it should be understood whether there was anything in the shape of new taxation in connection with the Bill. He thought the words of one clause widened the area of the Stamp Duty Bill, and that under Schedule C certain things were brought under the operation of the stamp duties which up to the present moment were not so. He therefore hoped the right hon. Gentleman the Chancellor of the Exchequer would state clearly whether there were any new taxes in the Bill; and, if there were any, what those taxes were?

THE CHANCELLOR OF THE EXCHEQUER said, so far as his understanding went, and so far as the intention of the Government went (although it was not for him to give any authoritative interpretation of the words to which objection had been taken), the only points in which taxation was to be raised by this Bill were as follow :—The principal point was the extension to policies of insurance, when made the subject of settlement, of liability of stamps *ad valorem.* This point would receive the particular attention of the Committee. There were no taxes to be laid or increased by this Bill excepting what he had mentioned in the financial statement. He remembered there would be an incidental application of the stamp duties in certain cases in connection with perpetual curacies which were brought under the same category as rectories, and would be similarly treated. If the right hon. Baronet would refer to any other point in particular upon which he wished information he would be happy to give him it.

Mr. HENLEY called attention to Clause 6, which proposed to grant licences at a reduced rate to persons occupying houses below a certain value, to be granted on the overseer's certificate of rating. Under the next clause the overseer was required to give a certificate in such cases, and he was liable to a penalty of £10 if the statement thus given was untrue in any particular. He (Mr. Henley) thought that, as the overseer was liable to this penalty, he ought to have facilities for extracting the information he required from the poor rate book, in order that a mistake might not be made between one John Smith and another John Smith, and thus the overseer become liable under the clause. He thought also they were entitled to some small fee on giving the certificate.

THE CHANCELLOR OF THE EXCHEQUER said, that he did not know whether the hon. Gentleman objected to the penalty or not ? [Mr. HENLEY: No.] As to the question of allowing a small fee for giving the certificate, he would consider the point and give an answer to it when he proposed to read the Bill a third time.

Clause 5 (Occasional Licences may be granted to Refreshment House Keepers, Wine Retailers, Beer Retailers, and Tobacco Dealers).

THE CHANCELLOR OF THE EXCHEQUER said, the hon. Member for Northamptonshire (Mr. Hunt) had given notice of an Amendment to this clause requiring the consent of a justice of the peace to the issuing of occasional licences under the Bill, and imposing restrictions as to hours. The House would remember that when occasional licences were granted, it was provided that they should only be granted with the approval of two magistrates. The law was subsequently modified to one magistrate. He first proposed by this clause simply to grant these occasional licences to publicans; but he now proposed to grant them to the other class of persons who had licences for wine and beer, and to place them under the same control as the other licences. He would add words to this effect to the end of the clause. This would probably meet the views of the hon. Member for Northamptonshire.

MR. HUNT said, he was perfectly satisfied with the alteration proposed.

Amendment agreed to.

SIR WILLIAM JOLLIFFE objected to the provision with respect to the mode in which penalties should be recovered. The clause was so worded that the penalty might be recovered even for an unintentional error.

THE CHANCELLOR OF THE EXCHEQUER said, that the penalties would not be recoverable by a private person, but by an officer of a public department subject to be called to account for any abuse of his powers. The same provision had been introduced into the other Revenue Acts, and when a system of penalties generally couched in form of expression pervaded the Revenue law, it was better to adhere to that form rather than introduce other expressions that might perplex the general administration of the Revenue laws. If it were said that all should be considered, that was another question; but he did not think they should consider it in a particular Bill. The hon. Member for Youghal (Mr. Butt) had suggested that the definition of goods, wares, and merchandize in the hands of manufacturers for sale was not complete. His hon. and learned Friend had observed that many accessory materials used in manufactures disappeared in the process, though they contributed to the result of the fully manufactured article. He did not think that there was anything doubtful in the provision; but as the suggestion had been made, he proposed to add words for the purpose of removing any doubt that might exist.

The clause was amended accordingly.

Mr. WALPOLE pointed out that a new *ad valorem* duty was imposed by the Bill on foreign and colonial stock.

THE CHANCELLOR OF THE EXCHEQUER said, the duty was imposed on the settlement of foreign and colonial stock, which up to the present time had not been taken cognizance of for the purpose of taxation. That was not the position that property held by a British subject abroad should be placed in, when compared with property of the same description held by him in this country. An anomaly, therefore, existed, which the present Bill proposed to remove.

Mr. MALINS said, that by a decision of the Court of Exchequer it had been held that a policy of assurance brought into settlement was not property and was not subject to *ad valorem* duty. The right hon. Gentleman now proposed to make these policies liable to the duty. But he contended that this was not a reasonable proposal; for where a man on his marriage insured his life for £5,000, and made this a subject of settlement, the policy had then no value whatever, and yet it was to pay the same duty as if it was so much money in the funds. It was true that a proviso had been added to that clause by which the policy was not made liable to duty unless in the deed of settlement there was a covenant to keeping it alive. But in every well-drawn instrument such a covenant was inserted. He would propose an Amendment in Clause 12, by which, when a policy of assurance was made the subject of settlement, the *ad valorem* duty would be payable only upon its value at the time of the settlement.

Amendment proposed, in page 6, to leave out from the word "if," in line 13, to the word "behalf," in line 15, both inclusive.—(*Mr. Malins.*)

THE CHANCELLOR OF THE EXCHEQUER said, he was sorry he could not accede to the Amendment of his hon. and learned Friend, which did not appear to be supported by any strong argument, either in principle or practice, and would introduce into the law a most invidious and arbitrary exemption. He saw no principle of justice to be urged in favour of the Motion. He would grant that, in the case of a policy where there was no covenant for keeping it alive, it might be fair to exempt it from the *ad valorem* duty; but as for a policy that had a covenant for keeping it up, that was equi-

The Chancellor of the Exchequer

valent to a bond given by the person bound to keep it up. With respect to the law and the practice, his hon. and learned Friend had said truly that there had been a judgment of the Court of Exchequer to the effect that life policies included in settlements were not chargeable with an *ad valorem* duty; but his hon. and learned Friend had not stated the whole of the question. The Government were not able to carry the judgment to a superior court on appeal, or they would have endeavoured to obtain its reversal. The Law Officers of the Crown had, however, been consulted from time to time, and they had given their opinions repeatedly to the effect that life policies were chargeable. They had also recommended the Government to continue to charge the duty, thereby challenging the parties on whom the duty had been levied to further try the question if they thought fit. On this being represented to him, he certainly was of opinion that it was not desirable that such an equivocal state of things should continue; and the Government had therefore thought it right to ask Parliament to construe the law in the sense for which they contended. The whole argument was, in principle, in favour of the proposal which the Government made. It appeared to him that, if the present practice was to be impeached on any ground at all, it was on the ground that taxation on settled personalty was exceedingly low compared with that on unsettled personalty. It paid only 5s. per cent ; it escaped the probate duty. [Mr. MALINS: It gets the succession duty.] Yes; but it escaped not only the probate duty but the legacy duty. He stated it moderately in estimating the taxation on one description of property at 5s. per cent, and that on the other at £2 10s. per cent. He could hardly, therefore, believe his hon. and learned Friend would make any serious opposition if he were to propose to raise the duty on settlements. He entirely objected to the proposition of his hon. and learned Friend.

Mr. HUNT thought it was very inconvenient to have those discussions on this stage of the Bill; but, notwithstanding what had been said by the Chancellor of the Exchequer, he was of opinion that it was desirable the House should adopt the Amendment of his hon. and learned Friend. He was astonished that the Law Officers of the Crown should have advised the Government to disregard the decision of a Court of Law. He made no charge against the Law Officers of any particular Administration, for he did not know under what Government the advice referred to by the right hon. Gentleman had been given.

THE ATTORNEY GENERAL said, he did not think the Law Officers of the Crown were bound to abide by the decision of a Court whose ruling was not final. He said so without any prejudice or personal feeling, because the present Law Officers of the Crown had not been consulted on this point. As to the Question before them, he contended that policies of Insurance ought to be taxed like other engagements. Suppose a man had not the means of paying down money to make a provision for his wife, but he hoped by his exertions to save money for that purpose. Well, he covenanted that after his death his executors should pay £5,000 for that purpose. Under the existing law the instrument by which he entered into that covenant paid duty, no matter whether the amount was covenanted to be paid the next day or not for years after. And what was the effect of a policy of Insurance ? It was simply a covenant that, instead of the insurer's executors paying a certain sum out of his estate upon his death, an Insurance Office should pay the money, and that the insurer should do everything necessary to be done on his part to make that payment absolutely certain. Therefore it was quite plain that the House would be acting with partiality if it refused to impose on policies of Insurance duties similar to those imposed on instruments containing analogous covenants.

MR. HENLEY would put a case. If A and B entered into a contract of marriage, and if C, father to A, gave a bond to pay a certain some of money at his death, the money agreed to be paid was hard money not coming from A to B, but from a third party, C. In the case of an Insurance the parties out of their annual income contracted to lay by a certain sum, all the product of which was paid to one of them when the other died. It was not by any means the same thing to persons marrying, because in one case they had a sum of money coming to them on bond, and in the other it was their own savings which were taxed. The two things were not the same in reality, and if the hon and learned Gentleman went to a division he should vote with him.

MR. HADFIELD also thought the two

cases were not on the same footing, and he should support the hon. and learned Member.

MR. THOMSON HANKEY thought that if there were to be any exemption, it should be for the bond, which was the least valuable instrument.

MR. PRICE also thought that if the bond was taxed, the Insurance, which was the more valuable instrument, ought to be taxed as well.

MR. NEATE supported the clause as it stood.

MR. COLLINS said, it was a monstrous proposition to tax a sum of money *in futuro* exactly as if it were in hand. He would support a proposition for the entire omission of the clause.

SIR BALDWIN LEIGHTON said, that the Attorney General would get few people to agree with him that it was not the duty of the Government to acquiesce in the decision of a superior Court of Law until it had been revised, and it was a gross act of tyranny to force the subject not only to go to that Court again, but to appeal to the House of Lords. If the Government were discontented with the law as laid down, it was their duty to come to Parliament.

SIR STAFFORD NORTHCOTE thought the two cases were *in pari materiâ,* and could see no reason in making a distinction between them.

Question put, " That the words proposed to be left out stand part of the Bill."

The House *divided :*—Ayes 161 ; Noes 124: Majority 37.

MR. J. B. SMITH : — I rise, Sir, to move words in Schedule A limiting the operation as to levying the duty on sugar, to the 1st August, 1865. The sugar duties have for many years past been annual, and my proposal is that they shall continue to be so, to give the House and the country opportunities for the further discussion of the question with which they are at present imperfectly acquainted. I am an older free trader than the Chancellor of the Exchequer, or than my hon. Friend the Member for Rochdale (Mr. Cobden). I had the honour to be the first to advocate, in the Manchester Chamber of Commerce, the total repeal of the Corn Laws, and also the equalization of the duties on foreign and colonial sugars ; but I take shame to myself that I have not, until recently, inquired into the effect of the

3 S

sugar duties upon the interest of the consumers of sugar. Having now done so, I am astounded to find that a gigantic monopoly has silently grown up, while we have been quietly flattering ourselves that all monopolies had been for ever swept away. The Chancellor of the Exchequer has truly observed of the discussions which have recently taken place in letters and pamphlets on the sugar duties, that "the literature is overwhelming." I can well understand hon. Gentlemen, who have complained to me that the more they read of the sugar literature the more they are bewildered ; for that was so much my own case, that I found the only course was to lay it aside, to get at facts, and reason them out in my own mind. I soon discovered that the sugar refiners and monopolists had raised a false issue ; they shouted lustily for free trade, but under cover of this cry, they endeavoured to blind us as to their real object by a bewildering "literature." I think I shall have no difficulty in showing that the real object of these pretended free traders is to prevent the consumer of sugar from buying it in the cheapest market. Let us see what was the origin of the existing state of the sugar question. Previously to 1845 there was only one rate of duty on sugar. In that year Sir Robert Peel brought in a Bill to change the mode of levying the duty on sugar to a classified rate of duties upon different qualities. It is quite clear that Sir Robert did not foresee the effects of his new measure, for he stated that he expected there would be an importation that year of about 85,000 tons of white clayed sugar ; the import, however, turned out to be only 1,161 tons. Since that time the consumption of sugar has more than doubled, and if Sir Robert Peel's estimate had been realized, we ought now to have an import of 170,000 tons of white clayed sugar ; but, instead of that, our import in 1863 was only 1,100 tons. The fact is, that Sir Robert Peel's Bill has had the effect of completely revolutionizing the sugar trade ; it has resulted in banishing the best qualities of sugar from the market and of supplying their place with sugars of the lowest qualities, which are unfit for consumption by the people of this country until they are made over again by the sugar refiners. The operation of the law in banishing good sugar from the market is very clearly shown by Mr. Hardman, a sugar planter, examined before a Committee of the House of Commons in

Mr. J. B. Smith

1848. Mr. Hardman stated that he had erected expensive machinery, on the most scientific principles, for making sugar, by means of which he was enabled to make a larger quantity and of better quality from the raw material than by the former process. That he sent three parcels of sugar, of different qualities, to London—all made from the same raw material, and all sold by auction the same day. The first parcel, which was yellow sugar, was sold for 51s., duty paid, and as the duty was 14s., he netted 37s. per cwt. ; the second, white clayed, sold for 53s. 6d., and the duty on this being 16s. 4d., netted him 37s. 2d. ; the third was called other refined, sold for 56s. ; the duty was 18s. 4d., netting him 37s. 8d. per cwt. As the importer paid the commission, and discount was allowed on the gross price, there was an actual difference of less than 2d. per cwt. between the best and the worst quality, so that although the best quality sold in the market for 5s. per cwt. more than the worst, the classified duty prevented him from netting more than an additional 2d. per cwt. for it. The consequence was, he said, "that the classification had operated to their absolute ruin." The law of classified duties, it is seen, prevents the planter from obtaining more for the highest class of sugars than for the lowest, and here is at once the explanation why white clayed sugar has ceased to be imported. It must not be supposed, however, that because these duties have had the effect of banishing the importation of white clayed sugar, its use has ceased ; on the contrary, it is now supplied from a different quarter. A new trade has been created by the classified duties which did not exist before. Formerly, the trade of the English sugar refiner was confined to refining raw sugar into loaf sugar ; now he carries on the new trade of re-making low qualities of raw sugar into cleaner looking moist sugar, resembling white clayed sugar. Before Peel's Bill enacting classified duties, the sugar refiners used about 100,000 tons of sugar per annum ; the new trade of re-making sugar has increased their consumption to 400,000 tons out of 500,000 tons, the total quantity of all kinds consumed. It is important to observe that the moist sugars furnished by the English refiners are inferior to those imported, because the re-making of sugar deteriorates the quality ; it is fair to look upon, but the process of re-making deprives it of a portion of its native sweetness, and the application of bullocks' blood and animal charcoal, which are not used when originally made, leave behind an unpleasant smell in re-made sugar. A law which excludes the importation of good sugar appears unnatural on the face of it. What, then, are the pretences for this law of classified duties ? That it is a kind of *ad valorem* duty on the quantity of crystallizable saccharine matter contained in each quality of sugar. But that this is a false and impracticable scheme was never more ably shown than by the Secretary of State for the Colonies (Mr. Cardwell) before he became a free trade backslider. When President of the Board of Trade in 1853, in answer to the complaints of the Governor of British Guiana of the injurious effects of the discriminating duties on sugar, the right hon. Gentleman forwarded a reply, stating that

"These discriminating rates of duty were fixed as an approximation to the *ad valorem* principle, it being held to be unfair to subject to the same duty sugars containing different qualities of saccharine matter. Although, in the opinion of my Lords, Customs duties proportioned to the value of imports, wherever practicable, are more just in principle, with reference to the incidence of taxation, than uniform rated duties, it has been found necessary, from a practical experience of the fraud to which such duties give rise, and the difficulty and cost of their collection, to adopt uniform duties upon so many important articles subject to Custom duties, that the retention of the *ad valorem* duties, which still remain in the British tariff, becomes comparatively unimportant. In the present instance my Lords are disposed to allow considerable weight to the arguments adduced by the Governor of Guiana ; and they would observe that the application of *ad valorem* duties on sugar appear to be in many respects less appropriate than to several other articles, in regard to which it has been found expedient to abandon them. To impose a discriminating duty upon distinct kinds of a given produce, such as the produce of vineyards varying in richness, different qualities of tea or tobacco would appear to be a legitimate application of *ad valorem* duties ; but to strike with a superior duty one pound of sugar which, by a better mode of manufacture, contains more saccharine matter than another pound obtained from the same raw material, is to inflict direct discouragement upon improvement."

This, then, is not a question of jaggery and crystallizable saccharine matter, as the Chancellor of the Exchequer would have us believe. That is a false issue raised by the sugar refiners to throw dust in our eyes. The real issue is, that having abolished all other monopolies, will you pass laws to throttle scientific improvements in sugar making in your colonies and elsewhere, and thus prevent the con-

sumers of sugar from buying the best qualities in the cheapest market, for the purpose of protecting the re-making of sugar in England ? But, Sir, this law is not only impracticable, but it is founded on a vicious principle. The valuation of sugar for the duty is not made on the quantity of saccharine matter it contains, for that cannot be ascertained but by comparing its appearance with certain standards provided by the Customs. This opens the door to fraud. All laws which tempt either merchants or Custom House officers to fraud are vicious in principle. I have had some experience in this way. There was formerly an *ad valorem* duty on raw cotton, by which the house with which I was connected were great losers. The law was that every importer entered his cotton at any valuation he chose, and the Customs could take it at that price, adding 5 per cent to it. It so happened that we were importers, not of low kinds worth 9*d*. per pound, but of the finest worth 1*s*. 6*d*. to 3*s*. 6*d*. ; and we found there were importers of this kind who, presuming upon the ignorance or dishonesty of the Custom House officers, entered the same qualities at half the price we entered ours. Thus the revenue was defrauded, the fair trader injured, and public morals not improved. The same temptations to fraud exist under the present system of levying the duties on sugar. The Custom House officer decides what duty any particular parcel of sugar shall pay, and it is notorious, not only that sugar which has paid the lowest rate of duty has sold at a higher price than that which has paid a higher duty, but that on the same kind of sugar different rates of duty have on the same day been imposed at Glasgow, Liverpool, and London. The sugar in any one cask is not of the same quality throughout. A sample taken at the top of the cask would be charged with a different rate of duty from a sample taken from the bottom. A fine field for chicanery ! Some years ago there were classified duties on tea, and every lot had to be examined by a Custom House officer, samples brewed in tea pots, and a value affixed according to the taste and flavour. It is a curious fact, that this system of duties had precisely the same effect in banishing good teas that the classified duties have had in banishing good sugar. We never had such bad tea as then ; when the duty was equalized, good teas immediately took the place of bad, and now such a quality as Bohea is unknown in the market. The notion that the interests of the consumers of sugar were consulted by the adoption of classified duties was effectually dissipated by the evidence before the Select Committee of 1862. Sir Thomas Freemantle, Chairman of the Board of Customs, gave it as his opinion—

"That the scale of duties has a tendency to act as a protection for the production of low-class West India sugars, and that if it is a question of protection, the consumers suffer. The West India proprietors claim the protection. They cannot stand the competition of Cuba and slave-producing countries."

Now, let us hear what the West India planters themselves say. Mr. Rennie, the representative of the largest West India house in England, was asked what would be the effect of one uniform duty. He answered—

"I think the immediate effect of it would be to put an end to the cultivation of all the estates making the low description of sugar. They are struggling now for existence with a protection of 1s. 2d., and if you took away that, they could not exist, and you would give a stimulus to a very large production of Cuba sugars, and all the finest West Indies sugars, and all the finest Mauritius and East Indies sugars; but you would lose the supply of the whole of the present low-class of West India sugar, that comes to this market to be refined here."

This evidence speaks for itself. There are planters who, availing themselves of scientific discoveries, have erected improved machinery for making sugar, by means of which they can make a larger quantity and of better quality than by the old machinery; but there is a large class of West India planters who, feeling great reverence for the wisdom of their ancestors, continue to make sugar after the manner of their great grandfathers, and they call out for protection against the new-fangled machinery, and insist that an extra duty shall be laid upon all the sugar it produces, and moreover they threaten us that if we do not comply with their demand, they will cease to grow sugar. Well, Sir, this is not the first time we have heard that kind of argument. There is an amusing similarity in protectionist arguments all the world over. When the people demanded the right to buy their corn in the cheapest market, the corn-growers told us a similar story: they said that the land would go out of cultivation. What say the sugar refiners?

"It was said by a London refiner, that if the 16s. duty was removed, not only would the fine sugars from the East Indies and the Mauritius come here, but that the much more preferable

white Havanah sugars would come in and supersede the sugars of the refiners, because they are white, and can be sent in any quantity. That such sugars are generally as cheap as any other sugars, but they are not used on account of the high duty. That if these fine sugars were imported, the business of the English refiner would be unjustly interfered with; that if the same duty is put upon the low sugars, containing molasses, water, and dirt, the refining trade would be at an end, because it is not their business to make white sugar whiter, but to make brown sugar into white. That refiners principally exist in this country on account of the large supply of low sugar; and if a better description is brought in and admitted at the same duty as low sugar, there will be less for them to do, as such pure sugars could be refined with the greatest ease and comfort, whereas, with the low sugars brought from the West Indies, the process is more difficult, and requires twice as many sugar houses as the other would."

Here is the key to the clamorous outcry of these pretended free traders—the sugar refiners. They unite in the cry with the West India planters for the exclusion of the good sugars of Cuba and the Mauritius, lest it should interfere with their remaking of bad sugar. The fact is, that these classified sugar duties have raised up a formidable monopoly interest, with which we shall have to struggle; and the struggle is rendered more difficult by the monopolists, strange to say, having enlisted on their side the Chancellor of the Exchequer and my hon. Friend the Member for Rochdale (Mr. Cobden). But I ask the Chancellor of the Exchequer, does he call the cry to be protected from Cuba and Mauritius free trade? I ask the right hon. Gentleman how he can reconcile his rejection of the claims of the silk manufacturers and those of the papermakers to be protected from the competition of the papermakers of France and Belgium, whose paper is admitted duty free, while a duty is imposed in those countries on the export of rags? He tells the papermakers—

"The claims of the consumers are paramount: they have the right to buy their paper in the cheapest markets."

Why does he not hold the same language to the West India planters and the English sugar refiners? The right hon. Gentleman said, on introducing this Bill—

"That no courage or ability can induce the Legislature to sanction a system of protection."

I quite agree with him, but I think I have shown that this Bill is "a system of protection," and I confidently predict that it will not be long ere it be repealed. When the people open their eyes to the fraud which has been practised upon them by

Mr. J. B. Smith

this Bill, they will insist with one voice upon their right to buy their sugar, as they buy everything else, in the cheapest market. I had not the honour of a seat in this House when Sir Robert Peel's Sugar Bill was introduced, but it was opposed by those consistent free traders, Mr. Hume, Mr. Ricardo, Mr. Bright, and Mr. Milner Gibson. My hon. Friend the President of the Board of Trade (Mr. Milner Gibson) was then Member for Manchester, and was considered a sort of free trade watch-dog, and a very wakeful watch-dog he was; his voice was always heard when there was the least approach of danger. We have not heard his opinion of the present Bill, but if he be about to become a free trade backslider, like his Colleague the Secretary for the Colonies (Mr. Cardwell), I hope he will have better reasons to offer for such a course than that right hon. Gentleman. The Secretary for the Colonies, who, when President of the Board of Trade in 1853, described the graduated scale of sugar duties as "inflicting a direct discouragement upon improvement," now turns round and thus defends them—

"He would show that since the graduated scale had been adopted, the consumption had gone on increasing until it was larger than ever."

I do not deny that our supplies of sugar have increased as stated, but does the right hon. Gentleman mean to say that if the classified duties had been abolished, the supply would not have equally increased? The increased consumption of sugar is not the consequence of a law which excludes good sugar, but in spite of it. The increased consumption of sugar is owing to the increased population, and the improved condition of the consumers of sugar. Then the right hon. Gentleman says—

"The object of the scale has been attained, because a quality of sugar most valuable to the consumer has been imported."

I deny that a valuable quality has been imported; good sugar is more valuable than bad, and the effect of the law has been to exclude good sugar. If, as the right hon. Gentleman says, the classification has brought us increased supplies of low sugar, does it follow that the converse of the proposition must be true, that the abolition of the standards and the adoption of one rate of duty would have diminished our supplies? It so happens that the experiment has been tried in France. In 1860 the graduated scale of duties was abolished, and all qualities of raw sugar were admitted at one rate of duty. Mark the results; the imports were in 1860, 60,496,812 kilogrammes; 1861, 95,802,687 kilogrammes; 1862, 129,167,182 kilogrammes. In England, under classified duties, the imports increased in eight years 25 per cent. In France, under one rate of duty, they increased in three years more than 100 per cent. But it is important to note that classified duties have brought us low rubbish, while an equal duty has brought France sugars of the most beautiful quality. The glory of the Bill, said the right hon. Gentleman the Secretary of the Colonies, is, that it admits the lowest class of sugars and excludes the best; and we are told this is for the benefit of the lower classes, who use low sugars. But why should the lower classes be compelled by law to consume the worst sugar? The lower classes desire good sugar as well as other folks. At one time they were content with oatmeal and barley bread, but now they are all aiming to get better bread and better meat and drink than before. Do you believe they prefer coarse sugar to fine, or bad tea to good? Time was, when bad tea was forced upon them by classified duties, as bad sugar is now; that scandalous law is now abolished, and the law forcing bad sugar upon them ought and must be abolished also. There has been a similar and instructive struggle going on in France on the sugar duties as in England. The sugar refiners in France have the monopoly of refining sugars for export, which are required to be refined from foreign sugar. The French beetroot sugar-makers justly claim an equal right to refine their sugar, and to receive the same drawback on exportation as the refiner. The French refiners, with whom are allied the shipowners, are little behind their brethren in England in sugar literature, but they sail on a different tack. In England, the refiners knowing the stigma attaching to protection, preach free trade. In France, free trade doctrines are less fashionable, and they tickle their countrymen, by affecting extraordinary concern for the safety and glory of France. If, say they, beetroot sugar be allowed to be exported, the import of foreign sugar will fall off, foreign commerce, the nursery of our seamen, will be diminished, and the safety of the nation will be imperilled, for if war should some day break out with "perfide Albion," you will have destroyed the arm (the seamen) by which their insolence would have been punished. The French Government have this year, by way of compromising the claims of the beetroot sugar-growers and the refiners, allowed the growers to export their sugar; but to pacify the refiners, have adopted two classifications, namely—a duty of 42 francs and 44 francs per kilo. on raw sugar. The Secretary for the Colonies told the House the other night that there had been a Conference at Paris of representatives from Holland, Belgium, France, and England, at which, although at first all except England were opposed to classified duties, at the close all were in favour of them except Belgium, and led us to expect that France would adopt our system. Well, France has adopted two classifications for raw sugar; England has four. The difference between the highest and the lowest rate of duty on raw sugars in France is 10*d.* per cwt.; what is the difference in England? Instead of 10*d.*, it is 3*s.* 6*d.* per cwt. I am sorry my hon. Friend the Member for Rochdale (Mr. Cobden) has not remained in the House, because I gave him notice that I intended to put him on his defence. I charge my hon. Friend with having been the cause of great mischief on this question, by silently allowing the Chancellor of the Exchequer and the sugar refiners to make use of his name as an approver of this Bill, without, I believe, having, with his usual shrewdness, inquired into its operations. The consequence has been that the free traders all over the country, confiding in his usually sound free trade opinions, have been lulled into a false security. My hon. Friend told the House the other night that our foreign Ambassadors and Consuls ought to be sent to school to learn political economy, and study Adam Smith. But some of my hon. Friend's constituents are of opinion that there are other persons besides our Ambassadors who ought to be sent to school. The grocers of Rochdale asked my hon. Friend's opinion on this question of the sugar duties, and the Chancellor of the Exchequer quoted the letter which my hon. Friend wrote to them as an evidence of his approval of his plan of classification. But the Chancellor of the Exchequer did not read to the House the answers of the Rochdale grocers, which showed that my hon. Friend ought to go to school again. My hon. Friend has been a great schoolmaster in his day, and he taught his scholars so well, that they immediately detected the sugar fallacies of their old

Mr. J. B. Smith

master. They reminded him, "These are not the doctrines we learnt from you; in considering this question, you have not put on your anti-Corn Law spectacles;" and so they beat him with the weapons he had taught them to handle. I contend, in the interest of the consumers, that the duty on sugar should operate in the same way as if there were no duty at all. If there were no duty at all, the West India planters would have to compete with sugar-growers all over the world; and if they chose to continue the system of their great grandfathers, and found themselves unable to compete with those who used the best machinery, and the most scientific processes of making sugar, they must take the consequences—they must go unpitied to the wall. The English sugar refiners would also have to compete with the colonial and foreign sugar refiners, and, under this competition, prices would soon regulate themselves, and the consumer would be supplied with the best sugar at the lowest price at which it could be afforded. It is proved that it is impossible to ascertain by inspection the quantity of crystallizable saccharine matter contained in any sample of sugar, and I hold, as the Secretary of State for the Colonies (Mr. Cardwell) formerly held, that—

"To strike with a superior duty one pound of sugar which, by a better mode of manufacture, contains more saccharine matter than another pound obtained from the same raw material, is to inflict direct discouragement upon improvement."

I am, therefore, in favour of one rate of duty, as the only just principle to adopt in the interest of consumers. One rate of duty on all qualities would attain the same object as no duty. But my hon. Friend the Member for Rochdale reminds me of the old anti-Corn Law cry, "A fixed duty is a fixed injustice." I quite agree with him that a fixed duty on corn is a fixed injustice; but I never advocated a fixed duty on corn, although my hon. Friend once did, and it is a curious historical fact, that he wrote a pamphlet in which he proposed a fixed duty on corn as a source of public revenue. Why was a fixed duty on corn a fixed injustice? Because if a fixed duty, say of 10*s.* a quarter, be laid on foreign corn, the price of home-grown corn would be proportionably raised to the consumer. Thus, an import of 2,000,000 quarters of foreign corn, at 10*s.* per quarter, would raise a revenue of £1,000,000, whilst the price of the 20,000,000 quarters of home-grown corn being raised by 10s. per quarter, the consumers would be taxed £10,000,000 for the purpose of putting £1,000,000 into the Exchequer. Let me remind my hon. Friend of another anti-Corn Law argument, which he has frequently used in former days, that if a duty be placed on foreign corn for purposes of revenue, a corresponding duty ought to be placed on home-grown corn. Let the House apply this principle to sugar. If the foreign and colonial planter paid a duty of 16s. per cwt. on their white sugar, why should not the English refiner pay a corresponding duty? But he pays no tax at all on his white sugar; he only pays a tax of 12s. 8d. on the lowest quality. It is said, no doubt, that the refiner pays on the "waste," but how does the House know what the "waste" is? Here is the juggle. Under the name of classified duties, the refiner gets a bounty on the low quality of sugar, which enables him to re-make it into white sugar, equal in appearance, but worse in quality, at a less price than the colonial planter, who has to pay a duty of 16s. instead of 12s. 8d. per cwt. The consequence is, that of the 500,000 tons of sugar which are consumed in this country, 400,000 tons pass through the hands of the sugar refiners, of which 300,000 tons pay the lowest rate of duty. Now, this 300,000 tons of sugar, paying 12s. 8d. duty, is re-made into sugar of a quality which, if imported by the sugar-planter, would pay duties of 16s. and 18s. 4d. per cwt. Is it just to make the planter pay a higher duty upon sugar of the same appearance, made by one single process, than the English refiner pays on that quality, because he puts it through the double process of making it over again? The fact is, this is a law to drive the planters of good sugar out of the market by high duties, and to give the English refiner, by means of low duties, almost the sole monopoly of the sale of sugar in this country. This is neither more nor less than a law to prevent the consumer from using cheap and good sugar, that the refiner may be protected in selling bad and dear sugar. No eloquence can long maintain this scandalous law. I trust I have shown sufficient reasons why it should be re-considered, and I therefore move, "That the duties on sugar be continued in force for one year only."

MR. LEATHAM: Sir, in rising to second the Motion of my hon. Friend, I do not rise with any intention or desire of expressing dissatisfaction with the propositions of the right hon. Gentleman; on the contrary, I cordially concur in the opinion which has been so generally expressed, that when we take into consideration the peculiar difficulties which at this moment beset this question, and especially the ill-informed and confused state of the public mind with respect to it, the right hon. Gentleman has dealt with it as satisfactorily as the House had any right to expect. In common with many who do not go quite so far as the right hon. Gentleman appears to go in their admiration of what we call *ad valorem* duties, and to whom simplicity in taxation has greater charms than complexity, I have observed with pleasure the step which the right hon. Gentleman has taken in the direction of equalization. And if the House will permit me, I should like to state the grounds upon which I think not only that the right hon. Gentleman was fully justified in taking that step, but would be fully justified if, on some early occasion, he should take other steps in the same direction. The right hon. Gentleman constructs his scale upon the principle, that the amount of the duty should correspond with the amount of crystallizable saccharine matter which is contained in the various sugars; and in order to show that the scale is just, we ought to be able to show that such is really the case. But with all due deference to the authority of the right hon. Gentleman, I cannot withhold my very grave doubts upon the fact. In the course of the very remarkable speech by which the right hon. Gentleman introduced his Budget, he had occasion to refer to the flood of literature with which this whole question has been inundated, and in which not only he but every hon. Member who takes a lively interest in great fiscal questions like this, has been hopelessly immersed during the last few weeks. Now, a peculiarity of that literature is, that the great bulk of it has proceeded from the pen of interested parties, and it seems almost necessary to disclaim at the outset (as I have much pleasure in being able to disclaim) the least personal interest in any particular solution of this question. Well, since I had no personal interest to guide me, the House may readily imagine how I floundered about in that Slough of Despond of controverted or conflicting facts which those who took part in this controversy contrived to place in the path of every pilgrim who set out on his journey with a single eye to arriving at the truth. But in the midst of this war of interests and conflict of opinion, there was one substantial fact which I was able to grasp firm hold of, and that was, that there exists the greatest diversity of opinion as to the amount of crystallizable saccharine matter contained in the various samples, and therefore the greatest possible doubt as to the justice of the scale. For example, I find Dr. Scoffern writing to the papers that

" He had on many occasions extracted upwards of 90 per cent of white pure sugar commercially equal to Dutch lumps from Indian khaur."

Now Indian khaur is the coarsest sugar known, and is practically identical with that Indian jaggery which the right hon. Gentleman selected when he put his extreme case the other night, and asked us whether it was fair to tax equally sugar nearly in a refined state, and Indian jaggery which contained only 50 per cent of crystallizable saccharine matter. I was astonished (having brought to the investigation the impression which I will engage to say prevails among ninety-nine out of every hundred Members of this House, that there exists the greatest disparity in the amount of crystallizable saccharine matter contained in the various samples) when I took up the Report of Professors Brande and Cooper, who conducted, at the instance of the Customs House, an analysis of 19 samples of sugar, embracing every kind known to the trade ; I was astonished, I say, to learn from that Report, that those learned gentlemen discovered in 15 out of the 19 samples no less than 90 per cent of crystallizable saccharine matter, and that in no one instance of the other four did the analysis disclose less than 85 per cent. Now if this be so, what becomes of the assertion (by which I venture to think the public mind has been grossly abused) that sugars are constantly imported containing 30 or 40 or 50 per cent of crystallizable saccharine matter only ? And what becomes of the justice of your scale which is based on some such assumption ? Surely, there must have been great ignorance or great delusion somewhere (to use no harsher term), either on the part of those who conducted this analysis, or on the part of those who, flying in the face of these results, still cling so tenaciously to a system of duties which they know to be so preposterously at variance with them. But I will call the refiners in order to prove

Mr. Leatham

the truth of what I say. And the refiners, at all events, are not obnoxious to the charge of giving *ex parte* evidence in favour of a uniform duty. Mr. Gaddesden, an eminent refiner, and in every sense an unimpeachable witness, in the course of his evidence before the Select Committee, proceeded to show how fraud would be committed if you refined in bond, and this is the illustration which he gave—

" I purchase," says Mr. Gaddesden, " West India sugar paying the 12s. 8d. duty, which contains of water about 5¼ per cent, dirt 1 per cent, total net sugar 6¼ per cent."

Mr. Gaddesden therefore speaks (as though it were a matter of daily occurrence) of purchasing West India sugar paying the very lowest duty, and containing 93¼ per cent of saccharine matter. Then Mr. Fryer (who is a great champion of the refiners, and a very able one) admits that he has bought sugar paying only the 13s. 10d. duty containing 95 per cent of crystallizable saccharine matter. Now, I do not wish to weary the House by needlessly multiplying proofs, but I should like to state a few facts with reference to the scale as it at present stands. My hon. Friend the Member for Carlisle (Mr. Potter), who has himself written very forcibly upon this question, obtained several samples of sugar which had passed the Customs House under the new scale, and transmitted them to an analytical chemist of great eminence, whose name if I were to mention it would be well known to the right hon. Gentleman, and the results I hold in my hand. There was one sample of sugar admitted under the highest duty but one, and this contained 94.5 per cent of crystallizable saccharine matter. There were two samples admitted under the 9s. 5d. duty (now the lowest but one) ; one of these contained 84.4 and the other 89 per cent of crystallizable saccharine matter. There were also two samples admitted under the lowest duty of all—the new duty recently added by the right hon. Gentleman in the scale in order to embrace the very lowest sugars ;—one of them contained 82 and the other 85 per cent of crystallizable saccharine matter. Now I have but little information beyond what I glean from publications which are the property of everybody ; I have no ends to serve beyond those of justice ; and what I want to know is, whether these facts (attested by the evidence of eminent analysts who must be presumed to be impartial witnesses, and by the evidence of eminent refiners, all whose interests point in a contrary direction)—I want to know whether these facts are facts or only so much gratuitous romance, because if they are facts I am at a loss to understand the justice of the scale. And do not let the right hon. Gentleman reply that it matters little how much crystallizable saccharine matter the samples contain if they do not yield that amount to the refiner, because, in the first place, this is not a refiner's but a consumer's question. In the second place, the right hon. Gentleman has admitted himself to be a disciple of the Manchester Chamber of Commerce, and the words of their memorial, as quoted by the right hon. Gentleman, are these—" that it is needful the duties be assessed upon the article in proportion to the amount of crystallizable saccharine matter which it contains," not which it may be made to yield; and in the third place, because the refiners themselves have stated that it is not their object to extract the greatest amount of sugar, but to extract it in the most tempting form. Thus Mr. Fairrie (and Mr. Fairrie is a perfect giant upon the field of saccharine literature), expressly states—

"That the refiner must carry on his manufacture in such a manner that he may obtain clear and bright crystals; which is not to be done if he makes it his principal or only object to get a large percentage of sugar. In this case his goods would be small in the grain, with a dingy look, and saleable only at a low price."

Now since my hon. Friend has not by his Motion distinctly raised the question of a uniform duty, I do not propose to go further now into the question of *ad valorem* duties as applied to sugar; but this I must say before I sit down, that if this artificial and capricious system is to be defended by analogy, it must be by much sounder analogies than those which the right hon. Gentleman strove to draw the other night. The right hon. Gentleman cited the case of wine, cocoa, coffee, corn and timber, as analogous to that of sugar. Now with the exception of wine, I cannot admit that any true analogy exists; and even in the case of wine, surely that man must be a poet who would call the wine duty an *ad valorem* duty, unless, indeed, he is prepared to throw overboard age, colour, bouquet and flavour, everything which constitutes the value of wine, and to value wine solely for the rapidity with which it will make him drunk. The right hon. Gentleman must be aware that at the same duty

are introduced brandies, quoted at 15*s.* proof, and rum at 15*d.*, and he knows perfectly well that at the same duty come in, side by side, the most silky Chateau Lafitte, at five or six guineas a dozen, and the most rasping Gladstonian, at 14*s.* But take the case of the other articles of import; the right hon. Gentleman states that cocoa paste pays a higher duty than cocoa nibs, roast coffee than green, flour than corn, and planks than timber; but what does this fact prove more than that your tariff sanctions the principle that the manufactured article ought to pay a higher duty than the raw product out of which it is manufactured? Cocoa nibs, green coffee, corn and timber, are all raw products, but sugar is never a raw product, it is always a manufactured article. No one imports sugar canes; and if the analogy is to prove anything, it must go much farther, and it must be shown that you strike the manufactured article with a higher and higher duty in proportion as it is further and further removed from the condition of the raw product out of which it is manufactured. Take the case of flour. The right hon. Gentleman ought to have shown that extra superfine pays a higher duty than superfine—superfine than fine—fine than seconds. But he can show nothing of the kind, and therefore I maintain that his analogy falls to the ground. And here is another point which is most material to this part of the question. The fact that these manufactured articles are liable to be charged with a higher duty than the raw products is instantly and of itself apparent. A blind man could tell the difference between roast coffee and green by the evidence of his nose, and by the use of his touch he could tell the difference between corn and flour, or between planks and timber; but in the case of sugar (and this is precisely where the shoe pinches) great technical knowledge and experience are requisite to assign the proper numbers; indeed, so nice and delicate an operation is it, that we are told the decision may be influenced by the shade of the sky, and by the state of the atmosphere, and that, too, in a climate and a country where two consecutive days were never yet known to be alike. And in the case of wine, the amount of duty to be charged is determined by the amount of alcohol which is present, and this is ascertained by the simplest operation known to science; but the analogous process in the case of sugar is an admitted failure—and in the evidence which the Customs House officers gave before the Committee, they stated that they judged solely by sight, by grain and colour. Well, the natural, the inevitable, and the notorious consequence has been, that strong sugars are constantly coloured in order that they may pass at a lower duty. So much, then, for the right hon. Gentleman's analogies. And, in conclusion, I would ask the right hon. Gentleman, and ask the House, what possible future can there be before a system of classified duties in defence of which even the right hon. Gentleman, with his vast stores of knowledge, with his keen ingenuity, and his wide range of illustration, is able to discover no sounder analogies than these?

Amendment proposed to Schedule (A), page 8, line 10, by adding after the words "sixty-four," the words "until the first day of August, one thousand eight hundred and sixty-five:"—(*Mr. John Benjamin Smith.*)

Mr. CAVE said, that having taken a somewhat active part in the Committee on the Sugar Duties, he desired to say a few words in opposition to the Motion which had been submitted to the House. He would be as short as possible, and avoid figures, which could not be tested in a debate; and if the subject were somewhat dry, and indeed scarcely intelligible to those who had no occasion to acquire a special knowledge of the details, he at least was not responsible for its having been forced a second time upon unwilling listeners. The hon. Member who had introduced this Motion had stated that he had only just given attention to the subject. That he (Mr. Cave) could well imagine. But the question had for a long time occupied the attention of others. According to the evidence of some of the witnesses before the Committee, this agitation arose from the dissatisfaction of certain wholesale grocers at their province being invaded by the refiners, who deprived them of the monopoly of supplying the retail trade. The fact was that a very great change had come over the taste of the great body of consumers, and large classes, who formerly never dreamt of using refined sugar, now did so habitually, owing chiefly to its increased variety and cheapness, and, perhaps, in some degree, to the publication some years ago in the *Lancet* of the magnified likenesses of *acari*, or raw sugar insects. This change of taste

Mr. Leatham

happened to be contemporaneous, in this country at least, with the new sugar duty scale, which was quite enough for the logical minds of a certain class of reasoners; but, unfortunately for them, in Scotland, where the same scale prevailed, scarcely any raw sugar had been used for more than twenty years. These "sugar insurgents," as they had been called, were joined by other highly respected houses, which had been trying the experiment of carrying the mountain to Mahomet, by refining in Mauritius and India, and did not find it pay. He fully believed the sincerity of these gentlemen, with some of whom he was well acquainted; and it would be absurd in him to say a word against interested motives. In such matters attack and defence were generally prompted by interested motives. The progress of the country was owing to various interests pressing forward, checking and being checked in turn. He was afraid that progress would be much retarded, did it depend upon public spirit alone. These gentlemen had among them a sort of newspaper, by means of which they instructed the people after the usual fashion of agitators, that is, by exaggerating the arguments on one side and suppressing those on the other; and it could not be denied that they had made many influential friends. Great were the advantages promised from a change of system. All profits, no losses! Sugar unknown to the present generation (though the scale was only ten years old) sparkling like Sinbad's valley of diamonds! But how was this saccharine paradise to be reached? Through the gate of a Parliamentary Committee. Give them but an opportunity of stating their case, and no reasonable man could fail to adopt their views. He need scarcely say the ordinary accessories of agitation were not wanting. They dressed up two lay figures, calling one free trade and the other protection, to frighten timid people, and the convenient poor man was pressed into the service, of whom agitators were so fond on platform and on paper, but whom they too often so utterly ignored everywhere else. The Committee was obtained by the aid of the hon. Gentleman the Member for the City of London. It might, therefore, be taken for granted, that its composition could not be challenged by those who adopted his views. The Chairman, the present Secretary for the Colonies, was supposed to be committed to the same opinions. After a long and patient inquiry, the Committee, by a large majority, adopted the Chairman's Report not against, but in favour of, an extension of the scale—in the main, in favour of the scale of this year's Budget—the adhesion of at least one Member of the Committee being caused by positive conversion from his former faith. The decision of the Committee was a blow to the agitators, who, however, soon consoled themselves by stigmatizing the majority, from chairman downwards, as people of intelligence much below par. They were sure the House of Commons would not adopt such an absurd decision. The appeal to the House of Commons came off last Session, under the auspices of his hon. Friend the Member for Sunderland. The result was certainly not triumphant; it was, however, easy then to abuse the House as a parcel of people who got there no one knew how; bad enough as individuals, still worse in their collective capacity. "There were, however, exceptions. The hon. Member for Rochdale would set the whole affair right, though it was scarcely worth troubling him about; scarcely *dignus vindice nodus*, so clear was the case." The hon. Member for Rochdale, however, thought otherwise, and then their opinion of his powers also changed; "he had overworked his brain, he was no longer quite himself. Was it not he who quarrelled with *The Times?*" A conference took place about this time on the duties between delegates from France, Belgium, Holland, and England. They concurred in a report in favour of classification; but his friends, the agitators, were very severe upon them as people with foregone conclusions, who merely wrote to order; "They were not worth thinking about. The Chancellor of the Exchequer would never perpetuate such enormities in his Budget." The right hon. Gentleman, he imagined, must have given some indication of his opinions, for it was hinted some time before Easter that his mind was too subtle to take a straightforward course, and his counsels "dark as Erebus." There was a last resource —the all-intelligent, all-powerful British public. There was to be a public meeting, but, in order to secure a proper expression of public opinion, only one side was to be heard. It was to be, in fact, a private meeting, disguised as a public one. It came off. His hon. Friend the Member for the City presided with his usual ability; but the British public intimated that they preferred hearing both sides, and eventually there was a scene much like that

which took place in the Rotunda in Dublin about the same time. The enemy were left in possession, and passed resolutions in favour of the Report of the Sugar Duties Committee. In spite of all this crushing weight of authority, the Member for the City would not give way, and he could not but admire the constancy with which his hon. Friend stood by a hopeless case.

"Victrix causa Diis placuit, sed victa Catoni."

And he deserved a better fate than that his able speech a few nights ago could induce only a forlorn hope of seventeen to follow him into the lobby.—What was the case of the other side? First, that the Customs' Officer could not judge accurately of the quality of the sugar from samples. They had had all this before the Committee—the dark day, the yellow fog, the bilious Custom House Officer; but it was proved that the trouble had been much exaggerated, the complaints few. The Committee could decide without proof, that if a bilious officer thought the sugar looked yellower than usual he would see the standard in the same light. Grocers, and specially refiners, settled the price they should give by tests similar to those by which the officer settled the duties, and if they could do so in a range of from 10s. to 15s., why should not he in a range of less than 5s.? The Dutch numbers, which were standards of value all over the world, were on the same principle, and more reliable than the samples which some hon. Members had, he understood, been carrying in their pockets ever since the Budget. But objection was taken to the principle of classification, even if it could be carried out in a perfect manner. The other side protested against taxing one pound of sugar more heavily than another. He (Mr. Cave) quite agreed with them. The late Mr. James Wilson had the same objection urged against his measure. Why do you have differential duties on sugar? His reply was, "We have not; we have only one; we tax sugar 13s. 4d. wherever we can get at it." So spirit was taxed at the same rate in cheap sherry and costly Lafitte. A person complaining that he paid a higher duty on his sugar simply complained that he had more sugar to pay for, like the man who on becoming rich grumbled that he had to pay more income tax. This was the principle of the sugar duties—to tax at one rate all the pure sugar which a refiner in the ordinary exercise of his trade could extract from that compound of various matters which was called the raw sugar of commerce. The duty would be strictly *ad valorem* if all sugar passed through refineries, but, practically, good grocery sugar—that is, sugar which came into consumption in a raw state, often fetched a higher price than the amount of pure sugar warranted, on account of its appearance—a kind of fancy price—and was, therefore, more lightly taxed according to its value; and sometimes a planter, in trying to improve his sugar, spoilt this appearance, and so lost the grocery market, which would have given him a better price for an intrinsically less valuable article. This accounted for some inequalities to which allusion had been made. It could not be too clearly stated that precisely the same considerations influenced the refiner in fixing the price he would give for sugar as the Customs' Officer in fixing the duty he would charge. Experience was a tolerably sure guide in both cases. The chemist might tell them that he got such and such percentage in his laboratory, just as he used to tell them after operating on a dozen ripe canes how much sugar they ought to grow to the acre. He remembered a story being told of an unhappy Jamaica planter going to air his grievances at the Colonial Office some years ago, when Mr. Hawes was Under Secretary, and while waiting in one of what the author of Philip Van Artevelde called the "sighing rooms," being asked by an enterprising clerk how much sugar he made to the acre? On replying that if the soil and weather were good and the negroes would work, he might get a ton all round, he was immediately met by the rejoinder, "Why, how can you expect to make both ends meet? our Under Secretary makes twice as much as that out of the worst soil upstairs!" The practical man knew that these calculations were worthless for ordinary life. If the refiner could get as much pure sugar profitably out of the lowest as out of the highest qualities, why did he give so much more for one than the other? A single illustration would suffice. In a Bristol refinery the other day, 12 lb. of actual mud was found in a cwt. of Brazilian sugar, which choked the filters, and caused much expense in reburning the animal charcoal. It was said, however, that the classification brought in this abominable stuff. "If it were not for this false system it would all be purified in the place of growth, and come in good sugar." [Mr. CRAWFORD: Hear, hear!] Well! but

Mr. Cave

would it? In order to test this, they must go to the place of growth. If they found there that the producer could only get as much for his good sugar as his bad, there would be at least a *prima facie* ground for this charge; but if they found, as they did, that the price of good sugar at the place of growth was always far higher than that of bad, what should induce the planter to make bad sugar except his incapacity, from various causes, to make better? Why should a man deliberately make what was worth 10*s*. when he could as easily, as they were told, make what was worth 20*s*.? Certainly not from fear of the duty, for he (Mr. Cave) was talking of prices at the place of growth. Possibly this was caused in some instances by want of means to make more than the rudest and simplest qualities; in others, by a conviction that the highest price was not always the most paying price, and that a colonial refinery, working only during crop, could not compete with one in England, working all the year round with every command of fuel, machinery, and reliable workmen. Just as it was cheaper for a West Indian planter to buy sawn planks from Canada than to cut down and saw up the splendid trees at his own door, so it was cheaper for him to send his sugar in a matrix of incongruous substances to be purified in London, Bristol, or elsewhere—very much as the Australian sent his copper ore to be smelted at Swansea. When Mr. Pitt said that the colonies should not make a nail, he pronounced an arbitrary edict for the benefit of the mother country; but, no doubt, it would not have been wise in the colonies to attempt it. When the hon. Member alluded to the decrease in the quantity of sugar equal to white clayed, as proved by the Returns, he forgot that the *standards* were altered in 1854, and that a great deal which formerly came in under that denomination now passed in the class below. This showed how dangerous it was for hon. Gentlemen to get up pamphlets, and then come down and make speeches on them. In truth, when they were told of the great increase in the lower qualities of sugar in this country, it was not that we had lost the better but that we had gained the others in addition. The greater part of the low sugars were foreign, and before 1846 excluded by a prohibitory duty. He did not defend the Act of 1846. He considered it a gross breach of national faith and national consistency, but as a free trade measure it was right; and as the duties on slave and free grown sugar gradually approximated under that Act, those from Brazil and Manilla, formerly excluded altogether, came in in great abundance, and the consumption rose from 17 lb. a head in 1841 to more than 36 lb. in the past year. He felt sure that the great demand consequent on this reduction of duty would cause fresh land to be brought into cultivation, and an increased supply of low sugar, which could be more quickly made to meet a sudden demand than high qualities. The hon. Member had talked of increased importation to France in a particular year, but that was caused by the failure of the beet root, and had nothing to do with duties. Certain fine qualities, no doubt, sought France rather than England, because the Government there chose to give them a high bounty in more ways than one. The result being that the net revenue derived from sugar as compared with the gross receipts was said to be as fifteen to forty-five, but when an uniform duty was recommended as likely to give the consumer a supply of good raw sugar, where was the proof of this in France? A Return, however, moved for this Session by the hon. Member for the City showed that last year the people of England got better sugar at a less price than the year before. It would be easy to show that if a scale was oppressive, because the lower qualities in each came so near the highest in the grade below, how much more oppressive, conversely, would be uniformity, which taxed at the same rate qualities differing in so much greater a degree. But he had already trespassed too long, and he would conclude by saying that, in his opinion, the most valuable of the Chancellor's proposals in respect of these duties was that which secured their permanence. Nothing was so injurious to a trade as that its operations should be unsettled for many weeks, year after year, by speculation on changes in the duties. For three years past the evil had been greatly aggravated by this mischievous agitation. He had heard that their fate at the next election depended on their course with reference to this question, but he hoped that hon. Members would disregard even this formidable threat. He trusted that that night this mere shadow of a shade might be laid for ever, and that it might be long before they had another debate on the sugar duties within those walls.

Mr. LINDSAY said, that the more he had examined this question the more he had come to the conclusion that the *ad valorem* or differential scale of duties—call it which you would—was not in the interest of the consumer. The room in the London Tavern in which the meeting was held, to which reference had been made, was packed with sugar refiners and their friends, and the advocates of an uniform duty were swamped by the Protectionists. He was much struck by hearing the same kind of arguments used on that occasion as had been used at former meetings in the same place concerning the Navigation Laws. The cry then was, "We shall not be able to compete with the foreigners, and ruin will fall upon us;" and now the sugar refiners said that an alteration in the sugar duties would ruin them. But many other traders who entertained similar fears had survived and prospered, and so, no doubt, would the sugar refiners. At any rate, the business of the House of Commons was to legislate not for the sugar refiners, but for the interests of the country at large. The Chancellor of the Exchequer said it was not fair to tax dirt; but surely it was expedient to discourage the importation of dirt under the disguise of sugar. The right hon. Gentleman said he aimed at taxing the saccharine matter. But if the principle upon which he went was sound his figures were wrong. Under the lower scale of duties there was 85 per cent of crystallizable saccharine matter which ought to be taxed, and 15 per cent of matter which ought not to be taxed. The 85 per cent paid 8s. 2d., while the 100 per cent paid 12s. 10d., being a difference of 35 per cent, while the difference in the percentage was only 15 per cent; consequently, a boon of 20 per cent was given to the sugar refiner. He had all along been an humble supporter of his right hon. Friend's policy, which was in the interest of the people, regardless of class; but his present proposition consulted the interests of the sugar refiners as against the consumer. He thought, however, that the right hon. Gentleman was taking a very arbitrary course in refusing to re-open the question. Moreover, practical difficulties would arise in the way of sampling sugar, which would be a great hindrance to trade. Consider the inconvenience which would arise supposing a 2,000 ton ship arrived carrying 16,000 bags of sugar, every ten bags of which would have to be sampled in order to see whether they came under the higher or lower scale of duty. At all events, he hoped the House would not allow their hands to be tied, but take care that the subject should be again discussed when the next budget was brought forward. He was quite sure the more the question was discussed, the more an *ad valorem* scale of duties would be seen to be a protection injurious to free commerce and disadvantageous to the consumer.

MR. CRAWFORD said, that the Chancellor of the Exchequer had stated in his Budget speech that the principle on which the duties on sugar should be levied in future was that stated in the Memorial of the Manchester Chamber of Commerce—according to the extractable saccharine value ; but this Bill involved an entire departure from that principle. So far from saccharine value only being taken, the third clause of the Bill enacted that " for facilitating the due assessment of the duties on sugar with reference to colour, grain, or saccharine matter, considered collectively," &c. He wished to know how the Chancellor of the Exchequer reconciled that clause with the principle laid down in the Manchester Memorial. Colour, grain, and saccharine matter collectively were now, it appeared, to be the criterion of value, and not saccharine matter only. Reference had been made to the meeting at the London Tavern. Now, having been one of the persons who convened it, he desired to say that that meeting was intended to be a meeting of those who were in favour of an equalization of the duty, and it was convened to consider a common course of action in discussing the question in that House. On arriving at the place, he found that the refiners had stolen a march upon them, occupied the room which others had hired, and conducted the business to their own entire satisfaction ; and they afterwards sent him the bill. The meeting, in short, was packed, and could afford no indication whatever of public feeling. It only showed the apprehensions which existed among the refining interest at the progress which had been made hostile to their views. The hon. Member for Shoreham (Mr. Cave) had referred to the small following he (Mr. Crawford) had the other evening into the lobby ; but if the division had taken place at an earlier hour he had the best reason to believe his following would have been much larger. He was also quite convinced that if the numbers were on one side the arguments were on

Mr. Lindsay

the other. He would remind the hon. Member for Shoreham that colour was not to be relied on—

" O formose puer, nimium ne crede colori."

He should support the hon. Member for Stockport (Mr. J. B. Smith)—if for no other reason, because of the great dissatisfaction that prevailed among the great body of consumers at the present scale of duties, which rendered it proper that this subject should be again brought under the notice of Parliament next Session, without leaving it to the arbitrary discretion of the Chancellor of the Exchequer to provide any opportunity for such consideration.

MR. CRUM-EWING said, he had failed to discover in the renewed discussion any fresh argument on either side ; he should, therefore, not reply to the speeches that had been made, but would confine himself to a statement of his own opinions. Being himself a large producer of sugar, and having upon his estates the most improved machinery, his own interests would rather lie in the direction of a single duty. As, however, he sat in that House to represent the interests of the community at large, he was bound to say that a uniform duty, without the privilege of refining in bond, would have the result of enhancing the cost of sugar to the consumer. The Committee of 1862 were strongly in favour of permitting refining in bond, but the Customs authorities declared there were extreme difficulties in the way of carrying out that plan. He was convinced, however, that if the Chancellor of the Exchequer would exercise a little pressure upon the Customs authorities those difficulties would be overcome. He believed the proposal of the Chancellor of the Exchequer to be a step in the right direction, and, therefore, he could not support the Amendment of the hon. Member for Stockport.

MR. MOFFATT said, that while he admitted that the plan now proposed was an improvement upon the original proposition, he still thought that the interests of the consumer had not been sufficiently considered. He would urge upon the Chancellor of the Exchequer the propriety of reverting to the old practice, and of allowing the sugar duties to be annually discussed and voted by that House. The effect of the graduated scale had been to revolutionize the sugar trade, and to constitute the refiners a very large and important body in this country, because the consumers had been compelled to purchase their sugars of the refiners, instead of from the original importers. The result of his experience, and of the evidence given before the Committee, was that the consumer had been placed at a disadvantage from the enhanced cost which was attributable to the operations of the refiners. He had heard from retailers, and the same point had been urged upon the Chancellor of the Exchequer, that there was another element in the sugar supplied by the refiners, for which the public had to pay largely, and that was water, which was present in proportions varying from 6 to 10 per cent. It was impossible that the present arrangement could be final, or that it would allay the agitation which prevailed ; and, therefore, he would press upon the right hon. Gentleman the expediency of making these duties the subject of annual discussion in Parliament. At present it was clear that the importation of the finer qualities of sugar was diminishing, while the introduction of low-class sugars was increasing ; and the consequence was, that our exportation of sugar was at a very low ebb. While France exported annually 70,000 tons, Holland 60,000 tons, and Belgium 24,000 tons, England with her vast mercantile marine, and extended commerce, only exported 7,000 tons. All these facts showed that the subject ought to be considered next Session, and he hoped the right hon. Gentleman would consent that an opportunity should be given for that purpose.

Mr. AYRTON said, it appeared as though the advocates for postponement thought they were the only depositories of the principles of free trade. He should be prepared to discuss the question, not in the interest of the refiners, but of the public. As far as his intercourse with those gentlemen enabled him to judge, he did not think that they adopted protection in the sense in which it was attributed to them. What they desired was the protection of a just and equal law against a system which would, in fact, give a large bounty to the foreign refiners against the refiners in this country. The principle which they maintained was, that the duty should be levied in such a manner as to make it the interest of no one to refine in one place more than in another. There was abundant evidence to show that it was not the interest, desire, or inclination of the persons who produced raw sugar to introduce it in a refined state. There were some few cultivators who had erected ma-

chinery for refining their sugar on the spot, and it was because of their failure that those persons were agitating for a new system which should be a protection and bounty to them ; but, in point of fact, ninety-nine out of every hundred knew that refining abroad could not be carried on with economy. It was not practically the case that there were persons in the East Indies who were desirous of producing refined sugar, but refining there was a distinct business as it was in London, and they wanted an uniform duty, because the raw material of the refiner would then be presented to them with an advantage which would be equivalent to a sum of 5s. or 10s. a cwt. The principle was the same elsewhere. The effect of the present system was to increase to the utmost the production of every description of sugar, and the effect of lowering the scale would be to bring into the market such coarse sugar as perhaps the African, who was incapable of the delicate operations of refining, might be able to produce from the cane. The hon. Member for the City of London had already brought forward the subject in an intelligible and reasonable form, and the opinion of the country had then been well expressed in that House, as well as at the meeting in the City, which was not packed as the hon. Gentleman described. With regard to the form in which this Amendment had been proposed, nothing could be more inconvenient than to keep any branch of industry in suspense. He had always felt it to be unjust to do so. But of all trades the sugar trade was the last in which they should desire to make an annual experiment. The production of sugar was not a matter of one year, but extended to three or four years, and it was not till the end of that period that the practical effect of any arrangement of the duties could be felt. It was of importance, therefore, if they would legislate on the matter, that some security should be given to those who traded on the basis of that arrangement that it should not be changed to-morrow. By creating an impression that the present system would be changed next year, they were levelling a blow at a large branch of industry, no matter where it might be carried on. His hon. Friend (Mr. J. B. Smith) had presented the question in a most impracticable form, and in one that would be most injurious to commerce. He hoped, therefore, the House would not accept the proposal submitted for its consideration. He was prepared at any time to discuss the question upon the principles of free trade, and he would undertake to satisfy any reasonable man who would accord to others, as well as to himself, some comprehension of the principles of free trade, that the duties as proposed by the right hon. Gentleman the Chancellor of the Exchequer, or any similar tariff, would give to every man the greatest possible latitude in his choice of operations, whether as a grower or refiner, consistently with the levying of those duties.

MR. BATHURST said, that he was a Member of the Committee on Sugar Duties; and as an allusion had been made to the corn duties, with reference to the sugar duties, he begged to remind the House that the question referred to the Committee was not the abolition of the sugar duty, but the question in what form it was most desirable to raise a certain amount of revenue. For himself, he was thoroughly convinced that the demands of justice and the benefit of the public required the maintenance in substance of a graduated scale of duties.

MR. BUCHANAN: I feel anxious to explain the reason why I followed the hon. Member for London when he led a "forlorn hope" into the lobby against the proposal of the Chancellor of the Exchequer for a graduated scale of sugar duties, and why I am again prepared to vote with the hon. Member for Stockport, in his proposal to restrict the new scale to one year only. The objection to the graduated scale of sugar duties which has the greatest weight, is that it has tended to the importation of one quality of sugar only, and that of the lowest and worst description. Whoever looks at the history of the sugar trade since the introduction of the graduated duties, cannot fail to perceive that, notwithstanding there are four different rates of duty on sugar, none, or at least small quantities only, have been imported of the two highest grades, and the importations have consisted of qualities not equal to brown clayed, and equal to brown clayed paying respectively 12s. 8d. and 13s. 10d. duty. The effect of this has been that all the sugar imported passed necessarily into the hands of the refiners, for the two lowest qualities are not fit for consumption as grocery sugars. A very small quantity of the 13s. 10d. kind, carefully prepared and coloured for the purpose, formed an exception to this rule, but of late years scarcely any importation of the 16s. and 18s. 4d. duty sugars has taken place. Besides this it is worth noticing that the quantity of the lowest

Mr. Ayrton

class at 12s. 8d. duty has been increasing from year to year till it has reached upwards of 80 per cent of the whole importation of the United Kingdom. It follows from this state of things, that the sugar importation of the country has been specially prepared and adapted for the refiner. Being the great, or rather the only buyers of sugar, the requirements of the refiner had to be met, as a matter of course they only wanted such sugars as had to be refined. The consequence has been that a regular toll has been levied in the interests of the refiner on all the consumption of the kingdom. What has been the amount of this toll it is not easy to say, but the refiners themselves in their anxiety to support a system of graduated duties have afforded certain data which enable us to form an estimate, if not exactly of their gain at least of the public loss. They have told us that sugars are imported containing only 50 per cent of crystallizable saccharine matter, the remaining 50 per cent being impurities of various kinds. If such sugars have been imported to any extent, it follows that the crushed and lump sugars prepared for the British market were manufactured under extraordinary difficulties. In the first place, such low sugars containing one half of foreign matter had to pay double freight and charges of every kind, as compared with pure sugars. Then there was the drainage on low half manufactured sugar always amounting to a large percentage of waste. But that was not all. If only one-half saccharine produce was obtained, duty being charged on the impure sugar as imported was equivalent to a charge of double duty. In addition to all this there was the refiner's profit to be allowed for, at whatever that may be estimated. But it is obvious there must be some mistake in such figures. No doubt the British consumer does pay dear enough for the weak crushed sugars which alone he uses, but he cannot be the victim of a system of manufacture so improvident and wasteful as this.

The solution of the difficulty is not far to seek. The refiner is master of the situation, because he is the only buyer in the sugar market, and the imports of sugar are carefully prepared to suit his wants and promote his profits. It has become the highest art of the sugar planter to hit the exact standard of colour and strength that will qualify for the lowest duty, and sugar of that description commands a certain and speedy sale. But it is a delusion to represent such sugars as containing only 50 per cent of saccharine. The truth is, that dry well made sugars, not subject to the drainage complained of, and containing from 80 to 90 per cent of pure sugar, are regularly imported at the lowest duty of the scale. Hence the difficulty of the refiner was by no means so great as he represented ; on the contrary, there is every reason to think that he carried on a very lucrative trade. It is no part of our business here to inquire into the secrets of trade, or to endeavour to estimate its profits; but there are two circumstances which afford at least a strong presumption that an unavowed and concealed profit was earned by the refiner. In the first place we know that there have been many new refineries built, as well as large additions made to old works during recent years ; and, in the second place, it is most suggestive of the cost which the British consumer must pay for his sugar, that not a pound of what has been prepared for his use can find a market elsewhere. Whatever may be the level of price in the sugar market of Europe, whatever may be the scarcity of cane or the failure of beetroot sugar, not one pound can be exported from our stocks of crushed sugars. It is not my wish to say a single word against a class so respectable as the British sugar refiners, nor do I make any charge against them either of one kind or another. My remarks are solely directed in the interests of the consumer and of the public revenue. There are various aspects of this argument which it is not necessary to enlarge upon, as the present debate must be regarded rather as a protest against an unsound principle than a serious attempt to overthrow it. But I cannot help noticing one remarkable effect of the late duties, and which will equally follow under the new scale, and that is, that the practical result in no way corresponds with the professed objects of its advocates. The main burden of the argument for a uniform duty so strongly put by the Chancellor of the Exchequer consisted in this, that varying qualities of sugar should be charged with varying duties, and that it is contrary to reason and sound policy to charge the same duty on khaur and jaggery as on the produce of the vacuum pan. We deprecate, said the right hon. Gentleman and his supporters, a uniform duty as contrary to common sense, as neither more nor less than a *reductio ad absurdum* as against one rate. But

would it be believed that the legislation embraced in the present Bill does in effect produce that very result ? One duty, and one duty only is levied at the Custom House, because only one kind of sugar is imported. We have heard much in late discussions about a "miscarriage of justice ; " this appears to be a case of a "miscarriage of legislation." The law not only does not accomplish what it proposes, but it accomplishes exactly the reverse. If a gradation of duties has any meaning at all, it means that sugar of various qualities should be imported, and that the consumer should have variety and assortment from which to choose. But the very opposite is the fact. Only one kind of sugar is imported, and only one duty levied. What, then, becomes of the arguments about adaptation of the scale to every quality of sugar, and the advantage of importing produce of all kinds and from all quarters ? The truth is, that the professed object of the graduated scale is an utter failure. One quality of sugar, and that the worst quality, has been imported, and will continue to be imported so long as the principle of the present Bill is adhered to. I therefore have no hesitation in voting with my hon. Friend the Member for Stockport.

THE CHANCELLOR OF THE EXCHEQUER said, there were two questions before the House—the one the merits of a classified as against an uniform scale of duties ; and the other, a proposal that the classified scale as now submitted should only continue for a year. He hailed with satisfaction the admission which had been freely made in the course of the debate by those who advocated an uniform duty— namely, that the scale of duties now proposed was an improvement upon the existing one. In that admission lay the answer to some part at least of the objections raised to a classified system of duties. It had been said by the hon. Member who spoke last (Mr. Buchanan) and by others, that the effect of the old scale was to drive out the superior kinds of raw sugar ; but that might be not because it was simply a classified scale—that we had yet to learn— but rather because it was a classified scale which might not be adapted to the several elements of the taxable material. The hon. Member who spoke last stated that the present scale favoured the introduction of only two descriptions of sugars—namely, those "equal to brown clayed " and those "not equal to brown clayed," and that it repelled from this country both sugars above and sugars below those classes. But the hon. Member also complained of the proposed multiplication of the number of steps in the scale, although one of the new steps was expressly intended to meet his objection that only two descriptions of sugar were encouraged, and to let in a description which was now shut out. As to the difficulties which were said to exist in carrying out the principle of a classified duty, those difficulties lay within very narrow limits, and were not such as rendered necessary any departure from the principle. The judgment of the House upon the main question should not depend upon this. His hon. Friend the Member for Stockport (Mr. J. B. Smith) had referred to the case of the papermakers, and asked how the conduct of the Government towards them could be justified. But he did justify it, and had no difficulty in doing so. What they had done in the case of the papermakers was this—they had declined to recognize foreign legislation as the basis of differences in English law. But if he had acted on the case set up by his hon. Friend he should have great difficulty in mitigating the case of the papermakers, because it would be in effect giving a bounty to the sugar refiners of one country over those of another. It was said that this was the case of the refiners against the people of England, and that the refiners declared their inability to compete with the foreigner; and then it was added that this complaint was analogous to other complaints made by interests which desired protection. Now, it was not true that the refiners had, as alleged, cried out for protection. The refiners said that a penalty was imposed upon them, as compared with the foreign refiners, by the limited margin allowed between refined and unrefined sugar. He did not admit this to be a well founded complaint, for he believed the scale to be a just scale. What the English refiners asked for, however, was not protection, but equality, and equality alone. The hon. Member for Huddersfield (Mr. Leatham), in seconding the Amendment, said, that the manufactured article should always be struck by a higher duty than the raw material. But sugar was always a manufactured article—nobody imported sugar canes—it was an article which was better or worse according to the amount of labour and capital bestowed upon it. Hon. Gentlemen admitted that no inducement should be given to parties to apply their

labour and capital in one country rather than in another, and to carry on the process of sugar refining upon the banks of the Ganges rather than upon the banks of the Thames. If, therefore, it paid importers to bring "dirty" sugar to be refined here on account of the superior machinery or the more abundant capital or the more highly skilled labour which were available in this country, Parliament had nothing to do with this result, unless it could be shown that Parliament offered inducements to importers to bring "dirt" to this country. What was wished for, apparently, was that Parliament should say to the English sugar refiners, "If you carry on your trade at all, you shall pay upon the refined sugar very much more than you would pay if you were carrying on this process upon the banks of the Ganges." The effect of a uniform duty had been well demonstrated by a gentleman (Mr. Reed) who had been a sugar refiner in this country, but who, seeing the advantage which a duty so levied afforded to the Indian refiner, transferred his operations to Calcutta. He saw that the Indian refiner could land sugar in England for 18s. 5d., for which the British refiner had to pay 25s. 3d.—exactly equivalent to a tax upon the British refiner of 6s. 10d. from which the Indian refiner was exempt. Others saw this, too, and began to open establishments at Calcutta; but unfortunately (said Mr. Reed) the Chancellor of the Exchequer made the same discovery, and the introduction of a system of the classified rates reduced the Indian refiners to an equality with those of England. The object of the Government was that the British refiner should be under no inducement whatever to fix himself abroad rather than in England, or in England rather than abroad. His hon. Friend (Mr. Leatham) had quoted him as having said that the duty ought to be on the extractable saccharine matter. If his hon. Friend had in view the main principle which ought to govern the duty, he did not deny that to be his opinion. Colour and grain were elements which must be taken into account; but the extractable saccharine matter was the main consideration on which the scale had been framed; and he contended that the nearest approximation to equality which the case admitted of was that at which the Government had arrived in the proposition now before the House. He could assure his hon. Friend that if they had departed from the principle of free trade in this

The Chancellor of the Exchequer

matter, their apostacy had not been a wilful apostacy; but it did appear to him that the principle of free trade was best exemplified and best applied by endeavouring to frame the law in such a manner as would remove all hope from all parties of adventitious advantages which capital and industry did not fairly place at their disposal. This question was one of great importance, and the decision at which the House had arrived on it was, on the whole, a very deliberate one. It had been arrived at after very full and deliberate discussion there, and, what was more, after most ample discussion in Committees of the House and out of doors, by pamphlets, and by the press in every shape; and that being so, it was best for all parties that a sufficient time should be allowed for the purpose of testing the merits of the newly-adopted measure. He did not say that they were for ever to shut their door against all improvement in legislation; but this he did say, that no more unwise course could be suggested than that Parliament, after having the subject before it for many years, and having arrived at a decision with, he might say, solemnity, but certainly with a knowledge of all the elements involved in the matter, should limit the operation of the new scheme to a period within which it was utterly impossible there could be any satisfactory experience. The fact that they could not have that experience in a year was a strong reason for allowing this question to be put to rest till those who took an interest in the question should have a better opportunity of urging their views by the light of the experience which might be accumulated in the interval. Since the year 1841 there had been numerous changes, and from that time the sugar duties had had nothing but a precarious existence. From his personal knowledge, he could say that throughout the tenure of their official existence the Government of Sir Robert Peel were anxious to make a permanent arrangement of the sugar duties, if it had been in their power to do so; and the Government of Lord John Russell, which succeeded to Sir Robert Peel's, attempted such an arrangement. Confusion, uncertainty, loss—heavy loss to the revenue, vexation, and bewilderment to producers abroad, partial paralysis pervading every ramification of one of the most important branches of our commerce, would be the result of adopting the Amendment of the hon. Member. Seeing the ability, energy, and zeal with which the hon. Member's side of the question was supported, they might safely conclude that the means would not be wanting for bringing it forward should the expectations of the Government be disappointed. He thought that, in the interests of those concerned in the sugar trade, and of the public generally, the House should decline to adopt the Amendment.

MR. J. B. SMITH rising to reply—

MR. SPEAKER said, that the hon. Member's proposition having been introduced as an Amendment he was not entitled to a reply.

Question put, "That those words be there added."

The House *divided* :—Ayes 14; Noes 97 : Majority 83.

AYES.

Barnes, T.	Moffatt, G.
Buchanan, W.	Pease, H.
Cobbett, J. M.	Potter, E.
Crawford, R. W.	White, J.
Denman, hon. G	Williams, W.
Hay, Sir J. C. D.	
Hubbard, J. G.	
Lawson, W.	TELLERS.
Lindsay, W. S.	Smith, J. B.
	Leatham, E. A.

NOES.

Ayrton, A. S.	Gibson, rt. hon. T. M.
Baillie, H. J.	Gilpin, C.
Barttelot, Colonel	Gladstone, rt. hon. W.
Bass, M. T.	Goldsmid, Sir F. H.
Bathurst, A. A.	Goschen, G. J.
Baxter, W. E.	Greaves, E.
Beecroft, G. S.	Gurney, J. H.
Berkeley, hon. C. P. F.	Hadfield, G.
Black, A.	Hartington, Marquess of
Blake, J.	Headlam, rt. hn. T. E.
Bridges, Sir B. W.	Henderson, J.
Briscoe, J. I.	Hennessy, J. P.
Butler, C. S.	Hornby, W. H.
Caird, J.	Hotham, Lord
Cardwell, rt. hon. E.	Howes, E.
Cave, S.	Hutt, rt. hon. W.
Chapman, J.	Jones, D.
Childers, H. C. E.	Kinglake, J. A.
Clifton, Sir R. J.	Kingscote, Colonel
Collier, Sir R. P.	Langton, W. H. G.
Cox, W.	Lee, W.
Dalglish, R.	Lyall, G.
Dawson, R. P.	Martin, P. W.
Dent, J. D.	Martin, J.
Disraeli, rt. hon. B.	Massey, W. N.
Duff, R. W.	Mills, J. R.
Dunbar, Sir W.	Moncreiff, rt. hon. J.
Dunlop, A. M.	Morris, D.
Dunne, Colonel	Morrison, W.
Ewart, J. C.	Norris, J. T.
Ewing, H. E. Crum-	O'Conor Don, The
Farquhar, Sir M.	O'Loghlen, Sir C. M.
Fenwick, E. M.	O'Reilly, M. W.
Fleming, T. W.	Padmore, R.
Floyer, J.	Paget, Lord C.
Foljambe, F. J. S.	Pakington, rt. hn. Sir J.

Parker, Major W.
Peel, rt. hon. Sir R.
Peto, Sir S. M.
Price, R. G.
Pugh, D.
Ridley, Sir M. W.
Robertson, H.
Selwyn, C. J.
Smith, A.
Smith, Sir F.
Somerset, Colonel
Somes, J.
Stansfeld, J.
Surtees, H. E.
Talbot, hon. W. C.

Taylor, P. A.
Trefusis, hon. C. H. R.
Turner, J. A.
Villiers, rt. hon. C. P.
Walcott, Admiral
Walsh, Sir J.
Whitbread, S.
White, hon. L.
Winnington, Sir T. E.
Wood, rt. hon. Sir C.

TELLERS.

Brand, hon. H. B. W.
Knatchbull-Hugessen, E.

THE CHANCELLOR OF THE EXCHE-QUER moved an Amendment, reducing the stamp duty upon powers of attorney given by seamen for the receipt of their wages from 20s. to 1s.

MR. HENNESSY said, when the Bill was in Committee he expressed the opinion that the duty was rather high, and urged its reduction. He was glad that the Chancellor of the Exchequer had knocked off 19s., and cordially accepted the Amendment.

Amendment *agreed to.*

THE CHANCELLOR OF THE EXCHE-QUER moved, that in that part of the Bill which regulates the duty on perpetual curacies, the words, "shall not exceed £100," should be inserted instead of the words "shall not amount to £100." The alteration was necessary in consequence of the Ecclesiastical Commissioners having adopted the system of raising the perpetual curacies to £300 a year, which, without this alteration, would be subject to a heavy duty.

Amendment *agreed to.*

Other Amendments made.

Bill to be read 3° *To-morrow.*

SUPPLY.

Order for Committee read.

Motion made, and Question proposed, "That Mr. Speaker do now leave the Chair."

RECREATION GROUND AT CHIGWELL.

QUESTION.

MR. COX said, that last year a Bill was introduced for the inclosure of a portion of Chigwell parish, and on looking into the matter it was found that it proposed to hand over to the Inclosure Commissioners some 600 or 700 acres of land, which, from time immemorial, had been used by the public, forming part of Hainault Forest. Petitions were presented against the Bill, and it was referred to a Select Committee, which added to it a clause, providing that fifty acres of ground should be set apart for public recreation. Relying on this clause, the public took very little further trouble in the matter; but some time afterwards it was found that the assistant valuer had set out fifty acres, of which two-thirds were swamp and the other third gravel. It was clear that if this project were sanctioned, the intention of the clause added by the Select Committee would be nullified. The Inclosure Commissioners had very properly at first refused their sanction to it; but within the last few weeks it had been rumoured that the sanction they had originally refused to the plan had now been given to it. In the same parish there had been, from time immemorial, opposite a house called the May Pole, very much frequented by the public, a large piece of green used for cricket and other purposes of recreation. He was told that the Commissioners had determined to enclose this green. He could not say whether it was a Village Green under the Act of Parliament; but, certainly, it had been used from time immemorial for purposes of recreation. He wished, therefore, to ask the Secretary to the Treasury, Whether it is now the intention of the Inclosure Commissioners to set out the fifty acres of Recreation Ground, under the Inclosure Act of last Session, for the parish of Chigwell, Essex, at the spot which they, in November, 1862 (in their Order to the Valuer), disapproved of, such spot being wet and swampy; and whether the Village Green, opposite the May Pole at Chigwell Row, is to be preserved (in accordance with the fifteenth section of the General Inclosure Act of 1845), as it has heretofore, from time immemorial, been a place for the recreation and enjoyment of the people?

MR. PEEL said, it was quite true that the provisional orders of the Inclosure Commissioners were sanctioned by Act of Parliament, with the Amendment that fifty acres of ground should be set apart in the parish for the purpose of public recreation. After the Act passed a valuer was appointed in the usual manner at a public meeting in the parish, and instructions were there drawn up for him. The Act of Parliament directed that the fifty acres should be at or near a spot marked A on the plans, and the instructions drawn up at the meeting directed the valuer to set them out within four given spots. The Inclosure Commissioners disallowed the instructions, not on the ground that the area was swampy, but because they considered that at that particular stage of the proceedings it was advisable that the discretion of the valuer should not be tied up, and that, under the circumstances, he should view the ground and form his own opinion. Since the valuer was appointed—a gentleman of great experience as a land surveyor—he had proceeded under the general supervision of the Inclosure Commissioners, and he was informed that his report was likely to be confirmed within the present year. On behalf of the Commissioners, however, he could assure the hon. Gentleman that the intentions of the Act of Parliament would not be nullified, and that the fifty acres would be of such a character as was contemplated when the clause was passed. Power was given to drain and level any land that might be set apart for the public; and if there were, as the hon. Gentleman suggested, any gravel pits within the area set out, care would be taken to fill them up, and to make the ground in every way available for the purpose of recreation. With regard to the second question, he was informed that the Assistant Commissioner had reported that there was no Village Green in the neighbourhood, nor had there been any claim of the sort made.

Motion *agreed to.*

SUPPLY—NAVY ESTIMATES.

SUPPLY *considered* in Committee.

(In the Committee.)

Motion made, and Question proposed,

"That a sum, not exceeding £449,298, be granted to Her Majesty, to defray the Charge of New Works, Improvements, and Repairs in the Naval Establishments, which will come in course of payment during the year ending on the 31st day of March, 1865."

MR. WYKEHAM MARTIN rose, pursuant to notice, to call attention to the manufacture of ropes by machinery in Her Majesty's dockyards. He had been told that neither in efficacy nor in economy was the system of rope making by machinery equal to the old hand-spun manufacture. He had been informed that the machine process of manufacture was precisely the same as that by which an old coat was turned into a new one in some of the cloth-making towns of Yorkshire. If hon. Members did not understand the process, he might be allowed to state that it consisted in putting the coat into a machine called a "devil," by means of which a material called "shoddy" was produced, which, although it bore the appearance of good cloth, yet had its fibre so damaged by the machinery that it was almost worthless, and was ready to drop to pieces after a few days' wear. Now, precisely the same effect was, he believed, produced on the hemp by the spinning machine in the manufacture of ropes, which were not at all equal in strength to those which were spun by hand. In support of that statement, he might observe that, in twenty-two trials which had taken place in Her Majesty's dockyards, while the machine-spun ropes broke at a strain of 8½ tons, it required a strain of 9½ to break the hand-spun. But, independent of that fact, there was in the machine-spun ropes the greatest irregularity in the number of strands in the same class of rope; in one sample it was stated that instead of 300 there were only 291, and in another 307 instead of 300. They were also open to objection on the score of economy, it being proved by experiments that there was in their case a loss of about 6½ per cent, which would amount to about £80,000 on the ropes used in our dockyards supposing Russian hemp to be at the price which it actually had reached, of £80 a ton. He might add that our most eminent shipowners — such, for example, as his hon. Friend the Member for Sunderland (Mr. Lindsay) and the Messrs. Green —would not use the machine-spun ropes; while the Secretary for India, on behalf of the Indian Government, declined to accept them after trial, notwithstanding that the noble Lord the Secretary for the Admiralty, his Colleague, employed them for the British navy. He was not, therefore, to be told that he was behind the age when he only proposed for the Government what the great private shipbuilders found good enough for themselves. The hon. Gentleman concluded by moving that the Vote should be reduced by £1,549, the amount asked for for the provision of additional accommodation for spinning machinery at Chatham.

Motion made, and Question proposed, "That the item of £1,549 be omitted from the proposed Vote."—(*Mr. Wykeham Martin.*)

MR. LINDSAY said, it was not strictly correct to say he never used any machine made rope. It was true he had a manufactory of hand-spun rope on the banks of the Thames; but that was a very small establishment, producing not more than seventy or eighty tons in the year. Rope was largely made by machinery; yarns were still spun by hand, but to a large extent yarns also were spun by machinery. Yarns spun by machinery, he believed, were not so strong, but were more regular than those spun by hand. He could not support the Motion of his hon. Friend, because he thought the Government were only following the example of large manufacturers, who found it much more economical to spin yarn for ropes by machinery than by hand.

Mr. CHILDERS said, that the question was not one of spinning ropes by machinery, but of spinning yarn by machinery. In 1857 the House voted a sum sufficient for establishing machinery at Chatham for spinning yarn of certain descriptions, and the result had been that not only had the cost of the machinery been paid for, but £4,000 had been saved to the country besides. Now the Government proposed to purchase new machines for £9,350; and it was demonstrable that in a very few years not only would the cost of the machines be repaid, but a saving to the country of £5,000 a year would be effected. The facts as to the expense, he thought, were conclusive; but other topics had been touched upon by his hon. Friend. He said that the hemp was bruised and crushed by the process. He hardly thought his hon. Friend could have seen the process. He (Mr. Childers) had seen it, and he could assure him that there was no bruising or crushing of any kind. It was true that the loss in weight was greater when yarn is machine-spun. The loss on hand-spun yarn was 2 per cent, and on machine-spun yarn 5 per cent, but the loss was an advantage, as it tended to the strength of the rope. Very careful experiments had been instituted to ascertain the relative strength of the two kinds of rope. At Woolwich the result of a large number of trials was 5 per cent in favour of rope made by machine-spun yarn, and at Devonport and Chatham the result was nearly the same. Then came the question of durability. Among other experiments this was tested on board the *Ariadne.* All the rope on the starboard side was made of machine-spun yarn, and all on the larboard of hand-spun yarn, and the result was that the rope made of

Mr. *Lindsay*

machine-spun yarn was in every respect equal, and, in some, superior in durability to that made of the latter. On the whole, it appeared that the general result of experiments was in favour of rope manufactured from machine-spun yarn; and he might say as regarded the opinion of the trade, that two of the largest steamship companies in this country were exclusively using rope of that description.

Mr. WYKEHAM MARTIN said, he held in his hand the result of fifty experiments, which showed that machine-spun rope was very inferior to hand-spun rope. The statement of the hon. Gentleman had, therefore, taken him by surprise. He would withdraw his Amendment.

Motion, by leave, *withdrawn.*

Original Question again proposed.

Mr. H. ROBERTSON said, he thought it desirable that some explanation should be given as to the item of £7,500 for "Preparations for Extending Portsmouth Dockyard." It was proposed to take 300 acres altogether for this extension, but it appeared that this item only extended to 100 acres with the possible future extension to 300 acres. Experience suggested that this item would commit us to operations of a much larger nature, and might, perhaps, prove only an instalment of £750,000. He doubted the wisdom of the Admiralty design, and thought that the employment of a competent engineer to report on the design and nature of the works would, in the end, turn out an economical expenditure.

Lord CLARENCE PAGET said, that there were two distinct proposals for extending the dockyard accommodation at Portsmouth—one the reclaiming a part of the harbour for the purpose of making basins and docks, and the other by adapting for Government purposes a large tract of waste land that was called the Pest House Fields, lately the property of the War Department, but which had been given up to the Admiralty. That land would require walling round, the construction of tramways, and preparations for the stacking of timber, and the sum of £7,500 asked for in these Estimates was mainly required for those purposes, though a small portion of it would be required for buying the plant for the purposes of what might be called the great sea extension of the dockyard; but as that was now under the consideration of a Committee upstairs, he need not then trouble the Committee with going into it. The proposition of the hon. Gentleman, that before they engaged in a work of that magnitude the Admiralty would consult some eminent engineers, was quite reasonable ; and he could assure the Committee that such advice would be taken.

MR. LINDSAY asked whether the £7,500 would complete the works referred to, and whether they would be distinct and complete in themselves, or whether it was only a part and parcel of a great plan to which the House had not yet given its sanction ?

LORD CLARENCE PAGET said, it was principally a Vote for what was required for the preparation of the Peat House Fields.

SIR FREDERIC SMITH said, that last year a sum of £8,000 was taken for the Naval Barracks at Portsmouth, but only £10 had been expended. Now the Admiralty asked for an additional £5,000. How much of this sum was intended to be spent ?

LORD CLARENCE PAGET said, the scheme of the Naval Barracks would depend very much upon the scheme now before the Committee upstairs, for if they extended the docks and basins in a northerly direction from the dockyard, it would be desirable to place the barracks in some place more contiguous to them.

COLONEL BARTTELOT rose to call attention to the situation of the new Marine Artillery barracks at Eastney. It was necessary that particular attention should be paid to them in connection with the enormous sums laid out at Portsmouth for the fortifications there, and he regretted that the noble Lord at the head of the Government, whom he held responsible for that expenditure, was not in his place in the House. The barracks at Eastney were erected in the very eye of the Channel, in going into Portsmouth Harbour, so that any ship attacking Portsmouth must fire into them. He feared there had been no harmony or concerted action between the Admiralty and the Defence Committee in carrying out those works. An enormous sum had been voted for fortifications at Portsmouth, and they had been asked to vote a large sum of money for the construction of barracks in a most untenable position. No doubt it might be said this was the only position where the Marine Artillery could practise the large guns ; and that might or might not be true ; but

all he could say was that a far better site might have been obtained for them inland, and where the troops might have been better protected. These barracks were intended to contain the wives and children of soldiers as well as the soldiers themselves belonging to the Marine Artillery, and that being so, Her Majesty's Government ought to have selected some safe and proper place whereon they could have erected these barracks, instead of where they had been erected, close to the shore and between two small forts that had been erected on the recommendation of the Defence Commissioners. Fort Cumberland, where the Marine Artillery now are, is bomb proof ; but these barracks were three stories high and were not bomb proof, and were not to be defended against shot and shell for a quarter of an hour ; and yet these barracks were intended to accommodate the Marine Artillery and their wives and children. Nothing could justify the erection of barracks in such a position. Then they had allowed public-houses and other dwellings to be built close round the barracks, and those buildings would perfectly command the barracks. The noble Lord at the head of the Government had made himself responsible for the fortifications at Portsmouth, and it was his bounden duty to see that all the works for the defence of the port were in harmony and concert with each other.

LORD CLARENCE PAGET said, that the barracks were placed on the best site that the Government could procure for the purpose which they had in view. One weighty reason which had influenced the site was, that the barracks were close to the sea and had a very good range for heavy guns. It was necessary that the young Marine artillerymen, who were constantly practising at this range, should reside in the neighbourhood of their guns. Another reason which influenced the site was, that the Admiralty obtained the ground at very little expense. The barracks were close to Fort Cumberland, and formed a chain of defence from that fort to Southsea Castle, so as to occupy the whole of the beach. The barracks had a very strong breast-work in front, and all round the rear was a crenellated wall, so that they were capable of a very respectable defence. It would not be occupied by any very great number of men in time of war, as Marine artillerymen generally embarked at such times for naval service. The barracks were, in fact, to be considered

principally as a place for the education
of young recruits in time of peace. They
were certainly exposed at present, but,
when the Spithead forts were completed,
the Admiralty trusted that Spithead would
be pretty well defended, and that the works
within Spithead would be comparatively
safe. No doubt it was very desirable to
find a safe place for the women and children; but they must submit to the fate
of their husbands and fathers. Then the
hon. and gallant Gentleman said these barracks were surrounded by public-houses.
Unfortunately that was true, but all our
barracks were equally surrounded by public-houses. Build them where they might,
there was no escaping the evil. He wished
they could put a stop to it.

SIR FREDERIC SMITH expected to
hear a better defence of the Vote than had
been made by the noble Lord. In the
whole course of his military experience, he
had never found a barrack worse situated.
It was said it was a link in the defence;
but it was a link of sand. A heavy weight
striking that barrack would carry all before
it. It could not stand for a minute before
the broadside of a man-of-war, so that it
could not be called a defence. His hon.
and gallant Friend stated that there could
have been no communication between the
Admiralty and the War Department on the
subject. But if that were so, and if there
had been no consultation with the Defence
Commission, it was a most flagrant instance of neglect. If considered as a defensive work, it was one of a most discreditable character; and if it was not a
defensive work, then it was placed in the
wrong position, and was a waste of public
money. He believed the total amount was
to be £167,801. But what he most found
fault with was that those who had devised
this plan had placed the officers under
a bomb-proof building [Lord CLARENCE
PAGET: That is only partly the case],
while the troops were put into that pack-
of-cards house.

MR. WHITBREAD thought the fort
on the Horse Shoe Sand had been left
out of sight by the gallant Officer. Did
any officer suppose it would be an agreeable position for any vessel to lie near that
fort for the purpose of shelling the barracks? The barracks were built, in the
first place, because the site was an eligible
one; and secondly, because it would afford
great facilities for practice in gunnery.
The gallant Officer was mistaken in supposing that the Admiralty had not com-

Lord Clarence Paget

municated with the authorities at the War
Office.

LORD CLARENCE PAGET said, the
hon. and gallant Officer ought to have
known better than to talk of the officers
being placed in a bomb-proof building while
the men were exposed in the barracks. No
doubt, some officers would reside with
their men in the bomb-proof; but there
was the proper arrangement to leave the
full complement of officers with the men in
the barracks.

SIR FREDERIC SMITH said, he went
upon the Estimate.

CAPTAIN JERVIS asked, what was the
good of having an unprotected barrack
between the two forts? The noble Lord
said they had got merely recruits, women,
and children there. [Lord CLARENCE PAGET
explained that what he meant was that, in
time of war, they would probably have
but a small number of Marine Artillery
there. They would go on shipboard.]
And leave their wives and children behind.
The great object should be to have the
barracks out of range of shot.

COLONEL NORTH would ask who were
to defend the forts upon which they were
spending millions of money? The noble
Lord the other night told them that these
forts would be defended by the Volunteers
and the militia. Why the Volunteers were
never intended to man the forts except
when the country was invaded. Now it
would seem that the women and children
were to be left to defend them. He could
see no use in spending money on these
forts if they were not to be properly defended.

LORD CLARENCE PAGET said, the
barracks were not for the Artillery, but
for the Marine Artillery in time of peace.
If there was a war to-morrow the probability would be that nearly every able-
bodied man in the Marine Artillery would
be on shipboard.

COLONEL DICKSON asked whether
they were to understand that they were to
lay out these enormous sums on barracks
as to which in time of war, when the
Marine Artillery were on shipboard, it did
not matter a jot whether they were to be
blown in pieces or not.

CAPTAIN JERVIS wanted to know how
much money had been spent on those barracks, and how much on the officers' quarters?

LORD CLARENCE PAGET replied,
that the total estimate for the work was
£167,000, the amount already voted was

£67,000, and the gross sum already expended on it was £56,000. The sum taken for the present year was £30,000, and the further estimate for completing the work was £73,000. He could not at the present moment say what were the particular sums out of that amount to be expended on the officers' quarters and on Fort Cumberland.

COLONEL BARTTELOT inquired, in the event of the Marine Artillery now in Fort Cumberland going into ships, what officers and men would then garrison that fort?

LORD CLARENCE PAGET said, that in the event of such an improbable matter as the bombardment of Spithead, Fort Cumberland would probably be garrisoned, in the absence of the Marine Artillery, by the Militia or Volunteers.

In reply to Sir FREDERIC SMITH,

MR. CHILDERS said, that it would be impossible to stop the works now, which were completed to a considerable extent, without the loss of all the money expended upon them under the sanction of the House during the last three years.

LORD CLAUD HAMILTON wished to know whether, supposing it to be inexpedient to alter the plan of the officers' and men's quarters, as far as it had gone, there was not yet time to locate the women's and children's quarters in a place not so very dangerous?

MR. CHILDERS presumed that the noble Lord would not propose that the women and children should be placed in a different spot from the place where their husbands and fathers were located.

COLONEL BARTTELOT said, that he should have divided the Committee against the whole Vote if he had seen the barracks sooner. The officers' quarters were unroofed.

SIR FREDERIC SMITH noticed that the former Estimate for constructing additional barrack accommodation at Plymouth was £76,000, and in the present Estimates the sum of £80,000 was put down for their further extension and completion. He thought that some explanation was necessary on this point. It was deceiving the House to bring forward a supplementary Estimate larger than the one originally proposed.

LORD CLARENCE PAGET said, that every day improvements were being made in the construction of barracks for the army, navy, and Marines, by means of additional ventilation and other accommoda-tion for the health and comfort of the men. Again, the Marines had been increased from 15,000 to 18,000 men, and, consequently, additional barrack accommodation was required for them. At Chatham, for instance, the barracks had been increased, and in order to furnish additional barrack accommodation it was sometimes necessary to throw down existing buildings.

SIR FREDERIC SMITH thought the noble Lord's explanation satisfactory.

LORD CLARENCE PAGET said, he now desired to call the attention of the Committee to a matter of considerable importance—the item for deepening the north-west basin and constructing a first-class dock at Malta. The original sum put in the Estimates for this purpose was £15,900; and he had now to move that that item be reduced by the sum of £5,000. It was right that he should state the grounds on which the Government had decided to make that reduction. The question was rather complicated, but a brief statement would explain the reasons of an agreement which the Admiralty had come to with the Maltese Government, and in which he was confident the Committee would concur. So far back as 1858 it became evident that the harbour used for Her Majesty's ships was entirely insufficient, on account of their increased size, especially as the trade of Malta had also augmented; and consequently proposals were made that a certain portion of the great harbour at Valetta, called the French Creek, should be appropriated to ships of the navy on certain conditions. The arrangement was that before Her Majesty's Government took possession of the French Creek, they should, as a preliminary condition, construct at the Marsa a harbour for merchant vessels, with quays and a basin. As originally proposed, the basin was to have had a depth of only twelve feet, and would consequently have been utterly useless for vessels of war. In the Resolution passed by the Council of Government of Malta on the 29th of May, 1859, it was distinctly laid down that—

"The merchant shipping shall continue in the possession of the creek, called the 'French Creek,' until all the works intended to be performed at the Marsa and in the said extensions shall have been completed."

There was a very clear understanding with the Maltese Government on that point, and up to the present time they had shown themselves desirous of acting in a spirit of the utmost good faith towards the Home

Government, who, on their part, were bound to take care that not a shadow of suspicion should rest on the integrity of their conduct in the matter. During the progress of the works the engineers suggested that it would be advantageous to deepen the basin to thirty feet instead of twelve feet, so as to permit vessels of war to make use of it, and to excavate the stone in that part of the harbour where it was supposed to be of a superior quality, employing the stone for the walls of the basin, and converting the quarry into a dock. Upon this the Maltese Government, after communicating with the Home Government, agreed to the following Resolution:—

"Resolved,—That the head of the Government of Malta be authorized and empowered to enter with the Imperial Government into an agreement to the following effect—namely, 'That if the Imperial Government will, at the charge of the Imperial Treasury, cause a repairing or graving dock capable of receiving a ship of the largest class in Her Majesty's navy to be formed in the proximity of the north-western basin referred to in the Resolution passed by this Council on the 25th of May, 1859, and to be furnished with the machinery and other appendages required to render such dock fit for use; and if, moreover, the said Imperial Government will agree to permit merchant vessels, at moderate charges, to be repaired in such dock, when the use of it may not be required for Her Majesty's ships, then the Government of Malta will consent that the work of deepening the said north-western basin to such extent, beyond the twelve feet established in the above quoted Resolution, as may be necessary for the easy passage to the said dock of a ship of the largest class in Her Majesty's navy be considered as part of the works mentioned in the said Resolution.'"

Accordingly the Maltese Government consented that a sum of about £10,000 should be applied to meeting any excess of expenditure in the works beyond the original estimate; but they were careful to insert a proviso to this effect—

"That the Government of Malta shall not be bound to pay any sum for the additional depth to be given, as aforesaid, to the said north-western basin before that depth shall have been attained, and the said dock shall have been formed and brought to a working condition, whatever may be the cause of either of those works remaining in an incomplete or insufficient state."

On the 13th of December, 1862, the Secretary to the Admiralty announced to the Colonial Office that my Lords were

"Prepared to propose to Parliament a Vote for constructing a first-class dock out of the north-west basin and in the line of the proposed canal, and to make the necessary deep water access to it, upon the conditions set forth in the Resolution passed by the Council of the Governor of Malta at sitting No. 34, on the 9th of May, 1862."

Lord Clarence Paget

Here there was a distinct agreement between the Home Government and that of Malta originally to construct this great work, afterwards to deepen the basin to thirty feet, and to construct a first-class dock, and the whole arrangement was based on the understanding that the French Creek was not to be occupied until the other works were completed. He believed no objection was made on the other side to the deepening of the basin. That work had been proceeded with, and was now in a forward state of progress; but the dock was not yet commenced. The basin was now in the course of excavation. [Sir JOHN PAKINGTON: How deep is it?] He was informed that the walls were nearly complete, and that round the edges the full depth had been attained in some places. He could not, however, say exactly how far down the excavation had been carried. Two distinguished naval officers, both well acquainted with Malta (Admirals Codrington and Sir William Martin) had reiterated objections to the scheme of the Government. Neither of these officers, he was sure, would give an opinion which he did not conscientiously believe to be right. Each of these gallant Admirals, however, had a pet scheme of his own, and that must not be forgotten. They alleged that the Marsa Dock was inconvenient on account of its distant situation, that it would be very difficult to get large ships through the merchants' vessels moored there, and there were other objections which he did not deny had all some force. He believed, however, that these two officers grounded their opposition on the impression that the Government were going to rest satisfied with the Marsa Dock, and that they were not going to make use of the other site. He wished to assure the Committee that the dock at the French Creek and that at the Marsa were not to be put into comparison for a moment. In his opinion, every day proved the necessity of constructing more extensive docks; and, although he could not give a distinct answer, he believed that if the Government were in a position to effect that object they would probably do so. Upwards of 2,000,000 tons of shipping went in and out of Malta harbour annually—and among them 100 steam ships of 1,000 tons each. Malta was becoming of more and more importance to this country. We had given up the Ionian Islands. With an increasing trade going on in Malta, and the probability of the Indian reliefs going by that route instead of by the Cape of Good Hope, would it be believed that no such thing as a merchant dock existed in Malta? And was it not then wise and right towards the colony that the Government should contribute to a magnificent work that would be at once beneficial to the colony, to commerce, and to the navy? The Duke of Somerset had sent out to Malta two able men—Sir Frederick Grey, the First Sea Lord of the Admiralty, and his hon. Friend the Member for Bedford (Mr. Whitbread), to inquire into this matter; and, after hearing both sides, Sir Frederick Grey came to the conclusion that the Government had taken a wise course. But Her Majesty had an opposition in Malta as well as in this country, and it was very strong there as well as here. The opposition in Malta was represented by four elected Members of the Council, who wrote a letter to the Duke of Somerset, dated 8th September, 1863, in which they stated—

"Having been informed that it has been asserted to the Home Government that the elected Members of the Council of this Island are opposed to the plan of a dock being constructed in the French Creek, we consider it our duty to deny the truth of that assertion, so far as we, the undersigned, are concerned. There is no reason why we should wish that a naval dock should be constructed at the Marsa (the north-western extension) rather than at the French Creek, since this creek must become naval property, according to the existing agreement for the harbour extension. As to whether such a work might be commenced immediately, we only desire that the merchant shipping be not disturbed in the use of the French Creek, before the new extension shall be ready to receive it. If arrangements can therefore be made to that effect, we see no objection to the commencement of the work immediately, with a view to its being completed by the time the French Creek will become naval property. We do not see how it can have been asserted that we are opposed to the construction of a dock in the French Creek, inasmuch as we have never been consulted on this subject, nor have we ever expressed any opinion which could warrant such an assertion."

They entirely repudiated the engagement that had been entered into with the Maltese Government. This caused great surprise in Malta. The other Councillors represented that they could not understand on what grounds they had come to that conclusion. The Governor, in a letter dated 29th of January, 1864, said—

"I am at a loss to understand what could have moved the Members of Council who signed the letter to the First Lord of the Admiralty to take that very unusual step, without previously referring to me for ascertaining whether, in what terms, and on what grounds, I had expressed my opinion in regard to any opposition that might be expected, in or out of the Council, to a grant to the Admiralty of any portion of the shore on the water of the French Creek, at the present moment; and I am still more surprised at the secresy in which those members kept that correspondence till, I might say, the eve of the opening of Parliament, to the extent even of not consulting their own colleagues, among whom are two of the wealthiest merchants in Malta. . . . It may also be worth noticing that that correspondence took place at a time when those four members of Council, and two of the merchants whom they consulted, were making every effort to obtain support to a petition against my administration. I cannot believe that the letter they addressed to the Duke of Somerset was unconnected with the agitation which existed at the time when that letter was written. That letter was evidently procured to contradict the statement made by myself and others acting under my direction, to the effect that strong opposition would be made to any grant to the Admiralty of any site in the French Creek. That statement was correct, and I firmly believe well founded, and I am satisfied that the very members who signed that letter (on learning the terms of the resolution of the 25th of May, 1859, which they seem to ignore, and on being informed by their predecessors of the reasons why the latter insisted on the insertion in that resolution of the clause establishing that the mercantile marine is to continue in the possession of the French Creek until the completion of the harbour works) would be the loudest in denouncing a breach of faith on the part of the Government, should any portion of the shore of that creek be now surrendered to the Naval Department for the construction of a dock. I cannot better show to your Grace what was the object of that clause than by a reference to the accompanying letters written to me on the subject by one of Her Majesty's Judges, Dr. Naudi, who, being then member of Council, moved the insertion of that clause in the resolution; and from another letter which, the next day after the publication of the correspondence in question, the other four elected members—one of whom, Dr. Randon, was also a member in 1859—thought it their duty to forward to me; your Grace will see how that important clause continues to be understood. For myself, who know that the resolution respecting the harbour works would not have received the assent of the Council, or at least of the elected members, without the positive assurance given on the part of the Government, and then embodied in the clause above alluded to—namely, that no portion of the shore or water of the French Creek would be made over to the Admiralty before the harbour works should be completed, I feel bound to submit to your Grace my strong opinion that any such grant at the present moment would be no less than an infraction of a promise solemnly made by the Government, and required by the Council as a guarantee for the performance of those works."

The letter of Judge Naudi said —

"The object of the clause unanimously adopted by the Council was that of keeping in the hands of the local authorities the French Creek as a security for the exact and total execution of the works contemplated in the resolution, and by that clause it was meant that no portion of the shore or of the wall of that creek, destined as it was for the use of merchant shipping, should be made over to the naval department before the works aforesaid should have been completed."

He had read these passages to show to the Committee that they were really bound to the Maltese Government to fulfil their engagements. Before engaging in these works they stated they would do so, provided Parliament granted the necessary funds. Last year he had brought the subject before the Committee, and the dock and basin had been sanctioned, and he would read a passage from the Governor's letter to show what were in his opinion the reasons for the delay that had taken place—

"For, to speak frankly, there can be no doubt, while Admiral Codrington was in command of the dockyard (and who made no disguise that his views were adverse to the plans which had been approved by the Admiralty), that prejudices were fostered which have not yet been altogether eradicated; and although I feel under great obligations to the straightforward, honourable, and very active support of Admiral Austin, yet obviously an undercurrent has shown itself among certain of the subordinates of the department, who, unable or unwilling to conquer their prejudices, prosecute their labours with a want of spirit and energy that is not to the advantage of the public service; indeed, I cannot better characterize my meaning than by saying that 'their heart is not in the work.'"

He had only further to say that he believed this to be a work of great national importance. It was important to Malta and to the commerce of the Mediterranean, and, above all, he believed we were under an engagement to the Maltese Government to proceed with it. It might be asked why he proposed to reduce the Vote. He had taken upon himself the responsibility of asking the Government to allow the Vote for the dock to be deferred; but he assured the House and the Maltese Government that he had not conceived that the Vote should be expunged, but merely deferred. He had done so because there was a Committee sitting to inquire into dock and basin accommodation at home and abroad, and this was a subject that could properly be considered by them. He was quite sure the hon. and gallant Gentlemen opposite would not bind themselves to a proposition that the Government should be guilty of a breach of faith. With respect to the basin, the works were in progress, and a great part of the money had been expended. He was sure that hon. Gentlemen would exercise their judgment, and not, because men of

Lord Clarence Paget

great weight and experience objected to the Marsa dock, oppose the Government plan, which was not objected to upon its own merits, but simply in comparison with another plan. The Government did not say that the Marsa dock would destroy the utility of a dock at the French Creek; on the contrary, they asserted that when the French Creek came into their possession it would be worthy of consideration whether a dock should be constructed there, and Mr. M'Clean had reported on the feasibility of constructing a dock in the French Creek by order of the Government. Under all these circumstances, he trusted the Committee would not incur the danger of anything like a breach of faith, and would allow the Vote to pass.

Motion made, and Question proposed, "That the Item of £15,900, for deepening the North-West Basin, and constructing a First-class Dock, be reduced by the sum of £5,000,"—(*Lord Clarence Paget,*)—put, and *agreed to.*

CAPTAIN TALBOT said, the speech of the noble Lord had given him great pleasure, because it showed that the trouble he had taken about this matter had not been thrown away; it had put a stop to the progress of a dock which he believed was not necessary for the Imperial service, nor for the mercantile marine. So far as the statement of the noble Lord was satisfactory; but beyond that there were subjects for remark. He had had a map prepared of the locality, and he trusted the House would look at it while listening to what he had to say. When it was determined to extend the harbour accommodation at Malta, the estimated cost, £125,000, was to be divided equally between the two Governments, and if that amount was exceeded, then to the extent of one-fourth of a limit of £42,000 the Government of Malta would be responsible. It was also agreed that when those extensions were made, the Maltese merchant shipping should give up the French Creek to the Imperial marine upon the water of the Marsa being deepened to a depth of thirty feet at the outer portion, and the remaining portion to a depth of not less than twenty-five feet. For a considerable time the Maltese Government had been desirous of having the dock made by private enterprise; but that plan was not carried out. The want of dock accommodation in the Mediterranean for British vessels had been long known to all naval officers, while at the same time they were well acquainted with the gigantic strides which the trade of France had made of late years in those waters. That Power had lately provided three docks in the Mediterranean, capable of receiving the largest ships, while at Marseilles ten docks were nearly available, and steps were probably being taken at Algiers in the same direction. Therefore it had been urged upon the Government, that more docks were wanted in the Mediterranean. The Governor of Malta, knowing those facts, proposed to the Government to make a first-class dock at the head of the harbour extension, capable of taking in our largest iron-clad ships—to make a dock inside the north-west basin, which, according to the harbour extension agreement, was only to have a depth of twelve feet, and, as an encouragement, the local Government offered, if any surplus remained from the Supplemental Estimate that was not required for the harbour extension, it should be expended in deepening the water beyond twelve feet. That proposal was an absurd one, because more than that sum would be required for the harbour extension itself. He had thought it right to call particular attention to the point, because it was of the utmost importance for them to have correct Estimates submitted to their consideration if they had any intention of practising economy. In the Estimates, the Admiralty had specified £50,000 for the construction of a dock, and for deepening of the north-western basin; from which sum they had subtracted £10,830 as a subscription from the Maltese Government. Of this latter sum, however, not a single farthing would be forthcoming, as it was only the savings of this sum which should be left after the harbour extension should be completed that the Maltese promised, and there was no doubt that the whole of it would be swallowed up in that work. An engineer, however, who had been lately sent out by the Admiralty for the purpose of inspecting the spot, had reported that it would be necessary to line the excavation with masonry, and to face it with hard stone. His estimate for the construction of the dock alone was £50,000; for the deepening of the basin, £41,000; and for the deepening of the harbour outside—a provision which the Admiralty and Mr. Scamp had entirely forgotten — £4,000. This would bring the total cost up to £95,000. One of the arguments urged in favour of this dock was its cheapness, but he believed that the House would now

perceive the fallacy of that reasoning. He regarded it as a most extraordinary circumstance that the Admiralty determined upon their plans without any reference to the opinions or advice of Admiral Sir William Martin, Commander-in-Chief of the Mediterranean station, or Rear Admiral Codrington, who had been the Admiral Superintendent for three or four years at Malta, and under whose attention, therefore, the question of the dock must undoubtedly have been brought during the period. Admiral Sir William Martin had made a proposition to the Admiralty, but his communication had not been well received. It was true that the Admiralty had written to Admiral Codrington, but not with the view of obtaining advice; and the first intimation that that officer received of the plans of the Government was through the instrumentality of a Maltese paper. The first objection to the formation of the proposed dock was its distance from the dockyard. The noble Lord had assured him upon a previous occasion, that the distance did not exceed half a mile, but he had subsequently ascertained that it was very nearly — within one-twelfth of—two miles. Not only would the conveyance of stores be a work of great labour and occasionally peril, but the difficulty of approach for the vessels themselves was very great. They would have to pass through crowds of merchant-shipping, and could hardly by any possibility reach their destination without a collision. The harbour-master looked upon the operation as a most hazardous one. Another objection was that they would have to build supplemental factories in the neighbourhood of the docks. This objection had been met on the part of the Admiralty by the supposition that the deficiency would be supplied by private enterprise, and that the factories which would necessarily be erected for the use of the mercantile marine could be made available for the necessities of Her Majesty's ships. He believed that supposition, however, to be a delusive one, for it could not be imagined that such factories (even were they erected, which was very problematical) would be of much service to our large class of vessels, or be at all capable of repairing our more powerful machinery. The two Admirals to whom he had referred had both pointed out the advantages of the French Creek, which was only 800 yards distant from the dockyard by water and 700 by land. The noble Lord had said that in consequence of the objections raised by the two Admirals, the First Sea Lord of the Admiralty, Sir Frederick Grey, and the hon. Member for Bedford (Mr. Whitbread) had been sent out, but he felt convinced that they had been sent on a foregone conclusion. ["No, no!"] They only remained at Malta two or three days, and he did not believe that they held any communication with the Admirals by whom the objections had been urged. The question was an important one, as affecting the efficiency and the safety of their Mediterranean fleet; and on a matter of that kind, when two Lords of the Admiralty were sent out to Malta, it was very remarkable that they should content themselves with a mere verbal report. That, he must say, appeared a very slovenly way of carrying on public business. One of his difficulties in dealing with that subject was, that he had to meet bare assertions. They had the bare assertion that the dock at the Marsa, with the approaches, was only to cost £50,000; and they were also told that the dock at the French Creek would be so expensive that they could not have it. That was entirely unsupported and erroneous. The noble Lord had conceded that the French Creek was the proper site for the dock; but it was only after toiling day after day and month after month that they had arrived at that position; because at first it was said that the distance was the same, that the expense would be much greater, and that the time occupied would also be much greater, if the French Creek were chosen instead of the Marsa. All these assertions, he was prepared to show, fell to the ground. He wished to call attention to the Report of Mr. M'Clean, the engineer lately sent out to the Mediterranean to report on that subject. The noble Lord had glanced lightly at that Report, and well he might, for it went entirely against the noble Lord's position. Mr. M'Clean entered into the different estimates, said the dock would cost so and so, the basins so and so, and he ended by very nearly doubling the estimates that had been laid on the table. Moreover, he said not one word in praise of the dock, but, on the other hand, he did say a great deal in favour of the site of the French Creek. It was true that that gentleman did not recommend the dock which Admiral Codrington recommended. That, however, was **not** the **point**; but he recommended that the dock should be made at the French Creek.

Captain Talbot

The noble Lord had referred to the four elected Members of the Council at Malta, and drew a comparison between the Opposition there and the Opposition in this House. Now, the position of parties in that House was not quite the same as it was at Malta, because the Government at Malta always had a working majority of fourteen against four. The Council at Malta was composed of eighteen Members; ten of them being official Members, who always voted with the Government on pain of losing their places. The remaining eight were elected Members, who were supposed to represent the public feeling of Malta; but two of the eight were large Government contractors, who had property round the very place where the dock was intended to be constructed, and no wonder they should support the Government. Besides these gentlemen, two more of the elected members went with the contractors and the Government. Therefore, there was a standing majority of fourteen, the other four members being the representatives of the people of Malta. Some months ago, when the noble Lord said, that if the Governor of Malta allowed them to make a dock at the French Creek, the Council and people of Malta would object to what the noble Lord erroneously called "breaking faith" with them,—when that was known at Malta, the freely elected Members of the Council wrote a letter to the Duke of Somerset, stating that they were not at all opposed to the construction of the dock at the French Creek. Those gentlemen were not content with sending their own opinions, but they wrote to the Chamber of Commerce of Malta, inviting the opinion of that body, and also that of the public of Malta. The Chamber of Commerce, in a letter dated Valetta, September 1, 1863, said they were not aware of any objection on the part of the public at Malta to the construction of the dock at the French Creek, and that they did not believe it existed. They also observed that they would not suffer, but rather gain by its construction there rather than at the Marsa. He was convinced that the real feeling of the people of Malta was that they would prefer the site of the French Creek being adopted without the disturbance of their mercantile waters. He had been surprised at the noble Lord quoting a passage in the letter of the Governor of Malta, throwing doubts on the character and motives of Admiral Codrington. Admiral Codrington was actuated by a regard for the public interest, and it was entirely ridiculous to say that he had left an animus among the subordinates in the dockyard at Malta. He was astonished that the noble Lord, himself an Admiral in Her Majesty's service, should have taken upon himself to endorse that statement. The noble Lord now proposed that the Vote should be reduced, and that the question of the docks should be submitted to a Committee sitting upstairs. Now, however that Committee might be constituted, he had such confidence in the strength of his case that he believed the dock would be condemned. If the case was to be referred to a Committee, it was only right that the whole case should be considered. Last year a Vote of £10,000 was taken ; this year, if the noble Lord's Motion were carried, £10,900 more would be voted ; and the Admiralty said that the sum of £10,800 had been subscribed by the Maltese Government. The whole of this money ought to be spent at once in providing proper dock accommodation at Malta, and in providing it, as soon as possible, in the proper place. The Admiralty had said lately that the French Creek was far superior as a site to the Marsa, but that the dock could not be made there without upsetting the arrangement with the Maltese Government. Now, no one wanted to disturb the merchant ships in the waters of the French Creek, and he contended that there was no impediment in the arrangement referred to which need prevent the Admiralty from carrying out the work as proposed, so that when we came into possession of the waters of the French Creek we should have a dock there complete.

MR. WHITBREAD said, that as his hon. and gallant Friend expressed his entire approval of Mr. M'Clean's plans and estimate, it must be a matter of satisfaction to him that he had not succeeded on a former occasion in carrying his Motion for the abandonment of the dock in the Marsa. The hon. and gallant Gentleman (Captain Talbot) had ignored the fact that the excess, which Mr. M'Clean's Report would lead the House to expect, upon the original estimate, had arisen from the proposal to commence new works which were for the benefit of the navy, and had to be undertaken solely at the expense of the Imperial Government. The whole question lay in a nutshell. The question had never been, which was the most desirable site, but which was the possible site ? Unless the

Government had been prepared to violate an agreement solemnly entered into, they had no choice but to build the dock in the Marsa. He had authority from Sir Frederick Grey to say, that when he recommended the Admiralty to go on with this dock it never entered into his head that it should be treated as a bar to the construction of a dock in the French Creek. In this opinion he entirely concurred, and it was shared by the Duke of Somerset and by the Board of Admiralty. The hon. and gallant Gentleman said that they had only just found this out, but they had really stated it all along. In their minds there was never any sort of comparison between the dock of the Marsa and that of the French Creek; what they looked to was the fact that the former was possible and that the latter was not possible. Then the hon. and gallant Gentleman said they ought to have written an elaborate report of the results of their visit to Malta with respect to this question. Now, the members of the Board of Admiralty had something to do besides writing letters to themselves, and it would have been idle to do so when they could explain themselves to their colleagues much better by word of mouth. As to Admiral Martin and Admiral Codrington, their opposition arose from a complete misapprehension. They believed all along that it was possible to go on with the dock in the French Creek, whereas it was considered by all the local authorities, that to take the necessary steps for this would have been a violation of the agreement which had been entered into. In his opinion it was owing to the persistent opposition of the two Admirals at Malta, backed by the right hon. Gentleman (Sir John Pakington), and of hon. and gallant Officers opposite, all of whom recognized the immense importance of providing additional dock accommodation at Malta, that there was not a dock in the Marsa at this moment, and they alone would be responsible if any inconvenience should result from the want of it. He believed that the original estimate of the cost was a sound one, and that it would not be exceeded—at any rate by more than a few thousand pounds, and deeply regretted that the noble Lord should have thought it proper to strike out any portion of the Vote.

SIR JOHN PAKINGTON thought there were passages in the report of Mr. M'Clean which did not bear out the interpretation which the hon. Gentleman put upon it. Hon. Gentlemen on his side of the House had no wish to break faith with the Maltese; on the contrary, they quite admitted the necessity of keeping faith with them; but our faith was not pledged with them for the construction of this dock. He hoped hon. Gentlemen would not run away with the idea that this was a question of £5,000 or £10,000. The question was one of the greatest importance to this country. He thought the Admiralty were much to blame. We had not a dock in a good position at Malta, and we ought to have constructed one years ago. As to the allegation of good faith in connection with the dock on the Marsa, what was the use of sending the hon. Gentleman to Malta, and of sending Mr. M'Clean there, if the Government were already pledged to the construction of that dock?

MR. WHITBREAD: I never said we were pledged to the construction of the dock.

SIR JOHN PAKINGTON: The hon. Gentleman implied it.

MR. WHITBREAD: Neither did I imply it.

SIR JOHN PAKINGTON would not, of course, say any more on that point. But the whole subject was an important one. No time ought to be lost in constructing a dock on the French Creek, and abandoning this dock on the Marsa, which was condemned by all the authorities. [" No, no!" "Hear, hear!"] He wished to ask the noble Lord what was their position at that moment? He did not understand from the noble Lord how they stood with regard to this Vote. What was the intention of the Admiralty in withdrawing the £5,000? Were they to understand that the construction of the dock on the Marsa was abandoned for this year?

LORD CLARENCE PAGET had said he was ready to refer the question to a Select Committee. He was quite sure that his right hon. Friend and his hon. and gallant Friends on the other side of the House would not, from any feelings of party, or any wish to criticise the acts of the Government, do anything unfair, or anything calculated to cause a breach of faith on the part of this country with Malta.

SIR JOHN PAKINGTON wanted to know why the noble Lord withdrew the £5,000, and what were his intentions with regard to the Marsa dock? He wanted to know how he intended to apply the £10,000, for he should object to deepening the north-west basin beyond

twelve feet. They were not pledged to deepen it beyond that depth.

LORD CLARENCE PAGET: The £5,000 was withdrawn for the present on account of the dock. The £10,900 would go on towards deepening the basin and completing the side walls of the basin where it had already been deepened. Considerable progress had already been made with the work.

COLONEL SOMERSET said, while he held the command of a regiment at Malta, he had given attention to this subject. The Government of Malta in 1858 was requested by the Admiralty to find the best harbour, and it was suggested that the Marsa was the only place. The merchant shipping there at the time were uneasy lest the Government should take the French Creek, which was the only place available for them. The question of this French Creek was mooted several times, but the expense was much greater. The dock at the Marsa was for the mercantile marine, and was a first-class one, on the principle of those of the Messrs. Laird. It was extraordinary that they had not a first-class dock in the Mediterranean for the navy; if they were going to war they would not have a dock there at which they could recruit.

SIR JAMES ELPHINSTONE said, no sailor could have recommended the project now before the Committee. It had been stated that the scheme was that of the Governor. No doubt the Governor wished to make things easy; but two Admirals were opposed to the plan. It was time that the House of Commons took up the question. The Committee had been told that the trade of Malta was immense; if so, the dock would always be occupied to the exclusion of Government vessels. The noble Lord said it was intended to send troops to India by way of the Mediterranean. If so, it was the duty of the Government to make the necessary provision.

CAPTAIN TALBOT wished the Committee clearly to understand the question at issue. Was the new dock not to be proceeded with before the next meeting of Parliament? He also wanted to know whether the north-west basin was to be deepened to the extent of thirty feet?

LORD CLARENCE PAGET had already stated that he proposed to withdraw the dock, referring it to the Committee now sitting upstairs. He was persuaded, in spite of what had been said, that he should have to bring forward a new Vote before the end of the present Session. All the money now asked for would be expended in deepening the basin.

SIR JOHN PAKINGTON was satisfied with the statement of the noble Lord that the dock would not be commenced until Parliament was again consulted.

Question put, and *agreed to.*

CAPTAIN TALBOT moved the omission of the whole item for deepening the basin and constructing the dock.

Motion made, and Question proposed, "That the Item so reduced be omitted from the proposed Vote."—(*Captain Talbot.*)

SIR JOHN PAKINGTON supported the Amendment on the ground that if the dock was not to be constructed there would be no necessity for deepening the basin.

LORD CLARENCE PAGET observed, that the importance of deepening the basin was admitted even by those who opposed the dock.

SIR JOHN HAY denied that the importance of deepening the basin to the extent of thirty feet was admitted. He himself regarded it as a waste of public money.

MR. CHILDERS remarked, that in the opinion of Mr. M'Clean the deepening of the basin to thirty feet was a matter of the greatest importance.

The Committee *divided :* — Ayes 93 ; Noes 111 : Majority 18.

Original Question, as amended, put, and *agreed to.*

£444,298, New Works, Improvements, and Repairs, also *agreed to.*

House *resumed.*

Resolution to be reported on *Tuesday* ; Committee to sit again on *Wednesday.*

RIVERS POLLUTION (SCOTLAND) BILL.

On Motion of The LORD ADVOCATE, Bill to prevent the discharge of Impure Water from Manufactories into Rivers in Scotland, *ordered* to be brought in by The LORD ADVOCATE, Sir GEORGE GREY, and Sir WILLIAM DUNBAR.

ADMIRALTY LANDS AND WORKS BILL.

On Motion of Lord CLARENCE PAGET, Bill to make provision respecting the acquisition of Lands required by the Admiralty for the public service, and respecting the use and disposition thereof, and the execution of Works thereon, *ordered* to be brought in by Lord CLARENCE PAGET and Mr. CHILDERS.

ADMINISTRATION OF TRUSTS (SCOTLAND) BILL.

On Motion of The LORD ADVOCATE, Bill to facilitate the Administration of Trusts, and to regulate the powers of Trustees in Scotland, *ordered* to be brought in by The LORD ADVOCATE, Sir GEORGE GREY, and Sir WILLIAM DUNBAR.

House adjourned at a quarter after One o'clock.

HOUSE OF LORDS,

Tuesday, May 3, 1864.

MINUTES.]—PUBLIC BILL — *Third Reading*— High Court at Bombay* (No. 57).

Their Lordships met ; and having gone through the business on the paper, without debate,

House adjourned at a quarter past Five o'clock, to Friday next, half past Ten o'clock.

HOUSE OF COMMONS,

Tuesday, May 3, 1864.

MINUTES.]—SELECT COMMITTEE—On Schools of Art*, Mr. Bruce *added.*
SUPPLY—*Resolutions* [May 2] *reported.*
PUBLIC BILLS—*Ordered* — Boiler Explosions* ; Public and Refreshment Houses (Metropolis) ; Street Music (Metropolis).
Second Reading—Insolvent Debtors [Bill 20].
Committee — Partnership Law Amendment [Bill 68].
Third Reading—Customs and Inland Revenue* [Bill 82].

PAYMENT OF RATES AND TAXES BY OFFICERS IN GOVERNMENT HOUSES.

QUESTION.

COLONEL NORTH said, he wished to ask the Under Secretary of State for War, Whether any decision has been arrived at by the War Department and Treasury as to the payment of Rates and Taxes by Officers of the Army occupying Government Houses in the performance of their duties?

THE MARQUESS OF HARTINGTON said, in reply, that no decision had yet been arrived at. It was a question in which the Admiralty were at least as much interested as the War Department, and it had been intended that the hon. Member for Halifax (Mr. Stansfeld) should confer with some officer of the War Department with a view to forwarding a joint recommendation to

3 U

the Treasury. In consequence of recent changes at the Admiralty that conference had not taken place, but he hoped that some arrangement would be made in a short time.

COLONEL NORTH said, he would give notice that he should take an early opportunity of moving an Address to the Crown praying that all Officers of Chelsea Hospital should be exempted from the payment of rates and taxes charged upon them for their residence in the Hospital for the due performance of their duties.

THE AUSTRIAN SQUADRON AND THE CHANNEL FLEET.—QUESTION.

MR. DARBY GRIFFITH said, he would beg to inquire of the Home Secretary, in the absence of the noble Lord the First Minister, Whether an Austrian Squadron has not arrived in the Downs and other of our harbours; and whether the Channel Fleet has not been ordered round to the Downs; and, if so, whether it is the intention of Her Majesty's Government to allow the Austrian ships of war to proceed to the Baltic or the North Sea without being accompanied by the Channel Fleet?

SIR GEORGE GREY: It is true, Sir, that three or four Austrian ships have arrived in the Downs, and we have reason to believe that a few others are on their passage from the Mediterranean to join them; but the Austrian Government have given the most distinct assurances to Her Majesty's Government that for the present the only orders given to the commander of that squadron are to protect German commerce in the North Sea, and to prevent a blockade of the Elbe and the Weser. The Channel Fleet is in the Downs, and the Admiral commanding will be fully informed of the movements of the Austrian squadron. Her Majesty's Government must decline to say what orders may be given to the commander of the Channel Fleet in the event of different instructions being given to the Austrian commander, but they have reason to entertain a confident expectation that the Austrian squadron will not enter the Baltic.

SEWAGE OF THE METROPOLIS.
QUESTION.

LORD ROBERT MONTAGU said, he wished to ask the First Commissioner of Works, Why the Return ordered by the House on 24th of July, 1863, on the Motion

The Marquess of Hartington

of Mr. Ayrton (namely, No. 67, Sewage (Metropolis), Copy of all Advertisements published by the Metropolitan Board of Works, &c.), has not been presented, and when it will be laid upon the table and printed?

MR. COWPER said, in reply, that the Return ordered in July, 1863, had not yet been made, but he was informed that it was nearly completed, and would speedily be laid before the House.

NEW LAW COURTS.
QUESTION.

MR. ARTHUR MILLS said, he wished to ask the First Commissioner of Works, When the Bill for the Concentration of the Courts of Justice which, on the 22nd of April, he stated would be brought forward in a few days, will be introduced by the Government?

MR. COWPER, in reply, said, the reintroduction of the Bill for the purchase of the site, of which he had charge last Session, must depend upon the introduction of another Bill for supplying the funds, which would be introduced by another Member of the Government. He was therefore unable to give the information asked for by the hon. Gentleman.

LAWS OF JERSEY.
QUESTION.

MR. PAULL said, he would beg to ask the Secretary of State for the Home Department, Whether his attention has been drawn to a Bill intituled "A Bill to amend the Constitution, Practice, and Procedure of the Courts of the Island of Jersey," purporting to deal with the Judicial Establishments and Taxation of the said Island, and also to ask whether such Bill has been introduced with the concurrence and approval of Her Majesty's Government?

SIR GEORGE GREY said, in reply, that of course his attention had been drawn to the Bill introduced by the hon. and learned Member for Southwark (Mr. Locke), but it had not been introduced with the concurrence of the Government, except so far that they offered no opposition to its introduction. Upon the second reading he had recommended the hon. and learned Gentleman to put off the Committee to a distant day, with a view of enabling the States of Jersey to take the subject into their own hands, and the hon. and learned Gentleman had consented to do so. Since then the hon. Member for Hampshire had moved for the production of the continuance of the Correspondence between the Government and the Lieutenant Governor of Jersey, and the hon. and learned Gentleman (Mr. Locke) had consented to postpone the Bill for another month in order that that Correspondence might be in the hands of Members.

MR. PAULL said, he thought the right hon. Gentleman had not answered his Question, whether the Bill proposing to deal with the Judicial Establishments of Jersey had been introduced with his concurrence.

SIR GEORGE GREY said, that the House permitted the introduction of a similar Bill three years ago. Upon the present occasion he had not dissented from the proposal to introduce the Bill, nor had the hon. Member or any one in that House done so.

MR. BRIGHT said, he thought the right hon. Gentleman might answer the Question more distinctly. The Question was whether of the House—at the Home Office—the right hon. Gentleman had expressed his approval of the Bill.

SIR GEORGE GREY said, he did not remember that, previous to the introduction of the Bill, any communication took place between his hon. and learned Friend (Mr. Locke) and himself. On the second reading he stated publicly the views he entertained with regard to it, and he had expressed no other opinion on it out of the House, except that he suggested to his hon. and learned Friend that it would be expedient that he should further postpone the future stage of the Bill till the Correspondence was placed in the hands of Members.

UNITED STATES—OUTRAGES BY THE SIOUX INDIANS.—QUESTION.

MR. HENNESSY rose to put a Question to the Secretary of State for the Colonies, and in order to make the subject intelligible to the House it was necessary he should make a brief statement of the circumstances. He held in his hand a letter from a respectable gentleman a Member of the Legislative Assembly of Canada, dated Quebec, April 16. That gentleman stated, that at a meeting of the Governor and Council of the Red River Settlement, held on the 12th of March, application was made by the Governor to the Council to permit Major Hatch, the Commander of the American troops in the vicinity of the frontier, to cross into British territory, in order to capture and destroy the Sioux Indians, who were at war with the United States. At the same time—

"The Governor further stated that he had received a message from the main body of the Sioux, on the Missouri, asking his advice as to making peace with the Americans, and hinting at a desire to visit the settlement in spring. He had returned an answer advising the Sioux to make peace with the Americans, or be prepared for a prosecution of the war with renewed vigour next summer."

It appeared that on the same day the Governor thought fit to grant to Major Hatch liberty to cross the frontier, and in his letter to Major Hatch he made only one reservation—

"I have no hesitation in complying with your request, stipulating only that in the event of active operations taking place within the settlements, you will communicate with the authorities and take such measures as will prevent bloodshed or violence in the houses or enclosures of the settlers, should any of the Sioux Indians take refuge there."

The gentleman whose letter he referred to said—

"A most extraordinary circumstance has lately occurred at Red River which must surely arouse the indignation of the British public, as it is the first time that British territory has been put into the occupation, under the protectorate it may be said, and hence at the mercy of a foreign soldiery. The cool reservation that the wretched savages are not to be butchered in the houses or enclosures of the inhabitants is meant, I suppose, as an apology for the outrage."

The Question he wished to ask was, Whether these statements were correct, and whether the right hon. Gentleman would lay the papers upon the table?

MR. CARDWELL said, in reply, that within the last few days he had received from the Governor of the Hudson's Bay Company a letter and enclosures which the Hudson's Bay Company had received from their Governor at the Red River Settlement. It appeared from these documents that the Commander of the United States forces upon the frontier requested permission from the Governor of the Red River Settlement to pursue and capture Sioux Indians who might cross the frontier. That permission was granted by the Governor of the Red River Settlement. The cause assigned for the request by the American Commander was to prevent the murder of women and children in the American territories, and the cause assigned by the Governor for the permission was the same. The stipulation made had been correctly described by the hon. Member. If the hon. Gentleman chose to move for the production of the official letters there would be no objection to lay them before the House.

CLOSING PUBLIC HOUSES ON SUNDAYS.

QUESTION.

MR. BAINES said, in order to remove some misapprehensions. that existed, he wished to ask the hon. Member for Hull, Whether the Bill which he proposed to introduce on Friday, is identical with the Bill of last Session ?

MR. SOMES said, the Bill was not the same as the Bill of last year, as he now proposed to allow public-houses to be open on Sundays from one to two and from eight to nine.

UNITED STATES—THE CRUISERS OF BELLIGERENTS.—QUESTION.

MR. PEACOCKE said, he would beg to ask the Secretary of State for the Colonies, Whether he is prepared to inform the House of the nature of the Instructions to be issued to the Colonial Authorities respecting the treatment to be pursued towards belligerent cruisers entering our harbours ?

MR. CARDWELL replied, that the Draft of Instructions intended to be sent to the Governors of our Colonies with reference to their treatment of belligerent cruisers had been submitted to the Law Officers of the Crown. The object of those Instructions was to give clear and precise directions to the Governors for their future guidance so far as the nature of the case would admit. As soon as the Instructions had been received back from the Law Officers, and approved by Her Majesty's Government, they would be laid upon the table of the House.

PUNISHMENT OF DEATH.—SELECT COMMITTEE MOVED FOR.

MR. W. EWART rose to move for a Select Committee to inquire into the expediency of maintaining the punishment of death. It is now nearly a quarter of a century that the opponents of capital punishment in this country have contended for its repeal. They hold it to be a great question of religion and civilisation. But, in a more practical point of view, and in one less connected with feeling and opinion, they support it, because they believe

Mr. Cardwell

it would give certainty to justice and punishment to crime—and they base that belief on this maxim of the illustrious Beccaria:—"The certainty of even a moderate punishment will always make a greater impression than the fear of a more severe punishment, which is accompanied by the expectation of impunity." We apply this maxim to our present system, and we maintain that ours is not the more "moderate" system which "makes the greater impression," but that it is the "severer system which is accompanied by the expectation of impunity." Are we not justified in saying that great inconsistency, great uncertainty, prevail under our present system of capital punishment ? Have we not arrived, with regard to cases of murder, at a similar position to that which we held with regard to other crimes punished capitally many years ago ? For a long time it was said of horse-stealing, sheep-stealing, stealing in a dwelling-house to the value of £5, and forging (all of them crimes which we remember to have been punished with death), "It is true you can seldom execute offenders for such crimes, but on occasions execution will suffice to terrify them." In those cases it was found that the "occasional system" induced, by its uncertainty, the very crime it was intended to prevent. For this reason capital punishment was, in those cases, repealed. Is not the case of murder in the same phase of its course at present ? That it is so has recently been proved by the able treatises of Mr. Amos and Lord Hobart—

"The practice (says Lord Hobart) really is, not to punish with death criminals who are murderers in the sight of the law, but to select a few such criminals for execution ; and the fate of a murderer depends, not on any fixed rite of penal legislation, but on the idiosyncrasy of a jury or of a Minister of the Crown."

The press very generally argues in a similar strain. Let us take a Whig paper— *The Globe. The Globe* says :—"Instead of a certainty, punishment for murder has become a lottery." Take a Tory paper— *The Standard.* "The law of the gallows (says *The Standard*) is a game of hazard between society and the criminal." If from opinions we turn to statistics, the logic of figures gives a similar result. First, let us take the evidence of one year only. In a paper read before the Society for the Amendment of the Law in 1856, it was shown that, out of every 100 persons tried for capital offences in 1852, only 32 were convicted (how much smaller a proportion must have been executed) ; while out of every 100 tried for offences—not capital—as many as 78 were convicted. The same result may easily be proved from other single years. But, next, let us take a period of three years. In 1861 Lord Hobart showed that, acccording to the judicial statistics of 1857-8-9, the chances of escape from the penalty awarded by law for crimes punishable with death was 4½ times greater than the chances of escape for crimes not so punishable. Next, let us take a period of five years. By a calculation which I now offer to your inspection, taken from the authorized "Judicial Statistics," it appears that, during a period of five years, the chances of escape in capital cases were, to the chances of escape in cases not capital, in the ratio of 5 to 1. Let us next take a period of ten years. A carefully prepared table (also compiled from the "Judicial Statistics") for the ten years ending with the year 1862, which I also offer for inspection, shows that, while the chances of escaping the punishment awarded by the law was, for all offences, as 1 to 4, the chances of escaping it for the capital case of murder as 5½ to 1. This result seems to correspond nearly with Lord Hobart's calculations, and with the Returns moved for by the hon. and learned Member for Clare (Sir Colman O'Loghlen); so that it is not unreasonable to conclude that the chances of a murderer escaping the punishment of death — to a great degree because it is the punishment of death—are as 4 or 5 to 1. Yet surely these cases, in which punishment fails to attain its end, are the most serious of all cases, and those which should be punished with the greatest certainty. So that, according to the administration of our law, the small offender is most certain to be punished; the great offender is least certain to be punished.

But it may be said, in the words of Lord Macaulay, "Statistics are mercenaries, and may be made to fight on either side." Let us then turn from figures to facts. Facts show the same results—great uncertainty arising from great fluctuation in punishment. For a certain time it appeared to be understood that women were not to be executed. Most of us remember the cases of Annette Meyer, Celestina Summers, and others, who, though guilty in law, escaped in fact. The policy of entirely exempting women from capital punishment was maintained, or suggested, by some of the leading journals. Then a sudden re-action took place. It was found

to be at once unjust and illogical to subject men to one punishment and women to another. The execution of women was recommenced. Women were again dragged shrieking and fainting to the scaffold; or we waited till a woman produced a child into the world, and then tried and executed her. Under such a system, guilty persons frequently escaped. Numerous cases might be cited—I have a long list here. In the first place, in cases of infanticide, the destroyer of her own offspring almost always escapes the punishment of death. Let me, however—though it is needless to cite examples, when examples are so many—give one instance of the practical effect of such examples. In 1851 a woman was tried for the murder of her child. The Judge said, "It was murder or nothing." The jury found her "not guilty,"—women outside the court were heard to exclaim, "We need not mind what we do now." But we cannot, perhaps, more strongly put the case of the inefficacy of the punishment of death, than by showing that the very same persons who are acquitted when tried for an act for which the law assigns capital punishment, are found guilty when tried for the same act on a charge which does not involve capital punishment. Three men, Barker, Breckon, and Raine, were tried at York, in 1846, for murder. They were acquitted. The same men were tried the next year for the same offence as a robbery only, which, of course, did not involve capital punishment. They were all found guilty. Joseph Travis was tried in 1848, at Lincoln, for murder. He was acquitted. He was tried again the next year for the same offence as a robbery. He was found guilty. At the Maidstone Assizes in 1855, Elizabeth Laws was tried for murder. She was acquitted. She was again tried for the same act on a charge for stealing only, and was found guilty. But, as she could only be tried for stealing, she escaped with six months' imprisonment. Had she been tried on the first trial on a charge of murder, for which the law had ceased to assign capital punishment, she would have been properly and effectively punished by penal servitude for life. If I were to pursue the list I could add very many more cases of acquittals by juries. Let us now, however, turn to cases brought before coroners. In their court no cases are so fearfully common as cases of infanticide. That crime has become painfully common in this country. Foreigners have observed its frequency. There is an article in the *Révue Chrétienne* which points to it. According to the *Globe* newspaper, 800 cases of infanticide, at least, occur yearly. Yet they continue to escape due punishment. Why? Because the law awards the punishment of death for infanticide. In October last Mr. Humphreys, the coroner for the Eastern division of Middlesex, said that the failure of justice in cases of infanticide is "attributable to the law. The legal punishment is death. The consequence is that all sorts of excuses are made rather than find the prisoner guilty." Dr. Lancaster, also another coroner, has recommended the repeal of the punishment of death, because it "made juries less willing to convict."

Let us now turn to the effect of maintaining the punishment of death on the minds of our Judges. As long ago as the year 1847, a Committee of the House of Lords examined the Judges by written inquiry on the subject; several of the Judges declined, or avoided giving an answer; but among them Baron Alderson admitted that "verdicts," in cases involving the punishment of death, "are continually given in the teeth of law and evidence." Mr. Justice Coltman was "disposed to think that imprisonment for life might be substituted for capital punishment." "Many guilty persons," he said, "now escape who would then be convicted." Mr. Justice Wightman says, "There can be little doubt that secondary punishment may be made so severe as to be a sufficient substitute for the punishment of death." Mr. Justice Perrin says, "I am convinced that, in many cases of murder, when juries have either acquitted or not agreed on a verdict, the apprehension of taking away life has been the cause." It is probable that a greater number of Judges would say so now. But, not only among juries, coroners, and Judges, but in the Home Office itself, there is reason to believe that conviction is forcing its way, and that some of our most eminent official men are convinced of the inexpediency of maintaining the punishment of death. A similar metamorphosis of opinion is taking place, as that which sprung up in our public offices during the agitation of the Corn Law Question. The most distinguished officers of the Board of Trade then became the most strenuous opponents of the Corn Laws. It is an ominous symptom when, in the language of Moore the poet,

"The extinguishers themselves take fire."

Mr. W. Ewart

But this conversion is natural; for in the public offices they see most clearly, and, as it were, inwardly, the effects of a faulty system, even more strongly than the great mass of observers outside. We have lately seen the effects of such cases as those of Townley, Wright, and Hall, at the Home Office. Can we say that, if Wright was fairly executed (which I deny), Townley was fairly exempted from execution? Hall, indeed, was wisely spared; but, if Hall was spared, ought Wright to have suffered the punishment of death? So argued the public. But why was Hall spared? Avowedly, and avowedly on the part of the Secretary of the Home Department, on account of the strong expression of popular feeling in his favour. I admit the propriety of the concession. But on what dangerous grounds was it made, and how dangerous a precedent was given to the public in favour of popular agitation against the sentences of the law? I boldly say that, when such a reason for infringing the law is not only acted on but avowed, the law ought to be altered; for the law can no longer be maintained consistently with its own consistency and dignity. Now, let us ask ourselves this question. Why do jurors, coroners, Judges, and the Home Office, and finally, the public itself, all act on these motives, and share in these opinions? It is because capital punishment differs from all other punishments. First, because it is irremediable. Every one shrinks from that which, when once done, cannot be repaired. Shakspeare, who rarely, or never, was wrong in sounding the depths of the human heart, *qui nil molitur inepté*, makes a character, familiar to us all, say to the lamp—

"If I quench thee, thou flaming minister,
I can again thy former light restore."

But who can restore the lamp of life, or revive its once-extinguished light? Another objection to the punishment of death is, that it admits of no gradations. There are different shades of criminality even in murder; yet the punishment is sternly, uniformly one. Another punishment may be adapted to the varying physical powers, or the varying nervous susceptibilities of the sufferer — the punishment of death cannot. The robust man, the feeble woman, the hardened offender who laughs at death, the trembling coward who shrinks from it, all undergo the same unvarying, unbending punishment. Therefore it has, besides being irremediable, this fault also, that it is an unequal punishment. Be-

cause it is unequal, it is therefore unjust. But it is unjust in another sense
also, for it overwhelms the innocent descendants of the criminal with an oppressive weight of infamy, and consigns them
to an heritage of disgrace, unknown to
any other punishment. A very important consideration here suggests itself.
Are these objections shown to exist among
jurymen, coroners, Judges, in the Home
Office, and among the public, likely
to increase, or is there a probability that
they may diminish? In all likelihood they
will increase. I think it is clear that such
objections uniformly increase with the progress of civilization. Increased sympathy
in the fate and fortunes of each other is
one of the tests and consequences of increased civilization. We also may observe
that, as time advances, minute distinctions
as to insanity are drawn, unknown to law
or medicine before. It is not the exposition
of the Judge, or the opinion of the jury
which decides the question of sanity, but
the opinion, perhaps the caprice, of the
doctor. So that if such an allusion may
be allowed on such an occasion, the scene
is like that in the *Malade Imaginaire* of
Molière, where authority is given to the
doctor, not only *medicandi, purgandi,* and
saigniandi, but also *occidendi.* Another
source of increasing uncertainty, in the
infliction of capital punishment, is to be
found in the increase of infanticide. Hence
arises this difficulty. If you maintain
capital punishment for infanticide, the
chances of escape will greatly increase. If
you abolish capital punishment for infanticide, how can you maintain it for other
kinds of murder? For what life more
justly claims our protection than that of
the infant which cannot protect itself?
Another cause of the increased uncertainty
of capital punishment may be found in the
increased facilities for poisoning which scientific chemistry affords. In 1861, Sir George
Lewis gave this opinion, "With all the
modern improvements in medical science,
it is still very difficult to form a judgment in
cases of medical poisoning." Here, again,
the varying opinions of medical men decide
the question. Supposing, then, that the
aversion to inflict capital punishment goes
on increasing, what remedies are proposed?
One remedy suggested is, no longer to
execute women; but such a distinction
between the sexes is at once illogical and
cruel. Another suggestion, also referring
to women, is no longer to execute them
for infanticide; but this distinction is also

forbidden by reason and humanity. A third
remedy suggested, is to establish a system
of private executions. This would only be
a palliative or concealment of the evil. It
would be a confession that we are ashamed
of what we are doing. The whole scene
of the execution, though excluded from the
public gaze, would re-appear, perhaps more
vividly, in the public press. But, even
were the desire to read of such horrors to
diminish (which I admit to be probable
owing to improved education and better
feeling) the precaution of private executions
would become needless. For, as the influence of civilization, above all of Christianity, extends, the people will voluntarily
withdraw themselves—they are even now
beginning to withdraw themselves — from
such

"Pomps of death, and theatres of blood."

Are we then to go on with a sort of legislative *vis inertia,* in the course we have
already followed? Can no remedy be proposed? I propose that we have a solemn
inquiry. Let us endeavour first to ascertain whether executions really do deter from
crime; secondly, with what results they
have been abolished in other countries;
thirdly, what would be the most effective
substitute for them? But it may be said,
"Go no further, let premeditated and
aggravated murder be an exceptional case,
reserved for capital punishment. There is
something so special in such a crime that
you should maintain it in this case, though
you abolish it in other cases." I answer,
there are other crimes of violence which,
for atrocity, can scarcely be distinguished
from murder, such as rape and violent
attempts to murder. Rape is sometimes a worse crime than murder. Attempts to murder are also sometimes as
bad as murder. If a man all but kill his
victim—if he leave him for dead, believing
that he has killed him—here the intent to
murder exists, and the act of murder is
merely prevented by an accident. Yet
you do not execute in such cases; and
society bears the exemption from execution
with safety. May you not, with equal
safety, extend the mitigation of punishment to cases of murder, which are many
of them scarcely distinguishable from the
cases I have mentioned? But, besides
this, capital punishment has been safely
abrogated in other countries. Our proceedings, our interest in this subject, are
not peculiar to this nation. In other countries there is the same shrinking from the
punishment of death. In France, we are

told, the juries persist in returning verdicts of murder, "with extenuating circumstances," which exempts the accused from execution. In Italy there is the same reluctance to return a verdict which involves a loss of life. Russia has long abolished capital punishment. I know it is said that capital punishment is virtually inflicted there, because its intended substitute, corporal punishment, is so severe that it kills the criminal. But I hold it impossible that in a civilized nation like Russia this can, except accidentally or exceptionally, be the case. Baden, Oldenburg, Louisiana followed the example of Russia. In Tuscany the abolition of capital punishment has been maintained consistently with public safety, and with a diminution of crime, for more than seventy years. During an interval when it was restored, the authorities had great difficulty in finding an executioner, and could not even raise the guillotine. A new one was procured from Paris, but it was never unpacked. In 1859 capital punishment was finally abolished; and all Tuscany heard with joy, throughout its length and breadth, the decree, *La Pena di Morte sarà abolita.* In Belgium, we are told, in four provinces, no execution has occurred since 1839. Yet the number of criminals has diminished. In Portugal it has been recently abolished. Will it be said that there are nations more refined than ours, and that the English are too barbarous to dispense with executions? Then we cite the case of a nation said to be even an exaggeration of ourselves—the United States—

"No execution now takes place in Maine, and capital punishment has been abolished by law in Alabama, Michigan, and Louisiana without any evil results."

Two of the cantons of Switzerland, Frieburg and Neufchatel, have also abolished it; and it is stated, in the Report of a Commission lately appointed in Frieburg, that, though for a short time after the repeal of capital punishment crime may increase, yet that, after an interval, the increased certainty of punishment begins to operate, and crime is diminished. In a journal ably conducted at Bologna by Signor Ellero (*Giornale per l'Abolizione della Pena di Morte*) a list is given of no less than seventeen countries or states where the punishment of death has been abolished, containing a population of many millions, without including Russia generally, but only the Grand Duchy of Finland.

One argument I desire to press before I

Mr. W. Ewart

close—that is, the effect of the retention of capital punishment on the administration of justice. In this country our boast has been the supremacy of the law, alike over the power of the Crown and the turbulence of the people. In the late case of Hall it was thought right to make the execution of the law give way before the strong expression of popular feeling. I think that Hall was justly reprieved. But is it expedient, is it not derogatory to the steady administration of justice, that these outbreaks of popular feeling, these incursions of public excitement into the calmer regions of justice and of law, should exist? And must you not expect such outbreaks and such excitement in certain cases if you maintain capital punishment? We are accustomed to think in this country, in the language of a distinguished lawyer and poet, that—

"Sovereign law, the State's collected will
    O'er thrones and globes elate,
Sits empress, crowning good, repressing ill."

But how can she firmly hold the balance, if popular impulse sways it; and how can you exclude popular impulse, if you maintain the punishment of death?

I have shown that figures, facts, and the tendency of the feelings of mankind are against the continuance of the punishment of death. I desire to express my own conviction that it is opposed to the spirit of Christianity and the progress of civilization. I have shown that the remedies usually proposed are inadequate to counteract the evil we complain of. I have shown that the objections to capital punishment go on increasing. Every passing and improving day, which makes man more deeply feel his own responsibility, will make him more averse to the punishment of death. This feeling is deeply seated in the mind, or rather in the soul, of man, and cannot be extinguished. Impressed by this conviction, impelled by these feelings, I once more ask you to reconsider this vital question, and inquire whether you cannot safely resign the awful attribute of disposing of human life into the hands of Him who gave it.

MR. DENMAN said, that in seconding the Motion, he would claim the indulgence of the House for a few minutes, as he could speak from considerable experience in criminal courts, both as a prosecuting counsel and as counsel retained to defend prisoners. He did not intend to argue this Question on the ground that the State had not a perfect power and a perfect right, if it was necessary for the protection of society, to inflict the punishment of death on those who had deserved it; but he would contend that the burden of proof lay on those who maintained the necessity of retaining that punishment, and that before they intrusted to any one the power of taking away the life of a human being they should have some probable ground for believing that doing so was necessary for the safety of the community. If it could be proved to his satisfaction that by the infliction of capital punishment murders had on the whole decreased, and not, as he thought, in all probability increased, he should give his vote for the retention of the punishment, at least to a certain extent. But from all he had seen and read, he believed that the punishment of death, instead of diminishing crime increased it. He need not consider the exceptional case of treason; and as, practically, capital punishment was inflicted for no other crime than that of murder, he should argue the question as one relating to punishment by death for murder only. In considering this question it was desirable that hon. Gentlemen should bear in mind how the crime of murder was defined by law—it was defined by law as of malice aforethought taking away the life of another; but when we come to consider what it was in practice, it turned out to be a very different thing. Under the expression "malice aforethought" every variety of murder, wilful and unwilful, was included. When we considered the various circumstances under which the offence was committed, we could not treat murder as an offence which was invariably uniform and equal in its gravity. He was told it might be suggested in the course of the debate that a Committee might be appointed, but with the limited object of considering whether murder ought not to be differently defined; whether, admitting that capital punishment ought to be retained in aggravated cases of murder, there were not other cases of murder in which it ought not to be resorted to. He hoped that no such course would be adopted; he hoped that the Committee would not be crippled or confined in that way, but that it should be at liberty to take evidence generally, and to consider whether capital punishment ought not to be abolished entirely. He had said that there were different cases of murder, and he should in the first instance take the worst. He would take those committed from the lowest passions, and with the most guilty motives;

and let the House consider whether the class who committed those murders were likely to be deterred from the commission of the crime by the small chance there was of their coming to the gallows. All experience of society and all knowledge of human nature led to the conclusion that they were not. Let them take the case of Palmer or that of the notorious poisoner, Mrs. Chesham, who poisoned her children, and was brought to trial on a charge of poisoning her husband. To the crimes of such persons, the lines of our great poet were peculiarly applicable—

> " Between the acting of a dreadful thing
> And the first motion, all the interim is
> Like a phantasma or a hideous dream."

And equally applicable to their case were the concluding lines—

> · " And the state of man,
> Like to a little kingdom, suffers then
> The nature of an insurrection."

The contemplation of the punishment of death was not likely to have the slightest deterring effect on the deliberate intention of those who were of a gambling, reckless disposition, and who were determined at all events to obtain their object. But suppose they did calculate the consequences, what would those consequences be, as such persons would be likely to look at them? A great chance of absolute impunity. In all other crimes the chances of escape were but 22 per cent on the committals, whereas in the case of murder the chances were 50 per cent. In the year 1852, which was a very fair year to choose as an illustration, there were eighty-one persons committed for murder. In the case of eight of these, the grand jury ignored the Bill; five were acquitted on the ground of insanity at the time of committing the offence; six on the ground of insanity at the time of trial; sixteen were convicted, and no less than forty-six were acquitted. The effect of the existence of capital punishment was to secure acquittals for the crime of murder enormously beyond the average of acquittals for other crimes. If criminals calculated upon anything, would they not calculate upon that? It had fallen to his lot to prosecute and defend many persons for murder, and he believed he spoke the experience of all who had been placed in a similar position, in saying that in cases of murder an amount of evidence was required far beyond anything required in other cases, owing to the extent to which Judges, juries, counsel, and all concerned in the administration of the law were constrained by the horror of sending a fellow-creature to death to distort the facts and strain the law. As to the encouragement which was thus given to crime, he believed there were few, if any, cases in which when a person had been found guilty of murder, and not receiving capital punishment, had been afterwards set at large, such a person had ever committed murder again. But there were cases in his own experience in which persons having been tried for murder and acquitted, because juries shrank from the infliction of capital punishment, had immediately gone to work to commit murder again. There was the case of Mrs. Chesham, who poisoned two children, and who was tried in 1847, and again in 1848. The evidence against her was very strong. Professor Taylor, the Professor of Chemistry at Guy's Hospital, proved that though he had not found arsenic in the stomachs of the children in quantity sufficient to cause death, yet its presence could only be accounted for on the supposition that it formed a portion of a larger quantity that had actually been administered; but because he would not say that he had found sufficient arsenic actually in the stomachs to cause death, she was found not guilty on both occasions. It was proved afterwards that on being taken into custody she had concealed the arsenic in the trunk of a hollow tree, and after the lapse of two years she went and got that arsenic and poisoned her husband with it. She was tried again before Lord Campbell. The evidence was precisely the same, except that the quantity of arsenic found in the stomach was rather smaller than that found in the stomachs of the children; in fact, as she afterwards acknowledged, she had taken a hint from the former trials, and administered the poison in smaller doses. The experienced counsel who conducted the prosecution, knowing the reluctance of juries to convict on capital offences, especially where it would lead to the execution of a woman, and calculating that the jury would most likely not know whether an attempt to murder was punishable capitally, deliberately advised that the prisoner should be indicted for poisoning with intent to murder, in the hope that it would be easier to get a conviction. The jury did find her guilty and she was executed. About the same time there were other similar cases tried on the same circuit. A woman named May was tried for the same offence of murdering her husband, who, it was shown, had

actually gone to consult Mrs. Chesham between the second and third trial as to how the thing was to be done. She was found guilty; but another woman, who was tried under precisely similar circumstances, was acquitted. These cases, he believed, were entirely owing to the encouragement given to crime by the acquittal of Mrs. Chesham. He believed that had Mrs. Chesham been tried in the first instance for a non-capital offence she would have been found guilty, and neither her own second crime nor the crimes of the other women would have been committed. It was a considerable time since the question had been considered by the House, and in that interval considerable changes had been made in the law. There was also a great lack of reliable statistics on the subject, and the proposed Committee would, he thought, do great service if they could throw light upon that part of the question, for in no country, he believed, in which capital punishment had been abolished, had it afterwards been re-imposed. M. Dupetiaux, the Inspector General of the Belgian Prisons in 1834, declared it to be his belief that the infliction of the punishment of death had the effect of increasing the number of murders. In support of that position he stated that, while in the five years ending 1804 there were in Belgium 235 executions, there were in the five years ending 1829 only 22 capital executions, the result being that there were in the latter period only 34 convictions for murder as against 150 in the former; there being no executions in the five years ending 1834, and only 20 convictions for murder. From a Return, he might add, which had lately been published on the Motion of the hon. Member for Clare (Sir Colman O'Loghlen), he found that there were in the year 1857 57 committals for murder, 28 acquittals, 10 no bills, and 11 sentences of death. In 1858 there were 16 sentences and 11 executions; in 1859, 18 sentences and nine executions; and in 1860, 17 sentences and nine executions. Those figures showed that for a considerable number of years the punishment of death had been inflicted only in a very limited number of cases and for very aggravated murders, and the number of those crimes showed during the same period a tendency to diminution. But for the last three or four years a change, he found, had for some reason taken place, and a tendency had sprung up to inflict the sentence of death in a

Mr. Denman

larger proportion as compared with the number of convictions. The result of that change was not to diminish, but rather to increase, the number of convictions for murder. In 1859 there were 18 persons convicted and 9 executed; while in the next year the proportions were 17 convicted and 12 executed. What followed? There were in 1861, 26 convictions for murder and 14 executions; in the following year, 28 convictions and 15 executions; and in 1863, 22 executions out of 29 convictions. It appeared, therefore, that for a period of 21 years there had not been so large a number of executions for murder as last year. From those statistics he was, he thought, entitled to argue that the carrying out capital punishment on a larger scale had had no tendency to diminish the number of murders. The uncertainty as to whether the sentence of the law would or would not be carried into effect acted, moreover, as a reason to induce the criminal to hope that he might offend with impunity. There were every day cases occurring in which the exercise of the prerogative of the Crown was discussed, and in which the propriety or impropriety of the action of the Home Secretary was canvassed, and all those circumstances operated to the encouragement of the criminal, by, among other things, inducing juries to hesitate before they convicted, inasmuch as they were uncertain what the effect of conviction might be. In his own experience he knew of instances in which jurors, whose recommendations to mercy had been set aside by the Home Secretary, had on subsequent occasions refused to convict of the capital offence; and more than this, he had known the same circumstance deter other jurors from convicting prisoners of murder. All these things tended greatly to diminish the efficacy of capital punishment, and to produce an impunity, or a belief in impunity, which, if there was any speculation in such matters, must encourage people to commit murders. And what was there in a public execution which could tend to the prevention of crime? Two almost opposite accounts had been given in that House of the effect which the recent execution of the five pirates produced upon those who witnessed it; but, whichever was correct, he was convinced that executions were mischievous. If they did not produce a feeling of sympathy for the criminal, they excited in the minds of the spectators a brutal feeling which was quite as injurious to public morality. He did not go to the execution to which he had just referred, but he saw hundreds and thousands of men and women coming away from it, and among them was a group of young girls from fourteen to eighteen years of age; and, so far from the spectacle having made a serious impression upon their minds, they were jeering and laughing and throwing themselves into contortions in imitation of the men who had just undergone the last sentence of law. That did not look as if they had been much impressed by the scene. It was illogical to retain the punishment of death for murder, after it had been abolished in the case of attempts to murder, leaving the punishment of the criminal to depend upon the accident whether his victim lived or died. If it was asked what were we to do with murderers, if we did not hang them, he replied "What do you do with them now?" From the year 1838 to 1852, 269 persons were convicted of murder, of whom 148 were executed. Of the rest, 92 were transported for life, and 29 were transported or imprisoned for short terms varying from seven years to six months; but he did not know that any of those persons had ever committed another murder. What did other countries do? He believed that upon inquiry it would turn out that in practice there were very few countries which adhered to capital punishment as a rule; and although we had lost a portion of our power of transportation, we were not worse, but rather better off in that respect than most other countries. All these matters were well worthy the consideration of a Committee of that House, or of a Royal Commission, and if such an inquiry resulted only in a diminution of the offences for which this punishment was inflicted, some advantage would have been gained. But if the Report was that capital punishment was a mistake, and if that Report led to its abolition, the statute which effected that reform would be the most glorious of all the beneficent enactments which had signalized the reign of our gracious Queen.

Motion made, and Question proposed,

"That a Select Committee be appointed to inquire into the expediency of maintaining the Punishment of Death."—(*Mr. William Ewart.*)

LORD HENRY LENNOX rose to move as an Amendment—

"That a Select Committee be appointed to inquire into the operation of the laws relating to capital punishment."

Whatever might be his own opinion, and he had a very strong one on the subject, he was not about, on that occasion, to attempt to advocate the abolition of capital punishment. All he should do was to give the House a truthful sketch of the operation of the laws relating to capital punishment since the last inquiry was made, now many years ago. He hoped that after he had laid before the House statements tending to confirm some of the views entertained by the hon. Member for Dumfries (Mr. Ewart) and the hon. and learned Member for Tiverton (Mr. Denman), on the subject, the right hon. Gentleman the Home Secretary would not hesitate to grant the inquiry which was asked. Capital punishment had been described by a high authority in English law (Blackstone) as not being of a retaliatory or vindictive nature, but as an example and a means to deter others from committing similar crimes. It must, therefore, be looked upon simply as a police regulation. The question then was, whether it fulfilled the requirements of a police law. One of the greatest requisites of healthy police regulation was certainty of the conviction of the guilty; and there could be no doubt that in many cases the difficulty in getting a jury to convict was occasioned by the penalty which it was known would follow upon their sentence. The House would excuse him if he stated to them the circumstances of a case which occurred some two years since in the city which he had the honour to represent in Parliament (Chichester), and which made at the time a profound impression on his mind. The circumstances were as follows: —An unfortunate young student at the Training College in that city was passing along a lane; when he reached a certain spot he was shot by a person in a soldier's dress, lingered for two days and died in great agony, so much so that he was unable to give any accurate account of the transaction. The shot was evidently not intended for this unfortunate youth, but for the colonel of one of the regiments stationed in the barracks, and whose wont it was to pass that spot at that hour. Suspicion at once fell upon a soldier in those barracks. He had been heard to vow vengeance against the officer in question. The corporal who slept in his room testified to the man leaving in the night, and to observing that in the place where the musket

Lord Henry Lennox

should have been it was not. He also heard the shot fired about the time the murder was committed. The soldier, shrinking with a guilty fear, instead of remaining in barrack to meet the charge, conscience-stricken fled across the fields, and was taken hiding himself in a ditch; his musket, with barrel exploded, was picked up in a neighbouring field. He was brought to trial. A stirring speech was made by his counsel, who threw doubts upon the circumstantial evidence, told the jury that if they convicted the man they would consign him to certain death, and was it not then much better that ten guilty men should escape rather than that one innocent man should suffer? The prisoner was acquitted. He (Lord Henry Lennox) felt at the time, and felt now, that a stronger instance could not be brought forward of the extreme difficulty of inducing jurymen to convict in capital cases. But can any man in his senses doubt, if the penalty had been one of penal servitude instead of capital punishment, that the jury would have returned a verdict of guilty? Now, if juries shrink from conviction in cases of adult murders, what shall we say of the cases of infanticide? No one who had watched the course of events for the last few years could doubt that this crime was greatly upon the increase. The public mind had lately been shocked by the accounts of dead bodies of infants stowed away wholesale in every cranny, and even in the coffins of adult strangers, in order to prevent the necessity of obtaining a medical certificate. Medical certificates were very properly designed as a protection to life by stating officially the cause of death; therefore he held that, when they found that these means were resorted to to avoid the ordeal of a medical certificate, they had *primâ facie* evidence for believing that, in many instances at least, those bodies had been the victims of foul play. After the cases brought forward by the hon. Member for Dumfries (Mr. Ewart), he would only trouble the House with one or two more. Some four or five years ago there was a remarkable case tried at Exeter. A woman named Boucher, tried at the spring assizes at Exeter last year, was found pressing the body of a new born infant in a tub—the child's neck bore marks of strangulation. The mother had been once before charged with a similar crime, but, having partially burnt the body, it could not be shown that the child had been born alive, and could only be found guilty of concealment of birth. Still more recently a young woman (Margaret Robinson) was tried for child murder at Carlisle. She had stuffed two rags down the child's throat; that they could have been there by accident was an utter impossibility. In addition to this, the infant had been strangled, and was found with a rope and a black mark round its neck. The jury, however, found her guilty of concealment of birth only, the verdict extracting from Mr. Baron Martin the exclamation of "Not guilty of murder, gentlemen!" These expressive words he used to show his surprise at such a verdict. He (Lord Henry Lennox) did not think that any one would deny that some inquiry was necessary after the remarkable speech which had lately been delivered by the Lord Chancellor, one of the most distinguished lawyers of this or any other times. He distinctly affirmed it as his conviction, that the time had come for a classification of cases of homicide. The hon. and learned Member for Tiverton (Mr. Denman) said truly that several crimes came under the category of murder, and that for those crimes there was but one punishment. He appealed to any Gentleman in the House whether it was possible to see a greater variation of vice, premeditation, and guilt than could be found in the capital cases tried at the assizes. Yet for one and all the sentence was death. What more could be said against the actual state of the law than this—that at present there is the same penalty attached to the case of him who, for a trifling gain with subtle skill, administers in small doses the deadly poison, and smiles upon the prolonged agonies of the fading victim, and for him who in a fit of drunken brawl, while the blood is heated with liquor, and some fancied wrong, if not in self-defence, destroys the life of his paramour or companion? What shall we say to the law which administers the same punishment to Palmer or Catherine Wilson, and the wretched man Wright? It was impossible for any one to say that that was a healthy state of the law, where two crimes so dissimilar in their character received the same punishment. A sentence, he thought, should rest upon such solid grounds that, once passed, it should be irreversible, and should not be dispensed with either at the caprice of the Minister or in obedience to popular clamour. From the speeches of the right hon. Gentleman the Secretary for the Home Department, he gathered that the existing law on the subject of capital punishment was as follows:—When a man was convicted and sentenced to death, the Judge wrote immediately to the Home Secretary apprising him of the fact. Thereupon his friends or the humanitarians got up a petition to the Home Office for the commutation of the sentence, and the Secretary of State referred the matter back to the Judge. According to theory, if the latter held that there was no ground for revising the sentence the matter was dropped, and the man went forth to be hanged. To the state of things represented by that description of the law he objected strongly. In the first place, it was putting too much upon the Judge, and, moreover, leaving the issue dependent very much on his personal character. There were some Judges who, like himself, shrank with horror from the thought of taking a human life; while others of stronger minds were known in the popular phrase as "hanging Judges." Even, therefore, supposing this were a fixed law, he should protest against it. The facts, however, were the reverse of what had been represented to the House, for the fiat of the Judge was not always final. The case of Jessie MacLachlan had caused the greatest dissatisfaction, and not twelve months ago a case occurred which was much discussed both in that House and out of it. The Judge confirmed the verdict, and not only that, but he applied to the senior Judge of the Court, who confirmed it also; the jury not only agreed upon their verdict, but afterwards with praiseworthy industry went through the evidence, and came to the same conclusion again. This double conclusion was in accordance with the opinion of the Judge, confirmed by that of the high functionary; yet the Secretary of State for the Home Department, who in other cases rested everything upon the fiat of the Judge, disregarded that and the opinion of the jury as well, and by the exercise of the irresponsible power committed to him rescued from execution one of the greatest criminals in the country. Since then they had had another case, in which he (Lord Henry Lennox) concurred in the course the Home Secretary had adopted. He alluded to the case of Hall. But what were the circumstances in connection with that case? Mr. Waddington, of the Home Office, wrote a reply to a memorial which had been addressed to the Home Secretary for a commutation of sentence in which the following words occurred:—

"There can be no doubt from the evidence that the murder was deliberate and premeditated. . . . . Sir George Grey feels that it would be of most dangerous consequences to society if such provocation as the prisoner received were held sufficient to exempt a man from the penalty attached by the law to deliberate and premeditated murder ; and therefore he regrets to be compelled to come to the conclusion that it would be inconsistent with his duty to recommend a commutation of the sentence."

What followed ? Yielding to the blandishments of some of his (Lord H. Lennox's) hon. Friends, the Secretary of State, at the last moment, respited Hall, and having pronounced that, in his matured judgment, the prisoner had been guilty of "deliberate and premeditated murder," he consented to forego that opinion in deference to popular opinion and to public clamour. If popular clamour and public opinion were to prevail, he would ask the right hon. Gentleman why they did not prevail a few weeks ago. Was there no popular clamour or public opinion in favour of Thomas Wright being reprieved ? Did not large bodies of his fellow-workmen press to the Home Office, and even go as far as the threshold of Windsor, to pray for the remission of the sentence on that man, but in vain ? He thought it much to be regretted that the right hon. Gentleman did not remit the sentence upon Wright. The noble words used by the right hon. Gentleman in the case of the woman Mac-Lachlan could not be too often repeated, and he would ask permission to read them to the House—

" I think it is most important that the administration of the law should not only be right, but that there should exist a general impression in the public mind of the country that it is right and just ; and especially in regard to capital punishment is it undesirable that it should be inflicted where there prevails a general, I may almost say a universal, feeling that there were circumstances in the case which rendered that coarse inexpedient."—[3 *Hansard*, clxx. 693.]

On another occasion the right hon. Gentleman said—

" I mention this to show that a case may be quite clear, and no ground for a commutation of the sentence may arise from any doubts as to the facts, and yet if you mean to retain capital punishments at all, it may not be expedient under some circumstances to let the law take its course. I think that capital punishments ought to be maintained, but I feel that they cannot be maintained if you stretch the law to the extreme, and execute every sentence without regard to its effect upon public opinion."—[3 *Hansard*, clxx. 694.]

There never was a case in the annals of capital punishment in which public opinion was so strongly enlisted as in favour of Wright. There were great apprehensions

Lord Henry Lennox

of a popular attempt at rescue. He died in a spirit of bravado, expressing his thanks to the crowd, amid uproarious expressions of sympathy. Even the wretched creatures in the opposite houses, who usually made money by letting their windows on those occasions, showed their sympathy by closing their windows and putting down their blinds. They were willing on that occasion to forego their unholy gains. With three such cases—of mistaken clemency in the instance of Jessie MacLachlan, of rightful clemency in the case of Hall, and wrongful severity in the case of Thomas Wright—it was reasonable to ask at the hands of the Home Secretary that he should grant the inquiry and enable the House to obtain that evidence which they had had no opportunity of acquiring on this subject since 1847. Whatever his opinions might be, and they were strongly against the continuance of capital punishment, he wished to point out to his hon. Friends near him, many of whom did not share his opinions, that even from their point of view there were strong grounds for this inquiry. Not many nights ago, in another place, one of the most talented and most vigorous-minded members of the House of Peers (the Earl of Ellenborough) moved the first reading of a Bill to alter the law in respect of the revision of capital sentences. He did so, saying that recent proceedings had shown the absolute necessity of a change in the present practice at the earliest period. The noble Earl contended that the practice of the law ought to be amended, so that the utmost authority and weight should attach to decisions in regard to capital sentences, and that the whole responsibility should not be thrown on the Home Secretary alone. The noble Earl added that—

" Unless the country was made to understand that entire confidence could be placed in the decisions on these questions, there would be some danger of our being forced to abandon a punishment which he believed to be necessary to the interests of society."—[3 *Hansard*, clxxiv. 1484.]

Being himself an advocate of the repeal of capital punishment, he (Lord H. Lennox) would appeal to his hon. Friends around him to follow the lead of the noble Earl in another place, and to join him in asking the Home Secretary to consent to this inquiry. The hon. and learned Member for Tiverton (Mr. Denman) had alluded to a statement he had made in that House relative to an execution some short time ago. He believed that his statement simply applied to the demeanour of the crowd on that occasion, which led him to suppose that those upon whom it was expected a salutary impression would be made were not in any way awed by the sight which they witnessed, but, on the contrary, viewed the spectacle with levity and indifference. Since then he had looked to the Report of the Lords' Committee, and found that it confirmed the opinion he had then expressed as to the effect of capital punishment upon the lower classes. The writer of a pamphlet which he held in his hand stated that the criminal classes expressed a deliberate preference of the violent death to the punishment of transportation for life. The Rev. James Amos, incumbent of St. Stephen's, Southwark, containing a population of 8,000, many of whom were of the lowest class, in a pamphlet which he held in his hand, stated that he had heard the punishment of hanging spoken of by that class with the most complete indifference, and that on the occasion of the execution of Wright nothing was heard except sympathy for the criminal and colloquial jokes among the crowd. If the right hon. Gentleman thought him incapable of deciding whether capital punishment should be retained or not, he could assure him he had not the slightest wish personally to take part in the deliberations of the Committee. He trusted, however, that there would be a Committee appointed, and that it would not be limited in its operations. He moved his Amendment with the view of widening the field of the inquiry, because he believed the Motion of the hon. Member for Dumfries (Mr. Ewart) to be far too confined to meet the object in view. He felt the most extreme confidence in the result of the deliberations of the Committee, because he believed that such an overwhelming mass of evidence would be brought forward as to compel the Committee to recommend to the House a change in the law, and thus remove from our country one of the greatest scandals that could possibly afflict it. The noble Lord concluded by moving, as an Amendment, that a Select Committee be appointed to inquire into the operation of the laws relating to capital punishments.

MR. MITFORD said, he would second the Amendment, because he thought it would open a much wider range of inquiry than the original Motion. They must all admire the spirit which animated the hon. and learned Member for Tiverton (Mr. Denman) during his speech; but, at the same time, as long as human nature was

what it was, he thought it would be necessary that capital punishment should be retained until they had devised some secondary punishment which would have the same deterring effect. He believed, however, that there was a strong feeling on the public mind in reference to the horrible spectacles sometimes presented at public executions, and the discussion in that House in February last, and the Report of the Select Committee of the House of Lords some years ago, had given great support to that feeling. In his opinion the hon. Member for Oldham (Mr. Hibbert) did good service in bringing this matter before the House last February. It was with much sorrow and disappointment he (Mr. Mitford) heard the right hon. Baronet the Home Secretary, treat on that occasion the Report of the Lord's Committee with apparently very little respect. That Report recommended that executions in public should be suppressed, whilst the utmost precaution at the same time should be taken to secure the due execution of the sentence. The right hon. Baronet said he thought that no Committee had ever come to a positive decision on a subject on less clear and conclusive grounds. Now this was an extraordinary observation, considering that some of the most eminent Members in the Upper House, including three Chancellors, were Members of that Committee. He need only mention the following names:—The Marquess of Lansdowne, Earl Stanhope, Earl Grey, the Bishop of Oxford, Lord Lyttelton, Lord Brougham, Lord Campbell, and Lord St. Leonards. Such men as these were not likely to put forth a Report on grounds that were not clear and conclusive. There was a time when the rotting carcases of malefactors might be seen swinging from gibbets on our highways; at another time it was thought that no better ornaments could be placed upon our city gates than the heads of traitors; and at those periods men in authority were found to advocate the practices, on the ground of their deterring effects. Happily we had lived to see those practices abolished without any of those evil results which had been anticipated. In like manner it was now argued that criminals should be publicly executed in order to deter others from the commission of dreadful crimes. But what evidence was there to show that public executions had a deterring effect? The right hon. Baronet said, "Who knows how many persons out of the crowd that witnessed those executions might be impressed with the sense of fear against the commission of murder who would otherwise be likely to fall into that crime?" Well, he (Mr. Mitford) echoed the right hon. Gentleman's language by asking—Who knows? But the evidence which had been given on the subject was all the other way. Public executions did not appear to impress any one on the spot with any good feeling whatever. They appeared to cause unmitigated evil by bringing together masses of people who, for reasons of policy and morality, should be kept isolated and dispersed. They knew that a place of execution was a scene of debauchery of the grossest nature. They knew that when the unfortunate criminals were brought on the scaffold men whistled and behaved as though in the gallery of a theatre, and while the attention of the spectators was attracted to what was going on their pockets were picked. He thought the practice of public executions was unworthy of the age, and he hoped the time would come when they would cease. He called the attention of the House to a letter on the subject from Mr. Charles Dickens, written since the execution of the pirates at Newgate. Mr. Dickens said he ventured to suggest that the question of public executions was not one to theorise about. No man's opinion on the subject was worth anything to him unless he had seen the shameful sight. He (Mr. Dickens) was, he said, outside of Newgate on the occasion of the execution to which he referred, and declared the scene was diabolical.

Amendment proposed,

To leave out from the word "The" to the end of the Question, in order to add the words "operation of the Laws relating to Capital Punishment,"—(*Lord Henry Lennox,*)

—instead thereof.

Question proposed, "That the words proposed to be left out stand part of the Question."

MR. ALDERMAN ROSE said, as the speeches had hitherto been all on one side, he thought something should be said on behalf of the public. As far as he could judge, the tendency of the speeches they had just heard was simply this—"Murder made easy." Having had some ten years' experience as Commissioner of the Central Criminal Court, he was bound to say that his idea of the conduct of juries was quite different from that of the hon. and learned Member for Tiverton (Mr. Denman). It was his belief that, in the main, juries

Mr. Mitford

performed their functions faithfully and honestly; they were, no doubt, always very jealous of the evidence upon which a man was to be convicted, and anxious to give the prisoner the full benefit of any doubt which might arise in their minds as to his actual guilt; but that was nothing more than what was in accordance with the law of the land and of humanity. Taking everything into account, it would be found that on the whole just verdicts were given. The hon. Member (Mr. Mitford) said that the punishment of death for murder must be retained until they had discovered some secondary punishment which should have an equally deterring effect. Well, did the hon. Member know what "secondary punishment" meant? It meant giving a convicted criminal a ticket-of-leave, entitling him to go about freely, perhaps to rejoin his old associates, and join in the perpetration of new crimes. Was secondary punishment applicable to such cases as Catherine Wilson, the notorious poisoner, who had succeeded for years in carrying her deadly designs into execution? or as Mrs. May's, or Mrs. Chesham's, or the notorious Palmer's? He believed the public out of doors would not think that kind of punishment the cure for that kind of crime. They were there to legislate for the people. He was quite aware that much sympathy was felt for the convicted murderer, and it was said "a hanged man was past recovery;" but so was the victim. It was quite right, no doubt, that every secondary punishment should be of such a nature that it should have a deterring effect; but it had been and always would be regarded as a deterring circumstance by the class of people who attended executions that the punishment of death should follow such crimes as that for which the man was hung yesterday. That man did not intend to commit murder, it was said. But what did he do? He got an iron bar, came behind his victim, and battered his skull in, whereas if he had only committed robbery he would have got off with secondary punishment. He happened to be Sheriff of London and Middlesex in 1856, and was instrumental in saving the life of a man who had murdered his wife while under the influence of drink. The execution was to have taken place on the Monday, but the reprieve came on Saturday night, and the man was consigned to penal servitude. But what was the effect of this secondary punishment? He believed the man had become penitent, and he had had several letters from him; but the man had actually made application to him to obtain a free pardon. But with what face could he (Alderman Rose) urge that that man, who had murdered his wife and ought to have been hanged according to law—but that there were mitigating circumstances in the case—should within seven or eight years be not only freed from the consequences of his crime, but enabled to come home to his family and enjoy his secondary punishment. The hon. and learned Member for Tiverton had quoted instances of a number of persons charged with murder who had been acquitted on the ground of insanity. But, then, these persons were sent to a lunatic asylum, and were to be kept there for life. But that was not secondary punishment. If a criminal was sane, and if he did as Mrs. Wilson, Mrs. Chesham, and Mrs. May had done, the only safeguard to society was to hang them out of the way, and free society from the chance of further injury from them.

MR. NEATE said, that as the forms of the House precluded him from moving the Amendment of which he had given notice (for an Address for the Appointment of a Royal Commission to inquire into the provisions and laws under which the punishment of Death is now inflicted), he desired to show that the terms of the Motion of his hon. Friend (Mr. Ewart), or of the noble Lord, would not give as comprehensive a scope to the inquiry as the circumstances warranted. The subject of inquiry ought to be not only the law as regarded murder, but also as regarded treason, which had been disposed of in a rather summary way as an offence not likely to occur. They had been so much accustomed to hear of the crime of murder, that it had come to be believed that it rested on the common law, without any reference to statute law. But this was not so, and the Criminal Law Commissioners, who had gone very fully into the subject, had pointed out how the Judges had departed from the plain meaning of the statute inflicting capital punishment, and suggested that there should be a better definition of the crime of murder, and they said that the construction put upon the words *malice prepense* was not that which was intended by those who framed the statute. He (Mr. Neate) thought it would be right to consider whether a distinction could not be established by law between aggravated cases of murder and other cases which were not of so deep a die. In other countries the juries were allowed to declare, if they so thought fit, that "extenuating circumstances" existed, and, in his opinion, that practice might be introduced into this country. With regard to the Amendment moved by the noble Lord (Lord Henry Lennox), the question arose whether the inquiry would not be better conducted by a Commission than by a Committee? Without any disrespect to the Committees of that House, he thought it would be difficult just now to appoint a Committee composed of men of sufficient authority who would be able to give up their time to an inquiry on the subject; and he also conceived it to be desirable that the inquiry should be conducted by a body less numerous than Committees generally were, and not so much by formal discussion as by the results of frequent suggestion and intercourse. On the other hand, if a Commission were appointed, the country might have the advantage of the presence of one or two of the Judges as members of that body. Still, whether by Commission or Committee, the subject ought to be inquired into. He believed that the first effect of doing away with capital punishment might probably be an increase in the number of crimes; but ultimately a decrease in the number was to be anticipated, as the Penal Servitude Commission had shown that generally crime had diminished within the last twenty years, during which period offences had been less severely punished. The number of exceptional cases had increased so much that it had become very difficult to draw the line between the exceptions and the rule; and the result must, sooner or later, be, that in attempting to deal with the exceptional cases it would be found necessary to give up capital punishment altogether. But however that might be, the time had come when it was essential that there should be inquiry.

· SIR GEORGE GREY : Sir, I will, with the permission of the House, state the course which the Government think it right to take on the important subject now under its consideration. Some years have now passed since my hon. Friend the Member for Dumfries (Mr. Ewart), who has always been a strenuous advocate of the abolition of the punishment of death, brought this question before the House. I think he acted wisely and with a sound discretion in discontinuing to pursue the course of annually submitting this Motion to Parliament; and, no doubt, he must have been aware that the object he had in view, "a declaration that the punishment of death ought to be entirely abolished," was contrary to the general feeling of the House and to the country. However a considerable interval has elapsed since he last brought forward this proposition. I think no one can find fault with him for now reviving the Question. It is a matter of the utmost gravity and importance, and one with respect to which I hope the House will exercise much caution before adopting any determination. Since the last Motion on this subject was made, a considerable change has taken place in the law with respect to capital punishment. For many years past capital punishment has been limited almost exclusively to cases of wilful murder, but there were, until lately, other crimes on the statute-book to which the penalty of death was attached. However, upon the consolidation of the criminal law in 1861 an important change was made, and the law was brought into harmony with what had been recently the practice, and the penalty of death was repealed, so far as concerned England and Ireland, in all cases except wilful murder and treason. Happily treason is a crime scarcely known in our country in modern days, and therefore we may treat the penalty as now attaching only to wilful murder. Under these circumstances, my hon. Friend asks the House to remit to the consideration of a Select Committee the important question whether it is or is not expedient that capital punishment should be maintained in the case of that crime. I must say at once, on the part of the Government, that I do not think this is a question which should be referred to the opinion of a Committee. It is a question of the gravest character, most seriously concerning the interests of society, and deeply affecting the security of human life. I do not say it is not a subject which the House should entertain. Far be it from me to set up my individual opinion against that of those who have come to the conclusion that capital punishment should be abolished; but I say it is a subject which, if it is to be dealt with at all, should be carefully and maturely considered by the House itself. It is a question which ought not to be referred to the judgment of fifteen gentlemen upstairs, and decided, perhaps, by an accidental majority in a Committee —more especially as after all the decision would not in the least degree bind the future action of the House. On the general ques-

Sir George Grey

tion I adhere to the opinion I have frequently before expressed in debates on this subject—that it would neither be safe nor expedient to abolish capital punishment altogether in all cases—even of the gravest kind—cases of wilful and deliberate murder. I believe that by its abolition you would remove a security which now protects human life; and while my hon. Friend (Mr. Neate) believes that the abolition would cause only a temporary increase in the number of murders, I believe that it would not only tend to increase the number of such crimes in the first instance, but that it would do so permanently, because the deterring effect which capital punishment now has, not on the criminal class only, but on those who are only just removed from it, would be lost. My hon. Friend the Member for Dumfries has referred to the Report of the Lords' Committee in 1847, who no doubt expressed an opinion in regard to capital punishment which is well worthy of consideration ; but I would observe to my hon. Friend that that Committee was appointed in different terms from what he proposes. It was a Committee to inquire generally into the execution of the criminal law, especially as regarded juvenile offenders and transportation. It was presided over by Lord Brougham, and questions were addressed to the Judges in England, Scotland, and Ireland. One of these questions was whether any form of secondary punishment could be devised as an effectual substitute for capital punishment. The answers given by the Judges, and, indeed, the evidence taken generally before the Committee, deserve the careful consideration of hon. Members. To my mind, the evidence fully bears out the opinion which, in one sentence of a very long Report, was expressed by the Committee. They say—

" Respecting the expediency of abolishing capital punishment the Committee found scarcely any difference of opinion. Almost all witnesses, and all authorities, agree in opinion that for offences of the gravest kind, the punishment of death ought to be retained."

I am satisfied that there is no punishment so much dreaded ; and whatever arguments to the contrary may be derived from statistics, I am afraid that they form rather an unsafe guide on this matter. Common sense tells us that capital punishment is looked upon with horror and dread ; and no one who has filled the office I have now the honour to hold, who knows how constantly efforts are made to obtain a commutation of the sentence, and how the most severe secondary punishment is gratefully received as a substitute for the extreme penalty, can doubt that it is so regarded. My hon. and learned Friend the Member for Tiverton (Mr. Denman) says that capital punishment exercises no deterring effect on that limited portion of the criminal population by whom murders are committed. On that point I would invite his attention to the replies which the Judges gave to the questions of the Lords' Committee. The Judges draw a distinction between one class of the community and the other. They point out that the deterring effect of punishment is not to be measured merely by its influence on men who are hardened in crime, who are actuated by evil passions, and who, from a total absence of all principle, are almost reckless of the consequences which they entail on themselves. The deterring effect on the great mass of the population who do not belong to the criminal class must also be considered. One of the most distinguished men who had adorned the judicial bench, Lord Denman, the father of the hon. and learned Member for Tiverton, in reply to the question as to whether a secondary punishment could safely be substituted for the capital penalty, declined to express any opinion, as he had not sufficiently considered the question.

Mr. DENMAN desired to explain. He had the opportunity of knowing that the reason why his father abstained from expressing an opinion was that, as a judge, daily called upon to execute the law, his views might have been quoted as a reason why the law should not be carried into effect.

Sir GEORGE GREY: I believe I stated correctly the answer which the late Lord Denman is recorded to have given. I did not cite his opinion as in favour of capital punishment. On the question of the deterring effect of that punishment, however, the late learned Lord said—

"I think I have seen many instances of forbearing to add aggravation to the criminal act from fear of the severer punishment. I allude in particular to burglary and highway robbery."

Again, Mr. Justice Cresswell, an authority of great experience, expressed this opinion—

"Where burglaries and robberies are committed with deliberation, I think that the fear of capital punishment often saves life."

The truth is that the saving the life of a criminal may, in certain cases, involve the sacrifice of an innocent person. That is, in my opinion, the only ground on which capital punishment can be maintained, and I believe it to be sufficient. If you can show me a punishment of a secondary kind which has the same effect in deterring from the perpetration of murder, I will, by all means, support its adoption; but till convinced that an effectual substitute can be found, I cannot consent to the total abolition of the punishment of death. As to its deterring effect on the population above the criminal class, we have the explicit opinion of Baron Rolfe, the present Lord Cranworth, who said—

"Capital punishment is now practically confined to cases of murder, and in such cases I think it ought to be retained. I think it very important to leave to every criminal the strongest possible motive for abstaining from murder, in whatever crimes he may be engaged. I think that the deterring effect of punishment generally is very great, not upon the actual criminal population, but upon the vast masses a little removed above guilt."

The late Lord Cockburn, an eminent Scotch Judge, also stated—

"I think the deterring effects of punishment very great, not on the hardened, or on those to whom the commission of crime has become a sort of necessity, but on those who are still guiltless."

A living Irish Judge, Chief Baron Pigot, expressed the following views:—

"I think the fear of punishment does substantially operate upon the large class of culprits who are tempted to crime, without the incentive of violent passion, and whose habits previous guilt has not depraved, including those who have not hitherto been at all engaged in crime."

My hon. and learned Friend the Member for Tiverton gave us some statistics as to Belgium. He stated that at one period executions there were very numerous, and convictions equally so; but that subsequently the executions diminished and so did the number of convictions. My hon. and learned Friend inferred that the decrease of convictions was due to the decrease of executions, and that there was less crime; but I would reverse the argument, and say that the executions were fewer because fewer persons were convicted. In speaking of the number of acquittals, my hon. and learned Friend also omitted an important consideration, which is that a man may be put on his trial for murder and acquitted of that charge, but convicted of manslaughter. The distinction between the two is in some cases almost imperceptible; and a man may be convicted on the less serious charge without an acquittal in the sense referred to by the hon. and learned Member, and without evidencing any disinclination on the part of the jury to convict. The hon. and learned Member had also alluded to cases of infanticide, in which it was difficult to obtain a conviction. But with regard to this crime, one of the Judges lately expressed the opinion that women were often committed on that charge on most insufficient evidence taken at the coroner's inquest ; and many of the cases cited by his hon. and learned Friend as cases of murder resolved themselves, on careful inquiry, into mere cases of concealment of birth. It is clear in like manner that in many cases of committal for murder the evidence was *primâ facie* sufficient to justify the committal on that charge ; but the result of the trial might show that murder was not the crime committed, and that manslaughter would, in accordance with the opinion of an honest jury, be the right verdict. With regard to the increase of the crime, I will not weary the House with statistics, but I must say that I do not think any one can allege that, looking to the vast and rapid increase in population, murders have increased. We know there has recently been an increase of crime of all descriptions, though we cannot very easily determine the cause, and there have been rather more murders committed in 1863 than there had been in some previous years ; but, compared with many years ago, murders have considerably diminished, and no one can say that the crime is substantially on the increase. Considering the vast increase of the population, I believe there has been a great decrease of this crime. There are very few cases in which, I think, you can say that the verdict of acquittal was actually against the evidence. Such cases occasionally happen ; but in ordinary cases the jury, acting under the direction of the Judge as to the law, return the proper verdict. I think any one who reads the charges of the Judges must say that nothing can be more fair and impartial than the manner in which they leave these cases to the consideration of juries ; and, speaking of juries generally, no complaint can be made of the manner in which they consider the facts before them, and there is no reason to charge them with any violation of the oath they have taken to return a verdict according to the evidence. No doubt there are cases in which the jury, acting on their conviction of duty and the evidence, and relying on the law

Sir George Grey

as laid down by the learned Judge, find the prisoner guilty and recommend him to mercy ; and it has been said that in such cases it is the duty of the Secretary of State to attend to that recommendation. The usual practice is, when such a recommendation is made by the jury, that the Judge asks the grounds on which it rests ; he reports it to the Secretary of State, and says whether, in his opinion, the recommendation is borne out by the facts, and is entitled to weight. It would be a most dangerous doctrine to hold that the recommendation of a prisoner to mercy by a jury must in all cases have that weight given to it, and that, irrespective of the grounds on which it rests, it should interfere with the execution of the sentence. Indeed, such a course would be fatal to the administration of the law. For these reasons I certainly am not prepared to assent to the Motion of my hon. Friend the Member for Dumfries, either for the introduction of a Bill to abolish capital punishment, as originally placed on the notice paper, or for a reference to a Committee of the simple question whether, in their opinion, capital punishments ought to be maintained or abolished. But two other notices have been given on this subject in the shape of Amendments—one of which has been moved by the noble Lord the Member for Chichester (Lord H. Lennox), and the other was intended to be moved by the hon. Member for Oxford (Mr. Neate). These Motions have the same object. They both evade the direct question. They do not ask the Committee to report whether capital punishments ought to be maintained or abolished, but they suggest an inquiry as to the operation of the law of capital punishments, and report whether any alteration should be made in it. Now, there are many points connected with capital punishments, and indeed with the law of homicide generally, which I think might usefully be the subject of inquiry. First of all, I would say there are certain homicides punishable with death in this country not so punishable in many of the Continental nations and in several of the States of America, although in those nations and states capital punishments form part of their criminal code in cases of crime of the gravest character. The definition of murder has been referred to ; and I would call the attention of the House to that definition—

" By the English law murder is the unlawfully killing another with malice aforethought, express or implied. 'Malice afterthought' is a mere technical term, and is frequently a conclusion of law, rather than a question of fact. No actual forethought or premeditation is required; if the wicked intent, which is not necessarily an intent to kill, is executed the moment it springs up in the mind, the act may yet be murder. The rules for determining when malice afterthought is to be implied from circumstances, and when not, are not laid down in any statute, but are to be collected from a great variety of cases to be found in the books, and though resting, sometimes, upon nice distinctions, are, upon the whole, pretty well settled and understood. The law always infers it when death is inflicted in the act of committing a felony, though there is neither premeditation nor intention to kill, or even to do serious injury to the person killed. And even when the wrongful act causing the death is not done in the prosecution of a felony, still, if it be done wilfully and deliberately (that is, with no such provocation as by law reduces murder to manslaughter), with a malicious and mischievous intention seriously to injure the person killed, or any other person in particular, or all persons indiscriminately, the crime amounts to murder.'

Now, it is obvious that under this large definition there must be a great variety in the degrees of guilt attaching to crimes which legally constitute murder according to the law of England; but, although there is this great variety in the nature of this crime, the law not only attaches to each the punishment of death without distinction, but it leaves no discretion to the Judge as to the punishment to follow conviction. A change in the law in this respect took place in 1861. Before 1861 the practice was for the Judge, when he thought the capital sentence ought not to take effect, although there had been a conviction for a crime to which the law attached the punishment of death, to direct that that sentence should be recorded, and he abstained from passing the sentence. .It was then perfectly understood at the time that the Judge, having presided over the trial, heard the evidence, weighed it, and considered the verdict of the jury, was of opinion that the extreme penalty ought not to follow, but that, although death was recorded, the sentence ought to be commuted; and the practice was for the Judge to write to the Secretary of State, report the case and sentence as recorded, and suggest to the Secretary of State that the sentence should be commuted, and a minor sentence adequate to the crime committed substituted for that which had been recorded. In the case of manslaughter, the next crime in gravity and guilt to murder, a discretion is left to the Judge. There are cases of manslaughter where the Judge assigns a merely nominal punish-

ment, such as imprisonment for a day, and others where he passes a sentence of penal servitude for life. With regard to murder, the Judge is required in every case, since the change in the law in 1861, to pass the capital sentence. Now, I think there is ample room for inquiry whether that change of the law has been beneficial. An instance occurred at the last assizes. A woman was tried for murder and convicted; the Judge passed sentence of death; she was carried away from the dock, and, to use the common term, left for execution. The crowd disperses; they have seen the Judge, in conformity with the law, and with all the solemnity observed on such an occasion, pass sentence of death, and they do not know whether that sentence is to be executed or not. The Judge then writes to the Secretary of State, reports the case, says that if he had had the power he should not have passed the sentence, and that he is perfectly satisfied it is a case in which no good result can follow from the sentence being executed; that, in fact, it ought not to be executed, and recommends a commutation. Well, that commutation of course takes place—for a sentence which the Judge said, if he had not been compelled by law he would not have passed, cannot be carried into effect. In accordance with the common practice, the Judge informed me what sentence he thought would have been adequate under the circumstances. Thus the discretion formerly exercised by Judges in capital cases is now taken away from them; they represent the matter to the Secretary of State, and upon him is thrown the whole responsibility of doing that which the Judge in any other case would have had the power of doing himself. It would, I think, be much better that the sentence should be passed by the Judge in the presence of those who heard the trial, rather than that he should make a private communication to the Secretary of State, who, acting on his recommendation, appears to the public to be overruling the sentence of the Judge, while, in fact, he is only carrying out the views of the Judge. This is a point connected with the subject of capital punishment which I should be glad to see inquired into. There are many difficulties attending the execution of this branch of the criminal law, and I think it would be advantageous, and would strengthen the hands of any person who fills the office I now occupy, if an inquiry took place which would show what the real practice is, and which at present is very little understood. There is another part of the subject which needs consideration, and that is the law of Scotland. I have already said that a change in the law of England and Ireland took place in 1861; but no alteration was made in the law of Scotland. In many instances the law of Scotland may be better than the law in England, but I think it would be well to ask whether it is necessary to retain upon the statute-book as crimes punishable in Scotland by death offences which have ceased to bear that penalty in England and Ireland. Practically there is no distinction between the three countries, because power is vested in the Lord Advocate to prevent a capital sentence being passed in cases where the nature of the offence does not demand the extreme penalty. I know it is not so easy to abolish capital punishment for all the crimes which are not now so punishable in England and Ireland; and those who have read the answers of the Scotch Judges to the questions of the Lords' Committee will observe that the subject needs very careful consideration. These and many other points might well be made the subjects of inquiry, and useful results would doubtless be arrived at. Then comes the question as between the Amendment of the noble Lord the Member for Chichester (Lord H. Lennox) and that of which my hon. and learned Friend the Member for Oxford (Mr. Neate) has given notice; and I cannot but think that as to the manner of inquiry, whether by a Committee or a Commission, the House would do well to adopt the proposition of the hon. and learned Gentleman. His proposition is not only to inquire into the operation of existing law, but, what is of very great importance, into the actual law of murder—that is, into the provisions of the law as well as into its operation. I am far from saying that this inquiry could not be conducted by a Committee. But let the House consider how we are placed in respect of Committees. I ascertained this morning that there are now no less than twenty-four Public Committees sitting. If this Committee should be appointed, it could not sit for a long time if members of weight and authority were to be placed upon it; and, indeed, I think it would be impossible to have a satisfactory inquiry by a Committee into this subject during the present Session. I also think there is great weight in what was said by the hon. and

learned Gentleman the Member for Oxford —that if you desire to give weight and authority to the opinion of the tribunal to which you intrust the inquiry, it should comprise some men who are or who have been Judges—men of experience in the criminal law; and I think an inquiry would be more satisfactorily conducted by such a body, and their conclusions would carry greater weight than the Resolutions of a Committee. If my hon. Friend the Member for Dumfries (Mr. Ewart) will accept such an inquiry instead of that which he has suggested, and if the noble Lord will withdraw his Amendment, I shall be quite ready to accept the Amendment of my hon. and learned Friend, and the Government will recommend Her Majesty to issue a Commission in accordance with its terms. I hope that course will be adopted, as all agree that this is a subject deserving of careful inquiry; and if we can come to an agreement as to the objects of the inquiry, it is very desirable that we should avoid the necessity for a division.

MR. BRIGHT: Sir, I shall not, after the discussion which has taken place, and which has been, I think, almost on one side, take up the time of the House by making a speech. But the right hon. Gentleman (Sir George Grey) has said something which I am obliged to contest to some extent. He has quoted the opinions of Judges upon this question, and he has laid, I think, more stress upon those opinions than they generally deserve. I think, if there is one thing more certain than another, it is this—that every amelioration of the criminal code of this country has been carried against the opinion of the majority of the Judges. And I may on this point quote the opinion of an eminent Irish Judge, who, I believe, is still living, and with whom I had some conversation in Ireland some fifteen years ago. The conversation turned on this very question. He said, "Beware of the Judges. If Parliament had acted on the opinion of the Judges we should have been hanging now for forgery, for horse stealing, and for I know not how many other offences for which capital punishment has long been abolished." Now the right hon. Gentleman proposes to have a Commission, as I understand, instead of a Committee. There was an inconsistency in his speech I thought, on that point ; for at first he seemed to say that the question, whether capital punishment should be continued or be abolished, was not one which a Committee of this House was fitted to consider ; but towards the close of his speech he moderated that by admitting that some of the points referred to in the Amendment, which is, I suppose, to be agreed to, might be considered by a Committee. I will undertake to say that if he were to inquire in every civilized country in the world where there is a representative legislative assembly, he would find that the changes which had been made in their laws have been made invariably in consequence of inquiries instituted by those Chambers and carried on by means of Committees formed amongst their members. I admit that the bulk of the Committees of this House are not fairly constituted. I served very assiduously on Committees for the first ten or fifteen years after I became a Member of this House, and I did not find out till about the year 1850 or 1853 that a Committee was generally of no use ; and from that time to this I have avoided, in nine cases out of ten, when I have been applied to, sitting upon a Committee. But that observation refers principally to questions where political interests are concerned. When, however, you come to a question of this nature, where we should necessarily take the opinion of Judges, to whom the right hon. Gentleman pays so much attention, and of those men of whose great authority he has spoken, and of a great many other men who are not wedded to existing systems, and of men who could give us the facts with regard to other countries, I say that a Committee of this House, so far at any rate as obtaining evidence is concerned, I think would be equal to any tribunal, or any court of inquiry, which the right hon. Gentleman could establish. The right hon. Gentleman has led the House away a little from the main question. The main question proposed by my hon. Friend the Member for Dumfries is whether capital punishment should be retained or abolished. The right hon. Gentleman has led the House into a discussion of a question somewhat personal to himself—in connection with recent cases. I know the right hon. Gentleman was justified in what he said in reference to the position which he holds in the performance of his painful duties with regard to the execution of the criminal law. But that is not exactly what is wanted — this Motion was not brought forward for that purpose. I think the House would agree with great unanimity if the right hon. Gentleman would

introduce a Bill proposing certain changes at which he has hinted. This country has always been the most barbarous of all civilized nations in its punishments ; and at this moment is the most barbarous still, notwithstanding what the right hon. Gentleman said about the punishment of death being inflicted only for the crime of murder. But did he not afterwards tell the House that this crime of murder is a net which includes cases as different in their quality as in their guilt and in their consequences to society, as the difference between the lowest class of murder which the law now includes and the pettiest larceny which is punishable before a single magistrate. Yet all these are part of the same list of crimes, and if a jury does its duty—that is what is always said, as if a jury had no other duty but inexorably to send a man to the scaffold—if a jury will find a verdict of guilty, the punishment is death, unless the right hon. Gentleman, importuned by a number of persons, or having examined into the case himself, will interfere to save the unfortunate wretch from the gallows. There can be no doubt whatever that if capital punishment be retained, and if it be absolutely necessary that there should be a crime called murder to which capital punishment attaches, it is no less necessary that there should be, as there are in some other countries, three or four degrees of manslaughter, and that for the highest degree of manslaughter there should be the highest kind of secondary punishment, and that the power should be placed in the hands of the jury of determining what should be the particular class in which the criminal should be placed. There is no doubt that this is necessary to be done. I think Voltaire—who said a good many things that were worth remembering—remarked that the English were the only people who murdered by law. And Mirabeau, when in this country, hearing of a number of persons who had been hanged on a certain morning, said, " The English nation is the most merciless of any that I have heard or read of." And at this very moment, when we have struck off within the last fifty years at least a hundred offences which were then capital, we remain still in this matter the most merciless of Christian countries. If anybody wishes to satisfy himself upon this point let him take those late cases in which the right hon. Gentleman has had so much trouble. Take the case of Townley ; take the case of Wright; take the case of Hall, of Warwick; and I will take the liberty of repeating—what I said to the right hon. Gentleman when I was permitted to see him on the case of the convict Hall—that there is not a country in Europe, nor a State among the Free States of America, in which either of those criminals would have been punished with death. Yet we have gone on leaving the law as it is; and the right hon. Gentleman, to my utter astonishment, every time this question has been discussed, has given us very much the same speech as he has addressed to us to-night: he has repeated the same arguments for continuing a law which drives him to distraction almost every time he has to administer it. I am surprised that the right hon. Gentleman, who has had to face the suffering which has been brought on him by this law, has never had the courage to come to this House and ask it fairly to consider, in the light of the evidence which all other Governments and the laws of all other countries afford, whether the time has not come when this fearful punishment may be abolished. The right hon. Gentleman says the punishment is so terrible that it will deter offenders from the commission of crime. Of course it is terrible to one just standing upon the verge of the grave; but months before, when the crime is committed, when the passion is upon the criminal, the punishment is of no avail whatsoever. I do not think it is possible to say too much against the argument that this is a dreadful punishment, and is very efficient to deter a criminal from the commission of crime. As the right hon. Gentleman proposes to give a Commission, I shall not trouble the House with the observations that I had intended to make. There are, however, two or three cases which have not been mentioned and which I should like to bring under the notice of the House. My hon. Friend the Member for Dumfries referred to Russia. Russia is a country in which capital punishments have for almost a hundred years been unknown. I was reading yesterday a very remarkable Report of a Committee of the Legislature of the State of New York, written in the year 1841. It states that the Empress Elizabeth determined that for twenty years there would be no capital punishments in Russia. The Empress Catherine, in giving her instructions for the new Grand Code, stated her opinion upon the subject in these words—

Mr. Bright

" Experience shows that the frequent repetition of capital punishment has never yet made men better. If, therefore, I can show that in the ordinary state of society the death of a citizen is neither useful nor necessary, I shall have pleaded the cause of humanity with success."

She then says what I think is worthy of hearing—

" When the laws bear quiet and peaceful sway, and under a form of government approved by the united voice of the nation, in such a state there can be no necessity for taking away the life of a citizen."

The exception is in the case of some great political offender whose incarceration did not destroy his power of doing mischief; and I believe that since the enactment of this law there have been only two cases of persons who have been put to death by law in Russia, and that these have been cases arising out of circumstances of a political and insurrectionary character. Count Ségur, the French Ambassador at St. Petersburgh, states that the Empress Catherine said to him—

" We must punish crime without imitating it. The punishment of death is rarely anything but a useless barbarity."

In reporting this to the French Government, Count Ségur stated that under the mildness of the law murders were very rare in Russia. My hon. Friend the Member for Dumfries referred to the case of Tuscany, where it is well known that for a lifetime capital punishment has never been inflicted. In the case of Belgium, to which reference was made by my hon. and learned Friend the Member for Tiverton, as one of the most remarkable, I think the right hon. Gentleman was not successful in getting rid of his figures. It happens, as I understand, the law in Belgium does not prohibit capital punishments; but the result of omitting to inflict capital punishment has been so satisfactory that now the law is literally obsolete, and that capital punishment is never inflicted. Take then the case of Bombay, which is of a very striking character. We have the evidence from the pen of Sir James Mackintosh, who says—

" It will appear that the capital crimes committed during the last seven years (1804 and 1811) with no capital executions, have in proportion to the population not been much more than a third of those committed in the first seven years (1756 to 1763) when forty-seven persons suffered death."

He adds—

" The intermediate periods lead to the same results."

The House ought to bear in mind, that to us who have examined this question for many years, no fact is more clearly demonstrated than this—that there is no country in the world, be it a great empire or be it a small state—where the law has been made milder, and capital punishment has been abolished, in which there is any proof that murders have been more frequent, and the security of life in the slightest degree endangered. If that be so—if I could convince every Member of this House that the abolition of capital punishment would not cause more murders than the average of the last ten years—if all that would be left would be that those ten or twelve wretches who are publicly strangled every year would be living in some prison, or engaged in some labour with a chance of penitence, and with life not suddenly cut off by law—is there a man in this House —I speak not of party, or to one side or the other—who durst demand that we should still continue these terrible punishments? There used to be in this House a venerable old Gentleman who represented the University of Oxford, who in the discussion on this subject constantly quoted a certain verse of a certain chapter in the Book of Genesis. I am delighted that in the seven or eight years that have elapsed since this question was last discussed, we have advanced so far that nobody has brought forward that argument. We have discussed it to-night by the light of proved experiments, of facts, and of reason. Seeing what has been done in this country by the amelioration of the Criminal Code, and what has been done in all other countries, is there any man with one particle of sense or the power of reason who believes that human life in this country is made more secure because ten or twelve men are publicly put to death every year? The security of human life does not depend upon any such miserable and barbarous provision as that. The security for human life depends upon the reverence for human life; and unless you can inculcate in the minds of your people a veneration for that which God only has given, you do little by the most severe and barbarous penalties to preserve the safety of your citizens. If you could put down what it is that secures human life in figures and estimate it at 100, how much of it is to be attributed to your savage law, and how much of it to the reverence of human life implanted in the human soul? No doubt

5 or 10 per cent out of the 100 may be owing, for aught I know, to the influence of the law; but 90 or 95 per cent is owing to that feeling of reverence for human life. Whenever you hang a man in the face of the public under the circumstances to which we are so accustomed in this country, if you do in the slightest degree deter from crime by the shocking nature of the punishment, I will undertake to say that you by so much—nay, by much more —weaken that other and greater security which depends upon the reverence with which human life is regarded. Since this notice of this Motion was given by my hon. Friend I took the liberty of writing to the Governors of three of the States of America in which capital punishment has for several years been abolished; and, with the permission of the House, I will read extracts from the answers which I have received. I think they are important in a discussion of this nature when we are attempting to persuade doubtful and timid people that we are not proposing a rash or dangerous change. In the State of Rhode Island, one of the small States of America, with a population of not more than 200,000, capital punishment has been abolished. The Governor, the Hon. J. Pye Smith, writing from the Executive Department, March 21, 1864, says—

"1. The death penalty was abolished in this State in the year 1852. 2. I do not think its abolition has had any effect upon the security of life. 3. Is the law against the death penalty sustained by the public opinion of the State? Very decidedly. 4. Are convictions and punishments more certain than before the change was made? I think they are. 5. What is the punishment now inflicted on such criminals as were formerly punished with death? Imprisonment for life at hard labour. I have conversed with one supreme Judge, State attorney, and warden of the State prison, and they support my own established views upon the subject."

In a second letter, dated April 4, and which I received a few days ago, he says—

"Our present able Chief Justice says:—'Although disposed to the present law when passed, I am equally opposed to a change in it until the experiment has been tried long enough to satisfy us that it has failed. I am clearly of opinion that the present state of the law is sustained by public opinion, and I believe it will continue to be until it is satisfactorily shown that crimes against life have been considerably increased in consequence of it. My observation fully justifies me in saying that conviction for murder is far more certain now in proper cases than when death was the punishment of it.'"

Here is the answer which I received from

the Hon. Austin Blair, the Governor of the State of Michigan—

Executive Office, Lansing, March 23, 1864.
" 1. The death penalty for murder was abolished March 1, 1847, when the revised statutes of 1846 went into effect. 2. Life is not considered less secure than before ; murders are probably less frequent in proportion to population. Twenty years ago the population of the State was 300,000, and we have now a population of about 900,000. Then it was chiefly agricultural, and now we have mines of copper, iron, coal, &c., bringing into proximity dissimilar classes, and increasing the probabilities of frequent crime. Before the abolition of the death penalty murders were not unfrequent, but convictions were rarely or never obtained. It became the common belief that no jury could be found (the prisoner availing himself of the common law right of challenge) which would convict. Since the abolition there have been in seventeen years thirty-seven convictions. 3. There can be no doubt that public opinion sustains the present law and is against the restoration of the death penalty. 4. Conviction and punishment are now much more certain than before the change was made. Murder requires a greater amount of proof than any other crime, and it is found practically that a trial for murder excites no very unusual interest."

It, therefore, does not make a hero of the criminal. The letter proceeds—

" 5. The punishment now is solitary confinement at hard labour for life. Since 1861 this class of prisoners have been employed as other prisoners, as it was found difficult to keep them at work in cells without giving them tools, and there was danger of their becoming insane. The reform has been successfully tried, and is no longer an experiment."

The last letter is from the Hon. J. S. Lewis, the Governor of Wisconsin, and is dated Madison, March 29, 1864—

" The evil tendency of public executions, the great aversion of many to the taking of life rendering it almost impossible to obtain jurors from the more intelligent portion of the community, the liability of the innocent to suffer so extreme a penalty and be placed beyond the reach of the pardoning power, and the disposition of courts and juries not to convict, fearing the innocent might suffer, convinced me that this relic of barbarism should be abolished. The death penalty was repealed in 1853. No legislation has since re-established it, and the people find themselves equally secure, and the public more certain than before. The population in 1850 was 305,000 ; in 1860 it was 775,000. With this large increase of population we might expect a large increase of criminal cases, but this does not appear to be the case."

If you take those two last States of Wisconsin and Michigan which have been comparatively recently settled, you will see that it was highly probable, as they are on the outskirts of advancing civilisation, that crimes of violence should not be uncom-

Mr. Bright

mon. But here, with the abolition of this punishment, crimes and violence are not more common than before; people are just as secure, the law is upheld by public opinion, and the elected Governors of those three States, after the experience of these years, are enabled to write me letters like these, so satisfactory and so conclusive with regard to the effect of the experiment as it has been tried with them. The special cases that have been mentioned to-night with regard to executions have not been by any means the most fearful that have occurred. There was a case last year at Chester of so revolting a nature that I should be afraid to state the details to the House. I think it is hardly conceivable that a Christian gentleman, a governor of a gaol, and a clergyman, another Christian gentleman, should be concerned in such a dreadful catastrophe as then took place. Sir, if there be fiends below, how it must rejoice them to discover that, after the law of gentleness and love has been preached on earth for 1,800 years, such a scene as that should be enacted in our day in one of the most civilized and renowned cities of this country. Well, but these are cases which will happen again if this law remains; and all the difficulties which the right hon. Gentleman has alluded to to-night and on previous occasions are difficulties inseparable from the continuance of this punishment. Now, the right hon. Gentleman has referred to one or two cases ; the noble Lord opposite (Lord Henry Lennox) has likewise referred to one or two. Why, the case at Glasgow, the case at Derby, the recent case in London, and the recent case at Warwick, are cases which move whole populations ; and, if that be so, how can any man argue that this law is in a satisfactory state, or that this punishment can be wisely and beneficially administered and executed in this country? Why, Parliament, unfortunately—we need not disguise it, and I will not at any rate conceal it—Parliament has been very heedless upon this question. Secretaries of States have gone on from year to year hobbling, as it were, through the performance of their duties in connection with great pain to themselves, and yet they have never had the courage to ask Parliament to consider whether the system might not be entirely abolished. Does not every man now feel that it is in opposition to the sentiment of what I will call—and I think I may say it without disparaging anybody

—the most moral and religious portion of the population of this country—the men who have led the advance during the past century in every contest that we have had with ignorance, and crime, and cruelty, in whatsoever shape it has shown itself? And every day they are becoming more and more estranged from the spirit and operation of this law. Whenever there are paragraphs floating about in the newspapers that on the 15th or the 25th of such a month such a one is to meet his doom for some crime, however foul, there is in every city, in every parish, and in almost every house in this country where there is any regard to humanity and to Christianity, a feeling of doubt as to whether this law is right, and a feeling of disgust and horror amongst hundreds of thousands of the best portion of our people. Now, merciful laws are, in my opinion, the very highest testimony to any Government, as I likewise think that they are the highest blessing a people can enjoy. I believe they give security to a Government, and they soften and humanise the people. Now, all the steps that have been taken in this direction have been so successful, that I wonder that even the late Lord Mayor of London should not himself have come to the conclusion that after all he would still sleep comfortably in our beds if men were not hanged; and that, if the law were gentle and merciful whilst it was just, he would find gradually growing up in the minds of all classes a greater dislike to crime and violence, and a greater reverence for human life. Benjamin Franklin, a great authority on matters of this nature, said that the virtues are all parts of a circle; that whatever is humane, is wise; whatever is wise is just; and whatever is wise, just, and humane, will be found to be the true interests of states, whether criminals or foreign enemies are the objects of their legislation. Would any one of us like to go back to the barbarism of that time when Charles Wesley wrote a note to the celebrated and excellent John Fletcher, the vicar of Madeley, in 1776. We were then trying to keep the empire together, and neglecting this great work at home. He says—

" A fortnight ago I preached a condemned sermon to about twenty criminals, and every one of them, I had good grounds to believe, died penitent. Twenty more must die next week."

And there were then cases in which twenty were hanged, not one of whom had been convicted or found guilty of the crime of murder. Have we not from that time made great and salutary and satisfactory advances in this question? Is there any man who wants to turn back to the barbarism of that day? But if you turn back to the Secretaries of State of that day, or to the Judges of that day, or even to the Bishops of that day, you will find that they had just the same sort of arguments in favour of the barbarism in which they were then concerned that the right hon. Gentleman, I suppose forced by the necessities of his office, has offered to the House to-night. I confess I wonder that all the right hon. Gentleman has gone through in these painful cases has not driven him stark mad many times. At any rate, I wonder that it has not driven him to the table of this House to propose, under the solemn feelings with which he must often have been impressed, that the House should take into consideration whether this vast evil—as I believe it to be—might not be put an end to. Is the Englishman worse than another man? Is this nation worse than other nations? Cannot the lenient laws practised with perfect safety in every other—not every other, but in many of the nations of the world—be practised in this nation, and at the same time leave us perfectly secure—at least as much so as we are at present? I say we may wash vengeance and blood from our code without difficulty and without danger. The right hon. Gentleman is going to appoint a Commission—he prefers it to a Committee, and I will not contest the point with him if the Commission be a fair Commission; but I should not like to see it a Commission of Judges. Mind I am not wishing to speak disrespectfully of Judges. I agree with what the right hon. Gentleman has said, that with the exception of a case or two, perhaps, in one's lifetime, we notice nothing on the bench but that which is honourable to the Judges of this country; and I would say that the Judges of this country may be compared with advantage probably with the Judges of any other country. But Judges are but men. Several of them, as a proof of that, have been Members of this House. And I am free to confess that the feelings I had when I was a schoolboy at York, and first went to an assize trial and saw that venerable old gentleman in his wig, were those of utter awe and astonishment; but those feelings have been considerably modified by my experience of many of the present Judges when they were Members of this House. But we know that Judges are like other men in this—they have trodden a certain path which has led them to the honourable position which they hold. They are there, however, not to make law, but to administer it; and they have tempered its severity, as the noble Lord said, as their judgments are merciful or otherwise. But they adhere to the law, for it is that which they have to administer. Some of them are not desirous, perhaps, to express an opinion, like the noble Lord, the father of the hon. and learned Member for Tiverton (Mr. Denman). They are strongly attached to that system which they have been administering; and, as I said at the beginning of the observations I have offered to the House, they have been in all past times—not all of them, but a majority of them—generally opposed to the amelioration of our Criminal Code. Although, therefore, I believe that at this moment there are more Judges on the bench who are in favour of the abolition of capital punishment, yet I should not like the right hon. Gentleman to leave the inquiry into this question entirely or even to a majority of the members of the bench. There is no reason to believe that a Judge is more competent to give an opinion on this question than any other intelligent, educated, and observing man; nor would I admit that the right hon. Gentleman himself, who is in his whole person the whole bench of Judges, is more capable of giving an opinion than any other Member of this House who has paid long and careful attention to this subject. Therefore, I hope that if the right hon. Gentleman does appoint a Commission he will put upon it—I do not say men who have not an opinion on one side or the other, for men who have no opinion at all are not likely to give any worth hearing—but men in whom the House and the country and those in the House who are against capital punishment shall have confidence, feeling that they would take evidence from every source whence it could be fairly offered to them, and that they would give to the House and the Government a fair opinion on that evidence in their Report. If that be done I am quite certain that the result will be a great improvement of the law, although it may not carry it to the point which my hon. Friend the Member for Dumfries has so long desired to carry it. But I should be very thankful if that much is accomplished; and if ever we come to that point, I have confidence

Mr. Bright

too that even you Gentlemen opposite, who are so very timid, always fancying that the ice is going to break, will be induced to go further than you seem inclined to do now; and perhaps the ten or twelve who are now hanged annually may be brought down to three or four, and at last we may come unanimously to the opinion, that the security of public life in England does not depend upon the public strangling of three or four poor wretches every year. This Parliament is about to expire, I suppose, before very long—though some say it is to endure during another Session; I should be glad indeed if it might be said of this Parliament at some future time, that it had dared to act upon the true lessons, and not upon the —what shall I say?—the superstitions of the past; and that this Parliament might be declared to be the Parliament which destroyed the scaffold and the gallows, in order that it might teach the people that human life is sacred, and that on that principle alone can human life be secured.

MR. NEWDEGATE: The House has just listened to the eloquent and carefully prepared speech of the hon. Member for Birmingham, and I think that the public will be a little surprised to hear that the hon. Member has declared that this country is one of the most barbarous in the world. [MR. BRIGHT: I said in its laws.] I can only refer to a note which I made when the hon. Member was speaking. It was a surprising announcement to me, for, in common with a large number of Her Majesty's subjects, I have been accustomed to believe that in England we enjoy a greater amount of personal freedom, a higher state of civilization, and a greater degree of personal safety than any other nation in the world. The hon. Member would have us doubt these facts, and upon what grounds? Upon this ground—that our law is unduly severe. Well, if that severity is necessary to the personal freedom, to the political freedom, and to the civilization which we enjoy—a freedom and a civilization enjoyed by a greater variety of classes, by persons in a greater variety of circumstances than are to be found in any other nation in the world—I am inclined to believe that the very severity of the law tends to the emancipation of the community; and I also feel this, that such is the pressure exercised by a certain section in favour of the mitigation of capital sentences, that it did high honour to the hon. Member for Southampton (Mr. Rose), that he should venture in a very plain-spoken, sensible, and prudent speech to vindicate the state of the law which the hon. Member for Birmingham denounces, but the blessings derived from which are patent to every class and in every home. The hon. Member in the course of his argument referred to various authorities in favour of the abolition of capital punishment for murder, and one was the Empress Catharine of Russia. Does he mean to hold up that powerful but misled woman for our imitation, either as a moralist or a philanthropist? Will he adduce the condition in which she found and left Russia as a condition of advancing civilization? Will he compare the condition of the people of Russia now with the condition of the people in this country, and constitute by such a comparison a preference for the opinion of Catharine of Russia against the opinion of his own countryman? He cited also Voltaire and Mirabeau; but what was the condition of France when their opinions were given? where was the freedom of France ere yet the ink was dry with which their opinions were recorded, and where is the freedom of France now? At this hour France is struggling under a despotism, that despotism being the consequence of the endorsement of the principles of those very authorities whom the hon. Member for Birmingham would have us adopt for the Government of England. I hope that we shall not pursue that path which the hon. Member desires to commend to us by a sympathy that is amiable in itself, but which has so often been proved mistaken when applied to the government of mankind. The hon. Member trusts to his hopes and his wishes for the advancement of mankind to a degree of morality which unfortunately has never yet been witnessed; and then basing his conclusions, not upon the actual state of humanity, but upon his hopes, he draws on his audience to conclusions which are amiable, but which have been proved in the history of the world to be fallacious, the fallacy of which is shown in the difference in the condition of the countries to which he refers, and that of this country existing under laws enacted by the will of the people, but which the hon. Member declares to be barbarous. The hon. Member condemned our Judges. I am convinced of this, that there are no men who feel more severely than do the Judges the painful responsibility which they incur in pronouncing sentence of death, and I am convinced that they concur in the convictions only under that sense of public duty that has made this country what it is. Judges, in acting as they always have done, do violence to their own sympathies, to those sympathies to which the hon. Member himself yields, and would induce the House to yield, to the detriment, aye, to the destruction of the blessings which we enjoy. These blessings this country gained gradually by an adherence to law. I believe that the respect for human life is greater in this country than in any other, and this respect is not only grounded upon religious conviction, but is also enforced by the dictates of that law which the hon. Member condemns. The hon. Member has quoted letters from various Governors of States in America; but will he say that there is in the United States the personal freedom that exists in this country? If the hon. Member were to state truly his opinion, I believe that he would say that, even before those convulsions which have lately occurred, the personal freedom of individuals and the security of life were as inferior in the United States to what we possess as it is possible to conceive. I have been there when an individual, during an election, dare not walk alone down the middle of the street, and in periods of excitement life itself is not safe. The hon. Member spoke of the convict Hall, but the hon. Member has been lauding the state of the law in the United States, and I ask him whether he is prepared to allow every man who has a cause for jealousy to exercise his own discretion as it was exercised by Mr. Sickles in New York? Is impunity for the commission of deliberate murder in open day and on the highway the kind of liberty he values? The truth is this, we are involved in the dangers of an advanced civilization, and I am afraid that this clamorous sympathy of which we have heard so much in this debate is sympathy rather for your own outraged sensibility — that with you sympathy for the sufferings of jurors and for the position of the Home Secretaries is far greater than for the welfare and the safety of the community at large. It appears to me to be most unfortunate that, just at the time when we are about to enter upon an experiment in the system of secondary punishments, and to make up our minds to retain among us those persons who are stained by crimes of a grievous character—I say that it is unfortunate at this very time we should be raising doubts whether it is prudent to continue the capital punishment for murder. Let me for a moment point to the tendency of this debate. There is always the danger, in a high state of civilization, that the legislation should lapse into refinements, should attempt definitions which cannot be justly carried out by law, should run after the impossible rather than the carrying out what is practically just in the administration of the law. We are asked to grant more discretionary powers; and why? Because difficulty has been found in reference to the discretionary power that exists at present. We always find two parties converging to one end; and here we have hon. Members who represent Democratic opinions assailing the law, and seeking to substitute for it discretionary power; and in this concurring with those on this side of the House, who scarcely disguisedly recommend an arbitrary system of Government very different from that which exists in this country. I deprecate the notion that the laws of this country with regard to capital punishment are barbarous. My belief is that he who deliberately takes human life owes his own to the community whom he robs of one of its citizens; and this opinion is supported, not only on the ground of abstract justice, but by the expressed will of the Almighty for the government of mankind. I hope the House will excuse these words, spoken with a view to vindicate the laws under which we live from the imputation that they are barbarous. The laws of England follow and protect each citizen from the cradle to the grave—in childhood, boyhood, manhood, and old age—and even care for each of us when we are consigned to the grave. The Home Secretary has so far yielded as to grant the Commission. I can only say that if he had thought fit to withstand the grievous pressure directed against him, I should have been prepared to support him, notwithstanding any clamour which might have been raised by those who affect a sympathy. I have been frequently applied to to make representations to the Home Office, and these applications I have refused. If there be any new facts I sift them to the best of my ability, and am ready to state them, but upon these facts I will express no opinion. I will use no influence that may interrupt the due course of law, and I hope no constituent of mine will approach me with a request to tamper with the law, the sanctity of which is the basis both of our freedom and of our civilization.

Mr. Newdegate

MR. GILPIN said, he did not intend to enter upon a defence of the hon. Member for Birmingham, who was well able to defend himself, but it was not a fact that his hon. Friend had condemned the Judges. All he said was that they were not better able to decide questions of this sort than other enlightened and intelligent men. The hon. Gentleman opposite (Mr. Newdegate) had talked of the democratic tendencies of the hon. Member for Birmingham; but that objection, if it could be accounted one, could not be brought against Dr. Lushington, who, in 1840, submitted a Motion for the abolition of capital punishments, which Motion was supported by the present President of the Poor Law Board and other distinguished Members. It was not for him to pretend to express the opinions of the Government, but upon the Treasury bench there were, besides the right hon. Gentlemen whom he had just mentioned, the President of the Board of Trade, the Judge Advocate, the Vice President of the Board of Trade, and several others, who had uniformly given their support not merely to an inquiry but to a Motion for the immediate abolition of capital punishments. No one could venture to say that the Judges were the best fitted to be upon the proposed Commission, far less to be the sole members of it. He could not forget that in 1811 the Recorder of London objected to the punishment of death being done away with for the crime of pocket-picking; that in 1813 the Lord Chancellor regretted the removal of the capital penalty for the offence of stealing property to the amount of 5s. from a dwelling house; that Lord Ellenborough thought it should be retained in the case of stealing linen from a bleaching ground; and that other Judges had advocated its retention in cases of forgery. He repudiated the idea of charging the advocates of the abolition of capital punishments with any sympathy with crime, with any mawkish sentimentality, with anything but a sincere desire to support that punishment which experience proved to be the most effective deterrent from crime. His right hon. Friend the Secretary of State had said that if any other punishment could be shown to be equally deterrent from crime, he would give up capital punishment; and he (Mr. Gilpin) said that the advocates of the abolition would give up their whole case if capital punishment could be shown to be best. He held that all punishments had, or ought to have, three objects in view of crime, restitution to the injured where—the security of society by the prevention ever possible, and he was not ashamed to add even in the case of the worst murderers, the reformation of the offender himself. Not one of these objects was accomplished by the punishment of death. Another important point for consideration was the fact that many innocent persons had suffered the penalty of death. The judgment of man was too weak and wavering to be intrusted with the infliction of an irrevocable punishment. Innocent men had been hanged; and their innocence had been established after their death. There was a case in which cries were heard from an apartment, and when it was reached, a man was found over a body with a weapon in his hand. This man was innocent.

MR. ROEBUCK: Was this an English case?

MR. GILPIN said it was.

MR. ROEBUCK: Who is the authority for it?

MR. GILPIN: Charles Dickens.

MR. ROEBUCK: He is no authority at all.

MR. GILPIN: The hon. and learned Gentleman may say that Mr. Dickens is no authority—some people may say that the hon. and learned Gentleman is no authority. I well recollect the late Daniel O'Connell relating in Exeter Hall, in 1844, the touching account of three brothers—

"I myself (said he) defended three brothers of the name of Cremming within the last ten years. They were indicted for murder. I sat at my window, as they passed by, after sentence had been pronounced. There was a large military guard taking them back to gaol, positively forbidden to allow any communication with the three unfortunate youths. But their mother was there, and she, armed with the strength of her affection, broke through the guard. I saw her clasp her eldest son, who was but twenty-two years of age; I saw her hang on her second, who was not twenty; I saw her faint, when she clung to the neck of the youngest son, who was but eighteen—and, I ask, what recompense could be made for such agony? They were executed—and—they were innocent."

"I think," said Sheriff Wilde in his examination (Report 1836, p. 101), "many innocent persons have suffered. I think that if the documents at the Home Office are examined, many instances will be found in which—by exertions of former sheriffs—the lives of many persons ordered for execution have been saved."

He was well authorized to say so. This most estimable gentleman is still alive, so we may not speak of him as we sincerely feel; but we shall chronicle his acts—they are his best eulogy. During the seven months of Mr. Wilde's shrievalty he saved the lives of six innocent persons who had been actually ordered for execution! The records and the documents are at the Home Office. These six men would have been hanged save for the volunteer philanthropy of this Christian man, who gave his time, his talents, his money, and his toil in behalf of hapless strangers. Where are we to find such men, at once so able and self-sacrificing? Let Sir Frederick Pollock answer—

"Though I believe undoubtedly the sheriffs of London are, in general, conspicuous for an active, humane, and correct discharge of their duty, they have not all, and cannot have, the means of bringing to the investigation of such subjects the same facility and the same unsparing exertion that Mr. Wilde afforded while he was sheriff. . . . It is impossible to speak in too high terms of the zeal, humanity, unsparing labour and expense which he bestowed upon those occasions, but the result satisfied me (says Sir Frederick Pollock) that the parties were in several instances guiltless of any crime, and in all, the cases were such as did not justify capital punishment; and Sir Robert Peel, after much labour in the investigation, was of the same opinion. . . . My impression is that several of these cases were cases of perfect and entire innocence, and that the others were cases of innocence as to the capital part of the charge. I had frequent communication (he adds) with Mr. Wilde on them as they proceeded."

The hon. Member quoted several other cases on the authority of Charles Dickens. He also instanced the case of the Cormacks, executed in Ireland in 1858, on which he had spoken shortly after coming into Parliament. Other cases there were also in which, whether the convicts were innocent or guilty, the strongest conviction prevailed among the public of their innocence; in these cases the whole end and object of the punishment was lost. He would only, in conclusion, call the attention of the House to this simple fact. We sentenced men to death as the last and greatest punishment of the law, and assumed to execute them for the sake of the example. He asked the House to consider for one moment what that example was. It was an example of revenge; an exemplification of what might be characterized the law of tit for tat; it was an example of life for life. In his opinion it was a reading backwards of the principles of the New Testament, and after paying great attention to the matter for the past twenty years he was convinced it did not prevent crime. It entailed the suffering of the innocent; it favoured the escape of the guilty; it was opposed to the spirit of Christianity and true civilisation; and he trusted the time was not far distant when the result of the inquiry of this Commission, and the opinion of the public, would be the entire abolition of the punishment of death.

MR. ROEBUCK said, that the speech of the hon. Gentleman who had just addressed the House ought to have been spoken twenty years ago. He had charged upon the administration of justice that it put to death people who were not guilty. That was not true. Could anybody assert that anybody had been hanged within the last ten years who was believed to be not guilty of the crime for which he suffered ? He allowed that heretofore the administration of justice in this country had been a bloody administration ; but now, so great had become the regard for human life, the tendency was entirely in the opposite direction. The Home Secretary would undoubtedly say that he had more difficulty in hanging a man now than former Secretaries had had in transporting one. What were the objects of punishment ? The first object of punishment was no doubt reformation. Hanging he allowed did not reform a man; but the next object was the putting out of danger the society in which a murderer lived. Hanging certainly did that. The removing of a man so dangerous to society—and very cheaply—was a thing to be considered by society. The murderer was hung, and there was an end of him. Society was in no more danger from him. The House was not chargeable with a mawkish sentimentality ; but if a man killed his own mother, people would be found to get up petitions to save him from death. He had no sympathy whatever with those petitions. He wished to see a man of that sort removed out of life—he had no hesitation in saying that. It was mock sentimentality to pray for that man's life. He had not thought of his mother's life, and why should we think of his ? Then came the question, would hanging him do any good ? We could not reform him—there was an end of him ; and what injury had been done to mankind ? The hon. Member for Birmingham had spoken with his usual eloquence to-night, and no one felt his power more or listened to him with more admiration than he did ; but still, as a practical legislator, he was bound to see what was best to be done for the advantage of society. He wished to vote with the hon. Member, and, as far as possible, to do away with the punishment of death ; but he was bound to consider the advantage of society. The hon. Member

Mr. Gilpin

had referred to the example of America, and he himself had paid much attention to the example of America. The hon. Gentleman said that men condemned to death went mad in confinement. That was true —but what had happened in America ? Many years ago Chancellor Livingstone wrote a code for Louisiana, and in that code he recommended the abolition of capital punishment and the condemnation of prisoners to solitary imprisonment for life. That was adopted, but all the prisoners went mad. Now, which was the more merciful, to kill the murderer outright at once, or to put him in a dungeon and condemn him to perpetual insanity ? Notwithstanding the writings of Mr. Dickens and others, who attempted to mislead mankind on this subject, he asserted that it was much more merciful to hang a man at once than to condemn him to insanity and lifelong solitary confinement.

SIR FRANCIS CROSSLEY said, he was sure the House would not put into the scale the cheapness of the process of getting rid of a criminal by hanging him against the value which they attached to human life. He should vote with the hon. and learned Member (Mr. Neate), because he did not believe that capital punishment was agreeable with the merciful character of the Christian dispensation ; and he believed it was not so deterrent as other punishments. He quite agreed that the murderer ought to be deprived of the opportunity of repeating his crime ; but he should be deterred from doing so by a punishment which, while it did not go so far as to produce insanity, should be effectual for its purpose. He thought that nothing less than a plain command given to us by the Creator himself could justify us in depriving a fellow-creature of life. No doubt civilization had greatly advanced since the days when men were hanged for stealing horses and sheep, and for forgery. Against the advance of civilization in one direction must be set the increase in population ; but, on the whole, no doubt these crimes had greatly diminished since capital punishment had been abolished as the penalty for them. The Secretary of State had admitted the necessity for inquiry by saying that if they could show that any other punishment was equally effectual in deterring from crime, he would give up capital punishment. He thought if a mode could be devised whereby they could deter the murderer from committing crime without taking his life, they were bound to adopt that mode ; and that for that purpose a most careful and anxious investigation ought to be pursued. So far he should support the proposition of the hon. and learned Member (Mr. Neate).

SIR JOHN WALSH deprecated the introduction into the discussion of the theological argument, on which he maintained the House of Commons was not a fitting tribunal to form an opinion. He might, however, incidentally remark that, before and since the foundation of Christianity, capital punishments had been almost universally adopted by mankind. But, passing to the point more immediately before the House,· whether a Committee or a Commission should be appointed to inquire into the subject, he must say that, for his own part, he should prefer a Commission. He might add that he had never been able to arrive at the conclusion that capital punishment was not on the whole the most deterrent of all. If a milder punishment could accomplish the same end, he would, of course, at once say, let it be adopted; but, then, other punishments did not exercise the same effect on the imagination, the feelings, and the fears of men. A fallacy ran through the whole of the arguments on this subject. The noble Lord the Member for Chichester (Lord Henry Lennox) had given the House an interesting account of the recent execution. In the interests of science, and in a desire to enlighten and benefit mankind, the noble Lord sacrificed his own feelings and personal convenience and attended the execution of the five pirates. The noble Lord's arguments went to show that the awful spectacle produced no effect on the 20,000 people who witnessed it; and the admirable and clever novelist (Charles Dickens) took the same view as the noble Lord as to the effect of public executions. Now, there could be no doubt that the spectators at such scenes did not belong to a very refined class, and that much coarseness and want of feeling were displayed by them; but it did not follow that because they indulged in unseemly levity in the public view they were not in the solitude of their own homes impressed by a deterrent influence against the crimes for which they had seen the punishment of death inflicted, and in the belief that that was so he was corroborated by the fact that what was called the criminal or dangerous class, seldom or never committed the crime of murder. They were stopped by something, and that something, he was disposed to think, was the fear of the gallows. Murders were, or almost all, committed by persons who were unknown to Sir Richard Mayne and to the Home Secretary as criminals. He did not agree with those who looked upon murder in the light of Hogarth in *The Idle Apprentice*, as a progressive crime, or that a youth began by picking pockets and ended at the gallows. On the contrary, the criminal class stopped at murder, because they knew and had calculated the consequences of the act. It was remarkable, and had not been sufficiently noticed, that the greater number of murders were committed by persons of a superior condition to the criminal class. To illustrate this, he need only mention Rush, Palmer, Mrs. Catherine Wilson, Mrs. Chesham, and the Mannings. It was also curious to observe that murders were almost always committed by solitary individuals. There were no gangs of men who associated themselves together for the purpose of murder. The fear of being hung not only prevented the criminal classes from committing murder, but it prevented murderers from seeking for accomplices. Those who dwelt upon the smallness of the deterrent influence which was exercised by capital punishment limited their consideration to the effect which an execution produced upon the few thousand persons who witnessed it. But he believed that it produced less effect upon those persons than upon the rest of the community. Every man who read *The Times* was affected by the detailed description of the last moments and of the execution of the five pirates. An execution produced an effect upon the fears of the whole nation; and it was impossible to trace the remote consequences of this deterrent principle. Early impressions produced sensible effects in after life, and the existence of capital punishment was no doubt of value in disciplining the passions, even in circles where such things as murders were hardly known. All experience confirmed the necessity of stringent punishment for grave crimes, and though others might be suggested which were more painful to individuals than that which was known to the law of England, none, he believed, had ever exercised so wholesome an effect on the imagination and feelings of mankind.

MR. HIBBERT, in opposition to the view taken by the hon. Baronet as to the deterrent effect of public executions, read a passage from the letter of a philanthropic gentleman in Manchester, who had attended more than fifty culprits to the scaffold, and who declared that means ought to be taken to put an end to the demoralizing effects of public executions, which hardened instead of softening the hearts of the spectators. At the execution of Taylor and Ward at Kirkdale, a young man named Thomas Edwards was present. In six days afterwards he was committed to gaol for taking the life of a young woman, and was the very next to suffer upon that scaffold.

MR. MAGUIRE said, he never heard a speech which so conclusively proved the case against capital punishment as that of the hon. Baronet. Every one who had studied the question knew that public executions had a brutalising effect upon the minds of those who witnessed them. Those Gentlemen who were in favour of private executions conceded half the argument against the punishment of death, because they admitted the injurious and demoralizing effect of executions in public. There was a time when stealing a piece of cloth was punished with death; but society had gone on very well since that was abolished. There had been much fewer forgeries since that crime ceased to be punished with death, and he believed that a still further beneficial effect would be produced by the entire abolition of the punishment. He thought the Government had acted wisely in consenting to a Commission, and he hoped that the present Parliament would, in its declining months, pass an Act on the subject which, while it satisfied the best feelings of the country, would do no injury to the interests of society.

MR. W. EWART, in reply, said, he would gladly accept the proposal of the Home Secretary that a Royal Commission should be appointed. He could not concur in the suggestion that the Judges should form part of the Commission. He felt confident that the right hon. Baronet would appoint a good Commission, composed of fair-minded and untrammelled men, and he would therefore withdraw his Motion.

Amendment, and Motion, by leave, *withdrawn.*

MR. NEATE then moved, as a substantive Resolution—

"That an humble Address be presented to Her Majesty, praying that she will be graciously pleased to issue a Royal Commission to inquire into the provisions and operation of the Laws under which the Punishment of Death is now inflicted in the United Kingdom, and the manner in which it is inflicted; and to report whether it is desirable to make any alteration therein."

Resolution *agreed to.*

Mr. Hibbert

PUBLIC AND REFRESHMENT HOUSES (METROPOLIS).—LEAVE.

SIR GEORGE GREY moved for leave to introduce a Bill for further regulating the closing of public-houses and refreshment houses within the Metropolitan Police district. He had stated some time since that it was his intention to bring in a Bill founded upon the representation of the inhabitants of certain parts of the metropolis, that great evils arose from the disorders occasioned by certain licensed victuallers and refreshment houses being kept open all night; and suggesting that if they were compelled to close between the hours of one and four o'clock in the morning, it would tend very much to public order and morality. It was only licensed victuallers' houses and certain refreshment houses licensed to sell wine which might be kept open all night, except Saturday and Sunday nights, beer houses being compelled to close at twelve o'clock; and the effect of this Bill would be to shut these houses on all other nights for three hours during the night. It was but right that he should state that he believed that the great majority of the licensed victuallers closed their houses during these hours, and he had been informed that they were generally perfectly satisfied with the regulations proposed to be enforced by the Bill. If the House consented to the introduction, he would fix the second reading for a time sufficiently distant for the provisions of the Bill to be well known.

LORD FERMOY thought there could not be the slightest objection to the Bill, and he believed the licensed victuallers as a body were favourable to it. The provisions could only apply to a very small minority of the licensed victuallers of the metropolis, as by far the greatest number of them closed before that time. The Bill would no doubt be productive of great good.

Motion *agreed to.*

Bill for further regulating the Closing of Public Houses and Refreshment Houses within the Metropolitan Police District; *ordered* to be brought in by Sir GEORGE GREY and Mr. BARING.

STREET MUSIC (METROPOLIS.)
LEAVE.

MR. BASS moved for leave to bring in a Bill for the better regulation of Street Music within the Metropolitan Police District. The particular evil against which the Bill was directed was this :—A street musician could be sent away on the ground of illness in a family or any " other reasonable cause." The magistrates of the metropolitan district differed, however, as to what was " reasonable cause," and what he desired was to specify what ought to be so considered. He did not propose, while doing this, to interfere with the reasonable recreation of the people.

MR. MAGUIRE said, he was sorry the hon. Member had not been more ample in his explanation. He would like to know what class of music the Bill referred to. Was the hon. Gentleman going to legislate in the interests of correct musical taste or in the spirit of Professor Babbage? He thought it would have been better to introduce a Bill that would cover the whole case, and send it to a Select Committee.

MR. ROEBUCK said, that this was properly a matter of police, and the most rational way of dealing with it would be to give the magistrate power to determine what was a nuisance and what was not. The police ought to be armed with the power of protecting society in this matter, and he would put it to the Home Secretary whether that was not the rational mode of meeting the difficulty. A lady or gentleman might be very ill, and a man would come there with a loud organ, knowing that his music would be bought off and intending to come back. If the Legislature would give the police magistrates the power to regulate the street music by means of the police, they would do much for the quiet and comfort of the metropolis.

SIR GEORGE GREY said, the police might be called upon to remove street musicians not only in the case of illness, but from any other reasonable cause. It was well known that Mr. Babbage alleged, and the magistrates agreed with him, that he was engaged in pursuits which street music was calculated seriously to disturb. The police magistrates, however, sometimes dismissed charges against street musicians if they did not consider the cause of removal reasonable. He was anxious to see the Bill that he might know how the hon. Gentleman defined what was " a reasonable cause;" but until he knew what its provisions were, he could not promise his support to it.

SIR JOHN SHELLEY said, this was just one of those subjects which the Government ought to take in hand. If it could be clearly shown that street music was a nuisance, the Home Secretary was the person to deal with it.

LORD FERMOY concurred with the hon. Baronet. It appeared to him the hon. Member for Derby (Mr. Bass) wished to abolish street music altogether. [Mr. BASS : No !] Then why ask for further powers than at present existed ? If this mode of legislation was adopted because some persons had a private grievance, they would by-and-by have some hon. Member proposing a Bill to put a stop to the noise occasioned by brewers' drays and beer barrels as they passed through the metropolis.

MR. AYRTON hoped the hon. Gentleman would give an intelligent explanation of the object of the Bill. He wanted to know what the hon. Member understood by a " reasonable cause."

SIR FRANCIS CROSSLEY said, the object of his hon. Friend was this—that where street music was not wanted, and the musicians refused to go away, they might be handed over to the police. It had come within his own knowledge that where persons were on their death-beds and the musicians were desired to go away, they refused, and the police when called upon said they had no power to interfere. When people paid for their houses they ought to be allowed to live in them in peace and quietness.

MR. BASS said, he had forborne to go at length into the subject, because on a former occasion he had explained his views to the House, and it was unusual for hon. Gentlemen when introducing a Bill upon well known matters to take up the time of hon. Members. In the Metropolitan Police Act "reasonable cause" was understood in different senses, and he had been informed that the magistrates themselves desired that what was meant by the words should be more strictly defined. He was also given to understand that the Commissioners of Police were in favour of some such measure as he sought to introduce, and the police felt themselves placed in this difficulty—that if a street musician refused to go away when desired, they could not take him into custody — they could only deal with him by summons. What he aimed at was to give the police power to arrest musicians who, upon receiving notice, refused to go away, and he held this to be " reasonable cause " that any person should be engaged in some serious occupation which required to be carried on without interruption.

Motion *agreed to.*

Bill for the Better Regulation of Street Music within the Metropolitan Police District; *ordered* to be brought in by Mr. BASS, Captain STACPOOLE, and Mr. CAVENDISH BENTINCK.

INSOLVENT DEBTORS BILL.—[BILL 20.]
SECOND READING.

Order for Second Reading read.

MR. PAULL, in moving the second reading of the Bill, said, its object was to extend the benefit of the present bankruptcy law to debtors under the sum of £20. As the law now stood debtors of small amounts, who came under the jurisdiction of the County Courts, had not the power of obtaining protection and final discharge from their liabilities; on the contrary, they were liable to be imprisoned again and again for the same debt. This was very frequently the case, and the number actually imprisoned in 1861 was 8,625, and 9,373 in 1862. The amounts for which these persons were committed to prison were sometimes ludicrously small. One man in Whitecross Street prison was committed five times for a debt the original amount of which was 8s. 6d. Another man was committed five times for a debt, and was in prison 110 days, and on his sixth committal the Governor of the prison paid the debt, the original amount of which was only 2s. 6d. Persons who contracted large debts were able to obtain a protection order in the first instance, and eventually a complete discharge from their debts, but the poor man who became indebted to a small amount might be imprisoned from time to time without any chance of release from the debt. The Bill proposed that when a judgment debtor of not more than £20, and who had not contracted his debts by means of any false pretence, breach of trust, or wilfully without reasonable expectation of paying, was summoned before a Small Debts' Court, he should be examined touching his estates and effects, and his means of paying, any judgment debt, and if it should appear to the Judge that he had not then, nor was likely to have, within a reasonable time, money or property of any kind, and that, taking into consideration his means of earning any money, there was no well founded expectation of his being able to pay and discharge his debts within a reasonable time, the Judge might make a preliminary order to the effect that within two months he would make, unless cause should be shown

Mr. Bass

to the contrary, a final order discharging the debtor from his debts and liabilities, of which he shall in the meantime disclose the amount and the names of the creditors.

Motion made, and Question proposed, "That the Bill be now read a second time."—(*Mr. Paull.*)

MR. DENMAN thought the principle of the Bill was open to grave doubt. The Judge would have to act upon the mere statement of the debtor himself, whose interest it would be to keep him in ignorance of the principal creditors, who were entitled to be present at his examination. He had had some experience as a County Court Judge, and he could not help observing that the Bill assumed that that was not the law which was the law already, because no Judge could commit a man to prison unless he was satisfied upon evidence that he had the means of paying his debts. He did not see what more could be fairly done in favour of the defendant. He did not think that at present County Court Judges were too ready to act in favour of the creditor against the debtor, and he saw no occasion for the Bill.

MR. AYRTON said, the object of the Bill was to make the law for the working man the same as the law for the man of higher rank. At present, a man might accumulate debts to any extent, and yet obtain a discharge; whereas the poor man, whose liabilities were under £20, was denied a release on the same terms. It was understood that the Government intended to introduce a Bill to rectify this anomaly; but as they had not done so, his hon. and learned Friend opposite deserved credit for bringing forward this measure. The House of Commons, which had made a special law as to debt for itself, ought to consider the hardships of the poorer classes in this respect. The fact was, the County Courts were greatly abused. The gaols were filled with poor people on account of small debts, while a special emissary was sent from the Bankruptcy Court to bring out any man who might have incurred vast debts and swindled the world from one end to the other.

MR. PAGET said, the same principle was to be found in the law for the rich as for the poor on this subject, and it was that a debtor should in the former case be made responsible in his estate, and in the other in his skill and labour. The Bill would do harm to the working classes because it would tend to a denial, or at least a restriction of the credit they were now able to get from the small shopkeepers in time of distress or sickness. He moved that it be read a second time that day six months.

Amendment proposed, to leave out the word "now," and at the end of the Question to add the words "upon this day six months."—(*Mr. Paget*).

Question proposed, "That the word 'now' stand part of the Question."

MR. LOCKE said, his hon. Friend (Mr. Paget) had been using the same arguments they had heard so often when they were reforming the law of bankruptcy. For his part he thought the labouring man at present got too much credit, not himself alone, but his wife, when they were away at work, through tallymen and others. It was the business of those who gave credit to look after the probability of getting their money without the law helping them by sending the debtor to gaol. The object of the Bill was to apply to small debtors the same provisions of law that were now applicable to debtors of a superior class. He thought the poor man had as good a right to the privilege of "white-washing" as the rich man, and therefore he thought this was a just and necessary measure. He trusted the Bill would now be read a second time.

Amendment, by leave, *withdrawn*.

Main Question put, and *agreed to*.

Bill read 2°, and *committed* for *Wednesday*, 8th June.

PARTNERSHIP LAW AMENDMENT BILL.
[BILL 68.] COMMITTEE.

Order for Committee read.

Motion made, and Question proposed, "That Mr. Speaker do now leave the Chair."

MR. T. BARING said, he could not but express his astonishment that a Bill upon a subject of such vast importance should not have been introduced by the Government. He could not help thinking that the President of the Board of Trade ought to have made himself responsible for this Bill, if the Government thought it was a measure that ought to be passed by the Legislature, and that it should not have been left in the hands of a private individual. The Bill was one of such importance for good or evil that he could not understand why the Government should have allowed it to reach its present stage without expressing their opinion upon its merits, or that of the Law Officers of the Crown. The effect of the Bill would be simply this—that whereas at present every partner was responsible to the extent of all he had to meet his liabilities, he would under this Bill be responsible only to the extent to which he had registered. That was a great change in the commercial legislation of this country. The right hon. Gentleman the Vice President of the Board of Trade had brought in several Bills to alter the law of partnership, but they had all been rejected. Last year a Bill was proposed on this subject by the hon. Member for Birmingham (Mr. Scholefield), which was subsequently referred to a Select Committee. The right hon. Gentleman the President of the Board of Trade was Chairman of that Committee, and although it was decided by that Committee that no evidence should be produced as to the alleged evil or the remedy for it, it was obvious that there were not three Members who knew exactly what was really wanted, or, if they did know it, how the want was really to be met. That Committee sat for some time, and reported in favour of a Bill which was afterwards brought before the House. They had not now the same Bill. [Mr. SCHOLEFIELD : Identically the same.] He was glad the hon. Gentleman knew something of the present measure, for when the former Bill was read the second time he confessed that he had not read all the clauses when he submitted it to the House. It appeared that though the Bill was one of the greatest importance, the interest it excited was very little indeed, considering the few Members that were then present, and how easily under such circumstances it would be to pass it through Committee. He (Mr. Baring) said it was not precisely the same Bill as the last, and he would ask why the President of the Board of Trade had not stated his views in respect to it before it was allowed to pass through the second reading. So far from his (Mr. Baring's) objections to the Bill being diminished they were rather strengthened, and he thought that the House ought to pause before they extended the principle of limited liability further. When they witnessed the many gambling speculations that were encouraged under this principle of limited liability, the House ought to be most cautious in allowing the law of limited liability to be stretched further. It was perhaps wise to recognize the principle of limited liability in cases where individual capital was not sufficient to carry out legitimate enterprise. It was, however, an unfounded argument to say, that because we adopted the principle of limited liability in regard to great companies and important enterprises, we should carry it out into the concerns of private partnerships. Although the principle was carried out to its fullest extent in France and the United States, there were nevertheless serious objections entertained against it. In the United States, for example, there was plenty of enterprise, but little capital. In this country, however, there was not only plenty of capital, but also great enterprise. There was no necessity for limited liability in a country when private enterprise could be carried out by private means. He was aware it was alleged that this measure was intended to effect benevolent purposes, by enabling a capitalist to advance money to a deserving tradesman without incurring the liability of partnership. But there were many other ways of assisting a young man without incurring this risk—for instance, by advancing money on interest. But he thought it absurd to represent this as a Bill for charitable purposes; it was a Bill that would encourage the love of gain —to limit the stake with the chances of the great winnings of the gaming table. There was no want of capital in this country for any legitimate purpose, and no want of power if they chose to apply that capital. The effect of this Bill would be to make trade all speculative, and give less security to trade than now existed. His great objection to applying this limited liability principle to private partnerships was that it diminished the responsibility of those in trade. Upon that responsibility rested the assurance of constant vigilance, caution, prudence, and attention. In this country, which was the greatest commercial community that existed, the system of credit was carried to the furthest possible extent. It had been stated (and he believed that the fact was underrated) that two-thirds of our trade was carried on upon credit, and that system of credit rested upon the security of our laws. That necessity rested upon this fact, that it was known that every individual who engaged in trade was responsible for the whole of his property—that his social position was involved, if not his very existence. Anything, then, which shook the security upon which that system of credit rested must

Mr. T. Baring

inflict injury upon the country. He wished to hear from the right hon. Gentleman (Mr. M. Gibson), whether he and the Government adopted this Bill; whether they were disposed to introduce any changes; whether the opinion of the Law Officers of the Crown had been taken as to the mode of carrying it into effect; and, for the purpose of giving the right hon. Gentleman the opportunity of explaining his views, he would move that the House go into Committee on the Bill that day six months.

Amendment proposed,

To leave out from the word "That" to the end of the Question, in order to add the words "this House will, upon this day six months, resolve itself into the said Committee,"—(*Mr. Thomas Baring,*)

—instead thereof.

Question proposed, "That the words proposed to be left out stand part of the Question."

MR. MILNER GIBSON said, that this was not the first appearance of the Bill before Parliament; and the Government had not thought it incumbent on them to interfere. The measure had received great attention from the hon. Member for Birmingham, and had been investigated last Session before a Select Committee; it had passed last year through all its stages, and had failed in the other House only he believed in consequence of the lateness of the Session. This Bill was mainly the same as that of last Session, and although there might be some small changes in the clauses they did not at all affect the principle. Some changes might be necessary in the Bill for the security of the commercial world, but these could all be effected in Committee; but the principle, which was that of limited liability, was already recognized and established. He quite agreed with the hon. Member for Huntingdon as to the importance of not introducing any measure which was calculated to shake the foundations of commercial credit in this country; but he denied that the Bill would have any such effect. On the contrary, he believed its effect would be to place the creditor in a better position than he was at present. The principle of the Bill was, that any person might lend his money, receiving a share of the profits, without thereby becoming a general partner. At present, if he lent his money at interest, and the firm became bankrupt, he came in as a creditor;

whereas if he were a partner under the provisions of this Bill on limited liability his money became assèts, and was impounded for the benefit of the creditors. Therefore the security to the creditor would be greater under the Bill than it was at present. At present any seven persons uniting together could limit their liability, and this Bill was therefore of less extent than the existing law. The House could hardly make a retrograde step from the policy of limited liability which they had already affirmed. He hoped, therefore, that, seeing that the Bill introduced no new principle, that it had received the sanction of that House in a former Session, and that the changes now introduced were of a kind that could be best considered in Committee, the right hon. Gentleman the Member for Huntingdon would not further oppose the progress of the Bill. He had no hesitation in saying, on behalf of the Government, that they adopted the principle of limited liability, and therefore he should give his support to this measure, without pledging himself to all the clauses in their present shape.

MR. HUBBARD said, he quite agreed with his hon. Friend the Member for Huntingdon that this was a subject which the Government ought to have grappled with, and not have left in the hands of a private Member. It was very true that the Government accepted the principle of limited liability; and they had adopted it in respect of this Bill, for they had left a subject of immense importance to the commercial world to be dealt with by a private Member until it had passed through all the most important stages. He could not think that the right hon. Gentleman had met the objections that had been raised. The real question at issue was, whether it was right to introduce into the commercial policy of this country a new principle, which gave to the unprincipled capitalist the opportunity of speculating with perfect impunity behind a man of straw—a medium through whom he could speculate to any extent, while he himself was shielded from all responsibility. That was an entirely new principle in our commercial legislation, and it had no parallel in what had been done in our legislation with regard to public companies, to whom the protection of liability was applied because it was only by that means we could get a number of individuals to combine and carry out those great works by which this country was distinguished. There was no analogy be-

tween that case and the application of limited liability to the undertakings of private partners. The principle was new, and it was one against which he strongly protested. He could not think that on a question of this kind the Government were justified in giving a silent vote. They ought to take a decided part on a measure which was giving a new character to the trade of the country, and the House in considering this subject should bear in mind that it was not under the limited liability system that this country had attained its commercial pre-eminence.

MR. GOSCHEN said, that so far from the Bill enabling a speculative capitalist to take shelter behind a man of straw, under its operation the whole world would know the amount put into a partnership by the capitalist, and to the extent of their capital the partners would be able to obtain credit. It was said that in these cases the profits were unlimited, while the loss would be limited to the amount invested ; but the profits would also be limited, for the whole trading community would be aware through the registry of the credit to which the partnership was entitled. Unscrupulous people were at present able to obtain much more credit than they would when a register was kept through which creditors would know the amount of the investments, and, therefore, under a system of limited partnership credit also would be limited. The present system was much more open to the charge than that which the Bill would introduce. The object of the Bill was to remove what was really a restriction upon trade, and to establish a natural state of things—to establish perfect freedom of contract ; and the onus of showing that it would lead to excessive credit rested with the opponents of the measure. It was not the business of the House to prevent or stimulate enterprise or speculation, but it was their business to clear the field so that individuals might take their own course.

MR. BUCHANAN said, he could not support the Bill, because he believed that its effect would be to place within available reach of the unscrupulous capitalist a powerful machinery for fraud. The registry would not show the real amount of *bonâ fide* capital invested, because parties might enter unsaleable goods, unseaworthy ships, and other property, at valuations which would be subject to no test.

MR. ALDERMAN SALOMONS reminded the House that it was impossible by this or any other measure to make people commercially moral when they chose to adopt an opposite course. He did not believe that any large firms would avail themselves of the provisions of the Act; and its real effect, as he regarded it, would be to strengthen weak firms without ruining the strong ones. He thought also that its effect would be to invite the assistance of enterprising traders to the small capitalists, and thus supersede the present undesirable method of raising money by bills.

Amendment, by leave, *withdrawn*.

Main Question put, and *agreed to*.

Bill *considered* in Committee.

(In the Committee.)

Clauses 1 and 2 *agreed to*.

Clause 3 (A Limited Partnership may be formed).

MR. T. BARING proposed the insertion of words requiring all such partnerships to be distinguished by the addition of the word "limited" to the name of the firm in all its dealings and transactions.

MR. GOSCHEN defended the clause as it stood.

MR. BUCHANAN said, the argument was that the great use of the Bill would be to enable young men to be supported by capitalists. This assumed that there would be no capital in the hands of the general partner, and that the only capital would be contributed by a person whose liability was limited. He thought that it was necessary to attach a mark to such a firm, but he suggested that, instead of the word "limited," the word "registered" should be employed.

MR. LINDSAY thought that when a certain firm changed their mode of conducting business the fact ought to be notified to the public.

MR. W. E. FORSTER thought that the objection of the hon. Member (Mr. T. Baring) would be met by Clauses 9 and 13.

MR. T. BARING would substitute the word "registered" for "limited," but he must divide the House if his Amendment was opposed.

Amendment proposed,

At the end of the Clause, to add the words "and all such partnership shall be distinguished by the addition of the word 'registered' to the name of the firm, in all its dealings and transactions."—(*Mr. Thomas Baring.*)

MR. ALDERMAN SALOMONS objected to the word registered, as putting him in mind of the shirt collars and trousers that were constantly advertised. [*Laughter.*]

MR. BRIGHT said, he was quite satisfied that if the Committee adopted Mr. T. Baring's suggestion they might as well get rid of the Bill altogether. If it were insisted that every firm under the provisions of the Bill should put on its signboard, as on its invoices, the word "registered" or "limited," that would interfere to a great extent, and probably altogether frustrate the objects of the Bill. The business of a firm affected its connections, and no one else; and those interested would take care to make the necessary inquiries. People in business were not so fast asleep as not to be alive to their interests in such matters. He hoped his hon. Colleague would not consent to the Amendment. He would advise him, in fact, not to go on with the Bill if such a proposition were carried.

MR. MILNER GIBSON thought the Amendment was quite unnecessary.

SIR FRANCIS GOLDSMID could not understand why the Amendment should be objected to, as the word "registered" was so often repeated in the Bill.

MR. HUBBARD thought the Amendment would give the *coup de grace* to the whole measure.

MR. DENMAN said, the Amendment was altogether beyond the scope of the Bill.

MR. T. BARING remarked that if, as stated by the hon. Member for Birmingham, the Amendment would prove fatal to the Bill, one could only infer that the object of the measure was deception.

Question put, "That those words be there added."

The Committee *divided*:—Ayes 12; Noes 20: Majority 8.

And it appearing on the Division that 40 Members were not present in the Committee; Mr. Speaker resumed the Chair.

House counted; and 40 Members not being present,

House adjourned at One o'clock.

[INDEX.

INDEX

TO

HANSARD'S PARLIAMENTARY DEBATES,

VOLUME CLXXIV.

SECOND VOLUME OF THE SESSION 1864.

EXPLANATION OF THE ABBREVIATIONS.

In Bills, Read 1°, 2°, 3°, or 1ª, 2ª, 3ª, Read the First, Second, or Third Time.—In Speeches, 1R., 2R., 3R., Speech delivered on the First, Second, or Third Reading.—*Amendt.*, Amendment.—*Res.*, Resolution.—*Comm.*, Committee.—*Re-Comm.*, Re-Committal.—*Rep.*, Report.—*Consid.*, Consideration.—*Adj.*, Adjournment or Adjourned.—*cl.*, Clause.—*add. cl.*, Additional Clause.—*neg.*, Negatived.—*M. Q.*, Main Question.—*O. Q.*, Original Question.—*O. M.*, Original Motion.—*P. Q.*, Previous Question.—*R. P.*, Report Progress.—*A.*, Ayes.—*N.*, Noes.—*M.*, Majority.—*1st. Div.*, *2nd. Div.*, First or Second Division.—*l.*, Lords.—*c.*, Commons.

☞ When in the Text or in the Index a Speech is marked thus *, it indicates that the Speech is reprinted from a Pamphlet or some authorized Report.

When in the Index a † is prefixed to a Name or an Office (the Member having accepted or vacated office during the Session) and to Subjects of Debate thereunder, it indicates that the Speeches on those Subjects were delivered in the speaker's private or official character, as the case may be.

When in this Index a * is added to the Reading of a Bill, it indicates that no Debate took place upon that stage of the measure.

VOL. CLXXIV. [THIRD SERIES.]   3 Z

[cont.

Copyright Bill
(*Mr. Black, Mr. Massey, Mr. Stirling*)
c. Bill withdrawn, *April 6*, 503   [Bill 34]

Copyright (No. 2) Bill
(*Mr. Black, Mr. Stirling, and Mr. Massey*)
c. Ordered*; read 1° *April 6*   [Bill 59]
Read 2°*, and referred to Select Committee, *April 15*
Committee nominated *April 26* :—Mr. Black, Mr. Massey, Mr. Walpole, Mr. Dunlop, Sir William Heathcote, Mr. Grant Duff, Mr. Cave, Earl Grosvenor, Mr. Maguire, Mr. Arthur Mills, Mr. Neate, Mr. Walter, Mr. Pollard-Urquhart, Mr. Lowe, and Mr. Whiteside ; and, on *May 11*, Mr. Milner Gibson added and Mr. Cave disch.

Cork, Earl of
Vestry Cess Abolition (Ireland), Comm. *cl.* 4, 9

Corn, Duty on
Question, Mr. Caird ; Answer, the Chancellor of the Exchequer, *April 18*, 1201

Corn Rents
Question, Mr. Hubbard ; Answer, Mr. C. P. Villiers, *April 18*, 1199

Corry, Rt. Hon. H. T. L., *Tyrone Co.*
Navy Estimates—Naval Stores, 420, 423, 426, 433 ;—Steam Machinery, 441
Navy—The Channel Fleet, 1472
Malta Dock, 395

Costs Security Bill
(*Mr. Butt and Mr. Murray*)
c. Ordered*; read 1° *Mar 18*   [Bill 58]

County Bridges Bill
(*Mr. Heygate, Mr. Evans, Mr. Hartopp*)
c. Ordered ; read 1°* *April 21*   [Bill 77]

County Courts (Ireland) Bill
(*Mr. Attorney General for Ireland, Sir Robert Peel, Sir George Grey*)
c. Read 1° *Feb.* 12 ; *Feb.* 26   [Bill 12]
Committee* ;—Report *April 14*, and recomm.
(*Afterwards entitled Civil Bill Courts Bill*)   [Bill 66]

County Franchise Bill
(*Mr. Locke King, Mr. Hastings Russell*)
c. Moved, "That the Bill be now read 2°" (*Mr. Locke King*) *April 13*, 916
After Debate, previous Question moved (*Mr. Knightley*)
After long Debate, previous Question put, A. 227, N. 254 ; M. 27, *April 13*   [Bill 33]

Court of Chancery Despatch of Business Bill
(*The Lord Chancellor*)
l. Read 2°* *Mar 18*   (No. 18)
Committee* ; Report, *April 5*
Read 3°* *April 8*
c. Read 1°* *April 14*   [Bill 69]
Read 2°* *April 19*
Committee* ; Report, *April 25*
Considered as amended* *April 26*
Read 3°* *April 28*

VOL. CLXXIV. [THIRD SERIES.]

Court of Chancery (Ireland) Bill
(*Mr. Attorney General for Ireland, Sir Robert Peel, and Sir George Grey*)
c. Motion for Leave (*Mr. Attorney General for Ireland*) *April 19*, 1376
Motion " That the Debate be now adjourned " (*Mr. Hennessy*)
After short Debate, Question put, A. 28, N. 57 ; M. 29. Original Question again proposed ; Motion, by leave, withdrawn
Motion for leave (*Mr. Attorney General for Ireland*), *April 25*, 1560
After long Debate, Motion " That the Debate be now adjourned"—(*Mr. Hennessy*)
Motion withdrawn ; Original Question put, and agreed to
Bill ordered ; read 1° *April 25*   [Bill 78]

Court of Justiciary (Scotland) Bill
c. Committee* ; Report, *April 21*   [Bill 81]

Courts of Justice
Question, Mr. Arthur Mills ; Answer, Mr. Cowper *April 15*, 1142

Cowper, Right Hon. W. F. (Chief Commissioner of Works), *Hertford*
Courts of Justice, 1142
National Gallery, 1776
New Law Courts, 1420, 1421, 2052
Patent Offices—Fife House, 182, 1954
Richard Cœur de Lion, Statue of, 1771
Sewage of the Metropolis, 2052
South Kensington, New Museums at, 1078, 1079, 1287
Victoria Tower, Improvements near the, 183

Cox, Mr. W., *Finsbury*
Chigwell, Recreation Grounds at, 2023
Customs and Inland Revenue, Comm. *cl.* 2, 1860
Stansfeld, Mr., and the Greco Conspiracy, Res. 283

Cranworth, Lord
Charitable Assurances Enrolment, 2R. 721
Land Securities Company, 2R. Amendt. 1280, 1281
Land Transfer Act, 1416
Rape, Punishment of, 2R. 861 ; Comm. *cl.* 1, 960, 961
Settled Estates Act Amendment, 2R. 534

Craufurd, Mr. E. H. J., *Ayr, &c.*
Court of Chancery (Ireland), Leave, 1378

Crawford, Mr. R. W., *London*
Customs and Inland Revenue, Comm. *cl.* 2, Proviso, 1836, 1860, Consid. Schedule A. 2011
Financial Statement—Ways and Means, Res. 601
Metropolitan Railways, 17
Sugar Duties and the Malt Duty, 959 ; Res. 991
*Ways and Means—Sugar Duties, Rep. Amendt. 1143, 1167, 1170, 1172

4 A

Government Annuities Bill
    c. Debate resumed *Mar* 17, 211   [Bill 11]
        Amendt. to leave out from "That" and add
        " the Bill be committed to a Select Com-
        mittee " (*Sir Minto Farquhar*), 211
    Question proposed, " That the words, &c."
    After long Debate, Debate further adjourned
    Debate further adjourned * *Mar* 18
    Debate resumed *April* 11, 789
    After long Debate, Question put and negatived
    Words added
    Main Question, as amended, put and agreed to
    Ordered, That the Bill be committed to a Select
        Committee
    Committee nominated *April* 21 :—The Chan-
        cellor of the Exchequer, Mr. Sotheron Est-
        court, Mr. Milner Gibson, Mr. Henley, Sir
        Minto Farquhar, Sir Stafford Northcote, Mr.
        Horsfall, Mr. Goschen, Mr. Charles Turner,
        Mr. Herbert, Mr. Hubbard, Mr. H. B.
        Sheridan, Mr. Ayrton, Mr. Hodgkinson, and
        Mr. Paget, 1473
    Motion, " That the Committee have power to
        send for persons, papers, and records " (*Sir
        Minto Farquhar*) *April* 21
    Question put, A. 104, N. 127 ; M. 23

Government Annuities Bill
    Question, Mr. Thomson Hankey ; Answer, The
        Chancellor of the Exchequer *Mar* 17, 177 ;
        Question, Sir Minto Farquhar ; Answer, Mr.
        Milner Gibson *Mar* 18, 343
    Mr. H. B. Sheridan, Personal Explanation,
        The Chancellor of the Exchequer, 191 ; Mr.
        H. B. Sheridan *Mar* 17, 198

[*cont.*

[cont.

PEASE, Mr. H., *Durham, S.*
County Franchise, 2R. 948
Harbours of Refuge, Res. 1677

PEEL, Right Hon. Sir R. (Chief Secretary for Ireland) *Tamworth*
Administration of Justice (Ireland)—The Queen *v.* Duigan and others, Papers moved for, 1270
Bishoprics in Ireland, 16
Court of Chancery (Ireland), Leave, 1877
Education, National (Ireland), 13
Galway (West District), Papers moved for, 1271
Grand Juries (Ireland), 2R. 1394
Indictable Offences (Ireland), Returns moved for, 1123, 1125, 1126, 1129
Ireland—The Constabulary, 184, 305, 967 ;—Additional at Lisburn, 970, 971 ;—District Lunatic Asylum, 187 ;—Brehon Laws, 1503
Landlord and Tenant (Ireland), 1976
National Schools (Ireland), 1199
Scientific Institutions of Dublin, 674, 677
Tenure and Improvement of Land Act (Ireland), 1775
Trespass (Ireland), Comm. 957, 1753, 1754

PEEL, Rt. Hon. Lt.-Gen. J., *Huntingdon*
Army Estimates—General Staff, &c. 809, 826 ; —Clothing, 834
Army — Instruction and Employment of Soldiers, Res. 626
Business of the House, 1776
Crawley, Colonel, Case of, Papers moved for, Amendt. 36, 69
Denmark and Germany — Bombardment of Sonderborg, 714

PEEL, Rt. Hon. F. (Joint Secretary to the Treasury), *Bury*
Bankruptcy Court (Dublin), 303
Chigwell, Recreation Grounds at, 2024
Civil Service Estimates, 17
Mails in the Provinces, Comm. moved for, 409 ;—from Southampton, 477
Post Office—Saturday Half Holiday, 1977
Public Lands and Buildings (Local Rates), Res. 488
Supply—Civil Services, 289
Treasury Regulations, 186
West India Mails, 1421, 1549

PEEL, Mr. J., *Tamworth*
Sugar Duties and the Malt Duty, Res. 986

Penal Servitude Acts Amendment Bill
(*Sir George Grey, Mr. Bruce*)
c. *Moved,* "That Mr. Speaker do now leave the Chair" *April* 18, 1250
Amendt. to leave out from "That" and add "this House is of opinion that the system of discharge of prisoners from Penal Servitude on licence without police supervision should no longer be continued" (*Mr. Adderley*)
After short Debate, Amendment withdrawn
Bill considered in Committee *April* 18, 1255
cl. 1 agreed to
cl. 2 (Length of Sentences of Penal Servitude), 1255
    After Debate, Clause agreed to
[cont.

Penal Servitude Acts Amendment Bill—cont.
cl. 3 (Punishment of Offences in Convict Prisons), 1258
    After short Debate, Clause agreed to
cl. 4 (Forfeiture of Licence), 1258
    Amendt. (Holder of Licence to report himself to Police) (*Mr. Hunt*), 1259
    After long Debate, Question put, "That those words be there added," A. 148, N. 120 ; M. 28
Clause, as amended, agreed to
Remaining Clauses agreed to
Schedule A.
    Amendment proposed after "large" to omit " in the United Kingdom " (*Mr. Hunt*)
    Amendment, withdrawn
    Schedule agreed to
new cl. (Licences may be granted in different form) (*Sir George Grey*)
cl. agreed to
Bill reported *April* 18
Bill, as amended, considered (*April* 29, 1961
new cl. (Application of Acts to Licence) (*Mr. Whitbread*), read 1°
    After Debate, Motion withdrawn
cl. 4 Amendments (*Mr. Hunt*) agreed to
cl., as amended, agreed to
Read 3°° *May* 2   [Bill 71]

Penal Servitude Acts Amendment Bill
Question, Mr. Maguire ; Answer, Sir George Grey *April* 15, 1077

PETO, Sir S. M., *Finsbury*
Chain Cables and Anchors, Comm. cl. 8, 514 ; cl. 9, 515
Navy Estimates—Naval Stores, 430, 439 ;—Steam Machinery, 442

Polish Refugees in Austria
Question, Mr. Yorke ; Answer, Viscount Palmerston *April* 18, 1200

POLLARD-URQUHART, Mr. W., *Westmeath Co.*
Grand Juries (Ireland), 2R. 1388
Penal Servitude Acts Amendment, Consid. add. cl. 1965
Sugar Duties and the Malt Duty, Res. 1003

Poor Law—Casual Poor
Question, Mr. Kekewich ; Answer, Mr. C. P. Villiers *Mar* 15, 15

Poor Law (Ireland) Acts Amendment Bill
(*Mr. Hennessy, Mr. Pollard-Urquhart*)
c. Ordered ; after short Debate, read 1° *Mar* 15, 99   [Bill 15]

Poor Law—Parochial Assessment
Committees, Question, Mr. Sutton Western ; Answer, Mr. C. P. Villiers *April* 21, 1421

Post Office
Mail Packet Contracts—The West India Colonies, Question, Mr. Cave ; Answer, Mr. Peel *April* 25, 1548
[cont.

Post Office—cont.

Mails, Departure of, from Southampton, Question, Mr. H. Berkeley ; Answer, Mr. Peel *April 5*, 477

Mails in the Provinces, Amendment on Comm. of Supply *April 4*, to leave out from 'That,' and add 'a Select Committee be appointed to inquire into the Post Office, with an especial view to the improvement of existing arrangements for the transmission of Mails in the Provincial Districts' (*Mr. Richard Long*), 402

    After long Debate, Question, "That the words, &c.," put, and agreed to

Post Office—*Saturday Half Holiday*

Question, Mr. O'Reilly ; Answer, Mr. Peel *May 2*, 1976

West India Mails—Question, Mr. Cave ; Answer, Mr. Peel *April 21*, 1421

POTTER, Mr. E., *Carlisle*

Ways and Means—Sugar Duties, Rep. 1164

POWELL, Mr. F. S., *Cambridge*

Church Building Acts, 184

Factory Inspectors, Reports of 1501

South Kensington, Buildings at, 1287

POWELL, Mr. J. J., *Gloucester*

Penal Servitude Acts Amendment, Comm. *cl.* 4, 1259

United States—Seizure of the "Tuscaloosa," Res. 1808

Prevention of Trespasses (Scotland) Bill
(*Duke of Argyll*)

l. Read 1° *April 26*   (No. 60)

PRICE, Mr. R. G., *New Radnor*

Customs and Inland Revenue, Consid. *cl.* 12, 1986

Private Bills

LORDS—

Ordered *April 21*, on Motion of Lord Redesdale, That no Private Bill brought from the House of Commons shall be read a Second Time after *Thursday*, the *30th Day of June next April 21*

Privilege—

See

    Government Annuities Bill
    Committee of Supply, April 29
    Under Secretaries of State

Promissory Notes and Bills of Exchange (Ireland) Bill
(*Sir Colman O'Loghlen, Captain Stacpoole*)

c. Ordered * ; read 1° *April 19*   [Bill 38]
Read 2°° *April 28*
Committee * and Report *May 2*

Prosecutions, Cost of

Question, Sir Jervoise Jervoise ; Answer, Sir George Grey, *April 14*, 968

Proxies, Stamp on

Question, Mr. Darby Griffith ; Answer, The Chancellor of the Exchequer, *April 14*, 971

Public Accounts—*Committee on*

Mr. Cobden disch. ; Lord Robert Montagu added, *April 8*

Public Houses, Closing on Sundays

Question, Mr. Baines ; Answer, Mr. Somes *May 3*, 2055

Public Lands and Buildings (Local Rates) —Resolution

Motion, " That, in the opinion of this House, all Lands and Buildings used and occupied for Public purposes should be assessed to Local Rates, and pay Rates accordingly" (*Mr. Alderman Salomons*) *April 5*, 479

After long Debate, Question put: A. 30, N. 52 ; M. 22

Public and Refreshment Houses (Metropolis) Bill
(*Sir George Grey, Mr. Baring*)

c. Ordered *May 23*, 119

PUGH, Mr. D., *Carmarthenshire*

Mails in the Provinces, Comm. moved for, 406

Sugar Duties and the Malt Duty, Res. 1004

Punishment of Death

Motion, " That a Select Committee be appointed to inquire into the expediency of maintaining the Punishment of Death" (*Mr. William Ewart*) *May 3*, 2055

Amendment, to leave out from " The" and add " operation of the Laws relating to Capital Punishment" (*Lord Henry Lennox*), 2070

Question, " That the words," &c. After long Debate, Amendment and Motion withdrawn

Resolved, " That an humble Address be presented to Her Majesty, praying that she will be graciously pleased to issue a Royal Commission to inquire into the provisions and operation of the Laws under which the Punishment of Death is now inflicted in the United Kingdom, and the manner in which it is inflicted ; and to report whether it is desirable to make any alteration therein" (*Mr. Neate*)

Punishment of Rape Bill
(*The Marquess of Westmeath*)

l. Bill read 2°, after short Debate, *April 12*, 859   (No. 22)

Considered in Committee, *April 14*

[cont.

Rose, Mr. Ald. W. A., *Southampton*
Church Rates Commutation, 2R. 1719
Death, Punishment of, Comm. moved for, 2079
Greco Conspiracy, The — M. Mazzini — Mr.
Stansfeld, 325
Thames Conservancy, 2R. 1559
War Department Clerks—Medical Assistance,
478

*Rule of the House—Questions to Private
Members*
Question, Captain Archdall ; Answer, Mr.
Speaker *April 29*, 1914

Russell, Earl (Secretary of State for
Foreign Affairs)
Confederate States, British Consuls in the, 457
Denmark and Germany—Affairs of, 293, 533 ;
—Bombardment of Sonderborg, 532, 1276 ;
Res. 754, 758, 772, 774, 776, 785 ; — The
Conference. 1417, 1419
Metropolitan Railways, 448
United States—The " Kearsarge " — Federal
Enlistments in Ireland, Papers moved for,
297, 299, 449, 533 :—Law of Prize, 1606 :—
Steam Rams in the Mersey, Papers moved
for, 1892, 1897, 1913

St. Germans, Earl of (Lord Steward of
the Household)
Vestry Cess Abolition (Ireland), Comm. *cl.* 4, 9

St. Mary's Burial Ground, Sydenham
Amendment on Committee of Supply *April* 8,
" To leave out ' That' and add ' a Select Com-
mittee be appointed to inquire into the Alle-
gations contained in the Petition of Mr.
Alfred Smee, which was presented upon the
19th day of February last, relative to the
Saint Mary's, Sydenham, Burial Ground ;
and further into the existence, increase, and
nature of the Conventual and Monastic
Communities, Societies, or Institutions in
England, Wales, and Scotland'" (*Mr. New-
degate*), 633
After long Debate, Question put, " That the
words &c." A. 113, N. 80 ; M. 33
Division List, Ayes and Noes, 661

Salisbury Cathedral
Question, Mr. Henry Seymour ; Answer, Mr.
Walpole *Mar* 17, 177

Salmon Fisheries Act
Question, Mr. Percy Wyndham ; Answer, Mr.
T. G. Baring *April 29*, 1915

Salomons, Mr. Ald. D., *Greenwich*
City of London Bye-Laws, 966
Navy Estimates—Medicines and Medical Stores,
442
Parochial Assessment Committees, 1422
Partnership Law Amendment, 2R. 1567 ;
Comm. 2126 ; *cl.* 3. 2128
Public Lands and Buildings (Local Rates), Res.
479, 509

Salt, Mr. T., *Stafford*
Government Annuities, Comm. 231

Sat First in Parliament
April 21. The Viscount Sidmouth, after the
Death of his Father

Scholefield, Mr. W., *Birmingham*
Partnership Law Amendment, 2R. 1559, 1568

Schools of Art — Select Committee. See
Art, Schools of

Scientific Institutions (Dublin)
Motion, That a Select Committee be appointed,
" to inquire into the condition of the Scientific
Institutions of Dublin which are assisted by
Government aid" (*Mr. Gregory*) *April* 11
Motion, " That the Debate be now adjourned"
(*Mr. Whiteside*) negatived
Original Question agreed to
Committee nominated* *April* 18 :—Mr.Gregory,
Lord Henry Lennox, Sir R. Peel, Mr. Luke
White, Mr. Lygon, Sir Colman O'Loghlen,
Mr. Cogan, The O'Conor Don, Mr. O'Reilly,
Mr. Dillwyn, Sir Edward Grogan, Mr. George,
Mr. Leader, Mr. Lefroy, and Mr. Waldron

Sclater-Booth, Mr. G., *Hampshire, N.*
Jersey—Royal Court at, 1772
Public Lands and Buildings (Local Rates), Res.
496

Scots Episcopal Fund Bill
l. Read 2° *April* 21   (No. 123)

Scourfield, Mr. J. H., *Haverfordwest*
Standing Orders (Parliamentary Deposits),
Comm. moved for, 1618

Scully, Mr. V., *Cork Co.*
Civil Bill Courts (Ireland), Comm. *cl.* 37,
Amendt. 1556
Court of Chancery (Ireland), Leave, 1376, 1592
Garibaldi, General, Departure of, 1423, 1425
Judgments, &c. Law Amendment, 2R. 101
Tests Abolition (Oxford), 2R. 143

Selwyn, Mr. C. J., *Cambridge University*
New Law Courts, 1420
New Zealand—War in, Papers moved for, 1656
Standing Orders (Parliamentary Deposits),
Comm. moved for, 1620
Tests Abolition (Oxford), 2R. 116, 137

Sentences of Death Bill
(*The Earl of Ellenborough*)
l. Read 1* after Debate *April 22*, 1438 (No. 58)